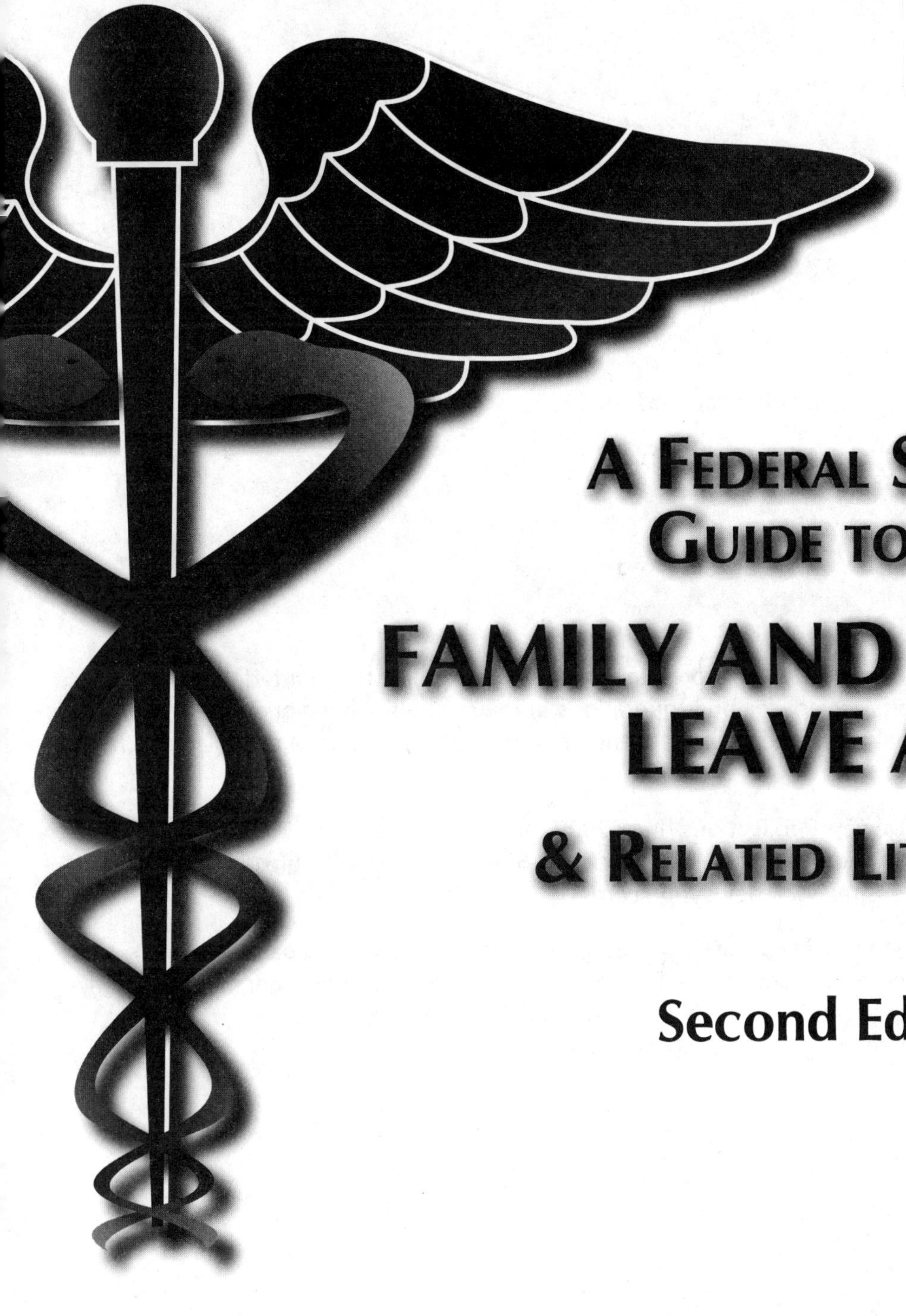

A Federal Sector Guide to the FAMILY AND MEDICAL LEAVE ACT & Related Litigation

Second Edition

Carl C. Bosland

 DEWEY PUBLICATIONS, INC.
ARLINGTON, VIRGINIA

Second Edition

Copyright 2007

Dewey Publications, Inc.

Arlington, Virginia

All Rights Reserved

No part of this book may be reproduced, stored in a retrieval system, or transmitted in any form or by any means, except for brief quotations in reviews, scholarly works, or administrative and judicial submissions, without the prior written permission of the publisher.

For information, address Dewey Publications, Inc., 2009 N. 14th Street, Suite 705, Arlington, VA 22201; telephone: 703–524–1355; fax: 703–524–1463; e–mail: info@deweypub.com; Internet website: www.deweypub.com.

This publication is designed to provide accurate and authoritative information in regard to the subject matter covered. It is sold with the understanding that the publisher and author are not engaged in rendering legal services. If legal advice or other expert assistance is required, the services of a competent professional person should be sought.

Library of Congress Control Number: 2007929211

ISBN 12: 978-1-932612-99-8

ISBN 10: 1-932612-99-8

Printed in the United States of America

HOW TO USE THIS GUIDE

Readers are cautioned to read full opinions, available through printed text, CYBERFEDS, PERSONNET/WESTLAW, and, LEXIS.

References are made to the Code of Federal Regulations, the United States Code, and a variety of other sources. These citations are current as of the time the guide went to press, in August 2007. Regulations, statutes, and guidance change. Readers should check the current edition of the sources to ensure the validity of a citation.

ACKNOWLEDGMENTS

I wish to extend my sincere thanks to my wife, family, and friends whose support and encouragement have sustained me these last few writing years. I particularly wish to acknowledge my nieces and nephews, Lindsey, Julie, Ellen, Ben, and Henry.

I also wish to thank Peter Broida, my publisher, and the first-class team at Dewey Publications, Inc., for giving me the opportunity to update the Guide.

SUMMARY TABLE OF CONTENTS

CHAPTER 1: OVERVIEW 1

CHAPTER 2: PURPOSES AND LEGISLATIVE HISTORY OF THE FMLA 13

CHAPTER 3: FMLA COVERAGE OF THE FEDERAL GOVERNMENT 21

CHAPTER 4: FEDERAL EMPLOYEES COVERED BY THE FMLA 41

CHAPTER 5: EMPLOYEE ELIGIBILITY FOR LEAVE 65

CHAPTER 6: COVERED FAMILY MEMBERS 117

CHAPTER 7: COVERED CONDITIONS 133

CHAPTER 8: NOTICE REQUIREMENTS 255

CHAPTER 9: DOCUMENTATION REQUIREMENTS 335

CHAPTER 10: LEAVE AMOUNT AND SCHEDULING 407

CHAPTER 11: SUBSTITUTION OF PAID LEAVE 473

CHAPTER 12: MAINTENANCE OF BENEFITS 505

CHAPTER 13: RETURN TO WORK FROM LEAVE 535

CHAPTER 14: RECORD-KEEPING REQUIREMENTS 611

CHAPTER 15: PROHIBITED ACTS, ENFORCEMENT, AND REMEDIES 625

CHAPTER 16: INTERACTION OF THE FMLA WITH OTHER FEDERAL LAWS, EMPLOYER PRACTICES, AND COLLECTIVE BARGAINING AGREEMENTS 745

APPENDIX 781

INDEX 793

TABLE OF CONTENTS

CHAPTER 1: OVERVIEW 1
- I. INTRODUCTION 1
  - A. FMLA BASICS 1
    1. The Four FMLA Variants 1
    2. Core Entitlements 2
    3. The Purpose of the FMLA 2
- II. DETERMINING WHETHER LEAVE QUALIFIES FOR THE PROTECTIONS OF THE FMLA 3
  - A. WHAT VARIANT OF THE FMLA APPLIES? 3
  - B. IS THE INDIVIDUAL REQUESTING LEAVE AN "EMPLOYEE" WITHIN THE MEANING OF THE FMLA? 3
    1. Title I 4
    2. Title II 4
    3. CAA 4
    4. PEOAA 4
  - C. IS THE EMPLOYEE ELIGIBLE FOR FMLA LEAVE? 4
    1. Title I 4
    2. Title II 5
    3. The CAA, and the PEOAA 5
  - D. DOES THE LEAVE INVOLVE A COVERED INDIVIDUAL? 5
  - E. DOES THE LEAVE INVOLVE A COVERED CONDITION? 5
  - F. DID THE EMPLOYER AND THE EMPLOYEE MEET THEIR NOTICE REQUIREMENTS? ... 6
    1. Title I, the CAA, and the PEOAA 6
    2. Title II 6
  - G. DID THE EMPLOYEE PROVIDE PROPER DOCUMENTATION TO SUBSTANTIATE THEIR NEED FOR FMLA LEAVE? 7
- III. OTHER FMLA ENTITLEMENTS AND OBLIGATIONS 8
  - A. LEAVE AMOUNT AND SCHEDULING 8
  - B. SUBSTITUTION OF PAID LEAVE 9
  - C. MAINTENANCE OF BENEFITS DURING LEAVE 10
  - D. RETURN TO WORK 11
  - E. ENFORCEMENT AND REMEDIES 11
- IV. CONCLUSION 12

CHAPTER 2: PURPOSES AND LEGISLATIVE HISTORY OF THE FMLA 13
- I. INTRODUCTION 13
- II. SOCIAL CONTEXT OF THE FMLA 13
  - A. INCREASED TIME DEMANDS OF WORK 13
  - B. SIGNIFICANT INCREASE OF WOMEN IN THE WORKFORCE 13
  - C. THE RISE OF SINGLE PARENT FAMILIES 14
  - D. THE AGING OF THE AMERICAN POPULATION AND PARENTAL CARE RESPONSIBILITIES 14
- III. LEGISLATIVE RESPONSES TO FAMILY AND MEDICAL NEEDS 15
  - A. FAMILY LEAVE LAWS AROUND THE WORLD 15
  - B. STATE FAMILY LEAVE LAWS 15
  - C. CREATION OF THE FEDERAL FAMILY MEDICAL LEAVE ACT 16
    1. The Parental and Disability Leave Act of 1985 16
    2. Parental and Medical Leave Act of 1986 17
    3. The Family and Medical Leave Act of 1987 17
    4. The Family and Medical Leave Act of 1989 17
    5. The Family and Medical Leave Act of 1991 17
    6. The Family and Medical Leave Act of 1993 18
- IV. FINDINGS AND PURPOSES OF THE FAMILY AND MEDICAL LEAVE ACT OF 1993 18
  - A. FINDINGS 18
    1. Strengthening the Family 18

		2.	Economic Advantages	18
	B.	PURPOSES		19
V.	AMENDMENT OF THE FEDERAL FAMILY AND MEDICAL LEAVE ACT			19
	A.	CONGRESSIONAL ACTION		19
	B.	PRESIDENTIAL ACTION		19
		1.	Calls for Congressional Action to Expand the FMLA Go Unheeded	19
		2.	Executive Directives Expand the FMLA	20
			a. Federal Employee Initiatives	20
			b. Use of Surplus State Unemployment Insurance to Subsidize FMLA Leave	20

CHAPTER 3: FMLA COVERAGE OF THE FEDERAL GOVERNMENT 21

I.	INTRODUCTION			21
II.	TITLE I FEDERAL EMPLOYERS: THE GOVERNMENT OF THE UNITED STATES			21
	A.	PUBLIC AGENCY EMPLOYERS AND EMPLOYEES		21
	B.	INDIVIDUAL MANAGERS AND SUPERVISORS AS COVERED EMPLOYERS		22
	C.	SUCCESSORS-IN-INTEREST		22
		1.	Responsibilities of Successor-in-Interest	23
		2.	Factors to Determine Successor-in-Interest	23
	D.	DETERMINING WHO IS A "COVERED EMPLOYER" WHERE THERE MAY BE MULTIPLE EMPLOYERS		24
		1.	Integrated Employer Test	25
		2.	Joint Employers	27
			a. Joint Employment Explained	28
			b. The FMLA Responsibilities of Primary and Secondary Employers	32
			c. Job Restoration	33
			d. Employee Eligibility in Joint Employment	33
			e. Prohibited Acts	34
	E.	EFFECT OF CONTRACT OR POLICY ON EMPLOYER COVERAGE		34
III.	TITLE II OF THE FMLA: FEDERAL CIVIL SERVICE EMPLOYEES			34
	A.	TITLE II FEDERAL AGENCIES		35
IV.	TITLE V: CONGRESS AS A COVERED EMPLOYER			35
	A.	CAA DEFINES FMLA "COVERED EMPLOYER"		35
	B.	INDIVIDUAL MANAGERS AND SUPERVISORS AS COVERED EMPLOYERS		36
	C.	SUCCESSOR-IN-INTEREST		36
	D.	DETERMINING WHO IS A COVERED EMPLOYER WHERE THERE MAY BE MULTIPLE EMPLOYERS		36
		1.	Integrated Employer Test	36
		2.	Joint Employment	37
			a. Joint Employment Explained	37
			b. Responsibilities of Primary and Secondary Employers	37
			c. Job Restoration	38
			d. Employer Coverage and Employee Eligibility	38
			e. Prohibited Acts	39
V.	FMLA COVERAGE OF THE EXECUTIVE OFFICE OF THE PRESIDENT			39
	A.	PEOAA DEFINES "COVERED EMPLOYER"		39
VI.	MIXED FMLA RESPONSIBILITIES OF FEDERAL SECTOR EMPLOYERS			39

CHAPTER 4: FEDERAL EMPLOYEES COVERED BY THE FMLA 41

I.	TITLE I COVERED EMPLOYEES		41
	A.	DEFINED	41
	B.	FEDERAL EMPLOYEES COVERED BY TITLE I	41
		1. Employees of the United States Postal Service and Postal Rate Commission	42
		2. Part-Time Federal Employees	42
		3. Intermittent Appointments of Less than One Year	43
		4. A Civilian in the Military	43
		5. Individuals Employed in a Nonappropriated Fund Instrumentality Under the Jurisdiction of the Armed Forces	43
		6. Employees of Other Executive Branch Agencies	44
		a. Executive Department	44

		b.	Government Corporation	45
			(1) Federal Home Loan Mortgage Corporation	45
			(2) Pension Benefit Guaranty Corporation	45
			(3) Tennessee Valley Authority	45
			(4) Smithsonian Institution	46
			(5) Federal Deposit Insurance Corporation	46
			(6) Radio Free Europe/Radio Liberty	46
			(7) Federal Reserve	46
			(8) Office of Inspector General, Justice Department	46
		c.	Independent Establishment of the Executive Branch	46
			(1) Factors	46
			(2) General Accounting Office	47
			(3) Atomic Energy Commission	47
			(4) Federal Energy Regulatory Commission	47
			(5) Parts of Larger Executive Departments Not Independent Establishments	47
			(6) White House	48
			(7) Judiciary	48
			(8) Postal Service	48
	7.	Legislative and Judicial Branch Employees		49

II. FEDERAL EMPLOYEES COVERED BY TITLE II 49
- A. COVERED EMPLOYEE DEFINED 49
  - 1. "Employee" as Defined in 5 USC 2105 49
    - a. Civil Service Employees, 5 USC 2105(a) 49
      - (1) Appointment in the Civil Service 50
      - (2) Authorized Official 52
      - (3) Serving a Federal Function 53
      - (4) Under Federal Supervision 53
  - 2. Specific Categories of Employees 55
    - a. CIA Proprietary Corporations 55
    - b. Cooperative Extension Services 56
    - c. Agricultural Stabilization and Conservation Service 56
    - d. Certain Employees of the Naval Academy, 5 USC 2105(b) 57
    - e. Employees of Armed Forces Nonappropriated Fund Instrumentalities 57
    - f. Employees of the Veterans Health Administration 58
    - g. Teachers for the Defense Department 58
    - h. Foreign Service Employees 59
  - 3. Other Employment Relationships 60
    - a. State Officials 60
    - b. Private Contractors 60
    - c. Illegal Appointments 60
- B. INDIVIDUALS EXCLUDED FROM TITLE II COVERAGE 60
  - 1. Title II Exclusions 60
    - a. Employees of the Government of the District of Columbia 60
    - b. Individuals Employed on a Temporary or Intermittent Basis 60
    - c. Employees Covered by Titles I and V of the FMLA 61
  - 2. 5 USC 6301(2) Employee Exclusions 61
    - a. Employees of the Government of the District of Columbia 61
    - b. Part–Time Employees 61
    - c. Temporary Construction Employees 61
    - d. Panama Canal Commission Employees 62
    - e. Employees of Congress 62
    - f. Farm Credit Administration 62
    - g. Alien or Noncitizen Employees 62
    - h. Presidential Appointed Executive Branch Officers 62
    - i. Presidential Designated Executive Branch Officers 63

		j.	Chief of Mission	63
		k.	Legislative or Judicial Branch Officers	63
	3.		Employee Exclusions Pursuant to 5 USC 2105	63

III. FEDERAL EMPLOYEES COVERED BY THE CAA FMLA 64
    A.   EMPLOYEE DEFINED 64

IV. FEDERAL EMPLOYEES COVERED BY THE PEOAA FMLA 64
    A.   EMPLOYEE DEFINED 64

CHAPTER 5: EMPLOYEE ELIGIBILITY FOR LEAVE 65

I. OVERVIEW 65
II. BASIC ELIGIBILITY STANDARDS 65
    A.   TITLE I ELIGIBILITY STANDARDS 65
    B.   TITLE II ELIGIBILITY STANDARDS..66
    C.   THE CAA ELIGIBILITY STANDARDS 66
    D.   PEOAA ELIGIBILITY STANDARDS 67
III. CALCULATING 12 MONTHS OF EMPLOYMENT 67
    A.   TITLE I CALCULATIONS 67
        1.   The Federal Government as Single Employer 67
        2.   Joint Employment 67
        3.   Successors-in-Interest 68
        4.   Nonconsecutive Employment 68
        5.   Effect of Leave on 12-Month Eligibility Requirement 69
        6.   Military Leave 69
        7.   Effect of Termination, Furloughs and Reductions In Force 70
        8.   Eligibility Determined at Leave Commencement 71
        9.   Federal Employees Stationed Outside the United States 72
        10.   Former Employees and Applicants 72
    B.   TITLE II CALCULATIONS 73
        1.   Federal Employment That Counts Toward 12-Month Eligibility Requirement 73
        2.   Joint Employment and Successor-in-Interest Doctrines 74
        3.   Nonconsecutive Employment 74
        4.   Effect of Leave on 12-Month Eligibility Requirement 74
        5.   Military Leave 75
        6.   Effect of Termination or Reduction In Force 75
        7.   Furloughs 76
        8.   When is Eligibility Determined? 76
    C.   CAA CALCULATIONS 76
        1.   What Federal Employment Counts Toward the 12-Month Eligibility Requirement? 76
        2.   Joint Employment and the Successor-in-Interest Doctrine 76
        3.   Nonconsecutive Employment 77
        4.   Effect of Leave on 12-Month Eligibility Requirement 77
        5.   Military Duty 77
        6.   Effect of Termination or Reductions in Force on 12-Month Eligibility Calculation 77
        7.   Effect of Furloughs on 12-Month Eligibility Requirement 78
        8.   Twelve-Month Eligibility Calculated at Leave Commencement 78
    D.   PEOAA CALCULATIONS 78
        1.   What Federal Employment Counts Toward the 12-Month Eligibility Requirement? 78
IV. DETERMINING 1,250 HOURS OF SERVICE DURING THE PREVIOUS 12 MONTHS 78
    A.   TITLE I: DETERMINING 1,250 HOURS 78
        1.   Hours Worked 79
            a.   FLSA Principles 80
                (1)   Historical Development 80
                (2)   To Suffer or Permit to Work 80
                (3)   On-Duty Work Time 80
                (4)   Off-Duty Time 81
                (5)   Rest Periods; Breaks 81
                (6)   Lunch Breaks and Other Meal Times 81

			(7)	On–Call Time	82
			(8)	Statutory Exclusions from Hours Worked	82
		b.		Overtime; Premium Pay	83
		c.		Paid or Unpaid Leave	83
		d.		Military Leave	84
		e.		Time Spent on Union Business	85
		f.		Preliminary and Postliminary Activities	85
		g.		Layover Time	86
		h.		Attending Training	87
		i.		Disciplinary Suspensions and Terminations	87
		j.		Other Employer Acts of Interference with "Hours Worked"	89
		k.		Layoffs and Furloughs	89
		l.		Lower Eligibility Requirement Per Employer Policy	90
		m.		Joint Employment	90
		n.		Successor–In–Interest	91
		o.		Stationed Outside the United States	91
		p.		Teachers	91
		q.		Proof Employee Worked 1,250 Hours	92
	2.			Preceding 12 Months	93
	3.			Leave Commencement	93
B.				TITLE II: DETERMINING 1,250 HOURS	95
C.				CAA: DETERMINING 1,250 HOURS	95
	1.			Hours Worked	95
		a.		What Federal Employment Counts Toward the 1,250–Hour Eligibility	95
		b.		Effect of Leave on 1,250–Hour Test	96
		c.		Military Duty	96
		d.		Joint Employment and Successor–in–Interest	96
		e.		Teachers	97
		f.		Stationed Outside the United States	97
		g.		Previous 12 Months	97
		h.		Commencement of Leave	97
D.				PEOAA	98
	1.			Hours Worked	98
V.				DETERMINING WHETHER AN EMPLOYING AGENCY EMPLOYS 50 OR MORE EMPLOYEES WITHIN 75 MILES OF THE EMPLOYEE'S WORKSITE	98
A.				WHEN THE DETERMINATION IS MADE	99
B.				DETERMINING THE NUMBER OF EMPLOYEES	99
	1.			The U.S. Government as a Single Employer	100
	2.			Eligible and Non–Eligible Employees	100
	3.			Effect of Leave	100
	4.			Part–Time and Full–Time Employees	101
	5.			Laid–Off Employees	101
	6.			Leaves of Absence and Suspensions	101
	7.			Employee Resignation	101
	8.			Military Duty	102
	9.			Joint Employment and Integrated Employers	102
	10.			Federal Employees Stationed Outside the United States	103
	11.			Teachers	103
	12.			Effect of More Generous Employer Policies	103
	13.			Proof of Number of Employees Maintained on Payroll	103
	14.			Employer Coverage Is Not the Same as Employee Eligibility	104
C.				75 MILE DISTANCE	104
D.				DETERMINING THE EMPLOYEE'S WORKSITE	105
	1.			General Worksite Rule	105
	2.			Single or Multiple Locations	105
	3.			Separate Facilities as Single Worksite	106

		4.	No Fixed Worksite	106
		5.	Personal Residence Not a Worksite	107
		6.	Worksite of Joint Employee	108
VI.	INDIVIDUALS WHO ARE "DEEMED ELIGIBLE" UNDER THE FMLA			110
	A.	GENERAL ELIGIBILITY NOTICE RULE		110
		1.	Notice Where Employee is Not Yet Eligible	110
		2.	Notice When Eligibility is Met	110
		3.	Eligibility Notice Before Leave Commences	111
		4.	Deemed Eligible: Employer Notice On or After Leave Commences	111
	B.	THE "DEEMED ELIGIBLE" PENALTY PROVISION IN THE COURTS		111
		1.	"Deemed Eligible" Due to Employer Failure to Timely Notify Employee of Ineligibility	111
	C.	ESTOPPEL AND ELIGIBILITY		112
		1.	Equitable Estoppel	112
			a. Silence as Misrepresentation	114
			b. Confirmation of Eligibility as Misrepresentation	115
		2.	Interference with FMLA Rights and Eligibility	116
		3.	Collateral Estoppel	116

CHAPTER 6: COVERED FAMILY MEMBERS 117

I.	OVERVIEW			117
II.	SPOUSE			117
	A.	MARRIAGE AND DIVORCE		117
		1.	Marriage	117
			a. Statutory Marriage	118
			b. Common-Law Marriages	118
		2.	Civil Union	119
		3.	Divorce	119
	B.	THE DEFENSE OF MARRIAGE ACT AND DOMESTIC PARTNERS		120
		1.	The FMLA and Domestic Partners	120
		2.	Defense of Marriage Act of 1996	120
			a. Full Faith and Credit Clause of the Constitution	120
			b. "Marriage" and "Spouse" Defined	121
			c. DOMA "Marriage" and "Spouse" and the FMLA	121
III.	SON OR DAUGHTER			122
	A.	RELATIONSHIP REQUIREMENT		122
		1.	***In Loco Parentis***	***122***
		2.	Current "Son or Daughter"	123
	B.	AGE REQUIREMENT		124
		1.	Children Under 18 Years of Age	124
		2.	Children 18 Years of Age or Older	124
			a. Incapable of Self-Care	124
			b. Physical or Mental Disability	125
			(1) Definitions	125
			(2) Pre-Existing Disability Not Required	126
			c. Case Law Interpreting FMLA "Disability"	127
IV.	PARENT			129
	A.	CURRENT OR PAST RELATIONSHIP		129
	B.	MULTIPLE PARENTS		129
V.	INDIVIDUALS WHO ARE NOT COVERED BY THE FMLA			130
	A.	PARENTS-IN-LAW		130
	B.	BROTHERS AND SISTERS		130
	C.	GRANDPARENTS		130
	D.	OTHER FAMILY MEMBERS		130
	E.	*IN LOCO PARENTIS* EXCEPTION		131
VI.	CONFIRMATION OF FAMILIAL RELATIONSHIP			132

CHAPTER 7: COVERED CONDITIONS 133

- I. OVERVIEW 133
- II. BIRTH, ADOPTION, OR FOSTER CARE PLACEMENT 134
  - A. BIRTH 134
    1. Title I, the CAA, and the PEOAA: BIRTH 134
       - a. General Rule 134
       - b. Prenatal Care 135
       - c. Leave Conclusion 136
       - d. Documentation 136
       - e. Availability of Childcare 137
       - f. Physical Ability to Return to Work Earlier 137
       - g. Multiple Births 137
       - h. Intermittent/Reduced Leave Schedule 137
       - i. Paid Leave Substitution 138
    2. Title II 138
       - a. General Rule 138
       - b. Prenatal Care 139
       - c. Leave Conclusion 139
       - d. Documentation 140
       - e. Availability of Childcare 140
       - f. Physical Ability to Return to Work Earlier 140
       - g. Multiple Births 140
       - h. Intermittent/Reduced Leave Schedule 141
       - i. Paid Leave Substitution 141
  - B. ADOPTION 141
    1. Title I, the CAA, and the PEOAA: ADOPTION 141
       - a. General Rule 141
       - b. Source of Adoption 144
       - c. Pre-Adoption Leave 144
       - d. Adoption of Older Children 145
       - e. Stepchildren 145
       - f. Leave Conclusion 145
       - g. Intermittent/Reduced Leave Schedule 146
    2. Title II: Adoption 146
       - a. General Rule 146
       - b. Source Not Relevant 147
       - c. Pre-Adoption Leave 147
       - d. Adoption of Older Children 147
       - e. Stepchildren 147
       - f. Leave Conclusion 148
       - g. Intermittent/Reduced Leave Schedule 148
  - C. FOSTER CARE PLACEMENT 148
    1. Title I, the CAA, and the PEOAA: Foster Care Placement 148
       - a. General Rule 148
       - b. Source Relevant 149
       - c. Pre-Placement Leave 149
       - d. Foster Care Placement of Older Children 150
       - e. Pay, Minimum Duration, and Multiple Foster Care Placements 150
       - f. Leave Conclusion 150
       - g. Intermittent/Reduced Leave Schedule 151
    2. Title II: Foster Care Placement 152
       - a. General Rule 152
       - b. Source Relevant 153
       - c. Pre-Placement Leave 153
       - d. Foster Care Placement of Older Children 153

- e. Pay, Minimum Duration, and Multiple Foster Care Placements 153
- f. Leave Conclusion 153
- g. Intermittent/Reduced Leave Schedule 154

III. SERIOUS HEALTH CONDITIONS 154
- A. INTRODUCTION 154
- B. WHOSE SERIOUS HEALTH CONDITION? 155
  1. Title I, the CAA, and the PEOAA 155
     - a. Needed to Care For a Covered Family Member 156
       - (1) General Rule 156
       - (2) "To Care For" the Living 159
       - (3) Availability of Other Caregivers 159
       - (4) Psychological and Physical Care of Covered Family Members 160
         - (a) Level of Care 160
         - (b) Traveling Care 161
         - (c) Evidence of Care 162
     - b. Unable to Work Due to Employee's Own Serious Health Condition 163
       - (1) General Rule 163
       - (2) Unable to Perform One or More 164
       - (3) Essential Job Functions 165
       - (4) Reasonable Accommodation; Light Duty 166
       - (5) Position Held 167
       - (6) Documentation of Essential Functions 168
       - (7) Receipt of Medical Treatment 168
  2. Title II 169
     - a. Needed to Care for a Covered Family Member 169
       - (1) General Rule 169
       - (2) Availability of Other Caregivers 169
       - (3) Participation in Care; Travel 170
       - (4) Medical Documentation 170
     - b. Unable to Work Due to Employee's Own Serious Health Condition 170
       - (1) General Rule 170
       - (2) Unable to Perform 171
       - (3) Essential Job Functions 171
       - (4) Reasonable Accommodation; Light Duty 171
       - (5) Position Held 172
       - (6) Documentation of Essential Functions 172
       - (7) Receipt of Medical Treatment 173
- C. TYPES OF SERIOUS HEALTH CONDITIONS 173
  1. Inpatient Care 174
     - a. Title I, the CAA, and the PEOAA 174
       - (1) General Rule 174
       - (2) Incapacity 174
       - (3) Treatment 175
       - (4) Illness, Injury, Impairment, or Physical or Mental Condition 176
       - (5) Hospital, Hospice, or Residential Medical Care Facility 176
       - (6) Overnight Stay 176
       - (7) Inpatient 177
       - (8) Subsequent Incapacity or Treatment 177
       - (9) Examples of Inpatient Care 177
     - b. Title II 178
       - (1) General Rule 178
       - (2) Key Terms 178
       - (3) Examples 178
  2. Continuing Treatment by a Health Care Provider 179
     - a. Introduction 179

		b.	Legislative History	179
		c.	Incapacity of More Than Three Consecutive Calendar Days Plus Health Care Provider Treatments	180
			(1) Title I, the CAA, and the PEOAA	180
			(a) General Rule	180
			(b) Regulatory Development	181
			(c) Incapacity	181
			(d) More Than Three Consecutive Calendar Days	185
			(e) Treatment	188
			(f) Subsequent Treatment/Incapacity	189
			(g) Health Care Provider Treatments	189
			(2) Title II	193
			(a) General Rule	193
			(b) Regulatory Development	193
			(c) Incapacity	194
			(d) More Than Three Consecutive Calendar Days	194
			(e) Treatment	194
			(f) Subsequent Treatment/Incapacity	195
			(g) Health Care Provider Treatments	195
			(h) Amount of FMLA Leave Available	197
		d.	Pregnancy, or Prenatal Care	197
			(1) Title I, the CAA, and the PEOAA	197
			(a) General Rule	197
			(b) Any Period	198
			(c) Incapacity	198
			(d) Treatment	199
			(e) Prenatal Care	200
			(f) Comparison With Birth and Care of a Newborn	201
			(g) Pregnancy as a Disability	201
			(2) Title II	203
			(a) General Rule	203
			(b) Any Period	203
			(c) Incapacity	203
			(d) Treatment	203
			(e) Pregnancy, Childbirth and Prenatal Care	204
			(f) Comparison to Birth as a Covered Condition	204
		e.	Chronic Serious Health Conditions	205
			(1) Title I, the CAA, and the PEOAA	205
			(a) General Rule	205
			(b) Regulatory Development	205
			(c) Any Period	206
			(d) Incapacity and Treatment for Incapacity	206
			(e) Chronic Serious Health Condition Defined	207
			(f) Periodic Visits	207
			(g) Nurse, Physician's Assistant; Direct Supervision	208
			(h) Episodic Incapacity	209
			(i) Extended period of time	210
			(2) Title II	210
			(a) General Rule	210
			(b) Regulatory Development	210
			(c) Any Period	211
			(d) Incapacity and Treatment for Incapacity	211
			(e) Chronic Serious Health Condition Defined	212
			(f) Periodic Visits	212

			(g)	Healthcare Provider; Direct Supervision	212
			(h)	Extended Period of Time; Recurring Episodes	213
			(i)	Episodic Incapacity	213
		f.	Permanent or Long Term Incapacity		213
			(1) Title I, the CAA, and the PEOAA		213
				(a) General Rule	213
				(b) Regulatory Development	214
				(c) Permanent or Long-Term	214
				(d) A Period	214
				(e) Incapacity	214
				(f) Treatment	215
				(g) Condition for Which Treatment May Not be Effective	216
			(2) Title II		216
				(a) General Rule	216
				(b) Regulatory Development	216
				(c) Permanent or Long-Term	217
				(d) A Period	217
				(e) Incapacity	217
				(f) Treatment	217
				(g) Condition for Which Treatment May Not be Effective	218
		g.	Multiple Treatments		218
			(1) Title I, the CAA, and the PEOAA		218
				(a) General Rule	218
				(b) Regulatory Development	219
				(c) Any Period	219
				(d) Absence to Receive	219
				(e) Multiple Treatments and Recovery	220
				(f) Health Care Provider	220
				(g) Restorative Surgery After an Accident or Other Injury	221
				(h) Condition That Would Likely Result in Incapacity of More Than Three Days	221
			(2) Title II		222
				(a) General Rule	222
				(b) Regulatory Development	222
				(c) Any Period	223
				(d) Absence	223
				(e) Multiple Treatments	223
				(f) Health Care Provider	224
				(g) Restorative Surgery After an Accident or Other Injury	224
				(h) Condition That Would Likely Result in Incapacity of More Than Three Days	224
	3.	Special Issues Concerning Serious Health Conditions			225
		a.	Minor Illnesses		225
			(1) General Rule		225
			(2) Complications		226
			(3) Minor Illnesses That Meet Definition of a Serious Health Condition: The DOL Flip-Flop		227
		b.	Cosmetic Treatments		230
			(1) General Rule		230
			(2) Cosmetic Treatments		230
			(3) Inpatient Care or Complications		230
		c.	Substance Abuse		230
			(1) Title I, the CAA, and the PEOAA		230
				(a) General Rule	230
				(b) Substance Abuse	231
				(c) Treatment v. Use	232

			(d)	Healthcare Provider	233
			(e)	Discipline for Employee's Own Substance Abuse	233
			(f)	Substance Abuse of a Covered Family Member	234
			(g)	Drug Testing on Return to Work	235
			(h)	Questions and Answers	235
		(2)	Title II		236
			(a)	General Rule	236
			(b)	Substance Abuse	236
			(c)	Treatment	237
			(d)	Health Care Provider	237
			(e)	Substance Abuse of Covered Family Members	237

- d. Mental Illness ... 237
  - (1) Title I, the CAA, and the PEOAA ... 237
- e. Combination Conditions ... 238
  - (1) Title II ... 239
- f. Routine Physical, Eye, and Dental Examinations; Regimen of Continuing Treatment ... 239
- g. Miscellaneous Illnesses and Procedures ... 240
- h. Retroactive Coverage of Absences ... 240

D. HEALTH CARE PROVIDER DEFINED ... 241
  1. Title I, the CAA, and the PEOAA ... 241
     a. Those Covered ... 241
     b. Scope of Practice ... 242
     c. Doctors and Osteopaths ... 243
     d. Podiatrists, Dentists, Clinical Psychologists, and Chiropractors ... 243
     e. Nurse Practitioners, Nurse Midwives and Clinical Social Workers ... 244
     f. Christian Science Practitioners ... 244
     g. Health Care Providers Recognized by Employer or Group Health Benefits Plan Manager ... 245
     h. Health Care Providers From Other Countries ... 246
  2. Title II ... 247
     a. Those Covered ... 247
     b. Doctors ... 247
     c. Physicians Serving on Active Duty in the Uniformed Services ... 247
     d. FEHBP Recognized Health Care Providers ... 247
     e. Licensed Health Care Providers Under Federal or State Law ... 248
     f. Health Care Providers Practicing in Another Country ... 248
     g. Christian Science Practitioners ... 248
     h. Native American Traditional Healers ... 248

E. SERIOUS HEALTH CONDITION BY PARTICULAR MEDICAL CONDITION ... 249
F. EVIDENCE OF SERIOUS HEALTH CONDITION ... 249
G. MEDICAL NECESSITY OF INTERMITTENT/REDUCED LEAVE SCHEDULE ... 250
  1. Title I, the CAA, and the PEOAA ... 251
     a. General Rule ... 251
     b. Medical Necessity ... 251
     c. Other Requirements and Uses of Leave ... 252
  2. Title II ... 253
     a. General Rule ... 253
     b. Medically Necessary ... 253
     c. Other Requirements ... 253

IV. AGENCIES WITH MIXED FMLA RESPONSIBILITIES ... 254

CHAPTER 8: NOTICE REQUIREMENTS ... 255

I. OVERVIEW ... 255
II. NOTICE OBLIGATIONS OF EMPLOYERS ... 255
  A. INTRODUCTION ... 255
  B. FMLA POSTER ... 255

		1.	Title I	255
		2.	CAA	258
		3.	PEOAA	258
		4.	Title II	258
	C.	HANDBOOKS, MANUALS, AND OTHER WRITTEN GUIDANCE		259
		1.	Title I and the CAA	259
		2.	PEOAA	261
		3.	Title II	261
	D.	ABSENCE OF AGENCY WRITTEN GUIDANCE		262
		1.	Title I and the CAA	262
		2.	PEOAA	263
		3.	Title II	263
	E.	SPECIFIC NOTICE OF EMPLOYEE RIGHTS AND OBLIGATIONS		263
		1.	Title I and the CAA	263
			a. General Rule	263
			b. Required Contents of Notice	264
			c. Language of Notice	265
			d. Manner, Timing, and Frequency of Providing Written Specific Notice	266
			e. Changed Circumstances and Specific Notice	266
			f. Specific Notice of Medical Certification or Fitness for Duty Requirement	267
			g. Employer's Duty to Answer Employee Questions	269
			h. Failure of Employing Agency to Provide Specific Notice	269
		2.	PEOAA	271
		3.	Title II	271
	F.	NOTICE OF EMPLOYEE ELIGIBILITY		272
		1.	Title I and the CAA	272
			a. General Rule	272
			b. When an Employing Agency Must Confirm Eligibility	272
			(1) Notice Where Employee is Not Yet Eligible	272
			(2) Notice When Eligibility is Met	273
			(3) Eligibility Notice Before Leave Commences	273
			(4) Deemed Eligible: Employer Notice On or After Leave Commences	273
		2.	PEOAA	273
		3.	Title II	274
	G.	DESIGNATION OF LEAVE AS FMLA		274
		1.	Title I and the CAA	274
			a. General Rule	274
			b. When Notice Must Be Given	276
			(1) General Rule	276
			(2) Before FMLA Leave Commences	277
			(3) After FMLA Leave Commences, But Before the Employee Returns to Work	277
			(4) Retroactive Designation After Employee Returns to Work	278
			c. Manner of Notice	279
			d. Failure of Agency to Provide Notice	280
			e. Note to the DOL and the Office of Compliance	284
		2.	PEOAA	284
		3.	Title II	284
	H.	MISCELLANEOUS AGENCY NOTICE REQUIREMENTS		285
		1.	Method of Calculation of 12-Month FMLA Leave Year	285
			a. Title I, the CAA, and the PEOAA	285
			b. Title II	286
		2.	Benefits	286
			a. Title I, the CAA, and the PEOAA	286
			(1) Employee Handbooks	287
			(2) Specific Written Notice	287
			(3) Changes to Group Health Plans	287

				(4)	Failure to Make Premium Payments	287
			b.	Title II		288
		3.	Notice Obligations Toward Key Employees			288
			a.	Title I, the CAA, and the PEOAA		288
			b.	Title II		289
		4.	Joint Employment			289
			a.	Title I, the CAA, and the PEOAA		289
			b.	Title II		289
		5.	Record Keeping			289
			a.	Title I		290
			b.	The CAA and the PEOAA		290
			c.	Title II		290
	I.	AGENCIES WITH MIXED FMLA RESPONSIBILITIES				290
III.	EMPLOYEE NOTICE OBLIGATIONS					290
	A.	INTRODUCTION				290
	B.	NEED FOR FMLA LEAVE				291
		1.	When Notice Must Be Given			291
			a.	Title I, the CAA, and the PEOAA		291
				(1)	Foreseeable Need for Leave	291
				(2)	Need for FMLA Leave is Not Foreseeable	294
				(3)	Effect of Employer Policies on Timing of Notice	296
			b.	Title II		298
				(1)	Foreseeable Need for Leave	298
				(2)	Need for Leave Is Not Foreseeable	299
				(3)	Effect of Employer Policies on Timing of Notice	300
		2.	Manner of Providing Notice			301
			a.	Title I, the CAA, and the PEOAA		301
				(1)	Who May Provide Notice	301
				(2)	Foreseeable Need for Leave	302
				(3)	Need for Leave Is Not Foreseeable	303
				(4)	Effect of Employer Policies	305
			b.	Title II		306
				(1)	General Rule	306
				(2)	Who May Provide Notice	306
				(3)	Notice and the Foreseeability of the Need for Leave	307
				(4)	Effect of Employer Policies on Notice	307
		3.	Adequacy of Notice			307
			a.	Title I, the CAA, and the PEOAA		307
				(1)	General Rule	308
				(2)	Employee Must Request Leave	315
				(3)	Notice Need Not Expressly Invoke FMLA	317
				(4)	Vague Requests for FMLA Leave	317
				(5)	Knowledge of Prior FMLA–Covered Condition	319
				(6)	Notice Based on Types of Covered Conditions	321
				(7)	False or Misleading Information	322
				(8)	Inability to Provide Notice	323
				(9)	Providing FMLA Leave/Medical Forms	323
				(10)	Miscellaneous Notice Issues	324
			b.	Title II		324
		4.	Failure of an Employee to Provide Notice as Required			325
			a.	Title I, the CAA, and the PEOAA		325
			b.	Title II		327
		5.	Additional Employee Notice Requirements			328
			a.	Changed Circumstances		328
				(1)	Title I, the CAA, and the PEOAA	328

			(2)	Title II	329
		b.	Paid Leave Substitution		329
			(1)	Title I, the CAA, and the PEOAA	329
			(2)	Title II	329
		c.	Consult with Employer on Medical Treatment Schedule		329
			(1)	Title I, the CAA, and the PEOAA	329
			(2)	Title II	330
		d.	Retroactive Notice of Need for Leave		330
			(1)	Title I, the CAA, and the PEOAA	330
			(2)	Title II	331
		e.	Maintenance of Benefits		331
			(1)	Title I, the CAA, and the PEOAA	331
			(2)	Title II	331
		f.	Return to Work from FMLA Leave		331
			(1)	Title I, the CAA, and the PEOAA	332
			(2)	Title II	332
		g.	Key Employee		332
			(1)	Title I, the CAA, and the PEOAA	332
			(2)	Title II	332
		h.	School Employees		333
			(1)	Title I and the CAA	333
			(2)	The PEOAA	333
			(3)	Title II	333
		i.	Joint Employees		333
IV.	MIXED AGENCY RESPONSIBILITIES AND EMPLOYEE NOTICE				334

CHAPTER 9: DOCUMENTATION REQUIREMENTS 335

I.	OVERVIEW				335
II.	MEDICAL CERTIFICATION				335
	A.	GENERAL RULE			335
		1.	Title I, the CAA, and the PEOAA		336
		2.	Title II		338
	B.	HEALTH CARE PROVIDER DEFINED			339
		1.	Title I, the CAA, and the PEOAA		339
		2.	Title II		340
	C.	EMPLOYER NOTICE OF MEDICAL CERTIFICATION REQUIREMENT			341
		1.	Title I, the CAA, and the PEOAA		341
			a.	Handbooks and Other Written Guidance	342
			b.	No Written Guidance Explaining Employee Benefits and Leave Requirements	342
			c.	Notice of Specific FMLA Expectations and Obligations	343
			d.	Failure of Employer to Provide Required Notice	344
		2.	Title II		346
	D.	TIME LIMITS FOR REQUEST OF MEDICAL CERTIFICATION			347
		1.	Title I, the CAA, and the PEOAA		347
		2.	Title II		348
	E.	TIME LIMITS FOR PROVIDING CERTIFICATION TO THE EMPLOYER			348
		1.	Title I, the CAA, and the PEOAA		348
			a.	General Rule	348
			b.	Foreseeable Need for FMLA Leave	349
			c.	Need for Leave is Not Foreseeable	349
			d.	Preliminary Designation of FMLA Leave	352
			e.	Paid Leave Substitution and Certification	352
			f.	More Generous Employer Requirements	353
			g.	Less Generous FMLA Leave Polices	353
		2.	Title II		353

			a.	General Rule	353
			b.	More Generous Employer Policies	354
			c.	Preliminary Designation	354
			d.	Paid Leave Substitution	354
	F.	CONTENTS OF MEDICAL CERTIFICATION			354
		1.	Title I, the CAA, and the PEOAA		354
			a.	Basic Certification Information	355
			b.	Employee's Own Serious Health Condition	357
			c.	Serious Health Condition of a Covered Family Member	357
			d.	Effect of Paid Leave Substitution	357
			e.	More Beneficial Employee Leave Requirements	358
		2.	Title II		358
			a.	Basic Certification Information	359
			b.	Serious Health Condition of a Covered Family Member	360
			c.	Employee's Own Serious Health Condition	360
			d.	Effect of Paid Leave Substitution	360
			e.	More Beneficial Employee Leave Requirements	360
		3.	Comparisons		361
			a.	Title I and Title II	361
			b.	Title II and the DOL WH 380	362
	G.	COMMON CERTIFICATION PROBLEMS			363
		1.	Medical Facts		363
		2.	Estimates of Probable Number of Absences and Leave Duration		363
		3.	Basis for Employee's Care for Covered Family Member		364
		4.	Essential Functions		364
	H.	INCOMPLETE CERTIFICATIONS			364
		1.	Title I, the CAA, and the PEOAA		364
		2.	Title II		369
	I.	COMPLETE CERTIFICATIONS; CLARIFICATION			369
		1.	Title I, the CAA, and the PEOAA		370
		2.	Title II		371
	J.	SECOND/THIRD OPINION PROCESS			372
		1.	Title I, the CAA, and the PEOAA		372
			a.	General Rule: Second Opinions	372
			b.	Christian Science Practitioners and Second/Third Opinions	375
			c.	Who is Initially Entitled to Second/Third Opinions?	375
			d.	Payment for Second Opinion	375
			e.	Preliminary Designation	376
			f.	Third Opinion	376
			g.	Selection of Third Opinion Health Care Provider	378
			h.	Payment for Third Opinions; Employee Expenses	378
			i.	Copies	379
			j.	Exclusivity of Second/Third Health Care Opinion Provider Process	379
			k.	Refusal to Cooperate in Second/Third Opinion Process	381
		2.	Title II		381
			a.	General Rule: Second Opinions	381
			b.	Christian Science Practitioners	382
			c.	Payment for Second Opinion	383
			d.	Entitlement to Second and Third Opinions	383
			e.	Time Frame for Receipt of Certification	383
			f.	Preliminary Designation of FMLA Leave	383
			g.	Third Opinion	384
			h.	Selection of Third Opinion Provider	384
			i.	Payment for Third Opinions	385
			j.	Copies	385

			k.	Exclusivity of Challenge Process	385

- K. EMPLOYEE FAILURE TO SATISFY CERTIFICATION REQUIREMENTS 385
  1. Title I, the CAA, and the PEOAA 385
  2. Title II 387
- III. RECERTIFICATION OF MEDICAL CONDITIONS 388
  - A. TITLE I, THE CAA, AND THE PEOAA 388
    1. Overview 388
    2. Circumstances Permitting Recertification 390
       - a. Pregnancy, Chronic, or Permanent/Long-Term Conditions 390
         - (1) General Rule 390
         - (2) Exceptions 391
       - b. Minimum Duration of Incapacity Exceeds 30 Days 391
         - (1) General Rule 391
         - (2) Exceptions 392
       - c. Intermittent or Reduced Leave Schedule 393
         - (1) General Rule 393
         - (2) Exceptions 394
       - d. All Other Circumstances 394
         - (1) General Rule 394
         - (2) Exceptions 394
    3. Time for Employee Submission of Recertification 395
    4. Selection of Medical Recertification Opinion Provider 395
    5. Form of Medical Recertification 395
    6. Notice of Requirement of Recertification 396
    7. Second and Third Opinions Prohibited on Recertifications 396
    8. Payment for Recertifications 396
    9. Failure to Provide Recertification 397
    10. Employer Violation of Recertification Rules 397
  - B. TITLE II 398
    1. Overview 398
    2. Circumstances Permitting Recertifications 398
       - a. Pregnancy, Chronic Conditions, or Long-Term Conditions 398
         - (1) General Rule 398
         - (2) Exceptions 398
       - b. All Other Circumstances 398
         - (1) Exceptions 399
    3. Time for Submission 399
    4. Selection of Medical Recertification Opinion Provider 399
    5. Form of Subsequent Medical Recertification 400
    6. Notice of Medical Recertification Requirement 400
    7. Second and Third Opinions 400
    8. Payment for Medical Recertifications 400
    9. Failure to Provide Medical Recertification 401
- IV. PERIODIC STATUS REPORTS DURING LEAVE 401
- V. CERTIFICATION OF AN EMPLOYEE'S FITNESS TO RETURN TO DUTY FROM LEAVE 401
- VI. DOCUMENTATION ESTABLISHING FAMILIAL RELATIONSHIPS 401
  - A. TITLE I, THE CAA, AND THE PEOAA 401
  - B. TITLE II 402
- VII. HIPAA AND FMLA CERTIFICATION 403
- VIII. DOCUMENTATION REQUIREMENTS IN AGENCIES WITH MIXED FMLA RESPONSIBILITIES 404

CHAPTER 10: LEAVE AMOUNT AND SCHEDULING 407

- I. OVERVIEW 407
- II. TWELVE-MONTH FMLA LEAVE YEAR 407
  - A. TITLE II: SETTING THE 12-MONTH LEAVE YEAR 407
    1. General Rule 407

		2.	Exception for Birth, Adoption, Foster Care Placement	408

- B. TITLE I, THE CAA AND THE PEOAA: ELECTION OF 12–MONTH YEAR 408
    1. Four Options 408
        a. Calendar and Other Fixed Leave Years 409
        b. Measuring Forward Leave Year 409
        c. Rolling Back Method 410
    2. Uniform Application 410
    3. Changing the 12–Month Period 411
    4. Notice of the Option Selected 411
        a. Initial Selection 411
        b. Notice at the Time FMLA Leave is Requested 413
        c. Change of Methodology 414
        d. Means and Adequacy of Notice 414
    5. Failure to Select One of the Four Options 415
    6. Expiration of 12–Month Period for Birth or Placement for Adoption or Foster Care 416
    7. More Generous Employer Policies 417
- C. THE 12–MONTH PERIOD IN AGENCIES WITH MIXED FMLA RESPONSIBILITIES 417

III. CALCULATING 12 WORKWEEKS OF FMLA LEAVE 417
- A. BASIC CALCULATION OF THE AMOUNT OF LEAVE AVAILABLE 418
    1. Title II 418
        a. Key Terms 418
        b. Amount of FMLA Leave Varies from Employee to Employee 419
        c. No Set Limit on Amount of FMLA Leave 420
        d. Deficiencies in Definition 420
            (1) Absence of Temporal Period 420
            (2) Point in Time of Calculation 420
    2. Title I, the CAA, and the PEOAA 421
        a. General Rule 421
        b. Deficiencies with the General Rule 422
            (1) Work Schedule 422
            (2) Absence of Temporal Period 423
            (3) No Fixed Starting Point for Calculation 423
- B. EMPLOYEES WORKING PART–TIME OR VARIABLE HOURS 425
    1. Title II 426
    2. Title I, the CAA, and the PEOAA 426
- C. EMPLOYEES WHOSE WORK SCHEDULES VARY FROM WEEK TO WEEK 426
    1. Title II 426
    2. Title I, the CAA, and the PEOAA 427
- D. FLSA–EXEMPT EMPLOYEES 428
- E. HOLIDAYS 429
    1. Title II 429
    2. Title I, the CAA, and the PEOAA 429
- F. TEMPORARY CESSATION OF BUSINESS ACTIVITIES 430
    1. Title II 430
    2. Title I, the CAA, and the PEOAA 430
- G. OVERTIME HOURS 430
    1. Title II 430
    2. Title I, the CAA, and the PEOAA 430
- H. CHANGES TO AN EMPLOYEE'S WORK SCHEDULE 431
    1. Title II 431
    2. Title I, the CAA, and the PEOAA 431
- I. HUSBANDS AND WIVES WHO WORK FOR THE SAME AGENCY: THE MARRIAGE PENALTY 433
    1. Title II 433
    2. Title I, the CAA, and the PEOAA 433
        a. General Rule 433
        b. Same Covered Employer 434

			c.	Valid Marriage	434
			d.	Siblings	435
			e.	Application of the Marriage Penalty	435
	J.	MORE GENEROUS EMPLOYER LEAVE BENEFITS			437
		1.	Title II		437
		2.	Title I, the CAA, and the PEOAA		438
	K.	EFFECT OF MIXED FMLA RESPONSIBILITIES			439
IV.	LEAVE SCHEDULING				439
	A.	BLOCK LEAVE			440
		1.	Smallest Increment of Leave		440
			a.	Title I, the CAA, and the PEOAA	440
			b.	Title II	440
			c.	Examples	441
		2.	Birth or Placement for Adoption or Foster Care		441
		3.	Serious Health Condition		441
	B.	INTERMITTENT AND REDUCED SCHEDULE LEAVE			441
		1.	Definitions		441
			a.	Intermittent Leave	441
				(1) Title II	441
				(2) Title I, the CAA, and the PEOAA	442
			b.	Reduced Leave Schedule	443
				(1) Title II	443
				(2) Title I, the CAA, and the PEOAA	443
			c.	Intermittent and Reduced Schedule Leave Treated the Same	444
		2.	Birth, Adoption, Foster Care Placement		444
		3.	Serious Health Conditions		445
			a.	Medically Necessary	446
				(1) Title II	447
				(2) Title I, the CAA, and the PEOAA	447
			b.	Employee Reasonable Efforts to Schedule Leave to Avoid Workplace Disruptions	449
				(1) Title II	449
				(2) Title I, the CAA, and the PEOAA	450
			c.	Notice	453
				(1) Title II	453
				(2) Title I, the CAA, and the PEOAA	453
			d.	Medical Certification	455
				(1) Title II	455
				(2) Title I, the CAA, and the PEOAA	455
			e.	When Intermittent or a Reduced Leave Schedule May Be Used for a Serious Health Condition	456
				(1) Title II	456
				(2) Title I, the CAA, and the PEOAA	456
		4.	Transfer to an Equivalent Alternative Position		457
			a.	Title II	458
			b.	Title I, the CAA, and the PEOAA	460
		5.	Leave Increments		462
			a.	Title II	463
			b.	Title I, the CAA, and the PEOAA	463
		6.	FLSA–Exempt Employees		464
			a.	Exemption from the FLSA Salary Basis Test	464
			b.	Fluctuating Workweek Method of Payment	465
			c.	Title II and FLSA Exemption	465
		7.	Determining the Amount of Intermittent or Reduced Leave Schedule Leave Taken		466
			a.	Title II	466
			b.	Title I, the CAA, and the PEOAA	466

		8.	Special School Rules	467
			a. Twenty Percent or More FMLA Leave	468
			b. Leave Taken Near the End of an Academic Term	468
			c. What Leave Counts Toward the 12-Week FMLA Leave Entitlement	469
			d. Return to Work	469
		9.	Impact of Intermittent or Reduced Leave Schedule on Other FMLA Requirements	470
			a. Eligibility	470
			b. Notice	470
			c. Medical Certification	470
			d. Return to Work	471
	C.	LEAVE SCHEDULING IN AGENCIES WITH MIXED FMLA RESPONSIBILITIES		471

CHAPTER 11: SUBSTITUTION OF PAID LEAVE ... 473

I.	OVERVIEW				473
II.	PAID LEAVE				473
	A.	SUBSTITUTION OF ACCRUED PAID LEAVE			473
		1.	Election of Paid Leave		473
			a. Order of Election		475
			b. Choice Among Paid Leave Balances		476
			c. Who Makes the Election?		477
			d. Notice of Election		478
			e. Timing of Election		479
				(1) Title II	479
				(2) Title I, the CAA, and the PEOAA	479
			f. Employee Election of Paid Leave, Not FMLA Leave		480
		2.	Substitution		481
		3.	Accrued Paid Leave		482
			a. Title II		482
				(1) Annual Leave	483
				(2) Sick Leave	483
				(a) Employee's Own Illness	484
				(b) To Care For An Ill Covered Family Member	485
				(c) Paid Sick Leave When No One is Sick: Adoptions and Funeral Arrangements	487
				(d) Paid Leave for Organ or Bone-Marrow Donation	488
				(e) Amount of Paid Sick Leave Available	488
				(3) Advanced Annual or Sick Leave	489
				(4) Leave Transfer	490
				(a) Voluntary Leave Transfer Program	490
				(b) Voluntary Leave Transfer Bank	491
			b. Title I, the CAA, and the PEOAA		491
				(1) Family Leave	492
				(2) Medical or Sick Leave	492
				(3) Vacation or Personal Leave	493
III.	COMPENSATORY OVERTIME, WORKERS' COMPENSATION, TEMPORARY DISABILITY LEAVE, FLEXIBLE WORK SCHEDULE CREDIT HOURS, AND UNEMPLOYMENT COMPENSATION				493
	A.	COMPENSATORY OVERTIME			493
		1.	Title II		493
		2.	Title I		495
		3.	The CAA		495
		4.	PEOAA		496
	B.	WORKERS' COMPENSATION			496
	C.	TEMPORARY DISABILITY LEAVE			497
	D.	FLEXIBLE WORK SCHEDULE AND ACCRUED CREDIT HOURS			498
	E.	UNEMPLOYMENT COMPENSATION			499
IV.	EFFECT OF PAID LEAVE ON FMLA PROCEDURAL REQUIREMENTS				500
	A.	TITLE I, THE CAA AND THE PEOAA			500

		1.	Paid Leave Substitution	500
			a. Less Stringent Paid Leave Procedural Requirements	500
			b. More Stringent Paid Leave Procedural Requirements	501
	B.	TITLE II		502
V.	MIXED FMLA RESPONSIBILITIES AND PAID LEAVE SUBSTITUTION			502

CHAPTER 12: MAINTENANCE OF BENEFITS 505

- I. OVERVIEW 505
- II. RETENTION OF ACCRUED EMPLOYMENT BENEFITS 505
  - A. GENERAL RULE 505
    1. Title II 505
    2. Title I 505
    3. CAA 505
    4. PEOAA 506
  - B. DEFINITIONS 506
    1. Employment Benefits 506
       a. Title I, the CAA, and the PEOAA 506
       b. Title II 506
    2. Accrued Benefits 507
    3. Leave Commencement 507
  - C. ACCRUAL OF SENIORITY AND EMPLOYMENT BENEFITS DURING FMLA LEAVE 509
    1. Title I, the CAA, and the PEOAA 509
    2. Title II 510
  - D. GREATER BENEFITS PROTECTION 510
- III. MAINTENANCE OF HEALTH BENEFITS 511
  - A. HEALTH PLANS DEFINED 511
    1. Group Health Plan 511
    2. FEHBP 511
    3. Multi-Employer Health Plan 512
  - B. GENERAL RULE REQUIRING MAINTENANCE OF HEALTH BENEFITS DURING FMLA LEAVE 512
    1. Title I 512
       a. Group Health Plans 512
       b. Multi-Employer Health Plans 513
       c. Fraud Exception 513
    2. Title II 513
    3. CAA 514
  - C. SCOPE OF HEALTH BENEFITS THAT MUST BE PROVIDED DURING LEAVE 514
    1. General Rule 514
       a. Title I, the CAA, and the PEOAA 514
          (1) Group Health Plans 514
          (2) Multi-Employer Health Plans 514
       b. Title II 514
    2. Effect of Changes in Health Plan Coverage 515
       a. Title I, the CAA, and the PEOAA 515
          (1) Group Health Plans 515
          (2) Multi-Employer Health Plans 515
       b. Title II 516
    3. Employer Notice to Employee of Health Plan Changes 516
       a. Title I, the CAA, and the PEOAA 516
          (1) Group Health Plans 516
          (2) Multi-Employer Health Plans 517
       b. Title II 517
  - D. ELECTION TO FOREGO GROUP HEALTH COVERAGE 517
    1. Title I, the CAA, and the PEOAA 517
       a. Group Health Plans 517
       b. Multi-Employer Health Plans 517

		2.	Title II	518
	E.	CESSATION OF HEALTH BENEFITS DURING FMLA LEAVE		518
		1.	Title I, the CAA, and the PEOAA	518
			a. Group Health Plans	518
			(1) Termination of Employee During FMLA Leave	518
			(2) Notice of Employee Intent Not to Return From FMLA Leave	519
			b. Multi-Employer Health Plans	519
		2.	Title II	519
	F.	CESSATION OF HEALTH BENEFITS OF A KEY EMPLOYEE		520
IV.	EMPLOYEE PAYMENT OF HEALTH BENEFIT PREMIUMS WHILE ON FMLA LEAVE			520
	A.	TITLE II		520
		1.	Agency Notice to Employee of Options	520
		2.	Employee Premium Payment Options	521
			a. Current Payment Method	521
			b. Payment Plan Method	521
		3.	Termination of Health Benefits	521
	B.	TITLE I, THE CAA AND THE PEOAA		521
		1.	Group Health Plan Benefits	521
			a. Changes to Premium Rates	521
			b. Substitution of Paid Leave	522
			c. Unpaid FMLA Leave	522
			d. Employer Notice	522
			e. Limitation on Requirements	523
			f. OWCP	523
		2.	Multi-Employer Health Benefit Plans	523
		3.	FEHBP	524
		4.	Other Health Benefit Plans	524
V.	CONSEQUENCES OF EMPLOYEE FAILURE TO MAKE TIMELY HEALTH PLAN PREMIUM PAYMENTS			524
	A.	TERMINATION OF EMPLOYER MAINTENANCE OBLIGATIONS		524
		1.	Title II	524
		2.	Title I, the CAA, and the PEOAA	525
			a. Group Health Plan	525
			(1) Employer Notice of Health Benefits Termination	525
			b. Retroactive Termination	525
		3.	Multi-Employer Health Plans	526
		4.	FEHBP	526
	B.	OTHER CONSEQUENCES		526
		1.	Non-Group Health Plans	526
		2.	Continuation of Other FMLA Obligations	526
		3.	Employer Payment of Employee Premiums	526
		4.	Re-Qualification of Group Health Plan Benefits	527
VI.	EMPLOYER RECOVERY OF COSTS OF MAINTAINING HEALTH CARE COVERAGE			527
	A.	TITLE II		528
	B.	TITLE I, THE CAA, AND THE PEOAA		528
		1.	Group Health Plans	528
			a. General Rule	528
			(1) Recovery of Payments Made on Behalf of Employee	528
			(2) Recovery of Employing Agency's Share of Premiums	528
			b. Amount of Recovery	528
			c. Exceptions	528
			(1) Serious Health Conditions	529
			(2) Other Circumstances	529
			d. When Has An Employee "Returned to Work"?	529
			e. Medical Certification of a Serious Health Condition	530
			f. Substituted Paid Leave	531
			g. OWCP and Other Forms of Compensation	531

		2.	Multi-Employer Health Plans	531
		3.	FEHBP	531
		4.	Self-Insured Health Plans	531
		5.	Other Non-Group Health Benefits	531
		6.	Method of Collection	532
		7.	Effect of Debt on Existing Obligations	532
VII.	MIXED RESPONSIBILITIES OF EMPLOYING AGENCIES TO MAINTAIN EMPLOYMENT BENEFITS DURING FMLA LEAVE			532

CHAPTER 13: RETURN TO WORK FROM LEAVE 535

- I. OVERVIEW 535
- II. EMPLOYEES' RIGHTS ON RETURN TO WORK FROM FMLA LEAVE 535
  - A. EMPLOYEE RETURN TO WORK FROM LEAVE 536
    1. Current Eligible Employee 536
       - a. Title I, the CAA, and the PEOAA 536
       - b. Title II 537
    2. Leave 537
       - a. Title I, the CAA, and the PEOAA 537
       - b. Title II 538
    3. Return 538
       - a. Title I, the CAA, and the PEOAA 538
         - (1) Defined 538
         - (2) What Constitutes an Employee's Return: Physical Presence or Notice? 540
         - (3) Employee's Obligation to Return 540
         - (4) Employer Delay of an Employee's Return to Work 541
       - b. Title II 543
  - B. SAME OR EQUIVALENT POSITION 543
    1. Same Position 543
       - a. Title I, the CAA, and the PEOAA 543
       - b. Title II 545
    2. Equivalent Position 546
       - a. Equivalency Generally 546
         - (1) Title I, the CAA, and the PEOAA 546
         - (2) Title II 547
       - b. Equivalent Pay, Including Bonuses 547
         - (1) Title I, the CAA, and the PEOAA 547
         - (2) Title II 549
       - c. Equivalent Benefits 549
         - (1) Title I, the CAA, and the PEOAA 549
         - (2) Title II 551
       - d. Equivalent Terms and Conditions of Employment 551
         - (1) Title I, the CAA, and the PEOAA 551
         - (2) Title II 552
       - e. ***De Minimis,*** Intangible, or Immeasurable Aspects of Job 553
         - (1) Title I, the CAA, and the PEOAA 553
         - (2) Title II 556
       - f. Lapsed Qualification for the Job; Licenses 556
         - (1) Title I, the CAA, and the PEOAA 556
         - (2) Title II 557
    3. Voluntary Move to Alternative Position; Light Duty 558
    4. Reasonable Accommodation 558
    5. Greater Employer Benefits 559
  - C. JOINT EMPLOYERS 559
- III. EMPLOYEES' PERFECTION OF RIGHT TO RETURN TO WORK 560
  - A. EMPLOYEE IS UNABLE TO PERFORM ALL ESSENTIAL JOB FUNCTIONS 561
    1. Title I, the CAA, and the PEOAA 561

		2.	Title II 565
	B.	FITNESS-FOR-DUTY MEDICAL CERTIFICATIONS 565	
		1.	Title I, the CAA, and the PEOAA 565
			a. General Rule.. 565
			b. Contents and Form of Certification 567
			c. Clarification of Certification 568
			d. Effect of Terms of Collective Bargaining Agreement 569
			e. DOT Requirements 571
			f. Interaction With ADA-Approved Medical Examinations 572
			g. Cost of Certification 574
			h. Employer Notice Requirements 574
			(1) Employee Handbook 574
			(2) Individual Notice 574
			(3) Specific Notice 575
			i. Failure to Provide Certification 575
			j. Second or Third Opinions 576
			k. Unfit to Return to Duty 576
			l. Fitness-for-Duty Exams After Employee Has Returned to Work 577
		2.	Title II 577
			a. General Rule.. 577
			b. Scope of Certification 578
			c. Clarification 578
			d. Collective Bargaining Agreements 579
			e. Cost 579
			f. Notice Requirements 579
			(1) Employee Handbook 580
			(2) Individual Notice 580
			(3) Specific Notice 580
			g. Failure to Provide Documentation 580
			h. Second and Third Opinions 581
			i. Unfit for Duty 581
			j. Medical Examination After the Employee Returns to Work 582
	C.	EXHAUSTION OF FMLA LEAVE 582	
		1.	Title I, the CAA, and the PEOAA 582
		2.	Title II 583
	D.	EMPLOYEE NOTICE OBLIGATIONS OF RETURN TO WORK 584	
		1.	Periodic Status Reports 584
			a. Title I, the CAA, and the PEOAA 584
			b. Title II 585
		2.	Notice of Intent to Return to Work Earlier than Anticipated 586
			a. Title I, the CAA, and the PEOAA 586
			b. Title II 587
		3.	Unequivocal Notice of Intent Not to Return to Work 587
			a. Title I, the CAA, and the PEOAA 587
			b. Title II 588
		4.	Form of Employee Notice 588
IV.	LIMITATIONS ON AN EMPLOYER'S OBLIGATION TO REINSTATE AN EMPLOYEE 588		
	A.	OVERVIEW 588	
	B.	GENERAL RULE 588	
	C.	EXAMPLES OF THE GENERAL RULE 589	
		1.	Discipline; Termination 589
		2.	Layoff/RIF 591
		3.	Shift Eliminated/Overtime Reduced 593
		4.	Employee Hired for Specific Term or Project 593
		5.	Workers' Compensation 594

		6.	Probationary Periods	594
		7.	Outside Employment	594
		8.	Fraud	595
V.	KEY EMPLOYEES			596
	A.	OVERVIEW		596
	B.	KEY EMPLOYEE DEFINED		596
		1.	Salaried Employee	596
		2.	Employer; Employing Office	597
			a. Title I	597
			b. CAA	597
		3.	Calculation of Highest Paid Ten Percent	598
		4.	When the "Key Employee" Determination is Made	598
	C.	SUBSTANTIAL AND GRIEVOUS ECONOMIC INJURY		598
		1.	General Rule	598
		2.	When the Determination is Made	599
		3.	Standard of Determination	599
		4.	Comparison with ADA "Undue Hardship Standard"	600
	D.	EMPLOYER NOTICE TO KEY EMPLOYEE		601
		1.	Initial Notice of Key Employee Qualification and Consequences	601
			a. General Rule	601
			b. When and How Initial Notice Must be Provided	601
			c. Consequences of Failure to Provide Initial Notice	602
		2.	Notice of Substantial and Grievous Economic Injury	603
			a. General Rule	603
			b. Timing and Manner of Notice	603
			c. Consequences of Employer Failure to Provide Notice	603
		3.	Notice of Denial of Restoration	604
			a. General Rule	604
			b. Timing and Method of Notice	604
			c. Consequences of Failure to Provide Notice	604
	E.	RIGHTS OF KEY EMPLOYEES		604
		1.	Return to Work	604
		2.	Maintenance of Health Benefits	605
	F.	BURDEN OF PROOF		605
VI.	SPECIAL RULES GOVERNING CERTAIN SCHOOLS			605
	A.	OVERVIEW		605
	B.	APPLICATION		605
		1.	Covered Schools	605
		2.	Covered School Employees	605
			a. Instructional Employees	605
			b. All Employees	606
	C.	RETURN TO WORK RIGHTS		606
		1.	Intermittent Leave or Leave on a Reduced Leave Schedule	606
		2.	Leave Near the End of Academic Term	607
			a. Leave Taken More Than Five Weeks From End of Academic Term	607
			b. Leave Taken Less Than Five Weeks From End of Academic Term	607
			c. Leave Begins Less Than Three Weeks Before End of Academic Term	607
			d. Leave Calculation and Return to Work	607
	D.	EQUIVALENT POSITION		608
		1.	General Rule	608
		2.	Notice to Employees	608
VII.	AGENCIES WITH MIXED FMLA RESPONSIBILITIES			609

CHAPTER 14: RECORD-KEEPING REQUIREMENTS 611

I.	OVERVIEW	611
II.	TITLE I RECORD-KEEPING REQUIREMENTS	611

	A.	GENERAL OBLIGATIONS	611
	B.	REQUIRED RECORDS	611
		1. Nonmedical Records	611
		a. Employing Agencies Without Eligible Employees	611
		b. Employing Agencies With Eligible Employees	612
		2. Medical Records	613
		3. Joint Employment	613
		4. FLSA–Exempt Employees and FMLA Record Keeping	614
		5. Employee Transfers and FMLA Record Keeping	614
	C.	FORM OF RECORDS AND RETENTION PERIOD	615
		1. Form of Records	615
		2. Location of Records	616
		3. Retention Period	616
III.	TITLE II RECORD-KEEPING REQUIREMENTS	616
	A.	GENERAL OBLIGATIONS	616
	B.	REQUIRED RECORDS	616
		1. Nonmedical Records	616
		2. Medical Records	617
		3. Joint Employment	618
		4. FLSA–Exempt Employees and FMLA Record Keeping	618
		5. Employee Transfers and FMLA Record Keeping	618
	C.	FORM OF RECORDS AND RECORDS RETENTION	618
IV.	FMLA RECORD-KEEPING UNDER THE CAA AND THE PEOAA	618
V.	DISCLOSURE OF FMLA RECORDS	618
	A.	GOVERNMENT INSPECTION OF FMLA RECORDS	619
		1. DOL	619
		2. OPM	619
		3. Other Government Agencies	619
	B.	OTHER DISCLOSURES	619
		1. Privacy Act	619
		a. Need to Know Within the Agency	621
		b. Routine Uses	621
		c. Congress	621
		d. Court Order	621
		2. Freedom of Information Act (FOIA)	621
		3. Disclosure to Supervisors	622
		4. Constitutional Right to Privacy	622
VI.	MIXED AGENCY FMLA RESPONSIBILITIES AND RECORD KEEPING	623

CHAPTER 15: PROHIBITED ACTS, ENFORCEMENT, AND REMEDIES 625

I.	OVERVIEW	625
II.	PROHIBITED ACTS	625
	A.	TITLE I, THE CAA AND THE PEOAA	625
		1. Introduction	625
		2. General Rule	625
		3. Interference	626
		a. Adequate Employee Notice Requirement	629
		b. Employer Notice Failures as Interference	630
		c. Employer Actions That "Chill" Employee FMLA Rights	631
		d. Manipulation	632
		e. Denial of Restoration and Interference	633
		4. Discrimination	634
		a. Use of FMLA Leave	634
		(1) General Rule	634
		(2) Benefits	636
		(3) Negative Factor	637

			(4)	"No Fault" Attendance Policies and Attendance-Based Bonus Plans 638

- b. Opposition to Unlawful Practices 639
  - (1) General Rule 639
  - (2) Legislative and Regulatory History 640
  - (3) Opposition 640
  - (4) Reasonable Belief of Unlawful Conduct 641
  - (5) Scope of Prohibition 641
  - (6) Enforcement 641
- c. Participation 642
  - (1) General Rule 642
  - (2) Legislative and Regulatory History 643
  - (3) Persons vs. Employing Offices 643
  - (4) Discriminating 643
  - (5) Individuals vs. Covered Employees 643
  - (6) Charges and Proceedings 644
  - (7) Information 644
  - (8) Testimony 645
  - (9) Enforcement 645

5. Waiver 645
   a. General Rule 645
   b. Regulatory Development 645
   c. Waiver or Rights 646
   d. Employee 648
   e. Collective Bargaining Representative 649
   f. Light Duty Exception 649
   g. Early Retirement 650
6. Posting Violations 650
   a. General Rule 650
   b. Violations 651

B. TITLE II 651
   1. Introduction 651
   2. General Rule 651
   3. Employee 651
   4. Intimidate, Threaten, or Coerce 652
   5. Intent 652

III. ENFORCEMENT 652
   A. TITLE I 653
      1. Introduction 653
      2. Employee Complaints to the U.S. Department of Labor 653
         a. Introduction 653
         b. Filing Administrative Complaints with DOL 653
            (1) General Rule 653
            (2) Effect of Filing DOL Complaint on Right to Bring Private Civil Action 653
            (3) Process for Filing Administrative Complaints 654
               (a) Who May File 654
               (b) Where to File 654
               (c) Form of Complaint 654
               (d) Time Frame for Filing Administrative Complaint 654
               (e) Post-Complaint Process 655
         c. Investigative Authority 655
            (1) General Authority 655
            (2) Enter and Inspect 656
            (3) Question Employees 656
            (4) Authority to Review FMLA Records 656
            (5) Subpoena Power and Employer Refusals to Cooperate with DOL Investigation 657

			(6)	Completion of the Investigation	657

- (6) Completion of the Investigation 657
- d. DOL Supervised Settlements 658
- e. Civil Actions Brought by the DOL 658
- f. Posting Violations 659
  - (1) General Rule 659
  - (2) Employer Appeals of Civil Penalty 659
- 3. Private Right of Action 660
  - a. General Rule 660
  - b. Who May Initiate a Private Action? 660
  - c. When Must a Private Civil Action Be Initiated? 661
    - (1) General Rule 661
    - (2) Extending the Time Period for Filing a Civil Action 664
  - d. Who Is the Defendant in a Private Civil Action for Violation of the FMLA? 665
  - e. Courts of Competent Jurisdiction 670
  - f. Limitations on Bringing a Private Civil Action 670
- 4. Other Enforcement Avenues 671
  - a. Grievance Process 671
  - b. MSPB 671
  - c. EEOC 672
  - d. Unfair Labor Practice Charges 673
- B. TITLE II 674
  - 1. General Rule 674
  - 2. Federal Court 675
  - 3. MSPB 676
  - 4. Unfair Labor Practice Charges 676
- C. CAA 677
  - 1. Introduction 677
    - a. Office of Compliance 677
    - b. FMLA Complaints 678
  - 2. Complaint Procedure 678
    - a. Exclusive Procedure 678
    - b. Counseling 678
      - (1) General Rule 678
      - (2) Key Terms 679
      - (3) Availability of Grievance Process 679
      - (4) Confidentiality 680
    - c. Mediation 680
      - (1) General Rule 680
      - (2) Mediation Process 680
      - (3) Mediation Period 680
      - (4) Confidentiality 681
    - d. Election of Proceedings 681
  - 3. Election of a Section 405 Administrative Complaint 681
    - a. General Rule 681
    - b. Hearing Officer 681
    - c. Dismissal 682
    - d. Discovery 682
    - e. Subpoenas 682
    - f. Conduct of Hearing 683
    - g. Settlement 683
    - h. Decision 683
    - i. Appeal to Office Board of Directors 683
    - j. Judicial Review of Office Board of Director Decisions 684
  - 4. Private Right to File a Civil Action 685
    - a. General Rule 685

- b. Time to File Suit ... 686
- c. Right to Jury Trial ... 686
- 5. Miscellaneous CAA Enforcement Provisions ... 686
  - a. Judicial Review of CAA Regulations ... 686
  - b. Other Judicial Review Prohibited; Wavier of Sovereign Immunity ... 687
  - c. Expedited Supreme Court Review of Certain Appeals ... 687
  - d. Settlements ... 688
  - e. Confidentiality ... 688
  - f. Savings Provisions ... 688
- D. PEOAA ... 689
  - 1. Introduction ... 689
  - 2. Complaint Procedure ... 689
    - a. Overview ... 689
    - b. Exclusive Procedure ... 689
  - 3. Counseling and Mediation ... 690
    - a. General Rule ... 690
    - b. Exhaustion Requirement ... 690
  - 4. Election of Proceedings ... 690
  - 5. Election of Administrative Appeal ... 690
    - a. General Rule ... 690
    - b. Exceptions ... 690
    - c. MSPB Consideration of Appeal ... 690
    - d. Judicial Review ... 691
  - 6. Election to File Civil Action ... 691
    - a. General Rule ... 691
    - b. Venue ... 691
    - c. Jury Trials ... 691
    - d. Effect of Failure to Issue Regulations ... 691
  - 7. Miscellaneous PEOAA Enforcement Provisions ... 692
    - a. Judicial Review of PEOAA Regulations ... 692
    - b. Expedited Supreme Court Review of Certain Appeals ... 692
- IV. REMEDIES ... 692
  - A. TITLE I ... 692
    - 1. Introduction ... 692
    - 2. Damages ... 692
      - a. Lost Wages, Salary, Employment Benefits, and Other Compensation ... 692
        - (1) General Rule ... 692
        - (2) Key Terms ... 693
          - (a) Eligible Employee ... 693
          - (b) Wages and Salary ... 693
          - (c) Employment Benefits ... 694
          - (d) Other Compensation ... 694
          - (e) Forms of Wages, Salary, Employment Benefits, and Other Compensation ... 694
            - i) Back Pay ... 694
            - ii) Overtime ... 696
            - iii) Front Pay ... 696
            - iv) Commissions ... 697
            - v) Bonuses ... 697
            - vi) Profit Sharing ... 697
            - vii) Benefits ... 697
        - (3) Punitive and Emotional Distress Damages ... 698
      - b. Actual Monetary Losses Other Than Lost Wages, Salary, Employment Benefits, and Other Compensation ... 698
        - (1) General Rule ... 698
        - (2) Key Terms ... 699

				(a)	Wages or Salary	699
				(b)	Actual Monetary Loss	699
				(c)	Direct Result	699
			(3)		The Problem of Requiring Actual Monetary Losses	700
		c.	Prejudgment Interest			700
		d.	Liquidated Damages			701
			(1)		General Rule	701
			(2)		Defense of Good Faith and Reasonable Grounds	702
		e.	Miscellaneous Rules on Title I Damages			705
			(1)		Special Rules Concerning Employees of Local Educational Agencies	705
			(2)		Damages Recovered by the Secretary of Labor	706
	3.	Equitable Relief				706
		a.	Private Civil Action			706
		b.	Secretary of Labor			707
	4.	Attorney's Fees and Costs				707
		a.	General Rule			707
		b.	Attorneys' Fees			707
		c.	Costs			711
			(1)		General Rule	711
			(2)		Recoverable Costs	712
	5.	MSPB Remedies				713

B. TITLE II ... 715
1. Introduction ... 715
2. General Rule ... 715
3. MSPB ... 716

C. CAA ... 718
1. Introduction ... 718
2. General Rule ... 718
3. Civil Penalties and Punitive Damages ... 718
4. Payments ... 718

D. PEOAA ... 718
1. Introduction ... 718
2. General Rule ... 719
3. Attorney's Fees, Expert Witness Fees, Costs, and Interest ... 719
4. Civil Penalties and Punitive Damages ... 720
5. Payments ... 720

V. MISCELLANEOUS LITIGATION MATTERS ... 720
A. INTRODUCTION ... 720
B. FMLA CLAIM OF DECEASED ... 720
C. REMOVAL ... 720
D. ADMINISTRATIVE EXHAUSTION ... 720
E. ARBITRATION OF FMLA CLAIMS ... 721
F. ISSUE PRECLUSION OR COLLATERAL ESTOPPEL ... 721
G. PLEADINGS ... 723
H. SERVICE OF PROCESS ... 724
I. JURY TRIAL ... 724
J. BURDEN OF PROOF ... 725
1. General Rule ... 725
2. Interference/Entitlement Theory ... 726
3. Retaliation/Discrimination Theory ... 729
   a. Adverse Employment Action ... 733
   b. Causal Connection ... 734
   c. Employer's Legitimate Non-Discriminatory Reason ... 737
   d. Honest Belief Defense ... 739
   e. Pretext ... 740

K. APPLICABLE REGULATIONS ... 741

	L.	NOMINAL DAMAGES	742
	M.	MITIGATION	742
	N.	AFTER ACQUIRED EVIDENCE	743

CHAPTER 16: INTERACTION OF THE FMLA WITH OTHER FEDERAL LAWS, EMPLOYER PRACTICES, AND COLLECTIVE BARGAINING AGREEMENTS 745

- I. OVERVIEW 745
- II. OTHER FEDERAL LAWS 745
  - A. INTRODUCTION 745
  - B. GENERAL RULE 745
    1. Title I 745
    2. Title II 746
    3. CAA 747
    4. PEOAA 747
  - C. REHABILITATION ACT/ADA 747
    1. Basics of Rehabilitation Act/ADA 748
    2. Key Requirements 750
       - a. Covered Employers 750
       - b. Eligibility for Leave 750
       - c. Basic Entitlement 751
       - d. Covered Conditions 751
       - e. Covered Individuals 754
       - f. Undue Hardship 754
       - g. Notice 755
       - h. Medical Documentation 756
       - i. How Leave May Be Taken 758
       - j. Paid Leave Substitution 759
       - k. Maintenance of Benefits During Leave 759
       - l. Return to Work 760
       - m. Confidentiality of Medical Records 762
  - D. PREGNANCY DISCRIMINATION ACT OF 1978 763
    1. Overview of PDA 763
    2. Comparison of PDA and FMLA 766
       - a. Eligibility 766
       - b. Excessive Absences 767
       - c. Intermittent/Reduced Leave Schedule 767
       - d. Return to Work 767
  - E. TITLE VII OF THE CIVIL RIGHTS ACT OF 1964 768
  - F. WORKERS' COMPENSATION 768
    1. FECA 769
    2. FECA/FMLA Interaction 769
       - a. Paid Leave Substitution 769
       - b. Maintenance of Health Benefits During FMLA Leave 769
       - c. Medical Information 770
       - d. Light Duty 770
  - G. FAMILY FRIENDLY LEAVE ACT 770
  - H. UNIFORMED SERVICES EMPLOYMENT AND REEMPLOYMENT RIGHTS ACT 770
  - I. DEPARTMENT OF TRANSPORTATION REQUIREMENTS 772
    1. Title I 772
- III. EMPLOYER PRACTICES AND COLLECTIVE BARGAINING AGREEMENTS 772
  - A. INTRODUCTION 772
  - B. TITLE I AND THE CAA 772
    1. General Rule 772
    2. Greater Family or Medical Leave Benefits 773
    3. Less Protection 775
    4. Modifications to Employee Family or Medical Leave Benefits 776

		5.	Existing Family and Medical Leave Act Policies	776
		6.	Collective Bargaining Agreements	777
			a. Effective Date of the FMLA	777
			b. Intermittent Leave and Employee Transfers	777
			c. Multi–Employer Health Plans	777
			d. Reinstatement of Laid–Off Employees	777
			e. Waiver of Rights	778
			f. Medical Certification	778
			g. Special School Rules	778
	C.	PEOAA		778
	D.	TITLE II		778
		1.	General Rule	778
		2.	Less Generous	779
		3.	Amendments	779
		4.	Existing Family and Medical Leave Act Policies	779
		5.	Collective Bargaining Agreements	779

APPENDIX 781

WH Publication 1420: Your Rights Under the Family and Meidcal Leave Act of 1993 783
WH-381: Employer Response to Employee Request for Family or Medical Leave 785
DOL USERRA-FMLA July 22, 2002 Memorandum 787
DOL USERRA-FMLA Questions and Answers 791

INDEX 793

CHAPTER 1
OVERVIEW

I. INTRODUCTION

Four different variants of the Family and Medical Leave Act of 1993 (FMLA or the Act) apply to the federal sector. Several variants of the FMLA may concurrently apply to the same federal employer. While the core entitlements of the four FMLA variants are substantially similar, there are many significant differences. As a result, compliance with one variant of the FMLA will not ensure compliance with others. Following the letter of the law of one variant may guarantee a violation of the Act when applied to employees covered by one of the other FMLA variants. To avoid that fate, federal employers must initially determine what variant of the FMLA applies in any given situation.

An added incentive to avoid violation of the FMLA is the very real prospect of personal liability. That means that an aggrieved federal employee may personally sue a manager or supervisor who incorrectly applies the requirements of this variant of the FMLA. The suit against the individual supervisor is in addition to the employee's ability to sue the employer for the same violation. Add the availability of double damages for willful violations (interpreted to include ignorance of the requirements of the FMLA), plus attorney fees and costs, and FMLA litigation can quickly become an operational and financial drain on individual supervisors and federal employers.

This book focuses on the FMLA as it applies to federal sector employment. It is intended to shed light and clarity on this often confusing and misunderstood entitlement. This book is not intended to champion the cause of either employees or employers. If it champions anything, it is for more guidance from the various regulatory bodies enforcing the requirements of the FMLA. Clarity is needed so that employees and federal employers are on notice of what is required of them in order to secure and abide by the protections and requirements of the Act.

This chapter has two purposes: first, it is designed to introduce the reader to federal sector FMLA leave. Second, it teaches the reader to ask the right questions in order to efficiently and accurately analyze fundamental FMLA issues. By knowing what questions to ask and in what order to ask them, the reader can quickly and methodically work their way through most FMLA problems.

A. FMLA BASICS

The foundation for understanding FMLA law begins with an introduction to the four FMLA variants applicable to the federal sector. This is followed by a short review of core entitlements common to all federal sector variants. The introduction concludes with a review of the purpose behind the FMLA.

1. The Four FMLA Variants

The four variants of the FMLA applicable to the federal sector are:

- *Title I of the FMLA*, 29 USC 2601 et. seq. This variant applies to every executive branch federal agency, but not every federal employee within the federal government. It applies to all non-civil service federal employees. Title I also applies to private sector employers.

- *Title II of the FMLA*, 5 USC 6301 et. seq., applies to all civil service employees.

- *Title V of the FMLA and the Congressional Accountability Act of 1995 (CAA)*, 2 USC 1301 et. seq. Before its repeal, Title V of the FMLA covered certain employees of the U.S. House of Representatives and the U.S. Senate. In 1996, Title V was replaced and the FMLA applied to certain employees of the House and Senate through the CAA, 2 USC 1312. The CAA regulations implementing the CAA most closely resemble those implementing Title I. There are, however, many significant differences.

- *Presidential and Executive Office Accountability Act of 1996 (PEOAA)*, 3 USC 401 et. seq. The PEOAA applies the FMLA to employees of the Executive Office of the President. 3 USC 412. It closely resembles the CAA, and follows Title I of the FMLA, with some differences.

There are regulations implementing the FMLA for three of the four federal sector variants. The Department of Labor issued final regulations implementing Title I effective April 6, 1995. *See* 29 CFR Part 825. The Office of Personnel Management (OPM) issued final regulations implementing Title II of the Act effective June 6, 1997. *See* 5 CFR Part 630. Regulations implementing the FMLA for purposes of the CAA were adopted on April 23, 1996. *See* S. Res. 242, Cong. Rec. S3959–S3997 (April 23, 1996). There are no regulations implementing the FMLA for purposes of the PEOAA. However, the PEOAA provides that §§ 101–105, and 107 of Title I of the FMLA apply to the PEOAA.

2. Core Entitlements

All federal sector variants of the FMLA allow eligible federal employees to take up to 12 weeks of job-protected, unpaid leave, each leave year under four general conditions. Those covered conditions are:

- The birth of a child and to care for the newborn child;
- The placement of a child with the employee for adoption or foster care;
- The care of a son, daughter, spouse, or parent with a serious health condition; or
- The employee's own serious health condition that renders the employee unable to perform essential job functions.

Where FMLA leave is due to a serious health condition, the law permits federal employers to require employees to timely provide adequate medical certification substantiating the need for FMLA leave. An employer who questions the validity of the employee's medical certification may require medical certification from a second and, ultimately, a third health care opinion provider. Federal employers may require an employee to update the original medical certification by means of medical recertifications.

During an employee's absence for FMLA leave, the law requires federal employers to maintain an employee's health benefits as if the employee remained at work. Under certain circumstances, an employee is also allowed to substitute accrued and available paid leave for unpaid FMLA leave.

The FMLA entitles employees to return to their same or equivalent position when FMLA leave is no longer needed or when the employees have exhausted their 12 weeks of FMLA leave. A federal employer may, under certain conditions, require an employee to submit a fitness for duty medical certification before accepting an employee's return to work from FMLA leave.

All federal sector variants of the FMLA protect an employee from adverse consequences for exercising rights under the Act. A federal employer may not discipline an employee for taking leave protected by the FMLA. Nor may an employer use the fact that an employee has taken FMLA leave to deny a promotion, bonus, transfer, job selection, or for any other negative reason impacting terms and conditions of employment. On the other hand, the FMLA will not protect an employee from discipline or other adverse actions for conduct or performance issues that are independent of the employee's use of FMLA leave.

The core entitlements identified above (which are discussed in more detail throughout this book), are common to all four federal sector variants of the FMLA. How these core entitlements are interpreted and applied may vary greatly among the four versions.

3. The Purpose of the FMLA

The FMLA is the product of more than eight years of legislative wrangling before being signed into law on February 5, 1993, the first piece of legislation of the newly elected Democratic President William Jefferson Clinton.

The FMLA was intended to balance the demands of the workplace with the needs of working families. Congress felt that re-balancing was needed in order to address the confluence of developing demographic trends with the competitive demands of the market economy, both of which were competing for limited employee time.

These demographic trends included the dramatic increase in the number of single parent and dual-income families, coupled with the new parental care demands of a growing aging population. The competitive demands imposed on American employers by the global market economy, as well as, the desire of employees to achieve a high standard of living, has resulted in American employees working the most hours and taking the least amount of vacation time, than employees in any other industrialized nation. Congress found that the time pressures placed on employees by the collision of the demographic trends and the increased time expected at work often placed employees in the position of having to choose between their job and family care responsibilities. These pressures, Congress found, were destabilizing the American family.

The FMLA was intended to promote the stability and economic security of families, and to promote national interests in preserving family integrity. The Act accomplished this by allowing employees to take up to 12 workweeks of job protected unpaid leave each year for their own illness or the illness of a covered family member. Employees are also entitled to this job protected leave to bond with a healthy newborn child, or a child placed with the employee through adoption or foster care. During leave, covered employers must maintain employee health benefits as if the employee remained at work. On the conclusion of leave, an employee must be returned to the same or an equivalent position. Finally, FMLA leave may not be used against an employee for any employment purpose, including discipline or as an impediment to advancement.

II. DETERMINING WHETHER LEAVE QUALIFIES FOR THE PROTECTIONS OF THE FMLA

The following is a series of questions that I generally ask to determine whether a request for leave falls within the protections of the FMLA. Determining whether leave is covered by the FMLA forms the foundation of any analysis.

I have ordered the questions in a way that efficiently raises and disposes of the most salient issues to determine whether leave qualifies for protection under the FMLA. Of course, I make no claim that this is the best or most logical ordering of issues, only that it has worked for me. Moreover, the questions should be used as an issue spotting guide only. The details of the FMLA, and there are many, must be considered and addressed with each request for FMLA leave.

A. WHAT VARIANT OF THE FMLA APPLIES?

The federal government is covered by the FMLA. This does not mean, however, that the same form of the FMLA applies throughout the federal sector. There are four variants of the FMLA that apply to different parts of the federal government. Titles I and II of the FMLA apply throughout the federal sector. Knowing which employees each variant covers is usually the more salient question. The two remaining forms of the FMLA, the CAA and the PEOAA, apply to a very limited number of federal employees who work for specific federal employers.

The four variants of the FMLA that apply to the federal sector, while similar, contain many significant differences. Because of these significant differences, it is crucial for an employer to determine which version of the FMLA applies in any given situation. This determination is complicated by the fact that, in many instances, more than one variant of the FMLA may apply to the same federal employer. Moreover, compliance with one variant of the FMLA does not ensure compliance with others. It is crucial to determine which variant(s) of the FMLA applies to the particular federal employer in question. [Federal employer coverage by the FMLA is addressed in more detail in Chapter 3, "FMLA Coverage of the Federal Government."]

B. IS THE INDIVIDUAL REQUESTING LEAVE AN "EMPLOYEE" WITHIN THE MEANING OF THE FMLA?

Having identified which FMLA variant applies to the leave request at issue, the next question is whether the individual requesting leave is an "employee" within the meaning of the FMLA. If not, you no longer have an FMLA issue. You may have an issue under another federal statute or pursuant to agency policy, such as the requirements of a collective bargaining agreement, but you do not have an FMLA issue. In order to be entitled to FMLA leave the individual requesting leave must be an "employee" within the meaning of the FMLA variant at issue.

The four federal sector FMLA laws define a covered "employee" differently. Proper identification of the individual as a covered employee under one of the four federal sector FMLA laws will have a major impact on the entitlements and obligations placed on the employee and the federal employer. Make a mistake here and a federal employer can find itself in deep trouble as it follows the requirements of one federal FMLA law, when it should be following completely different requirements of another federal FMLA law.

1. Title I

While Title I applies to the U.S. government as a whole, it only applies to certain non-civil service federal employees. Federal employees covered by Title I include employees of the United States Postal Service and the Postal Rate Commission. 29 CFR 825.109(b)(1)–(2). Title I also applies to certain employees serving under an intermittent or temporary appointment of one year or less, certain part–time employees, and employees of other federal executive agencies who are not covered by Title II. Finally, Title I applies to employees of the legislative or judicial branch, but only if they are employed in a unit which has employees in the competitive service, such as employees of the Government Printing Office and the US Tax Court.

2. Title II

Under Title II a covered "employee" is an appointed civil service employee, as defined in 5 USC 2105. This covers many, but by no means all, federal employees. There are many categories of employees that fall outside the definition of civil service employee, for purposes of Title II. Just because an individual is not an employee for purposes of Title II does not mean that they are not a covered employee for purposes of one of the other three federal sector variants of the FMLA. In fact, the regulations implementing Title I include a catch–all provision that says that Title I covers any federal employee who is not covered by Title II.

3. CAA

An "employee," for FMLA purposes of this variant, includes any employee of the House, the Senate, the Capitol Guide Service, the Capital Police, the Congressional Budget Office, the Office of the Architect of the Capitol, the Office of the Attending Physician, the Office of Compliance, and the Office of Technology. 2 USC 1301(3).

4. PEOAA

For purposes of the PEOAA, a covered employee is an employee of the Executive Office of the President. The Executive Office of the President includes the White House Office, the Executive Residence at the White House, the Office of the Vice President, the Office of Policy Development, the Council of Economic Advisors, the National Security Council, the Office of Management and Budget, and the Office of National Drug Control Policy. 3 USC 431(d)(2).

C. IS THE EMPLOYEE ELIGIBLE FOR FMLA LEAVE?

Having determined in the preceding questions what FMLA law applies to the federal employer and the employee, the next question is whether the employee meets the eligibility requirements for entitlement to FMLA leave. While all federal employees are covered by one of the four FMLA federal sector variants, not all covered employees are entitled to take FMLA leave. The FMLA adds another hurdle in order for an employee to take FMLA leave. To be entitled, an employee must meet certain eligibility requirements, which, while similar in some respects, are not identical among the variants.

If the employee does not meet the applicable eligibility requirements for FMLA coverage, the request for leave at issue is not covered by the FMLA. The request, of course, may be covered by another law, agency policy, or the requirements of a collective bargaining agreement, but it is not FMLA leave.

1. Title I

To be eligible for FMLA leave an employee must meet three requirements: (1) the individual must have been employed for at least 12 months before leave commencement; (2) the individual must have worked 1250 hours in the 12 months immediately preceding leave commencement; and (3) the individual must be employed in a worksite that has at least 50 employees within 75 miles at the time the employee requests leave.

2. Title II

Title II has only one eligibility requirement: the employee must have worked 12 months as a civil service employee before leave commencement. Moreover, this 12-month requirement is significantly narrower than the comparable requirement under Title I. As a result, any time spent working for the federal government outside the definition of a Title II civil service employee does not count towards employee eligibility for purposes of Title II. By comparison, time spent as an employee of the federal government in any capacity would count towards Title I eligibility.

3. The CAA, and the PEOAA

The CAA and PEOAA each impose two FMLA eligibility requirements: (1) employment for at least 12 months; and (2) that the employee has worked at least 1250 hours. These are essentially the same standards as those for Title I, with one important difference. Title I counts all time worked as an employee of the federal government towards the eligibility requirements. The CAA and PEOAA, on the other hand, only count time worked as an employee of a CAA or PEOAA-covered employer. For example, only the time spent as a Congressional employee would count towards the 12 months and 1250 hours CAA FMLA eligibility requirements. The employee's prior employment elsewhere in the federal government would not count for FMLA eligibility purposes.

D. DOES THE LEAVE INVOLVE A COVERED INDIVIDUAL?

The next question is whether the leave involves a *covered individual* within the meaning of the law. FMLA leave is available to an eligible employee to address the needs of certain individuals only. On this issue, all four federal sector variants of the FMLA are united. FMLA leave is available to an eligible employee because the following individuals have a covered condition:

- The eligible employee;
- A spouse;
- A son or daughter; or
- A parent.

If an eligible employee needs leave for an individual other than those identified above, the leave is likely not covered by the FMLA. Generally speaking, an employee is not entitled to FMLA leave to provide care for a brother, sister, grandparent, aunt, uncle, or anyone else, even if the individual is otherwise dependent on the employee.

The definitions of family members covered by the FMLA are, in some cases, broader than one might initially think. In other cases, the definitions are narrower. For example, a spouse includes common law marriages where such marriages are recognized. At this time, the term "spouse" does not include a partner in a same-sex marriage or civil union, even where such relationships are legally recognized. A parent, son, or daughter includes biological, legal, and extra-legal relationships. Extra-legal relationships, called *in loco parentis,* can involve individuals such as brothers, sisters, uncles, aunts, and grandparents who would not normally be covered by the FMLA.

These terms are defined in the respective FMLA statutes, and are further refined in the applicable regulations implementing each of the four FMLA federal sector variants. For the leave to be covered by the FMLA, it must involve a covered individual. An employer is prohibited from counting leave for an individual who is not covered by the FMLA from the employee's 12-week FMLA leave entitlement. Of course, an employer could provide leave to care for someone other than an FMLA-covered individual as a matter of policy.

E. DOES THE LEAVE INVOLVE A COVERED CONDITION?

In order for an eligible federal sector employee to be entitled to FMLA leave for a covered individual, the need for leave must be for a covered condition. There are four primary FMLA covered conditions:

- The birth of a son or daughter of the employee and in order to care for such son or daughter.

- The placement of a son or daughter with the employee for adoption or foster care.

- To care for the spouse, or a son or daughter, or parent, of the employee, if such spouse, son, daughter, or parent has a serious health condition.

- A serious health condition that renders the employee unable to perform the functions of his or her position.

The above statutory definitions are expanded upon, to different degrees, in their implementing regulations. These regulations, moreover, are at times identical and at other times significantly different. Because of these differences, great care must be exercised by federal employers, employees, unions, or other organizations representing the interests of employees, in determining whether the leave at issue is for a covered condition.

While broad, what constitutes a serious health condition, within the meaning of the FMLA is not limitless (although it often seems that way). Some illnesses will not ring the "serious health condition" bell, and are not protected by the FMLA. Generally, the FMLA does not specify illnesses that will always be considered a covered serious health condition. Employers should not assume that any particular condition is or is not covered by the FMLA. Rather, to determine whether an illness qualifies for FMLA protection, employers must compare the facts of each situation against the regulatory definition of a serious health condition for the applicable version of the FMLA.

F. DID THE EMPLOYER AND THE EMPLOYEE MEET THEIR NOTICE REQUIREMENTS?

The FMLA requires employees to notify their employer of the need for FMLA leave. The Act also requires employers to notify employees of FMLA entitlements and obligations. The notice requirements placed on employers and employees vary greatly depending on which variant of the FMLA applies.

1. Title I, the CAA, and the PEOAA

The notice requirements governing employees and employers are very specific. This is particularly true regarding the notice obligations imposed on employers. Generally, employers must post a notice of FMLA rights, include information on FMLA entitlements and benefits in employee handbooks or other written leave or benefit information, and periodically provide specific notice of FMLA rights and obligations at the time the employee requests FMLA leave. In some instances, the contents of such notices are dictated by regulation. An employer's failure to provide the employee with timely and adequate notice of FMLA rights and obligations may result in FMLA protections being extended to individuals who otherwise do not meet the eligibility requirements. As a consequence, the employer may also be unable to raise an employee's failure to meet FMLA requirements, where the requirement is contained in the notice the agency failed to provide.

The regulations also place notification obligations on employees. Employees must provide timely and adequate notice of the need for FMLA leave in order to perfect entitlement to the protections of the FMLA. The timeliness of employee notice depends on whether the need for leave is foreseeable or non–foreseeable. An employee's failure to provide timely notice may result in a delay of the start of FMLA leave. If an employee fails to provide adequate notice of the need for FMLA leave, leave may be denied altogether. For example, an employee who requests leave because they are "sick" may have failed to provide adequate notice of the need for FMLA leave. In that case, the leave would not be protected by the FMLA.

2. Title II

Compared with Title I, the CAA, and the PEOAA, the notice requirements of Title II are much less specific. Where there is specificity, the burden is placed on the employee rather than the employer. An employee must provide timely and adequate notice of their need for FMLA leave depending on whether the need for leave is foreseeable or non-foreseeable. The consequences of an employee's failure to provide such notice is denial of FMLA leave protections. That is certainly greater punishment than is imposed by comparable regulations implementing Title I, the CAA, and the PEOAA.

The notice requirements imposed on employers under Title II are far less onerous than the comparable requirements under Title I, the CAA, and the PEOAA. There is no requirement for an FMLA poster, or that a statement addressing FMLA leave benefits be included in an employee handbook or other written materials addressing leave or benefits. Nor is there a specific requirement that an employee be provided notice of FMLA rights and obligations at the time FMLA leave is requested. There is a generalized requirement that an employer notify an employee of FMLA rights and obligations. According to OPM, employers can satisfy this requirement by providing the employee with an OPM factsheet and brochure on the FMLA. The regulations do not specify when this needs to be done.

G. DID THE EMPLOYEE PROVIDE PROPER DOCUMENTATION TO SUBSTANTIATE THEIR NEED FOR FMLA LEAVE?

The FMLA permits employers to require that employees substantiate their need for FMLA leave due to a serious health condition with medical certification from a health care provider. The right is permissive, and an employee is not obligated to provide medical certification absent a request by the employer. Congress felt that the right of an employer to request medical certification was one of the strongest checks against employee leave abuse.

There are several medical certification requirements generally recognized by all four federal sector variants of the FMLA:

- Certification to substantiate the need for FMLA leave;
- Periodic status reports;
- Medical recertification; and
- Fitness to return to duty certification.

There are significant similarities and differences among the certification requirements of the four federal sector variants.

Generally speaking, an employee has a minimum of 15 days to provide an initial medical certification to substantiate the need for FMLA leave. That period of time may be extended where it is not practicable for an employee to provide the certification, as long as the employee makes a good faith effort to provide the certification. Under Title I, the CAA, and the PEOAA, there is no limit on the amount of time that an employee, acting in good faith, may have to provide the initial medical certification. Title II caps the time at 30 days from the date of the request.

The amount of medical information to which an employer is entitled is tightly regulated under all of the FMLA federal sector variants. The DOL has developed an optional form that meets the certification requirements. OPM has not developed a similar form. Rather, it makes the DOL form available for use with Title II employees.

Under all of the federal sector FMLA statutes, an employer who doubts the validity of the initial medical certification may, at the employer's expense, require the employee, or the employee's covered family member, to submit to a second health care opinion provider. If the certification from the second health care opinion provider differs from the first, the employer may, at its expense, require submission to a third health care opinion provider, whose opinion is final and binding.

An employee's failure to provide medical certification has different consequences depending on the federal sector FMLA law involved. The differences impact the length of time an employer must wait before it can declare that an employee has failed to timely provide medical certification. Under all federal sector FMLA variants, an employee that fails to provide the medical certification requested by an employer is not entitled to the protections of the FMLA. Under Title I, the CAA, and the PEOAA, an employer may delay the start or continuation of leave until certification is provided. The law does not specify the length of time an employer must wait. Under Title II, the employee has, at most, 30 days to provide the initial medical certification.

All of the federal sector FMLA laws permit employers to require employees to periodically update their medical certifications through medical recertification. The frequency of such a requirement differs substantially depending on the civil service status of the employee. In several instances, an employer is prohibited from requesting recertification more often than every 30 days. There are other instances where recertification may not be requested for periods in excess of 30 days. Exceptions permit an employer to require recertification more often than every 30 days or other applicable minimum period of time.

Finally, the four federal sector variants of the FMLA permit employers to require employees, as a condition of returning to work, to provide certification of fitness for duty. The requirements governing a return-to-work, fitness-for-duty certification, as with other areas, contain similarities and differences. Again, employers must exercise care to ensure that it is applying the appropriate FMLA requirements or risk violating the FMLA.

III. OTHER FMLA ENTITLEMENTS AND OBLIGATIONS

Where all of the above questions are answered in the affirmative, an eligible employee is likely entitled to FMLA leave. The determination that an eligible employee is entitled to FMLA leave raises issues regarding additional employee and employer rights and obligations. This section will provide an overview of some of these issues, highlighting basic rights and areas of difference among the four federal sector FMLA variants.

A. LEAVE AMOUNT AND SCHEDULING

All eligible federal employees covered by the FMLA are entitled to 12 workweeks of leave each leave year. The calculation of the FMLA leave year is different depending on which federal sector FMLA law applies. So too, the exact amount of leave that an employee is entitled to receive as part of their 12-week entitlement differs depending on the FMLA variant at issue.

With respect to calculating the 12-month FMLA leave year (during which employees are entitled to take their 12 weeks of leave), Title I, the CAA, and the PEOAA offer employers four options: (1) the calendar year; (2) any other fixed leave year; (3) the measuring forward method; and (4) the rolling back method. Only the measuring forward leave year is permitted under Title II. As discussed more fully in Chapter 10, "Leave Amount and Scheduling," there are benefits and drawbacks to each of the leave year calculation options.

Employers must calculate the exact amount of FMLA leave available to each employee, as the 12-workweek entitlement differs substantially between Title II and Title I, the CAA, and the PEOAA. Federal employers, employees, unions, and other employee organizations must carefully analyze the applicable standards for calculating the amount of FMLA leave available to each eligible employee. This is not an easy task, given the absence of key definitions in all of the federal sector FMLA regulations. What is clear, however, is that under all of the federal sector variants of the FMLA, the calculation of the exact amount of FMLA leave available to an eligible employee is made on a case-by-case basis. There is no uniform cap on the amount of FMLA leave available to all eligible employees during the FMLA leave year.

The leave that counts against the employee's 12-week FMLA entitlement differs under the various federal sector FMLA laws. For example, under Title II, a legal holiday that occurs during an eligible employee's FMLA leave does not count against the employee's 12-week entitlement. Under Title I, the CAA, and the PEOAA, a holiday that falls during a period of FMLA leave counts against the employee's 12-week entitlement.

Title I, the CAA, and the PEOAA also impose a penalty on married employees who work for the same agency. The "marriage penalty" reduces the total amount of FMLA leave available to both employees to a combined total of 12 weeks of leave for certain covered conditions. Title I does not impose a marriage penalty.

Leave scheduling has to do with how FMLA leave may be taken. Essentially, FMLA leave may be taken in one of three forms: (1) in a single block of time; (2) intermittently; or (3) on a "reduced leave schedule." Leave is taken in a single block of time where the absence is continuous for the same covered condition. Leave is taken intermittently where more than one absence is taken for the same underlying condition. A reduced leave schedule is where a full time employee works part time and is on leave part time. In a sense, a reduced leave schedule is simply a more systemic form of intermittent leave. For the most part, intermittent leave and leave on a reduced leave schedule are treated the same so the reader does not need to know the difference between these two forms of leave. It is more important, however, to know the difference between leave taken in a single block of time and leave taken in more than one block of time.

Whether leave is taken in a single block of time, intermittently, or on a reduced leave schedule impacts an employee's FMLA rights and obligations. For example, leave taken intermittently or on a reduced leave schedule following the birth, adoption, or foster care placement of a child can be denied outright by an employer. If the same leave were taken in a single block of time, the leave could not be denied, all other things being equal.

In order for an employee to take FMLA leave intermittently or on a reduced leave schedule for a serious health condition, the leave must be "medically necessary." The employee's health care provider generally determines whether leave is medically necessary. Employers confirm this fact by requesting medical certification from the employee. There are substantial similarities and differences between Title II and Title I, the CAA, and the PEOAA regarding the circumstances where intermittent or FMLA leave on a reduced leave schedule may be used for a serious health condition.

Where leave is taken intermittently or on a reduced leave schedule, the employee is required to make a reasonable effort to schedule the leave so as not to disrupt employer operations. A reasonable effort does not require success. On the other hand, an employee who fails or refuses to make a reasonable effort to structure their intermittent or reduced schedule leave in order to minimize workplace disruption will lose the protections of the FMLA.

An area of great difference among the four variants of the FMLA involves notice obligations where leave is taken on an intermittent or reduced leave schedule basis. Title I, the CAA, and the PEOAA impose specific notice obligations on employees and employers. Title II does not contain comparable notice obligations in these circumstances.

All federal sector variants of the FMLA permit employers to transfer the employee to an equivalent alternative position that better accommodates the employee's need for FMLA leave on an intermittent or reduced leave schedule basis. However, there are material differences among the four federal FMLA laws in how the implementing regulations apply this employer right.

B. SUBSTITUTION OF PAID LEAVE

FMLA leave is unpaid. In certain circumstances, however, a federal employee may be permitted to substitute paid leave for unpaid FMLA leave. The four federal sector variants of the FMLA differ regarding the circumstances permitting paid leave substitution, what paid leave may be used in substitution, and who makes the election, the employee or the employer.

More fundamentally, it is not clear what the term "substitute" means. The term is not defined in the FMLA statutes or implementing regulations. The majority position is that "substitute" should be read as meaning "in conjunction with" or "concurrent." That is, where paid leave is substituted for unpaid FMLA leave, the employee retains the benefits and protections of the FMLA but also draws on available paid leave for the absence. A minority view is that "substitute" means that the benefits and protections of the FMLA extinguish where paid leave is substituted for unpaid leave. The employee's leave is governed solely by the requirements of the substituted paid leave.

Under Title I, the CAA, and PEOAA, an eligible employee or the employer may elect to substitute paid leave for unpaid FMLA leave. There are rules, however, governing when an employer may elect to substitute paid leave. Under Title II, the election is solely the right of the eligible employee.

The timing of the paid leave election is another area of difference among the four federal sector FMLA laws. Under Title II, the eligible employee must make the election to substitute paid leave for unpaid FMLA leave before leave commences. Title I, the CAA, and the PEOAA do not have such a bright-line rule. Rather, the election must be made within two business days of when the employer is on notice that the leave is covered by the FMLA. In most instances, that will occur at the time the employee requests FMLA leave. In other instances, such as where additional information is needed from the employee to determine if the leave qualifies under the FMLA, it may be at some later time.

Federal sector FMLA laws permit the substitution of accrued paid leave for unpaid FMLA leave. The four variants of the FMLA differ, however, on what accrued leave is available for paid leave substitution. Under Title I, the CAA, and the PEOAA, the only limitation placed on the substitution of accrued paid leave is that the paid leave must be available for the FMLA leave at issue. For example, an employer with paid pregnancy leave benefits would not have to make paid leave available to an employee who is not pregnant simply because the employee is seeking to substitute paid leave for unpaid FMLA leave.

Title II, on the other hand, specifies exactly which paid leave programs are available for substitution with unpaid FMLA leave. No other accrued paid leave may be drawn upon for FMLA substitution purposes, even if the leave is accrued, available, and applicable to the need for FMLA leave at issue.

Note that the substitution of paid leave may affect the manner in which an employee may request FMLA leave. Pursuant to Title I, the CAA, and the PEOAA, if the paid leave program has less stringent procedural requirements (e.g., notice and certification) than those required by the FMLA, only the less stringent paid leave requirements apply. This is not the case under Title II. The substitution of paid leave for unpaid FMLA leave has no impact on notice, certification, or other FMLA procedural requirements under Title II. Rather, the procedural requirements of the FMLA and the paid leave are determined separately.

C. MAINTENANCE OF BENEFITS DURING LEAVE

The FMLA addresses what happens with employee benefits during the pendency of, and on an employee's return from, FMLA leave. Generally speaking, there are four issues in this area: (1) the retention of accrued benefits at the start of FMLA leave; (2) the accrual of benefits during FMLA leave; (3) the maintenance of health benefits during FMLA leave; and (4) the resumption of benefits on return from FMLA leave.

Eligible employees are entitled to retain all employment benefits accrued before the start of FMLA leave. The FMLA does not require the accrual of seniority or other employment benefits during FMLA leave. Where, however, an employer's policy permits the accrual of employment benefits when an employee is on paid or unpaid leave, then accrual while an employee is on FMLA leave is permitted. As an exception to this general rule, Title II does not explicitly prohibit the accrual of seniority during FMLA leave. Title I, the CAA, and the PEOAA do not require seniority to accrue during FMLA leave.

The provisions governing the maintenance of health benefits during FMLA leave differ among the four federal sector variants of the FMLA. The core differences among the federal sector implementing regulations are the types of benefits that must be maintained. Title II speaks only in terms of maintaining health benefits pursuant to the Federal Employees Health Benefits Program (FEHBP). Title I and the PEOAA do not mention that program at all, but require maintenance of any group health plan benefits or multi-employer health plans. The CAA splits the difference, requiring maintenance of benefits under the FEHBP or any group health plan.

Under all federal sector variants of the FMLA, an employer is required to maintain health benefits coverage during FMLA leave at the same level and under the same conditions as though the employee had been continuously employed. The regulations implementing Title I, the CAA, and the PEOAA detail what happens when changes occur to employment benefit programs and agency notice requirements. These matters are largely unaddressed by Title II.

An employee's obligation to pay their share of health benefits premiums, if any, continues during FMLA leave. The payment options and procedural requirements governing an employee's payment of health benefit premiums during FMLA leave are detailed in each of the four federal sector variants of the FMLA. Generally speaking, the requirements of Title II differ from those of Title I, the CAA, and the PEOAA.

Under all versions of the FMLA, an employee may forego health benefits coverage during FMLA leave. Employees may make such an election to avoid having to pay their share of health benefit plan premiums, which the FMLA would otherwise require. Employers often elect to pay the employee's share of health benefits payments in the interim in order to resume an employee's health benefits under the same conditions and terms as when the employee started FMLA leave.

Title I, the CAA, and the PEOAA regulate an employer's ability to collect premium payments it made on behalf of an employee to continue health benefits coverage during FMLA leave. The regulations issued under Title II on this matter are substantially different. For example, Title II offers two methods an employee may use to pay health benefit premiums during FMLA leave. Title I, the CAA, and the PEOAA, in contrast, offer five ways for an employee to make health benefit premium payments during the pendency of FMLA leave.

Under Title I, the CAA, and the PEOAA, an employer may terminate an employee's health benefits coverage during FMLA leave under certain limited circumstances. Title II does not specifically provide that an employer may terminate an employee's health coverage while the employee is out on FMLA leave.

Under all four federal sector variants of the FMLA, an employee returning from FMLA leave is entitled to the same level of employment benefits as they enjoyed before they took FMLA leave. Employees may not be required to submit to medical examination or other tests in order to re-qualify for health benefits coverage on return from FMLA leave. Changes in health benefits coverage during the employee's absence from FMLA leave are handled differently by the federal sector FMLA laws.

D. RETURN TO WORK

An employee is entitled to be returned to their same or an equivalent position on the conclusion of FMLA leave. To qualify for that right, an employee must satisfy certain conditions. Not surprisingly, there are differences among the four variants of the FMLA on this issue. A major difference is the right of return of an employee who is unable to perform all essential job functions at the conclusion of FMLA leave. Under Title I, the CAA, and the PEOAA, an employee who is unable to perform all essential job functions at the end of FMLA leave has no FMLA right to return to work. Of course, the employee may have the right to return to work pursuant to other laws, employer policy, or the terms of a collective bargaining agreement. On the other hand, Title II does not require, as a condition of an employee's FMLA right to return to work that the employee be able to perform all essential job functions.

The FMLA permits all federal employers to condition an employee's return to work from leave on the submission of a medical certification that the employee is fit to return to duty. Substantial differences exist between the procedural requirements for return to work attendant under Title I, the CAA, and the PEOAA, with the comparable requirements under Title II.

Under Title I, the CAA, and the PEOAA, an employee generally need only provide a short statement from a health care provider that an employee returning to work from FMLA leave due to his or her own serious health condition is fit for duty. Title II, on the other hand, permits employers to require employees to submit a complete medical certification. Under Title I, the CAA, and the PEOAA, the terms of a collective bargaining agreement may impose increased burdens on the medical information that an employer may require an employee to provide as a condition of returning to work. Title II does not have a similar provision permitting the terms of a collective bargaining agreement to alter the employee's right to return to work.

Another major area of difference involves the notification requirements imposed on employers of the requirement of a fitness-for-duty certification as a condition of an employee's return to work. For employers with non-civil service employees covered by Title I, the CAA, or the PEOAA, the obligation to provide notice of the requirement of a fitness to return to duty certification is detailed and specific. The comparable notice requirements under Title II are less onerous and less specific. This difference in notice requirements is problematic for federal employers with civil service and non-civil service employees covered by Titles I and II of the Act.

Generally, employers are not required to return an employee to the same or an equivalent position on the conclusion of FMLA leave if the employee would not have had a job had the employee not taken FMLA leave. For example, if an employee would have been terminated for cause, the fact that they took FMLA does not entitle the employee to be returned to work. Basically, an employee who takes FMLA leave has no greater right to return to work; they just don't have lesser rights because of their exercise of FMLA rights.

Finally, employers with employees covered by Title I, the CAA, and the PEOAA should be mindful of the return to work rules governing "key employees", and special rules governing certain educational employees. Title II does not contain rules regarding these groups of employees.

Key employees are employees in the highest paid top ten percent of all employees employed by the employer within 75 miles of the work site. The FMLA does not require an agency to return a key employee to work from FMLA leave where the employee's return (not the taking of FMLA leave) would cause substantial and grievous economic injury to the agency. It is a very limited right conditioned on notice to the employee and several opportunities to return from leave before a denial of job restoration may be imposed. The key employee exception is of questionable practical application in the federal service.

E. ENFORCEMENT AND REMEDIES

Violations of the FMLA are enforced differently under the four federal sector variants of the FMLA. Under Title I, an aggrieved employee may file a complaint with the Department of Labor or initiate a civil action in federal court. The FMLA does not require an employee to exhaust administrative remedies by first filing a complaint with DOL before filing suit. Rather, DOL can investigate the violation and recommend remedial relief to the employee, if warranted. DOL also has the power to subpoena documents in order to enforce FMLA regulations. DOL may file suit against the employer on behalf of the employee. In that event, the employee is unable to bring his or her own lawsuit.

As indicated previously, a civil action may name as defendants the federal employer and/or individual supervisors who allegedly violated the employee's FMLA rights. The employee must file the action within 2 years of the violation, or 3 years in the case of willful violations.

As a remedy, an employee may obtain damages in the amount of any wages, salary, employment benefits, or other compensation denied or lost by reason of the violation. This amount is doubled if the violation is willful. An employee is also entitled to equitable relief, such as being returned to their position in the event they were wrongfully terminated. Damages for emotional distress and punitive damages are not available. The Act provides for reasonable attorney fees and costs, which can be substantial in an FMLA case.

Title II does not permit employees to sue in federal court for violations of the Act. Rather, a civil service employee covered by Title II is limited to filing a grievance pursuant to the terms of an agency policy or an applicable collective bargaining agreement. The remedies available are limited to whatever is permitted by the grievance system.

The enforcement scheme under the CAA differs from Titles I and II and the PEOAA. Under the CAA, a congressional employee who believes that his or her FMLA rights have been violated must first file a request for counseling with the Congressional Office of Compliance. If counseling is not successful, the employee is given the right to make a request for mediation. The request is filed with the Office of Compliance. If mediation is unsuccessful, the employee has the right to elect to file a formal complaint with the Office of Compliance, or file a civil lawsuit in federal court.

If the administrative route is elected, the formal complaint is heard by a hearing officer, who renders a decision. The initial decision may be appealed to the Board of Directors of the Office of Compliance (Board). A decision of the Board may be appealed to the Court of Appeals for the Federal Circuit.

The PEOAA enforcement scheme has elements of both Title I and the CAA. According to the Act, the enforcement provisions of Title I apply to PEOAA. 3 USC 412(b) (incorporating §107 of Title I, 29 USC 2617, into PEOAA). Additionally, the PEOAA mandates an administrative exhaustion procedure initially requiring counseling and mediation efforts. The PEOAA specifically provides that these procedures must be substantially similar to those under the CAA.

If counseling and mediation are unsuccessful, an employee has the right to file an appeal with the MSPB. 3 USC 454. Judicial review of any administrative decision is made by appeal to the United States Court of Appeals for the Federal Circuit.

IV. CONCLUSION

The FMLA is sufficiently complicated that federal employers should exercise great care when addressing an employee's request for FMLA leave. This is particularly true of employers whose workforce contains a mixture of civil service and non-civil service employees. In many instances, the workforce of a federal agency is predominately made up of civil service employees covered by Title II, with a minority of non-civil service employees covered by Title I. Generally, employers should not apply the requirements of Title II to all employees, across the board. The requirements of the four federal sector variants of the FMLA often differ substantially. In many instances, compliance with requirements of Title II will constitute a violation of the law when applied to employees covered by Title I.

Employees, unions, and other organizations representing the interests of federal employees must also become familiar with the applicable FMLA requirements. Unions that advise employees how to comply with the requirements of Title II may be doing more harm than good if the employee is really covered by Title I, and vice versa.

This *Guide* is intended to aid employers, employees, unions, and other professionals to achieve a better understanding of the requirements of the FMLA as applied to the federal sector. I also hope that the questions raised throughout this book regarding various inadequacies with the current FMLA implementing regulations will spur the regulatory bodies to act to bring more clarity to this complicated entitlement.

CHAPTER 2
PURPOSES AND LEGISLATIVE HISTORY OF THE FMLA

I. INTRODUCTION

The Family and Medical Leave Act of 1993 (FMLA or the Act) was passed to address growing tensions caused by revolutionary changes in the composition of the workforce. These tensions pitted the increased time demands of work against employee family obligations and medical needs. The dramatic rise of women, particularly mothers, in the workforce to support two-income families, the rise of single parent families, and the parental care and medical needs of a large, rapidly-growing aging population placed competing time pressures on employees. In the absence of a federal statute providing job protection, employees were forced to choose between retaining their jobs and caring for their families. To alleviate this tension and shore up the family institution, Congress passed the FMLA.

This chapter provides an overview of the social context and legislative history that animated the enactment of the FMLA. Knowing the social and legislative background of the Act is important to understanding the intent and scope of the law, as it is currently constituted, and the form that future modifications of the law may take. Section II of this chapter discusses the social context that gave rise to the Act. Legislative responses to these social pressures by other nations, by the states, and by the federal government are addressed in Section III. The findings and purposes of Congress for the FMLA and expansions of the Act are set forth and discussed in Sections IV and V.

II. SOCIAL CONTEXT OF THE FMLA

The adverse impact on employees and families resulting from the confluence of four major societal and workplace demographic trends formed the backdrop to, and rationale for, enactment of the FMLA. *See generally* Report from the Committee on Labor and Human Resources, S. Rep. No. 3, 103d Cong., 1st Sess. 1–51 (1993) (hereinafter FMLA Legislative History Report). These trends, the increase in hours worked, the dramatic increase of women in the workforce, the rise of single parent families, and parental care responsibilities inherent in a growing aging population, along with the resulting time pressures they produced on employees, had been building for decades before the FMLA's enactment.

A. INCREASED TIME DEMANDS OF WORK

Americans spend significantly more time at work and less time at home than they have in the past. According to several studies, the average American in the 1990s worked a month more than their counterpart in the 1960s. Schorr, Juliet B., The Overworked American: The Unexpected Decline of Leisure (1993); Hochschild, Arlie, The Second Shift: Working Parents and the Revolution at Home (1989); and The Time Bind (1997). This extra month at work resulted in a 14% decrease (22 hours a week) in time available for parents to spend with their children. *Council of Economic Advisors, Families and the Labor Market, 1969–1999: Analyzing the Time Crunch* (1999).

Put another way, measured by time at work, American's are the hardest-working employees in the world. Employees in the United States average more work hours each year (1,966) than those in any other industrialized nation, including Japan (1,889), Canada (1,732), Britain (1,731), and Norway (1,399), the next four contenders. On average, Americans work 350 hours more per year (almost nine full workweeks) than Europeans. Wisensale, Steven K., Family Leave Policy: The Political Economy of Work and Family in America 89 (2001).

B. SIGNIFICANT INCREASE OF WOMEN IN THE WORKFORCE

In addition to longer work hours, the dramatic increase in the number of women, particularly wives and mothers, who entered the workforce in the decades preceding the enactment of the FMLA placed additional work-family time pressures on employees. Between 1950 and 1990, participation of women in the workforce more than tripled. FMLA Legislative

History Report at 7. In 1962, 43% of the female population was in the workforce. Bureau of Labor Statistics, U.S. Dept. of Labor, Bulletin No. 2385, Working Women: A Chartbook 31–34 (1991). By 1990, nearly 74% of women held jobs in the workforce. *Id*. According to a study conducted in 1987, approximately 80% of working women were of childbearing age. Of those women, 93% were predicted to become pregnant during their working lives. Caplan–Cotenoff, Scott A., *Parental Leave: The Need for a National Policy to Foster Sexual Equality*, 13 Am. J.L. & Med. 71–72 (1987). Between 1979 and 1990, women accounted for more than 62% of the increase in the workforce, with predictions that the female labor force participation rate would continue to increase through the following decade. FMLA Legislative History Report at 8.

Equally dramatic were the increases in the number of married women and mothers in the workforce. In 1960, only 31% of married women were in the workforce. By 1990, that figured nearly doubled to 61% of the workforce. Tauber, Cynthia M., Statistical Handbook on Women in America (2d ed. 1996). In 1993, the workforce included 56% of mothers with children under age six and 51% of mothers with children under the age of one. FMLA Legislative History Report, at 8. In 1975, only 36.7% of mothers with children under age six were in the labor force. Tauber, *supra*.

C. THE RISE OF SINGLE PARENT FAMILIES

The third major demographic trend that influenced the enactment of the FMLA was the dramatic increase in the number of single parent households. FMLA Legislative History Report at 8. In 1970, only 11% of families were headed by single parents. By 1993, due to divorce, separation, and a steady rise in out-of-wedlock births, 27% of families were headed by a single parent, mostly mothers. *Id.; see also* Wisensale, Family Leave Policy, at 17 (By 1997, 28% of all families were headed by a single parent.). By 1991, 69% of single mothers were in the workforce. Bureau of Labor Statistics, U.S. Dept. of Labor; Working Woman: A Chartbook 47 (1991). More importantly, children of single parent families were more than five times as likely to live below the poverty line as children of two-parent families. FMLA Legislative History Report at 8.

D. THE AGING OF THE AMERICAN POPULATION AND PARENTAL CARE RESPONSIBILITIES

Americans are living longer as a result of advances in medicine and health care. As a result, individuals over the age of 65 are the fastest-growing segment of the American population. FMLA Legislative History Report at 8. Between 1980 and 1990, the number of persons 65 or older increased from 25.5 million (11.3% of the population) to 31 million (12.5% of the population). U.S. Bureau of the Census: 65+ in the United States; Current Population Reports, Special Studies 23–190 (1996). In that same time period, the number of people aged 75 or older, the age group with significant health and other care needs, grew by nearly 33%. FMLA Legislative History Report at 8. Individuals over age 65 are projected to increase to 20.4% of the population by the year 2050. Wisensale, Family Leave Policy, at 20.

The health and other care needs of a growing elderly population fall increasingly on family members given the trend toward independent living or home care and away from institutionalization. As most family members (particularly parents) work, the care needs of the elderly add to the tension between work demands and family needs. The National Council on Aging estimated that 20 to 25% of the more than 100 million American workers have some caregiving responsibility for an older relative. Two-thirds of nonprofessional caregivers for older, chronically ill, or disabled persons were working women. FMLA Legislative History Report, at 8–9. A 1997 study confirmed that 25% of surveyed adults provided care for an elderly relative in the previous 12 months. The average caregiver was 45 years of age or older, and provided about 8 years of care. Wisensale at 20.

The impact of the confluence of these four social and workforce trends was best summed up in the FMLA Legislative History Report, at 9:

> The effect of these demographic changes has been far reaching. With men and women alike as wage earners, the crucial unpaid care-taking services traditionally performed by wives—care of young children, ill family members, aging parents—have become increasingly difficult for families to fulfill. When there is no one to provide such care, individuals can be permanently scarred as basic needs go unfulfilled. Families unable to perform their essential function are seriously undermined and weakened. Finally, when families fail, the community is left to grapple with the tragic consequences of emotionally and physically deprived children and adults.

III. LEGISLATIVE RESPONSES TO FAMILY AND MEDICAL NEEDS

A. FAMILY LEAVE LAWS AROUND THE WORLD

In addition to broad social and workforce demographic changes, the FMLA was also sparked by comparisons with the family leave policies of other nations. At the time of the FMLA's passage, the United States was one of the few remaining countries in the world without a national law mandating some form of family leave. In 1993, 135 countries provided some form of maternity benefits, 127 with at least partial wage replacement. FMLA Legislative History Report at 21.

Family leave policies in some industrialized nations have been in effect for more than a century. Germany, Sweden, France, Great Britain, and Italy have had family leave policies in effect since before World War I. Most other European countries have had maternity leave policies since 1919, when 33 countries signed the Maternity Protection Convention that provided 12 weeks of leave, job protection, and a wage benefit to be determined by each signatory nation. Wisensale, Family Leave Policy, at 217.

In September 1992, the European Community Commission issued a directive requiring that all member countries provide a standard minimum of 14 weeks paid maternity leave. FMLA Legislative History Report at 21. At the time, the average minimum paid leave in the major industrialized countries was 12 to 14 weeks, with the right to take unpaid, job-protected leave for at least one year. While the family leave policies of most industrialized nations covered maternity leave and illnesses, only a few covered absences for elder care. *Id.*

More recently, directives of the European Union (EU) the successor to the European Economic Community, have addressed family leave policies. It has 15 member states covering 373 million people who speak 11 different languages. The EU is the largest economic trading bloc in the world. It has its own flag, uniform passport, anthem, and currency. In June of 1996, the EU implemented its Directive on Parental Leave. It allows all workers, men or women, full or part-time, employed by any business of any size, three months of unpaid, job-protected leave for the birth, adoption, or care of a child up to eight years old. Both parents may use this leave separately or simultaneously. The Directive provides some local flexibility regarding notice and length-of-service requirements. Wisensale at 220-221. The European nations also have extensive sick and annual leave programs to cover illness. FMLA Legislative History Report at 21.

B. STATE FAMILY LEAVE LAWS

By the 1993 passage of the FMLA, 30 states, the District of Columbia and the Commonwealth of Puerto Rico had already passed some form of family and medical leave legislation. FMLA Legislative History Report at 22. These state initiatives varied greatly in the persons covered, the types of conditions that entitled employees to take leave, the amount of leave available, and the time frame in which the leave could be taken.

Approximately two-thirds of state family leave laws covered both public and private employers. One-third covered only state employees. The law in two-thirds of the states allowed time off from work for childbirth, adoption, or other limited purposes. The remaining third allowed time off for broader family responsibilities, similar to the FMLA. Wisensale, Family Leave Policy, at 118, 127-128. The state laws also varied greatly in the duration of the leave available and the period of time in which the leave could be taken.

Pennsylvania, for example, granted up to six months of parental leave each year for the birth or adoption of a child. Minnesota, on the other hand, granted only six weeks of leave each year for birth or adoption. Maine provided for eight weeks of unpaid leave every two years. The law in a few states granted different amounts of leave for different covered conditions. In Wisconsin, public employees were permitted up to six weeks of unpaid leave for the birth or adoption of a child, two weeks to care for a child, spouse or parent with a serious health condition, and two weeks personal medical leave within a 12-month period. FMLA Legislative History Report at 22.

Paid family leave was the exception rather than the rule in state family leave laws. Unpaid family and medical leave was the norm in all but six states. Rhode Island, California, New Jersey, New York, Puerto Rico, and Hawaii had long-standing temporary disability insurance policies that provided paid leave for pregnancy and childbirth. Wisensale at 119.

C. CREATION OF THE FEDERAL FAMILY MEDICAL LEAVE ACT

The spark for federal FMLA legislation can be traced to an unfavorable interpretation of a state maternity law. In 1984, the U.S. District Court for the Central District of California held that a 1978 California statute providing up to four months of job-protected maternity leave to women violated the equal protection provisions of Title VII of the Civil Rights Act of 1964 (Title VII) and the 1978 Pregnancy Discrimination Act (PDA). *California Federal Savings & Loan Assoc. v. Guerra*, No. 83-4927R, 1984 U.S. Dist. LEXIS 18387 (C.D. Cal. March 21, 1984), *rev'd*, 758 F.2d 390 (9th Cir. 1985), *aff'd*, 479 U.S. 272, 93 L. Ed. 2d 613, 107 S. Ct. 683 (1987). Specifically, the district court in *Garland* held that because the law only benefitted women, California employers who abided by the state law were subject to reverse discrimination suits under Title VII. Bernstein, Anya, The Moderation Dilemma: Legislative Coalitions and the Politics of Family and Medical Leave 92-94 (2001); Wisensale, Family Leave Policy, at 115-117.

Outraged, proponents of the California legislation, organizations representing the interests of women and labor, began to lobby politicians for redress while the *Garland* decision was appealed. These organizations, however, were fundamentally split on tactics. On the one side, women's and labor organizations, such as 9 to 5 National Association of Working Women (9 to 5) and the Coalition for Reproductive Equality in the Workplace (CREW), who supported laws like the California statute, argued only against the assumption that the maternity law did not discriminate against men. On the other side were groups, like the National Organization for Women (NOW) and the Women's Legal Defense Fund, who opposed "special treatment" laws for women. These groups favored laws providing equal treatment of men and women. Within the feminist community, the tactical debate between "special treatment" and "equal treatment" laws to advance the cause of women in the workplace simmered well before *Garland*. Bernstein at 92-94; Wisensale at 109-117.

The initial legislative foray began with members of the California congressional delegation, Representatives Howard Berman and George Miller. As a California State legislator, Berman was the author of the California maternity law at issue in *Garland*. One of Berman's campaign pledges, when he ran for Congress, was to introduce a similar maternity leave bill in Washington. When the federal district court issued its decision in *Garland* during the second year of his first term in Congress, Berman moved to introduce federal maternity leave legislation. He was quickly dissuaded from pursuing the matter further, not due to opposition from business groups, but from women's groups opposed to legislation that gave preferential treatment to women. These groups insisted that they would only support leave legislation that provided equal treatment for men and women. Because he was primarily interested in overturning the *Garland* decision, and he believed that broadening the bill from maternity to family medical leave would be more difficult, Berman turned the issue over to the Congressional Caucus on Women's Issues (CCWI), led by Representative Patricia Schroeder of Colorado. Bernstein at 92-94; Wisensale at 109-111, 137.

Meanwhile, Congressman Miller created the House Select Committee on Children, Youth, and Families. *Id.* at 137. Although they did not have real political power, select committees provided a forum for raising issue awareness among lawmakers. *Id.* In 1984, Miller's Select Committee on Children, Youth and Families conducted a comprehensive investigation of the issues involving families and child care and issued a report entitled Families and Child Care: Improving Options. The Select Committee unanimously recommended improving current leave policies, including the issue of job security. Report from the Committee on Education and Labor, H.R. 1, 103d Cong., 1st Sess. 19 (1993) (hereinafter Report on Education and Labor). Serious debate on family leave legislation began with the issuance of the Select Committee's report.

1. The Parental and Disability Leave Act of 1985

On April 4, 1985, Pat Schroeder introduced the first-ever bill proposing a national family and medical leave policy. The Parental and Disability Leave Act of 1985 (PDLA) applied to all employers and provided different amounts of job-protected leave over a two-year period, depending on the circumstances. If the leave was to care for a newborn or newly adopted child, employers were required to provide up to 18 weeks of unpaid leave to both mothers and fathers. For temporary disabilities unrelated to work or to care for a seriously ill child, the law mandated employers to provide up to 26 weeks of unpaid leave. The employer was required to continue the employee's health insurance and other benefits during the leave. Finally, the bill also called for the creation of a commission to investigate paid leave options. Bernstein, The Moderation Dilemma at 94-95; Wisensale, Family Leave Policy at 138-139.

While four hearings were held on the PDLA, the lack of a companion bill in the Senate, the absence of key cosponsors, and Schroeder's alienation of key committee chairmen by her vote against a favored plant-closing bill, stalled further consideration of the legislation that year. Elving, Ronald, Conflict and Compromise: How Congress Makes the Law 51–52 (1995); Wisensale at 138–140.

2. Parental and Medical Leave Act of 1986

Concerned that Schroeder might be unable to shepherd the bill through committee alone, supporters of federal leave legislation secured a powerful cosponsor in the House, William Clay, and a senator, Christopher Dodd, willing to sponsor a companion bill in the Senate. Wisensale, Family Leave Policy, at 141. On March 4, 1986, Representatives Clay and Schroeder introduced H.R. 4300, the Parental and Medical Leave Act of 1986 (PMLA). On April 6, 1986, Senator Dodd offered his nearly identical companion bill in the Senate. Report on Education and Labor at 18; Wisensale at 141–142.

The PMLA differed from the earlier PDLA in several important respects. First, at the urging of advocates for the handicapped, the name of the bill was changed by substituting "medical" for "disability." Second, only companies with 5 or more employees were covered. The PDLA originally applied to all employers regardless of size. Despite these and other changes made during the year and being successfully reported out of committee, the Democratic leadership in the House concluded that the bill was not ready for a floor vote before the 1986 elections and suggested that it be reintroduced in 1987. Wisensale at 143–144; Report on Education and Labor at 18. Efforts to enact the PMLA stalled for the 1986 elections.

3. The Family and Medical Leave Act of 1987

The 1986 elections swept the Democrats into the majority in the Senate, taking over the chairmanship of committees key to the passage of the FMLA. Democrats retained control of the House. Ronald Reagan remained President.

On February 3, 1987, Representatives Clay and Schroeder introduced H.R. 925, the Family and Medical Leave Act of 1987. Senator Dodd again introduced nearly identical companion legislation in the Senate, the Parental and Medical Leave Act of 1987, on January 6, 1987. Report on Education and Labor at 19; Wisensale, Family Leave Policy, at 144–145. Significant changes included another name change in the House bill, substituting "family" for "parental" to reflect a broadening of the bill to cover care for elderly parents and spouses as well as children.

During committee debates, a substitute bill offered by New Jersey Representative Marge Roukema was approved that substantially altered the bill. Roukema's amendments increased the cut-off for company size, reduced the duration of the leave, added a predetermined employment period for leave eligibility, and exempted the top 10% of company employees from the job security provisions of the law. Despite these and other changes, and being voted out of committee, with little movement on the companion Senate bill, the House leadership elected not to release the bill for a vote on the floor before the 1988 elections. Wisensale at 144–145; Report on Education and Labor at 19.

4. The Family and Medical Leave Act of 1989

Vice President George Bush won the 1988 presidential election. He campaigned against the FMLA and promised to veto the legislation if it were presented to him. The Democrats, however, retained control of the House and Senate.

On February 7, 1989, Representatives Clay, Roukema and Schroeder introduced H.R. 770, the Family and Medical Leave Act of 1989. Senator Dodd introduced the companion Senate bill (S. 345), renamed the Family and Medical Leave Act of 1989, on February 2, 1989. The House bill was modified to reduce the period of leave from 15 weeks a year for medical leave and 10 weeks every two years for family leave to 12 weeks per year for all circumstances covered in the bill. The House approved the FMLA bill on May 10, 1990. The Senate approved the House bill on June 14, 1990. As promised, President Bush vetoed the bill on July 25, 1990. The House subsequently failed to override the veto. Report on Education and Labor at 19.

5. The Family and Medical Leave Act of 1991

On January 3, 1991, Representatives Clay, Roukema, and Schroeder introduced H.R. 2, the Family and Medical Leave Act of 1991, which was identical to the bill vetoed by President Bush. Senator Dodd introduced his companion bill (S. 5) in the Senate on January 14, 1991. By this time, the House bill had 180 cosponsors and the Senate bill had 39 cosponsors. The House and Senate bills were modified to increase the eligibility threshold from 1000 to 1250 hours worked per year. Both bills added requirements of a 30-day notice to be provided by the employee before certain leave is taken, new employer protections against abuse of leave by employees, new restrictions on usage of intermittent leave, and a medical certification that an employee was needed to care for a seriously ill family member before the employee could take leave. Report on Education and Labor at 21.

The House and Senate subsequently passed their respective bills. On September 22, 1992, President Bush vetoed the legislation. The Senate overrode the veto by a vote of 68–31. The House vote failed to override the President's veto. *Id.*

6. The Family and Medical Leave Act of 1993

In November 1992, Democrat William Jefferson Clinton was elected President. The Democrats also held both the House and the Senate. Candidate Clinton campaigned that he would sign the FMLA, if elected.

On January 5, 1993, Representatives Clay, Roukema, and Schroeder, along with 170 cosponsors, introduced H.R.1, the Family and Medical Leave Act of 1993. The bill was identical to the one vetoed by President Bush. In the Senate, Senator Dodd introduced S.5, the Family and Medical Leave Act of 1991. Both chambers voted in favor of the legislation. President Clinton signed the Family and Medical Leave Act on February 5, 1993, the first bill the new President signed into law. Report on Education and Labor at 21.

IV. FINDINGS AND PURPOSES OF THE FAMILY AND MEDICAL LEAVE ACT OF 1993

A. FINDINGS

According to Congress, the enactment of the FMLA was predicated on two fundamental concerns—the needs of the American workforce and the development of high performance organizations. 29 CFR 825.101(b). Regarding the former, Congress recognized a need for legislation to strengthen families by relieving working parents, stretched thin by long work hours and family duties, from having to choose between keeping their job and meeting their personal or family obligations due to serious illness or to care for a newly-born or adopted child. 29 USC 2601(a)(1)–(4); 29 CFR 825.101(b). Congress found that legislation was needed at this time due to dramatic social and workplace demographic changes that developed over the preceding 40 years. Congress characterized these changes as "a demographic revolution…with profound consequences for the lives of working men and women and their families." FMLA Legislative History Report at 7.

1. Strengthening the Family

Congress found that significant increases in the number of working single parent and two-parent households and the lack of employment policies to accommodate working parents were undermining important child and family unit development. Employees were forced to choose between job security and participation in early child-rearing and caring for seriously ill family members. 29 USC 2601(a)(1)–(3). Congress also found that there was inadequate job security for employees with serious health conditions that prevented them from working for temporary periods. 29 USC 2601(a)(4). Congress recognized that job termination, due to an employee's own incapacitating illness, was unfair to the employee, devastating to the employee's family, and often resulted in the need for public assistance. FMLA Legislative History Report at 13–14. Congress also acknowledged that, as the primary caregiver in our society, working women were adversely affected more than working men by these demographic changes and the absence of job security legislation. 29 USC 2601(a)(5).

2. Economic Advantages

In addition to strengthening the family, economic advantages were cited by Congress in support of the enactment of a national family leave policy. A national family leave policy was found to benefit employers by encouraging loyal and skilled employees to remain with the company, improving employee morale, reducing turnover, and saving on costs for recruitment, hiring, and training. National legislation would also even the playing field so that no company would be at a competitive disadvantage by granting family leave. FMLA Legislative History Report at 18–20; 29 CFR 825.101(c). The enactment of national family leave legislation, according to Congress, would close a competitive gap between the United States and its major industrial competitors, virtually all of whom provided some form of national family leave. *Id.* at 21–22.

B. PURPOSES

Congress intended for the FMLA to promote and strengthen families by allowing employees to balance their work and family life through the availability of reasonable unpaid leave for medical reasons, for the birth or adoption of a child, and for the care of a child, spouse, or parent with a serious health condition. 29 USC 2601(b)(1)–(2); 29 CFR 825.101(a); *see also Englehardt v. S.P. Richards Co., Inc.*, 472 F.3d 1, 5 (1st Cir. 2006) (general purpose of the FMLA is to satisfy the "needs of the American workforce and the development of high-performance organizations); *Harrell v. USPS*, 445 F.3d 913, 919 (7th Cir. 2006) (Congress enacted the FMLA in order to assist workers in meeting the needs of their families and the demands of their jobs), *cert. denied*, 127 S. Ct. 845, 166 L. Ed. 2d 665 (2006); *Conoshenti v. Public Service Electric & Gas Co.*, 364 F.3d 135, 140–41 (3d Cir. 2004) (stated purposes of the FMLA are to "balance the demands of the workplace with the needs of families" and "to entitle employees to take reasonable leave for medical reasons"); *Babcock v. Bellsouth Advertising and Publishing Corp.*, 348 F.3d 73, 76 (4th Cir. 2003) (Congress enacted the FMLA in response to growing concerns about "inadequate job security for employees who have serious health conditions that prevent them from working for temporary periods"); *Moreau v. Air France,* 343 F.3d 1179, 1182 (9th Cir. 2003) (the FMLA was enacted, in part, "to balance the demands of the workplace with the needs of families…in a manner that accommodates the legitimate interests of employers.…"); *Cavin v. Honda of America Mfg., Inc.*, 346 F.3d 713, 719 (6th Cir. 2003) (Congress enacted the FMLA because, among other reasons, "there is inadequate job security for employees who have serious health conditions that prevent them from working for temporary periods."; the FMLA accommodates the important societal interest in assisting families by establishing minimum labor standards for leave. (Citations omitted.)); *Navarro v. Pfizer Corp.*, 261 F.3d 90, 94 (1st Cir. 2001) (Congress enacted the FMLA as a means of alleviating the tension that so often exists between the demands of earning a living and the obligations of family life); *Stekloff v. St. John's Mercy Health Systems*, 218 F.3d 858, 861 (8th Cir. 2000) (motivating force behind the adoption of the FMLA was Congress' concern with the inadequate job security for employees who have serious health conditions; the regulations emphasize the benefits of stable workplace relationships, noting that when workers can count on durable links to their workplace they are able to make their own full commitments to their jobs); *Cianci v. Pettibone Corp. et al.*, 152 F.3d 723, 728 (7th Cir. 1998) (Congress passed the FMLA to help balance the burdens of caretaking among family members and also to balance the demands of the workplace with the demands of the family); *Satterfield v. Wal–Mart Stores, Inc.*, 135 F.3d 973, 974 (5th Cir. Feb. 25, 1998), *cert. denied*, 525 U.S. 826, 119 S. Ct. 72 (1998) (same).

Congress intended that the Act would accomplish these purposes in a manner that accommodates the legitimate interests of employers, in a manner that, consistent with the Equal Protection Clause of the Fourteenth Amendment, minimizes the potential for employment discrimination on the basis of sex by providing leave on a gender–neutral basis, and in a manner that promotes equal opportunity for men and women. 29 USC 2601(b)(3)–(5); 29 CFR 825.101(a).

V. AMENDMENT OF THE FEDERAL FAMILY AND MEDICAL LEAVE ACT

A. CONGRESSIONAL ACTION

Every year bills are introduced in the House and Senate unsuccessfully seeking to amend the FMLA. Some amendments seek to expand the reach of the FMLA to smaller private sector employers, to broaden the definition of covered family members, and to increase the permissible reasons for leave. Others seek to shrink the reach of the FMLA. To date, the FMLA has not been amended.

B. PRESIDENTIAL ACTION

1. Calls for Congressional Action to Expand the FMLA Go Unheeded

During his tenure in office, President Clinton unsuccessfully petitioned Congress to expand the scope of the FMLA. In a 1997 radio address on the fourth anniversary of the FMLA, he called upon Congress to expand the law to allow employees to take 24 hours of unpaid leave a year to attend parent–teacher conferences or to take a child to dental or medical appointments. Congress did not pass any FMLA legislation in response. Two years later in his January 19, 1999, State of the Union address, President Clinton called for expansion of family leave to employees working for smaller companies. Again, while bills were introduced, Congress was unable to pass any responsive FMLA legislation. Wisensale, Family Leave Policy, at 185–186.

2. Executive Directives Expand the FMLA

Undeterred by his lack of legislative success, President Clinton used his executive authority to expand the FMLA. Executive expansions in 1997 and 1999 allowed federal employees to use FMLA leave for child school activities and routine medical treatments of children and elderly parents. They also allowed federal employees to substitute additional paid sick leave for FMLA leave purposes. President Clinton's executive FMLA expansions also sought the availability of state unemployment insurance funds for use by eligible employees, public or private, during FMLA leave.

a. Federal Employee Initiatives

On April 11, 1997, President Clinton issued a memorandum (the 1997 Memorandum) directing all executive departments and agencies to take immediate action to permit federal employees to take up to 24 hours of leave without pay each year for participation in a child's school activities or to take a child or elderly parent for routine medical appointments or other elderly care. The Memorandum noted that the President proposed that Congress make similar changes to the FMLA. It also noted that the Office of Personnel Management (OPM) would provide guidance on the implementation of the memorandum, which it did a few days later. April 11, 1997, Memorandum for the Heads of Executive Departments and Agencies from William J. Clinton, http://www.opm.gov/oca/leave/HTML/fampres.htm.

President Clinton announced the second executive expansion of federal employee FMLA rights at a commencement address at Grambling State University on May 23, 1999. The President's proposal allowed federal workers to use more sick leave to care for ill family members. He also called for the development of federal family–friendly workplace initiatives. May 24, 1999, White House Press Release, http://clinton4.nara.gov/WH/Work/052499.html; Wisensale, Family Leave Policy, at 186–187. The President told the graduates:

> I believe it is imperative that your country gives you the tools to succeed not only in the workplace but also at home. If you or any American has to chose between being a good parent and successful in your careers, you have paid a terrible price, and so has your country.

The following day, President Clinton issued a Memorandum (the 1999 Memorandum) that, among other things, directed OPM to propose government wide regulations to allow federal employees to use up to 12 weeks of accrued sick leave each year to care for a spouse, son, daughter, or parent with a "serious health condition," as that term is defined for purposes of applying the FMLA. "Currently," the 1999 Memorandum stated, "the amount of sick leave that can be used to care for a family member who is ill is limited to 13 days each year for most federal employees."

The President also directed OPM to establish an Intra–agency Family Friendly Workplace Working Group within 90 days to promote, evaluate, and exchange information on federal family–friendly workplace initiatives. The head of each executive agency and department was directed to appoint a family–friendly work/life coordinator to serve as a member of the Working Group. Working Group members were charged with the responsibility of ensuring that federal employees were made aware of the full range of options available to them to meet their personal and family responsibilities. May 24, 1999, White House Memorandum.

Pursuant to the 1999 Memorandum, OPM issued proposed regulations on February 9, 2000 (65 FR 6339–6341 (Feb. 9, 2000)), and final regulations on June 13, 2000 (65 FR 37233–37240 (June 13, 2000)).

Detailed analyses of these executive expansions in favor of federal employees are contained throughout this book, particularly Chapter 5, "Employee Eligibility for Leave"; Chapter 7, "Covered Conditions"; Chapter 9, "Documentation Requirements"; Chapter 10, "Leave Amount and Scheduling"; and Chapter 11, "Substitution of Paid Leave."

b. Use of Surplus State Unemployment Insurance to Subsidize FMLA Leave

During his 1999 commencement speech at Grambling State University and in the 1999 Memorandum, President Clinton directed the Department of Labor to develop model legislation to permit states to use surplus unemployment insurance funds to subsidize parents who use the FMLA to care for a newborn or newly adopted child. As a rationale for this action, the President noted that a 1996 study by the Commission on Family and Medical Leave found that "lost pay was the most significant barrier to parents taking advantage of unpaid leave after the birth or adoption of a child. This new step will help to give States the ability to eliminate a significant barrier that parents face in taking leave." 1999 Memorandum. Chapter 11, "Substitution of Paid Leave," will address this issue in more detail.

CHAPTER 3
FMLA Coverage of the Federal Government

I. INTRODUCTION

To be entitled to the benefits of the Family and Medical Leave Act (FMLA), a federal "employee" must work for a "covered employer." Fortunately for civilian federal employees, the federal government at large is a "covered employer" subject to the FMLA. However, the FMLA provisions that apply to the federal government are not uniform. Knowing which FMLA provisions apply to a given federal employer is critical to correctly determine the FMLA rights and responsibilities involved, as well as, the avenues of redress and remedies available in the event of a violation.

Most federal employees, if they are covered by the FMLA, are covered under Title II of the Act. Certain federal agencies and federal employees are covered under Title I of the FMLA, which also applies to employees in the private sector and those working for state and local government. The FMLA rights of employees of the Senate and the House of Representatives are contained in the Congressional Accountability Act of 1995 (CAA), 2 USC 1301, *et seq.*, which replaced Title V of the FMLA. Finally, the FMLA applies to employees of the Executive Office of the President through the Presidential and Executive Accountability Act (PEOAA), 3 USC 412.

Sections II, III, and IV of this chapter will identify and discuss which federal organizations are covered under the FMLA, the CAA, and the PEOAA. The impact of mixed FMLA responsibilities within federal organizations is set forth in Section V.

II. TITLE I FEDERAL EMPLOYERS: THE GOVERNMENT OF THE UNITED STATES

Title I of the FMLA defines a "covered employer" as any person engaged in commerce or in any industry or activity affecting commerce who employs 50 or more employees for each working day during each of 20 or more calendar workweeks in the current or preceding year. 29 USC 2611(4)(A)(I). DOL implementing regulations expand upon this statutory definition.

There are potentially five types of federal sector "covered employers" under Title I of the FMLA: (1) public agencies; (2) individuals who act in the interest of an employer to any employee; (3) successors-in-interest; (4) integrated employers; and (5) joint employers. 29 USC 2611(4)(A)(ii)–(iii); 29 CFR 825.104(a); 29 CFR 825.106; 29 CFR 825.107; 29 CFR 825.108. The first three types of employers are recognized in the statute. DOL FMLA regulations added integrated and joint employers.

A. PUBLIC AGENCY EMPLOYERS AND EMPLOYEES

For purposes of a "covered employer" under Title I, "public agency" is defined in accordance with section 3(x) of the Fair Labor Standards Act of 1938 (FLSA), 29 USC 203(x). *See* 29 USC 2611(4)(A)(iii). In relevant part, section 3(x) of the FLSA defines "public agency" as the Government of the United States. *See e.g.*, 29 CFR 825.108(a). As a "public agency, the US Government automatically meets the threshold requirement of "a person engaged in commerce or in an industry or activity affecting commerce." 29 USC 2611(4)(B); 29 CFR 825.104(a); 825.800 (public agency definition). The Government of the United States is covered regardless of the number of employees employed by any one federal employer. 29 USC 2611(4)(A)(3); 29 CFR 825.108(d); *see, e.g.*, *Fain v. Wayne County Auditor's Office*, 388 F.3d 257 (7th Cir. 2004). Private sector employers, in contrast, are covered by the FMLA only if they employ at least 50 employees for 20 or more weeks a year. 29 USC 26114)(A)(i); 29 CFR 825.104(a); *Walters v. Metropolitan Educational Enterprises, Inc.*, 519 US 202, 207, 117 S. Ct. 660, 664 (1997); *Walker v. Elmore County Bd. of Ed.*, 379 F.3d 1249 n.1 (11th Cir. 2004). The government of the Virgin Islands is a public agency employer within the meaning of Title I of the FMLA. *Smith v. Virgin Islands Port Authority*, No. 2002-227, 2005 U.S. Dist. LEXIS 56, at n.9 (D.V.I. Jan. 2, 2005). Title I of the FMLA applies to the Government of the United States in its entirety as an employer. This means that every federal employer, be it an agency, executive department, Congress, or the judiciary, is subject to Title I as a "covered employer." This does not mean, however, that Title I applies to all federal employees. As set forth more fully in Chapter 4, "Federal Employees Covered by the FMLA," Title I only applies to certain identified non-civil service employees within the federal sector. Other federal sector employees are covered by Title II or the FMLA as applied through the CAA or PEOAA.

B. INDIVIDUAL MANAGERS AND SUPERVISORS AS COVERED EMPLOYERS

Under Title I, the term "employer" includes "any person who acts, directly or indirectly, in the interest of an employer to any of the employees of such employer." 29 USC 2611(4)(A)(ii)(I); 29 CFR 825.104(a), (d); 29 CFR 825.800 (defining "employer"); *Modica v. Clare Taylor, et. al.*, 465 F.3d 174 (5th Cir. 2006); *Mitchell v. Chapman*, 343 F.3d 811, 827 (6th Cir. 2003), *cert. denied*, 542 U.S. 937 (2004); *Miller v. County of Rockingham, et. al.*, No. 5:06CV00053, 2007 U.S. Dist. LEXIS 23714 at *13 (W.D. Va. March 30, 2007); *Mueller v. J.P. Morgan Chase & Co., et. al.*, No. 1:05 CV 560, 2007 U.S. Dist. LEXIS 20828, at *66 (N.D. Ohio March 23, 2007); *Haybarger v. Lawrence County Ault Probation and Parole, et. al.*, No. 06-862, 2007 U.S. Dist. LEXIS 18314, at *17 (W.D. Pa. March 14, 2007); *Greenlee v. Christus Spohn Health Systems Corp., et. al.*, No. C-06-123, 2007 U.S. Dist. LEXIS 398, at *31 (S.D. Tex. Jan. 4, 2007); *Stuart v. Regis Corp., et. al.*, No. 1:05CV00016DAK, 2006 U.S. Dist. LEXIS 46719, at *20 (D. Ut July 10, 2006); *Heasley v. Carter's for Kids*, No. 3:05-0734, 2006 U.S. Dist. LEXIS 48140, at *6 (M.D. Tenn. July 5, 2006); *Stewart v. Willingboro Bd. of Ed., et al.*, 421 F. Supp. 2d 814, 817 (D.N.J. 2006); *Brown v. CBK, et, al.*, No. 1:05-1171-T-An, 2005 U.S. Dist. LEXIS 31960, at *6 (W.D. Tenn. Nov. 28, 2005); *Matukaitis v. Pennsylvania Coalition Against Domestic Violence, et. al.*, No. 4:CV 05-1146, 2005 U.S. Dist. LEXIS 31046, at *10 (M.D. Pa. Nov. 8, 2005); *Williamson v. Deluxe Financial Services, Inc.*, No. 03-2538-KHV, 2005 U.S. Dist. LEXIS 15293, at *27 (D. Kan. July 6, 2005); *Brewer v. Jefferson–Pilot Standard Life Ins. Co.*, 333 F. Supp. 2d 433 (M.D.N.C. 2004); *Whitney v. Wal-Mart Stores, Inc.*, Case No. 03–65–P–H, 2003 U.S. Dist. LEXIS 22629 (D. Me. Dec. 16, 2003); *Morrison v. Amway Corp.*, Case No. 6:01–cv–749–Orl–22JGG, 336 F. Supp. 2d 1193 (M.D. Fla. Sept. 17, 2003); *Johnson v. Fayette County, Tennessee*, 271 F. Supp. 2d 1068, 1070 (W.D. Tenn. 2003); *Lackey v. Jackson County Tennessee*, Case No. 2:01–0058, 2003 U.S. Dist. LEXIS 25686 (M.D. Tenn. Jan. 6, 2003), *aff'd*, 104 Fed. Appx. 483 (6th Cir. 2004).

The FMLA definition of "employer" is identical to the definition of "employer" in § 3(d) of the Fair Labor Standards Act (FLSA), 29 USC 203(d); 29 CFR 825.104(d). *Modica*, 465 F.3d at 174 (very similar); *Mitchell*. 343 F.3d at 827 (FMLA language mirrors FLSA's definition of employer in 29 USC 203(d)), *cert. denied*, 542 U.S. 937 (2004); *Mueller*, 2007 U.S. Dist. LEXIS 20828, at *66; *Stuart*, 2006 U.S. Dist. LEXIS 46719, at *20; *CBK, et.al.*, 2005 U.S. Dist. LEXIS 31960, at *7; *Brewer*, 333 F. Supp. 2d at 433 (courts have noted that the FMLA definition of employer closely resembles the definition of employer found in FLSA, 29 USC 203(d), and have looked to FLSA for guidance); *Fayette County, Tennessee*, 271 F. Supp. 2d at 1070–71 (looking to FLSA case law to interpret "employer" for purposes of FMLA). Under the FLSA, individual managers and supervisors acting in the interest of their employer have been found to be "employers." Preamble, 29 CFR 825.104; *Mitchell*, 343 F.3d at 826; *Brewer*, 333 F. Supp. 2d at 433.

The significance of including individuals within the definition of an "employer" is that Title I permits aggrieved employees to file suit against, and obtain damages from, a "covered employer." 29 USC 2617(a)(1)–(2). Courts, however, are split on whether individual public managers and supervisors are "employers" within the meaning of Title I of the FMLA. [The subject is addressed more fully in Chapter 15, "Prohibited Acts, Enforcement, and Remedies."]

C. SUCCESSORS–IN–INTEREST

The third definition of "employer" under Title I includes "any successor–in–interest of an employer." 29 USC 2611(4)(a)(ii)(II); 29 CFR 825.104(a), 825.107. *Grace v. USCAR, et al.*, No. 05-72847, 2006 U.S. Dist. LEXIS 72311, at n. 12 (E.D. Mich. Oct. 4, 2006). The term "successor–in–interest" is not defined in the Act. *Siciliano v. Cambridge Home Health Care Inc.*, 65 Fed. Appx. 542 (6th Cir. 2003). Generally, an employer is a successor–in–interest where one organization takes over some or all of the operations of another organization. While more prevalent in the private sector, the "successor–in–interest" rules apply to all federal employers. See *Rhoads v. FDIC*, 956 F. Supp. 1239, 1252 (D. Md. 1997) (FDIC held successor-in-interest to bank in receivership), *aff'd in part, vacated in part on other grounds*, 257 F.3d 373 (4th Cir. 2001), *cert. denied*, 535 U.S. 933, 152 L. Ed. 2d 219 (2002). The creation of the national Homeland Security Agency, through the absorption of existing federal agencies, likely implicates the "successor–in–interest" doctrine. Because, however, the U.S. Government is considered a single employer for purposes of employee eligibility, 29 CFR 825.109(e), the determination of "successor–in–interest" status in the federal sector does not have the practical importance that it does in the private sector. [The eligibility requirements for FMLA leave is discussed in Chapter 5, "Employee Eligibility for Leave."]

1. Responsibilities of Successor-in-Interest

The "successor-in-interest" determination is significant because successors are responsible for employee FMLA entitlements as if the predecessor and the successor were the same employer throughout. 29 CFR 825.107(c). This remains true even if the successor-in-interest is not itself a "covered employer" within the meaning of the FMLA. If the predecessor was covered by the FMLA, the successor must honor all of the predecessor's FMLA responsibilities, including allowing eligible employees to take requested FMLA leave, continue any FMLA leave that began while employed by the predecessor, restore employees at the conclusion of leave, and maintain group health benefits during leave. 29 CFR 825.107(c). The FMLA's obligations in such cases, however, are limited to completing the cycle of any FMLA requests initiated or begun by employees of the predecessor, where the employees met the eligibility criteria at the time the leave was requested. *See* Preamble, 29 CFR 825.107.

2. Factors to Determine Successor-in-Interest

The DOL regulations (29 CFR 825.107(a)) set out eight non-exhaustive factors to determine whether an employer qualifies as a successor-in-interest for purposes of Title I of the FMLA:

(1) Substantial continuity of the same business operations;

(2) Use of the same plant;

(3) Continuity of the work force;

(4) Similarity of jobs and working conditions;

(5) Similarity of supervisory personnel;

(6) Similarity in machinery, equipment, and production methods;

(7) Similarity of products or services; and

(8) The ability of the predecessor to provide relief.

Grace, 2006 U.S. Dist. LEXIS 72311, at n. 12. No one single factor is determinative. Rather, the "entire circumstances are to be viewed in their totality." 29 CFR 825.107(b). *Accord Siciliano*, 65 Fed. Appx. at 542; *Grace*, 2006 U.S. Dist. LEXIS 72311, at n. 3; *Carlson v. Rent-A-Center, Inc.*, 237 F. Supp. 2d 114, 125 (D. Me. 2002); *Barrilleaux v. Thayer Lodging Group, Inc.*, Case No. 97-3252 Section: e/1, 1999 U.S. Dist. LEXIS 8206 (E.D. La. May 26, 1999); *Vanderhoof v. Life Extension Institute et al.*, 988 F. Supp. 507, 513 (D.N.J. 1997); *Rhoads*, 956 F. Supp. at 1252-54. The FMLA regulations parallel those under Title VII of the Civil Rights Act, and the definition of "employer" should be liberally construed in favor of the employee. *Grace*, 2006 U.S. Dist. LEXIS 72311, at n. 3; *Barrilleaux*, 1999 U.S. Dist. LEXIS 8206, at n. 6.

The Sixth Circuit has found that a corporate merger or acquisition is not required to demonstrate that one entity succeeded another. *Cobb. v. Contract Trans., Inc.*, 452 F.3d 543 (6th Cir. 2006). In that case, Cobb worked for Byrd Trucking delivering mail for the U.S. Postal Service. As part of its regular two-year bid cycle, the Postal Service put the contract up for bid, and Contract Transport won, beating out Byrd Trucking. Ninety-five percent of Byrd drivers signed on with Contract Transport. Most drivers, including Cobb, continued to drive the exact same route they had with Byrd. In finding that Contract Transport was the successor to Byrd, the court noted that the merger or acquisition of one entity by another is a factor to consider, but it was not required. Rather, the court found succession based on the fact that Cobb performed the exact same job for three years notwithstandng the change in ownership.

The successor-in-interest determination is made by reference to a point in time near or shortly after the succession of the business. *Vanderhoof*, 988 F. Supp. at 513 & n. 2; *Rhoads*, 956 F. Supp. at 1239. Courts examine the DOL factors from the viewpoint of the aggrieved employee, asking whether an employee who has been retained by a successor would understandably view his or her job situation as essentially unaltered. *Vanderhoof*, 988 F. Supp. at 512-14. *Accord Barrilleaux*, 1999 U.S. Dist. LEXIS at 8206.

The analysis of the court in *Vanderhoof*, 988 F. Supp. at 513 & n.2, is instructive. There, a successor company purchased certain assets of the predecessor company, which operated various medical clinics. Although the successor closed a number of the clinics, Vanderhoof worked at a clinic that remained in operation. The successor denied her request for

FMLA leave believing that she was not eligible. The successor did not include the years Vanderhoof worked for the predecessor company in calculating eligibility. Vanderhoof sued alleging violation of the FMLA.

Addressing each of the eight successor-in-interest factors from the perspective of a predecessor employee at or near the time of the acquisition, the court found that the acquiring company was a successor-in-interest with FMLA responsibilities. Specifically, the court found that there was a continuity of business operations where no break in operations occurred on the day following the purchase, and the clinic continued to provide the same type of services to clients. The use of the same plant was satisfied as the clinic remained in the same building. The fact that the successor closed other clinics was not relevant to the issue because the clinic where Vanderhoof worked was the focus. Continuity of the workforce was satisfied as all of the employees at the clinic were retained. Similarity of the jobs and working conditions were satisfied even though minor changes were made in wage and benefits policies, and new management was put in place. The court stated that fundamental change in the nature of the business enterprise, more than the mere restructuring of the hours or conditions of work or new management, would be required to defeat successor-in-interest status. The court also found a similarity in the products and services offered, rejecting a change in the target clientele from low-priced to upscale as a basis for defeating successor-in-interest status. Finally, the court found a few of the eight factors inapplicable.

In *Siciliano v. Cambridge Home Health Care Inc.*, 65 Fed. Appx. 542 (6th Cir. 2003), the Sixth Circuit held that the employee failed to establish that Defendant Cambridge was an FMLA-covered successor-in-interest employer. Cambridge purchased the patient lists and records of Tri-County Private Hours, a multi-branch health care provider in Ohio. Plaintiff worked for Tri-County. The purchase agreement allowed Tri-County employees to apply for jobs with Cambridge, but Cambridge was under no obligation to hire Tri-County's employees. Cambridge opened some new offices or absorbed Tri-County's patients at its existing facilities, and it continued to operate one of Tri-County's offices. Cambridge hired plaintiff, who essentially performed the same job she had with Tri-County. Cambridge, however, did not hire all of Tri-County's former employees, although the exact number hired was never established. The court found that plaintiff failed to establish that Cambridge was a successor-in-interest to Tri-County for purposes of the FMLA based on lack of specific evidence addressing the eight factors. The lesson for employees is that to survive a motion to dismiss, employees must go beyond summary assertions and present specific factual evidence addressing the eight-factor successor-in-interest test.

D. DETERMINING WHO IS A "COVERED EMPLOYER" WHERE THERE MAY BE MULTIPLE EMPLOYERS

Covered employers are responsible for compliance with the requirements of Title I of the FMLA. The Act presumes that the legal entity that employs the employee is the employer under the FMLA. 29 CFR 825.104(c); *Englehardt v. S.P. Richards Co., Inc.*, No. 04-cv-120-PB, 2005 U.S. Dist. LEXIS 37118, at *5 (D.N.H. Dec. 29, 2005), *aff'd*, 472 F.3d 1 (1st Cir. 2006); *Schubert v. Bethesda Health Group, Inc.*, 319 F. Supp. 2d 963, 966 (E.D. Mo. 2004); *Cruz-Loco v. Ryder Systems, Inc.*, 298 F. Supp. 2d 1248, 1252 (S.D. Fla. 2003). Sometimes, however, determining who falls under the definition of a "covered employer" with FMLA responsibilities is complicated by various business arrangements, including the use of temporary or leased employees, joint ventures between federal agencies and between a federal agency and the private sector, and quasi-government agency relationships. To assure the protection of employees, the FMLA's statutory scheme makes it clear that an employee can be economically dependent on, and thus employed by, more than one entity at the same time. 29 CFR 825.104(c).

The DOL regulations implementing Title I of the FMLA provide two theories under which multiple entities can be determined to be the employer of an employee for purposes of the FMLA: (1) the "integrated employer" theory, and (2) the "joint employment" theory. *Id.* Under both theories, separate entities can be deemed to be parts of a single employer for purposes of the FMLA. 29 CFR 825.104(c); *Reichert v. Village of Greeley*, No. 4:06CV3026, 2006 U.S. Dist. LEXIS 35736, at *3 n. 3 (D. Neb. May 30, 2006); *Hulett v. America's Finest Service Co.*, No. 1:03 CV 2497, 2005 U.S. Dist. LEXIS 41952, at *33 (N.D. Ohio Sept. 14, 2005); *Fishman v. La-Z-Boy Furniture Galleries of Paramus, Inc., et. al.*, No. 04-749 (DRD), 2005 U.S. Dist. LEXIS 18088, at *19 (D.N.J. Aug. 17, 2005); *Cruz-Loco*, 298 F. Supp. 2d at 1252. The "integrated enterprise" test is designed to determine whether to treat two separate entities as a single covered employer for purposes of FMLA compliance. 29 CFR 825.104(c)(2). The "joint employment" test, on the other hand, seeks to apportion FMLA responsibilities between primary and secondary employers where two or more companies share control over the work or working conditions of an employee. 29 CFR 825.106.

The concepts of "integrated enterprise" and "joint employment" are currently of more practical importance in the private sector than in the federal sector. The reason is that the private and federal sectors are treated very differently under Title I in terms of employer coverage and employee eligibility, the two primary areas impacted by the results of these tests. In the federal sector, the significance of being an integrated or joint employer is limited to the impact on employee eligibility. In contrast, in the private sector, designation as an integrated or joint employer may be the difference between an employer meeting the minimum 50-employee complement requirement for FMLA coverage or not. Because all entities that make up the Government of the United States are FMLA-covered employers regardless of the number of employees employed, the addition of employees through designation as an integrated or joint employer is of little practical effect.

1. Integrated Employer Test

The "integrated employer" test is used to determine whether to treat apparently separate entities as a single "covered employer" for FMLA purposes. 29 CFR 825.104(c). Under the "integrated employer" test, several companies may be considered so interrelated that they constitute a single employer. *Hukill v. Autocare, Inc. et al.,* 192 F.3d 437, 442 (4th Cir. 1999), *cert. denied,* 529 U.S. 1116, 120 S. Ct. 1978 (2000); *Reichert,* 2006 U.S. Dist. LEXIS 35736, at n. 2; *Hulett,* 2005 U.S. Dist. LEXIS 41952, at *33; *Schubert v. Bethesda Health Group, Inc.,* 319 F. Supp. 2d 963, 966 (E.D. Mo. 2004). Where this test is met, the employees of all entities making up the integrated employer will be counted in determining employee eligibility. 29 CFR 825.104(c)(2); *Reichert,* 2006 U.S. Dist. LEXIS 35736, at n. 2; *Hulett,* 2005 U.S. Dist. LEXIS 41952, at *33; *Fishman,* 2005 U.S. Dist. LEXIS 18088, at *19; *Bowman v. Ameren Corp.,* No. 4:05 CV 399 DDN, 2005 U.S. Dist. LEXIS 34663, at *18 (E.D. Mo. July 20, 2005).

The integrated employer test was originally developed in the labor relations' context. *See Radio & Television Board Technicians Local 1264 v. Broadcast Serv. Of Mobile, Inc.,* 380 U.S. 255, 85 S. Ct. 876, 5 L. Ed. 789 (1965). It was subsequently incorporated into the employment discrimination context. *Hukill,* 192 F.3d at 442; *see also* Preamble, 29 CFR 825.104 (integrated employer test is based on established case law arising under Title VII of the Civil Rights Act of 1964 and the Labor Management Relations Act). Pursuant to its authority to promulgate regulations "necessary to carry out" the FMLA, *see* 29 USC 2654, the DOL adopted the "integrated employer" test. *Hukill,* 192 F.3d at 442 (citing 29 CFR 825.104(c)); *see also Smith v. Allen Health Systems, Inc. et al.,* No. C-99-2128, 2001 U.S. Dist. LEXIS 10547 (N.D. Iowa 2001) (citing *Hukill* that integrated employer test was adopted directly from NLRB's test for resolving issues of affiliate liability).

Four factors are considered in determining whether to treat multiple entities as a single employer: (1) common management; (2) interrelation between operations; (3) centralized control of labor relations; and (4) degree of common ownership/financial control. *Hukill,* 192 F.3d at 442 (citing 29 CFR 825.104(c)(2)); *Morrison v. Magic Carpet Aviation,* 383 F.3d 1253 (11th Cir. 2004); *Englehardt v. S.P. Richards Co., Inc.,* No. 04-cv-120-PB, 2005 U.S. Dist. LEXIS 37118, at *5 (D.N.H. Dec. 29, 2005), *aff'd,* 472 F.3d 1 (1st Cir. 2006); *Missak v. Lakeland Engineering Equipment Co.,* No. 8:04CV567, at *6 (D. Neb. Oct. 25, 2005); *Hulett,* 2005 U.S. Dist. LEXIS 41952, at *33; *Bowman,* 2005 U.S. Dist. LEXIS 34663, at *18; *Schubert,* 319 F. Supp. 2d at 966; *Cruz-Loco,* 298 F. Supp. 2d at 1252; *Cousin v. Harold,* 238 F. Supp. 2d 357, 364 (D. Mass. 2002); *Nott v. Woodstock Care Center, Inc. et al.,* No. C-3-99-133, 2000 U.S. Dist. LEXIS 9978 (S.D. Ohio 2000).

No single factor is conclusive. Rather, the entire relationship is to be viewed in its totality. 29 CFR 825.104(c)(2); *Hukill,* 192 F.3d at 442; *Englehardt v. S.P. Richards Co., Inc.,* No. 04-cv-120-PB, 2005 U.S. Dist. LEXIS 37118, at *5 (D.N.H. Dec. 29, 2005), *aff'd,* 472 F.3d 1 (1st Cir. 2006); *Hulett,* 2005 U.S. Dist. LEXIS 41952, at *33; *Bowman,* 2005 U.S. Dist. LEXIS 34663, at *18; *Cruz-Loco,* 298 F. Supp. 2d at 1252 (the "determination of whether or not separate entities are an integrated employer is not determined by the application of any single criterion, but rather the entire relationship is to be viewed in its totality").

Control of labor relations prong has traditionally been viewed as the most critical factor. *Englehardt v. S.P. Richards Co., Inc.,* No. 04-cv-120-PB, 2005 U.S. Dist. LEXIS 37118, at *5 (D.N.H. Dec. 29, 2005), *aff'd,* 472 F.3d 1 (1st Cir. 2006); *Allen Health Systems, Inc. et al.,* 2001 U.S. Dist. LEXIS 10547; *Schubert,* 319 F. Supp. 2d at 966 (citing *Schweitzer v. Advanced Telemarketing Corp.,* 104 F.3d 761, 764 (5th Cir. 1997)).

Common ownership alone is insufficient to find an integrated employer. *Magic Carpet Aviation,* 383 F.3d at 1253; *Schubert,* 319 F. Supp. 2d at 966 (citing *Frank v. U.S. West, Inc.,* 3 F.3d 1357, 1364 (10th Cir. 1993)); *Cruz-Loco,* 298 F. Supp. 2d at 1255. Several courts have had the opportunity to address the integrated employer test in the FMLA context, with mixed results.

The Fourth and the Eleventh Circuits addressed the FMLA integrated employer test. In *Hukill v. Auto Care, Inc. et al.,* 192 F.3d 437 (4th Cir. 1999), *cert. denied*, 120 S. Ct. 1978 (2000), after methodically addressing the facts as they relate to the four factors of the integrated employer test, the Fourth Circuit concluded that the several enterprises involved did not constitute an integrated employer. Critical in its decision was the court's determination that each of the entities controlled their own day–to–day labor relations operations. Since the one enterprise that was the employer did not meet the statutory minimum number of employees for FMLA coverage, the Fourth Circuit vacated the district court's judgment in favor of the employee and remanded the matter with instructions for dismissal of the case for lack of subject matter jurisdiction. *Id.* at 444–45. Because it concluded that the entities were not integrated, the court declined to decide the validity of 29 CFR 825.104(c). *Id.* at 443.

In *Morrison v. Magic Carpet Aviation,* 383 F.3d 1253, (11th Cir. 2004), the Eleventh Circuit found that three employers did not constitute an integrated employer. The employee, a pilot, was fired by Magic Carpet for requesting more than two weeks of leave for depression. The employee filed suit under the FMLA against three entities: (1) Magic Carpet Aviation, Inc.; (2) Amway Corporation, of which Magic Carpet was a wholly–owned subsidiary; and (3) RDV Sports, Inc., which owned the Orlando Magic NBA basketball team. Because Magic Carpet did not employ more than 50 employees within 75 miles of the employee's worksite, the employee alleged that RDV, Amway, and Magic Carpet were integrated employers. The combination of employers, the employee alleged, satisfied the 50/75 test for eligibility.

Reviewing the four–factor integrated employer test, the court found that Morrison failed to introduce any evidence regarding common management. The court held that the mere fact that RDV looked to Amway, among others, for advice in restructuring its operations failed to establish that the operations of the two entities were interrelated in any way. The court held that the request that Morrison attend an employee orientation program at RDV when he was first hired was "hardly enough to show centralized control over labor relations, much less that RDV and Magic Carpet were so integrated that they were, in effect, one entity." The court held that the employee satisfied the final prong of the test, as the DeVos family owns both Amway and TDV. The Fourth Circuit went on to hold, however, that common ownership alone is insufficient for a jury to conclude that two corporations are integrated into one operation for FMLA purposes. The Fourth Circuit encompasses Virginia, West Virginia, Maryland, North Carolina, and South Carolina.

Several courts have applied the Title VII integrated employer test to FMLA claims. In *Fishman v. La-Z-Boy Furniture Galleries of Paramus, Inc.,* No. 04-749 (DRD), 2005 U.S. Dist. LEXIS 18088, at *19 (D.N.J. Aug. 17, 2005), the court did not apply the four factor test set forth in the DOL regulations to determine whether separate entities were parts of one single integrated employer for FMLA purposes. Rather, the court applied a three-prong test used by the Third Circuit in Title VII cases for determining when multiple entities should be considered integrated. Under the three-prong test, to establish a *prima facie* case, an employee must provide that the defendants intentionally split the number of employees into multiple business entities in order to avoid liability under the statute. Second, when the companies sought to be aggregated for statutory purposes are in a parent-subsidiary relationship, the court will deem a parent and subsidiary a single employer when the parent has directed the subsidiary to perform the allegedly discriminatory act in question. Third, in determining whether to integrate the number of employees between parent and subsidiary, the court focuses on the degree of operational rather than financial entanglement. That is, whether the operations of the companies are so united that nominal employees of one company are treated interchangeably with those of another employee. Factors to make this determination include: (1) degree of unity between entities with respect to ownership, management, and business functions (e.g., hiring and personnel matters); (2) whether they present themselves as single company that third parties dealt with as one unit; (3) whether parent company covers salaries, expenses, or losses of its subsidiary; and (4) whether one entity does business exclusively with the other. The court concluded that LZB Paramus did not satisfy the three-prong test for an integrated employer.

In *Hulett v. America's Finest Service Co.,* No. 1:03 CV 2497, 2005 U.S. Dist. LEXIS 41952, at *34 (N.D. Ohio Sept. 14, 2005), the court noted the similarity of the FMLA integrated employer test with the integrated employer test developed under Title VII. Because the separate employers to a joint venture did not meet the Title VII integrated employer factors, the court concluded that these entities were not integrated employers for FMLA purposes. The Title VII factors were: (1) interrelated operations; (2) common management; (3) centralized control of labor relations; and (4) common ownership.

In *Bowman v. Ameren Corp., et. al.,* No. 04-cv-120-PB, 2005 U.S. Dist. LEXIS 37118, at *5 (D.N.H. Dec. 29, 2005) the court found that a parent and a subsidiary were not integrated employers. The court noted that the parent and subsidiary: (1) each had their own human resource departments; (2) each was solely responsible for its hiring and firing decisions; (3) one company managed the day-to-day operations of the facility where the plaintiff worked; (4) SPR's management made the decision to terminate Engelhardt without consulting anyone from the parent company. In those circumstances, the court found that the adoption by the subsidiary of a parent company's general policy statements regarding employment matters was not enough to demonstrate that the parent controlled labor relations.

The court in *Cruz–Loco v. Ryder Systems, Inc.,* 298 F. Supp. 2d 1248, 1252 (S.D. Fla. 2003), held that the plaintiff failed to establish that defendants Ryder System, Inc. (Ryder) and Ryder System Federal Credit Union (RSFCU) were integrated employers for purposes of the FMLA. Plaintiff was terminated after working fulltime for RSFCU for over four years. She sued alleging violations of the FMLA. Ryder moved for summary judgment arguing that they were not plaintiff's employer. RSFCU admitted that plaintiff was their employee, but also moved for summary judgment arguing that they were not a covered employer within the meaning of the FMLA because at all times they employed less than 50 people. Plaintiff alleged that Ryder and RCFSU constituted a "joint" or "integrated employer" of plaintiff for FMLA purposes.

RSFCU is a federally chartered bank with less than 20 employees. It provides banking and financial services to its members, which include the employees of Ryder and its subsidiaries. Ryder is a large company with many subsidiaries and affiliates employing hundreds, if not thousands, of employees. RSFCU pays Ryder to perform certain services, such as payroll processing. Ryder also provides certain employee benefits to RSFCU employees. RSFCU rents its office space from Ryder, and utilizes Ryder's human resource department on an *ad hoc* basis, which includes use of certain Ryder forms (including employment applications) and practices.

Applying the Fourth Circuit's analysis in *Hukill v. Auto Care, Inc.,* 192 F.3d 437 (4th Cir. 1999), the court analyzed the four–factor integrated employer test set forth in 29 CFR 825.104(c)(2). Regarding common management, the court noted that two factors governed: (1) who had control of the day–to–day operations of the business and; (2) who had the authority to hire and fire employees. The court found that RSFCU had day–to–day control of the operations of the business, because both Ryder and RSFCU had their own managers, officers, and directors. It also found that plaintiff's supervisor had and exercised the authority to hire and fire plaintiff, and she controlled all relevant terms of plaintiff's employment, including conducting performance appraisals and approving requests for leave. Regarding interrelation of operations, the court found that RSFCU's purchase of services from Ryder did not establish an integrated employer relationship where RSFCU could, at its discretion, obtain these services from outside vendors. The court also noted that RSFCU and Ryder are not in the same business. Because it had the sole authority to hire, fire, and supervise its employees, the court found no evidence of centralized labor relations even where RSFCU utilized Ryder's human resource department on an *ad hoc* basis. The court noted the absence of evidence that Ryder "gained control" over RSFCU's labor relations as a result of that arrangement. Finally, the court found that, while the plaintiff made some showing of common ownership in that RSFCU is owned by its members, which include employees of Ryder and its subsidiaries, such showing was not enough when viewed in light of the other elements. One court concluded that the integrated employer test was inapplicable in the FMLA context. *Diangi v. Valex, Inc. et al.,* 56 F. Supp. 2d 1023, 1024–25 (N.D. Ill. 1999). In deciding the permissible scope of pending discovery, the court found that it was necessary to determine whether the concept of "integrated enterprise" applied to claims under the FMLA. To make that determination, the court had to decide whether the FMLA was an anti–discrimination law or more similar to the National Labor Relations Act (NLRA). Precedent in the Seventh Circuit held that the integrated employer test did not apply to statutory discrimination claims, but did apply to claims arising under the National Labor Relations Act. *Id.* at 1024. The court found that the FMLA was "akin to the broad objectives of anti–discrimination statutes: to protect a class of employees form adverse employer action", (citing *Papa*, 56 F. Supp. 2d at 1025. The court found that the FMLA was "a far cry" from the NLRA, which the court distinguished by noting the flexibility inherent in the determination of an appropriate bargaining unit, which might be an enterprise, a plant, or a trade within a several plants, compared with the inflexibility of the FMLA. *Id.* Interestingly, the court made no mention of 29 CFR 825.104(c), which specifically applies the integrated employer test to the FMLA.

2. Joint Employers

Joint employment is the second method for determining FMLA responsibilities where multiple employers exercise some control over the same employee. Joint employment typically arises where a federal agency uses an employee from a temporary help or leasing agency. The determination of joint employment has two effects: (1) joint employees count for purposes of meeting the minimum employee complement requirements for FMLA coverage and eligibility; and (2) joint employers have different FMLA responsibilities to joint employees, depending on whether the employer is the primary or secondary employer. In the federal sector, the addition of joint employees to the complement of each joint employer has no impact on FMLA coverage of federal employers because all such entities are already covered as "public agencies" by Title I of the FMLA. Joint employment may, however, impact employee eligibility for leave and the FMLA responsibilities of a federal employer as a joint employer.

a. Joint Employment Explained

The FMLA does not address "joint employment." The term is, however, addressed in the regulations issued by the DOL to implement the requirements of the Act. 29 CFR 825.106; *see Moreau v. Air France*, 356 F.3d 942, 946 (9th Cir. 2004); *Schubert v. Bethesda Health Group, Inc.*, 319 F. Supp. 2d 963, 970 (E.D. Mo. 2004) (issue of joint employment is addressed in 29 CFR 825.106); *Cruz–Loco v. Ryder Systems, Inc.*, 298 F. Supp. 2d 1248, 1255 (S.D. Fla. 2003); *Miller v. Defiance Metal Products, Inc.*, 989 F. Supp. 945, 947 (N.D. Ohio 1997). "Joint employment" occurs where two or more employers share some control over an employee or the employee's working conditions. 29 CFR 825.106(a); *Taylor v. Texaco, Inc., et. al.*, No. 4:04-CV-212-JEC, 2007 U.S. Dist. LEXIS 22239, at *17 (N.D. Ga. March 28, 2007); *Moldenhauer v. Tazewell-Pekin Consolidated Communications Center*, No. 04-1169, 2006 U.S. Dist. LEXIS 93896, at *21 (C.D. Ill. Dec. 29, 2006); *Reichert v. Village of Greeley*, No. 4:06CV3026, 2006 U.S. Dist. LEXIS 35736, at n. 3 (D. Neb. May 30, 2006); *Heasley v. Carter's for Kids*, No. 3:05-0734, 2006 U.S. Dist. LEXIS 48140, at *4 (M.D. Tenn. July 5, 2006); *Hulett v. America's Finest Service Co.*, No. 1:03 CV 2497, 2005 U.S. Dist. LEXIS 41952, at *34 (N.D. Ohio Sept. 14, 2005); *Brown v. SBC Communications, Inc., et. al.*, No. 04-C-0290, 2005 U.S. Dist. LEXIS 41599, at *29 & N. 6 (E.D. Wis. Aug. 23, 2005); *Dinkins v. Varsity Contractors, Inc.*, No. 04 C 1438, 2005 U.S. Dist. LEXIS 6732, at *20 (N.D. Ill. March 10, 2005); *Defiance Metal Products, Inc.*, 989 F. Supp. at 947.

Joint employers are generally separate and distinct entities with separate ownership, management and facilities. 29 CFR 825.106(a); *see also Heasley*, 2006 U.S. Dist. LEXIS 48140, at *4; *Hulett*, 2005 U.S. Dist. LEXIS 41952, at *34; *SBC Communications, Inc., et. al.*, 2005 U.S. Dist. LEXIS 41599, at *29 & n.6; *Dinkins*, 2005 U.S. Dist. LEXIS 6732, at *20.

As set forth in 29 CFR 825.106(a), factors relevant to the determination of whether employers are engaged in a joint employment relationship include:

- Where two or more employers agree to share an employee's services or to interchange employees;

- Where one employer acts directly or indirectly in the interest of the other employer in relation to the employee; or

- Where the employers share control of the employee because one employer controls the other employer.

29 CFR 825.106(a); *accord Moreau* 356 F.3d at 946; *Texaco, Inc., et. al.*,2007 U.S. Dist. LEXIS 22239, at *17; *Moldenhauer*, 2006 U.S. Dist. LEXIS 93896, at *21; *SBC Communications, Inc., et. al.*, 2005 U.S. Dist. LEXIS 41599, at *29 & n. 6; *Dinkins*, 2005 U.S. Dist. LEXIS 6732, at *20;*Schubert*, 319 F. Supp. 2d at 970; *Cruz–Loco*, 298 F. Supp. 2d at 1255; *Phillips v. Leroy–Somer North America*, No. 01–1046–T, 2003 U.S. Dist. LEXIS 5349 (W.D. Tenn. March 28, 2003); *Thomas v. The Jewish Federation of Greater Philadelphia*, No. 01–CV–2415, 2003 U.S. Dist. LEXIS 4692 (E.D. Pa. March 18, 2003). No single factor, however, is determinative. Rather, the determination is made based on the totality of the relationship. *Texaco, Inc., et. al.*, 2007 U.S. Dist. LEXIS 22239, at *17; *Heasley*, 2006 U.S. Dist. LEXIS 48140, at *4.

The DOL regulation has been criticized for providing insufficient guidance regarding the boundaries of a joint employment relationship. *See Moldenhauer*, 2006 U.S. Dist. LEXIS 93896, at *23; *Dinkins*, 2005 U.S. Dist. LEXIS 6732, at *21; *Schube*, 319 F. Supp. 2d at 970; *Cruz–Loco*, 298 F. Supp. 2d at 1255. One court specifically declined to apply the four factors of the "integrated employer" test to the "joint employer" test. *Schubert*, 319 F. Supp. 2d at 970, n.9.

As an example, the use of an employee from a temporary or leasing agency will ordinarily create a joint employment relationship. 29 CFR 825.106(b); *Grace v. USCAR, et al.*, No. 05-72847, 2006 U.S. Dist. LEXIS 72311, at n. 3 (E.D. Mich. Oct. 4, 2006); *Mahoney v. Nokia, Inc.*, 444 F. Supp. 2d 1246 (M.D. Fla. 2006) (noting that the regulatory example constitutes "almost a presumption in favor of finding that" the leasing agency is the primary employer), *aff'd*, 2007 U.S. App. LEXIS 13644 (11th Cir. June 11, 2007); *Mackey v. Unity Health System*, Case No. 03–CV–6049T(F), 2004 U.S. Dist. LEXIS 8830 (W.D.N.Y. May 10, 2004) (finding joint employment between a hospital and Nurse Finders, a temporary employment agency for nurses); *Phillips*, 2003 U.S. Dist. LEXIS 5349 (W.D. Tenn. March 28, 2003) (joint employment relationship exists whenever a temporary agency provides employees for another employer); *Salgado v. CDW Computer Centers, Inc.*, No. 97-C–1975, 1998 U.S. Dist. LEXIS 1374 (N.D. Ill. Feb. 5, 1998); *Miller v. Defiance Metal Products, Inc.*, 989 F. Supp. 945, 947 (N.D. Ohio 1997). *But see Astrowsky v. First Portland Mortgage, Corp., Inc.*, 887 F. Supp. 332 (D. Me. 1995) (no joint employment relationship where leasing agency did not exercise sufficient control over employee on long-term lease assignment).

Employees on temporary detail assignments to other federal agencies, or seasonal employees, are additional examples of joint employment relationships.

There is little case law interpreting the question of joint employment under the FMLA. *Moldenhauer,* 2006 U.S. Dist. LEXIS 93896, at *23; *Dinkins,* 2005 U.S. Dist. LEXIS 6732, at *21. Courts that have addressed this issue ave looked to different sosurces for guidance in determining whether an entity was a joint employer for purposes of the FMLA.

A number of courts have looked to the FLSA for guidance on what constitutes joint employment. *Moreau,* 356 F.3d at 946-47; ; *Moldenhauer,* 2006 U.S. Dist. LEXIS 93896, at *21; *Dinkins,* 2005 U.S. Dist. LEXIS 6732, at *20; *Defiance Metal Products, Inc.,* 989 F. Supp. at 947. In support of this approach, courts have cited the FMLA's use of the FLSA definitions of "employee" and "employer." The JDOL has opined that the FLSA standard should apply. *See Moreau,* 356 F.3d at 946-47 (citing DOL WH Advisory Opinion letter, 2000 DOL FMLA LEXIS 4 (Sept. 11, 2000), that FLSA standards are to be used to determine joint employment under the FMLA), *aff'd,* 356 F.3d 942 (9th Cir. 2004). Under the FLSA, the "economic realities" test is used to determine the existence of an employer–employee relationship. *Goldberg v. Whitaker,* 366 U.S. 28, 33, 108 S. Ct. 933, 6 L. Ed. 2d 100 (1961); *Henderson v. Inter–Chem Coal Co., Inc.,* 41 F.3d 567, 570 (10th Cir. 1994); *Dinkins v. Varsity Contractors, Inc.,* No. 04 C 1438, 2005 U.S. Dist. LEXIS 6732, at *22 (N.D. Ill. March 10, 2005). The inquiry under this test is not limited to "traditional common law concepts of 'employee' or 'independent contractor' or contractual terminology." *Henderson,* 41 F.3d at 570; *Hale,* 993 F.2d at 1393. Rather, the focus is on the circumstances as a whole and the economic reality of the relationship. *Johns v. Stewart,* 57 F.3d 1544, 1559 n.21 (10th Cir. 1995). The determination of whether a joint employment relationship exists is based on the totality of the circumstances. 29 CFR 825.106(b); *Dinkins,* 2005 U.S. Dist. LEXIS 6732, at *20; *Defiance Metal Products, Inc.,* 989 F. Supp. At 945 n.1. The touchstone in analyzing an alleged employer/employee relationship is economic dependency. *Moreau v. Air France et al.,* No. C–99–4645–VRW, 2002 U.S. Dist. LEXIS 5665 (N.D. Ca. March 28, 2002), *aff'd,* 356 F.3d 942 (9th Cir. 2004).

Under the "economic realities" test, no single set of factors is determinative. *See Dinkins,* 2005 U.S. Dist. LEXIS 6732, at *20;

There is a split among the circuits regarding the precise factors a court should consider in determining joint employment under the FLSA. *Moldenhauer v. Tazewell-Pekin Consolidated Communications Center,* No. 04-1169, 2006 U.S. Dist. LEXIS 93896, at *23 (C.D. Ill. Dec. 29, 2006); *Dinkins,* 2005 U.S. Dist. LEXIS 6732, at *20. The First and Ninth Circuits apply a four-factor test that assesses whether the alleged employer: (1) had the power to hire and fire; (2) supervised and controlled employee work schedules or conditions of employment; (3) determined the rate and method of payment; and (4) maintained employment records. *See Baystate Alternative Staffing, Inc. v. Herman,* 163 F.3d 668, 675 (1st Cir. 1998); *Bonnett v. California Health & Welfare Agency,* 704 F.2d 1465, 1470 (9th Cir. 1983).

The Second Circuit has applied a six-factor test: (1) whether the plaintiff used the entity's premises and equipment for his work; (2) whether the labor contractor had a business that could or did shift as a unit from one putative joint employer to another; (3) the extent to which the plaintiff performed a discrete line-job that was integral to the entity's process of production; (4) whether responsibility under the labor contract could pass from one subcontractor; (5) the degree to which the entity or its agents supervised the plaintiff's work; and (6) whether the plaintiff worked exclusively or predominantly for the entity. *Zheng v. Liberty Apparel Co., Inc.,* 355 F.3d 72 (2d Cir. 2003).

The Ninth Circuit has noted that these factors are not etched in stone. *Bonnett v. California Health & Welfare Agency,* 704 F.2d 1465, 1470 (9th Cir. 1983). In fact, the Ninth Circuit applied other, albeit, similar factors in different factual situations. *See Torres–Lopez v. May,* 111 F.3d 633, 640 (9th Cir. 1997) (citing as factors (1) nature and degree of control of the workers; (2) the degree of supervision, direct or indirect, of the work; (3) the power to determine the pay rates or the methods of payment of the workers; (4) the right, directly or indirectly, to hire, fire, or modify the employment conditions of the workers; and (5) preparation of payroll and the payment of wages).

Congress intended the definitions of employer and employee in the FMLA to be broadly inclusive. *Defiance Metal Products, Inc.,* 989 F. Supp. at 947; *see also Nationwide Mutual Ins. v. Darden,* 503 U.S. 318, 326, 112 S. Ct. 1344, 117 L. Ed. 2d 581 (1992) (FLSA's definition of "employ" encompasses "striking breadth"); *Dinkins,* 2005 U.S. Dist. LEXIS 6732, at *20 (Supreme Court instructed courts to construe the terms "employer" and "employee" expansively under the FLSA); *Hale,* 993 F.2d at 1393 (Supreme Court has instructed that courts are to interpret the term "employ" in the FLSA expansively).

Finally, whether an employer/employee relationship exists is a question of law for the court to decide. *Bonnett,* 704 F.2d at 1469.

Two circuits addressed the impact of indirect supervision of employees through detailed contractual requirements on the establishment of joint employment. Both courts, on the facts before them, found such indirect supervision insufficient to establish a joint employment relationship. The effect of indirect supervision on joint employment appears to be an area ripe for conflict.

The Eleventh Circuit in *Morrison v. Magic Carpet Aviation*, 383 F.3d 1253 (11th Cir. 2004), relied on case law interpreting the Equal Pay Act to determine whether an entity was an individual's employer. The court gave no explanation for why it relied on case law interpreting the Equal Pay Act for this purpose. Morrison, a pilot for Magic Carpet Aviation, Inc., was fired when he requested more than the two weeks off he was granted to deal with depression. Morrison filed suit against three entities: (1) Magic Carpet; (2) Amway Corp., of which Magic Carpet was a wholly owned subsidiary; and (3) RDV Sports, Inc., which owned the Orlando Magic NBA team. RDV Sports contracted with Magic Carpet to fly the Orlando Magic NBA team to games. To meet the 50 employees within 75 miles eligibility test, Morrison needed to prove that RDV Sports was a joint employer with Magic Carpet.

The court applied three factors to determine if RDV Sports was Morrison's employer: (1) whether the employment took place on the premises of the alleged employer; (2) how much control the alleged employer exerted over the employee; and (3) whether the alleged employer had the power to fire, hire, or modify the employment contract. Addressing the first factor, the court concluded that RDV Sport's leasehold right to have its players flown around by Magic Carpet did not give RDV any meaningful direct control over the worksite (the plane). Regarding the third factor, the court concluded that, while RDV Sports, as a major client, could exert significant influence over Magic Carpet's employment decisions, it did not actually have the power to hire or fire Morrison directly. Finally, the court found insufficient evidence that RDV had control over Morrison. The court noted that the contract between RDV Sports and Magic Carpet specified that all crew members were under the exclusive control of Magic Carpet. The court concluded:

> [T]here is no evidence that RDV had direct control over Morrison, rather than the indirect control over a service provider's employees that a customer may obtain by contracting with that service provider. Such indirect control does not amount to an employment relationship because the customer is in privity of contract with the service provider (which is itself an independent contract of the customer), and not the service providers employees.

The Ninth Circuit looked to case law and regulations from the FLSA and the Migrant and Seasonal Agricultural Worker Protection Act (AWPA) to help it determine whether an entity was a joint employer for purposes of the FMLA. *Moreau v. Air France*, 356 F.3d 942, 946–947 (9th Cir. 2003). At least one other court has followed the lead of *Moreau* and applied FLSA joint employment principles in the FMLA context. *See Schubert v. Bethesda Health Group, Inc.*, 319 F. Supp. 2d 963, 970 (E.D. Mo. 2004). An Opinion Letter issued by the DOL specifically provides that "[t]he standards established under the Fair Labor Standards Act (FLSA) are used to determine joint employment under the FMLA." *See* DOL WH FMLA Advisory Opinion No.111 (September 11, 2000); *Schubert*, 319 F. Supp. 2d at 970, n.8.

In *Moreau v. Air France*, 356 F.3d 942, 946–947 (9th Cir. 2003), plaintiff was employed by Air France. Air France denied Moreau's request for 12 weeks of FMLA leave, explaining that Moreau was not eligible because Air France employed less than 50 employees within 75 miles of Moreau's worksite. Moreau contended that Air France should count certain ground handling company employees as joint employees of Air France. Moreau was fired after he took leave anyway. Moreau filed suit alleging that his termination violated the FMLA. The district court awarded summary judgment to Air France after finding that it was not a joint employer for FMLA purposes. Moreau appealed the decision.

The Ninth Circuit explained its application of FLSA principles to determine FMLA joint employment by noting that the FMLA employs a number of definitions from the FLSA, and the FMLA joint employer regulation mirrors the wording of the FLSA joint employment regulations. *Accord Schubert*, 319 F. Supp. 2d at 970. The AWPA, the court observed, relates to the FLSA as the AWPA regulations define joint employment by incorporation of the FLSA definition. *Moreau*, 356 F.3d at 947, n. 2.

Relying on FLSA case law, the court observed that the joint employment determination required consideration of the total employment situation, but focused primarily on four factors: whether the alleged employer (1) had the power to hire and fire employees; (2) supervised and controlled employee work schedules or conditions of payment; (3) determined the rate and method of payment; and (4) maintained employment records. *Id.* at 946–947. The district court relied solely on the above four factors. Moreau argued that the district court erred by applying only the four–factor test, and not the expanded considerations in the AWPA case law. The Ninth Circuit appears to agree that the four–factor FLSA test alone is overly restrictive and does not take into account the requisite totality of the circumstances and the economic reality of the situation. *Id.* at 953. The Ninth Circuit supplemented that analysis with additional factors based on regulations and case law interpreting the AWPA joint employment regulations.

Under Ninth Circuit case law interpreting joint employment for purposes of the AWPA, a non-exhaustive list of regulatory and non-regulatory factors is used to determine whether a joint employment relationship exits. The five regulatory factors include (20 CFR 500.20(h)(4)(ii)):

    (A) The nature and degree of control of the workers;

    (B) The degree of supervision, direct or indirect, of the work;

    (C) The power to determine the pay rates of the methods of payment of the workers;

    (D) The right, directly or indirectly, to hire, fire, or modify the employment conditions of the workers; and

    (E) Preparation of payroll and the payment of wages.

The Ninth Circuit in *Moreau* opined that the AWPA regulatory factors were roughly equivalent to the four FLSA factors. *Moreau*, 356 F.3d at 950. To these factors, the Ninth Circuit added eight "non-regulatory" factors that may be relevant in deciding whether a joint employment relationship exits:

    (1) Whether the work was a specialty job on the production line;

    (2) Whether responsibility under the contracts between a labor contractor and an employer pass from one labor contractor to another without material changes;

    (3) Whether the premises and equipment of the employer are used for the work;

    (4) Whether the employees had a business organization that could or did shift as a unit from one worksite to another;

    (5) Whether the work was piecework and not work that required initiative, judgment or foresight;

    (6) Whether the employee had an opportunity for profit or loss depending upon the alleged employee's managerial skill;

    (7) Whether there was permanence in the working relationship; and

    (8) Whether the service rendered was an integral part of the employer's business.

Id. at 947–948 (citing *Torres-Lopez v. May*, 111 F.3d 633, 639 (9th Cir. 1997)). The Ninth Circuit also considered two additional factors: (1) the use of shared premises by Air France with the ground handling companies; and (2) additional charges imposed by the ground handling companies to hold employees while waiting for an Air France aircraft to arrive. *Id.* at 952–953.

Applying these factors to the three ground handling companies at issue, the court concluded that Air France was not a joint employer of the ground handling service companies. The court noted that Air France lacked the ability to hire or fire ground handling company employees, it did not determine the rate or method of pay for these employees, it did not keep employment records for these employees, and it did not set or control the employees' work schedules, working conditions, or establish the conditions upon which the employees would receive payment. *Id.* at 950.

Significantly, the court noted that Air France's specificity regarding how it wanted the ground work performed and oversight to ensure that its standards were being met could, in some situations, constitute "indirect" supervision of the employee's performance. Such indirect supervision, the court opined, may constitute "some control over the work or working conditions of the employee" within the meaning of 29 CFR 825.106(a) of the FMLA joint employment regulations. The court, however, declined to find that such indirect supervision automatically means that a joint employment relationship is formed. Rather, the court noted that 29 CFR 825.106(b) indicates that in such circumstances, "the business[es] *may* be joint employers under the FMLA." Based on the totality of the circumstances, the court held that the supervision/control by Air France was minimal in contrast to the numerous other factors which negated a finding of a joint employment relationship on the facts of record. *Id.* at 951.

In *Taylor v. Texaco, Inc., et. al.*, No. 4:04-CV-212-JEC, 2007 U.S. Dist. LEXIS 22239, at *17 (N.D. Ga. March 28, 2007), the court found a joint employment relationship between Texaco-Shell Oil Company and an independent owner of a gas station based on the former's contractual ability to dictate employee dress, substance abuse policies, to send in inspectors to evaluate store operations, as well as, mystery shoppers who can evaluate employee performance. Under the Leave and Operating Agreement, the court noted that Shell-Texaco had the right to insist that the operator fire an employee.

Courts have readily found the existence of a joint employment relationship where temporary help agencies are involved. See *Mackey v. Unity Health System*, Case No. 03–CV–6049T(F), 2004 U.S. Dist. LEXIS 8830 (W.D.N.Y. May 10, 2004); *Phillips v. Leroy–Somer North America*, Case No. 01-1046-T, 2003 U.S. Dist. LEXIS 5349 (W.D. Tenn. March 28, 2003). Absent the presence of a temporary help agency, recent court decisions have found against a joint employment relationship. See *Schubert v. Bethesda Health Group, Inc.*, 319 F. Supp. 2d 963, 970 (E.D. Mo. 2004); *Cruz–Loco v. Ryder Systems, Inc.*, 298 F. Supp. 2d 1248, 1255 (S.D. Fla. 2003); *Thomas v. The Jewish Federation of Greater Philadelphia*, Case No. 01–CV–2415, 2003 U.S. Dist. LEXIS 4692 (E.D. Pa. March 18, 2003).

In *Thomas v. The Jewish Federation of Greater Philadelphia*, Case No. 01–CV–2415, 2003 U.S. Dist. LEXIS 4692 (E.D. Pa. March 18, 2003), the fact that plaintiff's employer described itself as a "constituent agency" of the larger Jewish Federation of Greater Philadelphia was not controlling on the issue of joint employment. Nor did the court find a joint employment relationship because the Federation makes charitable contributions to Hillel, or upon Hillel's dissolution the assets would be distributed to the Federation. The court noted that these organizations shared a common interest of working for the betterment of the Jewish Community. Otherwise, they were separate and distinct corporations, with separate employees who were not shared or exchanged and over whom there was no direct or indirect joint control.

In *Cruz–Loco v. Ryder Systems, Inc.*, 298 F. Supp. 2d 1248, 1255–1256 (S.D. Fla. 2003), the court relied on an eight–factor test developed by the Eleventh Circuit to determine joint employment for purposes of several federal labor statues. The eight factors are: (1) the nature and degree of the putative employer's control over the workers; (2) the degree of supervision, direct or indirect, of the work; (3) the right, directly or indirectly, to hire, fire, or modify the workers' employment conditions; (4) the power to determine the workers' pay rates or methods of payment; (5) the preparation of payroll and payment of workers' wages; (6) the ownership of the facilities where the work occurred; (7) whether the worker performed a line job integral to the end product; and (8) the relative investment in equipment and facilities. Applying these factors, the court found that Ryder System, Inc. was not a joint employer with Ryder System Federal Credit Union, plaintiff's direct employer.

At least one court has look to Title VII for guidance on what constitutes joint employment for FMLA purposes. In *Hulett v. America's Finest Service Co.*, No. 1:03 CV 2497, 2005 U.S. Dist. LEXIS 41952, at *34 (N.D. Ohio Sept. 14, 2005), the court applied the Title VII joint employment test rather than the FMLA test. Factors to consider include the authority to hire, fire and discipline employees, promulgation of work rules and conditions of employment, issuance of work assignments and instructions, and supervision of employees' day-to-day activities.

b. The FMLA Responsibilities of Primary and Secondary Employers

In a joint employment relationship, each employer's FMLA responsibilities depend on whether they are a "primary" or "secondary" employer. *Moreau v. Air France*, 356 F.3d 942, 946 (9th cir. 2004); *Mahoney v. Nokia, Inc.*, 444 F. Supp. 2d 1246 (M.D. Fla. 2006), aff'd, 2007 U.S. App. LEXIS 13644 (11th Cir June 11, 2007); *Salgado v. CDW Computer Centers, Inc.*, No. 97–C–1975, 1998 U.S. Dist. LEXIS 1374 (N.D. Ill. Feb. 5, 1998). Factors considered in favor of primary employer status include the authority to hire, fire, assign or place the employee, make payroll, and provide employment benefits. 29 CFR 825.106(c); *Mahoney*, 444 F. Supp. 2d at 1246. The primary employer is responsible for giving required notices to employees, providing FMLA leave, maintenance of health benefits during leave, and job restoration on the conclusion of leave. 29 CFR 825.106(c), (e); *Mahoney*, 444 F. Supp. 2d at 1246; *Salgado*, 1998 U.S. Dist. LEXIS 1374.

For employees of temporary help or leasing agencies, the placement agency most commonly would be the primary employer. 29 CFR 825.106(c); *Grace v. USCAR, et al.*, No. 05-72847, 2006 U.S. Dist. LEXIS 72311, at n.3 (E.D. Mich. Oct. 4, 2006). In *Mahoney*, the court found that Spherion, the leasing agency that supplied Mahoney to Nokia, was the primary employer. The court noted that Nokia played no role in Spherion's decision to hire Mahoney. Nokia employees lacked the authority to take corrective action or fire Mahoney. Mahoney was assigned to work at Nokia by Spherion. No one from Nokia interviewed or selected Mahoney before Spherion assigned him to work at Nokia. Spherion, not Nokia, paid Mahoney. Mahoney received his employment benefits from Spherion, which differed from the programs available to Nokia employees. The court also took notice that the employment agreement Mahoney signed clearly stated that

Spherion was his employer, and that he was not employed by Nokia. The responsibilities of secondary employers to joint employees are two-fold: (1) a conditional responsibility to accept their return from FMLA leave; and (2) compliance with the prohibited acts provisions of the FMLA. 29 CFR 825.106(e); *Mahoney*, 444 F. Supp. 2d at 1246; *Grace v. USCAR, et. al.*, No. 05-72847, 2006 U.S. Dist. LEXIS 72311, at n.3 (E.D. Mich. Oct. 4, 2006); *Miller v. Defiance Metal Products, Inc.*, 989 F. Supp. 945, 947 (N.D. Ohio 1997). It must always be remembered, however, that a secondary employer is still an employer of the employee even though it does not have the same FMLA obligations as the primary employer. *Mahoney*, 444 F. Supp. 2d at 1246; *Salgad,* 1998 U.S. Dist. LEXIS 1374.

c. Job Restoration

Job restoration is the responsibility of the primary employer, typically a temporary help or leasing agency. 29 CFR 825.106(e); *Mahoney,* 444 F. Supp. 2d at 1246. The secondary employer, however, is responsible for accepting the employee returning from FMLA leave if the secondary employer continues to utilize an employee from the temporary or leasing agency. 29 CFR 825.106(e); *Mahoney,* 444 F. Supp. 2d at 1246. The duty of a primary employer to restore a temporary employee to the same or an equivalent position on the conclusion of FMLA leave is not absolute. The FMLA does not entitle any employee, including a joint employee, to any right, benefit, or position which the employee would not have held or been entitled to had the employee not taken leave. *See* Preamble, 29 CFR 825.106; 825.216(a).

For example, if, by the time the employee was ready to return from FMLA leave, his or her services were no longer needed because of the completion or abandonment of the project for which he or she was hired, the primary employer (the leasing agency) would have no obligation to restore the employee to the temporary position he or she held with the secondary employer. For the same reason, the secondary employer would have no duty to accept the return of the joint employee. Otherwise, the employee would receive job restoration rights he or she would not have had if he or she had not taken FMLA leave and continued to work, which is not required by the Act.

Similarly, where the secondary employer discontinues the use of the services of the temporary agency altogether, or discontinues contracting for the particular services furnished by the temporary employee who took FMLA leave, the temporary agency (the primary employer) would not have an FMLA obligation to restore the employee returning from FMLA leave to the position he or she held with the secondary employer. Preamble, 29 CFR 825.106. In these circumstances, the Department of Labor endorses the idea that the primary employer (the temporary help or leasing agency) should follow a "head-of-the-line" approach by giving the returning employee priority consideration for possible placement in assignments with other client employers for which the employee is qualified. Preamble, 29 CFR 825.106.

The only time that a primary employer is legally obligated to restore a joint employee returning from FMLA leave to his or her temporary position with a secondary employer is where the primary employer provided the secondary employer with a replacement for the employee on FMLA leave. That the replacement employee might be dismissed as a result if the secondary employer elects not to retain both on the return of the employee from FMLA leave is both possible and required. 29 CFR 825.106(e).

Conversely, secondary employers, such as federal agencies that contract for temporary help, must accept a joint employee returning from FMLA leave if: (1) the secondary employer continues to utilize an employee of the temporary or leasing agency (the primary employer) for the particular services as those provided by the employee on FMLA leave; and (2) the temporary or leasing agency (the primary employer) elects to place the employee back with the secondary employer. 29 CFR 825.106(e). Under these circumstances, the secondary employer's duty to accept the return of a joint employee from FMLA leave continues, even if that means that a replacement employee must be dismissed. *Id.*

d. Employee Eligibility in Joint Employment

The general rule is that employees jointly employed must be counted by both employers, whether or not they are maintained on one of the employer's payroll, in determining employee eligibility. 29 CFR 825.106(d); *Mackey v. Unity Health System*, Case No. 03-CV-6049T(F), 2004 U.S. Dist. LEXIS 8830 (W.D.N.Y. May 10, 2004);*Salgado v. CDW Computer Centers, Inc.*, No. 97-C-1975, 1998 U.S. Dist. LEXIS 1374 (N.D. Ill. Feb. 5, 1998). For employee eligibility purposes, an employee's term of employment begins once assigned by the temporary agency, rather than when hired as a permanent employee. *Mackey,* 2004 U.S. Dist. LEXIS 8830 (citing *Miller v. Defiance Metal Products, Inc.*, 989 F. Supp. 945 (N.D. Ohio 1997)); *Phillips v. Leroy-Somer North America*, Case No. 01-1046-T, 2003 U.S. Dist. LEXIS 5349, at *10 (W.D. Tenn. March 28, 2003).

e. Prohibited Acts

Covered joint employers are subject to the FMLA's prohibitions against interfering with, restraining, or denying the exercise of or attempt to exercise any rights provided under the Act, or discharging or discriminating against an employee for opposing an unlawful practice under the FMLA. *See* 29 USC 2615; 29 CFR 825.106(e), 825.220(a); *Mahoney*, 444 F. Supp. 2d at 1246. A secondary employer that attempted to restrain or interfere with efforts by the primary employer (a temporary help or leasing agency) to restore an employee who was returning from FMLA leave to his or her previous position with the secondary employer would constitute prohibited interference if the primary employer was still providing the same services to the secondary employer by supplying a replacement employee. Preamble, 29 CFR 825.106.

It is not clear whether a secondary employer, such as a federal agency, would violate the Act if it terminated a contract with the primary employer and/or used a different temporary agency to replace the services being provided by the employee on FMLA leave. If the secondary employer's intention in replacing the employee on FMLA leave through another temporary agency was to avoid the responsibility to accept the employee returning from FMLA leave, it would appear that this would violate the spirit, if not the letter, of the FMLA.

The Act also applies the prohibitions to joint employees of secondary employers even if the secondary employer is not a covered employer within the meaning of the FMLA because it does not meet the minimum 50-employee threshold. 29 CFR 825.106(e).

As previously discussed above, because all Title I federal agencies are "covered" employers within the meaning of the Act regardless of size, the situation addressed by the rule would not come up in the federal sector. Of course, secondary employers, including those in the federal sector, are always responsible for compliance with all FMLA provisions with respect to their regular, permanent workforce. *Id.*

E. EFFECT OF CONTRACT OR POLICY ON EMPLOYER COVERAGE

Coverage as an FMLA "employer" is determined by statute and does not attach as a matter of policy or contract. This issue frequently arises in the private sector for small employers who fail to meet the 50 employee/20 weeks on the payroll requirement for FMLA coverage. 29 CFR 825.104(a); 29 CFR 825.105. Again, public agencies in the federal sector do not have a minimum complement requirement. 29 CFR 825.104(a). As an example, a private sector employer that does not meet the 50 employee/20 week payroll test has a policy that adopts the benefits and protections of the FMLA. The employer violates that policy and the employee sues, alleging violation of the adopted FMLA. The employer moves to dismiss the case, arguing that it is not a covered employer within the meaning of the Act. The employee responds that the employer has voluntarily agreed to be covered as a matter of policy. The courts faced with this issue have held that an employer cannot voluntarily agree to be a covered employer within the meaning of the Act where they otherwise do not meet the statutory requirements for FMLA coverage. *Bliss v. Jennifer Convertibles, Inc.*, Case No. 01 C 8661, 2003 U.S. Dist. LEXIS 17435 (N.D. Ill. Sept. 30, 2003) (citing *Thomas v. Pearle Vision, Inc.*, 251 F.3d 1132, 1136 (7th Cir. 2001)). At best, the employee might have a breach of contract claim against the employer.

The *Bliss* case is worth noting because it is another example that, although the FMLA permits employers to provide more generous benefits than the minimum required by the FMLA, the provision of more generous benefits does not necessarily extend FMLA benefits and protections to employers and employees. In the federal sector, the issue arises more frequently where an agency agrees to a lower eligibility threshold for FMLA benefits than the minimum required by the FMLA. [Employee eligibility is addressed in Chapter 5.]

III. TITLE II OF THE FMLA: FEDERAL CIVIL SERVICE EMPLOYEES

Title II of the FMLA applies to federal civil service employees. Unlike Title I, Title II of the Act does not define who is a covered employer. The term "employer" is simply not addressed as a defined term. However, like Title I, Title II does identify which federal employees are covered by these sections of the FMLA.

The Office of Personnel Management (OPM) issued regulations implementing Title II for federal civil service employees. 5 USC 6387. By statute, the regulations issued by OPM were to be consistent with the FMLA regulations issued by the U.S. Department of Labor implementing Title I of the Act. *See* 5 USC 6387. On July 23, 1993, OPM issued interim regulations (58 FR 39596) implementing sections 6381 through 6387 of Title 5, 5 USC 6381–6387. Final regulations implementing

Title II of the FMLA were published by OPM on December 5, 1996 (65 FR 37233), with an effective date of January 6, 1997. 5 CFR Parts 630 and 890.

A. TITLE II FEDERAL AGENCIES

Because it does not define "employer," Title II does not address the "successor-in-interest" doctrine or recognize individual managers and supervisors as "covered employers" within the meaning of the Act. Nor does Title II address the concept of an "integrated employer" or "joint employment." As addressed more fully in Chapter 4, "Federal Employees Covered by the FMLA," the absence of these concepts may adversely impact the eligibility of a Title II employee to take FMLA leave. Because Title II modifies Chapter 63 of Title V, Title II applies to all federal government employers that have "employees" within the meaning of Title II of the Act. Whether an individual is an employee within the meaning of the Title II is, therefore, critical to determining coverage. [The issue is addressed in detail in Chapter 4, "Federal Employees Covered by the FMLA."]

IV. TITLE V: CONGRESS AS A COVERED EMPLOYER

Employees of the United States Senate and House of Representatives (Congress) were originally covered by Title V of the FMLA until its repeal and replacement in 1996 by the Congressional Accountability Act of 1995 (CAA), 2 USC 60m, 60n, *repealed by*, 2 USC 1301, 1302, 1312, 1381–85, and 1401–1416. The CAA was adopted to make certain employment laws applicable to Congress. The FMLA was among the laws applied to Congress by the CAA. 2 USC 1302(a)(6), 1312; *Payne v. Meeks*, 200 F. Supp. 2d 200, 203 (E.D.N.Y. 2002). The CAA specifically adopts the rights and protections set forth in sections 101–105 of Title I of the FMLA, 29 USC 2611–2615. 2 USC 1312(a)(1). The FMLA provisions of the CAA became effective January 23, 1996, one year after the CAA's enactment. 2 USC 1312(e).

The CAA also provides for the enactment of FMLA implementing regulations. 2 USC 1312(d). The regulations were created by the Board of Directors of the Office of Compliance, an entity created to administer the various labor and employment laws applied to the legislative branch by the CAA. 2 USC 1301(2), 1312d)(1). [Additional information on the Board is addressed in Chapter 15, "Prohibited Acts, Enforcement, and Remedies."]

The CAA requires that any regulations issued by the Board be the same as the substantive regulations issued by the Department of Labor for Title I of the FMLA, except where the Board believes a modification would be more effective. 2 USC 1312(d)(2). Unlike federal agency regulations that are published in the Federal Register, the CAA mandates a different route for enactment of implementing regulations. *See generally* 2 USC 1384. The Board issued interim FMLA regulations effective January 23, 1996. *See Office of Compliance Manual*, § 6, Part IV, Method of Approval. The interim regulations were adopted as the final regulations on April 15, 1996. *See* S. Res. 242, Cong. Rec. S3959–S3997 (1996).

FMLA coverage pursuant to the CAA is accomplished by defining who constitutes an employer and employee. By defining who is a "covered employer," the FMLA provisions of the CAA share more in common with Title I of the FMLA than with Title II, which does not define the term "employer." There are, however, interesting differences between the FMLA provisions in the CAA, and Titles I and II of the FMLA.

A. CAA DEFINES FMLA "COVERED EMPLOYER"

The CAA modified the Title I definition of "employer" to mean an "employing office." 2 USC 1312(a)(1)(2)(A). The term "employing office", as set forth in 2 USC 1301(9), means

(1) The personal office of a Member of the House of Representatives or Senate;

(2) A committee or joint committee of the House of Representative or Senate;

(3) Any other office headed by a person with final authority to appoint, hire, discharge, and set the terms, conditions, or privileges of employment of an employee of the House of Representatives or the Senate;

(4) The Capitol Guide;

(5) The Capitol Police Board;

(6) The Congressional Budget Office;

(7) The Office of the Architect of the Capitol;

(8) The Office of the Attending Physician;

(9) The Office of Compliance; and

(10) The Office of Technology Assessment.

See Payne, 200 F. Supp. 2d at 203 (personal office of Representative Gregory Meeks qualifies as an "employing office" under CAA). An individual may only be a covered employee of one of those ten identified employing offices. *Moore v. Capitol Guide Bd.*, 982 F. Supp. 35, 39–40 (D.D.C. 1997).

The FMLA provisions of the CAA and Title I apply FMLA coverage regardless of employee complement. Title II of the FMLA does not define "employer" and, in that sense, also does not have a minimum employee complement before FMLA coverage attaches to the federal employer affected by that Title.

B. INDIVIDUAL MANAGERS AND SUPERVISORS AS COVERED EMPLOYERS

Like Title II, the CAA FMLA statute and regulations do not define individual managers or supervisors as covered employers within the meaning of the Act. Title I of the FMLA does recognize individual managers and supervisors as covered employers. 29 CFR 825.104(a), (d). Apparently, individual members of Congress were not interested in being personally sued for any FMLA transgressions they may inadvertently make.

C. SUCCESSOR-IN-INTEREST

Unlike Title I, but like Title II, the CAA FMLA statute and regulations do not address the "successor-in-interest" doctrine to determine who is a covered employer with FMLA responsibilities. As set forth more fully in Chapter 5, "Employee Eligibility for Leave," the absence of a successor-in-interest doctrine could, at least theoretically, adversely impact an employee's eligibility for FMLA leave. Presumably, Congress did not contemplate being dissolved or taken over by another entity anytime soon, thereby negating the necessity of the successor-in-interest doctrine.

D. DETERMINING WHO IS A COVERED EMPLOYER WHERE THERE MAY BE MULTIPLE EMPLOYERS

The CAA FMLA regulations use a modified form of the "integrated employer" and "joint employment" tests to determine who is a "covered employer" with FMLA responsibilities in multi-employer settings. S. Res. 242, Cong. Rec. S3959–S3997 (April 23, 1996); 29 CFR 825.104, 825.106. Like their counterparts in Title I, see 29 CFR 825.104(c), 825.106, the CAA FMLA regulations use the "integrated enterprise" test to determine whether to treat two separate entities as a single "covered employer" for purposes of FMLA compliance. *See* S. Res. 242, Cong. Rec. S3959–S3997 (April 23, 1996); 29 CFR 825.104(c). The "joint employment" test, on the other hand, seeks to apportion FMLA responsibilities between primary and secondary employers where two or more companies share control over the work or working conditions of an employee. *Id.*; 29 CFR at § 825.106.

1. Integrated Employer Test

The "integrated employer" test used by the CAA FMLA regulations is nearly identical to the test used by Title I. *Compare* 29 CFR 825.104(c), *with* S. Res. 242, Cong. Rec. S3959–S3997 (April 23, 1996), *and* 29 CFR 825.104(c). Factors to be considered in determining whether two or more entities are an integrated employer include: (1) common management; (2) interrelation between operations; (3) centralized control of labor relations; and (4) degree of common financial control. *Id.* These are the same factors as applied in the Title I "integrated employer" test. 29 CFR 825.104(c). Similarly, no single factor is determinative, but rather the entire relationship is viewed in its totality in establishing whether or not two separate entities are an integrated employer. 29 CFR 825.104(c).

The use of the term "separate entities" rather than "employing offices" to describe an integrated employer suggests that one of the "entities" may be from outside the Congress. Of course, to maintain coverage under the CAA FMLA regulations as a covered employer, it would appear that at least one of the entities must be an "employing office" within the meaning of the CAA FMLA regulations.

A significant difference in the CAA FMLA integrated employer test regulations from the Title I regulations is the effect of the integrated employer test. Under Title I, where the "integrated employer" test is met, all entities making up the integrated employer are counted in determining employee eligibility. 29 CFR 825.104(c)(2). Again, under Title I, employee eligibility is dependent, at least in some respects, on a minimum number of employees. *See* 29 CFR 825.104(a), 825.110(a)(3).

2. Joint Employment

Like Title I, the CAA FMLA regulations recognize the concept of "joint employment." S. Res. 242, Cong. Rec. S3959–S3997 (April 23, 1996); 29 CFR 825.106. The "joint employment" test under the CAA FMLA regulations shares many similarities with the same concept in Title I. There are, however, several noteworthy differences.

a. Joint Employment Explained

With the exception of the substitution of the term "employing office" for the Title I terms "businesses" and "employers," the explanation of "joint employment" in the CAA FMLA regulations and the Title I regulations are identical. *Compare* S. Res. 242, Cong. Rec. S3959–S3997 (April 23, 1996), *and* 29 CFR 825.106(a)–(b), *with* 29 CFR 825.106(a)–(b). This distinction, however, is significant. By limiting "joint employment" to arrangements between "employing offices," the CAA FMLA regulations exclude the possibility of joint employment arrangements between Congress and other federal agencies or private sector employers. Under the CAA, the most common form of joint employment under Title I, the use of a temporary or leasing agency to supply employees to a second employer, *see* 29 CFR 825.106(b), would be excluded. In contrast, the term "joint employment" under Title I does not contain a similar limitation but could arise between any two or more businesses, or a federal agency and a private sector business, such as a temporary employment or employee leasing agency.

Of course, the opposite is not true. That is, since Congress fits within the broad definition of a public agency employer under Title I, it is possible that federal agencies and private sector employers, including temporary help or leasing agencies, could be in a joint employment relationship with Congress under Title I, but not under the CAA. As a secondary employer under Title I, Congress could find itself subject to FMLA requirements that are very different from those under the CAA, including individual manager liability for violations.

b. Responsibilities of Primary and Secondary Employers

The FMLA responsibilities of "joint employers" under the CAA FMLA are dependent on whether the employing office is determined to be the primary or secondary employer. S. Res. 242, Cong. Rec. S3959–S3997 (April 23, 1996); 29 CFR 825.106(c). Title I divides FMLA responsibilities in joint employment similarly. *See* 29 CFR 825.106(c). There are significant similarities and differences between the CAA FMLA and Title I regarding the responsibilities of primary and secondary employers.

One significant difference is the manner in which primary and secondary employers are identified. Under the CAA FMLA, the employing offices may agree to designate one or the other to be the primary employing office, and the other or others to be the secondary office. Notice of this designation must be provided to the covered employee. S. Res. 242, Cong. Rec. S3959–S3997 (April 23, 1996); 29 CFR 825.106(c). Title I does not contain a provision permitting the parties to the joint employment relationship to designate one as the primary and one as the secondary employer. Nor does it impose a notice requirement on the designation of primary or secondary employer. Rather, the determination of primary and secondary employer status is made by analyzing various factors. *See* 29 CFR 825.106(c). Of course, there is nothing in the Title I FMLA regulations that would prohibit joint employers from making such a designation. Presumably, however, that designation would be subject to challenge if it were not made in accordance with the factors for primary and secondary employer status.

The allocation of responsibilities of primary and secondary employers is an area containing similarities and differences between Title I and the CAA FMLA. Identical to Title I, the primary employing office under the CAA FMLA is responsible for giving required notices to the covered employee, providing FMLA leave, and maintaining health benefits. *Compare* S. Res. 242, Cong. Rec. S3959–S3997 (April 23, 1996), *and* 29 CFR 825.106(d), *with* 29 CFR 825.106(c).

Secondary employers under the CAA FMLA, as under Title I, are responsible for accepting the return of the joint employee from FMLA leave. *Compare* S. Res. 242, Cong. Rec. S3959–S3997 (April 23, 1996), *and* 29 CFR 825.106(d), *with* 29 CFR 825.106(c).

Another significant difference is the allocation of FMLA responsibilities where employing offices fail to designate a primary employing office. Here, the CAA FMLA regulations impose joint and several liability on all employing offices for giving required notices to the employee, for providing FMLA leave, for assuring that health benefits are maintained, and for job restoration. S. Res. 242, Cong. Rec. S3959–S3997 (April 23, 1996); 29 CFR 825.106(d). Title I does not contain a similar clause.

c. Job Restoration

Job restoration under the CAA FMLA is the responsibility of the primary employing office. *Compare* S. Res. 242, Cong. Rec. S3959–S3997 (April 23, 1996), *and* 29 CFR 825.106(d), *with* 29 CFR 825.106(e). A secondary employer has a conditional responsibility to accept the return of the employee from FMLA leave. *Compare* S. Res. 242, Cong. Rec. S3959–S3997 (April 23, 1996), *and* 29 CFR 825.106(d), *with* 29 CFR 825.106(e). While similar in purpose, Title I and the CAA FMLA use different language to achieve that purpose. The difference in language, however, may demonstrate a difference in secondary employer responsibilities only.

Under the CAA FMLA, the responsibility of a secondary employer to accept the return of a joint employee from FMLA leave is expressly conditioned by incorporation of regulations limiting the obligation of an employing office to reinstate an employee. S. Res. 242, Cong. Rec. S3959–S3997 (April 23, 1996); 29 CFR 825.106(d). Pursuant to those regulations, an employee has no greater right to reinstatement or to other benefits and conditions of employment than if the employee had been continuously employed during the FMLA leave period. S. Res. 242, Cong. Rec. S3959–S3997 (April 23, 1996); 29 CFR 825.216.

The CAA FMLA regulations illustrate the concept with examples involving layoffs, elimination of a shift, or the hiring of an employee for a specific term or project, where the term has expired or the project has been completed. In these situations, the secondary employing office would have no obligation to accept the return of the employee, absent a collective bargaining agreement or other contractual obligations. *Id*. They also limit an employing office's obligation to reinstate a "key" employee, where the employee fails to produce a fitness for duty certificate, and where the employee is unable to return to work following a workers' compensation absence during which FMLA leave is taken concurrently. *Id*. [These concepts are addressed in more detail in Chapter 13, "Return to Work from Leave."]

The CAA FMLA regulations on the responsibility of a secondary employer to accept the return of a joint employee from FMLA leave differ in several respects from similar regulations under Title I. First, the Title I secondary employer regulations, 29 CFR 825.106(e), elected not to incorporate nearly identical regulations limiting the obligations of an employer to reinstate an employee from FMLA leave. *See* 29 CFR 825.216. Instead, the connection to 29 CFR 825.216 is referenced in the Preamble to 29 CFR 825.106, but not in the regulation itself. Because of the cursory reference, it is also unclear whether all of the exceptions to the obligation of an employer to reinstate an employee set forth in 29 CFR 825.216, apply to secondary employers rather than the limited exceptions mentioned in the Preamble. Arguably, the DOL, like the CAA, could have incorporated 29 CFR 825.216 into the secondary employer regulations, but elected not to. The absence of specific language of incorporation suggests DOL did not want all of the exceptions to reinstatement to apply to secondary employers.

Another distinction between the secondary employer regulations is the emphasis in Title I on replacing substitute employees. *See* 29 CFR 825.106(e). Under Title I, a secondary employer is obligated to accept the reinstatement of a returning employee if the secondary employer continues to utilize an employee from the secondary employer, most likely a temporary help agency. *Id*. The CAA FMLA secondary employer regulations do not mention the issue at all. *See* S. Res. 242, Cong. Rec. S3959–S3997 (April 23, 1996); 29 CFR 825.216. The absence in the CAA FMLA secondary employer regulations of the added requirement of the continued employment of a substitute employee before a secondary employer is obligated to accept the return of a joint employee from FMLA leave suggests that the CAA FMLA regulations are more demanding on secondary employers than are those of Title I.

d. Employer Coverage and Employee Eligibility

The CAA FMLA "joint employment" regulations differ dramatically from similar regulations in Title I regarding employer coverage and employee eligibility. Joint employees under Title I are counted toward each employer's complement for purposes of determining employer coverage and eligibility. Employer coverage and employee eligibility under Title I require a minimum number of employees. *See* 29 CFR 825.104(a); § 825.110. Undoubtedly because there is no minimum employee complement for purposes of employer coverage or employee eligibility under the FMLA, as made applicable by the CAA, the matter is simply not addressed in the CAA FMLA joint employment regulations.

e. Prohibited Acts

Another major difference between the CAA FMLA "joint employment" regulations and similar regulations implementing Title I involves the application of the prohibited acts provisions to secondary employers. The prohibited acts provisions of the FMLA define impermissible conduct in violation of the FMLA. [*See* Chapter 15, "Prohibited Acts, Enforcement, and Remedies," for a more detailed discussion.]

Under Title I, secondary employers are responsible for compliance with the prohibited acts provisions with respect to temporary/leased employees, whether or not the secondary employer is covered by the FMLA. 29 CFR 825.106(e). The CAA FMLA does not contain similar limiting language. The absence of this language may, however, be explained by the fact that, under the CAA, joint "employing offices" are both from Congress and, therefore, covered by the FMLA. That is, since the CAA limits joint employment internally to Congress, both the primary and secondary employers will always be covered by the prohibited acts provisions of the FMLA as applied by the CAA. In the private sector, joint employment could involve a secondary employer who was not independently covered by the prohibited acts provisions of the FMLA because that employer did not have the minimum requisite 50 employees for FMLA coverage.

V. FMLA COVERAGE OF THE EXECUTIVE OFFICE OF THE PRESIDENT

The Presidential and Executive Office Accountability Act of 1996 (PEOAA), like the CAA, applies certain labor and employment laws to the Executive Office of the President. 3 USC 401 *et seq.* The FMLA is one of the laws applied to the Executive Office of the President. 3 USC 402, 412. The effective date of the FMLA, as applied by the PEOAA, was the earlier of October 1, 1998, or the effective date of regulations issued to implement this section. To date, no regulations have issued.

A. PEOAA DEFINES "COVERED EMPLOYER"

The PEOAA defines "employer" for purposes of the FMLA as any "employing office." 3 USC 412(a)(2)(A). An "employing office" is defined in 3 USC 401(a)(4) as

1. each office, agency, or other component of the Executive Office of the President;
2. the Executive Residence at the White House; and
3. the official residence (temporary or otherwise) of the Vice President.

The individual offices covered by the PEOAA FMLA requirements include the White House Office, the Executive Residence at the White House, the Office of the Vice President, the Office of Policy Development, the Council of Economic Advisors, the National Security Council, the Office of Management and Budget, and the Office of National Drug Control Policy. *See, e.g.*, 3 USC 431(d)(2).

VI. MIXED FMLA RESPONSIBILITIES OF FEDERAL SECTOR EMPLOYERS

Depending on the composition of the workforce, federal employers may have mixed FMLA responsibilities. Mixed FMLA responsibilities result from the application of different versions of the FMLA to different employees working for the same federal employer. Because of the broad scope of federal employers covered by Titles I and II (essentially the entire federal sector), many, but by no means all, federal employers will need to abide by the FMLA requirements of at least one, and very likely two of these laws.

A federal employer that simply follows the requirements of one FMLA law runs the considerable risk of violating the very different requirements of other applicable FMLA laws. Knowing what FMLA laws apply to each federal employer is, therefore, very important.

CHAPTER 4
FEDERAL EMPLOYEES COVERED BY THE FMLA

The Family and Medical Leave Act (FMLA) only applies to a federal "employee." The FMLA laws applicable to the federal sector, Titles I and II, the CAA, and the PEOAA, each define a covered "employee" differently. Knowing what FMLA law applies to which federal employee is crucial to knowing the FMLA rights and responsibilities involved. This is particularly true in the federal sector where a federal employer may have multiple FMLA responsibilities to different groups of employees arising under several applicable FMLA laws.

Sections I, II, III and IV of this chapter discuss who is a "covered employee" under Titles I and II, and the FMLA as applied through the CAA and the PEOAA.

I. TITLE I COVERED EMPLOYEES

A. DEFINED

The term "employee" under Title I is defined the same as "employee" is defined under § 3(e) of the Fair Labor Standards Act of 1938 (FLSA), 29 USC 203(e). 29 USC 2611(3). The FLSA defines "employee" as any individual employed by an employer. 29 USC 203(e); 29 CFR 825.800 (employee definition). The FLSA defines "employ" broadly as "to suffer or permit to work." 29 USC 203(g); *see also* 29 USC 2611(3) (incorporating the FLSA definition of "employ" into the FMLA); 29 CFR 825.800 (definition of employ).

B. FEDERAL EMPLOYEES COVERED BY TITLE I

Federal employees within the jurisdiction of Title I of the FMLA, as set forth under 29 CFR 825.109(b)–(d) and 825.800 (employee definition), include:

- Employees of the United States Postal Service;
- Employees of the Postal Rate Commission;
- A part-time employee who does not have an established regular tour of duty during the administrative workweek;
- An employee serving under an intermittent appointment or temporary appointment with a time limitation of one year or less;
- Employees of the legislative or judicial branch of the United States, but only if they are employed in a unit which has employees in the competitive service, and excluding any employee covered by Title V. Examples include employees of the Government Printing Office and the U.S. Tax Court;
- A civilian in the military departments (as defined in § 102 of Title 5, United States Code);
- An individual employed in any executive agency (as defined in § 105 of Title 5, United States Code), excluding any federal officer or employee covered under Subchapter V of Chapter 63 of Title 5, United States Code;
- Any individual employed in a nonappropriated fund instrumentality under the jurisdiction of the Armed Forces; and
- Employees of other federal executive branch agencies who are not covered by Title II.

Title I of the FMLA does not apply to "any federal officer or employee" who is covered by Title II of the FMLA. *Hulett v. America's Finest Service Co., et. al.*, No. 1:03 CV 2497, 2005 U.S. Dist. LEXIS 41952 (N.D. Ohio, Sept. 14, 2005),

A brief review of each category of covered federal employees follows.

1. Employees of the United States Postal Service and Postal Rate Commission

Title I of the FMLA covers all employees of the United States Postal Service (Postal Service) and Postal Rate Commission (PRC). 29 CFR 825.109(b)(1)-(2). The reason all employees of the Postal Service and the PRC were singled out rests in the interplay between Titles I and II of the FMLA. In short, Title I covers federal employees who are not covered by Title II of the Act. *See* 29 CFR 825.109(c). Employees of the Postal Service and the PRC are specifically excluded from the civil service definition of "employee" used by Title II. *See* 5 USC 2105(e). Several cases confirm that postal employees fall within the coverage of Title I of the FMLA. *See Johnson v. USPS,* No. 1:97-CV-794, 1999 U.S. Dist. LEXIS 7981 (W.D. Mich. May 26, 1999); *Albert v. Runyon,* 6 F. Supp. 2d 57, 61 (D. Mass. 1998) (Title I of Act and implementing regulations apply to USPS); *Baber v. Runyon,* No. 97-CIV-4798 (DLC), 1998 U.S. Dist. LEXIS 20233 (S.D.N.Y. Dec. 28, 1998) (same); *Burge v. Dept. of Air Force,* 82 MSPR 75 (1999, *aff'd,* 2001 U.S. App. LEXIS 6756 (Fed. Cir. May 8 2001)); *Ramey v. USPS,* 70 MSPR 463, 466 (1996), *aff'd,* 178 F.3d 1312, 1999 U.S. App. LEXIS 657 (Fed. Cir. Jan. 8, 1999). Title I applies to all Postal Service and PRC employees regardless of how these employees are designated or categorized. For example, Title I of the FMLA applies with equal force to a Christmas Casual or Temporary Employee (TE) as it does to a full-time career employee of the Postal Service. Being a "covered employee" is not, however, the same as being an "eligible employee." As set forth more fully in Chapter 5, "Employee Eligibility for Leave," only "eligible" employees are entitled to take FMLA leave. While the Christmas Casual in this example may ultimately be less likely than the full-time career employee to meet the minimum eligibility requirements in order to invoke the benefits of the FMLA, as an initial matter, they are both covered employees within the meaning of the FMLA.

2. Part-Time Federal Employees

Title I covers all part-time federal employees who do not have an established regular tour of duty during the administrative workweek. 29 CFR 825.109(b)(3), 825.800 (employee definition). These part-time federal employees are specifically excluded from the definition of an employee for purposes of Title II. *See* 5 USC 6301(2)(B)(ii).

In *Lemily v. United States,* 190 Ct. Cl. 57, 418 F.2d 1337 (Ct. Cl. 1969), the United States Court of Claims explained the meaning of the phrase "part-time employee who does not have an established regular tour of duty" under 5 USC 6301(2)(B)(ii). In that case, the Court of Claims applied the part-time employee exemption to relief deck officers and engineers. The *Lemily* plaintiffs were temporary employees paid at an hourly rate on a "when actually employed" basis. *Id.* at 1338. Although they apparently worked the equivalent of a 40-hour workweek, the Court of Claims determined that the *Lemily* plaintiffs were part-time employees without a regular tour of duty. *Id.* at 1345.

In construing the section 6301 exclusion from the definition of "employee," the court in *Lemily,* 418 F.2d at 1344, stated:

> There is no evidence of a legislative intent to otherwise alter or relax the basic concept of a tour of duty as representing a specific period of time, regularly established in advance, during which an employee is unequivocally required to work.

To meet the "regular tour of duty" standard, a part-time employee must (1) work at specific times, and (2) in which the times are set in advance. *Cutright v. U.S.,* 953 F.2d 619, 621 (Fed. Cir. 1992). A "regular tour of duty" was described in a series of Comptroller General Decisions as requiring "definite and certain time, day and/or hour of any day, during the workweek when the employee regularly will be required to perform duty." *Id.* at 622 (citing 31 Comp. Gen. 581, 584 (1952)). The Comptroller General similarly determined that day-to-day variances in an employer's schedule prevented employee's (court reporters) from working a "regular tour of duty." *Id.* (citing 54 Comp. Gen. 251, 258 (1974)).

A part-time employee whose work schedule varies based on the needs of an employer or the availability of work does not satisfy the "regular tour of duty" standard. *Id.* at 623 (court reporter worked at convenience of court, not based on set work schedule); *Lemily,* 418 F.2d at 1344 (employer-employee relationship of mutual convenience wherein duty assignments resulted from a day-to-day and generally informal alignment of available work with individuals willing and able to do it failed to establish "regular tour of duty"). This is true even where the part-time employee either works the equivalent of a 40-hour workweek, or is guaranteed payment for a 40-hour week. *Cutright,* 953 F.2d at 623; *Lemily,* 418 F.2d at 1345.

3. Intermittent Appointments of Less than One Year

All federal employees serving an intermittent appointment of less than one year are covered by Title I. 29 CFR 825.109(b)(4), 825.800 (employee definition). These federal employees are specifically excluded from the definition of a covered employee for purposes of Title II. *See* 5 USC 6381(1)(A).

In *Hulett v. America's Finest Service Co., et. al.*, No. 1:03 CV 2497, 2005 U.S. Dist. LEXIS 41952 (N.D. Ohio, Sept. 14, 2005), the employee alleged that she was a temporary federal employee of the General Services Administration with an appointment of one year and, therefore, was covered by Title I of the FMLA. GSA argued that Hulett was an employee of a GSA contractor. For purposes of summary judgment, the court found sufficient evidence that Hulett was a Title I GSA employee. The court relied on language in the contract indicating that GSA significantly controlled the manner and means of plaintiff's performance as a security guard.

A former employee serving a temporary appointment of over 1 year with the Small Business Administration was found to be a federal employee covered by Title II of the FMLA rather than Title I. *See Sutherland v. Bowles*, 2 BNA WH Case 2d 1336 (E.D. Mich. 1995).

4. A Civilian in the Military

Title I of the FMLA applies to a civilian in the military departments. 29 CFR 825.800 (definition of employee). The Departments of the Army, Navy, and Air Force constitute the "military departments." 5 USC 102; *see also Corey v. U.S.A. et al.*, No. 96–6409, 1997 U.S. App. LEXIS 22258 (10th Cir. 1997) (unpublished) (5 USC 102 covers civilians in the "military departments," meaning the Army, Navy, and Air Force. It does not cover uniformed military personnel); *Rasmussen v. Dept. of Navy*, No. SF-0752-06-0837-I-1, 2006 MSPB LEXIS 7240, at *9 (MSPB Dec. 12, 2006) (federal civilian employee of Navy not covered by Title I because did not meet the 1250 work hours eligibility requirement).

National Guard technicians are considered civilian employees of the Departments of the Army and Air Force. *Sanford v. Connecticut Nat'l Guard*, 50 MSPR 120, 123–24 (1991); *Kostan v. Arizona Nat'l Guard*, 50 MSPR 182, 183–87 (1990); *see also* 32 USC 709(e). As such, National Guard technicians enjoy the benefits and burdens of Title I of the FMLA, not Title II.

5. Individuals Employed in a Nonappropriated Fund Instrumentality Under the Jurisdiction of the Armed Forces

An armed forces nonappropriated fund instrumentality (NAFI) is an entity created for the benefit of military personnel through an initial loan provided by the federal government. *Mann v. Haigh*, 120 F.3d 34, 35 (4th Cir. 1997); *Suarez v. OPM*, 58 MSPR 639 (1993). Repayment of the government loan and employee pay is made out of the income generated by the NAFI. *Id.* (citing *Dupo v. OPM*, 69 F.3d 1125, 1127 n.1 (Fed. Cir. 1995)). Military exchanges and similar entities are the major type of NAFIs. *Haigh*, 120 F.3d at 35; *see also Honeycutt v. Long*, 861 F.2d 1346, 1349 n.3 (5th Cir. 1988) (Army and Air Force Exchange Service is a nonappropriated fund instrumentality).

Both Title I and Title II of the Act claim to cover individuals employed in a NAFI of the armed forces. Title II of the Act, however, appears to have the stronger claim that it governs armed forces NAFI employees.

Title I does not expressly include armed services NAFI employees within the meaning of the term "employee." Nor are they referenced in § 109 of the Department of Labor (DOL) regulations, 29 CFR 825.109, addressing federal employees covered by Title I. Armed Services NAFI employees are referenced in the "Definitions" included in Subpart H of the DOL Title I regulations, 29 CFR 825.800. Subpart H defines "employee" as "any individual employed by the Government of the United States—(D) In a nonappropriated fund instrumentality under the jurisdiction of the Armed Forces...."

"Armed forces" is defined in 20 USC 101(a)(4) as the Army, Navy, Air Force, Marine Corps, and Coast Guard. *See also* 5 USC 2101(2) (defining "armed forces" the same as in § 101(a)(4) of Title 20, 20 USC 101(a)(4)). As defined, the term "armed forces" is broader than the term "military departments" contained in 5 USC 102, which is limited to the Army, Navy, and Air Force. *See Corey v. U.S.A. et al.*, No. 96–6409, 1997 U.S. App. LEXIS 22258 (10th Cir. Aug. 20, 1997) (unpublished). At least one court recognized a distinction between "military departments," defined as limited to civilian employees, and "armed forces," consisting of uniformed military personnel. *See Gonzales v. Dept. of Army*, 718 F.2d 926, 928 (9th Cir. 1983).

Title II also claims coverage of armed forces NAFI employees. As set forth more fully below, the definition of employee for purposes of Title II is, by cross-reference, contained in 5 USC 2105. *See* 5 USC 6381(1)(A); 5 USC 6301(2)(A). Armed forces NAFI employees are included as employees for purposes of Title II of the FMLA. *See* 5 USC § 2105(c)(1)(E); 5 CFR 630.1201(b)(ii)(D).

The only court to address the issue held that armed forces NAFI employees are subject to Title II of the FMLA. *Haigh*, 120 F.3d at 36–37. The *Haigh* plaintiff argued that both Title I and Title II of the FMLA applied to NAFI employees. *Id* at 36. The Fourth Circuit rejected the contention, finding that the inclusion of armed forces NAFI employees in the Title II definition of employee, 5 USC 2105, precluded their coverage by Title I, citing 29 USC 2611(2)(B)(I). This section specifically excludes from the Title I definition of employee any employee covered by Title II of the Act. Unfortunately, there was no mention in *Haigh* of the inclusion of armed forces NAFI employees in the Title I definition of employee contained in 29 CFR 825.800.

The issue of Title I or II coverage of armed forces NAFI employees will undoubtedly be the subject of continued litigation because of the consequences that flow from placement under either Title I or II of the FMLA. As will be discussed in Chapter 15, "Prohibited Acts, Enforcement, and Remedies," the chief consequence is that Title I employees can sue in court for violations of the FMLA, whereas Title II employees cannot. Until the definition in 29 CFR 825.800 is either rescinded by the DOL or invalidated by the courts, armed forces NAFI employees who want to have their complaint heard in court will likely argue that Title I permits them a judicial forum. In the contest between the clear language of Title II of the Act and the DOL regulation, armed forces NAFI employees will likely be held to coverage under Title II of the Act. Clear statutory language should trump agency interpretive regulations.

6. Employees of Other Executive Branch Agencies

Employees of any other executive agency, excluding any federal officer or employee covered under Subchapter V of Chapter 63 of Title 5, 5 USC 630, are covered by Title I of the FMLA. The term "executive agency" is defined by reference to 5 USC 105, and includes an "executive department," a "government corporation," and an "independent establishment."

a. Executive Department

The 14 executive departments, as set forth in 5 USC 101, are as follows:

- Department of State
- Department of Treasury
- Department of Defense
- Department of Justice
- Department of the Interior
- Department of Agriculture
- Department of Commerce
- Department of Labor
- Department of Health and Human Services
- Department of Housing and Urban Development
- Department of Transportation
- Department of Energy
- Department of Education
- Department of Veterans Affairs

As of this writing, it is unclear whether 5 USC 101 has been modified to include the newly created Department of Homeland Defense.

Courts appear to make the determination of whether a federal government entity is an "executive department" based solely on whether the institution at issue is one of the 14 listed in 5 USC 101. *See Lannan v. Bonner et al.,* No. 91-C-7555, 1993 U.S. Dist. LEXIS 119 (N.D. Ill. 1993) (because the DEA was not among the 14 cabinet-level departments listed in 5 USC 101, it was not an executive department).

b. Government Corporation

A "government corporation" is defined as a corporation owned or controlled by the Government of the United States. 5 USC 103(1). A "government controlled corporation," however, does not include a corporation owned by the Government of the United States. 5 USC 103(2).

Title 5 does not explain what a corporation owned by the Government of the United States is, but Congress classifies corporations elsewhere for budget and accounting purposes as either "mixed-ownership" corporations controlled by the Government of the United States or corporations that are "wholly owned" by the Government of the United States. *See Snead, Sr. v. Pension Benefit Guaranty Corp.,* 74 MSPR 501 (1997) (citing 31 USC 9101); *Dockery v. FDIC,* 64 MSPR 458 (1994). Corporations that are "wholly owned" by the Government of the United States are "government corporations" within the meaning of 5 USC 103; "mixed-ownership" corporations controlled by the Government of the United States are not. *Snead, Sr.,* 74 MSPR 501 (as a wholly owned government corporation, PBGC is a government owned corporation under 5 USC 103); *Dockery,* 64 MSPR at 458 (as a mixed-ownership government corporation, FDIC was not a government owned corporation for purposes of 5 USC 103).

The following are wholly owned government corporations within the meaning of 5 USC 103: (1) the Commodity Credit Corporation; (2) the Community Development Financial Institutions Fund; (3) the Export-Import Bank of the United States; (4) the Federal Crop Insurance Corporation; (5) Federal Prison Industries, Incorporated; (6) the Government National Mortgage Association; (7) the Overseas Private Investment Corporation; (8) the Pennsylvania Avenue Development Corporation; (9) the Pension Benefit Guaranty Corporation; (10) the Rural Telephone Bank, until the ownership, control, and operation of the Bank are converted under section 410(a) of the Rural Electrification Act of 1936; (11) the Saint Lawrence Seaway Development Corporation; (12) the Secretary of Housing and Urban Development when carrying out duties and powers related to the Federal Housing Administration Fund; (13) the Tennessee Valley Authority; (14) the Panama Canal Commission; (15) the Corporation for National and Community Service; and (16) the Overseas Private Investment Corporation. 31 USC 9101(3)(A)-(P).

Mixed-ownership corporations excluded from the definition of a government corporation in 5 USC 103 are: (1) the Central Bank of Cooperatives; (2) the Federal Deposit Insurance Corporation; (3) the Federal Home Loan Banks; (4) the Federal Intermediate Credit Banks; (5) the Federal Land Banks; (6) the National Credit Union Administration Central Liquidity Facility; (7) the Regional Banks for Cooperatives; (8) the Rural Telephone Banks when ownership, control and operation of the Bank are converted under § 410(a) of the Rural Electrification Act of 1936 (7 USC 950(a)); (9) the Financing Corporation; (10) the Resolution Trust Corporation; and (11) the Resolution Funding Corporation. 31 USC 9101(2)(A)-(K).

Courts have had the opportunity to decide whether various federal institutions constitute a "government corporation."

(1) Federal Home Loan Mortgage Corporation

The DC Circuit found Federal Home Loan Mortgage Corporation to be a government corporation within the meaning of 5 USC 103. *See McCauley v. Thygerson,* 732 F.2d 978, 982 (D.C. Cir. 1984).

(2) Pension Benefit Guaranty Corporation

The Pension Benefit Guaranty Corporation is a government corporation within the meaning of 5 USC 103. *See Pension Benefit Guaranty Corp. v. White Consolidated Industries, Inc.,* 72 F. Supp. 2d 547, 557 (W.D. Pa. 1999); *Snead, Sr. v. Pension Benefit Guaranty Corp.,* 74 MSPR 501 (1997) (PBGC is a government owned corporation under 5 USC 103).

(3) Tennessee Valley Authority

The TVA is a government corporation. *Richardson v. TVA,* 12 MSPR 319 (1982); *see also In the matter of Ervin Adams,* 1 MSPR 91 (1979) (TVA is an executive agency within the meaning of 5 USC 105).

(4) Smithsonian Institution

The court in *Rivera v. Heyman et al.*, 982 F. Supp. 932, 938–39 (S.D.N.Y. 1997), *aff'd*, 1998 U.S. App. LEXIS 20859 (2nd Cir. 1998), held the Smithsonian Institution was not a government corporation.

(5) Federal Deposit Insurance Corporation

The MSPB found the FDIC is not a "government controlled corporation." *Dockery v. FDIC*, 64 MSPR 458 (1994).

(6) Radio Free Europe/Radio Liberty

After a brief review of the historical development and surrounding legislative framework, Radio Free Europe/Radio Liberty was found not to be a "government controlled corporation." *Ralis v. RFE/RL, Inc.*, No. 83–1474, 1984 U.S. Dist. LEXIS 18767 (D.D.C. 1984), *aff'd*, 770 F.2d 1121 (D.C. Cir. 1985). In so holding, the court found that, although funded by the government through grants, RFE/RL was not government controlled. The court also noted that Congress, throughout the years, carefully stated that RFE/RL is a separate entity, and not a federal corporation, agency or instrumentality.

(7) Federal Reserve

The Board of Governors of the Federal Reserve System was found to be an executive agency. *Hadigian v. Bd. of Governors, Federal Reserve System*, 463 F. Supp. 437, 441 (D.D.C. 1978) (citing 5 USC 104 (government corporation), §105 (executive agency) in holding, without further analysis, that "[t]he Board is, of course, an executive agency"), *aff'd without op.*, 612 F.2d 586 (D.C. Cir. 1980).

Courts are split on whether regional Federal Reserve banks are government corporations. In *Katsiavelos v. Fed. Reserve Bank of Chicago et al.*, 859 F. Supp. 1183, 1185 (N.D. Ill. 1994), the court, following the EEOC's lead in an age discrimination case involving a local federal reserve bank, held that the regional reserve banks act with sufficient independence under private ownership and control such that they do not qualify as government corporations or independent establishments within the meaning of 5 USC 105).

With little analysis, the court in *Dorsey v. Federal Reserve Bank of St. Louis*, 451 F. Supp. 683, 84 (E.D. Mo. 1978), found, based on an examination of 5 USC 103–105, that the Federal Reserve Bank was an executive agency. The court never identified which specific definition it relied on in rendering its decision.

(8) Office of Inspector General, Justice Department

In *Fed. Labor Relations Authority v. U.S. Dept. of Justice et al.*, 137 F.3d 683, 689 (2nd Cir. 1997), the court held that the Office of Inspector General of the U.S. Department of Justice was "not an Executive department or a Government corporation."

c. Independent Establishment of the Executive Branch

An "independent establishment" means an establishment of the executive branch (other than the United States Postal Service or the Postal Rate Commission) that is not an executive department, military department, government corporation, or part thereof, or part of an independent establishment, and the General Accounting Office. 5 USC 104.

(1) Factors

In determining whether a federal entity is an "independent establishment" of the executive branch, the Merit Systems Protection Board appears to require that it be created by statute or Executive Order. *Hereford v. TVA*, 88 MSPR 201 (2001). The existence of language in the underlying legislation creating the independent establishment at issue has been one of the central factors addressed in determining whether the entity in an "independent establishment" for the purposes of 5 USC 104. *See Energy Research Foundation v. Defense Nuclear Research Facilities Safety Board*, 917 F.2d 581, 582–83 (D.C. Cir. 1990) (finding agency to be an independent establishment based on language in enabling statute describing agency as "independent establishment in the executive branch" and noting that other enabling statutes include similar language); *Di Lorio v. U.S. Holocaust Memorial Council*, 69 MSPR 100 (1995) (description in the enabling statute of the Council as an "independent Federal establishment" was cited as the reason for determining that the Council was an independent establishment within the meaning of 5 USC 104), *aff'd without op.*, 129 F.3d 135 (Fed. Cir. 1997); *Pessa v. Smithsonian Institution*, 60 MSPR 421 (1994) (Smithsonian is an independent establishment, citing enabling statute).

The presence of language in the enabling statute suggesting that the Smithsonian Institution is an independent establishment was insufficient to persuade a court from finding that the Smithsonian was not an independent establishment within the meaning of 5 USC 104. *Rivera v. Heyman et al.*, 982 F. Supp. 932, 938 (S.D.N.Y. 1997), *aff'd*, 1998 U.S. App. LEXIS 20859 (2d Cir. 1998). The *Rivera* court looked to the actual governing administrative structure of the Smithsonian in finding that it fell outside the definition of an independent establishment. Specifically, the court noted that the Board of Regents of the Smithsonian included members of all three branches of government; that Congress appointed all of the nine civilian members of the Board; and that 15 of the 17 members of the Board of Regents responsible for the administration of the Smithsonian were either members of Congress or appointed by Congress. The court opined that, while it could be a legislative entity, it was "clear that the Executive does not have the control over the Smithsonian necessary to classify the Institution" as an independent establishment of the executive branch. *Id. But see Pessa v. Smithsonian Institution*, 60 MSPR 421 (1994) (Smithsonian held to be an independent establishment based on language in the enabling statute).

The absence of language in an enabling statute has not, however, foreclosed further consideration of whether a federal entity is an independent establishment within the meaning of 5 USC 104. For example, in *Haddon v. Walters*, 43 F.3d 1488, 1490 (D.C. Cir. 1995), the court noted that the terms and conditions of employment of the White House were governed by different laws than those governing other Title 5 agencies, and looked to other laws distinguishing the White House from the term "independent establishment."

Similarly, in the absence of language in the enabling statute, the MSPB looked to other sources to determine whether an Office of Independent Counsel was an independent establishment of the executive branch. In *O'Brien v. Office of Independent Counsel*, 74 MSPR 192 (1997), the Board looked to characterizations made by the General Accounting Office as well as "implications" of the law's provisions, in finding that independent counsel are executive branch employees.

(2) General Accounting Office

The General Accounting Office (GAO) is a legislative support agency responsible for auditing, investigating, reporting on and proposing improvements to the programs and financial activities of executive agencies in the federal government. *See GAO v. GAO Personnel Appeal Board et al.*, 698 F.2d 516, 518 (D.C. Cir. 1982). Nevertheless, it is specifically included in the definition of an independent establishment of the executive branch. *Id.* at 521–22; *Lawrence v. Staats et al.*, 640 F.2d 427, 428–29 (D.C. Cir. 1978).

(3) Atomic Energy Commission

The former Atomic Energy Commission and one of its successors, the Energy Research and Development Administration, were found, with virtually no analysis, to be independent establishments within the meaning of 5 USC 104. *Nanfelt v. U.S.*, 1 Cl. Ct. 223, 224 (Cl. Ct. 1982).

(4) Federal Energy Regulatory Commission

The Federal Energy Regulatory Commission, on the other hand, was held not to be an independent establishment within the meaning of 5 USC 104. *Neubeiser v. FERC*, 41 MSPR 653 (1989) (although FERC is an independent regulatory commission, it was established within the Department of Energy and is, therefore, part of an executive department, and not an independent establishment).

(5) Parts of Larger Executive Departments Not Independent Establishments

A number of courts have found that various federal employers were not independent establishments of the executive branch because they were part of a larger executive department and, therefore, excluded from the definition of an independent establishment. *See Honeycutt v. Long*, 861 F.2d 1346, 1349 (5th Cir. 1988) (Army and Air Force Exchange

Service was not an independent establishment as it was part of the Department of Defense, an executive department); *Hancock v. Egger*, 848 F.2d 87, 88–89 (6th Cir. 1988) (IRS is not an independent establishment because it is clearly part of an executive department, the Department of the Treasury); *Lannan v. Bonner et al.*, No. 91–C–7555, 1993 U.S. Dist. LEXIS 119 (N.D. Ill. 1993) (DEA is not an independent establishment because it is part of an executive department, the Department of Justice); *Dean v. U.S. et al.*, 484 F. Supp. 888, 889 (D.N.D. 1980) (U.S. Marshall's Service and the Office of the U.S. Marshall in North Dakota are not independent establishments under 5 USC 102, 104, and 105 because they are part of a cabinet–level department, the Department of Justice); *Stephenson v. Simon et al.*, 427 F. Supp. 467, 470–71 (D.D.C. 1976) (because the Bureau of Alcohol, Tobacco and Firearms is part of the Department of the Treasury, an executive department, it is not itself an independent establishment).

At least one court has opined that a bureau of an executive department could be an independent establishment. See *Doolin Security Savings Bank, F.S.B v. Office of Thrift Supervision et al.*, 139 F.3d 203, 207 (D.C. Cir. 1998) (given the location of the Office of Thrift Supervision in the Treasury Department, the functions it performs and its statutory autonomy, it may fit the definition of an independent establishment of the executive branch within the meaning of 5 USC 104).

Whether the Office of the Inspector General (OIG) of a cabinet department is an independent establishment within the meaning of 5 USC 104 has split four circuit courts of appeals. The Second, Third and Eleventh Circuits read the definition of "independent establishment" as excluding "parts" of an executive department but as including the office of the OIG for that department. See *Fed. Labor Relations Authority v. DOJ.*, 137 F.3d 683, 689 (2nd Cir. 1997); *Defense Criminal Investigative Service, Dept. of Defense, et. al., v. FLRA.*, 855 F.2d 93, 98 (3rd Cir. 1988); *FLRA v. NASA*, 120 F.3d 1208, 1213 (11th Cir. 1997), *aff'd*, 525 U.S. 960 (1998). The District of Columbia Circuit, however, concluded that the OIG of the Department of Justice "plainly qualifies as an 'agency' because it is an 'independent establishment' and 'not' an Executive department." *DOJ v. FLRA*, 39 F.3d 361, 365 (D.C. Cir. 1994).

Because it was a part of the military department, the Puget Sound Naval Shipyard was not an independent establishment or federal agency within the meaning of 5 USC 104, 105. *Johnston et al. v. Captain R.B. Horne, Commander, Puget Sound Naval Shipyard et al.*, 875 F.2d 1415, 1420 (9th Cir. 1989). Similarly, the Kansas Army National Guard was held not to be an executive department, government corporation, or independent establishment within the meaning of 5 USC 105. *Blong v. Secretary of the Army et al.*, 877 F. Supp. 1494, 1496 (D. Kan. 1995).

(6) White House

The court in *Haddon v. Walters*, 43 F.3d 1488, 1490 (D.C. Cir. 1995), found the White House is not a 5 USC 104 "independent establishment." In that case, Mr. Haddon, the former assistant chef at the White House, alleged race discrimination when he was passed over for promotion. The case turned on whether the Executive Residence was an executive agency within the meaning of § 2000e–16 of Title VII of the Civil Rights Act of 1964. § 2000e–16 defines "executive agency" by reference to 5 USC 105. After summarily ruling out the definitions of government corporation or executive department, the court focused on whether the White House was an independent establishment. The court concluded that the White House was not an independent establishment after noting that Congress distinguished the White House from independent establishments, and proscribed a different pay system for employees of the White House in separate legislation.

Currently, employees of the White House are covered employees within the meaning of the FMLA, as applied through the PEOAA, not Title I.

(7) Judiciary

The federal judiciary is neither an "independent establishment" of the executive branch, nor a "federal agency." *LaPatourel et al., v. U.S.*, 430 F. Supp. 956, 960 (D. Neb. 1977), *rev'd on other grounds*, 571 F.2d 405 (8th Cir. 1978).

(8) Postal Service

The United States Postal Service, because it is specifically excluded from 5 USC 104, is not an "independent agency." *Van Werry, Jr. v. MSPB*, 995 F.2d 1048, 1052 (Fed. Cir. 1993); *Booker v. MSPB*, 982 F.2d 517, 519 (Fed. Cir. 1992); *Hagedor et al. v. U.S.P.S., et. al.*, No. 00–C–0172, 2001 U.S. Dist. LEXIS 19259 (N.D. Ill. 2001); *Knudtson v. OPM*, 59 MSPR 627 (1993) (USPS not an executive agency within the meaning of 5 USC 104–105). This is the case even though the Postal Reorganization Act of 1970 created the Postal Service as "an independent establishment of the Executive branch." 39 USC 201. Along with the creation of the Postal Service, the Postal Reorganization Act simultaneously modified the definition of independent establishment under 5 USC 104 to exclude the Postal Service. As a result, the Postal Service is specifically excluded from the definition of an independent establishment for the purposes of Title 5 since 1970. *Kane v. MSPB*, 210 F.3d 1379, 1381 (Fed. Cir. 2000). While it is not covered by Title I as an independent establishment of the executive branch, the Postal Service is specifically included within the requirements of Title I. *See* 29 CFR 825.109(b)(1).

7. Legislative and Judicial Branch Employees

Employees of the legislative or judicial branch of the United States are defined as Title I employees if they are employed in a unit that has employees in the competitive service, but excludes any employee covered by Title V. Examples include employees of the Government Printing Office and the U.S. Tax Court. 29 CFR 825.109(d).

The competitive service consists of three categories of employees, with exceptions. First, the competitive service consists of all civilian positions in the executive branch, except positions which are specifically excluded from the competitive service by law, positions which are made by nomination for confirmation by the Senate, unless the Senate directs otherwise, and positions in the Senior Executive Service. 5 USC 2102(a)(1).

Second, the competitive service consists of all civil service positions not in the executive branch, which are specifically included in the competitive service by statute. 5 USC § 2102(a)(2).

Third, the competitive service consists of positions in the government of the District of Columbia, which are specifically included in the competitive service by statute. 5 USC 2102(a)(3).

II. FEDERAL EMPLOYEES COVERED BY TITLE II

Most federal employees are covered by the FMLA under Title II. *See AFGE Local 2328 and VA Medical Center, Hampton, Virginia*, No. 0-AR-3971, 62 FLRA No. 18 n.1 (March 29, 2007); *AFGE Local 2006 and SSA, Philadelphia*, No. 0-AR-2887, 54 FLRA 110 n. 8 (April 30, 1998).

A. COVERED EMPLOYEE DEFINED

An "employee" covered by Title II of the FMLA, 5 USC 6381(1)(A), is defined the same as an "employee" for purposes of 5 USC 6301(2). The term "employee" in 5 USC 6301(2), in turn, is given two definitions. First, an "employee" is defined by cross-reference to 5 USC 2105. *See* 5 USC 6301(2)(A); 5 CFR 630.1201(b)(I). Second, 5 USC 6301(2)(xii) specifically includes in the definition of "employee" certain Foreign Service employees.

In addition to the definition of employee in 5 USC 2105, Title II covers two more groups of employees. 5 USC 6381(1)(A) ("…including any individual employed in a position referred to in clauses (v) and (ix) of section 6301(2)"). But for the specific incorporation of clauses (v) and (ix) into the definition of employee for purposes of Title II, 5 USC 6381(1)(A), individuals holding the referenced positions would not be covered employees. This is because clauses (v) and (ix) list individuals who are excluded from the definition of employee for purposes of 5 USC 6301(2).

This section will begin by reviewing the definition of employee in 5 USC 2105. Following this review, individuals holding positions covered in clauses (v) and (ix) of 5 USC 6301(2), and Foreign Service employees will be addressed.

1. "Employee" as Defined in 5 USC 2105

The term "employee" is defined in three ways in 5 USC 2105. There is a base definition of "employee" given in 5 USC 2105(a) and two more specific definitions addressed to particular employees of the U.S. Naval Academy and certain employees paid from nonappropriated fund instrumentalities of the armed forces, given in 5 USC 2105(b) and (c). As set forth more fully below, the remainder of 5 USC 2105 identifies individuals who either hold positions excluded from the definition of "employee" or who are "employees" for limited purposes other than the FMLA. *See* 5 USC 2105(c)–(f).

a. Civil Service Employees, 5 USC 2105(a)

The base definition of "employee" in 5 USC 2105(a) is as follows:

(a) For the purpose of this title, "employee," except as otherwise provided by this section or when specifically modified, means an officer and an individual who is—

   (1) appointed in the civil service by one of the following acting in an official capacity—

      (A) the President;

      (B) a Member or Members of Congress, or the Congress;

      (C) a member of a uniformed service;

      (D) an individual who is an employee under this section;

      (E) the head of a Government controlled corporation;

      (F) an adjunct general designated by the Secretary concerned under section 709(c) of title 32; and

   (2) engaged in the performance of a Federal function under authority of law or an Executive act; and

   (3) subject to the supervision of an individual named by paragraph (1) of this subsection while engaged in the performance of the duties of his position.

The civil service consists of all appointive positions in the executive, judicial, and legislative branches of the Government of the United States, except positions in the uniformed services. 5 USC 2101(1). "Uniformed services" means the armed forces, the commissioned corps of the Public Health Service, and the commissioned corps of the National Oceanic and Atmospheric Administration. 5 USC 2101(3). "Armed forces" means the Army, Navy, Air Force, Marine Corps, and the Coast Guard. 5 USC 2101(2).

All 3 elements that make up the definition of employee in 5 USC 2105 (appointment in the civil service by an authorized federal official, engagement in a lawful federal function, and supervision by an authorized federal official) have independent significance and are strictly construed in determining whether an individual is a federal employee. *Horner v. Acosta*, 803 F.2d 687, 691–92 (Fed. Cir. 1986). All three definitional requirements found in 5 USC 2105(a) must be met in order for an individual to be considered a federal employee. *Bisson v. OPM*, 908 F.2d 947, 949–950 (Fed. Cir. 1990); *Acosta*, 803 F.2d at 691–92; *Costner v. United States*, 229 Ct. Cl. 87, 665 F.2d 1016, 1020 (1981) ("[A]n abundance of federal function and supervision will not make up for lack of an appointment[.]"); *NTEU v. Reagan*, 663 F.2d 239, 246 (D.C. Cir. 1981); *Baker v. U.S.*, 614 F.2d 263, 266 (Ct. Cl. 1980).

(1) Appointment in the Civil Service

An appointment is necessary for a person to hold a government position and be entitled to its benefits. *Acosta*, 803 F.2d at 692; *accord Barrett v. SSA*, 309 F.3d 781, 787 (Fed. Cir. 2002); *Baker v. U.S.*, 614 F.2d at 268. To be effectuated, a significant degree of formality must surround an appointment. *Id* at 692–93. "Definite, unconditional action by an authorized federal official designating an individual to a specific civil service position is necessary to fulfill the appointment requirement of 5 USC 5120(a)." *Id* at. 693. Acceptance by the appointee is also an essential prerequisite to effectuate an appointment." That is, an individual cannot become a federal civil service employee in a passive manner, but must take some action, signaling acceptance of an appointment. *Watts v. OPM*, 814 F.2d 1576, 1580 (Fed. Cir. 1987), *cert. denied*, 484 U.S. 913 (1987).

Whether an appointment to the civil service has been effectuated is *not* determined based on the totality of the circumstances. *Acosta*, 803 F.2d at 693; *accord Bevans v. OPM*, 900 F.2d 1558, 1562 (Fed. Cir. 1990); *Watts*, 814 F.2d at 1580; *Costner v. U.S.*, 665 F.2d 1016, 1020 (Ct. Cl. 1981). Rather, factors evidencing the "significant degree of formality" that must surround an appointment include the execution of a SF 50 or 52 or any other standard form or document evidencing appointment. *Acosta*, 803 F.2d at 692; *see also Skalafuris v. U.S.*, 231 Ct. Cl. 173, 683 F.2d 383, 387 (Ct. Cl. 1982) (completion of an SF 50 or SF 52 personnel form is an important factor in determining whether an appointment has occurred); *Costner*, 665 F.2d at 1022 (Form 52 is the *sine qua non* to an appointment); *Goutos v. U.S.*, 212 Ct. Cl. 95, 98, 552 F.2d 922, 924 (Ct. Cl. 1976) (same); *Bridgewood v. VA*, 75 MSPR 480 (1997) (absence of SF 50 or SF 52 noted in finding individual was not appointed to civil service), *aff'd without op.*, 155 F.3d 565 (Fed. Cir. 1998). *But see NTEU v. Reagan*, 663 F.2d 239 (D.C. Cir. 1981) (addressed more fully below).

The lack of evidence that salary deductions were made for contributions to the civil service retirement fund has also been cited as "strong evidence that the employee did not have a civil service appointment." *Bevans*, 900 F.2d at 1562.

The failure to take the oath of office has been cited as evidence that an appointment was not effectuated. *See Watts*, 814, F.2d at 1580; *Costner*, 665 F.2d at 1023; *Bridgewood v. VA*, 75 MSPR 480 (1997) (there was no evidence that appellant was administered oath of office upon entering on duty), *aff'd without op.*, 155 F.3d 565 (Fed. Cir. 1998). In *Bevans*, however, the court held that, "even assuming that plaintiff was given the oath of office, the administration of an oath would not itself establish that he was appointed in the civil service because of other evidence indicating that he was not so appointed." *Bevans*, 900 F.2d at 1563–64 (other evidence included the absence of an official appointment form and the lack of salary deductions for civil service retirement, among others).

Courts have also considered and rejected various forms and identification cards offered to establish that an individual was appointed to the civil service. *See Id.* at 1562–64. Regarding the forms, while they may have appeared similar to official federal forms, they were not. In the case of picture identification, they indicated that the individual was an employee of the U.S. Government, but the identification failed to indicate that the individual was appointed to the civil service. "Not every person 'employed by the United States government' has been appointed in the civil service." *Id.* at 1564; *see also Lees v. Secretary of Commerce*, 31 Fed. Appx. 680 (Fed. Cir. 2002) (two letters were not evidence of appointment), *cert. denied*, 537 U.S. 884 (2002).

The usual factors cited as evidence of civil service appointment—official forms and oaths—are not exclusive, see *Watts*, 814 F.2d at 1580, and no single factor will determine whether an appointment has been effectuated. *See Bevans v. OPM*, 900 F.2d at 1563–64 (even assuming oath of office was administered, other factors cited in finding no civil service appointment).

The issue of when an appointment takes place was addressed in *NTEU v. Reagan*, 663 F.2d 239 (D.C. Cir. 1981). The case dealt with the legality of the federal hiring freeze ordered by President Reagan as it applied to individuals who had already been notified that they had been unconditionally selected for federal jobs and who had not begun work on or by January 20, 1981, the date of the hiring freeze. Plaintiffs contended that they were irrevocably appointed to the jobs in question, and the federal government was estopped from denying them employment. The federal government claimed that these individuals had not been appointed because no Form 50 or Form 52 was cut, and the employees had not subsequently entered on duty before the hiring freeze took effect. *Reagan*, 663 F.2d at 243.

The court in *Reagan*, 663 F.2d at 242, stated the rule on appointment as follows:

> For more than one hundred and seventy-five years, the rule as to when an appointment takes place has been clear: "when the last act to be done by the [appointing authority] was performed…." *Marbury v. Madison*, 5 USC (1 Cranch) 137, 156, 2 L. Ed. 60 (1803).

The court held that the receipt of a letter by members of the class stating that each had been selected for appointment and should report to work on a date certain was the "last act" of the appointing authority, and that they had been appointed to a position with the federal government. *Id.* at 242, 245–46.

In so holding, the court rejected the federal government's argument, based on provisions in the Federal Personnel Manual (FPM) issued by OPM, that the filling out of a Standard Form 50 or Standard Form 52, followed by the entrance of the "selectee" onto duty, was the last act within the meaning of *Marbury*. The court reasoned that the significance of these forms as basic documents of one's record of federal employment was both undisputed and irrelevant to whether their execution was a prerequisite to appointment. "The Government has cited no statute, regulation, or Personnel Manual provision to establish this point." *Id.* at 243.

The court also declined to defer to OPM's interpretation of its own regulations on this point because of inconsistencies between OPM's current construction (requiring an SF 50 or SF 52 as the last act for appointment) and prior constructions of the same provisions. These prior constructions indicated that the SF 50 was merely the document used to record personnel actions after they became effective. *Id.* at 244, n.6.

Finally, the court rejected the government's argument that "compelling circumstances" require that a SF 50 be filled out before an appointment occurs. *Id.* at 244. The government argued that an SF 50 should be required before an appointment occurs in order to fix a definite and easily ascertainable time when an appointment takes place; to assure that the appointment is made by someone with actual appointment authority, as opposed to those with only selection authority; and to condition appointment on budgetary considerations or successful completion of a background investigation. *Id*. The court noted that the argument established only that there were good reasons for a rule that the completion of a Form 50 was the "last act" necessary for an appointment. Those good reasons, however, did not establish that this was currently the rule, which the court found that it was not.

According to the court, *Reagan*, 663 F.2d at 245:

> Not one of the approximately 20,000 members of the class which is the subject of these cases received a letter stating that he had been conditionally selected, subject to budgetary factors. Not one received a letter stating that he had been conditionally selected, subject to the discretion of the appointing officer to change his mind at any time prior to the completion of the Standard Form 50. All class members received letters stating that they had been selected for employment and should report for work on a date certain in the future.

Under these circumstances, the court found that the completion of the Form 50 was not the "last act" required of the appointing authorities within the meaning of *Marbury*. *Id.* at 246. The members of the class, the court concluded, were appointed to the positions for which they were unconditionally selected. *Id*.

The court went on, however, to note that appointee status, by itself, does not confer any of the statutory protections due federal employees. To obtain the benefits of that protection, the class members must come within the definition of employee set forth in 5 USC 2105(a). *Id*. at 246. The court held that, while the class members satisfied the first criteria, appointment in the civil service, they did not satisfy the two remaining criteria as they were not engaged in the performance of a federal function nor were they subject to the supervision of a qualified federal employee while engaged in the performance of their duties. *Id*.

The court in *Goutos v. United States*, 552 F.2d 922, 925 (Ct. Cl. 1976), held that the "last act" required to perfect a promotion was the signature of the Civilian Personnel Officer (CPO) on the Form 50, and the failure of the CPO to sign the Form 50 meant that the plaintiff was never appointed.

In *Skalafuris v. U.S.*, 231 Ct. Cl. 173, 683 F.2d 383 (Ct. Cl. 1982), the court held that the action of an employer's supervisor initialing a routing slip does not constitute an appointment where the employee still had to be notified of the offer and to accept it, the department needed to request an appointment, and the Civil Service Commission had to certify the plaintiff, and the plaintiff had to take the oath of office.

To satisfy the definition of "employee" in 5 USC 2105(a), an appointment must be to a civil service position. 5 USC 2105(a). An individual who is hired for a non–civil service position is not, therefore, an "employee" for purposes of 5 USC 2105(a) and, by incorporation, for purposes of Title II of the FMLA. *See e.g., Lees v. Secretary of Commerce*, 31 Fed. Appx. 680 (Fed. Cir. 2002), *cert. denied*, 537 U.S. 884 (2002) (nonprecedential; hiring pursuant to personal services contract not a civil service appointment); *Wolcott et al. v. U.S.*, No. 97–192C LEXIS 87 (Ct. Cl. 1999) (Smithsonian trust fund employees not civil service employees as defined by 5 USC 2105(a)); *Bisson v. OPM*, 908 F.2d 947, 949–950 (Fed. Cir. 1990) (individual hired as "private roll" employee of Smithsonian was not appointed to "civil service" within the meaning of 5 USC 2105(a)); *Lees v. Secretary of Commerce*, 31 Fed. Appx. 680 (Fed. Cir. 2002), *cert. denied*, 537 U.S. 884 (2002).

(2) Authorized Official

To be effective, a civil service appointment must be by an appointing official "acting in an official capacity." 5 USC 2105(a)(1). The term "acting in an official capacity" means that the official is "a person authorized to make the appointment." *Costner v. U.S.*, 665 F.2d 1016, 1022 (Ct. Cl. 1981) (citing *Baker v. U.S.*, 614 F.2d 263, 268 (Ct. Cl 1980)). Those generally authorized to make civil service appointments are listed n 5 USC 2105(a)(1)(A)–(F):

- the President;
- a Member or Members of Congress or the Congress;
- a member of a uniformed service;
- an individual who is an employee under this section;
- the head of a government controlled corporation; or
- an adjunct general designated by the Secretary concerned under section 709(c) of Title 32.

If the individual is appointed by an individual authorized to make civil service appointments, this prong of the Title 5 "employee" test is satisfied. *See Contreras et al. v. U.S.*, 215 F.3d 1267, 1271 (Fed. Cir. 2000) (because members of the uniformed services appointed civilian employees of the military, they were Title 5 employees).

Most of the litigation involving an "authorized official" involves appointment by "an individual who is an employee under this section." 5 USC 2105(a)(1)(D). Because the category potentially grants any federal civil service employee the power to make civil service appointments, the cases focus on the actual authority of the individual who allegedly made the appointment.

Courts have looked to agency rules and regulations, accompanying documents, and employee affidavits to determine whether the federal employee had civil service appointment authority. *See Barrett v. SSA*, 309 F.3d 781, 784–787 (Fed. Cir. 2002) (Referral Sheet and SSA hiring instructions referred to by court to determine that SSA Hearing Office Director did not have civil service appointment authority; such authority was reserved for confirmation by Regional Personnel Office); *Costner*, 665 F.2d at 1022–1023 (finding no indication in record that the lieutenant or captain had authority to make civil service appointments; statements by officers did not indicate appointment authority, but only that they "accepted" the presence of the RCA contract employee).

Courts have also distinguished the authority of a federal employee to make a selection or hiring decision from the authority to make a civil service appointment. *Barrett*, 309 F.3d at 784–87 (federal ALJ had authority to select employee and schedule a tentative start date, but not effect a civil service appointment).

Joint employment and federal civil service employee status has been addressed by the courts in three situations: (1) service with government proprietary corporations or units engaged in intelligence work for the CIA; (2) employment with Cooperative Extension Service organizations; and (3) employment with the Agricultural Stabilization and Conservation Service.

(3) Serving a Federal Function

The second criterion for meeting the definition of a civil service "employee" is that the individual be engaged in the performance of a lawful federal function. 5 USC 2105(a)(2). This issue has not been the subject of extensive litigation. In *Costner v. U.S.*, 665 F.2d 1016, 1020 (Ct. Cl. 1981), the court opined that the plaintiff's efforts to show that he was doing tasks that would otherwise be performed by a federal employee demonstrated that he performed a federal function.

An employee does not perform a federal function by showing up at the worksite without performing any work. *Bilodeau v. American Battle Monuments Commission*, 39 MSPR 243 (1988), *aff'd*, 895 F.2d 1420 (Fed. Cir. 1990). The issue in *Bilodeau* was the effective date of appointment in order to determine whether the plaintiff completed his probationary period. Appellant contended that his employment began on February 1st, the date he reported to work as an Assistant Superintendent Trainee at Netherlands American Cemetery, pursuant to a letter notifying him of his selection. The effective date of his appointment was later changed to February 4th to coincide with the beginning of a pay period. This change was set forth in special orders, which plaintiff did not receive until he reported to work, and in the plaintiff's SF 50. Having determined that the change in the effective date was legitimate, the Board held that appellant was not an employee within the meaning of 5 USC 2105(a) effective February 1st simply by appearing at the Margraten Cemetery. The record, the court held, did not reflect that the appellant performed a federal function on February 1 or that he was supervised by a federal employee while performing his duties. At most, it appears that the appellant questioned the Cemetery Superintendent about the discrepancy between his letter of appointment and the special orders. *Id.* at n.7.

Employees working at University for Cooperative Extension Service (CES) met the federal function and supervision requirements of 5 USC 2105. *See Simmons et al. v. USDA*, 80 MSPR 380 (1998) (because CES Director's work is funded by the federal government and his program is jointly planned with the USDA Extension Services Administrator, Board found individual performed a function that was, at least partially, federal in nature under the supervision of a federal official, within the definition of employee for purposes of 5 USC 2105); *Steiner v. OPM*, 78 MSPR 53 (1998) (performance of services for CES of a land–grant college met federal function and supervision requirements).

(4) Under Federal Supervision

To be a federal "employee," an individual must be under the supervision of a qualified federal employee while performing his or her duties. 5 USC 2105(a)(3). The seminal case defining what constitutes such "supervision" is *Lodge 1858, AFGE et al. v. Webb et al.*, 580 F.2d 496 (D.C. Cir. 1978), *cert. denied*, 439 U.S. 927, 99 S. Ct. 311 (1978).

Lodge arose out of a 1967 RIF of NASA employees working at the Marshall Space Flight Center in Huntsville, Alabama (MSFC). NASA employed both government employees and technical service contractors at MSFC. The union and several former MSFC government employees displaced by the RIF brought suit alleging, essentially, that NASA was illegally employing technical service contract employees who, because of the degree of control exercised by NASA over their work, were functionally federal government employees. *Id*. at 498–99. The employment of these technical service contract employees, it was alleged, violated the Civil Service laws, the NASA statute, and the governing collective bargaining agreement with the union. As a remedy, the plaintiffs wanted the technical service contracts set aside and insisted that civil service employees, rather than being terminated by the RIF, should be permitted to take over the positions filled under the agreements with the contractors. *Id*. at 499.

In *Lodge*, the District Court found that 22 of the 33 contracts involved in the case were invalid, two more were partially invalid, and eight were permissible. The decision of the District Court rested in part on its determination that these technical service contractors were not independent contractors but federal employees because of the supervision provided by NASA over their work. In rendering its decision, the District Court applied a test that required a showing that the "inherent nature of the service, or the manner in which it is provided, reasonably requires, directly or indirectly, federal direction or supervision of contractor employees." *Id*. at 506–7. The Administrator of NASA and the intervener National Council of Technical Service Industries appealed the decision.

The court in *Lodge* determined that NASA did have the authority to enter into technical support service contracts. The narrower question addressed by the court was whether the contracts validly entered into were improperly administered so as to treat the contractor's employees as federal employees, who were required to be appointed in accordance with the civil service laws. *Id*. at 504. To do that, the court looked to the definition of "employee" contained in 5 USC 2105(a). *Id*.

In determining whether individuals furnished by independent contractors were employees of the contractors or of the United States, the district and appellate courts referenced the so-called "Pellerzi Standards." *Id*. at 499–500. In October of 1967, General Counsel Pellerzi of the U.S. Civil Service Commission issued an opinion concerning the legality of certain contracts at the Goddard Space Flight Center. That opinion set forth six specific criteria for determining whether the individuals furnished by independent contractors were employees of the contractors or of the United States. If all six criteria were present, an arrangement that had been considered an independent contract would instead, in the Commission's view, be treated as employment. *Id*. The Pellarzi Standards were subsequently supplemented by the successor General Counsel Mondello of the U.S. Civil Service Commission. *Id*.

The Court of Appeals for the District of Columbia agreed with the district court that all six Pellarzi Standards need not be present to determine the government status of contractor employees. *Id*. at 506. Rather, only one of the Pellerzi criteria overlaps with 5 USC 2105(a) for determining whether a person is an employee of the United States: the necessity for *supervision*. *Id*. at 504. Supervision is the third element of the definition of employee contained in 5 USC 2105(a)(3). *Id*. at 507. The Appellate Court, however, rejected the "supervision" test formulated by the district court to determine employee status. *Id*. at 506–7.

Principally, the court rejected the District Court's supervision test because, while it tracked some of the language in the Pellerzi opinion, it failed to incorporate an important feature added by the Mondello Supplement. The Mondello Supplement recognized that the "touchstone of legality under the personnel laws is whether the contract creates what is tantamount to an employer-employee relationship between the Government and the employee of the contractor." *Id*. at 507. If the contract terms permitted supervision of a contractor employee by a federal officer or employee, or if in the actual performance of the contract such supervision is conducted, the test is met. *Id*. Actual supervision by a federal employee was required by the Mondello Supplement. The district court's test looked only at what might be "reasonably required" and ignored "the always critical factor of who actually exercises the supervision over the manner and performance of the duties of the position." *Id*. at 507.

In determining what conduct would constitute supervision within the meaning of 5 USC 2105(a)(3), the court quoted approvingly from criterion 6 of the Pellerzi Standards. *Id*. at 504. The term "supervision" means control of the individual workman's physical conduct, not just oversight. It means control of the individual in the performance of his work and of the manner in which the work is done. *Id*. The principal element that differentiates employees and independent contractors in the common law and in the context of other federal statutes is the detail with which the party for whom the work is eventually produced actually supervises the manner and means by which the work is performed. *Id*. Merely giving an order for a specific service or article, with the right to reject the finished product or result, is not the type of supervision or control that converts an individual who is otherwise an independent contractor (such as an employee of a contractor) into a federal employee. *Id*. at 504–5.

As to the level of supervision needed, the court agreed with language requiring relatively close, continuous, day-to-day supervision of the details of the job performed. *Id*. at 507–8. In approving that standard, the court cited as controlling authority the decision of the Supreme Court in *Kelley v. Southern Pacific Co.*, 419 U.S. 318, 95 S. Ct. 472, 42 L. Ed. 2d 498 (1974). It also cited with approval the language in the Mondello Supplement.

Applying the above test to the facts at issue, the court found that appellants failed to establish that the contract employees were, in fact, employees of the United States. *Lodge*, 580 F.2d at 509. In each contract between NASA and the technical services companies, the company hired the individuals to perform certain tasks. The companies, not NASA, were to furnish the necessary management and personnel. It was the responsibility of each company to supervise, control, and direct the performance of its own employees in fulfilling the contract requirements. The contracts also required the companies to exercise their independent judgment. *Id*. at 505.

In actual operation, NASA generally gave specific orders, usually to the company supervisor, for certain articles or services. The contractor, not his employees, was told what to do, when to do it, how it was to be done, what qualifications were required for his key people, and how and when to report on his activities, etc. *Id*. at 505. The control over the performance of such requests and the responsibility for the manner in which they would be carried out was in the contracting party and its supervisors, not NASA. The specificity of the requests did not transcend the fact that the actual on-the-spot supervision employed to produce compliance was carried out by the contracting company and its employees, not NASA. *Id*. at 505–6.

In *Aluminum Co. of America et al. v. FTC*, 589 F. Supp. 169, 175–76 (S.D.N.Y. 1984), the court found that the FTC sufficiently supervised the activities of certain "special employees" hired to conduct research projects so that they satisfied the "supervision" criteria of 5 USC 2105(a). The court noted that researchers are supervised to prevent conflicts of interest. Research topics had to be accepted by a FTC committee that reviewed the relevance of the topic and the adequacy of the proposed research procedures. Papers written by special employees were reviewed and criticized on substantive aspects by other FTC economists. An unsatisfactory paper would not be forwarded for clearance, nor could a researcher prepare a second related paper based on FTC-acquired data without approval. Before a paper based on FTC-acquired data was disclosed outside the FTC, the manager of the program had to review it and certify that it did not identify individual company data. The FTC Chairman and other officials had to approve the paper's release.

In *Simmons et al. v. USDA*, 80 MSPR 380 (1998), the Board found that a Director of the University of Illinois Cooperative Extension Services (CES) performed a function which was, at least partially, federal in nature under the supervision of another federal official where the Director held a Schedule A excepted service appointment, the CES Director's work was funded by the federal government and his program was jointly planned with the ES Administrator, a federal employee.

An individual whose work is directly supervised by a nonfederal employer is not a federal civil service employee within the meaning of Title 5. *See Quarles v. Colorado Security Agency, Inc.*, 843 F.2d 557, 559 (D.C. Cir. 1988) (security guard for private company that provided services to HUD building was held not an employee within the meaning of 5 USC 2105(a)(3) where he was supervised by private security company; report of alleged inaccuracy in document submitted by private employer to HUD was insufficient to change the nature of supervision).

Again, satisfaction of the supervision test does not mean that an individual is a federal employee. All three tests set forth in 5 USC 2105(a) must be met for an individual to be considered a federal civil service employee. *See Costner v. U.S.*, 665 F.2d 1016, 1021–22 (Ct. Cl. 1981).

2. Specific Categories of Employees

a. CIA Proprietary Corporations

Individuals hired by persons jointly employed by the CIA and proprietary companies owned and operated by the CIA for intelligence purposes have been held not to be employees within the meaning of 5 USC 2105(a). *See Bevans v. OPM*, 900 F.2d 1558, 1562-1563 (Fed. Cir. 1990); *Watts v. OPM*, 814 F.2d 1576, 1580 (Fed. Cir. 1987), *cert. denied*, 484 U.S. 913 (1987).

Courts have rejected arguments that the mere fact that the appointing officials were both CIA employees as well as employees of the proprietary company was sufficient to establish that they had the authority to make civil service appointments. *Bevans*, 900 F.2d at 1563. Rather, the courts have looked to the authority actually exercised by the appointing officials to determine whether a civil service appointment was made.

In *Bevans*, the court supported its conclusion that although the individuals who hired the plaintiff for a legal position in Air America, a CIA-owned proprietary company, were both CIA employees and held positions with Air America, the evidence indicated that they were acting only for Air America when they hired the plaintiff. *Bevans*, 900 F.2d at 1563. The evidence included the letter offering Bevans the position, which was limited to employment with Air America. *Id*. It also included an affidavit of the individual who offered Bevans the position with Air America that indicated that, although he was a CIA employee, he did not have the authority to hire or fire a federal employee. *Id*.

The decision in *Watts* was based largely on the fact that the plaintiff did not know he was working for a CIA proprietary company. The court indicated that action denoting acceptance of a civil service appointment was necessary to establish an appointment and acceptance could not be made in a passive manner, such as where an individual is unaware that the private company he or she is working for is really a CIA operation. *Watts*, 814 F.2d at 1580. Regarding the lack of appointment authority of CIA officials in the proprietary company, the court noted that the CIA offered Watts a "career position" in the federal service. He refused, implying that neither he nor the CIA considered that Watts was already in the civil service, and that the CIA did not know how to create positions whose incumbents were "employees" within the statutory definition. *Watts*, 814 F.2d at 1580.

b. Cooperative Extension Services

Another area where the authority of an appointing official is at issue because of a joint employment arrangement involves Cooperative Extension Services (CES). The USDA is authorized to make excepted service Schedule A appointments for agents employed in field positions "the work of which is financed jointly by the [USDA] and cooperating persons, organizations, or government agencies outside the Federal service." 5 CFR 213.3113(a). State government, state universities and colleges are often the "cooperating" organization working jointly with the USDA.

Whether CES officials are qualified to make civil service appointments will depend on whether they are federal employees and on the scope of their authority. In *Simmons et al. v. USDA*, 80 MSPR 380, the Board found that both appellants were hired by federal officials with authority to make civil service appointments. These federal officials were either members of the excepted federal service or a USDA official. This conclusion was reached after examining USDA regulations, a Memorandum of Understanding (MOU) between the University of Illinois and the USDA, and an Administrative Handbook issued by the USDA regarding CES Employment. The Handbook and MOU indicated that CES agents were joint employees of the University and the USDA with a federal excepted service appointment without compensation. The excepted service is a part of the civil service. *See* 5 USC 2103(a).

The Board in *Steiner v. OPM*, 78 MSPR 53 (1998), found that an individual employed by a CES was not a civil service employee pursuant to 5 USC 2105(a). Here, OPM argued that in the absence of formal appointments by the USDA, the CES employees who perform services for the CES for a land-grant college such as the University of Rhode Island (URI) are state employees. As support, OPM submitted a letter from the URI Department of Human Resources stating that the appellant was employed by the University. The letter also stated that the appellant contributed to the State of Rhode Island Employees' Retirement System during his employment. The Board agreed with OPM.

c. Agricultural Stabilization and Conservation Service

The third category of joint federal-state employment involves employees in the Agricultural Stabilization and Conservation Service (ASCS). Again, the frequently litigated issue is whether these locally employed individuals are federal civil service employees within the meaning of Title 5. This issue generally turns on whether they were appointed to their position by a qualified federal official.

The ASCS was established pursuant to the Soil Conservation and Domestic Allotment Act of 1935, 16 USC 590(h). Today, the ASCS is part of the Consolidated Farm Service Agency. *See Moore v. Glickman et al.*, 113 F.3d 988, 990, n.1 (9th Cir. 1997). Generally speaking, under the law, the Secretary of Agriculture is authorized to develop a program of agricultural land stabilization and conservation. The Secretary was to accomplish this by forming local committees to advise the USDA in this task. Community members are elected by participating farmers to administer USDA programs such as price supports, agricultural conservation programs, and commodity loan programs. *Id.*

Because most of these locally employed ASCS individuals were hired by local, non–federal officials, they are not federal civil service employees. *See Bucholz v. Aldaya et al.*, 210 F.3d 862, 864 (9th Cir. 2000) (while ASCS employees are federal employees, they are not civil service employees because they are hired by county employees rather than appointed by a qualified federal official); *Moore v. Glickman et al.*, 113 F.3d 988, 992, n. 4 (9th Cir. 1997) (ASCS county employee was not civil service employee where she was appointed by county executive director, who in turn was not a federal employee because he was appointed by county committee composed of elected farmers, who themselves are not appointed federal civil service employees); *Hedman v. USDA*, 915 F.2d 1552, 1554–55 (Fed. Cir. 1990) (appointment by ASCS committee, a body of elected local farmers who are not themselves federal employees, does not satisfy § 2105(a)(1)(D) (definition for authorized federal official)); *Krueger v. Lying*, 733 F. Supp. 75, 77 (E.D. Mo. 1990) (plaintiff, who was appointed and served at the pleasure of the elected county committee, was not appointed in the civil service within the meaning of 5 USC 2105(a)(1)).

d.   Certain Employees of the Naval Academy, 5 USC 2105(b)

An "employee" for purposes of Title II, as made applicable by cross–reference to 5 USC 2105, includes an individual employed at the United States Naval Academy in the midshipmen's laundry, the midshipmen's tailor shop, the midshipmen's cobbler and barbershops, and the midshipmen's store, except an individual employed by the Academy dairy. To be covered, the individual must have commenced employment in one of these positions before October 1, 1996, and been uninterrupted in that position since that date. 5 USC 2105(b).

To be considered an employee under this subsection, an individual need only satisfy the requirements of 5 USC 2105(b). The individual need not meet the additional requirements of 5 USC 2105(a). *Suarez v. OPM*, 58 MSPR 639 (1993).

e.   Employees of Armed Forces Nonappropriated Fund Instrumentalities

A non–appropriated fund instrumentality (NAFI) is generally an entity created for the benefit of government personnel, typically in the form of a military exchange, through an initial loan provided by government. *Mann v. Haigh*, 120 F.3d 34, 35 (4th Cir. 1997). Repayment of the government loan and employee pay is made out of the income generated by the NAFI. *Id.* (citing *Dupo v. OPM*, 69 F.3d 1125, 1127 n.1 (Fed. Cir. 1995)).

Generally, an armed forces NAFI employee is not considered an "employee" for purposes of laws administered by the Office of Personnel Management. 5 USC 2105(c)(1); *see also Matthews et al. v. Commissioner of Internal Revenue*, 907 F.2d 1173, 1177 & n.3 (D.C. Cir. 1990) (NAFI personnel generally not considered employees for purposes of the civil services laws, except for laws listed as exceptions to general rule); *Suarez v. OPM*, 58 MSPR 639 (1993). Title II of the FMLA is administered by the OPM. *See* 5 USC 6387. An exception to this general rule, contained in 5 USC 2105(c)(1)(E), provides that armed forces NAFI employees are to be considered as employees for purposes of the laws administered by the OPM, specifically:

> Subchapter V of chapter 63 [5 USC 6381 et. seq.], which shall be applied so as to construe references to benefit programs to refer to applicable programs for employees paid from nonappropriated funds.

This provision was added when the FMLA was originally enacted. *See* 5 USC 6387(b). Subchapter V of Chapter 63 of Title 5 [5 USC 6381, *et. seq.*] is where Title II of the FMLA begins. As such, armed forces NAFI employees are subject to Title II of the FMLA. *Mann v. Haigh et al.*, 120 F.3d 34, 36 (4th Cir. 1997).

As set forth in 5 USC 2105(c), Title II covers employees paid from nonappropriated funds of the following:

- Army and Air Force Exchange Service;
- Army and Air Force Motion Picture Service;

- Navy Ship's Stores Ashore;
- Navy exchanges;
- Marine Corps exchanges;
- Coast Guard exchanges; and
- Other instrumentalities of the United States under the jurisdiction of the armed forces conducted for the comfort, pleasure, contentment, and mental and physical improvement of personnel of the armed forces.

To be an employee within the meaning of 5 USC 2105(c), an armed forces NAFI employee need only meet the requirements of subsection (c), and not the additional requirements of 5 USC 2105(a). *Suarez v. OPM*, 58 MSPR 639 n.5 (1993).

As noted previously, there is an argument that Title I covers armed forces NAFI employees. The DOL regulation defining "employee" includes within its definition NAFI employees under the jurisdiction of the armed forces. *See* 29 CFR 825.800 (definition of employee, subsection (2)(I)(D)). The only court that has addressed this issue, however, found that armed forces NAFI employees are governed by Title II of the Act, not Title I. *See Mann v. Haigh et al.*, 120 F.3d 34, 37 (4th Cir. 1997).

f. Employees of the Veterans Health Administration

By cross-reference to 5 USC 6301(2)(v), an "employee" covered by Title II of the FMLA includes a physician, dentist, or nurse in the Veterans Health Administration (VHA) of the Department of Veterans Affairs. 5 USC 6381(1)(A). The regulations implementing this section refer to section 7401(1) of Title 38 (38 USC 7401(1)). *See* 5 CFR 630.1201(b)(ii)(B). Section 7401(1) of Title 38 is a provision in the Veterans Affairs Health-Care Personnel Act of 1991, Pub. L. No. 102-40, 105 Stat. 210. *Pichon v. VA*, 67 MSPR 325 (1995). The regulations issued by the Office of Personnel Management implementing Title II of the FMLA appear to be incorrect regarding the coverage of physicians, dentists and nurses of the VHA. Rather than including VHA physicians, dentists and nurses as covered employees as required by the plain language of 5 USC 6381(1)(A), the OPM's regulations define the term "employee" solely by reference to 5 USC 6301(2). *See* 5 CFR 630.1201(b)(I). By its terms, subsection (v) of section 6301(2) *excludes* a physician, dentist, or nurse of the VHA. *See* 5 USC 6301(2)(B)(v). However, 5 USC 6381(1)(A) specifically included in the definition of "employee" individuals in positions covered by subsection (v) of section 6301(2). This change should be reflected in the OPM regulations implementing Title II, but it is not.

The OPM regulations do refer to VHA employees, but only for purposes of determining Title II employee eligibility for FMLA leave benefits. *See* 5 CFR 630.1201(b)(ii)(B). For that matter, the reference to VHA employees is not limited to physicians, dentists, and nurses of the VHA. *Id.* Appointments in the VHA include individuals holding positions other than physician, dentist, or nurse. *See* 38 USC 7401. This would also appear to be an incorrect application of Title II by the OPM. As set forth more fully in the next chapter, Title II requires a covered employee to have worked at least 12 months of service as an employee within the meaning of subparagraph A of section 6381, 5 USC 6381(1)(A)). With respect to the VHA, the term "employee" in subparagraph A is limited to physicians, dentists, and nurses. As such, the reference in the OPM regulation to appointed VHA employees beyond physicians, dentists, and nurses appears over broad.

In *AFGE Local 2328 and VA Medical Center, Hampton, Virginia*, No. 0-AR-3971, 62 FLRA No. 18 n.1 (March 29, 2007), the FLRA observed:

> Certain employees of the Department of Veterans Affairs, including nurses employed by the Veterans Health Administration under 38 USC 7401(1), are covered by regulations prescribed by the Secretary of Veterans Affairs, which must be consistent with Title I and II of the FMLA, see 5 CFR 630.1201(b)(3)(i), and follow the Department of Labor regulations for private sector employees, see 5 CFR 630.1201(b)(4).

g. Teachers for the Defense Department

A "teacher" or individual holding a "teaching position", as defined by section 901 of Title 20 (20 USC 901), is an employee within the meaning of Title II of the FMLA. 5 USC 6381(1)(A) (incorporating "employee" definition of 5 USC 6301(2)(ix)). Section 901 of Title 20, 20 USC 901, is the beginning section on the Overseas Teachers Pay and Personnel Practices Act.

A "teacher" is defined in 20 USC 901(2) as an individual

    (A) who is a citizen of the United States,

    (B) who is a civilian, and

    (C) who is employed in a teaching position described in paragraph 1.

A "teaching position" means those duties and responsibilities which

    (A) are performed on a school-year basis principally in a school operated by the Department of Defense in an overseas area for dependents of members of the Armed Forces and dependents of civilian employees of the Department of Defense, or are performed by an individual who carried out certain teaching activities identified in regulations prescribed by the Secretary of Defense; and

    (B) involve—

        (I) classroom or other instruction or the supervision or direction of classroom or other instruction; or

        (ii) any activity (other than teaching) which requires academic credits in educational theory and practice equal to the academic credits in educational theory and practice required for a bachelor's degree in education from an accredited institution of higher learning; or

        (iii) any activity in or related to the field of education notwithstanding that academic credits in educational theory and practice are not a formal requirement for the conduct of such activity.

The term "overseas" means any area situated outside the United States, including Hawaii, the Commonwealth of Puerto Rico, the Canal Zone, and the possession of the United States (excluding the Trust Territory of the Pacific Islands and Midway Islands). 20 USC 901(3)–(4). A guidance counselor stationed overseas has been found to be within the range of positions covered by 20 USC 901. *See Brown et al. v. DOD*, 12 MSPR 343 n.4 (1982).

As with the VHA, the regulations issued by the Office of Personnel Management implementing Title II of the FMLA appear to be incorrect regarding the coverage of Defense Department teachers and individuals in teaching positions. Rather than including Defense Department teachers and individuals in teaching positions as covered employees as required by the plain language of 5 USC 6381(1)(A), the OPM's regulations define the term "employee" solely by reference to 5 USC 6301(2). *See* 5 CFR 630.1201(b)(1)(I). By its terms, subsection (ix) of section 6301(2) *excludes* teachers or an individual holding a teaching position in the Department of Defense from the definition of employee. *See* 5 USC 6301(2)(B)(ix). However, 5 USC 6381(1)(A) specifically includes in the definition of employee individuals in positions covered by subsection (ix) of section 6301(2). This change should be reflected in the OPM regulations implementing Title II, but it is not.

The OPM regulations do refer to Defense Department teachers and individuals holding teaching positions, but only for purposes of determining Title II employee eligibility for FMLA leave benefits. *See* 5 CFR 630.1201(b)(ii)(C). Viewed alone, this reference would appear to be correct. Title II requires a covered employee to have worked at least 12 months of service as an employee within the meaning of subparagraph A of section 6381 (5 USC 6381(1)(A)). With respect to the DOD, the term "employee" in subparagraph A does cover teachers and individuals holding teaching positions. Again, however, the OPM regulation implementing subparagraph A of section 6381, 5 CFR 630.1201(b)(I), does not include teachers or individuals holding teaching positions within the definition of a Title II covered employee.

      h.   **Foreign Service Employees**

An "employee" for purposes of Title II, as incorporated from 5 USC 6301(2), includes

- any member of the Senior Foreign Service; or

- any Foreign Service officer (other than a member or officer serving as chief of mission or in a position which requires appointment by and with the advice and consent of the Senate); and

- any member of the Foreign Service commissioned as a diplomat or consular officer, or both, under section 312 of the Foreign Service Act of 1980.

Career members of the Senior Foreign Service and Foreign Service officers are appointed by the President, with the advice and consent of the Senate. 22 USC 3942(a)(1). Non-career Senior Foreign Service employees, consular officers, and diplomats are appointed by the Secretary of State. *See* 22 USC 3903(5), (7); 22 USC 3943.

3. Other Employment Relationships

a. State Officials

Because state government officials are not qualified federal officials, an individual appointed to his or her position by a state government official is not a federal civil service employee. *See Baker v. U.S.*, 614 F.2d 263, 268 (Cl. Ct. 1980).

b. Private Contractors

Individuals hired by private contractors performing federal work do not satisfy the statutory definition of employee in 5 USC 2105(a)(1) because they were not hired by a federal officer acting in an official capacity. *See Madridejo v. OPM*, 11 F.3d 1069 (Fed. Cir. 1993) (nonprecedential); *see also Oloroso v. OPM*, 951 F.2d 1266 (Fed. Cir. 1991) (hiring by a private contractor is not appointment by a qualified federal official; nonprecedential).

c. Illegal Appointments

An individual who is illegally employed in violation of an absolute statutory prohibition is not a civil service employee within the meaning of 5 USC 2105(a). *See Danespayeh v. Dept. of Air Force*, 57 MSPR 672 (1993) (U.S. citizen who was ordinary resident of Turkey was not employee as defined by the federal civil service laws based on a prohibition of such employment by the NATO Status of Forces Agreement), *aff'd without op.*, 17 F.3d 1444 (Fed. Cir. 1994).

B. INDIVIDUALS EXCLUDED FROM TITLE II COVERAGE

The list of federal employees excluded from coverage by Title II of the Act is long. Exclusion takes three forms: (1) exclusion from the definition of "employee" directly in Title II; (2) exclusion from the definition of "employee" by incorporation from 5 USC 6301(2); and (3) exclusions contained in 5 USC 2105. Of course, just because they are excluded from coverage by Title II of the Act does not mean that these federal employees may not be covered by other titles of the FMLA. Title I contains a catch–all provision which covers any federal employees not covered by Title II. *See* 29 CFR 825.109(c).

1. Title II Exclusions

Three groups of employees are excluded from the definition of "employee" for purposes of Title II.

a. Employees of the Government of the District of Columbia

All employees of the Government of the District of Columbia are excluded from Title II coverage. *See* 5 USC 6381(1)(A); 5 CFR 630.1201(b)(2)(I). Employees of the Government of the District Columbia are covered by Title I of the FMLA. *See* 29 CFR 108(a) (defining a "public agency employer" to include the District of Columbia).

b. Individuals Employed on a Temporary or Intermittent Basis

Title II also excludes from coverage any individual employed on a temporary or intermittent basis. *See* 5 USC 6381(1)(A).

Two categories of temporary or intermittent employees are addressed in the OPM regulations implementing Title II. An employee serving a temporary appointment with a time limitation of one year or less is excluded from coverage by Title II. 5 CFR 630.1201(b)(2)(ii). *See also* 5 CFR 316.401 (addressing temporary appointments generally). These employees are, however, included in the Title I definition of employee pursuant to 29 CFR 825.109(b)(4).

Also excluded from the reach of Title II are intermittent employees, as defined in 5 CFR 340.401(b). 5 CFR 630.1201(b)(2)(iii). "Intermittent employment" means employment without a regularly scheduled tour of duty. 5 CFR 340.401(b).

c. Employees Covered by Titles I and V of the FMLA

Employees covered by Titles I or V of the Act are excluded from the definition of a covered employee for purposes of Title II. 5 CFR 630.1201(2)(iv); *Hulett v. America's Finest Service Co., et. al.*, No. 1:03 CV 2497, 2005 U.S. Dist. LEXIS 41952 at *8 (N.D. Ohio, Sept. 14, 2005),

2. 5 USC 6301(2) Employee Exclusions

By incorporation of the definition of employee from 5 USC 6301(2), the following 11 additional categories of federal employees are excluded from coverage by Title II:

- A teacher or librarian of the public schools of the District of Columbia;
- A part–time employee who does not have an established regular tour of duty during the administrative workweek;
- A temporary employee engaged in construction work at an hourly rate;
- Employees of the Panama Canal Commission when employed on the Isthmus of Panama;
- A physician, dentist, or nurse in the Veterans Health Administration of the Department of Veterans Affairs;
- An employee of either House of Congress or of the two Houses;
- An employee of a corporation supervised by the Farm Credit Administration;
- An alien employee who occupies a position outside the United States, except as provided by section 6310 of Title 5;
- A "teacher" or an individual holding a "teaching position" as defined by section 901 of title 20;
- An officer in the executive branch or in the Government of the District of Columbia who is appointed by the President and whose rate of basic pay exceeds the highest rate payable under section 5332 of Title 5;
- An officer in the executive branch or in the Government of the District of Columbia who is designated by the President, except a postmaster, United States attorney, or United States marshal;
- A chief of mission (as defined in section 102(a)(3) of the Foreign Service Act of 1980); and
- An officer in the legislative or judicial branch who is appointed by the President.

a. Employees of the Government of the District of Columbia

As set forth previously, all employees, including teachers and officers of the Government of the District of Columbia, are excluded from coverage under Title II. They are covered by Title I of the FMLA as a "public agency." *See* 29 CFR 825.108(a).

b. Part–Time Employees

Part–time employees, who do not have a regular tour of duty during the administrative work week, are specifically excluded from coverage under Title II of the Act. They are specifically included in the definition of employee for purposes of Title I of the Act. *See* 29 CFR 825.109(b)(3).

c. Temporary Construction Employees

Title II specifically excludes any individual employed on a temporary or intermittent basis, see 5 USC 6381(1)(A), which would include temporary construction workers paid on an hourly basis. 5 USC 6301(2)(iii).

d. Panama Canal Commission Employees

Employees of the Panama Canal Commission when employed on the Isthmus of Panama are not employees within the meaning of Title II of the Act. 5 USC 6301(2)(iv).

e. Employees of Congress

Employees of either House of Congress or of the two Houses are excluded from the definition of a covered employee subject to Title II of the Act. 5 USC 6301(2)(vi). A "Congressional employee" is defined as an employee of either House of Congress, of a committee of either House, or of a joint committee of the two Houses. 5 USC 2107(1).

Employees of Congress are covered either by Title I or the CAA (formerly Title V of the Act). Title I only applies to employees of the legislative branch who are employed in a unit which has employees in the competitive service. 29 CFR 825.109(d). All other congressional employees would appear to be covered by the FMLA, as applied through the CAA.

f. Farm Credit Administration

An employee of a corporation supervised by the Farm Credit Administration is not an "employee" for purposes of Title II of the Act where private interests elect or appoint a member of the corporation's board of directors. 5 USC 6301(2)(vii). These employees are treated as if they were in the private sector, meaning that they may be subject to Title I of the Act provided they work for a covered employer and otherwise meet all of the prerequisites for Title I coverage. *See* Preamble, 29 CFR 825.109.

g. Alien or Noncitizen Employees

An alien or noncitizen of the United States who occupies a position outside the United States is not an employee within the meaning of Title II, except as provided by section 6310 of Title 5 (5 USC 6310). An "alien employee" means a non–U.S. citizen.

There is limited case law interpreting this exclusion. In *Ospino v. MSPB*, No. 97–3387, 1998 U.S. App. LEXIS 4376 (Fed. Cir. March 9, 1998). In that case, the appellant, a Panamanian citizen who occupied a position outside the United States, appealed to the Board seeking review of his removal from federal employment by the US Department of the Army. Board jurisdiction over adverse actions of employees of federal agencies, however, excluded certain employees, including alien or noncitizen employees occupying positions outside of the United States, as described in 5 USC 5102(c)(11).

The exception in 5 USC 6310 permits the head of an agency to grant a paid leave of absence, not in excess of the amount of annual and sick leave allowable to citizen employees under Subchapter 63 of Title 5, to alien employees who occupy positions outside the United States. 5 USC 6310.

Accounting for the exception and framed in the affirmative, a Title II "employee" includes an alien employee who occupies a position outside of the United States when the head of an agency grants the employee paid annual and sick leave, up to the amount of annual and sick leave available to citizen employees, as authorized by 5 USC 6310.

In terms of the FMLA, this means that an "alien employee" who occupies a position outside of the United States is a covered employee for purposes of Title II of the Act when the employee is granted paid annual or sick leave by the head of an agency. If all other prerequisites for leave are satisfied, an alien employee would be entitled to FMLA leave pursuant to Title II if, and only if, the employee was granted paid annual or sick leave pursuant to 5 USC 6310, and the leave was for a reason covered by the FMLA. In this circumstance, as discussed more fully in Chapter 11, "Substitution of Paid Leave," the alien employee's paid leave and unpaid FMLA leave would run concurrently.

h. Presidential Appointed Executive Branch Officers

Title II excludes from the definition of a covered employee an officer in the executive branch who is appointed by the President and whose basic pay exceeds the highest rate payable under section 5332 of Title 5 (5 USC 5332). 5 USC 6301(2)(B)(x). An "officer" means a justice or judge of the United States and an individual who is (1) appointed by the President; (2) engaged in the performance of a federal function under authority of the law or an executive act; and (3) is subject to the supervision of the President, a court of the United States, the head of an executive branch agency; or the Secretary of a military department. *See* 5 USC 2104(a). This definition of "officer" does not include officers of the United States Postal Service or of the Postal Rate Commission. 5 USC 2104(b).

Section 5332 of Title 5 (5 USC 5332) sets forth the General Schedule. The General Schedule is a schedule of annual rates of basic pay, consisting of 15 grades, designated GS–1 through GS–15, consecutively, with ten rates of pay for each such grade. As of January 2003, the highest GS rate of basic pay under § 5332 of Title 5 is $107,357.

Officers excluded from coverage under Title II of the Act are considered covered employees under Title I of the Act. *See* 29 CFR 825.109(c) (employees of other executive branch agencies are covered by Title I if not covered by Title II).

i. Presidential Designated Executive Branch Officers

Officers in the executive branch designated by the President, except a postmaster, United States attorney, or United States marshal, are not employees within the meaning of Title II of the FMLA. 5 USC 6301(2)(B)(xi). Officers excluded from coverage under Title II of the Act are considered covered employees under Title I of the Act. *See* 29 CFR 825.109(c) (employees of other executive branch agencies covered by Title I if not covered by Title II).

Read in the affirmative, postmasters, United States attorneys and United States marshals are employees within the meaning of Title II of the Act. All other executive branch officers designated by the President are not covered by Title II of the Act. As we have seen, Title II specifically excludes all employees of the Postal Service from coverage, which would include postmasters. *See* 5 USC 2105(e) (excluding employees of the Postal Service from the definition of employee. *See also* 29 CFR 825.109(b)(1) (Postal Service employees covered by Title I). This would appear to leave United States attorneys and United States marshals within the definition of employee for purposes of Title II.

j. Chief of Mission

A "chief of mission," as defined in section 102(a)(3) of the Foreign Service Act of 1980, is excluded from the definition of employee covered by Title II. 5 USC 6301(2)(B)(xii). A chief of mission is the principal officer in charge of a diplomatic mission of the United States or of a United States office abroad which is designated by the Secretary of State as diplomatic in nature, including any individual lawfully assigned to be temporarily in charge of a such a mission or office. 22 USC 3902(3).

k. Legislative or Judicial Branch Officers

Excluded from coverage by Title II is an officer in the legislative or judicial branch appointed by the President. 5 USC 6301(2)(B)(xiii). Whether these employees are covered by Title I or the CAA is not clear. Title I covers employees of the legislative or judicial branches only if they are employed in a unit which has employees in the competitive service. 29 CFR 825.109(d). Otherwise, these officers would appear to be covered by the FMLA, as applied through the CAA. *See* 5 CFR 630.1201(b)(2)(iv) (Title II does not apply to individuals covered by Titles I and V).

3. Employee Exclusions Pursuant to 5 USC 2105

Title II defines a covered employee by cross-reference to 5 USC 6301(2). *See* 5 USC 6381(1)(A). This section, in turn, defines an employee by reference to 5 USC 2105. *See* 5 USC 6301(2)(A).

Two groups of employees are specifically excluded from coverage by 5 USC 2105. An additional group is likely to be excluded given the very limited definition of employee provided for coverage. Specifically excluded from the definition of an employee for purposes of Title II are employees of the Postal Service and the Postal Rate Commission. 5 USC 2105(e).

A reservist in the armed forces who is either not on active duty or on active duty for training is deemed not an employee. 5 USC 2105(d). Of course, when a reservist goes on active duty, he or she is a member of the uniformed services of the armed forces, and is also excluded from coverage by Title II of the FMLA.

The final group of individuals excluded from coverage are those who do not meet the limited definition of employees of the Naval Academy. Only individuals whose employment began before October 1, 1996, and who have had uninterrupted employment since that date at the Naval Academy in the midshipmen's laundry, tailor ship, cobbler, barber shops, and the midshipmen's store, but not in the Academy dairy, are included within the definition of a Title II employee. Individuals outside those parameters may be covered by Title I of the Act under the catch–all provision. *See* 29 CFR 825.109(c).

III. FEDERAL EMPLOYEES COVERED BY THE CAA FMLA

A. EMPLOYEE DEFINED

The CAA FMLA, 2 USC 1301(3), defines a "covered employee" as any employee of:

1. the House of Representatives;
2. the Senate;
3. the Capitol Guide Service;
4. the Capital Police;
5. the Congressional Budget Office;
6. the Office of the Architect of the Capitol;
7. the Office of the Attending Physician;
8. the Office of Compliance; and
9. the Office of Technology Assessment.

An "employee" for purposes of the FMLA, as made applicable by the CAA, includes an applicant for employment and a former employee. 2 USC 1301(4).

An employee of the House includes all individuals who are paid by the Clerk of the House of Representatives, or another individual designated by the House, or individuals who hold any employment position in an entity that is paid with funds derived from the clerk–hire allowance of the House, but not individuals employed by any entity listed in numbers 3 through 9 above. 2 USC 1301(7).

An employee of the Senate includes any employee whose pay is disbursed by the Secretary of the Senate, but not any individual employed by any entity listed in numbers 3 through 9 above. 2 USC 1301(8).

An employee of the Office of the Architect of the Capitol includes any employee of the Office of the Architect of the Capitol, the Botanic Garden, or the Senate Restaurants. 2 USC 1301(5).

An employee of the Capitol Police includes any member or officer of the Capitol Police. 2 USC 1301(6).

Remember that employees of the legislative or judicial branches are covered by Title I if they are employed in a unit that has employees in the competitive service, such as the Government Printing Office and the U.S. Tax Court. 29 CFR 825.109(d).

IV. FEDERAL EMPLOYEES COVERED BY THE PEOAA FMLA

A. EMPLOYEE DEFINED

An "employee" is defined by the PEOAA to include an applicant for employment and a former employee. 3 USC 401(a)(3). A "covered employee" is defined as any employee of an employing office. 3 USC 401(a)(2). For purposes of the FMLA, a "covered employee" is synonymous with an "eligible employee." 3 USC 401(b)(2).

CHAPTER 5
EMPLOYEE ELIGIBILITY FOR LEAVE

I. OVERVIEW

Although the FMLA applies to all "covered" federal employees of the United States, only those employees who meet certain eligibility requirements have the right to take FMLA leave. *See McKim v. UPS, Inc.*, No. 3:97CV–153–H, 1997 U.S. Dist. LEXIS 22121 (W.D. Ky. Sept. 17, 1997) (FMLA does not protect "individuals," only "eligible employees").

The eligibility requirements of the four federal sector FMLA laws, while similar in some respects, contain many substantive differences. Because the workforce of a federal employer may include individuals covered by several of these FMLA laws, the correct determination of employee eligibility requires a thorough understanding of the eligibility requirements of each of these FMLA laws.

Section II of this chapter addresses the basic eligibility requirements of Titles I and II of the Act and the FMLA as applied by the CAA and the PEOAA. Sections III, IV and V of this chapter address in more detail the basic eligibility requirements. Notification of employee eligibility is addressed in Section VI and Chapter 9. Eligibility issues, such as pleading requirements and burdens of proof, are addressed in Chapter 15, "Prohibited Acts, Enforcement, and Remedies."

II. BASIC ELIGIBILITY STANDARDS

A. TITLE I ELIGIBILITY STANDARDS

To be an "eligible employee" under the FMLA, a Title I covered federal employee must have worked for the U.S. government (1) for at least 12 months; (2) for at least 1,250 hours during the 12–month period immediately preceding leave commencement; and (3) at a worksite where 50 or more employees are employed by the federal government within 75 miles of the employee's worksite. 29 USC 2611(2)(A), 2611(2)(B)(ii); *see also* 29 CFR 825.110(a); *Lackey v. Jackson County, Tennessee*, 104 Fed. Appx. 483 (6th Cir. 2004); *Pirant v. USPS*, No. 03 C 9383, 2006 U.S. Dist. LEXIS 89319, at *6 (N.D. Ill Dec. 7, 2006); *Gibson v. Transport Drivers, Inc.*, No. H-04-2083, 2006 U.S. Dist. LEXIS 12272, at *13 (S.D. Tex. March 8, 2006); *Nameth v. Celina Financial Corp.*, No. 1:04 CV 2282, 2006 U.S. Dist. LEXIS 8908, at *11 (N.D. Ohio March 2, 2006); *Washington v. Cooper Hospital/University Med. Center*, No. 03-5791 (RBK), 2005 U.S. Dist. LEXIS 31062, at *12 (D.N.J. Dec. 2, 2005); *Rivero v. United Airlines, Inc.*, No. 04 C 6514, 2005 U.S. Dist. LEXIS 29733, at *32 (N.D. Il. Nov. 22, 2005); *Kaniuka v. Good Shepherd Home*, No. 05-CV-02917, 2005 U.S. Dist. LEXIS 26963, at *14 (E.D. Pa. Nov. 3, 2005); *McInerney v. Moyer Lumber and Hardware, Inc.*, 244 F. Supp. 2d 393, 399 (E.D. Pa. 2002). An employee must satisfy each of these criteria independently to be eligible for FMLA leave. *Pirant*, 2006 U.S. Dist. LEXIS 89319, at *6; *Rivero*, 2005 U.S. Dist. LEXIS 29733, at *32.

Significantly, for employees covered by Title I, the U.S. Government is considered a single employer for purposes of determining employee eligibility. 29 CFR 825.109(e). Defining the entire U.S. Government as the "employer" for purposes of Title I employee eligibility has two main benefits. First, Title I covered federal employees carry with them the work time they have already spent with the federal government as they move from one federal agency to another. The ability to bank the time already worked will assist federal employees in meeting the 12 months and 1,250 hours of work requirements for Title I eligibility. Second, by defining eligibility in terms of the entire U.S. Government, Title I covered federal employees can count all federal employees, not just employees of their agency, in order to meet the minimum 50 employee requirement for Title I eligibility. This is of particular benefit to federal employees working in small field offices.

Of course, the portability of Title I covered federal employee eligibility, while a boon to employees, presents real challenges for federal agencies in the administration of their FMLA programs. To ensure compliance with the law, federal agencies will have to make a real effort to capture all previous federal employment by a Title I covered employee to determine Title I eligibility. At minimum, this will require the use of detailed application forms that are closely scrutinized by the employing federal agency in order to accurately determine an employee's Title I eligibility status.

B. TITLE II ELIGIBILITY STANDARDS

Title II has only one eligibility requirement, and it is not identified as an "eligibility requirement" *per se*. Rather, the eligibility requirement of Title II is incorporated directly into the definition of a "covered employee." *See* 5 USC 6381(1). Specifically, to be eligible for the benefits of the FMLA, a federal employee covered by Title II must have completed at least 12 months of service as an "employee." 5 USC 6381(1)(B); 5 CFR 630.1201(b)(ii); *Niimi–Montalbo v. White*, 243 F. Supp. 2d 1109, 1119 (D. Haw. 2003) (leave for federal civil service employees with more than 12 months of civil service is governed by Title II of the FMLA). Title II defines an "employee" by reference to 5 USC 6301(2), with a few additions and exclusions. 5 USC 6381(1)(A).

Notwithstanding the clear statutory and regulatory language that only 12 months of employment is required for Title II FMLA eligibility, the MSPB continues to erroneously apply the Title I eligibility standard to civil service employees covered by the very different eligibility standard of Title II. *See Stott v. DHHS*, No. DC-0752-07-0454-I-1, 2007 MSPB LEXIS 692, at *8 (May 30, 2007) (FMLA eligibility requires 12 months of employment and 1250-hours of service during the previous 12 months).

By limiting employee eligibility to time spent as an employee within the meaning of 5 USC 6301(2), as modified, Title II eligibility is significantly narrower than eligibility under Title I of the Act. For example, Title II would not credit any time spent by an individual as a Title I covered federal employee. A 15–year employee of the United States Postal Service who transferred to a career civil service position with another federal agency would not be credited any of those 15 years for purposes of Title II eligibility. Under Title I, however, a 15–year career civil service employee who transferred to a position in the Postal Service would have all of the time spent as a Title II covered employee credited towards their Title I FMLA eligibility in the Postal Service.

Eligibility for Title II covered federal employees is, however, portable within the confines of Title II. Title II covered federal employees who transfer to another Title II covered position in a different federal agency bring with them to the receiving federal agency, for Title II eligibility purposes, the time they spent with the losing federal agency. Time spent as an employee covered by Title I, the CAA, and the PEOAA, however, would not count toward Title II eligibility. Similarly, time spent as a Title I employee in the private sector would not count for FMLA eligibility purposes in the federal sector, with the possible limited exception of multi–employer situations, discussed in Section IV, A,1 of this chapter.

C. THE CAA ELIGIBILITY STANDARDS

The FMLA, as applied through the CAA, defines the term "eligible employee" to mean a covered employee who has been employed in any employing office for 12 months and for at least 1,250 hours of employment during the previous 12 months. 2 USC 1312(2)(B). As set forth more fully in the preceding chapter, a "covered employee" is defined as an employee of the House of Representatives, the Senate, the Capitol Guide Service, the Capitol Police, the Congressional Budget Office, the Office of the Architect, the Office of the Attending Physician, the Office of Compliance, or the Office of Technology Assessment. 2 USC 1301(3).

An "employing office" means the personal office of a Member of the House of Representatives or of a Senator; a committee of the House of Representatives, the Senate or a joint committee; any other office headed by a person with the final authority to appoint, hire, discharge, and set the terms, conditions, or privileges of the employment of an employee of the House of Representatives or the Senate, the Capital Guide Board, the Capitol Police, the Congressional Budget Office, the Office of the Architect of the Capitol, the Office of the Attending Physician, the Office of Compliance, and the Office of Technology Assessment. 2 USC 1301(9).

The scope of eligibility under the FMLA, as applied by the CAA, is narrower still. By limiting the calculation of CAA FMLA eligibility to an "employing office," employees covered by the CAA may only draw on their CAA–covered employment for purposes of meeting the CAA FMLA eligibility requirements. Any employment as a Title I, Title II, or PEOAA covered employee, no matter how extensive, does not count toward a CAA–covered employee's FMLA eligibility.

Eligibility under the CAA is, in one respect, broader than under Titles I and II of the Act. The CAA defines an "employee" to include an applicant for employment and a former employee. 2 USC 1301(4). Applicants for, and former employees of, an "employing office" within the meaning of the CAA are considered covered employees in addition to a current employee of those offices. As covered employees, applicants and former CAA employees would have access to the dispute resolution system under the CAA. *See* 2 USC 1361(e). In contrast, neither the statute nor the regulations implementing

Titles I and II of the Act define a covered employee as including applicants or former employees. As set forth more fully in Chapter 15, "Prohibited Acts, Enforcement, and Remedies," some courts have read Title I as including applicants and former employees.

D. PEOAA ELIGIBILITY STANDARDS

As applied through the PEOAA, the FMLA defines an "eligible employee" as a covered employee who has been employed in an employing office for 12 months and for at least 1,250 hours of employment during the previous 12 months. 3 USC 412(a)(2)(B). As set forth more fully in Chapter 4, "Federal Employees Covered by the FMLA," a "covered employee" means any employee of an employing office. 3 USC 401(a)(2)). Like the CAA, the term "employee" is defined to include applicants and former employees. 3 USC 401(3). An "employing office" is defined as each office, agency, or other component of the Executive Office of the President, the Executive Residence at the White House, and the official residence of the Vice President. 3 USC 401(a)(4).

Like the CAA, the scope of FMLA eligibility under the PEOAA is narrowly defined. Only employment in a PEOAA–defined "employing office" counts towards meeting the two eligibility criteria of the PEOAA. Time spent as a Title I or II covered employee does not count toward eligibility under the PEOAA. Nor does time spent as an employee covered by the FMLA, as applied through the CAA, count toward PEOAA eligibility. Conversely, time spent as a CAA–covered employee would count toward Title I eligibility, although it would not count toward eligibility under Title II and the CAA.

III. CALCULATING 12 MONTHS OF EMPLOYMENT

Twelve months of federal employment is a universal requirement for a covered federal employee to be eligible for FMLA leave under Titles I and II and the FMLA as applied through the CAA and the PEOAA. How those 12 months is determined, however, is not universal. The 12 months of employment requirement is calculated differently for each of the four types of FMLA laws applicable to the federal sector.

A. TITLE I CALCULATIONS

To be eligible for FMLA leave, a Title I covered federal employee must have worked at least 12 months for "the employer with respect to whom leave is requested." 29 USC 2611(2)(A)(I). An employee who has not worked the requisite 12 months for the employer is not an "eligible employee" within the meaning of Title II of the Act. *See Rucker v. Lee Holding Co.*, 471 F.3d 6 (1st Cir. 2006); *Walker v. Elmore County Bd. of Ed.*, 379 F.3d 1249 (11th Cir. 2004); *Babcock v. Bellsouth Advertising and Publishing Corp.*, 348 F.3d 73, 76–77 (4th Cir. 2003); *Dolese v. Office Depot, Inc.*, 231 F.3d 202 (5th Cir. 2000); *Garcia v. Blueberry Sales, L.P.*, No. EP-05-CA-0289-FM, 2006 U.S. Dist. LEXIS 7989, at *11 (W.D. Tex. Feb. 23, 2006); *Beffert v. Pennsylvania Dept. of Public Welfare*, No. 05-43, 2005 U.S. Dist. LEXIS 6681, at *7 (E.D. Pa. April 18, 2005); *Lopez v. Lone Star Beef Processors, L.P.*, No. 6:04–CV–020–C, 2004 U.S. Dist. LEXIS 20397, at *9 (N.D. Tex. Oct. 8, 2004), aff'd, 2005 U.S. App. LEXIS 17944 (5th Cir. 2005); *Ferrero v. Henderson*, 341 F. Supp. 2d 873, 904 (S.D. Ohio 2004); *McEachern v. Prime Hospitality Corp.*, No. 02–536 ADM.AJB, 2003 U.S. Dist. LEXIS 7997, at *9 (D. Minn. May 8, 2003); *Tornberg v. Business Interlink Services, Inc.*, 237 F. Supp. 2d 778, 784 (E.D. Mich. 2002); *Sewall v. Chicago Transit Authority*, No. 99–C–8372, 2001 U.S. Dist. LEXIS 330 (N.D. Ill. Jan. 16, 2001); *Scheidecker v. Arvig Enterprises, Inc.*, 122 F. Supp. 2d 1031 (D. Minn. 2000); *Jessie v. Carter Health Care Center, Inc.*, 926 F. Supp. 613, 616–717 (E.D. Ky. 1996).

1. The Federal Government as Single Employer

As set forth more fully in Chapter 3, "FMLA Coverage of the Federal Government," the term "employer" is defined generally as the U.S. Government as a whole rather than any particular federal employer. *See* 29 USC 2611(4)(B); 29 CFR 825.108(a), 825.109(e). Because the entire U.S. Government is considered to be the employer, employees covered by Title I of the Act may draw upon all previous federal employment to meet the 12–month eligibility requirement.

2. Joint Employment

Included in the 12–month calculation would be any time the individual spent as a joint employee of the federal government and a nonfederal entity, such as a temporary help or leasing agency. 29 CFR 825.106(d); *Miller v. Defiance Metal Products, Inc.*, 989 F. Supp. 945, 946–48 (N.D. Ohio 1997) (individual employee who worked as an employee of temporary agency at defendant's facility for eight months and was then hired by defendant and worked for another eight months was an eligible employee under Title I of FMLA); DOL WH Advisory Opinion No. 37 (July 7, 1994) (time that employee was employed by temporary help agency would be counted toward 12-month and 1,250-hours worked eligibility tests). Federal employment prior to the effective date of Title I must be counted toward the 12-month eligibility requirement. 29 CFR 825.110(e). Title I of the Act became effective on August 5, 1993, for most federal employers. If a collective bargaining agreement was in effect on that date, the Act became effective on the earlier of February 5, 1994, or the date the agreement expired. 29 CFR 825.102(a).

3. Successors-in-Interest

An employer who is a successor-in-interest to a covered employer must count the employee's time with the predecessor employer for purposes of the 12-month and 1,250-hour eligibility requirements. 29 CFR 825.107. When an employer is a successor-in-interest, employees' FMLA entitlements are the same as if the employment by the predecessor and the successor were continuous employment by a single employer. 29 CFR 825.107(c). [For a general discussion of the "successor-in-interest" doctrine of Title I, see Chapter 3, "FMLA Coverage of the Federal Government."]

Courts have addressed the interaction of eligibility with the successor-in-interest doctrine on several occasions. In *Rhoads v. FDIC,* 956 F. Supp. 1239 (D. Md. 1997), *aff'd in part, vacated in part on other grounds, remanded,* 257 F.3d 373 (4th Cir. 2001), *cert. denied,* 535 U.S. 933 (2002),, the district court held that the plaintiff was an eligible employee where her combined employment with the Standard Federal Savings Bank (SFSB) and the FDIC, as successor-in-interest to the SFSB when it took over the bank in receivership, met the 12-month employment eligibility requirement. The case provides a thorough analysis of the successor-in-interest doctrine generally.

Similarly, in *Vanderhoof v. Life Extension Institute et al.,* 988 F. Supp. 507 (D.N.J. 1997), the district court found that plaintiff met the 12-month eligibility requirement of Title I through her cumulative employment with Executive Health Group (EHG) and the Life Extension Institute, which the district court found to be the successor-in-interest to EHG when it purchased the clinic where plaintiff worked without interruption until her termination.

Finally, in another case involving a public agency, the court in *Joliffe v. Mitchell et al.,* 971 F. Supp. 1039 (W.D. Va. 1997), found that a newly elected County Sheriff was the "successor-in-interest" for FMLA purposes of employees of the former County Sheriff.

4. Nonconsecutive Employment

The 12 months of employment for Title I eligibility are cumulative, not consecutive. 29 CFR 825.110(b). *See Rucker v. Lee Holding Co.,* 471 F.3d 6 (1st Cir. 2006); *Tornberg v. Business Interlink Services, Inc.,* 237 F. Supp. 2d 778, 784 n.4 (E.D. Mich. 2002) (employee met eligibility requirement of 12 months of employment even though employment was sporadic). As such, previous periods of employment, even if separated by years, can be grouped together for purposes of determining whether the employee satisfies the 12-month eligibility requirement.

In *Rucker,* the First Circuit reversed the district court dismissing the case after finding that the employee's prior employment with the same employer did not count for purposes of the 12-month eligibility requirement. The district court reasoned that 825.110(b) only allowed for brief interruptions in an employee's attendance. It did not apply where an employee completely severed his or her relationship with an employer for a period of years, and then returned. The district court found that the prior employment, 5 years earlier, did not count for FMLA eligibility purposes. The First Circuit disagreed. Although it found the statutory and regulatory language on the issue ambiguous, the First Circuit deferred to the Department of Labor's interpretation that all periods of employment with an employer count towards the employee's 12-month FMLA eligibility requirement.

All periods of federal employment with any branch of the federal government, including part-time, seasonal, and intermittent employment, would count toward meeting the 12-month eligibility requirement of Title I. For purposes of determining whether occasional, intermittent, or casual employment satisfies the 12-month standard, 52 weeks is deemed to be equal to 12 months. 29 CFR 825.110(b).

5. Effect of Leave on 12–Month Eligibility Requirement

The 12–month eligibility requirement includes leaves of absence, whether paid or unpaid. 29 CFR 825.110(b); *see Rollins v. Wilson County*, 154 F.3d 626, 628 (6th Cir. 1998) (period of unpaid leave counted toward 12–month requirement where plaintiff remained on payroll and continued to receive employment benefits during medical leave); *Ruder v. Maine General Med. Center*, 204 F. Supp. 2d 16 (D. Me. 2002) (employee's two weeks of vacation at end of first year counted toward meeting 12–month eligibility requirement). If an employee is maintained on the payroll for any part of a week, including any period of paid or unpaid leave during which other benefits or compensation are provided by the employer (e.g., workers' compensation, group health plan benefits, etc.), the week counts as a full week of employment. 29 CFR 825.110(b); DOL WH Advisory Opinion No. 46 (October 14, 1994); *Nameth v. Celina Financial Corp.*, No. 1:04 CV 2282, 2006 U.S. Dist. LEXIS 8908, at *16 (N.D. Ohio March 2, 2006). In *Nameth*, the employer argued that the employee was not eligible because the employee's leave began on November 26, four days short of her one-year anniversary with the company. Nameth argued that the four days she missed work before her 12-month anniversary were approved absences, and her FMLA leave actually began on December 2. The evidence established that Celina maintained Nameth on its payroll and treated Nameth's four days absence from work before December 2 as approved absences. The court found that the four days absence from work counted as days of employment for purposes of FMLA eligibility. As such, the court found that Nameth met the 12-month eligibility requirement on December 2, when her FMLA leave commenced.

Theoretically, a federal employee could meet the 12–month eligibility standard through as little as 12 days of employment, provided the absences were spread over 12 different weeks and the individual received some unspecified "other benefits and compensation" from the federal employer during the remainder of the weeks he or she was out. Obviously, this would be highly unusual.

The reference to being "on the payroll" as a condition to receiving credit for a full week's employment towards the 12–month eligibility requirement for a partial week of work would appear to exclude some employees. Remember, Title I defines "employ" to mean "to suffer or permit to work." 29 CFR 825.105(a). Under this definition, "mere knowledge by an employer of work done for the employer by another is sufficient to create an employment relationship within the meaning of Title I." *Id.* Under this broad definition, an individual could be considered an employee but, according to the regulations, would not receive credit towards his or her 12–month eligibility if he or she were not maintained on the payroll. Curious.

6. Military Leave

For purposes of meeting the 12–month and 1,250–hour eligibility requirements, a Title I covered federal employee who is called to military service within the meaning of the Uniformed Services Employment and Reemployment Rights Act (USERRA), 38 USC 4301–4333, must be credited on his or her return to work for the months and hours he or she would have been employed but for the military service. *See* U.S. Dept. of Labor Memorandum, The Effect of the Uniformed Services Employment and Reemployment Rights Act on Leave Eligibility under the Family and Medical Leave Act (July 22, 2002) (hereinafter U.S. Dept. of Labor, USERRA–FMLA Memorandum), *reprinted in* 145 Daily Lab. Rep. BNA A–5 (July 29, 2002). [See Appendix—USERRA-FMLA Memorandum.]

USERRA is a federal law that provides reemployment rights for veterans and members of the National Guard and Reserve following qualifying military service. Significantly, it also requires that uniformed service members, who conclude their tours of duty and who are reemployed, are entitled to the "rights and benefits" of employment that they would have obtained if they have been continuously employed, except benefits that are considered a form of short–term compensation, such as accrued paid vacation. The "rights and benefits" protected by USERRA include those provided by employers and those required by statute, including the right to leave under the FMLA. Accordingly, a returning service member would be entitled to FMLA leave if the hours that he or she would have worked for the civilian employer during the period of military service would have met the FMLA eligibility threshold.

In determining whether a veteran meets the FMLA eligibility requirement, the months employed and the hours that were actually worked for the covered employer should be combined with the months and hours that would have been worked during the 12 months prior to the start of the leave requested for the military leave. *See* U.S. Dept. of Labor, USERRA–FMLA Memorandum, *reprinted in* 145 Daily Lab. Rep. BNA A–5 (July 29, 2002). [For a discussion of the interrelationship of the FMLA with other laws, including the USERRA, see Chapter 16, "Interaction of the FMLA with Other Federal Laws, Employer Practices, and Collective Bargaining Agreements."]

For purposes of calculating whether an employee returning from covered military service meets the 12-month employment eligibility test, each month served performing military service counts as a month actively employed by the employer. For example, an employee who has been employed by the federal government for nine months is ordered to active military service for nine months. On the conclusion of his or her military service, the individual is reemployed by the federal government. Upon reemployment, the individual must be considered to have been employed by the federal government for more than the required 12 months (9 months actually employed plus 9 months while serving in the military service) for purposes of FMLA eligibility. *See* U.S. Dept. of Labor USERRA-FMLA Questions and Answers (July 25, 2002), explaining the U.S. Dept. of Labor, USERRA-FMLA Memorandum. [See Appendix—USERRA-FMLA Questions and Answers.]

The U.S. Dept. of Labor USERRA-FMLA Memorandum and USERRA-FMLA Questions and Answers refer to a "civilian" employer covered by Title I. Similarly, elsewhere in these documents the DOL recognizes that Title I covers "persons employed by private employers, state and local governments, and the Postal Service." *See* U.S. Dept. of Labor, USERRA-FMLA Memorandum, at 2, lines 2-3; USERRA-FMLA Questions and Answers, answer to question 3. Of course, in addition to those employers, Title I applies to certain federal employees throughout the federal government. *See* 29 CFR 825.109. For a discussion of the federal government as a covered Title 1 employer and of the federal employees who are covered by Title I of the FMLA, see Chapters 3 and 4 respectively. The exclusion in the U.S. Dept. of Labor USERRA-FMLA memoranda of any reference to non-postal federal employees covered by Title I was not likely intended to relieve the federal government from calculating eligibility to include all USERRA-covered military service. The omission by the DOL was likely inadvertent.

7. Effect of Termination, Furloughs and Reductions In Force

The Title I regulations are not at all clear on how the termination or suspension of the employee/employer relationship impacts the calculation of the 12-month eligibility requirement. Certainly, the permanent cessation of federal employment would end the accumulation of time toward the 12-month eligibility requirement, as the individual would no longer be an "employee." *See* 29 CFR 825.112(f) (where the employer-employee relationship has been interrupted, such as in the case of an employee who has been on a layoff, the employee must be recalled or otherwise reemployed before being eligible for FMLA leave). What is unclear is how temporary layoffs or terminations that are reversed on appeal by the employee should be handled in terms of accumulating time toward the 12-month eligibility test.

Assistance with this issue may be found in the DOL implementing regulations regarding the calculation of the minimum number of private sector employees necessary for Title I coverage. *See* 29 CFR 825.105. As indicated in Chapter 3, "FMLA Coverage of the Federal Government," the U.S. Government is a covered employer for purposes of Title I regardless of the number of employees. 29 CFR 825.104(a).

With respect to layoffs or reductions-in-force (RIFs), the regulations provide that where there is no employee/employer relationship, such as when an employee is laid off, whether temporarily or permanently, the employee is not counted. 29 CFR 825.105(c). The DOL indicated that the test for determining who is an employee was based on a "continuing employment relationship." Preamble, 29 CFR 825.105. Under that principle, there was no continuing employee-employer relationship during a layoff, as evidenced by the fact that employees on layoff are entitled to unemployment benefits, and laid-off employees are not maintained on the payroll during such period. *Id.* In rejecting a proposed standard that would include employees on a temporary layoff in the minimum employee count, the DOL concluded, "based on [the] FMLA's legislative history, the regulations necessarily exclude all employees who are on a layoff, and the employment relationship terminated, whether the layoff is temporary, indefinite, or long-term." *Id.*

With respect to disciplinary suspensions or terminations, the DOL regulations on the minimum employee complement provide further assistance. Employees on paid or unpaid leave, including disciplinary suspensions, are counted as long as the employer has a reasonable expectation that the employee will later return to active employment. *See* 29 CFR 825.105(c). Because a federal employee on a suspension is still on the payroll, the time on suspension would count toward the 12-month requirement.

It gets trickier where the employee has been terminated, but is appealing that termination. Generally speaking, federal employers will often carry the employee on the payroll until the appeal has been exhausted. The question in these circumstances is whether this time counts towards the 12-month eligibility requirement. As set forth more fully in Section IV of this chapter, the short answer is that the courts are split on this issue, at least where the employee prevails and is returned to work.

The effect of an unlawful termination on the calculation of the 12-months eligibility requirement was briefly addressed by the court in *Schutze v. Financial Computer Software, L.P.*, No. 3:04–CV–0276–H, 2004 U.S. Dist. LEXIS 18606 (N.D. Tex. Sept. 14, 2004). In that case, the employee worked approximately 10 months for his employer before he was terminated. Schutze filed suit against his former employer alleging violation of the FMLA. FCS sought dismissal of the FMLA claim on the grounds that Schutze was not an eligible employee because he had not worked 12 months for FCS. Schutze admitted that he was employed by defendant for less than the required 12 months, but argued that he would have qualified as an FMLA eligible employee but for his termination by defendant. The court concluded that plaintiff's argument lacked merit. According to the court:

> The FMLA contains nothing in the way of an exception to the twelve months requirement. *See* 29 U.S.C. §§ 2601–2654. Congress' "clear statutory prerequisites for bringing an FMLA claim…did not provide for waiver of the minimum eligibility requirements when an employer has taken some action that allegedly precludes the employee from becoming statutorily eligible for protection under the Act." *Brown v. DaimlerChrysler Corp.* 1999 U.S. Dist. LEXIS 15189, No. CIV. A. 3:99–CV–1286–D, 1999 WL 766021 at *2 (N.D. Tex. Sept. 24, 1999).

Several circuit courts have addressed this issue with respect to the 1,250 hours of service eligibility requirement, with mixed results.

Where the employer–employee relationship is interrupted (e.g., layoff), the employee must recalled or otherwise be reemployed before being eligible for FMLA leave. 29 CFR 825.112(f). Where an employee is recalled from a layoff or other interruption in the employer–employee relationship, if the employee meets the eligibility requirements, the returning eligible employee is immediately entitled to FMLA leave for a qualifying reason. *Id.* That is, there is no minimum period of time an eligible employee returning to work from a layoff has to work before exercising their FMLA rights.

8. Eligibility Determined at Leave Commencement

The statute is silent regarding when eligibility is determined. DOL FMLA regulations state that eligibility is determined at leave commencement. *Babcock v. Bellsouth Advertising and Publishing Corp.*, 348 F.3d 73, 77 n.3 (4th Cir. 2003); *Flannery v. Nextgen Healthcare Information Systems, Inc.*, No. 05-6007, 2006 U.S. Dist. LEXIS 55738, at *8 (E.D. Pa. Aug. 10, 2006).

According to the DOL regulations, whether a Title I covered federal employee has met the 12-month eligibility requirement is determined at leave commencement. 29 CFR 825.110(d); *Moticka v. Weck Closure Systems*, 183 Fed. Appx. 343 (4th Cir. 2006); *Walker v. Elmore County Bd. of Ed.*, 379 F.3d 1249, at *11 n. 10 (11th Cir. 2004); *Babcock v. Bellsouth Advertising and Publishing Corp.*, 348 F.3d 73, 77 (4th Cir. 2003); *Roberts v. Ground Handling, Inc.*, No. 04 Civ. 4955 (WCC), 2007 U.S. Dist. LEXIS 23441, at *26 (S.D.N.Y. March 30, 2007); *Flannery v. Nextgen Healthcare Information Systems, Inc.*, No. 05-6007, 2006 U.S. Dist. LEXIS 55738, at *8 (E.D. Pa. Aug. 10, 2006); *Nameth v. Celina Financial Corp.*, No. 1:04 CV 2282, 2006 U.S. Dist. LEXIS 8908, at *11 (N.D. Ohio March 2, 2006); *Beffert v. Pennsylvania Dept. of Public Welfare*, No. 05-43, 2005 U.S. Dist. LEXIS 6681, at *7 (E.D. Pa. April 18, 2005); *Pennant v. Convergys Corp.*, 368 F. Supp. 2d 1307, 1310 (S.D. Fla. March 31, 2005); *Willemssen v. The Conveyor Co.*, 359 F. Supp. 2d 813, 818 (N.D. Iowa 2005); *McEachern v. Prime Hospitality Corp.*, No. 02-536 ADM.AJB, 2003 U.S. Dist. LEXIS 7997, at *9 (D. Minn. May 8, 2003).

In *Willemssen* 359 F. Supp. 2d at 818, whether the employee met the 12-month eligibility requirement depended on whether eligibility was calculated as of the date her leave commenced (in which case she was not eligible) or the date she was terminated (in which case she would have been eligible). In accordance with 29 CFR 825.110(d), the court held that 12 month eligibility is determined at leave commencement. Because she had not worked 12 months for her employer at the time, she was not eligible for FMLA leave. Because she was not eligible, her absence due to complications with her pregnancy was not covered by the FMLA. As such, her termination for taking excessive leave did not violate the FMLA.

Determining when FMLA leave "commences" is made more difficult because the critical term "leave" is not defined in Title I of the FMLA. *Babcock*, 348 F.3d at 77. Absent a statutory definition, the Fourth Circuit has held that "leave" in the employment context should carry its ordinary dictionary meaning requiring "an authorized absence or vacation from duty or employment." *Id.* at 77 (quoting *Webster's Third New Int'l Dictionary* 1287 (1976)). As demonstrated in *Babcock*, the limitation on "leave commencement" to approved leave for purposes of Title I eligibility has interesting results.

In *Babcock*, the plaintiff–employee began her employment with BellSouth on June 1, 1999. Due to health problems, Babcock was absent from work from May 18 to June 14, 2000. During her absence plaintiff called work and advised her supervisor that her physician recommended six weeks of leave. She also informed her supervisor that the physician would be faxing over supporting documents. Thinking that her six weeks of leave were approved, Babcock left town and did not return home until June 9. On her return, plaintiff found letters from her employer which advised her that: (1) she was approved short-term disability leave until May 27; (2) she was required to return to work no later than June 9; and (3) if she did not return to work by that date she could be terminated. Babcock called her employer that day to request more leave, which was denied. Babcock did not return to work and was subsequently terminated.

Babcock sued alleging that her termination violated the FMLA. BellSouth moved to dismiss the case on the grounds that Babcock did not meet the 12-month FMLA eligibility requirement. The Fourth Circuit found that Babcock did not meet the 12-month FMLA eligibility requirement, as of the start of her approved absence beginning May 18. The court also found that Babcock was not on approved leave from May 27 through June 9. Rather, this was an unexcused absence. According to the court, "[a]n employee cannot be both on leave and on an unexcused absence at the same time." Id. at 77. The court went on to find that Babcock met the 12-month eligibility requirement on June 9, when she requested additional leave, and affirmed the adverse judgment against BellSouth for denying Babcock's second request for FMLA leave and for her subsequent termination.

Although there was one continuous absence, because only approved leave counts for purposes of eligibility, the Fourth Circuit in *Babcock* found that the first approved absence ended, and the second request was treated independent of the first for purposes of calculating eligibility.

In *Barron v. Runyon*, 11 F. Supp. 2d 676 (E.D. Va. 1998), the court addressed whether "leave" is synonymous with "absence" for purposes of determining eligibility. [The matter is discussed more fully in Section IV, "Determining 1,250 Hours of Service During the Previous 12 Months", of this chapter.]

The courts are split on whether an employee who begins a leave of absence prior to meeting the 12-month eligibility requirement, but passes 12 months of employment while on leave, may immediately begin taking FMLA leave. Most courts have found that an employee must meet the 12-month eligibility requirement at leave commencement. If the employee does not meet the requirement at leave commencement, the fact that the employee passes 12 months of employment while on leave does not make an employee FMLA eligible. *See Flannery v. Nextgen Healthcare Information Systems, Inc.*, No. 05-6007, 2006 U.S. Dist. LEXIS 55738, at *8 (E.D. Pa. Aug. 10, 2006); *Garcia v. Blueberry Sales, L.P.*, No. EP-05-CA-0289-FM, 2006 U.S. Dist. LEXIS 7989, at *11 (W.D. Tex. Feb. 23, 2006); *McEachern v. Prime Hospitality Corp.*, No. 02-536 ADM.AJB, 2003 U.S. Dist. LEXIS 7997, at *9 (D. Minn. May 8, 2003); *Sewall v. Chicago Transit Authority*, No. 99-C-8372, 2001 U.S. Dist. LEXIS 330 (N.D. Ill. Jan. 16, 2001); *Briody v. American General Finance Co. et al.*, No. 98-2728, 1999 U.S. Dist. LEXIS 8405, at *21 (E.D. Pa. May 27, 1999).

The court in *Ruder v. Maine General Medical Center*, 204 F. Supp.2d 16 (D. Me. 2002), found that an employee who began sick leave after 51 weeks of work for the employer qualified to take FMLA leave as soon as the employee completed 12 months of service.

9. Federal Employees Stationed Outside the United States

Federal employees employed outside the United States and its territories and possessions are not eligible for FMLA leave. 29 CFR 825.105(b); DOL WH Advisory Opinion No. 9 (Oct. 18, 1993) (employees stationed in a foreign country on one- and two-year contracts are not eligible for benefits and protections of FMLA while stationed overseas).

10. Former Employees and Applicants

The circuits are split on whether the term "employee" is limited to current employees only, thereby excluding former employees and applicants. Some courts have found that the Act applies only to current employees. *See Hammon v. DHL Airways, Inc.*, 980 F. Supp. 919 (S.D. Ohio 1997) (former employee was not an eligible employee entitled to the benefits and protections of the FMLA), *aff'd*, 165 F.3d 441 (6th Cir. 1999); *Brohm v. JH Properties, Inc.*, 947 F. Supp. 299 W.D. Ky 1996) (ex-employee simply does not have a claim for FMLA leave after he has been lawfully terminated), *aff'd*, 149 F.3d 517 (6th Cir. 1998). The First Circuit has taken a contrary position, holding that the FMLA is not limited to current employees. *See Duckworth v. Pratt & Whitney*, 152 F.3d 1 (1st Cir. 1998) (job applicants are employees with private right of action for violations of FMLA). [For a discussion of who is a covered employee within the meaning of Title I, see Chapter 4, "Federal Employees Covered by the FMLA." For a discussion of who may bring a private cause of action under Title I, see Chapter 15, "Prohibited Acts, Enforcement, and Remedies."]

B. TITLE II CALCULATIONS

Unlike Title I, Title II does not label its eligibility requirements as such. Rather, the sole eligibility criterion under Title II is incorporated into the definition of a covered "employee." 5 USC 6382(a)(1).

To be considered an employee entitled to FMLA leave, an employee must have completed 12 months of service as an employee within the meaning of Title II of the Act. 5 USC 6381(1)(B); see Niimi–Montalbo v. White, 243 F. Supp. 2d 1109, 1119 (D. Haw. 2003) (leave for federal civil service employees with more than 12 months of civil service is governed by Title II of the FMLA); Humphrey v. Treasury, No. AT-0752-06-0187-I-1, 2006 MSPB LEXIS 1465, at *3 (MSPB April 4, 2006); Williams v. Treasury, No. DA-1221-02-0555-W-1, 2002 MSPB LEXIS 1412, at *12 (MSPB Oct. 31, 2002). [For a discussion of who is an employee within the meaning of Title II, see Chapter 4, "Federal Employees Covered by the FMLA."]

1. Federal Employment That Counts Toward 12–Month Eligibility Requirement

Only employment as an "employee" within the meaning of 5 USC 6301(2) counts toward the 12–month eligibility requirement. 5 USC 6381(1)(B); 5 CFR 630.1201(b)(ii). [For a discussion of who is an employee covered by Title II, see Chapter 4, "Federal Employees Covered by the FMLA".]

The regulations issued by OPM expand on this concept, although they add as much confusion as they do clarity. According to the regulations, 5 CFR 630.1201(b), Title II covers an employee, as defined under 5 USC 6301(2), with certain exceptions, who has completed at least 12 months of service as (1) an employee, as defined under 5 USC 6301(2), with some exclusions; (2) an appointed employee of the Veterans Health Administration (VHA) in occupations listed in 38 USC 7401(1); (3) a teacher or individual holding a teaching position within the meaning of 20 USC 901, or an employee paid from nonappropriated funds (NAFI), as identified in 5 USC 2105(c).

The regulatory definition of "employee" advanced by OPM does not comport with the statutory definition. Title II of the FMLA specifically includes within the definition of employee certain employees of the VHA, and Defense Department teachers and individuals holding teaching positions. See 5 USC 6381(1)(A). These individuals are generally *excluded* from the definition of a civil service employee. 5 USC 6301(2)(v), (ix). The 12–month eligibility requirement applies to individuals identified in 5 USC 6381(1)(A), which specifically includes VHA and DOD teachers and individuals holding teaching positions. 5 USC 6381(1)(B).

The way the OPM regulations read, VHA and DOD teachers remain excluded from the definition of a Title II covered employee, but any time spent working for those organizations can be counted toward the 12–month eligibility requirement of a 5 USC 6301(2) covered employee. This is clearly not what Title II of the Act requires. OPM's error appears to be in not modifying the definition of employee contained in 5 CFR 630.1201(b)(I) to include VHA and DOD teachers or individuals holding teaching positions, as suggested by 5 USC 6381(1)(A). Including VHA and DOD teachers or individuals holding teaching positions only for purposes of calculating the 12–month eligibility requirement has a completely different meaning.

For example, under the OPM regulations, assume a civil service employee of the Department of Education (DOE) is an employee covered by 5 USC 6301(2). A teacher for the DOD is not an employee within the meaning of 5 USC 6301(2) and, therefore, is generally excluded from Title II coverage. See 5 CFR 630.1201(b)(I). As written by OPM, a DOE employee could count any time spent as a teacher for the DOD for purposes of meeting the 12–month eligibility requirement of Title II. 5 CFR 630.1201(b)(ii)(C). A DOD teacher, however, could never be a Title II "employee" even if he or she met the 12–month eligibility requirement because OPM's regulations only refer to employees within the meaning of 5 USC 6301(2), which specifically excludes DOD teachers. Again, this would appear to be an incorrect application of 5 USC 6381(1)(A).

The reference in the OPM regulations to NAFI employees is correct, although unnecessarily confusing. NAFI employees are specifically included within the definition of a covered employee for purposes of Title II of the FMLA. See 5 USC 6387(b); 5 USC 6301(2)(A); 5 USC 2105(c)(2). Because they are considered employees within the meaning of 5 USC 6301(2), at least for purposes of Title II, any time spent as a NAFI employee would count toward the 12–month eligibility criteria. 5 USC 6381(1)(B). NAFI employees would, therefore, be included in 5 CFR 630.1201(b)(ii)(A). As such, there was no need for OPM to identify NAFI employees separately in 5 CFR 630.1201(b)(ii)(D).

The scope of employment that counts toward the 12–month eligibility requirement of Title II is much narrower than that of Title I. Title I employees can draw on any federal employment for purposes of eligibility. This would include time spent as a Title II employee. Title II employees, on the other hand, may not count any time spent as a Title I, CAA, or PEOAA-covered employee towards the Title II 12-month eligibility requirement. Only time spent as a Title II covered federal employee counts toward this requirement.

2. Joint Employment and Successor-in-Interest Doctrines

Title II does not recognize the concepts of joint employment or the successor-in-interest doctrine. These doctrines are recognized in Title I and the CAA. [See Chapter 3, "FMLA Coverage of the Federal Government."]

Absent recognition of joint employment, the time spent with the federal government as an employee of a temporary help or leasing agency will not be credited toward an individual's 12-month eligibility under Title II if the individual is ultimately hired as a civil service employee. This occurs because the individual, while employed by the federal government through a temporary help or employee-leasing agency, is not a civil service employee within the meaning 5 USC 6301(2). The 12-month eligibility requirement of Title II only counts time spent as a civil service employee. 5 USC 6381(1)(B).

This does not mean, however, that a civil service employee will necessarily lose time spent on a detail or other temporary assignment with another agency towards meeting the 12-month eligibility requirement. As long as the individual is a civil service employee within the meaning of 5 USC 6381(1)(A) of Title I when he or she is on the detail or temporary assignment, the time spent on the assignment will count toward the 12-month eligibility requirement. If, however, the employee takes a detail or assignment to a position outside of the civil service, the time spent would likely not count toward the 12-month eligibility requirement.

Whether the employee remains a civil service employee during the detail may depend on whether a Form 50 is issued placing the employee in the non-civil service position. If such a Form 50 is formally issued, placing the employee in a non-civil service position, such as with the Postal Service, it is likely that such time would not count toward the 12-month Title II eligibility requirement. In the absence of a Form 50 being issued, the employee remains on the rolls of the employing agency as a civil service employee and the time on a non-civil service detail should still count toward the 12-month requirement. The OPM regulations on this point, however, are nonexistent.

The same analysis applies to the successor-in-interest doctrine. As long as the employee remains a civil service employee within the meaning of Title II, the time spent working for a predecessor federal entity will count with the successor federal employer toward the 12-month eligibility requirement of Title II. The only way it would not count is if the successor federal employer were specifically excluded from the provisions of the FMLA, or were outside the confines of Title II of the FMLA.

3. Nonconsecutive Employment

The 12 months of civil service employment need not be 12 recent or consecutive months. 5 CFR 630.1201(b)(ii). As such, like under Title I, all periods of time spent as a federal civil service employee count toward the 12-month eligibility requirement.

While cumulative, the 12-month eligibility test only counts time spent as a federal civil service employee. An individual employed on a temporary or intermittent basis is specifically excluded from the definition of a Title II covered employee. 5 USC 6381(1)(A). As such, temporary and intermittent service is excluded as creditable service for determining the 12-month service requirement. Preamble, Employees Covered, 5 CFR 630. [Covered employees are discussed more fully in Chapter 4, "Federal Employees Covered by the FMLA."]

4. Effect of Leave on 12-Month Eligibility Requirement

Neither Title II nor the OPM regulations address the effect of leave on the 12-month eligibility requirement. In the absence of specific guidance, it would appear that leave would count towards the 12-month eligibility requirement. Again, because the 12-month eligibility test simply references being a covered federal civil service employee for the allotted time, as long as the individual is carried as a civil service employee during a leave of absence, whether paid or unpaid, this requirement would be satisfied. Similarly, under Title I, leave, whether paid or unpaid, counts towards the 12-month eligibility requirement.

Unlike Title I, Title II does not credit an employee a full week of employment towards the 12-month requirement even though the employee worked only part of a given week. *See* 29 CFR 825.110(b). For that matter, unlike Title I, Title II does not define the 12-month employment requirement as being equal to 52 weeks. Presumably, Title II covered employees must actually be employed by a federal agency for a full year before being eligible for FMLA leave. They will not receive credit for partial weeks of employment, although periods of paid or unpaid leave during a week would count.

5. Military Leave

The Office of Personnel Management (OPM) has not issued a memorandum or instructions governing the effect of military service on the calculation of 12 months of employment for purposes of Title II. It would seem, however, that the same rationale that motivated the DOL to add the time an employee served in the military to the eligibility of Title I federal employees would apply equally to all federal employees. The rationale advanced by the DOL was based on its interpretation of the requirement that, under USERRA, reemployed persons are entitled to the rights and benefits that they would have attained had they remained continuously employed. The ability to take FMLA leave was included in these USERRA rights. As USERRA applies to the federal government, 38 USC 4303(4)(A)(ii), (6), the same rationale would appear applicable to Title II covered federal employees.

Title II does not use the term "eligible employee." Rather, it defines a "covered employee" as an individual employed by a covered federal entity who also has worked for that covered federal entity for at least 12 months. It does not appear that absence of the term "eligible employee" would alter the application of the DOL USERRA–FMLA rule to Title II covered federal employees.

6. Effect of Termination or Reduction In Force

The effect of employee termination or reduction-in-force (RIF) is not addressed in Title II or the OPM implementing regulations. Presumably, an employee who has a Form 50 issued indicating his or her separation from the federal civil service as a result of a termination or RIF is, by definition, no longer a "civil service employee" and therefore, no longer accumulating time toward the 12-month employment eligibility test.

A related question is the effect of the reversal of a termination or RIF through a grievance, an appeal to the Merit Systems Protection Board, an Equal Employment Opportunity complaint, or a similar dispute resolution system on the accumulation of time for purposes of meeting the 12-month eligibility requirement. Title II fails to provide any guidance. The answer may partially depend on whether the employing agency issues a Form 50 separating the individual from civil service employment.

If the agency does not issue a Form 50 while the individual challenges the RIF or termination, arguably the individual is still serving under his or her civil service appointment. As such, the time would count toward the 12-month eligibility requirement. If the appeal is unsuccessful and a Form 50 is issued, unless it is backdated, arguably all the time the individual served under appointment would be counted toward the 12-month eligibility requirement. If the individual were to secure another civil service appointment, all of the time in this position would count toward future Title II FMLA eligibility.

If the employee's appeal is successful and the termination or RIF is reversed because a Form 50 was never issued, the time between the notice of termination or separation and the successful appeal would count toward the 12-month eligibility requirement.

The effect on the 12-month eligibility requirement is less clear where an employee successfully appeals a termination or RIF that was accompanied by the execution of a Form 50 formally severing the civil service appointment. Specifically, if the remedy awarded to the employee includes rescission of the separation with full back pay and benefits, does the time spent off work count toward the 12-month eligibility requirement? The short answer would appear to be that it would. Since the 12-month eligibility requirement does not deduct time spent on paid or unpaid leave, and the separation was completely reversed, it would appear that the entire time would count toward Title II eligibility.

If a termination accompanied by a Form 50 was, however, reversed, but reinstatement was prospective only, without back pay, arguably the time spent between the separation date and the return date would not count toward Title II eligibility. Because the individual was not serving a civil service appointment during this period of time, she was not an employee within the meaning of 5 USC 6381(1)(A), and this time would not count toward Title II eligibility. 5 USC 6381(1)(B).

7. Furloughs

A "furlough" means the placing of an employee in a temporary, nonduty, nonpay status because of lack of work or funds, or other nondisciplinary reasons. *Carita v. USPS*, 67 MSPR 277, 279 (1995) (emphasizing nonpay status of furloughed individual); *McCloud v. USPS*, 71 MSPR 508, 511 (1996) (furlough is the placement of an employee into a nonduty, nonpay status for nondisciplinary reasons). In many respects, it is the functional equivalent of a private sector layoff. The increased use of furloughs in recent years is largely attributable to budget and spending disagreements between the executive and legislative branches culminating in the "closing down" of the government and furloughing of federal employees.

There are two types of furloughs: (1) "adverse action" furloughs governed by 5 CFR 752.401; and (2) "reduction-in-force" (RIF) furloughs governed by 5 CFR 351.201. Adverse action or "short" furloughs involve work suspensions of less than 30 calendar days (22 work days). RIF furloughs involve suspensions from work of more than 30 calendar days, but less than one year. This type of furlough is governed by reduction-in-force regulations.

For purposes of the 12-month eligibility requirement, because the employee is still on the rolls of the federal government, although in a non-work status, the period of the furlough counts toward meeting the 12-month eligibility requirement. The time an employee is on furlough and not working would not count toward the 1,250-hour eligibility requirement, under Title I, the CAA or the PEOAA. Title II does not use the 1250-hour requirement.

8. When is Eligibility Determined?

Title II does not set a definite point in time or event on which the determination of whether the employee meets the 12-month eligibility requirement can be based. Title I and the CAA, on the other hand, set the date that leave is to commence as the point in time when employee eligibility is determined. *See* 29 CFR 825.110(d). Title II does, however, indicate that the regulations issued by OPM to implement Title II should "to the extent appropriate, be consistent with the regulations prescribed by the Secretary of Labor to carry out Title I of the Family and Medical Leave Act of 1993." 5 USC 6387. Absent anything suggesting it would not be appropriate, federal agencies should determine whether a Title II covered employee meets the 12-month eligibility requirement as of the date leave commences.

Like Title I, Title II does not define the term "leave." As such, Title II suffers from the same infirmities as Title I in determining when "leave" commences. [For more discussion on this issue, see discussion in this chapter, under the heading "Eligibility Determined at Leave Commencement".]

C. CAA CALCULATIONS

To be eligible for FMLA leave, a CAA-covered employee must have been employed in "any employing office for 12 months." 2 USC 1312(a)(2)(B); S. Res. 242, Cong. Rec. S3959–S3997 (April 23, 1996); 29 CFR 825.110(a).

1. What Federal Employment Counts Toward the 12-Month Eligibility Requirement?

The CAA limits the scope of federal employment that counts for purposes of meeting the 12-month eligibility requirement. Only employment in an "employing office" counts toward CAA eligibility. 2 USC 1312(a)(2)(B). The CAA limits the definition of an "employing office" to a small number of specifically enumerated offices within the authority and control of the House and Senate. *See* 2 USC 1301(9); S. Res. 242, 29 Rec. S3959–S3997 (April 23, 1996) 29 CFR 825.104. Federal employment other than in a CAA-defined "employing office" would not count towards the 12-month eligibility requirement. [See Chapter 3, "FMLA Coverage of the Federal Government" and Chapter 4, "Federal Employees Covered by the FMLA" for further discussion on "employing offices."]

2. Joint Employment and the Successor-in-Interest Doctrine

The CAA recognizes joint employment. *See* S. Res. 242, Cong. Rec. S3959–S3997 (April 23, 1996); 29 CFR 825.106. It does not, however, address the successor-in-interest doctrine.

The joint employment doctrine recognized by the CAA is much narrower in scope than is recognized in Title I. Joint employment under the CAA is limited to "employing offices." S. Res. 242, Cong. Rec. S3959–S3997 (April 23, 1996); 29 CFR 825.106(a). This effectively excludes time spent by private sector temporary or leased employees from calculation of the 12-month eligibility requirement. Joint employment under Title I, on the other hand, includes the time spent by temporary or leased employees who are later hired by the federal agency toward that Title's 12-month eligibility requirement. *See* 29 CFR 825.106(d). Similarly, by limiting joint employment to an employing office, the CAA also excludes all forms of joint employment involving federal employees who are not covered by the CAA.

For example, a Commerce employee and a Congressional Budget Office employee are detailed to work for a Congressional committee on a complex area of international trade. Both employees are retained on the payrolls of their respective employing agencies. The CBO employee is in a joint employment relationship while working on the Committee. As such, time spent on the committee counts for purposes of the CAA. Although the Commerce employee works shoulder-to-shoulder with the CBO employee during the detail, the Commerce employee is not in a joint relationship within the meaning of the CAA. Because the Commerce employee is retained on the payroll of the Commerce Department, an entity outside the definition of a CAA-covered "employing office," a joint employment relationship has not been formed. However, because the Commerce employee is retained on Commerce's payroll throughout the detail, the time the employee spent on the detail counts towards meeting the 12-month eligibility requirement under Title II.

3. Nonconsecutive Employment

The 12 months an employee must have been employed by an employing office need not be consecutive months. If an employee worked for two or more employing offices sequentially, the time worked will be aggregated to determine whether it equals 12 months. S. Res. 242, 29 Cong. Rec. S3959–S3997 (April 23, 1996), 29 § CFR 825.110(b).

Like Title I, the 12-month eligibility calculation does not set a time limit over which periods of CAA employment would be excluded. The period prior to the effective date of the application of FMLA rights and protections under the CAA are considered in determining employee eligibility. S. Res. 242, Cong. Rec. S3959–S3997 (April 23, 1996), 29 CFR 825.102(e); 825.110(e). The provisions of § 202 of the CAA that apply rights and protections of the FMLA to covered employees became effective on January 23, 1996. Prior to that, the FMLA applied to members of the House and Senate effective August 5, 1993. S. Res. 242, Cong. Rec. S3959–S3997 (April 23, 1996); 29 CFR 825.102(a)–(b).

4. Effect of Leave on 12-Month Eligibility Requirement

As long as the employee is maintained on the CAA payroll, the time an employee spends on leave, whether paid or unpaid, counts toward the 12-month eligibility requirement. Moreover, like Title I, if an employee is maintained on the payroll for any part of a week, including any periods of paid or unpaid leave (sick, vacation) during which other benefits or compensation are provided by the employer (e.g., workers' compensation, group health plan benefits, etc.), the entire week counts as a week of employment. S. Res. 242, Cong. Rec. S3959–S3997 (April 23, 1996); 29 CFR 825.110(b). For purposes of determining whether intermittent, occasional or casual employment qualifies as "at least 12 months"; 52 weeks is deemed to be equal to 12 months.

5. Military Duty

The Office of Compliance, the entity that enforces the provisions of the CAA, including the FMLA provisions, has not issued guidance governing the effect of military service on the calculation of 12 months of employment for purposes of the FMLA as applied through the CAA. It would seem, however, that the same rationale that motivated the DOL to add the time an employee served in the military to the eligibility of Title I federal employees would apply equally to federal employees covered by the CAA. The rationale advanced by the DOL was based on its interpretation of the requirement that, under USERRA, a person who is reemployed is entitled to the rights and benefits that he or she would have attained if he or she remained continuously employed. The ability to take FMLA leave was included in these USERRA rights. As USERRA applies to the federal government, including the legislative branch, 38 USC 4303(4)(A)(ii), (6), the same rationale would appear applicable to CAA-covered employees.

6. Effect of Termination or Reductions in Force on 12-Month Eligibility Calculation

Neither the CAA nor the implementing regulations address the effect of an employee's termination or suspension on the calculation of the 12-month eligibility requirement. Given the close similarity in language of the CAA and Title I regulations, however, the analysis previously provided on this issue for Title I should apply.

7. Effect of Furloughs on 12-Month Eligibility Requirement

As indicated previously, furloughs are essentially temporary layoffs, usually caused by a failure of the executive and legislative branches to agree on a budget. Because employees are retained on the payroll of the employing agency during this period of time, however, the period on furlough would count towards the employee's 12-month eligibility requirement.

8. Twelve-Month Eligibility Calculated at Leave Commencement

Whether a covered CAA employee meets the 12-month eligibility requirement of the CAA is calculated "as of the date leave commences." S. Res. 242, Cong. Rec. S3959–S3997 (April 23, 1996); 29 CFR 825.110(d). As with Title I, the CAA implementing regulations fail to define the terms "leave" or when the leave "commences." Given the close similarity in the wording of the eligibility regulations, the previous analysis in this section of this issue for Title I should be applicable to the CAA.

D. PEOAA CALCULATIONS

The FMLA as applied through the PEOAA defines an "eligible employee" as one that has been employed in any employing office for 12 months. 3 USC 412(a)(2)(B). An "employing office" is defined as several identified components of the Executive Office of the President. 3 USC 401(a)(4). [See Chapter 3, "FMLA Coverage of the Federal Government" for further discussion on "employing offices."]

1. What Federal Employment Counts Toward the 12-Month Eligibility Requirement?

Only employment within a PEOAA-covered "employing office" counts towards the 12-month eligibility requirement. Employment with any other federal government entity does not count towards the PEOAA 12-month eligibility requirement.

IV. DETERMINING 1,250 HOURS OF SERVICE DURING THE PREVIOUS 12 MONTHS

The second FMLA eligibility requirement under Title I, the CAA, and the PEOAA requires that a covered employee have worked at least 1,250 hours during the 12-month period preceding leave commencement. This requirement does not apply to employees covered by Title II. A review of the application of this requirement under Title I, the CAA, and the PEOAA follows.

A. TITLE I: DETERMINING 1,250 HOURS

To be eligible for the benefits and protections of the FMLA, a Title I covered federal employee must have been employed for at least 1,250 hours of service with a covered employer during the 12-month period immediately preceding the commencement of FMLA leave. *See* 29 USC 2611(2)(A)(ii); 29 CFR 825.110(a)(2), 825.800 (definition of "eligible employee"); a*ccord Moticka v. Weck Closure Systems*, 183 Fed. Appx. 343 (4th Cir. 2006); *Ricco v. Potter*, 377 F.3d 599, 603–604 (6th Cir. 2004); *Walker v. Elmore County Bd. of Ed.*, 379 F.3d 1249, at *2 (11th Cir. 2004); *Babcock v. Bellsouth Advertising and Publishing Corp.*, 348 F.3d 73, 77 (4th Cir. 2003); *Ross v. Kraft Foods North America, Inc.*, 347 F. Supp. 2d 200 (E.D. Pa. 2004); *Ammons-Lewis v. Metropolitan Water Reclamation District of Greater Chicago*, No. 885, 2004 U.S. Dist. LEXIS 21917, at *24 (N.D. Ill. Nov. 1, 2004), *aff'd*, 488 F.3d 739 (7th Cir. 2007); *Rasmussen v. Dept. of Navy*, No. SF-0752-06-0837-I-1, 2006 MSPB LEXIS 7240, at *10 (MSPB Dec. 12, 2006).

An employee who has not worked the requisite 1250 hours in the 12 months preceding leave commencement is not eligible for FMLA leave or protections. *See Ricco*, 377 F.3d at 603-04; *Kosakow v. New Rochelle Radiology Associates, P.C.*, 274 F.3d 706, 715–22 (2nd Cir. 2001) (vacating award of summary judgment in favor of employer after finding existence of genuine issues of material fact regarding periods of time that allegedly should have been counted toward 1,250 hour requirement); *Woodford v. Community Action of Greene County, Inc.*, 268 F.3d 51 (2nd Cir. 2001) (affirming award of summary judgment to employer because time sheets showed that employee had not worked requisite 1,250 hours); *Smith v. Midpointe Healthcare, Inc.*, No. 04-cv-6315 (PGS), 2007 U.S. Dist. LEXIS 10471, at *15 (D.N.J. Feb. 15, 2007); *Pirant v. USPS*, No. 03 C 9383, 2006 U.S. Dist. LEXIS 89319, at *7 (N.D. Ill. Dec. 7, 2006); *Rivero v. United Airlines, Inc.*, No. 04 C 6514,

2005 U.S. Dist. LEXIS 29733, at *32 (N.D. Il. Nov. 22, 2005); *Ross*, 347 F. Supp. 2d 200 (E.D. Pa. 2004) (employee who did not work minimum 1,250 hours could not maintain FMLA retaliation claim); *Ferrero v. Henderson*, 341 F. Supp. 2d 873, 904 (S.D. Ohio 2004) (because employee worked less than the total number of hours required to become an eligible employee under the FMLA, her FMLA claim fails); *Rasmussen,* 2006 MSPB LEXIS 7240, at *10.

An employee who falls short of the 1250-hour requirement by a *de minimis* amount is not eligible for FMLA leave. In *Pirant v. USPS*, No. 03 C 9383, 2006 U.S. Dist. LEXIS 89319, at *22 (N.D. Ill. Dec. 7, 2006), the employee was 1.2 hours short of meeting the 1250-hours requirement. The employee argued that the shortfall was *de minimis* and should be disregarded in favor of FMA eligibility. The court disagreed. The 1250-hour requirement, the court found, is strictly applied.

The three major components of this definition—hours worked, preceding 12 months, and leave commencement—are addressed below. Also addressed are record keeping and eligibility notice requirements.

1. Hours Worked

The FMLA does not define the term "hours of service" for purposes of the 1,250 hours requirement. *Ricco*, 377 F.3d at 604. The FMLA does, however, specify that the determination of whether an employee meets the 1,250 hours of service requirement is based on the legal standards developed under § 7 of the Fair Labor Standards Act (FLSA). 29 USC 207; 29 USC 2611(2)(C); 29 CFR 825.110(c); *Knapp v. America West Airlines*, 207 Fed. Appx. 896 (10th Cir. 2006); *Ricco*, 377 F.3d at 604 (6th Cir. 2004); *Plumely v. Southern Container, Inc.*, 303 F.3d 364, 369 (1st Cir. 2002); *Rivero v. United Airlines, Inc.*, No. 04 C 6514, 2005 U.S. Dist. LEXIS 29733, at *32 (N.D. Ill. Nov. 22, 2005); *Hastings v. Carlson Marketing Group, Inc.*, No. 04-3370 (DWF/JSM), 2005 U.S. Dist. LEXIS 25808, at *10 (D. Minn. Oct. 27, 2005); *Pennant v. Convergys Corp.*, 368 F. Supp. 2d 1307, 1310 (S.D. Fla. March 31, 2005).

Ironically, § 7 of the FLSA does not define the term "hours of service" either. *Ricco*, 377 F.3d at 603–604. In comments accompanying publication of the Title I FMLA regulations, the DOL stated that "the legislative history of the FMLA indicates that the minimum number of hours of service requirement is meant to be construed in a manner consistent with the legal principles established for determining hours of work for payment of overtime compensation." *Ricco*, 377 F.3d at 603–604 (quoting *Summary of Comments*, 60 Fed. Reg. 2186 (January 6, 1995); *Kosakow*, 274 F.3d at 715–22; *Robinson–Scott v. Delta Airlines, Inc.*, 4 F. Supp. 2d 1183 (N.D. Ga. 1998); *Cantrell v. Delta Airlines, Inc.*, 2 F. Supp. 2d 1460 (N.D. Ga. 1998). Pursuant to this standard, the determining factor is the number of hours the employee actually worked for the covered employer within the meaning of the FLSA. 29 CFR 825.110(c); *Ricco*, 377 F.3d at 604; *Plumley,* 303 F.3d at 367; *Rivero,* 2005 U.S. Dist. LEXIS 29733, at *32; *Rockwell v. Mack Trucks, Inc.*, 8 F. Supp. 2d 499, 502 (D. Md. 1998); *Nelson v. City of Cranston*, 116 F. Supp. 2d 260 (D.R.I. 2000). An employee's status as a full–time employee is not relevant in determining whether the employee has worked 1,250 hours. The question remains: how many hours the employee actually worked. *Plumley,* 303 F.3d at 372 (FMLA does not apply to all full–time employees of a covered employer; Congress chose to differentiate eligible employees from ineligible employees by the number of hours worked in the previous 12 months); *Lacoparra v. Pergament Home Centers, Inc.*, 982 F. Supp. 213, 219 (S.D.N.Y. 1997) (where plaintiff conceded that she did not work 1,250 hours in the prior 12 months, her status as a full–time employee was not probative of hours actually worked); *Nave v. Wooldridge Construction of Pennsylvania, Inc.*, No. 96–2891, 1997 U.S. Dist. LEXIS 9203 (E.D. Pa. June 30, 1997) (employee who worked 681 hours in 11 months of total employment preceding FMLA leave request not eligible for FMLA leave and benefits). Under the FLSA, "hours worked" does not include time paid, but only time spent working. *Pirant*, 2006 U.S. Dist. LEXIS 89319, at *7.

In the event that an employer does not maintain an accurate record of hours worked by an employee, including employees who are exempt from FLSA's requirement that a record be kept of their hours worked (e.g., *bona fide* executive, administrative, and professional employees as defined in FLSA Regulations, 29 CFR 541), the employer has the burden of showing that the employee has not worked the requisite hours. 29 CFR 825.110(c); *Pirant*, 2006 U.S. Dist. LEXIS 89319, at *7; *Rivero,* 2005 U.S. Dist. LEXIS 29733, at *34 (where the employer does not maintain an accurate record of hours worked, the employer must clearly demonstrate that the employee did not work the requisite 1,250 hours during the previous 12 months); *Hastings*, 2005 U.S. Dist. LEXIS 25808, at *10. In the event that the employer is unable to meet this burden, the employee is deemed to have met the 1,250–hour test. 29 CFR 825.110(c). [For a discussion of special FMLA record–keeping requirements for FLSA exempt employees, see Chapter 14, "Record Keeping Requirements."]

a. FLSA Principles

The following introduces some basic FLSA principles relevant to the determination of what employee activity constitutes "hours worked" for purposes of § 7 of the Act. It is not meant to be an exhaustive survey of the law. If more detailed information on the FLSA is needed, consult any of the many treatises available on this subject.

Section 7 of the FLSA (29 USC 207) generally provides that persons may not be employed for more than a stated number of hours a week without receiving at least one and one-half times their regular rate of pay for the overtime hours. 29 USC 207(a)(1); 29 CFR 785.1; 785.5. "Employ" is defined by the FLSA as "to suffer or permit to work." 29 USC 203(g); 29 CFR 785.6. The FLSA does not, however, define what constitutes "work." 29 CFR 785.6. Section 3(o) of the FLSA, 29 USC 203(o), contains a partial definition of "hours worked" in the form of a limited exception excluding clothes changing and wash-up time from "hours worked." *Id.*

(1) Historical Development

The United States Supreme Court originally stated that employees subject to the FLSA must be paid for all time spent in "physical or mental exertion (whether burdensome or not) controlled or required by the employer." 29 CFR 785.7 (citing *Tennessee Coal, Iron & Railroad Co. v. Muscoda Local No. 123*, 321 U.S. 590 (1944)). Subsequently, the Court ruled that there need be no exertion at all, and that all hours are hours worked, and that "an employer, if he chooses, may hire a man to do nothing, or to do nothing but wait for something to happen. Refraining from other activity often is a factor of instant readiness to serve, and idleness plays a part in all employments in a standby capacity. Readiness to serve may be hired, quite as much as service itself, and the time spent lying in wait for threats to the safety of the employer's property may be treated by the parties as a benefit to the employer." 29 CFR 785.7 (quoting *Armour & Co. v. Wantock*, 323 U.S. 126 (1944); *Skidmore v. Swift*, 323 U.S. 134 (1944)). The workweek ordinarily includes "all the time during which an employee is necessarily required to be on the employer's premises, on duty or at a prescribed workplace." 29 CFR 785.7 (quoting *Anderson v. Mt. Clemens Pottery Co.,* 328 U.S. 680 (1946)).

(2) To Suffer or Permit to Work

Working time includes not only the time an employer requires an employee to work, but also time spent by the employee working that was not requested by the employer but that the employer knows or has reason to believe that the employee is performing. In these circumstances, because the employer "suffered or permitted" the employee to work, it is considered compensable work time. 29 CFR 785.11. The principle applies even if the work is performed away from the premises or the job site, or even at home. 29 CFR 785.12. The reason why the employee works beyond the minimum time formally required by the employer is immaterial. 29 CFR 785.11. As long as the employer knows or has reason to believe that the employee continues to perform work, it is work time. *Id.*; 29 CFR 785.12. Management bears the burden through the exercise of its control to see that work is not performed if it wants to avoid compensating the employee for time worked that it does not desire. 29 CFR 785.13.

(3) On-Duty Work Time

An employee is on duty working when she is unable to use her time effectively for her own purposes because of work requirements imposed by an employer. *See* 29 CFR 785.15, 785.16. On-duty work time also includes short periods of inactivity in which the employee is waiting for work. 29 CFR 785.15. For example, a secretary who reads a book while waiting for an assignment, a fireman who does the crossword puzzle while waiting for a fire or a fire drill, or a production worker who talks to her colleagues while waiting for machinery to be repaired are all "working" within the meaning of the FLSA during these periods of inactivity. *Id.* In all of these examples, because the periods of inactivity are of short, unpredictable duration, the employees are unable to use the time effectively for their own purposes. It belongs to and is controlled by the employer. *Id.*

Of course, whether waiting time is time worked under the FLSA will depend on the particular circumstances of each case. 29 CFR 785.14; *Knapp v. America West Airlines*, 207 Fed. Appx. 896 (10th Cir. 2006). The determination involves a review of the contracts or other agreements between the particular parties, the conduct of the parties pursuant to those agreements, the nature of the activity at issue and its relation to the waiting time under the totality of the circumstances. 29 CFR 785.14; *Knapp*, 207 Fed. Appx. at 896; *Rivero v. United Airlines, Inc.*, No. 04 C 6514, 2005 U.S. Dist. LEXIS 29733, at *33

(N.D. Ill. Nov. 22, 2005). Facts may show that the employee was engaged to wait (compensable work time), or they may show that the employee was waiting to be engaged (nonwork time). *Knapp*, 207 Fed. Appx. at 896. The determination is made in accordance with "common sense and the general concept of work or employment." 29 CFR 785.14 (quoting *Central Mo. Tel. Co. v. Conwell*, 170 F.2d 641 (8th Cir. 1948)). The test is whether the time is spent predominantly for the employer's or for the employee's benefit. *Knapp*, 207 Fed. Appx. at 896; *Rivero*, 2005 U.S. Dist. LEXIS 29733, at *33. Where the employee is not required to remain on the employer's premises, the critical inquiry is whether the employee is able to use the time effectively for his or her own purposes. *Knapp*, 207 Fed. Appx. at 896.

In *Knapp*, 207 Fed. Appx. at 896, the employee was a pilot for American West Airlines. She was denied FMLA leave to care for her son. The district court held that Knapp was not eligible for FMLA leave because she had not accrued at least 1,250 hours of service in the 12-month period prior to the requested leave. The district court made its determination after reviewing four categories of working time: active-duty time, training time, layover time, and reserve-duty time. The district court counted active-duty time, layover time, and training time towards the 1,250-hour requirement. It did not count reserve time. Without reserve time, Knapp did not meet the 1,250-hour eligibility requirement. On appeal, the Tenth Circuit agreed that reserve time did not count. The court noted that restrictions on her during reserve time, a prohibition on drinking alcohol, and she had to be able to report to the airport within one hour of being called, were not so limiting that Knapp could not use the time effectively for her own purposes. The fact that she was compensated for this time, the court found, was not determinative of whether the time counted for FMLA eligibility purposes.

(4) Off-Duty Time

In general, periods during which an employee is completely relieved from duty and which are long enough to enable the employee to use the time effectively for his own purposes are not considered hours worked. 29 CFR 785.16(a). An employee is not completely relieved from duty and cannot use the time effectively for her own purposes unless she is definitely told in advance that she may leave the job, and that she will not have to commence work until a definitely specified hour has arrived. Whether the time is long enough to enable the employee to use the time effectively for her own purposes depends upon all of the facts and circumstances of the case. *Id.*

The FLSA, 29 CFR 785.16, provides the following example to illustrate on- and off- duty time:

> [For example,] a truck driver who has to wait at or near the job site for goods to be loaded is working during the loading period. If the driver reaches his destination and while waiting the return trip is required to take care of his employer's truck or good, he is also working while waiting. In both cases, the employee is engaged to wait. Waiting is an integral part of the job. On the other hand, for example, if the truck driver is sent from Washington D.C. to New York City, leaving at 6 a.m. and arriving at 12 noon, and is completely and specifically relieved from all duty until 6 p.m. when he again goes on duty for the return trip, the idle time is not working time. Instead, he is waiting to be engaged. (Citations omitted.)

(5) Rest Periods; Breaks

Rest periods of short duration, running from 5 minutes to about 20 minutes, must be counted as hours worked. 29 CFR 785.18. Compensable rest periods may not be offset against other working time, such as compensable waiting time or on-call time. *Id.*

(6) Lunch Breaks and Other Meal Times

Bona fide meal periods are not counted as hours worked. 29 CFR 785.19(a). *Bona fide* meal periods do not include coffee breaks or time for snacks, which are rest periods and count as hours worked. *Id.* A *bona fide* meal period is one in which the employee is completely relieved from duty for the purposes of eating regular meals. Ordinarily, 30 minutes or more is long enough for a *bona fide* meal period, although a shorter period may be long enough under some circumstances. *Id.* The employee is not relieved if he is required to perform any duties, whether active or inactive, while eating. For example, an office employee who is required to eat at his desk in order to answer the telephone is working while eating. That time must be counted as hours worked. *Id.*

It is not necessary to qualify as a *bona fide* meal period that an employee must be permitted to leave the premises if he is otherwise completely freed from duties during the meal period. 29 CFR 785.19(b).

(7) On-Call Time

An employee who is required to remain on call on the employer's premises or so close thereto that he cannot use the time effectively for his own purposes is working while "on call." 29 CFR 785.17. An employee who is not required to remain on the employer's premises but is merely required to leave word at his home or with company officials where he may be reached is not working while on call. 29 CFR 787.17.

(8) Statutory Exclusions from Hours Worked

The time involved in certain work-related activities has, by law, been excluded from the calculation of "hours worked." Exclusions are contained in the Portal-to-Portal Act and § 3(o) of the FLSA.

The Portal-to-Portal Act, 29 USC 251, *et. seq.*, eliminates from working time certain "preliminary" and "postliminary" activities performed "prior" or "subsequent" to the "workday" that are not otherwise made compensable by contract, custom, or practice. 29 CFR 785.9. The Portal-to-Portal Act does not, however, affect the computation of hours worked on "principal activities" within the "workday." *Id.*

The "workday" means the period between the time on any particular workday when an employee commences his principal activities and the time on any particular workday when the employee ceases such principal activities. *Id.* A "workday" may be longer than the employee's scheduled shift, hours, tour of duty, or time on the production line. Also, its duration may vary from day to day depending on when the employee commences and ceases his principal activities. *Id.*

By contract, custom or practice, time spent in "preliminary" or "postliminary" activities that is compensable must be counted as hours worked for purposes of the FLSA. *Id.* However, only the amount of time allowed by the contract, custom or practice is required to be counted. For example, if the time allowed for wash-up is 15 minutes but the activity takes 25 minutes, only 15 minutes is counted as "hours worked." *Id.* (citing *Galvin v. National Biscuit Co.*, 82 F. Supp. 535 (S.D.N.Y. 1949), *appeal dismissed*, 177 F.2d 963 (2d Cir. 1949)).

Section 3(o) of the FLSA, 29 USC 203, provides that "hours worked" for purposes of section 7 of the FLSA, excludes any time spent in changing clothes or washing at the beginning or end of each workday where such time is expressly excluded from measured working time during the workday by custom, practice, or the terms of a *bona fide* and applicable collective bargaining agreement. 29 CFR 785.9. If, however, a collective bargaining agreement, by its express terms, custom, or practice, includes wash time or time spent changing clothes at the beginning or end of the day as time worked, the time spent in those activities counts as "hours worked" for purposes of the FLSA.

In addition to the Portal-to-Portal Act, the FLSA, 29 USC 207(e)(2), excludes from the calculation of an employee's "regular rate," compensation for:

- Occasional periods when no work is performed due to vacation, holiday, illness, failure of the employer to provide sufficient work, or other similar cause.

- Reasonable payments for traveling expenses, or other expenses, included by an employee in the furtherance of his employer's interests and properly reimbursable by the employer.

- Other similar payments to an employee which are not made as compensation for his hours of employment.

The FLSA regulations implementing § 7(e) of the FLSA (29 CFR 778.218(b), (d)) explain:

> This provision of Section 7(e)(2) deals with the type of absences which are infrequent or sporadic or unpredictable. It has no relation to regular "absences" such as lunch periods nor to regularly scheduled days of rest…
>
> …
>
> The term "other similar cause" refers to payments made for periods of absence due to factors like holidays, vacations, sickness, and failure of the employer to provide work. Examples of "similar causes" are absences due to jury service, reporting to a draft board, attending a funeral of a family member, inability to reach the workplace because of weather conditions. Only absences of a nonroutine character which are infrequent or sporadic or unpredictable are included in the "other similar cause" category.

In *Ricco v. Potter*, 377 F.3d 599, 605 (6th Cir. 2004), the Sixth Circuit held that the time an employee would have worked but for an unlawful termination is not an "otherwise similar cause" within the meaning of § 7 of the FLSA because the hours an employee would have worked but for unlawful termination did not fit within the § 7(e)(2) exception to an employee's "regular rate" of compensation. Those hours, the Sixth Circuit went on to hold, counted for the purpose of determining an employee's "regular rate" and, as a result, for purposes of the FMLA's "hours of service" requirement.

The First Circuit came to the opposite conclusion in *Plumley v. Southern Container, Inc.*, 303 F.3d 364, 370–71 (1st Cir. 2002), observing:

> FLSA § 207(e) contains a list of remunerations that the regular rate "shall not be deemed to include." This compendium encompasses such things as "reward[s] for service, the amount of which are not measured by or dependent on hours worked, production, or efficiency [and] payment made for occasional periods when no work is being performed due to vacation, holiday, illness, failure of the employer to provide sufficient work, or other similar cause." 29 U.S.C. § 207(e)(1)–(2). These exclusions (and the statutory language used in their explication) illustrate that any compensation that is not paid for hours actually worked in the service and at the gain of the employer is not to be counted toward hours of service. It is surpassingly difficult to make a principled distinction between wages received for hours not worked because an employer has failed to provide sufficient work and wages received for hours not worked because an employer unjustifiably has kept the employee from working (and, thus, has failed to provide sufficient work).

b. Overtime; Premium Pay

Overtime hours are considered "hours worked" within the meaning of the FLSA and count toward the 1,250-hour eligibility requirement. *See* Preamble, 29 CFR 825.110 (because overtime hours worked are "hours worked" within the meaning of the FLSA, they are included). Only the amount of overtime actually worked, however, is included toward the 1,250-hour eligibility requirement. Payment of overtime at time-and-a-half, or payment for time worked in accordance with any other agreed upon premium pay formula in excess of straight time, does not add time to the amount of hours actually worked for determining the 1,250-hour eligibility requirement. Preamble, 29 CFR 825.110 (overtime hours are hours worked within the FLSA, and count towards 1,250-hour eligibility requirement); DOL Opinion Letter No. 70 (August 23, 1995) (no premium is applied to "hours actually worked" test under FMLA regardless of whether employee may have received overtime premium pay pursuant to federal or state law or the terms of a collective bargaining agreement).

c. Paid or Unpaid Leave

Leave, including vacation, personal leave, sick leave, FMLA leave, sabbaticals, and holidays, whether paid or unpaid, does not count toward the 1,250-hour eligibility requirement as leave is not considered to be actual "hours worked" within the meaning of the FLSA. Preamble, 29 CFR 825.110; DOL WH Advisory Opinion No. 18 (Nov. 15, 1993) (time spent on paid or unpaid leave are not "hours worked" within meaning of FLSA and, consequently, these hours are not counted in determining the 1,250-hour eligibility test); DOL WH Advisory Opinion No. 46 (Oct. 14, 1994) (paid or unpaid leave, sick days taken by the employee, even if paid, and sabbatical leave, even if the employee continues to receive some compensation during this period, are not counted toward FMLA eligibility); DOL WH Advisory Opinion No. 70 (Aug. 23, 1995) (annual or sick leave, paid or unpaid holidays, or FMLA leave are not counted as "hours worked" toward 1,250 hours for FMLA eligibility); *see also Sepe v. McDonnell Douglas Corp.*, 176 F.3d 1113, 1115 (8th Cir.) (time employee spent on medical leave does not count as "hours worked"), *cert. denied*, 528 U.S. 1062 (1999); *Pirant v. USPS*, No. 03 C 9383, 2006 U.S. Dist. LEXIS 89319, at *7 (N.D. Ill. Dec. 7, 2006); *Hastings v. Carlson Marketing Group, Inc.*, No. 04-3370 (DWF/JSM), 2005 U.S. Dist. LEXIS 25808, at *10 (D. Minn. Oct. 27, 2005) (hours/days of paid vacation and sick leave do not count in the computation of hours worked); *Aldrich v. Bobby Greg et al.*, 200 F. Supp. 2d 784, 788 (N.D. Ohio 2002) (paid vacations and holidays do not count toward 1,250-hour requirement); *Walters v. AP Supermarket Service et al.*, No. 3:98-CV-1222, 2001 U.S. Dist. LEXIS 2696 (M.D. Pa. Jan. 31, 2001) (time spent on FMLA leave does not count toward 1,250-hour eligibility requirement); *Nelson v. City of Cranston*, 116 F. Supp. 2d 260, 266–67 (D.R.I. 2000) (time spent on paid leave and LWOP did not count toward 1,250 hours); *Veal v. AT&T Corp*. No. 99-0370 § "K" (2), 2000 U.S. Dist. LEXIS 3863 (E.D. La. March 22, 2000) (disability leave does not count toward 1,250-hour eligibility requirement as it is not "hours worked"); *Rockwell v. Mack Trucks, Inc.*, 8 F. Supp. 2d 499, 502 (D. Md. 1998) (employee absences did not count toward "hours worked" in calculation of FMLA eligibility); *Clark v. Allegheny University Hospital*, No. 97-6113, 1998 U.S. Dist. LEXIS 2305 (E.D. Pa. 1998) (neither paid or unpaid leave is hours worked for purposes of determining FMLA eligibility); *Caruthers v. Proctor*

& Gamble Manufacturing, 961 F. Supp. 1484, 1490 (D. Kan. 1997) (time on leave does not count toward 1,250-hour eligibility requirement); Robbins v. Bureau of Nat. Affairs, 896 F. Supp. 18, 20–21 (D.D.C. 1995) (maternity leave did not count towards 1,250-hour eligibility requirement because, under FLSA, leave is not considered "work hours"); Rasmussen v. Dept. of Navy, No. SF-0752-06-0837-I-1, 2006 MSPB LEXIS 7240, at *10 (MSPB Dec. 12, 2006). Note that for purposes of determining whether a covered employee has met the 12 months of employment eligibility requirement, time on paid or unpaid leave counts as long as the employee is maintained on the payroll. Here, for purposes of the 1,250-hour eligibility requirement, leave, paid or unpaid, does not count; only the time actually worked by the employee counts.

d. Military Leave

Employees returning from military leave covered by the Uniformed Services Employment and Reemployment Rights Act (USERRA) must receive credit towards FMLA eligibility for the months and hours the employee should have worked but for the military leave.

For purposes of meeting the 12-month and 1,250-hour eligibility requirements, a Title I covered federal employee who is called to military service within the meaning of the USERRA, 38 USC 4301–4333, must be credited on his or her return to work for the months and hours he or she would have been employed but for the military service. See U.S. Dept. of Labor, USERRA–FMLA Memorandum, reprinted in 145 Daily Labor Report A–5 (July 29, 2002).

USERRA, as mentioned previously, is a federal law that provides reemployment rights for veterans and members of the National Guard and Reserve following qualifying military service. Significantly, it also requires that uniformed service members who conclude their tours of duty and who are reemployed are entitled to the "rights and benefits" of employment that they would have obtained if they have been continuously employed, with the exception of benefits that are considered a form of short-term compensation, such as accrued paid vacation. The "rights and benefits" protected by USERRA include those provided by employers and those required by statute, including the right to leave under the FMLA. Accordingly, a returning service member would be entitled to FMLA leave if the hours that he or she would have worked for the civilian employer during the period of military service would have met the FMLA eligibility threshold.

Therefore, in determining whether a veteran meets the FMLA eligibility requirement, the months employed and the hours that were actually worked for the covered employer should be combined with the months and hours that would have been worked during the 12 months prior to the start of the leave requested for the military leave. See U.S. Dept. of Labor, USERRA–FMLA Memorandum. Accordingly, a person reemployed following military service has the hours that would have been worked for the employer added to any hours actually worked during the previous 12-month period to meet the 1,250-hour requirement. In order to determine the hours that would have been worked during the period of military service, the employee's pre-service work schedule can generally be used for calculations. See U.S. Dept. of Labor, USERRA–FMLA, Questions and Answers, explaining U.S. Dept. of Labor, USERRA–FMLA Memorandum, answer to question 6. [For a discussion of the interrelationship of the FMLA with other laws, including the USERRA, see Chapter 16, "Interaction of the FMLA with Other Federal Laws, Employer Practices, and Collective Bargaining Agreements."]

For example, an employee who normally works a 40-hour week leaves civilian employment on November 5, 2001, to serve a tour of duty in Afghanistan, and is reemployed by the same employer on June 10, 2002. On July 1, 2002, the employee requests FMLA leave to commence immediately. The employee has only 840 hours of actual work performed for the employer in the 12 months prior to the leave request (18 weeks prior to the military service, and three weeks following reemployment, at 40 hours a week). If the employee is otherwise eligible for FMLA leave, the 1,240 hours that the employee would have worked but for his or her service in Afghanistan (31 weeks at 40 hours per week) should be added to the 840 hours actually worked, for a total of 2,080 hours in the 12 months preceding leave commencement. See U.S. Dept. of Labor, USERRA–FMLA Memorandum, at 2, ¶ 2.

The Department of Labor USERRA–FMLA Memorandum and USERRA–FMLA Questions and Answers refer to a "civilian" employer covered by Title I. Similarly, elsewhere in these documents the DOL recognizes that Title I covers "persons employed by private employers, state and local governments, and the Postal Service. See U.S. Dept. of Labor, USERRA–FMLA Memorandum, at 2, lines 2–3; U.S. Dept. of Labor, USERRA–FMLA Questions and Answers, answer to question 3. Of course, in addition to those employers, Title I applies to certain federal employees throughout the federal government. See 29 CFR 825.109. The exclusion in the DOL USERRA–FMLA memoranda of any reference to non-postal federal employees covered by Title I was not likely intended to relieve the federal government from calculating eligibility to include all USERRA-covered military service. The exclusion was probably inadvertent. [For a discussion of the federal government as a covered Title employer and what federal employees are covered by Title I of the FMLA, see Chapters 3, "FMLA Coverage of the Federal Government", and 4, "Federal Employees Covered by the FMLA" respectively.]

e. Time Spent on Union Business

Whether time spent adjusting grievances between an employer and employees counts as "hours worked" toward the 1,250-hour eligibility requirement will depend on the terms of any governing collective bargaining agreement. The matter is addressed in the regulations, implementing § 7 of the FLSA, 29 CFR 785.42, as follows:

> Time spent in adjusting grievances between an employer and employees during the time the employees are required to be on the premises is hours worked, but in the event a *bona fide* union is involved the counting of such time will, as a matter of enforcement policy, be left to the process of collective bargaining or to the custom or practice under the collective bargaining agreement.

The issue was addressed by the court in *Koontz v. USX Corp.*, No. 99-3191, 2001 U.S. Dist. LEXIS 9319 (E.D. Pa. July 2, 2001). The district court held that the time spent by one of the plaintiff's on "union business" processing grievances did not constitute "hours worked" for purposes of the FMLA. The evidence, according to the court, showed that USX neither tracked nor compensated the hours employees spent performing union business. The union paid the employee for time spent on "union business." The fact that the employer separately tracked and did not compensate for time spent on union business was sufficient to bring the matter within the collective bargaining agreement exception from "hours worked" for FLSA purposes, which the FMLA follows.

f. Preliminary and Postliminary Activities

Time spent by an employee preparing for work (preliminary) or preparing to leave work (postliminary) or excluded for purpose of the FMLA's 1250-hour eligibility requirement. The issue in these cases is whether an activity is preliminary or postliminary, or whether it counts as "hours worked" for purposes of the FLSA and, therefore, the 1250-hour eligibility requirement.

In *Pirant v. USPS*, No. 03 C 9383, 2006 U.S. Dist. LEXIS 89319, at *7 (N.D. Ill. Dec. 7, 2006), the court rejected the employee's argument that the several off-the-clock minutes she spent each day before and after work changing into and out of her work clothes, which included a work shirt, apron, gloves, and shoes, counted for purposes of meeting the 1250-work hours eligibility requirement. The court noted that the FMLA's standards for calculating hours of service are derived from the FLSA, which the Portal-to-Portal Act modified, to exclude such preliminary and postliminary activities. The court found Pirant's activities did not touch "upon the type of vital considerations of health, safety, or hygiene that would take Pirant's clothes changing activity out of the range of ordinary clothes changing and showering that need not be compensated under the FMLA."

In *Pennant v. Convergys Corp.*, 368 F. Supp. 2d 1307, 1312 (S.D. Fla. 2005), the court found that the time the employee allegedly spent each day clocking on and off was the type of preliminary or postliminary activity that did not count as time worked for purposes of the FLSA and, therefore, the FMLA. The court reasoned that clocking in and out did not count because it was not an integral part of the principal activity of a telephone sales representative.

The time spent by an employee at work before the workday officially begins, preparing machines and paperwork in order to open the office counted for purposes of the 1,250-hour eligibility requirement. In *Kosakow v. New Rochelle Radiology Associates, P.C.*, 274 F.3d 706 (2d Cir. 2001), plaintiff, a part-time radiological technologist, arrived 15 minutes early to work every day to prepare to open the office to receive patients. While there, she would turn on the X-ray machine, allow it to warm up, perform tests on the machine, and otherwise perform tasks to prepare the office to receive patients, such as pulling patient files. Plaintiff was granted medical leave for cancer surgery. When she attempted to return to work, she was told that her job was eliminated as a result of a downsizing. Plaintiff sued, alleging violation of the FMLA. The district court dismissed her claims after finding that she worked only 1,186.5 hours in the 12 months preceding the commencement of her leave, not the 1,250 hours required for eligibility. The district court did not include the 15 minutes a day she spent preparing the office to open, finding that such preliminary activities did not count as "work hours," citing the Portal-to-Portal Act, 29 USC 254.

On appeal, plaintiff argued that the district court erred when it found her ineligible for FMLA protections. Specifically, she argued that the 15 minutes each day she spent preparing the office to open should have been included toward FMLA eligibility. With that time added, she would meet the 1,250–hour eligibility requirement.

Disagreeing with the district court, the Second Circuit found that the 15 minutes the plaintiff spent preparing the office each morning constituted compensable "work hours." The court found that the activities performed were not preliminary activities but rather activities necessary for the proper performance of her job. The fact that she had not been instructed to perform this prepatory work was not material. Pursuant to the FLSA, time spent working outside of her scheduled shift was "work hours" even if the employer did not ask her to work during that time, as long as the employer "knows or has reason to believe that the employee is continuing to work" and the work was "suffered or permitted" by the employer. The court found that New Rochelle knew or had reason to believe that plaintiff was performing this prepatory work.

In *Rich v. Delta Airlines, Inc.*, 921 F. Supp. 767, 774 (N.D. Ga. 1996), the district court held that time spent by an employee in assisting with deplaning activities after her last flight of the day and in "debriefing" sessions with flight crews constituted "hours worked" under the FLSA because it was predominately for the benefit of her employer, and therefore counted toward the 1,250–hour eligibility requirement.

g. Layover Time

In *Rich v. Delta Airlines, Inc.*, 921 F. Supp. 767, 767 (N.D. Ga. 1996), the district court addressed the issue of whether layover time counted as "hours worked" for purposes of FMLA eligibility. In that case the plaintiff, a flight attendant, was terminated for attendance problems. She brought suit alleging that the absences that formed the basis of her dismissal were protected by the FMLA. In support of its motion for summary judgment, Delta Airlines argued that plaintiff was not an eligible employee because she had not worked the requisite 1,250 hours in the 12 months preceding the commencement of her leave. Time records produced by Delta Airlines indicated that plaintiff worked no more than 1,000 hours during the previous 12 months. Plaintiff, however, claimed that the records did not reflect the time she spent on layovers between flights and, if counted, the additional time would put her over the requisite 1,250–hour requirement. It was undisputed that, with layover time included, plaintiff would satisfy the 1,250–hour eligibility requirement.

To resolve the issue of whether layover time counted as "hours worked," the court looked to case law developed under the Fair Labor Standards Act. *Id.* at 772. Specifically, the court relied on a test enunciated by the U.S. Supreme Court for the computation of "hours worked." The court in *Rich* explained the test as follows:

> The [Supreme] Court has stated that the test for determining if an employee's time constitutes working time is whether the "time spent is predominantly for the employer's benefit or for the employee's." *Skidmore v. Swift & Co.*, 323 U.S. 134, 137, 65 S. Ct. 161, 89 L. Ed. 124 (1944); *Armour & Co. v. Wantock*, 323 U.S. 126, 133, 65 S. Ct. 165, 168, 89 L. Ed. 118 (1944). That test requires consideration of the agreement of the parties, the nature and extent of the restrictions, the relationship between services rendered and on–call time, and all surrounding circumstances. *Skidmore*, 323 U.S. at 137, 65 S. Ct. at 163. In other words, hours spent by an employee engaged in her principal work activities are considered to be hours worked under the FLSA. *Anderson v. Mt. Clemens Potter Co.*, 328 U.S. 680, 690, 66 S. Ct. 1187, 1194, 90 L. Ed. 1515 (1946). By contract, "[p]eriods during which an employee is completely relieved from duty and which are long enough to enable [her] to use the time effectively for [her] own purposes are not hours worked." 29 CFR 785.16. Whether a certain set of facts and circumstances constitutes work for purposes of the FLSA is a question of law. (citing *Birdwell v. City of Gadsden*, 970 F. 2d 802, 807 (11th Cir. 1992).

The court noted further that, in the Eleventh Circuit, it is "rare that an employee's off–duty time will constitute hours worked; as a result, an employee's free time must be severely restricted for off–time to be construed as work–time for purposes of the FMLA." *Id.* at 776 (citations omitted).

In *Rich v. Delta Airlines, Inc.*, 921 F. Supp. 767, 776–77 (N.D. Ga. 1996), the court held that the layover time did not count toward "hours worked" for purposes of the FLSA and FMLA eligibility. The court found that plaintiff was generally free to use the time on layover for her own purposes. The few restrictions imposed by Delta Airlines—not consuming alcohol or drugs for certain periods and having to call in to notify the airlines if she would be away from the hotel for more than six hours—were insufficient to convert layover time to "work hours."

h. Attending Training

In certain circumstances, time spent by an employee attending continuing education courses may be "hours worked" in accordance with the FLSA, and counted for purposes of meeting the 1,250-hour FMLA eligibility test. This issue was addressed by the Second Circuit in *Kosakow v. New Rochelle Radiology Associates, P.C.*, 274 F.3d 706, 720-22 (2d Cir. 2001), the facts of which are addressed at more length above. In that case, it was undisputed that plaintiff worked 1,186 hours in the 12 months preceding the commencement of her leave. To reach the minimum 1,250 hours, she argued that the time she spent attending continuing education courses in order to retain professional certification should count toward her eligibility. For guidance, the court looked to regulations promulgated under the FLSA.

Pursuant to those regulations, 29 CFR 785.27, the time an employee spends at lectures, meetings, training programs and similar activities need not be counted toward that employee's hours worked where

(1) Attendance is outside of the employee's regular working hours;

(2) Attendance is in fact voluntary;

(3) The course, lecture, or meeting is not directly related to the employee's job; and

(4) The employee does not perform any productive work during such attendance.

The court focused on New Rochelle's contention that the courses were voluntary and not related to plaintiff's job. With respect to the former, because New Rochelle required that plaintiff maintain professional certification, enrolled her in these courses, paid for the courses, and paid for some of her time at the courses, the court found that plaintiff's attendance at these courses was not voluntary. Finding that the courses were related to her job, the court held that the time plaintiff spent attending these continuing education courses should have counted toward meeting the 1,250-hour eligibility requirement.

In *Rich v. Delta Airlines, Inc.*, 921 F. Supp. 767, 773-77 (N.D. Ga. 1996) the district court held that, because it was predominately for the benefit of her employer, time spent by an employee in jet recurrent training constituted "hours worked" under the FLSA, and counted toward the 1,250-hour eligibility requirement.

i. Disciplinary Suspensions and Terminations

The period served by an employee as a result of a disciplinary suspension would not count toward meeting the 1,250-hour eligibility requirement because the employee has not performed work during this period within the meaning of the FLSA. *See Nelson v. City of Cranston et al.*, 116 F. Supp. 2d 260, 266-267 (D.R.I. 2000) (period of 20-day suspension not included in calculation of "hours worked" to meet 1250-hour eligibility requirement); *Thoele v. USPS*, 996 F. Supp. 818, 821-22 (N.D. Ill. 1998) (period of suspension not included in the calculation of 1,250 hours where employee failed to allege that his union breached the duty of fair representation in deciding not to arbitrate an issue, leaving the court without jurisdiction to review the propriety of the suspension).

The more difficult question involves the calculation of time toward meeting the 1,250-hour eligibility requirement for employees whose suspensions or terminations have been reversed. There is a split of authority on whether the rescission of the underlying action and award of back pay and benefits includes the projection of time that would have been worked "but for" the impermissible employer disciplinary action.

The First and Sixth Circuits, the only two circuits to address the issue, are split on whether the time an employee would have worked, but for his/her unlawful termination, should count toward the 1,250 hours of service eligibility requirement.

In *Plumley v. Southern Container, Inc.*, 303 F.3d 364 (1st Cir. 2002), the First Circuit held that the time an employee would have worked, but for an unlawful termination, did not count for purposes of the 1,250 hours of service requirement. Plumley performed only 851.25 hours of actual physical work for SCI in the 12-month period prior to the date of his discharge. The union he belonged to grieved Plumley's removal. An arbitrator vacated the removal in favor of a two-week suspension without pay and ordered that SCI compensate Plumley in full for the wages and benefits that he lost during the period while his grievance was being processed (minus the two-week unpaid suspension). Plumley received compensation for 400 hours of back wages. Within days of his return to work, Plumley called in and requested leave to visit his ill father. He did not show up to work. SCI fired Plumley shortly thereafter.

Plumley argued that his termination violated the FMLA, and that he was eligible because he worked for SCI for more than a year and, with the addition of the 400 hours awarded to him by the arbitrator, he met the 1,250 hours of service requirement at the time of his request for leave. SCI argued that Plumely was not eligible because the 400 hours were not hours he actually worked and, therefore, do not count toward the 1,250 hours of service requirement. The First Circuit agreed with SCI reasoning that, absent specific statutory definitions, the terms "employ" and "employment" for purposes of § 7 of the FLSA and, therefore, the FMLA, must be afforded their widely accepted legal definitions. Citing *Black's Law Dictionary* and Supreme Court precedent, the court found that the term "employment" means "work for which one had been hired and is being paid by an employer." "Work" is defined in its verb form as "to exert effort; to perform either physically or mentally." According to the court, *Plumley,* 303 F.3d at 370:

> Merging these definitions into one coherent sentence, we find that the statutory language, in a very technical sense, indicates that only those hours that an employer suffers or permits an employee to do work (that is, to exert effort, either physically or mentally) for which that employee has been hired and is being paid by the employer can be included as hours of service within the meaning of the FMLA.

After listing the identified exceptions for which no compensation is required (particularly periods when no work is performed due to the failure of an employer to provide sufficient work), the court went on to find that its interpretation was consistent with the exclusions from remuneration in § 7(e) of the FLSA.

A very different result was reached by the Sixth Circuit in *Ricco v. Potter*, 377 F.3d 599 (6th Cir. 2004). The Postal Service terminated Ricco in December 1997. By arbitration award of February 8, 1999, Ricco's termination was converted to a 30-workday suspension and Ricco was reinstated and made whole. After returning to work, Ricco requested FMLA leave in May 1999, due to depression and migraines after the death of her husband. The Postal Service denied her request for FMLA leave after concluding that Ricco did not meet the hours of service requirement. Ricco was subsequently terminated for attendance. She sued, alleging that her termination violated the FMLA. She argued that, but for her unlawful termination, she would have worked the requisite 1,250 hours in the 12 months before her FMLA leave.

The district court, relying on the decision of the First Circuit in *Plumley*, granted the Postal Service's motion to dismiss the FMLA complaint finding that Ricco did not meet the 1,250 hours of service requirement, because she did not actually work those hours. On appeal, the Sixth Circuit agreed with Ricco and reversed the decision of the district court.

The Sixth Circuit, unlike the First Circuit in *Plumley*, distinguished the situation faced by Ricco from the exceptions to compensation enumerated in § 7(e) of the FLSA. According to the court, *Ricco,* 377 F.3d at 605,:

> We conclude that time that an employee would have worked but for her unlawful termination is not an "other similar cause" within the meaning of § 207. Such hours are different from occasional hours of absence due to vacation, holiday, illness, and the employer's failure to provide work, etc., in that they are hours that the employee wanted to work but was unlawfully prevented by the employer from working. Section 207 does not clearly prevent such hours from counting, and the purpose of the FMLA's hours-of-service requirement is properly served by including these hours.

The court also justified its decision on equity. The court, *Ricco,* 377 F.3d at 605, noted that "[i]n such cases, the employer's unlawful conduct has prevented the employee from satisfying the hours of service requirement. Moreover, denying employees credit toward the hours of service requirement for hours that they would have worked, but for their unlawful termination, rewards employers for their unlawful conduct. We conclude that neither does the FMLA."

In *Pirant v. USPS*, No. 03 C 9383, 2006 U.S. Dist. LEXIS 89319, at *7 (N.D. Ill. Dec. 7, 2006), the employee argued that the Postal Service should have counted 2 hours towards the 1250-hour requirement when she was wrongfully suspended by her supervisor and directed to clock out early. The court disagreed, noting that there was no evidence that Pirant's suspension was wrongful. "Pirant's argument is based entirely on her own belief, which however honestly held is insufficient to warrant crediting her with the two hours she would have likely worked had she not been suspended."

In *Moore v. USPS*, 83 MSPR 533 (1999), the Board held that the award of full back pay and benefits by the MSPB included crediting an employee with the time he would have worked during the back pay period for purposes of determining the 1250-hour eligibility requirement. In *Moore*, the MSPB ordered the Postal Service to cancel the appellant's removal and reinstate him with back pay, interest, and other benefits under the Back Pay Act. The Postal Service complied with the Board's order. A week after his return to work, plaintiff requested FMLA leave as a result of an on-the-job back injury.

The Postal Service declined plaintiff's request for FMLA leave because Moore failed to meet the 1,250-hour eligibility requirement. Prior to reinstatement, Moore had not worked for the Postal Service for several years. The Postal Service subsequently removed Moore for additional absences after his restoration to work. Moore appealed his removal to the Board. He also moved to enforce the prior Board order reinstating him, alleging that the Postal Service violated that Order when it determined that he was not eligible for FMLA leave.

In finding that the Postal Service was not in compliance with its reinstatement Order, the Board focused on the provisions of the Back Pay Act. In relevant part, the Back Pay Act provides that a preference eligible veteran who is found to have been adversely affected by an unjustified or unwarranted personnel action resulting in loss of pay "for all purposes, is deemed to have performed service for the agency during that [back pay] period...." 5 USC 5596(b)(1); 5 CFR 550.805(a)(1). To be treated "for all purposes," as if he performed services for the Postal Service during the back pay period, the board held that Moore should have been credited with all work hours he would have worked but for his improper removal by the Postal Service. Because it failed to credit Moore with those hours (which exceeded the 1,250-hour eligibility requirement), the Postal Service was not in compliance with the prior Board Order reinstating Moore.

In rendering its decision, the Board rejected Postal Service arguments that FMLA eligibility was governed by FLSA standards, not by the Back Pay Act; the Back Pay Act applied to traditional employment benefits, not statutory mandates like the FMLA, and the calculation of time that Moore would have worked was speculative. Essentially, the Board answered all of these issues by concluding that the phrase in the Back Pay Act "for all purposes" encompassed the eligibility requirements of the FMLA.

Because Moore was eligible for FMLA leave for the absence underlying his removal, the Board reversed his removal and ordered his reinstatement.

The Board's determination effectively substitutes the Back Pay Act for the FLSA in calculating the 1,250-hour eligibility requirement. Since the Act specifically provides that FLSA principles govern eligibility, 29 USC 2611(2)(c), the decision of the Board is suspect. On the other hand, there is precedent (military time under the USERRA) for another federal statute trumping the FMLA and requiring time that was not actually worked for the employing agency to be counted towards meeting the 1250-hour requirement.

j. Other Employer Acts of Interference with "Hours Worked"

In addition to overturned suspensions and terminations, employees have sought to excuse their failure to meet the 1,250-hour eligibility requirement because of other employer acts that allegedly improperly interfered with their ability to work the requisite 1,250 hours. In *Brown v. Daimler-Chrysler Corp.* No. 3:99-CV-1286-D, 1999 U.S. Dist. LEXIS 15189 (N.D. Tex. Sept. 24, 1999), the plaintiff alleged that she would have worked the requisite 1,250 hours but for Chrysler's improper failure to allow her to perform light duty work. In rejecting the plaintiff's argument and finding that she was not eligible for FMLA leave, the district court stated, "Congress imposed clear statutory prerequisites for bringing an FMLA claim. It did not provide a waiver of the minimum eligibility requirements when an employer has taken some action that allegedly precludes the employee from becoming statutorily eligible for protection under the Act. Courts have resisted attempts to expand the class of employees eligible for relief under the FMLA."

k. Layoffs and Furloughs

Time spent on a layoff does not count toward the 1,250-hour eligibility requirement because, by definition, a layoff involves a suspension of work time. Preamble, 29 CFR 825.110 ("hours worked" does not include unpaid leave (of any kind) or periods of layoff).

A furlough is the placing of an employee in a temporary, nonduty, nonpay status because of lack of work or funds, or other nondisciplinary reasons. *McCloud v. USPS*, 71 MSPR 508, 511 (1996) (furlough is the placement of an employee into a nonduty, nonpay status for nondisciplinary reasons); *Carita v. USPS*, 67 MSPR 277, 279 (1995) (emphasizing nonpay status of furloughed individual). In many respects, it is the functional equivalent of a private sector layoff. The increased use of furloughs in recent years is largely attributable to budget and spending disagreements between the executive and legislative branches that have culminated in the "closing down" of the government and furloughing of federal employees.

There are two types of furloughs: (1) "adverse action" furloughs governed by 5 CFR 752; and (2) "reduction in force" (RIF) furloughs governed by 5 CFR 351.

Adverse action or "short" furloughs involve work suspensions of less than 30 calendar days (22 work days). RIF furloughs involve suspensions from work of more than 30 calendar days, but less than one year. This type of furlough is governed by reduction-in-force regulations.

For purposes of FMLA eligibility, because the employee is not actually performing work, the period of the furlough does not count toward meeting the 1,250-hour eligibility requirement. Employees who have been identified as "essential" to continued government operations pursuant to the Antideficiency Act, 31 USC 1341, *et. seq.*, and who continue to perform work during the period of a furlough, however, would accumulate time toward the 1,250-hour eligibility requirement.

Note that for purposes of meeting the 12-month eligibility requirement, furloughed employees, because they would still be listed on the payroll of the federal government, would continue to accumulate time toward meeting the 12-month eligibility requirement during the furlough period. Furloughed employees would not, however, accumulate time toward meeting the 1,250-hour eligibility requirement during the same furlough period because they would not be working during this period. [For a discussion of the impact of a layoff on a federal employer's obligations to continue an employee on FMLA leave, maintain group health benefits or restore the employee, see Chapter 10, "Leave Amount and Scheduling," Chapter 12, "Maintenance of Benefits," and Chapter 13, "Return to Work from Leave." *See also* 29 CFR 825.216(a).]

l.   Lower Eligibility Requirement Per Employer Policy

The district court in *Rich v. Delta Airlines, Inc.*, 921 F. Supp. 767, 773–74 (N.D. Ga. 1996), addressed whether the 1,250-hour eligibility requirement could be lowered by an employer policy or practice. Delta Airlines had a policy of providing leave benefits to those who work at least 540 hours. Plaintiff alleged that the 540-hour standard, as opposed to the 1,250-hour standard, should be utilized to determine plaintiff's eligibility for FMLA benefits and protections. As support, the plaintiff relied on 29 CFR 825.700, which addresses the interaction of an employer's internal policies and practices with an employee's rights under the FMLA. In relevant part, that section provides that "[a]n employer must observe any employment benefit program or plan that provides greater family or medical leave rights to employees than the rights established under the FMLA." 29 CFR 825.700(a). Rejecting this argument, the court held that 29 CFR 825.700 cannot be used to amend the explicit coverage provision adopted by Congress requiring 1,250 hours of work for eligibility by substitution of more generous eligibility requirements for the application of internal company policies. *Rich*, 921 F. Supp. at 773. The court went on to hold that 29 CFR 825.700 also does not create a separate cause of action to enforce more generous internal company FMLA policies. *Id*. at 773–74.

m.   Joint Employment

Included in the 1,250-hour eligibility calculation would be any time the individual spent as a joint employee of the federal government and a non-federal entity, such as a temporary help or leasing agency. 29 CFR 825.106(d); *Miller v. Defiance Metal Products, Inc.*, 989 F. Supp. 945, 946–48 (N.D. Ohio 1997) (individual employee who worked as an employee of a temporary agency at defendant's facility for eight months and was then hired by defendant and worked for another eight months was an eligible employee under Tile I of FMLA); DOL WH Advisory Opinion No. 37 (July 7, 1994) (time that employee was employed by temporary help agency would be counted toward 12-month and 1,250-hour eligibility tests). Federal employment prior to the effective date of Title I must be counted towards the 12-month eligibility requirement. 29 CFR 825.110(e). Title I of the Act became effective on August 5, 1993, for most federal employers. If a collective bargaining agreement was in effect on that date, the Act became effective on the earlier of February 5, 1994, or the date the agreement expired. 29 CFR 825.102(a). [Joint employment is discussed more fully in Chapter 3, "FMLA Coverage of the Federal Government."]

For purposes of Title I, joint employment is not limited to private sector temporary employees working for the federal government. Joint employment would also include arrangements involving federal employees who are not generally covered by Title I, but who are working on a detail or other temporary assignment with a Title I covered federal employer. However, in terms of Title I eligibility, the concept of joint employment is less important where the only employees involved in the "joint" enterprise are employees of the federal government. The reason is that, for purposes of eligibility, Title I considers the federal government to be a single employer. 29 CFR 825.109(e). This means that all hours worked by employees of the federal government count toward Title I eligibility, whether the employee is currently covered by

Title I or not. Given that the U.S. Government is considered a single employer for purposes of Title I eligibility, a joint employment relationship is simply not needed for the hours and months to count toward the 12-month and 1,250-hour eligibility requirements of a Title I federal employee.

n. Successor-In-Interest

When a federal employer is a "successor-in-interest," employees' FMLA entitlements are the same as if the employment by the predecessor and the successor were continuous employment by a single employer. 29 CFR 825.107(c). For Title I eligibility purposes, all federal agency successors must count the period of employment and hours worked for the predecessor for purposes of determining employee eligibility for FMLA leave. *Id.* [For a further discussion of the successor-in-interest doctrine, see Chapter 3, "FMLA Coverage of the Federal Government."]

As with joint employment, the impact of the successor-in-interest doctrine on Title I eligibility is muted where one federal entity succeeds or takes over another federal entity. Title I defines the U.S. Government as a single employer for purposes of determining Title I federal employee eligibility. 29 CFR 825.109(e). As such, the successor federal entity must count toward Title I eligibility the years of service and work hours retained federal employees spent with the predecessor federal entity as a matter of the Title I "covered employee" definition. The successor-in-interest doctrine is simply not necessary where the successor and the predecessor are already federal sector employers.

As set forth more fully above in this chapter regarding the 12-month eligibility requirement, the successor-in-interest doctrine has more viability where a federal entity takes over responsibility for a private sector predecessor. *See, e.g., Rhoads v. FDIC*, 956 F. Supp. 1239 (D. Md. 1997), *aff'd in part, vacated and remanded in part on other grounds*, 257 F.3d 373 (4th Cir. 2001), *cert. denied*, 535 U.S. 933 (2002).

o. Stationed Outside the United States

Federal employees employed outside the United States and its territories and possessions are not eligible for FMLA leave, nor are they counted for purposes of determining whether the 50-employee threshold has been met. 29 CFR 825.105(b); DOL WH Opinion No. 9 (Oct. 18, 1993) (employees stationed in a foreign country on one- and two-year contracts are not eligible for the benefits and protections of the FMLA while stationed overseas).

p. Teachers

Title I applies special rules for teachers of local educational agencies, as defined in the Elementary and Secondary Education Act of 1965, 20 USC 2891(12). *See* 29 USC 2618, 29 CFR 825.600. Basically, the special rules apply to instructional employees of public school boards and elementary and secondary schools under their jurisdiction, and private elementary and secondary schools. 29 CFR 825.600(a). The special rules, however, do not apply to other kinds of educational institutions, such as colleges and universities, trade schools, and preschools. *Id.* As such, educational institutions and employees not covered by the federal rules would be subject to the standard Title I FMLA rules and regulations.

With respect to eligibility, full-time teachers of an elementary or secondary school system, or an institution of higher education, are deemed eligible to meet the 1,250-hour test. 29 CFR 825.110(c). An employer must be able to clearly demonstrate that such an employee did not work 1,250 hours during the previous 12 months in order to claim that the employee is not "eligible" for FMLA leave. *Id.*

"Teacher" is defined to include an employee employed in an instructional capacity, or instructional employee. 29 CFR 825.800 (definition of "teacher"). "Teacher" means an employee employed principally in an instructional capacity by an educational agency or school whose principal function is to teach and instruct students in a class, small group, or an individual setting, and includes athletic coaches, driving instructors, and special educational assistants such as signers for the hearing impaired. *Id.* The term does not include teacher assistants or aides who do not have as their principal function actual teaching or instructing, nor does it include auxiliary personnel such as counselors and psychologists. *Id.*

The above regulations are not limited to the special rules for local educational agencies. Rather, all teachers of all educational institutions covered by Title I are "deemed" to meet the 1,250-hour eligibility requirement of Title I, unless an employer proves otherwise. As discussed more fully in Chapter 4, "Federal Employees Covered by the FMLA," individuals holding teaching positions with the Department of Defense are covered by Title II of the Act. *See* 5 USC 6381(1)(A). Federal employees in teaching positions who are not otherwise covered by Title II are likely covered by Title I. In that capacity, the "deemed eligible" provision of 29 CFR 825.110(c) would apply with respect to the 1,250-hour requirement.

As discussed more fully later in this chapter, the Supreme Court recently struck down a similar Title I regulation, 29 CFR 825.110(d), that "deemed" employees eligible for FMLA leave as a penalty for an employer's failure to timely notify an employee of FMLA leave eligibility. *See Ragsdale v. Wolverine World-Wide Inc.*, 535 U.S. 81, 152 L. Ed. 2d 167, 122 S. Ct. 1155 (2002). Because the "deemed eligible" regulation for teachers is not triggered as a penalty for an employer's failure to notify an employee of eligibility but merely shifts the burden of establishing non-eligibility to the employer, the Supreme Court decision may not undermine the validity of 29 CFR 825.110(c).

q. Proof Employee Worked 1,250 Hours

In determining whether an employee has met the 1,250-hour eligibility requirement, courts have relied on a variety of evidence offered in support of, or opposition to, a finding of eligibility. Uncontradicted employer affidavits have supported a court's decision that the employee did not meet the 1,250-hour eligibility requirement. *See Hinson v. Tecumseh Products Co.*, 234 F.3d 1268 (6th Cir. 2000); *Adams v. Honda America Mfg., Inc.*, No. C-2-01-0822, 2002 U.S. Dist. LEXIS 18787 (S.D. Ohio Sept. 19, 2002), *aff'd*, 2004 U.S. App. LEXIS 10110 (6th Cir. 2004); *Pinegar v. Baptist Memorial Hospital-Desoto County*, No. 2:96CV63-B-A, 1997 U.S. Dist. LEXIS 13510 (N.D. Miss. Aug. 19, 1997); *see also Nave v. Wooldridge Construction of Pennsylvania, Inc.* No. 96-2891, 1997 U.S. Dist. LEXIS 9203 (E.D. Pa. June 30, 1997) (court relied on statement in a memorandum of law in support of defendant's motion for summary judgment that employee worked only 681 hours to find employee was not eligible). Courts have also relied on uncontroverted payroll records in finding that an employee did not work the requisite 1,250 hours. *See Aldrich v. Bobby Greg et al.*, 200 F. Supp. 2d 784, 787-88 (N.D. Ohio 2002).

Employer affidavits containing mistakes regarding the amount of time an employee worked will not support a motion for summary judgment. *Sutherland v. Goodyear Tire & Rubber Co.*, 446 F. Supp. 2d 1203 (D. Kan. 2006).

Affidavits combined with employer records and court assumptions on the amount of time worked have also been used to defeat an employee claim that he or she met the 1,250-hour eligibility requirement. *See Ferrero v. Henderson*, 341 F. Supp. 2d 873, 904 (S.D. Ohio 2004) (court relied on a list demonstrating the number of hours Ferrero actually worked each pay period during the 12-month period before the date Ferrero claimed that she needed FMLA leave, as well as, testimony from a Postal Service official describing how the list was put together from data retrieved from payroll journals; data established that Ferrero worked 1,225.29 hours during the preceding 12-month period); *Rich v. Delta Air Line, Inc.*, 921 F. Supp. 767, 772-75 (N.D. Ga. 1996) (employer defeated presumption that FLSA-exempt employee met the requisite 1,250-hour eligibility requirement through a combination of employer records of the hours the employee worked, an affidavit of the time the employee spent performing deboarding activities where there were no records, and the application of the assumption of average time spent performing deboarding activities to number of flights worked, to calculate a time figure for these activities that would apply toward "hours worked"). Similarly, the court awarded summary judgment to an employer based on uncontradicted evidence in the form of attendance sheets and court assumptions showing that an employee did not work the requisite 1,250 hours. *Walters v. A & P Supermarket Service et al.*, No. 3: 98-CV-1222, 2001 U.S. Dist. LEXIS 2696 (M.D. Pa. 2001) (even if plaintiff worked 15 hours a day for the days in question, he still would not have even worked 1,000 hours, which is below the 1,250 hours required).

An employee's continuous full-time employment over a period of years may give rise to an inference that the employee has worked the requisite 1250 hours. *See Kaniuka v. Good Shepherd Home*, No. 05-CV-02917, 2005 U.S. Dist. LEXIS 26963, at *14 (E.D. Pa. Nov. 3, 2005) (court inferred that the employee met the 1250-hour requirement based on her continuous employment for 3 years).

An employee's mere allegation that she met the 1,250-hour requirement was insufficient to establish eligibility in *Hinson v. Tecumseh Products Co.*, 234 F.3d 1268 (6th Cir. 2000) (employee statement along with unsworn spreadsheet detailing hours worked, that, with the addition of an unspecified amount of overtime, employee met 1,250-hour requirement held insufficient to establish eligibility).

In *Woodford v. Community Action of Greene County, Inc. et al.*, 268 F.3d 51 (2d Cir. 2001), the circuit court rejected the plaintiff's personal log and diary showing that she worked the requisite 1,250 hours in favor of the time sheets offered by the employer that the plaintiff filled out and signed. The plaintiff contended that the official time sheets did not accurately reflect the hours she worked because her weekly salary was paid regardless of the number of hours she worked. Noting that the plaintiff recorded varying times on her official time sheets, the court opined that it "strains credulity to claim that, on the one hand, Woodford could not be bothered with accurately reporting her hours to her employer, yet on the other hand, each night she assiduously made accurate records for her own personal reference."

On the other hand, in Hastings v. Carlson Marketing Group, Inc., No. 04-3370 (DWF/JSM), 2005 U.S. Dist. LEXIS 25808, at *12 (D. Minn. Oct. 27, 2006), the court found there was a genuine issue of material fact as to whether the employee met the 1250-hour eligibility requirement based solely on the employee's statement that there were "many times" he worked more than 12 hours a day during the 12-month period preceding his request for leave. The court noted that it was possible he could reach the 1250-hour threshold depending on how "many" times he worked a more than 12 hour day.

2. Preceding 12 Months

A Title I federal employee must work the requisite 1,250 hours within the 12–month period immediately preceding the start of his or her requested FMLA leave. *See* 29 USC 2611(2)(A)(ii); 29 CFR 825.110(a)(2). Courts, on several occasions, have rejected employee and employer arguments for a different 12–month period to conduct the 1,250–hour eligibility calculation. *See Butler v. Owens–Brockway Plastic Products, Inc.,* 199 F.3d 314, 315–16 (6th Cir. Dec. 9, 1999) (court held that 1,250 hours of service must be performed in 12-month period prior to leave commencement, not 12-month period prior to the alleged adverse action in violation of the FMLA); *Duckworth v. Pratt & Whitney,* 152 F.3d 1, 8, (1st Cir. 1998) (same); *see also Corcino v. Banco Popular de Puerto Rico,* 200 F. Supp. 2d 507 (D.V.I. 2002) (rejecting the employee argument that the employer had to calculate FMLA eligibility over the same time period that it used to cite her numerous absences, the court held that the clear language of the statute requires that an employee worked at least 1,250 hours during the 12–month period immediately preceding leave commencement).

Depending on when the leave is scheduled to begin, the 12–month period for the calculation of the 1,250 hours may extend beyond the date when the employee made his or her request for FMLA leave. The inclusion of time in the 12–month period prior to leave commencement that the employee has not yet worked adds eligibility notice responsibilities that federal employers need to take into account.

3. Leave Commencement

Whether a covered employee has worked the requisite 1,250 hours in the 12–month period is determined as of the commencement of FMLA leave. 29 USC 2611(2)(A)(ii); 29 CFR 825.110(a)(2); *Moticka v. Weck Closure Systems,* 183 Fed. Appx. 343 (4th Cir. 2006). Neither the Act nor the DOL implementing regulations define what constitutes "leave" and when such leave "commences."

In the simple case where an employee requests a finite period of FMLA leave on a single occasion, the "leave" is the period the employee is absent, and the leave "commences" on the first day of the employee's absence. A federal employer would calculate whether the employee meets the Title I FMLA eligibility requirements on the occasion of the first day the employee is absent.

In addition to being taken in a single block of time, FMLA leave may be taken intermittently or on a reduced leave schedule. *See* 29 USC 2612(b); 29 CFR 825.203. Because FMLA leave may be taken intermittently or on a reduced leave schedule for the same covered condition, knowing whether "leave" is synonymous with "absence" or a "series of related absences" is critical for a federal employer to determine when leave has or will "commence" in order to accurately calculate and timely notify an employee as to whether she is eligible to take the FMLA leave she has requested. To rephrase this as a question, for eligibility purposes, does every intermittent absence covered by FMLA leave constitute the "commencement" of leave, even if all the absences are based on the same underlying covered condition? Or does a series of related intermittent FMLA absences constitute the "commencement" of only one period of "leave" requiring only one eligibility calculation? [For a discussion on intermittent leave, see Chapter 10, "Leave Amount and Scheduling."]

The district court in *Barron v. Runyon,* 11 F. Supp. 2d 676, 679–83 (E.D. Va. 1998), answered the above question. In that case, Willie Barron was terminated by the Postal Service for multiple unexcused absences. He claimed that all of his absences related to the care of his wife, who suffered from a back injury, and should have been covered as intermittent leave protected by the FMLA. The Postal Service countered that Barron did not meet the 1,250–hour eligibility requirement except for his first absence. The Postal Service calculated eligibility for each and every FMLA absence, including intermittent absences for the same underlying covered condition. Plaintiff maintained that eligibility for intermittent absences arising out of the same underlying covered condition should be calculated for the first absence only.

The court agreed with Barron, holding that an employee's eligibility for intermittent FMLA leave for the same underlying covered condition is determined only once—on the occasion of the first absence in each leave year—and not on the occasion of each subsequent absence. The court based its decision on its interpretations of the FMLA Statute and DOL implementing regulations. It found, essentially, that both the Act and the DOL regulations recognized that FMLA leave could be taken in two forms: intermittently (several absences based on the same underlying covered condition) or continuously (a single, uninterrupted absence). According to the court, if eligibility were required for each FMLA absence, there would be no such thing as intermittent leave; each absence would constitute a separate period of continuous absence.

Based on its legal determination, the court found that Barron was eligible for 12 of the 14 cited instances of absences without leave (AWOL). The court denied the Postal Service motion for summary judgment, finding questions of material fact as to whether the Postal Service would have terminated Barron for the two absences that were not FMLA protected because he was not eligible for those periods of FMLA leave. Ultimately, Barron's removal was upheld. *See Barron v. Runyon*, No. 99–1027, 2000 U.S. App. LEXIS 2887 (4th Cir. Feb. 28, 2000).

The DOL subsequently agreed with the analysis in *Barron*. *See* DOL WH Advisory Opinion No. 112 (September 11, 2000). In that Opinion Letter, the DOL provided the following helpful examples to explain eligibility in the context of intermittent leave:

1. Assume an employee is diagnosed with an FMLA-qualifying chronic condition, such as MS, as in your example that results in an employee needing intermittent leave due to the episodic nature of the condition. For example, if an employee with MS who was eligible to take intermittent FMLA leave in April and May needed leave again when the episodes of incapacity recurred in July and again in October, the employee would be entitled to FMLA leave without having to re-qualify under the 1,250-hour eligibility test so long as the absences occurred within the same 12-month period and the employee had not exhausted the 12-week leave entitlement for this or any other FMLA-qualifying reason. If the employee needed leave for MS again in a new 12-month period, the employee would have to re-qualify under the 1,250-hour eligibility test to be entitled to take FMLA leave for the same chronic condition in the new 12-month period.

2. Assume the same facts as in the first example, and, in addition, assume that the employee requests FMLA leave for up to six weeks for another serious health condition that requires major surgery and a subsequent period of recovery (e.g., a hysterectomy). If, at the time of this second and different FMLA-qualifying circumstances, the employee met the 1,250-hour eligibility test, the employee would be entitled to FMLA leave for *that* (i.e., second) reason. In addition, the employee would also continue to be eligible for intermittent FMLA leave for the chronic serious health condition (i.e., MS) for the remainder of the current 12-month period or until the 12-week leave entitlement has been exhausted.

3. Assume the same facts as in the second example, except that, at the time of the second and different FMLA-qualifying circumstances, the employee does *not* meet the 1,250-hour eligibility test. In this situation, the employee would not be entitled to FMLA leave for *that* (i.e., second) reason. Thus, it is possible that an employee could remain eligible for leave once for one FMLA-qualifying reason for which prior notice had been given when the employee met the 1,250-hour test (i.e., MS), but not be eligible for FMLA leave for a different FMLA-qualifying reason (i.e., surgery and recovery), and sue to the 1,250-hour test being re-calculated at the *commencement* of the subsequent and separate need for leave.

Although not binding, as an expression of the executive agency charged with enforcing the FMLA, DOL Opinion Letter 112 is entitled to deference by courts. *Sills v. Bendix Commercial Vehicle Systems, LLC*, N. 1:04-CV-149, 2005 U.S. Dist. LEXIS 25425, at n. 14 (N.D. Ind. Oct. 20, 2005).

The net effect of the *Barron* decision and DOL Opinion Letter 112 is that eligibility is determined for each covered condition that forms the basis of a request for FMLA leave. If that request is for intermittent or reduced schedule leave, eligibility is determined as of the first absence in the series for the remainder of the 12-month period selected by the employer. Eligibility is not calculated for any subsequent absences related to the first absence. If a wholly different FMLA-covered condition gives rise to the need for FMLA leave, however, eligibility for FMLA leave for that condition is calculated anew. Courts have followed *Barron* and DOL Opinion Letter 112. *See Roberts v. Ground Holding, Inc.*, No. 04 Civ. 4955 (WCC), 2007 U.S. Dist. LEXIS 23441, at *26 (S.D.N.Y. March 30, 2007); *Sills v. Bendix Commercial Vehicle Systems, LLC*, No. 1:04-CV-149, 2005 U.S. Dist. LEXIS 25425, at *26 (N.D. Ind. Oct. 20, 2005).

In another decision, a court held that the 1,250-hour requirement applied each time leave began. In holding that the employee was not eligible within the meaning of the FMLA because he did not meet the 1,250-hour test, the district court in *Adams v. Honda America Mfg., Inc.,* No. C-2-01-0822, 2002 U.S. Dist. LEXIS 18787 (S.D. Ohio Sept. 19, 2002), *aff'd,* 2004 U.S. App. LEXIS 10110 (6th Cir. 2004), rejected the plaintiff's argument that because she met the 1,250-hour test for a leave request in December 2000, she would also be eligible for FMLA leave in April 2001, as her subsequent request was related to the same condition as her earlier request. The court disagreed, holding that the "plain language of the statute and relevant implementing regulation tie the 1,250-hour requirement to the time leave begins," which was in April. The case does not refer to *Barron* or to the DOL WH Advisory Opinion referenced above.

It is also possible that the April 2001 leave occurred in a different leave year than the prior leave request in December, which, under *Barron,* would explain why meeting eligibility in December would not excuse not meeting eligibility in a subsequent leave year. The court, however, does not offer this explanation as justification for its decision.

B.   TITLE II: DETERMINING 1,250 HOURS

Title II does not have a minimum work hours requirement in order for a covered federal employee to be eligible for FMLA leave. The only "eligibility" requirement it has requires 12 months of employment as a Title II covered federal employee. 5 USC 6381(1)(B); *Niimi-Montalbo v. White,* 243 F. Supp. 2d 1109, 1119 (D. Haw. 2003) (MSPB erred by applying 1,250-hour eligibility requirement of Title I to employee covered by Title II). [For a discussion of the 12-month eligibility requirement of Title II, see Sections II,B, "Title II Eligibility Standards" and III,B, "Title II Calculations" of this chapter.]

C.   CAA: DETERMINING 1,250 HOURS

The 1,250-hours eligibility requirement applies to federal employees covered by the CAA. The term "eligible employee" means a covered employee who has been employed in any employing office for 12 months and for at least 1,250 hours of employment during the previous 12 months. 2 USC 1312(a)(2)(B); S. Res. 242, Cong. Rec. S3959–S3997 (April 23, 1996); 29 CFR 825.110(a).

The three major components of this definition—hours worked, previous 12 months, and leave commencement—are addressed below. Also addressed are record keeping and eligibility notice requirements.

1.   Hours Worked

The 1,250-hour test applied by the CAA is very similar to the test used by Title I. Significantly, the CAA's 1,250-hour test, like that of Title I, is determined according to the principles established for determining compensable hours of work under the FLSA. *See* S. Res. 242, Cong. Rec. S3959–S3997 (April 23, 1996); 29 CFR 825.110(c). As such, the case law interpreting § 7 of the FLSA, 29 USC 207, and the case law interpreting the 1,250-hour test under Title I should apply to the 1,250-hour test under the CAA. [For a discussion of "hours worked" under the FLSA and Title I, see Section IV.A.1, "Hours Worked" of this chapter.]

The determining factor is the number of hours an employee has worked for one or more employing offices. S. Res. 242, Cong. Rec. S3959–S3997 (April 23, 1996), 29 CFR 825.110(c). The determination is not limited by methods of record keeping, or by compensation agreements that do not accurately reflect all the hours an employee has worked for or been in service to the employing office. Any accurate accounting of actual hours worked may be used. *Id.*

Interestingly, unlike the similar regulations interpreting Title I, the CAA regulations do not include language "deeming" an employee to have met the 1,250-hour requirement, and shifting the burden to an employing office to prove otherwise, in the event that employment records do not accurately reflect the actual number of hours an employee has worked. *See* 29 CFR 825.110. Presumably, the absence of such language means that an employee will not be "deemed" eligible in the event of inaccurate CAA "employing office" records. Similarly, the absence of a burden-shifting provision in the event of inaccurate employer records suggests that the employee may well bear the burden of establishing that he or she worked the requisite 1,250 hours in order to establish that he or she is an "eligible employee" within the meaning of the CAA.

a.   What Federal Employment Counts Toward the 1,250-Hour Eligibility

A major difference between the 1,250-hour test as applied under Title I and under the CAA involves the scope of employment that counts toward meeting the test. Under the CAA, only employment as a "covered employee" in an "employing office" counts toward meeting the 1,250–hour test. 2 USC 1312(a)(2)(B); S. Res. 242, Cong. Rec. S3959–S3997 (April 23, 1996), 29 CFR 825.110(a). The terms "covered employee" and "employing office" are limited to very specific positions and congressional offices. 2 USC 1301(3) ("covered employee" defined), (9) ("employing office" defined); S. Res. 242, Cong. Rec. S3959–S3997 (April 23, 1996); 29 CFR 825.104 ("employing office" defined). Title I, on the other hand, counts all federal employment toward the eligibility of Title I covered employees. See 29 CFR 825.109(e). [For a discussion of covered employers and employees, see Chapters 3, "FMLA Coverage of the Federal Government," and 4, "Federal Employees Covered by the FMLA."]

A covered employee of an employing office under the CAA includes applicants and former employees. 2 USC 1301(4). It is not clear whether Title I covers applicants and former employees. [For a further discussion of who is a covered employee under Title I, see Chapter 4, "Federal Employees Covered by the FMLA."]

An intern is not a covered employee for purposes of the CAA. For purposes of the FMLA, the CAA applies FLSA principles, as set forth in § 203 of the CAA, 2 USC 1313. See Res. 242, Cong. Rec. S3959–S3997 (April 23, 1996), 29 CFR 825.110(c). Section 203 of the CAA specifically excludes an intern from the term "covered employee." 2 USC 1313(a)(2). Under Title I, all federal employment counts toward meeting the 1,250–hour eligibility test, including interns.

If an employee was employed by two or more employing offices, either sequentially or concurrently, the hours of service will be aggregated to determine whether the minimum of 1,250 hours has been reached. S. Res. 242, Cong. Rec. S3959–S3997 (April 23, 1996), 29 CFR 825.110(c).

b. Effect of Leave on 1,250–Hour Test

Based on the application of FLSA principles, time spent on leave, whether paid or unpaid, would not count toward the 1,250–hour eligibility requirement. Neither the Act nor the CAA implementing regulations address the effect of leave on the 1,250–hour test. [For a discussion of the effect of leave on the 1,250–hour test under Title I, see Section IV.A., "Title I: Determining 1,250 Hours" of this chapter.]

c. Military Duty

The Office of Compliance, the congressional entity created to enforce the CAA FMLA regulations, has not issued instructions on the effect of military duty on the accumulation of hours worked for purposes of the CAA's 1,250–hour eligibility test. As set forth previously in this section, the DOL issued a memorandum indicating that, for purposes of Title I, employees on military duty who return to federal employment are entitled to accumulate the hours they would have worked but for their military duty towards meeting the 1,250–hour test. The rationale for that position was based on an interpretation of the USERRA, which, by its terms, applies to the federal government, including the legislative branch. See 38 USC 4303(4)(A)(ii), (6). As such, the time spent by a CAA–covered employee on military duty should count toward that employee's 1,250 hours of work.

d. Joint Employment and Successor–in–Interest

Joint employment is recognized in the CAA. See S. Res. 242, Cong. Rec. S3959–S3997 (April 23, 1996), 29 CFR 825.106. The CAA does not incorporate the successor–in–interest doctrine. [For a further discussion of joint employment and the successor–in–interest doctrine, see Chapter 3, "FMLA Coverage of the Federal Government."]

Briefly, where two or more employing offices exercise some control over the work or working conditions of the employee, the employing offices may be joint employers under the FMLA, as made applicable by the CAA. See S. Res. 242, Cong. Rec. S3959–S3997 (April 23, 1996); 29 CFR 825.106(a). Joint employment can take the form of an employee performing work that simultaneously benefits two or more employing offices, or where the covered employee works for two or more employing offices at different times. Id.

For purposes of eligibility, if two or more employing offices have employed an employee, either sequentially or concurrently, the hours of service will be aggregated to determine whether the minimum 1,250 hours has been reached. See S. Res. 242, Cong. Rec. S3959–S3997 (April 23, 1996); 29 CFR 825.110(c).

By limiting joint employment to work for an "employing office," the CAA greatly restricts the scope of joint employment that will count toward meeting the 1,250–hour test. Employment outside the limitation definition of "employing office" would not count towards the 1,250–hour requirement. By comparison, joint employment under Title I would count the time spent by a Title I covered federal employee working in any joint employment relationship throughout the federal government. However, this has less to do with any differences in the concept of joint employment between Titles I and the CAA, and more to do with the fact that Title I counts all time spent in federal employment toward the eligibility of a Title I covered employee's FMLA eligibility. [For a further discussion of Title I employee eligibility and joint employment, see Section IV.A., "Title I, Determining 1,250 Hours" of this chapter.]

Because they are not CAA–covered employees, the time spent by individuals hired through a private sector temporary or leasing agent, who perform work in an employing office, would not count toward those individuals' 1,250–hour requirement, if they were eventually hired as employees within the meaning of the CAA. Again, under those circumstances, Title I would count the time toward the individuals' FMLA eligibility. *See* 29 CFR 825.106(d).

e. Teachers

Interestingly, the CAA has special eligibility rules for full–time teachers. *See* S. Res. 242, Cong. Rec. S3959–S3997 (April 23, 1996); 29 CFR 825.110(c). Like Title I, full–time teachers of an elementary or secondary school system, an institution of higher education, or another educational establishment or institution are deemed to meet the 1,250–hour eligibility test. *Id.* An employing office must be able to clearly demonstrate that such an employee did not work 1,250 hours during the previous 12 months in order to claim that the employee is not "eligible" for FMLA leave. *Id.*

The term "teacher" (or employee employed in an instructional capacity, or instructional employee) means an employee employed principally in an instructional capacity by an educational agency or school whose principal function is to teach and instruct students in a class, small group, or an individual setting, and includes athletic coaches, driving instructors, and special education assistants such as signers for the hearing impaired. S. Res. 242, Cong. Rec. S3959–S3997 (April 23, 1996); 29 CFR 825.800 (definition of teacher). The term does not include teacher assistants or aides who do not have as their principal function actual teaching or instruction, nor auxiliary personnel such as counselors, psychologists, curriculum specialists, cafeteria workers, maintenance workers, bus drivers, or other primarily noninstructional employees. *Id.*

Given the very limited definition of an employing office under the CAA, see 2 USC 1301(9), the inclusion in the CAA of the special teacher eligibility rule presupposes that Congress employs teachers. I would not have guessed that.

f. Stationed Outside the United States

The definitions of a covered employee and employing office under the FMLA regulations, as applied by the CAA, does not contain any geographic limitations. Therefore, unlike Title I, which excludes from coverage Title I employees stationed overseas, the CAA would apply to CAA covered employees who, for whatever reason, were stationed overseas. *Compare* 29 CFR 825.105(b) (Title I applies to employees within the United States, its territories and possessions) *with* S. Res. 242, Cong. Rec. S3959–S3997 (April 23, 1996), 29 CFR 825.105 (reserved).

g. Previous 12 Months

The "previous 12 months" means the 12 months immediately preceding the commencement of leave. S. Res. 242, Cong. Rec. S3959–S3997 (April 23, 1996), 29 CFR 825.110(d).

h. Commencement of Leave

The determinations of whether an employee has worked for an employing office for at least 1,250 hours in the previous 12 months and has been employed by an employing office for a total of at least 12 months must be made as of the date leave commences. S. Res. 242, Cong. Rec. S3959–S3997 (April 23, 1996), 29 CFR 825.110(d). Neither the CAA nor the implementing regulations define what "leave" is or when leave "commences." Given the close similarity between the requirements of the CAA and Title I, it is likely that developments under Title I will be relied on to interpret this section of the FMLA as applied by the CAA.

D. PEOAA

The FMLA, as applied by the PEOAA, has a 1,250–hour test. Specifically, the PEOAA defines an "eligible employee" as a covered employee who has been employed in any employing office for 12 months and for at least 1,250 hours of employment during the previous 12 months. 3 USC 412(a)(2)(B).

1. Hours Worked

A "covered employee" means any employee of an "employing office." 3 USC 401(a)(2). Interns and volunteers of an employing office are not considered to be covered employees. *See* 3 USC 413(a)(2). An "employing office" is defined in 3 USC 401(a)(4). For additional discussion of the term "employing office," see Chapter 3, "FMLA Coverage of the Federal Government."

V. DETERMINING WHETHER AN EMPLOYING AGENCY EMPLOYS 50 OR MORE EMPLOYEES WITHIN 75 MILES OF THE EMPLOYEE'S WORKSITE

The third eligibility requirement under Title I, and only Title I, is that the employee must work at a worksite where at least 50 employees are employed by the employer within 75 miles of that worksite. 29 USC 2611(2)(B)(ii); 29 CFR 825.110(a)(3); *Englehardt v. S.P. Richards Co.*, 472 F.3d 1 (1st Cir. 2006); *Hackworth v. Progressive Cas. Ins. Co.*, 468 F.3d 722, 726 (10th Cir. 2006), *cert. denied*, 127 S. Ct. 2883 (2007); *Bellum v. PCE Constructors Inc.*, 407 F.3d 734, 738 (5th Cir. 2005), *cert. denied*, 546 U.S. 1139 (2006); *Harbert v. Healthcare Services Group, Inc.*, 391 F.3d 1140 (10th Cir. 2004), *cert. denied*, 546 U.S. 822 (2005); *Humenny v. Genex Corp., Inc.*, 390 F.3d 901 (6th Cir. 2004); *Fain v. Wayne County Auditor's Office*, 388 F.3d 257, 259 (7th Cir. 2004); *Morrison v. Magic Carpet Aviation*, 383 F.3d 1253, 1254 (11th Cir. 2004); *Moreau v. Air France*, 356 F.3d 942, 945 (9th Cir. 2003); *Mason v. United Food and Commercial Workers International Union*, No. 04 C 7148, 2006 U.S. Dist. LEXIS 13929, at *12 (N.D. Il. March 7, 2006); *Knight v. Industrial Distribution Group, Inc.*, Case No. 04–182–SM, 2004 U.S. Dist. LEXIS 20474, at *3 (D.N.H. Oct. 12, 2004); *Bliss v. Jennifer Convertibles, Inc.*, No. 01–C–8661, 2003 U.S. Dist. LEXIS 17435, at *49 (N.D. Ill. Sept. 30, 2003); *Collingsworth v. Earthlink/OneMain, Inc.*, No. 03–2299–GTV, 2003 U.S. Dist. LEXIS 22304, at *9 (D. Kan. Dec. 4, 2003).

An employee who does not meet the 50/75 test is not eligible for FMLA benefits. *See Hackworth*, 468 F.3d at 726 & n. 4, *cert. denied*, 127 S. Ct. 2883 (2007); *Humenny*, 390 F.3d at 901 (employee who did not meet 50/75 test was not eligible for FMLA benefits and could not maintain FMLA retaliation claim); *McClain v. Lance, Inc.*, No. 8:05-3368-HMH-BHH, 2006 U.S. Dist. LEXIS 87747, at *7 (D.S.C. Nov. 30, 2006); *Connors v. Spectrasite Communications, Inc.*, 465 F. Supp. 2d 834 (S.D. Ohio 2006); *Gibson v. Transport Drivers, Inc.*, No. H-04-2083, 2006 U.S. Dist. LEXIS 12272, at *13 (S.D. Tex. March 8, 2006); *Lestarczyk v. Agri-Best Foods, Inc.*, No. 04 C 2551, 2005 U.S. Dist. LEXIS 18236, at *4 (N.D. Il. Aug. 24, 2005);

Courts have called this requirement the small employer, small operation, or satellite office exception. *Johnson v. Wabash Nat. Trailer Centers, Inc.*, No. 06-1688-KI, 2007 U.S. Dist. LEXIS 11017, at *6 (D. Ore. Feb. 15, 2007); *Leverne v. Shelby Group International, Inc.*, No. 04-2884 BP, 2005 U.S. Dist. LEXIS 29814, at *5 (W.D. Tenn. Nov. 14, 2005). Under the exception, a large employer with a relatively small satellite office in a particular area is relieved from having to provide FMLA leave to employees at that small facility. *Hackworth*, 468 F.3d 722, 727-28 (10th Cir. 2006), *cert. denied*, 127 S. Ct. 2883 (2007); *Podkovich v. Glazer's Distributors of Iowa, Inc.*, No. C04-4104-MWB, 2006 U.S. Dist. LEXIS 56069, at *36 (N.D. Iowa Aug. 11, 2006). Employees at such a small facility would not be eligible for FMLA leave. *Wabash Nat. Trailer Centers, Inc.*, 2007 U.S. Dist. LEXIS 11017, at *6. The FMLA excepts smaller companies who would unlikely be able to shoulder the burden. *Englehardt.*, 472 F.3d at 6.

The First Circuit in *Englehardt*, 472 F.3d at 5-6, described the small office exception as a threshold protecting smaller businesses from the onerous requirement of keeping an unproductive employee on the payroll in the form of redundant or absent employees, going without an employee for up to twelve weeks, or both. The First Circuit in *Englehardt*, 472 F.3d at 6, continued:

> Thus, the 75-mile rule protects those employers (and their employees) whose businesses require separate worksites from the cumbersome requirement of relocating or commuting over large distances to cover for an employee on leave. Moreover, the 75-mile requirement prevents companies from establishing separate worksites in order to circumvent obligations under the FMLA and other labor rules.

The 50/75 provision was specifically designed to accommodate employer concerns about the difficulties an employer may have in reassigning workers to geographically separate facilities. *Hackworth*, 468 F.3d 722, 727-28 (10th Cir. 2006), *cert. denied*, 127 S. Ct. 2883 (2007); *Moreau*, 356 F.3d at 945-46.

The court in *Leverne v. Shelby Group International, Inc.*, No. 04-2884 BP, 2005 U.S. Dist. LEXIS 29814, at *10 (W.D. Tenn. Nov. 14, 2005), observed:

> In creating the so-called "small employer" exclusion, "Congress has limited the effect of the [FMLA] on small businesses, and larger employers with smaller remote locations, perhaps due to Congress' desire not to burden small businesses by requiring them to operate without employees for an extended period of time or their determination that the effect upon commerce from the small companies is *de minimis*." (Citations omitted.)

A. WHEN THE DETERMINATION IS MADE

For purposes of eligibility, whether 50 employees are employed within 75 miles of the employee's worksite is determined when the employee gives notice of the need for leave. 29 CFR 825.110(f); *Hackworth v. Progressive Cas. Ins. Co.*, 468 F.3d 722, 726 (10th Cir. 2006), *cert. denied*, 127 S. Ct. 2883 (2007); *Moreau v. Air France*, 356 F.3d 942, 953, n.7 (9th Cir. 2003); *Johnson v. Wabash Nat. Trailer Centers, Inc.*, No. 06-1688-KI, 2007 U.S. Dist. LEXIS 11017, at *7 (D. Ore. Feb. 15, 2007); *Connors v. Spectrasite Communications, Inc.*, 465 F. Supp. 2d 834 (S.D. Ohio 2006); *Nameth v. Celina Financial Corp.*, No. 1:04 CV 2282, 2006 U.S. Dist. LEXIS 8908, at *11 (N.D. Ohio March 2, 2006); *Arvidson v. Wallace, Saunders, Austin, Brown & Enochs, Chartered*, No. 05-4025-JAR, 2006 U.S. Dist. LEXIS 6149, at *8 & n.19 (D. Kan. Feb. 16, 2006); *Lestarczyk v. Agri-Best Foods, Inc.*, No. 04 C 2551, 2005 U.S. Dist. LEXIS 18236, at *4 (N.D. Il. Aug. 24, 2005); *Missak v. Lakeland Engineering Equip. Co.*, No. 8:04CV567, 2005 U.S. Dist. LEXIS 40801, at *7 (D. Neb. Oct. 25, 2005); *Bliss v. Jennifer Convertibles, Inc.*, No. 01–C–8661, 2003 U.S. Dist. LEXIS 17435, at *49 (N.D. Ill. Sept. 30, 2003); *Grimsley v. Fiesta Salons, Inc.*, No. 01–10376–BC, 2003 U.S. Dist. LEXIS 298, at *12 (E.D. Mich. Jan. 7, 2003).

In contrast, the first two Title I eligibility requirements—12 months of employment and 1,250 hours of work—are determined at the time FMLA leave commences. *See* 29 CFR 825.110(d). *See McClain v. Lance, Inc.*, No. 8:05-3368-HMH-BHH, 2006 U.S. Dist. LEXIS 87747, at *7 (D.S.C. Nov. 30, 2006); *Nameth*, 2006 U.S. Dist. LEXIS 8908, at *11. The rationale for tying the worksite employee–count eligibility requirement to the employee's request for leave rather than to leave commencement was to avoid having both the employee and employer plan for leave, only to have it denied at the last moment before leave starts if fewer than 50 employees are employed within 75 miles of the worksite at leave commencement. Preamble, 29 CFR 825.110; *Johnson v. Wabash Nat. Trailer Centers, Inc.*, No. 06-1688-KI, 2007 U.S. Dist. LEXIS 11017, at *6 (D. Ore. Feb. 15, 2007) (later fluctuations in the headcount do not affect entitlement to leave for that specific notice); *Arvidson v. Wallace, Saunders, Austin, Brown & Enochs, Chartered*, No. 05-4025-JAR, 2006 U.S. Dist. LEXIS 6149, at *8 & n.21 (D. Kan. Feb. 16, 2006) (purpose of the rule is to fix the date for determination of an employee's eligibility for FMLA benefits and to protect employees who qualify for leave if there is a reduction in the workforce thereafter); *Grimsley v. Fiesta Salons, Inc.*, No. 01–10376–BC, 2003 U.S. Dist. LEXIS 298, at *12 (E.D. Mich. Jan. 7, 2003) ("purpose of this rule, as evident from the language of the regulations, is to fix the date for determination of an employee's eligibility if there is a reduction in the workforce thereafter").

B. DETERMINING THE NUMBER OF EMPLOYEES

The determination of how many employees are employed within 75 miles of a worksite is based on the number of employees "maintained on the payroll." 29 CFR 825.111(c); *Mason v. United Food and Commercial Workers International Union*, No. 04 C 7148, 2006 U.S. Dist. LEXIS 13929, at *13 (N.D. Il. March 7, 2006); *Arvidson*, 2006 U.S. Dist. LEXIS 6149, at *8 & n.20; *Missak*, 2005 U.S. Dist. LEXIS 40801, at *7; *Bliss*, 2003 U.S. Dist. LEXIS 17435, at *49. Pursuant to the payroll method, "any employee who appears on the employer's payroll will be considered employed each working day of the calendar year, and must be counted whether or not any compensation is received for the week." 29 CFR 825.105(b); *Bliss*, 2003 U.S. Dist. LEXIS 17435, at *49. In effect, the test of whether an individual is counted as an employee depends upon whether there is a continuing employment relationship, and being "maintained on the payroll" is used as a proxy for establishing the continuing nature of the relationship. Preamble, 29 CFR 825.110; *Mason*, 2006 U.S. Dist. LEXIS 13929, at *12.

The 50/75 test applies to public agency employers. That was the conclusion of the Seventh Circuit in *Fain v. Wayne County Auditor's Office*, 388 F.3d 257, 259 (7th Cir. Oct. 27, 2004). The court noted that, even though public agencies fall within Title I of the FMLA regardless of the number of employees, those employees cannot seek FMLA benefits unless the agency employees at least 50 employees within a 75–mile radius of the requesting employee's worksite.

1. The U.S. Government as a Single Employer

For Title I covered employees, the U.S. Government constitutes a single employer for purposes of determining employee eligibility. 29 CFR 825.109(e). *All* federal employees within 75 miles of the worksite of the Title I covered employee requesting leave are included in the calculation. The calculation is *not* limited to the employees of the federal entity employing the Title I covered individual requesting FMLA leave. As a result, for the vast majority of Title I covered employees, particularly those stationed in major metropolitan areas, meeting the minimum employee–worksite complement eligibility requirement will not be a problem. Title I covered employees stationed in very remote areas, however, may not meet this eligibility requirement.

The DOL has not provided guidance on how an employer is to determine whether there are 50 federal employees within 75 miles of the worksite of the employee requesting FMLA leave. Certainly, the first step a federal employer should take is to determine the number of employees on the payroll of the federal entity employing the Title I covered individual requesting FMLA leave. If there are 50 or more employees on the payroll within 75 miles of the impacted worksite at the time of the request, eligibility is met.

In the event the federal employer does not employ at least 50 employees within 75 miles of the worksite, the federal employer must determine whether federal personnel of other federal agencies are within the 75–mile area. Again, the DOL offers no guidance on how to accomplish this task or on the level of verification that a federal employer must undertake to confirm that an employee is "maintained on the payroll" of another federal agency.

For example, while as a practical matter it is very safe to assume that there are more than 50 federal employees within 75 miles of Washington D.C., New York, or San Francisco, can a federal employer "assume" satisfaction of this eligibility requirement, or must it do something more and, if so, what? If something more than a bare assumption were required, would a letter from another federal employer within the 75–mile area suffice? Or does the federal employer have to obtain copies of a sufficient number of Form 50s to verify federal employment in another federal agency? And what happens if the other federal agencies refuse to provide the requested information? Is a federal employer justified in denying FMLA leave because there was no evidence that there were 50 federal employees within 75 miles of the impacted worksite due to the refusal of other federal agencies to cooperate by providing the information?

Assuming that an employee meets this eligibility requirement is problematic because eligibility is mandated by statute. *See* 29 USC 2611(2)(B)(ii). It *must* be met in order for an employee to receive the benefits and protections of the Act. While at the time of applying for leave, most employees would not argue with a determination that they are eligible for FMLA leave based on an assumption that there are 50 federal employees within 75 miles of the impacted worksite, they may challenge that decision later, particularly if they are dismissed or disciplined for absenteeism or denied additional FMLA leave.

For federal employers with small worksites in remote areas who are trying to determine whether there are 50 federal employees within 75 miles, the U.S. Postal Service has employees in virtually every small town throughout the nation. Other federal employees who are frequently stationed in remote areas include the USDA, the U.S. Forest Service, employees of the national parks, and the military.

2. Eligible and Non-Eligible Employees

An employer must count all employees who are "maintained on the payroll," including eligible and non–eligible employees. Preamble, 29 CFR 825.110 *See, e.g.,* 29 CFR 825.105(c) (any employee, whose name appears on the employer payroll, counts towards the minimum 50-employee threshold for private sector Title I employer coverage). Again, because the U.S. Government is a single employer for purposes of eligibility, see 29 CFR 825.109(e), all federal employees who are "maintained on the payroll" count toward meeting the minimum worksite–employee complement eligibility requirement.

3. Effect of Leave

The employee count must include all employees of the employer who are maintained on the payroll, including employees on paid or unpaid leave of absence. Preamble, 29 CFR 825.110. *See, e.g.,* 29 CFR 825.105(c) (employees on paid or unpaid leave count toward meeting the minimum employee complement for purposes of private sector employer coverage under Title I).

4. Part-Time and Full-Time Employees

The employer count must include all employees of the employer who are "maintained on the payroll," including part-time and full-time employees. Preamble, 29 CFR 825.110. *See, e.g.,* 29 CFR 825.105(c) (part-time employees, like full-time employees, are considered toward meeting the private sector minimum employee complement for Title I employer coverage). Essentially, how a federal agency designates an employee is not determinative. What is determinative is whether the employee is "maintained on the payroll" of the Government of the United States.

5. Laid-Off Employees

Employees who have been laid off (whether temporary, indefinite, or long-term) are not included towards meeting the 50/75 requirement. Preamble, 29 CFR 825.110. *See, e.g.,* 29 CFR 825.105(c) (laid-off employee not counted toward meeting private sector minimum employee complement for Tile I coverage).

6. Leaves of Absence and Suspensions

The regulations on minimum employee worksite count do not address whether employees who are on long-term leaves of absence or have been suspended count towards eligibility. The short answer is that if these individuals are maintained on the payroll, they count. There may, however, be circumstances where employees maintained on the payroll might not count.

In the section of the Preamble addressing laid-off employees, the DOL refers to a discussion of related issues in 29 CFR 825.105. *See* Preamble, 29 CFR 825.110. This section addresses the minimum number of employees that are required to bring a private sector employer within the coverage of Title I. This section is generally not applicable to the federal sector as the federal sector is covered by Title I regardless of the number of employees. 29 CFR 108(d). The cross-reference suggests, however, that the analogous regulations in 29 CFR 825.105 may be relied upon to animate 29 CFR 825.110(f).

Under 29 CFR 825.105(c), employees on paid or unpaid leave, including FMLA leave, leaves of absence, disciplinary suspensions, etc., are counted as long as the employer has a reasonable expectation that the employee will later return to active employment. Applying that rule to the 50/75 requirement, an employer does not have to count an employee where the employer has a reasonable expectation that the employee will not be returning to active employment.

For example, a federal employer may not have to count an employee who has been suspended and will be terminated, as long as the agency reasonably believes that the employee will not be returning to active duty.

Similarly, an employee who is on disability leave with no apparent ability of returning may also be excluded from the 50/75 requirement, if there were no reasonable expectations that the employee would return to active duty. *See* Preamble, 29 CFR 825.105 ("An employee who is *permanently* disabled from work would not reasonably be expected to return to work and, therefore, may be excluded from the employee count"; the count referred to involved employer coverage, not employee complement). *See, e.g., Grimsley v. Fiesta Salons, Inc.,* No. 01-10376-BC, 2003 U.S. Dist. LEXIS 298 (E.D. Mich. Jan. 7, 2003) (court held that educational employees who have not returned from leaves of absence after receiving their last paycheck at the time an employee requests FMLA leave need not be counted toward meeting the 50/75 requirement).

Of course, what is reasonable will depend on the facts of each case. If an agency has a record of 0-30 on sustaining a particular suspension, it might not be reasonable for a federal employer to exclude a similarly suspended employee from the minimum employee worksite count.

7. Employee Resignation

In *Grimsley v. Fiesta Salons, Inc.,* No. 01-10376-BC, 2003 U.S. Dist. LEXIS 298 (E.D. Mich. Jan. 7, 2003), the district court held that at the time the plaintiff requested leave, unpaid educational employees who left their positions at the conclusion of the academic year and received their last paycheck and never returned did not count toward the 50/75 requirement. The court held that this was the case even if an employee counted on the payroll for purposes of employer coverage. If the employee no longer works for the employer at the time the plaintiff requests FMLA benefits, that employee should not be included toward meeting the 50/75 requirement.

8. Military Duty

The DOL regulations do not address whether an employee on military leave is counted for purposes of meeting the minimum number of employees at a worksite to meet the third Title I eligibility requirement. The issue also is not addressed in the DOL's recent Memorandum entitled *Protection of Uniformed Service Members' Rights to Family and Medical Leave* (July 22, 2002). [For additional discussion of the DOL USERRA–FMLA Memorandum, see Section III.A.6, "Military Leave" of this chapter.]

In the absence of specific guidance, whether an employer should count an employee on military leave would appear to be governed by the general "payroll" rule. If the employee on military leave is listed on the payroll at the time FMLA leave is requested, he should count toward meeting the minimum 50-employee complement at the worksite of the employee requesting FMLA leave. This will undoubtedly cover most short-term leaves for military duty.

Where the military deployment is likely to be long, it is possible, although by no means probable, that the individual need not be counted toward the minimum employee-worksite complement. The determination will depend on whether there is a reasonable expectation that the employee will return to work. *See* 29 CFR 825.105(c). Employees covered by the Uniformed Services Employment and Reemployment Rights Act (USERRA) have a statutory right to return to work for up to five years. As such, absent a direct, written indication from the employee that he or she has no intention of returning to work after their military duty has concluded, federal employers should "reasonably expect" that employees serving military duty will return to work. Therefore, federal employers should count employees still on the payroll who are on a long-term military assignment. If the individual is no longer on the payroll, she is not counted until she returns.

9. Joint Employment and Integrated Employers

In *Engelhardt v. S.P. Richards Co.*, 472 F.3d 1 (1st Cir. 2006), the employer argued that Englehardt was not eligible for FMLA leave because his employer, SPR, a wholly owned subsidiary of GPC, did not employ the requisite 50 employees within 75 miles of the Nashua facility where Englehardt was employed. Engelhardt argued that he was eligible because GPC and SPR should be considered integrated employers. GPC had more than 50 employees in Nashua. SPR adopted GPC's personnel policies on attendance. SPR's handbooks, benefits, brochures, information sheets, and paycheck stubs carried the GPC logo or letterhead rather than SPR's logo. SPR employees were eligible to participate in GPC administrated health insurance, life insurance, and pension plans. GPC issued SPR's payroll checks. The First Circuit affirmed the dismissal of Englehardt's suit after finding that SPR and GPC were not integrated employers. The court found that GPC did not control enough facets of SPR's business and operations to be considered an integrated employer. The court noted SPR was not under the same management as GPC. Nor was there evidence that the operations of the two companies were interrelated. They had separate headquarters, human resource functions, and record keeping. GPC, the court noted, is in the auto parts business, whereas SPR is in the office supply business. The use of GPC policies and forms, the court noted, "are reflective of SPR's desire to capitalize on certain economies of scale"; that is, it is cheaper for SPR to subscribe to the same policies. A small company that would otherwise be exempt from the FMLA should not be deprived of the exception just because it is a subsidiary of a larger company.

Joint employment occurs where two or more employers exercise some control over the work or working conditions of the employee. 29 CFR 825.106(a). Employees jointly employed by two employers must be counted by both employers, whether or not maintained on one of the employer's payroll, in determining employee eligibility. 29 CFR 825.106(d). An example of a joint employment relationship is where a federal agency hires a contract employee through a temporary help or employee-leasing agency. *See* 29 CFR 825.106(b). [For a discussion of joint employment, see Chapters 3 and 4.]

For purposes of determining Title I eligibility in the federal sector, joint employees must be counted as a federal employee for purposes of meeting the minimum 50-employee complement at the worksite of the Title I covered employee requesting FMLA leave. It does not matter that the temporary or leasing agency employee is not on the federal agencies' payroll, or whether he is covered by Title I of the FMLA. If he is a joint employee, he must be included in the employment complement to determine eligibility.

For example, if at the time FMLA leave is requested, a worksite of the U.S. Forest Service has 20 permanent federal smoke jumpers and jointly employs 40 more Hot Shots through a contract with an employee leasing agency, the worksite would meet the minimum 50-employee complement for FMLA eligibility. *See* 29 CFR 825.106(d).

In the same example, if the U.S. Forest Service employed 20 permanent smoke jumpers at the worksite, and jointly employed 30 more, with five on leave, the worksite would still meet the minimum employee complement for employee eligibility as long as there was a reasonable expectation that the five on leave would return to work for the Forest Service. Employees on leave count toward the minimum employee complement for purposes of Title I eligibility. *See* 29 CFR 825.106(d), 825.110(f).

A joint employment relationship may also exist between federal agencies. For example, a joint employment relationship may exist where an employee of one federal agency is on a detail with another federal agency. Because, however, the U.S. Government is considered a single employer for purposes of Title I eligibility, the concept of joint employment is unnecessary in order for the detailed federal employee to count. She would count anyway because all federal employees count for purposes of Title I eligibility, including meeting the minimum employee–worksite complement requirement.

10. Federal Employees Stationed Outside the United States

Federal employees employed outside the United States and its territories and possessions are not eligible for FMLA leave, nor are they counted for purposes of determining whether the 50/75 threshold has been met. 29 CFR 825.105(b); DOL WH Opinion No. 9 (Oct. 18, 1993) (employees stationed in a foreign country on one- and two-year contracts are not eligible for benefits and protections of FMLA while stationed overseas).

11. Teachers

Employees of educational institutions who are employed permanently or who are under contract are "maintained on the payroll" during any portion of the school year when school is not in session. 29 CFR 825.111(c). [For a discussion of special eligibility rules for teachers, see Chapter 10, "Leave Amount and Scheduling."]

12. Effect of More Generous Employer Policies

In *Thomas v. Pearle Vision, Inc.*, 251 F.3d 1132, 1136–1137 (7th Cir. 2001), Pearle Vision had a company FMLA policy that permitted employees with 12 months of employment and 1,250 hours of service prior to leave commencement to take FMLA leave. The policy did not mention the third eligibility requirement under Title I: that there be at least 50 employees within 75 miles of the worksite of the employee taking FMLA leave. Dr. Thomas worked at a Pearle Vision store that did not have 50 employees within 75 miles. The court held that, notwithstanding Pearle Vision's company FMLA policy, plaintiff was not an eligible employee within the meaning of the Act because Pearle Vision employed less than 50 employees within 75 miles of the store at which Dr. Thomas worked. The court, however, indicated that Dr. Thomas might have a breach of contract claim against his employer.

Thomas is yet another example of the proposition that more generous employer leave policies can not be used to expand statutory requirements.

13. Proof of Number of Employees Maintained on Payroll

Courts have looked to a variety of employer records to determine whether there were at least 50 employees within 75 miles of the worksite of the employee requesting FMLA leave.

In *Arvidson v. Wallace, Saunders, Austin, Brown & Enochs, Chartered*, No. 05-4025-JAR, 2006 U.S. Dist. LEXIS 6149, at *8 (D. Kan. Feb. 16, 2006), the court relied on the employer's 401K records, which listed each individual on the payroll during any given month, to find that the employer had 50 or more employees at the time the employee requested FMLA leave.

In *Gazda v. Pioneer Chlor Alkali Co., Inc.*, 10 F. Supp. 2d 656, 674–75 (S.D. Tex. 1997), the district court relied on comprehensive lists of all company employees who worked in Texas for the defendant or its affiliated companies at any time during the year of the FMLA leave request in dispute. The court noted that the lists were derived from the defendant's personnel, payroll, and benefits records, as attested to in the affidavit of Defendant's human resources manager. The court rejected arguments advanced by the plaintiff that employee W–2 records, 1099 forms, and two employment contracts suggested that additional employees were employed within the 75 mile area. Addressing each of the record categories advanced by plaintiff, the court essentially found that they failed to establish that the individuals identified in these records either lived or worked in the Houston area at the time in question.

The case should certainly give Title I employers a good idea of the type of information they can expect to produce in discovery to address the employee-worksite eligibility requirement. *See, e.g., In Grimsley v. Fiesta Salons, Inc.,* No. 01-10376-BC, 2003 U.S. Dist. LEXIS 298 (E.D. Mich. Jan. 7, 2003) (human resources manager's deposition testimony and affidavit, based on tax records and individual payroll audit reports to generate a list of employees who worked at the relevant employer locations during the pertinent time period); *Figueria v. Black Entertainment Television, Inc. et al.,* 944 F. Supp. 299, 308 (S.D.N.Y. 1996) (determination whether plaintiff is an eligible employee under the FMLA should be decided on a complete record, after both plaintiff and defendant have had an opportunity to conduct discovery, where the 50-employee threshold eligibility hinged on determination of whether individuals were employees or independent contractors).

14. Employer Coverage Is Not the Same as Employee Eligibility

Just because an employer admits that it is covered by Title I of the FMLA does not mean that it has admitted that its employees are eligible for FMLA leave. Employer "coverage" and "employee eligibility" are distinct concepts. They are, however, sometimes confused. This is particularly true in the private sector where employer coverage is determined based on whether the employer employed at least 50 employees over 20 workweeks within a given year. *See* 29 USC 2611(4)(a)(I). Employee eligibility is based, in relevant part, on whether a covered employer has, at leave commencement, at least 50 employees within 75 miles of the worksite of the employee requesting FMLA leave. While the private sector employer "coverage" standard and the "employee eligibility" standard are similar, they are not identical. *See Grimsley*, 2003 U.S. Dist. LEXIS 298 (employee eligibility definition not the same as covered employer definition); *Moreau v. Air France et al.,* Case 99-4645 VRW, 2002 U.S. Dist. LEXIS 5665 (N.D. CA. March 25, 2002) (parties conflate test for employer coverage with test for employee eligibility), *aff'd,* 343 F.3d 1179 (9th Cir. 2003); *Muller v. Hotsy Corp.,* 917 F. Supp. 1389, 1418 (N.D. Iowa 1996) (court held that plaintiff was not an eligible employee within the meaning of the Act because he worked at a worksite with less than 50 employees within 75 miles. court rejected plaintiff's argument that Hotsy waived the right to prove that it is not an "employer" under the terms of the FMLA because it already admitted that it was an employer under the Act, noting that "Hotsy is not claiming it is not an 'employer' under the FMLA; it is asserting that Muller is not an 'eligible employee' under the FMLA.").

Because Title I of the FMLA applies to the federal sector regardless of the number of employees, the confusion that sometimes arises as a result of similarities between the private sector employer coverage test and the third prong of the employee eligibility test is not an issue.

C. 75 MILE DISTANCE

The 75-mile distance is measured by surface miles, using surface transportation over public streets, roads, highways and waterways, by the shortest route from the facility where the eligible employee in need of leave is employed. 29 CFR 825.111(b). It is not measured by a 75-mile radius. *See* Preamble, 29 CFR 825.111 (deleting reference to 75-mile radius in favor of 75 surface miles); *Hackworth v. Progressive Cas. Ins. Co.,* 468 F.3d 722, 726 (10th Cir. 2006); *Englehardt v. S.P. Richards Co.,* 472 F.3d 1, 11 (1st Cir. 2006) *cert. denied*, 127 S. Ct. 2883 (2007). In the absence of available surface transportation between worksites, the distance is measured by using the most frequently utilized mode of transportation (e.g., airline miles). Preamble, 29 CFR 825.111

Note that the 75-mile distance is the shortest route, including public waterways. There is no priority in modes of transportation, so if a boat is shorter even though everyone drives, the calculation must be made by boat. Also, to achieve the "shortest" route, the calculation may have to include boats, trains and automobiles.

The Fifth and Tenth Circuits have sustained the validity of the DOL's 75 surface mile rule (29 CFR 825.111(b)). In *Hackworth v. Progressive Cas. Ins. Co.,* 468 F.3d 722, 726 (10th Cir. 2006), *cert. denied,* 127 S. Ct. 2883 (2007), the employee challenged the DOL regulation clarifying that surface miles are to be used in determining whether two worksites are "within 75 miles" of one another. The employer had more than 50 employees within a radius of 75 miles of Hackworth's worksite, but less than 50 employees within 75 surface miles. The statute simply requires 50 employees "within 75 miles" of the employee's worksite. The DOL regulation, 29 CFR 825.111(b), adds that the 75 miles must be determined by surface miles. Applying the standard for analyzing an agency's construction of a statute it administers developed by the Supreme Court in *Chevron USA, Inc. v. NRDC,* 467 U.S. 837 (1984), the court initially determined that Congress had not clearly expressed in the FMLA how one should measure the geographic proximity of two distinct worksites. Notwithstanding several references in the House and Senate Reports of the FMLA to a 75-mile "radius", the Tenth Circuit nevertheless sided with the DOL's interpretation. The court found the DOL regulation to be a reasonable interpretation of "within 75 miles" contained in the statute. The court did not consider the standard to be arbitrary merely because employee eligibility might depend on how straight a particular road is whether a particular road is under construction, or how many public roadways are located in a particular region.

A similar challenge to the DOL's 75 surface miles rule was mounted in *Bellum v. PCE Constructors Inc.*, 407 F.3d 734, 738-741 (5th Cir. 2005), *cert. denied*, 546 U.S. 1139 (2006), with the same result as in *Hackworth*, 468 F.3d at 726.

D. DETERMINING THE EMPLOYEE'S WORKSITE

Fixing the worksite of the Title I–covered employee requesting FMLA leave is important as it marks the point from which a federal employer must determine whether 50 or more federal employees are employed within 75 miles. The term "worksite" is not defined in the statute or in the DOL implementing regulations. *Harbert v. Healthcare Services Group, Inc.*, 391 F.3d 1140 (10th Cir. 2004), *cert. denied*, 546 U.S. 822 (2005). The term "worksite" is intended to be construed in the same manner as the term "single site of employment" under the regulations developed under the Worker Adjustment and Retraining Notification (WARN) Act. Preamble, 29 CFR 825.111; S. Rep. No. 103–3 at 23 (1993), *reprinted in* 1993 USCCAN 3, 25, H.R. Rep. No. 103–8(I) at 35. *See also Cobb v. Contract Transport, Inc.*, 452 F.3d 543, 558 (6th Cir. 2006); *Harbert*, 391 F.3d at 1140) (citing S. Rep. No. 103–3, at 23 (1993); H.R. Rep. No. 103–8(I), at 35 (1995)), *cert. denied*, 546 U.S. 822 (2005); *Cialini v. Nilfisk–Advance America, Inc. et al.*, No. 99–3954, 2000 U.S. Dist. LEXIS 2042 (E.D. Pa. Feb. 28, 2000) (because Congress intended the term "worksite" to be construed in the same manner as the term "single site of employment" under the WARN Act, the court looked to WARN Act regulations and case law to determine the worksite of a salesperson without a fixed office). The DOL's WARN Act regulations are codified at 20 CFR 639. The "single site of employment" regulations are set forth at 20 CFR 639.3(l).

1. General Worksite Rule

An employee's worksite under the FMLA will ordinarily be the site the employee reports to or, if none, from which the employee's work is assigned. 29 CFR 825.111(a); *see Podkovich v. Glazer's Distributors of Iowa, Inc.*, No. C04-4104-MWB, 2006 U.S. Dist. LEXIS 56069, at *37 (N.D. Iowa Aug. 11, 2006); *Leverne v. Shelby Group International, Inc.*, No. 04-2884 BP, 2005 U.S. Dist. LEXIS 29814, at *10 (W.D. Tenn. Nov. 14, 2005); *Collingsworth v. Earthlink/OneMain, Inc.*, Case No. 03–2299–GTV, 2003 U.S. Dist. LEXIS 22304, at *9 (D. Kan. Dec. 4, 2003); *Grimsley v. Fiesta Salons, Inc.*, No. 01–10376–BC, 2003 U.S. Dist. LEXIS 298, at *15 (E.D. Mich. Jan. 7, 2003); *Gazda v. Pioneer Chlor Alkali Co., Inc.*, 10 F. Supp. 2d 656, 674 (S.D. Tex. 1997) (determination of number of employees company had at or within 75 miles of Houston office, where plaintiff worked, as of leave commencement).

2. Single or Multiple Locations

Worksite can refer to either a single location or a group of contiguous locations. 29 CFR 825.111(a); *accord Mason v. United Food and Commercial Workers International Union*, No. 04 C 7148, 2006 U.S. Dist. LEXIS 13929, at *12 (N.D. Il. March 7, 2006); *Leverne*, 2005 U.S. Dist. LEXIS 29814, at *10; *Collingsworth*, 2003 U.S. Dist. LEXIS 22304, at *9; *Grimsley*, 2003 U.S. Dist. LEXIS 298, at *15.

Structures that form a campus or industrial park, or separate facilities in proximity with one another, may be considered a single site of employment. 29 CFR 825.111(a). Contiguous buildings, however, will not always constitute a single site of employment. Contiguous buildings owned by the same employer that have separate management, produce different products or services, and have separate workforces are considered separate single sites of employment. 20 CFR 639.3(l)(5).

Similarly, there may be several single sites of employment within a single building, such as an office building, if separate employers conduct activities within the building. 29 CFR 825.111(a); 20 CFR 639.3(l)(2). For example, an office building with 50 different businesses as tenants will contain 50 sites of employment. The offices of each employer will be considered separate sites of employment for purposes of the FMLA. *Id.*

3. Separate Facilities as Single Worksite

Separate buildings or areas that are not directly connected or in immediate proximity are a single worksite if they (1) are in reasonable geographic proximity, (2) are used for the same purpose, and (3) share the same staff and equipment. 29 CFR 825.111(a)(1).

For example, if the GSA manages a number of warehouses in a metropolitan area but regularly shifts or rotates the same employees from one building to another, the multiple warehouses would be a single worksite. 29 CFR 825.111(a)(1); *see also* 29 CFR 639.3(l)(3).

In *Mason v. United Food and Commercial Workers International Union*, No. 04 C 7148, 2006 U.S. Dist. LEXIS 13929, at *12 (N.D. Il. March 7, 2006), the court observed that Washington DC was not in reasonable geographic proximity to the employee's Schaumburg, Illinois home office within the meaning of the FMLA.

On the other hand, non-contiguous sites in the same geographic area that do not share the same staff or operational purpose should not be considered a single site. For example, postal facilities which are located on opposite sides of town, and which are managed by a single employer, are separate sites if they employ different workers. 29 CFR 639.3(l)(4).

4. No Fixed Worksite

For employees with no fixed worksite (e.g., construction workers, truck drivers, seamen, pilots, salespersons, etc.), the "worksite" is the site to which they are assigned as their home base, from which their work is assigned, or to which they report. 29 CFR 825.111(a)(2); 20 CFR 639.3(l)(6); *accord Cobb v. Contract Transport, Inc.*, 452 F.3d 543, 558 (6th Cir. 2006); *Harbert v. Healthcare Services Group, Inc.*, 391 F.3d 1140 (10th Cir. 2004), *cert. denied*, 546 U.S. 822 (2005); *Connors v. Spectrasite Communications, Inc.*, 465 F. Supp. 2d 834 (S.D. Ohio 2006); *Podkovich v. Glazer's Distributors of Iowa, Inc.*, No. C04-4104-MWB, 2006 U.S. Dist. LEXIS 56069, at *37-38 (N.D. Iowa Aug. 11, 2006); *Mason*, 2006 U.S. Dist. LEXIS 13929, at *12; *Leverne*, 2005 U.S. Dist. LEXIS 29814, at *10; *Grimsley*, 2003 U.S. Dist. LEXIS 298, at *15.

For example, if a federal wildfire crew stationed in Oregon opened a base camp in Colorado, and set up a mobile trailer on the site as the wildfire crew's on-site office, the mobile trailer in Colorado would be the worksite for any employees hired locally who reported to the mobile trailer/office daily for work assignments. If the Oregon wildfire crew also sent personnel such as a crew chief, firemen, and office personnel from Oregon to the job site in Colorado, those workers sent from Oregon would continue to have Oregon as their "worksite." The workers with Colorado as their worksite would not be counted in determining eligibility for employees whose home base is the Oregon worksite, but would be counted in determining eligibility for employees whose home base was the Colorado worksite. *See* 29 CFR 825.111(a)(2).

The converse, however, is not true. For workers with Colorado as their worksite, the federal employees from Oregon would count toward the 50-employee threshold for eligibility at the Colorado worksite. Again, the U.S. Government is considered a single employer for purposes of eligibility. 29 CFR 825.108(d); 825.109(e). As such, any federal employee within 75 miles of the impacted worksite is fair game to be counted toward meeting the 50-employee threshold, no matter where the worksite of this employee happens to be located.

For FMLA eligibility purposes, an employee who travels from one regional office to another is not permitted to "mesh each of these offices together in order to satisfy the 50 employee rule." *Mason v. United Food and Commercial Workers International Union*, No. 04 C 7148, 2006 U.S. Dist. LEXIS 13929, at *17 (N.D. Il. March 7, 2006). Rather, the worksite determination is made based on his home base where he regularly received work assignments.

For transportation employees, the worksite is the terminal to which they are assigned, report for work, depart, and return after completion of a work assignment. 29 CFR 825.111(a)(2). *But see Cobb v. Contract Transport, Inc.*, 452 F.3d 543, 558 (6th Cir. 2006). For example, an airline pilot may work for the Postal Service with headquarters in Washington D.C., but the pilot regularly reports from postal facilities located at the airport in Chicago and returns to Chicago at the completion of one or more flights to go off duty. The pilot's worksite is the facility in Chicago. 29 CFR 825.111(a)(2).

In *Cobb*, the Sixth Circuit found that the worksite of a truck driver was the place he received his work assignments and reported, and not the terminal where he was assigned. The court ruled that in order for a terminal to be a worksite the facility had to be owned by controlled by the employer. In *Cobb*, the terminal was "a public truck stop, a glorified gas station, over which the Defendant has no authority or control." Because the facility where his assignments were dispatched had more than 50 employees within 75 miles, Cobb was determined to be eligible for FMLA leave.

With respect to the "assignment" prong of this definition under the WARN Act, it has been noted that "the concern here is the source of the 'day–to–day' instructions received by the sales representatives notwithstanding centralized payroll and certain other centralized managerial or personnel functions." This inquiry requires the court "to distinguish the true source of instructions from mere conduits through which the instructions passed." *Peters v. Gilead Sciences, Inc.*, No. 1:04-cv-1338-JDT-TAB, 2006 U.S. Dist. LEXIS 84427, at *14 (S.D. Ind. Nov. 20, 2006); *Connors v. Spectrasite Communications, Inc.*, 465 F. Supp. 2d 834 (S.D. Ohio 2006); *Podkovich v. Glazer's Distributors of Iowa, Inc.*, No. C04-4104-MWB, 2006 U.S. Dist. LEXIS 56069, at *38 (N.D. Iowa Aug. 11, 2006); *Leverne v. Shelby Group International, Inc.*, No. 04-2884 BP, 2005 U.S. Dist. LEXIS 29814, at *11 (W.D. Tenn. Nov. 14, 2005); *Cialini v. Nilfisk–Advance America, Inc. et al.*, No. 99–3954, 2000 U.S. Dist. LEXIS 2042 (E.D. Pa. Feb. 28, 2000) (quoting *Ciarlante v. Brown & Williamson Tobacco Corp.*, 143 F.3d 139, 147 (3d Cir. 1998)).

Regarding the reporting function, the focus is on the location of the personnel who were primarily responsible for reviewing sales reports and other information sent by the sales representative, in order to record sales, assess employee performance, develop new sales strategies, and the like. *Peters*, 2006 U.S. Dist. LEXIS 84427, at *14; *Connors*, 465 f. Supp. 2d at 834 (quoting *Cialini*, 2000 U.S. Dist. LEXIS 2042); *Leverne*, 2005 U.S. Dist. LEXIS 29814, at *11.

In *Peters*, the employee worked as a sales representative for Gilead covering Indiana, Southern Illinois, and Western Michigan. Gilead is based in Foster City, California. More than 50 employees worked at Gilead's Foster City headquarters. Peters reported to a Regional Sales Director in St. Charles, Illinois. He received his assignments from his supervisor. Gilead had less than 50 employees within 75 miles of St. Charles. Gilead argued that St. Charles was Peters' worksite. Peters argued that Foster City was his worksite. The court agreed with Gilead. The fact that his supervisor used his personal residence in St. Charles as his worksite did not matter.

In *Connors*, the employee worked out of his home in Cincinnati, Ohio. He argued that he was eligible because he reported to Spectrasite's Cary, North Carolina headquarters, which had more than 50 employees. The employer argued that Connors reported to Spectrasite's Columbus, Ohio office, which had 12 employees. While Connors may have worked on a day-to-day basis with individuals in the Cary office, the court concluded that he actually reported and received assignments from his supervisor in the Columbus office. The court noted that Connor submitted his expense reports, attended quarterly sales meetings, and had his quarterly sales goals set by his supervisor in the Columbus office. His supervisor in Columbus also reviewed Connors' performance. In contrast, he worked on a daily basis with Spectrasite employees in Cary to ensure that work was completed for the client to lease space on Spectrasite's towers. The court found that Connors' worksite was Columbus, Ohio. As such, he was not FMLA eligible. For FMLA purposes, an employee's "worksite" may be at a different location than the physical office to which he or she is assigned. In *Podkovich v. Glazer's Distributors of Iowa, Inc.*, No. C04-4104-MWB, 2006 U.S. Dist. LEXIS 56069, at *43 (N.D. Iowa Aug. 11, 2006), the court found that Podkovich's worksite was in Des Moines, Iowa, even though she was physically assigned to Sioux City, Iowa, where she had an office. Des Moines had more than 50 employees whereas Sioux City had only a few employees. The court found that Des Moines was her worksite because she received her job assignments and authorizations from Des Moines, she reported to her supervisors in Des Moines, she received training in Des Moines, and her supervisors reviewed her sales performance in Des Moines. *Accord Leverne v. Shelby Group International, Inc.*, No. 04-2884 BP, 2005 U.S. Dist. LEXIS 29814, at *10 (W.D. Tenn. Nov. 14, 2005); *Collingsworth v. Earthlink/Onemain, Inc.*, No. Civ.A. 03-2299GTV, 2003 U.S. Dist. LEXIS 22304 (D. Kan. Dec. 4, 2003).

5. Personal Residence Not a Worksite

An employee's personal residence is not a worksite in the case of employees who travel a territory and who generally leave from home and return from work to their personal residence, or employees who telecommute to work from home. 29 CFR 825.111(a)(2); *Peters v. Gilead Sciences, Inc.*, No. 1:04-cv-1338-JDT-TAB, 2006 U.S. Dist. LEXIS 84427, at *24 (S.D. Ind. Nov. 20, 2006); *Connors v. Spectrasite Communications, Inc.*, 465 F. Supp. 2d 834 (S.D. Ohio 2006); *Podkovich*, 2006 U.S. Dist. LEXIS 56069, at *39; *Leverne*, 2005 U.S. Dist. LEXIS 29814, at *10. Rather, their worksite is the office to which they report and from which assignments are made. 29 CFR 825.111(a)(2); see 20 CFR 639.3(I)(6); *Peters*, 2006 U.S. Dist. LEXIS 84427, at *14; *Connors*, 465 F. Supp. 2d at 834; *Podkovich*, 2006 U.S. Dist. LEXIS 56069, at *39; *Leverne*, 2005 U.S. Dist. LEXIS 29814, at *10; *Grimsley v. Fieta Salon, Inc.*, No. 01-10376-BC, 2003 U.S. Dist. LEXIS 298, at *15–16 (E.D. Mich. Jan. 7, 2003) (finding that worksite of employee who worked from home was office in Ohio where she received her assignments); *Cialini v. Nilfisk–Advance America, Inc. et al.*, No. 99–3954, 2000 U.S. Dist. LEXIS 2042 (E.D. Pa. Feb. 28, 2000) (worksite of sales representatives was, by operation of 29 CFR 825.111(a)(2), not their personal residence, but the office to which they reported and where assignments were made). In order to be considered as an employee's worksite, the individual's contacts with that location must be based on something more than mere centralized management functions. *Podkovich*, 2006 U.S. Dist. LEXIS 56069, at *42.

6. Worksite of Joint Employee

When an employee is jointly employed by two or more employers, the employee's worksite is the primary employer's office from which the employee is assigned or reports. 29 CFR 825.111(a)(3). For employees of temporary help or leasing agencies, the placement agency most commonly would be the primary employer. 29 CFR 825.106(c). The employee is also counted by the secondary employer (the federal agency) to determine eligibility for the secondary employer's full-time or permanent employees. 29 CFR 825.106(d); 825.111(a)(3). [For a discussion of joint employment, see Chapters 3, "FMLA Coverage of the Federal Government," and 4, "Federal Employees Covered by the FMLA."]

Several courts have addressed the 50/75 requirement in the context of joint employment. The Tenth Circuit in *Harbert v. Healthcare Services Group, Inc.*, 391 F.3d 1140 (10th Cir. 2004), *cert. denied*, 546 U.S. 822 (2005), partially invalided 29 CFR 825.111(a)(3), which affixes the worksite of a joint employee as the site of the primary employer from which the employee is assigned or reports. Harbert was a joint employee of Healthcare Services (her primary employer) and Sunset Manor (her secondary employer), a convalescent/nursing facility in Brush, Colorado, where she worked. Harbert reported to her supervisor, who was stationed at Healthcare's regional office in Golden, Colorado. Golden, Colorado is more than 75 miles away from Brush, Colorado. Healthcare denied plaintiff's request for FMLA leave on the grounds that she was not eligible because Healthcare did not employ 50 or more employees within 75 miles of Brush, Colorado. Plaintiff sued Healthcare alleging that the denial of her request for leave violated the FMLA. Relying on 29 CFR 825.111(a)(3), the district court defined Healthcare's regional office in Golden, Colorado as plaintiff's "worksite." Because Healthcare employed more than 50 employees within 75 miles of its Golden office, the district court denied Healthcare's motion for summary judgment and, after a bench trial, found in plaintiff's favor. Healthcare appealed, arguing that the relevant portion of the DOL regulation defining the statutory term "worksite" was invalid.

The Tenth Circuit analyzed whether 29 CFR 825.111 was a valid construction of the FMLA pursuant to the two-step inquiry established by the Supreme court in *Chevron, U.S.A., Inc. v. Natural Resources Defense Council, Inc.*, 467 U.S. 837, 842–44, 104 S. Ct. 2778 (1984). In response to the first step, the court concluded that Congress had not clearly and directly spoken to the precise question at issue. Under the second step of *Chevron*, courts must give controlling weight to the agency's regulations unless they are arbitrary, capricious, or manifestly contrary to the statute. *Harbert*, 391 F.3d at 1149 (citing *Chevron*, 467 U.S. at 844)). The court concluded that "§ 825.111(a)(3), as applied to the situation of an employee with a fixed place of work, is arbitrary, capricious, and manifestly contrary to the FMLA." *Id.*

The court cited three indicia in support of its invalidation of 29 CFR 825.111(a)(3) as it applies to a joint employee with a fixed worksite. First, the court found that the DOL's definition of "worksite," as applied to plaintiff, runs contrary to the common meaning of that term. As commonly understood, "worksite" is the site where the employee works. Here, the plaintiff worked at Sunset Manor in Brush, Colorado. Under the ordinary meaning of the term, her "worksite," the court observed, would be Sunset Manor in Brush. However, under the joint employment regulations, 29 CFR 825.111(a)(3), plaintiff's "worksite" is Healthcare's regional office in Golden, a place where plaintiff only went occasionally for meetings. *Id.*

The second factor cited by the court to partially invalidate 29 CFR 825.111(a)(3) was that the DOL's definition of worksite, as applied to plaintiff, was contrary to the purpose underlying the 50/75 provision. As reflected in the legislative history, the 50/75 provision was designed to remove the burden of providing FMLA leave from employers, including the small operations of large employers, who do not have an abundant supply of temporary replacement in close geographic proximity to the employee requesting leave. The congressional purpose, the court observed, underlying the 50/75 provision is not affected if the "worksite" of an employee who has a regular place of work is defined as any site other than that place. Because 29 CFR 825.111(a)(3) defines plaintiff's "worksite" as defendant's regional office in Golden, the regulation did not affect the congressional purpose underlying the 50/75 provision. *Id.* at 1150.

Finally, the court found that 29 CFR 825.111(a)(3) creates an arbitrary distinction between sole employers and joint employers. The court illustrated its concerns as follows:

For example, if the employer is a company that operates a chain of convenience stores, the "worksite" of an employee hired to work at one of those convenience stores is that particular convenience store. *See* 58 Fed. Reg. 31794, 31798 (1993). If, on the other hand, the employer is a placement company that hires certain specialized employees to work at convenience stores owned by another entity (and therefore is considered a joint employer), the "worksite" of that same employee hired to work at that same convenience store is the office of the placement company. *See* 29 CFR 825.111(a)(3).

Assuming both employers employ more than 50 employees within 75 miles of their central office but fewer than 50 employees within 75 miles of the convenience store, the employee is ineligible for FMLA leave if the employer is a sole employer (e.g., the company that owns the convenience store chain) but eligible for FMLA leave if the employer is a joint employer (e.g., the placement company).

Id. The joint employment provision, the court continued, creates the possibility that an employer's responsibility to provide FMLA leave to an employee will depend exclusively on whether that employer is a sole employer or a joint employer, notwithstanding that neither employer has an abundant supply of nearby employees to temporarily replace the employee taking FMLA leave.

The court also addressed several counter-arguments advanced by the Secretary of the Department of Labor and the plaintiff. The Secretary argued that the joint employment provision is valid because it is patterned after the definition of "single site of employment" in the WARN Act as required by Congress. The court disagreed, holding that the WARN Act provision governs only employees without a fixed place of work and is not relevant to employees who, like plaintiff, do have a fixed place of work. *Id.* at 1151.

The Secretary also argued that because the legislative history suggests that the "worksite" of some employees may be some place other than their regular place of work, it was permissible for the agency to define the "worksite" of jointly-employed employees as some other location. The court disagreed. Congress, the court found, recognized that all employees, even those without a fixed worksite, must have a definable "worksite" so that their eligibility under the Act can be determined. For employees without a regular fixed worksite, it was necessary to identify a constructive worksite for purposes of FMLA eligibility. For employees with a fixed worksite, however, there is no need to identify a constructive worksite for purposes of the FMLA. *Id.* at 1152.

The court specifically noted that it did not question the validity of the joint employment provisions insofar as it applies to employees of temporary help agencies and joint employees without a fixed worksite. The court also indicated that it did not intend to cast doubt on 29 CFR 825.111(a)(2) defining the worksite of employees whose regular workplace is his or her home. *Id.* at 1153.

In *Moreau v. Air France et al.*, No. C-99-4645 VRW, 2002 U.S. Dist. LEXIS 5665 (N.D. Ca. March 28, 2002), *aff'd*, 343 F.3d 1179 (9th Cir. 2003), an airline employee sued alleging that the denial of his request for leave to care for his seriously ill father and his subsequent termination violated the FMLA. The central issue addressed in that case was whether the airline met the 50/75 requirement in order for plaintiff to be eligible for FMLA leave. Because the airline only had 43 of its own employees, whether the airline met the 50/75 test turned on whether ground service personnel employed by the airlines contractors were joint employees who could be attributed to the airline for purposes of FMLA eligibility. Applying the expansive FLSA definition of "employ," the district court applied the four-factor economic reality test used in the Ninth Circuit to the contract ground personnel. Because the airline did not have the power to hire and fire the contractor employees, did not determine individual work schedules, pay rates or methods of payment, and did not prepare the payroll for these employees, the court held that they were not joint employees within the meaning of the FMLA. As such, they were not included toward the 50/75 rule and, as a result, the plaintiff was not an eligible employee.

In *Morrison v. Magic Carpet Aviation*, 383 F.3d 1253, 1255 (11th Cir. 2004), the court found that an aircraft pilot's "worksite" was essentially the Boeing aircraft he flew. While undoubtedly correct as a practical matter, this determination is not in accord with the DOL regulations. Pursuant to 29 CFR 825.111(a)(2), the worksite of a transportation employee, such as a pilot, is the "site to which they are assigned as their home base, from which their work is assigned or to which they report." The decision is silent on this point.

In the case of a joint employment relationship involving a Title I covered federal employee on detail from one federal agency to another, the primary employer would be the federal agency where the employee is permanently stationed. The secondary employer would be the federal agency where the employee is serving the detail. For purposes of calculating eligibility of the federal employee on detail, the worksite would be their home office, which could be thousands of miles away. This can have interesting results.

For example, David is a Title I covered federal employee who is stationed in a remote part of Alaska. Within 75 miles of his Alaska worksite there are less than 50 federal employees, making him ineligible for FMLA leave. David accepts a detail in Washington D.C. Within 75 miles of his DC office there are easily in excess of hundreds of thousands federal workers. Still, if David requested FMLA leave while on his detail, he would not be eligible. The reason is that his worksite remains in Alaska, where there are less than 50 employees within 75 miles of his duty station.

VI. INDIVIDUALS WHO ARE "DEEMED ELIGIBLE" UNDER THE FMLA

The DOL regulations provide that an individual may be "deemed" to meet the eligibility requirements of Title I as a penalty for an employer's failure to timely notify an employee of whether he or she actually satisfies the eligibility criteria or not. *See* 29 CFR 825.110(d). While employer notice obligations will be addressed more fully in Chapter 8, "Notice Requirements," a brief review of the effect of the employer notice requirements as they apply to employee eligibility follows.

A. GENERAL ELIGIBILITY NOTICE RULE

An employer must notify an employee as to whether he or she is eligible for FMLA leave. Notice may be satisfied at three times.

1. Notice Where Employee is Not Yet Eligible

If an employee notifies the employer of the need for FMLA leave before the employee meets Title I eligibility requirements, the employer must either confirm the employee's eligibility based upon a projection that the employee will be eligible on the date leave would commence or must advise the employee when the eligibility requirement is met. 29 CFR 825.110(d). If the employer confirms eligibility at the time the notice for leave is received, the employer may not subsequently challenge the employee's eligibility. *Id.*

The regulations do not impose a separate time frame when notice prior to the time the employee is eligible must be given. As such, the regulations also do not impose a penalty for failure to timely provide advance notice based on a projection of whether the employee would be eligible as of the leave date. If an employer fails or declines to notify the employee based on a projection of eligibility as of the leave date, the regulations, by default, provide that notice should be given when eligibility is met.

At least one court has found 29 CFR 825.110(d) conditionally valid where an employer has confirmed eligibility before an employee commenced FMLA leave, only to determine later that the initial confirmation was erroneous. *See Gurley v. Ameriwood Industries, Inc.*, 232 F. Supp. 2d 969 (E.D. Mo. 2002) (after finding in apposite the cases invalidating the penalty provision in 29 CFR 825.110(d) where an employer fails to timely notify an employee of eligibility, the court held that "[t]o the extent the regulation [29 CFR 825.110(d)] mirrors the federal doctrine of equitable estoppel, it is valid"). The doctrine of equitable estoppel is discussed more fully below.

In *Freeman v. Sikorsky Aircraft Corp., et. al.*, No. 04-CV-0506-CVE-SAJ, 2006 U.S. Dist. LEXIS 58362, at *11 (N.D. Ok. Aug. 17, 2006), the court noted that the FMLA does not require an employer to notify an employee that he or she is ineligible because he or she is stationed outside of the United States, or because there are fewer than 50 employees near his or her worksite. The employee worked at a facility in Brazil.

2. Notice When Eligibility is Met

If an employer decides not to confirm eligibility based on a projection, the employer must advise the employee when eligibility is met. 29 CFR 825.110(d). The employer must advise the employee as soon as practicable after the date eligibility has been determined, which is generally two business days absent extenuating circumstances. *Id.* If an employer fails to timely notify an employee of eligibility as soon as practicable, the penalty imposed by the DOL regulations is that the employee will be "deemed" to have satisfied the notice requirements and the notice of leave is considered current and outstanding until the employer so advises. *Id.* An employer would not be able to challenge the timeliness or adequacy of the employee's notice to the employer of his or her need for leave until the employer notifies the employee of whether he or she is eligible for FMLA leave. [For a further discussion of employee notice obligations, see Chapter 8, "Notice Requirements."]

3. Eligibility Notice Before Leave Commences

Ultimately, an employer has until just before the date FMLA leave commences to notify an employee of whether he or she satisfies the eligibility criteria. Other than the inability to challenge the timeliness or adequacy of the employee's notice of the need for leave, if the employer does not notify the employee within two business days, there does not appear to be any additional penalty for waiting until the eve of leave commencement.

4. Deemed Eligible: Employer Notice On or After Leave Commences

If the employer fails to advise the employee as to whether the employee is eligible prior to the date the requested leave is to commence, the DOL regulations provide that the employee will be deemed eligible. 29 CFR 825.110(d). The employer may not, then, deny the leave. *Id.* Under the DOL regulations, the "deemed eligible" penalty for an employer's failure to notify an employee by leave commencement of whether he or she satisfied the eligibility criteria also applies where the employee gives as little as two business days notice of the need for FMLA leave. 29 CFR 825.110(d). Presumably, the DOL regulations mean that an employer may not deny the leave because the employee is not eligible, rather than, for example, because the leave is not for a covered condition within the meaning of the Act. In any event, as written, the regulations are not clear on this last point.

B. THE "DEEMED ELIGIBLE" PENALTY PROVISION IN THE COURTS

The courts have addressed the validity of 29 CFR 825.110(d) and employee eligibility where (1) the employer has failed to advise an employee within two business days of whether he or she is eligible for FMLA leave; and (2) the employer has (erroneously) confirmed eligibility based on a projection that the employee would be eligible by the time leave commenced.

1. "Deemed Eligible" Due to Employer Failure to Timely Notify Employee of Ineligibility

The penalty provision contained in 29 CFR 825.110(d) for an employer's failure to timely notify an employee of whether she satisfies the eligibility criteria before leave commences necessarily requires employers to provide FMLA leave to employees who do not meet the eligibility requirements mandated by the statute. *See* 29 USC 2611(2)(A), B (ii). For example, an employee who has not worked the requisite 12 months for an employer could be "deemed eligible" by operation of the DOL regulations if the employer fails to notify the employee requesting FMLA leave of whether he met the eligibility requirements before the employee's leave commenced.

Of course, if the employer does notify the employee as to whether he is eligible to take FMLA leave before the employee commences leave, the "deemed eligible" rule does not apply. *See McKim v. UPS, Inc.*, No. 3:97CV–153–H, 1997 U.S. Dist. LEXIS 22121 (W.D. Ky. Sept. 17, 1997).

The overwhelming majority of courts that have addressed this issue have found the "deemed eligible" penalty provision of 29 CFR 825.110(d) invalid, and have concluded that the DOL exceeded its "rule making powers by making eligible under the FMLA employees who do not meet the statute's clear eligibility requirements." *Evanoff v. Minneapolis Public Sch.*, 11 Fed. Appx. 670 (8th Cir. 2001); *Kosakow v. New Rochelle Radiology Assoc*iates, 274 F.3d 706, 724-25 (2d Cir. 2001); *Woodford v. Community Action of Greene County, Inc.*, 268 F.3d 51, 57 (2nd Cir. 2001); *Brungart v. BellSouth Telecommunications, Inc.*, 231 F.3d 791, 795–97 (11th Cir. 2000) (in finding 29 CFR 825.110(d) invalid, court stated that "Congress could have, but did not, conger the right to family medical leave on any employee who did not receive a prompt response from the employer to her leave request"), *cert. denied,* 532 U.S. 1037, 121 S. Ct. 1998 (2002); *Dormeyer v. Comerica Bank–Illinois,* 223 F.3d 579, 581–83 (7th Cir. 2000) (29 CFR 825.110(d) found "invalid", "unauthorized," and "unreasonable"); *Boyd v. City of Philadelphia*, No. 06-1524, 2007 U.S. Dist. LEXIS 21209, at *4-5 (E.D. Pa. March 22, 2007) (predicting Third Circuit would find "deemed eligible" penalty provision invalid); *Sinacole v. Igate Capital*, No. 2:04cv0921, 2006 U.S. Dist. LEXIS 91538, at *23 (W.D. Pa. Dec. 19, 2006) (predicting that Third Circuit would find penalty provision of 825.110(d) invalid); *Garcia v. Blueberry Sales, L.P.,* No. EP-05-CA-0289-FM, 2006 U.S. Dist. LEXIS 7989 at n.1 (W.D. Tex. Feb. 23, 2006); *Gurley v. Ameriwood*

Industries, Inc., 232 F. Supp. 2d 969 (E.D. Mo. 2002); *Nordquist v. City Finance Co.,* 173 F. Supp. 2d 537, 540 (N.D. Miss. 2001). Only one court has found the "deemed eligible" provision in 29 CFR 825.110(d) valid. *See Miller v. Defiance Metal Products, Inc.,* 989 F. Supp. 945, 948–49 (N.D. Ohio 1997). In a subsequent decision, however, the judge who rendered the decision in *Miller* joined the majority and refused to "deem" an employee eligible as a penalty for an employer's failure to timely notify the employee that he or she was not eligible for FMLA leave. *Rocha v. Sauder Woodworking Co. et al.,* 221 F. Supp. 2d 818, 819–820 (N.D. Ohio. 2002) ("Confronted, as I am, by the universal rejection of my decision and approach in *Miller*, I am persuaded that that decision was in error, and whatever impaired vitality it may still have should not be prolonged.").

The judicial demise of the penalty provision in 29 CFR 825.110(d) was no doubt hastened by the Supreme court's decision in *Wolverine World–Wide, Inc.,* 535 U.S. 81, 152 L. Ed. 2d 167, 122 S. Ct. 1155 (2002). As discussed more fully in Chapter 8, "Notice Requirements," the issue in that case was the validity of the DOL regulation contained in 29 CFR 825.700(a). The regulation provided that FMLA leave already taken would not count against an employee's yearly 12–workweek entitlement as a penalty where the employer failed to notify the employee that it designated the leave as protected by the FMLA. The effect of the penalty would grant an employee more than the 12 workweeks of leave the statute entitled the employee to receive. The Supreme court found the regulation invalid. The decision of the Supreme court in *Ragsdale* has been cited in support of the invalidation of 29 CFR 825.110(d). *See Gurley v. Ameriwood Industries, Inc.,* 232 F. Supp. 2d 969 (E.D. Mo. 2002).

While the penalty provision of 29 CFR 825.110(d) has been found invalid, the notice provision contained in that regulation remains valid. Pursuant to 29 CFR 825.110(d), an employer is required to timely notify employees who request FMLA leave of whether they meet the eligibility requirements for FMLA benefits and protections. The courts have not invalidated that provision. *See Kosakow v. New Rochelle Radiology Associates, P.C.,* 274 F.3d 706, 726, n.6 (2d Cir. 2001) (declining to address the validity of the penalty provision of § 110(d), the court opined, "[n]otwithstanding the resolution of that issue, the regulation is 'certainly valid insofar as it simply requires the employer to notify the employee whether her proposed leave is covered by the FMLA'"). Federal employers with Title I covered employees remain obligated to timely notify employees whose requests for leave may be covered by the FMLA of whether they satisfy the eligibility criteria for FMLA leave. While an employee may no longer be deemed eligible as a penalty, other doctrines, such as equitable estoppel (discussed below) may preclude an employer from challenging employee eligibility absent the required employer notice.

The penalty provision contained in 29 CFR 825.110(d) was not contained in the interim regulations that preceded the final regulations. The final DOL regulations (which contain the penalty provision) became effective on April 6, 1995. The final regulations are not applied retroactively. *See Bauer v. Varity Dayton–Walther Corp.,* 118 F.3d 1109, 1111 n.1 (6th Cir. 1997); *Thoele v. USPS,* 996 F. Supp. 818, 821 (N.D. Ill. 1998); *Lacoparra v. Pergament Home centers, Inc.,* 982 F. Supp. 213, 220 & n. 6 (S.D.N.Y. 1997); *Rollins v. Wilson County Government et al.,* 967 F. Supp. 990 (M.D. Tenn. 1997), *aff'd,* 154 F.3d 626 (6th Cir. 1998); *Caruthers v. The Proctor & Gamble Manufacturing Co.,* 961 F. Supp. 1484, 1490 (D. Kan. 1997); *Schlett v. Avco Financial Services,* 950 F. Supp. 823, 835 (N.D. Ohio 1996); *Robbins v. Bureau of Nat. Affairs, Inc.,* 896 F. Supp. 18, 21 (D.D.C. 1995).

C. ESTOPPEL AND ELIGIBILITY

Independent of the now discredited "deemed eligible" penalty provisions of 29 CFR 825.110(d), courts have applied the doctrines of equitable and collateral estoppel to determine whether an otherwise ineligible employee is, for all practical purposes, eligible within the meaning of the Act. One court applied an "interference" standard. All three areas are addressed below.

1. Equitable Estoppel

The majority of courts have applied the doctrine of equitable or promissory estoppel to determine whether an otherwise ineligible employee is "eligible" within the meaning of the Act. *See Duty v. Norton–Alcoa Proppants,* 293 F.3d 481 (8th Cir. 2002); *Kosakow v. New Rochelle Radiology Associates, P.C.,* 274 F.3d 706, 722–724 (2d Cir. 2001); *Dormeyer v. Comerica Bank– Illinois et al.,* 223 F.3d 579, 582–83 (7th Cir. 2000) (FMLA does not preclude application of doctrine of estoppel); *Brungart v. BellSouth Telecommunications, Inc.,* 231 F.3d 791, 797 & n. 4 (11th Cir. 2000), *cert. denied,* 532 U.S. 1037 (2001); *Fryman v. West Telemarketing, L.P.,* No. 06-CV-327-GKF-PJC, 2007 U.S. Dist. LEXIS 42591, at *6 (N.D. Okla. June 11, 2007) (predicting that Tenth Circuit would apply equitable estoppel to FMLA eligibility case); *Sinacole v. Igate Capital*, No. 2:04cv0921, 2006 U.S. Dist. LEXIS 91538, at *20-25 (W.D. Pa. Dec. 19, 2006) (predicting that Third Circuit would apply equitable estoppel in FMLA case); *Peters v. Gilead Sciences, Inc.*, No. 1:04-cv-1338-JDT-TAB, 2006 U.S. Dist. LEXIS 84427, at *14 (S.D. Ind. Nov. 20, 2006); *Garcia v. Blueberry Sales, L.P.*, No. EP-05-CA-0289-FM, 2006 U.S. Dist. LEXIS 7989, at *13-14 (W.D. Tex. Feb. 23, 2006) (predicting that Fifth Circuit will apply equitable estoppel to FMLA case); *Morgan v. Neiman-Marcus Group, Inc.*, No. 3:05-CV-0079-G, ECF, 2005 U.S. Dist. LEXIS 34541, at *14 (N.D. Tex. Dec. 20, 2005); *Gurley v. Ameriwood industries, Inc.*, 232 F. Supp. 2d 969 (E.D. Mo. 2002); *Rocha v. Sauder Woodworking Co. et al.*, 221 F. Supp. 2d 818, 820–21 (N.D. Ohio 2002); *Nordquist v. City Finance Co.*, 173 F. Supp. 2d 537, 540 (N.D. Miss. 2001). *But see Coen v. Sybron Dental Specialties*, 1 Fed. Appx. 386 (6th Cir. 2001) (court declined to apply estoppel to extend eligibility where there were not 50 employees within 75 miles of worksite).

Equitable estoppel is a judicial doctrine of equity that operates apart from any underlying statutory scheme. *Kosakow*, 274 F.3d at 724; see *Nordquist.*, 173 F. Supp. 2d at 540 (describing estoppel as a "uniquely judicial remedy"). If all the elements of equitable estoppel are met, an employer may be estoppel or prevented from challenging an employee's eligibility as a result of the employer's failure to provide the employee notice as to whether she is eligible for FMLA leave benefits and protections. *Id.*

Federal law principles of equitable estoppel apply to claims under the FMLA, a federal statute. *Kosakow*, 274 F.3d at 725 (citing *Wall v. Constr. & Gen, Laborers' Union, Local 230*, 224 F.3d 168, 176 (2nd Cir. 2000)); *Gurley v. Ameriwood Industries, Inc.*, 232 F. Supp. 2d 969 (E.D. Mo. 2002) (citing *Duty v. Norton–Alcoa Proppants*, 293 F.3d 481 (8th Cir. 2002)). The doctrine of equitable estoppel is properly invoked where the enforcement of the rights of one party would work an injustice upon the other party due to the latter's justifiable reliance upon the former's words or conduct. *Kosakow*, 274 F.3d at 725 (citing *In re Ionosphere Clubs, Inc.*, 85 F.3d 992, 999 (2d Cir. 1996)).

Similarly, the district court in *Blankenship v. Buchanan General Hospital, Inc.*, 999 F. Supp. 832, 837–38 (W.D. Va. 1998), described equitable estoppel as follows:

> Equitable estoppel is a device by which one, who by his statement induces detrimental reliance of another, will not be heard later to contradict the statement that induced the reliance. A person can be equitably estopped even when his earlier statement was not false. Fairness simply dictates that he should not be allowed to change his statement, which has been detrimentally relied upon.

The Second Circuit in *Kosakow v. New Rochelle Radiology Associates, P.C.*, 274 F.3d 706, 725 (2d Cir. 2001) described the factors involved in a claim of equitable estoppel:

> Under federal law, a party may be estopped from pursuing a claim or defense where: 1) the party to be estopped makes a misrepresentation of fact to the other party with reason to believe that the other party will rely upon it; 2) and the other party reasonably relies upon it; 3) to her detriment. See *Heckler v. Community Health Services of Crawford County, Inc.*, 467 U.S. 51, 59, 104 S. Ct. 2218, 2223, 81 L. Ed. 2d 42 (1984) (citing Restatement (Second) of Torts § 894(1979)); *Buttry v. Gen. Signal Corp.*, 68 F.3d 1488, 1493 (2d Cir. 1995). Whether equitable estoppel applies in a given case is ultimately a question of fact. *Bennett v. United States Lines, Inc.*, 64 F.3d 62, 65 (2d Cir. 1995).

Other courts have described equitable estoppel in the FMLA context similarly. See *Morgan v. Neiman-Marcus Group, Inc.*, No. 3:05-CV-0079-G, ECF, 2005 U.S. Dist. LEXIS 34541, at *14 (N.D. Tex. Dec. 20, 2005) (the doctrine is deeply rooted in the equitable principle that no one should be permitted to profit from his own wrongdoing in a court of justice); *Rocha v. Sauder Woodworking Co. et al.*, 221 F. Supp. 2d 818, 820–21 (N.D. Ohio 2002) (quoting the definition in § 894(1)(a) of the Restatement (Second) of Torts (1979), which was adopted by the Supreme court in *Heckler v. Community Health Services of Crawford County, Inc.*, 467 U.S. 51, 59, 81 L. Ed. 2d 42, 104 S. Ct. 2218 (1984)); *Blankenship v. Buchanan General Hospital, Inc.*, 999 F. Supp. 832, 837 (W.D. Va. 1998) (equitable estoppel arises when one party has made a misleading representation to another party and the other has reasonably relied to his detriment on that representation); *Gurley v. Ameriwood Industries, Inc.*, 232 F. Supp. 2d 969 (E.D. Mo. 2002) (equitable estoppel principles are applicable to estop an employee in an FMLA case from asserting an affirmative defense contesting an employee's entitlement to FMLA where the employer's representations misled the employee into relying on the leave (citing *Duty v. Norton–Alcoa Proppants*, 293 F.3d 481 (8th Cir. 2002)).

Estoppel requires a "material" or "definite" misrepresentation. *Kosakow*, 274 F.3d at 726 (citing Restatement (Second) of Torts, § 894(1)); *Fryman v. West Telemarketing, L.P.,* No. 06-CV-327-GKF-PJC, 2007 U.S. Dist. LEXIS 42591, at *7 (N.D. Ok. June 11, 2007); *Peters v. Gilead Sciences, Inc.*, No. 1:04-cv-1338-JDT-TAB, 2006 U.S. Dist. LEXIS 84427, at *14 (S.D. Ind. Nov. 20, 2006); *Blankenship,* 999 F. Supp. at 837 (misrepresentation must be proven by the party asserting equitable estoppel). A "definite misrepresentation" may be made by an affirmative statement or by silence. *Id.; see also Rocha v. Sauder Woodworking Co. et al.,* 221 F. Supp. 2d 818, 821 (N.D. Ohio 2002) (silence can be the basis of equitable estoppel (citing *Kosakow*)). An intention to deceive, however, is not required. *Kosakow,* 274 F.3d at 726; *Rocha,* 221 F. Supp. 2d at 818, 821 (silence can be the basis of equitable estoppel (citing *Kosakow*)). Estoppel "is appropriate even where the one making the representation believes that his statement is true," and, moreover, "it is immaterial whether the person making the representation exercised due care in making the statement." *Id.* (quoting Comment, Restatement (Second) of Torts, § 894(1)). As observed by the court in *Morgan v. Neiman-Marcus Group, Inc.*, No. 3:05-CV-0079-G, ECF, 2005 U.S. Dist. LEXIS 34541, at *14 (N.D. Tex. Dec. 20, 2005):

> [E]stoppel is any conduct, express or implied, which reasonably misleads another to his prejudice so that a repudiation of such conduct would be unjust in the eyes of the law. It is grounded not on subjective intent but rather on the objective impression created by the actor's conduct.

Because equitable estoppel is a "uniquely judicial remedy," courts should apply it "only when the facts of a particular case warrant its strong medicine." *Morgan v. Neiman-Marcus Group, Inc.*, 2005 U.S. Dist. LEXIS 34541, at *14-15. The party that seeks to invoke equitable estoppel has the burden of proof. *Morgan v. Neiman-Marcus Group, Inc.*, 2005 U.S. Dist. LEXIS 34541, at *17. In the Fifth Circuit, a litigant must establish that the party to be stopped: (1) made a material misrepresentation or concealment; (2) with actual or constructive knowledge of the facts; (3) with the intent that the misrepresentation or concealment be acted upon; (4) by a party without knowledge or means of knowledge of the true facts; and (5) who detrimentally relies or acts on the misrepresentation or concealment. *Morgan v. Neiman-Marcus Group, Inc.*, 2005 U.S. Dist. LEXIS 34541, at 18 (N.D. Tex. Dec. 20, 2005).

a. Silence as Misrepresentation

Several courts have applied the doctrine of equitable estoppel where the employer, by its silence, misled an employee concerning the employee's entitlement to FMLA leave, if the employee reasonably relied and was harmed as a result. *Garcia v. Blueberry Sales, L.P.,* No. EP-05-CA-0289-FM, 2006 U.S. Dist. LEXIS 7989, at *13-14 (W.D. Tex. Feb. 23, 2006). In *Kosakow v. New Rochelle Radiology Assocs.,* 274 F.3d 706, 722-27 (2d Cir. 2001), the court held that the plaintiff had a sufficient basis for involving the doctrine of equitable estoppel. The court reasoned that New Rochelle's silence with respect to plaintiff's eligibility constituted a definite misrepresentation given the legal duties imposed by the FMLA on New Rochelle to inform its employees of the protections of the FMLA and of the requirements necessary in order to qualify for those protections. The FMLA's employer notice regulations, the court found, indicate that an employee can generally assume she is protected by the FMLA unless informed otherwise. Because New Rochelle failed to fulfill its legal notice obligations, plaintiff was deprived of the opportunity to take her leave under the shelter of the FMLA. Kosakow testified that she would have delayed her long planned and non–emergent operation to gain the additional work time to meet the 1,250–hour requirement.

In *Rocha v. Sauder Woodworking Co. et al.,* 221 F. Supp. 2d 818, 820–21 (N.D. Ohio 2002), the court applied a different legal standard governing misrepresentation by silence as a basis for the application of equitable estoppel. According to the court, "for silence to work an estoppel, some evidence must exist to justify an inference that the silence was sufficiently misleading to amount to 'bad faith.'" *Id.* at 818, 821 (citing *RWM Manufacturing Co v. Dura Corp.,* 592 F.2d 346, 350 (6th Cir. 1979), *aff'd in part and rev'd in part on other grounds,* 722 F.2d 1261 (6th Cir. 1983)). In the Sixth Circuit, "estoppel requires more than a showing of mere silence on the part of the plaintiff; defendant must show that it had been mislead by plaintiff through actual misrepresentations, affirmative acts of misconduct, intentional misleading silence." *Id.* at 821 (quoting *Kellogg Co. v. Exxon Corp.,* 209 F.3d 562, 574 (6th Cir. 2000)). In *Rocha,* the court declined to estop the employer from challenging eligibility, finding that the plaintiff failed to establish that the employer acted in bad faith. *Id.* at 822. In this regard, the court accepted the testimony of the human resources manager of the company that he did not inform the plaintiff of whether she was eligible for FMLA leave because "it was not his job to know such information." *Id.*

In *Dormeyer v. Comerica Bank–Illinois et al.,* 223 F.3d 579, 582–83 (7th Cir. 2000), the court, in *dicta,* opined that an employer who by silence mislead an employee concerning the employee's entitlement to family leave might, if the employee reasonably relied on the employer's silence and was harmed as a result, be estopped to plead the defense of ineligibility to the employee's claim of entitlement to family leave. Because the plaintiff made no effort to establish the elements of estoppel, however, but relied on the "deemed eligible" provision of 29 CFR 825.110(d), which the court found invalid, equitable estoppel was not applied by the court.

In the absence of employee detrimental reliance on the employer's silence regarding eligibility for FMLA leave, a court will not estop an employer from challenging an employee's eligibility for FMLA leave. That was the conclusion of the circuit court in *Brungart v. Bellsouth Telecommunications, Inc.*, 231 F.3d 791, 797, n. 4 (11th Cir. 2000), *cert. denied*, 532 U.S. 1037 (2001). In that case, the plaintiff applied for FMLA leave to begin immediately so she could care for her mother, who was hospitalized for emergency heart surgery. Bellsouth denied the leave over a month later because the plaintiff had not worked 1,250 hours in the preceding 12 months. Regarding her argument that she should be deemed eligible, the court found 29 CFR 825.110(d) invalid. Regarding estoppel, the court held that, because the plaintiff did not reasonably rely to her detriment on BellSouth's failure to respond more promptly to her leave request, it would not estop BellSouth from challenging her eligibility. As evidence, the court cited the plaintiff's deposition testimony that she would have taken leave anyway, although she may not have taken as much leave as she did.

In *Sinacole v. Igate Capital*, No. 2:04cv0921, 2006 U.S. Dist. LEXIS 91538, at *20-25 (W.D. Pa. Dec. 19, 2006), the court declined to apply equitable estoppel where the employee's request for FMLA leave was met with silence and confusion. The employer, the court noted, did not misrepresent that the employee could take FMLA leave and then renege on is word.

b. Confirmation of Eligibility as Misrepresentation

Courts in several cases have addressed the application of the doctrine of equitable estoppel where an employer has made affirmative misrepresentations regarding eligibility. These affirmative representations are in the form of erroneous confirmations that an employee is eligible for FMLA leave.

In *Gurley v. Ameriwood Industries, Inc.*, 232 F. Supp. 2d 969 (E.D. Mo. Sept. 12, 2002), the plaintiff was not eligible for FMLA leave as she worked less than 12 months for Ameriwood. At the time of her leave request, plaintiff worked 11 months, three weeks and a day for Ameriwood. Nevertheless, Ameriwood told the plaintiff that she was eligible and gave her forms to fill out. Ameriwood subsequently argued that its prior representation to the plaintiff that she was eligible did not preclude it from now claiming that she was not eligible. The district court disagreed. Relying on the language in 29 CFR 825.110(d) that precludes an employer who affirmatively confirms an employee's eligibility from subsequently denying it "[t]o the extent that this provision mirrors the federal doctrine of equitable estoppel," the court found that "the plaintiff raised a genuine issue of fact with respect to the application of equitable estoppel." Note that there is nothing in the confirmation language in 29 CFR 825.110(d) that expressly incorporates equitable estoppel principles. The court, therefore, injected equitable estoppel into the language in 29 CFR 825.110(d).

If the employee would have taken leave whether the employer granted it as FMLA or not, the employer will not be estopped from subsequently challenging the employee's eligibility for FMLA leave, even if the employer previously notified the employee that she was eligible. That was the conclusion of the court in *Nordquist v. City Finance Co.*, 173 F. Supp. 2d 537 (N.D. Miss. Jan. 19, 2001).

In *Nordquist*, the employer affirmatively notified the employee that she was eligible even though it employed less than 50 employees within 75 miles of her worksite at the time of her request for leave. *Id.* at 539. After agreeing that 29 CFR 825.110(d) was invalid, the court found that the plaintiff had not established detrimental reliance on the misrepresentation. *Id.* at 540 ("Elementary to the application of estoppel is a finding that plaintiff detrimentally relied on defendant's determination that she was entitled to FMLA leave[.]"). According to the court, "[t]here is absolutely no evidence before the court that plaintiff, who requested leave for the birth her child, would not have taken leave even if defendant denied her application for FMLA leave." *Id.* Consequently, the court held that the defendant was not estopped from reversing its eligibility determination, and the employee was not eligible for FMLA leave.

The *Nordquist* decision suggests a line of inquiry that employing agencies should make in the event that it is discovered that the employee was erroneously advised that he or she met the eligibility requirements in order to take FMLA leave. Ironically, under *Nordquist*, equitable estoppel fails just when the employee needs it the most: in those extreme cases where the employee would have taken the leave under any circumstances, the employer's misrepresentation notwithstanding.

2. Interference with FMLA Rights and Eligibility

In *Lacoparra v. Pergament Home Center, Inc.*, 982 F. Supp. 213, 220 (S.D.N.Y. 1997), the district court, in *dicta*, opined that extension of eligibility could occur as a result of employer interference with FMLA rights. While similar, the test was not based on equitable estoppel. Rather, according to the court, even if an employee falls short of FMLA eligibility (Lacoparra fell short of the 1,250-hour requirement), the employee can overcome this infirmity if (1) the shortfall resulted from an employer failing to provide adequate notice of FMLA rights and obligations, and (2) the lack of information actually caused her to forfeit an FMLA entitlement. Relying on the decision of the court in *Fry v. First Fidelity Bancorp.*, No. 95-6019, 1996 U.S. Dist. LEXIS 875 (E.D. Pa. Jan. 30, 1996), the court found that an employer's failure to provide adequate notice of FMLA procedures may constitute interference with an employee's FMLA rights if it causes the employee to forfeit FMLA protections. Because Lacoparra alleged that, had she been notified, she would have worked the requisite 1,250-hour to secure FMLA eligibility before taking FMLA leave, the court opined that she alleged facts that were sufficient to defeat summary judgment. The court, however, ultimately ruled in favor of Pergament on other grounds.

The rationale underlying the decision in *Lacoparra* was severely challenged by the Second Circuit in *Kosakow v. New Rochelle Radiology Associates, P.C.*, 274 F.3d 706, 723–724 (2d Cir. 2001). Apparently, the trial court in *Kosakow* also relied on *Fry* as the basis for preventing the employer from challenging the plaintiff's eligibility. The Second Circuit found that *Fry* was not precisely on point because, in *Fry*, there was no question that the employee met the 1,250-hour requirement and was an eligible employee under the Act. *Fry*, according to the Second Circuit, "stands for the proposition that, under the proper circumstances, a distinct cause of action lies for an employer's failure to post a notice where that failure leads to some injury." *Id.* at 723. Because only an "eligible employee" is entitled to bring a claim for interference with the FMLA, the plaintiff in *Fry* (who was eligible) could bring a cause of action for violation of the notice provisions, whereas Kosakow could not because he was not eligible. *Id.* at 724. The Second Circuit then addressed the availability of the doctrine of equitable estoppel as a basis for preventing the employer from challenging Kosakow's eligibility.

3. Collateral Estoppel

One court has addressed the doctrine of collateral estoppel in the context of FMLA eligibility. Collateral estoppel applies if (1) the issue sought to be precluded is the same as that involved in the prior action; (2) the issue was actually litigated; (3) the determination of the issue was essential to the final judgment; and (4) the party against whom estoppel is invoked was fully represented. *Thoele v. USPS*, 996 F. Supp. 818, 821 N.D. Ill. 1998 (quoting *Havoco of Am. Ltd. V. Freeman, Atkins & Coleman, Ltd.*, 58 F.3d 303, 307 (7th Cir. 1995)).

In *Thoele*, the plaintiff argued that since the arbitrator found that an employee is deemed eligible for FMLA leave if he or she is not notified otherwise, the court was bound to apply collateral estoppel to find that Thoele was an eligible employee. *Id.* at 821. Addressing the elements, the district court found that the arbitrator's conclusory reference in a footnote on the issue of "deemed eligible" failed to establish that the employer notification issue was "actually litigated." Because the issue in the arbitration was "just cause," and not the propriety of Thoele's FMLA claim (which the arbitrator stated was immaterial to his decision), the court also found that any determination made by the arbitrator on the applicability of the FMLA was not "essential to the final judgment." As such, collateral estoppel did not apply. By analyzing the claim under collateral estoppel, however, the *Thoele* court implicitly sanctioned the application of that doctrine to FMLA eligibility claims.

CHAPTER 6
COVERED FAMILY MEMBERS

I. OVERVIEW

The FMLA entitles an eligible employee to take leave in order to care of certain family members, namely a spouse, a son or daughter, or a parent, of the employee, if these individuals have a serious health condition. All four federal sector FMLA laws limit the scope of the FMLA for leave to care for these individuals, and only these individuals. *Compare* 29 USC §§ 26111(7), (12), (13); § 2612(a)(1)(C); 29 CFR 825.113, *with* 5 USC 6381(3), (6); 5 CFR 630.1202 (definitions for *in loco parentis*: parent, son or daughter, spouse); 2 USC 1312(a)(1); 3 USC 412(a)(1), S. Res. 242, Cong. Rec. S3959–S3997 (April 23, 1996), 29 CFR 825.113. Of course, an eligible employee may be entitled to FMLA leave if he or she suffers from a serious health condition, or for the birth or adoption of the eligible employee's own son or daughter. \ [For a discussion of the conditions covered by the FMLA, see Chapter 7, "Covered Conditions."]

If the leave at issue is needed for an eligible employee to care for anyone other than a spouse, parent, son, or daughter of the employee, the leave is not covered by the FMLA. This is true even if the individual needing care is a member of the eligible employee's family and is suffering from a serious health condition. Of course, other laws or employer policies may permit more generous leave to care for individuals other than those identified in the FMLA. For example, annual leave is available for virtually any reason.

Because of the limited scope of the FMLA leave, it is important for federal employees and employers to know how the FMLA defines "spouse," "parent," and "son or daughter." Thankfully, all four federal sector FMLA laws use substantially similar language to define these terms. There are, however, some differences.

Section II, entitled "Spouse", of this chapter discusses who is considered a spouse. Section III of this chapter, entitled "Son or Daughter" identifies who is a son or daughter under the FMLA. Section IV of this chapter, "Parent", discusses who qualifies as a parent for purposes of FMLA coverage. Section V addresses "Individuals Who are not Covered by the FMLA." Section VI, "Confirmation of Familial Relationship", addresses the rights and responsibilities of employees and agencies to confirm the claimed covered family relationship.

II. SPOUSE

Title I and the CAA define the term "spouse" as a husband or wife as defined or recognized under state law for purposes of marriage in the state where the employee resides, including common law marriages in states where it is recognized. *See* 29 USC 2611(13); 29 CFR 825.113(a); DOL WH Advisory Opinion No. 98 (Nov. 18, 1998); S. Res. 242, Cong. Rec. S3959–S3997 (April 23, 1996), 29 CFR 825.113(a). The PEOAA applies the Title I definition of spouse.

The definition of spouse under Title II is similar, although not identical. "Spouse" means an individual who is a husband or wife pursuant to a marriage that is a legal union between one man and one woman, including common law marriage between one man and one woman in states where it is recognized. 5 CFR 630.1202 (definition of spouse).

A. MARRIAGE AND DIVORCE

1. Marriage

While included as part of the definition of a covered "spouse," the four federal sector FMLA statutes and their respective implementing regulations do not separately define the term "marriage." What constitutes a "marriage" is determined by reference to state law. That is, each state decides the requirements of a valid marriage contract, including who has the capacity to enter into a marriage, the duties and obligations resulting there from, and the grounds for dissolution. *See* Lisa Milot, Note, *Restitching the American Marital Quilt: Untangling Marriage from the Nuclear Family*, 87 Va. L. Rev. 701, 704 (2001) (citing *Loughran v. Loughran*, 292 U.S. 216, 223 (1933)). As a function of the Full Faith and Credit Clause of the

Constitution, a marriage or divorce obtained in one state has traditionally been valid in all others. *See Sherrer v. Sherrer*, 334 U.S. 343, 356 (1948); *Loughran v. Loughran*, 292 U.S. 216, 223 (1933). As set forth more fully below, the enactment of the Defense of Marriage Act of 1996 (DOMA), however, may have changed the interstate recognition of marriages. Milot, at n.14.

There are essentially two forms of marriage: statutory or common–law marriages.

a. Statutory Marriage

The form of marriage most commonly associated with the idea of marriage—statutory marriage—is state-regulated and generally involves some form of civil or religious solemnization. *See* Milot, *supra*, at 704. The barriers to entry into a statutory marriage are few; capacity qualifications generally involve a minimum age, a prohibition against marrying close family relatives, and, in most states, a short waiting period. *Id.* (citing Ira Mark Ellman et al., *Family Law: Cases, Text, Problems 56–57* (3d ed. 1998)). In all states, an individual can only be married to one spouse at a time.

b. Common–Law Marriages

Common–law marriage has been defined as "a marriage which does not depend for its validity upon any religious or civil ceremony but is created by the consent of the parties as any other contract." John B. Crawley, *Is the Honeymoon Over for Common–Law Marriage: A Consideration of the Continued Viability of the Common–Law Marriage Doctrine*, 29 Cumb. L. Rev. 399, 401, n.7 (1998/1999) (quoting Otto E. Koegel, *Common Law Marriage and Its Development in the United States*, at 7 (1922)). Under this doctrine, courts may recognize long–term relationships as valid marriages. Ariela R. Dubler, Note, *Governing Through Contract: Common Law Marriage in the Nineteenth Century*, 107 Yale L. J. 1885–1886 (1998). Once a common–law marriage has been established, it has the same legal force and effect of a statutory marriage. Milot, *supra* at 708; Crawley, at 410 (once a claimant has established the existence of a common–law marriage, the status of the claimant is forever changed as the claimant is married).

Presently, ten states and the District of Columbia recognize common–law marriage. Crawley, *supra*, at 403, n.25 (1998/1999). The jurisdictions allowing common–law marriage are Alabama, Colorado, Iowa, Kansas, Montana, Oklahoma, Pennsylvania, Rhode Island, South Carolina, Texas, Utah, and the District of Columbia. *Id.; see also* Milot, *supra* at 707–708, n.34.

While the laws of each state recognizing common–law marriage differ and, therefore, should be individually consulted, there are generally three requirements for recognition of a common–law marriage: (1) legal capacity to marry; (2) present agreement to enter into a marriage relationship; and (3) consummation of the marriage; that is, they must live in such a way as to gain public recognition that they are living as husband and wife. *See* Crawley, *supra* at 404.

Regarding legal capacity, states have held parties incapable of entering into a common law marriage if they are of unsound mind, are already married, or are underage. *See id.*, 405–406. If, however, the parties marry or attempt to marry when there is a legal impediment to the marriage, the law presumes the existence of a common–law marriage if the parties continue to live together as husband and wife after the removal of the legal impediment. *Id.*

A present agreement to enter into the marriage relationship does not require any particular words, and an agreement may be inferred from the circumstances. *Id.* at 407–408. A conditional agreement to marry, or an agreement to marry in the future is insufficient to establish this requirement. *Id.* at 406–407.

Finally, in order to perfect a common–law marriage, the parties must consummate the marriage; that is, once parties with legal capacity to marry presently agree to become husband and wife, they must live in a way that presents themselves as married. *See* Milot, *supra*, at 70, n.32; Crawley, *supra*, at 408–409; *see generally* Annotation, *Validity of Common–Law Marriage in American Jurisdictions*, 39 A.L.R. 538 (1925), supplemented by 60 A.L.R. 541 (1929); 94 A.L.R. 1000 (1935), 133 A.L.R. 758 (1941). Crawley, *supra*, at 409 describes the factors relevant to determining whether a marriage exists as follows:

> A sexual relationship between the parties is not an indispensable element of cohabitation, and consummation is not established by mere proof that the parties lived, ate, and slept together. Consummation can be proved by evidence that, among other things, the parties considered themselves married, shared household duties and expenses, maintained joint accounts, filed joint tax returns, used the same surname, referred to or introduced

each other as a spouse, listed themselves as "married" on legal and other documents, or reared children together. Perhaps the most crucial part of establishing the consummation requirement is proving that the parties gained public recognition of their status as husband and wife.

2. Civil Union

Vermont, Connecticut, California, Maine, Hawaii, New Jersey, and the District of Columbia legalized "civil unions," reciprocal benefits, or domestic partner laws. *See* Toni Lester, Adam and Steve vs. Adam and Eve: *Will the New Supreme court Grant Gay's the Right to Marry*, 14 Am. U.J. Gender Soc. Pol'y & L. 253, 263 & nn.59-65 (2006). While similar, civil unions and domestic partnerships are not marriages.

For example, under Vermont law, a "civil union" means that two eligible persons have established a relationship recognized under Vermont law and are entitled to receive the benefits and protections and be subject to the responsibilities of spouses. *Id.* To establish a civil union in Vermont, the parties must (1) not be a party to another civil union or a marriage; (2) be of the same sex and therefore excluded from the marriage laws of this state; and (3) meet the criteria and obligations set forth in 18 V.S.A. Chapter 106. 15 VT. STAT. ANN. § 1202. Vermont law, however, does not recognize a "civil union as a 'marriage.'" *Rosengarten v. Downes*, 71 Conn. App. 372, 376–77 (Ct. App. Ct. 2002). In Vermont, marriage is defined as "the legally recognized union of one man and one woman." 15 VT. STAT. ANN. § 1201(4). As such, a party to a civil union pursuant to Vermont law would not constitute a "spouse" for purposes of the FMLA. The FMLA looks to state marriage law to determine who is a spouse. *See* 29 CFR 825.113(a).

Because marriage is governed by state law, employers faced with claims of civil unions of same sex partners are well advised to consult the law of the state where the union is claimed to be legally sanctioned. As set forth more fully below in the discussion of "The Defense of Marriage Act and Domestic Partners", the reference to state marriage laws as the basis for determining who is a spouse is moot.

3. Divorce

As with its creation, state law governs the dissolution of a marriage. *See* Milot, Note, 87 Va. L. Rev., at 704, n. 13 (citing *Loughran v. Loughran*, 292 U.S. 216, 223 (1933)). Once entered into, a marriage, statutory or common law, can only be dissolved by death or divorce. *Id.* at 708; Crawley, Article, 29 Cumb. L. Rev., at 404 (describing Alabama law). There is no such thing as a common–law divorce by mutual agreement of the parties without state action to end the marriage. Milot, at 708; Crawley, at 405, 410 (describing Alabama law specifically). *See also* Theodore F. Haas, *The Rationality and Enforceability of Contractual Restrictions on Divorce*, 66 N.C. L. Rev. 879, 881 & n. 13 (1988).

For purposes of the FMLA, this means that, until divorce or death, an employee's spouse is the person whom he or she is married to, no matter what the status of the marriage. For example, although Robert is married to Amy, they have lived apart for five years. Robert lives in California and Amy lives in New York. Both have found other partners. For the past three years, Robert has lived with Cathy and her two children. Amy has lived with Don for about the same amount of time. Amy is pregnant and due in six months. Robert and Amy have not spoken for years. Robert asks for leave to care for Amy, who is hospitalized as a result of a difficult pregnancy. You believe that Robert just wants to go to New York for a few weeks during the summer, your busiest season. Is Robert entitled to FMLA leave?

Absent a divorce, Amy is still Robert's spouse and, all things being equal, he would be entitled to FMLA leave to care for Amy. Under similar circumstances, Robert could not take FMLA leave to care for Cathy even though he lives with her because he is still married to Amy, a legal impediment to the creation of a common–law marriage.

Similarly, because dissolution of a common–law marriage requires state action (generally in the form of a court decree), an employer should not accept an employee's representation that he or she needs FMLA leave to care for what amounts to the common–law spouse du jour. For example, Dan, a federal employee in Colorado (which recognizes common–law marriages) lived openly for 20 years as husband and wife with Jan, his high school sweetheart. They were never formally married. Jan left Dan to fulfill her lifelong dream of joining the circus. Dan has dated since Jan left. His current flame is Marsha, who moved in with Dan two months ago. Dan could not take FMLA leave to care for Marsha should she develop a serious health condition because he never divorced Jan. Dan could, however, take FMLA leave to care for Jan after she suffered severe injuries from a freak trapeze accident.

An agency is well-advised to have the employee identify in writing the name of his common-law spouse. Once identified, the employee will be forever married to that individual until they are formally divorced. As set forth more fully in Chapter 9, "Documentation Requirements," an employing agency can require both proof of a marriage, including a common-law marriage, and proof of a divorce or the death of a spouse, which also ends the marriage.

B. THE DEFENSE OF MARRIAGE ACT AND DOMESTIC PARTNERS

1. The FMLA and Domestic Partners

All of the federal sector FMLA laws define "spouse" to exclude domestic partners in committed relationships (including same-sex relationships). As set forth in the Preamble to Title I, see Preamble, 29 CFR 825.113, regarding the definition of "spouse" as meaning "a husband or wife, as the case may be," Senator Nickles noted in the Cong. Rec. S1347 (Feb. 4, 1993):

> This is the same definition that appears in Title 10 of the United States Code (10 U.S.C. 101).
>
> Under this amendment, an employer would be required to give an eligible female employee unpaid leave of care for her husband and an eligible male employee unpaid leave to care for his wife. No employer would be required to grant an eligible employee unpaid leave to care for an unmarried domestic partner.
>
> This simple definition will spare us a great deal of costly and unnecessary litigation. Without this amendment, the bill would invite lawsuits by workers who unsuccessfully seek leave on the basis of their unmarried adult companions.

2. Defense of Marriage Act of 1996

The enactment of the Defense of Marriage Act of 1996 (DOMA), Public Law 104-99 (1996) further solidified the limitation of the term "spouse" to married, heterosexual couples and the exclusion of domestic partners.

The DOMA has two provisions: (1) it clarifies that the Full Faith and Credit Clause of the Constitution does not require that same-sex marriages be recognized by other states; and (2) it defines the words "marriage" and "spouse", for purposes of federal law, as the union of one man and one woman. *See* 28 USC 1738C; 1 USC 7.

a. Full Faith and Credit Clause of the Constitution

The Constitution of the United States, U.S. Const., Article IV, § 1, requires

> [f]ull faith and credit shall be given in each State to the public Acts, Records, and judicial Proceedings of every other State.

Rosengarten v. Downes, 71 Conn. App. 372, 385-386, 802 A.2d 170, 178-179 (Ct. App. Ct. 2002), explained the operation of the Full Faith and Credit Clause as follows:

> That is, the full faith and credit clause, in its design to transform the States from independent sovereigns into a single unified Nation and, directs that a State, when acting as the forum for litigation having multistate aspects or implications, respect the legitimate interests of other States and avoid infringement upon their sovereignty, but because the forum State is also a sovereign in its own right, in appropriate cases it may attach paramount importance to its own legitimate interests. *The clause (and the comparable due process clause standards) obligates the forum State to take jurisdiction and to apply the law of another State, subject to the forum's own interest in furthering its public policy. In order "for a State's substantive law to be selected in a constitutionally permissible manner, that State must have a significant contact or significant aggregation of contacts, creating state interests, such that choice of its law is neither arbitrary nor fundamentally unfair."* (Emphasis in original). Congressional Research Service, Library of Congress, The Constitution of the United States of America, Analysis and Interpretation (J. Killian & G. Costello eds. 1996), Art. IV, Sec. 1, pp. 855-56, *citing Allstate Ins. Co. v. Hague*, 449 U.S. 302, 101 S. Ct. 633, 66 L. Ed. 2d 521 (1981); *Nevada v. Hall*, 440 U.S. 410, 99 S. Ct. 1182, 59 L. Ed. 2d 416 (1979); Carroll v. Lanza, 349 U.S. 408, 75 S. Ct. 804, 99 L. Ed. 1183 (1955); *Alaska Packers Assn. v. Industrial Accident Commission*, 294 U.S. 532, 55 S. Ct. 518, 70 L. Ed. 1044 (1935).

Addressing the Full Faith and Credit Clause of the Constitution, the DOMA, 28 USC 1738C, states:

> No State, territory, or possession of the United States, or Indian tribe, shall be required to give effect to any public act, record, or judicial proceeding of any other State, territory, possession, or tribe respecting a relationship between persons of the same sex that is treated as a marriage under the laws of such other State, territory, possession, or tribe, or a right or claim arising from such relationship.

According to the legislative history, the second provision in the DOMA was enacted to allow each state to decide for itself whether it wants to grant legal status to same-sex "marriages." The provision was necessary, according to the legislative history, because of the possibility that Hawaii might sanction same-sex "marriage" under its state law, and other states might be placed in the position of having to give "full faith and credit" to Hawaii's interpretation of what constitutes "marriage" pursuant to the "Effect" clause of Article IV, § 1 of the Constitution (the Full Faith and Credit Clause). Although "conflicts of law" principles did not necessarily compel that result, the legislative history indicates that a number of states were sufficiently alarmed at that prospect that they initiated legislation to defend themselves against being constitutionally compelled to acknowledge same-sex "marriage", and Congress decided to take federal action.

Prior to the enactment of the DOMA, the Supreme Court of Hawaii ruled that same sex marriages were legal. The decision was later overturned by an act of the Hawaii legislature.

Law review articles by advocates of same-sex marriage have roundly attacked the DOMA. David Orgon Coolidge, *Playing the Loving Card: Same-Sex Marriage and the Politics of Analogy*, 12 BYU J. Pub. L. 201, 229 & n.110 (1998). The DOMA has, thus far, survived constitutional attack. *See e.g., Rosengarten v. Downes*, 71 Conn. App. 372, 376–77 (Ct. App. Ct. 2002) (rejecting constitutional argument that Connecticut should give effect to Vermont civil union law for purposes of dissolution of the union under Connecticut family law).

b. "Marriage" and "Spouse" Defined

The DOMA established a federal definition of "marriage" and "spouse." Specifically, the DOMA, 1 USC 7, provides:

> In determining the meaning of any Act of Congress, or of any ruling, regulation, or interpretation of the various administrative bureaus and agencies of the United States, the word 'marriage' means only a legal union between one man and one woman as husband and wife, and the word 'spouse' refers only to a person of the opposite sex who is a husband or a wife.

c. DOMA "Marriage" and "Spouse" and the FMLA

The DOL subsequently adopted the DOMA definitions of the terms "marriage" and "spouse" for purposes of Title I of the FMLA. *See* DOL WH Advisory Opinion No. 98 (Nov. 18, 1999). The adoption of the DOMA definitions effectively negate the regulatory language interpreting Title I that defines "spouse" by reference to the law of the state where the employee resides for purposes of marriage. *See* 29 CFR 825.113(a). Because the DOMA mandates application of a uniform definition of "marriage" and "spouse" to all federal statutes, including all four federal sector FMLA laws, resorting to state marriage laws is no longer necessary.

The regulations interpreting the definition of "spouse" under Title II appear to incorporate the language of the DOMA. *See* 5 CFR 630.1202 (definition of "spouse"). As such, while Title II uses different language to define "spouse" than is used by Title I or the CAA, the practical effect is the same: domestic partners are excluded. Of course, leave, other than that protected by the FMLA, that might be available pursuant to agency policy or practice could be used. As such, leave, however, would not carry the job protections of the FMLA. Nor could it be counted against an employee's FMLA leave entitlement.

Since the enactment of the DOMA, the Massachusetts Supreme Court ruled that the state's ban on same-sex marriage was unconstitutional and gave the Massachusetts legislature 180 days to change the law. *See Goodrich v. Dept. of Public Health*, 798 N.E. 2d 941 (Mass. 2003). Massachusetts convened a constitutional convention, but ultimately failed to overturn Goodrich. Massachusetts is the first and only state to recognize same-sex marriages. For FMLA purposes, because DOMA is controlling, Massachusetts' recognition of same-sex marriages has no effect.

III. SON OR DAUGHTER

The uniform definition of "son or daughter" under the FMLA in the federal sector has two factors: relationship and age. A "son or daughter" means: (1) a biological, adopted, or foster child, a stepchild, a legal ward, or a child of a person standing *in loco parentis*, and (2) who is either under age 18, or age 18 or older and "incapable of self-care" because of a mental or physical disability. *See* 29 USC 2611(12); 29 CFR 825.113(c); 5 USC 6381(6); 5 CFR 630.1202 (definition of son or daughter); S. Res. 242, Cong. Rec. S3959–S3997 (April 23, 1996); 29 CFR 825.113(c); *accord Martin v. Brevard County Public Schools*, No. 6:05-cv-971-Orl.22KRS, 2007 U.S. Dist. LEXIS 9910, at *22 (M.D. Fla. Feb. 13, 2007); *Cool v. BorgWarner Diversified Transmission Products, Inc.*, No. IP 02–0960–C–B/S, 2004 U.S. Dist. LEXIS 570, n.3 (S.D. Ind. Jan. 12, 2004).

A. RELATIONSHIP REQUIREMENT

The relationship requirement included in the definition of the term "son or daughter" is broad, covering virtually every type of familial relationship involving a son or daughter. This is as intended. As set forth in the FMLA's legislative history, Preamble, 29 CFR 825.112:

> The terms "parent" and "son or daughter"…reflects the reality that many children in the United States today do not live in traditional "nuclear" families with their biological father and mother. Increasingly, those who find themselves in need of workplace accommodation of their child care responsibilities are not the biological parent of the children they care for, but their adoptive, step, or foster parents, their guardians, or sometimes simply their grandparents or other relatives or adults. This legislation deals with such families by tying the availability of "parental" leave to the birth, adoption, or serious health condition of a "son or daughter" and then defining the term "son or daughter" to mean "a biological, adopted, or foster child, a stepchild, a legal ward, or a child of a person standing in loco parentis.…"

Accord Novak v. MetroHealth Med. Center, No. 1:04CV2253, 2005 U.S. Dist. LEXIS 29677, at *11 (N.D. Ohio Nov. 28, 2005).

1. *In Loco Parentis*

A covered "son or daughter" includes a child of a person standing *in loco parentis*. *See* 29 CFR 825.113(c); 5 CFR 630.1202 (definition of "son or daughter"); S. Res. 242, Cong. Rec. S3959–S3997 (April 23, 1996); 29 CFR 825.113(c)(3). Persons who are *in loco parentis* include those with day–to–day responsibilities to care for and financially support a child. A biological or legal relationship is not necessary. 29 CFR 825.113(c)(3); 5 CFR 630.1202 (definition of *in loco parentis*); S. Res. 242, S3959–S3997 (April 23, 1996); 29 CFR 825.113(c)(3); *accord Brevard County Public Schools*, 2007 U.S. Dist. LEXIS 9910, at *22; *BorgWarner Diversified Transmission Products, Inc.*, 2004 U.S. Dist. LEXIS 570, n.3; *Krohn v. Forsting*, 11 F. Supp. 2d 1082, 1091 (E.D. Mo. 1998).

Note that the regulations have two requirements: day–to–day care responsibilities and financial support.

For example, Lori and her 12–year–old daughter, Nicole, live with Lori's parents. Lori's Army reserve unit is activated, and she leaves for Afghanistan. During her absence, Lori's parents take care of Lori's daughter, including making sure she does her homework, disciplining her when she misbehaves, paying for her food and giving her an allowance. While Lori is in Afghanistan, Nicole is injured in an accident requiring hospitalization. Lori's father, Steve, requests FMLA leave to comfort Nicole in the hospital. Although she is technically his granddaughter, Nicole would be considered to be Steve's "son or daughter" within the meaning of the FMLA, because he has day–to–day responsibility to care for and financially support Nicole during the period for which FMLA leave is requested.

There is no minimum period of time which an eligible employee must hold an *in loco parentis* relationship with a child for the child to qualify as that employee's son or daughter for purposes of the FMLA. Theoretically, an employee looking after a friend's child for a week while the friends are away could qualify. However, while there is no minimum temporal requirement to reach *in loco parentis* status, there is the requirement that the eligible employee have day–to–day responsibility for the care and financial support of the child.

In this example, the employee looking after the neighbor's children while the parents are away for the week would certainly meet the day–to–day care responsibility prong. Good arguments could be made both for and against a determination that the employee had day–to–day financial responsibility for the neighbor's child during the week.

Unfortunately, there is no case law or other guidance on this issue. In the absence of further guidance, federal employers should proceed with caution.

2. Current "Son or Daughter"

While potentially broad, the relationship requirement is tempered by the condition that an individual must qualify as a "son or daughter" of an employee *during the period for which FMLA leave is requested*. This temporal condition is demonstrated by the requirement that an eligible employee is entitled to FMLA leave to "care for the employee's spouse, son, daughter, or parent with a serious health condition." *See* 29 CFR 825.112(a)(3). Plainly, during the period of FMLA leave, the individual must be a "son or daughter" to the employee.

Whether an individual meets the definition of a son or daughter during the period of FMLA leave depends on the permanency of the relationship at issue. The relationships covered in the definition of an FMLA "son or daughter" range from quite temporary to permanent. For example, once paternity is established, a biological son or daughter of an employee is always the son or daughter of the employee, including during all periods of FMLA leave. With biological children of an eligible employee, the only real issue is whether the child meets the age requirements to be considered an FMLA covered "son or daughter."

In contrast to the stability of an established biological relationship, "son or daughter" relationships involving foster children, stepchildren, legal wards, adoptive children or *in loco parentis* relationships are often temporary. If this temporary relationship is extinguished before an eligible employee takes FMLA leave, the employee is not entitled to take FMLA leave to care for this individual because the individual no longer meets the definition of a covered son or daughter. The following examples illustrate the point.

- With the best of intentions, Mary adopts a severely disabled six-year-old child. The financial and personal demands prove to be too much, and Mary is forced to return the child to the foster home. The adoption is nullified. Mary subsequently learns that the child is severely ill and asks her federal agency employer for FMLA leave to be with the child before he dies. Because the child is not a covered "son or daughter" of the employee at the time of FMLA leave, Mary is not entitled to FMLA leave.

- Tom was married to Nancy for ten years. Nancy brought with her Zack, a child from a previous marriage. Tom became very close to Zack. Despite their best efforts, Tom and Nancy divorced. Tom remained close to Zack, frequently taking him fishing, hiking, and skiing. Tom also remained involved with Zack's school activities. Zack was injured in a playground accident. Tom requested FMLA leave to visit Zack in the hospital. Although Zack was Tom's stepchild for ten years, that relationship extinguished when Tom and Nancy divorced. As such, Tom is not entitled to FMLA leave.

- Joan and her husband take in minor foster children who the state has removed from their homes due to neglect. They are paid by the state for providing this service. The foster care placements generally do not last more than six months, after which the children are either returned to their parents, sent to live with relatives or sent to a more permanent state-run foster home. In ten years, Joan has had close to 35 foster children pass through her home. Joan requested FMLA leave to visit one of the children that passed through her home last year. The child is dying of cancer. Because the "son or daughter" relationship extinguished a year before the intended leave, Joan is not entitled to FMLA leave.

- Paula is a single mother of Benjamin, a four year old. Paula and Benjamin live with her parents, Walter and Jean. Paula is hopelessly addicted to heroin. Paula overdoses and is hospitalized. The state appoints Walter and Jean as the legal guardians of Benjamin while Paula cleans up her act. To avoid jail, Paula is remanded to a drug recovery program for 90 days, followed by close medical monitoring for six months in a halfway house.

    Paula recovers and is released by the courts. The court also terminated the legal guardianship of Walter and Jean, and Ben is returned to Paula. Ben subsequently falls ill with chickenpox and is bedridden. Walter asks for FMLA leave to visit Ben. Because the legal guardianship has ended, Ben is no longer a covered son or daughter of Walter at the time of the FMLA leave.

Of course, even in temporary relationships, changes do not always have to lead to the disqualification of a child from the definition of an FMLA-covered "son or daughter." For example, a child who was originally placed with a foster care family for a short period of time could later be adopted by that family. An eligible employee could be appointed legal guardian over a former stepchild.

The key to determining whether a son or daughter meets the current relationship requirement for FMLA coverage is to look at the relationship of the individual to the eligible employee at the time FMLA leave is to commence. For biological relationships, the individual will always meet the relationship requirement of the "son or daughter" definition, no matter what the quality of that relationship. For other than biological relationships, look at the status of the relationship at the time FMLA leave is to commence to determine whether the individual is a "son or daughter."

B. AGE REQUIREMENT

In addition to meeting the relationship requirement at the time leave commences, an individual must also meet the age requirements to be considered a "son or daughter" within the meaning of the FMLA. Two age requirements are contained in the FMLA: (1) children under 18 years of age; and (2) children 18 years of age or older. *Bagley v. Regis Corp.*, No. 3:03-CV-2908-M, 2004 U.S. Dist. LEXIS 24783, at *16 (N.D. Tex. Dec. 7, 2004).

1. Children Under 18 Years of Age

A "son or daughter" within the meaning of the FMLA includes all children of an eligible employee who are under 18 years of age, and who have a biological, adoptive, foster care, stepchild, legal ward, or *in loco parentis* relationship with the eligible employee at the time of FMLA leave. *See* 29 USC 2611(12)(A); 29 CFR 825.113(c); 5 USC 6381(6)(A); 5 CFR 630.1202 (definition of son or daughter); S. Res. 242, Cong. Rec. S3959-S3997 (April 23, 1996); 29 CFR 825.113(c).

2. Children 18 Years of Age or Older

The FMLA applies only to certain adult children of an eligible employee. Specifically, children age 18 or older fall within the definition of an FMLA-covered "son or daughter" only where the child is incapable of self-care because of a mental or physical disability. 29 USC 2611(12)(B); 29 CFR 825.113(c); 5 USC 6381(6)(B); 5 CFR 630.1202 (definition of son or daughter); S. Res. 242, Cong. Rec. S3959-S3997 (April 23, 1996); 29 CFR 825.113(c)(3); *see Novak v. MetroHealth Med. Center*, No. 1:04CV2253, 2005 U.S. Dist. LEXIS 29677, at *11 (N.D. Ohio Nov. 28, 2005); *Allender v. Raytheon Aircraft Co.*, 339 F. Supp. 2d 1196, 1203, n.2 (D. Kan. 2004) (FMLA leave not required if leave is requested to attend to a child who is not a minor, unless the child is incapable of self-care because of a mental or physical disability); *Blackburn v. Potter*, No. IP 01-1645-C-B/S, 2003 U.S. Dist. LEXIS 5269, at *14 (S.D. Ind. March 31, 2003).

a. Incapable of Self-Care

"Incapable of self-care" means that the age 18 or older child requires active assistance or supervision to provide daily self-care in three or more of the "activities of daily living" (ADLs) or "instrumental activities of daily living" (IADLs). 29 CFR 825.113(c)(1); 5 CFR 630.1202 (definition of son or daughter); S. Res. 242, Cong. Rec. S3959-S3997 (April 23, 1996); 29 CFR 825.113(c)(1).

ADLs include adaptive activities such as caring appropriately for one's grooming and hygiene, bathing, dressing and eating. 29 CFR 825.113(c)(1); 5 CFR 630.1202 (definition of "son or daughter"); S. Res. 242, Cong. Rec. S3959-S3997 (April 23, 1996); 29 CFR 825.113(c)(1); *See Bagley v. Regis Corp.*, No. 3:03-CV-2908-M, 2004 U.S. Dist. LEXIS 24783, at *16 (N.D. Tex. Dec. 7, 2004) (citing 29 CFR 825.113(c)(2)), *aff'd*, 2004 U.S. App. LEXIS 20578 (5th Cir. 2004).

IADLs include cooking, cleaning, shopping, taking public transportation, paying bills, maintaining a residence, using telephones and directories, using a post office, etc. 29 CFR 825.113(c)(1); 5 CFR 630.1202 (definition of son or daughter); S. Res. 242, Cong. Rec. S3959-S3997 (April 23, 1996); 29 CFR 825.113(c)(1). The list of IADLs does not appear to be exclusive. *See Navarro v. Pfizer Corp.*, 261 F.3d 90, 96 (1st Cir. 2001) (adding doing housework to the list of IADLs); *Bryan v. Delbar Products, Inc.*, 18 F. Supp. 2d 799, 803, n.2 (M.D. Tenn. 1998) (adding personal transportation to the list, the court appeared to give credence to plaintiff's argument that the list of IADLs provided in the regulation is not comprehensive). There are no similarly reported cases interpreting ADLs.

Note the use of the conjunctive "or" with respect to ADLs and IADLs. To be considered a covered "son or daughter," an age 18 or older child must require active assistance or supervision to provide daily self-care in 3 or more ADLs *or* IADLs. The adult child needs to have 3 or more ADLs *or* IADLs. *See Bryan v. Delbar Products, Inc. et al.*, 18 F. Supp. 2d 799, 803 (M.D. Tenn. 1998) (even assuming that Bryant could engage in ADLs, he satisfied the definition of "incapable of self-care" because he could not engage in IADLs). Nor does the regulation, by its terms, allow an individual to mix ADLs and IADLs to meet the three or more criteria.

To establish that an adult child is incapable of self-care, some medical evidence is necessary. *See Navarro*, 261 F.3d at 96 (1st Cir. 2001) (finding medical evidence that physician confined the child to bed); *Delbar Products, Inc. et al.*, 18 F. Supp. 2d at 803 (M.D. Tenn. 1998) (physician affidavit); *Sakellarion v. Judge & Dolph, Ltd.*, 893 F. Supp. 800, 807 (N.D. Ill. 1995) (absent medical records, plaintiff's own assertion that daughter was incapable of self-care held insufficient).

With a minimum of supporting medical evidence, the courts that have addressed this issue are willing to find that an adult child is incapable of self-care based on conjecture. For example, in *Bryan v. Delbar Products, Inc. et al.*, 18 F. Supp. 2d 799, 803 (M.D. Tenn. 1998), the court based its determination that the plaintiff's adult son was incapable of self-care based on conjecture. The court noted that, since a doctor's note established that the son was unable to perform IADLs after he was released from the hospital, "[i]t is only logical to conclude that [plaintiff's son] could not cook, clean, shop or take public transportation…while he was in the hospital."

Similarly, in *Navarro v. Pfizer Corp.*, 261 F.3d 90, 96 (1st Cir. 2001), after noting the "broad sweep" of the definitions of ADLs and IADLs, the court held that a doctor's note created a sufficient issue of material fact of whether the adult daughter could care for herself to preclude summary judgment. Specifically, based on her confinement to bed for the remainder of her pregnancy by her physician, the court opined, "such a prescription would appear to signal the patient's need for everyday activities such as cooking, cleaning, shopping, and doing housework."

In Novak v. MetroHealth Med. Center, No. 1:04CV2253, 2005 U.S. Dist. LEXIS 29677, at *11 (N.D. Ohio Nov. 28, 2005), the court found that the adult daughter was not incapable of self care where she suffered from post partum depression for only a week, which was treated with medication.

In *Bagley v. Regis Corp.*, No. 3:03-CV-2908-M, 2004 U.S. Dist. LEXIS 24783, at *16 (N.D. Tex. Dec. 7, 2004), *aff'd*, 2004 U.S. App. LEXIS 20578 (5th Cir. 2004), the court found that plaintiff failed to establish that her 18-year-old daughter was incapable of self-care within the meaning of Title I of the FMLA. Plaintiff, the court noted, explained in detail how her daughter was forced to use crutches and a wheelchair to get from point to point, but she failed to allege that her daughter was unable to perform any of her ordinary daily activities without assistance. Instead, plaintiff alleged her daughter was prevented from participating in some school activities, such as drill team. The court found that these were not the kinds of impairments the FMLA was intended to cover.

An employee's need to take leave to care for her 19-year-old daughter during her recovery from surgery for birth by C-section satisfied the "incapable of self-care" requirement for purposes of FMLA leave. In *Blackburn v. Potter*, No. IP 01-1645-C-B/S, 2003 U.S. Dist. LEXIS 5269, at *17 (S.D. Ind. March 31, 2003), the court credited the affidavit testimony of the daughter that she was instructed by her doctor that after delivery she would require regular assistance to clean and dress the incision, cook, bathe, and eat. The daughter further testified that her mother assisted with those tasks in the weeks following her surgery, along with her father, sister, and grandmother. According to the court, "[t]he inability to complete these basic tasks without assistance reasonably places Amanda's condition within the definition of 'incapable of self care.'"

b. Physical or Mental Disability

(1) Definitions

"Physical or mental disability" means a physical or mental impairment that substantially limits one or more of the major life activities of an individual. Regulations at 29 CFR 1630.2(h), (l), and (j), issued by the Equal Employment Opportunity Commission under the Americans with Disabilities Act (ADA), 42 USC 12101, *et. seq.*, define these terms. 29 CFR 825.113(c)(2); 5 CFR 630.1202 (definition of son or daughter); S. Res. 242, Cong. Rec. S3959–S3997 (April 23, 1996); 29 CFR 825.113(c)(2); *accord Novak*, 2005 U.S. Dist. LEXIS 29677, at *11.

A "physical or mental impairment" is defined under the ADA regulations, 29 CFR 1630.2(h), as follows:

(1) Any physiological disorder, or condition, cosmetic disfigurement, or anatomical loss affecting one or more of the following body systems: neurological, musculoskeletal, special sense organs, respiratory (including speech organs), cardiovascular, reproductive, digestive, genito-urinary, hemic and lymphatic, skin, and endocrine; or

(2) Any mental or psychological disorder, such as mental retardation, organic brain syndrome, emotional or mental illness, and specific learning disabilities.

The term "major life activities" is defined as follows under the ADA regulations, 29 CFR 1630.2(l):

Major Life Activities means functions such as caring for oneself, performing manual tasks, walking, seeking, hearing, speaking, breathing, learning, and working.

Note that the ADA definition of "major life activities" shares some similarities with the FMLA definition of "incapable of self-care," in that they both address an individual's ability to care for his or her self. *See* 29 CFR 825.113(c)(1).

The ADA regulation, 29 CFR 1630.2(j)(1), defines "substantially limits" as meaning:

(i) Unable to perform a major life activity that the average person in the general population can perform; or (ii) Significantly restricted as to the condition, manner or duration under which an individual can perform a particular major life activity as compared to the condition, manner, or duration under which the average person in the general population can perform that same major life activity.

With respect to the major life activity of working, the term "substantially limits" means significantly restricted in the ability to perform either a class of jobs or a broad range of jobs in various classes as compared to the average person having comparable training, skills, and abilities. 29 CFR 1630.2(j)(3).

The ADA regulation, 29 CFR 1630.2(j)(2), identifies factors that should be considered in determining whether an individual is substantially limited in a major life activity:

(i) The nature and severity of the impairment;

(ii) The duration or expected duration of the impairment; and

(iii) The permanent or long term impact, or the expected permanent or long-term impact of or resulting from the impairment.

Additional factors that need to be considered in determining whether an individual is substantially limited in the major life activity of "working" are set forth in 29 CFR 1630.2(j)(3)(ii):

(A) The geographic area to which the individual has reasonable access;

(B) The job from which the individual has been disqualified because of an impairment, and the number and types of jobs utilizing similar training, knowledge, skills or abilities, within that geographic area, from which the individual is also disqualified because of the impairment (class of jobs) and/or

(C) The job from which the individual has been disqualified because of an impairment, and the number and types of jobs utilizing similar training, knowledge, skills or abilities, within that geographic area, from which the individual is also disqualified because of the impairment (broad range of jobs in various classes).

For further elaboration on these subjects, *see* Ernest C. Hadley, *A Guide to Federal Sector Disability Discrimination Law and Practice* (Dewey Publications Inc. 2006) and Ernest C. Hadley, *A Guide to Federal Sector Equal Employment Law and Practice* (Dewey Publication, Inc. 2007).

(2) Pre-Existing Disability Not Required

The FMLA regulations do not require that the "mental or physical disability" exist prior to the child's reaching 18 years of age. *See* DOL WH Advisory Opinion No. 51 (Nov. 28, 1994) (the statute, by its terms, makes no distinction between children who were mentally or physically disabled prior to age 18 and those who became disabled after age 18); *Navarro v. Pfizer, Corp.*, 261 F.3d 90, 104 (1st Cir. 2001) (opining that evidence suggested that adult daughter may be disabled due to current, pregnancy–related complications); *Bryant v. Debar Products, Inc. et al.,* 18 F. Supp. 2d 799, 804 (M.D. Tenn. 1998) (adult child's current advanced kidney failure constituted FMLA "disability").

c. Case Law Interpreting FMLA "Disability"

The cases that have had the opportunity to address the adopted ADA definition of "disability" for purposes of determining whether an adult child is a covered "son or daughter" within the meaning of the FMLA have applied ADA case law to interpret key terms. *See Navarro v. Pfizer, Corp.,* 261 F.3d 90, 96–98 (1st Cir. 2001) (citing ADA and Rehabilitation Act case law to interpret "impairment" and "major life activity"); *Bryant v. Debar Products, Inc et al.,* 18 F. Supp. 2d 799, 804 (M.D. Tenn. 1998) (same). It is not clear, however, that the adoption of the ADA definition of "physical or mental disability" by the FMLA includes incorporation of all of the attributes and interpretations given to these terms for purposes of the ADA.

In the only circuit court decision to interpret the meaning of "physical or mental disability" for purposes of determining whether an adult child meets the definition of a covered "son or daughter," the court in *Navarro* held that courts should ignore EEOC interpretative guidance when determining whether an adult child has a disability.

In *Navarro*, Pfizer denied plaintiff's request for a three–month absence to care for her adult child. The adult child was restricted to bed rest by her physician due to high blood pressure in her 36th week of pregnancy. The restriction to bed rest rendered the adult child unable to care for her other children. When plaintiff's request was denied, she left work anyway and was terminated. The district court granted summary judgment to the employer, finding that the condition did not "substantially limit" a major life activity because the condition was temporary and of short duration. The district court relied on EEOC interpretative guidance for its conclusion.

On appeal, the First Circuit reversed the decision of the district court, but agreed with the lower court's findings on several key terms. The court found that plaintiff established that the adult child was "incapable of self–care" based on the child's confinement by her physician to bed rest for the remainder of her pregnancy, indicating the child's need for active assistance or supervision in the performance of everyday activities such as cooking, cleaning, shopping, and doing housework. *Id.* at 96. Analyzing the incorporated ADA regulations, the court found that high blood pressure and complications resulting from a pregnancy constituted "impairments," citing ADA case law. *Id.* The circuit court also found that working, caring for herself, and reproduction were "major life activities" within the meaning of the ADA. *Id.* at 97.

The circuit court disagreed with the lower courts determination that that adult child's impairments did not "substantially limit" the identified major life activities. Specifically, the court disagreed with the district court's reliance on the EEOC interpretive guidance that a "temporary, non–chronic impairment" did not constitute a disability because an impairment of such short duration did not "substantially limit" a major life activity. *Id.* at 99. In the case at hand, the adult child's impairment would last no more than a matter of a few weeks. *Id.*

The First Circuit cited several factors in support of its determination that the lower court erred by applying the EEOC Interpretive Guidance. First, the court determined that the EEOC interpretive guidance was not entitled to the *Chevron* deference when applied in the FMLA context. *Id.* at 99. The court found that to warrant *Chevron* deference, Congress must actually delegate authority to the agency, and the agency must invoke the authority. The EEOC, the court found, never had authority to promulgate regulations pursuant to the FMLA. The adoption by the Secretary of Labor of certain EEOC rules as her own (as happened here) does not automatically equate with the adoption of the EEOC's informal interpretations of those rules.

Second, the court analyzed whether the EEOC interpretive guidance was persuasive authority in accordance with *Skidmore v. Swift & Co.,* 323, U.S. 134, 89 L. Ed. 124 (1944). Under *Skidmore*, courts weigh the "thoroughness evident in [the guidance's] consideration, the validity of its reasoning, its consistency with earlier and later pronouncements, and all other factors which give it power to persuade, if lacking power to control." *Navarro,* 261 F.3d at 99 (citing *Skidmore,* 323 U.S. at 140). In finding "no thoroughness evident in the consideration of the guidance," the court noted that the guidance was not the product of notice–and–comment rulemaking or formal adjudication, that it was not meant to apply in the FMLA context, and that it bore little consistency with other EEOC pronouncements on the FMLA as the EEOC has made no such pronouncements. *Id.* at 100.

Additionally, the court noted that the interpretive guidance impermissibly gave equal weight to all factors that go into the "substantial limitation" determination. Rather, citing Supreme Court case law, the First Circuit held that the three factors contained in the borrowed regulatory definition of "substantially limits" should not be given equal weight, but will depend on the facts of each case based on the present, actual state of the condition. "In turn, this designated point of reference militates against according talismanic effect to factors such as duration and long-term impact, which may require the fact finder to hypothesize as to the future course of the impairment." *Id.* at 100–101.

Finally, and most importantly, the court found that the EEOC interpretive guidance could not be applied to the FMLA because it clashes with the underlying purposes of the FMLA. *Id.* at 101. According to the court, the "ADA and the FMLA have divergent aims, operate in different ways, and offer disparate relief. These dissimilarities argue convincingly that the trio of factors—particularly duration—must be treated somewhat differently in the FMLA context than in the ADA context." *Id.*

As support, the court noted that the concept of disability serves much different functions in the ADA than in the FMLA. In the ADA, a finding of disability is the key that "unlocks the storehouse of statutory protections." *Id.* In contrast, disability becomes relevant under the FMLA only in the relatively rare instance in which an employee seeks FMLA leave to care for a seriously ill child over the age of eighteen. Even then, disability provides only a partial answer to the question of whether the employee is entitled to leave. The minor role that the disability determination plays in the context of the FMLA indicates, "that very little weight should be placed on the duration of an impairment." *Id.* at 101–102.

The court also found that the much lower level of employer engagement and employee rewards in the FMLA (due to the short duration of the leave involved), than in the ADA suggested that Congress did not intend that FMLA litigants be required to make the same durational showing as ADA litigants. *Id.* at 102.

Having established that the differences between the ADA and the FMLA render the durational factor less important under the FMLA, the court held that the purposes of the statute would be frustrated by reading the "implementing regulations through the prism of the EEOC's interpretive guidance." *Id.* The court found that the primary purpose of the FMLA was to balance the demands of the workplace with the needs of families, to promote the stability and economic security of families, and to promote national interests in preserving family integrity. *Id.* (quoting 29 USC 2610(b)(1)). These objectives would be frustrated, the court held, by applying the rigid durational requirement of the EEOC interpretive guidance as it would necessarily require an employee to prove that an impairment is long-standing before it can furnish the basis for FMLA leave. *Id.*

The court concluded that whether an adult child's impairment substantially limits a major life activity should be determined by the application of the borrowed ADA regulations as written, and should consider (a) the nature and severity of the impairment, (b) its expected duration, (c) its anticipated long-term impact, and (d) any other relevant factors. This assessment must be performed on a case-by-case basis, balancing all factors in light of the FMLA's purpose, structure, and provisions for relief. The requisite test is a balancing test: apart from the severity of the impairment, no one factor is indispensable to finding that a disability exists for FMLA purposes. *Id.* at 104.

Applying this rule, the court held that the provisions of 29 USC 2611(12) were satisfied where the employee's adult child was suffering from a severe impairment which had a modest projected duration and as-yet-unquantified long-term impact.

Navarro comes complete with a thorough dissent by the Senior Circuit Judge. Anyone contemplating denying an FMLA leave request or defending the denial of an FMLA request because the adult child did not meet the ADA durational or long-term impact requirements to be considered "substantially limited" is well advised to closely review the dissenting opinion.

Essentially, the dissent argued that the plain words of the statute, as supported by the legislative history, demonstrated that Congress wanted to restrict leave benefits for parents to care for their adult children 18 years and older to only those special cases, where because of some mental or physical disability, the adult child is or remains especially dependent on the parent in the same ways minor children typically are dependent. *Id.* at 106. The dissent found it curious that the majority accepted the Secretary's borrowing from the ADA and the EEOC but then said that the same regulations should mean different things depending on whether used in an ADA case or in an FMLA case. The dissent predicted that the "balancing" approach advocated by the majority would destabilize the meaning of the FMLA in an area needing clarification, and amounted to a preference by the majority to liberally grant leave to parents with sick adult children regardless of Congressional intent. *Id.* at 109.

In *Novak v. MetroHealth Med. Center*, No. 1:04CV2253, 2005 U.S. Dist. LEXIS 29677, at *11 (N.D. Ohio Nov. 28, 2005), the court found that an adult child, who suffered through a difficult pregnancy and post-partum depression, was not disabled within the meaning of the ADA and was not a "daughter" within the meaning of the FMLA. The court noted that the majority of courts have determined that pregnancy is not an ADA-covered disability. It also observed that the post-partum depression for one week following the birth was treated with medication and otherwise did not render the daughter incapable of self acre.

IV. PARENT

"Parent" means a biological parent or an individual who stands or stood *in loco parentis* to an employee when the employee was an FMLA-covered "son or daughter." 29 USC 2611(7); 29 CFR 825.113(b); 5 USC 6381(3); 5 CFR 630.1202 (definition of parent); S. Res. 242, Cong. Rec. S3959–S3997 (April 23, 1996); 29 CFR 825.113(b). Curiously, the regulations defining "parent" do not simply repeat the list of relationships that are included in the definition of a covered "son or daughter." On the other hand, the definition of *in loco parentis* is sufficiently broad to encompass adoptive parents, foster parents, stepparents, and legal guardians as examples of individuals who assumed primary, day-to-day responsibilities to care for and financially support the employee now or during childhood. *See* 29 CFR 825.113(c)(3) (defining *in loco parentis*).

A. CURRENT OR PAST RELATIONSHIP

Parental coverage is broader than coverage of a son or daughter. For a son or daughter, the definition is limited to individuals who fit the definition of son or daughter at the time FMLA leave is taken by the employee. A parental relationship, on the other hand, may be either current or based on a past relationship with the employee. The only proviso to past relationships is that the employee must have been a son or daughter to the individual within the meaning of the FMLA. There is no additional requirement that a past parent have a current relationship with the employee.

For example, biological parents who put their newborn up for adoption immediately after giving birth and who extinguished all parental rights and never had anything to do with the child would still count as a parent under the FMLA 25 years later.

Nor is there a minimum temporal requirement that an individual had to be in the position of a parent to an employee when the employee was a son or daughter within the meaning of the FMLA. As long as the individual assumed primary, day-to-day responsibilities to care for and financially support the employee now (if the employee is below 18 years of age) or during childhood, the individual would satisfy the definition of an FMLA-covered "parent."

For example, when an employee, Kim, was 10 years of age she stayed with an appointed legal guardian, Kathy, for two weeks after a domestic dispute involving her parents. She was returned to her parents on the conclusion of the two-week period. Kathy, the appointed legal guardian, as long as she had the day-to-day responsibility to care for and financially support the employee, would be a parent within the meaning of the FMLA. As a parent, Kathy would be able to take FMLA leave to care for Kim, assuming Kim had a covered condition within the meaning of the Act.

Query whether the regulations' use of the phrase "day-to-day" could be interpreted to suggest a minimum period of time as a parent of two days. The matter has never been litigated.

B. MULTIPLE PARENTS

The FMLA's definition of "parent" permits an eligible employee to have more than two parents. Again, "parent" means a biological parent *or* an individual who stands or stood *in loco parentis* to an employee when the employee was an FMLA-covered "son or daughter."

For example, consider an employee whose biological parents split when he was five years old. The father simply abandoned the family. The mother remarried a year later, but the marriage ended in divorce when the employee was eight. The mother became involved with drugs and Social Services placed the employee with a foster family for six months. After that, the employee's grandparents were appointed to be his legal guardian, and he moved in with them for a year. His mother returned from rehabilitation, free from drug addiction, at which time the employee was reunited with her. When he was 12, his mother remarried and has remained married ever since. In this scenario, the employee has six parents. He has two biological parents, two step fathers from his mother's two marriages, and his two grandparents who served as his parents pursuant to a legal guardianship. All six would meet the definition of an FMLA-covered "parent."

An employee whose mother remarried when he was 18 years old would have only two parents, his biological mother and father. If the employee were subsequently incapable of self-care because of a mental or physical disability, which could occur years later, he would have three parents, as his stepfather would now count, assuming the stepfather had day-to-day responsibility to care for and financially support the disabled, adult child.

V. INDIVIDUALS WHO ARE NOT COVERED BY THE FMLA

To be covered by the FMLA, a federal sector employee's request for FMLA leave to care for someone else must involve a covered individual: a spouse, son or daughter, or parent. If the leave is to care for someone else and does not involve an individual who can fit within one of these definitions, then the leave is not covered by the FMLA. The fact that the individual whom the employee is going to care for is dependent on the employee does not change the outcome. FMLA leave is available to care for certain family members, and only those family members.

A. PARENTS-IN-LAW

In-laws are specifically excluded from coverage under the FMLA. *See* 29 CFR 825.113(b); 5 CFR 630.1202 (definition of parent); S. Res. 242, Cong. Rec. S3959–S3997 (April 23, 1996); 29 CFR 825.113(b); *Lewis v. Potter*, No. C 04-04716 CRB, 2005 U.S. Dist. LEXIS 10445, at *11 (N.D. Cal. May 25, 2006) (FMLA does not cover leave for parents-in law). The reason in-laws are excluded is that the leave entitlement under 102(a)(1)(C) of the FMLA, 29 USC 2612(a)(1)(C), is expressly limited to "care for the…parent, *of the employee*, if such…parent has a serious health condition" (emphasis added). As such, the FMLA does not apply to in-laws of a covered employee, but does apply to the employee's parents. *See* Preamble, 29 CFR 825.113.

B. BROTHERS AND SISTERS

The FMLA does not extend to employee absences to provide care to siblings with a serious health condition. DOL WH Advisory Opinion No. 73 (Oct. 26, 1995). Brothers and sisters are not covered individuals within the meaning of the FMLA.

C. GRANDPARENTS

The FMLA generally does not cover employee absences to care for grandparents with a serious health condition. *Dillion v. Maryland Nat. Capital Park and Planning Commission*, 382 F. Supp. 2d 777, 785 (D. Md. Aug. 18, 2005); *Krohn v. Forsting*, 11 F. Supp. 2d 1082 (E.D. Mo. 1998); *Campbell v. City of Prichard Police Department et al.*, No. 97-0496-AH-C, 1997 U.S. Dist. LEXIS 20463 (S.D. Ala. Nov. 19, 1997); *Bauer v. Dayton-Walther Corp.*, 910 F. Supp. 306, 308, n. 2 (E.D. Ky. 1996), *aff'd*, 118 F.3d 1109 (6th Cir. 1997); DOL WH Advisory Opinion No. 21 (Dec. 7, 1993).

D. OTHER FAMILY MEMBERS

The FMLA would not apply to employee absences to care for uncles, aunts, nephews, nieces, grandchildren, or any other relative or person unless that individual meets the FMLA definition of a spouse, son or daughter, or parent. *Novak v. MetroHealth Med. Center*, No. 1:04CV2253, 2005 U.S. Dist. LEXIS 29677, at *13 (N.D. Ohio Nov. 28, 2005) (FMLA leave not available to grandparent to care for grandchild); *Cool v. BorgWarner Diversified Transmission Products, Inc.*, No. IP 02-0960-C-B/S, 2004 U.S. Dist. LEXIS 570, n. 3 (S.D. Ind. Jan. 12, 2004) (same).

In *AFGE and Dept. of Navy*, 50 FLRA 637 (1995), the union filed a negotiability appeal under section 7105(a0(2)(E) of the Federal Service Labor-Management Relations Statute regarding the propriety of a provision extending FMLA leave benefits where the employee is needed to care for a dependent child regardless of age, an in-law, or grandparent of the employee. The FLRA found that, however beneficial to employees, the proposed extension of FMLA rights and benefits excessively interfered with management's rights. As a result, the provision was nonnegotiable.

E. *IN LOCO PARENTIS* EXCEPTION

The caveat to the general rule excluding all relatives and other individuals who do not meet the FMLA's definitions of a "spouse," "son or daughter," or "parent" is that the definitions of "son or daughter" and "parent" can be stretched to include individuals who stand (parent, son or daughter) or stood (parent) *in loco parentis* to the employee. Depending on the age and circumstances of the individual, he or she could meet the definition of a parent or son or daughter. A few examples will illustrate the point.

- A grandparent was appointed legal guardian of the employee for a period of time when the employee was below 18. The grandparent, who is usually not considered a covered individual within the meaning of the FMLA, is, under these circumstances, considered a covered parent.

- An older sibling takes over day-to-day responsibility for the care and financial support of a minor sister when their parents unexpectedly die. The younger sibling would meet the definition of a son or daughter and the older sibling would be considered a parent (*in loco parentis*) to the younger sister.

- An employee is the uncle to the under-age-18 son of his brother. The brother is called to service in Afghanistan and leaves his son with the employee. The employee has day-to-day care and financial responsibility for his nephew until his brother's return from Afghanistan. The employee is a parent within the definition of the FMLA.

- An employee's over-age-18 brother is paralyzed in a car accident. The paralyzed brother moves into the employee's home. The employee assumes day-to-day responsibility of care and financial responsibility for his brother. The employee requests FMLA leave to care for his paralyzed brother. The brother is an *in loco parentis* son or daughter of the employee, and the employee is the *in loco parentis* parent of his paralyzed brother.

In *Martin v. Brevard County Pub. Schs.*, No. 6:05-cv-971-Orl.22KRS, 2007 U.S. Dist. LEXIS 9910, at *22 (M.D. Fla. Feb. 13, 2007), Martin argued that he was the *in loco parentis* parent of his granddaughter. At the time, Martin lived with his wife and daughter, Brittany, and Brittany's five month old daughter, Hannah. Brittany attended school in addition to serving in the Army Reserves. In April 2004, Brittany's reserve unit was called up to active duty. Martin informed his staff that he would be taking leave to care for his granddaughter for 12 weeks starting May 7. The leave was approved as FMLA leave based on Martin's representations that the leave was FMLA-qualifying. Martin took the leave as scheduled, but Brittany was never called to active duty. Martin nevertheless stayed home and took care of Hannah while his daughter attended school. He also took care of his granddaughter during his daughter's three-day absence to attend Army Reserve drills. When his contract of employment was not renewed, Martin sued alleging violation of the FMLA. The court awarded summary judgment to the defendant employer after finding that Martin was not acting *in loco parentis* to his granddaughter. Looking to state law, the court opined:

> The key to determining whether the relationship of *in loco parentis* is established is found in the intention of the person allegedly *in loco parentis* to assume the status of a parent toward the child. The intent to assume such parental status can be inferred from the acts of the parties. Other factors which are considered in determining whether *in loco parentis* status has been assumed are (1) the age of the child; (2) the degree to which the child is dependent on the person claiming to be standing in loco parentis; (3) the amount of support, if any, provided; and (4) the extent to which duties commonly associated with parenthood are exercised.

The court observed that Brittany, the biological mother, remained at home at all times. The actual household dynamics, the court observed, did not change at all. Martin financially supported Brittany and Hannah both before and during his FMLA leave. He took care of Hannah when his daughter was away at school.

In *Dillion v. Maryland Nat. Capital Park and Planning Commission*, 382 F. Supp. 2d 777, 784 (D. Md. Aug. 18, 2005), the court found sufficient evidence in the record to preclude summary judgment to the employer where the grandmother was *in loco parentis* to the employee when the employee was a child. At the time, the employee provided her employer with a personal statement describing her relationship with her grandmother. It described how she and her mother (who was 16 at the time of the employee's birth) lived with her grandmother for all but a year of her life until high school, and then for an undetermined amount of time after the employee became pregnant at 16 years of age. The statement indicated that the grandmother was at all times financially responsible for the employee.

In *Cool v. BorgWarner Diversified Transmission Products, Inc.*, No. IP 02–0960–C–B/S, 2004 U.S. Dist. LEXIS 570, n.3 (S.D. Ind. Jan. 12, 2004), the employee argued that her grandchildren were her "son" and her "daughter" within the meaning of Title I of the FMLA because she was *in loco parentis*. Cool's son asked her to take care of his son and daughter because he was called up for deployment by the U.S. Navy. Cool's son signed a Special Power of Attorney giving Cool "full authority for the care, custody, and control of [his] minor children" as well as "the authority to act *in loco parentis*." The Special Power of Attorney went into effect on August 24. Cool traveled to Georgia on August 17 to begin care of the children in the home of her son. Unfortunately, the court elected not to decide whether Cool was an *in loco parentis* parent of her grandchildren. Rather, the court held that, regardless of whether Cool's grandchildren could qualify as her son and daughter under the FMLA, they could not justify her leave request because Cool did not give BorgWarner sufficient notice that the children suffered from a serious health condition.

In *Krohn v. Forsting*, 11 F. Supp. 2d 1082, 1091 (E.D. Mo. 1998), the court opined that while the FMLA does not authorize leave for the care of grandparents, plaintiff could be entitled to FMLA leave to care for her grandmother if the grandmother stood in *loco parentis* to plaintiff. Plaintiff failed to offer any evidence that her grandmother stood *in loco parentis* to her.

VI. CONFIRMATION OF FAMILIAL RELATIONSHIP

An employer is permitted to request documentation to confirm that the individual is the spouse, parent, or son or daughter of the employee as claimed. *See* 29 CFR 825.113(d); S. Res. 242, Cong. Rec. S3959–S3997 (April 23, 1996), 29 CFR 825.113(d). [For additional discussion of documentation requirements, see Chapter 9, "Documentation Requirements."]

CHAPTER 7
COVERED CONDITIONS

I. OVERVIEW

In order for an eligible employee to be entitled to the benefits and protections of the Act, the need for leave must be for a covered condition within the meaning of the FMLA. While broad, the circumstances that may fit within the scope of the FMLA covered conditions are not limitless. The four statutory situations for which FMLA leave is available are:

- Because of the birth of a son or daughter of the employee and in order to care for such son or daughter;

- Because of the placement of a son or daughter with the employee for adoption or foster care;

- In order to care for the spouse, or a son, daughter, or parent, of the employee, if such spouse, son, daughter, or parent has a serious health conditions; or

- Because of a serious health condition that makes the employee unable to perform the functions of the position of said employee.

29 USC 2612(a)(1)(A)–(D) (Title I); 5 USC 6382 (A)(1)(A)–(D) (Title II); 2 USC 1312(a)(1) (incorporating § 102 of Title I, 29 USC 2612, into CAA); 3 USC 412(a)(1) (incorporating § 102 of Title I, 29 USC 2612, into PEOAA); *See generally Urban v. Dolgencorp of Texas, Inc.*, 393 F.3d 572 (5th Cir. 2004); *Brockman v. Wyoming Dept. of Family Services*, 342 F.3d 1159, 1164 (10th Cir. 2003), *cert. denied*, 540 U.S. 1219 (2004); *McKinzie v. Sprint/United Management Co.*, No. 03–2348–GTV, 2004 U.S. Dist. LEXIS 23417, at *27 (D. Kan. Nov. 16, 2004); *Sabbrese v. Lowe's Home Centers, Inc.*, 320 F. Supp. 2d 311, 321 (W.D. Pa. June 9, 2004); *Jarjoura v. Ericsson, Inc.*, 266 F. Supp. 2d 519, 528 (N.D. Tex. 2003), *aff'd*, 2003 U.S. App. LEXIS 25515 (5th Cir. 2003); *Phillips v. Leroy-Somer North America*, No. 01–1046–T, 2003 U.S. Dist. LEXIS 5334, at *5 (W.D. Tenn. March 31, 2003).

Implementing regulations have further expanded the statutory covered conditions. *See* 29 CFR 825.112, 825.114–825.118, 825.800 (Title I); 5 CFR 630.1201, 630.1203 (Title II); and S. Res. 242, Cong. Rec. S3959, S3962–63, S3977 (April 23, 1996); 29 CFR 825.112, 825.114–825.118, 825.800; *see Lukacinsky v. Panasonic Service Co.*, No. 03–40141–FDS, 2004 U.S. Dist. LEXIS 25846, at *29, n.10 (D. Mass. Nov. 29, 2004) (DOL regulations provide a more comprehensive definition of FMLA "serious health condition"). The PEOAA has not issued regulations implementing application of the FMLA. For purposes of the FMLA, the PEOAA follows the regulations implementing Title I. *See* 3 USC 412(a)(1) (incorporating § 102 of Title I, 29 USC 2612 into PEOAA), § 455 (applying the most relevant substantive executive agency regulation promulgated to implement statutory provision at issue in a proceeding). As in other areas, there are substantial similarities and differences between the four federal sector variants of the FMLA when it comes to covered conditions.

If the need for leave does not fit within an FMLA–covered condition, the leave is not FMLA leave. A federal employer would not be able to deduct the leave from the employee's 12–week entitlement. Nor would the leave qualify for the protections of the Act. The leave would not be free from discipline, and the employee would not have the FMLA right to return to work to the same or an equivalent position. Absent FMLA protections, employee rights, if any, may be governed by other laws or federal employer policies. *See Jeremy v. Northwest Ohio Dev. Center*, 210 F.3d 372 (Table), No. 99–3253, 2000 U.S. App. LEXIS 6202 (6th Cir. March 30, 2000) (employee not entitled to FMLA leave because employee is going to jail); *Schaub v. Tech Data Corp.*, No. 4:00–CV–0357–A, 2001 U.S. Dist. LEXIS 2393 (N.D. Tex. March 8, 2001) (leave to attend birth of grandchildren, to attend anger management class, and to attend to personal business not covered by FMLA); *Evans v. Henderson*, No. 99–C–8332, 2001 U.S. Dist. LEXIS 962, at *7 (N.D. Ill. Feb. 5, 2001) (babysitting problems not a reason for FMLA leave); *Magiera v. Ford Motor Co.*, No. 97–C–0421, 1998 U.S. Dist. LEXIS 15792, at *31 (N.D. Ill. Sept. 30, 1998) (FMLA leave not available to allow employees to take time off from employment in order to resolve a dispute with employer over a job assignment).

Section II, "Birth, Adoption, or Foster Care Placement", of this chapter addresses the covered conditions of birth, adoption and foster care placement. Section III, "Serious Health Conditions", discusses covered conditions involving serious health conditions. "Agencies With Mixed FMLA Responsibilities" are addressed in Section IV.

II. BIRTH, ADOPTION, OR FOSTER CARE PLACEMENT

One myth about FMLA leave is that it is only available if someone is seriously ill. That is simply not true. Leave for the birth, adoption, or foster care placement of a son or daughter does not require that anyone be ill for FMLA benefits and protections to apply.

A. BIRTH

1. Title I, the CAA, and the PEOAA: BIRTH

a. General Rule

An eligible employee is entitled to FMLA leave because of the birth of a son or daughter, and to care for the newborn child. 29 USC 2612(a)(1)(A); 29 CFR 825.112(a)(1); 2 USC 1312(a)(1) (incorporating § 102 of Title I, 29 USC 2612, into CAA); S. Res. 242, Cong. Rec. S3959, S3962 (April 23, 1996); 29 CFR 825.112; 3 USC 412(a)(1) (incorporating § 102 of Title I, 29 USC 2612, into PEOAA); *see Hanger v. Lake County*, 390 F.3d 579, at *6 (8th Cir. 2004); *Walker v. Elmore County, Bd. of Ed.*, 379 F.3d 1249 (11th Cir. 2004) (FMLA requires employers to provide eligible employees with up to 12 weeks of unpaid leave to care for a newborn child); *Pharakhone v. Nissan North America, Inc.*, 324 F.3d 405, 407 (6th Cir. 2003); *Bila v. RadioShack Corp.*, No. 03-10177-BC, 2004 U.S. Dist. LEXIS 24649, at *22 (E.D. Mich. Nov. 23, 2004); *Hubins v. Operating Engineers Local Union No. 3*, No. C-04-3091 MMC (Docket No. 4), 2004 U.S. Dist. LEXIS 20376, at *9 (N.D. Cal. Sept. 29, 2004); *Batka v. Prime Charter, Ltd.*, 301 F. Supp. 2d 308, 316 (S.D.N.Y. 2004); *Johnson v. Morehouse College, Inc.,* 199 F. Supp. 2d 1345, 1354 (N.D. Ga. 2002); DOL WH FMLA Advisory Opinion No. 32 (March 24, 1994). [The FMLA terms "son or daughter" are addressed more fully in Chapter 6, "Covered Family Members."]

The statute and the regulations fail to define the key terms of "because of the birth" and "to care for." With respect to the former, the question is the scope of the phrase "because of the birth." The complication here is that incapacity due to pregnancy is also a form of serious health condition. *See* 29 CFR 825.114(a)(2)(ii); S. Res. 242, Cong. Rec. S3959, S3962 (April 23, 1996); 29 CFR 825.114(a)(2)(ii). Assuming that § 825.112(a)(1) is not redundant of § 825.114(a)(2)(ii), "because of the birth" in this context would appear to mean that an eligible employee is entitled to FMLA leave irrespective of whether the employee or employee's spouse suffers from a serious health condition due to pregnancy, child birth, or recovery. The question remains, however, whether "because of the birth" for purposes of § 825.112(a)(1) includes the right to take FMLA leave for prenatal care, for the actual birth of the child, and for recovery from childbirth, absent the presence of a serious health condition.

The issue of prenatal care is addressed below. Arguably, in the absence of further guidance, the phrase "because of the birth" would appear to encompass any need for leave by an eligible employee that is "because of the birth" of a son or daughter. Such needs arguably include prenatal leave, leave to attend to the delivery, and post-delivery leave.

The term "to care for" the newborn child is also undefined in § 825.112(a)(1). The similar term "needed to care for" is, however, defined for purposes of FMLA leave due to a serious health condition. 29 CFR 825.116; S. Res. 242, Cong. Rec. S3959, S3963 (April 23, 1996); 29 CFR 825.116. Given the difference in phrasing, it is not clear that the terms should be similarly interpreted. The argument would be that, if the "to care for" requirement in § 825.212(a)(1) was intended to be interpreted the same as § 825.116, it could have incorporated the definition of the latter by reference. The fact that it did not suggest a difference in meaning.

Those arguments notwithstanding, it is likely that the similarity in the terms will be favorably compared for purposes of determining the scope of the "to care for" requirement in § 825.212(a)(1). For purposes of § 825.116, "needed to care for" encompasses both physical and psychological care. 29 CFR 825.116(a); S. Res. 242, Cong. Rec. S3959, S3963 (April 23, 1996); 29 CFR 825.116(a). It also includes situations where the employee may be needed to fill in for others who are caring for the family member, or to make arrangements for changes in care. 29 CFR 825.116(b); S. Res. 242, Cong. Rec. S3959, S3963 (April 23, 1996); 29 CFR 825.116(b).

The regulations implementing § 825.112 do not address whether "to care for" includes both physical and psychological care. With respect to physical care, as there is nothing in the phrase "to care for" that would prohibit application to situations where physical care of a newborn is needed, it seems highly probable that physical care is a legitimate basis for FMLA leave. Again, such physical care does not require that the newborn son or daughter have a serious health condition within the meaning of the FMLA. If that were the case, the employee might also be entitled to FMLA leave pursuant to a serious health condition. Under § 825.112, the employee is entitled to FMLA leave to provide physical care for the newborn son or daughter even if the son or daughter is 100% healthy.

The legislative history of the FMLA and the comments to the final DOL regulations suggest that psychological care is covered. According to the legislative history, time off to bond with the newborn child was an important motivation for the FMLA. *See* Senate Report 103–3, p. 9. In pertinent part, the legislative history provides:

> These many personal accounts of the importance of family leave are corroborated by experts in the fields of child development and pediatrics. Dr. Ed Zigler, director of the Yale Bush Center on Child Development and Social Policy and former director of the Office of Child Development Policy at the then U.S. Department of Health, Education, and Welfare, testified in strong support of the legislation. The Yale Bush Center had convened a distinguished advisory committee to direct a [two]–year study of our Nation's infant care situation and to evaluate the impact of the changing composition of the workforce on families with infants.… The committee's primary recommendation was for an infant care policy that would allow employees an adequate period of time for parents to care for newborn or newly adopted infants and for mothers to recover from pregnancy and childbirth.… "Parental leave is critical to the healthy development of children and families."

> …Another world–recognized specialist in early childhood development, Dr. T. Berry Brazelton, from Harvard University and Children's Hospital in Boston, also stressed the importance of infant–parent bonding during the first few months of a child's life. He urged that at least one partner have the opportunity to care for a newborn in order to create a strong foundation for the child's later development. The early nurturing and attachment enables the parent to instill in the infant a sense of confidence and of being an important person.

The comments accompanying the issuance of the final DOL regulations implementing Title I of the FMLA also address the availability of bonding time to an eligible employee following the birth of a son or daughter, albeit in the context of adoption. *See* Preamble, 29 CFR 825.112. FMLA leave for adoption is addressed more fully in the next subsection of this chapter.

b. Prenatal Care

It is questionable whether "to care for" under of § 825.112(a) includes the right of an eligible employee to take FMLA leave for prenatal care. The confusion results from the interplay between § 825.212(a) and § 825.212(c). Section 825.212(a) does not define "for the birth of" a son or daughter. As a result, legitimate arguments could be made that "for the birth of" includes actions in preparation for the birth, such as prenatal care. Of course, a strict reading of the phrase "for the birth of" could limit the scope solely to the actual delivery of the baby.

Complicating matters is the language of § 825.212(c). That section recognizes circumstances may require that FMLA leave begin before the actual date of birth of a child. 29 CFR 825.112(c); S. Res. 242, Cong. Rec. S3959, S3962 (April 23, 1996); 29 CFR 825.112(c). An expectant mother may take FMLA leave pursuant to paragraph (a)(4) of this section before the birth of the child for prenatal care or if her condition makes her unable to work. 29 CFR 825.112(c); S. Res. 242, Cong. Rec. S3959, S3962 (April 23, 1996); 29 CFR 825.112(c). Subsection (a)(4) of § 825.112 provides that FMLA leave is available because of a serious health condition that makes the employee unable to perform the functions of the employee's job.

The language of § 825.212(c) suggests that prenatal care is only available when the mother has a serious health condition. That is, it is not available pursuant to § 825.112(a) where the mother does not have a serious health condition. A contrary argument would be that § 825.212(c) does not limit the availability of prenatal leave pursuant to § 825.212(a). Rather, by its terms, § 825.212(c) merely clarifies that leave for prenatal care is also available to the expectant mother/employee when the mother/employee has a serious health condition. *See Dormeyer v. Comerica Bank–Ill.*, No. 96–C–4805, 1997 U.S. Dist. LEXIS 10260, at *10, n.2 (Section 825.114 is unclear as to whether prenatal care received by the employee needs to result in incapacitation in order to be considered as a serious health condition).

Note that § 825.212(a) permits FMLA leave to an eligible employee. Section 825.212(c), on the other hand, limits prenatal care to an expectant mother/employee, not every eligible employee. Fathers who want to take FMLA leave for prenatal care should consider § 825.212(a) as grounds for such FMLA leave. This would be in line with the legislative intent that "[t]he right to take [FMLA] leave applies equally to male and female employees. A father, as well as a mother, can take family leave because of the birth or serious health condition of his child…" S. Rep. 103-3, p. 24.

Finally, neither the statute nor the regulations define "prenatal" for purposes of FMLA leave. Prenatal is defined as occurring, existing, or taking place before birth. Webster's Ninth New Collegiate Dictionary (Merriam-Webster Inc. 1988). It is unclear whether "prenatal" suggests a medical need for leave. Clearly the regulations do not explicitly make such a connection.

c. Leave Conclusion

An employee's entitlement to FMLA leave for the birth of a son or daughter expires at the end of the 12-month period beginning on the date of the birth or placement, unless the employer permits leave to be taken for a longer period. 29 USC 2612(a)(2); 29 CFR 825.201; S. Res. 242, Cong. Rec. S3959, S3964 (April 23, 1996); 29 CFR 825.201. [This subject is addressed more fully in Chapter 10, "Leave Amount and Scheduling."]

To receive the benefits and protections of the Act, leave pursuant to § 825.112(a) for the birth of a son or daughter, or to care for the newborn child must be concluded before the expiration of the 12-month period. There is no authority to provide by regulation that the leave need only begin within the statutory 12-month period. Preamble, 29 CFR 825.212. If an employer provides more generous policies, then the more generous policies would prevail, but such leave beyond what the FMLA requires would not count as FMLA leave. Preamble, 29 CFR 825.112.

The 12-month period for FMLA leave pursuant to § 825.112(a) begins on the date of birth. This is true even if the employee takes FMLA leave prior to the birth, such as for prenatal care. Preamble, 29 CFR 825.212. [For a further discussion of the impact of an employee's taking prenatal leave on the 12-month period in which an employee has to take leave "to care for" the newborn child, see Chapter 10, "Leave Amount and Scheduling."]

d. Documentation

The FMLA permits an agency to request, and an employee to provide, reasonable documentation or a statement confirming family relationship. 29 CFR 825.113(d); S. Res. 242, Cong. Rec. S3959, S3962 (April 23, 1996); 29 CFR 825.113(d). As the need for leave under § 825.212(a) involves the birth of a new family member, the documentation requirement applies. [Documentation of the need for FMLA leave is addressed more fully in Chapter 9, "Documentation Requirements." The matter is also addressed in Chapter 6, "Covered Family Members."]

The documentation may take the form of a simple statement from the employee, a court document, etc. 29 CFR 825.113(d); S. Res. 242, Cong. Rec. S3959, S3962 (April 23, 1996); 29 CFR 825.113(d). The employer is entitled to examine documentation provided, but the employee is entitled to the return of the official document submitted for this purpose. 29 CFR 825.113(d); S. Res. 242, Cong. Rec. S3959, S3962 (April 23, 1996); 29 CFR 825.113(d).

In terms of the birth or to care for the newborn child, the employer could require the employee to provide documentation of the need for such leave. Remember, such documentation would not be in the form of a § 825.306 medical certification, as § 825.112(a) does not require anyone to be ill in order for the eligible employee to be entitled to FMLA leave. However, it would appear permissible for an agency to require an employee to provide medical documentation to establish paternity, at least when the agency has a reasonable basis for the request. The "reasonable" qualifier on an agency's ability to require documentation confirming familial relationship arguably would preclude an agency from asking an eligible employee to produce evidence of paternity where the employee is in a legal marriage. The counter argument would be that "reasonable" only modifies "documentation" and not the agency's ability to request such documentation to confirm the familial relationship between the employee and newborn son or daughter. Why an agency would want to force an employee to confirm paternity when the birth is taking place in the confines of a valid marriage, on the other hand, is another question.

Where the need for leave is for bonding time, documentation confirming same appears scant. An agency might want to ask an employee for a statement that leave is needed for bonding time in order to confirm the purpose of the leave and when the leave begins. Leave for bonding time expires 12 months from the date of the birth. Of course, this may not be necessary if the reason for leave is noted in the leave records.

The regulations are not clear when an agency must request such documentation. The regulations reference an employee's notice of the need for FMLA leave as a pre-condition to an employer's right to request documentation of familial relationship. 29 CFR 825.113(d); S. Res. 242, Cong. Rec. S3959, S3962 (April 23, 1996); 29 CFR 825.113(d).

Presumably, the agency's request should occur shortly after the employee provides notice of the need for FMLA leave for the birth or to care for a newborn son or daughter. The regulations also fail to identify the time frame for an employee to provide such documentation, or the consequences when an employee fails to provide requested documentation of familial relationship. Arguably, an employee who fails to provide such documentation violated one of the prerequisites for the benefits and protections of the FMLA, and FMLA leave could be denied.

e. Availability of Childcare

The implementing regulations fail to address what impact, if any, the availability of child care has on an employee's entitlement to FMLA leave pursuant to § 825.112(a) in order "to care for" a newborn son or daughter. Based on comments in the legislative history, it appears that the availability of childcare has no impact on the employee's right to take FMLA leave. In pertinent part, the legislative history (S. Rep. 103–3, p. 24) provides:

> When both the father and mother, or more than one sibling, are involved in the care of a child…they can take leave at the same time, on an overlapping basis, or sequentially, as long as leave is taken "because of" one of the circumstances specified in Section 102(a). Section 102 makes it possible, among other things, for a father to take leave during his wife's childbirth and recovery, an especially crucial time, even if his wife is herself an employee who is also on leave.

The above suggests that an eligible employee is entitled to FMLA leave for the birth of a child, or to care for the newborn son or daughter irrespective of whether others are available to care for the newborn. Bonding time necessarily requires the presence of the employee, whether or not others are available to assist with care giving.

f. Physical Ability to Return to Work Earlier

The issue here is whether an agency may require a pregnant employee to return to work following childbirth earlier than originally requested because the employee is physically able to return to work. For example, may an employee who requested 12 weeks of FMLA leave for the birth of her child be required to return to work after six weeks of leave if the employee were well enough to return to work. In the comments accompanying the final regulations, the DOL answered in the negative. Because the FMLA allows up to 12 weeks of FMLA leave for the birth *and care* of a child, the DOL opined that an employee may not be required to return to work after six weeks if the employee desires 12 weeks of FMLA leave for the birth and care of a newborn child. Preamble, 29 CFR 825.212.

g. Multiple Births

An eligible employee is not entitled to more than 12 weeks of FMLA leave during the applicable 12-month leave year no matter how many births occur during that leave year. *See* DOL WH FMLA Advisory Opinion No. 45 (Oct. 14, 1994) (multiple births do not entitle the employee to additional FMLA leave beyond the 12 weeks in each leave year). Again, the amount of FMLA leave available to an eligible employee each leave year is fixed at 12 workweeks. The fact that an employee may have multiple opportunities during the leave year to use FMLA leave does not increase the total amount of FMLA leave available to the employee. [For a further discussion of the amount of FMLA leave available to an eligible employee during a leave year, see Chapter 10, "Leave Amount and Scheduling."]

h. Intermittent/Reduced Leave Schedule

Where FMLA leave is taken following the birth or placement of a child, an employee may take leave intermittently or on a reduced leave schedule only if the employer agrees. 29 USC 2612(b)(1); 29 CFR 825.203(b); S. Res. 242, Cong. Rec. S3959, S3964 (April 23, 1996); 29 CFR 825.203(b). If FMLA leave is taken in a single block of time, or if it is taken due to the serious health condition of the mother, son or daughter, the agency's agreement is not required. 29 CFR 825.203(b); S. Res. 242, Cong. Rec. S3959, S3964 (April 23, 1996); 29 CFR 825.203(b).

Note that the regulations apply following the birth of a child. This suggests that an employee need not obtain the agreement of the agency to take leave intermittently or on a reduced leave schedule prior to or on the actual birth date. Of course, this is a bit misleading as the employee needs the permission of the agency to take FMLA leave as he or she would any request for leave. Rather, what the regulation really provides is that an agency may legitimately veto an employee's request for FMLA leave after the birth of a child, where FMLA leave is to be taken on an intermittent or reduced leave schedule basis. The limitation to post–birth leave suggests that an agency may not deny FMLA leave to be taken on an intermittent or reduced leave schedule basis prior to the birth of the child.

It should be noted that the statute does not distinguish between leave taken before or after the birth of a child. *See* 29 USC 2612(b)(1). As such, an argument could be made by agency counsel that § 825.203(b) is invalid as it limits an agency's ability to veto an employee's request for FMLA leave on an intermittent or reduced leave schedule basis in post–birth situations, where such limitation is not reflected in the statute. Rather, consistent with the statute, agencies should be able to deny requests for intermittent or FMLA leave on a reduced leave schedule in all situations regarding the birth of a child and to care for the child, including pre–birth. [How FMLA leave may be taken is discussed more fully in Chapter 10, "Leave Amount and Scheduling."]

i. Paid Leave Substitution

FMLA leave is generally unpaid. 29 USC 2612(c); 29 CFR 825.207(a); S. Res. 242, Cong. Rec. S3959, S3965 (April 23, 1996); 29 CFR 825.207(a). However, the Act allows for the substitution of paid leave for unpaid FMLA leave where the employee has an applicable and accrued paid leave balance. 29 USC 2612(d)(2); 29 CFR 825.207; S. Res. 242, Cong. Rec. S3959, S3965–66 (April 23, 1996); 29 CFR 825.207. When an employee earns or accrues paid vacation, personal or family leave, that paid leave may be substituted for all or part of any (otherwise) unpaid FMLA leave relating to birth, placement of a child for adoption or foster care, or care for a spouse, child or parent who has a serious health condition. 29 CFR 825.207(b); S. Res. 242, Cong. Rec. S3959, S3965 (April 23, 1996); 29 CFR 825.207(b).

An employee is entitled to FMLA leave for the birth and to care for a newborn son or daughter even though the newborn child and/or the mother do not have a serious health condition. As such, in some instances, sick leave would not be an appropriate source from which to draw for substitution of paid leave for unpaid FMLA leave. This is because, generally, sick leave requires that someone be sick. Vacation, personal, or maternity leave are more often a more appropriate source for substitution of paid leave for unpaid FMLA leave in the absence of illness. *See* DOL WH FMLA Advisory Opinion No. 85 (Nov. 18, 1996); DOL WH FMLA Advisory Opinion No. 36 (May 18, 1994).

The Act and implementing regulations provide that the FMLA does not supersede any provision of state or local law that provides greater family and medical leave rights than those established under the FMLA as long as the state or local law has jurisdiction over the employer. DOL WH FMLA Advisory Opinion No. 36 (May 18, 1994). State or local law does not have jurisdiction over the federal government. *Id.* (Postal Service not subject to more generous Wisconsin State FMLA law as such state law would not apply to any federal government employee).

Of course, what accrued paid leave is available for substitution of unpaid FMLA leave will depend on the agency's paid leave policies. The Act neither requires nor prohibits an agency from allowing paid sick leave (or any other paid leave) to be used for the birth or to care for a newborn child. [For a more detailed discussion of paid leave substitution, see Chapter 11, "Substitution of Paid Leave."]

2. Title II

a. General Rule

Title II provides that an employee is entitled to FMLA leave because of the birth of a son or daughter of the employee and in order to care for such son or daughter. 5 USC 6382(a)(1)(A); 5 CFR 630.1203(a)(1); *Bradley v. VA*, No. CH-0752-04-0513-I-1, 2005 MSPB LEXIS 1194, at *11 (Feb. 16, 2005), *pet. denied*, 99 MSPR 402 (2005), *aff'd*, 2006 U.S. App. LEXIS 8506 (Fed. Cir. 2006). [The FMLA terms "son or daughter" are addressed more fully in Chapter 6, "Covered Family Members."]

As under the other federal sector variants of the FMLA, Title II and the OPM implementing regulations fail to define the key terms of "because of the birth" and "to care for." With respect to the former, it is unclear whether "because of the birth" is limited to the actual delivery of the baby, or whether it encompasses prenatal leave. Similarly, it is unclear what is included within the scope of "to care for" the son or daughter. It is therefore uncertain whether such leave is available for both physical and psychological care. Significantly, the statute, the implementing regulations, and the comments accompanying passage of the final regulations, fail to mention "bonding time" as a legitimate basis for an employee "to care for" a newborn child. Bonding time is specifically mentioned in the legislative history of the FMLA as a motivating factor for FMLA leave.

In the absence of further guidance from OPM, agencies are well advised to exercise caution when interpreting "because of the birth" and "to care for" for purposes of granting FMLA leave. Agencies should seriously consider applying the interpretations given to those terms for purposes of Title I. Title II, after all, was formed at the same time as Title I, and the statutory terms regarding leave for the birth and to care for a newborn child are virtually identical. *See e.g.,* 5 USC 6387 (OPM required to issue implementing regulations which, to the extent appropriate are consistent with the DOL regulations implementing Title I of the FMLA). Of course, agencies wanting to take a more restrictive posture could elect to interpret these provisions more narrowly than the comparable provisions under Title I. The argument would be that OPM created these regulations with full knowledge of the final DOL implementing regulations, but failed to incorporate key terms or explanations into the regulations or comments accompanying the final OPM implementing regulations. That failure was deliberate, and, as a result, the OPM regulations may mean something different than the comparable regulations interpreting Title I.

Even if the OPM regulations were viewed as distinct from the comparable regulations interpreting Title I, it would appear highly likely that such regulations will encompass situations involving the need for leave to provide physical comfort and/or care for the newborn child. Whether psychological needs may be stretched to include "bonding time" would appear to be the only issue truly at stake.

b. Prenatal Care

FMLA leave for the birth and care of a newborn son or daughter is available prior to or on the actual date of birth. 5 CFR 630.1203(d). Unlike Title I, the CAA, and the PEOAA, when there is doubt surrounding whether an eligible employee is entitled to FMLA leave prior to the birth absent the presence of a serious health condition, Title II clearly permits such leave. Moreover, the Title II regulation does not use the term "prenatal care" to describe leave prior to the birth of a son or daughter. To the extent that term may be interpreted for purposes of the other federal sector variants of the FMLA as being limited to medical care, such restrictions would not apply to the same leave for purposes of Title II.

c. Leave Conclusion

As under the other federal sector variants of the Act, the entitlement to FMLA leave because of the birth of a son or daughter and in order to care for such son or daughter expires at the end of the 12–month period beginning on the date of the birth. 5 USC 6382(a)(2); 5 CFR 630.1203(d).

OPM indicated that such leave must be finished within 12 months of the birth date, not simply commenced. In the comments to the final regulations (Preamble, 5 CFR 630.1203), OPM observed:

> Three organizations objected to requiring an employee to conclude FMLA leave taken for the birth or placement of a child within 12 months after the birth or placement. The organizations recommended revising the regulations to provide that an employee must commence FMLA leave, but not complete the leave, within one year of the birth or placement. Section 6382(a) states that the entitlement to leave for a birth or placement of a child, family leave must be taken within 12 months following the event. DOL, in its final regulations, also upholds that FMLA leave "must conclude within one year of the birth or placement."

The interaction of the regulations governing the availability of FMLA leave prior to birth combined with the method used to calculate the 12–month leave year and the expiration of the right to FMLA leave for the birth or to care for a newborn, is somewhat confusing and worthy of further explanation. [The matter is addressed more fully in Chapter 10, "Leave Amount and Scheduling."]

Under Title II, the 12–month leave year begins on the date an employee first takes FMLA leave. 5 CFR 630.1203(c). An employee is not entitled to 12 additional workweeks of FMLA leave until the previous 12–month period ends and an event or situation occurs that entitles the employee to another period of FMLA leave. 5 CFR 630.1203(c). Title II also allows an employee to take FMLA leave prior to the birth of a son or daughter. 5 CFR 630.1203(d). Finally, if FMLA leave is taken for the birth and to care for a newborn son or daughter, the right to such leave expires 12 months from the birth date.

According to OPM, the above provisions should *not* be read together as suggesting a new 12–month period. The new 12–week entitlement cannot begin until 12 months after the date of the birth or placement, even if the employee begins FMLA leave prior to the date of birth or placement. Nor should it be read as permitting an employee more than 12 weeks of unpaid leave during a 12-month leave year. *See* Preamble, 5 CFR 630.1203. "Rather, according to the OPM, the result of combining these provisions is that the time period in which an employee may use FMLA leave because of a birth or placement for adoption or foster care may extend into a succeeding 12-month period." Preamble, 5 CFR 630.1203. The OPM illustrated this issue (Preamble, 5 CFR 630.1203) with the following example:

> For example, if an employee invokes his or her entitlement to FMLA leave before the birth or placement for adoption or foster care, the 12-month period begins on that date and ends 12 months later (e.g., June 2, 1996, through June 1, 1997). In addition, the statutory entitlement to FMLA leave for one year after the actual birth or placement may permit an employee to use some FMLA leave in a second 12-month period for the birth or placement (e.g., June 14, 1996, through June 13, 1997). The second 12-month period begins immediately after the expiration of the first 12-month period. The employee may use up to a total of 12 weeks of FMLA leave during the first 12-month period for the birth or placement. During the second 12-month period, the employee would be entitled to use FMLA leave for care of the newborn or adopted child but only for the time period between the end of the first 12-month period and the expiration of the 12-month period after the date of the birth or placement (e.g., June 2, 1997, through June 13, 1997). During any 12-month period an employee may use no more than 12 weeks of FMLA leave. The final regulations have been clarified to state that leave taken for the birth of a child or placement for adoption or foster care may begin prior to or on the actual date of birth or placement.

As set forth more fully in Chapter 10, "Leave Amount and Scheduling," the DOL handles the above-situation differently than OPM.

d. Documentation

An agency may require that an employee's request for leave for the birth and care of a newborn son or daughter be supported by evidence that is administratively acceptable to the agency. 5 CFR 630.1206(f). The regulation fails to identify what might be "administratively acceptable" evidence of such a need for FMLA leave. Presumably, what is administratively acceptable is left to the discretion of the agency.

The regulations fail to identify a time frame for an agency to request administratively acceptable evidence, or for an employee to provide such evidence. An employee who does not comply with the notification requirements in § 630.1206 may not be entitled to FMLA leave. 5 CFR 630.1208(l). The equivocation is because the wording of the regulation links the failure of an employee to provide notice with the failure to provide a medical certification, suggesting that the penalty only applies if the employee fails to meet both the notice and medical certification requirements. [The consequences of an employee's failure to meet the notice requirements of Title II are addressed more fully in Chapter 8, "Notice Requirements."]

e. Availability of Childcare

The statute and the regulations do not address the impact of other caregivers on FMLA leave "for the birth of" or "to care for" a son or daughter. The availability of other caregivers would appear to have no impact on an employee's right to take FMLA leave for these purposes.

f. Physical Ability to Return to Work Earlier

The statute, implementing regulations, and comments accompanying the final implementing regulations do not address whether an employee, who takes leave "for the birth" of a son or daughter, may be required by an agency to return to work earlier when she is physically capable of returning, even though she wishes to take more available FMLA leave. In the absence of such authority, as under Title I, an agency may not require an employee who is physically capable to return to work earlier after delivering a baby if the employee wishes to take more available FMLA leave.

g. Multiple Births

The impact of an employee having multiple births on the amount of FMLA leave available is not addressed in Title II or the OPM implementing regulations. As under the other federal sector variants of the FMLA, the number of births that occur during an FMLA leave year would not increase the amount of FMLA leave available to an employee. That is, the 12 workweeks of FMLA leave an employee is granted each leave year is not calculated for each covered condition (so that an employee who experienced two births during a leave year would be entitled to 12 workweeks of FMLA leave for each birth). Rather, the 12 workweeks of FMLA leave each leave year is the total amount of FMLA leave available to the employee during that leave year no matter how many FMLA covered conditions occur during that leave year. [Calculation of the amount of FMLA leave available to an employee during a leave year is discussed more fully in Chapter 10, "Leave Amount and Scheduling."]

h. Intermittent/Reduced Leave Schedule

An employee is prohibited from taking FMLA leave on an intermittent or reduced leave schedule basis for the birth and to care for a son or daughter unless the employee and employing agency agree otherwise. 5 USC 6382(b)(1); 5 CFR 630.1204(a).

Unlike the other federal sector variants of the FMLA, Title II does not distinguish between leave taken before or after the birth of a child for purposes of gaining the approval from the employing agency to take leave on an intermittent or reduced leave schedule basis. Title II and the implementing regulations uniformly provide that the employee must gain the approval of his or her employing agency when FMLA leave is taken on an intermittent or reduced leave schedule basis for the birth and to care for a newborn child. [How FMLA leave may be taken is addressed more fully in Chapter 10, "Leave Amount and Scheduling."]

i. Paid Leave Substitution

Under Title II, FMLA leave is generally taken as leave without pay. 5 USC 6382(c); 5 CFR 630.1205(a). An employee may elect to substitute paid leave for any part of unpaid leave for the birth and care of a son or daughter, except that an agency is not required to provide paid sick leave in any situation in which the employing agency would not normally provide such paid leave. 5 USC 6382(c). The paid leave that may be drawn upon in substitution of leave without pay is specified in 5 CFR 630.1205(b). [Substitution of paid leave for leave without pay is addressed more fully in Chapter 11, "Substitution of Paid Leave."]

B. ADOPTION

1. Title I, the CAA, and the PEOAA: ADOPTION

a. General Rule

An agency must grant FMLA leave to an eligible employee because of the placement of a son or daughter with the employee for adoption. 29 USC 2612(a)(1)(B); 29 CFR 825.112(a)(2), 825.2202(a)(2); S. Res. 242, Cong. Rec. S3959, S3962–63 (April 23, 1996); 29 CFR 825.112(a)(2), 825.202(a)(2).

Neither the Act nor the implementing regulations define "adoption." Nor do they define what constitutes the "placement" of a son or daughter with the employee for adoption. Presumably, it means the intended permanent assignment of the child to the employee as a son or daughter. The Seventh Circuit in *Kelley v. Crossfield Catalysts*, 135 F.3d 1202 (7th Cir. 1998), held that an employee is entitled to FMLA leave to attend a custody hearing for adoption or foster care placement of a biological child, an admittedly rare occurrence.

The implementing regulations are in conflict regarding whether an eligible employee is entitled to FMLA leave "to care for" a newly adopted son or daughter. The conflict involves §§ 825.112(a)(2), 825.200(a)(2), and 825.212(a)(2). 29 CFR 825.112(a)(2), 825.212(a)(2); S. Res. 242, Cong. Rec. S3959, S3962 (April 23, 1996); 29 CFR 825.112(a)(2), 825.200(a)(2), and 825.212(a)(2).

Section 825.112 is titled with the question: "Under what kinds of circumstances are employers required to grant family or medical leave?" It would appear to be the main regulatory gateway addressing the subject of covered conditions entitling an employee to FMLA leave. In pertinent part, § 825.112(a) provides:

(a) Employers covered by FMLA are required to grant leave to eligible employees:

    (1) For birth of a son or daughter, and to care for the newborn child;

    (2) For placement with the employee of a son or daughter for adoption or foster care.

By its terms, § 825.112(a)(2) fails to include language similar to that contained in the preceding regulation governing birth that FMLA leave was also available "to care for" the newly adopted son or daughter. By limiting the scope of FMLA leave for adoption and foster care to "placement," § 825.112(a)(2) seriously calls into question whether leave for "bonding" time is available post-placement for adoption or foster care.

The possibility that "bonding" time was not available post-placement was seemingly further supported by comments made by the DOL accompanying publication of the final Title I regulations. The term "placement" is not defined. In the comments to the final regulations, however, the DOL interpreted "placement", for purposes of section 102(a)(1)(B) of the Act (29 USC 2612(a)(1)(B)), as relating only to the actual placement with the eligible employee of an adopted or foster child. The act of providing foster care, in and of itself, the DOL stated, "is not a qualifying reason for taking FMLA leave." Preamble, 29 CFR 825.112. Given the preceding definition, it would seem that the DOL would be hard pressed to expand the meaning of the term "placement" to mean something other than the "actual placement" with the eligible employee of an adopted son or daughter. However, that assumption is incorrect.

Notwithstanding the statutory and regulatory language limiting FMLA leave to the actual placement with the eligible employee of an adopted son or daughter, the DOL opined that leave for "placement" also includes "bonding time." As stated by the DOL in the comments to the final regulations (Preamble, 29 CFR 825.212):

> In response to the question on whether FMLA's leave entitlement for placement for adoption includes "bonding" time between the parent and child, we note from the legislative history's discussion of the need for family and medical leave legislation that:
>
>> Adoptive parents also face difficulties in the absence of a reasonable family leave policy. Most adoption agencies require the presence of a parent in the home—some for as long as four months—when a child is placed with the family to allow them adequate time for proper bonding.
>
> The legislative history's discussion of the leave provisions themselves provides:
>
>> Section 102(a)(2) required that leave provided under § 102(a)(1)(A) or (B) to care for a newborn child *or a child newly placed with the employee for adoption or foster care* be taken before the end of the first 12 months following the date of the birth or placement.
>
> ***
>
> Clearly, the intent of FMLA's leave entitlement in the case of leave for placement of a child with the employee for adoption or foster care includes "bonding" time with the newly-placed child, during the 12 months following the date of placement.

The DOL's comments make more sense in light of the language of §§ 825.200(a)(2) and 825.202(a)(2). 29 CFR 825.200(a)(2), 825.202(a)(2); S. Res. 242, Cong. Rec. S3959, S3962–64 (April 23, 1996); 29 CFR 825.200(a)(2), and 825.202(a)(2). Section 825.200 is titled with the question: "How much leave may an employee take?" In pertinent part, the regulation (29 CFR 825.200(a)(2); S. Res. 242, Cong. Rec. S3959, S3963 (April 23, 1996); 29 CFR 825.200(a)(2)) provides:

    (a) An eligible employee's FMLA leave entitlement is limited to a total of 12 workweeks of leave during any 12-month period for any one, or more, of the following reasons:

        (1) The birth of the employee's son or daughter, and to care for the newborn child;

        (2) The placement with the employee of a son or daughter for adoption or foster care, *and to care for the newly placed child* (emphasis added).

The same language is used in § 825.202(a) of the implementing regulations. Section 825.202 is titled: "How much leave may a husband and wife take if they are employed by the same employer?" The regulation (29 CFR 825.202(a)(2); S. Res. 242, Cong. Rec. S3959, S3964 (April 23, 1996); 29 CFR 825.202(a)(2)) provides:

> (a) A husband and wife who are eligible for FMLA leave and are employed by the same covered employer may be limited to a combined total of 12 weeks of leave during any 12-month period if the leave is taken:
>
> (1) for birth of the employee's son or daughter or to care for the child after birth;
>
> (2) for placement of a son or daughter with the employee for adoption or foster care, *or to care for the child after placement* (emphasis supplied).

Neither §§ 825.200 and 825.202 nor the comments accompanying publication of the final regulations explain the presence of the highlighted language in these sections. The presence of the added language is important as it fundamentally changes the scope of the FMLA leave entitlement involving the placement of a son or daughter with the employee for adoption or foster care.

Indeed, the presence of the added language in §§ 825.200(a)(2) and 825.202(a)(2) is even more puzzling as those sections were primarily focused on other issues. Section 825.200 is primarily concerned with the four methods for calculation of the FMLA leave year. The primary concern of § 825.202 is the special rules regarding the amount of FMLA leave available when spouses work for the same employer. In each case, the reference to the base right to take FMLA leave for purposes of adoption or foster care is ancillary to the main objective of each section. The primary concern of § 825.112, on the other hand, is the covered conditions that entitle an employee to FMLA leave. This is the section where one would think that the general rule regarding the scope of FMLA leave for adoptions and foster care would be completely laid out and discussed.

Whether FMLA leave for adoption or foster care placement includes leave "to care for" the newly adopted son or daughter after such placement fundamentally changes the scope of available leave. As discussed previously regarding birth, even though the term "to care for" is not defined by the regulations for purposes of adoption or foster care placement, it would seem sensible that such care would include physical or psychological comfort and care, particularly where the son or daughter does not have a serious health condition (which may be an independent basis for FMLA leave). Moreover, the term "to care for" would also appear to more easily encompass "bonding" time than "placement."

The conflict in the regulations regarding the scope of FMLA leave for adoption or foster care placement poses real problems for agencies. Agencies must now guess whether FMLA leave is available post-placement "to care for" a newly adopted/foster care placed son or daughter. Since the DOL provides that any violation of the regulations constitutes actionable interference with FMLA rights (29 CFR 825.220(b)), agencies need to be good guessers or suffer expensive legal fees and damage claims. Agencies have several choices when confronted with this issue.

First, agencies can follow the broader interpretation of adoption/foster care leave rights set forth in §§ 825.200(a)(2) and 825.202(a)(2) and permit eligible employees to take post-placement FMLA leave "to care for" a son or daughter. This would appear to be the DOL position. Following this course of action should keep most agencies out of trouble, at least for the time being. Of course, what will happen eventually is that an employee will be permitted post-adoption leave "to care for" a son or daughter. The leave will be deducted from the employee's 12-workweek FMLA leave entitlement. The employee will use up the available FMLA leave for that year, be fired for absenteeism, and then sue the agency. The employee will allege that, pursuant to § 825.112(a)(2), the agency illegally deducted FMLA leave as the Act does not cover post-placement "to care for" situations. The employee will claim that the reason he was terminated was covered by the FMLA leave and, with the leave that should not have been deducted, his or her absences were protected. The employee's termination for protected leave, the employee will argue, violated the Act.

The other alternative is that agencies can read the regulations narrowly, so that post-placement leave "to care for" a newly adopted/foster care placed son or daughter is not covered by the FMLA. The argument here relies on the language of the statute and § 825.112, both of which do not include "to care for" language permitting post-placement leave. We will call this the high-risk strategy as it is likely to result in litigation sooner rather than later.

Agencies that are currently in litigation can argue that because the regulations are in conflict they are not due any deference. The statute, 29 USC 2612(a)(1)(B), does not include "to care for" language when addressing adoption/foster care (but does when addressing birth), indicating that Congress did not intend that post-adoption/foster care leave "to care for" the newly adopted/foster care placed son or daughter be covered. The argument essentially seeks to invalidate §§ 825.200(a)(2) and 825.202(a)(2), and may result in doing away with "bonding" time in adoption/foster care placement situations.

As between the two strategies, agencies would be well advised to follow the former, at least until the DOL and the other enforcement bodies fix this situation. The DOL and the other enforcement agencies need to correct this issue before their regulations on this issue are invalidated.

Finally, "bonding" time is undefined in the Act and implementing regulation. It is unclear, then, exactly what constitutes "bonding" time. The issue is further complicated by the DOL's observations in the comments accompanying publication of the final regulations. According to the DOL, "placement" is limited to the actual placement with the employee of adoption, and not the act of providing care. *See* Preamble, 29 CFR 825.212. The latter observation by the DOL suggests that the "act of providing care," which is not a qualifying reason for taking FMLA leave, is different than "bonding" time, which is a qualifying reason. This, in turn, suggests that an employee simply staying at home, cooking, bathing, and engaging in other similar pursuits with the newborn or newly adopted/foster care placed son or daughter is not the basis of a legitimate request for FMLA leave to "bond" with a covered child. The DOL's observation in the comments suggests that it has some idea what it believes constitutes "bonding" time. The DOL needs to clarify this area so that agencies may properly credit FMLA leave.

b. Source of Adoption

The source of an adopted child (e.g., whether from a licensed placement agency or otherwise) is not a factor in determining eligibility for leave for purposes of the FMLA. 29 CFR 825.112(d); S. Res. 242, Cong. Rec. S3959, S3962 (April 23, 1996); 29 CFR 825.112(d). No explanation is provided in the regulations or comments accompanying the final DOL regulations regarding the purpose of this provision.

Note that the use of the term "eligibility" in § 825.212(d) does not appear to relate to the eligibility prerequisites for FMLA leave. *See* 29 USC 2611(2); 29 CFR 825.110(a); S. Res. 242, Cong. Rec. S3959, S3961 (April 23, 1996); 29 CFR 825.110(a). None of these eligibility requirements would be affected by the source of an adopted child. The term "eligibility" for purposes of § 825.212(d) appears more generic, suggesting that the source of an adopted child is not relevant to the determination of whether an employee is entitled to FMLA leave. Employee eligibility is addressed more fully in Chapter 5, "Employee Eligibility for Leave."

c. Pre-Adoption Leave

Employing agencies are required to grant FMLA leave for the placement of a son or daughter with the employee for adoption if an absence from work is required for the placement or adoption to proceed. 29 CFR 825.112(d); S. Res. 242, Cong. Rec. S3959, S3962 (April 23, 1996); 29 CFR 825.112(d). For example, the employee may be required to attend counseling sessions, appear in court, consult with his or her attorney or the doctor(s) representing the birth parent, or submit to a physical examination. 29 CFR 825.112(d); S. Res. 242, Cong. Rec. S3959, S3962 (April 23, 1996); 29 CFR 825.112(d).

Note that the regulation requires, in order for pre-adoption leave to be granted, that the need for such leave must be "required" for the placement or adoption to proceed. If the need for pre-adoption leave were permissive rather than required in order for the adoption to proceed, an agency would not be required to grant the leave.

The regulations fail to provide a mechanism for an agency to check to determine whether the employee's claimed need for pre-adoption leave is "required" in order for the adoption to proceed. For example, there is no specific regulation permitting an agency to require an employee to produce documentation substantiating the claim that the employee "requires" pre-adoption FMLA leave. One possibility is to read the requirement in § 825.113(d) to mean that an employee, on request, must provide reasonable documentation or a statement of familial relationship as covering the requirement for pre-adoption leave. Since the employee is requesting leave in order to establish a familial relationship with the adopted son or daughter, an agency should be permitted to inquire why pre-adoption leave is necessary as part of the familial confirmation process.

Another argument would be that, in the absence of a regulation prohibiting an agency from requiring an employee to provide documentation of the requirement for pre-adoption leave, an agency is permitted to request such documentation. Agencies would be well advised to exercise caution in this area by applying uniform policies requiring such documentation. This will avoid claims of disparate treatment, whether under the FMLA or other federal discrimination laws.

d. Adoption of Older Children

FMLA leave is not available for the adoption of a son or daughter who is 18 years of age or older and who is capable of self-care. Preamble, 29 CFR 825.112. This result is a function of the FMLA definition of "son or daughter." For purposes of the FMLA, a "son or daughter" is defined as a biological, adopted, or foster child, a stepchild, a legal ward, or a child of a person standing *in loco parentis*, who is either under age 18, or age 18 or older and incapable of self-care because of a mental or physical disability. 29 USC 2611(12); 29 CFR 825.113(c); S. Res. 242, Cong. Rec. S3959, S3962 (April 23, 1996); 29 CFR 825.113(c). Adoptions of over age 18 children frequently take place in a second marriage, where one spouse adopts the children of the other spouse. Such adoptions carry legal significance beyond the scope of the FMLA.

Conversely, FMLA leave is available for the adoption of a son or daughter who is age 18 or older and incapable of self-care because of mental or physical disability. Under this scenario, the statutory definition of "son or daughter" is met. Where the definition of a son or daughter is met, an eligible employee would be entitled to FMLA leave for the adoption of such son or daughter. [For a further discussion of when a son or daughter is incapable of self-care within the meaning of the FMLA, see Chapter 6, "Covered Family Members."]

e. Stepchildren

Absent an adoption, an eligible employee is not entitled to FMLA leave to "bond" with his or her new stepchildren. Preamble, 29 CFR 825.112. The Act permits FMLA leave only in certain instances, and, when the need for leave does not involve a serious health condition, those instances require a birth, adoption, or foster care placement. No other arrangements are recognized.

If, however, the stepson or stepdaughter had a serious health condition within the meaning of the FMLA, an eligible employee might be entitled to FMLA leave if the employee was needed to care for the son or daughter. The employee/stepparent would be entitled to leave absent adoption if the employee held an *in loco parentis* relationship with the stepson or daughter. 29 CFR 825.113(b); S. Res. 242, Cong. Rec. S3959, S3962 (April 23, 1996); 29 CFR 825.113(b). Persons who are *in loco parentis* include those with day-to-day responsibilities to care for and financially support a son or daughter or, in the case of an employee, who had such responsibility for the employee when the employee was a child. A biological or legal relationship is not necessary. 29 CFR 825.113(c)(3). [The definitions for FMLA covered family members, including parents, sons, or daughters, are discussed more fully in Chapter 6, "Covered Family Members."]

f. Leave Conclusion

As with leave for birth, FMLA leave for the placement of a son or daughter with the employee for adoption expires at the end of the 12-month period beginning on the date of placement. 29 USC 2612(a)(2); 29 CFR 825.201; S. Res. 242, Cong. Rec. S3959, S3964 (April 23, 1996); 29 CFR 825.201. Based on the wording of the statute, the DOL specifically rejected the argument that FMLA leave for placement of a son or daughter need only commence within the 12-month period from the placement date. *See* Preamble, 29 CFR 825.201 ("The Statute clearly states that the entitlement to leave *expires* at the end of one year following the date of birth or placement of the child. The leave must be concluded, (i.e., completed) within the statutory entitlement period.").

The regulations seemingly add an exception extending the expiration of FMLA leave as permitted by state law or as permitted by the employer. 29 CFR 825.201; S. Res. 242, Cong. Rec. S3959, S3964 (April 23, 1996); 29 CFR 825.201. In the comments to the final regulations, however, the DOL clarifies that what appear to be exceptions permitting the extension of FMLA leave beyond the 12-month period from the placement date, really are not. The DOL explained this (Preamble, 29 CFR 825.201) with the following example:

> If a State provision (as in the case in New Jersey) allows for a longer or more generous period, the more generous State provision would prevail but such leave would not count as FMLA leave....

Of course, the more generous provisions of state FMLA laws do not apply to federal employees. *See* DOL WH FMLA Advisory Opinion No. 36 (May 18, 1994) (FMLA does not supersede any provision of state or local law that provides greater family or medical leave rights than those established under the FMLA as long as the state law has jurisdiction over the employer. In this instance, the Wisconsin family and medical leave law does not have jurisdiction over the federal government and its provisions would not be applicable to any federal employee.).

Finally, the fact that an eligible employee is granted pre-adoption FMLA leave will not shorten the 12-month period measured from the placement date. *See* Preamble, 29 CFR 825.201. That is, the 12-month period in which an eligible employee must complete FMLA leave for the placement of a son or daughter with the employee for adoption is measured from the placement date, not from the date of any pre-placement FMLA leave that may have been taken to facilitate the adoption. [The amount of FMLA leave available to an eligible employee is addressed more fully in Chapter 10, "Leave Amount and Scheduling."]

g. Intermittent/Reduced Leave Schedule

The rules previously discussed for FMLA leave because of the birth and to care for a son or daughter apply equally where the need for FMLA leave is for the placement of a covered child with the employee for adoption. Essentially an employee needs the approval of his or her employing agency in order to take FMLA leave on an intermittent or reduced leave schedule basis for the placement of a son or daughter with the employee for adoption.

The statute and regulations differ regarding the circumstances when an agency may take FMLA leave for adoption placement. The statute provides that all intermittent or reduced leave schedule FMLA leave for adoption placement requires approval by the agency. *See* 29 USC 2612(b)(1). The regulations, on the other hand, provide that the requirement that an employee obtain the permission of the agency applies only if an intermittent or reduced leave schedule is sought after the placement of a covered child for adoption. 29 CFR 825.203(b); S. Res. 242, Cong. Rec. S3959, S3964 (April 23, 1996); 29 CFR 825.203(b).

The difference between the language of the statute and the regulations becomes important in pre-placement leave situations. The regulations suggest that an agency does not have the independent right to deny FMLA leave taken on an intermittent or reduced leave schedule basis for adoption placement prior to or on the actual date of placement. The statute, on the other hand, provides that agency permission is required in all circumstances involving intermittent/reduced leave schedule FMLA leave for adoption placement, including pre-placement leave. Agencies would appear to be on solid ground to argue that § 825.203(b) is too restrictive and fails to adequately reflect the clear statutory language allowing them veto authority over all requests for FMLA leave on intermittent/reduced leave schedule, whether the leave is to be taken before or after the adoption.

Finally, the placement with an employee of each child for adoption constitutes a separate FMLA-qualifying event. DOL WH FMLA Advisory Opinion No. 84 (Oct. 25, 1996). Subsequent placements, therefore, would not be subject to the restrictions on intermittent leave for foster care. 29 USC 2612(b); 29 CFR 825.203(b); S. Res. 242, Cong. Rec. S3959, S3964 (April 23, 1996); 29 CFR 825.203(b). Specifically, intermittent FMLA leave is leave taken in separate blocks of time for the same event and is available to care for a newborn or for a newly adopted or placed foster child only with the employer's agreement. DOL WH FMLA Advisory Opinion No. 84 (Oct. 25, 1996). By treating each adoption placement as a separate event, the employer does not have the discretion to deny the leave, but would be required to grant FMLA leave to an eligible employee for each placement, until such time as the 12 workweek leave entitlement is exhausted in the designated 12-month leave year. DOL WH FMLA Advisory Opinion No. 84 (Oct. 25, 1996).

In order for the agency to have the right to deny the employee permission to take FMLA leave on an intermittent or reduced leave schedule for the adoption placement of a son or daughter with the employee, multiple leave requests have to involve the same child.

2. Title II: Adoption

a. General Rule

An employee is entitled to a total of 12 administrative workweeks of FMLA leave during a leave year because of the placement of a son or daughter with the employee for adoption. 5 USC 6382(a)(1)(B); 5 CFR 630.1203(a)(2). Adoption is defined as a legal process in which an individual becomes the legal parent of another's child. 5 CFR 630.1202 (definition of "adoption"). The term "placement" is not defined.

It is unclear what circumstances would constitute "placement" of a child with an employee for adoption. The statute, the regulations, and comments by the OPM accompanying the final regulations, do not indicate that "placement" includes "bonding" time with the newly adopted son or daughter. Title II, like Title I, requires that such FMLA leave expire one year from the date of placement. 5 USC 6382(a)(2). The DOL used this as evidence that the term "placement" includes "bonding" time. *See* Preamble, 29 CFR 825.212. Moreover, since Title II shares a common legislative history with Title I, it is likely that an employee is entitled to take FMLA leave for "bonding" time with a newly adopted son or daughter.

The same concerns and issues involving FMLA leave for adoption that are addressed above for Title I, the CAA, and the PEOAA, also exist for Title II.

b. Source Not Relevant

The source of an adopted child—e.g., whether from a licensed placement agency or otherwise—is not a factor in determining eligibility for leave. 5 CFR 630.1202 (definition of "adoption"). The rule is identical to the comparable rules governing Title I, the CAA, and the PEOAA. *See* 29 CFR 825.112(d); S. Res. 242, Cong. Rec. S3959, S3962 (April 23, 1996); 29 CFR 825.112(d). The use of the term "eligibility" does not refer to any eligibility requirement for Title II, as, technically, there are no such requirements. The sole "eligibility" requirement for Title II is included in the definition of an employee, and requires 12 months of federal employment. *See* 5 USC 6381(1)(b). The source of an adopted son or daughter would not impact whether an employee meets the 12 months of employment test. For purposes of an adoption within the meaning of Title II, the term "eligibility" apparently means that an employee's entitlement to FMLA leave is not affected by the source of the adopted child.

c. Pre-Adoption Leave

Similar to the other federal sector variants of the FMLA, leave under Title II for the placement of a son or daughter with the employee for adoption may be taken prior to or on the actual date of placement for adoption. 5 CFR 630.1203(d). Title I, the CAA, and the PEOAA do not include language indicating that FMLA leave may be taken "on the actual date of placement." *See* 29 CFR 825.112(d); S. Res. 242, Cong. Rec. S3959, S3962 (April 23, 1996); 29 CFR 825.112(d).

Unlike Title I, the CAA, and the PEOAA, the ability of an employee to take pre-adoption FMLA leave under Title II is not conditioned on the absence from work being "required" for the placement to precede. *See* 29 CFR 825.112(d); S. Res. 242, Cong. Rec. S3959, S3962 (April 23, 1996); 29 CFR 825.112(d). The absence of the conditioned language suggests that it is easier for employees covered by Title II to take pre-adoption FMLA leave than eligible employees covered by Title I, the CAA, or the PEOAA.

d. Adoption of Older Children

Title II requires agencies to grant an employee FMLA leave for the placement of an age 18 or older son or daughter with the employee for adoption, but only if the child is incapable of self-care due to a mental or physical disability. 5 USC 6381(6); 5 CFR 630.1202 (definition of "son or daughter"). If the age 18 or older son or daughter is capable of self-care, or does not have a mental or physical disability within the meaning of the law, the employee is not entitled to FMLA leave for the adoption. Of course, an agency could grant the employee some other form of leave. [For further discussion of when a son or daughter is incapable of self-care within the meaning of the FMLA, see Chapter 6, "Covered Family Members."]

e. Stepchildren

Like Title I, the CAA, and the PEOAA, Title II provides that an agency must grant an employee FMLA leave for the placement of a son or daughter with the employee for adoption. Title II defines son or daughter to mean a biological, adopted, or foster child, a stepchild, a legal ward, or a child of a person standing *in loco parentis*, who is either under 18 years of age, or 18 years of age or older and incapable of self-care because of a mental or physical disability. 5 USC 6381(6); 5 CFR 630.1202 (definition of "son or daughter"). Absent an adoption, an employee would not be able to take time off to "bond" with a stepchild.

Of course, if the stepchild met the definition of a son or daughter, and the stepchild had a serious health condition within the meaning of the FMLA, the employee would be entitled to take FMLA leave if the employee were needed to care for the stepchild. *See* 5 USC 6382(a)(1)(C); 5 CFR 630.1203(a)(3).

f. Leave Conclusion

As with FMLA leave for the birth and care of a newborn son or daughter, FMLA leave for the placement of a son or daughter with an employee for adoption expires 12 months from the placement date. 5 USC 6382(a)(2); 5 CFR 630.1203(d). Again, because Title II fails to define "placement," it would appear difficult to determine when "placement" occurs.

An agency is permitted to require an employee requesting FMLA leave for the adoption of a son or daughter to provide evidence that is administratively acceptable to the agency. 5 CFR 630.1206(f). What constitutes "administratively acceptable" evidence is not defined or described. Presumably the agency has some discretion in this area. An agency should consider requesting that the employee provide documentation evidencing the adoption, preferably with an effective placement date. The regulations do not address when the agency may request such evidence after the employee's request, and how long the employee has to produce the evidence. The regulations also do not provide for what happens if an employee fails to provide administratively acceptable evidence of the adoption. Presumably, such a failure by the employee of a precondition to leave would result in FMLA leave being denied. *See e.g.*, 5 CFR 630.1208(l) (leave not covered by FMLA when employee fails to provide notice and medical certification).

The impact of pre–adoption leave on the calculation of the 12-month period for expiration of FMLA leave following the placement of a son or daughter with an employee for adoption follows the same rules as discussed previously for birth. Please refer to the above discussion for more on this subject. *See also* 5 CFR 630.1203(c), (d); Preamble, 5 CFR 630.1203.

g. Intermittent/Reduced Leave Schedule

FMLA leave for the placement of a son or daughter with the employee for adoption may not be taken by the employee on an intermittent or reduced leave schedule basis unless the employee and the employing agency of the employee agree otherwise. 5 USC 6382(b)(1); 5 CFR 630.1204(a).

Unlike the other federal sector variants of the FMLA, Title II does not distinguish between leave taken before or after the placement of a son or daughter with the employee for adoption for purposes of gaining the approval from the employing agency to take leave on an intermittent or reduced leave schedule basis. *Compare* 29 CFR 825.203(b); S. Res. 242, Cong. Rec. S3959, S3964 (April 23, 1996); 29 CFR 825.203(b). Title II and the implementing regulations uniformly provide that the employee must gain the approval of his or her employing agency when FMLA leave is taken on an intermittent or reduced leave schedule basis for the placement of a covered child with the employee for adoption. [How FMLA leave may be taken is addressed more fully in Chapter 10, "Leave Amount and Scheduling."]

C. FOSTER CARE PLACEMENT

1. Title I, the CAA, and the PEOAA: Foster Care Placement

a. General Rule

An eligible employee is entitled to FMLA leave because of the placement of a son or daughter with the employee for foster care. 29 USC 2612(a)(1)(B); 29 CFR 825.112(a)(2), 825.200(a)(2); S. Res. 242, Cong. Rec. S3959, S3962–63 (April 23, 1996); 29 CFR 825.112(a)(2), 825.200(a)(2). "Foster care" is not defined in the statute. The implementing regulations, however, define the term "foster care" as 24-hour care for children in substitution for, and away from, their parents or guardian. 29 CFR 825.112(e); S. Res. 242, Cong. Rec. S3959, S3962–63 (April 23, 1996); 29 CFR 825.112(e;. *see also* DOL WH FMLA Advisory Opinion No. 84 (Oct. 25, 1996).

As previously discussed regarding birth and adoption, the term "placement" is undefined for purposes of foster care. In the comments accompanying the final Title I regulations, the DOL rejected the argument that a parent of a drug addict who assumes the responsibility as primary caretaker for the addict's children is a form of "foster care" in which FMLA leave should be available to such parents. Preamble, 29 CFR 825.212. According to the DOL:

> Section 102(a)(1)(B) of FMLA entitles an eligible employee to take FMLA leave *"[b]ecause of the placement of a son or daughter with the employee for adoption or foster care* (emphasis added)." Thus, the entitlement to leave under this section of the Act relates only to the actual placement with the eligible employee of an adopted or foster child. The act of providing "foster care," in and of itself, is not a qualifying reason for taking FMLA leave under the Statute.

Foster care is included in the same regulation as adoption. As such, the previous discussion (in the section of this chapter regarding adoption) of the conflict in the regulations regarding whether FMLA leave is available post-placement "to care for" the newly placed child is directly applicable here.

b. Source Relevant

Foster care placements must be made by or with the agreement of the state as a result of a voluntary agreement between the parent or guardian that the child must be removed from the home, or pursuant to a judicial determination of the necessity for foster care, and involves agreement between the state and foster family that the foster family will take care of the child. 29 CFR 825.112(e); S. Res. 242, Cong. Rec. S3959, S3962 (April 23, 1996); 29 CFR 825.112(e); *see also* DOL WH FMLA Advisory Opinion No. 84 (Oct. 25, 1996). This would include placements made by a state through a state-approved agency. DOL WH FMLA Advisory Opinion No. 84 (Oct. 25, 1996) (Vermont Children's Aid Society cited as state-approved agency for foster care placements). Foster care may be with relatives of the child, but only if state action is involved in the removal of the child from parental custody. 29 CFR 825.112(e); S. Res. 242, Cong. Rec. S3959, S3962 (April 23, 1996); 29 CFR 825.112(e).

Note that the source of an adoption is not relevant for purposes of determining whether an employee is entitled to FMLA leave. The source of a foster care placement, on the other hand, is relevant, as such placement must be sanctioned by state action.

An agency could prove the legality of the source of the foster care placement by requiring the employee to provide documentation establishing the same. Section 825.213(d) of the implementing regulations (29 CFR 825.213(d); S. Res. 242, Cong. Rec. S3959, S3962 (April 23, 1996); 29 CFR 825.113(d)), permits agencies to require an eligible employee giving notice of the need for FMLA leave to provide reasonable documentation or a statement of family relationship. In the context of foster care placement, the documentation may take the form of a copy of the formal agreement between the state and the foster family. DOL WH FMLA Advisory Opinion No. 84 (Oct. 25, 1996). The employer would be able to examine the documents, but must return the document to the employee. *Id. See* 29 CFR 825.113(d); S. Res. 242, Cong. Rec. S3959, S3962 (April 23, 1996); 29 CFR 825.113(d). The regulations do not indicate how long the employer may retain the document before returning it to the employee. Nor does the regulation prohibit an agency from copying the document provided. The rules fail to address the penalty for an employee's failure to provide documentation confirming familial relationship. [For a further discussion of the FMLA's documentation requirements, see Chapter 9, "Documentation Requirements."]

c. Pre-Placement Leave

As with adoption, an agency must grant FMLA leave because of the placement of a son or daughter with the employee for foster care before the actual placement of the child if the absence from work is required for the placement for foster care to proceed. 29 CFR 825.112(d); S. Res. 242, Cong. Rec. S3959, S3962 (April 23, 1996); 29 CFR 825.112(d). For example, the employee may be required to attend counseling sessions, appear in court, consult with his or her attorney or doctors, or submit to a physical examination. 29 CFR 825.112(d); S. Res. 242, Cong. Rec. S3959, S3962 (April 23, 1996); 29 CFR 825.112(d).

An employee's right to take pre-foster care placement FMLA leave is predicated on the leave being "required" for the foster care placement to proceed. The regulations do not explicitly provide a mechanism by which an agency may verify or confirm that the claimed need for the pre-foster care placement leave is "required" in order for the placement to proceed. Agencies should consider using the ability to require employees to provide reasonable documentation or a statement confirming the familial relationship as the means of establishing that the pre-foster care placement leave is "required." Such use appears to be sanctioned by the DOL, which described the documentation requirement in § 825.113 as permitting an employer to request that employees provide reasonable documentation that verifies the legitimacy of an FMLA leave request, i.e., that the requested leave is for a qualifying statutory purpose. Preamble, 29 CFR 825.112. Documentation regarding foster care placement would include the formal agreement between the state and the foster family. DOL WH FMLA Advisory Opinion No. 84 (Oct. 25, 1996).

d. Foster Care Placement of Older Children

For purposes of entitlement to FMLA leave, the placement for foster care must be of a "son or daughter," as defined by the Act and implementing regulations. A "son or daughter" includes a foster child who is either under age 18, or 18 years of age or older who is incapable of self-care due to a mental or physical disability. 29 USC 2611(12) (definition of "son or daughter"); 29 CFR 825.113(c); S. Res. 242, Cong. Rec. S3959, S3962 (April 23, 1996); 29 CFR 825.113(c). Therefore, FMLA leave is available for the placement of an under age 18 son or daughter with the employee for foster care. It is also available for an age 18 or older son or daughter, if that son or daughter is incapable of self-care due to a mental or physical disability within the meaning of the FMLA. If an age 18 or older son or daughter is capable of self-care, or does not have a mental or physical disability within the meaning of the FMLA, an agency is not required to grant FMLA leave for the placement of that son or daughter with the employee for foster care. [For a further discussion of who is a "son or daughter" within the meaning of the FMLA, see Chapter 6, "Covered Family Members."]

e. Pay, Minimum Duration, and Multiple Foster Care Placements

Neither the statute nor the implementing regulations impose a minimum period of time or permanency in connection with a foster care placement for FMLA leave purposes. DOL WH FMLA Advisory Opinion No. 84 (Oct. 25, 1996). As long as the placement is the result of a foster care agreement between the foster parents and the state, leave to care for the newly placed foster child would be considered FMLA leave. DOL WH FMLA Advisory Opinion No. 84 (Oct. 25, 1996).

As long as they are sanctioned by state-action, multiple foster care placements with the employee do not affect the employee's entitlement to FMLA leave. The placement with an employee of each child for foster care is considered a separate FMLA-qualifying event. DOL WH FMLA Advisory Opinion No. 84 (Oct. 25, 1996). By treating each foster care placement as a separate event, the employer does not have the discretion to deny the leave, but would be required to grant FMLA leave to an eligible employee for each placement until such time as the 12 workweek leave entitlement is exhausted in the designated 12-month period. DOL WH FMLA Advisory Opinion No. 84 (Oct. 25, 1996). Remember, an eligible employee's entitlement is to a total of 12 weeks of FMLA leave each leave year. They do not get 12 weeks of FMLA leave each leave year for each foster child placement.

Finally, the fact that the employee receives compensation or other consideration for his or her services as a foster parent is not material for purposes of the employee's entitlement to FMLA leave. DOL WH FMLA Advisory Opinion No. 84 (Oct. 25, 1996).

f. Leave Conclusion

An eligible employee's entitlement to FMLA leave because of the placement of a son or daughter with the employee for foster care expires at the end of the 12-month period beginning on the placement date. 29 USC 2612(a)(2); 29 CFR 825.201; S. Res. 242, Cong. Rec. S3959, S3964 (April 23, 1996); 29 CFR 825.201.

The DOL interpreted the statute to require that such leave be concluded within the 12-month period, not merely commenced. *See* Preamble, 29 CFR 825.201 ("The Statute clearly states that that the entitlement to leave *expires* at the end of one year following the date of birth or placement of the child. Thus, the leave must be concluded, (i.e., completed) within the statutory entitlement period.").

Again, the absence of a definition for "placement" makes it more difficult for agencies to determine when "placement" occurred in order to calculate when the 12-month period expires. Because, however, such placement involves a legal process, agencies should be able to confirm the placement date by requiring that the employee provide reasonable documentation or a statement regarding the date of placement. 29 CFR 113(d); S. Res. 242, Cong. Rec. S3959, S3962 (April 23, 1996); 29 CFR 825.113(d).

The regulations seemingly add an exception extending the expiration of FMLA leave as permitted by state law or as permitted by the employer. 29 CFR 825.201; S. Res. 242, Cong. Rec. S3959, S3964 (April 23, 1996); 29 CFR 825.201. In the comments to the final regulations, however, the DOL clarifies that what appear to be exceptions permitting the extension of FMLA leave beyond the 12-month period from the placement date, really are not. The DOL explained this (Preamble, 29 CFR 825.201) with the following example:

If a State provision (as in the case in New Jersey) allows for a longer or more generous period, the more generous State provision would prevail but such leave would not count as FMLA leave....

Of course, the more generous provisions of state FMLA laws do not apply to federal employees. *See* DOL WH FMLA Advisory Opinion No. 36 (May 18, 1994) (FMLA does not supersede any provision of state or local law that provides greater family or medical leave rights than those established under the FMLA as long as the state law has jurisdiction over the employer. In this instance, the Wisconsin family and medical leave law does not have jurisdiction over the federal government and its provisions would not be applicable to any federal employee).

Finally, as discussed previously for FMLA leave due to the birth or adoption of a son or daughter, the fact that an eligible employee is granted pre-placement FMLA leave will not shorten the 12-month period measured from the placement date. *See* Preamble, 29 CFR 825.201. That is, the 12-month period in which an eligible employee must complete FMLA leave for the placement of a son or daughter with the employee for foster care is measured from the placement date, not from the date of any pre-placement FMLA leave that may have been taken to facilitate the foster care placement. [The amount of FMLA leave available to an eligible employee is addressed more fully in Chapter 10, "Leave Amount and Scheduling."]

g. Intermittent/Reduced Leave Schedule

As previously discussed regarding FMLA leave for birth and adoption, the statute and the regulations differ regarding the availability of intermittent/reduced leave schedule FMLA leave for foster care placement.

The statute provides that FMLA leave for the placement of a son or daughter with the employee may not be taken intermittently or on a reduced leave schedule unless both the employee and the employer agree otherwise. 29 USC 2612(b)(1). The regulations, on the other hand, provide that the requirement that an employee obtain the permission of the agency applies only when an intermittent or reduced leave schedule is sought after the placement of a covered child for adoption. 29 CFR 825.203(b); S. Res. 242, Cong. Rec. S3959, S3964 (April 23, 1996); 29 CFR 825.203(b).

The difference between the language of the statute and the regulations becomes important in pre-placement leave situations. The regulations suggest that an agency does not have the independent right to deny FMLA leave taken on an intermittent or reduced leave schedule basis for foster care placement prior to or on the actual date of placement. The statute, on the other hand, provides that agency permission is required in all circumstances involving intermittent/reduced leave schedule FMLA leave for foster care placement, including pre-placement leave. Agencies would appear to be on solid ground to argue that § 825.203(b) is too restrictive and fails to adequately reflect the clear statutory language allowing them veto authority over all requests for FMLA leave on intermittent/reduced leave schedule, whether the leave is to be taken before or after the foster care placement.

Finally, the placement with an employee of each child for foster care constitutes a separate FMLA-qualifying event. DOL WH FMLA Advisory Opinion No. 84 (Oct. 25, 1996. Subsequent placements, therefore, would not be subject to the restrictions on intermittent leave for foster care. 29 USC 2612(b); 29 CFR 825.203(b); S. Res. 242, Cong. Rec. S3959, S3964 (April 23, 1996); 29 CFR 825.203(b). Specifically, intermittent FMLA leave is leave taken in separate blocks of time for the same event and is available to care for a newborn or for a newly adopted or placed foster child only with the employer's agreement. DOL WH FMLA Advisory Opinion No. 84 (Oct. 25, 1996). By treating each foster care placement as a separate event, the employer does not have the discretion to deny the leave, but would be required to grant FMLA leave to an eligible employee for each placement, until such time as the 12 workweek leave entitlement is exhausted in the designated 12-month leave year. DOL WH FMLA Advisory Opinion No. 84 (Oct. 25, 1996).

In order for the agency to have the right to deny the employee permission to take FMLA leave on an intermittent or reduced leave schedule for the foster care placement of a son or daughter with the employee, multiple leave requests have to involve the same child. The regulations do not address when the same child is foster care placed with the same employee on multiple occasions. Presumably, each occasion the child is legally placed with the employee is a separate FMLA-qualifying event.

2. Title II: Foster Care Placement

a. General Rule

An employee covered by Title II is entitled to FMLA leave because of the placement of a son or daughter with the employee for foster care. 5 USC 6382(a)(1)(B); 5 CFR 630.1203(a)(2). Foster care is not defined in Title II. It is, however, defined in the implementing regulations. "Foster care" means 24-hour care for children in substitution for, and away from, their parents or guardian. 5 CFR 630.1202 (definition *of "foster care"*). The definition of "foster care" for purposes of Title II is the same as that under Title I, the CAA, and the PEOAA. *See* 29 CFR 825.112(e); S. Res. 242, Cong. Rec. S3959, S3964 (April 23, 1996); 29 CFR 825.203(b).

It is unclear whether post-placement leave is available to an employee "to care for" a recently placed foster son or daughter. Like Title I, the CAA, and the PEOAA, the statutory language does not include a right to take leave "in order to care for such son or daughter," as it does for birth. *Compare* 5 USC 6382(a)(1)(A) & (B). Unlike the regulations implementing the other federal sector variants of the FMLA, the regulations implementing Title II do not include "to care for" language. The regulation simply repeats the statutory language that FMLA leave is available for the placement of a son or daughter with the employee for foster care. 5 CFR 630.1203(a)(2). Moreover, unlike Title I, the CAA, and the PEOAA, there is no internal conflict in the Title II regulations on this point. Finally, the comments by the OPM accompanying the publication of the final regulations implementing Title II do not indicate that "bonding" time, or other circumstances where the employee is needed "to care for" the newly placed foster child, is covered by the FMLA.

A contrary argument that "bonding" time is covered by Title II of the FMLA can also be made. This argument tracks the argument used by the DOL (and referenced previously) to find that "bonding" time was available in post-adoption situations. *See* Preamble, 29 CFR 825.112. Essentially, the DOL referenced the legislative history, which indicated: "Most adoption agencies require the presence of a parent in the home—some for as long as four months—when a child is placed with the family to allow them adequate time for proper bonding." Preamble, 29 CFR 825.212 (*quoting* S. Rep. No. 103-3, p. 8.) The DOL also noted that the Act allows leave for placement of a son or daughter with an employee for foster care to expire 12 months from the date of placement, as evidence that post-placement "bonding time" leave was covered by the FMLA. The same two arguments are applicable to Title II. Title II shares a common legislative history with Title I. Additionally, Title II provides that FMLA leave for placement with an employee of a son or daughter for foster care expires 12 months after the placement date. 5 USC 6382(a)(2).

As with the other federal sector variants of the FMLA, the term "placement" is undefined. In the absence of even conflicting regulatory language inserting "and to care for" language to permit post-placement FMLA leave, the definition of "placement" becomes more important. Perhaps the DOL's reference to the legislative history that most placement agencies require the presence of at least one parent in the home for a minimum period of time in order to allow adequate bonding may be read more narrowly. Rather than an indication of wholesale "bonding" time, arguably the legislative history may be suggesting that "bonding" time is permitted up to a year after the placement, but only where such "bonding" time is required as a condition of the foster care placement. If "bonding" time is not a condition to perfect an adoption or foster care placement, the argument would be that it is not required for "placement" of the son or daughter with the employee and, therefore, not covered by the FMLA.

"Bonding" time is not defined by Title II. As such, similar to Title I, the CAA, and the PEOAA (where "bonding" time is also undefined), what constitutes "bonding" time is unclear.

Even if, for the reasons set forth above, "bonding" time is covered under Title II, it is not clear that such time would necessarily include leave to provide physical or psychological care to the newly placed foster child. This is of particular interest where the newly adopted foster child does not have a serious health condition within the meaning of the FMLA (which might be covered by another section of the Act). Of course, caring for a newly adopted child with the sniffles could be considered a "bonding" experience. But by the same token, almost anything could be considered a "bonding" experience. Making a bologna sandwich could be bonding, or not. The OPM, like the DOL and the other entities enforcing the FMLA, needs to declare whether "bonding" time is covered, and whether the simple act of providing primary care to a newly placed foster child constitutes a "bonding" experience.

b. Source Relevant

A foster care placement must be made by or with the agreement of the state as a result of a voluntary agreement by the parent or the guardian that the child be removed from the home, or pursuant to a judicial determination of the necessity for foster care, and involves agreement between the state and foster family to take the child. 5 CFR 630.1202 (definition of "foster care"). Although foster care may be with relatives of the child, state action is involved in the removal of the child from parental custody. 5 CFR 630.1202 (definition of "foster care").

An agency may verify the legitimacy of a request for FMLA leave for the placement of a son or daughter with the employee for foster care with documentation. An agency may require that an employee support his or her request for leave for the placement of a son or daughter with the employee for foster care with evidence administratively acceptable to the agency. 5 CFR 630.1206(f). What is "administratively acceptable" evidence is not described. Since, however, a foster care placement requires state action, agencies are well within their rights to request documentation verifying that state action.

c. Pre–Placement Leave

FMLA leave is available to an employee prior to or on the actual placement date of a son or daughter with the employee for foster care. 5 CFR 630.1203(d). Neither the regulation nor the comments by OPM accompanying the publication of the final regulation indicate what the purpose of such leave would be. Presumably, the leave would be used to facilitate the foster care placement. Unlike the comparable regulations governing Title I, the CAA, and the PEOAA (29 CFR 825.112(d); S. Res. 242, Cong. Rec. S3959, S3962 (April 23, 1996); 29 CFR 825.112(d)), the Title II regulation does not mandate that the pre–placement leave be "required" for the placement to proceed. As such, the Title II regulation would appear to be more flexible and available even when the pre–placement leave is optional, as long as it relates to the foster care placement.

d. Foster Care Placement of Older Children

FMLA leave is available for the foster care placement of an individual, as long as that individual meets the definition of "son or daughter." A "son or daughter" includes a foster child who is either under 18 years of age, or 18 years of age or older and incapable of self–care due to a mental or physical disability. 5 USC 6381(6); 5 CFR 630.1202 (definition of "son or daughter"). An employee would be entitled to FMLA leave for the placement of an age 18 or older son or daughter, only if that son or daughter was incapable of self–care due to a mental or physical disability. If the age 18 or older foster son or daughter was capable of self care, or did not have a mental or physical disability within the meaning of the FMLA laws, the employee would not be entitled to FMLA leave for the placement of such son or daughter with the employee for foster care. [Who is a covered "son or daughter," within the meaning of the FMLA, is addressed more fully in Chapter 6, "Covered Family Members."]

e. Pay, Minimum Duration, and Multiple Foster Care Placements

Title II does not impose requirements or restrictions, or otherwise address, the impact of the employee's receipt of compensation for being a foster parent. Nor does Title II impose a minimum duration of time the son or daughter must remain with the foster parent before FMLA leave is available. Finally, Title II does not treat employees differently because they have become foster parents multiple times during the course of any given leave year. It would appear, therefore, that Title II treats these matters the same for purposes of foster care as Title I, the CAA, and the PEOAA.

f. Leave Conclusion

As with FMLA leave for adoption and the birth and care of a newborn son or daughter, addressed previously, FMLA leave for the placement of a son or daughter with an employee for foster care expires 12 months from the placement date. 5 USC 6382(a)(2); 5 CFR 630.1203(d). Because Title II fails to define what "placement" is, it would appear difficult for an agency to determine when "placement" occurs.

As discussed previously, an agency is permitted to require an employee requesting FMLA leave for the adoption of a son or daughter to provide evidence that is administratively acceptable to the agency. 5 CFR 630.1206(f). What is "administratively acceptable" is not defined or described. Presumably, the agency has some discretion in this area. An agency should consider requesting the employee to provide documentation evidencing the foster care placement, preferably with an effective placement date. The regulations do not address when the agency may request such evidence after the employee's request, and how long the employee has to produce the evidence. The regulations also do not state any consequence if an employee fails to provide administratively acceptable evidence of the adoption. Presumably, such a failure by the employee of a precondition to leave would result in FMLA leave being denied. *See, e.g.,* 5 CFR 630.1208(l) (leave not covered by FMLA when the employee fails to provide notice and medical certification).

The impact of pre-placement foster care leave on the calculation of the 12-month period for expiration of FMLA leave following the placement of a son or daughter with an employee for adoption follows the same rules as discussed previously for adoption and birth. Please refer to the above discussion for more on this subject. *See also* 5 CFR 630.1203(c), (d); Preamble, 5 CFR 630.1203.

g. Intermittent/Reduced Leave Schedule

As with adoption, FMLA leave for the placement of a son or daughter with the employee for foster care may not be taken by the employee on an intermittent or reduced leave schedule basis unless the employee and the employing agency of the employee agree otherwise. 5 USC 6382(b)(1); 5 CFR 630.1204(a).

Unlike the other federal sector variants of the FMLA, Title II does not distinguish between leave taken before or after the placement of a son or daughter with the employee for foster care for purposes of gaining the approval of the employing agency to take leave on an intermittent or reduced leave schedule basis. *Compare* 29 CFR 825.203(b); S. Res. 242, Cong. Rec. S3959, S3964 (April 23, 1996); 29 CFR 825.203(b). Title II and the implementing regulations uniformly provide that the employee must gain the approval of his or her employing agency if FMLA leave is taken on an intermittent or reduced leave schedule basis for the placement of a covered child with the employee for foster care. [How FMLA leave may be taken is addressed more fully in Chapter 10, "Leave Amount and Scheduling."]

III. SERIOUS HEALTH CONDITIONS

A. INTRODUCTION

This section addresses the availability of FMLA leave when the employee, or the spouse, parent, son or daughter of the employee, is ill due to a serious health condition.

For FMLA leave to be available, the illness must meet all of the requirements of a serious health condition. If it does not, no matter how severe the illness, the employee generally will not be entitled to FMLA leave for that illness. *See* DOL WH FMLA Advisory Opinion No. 77 (Jan. 30, 1996) (an employee whose illness does not meet the statutory and regulatory definitions of a serious health condition will not be entitled to take FMLA leave even if the employee cannot perform any of the essential functions of his or her job). *But see Bauer v. Dayton-Walther Corp.,* 910 F. Supp 310 (E.D. Ky. 1996) (court opined, "[c]oncluding that [plaintiff's] condition does not fall within the regulatory definitions does not necessarily exclude his condition from coverage as a 'serious health condition' under the statute." The court went on, however, to find that the plaintiff's condition [rectal bleeding] was not an FMLA-covered serious health condition when viewed in light of the legislative history of the Act), *aff'd*, 118 F.3d 1109, 1111 (6th Cir. 1997).

The term "serious health condition" is defined by Title I to include "an illness, injury, impairment, or physical condition that involves either inpatient care or continuing treatment by a health care provider." 29 USC 2611(11). *Moorer v. First Baptist Mem. Health Care System*, 398 F.3d 469 (6th Cir. 2005); *Hoffman v. Professional Med Team*, 394 F.3d 414, 418 (6th Cir. 2005); *George v. Russell Stover Candies, Inc.*, 106 Fed. Appx. 946 (6th Cir. 2004); *Lackey v. Jackson County, Tennessee*, 104 Fed. Appx. 483 (6th Cir. 2004); *Brenneman v. MedCentral Health System*, 366 F.3d 412, 420–421 (6th Cir. 2004), *cert. denied*, 543 U.S. 1146 (U.S. 2005); *Perry v. Jaguar of Troy*, 353 F.3d 510, 514 (6th Cir. 2003); *Russell v. North Broward Hospital*, 346 F.3d 1335, 1338 (11th Cir. 2003).

The statute does not define continuing treatment or qualifying illnesses. *Russell v. North Broward Hospital*, 346 F.3d 1335, 1342 (11th Cir. 2003) (continuing treatment); *Wheeler v. Pioneer Dev. Services, Inc.*, 349 F. Supp. 2d 158, at *15 (D. Mass. 2004) (qualifying illnesses). The DOL regulations promulgated under the statute provide a more comprehensive description of the illnesses that qualify for FMLA leave. *See* 29 CFR 825.114(a); *North Broward Hospital*, 346 F.3d at 1342 (11th Cir. 2003); *Lackey v. Jackson County, Tennessee*, 104 Fed. Appx. 483 (6th Cir. 2004).

The courts are spit on the breadth of "serious health condition." Some courts believe that "serious health condition" was meant to be broad, and the FMLA's provisions should be interpreted to affect its remedial purpose. *Ruiz v. Ostbye & Anderson, Inc.*, No. 02–2954 (JNE/JGL), 2004 U.S. Dist. LEXIS 19890, at *11–12 (D. Minn. Sept. 28, 2004). Other courts opin that "serious health condition" is not intended to be broadly construed. These courts observe that "[t]his provision of the FMLA was aimed at genuinely serious and incapacitating conditions. It was not intended to mandate, as a matter of federal law, a uniform national sick leave policy for minor or temporary illnesses and discomforts." *Schmutte v. Resort Condominiums International, LLC*, 463 F. Supp. 2d 891, 908 (S.D. Ind. 2006); *see Merritt v. E.F. Transit, Inc.*, No. IP02–0393–C–H/K, 2004 U.S. Dist. LEXIS 4310, at *13 (S.D. Ind. March 11, 2004); *see also Lackey v. Jackson County, Tennessee*, 104 Fed. Appx. 483 (6th Cir. 2004) (not all medical problems are subject to the FMLA); *Bradley v. Mary Rutan Hospital Assoc.*, 322 F. Supp. 2d 926, 941–942 (S.D. Ohio 2004); *Wu v. Southeast–Atlantic Beverage Corp.*, No. 1:02–CV–505–CAP, 2003 U.S. Dist. LEXIS 25828, at *59 (N.D. Ga. Aug. 13, 2003) (not all leave requested or taken for medical reasons qualifies for the FMLA's protections).

Whether a condition is a "serious health condition" under the FMLA is a mixed question of fact and law. *Densmore v. Pilgrim's Pride Corp.*, No. 4:05CV00770-WRW, 2006 U.S. Dist. LEXIS 82285, at *12 & n.12 (E.D. Ark. Nov. 9, 2006); *Lubke v. City of Arlington*, No. 4:02–CV–188–Y, 2003 U.S. Dist. LEXIS 18816, at *9, n.5 (N.D. Tex. Sept. 9, 2003). Other courts have held that whether an illness qualifies as a serious health condition for purposes of the FMLA is a legal question, and a plaintiff may not avoid it by merely alleging his condition to be so. *Michels v. Sunoco Home Comfort Service*, No. 04–1906, 2004 U.S. Dist. LEXIS 25152, at *9 (E.D. Pa. Dec. 10, 2004).

While broad, particularly as amplified by the implementing regulations, the circumstances that will fit within the definition of an FMLA–covered "serious health condition" are not limitless. The burden, however, to determine whether an illness qualifies as a serious health condition falls largely on the agency. As will be discussed more fully in Chapter 8, "Notice Requirements," and Chapter 9, "Documentation Requirements," an employing agency is assisted in this process by the obligation of an employee to provide timely and adequate notice of the need for FMLA leave, and medical documentation to support that leave. At the end of the day, however, the FMLA requires employing agencies to designate the leave as FMLA–qualifying or not. In order to do that, employing agencies must have a thorough understanding of what circumstances will and will not be considered "serious health conditions" for purposes of FMLA protections and benefits.

As discussed throughout this book, there are substantial similarities and differences between the four federal sector variants of the FMLA. This is as true for serious health conditions as it is for other areas of the FMLA.

B.   WHOSE SERIOUS HEALTH CONDITION?

Whether a covered individual has a "serious health condition" within the meaning of the law involves two inquires: (1) who has the serious health condition; and (2) does the condition meet one of the definitions of an FMLA–covered "serious health condition." With respect to the first inquiry, an employee's entitlement to FMLA leave differs depending on whether the need for FMLA leave is due to the employee's own serious health condition, or whether the employee is needed to care for a covered family member with a serious health condition.

1.   Title I, the CAA, and the PEOAA

FMLA leave is available for the serious health condition of the employee, or the employee's spouse, parent, son or daughter. *See Overley v. Covenant Transport, Inc.*, 178 Fed. Appx. 488 (6th Cir. 2006); *Burnett v. LFW, Inc.*, 472 F.3d 471, 478 (7th Cir. 2006); *Dillon v. The Maryland-National Capital Park and Planning Commission*, 382 F. Supp. 2d 777, 789 (D. Md. 2005); *Wheeler v. Pioneer Dev. Services, Inc.*, 349 F. Supp 2d 158 (D. Mass. 2004); *Willis v. USPS*, No. 03 C 9185, 2004 U.S. Dist. LEXIS 18238, at *12 (N.D. Ill. Sept. 10, 2004); *Bailey v. Aetna Inc.*, No. 02–5153, 2003 U.S. Dist. LEXIS 19651, at *21 (E.D. Pa. Oct. 28, 2003). This section addresses the additional criteria for a valid claim for FMLA leave. Serious health conditions are addressed in the next section of this chapter.

a. Needed to Care For a Covered Family Member

(1) General Rule

An eligible employee is entitled to a total of 12 workweeks of leave during the 12-month leave year in order to care for a spouse, or a son, daughter, or parent, of the employee, if such spouse, son, daughter, or parent has a serious health condition. 29 USC 2612(a)(1)(C); 29 CFR 825.100(a), 825.101(a), 825.112(a)(3), 825.200(a)(3); S. Res. 242, Cong. Rec. S3959, S3960, S3962–63 (April 23, 1996); 29 CFR 825.100(a), 825.101(a), 825.112(a)(3), 825.200(a)(3); *see Overley*, 178 Fed. Appx. at 488; *Tellis v. Alaska Airlines, Inc.*, 414 F.3d 1045, 1047 (9th Cir. 2005); *Brockman v. Wyoming Dept. of Family Services*, 342 F.3d 1159, 1164 (10th Cir. 2003) (three of the four categories of qualified leave relate to the care of family members), *cert. denied*, 540 U.S. 1219 (2004); *Scamihorn, Jr. v. General Truck Drivers, Office, Food and Warehouse Union, Local 952 et al.*, 282 F.3d 1078, 1082 (9th Cir. 2002); *Navarro v. Gladys Navarro Pomares et al.*, 261 F.3d 90, 94–95 (1st Cir. 2001); *McGinnis v. Employer Health Services, Inc.*, No. 05-2219-JTM, 2006 U.S. Dist. LEXIS 35831, at *21 (D. Kan. May 31, 2006), *aff'd*, 2007 U.S. App. LEXIS 17336 (10th Cir. July 20, 2007); *Dillon*, 382 F. Supp. 2d at 789; *Bagley v. Regis Corp.*, No. 3:03–CV–2908–M, 2004 U.S. Dist. LEXIS 24783, at *15 (N.D. Tex. Dec. 7, 2004) (FMLA protects parents' right to take leave from work to care for son or daughter with serious health condition).

The FMLA does not provide leave for every family emergency. The reason for the leave must fall under the statute and accompanying regulations. *Overley*, 178 Fed. Appx. at 488.

The statute does not define what "in order to care for" means in this context. *Scamihorn, Jr. v. General Truck Drivers, Office, Food and Warehouse Union, Local 952 et al.*, 282 F.3d 1078, 1082 (9th Cir. 2002). The implementing regulations, however, do explain what "in order to care for" means. 29 CFR 825.116; S. Res. 242, Cong. Rec. S3959, S3963 (April 23, 1996); 29 CFR 825.116. *See Gradilla v. Ruskin Manufacturing*, 320 F.3d 951, 958 (9th Cir. 2003), *op withdrawn, dismissed*, 328 F.3d 1107 (9th Cir. 2003). By their terms, the regulations define the similar phrase "needed to care for." 29 CFR 825.116(a); S. Res. 242, Cong. Rec. S3959, S3963 (April 23, 1996); 29 CFR 825.116(a). According to the regulation, the term "needed to care for" is contained in the medical certification provisions. 29 CFR 825.116(a); S. Res. 242, Cong. Rec. S3959, S3963 (April 23, 1996); 29 CFR 825.116(a). The phrase is not contained in the regulations, *see* 29 CFR 825.306; S. Res. 242, Cong. Rec. S3959, S3972–73 (April 23, 1996); 29 CFR 825.306, but is used in the statute. *See* 29 USC 2613(b)(4) (for purposes of leave to care for a covered family member with a serious health condition, "a statement that the eligible employee is needed to care for the son, daughter, spouse, or parent…."). The DOL comments accompanying the publication of the final regulations indicate that § 825.116 addresses the "in order to care for" requirement of 29 USC 2612(a)(1)(C). *See* Preamble, 29 CFR 825.112 ("[a]n eligible employee may take FMLA leave "in order to care for" an immediate family member (spouse, son, daughter, or parent) with a serious health condition"). The DOL interprets the phrases "in order to care for" and "needed to care for" as having the same meaning.

Both physical and psychological care are encompassed within the meaning of "in order to care for" or "needed to care for." 29 CFR 825.116(a); S. Res. 242, Cong. Rec. S3959, S3963 (April 23, 1996); 29 CFR 825.116(a); *see Overley v. Covenant Transport, Inc.*, 178 Fed. Appx. 488 (6th Cir. 2006); *Tellis v. Alaska Airlines, Inc.*, 414 F.3d 1045, 1047 (9th Cir. 2005); *Gradilla v. Ruskin Manufacturing*, 320 F.3d 951, 958 (9th Cir. 2003), *op withdrawn, dismissed*, 328 F.3d 1107 (9th Cir. 2003); *Scamihorn, Jr. v. General Truck Drivers, Office, Food and Warehouse Union, Local 952 et al.*, 282 F.3d 1078, 1087 (9th Cir. 2002); *Bagley v. Regis Corp.*, No. 3:03–CV–2908–M, 2004 U.S. Dist. LEXIS 24783, at *16 (N.D. Tex. Dec. 7, 2004); *Aubuchon v. Knauf Fiberglass, GMBH*, 240 F. Supp. 2d 859, 865 (S.D. Ind. Jan. 10, 2003), *aff'd*, 359 F.3d 950 952 (7th Cir. 2004) (an employee who "hung out" in father's hospital room provided psychological care within the meaning of the FMLA, as confirmed by the father's affidavit that his son's hospital visits were comforting), *aff'd*, 359 F.3d 950 (7th Cir. 2004); *Hatch v. USPS*, No. AT-0752-07-0175-I-1, 2007 MSPB LEXIS 647, at *2-3 (June 1, 2007). A non–exclusive list of examples of physical care, 29 CFR 825.116(a); S. Res. 242, Cong. Rec. S3959, S3963 (April 23, 1996); 29 CFR 825.116(a)) includes situations where, because of a serious health condition, the covered family member is:

1. Unable to care for his or her own basic medical, hygienic, or nutritional needs or safety;

2. Unable to transport himself or herself to the doctor, etc.

See Overley, 178 Fed. Appx. at 488; *Gradilla*, 320 F.3d at 958; *McGinnis v. Employer Health Services, Inc.*, No. 05-2219-JTM, 2006 U.S. Dist. LEXIS 35831, at *21 (D. Kan. May 31, 2006), *aff'd*, 2007 U.S. App. LEXIS 17336 (10th Cir. July 20, 2007);

Wiseman v. Vanderbilt University, No. 3:04-0946, 2005 U.S. Dist. LEXIS 29000, at *28 (M.D. Tenn. Nov. 14, 2005); *Young v. USPS*, 79 MSPR 25 (1998).

The legislative history addresses the meaning of "to care for" as well:

> The phrase "to care for"…is intended to be read broadly to include both physical and psychological care. Parents provide far greater psychological comfort and reassurance to a seriously ill child than others not so closely tied to the child. In some cases there is no one other than the child's parents to care for the child. The same is often true for adults caring for a seriously ill parent or spouse.

S. Rep. No. 103–3, at p. 24 (reprinted in 1993 USCCAN at 26); *see Scamihorn, Jr.*, 282 F.3d at 1082.

Additional insight into the types of care that an employee may provide a covered family with a serious health condition for purposes of FMLA leave may be gleaned from the medical certification regulations. Specifically, § 825.306(b)(5)(I), addressing leave required to care for a family member with a serious health condition, provides that the medical certification must contain the following:

> (I) If leave is required to care for a family member of the employee with a serious health condition, whether the patient requires assistance for basic medical or personal needs or safety, or for transportation; or if not, whether the employee's presence to provide psychological comfort would be beneficial to the patient or assist in the patient's recovery. The employee is required to indicate on the form the care he or she will provide and an estimate of the time period.

Note that psychological comfort and care is only reached if the covered family member does not need assistance for basic medical or personal needs or safety, or for transportation. This interpretation is at odds with the similar language in § 825.116(a), discussed previously. There, physical and psychological care are identified as parts of the same definition of "needed to care for." No order of priority is suggested in the regulations. Again, the lack of consistency in the language used by the DOL creates unnecessary confusion. Agencies would be well advised to follow the requirements of § 825.116, as the medical certification provisions are directed at the health care provider, not the employer.

The DOL opined that a Care Conference, during which the covered family member's health care providers (nurses, dieticians, physical therapists, activity directors, or doctors) discuss the individual's condition, immediate needs, incidents, and general well–being, is "clearly essential to the employee's ability to provide appropriate physical or psychological care," and is covered by the FMLA. *See* DOL WH FMLA Advisory Opinion No. 94 (Feb. 27, 1998).

The use of the all–encompassing "etc." in § 825.116(a) is not particularly helpful to agencies or employees in determining whether the situation fits within the phrase "in order to care for." Agencies would be well advised to carefully compare the situation at hand to the examples provided in the regulations. Where the situation at hand compares favorably with the examples provided, agencies might conclude that the situation meets the "in order to care for" requirement. Where the situation does not compare favorably with the examples provided, agencies should seriously question whether the leave is needed "to care for" the covered family member. *See Gilbert v. Star Building Systems*, No. CIV–95–1932–L, 1996 U.S. Dist. LEXIS 22435, at *7–8 (W.D. Ok. Nov. 15, 1996) (FMLA leave "to care for" a spouse with serious health condition when the need for leave was to assist husband with employment action against former employer and union, not in caring for spouse because of an illness or disability); *Brown v. J.C. Penny Corp.*, 924 F. Supp. 1158, 1163 (S.D. Fla. 1996) (FMLA leave "to care for" a covered family member requires that the covered family member be alive; wrapping up the affairs of the deceased is not an included reason for leave covered by the FMLA).

The term also includes providing psychological comfort and reassurance that would be beneficial to a child, spouse or parent with a serious health condition who is receiving inpatient or home care. 29 CFR 825.116(a); S. Res. 242, Cong. Rec. S3959, S3963 (April 23, 1996); 29 CFR 825.116(a); *Tellis v. Alaska Airlines, Inc.*, 414 F.3d 1045, 1047 (9th Cir. 2005); *McGinnis v. Employer Health Services, Inc.*, No. 05-2219-JTM, 2006 U.S. Dist. LEXIS 35831, at *21 (D. Kan. May 31, 2006), *aff'd*, 2007 U.S. App. LEXIS 17336 (10th Cir. July 20, 2007); *Dillon v. The Maryland-National Capital Park and Planning Commission*, 382 F. Supp. 2d 777, 789 (D. Md. 2005). What constitutes "psychological comfort and reassurance" is not explained by the statute or regulations. Presumably, the term will be interpreted broadly. *See* S. Rep. 103–3, pg. 24 ("to care for" in § 102(a)(c) is intended to be read broadly to include both physical and psychological care).

Caring for a family member with a serious health condition involves some level of participation in ongoing treatment of that condition. *Tellis*, 414 F.3d 1045; *Marchisheck v. San Mateo County*, 199 F.3d 1068, 1076 (9th Cir. 1999), *cert. denied*, 530

U.S. 1214 (2000). Merely visiting a sick relative does not fall within the statutes parameters. *Fioto v. Manhattan Woods Golf Enters., LLC*, 270 F. Supp. 2d 401, 404 (S.D.N.Y. 2003), *aff'd*, 123 Fed. Appx. 26 (2d Cir. 2005); *Bright v. Colgate-Palmolive Co.*, No. 1:03-cv-01709-DFH-TAB, 2005 U.S. Dist. LEXIS 15470, at *44-45 (S.D. Ind. July 26, 2005) (no evidence of care during visit to father in hospital after suffering a stroke).

Inpatient care is a defined term, meaning an overnight stay in a hospital, hospice, or residential medical care facility. 29 CFR 825.114(a); S. Res. 242, Cong. Rec. S3959, S3962 (April 23, 1996); 29 CFR 825.114(a). "Home care" is not defined by the statute or the regulations. Based on the comments that accompany the final regulations, "home care" appears to refer to covered family members with a serious health condition who are literally at home. Preamble, 29 CFR 825.116. "Home care" does not appear to require anything more. *See, e.g., Scamihorn, Jr. v. General Truck Drivers, Office, Food and Warehouse Union, Local 952 et al.*, 282 F.3d 1078, 1088 (9th Cir. 2002) (employee/son care for parent who was at home with serious health condition).

In *Scamihorn, Jr. v. General Truck Drivers, Office, Food and Warehouse Union, Local 952 et al.*, 282 F.3d 1078, 1082 (9th Cir. 2002), the Ninth Circuit held that there were sufficient facts that the employee was providing both physical and psychological comfort and care to his parent with a serious health condition to warrant reversal of summary judgment for the employer. In that case, the employee took time off work to talk with his 73–year–old father who was at home grieving over the murder of his sister. The employee also performed various chores around the house, including shoveling snow, chopping firewood used to heat the house, clearing he backyard and cleaning the garage. He also drove his father to counseling sessions on four or five occasions.

Physical and psychological care also includes situations where the employee may be needed to fill in for others who are caring for the family member, or to make arrangements for changes in care, such as transfer to a nursing home. 29 CFR 825.116(a); S. Res. 242, Cong. Rec. S3959, S3963 (April 23, 1996); 29 CFR 825.116(a); *see Overley v. Covenant Transport, Inc.*, 178 Fed. Appx. 488 (6th Cir. 2006); *Marx v. Whirlpool Corp.*, No. 3:05-cv-108 RLY-WGH, 2006 U.S. Dist. LEXIS 86727, at *16 (S.D. Ind. Nov. 28, 2006); *McGinnis v. Employer Health Services, Inc.*, No. 05-2219-JTM, 2006 U.S. Dist. LEXIS 35831, at *21 (D. Kan. May 31, 2006), *aff'd*, 2007 U.S. App. LEXIS 17336 (10th Cir. July 20, 2007); *Dillon*, 382 F. Supp. 2d at 789; *Mora v. Chem Tronics, Inc.*, 16 F. Supp. 2d 1192, 1206 (S.D. Ca. 1998). For example, an eligible employee would be entitled to FMLA leave to visit assisted living facilities on behalf of a parent with a serious health condition.

In *Dillon v. The Maryland-National Capital Park and Planning Commission*, 382 F. Supp. 2d 777, 789 (D. Md. 2005), the court rejected the employer's argument that the employee's need for leave to look for better living conditions for her grandmother was not a sufficient reason for leave under the FMLA.

In order to be "needed to care for" an employee, there must be some evidence that the employee's need for leave is time sensitive. In *Overley v. Covenant Transport, Inc.*, 178 Fed. Appx. 488 (6th Cir. 2006), the court found that the employee was neither "needed to care for" her ill daughter, nor did she provide "care." In that case, the employee took leave to meet with the overseer of her ill daughter's trust. The court noted that, even if meeting constituted "care," there was no indication that it needed to occur on the day in question. The employee and trustee met for two hours during which they examined an empty plot of land where a possible future residence for the daughter might be built. The court found that the employee did not "need" leave for this activity as it was not time sensitive. The court also found that the meeting did not constitute "making arrangements for care" as there was no indication that the daughter was going to be moving anytime in the near future.

In *Marx v. Whirlpool Corp.*, No. 3:05-cv-108 RLY-WGH, 2006 U.S. Dist. LEXIS 86727, at *16 (S.D. Ind. Nov. 28, 2006), the court noted the absence of an imminent reason or emergency that required the employee to take off work to make the four telephone calls allegedly to make care arrangements for her ill son.

The fact that a covered family member may need assistance does not satisfy the "needed to care for" criterion of the FMLA. *Hatch v. USPS*, No. AT-0752-07-0175-I-1, 2007 MSPB LEXIS 647, at *2-3 (June 1, 2007); *Jones v. USPS*, 103 MSPR 561, 567 (2006).

Finally, § 825.116(a), while referencing medical certification, does not independently require an employee to provide certification verifying that the employee is "needed to care for" a covered family member with a serious health condition. An employer may, however, request that an employee provide such certification pursuant to § 825.306. *See Williams v. Shenango, Inc.*, 986 F. Supp. 309, 319 (W.D. Pa. 1997).

(2) "To Care For" the Living

An employee is only "needed to care for" an FMLA-qualifying "illness, injury, impairment, or physical or mental condition" of the living, not the deceased. *See Barone v. Leukemia Society of America*, 42 F. Supp. 2d 452, 460 (D.N.J. 1998) (bereavement leave or absence from work following the death of one's immediate family member is not protected by the FMLA); *Sharpe v. MCI Telecommunications Corp.*, 19 F. Supp. 2d 483, (E.D.N.C. 1998) (an employee's two-week absence following the death of her mother did not qualify as FMLA leave); *Lange v. Showbiz Pizza Time, Inc.*, 12 F. Supp. 2d 1150, 1153–54 (D. Kan. 1998) (bereavement leave following death of the mother not protected by FMLA); *Fisher v. State Farm Mutual Automobile Ins. Co.*, 999 F. Supp. 866, 869 (E.D. Tex. 1998) (former employee who took unauthorized leave following his father's death was not incapacitated and did not meet FMLA requirements for having a serious health condition and was not eligible for FMLA leave), *aff'd without op.*, 176 F.3d 479 (5th Cir. 1999); *Beal v. Rubbermaid Commercial Products, Inc.*, 972 F. Supp. 1216, 1226 (S.D. Iowa 1997) (finding that FMLA leave was not meant to be used for bereavement because deceased person has no basic medical, nutritional or psychological needs which need to be cared for), *aff'd*, 1998 U.S. App. LEXIS 9295 (8th Cir. 1998); *Brown v. J.C. Penny Corp.*, 924 F. Supp. 1158, 1161–63 (S.D. Fla. 1996) (finding that the language of the FMLA and relevant regulations indicate that "serious health condition" was limited to medical conditions affecting a living individual and the employee did not "care for" the father when he engaged in activities in connection with his father's affairs following his father's death); *Young v. USPS*, 79 MSPR 25 (1998) (death of a family member is not a statutory or regulatory reason for invoking the provisions of the FMLA).

Of course, if another covered family member (or the employee) were to suffer from a serious health condition due to the passing of loved one, provided all other conditions are met, the employee may be entitled to FMLA leave to provide care for the physical and/or psychological needs of other covered family members. *See e.g., Young v. USPS*, 79 MSPR 25 (1998) (Board noted lack of evidence that employee was incapacitated after father's death as a means to excuse employee's failure to return to work).

(3) Availability of Other Caregivers

Neither the statute nor the regulations address the affect of the availability of other care givers on an eligible employee's right to take FMLA leave "to care for" a covered family member. In comments accompanying the publication of the final regulations, however, the DOL clearly indicated that whether care is being provided through health care services or other family members is not relevant to the "to care for" determination. Responding to the comments suggesting that the final regulations should be changed to permit employers the discretion to consider whether other care is being provided to the covered family member, the DOL (Preamble, 29 CFR 825.116) stated:

> No further changes have been made in response to the remaining comments [including the one at issue]. The legislative history clearly reflects the intent of Congress that providing psychological care and comfort to family members with serious health conditions would be a legitimate use of FMLA's leave entitlement provisions. Because FMLA grants to eligible employees the absolute right to take FMLA leave for qualifying reasons under the law, employers have no discretion in this area and cannot deny the legitimate use of FMLA leave for such purposes without violating the prohibited acts section of the Statute.

Courts are split on the impact of the availability of other caregivers on the employees need for FMLA leave. Like the DOL, some have found that the availability of other caregivers has no affect on an eligible employee's entitlement to FMLA leave "to care for" a covered family member with a serious health condition. *See McGinnis v. Employer Health Services, Inc.*, No. 05-2219-JTM, 2006 U.S. Dist. LEXIS 35831, at *21 (D. Kan. May 31, 2006) (stepmother permitted to provide psychological care to stepdaughter even though biological parents present and also providing care), *aff'd*, 2007 U.S. App. LEXIS 17336 (10th Cir. July 20, 2007); *Dillon v. The Maryland-National Capital Park and Planning Commission*, 382 F. Supp. 2d 777, 789 (D. Md. 2005) (presence of aunt did not preclude employee from taking FMLA leave to care for seriously ill grandmother who served as in loco parentis parent of employee when employee was a child); *Bagley v. Regis Corp.*, No. 3:03-CV-2908-M, 2004 U.S. Dist. LEXIS 24783, at *16 (N.D. Tex. Dec. 7, 2004) (FMLA permits leave when the employee shares responsibility for the injured person's care with others, such as a former spouse); *Mora v. Chem Tronics, Inc.*, 16 F. Supp. 2d 1192, 1206 (S.D. Ca. 1998) ("[t]he term 'needed to care for' is statutorily defined and does not require an employee to demonstrate that no other caretakers be available before obtaining leave"). Other courts cite the availability of other caregivers in support of decisions to deny FMLA leave. *See Cianci v. Pettibone Corp. et al.*, 1997 U.S. Dist. LEXIS 4482 (N.D. Ill. April 7, 1997) (FMLA leave was not available to visit aging mother with serious health condition when the employee was not "needed to care for" the mother within meaning of the Act because the sister was performing those duties), *aff'd*, 152 F.3d 723 (7th Cir. 1998). In *Hatch v. USPS*, No. AT-0752-07-0175-I-1, 2007 MSPB LEXIS 647, at *2-3 (June 1, 2007), the Board cited the presence of the employee's brother with his seriously ill parents who could care for his parents as evidence that the employee was not "needed to care for" the parents within the meaning of the FMLA.

Given the absence of conditional language in the statute and implementing regulations, and the inclusion of psychological comfort and care in the legislative history and regulations as a legitimate reason for an employee to take FMLA leave "to care for" a covered family member, the better view is that the availability of other care givers has no bearing on the employee's entitlement to FMLA leave "to care for" a covered family member.

(4) Psychological and Physical Care of Covered Family Members

Three issues are addressed in this subsection: (1) what level of "care" must an employee provide to a covered family member with a serious health condition; (2) traveling with a covered family member to provide care; and (3) what evidence is needed to establish that the employee, in fact, provided care to the covered family member.

(a) Level of Care

There is a paucity of law on the subject of what constitutes the provision of physical or psychological care to a covered family member with a serious health condition. *Fioto v. Manhattan Woods Golf Enterprises, LLC et al.*, 270 F. Supp. 2d 401 (S.D.N.Y. 2003), *affd* 123 Fed. Appx. 26 (2d Cir. 2005). FMLA leave does not provide qualified leave to cover every family emergency. *Id.* FMLA leave is only available when an employee is needed "to care for" a covered family member with a serious health condition. *Id.* FMLA leave, therefore, does not cover absences that do not implicate giving physical or psychological care to a parent, spouse, son or daughter, as defined by the FMLA. *Id.*

FMLA leave "to care for" a covered family member is broadly construed. *Fioto v. Manhattan Woods Golf Enterprises, LLC et al.*, 270 F. Supp. 2d 401 (S.D.N.Y. 2003), *affd* 123 Fed. Appx. 26 (2d Cir. 2005). For example, it covers an employee's leave to assist in making medical decisions for a badly burned parent. *Id.* (citing *Brunell v. Cytec Plastics Inc.*, 225 F. Supp. 2d 67 (D.Me. 2002)). Merely visiting an ill family member with a serious health condition, however, does not fall within the protections of the FMLA. *Fioto v. Manhattan Woods Golf Enterprises, LLC et al.*, 270 F. Supp. 2d 401 (S.D.N.Y. 2003), *affd* 123 Fed. Appx. 26 (2d Cir. 2005). According to the Ninth Circuit, caring for a covered family member requires some level of participation by the eligible employee in ongoing medical or psychological treatment of that condition, either inpatient or at home. *Gradilla v. Ruskin Manufacturing*, 320 F.3d 951, 958 (9th Cir. 2003), *op. withdrawn, dismissed*, 328 F.3d 951 (9th Cir. 2003); *Scamihorn, Jr. v. General Truck Drivers, Office, Food and Warehouse Union, Local 952 et al.*, 282 F.3d 1078, 1082 (9th Cir. 2002); *Marchischeck v. San Mateo County*, 199 F.3d 1068, 1076 (9th Cir. 1999), *cert. denied*, 530 U.S. 1214 (200); *see also Fioto v. Manhattan Woods Golf Enterprises, LLC et al.*, 270 F. Supp. 2d 401 (S.D.N.Y. 2003), *affd* 123 Fed. Appx. 26 (2d Cir. 2005).

With respect to psychological comfort and care, the courts have found that even a minimal level of comfort of a covered family member with a serious health condition will fall within the protections of the Act. *Fioto*, 270 F. Supp. 2d 401 (S.D.N.Y. 2003), *affd* 123 Fed. Appx. 26 (2d Cir. 2005). For example, in *Plumley v. Southern Container, Inc.*, 2001 U.S. Dist. LEXIS 16040 (D.Me. Oct. 9, 2001), *aff'd*, 303 F.3d 364 (1st Cir. 2002), the plaintiff testified regarding the time spent with his father while the father was hospitalized. The plaintiff's father testified that this son was present with him and that the son's presence was comforting and reassuring. The Magistrate Judge concluded (*in dictum*) that this sufficed to meet the threshold of "psychological care" for FMLA purposes.

In *Overley v. Covenant Transport, Inc.*, 178 Fed. Appx. 488 (6th Cir. 2006), the court found that an employee who spent the day picking up her ill daughter's laundry (as she did every week), making a preliminary visit with a funeral home, and visiting her daughter to check on her care and condition, were routine activities that did not qualify as physical or psychological are under the FMLA, even under the broadest reading of the statute.

An employee did not provide psychological comfort and care for his wife who was having trouble with her pregnancy by leaving her in Seattle for almost four days to retrieve the family car from Atlanta. The court rejected arguments that the employee provided psychological comfort and care by calling his wife everyday from the road. The court found that, to constitute "caring for" a family member within the meaning of the FMLA, the employee must be in close and continuing proximity to the ill family member. *Tellis v. Alaska Airlines, Inc.*, 414 F.3d 1045 (9th Cir. 2005).

The MSPB similarly found that, in order to be "needed to care for" an ill family member, the employee must be in physical proximity to the family member. *See Hatch v. USPS*, No. AT-0752-07-0175-I-1, 2007 MSPB LEXIS 647, at *2-3 (June 1, 2007) (employee who was not with parents was not needed to care for parents); *Jones v. USPS*, 103 MSPR 561, 566 (2006) (employee on approved FMLA leave for dependent care who does not actually stay with seriously ill family member does not fall within the definition of "needed to care for" and, therefore, is not FMLA leave).

In *Bradley v. Mary Rutan Hospital Assoc.*, 322 F. Supp. 2d 926, 941–942 (S.D. Ohio 2004), the court found that the affidavits of the husband's doctor, the husband, and the employee, detailing how Mr. Bradley required basic medical assistance, assistance with his personal needs, and assistance to ensure his safety in that he could not walk, prepare meals, go to the restroom, or feed himself, was sufficient to demonstrate that the employee was needed to care for her husband.

In *Brunell v. Cytec Plastics, Inc.*, 225 F. Supp. 2d 67 (D.Me. 2002), the plaintiff was the son of a man who was critically burned in a fire. The plaintiff's father remained hospitalized for several months, enduring multiple surgeries, but ultimately died. During that period, the plaintiff kept vigil at his father's bedside. According to the testimony of the father's physician, the son helped doctors make decisions concerning the father's care. The court concluded that Brunelle satisfied the FMLA's "to care for" requirement.

In *Fioto v. Manhattan Woods Golf Enterprises, LLC et al.*, 270 F. Supp. 2d 401 (S.D.N.Y. 2003), *aff'd*, 123 Fed. Appx. 26 (2d Cir. 2005), the district court was agreeable to adopting modest standards interpreting the FMLA "to care for" requirement. Under those standards, the court held that there was no evidence in the record suggesting that Fioto did anything other than visit the hospital where his sick mother was staying. There was no evidence that he provided physical or psychological care to his mother. According to the court:

> Insofar as psychological care is concerned, the jury knows only that [the] plaintiff went to the hospital and did not see his mother after surgery. It was not told whether he saw his mother prior to surgery, or whether his mother was conscious or unconscious when [the] plaintiff arrived at the hospital. The jury did not even know whether [the] plaintiff's mother was aware that he was on the way to the hospital, or was capable of being aware of his imminent arrival.... Because the language of the [S]tatute does not guarantee employees FMLA leave to visit an ailing parent, it was incumbent on [the] plaintiff to demonstrate that he was doing something—anything—to participate in his mother's care. It would not have taken much to meet the very lose "psychological care" standard. The plaintiffs in *Brunell* and *Plumley* testified about their interaction with their parents and their doctors. Fioto did not.

The court agreed with the plaintiff that the phrase "to care for" should be read broadly to include both physical and psychological care. However, "it cannot be read so broadly that the concept of providing care is read out of the [S]tatute. If, on the basis of a bald statement that [the] plaintiff went to the hospital where his mother was having serious surgery, FMLA's 'to care for' provision was automatically implicated, the [S]tatute would protect mere visitation. By its terms it does not. Congress could have drawn the [S]tatute that broadly; nothing could more surely have been anticipated than the need of workers to visit their ailing relatives. It chose to limit FMLA's reach to absences that were occasioned by the provision of care."

The courts will undoubtedly continue to struggle over the distinction between mere "visitation" and "care." Employees and those that represent them would be well advised to include evidence of employee interaction with the covered family member or medical staff in order to satisfy the "to care for" requirement.

(b) Traveling Care

The FMLA does not cover leave to provide physical or psychological care whenever the covered family member with a serious health condition chooses to travel for non–medical reasons. *Gradilla v. Ruskin Manufacturing*, 320 F.3d 951, 958 (9th Cir. 2003), *op. withdrawn, dismissed*, 328 F.3d 951 (9th Cir. 2003). The issue was vetted in a series of Ninth Circuit cases.

In *Marchischeck v. San Mateo County*, 199 F.3d 1068 (9th Cir. 1999), *cert. denied*, 530 U.S. 1214 (2000), an employee left work to move her son to the Philippines. The son did not require medical or psychological treatment during his travel. The Ninth Circuit found no factual dispute on the question of whether her son had a serious medical condition under the FMLA. The court further held that even if the son had a serious medical condition, the employee was not entitled to FMLA leave because she was not moving her son so he could receive medical or psychological treatment. Indeed, the employee had no specific plans to seek medical attention for the son when she reached the Philippines, and he did not see a doctor of any kind for more than five months after he moved overseas. Moreover, there were no psychological services available within a three-hour drive of the rural area of the Philippines where the employee and son went. The employee moved the son for his safety as he had just been assaulted. *Marchischeck*, 199 F.3d at 1076.

In *Scamihorn v. General Truck Drivers*, 282 F.3d 1078 (9th Cir. 2002), the court held that the employee created a triable issue of fact regarding his eligibility for FMLA leave when the employee left work to move to his father's home because his presence in the home providing psychological support helped in the father's recovery from depression. *Gradilla*, 320 F.3d at 958 (*citing Scamihorn*, 282 F.3d at 1088). According to the court, "*Scamihorn* does not support the proposition that physical or psychological care by a spouse or parent is covered by the FMLA whenever the family member with a serious health condition chooses to travel for non-medical reasons." *Gradilla*, 320 F.3d at 958.

Finally, in *Gradilla v. Ruskin Manufacturing*, 320 F.3d 951, 953–54 (9th Cir. 2003), *op. withdrawn, dismissed*, 328 F.3d 951 (9th Cir. 2003), the employee's spouse had a serious health condition regarding heart problems. The wife's father died and she wanted her husband to accompany her to Mexico for the funeral. She claimed she needed her husband to care for her during the trip because her father's death and funeral were stressful, emotionally upsetting events that aggravated her heart condition. *Id*. They needed to leave for Mexico that afternoon. The employee was given permission to take leave to care for his wife, which he did during the absence by administering medication. Unfortunately, the employee missed more work than anticipated and failed to call in as required by the governing collective bargaining agreement. The employee was terminated on his return from leave.

The employee sued, alleging a violation of the California Family Rights Act (CFRA). The CFRA was modeled on the FMLA, and it incorporates FMLA regulations to the extent they do not conflict with California law. *Gradilla*, 320 F.3d at 956. The court found that there was no conflict between CFRA and FMLA law in this case, and applied federal FMLA leave to Gradilla's CFRA claim. *Id*.

After analyzing the decisions in *Marchischeck* and *Scamihorn*, the court in *Gradilla* (320 F.3d at 958) held as follows:

> The circumstances of the travel in this case, a funeral in Mexico, were sympathetic, unfortunate, and lawful. If we hold that the CFRA covered this situation, an employer would be required to grant family and medical leave whenever an employee has a spouse, parent, or child with a serious health condition, and that family member requested the employee's assistance while traveling. The travel could be for unlimited personal reasons, to any destination, for lawful or unlawful purposes, for business or vacation. Courts would then have to decide, in each case, the worthiness of the family member's travel motives. Such a broad scope finds no support in the Statute, regulations, or case law.

The court affirmed the judgment of the district court dismissing the CFRA claim.

The dissent in *Gradilla*, 320 F.3d at 960–65 should be read by those in favor of FMLA coverage of employees who take FMLA leave to care for a covered family member with a serious health condition while that covered family member travels. The opinion was subsequently withdrawn pursuant to the dismissal of the case by stipulation of the parties. *Gradilla v. Ruskin Manufacturing*, 328 F.3d 951 (9th Cir. 2003).

In *Dillon v. The Maryland-National Capital Park and Planning Commission*, 382 F. Supp. 2d 777, 789 (D. Md. 2005), the employee took FMLA leave to travel to Jamaica to care for her grandmother who just suffered a stroke. The court found sufficient material facts in dispute to deny summary judgment to the employer. While in Jamaica, the employee shared care giving responsibilities with an aunt. She spent some time looking for alternative living arrangements. The court found these to be permissible activities within the meaning of the FMLA. The court did not dwell on the fact that the activities took place in Jamaica.

(c)   Evidence of Care

One court addressed the evidentiary burden on an employee to establish that he or she provided "care" for a covered family member. In *Barrilleaux v. Thayer Lodging Group, Inc.*, No. 97-3252 § E/1, 1999 U.S. Dist. LEXIS 3436 (E.D. La. March 19, 1999), the court held that, while an employee must establish that he or she requested leave in order "to care for" a covered family member, the employee is not required to establish with evidence that the employee in fact provided "care for" the covered family member. The employer argued that the plaintiff failed to establish with evidence that she in fact "cared for" her seriously ill father. According to the court:

> Apparently Thayer believes that Barrilleaux must come forward with documentation clearly indicating that she cared for her father during her leave. Again, Thayer does not cite a single case to support the conclusion that this Court must require Barrilleaux to support her case with specific documentation that she "cared for" her father during the leave. The plain language of the FMLA requires that her leave request be for the purpose of caring for an ill parent, nothing more. Clearly, Barrilleaux has offered evidence that the purpose of her leave was "to care for" her father. Nothing in the [S]tatute or the legislative history of the FMLA requires a plaintiff to provide further specific documentation. This Court declines to require Barrilleaux to present specific evidence of the care that she undertook, under the facts of this case. The Court believes that the truly pertinent question is Barrilleaux's purported purpose at the time she requested the leave and not what she actually did during this time, especially since she was never actually given a "leave." The fact that Barrilleaux was unemployed as a result of her "termination" could clearly change Barrilleaux's entire outlook, as well as her corresponding activities during this time period. The fact that Barrilleaux may have cared for her children a lot of the time, or looked for a new job as a result of her termination does not change the fact that Barrilleaux offered documents indicating that her original purpose for requesting a leave of absence was to care for her ill father, which is a purpose that has been completely unrefuted by Thayer up until the current motion for reconsideration.

The decision's emphasis on what the intent of the leave was, rather than what the FMLA was actually used for, appears to invite abuse. While correct that the regulations do not specifically require an employee to provide documentation to establish that FMLA leave was actually used as intended "to care for" a covered family member, as addressed later in this chapter, the majority of courts have required an employee to establish that leave was for a serious health condition by the producing supporting medical evidence. After all, one of the conditions that must be met in order for an eligible employee to enjoy the benefits and protections of the FMLA is that the leave be taken "for the intended purpose" of the FMLA. 29 USC 2614(a)(1). The *Barrilleaux* court's holding that they do not care what an eligible employee actually did during the leave as long as he or she articulated at the time of the request that he or she wanted to care for a covered family member, appears to undermine the basic requirement that the leave must be used "for the intended purpose" within the meaning of the FMLA.

b. Unable to Work Due to Employee's Own Serious Health Condition

(1) General Rule

An eligible employee is entitled to FMLA leave because of a serious health condition that makes the employee unable to perform the functions of the position of such employee. 29 USC 2612(a)(1)(D); 29 CFR 825.115; S. Res. 242, Cong. Rec. S3959, S3963 (April 23, 1996); 29 CFR 825.116(c) *see Burnett v. LFW, Inc.*, 472 F.3d 471, 478 (7th Cir. Dec. 26, 2006); *Moorer v. First Baptist Mem. Health Care System*, 398 F.3d 469 (6th Cir. 2005); *Fogelman v. Greater Hazelton Health Alliance*, 122 Fed. Appx. 521 (3d Cir. 2004); *Urban v. Dolgencorp of Texas, Inc.*, 393 F.3d 572 (5th Cir. 2004); *Edmonsond v. The Brookwood Community*, 114 Fed. Appx. 148 (5th Cir. 2004); *Haley v. Alliance Compressor LLC*, 391 F.3d 644, 649 (5th Cir. 2004); *Babcock v. BellSouth Advertising and Publishing Corp.*, 348 F.3d 73, 76 (4th Cir. 2003); *Russell v. North Broward Hospital*, 346 F.3d 1335, 1342 (11th Cir. 2003); *Brockman v. Wyoming Dept. of Family Services*, 342 F.3d 1159, 1164 (10th Cir. 2003), *cert. denied*, 540 U.S. 1219 (2004); *Bryant v. American Airlines, Inc.*, 75 Fed. Appx. 699 (10th Cir. 2003), *cert. denied*, 540 U.S. 1219 (2002); *Levine v. Children's Museum of Indianapolis, Inc.*, 61 Fed. Appx. 298 (7th Cir. 2003); *Spangler v. Federal Home Loan Bank of Des Moines*, 278 F.3d 847, 851 (8th Cir. 2002); *Rhoads v. FDIC et al.*, 257 F.3d 373, 382 (4th Cir. 2001), *cert. denied*, 535 U.S. 933 (2002); *Rowe v. Laidlaw Transit, Inc.*, 244 F.3d 1115, 1118 (9th Cir. 2001*); Hodgens v. General Dynamics Corp.*, 144 F.3d 151, 164 (1st Cir. 1998*); Hebron v. USPS*, No. DC-0752-06-0319-I-1, 2006 MSPB LEXIS 2088, at *4 (May 25, 2006) (incorrectly citing 5 CFR Part 630).

The statute does not define the circumstances when a serious health condition would render an employee "unable to perform the functions of the position" of the employee's job. *Krohn*, 11 F. Supp. 2d at 1091. The implementing regulations, however, provide further guidance on this issue. 29 CFR 825.115; S. Res. 242, Cong. Rec. S3959, S3963 (April 23, 1996); 29 CFR 825.115.

The regulations provide two circumstances where an employee is "unable to perform the functions" of their position. First, an employee is "unable to perform the functions of the position" where the health care provider finds that the employee is unable to work at all or is unable to perform any one or more of the essential functions of the employee's position within the meaning of the Americans with Disabilities Act (ADA), 42 USC 12101, *et. seq.*, and the regulations at 29 CFR 1630.2(n). 29 CFR 825.115; S. Res. 242, Cong. Rec. S3959, S3963 (April 23, 1996); 29 CFR 825.115; *see Hurlbert v. St. Mary's Health Care System, Inc.*, 439 F.3d 1286, 1296 & n.14 (11th Cir. Feb. 16, 2006); *Rowe v. Laidlaw Transit, Inc.*, 244 F.3d 1115, 1118 (9th Cir. 2001); *Stekloff v. St. John's Mercy Health Systems*, 218 F.3d 858, 862 (8th Cir. 2000); *Klich v. Gabe's Construction Co.*, No. 05-C-1262, 2007 U.S. Dist. LEXIS 11988, at *31 (E.D. Wis. Feb. 20, 2007); *Hoffman v. Professional Med. Team*, No. 1:01–CV–3, 2003 U.S. Dist. LEXIS 11913, at *4 (W.D. Mich. June 5, 2003), *aff'd*, 394 F.3d 414 (6th Cir. 2005); *Lara v. Central Grocers Cooperative, Inc. et al.*, No. 00–C–7828, 2002 U.S. Dist. LEXIS 16745 (N.D. Ill. Sept. 6, 2002); *LeGrand v. Village of McCook*, No. 96–C–5951, 1998 U.S. Dist. LEXIS 5230 (N.D. Ill. April 15, 1998); *Harvender v. Norton Co.*, No. 96–CV–653 (LEK/RWS), 1997 U.S. Dist. LEXIS 21467 (N.D.N.Y. Dec. 15, 1997).

An employee who must be absent from work to receive medical treatment for a serious health condition is the second circumstance where an employee is considered to be unable to perform the essential function of the position during the absence for treatment. 29 CFR 825.115; S. Res. 242, Cong. Rec. S3959, S3963 (April 23, 1996); 29 CFR 825.115; *see Hodgens v. General Dynamics Corp.*, 144 F.3d 151, 164 (1st Cir. 1998) (under the interim DOL regulations, the court opined that "unable to perform" does not necessarily mean that an employee's physical condition itself "actually incapacitates" him and prevents him from working the statute could also be read to protect absences from work for whatever time the employee needs in order to be diagnosed and treated for a serious medical condition); *Swanson v. Senior Resource Connection*, 254 F. Supp. 2d 945, 951 (S.D. Ohio 2003).

Finally, for purposes of FMLA leave, the essential functions of the employee's position are determined with reference to the position the employee held at the time the employee gave notice of the need for FMLA leave, or leave commencement, whichever is earlier. 29 CFR 825.115; S. Res. 242, Cong. Rec. S3959, S3963 (April 23, 1996); 29 CFR 825.115.

The above requirements are addressed in more detail in the following subsections of this chapter.

(2) Unable to Perform One or More

According to the DOL comments accompanying publication of the final regulation (Preamble, 29 CFR 825.115):

> This section was intended to reflect that an employee would be considered "unable to perform the functions of the position" within the meaning of the regulations if the employee could not perform any *one* (or more) of the essential functions of the job held by the employee at the time the need for FMLA leave arose....

An employee does not have to be totally incapacitated or "too sick to work" to be considered "unable to perform his job." Rather, the employee need only be unable to perform one or more essential functions of the position for which the employee requests FMLA leave. *Wheeler v. Pioneer Dev. Services, Inc.*, 349 F. Supp. 2d 158 (D. Mass. 2004). An employee need not be found unable to perform each and every, or even most, job functions but only a single function, or some of several essential functions to meet this FMLA requirement. Preamble, 29 CFR 825.115. For example, an employee holds a position at the time of leave with three essential job functions: the ability to lift 75 pounds constantly for six hours a day, the ability to drive a commercial vehicle, and the ability to use a pen to confirm delivery orders. The employee would be entitled to FMLA leave if a serious health condition rendered the employee unable to use a pen, even though the employee could still lift 75 pounds for six hours a day and drive a commercial vehicle. *See e.g., Burnett v. LFW, Inc.*, 472 F.3d 471, 479 (7th Cir. 2006) (employee unable to lift heavy objects or engage in strenuous activity after biopsy, two tasks required of detailers); *Rowe*, 244 F.3d at 1118 (an employee met definition who was restricted in hours of work and in performing certain activities, including those that were an essential part of her job); *Lines v. City of Ottawa, Kansas*, No. 02–2248–KHV, 2003 U.S. Dist. LEXIS 10203, at *21 (D. Kan. June 16, 2003) (restriction from driving, an essential function of job, due to epilepsy seizures for more than three consecutive days arguably met definition of serious health condition).

Where an employee's health condition does not prevent the employee from performing the functions of her job or from obtaining alternative employment, FMLA protections should not apply. *See Hegre v. Alberto-Culver USA, nc.*, 485 F. Supp. 2d 1367 (S.D. Ga. 2007) (no evidence change in employee's mediation ever caused her to actually experience a period or episode of incapacity); *Bailey v. Aetna Inc.*, No. 02–5153, 2003 U.S. Dist. LEXIS 19651, at *21 (E.D. Pa. Oct. 28, 2003).

(3) Essential Job Functions

The FMLA regulations incorporate the ADA definition of "essential job functions." 29 CFR 825.115; S. Res. 242, Cong. Rec. S3959, S3963 (April 23, 1996); 29 CFR 825.115; *see Hurlbert v. St. Mary's Health Care System, Inc.*, 439 F.3d 1286, 1295 (11th Cir. 2006); *Harvender v. Norton Co.*, No. 96-CV-653 (LEK/RWS), 1997 U.S. Dist. LEXIS 21467 (N.D.N.Y. Dec. 15, 1997).

The ADA defines essential job functions in 29 CFR 1630.2(n), as:

> (n) Essential functions— (1) In general. The term essential functions means the fundamental job duties of the employment position the individual with a disability holds or desires. The term "essential functions" does not include the marginal functions of the position.
>
> (2) A job function may be considered essential for any of several reasons, including but not limited to the following:
>
> > (i) The function may be essential because the reason the position exists is to perform that function;
> >
> > (ii) The function may be essential because of the limited number of employees available among whom the performance of that job function can be distributed; and/or
> >
> > (iii) The function may be highly specialized in that the incumbent in the position is hired for his or her expertise or ability to perform the particular function.

Evidence of whether a particular function is essential includes, but is not limited to (42 USC 12111(8); 29 CFR 1630.2(n)(3)):

1. The employer's judgment as to which functions are essential;
2. Written job descriptions prepared before advertising or interviewing applicants for the job;
3. The amount of time spent on the job performing the function;
4. The consequences of not requiring the incumbent to perform the function;
5. The terms of a collective bargaining agreement;
6. The work experience of past incumbents in the job; and/or
7. The current work experience of incumbents in similar jobs.

Whether a job function is essential or marginal based on the above regulatory criteria will be a question of fact in each case. In any event, the issue is beyond the scope of this book. For those wanting to learn more about "essential job functions under the ADA," *see* Ernest C. Hadley, *A Guide to Federal Sector Disability Discrimination Law and Practice* (Dewey Publications, Inc. 2006).

The inability to work for FMLA purposes is not the same as the ADA inquiry whether a person is unable to perform the "major life activity of working." *Hurlbert v. St. Mary's Health Care System, Inc.*, 439 F.3d 1286, 1295 (11th Cir. 2006); *Stekloff v. St. John's Mercy Health Sys.*, 218 F.3d 858, 860-62 (8th Cir. 2000). While there are some parallels between the ADA and the FMLA, the applicable regulations state that the ADA's "disability" and the FMLA's "serious health condition" are different concepts, and must be analyzed separately. *Hurlbert*, 439 F.3d at 1295. Under the FMLA, the employees need only demonstrate that they are unable to work in their current job due to a serious health condition to show that they are incapacitated, even if that job is the only job they are unable to perform. *Hurlbert*, 439 F.3d at 1295 (quoting *Stekloff*, 218 F.3d at 861). Under the ADA, the inability to perform a single, particular job does not constitute a substantial imitation in the major life activity of working. *Stekloff*, 218 F.3d at 861.

Several cases have addressed the ability of a covered individual to perform essential job functions in the context of the FMLA. The inability to drive a vehicle due to epilepsy, a requirement of plaintiff's job, was sufficient evidence for the court in *Lines v. City of Ottawa, Kansas*, No. 02-2248-KHV, 2003 U.S. Dist. LEXIS 10203, at *15 (D. Kan. June 16, 2003) to find that plaintiff had a serious health condition.

In *Harvender v. Norton Co.*, No. 96-CV-653 (LEK/RWS), 1997 U.S. Dist. LEXIS 21467 (N.D.N.Y. Dec. 15, 1997), the court found that one essential function of a laboratory assistant is to work with and, as a result, be exposed to, chemicals. An eligible employee who could not be exposed to chemicals during pregnancy, the court held, could not perform an essential function of a laboratory assistant.

In *Reich v. The Standard Register Co.*, No. 96–0284–R, 1997 U.S. Dist. LEXIS 3021, at *8 (W.D. Va. Jan. 17, 1997), an employee could not work overtime because of arthritis. Overtime was frequently required by the employer. The employee sought FMLA leave from working overtime. He produced a medical certification limiting the employee to working 40 hours per week. Notwithstanding that overtime would appear to be an essential function of the job (a conclusion the court did not explicitly reach), the court nonetheless held that the employee did not have a serious health condition within the meaning of the FMLA. In pertinent part, the court found that the employee's ability to consistently work 40 or more hours a week did not meet the standard that the employee was "unable to perform the functions of the position of the employee," within the meaning of the FMLA. The decision of the court appears questionable, at least as a strict matter of application of the DOL regulations. Rather, the decision appears to be based more on the court's view that the employee's arthritis was not sufficiently "severe" to warrant FMLA coverage.

The base definition of "essential functions" includes the requirement that the individual be disabled. 29 CFR. § 1630.2(n)(1). Presumably, the DOL did not mean to suggest that "essential functions," for purposes of the FMLA, included the requirement that the eligible employee must be both disabled and unable to perform the essential functions of the position due to a serious health condition. *See, e.g.,* 29 CFR 825.702(b) (ADA's "disability" and FMLA's "serious health condition" are different concepts, and must be analyzed separately). That is, the reference to an "individual with a disability" should be replaced with "individual with a serious health condition," or dismissed altogether. Curiously, though, the DOL would incorporate § 1630.2(n) without modifying or clarifying the reference in that regulation to an individual with a disability. The fact that "individual with a disability" was incorporated along with the rest of § 1630.2(n) gives rise to the possibility of great mischief. It could be argued that, where the need for FMLA leave is due to the employee's own serious health condition, the employee must be both disabled and have an incapacitating serious health condition. That would drastically limit the reach of the FMLA. This is not likely the result the DOL intended when it incorporated § 1630.2(n) into the FMLA.

(4) Reasonable Accommodation; Light Duty

The ADA and the Rehabilitation Act require an employer to reasonably accommodate a disabled federal employee in certain circumstances. *See* 42 USC 12112(b)(5)(A). [The interaction of the leave requirements of the FMLA and the reasonable accommodation requirements of the ADA/Rehabilitation Act are addressed more fully in Chapter 16, "Interaction of the FMLA with Other Federal Laws, Employer Practices, and Collective Bargaining Agreements."]

For purposes of this discussion, however, the issue is whether an employee who is "unable to perform the essential functions" is with or without reasonable accommodation. If this view were accepted, FMLA leave could be denied to an employee with a serious health condition who, although unable to perform an essential job function, would be able, despite the serious health condition, to perform those functions if offered a "reasonable accommodation." For example, if we refer back to the delivery driver who could perform all of the essential job functions except the use of a pen. As a reasonable accommodation, the employer offers to allow the employee to use an ink stamp to certify delivery. The question is whether the employee remains entitled to FMLA leave because of the serious health condition that rendered the employee unable to perform an essential job function. According to the DOL, the answer is "yes". Reasonable accommodation is "irrelevant for purposes of FMLA." Preamble, 29 CFR 825.116.

The rule is that if the FMLA entitles an employee to leave, an employer may not, in lieu of FMLA leave entitlement, require an employee to take a job with a reasonable accommodation. 29 CFR 825.702(d)(1); S. Res. 242, Cong. Rec. S3959, S3976 (April 23, 1996); 29 CFR 825.702(d)(1); *see also* DOL WH FMLA Advisory Opinion No. 35 (April 19, 1994) (right to FMLA leave and ADA reasonable accommodation); DOL WH FMLA Advisory Opinion No. 29 (Feb. 7, 1994) (employee entitled to intermittent leave for serious health condition even if employee is unable to perform "essential functions" of job within meaning of ADA); DOL WH FMLA Advisory Opinion No. 17 (Nov. 15, 1993) (an employer cannot require an employee to take a job with reasonable accommodation in lieu of FMLA leave). While the ADA may require that an employer offer an employee the opportunity to take such a position, an employer may not change the essential functions of the job in order to deny FMLA leave. 29 CFR 825.702(d)(1); S. Res. 242, Cong. Rec. S3959, S3976 (April 23, 1996); 29 CFR 825.702(d)(1). This is because the leave provisions of the FMLA are wholly distinct from the reasonable accommodation obligations of employers covered by the ADA. DOL WH FMLA Advisory Opinion No. 97 (July 10, 1998); DOL WH FMLA

Advisory Opinion No. 55 (March 10, 1995). Such a change would constitute actionable interference with the employee's FMLA rights. 29 CFR 825.220(b)(2); S. Res. 242, Cong. Rec. S3959, S3970 (April 23, 1996); 29 CFR 825.220(b)(2).

When an eligible employee has both a serious health condition within the meaning of the FMLA and who is also a qualified individual with a disability under the ADA, "the requirements from both laws must be observed and applied in a manner that assures the most beneficial rights and protection." DOL WH FMLA Advisory Opinion No. 55 (March 10, 1995). See DOL WH FMLA Advisory Opinion No. 97 (July 10, 1998); DOL WH FMLA Advisory Opinion No. 82 (July 31, 1996). The DOL Advisory Opinion (No. 55) illustrates this statement as follows:

> For example, a reasonable accommodation under the ADA might be accomplished by providing an individual with a part-time job, which does not ordinarily provide health benefits. Under FMLA, an eligible employee would be permitted to work a reduced leave schedule for up to 12 workweeks of leave in any 12-month period with group health plan benefits maintained during this time. Once the FMLA leave had been exhausted in the 12-month period, the employer would have no further obligations under FMLA and would follow the requirements of ADA and other applicable law.

[For a further discussion of the interaction of the FMLA with the ADA, see Chapter 16, "Interaction of the FMLA with Other Federal Laws, Employer Practices, and Collective Bargaining Agreements."]

Similarly, an agency would not be able to force an employee on FMLA leave to return to work in a "light duty" (i.e., an unequal, modified, or restructured) position instead of continuing FMLA leave until the entitlement is exhausted. Preamble, 29 CFR 825.115; see also 29 CFR 825.702(d)(2); S. Res. 242, Cong. Rec. S3959, S3976 (April 23, 1996); 29 CFR 825.702(d)(2). DOL WH FMLA Advisory Opinion No. 75 (Nov. 14, 1995); DOL WH FMLA Advisory Opinion No. 55 (March 10, 1995). To do so would violate an employee's FMLA right to be restored to the same or an equivalent position. Preamble, 29 CFR 825.115. An employee retains the right to decline the "light duty" position and remain on FMLA leave, even if by so doing the employee loses workers' compensation benefits. Preamble, 29 CFR 825.116. See also 29 CFR 825.702(d)(2); S. Res. 242, Cong. Rec. S3959, S3976 (April 23, 1996); 29 CFR 825.702(d)(2). DOL WH FMLA Advisory Opinion No. 55 (March 10, 1995); DOL WH FMLA Advisory Opinion No. 38 (July 21, 1994); DOL WH FMLA Advisory Opinion No. 35 (April 19, 1994) (right to FMLA leave and light duty pursuant to workers' compensation laws). [The interaction of the FMLA with workers' compensation laws is addressed more fully in Chapter 16, "Interaction of the FMLA with Other Federal Laws, Employer Practices, and Collective Bargaining Agreements."]

(5) Position Held

As indicated above, the essential function(s) that an employee is unable to perform is determined by reference to the position the employee held either at the time notice is given or leave commenced, whichever is earlier. 29 CFR 825.115; S. Res. 242, Cong. Rec. S3959, S3963 (April 23, 1996); 29 CFR 825.115; see Stekloff v. St. John's Mercy Health Systems, 218 F.3d 858, 862 (8th Cir. 2000); Krohn v. Forsting et al., 11 F. Supp. 2d 1082, 1091 (E.D. Mo. July 17, 1998). The essential functions are measured against the job the employee held with his or her employer, not another employer. See Stekloff v. St. John's Mercy Health Systems, 218 F.3d 858, 862 (8th Cir. 2000) (nurse who could not perform essential functions of job with one hospital, even though evidence showed she was performing similar work for another hospital during FMLA leave).

The regulations fail to identify the source of the notice that is being given. As set forth more fully in Chapter 8, "Notice Requirements," employees and employing agencies are required to provide the other with certain notices regarding FMLA leave. Under these circumstances, the failure of the regulations to identify the source of the notice unnecessarily muddies what should otherwise be clear: that the source in this instance is the employee's notice of the need for FMLA leave.

Assuming that the source of the notice is the employee, in most, but not all, instances such notice of the need for FMLA leave will occur earlier than when leave commenced. This is almost certainly true where the need for leave is foreseeable, such as for planned medical treatment. When the need for leave is foreseeable, an employee may, in certain circumstances, have to provide up to 30 days advance notice of the need for FMLA leave. 29 CFR 825.302(a); S. Res. 242, Cong. Rec. S3959, S3971 (April 23, 1996), 29 CFR 825.302(a). If a 30-day notice is not possible, an employee must provide notice of the need for foreseeable FMLA leave as soon as practicable, which generally means within one to two business days. 29 CFR 825.302(a), (b); S. Res. 242, Cong. Rec. S3959, S3971 (April 23, 1996); 29 CFR 825.302(a), (b). In most instances, such notice will occur before FMLA leave commences.

Where the need for leave is not foreseeable, such as in exigent circumstances, an employee need only give notice of the need for FMLA leave as soon as practicable under the facts and circumstances of the particular case. 29 CFR 825.303(a); S. Res. 242, Cong. Rec. S3959, S3972 (April 23, 1996); 29 CFR 825.303(a). Again, this generally means within one or two working days of learning of the need for leave, except in extraordinary circumstances where such notice is not feasible. 29 CFR 825.303(a); S. Res. 242, Cong. Rec. S3959, S3972 (April 23, 1996); 29 CFR 825.303(a). Such notice may occur after the leave commenced and, indeed, after the employee returns to work. *See* 29 CFR 825.208(e)(1). Also, an employee may request an extension of leave because of an intervening event, such as an accident. *See* 29 CFR 825.208(d). Because such request was made after the leave commenced, whether the employee was unable to perform the essential functions would be determined at the time of leave commencement, not at the time of the request.

Note that the regulations do not require that the determination of whether an employee can perform the essential functions of the job must always be determined with respect to the employee's permanent position. That is, the employee could be on a detail or other special assignment at the time leave commences or the employee requests leave, whichever is earlier. In either case, whether the employee is able to perform the essential functions would be determined in reference to the detail position held rather than the employee's permanent position. This gives rise to the prospect that an employee may be entitled to FMLA leave because at the time of his or her leave request (which we will assume is earlier), the employee could not perform all of the essential functions of the detail position, even though at the time of leave commencement the employee has returned to his or her permanent position, and can perform all of the essential job functions.

(6) Documentation of Essential Functions

An employer has the option, if it requires certification from a health care provider confirming the employee's need for FMLA leave due to the employee's own serious health condition, of providing a statement of the essential functions of the employee's position for the health care provider to review. 29 CFR 825.115; S. Res. 242, Cong. Rec. S3959, S3963 (April 23, 1996); 29 CFR 825.115. Information regarding the essential functions of the position would assist the health care provider in providing required information in the medical certification to establish whether the employee is unable to perform any one or more of the essential functions of the employee's position. 29 CFR 825.306(b)(4)(ii); S. Res. 242, Cong. Rec. S3959, S3973 (April 23, 1996); 29 CFR 825.306(b)(4)(ii). Agencies would be well advised to provide this information to the health care provider to ensure that an accurate medical assessment is being made. [An agency's ability to require an employee to request medical certification in support of an employee's request for FMLA leave due to a serious health condition is discussed more fully in Chapter 9, "Documentation Requirements."]

(7) Receipt of Medical Treatment

The second manner in which an employee is "unable to perform the functions of the position of the employee" is when an employee must be absent from work to receive medical treatment for a serious health condition. 29 CFR 825.115; S. Res. 242, Cong. Rec. S3959, S3963 (April 23, 1996); 29 CFR 825.115. In this case, the inability of the employee to "perform the functions of the position of the employee" lasts "during the absence for treatment." 29 CFR 825.115; S. Res. 242, Cong. Rec. S3959, S3963 (April 23, 1996); 29 CFR 825.115.

It is unclear when an employee "must be" absent from work to receive medical treatment. Presumably, this is determined by the employee's health care provider. When planning medical treatment, an employee must consult with the employer and make a reasonable effort to schedule the leave so as not to unduly disrupt the employer's operations, subject to the approval of the health care provider. 29 CFR 825.302(e); S. Res. 242, Cong. Rec. S3959, S3972 (April 23, 1996); 29 CFR 825.302(e). Employees are ordinarily expected to consult with their employers prior to the scheduling of treatment in order to work out a treatment schedule which best suits the needs of both the employer and the employee. 29 CFR 825.302(e); S. Res. 242, Cong. Rec. S3959, S3972 (April 23, 1996); 29 CFR 825.302(e). [Employee notice obligations are discussed more fully in Chapter 8, "Notice Requirements."]

The term "medical treatment" is not defined in the statute or the regulations. For purposes of the definition of a serious health condition, "treatment" is defined to include (but is not limited to) examinations to determine if a serious health condition exits and evaluations of the condition. 29 CFR 825.114(b); S. Res. 242, Cong. Rec. S3959, S3963 (April 23, 1996); 29 CFR 825.114(b); *see Sloop v. ABTCO, Inc.*, No. 98–2440, 1999 U.S. App. LEXIS 8600, at *5 (4th Cir. May 6, 1999) (for purposes of FMLA, Sloop was "treated" at a detoxification center because his condition was evaluated by two physicians). "Treatment" does not include routine physical examinations, eye examinations, or dental examinations. 29 CFR 825.114(b); S. Res. 242, Cong. Rec. S3959, S3963 (April 23, 1996); 29 CFR 825.114(b).

A regimen of continuing treatment that includes taking over-the-counter medication (such as aspirin, antihistamines, or salves), bed-rest, drinking fluids, exercise, and other similar activities that can be initiated without a visit to a health care provider, is not, by itself, sufficient to constitute a regimen of continuing treatment for purposes of FMLA leave. 29 CFR 825.114(b); S. Res. 242, Cong. Rec. S3959, S3963 (April 23, 1996); 29 CFR 825.114(b); *see Miller v. AT&T et al.*, 250 F.3d 820, 828, n.6 (4th Cir. 2001) (a physician's instructions to an employee to rest, take over-the-counter medications, and increase fluid intake did not constitute a regimen of continuing treatment); DOL WH FMLA Advisory Opinion No. 87 (Dec. 12, 1996); DOL WH FMLA Advisory Opinion No. 86 (Dec. 12, 1996).

The DOL opined that treatment requires that the examination or evaluation be conducted by, or under the direction of a health care provider in person. DOL WH FMLA Advisory Opinion No. 87 (Dec. 12, 1996) (telephone conversation with doctor not considered "treatment" within the meaning of the FMLA). As the term "medical" is not defined for purposes of the FMLA, it is unclear whether the use of that term in this context means that an employee is only "unable to perform the essential functions of the position of the employee" because the employee must be absent from work to receive medical treatment administered by a licensed physician. As will be addressed later in this chapter, licensed physicians are not the only health care providers recognized by the FMLA for purposes of serious health conditions. *See* 29 CFR 825.118 (defining the term "health care provider"); S. Res. 242, Cong. Rec. S3959, S3963 (April 23, 1996); 29 CFR 825.118 (same).

By defining the period as "during the absence for treatment," it would appear that the entire time period, including travel to and from the location where medical treatment is to be administered, would fall within the period of time an employee is considered to be "unable to perform the functions of the employee's position."

2. **Title II**

   a. **Needed to Care for a Covered Family Member**

      (1) **General Rule**

A Title II employee is entitled to a total of 12 administrative workweeks of FMLA leave during any 12-month period in order to care for the spouse, or a son, daughter, or parent of the employee, if such spouse, son, daughter, or parent has a serious health condition. 5 USC 6382(a)(1)(C); 5 CFR 630.1203(a)(3); *see Covington v. Dept. of Army*, 85 MSPR 612 (2000), *pet. denied*, 90 MSPR 24 (2001).

Neither the statute nor the OPM's implementing regulations define what "in order to care for" means. However, the type of care that an employee may provide is suggested in the medical certification regulations. Specifically, 5 CFR 630.1207(b)(4), addressing leave taken by an employee to care for a covered family member with a serious health condition, provides:

   (i) A statement from the health care provider that the spouse, son, daughter, or parent of the employee requires psychological comfort and/or physical care; needs assistance for basic medical, hygienic, nutritional, safety, or transportation needs or in making arrangements to meet such needs; and would benefit from the employee's care or presence.

   (ii) A statement from the employee on the care he or she will provide and an estimate of the amount of time needed to care for his or her spouse, son, daughter, or parent.

The scope is substantially similar to comparable regulations governing Title I, the CAA, and the PEOAA. *See* 29 CFR 825.115, 825.306(b)(5)(I); S. Res. 242, Cong. Rec. S3959, S3962, S3973 (April 23, 1996); 29 CFR 825.115.

      (2) **Availability of Other Caregivers**

The statute and the regulations fail to address the impact, if any, the availability of other caregivers has on an employee's right to FMLA leave "in order to care for" a covered family member with a serious health condition. In the absence of any limitation, it would appear that, like Title I, the CAA, and the PEOAA, the availability and/or presence of other care givers, be they professional health care providers or family and friends, has no impact on an employee's right to take FMLA leave "in order to care for" a covered family member with a serious health condition.

(3) Participation in Care; Travel

Like the other federal sector variants of the FMLA, neither the statutory language of Title II nor the OPM implementing regulations address the location where an employee may provide care to a covered family member with a serious health condition. For example, there is no indication that an employee who is providing physical or mental care must be in the presence of the covered family member needing care. Arguably, psychological comfort and care could be provided over the telephone or by videophone. One could take the argument further that such care could be provided over the Internet or by taking time to write a letter.

Unlike the Ninth Circuit cases addressed previously governing Title I, there is no indication in the OPM regulations to prohibit an employee from traveling on vacation with a covered family member with a serious health condition, provided the employee meets all of the other requirements regarding FMLA leave. The employee could receive job-protected FMLA leave to provide psychological comfort and care while accompanying a family member with a chronic condition to the beaches of Hawaii, even though the chronic condition is not active while the family is vacationing in Hawaii.

(4) Medical Documentation

As indicated above, an agency may require an employee to provide a medical certification from a health care provider addressing, among other things, why the employee needs FMLA leave "in order to care for" a covered family member with a serious health condition. Specifically, the certification (5 CFR 630.1207(b)(4)), must include:

(i) A statement from the health care provider that the spouse, son, daughter, or parent of the employee requires psychological comfort and/or physical care; needs assistance for basic medical, hygienic, nutritional, safety, or transportation needs or in making arrangements to meet such needs; and would benefit from the employee's care or presence.

(ii) A statement from the employee on the care he or she will provide and an estimate of the amount of time needed to care for his or her spouse, son, daughter, or parent.

If leave is to be taken on an intermittent or reduced leave schedule for planned medical treatment, the certification must also include the dates (actual or estimates) on which such treatment is expected to be given, the duration of such treatment, and the period of recovery, if any, or specify that the serious health condition is a chronic or continuing condition with an unknown duration and whether the patient is presently incapacitated and the likely duration and frequency of episodes of incapacity. 5 CFR 630.1207b)(6).

In *Jefferies v. Dept. of Navy*, 78 MSPR 255 (1998), the Board held that the medical documentation submitted by the employee in support of his request for FMLA leave to care for his daughter was insufficient because the documentation did not demonstrate that the daughter's illness (bronchitis) involved inpatient care or continuous treatment by a health care provider for the charged period, it did not indicate the length of the daughter's illness, and it did not state that the appellant was required to care for his daughter during his absence from work.

b. Unable to Work Due to Employee's Own Serious Health Condition

(1) General Rule

An employee is entitled to take up to 12 administrative workweeks of FMLA leave during the leave year because of a serious health condition that makes the employee unable to perform the functions of the employee's position. 5 USC 6382(a)(1)(D); see *Ramseur v. Dept. of Navy*, DC-0752-06-0472-I-1, 2006 MSPB LEXIS 5852, at *7 (Oct. 4, 2006); *Jones v. Dept. of Navy*, No. DC-0752-06-0092-I-2, 2006 MSPB LEXIS 5031, at *4 (Sept. 5, 2006); *Kimbrough v. DOD*, No. DC-0752-06-0287-I-1, 2006 MSPB LEXIS 4379, at *11 (Aug. 1, 2006); *Cole v. DHHS*, No. DC-0752-05-0457-I-1, 2005 MSPB LEXIS 6825, at *7 (Nov. 1, 2005); *Williams v. Dept. of Navy*, No. DC-0752-05-0431-I-1, 2005 MSPB LEXIS 6866, at *3-4 (Oct. 17, 2005), pet. denied, 101 MSPR 133 (2006); *Dias v. VA*, No. NY-0752-04-0279-I-2, 2005 MSPB LEXIS 3926, at *13 (June 30,

2006); *Landahl v. Commerce*, 83 MSPR 40 (1999), *pet. denied*, 87 MSPR 530 (2000), *aff'd*, 2001 U.S. App. LEXIS 11774 (Fed. Cir. 2001); *Ellshoff v. Dept. of Interior*, 76 MSPR 54 (1997), *rev'd, remanded*, 78 MSPR 615 (1998). The OPM implementing regulations clarify the statutory language even further by providing that an employee is "unable to perform any one or more of the essential functions of his or her position." 5 CFR 630.1203(a)(4). "Essential functions" are defined in the regulations as meaning the fundamental job duties of the employee's position, as defined in 29 CFR 1630.2(n). The OPM regulations further provide that an employee who must be absent from work to receive medical treatment for a serious health condition is considered to be unable to perform the essential functions of the position during the absence for treatment. 5 CFR 630.1202 (definition of "essential functions"). The requirements under Title II are nearly identical to the comparable requirements under Title I, the CAA, and the PEOAA.

(2) Unable to Perform

As discussed previously in this chapter regarding the other federal sector variants of the FMLA, Title II also incorporates the ADA definition of "essential functions" set forth in 29 CFR 1630.2(n). However, the Title II regulation differs from the comparable regulations implementing Title I, the CAA, and the PEOAA in at least two respects. First, § 825.115 provides that the employee is either unable to work at all or is unable to perform any of the essential functions of the employee's position. The OPM regulation (§ 630.1202), in contrast, does not contain the alternative language "unable to work at all." Rather, § 630.1202 limits the phrase "unable to perform the functions of the position" to situations where the employee is unable to perform one or more essential job functions. *Romero v. Dept. of Interior*, No. SF-0752-05-0011-I-1, 2005 MSPB LEXIS 3147, at *10 (May 19, 2005). Since an employee who is unable to work at all is unable to perform all essential job functions, failure to include the phrase "unable to work at all" does not appear to have any practical effect. In that respect, the alternative language of § 825.115 is redundant.

Second, § 825.115 requires that a health care provider find that the employee is unable to work at all or is unable to perform any one of the essential functions of the employee's position within the meaning of the ADA. § 630.1202, on the other hand, does not require such a finding by a health care provider in order for an agency to consider an employee to be "unable to perform the functions of the position of the employee." Of course, an agency has discretion to request supporting medical certification. *See* 5 CFR 630.1207(a).

In *Ellshoff v. Dept. of Interior*, 76 MSPR 54 (1997), *rev'd, remanded*, 78 MSPR 615 (1998), the Board found that a medical certification sufficiently established that the employee was incapacitated within the meaning of the FMLA where it provided that the appellant's condition during her absence included "a complete inability to care for herself or her daily needs, anergy, anhedonia, impaired concentration, social withdrawal, and ultimately suicidal ideation and plan, which required hospitalization."

(3) Essential Job Functions

The FMLA regulations implementing Title II incorporate the ADA definition of "essential functions." 5 CFR 630.1202 (definition of "essential functions"). As the ADA regulatory definition of "essential functions" is fully addressed above in this chapter for purposes of Title I, the CAA, and the PEOAA, the reader is referred to that discussion for purposes of Title II.

(4) Reasonable Accommodation; Light Duty

The ADA and the Rehabilitation Act require an employer to reasonably accommodate a disabled federal employee in certain circumstances. *See* 42 USC 12112(b)(5)(A). The issue is whether the determination of whether an employee is "unable to perform the essential function" of his or her position is done with or without reasonable accommodation. If reasonable accommodation were factored into the determination, FMLA leave could be denied to an employee with a serious health condition who, although unable to perform one or more essential job functions, would be able, despite the serious health condition, to perform those functions if offered a "reasonable accommodation." For example, if an employee were detailed to an alternative or light–duty position and the employee were able to perform all of the essential functions of the alternative position, the employee would not be entitled to FMLA leave.

Like the DOL, OPM rejected the argument that an employee's inability to perform one or more essential job functions should be measured after the application of reasonable accommodation requirements, such as placement in an alternative position. The OPM responded to such an argument in the comments accompanying publication of the final Title II implementing regulations (Preamble, 5 CFR 630.1203 (leave entitlement)) as follows:

> The statute does not provide for placing an employee in an alternative or light-duty position in lieu of his or her entitlement under the FMLA. Therefore, the regulations were not revised.
>
> An agency should not confuse an employee's entitlement to leave under the FMLA with its ongoing obligation to provide reasonable accommodation under the Rehabilitation Act of 1973. While an agency cannot require an employee to accept an alternative position offer, an employee continues to maintain the right to request light duty assignment in lieu of unpaid leave under the FMLA.

[The interaction of the leave requirements of the FMLA and the reasonable accommodation requirements of the ADA/Rehabilitation Act are addressed more fully in Chapter 16, "Interaction of the FMLA with Other Federal Laws, Employer Practices, and Collective Bargaining Agreements."]

(5) Position Held

Neither the statute nor the OPM implementing regulations identify the "position" used as the basis for determining that the employee is "unable to perform the functions of the employee's position." As set forth previously in this chapter, the regulations implementing Title I, the CAA, and the PEOAA identify the means for determining what position is used for this calculation. Specifically, the essential functions are determined based on the position held by the employee at the time of notice or leave commencement, whichever is earlier. *See* 29 CFR 825.115; S. Res. 242, Cong. Rec. S3959, S3963 (April 23, 1996); 29 CFR 825.115. Again, no similar direction is given for purposes of Title II.

Absent further OPM direction, prudence suggests that agencies follow the requirements established by the DOL in 29 CFR 825.115 for purposes of employees covered by Title II. As discussed previously in this chapter, for purposes of Title I, the CAA, and the PEOAA, this means that whether an employee is unable to perform one or more essential job functions may be determined based on a detail or special assignment position held by the employee, rather than a permanent position, at the time of notice or leave commencement. To the extent that OPM does not like this result, and desires that the inability to perform one or more essential job functions be determined based on an employee's permanent position, the OPM needs to communicate that position.

(6) Documentation of Essential Functions

An employer may require that a request for FMLA leave for a serious health condition be supported by written medical certification issued by a health care provider of the employee. 5 USC 6383(a); 5 CFR 630.1207(a); *see Burge v. Dept. of Air Force*, 82 MSPR 75 (1999); *Jefferies v. Dept. of Navy*, 78 MSPR 255 (1998); *Ellshoff v. Dept. of Interior*, 76 MSPR 54 (1997), *rev'd, remanded*, 78 MSPR 615 (1998). If the agency elects to require an employee to submit a medical certification of the need for FMLA leave due to the employee's own serious health condition, the certification must include a statement from the health care provider that the employee is unable to perform one or more of the essential functions of his or her position or require medical treatment for a serious health condition. 5 USC 6383(b)(4)(B); 5 CFR 630.1207(b)(5). The statement of the health care provider must be on written information provided by the agency on the essential functions of the employee's position, or if not provided, discussion with the employee about the essential functions of his or her position. 5 CFR 630.1207(b)(5); *see Ellshoff v. Dept. of Interior*, 76 MSPR 54 (1997), *rev'd, remanded*, 78 MSPR 615 (1998).

Agencies would be well advised to provide a written description of the essential function of the employee's position rather than rely on what information the employee may provide. The regulations do not indicate whether the agency must provide the written description of the essential functions to the employee or directly to the employee's health care provider. In most cases, the agency should provide the written information to the employee with instructions that it be passed along to the health care provider for use in preparation of the medical certification. The employee should be advised that, in the event the medical certification does not address the essential job functions as described, the certification may be deemed incomplete. [An agency's ability to require an employee to request medical certification in support of an employee's request for FMLA leave due to a serious health condition is discussed more fully in Chapter 9, "Documentation Requirements."]

(7) Receipt of Medical Treatment

An employee is also "unable to perform the functions of the position of the employee" when the employee must be absent from work to receive medical treatment for a serious health condition. 5 CFR 630.1202 (definition of "essential functions"), 630.1207(b)(5). The inability of the employee to "perform the functions of the position of the employee" lasts "during the absence for treatment." 5 CFR 630.1202 (definition of "essential functions"). This provision is identical to comparable provisions (discussed previously in this chapter) for purposes of Title I, the CAA, and the PEOAA. *See* 29 CFR 825.115; S. Res. 242, Cong. Rec. S3959, S3963 (April 23, 1996); 29 CFR 825.115.

The statute and the OPM regulations fail to define key terms in this regulation. For example, the terms "medical" and "treatment," both separately and together, are undefined. One would think that, for purposes of the Family Medical Leave Act, someone would have defined what "medical" means. Unfortunately, that is not the case. Given the presence of non-medical professionals who are recognized as health care providers for purposes of the FMLA, the reference to "medical treatment" could suggest that not all health care providers are capable of providing "medical treatment." If that is correct, the regulation fails to identify which health care providers can provide "medical treatment."

It is also possible that when OPM referred to "medical treatment" it meant any treatment provided by an FMLA-recognized health care provider. Of course, the argument against this is that most states have laws limiting the practice of medicine to certain licensed medical practitioners. Others may be in the health care field, but they are not legally permitted to practice medicine and, therefore, could not dispense "medical treatment." They may, however, provide health care services. The OPM, as well as the DOL and the other FMLA enforcement agencies, need to provide better guidance on this issue.

Unlike Title I, the CAA, and the PEOAA (discussed previously in this chapter), Title II does not define what constitutes "treatment." In the comments to the final regulations implementing Title II, the OPM agreed that certain "treatments" should not be covered by the FMLA. The OPM indicated that it "added a paragraph at the end of the definition of 'serious health condition' to address those treatments and conditions that are not considered a serious health condition." Preamble, 5 CFR 630.1202 (definitions). In pertinent part, the last paragraph of the definition of a "serious health condition" (5 CFR 630.1202 (definition of "serious health condition")) provides:

> Serious health condition does not include routine physical, eye, or dental examinations; a regimen continuing treatment that includes the taking of over-the-counter medications, bed-rest, exercise, and other similar activities that can be initiated without a visit to a health care provider, a condition for which cosmetic treatments are administered, unless inpatient hospital care is required or unless complications develop....

The above definition does not consider the referenced health care services not to be "treatment." Rather, the regulation, by its terms, explains that they are treatments, but are not considered to fall within the definition of a FMLA-covered "serious health condition." Since the rule provides that the employee's absence to receive "medical treatment" must be for a "serious health condition," and the treatments identified above are not "serious health conditions," it follows that the absence for such treatments is not covered by the FMLA. Even though the employee may be absent to receive a routine dental examination, for purposes of the FMLA, the employee would not be "unable to perform the functions of the position" because the absence for a routine dental examination does not fall within the definition of a serious health condition.

C. TYPES OF SERIOUS HEALTH CONDITIONS

FMLA leave is available to an eligible employee in order to care for a covered family member with a serious health condition. It is also available to an eligible employee because the employee is unable to perform one or more of the essential functions of the employee's position.

This section discusses the types of serious health conditions that are recognized for purposes of FMLA leave. A serious health condition means an illness, injury, impairment, or physical or mental condition that involves: (1) inpatient care in a hospital, hospice, or residential medical care facility; or (2) continuing treatment by a health care provider. 29 USC 2611(11); 29 CFR 825.114; S. Res. 242, Cong. Rec. S3959, S3962-63 (April 23, 1996); 29 CFR 825.114; *see Spangler v. Federal Home Loan Bank of Des Moines*, 278 F.3d 847, 851 (8th Cir. 2002); *Navarro v. Gladys Navarro Pomares et al.*, 261 F.3d 90, 95 (1st Cir. 2001); *Marchisheck v. San Mateo County et al.*, 199 F.3d 1068, 1073-74 (9th Cir. 1999), *cert. denied*, 530 U.S. 1214 (2000); *Martyszenk v. Safeway, Inc.*, 120 F.3d 120, 122 (8th Cir. 1997); *Hodgens v. General Dynamics Corp.*, 144 F.3d 151, 161

(1st Cir. 1998); *Price v. Marathon Cheese Corp.,* 119 F.3d 330, 333–34 (5th Cir. 1997); *Bauer v. Varity Dayton–Walther Corp.,* 118 F.3d 1109, 1111 (6th Cir. 1997).

The regulations implementing the FMLA further divide "continuing treatment" into five types of serious health conditions.

If an employee is requesting FMLA leave for his or her own illness or the illness of a covered family member, that illness must meet one of the following definitions of a serious health condition in order for the absence to be covered by the FMLA. If the illness does not fit within one of the following definitions of a serious health condition, the leave is not covered by the FMLA no matter how "serious" the illness may be. While the definition of a "serious health condition" is broad, and many illnesses will fit within the definition, it is not limitless.

1. Inpatient Care

a. Title I, the CAA, and the PEOAA

(1) General Rule

The term "serious health condition" means an illness, injury, impairment, or physical or mental condition that involves inpatient care in a hospital, hospice, or residential medical care facility. 29 USC 2611(11); 29 CFR 825.114(a)(1); S. Res. 242, Cong. Rec. S3959, S3962 (April 23, 1996); 29 CFR 825.114(a)(1); *see Burnett v. LFW, Inc.,* 472 F.3d 471, 478 (7th Cir. Dec. 26, 2006); *Brenneman v. MedCentral Health System,* 366 F.3d 412, 420–421 (6th Cir. 2004), *cert. denied,* 543 U.S. 1146 (2005); *Haefling v. UPS, Inc.,* 169 F.3d 494, 498 (7th Cir. 1999), *cert. denied,* 528 U.S. 820 (1999); *Young v. USPS,* 79 MSPR 25 (1998).

The implementing regulations clarify the statutory language by indicating that inpatient care means an overnight stay. 29 CFR 825.114(a)(1); S. Res. 242, Cong. Rec. S3959, S3962 (April 23, 1996); 29 CFR 825.114(a)(1); *see Hicks v. Leroy's Jewelers, Inc.,* No. 98–6596, 2000 U.S. App. LEXIS 17568, at *8 (6th Cir. July 17, 2000); *Haefling v. UPS, Inc.,* 169 F.3d 494, 498–99 (7th Cir. 1999) (interim regulations), *cert. denied,* 528 U.S. 820 (1999); *Dominick v. Ver Halen, Inc.,* No. 02–C–375–X, 2003 U.S. Dist. LEXIS 11694 (W.D. Wis. March 10, 2003) (inpatient care for three days for treatment of alcoholic pancreatitis, pain management, and alcohol withdrawal covered); *Sanders v. The May Dept. Stores Co.,* No. 4: 00CV576–DJS, 2001 U.S. Dist. LEXIS 11495 (E.D. Mo. May 11, 2001); *Bryant v. Delbar Products, Inc. et al.,* 18 F. Supp. 2d 799, 802 (M.D. Tenn. 1998) (hospitalization for three days for kidney failure constitutes FMLA–covered serious health condition); *Skallarion v. Judge & Dolph, Ltd. et al.,* 893 F. Supp. 800, 807 (N.D. Ill. 1995) (no evidence of serious health condition where daughter did not require inpatient care); *Young v. USPS,* 79 MSPR 25 (1998) (father's hospitalization for several months qualified as inpatient care); DOL WH FMLA Advisory Opinion No. 87 (Dec. 12, 1996) (under the express statutory language, any absence involving inpatient care qualifies as a serious health condition).

The regulations also add that inpatient care includes any period of incapacity, or any subsequent treatment in connection with such inpatient care. 29 CFR 825.114(a)(1); S. Res. 242, Cong. Rec. S3959, S3962 (April 23, 1996); 29 CFR 825.114(a)(1).

Note that inpatient care covers "any period of incapacity" and any subsequent treatment in connection with such inpatient care. Many people erroneously believe that in order to receive the protections of the FMLA, an employee or covered family member must have a serious health condition for a minimum number of days. That is simply not true. Inpatient care does require at least one overnight stay in a hospital or other covered facility. Once an overnight stay in a covered facility is satisfied, inpatient care will cover "any period" of incapacity or for any subsequent treatments related to that inpatient care. That could be an hour, a day, or a week, up to the maximum 12 workweeks of FMLA leave available to an employee each leave year.

(2) Incapacity

Fortunately, the regulations define some of the key terms. A "period of incapacity" is defined to mean inability to work, attend school or perform other regular daily activities due to the serious health condition, treatment therefore, or recovery therefrom. 29 CFR 825.114(a)(1); S. Res. 242, Cong. Rec. S3959, S3962 (April 23, 1996); 29 CFR 825.114(a)(1). This definition, unfortunately, is not a model of clarity. In its effort to be inclusive of FMLA leave both for the employee's own serious health condition as well as the serious health condition of a covered family member, the definition unnecessarily confuses the two.

An employee is entitled to FMLA leave for his or her own serious health condition only if that condition renders the employee unable to perform one or more essential functions of the employee's position. As written, the regulation suggests that an employee who is fully capable of performing all essential functions of his or her job would nonetheless be able to take FMLA leave because the employee could not attend night school or perform other regular daily activities besides work. That is generally not the case, particularly when the employee is scheduled to work. In the context of inpatient care, these non–work related activities are mainly relevant to covered family members who, because of age or other reasons, may not be working when they are struck by a serious health condition.

Moreover, the definition of "incapacity" in § 825.114(a) may conflict with the similar, but by no means identical, definition of "unable to perform one or more essential job functions" in § 825.115. This is particularly true where an employee's own serious health condition renders the employee unable to work. There is no conflict if the employee suffers a serious health condition on his or her off days or while on leave. The matter is discussed below in more detail.

An employee "unable to perform the functions of the position" must be unable to work at all or unable to perform any one of the essential job functions of the employee's position. 29 CFR 825.115; S. Res. 242, Cong. Rec. S3959, S3963 (April 23, 1996); 29 CFR 825.115. For purposes of "incapacity," the requirement means "inability to work." 29 CFR 825.114(a)(1); S. Res. 242, Cong. Rec. S3959, S3963 (April 23, 1996); 29 CFR 825.114(a)(1). What is missing in § 825.114(a)(1) is the reference to "or unable to perform any one of the essential job functions.…" The difference in the regulations raises the possibility that an employee who is unable to perform one of the essential functions of his or her job due to a serious health condition may be found to be "unable to perform the functions of the position," but would simultaneously not be incapacitated because the employee is capable of work.

Where the need for leave is due to the employee's own serious health condition, agencies would be well advised to read "inability to work" for purposes of § 825.114(a)(1) to include "or unable to perform any one or more of the essential job functions of the employee's position," contained in § 825.115. If the leave is "in order to care for" a covered family member with a serious health condition, agencies could apply the more rigid "inability to work" language of § 825.114(a)(1), in addition to the examples of inability to attend school or perform other regular daily activities.

Sections 825.114(a)(1) and 825.115 are not always in conflict. At least with respect to the definition of incapacity regarding inability to attend school or perform other daily activities due to a serious health condition, the regulations would not be in conflict where the object is to determine the onset of the employee's serious health condition. For example, if an employee on annual leave initially falls seriously ill for several days, is admitted to an overnight stay in a hospital, and is released with a period of recovery, the entire period would meet the definition of incapacity for purposes of inpatient care. The ability of the employee to attend work is not relevant because the employee was on annual leave when this occurred. As a result, you look to the fact that the serious health condition of the employee rendered him or her unable to perform other regular daily activities in order to determine whether the all or some part of the annual leave qualified for FMLA.

(3) Treatment

"Treatment" includes (but is not limited to) examinations to determine if a serious health condition exists and evaluations of the condition. 29 CFR 825.114(b); S. Res. 242, Cong. Rec. S3959, S3963 (April 23, 1996); 29 CFR 825.114(b); see Miller v. AT&T Corp. et al., 250 F.3d 820, 831, 834 (4th Cir. 2001) (upholding regulatory definition of "treatment" against constitutional challenge that inclusion of examinations and evaluations is contrary to congressional intent). Treatment does not include routine physical examination, eye examinations, or dental examinations. The term "examination" is not further defined. Presumably, examinations must be conducted by an FMLA–covered health care provider.

In Dominick v. Ver Halen, Inc., No. 02–C–375–X, 2003 U.S. Dist. LEXIS 11694 (W.D. Wis. March 10, 2003), the court addressed the interaction of inpatient care and substance abuse as FMLA–covered serious health conditions. The court concluded that an employee's abuse of alcohol causing physical symptoms associated with that abuse resulting in inpatient care was covered by the FMLA.

There, the employee spent three days in a hospital after a drinking binge. When the employee checked in he smelled of alcohol. The employee was treated for alcoholic pancreatitis, pain management and the prophylactic administration of medicines designed to combat alcohol withdrawal symptoms. The employee argued that, because he spent an overnight stay in a hospital where he received treatment, he met all of the requirements for FMLA leave for these three days. The employer, on the other hand, argued (citing 29 CFR 825.114(d)) that these three days were not covered as the FMLA only applies to leave for treatment of substance abuse, not absences caused by the employee's substance use. In this case, the employee's hospital admission resulted from his binge drinking over the weekend.

While acknowledging that the employer's argument had "substantial curb appeal," the court concluded, "A plain reading of the regulation does not support the interpretation that 'treatment' is limited to treatment addressing chronic dependency issues as opposed to treatment for acute physical symptoms resulting from alcohol use." According to the court, the employer's interpretation "would exclude hospitalization for genuinely accidental alcohol poisoning (for instance, unwittingly drinking heavily spiked punch). At the other extreme, even inpatient treatment at a substance abuse rehabilitation center which Ver Halen would presumably concede constitutes qualified leave under the Act, occurs 'because of the employee's use' of a substance, and such dependency treatment could well involve treatment for physical symptoms associated with the use."

(4) Illness, Injury, Impairment, or Physical or Mental Condition

While regulatory definitions provide some clarity, many key terms are undefined and otherwise unexplained. For example, all serious health conditions require an illness, injury, impairment, or physical or mental condition. None of these terms is defined. Presumably, the terms apply as they are commonly understood. Moreover, the terms are so broad (e.g., physical or mental condition) as to be inclusive of virtually every ailment possible, however slight.

(5) Hospital, Hospice, or Residential Medical Care Facility

The terms "hospital," "hospice," or "residential medical care facility" are undefined. For most purposes, these terms are self-evident and will not present problems. However, it is suggested that the DOL and the other regulating entities should have specified that these facilities be duly licensed, where such licenses are required. This would exclude arguments that various forms of otherwise unlicensed and illegal "hospitals" operated out of homes and back rooms nevertheless constitute covered facilities. It would also relieve agencies of having to research other federal and state law definitions of these terms, if any.

(6) Overnight Stay

While an "overnight stay" sounds descriptive, it is unclear what it really means. Again, in most instances, it will be clear that the employee spent at least one overnight stay in a covered facility. As always, it is the marginal cases that test the limits of the law. For example, note that the regulation does not by its terms require that the employee actually be admitted to the hospital, hospice, or residential medical care facility.

An eligible employee's overnight stay in a hospital may not, of itself, establish entitlement to FMLA leave. That was the opinion of the Sixth Circuit in *Hicks v. Leroy's Jewelers, Inc.*, No. 98–6596, 2000 U.S. App. LEXIS 17568, at *8 (6th Cir. July 17, 2000). In that case, the employee was scheduled to begin 12 weeks of FMLA leave on August 28 following the expected birth of her child. She developed a kidney infection and spent an overnight stay in a hospital on August 8. Her employer began the 12 weeks of FMLA leave on August 8 instead of August 28. The employee could not return to work at the end of the 12 weeks of FMLA leave due to complications with her pregnancy and she was terminated.

The plaintiff sued, alleging that her termination violated the FMLA. Specifically, she alleged her hospitalization should not have been designated as FMLA leave because there was a genuine issue of material fact whether her hospitalization resulted from a temporary illness that qualified her only for paid sick leave, or from a "serious health condition" that qualified her for FMLA leave. The district court awarded summary judgment to Leroy's after finding that the employee's hospitalization automatically qualified her for FMLA leave because she spent an overnight stay in a hospital. On appeal, the Sixth Circuit opined in dictum that the decision of the district court may have been in error. The Sixth Circuit found that the employee's affidavit that she was able and willing to return to work after she was released from the hospital created a genuine issue of material fact whether her hospitalization automatically qualified her for FMLA leave. The Sixth Circuit, however, affirmed summary judgment in favor of the employer on the grounds that the employee was unable to return to work within 12 weeks of the time frame she was advocating.

(7) Inpatient

The term "inpatient" is not defined. This suggests that an employee who sits in the emergency room all night might qualify. For that matter, what does "overnight" mean? As it is stated in temporal terms, how much time must pass at night in order for the employee to be considered to have stayed overnight (e.g., an hour, two hours, four hours)? Finally, is "overnight" to be taken literally. What happens if an employee works nights, and is hospitalized from when the employee gets off in the early morning, all day, until the following evening? Such a stay would, for purposes of a "graveyard" shift employee, constitute overnight.

Note that the employee need not receive treatment during the overnight stay to be covered by this serious health condition. This would appear counterintuitive as the covered condition is called "inpatient care." Nevertheless, all that is required is that the employee has an illness, injury, impairment, or physical or mental condition and spends an overnight stay in a covered facility. Except for what it is entitled, neither the statute nor the implementing regulations mandate that any "care" actually be provided. Undoubtedly, the mere fact that the individual is in a hospital or other care facility suggests that, in some manner, the individual is under the "care" of that facility. In any event, "care" is not defined for purposes of "inpatient care."

(8) Subsequent Incapacity or Treatment

Finally, an FMLA–qualifying serious health condition includes not only the time spent in the hospital or other covered facility (if there was an overnight stay), but also periods of incapacity and subsequent treatment "in connection with" such inpatient care. The phrase "in connection with" is not defined. Presumably, the "connection" may be direct or indirect. Nor is there any indication of how strong a "connection" there must be in order for this rule to apply. For example, must the connection be medically proven in order for this to occur? Moreover, by its terms, an extremely "iffy" connection would suffice. Again, in most cases this will not be a problem as the connection will be readily apparent. In other cases, agencies will no doubt have to request medical certification to establish the "connection" between the present absence for incapacity or treatment and a prior overnight stay in a hospital or other covered facility.

(9) Examples of Inpatient Care

The simplest example of inpatient care is an employee who needs FMLA leave during the period the employee is hospitalized on an inpatient basis for an injury, illness, impairment, or physical or mental condition. An eligible employee who is injured in a car accident requiring a week of hospitalization would meet the inpatient care definition of a serious health condition. All other things being equal, the employee would be entitled to FMLA leave for the time the employee should have been at work which the employee spent in the hospital, where the hospital stay involved one or more overnight stays.

Additionally, inpatient care would apply to an employee or covered family member who spent an overnight stay in a hospital even though no serious health condition was found. For example, an employee goes to the emergency room complaining of chest pain. The hospital runs a series of tests and keeps the employee overnight for observation. The tests reveal that the employee did not suffer a heart attack. At best, the employee suffered a stress or panic attack. The overnight stay in the hospital would be covered as a serious health condition. *See Taylor v. Invacare Corp.*, 64 Fed. Appx. 516 (6th Cir. 2003).

As a serious health condition, inpatient care is defined to include leave beyond the actual time the employee or covered family member spends in the hospital. For example, Brian broke his hip in an automobile accident when he was a 24. He spent several weeks in the hospital where he received treatment. Twenty–five years later, Brain develops arthritis in his hip that occasionally flares up requiring him to miss work. Because his incapacitating arthritis attacks are connected to his overnight stay in a hospital, the attacks constitute an FMLA–qualifying serious health condition for inpatient care. There is no time limit placed by the statute or regulations on the overnight stay and the incapacity connected to that overnight stay.

As worded, the regulations do not require that an overnight stay in a covered facility occur first. For example, Mike and Laura have a 10–year–old son, Christopher. Christopher comes down with a cold and is unable to attend school for three days. He is seen by a doctor, who recommends bed rest for another two days. Christopher develops a high temperature, and is brought to the hospital, where he is diagnosed with pneumonia. Christopher spends two nights in the hospital, whereupon he is released to go home to recover for another three days. At the end of his recovery period Christopher is scheduled to see his doctor for an examination of his condition. Christopher clearly has a serious health condition in connection with his inpatient care. Because it is connected to his hospitalization, Christopher's incapacity prior to his going to the hospital would be covered. In addition, the time Christopher spent in the hospital, as well as his period of recovery and subsequent physician examination, would also be covered. Agencies need to think about this scenario, as it presents troublesome implications for the designation of FMLA leave.

When an employee or covered family member is claiming FMLA leave due to inpatient care, in addition to the actual time spent in the hospital, agencies need to look at absences that occur both before and after the overnight stay in a covered facility to determine whether those absences are also FMLA protected because they are connected to the inpatient care. *See Sanders v. The May Dept. Stores Co.*, No. 4: 00CV576–DJS, 2001 U.S. Dist. LEXIS 11495 (E.D. Mo. May 11, 2001) (an employee who spent seven days in the hospital for surgery, followed by two weeks convalescing, established sufficient facts of serious health condition to defeat summary judgment).

b. Title II

(1) General Rule

An FMLA–qualifying serious health condition means an illness, injury, impairment, or physical or mental condition that involves inpatient care in a hospital, hospice, or residential medical care facility. 5 USC 6381(5); 5 CFR 630.1202 (definition of "serious health condition"); *see Williams v. Dept. of Navy*, No. DC-0752-05-0431-I-1, 2005 MSPB LEXIS 6866, at *3-4 (Oct. 17, 2005), *pet. denied*, 101 MSPR 133 (2006); *Dias v. VA*, No. NY-0752-04-0279-I-2, 2005 MSPB LEXIS 3926, at *13 (June 30, 2006); *Marshall v. Dept. of Army*, No. DC-0752-05-0221-I-1, 2005 MSPB LEXIS 2901, at *11 (May 9, 2005); *Joos v. Treasury*, 74 MSPR 684 (1997), *rev'd* 102 MSPR 53 (2006), *appeal dismissed*, 2006 U.S. App. LEXIS 28961 (Fed. Cir. 2006), *vacated, reinstated* 2006 U.S. App. LEXIS 32257 (Fed. Cir. 2006), *aff'd*, 2007 U.S. App. LEXIS 11530 (Fed. Cir. May 8, 2007). As with the comparable definition under Title I, the CAA, and the PEOAA, the implementing regulations (5 CFR 630.1202 (definition of "serious health condition")) refine the statutory definition as follows:

> Inpatient care (i.e., an overnight stay) in a hospital, hospice, or residential medical care facility, including any period of incapacity or any subsequent treatment in connection with such inpatient care.

Accord Lenoir v. Dept. of Agriculture, No. DA-0752-04-0434-I-1, 2004 MSPB LEXIS 2755, at *5 (Oct. 29, 2004).

One difference between the regulation regarding inpatient care for purposes of Title II and comparable regulations (previously discussed) implementing inpatient care pursuant to Title I, the CAA, and the PEOAA, is the absence of a definition of "incapacity." *Compare* 5 CFR 630.1202 (definition of "serious health condition," Subsection (1)(I)) *with* 29 CFR 825.114(a)(1). Ultimately, however, these provisions have the same meaning, as the term "incapacity" for purposes of Title II is defined elsewhere (5 CFR 630.1202 (definition of "incapacity")) as:

> *Incapacity* means the inability to work, attend school, or perform other regular daily activities because of serious health condition or treatment for or recovery from a serious health condition.

As under Title I, the CAA, and the PEOAA, inpatient care covers "any period of incapacity" and any subsequent treatment in connection with such inpatient care.

(2) Key Terms

Because Title II and both the statute and implementing regulations use nearly identical terms in defining and describing a serious health condition due to inpatient care, the reader is referred to the observations made previously in this chapter for Title I, the CAA, and the PEOAA, regarding the strengths and weaknesses of key terms.

(3) Examples

Because Title II and both the statute and implementing regulations use nearly identical terms in defining and describing a serious health condition due to inpatient care, the reader is referred to the examples and observations made previously in this chapter for Title I, the CAA, and the PEOAA, illustrating the meaning of a serious health condition due to inpatient care.

2. Continuing Treatment by a Health Care Provider

a. Introduction

The second broad category of FMLA–qualifying serious health conditions falls under the general heading of "continuing treatment." Specifically, the term "serious health condition" means an illness, injury, impairment, or physical or mental condition that involves continuing treatment by a health care provider. 29 USC 2611(11); 5 USC 6381(5)(B); 2 USC 1312(a)(1) (incorporating § 101 of Title I, 29 USC 2611, into CAA); 3 USC 412(a)(1) (incorporating § 101 of Title I, 29 USC 2611, into PEOAA); see *Burnett v. LFW, Inc.*, 472 F.3d 471, 478 (7th Cir. 2006); *Dowell v. Indiana Heart Physicians, Inc.*, No. 1:03–cv–1410–DFH–TAB, 2004 U.S. Dist. LEXIS 26431, at *20 (S.D. Ind. Dec. 22, 2004); *Wheeler v. Pioneer Dev. Services, Inc.*, 349 F. Supp. 2d 158 (D. Mass. 2004); *Ruiz v. Ostbye & Anderson, Inc.*, No. 02–2954 (JNE/JGL), 2004 U.S. Dist. LEXIS 19890, at *11 (D. Minn. Sept. 28, 2004); *Lubke v. City of Arlington*, No. 4:02–CV–188–Y, 2003 U.S. Dist. LEXIS 18816, at *9 (N.D. Tex. Sept. 9, 2003); *Hendry v. GTE North, Inc.*, 896 F. Supp. 816, 827 (N.D. Ind. 1995) (Title I); *Ramseur v. Dept. of Navy*, DC-0752-06-0472-I-1, 2006 MSPB LEXIS 5852, at *7 (Oct. 4, 2006); *Jones v. Dept. of Navy*, No. DC-0752-06-0092-I-2, 2006 MSPB LEXIS 5031, at *4 (Sept. 5, 2006); *Kimbrough v. DOD*, No. DC-0752-06-0287-I-1, 2006 MSPB LEXIS 4379, at *11 (Aug. 1, 2006); *Hebron v. USPS*, No. DC-0752-06-0319-I-1, 2006 MSPB LEXIS 2088, at *4 (May 25, 2006) (incorrectly citing to 5 CFR Part 630), review denied, 104 MSPR 265 (2006); *Williams v. Dept. of Navy*, No. DC-0752-05-0431-I-1, 2005 MSPB LEXIS 6866, at *3-4 (Oct. 17, 2005); *Fisher v. DHHS*, No. DC-0752-05-0280-I-1, 2005 MSPB LEXIS 2653, at *8 (June 3, 2005), review denied, 101 MSPR 131 (2005); *Santiago v. USPS*, No. DA-0752-04-0128-B-1, 2005 MSPB LEXIS 2064, at *6 (April 28, 2005); *Jenifer v. USPS*, No. PH–0752–00–0344–I–2, 2001 MSPB LEXIS 1298 (March 14, 2001) (Title I); *Covington v. Dept. of Army*, 85 MSPR 612 (2000) (Title II), pet. denied, 90 MSPR 24 (2001), review dismissed, 2002 U.S. App. LEXIS 2559 (Fed. Cir. 2002); *Landahl v. Commerce*, 83 MSPR 40 (1999) (Tile II), pet. denied, 87 MSPR 530 (2000), aff'd, 2001 U.S. App. LEXIS 11774 (Fed. Cir. 2001); *Young v. USPS*, 79 MSPR 25 (1998) (Title II); *Gross v. DOJ*, 77 MSPR 83, 86 (1997) (Title II); *Joos v. Treasury*, 74 MSPR 684 (1997) (Tile II).

The FMLA does not define "continuing treatment by a health care provider." *Russell v. North Broward Hospital*, 346 F.3d 1335, 1338 (11th Cir. 2003); *Meadows v. Texar Federal Credit Union*, No. 5:05CV158, 2007 U.S. Dist. LEXIS 4456, at *57 (E.D. Tex. Jan. 22, 2007). The term is, however, defined in the implementing regulations. See 29 CFR 825.114(b), 825.800 (definition of "continuing treatment"); 5 CFR 630.1202 (definition of "serious health condition"); S. Res. 242, Cong. Rec. S3959, S3962–63, S3977 (April 23, 1996); 29 CFR 825.112, 825.114(b), 825.800 (definition of "continuing treatment"). Regulations have not been issued to implement the FMLA for purposes of the PEOAA. By operation of 3 USC 455, the PEOAA applies the implementing regulations of the most relevant substantive executive agency regulation promulgated to implement the statutory provision at issue. As the PEOAA incorporates the Title I statutory definition of a serious health condition due to continuing treatment by a health care provider, the regulations issued by the DOL interpreting "continuing treatment" will apply to employees covered by the PEOAA.

b. Legislative History

The legislative history of the FMLA addresses what is meant by a "serious health condition." According to the legislative history, the definition of "serious health condition" in § 101(1) (29 CFR 2611(1)) "is broad and intended to cover various types of physical and mental conditions." S. Rep. 103–3, 103rd Cong., 1st Sess. 129 (1993); see *Stekloff v. St. John's Mercy Health Systems*, 218 F.3d 858, 862 (8th Cir. 2000); DOL WH FMLA Advisory Opinion No. 87 (Dec. 12, 1996); *Washington v. Fort James Operating Co.*, 110 F. Supp. 2d 1325, 1334, n. 10 (D. Ore. 2000). A short review of the legislative history of the FMLA regarding what constitutes a "serious health condition" is instructive. The Senate Report goes on to list examples of what Congress considered to be serious health conditions:

> Examples of serious health conditions include but are not limited to heart attacks, heart conditions requiring heart bypass of valve operations, most cancers, back conditions requiring extensive therapy or surgical procedures, strokes, severe respiratory conditions, spinal injuries, appendicitis, pneumonia, emphysema, severe arthritis, severe nervous disorders, injuries caused by serious accidents on or off the job, ongoing pregnancy, miscarriages, complications or illnesses related to pregnancy, such as severe morning sickness, the need for prenatal care, childbirth and recovery from childbirth. All of these conditions meet the general test that either

the underlying health condition or the treatment for it requires that the employee be absent from work on a recurring basis or for more than a few days for treatment or recovery. They also involve either inpatient care or continuing treatment or supervision by a health care provider, and frequently involve both.

The above legislative language is often cited by the courts, particularly where the court finds that the illness at issue does not rise to the level of a serious health condition as contemplated by the Act. *See Hoban v. WBNCC Joint Venture*, No. 06-13142, 2007 U.S. Dist. LEXIS 25407, at *14 (E.D. Mich. April 5, 2007); *Brown v. Seven Seventeen HB Philadelphia Corp. No. 2*, No. 01-1741, 2002 U.S. Dist. LEXIS 15066, at *14 (E.D. Pa. Aug. 8, 2002); *Miller v. Venator Group, Inc. et al.*, No. 00-civ.-0454 (HB), 2000 U.S. Dist. LEXIS 6892, at *12-13 (S.D.N.Y. May 18, 2000); *Johnson v. USPS*, No. 1:97-CV-794, 1999 U.S. Dist. LEXIS 7981 (W.D. Mich. May 26, 1999); *Beal v. Rubbermaid Commercial Products, Inc.*, 972 F. Supp. 1216, 1226 (S.D. Iowa 1997), *aff'd*, 1998 U.S. App. LEXIS 9295 (8th Cir. 1998); *Mell v. Weyburn-Bartel, Inc.*, No. 1:96-CV-654, 1997 U.S. Dist. LEXIS 15758, at *10 (W.D. Mich. July 28, 1997); *Reich v. The Standard Register Co.*, No. 96-0284-R, 1997 U.S. Dist. LEXIS 3021, at *8 (W.D. Va. Jan. 17, 1997) (*citing* S. Rep. No. 103-3 in finding that employee's ability to work up to 40 hours a week does not suggest serious health condition as contemplated by Act); *Brown v. J.C. Penny Corp.* 924 F. Supp. 1158, 1162 (S.D. Fla. 1996); *Bauer v. Dayton-Walther Corp.*, 910 F. Supp. 306, 310-11 (E.D. Ky. 1996) *aff'd*, 118 F.3d 1109 (6th Cir. 1997); DOL WH FMLA Advisory Opinion No. 85 (Nov. 18, 1996) (citing portions of legislative history to establish that child birth and recovery from child birth are serious health conditions), *see also Olsen v. Ohio Edison Co.*, 979 F. Supp. 1159, 1163 (N.D. Ohio 1997) (citing similar language from legislative history obtained from House Report).

c. Incapacity of More Than Three Consecutive Calendar Days Plus Health Care Provider Treatments

(1) Title I, the CAA, and the PEOAA

(a) General Rule

For purposes of the FMLA, a "serious health condition" entitling an eligible employee to FMLA leave means an illness, injury, impairment, or physical or mental condition that involves continuing treatment by a health care provider, which includes:

(I) A period of incapacity (i.e, inability to work, attend school, or perform other regular daily activities therefore or recovery therefrom) of more than three consecutive calendar days, and any subsequent treatment or period of incapacity relating to the same condition that also involves:

(A) Treatment two or more times by a health care provider, by a nurse or physician's assistant under the direct supervision of a health care provider, or by a provider of health care services (e.g., physical therapist) under orders of, or on referral by, a health care provider; or

(B) Treatment by a health care provider on at least one occasion that results in a regimen of continuing treatment under the supervision of the health care provider.

29 CFR 825.114(a)(2)(I), 825.800 (definition of "serious health condition," subsection (1)(ii)(A)); S. Res. 242, Cong. Rec. S3959, S3962, S3978 (April 23, 1996); 29 CFR 825.114(a)(2)(I), 825.800 (definition of "serious health condition," subsection (1)(ii)(A)); DOL WH FMLA Advisory Opinion No. 43 Aug. 24, 1994); *see Hurlbert v. St. Mary's Health Care System, Inc.*, 439 F.3d 1286, 1294-95 (11th Cir. Feb. 16, 2006); *Lackey v. Jackson County, Tennessee*, 104 Fed. Appx. 483 (6th Cir. 2004); *Brenneman v. MedCentral Health System*, 366 F.3d 412, 428 (6th Cir. 2004), *cert. denied*, 543 U.S. 1146 (U.S. 2005); *Russell v. North Broward Hospital*, 346 F.3d 1335, 1338 (11th Cir. 2003); *Scamihorn, Jr. v. General Truck Drivers, Office, Food and Warehouse Union, Local 952 et al.*, 282 F.3d 1078, 1085 (9th Cir. 2002); *Rhoads v. FDIC et al.*, 257 F.3d 373, 382 (4th Cir. 2001), *cert. denied*, 535 U.S. 1309 (2002); *Stekloff v. St. John's Mercy Health Systems*, 218 F.3d 858, 860 (8th Cir. 2000); *Thorson v. Gemini, Inc.*, 205 F.3d 370, 378 (8th Cir. 2000), *cert. denied*, 531 U.S. 871 (2000); *Ahern v. Dept. of Treasury*, No. 99-3362, 1999 U.S. App. LEXIS 32461, at *3 (Fed. Cir. Dec. 13, 1999); *Haefling v. UPS, Inc.*, 169 F.3d 494, 498-99 (7th Cir. 1999), *cert. denied*, 528 U.S. 820 (1999); *Taylor v. AmeriTech Services, Inc.*, No. 05-C-952, 2007 U.S. Dist. LEXIS 28769, at *16 (E.D. Wis. April 18, 2007); *Stevens v. Advance Stores Co., Inc.*, No. 3-06-0537, 2007 U.S. Dist. LEXIS 28690, at 18 (M.D. Tenn. April 17, 2007); *Whitworth v. Consolidated Biscuit Co.*, No. 6:06-112-DCR, 2007 U.S. Dist. LEXIS 25971, at *14 (E.D. Ky. April 6, 2007); *Taylor v. Texaco, Inc.*, No. 4:04-CV-212-JEC, 2007 U.S. Dist. LEXIS 22239, at *28 (N.D. Ga. March 28, 2007); *Meadows v. Texar Federal Credit Union*, No. 5:05CV158, 2007 U.S. Dist. LEXIS 4456, at *57 (E.D. Tex. Jan. 22, 2007); DOL WH FMLA Advisory Opinion No. 86 (Dec. 12, 1996).

A discussion of the regulatory development of the final rule and the key terms contained therein follows.

(b) Regulatory Development

The regulatory development of the current standard provides additional context to understand this serious health condition. In confirming the propriety of this standard, the DOL addressed adverse public comments. The commentators (Preamble, 29 CFR 825.114) argued that:

1. A minimum durational limit is contrary to the statute and legislative history;

2. The "more than three days" test would encourage employees to remain absent from work longer than necessary in order to qualify for the protection of the Act;

3. The "more than three day" rule was unreasonably low, and trivialized the concept of seriousness; and

4. Calculating the "more than three day rule" based on calendar days should be changed to work days to better reflect the need for absence from work.

The DOL addressed these comments in the preamble to publication of the final Title I FMLA regulations. In pertinent part, the DOL (Preamble, 29 CFR 825.114) observed the following:

> Upon review, the Department has concluded that the "more than three days" test continues to be appropriate. The legislative history specifically provides that conditions lasting only a few days were not intended to be included as serious health conditions, because such conditions are normally covered by employers' sick leave plans. The Department has also concluded that it is not appropriate to change the standard to working days rather than calendar days because the severity of the illness is better captured by its duration rather than the length of time necessary to be absent from work. Furthermore, a working day's standard would be difficult to apply to serious health conditions of family members or part-time workers.

Notably, the DOL's comments did not address the argument that the unintended consequence of the "more than three day" standard would encourage employees with otherwise minor illnesses to stay out of work longer in order to capture the protections of the FMLA. Presumably, the DOL would respond that the ability of an employer to require medical certification substantiating the need for FMLA leave as claimed is an adequate counterweight to employees inappropriately extending their leave. While that may be true in most cases (most employees being basically honest), the position that medical certification will effectively check all employee abuse of the FMLA is undoubtedly an overstatement. Medical certifications are addressed in Chapter 9, "Documentation Requirements."

The repeated reference in the legislative history that an employee's absence from work "for more than a few days" suggests that the "more than three days" standard for a serious health condition would likely be found to be a legitimate construction of the Act. That is, the "more than three day" standard is probably not a prime candidate for invalidation due to DOL overreaching.

(c) Incapacity

As with inpatient care, "incapacity" is defined as the inability to work, attend school or perform other regular daily activities due to the serious health condition, treatment therefore, or recovery therefrom. 29 CFR 825.114(a)(2)(I); S. Res. 242, Cong. Rec. S3959, S3962 (April 23, 1996); 29 CFR 825.114(a)(2)(I); see *Whitworth v. Consolidated Biscuit Co.*, No. 6:06-112-DCR, 2007 U.S. Dist. LEXIS 25971, at *25 (E.D. Ky. April 6, 2007); *Lackey v. Jackson County, Tennessee*, 104 Fed. Appx. 483 (6th Cir. 2004); *Wheeler v. Pioneer Dev. Services, Inc.*, 349 F. Supp 2d 158 (D. Mass. 2004) ("incapacity" means that the patient cannot work due to the serious health condition, treatment therefore, or recovery therefrom); *Hobart v. Behavioral Connections of Wood County, Inc.*, No. 3:03CV7313, 2004 U.S. Dist. LEXIS 12051, at *19 (N.D. Ohio July 1, 2004) (inability to work); *Conrad v. Eaton Corp.*, 303 F. Supp. 2d 987, 1001 (N.D. Iowa 2004); *Peter v. Lincoln Technical Institute*, 255 F. Supp. 2d 417, 439 (E.D. Pa. 2002); *Scamihorn, Jr. v. General Truck Drivers, Office, Food and Warehouse Union, Local 952 et al.*, 282 F.3d 1078, 1085 (9th Cir. 2002); *Barnhill v. Farmland Foods, Inc.*, No. 98-4152-CM, 2001 U.S. Dist. LEXIS 5691 (D. Kan. April 19, 2001); *Stekloff v. St. John's Mercy Health Systems*, 218 F.3d 858, 861-62 (8th Cir. 2000); *Johnson v. USPS*, No. 1:97-CV-794, 1999 U.S. Dist. LEXIS 7981 (W.D. Mich. May 26, 1999); *LeGrand v. Village of McCook*, No. 96-C-5951, 1998 U.S. Dist. LEXIS 5230 (N.D. Ill. April 15, 1998); DOL WH FMLA Advisory Opinion No. 43 (Aug. 24, 1994). Again, incapacity is not limited to sick time, but includes time spent to receive treatment (a defined term addressed below) and to recover "therefrom." Presumably, in this context, "therefrom" means recovery from the serious health condition as well as treatment. There may be limitation on recovery from treatment.

Whether an employee suffers a "period of incapacity" within the meaning of the FMLA is a threshold consideration. *Caldwell v. Holland of Texas*, 208 F.3d 671, 674 (8th Cir. 2000); *Haefling v. UPS, Inc.*, 169 F.3d 494, 499 (7th Cir. 1999), *cert. denied*, 528 U.S. 820 (1999); *Murray v. Red Kap Industries, Inc.*, 124 F.3d 695, 698 (5th Cir. 1997); *Whitworth*, 2007 U.S. Dist. LEXIS 25971, at *14 (E.D. Ky. April 6, 2007); *Meadows v. Texar Federal Credit Union*, No. 5:05CV158, 2007 U.S. Dist. LEXIS 4456, at *61 (E.D. Tex. Jan. 22, 2007); *Bond v. Abbott Laboratories*, 7 F. Supp. 2d 967, 973 (N.D. Ohio 1998), *aff'd on other grounds*, 188 F.3d 506 (table), No. 98–3923, 1999 U.S. App. LEXIS 22242 (6th Cir. Sept. 9, 1999); *Olsen v. Ohio Edison Co.*, 979 F. Supp. 1159, 1164 (N.D. Ohio 1997) (before the court even considers the "continuing treatment" prong of the definition of serious medical condition, the employee must first demonstrate that he suffered from a period of incapacity within the meaning of that regulation).

An employee who fails to meet the "incapacitated" requirement will fail to establish a claim for FMLA leave. *Haefling v. UPS, Inc.*, 169 F.3d 494, 499 (7th Cir. 1999); *Meadows v. Texar Federal Credit Union*, No. 5:05CV158, 2007 U.S. Dist. LEXIS 4456, at *61 (E.D. Tex. Jan. 22, 2007); *Barnhill v. Farmland Foods, Inc.*, No. 98–4152–CM, 2001 U.S. Dist. LEXIS 5691 (D. Kan. April 19, 2001); *Olsen v. Ohio Edison Co.*, 979 F. Supp. 1159, 1164 (N.D. Ohio 1997). An employee is not required to demonstrate that s/he was totally incapacitated in order to avoid summary judgment. *Ruiz v. Ostbye & Anderson, Inc.*, No. 02–2954 (JNE/JGL), 2004 U.S. Dist. LEXIS 19890, at *12 (D. Minn. Sept. 28, 2004). The definition of incapacity, because it is the same as under inpatient care (previously discussed), contains some of the same infirmities. For example, incapacity is defined as the "inability to work." Absent any further qualification, the provision suggests that the incapacity must render the employee or covered family member unable to work at all. Where the need for leave is due to the employee's own serious health condition, "inability to work" may conflict with how the statute and regulations define "unable to perform the functions of the employee's position." "Unable to perform the functions of the employee's position" is satisfied if the employee is unable to work at all, or is unable to perform one or more essential functions of his or her position. *See* 29 CFR 825.115. Because it is not clear that an "inability to work" means the same thing as "unable to perform one or more essential functions of the job," the regulations unnecessarily sow confusion.

As applied to other covered family members, an "inability to work" appears to set a higher standard for "incapacity" than may be required of employees. That is, unless "inability to work" means the same thing as "unable to perform one or more essential job functions," it would appear that a covered family member must be completely unable to work due to a serious health condition. An employee, perhaps, need only be incapacitated from performing one or more essential job functions. Of course, to reach this result, "inability to work" would have a different meaning depending on whether the leave was for an employee's own serious health condition, or the serious health condition of a covered family member. Such inconsistent interpretations would not appear to be desirable.

Conservative agencies would be well advised to interpret "inability to work" for purposes of a serious health condition and "incapacity" the same as "unable to perform one or more essential job functions." This would be a consistent definition applicable to employees and covered family members where the incapacity renders the employee unable to work. If the incapacity renders the employee or covered family member unable to go to school or perform other regular daily activities, the standard would, obviously, not apply. More aggressive employers might consider interpreting "inability to work" literally, meaning inability to work at all. Such an interpretation would moot the alternative definition of "unable to perform one or more essential job functions" as a basis for FMLA leave. This is decidedly a high-risk strategy playing off the confusion in the FMLA regulations as a means of invalidating one or both regulations.

An employee who is able to work is not incapacitated within the meaning of the FMLA. In *Whitworth v. Consolidated Biscuit Co.*, No. 6:06-112-DCR, 2007 U.S. Dist. LEXIS 25971, at *14 (E.D. Ky. April 6, 2007), the employee claimed to be incapacitated from stress and anxiety due to the release of her former boyfriend from jail. However, she admitted that she could have and would have worked during the period in question if she had known that her request for leave would not be accepted. The court noted that it was well-settled that the possibility that a person can work removes FMLA protections.

An employee who is cleared to perform light duty work is not incapacitated within the meaning of the FMLA. In *Yansick v. Temple University Health System*, No. 04-4228, 2006 U.S. Dist. LEXIS 53789, at *42 (E.D. Pa. Aug. 3, 2006), the court found that "incapacity" does not mean the same thing as "unable to perform the functions" of the employee's job. Thus, an employee who is unable to perform one or more essential job functions is not automatically considered incapacitated within the meaning of a serious health condition.

The incapacity must be caused by the alleged serious health condition. In *Bradley v. Mary Rutan Hospital Assoc.*, 322 F. Supp. 2d 926, 942 (S.D. Ohio 2004), the court found that, while the employee was off work for more than three consecutive days following injuries she claims to have suffered when she knocked her right hand into a salad bar while walking past it, her incapacity was not caused by her injury. The court noted that the employee was released to return to work the very day she saw her doctor, albeit with restrictions not to use her right hand. The court also noted that the bulk of the time she was off work pursuant to her doctor's instructions was because Bradley erroneously told her doctor that Mary Rutan would not accommodate her original restrictions. "Consequently, to the extent that [p]laintiff was 'incapacitated' or 'unable to work' for more than three days, it still was not because of her injury; rather it was because she told Dr. Campbell that [d]efendant refused to accommodate her work restrictions."

In *Wheeler v. Pioneer Dev. Services, Inc.*, 349 F. Supp 2d 158 (D. Mass. 2004), the court qualified the requirement that the employee be unable to work due to the illness. The employee claimed that she had a serious health condition. The court noted that to prove incapacity, the employee need only show that she could not perform the job functions of her employer and continued to receive treatment for her illness. The employee was not required to show that she could not perform any work at all. The employee worked at another job during the continuation of her leave. The court found that "[t]he fact that Wheeler worked at another job during the continuation of her leave does not disprove her incapacity." The court held that the employee need only prove that she was incapacitated due to her illness for the first four days of her illness. What she did after that apparently did not matter.

Notwithstanding *Wheeler*, employees who perform other activities during FMLA leave may call into question whether they are truly "incapacitated" within the meaning of the FMLA. In *Ruiz v. Ostbye & Anderson, Inc.*, No. 02–2954 (JNE/JGL), 2004 U.S. Dist. LEXIS 19890, at *11 (D. Minn. Sept. 28, 2004), the court concluded that there were genuine issues of material fact with respect to whether and when Ruiz was incapacitated during the period of August 15 through August 22, precluding a determination (for purposes of summary judgment) of whether she was incapacitated for more than three days. On the one hand, plaintiff had a doctor's note advising she take that period of time off from work due to her illness (distress). On the other hand, during that time she attended a family reunion in another state and went on a shopping trip to Kmart.

In *Conrad v. Eaton Corp.*, 303 F. Supp. 2d 987, 1002–1003 (N.D. Iowa 2004), the court addressed whether an employee who was unable to work for the employer due to mental depression, but who could perform the same job for another employer and who performed household chores during leave, was "incapacitated" within the meaning of the FMLA. After reviewing and contrasting the purpose of the FMLA and the ADA, the court concluded that an employee's ability to perform the essential functions of his job focuses on his ability to perform those functions in his current environment. For purposes of the FMLA, "an inquiry into whether the employee was unable to work is limited to whether the employee was unable to work at the position [he or she] currently held." The fact that Conrad could perform his job functions at some hypothetical job is irrelevant.

Similarly, a family member that is able to engage in normal daily activities may not be incapacitated to support an employee's request for FMLA leave. In *Cool v. BorgWarner Diversified Transmission Products, Inc.*, No. IP-02-0960-C-B/S, 2004 U.S. Dist. LEXIS 570, at *19 (S.D. Ind. Jan. 12, 2004), the court found that a stress condition exhibited by crying, sullen acting out, and abdominal pain suffered by children did not reach the level of a serious health condition where the children attended school without disruption or accommodation and regularly participated in several extra curricular activities such as Cub Scouts and dance lessons. The court opined that while "childhood may at times be traumatic, a reasonable jury could not find that it was incapacitating under these circumstances."

Because the "more than three day" rule is calculated on consecutive calendar days, the non-work examples of incapacity (inability to attend school or perform other regular daily activities due to the serious health condition) equally apply to employees and other covered family members. Since consecutive calendar days could occur over the weekend or other non-scheduled workdays, a means of determining incapacity during these non-work hours is necessary for employees and covered family members where the claim is that the serious health condition rendered them unable to work. The non-work examples always made sense for covered family members whose incapacity did not impact on their ability to work, such as children rendered unable to go to school.

As defined, "incapacity" fails to distinguish between work and non-work activities. *Haefling v. UPS, Inc.*, 169 F.3d 494, 498–99 (7th Cir. 1999), *cert. denied*, 528 U.S. 820 (1999) (an employee could string together absences from work and absences from routine daily activities to establish a period of incapacity of more than three days). The lack of priority raised concerns among some that an employee who was still able to work might be entitled to FMLA leave because the employee was unable to go to a class after work. These concerns are largely unfounded. For example, the definition of incapacity does not make it clear whether an employee is incapacitated within the meaning of the FMLA where the employee is able to work, but cannot tend a garden after work. Even if the employee was viewed as being "incapacitated" for purposes of a serious health condition, the employee would nevertheless fail the requirement that he or she was "unable to perform one or more essential functions" of the employee's position. As a result, the employee would not be entitled to FMLA leave. The same, however, is not true when the need for leave is for a covered family member.

An employee, who is unable to work due to a serious health condition but able to perform other regular daily activities during leave, is nevertheless incapacitated within the meaning of the FMLA. In *Meadows v. Texar Federal Credit Union*, No. 5:05CV158, 2007 U.S. Dist. LEXIS 4456, at *63 (E.D. Tex. Jan. 22, 2007), the court rejected the employer's argument that an employee was not incapacitated where the employee was instructed not to work by their treating psychologist, but engaged in normal daily activities while on leave (also at the instruction of her treating physician). The court found that if an employee demonstrates that he or she is unable to perform one or more essential job functions due to a serious health condition, then he or she is incapacitated within the meaning of the FMLA. The employee need not also demonstrate that he or she is unable to perform daily activities nor does the performance of other regular daily activities negate the employee's claim that he or she has an FMLA-covered condition where the employee is unable to work due to that serious health condition.

An employee could still be "needed to care for" a covered family member who, although able to work, was incapacitated from performing other regular daily activities by the serious health condition, such as ensuring that he or she takes necessary medication. Since the employee is "needed to care for" the covered family member despite the covered family member's ability to work or perform some regular daily activities, the employee, all other things being equal, may be entitled to FMLA leave.

Note that "other daily activities" is not defined. In *Haefling v. UPS, Inc.*, 169 F.3d 494, 500 (7th Cir. 1999), *cert. denied*, 528 U.S. 820 (1999), the court indicated that eating, drinking, learning, taking care of oneself, and engaging in marital relations were a partial list of regular daily activities. According to the court, the burden is on the employee to establish inability to perform regular daily activities. "This showing would not be a difficult one." *Id*. The court also opined that an employee's inability to work due to a serious health condition does not automatically render the employee incapable of performing regular daily activities during his or her off-work hours. *Id*.

What constitutes the "other daily activities" of an infant was addressed by the court in *Caldwell v. Holland of Texas, Inc.*, 208 F.3d 671, 674–676 (8th Cir. 2000). There, the employee needed FMLA leave to care for her three-year-old son with a persistent ear infection. The court initially noted that the DOL regulations were an insufficient guide with respect to establishing "incapacity" as three year olds do not work, or attend school. Instead, the court held that "incapacity" should be judged based on whether the child's illness demonstrably affected his or her normal activity. *Id*. "In making this determination, the fact finder may consider a variety of factors, including but not limited to: whether the child participated in his daily routines or was particularly difficult to care for during that period, and whether a daycare facility would have allowed a child with Kejuan's illness to attend its sessions." *Id*. The court relied on medical records and the affidavit of the mother to find sufficient material issues of fact in dispute to reverse the award of summary judgment to the employer. The mother's affidavit indicated that her son did not participate in any of his normal activities, and that he was under constant care. The medical records established that the son was seeing doctors who prescribed prescription medications for well over three consecutive days, leading up to and after surgery.

The absence of a definition of "other daily activities" will also, no doubt, result in embarrassing and otherwise outrageous claims of incapacity entitling an employee to FMLA leave because the employee or covered family member could not participate in their "regular daily activity" of boozing, fishing, shooting guns, going to the go-go bars, watching soap operas, or eating potato chips.

Of course, such activities would have to be "daily." Note that no time frame is given for making such a determination. This leads to the question: How long a period of time must an activity be conducted to be considered a "regular daily activity"? A week? A month? A year? Agencies can verify a claim of incapacity from a "regular daily activity" by requiring medical certification from a health care provider. As discussed more fully in Chapter 9, "Documentation Requirements," the medical certification requires, among other things, identification of the serious health condition being claimed, and "the medical facts which support the certification, including a brief statement as to how the medical facts meet the criteria of the definition." 29 CFR 825.306(b)(1); S. Res. 242, Cong. Rec. S3959, S3972 (April 23, 1996); 29 CFR 825.306(b)(1). If the claim is that the employee or covered family member is incapacitated from performing "regular daily activities," the medical facts need to address this. Most will not, leaving the certification incomplete.

In *Haefling v. UPS, Inc.*, 169 F.3d 494, 499–500 (7th Cir. 1999), *cert. denied*, 528 U.S. 820 (1999), an employee's diary was used to discredit claims that the employee could not perform other regular daily activities during the time he was not scheduled to work. The diary simply indicated that the employee was "[s]till sick," which the court found insufficient evidence. The court also noted that the employee's deposition testimony indicated that during this time he was able to learn, care for himself, eat, drink and engage in marital relations. "While a list of routine daily activities would certainly encompass more than eating, drinking, and learning, Haefling has simply failed to adduce any evidence that would demonstrate a period of incapacity greater than three consecutive days."

In *Whitworth v. Consolidated Biscuit Co.*, No. 6:06-112-DCR, 2007 U.S. Dist. LEXIS 25971, at *28 (E.D. Ky. April 6, 2007), the employee's ability to do the laundry, travel to and from work, her lawyer's office, and her doctor's office demonstrated that she was capable of performing "other regular daily activities," and she was not incapacitated within the meaning of the FMLA.

Absent incapacity, a medical condition will not be considered a serious health condition within the meaning of the FMLA. *See Martyszenko v. Safeway, Inc.*, 120 F.3d 120 (8th Cir. 1997); *Bauer v. Dayton–Walther* Corp., 910 F. Supp. 306, 310 (E.D. Ky. 1996), *aff'd*, 118 F.3d 1109 (6th Cir. 1997); *Fisher v. State Farm Mutual Automobile Ins. Co.*, 999 F. Supp. 866, 869 (E.D. Tex. 1998), *aff'd without op.*, 176 F.3d 479, 1999 U.S. App. LEXIS 5516 (5th Cir. 1999); *Russo v. Jefferson Parish Water Dept.*, No. 96–2134–N, 1997 U.S. Dist. LEXIS 17951 (E.D. La. Nov. 6, 1997).

(d) More Than Three Consecutive Calendar Days

The "incapacity" of the employee or covered family member must be for more than three consecutive calendar days. 29 CFR 825.114(a)(2)(I); S. Res. 242, Cong. Rec. S3959, S3962 (April 23, 1996); 29 CFR 825.114(a)(2)(I); *see Scamihorn, Jr. v. General Truck Drivers, Office, Food and Warehouse Union, Local 952 et al.*, 282 F.3d 1078, 1085–86 (9th Cir. 2002); *Haefling*, 169 F.3d at 499; *Murray v. Red Kap Industries, Inc.*, 124 F.3d 695, 698 (5th Cir. 1997) (employee alleging that he has a serious health condition involving continuing treatment by a health care provider must first demonstrate a period of incapacity for at least four consecutive days*); Taylor v. Texaco, Inc.*, No. 4:04-CV-212-JEC, 2007 U.S. Dist. LEXIS 22239, at *28 (N.D. Ga. March 28, 2007); *Lottinger v. Shell Oil Co. et al.*, 143 F. Supp. 2d 743, 770–71 (S.D. Tex. 2001). Although they did not explicitly provide that the three days needed to be consecutive, courts have interpreted the interim regulations as requiring that the days be consecutive. *See Haefling*, 169 F.3d at 498–99.

The regulations fail to define what constitutes a "day." Absent any conditions, it would appear that the incapacity must last for more than three consecutive 24–hour periods. Presumably, the "more than three day" period is measured from the onset of the incapacity. The regulations are not clear on this point. The "more" is not quantified, so that any period (e.g., one–second) of time over the minimum three consecutive calendar days should satisfy the criteria.

The courts are all over the map as to whether partial days count for purposes of the "more than three day" incapacity requirement. The only circuit to address the issue found that the period of incapacity must be more than three 24 hour days to meet the "more than three day" requirement.

In *Russell v. North Broward Hospital*, 346 F.3d 1335, 1338 (11th Cir. 2003), the Eleventh Circuit addressed whether a covered individual must be incapacitated all day long for more than 72 continuous hours (three consecutive days) or whether more than three consecutive partial days of incapacity count. The court concluded that more than three consecutive whole days of incapacity are required. Partial days only count at the beginning or end of the period of incapacity in order to make up the "more than" element.

Russell suffered injuries as a result of a slip and fall at work. She was allowed and did return to work that day with restrictions. The next day, Russell worked two hours before leaving to go back to her physician because she was experiencing pain. She did not work the rest of that day or the following day. Russell left work the next day after working only an hour, again reporting pain. She claims she was in pain throughout the following weekend (which she was not scheduled to work). On Monday, she went to see a physician in the morning and worked the remaining four hours of her shift in the afternoon. Russell left work early on Tuesday and stayed at home on Wednesday at the direction of her supervisor while a doctor's appointment was being arranged. She worked all day Thursday. On Friday, Russell saw her doctor in the morning. She left the doctor's office and went home to get her medication before going to work. She fell asleep at home and never made it to work. She was fired the following Monday.

Russell argued that she met the incapacity requirement of more than three consecutive calendar days because she established seven consecutive partial days of incapacity. If not, she argued that the DOL regulatory requirement is invalid. It was undisputed that Russell was incapacitated for parts of more than three consecutive calendar days during the period at issue.

Interpreting § 825.114 as requiring full days of incapacity, the Eleventh Circuit in *Russell*, 346 F.3d at 1343–1344, reasoned:

> The plain language of § 825.114—"a period of incapacity…of more than three consecutive calendar days" (emphasis deleted)—points the way to resolution of this issue. A "period," in the sense relevant here, means "any specified division or portion of time." *Random House Unabridged Dictionary,* p. 1440 (2d ed. 1993). The specified portion of time in § 824.114 is "more than three consecutive calendar days." And a "calendar day" has a simple and universally understood meaning: "The period from one midnight to the following midnight." *Id.* at 296; *see also Black's Law Dictionary,* p. 401 (7th ed. 1999); *Webster's Third New International Dictionary,* p. 316 (1986) ("The time from midnight to midnight."). A "calendar day" thus refers to a whole day, not to part of a day, and it takes some fraction more than three whole calendar days in a row to constitute a "period of incapacity" required under § 825.114.
>
> If we interpret § 825.114 as requiring full days of incapacity, as we do, the requirement will ensure that "serious health conditions" are in fact serious, and are ones that result in an extended period of incapacity, as Congress intended. This interpretation adds certainty to the law by reading the regulation to set forth an objective, bright-line rule defining the period of incapacity necessary to invoke the protections of the FMLA.
>
> On the other hand, if we interpret § 825.114 as allowing partial days of incapacity to meet the requirement—a strained interpretation given the plain regulatory language—the objectivity and certainty that the regulation fosters will be undermined. Under the opposing interpretation, which Russell urges upon us, courts and juries would continually confront confounding issues about how much incapacity on a given day is enough for that day to count toward the regulatory requirement. Are five hours enough? Fifty minutes? Fifteen minutes? Five minutes? Does it depend on the circumstances? If so, how so?
>
> We are loath to adopt a strained interpretation of a regulatory provision that would result in employers, employees, and courts facing an uncertain and ever-shifting legal landscape. We think the better rule, and more importantly the rule that the language of § 825.114 indicates the Secretary of Labor has chosen, is the one that sets forth an objective standard of more than three consecutive full days of incapacity. Partial days do not count, except at the beginning or end of the "period of incapacity" in order to make up the "more than" element.

The court went on to reject the plaintiff's argument that the regulation is invalid if it requires more than three consecutive full days of incapacity. *Accord Taylor v. Texaco, Inc.,* No. 4:04-CV-212-JEC, 2007 U.S. Dist. LEXIS 22239, at *29 (N.D. Ga. March 28, 2007) (absence due to severe sinus infection lasting two consecutive days insufficient). In *Stevens v. Advance Stores Co., Inc.*, No. 3-06-0537, 2007 U.S. Dist. LEXIS 28690, at *18 (M.D. Tenn. April 17, 2007), the court found that the employee satisfied the incapacitation requirement even though the employee was not absent from work for more than three full consecutive days. Stevens called in sick on January 10, she remained ill on January 11, her scheduled day off. On January 12, Stevens came to work sick but was sent home by her employer after an undetermined period of time. She did not work January 13, 14, and 15. On these facts, the court found that, viewed in a light most favorable to the employee (for summary judgment purposes), a jury could find that she was ill for more than three consecutive days. The decision runs counter to *Russell v. North Broward Hospital*, 346 F.3d 1335, 1338 (11th Cir. 2003). The Eleventh Circuit would not count the day Stevens returned to work. Taking that partial day out of the mix, Stevens was not absent for "more than" three consecutive full days.

In *Barnhill v. Farmland Foods, Inc.*, No. 98-4152-CM, 2001 U.S. Dist. LEXIS 5691 (D. Kan. April 19, 2001), the court addressed the calculation of "more than three days." In that case, the plaintiff reported to work on August 5, working 90 minutes of her scheduled shift, and then left early. The plaintiff, the court noted, did not contend that she was unable to perform the functions of her job on August 5. The plaintiff was also absent from work on both August 6 and 7. Plaintiff returned to work on August 8. According to the court, "at most, [the] plaintiff was incapacitated for two full days and a portion of a third. This time period of less than three days is insufficient to meet the regulatory definition of serious health condition." Note that the court defined a "day," full or partial, in terms of a workday, not a 24-hour day.

In *Olsen v. Ohio Edison Co.*, 979 F. Supp. 1159, 1165 (N.D. Ohio Sept. 30, 1997), the court assumed, *arguendo*, that the days the employee worked on light duty counted as full days toward the "more than three days" requirement. The court ultimately concluded that the employee was not incapacitated for "more than three days."

As discussed above, by using "consecutive calendar days," the regulation necessarily includes weekends and other periods of time when the employee is not scheduled to work. Commentators to the final regulations opined that the test should be based on workdays as the leave was needed to excuse the employee from work. Preamble, 29 CFR 825.114. In response, the DOL stated that "it is not appropriate to change the standard to working days rather than calendar days because the severity of the illness is better captured by its duration rather than the length of time necessary to be absent from work. Furthermore, a 'working days' standard would be difficult to apply to serious health conditions of family members or part-time workers." Preamble, 29 CFR 825.114; *see also* DOL WH FMLA Advisory Opinion No. 43 (Aug. 24, 1994) (standard is consecutive calendar days, not workdays, and would include non-workdays such as the weekend when the employee was unable to carry out regular daily activities).

The length of time the employee's physician excused the employee establishes that the employee met the "more than three days" incapacity requirement. For example, in *Hobart v. Behavioral Connections of Wood County, Inc.*, No. 3:03CV7313, 2004 U.S. Dist. LEXIS 12051, at *21 (N.D. Ohio July 1, 2004), an employee who was excused from work by his physician for 14 days due to a medical condition exceeded the minimum 3 days required by the regulation.

Other courts have found the length of an employee's absence alone does not establish that they met the "more than three day" incapacity requirement. In *Bradley v. Mary Rutan Hospital Assoc.*, 322 F. Supp. 2d 926, 941–942 (S.D. Ohio 2004), the court opined that employee does not satisfy the "more than three days" requirement simply because she took off work for many days. The employee must be off work due to the alleged serious health condition. In *Bradley*, the court found that, while the employee was off work for more than three consecutive days following injuries she claims to have suffered when she knocked her right hand into a salad bar while walking past it, her incapacity was not caused by her injury.

The length of an employee's absence may, however, be sufficient to defeat an employer's motion for summary judgment. *See Carmen v. Unison Behavioral Health Group, Inc.*, 295 F. Supp. 2d 809, 814 (N.D. Ohio 2003) (employee who requested leave for four consecutive days and had a series of follow-up medical appointments relating to her condition adduced evidence sufficient to withstand summary judgment). In *Lines v. City of Ottawa, Kansas*, No. 02-2248-KHV, 2003 U.S. Dist. LEXIS 10203, at *21 (D. Kan. June 16, 2003), the court held that medical restrictions prohibiting an employee from driving, an essential function of the employee's job, due to epilepsy seizures for more than three consecutive days arguably met the "more than three days" requirement of a serious health condition under § 825.114(a)(2)(I). Always keep in mind that, if the leave is for an employee's own serious health condition, the condition must render the employee unable to perform one or more essential job functions in addition to meeting one of the FMLA "serious health condition" definitions.

When the period of incapacity does not exceed three consecutive calendar days, the absences cannot qualify for coverage under this definition of an FMLA-covered "serious health condition." *See Levine v. Children's Museum of Indianapolis, Inc.*, 61 Fed. Appx. 298 (7th Cir. 2003) (an employee's notice of a day and a half absence because he was sick insufficient to meet requirements of "more than three days" absence); *Collins v. NTN-Bowers Corp.*, 272 F.3d 1006, 1008 (7th Cir. 2001) (notice of two-day absence insufficient); *Taylor v. AmeriTech Services, Inc.*, No. 05-C-952, 2007 U.S. Dist. LEXIS 28769, at *24 (E.D. Wis. April 18, 2007); *Barnhill v. Farmland Foods, Inc.*, No. 98-4152-CM, 2001 U.S. Dist. LEXIS 5691 (D. Kan. April 19, 2001) (absences on August 5, 6, and 7 did not meet "more than three consecutive days" standard for coverage under FMLA); *Peterson v. Exide Corp.*, 123 F. Supp. 2d 1265, 1270 (D. Kan. 2000); *Laughlin v. Cardiovascular Institute of the South*, No. 99-3092 § "G", 2000 U.S. Dist. LEXIS 9586, at *12-13 (E.D. La. July 5, 2000), *aff'd*, 251 F.3d 157 (5th Cir. 2001); *Goodwin v. Rheem Manufacturing Co.*, 15 F. Supp. 2d 1197, 1204, n. 6 (M.D. Ala. 1998) (no evidence that employee's poison ivy resulted in any incapacity cited in finding employee did not have FMLA serious health condition); *Carter v. Rental Uniform Service of Culpepper, Inc. et al.*, 977 F. Supp. 753, 760-61 (W.D. Va. 1997); *Bauer v. Dayton-Walther* Corp., 910 F. Supp. 306, 310 (E.D. Ky. 1996) (one-day absence did not qualify for FMLA leave because it did not last more than three days), *aff'd*, 118 F.3d 1109 (6th Cir. 1997); *Seidle v. Provident Mutual Life Ins. Co.*, 871 F. Supp. 238 (E.D. Pa. 1994) (holding that when the plaintiff's child was examined only once by a physician and was not required to be absent from day care for more than three days, he had no serious health condition within the meaning of the FMLA); *Brannon v. Oshkosh B'Gosh, Inc.*,

897 F. Supp. 1028 (M.D. Tenn. 1995); *Jenifer v. USPS,* No. PH–0752–00–0344–I–2, 2001 MSPB LEXIS 1298 (March 14, 2001) (absences due to incapacity lasting less than three days where there is no evidence of continuing treatment by a health care provider not covered by FMLA).

(e) Treatment

Treatment is defined in the regulations for all serious health conditions. 29 CFR 825.114(b), 825.800 (definition of "serious health condition," Subsection (2)); S. Res. 242, Cong. Rec. S3959, S3963, S3978 (April 23, 1996); 29 CFR 825.114(b), 825.800 (definition of "serious health condition," Subsection (2)). Treatment includes, but is not limited to, examinations to determine if a serious health condition exists and evaluations of the conditions. 29 CFR 825.114(b), 825.800 (definition of "serious health condition," Subsection (2)); S. Res. 242, Cong. Rec. S3959, S3963, S3978 (April 23, 1996); 29 CFR 825.114(b), 825.800 (definition of "serious health condition," Subsection (2)); see *Taylor v. Invacare Corp.*, 64 Fed. Appx. 516 (6th Cir. 2003); *Miller v. AT&T Corp. et al.*, 250 F.3d 820, 830–31 (4th Cir. 2001) (where physician conducted a physical examination and drew blood to evaluate condition constituted "treatment" within the meaning of the FMLA); *Thorson v. Gemini, Inc.*, 205 F.3d 370, 378–79 (8th Cir. 2000) (employee satisfied "treatment" by undergoing examinations and evaluations even though ultimate diagnosis was of only minor ailments), *cert. denied*, 531 U.S. 871, 148 L. Ed. 2d 117, 121 S. Ct. 172 (2000); *Martinez v. Neiman Marcus Group, Inc.*, No. 3-05-CV-0422-P, 2006 U.S. Dist. LEXIS 3025, at *15 (N.D. Tax. Jan. 25, 2006); *Dowell v. Indiana Heart Physicians, Inc.*, No. 1:03–cv–1410–DFH–TAB, 2004 U.S. Dist. LEXIS 26431, at *20 (S.D. Ind. Dec. 22, 2004); *Wheeler v. Pioneer Dev. Services, Inc.*, 349 F. Supp 2d 158 (D. Mass. 2004); *Helfrich v. Leigh Valley Hospital*, No. 03–5793, 2003 U.S. Dist. LEXIS 23708, at *7 (E.D. Pa. Dec. 22, 2003) (Congress intended to allow employees in need of time off for medical evaluations to be protected under the FMLA).

In *Wheeler*, 349 F. Supp 2d at 158, the court credited the employee's initial visit to her doctor after the onset of her illness as "treatment" to determine if a serious health condition exists. The court also credited a second doctor visit for the same illness as treatment.

The regulations do not identify a time period in which the two treatments must occur. In *Hobart v. Behavioral Connections of Wood County, Inc.*, No. 3:03CV7313, 2004 U.S. Dist. LEXIS 12051, at *19 (N.D. Ohio July 1, 2004), the court found that two doctor visits where the plaintiff received treatment during the month of April was found to satisfy the numerical treatment requirement).

Treatment does not include routine physical, eye, or dental examinations. 29 CFR 825.114(b), 825.800 (definition of "serious health condition," Subsection (2)); S. Res. 242, Cong. Rec. S3959, S3963, S3978 (April 23, 1996); 29 CFR 825.114(b), 825.800 (definition of "serious health condition," Subsection (2)); see *Marchisheck v. San Mateo County et al.*, 199 F.3d 1068, 1075 (9th Cir. 1999), *cert. denied*, 530 U.S. 1214 (2000) (routine physical examinations not included).

The regulations do not define what constitutes a physical, dental, or eye examination. Note the absence of psychiatric examinations from the definition of treatment. For that matter, unless they are subsumed within physical examinations, there are a number of different types of examinations that are not mentioned (e.g., allergies, cardiac, brain scans, etc). On the other hand, all non–psychiatric examinations are, in a certain sense, physical examinations.

Nor do the regulations clarify when such examinations are "routine." This is further confused by the reference that covered treatments include examinations to determine if a serious health condition exists. Arguably, the point of every "routine" physical, dental, or eye examination is to determine the health of the individual, which necessarily includes whether the individual has a serious health condition. Because the regulations use the defined term "serious health condition," it could be argued that the examination must be intended to discover whether such a condition exists. This is probably the better interpretation. On the other hand, it raises the question whether such examinations include every non–routine (e.g., the yearly physical) visit to a doctor when an employee or covered family member feels ill, or is it limited to situations where the intention of the examination is to confirm the existence of a serious health condition only.

The term "examination" is not defined. Nor does the regulation identify who can conduct such an examination. There is nothing in the regulation that would limit such examinations to health care providers, as the term is defined in the statutes and regulations. Who is an FMLA–covered "health care provider" is discussed later in this chapter.

In *Marchisheck v. San Mateo County et al.*, 199 F.3d 1068, 1075 (9th Cir. 1999), *cert. denied*, 530 U.S. 1214 (2000), the Ninth Circuit held that, while "treatment'" is loosely defined under the DOL regulations, a drug counselor's single question during a drug counseling session about the son's black eye did not amount to an "examination" or "evaluation" of the son's injuries but, rather, "was plainly a passing expression of curiosity and concern."

(f) Subsequent Treatment/Incapacity

In order to establish a serious health condition under this regulation, in addition to more than three consecutive days of incapacity (of the eligible employee or covered family member), the individual with the serious health condition must incur subsequent treatment or incapacity relating to the same serious health condition that originally incapacitated the individual. 29 CFR 825.114(a)(2)(I), 825.800 (definition of "serious health condition," Subsection (1)((ii)(A); S. Res. 242, Cong. Rec. S3959, S3962, S3978 (April 23, 1996); 29 CFR 825.114(a)(2)(I), 825.800 (definition of "serious health condition," Subsection (1)(ii)(A)).

The regulation fails to identify a temporal limitation during which this "subsequent treatment or incapacity" must occur. As such, presumably years could go by between the initial period of incapacity of more than three consecutive calendar days and the required health care provider treatments. In most cases, that will not be the case. Most cases that fall under this provision will involve relatively tight time frames where an employee or covered family member falls ill, goes and sees a doctor, is prescribed medication and subsequently gets better, all within a matter of days or weeks. With that said, agencies need to be aware that there is no limitation period that governs this area. The greater the time span between the initial "more than three day" incapacity and the subsequent health care provider visits, the more an agency will have to rely on a medical certification to establish the relationship between the subsequent health care provider visits and the previous incapacity.

The regulation does not explain what "relating to" means in this context. For example, whether "relating to" requires a direct or indirect relationship is not addressed. Presumably, it simply means that the subsequent treatment or incapacity must bear some link or association with the prior serious health condition.

In *Hurlbert v. St. Mary's Health Care System, Inc.*, 439 F.3d 1286, 1295 (11th Cir. 2006), the court found that an employee's extended absence three years earlier due to a heart attack was not sufficiently related to his subsequent treatment for anxiety to count for purposes of requiring leave for more than three consecutive calendar days plus health care provider treatments. The court found that the employee was not prescribed medication as a result of his heart attack, but rather for his separate diagnosis for anxiety. The employee claimed his anxiety was due to his heart attack.

In *Beal v. Rubbermaid Commercial Products, Inc.*, 972 F. Supp. 1216, 1223 (S.D. Iowa 1997), *aff'd*, 1998 U.S. App. LEXIS 9295 (8th Cir. 1998), the court refused to count two appointments that the employee had with the company physician after returning to work from an absence of more than three days due to an alleged back injury. The court indicted that such appointments were at the request of the employee's supervisor and not for the purpose of further treatment. According to the facts of the case, on both occasions, the employee was sent to the company doctor "when his back went out." *Id.* at 1220. On both occasions the employee was told he could return to work, on one occasion with some restrictions. The company doctor would appear to have conducted an examination or evaluation of the employee's back problem, which was the cause of his previous incapacity of more than three days. Presumably, the court's rationale for distinguishing and excluding these appointments with the company physician was because such appointments were intended to determine if the employee could continue to work. They were not intended to determine the status of the employee's back injury that caused the more than three days of absence.

(g) Health Care Provider Treatments

Whether subsequent treatment or incapacity relating to the same serious condition is involved, at a minimum, that treatment or incapacity must involve one or more treatments by or under the supervision of a health care provider. Specifically, the employee or covered family member has two alternatives. The first alternative (29 CFR 825.114(a)(2)(i)(A); S. Res. 242, Cong. Rec. S3959, S3962, S3978 (April 23, 1996); 29 CFR 825.114(a)(2)(i)(A)) provides that the employee or covered family member must receive:

1. Treatment two or more times

    - By a health care provider;

    - By a nurse of physician's assistant under the direct supervision of a health care provider; or

- By a provider of health care services (e.g. physical therapist) under orders of, or on referral by, a health care provider.

An employee's assertion that he or she suffered from a serious health condition must be supported by evidence from a health care provider that the claimed condition, in that provider's professional opinion, actually prevented the employee from working. *Yansick v. Temple University Health System*, No. 04-4228, 2006 U.S. Dist. LEXIS 53789, at *42 (E.D. Pa. Aug. 3, 2006). The court in *Yansick*, 2006 U.S. Dist. LEXIS 53789, at *43, continued:

> It is not enough that, "in the employee's own judgment, he or she should not work, or even that it was uncomfortable or inconvenient for the employee to have to work." Generally, "a health care provider must instruct, recommend, or at least authorize an employee not to work for at least four consecutive days for that employee to be considered incapacitated." (Citations omitted.)

The same health care provider need not provide the treatment on two or more occasions. *Sims v. Alameda-Contra Cost Transit District et al.*, 2 F. Supp. 2d 1253, 1264–65 (N.D. Cal. 1998). In that case, the employer alleged that the employee was not treated two or more times by a "health care provider" because the employee was never treated twice by the same person for his health condition. Rather, he was treated by two different doctors at the same hospital. Disagreeing, the court observed:

> Defendant misconstrues the requirement that the employee be treated two more times by a health care provider. Continuing treatment by a health care provider does not require that the employee consult the same individual on two or more occasions. Rather, it means that the same health condition required care from a health care provider on two or more occasions.... This Court doubts that Congress intended to exclude from coverage those who, like Sims, subscribe to Health Maintenance Organizations that often assign different doctors to treat the same patients' ongoing medical condition.

While the same health care provider need not provide treatment on two or more occasions, the health care provider must provide treatment. In *Beal v. Rubbermaid Commercial Products, Inc.*, 972 F. Supp. 1216, 1223 (S.D. Iowa 1997), the court did not count the employee's subsequent appointments with the company physician as they were at the request of the employee's supervisor, and were not for the purpose of further treatment.

The regulations do not require that the two health care provider treatments follow the period of incapacity, but merely require two or more treatments and more than three days of incapacity. *Jones v. Willow Gardens Care Center et al.*, No. C98-0007 MJM, 2000 U.S. Dist. LEXIS 3559, at *40 (N.D. Iowa Jan. 28, 2000); *Summerville v. ESCO CO. Ltd. Part.*, 52 F. Supp. 2d 804, 810 (W.D. Mich. 1999); *George v. Associated Stationers*, 932 F. Supp. 1012, 1015 (N.D. Ohio 1996).

Courts have held that phone calls to a health care provider do not constitute "treatment" for purposes of the FMLA. See *Dowell v. Indiana Heart Physicians, Inc.*, No. 1:03-cv-1410-DFH-TAB, 2004 U.S. Dist. LEXIS 26431, at *23 (S.D. Ind. Dec. 22, 2004) (phone call by employee to doctor claiming depression and seeking FMLA leave not "treatment" where doctor did not conduct an examination or give a diagnosis of the patient, and did not even recommend that the employee take the time off); *Darst v. Interstate Brands Corp.*, No. IP01-0788-C-T/K, 2003 U.S. Dist. LEXIS 22200, at *12-16 (S.D. Ind. Sept. 30, 2003) (phone calls to schedule initial visit with health care provider not "treatment" for FMLA purposes); *Schmittou v. Wal-Mart Stores, Inc.*, No. 01-1763 (JRT/RLE), 2003 U.S. Dist. LEXIS 15767, at *19 (D. Minn. Aug. 22, 2003) (phone call in which doctor merely advised employee to continue administering Tylenol and the BRAT diet to a child are activities that could have been initiated without a visit to a health care provider and, therefore, did not constitute "treatment"). An employer's direction that an employee see a health care provider may not count towards the FMLA requirement that an employee see a health care provider two or more times. In *Johnson v. USPS*, No. 1:97-CV-794, 1999 U.S. Dist. LEXIS 7981 (W.D. Mich. May 26, 1999), the court found that an employee failed to establish that she received treatment "two or more times" by a health care provider where the employee saw her physician once and was directed to see a contract physician a second time to determine whether the restrictions imposed could be lifted. The court noted that the appointment with the contract physician was at the request of the employee's supervisor and, therefore, did not count.

Finally, the regulations fail to describe what "under orders of" a health care provider means. "Under orders" appears to be a military or police term with little practical application to civilian employment outside of health care emergencies.

In *Stubl v. T.A. Systems, Inc.*, 984 F. Supp. 1075, 1089 (E.D. Mich. 1997), the court expressed its skepticism whether two doctor visits should be considered "continuing treatment" for purposes of determining that an employee had an FMLA-qualifying "serious health condition." According to the court: "The breadth of the regulations in permitting two visits to a physician for the purpose of diagnosis to constitute 'continuing treatment' raises a serious question as to whether the regulations accurately reflect Congressional intent on the issue of what should constitute a 'serious health condition.'"

The second alternative requirement in order for a serious health condition for continuing treatment following a period of incapacity of more than three consecutive calendar days (29 CFR 825.114(a)(2)(i)(B); S. Res. 242, Cong. Rec. S3959, S3962, S3978 (April 23, 1996); 29 CFR 825.114(a)(2)(i)(B)) provides that the employee or covered family member must receive:

1. Treatment by a health care provider;

2. On at least one occasion;

3. Which results in a regimen of continuing treatment;

4. Under the supervision of the health care provider.

In contrast to the first alternative, the subsequent treatment in this case must be by a health care provider. A nurse, physician's assistant, or provider of health care services cannot, in the first instance, provide the treatment.

The alternative requires a minimum of one treatment by a health care provider, although it may be more. As a result, when there is more than one health care provider treatment, both alternatives are potentially available to determine whether the employee or covered family member has a serious health condition.

The initial treatment must result in a "regimen of continuing treatment." A regimen of continuing treatment" is a defined term. It includes (29 CFR 825.114(b); S. Res. 242, Cong. Rec. S3959, S3962, S3978 (April 23, 1996); 29 CFR 825.114(b)):

> [F]or example, a course of prescription medication (e.g., an antibiotic) or therapy requiring special equipment to resolve or alleviate the health condition (e.g., oxygen).

See Meadows v. Texar Federal Credit Union, No. 5:05CV158, 2007 U.S. Dist. LEXIS 4456, at *57 (E.D. Tex. Jan. 22, 2007); *Stevens v. Advance Stores Co., Inc.,* No. 3-06-0537, 2007 U.S. Dist. LEXIS 28690, at *20 (M.D. Tenn. April 17, 2007); *Dowell v. Indiana Heart Physicians, Inc.,* No. 1:03–cv–1410–DFH–TAB, 2004 U.S. Dist. LEXIS 26431, at *20 (S.D. Ind. Dec. 22, 2004); *Wheeler v. Pioneer Dev. Services, Inc.,* 349 F. Supp 2d 158 (D. Mass. 2004) (prescription by doctor of antibiotics constituted "regimen of continuing treatment"); *Ruiz v. Ostbye & Anderson, Inc.,* No. 02–2954 (JNE/JGL), 2004 U.S. Dist. LEXIS 19890, at *11 (D. Minn. Sept. 28, 2004); *Swanson v. Senior Resource Connection,* 254 F. Supp. 2d 945, 951, n. 3 (S.D. Ohio 2003); *Johnson v. USPS,* No. 1:97–CV–794, 1999 U.S. Dist. LEXIS 7981 (W.D. Mich. May 26, 1999); *Jenifer v. USPS,* No. PH–0752–00–0344–I–2, 2001 MSPB LEXIS 1298 (March 14, 2001) (prescription medication); *Young v. USPS,* 79 MSPR 25 (1998); DOL WH FMLA Advisory Opinion No. 86 (Dec. 12, 1996).

A course of prescription medication includes the provision of "sample" pharmaceuticals by a health care provider. In *Swanson v. Senior Resource Connection*, 254 F. Supp. 2d 945, 951, n. 2 (S.D. Ohio 2003), the court addressed whether a physician providing a patient with "sample" pharmaceuticals constituted a "regimen of continuing treatment." Finding that it did, the court noted that "sample" pharmaceuticals are no different than those offered via prescription, and it is common practice for physicians to have their patients try such before writing out a complete prescription. This allows a physician and patient to work together to identify a suitable drug treatment while at the same time sparing both the patient and her insurer unnecessary costs. Pharmaceutical companies supply physicians with such "samples" for this very reason, and it is splitting hairs for Senior Resource Connection to argue that the lack of an actual prescription, if that is even the case, negates a plaintiff's ability to show she received a course of "prescription medication."

The regulations describe what is not considered to fall within a "regimen of continuing treatment." The regulations (29 CFR 825.114(b); S. Res. 242, Cong. Rec. S3959, S3962, S3978 (April 23, 1996); 29 CFR 825.114(b)): provide:

> A regimen of continuing treatment that includes the taking of over–the–counter medications such as aspirin, antihistamines, or salves; or bed–rest, drinking fluids, exercise, and other similar activities that can be initiated without a visit to a health care provider, is not, by itself, sufficient to constitute a regimen of continuing treatment for purposes of FMLA leave.

See DOL WH FMLA Advisory Opinion No. 86 (Dec. 12, 1996); *accord Brenneman v. MedCentral Health System*, 366 F.3d 412, 428 (6th Cir. 2004), *cert. denied*, 543 U.S. 1146 (U.S. 2005); *Dowell v. Indiana Heart Physicians, Inc.*, No. 1:03–cv–1410–DFH–

TAB, 2004 U.S. Dist. LEXIS 26431, at *20 (S.D. Ind. Dec. 22, 2004). A regularly scheduled check-up does not constitute "treatment" for FMLA purposes. 29 CFR 825.114(b); *Schmittou v. Wal-Mart Stores, Inc.*, No. 01-1763 (JRT/RLE), 2003 U.S. Dist. LEXIS 15767, at *21 (D. Minn. Aug. 22, 2003).

The regulation does not indicate what else would be necessary to convert the items that are not ordinarily considered to constitute a regimen of continuing treatment into such a regimen. This prospect is suggested by the phrase "is not, by itself" sufficient to constitute a regimen of continuing treatment. It is unclear whether the fact that an FMLA-covered health care provider recommended such activities would convert those activities into a regimen of continuing treatment.

Finally, the regulations do not explain what "continuing supervision" means for purposes of the second alternative. In the comments to the final regulations (Preamble, 29 CFR 825.114), the DOL stated: "[I]t is envisioned that a patient would be under continuing supervision in this context, for example, where the patient is advised to call if the condition is not improved." Clearly, "continuing supervision" does not require active supervision. Note that the "continuing supervision" must be under "the health care provider." This suggests that the same health care provider that provided the initial treatment must also be the one who provides the "continuing supervision." The employee could not receive treatment by one health care provider and "continuing supervision" from another.

Absences attributable to incapacity under § 825.114(a)(2)(ii) qualify for FMLA leave even though the employee does not receive treatment from a health care provider during the absence, and even if the absence does not last more than three days. 29 CFR 825.114(c); *Lackey v. Jackson County, Tennessee*, 104 Fed. Appx. 483 (6th Cir. 2004).

In *Ruiz v. Ostbye & Anderson, Inc.*, No. 02-2954 (JNE/JGL), 2004 U.S. Dist. LEXIS 19890, at *14 (D. Minn. Sept. 28, 2004), the court rejected the argument that only "formal exams" counted as treatment by a health care provider. The court noted that Ostbye offered no authority holding that a doctor's visit does not qualify as treatment unless there is a formal exam. In support of the employee's claim that she was "treated," the court noted that plaintiff's doctor wrote Ruiz a prescription, offered his support, and referred Ruiz to the crisis counseling support line. Even if the initial visit did not qualify as "treatment," the court credited Ruiz's two subsequent visits to her therapist for her condition as "treatment" for purposes of the FMLA. The court found that it should consider both therapist visits, even though the second visit occurred after Ruiz's termination, for purposes of making the determination whether she suffered from a serious health condition.

Significantly, the court in *Bradley v. Mary Rutan Hospital Assoc.*, 322 F. Supp. 2d 926, 942-943 (S.D. Ohio 2004), found that a doctor visit does not necessarily constitute treatment by a health care provider. Bradley claimed injury as a result of knocking her hand against a salad bar while walking past it. In questioning whether this was the type of injury that Congress meant to cover when it enacted the FMLA, the court dismissed the diagnosis by her doctor that she could return to work that day, albeit with restrictions not to use her right hand. "Such 'diagnosis' or recommendation was not one that plaintiff could get only from a medical professional. *See, e.g.*, 29 CFR 825.114(b)." The court analogized the situation to bed rest, drinking fluids, exercise, and other similar activities that can be initiated without a visit to a health care provider.

Absent a regimen of continuing treatment, an employee who was incapacitated for more than three days and received treatment by a health care provider on one occasion does not meet the requirements for a serious health condition under this regulation. *Beal v. Rubbermaid Commercial Products, Inc.*, 972 F. Supp. 1216, 1223 (S.D. Iowa 1997), *aff'd*, 1998 U.S. App. LEXIS 9295 (8th Cir. 1998) (no regimen of continuing treatment where the employee could not recall if he was prescribed prescription medication and he was not following any treatment regimen such as physical therapy).

Similarly, the failure of an employee to follow a regimen of treatment resulted in the loss of FMLA coverage. *See Frazier v. Iowa Beef Processors, Inc.*, 200 F.3d 1190, 1195 (8th Cir. 2000) (no "continuing treatment" where an employee failed to return for scheduled follow-up visits with a health care provider, even where employee met with health care providers on two occasions); *Johnson v. USPS*, No. 1:97-CV-794, 1999 U.S. Dist. LEXIS 7981 (W.D. Mich. May 26, 1999) (an employee did not receive a prescription and did not follow treatment regimen to return to the health care provider for follow up); *Goodwin v. Rheem Manufacturing Co.*, 15 F. Supp. 2d 1197, 1204, n. 6 (M.D. Ala. 1998) (treatment for poison ivy on one occasion without medication prescribed for his condition not an FMLA-covered serious health condition); *Seidle v. Provident Mutual Life Ins. Co.*, 871 F. Supp. 238, 244 (E.D. Pa. 1994) (a plaintiff's son's otis media was not a serious health condition where the plaintiff did not schedule follow-up examination).

One court held that an employee need not produce evidence of compliance with a regimen of continuing treatment as directed by his health care provider in order to establish that the employee had a "serious health condition" within the meaning of the law. In *D'Amico v. Compass Group USA, Inc. et al.*, 198 F. Supp. 2d 18 (D. Mass. 2002), *aff'd*, 52 Fed. Appx.

524 (1st Cir. 2002), the employer argued that there was no evidence that D'Amico took the prescription medication and hence failed to follow a course of treatment. The district court held that "a patient's failure to cooperate with a prescribed regimen of care cannot reasonably be perceived to invalidate the doctor's diagnosis that the patient's medical condition is worthy of treatment." *D'Amico,* 198 F. Supp. at 23. Although affirming the district court's decision on the FMLA claim, it does not appear that the First Circuit agreed with the determination of the district court on this issue. Specifically, the court concluded, "the District Court did not err in granting summary judgment on the FMLA claim and we affirm the ruling essentially for the reasons expressed by the District Court in its opinion. We do not necessarily accept its conclusion that appellant met the FMLA threshold requirements of suffering from a 'serious health condition,' 29 USC 2612(a)(1)(D), or of being 'unable to perform the functions of [his] position.'"

The decision of the district court in *D'Amico* would appear to permit an employee the protections of the FMLA even though he or she has not satisfied all of the conditions of the Act. Under the interpretation advanced by the district court, an employee would satisfy the requirement that he or she is receiving "continuing treatment" whenever a health care provider prescribes such treatment, regardless of whether the employee actually engages in the continuing treatment. Arguably, this is not what is required by the FMLA. Employers covered by the Act are required to grant FMLA leave to an eligible employee where the employee or covered family member has a "serious health condition." The Act and the regulations define a "serious health condition" as one involving continuing treatment" by a health care provider. Continuing treatment, in turn, is defined to include a period of incapacity of more than three consecutive calendar days that also involves at least one health care provider treatment followed by a regimen of continuing treatment, such as a course of prescription medication. That a "course of prescription" requires the actual "taking of" medication is demonstrated in the DOL regulations defining what does not constitute a "regimen of continuing treatment." The "taking of" over-the-counter medications is not, by itself, sufficient to constitute a regimen of continuing treatment. The decision of the district court in *D'Amico* appears to have resulted from a combination of the presumptions afforded to the non-moving party in summary judgment and the fact that the court dismissed the FMLA claims on other grounds.

(2) Title II

(a) General Rule

The general rule under Title II is substantially the same as the requirements under Title I, the CAA, and the PEOAA. There are, however, a number of differences.

A serious health condition within the meaning of the FMLA means an illness, injury, impairment, or physical or mental condition that involves continuing treatment by a health care provider, that includes (5 CFR 630.1202 (definition of "serious health condition") one or more of the following:

(A) A period of incapacity of more than three consecutive calendar days, in including any subsequent treatment or period of incapacity relating to the same condition, that also involves–

(1) Treatment two or more times by a health care provider, by a health care provider under the direct supervision of the affected individual's health care provider, or by a provider of health care services under order of, or on referral by, a health care provider; or

(2) Treatment by a health care provider on at least one occasion which results in a regimen of continuing treatment under the supervision of the health care provider (e.g., a course of prescription medication or therapy requiring special equipment to resolve or alleviate the health condition).

A review of the key terms contained in the general rule follows.

(b) Regulatory Development

On July 23, 1993, the OPM published interim regulations (58 Fed. Reg. 39596) to implement the requirements of §§ 6381 through 6387 of Title 5, United States Code, as added by Title II of the FMLA. The interim OPM FMLA regulations remained in effect until January 6, 1997, when the final OPM regulations took effect. The final OPM FMLA regulations were issued on December 5, 1996 (61 Fed. Reg. 6441).

As reported, the comments received by OPM prior to the issuance of the final regulations regarding the definition of a "serious health condition" appear to be in line with the comments received by the DOL previously discussed in this chapter. In pertinent part, the commentators argued that the "more than 3 days" test was both too high and too low a standard for the determination of a "serious health condition." It was too high a standard as it would exclude many serious conditions of shorter duration. It was too low a standard because it would tend to include relatively minor illnesses, not the very serious health conditions outlined in the legislative history.

The OPM, like the DOL, responded to these comments by noting its belief that the minimum "more than three days" test "clarifies congressional intent" and, therefore, continues to be appropriate. Preamble, 5 CFR 630.1202 (comments regarding "serious health condition" definition). The OPM also noted that its position was consistent with DOL's final regulations. *Id.* Consistent with the DOL's final regulations, OPM significantly revised the definition of "serious health condition." *Id.*

(c) Incapacity

"Incapacity" means the inability to work, attend school, or perform other regular daily activities because of a serious health condition or treatment for or recovery from a serious health condition. 5 CFR 630.1202 (definition of "incapacity"). As this definition of "incapacity" is nearly identical with the definition of that term under Title I, the CAA, and the PEOAA, the reader is referred to the previous discussion interpreting "incapacity" under those statutes.

(d) More Than Three Consecutive Calendar Days

Title II, like the other federal sector variants of the FMLA, requires that the period of "incapacity" suffered by the employee or covered family member must be for more than three consecutive calendar days. 5 CFR 630.1202 (definition of "serious health condition," Subsection (1)(ii)(A)). Like its counterparts, the OPM regulations fail to define what constitutes a "day." Presumably, the regulation requires that the incapacity must last for more than three consecutive 24–hour periods. Nor does the regulation indicate the point that the "greater than three consecutive calendar day period" is measured. Presumably, it is measured from the onset of the incapacity. Finally, the term "more" is not quantified. Any period of time over the minimum three consecutive calendar days should satisfy the criteria.

(e) Treatment

Unlike Title I, the CAA, and the PEOAA, Title II does not define the term "treatment." Rather, it defines the term "continuing treatment" to include (but is not limited to) examinations to determine if there is a serious health condition and evaluations of such conditions if the examinations and evaluations determine that a serious health condition exists. 5 CFR 630.1202 (definition of "serious health condition," Subsection (1)(ii)).

The regulation is similar, although by no means identical, to the definition of treatment pursuant to Title I, the CAA, and the PEOAA. *See* 29 CFR 825.114(b); S. Res. 242, Cong. Rec. S3959, S3962, S3978 (April 23, 1996); 29 CFR 825.114(b). The primary difference between these definitions is that Title II appears to condition evaluations on the results of the initial examination to determine whether a serious health condition exits. "Treatment" for purposes of Title I, the CAA, and the PEOAA, on the other hand, does not condition evaluations on the results of the initial examination. Evaluations of the serious health condition are treated equally with examinations. *See* 29 CFR 825.114(b); S. Res. 242, Cong. Rec. S3959, S3962, S3978 (April 23, 1996); 29 CFR 825.114(b).

As with its counterparts in Title I, the CAA, and the PEOAA, "examination" is not defined. Nor does the regulation identify who can conduct such an examination. Unlike "treatment," however, "continuing treatment" requires the examination be conducted by a health care provider. Again, who is an FMLA–covered "health care provider" is discussed later in this chapter.

Another difference between "continuing treatment" under Title II and "treatment" for purposes of Title I, the CAA, and the PEOAA, is that the former does not exclude routine physical, dental, or eye examination from the definition the definition of "continuing treatment." However, routine physical, dental, and eye examinations are excluded from the definition of a "serious health condition." 5 CFR 630.1202 (definition of "serious health condition," Subsection (2)) ("[s]erious health condition does not include routine physical, eye, or dental examinations); *accord Marshall v. Dept. of Army*, No. DC-0752-05-0221-I-1, 2005 MSPB LEXIS 2901, at *11 (May 9, 2005). Presumably, since these terms are affirmatively excluded from the definition of a serious health condition, they are also excluded from inclusion as "continuing treatment." Remember, the Title II definition of "continuing treatment" was not exclusive ("includes, but is not limited to").

Finally, the terms "routine," "physical," "dental," and "eye" examinations are also undefined.

(f) Subsequent Treatment/Incapacity

In addition to more than three consecutive calendar days of incapacity, the employee or covered family member must also incur subsequent treatment or incapacity relating to the same serious health condition. 5 CFR 630.1202 (definition of "serious health condition," Subsection (1)(ii)(A)). As with the similar definition under Title I, the CAA, and the PEOAA discussed previously, the term "subsequent" does not include a temporal limitation. That means that days, weeks, months, or years could pass between the initial "more than three days" incapacity and the subsequent health care provider treatments and this definition of a serious health condition could be met.

The relationship between the subsequent health care provider treatments and the original incapacitating serious health condition is also undefined. It would appear that any relationship, however slight, between the subsequent health care provider treatments and the original "more than three days" incapacity would suffice.

(g) Health Care Provider Treatments

Employees covered by Title II, like employees covered by Title I, the CAA, and the PEOAA, may meet the subsequent treatment or incapacity requirement of this serious health condition in one of two ways. These two alternatives are similar, but by no means identical, to the two alternatives discussed previously in this chapter regarding the other federal sector variants of the FMLA.

First, the employee or covered family member, who is incapacitated for more than three consecutive calendar days, must (5 CFR 630.1202 (definition of "serious health condition," Subsection (1)(ii)(A)(1)) incur:

1. Treatment two or more times
2. By a health care provider
3. By a health care provider under the direct supervision of the affected individual's health care provider, or
4. By a provider of health care services under orders of, or on referral by, a health care provider.

Like the similar requirement for Title I, the CAA, and the PEOAA discussed previously in this chapter, the above alternative requires at least two treatments. Unlike the comparable regulation for the other federal sector variants of the FMLA, however, the term "treatment" is not defined for purposes of Title II. The OPM chose, instead, to define "continuing treatment." 5 CFR 630.1202 (definition of "serious health condition," Subsection (1)(ii)). "Continuing treatment by a health care provider" includes (but is not limited to) examinations to determine if there is a serious health condition and evaluations of such condition if the examinations or evaluations determine that a serious health condition exits." 5 CFR 630.1202 (definition of "serious health condition," Subsection (1)(ii)). The Title II definition of "continuing treatment" is the mirror image of the definition of "treatment" under Title I, the CAA, and the PEOAA. *Compare* 5 CFR 630.1202 (definition of "serious health condition," Subsection (1)(ii)), *with* 29 CFR 825.114(b); S. Res. 242, Cong. Rec. S3959, S3962, S3978 (April 23, 1996); 29 CFR 825.114(b). Presumably, removal of the requirement that the treatment be "continuing" will meet the definition of treatment.

As under Title I, the CAA, and the PEOAA, treatment may be provided by a health care provider. Note that subsequent treatment may be by "a" health care provider, which may not be the same provider that originally treated the employee or covered family member at the time of the "more than three days" period of incapacity.

Unlike the comparable regulation interpreting the other federal sector variants of the FMLA, Title II does not specifically provide that the employee may receive treatment from a nurse or physician's assistant. Rather, treatment can be obtained from a health care provider under the direct supervision of the affected individual's health care provider. Since the previous iteration did not require "the" health care provider to render subsequent treatment, but allowed "a" health care provider (i.e., any health care provider), the second iteration appears, at minimum, redundant. Given the use of a comma between the first iteration and second, it is doubtful that the second would be interpreted to modify the first iteration to read, as a practical matter "the" health care provider.

Addressing the second iteration, no indication is given as to how it is to be determined who is "the" affected individual's health provider. It is unclear whether this means any health care provider of the employee or covered family member with the serious health condition, or the original health care provider. It is not uncommon, after all, for people to have more than one health care provider. Presumably, it means any health care provider of the individual with the serious health condition can directly supervise another health care provider, who actually provides the treatment. "Direct supervision" is unexplained.

As with the comparable regulation interpreting Title I, the CAA, and the PEOAA (discussed previously in this chapter), the term "provider of health care services" is undefined. Given the proximity to the defined term "health care provider," it would appear that a "provider of health care services" is different than a "health care provider." Again, that difference is not explained.

The second alternative requirement to meet this definition of a serious health condition for continuing treatment following a period of incapacity of more than three consecutive calendar days (5 CFR 630.1202 (definition of "serious health condition," Subsection (1)(ii)(A)(2)) provides that the employee or covered family member must receive:

1. Treatment by a health care provider

2. On at least one occasion

3. Which results in a regimen of continuing treatment

4. Under the supervision of the health care provider (e.g., a course of prescription medication or therapy requiring special equipment to resolve or alleviate the health condition).

Examples of what constitutes a "regimen of continuing treatment" include a course of prescription medication or therapy requiring special equipment to resolve or alleviate the health condition. There is no indication that these are the exclusive means of meeting a "regimen of continuing treatment." The examples provided are substantially similar to the comparable examples given for purposes of Title I, the CAA, and the PEOAA. *See* 29 CFR 825.114(b); S. Res. 242, Cong. Rec. S3959, S3962 (April 23, 1996); 29 CFR 825.114(b).

Title II does not identify actions that fall outside of the scope of a "regimen of continuing treatment." In contrast, Title I, the CAA, and the PEOAA, do exclude certain activities as outside the definition of a "regimen of continuing treatment." *See* 29 CFR 825.114(b); S. Res. 242, Cong. Rec. S3959, S3962 (April 23, 1996); 29 CFR 825.114(b). However, Title II accomplishes virtually the same result by excluding certain activities from the definition of a "serious health condition." According to the regulation, "[s]erious health condition does not include a regimen of continuing treatment that includes the taking of over-the-counter medications, bed rest, exercise, and other similar activities that can be initiated without a visit to the health care provider." 5 CFR 630.1202 (definition of "serious health condition," Subsection (2)). The identified activities are identical to those excluded from the definition of a "regimen of continuing treatment" under Title I, the CAA, and the PEOAA. *See* 29 CFR 825.114(b); S. Res. 242, Cong. Rec. S3959, S3962 (April 23, 1996); 29 CFR 825.114(b).

Note, however, that the exclusion of these activities from the Title II definition of "serious health condition" is absolute. The same activities are not absolutely excluded from the definition of a "regimen of continuing treatment" for purposes of Title I, the CAA and the PEOAA. That regulation provides that such activities are not, by themselves, sufficient to constitute a "regimen of continuing treatment." 29 CFR 825.114(b); S. Res. 242, Cong. Rec. S3959, S3962, (April 23, 1996); 29 CFR 825.114(b). Such language suggests that these activities, in conjunction with some other unidentified activity, could constitute a "regimen of continuing treatment" within the definition of Title I, the CAA, and the PEOAA. Again, that would never be the case under Title II.

Finally, the second alternative does not define or otherwise describe the meaning of "under the supervision" or "under orders of." The former is slightly different than the comparable requirement under Title I, the CAA, and the PEOAA, which requires "continuing supervision." *See* 29 CFR 825.114(a)(2)(i)(B); S. Res. 242, Cong. Rec. S3959, S3962 (April 23, 1996); 29 CFR 825.114(a)(2)(i)(B). The DOL suggested in the preamble accompanying the publication of the final regulations that "continuing supervision" would be satisfied if the afflicted individual were advised to call the health care provider if the condition did not improve. Preamble, 29 CFR 825.114. It is unclear whether "under the supervision" for purposes of Title II has the same meaning as "continuing supervision" for purposes of Title I, the CAA, and the PEOAA. "Under the supervision" is also different than "direct supervision" in the first alternative form of this serious health condition. Again, the differences are unexplained.

(h) Amount of FMLA Leave Available

An employee who meets the minimum requirements for this serious health condition is entitled to use up to the full 12 workweeks of FMLA leave during the 12-month leave year. That is, once the minimum requirements of "more than three days" of incapacity and subsequent health care provider treatments are met, an employee may use as much FMLA leave as needed for subsequent treatments and incapacity related to the same serious health condition. Each incident of subsequent leave does not need to meet the "more than three days" requirement. Leave for subsequent treatments or incapacity may be in increments of hours, days, or weeks, up to a total of 12 workweeks of leave each leave year.

d. Pregnancy, or Prenatal Care

The second form of continuing treatment serious health condition involves pregnancy and prenatal care.

(1) Title I, the CAA, and the PEOAA

(a) General Rule

For purposes of the FMLA, a "serious health condition" entitling an employee to FMLA leave means an illness, injury, impairment, or physical or mental condition that involves continuing treatment by a health care provider. 29 USC 2611(11); 29 CFR 825.114(a)(2); S. Res. 242, Cong. Rec. S3959, S3962, S3978 (April 23, 1996); 29 CFR 825.114(a)(2). Continuing treatment by a health care provider includes one or more of the following:

(ii) Any period of incapacity due to pregnancy, or for prenatal care.

29 CFR 825.114(a)(2)(ii), 825.800 (definition of "serious health condition," Subsection (1)(ii)(B)); S. Res. 242, Cong. Rec. S3959, S3962, S3978 (April 23, 1996); 29 CFR 825.114(a)(2)(ii), 825.800 (definition of "serious health condition," Subsection (1)(ii)(B)); see *Navarro v. Gladys Navarro Pomares et al.*, 261 F.3d 90, 95 (1st Cir. 2001); *Hangar v. Lake County*, 390 F.3d 579 (8th Cir. 2004) (FMLA provides eligible employees the right to 12 weeks of maternity leave); *George v. Russell Stover Candies, Inc.*, 106 Fed. Appx. 946 (6th Cir. 2004); *Shepard v. Tyson Foods, Inc.*, No. 9:06cv84, 2007 U.S. Dist. LEXIS 27951, at *3 (E.D. Tex. April 16, 2007); *Hiemer v. Anthem Insurance Cos., Inc.*, No. C-1-05-124, 2007 U.S. Dist. LEXIS 21174, at *20 (S.D. Ohio March 26, 2007); *Snyder v. Yellow Transportation, Inc.*, 321 F. Supp. 2d 1127, 1132 (E.D. Mo. 2004); *Green v. New Balance Athletic Shoe, Inc.*, 182 F. Supp. 2d 128, 135 (D. Me. 2002); *Whitaker v. Bosch Braking Systems Div. of Robert Bosch Corp.*, 180 F. Supp. 2d 922, 926 (W.D. Mich. 2001); *Pendarvis v. Xerox Corp.*, 3 F. Supp. 2d 53, 55–56 (D.D.C. 1998); *Harvender v. Norton Co.*, No. 96–CV–653 (LEK/RWS), 1997 U.S. Dist. LEXIS 21467 (N.D.N.Y. Dec. 15, 1997); DOL WH FMLA Advisory Opinion No. 85 (Nov. 18, 1996) (childbirth and recovery from childbirth a "serious health condition" within the meaning of the FMLA).

The DOL noted in the preamble accompanying the publication of the final Title I regulations (Preamble, 29 CFR 825.114) that:

> It is clear from FMLA's legislative history that pregnancy was intended to be treated as a serious health condition entitling an individual to leave under the Act, and the definition therefore includes any period of incapacity due to pregnancy, or for prenatal care.

The legislative history provided examples of what Congress considered to be a serious health condition. Those examples included "ongoing pregnancy, miscarriages, complications or illnesses related to pregnancy, such as severe morning sickness, the need for prenatal care, childbirth and recovery from childbirth." S. Rep. 103-3 p. 29; see *Shepard v. Tyson Foods, Inc.*, No. 9:06cv84, 2007 U.S. Dist. LEXIS 27951, at *3 (E.D. Tex. April 16, 2007) (sickness due to pregnancy qualifies as a serious health condition under the FMLA); *Hiemer v. Anthem Insurance Cos., Inc.*, No. C-1-05-124, 2007 U.S. Dist. LEXIS 21174, at *20 (S.D. Ohio March 26, 2007) (absences due to nausea and light-headedness due to pregnancy covered by the FMLA); *Dowell v. Indiana Heart Physicians, Inc.*, No. 1:03–cv–1410–DFH–TAB, 2004 U.S. Dist. LEXIS 26431, at *18 (S.D. Ind. Dec. 22, 2004).

In *Dowell*, 2004 U.S. Dist. LEXIS 26431, at *18, the court declined to recognize depression as a pregnancy-related ailment that could qualify as a serious health condition without treatment from a health care provider. "While the language of the statute is expansive, it is still subject to the principle of *ejusdem generic*." As such, the specific terms used in the statute guided the court in its application. The court referred to the DOL regulations and legislative history to identify the types of pregnancy-related illnesses that Congress intended to cover and depression was not one of the listed illnesses.

A brief review of the key terms follows.

(b) Any Period

There is no minimum period of time that an employee or covered family member must be incapacitated due to pregnancy in order to meet this definition of a serious health condition. An employee or covered family member does not have to be incapacitated due to pregnancy or for prenatal care for "more than three" days, as was the case in the preceding covered condition. *See* 29 CFR 825.114(e) (absences attributable to incapacity under this section qualify for FMLA leave even though absence does not last more than three days); S. Res. 242, Cong. Rec. S3959, S3963 (April 23, 1996); 29 CFR 825.114(e) (same). The DOL addressed this distinction (Preamble, 29 CFR 825.114) as follows:

> Pregnancy is similar to a chronic condition in that the patient is periodically visiting a health care provider for prenatal care, but may be subject to episodes of severe morning sickness, for example, which may not require an absence from work of more than three days.

For example, an absence of four hours for an eligible employee to care for his wife who was suffering from severe morning sickness would fall within the definition of a qualifying serious health condition. *See, e.g.*, 29 CFR 825.114(e) (an employee who is pregnant may be unable to report to work because of severe morning sickness); S. Res. 242, Cong. Rec. S3959, S3963 (April 23, 1996); 29 CFR 825.114(e) (same; *see Pendavaris v. Xerox Corp.*, 3 F. Supp. 2d 53, 55–56 (D.D.C. 1998).

Moreover, any period of absence due to pregnancy would include subsequent periods of incapacity after the pregnancy is terminated, as long as the current incapacity is related to the pregnancy. *See Stiefel v. Allied Domecq Spirits & Wine U.S.A., Inc.* 184 F. Supp. 2d 886, 891 (W.D. Ark. 2002) (although it was ultimately determined that there was insufficient evidence to connect the absences, absences after miscarriage were considered as falling within this definition of FMLA leave if a health care provider could make the connection).

(c) Incapacity

"Incapacity" is not defined for purposes of this definition (birth and prenatal care) of a continuing treatment serious health condition. It is unclear whether previous descriptions of the term "incapacity" elsewhere in the regulations defining a serious health condition apply to birth and prenatal care. "Incapacity" is described by example in the definition of serious health condition of "inpatient care" and "continuing treatment" involving a minimum period of incapacity of at least three consecutive calendar days. Regarding the former, it is unclear whether the examples given for the meaning of incapacity for purposes of inpatient care apply to all serious health conditions, or only to inpatient care. The confusion stems from the prefatory language "for purposes of this section" before the examples are given. It is unclear whether "for purposes of this section" refers only to "inpatient care," or whether it generally applies to § 825.114, addressing all serious health conditions.

Absent further guidance on this issue, and given the consistency of the examples given of "incapacity" contained in § 825.114(a)(1) (inpatient care) and § 825.114(a)(2)(I) (continuing treatment), it would appear that the examples provided should apply to incapacity due to pregnancy or for prenatal care. Accordingly, "incapacity" means the inability work, attend school or perform other regular daily activities due to the serious health condition, treatment therefore, or recovery therefrom. *See* 29 CFR 825.114(a)(1), 825.114(a)(2)(I); S. Res. 242, Cong. Rec. S3959, S3962 (April 23, 1996); 29 CFR 825.114(a)(1), 825.114(a)(2)(I); *see Whitaker v. Bosch Braking Systems Div. of Robert Bosch Corp.*, 180 F. Supp. 2d 922, 926 (W.D. Mich. 2001) (applying definition of "incapacity" in § 825.114(a)(2)(I)).

Absent incapacity, pregnancy *per se* is not a serious health condition within the meaning of the FMLA. *Aubuchon v. Knauf Fiberglass, GMBH*, 240 F. Supp. 2d 859, 865 (S.D. Ind. Jan. 10, 2003), *aff'd*, 359 F.3d 950 952 (7th Cir. 2004) ; *Dowell v. Indiana Heart Physicians, Inc.*, No. 1:03–cv–1410–DFH–TAB, 2004 U.S. Dist. LEXIS 26431, at *17 (S.D. Ind. Dec. 22, 2004); *Whitaker v. Bosch Braking Systems Div. of Robert Bosch Corp.*, 180 F. Supp. 2d 922, 926 (W.D. Mich. 2001); *Dormeyer v. Comerica Bank-III.*, No. 96–C–4805, 1997 U.S. Dist. LEXIS 10260 (N.D. Ill. July 15, 1997). On the other hand, "incapacity" may result from work restrictions imposed by a health care provider on an employee even though the pregnancy is otherwise normal and the employee was physically able to perform the job. *Whitaker v. Bosch Braking Systems Div. of Robert Bosch Corp.*, 180 F. Supp. 2d 922, 926 (W.D. Mich. 2001). The delivery of a child constitutes a period of incapacity. *Aubuchon*, 240 F. Supp. 2d at 865 ("We have difficulty imagining delivery of a child that does not constitute a 'period of incapacity'"), *aff'd*, 359 F.3d 950 (7th Cir. 2004).

In *Aubuchon v. Knauf Fiberglass, GMBH*, 359 F.3d 950, 952 (7th Cir. 2004), the employee wanted to take FMLA leave to stay home with his wife until she gave birth. The employee did not give complications, false labor, or a serious health condition as the reason. The court observed, "[w]anting to stay home with one's wife until she has a baby, while understandable, is not the same thing as wanting to stay home to care for a spouse with a serious health condition," within the meaning of the FMLA.

(d) Treatment

The term treatment is not a term used in § 825.114(a)(2)(ii) regarding birth and prenatal care as a serious health condition. "Treatment" would apply by application of the definition of "incapacity" to birth and prenatal care. *See* 29 CFR 825.114(a)(1), 825.114(a)(2)(I); S. Res. 242, Cong. Rec. S3959, S3962 (April 23, 1996); 29 CFR 825.114(a)(1), 825.114(a)(2)(I).

While "treatment" is included in the definition of "incapacity" and could be the basis for FMLA leave due to pregnancy or prenatal care, it is not a requirement. An employee or covered family member is entitled to FMLA leave for incapacity due to pregnancy or for prenatal care even though the employee or covered family member does not receive treatment from a health care provider during the absence. 29 CFR 825.114(e); S. Res. 242, Cong. Rec. S3959, S3963 (April 23, 1996); 29 CFR 825.114(e); *see George v. Russell Stover Candies, Inc.*, 106 Fed. Appx. 946 (6th Cir. 2004); *Rhoads v. FDIC*, 257 F.3d 373, 382 (4th Cir. 2001), *cert. denied*, 535 U.S. 933 (2002). For example, an employee who is pregnant may be unable to report to work because the pregnant employee's health care provider advised the employee to stay home when her blood pressure reaches a certain level. The employee does not have to be treated by the health care provider during that absence, but may remain home and rest.

The absence of a "treatment" requirement for any particular absence due to incapacity caused by pregnancy or for prenatal care does not, however, mean that the employee or covered family member need not have any interaction with a health care provider. Remember, incapacity due to pregnancy or for prenatal care is a form of serious health condition that requires "continuing treatment" by a health care provider." 29 CFR 825.114(a)(2); S. Res. 242, Cong. Rec. S3959, S3962 (April 23, 1996); 29 CFR 825.114(a)(2). Unfortunately, the term "continuing treatment" is not defined for purposes of Title I, the CAA and the PEOAA. An explanation of what "continuing treatment" means in this context is, however, contained in the comments accompanying publication of the final Title I regulations. There, (Preamble, 29 CFR 825.114), the DOL observed that:

> The Department concurs with the comments that suggested that special recognition should be given to chronic conditions. The Department recognizes that certain conditions, such as asthma and diabetes, continue over an extended period of time (i.e., from several months to several years), often without affecting day-to-day ability to work or perform other activities of less than three days. *Although persons with such underlying conditions generally visit a health care provider periodically*, when subject to flare-up or other incapacitating episode, staying home and self-treatment are often more effective than visiting the health care provider (e.g., the asthma-sufferer who is advised to stay home and inside due to the pollen count being too high).

> ****

> Pregnancy is similar to a chronic condition in *that the patient is periodically visiting a health care provider* for prenatal care, but my be subject to episodes of severe morning sickness, for example, which may not require an absence from work of more than three days. (Emphasis supplied).

To be FMLA-qualifying, an employee or covered family member must "periodically visit" a health care provider for pregnancy or prenatal care. The employee or covered family member does not, however, have to visit the health care provider for any given incapacitating absence caused by the pregnancy or prenatal care.

No further explanation is provided in the comments to the final Title I regulations defining or otherwise describing the meaning of "visit" and "periodic." For example, it is unclear if a "visit" with a health care provider requires the actual meeting of the patient and health care provider, or whether a telephone or Internet consultation would suffice. Similarly left open is how many and how often such visits must be in order to be considered "periodic." At a minimum, the term "periodic" and the plural "visits" suggests that more than one visit with the health care provider is required to constitute "continuing treatment." Presumably, the period of pregnancy is the time frame used to determine when multiple "visits" become "periodic."

(e) Prenatal Care

"Prenatal care" is not defined in the statute or regulations. Comments accompanying the publication of the final Title I regulations suggest that "prenatal care" involves visits with a health care provider. For example, remarking about the similarity of pregnancy to chronic conditions, the DOL noted, "pregnancy is similar to visiting a health care provider for prenatal care, but may be subject to episodes of severe morning sickness, for example, which may not require an absence from work of more than three days." Preamble, 29 CFR 825.114. In another comment, the DOL addressed the "scheduling [of] prenatal care doctor's visits...." Preamble, 29 CFR 825.112.

There has been some debate over whether prenatal care requires the incapacitation of the employee or covered family member. *See Dormeyer v. Comerica Bank-Ill.*, No. 96-C-4805, 1997 U.S. Dist. LEXIS 10260, at *10, n. 2 (although § 825.114 is unclear as to whether prenatal care received by the employee needs to result in incapacitation in order to be considered a serious health condition, the court held that the statute itself is clear in requiring that any serious health condition that an employee suffers must result in an inability to perform the functions of an employee's position). The debate is raised as a result of the grammatical structure of the regulation. Specifically, the placement of a comma in between "incapacity due to pregnancy" and "or for prenatal care" could be read as limiting incapacity to pregnancy only. Prenatal care, on the other hand, would not require the employee or covered family member to be incapacitated in order for the leave to be covered by the FMLA. A similar distinction, without the use of a comma, exists in 29 CFR 825.112(c) (an expectant mother may take FMLA leave pursuant to paragraph (a)(4) [serious health condition of the employee] before the birth of the child for prenatal care or if her condition makes her unable to work). *See* S. Res. 242, Cong. Rec. S3959, S3962 (April 23, 1996); 29 CFR 825.114(c) (same).

As a practical matter, the debate is largely theoretical as, in either case, the employee or covered family member would be entitled to FMLA leave for prenatal care visits with a health care provider even if incapacitation was a prerequisite. *See Divizio v. Elmwood Care, Inc. et al.*, No. 97-C-8365, 1998 U.S. Dist. LEXIS 8398 (N.D. Ill. May 28, 1998) (the court found that the employee's early labor pains made her eligible for FMLA leave under §§ 825.112(c) and 825.114(a)(2)(ii) for prenatal care). As defined elsewhere for serious health conditions due to continuing treatment, "incapacity" includes treatment. 29 CFR 825.114(a)(2)(I). "Treatment" is defined to include evaluations of a serious health condition. 29 CFR 825.114(b). As "pregnancy" is considered to be a serious health condition, evaluations of that condition (prenatal care) would fit within the definition of incapacity for purposes of FMLA leave.

Weighing in on the debate, it appears that the statute, legislative and regulatory history are decidedly mixed. A review of the statute on this point would suggest that prenatal care must include incapacitation. The base definition of a serious health condition is of an illness, injury, impairment, or physical or mental condition that involves, in this case, continuing treatment by a health care provider. 29 USC 2611(11). "Prenatal care" is not itself an illness, injury, impairment, or physical or mental condition. "Prenatal care" is something that is needed because of pregnancy, which, at a minimum, is a physical condition. As such, "prenatal care" should not be considered a separate, stand-alone category entitling an employee to FMLA leave absent incapacitation. A number of courts have held that prenatal care requires incapacitation. *See Dormeyer v. Comerica Bank-Ill.*, No. 96-C-4805, 1997 U.S. Dist. LEXIS 10260, at *8-10 (N.D. Ill. July 15, 1997); *Gudenkauf v. Stauffer Communications, Inc. et al.*, 922 F. Supp. 465, 474 (D. Kan. 1996).

Notwithstanding the above, the legislative and regulatory history suggests that prenatal care is separate from incapacity caused by pregnancy-related illness. The legislative history listed examples of serious health conditions. S. Rep. 103-3, p. 29. In pertinent part, the Report lists "ongoing pregnancy, miscarriages, complications or illnesses related to pregnancy, such as severe morning sickness, the need for prenatal care, childbirth, and recovery from childbirth." S. Rep. 103-3, p. 29. By separating "prenatal care" from "complications or illnesses related to pregnancy," the legislative history could be read as suggesting that prenatal care is separate from incapacitation due to pregnancy.

The regulatory history also separates prenatal care and pregnancy-related incapacitation. In the passage quoted above, periodic visits to a health care provider for prenatal care are treated separately from the incapacitating episodes of severe morning sickness. Preamble, 29 CFR 825.114. Again, this suggests that "prenatal care" does not require incapacitation.

Finally, the DOL indicated that prenatal care does not require incapacitation. Specifically, the DOL (DOL WH FMLA Advisory Opinion No. 60 (May 2, 1995), observed the following:

> Because the Statute (Section 102(b)) permits intermittent leave or leave on a "reduced leave schedule" in cases of medical necessity, it is also clear that the Act contemplates that employees would be entitled to FMLA leave in some cases because of doctor's visits or therapy due to a condition that need not be incapacitating at that point. The legislative history explains that to receive treatment for early stage cancer, to receive physical therapy after a hospital stay or because of severe arthritis, etc., or for prenatal care are covered by the Act.

Again, the matter can be argued both ways and, in many respects, is more an academic point than a practical one.

(f) Comparison With Birth and Care of a Newborn

FMLA leave for the birth of a son or daughter, and to care for the newborn child does not require that anyone, not the employee, spouse, son or daughter, have a serious health condition in order for an eligible employee to be entitled to FMLA leave. On the other hand, to be eligible for FMLA leave due to pregnancy, or for prenatal care, the employee or covered family member of the employee must be incapacitated due to a serious health condition (pregnancy) within the meaning of the FMLA.

(g) Pregnancy as a Disability

A situation that comes up fairly frequently involves the request of an eligible employee/parent for FMLA to care for a pregnant daughter who is age 18 or older. In general, for an eligible employee to be entitled to take FMLA leave to care for a daughter with a serious health condition, the FMLA requires that the daughter meet the statutory definition of "daughter." DOL WH FMLA Advisory Opinion No. 51 (Nov. 28, 1994). A parent may be entitled to FMLA leave to care for an adult child with a serious health condition if the child has a physical or mental disability within the meaning of the ADA regulations, and is incapable of self-care. *Id.*; *see* 29 CFR 825.113(c) (definition of "son or daughter"); S. Res. 242, Cong. Rec. S3959, S3962 (April 23, 1996); 29 CFR 825.113(c). A parent is not entitled to FMLA leave to care for a child 18 years of age or older who is not disabled within the meaning of the ADA regulations, including a daughter age 18 or older who has a serious health condition because of pregnancy or is recovering from childbirth. DOL WH FMLA Advisory Opinion No. 51 (Nov. 28, 1994). *Id.* Pregnancy is generally not considered a "disability" within the meaning of the ADA. *Id.*

It should be noted that, while recognizing that pregnancy is normally not an ADA disability, the EEOC and some courts have recognized pregnancy as a disability in certain limited situations. *See* EEOC Compliance Manual § 902 (pregnancy not a disability absent complications); *Cerrato v. Durham, Heslin & Executive Health Group National Health Services*, 941 F. Supp. 388 (S.D.N.Y. 1996); *Patterson v. Xerox Corp.*, 901 F. Supp. 274 (N.D. Ill. 1995). Contrary to the position taken by the DOL, the First Circuit in *Navarro v. Gladys Navarro Pomares et al.*, 261 F.3d 90 (1st Cir. 2001), held that an employee/mother may take FMLA leave to care for her seriously ill adult child with high blood pressure as a result of the adult child's pregnancy. The court analyzed the claim by determining whether the adult child (1) had a serious health condition; (2) was incapable of self-care; and (3) was incapacitated because of a mental or physical disability. *Id.* at 95. The court quickly found that there was sufficient evidence to defeat summary judgment that the adult child was incapacitated due to pregnancy, a serious health condition. For similar reasons, the court noted that the adult child was "not capable of self-care" as defined in the regulations as she was confined to bed for the duration of her pregnancy. As such, she would need assistance or supervision with cooking, cleaning, shopping, and doing housework. *Id.* at 96. The crux of the issue, according to the court, was whether the adult child had a disability within the meaning of 29 USC 2612(12) of the FMLA. *Id.*

The court analyzed the disability claim pursuant to the regulations implementing the ADA, which were incorporated into the FMLA. *See* 29 CFR 825.113(c)(2). The ADA regulations ask three questions: (1) Is there a physical impairment? (2) What, if any, major life activity is implicated? (3) Does the impairment substantially affect the identified major life activity? The court quickly found that high blood pressure is a physical impairment, as are complications from pregnancy. The court also agreed that the employee established that working, caring for oneself, and reproduction are major life activities.

The core issue was whether the specified impairment substantially limits the identified major life activity. *Navarro*, 261 F.3d at 97–98. The issue within this issue was whether an impairment that may only last weeks could constitute such a substantial limitation. *Id.* at 98. The court concluded that it could.

According to the ADA regulations, "substantially limits" means that an individual is:

(i) Unable to perform a major life activity that the average person in the general population can perform; or

(ii) Significantly restricted as to the condition, manner or duration under which an individual can perform a particular major life activity as compared to the condition, manner, or duration under which the average person in the same general population can perform that same major activity.

29 CFR 1630.2(j)(1). For ADA purposes, the factors to be evaluated in assessing whether an individual is substantially limited in a major life activity include (1) the nature and severity of the impairment, (2) the duration or expected duration of the impairment, and (3) the permanent or long-term impact, or the expected permanent or long-term impact, of or resulting from the impairment. *Id*. § 1630.2(j)(2).

Focusing solely on the major life activity of caring for oneself, the court held that, for purposes of summary judgment, the adult child's high blood pressure constituted an impairment that substantially limited her in the major life activity of caring for herself. *Navarro*, 261 F.3d at 98. In so finding, the court rejected the district court's application of the FMLA to the EEOC's interpretive guidance that temporary, non-chronic impairments did not constitute a disability. *Id*. According to the court, the EEOC's interpretative guidance issued pursuant to the ADA was not entitled to deference when applied in the FMLA context. *Id*. at 99. The court opined that the EEOC interpretive guidance was inapplicable in the FMLA context because it clashed with the underlying purpose of the FMLA.

An additional consideration that led the court to the conclusion that factors such as duration must be accorded reduced significance in the FMLA context was that the FMLA deals in much lower levels of employer engagement and employee rewards than the ADA. *Id*. at 102. The court noted that, in contrast to the ADA, the FMLA implicates shorter time frames, the maximum FMLA benefit was limited to 12 weeks of leave, and the FMLA has no interactive process.

The court concluded that the question, under the FMLA, of whether an adult child's impairment substantially limits a major life activity is governed by a tripartite rule. First, the courts should apply the borrowed ADA regulation as written, ignore the EEOC's interpretive guidance, and consider (a) the nature and severity of the impairment, (b) its expected duration, (c) its anticipated long-term impact, and (d) any other relevant factors. *Id*. at 104. Second, the assessment must be performed on a case-by-case basis, balancing all factors in light of the FMLA's purpose, structure, and provisions for relief. Third, the requisite test is a balancing test: apart from the severity of the impairment, no one factor is indispensable in finding that a disability exists for FMLA purposes. *Id*.

The court in *Navarro*, 261 F.3d at 104, held:

> Applying this rule, we hold that the provisions of 29 U.S.C. § 2611(12)(B) may be satisfied by various combinations of factors. One such permissible combination entails, at least in certain circumstances, a showing that the employee's adult child is suffering from a severe impairment that has a modest projected duration and an as-yet-unquantified long-term impact. The case before us fits within the contours of that category. It follows that the Court below improvidently granted summary judgment for Pfizer.

In *Blackburn v. Potter*, No. IP-01-1645-C-B/S, 2003 U.S. Dist. LEXIS 5269 (S.D. Ind. March 31, 2003), the court similarly held that an eligible employee was entitled to FMLA leave (the employee requested two weeks) to care for an adult child who was recuperating at home after giving birth by Caesarian section. The court found that the daughter was "incapable of self-care" during her recovery period. The court, however, failed completely to address whether the daughter was disabled within the meaning of the FMLA. Instead the court repeated its presumption that "any incapacity due to pregnancy" is a serious health condition.

The facts of every request for FMLA leave must be carefully reviewed to determine whether the individual meets all of the prerequisites for leave, including whether a family member meets the requirements to be considered a "covered" family member for purposes of the FMLA. [For a further discussion of who is a "covered" family member within the meaning of the FMLA, see Chapter 6, "Covered Family Members."]

(2) Title II

(a) General Rule

An FMLA–qualifying "serious health condition" means an illness, injury, impairment, or physical or mental condition that involves continuing treatment by a health care provider includes one or more the following (5 CFR 630.1202 (definition of "serious health condition," Subsection (1)(ii)(B)):

> Any period of incapacity due to pregnancy or childbirth, or for prenatal care, even if the affected individual does not receive active treatment from a health care provider during the period of incapacity or the period of incapacity does not last more than three consecutive calendar days.

The definition is substantially similar, although not identical, to the comparable definition pursuant to Title I, the CAA, and the PEOAA discussed in the immediately preceding section of this chapter.

A review of the key terms of this serious health condition follows.

(b) Any Period

This serious health condition does not require a fixed minimum durational period of incapacity. Any period, however short, of incapacity due to pregnancy or childbirth is sufficient to meet the requirement of a serious health condition. Whether incapacity is required for prenatal care is discussed below.

Again, many people are of the misconception that FMLA leave is only available where an employee or covered family member is incapacitated for a minimum of more than three calendar days. This serious health condition expressly provides that the "more than three day" minimum does not apply, and that any period of incapacity will satisfy the incapacity requirement for pregnancy as a serious health condition.

(c) Incapacity

"Incapacity" means the inability to work, attend school, or perform other regular daily activities because of a serious health condition or treatment for or recovery from a serious health condition. 5 CFR 630.1202 (definition of "incapacity"). As this definition of "incapacity" is nearly identical to the definition of that term under Title I, the CAA, and the PEOAA, the reader is referred to the previous discussion in this chapter interpreting "incapacity" under those statutes for purposes of pregnancy as a serious health condition.

(d) Treatment

Title II does not define the term "treatment." Rather, it defines the term "continuing treatment" to include (but is not limited to) examinations to determine if there is a serious health condition and evaluations of such conditions if the examinations and evaluations determine that a serious health condition exists. 5 CFR 630.1202 (definition of "serious health condition," Subsection (1)(ii)).

The regulation is similar to, although by no means identical to, the definition of treatment pursuant to Title I, the CAA, and the PEOAA. See 29 CFR 825.114(b); S. Res. 242, Cong. Rec. S3959, S3962, S3978 (April 23, 1996); 29 CFR 825.114(b). The primary difference between these definitions is that Title II appears to condition evaluations on the results of the initial examination to determine whether a serious health condition exits. "Treatment" for purposes of Title I, the CAA, and the PEOAA, on the other hand, does not condition evaluations on the results of the initial examination. Evaluations of the serious health condition are treated equally with examinations. See 29 CFR 825.114(b); S. Res. 242, Cong. Rec. S3959, S3962, S3978 (April 23, 1996); 29 CFR 825.114(b).

Title II, like its counterparts in Title I, the CAA, and the PEOAA, fails to define what constitutes an "examination" or "evaluation." Under Title II, a health care provider must conduct such examinations and evaluations. That is not the case under Title I, the CAA, and the PEOAA (which fails to identify who can conduct examinations and evaluations). Who is an FMLA–covered "health care provider" is discussed later in this chapter.

Another difference between "continuing treatment" under Title II and "treatment" for purposes of Title I, the CAA, and the PEOAA, is that the former does not exclude routine physical, dental, or eye examination from the definition of "continuing treatment." However, routine physical, dental, and eye examination are excluded from the definition of a "serious health condition." 5 CFR 630.1202 (definition of "serious health condition," Subsection (2)) (serious health condition does not include routine physical, eye, or dental examinations). These terms are also undefined. Presumably, since these terms are affirmatively excluded from the definition of a serious health condition, they are also excluded from inclusion as "continuing treatment." Remember, the Title II definition of "continuing treatment" was not exclusive ("includes, but is not limited to").

Title II, like Title I, the CAA, and the PEOAA, does not require that "the affected individual receive active treatment from a health care provider during the period of incapacity." 5 CFR 630.1202 (definition of "serious health condition," Subsection (1)(ii)(B)). The term "active treatment" is undefined in the regulations, and unexplained in the comments accompanying the publication of the final OPM FMLA regulations. As discussed in the preceding section of this chapter regarding Title I, the CAA, and the PEOAA, presumably this means that the pregnant individual (employee or covered family member) must be under the care of, and periodically visit with, a health care provider during the pregnancy. This is necessary to satisfy the requirement that the individual be receiving "continuing treatment" by a health care provider. However, the affected (pregnant) individual need not see a health care provider for each and every absence due to incapacity during the pregnancy.

Finally, as structured, the regulation could be interpreted as requiring incapacity only for pregnancy and childbirth, but not for prenatal care. Neither the regulations nor comments accompanying publication of the final OPM regulations clarify this matter. A further discussion of this issue is presented in the preceding section of this chapter addressing "prenatal care" for purposes of Title I, the CAA, and the PEOAA.

(e)   Pregnancy, Childbirth and Prenatal Care

This serious health condition covers pregnancy, childbirth, and prenatal care. As discussed in the preceding section of this chapter, by comparison, Title I, the CAA, and the PEOAA only cover pregnancy and prenatal care. No explanation is given in the regulations or comments accompanying the publication of the final OPM regulations for the inclusion of childbirth. The terms "pregnancy," "childbirth," and "prenatal care" are undefined. Presumably, they mean what a reasonable person would expect them to mean. In any event, an agency could request a medical certification in support of such leave, which would address whether the leave was "due to" pregnancy or childbirth, or "for" prenatal care.

(f)   Comparison to Birth as a Covered Condition

FMLA leave for the birth of a son or daughter is available with or without the presence of a serious health condition. FMLA leave for the birth of a son or daughter is available. 5 CFR 630.1203(a)(1). An employee is entitled to such leave even if no one is incapacitated by a serious health condition. Given what is involved with childbirth, however, outside outlandish law school hypotheticals, virtually every childbirth will involve incapacitation within the meaning of the FMLA. As such, the birth would also constitute a serious health condition within the meaning of 5 CFR 630.1202 (definition of "serious health condition," Subsection (1)(ii)(B)). In sum, the birth of a child is a covered condition entitling an employee to FMLA leave under § 630.1203(a)(1), and as a serious health condition under either §§ 630.1203(a)(3) or (4).

A practical advantage of being considered a covered condition for purposes of FMLA leave involves an employee or covered family member who is not receiving continuing treatment by a health care provider within the meaning of the FMLA. This may occur for religious reasons, or the lack of available health care services in remote areas of the world. If the pregnant individual were not under the continuing treatment of a health care provider due to pregnancy, childbirth, or for prenatal care, the birth of the child would not be a covered serious health condition within the meaning of the law. As such, the employee would not be entitled to FMLA leave for the birth of the child as a serious health condition. The employee would, however, be entitled to FMLA leave for the birth of the child pursuant to § 630.1203(a)(1). That Subsection recognizes the birth of a child of the employee or covered family member as a covered condition without the necessity of the leave being considered a serious health condition.

e. Chronic Serious Health Conditions

(1) Title I, the CAA, and the PEOAA

(a) General Rule

An FMLA–qualifying "serious health condition" means an illness, injury, impairment, or physical or mental condition that involves continuing treatment by a health care provider including one or more the following:

> Any period of incapacity or treatment for such incapacity due to a chronic serious health condition.

29 CFR 825.114(a)(2)(iii), 825.800 (definition of "serious health condition," Subsection (1)(ii)(C)); S. Res. 242, Cong. Rec. S3959, S3962, S3978 (April 23, 1996); 29 CFR 825.114(a)(2)(iii), 825.800 (definition of "serious health condition," Subsection (1)(ii)(C)); *see Burnett v. LFW, Inc.*, 472 F.3d 471, 478 (7th Cir. Dec. 26, 2006); *Brenneman v. MedCentral Health System*, 366 F.3d 412, 421 (6th Cir. 2004), *cert. denied*, 543 U.S. 1146 (U.S. 2005); *Perry v. Jaguar of Troy*, 353 F.3d 510, 514 (6th Cir. 2003); *Rhoads v. FDIC et al.*, 257 F.3d 373, 382 (4th Cir. 2001), *cert. denied*, 535 U.S. 933 (2002); *Taylor v. Texaco, Inc.*, No. 4:04-CV-212-JEC, 2007 U.S. Dist. LEXIS 22239, at *28 (N.D. Ga. March 28, 2007); *Schmutte v. Resort Condominiums International, LLC*, 463 F. Supp. 2d 891, 909 (S.D. Ind. 2006); *Willis v. USPS*, No. 03–C 9185, 2004 U.S. Dist. LEXIS 18238, at *16 (N.D. Ill. Sept. 10, 2004); *Bradley v. Mary Rutan Hospital Assoc.*, 322 F. Supp. 2d 926, 941–942 (S.D. Ohio 2004); *Flanagan v. Keller Products, Inc.*, No. 00–542-M, 2002 DNH 47, 2002 U.S. Dist. LEXIS 3663 (D.N.H. Feb. 25, 2002); *Goodwin v. Rheem Manufacturing Co.*, 15 F. Supp. 2d 1197, 1204 & n.7 (M.D. Ala. 1998); *Hensley v. Baptist Hospital of East Tennessee, Inc. et al.*, No. 3:96–cv–789, 1997 U.S. Dist. LEXIS 22515, at *37 (E.D. Tenn. Oct. 27, 1997); *Beal v. Rubbermaid Commercial Products, Inc.*, 972 F. Supp. 1216, 1223, n.12 (S.D. Iowa 1997), *aff'd*, 1998 U.S. App. LEXIS 9295 (8th Cir. 1998); *Bauer v. Dayton–Walther Corp.*, 910 F. Supp. 306, 310 (E.D. Ky. 1996), *aff'd*, 118 F.3d 1109 (6th Cir. 1997); DOL WH FMLA advisory Opinion No. 60 (May 2, 1995).

A review of the regulatory history and key terms follows.

(b) Regulatory Development

Chronic serious health conditions were originally recognized in the interim DOL regulations as a serious health condition. *See* 58 Fed. Reg. 31794, 31817 (June 4, 1993) (29 CFR 825.114(a)(3)). However, the interim regulations required that the chronic condition either be incurable or so serious that, if not treated, it would likely result in a period of incapacity of more than three calendar days. *Id.*

Prior to the publication of the final implementing regulations, the DOL received numerous comments suggesting that the definition of "chronic conditions" was too restrictive. The commentators argued that "curability" was not a proper test for determining a "serious health condition" as many incurable disabilities require continuing treatment over long periods of time. Preamble, 29 CFR 825.114. The commentators also argued that the "more than three day" requirement made little sense when applied to chronic conditions because incapacitation from such conditions is infrequent and often of short duration (asthma attack). Preamble, 29 CFR 825.114; *see also* DOL WH FMLA Advisory Opinion No. 75 (Nov. 14, 1995).

In making revisions to the final regulations, the DOL concurred with the comments that "suggested that special recognition should be given to chronic conditions." Preamble, 29 CFR 825.114. The DOL continued:

> The Department recognizes that certain conditions, such as asthma and diabetes, continue over an extended period of time (i.e., from several months to several years), often without affecting day–to–day ability to work or perform other activities but may cause episodic period of incapacity of less than three days. Although persons with such underlying conditions generally visit a health care provider periodically, when subject to a flare–up or other incapacitating episode, staying home and self–treatment are often more effective than visiting the health care provider (e.g., the asthma–sufferer who is advised to stay home and inside due to the pollen count being too high). The definition has, therefore, been revised to include such conditions as serious health conditions, even if the individual episodes of incapacity are not or more than three days duration.

The DOL also did away with the requirement that chronic conditions be "incurable." Preamble, 29 CFR 825.114.

(c) Any Period

Absences due to incapacity caused by a chronic serious health condition are not required to last more than three consecutive days in order to be considered an FMLA-qualifying serious health condition under this definition. 29 CFR 825.114(b); S. Res. 242, Cong. Rec. S3959, S3963 (April 23, 1996); 29 CFR 825.114(b); DOL WH FMLA Advisory Opinion No. 60 (May 2, 1995); *see Barnett v. Revere Smelting & Refining Corp.*, 67 F. Supp. 2d 378, 384–85 (S.D.N.Y. 1999). Any absence, however short in duration, due to incapacity caused by a chronic serious condition is sufficient. Of course, the rule would not exclude periods of incapacity attributable to incapacity caused by a chronic serious condition that exceed three days in length from coverage.

(d) Incapacity and Treatment for Incapacity

The term "incapacity" is not defined in § 825.114(a)(2)(iii). "Incapacity" is consistently defined elsewhere for purposes of other serious health conditions as meaning an inability to work, attend school or perform other regular daily activities due to the serious health condition, treatment therefore, or recovery therefrom. 29 CFR 825.114(a)(1), 825.114(a)(2)(I); S. Res. 242, Cong. Rec. S3959, S3962 (April 23, 1996); 29 CFR 825.114(a)(1), 825.114(a)(2)(I).

If "incapacity" is similarly defined for purposes of a chronic serious condition, the inclusion of language in the regulation referring to "and treatment for such incapacity" would appear redundant. The term "incapacity" already includes "treatment therefore" of the serious health condition. Of course, an alternative explanation would be that the definition of "incapacity" elsewhere in the implementing regulations does not apply, as that term is used for purposes of a chronic serious health condition. Other than the absence of "incapacity" in § 825.114(a)(2)(iii), there is nothing in the regulations or comments accompanying the publication of the final regulations that would suggest such an interpretation. Moreover, the term would then be otherwise undefined.

"Treatment" is defined by the regulations as including examinations to determine if a serious health condition exists and evaluations of the condition. 29 CFR 825.114(b); S. Res. 242, Cong. Rec. S3959, S3963 (April 23, 1996); 29 CFR 825.114(b); *Burnett v. LFW, Inc.*, 472 F.3d 471, 478 (7th Cir. 2006); *Perry v. Jaguar of Troy*, 353 F.3d 510, 514 (6th Cir. 2003). Treatment does not include routine physical, eye, and dental examinations. 29 CFR 825.114(b); S. Res. 242, Cong. Rec. S3959, S3963 (April 23, 1996); 29 CFR 825.114(b). The terms "routine," "physical," "eye," and "dental" are undefined. In *Bauer v. Dayton–Walther Corp.*, 910 F. Supp. 306, 310 (E.D. Ky. 1996), *aff'd*, 118 F.3d 1109 (6th Cir. 1997), the district court opined that a "visual inspection" conducted by the employee's physician of his claim of rectal bleeding did not constitute "treatment."

Moreover, absences attributable to incapacity for a chronic serious health condition qualify for FMLA leave even though the employee or the immediate family member does not receive treatment from a health care provider during the absence, and even if the absence does not last more than three days. 29 CFR 825.114(c); S. Res. 242, Cong. Rec. S3959, S3963 (April 23, 1996); 29 CFR 825.114(c). *See Perry v. Jaguar of Troy*, 353 F.3d 510, 514 (6th Cir. 2003); *Rhoads v. FDIC et al.*, 257 F.3d 373, 382 (4th Cir. 2001); *Stekloff v. St. John's Health Systems*, 218 F.3d 858, 863 (8th Cir. 2000). For example, an employee with asthma may be unable to report for work due to the onset of an asthma attack or because the employee's health care provider advised the employee to stay home when the pollen count exceeds a certain level. 29 CFR 825.114(c); S. Res. 242, Cong. Rec. S3959, S3963 (April 23, 1996); 29 CFR 825.114(c). *See Rhoads v. FDIC et al.*, 257 F.3d 373, 382 (4th Cir. 2001), *cert. denied*, 535 U.S. 933 (2002).

An employee alleging a chronic serious health condition must establish that he or she is receiving treatment from a health care provider for that condition and that the condition, incapacitates the employee. *Perry v. Jaguar of Troy*, 353 F.3d 510, 514 (6th Cir. 2003). In *Perry*, the employee alleged that his 13-year-old son was incapacitated with ADD and ADHD. The court, however, found that plaintiff failed to prove that his son was unable to work, attend school, or perform other regular daily activities during the period of the employee's leave. During this time, the son attended school, rode the bus, rode bikes, swam, played video games, watched television, and played with neighborhood friends, just like other kids. Perry argued that his son was incapacitated because he could not perform regular daily activities when compared to other children without ADD and ADHD. Rejecting the claim, the court opined, "[t]he fact that a child with learning disabilities does not function at the same level as a child of the same age without learning disabilities sheds no light on whether that child can perform regular daily activities." That his son might need more supervision than other children, standing alone, "does not address the child's ability to engage in regular daily activities."

(e) Chronic Serious Health Condition Defined

A chronic serious health condition is defined in the regulations as one which:

1. Requires periodic visits for treatment

    - by a health care provider, or

    - by a nurse or physician's assistant under the direct supervision of a health care provider; and

2. Continues over an extended period of time (including recurring episodes of a single underlying condition); and

3. May cause episodic rather than a continuing period of incapacity (e.g., asthma, diabetes, epilepsy, etc.).

29 CFR 825.114(a)(2)(iii), 825.800 (definition of "serious health condition," Subsection (1)(ii)(C)); S. Res. 242, Cong. Rec. S3959, S3962, S3978 (April 23, 1996); 29 CFR 825.114(a)(2)(iii), 825.800 (definition of "serious health condition," Subsection (1)(ii)(C)); see *Burnett v. LFW, Inc.*, 472 F.3d 471, 478 (7th Cir. 2006); *Hoffman v. Professional Med Team*, 394 F.3d 414, 418 (6th Cir. 2005); *Brenneman v. MedCentral Health System*, 366 F.3d 412, 421 (6th Cir. 2004), cert. denied, 543 U.S. 1146 (U.S. 2005); *Perry v. Jaguar of Troy*, 353 F.3d 510, 514 (6th Cir. 2003); *Stoops v. One Call Communications, Inc.*, 141 F.3d 309, 312 (7th Cir. 1998); *Victorelli v. Shadyside Hospital*, 128 F.3d 184, 189 (3d Cir. 1997); *Taylor v. Texaco, Inc.*, No. 4:04-CV-212-JEC, 2007 U.S. Dist. LEXIS 22239, at *28 (N.D. Ga. March 28, 2007); *Schmutte v. Resort Condominiums International, LLC*, 463 F. Supp. 2d 891, 908 (S.D. Ind. 2006); *Willis v. USPS*, No. 03–C 9185, 2004 U.S. Dist. LEXIS 18238, at *16 (N.D. Ill. Sept. 10, 2004); *Bradley v. Mary Rutan Hospital Assoc.*, 322 F. Supp. 2d 926, 941–942 (S.D. Ohio 2004); *Brock v. United Grinding Technologies, Inc. et al.*, 257 F. Supp. 2d 1089, 1098–99 (S.D. Ohio 2003); *Flanagan v. Keller Products, Inc.*, No. 00–542–M, 2002 DNH 47, 2002 U.S. Dist. LEXIS 3663 (D.N.H. Feb. 25, 2002); *Vargo–Adams v. USPS*, 992 F. Supp. 939, 942 (N.D. Ohio 1998).

The court in *Willis v. USPS*, No. 03–C 9185, 2004 U.S. Dist. LEXIS 18238, at *16 (N.D. Ill. Sept. 10, 2004), found that chronic arthritis met this definition of serious health condition. The court noted that the undisputed evidence established that the employee obtained multiple physician notes diagnosing her condition as chronic arthritis, she visited her physician for the arthritis condition on multiple occasions over a period of time, and she had periods of incapacity.

In *Matthews v. Village Center Community Dev. District*, No. 5:05-cv-3440Oc-10GRJ, 2006 U.S. Dist. LEXIS 85906, at *63 (M.D. Fla. Nov. 28, 2006), the court found that keratoconus, a disease of the eyes, was chronic serious health condition because employee suffered from disease for a prolonged period of time, and her symptoms are more episodic rather than consistent in nature.

Many of the key terms of this definition are undefined and otherwise unexplained.

(f) Periodic Visits

The term "periodic" is not defined. It is therefore unclear how many visits and over what time frame these visits are necessary in order to meet the requirement that the employee or covered family member has made periodic visits for treatment. Combined with the plural "visits" the term "periodic" certainly suggests two or more visits is necessary in order for the requirement to be met.

It is also unclear whether "periodic" requires that such visits occur with certain regularity. This would appear to be the case based on the dictionary definition of "periodic." "Periodic" is defined as: 1: occurring or recurring at regular intervals. 2. A: Consisting of or containing a series of repeated stages, processes, or digits. B: Being a function any value of which recurs at regular intervals. Webster's Ninth New Collegiate Dictionary (Merriam–Webster, Inc. 1988). If this is the case, random visits to a health care provider may fail to be considered "periodic." What may be necessary is to determine the basis for the regular intervals. In the comments accompany publication of the final Title I regulations (Preamble, 29 CFR 825.114), the DOL makes the following observations:

> Although persons with such underlying [chronic serious] conditions generally visit a health care provider periodically, when subject to a flare–up or other incapacitating episode, staying home and staying home and self–treatment are often more effective than visiting he health care provider....

The comment suggests that "periodic visits" need not be scheduled, but can be based on flare–ups or incapacitating episodes. Complicating matters is that the regulations do not require an employee or covered family member to visit a health care provider in every instance that may otherwise be the basis for "periodic" visits. The language in the comments quoted above suggests that flare-ups of a chronic condition could be the basis of periodic visits, but then goes on to state that the individual with the chronic condition does not have to visit the health care provider with every flare-up. This will, no doubt, complicate an agency's ability to spot a recurring pattern of health care provider visits for the chronic condition.

No temporal period is given in which these "periodic visits" are measured. Absent an identified temporal period, such periodic visits could be separated by weeks, months or even years. It seems unreasonable to require individual managers to remember that ten years ago, and then again five years ago, the employee took leave for the same underlying condition in order to conclude that the current leave request is "periodic." Obviously, agencies will need to rely on their ability to request medical certification from the employee in order to verify that the employee or covered family member with the chronic serious condition meets the "periodic visits" requirement.

As with "periodic," the term "visits" is not defined. It is, therefore, unclear whether such a "visit" must be in person or may be conducted over the telephone, by videophone, or by e-mail. The matter can, therefore, be argued either way. It is also unclear whether a "visit" requires an examination, evaluation, or treatment. Presumably this is the case.

In *Schmutte v. Resort Condominiums International, LLC*, 463 F. Supp. 2d 891, 908 (S.D. Ind. 2006), the court found that a reasonable jury could find that the employee's depression and anxiety required periodic visits to her health care providers. Schmutte saw her doctor 4 times for medication management, and 11 times for therapy sessions during 2003. The court also noted Schmutte's hospital stay from September 19 through November 11, 2003, as evidence that she received periodic treatments.

An employee who did not see their allergist but took over the counter medications when she had a sinus flare-up twice a year did not establish that she had periodic treatments by a health care provider for her sinus condition. *Taylor v. Texaco, Inc.*, No. 4:04-CV-212-JEC, 2007 U.S. Dist. LEXIS 22239, at *32 (N.D. Ga. March 28, 2007).

In *Brock v. United Grinding Technologies, Inc. et al.*, 257 F. Supp. 2d 1089, 1098-99 (S.D. Ohio 2003), the court concluded eight visits with multiple doctors regarding the same underlying condition, depression and anxiety, was sufficient to create a material issue of fact whether the plaintiff suffered from a chronic serious health condition within the meaning of the FMLA.

(g) Nurse, Physician's Assistant; Direct Supervision

The individual with the chronic serious condition is required to periodically visit, for purposes of treatment, either a health care provider or a nurse or physician's assistant under the direct supervision of a health care provider. The terms "nurse" and "physician's assistant" are undefined. It is therefore unclear whether these individuals need to be duly licensed (at least in those states that require such a license) and practicing within the scope of their license. Presumably, that is the case.

The term "direct supervision" is also undefined. As a result, it is unclear what degree of supervision by the health care provider over the nurse or physician's assistant is required in order to constitute "direct supervision." While there are many dictionary definitions for the word "direct," the most pertinent in this regard would appear to be the following: "2 a: to regulate the activities or course of; b: to carry out the organizing, energizing, and supervising of; c: to dominate and determine the course of; d: to train and lead performance of." Webster's Ninth New Collegiate Dictionary (Merriam-Webster, Inc. 1988). Animated by the aforesaid dictionary definitions, it would appear that "direct supervision" requires active supervision of treatment administered by the nurse or physician's assistant by a health care provider.

Note that it is not required that the individual afflicted with a chronic serious health condition first see a health care provider before receiving treatment from a nurse or physician's assistant. According to the DOL, "An employee, however, may receive treatment by a physician's assistant or other health care professional under the supervision of a doctor or other health care provider without first seeing the health care provider and obtaining a referral." Preamble, 29 CFR 825.118. *See also* DOL WH FMLA Advisory Opinion No. 60 (May 2, 1995). Of course, the afflicted individual would generally need to be receiving continuing treatment by a health care provider to qualify for FMLA leave due to a chronic serious health condition. *See* 29 USC 2611(11)(B).

The second requirement of an FMLA-qualifying "chronic serious condition" is that it continues over an extended period of time. 29 CFR 825.114(a)(2)(iii), 825.800 (definition of "serious health condition," Subsection (1)(ii)(C)); S. Res. 242, Cong. Rec. S3959, S3962, S3978 (April 23, 1996); 29 CFR 825.114(a)(2)(iii), 825.800 (definition of "serious health condition," Subsection (1)(ii)(C)); see also DOL WH FMLA Advisory Opinion No. 60 (May 2, 1995), The regulation fails to define or otherwise describe what "continues" means, and what would constitute an "extended period of time." *Flanagan v. Keller Products, Inc.*, No. 00–542–M, 2002 DNH 47, 2002 U.S. Dist. LEXIS 3663, at *20 (D.N.H. Feb. 25, 2002) (regulations fail to define what is meant by an "extended period of time"). Absent further qualification, "continues" presumably means to remain in existence, no matter what the severity of the condition. A chronic serious condition that is still detectable in the body, but which has not flared-up in 20 years, would, presumably, meet the "continues" criteria.

It is unclear how long a chronic serious health condition must persist in order to meet the requirement that such condition continues for "an extended period of time." Nor is it clear whether "an extended period of time" is measured from the perspective of the afflicted individual, the medical community, or based strictly in temporal terms. Viewed from the perspective of the afflicted individual, an "extended period of time" could be a rather short time period. Presumably, agencies will have to rely on the medical certification from the health care provider to determine if the condition has or will continue over an "extended period of time," within the meaning of the FMLA.

In *Flanagan v. Keller Products, Inc.*, No. 00–542–M, 2002 DNH 47, 2002 U.S. Dist. LEXIS 3663, at *20 (D.N.H. Feb. 25, 2002), the court found that an employee's chipped tooth, which developed into dry socket, did not constitute a chronic serious health condition. The plaintiff received treatment from her physician on seven occasions during a one-month period before the ailment was resolved. The court's decision was based, in part, on its finding that the employee did not suffer from it or its side effects for a sufficiently lengthy period of time. Although acknowledging that the regulations fail to define what is meant by "an extended period of time," according to the court, "the language of the FMLA itself, its legislative history, and the regulations promulgated pursuant to the statute all suggest that to constitute a 'chronic' illness, the condition must exist for well more than a few weeks." As support, the court referenced the definition of chronic condition used by the U.S. National Center for Health Statistics as a condition lasting three months or longer. It also referenced the definition of "chronic" in Steadman Medical Dictionary as referring to a health-related state lasting a long time, and unfavorably compared the month-long duration of the plaintiff's dental condition to epilepsy, asthma, diabetes, and the other examples of chronic conditions listed in the regulation.

The Third Circuit in *Victorelli v. Shadyside Hospital*, 128 F.3d 184, 189 (3d Cir. 1997), found that the three-year duration of Victorelli's condition (peptic ulcer) constituted an "extended period of time" for purposes of an FMLA chronic serious health condition.

Eight visits with various health care providers from March 1999 through August 28, 1999, was held sufficient evidence to create a material issue of fact whether the employee suffered from a chronic serious health condition within the meaning of the FMLA. *See Brock v. United Grinding Technologies, Inc. et al.*, 257 F. Supp. 2d 1089, 1098–99 (S.D. Ohio 2003).

(h) Episodic Incapacity

The third requirement, that the chronic serious health condition may cause episodic rather than continuing periods of incapacity, reflects the DOL comments addressed above that the incapacity caused by chronic conditions may last for lengthy periods of time. *See* DOL WH FMLA Advisory Opinion No. 60 (May 2, 1995). Again, the term "episodic" is not defined, and fails to identify a time frame from which this may be judged. For example, is an employee who is incapacitated for 15 minutes once every ten years from the same chronic serious health condition suffering "episodic" periods of incapacity due to a "serious health condition"? Absent a time frame, the answer would appear to be yes. The broader question is whether this outcome is what Congress had in mind?

In *Burnett v. LFW, Inc.*, 472 F.3d 471, 478 (7th Cir. 2006), the court found that Burnett established that his need to take leave twice, once in January and a second time scheduled for February, confirmed that his condition might result in episodic periods of incapacity within the meaning of the FMLA.

In *Schmutte v. Resort Condominiums International, LLC*, 463 F. Supp. 2d 891, 908 (S.D. Ind. 2006), the court found that a reasonable jury could find that Schmutte's depression and anxiety caused her periods of incapacity. The court noted that she took three weeks of FMLA leave as a result of her condition in July 2002. From September 19, 2003, through November 11, 2003, Schumtte was in the Stress Center for depression and anxiety for 7 weeks. From her return to work on November 12, 2003, until her termination, she was out 4 more times due to depression and anxiety attacks.

In *Bauer v. Dayton–Walther Corp.*, 910 F. Supp. 306, 310 (E.D. Ky. 1996), *aff'd*, 118 F.3d 1109 (6th Cir. 1997), the District court found that the employee's condition, rectal bleeding, did not present the sort of episodic period of incapacity contemplated by the Act where his condition caused the employee to miss work one full day and leave early twice. "Bauer's condition falls far short of the sort of chronic serious health problems such as diabetes and epilepsy within the purview of the FMLA." *Id.*; *see Beal v. Rubbermaid Commercial Products, Inc.*, 972 F. Supp. 1216, 1224–25 (S.D. Iowa 1997), *aff'd*, 1998 U.S. App. LEXIS 9295 (8th Cir. 1998) (holding that although the plaintiff's eczema caused her to be incapacitated for more than one day and periodically forced her to leave work, it fell "far short of the sort of chronic problems entailing episodic periods of incapacity contemplated by the FMLA," such as diabetes and epilepsy).

(i) Extended period of time

The regulations do not identify what might constitute an extended period of time. In *Schmutte v. Resort Condominiums International, LLC*, 463 F. Supp. 2d 891, 908 (S.D. Ind. 2006), the court found that a reasonable jury could find that the employee's depression and anxiety continued over an extended period of time based on the fact that she first took FMLA leave for these conditions in July 2002, and she was still under medical treatment and still requesting FMLA leave because of depression and anxiety a year later.

An employee who suffered from kerotoconus [a degenerative eye disorder] since she was a young girl was found to have suffered from a chronic serious health condition for an extended period of time. *Matthews v. Village Center Community Dev. District*, No. 5:05-cv-3440Oc-10GRJ, 2006 U.S. Dist. LEXIS 85906, at *63 (M.D. Fla. Nov. 28, 2006),

(2) Title II

(a) General Rule

An FMLA–qualifying "serious health condition" means an illness, injury, impairment, or physical or mental condition that involves continuing treatment by a health care provider includes one or more the following (5 CFR 630.1202 (definition of "serious health condition," Subsection (1)(ii)(C)):

> Any period of incapacity or treatment for such incapacity due to a chronic serious health condition that—
>
> (1) Requires periodic visits for treatments by a health care provider or by a health care provider under the direct supervision of the affected individual's health care provider;
>
> (2) Continues over an extended period of time (including recurring episodes of a single underlying condition); and
>
> (3) May cause episodic rather than a continuing period of incapacity (e.g., asthma, diabetes, epilepsy, etc).

Accord Williams v. Dept. of Navy, No. DC-0752-05-0431-I-1, 2005 MSPB LEXIS 6866, at *3-4 (Oct. 17, 2005), *pet. denied*, 101 MSPR 133 (2006); *Davis v. Dept. of Homeland Security*, No. SF-0752-04-0760-I-1, 2005 MSPB LEXIS 898, at *27 (Feb. 22, 2005), *pet. denied*, 100 MSPR 62 (2005), *vacated, remanded*, 2007 U.S. App. LEXIS 12593 (Fed. Cir. May 30, 2007).

Note that, unlike Title I, the CAA, and the PEOAA, the term "chronic serious health condition" is not separately defined in the OPM regulation. Rather, language comparable to that used by Title I, the CAA, and the PEOAA to define a "chronic serious health condition" is incorporated directly into the requirements of § 630.1202 (definition of "serious health condition," Subsection (1)(ii)(C)). Either way, of course, the affect is the same: a chronic serious health condition under Title II, like the other federal sector variants of the FMLA, has three main requirements. Those requirements are substantially similar, although not identical to, the comparable requirements under Title I, the CAA, and the PEOAA.

A review of the regulatory history and key terms of a chronic serious health condition follows.

(b) Regulatory Development

The OPM received comments before the publication of the final regulations implementing Title II of the FMLA. As discussed previously regarding comments received by the DOL prior to the publication of the final Title I regulations, commentators argued that minimum durational periods failed to address the acute or episodic nature of chronic conditions. Preamble, 5 CFR 630.1202 (definition of "serious health condition"). The OPM agreed and, consistent with the DOL's final regulations, significantly revised the definition of "serious health condition." *Id*. According to the OPM, "A major change is the addition of chronic conditions, such as asthma, diabetes, and epilepsy, that continue over an extended period of time (i.e., from several months to several years), often without affecting day-to-day activities, but may cause episodic periods of incapacity of less than three days." *Id*.

(c) Any Period

There is no minimal durational period of incapacity required for a chronic serious health condition. Very short periods of incapacity (e.g., minutes, hours, or days) due to a chronic serious health condition would meet this requirement. Of course, longer periods of incapacity are not precluded and would also meet this requirement.

(d) Incapacity and Treatment for Incapacity

"Incapacity" means the inability to work, attend school, or perform other regular daily activities because of a serious health condition or treatment for or recovery from a serious health condition. 5 CFR 630.1202 (definition of "incapacity"). As this definition of "incapacity" is nearly identical to the definition of that term under Title I, the CAA, and the PEOAA, the reader is referred to the previous discussions in this chapter interpreting "incapacity" under those statutes for purposes of inpatient care, pregnancy, and chronic serious health conditions.

Since the definition of "incapacity" includes treatments, the wording of § 630.1202 (definition of "serious health condition," Subsection (1)(ii)(C)) in the alternative of "incapacity" or "treatment" would appear redundant. The comparable regulations interpreting Title I, the CAA, and the PEOAA did the same thing, also without explanation. 29 CFR 825.114(a)(2)(iii), 825.800 (definition of "serious health condition," Subsection (1)(ii)(C)); S. Res. 242, Cong. Rec. S3959, S3962, S3978 (April 23, 1996); 29 CFR 825.114(a)(2)(iii), 825.800 (definition of "serious health condition," Subsection (1)(ii)(C)).

Title II does not define the term "treatment." Rather, it defines the term "continuing treatment" to include (but is not limited to) examinations to determine if there is a serious health condition and evaluations of such conditions if the examinations and evaluations determine that a serious health condition exists. 5 CFR 630.1202 (definition of "serious health condition," Subsection (1)(ii)).

The regulation is similar to, although by no means identical to, the definition of treatment pursuant to Title I, the CAA, and the PEOAA. *See* 29 CFR 825.114(b); S. Res. 242, Cong. Rec. S3959, S3962, S3978 (April 23, 1996); 29 CFR 825.114(b). The primary difference between these definitions is that Title II appears to condition evaluations on the results of the initial examination to determine whether a serious health condition exits. "Treatment" for purposes of Title I, the CAA, and the PEOAA, on the other hand, does not condition evaluations on the results of the initial examination. Evaluations of the serious health condition are treated equally with examinations. *See* 29 CFR 825.114(b); S. Res. 242, Cong. Rec. S3959, S3962, S3978 (April 23, 1996); 29 CFR 825.114(b).

Title II, like its counterparts in Title I, the CAA, and the PEOAA, fails to define what constitutes an "examination" or "evaluation." Under Title II, a health care provider must conduct such examinations and evaluations. That is not the case under Title I, the CAA, and the PEOAA (which fails to identify who can conduct examinations and evaluations). Who is an FMLA-covered "health care provider" is discussed later in this chapter.

Another difference between "continuing treatment" under Title II and "treatment" for purposes of Title I, the CAA, and the PEOAA, is that the former does not exclude routine physical, dental, or eye examination from the definition of "continuing treatment." However, routine physical, dental, and eye examination are excluded from the definition of a "serious health condition." 5 CFR 630.1202 (definition of "serious health condition," Subsection (2)) (serious health condition does not include routine physical, eye, or dental examinations). These terms are also undefined. Presumably, since these terms are affirmatively excluded from the definition of a serious health condition, they are also excluded from inclusion as "continuing treatment." Remember, the Title II definition of "continuing treatment" was not exclusive ("includes, but is not limited to").

Title II, like Title I, the CAA, and the PEOAA, does not require that "the affected individual receive active treatment from a health care provider during the period of incapacity." 5 CFR 630.1202 (definition of "serious health condition," Subsection (1)(ii)(B); *Bhatti v. Dept. of Homeland Security*, No. SF-0752-06-0036-I-1, 2006 MSPB LEXIS 41, at *13 (Feb. 9, 2006), *review* *denied*, 102 MSPR 485 (2006). The term "active treatment" is undefined in the regulations, and unexplained in the comments accompanying the publication of the final OPM FMLA regulations. As discussed in the preceding section of this chapter regarding Title I, the CAA, and the PEOAA, presumably this means that the affected individual (employee or covered family member) must be under the care of, and periodically visit with, a health care provider while suffering from the chronic serious health condition. This is necessary to satisfy the requirement that the individual be receiving "continuing treatment" by a health care provider. However, the affected individual need not see a health care provider for each and every absence due to incapacity during the chronic serious health condition.

(e) Chronic Serious Health Condition Defined

Unlike the other federal sector variants of the FMLA, Title II does not separately define a "chronic serious health condition." Rather, the regulation incorporates directly into the regulation language substantially similar to the definition of "chronic serious condition" for purposes of Title I, the CAA, and the PEOAA. *Compare* 5 CFR 630.1202(a)(ii)(C)(1)–(3), *with,* 29 CFR 825.114(a)(2)(iii), 825.800 (definition of "serious health condition," Subsection (1)(ii)(C)); S. Res. 242, Cong. Rec. S3959, S3962, S3978 (April 23, 1996); 29 CFR 825.114(a)(2)(iii), 825.800 (definition of "serious health condition," Subsection (1)(ii)(C)).

The three requirements for a chronic serious health condition for purposes of Title II are:

1. Requires periodic visits for treatment

    - by a health care provider, or

    - by a health care provider under the direct supervision of the affected individual's health care provider;

   and

2. Continues over an extended period of time (including recurring episodes of a single underlying condition);

   and

3. May cause episodic rather than a continuing period of incapacity (e.g., asthma, diabetes, epilepsy, etc.).

Accord Bhatti v. DHS, No. SF-0752-06-0036-I-1, 2006 MSPB LEXIS 41, at *13 (Feb. 9, 2006), *review denied*, 102 MSPR 485 (2006); *Cole v. DHHS*, No. DC-0752-05-0457-I-1, 2005 MSPB LEXIS 6825, at *7 (Nov. 1, 2005) (illnesses such as asthma, diabetes, or epilepsy that cause episodic rather than continuing incapacity may be considered serious health conditions).

As with the comparable regulations implementing Title I, the CAA, and the PEOAA discussed in the preceding section of this chapter, many of the key terms of this definition are undefined and otherwise unexplained. These key terms are addressed in the subsections that follow.

(f) Periodic Visits

Both singularly and combined, the terms "periodic" and "visits" are undefined. For a further discussion of issues raised by the lack of definition for these terms, see the preceding section of this chapter regarding periodic visits for purposes of Title I, the CAA, and the PEOAA.

(g) Healthcare Provider; Direct Supervision

Title II requires that the periodic treatments received by the covered individual (employee or covered family member) affected by the chronic serious health condition must be provided by a health care provider. This differs from the comparable requirement under Title I, the CAA, and the PEOAA, which would allow non–health care providers (a nurse and physician's assistant) to provide such treatment, provided that they act under the direct supervision of a health care provider.

Title II requires that a health care provider issue the treatment to the affected individual in all cases. The regulations provide two alternatives for periodic treatment by health care providers. First, "a" health care provider may provide such periodic treatment. Second, a health care provider under the direct supervision of the affected individual's health care provider may provide the periodic treatments. It is unexplained how the health care provider in the second alternative who is providing treatment to a patient (the affected individual) is not the "affected individual's health care provider." The language of the second alternative also fails to suggest how an agency is supposed to determine whether a health care provider is not the "affected individual's health care provider."

For that matter, the first alternative does not require that the health care provider be the "affected individual's" primary health care provider. The language of the regulation clearly states "a" health care provider, not "the affected individual's" health care provider. Given the all-inclusive language of the first alternative that "a" or any health care provider can render periodic treatments, it would appear that the second, unclear alternative would rarely be used.

Finally, the second alternative does not explain what "direct supervision" means. This would appear to require a different approach than under the comparable regulation interpreting "direct supervision" for purposes of Title I, the CAA, and the PEOAA. The "direct supervision" under those statutes involved health care providers directly supervising non-healthcare provider nurses and physician's assistants. As the DOL noted in the preamble, "Physician's assistants are not included as health care providers because they are ordinarily only permitted to practice under a doctor's supervision." Preamble, 29 CFR 825.118. Presumably, the same is true for nurses. Title II, on the other hand, requires that the affected individual's health care provider directly supervise another health care provider in the administration of periodic treatments. Since the supervised health care provider could independently practice without such supervision, it would appear that "direct supervision" of one health care provider by another is of a different character than a health care provider supervising, in certain instances, non–health care providers.

(h) Extended Period of Time; Recurring Episodes

As with Title I, the CAA, and the PEOAA, Title II fails to define what would constitute an "extended period of time." Nor does it define what is meant by "recurring episodes." For a further discussion of these issues, the reader is referred to the preceding section of this chapter for Title I, the CAA, and the PEOAA.

In *Bhatti v. DHS*, No. SF-0752-06-0036-I-1, 2006 MSPB LEXIS 41, at *13 (Feb. 9, 2006), *review denied*, 102 MSPR 485 (2006), the Board found that a psychological condition did not involve an extended period of time where the evidence established that the employee was seen nine times before being diagnosed with personality and depressive disorders.

(i) Episodic Incapacity

Similar to "extended period of time," Title II fails to define what is meant by episodic periods of incapacity. Presumably, it means the incapacity caused by a chronic serious health condition need not meet any minimum durational period, such as the "more than three days" requirement discussed previously for another form of serious health condition. For a further discussion of these issues, the reader is referred to the preceding section of this chapter for Title I, the CAA, and the PEOAA.

f. Permanent or Long Term Incapacity

(1) Title I, the CAA, and the PEOAA

(a) General Rule

A "serious health condition" within the meaning of the FMLA means an illness, injury, impairment, or physical or mental condition that also involves continuing treatment by a health care provider for any one or more of the following:

> (iv) A period of incapacity that is permanent or long–term due to a condition for which treatment may not be effective.

29 CFR 825.114(a)(2)(iv), 825.800 (definition of "serious health condition," Subsection (1)(ii)(D)); S. Res. 242, Cong. Rec. S3959, S3962, S3978 (April 23, 1996); 29 CFR 825.114(a)(2)(iv), 825.800 (definition of "serious health condition," Subsection (1)(ii)(D)); *see Reich v. The Standard Register Co.*, No. 96–0284–R, 1997 U.S. Dist. LEXIS 3021, at *8 (W.D. Va. Jan. 17, 1997).

A review of the regulatory history and key terms of a chronic serious health condition follows.

(b) Regulatory Development

Long-term or permanent conditions were recognized as serious health conditions in the interim DOL regulations. *See* 58 Fed. Reg. 31794 (June 4, 1993), § 825.114(b)(3) (referred to as "serious long-term condition or disability"). Like chronic serious health conditions, the interim regulations required that a serious long-term condition either be incurable or so serious that, if not treated, it would likely result in a period of incapacity of more than three calendar days. *Id*.

The definition of a "serious long-term condition" received many critical comments prior to the DOL's publication of the final Title I regulations. As with chronic conditions (which serious long-term conditions was paired with in the interim regulations), the comments criticized the definition as too restrictive. Preamble, 29 CFR 825.114. They argued that application of the "more than three days" rule did not make sense in the context of a long-term or permanent condition, as such condition may only result in episodic periods of incapacity necessitating the need for leave. They also argued that "curability" was not a proper test determining a "serious health condition" because many incurable disabilities require continuing treatment over long periods of time. Preamble, 29 CFR 825.114.

In light of these and other comments, the DOL modified the requirements for long-term or permanent conditions in the final implementing regulations. With respect to long-term and permanent conditions in particular, the DOL (Preamble, 29 CFR 825.114) stated:

> The portion of the definition dealing with long-term chronic conditions such as Alzheimer's or a severe stroke has been modified to delete the reference to the condition being incurable, and to require instead that the condition involve a period of incapacity which is permanent or long-term and of which treatment may not be effective. Therefore, in this situation, as under the interim rule, it is only necessary that the patient be under the supervision of a health care provider, than receiving active treatment.

As with chronic serious health conditions, the DOL also eliminated the requirement that long-term or permanent conditions result in a period of incapacity of more than three days if not treated.

(c) Permanent or Long-Term

The terms "permanent" and "long-term" are not defined for purposes of the FMLA. "Permanent" presumably means that the serious health condition of the affected individual (employee or covered family member) is life-long. It is unclear what minimum length of time would be necessary for a condition to be considered "long-term." As animated by the requirement that treatment for the condition may not be effective and the examples provided (severe stroke, terminal stages of cancer, Alzheimer's), it would appear that "long-term" is measured in years, not a few months or weeks, or life-long, whichever is longer.

Again, this is an area where an agency should request and rely on the medical certification to establish that the condition is permanent or long-term.

(d) A Period

A "period" of incapacity is undefined. Presumably, it means the same thing as "any" period of incapacity. Again, the main point is that there is no minimum durational period of incapacity that must be met in order for an absence for a permanent or long-term condition to fall within the definition of an FMLA-qualifying serious health condition.

(e) Incapacity

"Incapacity" is not defined in § 825.114(a)(2)(iv). For other serious health conditions, incapacity is consistently defined to mean the inability to work, attend school or perform other regular daily activities due to the serious health conditions, treatment, therefore, and recovery therefrom. 29 CFR 825.114(a)(1), 825.114(a)(2)(I); S. Res. 242, Cong. Rec. S3959, S3962 (April 23, 1996); 29 CFR 825.114(a)(1), 825.114(a)(2)(I). The regulation fails to define its terms, particularly with regard to what would constitute "other regular daily activities."

Note that no minimum period of incapacity is required. Short periods of time (minutes, hours or days) would fall within this definition of a serious health condition if it meets the definition of incapacity. Of course, the definition would also cover long periods of incapacity of days, weeks, or months, up to the maximum of 12 workweeks of FMLA leave each leave year that an employee is entitled for all serious health conditions.

(f) Treatment

The term "incapacity" includes "treatment" for the permanent or long-term serious health condition. "Treatment" is a defined term that means examinations to determine if the condition exits and evaluations of the condition. 29 CFR 825.114(b); S. Res. 242, Cong. Rec. S3959, S3963 (April 23, 1996); 29 CFR 825.114(b). Treatment does not include routine physical, eye, or dental examination. 29 CFR 825.114(b); S. Res. 242, Cong. Rec. S3959, S3963 (April 23, 1996); 29 CFR 825.114(b). The terms "examinations," "evaluations," "routine," "physical," "eye," and "dental" are undefined. Nor does § 825.114 identify whether or not such "examinations" and "evaluations" must be performed by a health care provider within the meaning of the FMLA. Presumably, such "examinations" and "evaluations" must be performed by licensed a health care professional practicing within the scope of authority.

According to the regulation, the "employee or family member must be under the continuing supervision of, but need not be receiving active treatment by, a health care provider." 29 CFR 825.114(a)(2)(iv), 825.800 (definition of "serious health condition," Subsection (1)(ii)(D)); S. Res. 242, Cong. Rec. S3959, S3962, S3978 (April 23, 1996); 29 CFR 825.114(a)(2)(iv), 825.800 (definition of "serious health condition," Subsection (1)(ii)(D)). The key terms of this provision are not defined. An affected individual who is not under the "continuing treatment" of a health care provider is not covered by this definition of a serious health condition, even if the individual has a permanent or long-term condition. *See Reich v. The Standard Register Co.*, No. 96-0284-R, 1997 U.S. Dist. LEXIS 3021, at *8 (W.D. Va. Jan. 17, 1997) (an employee with arthritis did not have serious health condition absent evidence of inpatient care, incapacitation of more than three days, and where employee was no longer receiving active treatment).

What would constitute "continuing supervision" by a health care provider is not defined by the regulations. Nor is the term "active treatment" defined. The provision appears to respond to comments made before publication of the final DOL regulations. In pertinent part, the comment at issue (Preamble, 29 CFR 825.114) provides:

> Chicagoland Chamber of Commerce also considered the "continuing supervision" concept too vague, questioning whether "supervision" required the individual to actually be examined by the health care provider or to report in on some regular basis, or whether instructions to report in if the condition changes was sufficient. It considered treatment a definitive concept that could be proven, whereas "supervision" could not which would invite absence and litigation.

The DOL also noted in the comments (Preamble, 29 CFR 825.114) the following:

> It is envisioned that a patient would be under continuing supervision in this context, for example, where the patient is advised to call if the condition is not improved.

Viewed in light of the comments accompanying the publication of the final DOL regulations implementing Title I, it would appear that "continuing supervision" may be nothing more than a health care provider advising the affected individual with a permanent or long-term serious health condition that he or she should call if the condition is not improved. "Active treatment," meaning an actual examination of the affected individual by a health care provider, is not required. Of course, "continuing supervision" could involve more than an instruction to call if the condition worsens or flares-up, including actual treatment.

Note that the wording of the regulation does not tie "continuing supervision" of a health care provider to the affected individual (i.e., the person with the permanent or long-term condition). Rather, the regulation simply provides that either the employee or family member must be under the continuing supervision of a health care provider. This could result in a situation where, for example, a covered family member has a permanent or long-term serious health condition, but is not under the "continuing supervision" of a health care provider. The employee requesting FMLA leave "to care for" that individual is under the "continuing supervision" of a health care provider, but for a completely different illness. As currently written, this situation would satisfy the requirements for a permanent or long-term serious health condition. This result presumably is not what the drafters of § 825.114(a)(2)(iv) had in mind. Rather, the intended meaning of § 825.114(a)(2)(iv) is likely that the covered individual with the permanent or long-term serious health condition must be under the "continuing supervision" of a health care provider.

Finally, it is curious that the DOL chose to exclude "active treatment" directly in § 825.114(a)(2)(iv) rather than simply adding that section to § 825.114(e). That § (29 CFR 825.114(e)) provides that absences attributable to incapacity due to pregnancy or for chronic serious health conditions qualify even though the employee or immediate family member does not receive treatment from a health care provider during the absence. The failure of the DOL to add permanent or long-term serious health conditions to § 824.114(e) suggests that "active treatment" and "treatment from a health care provider during the absence" are not the same thing. The former is presumably broader than the latter.

(g) Condition for Which Treatment May Not be Effective

The regulation gives examples rather than a concrete definition of what is meant by a "condition for which treatment may not be effective." The examples include Alzheimer's, a severe stroke, or the terminal stages of cancer. 29 CFR 825.114(a)(2)(iv), 825.800 (definition of "serious health condition," Subsection (1)(ii)(D)); S. Res. 242, Cong. Rec. S3959, S3962, S3978 (April 23, 1996); 29 CFR 825.114(a)(2)(iv), 825.800 (definition of "serious health condition," Subsection (1)(ii)(D)). Some of these conditions were also cited by Congress as examples of serious health conditions. *See also* S. Rep. 103–3, g. 29 (strokes, most cancers).

One of the alternative definitions of a long-term serious health condition in the interim DOL regulation required that the condition be incurable. The term "incurable" was criticized as being an improper test for a serious health condition or continuing treatment. The commentators (Preamble, 29 CFR 825.114) noted that:

> [M]any incurable disabilities require continuing treatment that has nothing to do with during the condition. Some point out that conditions such as epilepsy, traumatic brain injury, and cerebral palsy are typically conditions which are not "curable" in the generally accepted sense, but are conditions for which training and therapy can help restore, maintain or develop function or prevent deterioration, and noted that people with disabilities have struggled for a generation or more to overcome the image that disabilities are, or should be viewed as, curable or incurable.

In response to such comments, the DOL changed the phrasing of the regulation from "incurable" to its current verbiage.

(2) Title II

Title II also recognizes a permanent or long-term condition as a serious health condition covered by the FMLA. The requirements are substantially the same as those under the comparable regulations implementing Title I, the CAA, and the PEOAA. There are, however, differences.

(a) General Rule

A serious health condition means an illness, injury, impairment, or physical or mental condition that also involves continuing treatment by a health care provider, including one or more of the following:

> (D) A period of incapacity that is permanent or long-term due to a condition for which treatment may not be effective.

5 CFR 630.1202 (definition of "serious health condition," Subsection (1)(ii)(D)); *Davis v. DHS*, No. SF-0752-04-0760-I-1, 2005 MSPB LEXIS 898, at *27 (Feb. 22, 2005), *pet. denied*, 100 MSPR 62 (2005), *vacated, remanded*, 2007 U.S. App. LEXIS 12593 (Fed. Cir. May 30, 2007).

A review of the regulatory development and key terms follows.

(b) Regulatory Development

Like Title I, the CAA, and the PEOAA, the interim OPM regulations also required long-term serious health conditions be incurable and, if untreated, result in a period of incapacity of more than three days. *See, e.g.*, 58 Fed. Reg. 39596 (July 23, 1993), § 630.1202 (definition of "serious health condition"). Like the DOL, the OPM received comments prior to the publication of the final regulations implementing Title II of the FMLA. 61 Fed. Reg. 64441 (December 5, 1996), Preamble,

5 CFR 630.1202 (definition of "serious health condition"). In response to those comments, and consistent with the DOL's final regulations, the OPM significantly revised the definition of "serious health condition." *Id*. In pertinent part, the OPM stated that:

> The definition of long-term, chronic conditions such as Alzheimer's or a severe stroke has been modified to delete the reference to the condition being incurable and to require instead that the condition involve a period of incapacity that is permanent or long term and for which treatment may not be effective.

The OPM also did away with the requirement that, if untreated, a permanent or long-term serious health condition had to cause more than three days of incapacity.

(c) Permanent or Long-Term

The terms "permanent" or "long-term" are undefined. These same terms were undefined for purposes of Title I, the CAA, and the PEOAA. The reader is referred to the analysis of what "permanent" and "long-term" may mean for purposes of the Title I, the CAA, and the PEOAA set forth in the preceding section of this chapter.

(d) A Period

A "period" of incapacity is undefined. Presumably, as with Title I, the CAA, and the PEOAA, "a period" means the same thing as "any period" of incapacity. Again, the main point is that there is no minimum durational period of incapacity that must be met in order for an absence for a permanent or long-term condition to fall within the definition of an FMLA-qualifying serious health condition.

(e) Incapacity

"Incapacity" means the inability to work, attend school, or perform other regular daily activities because of a serious health condition or treatment for or recovery from a serious health condition. 5 CFR 630.1202 (definition of "incapacity").

The term "inability" is undefined. It is not clear, then whether such "inability" must be total or whether something less would suffice. The meaning of "inability" with respect to work is important where the employee seeks leave for his or her own permanent or long-term serious health condition. An employee is only entitled to FMLA leave for his or her own serious health condition where such condition renders the employee unable to perform one or more essential functions of his or her position. 5 USC 6382(a)(1)(D); 5 CFR 630.1203(4). If "inability to work" does not mean the same thing as "one or more essential functions," an employee who could not perform one or more essential functions might still be precluded from taking FMLA leave where the condition did not render the employee unable to work. In that case, the employee would not have a serious health condition.

The phrase "perform other regular daily activities" is also undefined. The breadth of the phrase is presumably necessary to cover the full range of activities that might be enjoyed by employees themselves, as well as the employee's covered family members. That same breadth, however, lends itself to abuse. For example, the regular daily activity of a parent could be consuming large quantities of Twinkies. It is doubtful that the inability to consume large quantities of Twinkies because of a permanent or long-term serious health condition is what Congress had in mind when it enacted the FMLA.

(f) Treatment

"Treatment" is not a defined term under Title II. The similar term "continuing treatment," however, is defined in the regulations. "Continuing treatment" by a health care provider includes (but is not limited to) examinations to determine if there is a serious health condition and evaluations of such conditions if the examinations and evaluations determine that a serious health condition exists. 5 CFR 630.1202 (definition of "continuing treatment"). This definition is substantially similar to, although not identical to, the definition of treatment for purposes of Title I, the CAA, and the PEOAA. 29 CFR 825.114(b); S. Res. 242, Cong. Rec. S3959, S3963 (April 23, 1996); 29 CFR 825.114(b). Since "continuing" refers to duration, the definition of "continuing treatment" would appear to also define "treatment" for purposes of Title II.

The affected individual must be under the continuing supervision of, but need not be receiving active treatment by, a health care provider. 5 CFR 630.1202 (definition of "serious health condition," Subsection (1)(ii)(D)). The terms "continuing supervision" and "active treatment" are not defined or otherwise described in the regulations.

For a further discussion of this issue, the reader is referred to the previous section of this chapter addressing "treatment" for purposes of a permanent or long–term serious health condition under Title I, the CAA, and the PEOAA.

(g) Condition for Which Treatment May Not be Effective

Tile I does not further define the phrase "condition for which treatment may not be effective." The regulation does, however, provide the following examples of conditions that would fit within this definition. 5 CFR 630.1202 (definition of "serious health condition," Subsection (1)(ii)(D)). The examples, "Alzheimer's, severe stroke, or terminal states of a disease," are nearly identical to those cited in the comparable provisions implementing Title I, the CAA, and the PEOAA. *See* 29 CFR 825.114(a)(2)(iv) (Alzheimer's, a severe stoke, or the terminal stages of cancer), 825.800 (definition of "serious health condition," Subsection (1)(ii)(D) (same)); S. Res. 242, Cong. Rec. S3959, S3962, S3978 (April 23, 1996); 29 CFR 825.114(a)(2)(iv) (same), 825.800 (definition of "serious health condition," Subsection (1)(ii)(D) (same)).

For a further discussion of this issue, the reader is referred to the previous section of this chapter addressing conditions for which treatment may not be effective, for purposes of a permanent or long–term serious health condition under Title I, the CAA, and the PEOAA.

g. Multiple Treatments

Finally, a serious health condition for continuing treatment within the meaning of the FMLA includes absences to receive multiple treatments by a health care provider in two circumstances: (1) for restorative surgery; and (2) where the condition, if untreated, would likely result in a period of incapacity of more than three days. Here again, similarities and differences exist between the various federal sector variants of the FMLA.

(1) Title I, the CAA, and the PEOAA

(a) General Rule

A "serious health condition" within the meaning of the FMLA means an illness, injury, impairment, or physical or mental condition that also involves continuing treatment by a health care provider, including one or more of the following:

> (v) Any period of absence to receive multiple treatments (including any period of recovery therefrom) by a health care provider or a provider of health care services under orders of, or on referral by, a health care provider, either for restorative surgery after an accident or other injury, or for a condition that would likely result in a period of incapacity for more than three consecutive calendar days in the absence of medical intervention or treatment.

29 CFR 825.114(a)(2)(v), 825.800 (definition of "serious health condition," Subsection (1)(ii)(E)); S. Res. 242, Cong. Rec. S3959, S3962, S3978 (April 23, 1996); 29 CFR 825.114(a)(2)(v), 825.800 (definition of "serious health condition," Subsection (1)(ii)(E)); *see Williams v. Illinois Dept. of Corrections*, No. 05-cv-4227-JPG, 2007 U.S. Dist. LEXIS 17119, at *18 (S.D. Ill. March 9, 2007); *Merritt v. E.F. Transit, Inc.*, No. IP02–0393–C–H/K, 2004 U.S. Dist. LEXIS 4310, at *16 (S.D. Ind. March 11, 2004); *Washington v. Fort James Operating Co.*, 110 F. Supp. 2d 1325, 1333–34 (D. Ore. 2000); *Bauer v. Dayton–Walther Corp.*, 910 F. Supp. 306, 310 (E.D. Ky. 1996), *aff'd*, 118 F.3d 1109 (6th Cir. 1997).

Leave from work to receive kidney dialysis qualifies as an FMLA-covered serious health condition under this definition. *Williams v. Illinois Dept. of Corrections*, No. 05-cv-4227-JPG, 2007 U.S. Dist. LEXIS 17119, at *18 (S.D. Ill. March 9, 2007).

In *Merritt v. E.F. Transit, Inc.*, No. IP02–0393–C–H/K, 2004 U.S. Dist. LEXIS 4310, at *16 (S.D. Ind. March 11, 2004), the court found that the employee failed to establish that his condition satisfied the multiple treatment definition of a serious health condition. The court noted that the regulation clearly provides that FMLA leave taken by the employee must be for the employee "to receive multiple treatments" for the condition in question. The court found that Merritt "simply did not receive any treatments at all on the day that he attempted to use FMLA leave." He did not see his doctor or physical therapist or take his pain medication that day. According to the court, absent receipt of treatment, the FMLA does not "protect his unilateral decision to stay home."

A review of the regulatory development and key terms follows.

(b) Regulatory Development

The interim DOL regulations did not recognize this condition as a separate serious health condition. However, the elements of this definition may be found in the interim regulations for chronic or long-term health conditions. Specifically, the alternatives for FMLA coverage for a chronic or long-term health condition were that such condition was either incurable or "so serious that, if not treated, would likely result in a period of incapacity of more than three calendar days...." 58 Fed. Reg. 31794, 31817 (June 4, 1993), § 825.114(a)(3).

As discussed in previous section of this chapter for chronic and permanent or long-term conditions, comments received by the DOL prior to the publication of the final regulations implementing Title I criticized the aforesaid interim regulations governing chronic and long-term health conditions as too restrictive. Preamble, 29 CFR 8725.114. In response, the DOL significantly revised the FMLA definition of "serious health condition." With respect to § 825.114(a)(2)(v) in particular, the DOL (Preamble, 29 CFR 825.114) provided the following explanation:

> The Department has also included a definition to deal with serious health conditions which are not ordinarily incapacitating (at least at the current state of the patient's condition), but for which treatments are being given because the condition would likely result in a period of incapacity of more than three consecutive calendar days in the absence of medical intervention or treatment. The regulation requires multiple treatments, and includes as examples patients receiving chemotherapy or radiation for cancer, dialysis for kidney disease, or physical therapy for severe arthritis. Multiple treatments for restorative surgery after an accident or other injury are also specifically included. The previous requirement that the condition be chronic or long-term has been deleted because cancer treatments, for example, might not meet that test if immediate intervention occurs.

Finally, the creation of the regulation may be traced back to the examples of serious health conditions given in the legislative history. Those examples included a cancer patient's need for periodic leave for chemotherapy or radiation treatments. S. Rep. 103–3, p. 28. The legislative history gives the example of an individual who suffered a serious industrial accident who may require periodic physical therapy. *Id.*

(c) Any Period

By its terms, this serious health condition applies to any period of absence to receive or recover from treatments. "Any period" can be from minutes up to the entire 12 workweeks of FMLA leave than an eligible employee is entitled to receive during the course of any given leave year. *See Washington v. Fort James Operating Co.*, 110 F. Supp. 2d 1325, 1333–34 (D. Ore. 2000) (absences on two non-consecutive days may qualify as FMLA leave when taken for treatment of a condition that would likely result in a period of incapacity of more than three consecutive calendar days in the absence of medical intervention).

(d) Absence to Receive

The entitlement to leave under this serious health condition is for an "absence" to receive multiple treatments. The term "absence" is not defined in the regulations. The use of the term "absence," however, is significant. The other FMLA-qualifying serious health conditions for continuing treatment all required a period of "incapacity" caused by the serious health condition. "Incapacity" is a defined term which includes an inability to work, attend school, or perform other regular daily activities due to the serious health condition, treatment therefore, or recovery therefrom. *See* 29 CFR 825.114(a)(1), 825.114(a)(2)(I). "Incapacity" is not a requirement for a serious health condition due to multiple treatments.

The "absence" must be to receive or recover from multiple treatments. Note that the definition of "incapacity" also includes treatment and recovery as forms of incapacity. By process of elimination, it would appear that "absence" does not cover an inability to work, attend school, or perform other regular daily activities. It does however, cover multiple treatments for the serious health condition, and recovery from such treatments. In that sense, "absence" is similar to two of the three forms of "incapacity."

The lack of coverage for an employee or covered family member's inability to work, attend work or school, or perform other regular daily activities, is found in the regulatory history. The DOL indicated that a serious health condition for multiple treatments was created "to deal with serious health conditions which are not ordinarily incapacitating (at least at the current state of the patient's condition)..." Preamble, 29 CFR 825.114.

The bottom line is that, when you think of this form of serious health condition, the absence must be to receive treatments or recovery from such treatments. It is not because the serious health condition rendered the affected individual incapable of working or otherwise performing other regular daily activities. The latter situation may, however, be covered by other serious health conditions.

Note that the regulations fail to indicate "a period of absence" from what. That is, does it cover a period of absence from work? A period of absence from school? Presumably, the answer is that any absence to attend treatments would suffice. The term "absence," however, is an awkward fit when you apply it to examples of the performance of other regular daily activities. Most people would not consider someone "absent" when he or she is unable to perform their regular daily activity of watching television, or eating Twinkies. As commonly used "absence" connotes a certain responsibility to be somewhere doing something. I do not mean to imply that "absence" would not apply outside of work, school, or similar activities. It is quite possible for someone to be "absent" from his or her responsibility to clean the house, go on a planned fishing trip, or similar activity. It is simply harder for me to accept that someone could be "absent" from a completely unplanned and/or discretionary activity.

(e) Multiple Treatments and Recovery

The absence must be to receive multiple treatments, or to recover from such treatments. "Multiple" is not defined. Clearly, "multiple" means more than one treatment. *See Bauer v. Dayton–Walther* Corp., 910 F. Supp. 306, 310 (E.D. Ky. 1996) (an employee who did not receive multiple treatments not covered by this definition of FMLA "serious health condition"), *aff'd*, 118 F.3d 1109 (6th Cir. 1997). What is unclear is whether more than one treatment is needed during each absence, or whether treatment is required during each absence of multiple absences. The confusion stems from the actual wording, which is susceptible to alternative interpretations.

The wording of the regulation suggests that each absence must involve multiple treatments. In pertinent part, the regulation refers to any period (singular) of absence (singular) to receive multiple treatments (plural). Alternatively, the regulation could be read emphasizing "any period of absence." Essentially, the regulation would read, "any period of absence for the receipt of, or recovery from, multiple treatments...." Such an interpretation would appear to be what was intended. As amplified by the examples, nothing in the comments to the final regulation suggests that an affected individual absent to receive chemotherapy or kidney dialysis must incur two or more treatments during each absence in order for the definition to apply. Rather, it would appear from the listed examples that periodic absences will occur over time in order for the affected individual to receive treatment in order to avoid lengthy periods of incapacity.

The regulation fails to identify a time limit during which such multiple treatments must occur. The lack of a time period as the basis for measurement necessarily means that the determination whether an affected individual meets the requirement of multiple treatments may take place over months or even years. Like "periodic treatments" previously discussed, this may make it difficult for agencies to determine whether a condition will meet the "multiple" requirement, at least where such treatments are prospective. Again, agencies will have to rely on their ability to request medical certification from the employee in support of the request for leave to verify that "multiple treatments" are involved.

(f) Health Care Provider

The multiple treatments must be administered by:

1. A health care provider; or

2. By a provider of health care services under orders of, on referral by, a health care provider.

The term "health care provider" is addressed in detail later in this chapter. The term "provider of health care services" is undefined. The phrase "provider of health care services" was used regarding the first example of a serious health condition requiring continuing treatment. *See* 29 CFR 825.114(a)(2)(i)(A), 825.800 (definition of "serious health condition," Subsection (1)(ii)(A)(1)); S. Res. 242, Cong. Rec. S3959, S3962, S3978 (April 23, 1996); 29 CFR 825.114(a)(2)(i)(A), 825.800

(definition of "serious health condition," Subsection (1)(ii)(A)(1)). There, one example, a physical therapist, was provided. 29 CFR 825.114(a)(2)(i)(A), 825.800 (definition of "serious health condition," Subsection (1)(ii)(A)(1)); S. Res. 242, Cong. Rec. S3959, S3962, S3978 (April 23, 1996); 29 CFR 825.114(a)(2)(i)(A).

No explanation was given for use of the term "under orders of." Outside the military or a national emergency, it would appear unlikely that a health care provider could "order" a "provider of health care services," whoever that might be, to provide treatment. Although "referral" is not defined, it is commonly understood in this context to mean to send or direct for treatment.

(g) Restorative Surgery After an Accident or Other Injury

The periods of absence to receive or recover from multiple treatments provided by covered health care personnel must be for restorative surgery after an accident or other injury. The term "restorative surgery" is not defined by the Act or regulations. Clearly, however, at least for purposes of this alternative of multiple treatments, not all treatments are covered. Only those treatments involving "surgery" are covered. "Surgery" is defined as a branch of medicine concerned with diseases and conditions requiring or amenable to operative or manual procedures. Webster's Ninth New Collegiate Dictionary (Merriam–Webster, Inc. 1988). As more commonly understood, surgery is where a doctor cuts a patient in an attempt to improve the patient's physical condition. By using the term "surgery," the regulation necessarily diminishes the pool of "health care providers" who can provide or refer treatment.

Moreover, not all surgery is covered by this serious health condition. Only "restorative" surgery is covered. The term "restorative" is not defined. Turning again to my handy dictionary, "restorative" is defined as "of or relating to restoration." Webster's Ninth New Collegiate Dictionary (Merriam–Webster, Inc. 1988). "Restoration" is defined as "a bringing back to a former position or condition." An example is given of the replacement of missing teeth or crowns. *Id.*

Finally, the treatment or recovery from treatment as a result of restorative surgery is further limited to post–accident or injury situation. Surgery that does not fix that which was already impaired is not covered.

The terms "accident" and "other injury" are not defined. Note also that there is no time frame attached to when the accident or other injury occurred and when the restorative surgery takes place. Months, years, even decades could go by between when the accident or other injury was incurred and the absence to receive multiple treatments for restorative surgery.

(h) Condition That Would Likely Result in Incapacity of More Than Three Days

The second form of "multiple treatment" serious health condition involves conditions that would likely result in a period of incapacity of more than three consecutive calendar days in the absence of medical intervention or treatment. 29 CFR 825.114(a)(2)(v), 825.800 (definition of "serious health condition," Subsection (1)(ii)(E)); S. Res. 242, Cong. Rec. S3959, S3962, S3978 (April 23, 1996); 29 CFR 825.114(a)(2)(v), 825.800 (definition of "serious health condition," Subsection (1)(ii)(E)); *see Washington v. Fort James Operating Co.*, 110 F. Supp. 2d 1325, 1333–34 (D. Ore. 2000).

Let's be clear that this provision does *not* require that an employee or covered family member actually incur a period of incapacity of more than three consecutive calendar days. Rather, the preconditions that we discussed earlier—any period of absence, to receive multiple treatments, by a covered health care provider, etc.,—still apply. This condition applies for any period of absence (e.g., minutes, hours, days, or weeks). Those absences must be used to receive multiple treatments. The treatments must be administered or referred by covered health care providers.

This "multiple treatment" alternative adds that the affected individual (employee or covered family member) must have a "condition" that, in the absence of medical intervention or treatment, would likely result in a period of incapacity of more than three consecutive calendar days. The regulation necessarily asks agencies, with the assistance of supporting medical certifications, to make an educated guess whether, if the employee does not receive the multiple treatments, the condition will incapacitate the employee for more than three consecutive calendar days.

Note that the "condition" is undefined. The regulations do, however, provide a number of examples, including chemotherapy or radiation treatment for cancer, physical therapy for severe arthritis, and dialysis for kidney failure. Absent a defined list, all health conditions could potentially qualify as a serious health condition under this regulation, provided that all other conditions are met.

The regulations do not indicate how strong a likelihood there must be that more than three consecutive calendar days will result in the absence of medical intervention or treatment. Nor do the regulations indicate whether such likelihood is calculated based on a hypothetical "reasonable patient" or based on the specific facts of the affected individual on whom the request for FMLA leave is based. Courts have held that the condition must be evaluated based on what it actually was during the relevant period of time, not what it theoretically become. See Bauer v. Dayton–Walther Corp., 910 F. Supp. 306, 310 (E.D. Ky. 1996), aff'd, 118 F.3d 1109 (6th Cir. 1997); Seidle v. Provident Mut. Life Ins., Co., 871 F. Supp. 238, 246 (E.D. Pa. 1994) (same). At least one court stated that the courts and the employer should defer to the health care providers determination whether a condition qualifies as a serious health condition under this definition. See Washington v. Fort James Operating Co., 110 F. Supp. 2d 1325, 1333–34 (D. Ore. 2000).

No explanation is provided for the term "medical intervention" in addition to treatment. As this serious health condition only recognizes leave for absences to receive or recover from multiple treatments, "medical intervention" must either mean the same thing as "treatment," in which case it is covered, or it means something different than treatment, in which case it would not form the basis for a request for FMLA leave.

The use of the phrase "medical intervention or treatment" suggests that the calculation of whether the affected individual may incur more than three consecutive days of incapacity is based on the absence of "medical" treatment. The term "medical" is undefined. It is not at all clear that all FMLA–covered health care providers can provide "medical treatment." Most states have laws prohibiting the practice of medicine without a license. The provision of "medical treatment" or "medical intervention" would appear to require that the individual providing same be licensed to practice medicine. This potentially raises two issues.

First, the calculation of whether the absence of medical treatment may result in more than three days incapacity would appear to require a medical determination. Such a medical determination can only be made by licensed medical professional acting within the scope of the license. That would appear to exclude any number of FMLA–covered health care providers. As such, a certification from a health care provider who is not licensed to provide medical treatment would not be sufficient to confirm the existence of a serious health condition under this regulation.

Second, while a medical professional acting within the scope of authority is arguably needed to certify that the affected individual would suffer incapacity of more than three days absent medical treatment, an FMLA–covered health care provider can actually provide the multiple treatments. Again, the FMLA–covered health care provider may or may not be able to provide "medical treatment" as his or her license may limit what health services he or she can provide.

(2) Title II

Title II also recognizes multiple treatments as a qualifying serious health condition. The standard is substantially the same as previously discussed for purposes of Title I, the CAA, and the PEOAA. The only real difference relates to the issue of health care providers who can provide the multiple treatments.

(a) General Rule

An FMLA–qualifying serious health condition means an illness, injury, impairment, or physical or mental condition that also involves continuing treatment by a health care provider including one or more of the following:

(E) Any period of absence to receive multiple treatments (including any period of recovery) by a health care provider or by a provider of health care services under orders of, or on referral by, a health care provider, either for restorative surgery after an accident or other injury or for a condition that would likely result in a period of incapacity of more than three consecutive calendar days in the absence of medical intervention or treatment.

5 CFR 630.1202 (definition of "serious health condition," Subsection (1)(ii)(2)(E)).

(b) Regulatory Development

Absences to receive multiple treatments were not specifically recognized in the interim OPM regulations implementing Title II of the FMLA. See 58 Fed. Reg. 39596 (July 23, 1993). Rather, like Title I, elements of what would become the final OPM regulation recognize multiple treatments as a form of FMLA serious health condition in the definition of a "serious health condition." Specifically, one of the alternative definitions of a "serious health condition" contained in the OPM interim regulations included an illness, injury, impairment, or physical or mental condition that also included:

> Continuing treatment by (or under the supervision of) a health care provider for a chronic or long-term health condition that is incurable or so serious a health condition, if not treated, would likely result in a period of incapacity of more than three calendar days; or for prenatal care.

58 Fed. Reg. 39596, 39604 (July 23, 1993), § 630.1202 (definition of "serious health condition," Subsection (3)).

As under Title I, the OPM's definition of "serious health condition" set forth in the interim regulations was criticized as too restrictive. Consistent with the DOL's final regulations, OPM significantly revised the definition of "serious health condition" for purposes of Title II of the FMLA. Preamble, 5 CFR 630.1201 (definition of "serious health condition"). Among the changes made was recognition of serious health conditions that are not ordinarily incapacitating, but for which multiple treatments are being given because the condition would likely result in a period of incapacity of more than three consecutive calendar days in the absence of medical intervention or treatment (e.g., chemotherapy or radiation for cancer, dialysis for kidney disease, physical therapy for severe arthritis, or multiple treatments for restorative surgery after an accident or other injury). Preamble, 5 CFR 630.1202 (definition of "serious health condition").

On the surface, then, the OPM regulations defining this serious health condition share much of the same regulatory development as comparable regulations issued by the DOL.

(c) Any Period

Any period of absence is covered by this serious health condition. This serious health condition does not require a minimum period of incapacity or absence in order for the absence to be FMLA-qualifying. As long as the absence is for the purpose specified in the regulation, it is covered, no matter how short or long the absence, up to the maximum 12 administrative workweeks of leave available to an employee each leave year.

One of the two alternative forms of covered absences to receive or recover from multiple treatments does include a minimum durational requirement. That requirement, however, does not impose a minimum "more than three days" period of absence to receive or recover from multiple treatments. Rather, the rule is saying that, if the affected individual is not, for example, given a day off to receive kidney dialysis treatment, the affected individual is likely to suffer a period of incapacity of more than three days. The rule operates the same for all federal sector variants of the FMLA.

(d) Absence

The term "absence" is not defined by the Title II regulations. As discussed more fully in the preceding section of this chapter for multiple treatments under Title I, the CAA, and the PEOAA, the use of the word "absence" instead of the defined term "incapacity" would appear to be of significance. "Absence" to receive or recover from multiple treatments would appear to exclude absences for an affected individual's inability to work, attend school, or perform other regular daily activities. Absence, in that regard, is strictly limited to the receipt of multiple treatments, and to recover from such treatments. It is not intended for downtime caused by the underlying serious health condition itself. Of course, such downtime (e.g., inability to work, attend school, and perform other regular daily activities) could be covered by another FMLA-qualifying serious health condition, provided that the circumstances meet all the requirements of that other condition. The same rule applies for purposes of Title I, the CAA, and the PEOAA.

(e) Multiple Treatments

The OPM regulations do not set a minimum number of treatments in order to meet the "multiple" treatment requirement. The other federal sector variants of the FMLA also fail to define the meaning of "multiple" treatments. Two or more treatments, presumably, would be required to meet the definition of "multiple" treatments.

The OPM regulations also fail to provide a time frame in which these multiple treatments are to take place. As such, the multiple treatments could take place over the course of days, months, or even years. However, the examples given, chemotherapy, dialysis, physical therapy for severe arthritis, suggest a shorter time frame in between treatments. Again, the regulation does not provide a time frame, or require that the treatments be provided at regular intervals. The same rule applies to the other federal sector variants of the FMLA.

(f) Health Care Provider

The OPM regulations define who may provide multiple treatments to the affected individual differently than the comparable provisions (previously discussed in this chapter) implementing Title I, the CAA, and the PEOAA. For purposes of Title II, the multiple treatments must be provided either by:

1. A health care provider, or
2. A provider of health care services under orders of, or on referral by, a health care provider.

A "health care provider" is a defined term that is addressed more fully later in this chapter. The term "provider of health care services" is not a defined term. Neither the regulations nor the comments accompanying publication of the OPM final regulations identify examples of who or what might be considered to be a "provider of health care services." For purposes of Title I, the CAA, and the PEOAA, a physical therapist was identified as an example of a "provider of health care services." *See* 29 CFR 825.114(a)(2)(i)(A), 825.800 (definition of "serious health condition," Subsection (1)(ii)(A)(1)); S. Res. 242, Cong. Rec. S3959, S3962, S3978 (April 23, 1996); 29 CFR 825.114(a)(2)(i)(A). Of course, just because a physical therapist is an example of a "provider of health care services" for purposes of Title I, the CAA, and the PEOAA, it does not mean that it is an example for purposes of Title II (although that is probably the case).

Finally, the regulations do not explain what "under orders of" means. Outside of a state or national health emergency, or the military, it is difficult to imagine a health care provider "ordering" a provider of health care services to provide treatment to an affected individual. Although undefined "a referral" is generally understood to mean on the advice and direction of a health care provider. The same terms and issues are raised in Title I, the CAA, and the PEOAA.

(g) Restorative Surgery After an Accident or Other Injury

With the first of two alternative forms of serious health conditions to receive or recover from multiple treatments, the period of absence must be for restorative surgery after an accident or other injury. 5 CFR 630.1202 (definition of "serious health condition," Subsection (1)(ii)(E)). As discussed more fully in the preceding chapter for purposes of Title I, the CAA, and the PEOAA, by its terms this alternative definition of serious health condition is very limited. It does not apply to all forms of multiple treatments by a health care provider or provider of health care services. Rather, the multiple treatments must be for restorative surgery only. Moreover, not all restorative surgery is covered. Only restorative surgery after an "accident or other injury" is covered. While "accident or other injury" is not defined, it would appear to rule out, for example, restorative surgery resulting from a birth defect.

(h) Condition That Would Likely Result in Incapacity of More Than Three Days

An FMLA-qualifying serious health condition also includes any period of absence to receive multiple health care provider treatments for a condition that would likely result in a period of incapacity of more than three consecutive calendar days in the absence of medical treatment. 5 CFR 630.1202 (definition of "serious health condition," Subsection (1)(ii)(E)). This definition is the same as the comparable regulations previously discussed for purposes of Title I, the CAA, and the PEOAA.

The "condition" is not defined. Examples provided in the regulation include chemotherapy/radiation treatment for cancer, physical therapy for severe arthritis, and dialysis for kidney disease. These are the same examples used for purposes of Title I, the CAA, and the PEOAA. *See* 29 CFR 825.114(a)(2)(v), 825.800 (definition of "serious health condition," Subsection (1)(ii)(E)); S. Res. 242, Cong. Rec. S3959, S3962, S3978 (April 23, 1996); 29 CFR 825.114(a)(2)(v), 825.800 (definition of "serious health condition," Subsection (1)(ii)(E)). The examples are not exclusive, and virtually any physical or mental condition that meets the other requirements of this form of serious health condition would be covered.

Like the comparable regulations interpreting the other federal sector variants of the FMLA, the phrase "would likely result in" is not defined or otherwise explained. Absent further qualification (e.g., strong likelihood), it would appear that any likelihood that the absence of medical intervention or treatment would result in the affected employee incurring more than three days of incapacity would suffice.

The regulations also fail to explain whether the likelihood of incapacity is determined based hypothetically on the condition suffered by the affected individual or whether the actual health condition of the affected individual is the basis of this determination.

As discussed more fully in the preceding section of this chapter regarding this alternative form of serious health condition for multiple treatments, other terms that are not defined or explained include "medical intervention," and "medical treatment." The reader is referred to the preceding section of this chapter for a further discussion of those issues.

3. Special Issues Concerning Serious Health Conditions

All of the federal sector variants of the FMLA address special issues regarding serious health conditions within the meaning of the FMLA. Those issues include substance abuse and mental illness as serious health conditions, and what are not normally considered to be serious health conditions. These rules are in addition to the FMLA-qualifying serious health conditions addressed above. Differences, if any, between the various federal sector variants of the FMLA will be noted under each category.

a. Minor Illnesses

(1) General Rule

The FMLA was not intended to cover minor illnesses. As explained in the legislative history (S. Rep. 103-3, p. 28):

> The term "serious health condition" was not intended to cover short-term conditions for which treatment and recovery are very brief. It is expected that such conditions will fall within even the most modest sick leave policies. Conditions or medical procedures that would not normally be covered by the legislation include minor illnesses that last only a few days and surgical procedures that typically do not involve hospitalization and require only a brief recovery period. Complications arising out of such procedures that develop into "serious health conditions" will be covered by the Act.

See *Thorson v. Gemini, Inc.*, 205 F.3d 370, 379-380 (8th Cir. 2000), *cert. denied*, 531 U.S. 871, 148 L. Ed. 2d 117, 121 S. Ct. 172 (2000); *Flanagan v. Keller Products, Inc.*, No. 00-542-M, 2002 DNH 47, 2002 U.S. Dist. LEXIS 3663 (D.N.H. Feb. 25, 2002); *Bond v. Abbott Laboratories*, 7 F. Supp. 2d 967, 973 (N.D. Ohio 1998), *aff'd on other grounds*, 188 F.3d 506 (table), No. 98-3923, 1999 U.S. App. LEXIS 22242 (6th Cir. Sept. 9, 1999); *Olsen v. Ohio Edison Co.*, 979 F. Supp. 1159, 1163 (N.D. Ohio 1997); *Mell v. Weyburn-Bartel, Inc.*, No. 1:96-CV-654, 1997 U.S. Dist. LEXIS 15758, at *10 (W.D. Mich. July 28, 1997).

In *Bradley v. Mary Rutan Hospital Assoc.*, 322 F. Supp. 2d 926, 941-942 (S.D. Ohio 2004), the court observed:

> The slings and arrows of everyday life, in Congress' view, should not be the stuff of a federal statute, nor federal litigation based on it. Rather, Congress believed that quotidian afflictions like the common cold or flu should be covered by even the most modest of employer sick leave policies and chose not to legislate in that area.

The implementing regulations of all of the federal sector variants of the FMLA use nearly identical language to exclude minor illnesses as FMLA-qualifying conditions. Specifically, they provide that, ordinarily, unless complications arise, the following conditions do not meet the definition of an FMLA-qualifying serious health condition:

1. Common cold
2. Flu
3. Ear aches
4. Upset stomach
5. Minor ulcers
6. Headaches other than migraine
7. Routine dental or orthodontia problems
8. Periodontal disease
9. Etc.

29 CFR 825.114(b, 825.800 (definition of "serious health condition," Subsection (2)); S. Res. 242, Cong. Rec. S3959, S3962, S3978 (April 23, 1996); 29 CFR 825.114(b), 825.800 (definition of "serious health condition," Subsection (2)); 5 CFR 630.1202 (definition of "serious health condition," Subsection 2)); *see Brenneman v. MedCentral Health System*, 366 F.3d 412, 428 (6th Cir. 2004), *cert. denied*, 543 U.S. 1146 (U.S. 2005); *Miller v. AT&T Corp. et al.*, 250 F.3d 820, 831 (4th Cir. 2001); *Stevens v. Advance Stores Co., Inc.*, No. 3-06-0537, 2007 U.S. Dist. LEXIS 28690, at 19 (M.D. Tenn. April 17, 2007); *Plesha v. U.S. Steel Corp.*, No. 2:05-CV-201 PS, 2007 U.S. Dist. LEXIS 9230, at *27-28 (N.D. Ind. Feb. 7, 2007); *Wheeler v. Pioneer Dev. Services, Inc.*, 349 F. Supp. 2d 158 (D. Mass. 2004); *Ducharme v. Cape Industries, Inc.*, No. 01–74503, 2002 U.S. Dist. LEXIS 21926 (E.D. Mich. Oct. 8, 2002); *Brown v. Seven Seventeen HB Philadelphia Corp. No. 2*, No. 01–1741, 2002 U.S. Dist. LEXIS 15066, at *14 (E.D. Pa. Aug. 8, 2002) (routine dental); *Flanagan v. Keller Products, Inc.*, No. 00–542–M, 2002 DNH 47, 2002 U.S. Dist. LEXIS 3663 (D.N.H. Feb. 25, 2002); *Raymond v. Albertson's Inc.*, 38 F. Supp. 2d 866, 870 (D. Nev. 1999); *Mell v. Weyburn–Bartel, Inc.*, No. 1:96–CV–654, 1997 U.S. Dist. LEXIS 15758, at *10 (W.D. Mich. July 28, 1997) (flu); *Ramseur v. Dept. of Navy*, DC-0752-06-0472-I-1, 2006 MSPB LEXIS 5852, at *7 (Oct. 4, 2006); *Jones v. Dept. of Navy*, No. DC-0752-06-0092-I-2, 2006 MSPB LEXIS 5031, at *4 (Sept. 5, 2006); *Hebron v. USPS*, No. DC-0752-06-0319-I-1, 2006 MSPB LEXIS 2088, at *4 (May 25, 2006) (incorrectly citing to 5 CFR Part 630), *review denied*, 104 MSPR 265 (2006); *Williams v. Dept. of Navy*, No. DC-0752-05-0431-I-1, 2005 MSPB LEXIS 6866, at *3-4 (Oct. 17, 2005), *pet. denied*, 101 MSPR 133 (2006); *Fisher v. DHHS*, No. DC-0752-05-0280-I-1, 2005 MSPB LEXIS 2653, at *8 (June 3, 2005), *review denied*, 101 MSPR 131 (2005); *Santiago v. USPS*, No. DA-0752-04-0128-B-1, 2005 MSPB LEXIS 2064, at *6 (April 28, 2005); DOL WH FMLA Advisory Opinion No. 87 (Dec. 12, 1996); DOL WH FMLA Advisory Opinion No. 86 (Dec. 12, 1996). *But see Phillips v. Leroy–Somer North America et al.*, No. 01–1046–T, 2003 U.S. Dist. LEXIS 5334, at *15–16 (W.D. Tenn. March 31, 2003) (regulations setting forth examples of "ordinary" ailments that generally are not FMLA–qualifying unless complications arise are not a *per se* rule excluding all such ailments; defendant's assertion that the FMLA covers only "major" health conditions such as heart attacks, cancer, surgery and strokes is a misstatement of the law).

Note that this rule does not say that the listed minor illnesses can never constitute an FMLA–qualifying serious health condition. Rather, the rule is that "ordinarily" such minor illnesses will not be considered to be serious health conditions. That means that in extraordinary circumstances those same listed minor illnesses may be considered to be FMLA–qualifying serious health conditions. *See Stevens v. Advance Stores Co., Inc.*, No. 3-06-0537, 2007 U.S. Dist. LEXIS 28690, at *19 (M.D. Tenn. April 17, 2007) (cold or flu not normally considered FMLA serious health conditions, such conditions can be "serious" if "complications arise"); *Mell v. Weyburn–Bartel, Inc.*, No. 1:96–CV–654, 1997 U.S. Dist. LEXIS 15758, at *10 (W.D. Mich. July 28, 1997). The regulation serves as a reminder that, just as there is no "magic list" of illnesses that are always FMLA–qualifying serious health conditions, so there is no "black list" of minor illnesses that are never considered to be a serious health condition within the meaning of the FMLA. Each case is dependent on its own facts. Agencies can help themselves to determine whether minor illnesses are serious health conditions by requiring the employee requesting FMLA leave to provide supporting medical certification. According to the Sixth Circuit, sinusitis, bronchitis, and ear infections are routine, short term illnesses not covered by the FMLA. *Tafelski v. Novartis Pharmaceuticals*, No. 05-71547, 2007 U.S. Dist. LEXIS 22847, at *23-24 (E.D. Mich. March 28, 2007).

In *Bradley v. Mary Rutan Hospital Assoc.*, 322 F. Supp. 2d 926, 942 (S.D. Ohio 2004), the employee claimed that she had a serious health condition as a result of knocking her hand against a salad bar while walking past it. The court opined that "Congress did not have in mind to protect employees with injuries such as those occasioned by knocking one's hand into a salad bar while walking past it."

In *Brown v. Seven Seventeen HB Philadelphia Corp. No. 2*, No. 01–1741, 2002 U.S. Dist. LEXIS 15066, at *14 (E.D. Pa. Aug. 8, 2002), the court rejected the plaintiff's argument that her abscessed tooth was not a "routine" medical problem. The employee claimed that the infection of her tooth and prescription medication she received rendered her condition outside of the confines of routine dental work. The court disagreed, indicating that there was nothing in the legislative history to suggest that the plaintiff's dental work met the level of seriousness contemplated for FMLA protections.

(2)   Complications

The term "complications" is undefined. The term was referenced in the legislative history to illustrate that even minor illnesses may be considered an FMLA–qualifying serious health condition. Note that the literal language of the legislative history ties "complications" to medical or surgical procedures. *See* S. Rep. 103–3, p. 28 (quoted above). The implementing regulations do not limit "complications" to medical or surgical procedures. Presumably, then, "complications" could arise out of the condition itself, absent medical or surgical procedures.

The lack of a definition for "complications" raises the possibility that a minor illness could be considered to be an FMLA-covered serious health condition where a complication is involved, but the combination of the minor illness and the complication do not meet any of the definitions of an FMLA-qualifying serious health condition. For example, Andy suffers from a bout of the common cold. During the course of his cold, Andy develops an upset stomach. Both conditions are minor illnesses. Combined, they do not meet any other tests for an FMLA-qualifying serious health condition. But because complications (upset stomach) from the minor illness of a common cold developed, Andy arguably has a serious health condition within the meaning of the FMLA.

The legislative history of the Act provides a counter argument. First, as indicated above, "complications" need to be the result of medical or surgical procedures. Unfortunately, these terms are not defined either. In any event, there is nothing in the fact pattern provided to indicate that Andy was subjected to any medical or surgical procedures. Second, and more importantly, the legislative history suggests that the "complication" must develop into a "serious health condition." That is, the mere fact that a "complication" of a minor illness occurs does not end the inquiry. Rather, the complication must turn the condition into a "serious health condition" within the meaning of the FMLA. That means the complication must result in inpatient care or continuing treatment, as a "serious health condition" is defined in those terms. It is believed that this is the correct result. Complications alone will not turn an otherwise minor illness into an FMLA-covered serious health condition unless one or more of the definitions of a "serious health condition" is met.

The DOL addresses complications in DOL FMLA Advisory Opinion No. 87, Questions 1C and 3B (Dec. 12, 1996).

In *Brenneman v. MedCentral Health System*, 366 F.3d 412, 421 (6th Cir. 2004), *cert. denied*, 543 U.S. 1146 (2005), the court entertained a dual-condition theory that the employee's diabetes was a condition complicating his flu. The court, however, went on to find that because the doctor only treated him for one of the two conditions (the flu), the employee did not receive medical treatment "relating to that same condition" as required by 29 CFR 825.114(a)(2)(i) and, therefore, it was not covered by the FMLA.

In *Raymond v. Albertson's Inc.*, 38 F. Supp. 2d 866, 870 (D. Nev. 1999), the court held that the employee failed to establish sufficient facts that his daughter's flu was accompanied by complications. As support, the court cited two factors: (1) the failure of the daughter's doctor to testify as an expert witness on the employee's behalf; and (2) the fact that the physician prescribed an over-the-counter electrolyte maintenance solution for the daughter's flu. The court noted that the FMLA treated the use of over-the-counter medications as an indication of a less serious malady.

In *Brown v. Seven Seventeen HB Philadelphia Corp. No. 2*, No. 01-1741, 2002 U.S. Dist. LEXIS 15066, at *14 (E.D. Pa. Aug. 8, 2002), the court held that the plaintiff's toothache was a routine dental procedure. The plaintiff argued that it was a serious health condition as she was out for five days and was prescribed medication. The court's decision rests largely on the absence of medical evidence in support of the plaintiff's claim that she was incapacitated for five days. The employee's doctor testified that he only performed routine periodontal work, the dentist saw no need to refer the plaintiff to a specialist, and he did not authorize her to stay or otherwise conclude she was unable to work for more than three days. According to the court, the only relevant opinion whether the plaintiff was able to work belonged to her health care provider, not to the plaintiff or her supervisors.

Similarly, in *Bond v. Abbott Laboratories*, 7 F. Supp. 2d 967, 974 (N.D. Ohio 1998), *aff'd on other grounds*, 188 F.3d 506 (table), No. 98-3923, 1999 U.S. App. LEXIS 22242 (6th Cir. Sept. 9, 1999), the district court found that the extraction of three teeth without incident was a routine dental procedure outside of the protections of the FMLA. The decision rested largely on the testimony of the doctor that the tooth extraction was completely without complication. *Id.* at 975-976; see *Ducharme v. Cape Industries, Inc.*, No. 01-74503, 2002 U.S. Dist. LEXIS 21926 (E.D. Mich. Oct. 8, 2002) (citing *Abbott*, the court found routine tooth extraction exempted from FMLA leave, even where the employee been taking leave on recurring basis because of gum disease and recurring tooth abscesses).

(3) Minor Illnesses That Meet Definition of a Serious Health Condition: The DOL Flip-Flop

Whether an otherwise "minor" illness is considered to be an FMLA-qualifying "serious health condition" because it meets all of the requirements for one or more serious health conditions has met with mixed results. An argument in favor of FMLA-coverage is that, by meeting all of the requirements of one or more serious health conditions, the "ordinarily" minor illness is transformed into a covered condition entitling the eligible employee to FMLA leave.

The argument against FMLA coverage of otherwise minor illnesses is twofold: first, the Act was created with only serious health conditions in mind. The legislative history clearly excluded minor illnesses from coverage. Allowing minor illnesses recognition as an FMLA-covered "serious health condition" cuts against the purpose of the Act. Second, the implementing regulations clearly provide that, "unless complications arise," minor illnesses are not serious health conditions within the meaning of the FMLA. In light of the explicit regulatory language, to hold that minor illnesses, absent complications, can be covered by the FMLA as a serious health condition provided they meet all of the requirements for that serious health condition, essentially nullifies the plain language of § 825.114(c).

Faced with this conundrum, the DOL has, at one time or another, taken positions for and against allowing otherwise minor illnesses to be considered serious health conditions within the meaning of the FMLA where the condition otherwise meets all definitional requirements. Originally, the DOL opined that minor illnesses could not be converted into FMLA-covered serious health conditions simply because of the definitional requirement. The DOL (DOL WH FMLA Advisory Opinion No. 57 (April 7, 1995) opined:

> Regulations, 29 CFR Part 825, published as a Final Rule on January 6, 1995 and effective April 6, 1995, state that, unless complications arise, the common cold, the flu, ear aches, upset stomach, minor ulcers, headaches other than migraine, routine dental or orthodontia problems periodontal disease, etc., are examples of conditions that do not meet the definition of a serious health condition and therefore do not qualify for FMLA leave. *The fact that an employee is incapacitated for more than three days, has been treated by a health care provider on at least one occasion which has resulted in a regimen of continuing treatment prescribed by the health care provider does not convert minor illnesses such as the common cold into serious health conditions in the ordinary case (absent complications).*

(Emphasis supplied).

The DOL reversed its position 20 months later. According to the DOL, "Upon further review of this issue and of the conclusion expressed in our letter, we have determined that our letter [of April 7, 1995] expresses an incorrect view, being inconsistent with the Department's established interpretation of qualifying 'serious health conditions' under FMLA regulations." *See* DOL WH FMLA Advisory Opinion No. 86 (Dec. 12, 1996).

The DOL expressed its reasoning as follows:

> The FMLA regulations also provide examples, in [S]ection 825.114(c), of conditions that *ordinarily*, unless complications arise, would not meet the regulatory definition of a serious health condition and would not, therefore, qualifying for FMLA leave: the common cold, the flu, ear aches, upset stomach, minor ulcers, headaches other than migraine, routine dental or orthodontia problems, periodontal disease, etc. Ordinarily, these health conditions would not meet the definition of 825.114(a)(2), as they would not be expected to last for more than three consecutive calendar days and require continuing treatment by a health care provider as defined in the regulations. If, however, any of these conditions met the regulatory criteria for a serious health condition, e.g., an incapacity of more than three consecutive calendar days that also involves qualifying treatment, then the absence would be protected by the FMLA. For example, if an individual with the flu is incapacitated for more than three consecutive calendar days and receives continuing treatment, e.g., a visit to a health care provider followed by a regimen of care such as prescription drugs like antibiotics, the individual has a qualifying "serious health condition" for purposes of the FMLA.

See DOL WH FMLA Advisory Opinion No. 87 (Dec. 12, 1996); *see Wheeler v. Pioneer Dev. Services, Inc.*, 349 F. Supp. 2d 158 (D. Mass. 2004) (describing the DOL's opinion letter as "a more sensible" rule).

In the same Opinion Letter, the DOL went on to state, "Complications, *per se*, need not be present to qualify as a serious health condition if the regulatory 'more than three consecutive calendar days' period of incapacity and 'regimen of continuing treatment by a health care provider' are otherwise met. The regulations reflect the view that, *ordinarily*, conditions like the common cold and flu (etc.) would not be expected to meet the regulatory tests, *not* that such conditions could not routinely qualify under the FMLA where the tests are, in fact, met in particular cases." DOL WH FMLA Advisory Opinion No. 86 (Dec. 12, 1996). The DOL concluded by withdrawing its previous opinion letter (DOL WH FMLA Advisory Opinion No. 57 (April 7, 1995) as "an incorrect construction of the regulations."

The DOL's current position places considerable reliance on the thrice cited term "ordinarily." For all intents and purposes, the DOL's rationale greatly diminishes the utility of the term "absent complications" for purposes of minor illnesses.

The DOL's flip-flop on this issue has not gone unnoticed by the courts. See Miller v. AT&T Corp. et al., 250 F.3d 820, 830-31 (4th Cir. 2001) (addressing the DOL's reversal of opinion from Opinion letter 57 to Opinion Letter 86, the court noted that an agency's interpretation of a statute or regulation that conflicts with a prior interpretation is entitled to considerably less deference than a consistently held agency view); Thorson v. Gemini, Inc., 205 F.3d 370, 379 (8th Cir. 2000) (the court indicated that it was "far less inclined to yield to agency opinion if the administrative agency's interpretation of a matter appears to be inconsistent, as in this case...."), cert. denied, 531 U.S. 871, 148 L. Ed. 2d 117, 121 S. Ct. 172 (2000).

The flip-flop of the DOL notwithstanding, the Fourth Circuit in Miller v. AT&T Corp. et al., 250 F.3d 820, 830-31 (4th Cir. 2001), held that a minor ailment (such as the flu) that meets one of the serious health condition definitions will be considered an FMLA-covered serious health condition. The court, much like the DOL, reasoned:

> 29 CFR 825.114(c) provides that "ordinarily" the flu will not qualify as a serious health conditions. Presumably this is because the flu (and the other conditions listed in the regulations) ordinarily will not meet the objective criteria for a serious health condition, inasmuch as such an illness normally does not result in any inability to work for three or more consecutive calendar days or does not require continuing treatment by a health care provider. Section 825.114(c) simply does not automatically exclude the flu from coverage under the FMLA. Rather, the provision is best read as clarifying that some common illnesses will not ordinarily meet the regulatory criteria and thus will not be covered under the FMLA.

Note that the court did not require the existence of complications in order for these "ordinarily" minor illnesses to be considered FMLA-covered serious health conditions. All that is required is that the "ordinarily" minor illness (e.g., the flu) satisfies one of the FMLA serious health condition definitions. The Eighth Circuit reached a similar result. See Thorson v. Gemini, Inc., 205 F.3d 370, 380 (8th Cir. 2000), cert. denied, 531 U.S. 871, 148 L. Ed. 2d 117, 121 S. Ct. 172 (2000).

Some courts, without mentioning the DOL flip-flop, have held that minor illnesses could constitute a serious health condition. See Mell v. Weyburn-Bartel, Inc., No. 1:96-CV-654, 1997 U.S. Dist. LEXIS 15758, at *10 (W.D. Mich. July 28, 1997) (the regulations recognize that the flu can be a "serious health condition" by using the qualifiers "ordinarily" and "unless complications arise"; the court believed it would be incorrect to have a blanket exclusion under the Act for all cases of the flu).

The court in Miller v. AT&T Corp. et al., 250 F.3d 820, 833 (4th Cir. 2001), also addressed AT&T's general challenge to the validity of the definition of "serious health condition" in the DOL implementing regulations. Specifically, AT&T argued that Congress did not intend for the FMLA to cover relatively minor illness such as the flu. To the extent that the DOL implementing regulations recognized the flu as a covered serious health condition, AT&T argued that the regulations are invalid as contrary to congressional intent. As support, AT&T referred to the language in the legislative history that "serious health condition" was "not intended to cover short-term conditions for which treatment and recovery are very brief." Id. at 834. It also cited the examples of serious health conditions contained in the Senate Report. Id. at 834-35 (quoting S. Rep. No. 103-3, at 28-29).

Addressing those arguments, the Fourth Circuit opined:

> AT&T is correct, of course, that the legislative history indicates that in enacting the FMLA, Congress was focused on "major" illnesses, such as cancer, rather than relatively minor ailments. But, the passage in the Senate Report on which AT&T relies is not reflected in the statutory language. See Thorson, 205 F.3d at 380. Rather, the FMLA defines "serious health condition" broadly "and does not include any examples of conditions that either do or do not qualify as FMLA 'serious health conditions'". Id. Consistent with the statutory language, the regulations promulgated by the Secretary of Labor establish a definition of "serious health condition" that focuses on the effect of an illness on the employee and the extent of necessary treatment rather than on the particular diagnosis. This policy decision is neither unreasonable nor manifestly inconsistent with Congress' intent to cover illnesses that "require that the employee be absent from work on a recurring basis or for more than a few days for treatment or recovery" and involve "continuing treatment or supervision by a health care provider." S. Rep. No. 103-3, at 29, reprinted in 1993 U.S.C.C.A.N. at 31. It is possible, of course, that the definition adopted by the Secretary will, in some cases—and perhaps even in this one—provide FMLA coverage to illnesses that Congress never envisioned would be protected. We cannot say, however, that the regulations adopted by the Secretary are so manifestly contrary to congressional intent as to be considered arbitrary. See Thorson, 205 F.3d at 380.

Other courts have rejected similar attempts to invalidate the definition of "serious health condition" contained in the

DOL implementing regulations. *See Thorson v. Gemini, Inc.*, 205 F.3d 370, 380 (8th Cir. 2000), *cert. denied*, 531 U.S. 871, 148 L. Ed. 2d 117, 121 S. Ct. 172 (2000); *Phillips v. Leroy-Somer North America et al.*, No. 01-1046-T, 2003 U.S. Dist. LEXIS 5334, at *15-16 (W.D. Tenn. March 31, 2003) (§ 825.114(c) is not a *per se* rule excluding all such ailments from being FMLA-qualifying; assertion that FMLA covers only "major" health conditions such as heart attacks, cancer, surgery and strokes is a misstatement of law).

b. Cosmetic Treatments

(1) General Rule

Conditions for which cosmetic treatments are administered (such as most treatments for acne or plastic surgery) are not "serious health conditions" unless inpatient hospital care is required or unless complications arise. 29 CFR 825.114(b, 825.800 (definition of "serious health condition," Subsection (2)); S. Res. 242, Cong. Rec. S3959, S3962, S3978 (April 23, 1996); 29 CFR 825.114(b), 825.800 (definition of "serious health condition," Subsection (2)); 5 CFR 630.1202 (definition of "serious health condition," Subsection 2)).

A review of the key terms follows.

(2) Cosmetic Treatments

The term "cosmetic treatments" is undefined. The regulations provide examples of cosmetic treatments as including "most treatments" for acne or plastic surgery. It is unclear what "most treatments" means. As "most treatments" are not "all" treatments, presumably some acne and plastic surgery treatments are "serious health conditions." It is unclear what these "other" acne and plastic surgery treatments must involve in order to be considered "serious health conditions" apart from complications or inpatient care. Presumably, such cosmetic treatments must meet one or more of the other definitions of an FMLA-qualifying serious health condition.

(3) Inpatient Care or Complications

"Inpatient care" is a defined term under the statues and regulations. It involves an "overnight stay in a hospital, hospice, or residential medical care facility." Note that cosmetic treatments are only considered a serious health condition if treatments are administered in a hospital. A hospital is only one of three facilities recognized as being able to provide "inpatient care" within the meaning of the FMLA. *See* 29 CFR 825.114(a)(1), 825.800 (definition of "serious health condition," Subsection (1)(I)); S. Res. 242, Cong. Rec. S3959, S3962, S3978 (April 23, 1996); 29 CFR 825.114(a)(1), 825.800 (definition of "serious health condition," Subsection (2)); 5 CFR 630.1202 (definition of "serious health condition," Subsection (1)(I)). By process of elimination, cosmetic treatments performed in a hospice or residential medical care facility are not serious health conditions, even if an overnight stay were involved.

"Complications" is undefined. The analysis previously provided regarding the lack of a definition for "complications" applies equally in this context. The reader is referred to the prior analysis of "complications" provided earlier in this section of the chapter.

c. Substance Abuse

Substance abuse receives special attention in the regulations implementing the federal sector variants of the FMLA. The attention differs depending on which federal sector variant of the FMLA applies to the employee or affected individual.

(1) Title I, the CAA, and the PEOAA

(a) General Rule

Substance abuse may be a serious health condition if the condition meets the requirements of one or more of the other FMLA-qualifying serious health conditions. 29 CFR 825.114(c), 825.800 (definition of "serious health condition,"

Subsection (3)); S. Res. 242, Cong. Rec. S3959, S3963, S3978 (April 23, 1996); 29 CFR 825.114(c), 825.800 (definition of "serious health condition," Subsection (3)); see *Sloop v. ABTCo.*, No. 5:96CV83-V, 1998 U.S. Dist. LEXIS 16442, at *19–20 (W.D.N.C. Aug. 26, 1998), aff'd, 178 F.3d 1285, (4th Cir. 1999); *Lau v. Behr Heat Transfer System, Inc.*, 150 F. Supp. 2d 1017, 1021 (2001).

However, FMLA leave may only be taken for treatment for substance abuse by a health care provider or by a provider of health care services on referral by a health care provider. 29 CFR 825.114(c), 825.800 (definition of "serious health condition," Subsection (3)); S. Res. 242, Cong. Rec. S3959, S3963, S3978 (April 23, 1996); 29 CFR 825.114(c), 825.800 (definition of "serious health condition," Subsection (3)); see *Sloop*, 1998 U.S. Dist. LEXIS 16442, at *19–20; *Chalimoniuk v. Interstate Brands Corp. et al.*, 172 F. Supp. 2d 1055, 1059 (S.D. Ind. 2001); *Washington v. Bosch Braking Systems Corp. et al.*, No. 1:98-CV-855, 1999 U.S. Dist. LEXIS 21361, at *8 (W.D. Mich. Nov. 24, 1999); *Jeremy v. Northwest Ohio Development Center*, 33 F. Supp. 2d 635, 638–39 (N.D. Ohio 1999), aff'd, 210 F.3d 372 (6th Cir. 2000).

Absences because of the employee's use of the substance, rather than for treatment, do not qualify for FMLA leave. 29 CFR 825.114(c), 825.800 (definition of "serious health condition," Subsection (3)); S. Res. 242, Cong. Rec. S3959, S3963, S3978 (April 23, 1996); 29 CFR 825.114(c), 825.800 (definition of "serious health condition," Subsection (3)); see *Darst v. Interstate Brands Corp.*, No. IP01–0788–C–T/K, 2003 U.S. Dist. LEXIS 22200, at *10 (S.D. Ind. Sept. 30, 2003); *Sloop*, 1998 U.S. Dist. LEXIS 16442, at *19–20; *Chalimoniuk.*, 172 F. Supp. 2d at 1059; *Jeremy v. Northwest Ohio Development Center*, 33 F. Supp. 2d 635, 638–39 (N.D. Ohio 1999), aff'd, 210 F.3d 372 (6th Cir. 2000).

The issue in *Darst v. Interstate Brands Corp.*, No. IP01–0788–C–T/K, 2003 U.S. Dist. LEXIS 22200, at *12–16 (S.D. Ind. Sept. 30, 2003), was whether phone calls to health care providers over the course of several days during which the employee was absent from work constituted "treatment." Notwithstanding the opinion of plaintiff's doctors, the court held that such phone calls did not constitute treatment for purposes of the FMLA. The court found that whether something constitutes "treatment" was a legal matter for the courts to decide. The court found no evidence that prior to the employee's admission for inpatient treatment, he was subject to any examination or evaluation to determine if he had a serious health condition. The phone calls were to schedule appointments with health care providers. "The court concludes that a mere phone call to initiate contact with a health care provider and/or arrange for treatment or visit with such a provider simply does not constitute treatment under the FMLA."

Even assuming, *arguendo*, that such phone calls constitute treatment, the court went on to find that to qualify for FMLA coverage, the employee's treatment or substance abuse must have caused the absence. The court noted that plaintiff's phone calls were only minutes long each day, yet he remained absent for the entire day. As such, the court found that these absences were not "for treatment" and, consequently, were not covered by the FMLA.

However, where an employee's abuse of a substance causes the employee to meet one of the other definitions of an FMLA-covered serious health condition, the leave used by the employee may be covered by the FMLA See *Dominick v. Ver Halen, Inc.*, No. 02–C–375–X, 2003 U.S. Dist. LEXIS 11694 (W.D. Wis. March 10, 2003) (addressing the interaction of inpatient care and substance abuse as FMLA-covered serious health conditions, the court concluded that an employee's abuse of alcohol causing physical symptoms associated with that abuse and resulting in inpatient care was covered by the FMLA).

(b) Substance Abuse

The term "substance abuse" is undefined. Commentators, as opposed to the DOL, mentioned illegal drugs and alcohol in connection with the interim regulations regarding substance abuse. Preamble, 29 CFR 825.114. The comments made by the DOL in the preamble accompanying the publication of the final regulations used the term "substance abuse," without further refinement. Presumably, "substance abuse" means the abuse of illegal drugs and/or alcohol by an employee or covered family member. See *Dominick v. Ver Halen, Inc.*, No. 02–C–375–X, 2003 U.S. Dist. LEXIS 11694 (W.D. Wis. March 10, 2003) (alcohol); *Lau v. Behr Heat Transfer System, Inc.*, 150 F. Supp. 2d 1017, 1021 (2001) (alcohol); *Sloop v. ABTCo., Inc.*, No. 5:96CV83–V, 1998 U.S. Dist. LEXIS 16442, at *20–21 (W.D.N.C. Aug. 26, 1998), aff'd, 178 F.3d 1285, (4th Cir. 1999) (use of alcohol; the court cited approvingly Magistrate Judge's statement indicating that alcohol or any other substance resulting in impairment of the senses, was covered); *Jeremy v. Northwest Ohio Development Center*, 33 F. Supp. 2d 635, 638–39 (N.D. Ohio 1999) (alcohol), aff'd, 210 F.3d 372 (6th Cir. 2000).

(c) Treatment v. Use

If the employee or covered family member meets the definition of one or more FMLA-qualifying serious health conditions, FMLA leave is limited to absence for treatment. Absences because of the employee's use of the substances do not qualify for FMLA leave.

The term "absence" is not defined. As discussed regarding a serious health condition involving multiple treatments, the use of the term "absence" would appear to be in lieu of the more frequently used "incapacity" (at least for purposes of other serious health conditions). "Incapacity" has a three-fold definition: (1) an inability to work, attend school, or perform other regular daily activities; (2) treatment therefore; or (3) recovery therefrom. *See* 29 CFR 825.114(a)(1), 825.114(a)(2)(I). Arguably, the undefined term "absence" addresses one of the three definitions of incapacity: treatment.

Clearly, "absence" does not include any period of time where, because of the use of the abused substance, the affected individual is either unable to work, attend school or perform other regular daily activities, except to receive treatment. The regulation explicitly states that it does not cover absences due to use. In *Sloop v. ABTCo., Inc.*, No. 5:96CV83-V, 1998 U.S. Dist. LEXIS 16442, at *20-21 (W.D.N.C. Aug. 26, 1998), *aff'd*, 178 F.3d 1285, (4th Cir. 1999), the district court observed:

> Rather, the Court is confident that an employee's absence from work is justified under the FMLA only when the employee is seeking treatment from a health care provider for his substance abuse, and that treatment was not precipitated by the employee's recent use of the substance. Although the law pertaining to the FMLA is scarce in light of its recent enactment, the Court is certain that Congress, in drafting [Section] 825.114(d), did not intend for an employee to be entitled to leave for work missed due to his use of alcohol, subsequent intoxication, and involuntary commitment.

In *Sloop*, the employee, who had a history of absences due to alcoholism, missed one day of work due to his consumption of alcohol. He was thereafter involuntarily committed to an inpatient detoxification facility, where he remained for several months. During that time, he was terminated.

Time spent in jail as a result of an arrest for driving under the influence of alcohol is not protected by the FMLA as it relates to use, not treatment, for substance abuse. *Jeremy v. Northwest Ohio Development Center*, 33 F. Supp. 2d 635, 638-39 (N.D. Ohio 1999), *aff'd*, 210 F.3d 372 (Table) (6th Cir. 2000).

Treatment is not a defined term for purposes of § 825.114(c). By its terms, the definition of "treatment" that we have been referring to throughout this exploration of FMLA-covered serious health conditions is limited to § 825.114(a) of the implementing regulations. 29 CFR 825.114(b), 825.800 (definition of "serious health condition," Subsection (2)); S. Res. 242, Cong. Rec. S3959, S3963, S3978 (April 23, 1996); 29 CFR 825.114(b), 825.800 (definition of "serious health condition," Subsection (2)). At least one court applied the definition of treatment applicable to § 825.114(a) to substance abuse. *Sloop v. ABTCo.*, No. 5:96CV83-V, 1998 U.S. Dist. LEXIS 16442, at *19-20 (W.D.N.C. Aug. 26, 1998) (applying definition of treatment in § 825.114(a)), *aff'd*, 178 F.3d 1285 (4th Cir. 1999).

It is unclear whether recovery from treatment, as opposed to the abuse of the substance, is covered by the FMLA The regulation does not mention recovery, either in terms of the serious health condition or treatment. As such, an argument can be made that absences for recovery, including recovery from treatment, are not covered. The counter argument, of course, is that recovery from treatment is subsumed within "treatment."

A second argument for coverage of recovery from treatment rests on the application of the other definitions of a serious health condition. Substance abuse is not a separate type of FMLA-qualifying serious health condition. Rather, substance abuse only qualifies for FMLA leave if the circumstances fit within one or more of the other serious health conditions. Many of the other forms of serious health conditions include "incapacity" as one of the conditions for FMLA leave. "Incapacity" includes recovery from treatment. An employee who seeks FMLA leave for incapacity pursuant to an FMLA-qualifying serious health condition for substance abuse would appear to be entitled to FMLA leave for treatment and recovery from treatment, but not for use of the substance.

If, on the other hand, an employee were to seek FMLA leave under a serious health condition that did not include "incapacity," the employee would arguably not be entitled to FMLA leave to recover from treatment.

(d) Healthcare Provider

To be covered by the FMLA, the absence for treatment must be administered either by:

1. By a health care provider, or

2. By a provider of health care services on referral by a health care provider.

The term "provider of health care services" is undefined. Physical therapists were identified as one example of a "provider of health care services" for purposes of another continuing treatment serious health condition. *See* 29 CFR 825.114(a)(2)(A).

Note that this regulation does not use the phrase "under orders of" in addition to "on referral by" when describing the relationship of the health care provider and provider of health care services. In other regulations referencing a "provider of health care services," the phrase "under orders of" has also been used. *See* 29 CFR 825.825.114(a)(2)(i)(A), 825.114(a)(2)(v).

(e) Discipline for Employee's Own Substance Abuse

FMLA leave is available for treatment for substance abuse provided the conditions of § 825.114 have been met. However, treatment for substance abuse does not prevent an employer from taking an employment action (including discipline) against an employee. 29 CFR 825.112(g); S. Res. 242, Cong. Rec. S3959, S3962 (April 23, 1996); 29 CFR 825.112(g). The ability of an employer to take disciplinary action against an employee for substance abuse is not, however, unconditional.

An employer may take an employment action against an employee for substance abuse where the employer:

1. Has an established policy;

2. Communicated to all employees;

3. That provides that under certain circumstances an employee may be terminated for substance abuse; and

4. The policy is applied in a non-discriminatory way.

Where these conditions are met, an employer may discipline an employee, including termination, who violated that policy, whether or not the employee is presently taking FMLA leave, including leave for substance abuse treatment. 29 CFR 825.112(g); S. Res. 242, Cong. Rec. S3959, S3962 (April 23, 1996) 29 CFR 825.112(g); *see* DOL WH FMLA Advisory Opinion No. 69 (July 21, 1995).

The regulations do not address what would be considered an "established policy." What is clear is that, in the absence of an established policy, an agency would not be able to take disciplinary action against an employee who was taking leave for substance abuse treatment. DOL WH FMLA Advisory Opinion No. 69 (July 21, 1995). As such, agencies would be well advised to establish and maintain such a policy in a manner consistent with other agency employment policies. For example, if agency employment policies are contained in an employee handbook, manual or other written document, the substance abuse policy should also be included. Inclusion of the substance abuse policy in an employee handbook or manual, to the extent it involves FMLA rights and responsibilities, is arguably required by the FMLA 29 CFR 825.301(a)(1); S. Res. 242, Cong. Rec. S3959, S3971 (April 23, 1996); 29 CFR 825.301(a)(1); *see also Smith v. Eastman Kodak Co. et al.*, No. 95-4677 (DRD), 1999 U.S. Dist. LEXIS 17506 (D.N.J. Oct. 7, 1999), *aff'd*, 265 F.3d 159 (3d Cir. 2001) (absent contest by the plaintiff, distribution of a pamphlet to all employees regarding Kodak's Drug Awareness program indicating that violation of company substance abuse policy may result in termination, and inclusion of similar language in Employee handbook sufficient evidence of company substance abuse policy within the meaning of the FMLA). Employer notice obligations are addressed more fully in Chapter 8, "Notice Requirements."

The regulations do not specify how the policy is to be communicated to all employees. Agencies would be well advised to use multiple avenues to communicate of the substance abuse policy. For example, if the policy is new, it should be included in any employee handbook or manual. The revised manual should be re-distributed to all employees. Receipt of the manual should be acknowledged by each employee in writing. The substance abuse policy should be handed out at mandatory discussions conducted by management with all employees. Such discussions should be documented as to time, place, and attendance.

The regulation does not specify the circumstances under which an employer would be able to discipline an employee for substance abuse. Agencies are left with the discretion to craft their own policies.

The requirement that an agency apply the policy in a non-discriminatory way is intended to ensure that agencies do not misuse the policy as a pretext to discipline or terminate employees for exercising their right to take FMLA leave. An agency may not take action against an employee because the employee exercised his or her right to take FMLA leave for treatment. 29 CFR 825.112(g); S. Res. 242, Cong. Rec. S3959, S3962 (April 23, 1996); 29 CFR 825.112(g).

An alternative basis for taking disciplinary action for substance abuse was addressed in *Renaud v. Wyoming Dept. of Family Services*, 203 F.3d 723, 732 (10th Cir. 2000). The court sustained the termination of an employee for violation of the State of Wyoming's substance abuse policy for being intoxicated at work. The defendant terminated the employee just after it granted the employee leave to check himself in to an alcohol treatment program. In sustaining the termination, the court did not rely on (or even mention) the regulatory exception contained in § 825.112(g). Rather, the court relied on its previous holding that, "under the FMLA, an employee who requests leave or is on leave has no greater rights than an employee who remains at work." *Renaud*, 203 F.3d at 732. Applying the rule here, the court held that the plaintiff was terminated for using alcohol on the job, not for taking FMLA leave.

(f) Substance Abuse of a Covered Family Member

The regulations also address the rights of employees and employers where the need for FMLA leave involves the treatment of a covered family member for substance abuse. Specifically, an employee may take FMLA leave to care for an immediate family member who is receiving treatment for substance abuse. 29 CFR 825.112(g); S. Res. 242, Cong. Rec. S3959, S3962 (April 23, 1996); 29 CFR 825.112(g). As such, an employer may not take action against an employee who is providing care for an immediate family member receiving treatment for substance abuse. 29 CFR 825.112(g); S. Res. 242, Cong. Rec. S3959, S3962 (April 23, 1996); 29 CFR 825.112(g). These rules raise several interesting questions.

The unequivocal statement of a right to FMLA leave where an employee is needed to care for an immediate family member who is receiving treatment for substance abuse, appears to create a separate right to FMLA leave. Section 825.114(d) provides that substance abuse is not a serious health condition within the meaning of the FMLA unless it meets the requirements of one of the definitions of an FMLA-qualifying serious health condition. 29 CFR 825.114(d); S. Res. 242, Cong. Rec. S3959, S3963 (April 23, 1996); 29 CFR 825.114(d). This conflicts with the affirmative statement in § 824.112(g). Presumably, § 825.112(g) did not mean to usurp the requirement that the substance abusing immediate family member must independently meet one of the definitions of a covered serious health condition in order for the employee's leave to be FMLA-qualifying. Unfortunately, there is no evidence that this is the case. As worded, § 825.112(g) requires that the FMLA cover an employee's request for FMLA leave to care for an immediate family member receiving substance abuse treatment. Let the legal arguments begin.

Note that § 825.112(g) only protects from discipline an employee's FMLA leave to care for an immediate family member for substance abuse treatment. By process of elimination, an employee's leave to care for an immediate family member due to the use and/or recovery from use of such (unidentified) substances is not protected from discipline, at least not by the FMLA. This may not always be true. In addressing comments made by the EEOC regarding the FMLA's incorporation of the definition of "physical or mental disability" from the ADA in 29 CFR 825.113(c)(2) (addressing age 18 or older son or daughter within meaning of FMLA), the DOL (Preamble, 29 CFR 113) stated the following:

> An eligible employee's son or daughter who illegally uses drugs may be disabled for purposes of an eligible parent (employee) taking FMLA leave.

Of course, this only satisfies the requirement that an age 18 or older child is a "son or daughter" within the meaning of the FMLA. For FMLA leave to apply, the "son or daughter" would still need to meet the definition of a serious health condition, and the employee would have to be "needed to care for" the son or daughter. [The interaction of the FMLA and the ADA is addressed more fully in Chapter 16, "Interaction of the FMLA with Other Federal Laws, Employer Practices, and Collective Bargaining Agreements."]

Finally, § 825.112(g) uses the term "immediate family member." This is not a defined term. Presumably, an "immediate family member" means a spouse, parent, son or daughter, as defined in the FMLA. Of course, other interpretations are possible, but unlikely to succeed. The Act defines who is covered by the FMLA. Any individual who is not a spouse, parent, son or daughter is likely not going to be covered by § 825.112(g).

(g) Drug Testing on Return to Work

Some agencies require an employee to submit to on-going drug testing for a period of time as a condition of returning the employee to work pursuant to the terms of an employee assistance program for substance abuse. The issue is whether such a program complies with the requirements of the FMLA, particularly where the employee used FMLA leave to receive treatment for substance abuse. As set forth more fully in Chapter 13, "Return to Work from Leave," an employee is entitled to the same or an equivalent position on return to work from FMLA leave. The question is whether the imposition of drug testing violates that FMLA requirement that the employee be returned to the same or an equivalent position (as drug testing was not required prior to the employee's use of FMLA leave).

The DOL concluded that a return to work drug-testing policy as required by state or local law or the terms of a collective bargaining agreement, and in accordance with the ADA, does not violate the FMLA. *See* DOL WH FMLA Advisory Opinion No. 27 (Jan. 31, 1994). There, the issue was raised in the context of a drug-testing program mandated by Texas State workers' compensation law. The DOL concluded that it did not interpret the FMLA as creating a conflict with employers' substance abuse policies required under state workers' compensation laws. Drug testing was permitted pursuant to § 104(a)(4) of the FMLA (29 USC 2614(a)(5)), which provides that as a condition of restoring an eligible employee who takes leave for a personal serious illness, an employer may have a uniformly applied practice or policy that requires each such employee to receive certification from the employee's health care provider that the employee is able to resume work,…except that nothing in this paragraph shall supersede a valid state or local law or a collective bargaining agreement that governs the return to work of such employees." Moreover, the FMLA also provides that it is not to be construed as modifying or affected any federal law prohibiting discrimination on the basis of, among others, disability. 29 USC 2614(a)(1).

Of course, federal agencies are not subject to state or local law. They are, however, subject to federal disability law. Moreover, federal agencies are subject to the terms of applicable collective bargaining agreements that they enter. As such, drug-testing programs can be created that do not violate the terms of the FMLA.

(h) Questions and Answers

The following questions and answers are designed to illustrate the rules regarding FMLA. leave for substance abuse. The examples are derived from DOL WH FMLA. Opinion No. 59 (April 28, 1995).

Q1. An employee comes up for random testing and tests positive for illegal narcotics and the employee has never requested FMLA leave. Under the employer's policy this employee is subject to immediate termination. Is the employer obligated to provide FMLA leave to this employee?

A1. No. The FMLA does not require the employer to allow the employee the opportunity to seek treatment and be reinstated. Of course, an employer could allow the employee to seek treatment and reinstatement. Moreover, the terms of an applicable collective bargaining agreement may also govern the employee's rights and the employer's responsibilities in this situation.

Q2. The employer receives information that an employee is using illegal narcotics. As a result, the employee is requested to submit to a drug test under the "for cause" provisions of the testing policy. The employee tests positive for illegal narcotics and the employee has never requested FMLA leave. Under the provisions of the testing policy, the employee is subject to immediate termination. Does the FMLA require the employer to permit the employee to seek treatment in lieu of termination?

A2. No. The FMLA does not require the employer to allow the employee to seek treatment and be reinstated.

Q3. An employee comes forward and admits to the employer that he or she is addicted to drugs and indicates that a doctor is placing the employee in rehabilitative treatment. Again, the employer's policy requires immediate termination in this instance. Does the FMLA require the employer to permit the employee to seek treatment?

A3. No. The FMLA does not require the employee in this situation to seek treatment or be reinstated where the employee admits to the illegal use of drugs, and employer policy requires immediate termination.

Q4. An employee who tests positive for the presence of an illegal narcotic is granted FMLA leave and the terms and conditions of reinstatement include a requirement that the employee submit to weekly drug testing. If the employee tests positive a second time and has either not used all of his or her allowed FMLA leave time or has used all the allotted FMLA leave time, does the FMLA require that the employer allow the employee the opportunity to seek treatment and be reinstated for a second time?

A4.   No. The employer's policy could provide for termination of employment in either case, whether or not the employee has exhausted his or her FMLA leave allotment in the applicable 12-month leave year period.

Again, the fact that an employee has or will undergo treatment for substance abuse does not prevent an employer from taking an employment action (including discipline) against an employee. 29 CFR 825.112(g); S. Res. 242, Cong. Rec. S3959, S3962 (April 23, 1996); 29 CFR 825.112(g).

(2)   Title II

Title II also gives special recognition to substance abuse. Unlike Title I, the CAA, and the PEOAA discussed above, however, the regulations addressing substance abuse for purposes of Title II are far less comprehensive.

(a)   General Rule

A serious health condition within the meaning of the FMLA does not include an absence because of an employee's use of an illegal substance, unless the employee is receiving treatment for substance abuse by a health care provider or by a provider of health care services on referral by a health care provider. 5 CFR 630.1202 (definition of "serious health condition," Subsection (2)).

As reformulated in the affirmative, an absence for an employee to receive treatment by substance abuse by a health care provider or by a provider of health care services on referral by a health care provider is a serious health condition within the meaning of the FMLA Indeed, one could stretch that reformulation, based on the plain language of the regulation, to include an employee's absence due to use of an illegal substance, provided the employee is receiving health care provider treatment.

Notably, there is no regulation under Title II, comparable to that under Title I, the CAA, and the PEOAA, that provides, essentially, that treatment for an employee's substance abuse is not an independent form of "serious health condition," but meets the requirements of one or more of the other recognized serious health condition. Just the opposite. A plain reading of the regulation suggests that an employee's treatment for substance abuse is an independent "serious health condition."

Note too that the regulation is limited to an employee's absence for substance abuse treatment. There is no mention of an employee's need for FMLA leave "to care for" a covered family member's use or receipt of treatment for substance abuse. As such, it would appear that an employee's need for leave to care for a covered family member because of substance abuse requires that the situation fit within another definition of a "serious health condition." In contrast, the substance abuse rules of the other federal sector variants of the FMLA apply whether the need for leave is due to the employee's own substance problem, or that of a covered family member.

More importantly, if the circumstances fit within one of those definitions, there is no restriction that the FMLA leave is only available for an "absence" for treatment. Rather, it would appear that an employee would be entitled to take leave to provide care for a covered family member's use, treatment, and recovery from treatment of legal and illegal substances. In other words, if the circumstances met the definition of "incapacity" for purposes of a serious health condition, all things being equal, the employee would be entitled to leave for the covered family member's period of incapacity. This is very different from the comparable requirements under Title I, the CAA, and the PEOAA.

(b)   Substance Abuse

The regulation uses the terms "illegal substance" and "substance abuse." 5 CFR 630.1202 (definition of "serious health condition," Subsection (2)). Neither term is defined. The noteworthy point here is that, for purposes of Title II, the rule recognizing an employee's treatment for substance abuse as an FMLA-covered "serious health condition" is limited to "illegal" substances. Alcohol is legal. By comparison, while "substance abuse" is also undefined for purposes of Title I, the CAA, and the PEOAA, the term is not limited to "illegal" substances. Legal substances, such as alcohol, prescription and non-prescription medications, and inhalants such as glue, paint thinner, etc., are also covered.

(c) Treatment

"Treatment" is not defined for purposes of the substance abuse regulation or, for that matter, any other purpose in the OPM regulations. The term "continuing treatment" is described for purposes of a "serious health condition" as including, but not limited to, examinations to determine if there is a serious health condition and evaluations of such condition if the examinations or evaluations determine that a serious health condition exits. 5 CFR 630.1202 (definition of "serious health condition," Subsection (1)(ii)). Taking out the "continuing" requirement should reveal what Title II considers to constitute "treatment."

(d) Health Care Provider

A "health care provider" is a defined term under Title II. The phrase "provider of health care services" is undefined.

(e) Substance Abuse of Covered Family Members

Section 630.1202 (definition of "serious health condition," Subsection (2)), does not address an employee's need for FMLA leave to care for a covered family member with a substance abuse problem. As such, to be considered to be a serious health condition within the meaning of the FMLA, the circumstances must fit within one of the other Title II definitions of a serious health condition.

Title II defines a "mental or physical disability" for purposes of determining whether an adult child falls within the definition of a covered "son or daughter" by incorporation of the same ADA regulation as does Title I, the CAA, and the PEOAA. Title II does not address whether substance abuse by an adult child could constitute a disability for purposes of FMLA coverage. As such, the comments of the DOL regarding substance abuse as a disability for purposes of a parent's entitlement to FMLA leave should be reviewed. The reader is referred to the DOL's comments, which are addressed above. [The interaction of the FMLA with the ADA is addressed more fully in Chapter 16, "Interaction of the FMLA with Other Federal Laws, Employer Practices, and Collective Bargaining Agreements."]

d. Mental Illness

(1) Title I, the CAA, and the PEOAA

A serious health condition entitling an eligible employee to FMLA leave means an illness, injury, impairment, or physical or mental condition. 29 USC 2611(11); 29 CFR 825.114(a); S. Res. 242, Cong. Rec. S3959, S3962 (April 23, 1996); 29 CFR 825.114(a). Mental illness surely qualifies as a "mental condition." See *Stekloff v. St. John's Mercy Health Sys.*, 218 F.3d 858, 860 (8th Cir. 2000); *Whitworth v. Consolidated Biscuit Co.*, No. 6:06-112-DCR, 2007 U.S. Dist. LEXIS 25971, at *28 (E.D. Ky. April 6, 2007); *Hoban v. WBNCC Joint Venture*, No. 06-13142, 2007 U.S. Dist. LEXIS 25407, at *14 (E.D. Mich. April 5, 2007); *Schmutte v. Resort Condominiums International, LLC*, 463 F. Supp. 2d 891, 908 (S.D. Ind. 2006); *Marrero v. Camden County Bd. of Social Services et al.*, 164 F. Supp. 2d 455, 465 (D.N.J. 2001) (anxiety and depression); *Lau v. Behr Heat Transfer System, Inc.*, 150 F. Supp. 2d 1017, 1021 (2001) (depression and alcoholism); *Jefferies v. Dept. of Navy*, 78 MSPR 255 (1998) (depression and anxiety).

However, as with any other health condition, to be a "serious health condition" within the meaning of the FMLA, mental illness must also involve either inpatient care or continuing treatment. That is, mental illness is not an independent form of serious health condition. Rather, for an entitlement to FMLA leave, the mental illness must meet the requirements of one or more of the serious health condition definitions discussed throughout this chapter. 29 CFR 825.114(c); S. Res. 242, Cong. Rec. S3959, S3963 (April 23, 1996); 29 CFR 825.114(c); see *Whitworth v. Consolidated Biscuit Co.*, No. 6:06-112-DCR, 2007 U.S. Dist. LEXIS 25971, at *28 (E.D. Ky. April 6, 2007); *Hoban v. WBNCC Joint Venture*, No. 06-13142, 2007 U.S. Dist. LEXIS 25407, at *14 (E.D. Mich. April 5, 2007); *Jones. v. Willow Gardens Care Center et al.*, Case No C98–0007 MJM, 2000 U.S. Dist. LEXIS 3559, at *38 (N.D. Iowa Jan. 28, 2000) (indicating sufficient facts to establish that mental illness met requirements of § 825.114(a)(2)(I)); *Jefferies v. Dept. of Navy*, 78 MSPR 255 (1998) (depression and anxiety that cause more than three days incapacity and involved at least one doctor visit followed by regimen of prescription medication found an FMLA–covered serious health condition). Congress did not intend "[t]he slings and arrows of everyday life…to be the stuff of a federal statute, nor federal litigation based on it." *Whitworth v. Consolidated Biscuit Co.*, No. 6:06-112-DCR, 2007 U.S. Dist. LEXIS 25971, at *28 (E.D. Ky. April 6, 2007).

The term "mental illness" is undefined. Moreover, not all causes of mental illness may be considered an FMLA-qualifying serious health condition. The regulation provides that "mental illness resulting from stress" may be an FMLA-covered serious health condition provided all other conditions are met. "Stress" is undefined. Stated differently, mental illness not caused by stress may not be a serious health condition, even if all other conditions for a serious health condition are met. No explanation is offered to explain why mental illness not caused by stress will not be considered an FMLA-qualifying serious health condition. If this was not the DOL's intention, it needs to revise the regulations accordingly.

Indeed, the way the regulation reads, arguably mental illness caused by allergies may also be a serious health condition within the meaning of the FMLA In pertinent part, § 825.114(c) reads:

> Mental illness resulting from stress or allergies may be serious health conditions, but only if all the conditions of this section are met.

Absent a comma or other grammatical break in the sentence, it could be argued that mental illness may be a covered serious health condition if caused by stress or allergies, and if it otherwise meets the other requirements for a serious health condition. The regulatory history, however, suggests that "allergies" was meant to be read separately from mental illness. In the interim DOL regulations (Fed. Reg. 31794, 31817 (June 4, 1993), § 825.114(c), the provision read:

> Treatments for allergies or stress, or for substance abuse, are serious health conditions if all the conditions of the regulation are met.

In the comments accompanying the publication of the final regulations (Preamble, 29 CFR 825.114), the DOL observed:

> As suggested, the reference in the interim final rule to stress as a possible serious health condition has been revised to mental illness from stress.

An agency will have to request and rely on a supporting medical certification in determining whether a request for leave due to a mental illness caused by stress is an FMLA-covered serious health condition.

In *Hoban v. WBNCC Joint Venture*, No. 06-13142, 2007 U.S. Dist. LEXIS 25407, at *14-15 (E.D. Mich. April 5, 2007), the court found that the employee's claim that he was a "nervous wreck" following the death of his brother failed to establish that he had a serious health condition within the meaning of the FMLA. The court also noted that the employee did not seek medical attention for his condition, and that he returned to work the following day and was able to perform his job until he left for a dental appointment. The court found that being a "nervous wreck" did not rise to the level of an FMLA-covered serious health condition.

For cases addressing mental illness as an FMLA-covered serious health condition, see *Gay v. Gillman Paper Co.*, 125 F.3d 1432, 1434, n.3 (11th Cir. 1997); *Price v. City of Fort Wayne*, 117 F.3d 1022, 1023-24 (7th Cir. 1997); *Marrero v. Camden County Bd. of Social Services et al.*, 164 F. Supp. 2d 455, 465 (D.N.J. 2001); *Jones v. Willow Gardens Care Center et al.*, Case No C98-0007 MJM, 2000 U.S. Dist. LEXIS 3559, at *38 (N.D. Iowa Jan. 28, 2000); and *Jefferies v. Dept. of Navy*, 78 MSPR 255 (1998) (depression and anxiety).

e. Combination Conditions

A group of seemingly unrelated health conditions that combine to incapacitate an employee or covered individual may be considered together for purposes of determining whether, combined, they meet any one or more FMLA-qualifying serious health condition definitions. Each of the conditions did not have to be considered separately to determine whether one, by itself, was a "serious health condition." That was the conclusion of the court in *Price v. City of Fort Wayne*, 117 F.3d 1022 (7th Cir. 1997).

In *Price*, the plaintiff simultaneously suffered from "an assemblage of [conditions] including elevated blood pressure, hyperthyroidism, back pain, severe headaches, sinusitis, infected cyst, sore throat, swelling throat, coughing and feelings of stress and depression." *Id.* at 1022. There was no dispute that the plaintiff was incapacitated by that combination of conditions or that she underwent continuing treatment. She saw her doctor eight times over the relevant two-month period and underwent a thyroid ultrasound, a needle biopsy, and excision of a mass, and a CT scan. *Id.* at 1022. Again, the issue in *Price* was whether the conditions had to be analyzed separately or in combination for purposes of determining the existence of an FMLA-qualifying "serious health condition." *Id.* As indicated in the preceding paragraph, the court concluded that conditions that combine to incapacitate a person and to require continuing treatment can, together, constitute a "serious health condition." *Id.* at 1025.

In *Marchisheck v. San Mateo County et al.*, 199 F.3d 1068, 1075 (9th Cir. 1999), *cert. denied*, 530 U.S. 1214 (2000), the employee argued that her son (Shaun) suffered from a combination of physical and psychological conditions that rose to the level of a serious health condition. *Id.* at 1075. Shaun received counseling for mild depression and poor peer relations beginning in 1991 following an arrest for shoplifting. *Id.* at 1070. The final session ended on June 1, 1995. Shaun also attended six substance abuse counseling sessions in the period June through August 9, 1995. On August 5, 1995, Shaun was assaulted by several acquaintances. He was treated in the emergency room and released to go home with instructions to keep the area clean and apply ice. The plaintiff asked for five weeks of FMLA leave to move Shaun to the Philippines for his safety. When the leave was denied, the plaintiff went anyway. As a result, she was terminated.

The plaintiff argued that the combination of Shaun's incapacity resulting from the assault combined with the counseling sessions for his behavioral problems created a "combined condition" within the meaning of the FMLA. *Id.* at 1075. The court held that a "combined condition" did not exist in this situation. Specifically, the court opined, 199 F.3d at 1076,:

> The difficulty with applying the reasoning of *Price* here is that there is no competent evidence in the record to suggest that Shaun suffered from combined conditions that incapacitated him. Shaun received sporadic counseling beginning in 1991 and was assaulted in 1995, but there is nothing to suggest that Shaun ever was treated for a combination of physical and psychological symptoms, or that he was incapacitated by a combined condition. There simply is no basis in this record to conclude that Shaun's various behavioral and emotional problems ever "combined" with the passing physical effects of the assault to create a "serious health condition."

It would appear that not all unrelated, disparate treatment will be viewed as a "combined condition" for purposes of determining the existence of an FMLA-covered "serious health condition."

(1) Title II

Title II similarly recognizes mental illness as a serious health condition within the meaning of the FMLA. According to the implementing regulations, mental illness resulting from stress may be a serious health condition, but only if such condition requires inpatient care or continuing treatment by a health care provider. 5 CFR 630.1202 (definition of "serious health condition," Subpart (2)).

"Inpatient care" and "health care provider" are defined terms. *See* 5 CFR 630.1202 (definition of "serious health condition," Subsections (1)(i) (inpatient care) and 1(ii) (continuing treatment). Note that the regulation only refers to treatment by a "health care provider," and not a "provider of health care services," as permitted by some forms of continuing treatment serious health conditions. This discrepancy may be used to argue that only health care providers may provide treatment for mental illness as a serious health condition. By comparison, Title I, the CAA, and the PEOAA avoid this limitation by requiring that mental illness meet all of the conditions of a serious health condition, including who is allowed to treat the affected individual.

As under the other federal sector variants of the FMLA, the terms "mental illness," and "stress" are not defined. It is unclear whether this provision is designed to exclude mental illness based on reasons other than stress from being considered FMLA-qualifying serious health conditions, although such a position could certainly be argued.

f. Routine Physical, Eye, and Dental Examinations; Regimen of Continuing Treatment

The federal sector variants of the FMLA treat differently certain routine medical examinations and continuing treatment regimens. Title II provides that a serious health condition does not include routine physical, eye, or dental examinations. 5 CFR 630.1202 (definition of "serious health condition," Subsection (2)). Similarly, a regimen of continuing treatment that includes taking over-the-counter medications, bed-rest, exercise, and other similar activities that can be initiated without a visit to a health care provider, are not serious health conditions. *Id.*

Under Title I, the CAA, and the PEOAA, these same examinations and continuing treatment regimens are not excluded from the definition of a "serious health condition." Rather, routine physical, eye, and dental examinations are excluded from the definition of "treatment." *See* 29 CFR 825.114(b); S. Res. 242, Cong. Rec. S3959, S3963 (April 23, 1996); 29 CFR

825.114(b). Similarly, activities that can be initiated without a visit to a health care provider (e.g., over-the-counter medications, bed-rest, exercise, etc.) are excluded from the definition of a "regimen of continuing treatment," not a "serious health condition." The practical result, however, is virtually the same. "Treatment" and "regimen of continuing treatment" are terms used to describe aspects of most continuing treatment serious health conditions.

g. Miscellaneous Illnesses and Procedures

The regulations implementing all of the federal sector variants of the FMLA identify certain conditions that are serious health conditions, provided that these conditions satisfy the other requirements of a serious health condition. These conditions are:

1. Allergies
2. Restorative dental or plastic surgery after an injury
3. Removal of cancerous growths.

29 CFR 825.114(c); S. Res. 242, Cong. Rec. S3959, S3963 (April 23, 1996); 29 CFR 825.114(b); 5 CFR 630.1202 (definition of "serious health condition," Subsection (2)). See *Flanagan v. Keller Products, Inc.*, No. 00-542-M, 2002 DNH 47, 2002 U.S. Dist. LEXIS 3663 (D.N.H. Feb. 25, 2002) (restorative dental).

It is unclear whether this section creates new "serious health conditions" for these particular illnesses, or simply provides examples of illness that may fit within the definitions of existing serious health conditions. For example, restorative dental or plastic surgery after an injury would appear to fit within § 825.114(a)(2)(v) for purposes of Title I, the CAA, and the PEOAA, and 5 CFR 630.1202 (definition of "serious health condition," Subsection (1)(ii)(E)).

Finally, "allergies," "restorative dental or plastic surgery," and "cancerous growths" are undefined. Again, agencies are well advised to seek medical certification on these issues where they are the basis for an employee's request for FMLA leave.

h. Retroactive Coverage of Absences

A somewhat unusual feature of the FMLA is that it can retroactively protect employee absences. See *Lukacinsky v. Panasonic Service Co.*, No. 03-40141-FDS, 2004 U.S. Dist. LEXIS 25846, at *32 (D. Mass. Nov. 29, 2004). The court in *Lukacinsky* explained:

> Once the employee satisfies the standard of a "serious health condition," all *prior* absences that were necessary for the evaluation and treatment of the condition may become protected, even if they were not protected at the time they occurred. See *Hodgens*, 144 F.3d at 163, n. 13. Thus, once Lukacinsky's back problems became a "serious health condition" within the meaning of the statute, any prior absence for diagnosis or treatment of the condition is potentially protected FMLA leave.

The court further observed:

> The potential unfairness to the employer of this feature is considerably ameliorated by the prerequisite that the employee give notice to the employer before the protected status will attach. Otherwise, an employer who is unaware that an employee has a serious medical condition requiring leave might rebuke the employee for excessive absenteeism, only to find out afterwards that FMLA protection attached retroactively to those absences.

In order to be considered "unable to perform" his job, an employee does not have to be "too sick to work" or "incapacitated such that he cannot physically perform his work." Rather, an employee may be "unable to perform" his job if his absences from work are necessary for the diagnosis and treatment of his medical condition. An employee need only show that his medical appointments conflict with his work to satisfy this requirement. *Lukacinsky*, 2004 U.S. Dist. LEXIS 25846, at *33 n.13.

The court initially established that the employee had a serious health condition as of July 2000. Because of retroactivity, the court addressed whether Lukacinsky's intermittent absences before July 2000 were (1) attributable to a serious health condition that rendered him unable to perform the functions of his job; and (2) whether he complied with his FMLA-imposed duty to provide the company with appropriate notice of the medical need for those absences. The court concluded that at least some of the absences before July 2000 were attributable to his serious health condition (back problems). It also found that the employer was provided timely and adequate notice that these absences qualified for protection under the FMLA. This is at least sufficient to defeat summary judgment.

D. HEALTH CARE PROVIDER DEFINED

The federal sector variants of the FMLA substantively share the same definition of "health care provider." A "health care provider" means (a) a doctor of medicine or osteopathy who is authorized to practice medicine or surgery (as appropriate) by the state in which the doctor practices; and (b) any other person determined by (as appropriate) the DOL (Title I and the PEOAA), the OPM (Title II), or the Office of Compliance (CAA), to be capable of providing health care services. 29 USC 2611(6); 5 USC 6381(2); 2 USC 1312(a)(1) (incorporating § 101 of Title I, 29 USC 2611, into CAA); 3 USC 412(a)(1) (incorporating § 101 of Title I, 29 USC 2611, into PEOAA); *see Sims v. Alameda-Contra Costa Transit District et al.,* 2 F. Supp. 2d 1253, 1257 (N.D. Ca. 1998); *Harvender v. Norton Co.,* No. 96-CV-653 (LEK/RWS), 1997 U.S. Dist. LEXIS 21467 (N.D.N.Y. Dec. 15, 1997).

Regulations implementing the statutory definition of "health care provider" have been issued pursuant to Title I, Title II, and the CAA. *See* 29 CFR 825.118, 825.800 (definition of "health care provider"); 5 CFR 630.1202 (definition of "health care provider"); S. Res. 242, Cong. Rec. S3959, S3963, S3978 (April 23, 1996); 29 CFR 825.118, 828.800 (definition of "health care provider"); *see Sims v. Alameda-Contra Costa Transit District et al.,* 2 F. Supp. 2d 1253, 1257 (N.D. Ca. 1998). The PEOAA has not issued its own regulations implementing the FMLA. As a result, the PEOAA follows the regulations implementing Title I. *See* 3 USC 412(a)(1) (incorporating § 101 of Title I, 29 USC 2611 into PEOAA), 455 (applying the most relevant substantive executive agency regulation promulgated to implement statutory provision at issue in proceeding).

The definitions of "health care provider" in the implementing regulations contain some similarities and some differences.

Knowing who is considered an FMLA-covered health care provider is important for at least two reasons. First, agencies may require an employee to substantiate a request for FMLA leave due to a serious health condition (his or her own or a covered family member's) with a medical certification of a health care provider. Second, a serious health condition involving continuing treatment requires some form of health care provider involvement. Some forms of conditions, such as absences for treatment, require active health care involvement. Other forms allow a more passive form of health care provider involvement, such as periodic treatments. But all forms of FMLA-covered serious health conditions require health care provider involvement. Absent such health care provider involvement, the leave may not be covered by the FMLA.

Finally, there is no hierarchy among FMLA-covered health care providers. An employee need not obtain, and an employer may not insist that an employee obtain as an initial matter, treatment or certification from a specialist in lieu of the recognized health care provider being used by the employee. *See Matthews v. Fairview Health Services*, No. 01-2151 ADM/AJB, 2003 U.S. Dist. LEXIS 5901, at *11 (D. Minn. April 7, 2003) (employer not permitted to require certification from a specialist, as opposed to general practitioner); *Giuliani v. Minnesota Vikings Football Club, LLC*, No. 99-CV-1811 DDA/FLN, 2001 U.S. Dist. LEXIS 20207, at *8 (D. Minn. June 11, 2002) (employer request for certification from psychiatrist unnecessary because clinical psychologist was an FMLA-covered health care provider). An employer would have to utilize the second/third opinion process in order to require an employee to see a specialist. The second/third opinion process is discussed in Chapter 9, "Documentation Requirements."

1. Title I, the CAA, and the PEOAA

a. Those Covered

A "health care provider" means:

1. Doctor of medicine or osteopathy
2. Podiatrists

3. Dentists

4. Clinical psychologists

5. Optometrists

6. Chiropractors (limited to treatment consisting of manual manipulation of the spine to correct a subluxation as demonstrated by X-ray to exist)

7. Nurse practitioners

8. Nurse midwives

9. Clinical social workers

10. Christian Science Practitioners listed with the First Church of Christ, Scientist in Boston, Massachusetts

11. Any health care provider from whom an employer or the employer's group health plan's benefits manager will accept certification of the existence of a serious health condition to substantiate a claim for benefits; and

12. A health care provider listed above who practices in a country other than the United States, who is authorized to practice in accordance with the law of that country, and who is performing within the scope of his or her practice as defined under such law.

29 CFR 825.118, 825.800 (definition of "health care provider"); S. Res. 242, Cong. Rec. S3959, S3963, S3978 (April 23, 1996); 29 CFR 825.118, 828.800 (definition of "health care provider"); *see Silcox v. VIA Christi Oklahoma Regional Medical Center—Ponca City, Inc.*, 196 Fed. Appx. 658 (10th Cir. 2006*); Langlois v. City of Deerfield Beach, Florida*, 370 F. Supp. 2d 1233, 1242 & n. 15 (S.D. Fla. March 23, 2005) (clinical psychologist and doctor of medicine identified as "health care providers" for FMLA); *Sloop v. ABTCo., Inc.*, No. 5:96CV83-V, 1998 U.S. Dist. LEXIS 16442, at *20–21 (W.D.N.C. Aug. 26, 1998), *aff'd*, 178 F.3d 1285, (4th Cir. 1999); *Sims v. Alameda-Contra Costa Transit District et al.*, 2 F. Supp. 2d 1253, 1257 (N.D. Ca. 1998).

According to the DOL, the list was compiled from the statutory definition of "health care provider," as well as a review of "definitions under several programs, including rules of the U.S. Office of Personnel Management and Medicare...." Preamble, 29 CFR 825.118; DOL WH FMLA Advisory Opinion No. 63 (June 19, 1995). The DOL went on to indicate that it developed its regulatory definition of "health care provider" by "beginning with the definition of 'physician' under the Federal Employees' Compensation Act (5 U.S.C. 8101(2))...." Preamble, 29 CFR 825.118. The FECA definition of "physician" accounts for most of the FMLA definition of "health care provider." Preamble, 29 CFR 825.118. The DOL also noted that it added Christian Science Practitioners as FMLA-covered "health care providers" to "reflect Congressional intent that such practitioners be included (as expressed in colloquies on the floors of both the House and Senate, and as reflected in the Committee Report accompanying Title II of the FMLA applicable to Federal civil service employees)." Preamble, 29 CFR 825.118.

b. Scope of Practice

The regulations require that some of the health care providers identified above be authorized to practice by the state in which they practice. Some, but not all, also add that they must be performing within the scope of their authorized practice.

The phrase "authorized to practice" means that the provider must be authorized to diagnose and treat physical or mental conditions without supervision by a doctor or other health care provider. 29 CFR 825.118(c); S. Res. 242, Cong. Rec. S3959, S3963 (April 23, 1996); 29 CFR 825.118(c). Where a "health care provider" definition contains the phrase "authorized to practice in the state," if applicable state law does not permit the provider to both diagnose and treat physical or mental health conditions without supervision by a doctor or other health care provider, the individual is not an FMLA-covered "health care provider."

For example, if the law of state B allows a clinical social worker to diagnose and treat mental health conditions, but not physical conditions, the clinical social worker is not a "health care provider" within the meaning of the FMLA. The definition requires authority to diagnose and treat mental and physical conditions. This result would not appear to change even if the affected individual was treated for a mental condition (i.e., within the authority of state law).

Curiously, the key term "authorized" is not defined. Presumably, it means that the health care provider has met whatever educational, licensure and other requirements imposed by the state to diagnose and treat physical or mental conditions in a particular area of specialty. It also presumably means that the state authorized health care provider is practicing within the scope of his or her authorization. A health care provider practicing outside of the scope of state authorization would presumably be putting his or her license or other authorization to practice at risk.

It is significant that the definition of "health care provider" includes the requirement, in some instances, that such health care providers be state authorized and practicing within the scope off that authorization. The FMLA does not recognize specialization among health care providers. A Christian Science Practitioner and a licensed physician (say, the president of Harvard Medical School) are equal for purposes of being an FMLA-covered "health care provider." Absent the state authorization requirement, a podiatrist (foot doctor) is viewed equally with a psychiatrist for purposes of providing psychiatric treatment.

The state authorization requirement adds a certain base level of specialization to the equation. For example, absent authorization, a clinical social worker could be an FMLA-covered "health care provider" for purposes of performing surgery. If the state where the clinical social worker practices does not authorize clinical social workers to perform surgery, then the clinical social worker would not be a "health care provider" within the meaning of the FMLA for purposes of leave for surgery. This becomes important when determining whether medical certification is from a "health care provider." It is also important in determining whether "continuing treatment" is being performed by, or under the direction of, a health care provider. An individual may generally be a "health care provider" for purposes of the FMLA, but not for the treatment that is the reason for the request for leave where that treatment does not fall within the parameters of the health care provider's state authorization.

c. Doctors and Osteopaths

Doctors of medicine or osteopathy must be authorized to practice medicine or surgery (as appropriate) by the state in which the doctor practices. 29 CFR 825.118(a)(1); S. Res. 242, Cong. Rec. S3959, S3963 (April 23, 1996); 29 CFR 825.118(1)(1). DOL WH FMLA Advisory Opinion No. 63 (June 19, 1995); *see Matthews v. Fairview Health Services*, No. 01-2151 ADM/AJB, 2003 U.S. Dist. LEXIS 5901, at 11 (D. Minn. April 7, 2003) (internist is a health care provider); *Sloop v. ABTCo., Inc.*, No. 5:96CV83-V, 1998 U.S. Dist. LEXIS 16442, at *20-21 (W.D.N.C. Aug. 26, 1998), *aff'd*, 178 F.3d 1285 (4th Cir. 1999); *Sims v. Alameda-Contra Cost Transit District et al.*, 2 F. Supp. 2d 1253, 1264-65 (N.D. Cal. 1998) (chiropractor not a doctor authorized to practice medicine or surgery by State of California); *Harvender v. Norton Co.*, No. 96-CV-653 (LEK/RWS), 1997 U.S. Dist. LEXIS 21467, at n. 3 (N.D.N.Y. Dec. 15, 1997) (physician).

Note that, unlike other covered health care providers, this definition does not explicitly require that the doctor of medicine or osteopathy be performing within the scope of that authorization. In most cases, a doctor would not put his or her license to practice at risk by performing outside the scope of the state authorized practice. However, the absence of an explicit requirement that doctors must be performing within the scope of their state authorization, particularly where the requirement is included elsewhere in the definition of "health care provider," suggests that arguments can be made that doctors may be FMLA-covered "health care providers" even if acting outside of the scope of their state authorization. The fact that the doctor can get in trouble for practicing outside of state authorization is the doctor's problem, not the patient's, at least for purposes of the FMLA.

d. Podiatrists, Dentists, Clinical Psychologists, and Chiropractors

Podiatrists, dentists, clinical psychologists, optometrists, and chiropractors must be both authorized to practice in the state and performing within the scope of their practice as defined by state law. 29 CFR 825.118(b)(1); S. Res. 242, Cong. Rec. S3959, S3963 (April 23, 1996); 29 CFR 825.118(b)(1). DOL WH FMLA Advisory Opinion No. 63 (June 19, 1995); *see Giuliani v. Minnesota Vikings Football Club, LLC*, No. 99-CV-1811 D.A./FLN, 2001 U.S. Dist. LEXIS 20207, at *8 (D. Minn. July 11, 2001) (licensed clinical psychologist health care provider within meaning of FMLA); *Sloop v. ABTCo., Inc.*, No. 5:96CV83-V, 1998 U.S. Dist. LEXIS 16442, at *20-21 (W.D.N.C. Aug. 26, 1998), *aff'd*, 178 F.3d 1285 (4th Cir. 1999); *LeGrand v. Village of McCook*, No. 96-C-5951, 1998 U.S. Dist. LEXIS 5230 (N.D. Ill. April 15, 1998) (chiropractors for treatment limited to manual manipulation of the spine to correct a subluxation as demonstrated by X-ray to exist).

Neither the statute nor regulations explain why chiropractors are only considered to be FMLA-covered "health care providers" for treatment consisting of manual manipulation of the spine to correct a subluxation as demonstrated by

X-ray. Treatment by a chiropractor for something other than an X-ray verified subluxation of the spine is generally not covered by the FMLA. *Silcox v. VIA Christi Oklahoma Regional Medical Center—Ponca City, Inc.*, 196 Fed. Appx. 658 (10th Cir. 2006); *Sims v. Alameda-Contra Cost Transit District et al.*, 2 F. Supp. 2d 1253, 1264–65 (N.D. Cal. 1998); *Olsen v. Ohio Edison Co.*, 979 F. Supp. 1159, 1164 (N.D. Ohio 1997). Such treatment could be covered if the employer of the employer's health plan's benefits manager were to accept such services.

e. Nurse Practitioners, Nurse Midwives and Clinical Social Workers

An FMLA "healthcare provider" includes nurse practitioners, nurse midwives and clinical social workers who are authorized to practice under state law and who are performing within the scope of their practice as defined under state law. 29 CFR 825.118(b)(2); S. Res. 242, Cong. Rec. S3959, S3963 (April 23, 1996); 29 CFR 825.118(b)(2). *See Sloop v. ABTCo., Inc.*, No. 5:96CV83-V, 1998 U.S. Dist. LEXIS 16442, at *20–21 (W.D.N.C. Aug. 26, 1998), *aff'd*, 178 F.3d 1285 (4th Cir. 1999); DOL WH FMLA Advisory Opinion No. 63 (June 19, 1995) (noting that nurse practitioners and nurse mid-wives provide diagnosis and treatment of certain conditions, especially at health maintenance organizations and in rural areas where other health care providers may not be available).

The terms "nurse practitioner, nurse midwives," and "clinical social worker," are undefined. Presumably, these occupations are defined by state law.

The regulation is not clear what happens in the absence of state law. One interpretation of the regulation is that, in the absence of a state law authorization, nurse practitioners, nurse midwives, and clinical social workers will not be considered to be FMLA-covered health care providers. For example, say that state A has no laws on its books regulating midwives. The services performed by midwives in state A are neither illegal nor regulated. In that situation, it is unclear whether such a midwife would be an FMLA-recognized "health care provider." Arguments could be made either way.

Moreover, the addition of the term "nurse" to midwives would appear to limit the pool of midwives considered as covered by the FMLA. Most states regulate who is considered a "nurse." As such, even if a state did not regulate "mid-wives" but regulated who was a "nurse," the nurse would have to be acting within the scope of his or her state authorized authority and practice in order to be considered an FMLA-covered "health care provider."

The final permutation is where state A authorizes non-nurse midwives to perform certain health care services. Arguably, such non-nurse midwives, even though they are duly authorized by the state to perform certain health care services, would nevertheless not be considered an FMLA-covered "health care provider" because they are not "nurse midwives."

According to the comments accompanying publication of the final regulations, the DOL stated that it included clinical social workers as FMLA-covered health care providers "because our review reveals that they are ordinarily authorized to diagnose and treat without supervision under state law." Preamble, 29 CFR 825.118. It appears that the reference to "supervision" means supervision by doctors. *Id.* (The next sentence of the preamble provides: "Physician's assistants are not included as health care providers under the regulations because they are ordinarily only permitted to practice under a doctor's supervision.") It is unclear what would happen if the underlying assumption for the inclusion of clinical social workers were not true. That is, would a clinical social worker still be considered to be an FMLA "health care provider" if state law did not allow them to diagnose and provide treatment without a doctor's supervision?

f. Christian Science Practitioners

Christian Science Practitioners listed with the First Church of Christ, Scientist in Boston, Massachusetts are "health care providers" within the meaning of the FMLA. 29 CFR 825.118(b)(3); S. Res. 242, Cong. Rec. S3959, S3963 (April 23, 1996); 29 CFR 825.118(b)(3). *See Sloop v. ABTCo., Inc.*, No. 5:96CV83-V, 1998 U.S. Dist. LEXIS 16442, at *20–21 (W.D.N.C. Aug. 26, 1998), *aff'd*, 178 F.3d 1285 (4th Cir. 1999).

According to the DOL (DOL WH FMLA Advisory Opinion No. 63 (June 19, 1995):

> The FMLA's definition [of health care provider] includes Christian Science Practitioners to reflect the Congressional intent that such practitioners be included as expressed in colloquies on the floors of both the House and Senate, and reflected in the Committee report accompanying Title II of the FMLA applicable to Federal civil service employees.

It is unclear how an employing agency is supposed to confirm that the Christian Science Practitioner is, in fact, registered with the First Church of Christ, Scientist in Boston, Massachusetts. Such information is not required as part of information an agency is permitted to obtain as part of a medical certification. With respect to a health care provider, the WH 380 form created by the DOL includes a signature line identifying the health care provider and another blank line in which the health care provider could identify the type of practice. *See* 29 CFR 825.306(b). Identifying the "type of practice" does not appear to reach whether the practitioner is registered with the First Church of Christ, Scientist, in Boston, Massachusetts. Since an employer is prohibited by regulation from asking for more information than is permitted, it would appear that agencies have no means to verify a Christian Science Practitioner's status as an FMLA-covered health care provider.

An employee or covered family member receiving treatment from a Christian Science Practitioner may not object to an employer requirement that the employee or covered family member submit to an examination (though not treatment) to obtain a second or third certification from a health care provider other than a Christian Science Practitioner. 29 CFR 825.118(b)(3); S. Res. 242, Cong. Rec. S3959, S3963 (April 23, 1996); 29 CFR 825.118(b)(3). An exception to this rule would allow an employee or covered family member to refuse to submit to such an examination by a health care provider other than a Christian Science Practitioner where such refusal is permitted by applicable state or local law or the terms of a collective bargaining agreement. 29 CFR 825.118(b)(3); S. Res. 242, Cong. Rec. S3959, S3963 (April 23, 1996); 29 CFR 825.118(b)(3).

State or local law would not be applicable to the federal government as an employer pursuant to the doctrine of sovereign immunity. The terms of a collective bargaining agreement, however, would apply, at least to employees covered by such terms. Generally, that would exclude members of management. [For a further discussion of medical certifications and second and third medical opinions, see Chapter 9, "Documentation Requirements."]

g. Health Care Providers Recognized by Employer or Group Health Benefits Plan Manager

An FMLA-covered "health care provider" means any health care provider from whom an employer or the employer's group health plan's benefits manager will accept certification of the existence of a serious health condition to substantiate a claim for benefits. 29 CFR 825.118(b)(4); S. Res. 242, Cong. Rec. S3959, S3963 (April 23, 1996); 29 CFR 825.118(b)(4). DOL WH FMLA Advisory Opinion No. 63 (June 19, 1995); *see Washington v. Bosch Braking systems Corp. et al.*, No. 1:98-CV-855, 1999 U.S. Dist. LEXIS 21361, at *8-9 (W.D. Mich. Nov. 24, 1999) (evidence that substance abuse treatment clinic was state licensed, although not conclusive proof, sufficient to establish that program falls within definition of "health care provider" in § 825.118*(4) to defeat summary judgment).

In successfully lobbying for inclusion of this definition of "health care provider," the comments accompanying publication of the final DOL regulations (Preamble, 29 CFR 825.118) reflect the following:

> Federally Employed Women and the Women's Legal Defense Fund noted that [the] OPM's definition for Federal civil service employees under Title II of the FMLA includes those providers recognized by the Federal Employee's Health Benefits Program, and suggested a similar approach be used by [the] DOL for Title I. They contended that including any providers covered by the employer's health insurance plan avoids confusion as to whether the services would be reimbursed and ensures ease of administration.

Accepting this argument, the DOL (Preamble, 29 CFR 825.118) stated:

> After giving careful consideration to the numerous suggestions for changes in the definition of "health care provider," we have revised the final rule in the following respects. The definition will be expanded to include any health care provider that is recognized by the employer or accepted by the group health plan (or equivalent program) of the employer. To the extent that the employers or the employers' group health plans recognize any such individuals for certification of the existence of a health condition to substantiate a claim for health care and related services that are provided, they would be included in the revised definition of "health care provider."

It is unclear from the rule who is covered. By its terms, the rule defines a "health care provider" as "any health care provider" recognized by an employer or the employer's group health plan benefits manager. The confusion stems for the use of the term "health care provider." The term is a defined term in the statute and the implementing regulations. As such, it has a defined meaning. Because "health care provider" is a defined term, the regulation can be read as inserting all of the other statutory and regulatory definitions of "health care provider" into § 825.118(b)(4). Such a reading does not advance the definition of "health care provider" as it simply repeats the other definitions of "health care provider." That does not appear to be the intention of § 825.118(b)(4).

Based on the regulatory history, it would appear that the term "health care provider" in § 825.118(b)(4) should be read as "individual." That is, the intent of § 825.118(b)(4) appears to be to expand the definition of "health care provider" to individuals in addition to the health care providers listed in the statute and the regulations (e.g., doctors, dentists, podiatrists, nurse practitioners, clinical social workers, etc.). The thought behind the regulation, presumably, is that if an employer or benefits plan manager would accept a certification from such an individual that a serious health condition exits for purposes of a claim for benefits, who are we to argue?

The regulation does not provide that if an employer or group health plan would pay this individual for services rendered, the individual is automatically an FMLA-covered "health care provider." There are a few more hurdles than that. By its terms, the regulation is predicated on acceptance by the employer or employer's group health plan's benefits manager of certification of the existence of a serious health condition. The regulation does not convert any individual who the employer would pay for health services rendered into an FMLA-covered health care provider. The term "serious health condition" is a defined term in the statute and implementing regulations. The fact that the employer or health plan manager would also pay providers of health care services for services rendered does not mean that all services by all service providers constitute "serious health conditions" by the mere fact of payment by the employer or group health plan.

The term "certification" is not defined in § 825.118(b)(4). The term appears to refer to a medical certification, which is a defined term. *See* 29 CFR 825.305(a), 825.306. As such, the employer or health benefits plan manager must be willing to accept such certification of a serious health condition to substantiate a claim for benefits. Being "willing" to accept a certification does not appear to require that such a certification is actually provided.

The rule (as amplified by the comments to the final regulation) applies to a group health plan or equivalent program. This would appear to cover the Federal Employee's Health Benefits Program.

The affect of allowing employers or their group health plan benefits manager to recognize anyone as a health care provider may convert individuals who would otherwise not be recognized as FMLA-covered health care providers into covered "health care providers." For example, as discussed above, a chiropractor is only a "health care provider" under the FMLA for very limited purposes. If, however, an employer or the employer's health plan benefits manager were to accept a medical certification from a chiropractor in situations other than manipulation of the spine pursuant to an X-ray verified subluxation, the chiropractor would be a covered "health care provider" for whatever purpose the employer or health plan benefits manager was willing to accept. *See* DOL WH FMLA Advisory Opinion No 72 (Sept. 20, 1995) (physician's assistant may be "health care provider" if recognized by employer or employer's health plan benefits manager); DOL WH FMLA Advisory Opinion No. 63 (June 19, 1995) (same for chiropractor).

In *Silcox v. VIA Christi Oklahoma Regional Medical Center—Ponca City, Inc.*, 196 Fed. Appx. 658 (10th Cir. 2006), the Tenth Circuit refused to consider a chiropractor to be an FMLA-covered health care provider under 29 CFR 825.118(b)(4) where the chiropractor performed services without a diagnostic x-ray. The court opined that "Silox's attempt to invoke 29 CFR 825.118(b)(4) is specious given the Secretary's [of Labor] clear intent to limit coverage to chiropractic treatment that is accompanied by diagnostic x-rays."

h. Health Care Providers From Other Countries

An FMLA-covered "health care provider" means a health care provider listed above who practices in a country other than the United States, who is authorized to practice in accordance with the law of that country, and who is performing within the scope of his or her practice as defined under such law. 29 CFR 825.118(b)(5); S. Res. 242, Cong. Rec. S3959, S3963 (April 23, 1996); 29 CFR 825.118(b)(5).

By its terms, the regulation recognizes for purposes of the FMLA only those "health care providers" identified in § 825.118. The regulation does not set any minimum period of time during which the health care provider must practice in a country other than the United States. Finally, it is unclear how an agency would be able to determine whether a health care provider in another country is (1) authorized to practice in another country; (2) is practicing in another country; and (3) is performing within the scope of his or her practice.

Indeed, it is unclear who has the burden, the employer or the employee, of establishing the status of a health care provider as an FMLA-qualifying health care provider. Given the fact that entitlement to FMLA leave for a serious health condition involving continuing treatment requires that such treatment be performed by a health care provider, it would appear that the burden should be placed on the employee.

2. Title II

For purposes of Title II, the term "health care provider" is defined differently than under Title I, the CAA, and the PEOAA.

a. Those Covered

The OPM regulations implementing Title II of the FMLA define a "health care provider" as:

1. Doctor of medicine;
2. Doctor of osteopathy;
3. A physician who is serving on active duty in the uniformed services;
4. Any health care provider recognized by the Federal Employees Health Benefits Program;
5. Any health care provider who is licensed or certified under federal or state law to provide the service in question;
6. A health care provider who practices in another country other than the United States;
7. A Christian Science Practitioner listed with the First Church of Christ, Scientist, in Boston, Massachusetts; or
8. A Native American who is recognized as a traditional healing practitioner by native traditional religious leaders.

5 CFR 825.1202 (definition of "health care provider"). *See Burge v. Dept. of Air Force*, 82 MSPR 75 (1999), *pet. denied*, 86 MSPR 919 (2000).

A review of each of these definitions follows.

b. Doctors

A licensed Doctor of Medicine (M.D.) or Doctor of Osteopathy (O.D.) are "health care providers" within the meaning of Title II. 5 CFR 825.1202 (definition of "health care provider," Subsection (1)). The source of the license—federal, state, local, or outside of the country—is not specified. Note that there is no indication that the doctors must be performing in the scope of their licenses in order to be considered an FMLA-covered health care provider. Normally, of course, doctors will be performing within the scope of their license as to do otherwise would put their licenses at risk, and may render them outside of malpractice insurance protections.

c. Physicians Serving on Active Duty in the Uniformed Services

The term "physician" is undefined. Also undefined for purposes of the FMLA are the terms "active duty" and "uniformed services." 5 CFR 825.1202 (definition of "health care provider," Subsection (1)).

The "uniformed services" consist of the armed forces, the commissioned corps of the Public Health Service, and the commissioned corps of the National Oceanic and Atmospheric Administration. 5 USC 2101(3). "Armed forces" means the Army, Navy, Air Force, Marine Corps, and the Coast Guard. 5 USC 2101(2). Presumably, somewhere in the ocean of federal regulations, there are definitions governing the terms "active duty" and "physician" for purposes of the uniformed services.

d. FEHBP Recognized Health Care Providers

Any health care provider recognized by the Federal Employees Health Benefits Program is an FMLA-covered "health care provider." 5 CFR 825.1202 (definition of "health care provider," Subsection (2)). By comparison, the comparable regulation under Title I, the CAA, and the PEOAA adds requirements that the group health plan benefits manager has to be willing to accept certification from such "health care provider" of the existence of a serious health condition to substantiate a claim for benefits. These added restrictions apparently do not apply under Title II.

e. Licensed Health Care Providers Under Federal or State Law

Rather than list health care providers that fit within the Title II definition of an FMLA-covered "health care provider," the regulations include all health care providers who are licensed or certified under federal or state law to provide the service in question. 5 CFR 630.1202 (definition of "serious health condition," Subsection (2)).

Because the regulation basically defines an FMLA "health care provider" as a "health care provider," the regulation is less than clear. Arguably, because "health care provider" is a defined term in the statute and regulation, this regulation could be read as simply requiring the other identified "health care providers" in § 630.1202 to have a federal or state license or certificate. A second definition (and the one that was likely intended) is that an FMLA-covered "health care provider" includes any "health care provider" recognized and licensed (or certified) in accordance with federal or state law.

Assuming the latter definition is what was intended, the regulation assumes that federal or state law will identify certain occupations as "health care providers." Not all federal or state laws may do this. Moreover, federal or state licensure alone may not indicate whether an individual is a health care provider. Tattoo parlors and barbershops are licensed by most states. It would be difficult to imagine that they are "health care providers." The underlying problem stems from the failure of the OPM to include in the regulations a definition similar to § 825.118(c) that defines "authorized to practice" as meaning diagnosis and treatment.

f. Health Care Providers Practicing in Another Country

An FMLA-covered "health care provider" means a health care provider: (1) recognized by the Federal Employees Health Benefits Program; or (2) who is licensed or certified under federal or state law to provide the service in question, who practices in a country other than the United States, who is authorized to practice in accordance with the laws of that country, and who is performing within the scope of his or her practice as defined under such law. 5 CFR 630.1202 (definition of "serious health condition," Subsection (3)).

The regulation is not clear whether the individual must exclusively practice in a country other than the United States, or whether a practice both inside and outside the United States would be permissible. There is no indication of how an agency would go about verifying that the health care provider outside of the country is duly licensed and acting within the scope of his or her license.

g. Christian Science Practitioners

Christian Science Practitioners listed with the First Church of Christ, Scientist, in Boston Massachusetts, are "health care providers" within the meaning of Title II. 5 CFR 630.1202 (definition of "serious health condition," Subsection (4)).

h. Native American Traditional Healers

A "health care provider" within the meaning of Title II of the FMLA includes:

> A Native American, including an Eskimo, Aleut, and Native Hawaiian, who is recognized as a traditional healing practitioner by native traditional religious leaders who practices traditional healing methods as believed, expressed, and exercised in Indian religions of the American Indian, Eskimo, Aleut, and Native Hawaiians, consistent with Public Law 95–314, August 11, 1978 (92 Stat. 469), as amended by Public Law 103–344, October 6, 1994 (108 Stat. 3125).

5 CFR 630.1202 (definition of "serious health condition," Subsection (5)).

Title I, the CAA, and the PEOAA do not recognize Native American traditional healers as FMLA-covered "health care providers," unless the employer or a group health plan manager would so recognize them.

E. SERIOUS HEALTH CONDITION BY PARTICULAR MEDICAL CONDITION

Courts interpreting Title I of the FMLA have had the opportunity to find for and against the existence of an FMLA-qualifying serious health condition involving a wide variety of ailments. The better practice is to judge each ailment against the requirements for a "serious health condition," as set forth in the statute and implementing regulations. However, those who are inclined to search by ailment to determine what, if any, definitions of FMLA serious health conditions are implicated, are referred to Paula F. Wolff, Annotation, *What Constitutes "Serious Health Condition" Under § 101(11) or § 102(a)(1)(D) of Family and Medical Leave Act*, 29 USCA 2611(11), 29 USCA 2612(a)(1)(D), 169 ALR Fed. 369 (2001).

F. EVIDENCE OF SERIOUS HEALTH CONDITION

There is a split in the courts' recognition of an FMLA-qualifying serious health condition requiring supporting medical evidence, or whether the statements of the employee or covered family member alone are sufficient.

The majority of courts addressing this issue, hold that, absent confirmation by a health care provider, the lay assessment of an employee or covered family member that he or she is incapacitated is insufficient to establish the existence of an FMLA-covered serious health condition. See *Lackey v. Jackson County, Tennessee*, 104 Fed. Appx. 483 (6th Cir. 2004) (aside from the plaintiff's self-serving statements, the court had no medical evidence that he had any of the illnesses he claims to have; "We only know that he sometimes visited a doctor. We, however, do not know why he did."); *Brenneman v. MedCentral Health System*, 366 F.3d 412, 421 (6th Cir. 2004), *cert. denied*, 543 U.S. 1146 (U.S. 2005) (court credited medical certification and not plaintiff's testimony in finding that leave from work, rest, and fluids do not constitute a regimen of continuing treatment as required for FMLA coverage); *Haefling v. UPS, Inc.*, 169 F.3d 494, 500-501 (7th Cir. 1999), *cert. denied*, 528 U.S. 820 (1999) ("Haefling did not submit an affidavit from his own doctor or any other medical personnel demonstrating the necessity of the 'treatments' he supposedly received, and Haefling's own self-serving assertions regarding the severity of his medical condition and the treatment it required are insufficient to raise an issue of fact" that he had a serious health condition); *Dowell v. Indiana Heart Physicians, Inc.*, No. 1:03-cv-1410-DFH-TAB, 2004 U.S. Dist. LEXIS 26431, at *18 (S.D. Ind. Dec. 22, 2004) (court declined to accept an employee's claim of pregnancy-related depression without diagnosis or treatment by a health care professional); *Bickley v. FMC Technologies, Inc.*, No. 3:02CV7212, 2003 U.S. Dist. LEXIS 9489 (N.D. Ohio June 5, 2003) (plaintiff failed to provide any medical evidence that his "infection" could qualify as a "serious health condition"); *Brown v. Seven Seventeen HB Philadelphia Corp., No. 2*, No. 01-1741, 2002 U.S. Dist. LEXIS 15066, at *1113 (E.D. Pa. Aug. 8, 2002) (under the FMLA, the only relevant opinion about whether the plaintiff was able to work belongs to the plaintiff's health care provider, not to the plaintiff or the plaintiff's supervisors); *Stiefel v. Allied Domecq Spirits & Wine U.S.A., Inc.*, 184 F. Supp. 2d 886, 891 (W.D. Ark. 2002) (absent medical opinion, the employee's own testimony that she believed subsequent absences were related to her miscarriage four to nine months earlier insufficient to establish linkage); *Evans v. Henderson*, No. 99-C-8332, 2001 U.S. Dist. LEXIS 962, at *8 (N.D. Ill. Feb. 5, 2001) (employee's own testimony that he needed time off to care for his sick children insufficient to defeat summary judgment); *Austin v. Haacker*, 76 F. Supp. 2d 1213, 1221 (D. Kan. 1999) (the employee cannot rely on his own assessment of his health condition); *Johnson v. USPS*, No. 1:97-CV-794, 1999 U.S. Dist. LEXIS 7981, at *17 (W.D. Mich. May 26, 1999) (no evidence from a doctor or any other medical provider indicating that condition for which the plaintiff suffered—a trapezius strain—was incapacitating); *Joslin v Rockwell International Corp.*, 8 F. Supp. 2d 1158, 1161 (N.D. Iowa 1998) (employee's own testimony that she was unable to work for three days in a row insufficient to prove incapacitation); *Bond v. Abbott Laborato*ries, 7 F. Supp. 2d 967, 974 (N.D. Ohio 1998) (the plaintiff's self-serving statements that he was unable to perform routine daily activities during his scheduled off-days insufficient), *aff'd on other grounds*, 188 F.3d 506 (table), No. 98-3923, 1999 U.S. App. LEXIS 22242 (6th Cir. Sept. 9, 1999); *Olsen v. Ohio Edison Co.*, 979 F. Supp. 1159, 1166 (N.D. Ohio 1997) (employee's own judgment that he or she should not work, or even that it was uncomfortable or inconvenient for the employee to have to work insufficient. What is required is a medical assessment that the employee was prevented from working due to injury or illness); *Hensley v. Baptist Hospital of East Tennessee, Inc. et al.*, No. 3:96-cv-789, 1997 U.S. Dist. LEXIS 22515, at *37 (E.D. Tenn. Oct. 27, 1997) (employee's affidavit of medical need for intermittent leave insufficient to create issue of material fact where prior medical certification released the employee to return to work); *Gudenkauf v. Stauffer Communications, Inc. et al.*, 922 F. Supp. 465, 475-76 (D. Kan. 1996) (plaintiff's deposition testimony and affidavit are insufficient evidence to base a finding that the plaintiff's pregnancy and related conditions kept her from performing the functions of her job for more than one-half day); *Brannon v. OshKosh B'Gosh, Inc.*, 897 F. Supp. 1028, 1037 (M.D. Tenn. 1995) (plaintiff's own testimony that she was "too sick to work" held insufficient to prove that her absence from work was necessary); *Sakellarion v. Judge & Dolph, Ltd.*, 893 F. Supp. 800, 807 (N.D. Ill. 1995) (plaintiff's assertion that her adult daughter needed to stay in bed, without more, held insufficient evidence from which jury could infer that daughter was incapable of self-care); *Seidle v. Provident Mutual Life Ins. Co.*, 871 F. Supp. 238, 243–44 (E.D. Pa. 1994) (plaintiff's child was not incapacitated for more than three days where pediatrician told the plaintiff to keep the child at home for only three days and child's day-care center prohibited child from attending on fourth day because of their own policy against admitting children with a runny nose); *see also Stekloff v. St. John's Mercy Health Systems*, 218 F.3d 858, 861–62 (8th Cir. 2000) (sufficient evidence of serious health condition found based on physician testimony); *Frazier v. Iowa Beef Processors, Inc.*, 200 F.3d 1190, 1195 (8th Cir. 2000) (medical records completely devoid of any evidence the physician determined the plaintiff's injury was so severe he could not perform his job); *Swanson v. Senior Resource Connection*, 254 F. Supp. 2d 945, 951, n. 2 (S.D. Ohio 2003) (physician certification created material issue of fact whether the employee's depression constituted SHC); *Washington v. Fort James Operating Co.*, 110 F. Supp. 2d 1325, 1333–34 (D. Ore. 2000) (certification from the employee's physician *prima facie* proof that the employee's absence resulted from serious health condition).

Courts in a few cases, however, have found an employee's own statement concerning his or her medical condition sufficient to create a genuine issue of material fact concerning incapacity. *See Marchisheck v. San Mateo County*, 199 F.3d 1068, 1074 (9th Cir. 1999), *cert. denied*, 530 U.S. 1214 (2000) (even though no health care provider recommended that the plaintiff's son's activities be restricted following an assault, the court found that the son's declaration that he "did not and could not do anything for four or five days" sufficient to create a disputed issue of fact whether son was incapacitated during that time); *Rankin v. Segate Technologies, Inc.*, 246 F.3d 1145, 1148–49 (8th Cir. 2001) (summary judgment on issue of incapacity held inappropriate where the plaintiff's affidavit testimony that she was too sick to work on those days, combined with evidence that she told her nurse practitioner she suffered from the same symptoms for a week prior to seeking treatment, created a genuine issue of material fact concerning her incapacity on those dates); *Stiefel v. Allied Domecq Spirits & Wine U.S.A., Inc.*, 184 F. Supp. 2d 886, 891 (W.D. Ark. 2002) (the plaintiff competent to testify that she felt bad and couldn't work); *Barrilleaux v. Thayer Lodging Group, Inc.*, No. 97–3252 § E/1, 1999 U.S. Dist. LEXIS 3436 (E.D. La. March 19, 1999) (the employee did not need to provide medical evidence of serious health condition. "Under the plain language of the statute and the legislative history…a heart attack, and heart conditions requiring by-pass surgery are serious medical conditions. Barrilleauz offered sufficient evidence via affidavits of her and her father which, despite Thayer's contentions, would be admissible at trial, establishing that her father had a 'serious medical condition' as defined by the FMLA. Clearly a layman could testify that they had a 'heart attack', that [he] had 'by-pass surgery', and that [he was] under the care of a physician for a prolonged period of time. Clearly, based on that evidence alone, Barrilleaux met her summary judgment burden of showing that she could prove at trial that her father had a serious medical condition"); *Pendarvis v. Xerox Corp.*, 3 F. Supp. 2d 53, 55–56 (D.D.C. 1998) (medical evidence of an employee unable to perform essential job functions not necessary for pregnancy-related severe morning sickness).

A child's parents are competent to testify when an illness began and the duration of the illness. *Brannon v. OshKosh B'Gosh, Inc.*, 897 F. Supp. 1028, 1037 (M.D. Tenn. 1995).

While an employee's testimony alone may not establish incapacitation, the employee's actions can establish that the employee was not incapacitated, even if a health care provider certification says otherwise. In *Barnhill v. Farmland Foods, Inc.*, No. 98–4152–CM, 2001 U.S. Dist. LEXIS 5691 (D. Kan. April 19, 2001), the court held that an employee was not incapacitated within the meaning of the FMLA where the employee performed the functions of his position during a period of time when a medical certification provided by the employee said that he was unable to work at all.

G. MEDICAL NECESSITY OF INTERMITTENT/REDUCED LEAVE SCHEDULE

As discussed more fully in Chapter 10, "Leave Amount and Scheduling," an eligible employee may take FMLA leave all at once, intermittently, or on a so-called reduced leave schedule, up to the 12 workweek entitlement each leave year. *See Hoffman v. Professional Med Team*, No. 2003 U.S. Dist. LEXIS 11913, at *5 (W.D. Mich. June 5, 2003) (upon a showing of a "serious health condition" that renders an employee unable to perform the functions of the position of the employee, an employee may seek three kinds of leave: (1) all at once; (2) intermittent leave; or (3) leave on a reduced leave schedule). The availability of FMLA leave on an intermittent or reduced leave schedule basis for a serious health condition is not without condition. What follows is a brief overview of this area.

1. Title I, the CAA, and the PEOAA

a. General Rule

FMLA leave may be taken for an employee's own serious health condition or the serious health condition of a covered family member of the employee, provided four conditions are met:

1. The leave must be medically necessary;

2. The employee must try to schedule foreseeable leave based on planned medical treatment so as not to disrupt unduly the operations of the employer, subject to the approval of the health care provider;

3. The employee must provide the employer with not less than 30 days' notice of the need for leave before the leave is to begin or, if the date of the treatment requires leave to begin in less than 30 days, the employee must provide notice as soon as practicable; and

4. If the employer requires the employee to support the request for leave with medical certification, the certification must state the dates on which treatment is expected to be given and the duration of such treatment.

29 USC 2612(b)(1); 2 USC 1312(a)(1) (incorporating section 102 of Title I, 29 USC 2612, into CAA); 3 USC 412(a)(1) (incorporating § 102 of Title I, 29 USC 2612, into PEOAA); see *Dunning v. UPS*, 471 F. Supp. 2d 795 (E.D. Mich. Jan. 18, 2007); *George v. Russell Stover Candies, Inc.*, 106 Fed. Appx. 946 (6th Cir. 2004); *Adams v. Honda of America Mfg., Inc.*, 111 Fed. Appx. 353 (6th Cir. 2004); *Hoffman v. Professional Med Team*, No. 2003 U.S. Dist. LEXIS 11913, at *5 (W.D. Mich. June 5, 2003), aff'd, 394 F.3d 414 (6th Cir. 2005); *Caraballo v. Puerto Rico Telephone, Inc.*, 178 F. Supp. 2d 60, 65 (D.P.R. 2001); *Goodwin v. Rheem Manufacturing Co.*, 15 F. Supp. 2d 1197, 1204, n.6 (M.D. Ala. 1998); *Hensley v. Baptist Hospital of East Tennessee, Inc. et al.*, No. 3:96–cv–789, 1997 U.S. Dist. LEXIS 22515, at *37 (E.D. Tenn. Oct. 27, 1997); *Beal v. Rubbermaid Commercial Products, Inc.*, 972 F. Supp. 1216, 1223 (S.D. Iowa 1997), aff'd, 1998 U.S. App. LEXIS 9295 (8th Cir. 1998); *Kaylor v. Fannin Regional Hospital, Inc.*, 946 F. Supp. 988, 997 (N.D. Ga. 1996); DOL WH FMLA Advisor Opinion No. 60 (May 2, 1995); DOL WH FMLA Advisory Opinion No. 29 (Feb. 7, 1994) (describing effect of use of intermittent leave for serious health condition). The regulations implementing the FMLA further refine the above statutory definition. 29 CFR 825.116(c), 825.203; S. Res. 242, Cong. Rec. S3959, S3963 (April 23, 1996); 29 CFR 825.116(c), 825.203. The regulations provide several examples of what it means when an employee is "needed to care for" a family member:

(a) It includes situations where, for example, because of a serious health condition, the family member is unable to care for his or her own basic medical, hygienic, or nutritional needs or safety, or is unable to transport himself or herself to the doctor, etc. The term also includes providing psychological comfort and reassurance, which would be beneficial to a child, spouse, or parent with a serious health condition who is receiving inpatient or home care.

(b) The terms also includes situation where the employee may be needed to fill in for others who are caring for the family member, or to make arrangements for changes in care, such as transfer to a nursing home.

29 CFR 825.116(a)(7(b); S. Res. 242, Cong. Rec. S3959, S3963 (April 23, 1996); 291996); 29 CFR 825.116(a), (b); see *Gradilla v. Ruskin Manufacturing*, 320 F.3d 951, 958 (9th Cir. 2003); *Hensley v. Baptist Hospital of East Tennessee, Inc. et al.*, No. 3:96–cv–789, 1997 U.S. Dist. LEXIS 22515, at *37 (E.D. Tenn. Oct. 27, 1997); *Beal v. Rubbermaid Commercial Products, Inc.*, 972 F. Supp. 1216, 1223 (S.D. Iowa 1997), aff'd, 1998 U.S. App. LEXIS 9295 (8th Cir. 1998); *Young v. USPS*, 79 MSPR 25 (1998).

b. Medical Necessity

There are two requirements that must be met in order for an eligible employee to take FMLA leave on an intermittent or reduced leave schedule basis: (1) there must be a "medical need" for such leave; and (2) an intermittent or reduced leave schedule must be the best means of accommodating that medical need. *Hoffman v. Professional Med Team*, No. 2003 U.S. Dist. LEXIS 11913, at *5 (W.D. Mich. June 5, 2003).

"Medical need" is defined as something other than voluntary treatments and procedures. 29 CFR 825.117; S. Res. 242, Cong. Rec. S3959, S3963 (April 23, 1996); 291996); 29 CFR 825.116(c), 825.203. Specifically, § 825.117 provides:

For intermittent leave or leave on a reduced leave schedule, there must be a medical need for leave (as distinguished from voluntary treatments and procedures and it must be that such medical need can be best accommodated through an intermittent or reduced leave schedule.

Defining "medical need" by what it is not is not particularly enlightening. This is particularly true when the DOL's comments regarding "voluntary treatments" are taken into consideration. In the comments accompanying publication of the final regulations defining what is a FMLA-covered "serious health condition" (Preamble, 29 CFR 825.114), the DOL made the following observation:

> The regulations have also been revised in paragraph (c) to delete the reference to "voluntary" treatments for which treatment is not medically necessary, and restrict the exclusion to cosmetic treatments (unless inpatient care is required or complications develop). *The term "voluntary" was considered inappropriate because all treatments and surgery are voluntary.* (Emphasis supplied).

If, as the DOL contends, "all" treatments are voluntary, then defining "medical need" as being "not voluntary" would appear to be meaningless.

One court equated "medically necessary" with the requirement that the leave have some medical significance. In *Kaylor v. Fannin Regional Hospital, Inc.*, 946 F. Supp. 988, 997 (N.D. Ga. 1996), the court questioned, *in dictum*, whether the employee established that his need for intermittent leave for a medical appointment was "medically necessary." The employee had a degenerative back condition that qualified as a serious health condition. His back condition required periodic visits to his physician. The court questioned the medical necessity of leave on a particular occasion. The court noted that the employee's physician testified that the plaintiff's visit was not an emergency. The court further noted that the employee's physician stated that the visit was needed to order renewed prescriptions and "make sure nothing else was going on." *Id.* at 998. The court stated that it appeared that the plaintiff's visit was "routine," and of no special medical significance. Finally, the court noted that the plaintiff waiting so late to inform his supervisor of the appointment "underscores the doubt this court has as to whether the February 3, 1995, appointment was 'medically necessary.'" *Id.*

Ultimately, whether an employee has a "medical need" for FMLA leave on an intermittent or reduced leave schedule basis will generally be determined based on the health care provider of the employee or covered family member, as reflected in the medical certification that an agency may (and should request). 29 CFR 825.117. The language of § 825.117 is not as nearly pointed on this issue as are the DOL's comments accompanying publication of the final regulations. In pertinent part (Preamble, 29 CFR 825.117), the DOL states:

> The Department's [of Labor] medical certification form, as discussed in [Section] 825.306, is the vehicle for obtaining certification of the medical necessity of intermittent leave or leave on a reduced leave schedule, and such determinations are made exclusively by the health care provider of the employee or employee's family member (subject to an employer's right to request a second opinion at its own expense if it has reason to doubt the validity of the certification provided).

In light of the above comments, it is strongly recommended that agencies request medical certification whenever FMLA leave is requested for a serious health condition, and particularly where the leave is to be taken on an intermittent or reduced leave schedule. The failure to request such certification may restrict an agency's ability to later challenge the "medical need" for the leave.

In the absence of a "medical need," FMLA leave on an intermittent or reduced leave schedule basis is not available. For example, in *Hensley v. Baptist Hospital of East Tennessee, Inc. et al.*, No. 3:96-cv-789, 1997 U.S. Dist. LEXIS 22515, at *37 (E.D. Tenn. Oct. 27, 1997), the court found that the employee, who was released to return to work without restrictions, no longer had a medical need for intermittent leave. The court concluded that, as a result of her medical release to return to work without restrictions, the employee was not subsequently entitled to intermittent FMLA leave).

c. Other Requirements and Uses of Leave

The regulations also address the requirement that an employee needing FMLA leave on an intermittent or reduced leave schedule basis must attempt to schedule leave so as not to disrupt the employer's operations. 29 CFR 825.117; S. Res. 242, Cong. Rec. S3959, S3963 (April 23, 1996); 291996); 29 CFR 825.117c); *see Evans v. Barnes-Jewish Hospital,* 160 Fed. Appx. 549 (8th Cir. 2005); *Kaylor v. Fannin Regional Hospital, Inc.*, 946 F. Supp. 988, 998 (N.D. Ga. 1996); DOL WH FMLA Advisory Opinion No. 60 (May 2, 1995) (requirement that the employee consult with the employer prior to scheduling planned medical treatment where intermittent/reduced leave schedule involved attempts to accommodate legitimate interests of employers with purposes of FMLA); DOL WH FMLA Advisor Opinion No. 60 (May 2, 1995); DOL WH FMLA Advisory Opinion No. 29 (Feb. 7, 1994). The term "disrupt" is not otherwise defined or described.

An employee who fails to make a reasonable effort to reschedule intermittent leave that would be disruptive of an employer's operations is not entitled to FMLA leave. *Kaylor*, 946 F. Supp. at 997–98.

In *Evans*, 160 Fed. Appx. at 549, the court opined that the employer did not interfere with Evans's use of FMLA leave as a result of supervisor discussions with him about his use of FMLA leave to perform tasks that could have been done during his off-duty hours, such as picking up prescriptions.

Note that the employee is only obligated to "attempt" to schedule leave to avoid disruption to agency's operations. Presumably, this means a reasonable attempt. Such a reasonable "attempt" need not be successful. On the other hand, an employee who fails to make any attempt to schedule intermittent/reduced leave schedule FMLA leave will have failed to meet this precondition for FMLA leave. As addressed more fully in Chapter 10, "Leave Amount and Scheduling," the failure of an employee to attempt to schedule leave to avoid disrupting the agency's operations has led many courts to sustain the denial of FMLA leave.

Finally, an employee's intermittent leave or a reduced leave schedule to care for a family member includes not only a situation where the family member's condition itself is intermittent, but also where the employee is only needed intermittently—such as where other care is normally available, or care responsibilities are shared with another member of the family or a third party. 29 CFR 825.116(c); S. Res. 242, Cong. Rec. S3959, S3963–64 (April 23, 1996); 291996); 29 CFR 825.116(c).

2. Title II

a. General Rule

The statutory rule under Title II is nearly identical to that under Title I, the CAA, and the PEOAA. FMLA leave may be taken by an employee on an intermittent or reduced leave schedule basis for the employee's own serious health condition, or the serious health condition of a covered family member when medically necessary. 5 USC 6382 (b)(1)–(2).

b. Medically Necessary

Neither the statute nor the regulations define when FMLA leave on an intermittent or reduced leave schedule in order for an employee to care for a covered family member would be "medically necessary." *See* 5 CFR 630.1204(b). Presumably, like Title I, the CAA, and the PEOAA, FMLA leave taken by employees covered by Title II is "medically necessary" when a health care provider says it is medically necessary.

c. Other Requirements

The first condition on an employee's ability to take FMLA leave on an intermittent or reduced leave schedule basis for the serious health condition of a covered family member involves employee notice. According to the statute (5 USC 6382(e)(2):

> In any case in which the necessity for leave…is foreseeable based on planned medical treatment, the employee–
>
> > (A) shall make a reasonable effort to schedule the treatment so as not to disrupt unduly the operations of the employing agency, subject to the approval of the health care provider of the…son, daughter, spouse, or parent of the employee, as appropriate; and
> >
> > (B) shall provide the employing agency with not less than 30 days' notice, before the date the leave is to begin, of the employee's intention to take leave under such subparagraph, except that if the date of the treatment requires leave to begin in less than 30 days, the employee shall provide such notice as is practicable.

The above statutory language is also reflected in 5 CFR 630.1206(a)–(b). Employee notice requirements are addressed in Chapter 8, "Notice Requirements."

The second condition on an employee's ability to take FMLA leave on an intermittent or reduced leave schedule basis in order to care for a covered family member with a serious health condition involves medical certifications. Specifically, if an agency requires the employee to provide a medical certification in support of the employee's request for FMLA leave, in order for the certification to be considered sufficient, it must include the dates on which planned medical treatment are expected to be given and the duration of such treatment. 5 USC 6383(b)(5). [For a further discussion of the FMLA leave taken on an intermittent or reduced leave schedule basis, see Chapter 10, "Leave Amount and Scheduling."]

IV. AGENCIES WITH MIXED FMLA RESPONSIBILITIES

Federal agencies with employees covered by more than one variant of the FMLA must carefully review each request for FMLA leave to ensure that the leave is for a covered condition within the meaning of the applicable law. As discussed at length in this chapter, there are subtle and not–so–subtle differences between the requirements of each of these variants of the FMLA, particularly between Title II and Title I. Assuming that covered conditions for purposes of Title I are the same for Title II, for example, invites violation of the requirements of the applicable law.

CHAPTER 8
NOTICE REQUIREMENTS

I. OVERVIEW

The FMLA imposes notification obligations on employees and agencies. To perfect their claim to the protections of the Act, employees are required to provide their employing agencies with timely and adequate notice of the need for FMLA leave. Agencies are required to notify employees of their FMLA rights and obligations. The notice obligations of employees and agencies vary greatly depending on which federal sector variant of the FMLA applies, as do the consequences for failure to provide notice.

Section II of this chapter discusses the "Notice Obligations of Employers." "Employee Notice Obligations" are addressed in Section III. Finally, Section IV, "Mixed Agency Responsibilities and Employee Notice", compares and contrasts FMLA notice obligations in agencies with mixed FMLA responsibilities.

II. NOTICE OBLIGATIONS OF EMPLOYERS

A. INTRODUCTION

Depending on the federal sector variant of the FMLA, employing agencies may have to notify employees of FMLA rights and obligations in as many as 15 situations. Notice is an area where there are substantial differences between the federal sector variants of the FMLA, particularly between Title II, and Title I, the CAA, and the PEOAA. Courts describe the multiple notice requirements under Title I as highly ambiguous. *See Sarno v. Douglas Elliman–Gibbons & Ives, Inc. et al.*, 183 F.3d 155, 161 (2d Cir. 1999). Each employer notification requirement is addressed below.

B. FMLA POSTER

1. Title I

By statute, employers covered by Title I (29 USC 2619(a)) must:

> [P]ost and keep posted, in conspicuous places on the premises of the employer where notices to employees and applicants for employment are customarily posted, a notice, to be prepared or approved by the Secretary [of Labor], setting forth excerpts from, or summaries of, the pertinent provisions of this Title and information pertaining to the filing of a charge.

The posting requirement is the only employer notice provision required by the Act. *Ragdsale v. Wolverine World Wide, Inc.*, 535 U.S. 81, 88, 95, 122 S. Ct. 1155, 152 L. Ed. 167 (2002); *Sarno v. Douglas Elliman–Gibbons & Ives, Inc. et al.*, 183 F.3d 155, 161 (2d Cir. 1999); *Artis v. Palos Community Hosp.*, No. 02 C 8855, 2004 U.S. Dist. LEXIS 20150, at *25 (N.D. Ill. Sept. 23, 2004).

The regulations implementing Title I further address the statutory requirement. 29 CFR 825.300. *See Robinson v. Overnite Transportation Co.*, No. 95–3067, 1997 U.S. App. LEXIS 6574, at *24 (4th Cir. April 9, 1997); *Gilmore v. U. of Rochester Strong Mem. Hospital Div.*, No. 05-CV-6037L, 2005 U.S. Dist. LEXIS 38177, at *31 (W.D.N.Y. Sept. 1, 2005); *Marrero v. Camden County Board of Social Services et al.*, 164 F. Supp. 2d 455, 466 (D.N.J. 2001) (general posting requirement); *Biermann v. Aluminum Co. of America, Davenport Works*, No. 3:98–CV–20159, 2000 U.S. Dist. LEXIS 21964 (S.D. Iowa Jan. 21, 2000); *Santos v. Shields Health Group*, 996 F. Supp. 87, 92 (D. Mass. 1998); *Sims v. Alameda–Contra Cost Transit District et al.*, 2 F. Supp. 2d 1253, 1259 (S.D. Cal. 1998); *Reich v. Midwest Plastic Engineering, Inc.*, No. 1:94–CV–525, 1995 U.S. Dist. LEXIS 8772 (W.D. Mich. June 6, 1995). An employee is presumed to have actual notice of the Act's requirements regarding employee notice of the need for FMLA leave as a result of proper posting of the employer's notice. 29 CFR 825.304(c); *see Reich v. Midwest Plastic Engineering, Inc.*, No. 1:94–CV–525, 1995 U.S. Dist. LEXIS 8772 (W.D. Mich. June 6, 1995).

The poster must be displayed by federal employers whether or not the employer employs any Title I eligible employees. 29 CFR 825.800(a). *See e.g., Lackey v. Jackson County, Tennessee,* 104 Fed. Appx. 483 (6th Cir. 2004); *Taylor v. Invacare Corp.,* 64 Fed. Appx. 516 (6th Cir. 2003); *Artis v. Palos Community Hosp.,* No. 02 C 8855, 2004 U.S. Dist. LEXIS 20150, at *25 (N.D. Ill. Sept. 23, 2004); *Sahadi v. Per-Se Technologies, Inc.,* 280 F. Supp. 2d 689, 699 (E.D. Mich. 2003); *New York Metro Area Postal Union v. Potter,* No. 00–Civ. 8538 (LTS)(RLE), 2003 U.S. Dist. LEXIS 4904, at *4 (S.D.N.Y. March 31, 2003). Most federal agencies are not aware of this requirement and are, therefore, in violation of the Title I of the FMLA. There are monetary and non-monetary penalties for violation of this provision. The purpose of the poster is to call employees' attention to the basic requirements of the FMLA and provide information as to where employees may get additional information or file a complaint. Preamble, 29 CFR 825.300; *See Reifer v. Colonial Intermediate Unit 20,* 462 F. Supp. 2d 621, 638 (M.D. Pa. 2006) (purpose of FMLA notice regulations is to allow employees to make informed decisions about leave); *Tornberg v. Business Interlink Services, Inc.,* 237 F. Supp. 2d 778, 785 (E.D. Mich. 2002) ("Presumably the regulations include these notification provisions to ensure the employee has all of the information he or she needs to make an educated decision."); *Henthorn v. Olsten Kimberly Quality Care,* No. 97–C–50182, 1999 U.S. Dist. LEXIS 2029 (N.D. Ill. Feb. 24, 1999) (rejecting as contrary to purposes of FMLA the plaintiff's argument that the employer's failure to post notice did not deprive employee of notice of FMLA rights and obligations where employee knew of requirement to provide certification, as reflected in attorney's offer to provide medical documentation as soon as possible; Henthorn's interpretation of § 825.303(b), the court held, "is too broad and is rejected").

The notice must be posted prominently in conspicuous places on the employer's premises, where it can be readily seen by employees and applicants for employment. 29 USC 2619(a); 29 CFR 825.300(a); *Sanders v. May Department Stores Co.,* 315 F.3d 940, 945 (8th Cir. 2003), *cert. denied,* 539 U.S. 942 (2003) (court noted approvingly of placement of poster in May's human resources office); *Satterfield v. Wal-Mart Stores, Inc.,* 135 F.3d 973, 983 (5th Cir. 1998), *cert. denied,* 119 S. Ct. 72 (1998); *Robinson v. Overnite Transportation Co.,* No. 95–3067, 1997 U.S. App. LEXIS 6574 (4th Cir. April 9, 1997) (approving of posting of FMLA notice on permanent bulletin boards in the drivers' area); *Reifer v. Colonial Intermediate Unit 20,* 462 F. Supp. 2d 621, 637 (M.D. Pa. 2006); *Zawadowicz v. CVS Corp. et al.,* 99 F. Supp. 2d 518, 527 (D.N.J. 2000); *Kidwell v. Board of County Commissioners of Shawnee County,* 40 F. Supp. 2d 1201, 1224 (D. Kan. 1998), *aff'd,* 1999 U.S. App. LEXIS 1560 (10th Cir. 1999). The FMLA poster should be posted with other required legal notices. Agencies need to make sure that the FMLA poster is also conspicuously posted where applicants pick up applications. The First Circuit in *Dube v. J.P. Morgan Investor Services,* 201 Fed. Appx. 786 (1st Cir. 2006), found that posting the FMLA notice on the employer's intranet site which was available to all employees at work satisfied the conspicuous posting requirement. *See also; Smith v. MedPointe Healthcare, Inc.,* No. 04-cv-6315 (PGS), 2007 U.S. Dist. LEXIS 10471, at n. 6 (D.N.J. Feb. 15, 2007). In *Dube,* the employee complained that an intranet posting was not sufficient because the employee could not access the notice from home during his leave period. The court found that the FMLA only requires that the notice be posted at the workplace. An employer is not required to post the notice where it can be seen by employees from home.

The poster and the text must be large enough to be easily read and contain fully legible text. 29 CFR 825.300(a). The DOL decided not to prescribe the precise size of the required poster. Preamble, 29 CFR 825.300. To meet the requirement that the poster be large enough to be easily read, the DOL suggests that the poster be at least the size of a 8 ½ x 11 inch piece of paper. Preamble, 29 CFR 825.300. The DOL criticized some commercially available posters which attempt to address a number of posting requirements mandated by other laws in a single poster. According to the DOL, much of the information is not legible from any reasonable distance. Preamble, 29 CFR 825.300. "If the poster does not inform, it serves no useful purpose." *Id.*

The DOL created an acceptable poster that meets the requirements of Title I. The poster, WH Publication 1420, is available for free on the DOL's website and at the DOL offices nationwide. [See copy of WH 1420 in Appendix.] The sample poster does not mention the methods by which employers calculate leave eligibility. *Bachelder v. America West Airlines, Inc.,* 259 F.3d 1112, 1127, n.15 (9th Cir. 2001).

Failure to post the required DOL FMLA poster violates the FMLA. *Taylor v. Invacare Corp.,* 64 Fed. Appx. at 516, (6th Cir. 2003). There are two penalties for an employer's failure to post the required FMLA notice. First, an employer who willfully fails to post the required notice may be assessed a civil monetary penalty by the DOL Wage and Hour Division not to exceed $100 for each separate offense. 29 USC 2619(b); 29 CFR 300(b); *see Satterfield v. Wal-Mart Stores, Inc.,* 135 F.3d 973, 983 (5th Cir. 1998), *cert. denied,* 119 S. Ct. 72 (1998); *Zawadowicz v. CVS Corp. et al.,* 99 F. Supp. 2d 518, 527, n.6 (D.N.J. 2000); *Johnson v. USPS,* No. 1:97–CV–794, 1999 U.S. Dist. LEXIS 7981 (W.D. Mich. May 26, 1999); *Reich v. Midwest Plastic Engineering, Inc.,* No. 1:94–CV–525, 1995 U.S. Dist. LEXIS 8772 (W.D. Mich. June 6, 1995). It is unclear how "each separate offense" is calculated. Presumably, if an agency customarily posts notices in 100 locations in each of 100 facilities where the agency has employees, an agency that has not posted any Title I FMLA notices could be subject to a $10,000 per day fine ($100 fine x 100 locations x each day) in civil penalties.

The second penalty imposed by Title I for an employing agency's failure to post the required FMLA notice prohibits the agency from taking any adverse action against an employee, including denying leave, for failing to furnish the agency with advance notice of the employee's need to take FMLA leave. 29 CFR 825.300(b); *see Invacare Corp.*, 64 Fed. Appx. at 516; *Sanders v. May Department Stores Co.*, 315 F.3d 940, 945 (8th Cir. 2003), *cert. denied*, 539 U.S. 942 (2003); *Bachelder v. America West Airlines, Inc.*, 259 F.3d 1112, 1127, n.15 (9th Cir. 2001); *Ramey v. USPS*, No. 99–3327, 1999 U.S. App. LEXIS 657 (Fed. Cir. 1999); *Satterfield v. Wal-Mart Stores, Inc.*, 135 F.3d 973, 983 (5th Cir. 1998), *cert. denied*, 119 S. Ct. 72 (1998); *Taylor v. Texaco, Inc.*, No. 4:04-CV-212-JEC, 2007 U.S. Dist. LEXIS 22239, at *38 (N.D. Ga. March 28, 2007); *Sahadi v. Per-Se Technologies, Inc.*, 280 F. Supp. 2d 689, 699 (E.D. Mich. 2003); *Tornberg v. Business Interlink Services, Inc.*, 237 F. Supp. 2d 778, 785 & n.5 (E.D. Mich. 2002); *Johnson v. Moundsvista, Inc.*, No. 01–915 (DWF/AJB), 2002 U.S. Dist. LEXIS 16450, at n.7 (D. Minn. Aug. 28, 2002) (non-posting employer estopped from challenging adequacy of employee notice where need for leave is foreseeable). Note that this penalty only addresses situations where the employee failed to provide advance notice of a need for FMLA leave. *Kidwell v. Board of County Commissioners of Shawnee County*, 40 F. Supp. 2d 1201, 1224 (D. Kan. 1998), *aff'd*, 1999 U.S. App. LEXIS 15690 (10th Cir. 1999); *Henthorn v. Olsten Kimberly Quality Care*, No. 97-C-50182, 1999 U.S. Dist. LEXIS 2029 (N.D. Ill. Feb. 24, 1999); *Reich*, 1995 U.S. Dist. Lexis 8772 (employer's alleged failure to post notices was relevant only if employee was required to provide notice of intent to take leave). It would not apply where the need for FMLA leave was not foreseeable. *See Satterfield*, 135 F.3d at 983; *Gay v. Gilman Paper Co.*, 125 F.3d 1432, 1436, n. 6 (11th Cir. 1997); *Johnson v. Moundsvista, Inc.*, No. 01–915 (DWF/AJB), 2002 U.S. Dist. LEXIS 16450, at n.7 (D. Minn. Aug. 28, 2002). *But see Ramey v. USPS*, No. 99–3327, 1999 U.S. App. LEXIS 657 (Fed. Cir. 1999) (Ramey not prejudiced where MSPB found that the agency failed to post required notice and, pursuant to this finding, excluded from consideration those periods of unscheduled leave during which employee was eligible under the FMLA.).

Courts have held that an employee does not have a cause of action for monetary damages solely based on an employer's failure to comply with the posting requirement. *See Mullin v. Rochester Manpower, Inc. et al.*, 204 F. Supp. 2d 556, 563 (W.D.N.Y. 2002); *Johnson v. USPS*, No. 1:97–CV–794, 1999 U.S. Dist. LEXIS 7981 (W.D. Mich. May 26, 1999); *Kidwell*, 40 F. Supp. 2d at 1224 (D. Kan. 1998); *Knussman*, 16 F. Supp. 2d at 608, n.3; *Mitchell v. Continental Plastic Containers, Inc.*, No. C-1-97-412, 1998 U.S. Dist. LEXIS 21465 (S.D. Ohio March 3, 1998); *Blumenthal v. Murray*, 946 F. Supp. 623, 627 (N.D. Ind. 1996); *Jessie v. Carter Health Care Center, Inc.*, 926 F. Supp. 613, 617 (E.D. Ky. 1996); *Hendry v. GTE North, Inc.*, 896 F. Supp. 816, 828 (N.D. Ind. 1995).

However, an employer's failure to give adequate notice concerning an employee's rights and obligations under the FMLA may amount to interference with the employee's FMLA rights if such failure causes the employee to forfeit FMLA protections. *Biermann v. Aluminum Co. of America, Davenport Works*, No. 3:98–CV–20159, 2000 U.S. Dist. LEXIS 21964 (S.D. Iowa Jan. 21, 2000); *Goodwin-Haulmark v. Menninger Clinic, Inc.*, 76 F. Supp. 2d 1235, 1242 (D. Kan. 1999); *Mitchell v. Continental Plastic Containers, Inc.*, No. C–1–97–412, 1998 U.S. Dist. LEXIS 21465 (S.D. Ohio March 3, 1998).

In *Satterfield v. Wal–Mart Stores, Inc.*, 135 F.3d 973, 983 (5th Cir. 1998), *cert. denied*, 119 S. Ct. 72 (1998), the court noted that nothing in the DOL FMLA regulations placed the burden of proving compliance with the posting requirement of § 825.300(a) on the employer. In that case, the plaintiff alleged that, because Wal–Mart did not present evidence that it posted the required notice, it was prohibited from firing her, even if she failed to give notice of her need for FMLA leave.

When an employer's workforce is comprised of a significant portion of workers who are not literate in English, the employer must provide the posted FMLA notice in a language in which the employees are literate. 29 CFR 825.300(c). The regulations fail to provide guidance on what constitutes illiteracy in English. Does it mean reading and writing, or just oral comprehension? With oral comprehension, does it mean a complete inability to communicate in English, or something less?

The regulations do not require an employing agency to post an FMLA notice in a language other than English unless a "significant portion" of the employer's workforce is not literate in English. Unfortunately, the term "significant portion" is not defined in the regulation. Does that mean over 50 percent? At least a third?

Absent any guidance on these issues, agencies would be well advised to err on the side of caution and post notices in English and other languages when a relatively modest percentage of the workforce (10% or more) is not fluent in English. Agencies should also consider placing little weight on whether an individual is "literate" in English. Rather, agencies should make a practical determination based on whether the primary spoken language of a significant portion of the workforce is one other than English. If the answer is yes, the poster must also be in the language of the significant portion of employees. It is possible for a workforce to have several different significant portions of non–English speaking workers, necessitating posters in English and other languages.

The posting of a notice is only one of several required notices that employers are required to provide employees addressing FMLA entitlements and obligations. *Bachelder v. America West Airlines, Inc.*, 259 F.3d 1112, 1127, n.15 (9th Cir. 2001). As such, satisfaction of the posting requirement does not meet all of the employers' notice requirements. *Bachelder v. America West Airlines, Inc.*, 259 F.3d 1112, 1127, n. 15 (9th Cir. 2001).

2. CAA

The CAA does not require the posting of a notice to employees of their FMLA rights and responsibilities. The posting requirement of § 109 of Title I, 29 USC 2919, is not incorporated by reference into the CAA. The regulations interpreting the CAA, moreover, do not include a posting requirement. In fact, the comparable CAA regulation is marked "reserved." S. Res. 242, Cong. Rec. S3959, S 3971 (April 23, 1996); 29 CFR 825.300.

Remember, however, that employees of the legislative or judicial branches of the United States are covered by Title I if they are employed in a unit having employees in the competitive service, such as employees of the Government Printing Office. 29 CFR 825.109(d). CAA–covered employing offices must take this into consideration before deciding that no Title I required poster is required.

3. PEOAA

The PEOAA does not require a covered employing office to post a notice of FMLA rights and obligations. While it incorporates certain provisions of Title I of the FMLA, the posting requirement of § 2619 is not one of them. Moreover, as the Executive Office of the President is claiming that it does not have regulations implementing the FMLA, the posting requirement is not mandated by an implementing regulation either.

4. Title II

Title II does not include a requirement that agencies with covered employees post a notice of FMLA rights and obligations. Unlike Title I, the statutory language of Title II does not contain a posting requirement. Nor do the implementing regulations require agencies to post a notice advising employees of FMLA rights and responsibilities. With respect to notice, Title II (5 CFR 630.1203(g)) provides:

> Each agency shall inform its employees of their entitlements and responsibilities under this subpart, including the requirements and obligations of employees.

Accord Davis v. VA, No. CH-0752-06-0724-I-1, 2006 MSPB LEXIS 7394, at *16 (Dec. 12, 2006); *Cole v. DHHS*, No. DC-0752-05-0457-I-1, 98 MSPR 167 (2005); *Williams v. Dept. of Navy*, No. DC-0752-05-0431-I-1, 2005 MSPB LEXIS 6866, at *5 (Oct. 17, 2005), *pet. denied*, 101 MSPR 33 (2006); *Burge v. Dept. of Air Force*, No. AT-0752-97-0060-I-1, 82 MSPR 75 (1999); *Landahl v. Dept. of Commerce*, 83 MSPR 40 (1999); *Jeffries v. Dept. of Navy*, 78 MSPR 255 (1998).

To meet this requirement, OPM suggests that agencies may wish to provide employees access to the FMLA and OPM's implementing regulations or agency policies or guidance on implementing the FMLA. Also, agencies may provide employee's access to OPM's fact sheet and brochure, "*FMLA Employee Entitlements Under the Family and Medical Leave Act of 1993*" or "*Family–Friendly Leave Policies for Federal Employees*," both of which are available on OPM's website. Again, OPM does not require posting of FMLA rights and responsibilities.

The omission of a requirement that agencies notify employees of their FMLA entitlements and obligations by posting is not helpful to employees as it is one less means available to employees to learn of their employment rights and obligations. Federal agencies are often rightfully held to a higher standard in order to serve as a model employer. Requiring your local Burger Barn to post an FMLA notice to employees while at the same time leaving the overwhelming majority of federal employees in the dark hardly meets that higher "model" standard.

Moreover, the required Title I FMLA poster only partially mitigates the failure of the OPM to require a poster directed to employees covered by Title II of the Act. While some of the language in the Title I poster applies to Title II, other language is misleading at best, and wrong at worst when applied to Title II. For example, the Title I poster indicates that the DOL is authorized to investigate and resolve FMLA complaints, and that employees can also file a civil action for violations. Both of these statements are absolutely false when applied to employees covered by Title II of the Act.

Of course, enlightened agencies voluntarily, or as a negotiated requirement with a union, may want to post the OPM fact sheet or brochures in the same places that other similar employment notices are posted. This will aid employees in understanding their rights and obligations. It will also benefit agencies, which will be able to argue that the employee had actual or constructive notice of his or her FMLA rights because of postings. It will also demonstrate that the agency went the "extra mile" to inform employees of their FMLA rights and responsibilities.

C. HANDBOOKS, MANUALS, AND OTHER WRITTEN GUIDANCE

1. Title I and the CAA

If an FMLA-covered employing agency has any eligible employees and has any written guidance to employees concerning employee benefits or leave rights, such as in an employee handbook, information concerning FMLA entitlements and employee obligations under the FMLA must be included in the handbook or other written document. 29 CFR 301(a); S. Res. 242, Cong. Rec. S3959, S3971 (April 23, 1996); 29 CFR 825.301(a); *see Bachelder v. America West Airlines, Inc.*, 259 F.3d 1112, 1127 (9th Cir. 2001); *Thornton v. BASF*, No. 99-2243, 2000 U.S. App. LEXIS 15909, at n.2 (4th Cir. July 11, 2000); *Bond v. Abbott Laboratories*, No. 98-3923, 1999 U.S. App. LEXIS 22242 (6th Cir. Sept. 9, 1999); *Robinson v. Overnite Transportation Co.*, No. 95-3067, 1997 U.S. App. LEXIS 6574 (4th Cir. April 9, 1997) (applying interim regulations); *Reifer v. Colonial Intermediate Unit 20*, 462 F. Supp. 2d 621, 637 (M.D. Pa. 2006); *Fatima v. Laboratory Corp. of America*, No. 04-5739 (JAP), 2006 U.S. Dist. LEXIS 75724, at *11 (D.N.J. Oct. 18, 2006); *Dodaro v. Village of Glendale Heights*, No. 01-C-6396, 2003 U.S. Dist. LEXIS 5056 (N.D. Ill. March 31, 2003); *Tornberg v. Business Interlink Services, Inc.*, 237 F. Supp. 2d 778, 785 (E.D. Mich. 2002); *Marrero v. Camden County Bd. Of Social Services et al.*, 164 F. Supp. 2d 455, 466 (D.N.J. 2001). For example, if an employing agency provides employee handbooks to all employees that describe the agency's policies regarding leave, wages, attendance, and similar matters, the handbooks must incorporate information on FMLA rights and responsibilities and the employer's policies regarding the FMLA. 29 CFR 301(a); S. Res. 242, Cong. Rec. S3959, S3971 (April 23, 1996); 29 CFR 825.301(a).

Note that this obligation only applies to employing agencies with eligible employees. The poster requirement applies to all agencies, whether or not they have eligible employees. If an agency or employing office does not have any current eligible employees, the requirement does not apply. Of course, even if the employing agency does not have any current eligible employees, it could voluntarily decide to include FMLA statements in any written materials.

Under Title I, the inclusion of FMLA rights and obligations into the employer's written materials was supposed to be accomplished by the effective date of the FMLA. Preamble, 29 CFR 825.301. The effective date of the FMLA for most employers was August 5, 1993. For employers with active collective bargaining agreements the effective date of the FMLA was delayed until February 5, 1994. 29 CFR 825.102(a).

Neither the DOL nor the CAA prescribes particular language to be included in the employee handbook or other written materials. The DOL opined that there is no requirement that an employer include information regarding the process for filing complaints and advising the employees of their right to file a private civil suit. Preamble, 29 CFR 825.301. According to the DOL (Preamble, 29 CFR 825.301):

> The purpose of this provision is to provide employees the opportunity to learn from their employers of the manner in which that employer intends to implement FMLA and what company policies and procedures are applicable so that employees may make FMLA plans fully aware of their rights and obligations. It was anticipated that to some large degree these policies would be peculiar to that employer. Consequently, it would be of little use to incorporate the Department's Fact Sheet or a Department statement in the employer's handbook for employees.

Notwithstanding the above, informational publications describing the FMLA's provisions which may be incorporated in employing agency handbooks or written policies have been developed by, and are available from, the DOL (for employees covered by Title I) and the Office of Compliance (for employees covered by the FMLA as applied through the CAA).

A few courts addressed the substance of the FMLA notice language in an employee handbook. For example, in *Bitney v. Fred Meyer Jewelers, Inc.*, No. 02-1226-JE, 2004 U.S. Dist. LEXIS 19283, at *32 (D. Or. Sept. 17, 2004), the court found that although the employer's employee handbook noted the requirement that medical certifications must be provided in a "timely manner," it did not define the term. According to the court, "[f]ailure to set out the specific requirement that certification be provided within 15 days in written material explaining leave benefits violated legal requirements under the FMLA." This failure was significant, the court found, given that the employee's failure to timely provide the medical certification was the only reason provided at the time for denying plaintiff's request for leave, and given that plaintiff's termination was processed before plaintiff could provide the certification.

Bitney suggests that federal employers with eligible employees and employee handbooks or other written guidance regarding employee benefits or leave rights should spell out Title I and CAA employee FMLA rights and obligations in detail.

In *Fry v. First Fidelity Bancorporation*, No. 95-6019, 1996 U.S. Dist. LEXIS 875 (E.D. Pa. Jan. 31, 1996); the court found that the employer's FMLA notice contained in an employee handbook was inadequate. The employer in that case provided 16 weeks of family and medical leave; 4 weeks more than the minimum required by the Statute. In describing an employee's right to reinstatement from leave, however, the handbook did not mention or otherwise explain that an employee who takes more than the 12 weeks of FMLA leave permitted by the Statute is no longer guaranteed the right to reinstatement. Moreover, the court found that other provisions in the handbook were misleading as they indicated that the rights guaranteed therein were designed to provide an employee with equal or greater FMLA rights than those mandated by the FMLA. According to the district court:

> Thus, as a result of defendant's omission from the handbook of its policy concerning the designation of FMLA leave and the explicit statement therein and that it intends to confer rights equal to or greater than FMLA rights, an employee of defendant could be mislead into believing that he or she retains full FMLA rights even if he or she takes the full 16 weeks of leave offered by defendant. It is clear, therefore, that the handbook omits essential information concerning an employee's FMLA rights and the employer's FMLA policies. Hence, defendant's employee handbook does not comport with the notice provisions of 29 CFR 825.301, and, therefore, may violate the FMLA by interfering with an employee's right to invoke the reinstatement protections of the statute by electing to take only [12] weeks of leave.

At minimum, *Fry* stands for the proposition that the notice of FMLA rights in an employee handbook must be accurate and not misleading. The interaction of employee policies with statutory rights must be clearly explained. *See Kruse v. Laguardia Hospital*, No. 95-CV-4467 (JG), 1996 U.S. Dist. LEXIS 22433 (E.D.N.Y. Nov. 6, 1996) (applying *Fry*, the court held that employer notice was inadequate where it failed to clearly differentiate FMLA rights with similar, but not equal, rights pursuant to the employer's Leave of Absence policy).

Note that *Fry* went on to hold that the failure of the employer to provide adequate notice in an employee handbook did not automatically amount to a statutory violation. Rather, a violation of the handbook notice provision is actionable only if the inadequate notice effectively interfered with the plaintiff's statutory rights. The district court further indicated that a violation of the handbook notice provision could be cured by providing complete and adequate specific notice of FMLA rights and obligations, as required by § 825.301(c).

A number of courts have held that employer notice violations are actionable only if they deprive an employee of FMLA entitlements. *See Hunt v. Rapides Healthcare System, LLC*, 277 F.3d 757, 768 (5th Cir. 2001) (no actionable FMLA claim regardless of the quality of employer notice of FMLA rights and obligations where employee received all entitlements under Act); *Sarno v. Douglas Elliman-Gibbons & Ives, Inc.*, 17 F. Supp. 2d 271, 275 (S.D.N.Y. 1998), *aff'd*, 183 F.3d 155 (2d Cir. 1999); *Lacoparra v. Pergament Home Centers, Inc.*, 982 F. Supp. 213, 223 (S.D.N.Y. 1997); *Dodgens v. The Kent Manufacturing Co.*, 955 F. Supp. 560, 564-65 (D.S.C. 1997) (although the employer's failure to include statement of FMLA rights in the employee handbook clearly violated FMLA, the court found that it "would be elevating form over substance" to permit this claim to go forward in light of the fact that Dodgens received all of the leave benefits he was guaranteed pursuant to the FMLA); *Kruse v. LaGuardia Hospital*, No. 95-CV-4467 (JG), 1996 U.S. Dist. LEXIS 22433 (E.D.N.Y. Nov. 6, 1996) (to be actionable, deficiencies in the employer written FMLA guidance must cause the employee to forfeit FMLA rights).

In finding that the employer provided sufficient notice to its employees of their rights under the FMLA, the circuit court in *Robinson v. Overnite Transportation Co.*, No. 95-3067, 1997 U.S. App. LEXIS 6574 (4th Cir. April 9, 1997), noted approvingly that, within a few weeks of the effective date of the FMLA, Overnite revised its family and medical leave policy and disseminated the policy to all employees during employee meetings held to discuss the new policy or was provided with their paychecks. The court further noted that FMLA notices were posted on permanent bulletin boards in the drivers' areas, and a FMLA notice was contained in the first employee handbook that was distributed in June 1994, following the effective date of the FMLA. There was, the circuit court held, sufficient evidence from which the district court could conclude that Overnite fully complied with its notice requirements under the interim regulations, both by providing notice of the FMLA at the time of the effective date and by including information about the FMLA in its first handbook issued after the effective date. The circuit court did not address the substance of the notice.

An employer's satisfaction of the requirement to include notice in a handbook or manual of employee FMLA rights and responsibilities does not also satisfy an employer's responsibility to provide the employee with written notice "detailing the specific expectations and obligations of a failure to meet these obligations." *Henthorn v. Olsten Corp.*, No. 97–C–50182, 1999 U.S. Dist. LEXIS 2029 (N.D. Ill. Feb. 24, 1999). According to the *Henthorn* court:

> Section 301 addresses two types of notices: general (section 301(a)) and specific (section 301(b)). While Olsten's handbook satisfies section 301(a)'s general notice provisions because it includes a detailed explanation of the FMLA, it does not satisfy Section 301(b). Section 301(b) addresses written notices to be given to an employee who has requested an FMLA leave. Such a notice is to include specific information about that particular employee.

Several courts have held that a violation of the FMLA's handbook notice provision in 29 CFR 825.301(a) is actionable only if the employer's inadequate notice effectively interfered with an employee's statutory rights since a violation of 29 CFR 825.301(a) may be cured by proper notice under 29 CFR 825.301(c). *LeGrand v. Village of McCook*, No. 96–C–5951, 1998 U.S. Dist. LEXIS 5230 (N.D. Ill. April 15, 1998); *Fry v. First Fidelity Bancorporation*, No. CIV. A. 95–6019, 1996 U.S. Dist. LEXIS 875 (E.D. Pa. Jan. 30, 1996).

2. PEOAA

A PEOAA–covered employing office is not required to incorporate written notice of FMLA rights and obligations into employee handbooks or other written materials comparable to the requirements of Title I and the CAA. This conclusion results from the manner in which the PEOAA handles the absence of regulations implementing the FMLA.

Absent FMLA implementing regulations, the PEOAA provides (3 USC 455):

> In any proceeding under section 453(1), if the President, or the designee of the President, has not issued a regulation on a matter for which this chapter requires a regulation to be issued, the administrative agency shall apply, to the extent necessary and appropriate, the most relevant substantive executive agency regulation promulgated to implement the statutory provision at issue in the proceeding.

A proceeding under section 453(1), 3 USC 453(1), permits an employee to file a complaint with the MSPB alleging a violation of the FMLA. The MSPB is directed to apply the "most relevant substantive executive agency regulation promulgated to implement the FMLA."

Regulations implementing the FMLA for purposes of the PEOAA must "be the same as substantive regulations promulgated by the Secretary of Labor to implement the statutory provisions referred to in subsections (a) and (b)." 3 USC 412(c)(2). The referenced statutory provisions, 29 USC 2611–2615, 2617, do not include a requirement that an agency notify employees of FMLA rights or obligations. As a result, it does not appear that the MSPB could rely on the agency notification regulations implementing Title I for complaints alleging violation of the PEOAA. Stated more broadly, there is no PEOAA obligation to include a notice of FMLA rights and obligations in an employee handbook, manual, or other written material regarding employee leave and benefits.

Of course, just because the PEOAA does not require inclusion of FMLA information in an employee handbook or other written material regarding employee benefits and leave, does not mean that PEOAA–covered employers are precluded from voluntarily including such information. Unions and other organizations representing employees may also wish to bargain for the inclusion of such language.

3. Title II

Title II does not specifically require agencies to include a statement of FMLA rights and obligations into an employee handbook or other written materials. Rather, as addressed above, the regulations implementing Title II generally require an agency to inform employees of their FMLA entitlements and responsibilities. 5 CFR 630.1203(g); *Dias v. VA*, No. NY-0752-04-0279-I-2, 2005 MSPB LEXIS 3926, at *15 (June 30, 2005), *rev'd*, 102 SPR 53 (2006), *appeal dismissed*, 2006 U.S. App. LEXIS 28961 (Fed. Cir. 2005), *vacated, reinstated*, 2006 U.S. App. LEXIS 32257 (Fed. Cir. 2006), *aff'd*, 2007 U.S. App. LEXIS 11530 (Fed. Cir. 2007). There is some suggestion in the comments to the final OPM regulations that agencies may meet this general notice requirement by including written guidance in agency policies. Specifically, the comments (Preamble, 5 CFR 1203) provide that:

> To meet this [notice] requirement, agencies may wish to provide employees access to the FMLA and [the] OPM's implementing regulations or agency policies or guidance on implementing the FMLA.

The comments to the OPM implementing regulations also provide that agencies may meet the general notice requirement by providing employees access to the OPM's fact sheet and brochure, "Federal Employee Entitlements Under the Family and Medical Leave Act of 1993" or "Family–Friendly Leave Policies for Federal Employees." There is no indication in the regulations how an agency is to "provide" an employee access to these documents. Presumably, access could be provided by incorporating these documents into agency handbooks or other written materials describing employee leave and benefits, including FMLA benefits.

In *Dias v. VA*, No. NY-0752-04-0279-I-2, 2005 MSPB LEXIS 3926, at *17 (June 30, 2005), *rev'd*, 102 SPR 53 (2006), *appeal dismissed*, 2006 U.S. App. LEXIS 28961 (Fed. Cir. 2005), *vacated, reinstated*, 2006 U.S. App. LEXIS 32257 (Fed. Cir. 2006), *aff'd*, 2007 U.S. App. LEXIS 11530 (Fed. Cir. 2007), the Board found that, without further explanation, the employer's request that the employee provide "appropriate supportive documentation" failed to adequately inform the employee as to what medical documentation would be acceptable.

D. ABSENCE OF AGENCY WRITTEN GUIDANCE

1. Title I and the CAA

In the unlikely event that an employing agency does not have written policies, manuals, or handbooks describing employee benefits and leave provisions, the employing agency must provide written guidance to an employee concerning all of the employee's rights and obligations under the FMLA. 29 CFR 825.301(a)(2); S. Res. 242, Cong. Rec. S3959, S3971 (April 23, 1996); 29 CFR 825.301(a)(2); *see Conoshenti v. PSE&G Gas Co.*, 364 F.3d 135, 142 (3d Cir. 2004); *Bachelder v. America West Airlines, Inc.*, 259 F.3d 1112, 1127, n.14 (9th Cir. 2001); *Bond v. Abbott Laboratories*, No. 98–3923, 1999 U.S. App. LEXIS 22242 (6th Cir. Sept. 9, 1999); *Dodaro v. Village of Glendale Heights*, No. 01–C–6396, 2003 U.S. Dist. LEXIS 5056, at n. 7 (N.D. Ill. March 31, 2003); *Sims v. Alameda–Contra Cost Transit District et al.*, 2 F. Supp. 2d 1253, 1259 (S.D. Cal. 1998).

What constitutes such "written policies" was addressed by the circuit court in *Bond*, 1999 U.S. App. LEXIS 22242. There, the employee argued that the employer's attendance control policy constituted a "written policy" bringing the employer within the requirements of § 825.301(a)(1). Because the attendance control policy did not contain the required notice of FMLA rights and responsibilities, the employee alleged that the employer was in violation of the Act. Disagreeing, the court found that the attendance control policy did not constitute a "written policy" within the meaning of § 825.301(a)(1). According to the court, the attendance control policy "did not function as, nor was it intended to provide, written guidance to employees concerning their general benefits and leave rights. The sole purpose of Abbott's Attendance Control Program was to provide a system of progressive discipline for unexcused absences. By the express terms of [Section] 825.301(a)(1), information concerning FMLA entitlements and employee obligations was not required to be included in the program."

The DOL and the Office of Compliance do not prescribe the contents of such written guidance. To meet this requirement, agencies may duplicate and provide a copy of the FMLA Fact Sheet available from the DOL (for Title I employees) or Office of Compliance (for employees covered by the CAA). 29 CFR 825.301(a)(2); S. Res. 242, Cong. Rec. S3959, S3971 (April 23, 1996); 29 CFR 825.301(a)(2). This would appear the better course of action for agencies to take as it is otherwise unclear what an agency would need to provide in order to meet the requirement that the written guidance notify employees of "all" employee FMLA rights and obligations.

Employing agencies must provide this written guidance to employees each time notice is given pursuant to §

825.301(a)(2), and in accordance with those provisions. 29 CFR 825.301(a)(2); S. Res. 242, Cong. Rec. S3959, S3971 (April 23, 1996); 29 CFR 825.301(a)(2). The requirements of § 825.301(b) are addressed more fully below.

2. PEOAA

Absent implementing regulations requiring notification, there does not appear to be any legal obligation on a PEOAA-covered employing office to provide written guidance to employees of their FMLA rights and obligations.

3. Title II

Title II of the FMLA, as discussed previously, does not specifically require an agency to provide written guidance to an employee of FMLA rights and obligations. That the examples given by the OPM for how an agency may meet the general notice requirement involves FMLA fact sheets, brochures, and other forms of written guidance. The general agency notice obligation does not indicate the manner, frequency, or means of agency notice.

E. SPECIFIC NOTICE OF EMPLOYEE RIGHTS AND OBLIGATIONS

1. Title I and the CAA

a. General Rule

In addition to a poster (Title I only), information where a federal employer has eligible employees, and written guidance on employee benefits and leave right, federal employers are required to provide each employee with written notice detailing the specific expectations and obligations of the employee and explaining any consequences of a failure to meet these obligations. 29 CFR 825.301(b)(1); S. Res. 242, Cong. Rec. S3959, S3971 (April 23, 1996); 29 CFR 825.301(b)(1); *see Conoshenti v. PSE&G Gas Co.*, 364 F.3d 135, 142 (3d Cir. 2004); *Fogelman v. Greater Hazelton Health Alliance*, 122 Fed. Appx. 521 (3d Cir. 2004); *Perry v. Jaguar of Troy*, 353 F.3d 510, 514 (6th Cir. 2003); *Rager v. Dade Behring, Inc.*, 210 F.3d 776, 777 (7th Cir. 2000) (written notice must address the requirement to timely submit medical certification and consequences of failure to provide certification); *Robinson v. Overnite Transportation Co.*, No. 95-3067, 1997 U.S. App. LEXIS 6574 (4th Cir. April 9, 1997) (applying interim regulations); *Bitney v. Fred Meyer Jewelers, Inc.*, No. 02-1226-JE, 2004 U.S. Dist. LEXIS 19283, at *24 (D. Or. Sept. 17, 2004); *Conrad v. Eaton Corp.*, 303 F. Supp. 2d 987, 999 (N.D. Iowa 2004); *Smith v. Blue Dot Co.*, 283 F. Supp. 2d 1200, 1204 (D. Kan. 2003). The requirement that an employer provide such written specific notice is conditioned on proper notification by the employee of the need for FMLA leave. *Levine v. The Children's Museum of Indianapolis, Inc.*, No. 02-3013, 2003 U.S. App. LEXIS 5755 (7th Cir. March 24, 2003); *Sanders v. May Department Stores Co.*, 315 F.3d 940, 945 (8th Cir. 2003), *cert. denied*, 539 U.S. 942 (2003); *Lara v. Central Grocers Cooperative, Inc. et al.*, No. 00-C-7828, 2002 U.S. Dist. LEXIS 16745 (N.D. Ill Sept. 6, 2002); *Lara*, 2002 U.S. Dist. LEXIS 16745. If an employee fails to provide his or her employer with adequate notice of the need for FMLA leave, the employer is under no obligation to provide specific notice as required by § 825.301(c). *Sanders*, 315 F.3d at 945 *Bachelder v. America West Airlines, Inc.*, 259 F.3d 1112, 1131 (9th Cir. 2001), *cert. denied*, 539 U.S. 942 (2003); *Strickland v. Water Works & Sewer Bd.*, 239 F.3d 1199, 1207 (11th Cir. 2001) (affirming summary judgment for employer as there was no evidence that the employee told the supervisor he was leaving work for medical reasons); *Brungart v. Bellsouth Telecommunication, Inc.*, 231 F.3d 791, 800 (11th Cir. 2000), *cert. denied*, 532 U.S. 1037 (2001) (holding that employer was not liable because the decision maker who fired the plaintiff did not know that she was about to take leave at all, protected or otherwise); *Bailey v. Amsted Indus. Inc.*, 172 F.3d 1041 (8th Cir. 1999) (affirming judgment for the employer because it lacked notice that the plaintiff's frequent absences were for medical reasons); *Robinson v. Overnite Transportation Co.*, No. 95-3067, 1997 U.S. App. LEXIS 6574 (4th Cir. April 9, 1997) (the employer § 825.301(c) notice obligation never triggered when the employee failed to notify the employer of a need for FMLA leave).

The use of the term "also" suggests that the specific notice is in addition to written guidance. *Wilson v. Lemington Home for the Aged*, 159 F. Supp. 2d 186, 193-94 (W.D. Pa. 2001) ("also" interpreted to mean that requirement of specific written notice is in addition to notice in an employee handbook). Note that this will require an employing agency that does not have written policies, a manual, or handbooks describing employee benefits and leave provisions (a rarity in the federal sector) to provide two notices to the employee: the notice required by § 825.301(a)(2) and the specific notice required by § 825.301(b). The former is satisfied by provision of the DOL FMLA Fact Sheet. The latter is satisfied by providing specific notice in conformance with the requirements of § 825.301(b).

Finally, in the category of no good deed goes unpunished, the district court in *Barnhill v. Farmland Foods, Inc.*, No. 98-4152-CM, 2001 U.S. Dist. LEXIS 5691 (D. Kan. April 19, 2001), rejected the plaintiff's claim of retaliation based on the employer's provision of FMLA forms because the employee had not requested them. In rejecting the claim, the court noted that an employer is required to provide employees who may qualify for leave with written notice of their rights and obligations under the FMLA, citing §§ 825.301(b) & (c).

b. Required Contents of Notice

The contents of the specific written notice that an employing agency must provide an eligible employee covered by Title I or the CAA is prescribed. Specifically, the notice must include the following:

- That the leave will be counted against the employee's annual FMLA leave entitlement (see § 825.208);

- Any requirements for the employee to furnish medical certification of a serious health condition and the consequences of failing to do so (see §825.305);

- The employee's right to substitute paid leave and whether the employer will require the substitution of paid leave, and the conditions related to any substitution;

- Any requirement for the employee to make any premium payments to maintain health benefits, the arrangements for making such payments, and the possible consequences of failure to make such payments on a timely basis (i.e., the circumstances under which coverage may lapse) (see § 825.210);

- Any requirement for the employee to present a fitness-for-duty certificate to be restored to employment (see § 825.310);

- The employee's status as a "key employee" and the potential consequences that restoration may be denied following FMLA leave, explaining the conditions required for such denial (see § 825.218);

- The employee's right to restoration to the same or an equivalent job upon return from leave (see §§ 825.214 and 825.604); and

- The employee's potential liability for payment of health insurance premiums by the employer during the employee's unpaid FMLA leave if the employee fails to return to work after taking FMLA leave (see § 825.213).

29 CFR 825.301(b)(1)(i)-(viii); S. Res. 242, Cong. Rec. S3959, S3971 (April 23, 1996); 29 CFR 825.301(b)(1)(i)-(viii); *see Conoshenti v. PSE&G Gas Co.*, 364 F.3d 135, 142 (3d Cir. 2004); *Fogelman v. Greater Hazelton Health Alliance*, 122 Fed. Appx. 521 (3d Cir. 2004); *Fatima v. Laboratory Corp. of America*, No. 04-5739 (JAP), 2006 U.S. Dist. LEXIS 75724, at *11 (D.N.J. Oct. 18, 2006) (employer notice obligation limited to 8 items specified in the regulations); *Bitney v. Fred Meyer Jewelers, Inc.*, No. 02-1226-JE, 2004 U.S. Dist. LEXIS 19283, at *24 (D. Or. Sept. 17, 2004); *Wilson v. Lemington Home for the Aged*, 159 F. Supp. 2d 186, 192093 (W.D. Pa. 2001); *see also Plesha v. U.S. Steel Corp.*, No. 2:05-CV PS, 2007 U.S. Dist. LEXIS 9230, at *16 (N.D. Ind. Feb. 7, 2007); *Fatima v. Laboratory Corp. of America*, No. 04-5739 (JAP), 2006 U.S. Dist. LEXIS 75724, at *11 (D.N.J. Oct. 18, 2006) (notice must include 8 items listed in 29 CFR 825.301(b)(1)); *Rager v. Dade Behring, Inc.*, 210 F.3d 776, 777 (7th Cir. 2000) (written notice required of 15-day deadline for submission of medical certification and consequences of failure to provide certification); *Stewart v. Sears, Roebuck and Co.*, No. CV-04-428-HU, 2005 U.S. Dist. LEXIS 42371, at *29 (D. Ore. March 7, 2005); *Karnes v. Central Texas Mental Health/Mental Retardation Center*, No. 6:01-CV-045-C, 2002 U.S. Dist. LEXIS 2951 (N.D. Tex. Feb. 22, 2002) (employer letter sufficiently advised employee of obligation/consequences regarding health care premium payments during FMLA leave). While not required by the regulations, the Third Circuit recommended that employers include information on the availability of intermittent leave as part of their FMLA notice to employees. *See Weisman v. Buckingham Township*, No. 04-CV-4719, 2005 U.S. Dist. LEXIS 11696, at *19 (E.D. Pa. June 14, 2005).

Employers are not required to inform employees that the right to take FMLA leave to care for a sick family member expires on the death of that family member. *Fatima v. Laboratory Corp. of America*, No. 04-5739 (JAP), 2006 U.S. Dist. LEXIS 75724, at *19 (D.N.J. Oct. 18, 2006).

In *Alexander v. Ford Motor Co.*, 204 F.R.D. 314, 319 2001 U.S. Dist. LEXIS 19180 (E.D. Mich. Nov. 5, 2001), the plaintiff alleged that Ford did not provide its employees with adequate notice of their FMLA rights. The court found that Ford's "Family and Medical Leave Act of 1993 Notice" incorporates all of the required provisions. The district court observed:

> The notice instructs the employee that he or she has 15 days to provide medical certification, and that the failure to provide this certification in a timely manner could delay the leave, result in AWOL classification, jeopardize FMLA rights and/or result in discharge...The notice also advises that the leave will not be counted against FMLA entitlement if Accident & Sickness coverage is available. The noticed also informs employees of both reinstatement rights and fitness-for-duty requirements. Moreover, it is Ford's policy to expressly require that this notice be provided to the employee with the original medical certification form and with every recertification form. If the Plaintiff was not provided with proper notification of his or her FMLA rights, it was not due to a Ford policy.

The specific notice may also include other information, such as whether the employing agency will require periodic reports of the employee's status and intent to return to work, but is not required to do so. 29 CFR 825.301(b)(2); S. Res. 242, Cong. Rec. S3959, S3971 (April 23, 1996); 29 CFR 825.301(b)(2). There is nothing in the regulation that precludes the employer from providing more information than required, only from providing less. Preamble, 29 CFR 825.301.

The DOL (for employees covered by Title I) and the Office of Compliance (for employees covered by the FMLA as applied through the CAA) have created a prototype notice for use by employing agencies, which employers may adapt for their use to meet these specific notice requirements. 29 CFR 825.301(b)(2); S. Res. 242, Cong. Rec. S3959, S3971 (April 23, 1996); 29 CFR 825.301(b)(2). Provision of the prototype notice satisfies the employer's specific notice obligation. *Stonum v. U.S. Airways, Inc.*, 83 F. Supp. 2d 894, 900–901 (S.D. Ohio 1999). [See Appendix, DOL WH 381 and Office of Compliance Prototype Notices.]

Note that the prototype notices require agencies to add information unique to each employee requesting FMLA leave. An employing agency that decides to create its own form rather than use the prototype forms must avoid using a static form for all occasions. A static form that requires no individualized input will likely fail to satisfy all of the content requirements of the FMLA. *See* Preamble, 29 CFR 825.301 (It would be inappropriate to use a generic notice as much of the information may be employee specific, particularly the arrangements for payment of insurance co-payments). Agencies are well advised to use the approved prototype forms to avoid the prospect that forms they create fail to meet the requirements of the FMLA. With respect to paid leave substitution, an employer's notice that simply repeats the regulatory language that the FMLA permits an employee to substitute paid leave for unpaid leave fails to notify the employee that the employer will substitute paid leave for unpaid leave, and is legally deficient. *Chan v. Loyola University Medical Center*, No. 97-C-3170, 1999 U.S. Dist. LEXIS 2790 (N.D. Ill. March 3, 1999).

c. Language of Notice

The employing agency must provide the employee with specific written notice in a language in which the employee is literate. 29 CFR 825.301(b)(1); S. Res. 242, Cong. Rec. S3959, S3971 (April 23, 1996); 29 CFR 825.301(b)(1). Note that this will require agencies to tailor the specific notice to the language literacy of every employee requesting FMLA leave. The FMLA poster requirement, you may recall, required agencies to post FMLA notices in languages other than English only where a "significant portion" of the workforce is not literate in English.

The regulation fails to define what "literate" means for purposes of the specific FMLA notice requirement. Presumably, it means the ability to read and comprehend the language of the written specific notice. The regulations fail to indicate what obligation, if any, the agency has to determine the language literacy of each employee. Absent a more specific literacy-testing requirement, presumably an agency may satisfy this requirement through informal means. Where there is a question regarding the employee's language literacy, an agency should inquire further in order to determine what language it must provide the specific written notice of FMLA rights and obligations. An agency that assumes that all employees are literate in English where the actual language literacy could be readily determined, may find itself in violation of this provision.

Employee literacy for FMLA notice purposes was addressed in *Chan v. Loyola University Medical Center*, No. 97-C-3170, 1999 U.S. Dist. LEXIS 2790 (March 3, 1999). There, the employee was bi-lingual. The employee alleged that the specific notice provided by the employer was inadequate because Chan's Chinese language skills were better than her English language skills. This argument, the district court noted, may be based on 29 CFR 825.301(b)(1), which requires that "the written notice must be provided to the employee in a language in which the employee is literate." The court went on to hold that Chan failed to provide evidence that she is not literate in English. In her deposition, Chan testified that she did not have a problem reading or understanding English. Moreover, she worked as a pharmacist for Loyola since 1977. The decision is noteworthy in that it places the burden of proof on language literacy on the employee.

Note also that, unlike the FMLA poster requirement, illiteracy in English is not a precondition for the requirement. An employee literate in multiple languages could be provided a specific written notice in a language other than English, even though English is the individual's primary language.

Employers furnishing FMLA-required notices to sensory impaired individuals must also comply with all applicable requirements under federal law. 29 CFR 825.301(e); S. Res. 242, Cong. Rec. S3959, S3971 (April 23, 1996); 29 CFR 825.301(e). Presumably, that means that specific written notice needs to be provided to the employee in Braille, if the employee reads Braille. Agencies need to be careful in this area not to treat sensory-impaired employees differently than non-sensory impaired employees. Agencies may not meet this requirement by orally advising the sensory-impaired employee of his or her FMLA rights, while non-sensory impaired employees are provided written notice. Moreover, such disparate treatment may run afoul of the disability laws, such as the Rehabilitation Act.

d. Manner, Timing, and Frequency of Providing Written Specific Notice

Written specific notice (and the notice required by § 825.301(a)(2)) must be provided to the employee no less often than the first time in each six-month period that an employee gives notice of the need for FMLA leave, if FMLA leave is taken during the six-month period. 29 CFR 825.301(c); S. Res. 242, Cong. Rec. S3959, S3971 (April 23, 1996); 29 CFR 825.301(c); *see Sanders v. May Department Stores Co.*, 315 F.3d 940, 945 (8th Cir. 2003), *cert. denied*, 539 U.S. 942 (2003); *Stewart v. Sears, Roebuck and Co.*, No. CV-04-428-HU, 2005 U.S. Dist. LEXIS 42371, at *29 (D. Ore. March 7, 2005). This means that specific notice need not be given each time an employee takes FMLA leave. Preamble, 29 CFR 825.301.

The specific notice must be given within a reasonable time after notice of the need for leave is given by the employee, which generally means within one or two business days, if feasible. 29 CFR 825.301(c); S. Res. 242, Cong. Rec. S3959, S3971 (April 23, 1996); 29 CFR 825.301(c); *see Ragdsale v. Wolverine World Wide, Inc.*, 535 U.S. 81, 122 S. Ct. 1155, 152 L. Ed. 167 (2002); *Perry v. Jaguar of Troy*, 353 F.3d 510, 514 (6th Cir. 2003) (employer must give specific written notice of FMLA rights and obligations when an employee first asks for FMLA leave); *Plesha v. U.S. Steel Corp.*, No. 2:05-CV PS, 2007 U.S. Dist. LEXIS 9230, at *16 (N.D. Ind. Feb. 7, 2007); *Kent v. Maryland Transportation Auth.*, No. CCB-06-2351, 2006 U.S. Dist. LEXIS 94832, at *9 (D. Md. Dec. 21, 2006), *aff'd* 2007 U.S. App. LEXIS 16228 (4th Cir. July 9, 2007); *McCarthy v. Eschelon Telecom, Inc.*, No. 04-4842 (JRT/FLN), 2006 U.S. Dist. LEXIS 58623, at *9 (D. Minn. Aug. 18, 2006); *Shivakumar v. Abbott Laboratories et al.*, No. 99-7861, 2001 U.S. Dist. LEXIS 9628 (N.D. Ill. July 10, 2001). If leave has already begun, the specific written notice should be mailed to the employee's address of record. 29 CFR 825.301(c); S. Res. 242, Cong. Rec. S3959, S3971 (April 23, 1996); 29 CFR 825.301(c).

e. Changed Circumstances and Specific Notice

If the specific information provided by the notice changes with respect to a subsequent period of FMLA leave during the six-month period, an employing agency must, within one or two business days of receipt of the employee's notice of a need for FMLA leave, provide written notice referencing the prior notice and setting forth any of the information in § 825.301(b) that has changed. 29 CFR 825.301(c)(1); S. Res. 242, Cong. Rec. S3959, S3971 (April 23, 1996); 29 CFR 825.301(c)(1); *see Wilson v. Lemington Home for the Aged*, 159 F. Supp. 2d 186, 193-94 (W.D. Pa. 2001). For example, if the initial leave period were paid leave and the subsequent leave period would be unpaid leave, the employing agency may need to give notice of the arrangements for the employee to make group health care premium payments. 29 CFR 825.301(c); S. Res. 242, Cong. Rec. S3959, S3971 (April 23, 1996); 29 CFR 825.301(c).

The regulations are not clear regarding how this requirement works where FMLA leave is taken on an intermittent or reduced leave schedule. Where leave is taken intermittently or on a reduced leave schedule for the same underlying covered condition, the employee need only give notice of the need for leave once at the beginning of the leave period. 29 CFR 825.302(a); S. Res. 242, Cong. Rec. S3959, S3971 (April 23, 1996); 29 CFR 825.302(a); *see Bailey v. Amsted Industries, Inc.*, 172 F.3d 1041, 1045-46 (8th Cir. 1999) (notice need only be given one time); *Collins v. The U.S. Playing Card Co.*, 466 F. Supp. 2d 954, 965 (S.D. Ohio Nov. 6, 2006). Because the employee need not give notice of the need for additional intermittent FMLA leave, the employing agency would not be obligated to provide notice referencing any changes from the original specific written notice. Where, however, the subsequent request for FMLA leave is independent of any previous FMLA leave taken in the six-month period, the agency would be obligated to provide specific written notice of any changes in the prior notice, as required by § 825.301(c)(1).

The above result is clearly suggested by the DOL and CAA regulations, particularly in light of the way the DOL defines "leave." See DOL WH FMLA Advisory Opinion No. 112 (Sept. 11, 2000) (for purposes of calculation of employee eligibility, "leave" commences on first absence in series of intermittent period of FMLA leave, not on every individual absence). Under this interpretation, even where substantial changes have occurred since the employee's original notice of the need for FMLA leave, an agency would technically not be obliged to provide specific written notice of such changes to an employee when leave is taken on an intermittent or reduced leave schedule basis.

With that said, there is nothing prohibiting agencies from providing specific written notice more often than the minimum required by the Act. Agencies should seriously consider ignoring the distinction between leave taken in a single block and leave taken on an intermittent or reduced leave schedule basis for purposes of subsequently providing specific written notice of changes occurring since issuance of the agencies original specific written notice. The intent of the regulations appears to be to require employing agencies to keep employees current on their FMLA rights and obligations. In that sense, the exclusion of updates for employees on intermittent or reduced schedule FMLA leave until those periods have expired (and some may never expire) appears unhelpful to employees and agencies. Agencies and employees would be better served if an agency were to provide the employee with specific written notice of changes from the original specific written notice whenever those changes occur, including during an absence that forms a part of a series of absences during a period of FMLA leave taken on an intermittent or reduced leave schedule basis.

f. Specific Notice of Medical Certification or Fitness for Duty Requirement

As a general rule, an employing agency must provide specific written notice to the employee that a medical certification or "fitness-for-duty" report is required with respect to each employee notice of the need for leave. 29 CFR 825. (2)(I); S. Res. 242, Cong. Rec. S3959, S3971 (April 23, 1996); 29 CFR 825.301(c)(2)(I); see Perry v. Jaguar of Troy, 353 F.3d 510, 514, n.1 (6th Cir. 2003); Rager v. Dade Behring, Inc., 210 F.3d 776, 777 (7th Cir. 2000) (written notice must address the requirement to timely submit medical certification and consequences of failure to provide certification); Covucci v. Service Merchandise Co., Inc., No. 97–4472, 1999 U.S. App. LEXIS 2073 (6th Cir. Feb. 8, 1999) (interim regulations); Tenney v. Total Renal Care, Inc., No. 8:05-CV-662, T-23MAP, 2006 U.S. Dist. LEXIS 52730, at *12 (M.D. Fla. June 22, 2006); Bitney v. Fred Meyer Jewelers, Inc., No. 02–1226–JE, 2004 U.S. Dist. LEXIS 19283, at *33 (D. Or. Sept. 17, 2004); Conrad v. Eaton Corp., 303 F. Supp. 2d 987, 999 (N.D. Iowa 2004); Tornberg v. Business Interlink Services, Inc., 237 F. Supp. 2d 778, 785, n.5 (E.D. Mich. 2002); Shtab v. The Greate Bay Hotel and Casino, Inc., 173 F. Supp. 2d 255, 264 (D.N.J. 2001); Wilson v. Lemington Home for the Aged, 159 F. Supp. 2d 186, 193–94 (W.D. Pa. 2001); Michelle v. SMC Pneumatics, Inc., No. IP99-1285-C-T/G, 2000 U.S. Dist. LEXIS 12478 (S.D. Ind. Aug. 21, 2000).

Use of the term "each time" indicates that the employer is required to notify the employee on a per occasion basis of the need for medical certification to substantiate the FMLA leave. A general notice in an employee manual that the employer wants medical certification for an absence is insufficient. See Tenney v. Total Renal Care, Inc., No. 8:05-CV-662, T-23MAP, 2006 U.S. Dist. LEXIS 52730, at *12 (M.D. Fla. June 22, 2006); Harcourt v. Cincinnati Bell Tel. Co., 383 F. Supp. 2d 944, 961 (S.D. Ohio Aug. 18, 2005).

Employers must provide the employee with specific written notice of the return-to-work certification requirement either at the time notice of the need for leave is given or immediately after leave commences and the employer is advised of the medical circumstances requiring the leave. 29 CFR 825.301(b)(1)(v); 29 CFR 825.310(e); Bobel v. Bolingbrook's Park District, No. 05 C 2482, 2006 U.S. Dist. LEXIS 44851, at *9 (N.D. Ill. June 19, 2006).

Such written notice must detail the specific expectations and obligations of the employee and explain any consequences of a failure to meet these obligations. Lipscomb v. Electronic Data Systems, Corp., 462 F. Supp. 2d 581, 588 (D. De. Nov. 28, 2006); Conrad v. Eaton Corp., 303 F. Supp. 2d 987, 999 (N.D. Iowa 2004).

An employer must give notice of a requirement for medical certification each time a certification is required. 29 CFR 825.305(a); Perry v. Jaguar of Troy, 353 F.3d 510, 514, n.2 (6th Cir. 2003); Conrad, 303 F. Supp. 2d at 999. Subsequent written notifications are not required if notice is given after the employee first requests leave, and the employee handbook clearly provides that certification is required. 29 CFR 825.301(c)(2)(ii); Jaguar of Troy, 353 F.3d at 514, n.1. Specific notice that a medical certification is required and the consequences of failing to provide same may be gleaned from a number of sources. In *Ridings v. Riverside Medical Center*, No. 05-2134, 2006 U.S. Dist. LEXIS 86991, at *14-15 (C.D. Ill. Nov. 30, 2006), the court found that the employer provided the employee with sufficient written notice of the obligation to provide medical certification and of the consequences of failing to do same based on several documents. The medical certification form supplied to the employee indicated that she had 15 days to provide the certification, or the leave could be delayed. After 15 days passed, the employer issued a written corrective action report indicating that the employee was not authorized to work reduced hours, and that if she continued to fail to report for full duty she could be disciplined. *See also Hurt v. EcoLab, Inc.*, No. 3-05-CV-1508-BD, 2006 U.S. Dist. LEXIS 47564, at *9 (N.D. Tex. July 13, 2006) (letter and accompanying materials, including physician's statement of disability and cover letter warning that failure to provide proper medical certification may result in discipline found sufficient notice).

Where an employer fails to inform an employee of FMLA rights and obligations as required, an employee's failure to provide acceptable medical documentation will not preclude the employee from being covered under the FMLA. *Cooper v. Fulton County, Georgia*, 458 F.3d 1282, 1285 (11th Cir. 2006); *Bitney v. Fred Meyer Jewelers, Inc.*, No. 02–1226–JE, 2004 U.S. Dist. LEXIS 19283, at *24 (D. Or. Sept. 17, 2004); *Tornberg v. Business Interlink Services, Inc.*, 237 F. Supp. 2d 778, 785 (E.D. Mich. 2002) (employer failed to provide specific written notice detailing obligations regarding leave and consequences of failure to supply medical certification); *Shivakumar v. Abbott Laboratories et al.*, No. 99–7861, 2001 U.S. Dist. LEXIS 9628 (N.D. Ill. July 10, 2001) (same).

An employer's failure to provide such notice may constitute actionable interference with an employee's FMLA rights. *Saroli v. Automation & Modular Components, Inc.*, 405 F.3d 446, 454 (6th Cir. 2005) (demand that employee present fitness-for-duty certification without prior notice violates the Act); *Tenney v. Total Renal Care, Inc.*, No. 8:05-CV-662, T-23MAP, 2006 U.S. Dist. LEXIS 52730, at *12 (M.D. Fla. June 22, 2006); *Michelle v. SMC Pneumatics, Inc.*, No. IP99–1285–C–T/G, 2000 U.S. Dist. LEXIS 12478 (S.D. Ind. Aug. 21, 2000). It also renders unlawful any action against the employee for failure to comply with the 15–day time limit. *Jaguar of Troy*, 353 F.3d at 514; *Bitney*, 2004 U.S. Dist. LEXIS 19283, at *24. A few courts have excused an employer's failure to provide written notice of an employee's obligation to provide a medical certification where the employee was already aware of the requirement prior to requesting leave. *See Harrell v. USPS*, 445 F.3d 913, 915-916 (7th Cir. 2006); *Schimek v. MCI, Inc.*, No. 3-05-CV-0045-P, 2006 U.S. Dist. LEXIS 54747, at *37 & n.11 (N.D. Tex. Aug. 7, 2006) (citing *Allendar v. Raytheon Aircraft Co.*, 339 F. Supp. 2d 1196, 1205 (D. Kan. 2004)); *Bobel v. Bolingbrook's Park District*, No. 05 C 2482, 2006 U.S. Dist. LEXIS 44851, at *10-12 (N.D. Ill. June 19, 2006). *But see Bitney v. Fred Meyer Jewelers, Inc.*, No. 02-1226-JE, 2004 U.S. Dist. LEXIS 19283, at *35 (D. Or. Sept. 17, 2004) (employee's independent knowledge of the 15-day requirement to provide medical certification does not trump the requirement that such notice be provided in writing).

According to several courts, an employer's failure to provide written notice to an employee of the consequences of failing to provide medical certification does not necessarily bar an employer from taking adverse action against an employee who fails to provide medical certification. *Lubke v. City of Arlington*, 455 F.3d 489, 497-98 (5th Cir. 2006); *Curry v. Neumann*, No. 98–8969–CIV–JORDAN, 2000 U.S. Dist. LEXIS 14758 (S.D. Fla. April 3, 2000); *Henthorn v. Olsten Corp.*, No. 97–C–508182, 1999 U.S. Dist. Lexis 2029 (N.D. Ill. Feb. 24, 1999); *Cox v. Autozone, Inc.*, 990 F. Supp. 1369, 1375–80 (M.D. Ala. 1998), *aff'd*, 180 F.3d 1305 (11th Cir. 1999).

In *Lubke*, the Fifth Circuit opined *in dicta*, that the Supreme Court's reasoning in *Ragsdale v. Wolverine World Wide*, 535, U.S. 81 (2002), counsels against the validity of the sanction in 29 CFR 825.301(f) if the consequences would afford the employee an FMLA remedy to which he or she would not otherwise be entitled. An exception to the general rule frees agencies from the obligation to provide specific written notice of the requirement of a medical certification or "fitness–for–duty" report each time an employee notifies an agency of the need for FMLA leave. Such notice is not required when the initial notice in the six–month period and the employer's handbook or other written materials (if any) describing the employer's leave policies, clearly provide that certification or a "fitness–for–duty" report is required. 29 CFR 825.301(c)(2)(ii); S. Res. 242, Cong. Rec. S3959, S3971 (April 23, 1996); 29 CFR 825.301(c)(2)(ii); *see Wilson v. Lemington Home for the Aged*, 159 F. Supp. 2d 186, 193–94 (W.D. Pa. 2001). For example, the statement should clearly state that certification would be required in all cases, by stating that certification would be required in all cases in which leave of more than a specified number of days is taken, or by stating that a "fitness–for–duty" report would be required in all cases for back injuries in a certain occupation. 29 CFR 825.301(c)(2)(ii); S. Res. 242, Cong. Rec. S3959, S3971 (April 23, 1996); 29 CFR 825.301(c)(2)(ii).

Agencies, however, are not let completely off the notice hook under this exception. Where the above exception applies and agencies are relieved of providing subsequent written notice of the requirement of a medical certification or "fitness–for–duty" report each time an employee notifies an employing agency of the need for FMLA leave, the agency remains obligated to provide oral notice of the requirement. 29 CFR 825.301(c)(2)(ii); S. Res. 242, Cong. Rec. S3959, S3971 (April 23, 1996); 29 CFR 825.301(c)(2)(ii). Of course, in these litigious days, agencies would be well advised to memorialize such oral notice in writing, thereby, as a practical matter, rendering the exception moot.

Again, note that the specific written notice requirement of a medical certification or "fitness–for–duty" report is tied to an employee's notice to the agency of the employee's need for FMLA leave. An employee need only notify an agency once of the need for FMLA leave, even if that leave involves multiple absences taken intermittently or on a reduced leave schedule basis. As such, an agency does not have to provide an employee with such written notice every time an employee is absent intermittently or on a reduced leave schedule. The agency would only have to provide such notice where the employee's notice of the need for FMLA leave involves a new request for FMLA leave separate and apart from any FMLA leave that was previously taken. It is believed this is the correct interpretation.

It is unclear whether the DOL and the Office of Compliance really mean the above. An alternative interpretation would interpret "leave" as being equivalent to "absence." Such an interpretation would be contrary to the DOL's stated definition of "leave," at least for purposes of employee eligibility. *See* DOL WH FMLA Advisory Opinion No. 112 (Sept. 11, 2000). Under this interpretation, agencies would be obligated to provide written notice of the requirement of a medical certification or "fitness–for–duty" report every time an employee was absent on FMLA leave, including multiple absences where leave was taken intermittently or on a reduced leave schedule basis related to the same underling covered condition. The underlying problem is that the central term "leave" is not defined in the statutes or implementing regulations.

Until further guidance is provided by the DOL and Office of Compliance, cautious agencies should consider giving the required written notice every time an employee requests an absence that is covered by the FMLA where the agency requires a medical certification or a "fitness–for–duty" report. Doing more than the minimum required by the regulations is rarely a bad idea.

g. Employer's Duty to Answer Employee Questions

Employing agencies are expected to responsively answer questions from employees concerning their rights and responsibilities under the FMLA. 29 CFR 825.301(d); S. Res. 242, Cong. Rec. S3959, S3971 (April 23, 1996); 29 CFR 825.301(d); *Stewart v. Sears, Roebuck and Co.*, No. CV-04-428-HU, 2005 U.S. Dist. LEXIS 42371, at *30 (D. Ore. March 7, 2005). No further guidance is provided regarding this requirement. Presumably, an agency has a reasonable period of time to answer the employee's questions. While there is no requirement that an agency provide its answers in writing, prudent agencies should make a written record of the question, the date it was asked, the date it was answered, and the answer given.

h. Failure of Employing Agency to Provide Specific Notice

If an employing agency fails to provide notice in accordance with the provisions of § 825.301, the employing agency may not take action against an employee for the employee's failure to comply with any provision required to be set forth in the notice. 29 CFR 825.301(f); S. Res. 242, Cong. Rec. S3959, S3971 (April 23, 1996); 29 CFR 825.301(f); *see Tenney v. Total Renal Care, Inc.*, No. 8:05-CV-662, T-23MAP, 2006 U.S. Dist. LEXIS 52730, at *12 (M.D. Fla. June 22, 2006); *Hurt v. Ecolab, Inc.*, No. 3-05-CV-1508-BD, 2006 U.S. Dist. LEXIS 47564, at *9 (N.D. Tex. July 13, 2006); *Bitney v. Fred Meyer Jewelers, Inc.*, No. 02-1226-JE, 2004 U.S. Dist. LEXIS 19283, at *24 (D. Or. Sept. 17, 2004); *Dodaro v. Village of Glendale Heights*, No. 01-C-6396, 2003 U.S. Dist. LEXIS 5056 (N.D. Ill. March 31, 2003); *Shivakumar v. Abbott Laboratories et al.*, No. 99-7861, 2001 U.S. Dist. LEXIS 9628 (N.D. Ill. July 10, 2001); *Wilson v. Lemington Home for the Aged*, 159 F. Supp. 2d 186, 193–94 (W.D. Pa. 2001); *Sims v. Alameda–Contra Cost Transit District et al.*, 2 F. Supp. 2d 1253, 1259 (S.D. Cal. 1998).

In order for an employee to succeed on a claim of actionable interference with FMLA rights as a result of an employer's failure to provide the employee with specific notice of FMLA obligations, the employee must establish both a failure to provide specific notice and prejudice resulting from such failure. *Harrell v. USPS*, 445 F.3d 913, 930 (7th Cir. 2006), *cert. denied*, 127 S. Ct. 845 (2006) (employee failed to demonstrate harm by employer's failure to timely inform employee of return-to-work fitness for duty obligations); *Conoshenti v. PSE&G Gas Co.*, 364 F.3d 135, 142–145 (3d Cir. 2004) (citing *Ragsdale v Wolverine World Wide*, Inc., 535 U.S. 81, 122 S. Ct. 1155 (2002); *Fogelman v. Greater Hazelton Health Alliance*, 122 Fed. Appx. 521 (3d Cir. 2004); *Kent v. Maryland Transportation Auth.*, No. CCB-06-2351, 2006 U.S. Dist. LEXIS 94832, at *9 (D. Md. Dec. 21, 2006), *aff'd*, 2007 U.S. App. LEXIS 16228 (4th Cir. July 9, 2007); *Reifer v. Colonial Intermediate Unit 20*, 462 F.

Supp. 2d 621, 638 (M.D. Pa. 2006); *McCarthy v. Eschelon Telecom, Inc.*, No. 04-4842 (JRT/FLN), 2006 U.S. Dist. LEXIS 58623, at *9-10 (D. Minn. Aug. 18, 2006); *Capilli v. Whitesell Construction Co.*, No. 04-5777, 2006 U.S. Dist. LEXIS 44453, at *21-22 (D.N.J. June 21, 2006); *Stewart v. Sears, Roebuck and Co.*, No. CV-04-428-HU, 2005 U.S. Dist. LEXIS 42371, at *29 (D. Ore. March 7, 2005). *Felder v. Winn-Dixie Louisiana, Inc.*, No. 03-1438 Section "N" (2), 2003 U.S. Dist. LEXIS 22535, at *5 (E.D. La. Dec. 16, 2003) (analyzing the employee's claim that the employer failed to give required notices pursuant to *Ragsdale v. Wolverine World Wide, Inc.*, 535 U.S. 81, 122 S. Ct. 1155 (2002)).

In *Conoshenti v. PSE&G Gas Co.*, 364 F.3d 135, 142 (3d Cir. 2004), it was uncontested that the employer failed to provide Conoshenti specific notice of his FMLA rights and obligations. Conoshenti argued that he would have been able to make an informed decision about structuring his leave and would have structured it, and his plan of recovery, in such a way as to preserve the job protections afforded by the Act (i.e., not let the 12 weeks of leave run out). The record, according to the court, contained "some support" for Conoshenti's assertion that he could have returned to work within 12 weeks and delayed the surgery until another time. Based on that record, the Third Circuit reversed the award of summary judgment in favor of the employer.

In *Fogelman v. Greater Hazelton Health Alliance*, 122 Fed. Appx. 521 (3d Cir. 2004), the employee failed to show prejudice as a result of the employer's failure to advise her of her FMLA rights or the consequences of failing to provide a medical leave form. Specifically, the court found that the employee failed to establish that she would have been able to return to work at the end of the 12-week period without accommodation of her medical condition. *Accord Sarno v. Douglas Elliman-Gibbons & Ives, Inc. et al.*, 183 F.3d 155, 161 (2d Cir. 1999) (the employer's failure to notify the employee that entitlement was for up to 12 workweeks of leave did not interfere with employee's right to reinstatement when it was undisputed that such inability continued for two months after the end of the 12-week FMLA leave period); *Dodaro v. Village of Glendale Heights*, No. 01-C-6396, 2003 U.S. Dist. LEXIS 5056, at *31 (N.D. Ill. March 31, 2003).

In *Reifer v. Colonial Intermediate Unit 20*, 462 F. Supp. 2d 621, 638 (M.D. Pa. 2006), even though the employer failed to inform Reifer of her FMLA rights, the court awarded summary judgment to the employer due to the employee's failure to establish that she was prejudiced by the notice failure. Reifer argued that, had she known her FMLA rights, she would have structured her leave differently. The record evidence, the court found, established that Reifer could not work at all due to her injuries until well after the running of 12 weeks of FMLA leave. As such, she could not have structured her leave to return to work before the expiration of her FMLA leave.

In *Felder v. Winn-Dixie Louisiana, Inc.*, No. 03-1438 Section "N" (2), 2003 U.S. Dist. LEXIS 22535, at *5 (E.D. La. Dec. 16, 2003), the court, relying on the decision of the Supreme Court in *Ragsdale v. Wolverine World Wide, Inc.*, 535 U.S. 81, 122 S. Ct. 1155 (2002), found invalid the penalty provision of 29 CFR 825.301(f) for an employer's failure to provide employees with specific notice of FMLA rights and obligations. The court concluded that "the only available penalty for an employer's violation of the general notice provision is for the Secretary to impose a fine. Felder has no right to sue Winn-Dixie for its violation."

At least one circuit court, however, suggested that a mere violation of the employer specific notice provisions is sufficient to state a cause of action. *See Tate v. Farmland Industries, Inc.*, 268 F.3d 989, 997 (10th Cir. 2001).

The failure of an agency to provide specific notice to an employee of FMLA rights and obligations may take the form of misleading, inaccurate or otherwise erroneous information provided by the agency to the employee regarding FMLA rights and responsibilities. *Schober v. SMC Pneumatics, Inc.*, No. IP-99-1285-C T/G, 2000 U.S. Dist. LEXIS 19088 (S.D. Ind. Dec. 4, 2000) (misleading or giving incorrect information to an employee by an employer about the employee's FMLA rights or obligations constitutes actionable interference if the incorrect information causes the employee to forfeit FMLA protections). In *Schober*, the district court denied an attempt by the employer to exclude evidence that the employer advised the employee that only a certain physician could complete the employee's medical certification form. The court found that such an instruction would violate the employee's right to obtain certification from any health care provider. The trier of fact could find from this evidence that the misinformation given to the employee about who could complete the medical certification contributed to termination.

Courts in other cases have reached similar results. *See Covey v. Methodist Hospital of Dyersburg, Inc.*, 56 F. Supp. 2d 965 (W.D. Tenn. 1999); *Kruse v. LaGuardia Hospital*, No. 95-CV-4467, 1996 U.S. Dist. LEXIS 22433 (E.D.N.Y. Nov. 6, 1996); *Mora v. Chem-Tronics, Inc.* 16 F. Supp. 2d 1192 (S.D. Ca. 1998). In *Covey*, the plaintiff alleged that the employer incorrectly advised her that her FMLA leave would expire by a certain date. She claimed that the date provided was incorrect. The district court stated that in order for the plaintiff to prevail on her failure to inform claim, she had to demonstrate that: (1) the defendants failed to correctly inform her of her FMLA rights; and (2) that failure to do so caused her to forfeit protections provided by the Act. The court concluded that the employer correctly informed the employee when her FMLA leave would expire. In so finding, the court implied that the giving of incorrect information regarding an employee's FMLA rights and obligations constitutes interference of those rights, provided the incorrect information caused the employee to forfeit FMLA protections.

In *Kruse*, the employer failed to advise the employee that if the employee took more than 12 weeks of FMLA-protected leave, the employee could be terminated. The employee took leave pursuant to the employer's maternity policy, which allowed unprotected leaves of absence of up to nine months. The district court concluded that the employer had a duty to notify its employees of the differences between the two policies and, specifically, to notify the plaintiff that she gave up reinstatement rights by taking the nine-month leave.

In *Mora*, the plaintiff alleged his employer failed to provide him sufficient notice of his rights and obligations under the FMLA in several ways. The district court noted that the defendant failed to give written notice of the employee's FMLA rights and obligations, including the right to take intermittent leave. The court also noted that the employee's supervisors were not trained in and did not provide adequate information about his rights and responsibilities under the Act. The court commented that an employee could be discouraged from exercising FMLA rights if the employer gives misinformation about the FMLA rights and obligations or fails to give such information at all. *Mora*, 16 F. Supp. 2d at 1229.

An employer's § 825.301b)(1) obligation to notify an employee of the consequences of failing to provide a medical certification does not include the requirement to "seek clarification" of such certification from the employee before an employer may hire an investigator or terminate the employee for abuse of leave. *Stonum v. U.S. Airways, Inc.*, 83 F. Supp. 2d 894, 900–901 (S.D. Ohio 1999). In *Stonum*, the employer approved the plaintiff's application for FMLA leave on a reduced leave schedule so that the employee could spend more time assisting her mother. Subsequently, a co-worker advised the employer that the employee stated that she used FMLA leave for purposes other than assisting her mother. Management initiated an investigation. The investigation revealed that on days she requested FMLA leave, the plaintiff spent little if any time with her mother. U.S. Airways subsequently fired the plaintiff for abuse of leave. The plaintiff alleged that her termination violated the FMLA because U.S. Airways should have sought additional information from her regarding the medical certification supporting her request for leave before initiating an investigation. The district court disagreed. The court held that U.S. Airways complied with its specific notice obligation by providing the prototype DOL notice of FMLA rights and obligations. The notice indicated that violation of its leave policies would constitute grounds for termination. No further notice was required. "Nothing in 29 CFR 825.301 obligates an employer to 'seek clarification' when it suspects that an employee is abusing leave granted under the FMLA" *Stonum*, 83 F. Supp. 2d at 901. Moreover, the court noted that the employer did afford the employee several opportunities to explain her actions before terminating her. The employer simply found her explanations unconvincing.

It is unclear whether the penalty provision applies when an agency fails to answer employee questions concerning the employee's rights and responsibilities. Technically, this does not appear to be a "notice" requirement. On the other hand, the duty to answer employee questions is contained in § 825.301, giving rise to the argument that the penalty provision should apply.

2. PEOAA

The PEOAA does not require specific written notice of employee rights and obligations comparable to what is required under Title I and the CAA.

3. Title II

Title II does not require an agency to provide employees with specific written notice of employee FMLA rights and obligations comparable to the requirements of Title I and the CAA. Title II does, however, require agencies to inform employees of their entitlements and responsibilities. 5 CFR 630.1203(g); *see Wiliams v. Dept. of Navy*, No. DC-0752-05-0431-I-1, 2005 MSPB LEXIS 6866, at *5 (Oct. 17, 2005), *pet. denied*, 101 MSPR 133 (2006).

The OPM suggests, in the final comments to the regulations, that agencies may wish to meet this requirement by providing the employee with access to the FMLA and OPM's implementing regulations or agency policies or guidance on implementing the FMLA. Preamble, 5 CFR 630.1203. Agencies may also provide employees access to the OPM's fact sheet and brochure, "Federal Employee Entitlements Under the Family and Medical Leave Act of 1993," or "Family–Friendly Leave Policies for Federal Employees." These publications are available on the OPM's website. The OPM fails to suggest whether "access" means the agency must actually provide the employees with the identified documents, or whether providing the employee with access to a computer so that the documents can be obtained from the OPM's website will suffice.

Moreover, there is no indication that the agency must provide the employee "access" to the referenced documents under comparable circumstances and times as the specific written notice requirement of Title I or the CAA.

Finally, the OPM regulations fail to identify a penalty for an agency's failure to inform employees of their FMLA entitlements and responsibilities.

In *Wiliams v. Dept. of Navy*, No. DC-0752-05-0431-I-1, 2005 MSPB LEXIS 6866, at *8 (Oct. 17, 2005), *pet. denied*, 101 MSPR 133 (2006), the Board favorably reported the Navy's letter and other materials notifying the employee of his or her FMLA rights and obligations, including how to properly request leave.

In *Dias v. VA*, No. NY-0752-04-0279-I-2, 2005 MSPB LEXIS 3926, at *15 (June 30, 2005), *rev'd*, 102 MSPR 53 (2006), *appeal dismissed*, 2006 U.S. App. LEXIS 28961 (Fed. Cir. 2006), *vacated, reinstated*, 2006 U.S. App. LEXIS 32257 (Fed. Cir. 2006), *aff'd*, 2007 U.S. App. LEXIS 11530 (Fed. Cir. 2007), the Board found that, absent further explanation, the employer's notice that the employee must provide "appropriate medical documentation failed to inform the employee what medical documentation would be acceptable."

F. NOTICE OF EMPLOYEE ELIGIBILITY

1. Title I and the CAA

a. General Rule

Employing agencies are required to notify employees whether they meet the eligibility requirements for FMLA leave. 29 CFR 825.110(d); S. Res. 242, Cong. Rec. S3959, S3961–62 (April 23, 1996); 29 CFR 825.110(d). Interestingly, the requirement is not identified as a mandatory subject of the specific written notice that must be provided to employees on the first request for leave in each six–month segment of the FMLA leave year. The eligibility determination would, however, fall within the requirement that the specific written notice inform employees whether the leave will be counted against the employee's annual FMLA leave entitlement. 29 CFR 825.301(b)(1)(I); S. Res. 242, Cong. Rec. S3959, S3971 (April 23, 1996); 29 CFR 825.301(b)(1)(I). The DOL approved prototype employer notice form includes a question addressing whether an employee is eligible for FMLA leave. [Eligibility is addressed more fully in Chapter 5, "Employee Eligibility for Leave."]

b. When an Employing Agency Must Confirm Eligibility

There are three circumstances that trigger an employing agency's obligation to notify an employee whether the employee is eligible for FMLA leave.

(1) Notice Where Employee is Not Yet Eligible

If an employee notifies the employer of the need for FMLA leave before the employee meets the eligibility requirements, the employer must either confirm the employee's eligibility based upon a projection that the employee will be eligible on the date leave would commence or must advise the employee when the eligibility requirement is met. 29 CFR 825.110(d); S. Res. 242, Cong. Rec. S3959, S3961–62 (April 23, 1996); 29 CFR 825.110(d). If the employer confirms eligibility at the time the notice for leave is received, the employer may not subsequently challenge the employee's eligibility. 29 CFR 825.110(d); S. Res. 242, Cong. Rec. S3959, S3961–62 (April 23, 1996); 29 CFR 825.110(d).

The regulations do not impose a separate time frame when notice prior to the time the employee is eligible must be given. As such, the regulations also do not impose a penalty for failure to timely provide advance notice based on a projection of whether the employee would be eligible as of the leave date. If an employer fails or declines to notify the employee based on a projection of eligibility as of the leave date, the regulations, by default, provide that notice should be given when eligibility is met.

At least one court found 29 CFR 825.110(d) conditionally valid where an employer confirmed eligibility before an employee commenced FMLA leave, only to determine later that the initial confirmation was erroneous. *See Gurley v. Ameriwood Industries, Inc.*, 232 F. Supp. 2d 969 (E.D. Mo. 2002) (after finding in apposite the cases invalidating the penalty provision in 29 CFR 825.110(d) where an employer fails to timely notify an employee of eligibility, the court held, "[t]o the extent the regulation [29 CFR 825.110(d)] mirrors the federal doctrine of equitable estoppel, it is valid").

(2) Notice When Eligibility is Met

If an employer decides not to confirm eligibility based on a projection, the employer must advise the employee when eligibility is met. 29 CFR 825.110(d); 29 CFR 825.110(d); S. Res. 242, Cong. Rec. S3959, S3961–62 (April 23, 1996); 29 CFR 825.110(d). The employer must advise the employee as soon as practicable after the date eligibility is determined, which is generally two business days absent extenuating circumstances. 29 CFR 825.110(d); 29 CFR 825.110(d); S. Res. 242, Cong. Rec. S3959, S3961–62 (April 23, 1996); 29 CFR 825.110(d). If an employer fails to timely notify an employee of eligibility as soon as practicable, the penalty imposed by the DOL regulations is that the employee will be "deemed" to have satisfied the notice requirements and the notice of leave is considered current and outstanding until the employer so advises. 29 CFR 825.110(d); 29 CFR 825.110(d); S. Res. 242, Cong. Rec. S3959, S3961–62 (April 23, 1996); 29 CFR 825.110(d). An employer would not be able to challenge the timeliness or adequacy of the employee's notice to the employer of his or her need for leave until the employer notifies the employee whether he or she is eligible for FMLA leave. [For a further discussion of employee notice obligations, see Chapter 8, "Notice Requirements."]

(3) Eligibility Notice Before Leave Commences

Ultimately, an employer has until just before the date FMLA leave commences to notify an employee whether he or she satisfies the eligibility criteria. Other than the inability to challenge the timeliness or adequacy of the employee's notice of the need for leave, if the employer does not notify the employee within two business days, there does not appear to be any additional penalty for waiting until the eve of leave commencement.

(4) Deemed Eligible: Employer Notice On or After Leave Commences

If the employer fails to advise the employee whether the employee is eligible prior to the date the requested leave is to commence, the regulations provide that the employee will be deemed eligible. 29 CFR 825.110(d); 29 CFR 825.110(d); S. Res. 242, Cong. Rec. S3959, S3961–62 (April 23, 1996); 29 CFR 825.110(d). The employer may not, then, deny the leave. 29 CFR 825.110(d); 29 CFR 825.110(d); S. Res. 242, Cong. Rec. S3959, S3961–62 (April 23, 1996); 29 CFR 825.110(d). Under the regulations, the "deemed eligible" penalty for an employer's failure to notify an employee by leave commencement whether he or she satisfied the eligibility criteria also applies where the employee gives as little as two business days notice of the need for FMLA leave. 29 CFR 825.110(d); S. Res. 242, Cong. Rec. S3959, S3961–62 (April 23, 1996); 29 CFR 825.110(d). 29 CFR 825.110(d). Presumably, the regulations mean that an employer may not deny the leave because the employee is not eligible, rather than, for example, because the leave is not for a covered condition within the meaning of the Act. In any event, as written, the regulations are not clear on this last point. [For a further review of the deemed eligible requirement, see Chapter 5, "Employee Eligibility for Leave."]

2. PEOAA

The PEOAA requires an employing office to notify employees whether they meet the eligibility requirements for FMLA leave. The PEOAA incorporates the eligibility notice requirements of Title I. The PEOAA incorporates §§ 101–105 of Title I, 29 USC 2611–15. 3 USC 412(a)(1). The eligibility requirements of Title I are set forth in 29 USC 2611(2) (defining eligible employee). In the absence of regulations implementing the FMLA, the PEOAA directs, "to the extent necessary and appropriate, the most relevant substantive executive agency regulations promulgated to implement the statutory provision at issue." The Executive Office of the President indicated that it does not have regulations implementing the FMLA for purposes of the PEOAA. As such, the most relevant substantive executive agency regulations are those implementing Title I, the Statute specifically incorporated into the PEOAA. The PEOAA also indicates that regulations implementing the FMLA should "be the same as substantive regulations promulgated by the Secretary of Labor." 3 USC 412(c)(2).

3. Title II

Title II does not require that an agency notify employees whether they are eligible for FMLA leave. Title II does not have an eligibility requirement *per se*. As discussed more fully in Chapter 5, "Employee Eligibility for Leave," the eligibility requirement is incorporated into the definition of an employee. To be an "employee" covered by Title II, the individual must have completed at least 12 months of service as a federal civil service employee, as that term is defined in Title II. 5 USC 6381(1)(B); 5 CFR 630.1201(b)(ii).

Absent a specific provision requiring notice of eligibility, an agency's responsibility to notify employees of their FMLA rights and obligations is governed by the general notice provisions of 5 CFR 630.1203(g). An agency must inform employees of their entitlements and responsibilities under the FMLA. 5 CFR 630.1203(g). Neither the regulations nor the OPM comments in the Preamble to the final regulations indicate that such notice includes notice of FMLA eligibility. Rather, an agency may meet this general notice requirement by providing the employee with access to various identified OPM documents explaining FMLA rights.

Of course, because Title II does not require an agency to notify an employee if he or she is eligible for FMLA leave, it does not mean that an agency is prohibited from providing such notice. Unions and other organizations representing the interests of employees should consider bargaining for a requirement that an agency notify employees of FMLA eligibility.

G. DESIGNATION OF LEAVE AS FMLA

1. Title I and the CAA

a. General Rule

In all circumstances, employing agencies are responsible for designating leave, paid or unpaid, as FMLA-qualifying, and must give notice of the designation to the employee. 29 CFR 825.208(a); S. Res. 242, Cong. Rec. S3959, S3966 (April 23, 1996); 29 CFR 825.208(a); *see Ragdsale v. Wolverine World Wide, Inc.*, 535 U.S. 81, 87–88, 122 S. Ct. 1155, 152 L. Ed. 167 (2002); *Conoshenti v. PSE&G Gas Co.*, 364 F.3d 135, 142 (3d Cir. 2004); *Katekovich v. Team Rent A Car of Pittsburgh, Inc. et al.*, 36 Fed. Appx. 688 (3rd Cir. 2002); *Hicks v. LeRoy's Jeweler's, Inc. et al.*, No. 98–6596, 2000 U.S. App. LEXIS 17568, at n.7 (6th Cir. July 17, 2000); *Thornton v. BASF*, No. 99–2243, 2000 U.S. App. LEXIS 15909 (4th Cir. July 11, 2000); *Plant v. Morton International, Inc.*, 212 F.3d 929, 934–35 (6th Cir. 200); *McGregor v. Autozone, Inc.*, 180 F.3d 1305, 1307 (11th Cir. 1999); *Gay v. Gilman Paper Co.*, 125 F.3d 1432, 1434 (11th Cir. 1997); *Price v. City of Fort Wayne, Ind.*, 117 F.3d 1022, 1025–26 (7th Cir. 1997); *Hackney v. Central Ill. Public Service Co.*, No. 04-3204, 2006 U.S. Dist. LEXIS 51850, at *21 (C.D. Ill. July 27, 2006); *Uthell v. Mid-Illinois Concrete, Inc.*, No. 05-4034-JLF, 2006 U.S. Dist. LEXIS 89314, at *12 (S.D. Ill. Dec. 11, 2006); *Sisturn v. Time–Warner Cable*, No. 02–CV-8023, 2004 U.S. Dist. LEXIS 16681, at *41 (E.D. Pa. Aug. 19, 2004).

Notice that the leave is designated as FMLA-qualifying and, therefore, will be counted against the employee's 12-week FMLA leave entitlement and is included in the specific written notice which agencies are required to provide employees. 29 CFR 825.301(b)(1)(I); S. Res. 242, Cong. Rec. S3959, S3971 (April 23, 1996); 29 CFR 825.301(b)(1)(I). Such information is also reflected in the DOL and Office of Compliance prototype written notice.

This designation notice requirement is not statutory but is contained in the DOL and CAA implementing regulations. 29 CFR 825.208; S. Res. 242. CONG. REC. S3959, S3966 (April 23, 1996); 29 CFR 825.208(a); *Smith v. Blue Dot Co.*, 283 F. Supp. 2d 1200, 1204 (D. Kan. 2003); *Farina v. Compuware Corp.*, 256 F. Supp. 2d 1033, 1054 (D. Az. 2003).

The employer's designation decision must be based only on information received from the employee or the employee's spokesperson (e.g., if the employee is incapacitated, the employee's spouse, adult child, parent, doctor, or others, may provide notice to the employer of the need to take FMLA leave). 29 CFR 825.208(a); S. Res. 242, Cong. Rec. S3959, S3966 (April 23, 1996); 29 CFR 825.208(a); *see Covucci v. Service Merchandise Co., Inc.*, No. 97–4472, 1999 U.S. App. LEXIS 2073 (6th Cir. Feb. 8, 1999) (interim regulations); *Stoops v. One Call Communications, Inc.*, 141 F.3d 309, 312 (7th Cir. 1998); *Gay v. Gilman Paper Co.*, 125 F.3d 1432, 1434 (11th Cir. 1997) (employee's husband); *Carmen v. Unison Behavioral Health Group, Inc.*, 295 F. Supp. 2d 809, 814 (N.D. Ohio 2003); *Manns v. ArvinMeritor, Inc.*, 291 F. Supp. 2d 655, 660 (N.D. Ohio 2003); *De Hoyas v. Bristol Laboratories Corp. et al.*, 218 F. Supp. 2d 222, 225–26 (D.P.R. 2002).

In *Stoops v. One Call Communications, Inc.*, 141 F.3d 309, 312 (7th Cir. 1998), the Seventh Circuit held that the above provision does not require that an "employer base its decision solely on information provided by the employee *at the time of the request for leave*; nor does the regulation prohibit an employer from basing its decision on a prior [medical] certification by the employee's physician that the employee was not qualified for FMLA leave." (emphasis in original). *Stoops* permits employers to rely on a prior so-called "negative certification" in addition to information from the employee in making the designation decision. Negative certifications are discussed in the next section of this chapter under adequacy of employee notice.

Note that the regulations technically require an agency to accept information from someone other than the employee only when the employee is *incapacitated*. The term "incapacitated" is not defined in this section of the regulations. While "incapacitated" is not formally defined elsewhere in the regulations, it is described as an inability to work, attend school or perform other regular daily activities due to a serious health condition, treatment therefore, or recovery therefrom. *See* 29 CFR 825.114(a)(1), (2)(I); S. Res. 242, Cong. Rec. S3959, S3962 (April 23, 1996); 29 CFR 825.208(a). Presumably, that description applies in the context of the designation decision.

The regulations do not explain how someone becomes an employee's *spokesperson*. There is no indication that a formal appointment must be made. Nor is there any indication that an agency may ask an employee for written confirmation that the individual is authorized to serve as the employee's spokesperson. On the other hand, the regulations do not prohibit an agency from asking for written confirmation either. Agencies may want to consider asking for written confirmation of authorization where there is a legitimate question as to whether the individual is authorized to represent the employee.

The regulations do not indicate what happens if more than one spokesperson is involved. For example, a spouse and a union steward claim to be the spokesperson of an incapacitated employee. It seems appropriate in these circumstances to require written authorization from the employee indicating who will serve as spokesperson. If that is not possible, the employer should abide by the legal and contractual requirements with the union in terms of its representation of individuals in its bargaining unit. The employer may also have to deal with a spouse or other family member. Technically, by using the singular "spokesperson," the regulations suggest that only one spokesperson need be recognized.

Similarly, the regulations do not indicate what will happen if an employee subsequently disagrees with the decisions of the spokesperson. Presumably, a spokesperson stands in the shoes of the employee and has all of the authority of the employee while serving as spokesperson. Decisions by the spokesperson should stand, and an agency should be able to make decisions based on the information provided by the spokesperson.

Agencies need to be careful in situations where a physician serves as the employee's spokesperson. Because of the prohibitions against agencies having contact with the employee's physician, this is a situation where written confirmation of the physician's appointment as the employee's spokesperson should, if possible, be obtained from the employee. If the employee is incapacitated and cannot provide such written authorization, the agency should consider requesting the same from the employee's physician. At a minimum, the agency should send a confirming letter to the physician that the physician is serving as the employee's spokesperson. Finally, it is unclear whether a physician automatically becomes the "spokesperson" of an employee by virtue of providing a medical certification. This seems unlikely, as a spokesperson serves a different role than a physician.

In circumstances where the employer does not have sufficient information regarding the reason for an employee's use of paid leave, the employer should inquire further of the employee or the spokesperson to ascertain whether the paid leave is potentially FMLA-qualifying. 29 CFR 825.208(a); S. Res. 242, Cong. Rec. S3959, S3966 (April 23, 1996); 29 CFR 825.208(a); *see Plant v. Morton International, Inc.*, 212 F.3d 929, 935–36 (6th Cir. 2000); *Stoops v. One Call Communications, Inc.*, 141 F.3d 309, 312, 1026 (7th Cir. 1998); *Gay v. Gilman Paper Co.*, 125 F.3d 1432, 1434 (11th Cir. 1997); *Price v. City of Fort Wayne, Ind.*, 117 F.3d 1022, 1025–25 (7th Cir. 1997); *Carmen v. Unison Behavioral Health Group, Inc.*, 295 F. Supp. 2d 809, 814 (N.D. Ohio 2003); *Farina v. Compuware, Corp.*, 256 F. Supp. 2d 1033, 1054 (D. Az. 2003); *Michelle v. SMC Pneumatics, Inc.*, No. IP99-1285-C-T/G, 2000 U.S. Dist. LEXIS 12478 (S.D. Ind. Aug. 21, 2000); *Goodwin-Haulmark v. Menninger Clinic, Inc.*, 76 F. Supp. 2d 1235, 1242 (D. Kan. 1999). An employer's duty to make further inquiry may be made less likely when the employee provided notice on multiple occasions, none of which implicated the need for FMLA leave. *See Aubuchon v. Knauf Fiberglass, GMBH*, 240 F. Supp. 2d 859, 866 (S.D. Ind. 2003), *aff'd*, 359 F.3d 950 (7th Cir. 2004) (employee who provided notice on three occasions "may have made it less likely that the employer would need to inquiry further, since notice failed to mention facts suggesting need for exigent FMLA leave").

It is expected that the employer will obtain any additional required information through informal means. 29 CFR 825.303(b); S. Res. 242, Cong. Rec. S3959, S3972 (April 23, 1996); 29 CFR 825.303(b); *See Peeples v. Coastal Office Products, Inc.*, 64 Fed. Appx. 860 (4th Cir. 2003); *Price v. City of Fort Wayne, Ind.*, 117 F.3d 1022, 1025–26 (7th Cir. 1997); *Michelle v. SMC Pneumatics, Inc.*, No. IP99–1285–C–T/G, 2000 U.S. Dist. LEXIS 12478 (S.D. Ind. Aug. 21, 2000); *Biermann v. Aluminum Co. of America*, No. 3:98–CV–20159, 2000 U.S. Dist. LEXIS 21964 (S.D. Iowa Jan. 21, 2000).

In *McCarron v. British Telecom et al.*, No. 00–CV–6123, 2002 U.S. Dist. LEXIS 15151 (E.D. Pa. Aug. 7, 2002), the district court found that the employer satisfied its obligation to obtain additional information through informal means by leaving two telephone messages with the plaintiff. The employee originally requested FMLA leave to "remedy a family situation." The employer left two voice mail messages for the plaintiff, offering to assist him in processing the necessary forms, requesting that he call her, and warning him of the consequences of not providing a reason for leave. The employee responded to the first message by refusing to provide details and telling the employer to leave him alone. The employee did not respond to the second telephone message.

An employee, who takes leave before receiving notice of its approval, may not be covered by the FMLA. The situation was addressed by the Sixth Circuit in *George v. Russell Stover Candies, Inc.*, 106 Fed. Appx. 946, (6th Cir. 2004). The employee applied for a reduced leave schedule. The employer, Russell Stover, granted her request. However, neither the employee nor her supervisor was notified of the approval. The employee had no knowledge that her request to work a reduced leave schedule was granted when she left work early (which resulted in her termination). The employee sought to benefit from the approval of her reduced leave schedule *post facto*. The court disagreed. According to the court, "[i]n the absence of extraordinary circumstances, an employee has a positive duty to wait until she is notified that her request for reduced leave had been granted." The court found that such extraordinary circumstances did not exist in the case because working on the day in question did not violate the plaintiff's medical restrictions. Because she did not attempt to work out her reduced leave schedule with her employer pursuant to company policy, the court concluded that plaintiff's "unilateral decision to take the day off prior to being notified that her reduced schedule had been approved, rendered her ineligible for FMLA protection."

b. When Notice Must Be Given

The regulations governing the circumstances and timing of an agency's obligation to notify an employee that it has designated leave as FMLA–qualifying are unnecessarily confusing. The obligation of covered agencies to designate leave as FMLA–qualifying and notify the employee of that designation differs depending on the point in time when the determination is made: (1) before FMLA leave commences; (2) after leave commences, but before the employee returns to work; and (3) after the employee returns to work. The regulations further divide these areas depending on whether the FMLA leave is unpaid, or paid leave is substituted.

(1) General Rule

Generally, an agency must notify an employee that it has designated paid leave as FMLA–qualifying within two business days, absent extenuating circumstances, of when the agency acquired knowledge from the employee or the employee's spokesperson that the leave is being taken for an FMLA required reason. 29 CFR 825.208(b)(1); S. Res. 242, Cong. Rec. S3959, S3966 (April 23, 1996); 29 CFR 825.208(b)(1); *see Plant v. Morton International, Inc.*, 212 F.3d 929, 935 (6th Cir. 2000); *Covucci v. Service Merchandise Co., Inc.*, No. 97–4472, 1999 U.S. App. LEXIS 2073 (6th Cir. Feb. 8, 1999) (under interim regulations, the employer is required to immediately notify the employee that paid leave is designated as FMLA leave); *Cline v. Wal–Mart Stores, Inc.*, 144 F.3d 294, 300 (4th Cir. 1998); *Wright v. Owens–Illinois*, No. 2:02–cv–223–LJM–WGH, 2004 U.S. Dist. LEXIS 8535, at *20 (S.D. Ind. May 14, 2004); *Roberts v. Owens–Illinois*, No. 2:02–cv–207–LJM–WGH, 2004 U.S. Dist. LEXIS 8534, at *16 (S.D. Ind. May 14, 2004); *Whitney v. Wal–Mart Stores, Inc.*, No. 03–65–P–H, 2003 U.S. Dist. LEXIS 22629, at *40 (D. Me. Dec. 16, 2003); *Donahoo v. Master Data Center*, 282 F. Supp. 2d 540, 554 (E.D. Mich. 2003).

Note that the regulations technically speak only in terms of the designation of paid leave. The rule has, however, been applied generally to the designation of leave, whether paid or unpaid. Obviously, an argument can be made that the paid leave notice requirement does not apply to the designation of unpaid FMLA leave.

The regulations are designed to resolve the question of FMLA designation as early as possible in the leave request process, to eliminate protracted "after the fact" disputes. Preamble, 29 CFR 825.208. That is, the designation of leave as being FMLA–qualifying is expected to take place "up front" whenever possible. Preamble, 29 CFR 825.208.

(2) Before FMLA Leave Commences

An employing agency's obligation to designate leave as FMLA-qualifying and notify the employee of that designation before leave commences depends on whether the leave is paid or unpaid.

Where FMLA leave is paid, an employer's designation decision generally must be made before the start of the employee's FMLA leave. 29 CFR 825.208(c); S. Res. 242, Cong. Rec. S3959, S3966 (April 23, 1996); 29 CFR 825.208(c). If the employer requires paid leave to be substituted for unpaid leave, or that paid leave taken under an existing leave plan be counted as FMLA leave, the designation decision must be made by the employer within two business days of the time the employee gives notice of the need for leave. 29 CFR 825.208(c); S. Res. 242, Cong. Rec. S3959, S3966 (April 23, 1996); 29 CFR 825.208(c); see Farina v. Compuware, Corp., 256 F. Supp. 2d 1033, 1054 (D. Az. 2003). If the employer does not initially have sufficient information to designate paid leave as FMLA-qualifying at the time the employee gives notice of the need for the leave, the agency must make the designation determination when the employer determines that the leave qualifies as FMLA leave. 29 CFR 825.208(c); S. Res. 242, Cong. Rec. S3959, S3966 (April 23, 1996); 29 CFR 825.208(c). Again, once the employing agency determines that the leave qualifies as FMLA leave, it must notify the employee within two business days, absent extenuating circumstances, of the fact that the leave is designated as FMLA leave.

Note that the obligation of an agency to notify an employee that it has designated paid leave as FMLA-qualifying is in addition to the § 825.301(b)(1) requirement that an agency provide specific written notice to the employee of the employee's FMLA rights and obligations. Although the specific written notice includes information that the leave will count against the employee's FMLA leave entitlement, the notice need only be given to the employee the first time the employee requests leave in each six-month segment of the FMLA leave year. 29 CFR 825.301(c); S. Res. 242, Cong. Rec. S3959, S3966 (April 23, 1996); 29 CFR 825.208(c). The notice of paid leave designation, in contrast, must be given in most instances within two business days after the employee requests FMLA leave, which may be more than once in each six-month leave year period.

As with paid leave, where FMLA leave is unpaid an employing agency is required to designate the leave as FMLA-qualifying and notify the employee of the designation. 29 CFR 825.208(a); S. Res. 242, Cong. Rec. S3959, S3966 (April 23, 1996); 29 CFR 825.208(c). The regulations fail, however, to specify a time frame within which an employer must designate unpaid leave as FMLA-qualifying, and when it must notify the employee that it has so designated the leave. The two-day time frame is specifically tied to situations where paid leave is designated as FMLA-qualifying.

In the absence of a specific time frame before leave commences within which an agency is required to notify an employee that it designated the leave as FMLA-qualifying, an employing agency can meet its notice requirement by compliance with the specific written notice provisions of § 825.301(b)(1). The agency notice includes information whether the leave will be counted against the employee's annual FMLA leave entitlement. 29 CFR 825.301(b)(1)(I); S. Res. 242, Cong. Rec. S3959, S3971 (April 23, 1996); 29 CFR 825.301(b)(1)(I). Specific written notice must be given no less often than the first time in each six-month period that an employee gives notice of the need for FMLA leave. 29 CFR 825.301(b)(1)(I); S. Res. 242, Cong. Rec. S3959, S3971 (April 23, 1996); 29 CFR 825.301(b)(1)(I).

The distinction in the regulations between paid and unpaid leave, in terms of when an agency must notify the employee that it designated the leave as FMLA-qualifying, is not explained. The distinction certainly violates the stated intention of the DOL that the designation decision, and the corresponding agency notice to the employee, take place sooner rather than later. It should be noted that the distinction is often read out of the regulations, and the two-day notice rule for the designation of paid leave is applied to unpaid leave. Again, agencies may provide more notice to an employee of FMLA rights and responsibilities than the minimum required by the FMLA.

(3) After FMLA Leave Commences, But Before the Employee Returns to Work

An employer may designate leave, paid or unpaid, after leave commences where the employer did not have sufficient information as to the employee's reason for taking the leave until after the leave began. 29 CFR 825.208(c), (d); S. Res. 242, Cong. Rec. S3959, S3966–67 (April 23, 1996); 29 CFR 825.208(c), (d).

If the employer learns that leave, paid or unpaid, is for an FMLA purpose after leave begins, such as when an employee gives notice of the need for an extension of the paid leave with unpaid FMLA leave, the entire or some portion of the paid leave period may be retroactively counted as FMLA leave, to the extent that the leave period qualified as FMLA leave. 29 CFR 825.208(d); S. Res. 242, Cong. Rec. S3959, S3967 (April 23, 1996); 29 CFR 825.208(d). For example, Eric is initially granted two weeks paid annual leave for a skiing trip. In the middle of the second week, Eric contacts his employer for an extension of leave as unpaid leave and advises that at the beginning of the second week of paid vacation leave he took a tumble down the slopes, suffering injuries requiring hospitalization. The employer may notify Eric that both the extension and the second week of paid vacation leave (from the date of the injury) are designated as FMLA leave. 29 CFR 825.208(d); S. Res. 242, Cong. Rec. S3959, S3967 (April 23, 1996); 29 CFR 825.208(d). On the other hand, if an employee takes sick leave that turns into a serious health condition (e.g., bronchitis that turns into bronchial pneumonia) and the employee gives notice of the need for an extension of leave, the entire period of the serious health condition may be counted as FMLA leave. 29 CFR 825.208(d); S. Res. 242, Cong. Rec. S3959, S3967 (April 23, 1996); 29 CFR 825.3208(d).

For purposes of notice of the designation of leave as FMLA-qualifying, the rules continue to differentiate between paid and unpaid FMLA leave. Where the leave is paid, an employer, with knowledge that the leave is for an FMLA-covered reason, must promptly (within two business days, absent extenuating circumstances) notify the employee that it designated the leave as FMLA-qualifying and that the leave will count against the employee's FMLA leave entitlement. 29 CFR 825.208(c); S. Res. 242, Cong. Rec. S3959, S3971 (April 23, 1996); 29 CFR 825.208(c).

Where the agency learns that unpaid leave is for an FMLA-covered reason after leave commences, the regulations fail to indicate when an agency must notify an employee that the agency designated the leave as FMLA-qualifying. As with the designation of unpaid leave before leave commences, the employing agency's notice obligation would appear to be limited to compliance with the specific written notice requirements of § 825.301(c).

(4) Retroactive Designation After Employee Returns to Work

Generally, employers are prohibited from designating leave, paid or unpaid, as FMLA leave after the employee returns to work. 29 CFR 825.208(e); S. Res. 242, Cong. Rec. S3959, S3967 (April 23, 1996); 29 CFR 825.208(e); *see Sims v. Schultz*, 305 F. Supp. 2d 838, 845 (N.D. Ill. 2004); *Donahoo v. Master Data Center*, 282 F. Supp. 2d 540, 554 (E.D. Mich. 2003); *Cavin v. Honda of America Mfg., Inc.*, No. C2-00-400, 2002 U.S. Dist. LEXIS 19601 (S.D. Ohio Feb. 22, 2002), *aff'd in part, rev'd in part, remanded*, 346 F.3d 713 (6th Cir. 2003). There are two exceptions. *Uthell v. Mid-Illinois Concrete, Inc.*, No. 05-4034-JLF, 2006 U.S. Dist. LEXIS 89314, at *13 (S.D. Ill. Dec. 11, 2006);

The first exception to the general rule applies when an employee is absent for a FMLA reason and the employer did not learn of the reason for the absence until the employee's return (e.g., where the employee was absent for only a brief period), the employer may, upon the employee's return to work, promptly (within two business days of the employee's return to work) designate the leave retroactively with appropriate notice to the employee. 29 CFR 825.208(e)(1); S. Res. 242, Cong. Rec. S3959, S3967 (April 23, 1996); 29 CFR 825.208(e)(1); *see Cavin v. Honda of America Mfg., Inc.*, No. C2-00-400, 2002 U.S. Dist. LEXIS 19601 (S.D. Ohio Feb. 22, 2002), *aff'd in part, rev'd in part, remanded*, 346 F.3d 713 (6th Cir. 2003). In this situation, the employee is obligated to notify the employer within two business days of returning to work of the FMLA-qualifying reason for the leave. 29 CFR 825.208(e)(1); S. Res. 242, Cong. Rec. S3959, S3967 (April 23, 1996); 29 CFR 825.208(e)(1). In the absence of such timely notification by the employee, the employee may not subsequently assert FMLA protections for the absence. 29 CFR 825.208(e)(1); S. Res. 242, Cong. Rec. S3959, S3967 (April 23, 1996); 29 CFR 825.208(e)(1).

Note that in the first exception an agency is obligated to designate the leave within two business days of the employee's return to work. There is no indication that extenuating circumstances can extend that period of time. Nor is there any indication of what "appropriate notice to the employee" means. Presumably, it means that the general rules regarding employee notification of FMLA leave designation apply. As such, if the leave is retroactively designated as paid leave, the agency must notify the employee within two business days of the when the agency learned of the FMLA-qualifying nature of the leave. *See* 29 CFR 825.208(b)(1); S. Res. 242, Cong. Rec. S3959, S3966 (April 23, 1996); 29 CFR 825.208(b)(1). Where the leave is unpaid, the specific written notice provisions should apply. 29 CFR 825.301(c); S. Res. 242, Cong. Rec. S3959, S3971 (April 23, 1996); 29 CFR 825.301(c). Of course, one could make the argument that "appropriate notice" means something else.

The second exception to the general prohibition on retroactive designation of FMLA leave after an employee returns to work occurs in three circumstances where the employer knows the reason for the leave:

- The employer has been unable to confirm that the leave qualifies under the FMLA;
- The employer has not received requested medical certification; or
- The parties are in the process of obtaining a second or third medical opinion.

29 CFR 825.208(e)(2); S. Res. 242, Cong. Rec. S3959, S3967 (April 23, 1996); 29 CFR 825.208(e)(2).

Where these circumstances exist, an employer should make a preliminary designation that the leave, paid or unpaid, is FMLA-qualifying, and so notify the employee at the time leave begins, or as soon as the reason for the leave becomes known. 29 CFR 825.208(e)(2); S. Res. 242, Cong. Rec. S3959, S3967 (April 23, 1996); 29 CFR 825.208(e)(2).

Upon receipt of the requisite information from the employee or of the medical certification, confirming that the leave is for an FMLA reason, the preliminary designation becomes final. 29 CFR 825.208(e)(2); S. Res. 242, Cong. Rec. S3959, S3967 (April 23, 1996); 29 CFR 825.208(e)(2). If the medical certifications fail to confirm that the reason for the absence was an FMLA reason, the employer must withdraw the designation (with written notice to the employee). 29 CFR 825.208(e)(2); S. Res. 242, Cong. Rec. S3959, S3967 (April 23, 1996); 29 CFR 825.208(e)(2).

The notice requirements under this exception are schizophrenic. The notice regulations regarding the preliminary designation of leave as FMLA leave are clear. An agency must notify an employee that it has made a preliminary designation that the leave is FMLA-qualifying, pending receipt of further information. That notice must be made either at the time leave begins or as soon as the reason for the leave becomes known. The rule makes no distinction between paid and unpaid leave. The rule does not specifically apply the two business day rule for notice.

The notice requirements are decidedly unclear when the agency receives the information intended to confirm that the reason for the leave is FMLA-qualifying. For example, there is no requirement that the agency notify the employee that the preliminary designation is final because of the receipt of information confirming that the leave was for an FMLA-qualifying reason.

On the other hand, if the information fails to confirm that the leave is for an FMLA-qualifying reason, the agency must notify the employee in writing of its withdrawal of the preliminary designation of FMLA leave. The rule does not distinguish between paid and unpaid leave when it comes to notice. It also fails to provide any guidance on when such notice must be provided to the employee. It would appear that notice must be provided on receipt of the information that fails to establish that the leave is for an FMLA-qualifying reason.

c. Manner of Notice

Generally, the employer's notice to the employee of the leave designation as FMLA leave may be oral or in writing. 29 CFR 825.301(b)(2); S. Res. 242, Cong. Rec. S3959, S3966 (April 23, 1996); 29 CFR 825.208(b)(2). Written notice is required when an agency withdraws a preliminary designation of leave as FMLA-qualifying because subsequent information failed to substantiate that the leave fell within the protections of the FMLA.

If the notice is oral, it must be confirmed in writing, no later than the following payday (unless the payday is less than one week after the oral notice, in which case, it must be no later than the subsequent payday). 29 CFR 825.301(b)(2); S. Res. 242, Cong. Rec. S3959, S3966 (April 23, 1996); 29 CFR 825.208(b)(2); *see Uthell v. Mid-Illinois Concrete, Inc.*, No. 05-4034-JLF, 2006 U.S. Dist. LEXIS 89314, at *13 (S.D. Ill. Dec. 11, 2006); *Chan v. Loyola University Medical Center*, No. 97-C-3170, 1999 U.S. Dist. LEXIS 2790 (N.D. Ill. March 3, 1999). The written notice may be in any form, including a notation on the employee's pay stub. 29 CFR 825.301(b)(2); S. Res. 242, Cong. Rec. S3959, S3966 (April 23, 1996); 29 CFR 825.208(b)(2). Note that there is no requirement that the notice be in a language in which the employee is literate. The employee bears the burden of proof that the employer failed to follow up oral notice with timely written confirmation. *Chan v. Loyola University Medical Center*, No. 97-C-3170, 1999 U.S. Dist. LEXIS 2790 (N.D. Ill. March 3, 1999).

What constitutes oral notice and written confirmation was addressed in *Chan v. Loyola University Medical Center*, No. 97-C-3170, 1999 U.S. Dist. LEXIS 2790 (N.D. Ill. March 3, 1999). In *Chan*, the district court found that an employer failed to adequately notify the employee that leave had been designated as FMLA-qualifying. The court appeared to favorably indicate that the employer met the oral designation prong when management advised the employee that it would send her FMLA forms. The packet of materials Loyola sent Chan, which included a "Family/Medical Leave Request for FMLA Leave Form" and a summary of various provisions of the FMLA, still failed to adequately designate the leave as FMLA-qualifying. The court noted that the written notice may be in any form, providing flexibility to the employer in terms of notice. However, because Chan was not explicitly told that she was on FMLA leave, and the employer's communications came before she even filled out the FMLA leave request form, the court held that it could not find as a matter of law that Loyola's communications did or did not constitute adequate notice. The question was left to the jury.

Separately, the court in *Chan* also addressed whether a notation on a pay stub satisfied the employer's designation notice obligation. The employer argued that notice that her paid sick leave and vacation time was being run concurrently with her FMLA leave was reflected in the employee's pay stub. Specifically, Loyola argued that because Chan's paycheck stubs during her initial leave identified her earnings type as "sick pay," and "vacation," and/or "holiday", Chan received notice that her accumulated sick pay and vacation pay would be run concurrently with her FMLA leave. According to the court, the paycheck stubs failed to establish that Loyola provided Chan with the required notice. "A close inspection of Chan's paycheck stubs reveals that there is no language *explicitly informing* Chan that her paid leave is running concurrently with her FMLA leave." *Chan v. Loyola University Medical Center*, No. 97–C–3170, 1999 U.S. Dist. LEXIS 2790 (N.D. Ill. March 3, 1999) (emphasis added). Rather, the stubs merely indicated that the balance of Chan's paid sick leave, vacation, and personal time were decreasing during her initial leave of absence.

In *Bala v. Jacobson Stores, Inc.*, No. 99–10482–BC, 2001 U.S. Dist. LEXIS 19866 (E.D. Mich. Nov. 27, 2001), the district court rejected the plaintiff's argument that the employer's written confirmation of FMLA leave needed to be in the form of a countersignature on the Application for Family Medical Leave he originally submitted. In rejecting this claim, the court observed the following:

> The DOL regulations for designating FMLA leave are not intended to create hyper technical requirements designed to trap employers or confuse employees. Once oral approval is given, the requirement of written confirmation of FMLA leave may be as simple as a notation on a pay stub. 29 CFR 825.208(b)(2). There is no requirement for countersignatures or formal declarations.
>
> ****
>
> The facts in this case establish that plaintiff asked for time off under the FMLA (a request with which he was familiar having done it before), his request was verbally granted, and within reasonable time paperwork—which included a precise description of his rights and responsibilities under the FMLA and his employer's policy—was sent to him. He acknowledges receiving this written documentation. Neither the FMLA nor the implementing regulations require more.

An agency generally need only notify an agency once that the employee's request for leave is designated as FMLA–qualifying. This is true whether the leave is taken in a single block of time, intermittently or on a reduced leave schedule. 29 CFR 825.208(a); S. Res. 242, Cong. Rec. S3959, S3966 (April 23, 1996); 29 CFR 825.208(a). An employing agency must notify employees more than once that leave is designated as FMLA–qualifying where leave is taken intermittently or on a reduced leave schedule and circumstances regarding the leave have changed. 29 CFR 825.208(a); S. Res. 242, Cong. Rec. S3959, S3966 (April 23, 1996); 29 CFR 825.208(a).

d.   Failure of Agency to Provide Notice

There are penalties imposed on agencies that fail to timely notify the employee that leave is FMLA–qualifying in some instances, and no penalties in others.

If the employer has the requisite knowledge to make a determination that the paid leave is for an FMLA reason at the time the employee either gives notice of the need for leave or commences leave and fails to designate the leave as FMLA leave (and so notify the employee in accordance with § 825.208(b)), the employer may not designate leave as FMLA leave retroactively, and may designate only prospectively as of the date of notification to the employee of the designation. 29 CFR 825.208(c); S. Res. 242, Cong. Rec. S3959, S3966 (April 23, 1996); 29 CFR 825.208(c).; *Sims v. Schultz*, 305 F. Supp. 2d 838, 845 (N.D. Ill. 2004); *Donahoo v. Master Data Center*, 282 F. Supp. 2d 540, 554 (E.D. Mich. 2003); *Farina v. Compuware, Corp.*, 256 F. Supp. 2d 1033, 1054 (D. Az. 2003). In that case, the employee is subject to the full protections of the Act, but none of the absences preceding the notice to the employee of the designation may be counted against the employee's 12–week FMLA leave entitlement. 29 CFR 825.208(c); S. Res. 242, Cong. Rec. S3959, S3966 (April 23, 1996); 29 CFR 825.208(c).

The penalty provision in § 825.208(c) is similar to the provision contained in § 825.700(a). 29 CFR 825.700(a); S. Res. 242, Cong. Rec. S3959, S3976 (April 23, 1996); 29 CFR 825.700(a). In pertinent part, § 825.700(a) provides:

> If an employee takes paid or unpaid leave and the employer does not designate the leave as FMLA leave, the leave taken does not count against an employee's FMLA leave entitlement.

One of the consequences of the penalty provision in § 825.700(a) was that an employee could receive more than the statutory 12 workweeks of FMLA leave in a leave year as a penalty for an employer's failure to designate the leave as FMLA-qualifying. Because of that consequence, the Supreme Court in *Ragsdale v. Wolverine World Wide, Inc.*, 535 U.S. 81, 122 S. Ct. 1155, 152 L. Ed. 167 (2002), held that § 825.700(a) was invalid. Specifically, the Supreme Court held that, among other reasons, the regulation amended the FMLA's most fundamental substantive guarantee—the employee's entitlement to a total of 12 workweeks of leave during any 12-month period. The DOL's penalty, a grant of an additional 12 workweeks of leave for an employer's failure to designate the leave as FMLA-qualifying, subverts the careful balance achieved by Congress, by giving certain employees a right to more than 12 weeks of FMLA-compliant leave in a given one-year period. *Ragsdale*, 535 U.S. at 94. In its decision, the Court also found that § 825.700(a) was invalid because the penalty was automatic regardless of whether the employee actually suffered harm as a result of the employer's failure to properly notify the employee of the designation of leave as FMLA-qualifying.

Note that the decision of the Supreme Court does not invalidate the requirement that an employer notify the employee of the leave as FMLA-qualifying. The Supreme Court only invalidated the penalty provision where an employer fails to so notify an employee.

Since the Supreme Court's invalidation of the penalty provision in 29 CFR 825.700(a) in *Ragsdale v. Wolverine World Wide, Inc.*, 535 U.S. 81, 122 S. Ct. 1155 (2002), courts are split on whether the penalty provisions of the notice requirements of 29 CFR 825.208 are valid or in contravention of the FMLA statutory language. *Farina v. Compuware, Corp.*, 256 F. Supp. 2d 1033, 1055 (D. Az. 2003).

Post-*Ragsdale*, many courts invalidated the penalty provision of 29 CFR 825.208(c). *Katekovich v. Team Rent A Car of Pittsburgh, Inc. et al.*, 36 Fed. Appx. 688 (3rd Cir. 2002) (Katekovich was not entitled to more leave than she received because of the employer's failure to notify her that it designated the leave as FMLA-qualifying. The court essentially held that the penalty provision of § 825.208(c) is constitutionally invalid); *Brown v. Dollar General Stores, Ltd.*, No. 1:04CV-107-M, 2006 U.S. Dist. LEXIS 6746, at *14 (W.D. Ky. Feb. 21, 2006); *Sisturn v. Time-Warner Cable*, No. 02-CV-8023, 2004 U.S. Dist. LEXIS 16681, at *41 (E.D. Pa. Aug. 19, 2004) (an employer's failure to designate leave as FMLA-qualified does not mean that the leave taken does not count against an employee's FMLA entitlement); *Wright v. Owens-Illinois*, No. 2:02-cv-223-LJM-WGH, 2004 U.S. Dist. LEXIS 8535, at *25 (S.D. Ind. May 14, 2004); *Roberts v. Owens-Illinois*, No. 2:02-cv-207-LJM-WGH, 2004 U.S. Dist. LEXIS 8534, at *15 (S.D. Ind. May 14, 2004); *Sims v. Schultz*, 305 F. Supp. 2d 838, 845 (N.D. Ill. 2004) (Section 825.208 validity may be fairly questioned after *Ragsdale*); *Whitney v. Wal-Mart Stores, Inc.*, No. 03-65-P-H, 2003 U.S. Dist. LEXIS 22629, at *40-41(D. Me. Dec. 16, 2003); *Felder v. Winn-Dixie Louisiana, Inc.*, No. 03-1438 Section "N" (2), 2003 U.S. Dist. LEXIS 22535, at *12 (E.D. La. Dec. 16, 2003); *Smith v. Blue Dot Co.*, 283 F. Supp. 2d 1200, 1206 (D. Kan. 2003); *Donahoo v. Master Data Center*, 282 F. Supp. 2d 540, 554 (E.D. Mich. 2003).

Other courts have not completely done away with all penalties for an employer's failure to notify an employee that it designated the requested leave as FMLA-qualifying. These courts read *Ragsdale* as effectively invalidating the automatic penalty provision of § 825.208(c). However, they also read the Supreme Court's decision as leaving open the possibility that employees could recover for notice violations on a "case-by-case" basis. *Farina v. Compuware Corp.*, 256 F. Supp. 2d 1033, 2003 U.S. Dist. LEXIS 5983 (D. AZ. March 31, 2003). In *Farina*, the court relied on statements made by the Supreme Court indicating that an employee could recover for notice violations on a case-by-case basis where an employee could demonstrate that he suffered actual harm as a result of an employer's violation of the notice provision. *Id.* (citing *Ragsdale*, 122 S. Ct. at 1162). The court also noted that another post-*Ragsdale* district court held that a plaintiff must show detrimental reliance and prejudice to prevail on an FMLA notice violation. *Id.* (citing *Summers v. Middleton & Reutlinger, P.S.C.*, 214 F. Supp. 2d 751 (W.D. Ky. 2002)). In *Farina*, even though the employer notified the employee of the wrong date her FMLA leave would end, the district court found that the plaintiff failed to establish detrimental reliance and prejudice where her 12 weeks of FMLA leave had expired by the time she received the errant notice of additional FMLA leave.

Farina and similar decisions rely on several rationales expressed by the Supreme Court for invalidating the penalty provision contained in § 825.700(a). The interesting question is what happens if there is detrimental reliance and prejudice, but the penalty imposed would extend the leave beyond the statutory 12 weeks? The Supreme Court in *Ragsdale* based its decision, in part, on the argument that the DOL exceeded its authority by imposing a penalty for an employer's failure to provide notice of leave designation that effectively increased the amount of FMLA leave to an employee beyond the statutory 12 workweeks. Perhaps the *Farina* line of cases is limited to situations where the employee would not receive more than the statutory 12-week entitlement. This is certainly a viable argument given the multiple bases for the *Ragsdale* decision.

Post–*Ragsdale*, to establish an actionable claim of interference as a result of an employer's failure to notify an employee that it designated the leave as FMLA–qualifying, the employee must prove both that the employer failed to give notice as required, and that the employee's FMLA rights were prejudiced as a result. *See Dube v. J.P. Morgan Investor Services*, 201 Fed. Appx. 786 (1st Cir. 2006); *Fiato v. Keala*, 191 Fed. Appx. 551 (9th Cir. 2006); *Moticka v. Weck Closure Systems*, 183 Fed. Appx. 343 (4th Cir. 2006); *Wilkerson v. Autozone, Inc.*, 152 Fed. Appx. 444 (6th Cir. 2005); *Conoshenti v. PSE&G Gas Co.*, 364 F.3d 135, 142 (3d Cir. 2004); *Reed v. Buckeye Fire Equip. Co.*, 422 F. Supp. 2d 570, 577 & n.4 (W.D.N.C. March 22, 2006), *aff'd in part, rev'd and remanded on other grounds*, 2007 U.S. App. LEXIS 18120 (4th Cir. July 30, 2007); *Mondaine v. American Drug Stores, Inc.*, 408 F. Supp. 2d 1169, 1204 (D. Kan. Jan. 11, 2006); *Sisturn v. Time–Warner Cable*, No. 02–CV–8023, 2004 U.S. Dist. LEXIS 16681, at *41 (E.D. Pa. Aug. 19, 2004); *Wright v. Owens–Illinois*, No. 2:02–cv–223–LJM–WGH, 2004 U.S. Dist. LEXIS 8535, at *27 (S.D. Ind. May 14, 2004) (after *Ragsdale*, an employer's failure to give notice designating leave as FMLA qualifying, standing alone, does not violate the FMLA); *Sims v. Schultz*, 305 F. Supp. 2d 838, 845 (N.D. Ill. 2004), *Roberts v. Owens–Illinois*, No. 2:02–cv–207–LJM–WGH, 2004 U.S. Dist. LEXIS 8534, at *15 (S.D. Ind. May 14, 2004); *Smith v. Blue Dot Co.*, 283 F. Supp. 2d 1200, 1204 (D. Kan. 2003) (*Ragsdale* instructs courts to take into consideration the reality of what would have happened had the notice been given, including whether or not the employee would have returned to work after taking leave); *Wright v. Owens–Illinois*, No. 2:02–cv–223–LJM–WGH, 2004 U.S. Dist. LEXIS 8535, at *27 (S.D. Ind. May 14, 2004); *Roberts v. Owens–Illinois*, No. 2:02–cv–207–LJM–WGH, 2004 U.S. Dist. LEXIS 8534, at *15 (S.D. Ind. May 14, 2004); *Sims v. Schultz*, 305 F. Supp. 2d 838, 845 (N.D. Ill. 2004); *Whitney v. Wal–Mart Stores, Inc.*, No. 03–65–P–H, 2003 U.S. Dist. LEXIS 22629, at *40 (D. Me. Dec. 16, 2003); *Donahoo v. Master Data Center*, 282 F. Supp. 2d 540, 554 (E.D. Mich. 2003).

Prejudice exists where the employee loses compensation or benefits "by reason of the violation;" sustains "other monetary loses" as a result of the violation; or suffers some loss in employment status remediable through "appropriate equitable relief." *Reed v. Buckeye Fire Equip. Co.*, No. 06-1481, 2007 U.S. App. LEXIS 18120, at *17 (4th Cir. July 30, 2007).

These cases typically involve an employee who used up some or all of his or her 12 weeks of FMLA leave before learning that the employer counted that protected leave toward the employee's 12 weeks of FMLA leave. An employee can survive a motion for summary judgment by establishing both that the employer failed to notify the employee of the FMLA leave designation, and that the employee suffered prejudice as a result of that notice failure. Prejudice can be established by showing that the employee could have structured his or her leave in a way that he or she would not have run out of job–protected FMLA leave. *Conoshenti v. PSE&G Gas Co.*, 364 F.3d 135, 142 (3d Cir. 2004); *Parsley v. City of Columbus, Ohio*, 471 F. Supp. 2d 858 (S.D. Ohio 2006); *Menzies v. La Veta School District RE-2*, No. 05-cv-00287-MSK-MJW, 2006 U.S. Dist. LEXIS 33996, at 822 (D. Colo. May 26, 2006); *Reed v. Buckeye Fire Equip. Co.*, 422 F. Supp. 2d 570, 577 & n.4 (W.D.N.C. March 22, 2006), *aff'd in part, rev'd and remanded in part*, 2007 U.S. App. LEXIS 18120, at *17 (4th Cir. July 30, 2007) (employee would have returned to work before expiration of 12 weeks had employee been given notice leave designated as FMLA); *Mondaine v. American Drug Stores, Inc.*, 408 F. Supp. 2d 1169, 1204 (D. Kan. Jan. 11, 2006); *Sisturn v. Time–Warner Cable*, No. 02–CV–8023, 2004 U.S. Dist. LEXIS 16681, at *41 (E.D. Pa. Aug. 19, 2004); *Sims v. Schultz*, 305 F. Supp. 2d 838, 845 (N.D. Ill. 2004) (conceivable that, had defendants promptly designated employee's leave as FMLA leave, he may have taken intermittent or part time leave so as not to exceed 12–week entitlement).

In *Sims v. Schultz*, 305 F. Supp. 2d 838, 845 (N.D. Ill. 2004), the employer failed to designate the employee's sick leave as FMLA leave until after 12 weeks passed. After noting the questionable validity of the penalty provision of § 825.208 after *Ragsdale*, the court found sufficient evidence of prejudice from the employer's failure to designate the leave as FMLA leave to preclude summary judgment. In so doing, the court rejected as overly broad the employer's argument that *Ragsdale* permitted an employer to retroactively designate medical leave as FMLA leave as long as the employee was given at least 12 weeks.

Similarly, in *Roberson v. Cendant Travel Services, Inc.*, 252 F. Supp. 2d 573, 577–79 (M.D. Tenn. 2002), the district court indicated that an employer's failure to notify an employee that it designated leave as FMLA–qualifying was not itself a violation of the Act. However, the employer's failure to notify the employee of FMLA leave designation pushed back the date when FMLA leave started. The court found no FMLA violation, despite the employer using the wrong date for expiration of the 12–week FMLA leave entitlement, because the employee was unable to return to work on the date leave should have ended, and she had no right of restoration to her former position. The plaintiff argued that, had she known when the FMLA leave was going to expire, she would have returned to work earlier. The court rejected this argument because the medical evidence indicated that she could not return to work on the date she calculated her FMLA leave would run out. As such, she could not show that she was injured as a result of the defendant's actions. *See Reynolds v. Phillips & Temro Industries, Inc.*, 195 F.3d 411, 414 (8th Cir. 1999); *Holmes v. E.Spire Communications*, 135 F. Supp. 2d 657 (D. Md. 2001). [Return to work issues are addressed in Chapter 13, "Return to Work from Leave."]

In *Wright v. Owens–Illinois*, No. 2:02–cv–223–LJM–WGH, 2004 U.S. Dist. LEXIS 8535, at *27 (S.D. Ind. May 14, 2004), the employer failed to notify the employee that it designated the employee's ten weeks of leave and eight weeks of "light duty" as FMLA–qualified. The court concluded that, under the circumstances, the employee received all of the benefits to which he was entitled pursuant to the FMLA. The court noted that, even if the eight weeks of light duty did not count toward his FMLA leave and Wright consequently only received ten weeks of medical leave, it would elevate form over substance to provide him with two remaining weeks of medical leave where the employee was on permanent medical restrictions and could not perform the essential functions of his job.

In *Roberts v. Owens–Illinois*, No. 2:02–cv–207–LJM–WGH, 2004 U.S. Dist. LEXIS 8534, at *15 (S.D. Ind. May 14, 2004), the court held that the "underpinnings of *Ragsdale* still militate against" plaintiff. The employer terminated the employee once it learned that the employee's medical restrictions were permanent. The employer also failed to notify the employee that it designated leave and "light duty" as FMLA–qualified. The court, however, found that plaintiff failed to establish that she suffered any prejudice, because the employer eventually reinstated the employee with back pay and benefits. The court concluded that this was all she was entitled to receive under the FMLA.

The employee in *Whitney v. Wal–Mart Stores, Inc.*, No. 03–65–P–H, 2003 U.S. Dist. LEXIS 22629, at *40 (D. Me. Dec. 16, 2003), alleged that the premature exhaustion of his FMLA leave constituted prejudice resulting from his employer's failure to inform him that he could work 40 hours a week and use FMLA leave for any hours of work over that amount. The court found sufficient information in the record to preclude an award of summary judgment to the employer.

In *Felder v. Winn–Dixie Louisiana, Inc.*, No. 03–1438 Section "N" (2), 2003 U.S. Dist. LEXIS 22535, at *12–14 (E.D. La. Dec. 16, 2003), the employee was terminated while on maternity leave. At the time of her termination, Felder had been on leave for more than 12 weeks. Felder sought reinstatement, alleging that Winn–Dixie failed to inform her that it designated her leave as FMLA qualifying. She did not argue that she was entitled to more leave pursuant to 29 CFR 825.208(c). The court observed that "[a]lthough plaintiff acknowledges the holding in *Ragsdale* and avoids seeking any additional leave, the result of accepting her argument that she can seek reinstatement based on defendant's failure to comply with the notice regulations would create a situation virtually identical to the one that the Supreme Court held was contrary to the FMLA." The court concluded: "Just as *Ragsdale* would not permit Felder to obtain an additional 12 weeks of leave because of the lack of notice, she is not entitled to any of the other penalties or benefits provided by the FMLA, such as reinstatement or back pay."

An employee who is unable to return to work after 12 weeks and who would have been returning from the employer's own disability leave plan, not FMLA leave, suffers no prejudice as a result of her employer's failure to notify her that the leave was designated as FMLA leave. *Mondaine v. American Drug Stores, Inc.*, 408 F. Supp. 2d 1169, 1204 (D. Kan. Jan. 11, 2006); *Donahoo v. Master Data Center*, 282 F. Supp. 2d 540, 554 (E.D. Mich. 2003).

Absent prejudice, an employee who was erroneously told by her employer that her FMLA leave would end on a certain date does not have a viable FMLA claim. In *Farina v. Compuware, Corp.*, 256 F. Supp. 2d 1033, 1057 (D. Az. 2003), the employee was properly advised that her FMLA leave would run concurrently with long–term disability leave. Plaintiff was protected for 12 weeks, until February. After the 12 weeks of FMLA leave ran out, the employer erroneously sent the employee another letter in March indicating that her FMLA leave expired in May. According to the court, even if plaintiff relied on the March letter, that reliance was not detrimental to her FMLA rights. "By March, plaintiff was no longer protected by the provisions of the FMLA. She lost her FMLA protections on February 16, before she was told by Defendant that she could remain on FMLA leave." Therefore, plaintiff fully exercised her FMLA rights notwithstanding her employer's actions. Defendant's "representation that the additional leave time was mandated by the FMLA does not create a cause of action for Plaintiff under the statute."

There are no penalties imposed by the regulations where the agency fails to inform an employee that it has designated unpaid leave as FMLA qualifying. *Rowe v. Laidlaw Transit, Inc.*, 244 F.3d 1115, 118 (9th Cir. 2001). In *Rowe*, the Ninth Circuit indicated that unpaid leave is treated the same as paid leave for purposes of an employer's failure to notify the employee that it designated the leave as FMLA–qualifying. The case was formally concerned with whether an employee exempt from the overtime requirements became non–exempt by virtue of being placed on an FMLA reduced leave schedule. The court answered that question in the negative. The case was complicated by the fact that the leave was not formally designated as FMLA qualifying. The court held that the employer's failure to designate the leave as FMLA–qualifying did not alter the conclusion that the employee was on FMLA leave. The court noted that paid leave is still protected by the Act even where the employer fails to designate the leave as FMLA–qualifying, citing § 825.208(c). In pertinent part, the court noted that Rowe was on unpaid leave. Section 825.208(c), the court noted, specifically applied to paid leave. The court, however, held that "FMLA-qualifying unpaid leave is entitled to FMLA protection in the same fashion as paid leave, that is regardless of notification by employer or employee. Rowe's unpaid leave, granted in the form of a reduced schedule, qualified as FMLA leave, and under the FMLA, providing unpaid FMLA-qualifying leave does not effect an employee's exempt status."

The *Rowe* decision opens the door for application of § 825.208(c) penalties to be applied where an employer fails to designate unpaid leave as FMLA-qualifying. It is curious that *Rowe* did not rely on § 825.700(a), which applies to both paid and unpaid leave.

Nor are there penalties imposed for an employing agency's failure to timely notify an employee that it designated leave, paid or unpaid, as FMLA-qualifying where the employer does not have the requisite knowledge at the time leave commences. This may arise where the agency learns that leave is for an FMLA purpose after leave has begun (§ 825.301(d)), or where subsequent information failed to confirm that the leave was for an FMLA-covered reason (§ 825.301(e)(2)). Of course, a failure to provide such notice may independently support a claim of interference with FMLA rights. *Klaus v. Builders Concrete Co.*, No. 00-C-7757, 2002 U.S. Dist. LEXIS 1919 (N.D. Ill. Feb. 7, 2002).

Finally, there is no requirement that an employer notify an employee that it has not designated the leave as FMLA-qualifying. *Thornton v. BASF*, No. 99-2243, 2000 U.S. App. LEXIS 15909 (4th Cir. July 11, 2000) (because the employee's leave was not classified as FMLA leave, the employer had no obligation to further notify the employee of that fact; the employer designated leave as paid sick leave, not concurrently covered by the FMLA).

e. Note to the DOL and the Office of Compliance

The designation notice regulations of Title I and the CAA are hopelessly vague and unnecessarily complicated. The DOL and the Office of Compliance need to replace these regulations with new regulations. The new regulations must:

- Clearly identify the circumstances when employer notice of the designation of leave as FMLA-qualifying is required;
- Identify any differences in notice depending on whether the leave is paid or unpaid;
- State how long the employer has to provide such notice to the employee in each circumstance; and
- Specify the manner in which such notice is provided (oral or in writing, and in what language).

Until this is accomplished, agencies will undoubtedly continue to stumble along by applying the two-business day rule for paid leave prior to leave commencement in all circumstances. A close reading of the current regulations reveals that such a practice is not correct.

2. PEOAA

The PEOAA does not require an employing office to notify an employee that it has designated leave, paid or unpaid, as FMLA qualifying. The Office of Administration indicated that it has not issued regulations implementing the FMLA for purposes of the PEOAA. As a result, FMLA as applied by the PEOAA is governed solely by the statutory language of the PEOAA. The PEOAA provides that §§ 101-105, and 107 of Tile I of the FMLA (29 USC 2611-2615, 2617) apply to the PEOAA. 3 USC 412(a). Those sections do not address an employer's obligation to designate leave, paid or unpaid, as FMLA-qualifying. Nor does the PEOAA otherwise address notice of the designation of FMLA leave. As a result, the PEOAA does not require an employing office to notify the employee of such designation. Of course, because an agency is not required to provide notice does not mean that an agency is prohibited from notifying employees whether leave is FMLA-qualifying.

3. Title II

Title II requires an agency to notify an employee of its intention to designate leave as FMLA-qualifying by confirming that the employee wants the FMLA protection to apply to such leave. An agency may not put an employee on family and medical leave and may not subtract leave from an employee's 12-week entitlement unless the agency obtains confirmation from the employee of his or her intent to invoke entitlement to FMLA leave. 5 CFR 630.1203(h). An employee's notice of his or her intent to take leave pursuant to § 630.1206 may suffice as the employee's confirmation. 5 CFR 630.1203(h). In that case, the employer effectively has no duty to separately notify the employee that the leave is FMLA-qualifying.

H. MISCELLANEOUS AGENCY NOTICE REQUIREMENTS

What follows is an assortment of notice requirements imposed on employing agencies by some of the federal sector variants of the FMLA.

1. Method of Calculation of 12-Month FMLA Leave Year

a. Title I, the CAA, and the PEOAA

Employing agencies must notify employees how the 12-month FMLA leave year is calculated. All federal sector variants of the FMLA provide that an eligible employee is entitled to take up to 12 workweeks of leave each leave year for a covered condition, all other requirements being met. As addressed more fully in Chapter 10, "Leave Amount and Scheduling," the definition of an FMLA "leave year" differs under the four federal sector variants of the FMLA.

Employing agencies with employees covered by Title I, the CAA, or the PEOAA, have four options for calculating the FMLA leave year. The four options are reflected in the regulations implementing Title I and the CAA. 29 CFR 825.200(b); S. Res. 242, Cong. Rec. S3959, S3963-64 (April 23, 1996); 29 CFR 825.200(b). By a more circuitous route, the PEOAA provides employing offices with the same four options.

The Executive Office of the President indicated that regulations have not been issued by the President or a designee of the President to implement the FMLA for purposes of the PEOAA. Absent such regulations, the PEOAA directs that, to the extent necessary and appropriate, the most relevant substantive executive agency regulations promulgated to implement the statutory provision at issue must be applied for purposes of interpreting the PEOAA. 3 USC 455. The PEOAA applies §§ 101-105 of Title I of the FMLA, 29 USC 2611-2615. 3 USC 412(a)(1). Section 102 of Title I, 29 USC 2612(a)(1), provides the basic entitlement of an eligible employee to 12 workweeks of FMLA leave "during any 12-month period." Regulations implementing this section of Title I, particularly regarding the method for calculating what constitutes "any 12-month period," are found at 29 CFR 825.200(b). By operation of law, § 825.200(b) applies to the PEOAA.

The implementing regulations do not explicitly require an employing agency to inform employees of the 12-month FMLA leave year initially selected. According to at least one court, agencies must notify employees which of the four options for calculating the FMLA leave year will be used. *See Bachelder v. America West Airlines, Inc.*, 259 F.3d 1112, 1128 (9th Cir. 2001); *Dodaro v. Village of Glendale Heights,* No. 01-C-6396, 2003 U.S. Dist. LEXIS 5056 (N.D. Ill. March 31, 2003); *see also* Preamble, 29 CFR 825.200 ("Employers must inform employees of the applicable method for determining FMLA leave entitlement when informing employees of their FMLA rights). *But see Phillips v. Leroy-Somer North America et al.*, No. 01-1046-T, 2003 U.S. Dist. LEXIS 5349 (W.D. Tenn. March 28, 2003). Such notice would also appear to fit within the requirement that employing agencies with written guidance to employees concerning benefits or leave rights (i.e., most federal employers) must include information concerning FMLA entitlements and employee obligations in the employee handbook or other written document. 29 CFR 825.301(a)(1); S. Res. 242, Cong. Rec. S3959, S3971 (April 23, 1996); 29 CFR 825.301(a)(1); *see Bachelder*, 259 F.3d at 1128.

It does not appear that information regarding an agency's initial election of an option for calculating the FMLA leave year must be included in the required FMLA poster or specific written notice of FMLA rights and obligations. 29 CFR 825.300, 825.301(b)(1); S. Res. 242, Cong. Rec. S3959, S3971 (April 23, 1996); 29 CFR 825.300, 825.301(b)(1). *But see* Preamble, 29 CFR 825.200 ("Employers must inform employees of the applicable method for determining FMLA leave entitlement when informing employees of their FMLA rights). These provisions do not require publication of the FMLA leave year selected by the employing agency.

The regulations require employing agencies to notify employees of changes to the method for calculating the FMLA leave year. The notice obligation arises in two circumstances: (1) where the employer initially fails to select from one of the four FMLA leave year options; and (2) where the employer wishes to change the FMLA leave year currently in use to an alternative method. The method for notification of change is similar under both methods.

Where an employing agency fails to select one of the four available options for measuring the 12-month FMLA leave year, the option that provides the most beneficial outcome for the employee is applied. 29 CFR 825.200(e); S. Res. 242, Cong. Rec. S3959, S3964 (April 23, 1996); 29 CFR 825.200(e). The employer may subsequently select an option only by providing at least 60 days' notice to all employees of the option the employer intends to implement. 29 CFR 825.200(e); S. Res. 242, Cong. Rec. S3959, S3964 (April 23, 1996); 29 CFR 825.200(e). During the running of the 60-day period any other employee who needs FMLA leave may use the option providing the most beneficial outcome to that employee. 29 CFR 825.200(e); S. Res. 242, Cong. Rec. S3959, S3964 (April 23, 1996); 29 CFR 825.200(e). At the conclusion of the 60-day period the employer may implement the selected option. 29 CFR 825.200(e); S. Res. 242, Cong. Rec. S3959, S3964 (April 23, 1996); 29 CFR 825.200(e).

Similarly, an employing agency that wishes to change from the FMLA leave year option currently in use to another alternative must give at least a 60-day notice to all employees, and the transition must take place in such a way that the employees retain the full benefit of 12 weeks of leave under whichever method affords the greatest benefit to the employee. 29 CFR 825.200(d)(1); S. Res. 242, Cong. Rec. S3959, S3964 (April 23, 1996); 29 CFR 825.200(d)(1).

The regulations fail to specify the means of notification that an employing agency must use to effectuate the 60-day notice requirement to all employees. At minimum, such a change should be reflected in employee handbooks, manuals, or other written guidance addressing employee leave or benefits. Employing agencies should strongly consider multiple means of notifying all employees of such a change to the method of calculating the 12-month FMLA leave year. Methods to consider would include redistribution of a modified employee handbook or manual, conspicuous posting of notice of such change on employee bulletin boards where similar notices are posted, posting on an agency website, or inclusion of information in the paycheck of all employees.

In *Coker v. McFaul*, No. 06-3587, 2007 U.S. App. LEXIS 16565, at 822-26, 2007 FED App. 0466N (6th Cir. June 29, 2007), the Sixth Circuit, relying on the Supreme Court's decision in *Ragsdale v. Wolverine World Wide, Inc.*, 535 U.S. 81, 122 S. Ct. 1155 (2002), found that an employee must demonstrate prejudice as a result of an employer's failure to notify the employee of the method used for calculating the 12-month FMLA leave year (assuming, *arguendo*, that an employer has a duty to notify the employee).

b. Title II

Title II mandates the method for the calculation of the 12-month FMLA leave year; there are no other options available. 5 CFR 630.1203(c). There is no specific requirement that an agency notify employees covered by Title II of the method for calculating the FMLA leave year. Agencies are, however, generally required to inform employees of their entitlements and responsibilities under the FMLA. 5 CFR 1203(g). The OPM suggests that agencies may meet this obligation by, among other methods, providing employees access to the FMLA and OPM's implementing regulations. Preamble, 5 CFR 630.1203. As the method of calculation of the FMLA leave year is set forth in the OPM implementing regulations, providing the employee with a copy of the regulations would notify the employee how the agency calculates the FMLA leave year.

2. Benefits

a. Title I, the CAA, and the PEOAA

Employing agencies are required to notify employees of entitlements and obligations regarding employment benefits. As with notice of the method for calculating the FMLA leave year, the notice requirements are set forth in the regulations implementing Title I and the CAA. See 29 CFR 825.209, 825.210, 825.212, 825.213; S. Res. 242, Cong. Rec. S3959, S3967–S3969 (April 23, 1996); 29 CFR 825.209, 825.210, 825.212, 825.213. In the absence of its own implementing regulations, the PEOAA requires application of the most relevant and substantive regulation issued by the DOL to implement Title I of the FMLA to implement the statutory provision at issue. 3 USC 455. The PEOAA incorporates §§ 101 and 104 of Title I, 29 USC 2611, 2614, both of which address employment benefits and the FMLA. As such, the Title I FMLA regulations regarding employment benefits apply to employees covered by the PEOAA.

Chapter 12 addresses the "Maintenance of Benefits" during FMLA leave. What follows addresses the agency notice requirements regarding employment benefits under the FMLA.

(1) Employee Handbooks

If, as is highly likely, an employing agency with eligible employees issues any written guidance to employees concerning employee benefits or leave rights, such as in an employee handbook, information concerning FMLA entitlements and employee obligations under the FMLA must be included in the handbook or other document. 29 CFR 825.301(a)(1); S. Res. 242, Cong. Rec. S3959, S3971 (April 23, 1996); 29 CFR 825.301(a). As FMLA entitlements and obligations include rights regarding employment benefits during and on the return from FMLA leave, notification of those rights must be included in the employee handbook or other written materials.

(2) Specific Written Notice

The FMLA requires that employing agencies provide eligible employees with specific written notice of FMLA rights and obligations. 29 CFR 825.301(b); S. Res. 242, Cong. Rec. S3959, S3971 (April 23, 1996); 29 CFR 825.301(a). The specific written notice must inform the employee of any requirement for the employee to make any premium payments to maintain group health benefits, the arrangements for making such payments, and the consequences of failure to make such payments on a timely basis (i.e., the circumstances under which coverage may lapse). 29 CFR 825.210(d), 825.301(b)(1)(iv); S. Res. 242, Cong. Rec. S3959, S3968, S3971 (April 23, 1996); 29 CFR 825.210(d), 825.301(b)(1)(iv). The frequency of such notice is addressed in § 825.301(c). 29 CFR 825.301(c); S. Res. 242, Cong. Rec. S3959, S3971 (April 23, 1996); 29 CFR 825.301(c). [The topic is addressed more fully previously in this chapter, as well as in Chapter 12, "Maintenance of Benefits."]

(3) Changes to Group Health Plans

During any FMLA leave, an employing agency is required to maintain the employee's coverage under any group health plan on the same conditions as coverage would have been provided if the employer continuously employed the employee during the entire leave period. 29 CFR 825.209(a); S. Res. 242, Cong. Rec. S3959, S3967 (April 23, 1996); 29 CFR 825.209(a). If the employing agency provides a new health plan or benefits or changes health benefits or plans while an employee is on FMLA leave, the employee is entitled to the new or changed plan/benefits to the same extent as if the employee were not on leave. 29 CFR 825.209(c); S. Res. 242, Cong. Rec. S3959, S3967 (April 23, 1996); 29 CFR 825.209(c). For example, if an employing agency changes a group health plan so that dental coverage becomes covered under the plan, the employee on FMLA leave must be given the same opportunity as other employees to receive (or obtain) the dental coverage. 29 CFR 825.209(c); S. Res. 242, Cong. Rec. S3959, S3967 (April 23, 1996); 29 CFR 825.209(c).

The FMLA requires that "[n]otice of any opportunity to change plans or benefits must be given to an employee on FMLA leave." 29 CFR 825.209(d); S. Res. 242, Cong. Rec. S3959, S3967 (April 23, 1996); 29 CFR 825.209(d). The regulations do not identify who bears the responsibility for providing such notice. Presumably, the responsibility is borne by the employing agency. The regulations also fail to provide any additional guidance on the timing or method of notice. A prudent employing agency would provide such notice within a reasonable period of time of the change to the employment benefit plan. It would also provide such notice in writing, detailing what the employee needs to do, and when it must be done, in order to perfect the right to the change in group health plans.

(4) Failure to Make Premium Payments

An agency's obligation to maintain group health benefits during an employee's FMLA leave on the same terms as if the employee were continuously employed during the leave period, places concomitant responsibilities on employees to continue to pay their share (if any) of group health plan premiums during the FMLA leave period. 29 CFR 210(a); S. Res. 242, Cong. Rec. S3959, S3967 (April 23, 1996); 29 CFR 825.210(a). Agencies are required to notify employees of the terms and conditions by which these payments must be made. 29 CFR 825.210(d); S. Res. 242, Cong. Rec. S3959, S3967 (April 23, 1996); 29 CFR 825.210(a).

An agency's responsibility to maintain group health plan coverage ceases under the FMLA if an employee's premium payment is more than 30 days late. 29 CFR 825.212(a)(1); S. Res. 242, Cong. Rec. S3959, S3968 (April 23, 1996); 29 CFR 825.212(a). In order to drop group health plan coverage where an employee's premium payment is late, the employing agency must provide written notice to the employee that the payment was not received. 29 CFR 825.212(a)(1); S. Res. 242, Cong. Rec. S3959, S3968 (April 23, 1996); 29 CFR 825.212(a). Such notice must be mailed to the employee at least

15 days before coverage is to cease, advising that coverage will be dropped on a specified date at least 15 days after the date of the letter unless the payment is received by that date. 29 CFR 825.212(a)(1); S. Res. 242, Cong. Rec. S3959, S3968 (April 23, 1996); 29 CFR 825.212(a); see Karnes v. Central Texas Mental Health/Mental Retardation Center, No. 6:01–CV–045–C, 2002 U.S. Dist. LEXIS 2951 (N.D. Tex. Feb. 22, 2002).

The regulations do not identify what penalty, if any, an employer would incur for failure to provide the required notice. At minimum, an agency's failure to provide such notice would constitute an actionable claim of interference with FMLA rights.

b. Title II

Title II provides that employees on LWOP may maintain health benefits coverage, and that they must make arrangements to continue to make contributions. 5 CFR 630.1209. The regulation does not require an agency to notify employees about changes to the FEHBP during FMLA leave. Nor does it require that agencies notify employees of the obligation to make premium payments during leave, or the consequences of failing to make premium payments. Finally, Title II does not require agencies to give employees advance notice that the agency will terminate health benefits coverage due to untimely premium payments.

The general notice provision of Title II requires agencies to inform employees of their entitlements and responsibilities under the FMLA. 5 CFR 630.1203(g). One of the ways that the OPM suggests that this may be accomplished is for an agency to provide employees with access to the FMLA and OPM implementing regulations. 5 CFR 630.1203(g). The regulations do not define what "access" means in terms of frequency or timing of such notice.

3. Notice Obligations Toward Key Employees

a. Title I, the CAA, and the PEOAA

The FMLA provides that an eligible employee is entitled to return to the same or an equivalent position on conclusion of FMLA leave. 29 USC 2614(a)(1); 2 USC 1312(a)(1) (incorporating § 104, 29 USC 2614, into CAA); 3 USC 412(a)(1) (incorporating § 104, 29 USC 2614, into PEOAA). A limited exception to that right permits employing agencies to deny job restoration to certain highly compensated or "key" employees. 29 USC 2614(b). Restoration may be denied when an employing agency determines that it is necessary to avoid substantial and grievous economic injury if the employee returns. 29 USC 2614(b)(1)(A). [For a more developed discussion of the job restoration rights of key employees, see Chapter 13, "Return to Work from Leave."] This section will address the notification provisions only with respect to key employees.

Employing agencies have three notice obligations when it comes to the denial of restoration of a key employee. First, an employer who believes that reinstatement may be denied to a key employee must give written notice to the employee at the time the employee gives notice of the need for FMLA leave (or when FMLA commences, if earlier) that the employee qualifies as a key employee. If the agency is unable at that time to determine whether the individual is a key employee, the agency must notify the employee as soon as practicable. 29 CFR 825.219(a); S. Res. 242, Cong. Rec. S3959, S3970 (April 23, 1996); 29 CFR 825.219(a); see Oby v. Baton Rouge Marriott, 329 F. Supp. 2d 772, 782 (M.D. La. 2004); Woodford v. Community Action of Greene County, Inc. et al., 103 F. Supp. 2d 97, 100–101 (N.D.N.Y. 2000) (the employer notified the employee of "key" employee determination and that reinstatement would be denied within two to three days; the employee's request for leave provided notice "as soon as practicable" within the meaning of the regulation).

The notice must also fully inform the employee of the potential consequences of that determination with respect to reinstatement and maintenance of health benefits if the employer should also determine that substantial and grievous economic injury to the agencies operations would result if the employee is reinstated from FMLA leave. 29 CFR 825.219(a); S. Res. 242, Cong. Rec. S3959, S3970 (April 23, 1996); 29 CFR 825.219(a).

The second notice that an employing agency must give to a key employee, should it want to deny reinstatement to that employee, is that substantial and grievous economic injury to its operations will result if the key employee is reinstated. The notice must also inform the employee that it cannot deny FMLA leave to the employee, and that it intends on denying job restoration to the key employee on completion of FMLA leave. 29 CFR 825.219(b); S. Res. 242, Cong. Rec. S3959, S3970 (April 23, 1996); 29 CFR 825.219(b). This notice must also explain the basis of the employer's determination that substantial and grievous economic injury will result, and, if leave has commenced, must provide the employee a reasonable time in which to return to work, taking into account the circumstances, such as the length of the leave and the urgency of the need for the employee to return. 29 CFR 825.219(b); S. Res. 242, Cong. Rec. S3959, S3970 (April 23, 1996); 29 CFR 825.219(b).

This notice must be in writing, and served on the employee in person or by certified mail. 29 CFR 825.219(b); S. Res. 242, Cong. Rec. S3959, S3970 (April 23, 1996); 29 CFR 825.219(b). It is anticipated that an employer will ordinarily be able to give such notice prior to the employee starting leave. 29 CFR 825.219(b); S. Res. 242, Cong. Rec. S3959, S3970 (April 23, 1996); 29 CFR 825.219(b). Nothing prohibits an agency from combining the first and second notices.

The third and final notice an agency must provide a key employee comes after the conclusion of the key employee's FMLA leave. After receiving notification that substantial and grievous economic injury will result if the employee is reinstated to employment, an employee is still entitled to request reinstatement at the end of the leave period even if the employee did not return to work in response to the employer's prior notice. 29 CFR 825.219(d); S. Res. 242, Cong. Rec. S3959, S3970 (April 23, 1996); 29 CFR 825.219(d). The employer must again determine whether there will be substantial and grievous economic injury from reinstatement, based on the facts at that time. 29 CFR 825.219(b); S. Res. 242, Cong. Rec. S3959, S3970 (April 23, 1996); 29 CFR 825.219(b). If it is determined that substantial and grievous economic injury will result, the employer must notify the employee in writing (in person or by certified mail) of the denial of restoration. 29 CFR 825.219(b); S. Res. 242, Cong. Rec. S3959, S3970 (April 23, 1996); 29 CFR 825.219(b).

b. Title II

Agencies do not have any notification responsibilities to "key employees" as Title II does not recognize the concept of a "key employee."

4. Joint Employment

a. Title I, the CAA, and the PEOAA

Covered employers within the meaning of the FMLA include so-called joint employers. 29 USC 2611(4); 29 CFR 825.106; 2 USC 1312(a) (incorporating § 101, 29 USC 2611 into the CAA); S. Res. 242, Cong. Rec. S3959, S3961 (April 23, 1996); 29 CFR 825.106; 3 USC 412(a)(1) (incorporating § 101, 29 USC 2611 into the PEOAA). As discussed more fully in Chapter 3, "FMLA Coverage of the Federal Government," joint employment occurs where two or more entities exercise some control over the work or working conditions of the employee. 29 CFR 825.106; S. Res. 242, Cong. Rec. S3959, S3961 (April 23, 1996); 29 CFR 825.106. Under Title I and the PEOAA, a joint employment relationship will ordinarily be found to exist when a temporary or leasing agency supplies employees to a second employer. 29 CFR 825.106(b). Under the CAA, the joint employment relationship may only exist between CAA-covered employing offices. S. Res. 242, Cong. Rec. S3959, S3961 (April 23, 1996); 29 CFR 825.106.

In joint employment relationships, only the primary employer is responsible for giving required notices to employees. 29 CFR 825.106(c); S. Res. 242, Cong. Rec. S3959, S3961 (April 23, 1996); 29 CFR 825.106(c). Under Title I and the PEOAA, the primary employer generally has the authority to hire and fire, assign/place the employee, make payroll, and provide employment benefits. 29 CFR 825.106(c); S. Res. 242, Cong. Rec. S3959, S3961 (April 23, 1996); 29 CFR 825.106(c). Under the CAA, the parties to the joint employment relationship can designate who is the primary and who is the secondary employer. S. Res. 242, Cong. Rec. S3959, S3961 (April 23, 1996); 29 CFR 825.106(c).

b. Title II

Title II does not recognize joint employment. As a result, it does not have any notice provisions addressing that concept.

5. Record Keeping

The record keeping requirements of the FMLA are discussed in detail in Chapter 14, "Record Keeping Requirements."

a. Title I

The FMLA requires that covered employing agencies keep and preserve records pertaining to their obligations under the Act. 29 USC 2616(b); 29 CFR 825.500(a). Covered employers who have eligible employees must maintain and retain copies of all general and specific written notices given to employees as required by the FMLA and the implementing regulations. 29 CFR 825.500(c)(4).

b. The CAA and the PEOAA

Neither the CAA nor the PEOAA require covered agencies to retain copies of written notices given to employees pursuant to the FMLA, as applied through the CAA or the PEOAA. This result is not surprising as the CAA and the PEOAA both apply the FMLA by incorporation of §§ 101–105 and 107 (29 USC 2611–2615, 2617) of Title I. 2 USC 1312(a)(CAA); 3 USC 412(a)(1) (PEOAA). The record keeping requirement of Title I is contained in § 106, 29 USC 2616. That section is not incorporated into the CAA or the PEOAA. As a result, the regulations implementing the CAA do not include a record–keeping requirement. The PEOAA, as we have seen, does not have implementing regulations.

c. Title II

Title II requires that agencies maintain certain records on the employee's use of FMLA leave. 5 CFR 630.1211. Agency notice to employees of FMLA rights and obligations are not included in the records that must be maintained by agencies.

I. AGENCIES WITH MIXED FMLA RESPONSIBILITIES

Agencies whose workforce consists of a mixture of FMLA coverages must exercise great care to ensure that they satisfy the notice requirements of each FMLA constituency. This is particularly true in the majority of federal agencies whose workforce predominately consists of employees covered by Title II of the Act, and a minority covered by Title I. In terms of an agency's responsibility to notify employees of FMLA rights and responsibilities, Titles I and II of the Act are substantially different.

Title II contains a general agency notice requirement that may be satisfied by providing an employee access to FMLA regulations, agency FMLA policies, and various OPM FMLA fact sheets and brochures. The employer notification requirements of Title I, in contrast, are numerous and specific. They include the requirement of agencies to post FMLA notices, incorporate notice of FMLA rights and responsibilities in employee handbooks, and periodically provide employees with specific written notice of FMLA rights and responsibilities. Title I agency notice obligations detail when and how notice must be given. Written notice is required in certain instances, and not in others. There are also legal consequences for agencies that violate the Title I notice requirements, including civil penalties, the inability to assert employee violations of the FMLA to deny leave, and civil liability for interference with an employee's FMLA rights.

Agencies with a majority of Title II employees who apply the notification requirements of Title II to all employees, including those covered by Title I, stand an excellent chance of violating the FMLA rights of employees covered by Title I. Indeed, because most federal agencies have likely not posted the DOL FMLA poster, which all agencies are required to post whether they have covered employees or not, it is highly likely most federal agencies are currently in violation of Title I of the FMLA. At $100 per offense, given the number of employee bulletin boards in every office of every federal agency across the country that is not adorned with the DOL FMLA poster, that quickly adds up to some real, unbudgeted money.

III. EMPLOYEE NOTICE OBLIGATIONS

A. INTRODUCTION

Employees, like agencies, have multiple notice obligations in the exercise of FMLA entitlements. The notice obligations of the four federal sector variants of the FMLA have substantial similarities and differences. The failure of an employee to fulfill the responsibility to notify the employer in accordance with the requirements of the FMLA may, in some instances, result in the loss of the benefits and protections of the Act.

B. NEED FOR FMLA LEAVE

Central to an employee's ability to gain the benefits and protections of the FMLA is the responsibility to notify his or her employing agency of the need for FMLA leave. The timing, adequacy, and manner of notice is strictly prescribed by some federal sector variants of the FMLA, and more loosely referenced in others. As with other areas of federal sector FMLA law, agencies, employees, unions, and other organizations representing the interests of employees must appreciate these differences in order to properly apply the requirements of the FMLA.

1. When Notice Must Be Given

a. Title I, the CAA, and the PEOAA

To perfect their right to FMLA leave, eligible employees must provide their employer with timely notice of the need for FMLA leave. *See* 29 USC 2612(e); 2 USC 1312(a)(1) (incorporating § 102 of Title I, 29 USC 2612, into the CAA); 3 USC 412(a)(1) (incorporating § 102 of Title I, 29 USC 2612, into the PEOAA); *see Brenneman v. MidCentral Health System*, 366 F.3d 412, 421 (6th Cir. 2004) (an eligible employee must give the employer notice of the need for FMLA leave within the requisite time frame), *cert. denied*, 534 U.S. 1146 (2005); *Wheeler v. Pioneer Dev. Services, Inc.*, 349 F. Supp. 2d 158 (D. Mass. 2004) (employee must give employer appropriate notice of need for FMLA leave*); Lukacinsky v. Panasonic Service Co.*, No. 03–40141–FDS, 2004 U.S. Dist. LEXIS 25846, at *38 (D. Mass. Nov. 29, 2004).

Courts have opined on the purpose and utility of the employee notice requirement. The court in *Lukacinsky v. Panasonic Service Co.*, No. 03–40141–FDS, 2004 U.S. Dist. LEXIS 25846, at *40–41 (D. Mass. Nov. 29, 2004) (citations omitted) observed:

> The notice requirement thus furthers the FMLA's goal of providing leave to employees in a manner that accommodates the legitimate needs of employers.… Employers obviously are entitled to an explanation of their employees' absences.… Furthermore, without notice, employers would be uncertain whether to punish an absence or provide accommodation to the employee.

The Seventh Circuit similarly opined that, "Conditioning the right to take FMLA leave on the employee's giving the required notice to his employer is the *quid pro quo* for the employer's partial surrender of control over his work force." *Aubuchon v. Knauf Fiberglass, GMBH*, 359 F.3d 950, 951–952 (7th Cir. 2004); *accord Gilliam v. UPS*, 233 F.3d 969, 971 (7th Cir. 2000); *Maynard v. Total Image Specialists, Inc.*, 478 F. Supp. 2d 993 (S.D. Ohio 2007); *Williams v. Illinois Dept. of Corrections*, No. 05-cv-4227-JPG, 2007 U.S. Dist. LEXIS 17119, at *9-10 (S.D. Ill. March 9, 2007) ("Notice minimizes the disruptive effect of an employee's absence and enables an employer to keep its business operating smoothly by bringing in substitutes or hiring temporary help"). Regulations implementing this requirement have been promulgated pursuant to Title I (29 CFR 825.302–303) and the CAA (S. Res. 242, Cong. Rec. S3959, S3971–72 (April 23, 1996); 29 CFR 825.302–303). Because regulations have not been issued to implement the FMLA for purposes of the PEOAA, the regulations issued pursuant to Title I governing employee notice responsibilities apply to employees covered by the PEOAA. 3 USC 455.

When an employee must provide notice to his or her employer of the need for FMLA leave depends on whether the need for leave is foreseeable. *Maynard v. Total Image Specialists, Inc.*, 478 F. Supp. 2d 993 (S.D. Ohio 2007); *Cool v. BorgWarner Diversified Transmission Products, Inc.*, No. IP 02–0960-C-B/S, 2004 U.S. Dist. LEXIS 570, at *16 (S.D. Ind. Jan. 12, 2004) (federal regulations, specifically 29 CFR 825.302(a), provide for two kinds of notice: notice of a foreseeable leave, and notice of leave that is not foreseeable).

(1) Foreseeable Need for Leave

An employee must provide his or her employer at least 30 days advance notice before FMLA leave is to begin if the need for the leave is foreseeable based on an expected birth, placement for adoption or foster care, or planned medical treatment for a serious health condition of the employee or of a covered family member. 29 USC 2612(e); 29 CFR 825.301(a); S. Res. 242, Cong. Rec. S3959, S3971 (April 23, 1996); 29 CFR 825.302(a); *see Moorer v. Baptist Mem. Health Care System*, 398 F.3d 469 (6th Cir. 2005); *Brenneman v. MidCentral Health System*, 366 F.3d 412, 421 (6th Cir. 2004), *cert. denied*, 543 U.S. 1146 (2005); *Aubuchon v. Knauf Fiberglass, GMBH*, 359 F.3d 950, 951–952 (7th Cir. 2004); *Perry v. Jaguar of Troy*, 353 F.3d 510, 513 (6th Cir. Dec. 30, 2003*); Spangler v. Federal Home Loan Bank of Des Moines*, 278 F.3d 847, 852 (8th Cir. 2002); *Bailey v. Southwest Gas Co.*, 275 F.3d 1181, 1185 (9th Cir. 2002); *Bachelder v. America West Airlines, Inc.*, 259 F.3d 1112, 1130

(9th Cir. 2001); *Bailey v. Amsted Industries, Inc.*, 172 F.3d 1041, 1045–46 (8th Cir. 1999); *Tafelski v. Novartis Pharmaceuticals*, No. 05-71547, 2007 U.S. Dist. LEXIS 22847, at 15 (E.D. Mich. March 28, 2007); *Maynard v. Total Image Specialists, Inc.*, 478 F. Supp. 2d 993 (S.D. Ohio 2007); *Williams v. Illinois Dept. of Corrections*, No. 05-cv-4227-JPG, 2007 U.S. Dist. LEXIS 17119, at *9-10 (S.D. Ill. March 9, 2007); *Sons v. Henry County*, No. 1:05-cv-0516-DFH-TAB, 2006 U.S. Dist. LEXIS 79604, at *24 (S.D. Ind. Oct. 31, 2006). For example, the daughter of an eligible employee is scheduled to have knee surgery following a bicycling accident. The employee is advised of the surgery 60 days before it is scheduled to take place. The employee is needed to take the daughter to surgery, and accompany her while she recovers. To provide timely notice of the need for FMLA leave, the employee must notify his or her employer no less than 30 days prior to when the leave is to begin. Of course, the employee could give more notice than the minimum 30 days notice required by the FMLA.

In *Tafelski v. Novartis Pharmaceuticals*, No. 05-71547, 2007 U.S. Dist. LEXIS 22847, at 15 (E.D. Mich. March 28, 2007), the court found that because the employee knew that his wife was pregnant and her due date months before the event, he was subject to the 30-day notice requirement.

In *Hughes v. City of Bethlehem*, No. 05-5444, 2007 U.S. Dist. LEXIS 22409, at *36 (E.D. Pa. March 27, 2006), the employee was scheduled to work September 24, 25, and 26 following three days of vacation. While on vacation she planned to have cosmetic surgery. She originally planned to have the surgery on September 24, recuperate on the 25th, and return to work September 26. She did not get those days off. She had her surgery on the 24th anyway. Hughes called in sick on the 24th and 25th. Her airline ticket had her returning to the state on the 25th, the second day she was scheduled to be at work. The court observed that Hughes could have told her employer 30 days in advance of the trip that she needed leave for those two days for surgery.

If 30 days notice is not practicable, such as because of a lack of knowledge of approximately when leave will be required to begin, a change in circumstances, or a medical emergency, the employee must notify his or her employer as soon as practicable. 29 USC 2612(e); 29 CFR 825.301(a); S. Res. 242, Cong. Rec. S3959, S3971 (April 23, 1996); 29 CFR 825.302(a); *see Moorer v. Baptist Mem. Health Care System*, 398 F.3d 469 (6th Cir. 2005); *Spangler v. Federal Home Loan Bank of Des Moines*, 278 F.3d 847, 852 (8th Cir. 2002); *Bailey v. Amsted Industries, Inc.*, 172 F.3d 1041, 1045–46 (8th Cir. 1999); *Tafelski v. Novartis Pharmaceuticals*, No. 05-71547, 2007 U.S. Dist. LEXIS 22847, at 15 (E.D. Mich. March 28, 2007); *Maynard v. Total Image Specialists, Inc.*, 478 F. Supp. 2d 993 (S.D. Ohio 2007); *Lukacinsky v. Panasonic Service Co.*, No. 03–40141–FDS, 2004 U.S. Dist. LEXIS 25846, at *38 (D. Mass. Nov. 29, 2004); *Tambash v. St. Bonaventure Univ.*, No. 99CV967, 2004 U.S. Dist. LEXIS 19914, at *30 (W.D.N.Y. Sept. 24, 2004); *Sabbrese v. Lowe's Home Centers, Inc.*, 320 F. Supp. 2d 311, 321 (W.D. Pa. 2004); *Loring v. Advanced Foods, Inc.*, No. C02–4067–PAZ, 2004 U.S. Dist. LEXIS 6172, at *16 (N.D. Iowa April 9, 2004), aff'd, 2005 U.S. App. LEXIS 4124 (8th Cir. 2005).

As soon as practicable means as soon as both possible and practical, taking into account all of the facts and circumstances in the individual case. 29 USC 2612(e); 29 CFR 825.301(a); S. Res. 242, Cong. Rec. S3959, S3961 (April 23, 1996); 29 CFR 825.302(a); *see Spangler*, 278 F.3d at 852; *Bailey v. Amsted Industries, Inc.*, 172 F.3d 1041, 1045–46 (8th Cir. 1999); *Tambash*, 2004 U.S. Dist. LEXIS 19914, at *30.

For foreseeable leave where it is not possible to give as much as 30 days notice, *as soon as practicable* ordinarily would mean at least verbal notification to the employer within one or two business days of when the need for leave becomes known to the employee. 29 USC 2612(e); 29 CFR 825.301(a); S. Res. 242, Cong. Rec. S3959, S3971 (April 23, 1996); 29 CFR 825.302(a); *see Tambash*, 2004 U.S. Dist. LEXIS 19914, at *30; *Sabbrese*, 320 F. Supp. 2d at 321; *McCarron*, 2002 U.S. Dist. LEXIS 15151. Absent extraordinary circumstances that prevented the employee from providing notice earlier, notice "as soon as practicable" does not mean ten business days. *Clifton v. N.J. Transit Corp.*, No. 03-3725 (JAP), 2005 U.S. Dist. LEXIS 21420, at *19 (D.N.J. Sept. 22, 2005).

For example, a tumor was discovered during a routine medical examination of the spouse of an eligible employee. The spouse schedules surgery to remove the tumor in two weeks. Obviously, even through the need for leave is foreseeable, the employee cannot give 30 days notice because the need will arise before the expiration of 30 days. In these circumstances, because the need for leave is foreseeable, the employee is required to provide his or her employer with at least verbal notice as soon as possible or practicable, which ordinarily means within one or two business days of when the employee first learned of the leave. In this case, all things being equal, if the employee learned of the need for leave 14 days before the leave would begin, the employee must at least provide verbal notice no later than 12 days before the leave is to begin.

It is unclear just how "foreseeable" the need for leave must be in order for this rule, rather than the rules (addressed below) governing situations where the leave is not foreseeable, to apply. This is largely due to the fact that the term "foreseeable" is not defined by the statutes or regulations. The dictionary definition of the root of that term, "foresee," means to know beforehand. Webster's Ninth New Collegiate Dictionary (Merriam–Webster Inc. 1988). An individual may have knowledge of something years, months, days, hours, or minutes beforehand. Regarding the absence of a definition of "foreseeable" leave, the court in *Spraggins v. Knauf Fiber Glass, Inc.*, 401 F. Supp. 2d 1235, 1239 (D. Ala. Nov. 21, 2005) observed:

> As the parties frame the question, then, the critical inquiry would be whether the leave here was foreseeable or unforeseeable. Except for the 30-day notice provision, however, §§ 825.302 and 825.303 do not clearly explain when leave is to be viewed as "foreseeable" or "unforeseeable." For example, if an employee learns of the need for leave only a day before the work day begins, is the need viewed as "foreseeable" or "unforeseeable?" What about a half day? Or two hours? Section 825.302 and 828.303 do not answer these questions. In fact, the regulations blur the distinction between the two because both, at bottom, require that an employee give notice as soon as practicable under the individual circumstances of the case. Regrettably, §§ 825.302 and 828.303 actually do more to confuse than to clarify the FMLA's requirements.

I couldn't agree more.

In *Waalkes v. Global Futures & Forex, Ltd.*, No. 1:05-CV-439, 2006 U.S. Dist. LEXIS 44855, at *13 & n. 13 (W.D. Mich. June 29, 2006), the court found absurd the employer's suggestion that the employee's need for FMLA leave for panic attacks was foreseeable. "Plaintiff could not better predict when he would suffer a panic attack than he could predict when he would suffer a heart attack or be involved in a car accident."

It is doubtful that the requirement that an employee provide *notice as soon as practicable* sets the minimum period of foreknowledge that an eligible employee must have in order to fall within the requirements governing a foreseeable need for leave. That is, because *as soon as practicable* ordinarily means up to two business days, it does not follow that notice of a need for leave of less than two business days automatically means the leave is governed by the requirements where the need for leave is not foreseeable. This result arguably follows from the use of the term "ordinarily." The use of that term suggests that extraordinary circumstances may increase or decrease the time within which an employee must provide notice, taking into account all of the facts and circumstances in an individual case.

For example, an eligible employee is called into his supervisor's office to take a telephone call from his wife. His wife informs the employee that their ten-year-old son was hit by a car while crossing the street. She indicates that the son is at home resting, but the doctor wants the son to return tomorrow morning for additional tests. The employee hangs up the phone. He looks at the supervisor, who was sitting ten feet away through the whole conversation. The employee does not inform the supervisor that he needs FMLA leave at that time. Rather, he calls the next morning and asks for the day off to take his son to the hospital. The question is whether the employee timely provided notice of a need for FMLA leave. The legal answer depends on whether the leave was foreseeable. Clearly the employee had notice of the need for leave a day before the leave was to begin. As such, the leave was foreseeable. Moreover, the employee arguably did not inform the employer of the need for leave as soon as practicable, taking into account all of the facts and circumstances in the individual case. The employee was ten feet from the supervisor when he learned of the need for FMLA leave. The employee could have told him then. Instead, the employee informed the employer the next day. Even though the employee informed the employer within one or two business days, under these circumstances, the employee arguably failed to timely inform the employer of the need for leave.

Note that this notice requirement only applies for certain covered conditions, not all. Presumably, if the need for leave is foreseeable, but is not for planned medical treatment, the rule would not apply. The regulations do not explain what the phrase "planned medical treatment" means, nor is that term defined elsewhere in the statute or regulations. Again, it is not clear how far in advance treatment has to be contemplated in order for it to be planned. Nor is it clear whether treatment must be scheduled with a health care provider in order for it to be considered "planned." Finally, the regulation fails to define what is considered "treatment." Elsewhere, "treatment" is defined for purposes of a "serious health condition" to include examinations, to determine if a serious health condition exists, and evaluations of the condition. 29 CFR 825.114(b); S. Res. 242, Cong. Rec. S3959, S3963 (April 23, 1996); 29 CFR 825.114(a). Presumably, the same definition applies for purposes of notice.

In the absence of guidance on when leave is or is not "foreseeable," agencies, employees, unions, and other organizations representing employees should closely examine when the employee learned of the need for leave. If there is any foreknowledge by the employee of a need for leave, the critical question will be whether the employee provided the employer with notice of the need for leave *as soon as practicable*. Based on the circumstances, that may be more than one or two business days, or it may be less. The point is that the one or two business day rule is not static.

One court found that an employee timely requested FMLA leave to avoid a drug test she knew she would fail. In *Sons v. Henry County*, No. 1:05-cv-0516-DFH-TAB, 2006 U.S. Dist. LEXIS 79604, at *24 (S.D. Ind. Oct. 31, 2006), the court found that the employee provided timely notice of the need for leave. The employee asked for FMLA leave shortly before she was scheduled to take a drug test that she knew she would fail. The court noted that, although Sons did not give the County 30 days warning, she might have provided notice as soon as practicable. A jury, the court observed, "could reasonably conclude that the gravity of Sons' substance abuse problem was not apparent to her until she was actually faced with the prospect of a drug test."

In *Moorer v. Baptist Mem. Health Care System*, 398 F.3d 469 (6th Cir. 2005), the court found that the employee provided notice of his need for leave "as soon as practicable." The employer threatened the employee with termination if he did not meet with an EAP counselor. The employee met with the counselor and was directed to enter an alcoholism treatment facility immediately. Moorer had only two days' notice of his need for extended medical leave. The court found that the employer knew of the employee's anticipated leave as it demanded that he go to EAP and follow through on the recommended course of treatment.

(2) Need for FMLA Leave is Not Foreseeable

When the approximate timing of the need for leave is not foreseeable, an employee should give notice to the employer of the need for FMLA leave as soon as practicable under the facts and circumstances of the particular case. 29 USC 2612(e); 29 CFR 825.303(a); S. Res. 242, Cong. Rec. S3959, S3972 (April 23, 1996); 29 CFR 825.303(a); *see Brenneman v. MidCentral Health System*, 366 F.3d 412, 421 (6th Cir. 2004), cert. denied, 543 U.S. LEXIS 1146 (2005); *Aubuchon v. Knauf Fiberglass, GMBH*, 359 F.3d 950, 951–952 (7th Cir. 2004); *Levine v. The Children's Museum of Indianapolis, Inc.*, No. 02–3013, 2003 U.S. App. LEXIS 5755 (7th Cir. March 24, 2003); *Spangler v. Federal Home Loan Bank of Des Moines*, 278 F.3d 847, 852 (8th Cir. 2002); *Bachelder v. America West Airlines, Inc.*, 259 F.3d 1112, 1130 (9th Cir. 2001); *Rhoads v. FDIC*, 257 F.3d 373, 383 (4th Cir. 2001); *Medina v. Coors Brewing Co.*, No. 99–1463, 2000 U.S. App. LEXIS 27577 (10th Cir. Nov. 3, 2000); *Gay v. Gilman Paper Co.*, 125 F.3d 1432, 1435 (11th Cir. 1997); *Tafelski v. Novartis Pharmaceuticals*, No. 05-71547, 2007 U.S. Dist. LEXIS 22847, at 15 (E.D. Mich. March 28, 2007); *Maynard v. Total Image Specialists, Inc.*, 478 F. Supp. 2d 993 (S.D. Ohio 2007); *Wheeler v. Pioneer Dev. Services, Inc.*, 349 F. Supp. 2d 158 (D. Mass. 2004); *Sabbrese v. Lowe's Home Centers, Inc.*, 320 F. Supp. 2d 311, 321 (W.D. Pa. 2004); *Loring v. Advanced Foods, Inc.*, No. C02–4067–PAZ, 2004 U.S. Dist. LEXIS 6172, at *16 (N.D. Iowa April 9, 2004), aff'd, 2005 U.S. App. LEXIS 4124 (8th Cir. 2005); *Phillips v. Leroy–Somer North America et al.*, No. 01–1046–T, 2003 U.S. Dist. LEXIS 5334 (W.D. Tenn. March 31, 2003).

It is expected that an employee will give notice to the employer within no more than one or two working days of learning of the need for leave, except in extraordinary circumstances where such notice is not feasible. 29 USC 2612(e); 29 CFR 825.303(a); S. Res. 242, Cong. Rec. S3959, S3972 (April 23, 1996); 29 CFR 825.303(a). *See Brenneman*, 366 F.3d at 421; *Cavin*, 346 F.3d at 720; *Medina v. Coors Brewing Co.*, No. 99–1463, 2000 U.S. App. LEXIS 27577 (10th Cir. Nov. 3, 2000); *Wheeler*, 349 F. Supp. 2d 158; *Sabbrese*, 320 F. Supp. 2d at 321; *Loring*, 2004 U.S. Dist. LEXIS 6172, at *16; *Henson v. Bell Helicopter Textron, Inc.*, No. 4:01–CV–1024–Y, 2004 U.S. Dist. LEXIS 1630, at *38 (N.D. Tex. Feb. 6, 2004), aff'd, 2005 U.S. App LEXIS 660 (5th Cir. 2005). Again, the precondition for application of this rule is the inability of an employee to foresee the approximate timing of the need for leave. Generally, this will involve emergency circumstances where the need for leave was both unanticipated and immediate. Arguably, it might also cover situations where the employee knows that he or she will need leave, but does not know the approximate timing of the need for leave. Foreseeability is determined from the perspective of the employee, not the employer. *Barngrover v. W.W. Transport*, No. 3:02–cv–40020, 2003 U.S. Dist. LEXIS 13145, at *22 (S.D. Iowa July 24, 2003).

For example, an eligible employee suffers from severe migraine headaches. While the employee knows that she will need leave when the migraine occurs, the employee is unable to predict exactly when the migraine will occur, and the employee is unable to foresee the exact the timing of the need for leave. When the migraine arrives, the employee's need for leave would not be foreseeable. As such, the employee would be expected to give notice to the employer within one or two working days of learning of the need for leave, in this case, by the onset of an incapacitating migraine headache.

An employee taking intermittent leave is required to notify the employer as soon as practicable of her intent to take leave on particular dates if those dates are initially unknown. *Anderson v. New Orleans Jaxx & Heritage Festival and Foundation, Inc.*, 464 F. Supp. 2d 562, 566 (E.D. La. Nov. 22, 2006).

Unlike foreseeable leave, the notice provisions applied when the need for leave is not foreseeable are not limited to certain covered conditions. As such, they should apply to all covered conditions, including those expressly covered where the need for leave is foreseeable (i.e. birth, adoption/foster care placement, or planned medical treatment). In certain respects, the rules apply the same one to two day notice standard where the timing of the need for leave is not foreseeable. In other respects, the rules may be different.

For example, in the case of a medical emergency involving an otherwise planned medical treatment, an employee is "ordinarily" required to notify the employer within one or two business days of the need for FMLA leave. In the same situation, the rules regarding the need for leave where the approximate timing is not foreseeable would require the employee to provide notice to the employer within no more than one or two business days, except in extraordinary circumstances where such notice is not feasible. The standards of "ordinarily" and "extraordinary" could be the same. That is, something that is not ordinary may, by definition, be extraordinary. Another way of defining extraordinary is that something is exceptionally different than ordinary. Under this second definition, you could have something that is not ordinary, but not exceptionally so. In any event, the ambiguities in the definitions may give rise to arguments on the meanings of these otherwise undefined terms.

An employee who provided his employer with a doctor's note the same day that the employee was sent home from work indicating "no work until further notice," timely apprised the employer of the employee's unforeseeable need for FMLA leave. *Conrad v. Eaton Corp.*, 303 F. Supp. 2d 987, 997 (N.D. Iowa. 2004); accord *Lincoln v. Sears Home Improvement Products, Inc.*, No. 02–840 (DWF/SRN), 2004 U.S. Dist. LEXIS 402, at 15 (D. Min. Jan. 9, 2004) (employee provided timely notice as soon as he learned of the surgery date and within 24 to 48 hours prior to his father's surgery).

If the required notice, whether 30 days or "as soon as practicable," is not given, the employer can deny leave even if all other FMLA requirements are met. *Aubuchon v. Knauf Fiberglass, GMBH*, 359 F.3d 950, 951–952 (7th Cir. 2004); *Williams v. Illinois Dept. of Corrections*, No. 05-cv-4227-JPG, 2007 U.S. Dist. LEXIS 17119, at *9-10 (S.D. Ill. March 9, 2007).

In *Brenneman v. MidCentral Health System*, 366 F.3d 412, 421 (6th Cir. 2004), cert. denied, 543 U.S. 1146 (2005), the court concluded that the employee failed to provide notice of his need for unforeseeable FMLA leave "as soon as practicable." Brenneman originally called in to request leave, stating that he "wasn't doing well." He failed to link his absence to his known diabetic condition. He was absent for one day. He returned and worked the next two days. He also failed to link his one–day absence with his diabetic condition at a meeting with his supervisors regarding his attendance problems. Five days after the absence, plaintiff's wife called and told his supervisor that plaintiff's one–day absence was due to his diabetic condition. Plaintiff confirmed this the next day and presented a note from his doctor as support. Brenneman argued that he did not provide the doctor's note within two days of his absences because the absences occurred over the weekend, which were not normal workdays for doctors. The court noted that "the applicable regulation imposes no qualification that only the normal working days of physicians be counted in determining the timeliness of an employee's notice." The court also found no extraordinary circumstances that rendered it unfeasible for Brenneman to give defendant the necessary notice within two days of his absence. The court rejected Brenneman's argument that he was unable to timely inform the defendant due to physical illness from his diabetes. The court noted plaintiff's contrary testimony that on his return to work the day after his absence he was "stabilized and fine." Because he was physically able to give his employer sufficient notice on or before the passage of two days from his absence, the court found that his notice several days later was untimely.

Similarly, the court in *Henegar v. DaimlerChrysler Corp.*, 280 F. Supp. 2d 680, 685 (E.D. Mich. 2003), concluded that the employee failed to notify his employer of his need for FMLA leave as soon as practicable. The court initially found that selecting the "ill" option on the company's automated telephone attendance system was insufficient notice. The court also rejected the employee's argument that the doctor's note he provided on his return to work from leave two weeks later was sufficient and timely notice. The court noted that DOL regulations contemplate notice within one or two days, not two weeks. The court also cited the fact that during this two–week period, plaintiff drove to work to pick up his paycheck one day, and played golf with the company golf league another day. "Obviously, it was feasible for the Plaintiff to give notice before April 24, 2001."

In *Cool v. BorgWarner Diversified Transmission Products, Inc.*, No. IP 02–0960–C–B/S, 2004 U.S. Dist. LEXIS 570, at *17 (S.D.

Ind. Jan. 12, 2004), the court found that "a change in circumstances" for purposes of the FMLA refers to circumstances requiring an otherwise qualifying leave to begin sooner than originally anticipated.

(3) Effect of Employer Policies on Timing of Notice

Employer policies may affect the time frame that employees have to provide notice of the need for FMLA leave. An employer may not require compliance with stricter FMLA notice requirements where the provisions of a collective bargaining agreement or applicable leave plan allows less advance notice to the employer than required by the FMLA. 29 CFR 825.302(g); S. Res. 242, Cong. Rec. S3959, S3972 (April 23, 1996); 29 CFR 825.302(g). If an employee elects, or an employer requires, the substitution of paid leave for unpaid FMLA leave, and the employer's procedural requirements for taking that kind of leave are less stringent than the requirements of the FMLA, only the less stringent requirements may be imposed. 29 CFR 825.207(h), 825.302(g); S. Res. 242, Cong. Rec. S3959, S3966, S3972 (April 23, 1996); 29 CFR 825.207(h), 825.302(g). For example, if an employee elects (or an employer requires) to substitute paid annual leave for unpaid FMLA leave, and the employer's paid annual leave plan imposes no prior notification requirements for taking annual leave, no advance notice may be required for the FMLA leave taken in these circumstances.

The same concept equally applies where the employee takes unpaid FMLA leave. Here, the FMLA notice requirements would apply, unless the employer imposes lesser notice requirements on employees taking leave without pay. 29 CFR 825.302(g); S. Res. 242, Cong. Rec. S3959, S3972 (April 23, 1996); 29 CFR 825.302(g). If FMLA is taken on LWOP, and the LWOP requirements for advance notice of the need for leave are less than those for FMLA leave, only the LWOP notice requirements may be applied. In light of this rule, agencies would be well-advised to take a close look at their LWOP employee notice policies.

An employer may require an employee to comply with the employer's usual and customary notice and procedural requirements for requesting leave. 29 CFR 825.302(d); S. Res. 242, Cong. Rec. S3959, S3972 (April 23, 1996); 29 CFR 825.302(d); *see Spangler v. Federal Home Loan Bank of Des Moines*, 278 F.3d 847, 852 (8th Cir. 2002); *Lewis v. Holsum of Fort Wayne, Inc.*, 278 F.3d 707, 710–11 (7th Cir. 2002); *Gilliam v. UPS*, 233 F.3d 969, 971–72 (7th Cir. 2000); *Williams v. Illinois Dept. of Corrections*, No. 05-cv-4227-JPG, 2007 U.S. Dist. LEXIS 17119, at *10 (S.D. Ill. March 9, 2007); *Cobb v. Contract Transport, Inc.*, No. 04-305-KSF, 2007 U.S. Dist. LEXIS 4531, at *14-15 (E.D. Ky. Jan. 22, 2007); *Sons v. Henry County*, No. 1:05-cv-0516-DFH-TAB, 2006 U.S. Dist. LEXIS 79604, at *25 (S.D. Ind. Oct. 31, 2006); *Honeycutt v. Baltimore County*, No. JFM-06-0958, 2006 U.S. Dist. LEXIS 49315, at *11 (D. Md. July 7, 2006); *Bones v. Honeywell, Inc.*, 223 F. Supp. 2d 1203, 1217 (D. Kan. 2002), aff'd, 366 F.3d 869 (10th Cir. 2004) (requirement that the employee provide notice of need for leave to the supervisor upheld as the employer's "usual and customary" notice and procedural requirement; the regulations fail to define what would fall within the scope of an employer's "usual and customary notice and procedural requirements for requesting leave"); *Alexander v. Ford Motor Co.*, No. 01–70051, 204 F.R.D. 314, 2001 U.S. Dist. LEXIS 19180 (E.D. Mich. Nov. 5, 2001) (five-day "quit notice" rule for employees who do not notify the employer of absence).

An employer's "usual and customary" reporting requirements may include the requirement that an employee call in to work every day that she is unable to report for duty. That was the conclusion of the court in *Lewis v. Holsum of Fort Wayne, Inc.*, 278 F.3d 707, 710–11 (7th Cir. 2002). There, company policy and the terms of the applicable collective bargaining agreement provided that an employee must call into work not less than one hour before the scheduled reporting time when unable to report for duty. If an employee fails to so report for three working days, absent impossibility, the employee is subject to termination. The court found that Holsum's company rules and Attendance Policy are "usual and customary" requirements. *Id* at. 710. The employee, who admitted she knew the company policy, did not call into to work as required on three consecutive days. It was not impossible for her to call as the employee admitted that she had access to her telephone on these days, and her husband, who also worked at Holsum, was at work on those days and could have notified Holsum of the employee's need to be absent.

Similarly, in *Gilliam v. UPS, Inc.*, 233 F.3d 969, 971–72 (7th Cir. 2000), the circuit court held that the FMLA does not "authorize employees on leave to keep their employers in the dark about when they will return." *Id.* at 971. Gilliam requested leave to visit his finance and newborn child on a Friday. *Id. at* 970. The UPS granted his request for leave for this purpose. *Id.* Gilliam did not contact his employer until the following Thursday morning, at which point Gilliam was informed that his employment with UPS was terminated as of Tuesday morning. *Id.* Gilliam failed to follow an applicable collective bargaining agreement provision that required an employee on leave to call his or her supervisor no later than the beginning of the third day of leave, in order to let the supervisor know how much more leave would be required. *Id.* at 970–71. The circuit court held that the UPS notice requirement was a valid "usual and customary" notice requirement.

In *Spraggins v. Knauf Fiber Glass, Inc.*, 401 F. Supp. 2d 1235 (D. Ala. Nov. 21, 2005), the court held that the FMLA allows an employer to require an employee to provide notice one hour before the employee's shift begins, as long as it is reasonable to expect the employee, under the individual circumstances, to give such notice. But if the employee cannot meet the one-our requirement, then, under the FMLA, the employee must give notice as soon as practicable, up to one or two days after learning of the need for leave, unless giving notice within the one-or two-day period is impracticable as well.

Several cases have addressed to whom employee notice must be provided, with mixed results. In *Cavin v. Honda of Am. Mfg.*, 346 F.3d 713, 720 (6th Cir. 2002), the employer's policy permitted employees to call security to report one-day absences, but for any absences beyond one-day, employees were directed to call the leave coordination department. Cavin called the security department daily for two weeks to report his absence due to a motorcycle accident. The Sixth Circuit found that Cavin was not obligated to comply with Honda's requirement that he notify the leave coordination department because the content of the notice apprised Honda that the leave was FMLA-qualifying.

In *Walton v. Ford Motor Co.*, 424 F.3d 481 (6th Cir. 2005), the Sixth Circuit held that plaintiff's notice to security was not sufficient. In *Walton*, the employee called the security department the day after he suffered an injury at work. Walton told the security office that he would not be able to return to work for 4 days. He did not contact his supervisor or the labor relations department, or the medical department per company policy. He was fired shortly after he notified the security department that his doctors put him off work for 4 weeks. The Sixth Circuit noted that Walton previously properly requested leave, so he knew the employer's requirements. Moreover, security at Ford was provided by independent contractors. Therefore, Walton, the court found, did not provide Ford with notice of his need for FMLA leave. Third, Walton never explained the extent of his injuries. Finally, no one at Ford had actual notice that his injury was a serious health condition.

In *Cobb v. Contract Transport, Inc.*, No. 04-305-KSF, 2007 U.S. Dist. LEXIS 4531, at *14-15 (E.D. Ky. Jan. 22, 2007), Cobb called and told his dispatcher that he would be having gallbladder surgery on the following Monday. The dispatcher told Cobb he needed to call two named supervisors to request extended leave. Cobb failed to do this. One of the supervisors, however, had actual notice of Cobb's request for leave for gallbladder surgery. Under these facts, the court found that the information imparted to the employer was sufficient to reasonably apprise the employer of the employee's request for FMLA leave.

In *Caskey v. Colgate-Palmolive Co.*, 438 F. Supp. 2d 954, 968 (S.D. Ind. 2006), the employee's admission that she did not communicate her absence to her team leader as required by employer policy presented a stronger case for denying FMLA leave.

Where an employer's internal policies conflict with the provisions of the FMLA, the FMLA controls, and an employee need only comply with the requirements of the Act to invoke its protections. *See Cavin v. Honda of America Mfg., Inc.*, 346 F.3d 713, 723 (6th Cir. 2003).

There is a split in the circuits over whether an employer can require an employee to abide by the employer's notice reporting requirements where the need for leave is not foreseeable. The Seventh and Tenth Circuits have interpreted § 825.303 to permit an employer to require employees to abide by leave reporting requirements. In *Holmes v. Boeing Co.*, No. 98–3056, 1999 U.S. App. Lexis 377 (10th Cir. Jan. 12, 1996), the Tenth Circuit interpreted § 825.303 to mean that the FMLA prohibits an employer from enforcing only its requirement of advanced written notice and, even then, only in the context of emergencies. The Tenth Circuit reasoned that "the FMLA does not prohibit an employer from requiring its employees to give notice to specific company supervisors on the day the employee is going to be absent in a non–emergency situation, as in this case." The *Holmes* court concluded that an employee cannot seek FMLA relief in the event of his noncompliance with his employer's specific notice requirements absent an "allegation that his physical condition was such that he could not comply with the defendant's reasonable notice requirements."

Similarly, the Seventh Circuit in *Lewis v. Holsum of Fort Wayne, Inc.*, 278 F.3d 706, 710 (7th Cir. 2002), concluded that an employer did not violate the FMLA by discharging an employee who failed to comply with applicable company rules and policies regarding leave notice where it was not "impossible" for her to do so.

The Fourth Circuit in *Cavin v. Honda of America Mfg., Inc.*, 346 F.3d 713, 722 (6th Cir. 2003), rejected the positions of the Tenth and Seventh Circuits as misinterpretations of the FMLA's notice requirements, finding their positions "contrary to the goals of the FMLA and inconsistent with the regulation of notice in situations where an employee has a foreseeable need for leave." The court found that Congress intended to prohibit employers from disallowing or delaying an employee's taking FMLA leave for failure to comply with internal employer procedures in the context of foreseeable and unforeseeable leave. The court found that to hold otherwise would be illogical. It also found that this interpretation was consistent with the purpose of the FMLA to remedy inadequate job security. Where, as here, the employer's policy had more stringent timing requirements for FMLA leave where the need was not foreseeable, the determination of whether an employee provided timely notice is judged on the FMLA standard only. *Accord Cobb v. Contract Transport, Inc.*, No. 04-305-KSF, 2007 U.S. Dist. LEXIS 4531, at *14-15 (E.D. Ky. Jan. 22, 2007) (employer's cannot deny FMLA leave on grounds that an employee failed to comply with internal procedures, as long as the employee gives timely verbal or other notice).

b. Title II

As with the other federal sector variants of the FMLA, the timing of an employee's notice of the need for FMLA leave depends on whether the need is foreseeable or not foreseeable. 5 USC 6382(e).

(1) Foreseeable Need for Leave

If the leave taken is foreseeable based on an expected birth, placement for adoption or foster care, or planned medical treatment, the employee must notify the agency of his or her intention to take FMLA leave not less than 30 calendar days before the date leave is to begin. 5 USC 6382(e)(1); 5 CFR 630.1206(a); *Davis v. VA*, No. CH-0752-06-0724-I-1, 2006 MSPB LEXIS 7394, at *14 (Dec. 12, 2006); *Romero v. Dept. of Interior*, No. SF-0752-05-0011-I-1, 2005 MSPB LEXIS 3147, at *10-11 (May 19, 2005); *Bradley v. VA*, No. CH-0752-04-0513-I-1, 2005 MSPB LEXIS 1194, at *12 (Feb. 16, 2005), pet. denied, 99 MSPR 402 (2005), *aff'd*, 2006 U.S. App. LEXIS 8506 (Fed. Cir. 2006); *Gross v. DOJ*, 77 MSPR 83 (1997). If the date of birth or placement or planned medical treatment requires leave to begin within 30 calendar days, the employee must provide notice as soon as practicable. 5 USC 6382(e)(1); 5 CFR 630.1206(a); *see Anderson v. VA*, No. PH-0752-06-0341-I-1, 2006 MSPB LEXIS 6777, at *13 (Nov. 16, 2006); *Cole v. DHHS*, No. DC-0752-05-0457-I-1, 2005 MSPB LEXIS 6825, at *8 (Nov. 1, 2005); *Wiliams v. Dept. of Navy*, No. DC-0752-05-0431-I-1, 2005 MSPB LEXIS 6866, at *5 (Oct. 17, 2005), *pet. denied*, 101 MSPR 133 (2006); *Bradley*, 2005 MSPB LEXIS 1194, at *12.

The above rule is comparable to the nearly identical rule under the other three federal sector variants of the FMLA. A major substantive difference between this rule and the comparable federal sector variants involves situations where the leave must begin in less than 30 calendar days. Under Title II, the covered condition must "require" that the leave commence within 30 days. Under Title I, the CAA, and the PEOAA, less than 30 days notice is not conditioned on the requirement that leave will commence in 30 days (although that is undoubtedly the case). Rather, less than 30 days notice is permissible when more than 30 days notice is not practicable under the circumstances. While there will certainly be a high degree of overlap, there may be situations where what is "not practicable" is different than what is "required." For that matter, "required" in whose judgment?

When the need for leave is foreseeable but in less than 30 calendar days, Title II requires that an employee provide notice to the agency of the need for leave "as is practicable." 5 USC 6382(e)(1); 5 CFR 630.1206(a). Title I, the CAA, and the PEOAA, use the phrase "as soon as practicable" to define the comparable employee notice obligation. The Title II phrase is in keeping with the statutory language. Although the statutory language is identical, Title I (and therefore, the CAA and the PEOAA) change the phrase from "as is practicable" to "as soon as practicable." The change is interesting in that it injects a temporal requirement that does not exist in the statutory language. The MSPB uses "as soon as practicable," and "as is practicable" interchangeably. *See Bradley v. VA*, No. CH-0752-04-0513-I-1, 2005 MSPB LEXIS 1194, at *13 (Feb. 16, 2005), *pet. denied*, 99 MSPR 402 (2005), *aff'd*, 2006 U.S. App. LEXIS 8506 (Fed. Cir. 2006).

"As soon as practicable" is a defined term in the regulations implementing Title I, the CAA, and the PEOAA. "As is practicable" is not a defined term in the regulations implementing Title II. It is unclear whether the terms mean the same thing. It certainly would have been easy enough for the OPM to adopt the DOL definition of "as soon as practicable" for "as is practicable." It is noteworthy that the OPM did not elect to do that, or otherwise define the term. This is in contrast to OPM's interpretation of the similar, but by no means identical phrase "within a reasonable period of time appropriate to the circumstances involved" for purposes of notice where the need for leave is not foreseeable.

(2) Need for Leave Is Not Foreseeable

Where the need for leave is not foreseeable and the employee cannot provide 30 calendar days' notice of his or her need for leave, the employee must provide notice within a reasonable period of time appropriate to the circumstances involved. 5 CFR 630.1206(c); *Davis v. VA*, No. CH-0752-06-0724-I-1, 2006 MSPB LEXIS 7394, at *14 (Dec. 12, 2006); *Cole v. DHHS*, No. DC-0752-05-0457-I-1, 2005 MSPB LEXIS 6825, at *8 (Nov. 1, 2005); *Wiliams v. Dept. of Navy*, No. DC-0752-05-0431-I-1, 2005 MSPB LEXIS 6866, at *5 (Oct. 17, 2005), *pet. denied*, 101 MSPR 133 (2006); *Romero v. Dept. of Interior*, No. SF-0752-05-0011-I-1, 2005 MSPB LEXIS 3147, at *10-11 (May 19, 2005); *Crayton v. Dept. of Navy*, No. DC-0752-05-0235-I-1, 2005 MSPB LEXIS 2632, at *11 (May 5, 2005), *pet. denied*, 100 MSPR 61 (2005); *Gross v. DOJ*, 77 MSPR 83 (1997). As examples, the regulations implementing Title II cite a medical emergency or the unexpected availability of a child for adoption or foster care. 5 CFR 630.1206(c); *See Gross*, 77 MSPR 83.

The OPM appears to interpret the phrase "notice within a reasonable period of time appropriate to the circumstances involved" as having the same meaning as the DOL phrase "as soon as practicable." In the comments accompanying publication of the final Title II regulations, OPM addressed application of the DOL rule for the need for leave that is not foreseeable. Specifically, OPM (Preamble, 5 CFR 630.1206) observed:

> Section 630.1206(g) requires that if the need for leave is not foreseeable and an employee cannot provide 30 days notice, he or she must provide notice within a reasonable period of time appropriate to the circumstances involved. One commentator suggested that a time limit for such notification be established similar to the time limit set by [the] DOL—i.e. [one] or [two] working days after learning of the need for leave. Agencies are responsible for the administration of the FMLA and may establish such time limitations in their agency policies. Therefore, the regulations have not changed.

The above phrasing is interesting as it can be interpreted in a number of ways. First, it can be interpreted as meaning that the DOL definition of "as soon as practicable" applies under Title II where the need for leave is not foreseeable. This interpretation views the phrase "such time limitations" as referring to the DOL rule allowing notice in one or two business days when the need for leave is not foreseeable. 29 CFR 825.303(a). The fact that the OPM is saying it won't change the regulation even though it approves the application of the DOL definition does not alter the fact that the OPM approves of the DOL definition. Alternatively, the phrase "such limitations" can be interpreted to approve not only the DOL definition, but any similar period of limitations, as the commentator was addressing the need for a time limitation for such notification similar to the limit set by the DOL.

In either case, OPM appears to accept that, where the need for leave is not foreseeable, an employee must notify the agency of the need for leave as soon as reasonable under the circumstances, which normally means one or two business days.

As a final note on this topic, because OPM uses different terms when addressing employee notice where the need for leave is foreseeable and where it is not, it is decidedly unclear that "as is practicable" has the same meaning as "within a reasonable period of time appropriate to the circumstances involved." Clearly, OPM could have used the same terms had it intended the same meaning. Title I, in contrast, uses the same phrase, "as soon as practicable," whether the need for leave is foreseeable or is not foreseeable. *See* 29 CFR 825.302(b), 303(a). As such, it is doubtful that "as is practicable" has the same meaning as "within a reasonable period of time appropriate to the circumstances." It follows, then, that "as is practicable" may not have the same meaning as the Title I phrase "as soon as practicable," the latter having only been identified by the OPM as applying to Title I when the need for leave is not foreseeable.

An employer may not delay or deny an employee's request for FMLA leave if the need is unforeseeable and the employee is unable, for circumstances beyond her control, to give notice at all. *Davis v. VA*, No. CH-0752-06-0724-I-1, 2006 MSPB LEXIS 7394, at *14 (Dec. 12, 2006).

An employee's request for FMLA leave months after the absence and the notice of proposed removal was not within a reasonable time. *Cole v. DHHS*, No. DC-0752-05-0457-I-1, 2005 MSPB LEXIS 6825, at *9 (Nov. 1, 2005).

In *Crayton v. Dept. of Navy*, No. DC-0752-05-0235-I-1, 2005 MSPB LEXIS 2632, at *11 (May 5, 2005), *pet. denied*, 100 MSPR 61 (2005), the Board found that an employee's letter to the agency requesting leave four days after the employee's absence began was within a reasonable period of time given that the employee was suffering from a medically documented, disabling psychiatric condition. An employee or representative who is physically or mentally incapable of providing notice of the need for FMLA leave may invoke the right to FMLA leave within two working days after returning to work, provided the incapacity is documented by a health care provider and the employee provides documentation acceptable to the agency explaining the inability of the personal representative to contact the agency and invoke the employee's entitlement to FMLA leave. *Bradley v. VA*, No. Ch-0752-04-0513-I-1, 2005 MSPB LEXIS 1194, at *12 (Feb. 16, 2005), *pet. denied*, 99 MSPR 402 (2005), *aff'd*, 2006 U.S. App. LEXIS 8506 (Fed. Cir. 2006).

(3)　Effect of Employer Policies on Timing of Notice

Agency policies may impact the timing of employee notice of FMLA leave. Like the other federal sector variants of the FMLA, an agency must comply with any collective bargaining agreements or any agency employment benefit program or plan that provides greater family or medical leave entitlements to employees than those provided by Title II. 5 CFR 630.12109(a), (c). Conversely, the entitlements established under Title II of the FMLA may not be diminished by any collective bargaining agreement or any employment benefit plan or program. 5 CFR 630.1210(b). An agency could adopt a policy wherein employees may provide notice of the need for foreseeable FMLA leave no less than 20 days from when the leave is to begin, except where that is not practicable. Such a policy would be more generous that the FMLA, which requires a minimum of 30 days notice under similar conditions. Agency policy or the terms of a collective bargaining agreement could not, however, mandate 40 days' notice in similar circumstances. Such a requirement would be more stringent than the comparable requirement under the FMLA.

Where the need for leave is foreseeable, an agency may waive the FMLA notice requirements and instead impose the agency's usual and customary policies or procedures for providing notification of leave. 5 CFR 630.1206(e); *Dias v. VA*, No. NY-0752-04-0279-I-2, 2005 MSPB LEXIS 3926, at *15 (June 30, 2005), *rev'd*, 102 MSPR 53 (2006), *appeal dismissed*, 2006 U.S. App. LEXIS 28961 (Fed. Cir. 2006), *vacated reinstated*, 2006 U.S. App. LEXIS 32257 (Fed. Cir. 2006), *aff'd*, 2007 U.S. App. LEXIS 11530 (Fed. Cir. May 30, 2007); *Fisher v. DHHS*, No. DC-0752-05-0280-I-1, 2005 MSPB LEXIS 2653, at *15 (June 3, 2005), *rev. denied*, 101 MSPR 131 (2005); *Gross v. DOJ*, 77 MSPR 83 (1997).

Up to this point, the Title II regulations are sounding like comparable regulations under Title I. *See* 29 CFR 825.1206(e). Unfortunately, from this point the regulations take a detour into irrelevance. According to the regulations, the agency's "usual and customary policies or procedures or providing notification of leave" must not be more stringent than the notice requirements of the FMLA. 5 CFR 630.1206(e). *Dias v. VA*, 2005 MSPB LEXIS 3926, at *15; *Fisher v. DHHS*, 2005 MSPB LEXIS 2653, at *15; *Crayton v. Dept. of Navy*, No. DC-0752-05-0235-I-1, 2005 MSPB LEXIS 2632, at *11 (May 5, 2005): *Wirzberger v. Treasury*, No. PH-0752-04-0154-I-2, 2004 MSPB LEXIS 1980, at *7 (Oct. 20, 2004), *rev. dismissed*, 101 MSPR 448 (2006); *Burge v. Dept. of Air Force*, No. AT-0752-97-0060-I-1, 82 MSPR 75 (1999); *Gross v. DOJ*, 77 MSPR 83 (1997), *aff'd*, 250 F.3d 762 (Fed. Cir. 2000). Recapping, an agency can waive the FMLA employee notice requirements to impose its own. But whatever is imposed cannot be more stringent than the requirements of the FMLA. By process of elimination, that means that an employee could waive more demanding employee notice requirements to impose less demanding requirements. Exactly why employers would want to do this is unclear. Unions and other organizations representing the interests of employees, on the other hand, will want to bargain to obtain less stringent notice requirements. The odd thing is that the OPM did not create this regulation in order to reach this result. Other OPM FMLA regulations reach the same result by allowing employers to provide greater FMLA leave benefits. *See* 5 CFR 630.1210.

The final piece to this odd puzzle is that an agency cannot enforce its "usual and customary" notice rules. An employee who requests FMLA leave that is foreseeable may not have that leave delayed or denied if the employee fails to follow such agency policies or procedures. 5 CFR 630.1206(e). *Dias v. Dept. of Veterans Affairs*, No. NY-0752-04-0279-I-2, 2005 MSPB LEXIS 3926, at *15 (June 30, 2005), *rev'd*, 102 MSPR 53 (2006), *appeal dismissed*, 2006 U.S. App. LEXIS 28961 (Fed. Cir. 2006), *vacated reinstated*, 2006 U.S. App. LEXIS 32257 (Fed. Cir. 2006), *aff'd*, 2007 U.S. App. LEXIS 11530 (Fed. Cir. May 30, 2007); *Wirzberger v. Dept. of Treasury*, No. PH-0752-04-0154-I-2, 2004 MSPB LEXIS 1980, at *7 (Oct. 20, 2004), *rev. dismissed*, 101 MSPR 448 (2006). So, recapping again, under the FMLA regulations, if an employee fails to provide timely notice where the need for leave is foreseeable, the agency may delay the start of the leave. 5 CFR 630.1206(d). The agency could, however, waive this notice requirement and impose its own. The agency's own notice requirement, cannot be more stringent than the FMLA notice requirement (i.e. the one it just waived). Moreover, as added incentive, if an agency were to waive the notice requirement and impose its own, it cannot delay nor deny FMLA leave if the employee completely ignores the agency's "usual and customary" notice requirement. This regulation appears to be a test to determine whether agencies are asleep or awake.

The regulation appears to be a poor cousin to the comparable regulation under Title I. *See* 29 CFR 825.302(d). The comparable regulation under Title I differs from Title II in two major respects. First, the Title I regulation allows the imposition of more stringent requirements pursuant to agency policy. The example given to illustrate the rule is that an employer may require written notice by an employee of the need for leave where such notice is part of the employer's "usual and customary" notice and procedural requirements for requesting leave. Absent such a policy, an employee covered by Title I is only required to give verbal notice of the need for FMLA leave. Title II, by contrast, prohibits the imposition of any more stringent agency notice policies pursuant to an agencies "usual and customary" notice and procedural requirements.

Second, under Title I, an employee fails to provide notice pursuant to the employer's "usual and customary" notice requirements may not have his or her FMLA leave delayed or denied (where verbal notice was given in accordance with the requirements of the FMLA), but may be disciplined for an infraction of the agency's policies. Under Title II, the regulations do not give express permission for an agency to discipline an employee who fails to follow the agencies "usual and customary" notice requirements.

OPM needs to clarify what § 630.1206(e) means or it will simply not be utilized. If OPM intended that the regulation operate the same as the comparable regulation under § 825.302(d), then OPM needs to clearly state so.

Title II does not have a specific policy comparable to that of the other federal sector variants of the FMLA which reduces the timing of notice an employee is required to provide of the need for FMLA leave where the employer's leave plan or the terms of a collective bargaining agreement allow less advance notice to employers for paid leave. Absent this bridge linking the less stringent notice requirements for paid leave with unpaid FMLA leave, Title II appears to require that the employee meet the notice and procedural requirements of both the FMLA and paid leave to enjoy the benefits of both. This, in turn, will depend on what the term "substitution" means. [The substitution of paid leave for unpaid FMLA leave is addressed in Chapter 11, "Substitution of Paid Leave."]

In *Crayton v. Dept. of Navy*, No. DC-0752-05-0235-I-1, 2005 MSPB LEXIS 2632, at *11 (May 5, 2005), *pet. denied*, 100 MSPR 61 (2005), the Board rejected the employer's argument that FMLA leave was not appropriate because the employee failed to request leave in writing in advance in accordance with agency policy. The Board found that, while an agency may apply its own leave procedure to a leave request under the FMLA, it may not apply a more restrictive leave policy than provided by the FMLA. Here, the agency improperly denied FMLA leave for the employee's failure to comply with the agency's additional procedures for requesting FMLA leave where the employee provided timely notice of the unforeseeable need for leave within a reasonable period of time under the circumstances.

2. Manner of Providing Notice

a. Title I, the CAA, and the PEOAA

Who may provide notice of an employee's need for FMLA leave, and the manner in which notice may be provided is regulated. The manner of notice is dependent on whether the need for leave is foreseeable or not. It may also be affected by the usual and customary notice and procedural requirements for requesting leave.

(1) Who May Provide Notice

Notice of an employee's need for FMLA leave may be provided by the employee or the employee's spokesperson. *See* 29 CFR 825.208(a) (the employer's decision to designate leave as FMLA–qualifying may only be based on information received from the employee or the employee's spokesperson); S. Res. 242, Cong. Rec. S3959, S3966 (April 23, 1996); 29 CFR 825.208(a) (same). *See Stoops v. One Call Communications, Inc.*, 141 F.3d 309, 312–313 (7th Cir. 1998); *Morran v. Nevada System of Higher Ed.*, No. 3:05-CV-00577-ECR (RAM), 2007 U.S. Dist. LEXIS 27796, at *18 (D. Nev. March 30, 2007); *Meadows v. Texar Fed. Credit U.*, No. 5:05CV158, 2007 U.S. Dist. LEXIS 4456, at *51 (E.D. Tex. Jan. 22, 2007); *Kaniuka v. Good Shepherd Home*, No. 05-CV-02917, 2006 U.S. Dist. LEXIS 57403, at *38 (E.D. Pa. Aug. 15, 2006); *Miller v. GB Sales & Service, Inc.*, 275 F. Supp. 2d 823, 829 (E.D. Mich. 2003). *McCarron v. British Telecom et al.*, No. 00–CV–6123, 2002 U.S. Dist. LEXIS 15151 (E.D. Pa. Aug. 7, 2002). For example, in the event an employee is incapacitated, the employee's spouse, adult child, parent, or doctor, may provide notice to the employer of the need to take FMLA leave. 29 CFR 825.208(a); S. Res. 242, Cong. Rec. S3959, S3966 (April 23, 1996); 29 CFR 825.208(a). *Browning v. Liberty Mutual Insurance Co.*, 178 F.3d 1043, 1049 (8th Cir.) (sister telephoned the employer), *cert. denied* 120 S. Ct. 588 (1999); *Hobart v. Behavioral Connections of Wood County, Inc.*, No. 3:03CV7313, 2004 U.S. Dist. LEXIS 12051, at *10 (N.D. Ohio July 1, 2004) (notice sent by an employee's attorney requesting leave sufficient for purposes of the FMLA).

Where notice is provided by the employee, courts are only concerned with the notice given during the course of employment, not after the employee has been terminated. "The use of the word "employee" in the FMLA illuminates a significant limitation on the timing of the required notice: It must be provided *during* the employment relationship, not after the employee has been terminated.... Thus, for purposes of FMLA notice, the Court must ignore Plaintiff's post-termination claims of health problems, including all of those made during her deposition and in her filings. What is relevant at this stage are Plaintiff's statements to Defendant during the course of her employment relationship." *McFall v. BASF Corp.*, 406 F. Supp. 2d 763, 768 (E.D. Mich. Dec. 20, 2005).

The DOL comments to the final regulations implementing Title I (Preamble, 29 CFR 825.208) suggest that an employee may designate a spokesperson in situations other than the employee's incapacity. Specifically, the DOL states:

> Employers must still base their designations of FMLA leave on information obtained directly from the employee or the employee's spokesperson (in the event the employee is incapacitated or otherwise designates a point of contact, e.g. an immediate family member.).

The above language suggests that an immediate family member of the employee, e.g., a spouse, adult child, or parent, may speak for the employee without a formal designation by the employee. Persons other than immediate family members must be designated by the employee in order to speak for the employee. The regulations fail to address what information, if any, may be obtained to establish that an individual other than an immediately family member legitimately serves as a spokesperson for the employee. Certainly, the comments to the regulation call into question the ability of an individual other than an immediately family member to serve as a spokesperson for an employee regarding a request for FMLA leave without some type of formal designation. A possible exception involves employees in bargaining units who are represented by union officials for purposes of wages, hours, and terms and conditions of employment. Such terms and conditions of employment would certainly cover leave issues.

Notice may be provided by a telephone call from the parent of an employee. *McLaughlin v. Innovative Logistics Group, Inc.*, No. 05-72305, 2007 U.S. Dist. LEXIS 6363, at *14 (E.D. Mich. Jan. 30, 2007) (voicemail message from mother explaining that daughter was hospitalized sufficient).

(2) Foreseeable Need for Leave

Where the need for leave is foreseeable based on an expected birth, placement for adoption or foster care, or planned medical treatment, the employee must provide at least verbal notice sufficient to make the employer aware that the employee needs FMLA qualifying leave. 29 CFR 825.302(c); S. Res. 242, Cong. Rec. S3959, S3971 (April 23, 1996); 29 CFR 825.302(c); *see Rhoads v. FDIC*, 257 F.3d 373, 382–83 (4th Cir. 2001), *cert. denied*, 535 U.S. 933 (2002); *Bailey v. Amsted Industries, Inc.*, 172 F.3d 1041, 1045–46 (8th Cir. 1999).

The regulations do not address to whom in the employing agency the employee needs to provide the required notice. *Bones v. Honeywell International, Inc.*, 223 F. Supp. 2d 1203, 1217 (D. Kan. Sept. 20, 2002), *aff'd*, 366 F.3d 869 (10th Cir. 2004). Providing clear guidance on this issue is important to avoid situations where employees or spokespersons, deliberately or through inadvertence, provide notice of the need for FMLA leave to individuals who are not in a position to accurately determine whether the leave is FMLA-qualifying. For example, an employee telephones the head of the agency and notifies a secretary orally that the employee needs FMLA leave. The head of the agency is in no position to act on such a request. In all likelihood, the head of the agency has no idea who the employee is, let alone whether the employee meets the eligibility requirements.

Fortunately, the DOL provides guidance on this issue in the comments accompanying the issuance of the final FMLA regulations. *See* Preamble, 29 CFR 825.302. According to the DOL, an employee is required to provide notice of the need to take FMLA leave to the same person(s) within the agency that the employee ordinarily contacts to request other forms of leave, usually the employee's supervisor. Preamble, 29 CFR 825.302. The DOL continues:

> It is the responsibility of the supervisor either to refer the employee who needs FMLA leave to the appropriate person, or to alert that person to the employee's notice. Once the employee has provided notice to the supervisor or other appropriate person in the usual manner, the employee's obligation to provide notice of the need for FMLA leave has been fulfilled.

The DOL does not explain why the above guidance was not formally incorporated into the regulations.

In *Bones v. Honeywell International, Inc.*, 223 F. Supp. 2d 1203, 1215–18 (D. Kan. 2002), *aff'd*, 366 F.3d 869 (10th Cir. 2004), the employee did not provide notice of the need for FMLA leave to the employee's supervisor, as required by company regulations. Rather, the employee notified the company's medical department of the need for FMLA leave. The employer argued that, pursuant to § 825.302(d), the employee was required to comply with the company's usual and customary notice and procedural requirements for requesting leave. The employer's usual and customary notice requirements mandated that employees provide notice as required by their department. This generally meant to the employee's immediate supervisor. Company policy clearly provided that notice to the medical unit was insufficient and would not be forwarded. After a thorough review of the employer's policies and the FMLA implementing regulations, the district court concluded that, absent proof that the plaintiff's physical condition prevented her from complying with the company's reasonable notice requirements, an employer may require employees seeking FMLA leave to notify a particular department or a particular supervisor. By failing to comply with that known requirement, the plaintiff failed to give proper notice under the FMLA.

Other cases have similarly concluded that an employer may designate the person(s) within the company with whom an employee must provide notice of the need for FMLA leave. *See Holmes v. The Boeing Co.*, 166 F.3d 1221 (10th Cir. 1999) (FMLA does not prohibit an employer from requiring its employees to give notice to specific company supervisors on the day the employee is going to be absent in a non–emergency); *Gilliam v. United Parcel Service, Inc.*, 233 F.3d 969, 972 (7th Cir. 2000) (upholding termination of an employee who failed to call the supervisor pursuant to requirements of collective bargaining agreement); *Lewis v. Holsum of Fort Wayne, Inc.*, 278 F.3d 706 (7th Cir. 2002) (discussing no call no show rule in context of FMLA); *Alexander v. Ford Motor Co.*, 204 F.R.D. 314, 318 (E.D. Mich. 2001) (finding the employer's rule requiring employees to notify the company of their intentions within five days of conclusion of leave not violative of FMLA because it requires only that the employee notify the employer when he or she needs to be absent); *Cavin v. Honda of America Mfg. Inc.*, 2002 U.S. Dist. LEXIS 19601 (S.D. Ohio, Feb. 22, 2002), *aff'd in part, rev'd and remanded on other grounds*, 346 F.3d 713 (6th Cir. 2003) (notice to particular supervisor pursuant to company policy upheld).

In *Holmes v. Boeing Co.*, 166 F.3d 1221 (10th Cir. 1999), the company policy required employees to speak directly with a supervisor or a personnel representative. The plaintiff complied with that request on several occasions. On the 12–day absence leading to his termination, however, the plaintiff did not call his supervisor or personnel representative. Instead, he contacted his union steward and informed him of his need for leave. He also called an automated absentee reporting line. The plaintiff alleged that calling his union steward and the automated line was sufficient notice to the defendant of the need for FMLA leave. He alleged that the additional requirement that he contact his supervisor or a personnel representative violated § 825.303(a). He argued that § 825.303(a) allows an ill employee at least two working days to give notice to an employer of the need for FMLA leave when the need for leave is not foreseeable and prohibits an employer from imposing additional requirements. The Tenth Circuit disagreed. Only in emergencies, the court held, are an employer's advance written notice requirements precluded by § 825.303(a), and the "no more than" one to two day delay in notifying an employer is the outer limit of reasonable notice. The FMLA does not prohibit an employer from requiring its employees to give notice to specific company supervisors on the day the employee is going to be absent in a non–emergency situation, as in this case.

(3) Need for Leave Is Not Foreseeable

If the need for leave is not foreseeable, an employee may provide oral notice to the employer of the need for FMLA leave. Ironically, this fact is not directly contained in the regulations governing the manner of notice where the need for leave is not foreseeable. Rather it is gleaned from the comments to the final regulations implementing Title I. According to those comments (Preamble, 29 CFR 825.303):

> Two commentators indicated that verbal notice is not sufficient and the employer should be permitted to require written notice requesting leave and providing a general reason for leave if FMLA. They suggested that if an employee needs to request leave in an emergency, oral notice should be sufficient but only if the employee confirms that request in writing within two working days.

> Nothing in the regulations prohibits an employer from requiring written notice to take or request leave if this is the employer's usual procedure. The employer may request written notice for all leave. The employer, however, may not deny or delay FMLA-qualifying leave when the employee provides verbal notice as soon as practicable.

Again, there is nothing to explain why the DOL did not include the requirement that employees need only provide verbal notice when the need for leave is not foreseeable.

This issue was addressed by the Seventh Circuit in *Collins v. NTN–Bower Corp. et al.*, 272 F.3d 1006, 1008 (7th Cir. 2001). There, the issue was whether an employee complied with the requirement that she notify her employer of the need for FMLA leave when she called in sick. The plaintiff argued that her calling in sick complied with the notice provisions where the need for leave is not foreseeable. She noted the difference between the language used in § 825.303, governing situations where the need for leave is not foreseeable, and § 825.302(c), which sets forth the employee notice requirements where the need for leave is foreseeable. Specifically, where the need for leave is foreseeable, an employee must provide at least verbal notice sufficient to make the employer aware that the employee needs FMLA qualifying leave, and the anticipated timing and duration of the leave. 29 CFR 825.302(c). No comparable language appears in § 825.303. This means, the plaintiff argued, that when time is short an employee need not let the employer know that the leave is FMLA–qualifying—in other words, need not ever let the employer know that the medical condition is "serious." According to the court in *Collins*:

> This is a lot to read into silence, especially when the premise of the argument is so doubtful. Collins treats [Section] 825.302 as handling exclusively those situations in which advance notice is possible. Yet its language is not so limited; it deals with all particulars of notice, and then [Section] 825.303 states an *exception to the timing rule*. On this understanding the substance and other particulars of notice must conform to [Section] 825.302, and only the timing of its delivery is affected by [Section] 825.303. *See Satterfield v. Wal–Mart Stores, Inc.*, 135 F.3d 973 (5th Cir. 1998).

Interestingly, the court went on to find that Collins' need for leave due to depression was not unforeseeable. According to the court, because her depression had been developing for years, once Collins knew she had a problem, she could predict that this would lead her to miss work on occasion, and she could have given notice contemplated by § 825.302 long before the incident at issue. "Then when depression incapacitated her on a particular day she could have made clear the 'serious' nature of her condition by referring to knowledge already in the employer's possession. A reference to being 'sick' not only withheld important information from the employer but likely threw it off the scent. Certainly, it did not suggest to the employer that the medical condition might be serious or that the FMLA otherwise could be applicable." *Collins*, 272 F.3d at 1008–1009.

The employee may provide notice to the employer either in person or by telephone, telegraph, facsimile (fax) machine or other electronic means. 29 CFR 825.303(b); S. Res. 242, Cong. Rec. S3959, S3971 (April 23, 1996); 29 CFR 825.302(b); *see Spangler v. Federal Home Loan Bank of Des Moines*, 278 F.3d 847, 852 (8th Cir. 2002); *Browning v. Liberty Mutual Insurance Co.*, 178 F.3d 1043, 1049 (8th Cir. 1999) (telephone notice), *cert. denied*, 120 S. Ct. 588 (1999); *Gay v. Gillman Paper Co.*, 125 F.3d 1432, 1434 (11th Cir. 1997); *Meadows v. Texar Fed. Credit U.*, No. 5:05CV158, 2007 U.S. Dist. LEXIS 4456, at *51 (E.D. Tex. Jan 22, 2007); *Snelling v. Stark Properties, Inc.*, No. 5:05-CV-46 (DF), 2006 U.S. Dist. LEXIS 50272, at *22 (M.D. Ga. July 24, 2006); *Wheeler v. Pioneer Dev. Services, Inc.*, 349 F. Supp. 2d 158 (D. Mass. 2004); *Conrad v. Eaton Corp.*, 303 F. Supp. 2d 987, 997 (N.D. Iowa 2004); *Henegar v. DaimlerChrysler Corp.*, 280 F. Supp. 2d 680, 686 (E.D. Mich. 2003); *Miller v. GB Sales & Service, Inc.*, 275 F. Supp. 2d 823, 829 (E.D. Mich. 2003); *Phillips v. Leroy–Somer North America et al.*, No. 01–1046-T, 2003 U.S. Dist. LEXIS 5334 (W.D. Tenn. March 31, 2003). Neither the regulations nor the comments to the final regulations limit who the employee may notify in the employing agency of the need for FMLA leave. Where the need for leave is foreseeable, the comments to the final regulations indicated that notice must be provided to the same persons within the company that the employee ordinarily contacts to request other forms of leave. Preamble, 29 CFR 825.302. That is not the case with respect to leave that is not foreseeable. Agencies will need to address this matter by policy in order to avoid arguments that the employee properly notified the agency by sending a telegraph message to an unknown employee of the agency located in a different office under different supervision 2000 miles away.

Absent employer policies, the FMLA regulations do not express a preference for one means of notice over another. Agencies may want to express such a preference by policy. While it is doubtful that an agency could outright prohibit notice by telegraph or email given their presence in the regulation, agencies should be able to request that employees use particular means over others. Most employees will comply with the agency's request, which would ease the administrative burden on agencies to be simultaneously monitoring multiple means of communication.

The regulations do not address the circumstances when an employee might be "unable to provide notice personally" thereby justifying the acceptance of notice by a spokesperson for the employee. It is unclear whether the employee's inability to provide notice personally requires physical or psychological incapability, or whether the employee's mere unwillingness to provide notice personally is sufficient. Nor is it clear what an employer could do to verify that the employee was "unable" to provide notice personally. Certainly, the regulations do not permit any sort of certification or other documentation in support of such a claim. Nor, for that matter, does the regulation address whether an employer may ask for proof that the individual claiming to be the employee's spokesperson is, in fact, the duly authorized spokesperson for the employee. Apparently agencies are supposed to take the word of the spokesperson. Again, this is an area that agencies should consider addressing as a matter of leave administration policy.

(4) Effect of Employer Policies

The regulations governing FMLA leave where the need for leave is not foreseeable apply the same rules regarding the affect of employer policies as where the need for leave is foreseeable. Unlike where the need for leave is foreseeable, however, the rules are not directly incorporated into the regulations governing leave where the need is not foreseeable. Rather, the rules are located elsewhere in the regulations. For example, the regulations governing situations where the need for leave is foreseeable (§ 825.302) directly contain requirements addressing application of the employer's "usual and customary" notice and procedural requirements (§ 825.302(d)), and substitution of paid leave (§ 825.302(g). These rules are not incorporated into the regulations governing situations where the need for leave is not foreseeable (§ 825.303). *See Moore v. Potter*, 353 F. Supp. 2d 419 (E.D.N.Y. 2005).

That an employee is required to comply with an employer's "usual and customary" notice and procedural requirements for requesting leave is addressed in the comments accompanying the publication of the final DOL regulations (Preamble, 29 CFR 825.303). In pertinent part, the regulations provide:

> Nothing in the regulations prohibits an employer from requiring written notice to take or request leave if this is the employer's usual procedure. The employer may request written notice for all leave. The employer, however, may not deny or delay FMLA–qualifying leave when the employee provides verbal notice as soon as practicable.

The above would appear to reflect the content of § 825.302(d), although there are some differences. For example, the above language may be viewed more narrowly than § 825.302(d) in that it only addresses written notice, rather than all notice and procedural requirements for requesting leave. Clearly, however, the DOL is indicating that written notice may be required of an employee where the need for leave is not foreseeable if that is the employer's usual procedure. Once again, the regulations do not incorporate this requirement, giving rise to questions whether employers may actually require such written notice.

When paid leave is substituted for unpaid FMLA leave, the employer's procedural requirements for taking that kind of leave apply. The regulation does not distinguish based on the foreseeability of the need for FMLA leave. If the employer's procedural requirements for taking the substituted paid leave are less stringent that requirements of the FMLA (e.g. notice or certification), only the less stringent requirements may be imposed. 29 CFR 825.207(h); S. Res. 242, Cong. Rec. S3959, S3966 (April 23, 1996); 29 CFR 825.207(h).

Similarly, an employer must observe any employment benefit program or plan that provides greater family or medical leave rights to employees than the rights established by the FMLA. 29 CFR 825.700(a); S. Res. 242, Cong. Rec. S3959, S3976 (April 23, 1996); 29 CFR 825.700(a). Conversely, the rights established by the Act may not be diminished by any employment benefit program or plan. 29 CFR 825.207(h); S. Res. 242, Cong. Rec. S3959, S3966 (April 23, 1996); 29 CFR 825.207(h). The same rule applies where the need for leave is foreseeable.

In *Moore v. Potter*, 353 F. Supp. 2d 419 (E.D.N.Y. 2005), plaintiff, a supervisor, was instructed that the proper call–in procedure for leave requests required that, prior to taking any kind of leave, employees were required to speak to their supervisor. If they did not speak with their supervisor, they would be charged AWOL. On the day in question, plaintiff called in sick and did not ask to speak with his supervisor. He was charged with AWOL and issued a letter of warning in lieu of suspension. Plaintiff admitted that he did not speak to his supervisor before taking leave. He explained that he did not call his supervisor because she was disrespectful towards him. On that record, the court found that plaintiff did not follow proper procedures and that the defendant's suspension did not violate the FMLA.

In the case of a medical emergency requiring leave because of an employee's own serious health condition or to care for a family member with a serious health condition, written advance notice pursuant to an employer's internal rules and procedures may not be required when FMLA leave is involved. 29 CFR 825.303; *Sabbrese v. Lowe's Home Centers, Inc.*, 320 F. Supp. 2d 311, 321–322 (W.D. Pa. June 9, 2004); *Miller v. GB Sales & Service, Inc.*, 275 F. Supp. 2d 823, 829 (E.D. Mich. 2003).

In *Meadows v. Texar Fed. Credit U.*, No. 5:05CV158, 2007 U.S. Dist. LEXIS 4456, at *51 (E.D. Tex. Jan. 22, 2007), the employer's usual and customary notice and leave policies required an employee on leave to contact his or her supervisor or the personnel administrator on at least a weekly basis every Friday. Plaintiff failed to call in herself. Instead, she sent in written status reports from her treating health care provider on a weekly basis. The court found the doctor reports sufficient to satisfy the periodic report requirement.

b. Title II

(1) General Rule

An employee covered by Title II must invoke his or her entitlement to family and medical leave, subject to the notification requirements of § 630.1206. 5 CFR 630.1203(b); *Bradley v. VA*, No. CH-0752-04-0513-I-1, 2005 MSPB LEXIS 1194, at *11 (Feb. 16, 2005), *pet. denied*, 99 MSPR 402 (2005), *aff'd*, 2006 U.S. App. LEXIS 8506 (Fed. Cir. 2006). The OPM indicates in the comments to the final regulations implementing Title II that, consistent with all other federal leave programs and policies, employees who choose to take leave under the FMLA must initiate the action to take such leave. Preamble, 5 CFR 630.1203. It would appear that the manner in which an employee covered by Title II invokes entitlement to FMLA leave is dependent on what is allowed as a matter of agency leave programs and policies. Agency policies may permit verbal notice of the need for FMLA leave. Unlike Title I, the CAA, and the PEOAA, verbal notice alone may not be sufficient for a Title II–covered employee to invoke the right to FMLA leave if the agency's FMLA leave programs or policy requires written notice.

In *Cole v. DHHS*, No. DC-0752-05-0457-I-1, 2005 MSPB LEXIS 6825, at *8 (Nov. 1, 2005), the Board sustained the removal charge that the employee failed to follow leave procedures for requesting FMLA leave. The employee was repeatedly notified of the correct procedures. The employee left the office for a doctor's appointment without requesting leave from her supervisor as required by established leave procedures. On six occasions, the employee similarly failed to request leave by contacting her supervisor in accordance with agency leave procedures. The employee did not deny that she knew the correct procedure for requesting leave or that she did not follow that procedure.

(2) Who May Provide Notice

Although less than clear, it appears that the employee or a personal representative of the employee may invoke the employee's right to FMLA leave benefits. The ability of a personal representative to invoke an employee's entitlement to FMLA leave is raised twice in the OPM regulations. 5 CFR 630.1206(c) addresses situations where the need for leave is not foreseeable. The availability of a personal representative is also discussed in 5 CFR 630.1203(b), addressing retroactive invocation of the entitlement to FMLA leave.

Where the need for leave is not foreseeable—e.g. a medical emergency or the unexpected availability of a child for adoption or foster care—and the employee cannot provide 30 calendar days' notice of his or her need for leave, the employee must provide notice within a reasonable period of time appropriate to the circumstances involved. 5 CFR 630.1206(c). If necessary, notice may be given by an employee's personal representative (e.g. a family member or other responsible party). 5 CFR 630.1206(c). The regulations do not define or otherwise provide guidance on when it may become "necessary" for notice of a need for leave to be provided by a personal representative.

The Board did not object to a request for FMLA leave by a union official on behalf of the employee in *Dias v. VA*, No. NY-0752-04-0279-I-2, 2005 MSPB LEXIS 3926, at *15 (June 30, 2005), *rev'd*, 102 MSPR 53 (2006), *appeal dismissed*, 2006 U.S. App. LEXIS 28961 (Fed. Cir. 2006), *vacated, reinstated*, 2006 U.S. App. LEXIS 32257 (Fed. Cir. 2006), *aff'd*, 2007 U.S. App. LEXIS 11530 (Fed. Cir. 2007).

The second area where the regulations permit a personal representative of an employee to invoke the employee's entitlement to FMLA leave occurs when the right to leave is being invoked retroactively. Generally, an employee may not retroactively invoke his or her entitlement to family and medical leave. 5 CFR 630.1203(b). However, if an employee and his or her personal representative are physically or mentally incapable of invoking the employee's entitlement to

FMLA leave *during the entire period* in which the employee is absent, the employee may retroactively invoke his or her entitlement to FMLA leave within two workdays after returning to work. 5 CFR 630.1203(b). In such cases, the incapacity of the employee must be documented by a written medical certification from a health care provider. 5 CFR 630.1203(b). Additionally, the employee must provide documentation acceptable to the agency explaining the inability of his or her personal representative to contact the agency and invoke the employee's entitlement to FMLA leave during the entire period in which the employee was absent from work for an FMLA-qualifying purpose. 5 CFR 630.1203(b).

The term "personal representative" is not formally defined in the Statute or implementing regulations. Nor is it clear whether a personal representative may be used in a context other than where the need for leave is not foreseeable or retroactive invocation of the employee's entitlement to FMLA leave. Finally, the regulations do not address how an individual becomes an employee's "personal representative," or whether the agency may obtain information verifying such a relationship. Unlike the other federal sector variants of the FMLA, the regulations do not use the term "designate" when referencing how an individual becomes a personal representative. This suggests a lower level of formality surrounding the appointment of a personal representative than is involved with the appointment of a spokesperson.

(3) Notice and the Foreseeability of the Need for Leave

Generally, the foreseeability of the need for FMLA leave does not affect the manner in which an employee must invoke entitlement to FMLA leave. That is, the employee remains obligated to invoke his or her entitlement to family and medical leave, consistent with all other federal leave programs and policies. 5 CFR 630.1203(b).

Where the need for leave is not foreseeable, a personal representative, where necessary, can invoke the employee's right to FMLA leave. That is not the case if the need for leave is foreseeable. Additionally, where the need for leave is foreseeable based on planned medical treatment, the employee must consult with the agency and make a reasonable effort to schedule medical treatment so as not to disrupt unduly the operations of the agency, subject to the approval of the health care provider. 5 CFR 630.1206(b).

(4) Effect of Employer Policies on Notice

The regulations implementing Title II require an agency to abide by the less stringent requirements of any collective bargaining agreement or any agency employment benefit program or plan that provides greater family or medical leave entitlements to employees than those provided by the FMLA. 5 CFR 630.1210(a), (c).

When the need for FMLA leave is foreseeable, agencies may also waive the notice requirements of the FMLA and instead impose the agency's "usual and customary" policies and procedures for providing notification of leave. 5 CFR 630.1206(e). The advantages and disadvantages of this exercise are addressed more fully above.

3. Adequacy of Notice

An eligible employee's entitlement to the benefits and protections of the FMLA is predicated on a leave request that contains sufficient information to apprize an informed employer that the leave may fall within the coverage of the Act. The adequacy of the employee's notice to the employer of the need for FMLA leave is one of the most heavily litigated subjects under the Act.

a. Title I, the CAA, and the PEOAA

In addition to being timely, to perfect entitlement to FMLA leave an employee must include sufficient information in the request for FMLA leave so as to alert the employer that the leave may be FMLA-qualifying. *Cavin v. Honda of America Mfg., Inc.*, 346 F.3d 713, 723 (6th Cir. 2003); *Peeples v. Coastal Office Products, Inc.*, 64 Fed. Appx. 860 4th Cir. 2003) (an employee must give timely and adequate notice of the need for FMLA leave); *Levine v. The Children's Museum of Indianapolis, Inc.*, No. 02-3013, 2003 U.S. App. LEXIS 5755 (7th Cir. March 24, 2003); *Collins v. NTN-Bower Corp.*, 272 F.3d 1006, 1008 (7th Cir. 2001); *Stoops v. One Call Communications, Inc.*, 141 F.3d 309, 312 (7th Cir. 1998); *Carter v. Ford Motor Co.*, 121 F.3d 1146, 1148 (8th Cir. 1997); *Artis v. Palos Community Hosp.*, No. 02 C 8855, 2004 U.S. Dist. LEXIS 20150, at *16 (N.D. Ill. Sept. 23, 2004); *Daoud v. Avamere Staffing, LLC*, 336 F. Supp. 2d 1129, 1139 (D. Ore. 2004); *Hobart v. Behavioral Connections of Wood County, Inc.*, No. 3:03CV7313, 2004 U.S. Dist. LEXIS 12051, at *21 (N.D. Ohio July 1, 2004); *Loring v.*

Advanced Foods, Inc., No. C02–4067–PAZ, 2004 U.S. Dist. LEXIS 6172, at *16 (N.D. Iowa April 9, 2004), *aff'd*, 2005 U.S. App. LEXIS 4124 (8th Cir. 2005); *Wu v. Southeast-Atlantic Beverage Corp.*, 321 F. Supp. 2d 1317, 1340 (N.D. Ga. 2003); *De Hoyas v. Bristol Laboratories, Corp.*, 218 F. Supp. 2d 222, 225–26 (D.P.R. Aug. 19, 2002) (under the Act, an employee is responsible for alerting the employer of the need for FMLA leave).

Whether an employee has given adequate notice of the need for FMLA leave is generally an issue of fact for the jury to decide. *Burnett v. LFW, Inc.*, 472 F.3d 471, 479 (7th cir. Dec. 26, 2006); *Williams v. Schuller International, Inc. et al.*, 29 Fed. Appx. 306 (6th Cir. 2002); *Hopson v. Quitman County Hosp. & Nursing home, Inc.*, 126 F.3d 635, 640 (5th Cir. 1997); *De Hoyas v. Bristol Laboratories, Corp.*, 218 F. Supp. 2d 222, 225–26 (D.P.R. Aug. 19, 2002); *Zawadowicz v. CVS Corp.*, 99 F. Supp. 2d 518, 529 (D.N.J. 200); *Mora v. Chem-Tronics, Inc.*, 16 F. Supp. 2d 1192, 1209 (S.D. Cal. 1998). The burden of providing notice is not onerous. *Cavin* 2002 U.S. Dist. LEXIS 19601; *see also Brooks v. Lowe's Home Centers, Inc.*, No. C2-04-740, 2006 U.S. Dist. LEXIS 17003, at *24 (S.D. Ohio March 27, 2006); *McNeela et al. v. United Air Lines, Inc.*, No. 98–C–1433, 1999 U.S. Dist. LEXIS 20042, at *16 (N.D. Ill. May 13, 1999) (FMLA affords substantial deference to employees with respect to notice of their need for FMLA leave).

The adequacy of employee notice of the need for FMLA leave is not addressed in the Statute itself. *See Hensley v. Baptist Hospital of East Tennessee, Inc. et al.*, No. 3:96–cv–789, 1997 U.S. Dist. LEXIS 22515 (E.D. Tenn. Oct. 27, 1997) (the Act is silent regarding the notice an employee must provide when the need for leave is not foreseeable); *Reich v. Midwest Plastic Engineering, Inc.*, No. 1:94–CV–525, 1995 U.S. Dist. LEXIS 8772 (W.D. Mich. June 6, 1995) (same). Rather, what requirements exist regarding the adequacy of an employee's notice of the need for FMLA leave are contained in the implementing regulations and the case law interpreting those regulations. *See* 29 CFR 825.302–303; S. Res. 242, Cong. Rec. S3959, S3971 (April 23, 1996); 29 CFR 825.302–303. Because regulations have not been enacted to implement the FMLA for purposes of the PEOAA, the DOL employee notice regulations implementing Title I apply. 3 USC 455.

(1) General Rule

The adequacy of employee notice of the need for FMLA leave is dependent on whether the leave is paid or unpaid, and whether the leave is foreseeable or not foreseeable. While these two groups of employee notice provisions largely work in tandem, they sometimes appear to be in conflict with one another.

The need for leave, paid or unpaid, may either be foreseeable or not foreseeable. Employee notice rules regarding paid and unpaid leave, at least as an initial matter, apply equally whether the need for leave is foreseeable or is not foreseeable.

An employee giving notice of the need for unpaid FMLA leave does not need to expressly assert rights under the Act or even mention the FMLA to meet his or her obligation to provide notice, though the employee would need to state a qualifying reason for the needed leave. 29 CFR 825.208(a)(2); S. Res. 242, Cong. Rec. S3959, S3966 (April 23, 1996); 29 CFR 825.208(a)(2); *see Burnett v. LFW, Inc.*, 472 F.3d 471, 478 (7th Cir. 2006); *Moorer v. Baptist Mem. Health Care System*, 398 F.3d 469 (6th Cir. 2005); *Hoffman v. Professional Med Team*, 394 F.3d 414, 418 (6th Cir. 2005); *Perry v. Jaguar of Troy*, 353 F.3d 510, 513 (6th Cir. 2003); *Babcock v. BellSouth Advertising and Publishing Corp.*, 348 F.3d 73, 78, n.5 (4th Cir. 2003); *Cavin*, 346 F.3d 713, 723; *Peeples*, 64 Fed. Appx. 860; *Bailey v. Southwest Gas Co.*, 275 F.3d 1181, 1185–86 (9th Cir. 2002); *Bachelder v. America West Airlines, Inc.*, 259 F.3d 1112, 1130–31 (9th Cir. 2001); *Stoops v. One Call Communications, Inc.*, 141 F.3d 309, 312–313 (7th Cir. 1998) (an employee can be completely ignorant of the benefits conferred by the FMLA; it is sufficient notice if the employee provides the employer with enough information to put the employer on notice that FMLA-qualifying leave is needed); *Tafelski v. Novartis Pharmaceuticals*, No. 05-71547, 2007 U.S. Dist. LEXIS 22847, at 15 (E.D. Mich. March 28, 2007); *Maynard v. Total Image Specialists, Inc.*, 478 F. Supp. 2d 993 (S.D. Ohio 2007). The employee notice requirements of the FMLA are not onerous. *Burnett v. LFW, Inc.*, 472 F.3d 471, 478 (7th Cir. 2006); *Leonard v. Uhlich Children's Advantage Network*, No. 05 C 5647, 2007 U.S. Dist. LEXIS 27099, at *8 (N.D. Ill. April 12, 2007). Employee notice requirements should not be rigid. *Morran v. Nevada System of Higher Ed.*, No. 3:05-CV-00577-ECR (RAM), 2007 U.S. Dist. LEXIS 27796, at *14 (D. Nev. March 30, 2007); *Brooks v. Lowe's Home Centers, Inc.*, No. C2-04-740, 2006 U.S. Dist. LEXIS 17003, at *24 (S.D. Ohio March 27, 2006).

An employee giving notice of the need for unpaid FMLA leave must explain the reasons for the needed leave so as to allow the employer to determine whether the leave qualifies under the Act. 29 CFR 825.208(a)(1); S. Res. 242, Cong. Rec. S3959, S3966 (April 23, 1996); 29 CFR 825.208(a)(1); *see Sherrod v. Philadelphia Gas Works*, 57 Fed. Appx. 68 (3d Cir. 2003). The critical question is whether the information imparted to the employer is sufficient to reasonably apprise it of the employee's request to take time off for a covered condition. *See Moorer v. Baptist Mem. Health Care System*, 398 F.3d 469 (6th Cir. 2005); *accord Hoffman v. Professional Med Team*, 394 F.3d 414, 418 (6th Cir. 2005) (employee must give employer notice of the request for leave stating a qualifying reason for the needed leave); *Brenneman v. MidCentral Health System*, 366 F.3d 412, 421 (6th Cir. 2004), *cert. denied*, 2005 U.S. LEXIS 1474 (U.S. 2005); *Perry v. Jaguar of Troy*, 353 F.3d 510, 513 (6th Cir. 2003) (employee gives sufficient notice when he provides enough information for the employer to reasonably conclude that an event described in § 2612(a)(1) occurred); *Cavin v. Honda of America Mfg., Inc.*, 346 F.3d 713, 723 (6th Cir. 2003); *Spangler v. Federal Home Loan Bank of Des Moines*, 278 F.3d 847, 852 (8th Cir. 2002); *Brohm v. JH Props., Inc.*, 149 F.3d 517, 523 (6th Cir. 1998); *Stoops v. One Call Communications, Inc.*, 141 F.3d 309, 312 (7th Cir. 1998) (an employee must provide the employer with enough information to put the employer on notice that FMLA–qualifying leave is needed); *Price v. City of Fort Wayne, Inc.*, 117 F.3d 1022, 1026 (7th Cir. 1997) (holding that sufficient notice is given when the employee requests leave for a covered condition); *Manuel v. Westlake Polymers Corp.*, 66 F.3d 758, 764 (5th Cir. 1995) (stating that sufficient notice is given when the information provided can reasonably apprise the employer of the employee's request to take time off for a serious health condition); *Williams v. Illinois Dept. of Corrections*, No. 05-cv-4227-JPG, 2007 U.S. Dist. LEXIS 17119, at *10 (S.D. Ill. March 9, 2007); *Tambash v. St. Bonaventure Univ.*, No. 99CV967, 2004 U.S. Dist. LEXIS 19914, at *30 (W.D.N.Y. Sept. 24, 2004) (under the FMLA, the employer's duties are triggered when the employee provides enough information to put the employer on notice that the employee may be in need of FMLA leave).

As observed by the court in *Aubuchon v. Knauf Fiberglass, GMBH*, 359 F.3d 950, 951–952 (7th Cir. 2004):

> So that the scope of our holding is clear, we emphasize that the employee's duty is merely to place the employer on notice of a probable basis for FMLA leave. He doesn't have to write a brief demonstrating legal entitlement. He just has to give the employer enough information to establish probable cause, as it were, to believe that he is entitled to FMLA leave.

Accord Burnett v. LFW, Inc., 472 F.3d 471, 479 (7th Cir. 2006) (employee's duty is merely to place employer on notice of a probable basis for FMLA leave); *Maynard v. Total Image Specialists, Inc.*, 478 F. Supp. 2d 993 (S.D. Ohio 2007).

An employee need only provide his or her employer with notice of a reason for leave that *potentially* qualifies for FMLA leave. An employee is not required to provide his or her employer with information sufficient show that the stated reason actually qualifies for FMLA protection. *Snelling v. Stark Properties, Inc.*, No. 5:05-CV-46 (DF), 2006 U.S. Dist. LEXIS 50272, at *22 (M.D. Ga. July 24, 2006); *Seachrist v. Harris Steel Co.*, No. 03 C 6197, 2005 U.S. Dist. LEXIS 30161, at *12 (N.D. Il. Nov. 30, 2005).

An employee does not even have to be aware of his or her FMLA rights to request FMLA leave. *Burnett*, 472 F.3d at 478; *Lucterhand v. Granite Microsystems, Inc.*, No. 05-CV-1047, 2007 U.S. Dist. LEXIS 15072, at *20 (E.D. Wis. March 2, 2007); *Wheeler v. Pioneer Dev. Services, Inc.*, 349 F. Supp. 2d 158 (D. Mass. 2004). Some courts reject the articulation of categorical rules governing the content of notices, instead recognizing that "what is practicable, both in terms of the timing of the notice and its content, will depend upon the facts and circumstances of each individual case." *Cavin v. Honda of America Mfg., Inc.*, 346 F.3d 713, 720 (6th Cir. 2003) (quoting *Manuel v. Westlake Polymers Corp.*, 66 F.2d 758, 764 (5th Cir. 1995)).

An employee who expressly asserts that he wants to take FMLA leave adequately alleges that he requested leave under the FMLA. *Cooper v. Fulton County, Georgia*, 458 F.3d 1282, 1286 (11th Cir. 2006) (employer request for family leave due to blurred vision, extreme headaches, and passing out sufficient); *Hubins v. Operating Engineers, Local Union No. 3*, No. C–04–3091 MMC (Docket No. 4), 2004 U.S. Dist. LEXIS 20376, at *12 (N.D. Cal. Sept. 29, 2004).

To be valid, a request for FMLA leave does not have to be made by submission of a medical certification. *Lucterhand v. Granite Microsystems, Inc.*, No. 05-CV-1047, 2007 U.S. Dist. LEXIS 15072, at *25 (E.D. Wisc. March 2, 2007).

Similarly, to gain the protections of the FMLA, an employee requesting to use paid leave for an FMLA–qualifying condition must inform the employer of the reason for the leave. 29 CFR 825.208(a); S. Res. 242, Cong. Rec. S3959, S3966 (April 23, 1996); 29 CFR 825.208(a). As with unpaid leave, an employee requesting to use accrued paid leave, even if for a purpose covered by the FMLA, need not expressly assert rights under the Act or even motion the FMLA to meet his or her obligation to provide notice of a need for FMLA leave. 29 CFR 825.208(a)(2); S. Res. 242, Cong. Rec. S3959, S3966 (April 23, 1996); 29 CFR 825.208(a)(2); *see Sanghvi v. Frendel et al.*, No. 00–7538, 2000 U.S. App. LEXIS 31757 (2nd Cir. Dec. 7, 2000); *Medina v. Coors Brewing Co.*, No. 99–1463, 2000 U.S. App. LEXIS 27577 (10th Cir. Nov. 3, 2000). "The critical question is whether the information imparted to the employer is sufficient to reasonably apprise it of the employee's request to take time off for a serious health condition." *Manual v. Westlake Polymers Corp.*, 66 F.3d 758, 762 (5th Cir. 1995); *see Medina*, 2000 U.S. App. LEXIS 27577; *Gay v. Gilman Paper Co.*, 125 F.3d 1432, 1435 (11th Cir. 1997).

In determining whether an employee imparted sufficient information, an employer is not required to be clairvoyant. *Levine v. The Children's Museum of Indianapolis, Inc.*, No. 02–3013, 2003 U.S. App. LEXIS 5755 (7th Cir. March 24, 2003); *Satterfield v. Wal–Mart Stores*, 135 F.3d 973, 980 (5th Cir. 1998), *cert. denied*, 119 S. Ct. 72 (1998); *Greenwell v. State Farm Ins. Co.*, No. 04-2427, 2006 U.S. Dist. LEXIS 14591, at *14 (W.D. La. March 13, 2006), *aff'd*, 486 F.3d 840 (5th Cir. 2007); *Mullin v. Rochester Manpower, Inc. et al.*, 204 F. Supp. 2d 556, 562 (W.D.N.Y. 2002); *Johnson v. Primerica*, No. 94 Civ. 4869, 1996 U.S. Dist. LEXIS 869 (S.D.N.Y. Jan. 30, 1996).

An employee using accrued paid leave, especially vacation or personal leave, may in some cases not spontaneously explain the reasons or plans for using accrued leave. 29 CFR 825.208(a)(1); S. Res. 242, Cong. Rec. S3959, S3966 (April 23, 1996); 29 CFR 825.208(a)(1). If the employee fails to explain the reasons for taking paid leave, FMLA leave may be denied. 29 CFR 825.208(a); S. Res. 242, Cong. Rec. S3959, S3966 (April 23, 1996); 29 CFR 825.208(a); *see Russell v. First Health Services et al.*, 11 Fed. Appx. 221 (4th Cir. 2001) (employee failure to provide adequate notice of the need for FMLA leave permitted the employer to terminate the employee); *Sanghvi v. Frendel et al.*, No. 00–7538, 2000 U.S. App. LEXIS 31757 (2d Cir. Dec. 7, 2000) (employee request for two months vacation to visit father in India as his mother recently died insufficient notice of need for FMLA–qualifying leave).

If an employee requesting to use paid leave for an FMLA–qualifying purpose does not explain the reason for the leave—consistent with the employer's established policy or practice—and the employer denies the employee's request, the employee will need to provide sufficient information to establish an FMLA qualifying reason for the needed leave so that the employer is aware of the employee's entitlement (i.e. the leave may not be denied) and then may designate that the paid leave be appropriately counted against (substituted for) the employee's 12–week entitlement. 29 CFR 825.208(a)(2); S. Res. 242, Cong. Rec. S3959, S3966 (April 23, 1996); 29 CFR 825.208(a)(2).

Similarly, an employee using accrued paid vacation leave who seeks an extension of unpaid leave for an FMLA–qualifying purpose will need to state the reason. 29 CFR 825.208(a)(2); S. Res. 242, Cong. Rec. S3959, S3966 (April 23, 1996); 29 CFR 825.208(a)(2); *see De Hoyas Bristol Laboratories, Corp.*, 218 F. Supp. 2d 222, 226–27 (D.P.R. 2002) (an employee who asked for "floating day" and for extension of accrued paid vacation not entitled to FMLA protections where employee never indicated that leave was to care for mother's deteriorating health condition). If this is due to an event that occurred during the period of paid leave, the employer may count the leave used after the FMLA–qualifying event against the employee's 12–week entitlement. 29 CFR 825.208(a)(2); S. Res. 242, Cong. Rec. S3959, S3966 (April 23, 1996); 29 CFR 825.208(a)(2).

The requirement of employee notice is not satisfied by the employee merely demanding leave. He must give the employer a reason to believe he's entitled to it. If an employee has brain cancer but only tells his employer that he has a headache, he has not given the notice required by the Act. *Aubuchon v. Knauf Fiberglass, GMBH*, 359 F.3d 950, 951–952 (7th Cir. 2004); *Williams v. Illinois Dept. of Corrections*, No. 05-cv-4227-JPG, 2007 U.S. Dist. LEXIS 17119, at *10 (S.D. Ill. March 9, 2007).

In *Ruiz v. Ostbye & Anderson, Inc.*, No. 02–2954 (JNE/JGL), 2004 U.S. Dist. LEXIS 19890, at *9 (D. Minn. Sept. 28, 2004), the court found that the employee provided adequate notice of his need for FMLA leave when the employee informed her supervisor: (1) she was having a mental breakdown; (2) she was seen by a doctor who excused her from work for four days; and (3) she was prescribed medication.

In *Carmen v. Unison Behavioral Health Group, Inc.*, 295 F. Supp. 2d 809, 813 (N.D. Ohio 2003), the court found that the employee provided sufficient notice of the need for FMLA leave where the employee notified her employer that she would be off work for four days and required continuing medical treatment for her condition. The court rejected the employer's argument that she asked for and was granted sick leave. The employee argued that she merely filled out the sick leave forms that the employer required.

In *Cavin v. Honda of America Mfg., Inc.*, 346 F.3d 713, 725 (6th Cir. 2003), the court found that an employee's statement that he was injured in a motorcycle accident and just left the hospital was sufficient notice of the need for FMLA leave.

An employee's request for leave to care for her grandchildren because her son (the father) was called up for deployment, was held insufficient notice of the need for FMLA leave for a covered condition. *Cool v. BorgWarner Diversified Transmission*

Products, Inc., No. IP 02–0960–C–B/S, 2004 U.S. Dist. LEXIS 570, at *22 (S.D. Ind. Jan. 12, 2004). No mention was made that the children were ill.

An employer must consider the context surrounding an employee's request for leave when determining whether the request may be FMLA-qualifying. In *Burnett v. LFW, Inc.*, 472 F.3d 471, 480 (7th Cir. 2006), the employee stated that he was sick and wanted to go home. The employer argued that this was insufficient notice of the need for FMLA leave. The court disagreed finding that the employer must view the employee's remarks in light of the surrounding context. Over a four month period, the court noted, the employee informed his employer that he suffered from a weak bladder, he recently had a biopsy and requested help with work duties, he repeatedly stated he felt sick, and he was on a trajectory of increased medical visits and testing. The court found that, in context, the employee's request for leave because he was "sick" was sufficient notice that the leave might be FMLA-qualifying.

In contrast, the court in *Ireland v. Borough of Haddonfield*, No. 04-5372(NLH), 2006 U.S. Dist. LEXIS 65286, at *13 & n. 5 (D.N.J. Sept. 1, 2006), declined to find sufficient notice based on the employee's intermittently "calling out sick for knee injuries and other ailments over the course of three years of employment."

In *Rodriguez v. Ford Motor Co.*, 382 F. Supp. 2d 928, 934 (E.D. Mich. Aug. 12, 2005), the court found sufficient notice where the employer was aware that the employee suffered an occupational injury at the plant, was taken to the hospital, remained there for almost three days, suffered a broken foot, had a large bandage on his foot, needed crutches, was determined by the company not to be able to perform his regular job, was reassigned to a seated, non-production position and, after his foot allegedly began to well and cause pain, requested leave.

In *Stevens v. Advance Stores, Inc.*, No. 3-06-0537, 2007 U.S. Dist. LEXIS 28690, at *15-16 (M.D. Tenn. April 17, 2007), the court found sufficient notice based on the employer's knowledge that plaintiff was sent home after she was observed as being ill at work, a doctor prescribed medication, she was sent home ill a few days later and marked absent due to illness, and the employer's records marked Stevens as being ill for four consecutive days.

Adequate notice will be found where the employer indicates that FMLA leave was more appropriate than the employee's original request to take vacation time for cataract surgery. *See Basick v. Huron Valley Hosp., Inc.*, No. 06-11847, 2007 U.S. Dist. LEXIS 3650, at *18 (E.D. Mich. Jan. 18, 2007). Similarly, an employer's approval of leave as FMLA leave establishes that the employee provided adequate notice. *Williams v. Air Products & Chemicals, Inc.*, No. 3:04cv93/LAC, 2005 U.S. Dist. LEXIS 23131, at *11 (N.D. Ill. Aug. 16, 2005).

The length of an absence is generally not considered adequate employee notice that the leave might be FMLA qualifying. *Phillips v. Quebecor World RAI, Inc.*, 450 F.3d 308, 311 (7th Cir. 2006); *Maynard v. Total Image Specialists, Inc.*, 478 F. Supp. 2d 993 (S.D. Ohio 2007).

If an employer feels it does not have sufficient information to determine whether the employee's reasons for requesting leave are encompassed by the FMLA, the employer should inquire further of the employee to ascertain whether the leave is potentially FMLA-qualifying. 29 CFR 825.208(a); *see Brenneman v. MidCentral Health System*, 366 F.3d 412, 422 (6th Cir. 2004), *cert. denied*, 2005 U.S. LEXIS 1474 (U.S. 2005); *Aubuchon v. Knauf Fiberglass, GMBH*, 359 F.3d 950, 951–952 (7th Cir. 2004) (employer duty to investigate further triggered when employee provides notice of probable basis for FMLA leave); *Tafelski v. Novartis Pharmaceuticals*, No. 05-71547, 2007 U.S. Dist. LEXIS 22847, at 15 (E.D. Mich. March 28, 2007); *Williams v. Illinois Dept. of Corrections*, No. 05-cv-4227-JPG, 2007 U.S. Dist. LEXIS 17119, at *11 (S.D. Ill. March 9, 2007); *Tambash v. St. Bonaventure Univ.*, No. 99CV967, 2004 U.S. Dist. LEXIS 19914, at *30 (W.D.N.Y. Sept. 24, 2004); *Artis v. Palos Community Hosp.*, No. 02 C 8855, 2004 U.S. Dist. LEXIS 20150, at *16 (N.D. Ill. Sept. 23, 2004); *Daoud v. Avamere Staffing, LLC*, 336 F. Supp. 2d 1129, 1139 (D. Ore. 2004); *Wheeler v. Pioneer Dev. Services, Inc.*, 349 F. Supp. 2d 158 (D. Mass. 2004); *Hobart v. Behavioral Connections of Wood County, Inc.*, No. 3:03CV7313, 2004 U.S. Dist. LEXIS 12051, at *10 (N.D. Ohio July 1, 2004); *Henson v. Bell Helicopter Textron, Inc.*, No. 4:01–CV–1024–Y, 2004 U.S. Dist. LEXIS 1630, at *38 (N.D. Tex. Feb. 6, 2004), *aff'd*, 2005 U.S. App. LEXIS 6600 (6th Cir. 2005).

Stated differently, once the employee furnishes adequate information, the burden shifts to the employer to obtain any additional required information through informal means. 29 CFR 825.303(b); *see Maynard v. Total Image Specialists, Inc.*, , 478 F. Supp. 2d 993 (S.D. Ohio 2007); *Sons v. Henry County*, No. 1:05-cv-0516-DFH-TAB, 2006 U.S. Dist. LEXIS 79604, at *23 (S.D. Ind. Oct. 31, 2006); *Snelling v. Stark Properties, Inc.*, No. 5:05-CV-46 (DF), 2006 U.S. Dist. LEXIS 50272, at *22 (M.D. Ga. July 24, 2006); *Lukacinsky v. Panasonic Service Co.*, No. 03–40141–FDS, 2004 U.S. Dist. LEXIS 25846, at *38 (D. Mass. Nov. 29, 2004); *Hubins v. Operating Engineers, Local Union No. 3, et. al.*, No. C–04–3091 MMC (Docket No. 4), 2004 U.S. Dist. LEXIS

20376, at *12 (N.D. Cal. Sept. 29, 2004); *Carmen v. Unison Behavioral Health Group, Inc.*, 295 F. Supp. 2d 809, 813 (N.D. Ohio 2003); *Miller v. GB Sales & Service, Inc.*, 275 F. Supp. 2d 823, 829 (E.D. Mich. 2003).

Courts have not clearly defined the precise contours of what constitutes sufficient notice to shift the burden of inquiry. *Jennings v. Parade Publications*, No. 01 Civ. 8590 (TPG), 2003 U.S. Dist. LEXIS 17088, at *8 (S.D.N.Y. Sept. 30, 2003). The court in *Jennings* noted: "At one end of the spectrum, notice has been held insufficient where an employee requested leave to deal with "some family matters," and referred to a family business.... On the other hand, courts have held that an employer with some prior knowledge of an employee's medical situation may not rely on an unspecific request for FMLA leave to avoid the duty to inquiry further into whether the request is FMLA–qualifying."

In *Cruz v. Publix Super Markets, Inc.*, 428 F.3d 1379, 1385 (11th Cir. 2005), an employee's statement that she needed leave based on her own belief that her daughter was going into labor, her son-in-law had a broken collarbone, and that her daughter needed her help was insufficient notice to shift the burden to Publix to request further information. "We cannot expect Publix to undergo an investigation to uncover possible circumstances under which Cruz would be entitled to FMLA leave when Cruz never raised any such circumstances."

The employer must seek this additional information only from the employee requesting leave. *Hobart v. Behavioral Connections of Wood County, Inc.*, No. 3:03CV7313, 2004 U.S. Dist. LEXIS 12051, at *10 (N.D. Ohio July 1, 2004).

In *Aubuchon v. Knauf Fiberglass, GMBH*, 359 F.3d 950, 951–952 (7th Cir. 2004), the employee requested leave to be with his wife until she gave birth. He failed to mention that his wife was experiencing complications due to the pregnancy or any other serious health condition. His leave was denied. He absented himself from work anyway and was fired. Thereafter, Aubuchon produced a note from his wife's doctor stating that she had complications from pregnancy. The court found that the production of the note was too late. "Employees should not be encouraged to mousetrap their employers by requesting FMLA leave on patently insufficient grounds and then after the leave is denied obtaining a doctor's note that indicates that sufficient grounds existed, though they were never communicated to the employer."

The court also found that, under the circumstances, the employer was not required to inquire further pursuant to 29 CFR 825.302(c), 303(b). Plaintiff argued that an employee who bases a request for leave on patently insufficient grounds should operate as a signal to the employer that the employee may not understand the contours of the duty of notice. The court observed:

> Some of the regulations that the Department of Labor has issued suggest that merely by demanding leave, the employee triggers a duty on the part of the employer to determine whether the requested leave is covered by the FMLA. *See* 29 CFR§ 825.302(c), 303(b). That is an extreme position, as most leaves requested by employees are not based on a ground entitling them to leave under the FMLA, so that if the position were accepted the consequence would be to place a substantial and largely wasted investigative burden on employers.

In *Barngrover v. W.W. Transport*, No. 3:02–cv–40020, 2003 U.S. Dist. LEXIS 13145, at *26–28 (S.D. Iowa July 24, 2003), because the employee never complained that she was being worked outside of her known medical restrictions, the court found that the employer was under no duty to inquire further whether the employee needed FMLA leave to avoid work outside her restrictions.

An employee's request for time off for a European vacation "plainly does not give defendant notice of any intention to take leave for a qualified reason." *Daoud v. Avamere Staffing, LLC*, 336 F. Supp. 2d 1129, 1140 (D. Ore. 2004).

In the case of intermittent leave or leave on a reduced leave schedule that is medically necessary, an employee must advise the employer, upon request, of the reasons why the intermittent/reduced leave schedule is necessary and of the schedule for treatment, if applicable. 29 CFR 825.302(f); *see George v. Russell Stover Candies, Inc.*, 106 Fed. Appx. 946 (6th Cir. 2004).

An employer's denial of FMLA leave indicates that the employee provided the employer with sufficient evidence that the leave was not for an FMLA–qualifying need. *Perry v. Jaguar of Troy*, 353 F.3d 510, 513 (6th Cir. Dec. 30, 2003*)*. Similarly, courts have cited to an employer's admission that it was considering an employee's current leave under the FMLA as evidence that the employee provided adequate notice of the need for FMLA leave. *Conrad v. Eaton Corp.*, 303 F. Supp. 2d 987, 998 (N.D. Iowa 2004); *Jennings v. Parade Publications*, No. 01 Civ. 8590 (TPG), 2003 U.S. Dist. LEXIS 17088, at *8–12 (S.D.N.Y. Sept. 30, 2003) (court cited that the employer considered employee's leave request seriously enough to inquire of company's lawyers whether condition was covered by the FMLA in denying summary judgment to employer due to insufficient employee notice).

The Sixth Circuit in *Cavin v. Honda of America Mfg., Inc.*, 346 F.3d 713, 725–726 & n.8 (6th Cir. 2003), also addressed what constitutes "notice to an employer." Cavin notified the security office that he would be absent due to injuries suffered in a motorcycle accident. Honda did not contest that notice to the security department rather than the Leave Coordination Department constituted notice to the "employer." Honda permitted employees to report one day absences to the security department. An employee seeking a leave of absence of more than one day was supposed to contact the Leave Coordination Department. With regard to Honda's leave policy, the court noted:

> We recognize that it is both appropriate and efficient for Honda to delegate the management of all FMLA claims to one department and that it has chosen the Leave Coordination Department for this purpose. ... However, we are not persuaded that notice to security constitutes notice to Honda only [in] the event of an absence, but not of a need for a leave of absence.

The court held plaintiff's supervisor had actual notice of Cavin's need for leave, and such notice should be imputed to Honda management.

In the Sixth Circuit, whether an employee provided adequate notice of the need for FMLA leave is a finding of mixed fact and law. *Cavin*, 346 F.3d at 723. In the Fifth Circuit, whether an employee gave adequate notice of a need for FMLA leave is generally an issue of fact for the jury to decide. *Lubke v. City of Arlington*, No. 4:02–CV–188–Y, 2003 U.S. Dist. LEXIS 18816, at *14 (N.D. Tex. Sept. 9, 2003).

Overlapping with the notice provisions governing unpaid or, with substitution, paid FMLA leave, are notice requirements based on the foreseeability of the need for leave. There are similarities and differences between the foreseeability-based notice provisions and the notice provisions based on whether FMLA leave is paid or unpaid. *Ode v. Mount Sinai Med. Center*, No. 04-CIV. 9632 (DLC), 2006 U.S. Dist. LEXIS 41479, at *14 (S.D. N.Y. June 22, 2006) (regulations for foreseeable and unforeseeable leave differ regarding the content of the notice that an employee should give).

When the need for leave is foreseeable, an employee must provide at least verbal notice sufficient to make the employer aware that the employee needs FMLA–qualifying leave, as well as the anticipated timing and duration of the leave. 29 CFR 825.302(c); S. Res. 242, Cong. Rec. S3959, S3971 (April 23, 1996); 29 CFR 825.302(c); *see Bailey v. Southwest Gas Co.*, 275 F.3d 1181, 1185 (9th Cir. 2002); *Bailey v. Amsted Industries, Inc.*, 172 F.3d 1041, 1045 (8th Cir. 1999); *Howard v. Garage Door Group, Inc.*, 197 F. Supp. 2d 1297, 1308–1309 (D. Kan. 2002), *aff'd*, 2005 U.S. App. LEXIS 3509 (10th Cir. 2005); *Williams v. Shenango, Inc.*, 986 F. Supp. 309, 319–20 (W.D. Pa. 1997).

The employee need not expressly mention the FMLA, but may only state that leave is needed for a covered condition. 29 CFR 825.302(c); S. Res. 242, Cong. Rec. S3959, S3971 (April 23, 1996); 29 CFR 825.302(c); *see Bailey v. Southwest Gas Co.*, 275 F.3d at 1185; *Tate v. Farmland Industries, Inc.*, 268 F.3d 989, 997 (10th Cir. 2001); *Sanghvi v. Frendel et al.*, No. 00–7538, 2000 U.S. App. LEXIS 31757 (2d Cir. Dec. 7, 2000); *Ode*, 2006 U.S. Dist. LEXIS 41479, at *14; *Lazano v. Kay Mfg., Co.*, No. 04 C 2784, 2005 U.S. Dist. LEXIS 26930, at *14 (N.D. Ill. Nov. 3, 2005); *Williams v. Shenango, Inc.*, 986 F. Supp. 309, 319–20 (W.D. Pa. 1997) (the Act does not require the employee to use "magic words" when invoking the need for FMLA leave). Courts cite to the fact that an employee used the term FMLA when requesting leave as evidence that the leave requested by the employee may be FMLA-qualifying. *See Michelle v. SMC Pneumatics, Inc.*, No. IP99–1285–C–T/G, 2000 U.S. Dist. LEXIS 12478, at *27 (S.D. Ind. Aug. 21, 2000).

The employer should inquire further of the employee if it is necessary to have more information about whether FMLA leave is being sought by the employee, and obtain the necessary details of the leave to be taken. 29 CFR 825.302(c); S. Res. 242, Cong. Rec. S3959, S3971 (April 23, 1996); 29 CFR 825.302(c); *see Bailey v. Southwest Gas Co.*, 275 F.3d 1181, 1185–86 (9th Cir. 2002); *Rhoads v. FDIC*, 257 F.3d 373, 382–83 (4th Cir. 2001), *cert. denied*, 535 U.S. 933 (002); *Stoops v. One Call Communications, Inc.*, 141 F.3d 309, 312 7th Cir. 1998); *Ode v. Mount Sinai Med. Center*, No. 04-CIV. 9632 (DLC), 2006 U.S. Dist. LEXIS 41479, at *14-15 (S.D. N.Y. June 22, 2006); *Williams v. Shenango, Inc.*, 986 F. Supp. 309, 319–20 (W.D. Pa. 1997).

While the employer's duty to inquiry may be predicated on statements made by the employee, the employer is not required to be clairvoyant. *Mullin v. Rochester Manpower, Inc. et al.*, 204 F. Supp. 2d 556, 562 (W.D.N.Y. 2002); *Johnson v. Primerica*, No. 94 Civ. 4869, 1996 U.S. Dist. LEXIS 869 (S.D.N.Y. Jan. 30, 1996). An employee is obligated to respond to an employer's inquiries, and must explain the reasons justifying the requested leave so as to allow the employer to determine whether the FMLA is implicated. *Peeples v. Coastal Office Products, Inc.*, 64 Fed. Appx. 860 (4th Cir. 2003); *Bailey v. Southwest Gas Co.*, 275 F.3d 1181, 1185–86 (9th Cir. 2002).

In the case of intermittent leave or leave on a reduced leave schedule that is both foreseeable and medically necessary, an employee must advise the employer, upon request, of the reasons why the intermittent leave or reduced leave schedule is necessary and of the schedule for treatment, if applicable. 29 CFR 825.302(f); Res. 242, Cong. Rec. S3959, S3972 (April 23, 1996); 29 CFR 825.302(f). Note that the notice provisions based on whether FMLA leave was paid or unpaid do not have a similar requirement.

Where the need for leave is not foreseeable, the notice requirement is less extensive. *Ode*, 2006 U.S. Dist. LEXIS 41479, at *15. The regulations provide that an employee need not expressly assert rights under the FMLA or even mention the FMLA, but may only state that leave is needed for an FMLA-covered reason. 29 CFR 825.303(b); Res. 242, Cong. Rec. S3959, S3972 (April 23, 1996); 29 CFR 825.303(b); see *Medina v. Coors Brewing Co.*, No. 99-1463, 2000 U.S. App. LEXIS 27577 (10th Cir. Nov. 3, 2000); *Levine v. Children's Museum of Indianapolis, Inc.*, No. IP 00-0715-C G/H, 2002 U.S. Dist. LEXIS 14738 (S.D. Ind. July 1, 2002), aff'd, No. 02-3013, 2003 U.S. App. LEXIS 5755 (7th Cir. March 24, 2003); *Odenter*, No. 04-CIV. 9632 (DLC), 2006 U.S. Dist. LEXIS 41479, at *15 (S.D. N.Y. June 22, 2006). The critical question is whether the information imparted to the employer is sufficient to reasonably apprise it of the employee's request to take time off for a serious health condition. *Manuel v. Westlake Polymers Corp.*, 66 F.3d 758, 764 (5th Cir. 1995); see *Satterfield v. Wal–Mart Stores, Inc.*, 135 F.3d 973, 977 (5th Cir. 1998), cert. denied, 119 S. Ct. 72 (1998).

The employer will be expected to obtain any additional required information through informal means. 29 CFR 825.303(b); S. Res. 242, Cong. Rec. S3959, S3972 (April 23, 1996); 29 CFR 825.303(b); see *Price v. City of Fort Wayne, Ind.*, 117 F.3d 1022, 1025–26 (7th Cir. 1997); *Lara v. Central Grocers Cooperative, Inc. et al.*, No. 00-C-7828, 2002 U.S. Dist. LEXIS 16745 (N.D. Ill. Sept. 6, 2002); *Biermann v. Aluminum Co. of America*, No. 3:98-CV-20159, 2000 U.S. Dist. LEXIS 21964 (S.D. Iowa Jan. 21, 2000); *McCarron v. British Telecom et al.*, No. 00-CV-6123, 2002 U.S. Dist. LEXIS 15151 (E.D. Pa. Aug. 7, 2002). The employee or spokesperson will be expected to provide more information when it can readily be accomplished as a practical matter, taking into consideration the exigencies of the situation. 29 CFR 825.303(b); S. Res. 242, Cong. Rec. S3959, S3972 (April 23, 1996); 29 CFR 825.303(b); see *Phillips v. Leroy-Somer North America et al.*, No. 01-1046-T, 2003 U.S. Dist. LEXIS 5334 (W.D. Tenn. March 31, 2003); *Bonilla v. Small Assemblies Co.*, No. 99-C-6675, 2001 U.S. Dist. LEXIS 7342 (N.D. Ill. May 31, 2001).

The duty of an employee to provide additional information may be substantial. In *Bonilla v. Small Assemblies Co.*, No. 99-C-6675, 2001 U.S. Dist. LEXIS 7342 (N.D. Ill. May 31, 2001), the employee took an approved two-week vacation to visit her family in Honduras. During the visit the employee's mother became ill. The employee called the employer and requested additional leave to care for her ill mother. The employee advised the employer that she did not know the nature of her mother's illness. The employer required that the employee call back on the last day of her scheduled vacation to inform the employer of her status. The employee never called, but returned to work 13 days after the expiration of her vacation. The employer argued that the employee failed to make a reasonable effort after the initial telephone conversation to provide additional information in order for the employer to determine whether the leave was FMLA-qualifying. The employee responded that she did not call as she would have to travel 30 miles each way to get to a telephone and that she was the only person able to take care of her mother. Because the employee's father and sister, who lived with the mother, were able to care for the mother while the employee went to make a phone call, a reasonable jury, the court held, could conclude that the employee failed to give sufficient information to the employer.

It is unclear how the above notice requirement where the need for leave is not foreseeable, interacts with the notice requirements based on whether the leave is paid or unpaid. Specifically, the regulations differ as to the quality of notice required of the employee. Whether leave is paid or unpaid, the employee is required to provide the employer with sufficient information so that the employer can determine whether the leave is FMLA-qualifying. The notice requirement where the need for leave is not foreseeable is that the employee need only state that leave is needed. Stating that "leave is needed" appears to require less information than the requirement that sufficient facts be provided for an employer to judge whether the leave is FMLA-qualifying.

At minimum, when the need for leave is not foreseeable, the regulations may be signaling that an employee may initially provide an employer with less information due to the exigencies of the situation. Such a reading necessarily assumes that § 825.303(b) modifies the notice requirements for paid or unpaid leave contained in § 825.208. There is no express statement in the regulations or the comments accompanying the regulations that this is the case. One could argue that, as a matter of regulatory construction, because § 825.303(b) occurs after § 825.208, the former assumes the later, and modifies it where the need for leave is not foreseeable. An equally valid argument could be made for the opposite proposition.

As a practical matter, the regulations seem to suggest that, where the need for leave is not foreseeable due to the exigencies of the situation, an employer should hold off making an immediate decision whether the leave is FMLA-qualifying until additional information is obtained. Indeed, when in doubt, employers may want to provisionally designate the leave as FMLA-qualifying until that additional information is both requested and promptly provided by the employee or spokesperson. Ultimately, however, the employee is responsible for providing the employer sufficient information on which to base a final determination whether the leave is FMLA-qualifying.

(2) Employee Must Request Leave

Generally, to receive the benefits and protections of the Act, an eligible employee must first request leave. See *Johnson v. Thru Point Inc.*, 160 Fed. Appx. 159 (3d Cir. 2005) (insufficient notice where employee did not tell employer of his PTSD, take or request leave, but signaled he was ready and able to work); *Brenneman v. MidCentral Health System*, 366 F.3d 412, 421 (6th Cir. 2004), cert. denied, 2005 U.S. LEXIS 1474 (U.S. 2005); *Bailey v. Southwest Gas Co.*, 275 F.3d 1181, 1185 (9th Cir. 2002) (an employee who never requested FMLA leave does not have a basis for arguing that employer interfered with the exercise of FMLA rights); *Seaman v. CSPH, Inc. et al.*, 179 F.3d 297, 302 (5th Cir. 1999) (an employee never requested leave within the meaning of the FMLA by mentioning he may suffer from bipolar disorder and may need to see a doctor, but he failed to follow up by scheduling an appointment or otherwise informed employee that he would be off duty seeking medical attention); *Williams v. The Thomson Corp.*, No. 00-2256, 2003 U.S. Dist. LEXIS 4481, at *39 (D. Minn. March 21, 2003) (employee has affirmative duty to request some kind of leave in order for FMLA to be implicated); *Howard v. Garage Door Group, Inc.*, 197 F. Supp. 2d 1297, 1308-1309 (D. Kan. 2002), aff'd, 2005 U.S. App. LEXIS 3509 (10th Cir. 2005) (the employer's obligation to notify employee of potential FMLA coverage never invoked where employee never expressed desire to take leave); *Tornberg v. Business Interlink Services, Inc.*, 237 F. Supp. 2d 778, 784 (E.D. Mich. 2002) (§ 2612(e)(2)(B) requires an employee to provide notice to the employer, expressing his or her intention to take leave); *Cole v. Uni-Marts, Inc.*, 88 F. Supp. 2d 67 (W.D.N.Y. 1999).

An employee need not use the word "leave" to request leave. In *Cavin v. Honda of America Mfg., Inc.*, 346 F.3d 713, 720 (6th Cir. 2003), the employee called in stating that he could not work because the hospital had just released him after a motorcycle accident. According to the *Cavin* court:

> However, we conclude that Cavin's failure to use the word "leave" or the phrase "leave of absence" is of no consequence in assessing whether Honda received sufficient notice of his request for FMLA. Just as an employee can give an employer notice of his request for FMLA-qualifying leave without invoking the FMLA…an employee can give notice sufficient to make his employer aware that he needs FMLA-qualifying leave without using the words "leave" or "leave of absence."

Accord *Rodriguez v. Ford Motor Co.*, 382 F. Supp. 2d 928, 933 (E.D. Mich. 2005).

A request for a reduced-work schedule may qualify as FMLA leave. *Daoud v. Avamere Staffing, LLC*, 336 F. Supp. 2d 1129, 1139 (D. Ore. 2004).

Notice that an employee may need to take time off from work due to a serious health condition at some unspecified date in the future is not a "request for leave" within the meaning of the FMLA. See *Artis v. Palos Community Hosp.*, No. 02 C 8855, 2004 U.S. Dist. LEXIS 20150, at *16 (N.D. Ill. Sept. 23, 2004); *Barngrover v. W.W. Transport*, No. 3:02-cv-40020, 2003 U.S. Dist. LEXIS 13145, at *24 (S.D. Iowa. July 24, 2003).

In *Artis*, the employee argued that her employer was put on notice of the potential need for FMLA leave when plaintiff informed the hospital of her need for time off following two surgeries. Plaintiff, however, elected to continue to work on limited duty rather than take leave. According to the court, plaintiff's "continued working, albeit in limited duty, militates against the conclusion that the Defendant knew of her need for FMLA leave."

In *Mullin v. Rochester Manpower, Inc. et al.*, 204 F. Supp. 2d 556, 562-63 (W.D.N.Y. 2002), the employee told her supervisor that she was pregnant and was due in January. The employee claimed that this was sufficient notice of a need for FMLA leave. The employer argued that an employer's FMLA obligations are only triggered when an employee requests leave, and to constitute such a "request" the employee must ask for an actual leave of absence from employment. The employer argued that notification that an employee has a covered condition that might require leave at some undetermined point in the future is insufficient. The district court agreed, holding, as a matter of law, that the plaintiff's notice was inadequate. See also *Klaus v. Builders Concrete Co.*, No. 00-C-7757, 2002 U.S. Dist. LEXIS 1919, at *13 (N.D. Ill. Feb. 7, 2002) (the employee did not request FMLA leave by merely informing the employer that the employee might require certain medical procedures—which would be performed at a time when the plaintiff was not even employed by the employer–is not a request for FMLA leave; the evidence does not demonstrate that the plaintiff informed the defendant that it was foreseeable that he would require leave prior to his lay off). An employee who does not request leave of any kind generally does not have a viable claim against an employer for denial of the employee's FMLA leave request. *See Artis v. Palos Community Hosp.*, No. 02 C 8855, 2004 U.S. Dist. LEXIS 20150, at *16 (N.D. Ill. Sept. 23, 2004) (employee admission that she never made a request for leave); *accord Loring v. Advanced Foods, Inc.*, No. C02–4067–PAZ, 2004 U.S. Dist. LEXIS 6172, at *17 (N.D. Iowa April 9, 2004), *aff'd*, 2005 U.S. App. LEXIS 4124 (5th Cir. 2005); *Barngrover v. W.W. Transport*, No. 3:02–cv–40020, 2003 U.S. Dist. LEXIS 13145, at *26–28 (S.D. Iowa. July 24, 2003).

There are two exceptions to the general requirement that an employee must provide notice of the need for leave due to a serious health condition. *Burnett v. LFW, Inc.*, 472 F.3d 471, 479 (7th Cir. 2006); *Leonard v. Uhlich Children's Advantage Network*, 481 F. Supp. 2d 931 (N.D. Ill. 2007). An employee may request FMLA leave where circumstances provide the employer with sufficient notice of the need for leave or when the employee is incapable of providing such notice. *Burnett*, 472 F.3d at 479; *Leonard*, 2007 U.S. Dist. LEXIS 27099, at *8.

An employee may "request" leave by engaging in unusual behavior. That was the conclusion of the Seventh Circuit in *Byrne v. Avon Products, Inc.*, 328 F.3d 379, 381 (7th Cir. 2003), *cert. denied*, 540 U.S. 881 (2003). In that case, a model employee began to act unusually by sleeping on the job and spending long hours in a back room. He subsequently was diagnosed with depression, causing him to hallucinate. The employee was fired for sleeping on the job. In vacating judgment for the employer, the court held that an employee's unusual behavior alone was all the notice required in order for an employee to be entitled to the benefits and protections of the FMLA. According to the court:

> It is not beyond the bounds of reasonableness to treat a dramatic change in behavior as notice of a medical problem. That's clear enough if a worker collapses: an employer might suspect a stroke, or a heart attack, or insulin deficiency, or some other serious condition. It would be silly to require the unconscious worker to inform the employer verbally or in writing. Unusual behavior gives all the notice required, and no employer would be allowed to say, "I fired this stricken person for shirking on company time, and by the time a physician arrived and told me why the worker was unconscious it was too late to claim FMLA leave." A sudden change may supply notice even if the employee is lucid: someone who breaks an arm obviously requires leave. It is enough under the FMLA if the employer knows of the employee's need for leave; the employee need not mention the Statute or demand its benefits. *See, e.g., Price v. Ft. Wayne,* 117 F.3d 1022, 1026 (7th Cir. 1997).

Accord Burnett v. LFW, Inc., 472 F.3d 471, 478 (7th Cir. 2006) (unusual behavior may provide notice where employee's illness impedes employee's ability to communicate need for FMLA leave); *Williams v. Illinois Dept. of Corrections*, No. 05-cv-4227-JPG, 2007 U.S. Dist. LEXIS 17119, at *17 (S.D. Ill. March 9, 2007) (dramatic change in employee's behavior may be sufficient to alert an employer that an employee suffers from a serious health condition for which FMLA leave may be appropriate); *Lozano v. Kay Mfg., Co.*, No. 04 C 2784, 2005 U.S. Dist. LEXIS 26930, at *17 (N.D. Ill. Nov. 3, 2005) (performance evaluation drop from meets expectations to meets expectations minus sufficient to raise material issue of fact regarding whether employer on notice employee needed FMLA leave for mental condition precluding summary judgment).

An employer after *Byrne* must now be clairvoyant. The employer must determine whether an employee's "unusual behavior" is such that FMLA leave is implicated. The case transfers the onus of requesting FMLA leave, at least where the need for leave is not foreseeable, from the employee to the employer. The decision represents the opening of a Pandora's box of problems for employers who now must guess that an employee who is acting "unusually" has a serious health condition within the meaning of the FMLA and that it is "obvious" that the employee needs job-protected leave. Of course, for employees, the case presents an opportunity to argue that their employer failed to divine notice from the circumstances.

In *McNeela et al. v. United Airlines, Inc.*, No. 98–C–1433, 1999 U.S. Dist. LEXIS 20042 (N.D. Ill. May 13, 1999), the court held that an employee was excused from requesting leave where the employee was angry about being injured at work, and was advised by his attorneys not to have any contact with anyone at United. The court held that since United knew that this individual was injured at work (having visited him in the Hospital), and that he may need leave, a question of fact exited whether the employee provided sufficient notice of the need for FMLA-qualifying leave.

(3) Notice Need Not Expressly Invoke FMLA

Whether paid or unpaid, the request for FMLA leave need not expressly invoke the FMLA by name in order to receive the protections of the Act. *See Burnett v. LFW, Inc.*, 472 F.3d 471, 478 (7th Cir. Dec. 26, 2006); *Phillips v. Quebecor World RAI Inc.*, 450 F.3d 308, 311 (6th Cir. 2006); *Moorer v. Baptist Mem. Health Care System*, 398 F.3d 469 (6th Cir. 2005); *Hoffman v. Professional Med Team*, 394 F.3d 414, 418 (6th Cir. 2005); *Spangler v. Federal Home Loan Bank of Des Moines*, 278 F.3d 847, 852 (8th Cir. 2002); *Bailey v. Southwest Gas Co.*, 275 F.3d 1181, 1185 (9th Cir. 2002); *Sanghvi v. Frendel et al.*, No. 00–7538, 2000 U.S. App. LEXIS 31757 (2d Cir. Dec. 7, 2000); *Medina v. Coors Brewing Co.*, No. 99–1463, 2000 U.S. App. LEXIS 27577 (10th Cir. Nov. 3, 2000); *Thorson v. Gemini, Inc. et al.*, 205 F.3d 370, 381 (8th Cir. 2000), *cert. denied*, 531 U.S. 871 (2000); *Price v. City of Fort Wayne, Ind.*, 117 F.3d 1022, 1025–26 (7th Cir. 1997); *Manuel v. Westlake Polymers Corp.*, 66 F.3d 758, 763–764 (5th Cir. 1995) (the court rejected contention that FMLA requires employees to invoke the Act by name, and to specific subparagraphs therein, stating, "These are workers, not lawyers"); *Morran v. Nevada System of Higher Ed.*, No. 3:05-CV-00577-ECR (RAM), 2007 U.S. Dist. LEXIS 27796, at *14 (D. Nev. March 30, 2007); *Tambash v. St. Bonaventure Univ.*, No. 99CV967, 2004 U.S. Dist. LEXIS 19914, at *31 (W.D.N.Y. Sept. 24, 2004)

(4) Vague Requests for FMLA Leave

The quality of the notice provided by the eligible employee of the need for FMLA leave is a frequently litigated issue. In these cases the issue frequently is whether the employee imparted sufficient information to shift the burden of further inquiry to the employer. An employee bears the initial burden of providing the employer with sufficient notice to make the employer aware that the employee needs FMLA-qualifying leave. If additional information is needed in order to determine whether the leave is FMLA-qualifying, the employer is required to ask for that information. The courts are all over the place on the quality and quantity of information that an employee may impart in order to shift the burden to the employer to make further inquiry. If the court determines that the burden shifted to the employer and the employer did not make further inquiry, the employer will be found in violation of the Act.

A large number of the litigated cases involve employee notice consisting of statements that the employee or a covered family member is sick, ill, not feeling well on, is going to see the doctor. Although these issues are highly specific to the circumstances in each case, a majority of cases have found these types of employee requests to be vague and otherwise insufficient to meet the employee's initial burden to notify the employer that the employee needs FMLA-qualifying leave. *See Burnett v. LFW, Inc.*, 472 F.3d 471, 478 (7th Cir. Dec. 26, 2006) (employee reference to being "sick" generally insufficient notice of the need for FMLA leave); *Woods v. DaimlerChrysler Corp.*, 409 F.3d 984, 991 (8th Cir. 2005); *Brenneman v. MidCentral Health System*, 366 F.3d 412, 421 (6th Cir. 2004), *cert. denied*, 2005 U.S. LEXIS 1474 (U.S. 2005) (employee's call indicating that "he wasn't doing well and wouldn't be in today" was found to be insufficient notice of the need for FMLA-qualifying leave); *Peeples v. Coastal Office Products, Inc.*, 64 Fed. Appx. 860 (4th Cir. 2003); *Levine v. The Children's Museum of Indianapolis, Inc.*, No. 02–3013, 2003 U.S. App. LEXIS 5755 (7th Cir. March 24, 2003); *Collins v. NTN-Bower, Corp.*, 272 F.3d 1006, 1008–1009 (7th Cir. 2001) ("sick" does not imply an FMLA-covered serious health condition); *Medina v. Coors Brewing Co.*, No. 99–1463, 2000 U.S. App. LEXIS 27577 (10th Cir. Nov. 3, 2000) (an employee stipulation that absences were due to personal business and to being "sick" failed to furnish Coors with sufficient information to apprise it of the employee's need for leave due to a potentially FMLA-qualifying reason); *Seaman v. CSPH, Inc. et al.*, 179 F.3d 297, 302 (5th Cir. 1999) (an employee who never requested leave but merely informed employer that he might be suffering from bipolar disorder and needed time off to see a doctor, but who never scheduled a doctor's appointment nor requested leave for a certain day following conversation failed to provide adequate notice of need for FMLA leave); *Browning v. Liberty Mutual Insurance Co.*, 178 F.3d 1043, 1049 (8th Cir.,) (notice that an employee's arm went numb insufficient notice), *cert. denied*, 120 S. Ct. 588 (1999); *Satterfield v. Wal-Mart Stores, Inc.*, 135 F.3d 973, 980 (5th Cir. 1998) (reversing judgment for the plaintiff where, as a matter of law, notes stating that the plaintiff had pain in her side and would not be able to work that day, combined with report to manager that the plaintiff was "sick," insufficient to apprise employer of request to take time off for a "serious health condition"), *cert. denied*, 119 S. Ct. 72 (1998); *Carter v. Ford Motor Co.*, 121 F.3d 1146, 1148–49 (8th Cir. 1997) (statement that the employee was sick and unable to work insufficient notice of need for FMLA leave); *Rask v. Fresenius Med. Care North America*, No. 05-1267, 2006 U.S. Dist. LEXIS 78251, at *49 (D. Minn. Oct. 26, 2006) (vague comments about medication and calling-in sick insufficient notice); *Nicolatos v. Sprint/United Management Co.*, No. 1:05-CV-1722-RLV, 2006 U.S. Dist. LEXIS 76628, at *8-11 (N.D. Ga. Oct. 19, 2006) (employee telling employer he fell, was in a lot of pain, hit his head, and was having x-rays, without a request for leave, found insufficient notice); *Medina-Salas v. Tyson Fresh Meats, Inc.*, No. 4:05CV3211, 2006 U.S. Dist. LEXIS 67612, at *25 (D. Neb. Sept. 20, 2006) (indicating to an employer that employee is "sick" or "ill" insufficient notice); *Blazier v. St. John Med. Center, Inc.*, No. 05-CV-

0466-TCK-FHM, 2006 U.S. Dist. LEXIS 64607, at *8 (N.D. Okla. Sept. 7, 2006) (calling in "sick" insufficient notice).

A minority of cases have either held that notice that an employee or covered family member is sick, ill, not feeling well, going to visit the doctor, etc. is sufficient to shift the burden of inquiry to the employer, or such notice was at least sufficient to defeat a motion for summary judgment. See *Price v. City of Fort Wayne, Ind.*, 117 F.3d 1022, 1025 (7th Cir. 1997) (an employee who cited "medical need" as reason for leave on the employer's leave form and who attached a doctor's notice stating that the plaintiff could not work put the employer on notice that leave might be for FMLA reasons); *Ode v. Mount Sinai Med. Center*, No. 04 Civ. 9632 (DLC), 2006 U.S. Dist. LEXIS 41479, at *15-16 (S.D.N.Y. June 22, 2006) (calling in sick three consecutive days with doctors note indicating employee was unable to work due to severe neck pain sufficient to trigger employers' duty to inquire further); *Barr v. New York City Transit Authority*, No. 99–CV–7927 (FB), 2002 U.S. Dist. LEXIS 2968 (E.D.N.Y. Feb. 20, 2002) (an employee notice of "swelling an tightness in legs" sufficient to apprise employer of need to take time off for a serious health condition); *Mann v. Mass. Correa Electric et al.*, No. 00 CIV. 3559 (DLC), 2002 U.S. Dist. LEXIS 949 (S.D.N.Y. Jan. 23, 2002) (an employee notice that she was experiencing "acute lumbosacral sprain" sufficient to raise issue of fact whether she provided adequate notice of need for FMLA leave); *Sims v. Alameda–Contra Costa Transit District et al.*, 2 F. Supp. 2d 1253, 1267–68 (N.D. Cal. 1998) (an employee telephone instruction that he be placed in the "sick book" along with doctor's notes sufficient to trigger employer duty to inquire further); *McClain v. Southwest Steel Co.*, Inc., 940 F. Supp. 295, 299–300 (N.D. Ok. 1996) (material issue of fact whether plaintiff provided sufficient notice when she called her employer and reported herself ill with a migraine headache); *Wilson v. Lemington Home of the Aged*, 159 F. Supp. 2d 186, 191–92 (W.D. Pa. 2001) (an employee's phone call to supervisor that she was taking personal leave because she was suffering chest pains, was vomiting and had diarrhea was sufficient notice under FMLA); *Shivakumar v. Abbott Labs. et al.*, No. 99 7861, 2001 U.S. Dist. LEXIS 9628 (N.D. Ill. July 10, 2001) (an employee statement that she "could not work" was both a request for leave and created genuine dispute whether the employer's obligations to inquire further were triggered under the FMLA); *Bell v. Jewell Food Store*, 83 F. Supp. 2d 951, 957 (N.D. Ill. 2000) (suggesting that the employer might have had duty to inquire further where the employee simply called in sick, without explaining how he was sick); *Routes v. Henderson*, 58 F. Supp. 2d 959, 981 (S.D. Ind. 1999) (an employee's notice that he needed time off to be treated for severe headaches on an inpatient basis at a hospital sufficient notice that leave might qualify for FMLA protections); *Mitchell v. Continental Plastic Containers, Inc.*, No. C–1–97–412, 1998 U.S. Dist. LEXIS 21465 (S.D. Ohio March 3, 1998) (although an employee notice failed to state reason for leave, doctor's note indicating "Off work from October 17–20" sufficient to create material issue of fact whether employee provided adequate notice of need for FMLA leave); *Bryant v. Delbar*, 18 F. Supp. 2d 799 (M.D. Tenn. 1998) (statement that the employee's son was in the hospital and the employee had to work things out held sufficient to shift burden to the employer to inquiry further); *Vincent v. Wells Fargo Guard Services, Inc. of Florida*, 3 F. Supp. 2d 1045 (S.D. Fla. 1998) (notice by an employee's wife that the employee was being hospitalized sufficient); *Brannon v. Oshkosh B'Gosh, Inc.*, 897 F. Supp. 1028, 1039 (M.D. Tenn. 1995) (an employee who told the employer that the employee's daughter was sick on two successive days and on return to work the third day provided sufficient notice that leave may be FMLA–qualifying).

Of course, employees who offer reasons for leave that are not covered conditions within the meaning of the FMLA have not provided adequate notice of the need for FMLA leave. See *Russell v. First Health Services et al.*, 11 Fed. Appx. 221 (4th Cir. 2001) (an employee request of "personal leave" insufficient notice of need for FMLA leave); *Sanghvi v. Frendel et al.*, No. 00–7538, 2000 U.S. App. LEXIS 31757 (2d Cir. Dec. 7, 2000) (an employee request for vacation to visit the employee's father in India after death of mother held insufficient notice of need for FMLA leave); *Hoban v. WBNCC Joint Venture*, No. 06-13142, 2007 U.S. Dist. LEXIS 25407, at *12 (E.D. Mich. April 5, 2007) (request for leave to take care of affairs of deceased brother); *De Hoyas Bristol Laboratories, Corp.*, 218 F. Supp. 2d 222, 226–27 (D.P.R. 2002) (an employee who asked for "floating day" and for extension of accrued paid vacation not entitled to FMLA protections where the employee never indicated that the leave was to care for the mother's deteriorating health condition); *McCarron v. British Telecom et al.*, No. 00–CV–6123, 2002 U.S. Dist. LEXIS 15151 (E.D. Pa. Aug. 7, 2002) (the employee requesting leave to "remedy a family situation" insufficient notice, particularly where the employee refused to respond to the employer's subsequent inquires to clarify whether leave was FMLA–qualifying); *Davila v. Hilton International of Puerto Rico, Inc.*, 165 F. Supp. 2d 94 (D.P.R. 2001) (employee request for leave to make repairs to home due to damage caused by hurricane insufficient notice of need for FMLA leave); *Oracle Corp. v. Curtis et al.*, No. 00–1650–HA, 2001 U.S. Dist. LEXIS 10937 (D. Ore. July 13, 2001) (reasonable jury could conclude that the employee failed to provide Oracle with sufficient information about his need for leave to trigger any obligation by Oracle to inquire further where the employee told his supervisor he was disenchanted with Oracle and needed some time off); *Niese v. General Electric Co.*, No. IP 99–1457–C–T/G, 2001 U.S. Dist. LEXIS 5352 (S.D. Ind. Jan. 31, 2001) (request for leave for "personal problems and child care issues").

Inadequate employee notice of a need for FMLA leave may also result from vagueness regarding when leave may be taken and the amount of that leave. In *Bailey v. Amsted Industries, Inc.*, 172 F.3d 1041, 1045–46 (8th Cir. 1999), the employee suffered from depression and hypothyroidism. Bailey alleged that he provided sufficient notice of the need for FMLA leave by his employer's knowledge that he had serious health conditions, was under medical care, and needed to miss work "from time to time." The Eighth Circuit disagreed, holding that:

> An attempt to satisfy the notice requirements by an indication that he might have to be absent at some unforeseen time in the future satisfies neither the requirement of notice of "the anticipated timing and duration of the leave," 29 CFR 825.302(c), nor the requirement of notice "as soon as practicable if dates…were initially unknown," 29 CFR 825.302(a).

The case should prove helpful to employers with so-called "blank check" requests for FMLA leave at undetermined times in the future.

(5) Knowledge of Prior FMLA–Covered Condition

A number of courts have addressed whether an employer had knowledge that an employee or a covered family member suffered from a serious health condition prior to an employee's notice of a need for leave. Again, the courts are split on the impact of this prior knowledge on the quality of notice the employee must initially provide in order to tip the burden on to the employer to make further inquiry.

In evaluating whether adequate notice was given, courts consider the totality of the circumstances, including whether the employer was aware that the employee suffered from a serious health condition and whether the employee previously requested FMLA leave. *Goodman v. Bestbuy, Inc.*, No. 05-157 (DSD/JJG), 2006 U.S. Dist. LEXIS 88093, at *11 (D. Minn. Dec. 4, 2006); *Hansen v. Mannheim Services Corp.*, No. 04-4775(DSD/SRN), 2006 U.S. Dist. LEXIS 1919, at *12 (D. Minn. Jan 9, 2006). The better reasoned decisions have held that employee notice in these circumstances must at least allude to the prior covered condition in order to meet the employee's initial burden to provide sufficient information that the employee may be requesting FMLA–qualifying leave, thereby shifting the burden of inquiry to the employer. For example, in *Medina v. Coors Brewing Co.*, No. 99–1463, 2000 U.S. App. LEXIS 27577 (10th Cir. Nov. 3, 2000), the circuit court rejected the plaintiff's contention that his employer should have known that his absence was due to depression because the employer previously granted FMLA leave for that condition. In rejecting this argument, the court noted that the employee's prior leave of absence ended when his doctor released him to return to work, and the employee never subsequently indicated that his inability to work was due to depression. Clearly, the court was saying that an employer's prior knowledge that the employee suffered from a serious health condition in the past does not relieve the employee from properly notifying the employer of a present need for FMLA leave absent a connection or reference to the previous covered condition. *Accord Cruz v. Publix Super Markets, Inc.*, 428 F.3d 1379, 1385 (11th Cir. 2005); *Adams v. Honda of America Mfg., Inc.*, 111 Fed. Appx. 353 (6th Cir. 2004); *Spangler v. Federal Home Loan Bank of Des Moines*, 278 F.3d 847, 852 (8th Cir. 2002); *Paulson v. Superior Plating, Inc.*, No. 03–3118 (RHK/AJB), 2004 U.S. Dist. LEXIS 19383, at *12 (D. Minn. Sept. 27, 2004); *Tambash v. St. Bonaventure Univ.*, No. 99CV967, 2004 U.S. Dist. LEXIS 19914, at *30 (W.D.N.Y. Sept. 24, 2004); *Henson v. Bell Helicopter Textron, Inc.*, No. 4:01–CV–1024–Y, 2004 U.S. Dist. LEXIS 1630, at *39–40 (N.D. Tex. Feb. 6, 2004), aff'd, 2005 U.S. App. LEXIS 6600 (5th Cir. 2005); *Jennings v. Parade Publications*, No. 01 Civ. 8590 (TPG), 2003 U.S. Dist. LEXIS 17088, at *8–12 (S.D.N.Y. Sept. 30, 2003); *Barngrover v. W.W. Transport*, No. 3:02–cv–40020, 2003 U.S. Dist. LEXIS 13145, at *26–28 (S.D. Iowa July 24, 2003); *Miller v. GB Sales & Service, Inc.*, 275 F. Supp. 2d 823, 829–830 (E.D. Mich. 2003).

The court in *Schmuttee v. Resort Condominiums International, LLC*, 463 F. Supp. 2d 891, 911 (S.D. Ind. Nov. 29, 2006), held that an employer with prior knowledge of an employee's medical situation has the duty to inquire further where the employee requests medical leave. Absent linkage of each absence to the known FMLA–covered condition, an employee does not have the right to take unscheduled leave at a moment's notice. *Henson v. Bell Helicopter Textron, Inc.*, No. 4:01–CV–1024–Y, 2004 U.S. Dist. LEXIS 1630, at *38 (N.D. Tex. Feb. 6, 2004), aff'd, 2005 U.S. App. LEXIS 6600 (5th Cir. 2005).

In *Collins v. The U.S. Playing Card Co.*, 466 F.3d 954, 965-66 (S.D. Ohio 2006), the employee provided sufficient information of the need for intermittent FMLA leave where he previously advised his employer that he was diabetic and would need intermittent leave. His subsequent request (for which he was disciplined) to take an early break to eat because of his diabetes let the employer know that he needed leave due to his known serious health condition.

In *Hastings v. Carlson Marketing Group, Inc.*, No. 04-3370 (DWF/JSM), 2005 U.S. Dist. LEXIS 25808, at *18-20 (D. Minn. Oct.

27, 2005), the court found that the employee failed to notify his employer he needed FMLA-qualifying leave. At the time the employee was out on FMLA leave for depression. On the day the employee was scheduled to return to work he called and informed his supervisor that he had a toothache and was going to an emergency dentist appointment. The court found that, by stating that he suffered from a toothache, the employee "dispelled any assumption that his absence was related to his previous medical leave for depression."

In *Tambash v. St. Bonaventure Univ.*, No. 99CV967, 2004 U.S. Dist. LEXIS 19914, at *32–35 (W.D.N.Y. Sept. 24, 2004), the court found that the employee's present request for leave was "somewhat equivocal," however, because the employer was aware that the employee was being treated for anxiety and depression and took time off in the past for same, the employee's statement to his supervisor that he could no longer work due to mental anguish and that he wanted sick leave was held to be sufficient notice of a need for FMLA leave.

Where the employee with a known FMLA-covered condition fails to link the present need for FMLA leave with that condition, courts are less inclined to find that an employee provided adequate notice of the need for FMLA leave. For example, in *Brenneman v. MidCentral Health System*, 366 F.3d 412, 421 n.9 (6th Cir. 2004), *cert. denied*, 2005 U.S. LEXIS 1474 (U.S. 2005), a known diabetic employee called in sick stating that "he wasn't doing well and wouldn't be in today." He never mentioned that his illness was related to his known diabetic condition until after his termination. According to the court, "even if plaintiff's assertions were true—that defendant knew of plaintiff's diabetes and his past need for FMLA leave for diabetes-related absences, they are insufficient to create a genuine issue of material fact as to whether plaintiff's 'call-in' gave defendant sufficient notice that his March 31st absence was FMLA-qualifying."

In *Adams v. Honda of America Mfg., Inc.*, 111 Fed. Appx. 353 (6th Cir. 2004), the employee had a FMLA certification on file that, she argued, notified the employer that she may need to take intermittent leave. The employee claimed that this was sufficient notice to cover the absences at issue. The court concluded that the employee failed to establish that the absences at issue were related to the same qualifying medical condition.

In *Hobart v. Behavioral Connections of Wood County, Inc.*, No. 3:03CV7313, 2004 U.S. Dist. LEXIS 12051, at *23–24 (N.D. Ohio July 1, 2004), the court found that the employee provided adequate notice of the need for FMLA leave. Although the medical note from his doctor did not describe the health condition that generated the doctor's request that the employee be excused from work for 14 days, the court found the doctor's note was sufficient to shift the burden of inquiry on to the employer to request further information. This was particularly true, the court found, where the employer knew that in the past year the employee incurred several health-related absences, which were supported by medical documentation referencing ongoing treatment. According to the court, "[t]his information suggests that defendant knew, or at the very least, should have presumed, that plaintiff's request for leave might be FMLA-qualifying." The court denied the employer's motion for summary judgment.

An employer's prior knowledge of an employee's serious health condition does not relieve the employee from having to request leave. In *Loring v. Advanced Foods, Inc.*, No. C02-4067-PAZ, 2004 U.S. Dist. LEXIS 6172, at *17 (N.D. Iowa April 9, 2004), *aff'd* 2005 U.S. App. LEXIS 4124 (8th Cir. 2005), the court rejected the employee's argument that, although he did not request leave of any kind, the employer had notice of his need for FMLA leave because it knew he had a serious health condition, he was under medical care, and he could not perform his current duties. The employee had medical restrictions, which prohibited him from prolonged exposure to cold. He worked in the cold as a laborer at a meat processing plant. Because the employer had no work at the plant within his medical restrictions, the employee was terminated. Loring argued that had his employer granted FMLA leave, he could have recovered sufficiently to resume full-time work in the cold. Rejecting the employee's argument as an attempt to shift the notice burden to the employer, the court noted this "satisfies neither the requirement of notice of the anticipated timing and duration of the leave, nor the requirement of notice as soon as practicable if dates…were initially unknown."

Courts also allow employers to rely on so-called "negative certifications" as a basis for deciding whether an employee advanced an FMLA-qualifying reason for leave. In *Stoops v. One Call Communications, Inc.*, 141 F.3d 309, 312–313 (7th Cir. 1998), the circuit court found that an employee failed to provide sufficient information to alert the employer that the FMLA-qualifying leave was being requested. Stoops previously submitted a medical certification indicating that his chronic fatigue syndrome was not an FMLA-covered condition as it was not presently incapacitating. Stoops was informed that his absences for chronic fatigue syndrome were not FMLA-qualifying. Stoops continued to be absent from work for chronic fatigue. The absences were not designated as FMLA-qualifying. The employer eventually fired Stoops for attendance. Stoops sued, alleging that his requests were for FMLA leave. The employer did not disagree that Stoops provided sufficient notice that he needed FMLA leave. Rather, the employer alleged that Stoops never provided it with notice that his absences were due to an FMLA-qualifying reason. The employer relied on the prior medical certification that indicated that the chronic fatigue syndrome Stoops suffered from was not FMLA-qualifying. The court rejected Stoops' argument that the employer could only rely on information he provided, and if it had a question regarding this it had to make further inquiry or request another medical certification. Rather, the court held that the employer could rely on a prior negative medical certification that Stoops already provided. *Accord Nawrocki v. United Methodist Retirement Communities, Inc.*, 174 Fed. Appx. 334 (6th Cir. 2006); *Brown v. Goodyear Tire and Rubber Co.*, No. 4:04CV327, 2006 U.S. Dist. LEXIS 23100, at *37 (D. Neb. April 24, 2006); *Collins v. Merck-Medco RX Services of Texas, LLC*, No. 3:00-CV-1852-X, 2001 U.S. Dist. LEXIS 15143 (N.D. Tex. Sept. 24, 2001).

Closely related to the "negative certification" cases are those where doctors have cleared an employee to return to work and following the return to work, the employee needs leave. The employee claims that the employer should have known that the leave was FMLA-qualifying based on knowledge of the prior condition. Courts, however, have held that, absent new information, the medical clearance of an employee to return to work may negate any inference that a subsequent request for leave was FMLA-qualifying. *See Browning v. Liberty Mutual Insurance Co.*, 178 F.3d 1043, 1049 (8th Cir. 1999) (the employee failed to provide sufficient notice of the need for FMLA leave where medical certification cleared the employee to return to work and the employee notice of the need for leave related to cleared medical condition), *cert. denied* 120 S. Ct. 588 (1999); *Robinson v. Overnite Transportation Co.*, No. 95-3067, 1997 U.S. App. LEXIS 6574 (4th Cir. April 9, 1997); *Niese v. General Electric Co.*, No. IP 99-1457-C-T/G, 2001 U.S. Dist. LEXIS 5352 (S.D. Ind. Jan. 31, 2001) (release to return to work without medical restrictions from depression prevented the employer from guessing that request for leave for "personal problems and child care issues" was a request for FMLA leave due to depression).

Other courts have been more forgiving to employees. These courts have not required the initial employee notice to refer, however obliquely, to the known covered condition. Rather, these cases tend to emphasize the employer's duty to make further inquiry where it is known that the employee has been eligible for FMLA leave in the past due to a covered condition. *See Rhoads v. FDIC*, 956 F. Supp. 1239 (D. Md. 1997), *aff'd in part, rev'd and remanded on other grounds*, 257 F.3d 373 (4th Cir. 2001), *cert. denied*, 535 U.S. 933 (2002) (issue of fact whether the employee with known asthma condition who notified the employer of need to extend leave because she still did not feel well enough to work).

The cases that require linkage of the prior FMLA covered condition with the present notice of the need for leave are better reasoned because they treat employees who have used FMLA leave in the past no better or worse than employees who have not used FMLA leave. Like anyone else, employees who have used FMLA leave in the past are just as likely to get flat tires, go to the ball game rather than to work, get a cold, or otherwise not show up to work for reasons having nothing to do with the FMLA. Absent linkage to the past covered condition, these employees should be treated the same as any other employee requesting leave. The cases that do not require the establishment of a linkage between the past use of FMLA leave and the current notice of a need for leave are overly paternalistic and invite discriminatory treatment. By requiring less initial employee notice and quickly shifting the burden of inquiry to employers, these cases inadvertently encourage employers to make inquiries, for example, of why an employee is requesting to use annual leave that would not be made to another employee. Such disparate treatment is prohibited by the Act and should be discouraged rather than encouraged.

(6) Notice Based on Types of Covered Conditions

A number of courts have found that employees satisfy their initial burden of providing sufficient information of the need for FMLA leave, thereby shifting the burden of inquiry to the employer, by explicit reference to specific covered conditions. *See Williams v. Illinois Dept. of Corrections*, No. 05-cv-4227-JPG, 2007 U.S. Dist. LEXIS 17119, at 17 (S.D. Ill. March 9, 2007) (employee request for leave due to very ill mother needing kidney dialysis should have alerted employer that leave was covered by the FMLA; kidney disease requiring dialysis clearly qualifies as a serious health condition); *Darboe v. Staples, Inc. et al.*, 243 F. Supp. 2d 5, 2003 U.S. Dist. LEXIS 2068 (S.D.N.Y. Feb. 7, 2003) (an employee notice to the employer of the need for leave for surgery sufficient notice of the need for FMLA leave to defeat motion for summary judgment); *Tornberg v. Business Interlink Services, Inc.*, 237 F. Supp. 2d 778, 785 (E.D. Mich. 2002) (an employee notice to an employer of the need for leave due to kidney stone sufficient notice to shift burden to the employer to request additional information); *Wilson v. Lemington Home for the Aged*, 159 F. Supp. 2d 186, 192 (W.D. Pa. 2001) (an employee notice of vomiting, diarrhea, and chest pains coupled with verbal report by doctor indicating that the employee needed leave for a month sufficient notice of the need for FMLA leave); *Routes v. Henderson*, 58 F. Supp. 2d 959, 981 (S.D. Ind. 1999) ("When Routes notified

Gould that he needed time off from work to be treated for his severe headaches on an inpatient basis at a hospital, he supplied sufficient notice to his employer that his leave might qualify for FMLA-protection); *Mora v. Chem-Tronics, Inc.*, 16 F. Supp. 2d 1192, 1212 (S.D. Cal. 1998) (notice that employee's son was HIV positive, had very high fever, and that the employee could not leave the son when he is so ill sufficient); *Barone v. Leukemia Society of America*, 42 F. Supp. 2d 452, 460 (D.N.J. 1998) (notice of kidney stone and diagnosis of husband with terminal cancer sufficient); *Bryant v. Delbar*, 18 F. Supp. 2d 799 (M.D. Tenn. 1998) (statement that "My son is in the hospital and I've got to work things out" sufficient notice of potential need for FMLA leave); *Vincent v. Wells Fargo Guard Services, Inc., of Fla.*, 3 F. Supp. 2d 1405 (S.D. Fla. 1998) (notice by wife of employee that employee was being hospitalized held sufficient notice); *Vargo-Adams v. USPS*, 992 F. Supp. 939 (N.D. Ohio 1998) (question of fact whether an employee's notice that absences were due to migraine headaches was sufficient to put the employer on notice leave may be FMLA-qualifying); *Viereck v. City of Gloucester City*, 961 F. Supp. 703, 707 (D.N.J. 1997) (an employee's telephone call informing the employer that the employee was hospitalized and would be unable to return to work for some time due to her medical condition held sufficient notice of need for FMLA leave).

Courts have split on whether notice is sufficient based on the same serious health condition. In *Reich v. Midwest Plastic engineering, Inc.*, No. 1:94-CV-525, 1995 U.S. Dist. LEXIS 8772 (W.D. Mich. June 6, 1995), the district court held that an employee's notice that she missed work due to chicken pox was insufficient. In *George v. Associated Stationers*, 932 F. Supp. 1012 (N.D. Ohio 1996); the district court held that the employee's notice that he missed work due to chicken pox was sufficient to shift the burden to the employer to request additional information to determine if the need for leave was FMLA-qualifying.

The Seventh Circuit held that notice that an employee suffers from multiple conditions is sufficient to put an employer on notice that the employee is requesting FMLA leave. The employer then had an obligation to inquire further. *Price v. City of Fort Wayne, Ind.*, 117 F.3d 1022, 1025-26 (7th Cir. 1997) (the employee filled out the employer's leave request form and indicated that the case was medical need; she also attached doctor's note explaining multiple conditions necessitating a need for leave).

(7) False or Misleading Information

Employers are entitled to truthful information in order to determine whether an employee's request for leave is FMLA-qualifying. An employee may not provide an employer with false information for the need for leave that fits within the protections of the FMLA, even if the real reason also fits within the definition of the FMLA. In *Gay v. Gilman Paper Co.*, 125 F.3d 1432, 1434 (11th Cir. 1997), the employee was admitted to a Houston psychiatric hospital to receive treatment for a nervous breakdown. The employee's husband called Gilman Paper and advised them that the employee was in an Atlanta hospital having some tests run. The husband subsequently admitted that he lied to Gilman Paper about his wife's whereabouts and condition. He also admitted that he instructed his sons not to give Gilman Paper any information regarding Gay's condition or location. Gay argued that her husband's assertion that she was in the hospital for tests was sufficient to put Gilman on notice that her condition was potentially FMLA-qualifying, shifting the burden to Gilman to make further inquiry as to whether her absence was in fact qualified for treatment under the FMLA. *Gay*, 125 F.3d at 1434. The circuit court disagreed. The court found that, not only was there a dearth of information provided, but the information that was provided was false. According to the court:

> Gay's husband deliberately withheld information concerning the true nature of her condition and instructed his sons to do the same. Under these circumstances, the burden to request further information never shifted to Gilman because Gilman could not reasonably be expected to conclude that Gay's absence might have qualified for treatment under the FMLA.

The case appears to stand for the proposition that an employee is obligated to provide all of the information it has on hand regarding the condition in order for the employer to determine whether the leave is FMLA-qualifying. An employee that deliberately withholds information that might be useful to the employer in determining whether to designate the leave as FMLA leave fails to impart sufficient information to reasonably apprise the employer of the employee's request to take time off for a serious health condition. This is true even if the information that is imparted was at least sufficient to trigger further inquiry on the part of the employer. Presumably, the court's decision is designed to do away with gamesmanship in the notice process by requiring complete disclosure of all known relevant facts regarding the covered condition that forms the basis of the request for FMLA leave.

The Fourth Circuit also found that employee notice that is deliberately evasive and misleading was insufficient to inform the employer that the employee was requesting FMLA leave. In *Peeples v. Coastal Office Products, Inc.*, 64 Fed. Appx. 860 (4th Cir. 2003), despite repeated requests, the employee gave only the vaguest statements about his diagnosis and possible return date. He falsely indicated that his medical condition was related to a thyroid disorder. At no time did Peoples or his physician advise Coastal that Peeples was suffering from a psychiatric condition. The court found that Coastal was "utterly incapable of making a preliminary determination whether Peeples' absence was justified…because Peeples and his doctor were providing incomplete responses, indeed dishonest responses, to defendant's informal requests for information." As a result, Peeples' termination did not violate the FMLA.

Other courts have not harped on an employee's lack of honesty when notifying the employer of the need for FMLA leave. Rather, the courts in these cases simply analyze the sufficiency of the notice provided by the employee. For example, in *McCarron v. British Telecom et al.*, No. 00–CV-6123, 2002 U.S. Dist. LEXIS 15151 (E.D. Pa. Aug. 7, 2002), the employee left a voicemail message requesting "Family Leave" to deal with a "family situation." It was undisputed that this was not the real reason for the leave. Rather, the leave apparently had to do with psychological problems suffered by the plaintiff. The employer granted the plaintiff FMLA leave for psychological problems a year before this request. The employee also rebuffed the efforts of the employer to obtain additional information regarding the employee's need for FMLA leave. The district court did not concentrate on the employee's lack of honesty, but analyzed the case based on the information imparted by the employee. The court found that information lacking, and held that the employee failed to give the employer adequate notice of the need for FMLA leave. As a result, FMLA protections did not apply, and the employee's termination did not violate the FMLA.

In *Larson v. Endodontic & Periodontic Assoc., Ltd.*, No. 04 C 7305, 2006 U.S. Dist. LEXIS 53541, at *15 (N.D. Ill. July 17, 2006), the employee informed her employer that she needed leave for treatment for Graves disease. She did not have Graves disease. Larson had a similar, but less serious, thyroid disease. The court noted that Larson gave the employer sufficient notice of an FMLA-qualifying condition by providing the employer a reason to believe that Larson might need medical treatment for a thyroid condition that would require her to be away from work for an extended period of time. The court cited the fact that Larson stated a condition that was more serious than the condition she actually suffered as a factor in favor of its determination that the employee provided adequate notice of her need for FMLA leave. Interestingly, it is unclear from the case why Larson believed she had Graves disease.

(8) Inability to Provide Notice

A person who is unable to provide notice of a need for FMLA leave is excused from doing so. *Byrne v. Avon Products, Inc.*, 328 F.3d 379, 382 (7th Cir. 2003), *cert. denied*, 540 U.S. 881 (2003). In *Byrne*, the court interpreted the provision in § 825.303(a) that an employee need not give notice of the need for FMLA–qualifying leave within no more than one or two working days of learning of the need for leave, *except in extraordinary circumstances where such notice is not feasible.* (emphasis in original). According to the court, if a person (such as Byrne) with "major depression could not have told his employer about the problem and requested leave, then notice was not 'feasible' and was unnecessary." This was true even if the employee's change in behavior was not enough to alert the employer to a need for medical leave.

The rule is limited to "extraordinary circumstances." In *Byrne*, the employee began sleeping on the job and spending hours in a back room. It was subsequently determined that he suffered from "major depression," and that such depression manifested itself in hallucinations and suicide attempts at about the time the employee was sleeping at work.

The above decision will open the floodgates for arguments that employees who failed to provide notice of the need for FMLA–qualifying leave were prevented from doing so due to psychiatric problems.

(9) Providing FMLA Leave/Medical Forms

Adequate notice of an employee's need for FMLA leave may be provided in the form of a doctor's note. *See Brenneman v. MidCentral Health System*, 366 F.3d 412, 423 (6th Cir. 2004), *cert. denied*, 2005 U.S. LEXIS 1474 (U.S. 2005); *Aubuchon v. Knauf Fiberglass, GMBH*, 359 F.3d 950, 953–954 (7th Cir. 2004); *Kaniuka v. Good Shepherd Home*, No. 05-CV-02917, 2006 U.S. Dist. LEXIS 57403, at *38 (E.D. Pa. Aug. 15, 2006); *EEOC v. Pepsiamericas, Inc.*, No. 03 C 6576, 2005 U.S. Dist. LEXIS 13068, at *11 (N.D. Ill. June 21, 2005); *Hobart v. Behavioral Connections of Wood County, Inc.*, No. 3:03CV7313, 2004 U.S. Dist. LEXIS 12051, at *10 (N.D. Ohio July 1, 2004); *Conrad v. Eaton Corp.*, 303 F. Supp. 2d 987, 998 (N.D. Iowa 2004).

Similarly, a doctor's note combined with information imparted by the employee may be sufficient notice that the leave may be FMLA-qualifying to shift the burden of inquiry to the employer. In *Ode v. Mount Sinai Med. Center*, No. 04-CIV. 9632 (DLC), 2006 U.S. Dist. LEXIS 41479, at *14-16 (S.D. N.Y. June 22, 2006), the court found that the employee's calling in "sick" coupled with his doctor's note the next day that the employee was "unable to work due to severe neck pain" was found sufficient to create a material issue of fact as to whether these statements triggered the employer's duty to conduct further inquiry into whether Ode's medical condition qualified as an FMLA-covered serious health condition.

Medical documentation alone, of course, may also be insufficient notice of the need for FMLA leave. In *Barngrover v. W.W. Transport*, No. 3:02–cv–40020, 2003 U.S. Dist. LEXIS 13145, at *26–28 (S.D. Iowa July 24, 2003), the employee argued that her employer's prior knowledge of her medical restrictions was sufficient notice of her need for FMLA leave. The court disagreed, finding that because the employee never complained that she was working outside of her medical restrictions, the employer did not have an obligation to inquire further to determine if the employee needed FMLA leave.

The Sixth Circuit found that an employer providing FMLA leave forms to an employee requesting leave is evidence that the employee provided adequate notice of the need for FMLA leave. *Walton v. Ford Motor Co.*, 424 F.3d 481, 486-87 (6th Cir. 2006); *see also Maynard v. Total Image Specialists, Inc.*, 478 F. Supp. 2d 933 (S.D. Ohio 2007); *Hemenway v. Albion Public Schools*, No. 4:05-CV-7, 2006 U.S. Dist. LEXIS 83076, at *12-13 (W.D. Mich. Nov. 15, 2006) (employee supplying doctor's note stating "please excuse patient for 3 weeks," making a request for FMLA papers, and providing notice that she did not feel well and that she needed to see her doctor found sufficient notice that leave may be FMLA-qualifying and defeats motion for summary judgment); *O'Hara v. Mt Vernon Bd. of Education*, 16 F. Supp. 2d 868, 890 (S.D. Ohio 1998. Other courts, however, have concluded that the provision of FMLA leave forms does not preclude a finding that the employee failed to provide adequate notice that leave may be FMLA–qualifying. *See Carter v. Ford Motor Co.*, 121 F.3d 1146 (8th Cir. 1997) (notice that employee was sick and would be out for a few days insufficient where employee failed turn in provided FMLA leave request forms); *Sampson v. Citibank*, FSB, 53 F. Supp. 2d 13, 19 (D.D.C. 1999), *aff'd without op.*, 221 F.2d 196 (D.C. Cir. 2000), *cert. denied*, 531 U.S. 970 (2000) (employee, advised in writing of FMLA option on at least three occasions, failed to request FMLA leave).

In light of the case law, agencies that provide FMLA leave forms as a matter of routine when an employee requests leave should consider including language that provides that merely providing the FMLA leave forms does not indicate that the employer considers the employee to have provided adequate notice of the need for FMLA leave, or that the leave is FMLA–qualifying.

(10) Miscellaneous Notice Issues

The requirement that an employee must explain the reasons for leave so as to allow the employer to determine that the leave qualifies for FMLA protections includes the requirement to address the employee's relationship with a covered family member, at least where it is not obvious how the individual is covered within the meaning of the FMLA. For example, in *Sherrod v. Philadelphia Gas Works*, 57 Fed. Appx. 68 (3d Cir. 2003), the employee requested FMLA leave to care for an ill grandmother. Grandmothers generally are not covered individuals within the meaning of the Act. They may, however, be covered individuals if, for example, the grandmother stood *in loco parentis* to an employee when the employee was a son or daughter. In this case, the circuit court held that because the employee failed to initially tell her employer that her grandmother raised her (making the grandmother an *in loco parentis* parent covered by the FMLA), the employee failed to sufficiently explain her reasons for the needed leave so as to allow the employer to determine that her request was covered by the FMLA. Therefore, the initial denial of leave was not improper, nor did it interfere with the employee's FMLA rights.

b. Title II

An employee is not required to explicitly invoke the FMLA in order to request FMLA leave. *See Romero v. Dept. of Interior*, No. SF-0752-05-0011-I-1, 2005 MSPB LEXIS 3147, at *10-11 (May 19, 2005); *Burge v. Dept. of Air Force*, 82 MSPR 75 (1999), *pet. denied*, 86 MSPR 688 (2000); *Jeffries v. Dept. of Navy*, 78 MSPR 255 (1998); *Ellshoff v. Dept. of Interior*, 76 MSPR 54, 76 (1997), *rev'd, remanded*, 78 MSPR 615 (1998). Rather, an employee need only provide the employer with sufficient information that the leave might be covered by the FMLA. *Landahl v. Commerce*, 83 MSPR 40 (1999), *pet. denied*, 87 MSPR 530 (2000), *aff'd*, 2001 U.S. App. LEXIS 11774 (Fed. Cir. 2001); *Burge*, 82 MSPR 75.

In *Ellshoff*, 76 MSPR at 76, the Board noted that the statute and OPM regulations do not specifically require an employee to invoke the FMLA. The Board relied on the analysis of the Fifth Circuit in *Manual v. Westlake Polymers Corp.*, 66 F.3d 758,

762 (5th Cir. 1995). Although *Manual* involved Title I of the FMLA, the Board found that "the notice provisions under title I and Title Ii are identical in material respects...and we therefore find that *Manual* constitutes persuasive authority on this issue." The Board went on to find that Ellshoff satisfied the notice requirement even though she did not invoke the FMLA when she initially requested FMLA leave. The notices in that case involved written documentation and telephone conversations between the employee's treating psychiatrist and the agency that Ellshoff was disabled by depression and hospitalized.

In *Landahl*, 83 MSPR 40, the Board found that the employee arguably provided adequate notice that his request for extended leave may have been covered by the FMLA. The employee alleged that his supervisors were aware that he suffered from depression, was taking medication for his condition, and was considering a medical disability retirement. In a meeting wherein the agency asked him to provide medical documentation to support his absences, the employee informed his supervisors that he asked for extended sick leave, which request was denied.

In *Burge*, 82 MSPR 75, the Board found that the employee provided adequate notice of the need for FMLA leave even though he did not specifically invoke the FMLA by name. The Board found that the notice placed the agency on notice of his possible entitlement to leave under the FMLA based on one letter requesting 6 months of LWOP due to his medical condition, and a completed leave request form requesting a month of leave due to his "condition."

In *Jeffries v. Dept. of Navy*, 78 MSPR 255 (1998), the Board found that the agency was placed on notice that the employee was requesting FMLA leave even though the employee first raised the issue of possible entitlement to FMLA leave during his oral reply to the proposed removal several months after the conclusion of his leave. The Board subsequently taken the position that an employee may not establish entitlement to FMLA leave for the first time on appeal when the agency provided notice to the employee of FMLA requirements. *See Brown v. Dept. of Treasury*, No. DC-0752-06-0669-I-1, 2006 MSPB LEXIS 5903, at *14 (Oct. 19, 2006); *Dias v. Dept. of Veterans Affairs*, 102 MSPR 53 (2006).

The Board's adoption of the Title I standard to determine whether an employee provided adequate notice of the need for FMLA leave has broad implications for agencies. To avoid FMLA violations, employers need to closely follow developments in Title I of the FMLA regarding the adequacy of employee notice of the need for FMLA leave.

Notice that an employee is "ill" is insufficient to invoke the protections of the FMLA. *See Williams v. Dept. of Navy*, No. DC-0752-05-0431-I-1, 2005 MSPB LEXIS 6866, at *7 (Oct. 17, 2005), *pet. denied*, 101 MSPR 133 (2006).

In *Cole v. DHHS*, No. DC-0752-05-0457-I-1, 2005 MSPB LEXIS 6825, at *8 (Nov. 1, 2005), the employee's notice that she was "waiting for a scheduled date to have surgery, and would like to be placed on the donated leave request," was found insufficient notice that she needed FMLA leave.

An employee's request for leave because she could not find her eyeglasses did not provide adequate notice that the leave may be FMLA-qualifying. *Cole v. DHHS*, No. DC-0752-05-0457-I-1, 2005 MSPB LEXIS 6825, at *9 (Nov. 1, 2005).

4. Failure of an Employee to Provide Notice as Required

Penalties are imposed against employees who fail to meet their notice responsibilities. As with other areas, the penalties imposed differ among the four federal sector variants of the FMLA.

a. Title I, the CAA, and the PEOAA

An employer has several options to address an employee's failure to timely provide adequate notice of the need for FMLA leave. First, if the employee fails to provide adequate notice sufficient to inform the employer that the leave qualifies under the Act, the leave may be denied. 29 CFR 825.208(a)(1)–(2); S. Res. 242, Cong. Rec. S3959, S3966 (April 23, 1996); 29 CFR 825.208(a)(1)–(2); *Mollison v. Stein*, No. 97-3487, 1998 U.S. App. LEXIS 10773 (6th Cir. 1998) (failure to provide notice to the employer of the reason for absence precludes an employee from claiming the protection of the Statute); *Alexander v. Ford Motor Co.*, No. 01–70051, 204 F.R.D. 314, 2001 U.S. Dist. LEXIS 19180 (E.D. Mich. Nov. 5, 2001); *Slaughter v. American Building Maintenance*, 64 F. Supp. 2d 319, 329 (S.D.N.Y. 1999) (an employee who failed to provide notice of the need for unforeseeable leave within two days was not entitled to protection under the FMLA).

Second, an employer may waive employees' FMLA notice obligations or the employer's own internal rules on leave notice requirements. 29 CFR 825.302(g), 825.304(a); S. Res. 242, Cong. Rec. S3959, S3972 (April 23, 1996); 29 CFR 825.302(g),

825.304(a); see *Bailey v. Miltope Corp.*, No. 2:05-cv-1061-MEF (WO), 2007 U.S. Dist. LEXIS 1760, at *21 (M.D. Alabama Jan. 8, 2007); *Rodriguez v. Ford Motor Co.*, 383 F. Supp. 2d 928, 934 (E.D. Mich. 2005). That is, an employer can simply choose to ignore the employee's failure to meet the notice obligations and grant the leave or other FMLA entitlements as requested.

Third, where the employee fails to give at least 30 days' notice for foreseeable leave with no reasonable excuse for the delay, the employer may delay the taking of FMLA leave until at least 30 days after the date the employee provides notice to the employer for the need for FMLA leave. 29 CFR 825.304(b), 825.312(a); S. Res. 242, Cong. Rec. S3959, S3972, S3974 (April 23, 1996); 29 CFR 825.304(a), 825.312(a). An employer is not permitted to deny FMLA leave as a penalty for an employee's failure to timely provide notice of the need for FMLA leave that is foreseeable. Preamble, 29 CFR 825.304; See *Killian v. Yorozu Automotive Tennessee, Inc.*, 454 F.3d 549, 554 (6th Cir. 2006); *Bailey v. Miltope Corp.*, No. 2:05-cv-1061-MEF (WO), 2007 U.S. Dist. LEXIS 1760, at *21 (M.D. Alabama Jan. 8, 2007); *Williams v. Ill. Dept. of Corrections*, No. 05-cv-4227-JPG, 2007 U.S. Dist. LEXIS 17119, at *10 (S.D. Ill. March 9, 2007).

In order for the onset of FMLA leave to be delayed due to the lack of required notice, two requirements must be met. First, it must be clear that the employee had actual notice of the FMLA notice requirements. 29 CFR 825.304(c); S. Res. 242, Cong. Rec. S3959, S3972 (April 23, 1996); § 825.304(c). Actual notice may be satisfied by the employer's proper posting of the required notice at the worksite where the employee is employed. 29 CFR 825.304(c); S. Res. 242, Cong. Rec. S3959, S3972 (April 23, 1996); § 825.304(c). The regulations do not exclude actual notice by other means.

Second, the need for leave and the approximate date leave would be taken must have been clearly foreseeable to the employee 30 days in advance of the leave. 29 CFR 825.304(c); S. Res. 242, Cong. Rec. S3959, S3972 (April 23, 1996); 29 CFR 825.304(c). For example, knowledge that an employee would receive a telephone call about the availability of a child for adoption at some unknown point in the future would not be sufficient. 29 CFR 825.304(c); S. Res. 242, Cong. Rec. S3959, S3972 (April 23, 1996); § 825.304(c). Presumably, a date certain for a scheduled medical treatment would satisfy this criterion if known by the employee.

Note that the regulations indicate that an employer may delay the taking of FMLA leave "until at least 30 calendar days" after the employee gives notice. The language suggests that the minimum period of delay is 30 calendar days, and agencies are authorized to require even greater delays (there is no stated limit in the regulation). Agencies should tread carefully in this area and not impose lengthy delays beyond the 30 calendar days without legitimate, non–discriminatory business reasons.

An employer is not required to establish that it suffered actual prejudice due to the employee's failure to timely notify the employer of the need for FMLA leave in order to exercise the right to delay the start of the leave. Preamble, 29 CFR 825.304.

An employee's failure to strictly comply with the FMLA notice time-frames is not fatal to the employee's ability to bring a claim for denial of FMLA leave. In *Lester v. Wayne County*, No. 04-74109, 2006 U.S. Dist. LEXIS 32450, at *15 (E.D. Mich. May 23, 2006), the court rejected the employer's argument that an employee could be precluded from asserting an FMLA violation because she did not strictly observe the time frames set forth in the FMLA regulations for notifying the employer of the need for leave, where the employer knew that the employee was requesting FMLA leave. Relying on *Breneman v. Medcentral Health System*, 366 F.3d 412 (6th Cir. 2004), cert. den., 543 U.S. 1146 (2005), the court found that the timeliness of an employee's notice should only be considered with regard to when and whether sufficient substantive notice was given to allow the employer to timely assess the FMLA claim.

An employer may require an employee to comply with the employer's "usual and customary" notice and procedural requirements for requesting leave that is foreseeable. 29 CFR 825.302(d); S. Res. 242, Cong. Rec. S3959, S3971–72 (April 23, 1996); § 825.302(d); see *Spangler v. Federal Home Loan Bank of Des Moines*, 278 F.3d 847, 852 (8th Cir. 2002). The same rule may apply when the need for leave is not foreseeable. Preamble, 29 CFR 825.303. Where an employee fails to follow such internal employer procedures, the employer is not permitted to disallow or delay an employee's taking of FMLA leave if the employee gives timely verbal or other notice. 29 CFR 825.302(d); S. Res. 242, Cong. Rec. S3959, S3971–72 (April 23, 1996); § 825.302(d); see *Cavin v. Honda of America Mfg., Inc.* 346 F.3d 713 (6th Cir. 2003); *Spangler v. Federal Home Loan Bank of Des Moines*, 278 F.3d 847, 852 (8th Cir. 2002); *Ryl-Kuchar v. Care Centers, Inc.*, No. 05-3223, 2006 U.S. Dist. LEXIS 87853, at *17 (N.D. Ill. Dec. 4, 2006); *Wood v. AT&T Corp.*, No. 2:05 CV 131, 2006 U.S. Dist. LEXIS 76148, at *16 (D. Ut. Oct. 18, 2006); *McClain v. Detroit Entertainment, LLC*, 458 F. Supp. 2d 427 (E.D. Mich. 2006). The employer may, however, take appropriate disciplinary action for the employee's failure to follow proper procedure. Preamble, 29 CFR 825.302. Of course, such discipline would have to be issued in a way that does not discriminate against those who take FMLA leave.

Issuance of discipline, while permitted, will likely invite retaliation claims for exercising FMLA rights. Agencies should exercise great care before issuing discipline in this area.

In *McClain v. Detroit Entertainment, LLC,* 458 F. Supp. 2d 427 (E.D. Mich. 2006), the court found that the employer's discipline, for failure to request leave pursuant to the employer's policy, of an employee granted intermittent FMLA leave violated the FMLA. Because the employer already approved the FMLA leave, the court found that the employer failed to establish why the employee needed to secure its approval for a leave of absence covering the exact same period.

The regulations do not provide a penalty when an employee fails to timely provide notice as soon as practicable where the need for FMLA leave was not foreseeable. Courts that have addressed this situation have found that the employee was not entitled to the benefits and protections of the FMLA where the employee failed to timely provide notice of the need for leave as soon as practicable. *See Russell v. First Health Services et al.,* 11 Fed. Appx. 221 (4th Cir. 2001) (the employer did not violate the FMLA by terminating employee on third day because the employee failed to provide timely notice of the need for FMLA leave that was not foreseeable within two days of her absence).

If the required notice, whether 30 days or "as soon as practicable," is not given, the employer can deny leave even if all other FMLA requirements are met. *Aubuchon v. Knauf Fiberglass, GMBH,* 359 F.3d 950, 951–952 (7th Cir. 2004); *accord Loring v. Advanced Foods, Inc.,* No. C02–4067–PAZ, 2004 U.S. Dist. LEXIS 6172, at *17 (N.D. Iowa April 9, 2004), *aff'd,* 2005 U.S. App. LEXIS 4124 (8th Cir. 2005) (no FMLA claim where employee did not request leave of any kind); *Henson v. Bell Helicopter Textron, Inc.,* No. 4:01–CV–1024–Y, 2004 U.S. Dist. LEXIS 1630, at *38 (N.D. Tex. Feb. 6, 2004), *aff'd,* 2005 U.S. App. LEXIS 6600 (5th Cir. 2005); *Henegar v. DaimlerChrysler Corp.,* 280 F. Supp. 2d 680, 686 (E.D. Mich. 2003); *Williams v. The Thomson Corp.,* No. 00–2256, 2003 U.S. Dist. LEXIS 4481, at *39 (D. Minn. March 21, 2003).

b. Title II

Title II generally provides that an employee who does not comply with the notification requirements of § 630.1206 and does not provide medical certification signed by the health care provider that includes all of the information required in § 630.1207(b) is not entitled to family and medical leave. 5 CFR 630.1208(l). The use of the conjunctive suggests that the loss of entitlement to FMLA leave requires both that the employee failed to provide notice of a need for leave as required *and* also failed to provide a complete and signed medical certification. If an employee only failed to provide notice or the medical certification, the regulation would not disenfranchise an employee from entitlement to FMLA leave.

Title II does not set forth a separate penalty for an employee's failure to invoke his or her entitlement to FMLA leave. Presumably, an agency may deny FMLA leave to an employee who fails to invoke entitlement to FMLA leave as required.

The regulations implementing Title II also address the penalty for an employee's failure to timely provide notice of a need for FMLA leave. If the need for leave is foreseeable, and the employee fails to give 30 calendar days' notice with no reasonable excuse for the delay of notification, the employer may delay the taking of FMLA leave until at least 30 calendar days after the date the employee provides notice of his or her need for FMLA leave. 5 CFR 630.1206(d).

The regulations fail to provide further guidance on what circumstances might constitute a "reasonable excuse" for the delay of notification. Presumably, where the need for leave is foreseeable, but in less than 30 days, that would excuse an employee from giving 30 calendar days' notice.

Like Title I, the regulations provide that an employer may delay the taking of FMLA leave "until at least 30 calendar days" after the employee gives notice. The language ("until at least…") suggests that the minimum period of delay is 30 calendar days, and employers are authorized to require even greater delays (there is no stated limit in the regulation). Agencies should tread carefully in this area and not impose lengthy delays beyond the 30 calendar days without legitimate, non–discriminatory business reasons.

An employer may waive the employee notice requirements where the need for leave is foreseeable and instead impose the agency's usual and customary policies or procedures for providing notification of leave. 5 CFR 630.1206(e). The agency's policies or procedures for providing notification of leave must not be more stringent than the requirements in this section. 5 CFR 630.1206(e). Moreover, an employer may not deny an employee's entitlement to FMLA leave if the employee fails to follow such agency policies or procedures. 5 CFR 630.1206(e). Note that the prohibition does not extend to discipline or delaying the start of FMLA leave.

The above regulation, while sounding similar to comparable regulations implementing Title I, the CAA, and the PEOAA (§§ 825.302(g), 825.304(a)), is actually quite different. The comparable regulations implementing the three other federal sector variants of the FMLA allow an agency to outright waive any deficiency in employee notice. Section 630.1206(e), on the other hand, only allows waiver in order for an employer to impose the employer's "usual and customary" policies and procedures for an employee to provide notice of a need for FMLA leave. The Title II regulation is not a general waiver provision that an agency may use to forgive individual employee FMLA notice violations.

Waiver of specific employee notice deficiencies would appear to be allowed if they were contained in a collective bargaining agreement or an employer benefit program or plan. Under Title II, an employer must abide by the requirements of a collective bargaining agreement or benefit program or plan that provides greater family or medical leave entitlements to employees than those provided by Title II. 5 CFR 630.1210(a), (c). As Title II does not permit an agency to waive notice violations of individual employees, such a provision in a collective bargaining agreement or employer policy would be more generous than the rights provided by Title II.

In *Anderson v. VA*, No. PH-0752-06-0341-I-1, 2006 MSPB LEXIS 6777, at *13 (Nov. 16, 2006), the MSPB sustained the removal of an employee for unauthorized absence and failure to follow leave requesting procedures. The Board found that the FMLA did not apply. Even if it applied, the Board found that the employee was not entitled to the protections of the FMLA where the need or leave was foreseeable, and the employee failed to schedule his absences in advance. In *Bradley v. VA*, No. CH-0752-04-0513-I-1, 2005 MSPB LEXIS 1194, at *12 (Feb. 16, 2005), *pet. denied*, 99 MSPR 402 (2005), *aff'd*, 2006 U.S. App. LEXIS 8506 (Fed. Cir. 2006), the Board sustained the removal of the employee for AWOL and failure to follow proper leave procedures. The Board found that the employee failed to provide 30 days advance notice of her need for leave or notice as soon as practicable incident to the birth of the employee's child.

Finally, if the need for FMLA leave is not foreseeable (e.g. a medical emergency or the unexpected availability of a child for adoption or foster care), and the employee is unable, due to circumstances beyond his or her control, to provide notice of his or her need for leave, the leave may not be delayed or denied. 5 CFR 630.1206(c); *see Cole v. DHHS*, No. DC-0752-05-0457-I-1, 2005 MSPB LEXIS 6825, at *9 (Nov. 1, 2005).

The regulations do not indicate what happens if the employee's failure to timely provide notice where the need for leave is not foreseeable, was not due to circumstances beyond his or her control. Presumably, the agency could deny or delay FMLA leave.

Technically, the regulation only applies where the employee altogether fails to provide notice when the need for leave is not foreseeable. An argument could be made that it does not apply when the employee provides untimely notice where the need for leave is not foreseeable. Again, no penalty is identified where an employee's request for leave that is not foreseeable is untimely.

The penalties imposed for an employee's failure to provide timely notice where the need for FMLA leave is not foreseeable are subject to modifications if the terms of a collective bargaining agreement or employment benefit program or plan provide greater family or medical leave benefits than the minimum required by the FMLA, including notice. 5 CFR 630.1210(a), (c).

5. Additional Employee Notice Requirements

One or more federal sector variants of the FMLA impose notice requirements on employees in addition to the obligation to request FMLA leave. While these notice requirements are discussed in more detail in other chapters in this book, a quick survey of these requirements are provided below.

a. Changed Circumstances

(1) Title I, the CAA, and the PEOAA

An employee is obligated to notify his or her employer when circumstances have changed necessitating the need for more or less FMLA leave. In both of these situations, the employer may require that the employee provide the employer reasonable notice (i.e. within two business days) of the changed circumstances where foreseeable. 29 CFR 825.309(c); S. Res. 242, Cong. Rec. S3959, S3973–74 (April 23, 1996); § 825.309(c); *Killian v. Yorozu Automotive Tennessee, Inc.*, 454 F.3d

549, 554 (6th Cir. 2006). The employer may also obtain information on such changed circumstances through requested status reports. 29 CFR 825.309(c); S. Res. 242, Cong. Rec. S3959, S 3973–74 (April 23, 1996); § 825.309(c); *Hoge v. Honda of America Mfg., Inc.*, 384 F.3d 238, (6th Cir. 2004). Note that this obligation is not self–executing on the part of employees. That is, an employee is only required to notify his or her employer of changed circumstances necessitating more or less FMLA leave where the employer has made this a requirement. Employing agencies should seriously consider imposing such a requirement to maximize the information it has regarding an employee's FMLA leave status. Agencies with collective bargaining agreements may have to bargain over this issue.

Absent special regulations, an employee's failure to timely provide notice of changed circumstances would appear to be governed as any employee failure to provide notice of the need for leave. In any event, there are no penalties specifically imposed by the regulations for an employee's failure to provide notice of changed circumstances.

(2) Title II

Title II does not have a similar requirement governing employee notice where changed circumstances have increased or decreased the employee's continuing need for FMLA leave. Presumably, the matter is governed by the basic rules governing employee notice. *See* 5 CFR 630.1206.

b. Paid Leave Substitution

(1) Title I, the CAA, and the PEOAA

An employee may elect, or an employer may require the employee, to substitute any accrued paid leave of the employee for unpaid FMLA leave. 29 USC 2612(d)(2)(A); 29 CFR 825.207(a). As set forth more fully in Chapter 11, "Substitution of Paid Leave," neither the statutes nor implementing regulations specifically address the manner in which such election is communicated to the employer. Presumably, notice of an employee election to substitute paid leave for unpaid FMLA leave may be provided verbally, consistent with the general employee notice requirements. *See* 29 CFR 825.208.

(2) Title II

An employee is required to notify the agency of his or her intent to substitute paid leave for FMLA taken on leave without pay. 5 CFR 630.1205(e). The employee must notify the agency of the desired substitution prior to the date such paid leave commences. 5 CFR 630.1205(e). An employee may not retroactively substitute paid leave taken for FMLA leave previously taken as leave without pay. 5 CFR 630.1205(e).

It is unclear whether retroactive substitution of paid leave for FMLA leave previously taken as LWOP would be permissible (indeed required) if such a policy were incorporated into the terms of a collective bargaining agreement or employment benefit plan or program. Under these circumstances, retroactive substitution pursuant to agency policy could be considered a greater family or medical leave benefit then an agency is required to comply with. 5 CFR 630.1210. The argument against an agency permitting retroactive substitution of paid leave for FMLA leave already taken as LWOP is set forth by OPM in the preamble to the final regulations. The OPM (Preamble, 5 CFR 630.1205) states:

> The right to substitute paid leave for leave without pay under the FMLA applies only to leave that is to be taken in the future. The legislative history provides an intent to authorize the use of leave "to be taken" under the FMLA. Therefore, the substitution of paid leave for unpaid FMLA leave can be accomplished only on a prospective basis.

[Substitution of paid leave is addressed more fully in Chapter 11, "Substitution of Paid Leave."]

c. Consult with Employer on Medical Treatment Schedule

(1) Title I, the CAA, and the PEOAA

An employee is required to consult with his or her employer when planning medical treatment and make a reasonable effort to schedule the leave so as not to unduly disrupt the employer's operations, subject to the approval of the health care provider. 29 USC 2612(e)(2)(A); 29 CFR 825.302(e); S. Res. 242, Cong. Rec. S3959, S 3972 (April 23, 1996); 29 CFR 825.302(e). Employees ordinarily are expected to consult with their employers prior to the scheduling of treatment in order to work out a treatment schedule which best suits the needs of both the employer and the employee. 29 CFR 825.302(e); S. Res. 242, Cong. Rec. S3959, S 3972 (April 23, 1996); 29 CFR 825.302(e).

If an employee who provides notice of the need to take FMLA leave on an intermittent basis for planned medical treatment neglects to consult with the employer to make a reasonable attempt to arrange the schedule of treatments so as not to unduly disrupt the employer's operations, the employer may initiate discussions with the employee and require the employee to attempt to make such arrangements, subject to the approval of the health care provider. 29 CFR 825.302(e); S. Res. 242, Cong. Rec. S3959, S 3972 (April 23, 1996); 29 CFR 825.302(e).

There is no penalty identified in the regulations for an employee's failure to consult with an employer regarding the employee's schedule of medical treatments. The courts, however, have upheld the denial of FMLA leave protections where an employee fails to consult with an employer and otherwise attempt to arrange medical treatment schedule so as not to unduly disrupt the employer's operations.

(2) Title II

Where FMLA leave is needed due to a serious health condition which is foreseeable based on planned medical treatment, an employee is required to consult with the agency and make a reasonable effort to schedule medical treatment so as not to unduly disrupt the operations of the agency, subject to the approval of the health care provider. 5 USC 6382(e)(2)((A); 5 CFR 630.1206(b). The agency may, for justifiable cause, request that an employee reschedule medical treatment, subject to the approval of the health care provider. 5 CFR 630.1206(b).

Neither the Statute nor the implementing regulation contains a penalty for an employee's failure to consult with an agency on the medical treatment scheduled as required.

d. Retroactive Notice of Need for Leave

The rules governing an employer's retroactive designation of leave as FMLA–qualifying were addressed previously in this chapter. The flip side to those rules addresses the employee's notice obligations after FMLA leave begins. Those rules are addressed below.

(1) Title I, the CAA, and the PEOAA

In order to gain the protections of the Act, an employee must timely notify the employer of the need for FMLA leave. Such notice may occur before, during, or after the employee takes leave. Retroactive employee notice occurs where the employee notifies his or her employer during a leave of absence, or after the employee returns from leave, that some or all of the leave should be designated as FMLA–qualifying.

For example, an employee is initially granted two weeks of paid annual leave. During this time the employee goes scuba diving in the Caribbean. Unfortunately, mid–week of the second week the employee contacts the employer for an extension of leave. The employee developed a serious ear infection requiring hospitalization followed by a course of prescription medication. The agency may notify the employee that it is designating the leave from the date of hospitalization and after as FMLA–qualifying. *See* 29 CFR 825.208(d).

Note that the regulations do not mandate that the employee contact his or her employer during leave to inform the employer that something unexpected happened that qualifies for FMLA leave protections. Rather, the employee notice in this instance was due to the employee needing more leave. The request was required by the employer's normal leave reporting requirements, as the employee needed additional leave in order to avoid being considered AWOL. To gain the protections of the FMLA, the employee must provide timely and adequate notice of the need for leave that qualifies for coverage under the Act. If the need for FMLA leave was not foreseeable, notice must be given as soon as practicable, generally within one or two business days of when the employee learned of the need for FMLA leave. 29 CFR 825.303(a). In the hypothetical, the employee accomplished this by imparting sufficient information when requesting an extension of leave to alert the employer that both the extension and some of the prior annual leave should be retroactively designated as FMLA leave.

An employee may also retroactively notify an employee of the need for FMLA leave after the employee returns to work. If leave is taken for an FMLA reason but the employer was not aware of the reason, and the employee desires that the leave be counted as FMLA leave, the employee must notify the employer within two business days of returning to work of the reason for the leave. 29 CFR 825.208(e)(1); S. Res. 242, Cong. Rec. S3959, S3967 (April 23, 1996); 29 CFR 825.208(e)(1).

The above is not a catchall designed to rescue employees who have failed to otherwise provide timely notice of the need for FMLA leave. Rather, the regulation is designed to cover those situations where an employee is absent for only a brief period of time before returning to work, and the employee was unable to provide notice before or during FMLA leave. 29 CFR 825.208(e)(1); S. Res. 242, Cong. Rec. S3959, S3967 (April 23, 1996); 29 CFR 825.208(e)(1); *see Lukacinsky v. Panasonic Service Co.*, No. 03–40141–FDS, 2004 U.S. Dist. LEXIS 25846, at *38 (D. Mass. Nov. 29, 2004) (employee notification of the need for FMLA leave does not operate retroactively to excuse previously unexplained absences unless it is given as soon as practicable after an emergency or unforeseeable medically-related absence).

(2) Title II

Title II does not have any regulations specifically addressing employee notice and retroactive designation of FMLA leave.

e. Maintenance of Benefits

Maintenance of health benefits during an employee's use of FMLA leave is addressed in Chapter 12, "Maintenance of Benefits." What follows is an overview highlighting employee obligations broadly construed as notification requirements.

(1) Title I, the CAA, and the PEOAA

Loosely defined, employees are responsible for notifying employers on several issues involving the continuation of health care benefits during the course of an employee's use of FMLA leave. Employee notice includes requests involving new or changed benefit plan coverage, election not to continue group health plan coverage, and the termination of health care coverage.

An employer is required to inform employees on FMLA leave of any changes to health benefits or plans as the employee is entitled to the new or changed plan or benefits to the same extent as if the employee were not on leave. 29 CFR 825.209(c). If the employee requests the changed coverage it must be provided by the employer. 29 CFR 825.209(c).

An employee may choose not to retain group health plan coverage during FMLA leave. 29 CFR 825.209(d). Presumably, the employee must communicate his or her decision not to continue group health plan coverage during FMLA leave to his or her employer. No specific rule, however, requires such notice.

Finally, an employer's obligation to continue group health care coverage ceases when the employee informs the employer of his or her intention not to return to work from FMLA leave. 29 CFR 825.209(f), 825.211(e)(3), 825.312(e). [Maintenance of health benefits during FMLA leave is addressed in Chapter 12, "Maintenance of Benefits."]

(2) Title II

An employer whose employee is enrolled in a health benefits plan under 5 USC 8901, *et. seq.*, and is placed in a leave status under § 6382(d) may elect to continue the health benefits enrollment of the employee while in FMLA leave and arrange to pay appropriate employee contributions into the Employee Health Benefits Fund. 5 USC 6386; 5 CFR 630.1209. There are no specific employee notice requirements set forth in the statute or the implementing regulations regarding continuation of employment benefits during the course of FMLA leave. Presumably, an employee may elect not to continue health benefits coverage, which election would have to be communicated to the employer. Any other employee notices regarding continuation of health benefits coverage would appear to be governed by the health benefits plan.

f. Return to Work from FMLA Leave

The requirements governing an employee's return to work from FMLA leave are addressed more fully in Chapter 13,

"Return to Work from Leave." This section provides an overview of employee notice requirements regarding an employee's return to work.

(1) Title I, the CAA, and the PEOAA

An employee may provide notice to the employer of his or her intention to return to work. Such employee notice may be required in response to an employer's request that the employee report periodically on the employee's status and intention to return to work. 29 CFR 825.312(e), 825.309(a), 825.209(f). An employee who fails to provide such notice is not entitled to the protections of the FMLA. *See Hoge v. Honda of America Mfg., Inc.*, 384 F.3d 238 6th Cir. 2004); *Peeples v. Coastal Office Products, Inc.*, 64 Fed. Appx. 860 (4th Cir. 2003).

In *Hoge*, the court found that when the employee showed up at work at the beginning of the work day, it constituted notice to Honda that the employee was ready and capable to return to work sooner than expected. If the employee's actual return did not give Honda reasonable notice as required, Honda could delay the employee's return to work for two days. Conversely, if the employee's earlier return to work was reasonable notice, Honda could not delay the employee's return to work.

An employer may also require an employee on FMLA leave to report periodically on the employee's status and intent to return to work. 29 CFR 825.309(a); *Hoge v. Honda of America Mfg., Inc.*, 384 F.3d 238, (6th Cir. 2004).

Where an employee gives unequivocal notice of intent not to return to work, the employer's obligations under the FMLA to maintain health benefits and to restore the employee ceases. 29 CFR 825.312(e), 825.309(a). However, these obligations may continue when, for example, the employee takes paid leave pursuant to an employer policy. 29 CFR 825.312(e).

(2) Title II

Notice of an employee's intention not to return to work is not addressed in the Statute or the regulations implementing Title II.

g. Key Employee

The rights of certain highly compensated or "key" employees are addressed more fully in Chapter 13, "Return to Work from Leave." Employee notice issues are briefly addressed below.

(1) Title I, the CAA, and the PEOAA

An employing agency can deny job restoration to a key employee on the conclusion of FMLA leave if the return of the employee would cause substantial and grievous economic injury to the operations of the employer. 29 USC 2614(b); 29 CFR 825.218. A key employee is a salaried FMLA–eligible employee who is among the highest paid ten percent of all employees employed by the employer within 75 miles of the employee's worksite. 29 CFR 825.218(a).

Basically, an agency must notify an employee that the employer considers the employee to be a "key" employee and that the employee's return would result in substantial and grievous economic injury. The notice further advises the employee that the employer intends to deny job restoration on the conclusion of FMLA leave. If the employee is out on leave when this employer notice is received, the employee has a right to return to work within a reasonable period of time. If the employee does not return to work on receipt of such notice, the employer must continue to maintain health benefits and the employer may not recover its cost of health benefit premium, if any.

A key employee's rights under the FMLA continue unless and until the employee either gives notice that he or she no longer wishes to return to work, or the employer actually denies reinstatement at the conclusion of the leave period. 29 CFR 825.219(c).

(2) Title II

Title II does not recognize the concept of a "key" employee.

h. School Employees

Chapter 10, "Leave Amount and Scheduling," addresses the rules governing certain employees of educational institutions in more detail. Employee notice requirements follow.

(1) Title I and the CAA

Certain special rules apply to employees of local educational agencies. 29 USC 2618; 29 CFR 825.500(a). Generally speaking, the rules regulate the return of an employee to work from FMLA leave at certain points during the academic year. In terms of employee notice of the need for FMLA leave, the usual rules for employee notice continue to apply. The penalty for an employee's failure to notify an employer where the need for leave is foreseeable is modified in one instance.

Specifically, if an instructional employee needs intermittent leave or leave on a reduced leave schedule due to his or her own serious health condition or the serious health condition of a covered family member, which is foreseeable based on planned medical treatment, and the employee would be on leave for more than 20 percent of the total working days over the period the leave would extend, the employee must provide notice of the need for the leave in accordance with § 825.302. 29 CFR 825.601(b). If an instructional employee fails to give such notice, the employer may require the employee to take leave of a particular duration, or to transfer temporarily to an alternative position. 29 CFR 825.601(b). Alternatively, the employer may require the employee to delay the taking of leave until the notice provision is met. 29 CFR 825.601(b).

Leaves of a particular duration mean a block, or blocks of time beginning no earlier than the first day for which leave is needed and ending no later than the last day on which leave is needed, and may include one uninterrupted period of leave. 29 CFR 825.601(a)(2).

(2) The PEOAA

The PEOAA does not incorporate the special rules governing certain school employees from Title I. As such, those rules are not applicable to employers or employees covered by the PEOAA.

(3) Title II

Title II does not have special rules for certain school employees comparable to Title I and the CAA.

i. Joint Employees

Joint employment is discussed in detail in Chapter 3, "FMLA Coverage of the Federal Government," and Chapter 4, "Federal Employees Covered by the FMLA."

Title II does not recognize the concept of joint employment. Joint employment is recognized for purposes of Title I, the CAA, and the PEOAA.

Joint employment occurs when two or more entities exercise some control, over the work or working conditions of the employee. 29 CFR 825.106(a). A typical joint employment relationship occurs when an agency hires a temporary worker through a temporary or employee–leasing agency. In that situation, the primary employer is usually the temporary help agency. The secondary employer is the federal agency that contracted with the temporary help agency for the services of a temporary worker. 29 CFR 825.106(b).

The regulations provide that the primary employer is responsible for giving required notices to its employees, providing FMLA leave, and maintenance of health benefits. The secondary employer is responsible for accepting the return of the joint employee, provided the employer continues to utilize an employee from the temporary or leasing agency. 29 CFR 825.106(e).

Ironically, the regulations fail to indicate what the notice obligations of an employee in a joint employment relationship are. Presumably, the employee's notice obligations run only to the primary employer.

IV. MIXED AGENCY RESPONSIBILITIES AND EMPLOYEE NOTICE

In terms of notice, profound differences exist between the four federal sector variants of the FMLA. This is particularly true between the requirements of Title II and the requirements of Title I, the CAA, and the PEOAA. For example, Title II requires that an employee affirmatively invoke his or her desire to take FMLA leave. Employees covered by Title I, the CAA, and the PEOAA, on the other hand, are not required to invoke the protections of the FMLA. In fact, they don't have to mention to FMLA at all or even know of the Act's existence. An employee is only required to provide timely and adequate notice of a need for leave that may be FMLA-qualifying. To be adequate, the notice need only provide sufficient facts to alert a vigilant employer that the employee's leave might qualify under the FMLA. The employee is not even required to provide facts that meet all of the requirements of FMLA leave. If sufficient facts are produced, even if he or she does not meet all of the requirements for FMLA leave, the burden of inquiry may shift to the employer to obtain additional information in order for the employer to determine whether the leave is FMLA-qualifying.

An agency with a workforce that predominately consists of employees covered by Tile II must avoid applying the employee notice provisions of that Act to employees covered by Title I. An agency that denies FMLA leave to an employee covered by Title I because the employee failed to affirmatively invoke his or her right to take FMLA leave will be in violation of Title I if the employee provided sufficient facts suggesting that the leave was FMLA-qualifying.

As with other areas of the FMLA, employee notice obligations are varied and complex. Employees, unions, and other organizations representing employees need to thoroughly understand this obligations in order to ensure that employees know how to perfect their right to job-protected FMLA leave. Employers too need to train their supervisors and personnel responsible for handling employee leave requests on the rules governing timely and adequate employee notice. Employers need to know these rules in order to manage leave within the requirements of the law. Employees who fail to provide timely and/or adequate notice of a need for FMLA have failed to perfect their right to the benefits and protection of the Act. Such failure has consequences that an employer may wish to exploit. Employing agencies who fail to appreciate requirements, similarities and differences in the employee notice obligations under all of the federal sector FMLA laws applicable to their agency run the considerable risk of violating those laws, subjecting the agency and, in some cases, individual supervisors and managers, to substantial monetary liability.

CHAPTER 9
DOCUMENTATION REQUIREMENTS

I. OVERVIEW

The FMLA permits employers to require employees to provide documentation in support of requests for, or to establish fitness to return from, FMLA leave. Medical and non-medical documentation may be requested to support an employee's request for leave. There are four types of medical documentation: certifications, recertifications, periodic status reports, and certification of fitness to return to duty. The Act identifies when and how an employer may request supporting documentation, the responsibilities of employees to respond to such requests, and the consequences for the failure of an employer and employee to properly make and respond to requests for verifying documentation.

Section II of this chapter addresses medical certifications. Recertifications are discussed in Section III. Section IV addresses periodic status reports. Certification of fitness to return to duty from FMLA leave is discussed in Section V. Documentation certifying familial relationships is discussed in Section VI. Section VII addresses HIPAA and the FMLA Finally, Section VIII compares the documentation requirements in agencies with mixed FMLA responsibilities.

II. MEDICAL CERTIFICATION

This section addresses the basic requirement that, under certain circumstances, an employee must timely comply with a request to provide adequate medical certification in support of the need for FMLA leave.

A. GENERAL RULE

An employer *may* require that a request for FMLA leave for the employee's own serious health condition, or for the serious health condition of the employee's covered spouse, parent, son or daughter, be supported by a certification issued by the appropriate health care provider. 29 USC 2613(a); 5 USC 6383(a); 2 USC 1312(a)(1) (incorporating 29 USC 2613 into CAA); 3 USC 412(a)(1) (incorporating 29 USC 2613 into PEOAA). From this virtually identical language, the regulations implementing this requirement for each of the FMLA statutes applicable to the federal sector contain substantial differences.

Congress described the rationale for this provision in the original Act (which, at the time, contained the basis for Title II and the CAA) as a "check against employee abuse of leave." S. Rep. No. 103–03, at 25; DOL WH FMLA Advisory Opinion No. 16 Nov. 15, 1993); *see Thorson v. Gemini, Inc. et al.*, 205 F.3d 370, 381 (8th Cir. 2000), *cert. denied*, 531 U.S. 871 (2000) (to prevent abuse of FMLA leave, employer may require second health care provider opinion); *Hemensay v. Albion Public Schools*, No. 4:05-CV-7, 2006 U.S. Dist. LEXIS 36231, at *7 -8 (W.D. Mich. Jan. 12, 2006) (purpose of the verification section is to guard against employee abuse of FMLA leave); *Cavin v. Honda of America MFG., Inc.*, No. C2–00–400, 2002 U.S. Dist. LEXIS 19601 (S.D. Ohio Feb. 22, 2002), *aff'd in part, rev'd in part, remanded on other grounds*, 346 F.3d 713 (6th Cir. 2003) (to prevent abuse of the FMLA, statute permits employers to require medical certification); *Shtab v. The Greate Bay Hotel and Casino, Inc. et al.*, 173 F. Supp. 2d 255, 264 (D.N.J. 2001) (in order to safeguard the interests of employers and prevent abuses by employees, Congress included a provision in the FMLA which entitled employers to request medical certification from an employee requesting leave); *Washington v. Fort James Operating Co.*, 110 F. Supp. 2d 1325, 1330 (D. Ore. 2000); *Vanderpool v. Inco Alloys International, Inc.*, No. 3:98–0449, 1999 U.S. Dist. LEXIS 12363 (S.D. W.Va. June 3, 1999) (FMLA and regulations do not require an employer to blindly accept an employee's claim that he or she requires leave; the employer may request certification and even seek a second opinion); *Pendarvis v. Xerox Corp.*, 3 F. Supp. 2d 53, 56 (D. D.C. 1998).

Note that the term "certification" is not defined in the statutes or regulations implementing the FMLA. The permissible content of such a certification is addressed in the statute and regulations, but the term itself remains undefined.

The regulations do not permit an employer to request medical certification if the need for FMLA leave does not involve a serious health condition. Where the need for FMLA leave is due to the birth, adoption, or foster care placement of a covered son or daughter, an employer would not be entitled to request medical certification to verify the employee's need for FMLA leave. An employer who requests medical certification where the need for FMLA leave was for a reason other than a serious health condition would likely find itself in violation of the FMLA. Moreover, the employer might also be in violation of the Rehabilitation Act, as there would appear to be no legitimate business necessity for medical documentation when the need for FMLA leave does not involve an employee's illness.

Finally, note that an employer is not required to ask an employee for certification, and an employee is not automatically required by law to provide certification every time the need for FMLA leave for a serious health condition arises. Rather, an employee is only required to provide medical certification in support of a request for FMLA leave if asked by the employer to provide such certification.

1. Title I, the CAA, and the PEOAA

As set forth in the implementing regulations, an employer *may* require that an employee's leave to care for the employee's seriously ill spouse, son, daughter, or parent, or due to the employee's own serious health condition that makes the employee unable to perform one or more essential functions of the employee's position, be supported by a certification issued by the health care provider of the employee or the employee's ill family member. 29 CFR 825.305)(a); S. Res. 242, Cong. Rec. S3959, S3972 (April 23, 1996); 29 CFR 825.305(a); *see Lubke v. City of Arlington*, 455 F.3d 489, 496 (5th Cir. 2006); *Phillips v. Quebecor World Rai Inc.*, 450 F.3d 308, 312 (7th Cir. 2006); *Edgar v. JAC Products, Inc.*, 443 F.3d 501, 506 (6th Cir. 2006); *Buettner v. North Oklahoma County Mental Health Center*, 158 Fed. Appx. 81 (10th Cir. 2005); *Kauffman v. Federal Express Corp.*, 426 F.3d 880, 885 (7th Cir. 2005); *Hoffman v. Professional Med Team*, 394 F.3d 414, 418 (6th Cir. 2005); *Urban v. Dolgencorp of Texas, Inc.*, 393 F.3d 572, 574 (5th Cir. 2004); *George v. Russell Stover Candies, Inc.*, 106 Fed. Appx. 946 (6th Cir. 2004); *Brenneman v. MedCentral Health System*, 366 F.3d 412, 422 (6th Cir. 2004), *cert. denied*, 2005 U.S. LEXIS 1474 (U.S. 2005); *Bailey v. Southwest Gas Co.*, 275 F.3d 1181, 1185–86 (9th Cir. 2002); *Rhoads v. FDIC et al.*, 257 F.3d 373, 383 (4th Cir. 2001), *cert. denied*, 535 U.S. 922 (2002); *Rager v. Dade Behring, Inc.*, 210 F.3d 776, 777 (7th Cir. 2000); *Thorson v. Gemini, Inc. et al.*, 205 F.3d 370, 381–382 (8th Cir. 2000), *cert. denied*, 521 U.S. 871 (2000); *Harrington v. Boysville of Michigan, Inc. et al.*, No. 97–1862, 1998 U.S. App. LEXIS 9796 (6th Cir. May 13, 1998); *Stoops v. One Call Communications, Inc.*, 141 F.3d 309, 312 (7th Cir. 1998); *Dittle v. USPS*, No. 04–146 (PAM/RLE), 2005 U.S. Dist. LEXIS 1487, at *15 (D. Minn. Feb. 2, 2005); *Smith v. V.I. Port Authority*, No. 2002–227, 2005 U.S. Dist. LEXIS 56, at *36 (D.V.I. Jan. 2, 2005); *Dowell v. Indiana Heart Physicians, Inc.*, No. 1:03–cv–1410–DFH–TAB, 2004 U.S. Dist. LEXIS 26431, at *14 (S.D. Ind. Dec. 22, 2004); *Wheeler v. Pioneer Dev. Services, Inc.*, 349 F. Supp 2d 158 (D. Mass. 2004); *Lukacinsky v. Panasonic Service Co.*, No. 03–40141–FDS, 2004 U.S. Dist. LEXIS 25846, at *29 (D. Mass. Nov. 29, 2004); *Austin v. USPS*, No. SF-0752-06-0856-I-1, 2006 MSPB LEXIS 7717, at *9 (Dec. 26, 2006).

An employer is not required to ask for medical certification, and may dispense with the requirement altogether. *Rager v. Dade Behring, Inc.*, 210 F.3d 776, 777 (7th Cir. 2000) (citing *Thorson v. Gemini, Inc.*, 205 F.3d 370 (8th Cir. 2000)); *Fernandes v. Wal-Mart Stores, Inc.*, No. 03-11933-RGS, 2007 U.S. Dist. LEXIS 14618, at *11 (D. Mass. March 1, 2007); *Carpenter v. Kaiser Permanente*, No. 1:04 cv 1689, 2006 U.S. Dist. LEXIS 69564, at *32 (N.D. Ohio Sept. 27, 2006) ("while it is true that submission of a medical certification as a prerequisite to a grant of FMLA leave is an 'option' rather than a "requirement," it is an option which belongs to the employer"); *Electrolux Home Products, Inc. v. UAW*, 343 F. Supp. 2d 747, at *35 (N.D. Iowa 2004); *Hemensay v. Albion Public Schools*, No. 4:05-CV-7, 2006 U.S. Dist. LEXIS 36231, at *6 (W.D. Mich. Jan. 12, 2006); *Carmen v. Unison Behavioral Health Group, Inc.*, 295 F. Supp. 2d 809, 813 (N.D. Ohio 2003).

In all instances, it is the responsibility of the employer to request FMLA certification. *Conrad v. Eaton Corp.*, 303 F. Supp. 2d 987, 999–1000 (N.D. Iowa 2004); *McCarron v. British Telecom et al.*, No. 00-CV-6123, 2002 U.S. Dist. LEXIS 15151 (E.D. Pa. Aug. 7, 2002); *Levine v. Children's Museum of Indianapolis Inc.*, No. IP–00–0715–C G/H, 2002 U.S. Dist. LEXIS 14738 (S.D. Ind. July 1, 2002), *aff'd*, 61 Fed. Appx. 298 (7th Cir. 2003); *Washington v. Fort James Operating Co.*, 110 F. Supp. 2d 1325, 1330 (D. Ore. 2000); *Curry v. Neumann*, No. 98-8969-CIV-JORDAN, 2000 U.S. Dist. LEXIS 14758 (S.D. Fla. April 3, 2000); *Pendarvis v. Xerox Corp.*, 3 F. Supp. 2d 53, 56 (D. D.C. 1998); *LeGrand v. Village of McCook*, No. 96–C–5951, 1998 U.S. Dist. LEXIS 5230 (N.D. Ill. April 15, 1998); *Sims v. Alameda–Contra Costa Transit District et al.*, 2 F. Supp. 2d 1253, 1257 (N.D. Cal. 1998).

The responsibility to request FMLA certification is the employer's, not the employee's. *Thorson v. Gemini, Inc. et al.*, 205 F.3d 370, 381 (8th Cir. 2000); *Seachrist v. Harris Steel Co.*, No. 03 C 6197, 2005 U.S. Dist. LEXIS 30161, at *10 & n.6 (N.D. Ill. Nov. 30, 2005) (employee has no duty to provide medical certification where employer never asked for one); *Cook v. Electrolux Home Products, Inc.*, No. C04-3036-MWB, 2005 U.S. Dist. LEXIS 29828, at *34 (N.D. Iowa Nov. 28, 2005); *Marrero*

v. *Camden County Bd. of Social Services, et al.*, 164 F. Supp. 2d 455, 463–64 (D. N.J. 2001) (employee under no duty to provide any medical documentation of her condition unless and until requested by employer); *Shivakumar v. Abbott Laboratories et al.*, No. 99–7861, 2001 U.S. Dist. LEXIS 9628 (N.D. Ill. July 10, 2001) (until requested by employer, employee is under no obligation to provide medical certification); *Zawadowicz v. CVS. Corp et al.*, 99 F. Supp. 2d 518, 530 (D. N.J. 2000) (employees not required by statute or regulations to substantiate need for FMLA leave with medical certification unless requested by employer); *Michelle v. SMC Pneumatics, Inc.*, No. IP99–1285–C–T/G, 2000 U.S. Dist. LEXIS 12478 (S.D. Ind. Aug. 21, 2000); *Pendarvis v. Xerox Corp.*, 3 F. Supp. 2d 53, 56 (D. D.C. 1998); *Salgado v. CDW Computer Center, Inc.*, No. 97–C–1975, 1998 U.S. Dist. LEXIS 1374 (N.D. Ill. Feb. 5, 1994). But see *Diaz v. Fort Wayne Foundry Corp.*, 131 F.3d 711, 713 (7th Cir. 1997) (to establish existence of serious health condition an employee must submit medical certification).

An employer is not precluded from challenging whether the employee suffered from a serious health condition if the employer did not request medical certification at the time that the employee notified the employer of the need for leave. See *Levine*, 61 Fed. Appx. 298; *Hemensay v. Albion Public Schools*, No. 4:05-CV-7, 2006 U.S. Dist. LEXIS 36231, at *6 (W.D. Mich. Jan. 12, 2006); *Porter v. NYU School of Law*, No. 99 Civ. 4693 (TPG), 2003 U.S. Dist. LEXIS 14674, at *18–29 (S.D.N.Y. Aug. 25, 2003), *aff'd*, 392 F.3d 530 (2d Cir. 2004).

In *Levine v. Children's Museum of Indianapolis Inc.*, No. IP–00–0715–C G/H, 2002 U.S. Dist. LEXIS 14738 (S.D. Ind. July 1, 2002), *aff'd*, 61 Fed. Appx. 298 (7th Cir. 2003), the plaintiff argued that the employer was precluded from challenging whether he had a serious health condition within the meaning of the FMLA because the employer never asked for medical certification, as was its right. The district court found that the employer was not required to request certification because the notice provided by the employee only indicated that the employee was requesting leave due to "illness." The District court found that the Museum could not have reasonably considered FMLA certification as an option. The decision appears to either misapply or expand the holdings of some courts that require the use of the second and third opinion process as the exclusive means of challenging whether the employee has a serious health condition within the meaning of the law.

The regulation tracks the language of the Statute, with two exceptions. First, the reference to an employee's seriously ill covered family member is not accurate. In order for an eligible employee to be entitled to FMLA leave, the covered family member must have a serious health condition, within the meaning of the law. While, presumably, the phrase "seriously ill" means the same thing as "serious health condition," because the correct statutory language was not used the phrase could be interpreted differently. Agencies, however, are well advised to treat the term "seriously ill" as if it means "serious health condition."

Second, as written, the regulation does not clearly provide that the certification must be from an appropriate health care provider based on whether the need for FMLA leave was due to the employee's own serious health condition, or to care for a covered family member with a serious health condition. That is, the regulation should be read as permitting an employer to request, and an employee to provide, a certification from his or her own health care provider if the need for FMLA leave is due to the employee's own serious health condition. If the need for FMLA leave is due to the serious health condition of a covered family member of the employee, the medical certification should be from the covered family member's health care provider. While this was undoubtedly the intent of the drafters, as currently written, the regulation could be read to permit an employee to provide certification from their own health care provider even when the issue is whether the covered family member has an FMLA–covered serious health condition. The statutes address this matter by use of the term "as appropriate" to signify that the certification must be from the health care provider of the employee or the covered family member, depending on who has the serious health condition. See 29 USC 2613(a); 5 USC 6383(a); 2 USC 1312(a)(1) (incorporating 29 USC 2613 into CAA); 3 USC 412(a)(1) (incorporating 29 USC 2613 into PEOAA).

This is more than mere semantics. By requiring an employee to provide certification from the *appropriate* health care provider, an employer may avoid having to go through the time and expense of securing a second or third opinion to challenge a certification from an inappropriate health care provider. For example, an employee requests FMLA leave to care for a covered spouse with a serious health condition and the employer requests medical certification in support of the leave. Instead of producing a certification from the health care provider of the employee's spouse, the employee provides a complete certification from the employee's own health care provider. The employee's health care provider has never seen or treated the spouse. As currently written, the regulations would require the employer to accept that certification. The agency's only means to challenge the certification is to go through the expense of having to pay for a second and, perhaps, third medical opinion process.

Federal employers faced with this situation should seriously consider returning the certification to the employee, advising the employee of the reasonable opportunity to obtain certification from an appropriate health care provider. If the employee fails or refuses to obtain appropriate certification, the employer can deny FMLA leave. If challenged by citation to the implementing regulations, the employer should cite the statutory requirement that certification be from the *appropriate* health care provider. To the extent that the regulation permits a different result, it is void as the statutory language is crystal clear on this point. Of course, agencies contemplating such action should consult with counsel beforehand.

The regulations do not clearly indicate whether the employer may directly provide the certification to the health care provider, or must provide the form to the employee who delivers it to the health care provider. Because an employee is obligated to return the form within, in most cases, 15 days, the inference is that employers should provide the certification to the employee to provide to the health care provider. In *White v. Interstate Brake Products, Inc.*, No. 3:96–CV5–S–A, 1997 U.S. Dist. LEXIS 10921 (N.D. Miss. June 2, 1997), however, the court held that an employer did not violate the FMLA, as a matter of law, by simply mailing a medical certification directly to the employee's physician. In most cases, agencies should not contact the employee's or covered family member's physician directly, but should provide the requested certification to the employee to obtain from the health care provider.

The medical certification must be from a health care provider. *Gulan v. Federal Reserve Bank of Cleveland*, No. 1:01 CV 1784, 2003 U.S. Dist. LEXIS 15749, at *15 (N.D. Ohio July 31, 2003). Affidavits from the employee and from friends to support the conclusion that she was absent from work due to her hemorrhoids is, therefore, insufficient. The "requirement that a health care provider furnish certification does not mean that, in the employee's own judgment, he or she should not work, or even that it was uncomfortable or inconvenient for the employee to have to work. Rather, it means that a 'health care provider' has determined that, in his or her professional medical judgment, the employee…could not have worked because of the illness. If it were otherwise, a note form a spouse, parent, or even one's own claim that one cannot work because of illness would suffice." *Id.* at *15–16 (quoting *Olsen v. Ohio Edison Co.*, 979 F. Supp. 1159, 1166 (N.D. Ohio 1997)).

The initial medical certification must be from a health care provider of the employee's choosing. An employer may not rely on the medical opinion of its own physician for purposes of granting an employee's request for FMLA leave. *Krohn v. Forsting et al.*, 11 F. Supp. 2d 1082, 1090 (E.D. Mo. 1998).

2. Title II

The regulations implementing the medical certification provision of Title II do not suffer from the same infirmities as those discussed above implementing Title I, the CAA, and the PEOAA. In pertinent part, the regulation, 5 CFR 630.1207(a), provides:

> An employer may require that a request for leave under § 630.1203(a)(3) (care or spouse, son, daughter, or patent with a serious health condition) or (4) (employee's own serious health condition) be supported by written medical certification issued by the health care provider of the employee or the health care provider of the spouse, son, daughter, or parent of the employee, as appropriate.

Accord Hatch v. USPS, No. AT-0752-07-0175-I-1, 2007 MSPB LEXIS 647, at *3 (June 1, 2007); *Slaughter v. USDA*, No. DC-0752-06-0624-I-1, 2006 MSPB LEXIS 6978, at *11 (Nov. 20, 2006); *Brown v. Treasury*, No. DC-0752-06-0669-I-1, 2006 MSPB LEXIS 5903, at *14 (Oct. 19, 2006); *Franklin v. Dept. of Air Force*, No. AT-0752-05-0355-I-2, 2005 MSPB LEXIS 8069, at *36 (Dec. 27, 2005); *Cole v. DHHS*, No. DC-0752-05-0457-I-1, 2005 MSPB LEXIS 6825, at *8 (Nov. 1, 2005); *Williams v. Dept. of Navy*, No. DC-0752-05-0431-I-1, 2005 MSPB LEXIS 6866, at *4 (Oct. 17, 2005), *pet. denied*, 101 MSPR 133 (2006); *Dias v. VA*, No. NY-0752-04-0279-I-2, 2005 MSPB LEXIS 3926, at *14 (June 30, 2005), *rev'd*, 102 MSPR 53 2006), *appeal dismissed*, 2006 U.S. App. LEXIS 28961 (Fed. Cir. 2006), *vacated, reinstated*, 2006 U.S. App. LEXIS 32257 (2006), *aff'd*, 2007 U.S. App. LEXIS 11530 (May 8, 2007); *Romero v. Dept. of Interior*, No. SF-0752-05-0011-I-1, 2005 MSPB LEXIS 3147, at *12-13 (May 19, 2005); *Jeffries v. Dept. of Navy*, 78 MSPR 255, at *5 (1998).

By cross-referencing regulations that define serious health conditions, OPM's regulations avoid any confusion regarding the circumstances under which an employer may request medical certification. The regulations also accurately track the Statute requiring that the certification be provided from the appropriate health care provider, depending on who has the serious health condition giving rise to the need for FMLA leave.

Note that the OPM regulations clearly provide that an employer may request that the health care certification be in writing. The regulations implementing Title I, the CAA, and the PEOAA do not specifically provide that the certification be in writing, although that would appear to be the intent.

B. HEALTH CARE PROVIDER DEFINED

The medical certification that an employer may require of an eligible employee in support of their request for FMLA leave must be from a health care provider. Not surprisingly, the FMLA statues and regulations do not have a uniform definition of which members of the medical profession fall within the definition of a "health care provider," for purposes of the FMLA. As this matter was discussed in detail in Chapter 7, "Covered Conditions," an overview of this area follows.

1. Title I, the CAA, and the PEOAA

The term "health care provider" means a doctor of medicine or osteopathy who is authorized to practice medicine or surgery (as appropriate) by the state in which the doctor practices, and any other person determined by the Secretary of Labor (in the case of Title I) to be capable of providing health care services. 29 USC 2611(6); 29 CFR 825.118(a)(1)–(2); 2 USC 1312(a)(1) (incorporating 29 USC 2613 into CAA); S. Res. 242, Cong. Rec. S3959, S3963 (April 23, 1996); 29 CFR 825.118(a)(1)(i)–(ii); 3 USC 412(a)(1) (incorporating 29 USC 2613 into PEOAA).

The implementing regulations define what "others" are capable of providing health care services. 29 CFR 825.118(b); S. Res. 242, Cong. Rec. S3959, S3963 (April 23, 1996); 29 CFR 825.118(a)(2). These others include the following individuals who are authorized to practice by the state and are performing within the scope of their practice:

- Podiatrists;
- Dentists;
- Clinical psychologists;
- Optometrists;
- Chiropractors, but only for treatment consisting of manual manipulation of the spine to correct a subluxation as determined by x–ray to exist;
- Nurse practitioners;
- Nurse midwives;
- Clinical social workers.

Individuals providing health care services that do not have to be authorized by the state and practicing within the scope of their legal authority include:

- Christian Science practitioners listed with the First Church of Christ, Scientists in Boston, Massachusetts;
- Any health care provider from whom an employer or the employer's group health plan's benefits manager will accept certification of the existence of a serious health condition to substantiate a claim for benefits; and
- A health care provider listed above who practices in a country other than the United States, who is authorized to practice in accordance with the law of that country, and who is performing within the scope of his or her practice as defined under such law.

A Nurse Practitioner is specifically recognized as a "health care provider" under DOL's regulations. *Electrolux Home Products, Inc. v. UAW*, 343 F. Supp. 2d 747 (N.D. Iowa 2004), *aff'd*, 416 F.3d 848 (8th Cir. 2005).

The phrase "authorized to practice in the state" as used above means that the health care provider must be authorized to diagnose and treat physical or mental health conditions without supervision by a doctor or other health care provider. 29 CFR 825.118(c); S. Res. 242, Cong. Rec. S3959, S3963 (April 23, 1996); 29 CFR 825.118(c).

Employers can get into trouble when they demand that an employee provide medical certification in support of the leave, the employee does, and the employer insists that the employee obtain another certification from an expert or specialist. *See Giuliani v. Minnesota Vikings Football Club, LLC*, No. 99–CV–1811 DDA/FLN, 2001 U.S. Dist. LEXIS 20207 (D. Minn. June 11, 2001) (employer's rejection of certification from licensed clinical psychologist and insistence that employee obtain certification from psychiatrist invalid because the former was a health care provider for purposes of FMLA). If the employee provides a complete certification and the individual who signed it is a health care provider within the meaning of the law, the employer must accept it, clarify it, or challenge it through the second and third health care opinion provider process. Insisting that the employee go out and obtain another certification from a specialist is not an option.

In *Schober v. SMC Pneumatics, Inc.*, No. IP 99–1285–C T/G, 2000 U.S. Dist. LEXIS 19088 (S.D. Ind. Dec. 4, 2000), the court found that an employer interfered with the employee's FMLA rights when it erroneously advised the employee that the employee may only obtain the FMLA medical certification from a named health care provider, who was the covered family member's primary care physician. The court noted that 29 CFR 825.305(a) provides that if medical certification is required by an employer, such certification may be issued by "the health care provider" of "the employee's ill family member." *Id*. The regulation does not require that the certification be completed by the employee's ill family member's primary care physician only.

Similarly, certifications need not be submitted by the same health care provider. *Sims v. Alameda–Contra Costa Transit District et al.*, 2 F. Supp. 2d 1253, 1264–65 (N.D. Cal. 1998) (for purposes of determining if employee received "continuing treatment from a health care provider," the term "health care provider" does not require that an employee be treated twice by the same doctor; an employee who submitted certifications from different physicians in same Health Maintenance Organization satisfied certification requirement).

2. Title II

The statutory definition of a health care provider under Title II is virtually identical to that of Title I, the CAA, and the PEOAA. Title II, 5 USC 6381(2), defines "health care provider" as a doctor of medicine or osteopathy who is authorized to practice medicine or surgery (as appropriate) by the state in which the doctor practices, or any other person determined by the Director of OPM to be capable of providing health care services.

The regulations implementing Title II clarifies the definition of health care provider. 5 CFR 630.1201 (definition of health care provider). The definition is substantially different than the way the term is defined for purposes of Title I, the CAA, and the PEOAA. For purposes of employees covered by Title II, "health care provider" means:

- A licensed Doctor of Medicine;
- A licensed Doctor of Osteopathy;
- A physician serving on active duty in the uniformed services and who is designated by the uniformed service to conduct examinations under this subpart;
- Any health care provider recognized by the Federal Employees Health Benefits Program;
- Any health care provider who is licensed or certified under federal or state law to provide the service in question;
- A health care provider recognized by the FEHBP or licensed or certified under federal or state law to provide the service in question, who practices in a country other than the United States, who is authorized to practice in accordance with the laws of that country, and who is performing within the scope of his or her practice as defined under such law;
- A Christian Science practitioner listed with the First Church of Christ, Scientist, in Boston, Massachusetts;
- A Native American, including an Eskimo, Aleut, and Native Hawaiian, who is recognized as a traditional healing practitioner by native traditional religious leaders who practices traditional healing methods as believed, expressed, and exercised in Indian religions of the American Indian, Eskimo, Aleut, and Native Hawaiians, consistent with Public Law 95–314, August 11, 1978 (92 Stat. 469), as amended by Public Law 103–344, October 6, 1994 (108 Stat. 3125).

Accord Burge v. Dept. of Air Force, 82 MSPR 75 (1999), *pet. denied*, 86 MSPR 688 (2000).

The regulations defining the term "health care provider" for purposes of Title II, while often similar, contain several substantial differences from the comparable regulations implementing Title I, the CAA, and the PEOAA. For example, Title II specifically includes within the definition of a health care provider certain authorized physicians who are serving on active duty in the uniformed services. It also includes certain Native American traditional religious leaders practicing traditional healing methods. Neither category is specifically recognized as "health care providers" pursuant to Title I, the CAA, and the PEOAA.

The definitions of certain other health care providers under Title II are slightly modified from the comparable definitions under Title I, the CAA, and the PEOAA, giving them a different meaning. For instance, under Title I, an individual will be recognized as a health care provider if the employer's group health plan's benefits manager would accept certification of the existence of a serious health condition to substantiate a claim for benefits. Under Title II, the similar regulation changes the phrase "group health plan's benefits manager" to anyone recognized by the Federal Employees Health Benefits Program. These may not be the same entities. The CAA modifies this further to include any health care provider from whom an employing office or the employing office's group health plan's benefits manager would accept such certification. [For a further discussion comparing the similarities and differences between defined FMLA health care providers, see Chapter 7, "Covered Conditions."]

C. EMPLOYER NOTICE OF MEDICAL CERTIFICATION REQUIREMENT

In order to require an employee to provide medical certification in support of a request for FMLA leave, the employer must first notify the employee of this requirement. This requirement is not set forth directly in the language of the federal sector FMLA statutes. Rather, this employer notice requirement is contained in the regulations implementing the FMLA. Because employer notice obligations are addressed in Chapter 8, "Notice Requirements," an overview of the matter follows.

1. Title I, the CAA, and the PEOAA

An employer must give written notice of a requirement for medical certification each time a certification is required. 29 USC 2613(a); 29 CFR 825.305(a); S. Res. 242, Cong. Rec. S3959, S3972 (April 23, 1996); 29 CFR 825.305(a); *see Cooper v. Fulton County*, 458 F.3d 1282, 1285 (11th Cir. 2006); *Lubke v. City of Arlington*, 455 F.3d 489, 496-97 (5th Cir. 2006); *Rhoads v. FDIC et al.*, 257 F.3d 373, 383 (4th Cir. 2001), *cert. denied*, 535 U.S. 933 (2002); *Urban v. Dolgencorp of Texas, Inc.*, 393 F.3d 572, 574 (5th Cir. 2004); *Rager v. Dade Behring, Inc.*, 210 F.3d 776, 777 (7th Cir. 2000); *Dittle v. USPS*, No. 04–146 (PAM/RLE), 2005 U.S. Dist. LEXIS 1487, at *15 (D. Minn. Feb. 2, 2005); *Smith v. V.I. Port Authority*, No. 2002–227, 2005 U.S. Dist. LEXIS 56, at *36 (D.V.I. Jan. 2, 2005); *Wheeler v. Pioneer Dev. Services, Inc.*, 349 F. Supp 2d 158 (D. Mass. 2004); *Electrolux Home Products, Inc. v. UAW*, 343 F. Supp. 2d 747, at *26 (N.D. Iowa 2004), *aff'd*, 416 F.3d 848 (8th Cir. 2005); *Baldwin–Love v. Electronic Data Systems, Corp.*, 307 F. Supp. 2d. 1222, 1229 (M.D. Ala. 2004); *Conrad v. Eaton Corp.*, 303 F. Supp. 2d 987, 999 (N.D. Iowa 2004); *Porter v. NYU School of Law*, No. 99 Civ. 4693 (TPG), 2003 U.S. Dist. LEXIS 14674, at *15 (S.D.N.Y. Aug. 25, 2003), *aff'd*, 392 F.3d 530 (2d Cir. 2004); *Gulan v. Federal Reserve Bank of Cleveland*, No. 1:01 CV 1784, 2003 U.S. Dist. LEXIS 15749, at *11 (N.D. Ohio July 31, 2003).

Dittle v. USPS, No. 04–146 (PAM/RLE), 2005 U.S. Dist. LEXIS 1487, at *15 (D. Minn. Feb. 2, 2005), addressed the adequacy of the employer's request for a medical certification. Dittle had an existing medical certification for intermittent leave of one to three days in length due to post–traumatic stress disorder. He was subsequently absent for several weeks. The Postal Service FMLA coordinator contacted Dittle and asked him to resubmit a certification within 15 days as his current FMLA certification covered only intermittent leave, up to three days. Because he had not reported to work in more than two weeks, the Coordinator requested that Dittle's physician specifically address the issue of whether Dittle's medical condition warranted extended periods of absence. The coordinator also warned that failure to provide complete medical certification could result in delaying his FMLA protected leave and, if he failed to comply, his absences may not be FMLA protected and could be used as discipline. When he failed to timely provide the requested medical certification, the Postal Service denied Dittle's FMLA leave request and notified him of same. Dittle was subsequently fired as a result of his absence.

Dittle argued that he was provided insufficient notice through the Postal Service's request for a certification that covered his extended period of absence. The court disagreed. The court noted that the e-mail notice apprised Dittle that his earlier certification covered only intermittent leave and his paperwork needed to be updated to cover a period of absence exceeding three days. It also informed Dittle that his physician should identify the duration and frequency of Dittle's medical condition. According to the court, the "notice was sufficiently clear to notify Dittle that the January 2002 certification did not cover his extended period of absence, and that a new certification was needed."

Dittle also argued that the notices he received were insufficient because they did not explicitly warn that Dittle would be discharged if he did not provide certification. The court disagreed. The court found that the notice was sufficient as it informed Dittle that he could face adverse action if he did not provide a certification.

The court in *Conrad v. Eaton Corp.*, 303 F. Supp. 2d 987, 999 (N.D. Iowa 2004), found the employer's request for medical certification sufficiently ambiguous to deny summary judgment to the employer. The employer in that case provided the employee with a FMLA summary, which, in pertinent part, provided:

> Medical certification will be required to support a request to leave because of "serious health condition,"...

The court questioned whether the language was sufficient to rise to the level of a specific request by Eaton that Conrad fill out a medical certification.

a. Handbooks and Other Written Guidance

FMLA-covered employers (including all federal agencies) with eligible employees must include information concerning FMLA entitlements and obligations in any written guidance to employees regarding employee benefits and leave rights, such as in employee handbooks. 29 CFR 825.301(a)(1); S. Res. 242, Cong. Rec. S3959, S3971 (April 23, 1996); 29 CFR 825.301(a)(1); *see Konipol v. Restaurant Associates*, No. 01–Civ. 7857 (GEL), 2002 U.S. Dist. LEXIS 22439 (S.D.N.Y. Nov. 20, 2002); *Tornberg v. Business Interlink Services, Inc.*, 237 F. Supp. 2d 778, 785 n.5 (E.D. Mich. 2002); *Curry v. Neumann*, No. 98–8969–CIV–JORDAN, 2000 U.S. Dist. LEXIS 14758 (S.D. Fla. April 3, 2000). While not specifically mentioned, prudent employers should include the agencies policy regarding an employee's obligation to provide medical certification in support of the need for FMLA leave, and the consequences of failure to provide certification.

In *Henderson v. Whirlpool Corp.*, 17 F. Supp. 2d 1238, 1247 (N.D. Okla. 1998), the court held that an employer did not satisfy the requirement that it give "notice of a requirement of a medical certification each time a certification is required" solely by including notice of the requirement in an employee handbook. According to the court, *id*. at 1248:

> By claiming that a statement in the policy manual is a blanket requirement to provide medical certification each time an absence is taken shifts the burden in this context from the employer to the employee and results in a significant modification of the Statute. The effect would be to write into the law a trip to the doctor ever time an employee requests medical leave. This result is contrary to the terms of the statute, illogical, and inconsistent with the legislative intent. Therefore, the Court concludes, as a matter of law, that a blanket requirement for medical certification in the policy manual cannot satisfy an employer's obligation to notify an employee that medical certification is requested "each time a certification is required." The law mandates that an employer communicate its desire for medical certification in each instance that it deems it necessary to meet its legal obligation to determine whether the leave sought qualifies.

Where the certification requirement is set forth in a handbook, but the handbook is given to the employee when leave is requested, if the notice otherwise satisfies the FMLA requirements, that employer may meets its certification notice obligations. *Stubl v. T.A. Sys., Inc.*, 984 F. Supp. 1075, 1086–87 (E.D. Mich. 1997).

b. No Written Guidance Explaining Employee Benefits and Leave Requirements

In the unlikely event that a federal employer does not have written policies, manuals, or handbooks describing employee benefits and leave provisions, the federal employer must provide the employee with written guidance concerning the employee's FMLA rights and obligations. 29 CFR 825.301(a)(2); S. Res. 242, Cong. Rec. S3959, S3971 (April 23, 1996); 29 CFR 825.301(a)(2). Again, the regulation does not specifically require that such notice include information regarding medical certifications. Prudent federal employers, however, will include such a statement of its medical certification policy or practice. This written notice must be given no less often than the first time in each six-month period that an employee gives notice of the need for FMLA leave, if FMLA leave is taken during the six-month period. 29 CFR 825.301(a)(2), 825.301(c); S. Res. 242, Cong. Rec. S3959, S3971 (April 23, 1996); 29 CFR 825.301(a)(2), 825.301(c); *see*

Frazier v. Honda of America Mfg., Inc., 431 F.3d 563, 566 (6th Cir. 2005). In lieu of creating its own form of notice, the employer may provide employees with a copy of the FMLA Fact Sheet available through the DOL (for Title I), or the Office of Compliance (for the CAA). 29 CFR 825.301(a)(2), 825.301(c); S. Res. 242, Cong. Rec. S3959, S3971 (April 23, 1996); 29 CFR 825.301(a)(2), 825.301(c).

c. Notice of Specific FMLA Expectations and Obligations

In addition to notice by way of a written employee handbook, manual, or other written guidance regarding employee benefits or leave rights, employers must provide the employee with written notice detailing the specific expectations and obligations of the employee and explaining the consequences of a failure to meet these obligations. 29 CFR 825.301(b)(1); S. Res. 242, Cong. Rec. S3959, S3971 (April 23, 1996); 29 CFR 825.301(b)(1); *see Cooper v. Fulton County,* 458 F.3d 1282, 1285 (11th Cir. 2006); *Lubke v. City of Arlington,* 455 F.3d 489, 497 (5th Cir. 2006); *Rhoads v. FDIC et al.,* 257 F.3d 373, 383 (4th Cir. 2001) (under Interim DOL regulations), *cert. denied,* 535 U.S. 933 (2002); *Rager v. Dade Behring, Inc.,* 210 F.3d 776, 777 (7th Cir. 2000); *Konipol v. Restaurant Associates,* No. 01–Civ. 7857 (GEL), 2002 U.S. Dist. LEXIS 22439 (S.D.N.Y. Nov. 20, 2002); *Tornberg v. Business Interlink Services, Inc.,* 237 F. Supp. 2d 778, 785 n.5 (E.D. Mich. 2002); *Peter v. Lincoln Technical Institute,* No. 01–5949, 2002 U.S. Dist. LEXIS 17345 (E.D. Pa. Aug. 29, 2002); *Peeples v. Coastal Office Products, Inc.* 203 F. Supp. 2d 432, 449 (D. Md. 2001), *aff'd,* 2003 U.S. App. LEXIS 8644 (4th Cir. 2003); *Robinson v. Franklin County Bd. of Commissioners et al.,* No. 99–CV–162, 2002 U.S. Dist. LEXIS 25681 (S.D. Ohio Jan. 28, 2002); *Shtab v. The Greate Bay Hotel and Casino, Inc. et al.,* 173 F. Supp. 2d 255, 264 (D. N.J. 2001).

The written notice must be provided to the employee in a language in which the employee is literate. 29 CFR 825.301(b)(1); S. Res. 242, Cong. Rec. S3959, S3971 (April 23, 1996); 29 CFR 825.301(b)(1).

With one pertinent exception, such notice must also be provided to the employee no less often than the first time in each six–month period that an employee gives notice of need for FMLA leave. 29 CFR 825.301(b)(1); S. Res. 242, Cong. Rec. S3959, S3971 (April 23, 1996); 29 CFR 825.301(b)(1); *see Frazier v. Honda of America Mfg.,* Inc., 431 F.3d 563, 566 (6th Cir. 2005). Where the employer requires medical certification or a fitness–for–duty report, written notice of the requirement must be provided to the employee each time the employee requests FMLA leave. 29 CFR 825.301(c)(2)(I); S. Res. 242, Cong. Rec. S3959, S3971 (April 23, 1996); 29 CFR 825.301(c)(2)(I).

Specific written notice that the employer is requiring medical certification or a fitness–for–duty report is not required each time an employee requests FMLA leave if: (1) the initial written notice is in the six–month period; and (2) the employer handbook or other written documents (if any) describing the employer's leave policies, clearly provides the circumstances under which such certification or a fitness–for–duty report is required. 29 CFR 825.301(c)(2)(ii); S. Res. 242, Cong. Rec. S3959, S3971 (April 23, 1996); 29 CFR 825.301(c)(2)(ii); *see Frazier v. Honda of America Mfg.,* Inc., 431 F.3d 563, 566 (6th Cir. 2005). For example, if the initial written notice in the six–month period and the handbook clearly provided that medical certification was required in all cases, or in cases where an employee was out more than a specified number of days, or for all back injuries. 29 CFR 825.301(c)(2)(ii); S. Res. 242, Cong. Rec. S3959, S3971 (April 23, 1996); 29 CFR 825.301(c)(2)(ii). Where subsequent written notice is not required, the employer must still orally request that the employee provide certification. 29 CFR 825.301(c)(2)(ii), 825.305(a); S. Res. 242, Cong. Rec. S3959, S3971–S3972 (April 23, 1996); 29 CFR 825.301(c)(2)(ii), 825.305(a); *see Frazier v. Honda of America Mfg.,* Inc., 431 F.3d 563, 566 (6th Cir. 2005).

In *Frazier v. Honda of America Mfg.,* Inc., 431 F.3d 563, 566 (6th Cir. 2005), the employer orally requested medical certification on July 26. On July 31, Frazier received a packet of FMLA information containing written notice of FMLA rights and obligations. Because Honda repeatedly provided written notice to Frazier in the six month period prior to the request for leave, the court found that the oral request for medical certification was sufficient, thereby triggering the 15-day period for the employee to provide medical certification.

Agencies are well advised to provide written notice of the employee's need to provide medical certification or a fitness–for–duty report each and every time the employee requests FMLA leave. When it comes to litigation, oral notice is generally not worth the paper it's not printed on.

The contents of the notice of specific FMLA expectations and obligations must include, as appropriate, 29 CFR 825.301(b)(1); S. Res. 242, Cong. Rec. S3959, S3971 (April 23, 1996); 29 CFR 825.301(b)(1), the following:

- Any requirements for the employee to furnish medical certification of a serious health condition and the consequences of failing to do so;

- The employee's right to substitute paid leave and whether the employer will require the substitution of paid leave, and the conditions related to any substitution;

- Any requirement for the employee to make premium payments to maintain health benefits, the arrangements for making such payments, and the possible consequences of failure to make such payments on a timely basis;

- Any requirement for the employee to present a fitness-for-duty certificate to be restored to employment;

- The employee's status as a "key employee" and the potential consequences that restoration may be denied following FMLA leave, explaining the conditions required for such denial;

- The employee's right to restoration to the same or an equivalent job upon return from leave;

- The employee's potential liability for payment of health insurance premiums paid by the employer during the employee's unpaid FMLA leave if the employee fails to return to work after taking FMLA leave.

Written notice pursuant to § 825.301(b), providing specific expectations and obligations of the employee, must be given within a reasonable time after notice of the need for FMLA leave is given by the employee, generally within one or two business days if feasible. 29 CFR 825.301(c); S. Res. 242, Cong. Rec. S3959, S3971 (April 23, 1996); 29 CFR 825.301(c). The regulations do not identify the time frame that an employee has when the employer must notify the employee each and every time that medical certification is required. Nor does the regulation specify what the time frame is for an employer to orally notify an employee that medical certification is required, where written notice is not required pursuant to § 825.301(c)(2)(ii). Presumably, the time frame is also a reasonable period of time, if feasible.

The regulations generally do not prescribe the means an employer may use to provide notice of the certification requirement. Presumably, an employer should use a reasonable means of notification. Where leave has already begun, the regulations provide that notice should be mailed to the employee's address of record. 29 CFR 825.301(c); S. Res. 242, Cong. Rec. S3959, S3971 (April 23, 1996); 29 CFR 825.301(c).

d. Failure of Employer to Provide Required Notice

If an employer fails to provide notice of the requirement that an employee provide medical certification in accordance with the provisions of the regulations, the employer may not take action against an employee for failure to comply with any provision required to be set forth in the notice. 29 CFR 825.301(f); S. Res. 242, Cong. Rec. S3959, S3971 (April 23, 1996); 29 CFR 825.301(f); see Lubke v. City of Arlington, 455 F.3d 489, 497 (5th Cir. 2006); Tornberg v. Business Interlink Services, Inc., 237 F. Supp. 2d 778, 785 n.5 (E.D. Mich. 2002) (employer's failure to provide employee with required notice of medical certification excused employee's failure to provide certification, and employee was not precluded from being covered by the FMLA); Shivakumar v. Abbott Laboratories et al., No. 99-7861, 2001 U.S. Dist. LEXIS 9628 ((N.D. Ill. July 10, 2001); Michelle v. SMC Pneumatics, Inc., No. IP99-1285-C-T/G, 2000 U.S. Dist. LEXIS 12478 (S.D. Ind. Aug. 21, 2000); Curry v. Neumann, No. 98-8969-CIV-JORDAN, 2000 U.S. Dist. LEXIS 14758 (S.D. Fla. April 3, 2000). Given the breadth of the notice requirements, the failure of an employer to meet these notice requirements may excuse an employee's failure to timely provide a complete medical health care provider certification in support of the employee's request for FMLA leave.

In Lubke v. City of Arlington, 455 F.3d 489, 496-97 (5th Cir. 2006), the Fifth Circuit questioned the validity of the sanction in 825.301(f). The district court prohibited the employer from contending that Lubke failed to submit timely medical documentation for FMLA lave because the employer failed to notify the employee of the FMLA certification requirements and consequences. On appeal, the Fifth Circuit, relying on the Supreme Court's decision in Ragsdale v. Wolverine World Wide, Inc., 535 U.S. 81, 122 S. Ct. 1155 (2002), opined that the district court should not apply the sanction in 825.301(f) if the consequence of doing so would afford Lubke an FMLA remedy to which he was not otherwise entitled. The Fifth Circuit went on to find that the district court's application of 825.301(f) resulted in harmless error because it did not deprive the City of medical documentation (the City received the documentation late).

The adequacy of an employer's notice of the employee's obligations to timely obtain certification, and consequences for failing to do so, is an oft-litigated subject. In Shtab v. The Greate Bay Hotel and Casino, Inc. et al., 173 F. Supp. 2d 255, 264 (D. N.J. 2001), the court indicated that the wording of the notice was not sufficiently clear with respect to the consequences that might result from an employer's failure to timely provide a requested medical certification. Because an employee reading the form could conclude that an insufficient medical certification would result in immediate termination or the employer might ask the employee to provide additional information, the court found that sufficient questions were raised as to the sufficiency of the notice that it denied the employer's motion for summary judgment on this issue. Employers clearly need to be careful to clearly spell out the consequences. This is no easy task since the regulations require an employer to allow an employee a reasonable opportunity to cure any deficiency in an incomplete form. It appears that the employer in *Shtab* attempted to cover both of those bases, albeit unsuccessfully.

In *Rager v. Dade Behring, Inc.*, 210 F.3d 776, 779 (7th Cir. 2000), although the court noted that the employer's communication to the employee regarding the 15-day deadline for submitting the certification was "clumsy and potentially confusing," the court nevertheless concluded that the document did give the employee 15 days to submit documentation (it never said she had 15 days in so many words) and told her that if she did not provide the form by the due date she could be fired. The court held that, under the circumstances, she was provided sufficient notice.

Similarly, in *Robinson v. Franklin County Bd. of Commissioners et al.*, No. 99-CV-162, 2002 U.S. Dist. LEXIS 25681 (S.D. Ohio Jan. 28, 2002), the court held that the employer complied with its obligation to notify the employee that medical certification would be required when the employer sent the employee a letter indicating the he must provide medical certification for the leave to be FMLA designated. The letter advised him that he had 15 days to provide the certification, and attached a copy of the certification form for the employee to send to his doctor. The employee never returned the form. The court also rejected the plaintiff's argument that his failure to provide the certification should be excused because a manager told him that he would not certify FMLA leave no matter what. See also *Alexander et al., v. Ford Motor Co.*, 204 F.R.D. 314, 318-19 (E.D. Mich. 2001) (approving Ford's notice policies regarding medical certification requirement); *Curry v. Neumann*, No. 98-8969-CIV-JORDAN, 2000 U.S. Dist. LEXIS 14758 (S.D. Fla. April 3, 2000) (Sheriff Neumann gave adequate notice of certification requirement where employee given written notice employee must provide certification, employee received a handbook that also set forth certification requirement, and employee signed FMLA application that stated leave for serious health condition must be accompanied by certification).

In *Peter v. Lincoln Institute*, 255 F. Supp. 2d 417 (E.D. Pa. 2002), the employer failed to advise the employee that the employee had at least 15 days to provide the certification. Rather, the employer informed the employee that he must provide certification "as-soon-as-possible." The failure of an employer to provide a deadline creates a question of fact whether the employer met its notification obligations under the FMLA. *Id.*; see *Rager v. Dade Behring, Inc.*, 210 F.3d 776, 776 (7th Cir. 2000); *Marrero v. Camden County Bd. of Social Services et al*, 164 F. Supp. 2d 455463-64 (D. N.J. 2001) (employer's medical certification notice deficient because it did not state that employee had 15 days to provide notice). But see *Curry v. Neumann*, No. 98-8969-CIV-JORDAN, 2000 U.S. Dist. LEXIS 14758 (S.D. Fla. April 3, 2000) (neither the FMLA nor the regulations include any specific requirement that the employer give notice to the employee as to the deadline for producing medical certification).

An employer that notified an employee that certification was due in less than the minimum 15 days is in violation of the Act. *LeGrand v. Village of McCook*, No. 96-C-5951, 1998 U.S. Dist. LEXIS 5230 (N.D. Ill. April 15, 1998) (requests for medical certification failed to comply with FMLA as one request advised that the employee had four days to provide certification or the employer would consider employee to have resigned; request for certification within 14 days also failed to meet minimum 15-day FMLA standard); *Reich v. Midwest Plastic Engineering, Inc. et al.*, No. 1:94-CV-525, 1995 U.S. Dist. LEXIS 8772 (W.D. Mich. June 6, 1995).

The courts are split when the employer's notice fails to indicate the consequences of an employee's failure to timely provide supporting medical certification, such notice was arguably deficient. Several courts have found such notice to be legally deficient. See *Chenoweth v. Wal-Mart Stores, Inc.*, 159 F. Supp. 2d 1032, 1037 (S.D. Ohio 2001); *Washington v. Fort James Operating Co.*, 110 F. Supp. 2d 1325, 1330 (D. Ore. 2000) (notice provided by employer did not address consequences of employee's failure to timely provided certification; employer bears burden of demonstrating a factual issue whether employer notified employee of consequences before imposing those consequences); *Uema v. Nippon Express Hawaii, Inc. et al.*, 26 F. Supp. 2d 1241 (D. Hawaii 1998) (language in notice that stated that leave could be delayed if certification not received within 15 days deficient as reasonable person could conclude that it did not apply where leave already commenced); *Reich*, 1995 U.S. Dist. LEXIS 8772.

Other courts have held that, notwithstanding the requirement of the regulations, an employer's failure to notify an employee of the consequences of failing to timely provide certification does not necessarily bar an employer from taking adverse action against an employee who fails to provide medical certification. *Curry*, 2000 U.S. Dist. LEXIS 14758;

Henthorn v. Olsten Corp., No. 97–C–508182, 1999 U.S. Dist. LEXIS 2029 (N.D. Ill. Feb. 24, 1999). In *Henthorn*, the court reasoned that "to read such a penalty into the regulation could effectively nullify § 2613 of the FMLA, which authorizes an employer to require an employee with a serious health condition to supply the appropriate medical certifications." In *Curry*, the court found that, even if the employer failed to notify the employee of the consequences of failing to provide certification, the employee failed to demonstrate a triable issue of fact where the employee was unable to return to her assigned job. Employers can also violate the Act by providing incorrect notice to the employee regarding FMLA rights and obligations with respect to medical certification. In *Schober v. SMC Pneumatics, Inc.*, No. IP 99–1285–C T/G, 2000 U.S. Dist. LEXIS 19088 (S.D. Ind. Dec. 4, 2000), the court found that the employer violated the Act when it erroneously advised the employee that only the primary care physician of the covered family member could sign the certification.

At least one court has held that an employer's failure to provide written notice regarding the medical certification requirement rendered the notice inadequate. *Reich v. Midwest Plastic Engineering, Inc. et al.*, No. 1:94–CV–525, 1995 U.S. Dist. LEXIS 8772 (W.D. Mich. June 6, 1995).

An employer's failure to provide the required notice regarding medical certification requirements also constitutes "interfering with, restraining, or denying the exercise of rights provided by the Act." 29 CFR 825.200; S. Res. 242, Cong. Rec. S3959, S3971 (April 23, 1996); 29 CFR 825.301(f); see *Rager v. Dade Behring, Inc.*, 210 F.3d 776, 777 (7th Cir. 2000); *Peter v. Lincoln Institute*, 255 F. Supp. 2d 417 (E.D. Pa. 2002); *Robinson v. Franklin County Bd. of Commissioners et al.*, No. 99–CV–162, 2002 U.S. Dist. LEXIS 25681 (S.D. Ohio Jan. 28, 2002); *Chenoweth v. Wal–Mart Stores, Inc.*, 159 F. Supp. 2d 1032, 1037 (S.D. Ohio 2001); *Schober v. SMC Pneumatics, Inc.*, No. IP 99–1285–C T/G, 2000 U.S. Dist. LEXIS 19088 (S.D. Ind. Dec. 4, 2000) (providing a fairly thorough analysis of employer misinformation as actionable interference); *Curry v. Neumann*, No. 98–8969–CIV–JORDAN, 2000 U.S. Dist. LEXIS 14758 (S.D. Fla. April 3, 2000); *Lacoparra v. Pergament Home Centers, Inc.*, 982 F. Supp. 213, 220 (S.D.N.Y. 1997); *Fry v. First Fidelity Bancorporation*, No. Civ. A. 95–6019, 1996 U.S. Dist. LEXIS 875 (E.D. Pa. Jan. 30, 1996).

Courts have applied equitable principles, particularly equitable estoppel and equitable tolling, to address an employee's failure to timely provide medical certification when the employer has failed to notify the employee of the obligation to provide certification and the consequences of failing to do so. See *Rager v. Dade Behring, Inc.*, 210 F.3d 776, 779 (7th Cir. 2000) (addressing potential application of equitable doctrines, but finding they were of no assistance as the plaintiff made no effort to establish elements of equitable claims); *Peter v. Lincoln Institute*, 255 F. Supp. 2d 417 (E.D., 2002).

Equitable estoppel rests on a claim of detrimental reliance, both actual and reasonable, on the representations or actions of another, in this case the employer. *Rager*, 210 F.3d at 779. Equitable tolling does not require any misleading conduct by the defendant, only that, under the circumstances, the employer could not reasonably have expected the plaintiff to act within the deadline. *Id.* at 779.

An employer's failure to notify an employee of the FMLA's certification requirements and consequences does not render an employee automatically covered under the Statute or provide the employee an independent cause of action. *Johnson v. USPS*, No. 1:97–CV–794, 1999 U.S. Dist. LEXIS 7981 (W.D. Mich. May 26, 1999).

2. Title II

The regulations implementing Title II do not specifically address or require an employer to notify an employee that the employer will require the employee to provide medical certification from a health care provider confirming the employee's need for FMLA leave, or the consequences of failure to provide such certification. The regulations do, however, generally provide that each employer must inform its employees of their entitlements and responsibilities pursuant to the implementing regulations, including the requirements and obligations of employees. 5 CFR 630.1203(g). The preamble to the implementing regulations, 5 CFR 630.1203 (leave entitlement), provides that agencies may meet this requirement by providing employees access to the FMLA and OPM's implementing regulations or agencies policies or guidance implementing the FMLA. The preamble continues that agencies may also provide employees access to OPM's fact sheet and brochure, "Federal Employee Entitlements Under the Family and Medical Leave Act of 1993" or "Family Friendly Leave Policies for Federal Employees," which are available on OPM's website: www.opm.gov.

In *Williams v. Dept. of Navy*, No. DC-0752-05-0431-I-1, 2005 MSPB LEXIS 6866, at *4 (Oct. 17, 2005), *pet. denied*, 101 MSPR 133 (2006), the Board found that the employee was repeatedly notified by the employer that she needed to provide acceptable medical documentation for her medical absences. The Board noted that the employer provided the employee several letters containing specific instructions of the kind of details she needed to provide in all documentation presented to justify an absence due to illness.

As the OPM materials will not set forth whether the employer is requesting that the employee provide medical certification to support a particular leave request, it is recommended that federal agencies include notice of employer policy on this matter in employee handbooks or manuals, and provide separate notice each and every time an employee requests FMLA leave. The notice should set forth the agency's policies regarding the requirement that an employee timely provide adequate medical certification, and the consequences of an employee's failure to provide such certification. An employer is well advised to provide written notice to the employee by reasonable means.

D. TIME LIMITS FOR REQUEST OF MEDICAL CERTIFICATION

The federal sector FMLA statues do not address when an employer should request an employee to provide medical certification supporting the employee's need for FMLA leave. The matter is addressed in some of the implementing regulations.

1. Title I, the CAA, and the PEOAA

There are four points in time when an employer may request medical certification to support an employee's request for FMLA leave. In most cases, the employer should request that an employee furnish certification from a health care provider at the time the employee gives notice of the need for FMLA leave or within two business days thereafter. 29 CFR 825.305(c); S. Res. 242, Cong. Rec. S3959, S3972 (April 23, 1996); 29 CFR 825.305(c); *see Lubke v. City of Arlington*, 455 F.3d 489, 496-97 (5th Cir. 2006); *Myers v. Dolgencorp., Inc.*, No. 04-4137-JAR, 2006 U.S. Dist. LEXIS 14108, at *6 (D. Kan. March 25, 2006); *Wheeler v. Pioneer Dev. Services, Inc.*, 349 F. Supp 2d 158 (D. Mass. 2004); *Konipol v. Restaurant Associates*, No. 01–Civ. 7857 (GEL), 2002 U.S. Dist. LEXIS 22439 (S.D.N.Y. Nov. 20, 2002); *Zawadowicz v. CVS. Corp. et al.*, 99 F. Supp. 2d 518, 530 (D. N.J. 2000); *Michelle v. SMC Pneumatics, Inc.*, No. IP99–1285–C–T/G, 2000 U.S. Dist. LEXIS 12478 (S.D. Ind. Aug. 21, 2000); *Uema v. Nippon Express Hawaii, Inc. et al.*, 26 F. Supp. 2d 1241 (D. Hawaii 1998); *Sims v. Alameda–Contra Costa Transit District et al.*, 2 F. Supp. 2d 1253, 1257 (N.D. Cal. 1998); *Austin v. USPS*, No. SF-0752-06-0856-I-1, 2006 MSPB LEXIS 7717, at *9 (Dec. 26, 2006).

When the need for FMLA leave is unforeseen, within two business days after FMLA leave has commenced, the employer may request that the employee provide medical certification. 29 CFR 825.305(c); S. Res. 242, Cong. Rec. S3959, S3972 (April 23, 1996); 29 CFR 825.305(c); *see Lubke v. City of Arlington*, 455 F.3d 489, 496-97 (5th Cir. 2006); *Zawadowicz v. CVS. Corp. et al.*, 99 F. Supp. 2d 518, 530 (D. N.J. 2000); *Michelle v. SMC Pneumatics, Inc.*, No. IP99–1285–C–T/G, 2000 U.S. Dist. LEXIS 12478 (S.D. Ind. Aug. 21, 2000); *Austin*, 2006 MSPB LEXIS 7717, at *9. For FMLA leave of a short duration (one or two days), this may mean that an employer may request certification to support an employee's need for FMLA leave after the employee has returned to work.

Several courts have found that 29 CFR 825.305(c) is permissive, and does not mandate that an employer request medical certification within two business days of the employee's request for leave. *See Dolgencorp, Inc.*, 2006 U.S. Dist. LEXIS 14108, at *7-10 (rejecting argument that employer waived its right to require medical certification by unduly delaying its request for certification); *Brown v. SBC Communications, Inc.*, No. 04-C-0290, 2005 U.S. Dist. LEXIS 41599, at *6 (E.D. Wis. Aug. 23, 2005); *Poteet v. Potter*, No. IP00-0712-C-Y/S, 2005 U.S. Dist. LEXIS 8658, at *18 (S.D. Ind. March 28, 2005).

An employer who fails to timely request certification may have interfered with the employee's FMLA rights. *Michelle v. SMC Pneumatics, Inc.*, No. IP99–1285–C–T/G, 2000 U.S. Dist. LEXIS 12478 (S.D. Ind. Aug. 21, 2000).

Remember that, for purposes of Title I, FMLA leave commences on the first absence of FMLA leave for each covered condition during the leave year. For intermittent or FMLA leave on a reduced leave schedule, the FMLA leave commences only once, on the first absence in the series of FMLA absences for the same covered condition during the leave year.

The employer may also request certification at some later date if the employer has reason to question the appropriateness of the leave or its duration. 29 CFR 825.305(c); S. Res. 242, Cong. Rec. S3959, S3972 (April 23, 1996); 29 CFR 825.305(c); *see Lubke*, 455 F.3d at 497; *Ausler v. Engineered Polymer Solutions*, No. 01–C 50439, 2003 U.S. Dist. LEXIS 13114, at *4 (N.D. Ill. July 28, 2003); *Konipol* 2002 U.S. Dist. LEXIS 22439.

In *Ausler*, the employee argued that his employer should be estopped from claiming that his absence (for which he was terminated) was not covered by the FMLA because defendant did not ask for the certification within two business days (waiting until the third business day to make the request). The court disagreed. The court reasoned that the employee provided the employer with a doctor's note that called into question his eligibility for FMLA leave. Pursuant to 29 CFR 825.305(c), the employer's subsequent request for additional medical certification was timely because that section permits an employer to request certification "at some later date" if the employer has reason to question the appropriateness of the leave. Thus, "the timing of defendant's request for certification does not estop defendant from making the claim that the absence was not covered by the FMLA."

Note that the regulation is worded in such a way that would not prohibit an employer from requesting certification "at some later date" even if it previously requested that the employee submit a certification. As such, barring harassment, there is nothing in the regulations prohibiting an employer from being able to request multiple certifications for the same FMLA leave period, at least where the employer later has reason to question the appropriateness of the leave or its duration.

2. Title II

Unlike Title I, the regulations implementing Title II do not place a time limit on when an employer may request that an employee provide a medical certification in support of a need for FMLA leave. As such, agencies are well advised to make such a request within a reasonable period of time of when the employer determines that it needs the medical certification in order to determine whether the request qualifies as a serious health condition for purposes of FMLA leave.

Note that, like Title I and the CAA, the absence of limitations on this point suggests that Title II would permit agencies to request more than one medical certification for the same period of FMLA leave. Again, agencies should proceed with caution in this area and limit such requests to situations, like under Title I, where the employer has reason to question the appropriateness of the leave or its duration based on all of the facts.

E. TIME LIMITS FOR PROVIDING CERTIFICATION TO THE EMPLOYER

The federal sector FMLA statues do not set forth the time limit that an employee has to provide an employer with a medical certification. Limitations are, however, contained in the implementing regulations.

1. Title I, the CAA, and the PEOAA

How much time an employee has to provide a medical certification in response to an employee's request for medical certification depends on whether the need for leave is foreseeable or not foreseeable. It also depends on whether the employer has extended the minimum time frames by policy.

a. General Rule

The FMLA requires an employee to provide, in a timely manner, a copy of such certification to the employer. 29 USC 2613(a); *see Baldwin–Love v. Electronic Data Systems, Corp.*, 307 F. Supp. 2d. 1222, 1229 (M.D. Ala. 2004). The DOL regulations are more specific. *Id.*

Where the need for FMLA leave is foreseeable and at least a 30-day notice is provided, the employee should provide the medical certification before the leave begins. 29 CFR 825.305(b); S. Res. 242, Cong. Rec. S3959, S3972 (April 23, 1996); 29 CFR 825.305(b); *see Killian v. Yorozu Automotive Tennessee, Inc.*, 454 F.3d 549, 554 (6th Cir. 2006); *Wheeler v. Pioneer Dev. Services, Inc.*, 349 F. Supp 2d 158 (D. Mass. 2004); *Konipol v. Restaurant Associates*, No. 01–Civ. 7857 (GEL), 2002 U.S. Dist. LEXIS 22439 (S.D.N.Y. Nov. 20, 2002); *Robinson v. Franklin County Bd. of Commissioners et al.*, No. 99–CV–162, 2002 U.S. Dist. LEXIS 25681 (S.D. Ohio Jan. 28, 2002); *Toro v. Mastex Industries et al.*, 32 F. Supp. 2d 25, 29 (D. Mass. 1998); *Uema v. Nippon Express Hawaii, Inc. et al.*, 26 F. Supp. 2d 1241, 1247–48 (D. Hawaii 1998); *Austin v. USPS*, No. SF-0752-06-0856-I-1, 2006 MSPB LEXIS 7717, at *9 (Dec. 26, 2006).

When this is not possible, the employee must provide the requested certification to the employer within a minimum period of 15 calendar days after the employer's request, or such other greater time period as requested by the employer, unless it is not practicable under the particular circumstances to do so despite the employee's diligent, good faith efforts.

29 CFR 825.305(b); S. Res. 242, Cong. Rec. S3959, S3972 (April 23, 1996); 29 CFR 825.305(b); see *Cooper v. Fulton County*, 458 F.3d 1282, 1285 (11th Cir. 2006); *Killian v. Yorozu Automotive Tennessee, Inc.*, 454 F.3d 549, 554 (6th Cir. 2006); *Lubke v. City of Arlington*, 455 F.3d 489, 496-97 (5th Cir. 2006); *Edgar v. JAC Products, Inc.*, 443 F.3d 501, 506 (6th Cir. 2006); *Kauffman v. Federal Express Corp.*, 426 F.3d 880, 885 (7th Cir. 2005); *Urban v. Dolgencorp of Texas, Inc.*, 393 F.3d 572, 574 (5th Cir. 2004); *Rhoads v. FDIC et al.*, 257 F.3d 373, 383 (4th Cir. 2001), cert. denied, 535 U.S. 933 (2002); *Rager v. Dade Behring, Inc.*, 210 F.3d 776, 777 (7th Cir. 2000); *Dittle v. USPS*, No. 04–146 (PAM/RLE), 2005 U.S. Dist. LEXIS 1487, at *15 (D. Minn. Feb. 2, 2005); *Smith v. V.I. Port Authority*, No. 2002–227, 2005 U.S. Dist. LEXIS 56, at *36 (D.V.I. Jan. 2, 2005); *Wheeler v. Pioneer Dev. Services, Inc.*, 349 F. Supp 2d 158 (D. Mass. 2004); *Electrolux Home Products, Inc. v. UAW*, 343 F. Supp. 2d 747, at *25 (N.D. Iowa 2004); *Peter v. Lincoln Institute*, 255 F. Supp. 2d 417 (E.D. Pa. 2002); *Robinson v. Franklin County Bd. of Commissioners et al.*, No. 99–CV–162, 2002 U.S. Dist. LEXIS 25681 (S.D. Ohio Jan. 28, 2002); *Michelle v. SMC Pneumatics, Inc.*, No. IP99–1285–C–T/G, 2000 U.S. Dist. LEXIS 12478 (S.D. Ind. Aug. 21, 2000); *Washington v. Fort James Operating Co.*, 110 F. Supp. 2d 1325, 1330 (D. Ore. 2000); *Toro v. Mastex Industries et al.*, 32 F. Supp. 2d 25, 29 (D. Mass. 1998); *Uema v. Nippon Express Hawaii, Inc. et al.*, 26 F. Supp. 2d 1241, 1247–48 (D. Hawaii 1998); *Morris v. VCW, Inc.*, No. 95–0737–CV–W–3–6, 1996 U.S. Dist. LEXIS 11124 (W.D. Mo. July 24, 1996) (certificate that an employer is entitled to request is not one that must be instantaneously produced on oral request; under the regulations, a written request seems the trigger the duty, with at least a 15–day time limit); *Austin v. USPS*, No. SF-0752-06-0856-I-1, 2006 MSPB LEXIS 7717, at *9 (Dec. 26, 2006).

A closer examination of the above rule follows.

b. Foreseeable Need for FMLA Leave

As set forth more fully in Chapter 8, "Notice Requirements," the regulations governing when an employee must provide medical certification responsive to an employer's request suffer from terminal vagueness. First, it not clear when the DOL or other regulatory bodies will consider FMLA leave to be foreseeable. The issue here is how much advance notice of the need for FMLA leave an employee must have for it to be considered foreseeable. Certainly, medical treatment planned weeks in advance is foreseeable. The determination becomes more difficult where the need for leave is known only days or hours in advance. Technically speaking, the need for FMLA leave is foreseeable whenever there is any time interval between when an employee knows he or she will need FMLA leave and when the leave actually begins.

The reference in the regulations to the requirement that "at least 30–days notice has been given" would appear to refer to notice of the need for FMLA leave given by the employee. That 30–days notice must be given by the employee as a condition for application of this requirement suggests that the need for leave must be foreseeable to the employee at least 30 days in advance of when leave commences.

The requirement that an employee provide the medical certification before leave *begins* raises the issue of whether there is a difference between when leave *commences* and when it *begins*. Presumably, they mean the same thing. Again, remember, that under Title I, leave taken on an intermittent or reduced leave schedule basis *begins* or *commences* only once, on the occasion of the first absence in the series of related absences. That day begins the running of the limitations period in which an employee must provide a medical certification at the request of an employer.

c. Need for Leave is Not Foreseeable

The alternative time period for an employee to provide medical certification comes into play "when this is not possible." Presumably, the reference to "this" means that it is not possible that: (1) the need for leave is foreseeable; and (2) the employee is unable to provide at least 30–days advance notice of the need for FMLA leave; and (3) the employee should provide the medical certification before the leave begins. Note that it must be *impossible* for the employee to provide the certification before leave begins in order for the alternative 15 or more calendar day limitations period to become effective. *Impossibility* is a very difficult standard for employees to meet. If the employee had notice of the need for leave more than 30 days from when the leave is to commence, as a result of application of the impossibility standard, it would be highly unlikely, under normal circumstances, for this alternative limitations period to apply.

The alternative time period is really geared toward situations where an employee is made aware of the need for FMLA leave within 30 days of when the leave must begin. While this certainly would include situations where the need for leave was immediate and unforeseen, such as a result of an accident, it would also include situations that are less emergent as the employee may have up to 29–days advance notice.

The alternative time period provides a minimum time period of 15 calendar days. 29 CFR 825.305(b); *see Wheeler v. Pioneer Dev. Services, Inc.*, 349 F. Supp 2d 158 (D. Mass. 2004) (where employee's need for FMLA leave is not foreseeable, employer must give employee a minimum of 15 days to comply).

An employee has 15 full days to provide the medical certification, measured from the date and time of the employee's request. In *Kauffman v. Federal Express Corp.*, 426 F.3d 880, 885 (7th Cir. 2005), the employer requested medical certification at 6:00 p.m. on January 7. The employee therefore had until 6:00 p.m. on January 22, to submit the certification.

An employer may, however, allow the employee more than 15 calendar days to provide the certification. Again, an employer may offer more generous leave benefits than the minimum required by the FMLA. *See* 29 CFR 825.700(b); S. Res. 242, Cong. Rec. S3959, S3976 (April 23, 1996); 29 CFR 825.700(a). Allowing more than the minimum period of time for an employee to provide medical certification would be a more generous employer benefit. With that said, most employers adhere to the minimum 15-day time period in order to keep the process moving. Unions and other organizations representing the interests of employees, on the other hand, will want to expand the minimum period in order to give employees as much time as possible to provide certification.

An employer who requires an employee to provide medical certification in less than 15 days violates the FMLA. *See Killian v. Yorozu Automotive Tennessee, Inc.*, 454 F.3d 549, 554 (6th Cir. 2006); *Cooper v. Fulton County*, 458 F.3d 1282, 1286 (11th Cir. 2006) (employer violated FMLA by giving employee 6 days to provide medical certification).

An employee, who is asked to provide medical certification but then is terminated before the passage of the 15 days, has a colorable claim against the employer for violation of the FMLA. *See Killian v. Yorozu Automotive Tennessee, Inc.*, 454 F.3d 549, 554 (6th Cir. 2006) (employer violated FMLA by terminating employee 6 days after requesting medical certification); *Chenoweth v. Wal-Mart Stores, Inc.*, 159 F. Supp. 2d 1032, 1037 (S.D. Ohio 2001) (denying employer's motion for summary judgment because employee was not given 15 days to return certification, but was terminated six days after receipt of the FMLA medical certification form); *Giuliani v. Minnesota Vikings Football Club, LLC*, No. 99–CV–1811 DDA.FLN, 2001 U.S. Dist. LEXIS 20207 (D. Minn. June 11, 2001) (employer did not follow FMLA certification requirements when it terminated employee a few days after request to obtain certification); *Michelle v. SMC Pneumatics, Inc.*, No. IP99–1285–C–T/G, 2000 U.S. Dist. LEXIS 12478 (S.D. Ind. Aug. 21, 2000) (employee terminated only 14 days after request for certification has colorable FMLA interference claim).

In *Bass v. Potter*, No. 05-CV-220-TCK-FHM, 2006 U.S. Dist. LEXIS 37834, at *16 & n.8 (N.D. Ok. June 7, 2006), the court declined to find that the employer willfully violated the FMLA when it gave the employee 14 rather than 15 days to provide medical certification. The court noted that the defendant, at most, was negligent. "This type of error by an employer simply does not evidence the type of intentional or reckless disregard that is required for a 'willful' violation."

An employer does not have to wait the 15 calendar days for a medical certification if the employee provided medical certification in support of FMLA leave, but the certifications the employee provided failed to indicate that the leave was FMLA-qualifying. In *Boyd v. State Farm Insurance Companies et al.*, 158 F.3d 326, 332 (5th Cir. 1998), *cert. denied*, 526 U.S. 1051 1999), the employer approved the employee's FMLA leave for stress, but notified the employee of the requirement that he obtain medical certification. In response to numerous requests for medical certification during his five-day absence, Boyd submitted a total of three letters by physicians and psychologists. Each time Boyd submitted a letter, State Farm informed him that the letters were insufficient and that he should return to work immediately. When he was informed that he was now being carried as AWOL and that he must submit medical certification, Boyd submitted another note from his psychologist, which again failed to indicate that his leave of absence was medically required. Nine days after he started leave, Boyd was fired.

Boyd sued alleging, in pertinent part, that his termination violated the FMLA because State Farm failed to wait 15 days after the written request for medical certification to terminate him. The court (158 F.3d at 332) addressed the matter as follows:

> The regulation at issue, 29 CFR 825.305(b), simply provides that an employee must be allowed a minimum of fifteen days to respond to an employer's written request for medical certification. Here, Boyd submitted the medical information in approximately five days after he received State Farm's written request, and consequently, did not need the full fifteen days in which to respond. In such situations, we hold as a matter of law, that when an employee submits medical information in response to an employer's written request, 29 CFR 825.305(b) is no longer implicated and the employer is not required to wait fifteen days before taking action on the employee's request for medical leave.

A number of cases have addressed the circumstances under which it is not practicable for an employee, despite good faith, diligent efforts, to provide certification within 15 calendar days (or the more generous time period selected by the employer) of the employer's request that the employee provide a medical certification in support of the need for FMLA leave. In general, what is practicable in terms of timing is based on the facts and circumstances of each case and is a question for the jury. *Peter v. Lincoln Institute*, 255 F. Supp. 2d 417 (E.D. Pa. 2002). Good faith requires "at least that the employee contact his employer by telephone and make it aware that he is unable to return his certification before the deadline." *Id.* (quoting *Washington v. Fort James Operating Co.*, No. CIV–9901300–JO, 2000 U.S. Dist. LEXIS 17859 (D. Or. Nov. 7, 2000)).

Courts excuse the failure of employees to timely provide medical certification due to physician delays in getting the paperwork done. *Id.*; *Toro v. Mastex Industries et al.*, 32 F. Supp. 2d 25, 29 (D. Mass. 1998) (failure of Columbia doctor to return medical forms provided by employee that were required by employer might be excused by jury under circumstances); *Ueme v. Nippon Exp. Hawaii, Inc.*, 26 F. Supp. 2d 1241, 1248 (D. Hawaii 1998) (jury could find that employee's failure to timely provide certification was excused because physician went on vacation); *Chenoweth v. Wal–Mart Stores, Inc.*, 159 F. Supp. 2d 1032, 1039 (S.D. Ohio 2001) (equitable provision triggered when employee's spouse's physician could not complete certification and home health aide delayed until after employee was terminated).

In *Taylor v. Ameritech Services, Inc.*, No. 05-C-952, 2007 U.S. Dist. LEXIS 28769, at *20-24 (E.D. Wis. April 18, 2007), the court rejected the doctor's explanation that he faxed medical certifications to the employer on several occasions where the doctor failed to indicate that date he faxed the certifications.

On the other hand, the burden to provide a completed medical certification is on the employee, not the doctor. *Rigel v. Wilks*, No. 1:03-CV-971, 2006 U.S. Dist. LEXIS 93659, at *53 (M.D. Pa. Dec. 28, 2006) (rejecting the employee's argument that completeness of the certification was the doctor's responsibility, not his).

Courts have taken the physical condition of the employee into consideration in determining whether the employee made a good faith attempt to timely obtain the certification. *Konipol v. Restaurant Associates*, No. 01–Civ. 7857 (GEL), 2002 U.S. Dist. LEXIS 22439 (S.D.N.Y. Nov. 20, 2002) (reasonable jury could conclude that given the employee's cancer-related fatigue employee's attempts to provide timely and adequate certification were made in good faith).

In *Muriekes v. Boeing Co.*, 111 Fed. Appx. 483 (9th Cir. 2004), the court held that a clerical error on the part of the employee's physician did not justify application of the exception to the 15–day rule for the employee to provide supporting medical certification to his/her employer because it was "not practicable under the particular circumstances." The court noted that the regulatory exception "is directed to known and objective circumstances (such as the employee being hospitalized for the 15–day period) which makes compliance impracticable—not to circumstances where notice is timely received and (insofar as the record shows) noncompliance with the 15–day requirement is due to some oversight, such as clerical error." The court found that by waiting nearly three months before she provided the requested medical certification plaintiff did not provide the documentation "as soon as reasonably possible" pursuant to 29 CFR 825.311(b).

In *Electrolux Home Products, Inc. v. UAW*, 343 F. Supp. 2d 747 (N.D. Iowa 2004), *aff'd*, 416 F.3d 848 (8th Cir. 2005), the district court rejected the employer's attempt to vacate an arbitration award favorable to the employee. The employer argued that the arbitrator's decision was based on manifest disregard of the law because the employee did not submit a complete FMLA certification form indicating that the employee was incapacitated on the day in question. Electrolux failed to give the employee 15 days in which to submit medical certification (it terminated the employee the day after its request) and failed to give the employee a reasonable period of time to cure the deficiency. According to the court, "where the employer who requested medical certification itself failed to follow the implementing regulations, the arbitrator's decision that the medical certification Cook had submitted was 'close enough to qualify' for FMLA leave and was not a manifest disregard for the law."

In *Baldwin–Love v. Electronic Data Systems Corp.*, 307 F. Supp. 2d 1222, 1230 (M.D. Ala. 2004), the court declined to impose DOL regulations applicable to a 15–day window (longer if that time period is impracticable) to second, third, and fourth opportunities given to an employee to submit a certification. In that case, the employee was repeatedly given opportunities by her employer to provide a competed medical certification in April, May, June, and early July, with warnings that if she did not do so her absences would not be protected by the FMLA. According to the court, in "effect, the Plaintiff is seeking to punish the Defendant for allowing her additional chances after she failed to provide the certification earlier as requested." The court went on to find that Love's failure to pursue this certification for months "cannot fairly be described as having acted diligently" within the meaning of 29 CFR 825.305(d).

In *Hite v. USPS*, No. AT–0752–04–0598–I–1, 2004 MSPB LEXIS 1300 (Aug. 9, 2004), *pet. denied*, 98 MSPR 677 (2005), the administrative judge considered medical documentation the employee provided more than a month after the 15-day deadline. The employer refused to consider the documentation because it was untimely. Although the administrative judge found that the employee bore some responsibility for the delay, he considered the documentation because there was no evidence that the employee consciously evaded receiving the agency's information request, citing 29 CFR 825.305(b), among other regulations. There was also some evidence that the Postal Service permitted extension of the time to submit documents where the delay is outside the employee's control. There was no question that the FMLA documentation covered some of the absences at issue, which were subsequently dropped from consideration of the propriety of the penalty.

d.   Preliminary Designation of FMLA Leave

The employer is responsible for the designation of leave, paid or unpaid, as FMLA leave. 29 CFR 825.208(a); S. Res. 242, Cong. Rec. S3959, S3966 (April 23, 1996); 29 CFR 825.208(a). Generally, the employer must make this determination within two business days of the time the employee gives notice of the need for leave, or, where the employer does not initially have sufficient information to make a determination, when the employer determines that the leave qualifies as FMLA leave if this happens later. 29 CFR 825.208(c); S. Res. 242, Cong. Rec. S3959, S3966 (April 23, 1996); 29 CFR 825.208(c). The employer's designation must be made before the leave starts, unless the employer does not have sufficient information as to the employee's reason for taking the leave until after the leave commenced. 29 CFR 825.208(c); S. Res. 242, Cong. Rec. S3959, S3966 (April 23, 1996); 29 CFR 825.208(c). Where the employer has requested medical certification not yet received or the parties are in the process of obtaining a second or third medical opinion, the employer should make a preliminary designation, and so notify the employee, at the time leave begins, or as soon as the reason for the leave becomes known. 29 CFR 825.208(e)(2); S. Res. 242, Cong. Rec. S3959, S3967 (April 23, 1996); 29 CFR 825.208(e)(2); *see Bohman v. County of Wood*, No. 03–C–571–C, 2004 U.S. Dist. LEXIS 13082, at *12 (W.D. Wis. July 7, 2004). [For a further discussion of the requirements of an employee to designate the leave as covered by the FMLA, see Chapter 8, "Notice Requirements."]

e.   Paid Leave Substitution and Certification

The taking of FMLA leave concurrently with paid leave may have a substantial impact on an employer's ability to require the employee to provide medical certification. If the employer's sick or medical leave plan imposes medical certification requirements that are less stringent than the certification requirements of the FMLA implementing regulations, and the employee or employer elects to substitute paid sick, vacation, personal or family leave for unpaid FMLA leave where authorized, only the employer's less stringent sick leave certification requirements may be imposed. 29 CFR 825.305(e), 825.207(h); S. Res. 242, Cong. Rec. S3959, S3967, S3972 (April 23, 1996); 29 CFR 825.305(e), 825.207(h).

Note that the regulations do not prohibit an employer from having more stringent paid leave policies than those required by the FMLA. The regulations simply say that if the employees' paid leave policies are less stringent on certification, those less stringent policies apply if that paid leave policy is substituted for unpaid FMLA leave. If the paid leave policies are more stringent, then the FMLA requirements are the minimum for determining whether unpaid FMLA leave is granted. If the employee meets the FMLA requirements, the employee is entitled to unpaid FMLA leave. If the employee who meets the minimum FMLA leave requirements does not meet the more stringent requirements for paid leave, then the employee is entitled to unpaid FMLA leave.

Employers who are contemplating requiring employees to substitute paid leave for unpaid FMLA leave must weigh the pros and cons of that action against their current paid leave procedural policies, including the policy to provide medical certification to support a request for FMLA leave. If, for example, an employer decides to require an employee to use annual leave concurrent with unpaid FMLA leave, the employer may lose the ability to request medical certification. Generally speaking, most annual leave policies do not require an employee to provide a medical certification to support a request for leave. As such, in an effort to discourage the abuse of FMLA leave by requiring an employee to concurrently use annual leave; the employer may have inadvertently put itself in the position of being unable to challenge the medical legitimacy of the need for FMLA leave. If the employer cannot ask for a medical certification in support of the leave, it is also arguably prohibited from utilizing the second and third opinion process to challenge the legitimacy of the medical certification and, ultimately, the need for the leave. This may be a disaster if the employee is requesting leave intermittently on an indefinite basis.

Employers are not prohibited from having paid leave policies that include certification or other procedural requirements that meet or exceed the minimum requirements of the FMLA. Such policies may not, however, discriminate against individuals because they have taken FMLA leave. For example, a policy that says that employees taking annual leave need not provide a medical certification, except those taking FMLA leave, is discriminatory and in violation of the FMLA.

Generally, employers will want to review their policies to ensure that they may obtain medical certification where an employee elects, or an employer requires substitution of paid leave for unpaid FMLA leave. Unions and other organizations representing the interests of employees, on the other hand, will want to make sure that only employees get to elect paid leave substitution, and when that occurs the employee is subject to less stringent certification and other procedural requirements than the minimum mandated by the FMLA. [For a further discussion of the effects of paid leave substitution on certification and other procedural requirements, see Chapter 11, "Substitution of Paid Leave."]

f. More Generous Employer Requirements

An employer may also provide a more generous deadline or dispense with the certification requirement in its entirety. 29 USC 2613; 29 CFR 305(b), 825.700(a); *accord Electrolux Home Products, Inc. v. UAW*, 343 F. Supp. 2d 747 (N.D. Iowa 2004), *aff'd*, 416 F.3d 848 (8th Cir. 2005); *Baldwin–Love v. Electronic Data Systems, Corp.*, 307 F. Supp. 2d. 1222, 1229 (M.D. Ala. 2004); *Rager v. Dade Behring, Inc.*, 210 F.3d 776, 777 (7th Cir. 2000).

g. Less Generous FMLA Leave Polices

The FMLA provides that the rights created therein "shall not be diminished by any collective bargaining agreement or any employment benefit program or plan." 29 USC 2652(b). Where an employer's internal policies conflict with the provisions of the FMLA, the FMLA controls and an employee need only comply with the requirements of the Act to invoke its protections. For example, where the terms of a collective bargaining agreement provide that all absences of over five consecutive days be supported by a doctor's certificate, the FMLA provides that an employee has 15 days to provide the certificate if the leave is covered by the FMLA. *Marrero v. Camden County Bd. of Social Services et al.*, 164 F. Supp. 2d 455, 463–64 (D. N.J. 2001). An employer's certification policies do not necessarily conflict with the requirements of the FMLA simply because they do not expressly contain all of the provisions of the law. In *Washington v. Fort James Operating Co.*, 110 F. Supp. 2d 1325, 1330–32 (D. Ore. 2000), the court found that the employer's written policy disqualifying FMLA eligible absences accruing more than 15 days prior to receipt of the employee's completed certification was not facially invalid because it did not expressly contain the unusual circumstances exception to the 15–day rule. The regulation, 29 CFR 825.311(b), requires an employees whose need for FMLA leave was not foreseeable to provide certification at the request of an employer within 15 days, or as soon as possible under particular facts and circumstances. The court held that "[n]othing in the FMLA requires that an employer's leave policy list every right and remedy under the FMLA in order to be valid." The court noted that, while the policy did not expressly provide for waiver of the 15–day certification requirement, the policy's silence on the matter did not preclude consideration of unusual circumstances either. Additionally, the policy provided that the actual law supersedes the company's guidelines.

2. Title II

a. General Rule

An employee must provide a written medical certification, signed by the health care provider, no later than 15 calendar days after the date the employer requests such medical certification. 5 CFR 630.1207(h); *see Edwards v. VA*, 100 MSPR 437, at P8 (2005), *aff'd*, 2006 U.S. App. LEXIS 11323 (Fed. Cir. 2006). If this is not practicable under the particular circumstances despite the employee's diligent, good faith efforts, the employee must provide the medical certification within a reasonable period of time under the circumstances involved, but no later than 30 calendar days after the date the employer requests such medical certification. 5 CFR 630.1207(h); *see Edwards v. VA*, 100 MSPR 437, at P8 (2005), *aff'd*, 2006 U.S. App. LEXIS 11323 (Fed. Cir. 2006).

Unlike the regulations implementing Title I, the CAA, and the PEOAA, the determination of when an employee must provide certification is not conditioned on whether the need for leave was foreseeable within a certain period of time. Under Title II, an employee must make diligent, good faith efforts to provide the medical certification within 15 calendar days of the agency's request. If that is not practicable, the employee must provide the certification within a reasonable period of time, not to exceed a maximum of 30 calendar days from the request. Under Title I, the CAA, and the PEOAA, the period that an employee has to provide a certification is uncapped and, therefore, potentially limitless and the matter could drag on for months. That is not the case under Title II.

In *Edwards v. VA*, 100 MSPR 437, at P8 (2005), *aff'd*, 2006 U.S. App. LEXIS 11323 (Fed. Cir. 2006), the employer gave the employee less than 15 days to provide medical certification. The Board declined to find this a violation of the FMLA where the employee failed to provide responsive medical documentation during the seven-month period between the employee's removal and the arbitration hearing.

b. More Generous Employer Policies

Title II, like its counterparts in Title I, the CAA, and the PEOAA, allow agencies to adopt and comply with leave policies that are more generous than the minimum requirements provided by the FMLA. 5 CFR 630.1210(a), 630.1210(c). For example, an employer could provide that an employee has 45 calendar days to provide medical certification under all circumstances. Such a policy is more generous than the minimum requirements of the FMLA.

Generally speaking, agencies are more apt to adopt the minimum requirements of the FMLA as their policy. Unions and other entities representing the interests of employees are more inclined to negotiate for more generous leave policies, including more time for an employee to provide a requested medical certification in support of the employee's request for FMLA leave.

c. Preliminary Designation

If the employee is unable to provide the requested medical certification before leave begins, or if the employer questions the validity of the original certification provided by the employee and the medical treatment requires the leave to begin, the employer must grant provisional leave pending final written medical certification. 5 CFR 630.1207(g). [For a further discussion of the requirements regarding the designation of leave as being covered by the FMLA, see Chapter 8, "Notice Requirements."]

d. Paid Leave Substitution

Title II allows an employee under certain circumstances to elect to substitute paid leave for unpaid FMLA leave. *See* 5 USC 6382(d); 5 CFR 630.1205. Unlike the comparable regulations implementing Title I, the CAA, and the PEOAA, Title II does not provide that an employer is required to abide by any less stringent procedural requirements, including the requirement to provide medical certification at the request of an employer, pursuant to the agencies substituted paid leave policies. As a result, employees arguably must separately satisfy the procedural requirements of the FMLA and the substituted paid leave policies in order to receive the protections of that Act and receive pay. Both requirements must be met (or the employer must waive the employee meeting both) whether the requirements for paid leave are more or less stringent than those of the FMLA. [For a further discussion of the FMLA when paid leave is substituted, see Chapter 11, "Substitution of Paid Leave."]

F. CONTENTS OF MEDICAL CERTIFICATION

Employers are limited as to the scope of information that they may obtain in the medical certification an employee must provide in support of FMLA leave. The permissible contents of a medical certification are set forth in the FMLA statues and the regulations implementing the FMLA. As with most other provisions, there are substantial differences between the various federal sector FMLA laws regarding the scope of information that an employer may receive in the medical certification.

1. Title I, the CAA, and the PEOAA

The contents of a medical certification are strictly regulated by the FMLA. An employer is prohibited from requiring any additional information beyond the information specifically identified as permissible for purposes of the FMLA. 29 CFR 825.306(b); S. Res. 242, Cong. Rec. S3959, S3972 (April 23, 1996); 29 CFR 825.306(b). In all circumstances, the medical information collected in the certification must relate only to the serious health condition for which the current need for leave exists. 29 CFR 825.306(b); S. Res. 242, Cong. Rec. S3959, S3972 (April 23, 1996); 29 CFR 825.306(b).

The DOL and the Office of Compliance created optional forms for use in obtaining medical certification. 29 CFR 825.306(a)–(b); S. Res. 242, Cong. Rec. S3959, S3972 (April 23, 1996); 29 CFR 825.306(a)–(b); *see Hoffman v. Professional Med Team*, 394 F.3d 414, 418 (6th Cir. 2005); *Snelling v. Stark Properties, Inc.*, No. 5:05-CV-46 (DF), 2006 U.S. Dist. LEXIS 50272, at *31 (M.D. Ga. July 24, 2006) (WH-380 constitutes a medical certification within the meaning of 29 CFR 825.306); *Willis v. USPS*, No. 03 C 9185, 2004 U.S. Dist. LEXIS 18238, at *13 (N.D. Ill. Sept. 10, 2004); *Konipol v. Restaurant Associates*, No. 01–Civ. 7857 (GEL), 2002 U.S. Dist. LEXIS 22439 (S.D.N.Y. Nov. 20, 2002); *Peeples v. Coastal Office Products, Inc.*, 203 F. Supp. 2d 432, 450 (D. Md. 2002), *aff'd*, 2003 U.S. App. LEXIS 8644 (4th Cir. 2003). The advantage of these forms is that DOL has already approved them for compliance with the FMLA. These forms, however, are optional. An employer is not required to use Form WH–380; however, if the form is used "no additional information may be required." 29 CFR 825.306(b); *see Willis v. USPS*, No. 03 C 9185, 2004 U.S. Dist. LEXIS 18238, at *13 (N.D. Ill. Sept. 10, 2004). An employer may create and use other forms, provided that no additional information is required. 29 CFR 825.306(b); S. Res. 242, Cong. Rec. S3959, S3972 (April 23, 1996); 29 CFR 825.306(b); *see Rager v. Dade Behring, Inc.*, 210 F.3d 776, 777 (7th Cir. 2000) (DOL form available, but employer is not required to use it); *Konipol*, 2002 U.S. Dist. LEXIS 22439 (finding that several doctors letters, taken together, created material fact issue for jury whether employee met medical certification requirement). Absent a compelling reason not to, agencies are well advised to use the pre–approved forms. Additions to the forms should be carefully scrutinized to determine that they do not require any additional information. Note that the prohibition of "no additional information" includes medical and non–medical information. However, the forms are not perfect and exclude information that the regulations indicate is permissible.

The DOL medical certification form tracks the language of the statute and implementing regulations regarding the permissible content of FMLA medical certifications, with one exception. *Hoffman v. Professional Med Team*, 394 F.3d 414, 418 (6th Cir. 2005). In *Hoffman*, the court addressed differences in the language of 29 CFR 825.306(b)(2)(ii) and the DOL WH–380 form regarding intermittent FMLA leave. According to the court, while "the regulation requires that intermittent leave applicants establish the medical necessity of 'taking leave intermittently,' question 5.b on the form asks whether it will be medically necessary for the employee to 'take work only intermittently or to work on a less than full schedule'...." Hoffman answered "no" to question 5.b of the WH–380. The employer claimed that it was confused by that response as it could be interpreted to mean that the employee's serious health condition did not require the employee to miss work. The employer asked Hoffman to correct her certification to clear up the confusion. Hoffman did not feel that the form needed to be corrected. The matter escalated into a heated exchange complete with profanities. Hoffman was terminated for her inappropriate conduct. The Sixth Circuit affirmed the decision of the district court that the termination of Hoffman for her use of inappropriate language did not violate the FMLA.

The information that may be obtained in a medical certification may be divided into three main categories: (1) basic information; (2) information where the employee's need for FMLA leave is due to his or her own serious health condition; and (3) information where the employee's need for FMLA leave is to care for a covered family member with a serious health condition. These categories are addressed below.

a. Basic Certification Information

This information may be required as part of any medical certification in support of an employee's request for FMLA leave. This information includes:

- The identity of the health care provider and the type of medical practice (including pertinent specialization, if any) (29 CFR 825.306(b); S. Res. 242, Cong. Rec. S3959, S3972 (April 23, 1996); 29 CFR 825.306(b));

- A certification as to which part of the definition of "serious health condition," if any, applies to the patient's condition, and the medical facts which support the certification, including a brief statement as to how the medical facts meet the criteria of the definition (29 USC 2613(b)(3); 29 CFR 825.306(b); S. Res. 242, Cong. Rec. S3959, S3972 (April 23, 1996); 29 CFR 825.306(b));

- The approximate date the serious health condition commenced, and its probable duration, including the probable duration of the patient's present incapacity (defined as inability to work, attend school or perform other regular daily activities due to the serious health condition, treatment therefore, or recovery there from) if different (29 USC 2613(b)(1)–(2); 29 CFR 825.306(b)(2)(i); S. Res. 242, Cong. Rec. S3959, S3972 (April 23, 1996); 29 CFR 825.306(b)(2)(i));

- Whether it will be necessary for the employee to take leave intermittently or to work on a reduced leave schedule basis as a result of the serious health condition, and if so, the probable duration of such schedule (29 USC 2613(b)(5)–(7); 29 CFR 825.306(b)(2)(ii); S. Res. 242, Cong. Rec. S3959, S3972 (April 23, 1996); 29 CFR 825.306(b)(2)(ii));

- If the serious health condition is pregnancy or a chronic condition, whether the patient is presently incapacitated and the likely duration and frequency of episodes of incapacity (29 CFR 825.306(b)(2)(iii); S. Res. 242, Cong. Rec. S3959, S3972 (April 23, 1996); 29 CFR 825.306(b)(2)(iii));

- If additional treatments will be required for the condition, an estimate of the probable number of such treatments (29 CFR 825.306(b)(3)(I)(A); S. Res. 242, Cong. Rec. S3959, S3972 (April 23, 1996); 29 CFR 825.306(b)(3)(I)(A));

- If the patient's incapacity will be intermittent, or will require a reduced leave schedule, an estimate of the probable number and interval between such treatment, actual or estimated dates of treatment if known, and period required for recovery, if any (29 USC 2613(b)(5)–(7); 29 CFR 825.306(b)(3)(i)(B); S. Res. 242, Cong. Rec. S3959, S3972 (April 23, 1996); 29 CFR 825.306(b)(3)(i)(B));

- If any treatments will be provided by another provider of health care services (e.g., physical therapist) and the nature of the treatments (29 CFR 825.306(b)(3)(ii); S. Res. 242, Cong. Rec. S3959, S3972 (April 23, 1996); 29 CFR 825.306(b)(3)(ii));

- If a regimen of continuing treatment by the patient is required under the supervision of the health care provider, a general description of the regimen (29 CFR 825.306(b)(3)(iii); S. Res. 242, Cong. Rec. S3959, S3972 (April 23, 1996); 29 CFR 825.306(b)(3)(iii)).

A medical certification is considered sufficient if it contains certain information, including: (1) the date on which the serious health condition commenced; (2) the probable duration of the condition; (3) the appropriate medical facts within the knowledge of the health care provider regarding the condition; and (4) if the leave is for the employee's own serious health condition, a statement that the employee is unable to perform the functions of his or her job. 29 USC 2613(b); *Urban v. Dolgencorp of Texas, Inc.*, 393 F.3d 572, 574 (5th Cir. 2004); *Brenneman v. MedCentral Health System*, 366 F.3d 412, 422 (6th Cir. 2004) *cert. denied*, 2005 U.S. LEXIS 1474 (U.S. 2005); *Taylor v. Ameritech Service, Inc.*, No. 05-C-952, 2007 U.S. Dist. LEXIS 28769, at *17 (E.D. Wis. April 18, 2007); *Schumtte v. Resort Condominiums Intl., LLC*, No. 463 F. Supp. 2d 891, 912 (S.D.I nd. Nov. 29, 2006); *Ransell v. Heritage Enterprises, Inc.*, No. 04-1209, 2006 U.S. Dist. LEXIS 82979, at *13 (C.D. Ill. Nov. 14, 2006); *Dowell v. Indiana Heart Physicians, Inc.*, No. 1:03–cv–1410–DFH–TAB, 2004 U.S. Dist. LEXIS 26431, at *14 (S.D. Ind. Dec. 22, 2004); *Smith v. V.I. Port Authority*, No. 2002–227, 2005 U.S. Dist. LEXIS 56, at *36 (D.V.I. Jan. 2, 2005); *Electrolux Home Products, Inc. v. UAW*, 343 F. Supp. 2d 747 (N.D. Iowa 2004); *Porter v. NYU School of Law*, No. 99 Civ. 4693 (TPG), 2003 U.S. Dist. LEXIS 14674, at *15 (S.D.N.Y. Aug. 25, 2003), *aff'd*, 392 F.3d 530 (2d Cir. 2004); *Baldwin–Love v. Electronic Data Systems, Corp.*, 307 F. Supp. 2d. 1222, 1229 & n.4 (M.D. Ala. 2004); *Cool v. BorgWarner Diversified Transmission Products, Inc.*, No. IP 02–0960–C–B/S, 2004 U.S. Dist. LEXIS 570, at *25 (S.D. Ind. Jan. 12, 2004); *Carmen v. Unison Behavioral Health Group, Inc.*, 295 F. Supp. 2d 809, 813 (N.D. Ohio 2003); *Smith v. Univ. of Chicago Hospitals*, No. 02 C 0221, 2003 U.S. Dist. LEXIS 20965, at *22 (N.D. Ill. Nov. 24, 2003); *Gulan v. Federal Reserve Bank of Cleveland*, No. 1:01 CV 1784, 2003 U.S. Dist. LEXIS 15749, at *11 (N.D. Ohio July 31, 2003); *Austin v. USPS*, No. SF-0752-06-0856-I-1, 2006 MSPB LEXIS 7717, at *9 (Dec. 26, 2006).

The FMLA certification does not require disclosure of the diagnosis, the nature of treatment provided, (in most cases) or the dates on which the employee was seen by the health care provider. *Schumttee v. Resort Condominiums Intl., LLC*, No. 1:05-cv-0311-LJM-WTL, 2006 U.S. Dist. LEXIS 86262, at *55-56 (S.D. Ind. Nov. 29, 2006); *O'Reilly v. Rutgers, the State University*, No. 04-5787 (FSH), 2006 U.S. Dist. LEXIS 2341, at *21 (D.N.J. Jan. 19, 2006), *aff'd*, 2007 U.S. App. LEXIS 9530 (3d Cir. 2007).

In *Sconfienza v. Verizon Pennsylvania, Inc.*, No. 3:05cv272, 2007 U.S. Dist. LEXIS 29709, at *65-66 (M.D. Pa. April 23, 2007), the court refused to find that the employer's requirement that the employee submit a signed certification attesting that the employee absence was due to the previously accepted need for intermittent FMLA leave. If an employee did not return the signed certification, Verizon denied FMLA leave. The court found that requiring employee's to file paperwork to seek leave and to verify the reasons for absences is not harassment, but a necessary part of ensuring that the employer's FMLA leave program works equitably for all involved.

b. Employee's Own Serious Health Condition

Where the need for leave is due to the employee's own serious health condition, including absences due to pregnancy or a chronic condition, the Statute and regulations allow an employer to require an employee to provide additional information as part of the medical certification. That additional information includes the following:

- Whether the employee is unable to perform work of any kind (29 USC 2613(4)(B); 29 CFR 825.306(b)(4)(i); S. Res. 242, Cong. Rec. S3959, S3972 (April 23, 1996); 29 CFR 825.306(b)(4)(i));

- Whether the employee is unable to perform any one or more of the essential functions of the employee's position, including a statement of the essential functions the employee is unable to perform, based on either information provided on a statement from the employer of the essential functions of the position or, if not provided, discussion with the employee about the employee's job functions (29 USC 2613(4)(B); 29 CFR 825.306(b)(4)(I); S. Res. 242, Cong. Rec. S3959, S3972 (April 23, 1996); 29 CFR 825.306(b)(4)(I).

An employer may not request additional information from the employee's health care provider. 29 CFR 825.307(a); see Smith v. Univ. of Chicago Hospitals, No. 02 C 0221, 2003 U.S. Dist. LEXIS 20965, at *24 (N.D. Ill. Nov. 24, 2003).

c. Serious Health Condition of a Covered Family Member

Where FMLA leave is required to care for a covered son, daughter, spouse, or parent with a serious health condition, the Statute and regulations allow an employer to require the following additional information as part of the medical certification:

- Whether the patient requires assistance for basic medical or personal needs or safety, or for transportation (29 USC 2613(b)(4)(A); 29 CFR 825.306(b)(5)(i); S. Res. 242, Cong. Rec. S3959, S3972 (April 23, 1996); 29 CFR 825.306(b)(5)(i));

- If the patient does not require assistance for basic medical, personal needs, safety, or transportation, whether the employee's presence to provide psychological comfort would be beneficial to the patient or assist in the patient's recovery (29 CFR 825.306(b)(5)(i); S. Res. 242, Cong. Rec. S3959, S3972 (April 23, 1996); 29 CFR 825.306(b)(5)(i));

- The employee is required to indicate on the form the care he or she will provide and an estimate of the time period (29 CFR 825.306(b)(5)(i); S. Res. 242, Cong. Rec. S3959, S3972 (April 23, 1996); 29 CFR 825.306(b)(5)(i));

- If the employee's family member will need care only intermittently or on a reduced leave schedule basis, the probable duration of the need. (29 USC 2613(b)(7); 29 CFR 825.306(b)(5)(ii); S. Res. 242, Cong. Rec. S3959, S3972 (April 23, 1996); 29 CFR 825.306(b)(5)(ii)).

See Bailey v. Southwest Gas Co., 275 F.3d 1181, 1185–86 (9th Cir. 2002); Konipol v. Restaurant Associates, No. 01 Civ. 7857 (GEL), 2002 U.S. Dist. LEXIS 22439 (S.D.N.Y. Nov. 20, 2002); Peeples v. Coastal Office Products, Inc. 203 F. Supp. 2d 432, 449 (D. Md. 2001) (DOL WH 380 requirements), aff'd, 2003 U.S. App. LEXIS 8644 (4th Cir. 2003); Shtab v. The Greate Bay Hotel and Casino, Inc. et al., 173 F. Supp. 2d 255, 264 (D.N.J. 2001) (contents of certification as set forth in 29 USC 2613(b); Washington v. Fort James Operating Co., 110 F. Supp. 2d 1325, 1330 (D. Ore. 2000); Vanderpool v. Inco Alloys International, Inc., No. 3:98–0449, 1999 U.S. Dist. LEXIS 12363 (S.D. W.Va. June 3, 1999); Johnson v. USPS, No. 1:97–CV-794, 1999 U.S. Dist. LEXIS 7981 (W.D. Mich. May 26, 1999); Henthorn v. Olstgen Corp., No. 97–C–50182, 1999 U.S. Dist. LEXIS 2029 (N.D. Ill. Feb. 24, 1999); Sims v. Alameda–Contra Costa Transit District et al., 2 F. Supp. 2d 1253, 1257 (N.D. Cal. 1998); Sicoli v. Nabisco Biscuit Co., No. 96–6053, 1998 U.S. Dist. LEXIS 8429 (E.D. Pa. June 8, 1998).

d. Effect of Paid Leave Substitution

The permissible contents of a medical certification may be reduced where paid leave is substituted for unpaid FMLA leave. If the employer's sick or medical leave plan requires less information to be furnished in medical certifications than the certification requirements of the FMLA regulations, and the employee or employer elects to substitute paid sick leave, vacation, personal or family leave for unpaid FMLA leave, where authorized, only the employer's lesser sick leave certification requirements may be imposed. 29 CFR 825.306(c); S. Res. 242, Cong. Rec. S3959, S3972 (April 23, 1996); 29 CFR 825.306(c).

This poorly written regulation is susceptible to a number of interpretations. However, as set forth in the preamble to the final DOL regulations (Preamble, 29 CFR 825.307), the regulation simply means that, when the employer's paid leave plan contains lesser obligations than the FMLA, only the employer's lesser certification requirements may be imposed when paid leave is substituted for FMLA leave. In that sense, the laundry list of types of paid leave contained in the body of the actual regulation (sick leave, vacation, personal or family leave) is illustrative, not limiting. That is, if an employee elects to substitute available paid leave that is not sick leave, vacation, personal or family leave, the lesser certification requirements of the selected paid leave nevertheless apply.

Similarly, as currently written, the regulation requires an employer to substitute the lesser sick leave certification requirements even if the employee has substituted paid vacation leave. Based on the explanation in the preamble, this would not appear to be the intent of the regulation. Rather, the regulation presumably should be read as requiring application of any lesser certification requirements of whatever paid leave plan is substituted for unpaid FMLA leave.

e. More Beneficial Employee Leave Requirements

The FMLA permits employers to adopt employment benefit programs or plans that provide greater FMLA rights to employees than the rights established by the FMLA. 29 USC 2652(a); 29 CFR 825.700(a); S. Res. 242, Cong. Rec. S3959, S3976 (April 23, 1996); 29 CFR 825.700(a). For purposes of the contents of medical certification, an employer by policy could agree to require less information than the maximum allowed by the FMLA. *See Miller v. AT&T et al.*, 250 F.3d 820, 836 (4th Cir. 2001) (employer whose medical certification form did not require health care provider to provide medical facts in support of employee's claim of a serious health condition was not entitled to the information; the failure of the employee's health care provider to include such information did not render the certification incomplete).

Employers are well advised to obtain as much medical information possible, up to the maximum allowed by law, in order to confirm that an employee who claims to have a serious health condition, or a covered family member with a serious health condition, that will require intermittent leave at unexpected times and for an undetermined length of time (or for life) actually is entitled to FMLA leave. Employers who forego obtaining all of the information they are entitled to receive up front may be unable to challenge the legitimacy of the leave, absent blatant fraud.

Unions and other organizations representing the interests of employees, on the other hand, spurred on by the privacy concerns of their constituents, generally want to restrict the contents of medical information available to an employer.

2. Title II

Title II also defines the permissible contents of a medical certification. Like Title I, the CAA, and the PEOAA, the information on the medical certification must relate only to the serious health condition for which the current need for FMLA leave exists. 5 CFR 630.1207(c). An employer may not require any personal or confidential information in the written medical certification other than what is required by the OPM FMLA regulations. *Id.* The phrase "personal or confidential information" is not defined. Presumably, it means that an employer may not ask for any information beyond that which is specifically permitted by the Statute and OPM regulations.

The OPM regulations are phrased differently than the comparable regulations under Title I. The OPM regulations specify what information must be in the certification. The similar DOL regulations under Title I do not mandate the contents of a certification. Rather, they identify the maximum amount of information that an employer is entitled to receive.

In *Burge v. Dept. of Air Force*, 82 MSPR 75, P16 (1999), *pet. denied*, 86 MSPR 688 (2000), the employer required the employee to provide more medical information as part of the medical certification than was permitted by the FMLA. The Board found, however, that the employer did not harm the employee's rights under the FMLA because not only did the employee fail to comply with the agency's request for medical documentation, but he also failed to comply with the medical certification requirements of the FMLA.

OPM has not produced its own pre-approved medical certification form like the one developed by the DOL. OPM has indicated that it does not believe that it would be cost-effective to develop a medical certification form for the federal sector in addition to the DOL form. Preamble, 5 CFR 630.1207 (Medical Certification). Rather, OPM has made the DOL form available to agencies on the OPM website. *Id.* Presumably, this constitutes an endorsement of DOL's form for use by agencies requesting information from employees covered by Title II of the Act. This is somewhat surprising since the information that may be gathered for purposes of Title I is not the same as the information that may be gathered for purposes of Title II.

Finally, like Title I, the information that may be obtained in a medical certification under Title II may be divided into three main categories: (1) basic information; (2) information where the employee's need for FMLA leave is due to his or her own serious health condition; and (3) information where the employee's need for FMLA leave is to care for a covered family member with a serious health condition. These categories are addressed below.

a. Basic Certification Information

The written medical certification must include (5 CFR 630.1207(b)(1)–(3)) the following information:

- The date the serious health condition commenced;

- The probable duration of the serious health condition or a statement that the serious health condition is a chronic or continuing condition with an unknown duration and whether the patient is presently incapacitated and the likely duration and frequency of episodes of incapacity;

- The appropriate medical facts within the knowledge of the health care provider regarding the serious health condition, including a general statement as to the incapacitation, examination, or treatment that may be required by a health care provider.

Brown v. Treasury, No. DC-0752-06-0669-I-1, 2006 MSPB LEXIS 5903, at *14 (Oct. 19, 2006); *Kimbrough v. DOD*, No. DC-0752-06-0287-I-1, 2006 MSPB LEXIS 4379, at *13-16 (Aug. 1, 2006); *Cole v. DHHS*, No. DC-0752-05-0457-I-1, 2005 MSPB LEXIS 6825, at *8 (Nov. 1, 2005); *Williams v. Dept. of Navy*, No. DC-0752-05-0431-I-1, 2005 MSPB LEXIS 6866, at *4 (Oct. 17, 2005), *pet. denied*, 101 MSPR 133 (2006); *Fisher v. DHHS*, No. DC-0752-05-0280-I-1, 2005 MSPB LEXIS 2653, at *9-10 (June 3, 2005), *review den.*, 101 MSPR 131 (2005); *Santiago v. USPS*, No. DA-0752-04-0128-B-1, 2005 MSPB LEXIS 2064, at *8 (April 28, 2005) (incorrectly citing OPM's FMLA regulations rather than the DOL regulations); *Burge v. Dept. of Air Force*, 82 MSPR 75, P16 (1999), *pet. denied*, 86 MSPR 688 (2000).

Appropriate medical facts must describe how the condition prevents the employee from performing his or her duties. *Kimbrough v. DOD*, No. DC-0752-06-0287-I-1, 2006 MSPB LEXIS 4379, at *13-16; *Fisher v. DHHS*, 2005 MSPB LEXIS 2653, at *10; *Romero v. Dept. of Interior*, No. SF-0752-05-0011-I-1, 2005 MSPB LEXIS 3147, at *13 (May 19, 2005).

In *Kimbrough v. Dept. of Defense*, No. DC-0752-06-0287-I-1, 2006 MSPB LEXIS 4379, at *13-16 (Aug. 1, 2006), the Board found a medical certification deficient where it did not state the probable duration of the condition or incapacity, but merely indicated that the issue would be determined in the future consultation with the orthopedic surgeon. The Board characterized the response as "I don't know." The Board cited the employee's failure to obtain responsive information from his orthopedic specialist.

In *Williams v. Dept. of Navy*, No. DC-0752-05-0431-I-1, 2005 MSPB LEXIS 6866, at *4 (Oct. 17, 2005), *pet. denied*, 101 MSPR 133 (2006), the Board found that the doctors notes supplied by the employee, a slip on hospital letterhead stating "work excuse 3/31/, 4/1-2/04 (Wed-Fri)", and a hospital discharge slip documenting treatment in the emergency room on September 15 for vomiting and gastritis were insufficient to support the employee's request for FMLA leave.

In *Romero v. Dept. of Interior*, No. SF-0752-05-0011-I-1, 2005 MSPB LEXIS 3147, at *13 (May 19, 2005), the Board found that doctors' notes submitted by the employee fell far short of the required certification under the FMLA. The Board noted that the notes provided no medical reason for the absences, they did not include the date the serious health condition commenced, the probable duration of the condition, or whether the condition was chronic or continuing, whether the appellant was incapacitated, or the likely duration and frequency of incapacitation. They also did not include a statement of appropriate medical facts.

b. Serious Health Condition of a Covered Family Member

Where the FMLA leave is taken for the care of a spouse, son, daughter, or parent of the employee with a serious health condition, the written medical certification must also include, 5 CFR 630.1207(b)(4), (6):

- A statement from the health care provider that the spouse, son, daughter, or parent of the employee requires psychological comfort and/or physical care; needs assistance for basic medical, hygienic, nutritional, safety, or transportation needs or in making arrangements to meet such needs; and would benefit from the employee's care or presence;

- A statement from the employee on the care he or she will provide and an estimate of the amount of time needed to care for his or her spouse, son, daughter, or parent; and

- In the case of certification for intermittent leave or leave on a reduced leave schedule for planned medical treatment, the dates (actual or estimates) on which such treatment is expected to be given, the duration of such treatment, and the period of recovery, if any, or specify that the serious health condition is a chronic or continuing condition with an unknown duration and whether the patient is presently incapacitated and the likely duration and frequency of episodes of incapacity.

c. Employee's Own Serious Health Condition

Where the FMLA leave is taken for a serious health condition of the employee that renders the employee unable to perform any one or more of the essential functions of his or her position, the written medical certification must include, 5 CFR 630.1207(b):

- A statement that the employee is unable to perform one or more of the essential functions of his or her position or requires medical treatment for a serious health condition, based on written information provided by the employer on the essential functions of the employee's position or, if not provided, discussion with the employee about the essential functions of his or her position;

- In the case of certification for intermittent leave or leave on a reduced leave schedule for planned medical treatment, the dates (actual or estimates) on which such treatment is expected to be given, the duration of such treatment, and the period of recovery, if any, or specify that the serious health condition is a chronic or continuing condition with an unknown duration and whether the patient is presently incapacitated and the likely duration and frequency of episodes of incapacity.

Brown v. Treasury, No. DC-0752-06-0669-I-1, 2006 MSPB LEXIS 5903, at *14 (Oct. 19, 2006); *Jones v. Dept. of Navy*, No. DC-0752-06-0092-I-2, 2006 MSPB LEXIS 5031, at *5-6 (Sept. 5, 2006); *Kimbrough v. DOD*, No. DC-0752-06-0287-I-1, 2006 MSPB LEXIS 4379, at *13-16 (Aug. 1, 2006); *Ellshoff v. Dept. of Interior*, 76 MSPR 54, at *37 (1997), *rev'd, remanded on other grounds,* 78 MSPR 615 (1998).

d. Effect of Paid Leave Substitution

The OPM regulations do not address what impact, if any, the employee's election to substitute paid leave for unpaid FMLA leave has on the medical certification requirement. Under Title I, the CAA, and the PEOAA, an employee who substitutes paid leave for unpaid FMLA need only be required to abide by the lesser paid leave requirements regarding medical certification.

Because the OPM regulations do not provide that an employee need only abide by the lesser certification requirements where paid leave is substituted for unpaid FMLA leave, employees covered by Title II must separately abide by the certification requirements, if any, of the substituted paid leave. They must also abide by the certification requirements of the FMLA.

e. More Beneficial Employee Leave Requirements

An employer must comply with any collective bargaining agreement or an employment benefit program or plan that provides greater family or medical leave entitlements to employees than those provided under the OPM FMLA regulations. 5 CFR 630.1210(a), (c). For example, an employer could adopt a family or medical leave entitlement that does not require medical certification in some instances, or requires medical certification, but with less detail than is currently allowed.

3. Comparisons

The following makes several comparisons involving the medical certification requirements. The first comparison is between the medical certification provisions of Title I and Title II. The second comparison is between the requirements of Title II and the DOL WH 380 Form. Finally, the DOL WH 380 is examined to determine whether it captures all of the information that an employer needs and is permitted to obtain under Title I in order to determine if an employee's request for FMLA leave is covered by the Act.

a. Title I and Title II

Title I allows an employer to collect significantly more information in a medical certification than its counterpart in Title II. Information that may be collected in Title I that may not be collected under Title II includes the following:

- The identity of the health care provider and the type of medical practice, including pertinent specialization, if any;
- Certification as to which part of the definition of "serious health condition," if any, applies to the patient's condition;
- If the serious health condition is pregnancy, whether the patient is presently incapacitated and the likely duration and frequency of episodes of incapacity;
- If additional treatments will be required for the condition, an estimate of the probable number of such treatments;
- Whether it will be necessary for the employee to take leave intermittently or work on a reduced leave schedule;
- If any treatments will be provided by another provider of health care services, the nature of the treatments;
- If a regimen of continuing treatment is required under the supervision of the health care provider, a general description of the regimen; and
- Whether the employee is unable to perform work of any kind.

There are also a number of subtle differences between the two regulations regarding the type and amount of information that may be collected. For example, Under Title I, an employer is entitled to information indicating whether a patient requires assistance for basic medical or personal needs, safety, or for transportation. If not, the employer is entitled to know whether the employee's presence to provide psychological comfort would be beneficial. Under Title II, the employer's entitlement to information from the health care provider demonstrating that the patient requires psychological comfort is not conditioned on the absence of a need for physical care.

Additional differences between Titles I and II include:

- Title I permits a statement regarding the approximate date the serious health condition commenced. Title II requires the actual date the serious health condition commenced.
- Under Title I, the certification may include a statement of the probable duration of the serious health condition, including the probable duration of the patient's present incapacity. Title II requires that the certification provide the probable duration of the serious health condition *or* specify that the serious health condition is a chronic or continuing condition with an unknown duration and whether the patient is presently incapacitated and the likely duration and frequency of episodes of incapacity.

Finally, Title I provides that substitution of paid leave for unpaid FMLA leave may impact whether medical certification is allowed, and the contents of that certification. Essentially, where paid leave is substituted for unpaid FMLA leave, Title I only permits medical certification to the extent allowed under the paid leave policy, and then only if the requirements of the paid leave policy have less stringent certification requirements than those of the FMLA Title II does not have a similar policy.

b. Title II and the DOL WH 380

Given the substantial differences between Titles I and II regarding the contents of medical certification, the OPM's encouragement of agencies to use the DOL medical certification form (WH 380) for purposes of Title II is somewhat surprising. It is particularly surprising given OPM's admonition that agencies may not require any other information than what is permitted by the OPM medical certification regulations. 5 CFR 630.1207(c). The DOL medical certification form WH 380) permits the collection of information beyond the permissible confines of the OPM medical certification regulations.

Based on comparison of the DOL WH 380 Form and the OPM regulations, the following information is sought on the form that is not specifically sanctioned by the OPM regulations:

- The name of the employee (WH 380, #1);
- The name of the patient (if not the employee) (WH 380, #2);
- Certification as to which part of the definition of "serious health condition" applies (WH 380, #4);
- Statement as to how the medical facts meet the criteria of the definition (WH 380, #4);
- The approximate date the conditioned commenced (WH 380, #5.a);
- The probable duration of the condition (WH 380, #5.a);
- Whether it will be necessary for the employee to work only intermittently or to work on a less than full schedule as a result of the condition (including for treatment described in Item 6 below) (WH 380, #5.b);
- If the condition is pregnancy, state whether the patient is presently incapacitated and the likely duration and frequency of episodes of incapacity (WH 380, #5.c);
- If additional treatments will be required for the condition, provide an estimate of the probable number of such treatments (WH 380, #6.a);
- If any of these treatments will be provided by another provider of health services (e.g., physical therapist), please state the nature of the treatments (WH 380, #6.c);
- If a regimen of continuing treatment for the patient is required under your supervision, provide a general description of such regimen (e.g., prescription drug, physical therapy requiring special equipment) (WH 380, #6.c);
- If medical leave is required for the employee's absence from work because of the employee's own serious health condition, state whether the employee unable to perform work of any kind (WH 380, # 7.a);
- If neither 7 a. nor b. applies, state whether it will be necessary for the employee to be absent from work for treatment (WH 380, #7.c);
- If the patient will need care only intermittently or on a part–time basis, please indicate the probable duration of the need (applies to all reasons; OPM regulations [§ 630.1207(b)(6)] limited to intermittent or reduced leave schedule for planned medical treatment) (WH 380, #8.c);
- Signature of health care provider; address, type of practice, and telephone number.

An employer that requires an employee covered by Title II of the Act to provide responsive information to the DOL WH 380, as suggested by OPM, will violate OPM certification requirements. Agencies are well advised to create their own form based on OPM regulations. Because, however, OPM regulations do not specifically provide that the certification may include the identity of the employee, the patient, and the health care provider, strict adherence to OPM's prohibition against including any additional personal or confidential information would appear to be impossible. In order to be of any practical use, the certification needs to identify the employee, the patient, if different than the employee, and the identification information regarding the health care provider who is signing the form.

G. COMMON CERTIFICATION PROBLEMS

Problems with medical certifications submitted by employees are as varied as the health care providers who fill out the forms. Most of the problems involve incomplete certifications. The high incidence of incomplete certifications is largely explained by the fact that physicians are often not paid for the time they spend filling out the certification forms. As a result, the certifications are often illegible and perfunctory. I have grouped the most common certification problems into the following categories.

1. Medical Facts

All of the federal regulations implementing the FMLA require a health care provider to describe the medical facts that support the claim that the employee or covered family member has a serious health condition. On the DOL Form, this information is requested in Question 4. More often than not, the information provided in the certification fails to describe any medical facts or describe how those facts meet the claimed serious health condition definition. Rather, at best, in a few short words the "facts" may repeat the serious health condition being claimed, without a single medical fact being discussed. This is non-responsive and fails to provide the employer with the information it is entitled to receive and needs to determine whether the leave falls within the protections of the FMLA.

Of course, since employers may altogether waive the requirement that an employee provide certification, they may also accept a certification with insufficient facts. Employers should take great care when doing so. One of the few checks permitted by the FMLA on employee abuse of leave is the ability to request certification from a health care provider attesting to the *bona fides* of the need for the claimed leave. Given the disruption inherent in lengthy or intermittent absences, an employer should thinking carefully before waiving one of the only real tools it has to ensure that the employee is legitimately exercising the rights under the FMLA.

2. Estimates of Probable Number of Absences and Leave Duration

The regulations, in several places, require the health care provider to provide estimates of the probable number, intervals, actual or estimated treatment dates, and probable duration of incapacity and leave. The health care provider must identify the actual dates of treatment or other absences, if known. More than likely, the health care provider may only know when the next few appointments will be. The health care provider will not know the exact number of absences that may occur in a given period of time.

Employers, on the other hand, will want specific information on the number of and frequency of absences anticipated. With this information, an employer can plan to get the work done around the employee's schedule. More specific information would also allow the employer to determine whether transferring the employee to an alternative equivalent position during the duration of the need for FMLA leave would be appropriate. It would also give the employer a base line of expected absences for purposes of requesting subsequent medical certifications (recertifications are discussed later in this chapter).

The problem here comes when health care providers fail to provide a numerical estimate of anticipated absences. Rather, they will say something like "indeterminate." Alternatively, they may say that the employee may be absent from 0–30 times a month for the foreseeable future. This type of information is almost always non-responsive. The frequency of absences may often be projected based on the past experience of the employee, or the experience of the doctor with patients with similar conditions. Unless employers are willing to live with this type of "blank check" certification, they should seriously consider requiring the employee to return the form to the health care provider at least once with a request for more concrete information regarding the probable number, frequency, and duration of absences. The health care provider should be asked to provide this information based on the patient's past history, or the professional experience of the health care provider. Many health care providers will put down estimated numbers if pressed ever so slightly. Many, however, will not. It is not recommended that you go back more than once to a health care provider that simply refuses to give any estimates. There are some conditions that are simply not susceptible to such medical estimations. Agencies will have to either live with those ambiguities, or send the employee for a second opinion (as discussed later in this chapter). *See Peter v. Lincoln Institute*, 255 F. Supp. 2d 417 (E.D. Pa. 2002) (even if certification that probable duration of condition was "indefinite" fails to satisfy criteria for identifying probable duration of incapacity, proper course for employer was to return certification to employee and allow him or her a reasonable opportunity to cure deficiency, not termination).

3. Basis for Employee's Care for Covered Family Member

All of the FMLA regulations require the employee to indicate the care he or she will provide and an estimate of the time period the employee will need such leave. This is contained on the bottom of the DOL WH 380 form, as it is not for the health care provider to fill out. More often than not, the health care provider fills this out, which is technically incorrect; the employee is supposed to fill this out. Frequently, neither the health care provider nor the employee completes this section.

Even if it is completed, the scant information provided is usually not responsive to the question. Employers are entitled to this information, as it will help them plan to get the work done while the employee is out on leave. Employers need to remember, however, that the employee, not the health care provider, provides this information. That is why on the DOL WH 380 form the question appears after the health care provider's signature. Employers should not require an employee to obtain this information from the health care provider, as that might constitute a technical violation of the FMLA.

4. Essential Functions

Another area in which medical certifications often fall short involves the inclusion of a statement of the essential functions the employee is unable to perform where the need for FMLA leave is due to the employee's own serious health condition. Health care providers frequently fail to address this matter at all. This frequently happens because employers fail to provide a job description to the health care provider setting forth in detail the essential functions of the job. Employers are well advised to provide the health care provider with such information, rather than rely on the employee to communicate this information. Employees may not accurately communicate all of the essential functions to the health care provider, potentially leading to erroneous certifications that the employee has a serious health condition when, in fact, the employee does not. As is said, garbage in, garbage out. One way that an employer can reduce the potential for a certification that the employee has a serious health condition is to take advantage of the right to provide a job description setting forth the essential functions of the employee's position, as determined by the employer.

H. INCOMPLETE CERTIFICATIONS

This section addresses the options available to an employer when an employee provides a medical certification that is incomplete. The available options depend on what FMLA requirements apply.

1. Title I, the CAA, and the PEOAA

The regulations provide employers with two options when in receipt of an incomplete medical certification. First, the employer can waive the deficiency and accept the certification as is. Remember, that because requiring a medical certification is optional on the part of the employer in the first place, the employer can waive any deficiency in any certification provided. Moreover, pursuant to § 825.700(a), (c), an employer can provide greater family or medical leave benefits than the minimum required by the Act. 29 CFR 825.700(a), (c); S. Res. 242, Cong. Rec. S3959, S3976 (April 23, 1996); 29 CFR 825.700(a), (c). The greater benefit would, in this instance, take the form of a less stringent medical certification requirement.

The second option comes into play where the employer is not willing to accept the incomplete certification provided by the employee. According to the regulations, 29 CFR 825.305(e); S. Res. 242, Cong. Rec. S3959, S3972 (April 23, 1996); 29 CFR 825.305(e), an employer:

> [m]ust advise an employee whenever the employer finds a certification incomplete, and provide the employee a reasonable opportunity to cure any such deficiency.

See *Phillips v. Quebecor World Rai Inc.*, 450 F.3d 308, 312 (7th Cir. 2006); *Kauffman v. Federal Express Corp.*, 426 F.3d 880, 886 (7th Cir. 2005); *Hoffman v. Professional Med Team*, 394 F.3d 414, 418 (6th Cir. 2005); *Sorrell v. Rinker Materials Corp.*, 395 F.3d 332, 337 (6th Cir. 2005); *Urban v. Dolgencorp of Texas, Inc.*, 393 F.3d 572, 574 (5th Cir. 2004); *Rhoads v. FDIC et al.*, 257 F.3d 373, 383 (4th Cir. 2001), *cert. denied*, 535 U.S. 933 (2002); *Miller v. AT&T et al.*, 250 F.3d 820, 836 (4th Cir. 2001); *Strickland v. Water Works and Sewer Bd. of the City of Birmingham*, 239 F.3d 1199, 1209 n.12 (11th Cir. 2001); *Dittle v. USPS*, No. 04–146 (PAM/RLE), 2005 U.S. Dist. LEXIS 1487, at *15 (D. Minn. Feb. 2, 2005); *Wheeler v. Pioneer Dev. Services, Inc.*, 349 F. Supp. 2d 158 (D. Mass. 2004); *Electrolux Home Products, Inc. v. UAW*, 343 F. Supp. 2d 747, at *25 (N.D. Iowa 2004), *aff'd*, 416 F.3d 848 (8th Cir 2005); *Willis v. USPS*, No. 03 C 9185, 2004 U.S. Dist. LEXIS 18238, at *13 (N.D. Ill. Sept. 10, 2004); *Porter v. NYU School of Law*, No. 99 Civ. 4693 (TPG), 2003 U.S. Dist. LEXIS 14674, at *15 (S.D.N.Y. Aug. 25, 2003), *aff'd*, 392 F.3d 530 (2d Cir. 2004); *Neppl v. Signature Flight Support Corp.*, 234 F. Supp. 2d 1016, 1027 (D. Minn. 2002); *Konipol v. Restaurant Associates*, No. 01–Civ. 7857 (GEL), 2002 U.S. Dist. LEXIS 22439 (S.D.N.Y. Nov. 20, 2002); *Peter v. Lincoln Institute*, 255 F. Supp. 417 (E.D. Pa., 2002); *Morris v. VCW, Inc.*, No. 95–0737–CV–W–3–6, 1996 U.S. Dist. LEXIS 11124 (W.D. Mo. July 24, 1996) (in the real world, it is not to be supposed that doctors will always answer in full compliance with the statute on the first inquiry; as such, the Statute and regulations contemplate follow-up requests by the employer for more information until a "complete certification" is supplied).

The regulation imposes an affirmative, rather than permissive, duty on the employer to inform the employee and permit a reasonable opportunity to cure the deficiency where it finds a medical certification incomplete. *Sorrell v. Rinker Materials Corp.*, 395 F.3d 332, 337 (6th Cir. 2005). Employers have no responsibility, however, to conduct further investigation where a certification is facially invalid. *Sorrell v. Rinker Materials Corp.*, 395 F.3d 332, 337 (6th Cir. 2005); *Hoffman v. Professional Med Team*, 394 F.3d 414, 419 (6th Cir. 2005) (citing *Stoops v. One Call Communications, Inc.*, 141 F.3d 309, 313 (7th Cir. 1998)); *Brady v. Potter*, 476 F. Supp. 2d 745 (N.D. Ohio Feb. 7, 2007).

Termination is not an appropriate response for an inadequate certification. *Jiminez v. Velcro USA, Inc.*, No. 01–001–JD, 2002 U.S. Dist. LEXIS 3900 (D. N.H. March 4, 2002); *Shtab v. The Greate Bay Hotel and Casino*, Inc. et al., 173 F. Supp. 2d 255, 264 (D. N.J. 2001); *Marrero v. Camden City, Bd. Of Social Services*, 164 F. Supp. 2d 455, 466 (D. N.J. 2001); *Sims v. Alameda–Contra Costa Transit Dist.*, 2 F. Supp. 2d 1253, 1268 (N.D. Cal. 1998); *Marrero v. Camden County Bd. of Social Services et al.*, 164 F. Supp. 2d 455, 466 (D. N.J. 2001); *Morris v. VCW, Inc.*, No. 95–0737–CV–W–3–6, 1996 U.S. Dist. LEXIS 11124 (W.D. Mo. July 24, 1996). Nor is discipline. *Washington v. Fort James Operating Co.*, 110 F. Supp. 2d 1325, 1332–33 (D. Ore. 2000) (employer cannot discipline employee for submitting incomplete certification unless it gives the employee a reasonable opportunity to cure any deficiencies in the certification).

The regulations fail to give any guidance on what might constitute a reasonable opportunity to cure. *Cavin v. Honda of America MFG., Inc.*, No. C2–00–400, 2002 U.S. Dist. LEXIS 19601 (S.D. Ohio Feb. 22, 2002), *aff'd in part, rev'd in part, remanded*, 346 F.3d 713 (6th Cir. 2003). For example, must an employer give the employee a single chance to cure the deficiency? Two chances? A dozen? Presumably, DOL would respond that what constitutes a reasonable opportunity will depend on all of the circumstances of a particular case. *Cavin v. Honda of America MFG., Inc.*, No. C2–00–400, 2002 U.S. Dist. LEXIS 19601 (S.D. Ohio Feb. 22, 2002) (what constitutes a reasonable opportunity must be determined on a case by case basis).

In *Muhammad v. Indiana Bell Tel. Co., Inc.*, 182 Fed. Appx. 551 (7th Cir. 2006), the Seventh Circuit found that the 15-day period the employer gave the employee to cure the identified deficiency in the medical certification was reasonable. *Accord Brady v. Potter*, 476 F. Supp. 2d 745 (N.D. Ohio 2007); *Rigel v. Wilks*, No. 1:03-CV-971, 2006 U.S. Dist. LEXIS 93659, at *54 (M.D. Pa. Dec. 28, 2006).

In *Boyd v. State Farm Insurance Companies et al.*, 158 F.3d 326, 332 (5th Cir. 1998), *cert. denied*, 526 U.S. 1051 (1999), the court did not address this issue directly. However, in finding in favor of the employer, the court noted that the employee provided State Farm with insufficient certifications on three occasions, and on each occasion State Farm notified the employee of the insufficiency and that he needed to supply sufficient certification or be considered AWOL. When he failed on the third and last occasion to provide a certification that stated that the leave was covered by the FMLA, State Farm terminated Boyd's employment. The court found that State Farm provided sufficient notice of what Boyd needed to do and the consequences if he failed to do it. As such, his termination did not violate the FMLA. We are indeed a baseball society; three strikes and you're out.

Similarly, the Ninth Circuit in *Bailey v. Southwest Gas Co.*, 275 F.3d 1181, 1185–86 (9th Cir. 2002), did not address the employee's submission of a physically incomplete certification by direct reference to the opportunity to cure requirement. In that case, the employer met with the employee on receipt of a physically incomplete certification form. When the employer requested that the employee obtain the remaining information, the employee refused. Under those circumstances, the court found that the certification was incomplete, that Southwest complied with its duties and responsibilities under the FMLA, and that the employee did not shoulder her burden. As a result, the employee failed to establish her claim that the employer interfered with her FMLA rights.

In *Cavin v. Honda of America MFG., Inc.*, No. C2–00–400, 2002 U.S. Dist. LEXIS 19601 (S.D. Ohio Feb. 22, 2002), *aff'd in part, rev'd in part, remanded*, 346 F.3d 713 (6th Cir. 2003), the district court held that, even if the employee made a good faith effort to timely provide information missing from a certification, because it was not impossible or impracticable to comply with the employer's deadline to provide such information, the employee did not satisfy the requirements of the FMLA and would not be covered by its protections.

The district court further held that Honda gave the employee a reasonable opportunity to cure the deficiency. Once the employer discovered that the certification was incomplete, the employer notified the employee of the deficiency. Because it was unclear that the employer advised the employee that the deficiency had to be cleared within two days, it gave him additional time. Ultimately, the employer gave the employee seven days to cure the deficiency. Even though the employee timely asked his physician to fax the certification before the deadline expired, the physician sent it five days later (12 days after notice that the certification was incomplete). Here, the court held that the employee failed to show that it was either impossible or impractical to comply with the deadline. Interestingly, the court cited the employee's failure to watch his physician fill out the fax cover sheet or send the fax. The employee admitted that he could have hand-delivered the certification to his employer, but chose not to do so. Under those circumstances, and notwithstanding his good faith efforts, the court held that the employee failed to provide timely medical certification of his need for FMLA leave.

In *Johnson v. USPS*, No. 1:97–CV–794, 1999 U.S. Dist. LEXIS 7981 (W.D. Mich. May 26, 1999), the court found that the employer did provide the employee a reasonable opportunity to cure a deficient certification when the employer almost immediately requested additional information upon being notified of the plaintiff's absence. The plaintiff was advised to complete the workers' compensation forms before leaving the building, and failed to do so. Had the employee done so, the USPS would have had the information it needed.

Once the employee submits sufficient medical certification, the employee is entitled to protection under the FMLA, unless and until there is contrary medical evidence. *Wheeler v. Pioneer Dev. Services, Inc.*, 349 F. Supp 2d 158 (D. Mass. 2004). An employer may not assert incompleteness of a medical certification as grounds for disciplining an employee where the employer never notified the employee of the problem or gave him an opportunity to cure it. *Sorrell v. Rinker Materials Corp.*, 395 F.3d 332, 337 (6th Cir. 2005).

The regulations also fail to define when a certification is "incomplete." "An incomplete certification is tantamount to an insufficient or inadequate certification or a certification that does not provide the information requested by the employer." *Jacks v. Conair Corp.*, No. 04-2230, 2006 U.S. Dist. LEXIS 42569, at *10 (C.D. Ill. June 23, 3006); *see Daugherty v. Mikart, Inc.*, No. 1:05-CV-0384-JOF, 2006 U.S. Dist. LEXIS 24357, at *7 & n.3 (N.D. Ga. April 26, 2007), *aff'd*, 2006 U.S. App. 31472 (11th Cir 2006). The courts are split on the circumstances which may give rise to an employer's obligation to inform an employee that the certification submitted in support of a request for FMLA leave is incomplete, requiring the employer to allow the employee a reasonable opportunity to cure the deficiency.

There is no controversy that a certification is incomplete if it is physically missing information that an employee is entitled to receive. *See Muhammad v. Indiana Bell Tel. Co., Inc.*, 182 Fed. Appx. 551 (7th Cir. 2006) (certification stating unknown frequency and intermittent leave of 1-2 days duration was incomplete because it did not identify how long employee would need intermittent leave or how frequently she would need it); *Bailey v. Southwest Gas Co.*, 275 F.3d 1181, 1185–86 (9th Cir. 2002). Of course, if the certification is missing information that is not relevant to the case at hand, it is not incomplete. *Miller v. AT&T et al.*, 250 F.3d 820, 836 (4th Cir. 2001) (certification not incomplete where AT&T did not request the information, and health care provider was not required to fill out item 4 because that item specified that it was to be completed "only for a 'serious health condition' of an employee's spouse, child, or parent," which was not relevant for the employee's own serious health condition); *Ridings v. Riverside Med. Center*, No. 05-2134, 2006 U.S. Dist. LEXIS 86991, at *13 (C.D. Ill. Nov. 30, 2006) (certification that did not contain dates on which treatment was expected to be given, duration of such treatment, or statement of necessity of intermittent leave incomplete). One court held that "incomplete" and "non–existent" are not synonymous. *Neppl v. Signature Flight Support Corp.*, 234 F. Supp. 2d 1016, 1027

(D. Minn. 2002) ("an employer cannot 'find a certification incomplete' if the employer cannot find it at all because the employee has not produced it").

An employer may be barred from relying on absences not covered by the submitted medical certifications as a penalty for the employer's failure to notify the employee that the employer considered the certifications insufficient. *See Sims v. Alameda–Contra Costa Transit District et al.*, 2 F. Supp. 2d 1253, 1257 (N.D. Cal. 1998) (two-day insufficiency in certification could not be properly used as grounds for discipline against employee because employer never notified employee that certification was inadequate).

In *McCray v. H&R Block Eastern Enterprises, Inc.*, No. 04-12232-PBS, 2006 U.S. Dist. LEXIS 29068, at *23 (D. Mass. May 10, 2006), the court found that the leave was protected by the FMLA where the employer failed to notify the employee that the medical certification was incomplete, and failed to give the employee a reasonable opportunity to cure the deficiency.

The courts are split regarding whether a certification that is physically complete may nevertheless be considered "incomplete" because it does not support the employee's request for FMLA leave. A number of courts have held that an employer may rely on a physically complete certification that fails to support the FMLA leave period intended by the employee. *See Cash v. Smith et al.*, 231 F.3d 1301 (11th Cir. 2002), *cert. denied*, 539 U.S. 909 (2003) (affirming award of summary judgment to employer where certification provided by employee's health care provider indicated that employee did not have a serious health condition within the meaning of the FMLA); *Stoops v. One Call Communications, Inc.*, 141 F.3d 309 (7th Cir. 1998) (employer did not violate the Act when it denied leave based on prior medical certification that employee's illness did not meet the definition of an FMLA serious health condition); *Collins v. Merck–Medco RX Servs. Of Tex., LLC*, No. 3:00–CV–1852–X, 2001 U.S. Dist. LEXIS 15143 (N.D. Tex. Sept. 24, 2001) (employer did not violate the Act when it denied FMLA leave to employee whose medical certification did not support employee's leave request); *Dillon v. Carlton*, 977 F. Supp. 1155, 1158–59 (M.D. Fla. 1997), *aff'd without op.*, 161 F.3d 21 (11th Cir. 1998) (clear statement by doctor on certification that employee did not have a serious health condition); *Sicoli v. Nabisco Biscuit Co.*, No. 96–6053, 1998 U.S. Dist. LEXIS 8429 (E.D. Pa. June 8, 1995) (employer could rely on certification stating that employee was able to perform functions of position and, therefore, the employee was not entitled to FMLA leave). An employer has an obligation to allow an employee to cure an inadequate certification only if it is physically incomplete.

Another line of cases has held that a physically complete certification may nevertheless be incomplete if it fails to support the employee's request for FMLA leave. *See Jiminez v. Velcro USA, Inc.*, No. 01–001–JD, 2002 U.S. Dist. LEXIS 3900 (D. N.H. March 4, 2002); *Shtab v. The Greate Bay Hotel and Casino, Inc.*, 173 F. Supp. 2d 255, 265 (D. N.J. 2001); *Washington v. Fort James Operating Co.*, 110 F. Supp. 2d 1325, 1333 (D. Or. 2000); *Zawadowicz v. CVS Corp.*, 99 F. Supp. 2d 518, 524 (D. N.J. 2000); *Sims v. Alameda–Contra Costa Transit Dist.*, 2 F. Supp. 2d 1253, 1266 (N.D. Cal. 1998). Because the certification is considered incomplete, an employer is required to so advise the employee and give the employee a reasonable opportunity to cure "any such deficiency."

The decision in *Jiminez* is instructive regarding the line of cases holding that a physically complete certification is nonetheless incomplete if it fails to support the employee's request for FMLA leave. Alex Jiminez worked for Velcro. Velcro policy requires that requests for paid leave be submitted in advance on an absence form. The form clearly has an entry for FMLA leave. Although Jiminez submitted over 20 of the forms in 2000, he only indicated on one form, the last one, that he was requesting FMLA leave.

Under Velcro's absenteeism policy, an employee who accumulates 56 hours of absences receives verbal counseling, followed by a written warning at 72 hours. After 80 absentee hours, an employee is brought before a Review Board, which may take disciplinary action including termination.

Between February and November 2000, Jiminez accrued 80 absentee hours. Along the way, he was reminded no fewer than four times that he needed to provide medical certification in order to gain the protections of the FMLA. He was provided a copy of the FMLA certifications form on several occasions. On November 14, 2000, Jiminez submitted medical certification. In pertinent part, under the section in the certification asking for the date the condition commenced, the phrase "commence 1990" is legible, but crossed out. Instead, the certification states that the condition commenced on October 27, 2000, and the expected period of incapacity was three to four days. As written, the certification did not support the plaintiff's absences from February 2000 to October 26, 2000. Jiminez was subsequently terminated for poor attendance.

According to the court, § 825.305(d) of the DOL FMLA regulations requires an employer to advise an employee when it finds a certification incomplete, and to provide that employee with a reasonable opportunity to cure "any such deficiency." Whether a certification is incomplete is not, the court found, limited to situations where the documentation is physically complete. Rather, § 825.305(d) speaks of curing "any such deficiency" which results in an incomplete certification. The court referred to the Concise Oxford Dictionary to define "deficiency" as "a lack or shortage." The court also relied on the decisions of other courts, which found that any type of deficiency in a certification that operates to defeat an employee's request for medical leave is incomplete.

Here, Jiminez's request for medical leave prior to October 27, 2000, was unsuccessful because his health care provider did not include those dates in the certification. As such, the certification was deficient. The employer was required by law to notify Jiminez of that deficiency, and give him a reasonable opportunity to cure it. Because he was not given that chance, the court refused to award summary judgment to the employer.

The *Jiminez* line of cases appears a bit overbroad. In the absence of a regulatory definition of what constitutes an incomplete certification, what constitutes an incomplete certification may be derived from the definition of "certification." Section 825.306 goes into painstaking detail on what information an employer may and may not receive as part of a medical certification. Contrary to the underlying rationale of the *Jiminez* line of cases, nowhere in this regulation or in the certification form created by the DOL (WH 380) is there any mention of the intent of the employee requesting FMLA leave.

An equally valid interpretation of when a certification is incomplete is if an employer believes that it needs more information to determine whether the leave qualifies for FMLA protections, up to the maximum allowable information that may be requested as a certification. Since employee intent is not part of the information contained in a certification, it follows that the failure of a certification to support an employee's intended leave does not render the certification incomplete. Whether agencies will follow the lead of the *Jiminez* or *Cash* line of cases on certification incompleteness is a decision that should be made in consultation with counsel.

A fraudulent certification is not an incomplete certification. *Daugherty v. Mikart, Inc.*, No. 1:05-CV-0384-JOF, 2006 U.S. Dist. LEXIS 24357, at *7 & n.3 (N.D. Ga. April 26, 2007), *aff'd*, 2006 U.S. App. LEXIS 31472 (11th Cir. 2006).

The adequacy of the employer's notice of deficiency was addressed by the court in *LeGrand v. Village of McCook*, No. 96–C–5951, 1998 U.S. Dist. LEXIS 5230 (N.D. Ill. April 15, 1998). There, the employer advised the employee that, although the certification the employee provided "does not specifically state that your present condition precludes you performing the essential functions of your job, the Village is willing to give you the benefit of the doubt." The court held that the letter did not advise LeGrand that his employer found the health care provider's certification incomplete. Specifically, the court found that the letter did not "clearly apprise the plaintiff of the information necessary to meet the certification requirement, and actually service[d] to muddy the waters as to what information was necessary." When informing employees of incomplete or inadequate certification, agencies need to clearly and specifically identify the deficiencies.

Some courts equate "incomplete" with the term "inadequate." *Sorrell v. Rinker Materials Corp.*, 395 F.3d 332, 338 (6th Cir. 2005). Whether a medical certification is complete is a question of material fact for the jury to decide. *Sorrell*, 395 F.3d at 337 (citing *Shtab v. Greate Bay Hotel & Casino, Inc.*, 173 F. Supp. 2d 255, 265 (D.N.J. 2001)).

In *Urban v. Dolgencorp of Texas, Inc.*, 393 F.3d 572, 574 (5th Cir. 2004), the Fifth Circuit addressed whether the curing provision of § 825.305(d) applies where an employee fails to submit a medical certification to the employer altogether. That is, whether a non-existent medical certification equates to an "incomplete" certification. The court found that it did not. The employer requested that the employee provide medical certification to support her request for leave and gave her more than 15 days to do so. The employer also properly notified Urban of the consequences of failing to provide the medical certification. Urban provided the medical certification form to her doctor, who promptly lost it. Urban was first informed that her employer did not receive the completed medical certification from her physician when she was terminated approximately 30 days into her leave. Urban argued that her employer should have told her that it did not receive her medical certification and, at that point, given her a reasonable opportunity to cure the deficiency. Her employer argued that it fully complied with all relevant statutory and regulatory requirements. It was Urban's responsibility, not her employer's, as an employee seeking the protections of the FMLA, to ensure that her medical certification was timely filed. The court agreed.

The court distinguished several cases advanced by Urban suggesting that a non-existent certification was an "incomplete" certification requiring employer notice and a reasonable opportunity to cure. In both cases, unlike in *Urban*, the employee actually submitted a medical certification to the employer before adverse action was taken. As a policy matter, the court declined to equate a non-existent medical certification to an "incomplete" one. The court opined that such a reading would upset the balance of employee and employer interests underlying the FMLA.

> Were this Court to adopt Urban's proposed application of § 825.305(d), an employer could never set a real deadline for the return of a medical certification. In effect, whenever an employee failed to return a medical certification within the appropriate time period, the employer would be required to notify the employee of that fact and provide the employee with an opportunity to cure the deficiency by allowing the employee to submit the certification within a new, extended deadline—a scenario that could, in theory, repeat itself ad infinitum.

Accord Baldwin-Love v. Electronic Data Systems Corp., 307 F. Supp. 2d 1222, 1230 (M.D. Ala. 2004).

In Porter v. NYU School of Law, No. 99 Civ. 4693 (TPG), 2003 U.S. Dist. LEXIS 14674, at *16–19 (S:D.N.Y. Aug. 25, 2003), aff'd, 392 F.3d 530 (2d Cir. 2004), the employee claimed that NYU failed to explain why his medical certification was insufficient and did not permit him a reasonable opportunity to submit more materials. The court disagreed. After the employee initially faxed the note from his chiropractor substantiating his request for leave, NYU called Porter the next day and told him the note was insufficient to justify FMLA leave. A "full, detailed report" was requested by NYU. NYU promptly sent Porter an FMLA application that included a certification form for his doctor to complete and general instructions. At the same time, NYU sent a letter which again explained in writing that the chiropractor's note was insufficient to verify his alleged illness, and that it lacked information on the probable duration and treatment of his condition. The day after Porter resubmitted his certification, NYU sent him a letter stating that the certification did not provide information showing that Porter's doctor certified him unable to work, and that the certification showed that the condition commenced in January 1995 with a probable duration of six months. The certification was submitted 17 months after the condition commenced. NYU required the employee to submit to a second health care provider opinion, and told Porter that approval of his request for FMLA leave was contingent on the results of his examination.

Porter was advised that the second medical opinion provider determined that he could return to work. When Porter stated that his own doctor gave him different advice, he was informed that he could submit more documentation to substantiate his claim. Porter did not submit additional medical documentation. Based on the above facts, the court concluded that NYU did not fail to advise the employee that a certification was incomplete or provide the employee a reasonable opportunity to cure any deficiency.

An employer that failed to notify an employee that it had problems with the medical certification provided may still challenge whether the employee has a serious health condition. See Pleasha v. U.S. Steel Corp., No. 2:05-CV-201 PS, 2007 U.S. Dist. LEXIS 9230, at *18-19 (N.D. Ind. Feb. 7, 2007).

2. Title II

Title II does not have any special requirements that would require employers to notify employees when certification is incomplete and allow the employee a reasonable opportunity to cure any deficiency. On the contrary, an employee who does not provide the medical certification from a health care provider that includes all of the information required in § 630.1207(b) is not entitled to FMLA leave. 5 CFR 630.1208(l).

Of course, an employer could waive any deficiencies in the medical certification provided by the employee. Like Title I, such waiver is possible because an employer is not required to request medical certification in the first place. Additionally, an employer may provide greater family or medical leave benefits than the minimum required by the FMLA. Such greater benefits could include a relaxation of the content requirements for medical certifications.

Unions and other organizations representing the interests of employees should consider bargaining for rights to notification and a reasonable opportunity to cure deficiencies in medical certifications similar to those enjoyed by employees covered by Title I, the CAA, and the PEOAA.

I. COMPLETE CERTIFICATIONS; CLARIFICATION

The FMLA provides employers with certain rights when it questions the adequacy of a medical certification submitted by the employee that is complete.

1. Title I, the CAA, and the PEOAA

An employer has two options when it questions the adequacy of an otherwise complete medical certification: (1) it may seek clarification; and (2) it may invoke the second/third opinion process. [The "Second/Third Opinion Process" is the subject of the next section of this chapter.]

If an employee submits a complete certification signed by the health care provider, the employer may not request additional information from the employee's health care provider. 29 CFR 825.307(a); S. Res. 242, Cong. Rec. S3959, S3973 (April 23, 1996); 29 CFR 825.307(a); see *Konipol v. Restaurant Associates*, No. 01–Civ. 7857 (GEL), 2002 U.S. Dist. LEXIS 22439 (S.D.N.Y. Nov. 20, 2002). However, a health care provider representing the employer may contact the employee's health care provider, with the employee's permission, for purposes of clarification and authenticity of the medical certification. 29 CFR 825.307(a); S. Res. 242, Cong. Rec. S3959, S3973 (April 23, 1996); 29 CFR 825.307(a); see *Harcourt v. Cincinnati Bell Tel. Co.*, 383 F. Supp. 2d 944, 955 (S.D. Ohio Aug. 18, 2005); *Willis v. USPS*, No. 03 C 9185, 2004 U.S. Dist. LEXIS 18238, at *13, 22–23 (N.D. Ill. Sept. 10, 2004); *Cool v. BorgWarner Diversified Transmission Products, Inc.*, No. IP 02–0960–C–B/S, 2004 U.S. Dist. LEXIS 570, at *26, n. 5 (S.D. Ind. Jan. 12, 2004); *Lara v. Central Grocers Cooperative, Inc. et al.*, No. 00–C–7828, 2002 U.S. Dist. LEXIS 16745, at n. 4 (N.D. Ill. Sept. 6, 2002); *Shtab v. The Greate Bay Hotel and Casino, Inc. et al.*, 173 F. Supp. 2d 255, 264 (D. N.J. 2001); *Whitaker v. Bosch Braking Systems Div. of Robert Bosch Corp.*, 180 F. Supp. 2d 922, 932 (W.D. Mich. 2001). In other words, the statute and the regulation establish that the medical certification provided by the employee is presumptively valid provided it contains the required information and is signed by the health care provider. The burden is on the employer to establish that the certification is invalid or inauthentic. *Harcourt v. Cincinnati Bell Tel. Co.*, 383 F. Supp. 2d 944, 955-56 (S.D. Ohio Aug. 18, 2005).

The clarification provision was added in response to requests by employers that the absence of an opportunity by the employer's health care provider to contact the employee's health care provider to ask clarifying questions could result in unnecessary costs to the employer (who would be forced to use the second opinion process) and additional discomfort to an employee who may be asked to submit to a second opinion while on FMLA leave. Preamble, 29 CFR 825.307.

An employer may ask the employee to obtain clarification from the health care provider. In *Rutschke v. Northwest Airlines, Inc.*, No. 04-3212 (RHK/AJB0, 2005 U.S. Dist. LEXIS 18725, at *20-21 (D. Minn. Aug. 30, 2005), the court found that the employer did not interference with the employee's FMLA rights by asking the employee to take the certification back to his physician for clarification regarding some identified inconsistencies in the original medical certification.

Absent evidence of prejudice or actual damages, an employee will not have a cause of action for an employer's improper contact with the employee's health care provider. See *Harrell v. USPS*, 445 F.3d 913, 928-29 (7th Cir. 2006), cert. denied, 127 S. Ct. 845 (2006); *Moticka v. Weck Closure Systems*, 183 Fed. Appx. 343 (4th Cir. 2006); *Sons v. Henry County*, No. 1:05-cv-0516-DFH-TAB, 2007 U.S. Dist. LEXIS 20574, at *6-9 (S.D. Ind. March 13, 2007);

In *Cool v. BorgWarner Diversified Transmission Products, Inc.*, No. IP 02–0960–C–B/S, 2004 U.S. Dist. LEXIS 570, at *26, n.5 (S.D. Ind. Jan. 12, 2004), the court found that the employer's health care provider did not have permission to contact the employee's health care provider to clarify information in the medical certification. As a penalty, the court excluded the clarification gained by the employer's physician in its analysis of the issue, even though it supported the court's conclusion.

An employer's contact with the employee's physician without the employee's permission is evidence of discriminatory or retaliatory motive. *Hite v. Vermeer Mfg., Co.*, 361 F. Supp. 2d 935, 951 (S.D. Iowa 2005), aff'd, 446 F.3d 858 (8th Cir. 2006).

The provision prohibiting an employer from seeking "additional information" is further clarified in the preamble as prohibiting an employer from seeking additional information regarding the employee's condition. Preamble, 29 CFR 825.305.

In the event the employee refuses to give permission for the employer to clarify, the employer may then require certification from a second health care provider. Preamble, 29 CFR 825.305. The second opinion is at the expense of the employer. There is nothing in the regulations that requires the employee to act reasonably or otherwise have a legitimate reason for denying an employer permission to clarify the submitted certification.

Note that the prohibition against an employer seeking clarification, with the employee's permission, includes confirmation of the authenticity of the certification. That is, if the employer suspects that the employee has submitted a forged or altered certification, the employer must ask the employee's permission before contacting the listed health care provider. Absent that permission, the employer must go through the expense of the second opinion process.

There is no stated rationale to explain why questions concerning the authenticity of the document requires an employer to obtain the employee's permission before confirming the issue with the health care provider. According to the Preamble, contact by a health care provider of the employer adequately addressed concerns regarding the privacy of the employee and the ethical considerations of the employee's health care provider furnishing information to a non–medical person. Preamble, 29 CFR 825.305. Both of these stated concerns do not appear, to be relevant where the issue is whether the health care provider submitted any documentation at all. Whether the health care provider did or did not submit the certification at issue does not delve into the medical privacy of the employee. The existence of the medical relationship, if any, was revealed in the certification. Confirming that fact does not impinge a privacy interest. Moreover, if the health care provider did not provide the certification, there is no medical privacy issue at all.

The irony here is that, while the DOL regulations profess that FMLA obtained by fraud is not protected by the FMLA, the regulations place a giant roadblock in the way of an employer's ability to establish that the employee fraudulently obtained FMLA leave by means of a forged or altered certification. All of this is done in the name of employee privacy. Such privacy, moreover, is not implicated since the existence of the certification in the possession of the employer has already waived that privacy, at least to the extent that the employee is claiming that an identified health care provider signed the certification as represented.

Agencies that suspect fraud need to think carefully before turning the matter over to internal affairs or the Inspector General. If the investigation includes contacting the health care provider without first obtaining the employee's permission, the employer may well find itself in violation of the FMLA.

In *Kitts v. General Telephone North, Inc.*, No. 2:04-cv-173, 2005 U.S. Dist. LEXIS 20421, at *30 (S.D. Ohio Sept. 19, 2005), the court found the FMLA does not prohibit an employer from investigating allegations of employee dishonesty involving the use of FMLA leave. The court observed that the FMLA does not require an employer to seek "clarification" when it suspects that an employee is abusing leave granted under the FMLA. The employer hired a private investigator when it became suspicious that the employee did not use FMLA leave for the stated purpose. An exception to the "no clarification without permission" rule involves situations where the employee is on FMLA leave running concurrently with a workers' compensation absence. Where the provisions of the workers' compensation statute permit an employer or the employer's representative to have direct contact with the employee's workers' compensation health care provider, the employer may follow the workers' compensation provisions. 29 CFR 825.307(a)(1); S. Res. 242, Cong. Rec. S3959, S3973 (April 23, 1996); 29 CFR 825.307(a)(1).

Finally, note that the regulations do not require that the employee's permission be in writing. Prudent employers, however, should require written consent before contact with the health care provider for purposes of clarification is made. Preamble, 29 CFR 825.307.

2. Title II

The regulations implementing Title II also allow an employer to seek clarification of the contents of a complete medical certification. The regulations, 5 CFR 630.1207(c), provide that:

> If an employee submits a completed medical certification signed by the health care provider, the agency may not request new information from the health care provider. However, a health care provider representing the agency, including a health care provider employed by the agency or under administrative oversight of the agency, may contact the health care provider who completed the medical certification, with the employee's permission, for purposes of clarifying the medical certification.

See *Franklin v. Dept. of Air Force*, No. AT-0752-05-0355-I-2, 2005 MSPB LEXIS 8069, at *39 (Dec. 27, 2005).

In *Franklin*, the Board found that the employer did not have the right to order the employee to sign a document authorizing the agency's physician to talk directly with the employee's health care provider. The Board found that the directive was prohibited by the FMLA.

In the preamble to the final regulations, OPM explained that the clarification of the medical certification pertained to the condition. Preamble, 5 CFR 630.1207 (medical certification). Arguably, an employer is not prohibited from contacting the employee's health care provider without the employee's permission to confirm the authenticity of the certifications, i.e., that the health care provider signed the certification. The actual wording of the regulation prohibits an employer form contacting the health care provider who completed the certification for purposes of clarifying the medical certification. The question remains whether the phrase "clarifying the certification" includes confirming the authenticity of the document, as it does under Title I.

The argument that it does not include confirming the authenticity of the document is twofold: (1) the OPM regulations came out after the DOL regulations, which explicitly included authenticity. The absence in the OPM regulations, therefore, suggests that authenticity was deliberately not included; and (2) the preamble to the final DOL regulations speaks in terms of "the condition," not authenticity. Since authenticity of the document does not address the employee's condition, checking on the legitimacy of the certification presented should not require an employee's prior consent. Agencies are well advised to seek the advice of counsel before assuming that checking the authenticity of a Title II employee's certification does not require the prior consent of the employee.

Title II does not contain a provision that would permit an employer to have direct contact with the employee's workers' compensation health care provider where the employee's FMLA leave is being run concurrently with a workers' compensation absence. This would appear to present major problems for agencies processing OWCP claims for Title II employees. If the agencies processing these claims are contacting the employees health care providers directly, and those health care providers were the same ones who signed the FMLA certification form, those contacts are in violation of the FMLA, absent the consent of the employee.

J. SECOND/THIRD OPINION PROCESS

In addition to clarification, the FMLA permits employers to address concerns regarding a medical certification by requiring a second and, ultimately, a third medical opinion.

1. Title I, the CAA, and the PEOAA

a. General Rule: Second Opinions

An employer who has reason to doubt the validity of a medical certification may require the employee to obtain a second medical opinion. 29 USC 2613(1); 29 CFR 825.307(a)(2); S. Res. 242, Cong. Rec. S3959, S3973 (April 23, 1996); 29 CFR 825.307(a)(2); see Bailey v. Southwest Gas Co., 275 F.3d 1181, 1186 (9th Cir. 2002); Rhoads v. FDIC et al., 257 F.3d 373, 383 (4th Cir. 2001), cert. denied, 535 U.S. 933 (2002); Thorson v. Gemini, Inc. et al., 205 F.3d 370, 381 (8th Cir. 2000), cert. denied, 531 U.S. 871 (2000) (to prevent abuse of FMLA leave, employer may require a second opinion); Stoops v. One Call Communications, Inc., 141 F.3d 309, 312 (7th Cir. 1998); Diaz v. Fort Wayne Foundry Corp., 131 F.3d 711, 713 (7th Cir. 1997); Whitworth v. Consolidated Biscuit Co., No. 6:06-112-DCR, 2007 U.S. Dist. LEXIS 25971, at *17 (E.D. Ky. April 6, 2007); Smith v. V.I. Port Authority, No. 2002–227, 2005 U.S. Dist. LEXIS 56, at *37 (D.V.I. Jan. 2, 2005); Dowell v. Indiana Heart Physicians, Inc., No. 1:03–cv–1410–DFH–TAB, 2004 U.S. Dist. LEXIS 26431, at *14 (S.D. Ind. Dec. 22, 2004); Wheeler v. Pioneer Dev. Services, Inc., 349 F. Supp 2d 158 (D. Mass. 2004); Willis v. USPS, No. 03 C 9185, 2004 U.S. Dist. LEXIS 18238, at *13 (N.D. Ill. Sept. 10, 2004); Dillaway v. Ferrante, No. 02–715 (JRT/JSM), 2003 U.S. Dist. LEXIS 23468, at *22 (D. Minn. Dec. 9, 2003); Smith v. Univ. of Chicago Hospitals, No. 02 C 0221, 2003 U.S. Dist. LEXIS 20965, at *22 (N.D. Ill. Nov. 24, 2003); Porter v. NYU School of Law, No. 99 Civ. 4693 (TPG), 2003 U.S. Dist. LEXIS 14674, at *16 (S.D.N.Y. Aug. 25, 2003), aff'd, 392 F.3d 530 (2d Cir. 2004).

If the second opinion differs from the first, an employer may require the employee or the employee's covered family member to undergo an examination from a third health care opinion provider. 29 USC 2613(d)(1); Whitworth v. Consolidated Biscuit Co., No. 6:06-112-DCR, 2007 U.S. Dist. LEXIS 25971, at *17 (E.D. Ky. April 6, 2007); Shtab v. The Greate Bay Hotel and Casino, Inc. et al., 173 F. Supp. 2d 255, 264 (D. N.J. 2001); Washington v. Fort James Operating Co., 110 F. Supp. 2d 1325, 1330 (D. Ore. 2000).

The regulations do not explain or otherwise give guidance on what circumstances would legitimately give rise to an employer having a "reason to doubt the validity" of the medical certification provided by the employee. See Albert v. Runyon, 6 F. Supp. 2d 57, 63–65 (D. Mass. 1998) (what constitutes a "reason to doubt the validity" of a medical certification is not well-established). One court observed that "'validity' means that there is some reason for the employer to believe that [the] health care provider's opinion is wrong." See Harcourt v. Cincinnati Bell Tel. Co., 383 F. Supp. 2d 944, 955 (S.D. Ohio Aug. 18, 2005). In Harcourt, the court opined that an employer would have a reason to doubt the validity of a medical certification where the certification indicates that the employee needs six months of continuous leave to recuperate from a tonsillectomy when one would reasonably expect recovery to take two weeks, at most.

In *Dillon v. Carlton*, 977 F. Supp. 1155, 1159 (M.D. Fla. 1997), *aff'd without op.*, (11th Cir. 1998), the court held that the employer did not have a reason to doubt the validity of a certification where the certification clearly indicated that the employee did not have an FMLA–covered serious health condition. As a result, the employer was not required to challenge the validity of the certification provided through the second and third opinion process before denying the request for FMLA leave.

The disparity between the medical opinions rendered by an employee's two physicians may be grounds for an employer to have reason to doubt the validity of the certification. In *Diaz v. Fort Wayne Foundry Corp.*, 131 F.3d 711, 713 (7th Cir. 1997), the employer gave the employee one month's FMLA leave based on a certification from his physician that the employee had bronchitis. When his employer told the employee to return to work, the employee indicated that he was receiving medical treatment in Mexico and would submit a certification. The second certification from a different physician indicated that the employee suffered from irritable bowel syndrome, hiatal hernia, gastro esophageal reflux, and a duodenal peptic ulcer, requiring a month and a half of rest. These conditions, the court found, are unrelated to bronchitis, and legitimately raised the employer's suspicions justifying a second opinion.

In *Albert v. Runyon*, 6 F. Supp. 2d 57, 63–65 (D. Mass. 1998), the court found that the employer failed to articulate a reason to doubt the validity of the certification provided by the employee. The analysis of the court is instructive. In rejecting the argument by the Postal Service that it had the right to require the employee to undergo a psychiatric examination as a second opinion, the court noted that the Postal Service failed to identify any problems with the certification provided until the onset of litigation. *Id.* at 63. Moreover, the court dismissed the Postal Service's arguments that the certification omitted information, noting that the information that the Postal Service sought was beyond the bounds of what it was entitled to receive. *Id.* at 64.

The court further noted that Postal Service's criticisms of the certifications submitted by the employee's health care provider "may have stemmed from a misapprehension of its own role." *Id.* The court continued:

> At times, the Service writes as if it needs sufficient information to independently assess Albert's condition or to evaluate Dr. Smith's diagnosis. However, an employer is not entitled to require information beyond that alleged by 29 USC 2613, in order to make its own assessment. *See* 29 CFR 825.306(b) ("[n]o additional information may be required"). Moreover, the limited information that the FMLA permits an employer to demand shows that the [S]tatute does not authorize an employer to make an independent assessment of the employee's medical condition. Instead, the employer should determine whether the provided information demonstrates that the diagnosed condition is a serious health condition within the meaning of the FMLA.

The Postal Service, according to the court, needed a specific reason to doubt the validity of the employee's certification in order to demand a second examination. *Id.* at 64. In addition to making a timely demand, the court noted the lack of any suggestion that the certifications submitted by the employee were deficient, and that they provided no reason to doubt the validity of these certifications. With respect to the reason offered by the Service after litigation ensued, that it doubted the objectivity of the plaintiff's physician, the court noted that there was no basis for concluding that this newly asserted claim was a motivating factor for the Service's instruction that the employee undergo a second opinion, or that its vague allegation provides "reason to doubt the validity" of the original certification. According the court, *Id.* at 65:

> In providing that an employee's health care provider should furnish her medical certification, the FMLA does not contemplate an adversarial investigation into a patient's symptoms and complaints.
>
> ....
>
> While what constitutes a "reason to doubt the validity" of a medical certification is not well established, it is difficult to conclude that the fact that a health care provider follows generally accepted treating practices provides such a reason. *Cf. Diaz v. Fort Wayne Foundry Corp.* 131 F.3d 711 (7th Cir. 1997) (employer ordered second opinion to resolve conflict between certifications provided by employee's two physicians); *Patterson v. Dept. of Air Force*, 74 M.S.P.R. 648 (1997) (finding that the fact that employee's physician never "contacted [her] supervisor to evaluate [her] version of events, and that [the doctor's] letters put the employer in a difficult position because accepting that her 'maltreatment' would compromise its position in her equal employment opportunity complaints" did not justify the agency's reject[ion of the] medical evidence).

The employer is permitted to designate the health care provider to furnish the second opinion. 29 USC 2613(1); 29 CFR 825.307(a)(2); S. Res. 242, Cong. Rec. S3959, S3973 (April 23, 1996); 29 CFR 825.307(a)(2); *see Thorson v. Gemini, Inc. et al.*, 205 F.3d 370, 381 (8th Cir. 2000), *cert. denied*, 531 U.S. 871 (2000); *Diaz. v. Fort Wayne Foundry Corp.*, 131 F.3d 711, 713 (7th Cir. 1997). However, the health care provider selected by the employer for the second opinion may not be employed on a regular basis by the employer. 29 USC 2613(1); 29 CFR 825.307(a)(2); S. Res. 242, Cong. Rec. S3959, S3973 (April 23, 1996); 29 CFR 825.307(a)(2); *see Diaz*, 131 F.3d 711, 713 (7th Cir. 1997); *Smith v. V.I. Port Authority*, No. 2002–227, 2005 U.S. Dist. LEXIS 56, at *37 (D.V.I. Jan. 2, 2005); *Wheeler v. Pioneer Dev. Services, Inc.*, 349 F. Supp 2d 158 (D. Mass. 2004); *Smith v. Univ. of Chicago Hospitals*, No. 02 C 0221, 2003 U.S. Dist. LEXIS 20965, at *22 (N.D. Ill. Nov. 24, 2003); *Porter v. NYU School of Law*, No. 99 Civ. 4693 (TPG), 2003 U.S. Dist. LEXIS 14674, at *16 (S.D.N.Y. Aug. 25, 2003), *aff'd*, 392 F.3d 530 (2d Cir. 2004); *Pollard v. City of Northwood et al.*, 161 F. Supp. 2d 782, 794 (N.D. Ohio 2001); *Krohn v. Forsting et al.*, 11 F. Supp. 2d 1082, 1090 (E.D. Mo. July 17, 1998). Nor is the employer allowed to select a health care provider for the second opinion that the employer regularly contracts with or otherwise regularly utilizes the services of that health care provider, unless the employer is located in an area where access to health care is extremely limited (e.g., a rural area where no more than one or two doctors practice in the relevant specialty in the vicinity). 29 CFR 825.307(b); S. Res. 242, Cong. Rec. S3959, S3973 (April 23, 1996); 29 CFR 825.307(b).

In *Pollard v. City of Northwood et al.*, 161 F. Supp. 2d 782, 794 (N.D. Ohio 2001), the court held that, even while the employer used a second opinion health care provider whom the employer regularly contracted with, the employer was entitled to summary judgment on the plaintiff's claim because the second opinion supported the employee's request for FMLA leave.

The ability of an employer to select the second opinion provider allows employers to select specialists in the field to determine whether the individual has a serious health condition and, if so, the probable frequency of absences and duration of the condition. Very often, the initial certification provided by the employee is from a general medical practitioner who may or may not have expertise regarding the claimed serious health condition. Requiring the individual with the serious health condition, whether the employee or a covered family member of the employee, to get a second opinion enables employers to ensure that the condition qualifies for FMLA leave.

An employer has the right to require a second or third opinion from a health care provider even if meeting that requirement would be onerous or burdensome to the employee or the employee's covered family member. Addressing comments seeking an exemption from the requirements for a second or third opinion where securing same would be onerous or unduly burdensome, the DOL (Preamble, 29 CFR 825.307) stated the following:

> The right of the employer to require a second medical opinion when the employer has reason to question the validity of the original medical certification is statutory. Consequently, the employer is entitled to the second opinion, and the third opinion if the second disagrees with the original opinion. The alternative is for the employee to forego FMLA leave.

The regulations do not address the timing or method of notice of the second opinion process. That is, how much notice must an employee have before the appointment with the second (and presumably third) health care opinion provider? In *Diaz v. Fort Wayne Foundry Corp.*, 131 F.3d 711, 714 (7th Cir. 1997), the court stated that "[d]oubtless the FMLA implies a duty to set a reasonable time for the [second] medical examination." In that case, the employer directed the employee to attend the second medical examination that was scheduled in approximately eight days. The employee, however, claimed not to receive notice of this direction because the employer sent the letter to his home in Indiana, when the employee was in Mexico. The court, however, agreed that the employer properly notified the employee at the employee's last address of record, as required by terms of the governing collective bargaining agreement. It was incumbent on the employee, the court found, to make arrangements to have his mail opened while he was away from home, or provide the employer with an address where the employee could be reached. Because the employee did neither, the fact that he did not receive timely notice of the second opinion process is his own fault, not that of the employer.

The case should motivate unions and other organizations representing employees to modify the typical "address of record" notice requirement so that the employee receives actual notice. This can be accomplished by requiring service of the notice on the union as well as the employee (if the union wants to assume that responsibility). Alternatively, the employee can be provided the opportunity to notify the employer of temporary addresses where notice can be sent during periods of medical treatment/leave.

b. Christian Science Practitioners and Second/Third Opinions

Christian Science practitioners listed with the First Church of Christ, Scientist in Boston, Massachusetts, are health care providers within the meaning of the FMLA. 29 CFR 825.118(b)(3); S. Res. 242, Cong. Rec. S3959, S3963 (April 23, 1996); 29 CFR 825.307(e). Where an employee or covered family member is receiving treatment from a Christian Science practitioner, the employee may not object to any requirement from an employer that the employee or covered family member submit to examination (though not treatment) to obtain a second or third certification from a health care provider other than a Christian Science practitioner, except as otherwise provided under applicable state or local law or collective bargaining agreement. 29 CFR 825.118(b)(3); S. Res. 242, Cong. Rec. S3959, S3963 (April 23, 1996); 29 CFR 825.118(b)(3).

Generally speaking, absent a specific wavier of sovereign immunity, state or local law does not bind the federal government. Unions frequently bargain for language that would restrict an agency's ability to require an employee seeking treatment from a registered Christian Science practitioner from having to undergo a second or third opinion examination from anyone other than a Christian Science practitioner. Agencies are well advised to not agree to such language. It is very important for an employer to retain the ability to require an employee claiming to have a serious health condition to undergo examination by a medical specialist.

c. Who is Initially Entitled to Second/Third Opinions?

The regulations do not clearly provide whether the second and third health care provider opinions are provided directly to the employee, or to the employer who is paying for them. Since the second and third opinion process is for the benefit of the employer, who is paying, it makes sense that the opinions are initially provided to the employer, not the employee. This explains why the regulations fail to place any time frame on the employee to provide these certifications.

That the second and third opinions are delivered to the employer rather than the employee is reflected in the requirement that, on request, the employer must provide copies of the second and third opinions to the employee. 29 CFR 825.307(e); S. Res. 242, Cong. Rec. S3959, S3973 (April 23, 1996); 29 CFR 825.307(e). In contrast, an employer is not required by the FMLA to provide a copy of the original certification to the employee. The DOL explained the rationale for this distinction in the preamble (Preamble, 29 CFR 825.305), as follows:

> As the employee is providing the certification to the employer, if the employee wishes to have a copy he/she may make a copy before submission to the employer. The regulations have been amended to provide for copies of a second or third opinion to be provided by the employer to the employee upon the employee's request.

The inference to be drawn from the above is that the employee is not provided the second or third certification, which he or she then hands over to the employer. Rather, the second or third opinion provider receives the second or third opinion directly. If the employee requests a copy of the second or third opinion, the employer is obligated to provide copies.

d. Payment for Second Opinion

The employer pays the health care provider for the expense of the second opinion. 29 USC 2613(1); 29 CFR 825.307(b); S. Res. 242, Cong. Rec. S3959, S3973 (April 23, 1996); 29 CFR 825.307(b); see Rhoads v. FDIC et al., 257 F.3d 373, 383 (4th Cir. 2001); Smith v. V.I. Port Authority, No. 2002–227, 2005 U.S. Dist. LEXIS 56, at *37 (D.V.I. Jan. 2, 2005); Smith v. Univ. of Chicago Hospitals, No. 02 C 0221, 2003 U.S. Dist. LEXIS 20965, at *22 (N.D. Ill. Nov. 24, 2003); Porter v. NYU School of Law, No. 99 Civ. 4693 (TPG), 2003 U.S. Dist. LEXIS 14674, at *16 (S.D.N.Y. Aug. 25, 2003), aff'd, 392 F.3d 530 (2d Cir. 2004); Washington v. Fort James Operating Co., 110 F. Supp. 2d 1325, 1330 (D. Ore. 2000). The employer must also reimburse the employee or family member for any reasonable out-of-pocket travel expenses incurred to obtain the second opinion. 29 CFR 825.307(e); S. Res. 242, Cong. Rec. S3959, S3973 (April 23, 1996); 29 CFR 825.307(e); see Kent v. Maryland Transportation Authority, No. CCB-06-2351, 2006 U.S. Dist. LEXIS 94832, at *8 & n.3 (D. Md. Dec. 21, 2006), aff'd, 2007 U.S. App. LEXIS 16228 (4th Cir. July 9, 2007). An employer may not require the employee or family member to travel outside normal commuting distance for purposes of obtaining the second medical opinion except in very unusual circumstances. 29 CFR 825.307(e); S. Res. 242, Cong. Rec. S3959, S3973 (April 23, 1996); 29 CFR 825.307(e); see Kent, 2006 U.S. Dist. LEXIS 94832, at *8 & n.3. What constitutes a "normal" commuting distance and "very unusual circumstances" is undefined. As with most ambiguous legal matters, agencies should proceed with caution.

The FMLA does not require that an employee must be paid for the time spent in acquiring the required second opinion. According to comments in the preamble to the final regulations, Preamble, 29 CFR 825.307:

> The Department [of Labor] has...concluded that Congress did not intend that employees on unpaid FMLA leave be paid for the time spent obtaining second and third opinion. Section 825.307(d) has been amended, however, to make it clear that an employer must in all cases reimburse an employee or family member for any reasonable "out of pocket" travel expenses incurred in obtaining the required second and third opinions.

Of course, an employer could adopt a policy that provided that employees are paid for the time they spend obtaining second and third opinions at the request of the agency. Some agencies may already have agreed to this as part of a collective bargaining agreement. Many collective bargaining agreements have provisions requiring the payment of wages to an employee for attending fitness for duty and other required medical examinations. Agencies and unions should closely scrutinize the language in these agreements to determine whether they would apply to a second medical opinion for purposes of leave. Note that a fitness for duty report generally serves a different function than a second or third medical opinion. The former is used to determine if the employee is fit to work. The latter is used to determine if the employee is entitled to take FMLA leave due to a serious health condition.

e. Preliminary Designation

Pending receipt of the second opinion, the employee is provisionally entitled to the benefits of the Act, including maintenance of group health benefits. 29 CFR 825.307(a)(2); S. Res. 242, Cong. Rec. S3959, S3973 (April 23, 1996); 29 CFR 825.307(a)(2); see Smith v. V.I. Port Authority, No. 2002-227, 2005 U.S. Dist. LEXIS 56, at *37 (D.V.I. Jan. 2, 2005); Smith v. Univ. of Chicago Hospitals, No. 02 C 0221, 2003 U.S. Dist. LEXIS 20965, at *24 (N.D. Ill. Nov. 24, 2003). The leave is provisionally designated as FMLA leave. 29 CFR 825.208(e)(2); S. Res. 242, Cong. Rec. S3959, S3966 (April 23, 1996); 29 CFR 825.208(e)(2). Ultimately, if the certifications do not establish the employee's entitlement to FMLA leave, the leave may not be designated as FMLA leave but may be treated as paid or unpaid leave under the employer's established policy. 29 CFR 825.307(a)(2); S. Res. 242, Cong. Rec. S3959, S3973 (April 23, 1996); 29 CFR 825.307(a)(2); see V.I. Port Authority, 2005 U.S. Dist. LEXIS 56, at *38.

f. Third Opinion

If the opinions of the health care providers for the employee and the employer differ, the employer may require the employee to obtain certification from a third health care provider, again at the employer's expense. 29 USC 2613(d)(2); 29 CFR 825.307(c); S. Res. 242, Cong. Rec. S3959, S3973 (April 23, 1996); 29 CFR 825.307(c); see Rhoads v. FDIC et al., 257 F.3d 373, 383 (4th Cir. 2001), cert. denied, 535 U.S. 933 (2002); Thorson v. Gemini, Inc. et al., 205 F.3d 370, 381 (8th Cir. 2000), cert. denied, 531 U.S. 871 (2000); Stoops v. One Call Communications, Inc., 141 F.3d 309, 312 (7th Cir. 1998); V.I. Port Authority, 2005 U.S. Dist. LEXIS 56, at *38; Wheeler v. Pioneer Dev. Services, Inc., 349 F. Supp 2d 158 (D. Mass. 2004); Willis v. USPS, No. 03 C 9185, 2004 U.S. Dist. LEXIS 18238, at *14 (N.D. Ill. Sept. 10, 2004); Dillaway v. Ferrante, No. 02-715 (JRT/JSM), 2003 U.S. Dist. LEXIS 23468, at *22 (D. Minn. Dec. 9, 2003); Univ. of Chicago Hospitals, 2003 U.S. Dist. LEXIS 20965, at *23; Porter v. NYU School of Law, No. 99 Civ. 4693 (TPG), 2003 U.S. Dist. LEXIS 14674, at *16 (S.D.N.Y. Aug. 25, 2003), aff'd, 392 F.3d 530 (2d Cir. 2004); Washington v. Fort James Operating Co., 110 F. Supp. 2d 1325, 1330 (D. Ore. 2000).

This third opinion is final and binding. 29 USC 2613(d)(2); 29 CFR 825.307(c); S. Res. 242, Cong. Rec. S3959, S3973 (April 23, 1996); 29 CFR 825.307(c); see Rhoads, 257 F.3d at 384; Thorson, 205 F.3d at 381; Stoops, 141 F.3d at 312; V.I. Port Authority, 2005 U.S. Dist. LEXIS 56, at *38; Dillaway, 2003 U.S. Dist. LEXIS 23468, at *22; Porter 2003 U.S. Dist. LEXIS 14674, at *16; Washington v. Fort James Operating Co., 110 F. Supp. 2d at 1330.

While the language is permissive, agencies are well advised to treat the requirement to seek a third medical opinion whenever the first and second health care opinions differ as mandatory. The intent of the regulation appears to require an employer to seek a third opinion whenever the second health care opinion differs from the initial certification provided by the employee. Preamble, 29 CFR 825.307 ("The third medical opinion becomes necessary only when the second opinion disagrees with the original opinion."); see Stoops v. One Call Communications, Inc., 141 F.3d 309, 312 (7th Cir. 1998) ("A binding third opinion must be gotten to resolve a conflict between the first and second opinions.").

The regulations do not clearly define the circumstances that would justify an employer to require a third medical opinion. The regulations provide that a third opinion may be required when the first and second health care opinions differ. DOL described this in the preamble as arising when the second opinion disagrees with the original certification. Needless to say, these are not necessarily the same standard. That is, the original and second certifications could be in agreement, yet differ. Since the actual regulation uses the term "differ," agencies should apply that standard.

The regulations also do not make any further distinctions regarding the type or degree of difference necessary in order to perfect the agency's right to require a third medical opinion. As such, the slightest difference, even if not particularly substantive, would allow an employer to require a third medical opinion. Of course, substantive differences, such as a more accurate estimate in the second opinion of the number of days that an employee may need intermittent absences a month, would also justify an employer to seek a third medical opinion.

It is unclear exactly what the phrase "final and binding" means with respect to the third medical opinion. The ultimate question is whether "final and binding" attaches to the serious health condition, a particular request for leave (which, of course, may be the same as the serious health condition, based on the scope of the original request for FMLA leave), a temporal period, or some combination thereof.

Presumably, final and binding means that the third opinion is binding on all aspects of the certification, including the duration of the condition, the number of permissible absences within a given time frame, and the length of particular absences. It is unclear how a third opinion interacts with subsequent changes in the need for FMLA leave. For example, if an employee needs FMLA leave to care for a parent with a long-term condition that is getting progressively worse over time, it stands to reason that the employee's need for FMLA leave should increase over time. If, however, the third medical opinion had a fixed number of absences per month, arguably, as a final and binding opinion, the employee would not be entitled to any additional FMLA leave beyond that which is set forth by the third opinion. Of course, the employee could take any non–FMLA leave that was available, but such leave would not be protected by the FMLA and could be the basis for disciplinary action.

Similarly, a third opinion could fix a higher number of absences each month than may be necessary due to improvement in the serious health condition. If the third opinion is final and binding, arguably, the employee may be entitled to more leave than is really necessary. The counter argument, of course, is that all absences have to meet all of the requirements of the FMLA, so that an employee would not be entitled to FMLA protections for absences that were not for a serious health condition, even if they fit within the final and binding number of absences of a third opinion.

Generally, the meaning of final and binding is tested where a third medical opinion provides a lower number of intermittent absences than the original certification. The third opinion is final and binding by operation of law. Subsequently, the employee provides a new certification indicating that the condition has changed, necessitating an increased (or unlimited number of absences) for the foreseeable future. This new certification is, surprise, surprise, signed by the health care provider who signed the original certification way back when. Absent guidance on this issue, an employer may find itself at a loss as to how to proceed.

If the new certification provided by the employee trumps a final and binding third opinion, then the entire second and third opinion process is called into question. An employer would have to ask itself whether it is worth the great expense (these second and third opinions are not cheap) of going through the second and third opinion process only to be trumped by the employee in the end. On the other hand, the FMLA contemplates that some forms of leave are for serious health conditions, which will almost certainly get worse, necessitating an increased need for FMLA leave. By forever restricting the number of absences based on a final and binding third opinion, an employee may be denied the right to take FMLA leave in situations where all of the conditions for such leave are otherwise met.

The requirement that a third opinion is final and binding is statutory. 29 USC 2613(d)(2); 2 USC 1312(a)(1) (incorporating 29 USC 2613 into CAA); 3 USC 412(a)(1) (incorporating 29 USC 2613 into PEOAA). Although the legislative history on this point is not particularly enlightening, it seems reasonable to assume that Congress meant what it said: the third opinion is final and binding. Congress opted for finality on this issue by including the "final and binding" language in the Statute. If that means anything, it means that an employer is well within its rights to provide FMLA leave to an employee as specified by the third opinion. Absences for the same condition in excess of those permitted by the third opinion, even if they otherwise meet the requirements for FMLA leave, need not be granted. Such absences could, of course, be covered by an agency's usual leave policies. They would not, however, be covered by the protections of the FMLA.

In the example previously given, an employee who brought in a new certification covering the same serious health condition seeking to modify the requirements of a final and binding third opinion by claims of a change in the underlying serious health condition would be unsuccessful.

It is unclear whether an employer could grant FMLA leave to an employee, notwithstanding that the leave falls outside the requirements of a third opinion. The Statute and the regulations are unequivocal that a third opinion is final and binding on the parties. Neither the Statute nor the regulations provide that the parties may decide to ignore the final and binding nature of the third opinion. While the Statute and the regulations do allow employers to provide more generous family and medical leave benefits than are provided by the Act, it is unclear that this generosity extends to allowing FMLA leave in circumstances where a binding third opinion says that FMLA leave is not warranted. Like extending eligibility to those who do not meet the minimum statutory threshold, it would seem more likely that an employer could agree to allow an employee leave pursuant to employer policy, and even agree that such leave would not be the subject of discipline. That leave, however, would not be subject to the protections of the FMLA where it falls outside of the parameters of a final and binding third opinion.

g. Selection of Third Opinion Health Care Provider

The third health care provider must be designated or approved jointly by the employer and the employee. 29 CFR 825.307(c); S. Res. 242, Cong. Rec. S3959, S3973 (April 23, 1996); 29 CFR 825.307(c); *see Smith v. V.I. Port Authority*, No. 2002-227, 2005 U.S. Dist. LEXIS 56, at *38 (D.V.I. Jan. 2, 2005); *Smith v. Univ. of Chicago Hospitals*, No. 02 C 0221, 2003 U.S. Dist. LEXIS 20965, at *22 (N.D. Ill. Nov. 24, 2003); *Washington v. Fort James Operating Co.*, 110 F. Supp. 2d 1325, 1330 (D. Ore. 2000). The employer and the employee must each act in good faith to attempt to reach agreement on whom to select as the third health care opinion provider. 29 CFR 825.307(c); S. Res. 242, Cong. Rec. S3959, S3973 (April 23, 1996); 29 CFR 825.307(c). If the employer does not attempt in good faith to reach agreement, the employer will be bound by the first certification. 29 CFR 825.307(c); S. Res. 242, Cong. Rec. S3959, S3973 (April 23, 1996); 29 CFR 825.307(c). If the employee does not attempt in good faith to reach agreement, the employee will be bound by the second certification. 29 CFR 825.307(c); S. Res. 242, Cong. Rec. S3959, S3973 (April 23, 1996); 29 CFR 825.307(c). For example, an employee who refuses to see a doctor in the specialty in question may be failing to act in good faith. 29 CFR 825.307(c); S. Res. 242, Cong. Rec. S3959, S3973 (April 23, 1996); 29 CFR 825.307(c). On the other hand, an employer that refuses to agree to any doctor on a list of specialists in the appropriate field provided by the employee and whom the employee has not previously consulted may be failing to act in good faith. 29 CFR 825.307(c); S. Res. 242, Cong. Rec. S3959, S3973 (April 23, 1996); 29 CFR 825.307(c).

Note that the prohibition against using a health care provider regularly employed by the employer does not apply to the selection of the health care provider to render the third medical opinion, subject to the agreement of the employee. Preamble, 29 CFR 825.307.

In circumstances where the employee or the covered family member is visiting another country, or a family member resides in another country, and a serious health condition develops, the employer must accept a medical certification as well as second and third opinions from a health care provider who practices in that country. 29 CFR 825.307(f); S. Res. 242, Cong. Rec. S3959, S3973 (April 23, 1996); 29 CFR 825.307(f).

h. Payment for Third Opinions; Employee Expenses

Like second opinions, the third opinion is at the expense of the employer. 29 USC 2613(d)(1); 2 USC 1312(a)(1) (incorporating 29 USC 2613 into CAA); 3 USC 412(a)(1) (incorporating 29 USC 2613 into PEOAA); *see Rhoads v. FDIC et al.*, 257 F.3d 373, 383 (4th Cir. 2001), *cert. denied*, 535 U.S. 933 (2002); *Smith v. V.I. Port Authority*, No. 2002-227, 2005 U.S. Dist. LEXIS 56, at *38 (D.V.I. Jan. 2, 2005); *Smith v. Univ. of Chicago Hospitals*, No. 02 C 0221, 2003 U.S. Dist. LEXIS 20965, at *22 (N.D. Ill. Nov. 24, 2003).

The employer must also reimburse the employee or covered family member for any reasonable out-of-pocket travel expenses incurred to obtain the third opinion. 29 CFR 825.307(e); S. Res. 242, Cong. Rec. S3959, S3973 (April 23, 1996); 29 CFR 825.307(e). The employer may not, absent very unusual circumstances, require the employee or covered family member to travel outside normal commuting distance for purposes of obtaining the third medical opinion. 29 CFR 825.307(e); S. Res. 242, Cong. Rec. S3959, S3973 (April 23, 1996); 29 CFR 825.307(e).

As with second opinions, the FMLA does not require an employer to compensate the employee or covered family member for the time spent in obtaining the third opinion. Frequently, unions and other organizations representing the interests of employees bargain to modify this rule so that, at minimum, employees are paid for their time to obtain these documents. Agencies entertaining acceptance of such a proposal should structure payment so that the employee is not considered to be on the clock while driving around or otherwise attempting to obtain the second or third medical opinion. The employer needs to structure this in a way to avoid tort claims or workers' compensation if the employee is involved in an accident or is otherwise injured while attempting to obtain the second or third opinion.

The regulations do not address what constitutes a normal commuting distance. Presumably, for the employee, it means that the employee may not be asked to travel more distance for the second or third opinion than the employee travels to work. The concept is more difficult where the covered family member does not work, such as an underage child or retired parent. In these circumstances, agencies are well advised to keep the travel distance to the second or third opinion provider low, certainly less than the distance the employee usually travels to work, if that is at all possible.

The regulations also fail to identify the unusual circumstances that permit an employer to require an employee or covered family member to travel a greater distance than the normal commuting distance. Access to medical specialists would, in some circumstances, constitute such unusual circumstances. For example, employees in rural areas with limited health care providers might be required to travel beyond normal commuting distance in order to be examined by a health care provider who is a specialist in the field. On the other hand, requiring an employee to travel beyond normal commuting distances to see a particular specialist, where there are any number of such specialists within the employee's normal commuting range, would appear to fall outside of the permissible requirements of the FMLA.

i. Copies

The employer is required to provide the employee with a copy of the second and third medical opinions, where applicable, upon request by the employee. 29 CFR 825.307(d); S. Res. 242, Cong. Rec. S3959, S3973 (April 23, 1996); 29 CFR 825.307(d). The requested copies must be provided within two business days, absent extenuating circumstances. 29 CFR 825.307(d); S. Res. 242, Cong. Rec. S3959, S3973 (April 23, 1996); 29 CFR 825.307(d). Presumably, where extenuating circumstances prevent the provision of copies of the second and third medical opinions within two business days, the employer should provide such copies as soon as practicable.

Note that the regulations do not mandate a method for providing the employee with copies of the second and third opinions. An employer could provide the copies in person or by mail. It is unclear whether mailing the employee the certification within the required two business days satisfies the requirement that the copies are "to be provided" within that time frame. On the other hand, there is nothing in the regulations that specifically states that the requirement is measured by the date of receipt by the employee, and not the date of mailing. To be on the safe side, agencies should attempt to ensure that the employee receives the copy with two business days.

Whatever method of delivery is used, the employer should keep a record of what was sent (including a copy of the actual document sent). If delivery is made in person, the employee should be required to sign a document acknowledging receipt. If the employee refuses to sign such a document, a notation should be made indicating when the document was handed to the employee, by whom, and that the employee refused to sign acknowledging receipt. Having a witness to the transaction would be an added precaution.

If delivery is made by mail, the documents should be sent by certified mail, return receipt requested, or by some other means where receipt is acknowledged by the employee.

An employer is not required to provide the employee a copy of the original certification. Preamble, 29 CFR 825.305 ("As the employee is providing the certification to the employer, if the employee wishes to have a copy he/she may make a copy before submission to the employer."). Of course, the employee may be able to obtain a copy from the employer pursuant to employer policy. Certainly, in most instances, the employee would be entitled to a copy of his or her own medical file pursuant to the Privacy Act.

j. Exclusivity of Second/Third Health Care Opinion Provider Process

The courts are split regarding whether the exclusive means available to an employer for challenging an employee's claim of a serious health condition is the second/third health care opinion provider process. The issue generally arises where an employer seeks to challenge the employee's claim that he or she or a covered family member had a serious health condition, within the meaning of the FMLA, in court.

According to the Second, Fourth, Seventh, and Eighth Circuits, an employer may challenge the existence of a serious health condition at trial even though it did not utilize the second/third health care opinion provider process. *See Porter*

v. *NYU School of Law*, No. 99 Civ. 4693 (TPG), 2003 U.S. Dist. LEXIS 14674, at *19–20 (S.D.N.Y. Aug. 25, 2003), *aff'd*, 392 F.3d 530 (2d Cir. 2004); *Rhoads v. FDIC*, 257 F.3d 373, 386 (4th Cir. 2001), *cert. denied*, 535 U.S. 933 (2002); *Stekloff v. St. John's Mercy Health Sys.*, 218 F.3d 858, 860 (8th Cir. 2000); *Levine v. Children's Museum of Indianapolis, Inc.*, 61 Fed. Appx. 298 (7th Cir. 2003). A number of federal district courts have followed the decisions. See *Whitworth v. Consolidated Biscuit Co.*, No. 6:06-112-DCR, 2007 U.S. Dist. LEXIS 25971, at *15-23 (E.D. Ky. April 6, 2007); *In re U.S. Airways, Inc.*, No. 04-13819-SSM, 2006 Bankr. LEXIS 1000, at *21-22 & n.8 (Bankr. E.D. Va. April 27, 2006); *Cool v. Borg Warner Diversified Transmission Products, Inc.*, No. IP 02-0960-C-B/S, 2004 U.S. Dist. LEXIS 570, at *25 (S.D. Ind. Jan. 12, 2004); *Dillaway v. Ferrante*, No. 02-715 (JRT/JSM), 2003 U.S. Dist. LEXIS 23468, at *22 (D. Minn. Dec. 9, 2003); *Darst v. Interstate Brands Corp.*, No. IP01-0788-C-T/k, 2003 U.S. Dist. LEXIS 22200, at *19–20 (S.D. Ind. Sept. 30, 2003) (following *Rhoads* and *Stekloff*).

In *Porter v. NYU School of Law*, No. 99 Civ. 4693 (TPG), 2003 U.S. Dist. LEXIS 14674, at *19–20 (S.D.N.Y. Aug. 25, 2003), *aff'd*, 392 F.3d 530 (2d Cir. 2004), the employee alleged that an employer who obtains a second health care provider opinion that differs from the initial certification is required to obtain an opinion from a third health care provider. The court disagreed. Following decisions of three circuit courts, the court found that the language in § 2613 of the FMLA that an employer "may" require a second or third medical opinion is permissive rather than mandatory. As such, an employer can challenge the validity of an employee's medical certification without seeking a second or third opinion.

In *Dowell v. Indiana Heart Physicians, Inc.*, No. 1:03-cv-1410-DFH-TAB, 2004 U.S. Dist. LEXIS 26431, at *16 (S.D. Ind. Dec. 22, 2004), the court distinguished the cases finding an employer could not challenge the existence of a serious health condition at trial if the employer did not apply the second/third health care opinion process. The court noted that the rule applied only if the initial certification was complete. In *Dowell,* the court noted that the initial certification was incomplete on its face because it failed to provide any medical facts which supported the certification, as required by 29 CFR 825.306(b)(1), and failed to show any course of treatment.

According to several district courts, the second and third health care opinion provider process is the exclusive means for challenging the validity of an initial certification. An employer who did not invoke that process was precluded from subsequently challenging the validity of the certification and, therefore, the existence of a serious health condition within the meaning of the law. See *Wheeler v. Pioneer Dev. Services, Inc.*, 349 F. Supp 2d 158 (D. Mass. 2004); *Willis v. USPS*, No. 03 C 9185, 2004 U.S. Dist. LEXIS 18238, at *21 (N.D. Ill. Sept. 10, 2004) (third opinion is required if the first and second opinions contradict one another); *Smith v. Univ. of Chicago Hospitals*, No. 02 C 0221, 2003 U.S. Dist. LEXIS 20965, at *22–26 (N.D. Ill. Nov. 24, 2003); *Miller v. AT&T*, 60 F. Supp. 2d 574, 580 (S.D. W.Va. 1999), *aff'd on other grounds*, 250 F. 3d 820, 836 n.13 (2001) (not addressing the issue on appeal); *Sims v. Alameda–Contra Costa Transit District*, 2 F. Supp. 2d 1253, 1260–63 (N.D. Cal. 1998); *see also Konipol v. Restaurant Associates*, No. 01-Civ. 7857 (GEL), 2002 U.S. Dist. LEXIS 22439 (S.D.N.Y. Nov. 20, 2002) (legitimate factual dispute whether the employer sufficiently satisfied its FMLA responsibilities either because the employer did not seek available, alternative means of collecting the required information, either through clarification or use of the second/third opinion process).

In *Smith v. Univ. of Chicago Hospitals*, No. 02 C 0221, 2003 U.S. Dist. LEXIS 20965, at *22 (N.D. Ill. Nov. 24, 2003), the court held that an employer choosing not to utilize the second and third opinion procedure for contesting an employee's entitlement to FMLA leave for a serious health condition may not later seek discovery of an employee's medical records to challenge the employee's entitlement to the leave in a civil action. The court granted Smith's motion for a protected order covering her confidential medical records and communications with her health care providers.

In *Peeples v. Coastal Office Products, Inc.* 203 F. Supp. 2d 432, 449 (D. Md. 2001), *aff'd*, 2003 U.S. App. LEXIS 8644 (4th Cir. 2003), the district court rejected the employee's argument that the only means at the disposal of an employer to obtain more information from an employee regarding the employee's need for FMLA leave was through the formal certification process, not asking the employee more questions where the employee notified the employee of the need for FMLA leave. Rather, the district court held that Peeples "crabbed, indeed, outright false, responses to Coastal's repeated efforts to obtain information from him" failed to meet the notice requirements of 29 CFR 303(b). In so holding, the court observed that:

> It is easy to see why an employer might not wish to resort to the medical certification procedure, particularly for a management level employee whose maturity and judgment might not be thought to require such verification. Thus, the availability of an informal mechanism to verify the legitimacy of FMLA leave is not a trivial matter.
>
> ....
>
> As can readily be seen, it would redound to the benefit of both employer and employee (and certainly beleaguered health care professionals flooded with paperwork) to avoid resort to the formal certification process whenever

it is possible to do so. No doubt, this consideration animates, in part, the admonishment in the regulations that "the employer will be expected" to proceed informally. 29 CFR 303(b)

Peeples reminds us that employers may be able to get sufficient medical information as part of the employee's notice obligation, and do not always have to resort to the requirement of a medical certification. [Employee notice obligations are addressed in Chapter 8, "Notice Requirements."]

k. Refusal to Cooperate in Second/Third Opinion Process

An employee who fails to cooperate with the second and third health care opinion process loses the benefit of FMLA leave. In *Diaz v. Fort Wayne Foundry Corp.*, 131 F.3d 711, 713 (7th Cir. 1997), the employer directed the employee to report for a second medical opinion with a physician the employer selected. The scheduled appointment gave the employee approximately eight–days notice. The employee did not attend the second opinion appointment. The Seventh Circuit held that missing the appointment constituted a failure to cooperate with the second opinion process. The employee lost entitlement to the protections of the FMLA. As a result, the employee was AWOL and could not invoke the FMLA to avoid discharge.

The court rejected the plaintiff's argument that he should be excused from missing the appointment because the Foundry sent the notice to his home in Indiana rather than Mexico. The court agreed that the Foundry properly notified the employee pursuant to the requirements of the governing collective bargaining agreement, which mandated that such notices be sent to the employee's address of record. "Federal labor law requires employers to adhere to collective bargaining agreements; nothing in the FMLA entitles employees to variance from neutral rules." *Diaz*, 131 F.3d at 713–14. The court found that the employee was obligated to either make arrangements for his mail to be opened in Indiana, or advise his employer of his new address. He did neither. The court went on to hold that "[a] firm safely may use the method [of notice] prescribed by collective bargaining agreements or some other source of rules."

Finally, the court opined that "the FMLA implies a duty to set a reasonable time for the [second–opinion] medical examination; the Foundry would have had to allow Diaz a few days to return from Mexico, but he did not ask for more time. As far as the FMLA is concerned, his leave was over. So is this case."

Snelling v. Stark Properties, Inc., No. 5:05-CV-46 (DF), 2006 U.S. Dist. LEXIS 50272, at *31 (M.D. Ga. July 24, 2006), addressed the pitfalls of using certified rather than regular mail to notify an employee that the employer is requesting a second health care opinion The employer sent a certified letter to Snelling's home address. The letter directed Snelling to contact the employer to arrange for a second health care provider opinion. The certified letter was returned as unclaimed. The court held that the employer's "failure to ensure that its request for a second medical certification was actually communicated to Snelling puts JPC in the same position as if it had never made the request at all. Unable to show that Snelling had notice of its request, JPC cannot assert her noncompliance with the request as a reason why it is entitled to prevail as a matter of law on her interference claim." The court went on to observe that certified mail may be less useful to establish delivery than regular mail because certified mail must be signed for, whereas, regular mail can be left behind.

2. Title II

Title II also has a second and third medical opinion process available to an employer that doubts the validity of the certification provided by the employee. While similar, that process is not the same as the process governing employees subject to Title I, the CAA, and the PEOAA.

a. General Rule: Second Opinions

If an employer doubts the validity of the original certification provided by the employee, the employer may require that the employee obtain the opinion of a second health care provider. 5 USC 6383(c)(1); 5 CFR 630.1207(d); *see Franklin v. Dept. of Air Force*, No. AT-0752-05-0355-I-2, 2005 MSPB LEXIS 8069, at *36 (Dec. 27, 2005). The scope of the examination conducted by the second health care opinion provider is limited to the information certified under § 630.1207(b). 5 CFR 630.1207(d). The referenced subsection addresses the contents of the original medical certification.

Neither the Statute nor the regulations explain what circumstances would cause an employer to doubt the validity of the original certification.

The employer is permitted to designate or approve the second health care opinion provider. 5 USC 6383(c)(1); 5 CFR 630.1207(d). However, any health care provider designated or approved by the employer cannot be employed by the employer or be under the administrative oversight of the employer on a regular basis unless the employer is located in an area where access to health care is extremely limited, e.g., a rural area or an overseas location where no more than one or two health care providers practice in the relevant specialty, or the only health care providers available are employed by the agency. 5 CFR 630.1207(d); see Franklin, 2005 MSPB LEXIS 8069, at *36.

The above rule is different from the comparable rule under Title I in several respects. First, the regulations implementing Title II are more faithful to the statutory language, which provide (both for Title I and Title II) that an employer may designate or approve the second health care opinion provider. The regulations under Title I provide only that an employer may designate the second health care opinion provider. Under Title II, the employer may designate or approve. Presumably, an employer under Title I could designate a health care provider by approving one offered by the employee.

Second, Title II differs as to who is generally excluded as a second health care opinion provider. Under Title II, an employer may not employ or be under administrative oversight of the employer on a regular basis. Under Title I, the exclusion does not apply to entities that are under the administrative oversight of the employer. Rather, the exclusion applies to those second opinion health care providers with whom the employer regularly contracts or otherwise regularly utilizes the services of. Nothing is said about entities under the administrative oversight of the employer. Of course, if such an entity were regularly utilized by the employer, it would be excluded from consideration as well, absent application of the rural exception.

Note that under both Titles I and II, it does not matter whether the services that are regularly contracted, utilized, or employed have to do with second medical opinions. The same goes for health care providers who are under the administrative oversight of the employer. As long as they are health care providers and they are regularly contracted, employed, or utilized, they are excluded, subject to the rural exception.

Third, the rural exception allowing use of certain otherwise prohibited second health care opinion providers is different under Titles I and II. The chief difference is that, in addition to allowing the use of a second health care opinion provider who the employer regularly uses, contracts with, or employs, Title II also allows the use of such individuals where the only health care providers available are employed by the agency. As long as the employer regularly utilized the services of the second health care opinion provider, Title I would appear to allow an employer to use employees to provide second opinions, provided all other conditions of the rural exception are met.

The right of an employer to select the second health care opinion provider should not be underestimated. That right allows agencies to select medical specialists in the field to examine the employee or the covered family member claiming to have a serious health condition. Many times the original certification is from a general medical practitioner rendering an opinion on issues well outside his or her area of expertise. Typical is the situation in which a general family practitioner signs a certification that the employee is suffering from a psychological condition, such as stress. The employer is well advised to go through the expense of a second opinion if the original certification is well outside the area of expertise of the original FMLA health care provider.

As a general rule, it is recommended that agencies seriously consider sending an employee for a second opinion when at least one of two conditions are present: (1) the original certification gives the employee a "blank check" to take intermittent leave of undetermined frequency and duration over an extended period of time; or (2) the further the original health care provider is outside of his or her area of medical expertise (if any), the more interested an employer should be in sending the employee to a medical specialist.

b. Christian Science Practitioners

A Christian Science practitioner listed with the First Church of Christ, Scientist, Boston, Massachusetts, is a health care provider for purposes of Title II. 5 CFR 630.1201 (definition of "health care provider"). The similarities with Title I end here. Unlike Title I, there are no special rules addressing Christian Science practitioners for purposes of second and third opinions. Compare, 29 CFR 825.118(b)(3). As such, a Christian Science practitioner is treated like other health care providers for purposes of abiding by the requirement to undergo an examination by a second or third health care opinion provider.

The comparable rule under Title II provides that for an employee to remain entitled to family and medical leave, an employee or the employee's spouse, son, daughter, or parent must comply with any requirement from an employer that he or she submit to examination (although not treatment) to obtain a second or third medical certification from health care provider other than the individual's health care provider. 5 CFR 630.1207(f).

c. Payment for Second Opinion

The Statute and regulations provide that the second health care opinion provider is "at the expense of the agency." 5 USC 6383(c)(1); 5 CFR 630.1207(d); see Franklin v. Dept. of Air Force, No. AT-0752-05-0355-I-2, 2005 MSPB LEXIS 8069, at *36 (Dec. 27, 2005). Neither the Statute nor the regulations define what the phrase "at the expense of the agency" means. Presumably, this means the fee charged by the second health care opinion provider. What is unclear is whether it means that the employer must pay the employee for the time spent in obtaining the second and third opinion. It is also unclear whether "at the expense of the agency" also includes any travel–related costs incurred by a covered family member to obtain the second health care provider opinion. An employer is required under Title I to reimburse an employee or a covered family member for reasonable out–of–pocket" travel expenses incurred in obtaining a second or third opinion. See 29 CFR 825.307(e).

Given the prior existence of the DOL regulations, the absence of a similarly specific requirement in the OPM regulations requiring reimbursement of out–of–pocket travel expenses strongly suggests that an employer is not legally obligated to reimburse such expenses under Title II. Similarly, since "expense" is rarely equated with "pay," it would appear that an employer is not obligated by Title II of the Act to compensate an employee for time spent securing a required second health care provider opinion. Of course, pursuant to 5 CFR 620.1210(a), (c), an employer could adopt more generous family and medical leave policies, including compensation for employee time and reasonable out–of–pocket outlays incurred in obtaining a second or third health care provider opinion.

d. Entitlement to Second and Third Opinions

The regulations do not specify who, the employer or the employee, is entitled to receive the opinion of the second or third health care provider. It appears that the employee receives the certification directly from the second or third health care opinion provider. This appearance is derived from the requirement that the employee must provide the initial medical certification, and the second and third health care opinion provider certifications, to the employer within the same time period. 5 CFR 630.1207(h). Under Title I, although not specifically stated, it appears that the employer receives the certification directly from the second and third health care opinion providers.

e. Time Frame for Receipt of Certification

Employees are required to provide the initial medical certification, and the certifications resulting from the second and third health care opinion providers no later than 15 calendar days after the date the employer requests the certification. 5 CFR 630.1207(h). If it is not practicable under the particular circumstances for the employee to provide the certification within 15 calendar days from the date of the employer request despite the employee's diligent, good faith efforts, the employee must provide the medical certification within a reasonable period of time under the circumstances, but no later than 30 calendar days after the date the employer requests such medical certification. 5 CFR 630.1207(h).

By comparison, Title I does not provide a time frame within which an employee must provide the certification prepared by the second or third health care opinion provider. Rather, although not directly stated in the regulations, the inference that may be drawn from the absence of such guidance, as well as other evidence, is that the employer receives the second and third opinion provider certification results directly from the health care provider.

f. Preliminary Designation of FMLA Leave

If the employer questions the validity of the original certification provided by the employee and the medical treatment requires the leave to begin, the employer must grant provisional leave pending final written medical certification. 5 CFR 630.1207(g). If, after the leave has commenced, the employee fails to provide the requested medical certification, the employer may either: (1) charge the employee as being AWOL; or (2) allow the employee to request that the provisional leave be charged as leave without pay or charged to the employee's annual and/or sick leave account, as appropriate. 5 CFR 630.1207(l).

It is less than clear whether the provisional leave is FMLA leave or not. If it is FMLA leave, it hardly seems appropriate that the employee should be charged with AWOL during the 15- to 30-day period before the medical certification is provided. If the leave is provisionally designated as FMLA leave pending receipt of medical certification, by definition, the leave is not absence without leave. Provisional leave is not absence without leave.

Perhaps the better reading of the regulation is that it applies when an employer has provisionally granted FMLA leave, and the employee subsequently never provides the requested certification. Under those circumstances, the employer would have the option of charging the employee AWOL or converting the provisional FMLA leave into some other paid or unpaid leave.

While the above may be the better reading, there is nothing to prevent an employer from charging an employee with AWOL if the employee has not provided the medical certification before leave commences, even where that leave is provisionally designated as FMLA leave. Presumably, if the employee provides acceptable certification, the employer must convert the AWOL to FMLA leave.

While the regulation permits an employer to charge an employee with AWOL pending receipt of medical certification where FMLA leave has commenced, it is not recommended that agencies do this. The regulation appears to violate the one of the most basic precepts of the FMLA: that leave under the Statute is protected from adverse consequences.

g. Third Opinion

If the opinion of the second health care provider differs from the original medical certification provided by the employee, the employer may require that the employee obtain the opinion of a third health care provider designated or approved jointly by the employer and the employee. 5 USC 6383(c)(2); 5 CFR 630.1207(e). The scope of the examination by the third health care opinion provider is limited to the information certified under § 630.1207(b). *Id.* That section addresses the contents of the original medical certification.

Absent further guidance, any difference between the original certification submitted by the employee and the second health care opinion provider would justify an employee's use of a third health care provider to decide the issue. For example, a difference in the number of expected absences, the duration of those expected absences, and the duration of the underlying serious health condition, would justify resort to a third, final and binding, health care opinion provider certification.

Note that, like under Title I, the language regarding resort to a third opinion provider is permissive. An employer may require the employee to obtain certification from a third health care opinion provider. Unless it is going to fully adopt the results of the original certification, an employer is well advised to utilize a third health care opinion provider to finally resolve any differences between the original and second health care opinion provider certifications. An employer is asking for trouble if it seeks to impose a more favorable second medical opinion that differs from the original certification, with the argument that "may" does not mean "must" when it comes to a third opinion to break the tie.

The regulations interpreting Title II are similarly devoid of guidance on exactly what the phrase "final and binding" means. Agencies certainly can use that language to argue that final and binding means just what it says, and the employee is bound by the results of the third opinion for as long as the third opinion states that the employee will need FMLA leave to address the serious health condition at issue. Unions and other organizations representing employees may want to consider arguments that "final and binding" is attached only to the scope of the leave request at issue, not FMLA leave requests not contemplated or made.

h. Selection of Third Opinion Provider

The third health care opinion provider is designated or approved jointly by the employer and the employee. 5 CFR 630.1207(f). Unlike Title I, the regulations fail to specify what happens if the employer and the employee are unable to agree on a third health care opinion provider. Nor do the regulations provide a penalty if the failure to agree on a third health care provider is the result of the employer or the employee failing to act in good faith. For example, the employee insists that the third health care opinion provider be the health care provider that issued the original certification.

In these instances, the better developed rules under Title I should be referred to and applied. The party who was at fault for the failure to reach agreement on the third health care opinion provider should lose the right to assert the medical certification it favors. The other party may apply the results of the medical certification it favors.

i. Payment for Third Opinions

Like second opinions, the third health care provider opinion is at the expense of the agency. 5 CFR 630.1207(e), and it is unclear what expenses are to be paid by the agency, if any, beyond the actual cost of the third health care provider opinion.

j. Copies

Unlike Title I, Title II does not require an agency, on request, to provide a copy of the second or third health care opinion provider certification to the employee. However, pursuant to the Privacy Act, agencies will likely be required to make these records available for inspection and copying by employees as the certifications will likely be maintained in a system of records accessible to the employee.

k. Exclusivity of Challenge Process

In *Franklin v. Dept. of Air Force*, No. AT-0752-05-0355-I-2, 2005 MSPB LEXIS 8069, at *36 (Dec. 27, 2005), the employer noted that the proper procedure to challenge a medical certification provided by the employee is to require the employee to submit to a second health care provider opinion. The employer in that case ordered the employee to either sign a form authorizing the employee's physician to talk with the agency's physician, or submit additional information. The employee refused. The Board found that the agency's order violated the FMLA. The decision could be construed to suggest that the process set forth in 5 CFR 630.1202(d) is the exclusive means to challenge a complete medical certification.

K. EMPLOYEE FAILURE TO SATISFY CERTIFICATION REQUIREMENTS

1. Title I, the CAA, and the PEOAA

What happens if an employee fails to satisfy the medical certification requirements depends on whether the need for leave was or was not foreseeable. In the case of foreseeable leave, an employer may delay the taking of FMLA leave where an employee fails to timely provide medical certification requested by the agency, until the certification is provided. 29 CFR 825.311(a), 825.312(b); S. Res. 242, Cong. Rec. S3959, S3974 (April 23, 1996); 29 CFR 825.311(a), 825.312(b).

If the employee never produces the certification, the leave is not protected by the FMLA. 29 CFR 825.312(b); S. Res. 242, Cong. Rec. S3959, S3974 (April 23, 1996); 29 CFR 825.312(b); see *Killian v. Yorozu Automotive Tennessee, Inc.*, 454 F.3d 549, 555 (6th Cir. 2006); *Perry v. Jaguar of Troy*, 353 F.3d 510, 514 (6th Cir. Dec. 30, 2003); *Harrington v. Boysville of Michigan, Inc. et al.*, No. 97–1862, 1998 U.S. App. LEXIS 9796 (6th Cir. May 13, 1998) (employee who failed to provide certification not protected by FMLA, and termination for unexcused absence does not constitute a violation of the Act); *Carpenter v. Kaiser Permanente*, No. 1:04 cv 1689, 2006 U.S. Dist. LEXIS 69564, at *35 (N.D. Ohio Sept. 27, 2006) (an employee is not eligible for leave under the FMLA if he does not submit the proper FMLA medical certification to his employer as requested); *Baldwin–Love v. Electronic Data Systems, Corp.*, 307 F. Supp. 2d. 1222, 1229 (M.D. Ala. 2004); *Gulan v. Federal Reserve Bank of Cleveland*, No. 1:01 CV 1784, 2003 U.S. Dist. LEXIS 15749, at *11 (N.D. Ohio July 31, 2003); *Wilson v. Ameritech*, No. 01 C 9511, 2003 U.S. Dist. LEXIS 8033, at *22 (N.D. Ill. May 12, 2003); *Konipol v. Restaurant Associates*, No. 01–Civ. 7857 (GEL), 2002 U.S. Dist. LEXIS 22439 (S.D.N.Y. Nov. 20, 2002).

If uncertified, hence unprotected, absences violate an attendance policy, an employer may terminate an employee without violating the FMLA. *Baldwin–Love*, 307 F. Supp. 2d. at 1229–1230; *Gulan*, 2003 U.S. Dist. LEXIS 15749, at *11.

When the need for FMLA leave is not foreseeable, an employee must provide certification within the time frame requested by the employer (which must allow at least 15 calendar days after the employer's request) or as soon as reasonably possible under the particular facts and circumstances. 29 CFR 825.311(b); S. Res. 242, Cong. Rec. S3959, S3974 (April 23, 1996); 29 CFR 825.311(b); see *Killian*, 454 F.3d at 554. In the case of a medical emergency, it may not be practicable for an employee to provide the required certification within 15 calendar days. 29 CFR 825.311(b); S. Res. 242, Cong. Rec. S3959, S3974 (April 23, 1996); 29 CFR 825.311(b). If an employee fails to provide medical certification within a reasonable period of time under the pertinent circumstances, the employer may delay the employee's continuation of FMLA leave. 29 CFR 825.311(b); S. Res. 242, Cong. Rec. S3959, S3974 (April 23, 1996); 29 CFR 825.311(b); see *Killian*, 454 F.3d at 554.

If the employee never produces the certification, the leave is not FMLA leave. 29 CFR 825.311(b); S. Res. 242, Cong. Rec. S3959, S3974 (April 23, 1996); 29 CFR 825.311(b); *Killian v. Yorozu Automotive Tennessee, Inc.*, 454 F.3d 549, 554 (6th Cir. 2006); *Ridings v. Riverside Med. Center*, No. 05-2134, 2006 U.S. Dist. LEXIS 86991, at *13 (C.D. Ill. Nov. 30, 2006); *Fuller v. Alliant Energy Corp. Services, Inc.*, No. C 05-92-MWB, 2006 U.S. Dist. LEXIS 75497, at *74 (N.D. Iowa Oct. 16, 2006); *Carpenter*, 2006 U.S. Dist. LEXIS 69564, at *31, 35; *Schimek v. MCI, Inc.*, No. 3:05-CV-0045-P, 2006 U.S. Dist. LEXIS 54747, at *37 (N.D. Tex. Aug. 7, 2006) (failure to provide appropriate medical certification is fatal to FMLA claim); *Caskey v. Colgate-Palmolive Co.*, 438 F. Supp. 2d 954, 964 (S.D. Ind. 2006) (if employer requests medical certification and employee never produces the certification, the absences need not be treated as FMLA leave); *Toro v. Mastex Industries*, 32 F. Supp. 2d 25, 29 (D. Mass. 1999).

Employers with employees who fail to timely provide medical certification as requested may not, under these regulations, simply deny the leave and/or take disciplinary action for leave that has already commenced. There is no set time limit placed on the delay that an employer must impose on an employee until medical certification is received. Moreover, the unfortunate use of the word "never" to describe when it would be appropriate for an employer to deny FMLA leave and/or take disciplinary action for an absence provisionally granted as FMLA leave pending certification, which certification never came, further restricts employers ability to act. "Never" encompasses a potentially infinite period of time.

The regulations do provide, however, that the employee must be given a reasonable opportunity to cure any deficiency in the certification. 29 CFR 825.305(e); S. Res. 242, Cong. Rec. S3959, S3974 (April 23, 1996); 29 CFR 825.305(e). Technically, this regulation assumes that the employee provided a certification. Arguably, therefore, it does not directly apply where, as here, the employee has failed to timely provide a requested certification.

By analogy, the regulation suggests that an employee does not have an indefinite period within which to provide the certification, but only a reasonable period of time taking into account all of the circumstances to provide the certification. During this reasonable period of time, the employer cannot deny the request for FMLA leave, but may delay the start of the leave or, where leave has already begun, delay the continuance of the leave until acceptable certification is provided. If, after a reasonable period of time, the employee fails to provide the certification, FMLA leave may be denied.

A reasonable period of time under all of the circumstances necessarily requires agencies to take into account any delays that are not the responsibility of the employee. The employee must be acting diligently and in good faith to secure the certification as soon as practicable. An employee, who can demonstrate that he or she diligently attempted to obtain the certification, but was having difficulty with obtaining the cooperation of the health care provider, may have a legitimate excuse. An employee who cannot articulate or demonstrate what was done to timely obtain the certification may be denied leave.

A potential problem arises from the unfortunate use of the word "never" in the regulation. For example, the employee unquestionably failed to act in good faith and did not timely secure a requested medical certification. The employer denies the leave. The employer also seeks to discipline the employee for the absence already taken for the same condition. The employee, months later, hands in a certification from a health care provider that seeks to excuse the prior absence. According to the regulations, since the employee did hand in a certification, it cannot be said that the employee "never" submitted a certification and, the argument goes, the regulations did not permit the employer to deny the employee leave. Since the employer did deny the leave and took disciplinary action, the employer is in violation of the law.

The meaning of the word "never" was addressed by the court in *Cavin v. Honda of America MFG., Inc.*, No. C2–00–400, 2002 U.S. Dist. LEXIS 19601 (S.D. Ohio Feb. 22, 2002), *aff'd in part, rev'd in part, remanded*, 346 F.3d 713 (6th Cir. 2003). In that case, despite good faith efforts, the employee nevertheless missed the deadline for submitting a complete medical certification. The employer notified the employee that the original certification provided by the employee was incomplete and gave the employee two days to return a complete certification. After seven days, the employee still had not turned in the certification. The certification arrived 12 days after it was requested. The employee's request for FMLA leave was denied, and he was terminated. The employee argued that an employer can only deny an employee FMLA leave if the employee *completely fails* to submit certification. As long as an employee ultimately provides proper medical certification, pursuant to §§ 825.305 and 825.311, the employer cannot deny the employee FMLA leave.

The court noted that a similar argument was made and rejected in *Washington v. Fort James Operating Co.*, 110 F. Supp. 2d 1325 (D. Ore. 2000). In that case, *Id.* at 1331–32, the court noted:

The requirement that an employee returns his FMLA certification within a reasonable time or else loses his entitlement to FMLA fulfills Congress' desire to balance the demands of the workplace with the needs of families. The FMLA protects an employee from losing his leave when his certification is reasonably delayed and protects an employer from the unreasonable burden of indefinitely maintaining records of potentially eligible but unclaimed FMLA leave. *See* S. Rep. No. 103-3, at 2 (1993), 1993 U.S.C.C.A.N. 3. Accordingly, the Court concludes that an employer may deny FMLA leave where the employee has failed to timely submit the required certification unless timely submission was not reasonably possible under the employee's particular facts and circumstances.

The court in *Washington* found this reasoning extremely persuasive. In the court's view, "although the regulations *permit* the employer to extend the established deadline they cannot be read to *require* an employer to wait indefinitely for medical certification of a need for leave." (Emphasis in original).

Agencies must decide for themselves whether they wish to litigate this issue. Where the employee failed to act diligently or, even acted diligently, if the employee was given a reasonable opportunity to provide the certification and still failed, it would seem that the employer did all that is required, the regulation notwithstanding. If the matter is litigated, in addition to citing *Washington* and *Cavin*, the employer should strongly consider attacking the constitutional validity of the regulation. Nothing in the Statute suggests that an employer must delay a decision on FMLA leave for time immemorial so that the employee can obtain a medical certification.

Of course, unions and other organizations representing employees will likely argue the literal interpretation of the regulation. In that case, unions are wise to make that an alternative argument, and attempt to demonstrate all of the good faith efforts of the employee to timely provide the certification, and the unreasonableness of the opportunity to cure. To that end, given the short deadlines involved, *Cavin* will be a tough case to distinguish.

Employees may also seek to justify their failure to provide certification alleging futility; that whatever they produced would be rejected anyway by hostile management. The court in *Robinson v. Franklin County Bd. of Commissioners et al.*, No. 99-CV-162, 2002 U.S. Dist. LEXIS 25681 (S.D. Ohio Jan. 28, 2002), addressed such an argument. In that case, the court rejected the employee's argument that his failure to provide the certification should be excused because a high-ranking manger indicated that the manager would not approve FMLA leave, no matter what. The court found that the employee's reliance on the manager's statement did not justify his failure to comply with the written notice he received stating that he must provide medical certification in order to have his absences covered by the FMLA.

A public employee's constitutional right to privacy does not defeat an employer's right to medical information to support the employee's request for FMLA leave. *See O'Reilly v. Rutgers*, No. 04-5787 (FSH), 2006 U.S. Dist. LEXIS 2341, at *18-22 (D.N.J. Jan. 19, 2006), *aff'd*, 2007 U.S. App. LEXIS 9530 (3d Cir. 2007).

An employee's FMLA claims may be dismissed where the employee fails to provide medical certification requested by the employer in support of FMLA leave. *Muriekes v. Boeing Co.*, 111 Fed. Appx. 483 (9th Cir. 2004); *Gulan v. Federal Reserve Bank of Cleveland*, No. 1:01 CV 1784, 2003 U.S. Dist. LEXIS 15749, at *16 (N.D. Ohio July 31, 2003); *Wilson v. Ameritech*, No. 01 C 9511, 2003 U.S. Dist. LEXIS 8033, at *22 (N.D. Ill. May 12, 2003).

2. Title II

When it comes to an employee's failure to timely provide a requested medical certification, Title II is not nearly as coddling as Title I. An employee who does not provide medical certification signed by the health care provider, containing all of the permissible information is not entitled to FMLA leave. 5 CFR 630.1208(l); *see Slaughter v. USDA*, No. DC-0752-06-0624-I-1, 2006 MSPB LEXIS 6978, at *13-14 (Nov. 20, 2006); *Jones v. Dept. of Navy*, No. DC-0752-06-0092-I-2, 2006 MSPB LEXIS 5031, at *5-6 (Sept. 5, 2006); *Kimbrough v. DOD*, No. DC-0752-06-0287-I-1, 2006 MSPB LEXIS 4379, at *13-16 (Aug. 1, 2006); *Cole v. DHHS*, No. DC-0752-05-0457-I-1, 2005 MSPB LEXIS 6825, at *8 (Nov. 1, 2005); *Burge v. Dept. of Air Force*, 82 MSPR 75, P16 (1999), *pet. denied*, 86 MSPR 688 (2000).

In *Jones v. Dept. of Navy*, No. DC-0752-06-0092-I-2, 2006 MSPB LEXIS 5031, at *5-6 (Sept. 5, 2006), the Board found that the employee's provision of a simple note from her physician indicating that the employee was seen by the physician and should refrain from working for a period of time was insufficient to establish that the employee had an FMLA-covered serious health condition.

In *Kimbrough v. DOD*, No. DC-0752-06-0287-I-1, 2006 MSPB LEXIS 4379, at *13-16 (Aug. 1, 2006), in finding the medical certification insufficient, the Board noted: (1) the certification was signed by his family practice physician and not the orthopedic specialist who performed the knee surgery; (2) the medical facts section described common conditions rather than the conditions that prevented the employee from performing the duties of his position; (3) the physician made no attempt to identify the date that the employee's condition commenced; and (4) the physician indicated that the probable number of treatments and periods of recovery would be determined in consultation with the employee's orthopedic surgeon.

The failure to provide a medical certification that satisfies the requirements of the FMLA may not be fatal to an employee's FMLA claim, In *Ellshoff v. Dept. of Interior*, 76 MSPR 54, at *37 (1997), *rev'd, remanded*, 78 MSPR 615 (1998), the Board found that, even if the employee's medical certification did not meet the technical requirements of the FMLA, it was sufficient to entitle the employee to FMLA leave because it clearly showed that the employee was incapacitated for her essential job functions. The employee's physician indicated that, during the absence, the employee was completely unable to care for her herself or her daily needs, which required hospitalization. The certification was sufficient because it "was adequate to show...incapacitation."

The cut off for providing the medical certification, be it an original, second, or third opinion, is 30 calendar days, no matter what. The regulations do not require an employer to delay a decision on an employee's FMLA leave while waiting to see if the employee never provides the medical certification.

An employer that applies the Title II rule regarding failure to provide medical certification to Title I employees, however, may quickly find itself in violation of Title I of the Act. Again, agencies must determine in each case what FMLA rules apply to the employee in question. An employer that assumes that adherence to the requirements of Title II will necessarily comply with the requirements for Title I may be in for an unpleasant surprise.

III. RECERTIFICATION OF MEDICAL CONDITIONS

All of the major federal sector FMLA laws allow an employer to require an employee to periodically provide medical recertification of the need for FMLA leave due to a serious health condition. The rules regarding medical recertifications are addressed below.

A. TITLE I, THE CAA, AND THE PEOAA

1. Overview

The case law regarding recertification is sparse. *Geromanos v. Columbia Univ., College of Physicians and Surgeons*, 322 F. Supp. 2d 420, 431 (S.D.N.Y. 2004).

An employer may require that an eligible employee obtain subsequent recertifications on a reasonable basis. 29 CFR 2613(e); 2 USC 1312(a)(1) (incorporating 29 USC 2613 into CAA); 3 USC 412(a)(1) (incorporating 29 USC 2613 into PEOAA); see *Brumbalough v. Camelot Care Centers, Inc.*, 427 F.3d 996, 1001 (6th Cir. Nov. 2, 2005); *Williams v. The Boeing Co.*, No. 97-36098, 1999 U.S. App. LEXIS 785 (9th Cir. 1999); *Stoops v. One Call Communications, Inc.*, 141 F.3d 309, 312 (7th Cir. 1998); *Parsley v. City of Columbus, Ohio*, No. 2:05-cv-00229, 2006 U.S. Dist. LEXIS 72185, at *9-10 (S.D. Ohio Oct. 3, 2006); *Hurt v. Ecolab, Inc.*, No. 3-05-CV-1508-BD, 2006 U.S. Dist. LEXIS 32373, at *10 (N.D. Tex. May 23, 2006); *Kitts v. General Tel. North, Inc.*, No. 2:04-cv-173, 2005 U.S. Dist. LEXIS 20421, at *30 (S.D. Ohio Sept. 19, 2005); *Brown v. SBC Communications, Inc.*, No. 04-C-0290, 2005 U.S. Dist. LEXIS 41599, at *4 (E.D. Wis. Aug. 23, 2005); *Bohman v. County of Wood*, No. 03–C–571–C, 2004 U.S. Dist. LEXIS 13082, at *10 (W.D. Wis. July 7, 2004); *Geromanos v. Columbia Univ., College of Physicians and Surgeons*, 322 F. Supp. 2d 420, 431 (S.D.N.Y. 2004); *Hanson v. The Sports Authority*, 256 F. Supp. 2d 927 (W.D. Wis. 2003); *Lara v. Central Grocers Cooperative, Inc. et al.*, No. 00–C–7828, 2002 U.S. Dist. LEXIS 16745, at n.4 (N.D. Ill. Sept. 6, 2002); *Alexander et al., v. Ford Motor Co.*, 204 F.R.D. 314, 317, 2001 U.S. Dist. LEXIS 19180 (E.D. Mich. 2001); *Vanderpool v. Inco Alloys International, Inc.*, No. 3:98–0449, 1999 U.S. Dist. LEXIS 12363 (S.D. W.Va. June 3, 1999).

Neither the Statute nor the regulations define what constitutes "recertification." According to the comments in the final DOL regulations (Preamble, 29 CFR 308), recertification addresses the "appropriate length of time that a medical certification should be valid."

The statute does not define "reasonable basis." *Parsley v. City of Columbus, Ohio*, 471 F. Supp. 2d 858 (S.D. Ohio Oct. 3, 2006); *accord Geromanos v. Columbia Univ., College of Physicians and Surgeons*, 322 F. Supp. 2d 420, 431 (S.D.N.Y. 2004). Although the Act does not specify what constitutes a reasonable basis, the regulations implementing the FMLA provide that an employer "may request recertification at any reasonable interval, but not more often than every 30 days, unless: (1) The employee requests an extension of leave; (2) Circumstances described by the previous certification have changed significantly (e.g., the duration of the illness, the nature of the illness, complications); or (3) The employer receives information that casts doubt upon the continuing validity of the certification." 29 CFR 825.308(c).

This limitation prevents employers from requiring plaintiffs to repeatedly prove that they do in fact suffer from a serious health condition entitling them to leave. *Geromanos*, 322 F. Supp. 2d at 431; *Conrad v. Eaton Corp.*, 303 F. Supp. 2d 987, 999 (N.D. Iowa 2004) (FMLA permits an employer to require recertification when an employee requests an extension of leave, provided that such recertification is not required prior to 30 days after the employer's previous receipt of medical certification).

The court in *Geromanos v. Columbia Univ., College of Physicians and Surgeons*, 322 F. Supp. 2d 420, 431 (S.D.N.Y. 2004), addressed whether weekly progress reports on an employee's outpatient treatment for substance abuse was a "reasonable interval" for recertification. The court concluded that because the employee was on paid leave, Columbia was free to impose whatever conditions it chose as a condition of continuing plaintiff's salary while she was not working, including the provision of reports detailing her cooperation and progress in the substance abuse program she was attending.

The DOL issued an FMLA Advisory Opinion on May 25, 2004, addressing recertification where the minimum duration of incapacity is long-term or indefinite, and where the FMLA leave pattern involves Mondays/Fridays. The advisory opinion is posted on DOL's website at http://www.dol.gov/esa/whd/opinion/FMLA/200405252FMLA.html. The Opinion Letter addresses three issues:

1. Minimum recertification period when no minimum duration of capacity is specified in the medical certification.

   You understand that the FMLA allows an employer to request recertification every 30 days for pregnancy, chronic or permanent/long term conditions, citing four scenarios involving such conditions, none of which have a minimum duration or incapacity specified in the certification.

   Scenario One: An employee's Health Care Provider (HCP) certifies her migraine headaches will last indefinitely.

   Scenario Two: An employee's HCP certifies a chronic serious health condition (diabetes) and provides no time frame for the duration of the condition.

   Scenario Three: The employee's chronic serious health condition (asthma) is certified to last for an indefinite period, with possible episodes of incapacity (coinciding with pollen season) over a three-month period.

   Scenario Four: The certification again specifies an indefinite period, and indicates a need for breathing tests and treatments to be conducted over the next three months.

   We agree with your understanding, provided the recertification is requested in connection with an absence. Section 103(e) of the FMLA states the employer may require subsequent recertifications "on a reasonable basis." The FMLA regulations at § 825.308(a) limit recertification for pregnancy, chronic, or permanent/long-term serious health conditions, when no minimum duration of incapacity is specified on the medical certification (as discussed in § 825.308(b)), to no more often than every 30 days, provided the recertification is done only in connection with an absence. If circumstances have changed significantly, or the employer receives information which casts doubt upon the continuing validity of the certification, recertification may be requested more frequently than every 30 days.

2. Minimum recertification period with Friday/Monday absence pattern.

   You understand that a pattern of Friday/Monday absences can constitute "information that casts doubt upon the employee's stated reason for the absence" (§ 825.308(a)(2)), thus allowing an employer to request recertification more frequently than every 30 days.

   We agree with your understanding, provided there is no evidence that provides a medical reason for the timing of such absences and the request for recertification is made in conjunction with an absence. A recertification under these circumstances could thus be justified, for example, if a medical certification indicated the need for intermittent leave for two or three days a month due to migraine headaches, and the employee took such leave every Monday or Friday (the first and last days of the employee's work week).

3. Informing medical provider of pattern of Monday/Friday or apparent excessive absences, and asking for clarification.

You understand that an employer, when requesting medical certification, may inform the health care provider that the employee has a pattern of Friday/Monday or apparent excessive absences. You add that you understand that an employer who has observed such a pattern of potential abuse may ask the health care provider, as part of the certification (and subsequent recertification) process, if this pattern of absence is consistent with the employee's serious health condition. You recognize that an employer's direct contact with the employee's health care provider is prohibited, but you understand that his question could be added to the medical certification form given to the employee for completion by the health care provider.

The FMLA does not prohibit an employer from including a record of an employee's absences along with the medical certification form for the health care provider's consideration in determining the employee's likely period of future absences. Nor does the FMLA prohibit an employer from asking, as part of the recertification process, whether the likely duration and frequency of the employee's incapacity due to the chronic condition is limited to Mondays and Fridays.

Under the Health Insurance Portability and Accountability Act (HIPPA), 104 P.L. 191, 42 U.S.C. § 1320d, covered entities (such as HCPs) are subject to certain standards regarding the use and disclosure of an individual's protected health information (See 45 C.F.R. Parts 160 and 164, administered by the U.S. Department of Health and Human Services, Office for Civil Rights). In general, the HIPPA does not prohibit covered entities form releasing an individual's protected health information to that individual. An employee's failure to provide information an employer is entitled to under the FMLA could jeopardize the employee's FMLA leave entitlement.

The prefix "re" in this instance appears to mean anew, as in retell. Webster's Ninth New Collegiate Dictionary (Merriam–Webster Inc., 1988). The term "certification," while not specifically defined, is certainly described in the Statute and regulations. 29 USC 2613; 29 CFR 825.306; S. Res. 242, Cong. Rec. S3959, S3974 (April 23, 1996); 29 CFR 825.306. In the FMLA context, recertification would appear to mean a renewal of the original certification, which has grown stale over time.

A certification is not a recertification if the employee has returned to work and the need for FMLA leave has ceased. At that point, a subsequent request for medical documentation to support a request is considered a new certification. *Dillon v. Carlton*, 977 F. Supp. 1155, 11–58–59 (M.D. Fla. 1997), *aff'd without op.*, 161 F.3d 21 (11th Cir. 1998).

Where the original certification is insufficient on its face, the FMLA's provisions governing an employer's request for recertification where it "has a reason to doubt the validity of the certification" are inapposite. *Brenneman v. MedCentral Health System*, 366 F.3d 412, 428 (6th Cir. 2004), *cert. denied*, 2005 U.S. LEXIS 1474 (U.S. 2005).

2. Circumstances Permitting Recertification

From the simple statement in the Statute that an employer may obtain subsequent recertifications from the employee on a reasonable basis, the regulations have derived four different recertification circumstances.

a. Pregnancy, Chronic, or Permanent/Long-Term Conditions

(1) General Rule

Where the serious health condition of the employee or a covered family member of the employee involves pregnancy, a chronic condition, or permanent/long-term conditions under the continuing supervision of a health care provider (as defined in §§ 825.114(a)(2ii), (iii), or (iv)), an employer may request recertification no more often than every 30 days and only in connection with an absence by the employee. 29 CFR 825.308(a); S. Res. 242, Cong. Rec. S3959, S3973 (April

23, 1996); 29 CFR 825.308(a); *see Muhammad v. Indiana Bell Tel., Co.*, 182 Fed. Appx. 551 (7th Cir. 2006); *Stoops v. One Call Communications, Inc.*, 141 F.3d 309, 312 (7th Cir. 1998). The statute does not define "reasonable basis." *Parsley v. City of Columbus, Ohio*, 471 F. Supp. 2d 858 (S.D. Ohio 2006); *McClain v. Detroit Entertainment, LLC*, 458 F. Supp. 2d 427 (E.D. Mich. 2006); *Yntema v. USPS*, No. 3:04CV7360, 2006 U.S. Dist. LEXIS 18816, at *12-13 (N.D. Ohio March 1, 2006); *Henderson v. Whirlpool Corp.*, 17 F. Supp. 2d 1238, 1248, n. 5 (N.D. Okla. 1998).

An employer may not, under this regulation, simply request that the employee supply medical recertification every 30 days where the need for leave involves the serious health conditions of pregnancy, a chronic condition, or a permanent/long–term condition. An employer must wait for the first absence on day 30 and beyond before the employer may require a subsequent medical recertification. Note also that the regulation does not require that this first absence be covered by the FMLA. Any absence would trigger an employer's entitlement to request medical recertification, whether the absence is covered by the FMLA or not.

In *Muhammad v. Indiana Bell Tel., Co.*, 182 Fed. Appx. 551 (7th Cir. 2006), the court found that the employer properly requested recertification. The original certification indicated that the employee may be absent one to two days a month. Because more than 30 days had passed since her last absence in July, the court found that the employer had the right to request recertification. The original certification did not, the court found, provide a longer minimum period of intermittent leave than 30 days.

(2) Exceptions

The FMLA regulations (29 CFR 825.308(a)(1)–(2); S. Res. 242, Cong. Rec. S3959, S3973 (April 23, 1996); 29 CFR 825.308(a)(1)–(2)) permit an employer to require an employee to provide recertification of a serious health condition involving pregnancy, a chronic condition, or a permanent/long–term condition more often than every 30 days and even though the leave is not connected with an absence where:

1. Circumstances described by the previous certification have changed significantly (e.g., the duration or frequency of absences, the severity of the condition, complications); or

2. The employer receives information that casts doubt upon the employee's stated reason for the absence.

Parsley, 471 F. Supp. 2d 858; *McClain*, 458 F. Supp. 2d 427; *Yntema*, No. 3:04CV7360, 2006 U.S. Dist. LEXIS 18816, at *12-13.

For example, say the original certification provided by the employee indicated that the employee would be out three times per month to care for a parent with a chronic serious health condition. The employee actually was out five times in one month. The extra two absences constitute a 66 percent increase in the expected frequency of absences. While the regulations fail to define what "significantly" means in percentage terms, a 66 percent increase would appear to meet that criterion.

An employer must point to "information that cases doubt" upon the employee's claim of an FMLA leave related absence in order to demand recertification by the employee's physician within 30 days of the initial certification. *McClain*, 458 F. Supp. 2d 427.

The above illustrates why it is important for employers to get information that is as specific as possible regarding the duration or frequency of absences necessitating FMLA leave in the original, second, or third opinion provider certification. Those numbers will serve as a baseline for determining whether and when an employer may require subsequent recertifications in order for the employer to stay abreast of the situation and plan for the employee's FMLA absences. The failure to obtain specific information in the original certification may severely hamper subsequent efforts to obtain medical recertifications.

b. Minimum Duration of Incapacity Exceeds 30 Days

(1) General Rule

Where the minimum duration of the period of incapacity specified on a certification furnished by the health care provider is more than 30 days, the employer may not request recertification until that minimum duration has passed. 29 CFR 825.308(b)(1); S. Res. 242, Cong. Rec. S3959, S3973 (April 23, 1996); 29 CFR 825.308(b)(1). *See Muhammad v. Indiana*

Bell Tel., Co., 182 Fed. Appx. 551 (7th Cir. 2006); *Brady v. Potter*, 476 F. Supp. 2d 745 (N.D. Ohio 2007); *Pande v. Chevron Corp.*, No. C 04-5107 CW, 2007 U.S. Dist. LEXIS 3247, at *24 (N.D. Ca. Jan. 17, 2007); *Parsley v. City of Columbus, Ohio*, 471 F. Supp. 2d 858 (S.D. Ohio 2006); *Hurt v. Ecolab, Inc.*, No. 3-05-CV-1508-BD, 2006 U.S. Dist. LEXIS 32373, at *10 (N.D. Tex. May 23, 2006); *Yntema v. USPS*, No. 3:04CV7360, 2006 U.S. Dist. LEXIS 18816, at *12-13 (N.D. Ohio March 1, 2006).

"Incapacity" is not defined in the Statute. The term is defined in the certification section of the regulations to mean inability to work, attend school or perform other regular daily activities due to the serious health condition. 29 CFR 825.306(b)(2)(I); S. Res. 242, Cong. Rec. S3959, S3973 (April 23, 1996); 29 CFR 825.306(b)(2)(I). Note that the period of incapacity may not be the same as the period of time an employee may have the serious health condition (which potentially could be a lifetime).

For example, if the original certification submitted by the employee's health care provider provided that the employee would need 45 days of FMLA leave in a single block of time to undergo and recover from surgery. Thereafter, the employee might need FMLA leave occasionally until the employee's strength returns. The employer could not require the employee to submit a medical recertification within the initial 45 days of FMLA leave. The earliest that the employer could require the employee to submit a medical recertification is on day 46, the day after the minimum period duration of incapacity set forth on the original certification.

Similarly, if the original certification submitted by the employee provided that the employee would be incapacitated for at least 31 days, and possibly 45 days, the earliest the employer is able to request recertification is on day 31. That is, one day after the minimum period of incapacity set forth on the original certification.

In *Hurt v. Ecolab, Inc.*, No. 3-05-CV-1508-BD, 2006 U.S. Dist. LEXIS 32373, at *10 (N.D. Tex. May 23, 2006), the original certification indicated the minimum period of incapacity was six weeks, Because the minimum period was more than 30 days, the employer could not require the employee to provide medical updates every two weeks as a condition of receiving FMLA leave. On the contrary, the employee was not obligated to provide further information to substantiate his request for medical leave until that six-week period passed.

When the employee's doctor specifies a duration for intermittent leave or a reduced lave schedule for a chronic condition, 825.308(b) trumps 825.308(a). Subsection (a) of 825.308 applies when a doctor does not specify a duration for a chronic illness, long-term condition, or pregnancy. *See Yntema v. USPS*, No. 3:04CV7360, 2006 U.S. Dist. LEXIS 18816, at *12-13 (USPS violated FMLA by requiring certification every 30 days instead of in 90 day intervals, the period of incapacity specified by the employee's doctor); *Harcourt v. Cincinnati Bell Tel. Co.*, 383 F. Supp. 2d 944, 957 (S.D. Ohio 2005) (employer policy requiring employees to recertify every 90 days regardless of whether health care providers certification indicates that the need for leave will be longer violates FMLA).

The minimum period of incapacity is not the same as the minimum duration of the health condition. In *Parsley v. City of Columbus, Ohio*, 471 F. Supp. 2d 858 (S.D. Ohio 2006), the employee argued that her employer was prohibited from requiring her to recertify every 30 days because her condition was lifelong. The court disagreed, finding that the employee's lifetime back condition fell squarely within the recertification requirements for a chronic condition. As such, the employer was permitted to require the employee to recertify every 30 days. Because the employee failed to timely submit recertification, the court awarded summary judgment to the employer.

(2) Exceptions

An employer may request recertification before the passage of the period of incapacity in excess of 30 days (29 CFR 825.308(b)(1); S. Res. 242, Cong. Rec. S3959, S3973 (April 23, 1996), 825.308(b)(1)) where:

1. The employee requests an extension of leave;

2. Circumstances described in the previous certification have changed significantly (e.g., the duration of the illness, the nature of the illness, complications); or

3. The employer receives information that casts doubt upon the continuing validity of the certification.

Parsley v. City of Columbus, Ohio, 471 F. Supp. 2d 858 (S.D. Ohio 2006); *Hurt v. Ecolab, Inc.*, No. 3-05-CV-1508-BD, 2006 U.S. Dist. LEXIS 32373, at *10 (N.D. Tex. May 23, 2006); *Yntema v. USPS*, No. 3:04CV7360, 2006 U.S. Dist. LEXIS 18816, at *12-13 (N.D. Ohio March 1, 2006).

Two of the exceptions have been previously discussed. Added to those exceptions is the right of an employer to request medical recertification before the passage of the minimum period of incapacity, in excess of 30 days, where the employee requests an extension of leave. Absent further guidance, it would appear that the agency's ability to request recertification is triggered by the employee's request for an extension of leave, whether that leave is actually taken or not.

The regulations do not define what constitutes a "request." Presumably, whether an employee has made a request for an extension of leave, or merely floated an inquiry that this might be a possibility, will depend on all of the surrounding circumstances. As the FMLA does not require that such employee requests be made in writing, agencies are well advised to obtain such requests in writing. If the employee fails to submit the request in writing, the employer could memorialize the request in a confirming letter to the employee.

An extension of leave is undefined. Note, however, that the request is for an extension of leave, which may be different than a single period of incapacity. Presumably, an extension of leave occurs whenever more FMLA leave is needed than previously planned. For example, if an employee initially requested 45 days of FMLA leave and, on day 20 of the leave, the employee requested an additional 10 days to be tacked on to the end, the request is for an extension of leave. The employer is entitled to request medical recertification on day 20; the day the employee requested an extension of leave.

c.   Intermittent or Reduced Leave Schedule

(1)   General Rule

For FMLA leave taken intermittently or on a reduced leave schedule basis, the employer may not request recertification in less than the minimum period specified on the certification as necessary for such leave (including treatment). 29 CFR 825.308(b)(2); S. Res. 242, Cong. Rec. S3959, S3973 (April 23, 1996); 29 CFR 825.308(b)(2); *see Muhammad v. Indiana Bell Tel., Co.*, 182 Fed. Appx. 551 (7th Cir. 2006); *Brady v. Potter*, 476 F. Supp. 2d 745 (N.D. Ohio 2007). The statute does not define "reasonable basis." *Parsley v. City of Columbus, Ohio*, 471 F. Supp. 2d 858 (S.D. Ohio 2006); *Kitts v. General Tel. North, Inc.*, No. 2:04-cv-173, 2005 U.S. Dist. LEXIS 20421, at *30 (S.D. Ohio Sept. 19, 2005); *Zawadowicz v. CVS. Corp. et al.*, 99 F. Supp. 2d 518, 530 (D. N.J. 2000).

Read literally, the above rule would prohibit an employer from being able to require an employee to submit medical certification for as long as the employee needs FMLA leave intermittently or on a reduced leave schedule. If the employee or the covered family member had a serious health condition that would require the use of intermittent or reduced leave schedule FMLA for the remainder of that person's working life, the employer would theoretically be unable to request medical certification.

It is unclear how the general rule regarding intermittent or FMLA leave on a reduced leave schedule interacts with the general rule governing pregnancy, chronic, or permanent/long–term serious health conditions. Neither the regulations themselves nor the comments accompanying the publication of the final employer regulations provide any guidance regarding which of these general rules governs when the need for intermittent or FMLA leave on a reduced leave schedule is due to pregnancy, chronic, or a permanent/long–term condition.

Nothing in the general recertification rule governing pregnancy, chronic or permanent/long–term serious health conditions excludes leave taken on an intermittent or reduced leave schedule basis. Nor does the general rule governing recertification exclude leave taken due to pregnancy, chronic, or permanent/long–term conditions from its reach. Given the differences in the rules regarding when an employer may safely request medical recertification, agencies must exercise great care when requesting medical recertification where these two rules are implicated.

For what it is worth, as a matter of regulatory construction, it would seem the general rule governing intermittent and reduced leave schedule FMLA leave would govern where the need for FMLA leave was due to pregnancy, chronic, or a permanent/long–term condition. The regulation follows the earlier general rule regarding pregnancy, chronic, or permanent/long–term conditions. As such, the intermittent/reduced leave schedule general recertification rule takes into consideration the preceding regulations, including the general rule on recertification where the need for leave involves pregnancy, chronic, or permanent/long–term conditions. The result of this interpretation is to limit the general recertification rule in § 825.308(a) to pregnancy, chronic, or permanent/long–term conditions when the leave is taken in a single block of time.

(2) Exceptions

An employer may require an employee who is taking FMLA leave on an intermittent or reduced leave schedule basis to provide medical recertification before the expiration of the minimum period specified on the certification as necessary for such leave under three circumstances 29 CFR 825.308(b)(2), (c); S. Res. 242, Cong. Rec. S3959, S3973 (April 23, 1996); 29 CFR 825.308(b)(2), (c). *The three circumstances are:*

1. The employee requests an extension of leave;
2. Circumstances described in the previous certification have changed significantly (e.g., the duration of the illness, the nature of the illness, complications);
3. The employer receives information that casts doubt on the continuing validity of the certification.

See *Zawadowicz v. CVS. Corp. et al.*, 99 F. Supp. 2d 518, 530–31 (D. N.J. 2000).

d. All Other Circumstances

(1) General Rule

Where the employee's need for leave due to his or her own serious health condition, or to care for a covered family member with a serious health condition, does not involve the serious health conditions of pregnancy, chronic, or permanent/long-term conditions, and/or does not involve an employee's use of FMLA leave on an intermittent or reduced leave schedule basis, an employer may request medical recertification at any reasonable interval, but not more often than every 30 days. 29 CFR 825.308((c); S. Res. 242, Cong. Rec. S3959, S3973 (April 23, 1996); 29 CFR 825.308(c); see *Brumbalough v. Camelot Care Centers, Inc.*, 427 F.3d 996, 1002 (6th Cir. 2005); *Williams v. The Boeing Co.*, No. 97-36098, U.S. App. LEXIS 785 (9th Cir. 1999); *Parsley v. City of Columbus, Ohio*, 471 F. Supp. 2d 858 (S.D. Ohio 2006); *Zawadowicz v. CVS Corp. et al.*, 99 F. Supp. 2d 518, 530–31 (D. N.J. 2000).

Stated differently, this general rule applies when the need for FMLA leave is due to the following serious health conditions:

- Inpatient care (825.114(a)(1));
- Continuing treatment by a health care provider involving a period of incapacity of more than three consecutive calendar days, plus one or more health care provider treatments (825.114(2)((I)); or
- Any period of absence to receive multiple treatments by a health care provider either for restorative surgery after an accident or other injury, or for a condition that would likely result in a period of incapacity of more than three consecutive calendar days in the absence of medical intervention (825.114(2)(v)).

It is unclear how this rule interacts with the general rules governing pregnancy, chronic, or permanent/long-term conditions where, for example, inpatient care is due to the serious health condition of pregnancy. Presumably, the "all other circumstances" rule would not apply where FMLA coverage is due to two or more categories of FMLA serious health conditions, provided one of the conditions is set forth in §§ 825.308(a) or (b). This is because § 825.308(c) only applies where the circumstances are "not covered by paragraphs (a) or (b)" of § 825.308.

The regulations do not establish what constitutes a reasonable interval for an employer to request medical certification, other than it must be no more often than once every 30 days. Because the term "reasonable" is included in the regulation, agencies are well advised to consider all of the facts and circumstances of each case rather than establishing a uniform rule in these matters (e.g., every 31 days). Presumably, the reference to 30 days means 30 calendar days.

(2) Exceptions

An employer may require an employee who is taking FMLA leave due to a serious health condition requiring inpatient care, continuing treatment, or for any period of absence to receive multiple treatments by a health care provider following restorative surgery for accident or other injury, or for a condition that would likely result in a period of incapacity of more than three consecutive calendar days in the absence of medical intervention, to provide on request medical recertification more frequently than at any reasonable interval in excess of 30 days (29 CFR 825.308(c), (c); S. Res. 242, Cong. Rec. S3959, S3973 (April 23, 1996); 29 CFR 825.308(c)), where:

- The employee requests an extension of leave;
- Circumstances described in the previous certification have changed significantly (e.g., the duration of the illness, the nature of the illness, complications);
- The employer receives information that casts doubt on the continuing validity of the certification.

Parsley v. City of Columbus, Ohio, 471 F. Supp. 2d 858 (S.D. Ohio 2006). *But see Junker v. Amana Co., L.P.,* 240 F. Supp. 2d 894, 900 (N.D. Iowa 2003) (holding that an employer is entitled to request recertification where an employee has requested an extension of leave, provided that such recertification is not required prior to 30 days after the employer's previous receipt of medical recertification).

This means, for example, that an employee who is supposed to be recovering at home from inpatient surgery for 60 days may be required to provide medical recertification if, for example, the employee is spotted at the local bowling alley, but was limited to bed rest in the initial certification. Whether an employer would want to request recertification in this circumstance is addressed later in this chapter.

3. Time for Employee Submission of Recertification

An employee must provide the requested medical recertification to the employer within the time frame requested by the employer (which must allow at least 15 calendar days after the employer's request), unless it is not practicable under the particular circumstances to do so despite the employee's diligent, good faith efforts. 29 CFR 825.308(d); S. Res. 242, Cong. Rec. S3959, S3973 (April 23, 1996); 29 CFR 825.308(d); *see Muhammad v. Indiana Bell Tel., Co.*, 182 Fed. Appx. 551 (7th Cir. 2006); *Brumbalough v. Camelot Care Centers, Inc.*, 427 F.3d 996, 1002 (6th Cir. 2005); *McClain v. Detroit Entertainment, LLC*, 458 F. Supp. 2d 427 (E.D. Mich. Sept. 28, 2006); *Roupp v. Susquehanna Health System*, No. 4:CV-04cv2020, 2006 U.S. Dist. LEXIS 4542, at *10 (M.D. Pa. Jan. 13, 2006); *Brown v. SBC Communications, Inc.*, No. 04-C-0290, 2005 U.S. Dist. LEXIS 41599, at *4 (E.D. Wis. Aug. 23, 2005); *Alexander et al., v. Ford Motor Co.*, 204 F.R.D. 314, 317 (E.D. Mich. 2001). This is the same time frame required for submission of the original certification. An employer who requires an employee to submit a recertification in less time, absent application of an exception, is in violation of the FMLA. *LeGrand v. Village of McCook*, No. 96-C-5951, 1998 U.S. Dist. LEXIS 5230 (N.D. Ill. April 15, 1998) (if employer requirement that employee must provide certifications every 14 days is considered a recertification, the request violated the FMLA).

4. Selection of Medical Recertification Opinion Provider

It is unclear who, the employee or the agency, gets to select the health care provider for the medical recertification. The lack of clarity is due to the fact that neither the Statute nor the regulations specify who makes the selection. In the absence of further guidance, agencies should treat recertifications as if they were original certifications, and allow the employee to make the selection.

Allowing an employee to select the health care provider for medical recertification is consistent with the Statute and the regulations. Unlike second opinions, which the Statute specifically permits employers to select, the statute does not allow employers to select the medical recertification health care provider. Moreover, the regulations specifically provide that the employer may request that the employee provide medical recertification. The scope of an agency's authority is limited to making the request. The regulations say nothing that would authorize an employer to select the health care provider the employee must use to provide the medical recertification.

5. Form of Medical Recertification

Ironically, while an employer is allowed to request medical recertification, the regulations fail to address the permissible contents of that recertification. Because this is a recertification, employers are well advised to limit the contents of the certification to that permitted pursuant to 29 CFR 825.306; S. Res. 242, Cong. Rec. S3959, S3973 (April 23, 1996); 29 CFR 825.306. In fact, employers should provide the covered employee with a copy of the DOL approved WH 380 medical certification form when requesting medical recertifications.

6. Notice of Requirement of Recertification

Agencies are not specifically required to notify employees that they may have to provide a medical recertification at the request of the agency. The individual notice that must be provided to employees does not mandate that medical recertifications be addressed. *See* 29 CFR 825.301(b)(1); S. Res. 242, Cong. Rec. S3959, S3971 (April 23, 1996); 29 CFR 825.301(b)(1); *see Muhammad v. Indiana Bell Tel., Co.*, 182 Fed. Appx. 551 (7th Cir. 2006). Presumably, medical recertifications are a permissive subject of such notices, although recertifications are not mentioned in the regulation allowing additional information in the required notice either. 29 CFR 825.301(b)(2); S. Res. 242, Cong. Rec. S3959, S3973 (April 23, 1996); 29 CFR 825.301(b)(2).

Unlike medical certifications, because agencies are not specifically required by the FMLA regulations to notify an employee of the medical recertification requirement, the failure of an employer to include specific notice of any recertification requirement would not be grounds for precluding an employer from taking action against the employee for failure to provide recertification. *See* 29 CFR 825.301(e); S. Res. 242, Cong. Rec. S3959, S3973 (April 23, 1996); 29 CFR 825.301(a)(1).

Of course, because an employer is not required to notify employees that medical recertification may be required does not mean that employers are prohibited from including such information in any written notice that is required to be provided to the employee. Agencies should seriously consider including information regarding any medical recertification requirements as part of the written notice the employer must otherwise provide the employee regarding FMLA rights and obligations. Notice avoids misunderstandings. Misunderstandings are the seed of many a lawsuit.

Notice that an employee may be required to provide a medical recertification appears to be a necessary part of any written guidance the employer provides regarding employee leave and benefits. According to the notice rules, an employer that has any eligible employees and has any written guidance for employees, such as an employee handbook or manual, must include information concerning "FMLA entitlements and employee obligations under the FMLA" 29 CFR 825.301(a)(1); S. Res. 242, Cong. Rec. S3959, S3973 (April 23, 1996); 29 CFR 825.301(a)(1). If an employer is going to exercise its right to require an employee to provide a medical recertification, notice of that obligation must be included in the employee handbook, manual, or other written guidance on employee leave or benefits.

7. Second and Third Opinions Prohibited on Recertifications

Second and third opinions are not permitted on medical recertifications. 29 CFR 825.308(e); S. Res. 242, Cong. Rec. S3959, S3973 (April 23, 1996); 29 CFR 825.308(e). The prohibition on an agency's ability to challenge the validity of a medical recertification should give agencies pause before using this tool to update an employee's medical condition.

Agencies that do not have a reason to doubt the validity of an original certification are not permitted to challenge the validity of that certification by requiring certification by a second or third health care opinion provider. If an employer who has not challenged the original certification through the second and third health care opinion provider process requests medical recertification, the employer will be forever barred from challenging the original certification. Because a recertification updates the now stale certification that preceded it, it follows that the stale certification falls by the wayside. Where the recertification is preceded by the original certification, the original certification lapses and the newer medical recertification stands in its place. Because second and third opinions are prohibited on recertifications, an employer who failed to challenge the validity of the original certification may be forever barred from making such a challenge, absent fraud.

DOL representatives may orally indicate that challenges to an original certification may be maintained even after a medical recertification. Such a position assumes that the original certification survives the recertification process. In the absence of further guidance on this issue, agencies are well advised to proceed with caution. They should check the policy of the local DOL office on second and third opinions after a recertification is provided. Unions and other organizations representing the interests of employees, on the other hand, will want to limit the ability of employers to invoke the second and third health care opinion provider process where a recertification has been submitted.

8. Payment for Recertifications

Recertifications requested by the employer must be obtained at the employee's expense, unless the employer voluntarily provides otherwise. 29 CFR 825.308(e); S. Res. 242, Cong. Rec. S3959, S3973 (April 23, 1996); 29 CFR 825.308(e). The DOL explained (Preamble, 29 CFR 825.308) that:

Congress did not include such a requirement [that the employer bear the cost of a medical recertification it has requested] regarding recertifications; consequently, there is no basis for the Department [of Labor] to impose costs on the employer by regulation.

Employers generally like the fact that recertifications are at the employee's expense. They use it as a tool to prevent abuse of FMLA leave. Agencies must take great care, however, to avoid claims of harassment when requesting medical recertifications. Unions and other organizations representing employees, on the other hand, generally seek modification of employer policies to require payment for the recertification, payment of employee or family member expenses in securing the recertification, as well as compensation for the employee's time.

9. Failure to Provide Recertification

The regulations are less than clear regarding the consequences for an employee's failure to timely provide a requested recertification. The lack of clarity stems from the inclusion of "recertification" in the title of the pertinent regulation, but only one reference is made in the body of the regulation. The regulation, 29 CFR 825.311;S. Res. 242, Cong. Rec. S3959, S3973 (April 23, 1996); 29 CFR 825.311, is entitled:

> What happens if an employee fails to satisfy the medical certification and/or recertification requirements?

The above title suggests that the rules that follow apply where an employee fails to provide a medical certification or medical recertification. Only one of the regulations that follow the title, however, actually indicates that it applies to recertifications. The regulation provides that when the need for leave is not foreseeable, or in the case of recertification, an employee must provide certification (or recertification) within the time frame requested by the employer (which must allow at least 15 days after the employer's request) or as soon as reasonably possible under the particular facts and circumstances. 29 CFR 825.311(b); S. Res. 242, Cong. Rec. S3959, S3973 (April 23, 1996); 29 CFR 825.311(b).

The regulation goes on to provide that in the event an employee fails to provide a medical certification within a reasonable time under the pertinent circumstances, the employer may delay the employee's continuation of FMLA leave. 29 CFR 825.311(b); S. Res. 242, Cong. Rec. S3959, S3973 (April 23, 1996); 29 CFR 825.311(b). If the employee never produces the certification, the leave is not FMLA leave. 29 CFR 825.311(b); S. Res. 242, Cong. Rec. S3959, S3973 (April 23, 1996); 29 CFR 825.311(b); *see Muhammad v. Indiana Bell Tel. Co. Inc.*, 182 Fed. Appx. 551 (7th Cir. 2006) (as a result of employee's failure to provide recertification, employer reasonably concluded absences were unexcused and could be the basis of disciplinary action, including termination); *Brumbalough v. Camelot Care Centers, Inc.*, 427 F.3d 996, 1002 (6th Cir. 2005); *Hurt v. Ecolab, Inc.*, No. 3-05-CV-1508-BD, 2006 U.S. Dist. LEXIS 32373, at *10 (N.D. Tex. May 23, 2006) (failure to provide an appropriate recertification is fatal to a claim under the FMLA).

Presumably, the reference to "medical certification" and "certification" when the regulation addresses the consequences for an employee's failure to provide the requested medical certification includes recertification. *Brumbalough*, 427 F.3d at 1002.

10. Employer Violation of Recertification Rules

The regulations do not include a penalty in the event an employer violates the recertification rules, typically by requiring an employee to provide medical documentation more often than permitted. As a violation of the FMLA regulations, an employer that requires an employee to recertify more often than permitted interferes with the exercise of an employee's FMLA rights. 29 CFR 825.220(b). However, to have an actionable claim, an employee must establish that he or she suffered prejudice or monetary harm as a result of the employer's requirement that the employee recertify his or her serious health condition more often than allowed by the FMLA. *Mueler v. J.P. Morgan Chase & Co.*, No. 1:05CV 560, 2007 U.S. Dist. LEXIS 20828, at *52 (N.D. Ohio March 23, 2007).

Notice to the employee that he or she may be required to provide recertification in the event he or she requests an extension of leave does not violate the FMLA. *Pande v. Chevron Corp.*, No. C 04-5107 CW, 2007 U.S. Dist. LEXIS 3247, at *24 (N.D. Ca. Jan. 17, 2007).

A request that an employee provide periodic status reports on the employee's status and intent to return to work during leave every 30 days is not a request for recertification, and is specifically permitted by the FMLA, 29 CFR 825.309(a); *see Pande v. Chevron Corp.*, No. C 04-5107 CW, 2007 U.S. Dist. LEXIS 3247, at *24 (N.D. Ca. Jan. 17, 2007).

B. TITLE II

1. Overview

Title II also allows employers to require that an employee obtain subsequent recertifications on a reasonable basis. 5 USC 6383(e); 5 CFR 630.1207(j). As with Title I, the CAA, and the PEOAA, neither the Statute nor the regulations define what constitutes a recertification. Presumably, it means the same thing as under Title I, a renewed medical certification updating a previous certification that has grown stale.

2. Circumstances Permitting Recertifications

There are two circumstances where an employer may request medical recertification from an employee.

a. Pregnancy, Chronic Conditions, or Long-Term Conditions

(1) General Rule

For pregnancy, chronic conditions, or long-term conditions, as those terms are defined in 5 CFR 630.1202, an employer may require subsequent medical recertification on a periodic basis, but not more often than once every 30 calendar days. 5 CFR 630.1207(j).

(2) Exceptions

An employer may require an employee to provide subsequent medical recertification more often than once every 30 calendar days if the employee, 5 CFR 630.1207(j):

- Requests that the original leave period be extended;
- The circumstances described in the original medical certification have changed significantly; or
- The employer receives information that casts doubt upon the continuing validity of the medical certification.

The exceptions identified above are very similar to those set forth in § 825.308(c)(1)–(3) of the Title I regulations, 29 CFR 825.301(c)(1)–(3).

As with Title I, the regulations fail to describe key terms. For example, under what circumstances will the original medical certification be considered to have changed significantly? Similarly, what information may an employer receive that casts doubt on the continuing validity of the medical certification? Some guidance in these areas would be helpful to agencies.

b. All Other Circumstances

For FMLA leave taken for all other serious health conditions (excluding pregnancy, chronic, and long-term conditions), and including leave taken on an intermittent or reduced leave schedule, if the health care provider has specified on the medical certification a minimum duration of the period of incapacity, the employer may not request recertification until that period has passed. 5 CFR 630.1207(j).

This regulation resembles a combination of 29 CFR 825.308(b)(1) and (2). The chief difference is that, under § 825.308(b)(2), where FMLA leave is taken intermittently or on a reduced leave schedule, an employer is prohibited from requesting medical recertification before the expiration of the minimum period specified on the certification as necessary for such leave. Under Title II, an employer is not permitted, absent exceptions, to request recertification more often than the minimum period of incapacity, even if leave is taken intermittently or on a reduced leave schedule.

As explained in the section of this chapter addressing recertification under Title I, this is a significant difference. The difference between a minimum period of incapacity and the minimum duration of leave can be days, weeks, months, or years. Incapacity is generally the inability of the employee or covered family member to attend work, school, or otherwise assume his or her normal activities of living. Leave, on the other hand, may be an entire series of absences due to incapacity or treatment related to the same underlying condition. An employee may, for example, need intermittent leave for the remainder of his or her working life. In contrast, the maximum amount of time an employee may be incapacitated during any given leave year is 12 workweeks. After that, the leave is not covered by the FMLA.

Because of these differences, agencies with employees covered by both Title I and Title II of the Act must be careful to apply the correct standard. An employer that simply applies the Title II recertification regulations to all employees, including Title I employees, runs the considerable risk of violating Title I. This is particularly true when the employee has requested intermittent or FMLA leave on a reduced leave schedule.

(1) Exceptions

An employer may require subsequent medical recertifications more often than the minimum period of incapacity specified on the medical certification (5 CFR 630.1207(j)) if:

- The employee requests that the original leave period be extended;
- The circumstances described in the original medical certification have changed significantly; or
- The employer receives information that casts doubt upon the continuing validity of the medical certification.

The above exceptions are substantially the same as those contained in 29 CFR 825.308(c)(1)–(3).

3. Time for Submission

The regulations fail to identify how long an employee has, after the agency's request, to provide the subsequent medical recertification. The regulations do not provide a minimum or maximum period of time. Nor do they set a standard for this determination, such as a reasonable period of time.

In the absence of any guidance on this issue, agencies are well advised to allow the employee a reasonable period of time under the circumstances to provide the certification. Agencies should be cautious in applying the temporal limitations for submission of the original medical certification contained in 5 CFR 630.1207(h). Generally speaking, the provision allows an employer 15 calendar days after the date the employer requests certification. If that is not practicable under the circumstances, the employee must provide the certification within a reasonable period of time, but under no circumstances later than 30 calendar days from the request.

The advantage of the use of these criteria is that they are sanctioned for the closely related area governing the collection of the original certification, as well as second and third opinions. The downside is that an argument could be made that the drafters of the regulations were aware of the general certification regulations when they created the recertification regulations. The fact that the recertification regulations do not incorporate the time frames for submission of the general certification regulations could suggest that the drafters did not want those time frames to apply.

A little help from OPM would go a long way in clarifying this area so that agencies have a sporting chance of abiding by the requirements of the law.

4. Selection of Medical Recertification Opinion Provider

It is unclear who, the employee or the agency, gets to select the health care provider for the medical recertification. The lack of clarity is due to the fact that neither the Statute nor the regulations specify who makes the selection. In the absence of further guidance, agencies should treat recertifications as if they were original certifications, and allow the employee to make the selection.

Allowing an employee to select the health care provider for medical recertification is consistent with the Statute and the regulations. Unlike second opinions, which the Statute specifically permits employers to select, the Statute does not allow employers to select the medical recertification health care provider. Moreover, the regulations specifically provide that the employer may request that the employee provide medical recertification. The scope of an agency's authority is limited to making the request. The regulations say nothing that would authorize an employer to select the health care provider the employee must use to provide the medical recertification.

5. Form of Subsequent Medical Recertification

The regulations do not identify the form or permissible contents of the subsequent medical recertification. Presumably, the contents of a recertification are the same as the original certification. Agencies are well advised not to ask for any more information for purposes of a medical recertification than is permitted by Title II for purposes of an original certification.

6. Notice of Medical Recertification Requirement

Title II does not specifically require an employer to notify an employee of the obligation to submit subsequent medical certifications. However, arguably, agencies should notify employees that they may be obligated to provide a subsequent medical recertification pursuant to the general notice requirements. Those requirements provide that each employer inform its employees of their FMLA entitlements and responsibilities. 5 CFR 630.1203(g). Although not specifically required pursuant to the general notice provisions, agencies are well advised to include in any employee handbook, manual or other written documentation explaining employee leave or benefits FMLA entitlements and obligations, including the obligation to submit a medical recertification on request.

7. Second and Third Opinions

The regulations implementing Title II do not address whether second or third opinions are available where an employer doubts the validity of the original certification. Title I specifically bars the use of second and third opinions to challenge the validity of a recertification. 29 CFR 825.308(e). Because the Statute does not provide for second or third opinions for recertification, the DOL explained that no such opinions may be required. Preamble, 29 CFR 825.308. The same rationale would apply to Title II. That is, the Statute, using virtually identical language as in Title I, does not provide for second or third opinions on subsequent medical recertifications.

For the more daring, the argument could be made that, since the regulations do not specifically bar second and third opinions on recertifications, they are permissible. The problem with that argument is that a second and third opinions process is contained in the Statute and regulations for the original certification, but does not include recertifications. On balance, it is not recommended that Title II agencies use the absence of a prohibition against second and third opinions as a signal that they are permissible.

8. Payment for Medical Recertifications

Recertifications are at the expense of the agency. 5 USC 6383(e); 5 CFR 630.1207(j). The regulations do not define what constitutes an "expense." It is, therefore, unclear whether the employer is required to compensate the employee for the time the employee or the employee's covered family member spent in securing the medical recertification. Compensation is generally not thought of as an employer "expense."

It is more likely that the employer must pay the cost of the medical recertification (the fee of the health care provider). It is also quite possible that the employer will have to reimburse the employee for any expenses incurred by the employee or covered family member in securing the recertification, such as parking, tolls, etc.

Note that there is no penalty for an agency's failure to pay such expenses. Presumably, if the employee's failure to secure a medical recertification is due to the employer's failure or refusal to pay the expense of the recertification the employee should be relieved of the consequences for failing to provide the recertification. The employer would also be in violation of the requirements of the FMLA.

9. Failure to Provide Medical Recertification

Neither the Statute nor the regulations specify the consequences for an employee's failure to provide a requested medical recertification. Presumably, since a recertification is still a certification, the rules governing the employee's failure to provide a certification would apply. An employee who does not provide a certification signed by a health care provider that includes all of the information specified in § 630.1207(b) is not entitled to FMLA leave. 5 CFR 630.1208(l).

IV. PERIODIC STATUS REPORTS DURING LEAVE

Periodic status reports are addressed in Chapter 13, "Return to Work from Leave."

V. CERTIFICATION OF AN EMPLOYEE'S FITNESS TO RETURN TO DUTY FROM LEAVE

The requirement that an employee submit a fitness for duty certification attesting to his or her medical ability to return to work is addressed in Chapter 13, "Return to Work from Leave."

VI. DOCUMENTATION ESTABLISHING FAMILIAL RELATIONSHIPS

An eligible employee is entitled to FMLA leave where a covered family member, a spouse, son, daughter, or parent, has a serious health condition and the employee is needed to provide care for that individual. Employers may, in certain circumstances, require employees to provide documentation in support of their claimed familial relationship with a covered family member for purposes of FMLA leave.

A. TITLE I, THE CAA, AND THE PEOAA

To confirm a covered family relationship, an employer may require an employee giving notice of the need for leave to provide reasonable documentation or a statement of family relationship. 29 CFR 825.113(d); S. Res. 242, Cong. Rec. S3959, S3962 (April 23, 1996); 29 CFR 825.113(d). The documentation may take the form of a simple statement from the employee, or a child's birth certificate, a court document, etc., but the employee is entitled to the return of the official document submitted for this purpose. 29 CFR 825.113(d); S. Res. 242, Cong. Rec. S3959, S3962 (April 23, 1996); 29 CFR 825.113(d).

The regulations do not provide when or how an employer may request documentation of familial relationship. Presumably, an employer should make such a request within a reasonable period of time from when the employee initially requests leave, or when the employer acquires information that casts doubt on the validity of the familial relationship after leave has commenced. An employer is well advised to request such documentation in writing.

The scope of the documents that may be requested to establish a covered family relationship is broad. In addition to examples identified in the regulations, agencies may request other records, such as tax records, marriage certificates or divorce orders. In the case of common–law marriages, agencies interested in confirming the existence of such a relationship should consider tax records, joint bank account records, joint mortgage records, and similar indicia of a common–law marriage.

Having said that, employers generally do not need this type of documentation. In most cases, the employer will have a record of who is a spouse, son, daughter, and perhaps parent in the employee's health benefits, insurance, and other employment records. A statement from the employee that the claimed individual is a covered family member is sufficient in most cases.

It is unclear how far agencies may push this issue. For example, could an employer require a paternity test to determine whether a son or daughter is the child of the employee, where the employee has offered a birth certificate certifying paternity? Agencies are well advised to avoid pushing the envelope on paternity.

The regulation does not specify the amount of time an employee has within which to provide the documentation once requested by the employer. In the absence of guidance, the employer should allow the employee a reasonable period of time to provide the documentation. As a general rule, the employer may initially want to give the employee 15 calendar days from the request to provide the requested documentation, absent extenuating circumstances. This is the same period that an employee is allowed to provide a medical certification. Of course, if the employee has a legitimate reason to explain why he or she cannot obtain the requested documentation within that period of time, the employee should be given an additional reasonable period of time. Employers should avoid short, uniform deadlines that do not take into account all of the surrounding circumstances.

The regulations do not specifically address what notice, if any, an employer must provide an employee regarding the obligation to provide documentation of familial relationship. The specific notice requirements of § 825.301(b)(1) do not require that an employer advise employees of the familial documentation requirement. 29 CFR 825.301(b)(1); S. Res. 242, Cong. Rec. S3959, S3971 (April 23, 1996); 29 CFR 825.301(b)(1). Because an employer that has an employee handbook or manual is required to include information regarding FMLA entitlements and obligations, the obligation of an employee to provide documentation, on request, of familial relationship should be included in the employee handbook, manual, or other written guidance regarding employee leave and benefits.

The cost to employees of obtaining documentation of familial relationships is addressed in the implementing regulations or the Statute. As such, it appears that such cost is borne by the employee, absent a more generous employer policy.

Finally, the regulations do not address the consequences of an employee's failure to provide such documentation. Absent further guidance, an employee who fails to provide written documentation establishing familial relationship should be treated the same as if the employee failed to provide medical certification. That is, an employee who fails to provide documentation is not protected by the FMLA.

B. TITLE II

It is unclear whether Title II contains a provision for an employer to require an employee to provide documentation to confirm a claimed familial relationship. The lack of clarity is due to the wording of the regulation. To the extent that the wording may be construed to permit such documentation, the requirement is different than that contained in Title I.

Title II allows an employer to require that a request for leave under § 630.1203(a)(1) and (2) be supported by evidence that is administratively acceptable to the agency. 5 CFR 630.1206(f). Sections 630.1203(a)(1)–(2), 29 CFR 630.1203(a)(1), provide that an employee is entitled to FMLA leave for the birth of a son or daughter of the employee, and the care of such son or daughter. Section 630.1203(a)(2) provides that an employee is entitled to FMLA leave for the placement of a son or daughter with the employee for adoption for foster care.

The regulations do not permit an employer to establish the existence of a covered family relationship *per se*. However, they may be read as permitting an employer to require an employee to establish that a son or daughter of the employee is being born or needs the employee's care, or is being placed with the employee for adoption or foster care. This would appear to be the functional equivalent of permitting an employer to require that an employee establish a covered family relationship with a son or daughter.

Note that Title II does not allow agencies to require an employee to establish a covered family relationship with a parent or spouse. This could prove to be a problem for agencies given that spouse is defined to include common–law marriages, and parent includes individuals who stands or stood in loco parentis to an employee when the employee was a son or daughter. These are not necessarily the easiest or clearest determinations to be made. Apparently, for purposes of the FMLA, an employer simply has to take the employee's word on these issues. Agencies may be able to make up most of the difference by having policies requiring this information when the employee seeks paid leave.

The reference in the regulations to the documentation being "administratively acceptable" would appear to give agencies a lot of leeway in what documents they may require.

Note that the regulation does not address a number of topics. First, there is no time limit placed on when an employer may request such documentation, and when an employee must respond. Presumably, both must be within a reasonable period of time under the circumstances.

Second, there is nothing specifically contained in the regulations regarding employer notification of employees that this type of documentation may be required. Pursuant to the general notice requirement compelling agencies to notify employees of their FMLA entitlements and responsibilities, 5 CFR 630.1203(g), an employer is well advised to include notice of this obligation in all written FMLA materials outlining employee rights and obligations.

The regulations also fail to indicate what penalty, if any, an employer may suffer if it fails to notify the employee of his or her FMLA obligations, including the obligation to provide documentation of the birth, adoption, or foster care placement of a son or daughter. Agencies will argue that, since the regulations did provide a penalty, there should not be any. Employees will likely argue that they were unaware of this responsibility and, therefore, should not be held strictly accountable for failing to meet this requirement. Unions and organizations representing employees should consider bargaining for employer policies requiring notice and imposing a penalty.

Third, the cost of obtaining such documentation is not addressed in the regulation. As such, it would appear that employees must bear the costs of obtaining this documentation. Unions and other organizations representing employees should be expected to bargain to shift the cost of obtaining such documentation at the agency's request to the agency.

Fourth, the regulations fail to indicate whether an employer may delay the commencement or continuation of leave pending receipt of this documentation. Presumably, the absence of a regulation permitting an employer to take such action indicates that agencies may not delay the start or continuation of leave pending receipt of such documentation.

Finally, the regulations fail to provide a penalty for an employee's failure to provide such documentation. Since the regulations allow agencies to require the documentation, the employee's failure to provide it should be treated the same as if the employee failed to provide medical documentation. That is, an employee who fails to provide such documentation is not entitled to the protections of the FMLA. Unions and other organizations representing employees will want to bargain to obtain a less onerous penalty.

VII. HIPAA AND FMLA CERTIFICATION

The final privacy regulations implementing the Health Insurance Portability and Accountability Act of 1996, Public Law 104-91, will impact the ability of agencies to obtain FMLA medical information about employees. The final privacy regulations were issued by the U.S. Department of Health and Human Services effective April 14, 2003, requiring, among other things, employee authorization before a covered health care provider may disclose protected health information. *See* 68 Fed. Reg. 8333. The interaction of HIPAA with the FMLA is discussed more fully in Chapter 16, "Interaction of the FMLA with Other Federal Laws, Employer Practices, and Collective Bargaining Agreements." An overview of the HIPAA privacy requirements is provided below.

The HIPAA privacy regulations do not directly apply to employers or employment records. However, because the rules apply to government-funded health plans (including the Federal Employees Health Benefit Program) and all health care providers (e.g., physicians, hospitals, labs, pharmacies, etc.), federal agencies will be indirectly impacted by the rules, particularly in their ability to obtain medical information regarding an employee or a covered family member for purposes of the FMLA.

Under the HIPAA privacy rules, a covered health care provider may release protected health information to an employer only with the express written authorization of the employee, and only for the purpose authorized. The HIPAA privacy rules do not apply where the employee requests medical information regarding the employee from a HIPAA covered health care provider. Typically, where an employer requires an employee to provide medical certification, the HIPAA rules will not apply. Where, however, the employer requires an employee to submit to an examination by a second or third health care opinion provider, or the employer seeks to clarify the contents of a certification, the health care provider is prohibited from disclosing such information unless he or she is provided a proper, written HIPAA privacy authorization.

The written authorization must conform to certain very specific standards mandated by the HIPAA privacy rule. For example, the authorization must be written in plain language, and must specifically describe the protected information to be disclosed, identify the person or class of persons who are to receive the information, describe the purpose of the disclosure, the date or event that will end the authorization, and outline the individual's right to revoke the authorization, among other items. The authorization must be on a form separate from any other form, such as the DOL WH 380.

The HHS has not developed a complaint authorization form. Agencies are well advised to create such authorization and provide them to employees when needed for FMLA purposes.

The HIPAA privacy rules also govern the maintenance of HIPAA-covered medical records. Basically, they must be kept separate from other personnel files and employee records. This includes separating FMLA medical certifications that are not protected by HIPAA (such as certifications obtained by the employer directly from the employee) from FMLA medical certifications that are covered by HIPAA. Both paper and electronic files containing HIPAA records must be protected, and access to the files must be limited to those with authorization.

Agencies will want to comply with the HIPAA privacy rules as the law provides for substantial fines, penalties, and for some violations, imprisonment.

VIII. DOCUMENTATION REQUIREMENTS IN AGENCIES WITH MIXED FMLA RESPONSIBILITIES

There are significant differences between the requirements of Titles I and II of the Act regarding documentation requirements. As a result of these differences, most agencies with a majority of employees covered by Title II must avoid simply applying the documentation requirements of Title I to all employees. Adherence to the documentation entitlements and obligations of Title II will not ensure compliance with the comparable entitlements and obligations under Title I. Unlike Title II, violation of Title I can result in costly federal court litigation for the employer and the individual supervisor who made the errant decision.

One of the significant differences between Titles I and II involves the requirement that an employer notify an employee of the obligation to provide medical certification in support of a request for FMLA leave, and the consequences of an employee's failure to provide such documentation. Title II contains a general requirement that obligates agencies to notify employees at no particular time and in no particular manner of the employees' entitlements and obligations. The OPM suggests that an employer can meet this obligation by providing the employee with a copy of the OPM's FMLA regulations and/or by referring the employee to the OPM's FMLA Fact Sheet.

Title I also requires agencies to notify employees of their FMLA entitlements and obligations, including the obligation to provide medical certification in support of a request for FMLA leave. The regulations implementing the notice requirements sets forth very specific employer obligations governing when, how, and the content of such employer notice. An employer that notifies Title I employees of the obligation to provide medical certification in support of FMLA leave in compliance with the requirements of Title II will almost certainly violate the requirements of Title I.

Significant differences between Titles I and II are also found in the amount of time an employee has to provide medical certification. Under Title II, under all circumstances, an employee must provide the supporting medical certification within 30 calendar days of the agency's request. Title I does not have a 30–day cut–off governing an employee's submission of a medical certification. Under Title I, the employee may take more than 30 calendar days if, despite the employee's good faith and diligent efforts, medical certification cannot be secured before then. An employer that applies the 30–day cut–off under Title II to a Title I employee risks violating Title I if the circumstances justify the employee's taking more than 30 calendar days.

The consequences of an employee's untimely submission of a supporting medical certification differs substantially under Titles I and II. Under Title II, if the employee has not timely provided certification the leave is not protected by the FMLA. Under Title I, an employer must first delay the start or continuation of FMLA leave until certification is provided. Only where the employee never provides the certification is the leave unprotected by the FMLA. The Title I regulations do not define how long an employee must delay the start or continuation of FMLA before it can decide that the employee has never provided the certification. An employer that applies the Title II rule to Title I employees without first delaying the start or continuation of FMLA leave may well find itself in violation of Title I.

Title I also provides that an employer must abide by any less stringent certification requirements if the employee or employer elects to substitute paid leave for the unpaid FMLA leave. For example, if an employee elects to substitute paid annual leave for unpaid FMLA leave, and employer policy has no certification requirement for annual leave, the Title I employee is relieved of having to provide any certification in support of FMLA leave. Title II does not have such a provision. Under Title II, an employer may require an employee who has substituted paid leave for FMLA leave on LWOP to provide medical certification in support of the need for FMLA leave. An employer with a majority of Title II employees that attempts to require a Title I employee to provide medical certification where the employee has elected to substitute paid leave will be in violation of the Act.

The permissible contents of medical certification forms differ under Titles I and II. Title I allows agencies to collect significantly more information than is allowed under Title II. Because of these differences, OPM's failure to produce its own form, and direction to agencies to use the medical certification form (WH 380) approved by the DOL, is problematic. Agencies that use the DOL WH 380 for Title II employees will routinely violate Title II.

How agencies address incomplete medical certifications differs under Titles I and II. Under Title I, an employer is required to notify an employee that a certification is incomplete, and allow the employee a reasonable opportunity to cure the deficiency. Title II has no such requirement. Agencies with employees covered by Titles I and II must be aware of this difference in order to avoid inadvertent violations of Title I, such as by denial of FMLA leave without giving the employee notice and a reasonable opportunity to cure the deficiency, when the employee submits an incomplete certification.

Agencies that seek to determine whether the employee has submitted a forged or otherwise fake medical certification must be aware of the different requirements to establish the authenticity of the document. Under Title I, as ridiculous as it sounds, the regulations require the employer to ask the employee for permission to contact the health care provider to confirm the authenticity of the document. If the employee refuses, the employer presumably must spend thousands of dollars for a second opinion. Under Title II, the regulations do not specifically require an employer to obtain the employee's permission before contacting the employee's health care provider regarding the authenticity of the certification. Agencies who apply the Title II standard and contact a health care provider without the Title I employee's prior consent are in violation of the FMLA.

Both Titles I and II contain a second and third health care opinion provider process where the employer challenges the validity of the original medical certification provided by the employee. While similar, these processes are not the same under Titles I and II. For example, what health care providers are excluded from being able to serve as a second health care opinion provider differs under Titles I and II. Likewise, exceptions that allow certain health care providers who are otherwise excluded from performing second opinions differ.

Title II provides that the employee bears the responsibility to ensure that the certification prepared by the second and/or third health care opinion provider is timely given to the agency. This may presuppose that the second or third health care opinion provider must serve the results of his or her examination on the employee. Under Title I, while less clear, there is no requirement imposed on the employee to ensure that the second or third health care opinion provider certification is timely served on the agency.

The regulations implementing Title I also provide detailed instructions on various other rights and obligations not found in Title II. For example, Title I addresses the consequences where an employee and employer cannot agree on a third health care opinion provider. Title II is silent on this issue. Tile I requires an employer to provide the employee with copies of the second and third health care opinion provider certification. Title II is silent on this issue.

Both Titles I and II allow an employer to require an employee to provide medical recertification to update the need for FMLA leave due to a serious health condition. The circumstances permitting recertification, however, differ under Titles I and II. Significantly, Title I contains four circumstances where an employer may request medical recertification; Title II has two circumstances. While the two circumstances under Title II are substantially similar to the four circumstances permitted by Title I, they are not identical.

Recertifications under Titles I and II differ in two significant ways. First, under Title I, an employer may not require an employee on intermittent or a reduced leave schedule to provide medical recertification, absent some exceptions, before the minimum period specified on the original certification expires. Remember, some employees may need FMLA leave on an intermittent or reduced leave schedule basis for the remainder of their working lives. Under Title II, employees on intermittent or a reduced leave schedule may not be required to provide medical recertification for the minimum period of incapacity, as specified on the original certification. The minimum period of incapacity may be significantly less than the minimum period of the need for leave. Agencies must be careful not to apply the Title II rule, which is centered on minimum period of incapacity to Title I employees, as the rule is completely different.

Second, under Title II, medical recertifications are at the expense of the agency. Under Title I, they are at the expense of the employee. Agencies may apply the more generous Title II rules to Title I employees.

Finally, both Titles I and II allow agencies to request documentation to substantiate an employee's claim of familial relationship with a covered family member for purposes of FMLA leave. Again, Titles I and II differ significantly in the application of these rules. For example, Title I allows an employer to require documentation to substantiate all familial relationships claimed by the employee, son, daughter, parent, and spouse.

Title II, on the other hand, only allows verification of the relationship of the employee to a son or daughter, and only in certain circumstances. There is no provision permitting an employer to require the employee to submit documentation verifying a claimed common-law marriage or an in loco parentis relationship with a parent. Agencies have an opportunity *vis a vis* their Title I employees to obtain information that is not available in terms of their Title II employees.

CHAPTER 10
LEAVE AMOUNT AND SCHEDULING

I. OVERVIEW

The FMLA provides that an eligible employee is entitled to a maximum of 12 workweeks of protected leave for one or more covered conditions during a specified 12–month period. There are substantial similarities and differences in how the 12–month FMLA leave period is set, how the 12 weeks of FMLA leave are calculated, and how FMLA leave may be taken under the federal sector FMLA statutes.

Section II, "Twelve-Month FMLA Leave Year", of this chapter addresses the identification of a 12-month leave period. Section III, "Calculating 12 Workweeks of FMLA Leave", discusses the calculation of 12 workweeks of FMLA leave within a 12-month leave period. Section IV addresses "Leave Scheduling". Specifically, this section explores the three ways that FMLA leave may be taken by an eligible employee (block, intermittent and reduced leave schedule), and special rules that may apply.

II. TWELVE-MONTH FMLA LEAVE YEAR

In the federal sector, eligible employees are entitled to 12 workweeks of FMLA leave for covered conditions in a specified 12–month period. 29 USC 2612(a) (Title I); 29 CFR 825.200 (same); 5 USC 6382(a)(1) (Title II); 5 CFR 630.1201(a), 1203(a) (same); 2 USC 1312(a)(1) (incorporating § 102 of Title I, 29 USC 2612 into CAA); S. Res. 242, Cong. Rec. S3959, S3964 (April 23, 1996); 29 CFR 825.200(a); 3 USC 412(a) (incorporating § 102 of Title I, 29 USC 2612 into PEOAA); *accord Miller v. Personal-Touch of Virginia, Inc.*, 342 F. Supp. 2d 499, 511 (E.D. Va. Nov. 2, 2004); *Sabatino v. Flik International Corp.*, 286 F. Supp. 2d 327, 336 (S.D.N.Y. 2003) (Title I); *Panto v. Palmer Dialysis Center/Total Renal Care*, No. 01–6013, 2003 U.S. Dist. LEXIS 5663, at *17 (E.D. Pa. April 7, 2003) (Title I); *Jennings v. Mid-America Energy Co.*, 282 F. Supp. 2d 954, 959–960 (S.D. Iowa 2003) (FMLA entitles employees to an annual total of 12 weeks of leave for a number of reasons); *Thomas v. DHS*, No. DA-0752-06-0522-I-1, 2006 MSPB LEXIS 6513, at 8 & n.3 (Oct. 26, 2006); *Cole v. DHHS*, No. DC-0752-05-0457-I-1, 2005 MSPB LEXIS 6825, at *7 (Nov. 1, 2005); *Williams v. Dept. of Navy*, No. DC-0752-05-0431-I-1, 2005 MSPB LEXIS 6866, at *3 (Oct. 17, 2005), *pet. denied*, 101 MSPR 133 (2006).

This section addresses the options available to some employers in setting the base 12–month period.

A. TITLE II: SETTING THE 12-MONTH LEAVE YEAR

With respect to eligible employees covered by Title II, the 12–month base period is fixed by statute; no other options are available. Federal employers with employees covered by Title I, the CAA, or the PEOAA, however, have a greater range of options in selecting the 12–month base period. The various options have advantages and disadvantages to eligible employees and employers.

1. General Rule

The 12–month base period begins on the date an employee first takes leave for a covered family or medical need, and continues for 12 months. 5 CFR 630.1203(d); *see Kimbrough v. Dept. of Defense*, No. DC-0752-06-0287-I-1, 2006 MSPB LEXIS 4379, at *17 (Aug. 1, 2006). During this 12–month period, a Title II employee has the right to use up to a maximum of 12 workweeks of FMLA leave. After the expiration of that 12–month period, with one exception, a new 12–month period generally would not commence until the first time an employee takes covered FMLA leave, and so on.

Note that the beginning of the base 12–month period is triggered, subject to the exception addressed below, when an eligible employee takes FMLA leave. The regulations do not specifically define what *takes* means. That is, does it mean notice of a need for FMLA leave, or does it require the employee to actually begin an FMLA absence from work? It would appear that the term "takes" means that the eligible employee must actually begin an FMLA leave absence before the

12–month base period for the calculation of 12 workweeks of leave begins to run. *See Kimbrough v. DOD*, No. DC-0752-06-0287-I-1, 2006 MSPB LEXIS 4379, at *17 (Aug. 1, 2006) (12-month period being on the date employee begins FMLA leave of absence).

2. Exception for Birth, Adoption, Foster Care Placement

This exception applies to leave following the birth, placement for adoption or foster care of a covered son or daughter. 5 CFR 630.1203(d). Remember that an eligible employee may take leave in these circumstances even though the son or daughter does not have a covered serious health condition. Think of this as leave to bond with the son or daughter. Leave taken following the birth, placement for adoption or foster care of a covered son or daughter may begin *prior to* or on the actual date of birth, placement for adoption or foster care, and the 12–month period begins to run on that earlier date. *Id.* (emphasis added).

For example, if an employee invokes his or her entitlement to FMLA leave before the birth or placement for adoption or foster care, the 12–month period begins on that date and ends 12 months later. As set forth more fully in Section III, "Calculating 12 Workweeks of FMLA Leave", of this chapter, because an eligible employee's entitlement to 12 workweeks of leave following the birth, placement for adoption or foster care expires one year from the birth or placement date, 5 U. S. C. 6382(a)(2), an eligible employee may be permitted to use some FMLA leave in a second 12-month period, which begins immediately after the expiration of the first 12-month period. The employee may use up to a total of 12 weeks of FMLA leave during the first 12-month period for the birth or placement. During the second 12-month period, the employee is entitled to use FMLA leave for the care of the newborn or newly adopted child, but only for the time period between the end of the first 12-month period and the expiration of the 12-month period after the date of birth or placement. During any 12-month period an employee may use no more than 12 workweeks of FMLA leave.

The exception distinguishes the actual taking of FMLA leave and the invocation of the right to take leave before the actual need for FMLA leave arises. This distinction suggests that the term "takes" under the general rule requires the actual absence for FMLA leave, rather than the limited exception allowing notice of the need for leave for birth or placement.

B. TITLE I, THE CAA AND THE PEOAA: ELECTION OF 12–MONTH YEAR

Federal employers with employees covered by Title I, the CAA, and/or the PEOAA may choose among any of four options for calculating the 12–month base period during which an eligible employee may use up to 12 workweeks of FMLA leave for a covered condition. 29 CFR 825.200; S. Res. 242, Cong. Rec. S3959, S3964 (April 23, 1996); 29 CFR 825.200(a). *See Hunt v. Rapides Healthcare System, LLC*, 277 F.3d 757, 765 (5th Cir. 2002) (employer choice of four methods for calculating 12–month FMLA leave year); *Bachelder v. America West Airlines, Inc.*, 259 F.3d 1112, 1120 (9th Cir. 2001); *Roberts v. Ground Handling, Inc.*, No. 04 Civ. 4955 (WCC), 2007 U.S. Dist. LEXIS 23441, at *35-36 (S.D. N.Y. March 30, 2007); *Sabatino v. Flik International Corp.*, 286 F. Supp. 2d 327, 336 (S.D.N.Y. 2003); *Panto v. Palmer Dialysis Center/Total Renal Care*, No. 01–6013, 2003 U.S. Dist. LEXIS 5663 (E.D. Pa. April 7, 2003); *Dodaro v. Village of Glendale Heights*, No. 01–C-6396, 2003 U.S. Dist. LEXIS 5056 (N.D. Ill. March 31, 2003); *Karnes v. Central Texas Mental Health–Mental Retardation Center*, No. 6:01–CV–245–C, 2002 U.S. Dist. LEXIS 2951 (N.D. Tex. Feb. 22, 2002); *Krohn v. Forsting et al.*, 11 F. Supp. 2d 1082, 1092 (E.D. Mo. 1998).

According to the DOL, the "choice of options was intended to give maximum flexibility for ease in administering FMLA in conjunction with ongoing employer leave plans." Preamble, 29 CFR 825.200.

A review of the various options and related rules follows.

1. Four Options

An employer is permitted (29 CFR 825.200(b); S. Res. 242, Cong. Rec. S3959, S3963–64 (April 23, 1996); 29 CFR 825.200(b)) to choose any one of the following methods for determining the 12-month period in which the 12 weeks of FMLA leave entitlement occurs:

- The calendar year;
- Any fixed 12–month "leave year," such as a fiscal year, or a year starting on an employee's "anniversary" date;

- The 12-month period measured forward from the date any employee's first FMLA leave begins;
- A "rolling" 12-month period measured backward from the date an employee uses any FMLA leave.

Davis v. Michigan Bell Tel. Co., No. 06-10513, 2007 U.S. Dist. LEXIS 18940, at *6 (E.D. Mich. March 19, 2007); *Price v. Diamond Services Co.*, No. CIV-05-1081-M, 2006 U.S. Dist. LEXIS 87687, at *7-8 (W.D. Okla. Dec. 4, 2006); *Sjoblom v. Jersey Shore Med. Center*, No. 05-1042 (SC), 2006 U.S. Dist. LEXIS 27467, at *7-8 (D. N.J. May 4, 2006); *Dortman v. ACO Hardware, Inc.*, 405 F. Supp. 2d 812, 820 (E.D. Mich. June 14, 2005); *Bofield v. Nebraska Pork Partners*, No. 4:05CV3218, 2006 U.S. Dist. LEXIS 18532, at *7 (D. Neb. April 5, 2006); *Hill v. Underwood Mem. Hosp.*, 365 F. Supp. 2d 602, 606 (D.N.J. April 20, 2005); *Sabatino v. Flik International Corp.*, 286 F. Supp. 2d 327, 336 (S.D.N.Y. 2003); *Panto v. Palmer Dialysis Center/Total Renal Care*, No. 01-6013, 2003 U.S. Dist. LEXIS 5663, at *17 (E.D. Pa. April 7, 2003).

a. Calendar and Other Fixed Leave Years

Under a calendar or other fixed 12-month leave year plan, an employee is entitled up to 12 weeks of FMLA leave at any time in the fixed 12-month leave year. 29 CFR 825.200(c); S. Res. 242, Cong. Rec. S3959, S3963-64 (April 23, 1996); 29 CFR 825.200(c). If a calendar year is selected, the 12-month FMLA leave year begins on January 1 of each year. Under a fixed year method, an employer simply selects any 12-month period as the FMLA leave year. In addition to a calendar year, examples of a fixed leave year include a fiscal year (September 1 to October 31) and an employee's anniversary date.

The calendar or other fixed year method allows an employee to stack FMLA leave and take up to 24 consecutive weeks of leave. 29 CFR 825.200(c); S. Res. 242, Cong. Rec. S3959, S3963-64 (April 23, 1996); 29 CFR 825.200(c); *see Bachelder v. America West Airlines, Inc.*, 259 F.3d 1112, 1126 (9th Cir. 2001); *Gentry v. Data Core, Inc.*, No. 06-2218-CN, 2006 U.S. Dist. LEXIS 68577, at *5-6 (D. Kan. Sept. 22, 2006); *McKiernan v. Smith-Edwards-Dunlap Co. et al.*, No. 95-1175, 1995 U.S. Dist. LEXIS 6822 at *4 (E.D. Pa. May 17, 1995); DOL WH FMLA Advisory Opinion No. 74 (Oct. 30, 1995).

For example, Jay works for the Postal Service, which has a fixed 12-month leave year for FMLA purposes. Jay suffered injuries requiring an extended hospital stay and recuperation. Jay, who is an eligible employee, requests 12 weeks of FMLA leave to commence at the end of this leave year and continue through the first 12 weeks at the beginning of next FMLA leave year. This stacking of FMLA leave by taking leave straddling the end of one leave year and the beginning of the next fixed leave year is permitted under the rules. *See Bachelder v. America West Airlines, Inc.*, 259 F.3d 1112, 1126 (9th Cir. 2001) ("For example, an employee whose employer had adopted the calendar year method could, consistently with the Act, take 12 weeks of leave at the end of the leave year and 12 weeks of leave at the beginning of leave year."). Again, an eligible employee is entitled to 12 workweeks of FMLA leave each leave year.

The calendar or other fixed leave year method is generally the easiest to administer, particularly where the fixed year is something other than an individual employee's anniversary date. However, the ability to stack FMLA leave to take 24 weeks of continuous leave makes a calendar or fixed leave year less desirable for federal employers. Conversely, employees and their representatives might enjoy the greater leave benefits available by being able to stack leave at the end of one leave year and the beginning of the next.

b. Measuring Forward Leave Year

Under the measured forward method, the 12-month FMLA leave year begins on the first date FMLA leave is taken. 29 CFR 825.200(c); S. Res. 242, Cong. Rec. S3959, S3963-64 (April 23, 1996); 29 CFR 825.200(c); *accord Sabatino v. Flik International Corp.*, 286 F. Supp. 2d 327, 336-337(S.D. N.Y. 2003). The next leave year begins on the first occasion that the employee takes FMLA leave following completion of the current leave year.

For example, Lori Weber is an eligible Title I employee with the Forest Service. On March 15, 2002, she takes her first FMLA leave. Under the measuring forward method, her FMLA leave year begins on March 15, 2002, and will run until March 14, 2003. Her next leave year will begin the first day, after March 14, 2003, in which she uses FMLA leave.

Like fixed leave years, the measuring forward method allows an employee to stack FMLA leave over two leave years, although to a more limited degree. *See* DOL WH FMLA Advisory Opinion No. 74 (Oct. 30, 1995). The limitation is that the first FMLA absence sets the leave year. Therefore, two absences are necessary in order for there to be FMLA leave straddling two leave years.

In our example above, Lori's initial taking of FMLA leave on March 15 sets the leave year as March 15, 2002, to March 14, 2003. If Lori took all 12 weeks of FMLA leave in a row beginning March 15, she would not have any more FMLA leave as of March 14, 2003, to stack with her next 12 weeks of FMLA leave beginning with her first FMLA absence after March 14, 2003. If, however, she were to take only a day of FMLA leave on March 15, 2002, and she took no other FMLA leave, Lori would have 11 weeks and four days worth of FMLA leave she could use in the period immediately preceding March 14, 2004. If she were eligible and entitled to FMLA leave beginning March 15, 2003, she could use up to 12 weeks of FMLA leave. Although she could not assemble 24 consecutive weeks of FMLA leave under the measuring forward method as under the fixed or calendar leave method, she could come very close.

Because it is customized for each eligible employee, the measuring forward method is more difficult to administer than other methods. This creates headaches for both agencies and employees. On the other hand, because it allows the stacking of FMLA leave straddling two leave years, employees generally benefit from application of the measuring forward method.

The measured forward method is the exclusive method for fixing the 12-month leave year for employees covered by Title II of the Act. In the absence of an employer election to apply another method, employees covered by Title I of the FMLA in federal agencies predominately staffed with Title II covered employees may be subject to the measuring forward method; a further benefit to these employees. This issue is addressed in more detail below.

c. Rolling Back Method

The only method that prevents employee leave stacking is the rolling back method. Under the rolling back 12-month period, each time an employee takes FMLA leave the remaining leave entitlement will be any balance of the 12 weeks not used during the immediately preceding 12 months. *Batchelder v. America West Airlines, Inc.*, 259 F.3d 1112, 1126 (9th Cir. 2001); *Smith v. Medpointe Healthcare, Inc.*, No. 04-cv-6315 (PGS), 2007 U.S. Dist. LEXIS 10471, a *10 & n.2 (D. N.J. Feb. 15, 2007); *Russell v. Verizon Communications, Inc.*, No. 01-CV-0752A, 2007 U.S. Dist. LEXIS 16779, at *15-16 (W.D.N.Y. Jan. 30, 2007), adopted, summ. judgment granted, 2007 U.S. Dist. LEXIS 11721 (W.D.N.Y. Feb. 20, 2007); *Chrisman v. Rapid-Line, Inc.*, No. 1:04-CV-509, 2005 U.S. Dist. LEXIS 43664, at *2-3 (W.D. Mich. June 21, 2005); *Smith v. ACO, Inc.*, 368 F. Supp. 2d 721, 725 (E.D. Mich. April 22, 2005); *Plato v. Palmer Dialysis Center/Total Renal Care*, No. 01–6013, 2003 U.S. Dist. LEXIS 5663, at 18–19 (E.D. Pa. April 7, 2003).

For example, if an employee takes eight weeks of leave during the past 12 months, an additional four weeks of leave could be taken. If an employee used four weeks beginning February 1, 2000, four weeks beginning June 1, 2000, and four weeks beginning December 1, 2000, the employee would not be entitled to any additional leave until February 1, 2001. However, beginning on February 1, 2001, the employee would be entitled to four weeks of leave, on June 1, 2001, and so on. 29 CFR 825.200(c); S. Res. 242, Cong. Rec. S3959, S3963–64 (April 23, 1996); 29 CFR 825.200(c).

The rolling back method was described by the DOL as a "snapshot of the 12-month period that changes daily" (i.e., as each new day is added to the 12-month period, one day from 12-months ago is eliminated). Preamble, 29 CFR 825.200. The DOL went on to note that "[w]hile many comments were received opposing this method, it has been retained as one of the available options because it is the one method that most literally tracks the statutory language." *Id.*

The rolling back method is somewhat difficult to administer and fairly confusing for employees. It is, however, the only method available that prevents employee stacking of FMLA leave. Employers that are interested in controlling long periods of absenteeism should seriously consider electing this option. Organizations representing employees, on the other hand, will want to avoid application of this method in order to provide greater benefits to employees.

2. Uniform Application

Employers are allowed to choose any one of the four alternative methods provided the alternative chosen is applied consistently and uniformly to all employees. 29 CFR 825.200(d)(1); S. Res. 242, Cong. Rec. S3959, S3963–64 (April 23, 1996); 29 CFR 825.200(d)(1); see *Hunt v. Rapides Healthcare System, LLC*, 277 F.3d 757, 765 (5th Cir. 2001); *Bachelder v. America West Airlines, Inc.*, 259 F.3d 1112, 1126 (9th Cir. 2001); *Dortman v. ACO Hardware, Inc.*, 405 F. Supp. 2d 812, 820 (E.D. Mich. June 14, 2005); *Hill v. Underwood Mem. Hosp.*, 365 F. Supp. 2d 602, 606 (D. N.J. April 20, 2005); *Dodaro v. Village of Glendale Heights*, No. 01-C-6396, 2003 U.S. Dist. LEXIS 5056, at *18 (N.D. Ill. March 31, 2002); *Phillips v. Leroy-Somer North America et al.*, No. 01–1046, 2003 U.S. Dist. LEXIS 5349, at *12 (W.D. Tenn. March 28, 2003); *Karnes v. Central Texas*

Mental Health–Mental Retardation Center, No. 6:01–CV–045–C, 2002 U.S. Dist. LEXIS 2951, at *11 (N.D. Tex. Feb. 22, 2002); *McKiernan v. Smith–Edwards–Dunlap Co. et al.*, No. 95–1175, 1995 U.S. Dist. LEXIS 6822, at *4–*6 (E.D. Pa. May 17, 1995); DOL WH FMLA Advisory Opinion No. 88 (Dec. 13, 1996).

3. Changing the 12-Month Period

Employers may change from one alternative method of calculating the 12–month period to any of the other approved methods. 29 CFR 825.200(d)(1); S. Res. 242, Cong. Rec. S3959, S3963–64 (April 23, 1996); 29 CFR 825.200(d)(1). *See Dodaro v. Village of Glendale Heights*, No. 01–C–6396, 2003 U.S. Dist. LEXIS 5056, at *18 (N.D. Ill. March 31, 2003). An employer wishing to change to another alternative method is required to give at least 60–days notice to all employees, and the transition must take place in such a way that the employees retain the full benefit of 12 weeks of leave under which ever method affords the greatest benefit to the employee. 29 CFR 825.200(d)(1); S. Res. 242, Cong. Rec. S3959, S3963–64 (April 23, 1996); 29 CFR 825.200(d)(1).

It is unclear from the language employed in the regulation which of the four alternative methods is considered to determine which provides the "greatest benefit" to the employee during the transition period from one alternative to the next. One would think that this determination is decided by comparing the old and new methods for calculating the 12–month period. The regulatory language, however, is susceptible to an interpretation suggesting that all methods for calculating the 12–month period (i.e., whichever method), not just the two directly involved in the transition, may be considered in determining which provides the greatest benefits to the employee. Although the matter is not clarified in the preamble to the final DOL regulations, this interpretation would make little sense as it would effectively impose an unintended third 12–month period during the 60–day transition from one identified method of calculation to another.

Under no circumstances may a new method be implemented in order to avoid the Act's leave requirements. 29 CFR 825.200(d)(1); S. Res. 242, Cong. Rec. S3959, S3963–64 (April 23, 1996); 29 CFR 825.200(d)(1); *see Dodaro v. Village of Glendale Heights*, No. 01–C–6396, 2003 U.S. Dist. LEXIS 5056, at *18 (N.D. Ill. March 31, 2003). A comment noted in the Preamble to the final DOL regulations suggests that this provision was intended to prevent employers from switching methods to deny employees FMLA leave. Preamble, 29 CFR 825.200.

The inclusion of this provision limiting an employer's right to switch methods for calculating the 12–month period is somewhat perplexing. An employer that switches to the rolling back method from any of the other three methods, or from having no identified method to any of the four identified methods will, as a matter of course, avoid some of the Act's greater leave requirements. Switching from a fixed or measured forward method to the rolling back method will avoid the requirement that employees are allowed to stack FMLA leave straddling two leave years. In fact, that is precisely why an employer would want to switch.

Presumably, the limitation is restricted to situations where an employer is switching methodologies to avoid granting a particular employee FMLA leave. The time and expense of such a move would appear to make such an employer motivation slim, particularly in the federal sector. Otherwise, as generally applied, the restriction would effectively eliminate all changes to the method of calculating the 12–month period, because any change may adversely affect an employee's right to take FMLA leave under the more generous provisions of the existing scheme, if any.

4. Notice of the Option Selected

The extent of an employer's duty to inform employees what method it chooses to calculate the 12–month FMLA leave year period is unclear. What follows will examine the notice obligation at three points in time: (1) the initial selection; (2) notice on the occasion of a request for FMLA leave; and (3) notice when a change in the method of calculation is made. Finally, we will examine the method of notification.

a. Initial Selection

The regulations do not specifically provide that an employer must notify its employees of the method initially selected to calculate the 12–month FMLA leave year. *Bachelder v. America West Airlines, Inc.*, 259 F.3d 1112, 1127 (9th Cir. 2001) ("The regulations allow employers to choose among four methods for calculating their employees' eligibility for FMLA leave, but they do not specifically state how an employer indicates its choice."); *Phillips v. Leroy–Somer North America et al.*, No. 01–1046–T, 2003 U.S. Dist. LEXIS 5349, at *12 (W.D. Tenn. March 28, 2003) ("[N]o notice of the method initially selected is required."); *Dodaro v. Village of Glendale Heights*, No. 01–C–6396, 2003 U.S. Dist. LEXIS 5056, at *18–*19 (N.D. Ill. March 31, 2003) ("Section 825.200 itself does not delineate the particular means by which the employer may elect one of the methods of counting the 12–month period."). Notwithstanding the absence of specific statutory or regulatory language requiring an employer to notify an employee of the method selected for the calculation of the 12–month FMLA year, some courts have found such an obligation. Others have come to the opposite conclusion.

The leading case in this area is the Ninth Circuit's decision in *Bachelder v. America West Airlines, Inc.*, 259 F.3d 1112 (9th Cir. 2001). After initially acknowledging that the regulations do not specifically require that employees be informed of an employer's initial selection, the court went on to hold that such notice was nevertheless required. Specifically, the court held that the initial selection of a method for calculating the FMLA leave year must be an open—not a secret—one before it can be applied to an employee's disadvantage. *Id.* at 1128.

In rendering its decision, the court relied heavily on the general employer notice requirement contained in 29 CFR 825.301(a)(1). This regulation requires employers with eligible employees to include information concerning FMLA entitlements and employee obligations into any written guidance the employer may have on employee benefits and leave, such as in an employee handbook. Citing several other provisions that allow employer choice in how to comply with the statute, the court noted that the purpose of the general notice provision, as expressed by the DOL, was to "provide employees the opportunity to learn from their employers of the manner in which that employer intends to implement FMLA and what company policies and procedures are applicable so that employees may make FMLA plans fully aware of their rights and obligations." *Id.* at 1127 (citing Preamble, 29 CFR 301, 60 Fed. Reg. at 2219).

The court also relied on its reading of the regulations as a whole, particularly those regulations that did explicitly require employer notification of the method selected for calculating the 12–month FMLA leave year. *Id.* at 1128. The court concluded that the two instances where the regulations do require an employer to notify employees of the method of leave year calculation (a change in the method of calculation or where the employer initially failed to select a method and now wants to select an option) presuppose the awareness of the employee of the leave year method currently in use. As stated by the court, "notifying employees of a change of methods is only meaningful if they are aware that another method was previously in use." *Id.*

Concluding that specific notice of the method chosen to calculate the FMLA leave year was required, the Ninth Circuit opined that the notice requirements "would be meaningless if the regulations…allowed employers to conceal the initial selection from their employees," and that "employees cannot reasonably act in reliance on an employer's initial policy choice if the choice was kept secret from them." *Id.*

Since the decision of the Ninth Circuit in *Bachelder*, two district courts (both from outside the Ninth Circuit) have had the opportunity to address this issue, reaching different conclusions.

Expanding on the lead of the Ninth Circuit, the court in *Dodaro v. Village of Glendale Heights*, No. 01–CC–6396, 2003 U.S. Dist. LEXIS 5056 (N.D. Ill. March 31, 2003), held that an employer's failure to include notification of the method selected for calculating the 12–month leave year in the employee handbook as required by the general notice provision of 29 CFR 825.301(a)(1) amounted to an improper election. The district court was not swayed, moreover, by the fact that the employer provided the employee with a separate written document stating the employer's FMLA leave policy, including an express statement that the rolling method would be used in determining eligibility for FMLA leave. *Dodaro*, 2003 U.S. Dist. LEXIS 5056, at *22. The document was provided to the employee both when the policy was first instituted and when she first applied for FMLA leave.

The court's decision rests on a parsing of the wording of 29 CFR 825.301(a)(1). In pertinent part, that regulation provides, "if [there is] any written guidance, such as in an employee handbook or other document." This, the court opined, could be read as meaning that, if a handbook exists, it is sufficient to include the information in either "the handbook or other document." Alternatively, it could mean that, if there is a handbook, the information must be in the handbook, whereas if there is no handbook, but some other type of document that constitutes written guidance, the information must be in that other document. The court concluded that "[t]o be consistent with a goal of enabling employees to stay aware of the applicable rules, the regulation should be construed as requiring that the election be incorporated in a permanent written document such as a handbook, not simply conveyed in what could be a one-time, stand-alone "other document." Finding that the employer did not properly elect the rolling method and citing to 29 CFR 825.200(e), the court held that the method more favorable to plaintiff must be employed.

The district court in *Phillips v. Leroy-Somer North America et al.*, No. 01-1046-T, 2003 U.S. Dist. LEXIS 5349 (W.D. Tenn. March 28, 2003), reached a different conclusion. In that case, plaintiff argued that her employer failed to provide her with the required notice of the method that it chose to use in calculating the FMLA leave year, and that such failure constituted actionable interference with her FMLA rights. The plaintiff was out on maternity leave from September 28, 1998, until February 22, 1999, a twenty-two week period. Pursuant to company policy, maternity leave ran concurrently with FMLA leave. On her return she was placed in a position with less pay, prompting her claim that the new position was not equivalent to the one she had when she went on leave.

Her employer argued that it did not violate the Act by placing her in this position on her return because the plaintiff had no FMLA rights at that point. She had no FMLA rights because it was undisputed that she was unable to return to work at the end of her 12 weeks of leave, and therefore, her employer had no FMLA duty to return her to the same or an equivalent position when she did return to work. The plaintiff appears to have argued that, pursuant to *Bachelder*, the failure to notify her of the method of calculating the FMLA leave year is the equivalent of failing to select a method. By operation of the regulations, she is entitled to the option that provides the most beneficial outcome for the employee. 29 CFR 825.200(e). Excluding the two weeks when the plant was shut down (29 CFR 825.200(f)), the plaintiff's original 12 weeks of FMLA leave expired in early January 1999. Applying the calendar year method, the plaintiff is entitled to another 12 weeks of FMLA leave, which would take her through her return on February 22, 1999.

Disagreeing with the Ninth Circuit in *Bachelder*, the district court opined that 29 CFR 825.301(a)(1) "does not go so far as to require the specific notice to which the Ninth Circuit refers." The court went on to note the absence of evidence suggesting that the plaintiff's employer concealed its method of calculating the FMLA leave year, or kept it secret from its employees. Furthermore, the court continued, there was no evidence that the plaintiff mistakenly believed, at that time, that she is entitled to an additional twelve weeks of FMLA leave beginning January 1, 1999. The court concluded:

> Finally, there is no evidence that [the] plaintiff would have, or could have, returned to work any sooner than she did, regardless of Magnetek's method of calculating her FMLA leave. Thus, there is no evidence that [the] plaintiff suffered any prejudice because of Magnetek's lack of notice regarding the method it selected.

With all due respect, if notice of the method of calculation initially selected by the employer is required, and the absence of such notice constitutes a failure to make an election, then the plaintiff was prejudiced by the outcome. In the absence of an employer election of the method of leave year calculation, the regulations require that the most beneficial method be applied. Applying the calendar year method, the plaintiff's return to work on February 22 was well within the 12-week entitlement for that year. As a result, her employer would have been obligated to give her back the same or an equivalent job, which it did not. The decision is a likely candidate for reversal on appeal, provided the Sixth Circuit (the appellate court covering Tennessee) agrees with the Ninth Circuit that the general employer notice provision includes notification of the initial method selected by the employer for the calculation of the leave year.

In *Sabatino v. Flik International Corp.*, 286 F. Supp. 2d 327, 336 (S.D.N.Y. 2003), the court rejected plaintiff's argument that her employer's FMLA policy was ambiguous as to when the 12-month period begins by reference to the following language in the company's written FMLA policy: "once it is determined that the associate qualifies for a leave of absence he/she will be provided up to sixteen (16) weeks of unpaid leave in the twelve (12) month period, *beginning from the first day of the schedule [sic] leave*." The court characterized the emphasized language as clearly indicating "that the twelve-month period is measured forward from the date FMLA leave begins. Plaintiff cannot now argue that one could reasonably interpret it to mean a calendar year."

An employee's prior knowledge of the method of calculation as a result of prior use of FMLA leave provided the employee with adequate notice of the FMLA leave year selected by the employer. *Sjoblom v. Jersey Shore Med. Center*, No. 05-1042 (SC), 2006 U.S. Dist. LEXIS 27467, at *7-8 (D.N.J. May 4, 2006) (noting that the Third Circuit had not spoken on the issue of notice addressed in *Bachelder*); accord *Hill v. Underwood Mem. Hosp.*, 365 F. Supp. 2d 602, 609 (D.N.J. April 20, 2005).

b. Notice at the Time FMLA Leave is Requested

It is unclear whether an employer must also notify employees of the applicable method for determining the 12-month period for FMLA leave when informing employees of their FMLA rights. The lack of clarity on this issue stems from the absence of such language in the notice regulations, but inclusion of such a requirement in the DOL's Preamble comments to the notice regulations.

The regulations require employers to provide written notice to employees detailing the specific expectations and obligations of the employee and explaining any consequences of a failure to meet these obligations. 29 CFR 825.301(b)(1); S. Res. 242, Cong. Rec. S3959, S3971 (April 23, 1996); 29 CFR 825.301(b)(1). The regulation fails to specifically provide that the method selected by the employer for the calculation of the FMLA leave year must be addressed as part of this notice. However, in light of the Ninth Circuit's parsing of the wording of regulations in *Bachelder*, it is noted that one of the required topics for this notice is that "the leave will be counted against the employee's annual FMLA leave entitlement (see § 825.208)." 29 CFR 825.301(b)(1)(I); S. Res. 242, Cong. Rec. S3959, S3971 (April 23, 1996); 29 CFR 825.301(b)(1)(I). An argument could be made that provision of the required information would only be useful to employees if they knew which methodology was applied with respect to annual FMLA leave entitlement. Stay tuned.

The potential that the written notice required by § 825.301(b)(1) includes notice of the methodology selected by the employer for calculating the FMLA leave year is buttressed by language contained in the Preamble to the final DOL regulations implementing Title I. There, the DOL affirmatively states, "[e]mployers must inform employees of the applicable method for determining FMLA leave entitlement when informing employees of their FMLA rights." Preamble, 29 CFR 825.200. As discussed more fully in Chapter 8, "Notice Requirements," the employer's obligations to inform employees of their FMLA rights are contained in 29 CFR 825.300, 825.301; S. Res. 242, Cong. Rec. S3959, S3971 (April 23, 1996); 29 CFR 825.301. Those regulations provide for the communication of FMLA rights and responsibilities by posting, inclusion in any written handbook, manual or other documents explaining employee benefits and leave, and the provision of individual notices to employees requesting FMLA leave.

To be on the safe side, employers are well-advised to review their 825.300(b)(1) FMLA leave notices to ensure they contain language identifying the methodology used to calculate the 12-month FMLA leave year.

Note that the district court in *Dodaro v. Village of Glendale Heights*, No. 01–C–6396, 2003 U.S. Dist. LEXIS 5056 (N.D. Ill. March 31, 1998), held that where an employee has a handbook or manual, the obligation to notify an employee of the methodology selected for calculation of the leave year is not satisfied solely by giving the employee individual written notice of the methodology employed. In addition to the § 825.300(b)(1) notice, employers should modify their exiting employee handbook, manual or other written documents setting forth benefit and leave policies to identify the method for calculating the FMLA leave year.

In *Sabatino v. Flik International Corp.*, 286 F. Supp. 2d 327, 336 (S.D.N.Y. 2003), the court rejected plaintiff's argument that her employer's FMLA policy was ambiguous on the method elected to calculate the 12-month FMLA leave period based on the inclusion of language in the company's written FMLA policy electing the measured-forward method, and direction that plaintiff consult such policy in the letter approving her request FMLA leave.

c. Change of Methodology

In two instances, the regulations specifically require an employer to notify employees of the methodology elected by the employer for the calculation of the FMLA leave year. *Bachelder v. America West Airlines, Inc.*, 259 F.3d 1112, 1128 (9th Cir. 2001). An employer is required to notify all employees of the method used to calculate the 12-month base period for FMLA leave when the employer is changing from one method to another. 29 CFR 825.200(d)(1); S. Res. 242, Cong. Rec. S3959, S3963–64 (April 23, 1996); 29 CFR 825.200(d)(1). Similarly, if an employer initially failed to select one of the four options, the employer may subsequently select an option only by providing 60-days notice to all employees of the option the employer intends to implement. 29 CFR 825.200(e); S. Res. 242, Cong. Rec. S3959, S3963–64 (April 23, 1996); 29 CFR 825.200(e).

d. Means and Adequacy of Notice

The regulations fail to indicate what constitutes adequate notice of the employer's selection of the method used to calculate the 12-month leave year. Adequate notice refers to the content, timing, and means of notification. The case law, however, provides some guidance.

Simply parroting the statutory language is insufficient notice of the methodology selected for the calculation of the 12-month leave year, according to the Ninth Circuit. For example, in *Bachelder*, 259 F.3d at 1129, the Ninth Circuit held that the following language contained in the employee handbook failed to adequately inform employees that America West selected the rolling leave year method: "entitled to up to [12] calendar weeks of unpaid FMLA leave within any [12] month period." According to the court, because the regulation permits employers to use any of four calculating methods, "merely parroting the statutory language cannot possibly inform employees of the method the employer has chosen. By paraphrasing the statutory language, in other words, America West has done no more than announce its intention to comply with the Act." Because it failed to adequately inform employees of the calculating method it selected in the employee handbook as required by 29 CFR 825.301(a)(1), the court held that America West failed to select a calculating method. By operation of 29 CFR 825.200(e), the court applied the option that provided the most beneficial outcome for the employee.

Actual written notice of the leave year method selected by the employer has been held inadequate due to the means of notification. In *Dodaro v. Village of Glendale Heights*, Case No 01–C–6396, 2003 U.S. Dist. LEXIS 5056 (N.D. Ill. March 31, 2003), the employee manual stated that "an employee is entitled to leave of absence without pay in accordance with the terms of the FMLA." Separately, both at the time the employer elected the rolling method and when the employee first applied for FMLA leave, the employee was provided with a written document specifically advising the employee that the rolling method would be used in determining eligibility for FMLA leave. Despite actual notice before and at the time of her first request for FMLA leave (eight months earlier than the leave at issue), the district court nevertheless held that the employer failed to adequately inform the employee of the method elected to calculate the FMLA leave year. The court based its decision on this interpretation of the general notice provisions of 29 CFR 825.301(a)(1), requiring adequate notice in the employee manual as a permanent record of the policy. Because the employee manual did not identify the rolling leave year as the applicable method for calculating the FMLA leave year, by operation of the regulations, the court applied the method more favorable to the employee.

It is doubtful that the Ninth Circuit would agree with the decision of the district court in *Dodaro*. The focus of the Ninth Circuit was that the employer's selection of one of the four calculation methods would be open and known to employees, not a secret. *Bachelder*, 259 F.3d at 1127. If an employee was informed of the method for calculating the leave year "before it can be applied to an employee's disadvantage," the Ninth Circuit would not find a violation. Actual written notice to an employee of the leave year method used by the employer prior to the use of FMLA leave would appear to satisfy that condition.

Employers should include clear statements in any employee handbook or manual identifying the method used to calculate the FMLA leave year. A clear statement would identify the method selected, and repeat verbatim the DOL regulation defining or describing that method. Inclusion of an accurate example of the operation of the method (preferably the example would be taken directly from the regulations), particularly if the measured forward or rolling back methods are selected, should seriously be considered.

If the employer does not have an employee handbook or manual but does have other written guidance to employees concerning employee benefits or leave rights, by operation of 29 CFR 825.301(a)(1), information regarding FMLA entitlements and obligations, including the method selected for calculating the FMLA leave year, should be included in those documents and distributed to employees. The regulations fail to define or otherwise describe what constitutes written guidance regarding employee benefits and leave. Employers are well-advised to interpret "written guidance" broadly.

Even in the slim chance that an employer does not have written guidance describing employee benefits and leave provisions, it must still provide written guidance to employees on their FMLA rights and obligations. 29 CFR 825.301(a)(2). Given the interpretation taken by the *Bachelder* and *Dodaro* courts of 825.301(a)(1), it is highly likely that 825.301(a)(2) will be interpreted to include written guidance on the method selected by the employer to calculate the leave year.

Finally, as indicated above, employers are well advised to identify the method selected to calculate the leave year in the notice required by 29 CFR 825.301(b)(1).

5. Failure to Select One of the Four Options

If an employer fails to select one of the four options for measuring the 12–month period, the option that provides the most beneficial outcome for the employee will be used. 29 CFR 825.200(e); S. Res. 242, Cong. Rec. S3959, S3964 (April 23, 1996); 29 CFR 825.200(e); accord *Hunt v. Rapides Healthcare System, LLC*, 277 F.3d 757, 765 (5th Cir. 2001); *Roberts v. Ground Handling, Inc.*, No. 04 Civ. 4955 (WCC), 2007 U.S. Dist. LEXIS 23441, at *34, 36 (S.D.N.Y. March 30, 2007); *Price v. Diamond Services Co.*, No. CIV-05-1081-M, 2006 U.S. Dist. LEXIS 87687, at *7-8 (W.D. Okla. Dec. 4, 2006); *Gentry v. Data Core, Inc.*, No. 06-2218-CN, 2006 U.S. Dist. LEXIS 68577, at *6 (D. Kan. Sept. 22, 2006); *Bofield v. Nebraska Pork Partners*, No.

4:05CV3218, 2006 U.S. Dist. LEXIS 18532, at *7 (D. Neb. April 5, 2006); *Hill v. Underwood Mem. Hosp.*, 365 F. Supp. 2d 602, 606 (D.N.J. April 20, 2005).

The Ninth Circuit in *Bachelder v. America West Airlines, Inc.*, 259 F.3d 1112, 1126 (9th Cir. 2001), offered the following rationale where an employer failed to select a method for calculating the 12-month FMLA leave year:

> By preventing employers from calculating FMLA leave eligibility in their own favor on an *ad hoc*, employee-by-employee basis, the "leave year" regulation encourages the employer to choose its calculating method prospectively. By doing so, the regulation not only prevents unfairness to employees, through retroactive manipulation of the "leave year," but also encourages a system under which both employees and employers can plan for future leaves in an orderly fashion.

The rules permit an employer that initially failed to elect one of the four methods for calculating the "leave year" to subsequently select an option. This selection, however, is conditioned on the employer providing the 60-day notice to all employees of the option the employer intends to implement. 29 CFR 825.200(e); S. Res. 242, Cong. Rec. S3959, S3964 (April 23, 1996); 29 CFR 825.200(e). During the running of the 60-day period, any other employee who needs FMLA leave may use the option providing the most beneficial outcome to that employee. 29 CFR 825.200(e); S. Res. 242, Cong. Rec. S3959, S3964 (April 23, 1996); 29 CFR 825.200(e). At the conclusion of the 60-day period, the employer may implement the selected option. 29 CFR 825.200(e); S. Res. 242, Cong. Rec. S3959, S3964 (April 23, 1996); 29 CFR 825.200(e).

One court held that the failure of an employer to select one of the four methods for calculating the 12-month leave period did not create actionable substantive rights. In *Krohn v. Forsting et al.*, 11 F. Supp. 2d 1082, 1092 (E.D. Mo. 1998), the district court found that the plaintiff was not entitled to FMLA leave to care for her son who did not have a serious health condition, because the entitlement expired one year after the son's birth. The court rejected the plaintiff's assertion that the failure of her employer to select a method for calculating the 12-month leave year somehow gave her the right to leave or, in the alternative, an independent cause of action.

In *Roberts v. Ground Handling, Inc.*, No. 04 Civ. 4955 (WCC), 2007 U.S. Dist. LEXIS 23441, at *35-36 (S.D.N.Y. March 30, 2007), the employer did not initially select the method for calculating the 12-month FMLA leave year. The court found that the calendar leave year method was the most beneficial. Applying that method, the court found that the employee had 6 weeks of FMLA leave available for the remainder of the calendar year. The court opined that an employee must use the same method for calculating eligibility as it does to determine leave entitlement to determine which method secures the best result for the employee.

In *Price v. Diamond Services Co.*, No. CIV-05-1081-M, 2006 U.S. Dist. LEXIS 87687, at *7-8 (W.D. Okla. Dec. 4, 2006), the employer failed to select a method for calculating the 12-month FMLA leave year. After applying four methods, the court concluded that the employee was not eligible for FMLA leave for the absence at issue and, therefore, did not have the FMLA right to return to work at the conclusion of his absence.

6. Expiration of 12-Month Period for Birth or Placement for Adoption or Foster Care

Title I, the CAA, and the PEOAA treat the expiration of the 12-month period differently from Title II regarding the birth or placement with the employee of a son or daughter for adoption or foster care.

Like its counterpart in Title II, the leave entitlement of an employee covered by Title I, the CAA, and the PEOAA for the birth or placement for adoption or foster care of a son or daughter expires at the end of the 12-month period beginning on the date of the birth or placement. 29 USC 2612(a)(2); 29 CFR 825.201; S. Res. 242, Cong. Rec. S3959, S3964 (April 23, 1996); 29 CFR 825.201; see *Krohn v. Forsting et al.*, 11 F. Supp. 2d 1082, 1092-1093 (E.D. Mo. 1998). Any such FMLA leave must be concluded within this one-year period. 29 CFR 825.201; S. Res. 242, Cong. Rec. S3959, S3964 (April 23, 1996); 29 CFR 825.201. Also like Title II, prenatal and pre-placement leave is available. 29 CFR 825.112(c); S. Res. 242, Cong. Rec. S3959, S3962 (April 23, 1996); 29 CFR 825.112(c).

Unlike Title II, even if prenatal or pre-placement leave is used, the 12-month period runs from the date of the birth or placement. Preamble, 29 CFR 825.201 (no authority exists to shorten the statutory 12-month period under the regulations where an employee begins leave for the birth or placement prior to the actual birth or placement). Under Title II, the 12-month period would begin to run on the date an employee used prenatal or pre-placement leave, not the actual birth date.

Because the 12-month period is measured from the actual date of birth or placement regardless of whether prenatal or pre-placement leave is used, an employee must use all of his or her leave entitlement for these covered conditions before the expiration of the 12-month period or the unused leave is lost. For example, an employee who waits ten months from the date of birth to take FMLA leave to bond with a newborn or newly adopted child will have lost approximately four weeks of available FMLA leave. An employee cannot extend the 12-week period by simply beginning this leave within 12 months of the birth or placement. Preamble 29 CFR 825.201 (no authority exists to provide by regulation that the leave need only begin with the statutory 12-month period). The leave must be concluded (i.e., completed) within the statutory 12-month period from the birth or placement. *Id*. This is a "use it or lose it" regulation.

In *Bocalbos v. National Western Life Insurance Company*, 162 F.3d 379, 384 (5th Cir. 1998), *cert. denied*, 528 U.S. 872 (1999), the circuit court held that the 12-month period began to run when the children were placed with the employee for adoption, not when the employee actually retrieved the children years later from the country they remained in after the adoption. According to the court, "Congress placed a 12-month limitation on the eligibility so that the period of time for employees to request leave would not be indefinite or too far removed from the actual adoption." *Id*. [Chapter 7, "Covered Conditions," addresses FMLA leave for eligible employees to adopt a son or daughter.]

7. More Generous Employer Policies

The FMLA does not prohibit employers from adopting more generous employer policies regarding family and medical leave benefits. This is true under Title I, Title II, the CAA, and the PEOAA. 29 CFR 825.700(b) (Title I); 5 CFR 630.1210 (Title II); S. Res. 242, Cong. Rec. S3959, S3976 (April 23, 1996); 29 CFR 825.700(b) (CAA). Presumably, this would also apply to the calculation of the 12-month FMLA leave period. For example, under Title I, the CAA, and the PEOAA, an employer interested in changing from one method to another may agree to provide 90 days notice to all employees of the impending change, not the 60 days required by the Act.

C. THE 12-MONTH PERIOD IN AGENCIES WITH MIXED FMLA RESPONSIBILITIES

Federal agencies whose workforce contains a mix of employees covered by Titles I and II of the FMLA have a choice of whether to extend the use of the measured forward method mandated for Title II employees to employees covered by Title I. Assuming that the workforce of most federal agencies is made up of a majority of employees covered by Title II and a minority covered by Title I, agencies must weigh the administrative ease of simply applying the measured forward method to all employees, against the added burden of employee FMLA leave stacking. When given a choice, most employers in the private sector opt for the rolling back method to avoid lengthy absences resulting from employee FMLA leave stacking.

Unions and other organizations representing employees, on the other hand, need to consider the interests of their members. Generally speaking, the rolling back method is least favorable to their membership as it prevents leave stacking. Some employees may need that leave back-to-back to care for ill family members or to recover from their own lengthy FMLA illnesses. As a term and condition of employment, FMLA leave is a required subject of collective bargaining negotiations. Unions should bargain to obtain an FMLA method for calculating the leave year that permits employees to stack FMLA leave. [For a further discussion of this issue, see Chapter 16, "Interaction of the FMLA with Other Federal Laws, Employer Practices, and Collective Bargaining Agreements."]

Another area warranting attention is the difference in treatment regarding the amount of FMLA leave available for the birth or placement for adoption/foster care of a covered son or daughter. Titles I and II have different requirements. Under Title II, the 12-month entitlement to FMLA leave following the birth or placement may begin on the first date prenatal or pre-placement leave is used. Under Title I, the 12-month period begins to run on the date of the actual birth or placement, although prenatal and pre-placement leave are available. An employer, therefore, that began the calculation of the 12-month period of a Title I employee on the date prenatal leave began would violate that employee's FMLA rights.

III. CALCULATING 12 WORKWEEKS OF FMLA LEAVE

The FMLA provides that eligible employees are entitled to a total of 12 weeks of protected FMLA leave during a 12-month leave year for one or more covered conditions. This section addresses the amount (hours) of FMLA leave available within those 12 weeks, and the way leave is counted in order to ensure that an eligible employee receives all of the FMLA leave he or she is entitled to during the 12-month leave year.

A. BASIC CALCULATION OF THE AMOUNT OF LEAVE AVAILABLE

Although the FMLA provides for 12 weeks of leave during a 12-month period, the exact number of hours of leave available to an eligible federal employee is determined on a case-by-case basis for each employee. While the terms used by Title I, Title II, the CAA, and the PEOAA differ somewhat they share a great deal in common.

1. Title II

Title II provides that an employee is entitled to a total of 12 administrative workweeks of leave during any 12-month period for a covered condition. 5 USC 6382(a)(1); 5 CFR 630.1203(a). The 12 administrative workweeks of leave are available to both full- and part-time employees equally in direct proportion to the number of hours in an employee's regularly scheduled administrative workweek. 5 CFR 630.1203(e). The 12 administrative workweeks of leave are calculated on an hourly basis and equal 12 times the average number of hours in the employee's regularly scheduled administrative workweek. *Id.*

a. Key Terms

The key terms "administrative workweek," "regularly scheduled," and "regularly scheduled administrative workweek" are defined by cross-reference in the OPM regulations implementing Title II of the FMLA. 5 CFR 630.1202. Administrative workweek is defined by reference to the meaning given to that term in 5 CFR 610.102. That section defines "administrative workweek" as meaning any period of seven consecutive 24-hour periods designated in advance by the head of the agency pursuant to 5 USC 6101.

"Regularly scheduled" is defined by cross reference to 5 CFR 610.102, and means work that is scheduled in advance of an administrative workweek under an agency's procedures for establishing workweeks in accordance with § 610.111, 5 CFR 610.111.

A regularly scheduled administrative workweek differs for full- and part-time employees. 5 CFR 630.1202 (cross-referencing 5 CFR 610.102). For a full-time employee, a regularly scheduled administrative workweek means the period within an administrative workweek established pursuant to 5 CFR 610.111, within which the employee is regularly scheduled to work. 5 CFR 610.102. For a part-time employee, it means the officially prescribed days and hours within an administrative workweek during which the employee is regularly scheduled to work. *Id.*

Workweeks are established in accordance with 5 CFR 610.111. There are five different types of workweeks that an agency may establish depending on the circumstances.

An agency must establish for each full-time employee a written policy setting forth a basic workweek of 40 hours extending over six of any seven consecutive days, specifying the days and hours within the administrative workweek that constitute the basic workweek. 5 CFR 610.111(a)(1). The agency must also establish for each full-time employee a written policy statement setting forth a regularly scheduled administrative workweek that consists of the 40-hour basic workweek, plus the period of regular overtime work, if any, required of each employee. 5 CFR 610.111(a)(2). Again, the written agency policy statement must specify the days and hours of each day included in the regularly scheduled administrative workweek that do not constitute the basic workweek. *Id.*

If it is impracticable to prescribe a regular schedule of definite hours of duty for each workday of a regularly scheduled administrative workweek, the agency may establish the first 40 hours of duty performed within not more than six of seven days of the administrative workweek as the basic workweek. 5 CFR 610.111(b). The first 40 hours of work, without specificity as to days and hours of work, is considered the regularly scheduled work for purposes of premium pay and hours of duty purposes. Any additional hours of officially ordered or approved work within the administrative workweek are overtime work hours. *Id.*

When an employee is paid additional pay under § 5545(c)(1) of Title 5, 5 USC 5545(c)(1), the employee's regularly scheduled administrative workweek is the total number of regularly scheduled hours of duty a week. Section 5545 of Title 5 addresses night, standby, irregular, and hazardous duty differential pay. Subsection (c)(1) of § 5545, 5 USC 5545(c)(1), provides that the head of an agency, with the approval of the Office of Personnel Management, may provide that

> an employee in a position requiring him regularly to remain at, or within the confines of, his station during longer than ordinary periods of duty, a substantial part of which consists of remaining in a standby status rather than performing work, shall receive premium pay provided for this duty on an annual basis instead of premium pay provided by other provisions of this subchapter, except for irregular, unscheduled overtime duty in excess of his regularly scheduled weekly tour. Premium pay under this paragraph is determined as an appropriate percentage, not in excess of 25 percent, of such part of the rate of basic pay for the position as does not exceed the minimum rate of basic pay for GS–10 (including any applicable locality–based comparability payment under section 5304 or similar provision of law and any applicable special rate of pay under section 5305 or similar provision of law or, for a position described in section 5542(a)(3) of this title, of the basic pay of the position), by taking into consideration the number of hours of actual work required in the position, the number of hours required in a standby status at or within the confines of the station, the extent to which the duties of the position are made more onerous by night, Sunday, or holiday work, or by being extended over periods of more than 40 hours a week, and other relevant factors.

When an employee has a tour of duty which includes a period during which the employee remains at or within the confines of the employee's station in a standby status rather than performing actual work, the employee's administrative workweek is the total number of regularly scheduled hours of duty a week, including time in a standby status except that allowed for sleep and meals by a written agency policy statement. 5 CFR 610.111(c)(2).

Finally, when an agency establishes a flexible or compressed work schedule under 5 USC 6121 or 6122, the flexible or compressed work schedule is a scheduled tour of duty and all work performed by an employee within the basic work requirement is considered regularly scheduled work for premium pay and hours of duty purposes. 5 CFR 610.111(d).

b. Amount of FMLA Leave Varies from Employee to Employee

Under Title I, although all eligible employees are entitled to 12 workweeks of FMLA leave for a qualifying condition each year, the actual amount (hours) of FMLA leave will vary from one employee to the next. The reason is that the basic calculation of the amount of FMLA leave rests, in part, on the average number of hours in the employee's regularly scheduled workweek, which may vary from one employee to the next.

For example, if employee A's average regularly scheduled workweek were 60 hours a week, employee A is entitled to 720 hours (12 x 60 hours/week) of FMLA leave as his 12–week entitlement during the 12–month leave year. Employee B, who works in the office next to employee A, averages only 40 hours a week during her regularly scheduled administrative workweek. Employee B is entitled to only 480 hours of FMLA leave during the 12–month FMLA leave year.

The agency's choice of which method to use to calculate the employees workweek will determine whether the calculation of available FMLA leave reflects the actual hours the employee worked, or some lesser amount of time. For example, the agency elects to calculate an employee's workweek as a basic workweek of 40 hours, plus a period of regular overtime. This figure, say, 50 hours, is multiplied by 12 to calculate the total number of FMLA leave hours available to the employee, in this case 600 hours. The employee is entitled to 600 hours whether the employee actually worked less time (say, 40 hours), or substantially more time (60 hours). This is because the amount of FMLA leave available is determined by reference to the regularly scheduled administrative workweek, and one of the methods an agency can use to calculate the workweek includes a set period of time.

Under another permissible method for calculation of the workweek, the hours an employee actually works could be used to determine the amount of FMLA leave available. For example, if it is impractical to prescribe a regular schedule of definite hours of duty for each workday of a regularly scheduled administrative workweek, the regulations allow an agency to establish that the first 40 hours is the basic workweek, and anything over that is considered regularly scheduled overtime. Pursuant to this method, the amount of FMLA leave available to an employee would accurately reflect the number of hours actually worked, rather than the hours that the employee was scheduled to work.

Agencies should carefully consider the method they use to calculate an employee's regularly scheduled administrative workweek. Unions and other organizations representing employees would also be well–advised to determine the most beneficial method for calculating the employees' workweek in order to maximize FMLA leave benefits.

c. No Set Limit on Amount of FMLA Leave

The number of hours of FMLA leave available to an employee during the 12-month leave year is only limited based on the employee's average weekly schedule. There is no technical limitation that puts 480 hours or some other number as the upper limit of available FMLA leave. The only limit real limit is the number of hours in a regularly scheduled administrative workweek. For example, an employee who worked 80 hours a week as his or her regularly scheduled administrative workweek would have 960 hours of FMLA leave available during the 12-month FMLA leave year.

d. Deficiencies in Definition

There are at least two major definitional issues resulting from the language used to describe how the amount of FMLA leave is calculated under Title II: (1) the absence of a temporal period to determine the average number of hours in the employee's regularly scheduled administrative workweek; and (2) the point in time at which these calculations are made and how often they may be made.

(1) Absence of Temporal Period

Where an employee's regularly scheduled administrative workweek does not vary, the regulation requires that the number of hours of FMLA leave must be calculated as 12 times the average number of hours in an employee's regularly scheduled administrative workweek. First, if the number of hours does not vary, by definition, all workweeks will have the same hours. There is no need to calculate an average if every week the employee works the exact same number of hours. For example, if employee A works 40 hours as her regularly scheduled administrative workweek and the number of hours never varies, the average number of hours that employee A will work over any time period will be 40 hours a week. Basically, in this context, the term "average" is superfluous.

To the extent the term" average" is not superfluous where an employee's regularly scheduled administrative workweek does vary, the absence of a standard temporal period in which to judge what constitutes an employee's average regularly scheduled workweek is fatal to the calculation. An average is the result obtained by dividing the sum total of a set of figures by the number of figures. Webster's Ninth New Collegiate Dictionary (Merriam-Webster, Inc. 1988).

To have a coherent policy, the FMLA needs to define how the average is obtained. One way to do that is to identify an agreed-upon time period to judge the average number of hours worked. For example, Title II calculates the number of hours of FMLA leave available where an employee's work schedule varies by taking the average number of hours worked in the 12 weeks preceding leave commencement. 5 CFR 630.1203(e). This is not the case where the employee's work schedule does not vary. Where the employee's workweek does not vary, there is no set time frame in the regulations to determine the employee's average regularly scheduled workweek.

In the absence of an identified time period, employers are well-advised to obtain advance written agreement from the employee on the total amount of FMLA leave available based on the average number of hours in the employee's regularly scheduled administrative workweek. This agreement should be based on the employers review of hours worked during the employee's regularly scheduled administrative workweek over the 12 weeks preceding leave commencement. If the number of hours in the employee's workweek does not vary from week to week, an average should be calculated over a uniform time period. In the absence of specific guidance, the time period should be at least the 12 weeks prior to leave commencement.

If the records show that the number of hours in an employee's workweek varies from week to week, a different method of calculation must be used. This method is discussed more fully below.

(2) Point in Time of Calculation

The issues here are (1) at what point in time is the calculation of the amount of FMLA leave made, and (2) how often may that calculation be made during the course of the 12-month leave year.

Regarding the former, the regulation fails to define when the average number of hours in the employee's regularly scheduled administrative workweek is calculated, where the number of hours does not vary from week to week. The calculation could be made on the employee's notice of the need for FMLA leave. Alternatively, the calculation might be made as of the employee's commencement or start of leave. The regulation fails to provide a point in time at which the calculation is made.

Where the number of hours in an employee's workweek varies from week to week, the calculation of the amount of FMLA leave is made as of leave commencement. This begs the question, however, of when does FMLA leave commence? The DOL takes the position that, under Title I, FMLA leave commences on the date of the first absence of FMLA leave for each covered condition during the leave year. If leave is taken in a single block of time, the leave commences with the start of the absence. If, however, a series of intermittent or reduced schedule leave is taken related to the same underlying condition, the leave commences on the date of the first absence only. For the remainder of the 12-month leave year, subsequent absences related to the same condition are not considered separate periods of leave. The question is whether Title II will follow the DOL's definition of "commence," or whether it will do something else.

A related issue has to do with the number of times during the 12-month leave year that the amount of leave may be recalculated. This issue results from the absence of a requirement that fixes the amount of FMLA leave during any given leave year as of, for example, the first FMLA absence of the leave year. To illustrate, assume that as of the first FMLA leave during a 12-month leave year, employee A worked an average of 40 hours per week on a weekly schedule that varied. Employee A is entitled to 480 hours of FMLA leave for the rest of the leave year.

However, the regulations do not provide that the amount of leave year is static based on a fixed point in time. As a result, the employee's entitlement to FMLA leave will always change throughout the leave year. It may go up or down depending on the average number of work hours calculated. For example, if the number of hours in the employee's workweek varies from week to week, whether due to FMLA leave usage or overtime, potentially the amount of FMLA leave available to the employee could change drastically throughout the leave year (as often as every 12 weeks) regardless of whether the employee actually used any FMLA leave.

In our previous example, at the time of his first FMLA absence, employee A may have been entitled to 480 hours of leave. Let's say he took 80 hours. Three months later employee A needs FMLA leave for a completely different reason. Other than the 80 hours, employee A took no FMLA leave during this three-month period. He did, however, use a lot of annual and sick leave. You might think that employee A had 400 hours of FMLA leave at this time. You would be wrong. Considering the annual and sick leave used in the 12 weeks preceding his second leave request, employee A's average hours of scheduled work was only 20 hours per week. Employee A is now entitled to a maximum of 240 hours of FMLA leave. From this, 80 hours must be subtracted, leaving the employee 160 hours of FMLA leave only 12 weeks after the initial calculation put the number at 480 hours.

The above definitional problems persist in the regulations implementing Title I, the CAA, and the PEOAA.

2. Title I, the CAA, and the PEOAA

a. General Rule

Like Title II, the amount of FMLA leave available to eligible employees covered by Title I, the CAA, and the PEOAA may be different for each employee. Section 102 of Title I of the FMLA, 29 USC 2612(a)(1), provides that each eligible employee is entitled to a "total of 12 workweeks of leave" during the 12-month leave period. The term "workweek" is the employee's usual or normal schedule (hours/days per week) prior to the start of FMLA leave, and is the controlling factor for determining how much leave an employee is entitled. Preamble, 29 CFR 825.205; DOL WH FMLA Advisory Opinion No. 107 (July 19, 1999). Because this determination is based on the actual work history of each eligible employee, the number of days and/or hours that constitute an employee's usual or normal work schedule may vary from employee to employee.

If an employee normally works overtime as part of the usual or normal work schedule, then such overtime hours form part of the usual and normal workweek schedule of the employee and are included in calculating the amount of FMLA leave available to the employee. DOL FMLA WH Advisory Opinion No. 107 (July 19, 1999). If, on the other hand, overtime hours are not part of the employee's usual or normal workweek, such as where overtime is made available on an as-needed basis or is voluntary, such hours are not part of the employee's usual or normal workweek and would not be counted toward the calculation of the amount of FMLA leave available to the employee. *Id.*

One of the greatest myths about the FMLA is that 480 hours is the maximum amount of leave available to an eligible employee during a leave year. Nothing in the Act or its legislative history suggests that the maximum amount of leave available to an employee is 480 hours. Preamble, 29 CFR 825.205. If an employee's normal workweek exceeds 40 hours, the calculation of total FMLA leave available for pro rata reduction of total leave entitlement is based on the employee's normal workweek, even if it exceeds 40 hours. *Id.*

For example, Dan is a hard working labor–relations specialist with the Postal Service. Before taking FMLA leave to care for his ill mother, Dan's usual and normal work schedule was 60 hours a week. Dan is entitled to 720 hours (12 workweeks x 60 hours) of FMLA leave during the course of the 12–month FMLA leave year. Mike, a colleague of Dan, worked 50 hours a week as his "usual and normal" work schedule prior to his need for FMLA leave. Mike is entitled to only 600 hours (12 workweeks x 50 hours) of FMLA leave during the same leave year that Dan, his colleague down the hall, is entitled to 720 hours.

b. Deficiencies with the General Rule

The basic calculation of the amount of FMLA leave available to an eligible employee suffers from the absence of three critical elements: (1) it fails to identify what constitutes an employee's schedule; (2) it lacks a specified temporal period in order to determine an eligible employee's usual or normal work schedule; and (3) it fails to address at what point in time the employer must make this determination. The absence of these critical terms undermines the legitimacy of all but the most obvious or agreed–upon determinations of an employee's usual or normal work schedule.

(1) Work Schedule

The calculation of the actual amount of FMLA leave available as part of the 12–week entitlement is based on each eligible employee's usual or normal work schedule. The term "work schedule" is not defined in the statute or the implementing regulations. The lack of definition raises several issues. First, does the term mean the actual amount of hours the employee works, or is it the hours scheduled to work, which may be more or less than the time the employee actually worked? The term "schedule" suggests a pre–planned work schedule.

This is consistent with the way unplanned overtime hours are treated. *See* DOL WH FMLA Advisory Opinion No. 107 (July 19, 1999) (overtime hours on a voluntary or as–needed basis are not part of the employee's usual or normal workweek). If an employee's work schedule is not necessarily the same as the actual hours worked, the number of hours used to calculate the amount of FMLA leave may be significantly more or less than the number of hours actually worked during the 12–week measuring period.

For example, an employee is scheduled to work 40 hours each workweek during the 12–week measuring period. The employee actually works 50 hours each week. The employee is entitled to only 480 hours of FMLA leave based on the scheduled work. If the unscheduled work counted, the employee's FMLA leave entitlement is 600 hours (50 x 12).

Alternatively, the employee's usual or normal work schedule has her working 50 hours a week. The employee actually works 40 hours a week. According to the regulations, the amount of FMLA leave is based on 50 hours a week as the employee's usual or normal work schedule.

If work schedule means a pre–planned work schedule, it is not clear who gets to determine what the employee's work schedule is: the employer or the employee. For example, may an employer set an employee's work schedule as 40 hours a week, regardless of how much time the employee actually works? Similarly, may an employer set an employee's work schedule at 40 hours a week for purposes of the FMLA, even if the employer really has nothing to do with setting the employee's actual day–to–day work schedule?

Finally, how does an employer establish what constitutes the employee's usual or normal work schedule, particularly for employees whose time is not recorded? Other than mass edicts by an employer, there appears to be some problem regarding the ability of an employer to establish what the employee's usual or normal work schedule is, in the event the employer and employee cannot come to an agreement on the issue.

(2) Absence of Temporal Period

Neither the Act nor the implementing regulations identify the temporal period that an employer should consider to determine what constitutes an employee's usual or normal work schedule prior to the start of FMLA leave. The only temporal reference made refers to the period of time prior to the start of FMLA leave. Preamble, 29 CFR 825.205; DOL FMLA Advisory Opinion No. 107 (July 19, 1999). Normally, where there is no dispute about an employee's work schedule, such as where the schedule is clearly documented or the employer and employee agree on the employee's usual or normal work hours, the absence of a more specific method for determining an employee's usual or normal work schedule would not be an issue.

Where, however, the employee and employer cannot agree on the number of hours that constitute an employee's usual or normal work schedule, the absence of further direction quickly becomes a major problem. While some of the problem is mitigated by better guidance provided where employees work on a schedule that varies from week-to-week, the absence of a base temporal period unnecessarily complicates the critical calculation of the number of hours of protected FMLA leave an employee has available during the course of a leave year.

If the temporal period is relatively short and encompasses summer months with significant vacation time, the employee's usual or normal work schedule is apt to appear relatively meager. In that case, the direct result of the use of a short time span to judge what constitutes an employee's usual or normal work schedule is the loss of available FMLA leave. Conversely, a short temporal period might overstate an employee's usual or normal work schedule. For example, if an employee worked on a project for the last three months that required a great deal of time, far and above the employee's normal work schedule, an employer is legally obliged to provide an employee far more FMLA leave than it would if the employee's usual or normal work schedule were judged with a longer time frame.

On the other hand, a five-year snapshot of the employee's usual or normal work schedule might lower the amount of FMLA leave that may be available to an employee as such a lengthy period of time would tend to average out a very high amount of hours routinely worked by the employee in the preceding year and a half. Of course, the opposite might be true. An employee may have been working relatively modest hours recently, but was putting in Herculean hours for years. In that case, the employee's usual or normal work hours might benefit from consideration of a longer time frame.

There is nothing in the regulations to prevent an employer or employee from arguing that the "usual or normal" work schedule is better reflected in a time period other than the time immediately preceding leave commencement. For example, if an employee took significant amounts of vacation or FMLA leave in the six weeks immediately preceding the start of FMLA leave, the employee might argue that an earlier time period was the correct period. Employers, of course, could play the same game.

In the absence of official direction on this issue, employers are well advised to attempt to reach a written agreement with the employee regarding the number of hours in a normal workweek. Absent agreement, employers could calculate what a normal workweek consists of based on available time or pay records. As for a time frame for such a calculation, the employers should consider looking back at least 12 weeks prior to the start of the first FMLA leave taken during the leave year. This is the period permitted to determine the amount of FMLA leave available for an employee whose schedule varies from week to week. 29 CFR 825.205; S. Res. 242, Cong. Rec. S3959, S3965 (April 23, 1996); 29 CFR 825.205(d). As the only definite period provided in the regulations, it is the best estimate of what might be a reasonable time frame.

(3) No Fixed Starting Point for Calculation

Another major issue with the determination of the amount of available FMLA leave is the absence of a definitive starting point for the calculation. The starting point is described as the "employee's normal workweek *prior to the start of FMLA leave.*" Preamble, 29 CFR 825.205 (emphasis supplied); DOL FMLA Advisory Opinion No. 107 (July 19, 1999). This phrasing raises two related questions: (1) when does FMLA leave start, and (2) how often is the amount of FMLA leave calculated?

Regarding when FMLA leave starts, the question is whether the term "start" has the same meaning as "commence" or whether it means something else, such as each and every FMLA absence or the first absence in a leave year. Which definition is chosen will greatly impact the amount of FMLA leave available to an employee during the course of a 12-month leave year.

As discussed previously in Chapter 5, "Employee Eligibility for Leave," and as will be discussed subsequently in Section IV, "Leave Scheduling," the DOL interpreted the similar term "commencement of leave" for purposes of employee eligibility. The issue before the DOL was whether employee eligibility for FMLA leave at the time of leave commencement meant a new calculation for each and every FMLA absence, or, for leave taken on an intermittent or reduced leave schedule, whether leave commencement began at the start of a series of absences related to the same underlying covered condition. For example, as in the case of an eligible employee requiring intermittent absences over the course of a leave year to receive dialysis treatment.

The DOL, following the lead of the district court in *Barron v. Runyon*, 11 F. Supp. 2d 676 (E.D. Va. 1998), opined that "leave" encompassed all FMLA leave for the same covered condition. DOL FMLA WH Advisory Opinion No. 112 (Sept. 11, 2000). For FMLA leave taken on an intermittent or reduced leave schedule that is caused by the same underlying covered condition, eligibility is calculated once at the commencement of the series of related leave. *Id*. Eligibility for unrelated leave would be calculated separately at the start of each separate covered condition.

The term "start" is synonymous with "commence." The Random House Thesaurus: College Edition (Random House Inc. 1989). If that is the case, applying the definition of leave commencement for employee eligibility, an employer should calculate the amount of FMLA leave available to an eligible employee at the start of each FMLA absence for a separate covered condition. For a series of related FMLA absences, the calculation of leave amount is made at the start of the first absences in the series during each leave year.

The above suggests that the amount of leave an employee may have during the course of a 12–month leave year is not static. While an eligible employee is entitled to 12 workweeks of FMLA leave, the number of actual hours of leave that make up the 12 workweeks is not fixed, but may fluctuate during the course of a leave year.

For example, Elaine is an eligible employee covered by Title I. She works for an agency that uses the calendar year as the FMLA leave year. In January, Elaine notifies her employer that she needs intermittent FMLA leave to care for her husband, who has a serious health condition. Based on her 40 hours a week schedule for the preceding 12 weeks, Elaine is entitled to 480 hours of FMLA leave. In March, Elaine notifies her employer that she no longer needs intermittent leave to care for her husband as he has recovered. She returns to work and resumes working 40 hours a week. In April, Elaine notifies her employer of her diagnosis with cancer and her need for intermittent leave. Because of her previous FMLA absences to care for her husband, Elaine only worked 25 hours a week in the 12 weeks preceding the start of her FMLA leave in April. At this time, Elaine is only entitled to a maximum of 300 hours of FMLA leave, minus whatever leave she has already used to care for her husband.

That the amount of FMLA leave available to an employee may be adjusted during the course of an FMLA leave year based on changes in the employee's "usual or normal" work schedule is suggested by the requirements for employees whose work schedules vary from week to week. 29 CFR 825.205(d); S. Res. 242, Cong. Rec. S3959, S3965 (April 23, 1996); 29 CFR 825.205(d). The calculation of the amount of FMLA leave available to an employee whose work schedule varies from week to week is based on a weekly average of the number of hours worked over the 12 weeks prior to the beginning of leave. *Id*. As there are at least four 12-week periods during the course of a 12–month leave year, the regulation suggests that multiple revisions to the amount of FMLA leave available to an employee are not only permissible, but also required.

Of course, a counter argument is that multiple revisions are limited to the circumstances set forth in 29 CFR 825.205(d). Employees whose work schedules do not vary from week to week are not limited to a 12-week period to determine what an employee's usual or normal work schedule was prior to the start of FMLA leave. That may well be the case, but if it is, it begs the question of which temporal period applies.

The above result is further amplified if the "start of FMLA leave" means each and every FMLA leave absence, including multiple absences taken on an intermittent or reduced leave schedule related to the same underlying covered condition. The amount of FMLA leave available to an eligible employee would have to be recalculated at the time of every FMLA absence. For employees who take a significant amount of FMLA or other leave between FMLA absences, this could greatly reduce the amount of FMLA leave available to an employee during the course of a year.

Finally, the phrase "start of FMLA leave" could be interpreted to mean the first FMLA absence during the 12–month leave year. Under this interpretation, the amount of FMLA leave an employee is entitled to receive for the entire leave year would be fixed as of the first FMLA leave absence. For example, Wendy advises her employer that she needs FMLA leave to care for her husband Brent, who has been diagnosed with a serious health condition. This is the first time this leave year that Wendy sought FMLA leave for any reason. Wendy works for an agency with a fixed leave year. In the 12 weeks prior to her leave, Wendy worked her usual or normal 50 hours a week. Wendy's entitlement to 12 workweeks of FMLA leave would translate into 600 hours of leave (50 hours/week x 12 weeks). The 600 hours would remain fixed throughout the leave year, no matter how much more Wendy did or did not work the remainder of the year.

The benefit of fixing the amount of FMLA leave available to an employee as of the first FMLA absence of the leave year is it brings certainty to the employee's entitlement. Employees know what their FMLA entitlement is for the remainder of the leave year, and employers can plan around known leave numbers. The downside of not permitting multiple calculations throughout the leave year is that it punishes employees who dramatically increase the amount of work they perform after the first FMLA absence of the leave year. Because the amount of FMLA leave available is fixed as of the first FMLA absence, the employee's increased usual or normal work schedule cannot be reflected in the amount of leave available to them until the next leave year. Employers also lose the ability to revise downward the number of hours an employee is entitled to as FMLA leave during the course of a leave year.

Again, the basic rule lacks a temporal period and guidance on whether the amount of leave available is fixed as of the first FMLA absence of the leave year, or may be adjusted throughout the course of the leave year. The DOL and other regulatory entities that enforce Title I, the CAA, and the PEOAA should identify the appropriate starting point and time frame for employers to determine an employee's usual or normal work schedule. Given the central importance that this number plays in the accurate determination of the number of hours that make up an employee's 12 workweek entitlement during a leave year, these regulatory bodies simply cannot leave this problem unresolved.

Additionally, the DOL and other regulating entities should use the same terms to describe the same event. As a matter of regulatory construction, if "start" means the same thing as "commence," it is better for all concerned if only one of these terms was used throughout. Alternatively, the terms could be defined as meaning the same thing. Using different terms without defining them as having the same meaning necessarily raises the question of whether a different meaning was meant to be attached. This results in unnecessary confusion. Unfortunately, the regulations implementing Title I, the CAA, and the PEOAA use the terms "commencement of," "start of," and "beginning of" to describe the point in time when eligibility and leave amount calculations are to be made. Because different language is used, it is unclear if these terms are meant to be synonymous or have different meanings. Litigation is an awfully expensive way to figure out the meaning of basic phrases.

Until further guidance is provided, employers should apply a uniform temporal period of not less than 12 weeks prior to the commencement of leave for determining an employee's usual or normal work schedule prior to the commencement of leave. Except for eligible employees whose work schedule varies from week to week, employers might consider looking back one year from the start of the employee's FMLA leave. This is the same time period that the 1,250-hour eligibility requirement is considered. [See Chapter 5, "Employee Eligibility for Leave."] The amount of leave available for eligible employees whose work schedule varies from week to week is governed by regulation. 29 CFR 825.205(d); S. Res. 242, Cong. Rec. S3959, S3965 (April 23, 1996); 29 CFR 825.205(d).

Whether the amount of FMLA leave is determined as of the first FMLA leave absence during the leave year or is recalculated with the subsequent taking of FMLA leave, my educated guess is that the DOL and other regulating entities will opt for a fixed amount of leave calculated as of the first FMLA absence of the leave year, with the exception of employees whose schedules vary from week to week, which may fluctuate during the leave year. My educated guess is based simply on the assumption that certainty in this area will triumph over uncertainty.

Currently, a strict reading of the regulations requires employers to recalculate the amount of FMLA leave available to an eligible employee at the start of each new FMLA leave period during the leave year.

B. EMPLOYEES WORKING PART-TIME OR VARIABLE HOURS

The calculation of the amount of FMLA leave available and, therefore, the amount used by an eligible employee, is different for some eligible employees working part-time or variable hours.

1. Title II

The calculation of the amount of FMLA leave is the same for full- and part-time employees. 5 CFR 630.1203(e). The 12 administrative workweeks of leave are calculated on an hourly basis and equal 12 times the average number of hours in the employee's regularly scheduled administrative workweek. *Id.* The administrative workweek for part-time employees means the officially prescribed days and hours within an administrative workweek during which the employee is regularly scheduled to work. 5 CFR 1202 (incorporating definition contained in 5 CFR 610.102).

I note that the term "part-time employee" is not defined in the referenced regulations. Presumably, it means an employee whose regularly scheduled workweek is less than 40 hours per week. In contrast, the basic workweek of a full-time employee is 40 hours. 5 CFR 610.102 (basic workweek defined). [The issue of variable hours under Title I is addressed in Section III, "Calculating 12 Workweeks of FMLA Leave", this chapter.]

2. Title I, the CAA, and the PEOAA

Where an employee normally works a part-time schedule or variable hours, the amount of leave to which that employee will be entitled is determined on a pro rata or proportional basis by comparing the new schedule with the employee's normal schedule. 29 CFR 825.205(b); S. Res. 242, Cong. Rec. S3959, S3965 (April 23, 1996); 29 CFR 825.205(b). For example, if an employee who normally works 30 hours per week works only 20 hours under a reduced leave schedule, the employee's ten hours of leave would constitute one-third of a week of FMLA leave for each week the employee works the reduced leave schedule. *Id.* Under this example, it would take the employee 24 weeks to exhaust his or her entitlement if no other FMLA leave were taken during the 12-month period. Preamble, 29 CFR 825.205.

As under Title II, the term "part-time schedule" under Title I is undefined. Presumably, it means an employee whose usual or normal work schedule is less than 40 hours per week. The term "variable hours" is also undefined. It is unclear whether "variable hours" modifies the term "schedule," which would limit the reach of the regulations to part-time employees working variable hours. Alternatively, "variable hours" could be interpreted as modifying the entire phrase "part-time schedule," which would mean that the regulation is not limited to part-time employees, but would include any eligible employee who normally works variable hours. The latter interpretation is likely correct as a matter of regulatory construction.

What constitutes "normally" is undefined, except that it involves the comparison of an undefined period prior to the taking of FMLA leave with the period during which the employee is taking intermittent or reduced schedule FMLA leave. The problems associated with the lack of an identified temporal period to establish the employee's "normal" pre-FMLA leave part-time schedule or variable hours exist in this scenario.

Also present is the issue of whether the amount of FMLA leave available to an employee who normally works a part-time schedule or variable hours is fixed as of the first FMLA leave taken during any given leave year, or whether it is recalculated each time such an employee takes FMLA leave. The example given in the regulation is ambiguous, as it does not indicate that the amount of leave either is or is not recalculated for each FMLA absence that falls below the employee's "normal" part-time schedule or variable hours. What is clear is that only the amount of leave actually taken by an eligible employee on intermittent or reduced schedule leave may be counted toward the 12 workweeks of FMLA leave entitlement each leave year. 29 CFR 825.205(a); S. Res. 242, Cong. Rec. S3959, S3965 (April 23, 1996); 29 CFR 825.205(a). *See* DOL WH FMLA Advisory Opinion No. 42 (August 23, 1994). Again, the temporal period to judge what is "normal" and how often an employer is required to make that judgment during the course of the leave year remains unresolved.

C. EMPLOYEES WHOSE WORK SCHEDULES VARY FROM WEEK TO WEEK

Special rules govern the calculation of the amount (hours) of FMLA leave available to an eligible employee whose schedule varies from week to week.

1. Title II

The regulation governing the calculation of the amount of FMLA leave available to an eligible employee whose work hours vary, 5 CFR 630.1203(e), provides:

If the number of hours in an employee's workweek varies from week to week, a weekly average of the hours scheduled over the 12 weeks prior to the date leave commences shall be used as the basis for this calculation.

The regulation is confusing because of its use of the terms "workweek" and "scheduled." The regulation is susceptible to several interpretations.

The regulation appears to be saying that if the number of hours an employee actually works during a workweek varies from week to week, the employer calculates the amount of FMLA leave available, not based on the hours actually worked, but on the 12-week average of scheduled hours of work. That suggests the possibility that the scheduled amount of work might be less than the actual hours worked over the 12-week period, lowering the total amount of FMLA leave available to the employee.

Another possible interpretation is suggested by the regulation. If scheduled hours mean the same as actual hours worked, then the amount of FMLA leave available to the employee is calculated as the average of the actual variable hours worked by the employee during the 12-week measuring period. Under this interpretation, actual hours worked are used to trigger the rule. The benefit of this interpretation is that it is internally consistent. The rule, however, ignores actual hours worked by the employee in favor of an average of the scheduled hours of work.

The term "schedule" suggests a limitation on the hours considered toward the calculation. What is not planned is generally not "scheduled." Actual hours worked that are unplanned, therefore, should not count toward the amount of FMLA leave available to the employee. However, because unplanned work may cause a variation in the number of hours in an employee's workweek from week to week, this unplanned work could be the basis for application of the variation calculation rule.

2. Title I, the CAA, and the PEOAA

The regulations interpreting Title I, the CAA and the PEOAA regarding an eligible employee whose work schedule varies from week to week is every bit as confusing as the regulation under Title II.

The amount of leave available to an eligible employee whose work schedule varies from week to week prior to taking FMLA leave is based on the employee's average workweek over the 12 weeks prior to beginning a leave period. 29 CFR 825.205(d); S. Res. 242, Cong. Rec. S3959, S3965 (April 23, 1996); 29 CFR 825.205(a). The calculation establishes the employee's "normal" work schedule. Preamble, 29 CFR 825.205. For example, an eligible employee works the following schedule in the 12 weeks preceding the start of FMLA leave:

	Hours Worked
Week 1:	45
Week 2:	45
Week 3:	40
Week 4:	50
Week 5:	40
Week 6:	35
Week 7:	20
Week 8	20
Week 9:	50
Week 10:	50
Week 11:	45
Week 12:	40
	470

To get the average hours worked for this 12-week period, divide 470 (the total number of hours worked during the 12-week period) by 12 weeks, which equals 49.17 hours as the average week. The employee is entitled to a total of 470 hours of FMLA leave during the leave year. It would take an eligible employee who worked 20 hours per week on an intermittent or reduced leave schedule over 23.5 weeks to exhaust her FMLA leave entitlement, if no other FMLA leave was used during the leave year.

The regulations suffer from the same deficiencies as previously discussed. For example, it is unclear what temporal period is used to judge whether an employee's schedule varies from week to week. A month? A year? Three years? Whether an employee's schedule varies from week to week will depend on the time period chosen. In the absence of guidance, it is recommended that employers select a uniform time period and apply that to all employees. At minimum, the time period should be 12 weeks from the date FMLA leave is to commence. On the other end of the spectrum, an agency should not need to go back more than a year. Obtaining written agreement with the employee on this issue is helpful.

A second deficiency arises from the absence of a definition of what constitutes a variation in an employee's schedule. As currently written, any variation in an employee's week-to-week schedule, however slight, would bring the employee within the reach of the rule. For example, a schedule that varied by one minute in one of twelve weeks is sufficient for application of the rule.

The term "schedule" is undefined. If an employee's work schedule is the same, but the employee actually works different hours from week to week, is the rule implicated? Is an employee's schedule synonymous with the hours actually worked, or does it mean something else? According to my handy dictionary, the term "schedule" means "to appoint, assign, or designate for a fixed time." Webster's Ninth Collegiate Dictionary (Merriam-Webster, Inc. 1988). Listed synonyms for the term "schedule" include "set the time for, slate, fix, plan, book, appoint, set down, fit in," and "put down." The Random House Thesaurus: College Edition (Random House, Inc. 1989). None of these terms sound, to me, like they mean whatever hours an employee happened to work, whether planned or unplanned. Rather, they suggest that only the planned hours of work each week are used to consider whether there is any variation on the employee's week-to-week work schedule. That is consistent with the way unplanned overtime hours are treated. *See* DOL WH FMLA Advisory Opinion No. 107 (July 19, 1999) (overtime hours on a voluntary or "as needed" basis are not part of the employee's usual or normal workweek).

This gives rise to another issue. Who gets to decide what constitutes the employee's schedule: the employer or employee? If the employer gets to set the employee's schedule, what happens if the set schedule bears no relationship with the actual schedule worked by the employee?

If, as it appears, the required variation must be to the employee's work schedule and not the actual hours worked, the number of hours used to calculate the amount of FMLA leave may be significantly more or less than the number of hours actually worked during the 12-week measuring period. For example, an employee is scheduled to work 40 hours each workweek during the 12-week measuring period. The employee actually works 50 hours each week. The employee would only be entitled to 480 hours of FMLA leave based on the scheduled work. If the unscheduled work counted, the employee's FMLA leave entitlement is 600 hours (50 x 12). Conversely, if the employee were to scheduled to work 50 hours a week, but only worked 40, the employee is entitled to 600 hours of FMLA leave (50 x 12) of FMLA leave, not the 480 hours based on the time the employee actually worked.

Proving what constitutes an employee's work schedule appears problematic. It is unclear whether an employer's policy or position description generally describing an employee's normal work schedule would suffice. If not, employers would have to require employees to submit weekly or monthly work schedules in order to have some control over this issue. Otherwise, the actual work schedule of the employee might govern this issue. Since these schedules are not uniformly maintained, employers and employees would appear to have significant proof problems.

Of course, not everything about this regulation is bad. In this instance, the regulations clearly establish the temporal period (12 weeks) used to establish the employee's usual or normal work schedule prior to beginning FMLA leave. That helps.

D. FLSA-EXEMPT EMPLOYEES

In the federal sector, the FMLA does not contain special provisions governing the calculation of the amount of FMLA leave available for employees who are exempt from the overtime reporting requirements of the Fair Labor Standards Act (FLSA). Generally speaking, *bona fide* executives, administrative, and professional employees are exempt from the FLSA's requirement that a record be kept of their hours worked. *See* 29 CFR Part 541.

Because employers are not required by the FMLA or the FLSA to keep time records of the hours worked for these classes of employees, it will be difficult to determine with a high degree of accuracy the number of hours the employee worked over any meaningful period of time. This, in turn, will make it difficult to determine the employee's usual or normal workweek hours. Difficulties aside, employers must take reasonable steps to determine the number of hours worked by FLSA-exempt employees in order to determine their FMLA entitlement. Simply assigning an average based on pure guesswork will not do.

Employers first must determine if the employee's work hours vary from week to week. This is very likely to be the case for most FLSA-exempt employees. In such situations, the employer must apply the rules governing the calculation of FMLA leave for employees on a schedule that varies from week to week. The hallmark of that rule is that the employer must calculate the amount of FMLA leave available by looking at the hours worked in the 12 weeks prior to the commencement of FMLA leave. Again, no easy trick without time and attendance records.

Employers need to reach an agreement with the employee on the calculation of the amount of FMLA leave available to the FLSA-exempt employee. The employer should seriously consider asking the employee to calculate the number of hours worked in the 12-week period prior to leave commencement. The employer could then verify the accuracy of the employee' estimate with the employee's supervisor. If an acceptable agreement can be reached, it should be reduced to writing.

If the employer and the employer are unable to come to an agreement, the employer remains responsible for calculating the amount of FMLA leave available to the employee. The employer should use all reasonable means to make that determination, including reasonable inquires of the employee, the employee's subordinates, peers, clients, contractors, or anyone else who might have knowledge of the work hours spent by the employee during the 12-week period. Such employer inquiries should be discrete, and limited to determining the hours the employee worked. Because the employee can challenge the calculation of the amount of FMLA leave available, employers should give the employee the benefit of the doubt on the number of hours worked during the relevant time period.

E. HOLIDAYS

1. Title II

Any holidays authorized under 5 USC 6103 or by Executive Order and non-workdays established by federal statute, executive order, or administrative order that occur during the period in which the employee is on family and medical leave may not be counted toward the 12-week entitlement to FMLA leave. 5 CFR 630.1203(e).

For example, an eligible federal employee takes five weeks of FMLA leave for a serious health condition beginning Monday, December 22, and ending Monday, January 26. The employee's usual and normal work schedule is 40 hours per week, Monday through Friday, 9:00 a.m. to 5:00 p.m. During the five-week FMLA leave period, the ten weekend days would not count toward the employee's 12-week FMLA leave entitlement because the employee is not normally scheduled to work on those days. The three holidays included in that time period, Christmas Day, New Year's, and Martin Luther King, Jr. Day would also not count against the employee's FMLA leave entitlement. The employee is charged 176 hours toward his or her 12-week FMLA leave entitlement (5 weeks x 40 hours per week minus 24 hours for the three holidays = 176 FMLA leave hours).

The federal government established the following legal public holidays:

New Year's Day	January 1
Martin Luther King Jr.'s Day	3rd Monday in January
Washington's Birthday	3rd Monday in February
Independence Day	July 4
Labor Day	1st Monday in September
Columbus Day	2nd Monday in October
Veterans Day	November 11
Thanksgiving Day	4th Thursday in November
Christmas Day	December 25

2. Title I, the CAA, and the PEOAA

When determining the amount of FMLA leave taken, a holiday occurring within a week of FMLA leave has no effect—the week is still counted as a week of FMLA leave. 29 CFR 825.200(f); S. Res. 242, Cong. Rec. S3959, S3964 (April 23, 1996); 29 CFR 825.200(f). Using the above example, because the three holidays occurred during the employee's five-week FMLA leave absence, they are counted toward the employee's 12-workweek FMLA leave entitlement. The employee would be charged with 200 hours of FMLA leave. Note that an eligible employee covered by Title II would be charged 176 hours for the same time period because holidays are not counted toward the 12-week FMLA entitlement under Title II.

F. TEMPORARY CESSATION OF BUSINESS ACTIVITIES

1. Title II

Non-workdays established by federal statute, executive order, or administrative order that occur during the period in which the employee is on family and medical leave may not be counted toward the employee's 12-week FMLA leave entitlement. 5 CFR 630.1203(e). For example, if the federal government is closed as a result of a snow storm while an employee is out on FMLA leave, the time the federal government was closed would not count toward the employee's 12-week FMLA leave entitlement.

2. Title I, the CAA, and the PEOAA

If, for some reason, the employer's operations have temporarily ceased and employees generally are not expected to report for work for one or more weeks (e.g., a school closing two weeks for the Christmas/New Year holiday or the summer vacation or an employer closing a plant for retooling or repairs), the days the employer's activities have ceased do not count against the employee's FMLA leave entitlement. 29 CFR 825.200(f); S. Res. 242, Cong. Rec. S3959, S3964 (April 23, 1996); 29 CFR 825.200(f); see Phillips v. Leroy-Somer North America et al., No. 01-1046-T, 2003 U.S. Dist. LEXIS 5349 (W.D. Tenn. March 28, 2003) (two-week period of plant closing not counted toward employee's 12-week FMLA leave entitlement).

Note the distinction made by the regulations between a holiday that does count toward the 12-week FMLA leave entitlement, and the cessation of business activity "for one or two weeks," which does not count against the 12-week leave entitlement. Although both examples may involve periods of time that employees generally are not expected to report to work, only where the cessation is a week or more will an employee's concurrent absence not count against the employee's 12-week FMLA leave entitlement. No further explanation is given for this distinction.

G. OVERTIME HOURS

1. Title II

Overtime hours may be included in the calculation of the amount of FMLA leave available to an eligible employee as part of the 12-administrative workweek entitlement. For overtime hours to be included toward the calculation of FMLA leave available to an eligible employee, overtime must be included as part of the employee's regularly scheduled administrative workweek. In the case of the calculation of the amount of FMLA leave where the number of hours in an employee's workweek does not vary from week to week, the calculation is based on the average number of hours in the employee's regularly schedule workweek. 5 CFR 630.1203(e). As defined, a workweek may include overtime hours. 5 CFR 610.111.

Where the number of hours in an employee's workweek varies from week to week, the amount of FMLA leave is calculated based on the weekly average of the hours scheduled over the 12 weeks prior to the date leave commences. 5 CFR 610.1203(e). Overtime is not excluded from this calculation, and is very likely the cause of the variation in work hours.

2. Title I, the CAA, and the PEOAA

Whether overtime hours are counted for purposes of calculating the amount of an eligible employee's FMLA leave entitlement or charged to the employee's FMLA leave entitlement depends on whether overtime hours are part of the employee's usual or normal workweek prior to the start of FMLA leave. DOL WH FMLA Advisory Opinion No. 107 (July 19, 1999).

If an employee's usual or normal workweek is greater than 40 hours, hours worked above 40 hours must be included in determining the maximum amount of leave available to the employee as part of the employee's 12–workweek entitlement. *Id*. For example, if an employee normally works overtime in three of every four weeks, then such overtime hours are part of the employee's usual and normal workweek schedule and are included in calculating the amount of FMLA leave available to the employee. *Id*.

If overtime hours are part of an eligible employee's usual or normal workweek and the employee is unable to work overtime hours because of an FMLA qualifying reason, then any overtime hours not worked may be counted against the employee's FMLA leave entitlement, as long as the employer designates the absence as FMLA leave. *Id*.

For example, assume that an employee's schedule over the 12 weeks before starting FMLA leave shows five weeks at 50 hours, four weeks at 60 hours, and three weeks at 40 hours for a total of 610 hours, or an average of 50.8333 hours per week. Under the FMLA, only the amount of leave actually taken may be counted toward the 12-week leave entitlement. If the employee was not able to work overtime hours over the 12-week period due to an FMLA-qualifying reason, then up to 130 hours (610–480 [40 x 12]) may be charged to the employee's FMLA leave entitlement. Any pro-rata reduction in total leave entitlement during intermittent or reduced schedule FMLA leave should be based on the employee's normal workweek, even if it exceeds 40 hours. *Id*.

Conversely, if overtime hours are on a voluntary or as-needed basis and are not part of the employee's usual or normal workweek, such hours would not be counted to calculate the amount of the employee's FMLA leave entitlement. *Id*. Where, however, overtime hours are not part of an employee's usual or normal workweek prior to the start of FMLA leave, overtime hours that an employee is unable to work due to an FMLA-covered condition may be charged against the employee's FMLA leave entitlement, up to the maximum of 12 workweeks in a 12-month leave period. *Id*. In that case, disciplinary action may not be taken against an employee for being unable to work overtime due to an FMLA-covered condition.

H. CHANGES TO AN EMPLOYEE'S WORK SCHEDULE

1. Title II

If the number of hours in an employee's regularly scheduled administrative workweek is changed during the 12-month FMLA leave period, the employee's entitlement to any remaining FMLA leave will be recalculated based on the number of hours in the employee's current regularly scheduled administrative workweek. 5 CFR 630.1203(f).

For example, at the beginning of the current FMLA leave year an employee's regularly scheduled administrative workweek called for a basic 40-hour workweek and ten hours per week of overtime. The employee is now entitled to a maximum of 600 hours (50 hours x 12) of FMLA leave during the measured forward FMLA leave year. During the course of the same FMLA measured forward leave year, the employer changes the employee's regularly scheduled administrative workweek to a basic 40-hour workweek with no overtime. As of the change in the employee's regularly scheduled workweek, the employee would not be entitled to 480 hours of total FMLA leave, minus whatever FMLA leave the employee has already taken. Presumably, such a recalculation could deprive an employee of any further FMLA leave for the remainder of the employee's measured forward FMLA leave year.

Note that any change to an employee's regularly scheduled administrative workweek should be for legitimate operational reasons independent of the employee taking FMLA leave. An employer that changed an employee's regularly scheduled administrative workweek to reduce FMLA leave benefits is in violation of the Act.

2. Title I, the CAA, and the PEOAA

If an employer makes a permanent or long-term change in the employee's schedule (for reasons other than FMLA, and prior to the notice of need for FMLA leave), the hours worked under the new schedule are used for making this calculation. 29 CFR 825.205(c); S. Res. 242, Cong. Rec. S3959, S3965 (April 23, 1996); 29 CFR 825.200(f).

Unlike the similar rule under Title II, before changes to an employee's usual or normal work schedule may be used to calculate the amount of FMLA leave that an eligible employee has remaining, several conditions must be met. First, the changes to the employee's usual or normal work schedule must be permanent or long-term. The key terms "permanent" or "long-term" are undefined. Specifically, no guidance is provided to identify the length of time a change to an employee's work schedule must last in order to be considered long-term. Presumably, to be considered permanent, no change in the employee's schedule must be contemplated. I doubt the term means that an employer must issue a statement to the effect that the employee's schedule will never change for the remainder of the employee's career.

In addition to being permanent or long-term, the second condition placed on modification of the amount of FMLA leave available to an employee is that the change in work schedule must occur before the employee provides notice of the need for FMLA leave. [Employee notice obligations are addressed in Chapter 8, "Notice Requirements."] Briefly, an eligible employee must provide timely notice to his or her employer of the need for FMLA leave. 29 CFR 825.302, 825.303; S. Res. 242, Cong. Rec. S3959, S3971–S3972 (April 23, 1996); 29 CFR 825.302, 825.303.

Although it also requires an employee to notify an agency of the need for FMLA leave, Title II does not contain a similar bar preventing an employer from recalculating the amount of an employee's remaining leave entitlement when the employee has given notice of the need for FMLA leave. Under Title II, an employer can recalculate an employee's FMLA leave entitlement based on any changes to the employee's work schedule, whether the employee has already given notice of the need for FMLA leave.

If a long-term or permanent change to the employee's usual or normal work schedule is made before the employee provides notice of a need for FMLA leave, the condition is met and, all things being equal, the employer may recalculate the available leave based on the new schedule. If, however, the long-term or permanent change to the employee's work schedule is instituted after the employee has given notice of the need for FMLA leave, the employer may not recalculate the amount of leave based on the employee's new work schedule. Rather, the amount of FMLA leave (hours) the employee is entitled to receive is calculated based on the employee's usual or normal work schedule prior to the change to the employee's work schedule.

Under certain circumstances, an employer may recalculate an employee's FMLA leave entitlement based on a permanent or long-term change in an employee's work schedule after the employee begins FMLA leave. This is permitted because, in certain limited circumstances, an employee may notify an employer of the need for FMLA leave after the leave begins. For example, in the case of a medical emergency requiring an employee's immediate absence from work, the employee's obligation is to give notice of the need for FMLA leave within one or two working days of learning of the need for FMLA leave, which could occur after the leave begins (or ends). 29 CFR 825.303(a). If the employer, for reasons other than the employee's taking of FMLA leave, were to effect a permanent or long-term change to the employee's work schedule during the period between the employee's absence from work and notice of the need for FMLA leave, the employer would be able to recalculate the amount of FMLA leave available to the employee based on the new schedule.

Employers must exercise great care in implementing long-term or permanent changes to an employee's work schedule when the employee gives notice of a need for intermittent or reduced schedule leave. Whether FMLA leave is taken all at once, intermittently, or on a reduced leave schedule, an eligible employee is only required to give notice of a need for that leave once, but must advise as soon as practical if dates of scheduled leave change or are extended, or were initially unknown. 29 CFR 825.302(a); DOL WH FMLA Advisory Opinion No. 101 (Jan. 15, 1999); S. Res. 242, Cong. Rec. S3959, S3971 (April 23, 1996); 29 CFR 825.302, 825.302(a). Because DOL defines "leave" to include a series of intermittent absences (or absences on a reduced leave schedule) related to the same underlying condition (see DOL WH FMLA Advisory Opinion No. 112 (Sept. 11, 2000)), employers may not effect a long-term or permanent change to an employee's work schedule during the pendency of intermittent or reduced schedule leave during a given 12-month leave year.

For example, an employer has a fixed FMLA leave year as the calendar year. Our employee's usual or normal work schedule is Monday through Friday, 8:00 am to 5:00 p.m. The agency is not open over the weekend. Our employee, who is eligible for FMLA leave, notifies the employer on January 7 of the need for intermittent FMLA leave for eight hours per week every Friday to receive dialysis treatment. The employee has 480 hours of FMLA leave available.

The employee's notification of the employer on January 7 of the need for intermittent FMLA leave freezes the employer's ability to recalculate the amount of FMLA leave available to an employee based on a planned, permanent, or long-term change to the employee's work schedule (unrelated to the employee's use of FMLA leave) until the employee no longer needs to use intermittent FMLA leave. At 8 hours per week, the employee could be out intermittently for the remainder of the leave year without exhausting all available FMLA leave. If the employee's need for intermittent FMLA leave continued, the employer might be able recalculate the amount of FMLA leave available based on the changed schedule between the last use of FMLA leave in the current leave year, and the first use of FMLA leave in the following leave year. If, however, the employee were to notify the employer 30 days in advance, as required of a foreseeable need for intermittent FMLA leave continuing during the next leave year, the employer may continue to be blocked from recalculating the amount of FMLA leave available based on the employee's new work schedule. Theoretically, this could go on indefinitely as the employee receives a new entitlement to FMLA leave each leave year, assuming the employee meets all the eligibility requirements.

Note that the employer is not prohibited from changing the employee's work schedule. Rather, the agency is simply prohibited from recalculating the amount of FMLA leave available to the employee based on that new schedule until all of the conditions are met.

I. HUSBANDS AND WIVES WHO WORK FOR THE SAME AGENCY: THE MARRIAGE PENALTY

1. Title II

There are no special rules governing the calculation of the amount of FMLA leave available to eligible employees who are husband and wife working for the same employer. As such, the amount of FMLA leave (hours) credited toward the 12-week entitlement is calculated separately for each eligible employee based on each employee's pre-leave regularly scheduled administrative workweek; their status as husband and wife does not enter into the calculation.

2. Title I, the CAA, and the PEOAA

Under certain circumstances, a husband and wife who are employed by the same covered employer and who are eligible for FMLA leave suffer a "marriage penalty" reducing the total amount of FMLA leave available to both. 29 USC 2612(f); 2 USC 1312(a)(1) (incorporating 29 USC 2612). According to the legislative history, the limitation on leave taken by spouses who work for the same employer was intended to eliminate any employer incentive to refuse to hire married couples. Preamble, 29 CFR 202; DOL WH FMLA Advisory Opinion No. 99 (January 12, 1999); DOL WH FMLA Advisory Opinion No. 66 (July 19, 1995). Addressing criticisms of the regulations implementing this section, the DOL noted that it lacked the authority to modify or eliminate the marriage penalty by regulation because it is clearly set forth in the statute. *Id*.

a. General Rule

As set forth in the regulations (29 CFR 825.202(a); S. Res. 242, Cong. Rec. S3959, S3964 (April 23, 1996); 29 CFR 825.202(a)), a husband and wife who are eligible for FMLA leave and are employed by the same covered employer may be limited to a combined total of 12 weeks of leave during any 12-month period if the leave is taken:

- For the birth of the employee's son or daughter or to care for the child after birth;
- For placement of a son or daughter with the employee for adoption or foster care, or to care for the child after placement;
- To care for the employee's parent with a serious health condition.

By process of elimination (see also Preamble, 29 CFR 825.202; DOL WH FMLA Advisory Opinion Nos. 99 (Jan. 12, 1999), 42, 7 (Aug. 23, 1994)), the marriage penalty does not apply to FMLA leave taken for the following covered conditions:

- Because of a serious health condition that makes the employee unable to perform the functions of the employee's job;
- To care for the employee's spouse, son or daughter with a serious health condition.

Where the husband and wife both use a portion of the total 12-week FMLA leave entitlement for one of the purposes covered by the marriage penalty, the husband and wife would each be entitled to the difference between the amount he or she has taken individually and the 12 weeks for FMLA leave for a purpose other than those covered by the marriage penalty. 29 CFR 825.202(c); S. Res. 242, Cong. Rec. S3959, S3964 (April 23, 1996); 29 CFR 825.202(a).

The marriage penalty is strictly applied, and only to leave that is taken for a purpose that is expressly subject to the limitation. Preamble, 29 CFR 825.202. If the leave is not covered by the marriage penalty, the employees, even if husband and wife, are treated separately for purposes of entitlement to FMLA leave.

Examples illustrating the basic rules are set forth below.

b. Same Covered Employer

Whether a husband and wife are considered to be working for the same covered employer depends on whether they are covered by Title I, the CAA, or the PEOAA.

Title I covers all "public agency" employers, as defined in section 3(x) of the Fair Labor Standards Act (FLSA), 29 USC 203(x). 29 USC 2611(4)(iii); 29 CFR 825.108(a). Section 3(x) of the FLSA defines "public agency" as the government of the United States; the government of a State or political subdivision of a State; or an agency of the United States; a State, or a political subdivision of a State; or any interstate governmental agency. 29 CFR 825.108(a). Clearly, the entire federal government is covered by Title I. [For a further discussion of coverage of the federal government as a Title I employer, see Chapter 4, "Federal Employees Covered by the FMLA."]

It appears that the "same covered employer" means that the husband and wife must work for the same employer, not the federal government as a whole. For purposes of eligibility, the U.S. Government is considered a single employer. 29 CFR 825.109(e). It does not appear that the U.S. Government is considered a single employer for purposes of the marriage penalty.

The same employer marriage penalty under Title I applies even though the spouses are employed at two different worksites located more than 75 miles apart, or by two different operating divisions of the same company.

The CAA contains a marriage penalty, but that penalty is limited to a husband and wife who are employed by the same employing office. 2 USC 1312(a)(1) (incorporating 29 USC 2612); S. Res. 242, Cong. Rec. S3959, S3964 (April 23, 1996), 825.202(a). For employees covered by the CAA, the term "employer" is limited to an employing office. 2 USC 1312(a)(2)(A); S. Res. 242, Cong. Rec. S3959, S3961 (April 23, 1996); 29 CFR 825.104(a)). The term "employing office" is defined in the statute and regulations as a specific entity within the Office of the House and Senate. 2 USC 1301(9); S. Res. 242, Cong. Rec. S3959, S3961 (April 23, 1996); 29 CFR 825.104(a)). Presumably, the term "same employing office" means that the husband and wife must be employed in the exact same employing office and not just in any employing office covered by the CAA.

Like Title I, the "same employing office" marriage penalty under the CAA applies even though the spouses are employed at two different work sites of an employing office. S. Res. 242, Cong. Rec. S3959, S3964 (April 23, 1996); 29 CFR 825.202(a). The PEOAA incorporates § 102 of Title I, which includes the marriage penalty. 3 USC 412(a)(1). Like the CAA, the PEOAA limits the definition of a covered employer to any employing office. 3 USC 412(a)(2)(A). An "employing office" is defined as certain identified offices within the Executive Office of the President. 3 USC 401(4).

c. Valid Marriage

The marriage penalty only applies to employees who are currently husband and wife. The penalty does not apply to unmarried parents employed by the same employer. Preamble, 29 CFR 825.202; DOL WH FMLA Advisory Opinion No. 66 (July 19, 1995). Nor does it apply where the employees have been legally divorced. If the employees have separated but have not been legally divorced, they are still married and the penalty remains applicable. While some states recognize common law marriages, no state recognizes a common law divorce. Divorce requires a legal act ending the marriage.

The use of the term "spouse" to describe a husband and wife negates the possibility that the marriage penalty applies to same-sex marriages. The regulations do not define the term "husband and wife" as meaning spouse, which is a defined term for purposes of coverage under the Act. However, the regulations appear to use husband and wife interchangeably with spouse throughout the regulation. See 29 CFR 825.202(b), (c). [For a further discussion of spousal coverage under the FMLA, see Chapter 6, "Covered Family Members."]

A "spouse" is defined as a husband or wife as defined or recognized under State law for purposes of marriage in the State where the employee resides, including common law marriage in states where it is recognized. 29 USC 2611(13); 29 CFR 825.113(a), 825.800; S. Res. 242, Cong. Rec. S3959, S3962 (April 23, 1996); 29 CFR 825.113(a), 825.800. No state currently recognizes same-sex marriages. Vermont recognizes same-sex civil unions, but expressly provides that such unions are not marriages. [For a further discussion of same-sex marriages in the context of the FMLA, see Chapter 6, "Covered Family Members."]

The Defense of Marriage Act ("DOMA"), 28 USC 1738C, defines spouse, for purposes of federal law, as referring only to a person of the opposite sex who is a husband or a wife. The DOMA defines marriage as meaning only a legal union between one man and one woman as husband and wife. *Id*. The term "marriage" is not contained in the marriage penalty regulations, although it is mentioned in the Preamble to the final Title I regulations. *See* Preamble, 29 CFR 825.202 (marriage penalty limitation does not apply to unmarried parent).

If, as it appears, the term "husband and wife" is synonymous with "spouse," then all of the limitations of that term would apply. The marriage has to be recognized in the state where the employee resides, including common law marriage in states where it is recognized. 29 USC 2611(13); 29 CFR 825.113(a), 825.800; S. Res. 242, Cong. Rec. S3959, S3962 (April 23, 1996), 29 CFR 825.113(a), 825.800. [For a further discussion of recognized marriages, see Chapter 6, "Covered Family Members."]

d. Siblings

The marriage penalty only applies to a currently married husband and wife who work for the same employer. The penalty does not apply to other combinations of relatives who happen to work for the same employer, such as siblings. *See* Preamble, 29 CFR 202 (marriage penalty does not apply to siblings); DOL WH FMLA Advisory Opinion No. 99 (Jan. 12, 1999) (marriage penalty does not apply to siblings who work for the same employer).

e. Application of the Marriage Penalty

At first blush, the marriage penalty does not appear to be particularly complex. In application, however, the marriage penalty requires employers to exercise additional care to ensure that both spouses receive all the FMLA leave to which they are entitled. The following examples illustrate application of the marriage penalty. All examples assume a valid marriage.

Example 1

Hal and Daryl Alpine are both FMLA eligible employees of the Postal Service. The Postal Service uses a fixed 12-month leave year. During the leave year, Daryl took eight weeks of FMLA leave to bond with the couple's newly adopted infant daughter.

The FMLA leave taken by Daryl is subject to the marriage penalty (care for child after adoption placement). As a result, for the remainder of the leave year, Hal is limited to four weeks of FMLA leave for any other reason covered by the marriage penalty. Hal could take up to four weeks of FMLA leave to bond with his newly adopted infant daughter, for the birth of another son or daughter, or to care for the employee's parent with a serious health condition.

Whether Hal takes the four weeks subject to the marriage penalty, he remains entitled to eight weeks of FMLA leave during the leave year for FMLA conditions not covered by the marriage penalty. Hal could use his eight weeks of FMLA leave if he fell ill with a serious health condition, to care for Daryl if she were to suffer a serious health condition, or to care for Hal's son or daughter, including the newly adopted daughter, if they were to suffer from a serious health condition.

Example 2

Same facts as above, except that Hal took 12 weeks of FMLA leave to care for his mother who suffers from a serious health condition.

Because Hal took FMLA leave to care for his mother with a serious health condition, the marriage penalty applies. By taking the maximum amount of combined leave available for a condition subject to the marriage penalty, Hal does not have any FMLA leave to use to care for his father in the event of a serious health condition. Hal would also not have any FMLA leave to bond with a child following the birth or placement for adoption or foster care of a son or daughter. Daryl remains entitled to a full 12 workweeks of FMLA leave during the same leave year for a condition that is not subject to the marriage penalty. Daryl could use any or all of her 12 workweeks of FMLA leave for her own serious health condition, for the serious health condition of her son or daughter, or to care for Hal should he have a serious health condition.

Example 3

Same facts as above, except that Hal is an FMLA-eligible employee and Daryl is not. During the leave year, Daryl takes two weeks of paid family leave to bond with their newly adopted five-year old son. Hal plans on taking eight weeks of FMLA leave at the same time to bond with their son.

The marriage penalty does not apply because Daryl is not eligible for FMLA leave. Note that this is true even though the reason for the leave, bonding time with a newly adopted child, would normally fall within the marriage penalty. Because the marriage penalty does not apply, Hal gets his full 12 workweeks of FMLA leave during the leave year.

Example 4

Same facts as above, except that Hal and Daryl work for the U.S. Forest Service. Hal is an eligible employee under Title II of the FMLA Daryl is an eligible employee under Title I of the FMLA Hal and Daryl each ask for six weeks of FMLA leave to run at the same time to bond their newly adopted five-year old son.

It is unclear whether the marriage penalty would apply in this situation, although it is probably doubtful. According to the regulations implementing Title I, if one spouse is ineligible for FMLA leave, the other spouse is entitled to a full 12 weeks of FMLA leave. 29 CFR 825.202(b). Neither the regulations nor the Preamble state that ineligibility is determined solely by reference to Title I. In this case, the argument would be that Hal is not ineligible for FMLA leave because he is eligible under Title II. A counter argument would be that the ultimate form of ineligibility is the inapplicability of the statute (Title I) applying the marriage penalty. Title II does not impose a marriage penalty.

The regulation should be read to include a requirement that eligibility for purposes of applying the marriage penalty is determined by reference to the underlying statute, not similar statutes that do not include a marriage penalty. In this case, because Hal is not an eligible employee under Title I, the marriage penalty does not apply. As such, Daryl is entitled to the six weeks of FMLA leave she requested. Hal would also be entitled to six weeks of FMLA leave under Title II, which does not have a marriage penalty.

The example also illustrates the need for the DOL, OPM, and other regulating entities to cooperate on how these similar, but different, FMLA laws interact with one another.

Example 5

Same facts as above, except that Hal and Daryl are both eligible employees under Title I of the FMLA Hal's usual or normal work schedule is 60 hours in a five-day workweek, Monday through Friday. Daryl also works Monday through Friday, for 40 hours per week. During the fixed 12-month leave year, Daryl took 60 hours of FMLA leave for her own serious health condition, 20 hours to care for Hal, who was laid up with a serious health condition, and 20 hours to care for Greg, their 16-year old son who also had a serious health condition.

During the same leave year, Hal took 32 hours of FMLA leave for his own serious health condition, and 20 hours to care for Daryl, who was laid up with a serious health condition. Hal also took 120 hours of FMLA leave to care for his mother, who has a long-term serious health condition.

Daryl requested 100 hours of FMLA leave to care for her father, who is suffering with a serious health condition. Hal also needs 100 hours of FMLA leave for further care for his mother.

Under the marriage penalty, an eligible husband and wife are limited to a combined total of 12 weeks of leave during any 12-month period for FMLA taken for a covered condition subject to the marriage penalty. In this example, Daryl is entitled to 480 hours of FMLA leave during the 12-month leave year. She has already used 100 hours, leaving her with 380 hours. However, that amount is further reduced for the 120 hours of FMLA leave taken by Hal to care for his seriously ill mother. That leave is subject to the marriage penalty. Subtracting the 120 marriage penalty hours used by Hal from the 380 hours of FMLA leave Daryl has remaining, leaves 260 hours left for further use. Subtracting the 100 hours she plans to use and the 100 hours Hal plans to use, both of which are subject to the marriage penalty, leaves Daryl with 60 additional FMLA hours she could use during the remainder of the leave year.

Hal's total FMLA leave entitlement for the year is 720 hours (60 x 12). He used 172 hours of FMLA leave so far, leaving him with 548 hours. None of the 100 hours of leave Daryl has taken so far involves the marriage penalty. Even including the 100 hours that Daryl plans on taking to care for her father, which hours are subject to the marriage penalty, Hal would still have 448 hours of FMLA leave remaining. Subtracting the 100 hours Hal plans on using to care for his mother, which are also subject to the marriage penalty, Hal has 328 hours of FMLA leave for use.

J. MORE GENEROUS EMPLOYER LEAVE BENEFITS

The FMLA sets the minimum requirements for the provision of family and medical leave by employing agencies. Agencies may, however, offer more generous family and medical leave benefits than the minimum required by the FMLA.

1. Title II

An agency must comply with any collective bargaining agreement or any agency employment benefit program or plan that provides greater family or medical leave entitlements to employees than those required by Title II. 5 CFR 630.1210(a). To that end, employers may amend any employment benefit program or plan provided the amended policies, at minimum, comply with the requirements of Title II. 5 CFR 630.1210(a). Conversely, the rights established by the FMLA may not be diminished by any agency leave policies or the terms of a collective bargaining agreement. 5 CFR 630.1210(b).

An agency that adopts leave policies more generous than the legal minimum required by Title II is prohibited from providing paid time off in an amount greater than that otherwise authorized by law or provide sick leave in any situation in which sick leave would not normally be allowed by law or regulation. 5 CFR 630.1210(c). For example, an employer may not provide by agency policy that an employee may receive more than seven days of paid leave for bone marrow donation. [For a further discussion of paid leave substitution under the FMLA, see Chapter 11, "Substitution of Paid Leave."]

In the context of the amount of FMLA leave available to an eligible employee, the ability to adopt more generous employment benefit programs or plans to provide greater family and medical leave entitlements than those required by Title II allows employers to provide more than 12 workweeks of leave each 12-month leave year. Because these more generous family and medical leave policies may be enacted pursuant to the terms of a collective bargaining agreement, unions representing employees may bargain for more than the minimum 12 workweeks of FMLA leave guaranteed to eligible employees by law.

The regulations implementing Title II, unlike those discussed below implementing Title I, the CAA, and the PEOAA, are less clear regarding the treatment of these more generous family and medical leave benefits. That is, are these more generous benefits covered by the protections of the FMLA, or are they outside the protections of the FMLA? I argue that these extra benefits are not covered by the protections of the FMLA.

While an employer may adopt employment policies providing more generous family and medical leave entitlements, these more generous leave entitlements are not covered by the FMLA. By statute, the FMLA provides for 12 workweeks of protected FMLA leave for certain covered conditions. If, for example, a union were able to secure an additional four weeks of unpaid leave each year for family and medical purposes, that extra four weeks of leave would not be protected by the FMLA. Rather, the four extra weeks of leave are only covered by whatever protections exist under agency policy. This remains the case even if the employer's policy applies all of the definitions and procedural requirements of the FMLA to these extra four weeks.

The regulation allowing more generous family and medical leave entitlements (5 CFR 630.1210) should not be read as expanding statutory entitlements and protections, which it cannot do. The 12-workweek FMLA leave entitlement is a statutory entitlement. Rather, the regulation should be read as allowing agencies to adopt, and union or other employee organizations to advocate for, more generous family and medical leave policies. Such polices, however, are just that: agency policies.

An employer could adopt policies so similar to the FMLA that, as a practical matter, they carry the same protections as the FMLA. Such policies, however, would never be exactly like the FMLA. Take our example where a union successfully negotiated for four additional weeks of LWOP for family and medical leave purposes. Also assume that the same definitions, procedural requirements, and protection from discipline or adverse action are applied to those four weeks, as a matter of agency policy. A violation of 12 weeks of FMLA leave would be protected by the FMLA and agency policy. Regarding the additional four weeks, only the protections afforded by agency policy would apply.

Unions and other organizations representing the interests of federal employees will likely bargain for the availability of more generous family and medical leave benefits. Agencies need to be careful to tailor any agreement for more generous family and medical leave benefits so that it can readily identify what leave is covered by the FMLA and what leave is covered only by the agencies' more generous leave policies. The agency does not want to get into a situation where it cannot tell whether the leave benefits being applied are covered by the FMLA or agency policy. For example, an agency that is willing to provide more family and medical leave benefits than the minimum 12 workweeks may want to stipulate that the first 12 weeks of such leave are drawn from the FMLA (assuming all conditions are met), and then the added amount of leave is drawn under company policy.

2. Title I, the CAA, and the PEOAA

Title I, the CAA, and the PEOAA contain similar provisions that permit employers to provide more generous FMLA leave benefits than those required by the Act. Specifically, an employer must observe any employment benefit program or plan that provides greater family or medical leave rights to employees than the rights established by the FMLA. 29 CFR 825.700(a); S. Res. 242, Cong. Rec. S3959, S3976 (April 23, 1996); 29 CFR 825.700(a). To that end, employers may amend existing employment benefit programs or plans provided the amended policies, at minimum, comply with the requirements of Act. 29 CFR 825.700(b); S. Res. 242, Cong. Rec. S3959, S3976 (April 23, 1996); 29 CFR 825.700(b). Conversely, the rights established by the FMLA may not be diminished by any employment benefit program or plan, including the terms of a collective bargaining agreement. 29 CFR 825.700(a); S. Res. 242, Cong. Rec. S3959, S3976 (April 23, 1996); 29 CFR 825.700(a). For example, a union could not agree to limit eligible employees to a maximum of 11 workweeks of FMLA leave each leave year.

If an employer provides greater unpaid family and medical leave rights than are afforded by the FMLA, the employer is not required to extend additional rights afforded by the FMLA to the additional leave period not covered by the FMLA. 29 CFR 825.700(a); S. Res. 242, Cong. Rec. S3959, S3976 (April 23, 1996); 29 CFR 825.700(a). Unlike Title II, this provision clearly indicates that the greater unpaid family and medical leave benefits are governed by agency policy, and not the FMLA. *See Green v. New Balance Athletic Shoe, Inc.*, 182 F. Supp. 2d 128, 135 (D. Me. 2002); *Covey v. Methodist Hospital of Dyersburg, Inc.*, 56 F. Supp. 2d 965, 970 (W.D. Tenn. 1999) (employer policy can provide more than 12 workweeks of leave each leave year, but the extra leave is covered by employer policy, not the FMLA).

For example, an employer with a more generous family and medical leave plan may permit an employee to take up to 52 weeks of medical leave and return to work. Under the plan, if the employee fails to return to work within the 52 weeks of medical leave, the employer may terminate the employee's employment. The FMLA, in contrast, only requires 12 workweeks of leave during a 12-month period. The employer in this example would have an obligation under its own "medical leave or absence" policies to extend leave benefits for up to 52 weeks, but not beyond 52 weeks. If the medical leave of absence also qualifies as a serious health condition within the meaning of the FMLA, the employer may designate up to 12 weeks of that absence as FMLA leave, provided the employee also meets the eligibility and other requirements of the Act. The 12 weeks of absence designated as FMLA are covered by the protections of the Act. The FMLA would not, however, require an employer to extend those benefits beyond 12 workweeks. Where an employer has extended family and medical leave benefits beyond the 12 weeks required by the FMLA, such leave would be governed by the employer's policies, not the FMLA. *See* DOL WH FMLA Advisory Opinion No. 103 (March 26, 1999).

In *Panto v. Palmer Dialysis Center/Total Renal Care*, No. 01-6013, 2003 U.S. Dist. LEXIS 5663, at *18 (E.D. Pa. April 7, 2003), the court addressed the interaction of the FMLA with a more generous company leave policy. In pertinent part, the company policy provided:

> The Company recognizes that there may be times when you are required to be away from your job an extended period of time. Leaves of absence will be administered in compliance with the Family and Medical Leave Act "FMLA"... Additionally, a qualified leave of absence, upon prior approval, may be extended for an additional three (3) months (not to exceed a total six months).

Panto did not deny that she exhausted 12 weeks of FMLA leave. She argued, however, that her employer should be estopped from asserting that her leave was confined to 12 weeks because defendant's policy allowed for up to six months medical leave under the FMLA. The court disagreed. According to the court, "[a]lthough Defendant's policy contemplates an additional three months 'qualified leave of absence,' the FMLA does not create a federal cause of action to enforce the voluntary employer policies of providing benefits that exceed those required by the FMLA."

K. EFFECT OF MIXED FMLA RESPONSIBILITIES

Federal agencies with mixed FMLA coverage under, in most instances, Title I and II of the Act, must be cognizant of differences between the statutes regarding the calculation of FMLA leave. Failure to take these differences into account, such as by applying the requirements of Title II to all employees, even those covered by Title I, may lead to inadvertent violations of Title I of the Act. Such violations can form the basis of costly and time-consuming litigation, including lawsuits against individual managers and supervisors. Those differences also include a choice of options more beneficial to employers under Title I than are permitted under Title II.

Regarding the calculation of the amount of FMLA leave available to an eligible employee, some of the major differences between Title I and Title II of the Act include the application of the marriage penalty. Title I allows employers to limit the total amount of FMLA absences where a husband and wife work for the same agency. Title II does not have such a limitation. To limit FMLA leave absences, an employer with Title I employees should consider applying the marriage penalty to those employees. Union and other organizations representing employees covered by Title I, on the other hand, should bargain for more generous employer family and medical leave benefits, including elimination of the marriage penalty. Elimination of the marriage penalty is permitted under Title I, the CAA, and the PEOAA as application of the penalty is permissive, rather than mandatory.

Additionally, the calculation of the amount of FMLA leave under Title I, the CAA, and the PEOAA is determined by reference to the employee's usual or normal workweek. Title II, on the other hand, references the employee's regularly scheduled administrative workweek as the basis for the calculation of the amount of FMLA leave. These terms may not mean the same thing. Employers and organizations representing employees must be cognizant of these differences. An employer that calculates the amount of FMLA leave available to a Title I employee based on that employee's regularly scheduled administrative workweek may find itself in violation of Title I of the Act.

Holidays are treated differently in calculating the amount of FMLA leave used by an eligible employee. Under Title II, holidays are specifically excluded from the 12-workweek entitlement. Title I, on the other hand, includes a holiday that falls within an FMLA leave absence toward the employee's 12 workweeks of FMLA leave. Employers with Title I employees who wish to reduce employee absences are well advised to apply the holiday penalty rather than the more generous Title II provisions. Unions and other employee organizations, on the other hand, should bargain for general application of the Title II holiday calculation rule, a more generous family and medical leave policy.

Another area where subtle differences between Title I and Title II of the Act can lead to potential problems for employers involves changes to an employee's work schedule. Under Title II, any change to the employee's work schedule during the 12-month FMLA leave year requires recalculation of the employee's remaining FMLA leave entitlement based on the new schedule. Under Title II, only long-term or permanent changes to an employee's work schedule warrant recalculation of the amount of FMLA leave available to an eligible Title I employee. An employer that recalculates the amount of FMLA leave available to a Title I employee for a short-term change in schedule (as permitted by Title II) is in violation of Title I.

To avoid the pitfalls resulting from subtle differences between Title I and Title II of the FMLA, employers must carefully determine what rules apply to each eligible employee exercising rights under the FMLA. An employer that rotely applies the requirements of Title I to all employees, including those covered by Title II, may violate that employee's FMLA rights. Similarly, to effectively represent their constituents, unions and other organizations representing federal employees must gain an appreciation for the differences in the requirements of the FMLA laws. In application to the federal workforce, the FMLA is not a one-size-fits-all law.

IV. LEAVE SCHEDULING

This section explains how an eligible employee may take FMLA leave. As we have seen, the FMLA permits an eligible employee up to 12 weeks of FMLA each 12-month leave year for various covered conditions. 29 USC 12(a)(1) (Title I); 5 USC 6382(a); 2 USC 1312(as)(1) (incorporating 12-week leave entitlement of Title I into CAA); 3 USC 412(a)(1) (incorporating 12-week leave entitlement of Title I into PEOAA). Eligible federal employees may take FMLA leave in one of three ways: (1) in a single block of time; (2) intermittently; or (3) on a reduced leave schedule. While similar, the rules governing how FMLA leave may be taken are not identical. *Hoffman v. Professional Med Team*, 394 F.3d 414, 418 (6th Cir. 2005).

A. BLOCK LEAVE

An eligible employee may take any or all of his or her 12-week FMLA leave entitlement in the form of a single continuous block of time during which the employee is absent for the same covered condition. *Hoffman*, 394 F.3d at 418 (FMLA leave may be taken in one block of 12 or fewer weeks); *Adams v. Honda of America Mfg.*, 111 Fed. Appx. 353 (6th Cir. 2004) (when medically necessary, an employee may take "continuous" or "intermittent" leave for a serious health condition; continuous leave is leave taken as one continuous period of time).

The concept of a single block of FMLA leave is not mentioned in Title I, Title II, the CAA, or the PEOAA. However, the concept was originally mentioned in the legislative history of the original Act (which contained Titles I, II, and Title V, which would become the CAA). As justification for the availability of FMLA leave on an intermittent or reduced leave schedule basis, the Congressional Committee Reports recognize that some serious health conditions require that an employee be "absent from work on a recurring basis" rather than for a single block of time, and that "continuing treatment or supervision may sometimes take the form of intermittent visits to a doctor." DOL WH FMLA Advisory Opinion No. 112, n. 2 (Sept. 11, 2000) (citing Report from the Committee on Labor and Human Resources (S.5), Report 105-3, January 27, 1993, pp. 27–29; Report from the Committee on Education and Labor (H.R. 1), Report 103-8, Part 1, February 2, 1993, pp. 27, 40–41).

The regulations implementing Title II define intermittent leave as leave taken in separate blocks of time, rather than for one continuous period of time. 5 CFR 630.1201 (definition of intermittent leave). A similar definition is included in the regulations implementing Title I, 29 CFR 825.800 (definition of intermittent leave), and the CAA. S. Res. 242, Cong. Rec. S3959, S3977 (April 23, 1996); 29 CFR 825.800 (definition of intermittent leave).

It is curious that the FMLA addresses leave taken in a single block of time for the same covered condition, one of only three ways that FMLA leave may be taken, by absentia. That is, the FMLA describes the rules regarding FMLA leave taken on an intermittent or reduced leave schedule. If those rules do not apply because the leave is for a single block of time, we get to go on a treasure hunt to figure out what rules do apply. Sounds like fun, doesn't it?

1. Smallest Increment of Leave

a. Title I, the CAA, and the PEOAA

Because of the absence of regulatory guidance, it is unclear what the smallest increment of time an employee may take as FMLA leave in a single block of time. Under Title I, the CAA, and the PEOAA, there is no limit on the size of an increment of leave when an employee takes intermittent leave or leave on a reduced leave schedule. However, an employer may limit leave increments to the shortest period of time that the employer's payroll system uses to account for absence or use of leave, provided it is one hour or less. 29 CFR 825.203(d); S. Res. 242, Cong. Rec. S3959, S3964 (April 23, 1996); 29 CFR 825.203(d). If that is the rule for intermittent and reduced schedule leave, what is the rule for leave taken in a single bock of time for a covered condition? The answer: unknown.

In the absence of clear direction in the regulations, employers governed by Title I, the CAA, and the PEOAA who wish to play it conservatively are well advised to apply the intermittent and reduced schedule leave rule to FMLA leave taken in a single block of time. That is, the smallest increment of FMLA leave that an employee may take in a single block of time for a covered condition is equal to the smallest increment of time that an employer payroll system uses to account for absences or use of leave, provided it is one hour or less.

b. Title II

The regulations implementing Title II are better at addressing the smallest increment of leave that may be taken for a single block of FMLA leave. An employee may not take any more leave than necessary to manage the circumstances that prompted the need for FMLA leave. 5 CFR 630.1203(b). Taken literally, an employee who only needs five minutes of FMLA leave to make arrangements to drive a parent for a post–operative physical could not take any more FMLA leave. The regulation presupposes that the smallest increment of FMLA leave available is the increment of time needed by the employee, and nothing more. This, in turn, presupposes that an employer is obligated to record and manage these small amounts of FMLA leave.

c. Examples

Examples of FMLA leave taken in a block of time include the following:

- Twelve weeks to bond with a newly adopted son or daughter;
- Six weeks to care for a terminally ill parent;
- Three days for an eligible employee to recover from his or her own serious health condition;
- Two hours to drive a parent for a post-operative follow-up visit with a doctor.

Again, for Title I, the CAA, and the PEOAA, the above examples assume the application of the rules governing the smallest increment of time, for purposes of intermittent or reduced leave schedule. For Title II, the examples work applying a literal reading of the requirement that an employee is entitled to the exact amount of FMLA leave needed, no matter what that amount is, and no more.

2. Birth or Placement for Adoption or Foster Care

Where FMLA leave is taken in a single block of time for the birth or to care for a newborn son or daughter, or for the placement with the employee of a son or daughter for adoption or foster care, the employee does not need the agreement of the agency to be entitled to take the leave. The above is an example of a rule that is not set forth in the implementing regulations, but is derived from limitations placed on leave for the same covered condition (birth or placement) taken on an intermittent or reduced leave schedule basis.

3. Serious Health Condition

Where FMLA leave is taken in a single block of time due to the serious health condition of a covered family member, or because of the employee's own serious health condition, an employee may take the leave without further conditions, such as the agreement of the agency. Again, this is an example of a rule that is not set forth in the implementing regulations, but is derived from limitations placed on leave for the same covered condition (serious health condition) taken on an intermittent or reduced leave schedule basis.

B. INTERMITTENT AND REDUCED SCHEDULE LEAVE

In addition to a single block of time, an eligible employee may take FMLA leave intermittently or on a reduced leave schedule under certain circumstances. 29 USC 2612(b) (Title I); 29 CFR 825.203; 5 USC 6382(b) (Title II); 5 CFR 630.1204; 2 USC 1312(a)(1) (adopting § 2612 of Title I into CAA); S. Res. 242, Cong. Rec. S3959, S3964 (April 23, 1996); 29 CFR 825.203; 3 USC 412(a)(1) (adopting § 2612 of Title I into PEOAA). The rules governing the circumstances under which an employee may take FMLA leave intermittently or on a reduced leave schedule, while similar under the various federal sector FMLA statutes, are not identical.

1. Definitions

a. Intermittent Leave

"Intermittent leave" or "leave taken intermittently" is defined several different, although substantially similar, ways for purposes of federal sector FMLA. The term is not defined in any of the statutes.

(1) Title II

For purposes of Title II, intermittent leave or leave take intermittently means leave taken in separate blocks of time, rather than for one continuous period of time. 5 CFR 630.1202 (definition).

Note that the above definition does not require that leave taken in separate blocks of time be due to the same FMLA covered condition. This would appear to be a critical omission, as the gravamen of intermittent leave is that multiple absences are permitted for the same underlying FMLA condition. The omission of the proviso that intermittent leave is related to the same underlying covered condition raises the specter that multiple, unrelated FMLA absences could be argued to constitute intermittent FMLA leave, justifying application of the intermittent FMLA leave limitations. While it does not appear that was the intent of the regulations (particularly when compared to how Title I, the CAA, and the PEOAA address this area), the argument is available.

The Title II definition of intermittent leave or leave taken intermittently also fails to tie such leave to a covered condition. Again, since all FMLA leave must, by definition, be for a covered condition, the inclusion of such language is probably unnecessary. By comparison, the similar regulations for Title I, the CAA, and the PEOAA include the tie to covered conditions.

(2) Title I, the CAA, and the PEOAA

Intermittent leave is defined in two different, yet similar, ways under Title I, the CAA, and the PEOAA. In the definition section of the regulations (29 CFR 825.800; S. Res. 242, Cong. Rec. S3959, S3977 (April 23, 1996); 29 CFR 825.800), intermittent leave means:

> [L]eave taken in separate periods of time due to a single illness or injury, rather than for one continuous period of time, and may include leave of periods from an hour or more to several weeks. Examples of intermittent leave would include leave taken on an occasional basis for medical appointments, or leave taken several days at a time spread over a period of six months, such as for chemotherapy.

Accord George v. Russell Stover Candies, Inc., 106 Fed. Appx. 946 (6th Cir. 2004); *Adams v. Honda of America Mfg.*, 111 Fed. Appx. 353 (6th Cir. 2004) (intermittent leave is leave taken in separate blocks of time for a single qualifying reason); *Roberts v. Ground Handling, Inc.*, No. 04 Civ. 4955 (WCC), 2007 U.S. Dist. LEXIS 23441, at *27-28 (S.D.N.Y. March 30, 2007); *Karl v. City of Chicago*, No. 05 C 6632, 2007 U.S. Dist. LEXIS 6873, at *9 (N.D. Ill. Jan. 25, 2007); *Dupee v. Klaff's Inc.*, 462 F. Supp. 2d 233, 242 (D. Conn. Nov. 8, 2006); *Sabrese v. Lowe's Home Centers, Inc.*, 320 F. Supp. 2d 311, 321 (W.D. Pa. 2004) (Title 1); *Wu v. Southeast-Atlantic Beverage Corp.*, No. 1:02-CV-505-CAP, 2003 U.S. Dist. LEXIS 25828, at *60 (N.D. Ga. Aug. 13, 2003) (FMLA leave need not be taken as a 12-week block, but may be taken "intermittently or on a reduced leave schedule when medically necessary"), *approved, adopted, summary judgment granted*, 2003 U.S. Dist. LEXIS 25827 (N.D. Ga. Sept. 12, 2003).

Elsewhere, the regulations define intermittent leave as FMLA leave taken in several blocks of time due to a single qualifying reason. 29 CFR 825.203(a); S. Res. 242, Cong. Rec. S3959, S3964 (April 23, 1996); 29 CFR 825.203(a); *see Plautz v. Potter*, 156 Fed. Appx. 812 (6th Cir. 2005); *Hoffman v. Professional Med Team*, 394 F.3d 414, 418 (6th Cir. 2005); *Roberts v. Ground Handling, Inc.*, No. 04 Civ. 4955 (WCC), 2007 U.S. Dist. LEXIS 23441, at *27-28 (S.D.N.Y. March 30, 2007); *Collins v. U.S. Playing Card Co.*, 466 F. Supp. 2d 954, 964 (S.D. Ohio Nov. 6, 2006); *Price v. GKN Aerospace North America, Inc.*, No. 4:05CV01147 ERW, 2006 U.S. Dist. LEXIS 76392, at *13 & n.11 (E.D. Mo. Oct. 20, 2006); *Underhill v. Willamina Lumber Co. et al.*, No. 98-630-AS, 1999 U.S. Dist. LEXIS 9722, at n.1 (D. Ore. June 17, 1999); *Giles v. Christian Care Centers, Inc. et al.*, No. 3:96-CV-2168-G, 1997 U.S. Dist. LEXIS 20351, at n.1 (N.D. Tex. Dec. 11, 1997); *Hendry v. GTE North, Inc.*, 896 F. Supp. 816, 828 (N.D. Ind. 1995).

In addition to the examples given in the definition section cited above, a pregnant employee may take leave intermittently for prenatal examinations or for her own conditions, such as for periods of severe morning sickness. 29 CFR 825.203(c)(1); S. Res. 242, Cong. Rec. S3959, S3964 (April 23, 1996); 29 CFR 825.203(c)(1); *see McClain v. Detroit Entertainment, LLC*, 458 F. Supp. 2d 427 (E.D. Mich. 2006); *Nance v. Buffalo's Café of Griffin, Inc.*, No. 1:03-cv-2887-WSD, 2005 U.S. Dist. LEXIS 20429, at *13 (N.D. Ga. March 30, 2005).

The internal differences in the above regulations are worth addressing. First, note the use of the phrase "separate periods of time" in the definition section with the term "several blocks of time" elsewhere in the regulations. Presumably, the terms "blocks" and "periods," when describing time, mean the same thing.

Second, note that the use of the phrase "due to a single injury or illness" in the definition section. Elsewhere, the regulations use the phrase "due to a single qualifying reason." Presumably, the terms mean the same thing. On the other hand, absent a tie to covered conditions (like the reference to a qualifying reason), the phrase "injury or illness" does not, in and of itself, require that the reason for intermittent FMLA leave be due to a covered condition. That is, not every injury or illness will rise to the level of a serious health condition within the meaning of the Act. Moreover, reference to an injury or illness necessarily excludes the possibility of FMLA leave for covered conditions that do not involve illness, such as to bond with a newborn or to adopt a son or daughter. Of course, an eligible employee only gets to take FMLA leave if the reason is a condition covered by the Act.

The above point is not made because much mischief can be made of these particular semantic differences, but to demonstrate the problem with using different regulatory terms to describe the same thing. Regulatory language needs to be consistent. The easiest and clearest way to be consistent is to use the same regulatory terms to describe the same phenomena.

In *Roberts v. Ground Handling, Inc.*, No. 04 Civ. 4955 (WCC), 2007 U.S. Dist. LEXIS 23441, at *27-28 (S.D.N.Y. March 30, 2007), the court found that because the employee's absences commencing in October 2002 and March 2003 were both due to peritonitis, her absences must be considered part of a single, intermittent leave.

Intermittent leave involves intermittent periods of leave and work, not FMLA leave interspersed with other forms of leave. *Miller v. Personal–Touch of Virginia, Inc.*, 342 F. Supp. 2d 499, 512–513 (E.D. Va. 2004). In *Miller*, plaintiff argued that because she was not required to substitute paid leave for unpaid FMLA leave under her understanding of her employer's policy, she could use FMLA leave intermittently with periods of paid leave during her FMLA—covered absence, thereby extending the amount of FMLA leave available to cover her absence. The court disagreed, finding that "it is beyond the intent of the FMLA to have permitted the plaintiff to switch back and forth, between FMLA unpaid leave and paid leave not taken pursuant to the FMLA, when the reason for either form of leave was the same—complications due to and following her pregnancy." Intermittent leave, the court found, is designed to be interspersed with periods of work, not with periods of other leave. The court concluded:

> The plaintiff's purported structuring of her paid leave and FMLA leave did not constitute intermittent use of FMLA leave as the leave amounted to one continuous period for the same medical need. Such leave cannot, as a matter of law, be characterized as intermittent such that the plaintiff could intersperse paid leave with unpaid FMLA leave.

The case supports the majority view that "substitution" of paid leave for unpaid FMLA leave means that paid leave will run concurrently with unpaid FMLA.

b. Reduced Leave Schedule

The term "reduced leave schedule" is defined in the statues. It means a leave schedule that reduces the usual number of hours per workweek, or hours per workday, of an employee. 29 USC 2611(9) (Tile I); 5 USC 6381(4); 2 USC 1312(a)(1) (adopting § 2611 of Title I into CAA); 3 USC 412(a)(1) (adopting § 2611 of Title I into PEOAA).

If you are confused by the term "reduced leave schedule," you are not alone. One commentator to the final OPM FMLA regulations asked that the phrase "reduced leave schedule" be changed to "reduced work schedule," because the hours of work are reduced and supplemented by FMLA leave. Preamble, 5 CFR 630.1204, Intermittent or reduced schedule leave. OPM rejected the suggestion after noting that "reduced leave schedule" was the phrase used in the statute. *Id*.

The regulations implementing the FMLA further refine the definition of "reduced leave schedule." While the language of the various statutes define the phrase exactly the same, the regulatory definitions do not.

(1) Title II

"Reduced leave schedule" means a work schedule under which the usual number of hours of regularly scheduled work per workday or workweek of an employee is reduced. 5 CFR 630.1202 (definition of reduced leave schedule). "Regularly scheduled" is defined by cross–reference to 5 CFR 610.102. It means work that is scheduled in advance of an administrative workweek under agency procedures for establishing workweeks in accordance with 5 CFR 610.111. An "administrative workweek" means any period of seven consecutive 24–hour periods designated in advance by the head of an agency. 5 CFR 610.102 (definition).

(2) Title I, the CAA, and the PEOAA

The regulations define a "reduced leave schedule" in two ways. First, they repeat the statutory definition. 29 CFR 203(a), 825.800 (definition of reduced leave schedule); S. Res. 242, Cong. Rec. S3959, S3964, S3978 (April 23, 1996); 29 CFR 825.203(a), 825. 800 (definition of reduced leave schedule). The regulations add that a reduced leave schedule is a change in the employee's schedule for a period of time, normally from full-time to part-time. 29 CFR 203(a); S. Res. 242, Cong. Rec. S3959, S3964 (April 23, 1996); 29 CFR 825.203(a); *see Hoffman v. Professional Med Team*, 394 F.3d 414, 418 (6th Cir. 2005); *George v. Russell Stover Candies, Inc.*, 106 Fed. Appx. 946 (6th Cir. 2004); *Metzler v. Federal Home Loan Bank of Topeka*, No. 03-4024-SAC, 2004 U.S. Dist. LEXIS 21647, at *15 (D. Kan. Sept. 21, 2004), aff'd, 464 F.3d 1164 (10th Cir. 2006) (indicating that a reduced leave schedule is equivalent to a part-time schedule); *Dressler v. Community Service Communications, Inc.*, 275 F. Supp. 2d 17, n.11 (D. Me. 2003) (reduced leave schedule is a change in the employee's schedule for a period of time, normally from full-time to part-time), aff'd, 115 Fed. Appx. 452 (1st Cir. 2004); *Green v. New Balance Athletic Shoe, Inc.*, 182 F. Supp. 2d 128, 136 (D. Me. 2002); *Giles v. Christian Care Centers, Inc. et al.*, No. 3:96-CV-2168-G, 1997 U.S. Dist. LEXIS 20351, at n. 1 (N.D. Tex. Dec. 11, 1997).

An example of an employee taking leave on a reduced leave schedule is an employee who is recovering from a serious health condition and is not strong enough to work a full-time schedule. 29 CFR 203(c)(1); S. Res. 242, Cong. Rec. S3959, S3964 (April 23, 1996); 29 CFR 825.203(c)(1).

For all intents and purposes, a reduced leave schedule is simply a more systematic form of intermittent leave. That is, like intermittent leave, a reduced leave schedule involves multiple absences for the same underlying covered condition. Unlike the randomness of intermittent leave, the multiple FMLA leave absences in a reduced leave schedule are taken more systematically, such as every Friday, or working part-time rather than full-time.

c. Intermittent and Reduced Schedule Leave Treated the Same

You do not need to master the differences between the definitions of intermittent or reduced leave schedule because these types of leave are treated the same for purposes of the FMLA. For the most part, the only real difference you need to be aware of for purposes of treatment under the FMLA is between leave taken in a single block of time, and leave taken in multiple blocks of time for the same underlying condition, either intermittently or on a reduced leave schedule.

2. Birth, Adoption, Foster Care Placement

An eligible employee must obtain the permission of an employer in order to take FMLA leave on an intermittent or reduced leave schedule basis for or following the birth of a son or daughter, or the placement of a son or daughter for adoption or foster care. 29 USC 2612(b)(1); 29 CFR 825.203(b); 5 USC 6382(b)(1); 5 CFR 630.1204(a); 2 USC 1312(a)(1) (incorporating § 2612 of Title I into CAA); S. Res. 242, Cong. Rec. S3959, S3964 (April 23, 1996); 29 CFR 825.203(b); 3 USC 412(a)(1) (incorporating § 2612 of Title I into PEOAA); accord *Maynard v. Town of Monterey, Tennessee*, 75 Fed. Appx. 491 (6th Cir. 2003) (FMLA claim properly dismissed where no agreement existed between employee and employer permitting employee to take intermittent leave to care for infant daughter); *Ryl-Kuchar v. Care Centers, Inc.*, No. 05-3223, 2006 U.S. Dist. LEXIS 87853, at *15 (N.D. Ill. Dec. 4, 2006); *Miller v. Personal-Touch of Virginia, Inc.*, 342 F. Supp. 2d 499, 512-513 (E.D. Va. 2004).

Remember that an employee is entitled to leave for or following the birth, adoption, or foster care placement of a son or daughter, even though the son or daughter is not sick at all, or whose illness does not rise to the level of a serious health condition within the meaning of the FMLA. An eligible employee is entitled to take FMLA leave simply to bond with his or her new son or daughter. [For a further discussion of this issue, see Chapter 7, "Covered Conditions."]

Distinguished from the above is the situation where the newborn or newly adopted or foster care placed son or daughter has a serious health condition. In that case, an eligible employee requesting FMLA leave on an intermittent or reduced leave schedule does *not* need the permission of the employer. 29 CFR 825.203(b); S. Res. 242, Cong. Rec. S3959, S3964 (April 23, 1996); 29 CFR 825.203(b); *see Ryl-Kuchar v. Care Centers, Inc.*, No. 05-3223, 2006 U.S. Dist. LEXIS 87853, at *15 (N.D. Ill. Dec. 4, 2006). Different rules apply when FMLA leave is sought on an intermittent or reduced leave schedule basis involving a serious health condition.

Employer permission to authorize the use of FMLA leave on an intermittent or reduced leave schedule basis frequently arises in situations involving the birth, adoption, or foster care placement with the employee of a son or daughter. For example, an employee needs four hours of pre-placement FMLA leave to meet with a lawyer to arrange for a Russian adoption. Gleaning from Chapter 7, "Covered Conditions," pre-placement FMLA leave is available to an eligible employee. You grant the employee the leave. Five months later, the employee requests ten weeks of FMLA leave in order to fly to Russia to formalize the adoption, return to the states, and bond with the child. As this is the second request for FMLA leave for the same covered condition, the employee has requested intermittent FMLA leave. The employer could deny the second request for leave.

You would think that the same logic would apply to an employee who initially requested time off for prenatal care followed by a request for FMLA leave on an intermittent or reduced leave schedule basis subsequent to the birth, but you would be wrong. As set forth more fully in Chapter, 7, "Covered Conditions," FMLA leave for prenatal care is available to an eligible employee. However, prenatal care, unlike pre-placement leave, requires the expectant mother to have a serious health condition. *See* 29 CFR 825.112(c); S. Res. 242, Cong. Rec. S3959, S3962 (April 23, 1996); 29 CFR 825.112(c). Because the request for prenatal care was for a serious health condition, and the subsequent request was for bonding time with the newborn, which does not require the existence of a serious health condition, the two requests are treated separately. As such, the two requests do not meet the definition of intermittent leave, and the employer's agreement for the second request is not required. Rather, each request, for a single instance of prenatal leave and a single instance of bonding time, are separately considered as requests for a block of FMLA leave.

The regulations do not address the basis for an employer's refusal to agree to an eligible employee's request to take FMLA leave on an intermittent or reduced leave schedule basis for or following the birth, adoption, or foster care placement of a son or daughter. It is illegal to interfere with or discriminate against an employee for exercising rights under the FMLA. Under these circumstances, an employer is well advised to grant an employee's request for FMLA leave on an intermittent or reduced leave schedule basis unless it has a legitimate, nondiscriminatory reason for its decision. An employer should not deny an employee's request for FMLA leave as a form of retaliation for the employee's prior use of FMLA leave, because the supervisor does not like the FMLA, or simply because the employer can deny the request. In addition to legal restrictions, employers also need to think about the morale of this employee and the morale of the office if FMLA leave is denied without a legitimate basis.

There is a practical limitation on an employer's perceived arbitrary denial of a request for FMLA leave on an intermittent or reduced leave schedule basis in these circumstances. An eligible employee, denied intermittent or reduced leave schedule FMLA leave for or following the birth, adoption, or placement of a son or daughter, can always request to take the leave in a single block of time. In that circumstance, the employer's agreement is not required. For example, an eligible employee requests a reduced leave schedule from a full-time to a part-time schedule for 16 weeks to bond with a newborn child. Because this is the busy season, the employer denies the request. Incensed, the employee immediately requests to use the full 12 weeks of FMLA leave all at once. As a request for FMLA leave in a single block of time, the employer's permission is not required. All things being equal, the employee gets the leave, and the employer's work does not get done.

The above suggests that, while employers do have the legal authority to deny requests for FMLA leave on an intermittent or reduced leave schedule basis for following the birth, adoption, or foster care placement of a son or daughter, the arbitrary exercise of that right can be easily trumped by the employee. Employers are well advised to work with eligible employees in these circumstances to reach an agreement on a schedule that gets the employee what he or she wants, and ensures the agency that its critical needs are being met.

Unions and other organizations representing employees often seek to modify (out of existence) the requirement that an employee must obtain the permission of an employer in order to take FMLA leave on an intermittent or reduced leave schedule basis for birth, adoption, or foster care placement. Such a modification would constitute a more generous family and medical leave plan, which is permitted by the FMLA.

3. Serious Health Conditions

Under certain circumstances, FMLA leave is available on an intermittent or reduced leave schedule basis when the employee or a covered family member has a serious health condition. *George v. Russell Stover Candies, Inc.*, 106 Fed. Appx. 946 (6th Cir. 2004); *Adams v. Honda of America, Mfg.*, 111 Fed. Appx. 353 (6th Cir. 2004); *Dunning v. UPS*, 471 F. Supp. 2d 795, at *33 (E.D. Mich. 2007); *Dupee v. Klaff's Inc.*, 462 F. Supp. 2d 233, 242 (D. Conn. Nov. 8, 2006); *Metzler v. Federal Home Loan Bank of Topeka*, No. 03–4024–SAC, 2004 U.S. Dist. LEXIS 21647, at *15 (D. Kan. Sept. 21, 2004), aff'd, 464 F.3d 1164 (9th Cir. 2006); *Willis v. USPS*, No. 03 C 9185, 2004 U.S. Dist. LEXIS 18238, at *19 (N.D. Ill. Sept. 10, 2004) (for instance, employee with cancer may need intermittent leave for chemotherapy); *Sabbrese v. Lowe's Home Centers, Inc.*, 320 F. Supp. 2d 311, 321 (W.D. Pa. 2004); *Henson v. Bell Helicopter Textron, Inc.*, No. 4:01–CV–1024–Y, 2004 U.S. Dist. LEXIS, at 1630 *36 (N.D. Tex. Feb. 6, 2004), aff'd, 2005 U.S. App. LEXIS 6600 (5th Cir. April 18, 2005); *Jennings v. Mid-American Energy Co.*, 282 F. Supp. 2d 954, 960 (S.D. Iowa 2003); *Wu v. Southeast-Atlantic Beverage Corp.*, No. 1:02–CV–505–CAP, 2003 U.S. Dist. LEXIS

25828, at *60 (N.D. Ga. Aug. 13, 2003), *approved, adopted, summary judgment granted*, 2003 U.S. Dist. LEXIS 25827 (N.D. Ga. Sept. 12, 2003) (FMLA leave need not be taken as a 12-week block, but may be taken "intermittently or on a reduced leave schedule when medically necessary").

In *Sabbrese v. Lowe's Home Centers, Inc.*, 320 F. Supp. 2d 311, 321 (W.D. Pa. 2004), the court found that leave taken by a diabetic in order to eat to correct low blood sugar when medically necessary may qualify as intermittent leave under the FMLA.

The court in *Carmen v. Unison Behavioral Health Group, Inc.*, 295 F. Supp. 2d 809, 813 (N.D. Ohio 2003), inexplicably (and incorrectly) cited the need for agreement in order for an employee to take FMLA leave intermittently in a case involving a serious health condition.

The right to intermittent leave in these circumstances, however, is not absolute. *Palazzolo v. Galen Hospitals of Texas, Inc.*, No. 1: 96-CV-2550-TWT, 1997 U.S. Dist. LEXIS 21915, at *14–15 (N.D. Ga. Nov. 25, 1997). In order to be granted intermittent or a reduced leave schedule under the FMLA for a serious health condition, "an employee must pass through a series of substantive requirements and procedural hoops as provided by the statute." *Kaylor v. Fannin Regional Hospital, Inc.*, 946F. Supp. 988, 997 (N.D. Ga. 1996). These statutory requirements and procedures include: (1) the leave must be "medically necessary" for a "serious health condition" (29 USC 2612(b)(1)); (2) the employee must make a reasonable effort to schedule the treatment so as not to "disrupt unduly the operations of the employer" (29 USC 2612(e)(2)(a)); (3) the employee must give timely and adequate notice of the need for FMLA leave on an intermittent or reduced leave schedule basis (29 USC 2612(e)(2)(b)); and (4) if requested, the employee must timely provide medical certification in support of the "medical necessity" of the employee's need for FMLA leave on an intermittent or reduced leave schedule basis (29 USC 2613(b)(5)). *See Goodwin v. Rheem Manufacturing Co.*, 15 F. Supp. 2d 1197, 1205 (M.D. Ala. 1998) (FMLA required plaintiff seeking intermittent leave to fulfill certain statutory requirements, namely the employee must provide the employer with notice and certification regarding the reason for leave); *Rocky v. Columbia Lawnwood Regional Medical Center et al.*, 54 F. Supp. 2d 1159, 1170 (S.D. Fla. 1999).

An employee who fails to meet all of the above requirements is not entitled to intermittent or reduced leave schedule FMLA leave. *Kaylor v. Fannin Regional Hospital, Inc.*, 946 F. Supp. 988, 997 (N.D. Ga. 1996). Even if all of these requirements are met, FMLA leave on an intermittent or reduced leave schedule basis is limited to certain circumstances.

a. Medically Necessary

FMLA leave may be taken on an intermittent or reduced leave schedule basis when medically necessary because of a serious health condition that renders the employee unable to perform the functions of his or her position, or because the employee is needed to care for a spouse, son, daughter, or parent with a serious health condition. 29 USC 2612(b)(1); 5 USC 6382(b)(1); 2 USC 1312(a)(1) (incorporating § 2612 of Title I into CAA); 3 USC 412(a)(1) (incorporating § 2612 of Title I into PEOAA); *see Ryl-Kuchar v. Care Centers, Inc.*, No. 05-3223, 2006 U.S. Dist. LEXIS 87853, at *15 (N.D. Ill. Dec. 4, 2006). The statutes do not define the term "medically necessary." In *Dunning v. UPS*, 471 F. Supp. 2d 795 (E.D. Mich. 2007), the court found that the employee's need for intermittent FMLA leave was not "medically necessary." Dunning argued that he was entitled to intermittent leave where his shoulder problem rendered him unable to perform the essential functions of his truck driver position on the few occasions that a manual, as opposed to power, steering truck is assigned to his route. The court opined:

> A fair reading of the statute and regulations compels the conclusion that intermittent leave may be allowed under the FMLA when a chronic conditions suffered by the worker is exacerbated by a physical or an environmental factor, as in the example of a rise in pollen count triggering an asthmatic reaction, cited by the plaintiff. *See* 29 CFR 825.114(e)

The court found the plaintiff's circumstances were different. Plaintiff's claim that he was entitled to leave when a power-steering-equipped truck was not available to him because his shoulder condition prevented him from driving a manual-steering truck does not represent a relapsing-remitting condition as contemplated, but rather suggests in inability to do the job without an equipment accommodation. It is not a period of incapacity due to a change in the plaintiff's own condition, but results from circumstances entirely external to the plaintiff and calls into question whether the plaintiff can perform the changing functions of the job. Employees who cannot perform the essential functions of the job are not protected by the FMLA.

In *Sabbrese v. Lowe's Home Centers, Inc.*, 320 F. Supp. 2d 311, 321 (W.D. Pa. 2004), the issue was whether leave taken by an employee qualified as FMLA-protected unforeseeable intermittent leave because the leave also served as the employee's lunch break. As a diabetic, Sabbrese had to eat on scheduled intervals in order to control his blood sugar, a fact known by his employer. If he did not maintain this schedule, he became ill. By company policy, Sabbrese coordinated his lunch break with Grayson, his co-worker, to ensure coverage. On the day in question, Grayson took his lunch hour first. An hour came and went and Grayson had not returned. Feeling weak and that he might get sick if he waited any longer, Sabbrese went to lunch before Grayson returned. Before going he tried to page Grayson and asked the manager of an adjacent department to watch the appliance department until Grayson returned. Sabbrese was given a verbal warning for leaving the department unattended. He was subsequently terminated as a result of a physical altercation with his supervisor. Sabbrese sued alleging that the verbal warning and termination were in retaliation for his exercise of FMLA rights.

Lowe's argued that Sabbrese's claim for retaliation under the FMLA must fail because Sabbrese did not take actual "leave" under the FMLA and thus was not exercising a right under the FMLA. Lowe's contended that Sabbrese was not taking intermittent FMLA leave on the day in question, but was simply leaving for lunch, not FMLA-protected leave. The court disagreed. The court concluded, *id. at* 322,:

> After reviewing the statutory language of the FMLA, as well as the implementing regulations, the court finds that leave taken by a diabetic employee in order to eat to correct low blood sugar when medically necessary may qualify as intermittent leave under the FMLA. As noted above, the statute and regulations provide that an employee may take intermittent FMLA leave when medically necessary. In this case, there is no dispute that plaintiff was required to eat in order to control his blood sugar. Defendant cites no cases for the proposition that, where it is medically necessary to consume food due to a diabetic or other condition, a lunch break or other type of break cannot also qualify as intermittent leave. The fact that an employee receives daily lunch and other breaks is not dispositive because there may be situations, such as the present case, where a diabetic (or otherwise impaired) employee faces a medical emergency and is unable to comply with his employer's break policies, yet still must take unforeseeable intermittent leave.... [A] reasonable finder of fact may determine that, even if Sabbrese violated company policy by leaving before his co-worker returned from lunch, he still qualified for FMLA intermittent leave.

Note that the agreement of the employer is not required for an eligible employee to take FMLA leave on an intermittent or reduced leave schedule basis where the reason for the leave involves a serious health condition. FMLA leave on an intermittent/reduced leave schedule for or following the birth, adoption, or foster care placement of a son or daughter requires the agreement of the employer.

(1) Title II

While Title II uses the term "medically necessary" as a condition on an employee's use of FMLA leave on an intermittent or reduced leave schedule for a serious health condition, neither the statute nor the regulations define what that term means. Ironically, although Title II permits an employer to require an employee to substantiate his or her request for FMLA leave due to a serious health condition with a medical certification, the medical necessity of such leave is not one of the permitted inquiries. 5 CFR 630.1207. Presumably, an intermittent or reduced leave schedule is medically necessary if a health care provider sets forth an intermittent or reduced leave schedule on the form, without ever stating unequivocally that such leave is medically necessary. *See, e.g.*, 29 CFR 825.700.

In the absence of additional guidance, employers with Title II employees are well advised to rely on health care provider certifications to determine whether an intermittent or reduced leave schedule involving a serious health condition is medically necessary. The safe course is to assume that the use of the term "medical" was designed to restrict the determination to the medical community, not untrained human resources personnel, line supervisors, or managers.

Employers with Title II employees are also well advised to follow developments in this area under Title I, the CAA, and the PEOAA, where the term "medically necessary" is given more attention.

(2) Title I, the CAA, and the PEOAA

The FMLA permits eligible employees to take leave for a covered serious health condition intermittently or on a reduced leave schedule when medically necessary. The term "medically necessary" is not defined in the statute or implementing regulations. The regulations do, however, define the related term "medical necessity" when describing an employee seeking intermittent FMLA leave or leave on a reduced leave schedule. 29 CFR 825.117; S. Res. 242, Cong. Rec. S3959, S3963 (April 23, 1996); 29 CFR 825.117.

For intermittent leave or leave on a reduced leave schedule for a serious health condition, there must be a medical need for leave and it must be that such medical need can be best accommodated through an intermittent or reduced leave schedule. Voluntary treatments and procedures are deemed to be not medically necessary. 29 CFR 825.117; S. Res. 242, Cong. Rec. S3959, S3963 (April 23, 1996); 29 CFR 825.117; see *Hatchett v. Philander Smith College et al.*, 251 F.3d 670, 676–77 (8th Cir. 2001); *Haggard v. Levi Straus & Co.*, 8 Fed. Appx. 599 (8th Cir. 2001); *Brunelle v. Cyro Industries et al.*, 225 F. Supp. 2d 67, 76 (D. Me. 2002); *Flanagan v. Keller Products, Inc.*, No. 00–542–M, 2002 U.S. Dist. LEXIS 3663 (D. N.H. Feb. 25, 2002); *Caraballo v. Puerto Rico Telephone, Inc.*, 178 F. Supp. 2d 60, 65 (D. P.R. 2001); *Rocky v. Columbia Lawnwood Regional Medical Center et al.*, 54 F. Supp. 2d 1159, 1170 (S.D. Fla. 1999); *Parker v. Sony Pictures Entertainment et al.*, 19 F. Supp. 2d 141, 154 (S.D.N.Y. 1998), aff'd in part, vacated and remanded on other grounds, 204 F.3d 326 (2d Cir. 2000); *Palazollo v. Galen Hospitals of Texas, Inc.*, No. 1:96–CV–2550–TWT, 1997 U.S. Dist. LEXIS 21915 (N.D. Ga. Nov. 25, 1997); *Hensley v. Baptist Hospital of East Tennessee et al.*, No. 3: 96–CV–789, 1997 U.S. Dist. LEXIS 22515, at *36–37 (E.D. Tenn. Oct. 27, 1997); *Kaylor v. Fannin Regional Hospital, Inc.*, 946 F. Supp. 988, 997 (N.D. Ga. 1996); *Hendry v. GTE North, Inc.*, 896 F. Supp. 816, 828 (N.D. Ind. 1995). When there is no longer a medical need, such as where a physician has released the employee o return to work, the employee is not entitled to FMLA leave on an intermittent or reduced leave schedule basis. *Hensley*, 1997 U.S. Dist. LEXIS 22515, at *36–37.

The determination of the medical necessity for intermittent or reduced leave schedule is made exclusively by the health care provider of the employee or employee's family member (subject to the second and third opinion process where the employer has reason to doubt the validity of the certification). Preamble, 29 CFR 825.117. Voluntary treatments and procedures, however, are not considered to fall within the definition of "medical need." 29 CFR 825.117; S. Res. 242, Cong. Rec. S3959, S3963 (April 23, 1996); 29 CFR 825.117. The DOL's medical certification form, or other form meeting the DOL's certification requirements [as discussed in Chapter 9, "Documentation Requirements" and 29 CFR 825.306], is the vehicle by which employers may learn of the medical necessity for intermittent or a reduced leave schedule due to a serious health condition. 29 CFR 825.117; S. Res. 242, Cong. Rec. S3959, S3963 (April 23, 1996); 29 CFR 825.117.

Note that, while the medical certification form is used to determine the medical necessity of an intermittent or reduced leave schedule, there is no guidance in the regulations on how an employer satisfies the second requirement: that the medical need is best accommodated through an intermittent or a reduced leave schedule. Presumably, employers should also rely on the medical certification for this determination as well, but that is not what the regulations require. Agencies are well advised, however, to proceed with caution in this area and avoid making medical need judgments outside of the second and third opinion challenge process. [For additional discussion of challenging medical certification forms, see Chapter 9, "Documentation Requirements."]

Several courts have addressed the medical necessity of intermittent leave or FMLA leave on a reduced leave schedule. Two (from the same district) have suggested that medical necessity equates with medical emergency. *Palazzolo v. Galen Hospitals of Texas, Inc.*, No. 1: 96–CV–2550–TWT, 1997 U.S. Dist. LEXIS 21915, at *14–15 (N.D. Ga. Nov. 25, 1997) (medical necessity denotes a certain sense of urgency; court found that routine examination and blood work were not sufficiently urgent to be considered medically necessary); *Kaylor v. Fannin Regional Hospital, Inc.,* 946. F. Supp. 988, 997 (N.D. Ga. 1996) (in dicta, court credited testimony of plaintiff's physician that medical appointment was not an emergency visit, but was routine and holding no special medical significance; the purpose of the visit was to renew prescriptions and to "make sure nothing else was going on").

Other factors cited by the courts in support of a determination that intermittent or reduced leave schedule was not medically necessary include the employee's election to reschedule the appointment, (see *Palazzolo*, 1997 U.S. Dist. LEXIS 21915, at *14–15), plaintiffs waiting to inform the employer of the need for leave until just before the appointment, (see *Kaylor v. Fannin Regional Hospital, Inc.,* 946. F. Supp. 988, 997 (N.D. Ga. 1996)), and the testimony of plaintiff's physician that plaintiff would have been able to "function in his job" that day. *Id.; see also Haggard v. Levi Strauss & Co.*, 8 Fed. Appx. 599 (8th Cir. 2001) (failure of physicians note to explain medical necessity cited in support of finding that intermittent leave was not justified).

The decision of the district court in *Brunelle v. Cyro Industries et al.*, 225 F. Supp. 2d 67, 77 (D. Me. 2002), found that an employee's absence from work while drinking at the local bar was medically necessary. Brunelle had been out intermittently for months to provide care for his parent who was in the hospital as a result of serious injuries suffered in a house fire. Brunelle was scheduled to work a 12-hour shift at 7:00 p.m. on the night in question. He did not show or call. Brunelle had been at the hospital since 7:00 a.m. that day providing comfort and care to his critically ill father and assisting in medical decision-making regarding surgery. He left the hospital at 5:00 p.m. and met his girlfriend and several others at a local restaurant/pub, where he was seen by a co-worker. The co-worker reported seeing Brunelle drinking with others to management. Plaintiff was subsequently terminated.

Plaintiff filed suit, alleging that his absence was covered by the FMLA. The employer argued that the leave from work was not medically necessary and, therefore, not covered by the FMLA. Characterizing the employer's argument as a "crabbed view of the facts," the court held that, although he was discovered drinking with friends, his daylong vigil at his critically ill father's bedside, assisting in medical-decision making, provided "care or psychological comfort to an immediate family member with a serious health condition" and was, therefore, medically necessary within the meaning of 29 CFR 825.203(c). No more, the court held, was required. *Id.* at 77.

The court further found that it did not matter that Brunelle "technically was available to work, having left the hospital prior to the start of his shift, and was discovered having drinks with friends instead." *Id.* at 77 & n.13. The court reasoned that, because he stood vigil from 7:00 a.m. that morning, had not slept all day, and would have been required to work a 12-hour shift starting at 7:00 p.m., "[I]t is a reasonable inference that, while he was able to unwind with friends, he was not prepared to work." *Id.*

And there you have it. "Medically necessary" means a court's opinion, based on inference not medical facts (there were none presented), that an employee is too tired to work a shift he or she could have made, but was not too tired to go out and knock down some drinks with friends. As much compassion and respect as one may have for Mr. Brunelle's decision to stand vigil at his father's hospital bed, legally, it is hard to see how the absence was medically necessary. At the time Mr. Brunelle was at the bar he was no longer caring for his father in any meaningful FMLA sense. Since his absence was not to care for his father (i.e., active sense), but was to recover from caring for his father, it was not medically necessary. As a result, the court should not have found that the leave was covered by the FMLA.

b. Employee Reasonable Efforts to Schedule Leave to Avoid Workplace Disruptions

All federal employees are required, under certain circumstances, to make reasonable efforts to schedule their FMLA leave to avoid disruption to the workplace. The circumstances in which this requirement arises differ, however, depending on what FMLA statute applies to a given eligible employee.

(1) Title II

Eligible employees covered by Title II of the Act are required to consult with the agency and make reasonable efforts to schedule foreseeable, planned medical treatment for their own serious health condition or that of a covered family member, so as not to unduly disrupt the operations of the agency, subject to the approval of the health care provider. 5 CFR 630.102(b). The agency may, for justifiable cause, request that an employee reschedule medical treatment, subject to the approval of the health care provider. *Id.*

Note that the responsibility of an employee to make reasonable efforts to schedule his or her FMLA leave applies whether the leave is taken in a block of time, intermittently, or on a reduced leave schedule. This obligation on Title II-covered employees is broader than what is required of Title I employees.

There are several conditions that must exist before a Title II employee is obligated to make reasonable efforts to reschedule leave. First, the responsibility only arises in the context of a serious health condition, not leave for or following the birth, adoption or foster care placement of a son or daughter.

Second, in addition to the limitation to serious health conditions, the employee's reasonability only arises when the need for leave is foreseeable based on planned medical treatment. It is unclear if planned means that the employee must have a scheduled appointment, or if it means something less.

Third, the planned medical treatment must be such as to unduly disrupt the operations of the agency if not rescheduled. No explanation is offered to explain under what circumstances an FMLA absence might unduly disrupt agency operations. Presumably, reference to the agency does not require that the absence would disrupt the agency as a whole, but merely the particular office, department, or unit involved. Similarly, as undefined, the term "unduly" provides little practical guidance on the level or intensity of disruption necessary before the rescheduling requirement applies. To address this issue, agencies need to articulate adverse consequences stemming from the employee's present schedule, such as the need to hire replacements, payment of overtime to make up the work, or other real-world consequences caused by the present medical treatment schedule.

Note that the employee bears the burden of making a reasonable effort to schedule medical treatment so as not to disrupt unduly the operations of the agency. Whether an employee has made a reasonable effort will depend on the circumstances of any given case. An employee can make a reasonable effort that does not succeed. That is, "effort" is not the same as "result." Clearly, however, an employee who fails to make any effort will not meet these criteria. When an employee fails to make any effort to schedule leave so as not to disrupt the agency's operations, employers should expect to see challenges to the existence of the other pre-conditions of the requirement in order to excuse the employee's nonperformance.

An employer, for justifiable cause, may request that an employee reschedule medical treatment, subject to the approval of the health care provider. "Justifiable cause" is not defined. Presumably it includes the failure of an employee, in the first instance, to consult with the agency and schedule leave so as not to unduly disrupt the operations of the agency. It may also include other reasons.

The regulations fail to identify the penalty imposed upon an employee who fails to make a reasonable effort to schedule FMLA leave to avoid undue disruptions to the agency. Under Title I, the courts have not been kind to employees who have failed to make such reasonable efforts.

Ultimately, the employee or covered family member's health care provider gets to make the call, subject, in some cases, to the employer's ability to invoke the second and third opinion process. [For a discussion of the second and third opinion process, see Chapter 7, "Covered Conditions."]

(2) Title I, the CAA, and the PEOAA

Under Title I, the CAA, and the PEOAA, an eligible employee who requires intermittent FMLA leave or leave on a reduced leave schedule must make some effort to schedule leave so as not to disrupt the employer's operations. 29 CFR 825.117; S. Res. 242, Cong. Rec. S3959, S3963 (April 23, 1996); 29 CFR 825.117; see DOL WH FMLA Advisory Opinion No. 101 (January 15, 1999); DOL WH FMLA Advisory Opinion No. 60 (May 2, 1995); see also Whitney v. Wal-Mart Stores, Inc., No. 03-65-P-H, 2003 U.S. Dist. LEXIS 22629, at *28 (D. Me. Dec. 16, 2003). This requirement applies whenever FMLA leave is taken on an intermittent or reduced leave schedule basis. See 29 CFR 825.302(e)-(f); S. Res. 242, Cong. Rec. S3959, S3972 (April 23, 1996); 29 CFR 825.302(e)-(f). Both the text of the FMLA and its legislative history indicate that the cooperation of the employee and employer in scheduling intermittent leave is vital in implementing the goals of the FMLA. *Kaylor v. Fannin Regional Hospital, Inc.*, 946 F. Supp. 988, 998 (N.D. Ga. 1996).

There are two regulations that address this issue. 29 CFR 825.117, 825.302(e)-(f); S. Res. 242, Cong. Rec. S3959, S3963, S3972 (April 23, 1996); 29 CFR 825.117, 825.302(e)-(f). Unfortunately, they do not use the same terms to describe the requirements. Again, this leads to unnecessary confusion. A review of the major components of the regulations follows.

Both regulations appear to apply where the employee needs intermittent leave or FMLA leave on a reduced leave schedule for a serious health condition. Section 825.117 requires that there be a medical need for leave on an intermittent or reduced leave schedule basis. The term "medically necessary" is used in the statue to justify the taking of FMLA leave on an intermittent or reduced leave schedule due to a serious health condition. 29 USC 2612(b)(1). Section 825.302(e) speaks in terms of "planned medical treatment." There is nothing, however, in either regulation that limits application to FMLA leave taken for a serious health condition. For example, an employee requesting intermittent FMLA leave following the birth of a son or daughter for planned medical treatment that does not rise to the level of a serious health condition, would appear to be subject to one or both regulations.

Note that "planned medical treatment" and "medical need for leave" are not necessarily the same thing. Section 825.117 identifies voluntary treatments and procedures as not being medically necessary. No such limitation is placed on the definition of "planned medical treatments" contained in § 825.302(e). One could, therefore, have a situation where an employee needs intermittent leave for a planned medical treatment that is elective surgery. The provisions of § 825.302(e) would continue to apply, but the requirements of § 825.117 would not. Conversely, an employee might only be covered by § 825.117 when the need for intermittent leave was not for a planned medical treatment, but was medically necessary. Finally, there may be situations where both regulations arguably apply. For example, an employee needs intermittent leave for planned medical treatments that are medically necessary and are not voluntary.

Presumably, the undefined term "voluntary" means elective treatments or procedures. Except in cases of children, adjudicated incompetents, or the unconscious, most medical treatments are voluntary in the sense they are not compelled by state action.

The effort that an eligible employee is required to make, in order to avoid workplace disruptions, is described differently in the regulations. In § 825.117, the effort is described as an attempt to schedule. In § 825.302(e), the standard is identified as twofold: the employee must consult with the employer, and make a reasonable effort to schedule leave so as not to unduly disrupt the employer's operations. When the need for intermittent leave or FMLA leave on a reduced leave schedule is medically necessary, but not due to planned medical treatment, the employee apparently only need make an attempt to schedule leave to avoid disrupting the employer's operations. There is nothing in § 825.117 that requires the employee to consult with the employer.

Moreover, § 825.302(e) goes on to impose additional requirements that are not contained in § 825.117. Employees are ordinarily expected to consult with their employers prior to the scheduling of treatment in order to work out a treatment schedule which best suits the needs of both the employer and the employee. 29 CFR 825.302(e); S. Res. 242, Cong. Rec. S3959, S3972 (April 23, 1996); 29 CFR 825.117, 825.302(e).

The level of effort required of an employee is described differently under the regulations. Section 825.117 requires only that the employee *attempt* to schedule leave to avoid disruptions. Section 825.302(e) requires that the employee make a *reasonable effort*. It is, however, highly likely that the courts will impose a standard of reasonableness into § 825.117, bringing the regulations into harmony. In *Palazzolo v. Galen Hospital of Texas, Inc.*, No. 1:96-CV-2550-TWT, 1997 U.S. Dist. LEXIS 21915, at *15-*16 (N.D. Ga. Nov. 25, 1997), the district court found that the employee failed to make the required effort. The court described the rule as follows:

> In addition, the FMLA envisions a cooperative effort between the employer and employee to ensure that the employee gets leave necessary for medical treatment while not unduly disrupting the employer's operations. *Kaylor*, 946 F. Supp. 988. To that end, every employee must avoid imposing upon the employer whenever possible.

The court found the plaintiff did not try to avoid disrupting the hospital's operations. Although he knew he was often the only closing chef, and that his role was essential to proper operation of the kitchen, he did not try to ensure that the hospital would have at least one closing chef available on the day in question. The court noted that the plaintiff previously been rescheduled his appointments to avoid conflicts with his duties. It also noted that the plaintiff did not attempt to find an appointment date that did not conflict with his work schedule, and he did not offer to reschedule his appointment when he was told that the hospital would be left without a closing chef. The court also noted that the plaintiff's "statements on the day of the appointment underscore his total disregard for the effects of his absence on the hospital." The plaintiff said that he was going to keep the appointment "come hell or high water" and that the "hospital's staffing issues were not his problem." *Id.*

Another example of a case in which an employee failed to make reasonable efforts to reschedule leave to avoid disrupting the employer's operations was addressed by the court in *Kaylor v. Fannin Regional Hospital, Inc.*, 946 F. Supp. 988, 998 (N.D. Ga. 1996). The district court noted the plaintiff's failure to reasonably attempt to reschedule his medical appointment after he was told that his absence would leave the hospital without adequate staffing in the radiology department. The court cited the lack of evidence that the plaintiff contacted his physician about rescheduling. As further evidence that the plaintiff never intended to make a "reasonable effort" to reschedule at all, the court noted that the plaintiff continually mislead his supervisor by claiming he would be available to attend work on the day of his appointment, but never cancelled his appointment. According to the court, 946 F. Supp. at 998:

> Plaintiff's actions indicate he intended to attend the February 3 appointment regardless of the effect upon staffing at Fannin Hospital. In contrast to the "reasonable effort" required by the FMLA, plaintiff made no effort whatsoever to cooperate with Fannin Hospital.

The requirement that an eligible employee attempt or make a reasonable effort to schedule intermittent or reduced leave to avoid workplace disruptions does not mean that the employee must be successful in the attempt. An employee who makes a good faith attempt to schedule intermittent or reduced schedule FMLA leave to avoid workplace disruptions satisfies this condition, whether successful in the attempt or not. Whether an employee has made a good faith effort will depend on the facts in each case. Preamble, 29 CFR 825.117.

An employee's ability to schedule intermittent or reduced schedule FMLA leave so as not to disrupt the workplace presupposes that the leave is capable of being scheduled at all. Planned medical treatments would seem to be prime candidates for application of both regulations. Section 825.117, however, is not limited to planned medical treatments. It applies whenever intermittent or reduced leave schedule FMLA leave is susceptible to being scheduled. The term "schedule" is not defined.

Nor is there any minimum advance time that an employee is given in order to schedule the leave. As such, an employer may be able to argue that the employee failed to schedule the intermittent or reduced schedule FMLA leave even in situations where the need for leave came with relatively short notice.

The implementing regulations arguably give two different standards for the level of disruption that will be imposed on an employer due to the use of intermittent leave or FMLA leave on a reduced leave schedule. Under § 825.117, the level of interference is described as *so as not to disrupt the employer's operations* (emphasis supplied). Arguably, the language prohibits all disruptions to the employer's operations, no matter how slight. Section 825.302(e), by comparison, adds the qualifier *unduly* to describe the disruption caused by the employee's use of intermittent or FMLA leave on a reduced leave schedule. *See Rocky v. Columbia Lawnwood Regional Medical Center et al.*, 54 F. Supp. 2d 1159, 1170 (S.D. Fla. 1999) (stating general rule, using "unduly" term). Although undefined, the term "unduly" clearly adds a level of disruption that is not present in § 825.117.

The level of disruption to an employer's operations caused by the employee's absence, necessary to trigger the requirement that the employee make reasonable efforts to reschedule the FMLA leave, appears modest. In *Kaylor*, 946 F. Supp. at 998, the disruption took the form of understaffing of the employee's department for the day of the appointment. According to the court, the understaffing caused several patients to be rescheduled for cat–scans, and the remaining radiology staff was forced to cover for the plaintiff. *Kaylor*, 946 F. Supp. at 994.

Similarly, in *Palazzolo v. Galen Hospital of Texas, Inc.*, No. 1:96–CV–2550–TWT, 1997 U.S. Dist. LEXIS 21915, at *15–*16 (N.D. Ga. Nov. 25, 1997), plaintiff was advised that his absence would leave the hospital without a closing chef. The case does not indicate what the actual impact of the employee's leaving work a few hours early had on hospital operations. The court nevertheless found that plaintiff's absence disrupted the hospital's operations.

Finally, the regulations differ as to the options available to an employer in the event the employee fails to satisfy the burden to reasonably avoid disrupting the employer's operations. Section 825.117 does not address this issue. Section 825.302(e) provides:

> If an employee who provides notice of the need to take FMLA leave on an intermittent basis for planned medical treatment neglects to consult with the employer to make a reasonable attempt to arrange the schedule of treatments so as not to unduly disrupt the employer's operations, the employer may initiate discussions with the employee and require the employee to attempt to make such arrangements, subject to the approval of the health care provider.

The regulation is interesting in several respects. First, it only applies where intermittent leave is involved, not when FMLA leave is taken on a reduced leave schedule. Second, the employer's remedy for an employee's failure to consult about the schedule of treatments is limited to requiring the employee to attempt to reschedule the intermittent leave. This presupposes that the employer could not require this in the first instance. Note that an employer *may* require an employee to attempt to reschedule the intermittent leave; an employer is not required to initiate such discussions with the employee before taking other action, such as denial of FMLA leave.

The ability of an employer to require an employee to attempt to schedule intermittent or reduced schedule leave to minimize workplace disruptions should not be underestimated. FMLA leave taken on an intermittent or reduced leave schedule is frequently the most disruptive form of FMLA leave to operations. The FMLA does not provide a wealth of opportunities to employers to control intermittent or reduced leave schedule FMLA leave. As such, employers should seriously consider aggressive use of this technique to control FMLA absences. You would be amazed how the use of FMLA leave decreases if the employee's preferred intermittent schedule, every Friday afternoon off for therapy, becomes every Wednesday before or after work.

Employees frequently balk at asking their health care providers to schedule leave for their employer's convenience and not their own. Employees who refuse to make a good faith effort to reschedule their leave in these situations run the considerable risk of losing FMLA protections. The courts have upheld the denial of FMLA leave and termination of employees who failed or refused to make even a good faith attempt at rescheduling leave. *See Palazollo v. Galen Hospitals of Texas, Inc.*, No. 1:96–CV–2550–TWT, 1997 U.S. Dist. LEXIS 21915, at *15–18 (N.D. Ga. 1997) (employee failed to attempt to schedule leave so as not to disrupt hospital's operations where employee stated that he would make his medical appointment "come hell or high water," and that his employer's staffing issues were not his problem); *Kaylor v. Fannin Regional Hospitals, Inc.*, 946 F. Supp. 988, 998–99 (N.D. Ga. 1996). Note that the regulations do not prescribe the penalty for an employee's failure to attempt to schedule intermittent or reduced leave so as not to disrupt the employer's operations.

In light of the decisions of the courts, unions and organizations representing Title I employees are well-advised to ensure that employees at least make a good faith attempt to schedule FMLA leave taken on an intermittent or reduced leave schedule basis so as not to disrupt the employer's operations.

c. Notice

In some cases, the regulations impose special notice obligations on employees when FMLA leave will be taken intermittently or on a reduced leave schedule basis. Employee notice is generally addressed in Chapter 8, "Notice Requirements." A brief review of the notice rules where FMLA leave is taken intermittently or on a reduced leave schedule follows.

(1) Title II

There are no special employee notice rules that apply when an employee takes FMLA leave on an intermittent or reduced leave schedule basis. As set forth more fully in Chapter 8, "Notice Requirements," the general rules requiring timely employee notice of the need for FMLA leave apply where the leave is taken intermittently or on a reduced leave schedule. *See* 5 CFR 630.1206.

An employee who fails to comply with the notification requirements is not entitled to FMLA leave. 5 CFR 630.1208(l).

(2) Title I, the CAA, and the PEOAA

There are special employee notice rules that apply when an employee takes FMLA leave on an intermittent or reduced leave schedule basis.

The Act and the regulations require an employee to give timely and adequate notice of the need for FMLA leave, including leave taken on an intermittent or reduced leave schedule basis. 29 USC 2612(e)(2)(b); 29 CFR 825.303(a); 2 USC 1312(a)(2) (incorporating 29 USC 2612 into CAA); S. Res. 242, Cong. Rec. S3959, S3972 (April 23, 1996); 29 CFR 825.303(a); *see Whitney v. Wal-Mart Stores, Inc.*, No. 03–65–P–H, 2003 U.S. Dist. LEXIS 22629, at *28 (D. Me. Dec. 16, 2003); *Rocky v. Columbia Lawnwood Regional Medical Center et al.*, 54 F. Supp. 2d 1159, 1170 (S.D. Fla. 1999); *Goodwin v. Rheem Manufacturing Co.*, 15 F. Supp. 2d 1197, 1205 (M.D. Ala. 1998); *Palazollo v. Galen Hospitals of Texas, Inc.*, No. 1:96–CV–2550–TWT, 1997 U.S. Dist. LEXIS 21915, at *15–18 (N.D. Ga. 1997); *Kaylor v. Fannin Regional Hospitals, Inc.*, 946 F. Supp. 988, 998–99 (N.D. Ga. 1996).

In *Whitney*, the court found that, absent an employee request for FMLA leave on an intermittent or reduced leave schedule basis, 29 CFR 825.302 does not require an employer to offer intermittent leave on its own. Plaintiff argued that Wal-Mart violated the FMLA by failing to alert Whitney that he could take FMLA leave on an intermittent basis, causing Whitney to prematurely exhaust his 12 weeks of FMLA. Whitney would have used intermittent FMLA leave to cover hours of work in excess of 45 per week that his doctor indicated he should not work. Rejecting plaintiff's argument, the court noted the absence of evidence that plaintiff suggested or asked for intermittent FMLA leave.

There are three rules to remember about employee notice of the need for FMLA leave on an intermittent or reduced leave schedule basis. First, as with any FMLA leave, the employee must provide timely notice to the employer of the need for FMLA leave on an intermittent or reduced leave schedule. When the need for intermittent or reduced leave schedule is foreseeable, the employee must provide at least 30 days advance notice before FMLA leave is to begin. 29 USC 2612(e)(20(b); 29 CFR 825.302(a); S. Res. 242, Cong. Rec. S3959, S3972 (April 23, 1996); 29 CFR 825.302(a). If 30 days advance notice is not practicable, the employee must advise the employer as soon as practicable (ordinarily, one or two business days). Where the need for leave is not foreseeable, an employee must give notice of the need for FMLA leave as soon as practicable under the facts. 29 CFR 825.303(a); S. Res. 242, Cong. Rec. S3959, S3972 (April 23, 1996), 825.303(a); see *George v Russell Stover Candies, Inc.*, 106 Fed. Appx. 946 (6th Cir. 2004); *Sabbrese v. Lowe's Home Centers, Inc.*, 320 F. Supp. 2d 311, 321–322 (W.D. Pa. 2004); *Rocky v. Columbia Lawnwood Regional Medical Center et al.*, 54 F. Supp. 2d 1159, 1170 (S.D. Fla. 1999).

The rules regarding employee notice of the need for FMLA leave on an intermittent or reduced leave schedule basis were summarized by the court in *Sabbrese v. Lowe's Home Centers, Inc.*, 320 F. Supp. 2d 311, 321–322 (W.D. Pa. 2004), as follows:

> All FMLA leave, whether intermittent or not, falls into two categories: foreseeable intermittent leave and unforeseeable intermittent leave. The degree of notice required to be given to an employer depends upon whether the leave is foreseeable. If intermittent leave is foreseeable, an employee is required to give the employer 30-days advance notice, or, if 30-days advance notice is impossible under the circumstances, notice must be given as soon as practicable. 29 U.S.C. § 2612(e)(1); 29 C.F.R. § 825.302. The phrase "as soon as practicable" is defined under the regulations as "as soon as both possible and practical, taking into account all of the facts and circumstances in the individual case…[and] ordinarily would mean at least verbal notification to the employer within one or two business days of when the need for leave becomes known to the employee." 20 C.F.R. § 825.302(b). If leave is unforeseeable, an employee must give notice to the employer within one or two days of learning of the need for leave, except where extraordinary cases prevent such notice. 29 C.F.R. § 825.303. The regulations with respect to unforeseeable leave further state:
>
> > In the case of a medical emergency requiring leave because of an employee's own serious health condition or to care for a family member with a serious health condition, written advance notice pursuant to an employer's internal rules and procedures may not be required when FMLA leave is involved.

In *Rocky v. Columbia Lawnwood Regional Medical Center et al.*, 54 F. Supp. 2d 1159, 1170 (S.D. Fla. 1999), the court found that the employee failed to provide adequate notice of the need for intermittent leave. There, the plaintiff relied on an understanding she had with a supervisor that Columbia would work with the plaintiff regarding the plaintiff's need to take time off to care for her son. The plaintiff asserted that she interpreted this to mean she had unlimited permission to work at any time and for any length of time in order to care for her son. *Id.* at 1170. The court found, regardless of the plaintiff's stated objective beliefs, "no rational jury could conclude that the [p]laintiff had received [d]efendant's permission to be absent or tardy whenever and as often as she desired. Therefore, the Court finds that the [p]laintiff has failed to satisfy any of FMLA notice requirements based on this alleged understanding." *Id.*

A request for a flexible work schedule to care for a spouse with a back injury was held insufficient notice of the need for FMLA leave. *Giles v. Christian Care Centers, Inc. et al.*, No. 3:96–CV–2168–G, 1997 U.S. Dist. LEXIS 20351 (N.D. Tex. Dec. 11, 1997) ("Because Giles did not ask for leave, she has no viable FMLA claim.").

Second, an employee need only give the employer notice of the need for leave on an intermittent or reduced leave schedule basis one time, but the employee must advise the employer as soon as practicable if dates of scheduled leave change, are extended, or were initially unknown. 29 CFR 825.302(a); S. Res. 242, Cong. Rec. S3959, S3972 (April 23, 1996); 29 CFR 825.302(a). For example, an employee with a serious health condition learns on February 1 that he will need intermittent FMLA leave for a half-day, one day per week for physical therapy. The therapy begins in two weeks. Within one or two business days of February 1, the employee would have to notify the employer of the need for intermittent leave. Thereafter, the employee would not have to notify the employer every week that the leave was needed, unless the schedule changed. If the schedule changed, say to once every two weeks, the employee would have to inform the employer within one or two business days of learning of the change in schedule.

Third, employees are required to provide additional information to the employer when taking FMLA leave on an intermittent or reduced leave schedule basis. Generally, an employee must provide notice sufficient to make the employer aware that the employee needs FMLA–qualifying leave, and the anticipated timing and duration of the leave. 29 CFR 825.302(c); S. Res. 242, Cong. Rec. S3959, S3972 (April 23, 1996); 29 CFR 825.302(a). In the case of intermittent leave or leave on a reduced schedule which is medically necessary, an employee must also advise the employer, upon request, of the reasons the intermittent or reduced leave schedule is necessary, and of the schedule for treatment, if applicable. 29 CFR 825.302(f); S. Res. 242, Cong. Rec. S3959, S3972 (April 23, 1996); 29 CFR 825.302(f).

An employee's failure to timely notify an employer of the need for intermittent leave or a reduced leave schedule may justify the denial of leave and result in the loss of FMLA protections for the absence. See *Kaylor v. Fannin Regional Hospital*,

Inc., 946. F. Supp. 988, 998–99 (N.D. Ga. 1996) (employer did not violate the FMLA by denying plaintiff requested leave for medical appointment where plaintiff knew of the appointment for three months, but waited until four days before the appointment before requesting the day off).

d. Medical Certification

The FMLA permits an employer to require an employee to support a request for FMLA leave due to a serious health condition with a medical certification. Some special rules apply when FMLA leave is taken on an intermittent or reduced leave schedule basis. The requirements for an employee to support a request for FMLA leave with medical documentation is addressed more fully in Chapter 9, "Documentation Requirements." A brief review of the medical documentation requirements, as they relate to intermittent or reduced leave schedule, follows.

(1) Title II

An agency may require that a request for FMLA leave due to a serious health condition be supported by written medical certification. 5 USC 6383(a); 5 CFR 1607(a). When FMLA leave due to a serious health condition is taken on an intermittent or reduced leave schedule basis for planned medical treatment, the agency may require that the supporting medical certification identify the dates (actual or estimated) on which the treatment is expected to be given, the duration of such treatment, and the period of recovery, if any. Alternatively, an employee may specify that the serious health condition is a chronic or continuing condition with an unknown duration, and whether the patient is presently incapacitated, if the likely duration and the frequency of episodes of incapacitation are unknown. 5 USC 6383(b)(6); 5 CFR 630.1207(b)(6).

An employee who fails to provide medical certification that includes all of the required information, including the information addressing the need for FMLA leave on an intermittent or reduced leave schedule, is not entitled to FMLA leave. 5 CFR 630.1208(l).

(2) Title I, the CAA, and the PEOAA

An employer may require an eligible employee who is requesting FMLA leave for his or her own serious health condition, or the serious health condition of a covered family member, to support that request with a medical certification. 29 USC 2613(a); 29 CFR 825.305(a); 2 USC 1312(a)(1) (incorporating 29 USC 2613 into CAA); S. Res. 242, Cong. Rec. S3959, S3972 (April 23, 1996); 29 CFR 825.305(a).

There are four medical certification rules that are pertinent to this discussion of FMLA leave taken on an intermittent or reduced leave schedule basis.

First, in addition to the usual requirements governing the permissible content of supporting medical documentation, an employer is entitled to additional information when the employee needs intermittent or reduced leave schedule FMLA leave. Specifically, an employer may insist that the medical documentation state whether it will be necessary for the employee to take leave intermittently or to work on a reduced leave schedule basis as a result of a serious health condition. 29 CFR 825.306(b)(2)(ii);); S. Res. 242, Cong. Rec. S3959, S3972 (April 23, 1996); 29 CFR 825.306(b)(2)(ii); *see Goodwin v. Rheem Manufacturing Co.*, 15 F. Supp. 2d 1197, 1205 (M.D. Ala. 1998). If so, the employer may require the certification to identify the probable duration of such schedule, an estimate of the probable number and interval between treatments, actual or estimated dates of treatment, if known, and the period required for recovery, if any. 29 CFR 825.306(b)(3)(i)(B); S. Res. 242, Cong. Rec. S3959, S3972 (April 23, 1996); 29 CFR 825.306(b)(3)(i)(B). If the employee will need leave intermittently or on a reduced leave schedule basis to care for a covered family member, the probable duration of the leave may be required. 29 CFR 825.306(b)(5)(ii); S. Res. 242, Cong. Rec. S3959, S3972 (April 23, 1996); 29 CFR 825.306(b)(5)(ii).

Second, normally an employer is required to request that the employee furnish medical certification at the time the employee gives notice of the need for leave or within two business days thereafter. 29 CFR 825.305(c); S. Res. 242, Cong. Rec. S3959, S3972 (April 23, 1996); 29 CFR 825.305(c). As currently interpreted by the DOL, "leave" is defined to include a series of absences taken on an intermittent or reduced leave schedule basis for the same underlying covered condition during the course of an FMLA leave year. *See* DOL WH FMLA Advisory Opinion No. 112 (Sept. 11, 2000). As such, an employer is generally restricted from asking for medical certification for each and every intermittent or reduced leave schedule absence. Rather, the employer is supposed to request medical certification for the entire series of absences on notice of the need for intermittent or reduced leave schedule FMLA leave. An employer may request medical certification at some later date if the employer later has reason to question the appropriateness of the leave or its duration. 29 CFR 825.305(c); S. Res. 242, Cong. Rec. S3959, S3972 (April 23, 1996); 29 CFR 825.305(c).

Third, for FMLA leave taken intermittently or on a reduced leave schedule basis, the employer may not request recertification in less than the minimum period specified on the certification as necessary for such leave (including treatment), unless one of three exceptions apply. 29 CFR 825.308(b)(2); S. Res. 242, Cong. Rec. S3959, S3973 (April 23, 1996); 29 CFR 825.306(b)(2)(ii).

Fourth, an employer is not entitled to request a medical certification that the employee is fit to return to duty when the employee takes intermittent leave. 29 CFR 825.310(g); S. Res. 242, Cong. Rec. S3959, S3974 (April 23, 1996); 29 CFR 825.306(b)(2)(ii). Note the absence of any reference to FMLA leave taken on a reduced leave schedule basis.

In *Hoffman v. Professional Med Team*, 270 F. Supp. 2d 954, 961 (W.D. Mich. 2003), *aff'd*, 394 F.3d 414, 418 (6th Cir. 2005), the court addressed an incomplete medical certification for intermittent FMLA leave. The employer properly requested that the employee submit a medical certification in support of her request for FMLA leave. The physician's certification indicated that the employee's qualifying serious health condition would not require intermittent leave or a reduced leave schedule. Because plaintiff indicated that she wanted FMLA leave on an intermittent or reduced leave schedule, the employer considered the certification contradictory and not a valid request for intermittent FMLA leave. The employer informed the employee of the discrepancy and gave the employee multiple opportunities to correct the answer to the intermittent/reduced leave schedule question, to no avail. The court concluded that the employer was correct to rely on the negative certification and deny the employee FMLA leave.

In another case involving a contradictory medical certification, *Willis v. USPS*, No. 03 C 9185, 2004 U.S. Dist. LEXIS 18238, at *18–19 (N.D. Ill. Sept. 10, 2004), the medical certification indicated that the employee would need to be absent from work on an intermittent basis. However, there were negative responses to questions regarding whether the employee was unable to work at all, and whether she was unable to perform one or more of the essential functions of her job. The employer argued that the certification did not support plaintiff's request for 30 days of FMLA leave. Viewing the certification in its entirety, the court concluded that the certification supported her claim for leave based on a serious health condition. The court appears to be saying that the requested 30 days of leave might constitute intermittent leave and, therefore, the negative responses relied on by the employer would not apply as the employee is able to perform the essential function of her job at times. [Medical certifications are discussed more fully in Chapter 9, "Documentation Requirements."]

e. When Intermittent or a Reduced Leave Schedule May Be Used for a Serious Health Condition

The regulations implementing the various federal sector FMLA laws vary greatly regarding the availability of FMLA leave on an intermittent or a reduced leave schedule for a serious health condition.

(1) Title II

The regulations implementing Title II appear to be the most faithful to the statute regarding the availability to an eligible employee of intermittent or a reduced leave schedule for a serious health condition. Like the statute, the implementing regulation simply provides that FMLA leave for a covered serious health condition is available to an eligible employee on an intermittent or reduced leave schedule when medically necessary, all other requirements being satisfied. 5 CFR 630.1204.

(2) Title I, the CAA, and the PEOAA

The regulations implementing Title I, the CAA, and the PEOAA place limitations on the use of FMLA leave on an intermittent or reduced leave schedule for a serious health condition that are not obvious from the wording of the statute. Again, the statute simply provides that FMLA leave for serious health conditions may be taken intermittently or on a reduced leave schedule when medically necessary. 29 USC 2612(b)(1); 2 USC 1312(a)(1) (incorporating § 2612 of Title I into CAA); 3 USC 412(a)(1) (incorporating § 2612 of Title I into PEOAA).

The regulations (29 CFR 825.203(c); S. Res. 242, Cong. Rec. S3959, S3964 (April 23, 1996); 29 CFR 825.203(c)) have interpreted that language as allowing an eligible employee to take FMLA leave intermittently or on a reduced leave schedule when medically necessary for his or her own serious health condition, or to care for a covered family member with a serious health condition for:

- Planned and/or unplanned medical treatment of a related serious health condition by or under the supervision of a health care provider;

- Recovery from treatment;

- Recovery from a serious health condition;

- Care or psychological comfort to an immediate family member with a serious health condition;

- Incapacity or inability to perform the essential functions of the position due to a chronic serious health condition, even if he or she does not receive treatment by a health care provider.

The above regulations are interesting, as they do not completely replicate the various serious health conditions recognized under the FMLA. This raises the question of whether FMLA leave on an intermittent or reduced leave schedule is available in those instances where the above terms are not included in the definition of the applicable serious health condition. Alternatively, it raises the question of whether the regulation regarding intermittent or reduced leave schedule modifies the definitions of covered serious health conditions (which seems dubious on its face).

Before we analyze the above, however, a few terms need to be defined. "Treatment" includes (but is not limited to) examinations to determine if a serious health condition exists and evaluations of the condition. 29 CFR 825.114(b); S. Res. 242, Cong. Rec. S3959, S3963 (April 23, 1996); 29 CFR 825.114(b). "Incapacity" is defined as an inability to work, attend school or perform other regular daily activities due to the serious health condition, treatment therefore, or recovery therefrom. 29 CFR 825.114(a)(2)(I); S. Res. 242, Cong. Rec. S3959, S3962 (April 23, 1996); 29 CFR 825.114(a)(2)(I).

Note that, with the exception of a chronic serious health condition, incapacity or an inability of an employee to perform an essential job function is generally *not* a permissible reason for intermittent or reduced leave schedule.

Related to incapacity, FMLA leave on an intermittent or reduced leave schedule is available for recovery from a serious health condition. The term recovery is undefined. Recovery from a serious health condition is one of several definitions given to the term "incapacity," provided it prevents a covered individual from working, attending school, or performing other regular daily activities. As a practical matter, it may prove very difficult to determine when an FMLA absence is to recover from a serious health condition, or when it is due to incapacity resulting from a serious health condition.

For example, an employee who is in the hospital bed recovering from cancer surgery could be said to be recovering from a serious health condition or treatment for a serious health condition. In that instance, the employee is entitled to FMLA leave on an intermittent or a reduced leave schedule. It becomes more difficult, however, to determine when an employee or covered family member is recovering from a serious health condition where, for example, a severe flu incapacitates the employee so that she is unable to work for more than three consecutive days. That is, rest or convalescence is a form of recovery that looks a lot like incapacity. Again, recovery is a permissible basis for intermittent or reduced leave schedule, while incapacity, with the exception of a serious chronic condition, is not.

Ultimately, the way employers will determine whether intermittent or reduced leave schedule is appropriate will be based on the medical certification submitted by the employee to justify the absence. Arguably, an employer faced with a request for intermittent or a reduced leave schedule must request medical certification, as, according to the regulations, it is the only vehicle allowed to make this determination. An employer that elects not to request medical certification may have no choice but to allow an intermittent or reduced schedule leave.

4. Transfer to an Equivalent Alternative Position

An employer, under certain conditions, may transfer an eligible employee who needs FMLA leave on an intermittent or reduced leave schedule basis to an equivalent alternative position that better accommodates recurring periods of leave than does the employee's regular position. 29 USC 2612(b)(2); 5 USC 6382(b)(2); 2 USC 1312(a)(1) (incorporating § 2612 of Title I, 29 USC 2612, into CAA); 3 USC 401(a)(1) (incorporating § 2612 of Title I, 29 USC 2612, into PEOAA). The criteria governing when an employer may transfer an eligible employee into an equivalent alternative position is different under the federal sector FMLA law.

According to the legislative history of the original Act, Preamble, 29 CFR 825.204:

> [T]his provision was intended to give greater staffing flexibility to employers by enabling them temporarily to transfer employees who need intermittent leave or leave on a reduced leave schedule to positions more suitable for recurring periods of leave. At the same time, it ensures that employees will not be penalized for their need for leave by requiring that they receive equivalent pay and benefits during the temporary transfer. Congress anticipated that a reduced leave schedule would often be perceived as desirable by employers who would prefer to retain a trained and experienced employee part-time for the weeks that the employee is on leave rather than hire a full-time temporary replacement.

a. Title II

An employer has the authority under Title II to place an eligible employee taking FMLA leave on an intermittent or reduced leave schedule basis into an equivalent alternative position. An equivalent alternative position need not consist of equivalent duties, but according to 5 CFR 630.1204(d), the position must be:

- in the same commuting area;
- at an equivalent grade or pay level, including applicable locality pay under 5 USC 5304, special rate pay for law enforcement officers or special pay adjustments for law enforcement officers under Sections 403 and 404 of the Federal Employees Pay Comparability Act of 1990, respectively; continued rate of pay under Subpart G of Part 531 of Title 5; or special salary rate under 5 USC 5305 or similar provision of law;
- the same type of appointment, work schedule, status, and tenure;
- the same employment benefits made available to the employee in his or her previous position (e.g., life insurance, health benefits, retirement coverage, and leave accrual).

The authority of an employer to place (i.e., with or without the employee's consent) an employee into an equivalent alternative position is heavily conditioned.

First, such placement is permitted only when the eligible employee uses intermittent or reduced schedule FMLA leave. An agency does not have the authority under Title II to place an employee who takes FMLA leave in a single block of time into an alternative position during the pendency of FMLA leave.

Second, the intermittent or reduced schedule FMLA leave must be for the serious health condition of the employee, or to care for a covered family member with a serious health condition. 5 CFR 630.1204(c). An agency is not authorized by Title II to transfer an eligible employee to an equivalent alternative position where the employee's need for FMLA leave is based on the birth, adoption, or foster care placement of a son or daughter.

Third, the need for FMLA leave on an intermittent or reduced leave schedule basis due to a serious health condition must be foreseeable based on planned medical treatment or recovery from a serious health condition. If the need for FMLA leave is not foreseeable based on planned medical treatment or recovery from a serious health condition, an employer lacks the authority to place the employee into an alternative equivalent position. Note that the terms "foreseeable," "planned," "medical treatment" and "recovery" are undefined. Nor is any direction given on whether this requirement is judged from the perspective of the employee or employer. The use of the term "planned" suggests that this requirement is judged based on the perspective of the employee or the employee's covered family member. Evidence showing whether medical treatment is planned should be available in the supporting medical certification provided by the employee in support of the leave request.

The regulatory language also excludes recovery from treatment as a condition permitting an employer to transfer an employee to an equivalent alternative position. Transfer is only permitted for planned medical treatment or recovery from a serious health condition. Query whether recovery from a serious health condition includes recovery from treatment for that condition. Probably so.

Fourth, the agency may only place the employee into the equivalent alternative position temporarily. Presumably, temporarily means until the employee returns from leave. According to the rule, upon returning from leave, the employee shall be entitled to be returned to his or her permanent position or an equivalent position. 5 CFR 630.1204(c). This raises the thorny issue we have grappled with elsewhere in this book: what is leave? Is leave the entire series of intermittent or reduced schedule leave? Or is it any particular absence in a series of related intermittent or reduced leave schedule absences?

Under the prevailing Title I interpretation, the term "leave" would include the entire series of intermittent or reduced schedule leave based on the same underlying covered condition, at least for the period of the leave year. In that case, an employer could place an employee who needs intermittent FMLA leave for a serious health condition into an equivalent alternative position until the employee returns from leave. If the need for FMLA leave will be throughout the year, the employer is within its rights to keep the employee in the alternative position for that period of time. If the employee had a lifelong condition, arguably, the employer could keep the employee in the position for the remainder of the employee's career because the employee has not yet returned from leave. Although a lifetime placement into an equivalent alternative position hardly seems temporary, this would appear to be a permissible result under the regulations.

Another situation that may come up is when the employee still needs intermittent leave for a serious health condition, but the employee does not like the equivalent alternative position. The employee submits a health care provider certification indicating he should be moved back into his old job, with modifications. Assuming the employee can medically perform the equivalent alternative position, as long as the employee continues to require intermittent leave, the employer would appear to have the right to keep the employee in the alternative position. The employee, again, has not yet returned from FMLA leave. Of course, as a practical matter an employer might want to move the employee anyone to keep him or her productive.

The rules fail to address what happens if the employee outright refuses a transfer to an equivalent alternative position. Presumably, at minimum, the employee will forfeit FMLA protections.

Fifth, the employee has to be qualified for the equivalent alternative position. The term "qualified" is undefined. Presumably, it means that the employee may have held the position in the past, or otherwise has the requisite knowledge, skills, and abilities to meet the minimum qualifications for the position.

Sixth, the equivalent alternative position must be available and must better accommodate the employee's recurring need for leave. No guidance is offered on how an employer is to judge whether the alternative position better accommodates the employee's need for FMLA leave on an intermittent or reduced leave schedule. It begs the question: better from whose perspective? Since the employer may require an employee to transfer to the alternative position, presumably better is judged from the perspective of the employer.

Nor is the term "available" defined or otherwise explained. It is unclear if available means that there must be a funded, vacant position, or whether an agency can simply create a temporary position that fits the employee's skills, abilities and schedule. If the former interpretation is correct, it would amount to a significant limitation on the ability of an agency to transfer employees to an equivalent alternative position.

Employers must determine the available alternative position that has equivalent pay and benefits consistent with federal laws, including the Rehabilitation Act of 1973, 29 USC 701, and the Pregnancy Discrimination Act of 1978, 42 USC 2000e. 5 CFR 630.1204(f). Basically, if the employee who requested FMLA leave due to a serious health condition is also disabled within the meaning of the law, the above regulation provides that the employer may also have to factor in the reasonable accommodation requirements of the Rehabilitation Act when considering an alternative position that better accommodates the employee's intermittent or reduced leave schedule. Pursuant to the Pregnancy Act, the employer must make sure that pregnant women receive equal treatment in terms of available leave. [For a further discussion of the interaction of the FMLA with a collective bargaining agreement, see Chapter 16, "Interaction of the FMLA with Other Federal Laws, Employer Practices and Collective Bargaining Agreements."]

Because collective bargaining in the federal sector is governed by federal law, an employer's ability to transfer an employee to an equivalent alternative position must be accomplished in compliance with any applicable collective bargaining agreement. If the applicable collective bargaining agreement precludes such transfers, the employer will not be able to exercise this FMLA right. If, on the other hand, the collective bargaining agreement allows such transfers, but provides fewer protections than those afforded by the FMLA, the FMLA protections will apply. [This topic is also discussed in more detail in Chapter 16, "Interaction of the FMLA with Other Federal Laws, Employer Practices and Collective Bargaining Agreements."]

Finally, upon returning from FMLA leave, the employee shall be returned to his or her permanent position or an equivalent position, as provided in 5 CFR 630.1208(a). The cited regulation generally defines the right of an eligible employee to return to work from FMLA leave. [For a further discussion of an employee's rights on return from FMLA leave, see Chapter 13, "Return to Work from Leave."]

b.   Title I, the CAA, and the PEOAA

Employers enjoy broader authority to transfer eligible employees covered under Title I, the CAA, and the PEOAA to equivalent alternative positions during the pendency of FMLA leave than they have for employees covered by Title I.

If an employee needs intermittent leave or leave on a reduced leave schedule that is foreseeable based on planned medical treatment for the employee or a family member, including during a period of recovery from a serious health condition, or if the employer agrees to permit intermittent or reduced schedule leave for the birth of a child or for placement of a child for adoption or foster care, the employer may require the employee to transfer temporarily, during the period that the intermittent or reduced leave schedule is required, to an available alternative position for which the employee is qualified and which better accommodates recurring periods of leave than does the employee's regular position. 29 CFR 825.204(a); S. Res. 242, Cong. Rec. S3959, S3964 (April 23, 1996); 29 CFR 825.204(a); *see Metzler v. Federal Home Loan Bank of Topeka*, No. 03–4024–SAC, 2004 U.S. Dist. LEXIS 21647, at *15 (D. Kan. Sept. 21, 2004), *aff'd*, 464 F.3d 1164 (10th Cir. 2006); *Hoffman v. Professional Med Team*, 270 F. Supp. 2d 954, 961 (W.D. Mich. 2003), *aff'd*, 394 F.3d 414, 418 (6th Cir. 2005); *Covey v. Methodist Hospital of Dyersburg et al.*, 56 F. Supp. 2d 965, 968 (W.D. Tenn. 1999); *Summerville v. ESCO CO., Ltd*, 52 F. Supp. 2d 804, 816 (W.D. Mich. 1999); *Hensley v. Baptist Hospital of East Tennessee, Inc. et al.*, No. 3:96–CV–789, 1997 U.S. Dist. LEXIS 22515, at *38 (E.D. Tenn. Oct. 27, 1997).

The alternative position must have equivalent pay and benefits, but need not have equivalent duties. 29 CFR 825.204(c); S. Res. 242, Cong. Rec. S3959, S3965 (April 23, 1996); 29 CFR 825.204(c); *see Metzler*, 2004 U.S. Dist. LEXIS 21647, at *15; *Hoffman* 270 F. Supp. 2d at 961; *Covey*, 56 F. Supp. 2d at 968; *Summerville*, 52 F. Supp. 2d at 816; *Hensley*, 1997 U.S. Dist. LEXIS 22515, at *38.

In *Metzler*, the court found that plaintiff's employer did not violate the FMLA by failing to restore her to an equivalent position on her return from FMLA leave. The court found that Metzler was on an approved reduced leave schedule at the time of her termination. As such, the court found that she had no entitlement to the same or equivalent duties she previously held because she had not returned from FMLA leave to full-time work status. Because she was receiving her same pay and benefits, the court found that the defendant had every right under the FMLA to transfer plaintiff to a completely different position while she was on an approved FMLA reduced leave schedule.

To ensure such equivalency, an employer may increase the pay and benefits of an existing alternative position, so as to make them equivalent to the pay and benefits of the employee's regular job. Alternatively, the employer may also transfer the employee to a part-time job with the same hourly rate of pay and benefits, provided the employee is not required to take more leave than is medically necessary. 29 CFR 825.204(c); S. Res. 242, Cong. Rec. S3959, S3965 (April 23, 1996); 29 CFR 825.204(c).

For example, if a full-time employee switches to a part-time or reduced leave schedule under the FMLA, the employee must continue to receive the same (full) level of benefits that the employee enjoyed before starting FMLA leave, and may not be required to pay more to maintain that same level of benefits enjoyed prior to the start of the FMLA leave, regardless of any employer policy applicable to part-time employees that would suggest a different result. Preamble, 29 CFR 825.204. To permit otherwise would result in the employee not receiving equivalent pay and benefits as required by the FMLA. *Id*. An employer may, however, proportionately reduce the benefits that are computed on the basis of the number of hours worked during the period, e.g., vacation or sick leave, insurance or other benefits that are determined by the amount of earnings. *Id*.

An employer may not transfer the employee to an alternative position in order to discourage the employee from taking leave or otherwise work a hardship on the employee. 29 CFR 825.204(d); S. Res. 242, Cong. Rec. S3959, S3965 (April 23, 1996); 29 CFR 825.204(d); *see Metzler v. Federal Home Loan Bank of Topeka*, No. 03–4024–SAC, 2004 U.S. Dist. LEXIS 21647, at *15 (D. Kan. Sept. 21, 2004); *Hoffman v. Professional Med Team*, 270 F. Supp. 2d 954, 961 (W.D. Mich. 2003) (if the employer submitted a complete request for intermittent leave under the FMLA, and as a result, the employer reduced plaintiff to a part-time employee and used plaintiff's reduced schedule as a means to deprive her of future FMLA leave or terminate her, plaintiff would have had grounds to sue her employer for violating the FMLA), *aff'd*, 394 F.3d 414, 418 (6th Cir. 2005). For example, a white-collar employee may not be assigned to perform laborers' work; an employee working the day shift may not be reassigned to the graveyard shift; and an employee working in the headquarters facility may not be reassigned to a branch a significant distance away from the employee's normal job locations. 29 CFR 825.204(d); S. Res. 242, Cong. Rec. S3959, S3965 (April 23, 1996); 29 CFR 825.204(d). An employer that even attempts to make such a transfer will be considered in violation of the Act. 29 CFR 825.204(d); S. Res. 242, Cong. Rec. S3959, S3965 (April 23, 1996); 29 CFR 825.204(d).

In *Summerville v. ESCO Co., Ltd. Partnership*, 52 F. Supp. 2d 804, 816 (W.D. Mich. 1999), the district court found that the employer properly transferred the employee to an equivalent alternative position as permitted by the FMLA. Specifically, the court found that:

> ESCO had a legitimate nondiscriminatory reason for removing Summerville from his centrifuge position as three of the four centrifuge operators were moved for legitimate business purposes as a result of ESCO's preparations to open a new plant. The Court also finds that, because of Summerville's attendance problems prior to his FMLA-protected leave and Summerville's indication that he was not going to have surgery for his heel spur, it was a reasonable business decision for Summerville's not to be assigned to running the RX 101–103 kettles. The temporary assignment of Summerville to drying and packing better accommodated the substantial possibility that Summerville would require leave for his bone spur again, as drying and packing was not a crucial job requiring strict attendance and allowed Summerville to rest his foot when needed. Summerville did not suffer a loss of pay or benefits during this reassignment and in fact had previously done drying and packing. Finally, the reassignment lasted only two months, at which time Summerville was moved to a permanent position comparable to his job as centrifuger after another employee left in May of 1996. Accordingly, ESCO has offered a legitimate nondiscriminatory reason for the change in Summerville's duties.

Several lessons may be drawn from *Summerville*. First, the court determined whether the transfer was proper based on a determination that it was made based on legitimate, nondiscriminatory business reasons. Second, the court cited the benefit to the employer (movement into a less attendance-sensitive position) of moving Summerville to the alternative position. It also noted the benefit to Summerville (ability to rest heel).

Like Title II, transfer to an alternative position under Title I, the CAA, and the PEOAA may require compliance with any applicable collective bargaining agreement and federal law (such as the Americans with Disabilities Act). 29 CFR 825.204(b); S. Res. 242, Cong. Rec. S3959, S3965 (April 23, 1996); 29 CFR 825.204(d); DOL WH FMLA Advisory Opinion No. 42 (Aug. 23, 1994) (transfer to alternative position may require compliance with applicable collective bargaining agreement, and the transferred employee retains the same level of benefits in the transferred position, if required by the collective bargaining agreement). Transfer to an alternative position may include altering an existing job to better accommodate the employee's need for intermittent or reduced leave. 29 CFR 825.204(b); S. Res. 242, Cong. Rec. S3959, S3965 (April 23, 1996); 29 CFR 825.204(b); *see also* DOL WH FMLA Advisory Opinion No. 29 (Feb. 7, 1994).

When an employee, who is taking FMLA leave intermittently or on a reduced leave schedule and is transferred to an alternative position, no longer needs to continue on leave and is able to return to full-time work, the employee must be placed in the same or equivalent job as the job he or she left when the leave commenced. 29 CFR 825.204(e); S. Res. 242, Cong. Rec. S3959, S3965 (April 23, 1996); 29 CFR 825.204(d); *see Metzler v. Federal Home Loan Bank of Topeka*, No. 03-4024-SAC, 2004 U.S. Dist. LEXIS 21647, at *15 (D. Kan. Sept. 21, 2004). An employee may not be required to take more leave than necessary to address the circumstances that precipitated the need for leave. 29 CFR 825.204(e); S. Res. 242, Cong. Rec. S3959, S3965 (April 23, 1996); 29 CFR 825.204(d); *see Matthews v. Village Center Community Dev. District*, No. 5:05-cv-344-Oc-10GRJ, 2006 U.S. Dist. LEXIS 85906, at *56 (M.D. Fla. Nov. 28, 2006); *Nance v. Buffalo's Café of Griffin, Inc.*, No. 1:03-cv-2887-WSD, 2005 U.S. Dist. LEXIS 20429, at *13 (N.D. Ga. March 30, 2005).

The above rules differ from similar rules under Title II in several noteworthy respects. First, an employer may require an employee to transfer to an equivalent alternative position in more situations than is permitted under Title II. In addition to serious health conditions, an employer may require an employee to transfer to an equivalent alternative position for the birth, adoption, or foster care placement of a son or daughter. Note, however, that this ability is somewhat circumscribed. The transfer regulation only applies for the birth or for the placement of a child. The covered conditions provide "for the birth…and to care for" a newborn son or daughter. 29 CFR 825.112(a)(1); S. Res. 242, Cong. Rec. S3959, S3962 (April 23, 1996); 29 CFR 825.112(a)(1). Arguably, an employer does not have the authority to transfer an employee to an alternative position to care for a newborn child.

Second, employers may proportionately reduce pay and some benefits to eligible employees covered by Title I, the CAA, and the PEOAA who have been transferred to an equivalent alternative position with reduced hours. The pay can be proportionately reduced based on the hourly rate of the old position multiplied by the number of hours worked. *Green v. New Balance Shoe, Inc.*, 182 F. Supp. 2d 128, n. 2 (D. Me. 2002). Benefits that are normally calculated based on the number of hours worked may also be proportionately reduced. The regulations implementing Title II do not specifically authorize the proportionate reduction of pay and benefits during the period of FMLA leave on an intermittent or reduced leave schedule.

Third, the obligation to return an employee from the alternative position is different depending on which federal sector FMLA regulations apply. For eligible employees covered by Title II, at the conclusion of leave the employee must be returned to his or her permanent position or an equivalent position. 5 CFR 630.1204(c). Under Title I, the CAA, and the PEOAA, the right of return is conditioned on the employee's ability to return to full-time work. Presumably, this means that the employee may return to work without the need for additional leave. The regulation could, of course, be read to exclude part-time employees who are eligible for FMLA from the right to be returned from their transfer position to the same or equivalent position on the conclusion of their need for FMLA leave. While I do not advocate such an interpretation, the possibility serves as yet another reminder of the inadequacies of the current FMLA regulations.

Note also that the entitlement of Title II employees is return to their permanent position. It is less than clear to what position the employee has a right of return under Title I, the CAA, and the PEOAA. The regulations provide that an employee's right of return is to the same job he or she held prior to taking leave. The preamble to the final Title I regulations, however, provides that the employer must restore the employee to his or her original position. Query whether "job" and "position" mean the same thing. As used, it appears that an employee's original position is the same job the employee held at the time he or she was transferred to an equivalent alternative position. If the employee held a position other than his or her permanent position when he or she left for FMLA leave (i.e., a light duty position or a position held while on a detail), the employee's right to return under Title II is to the permanent position, while under Title I, the CAA, and the PEOAA, it is to the position left, whether permanent or otherwise.

Fourth, the regulations implementing Title I, the CAA, and the PEOAA also differ from Title II in that they permit an employer to alter an existing job to better accommodate the employee's need for FMLA leave on an intermittent or reduced leave schedule. Title II does not contain similarly explicit language. Because it is stated immediately after the regulatory language confirming an employer's continuing obligation to comply with existing federal laws, including the disabilities laws, it is unclear whether the accommodation language is a separate FMLA requirement or is part and parcel of the duty to reasonably accommodate a disabled employee who also happens to require FMLA leave. Since the right to transfer an employee is one held by an employer, however, the language permitting an employer to alter an existing job to better accommodate the employee's need for FMLA leave on an intermittent or reduced leave schedule might not create a formal FMLA reasonable accommodation right which can be exercised by an employee. It is, however, an intriguing thought, and the language is sufficiently poorly presented that employee and union organizations should be able to make some mischief of it.

The regulations implementing Title I, the CAA, and the PEOAA also share many similarities with those under Title II. Specifically, the regulations use of many of the same terms, such as "foreseeable," "planned medical treatment," and "better accommodates" as conditions on an agency's ability to exercise its authority to transfer an employee to an equivalent alternative position. As in Title II, the terms are undefined.

The regulations also add some new definitional ambiguities. For example, an employee may not be reassigned to another office a significant distance from the employee's original job location. No guidance is offered on how a significant distance is determined. Whether the determination is based on the subjective view of the impacted employee or the objective view of the hypothetical reasonable person may greatly impact the outcome of the decision. Similarly, it is possible that very small distances may be considered significant where, for example, the absence of public transportation renders impossible a three-mile diversion to another office that is physically closer to the employee's home. Employers should tread carefully when a transfer is to another location.

5. Leave Increments

The size or length of a period of FMLA leave taken on an intermittent or reduced leave schedule is regulated. The smaller the increment in which FMLA leave may be taken on an intermittent or reduced leave schedule basis, the more burdensome it is for employers to administer that leave. As we have seen with other provisions, there are differences between the various federal sector FMLA schemes on this matter.

a. Title II

Theoretically, only the amount of leave taken intermittently or on a reduced leave schedule may be subtracted from the employee's total 12-month FMLA leave entitlement. 5 CFR 630.1204(f). The requirement is theoretical because practical limitations on the agency's recording of leave time may result in the subtraction of more FMLA leave than was precisely taken. This is particularly true in the case of intermittent leave.

Intermittent leave means leave taken in separate blocks of time, and may include leave periods of one hour to several weeks. 5 CFR 630.1202 (definition of intermittent leave). Leave may be taken for periods of less than one hour if agency policy provides for a minimum charge for leave of less than one hour. *Id.* An agency's ability to establish leave periods of less than an hour is governed by 5 CFR 630.206. Unless an agency establishes a minimum charge of less than one hour, or establishes a different minimum charge through negotiations, the minimum charge of leave is one hour, and additional charges are in multiples thereof. 5 CFR 630.1206(a).

Note that the base agency policy is that all leave, including FMLA leave, is taken in one-hour increments, unless the agency has agreed to a different policy. That means even if an employee only needed 15 minutes of incremental FMLA leave (perhaps to recover from a dizzy spell due to medication for a covered condition), the minimum charge would be one hour (assuming you charged the employee for this time at all). Technically, this is more than the actual leave needed and, perhaps, taken. The Title II regulations, however, allow this for intermittent leave.

The rules governing FMLA leave taken on a reduced leave schedule are unclear. The lack of clarity is due to the fact that the definition does not include any reference to leave periods of an hour or less. According to the definition, a reduced leave schedule is one in which the usual number of hours of regularly scheduled work per workday or workweek of an employee is reduced. The number of hours by which the daily or weekly tour of duty is reduced is counted as leave for purposes of the FMLA. 5 CFR 630.1202 (definition of reduced leave schedule). Unlike intermittent leave, the definition does not contain a cross-reference to 5 CFR 630.206, governing a minimum charge of leave. Add in the requirement that an agency may only subtract the amount of leave taken (5 CFR 630.1204(f)), the strong implication is that the exact period of time an employee takes reduced leave schedule must be subtracted from an employee's FMLA leave entitlement.

For example, Chip is an eligible employee with a serious chronic back condition which flares up on occasion. Everyday, Chip unloads the same truck that arrives during his last half-hour of work. On occasion, Chip aggravates his back while unloading the truck. The pain subsides quickly, allowing him to resume work in 30 minutes. If the agency Chip works for has not agreed to a smaller minimum leave charge, even if Chip only needed 35 minutes of leave to rest his aching back. If Chip wanted to avoid aggravating his back altogether, he might be able to have his doctor arrange a reduced leave schedule for the last half-hour of the day. In that case, only a half-hour each day (rather than the hour minimum for intermittent leave) would be charged.

To avoid the potential burden of recording many very small amounts of FMLA leave, agencies are well advised to review their current leave policies to determine whether minimum leave charges of less than an hour are worth the administrative headaches. Unions and organizations representing employees, on the other hand, should also review current agency policies regarding the minimum leave charge. Generally speaking, the ability to take leave in smaller amounts gives employees added flexibility and opportunity to use their FMLA leave entitlement.

b. Title I, the CAA, and the PEOAA

The general rule is that an employee may not be required to take more FMLA leave than necessary to address the circumstances that precipitated the need for the leave. 29 CFR 825.209(d); S. Res. 242, Cong. Rec. S3959, S3964 (April 23, 1996); 29 CFR 825.203(d); *see Whitney v. Wal-Mart Stores, Inc.*, No. 03-65-P-H, 2003 U.S. Dist. LEXIS 22629, at *28 (D. Me. Dec. 16, 2003). To that end, the regulations provide that there is no limit on the size of an increment of leave when an employee takes intermittent or leave on a reduced leave schedule. 29 CFR 825.203(d); S. Res. 242, Cong. Rec. S3959, S3964 (April 23, 1996); 29 CFR 825.203(d); *see Dupee v. Klaff's Inc.*, 462 F. Supp. 2d 233, 242 (D. Conn. Nov. 8, 2006); *Collins v. U.S. Playing Card Co.*, 466 F. Supp. 2d 954, 964 (S.D. Ohio Nov. 6, 2006); *Whitney v. Wal-Mart Stores, Inc.*, No. 03-65-P-H, 2003 U.S. Dist. LEXIS 22629, at *28 (D. Me. Dec. 16, 2003); *Dressler v. Community Service Communications, Inc.*, 275 F. Supp.

2d 17, n. 11 (D. Me. 2003), *aff'd*, 115 Fed. Appx. 452 (1st Cir. 2004). Of course, the statement is somewhat exaggerated.

At the upper end of the spectrum, in order to constitute intermittent or reduced leave schedule, there must be multiple absences of FMLA leave. Multiple absences of FMLA leave require at least two periods of FMLA leave during the course of a 12-month leave year. For there to be two absences in an FMLA leave, no one FMLA leave absence can be more than 12 workweeks of leave in length.

At the other end of the spectrum, the regulations provide that an employer may limit leave increments to the shortest period of time that the employer's payroll system uses to account for absences or use of leave, provided it is one hour or less. 29 CFR 825.203(d); S. Res. 242, Cong. Rec. S3959, S3964 (April 23, 1996); 29 CFR 825.203(d); *see Dressler v. Community Service Communications, Inc.*, 275 F. Supp. 2d 17, n. 11 (D. Me. 2003), *aff'd*, 115 Fed. Appx. 452 (1st Cir. 2004).

In *Collins v. U.S. Playing Card Co.*, 466 F. Supp. 2d 954, 964 (S.D. Ohio Nov. 6, 2006), the court found that FMLA protects an employee's right to take intermittent leave in increments of only a few minutes duration. Collins, a diabetic, left his work station a few minutes early in order to get something to eat to control his blood sugar level.

6. FLSA-Exempt Employees

This section addresses the impact of deducting unpaid FMLA leave of otherwise exempt, salaried employees for FMLA leave taken for partial day absences. Title II does not address this issue at all. Unless otherwise stated, what follows applies to employees covered by Title I, the CAA, and the PEOAA.

a. Exemption from the FLSA Salary Basis Test

Section 102(c) of the FMLA, 29 USC 2612(c), expressly provides that when an employee is otherwise exempt from the Fair Labor Standards Act's (FLSA) requirements for payment of minimum wage and overtime compensation for hours worked over 40 per week (the exemption for "executive, administrative, and professional" employees under FLSA 13(a)(1)), compliance by an employer with the FMLA's requirement to provide unpaid leave will not affect the exempt status of the employee under the FLSA exemption and its regulations (29 CFR Part 541). Employers can dock the pay of otherwise exempt, salaried employees for FMLA leave taken for partial day absences. Preamble, 29 CFR 825.206. If a FLSA-exempt employee needs to work a reduced leave schedule under the FMLA, the employer may deduct from the employee's salary partial-day absences for any hours taken as intermittent or reduced schedule FMLA leave within the workweek without causing loss of the employee's except status under 29 CFR Part 541. By operation of the statute, this exception to the FLSA salary basis test extends only to leave that qualifies as FMLA leave (i.e., FMLA-eligible employees, working for FMLA-covered employers, who take FMLA leave only for reasons which qualify as FMLA leave). *Rowe v. Laidlaw Transit, Inc.*, 244 F.3d 1115, 1118 (9th Cir. 2001) (pivotal question on employee's claim for overtime compensation for hours worked as a supervisor is whether her reduced schedule while recovering from an injury was FMLA-qualifying leave or an indicia of hourly compensation).

This means that under FLSA regulations currently in effect, when an employee meets the specified duties test, is paid on a salary basis, and is paid a salary of at least the amount specified in the FLSA regulations, an employer may make deductions from the employee's salary for any hours taken as intermittent or reduced schedule FMLA leave within a workweek, without affecting the status of the employee as exempt from minimum wage and overtime requirements. 29 CFR 825.206(a); S. Res. 242, Cong. Rec. S3959, S3965 (April 23, 1996); 29 CFR 825.206(a); *see Rowe v. Laidlaw Transit, Inc.*, 244 F.3d 1115, 1118 (9th Cir. 2001); *Furlong v. Johnson Controls World Services, Inc.*, 97 F. Supp. 2d 1312, 1316 (S.D. Fla. 2000)(an employer may deduct an employee's salary for hours taken as intermittent or reduced leave under the FMLA without losing the exempt status of the employee); *see also* DOL WH FMLA Advisory Opinion No. 59 (July 3, 1997) (describing operation of FMLA and FLSA salary basis test).

In *Rowe*, the Circuit court found that the plaintiff's reduced leave schedule, during which she was paid on an hourly basis while she recovered from a serious ankle injury, was FMLA-qualifying leave. *Rowe*, 244 F.3d at 1118–1119. Rowe argued that, although she was a supervisor, because she was paid on an hourly basis during a period of time that she worked a part-time schedule to recover from an ankle injury, she was no longer an exempt employee. She claimed entitlement to unpaid overtime. The court rejected the plaintiff's argument that her part-time schedule was not FMLA-qualifying leave because Laidlaw had not designated it as FMLA leave prior to accepting her proposal for a reduced leave schedule. The court concluded that FMLA-qualifying unpaid leave is entitled to FMLA protection in the same fashion as paid leave, that is, regardless of notification by employer or employee. Rowe's unpaid leave, granted in the form of a reduced schedule, qualified as FMLA leave, and under the FMLA, providing unpaid FMLA-qualifying leave does not affect an employee's exempt status. *Id.* at 1119.

b. Fluctuating Workweek Method of Payment

For an employee paid in accordance with the fluctuating workweek method of payment for overtime (see 29 CFR 778.114), the employer, during the period in which intermittent or reduced schedule FMLA leave is scheduled to be taken, may compensate an employee on an hourly basis and pay only for the hours the employee works, including time and one-half of the employee's regular rate for overtime hours. 29 CFR 825.206(b); S. Res. 242, Cong. Rec. S3959, S3965 (April 23, 1996); 29 CFR 825.206(b). The change of payment on an hourly basis would include the entire period during which the employee is taking intermittent leave, including weeks in which no leave is taken. 29 CFR 825.206(b); S. Res. 242, Cong. Rec. S3959, S3965 (April 23, 1996); 29 CFR 825.206(b). The hourly rate is determined by dividing the employee's weekly salary by the employee's normal or average schedule of hours worked during weeks in which FMLA leave is not being taken. 29 CFR 825.206(b); S. Res. 242, Cong. Rec. S3959, S3965 (April 23, 1996); 29 CFR 825.206(b).

If an employer elects to follow this exception from the fluctuating workweek method of payment, the employer must do so uniformly, with respect to all employees paid on a fluctuating workweek basis for whom FMLA leave is taken on an intermittent or reduced leave schedule basis. 29 CFR 825.206(b); S. Res. 242, Cong. Rec. S3959, S3965 (April 23, 1996); 29 CFR 825.206(b). If an employer does not elect to convert the employee's compensation to hourly pay, no deduction may be taken for FMLA leave absences. 29 CFR 825.206(b); S. Res. 242, Cong. Rec. S3959, S3965 (April 23, 1996); 29 CFR 825.206(b). Once the need for FMLA leave on an intermittent or reduced leave schedule is over, the employee may be restored to payment on a fluctuating workweek basis. 29 CFR 825.206(b); S. Res. 242, Cong. Rec. S3959, S3965 (April 23, 1996); 29 CFR 825.206(b).

This special exception to the salary basis requirements of the FLSA exemption or fluctuating workweek payment requirements applies only to employees of covered employers who are eligible for FMLA leave, and to leave which qualifies as FMLA leave. 29 CFR 825.206(c); S. Res. 242, Cong. Rec. S3959, S3965 (April 23, 1996); 29 CFR 825.206(c). Hourly or other deductions, which are not in accordance with 29 CFR Part 541 or 29 CFR 778.114, may not be taken. For example, the special exception would not apply to an employee who did not meet the 12 months and 1,250 hours eligibility requirement.

Nor may deductions which are not permitted by 29 CFR Part 541 or 29 CFR 778.114 be taken from such an employee's salary for any leave which does not qualify as FMLA leave. 29 CFR 825.206(c); S. Res. 242, Cong. Rec. S3959, S3965 (April 23, 1996); 29 CFR 825.206(c). For example, deductions from an employee's pay for leave to care for a sibling with a serious health condition, or a parent with a non-serious health condition, would not be permitted. In these non-FMLA circumstances, the employer may comply with the employer's own policy or practice and maintain the employee's eligibility for exemption or for the fluctuating workweek method of pay by not taking hourly deductions from the employee's pay, in accordance with FLSA requirements, or may take such deductions, treating the employee as an hourly employee and pay overtime premium pay for hours worked over 40 in a workweek. 29 CFR 825.206(c); S. Res. 242, Cong. Rec. S3959, S3965 (April 23, 1996); 29 CFR 825.206(c).

c. Title II and FLSA Exemption

There is nothing in Title II, neither the statute nor the implementing regulations, that exempts the deduction of hourly amounts of unpaid FMLA leave from the requirements of the FLSA. Because Title II provides that unpaid FMLA leave may be taken on an intermittent or reduced leave schedule, the absence of statutory or regulatory language excepting such FMLA leave from the FLSA requirements means that compliance with the FMLA may result in the loss of FLSA-exempt status. The loss of FLSA-exempt status transforms salaried employees to hourly employees for payment of overtime premium pay for hours worked over 40 in a workweek.

Think about it. Employers that abide by the requirements of Title II and deduct hourly amounts of unpaid FMLA leave taken on an intermittent or reduced leave schedule basis may be exposing themselves to massive FLSA problems. Employees who have had intermittent or reduced leave schedule amounts deducted may be able to argue that they are not exempt from the FLSA overtime requirements because they are really hourly employees. The evidence, again, would be the deduction of hourly amounts of unpaid FMLA leave.

7. Determining the Amount of Intermittent or Reduced Leave Schedule Leave Taken

This section addresses how an employer accounts for FMLA leave taken on an intermittent or reduced leave schedule basis.

a. Title II

Under Title II, in the case of an employee who takes leave intermittently or on a reduced leave schedule, any hours of leave taken by such employee must be subtracted from the total amount of leave remaining available to such employee for the duration of the leave year, on an hour–for–hour basis. 5 USC 6382(b)(1). Only the amount of leave taken intermittently or on a reduced leave schedule basis may be subtracted from the total amount of leave available to the employee. 5 CFR 630.1204(f).

b. Title I, the CAA, and the PEOAA

If an employee takes leave on an intermittent or reduced leave schedule basis, only the amount of leave actually taken may be counted toward the 12 weeks of leave to which an eligible employee is entitled. 29 CFR 825.205(a); S. Res. 242, Cong. Rec. S3959, S3965 (April 23, 1996); 29 CFR 825.205(a); *see Counsell v. Nystrom & Assoc., Ltd.*, No. 05-2315 (PJS/JJG), 2007 U.S. Dist. LEXIS 10759, at *18 & n.5 (D. Minn. Feb. 13, 2007) (intermittent leave is calculated on a *pro rata* basis according to the employee's schedule); *Price v. GKN Aerospace North America, Inc.*, No. 4:05CV01147 ERW, 2006 U.S. Dist. LEXIS 76392, at *13 & n.11 (E.D. Mo. Oct. 20, 2006). For example, if an employee who normally works five days per week takes off one day, the employee would use one–fifth of a week of FMLA leave. Similarly, if a full–time employee who normally works eight–hour days now works four–hour days under a reduced leave schedule, the employee would use one–half week of FMLA leave. 29 CFR 825.205(a); S. Res. 242, Cong. Rec. S3959, S3965 (April 23, 1996); 29 CFR 825.205(a).

When an employee normally works a part–time schedule or variable hours, the amount of leave to which an employee is entitled is determined on a pro rata or proportional basis by comparing the new schedule with the employee's normal schedule. 29 CFR 825.205(a); S. Res. 242, Cong. Rec. S3959, S3965 (April 23, 1996); 29 CFR 825.205(a). For example, if an employee who normally works 30 hours per week works only 20 hours a week under a reduced leave schedule, the employee's ten hours of leave would constitute one–third of a week of FMLA leave for each week the employee works the reduced leave schedule. 29 CFR 825.205(b); S. Res. 242, Cong. Rec. S3959, S3965 (April 23, 1996); 29 CFR 825.205(b).

If an employee's schedule varies from week to week, a weekly average of the hours worked over the 12 weeks prior to the beginning of the leave period would be used for calculating the employee's normal workweek. 29 CFR 825.205(c); S. Res. 242, Cong. Rec. S3959, S3965 (April 23, 1996); 29 CFR 825.205(c).

Similarly, an employee generally may not be required to take more FMLA leave than necessary to address the circumstances that precipitated the need for the leave. 29 CFR 825.203(d), 825.309(c); S. Res. 242, Cong. Rec. S3959, S3964, S3973 (April 23, 1996); 29 CFR 825.203(d), 825.309(c); *see Green v. New Balance Athletic Shoe, Inc.*, 182 F. Supp. 2d 128, 136 (D. Me. 2002). For example, the death of a covered family member will end the employee's need for FMLA to care for the now deceased family member. *Brown v. J.C. Penny Corp.*, 924 F. Supp. 1158 (S.D. Fla. 1996). When FMLA concludes, the issue becomes the right of an employee to return to the same or an equivalent position, the subject of Chapter 13, "Return to Work from Leave."

Note that the above rules prohibiting the subtraction of more FMLA leave than was actually taken are subject to the rules regarding increments of leave previously discussed in this chapter. In limited circumstances, those rules allow for the reduction of more FMLA leave than was actually taken, depending on how the employer records employee time for purposes of leave and benefits.

The taking of leave intermittently or on a reduced leave schedule does not result in a reduction in the total amount of leave to which the employee is entitled to under the FMLA beyond the amount of leave actually taken. 29 USC 2612(b)(1); 2 USC 1312(a)(1) (incorporating 29 USC 2612 into CAA); *see Sabbrese v. Lowe's Home Centers, Inc.*, 320 F. Supp. 2d 311, 321 (W.D. Pa. 2004). That means that an eligible employee's entitlement to 12 workweeks of FMLA leave each leave year remains the same whether the employee takes the leave in a single block of time, intermittently, or on a reduced leave schedule basis. Even though leave taken on an intermittent or reduced leave schedule basis may be more disruptive to an employer and may extend throughout the entire leave year, the FMLA does not impose any sort of penalty, in the form of a reduction in the amount of total leave available to an employee based on how the leave is taken.

Conversely, intermittent leave does not entitle an employee to additional FMLA leave time. *Price v. GKN Aerospace North America, Inc.*, No. 4:05CV01147 ERW, 2006 U.S. Dist. LEXIS 76392, at *13 & n.11 (E.D. Mo. Oct. 20, 2006).

Finally, the impact of work at home during the course of intermittent or reduced schedule leave on the amount of FMLA leave that may be subtracted from an eligible employee's 12-week entitlement was addressed by the court in *Parker v. Sony Pictures Entertainment Inc. et al.*, 19 F. Supp. 2d 141, 154–55 (S.D.N.Y. 1998), *aff'd in part, vacated and remanded in part on other grounds*, 204 F.3d 326 (2d Cir. 2000). The district court held that "to the extent that Parker worked at home, whether at the request of his employer or not, the time he spent cannot be counted as part of the 12 week leave to which he was entitled."

In rendering its decision, the court cited a DOL advisory opinion. *Parker*, 19 F. Supp. 2d at 154, n. 122. DOL WH FMLA Advisory Opinion No. 67 (July 21, 1995) addressed this matter as follows:

> Issue 1
>
> Q. Where an employer and employee have agreed that the employee would continue to work out of the office between the time spent caring for a seriously ill child, is it proper to include the hours the employee worked when on leave toward the employee's 12 week maximum under the FMLA?
>
> A. No. Only the amount of leave actually taken may be charged as FMLA leave. The amount of time that the employee is "suffered and permitted" to work for the employer, whether requested or not by the employer, must be counted as "hours worked" pursuant to the Fair Labor Standards Act (FLSA) Interpretative Bulletin, section 785.11 of 29 C.F.R. Part 785. This means that the eight hours per day in the hospital and the time at home that the employee was "suffered and permitted" to work would be considered hours worked under the FLSA (see 29 C.F.R. 785.12 for work performed away from the premises or job site) and this amount of time could not be counted against the employee's 12-week FMLA leave allowance.

8. Special School Rules

Title I, the CAA, and the PEOAA have special rules that apply to "local educational agencies," including public school boards and elementary and secondary schools under their jurisdiction, and private elementary and secondary schools. 29 USC 2612(c);2 USC 1312(a)(1) (incorporating 29 USC 2618(a) for purposes of the CAA); 3 USC 412(a)(1) (incorporating 29 USC 2612 of Title I into PEOAA). The special rules do not apply to other kinds of educational institutions, such as colleges and universities, trade schools, and preschools. 29 CFR 825.600(a)); S. Res. 242, Cong. Rec. S3959, S3975 (April 23, 1996); 29 CFR 825.600(a). It is unclear, at least to me, why the CAA and the PEOAA would incorporate such rules. Presumably, somewhere in Congress and the Executive Office of the President there must be a school within the definition of the regulations for those entities.

The special rules affect the taking of FMLA leave on an intermittent or reduced leave schedule, or leave near the end of an academic term (semester), by instructional employees. Instructional employees are those whose principal function is to teach and instruct students in a class, a small group, or an individual setting. 29 CFR 825.600(c); S. Res. 242, Cong. Rec. S3959, S3975 (April 23, 1996); 29 CFR 825.600(c). The term includes teachers, athletic coaches, driving instructors, and special education assistants such as signers for the hearing impaired. 29 CFR 825.600(c); S. Res. 242, Cong. Rec. S3959, S3975 (April 23, 1996); 29 CFR 825.600(c). It does not include, and the special rules do not apply to, teacher assistants or aides who do not have as their principal job actual teaching or instructing, nor does it include auxiliary personnel such as counselors, psychologists, curriculum specialists, cafeteria workers, maintenance workers, or bus drivers. 29 CFR 825.600(c); S. Res. 242, Cong. Rec. S3959, S3975 (April 23, 1996); 29 CFR 825.600(c).

Limitations are placed on the taking of FMLA leave intermittently or on a reduced leave schedule in two instances: (1) taking leave in excess of 20 percent of the working days over the leave period; and (2) taking FMLA leave near the end of an academic term.

a. Twenty Percent or More FMLA Leave

If an eligible instructional employee needs intermittent leave or leave on a reduced leave schedule to care for his or her own serious health condition, or to care for a covered family member with a serious health condition, which is foreseeable based on planned medical treatment, and the employee would be on leave for more than 20 percent of the total number of working days over the period the leave would extend, the employer may require (29 USC 2618(c)(1); 29 CFR 825.601(a)(1); S. Res. 242, Cong. Rec. S3959, S3975 (April 23, 1996); 29 CFR 825.600(a)(1)) the employee to choose either to:

- Take leave for a period or periods of a particular duration, not greater than the duration of the planned treatment; or

- Transfer temporarily to an available alternative position for which the employee is qualified, which has equivalent pay and benefits and which better accommodates recurring periods of leave than does the employee's regular position.

A "period of particular duration" means a block, or blocks, of time beginning no earlier than the first day for which leave is needed and ending no later than the last day on which leave is needed, and may include an uninterrupted period of leave. 29 CFR 825.601(a)(2); S. Res. 242, Cong. Rec. S3959, S3975 (April 23, 1996); 29 CFR 825.601(a)(2).

For example, if an instructional employee who normally works five days each week needs to take two days of FMLA leave per week over a period of several weeks, the special rules would apply. Employees taking leave which constitutes 20 percent or less of the working days during the leave period would not be subject to transfer to an alternative position. 29 CFR 825.601(a)(2); S. Res. 242, Cong. Rec. S3959, S3975 (April 23, 1996); 29 CFR 825.601(a)(2).

Note that the employer may require the employee to choose between the two alternatives, but the choice of which alternative remains with the employee. The employer is not authorized to choose which alternative for the employee.

An employer has three options when an instructional employee fails to give timely and adequate notice of his or her need for FMLA leave on an intermittent or reduced leave schedule for planned medical treatment. 29 CFR 825.601(b); S. Res. 242, Cong. Rec. S3959, S3975 (April 23, 1996); 29 CFR 825.601(b). The employer may require the employee to take leave of a particular duration, or to transfer temporarily to an alternative position. 29 CFR 825.601(b); S. Res. 242, Cong. Rec. S3959, S3975 (April 23, 1996); 29 CFR 825.601(b). The employer may also require the employee to delay the taking of leave until the notice provision is met. 29 CFR 825.601(b); S. Res. 242, Cong. Rec. S3959, S3975 (April 23, 1996); 29 CFR 825.601(b). [Employee notice obligations are addressed more fully in Chapter 8, "Notice Requirements."]

b. Leave Taken Near the End of an Academic Term

There are special rules that apply depending on the covered condition involved and the length of time from the end of the academic term that the leave both begins and ends. 29 CFR 825.602(a)(1); S. Res. 242, Cong. Rec. S3959, S3975 (April 23, 1996); 29 CFR 825.601(a)(1). There are three periods of time to keep in mind: (1) leave that begins more than five weeks from the end of the academic terms; (2) leave that begins less than five weeks before the end of the academic term; and (3) leave that begins less than three weeks before the end of the academic term. "Academic term" means the school semester. 29 CFR 825.602(b); S. Res. 242, Cong. Rec. S3959, S3975 (April 23, 1996); 29 CFR 825.601(b). For purposes of the FMLA, a school may not have more than two academic terms or semesters each year. 29 CFR 825.602(b); S. Res. 242, Cong. Rec. S3959, S3975 (April 23, 1996); 29 CFR 825.601(b).

When an instructional employee begins FMLA leave (block, intermittent or reduced leave schedule) more than five weeks before the end of the academic term, the employer may require the employee to continue taking leave until the end of the term if: (1) the leave will last at least three weeks; and (2) the employee would return to work during the three-week period before the end of the term. 29 CFR 825.602(a)(1); S. Res. 242, Cong. Rec. S3959, S3975 (April 23, 1996); 29 CFR 825.601(a)(1).

For example, an instructional employee begins FMLA leave eight weeks from the end of the academic term. The FMLA leave is taken in a block of time and will continue for six weeks. Because the employee began leave more than five weeks from the end of the academic term and is scheduled to return from FMLA leave within the three-week period before the academic terms ends, the employer is within its rights to require the employee to continue taking leave until the end of the academic term.

Where an employee begins FMLA leave (block, intermittent, or reduced leave schedule) for a purpose other than the employee's own serious health condition during the five-week period before the end of the academic term, the employer may require the employee to continue taking leave until the end of the term if: (1) the leave will last more than two weeks; and (2) the employee would return to work during the two-week period before the end of the term. 29 CFR 825.602(a)(2); S. Res. 242, Cong. Rec. S3959, S3975 (April 23, 1996); 29 CFR 825.602(a)(2).

For example, an instructional employee takes FMLA leave on a reduced leave schedule beginning four weeks before the end of the academic term to care for a parent with a serious health condition. The leave is to last three weeks. Because the leave is not for the employee's own serious health condition, it began within five weeks from the end of the academic term, and the employee is set to return within the two-week period before the end of the academic term, the employer could require the employee to remain on leave until the end of the academic term.

When the employee begins FMLA leave for a purpose other than the employee's own serious health condition during the three-week period before the end of the academic term, and the leave will last more than five working days, the employer may require the employee to continue taking leave until the end of the academic term. 29 CFR 825.602(a)(3); S. Res. 242, Cong. Rec. S3959, S3975 (April 23, 1996); 29 CFR 825.602(a)(3).

For example, an employee begins FMLA leave for ten working days within the three-week period prior to the end of an academic term to care for a son or daughter with a serious health condition. Because the leave began within the three-week period at the end of an academic term and would last more than five working days, the employer could require the employee to remain on leave until the end of the academic term.

Note that the above special rules apply whether FMLA leave is taken in a single block of time, intermittently, or on a reduced leave schedule. This may lead to some strange results. For example, applying the first scenario, an instructional employee begins a period of intermittent FMLA leave 12 weeks from the end of a semester. The leave will last at least six weeks, consisting of the first absence for one-half hour to make telephone calls to try to place a parent in a retirement home, and a second absence for two hours to drive the parent to the retirement home. The second absence takes place six weeks after the first, and within the three-week period before the end of the term. Even though the employee will be out on FMLA leave for a grand total of two and one-half hours, the employer has the right to require the employee to sit out the entire 12-week period. Of course, an employer would be silly to require an employee to sit out the remainder of the term under those circumstances. Nevertheless, the employer has the legal authority to do so.

c. What Leave Counts Toward the 12-Week FMLA Leave Entitlement

Under the special school rules, only certain leave counts towards an eligible instructional employee's FMLA leave entitlement.

If an employee chooses to take leave "for periods of a particular duration" in the case of intermittent or reduced schedule leave, the entire period of leave taken will count as FMLA leave. 29 CFR 825.603(a); S. Res. 242, Cong. Rec. S3959, S3975 (April 23, 1996); 29 CFR 825.603(a).

In the case of an employee who is required to take leave until the end of an academic term, only the period of leave until the employee is ready and able to return to work shall be charged against the employee's FMLA leave entitlement. 29 CFR 825.603(b); S. Res. 242, Cong. Rec. S3959, S3975 (April 23, 1996); 29 CFR 825.603(b). Because the employer has the option not to require the employee to stay on leave until the end of the semester, any additional leave required by the employer to the end of the school term is not counted as FMLA leave. 29 CFR 825.603(c); S. Res. 242, Cong. Rec. S3959, S3975 (April 23, 1996); 29 CFR 825.603(c).

d. Return to Work

The rules governing the right of an instructional employee to return to work on the conclusion of absences involving FMLA leave are incomplete.

In the case of an employee who is required to take leave until the end of an academic term, even though the additional leave an employee is required to take beyond the point where he or she is ready and able to return to work is not considered FMLA leave, the regulations nonetheless require that the employer maintain group health benefits during this period, and restore the employee to the same or an equivalent job. 29 CFR 825.603(b); S. Res. 242, Cong. Rec. S3959,

S3975 (April 23, 1996); 29 CFR 825.603(b). It is unclear what rules govern this restoration right because the right to return to work is generally phrased in reference to an employee returning from FMLA leave. These instructional employees are not, however, on FMLA leave. Therefore, arguably, the regulations, such as 29 CFR 825.604, do not technically apply. While the return-to-work rules do not technically apply, employers are well advised to treat employees as if they do apply for purposes of determining return to the same or an equivalent position.

The regulations do not provide any special rules governing the return of an employee who chooses a temporary transfer to an equivalent available alternative position for which the employee is qualified to accommodate a need for FMLA leave on an intermittent or reduced leave schedule. Presumably, the employee's right to return to work is governed by the general rules governing an employee's return to work from FMLA leave. These rules, however, are less than clear. The special school regulations address what an equivalent position means. 29 CFR 825.604; S. Res. 242, Cong. Rec. S3959, S3975 (April 23, 1996); 29 CFR 825.604. What they do not do is restate the rule that an employee is entitled to be restored to his or her same or an equivalent position at the conclusion of the need for FMLA leave. The statute, however, clearly provides that the rights, remedies, and procedures under the Act apply to instructional employees of covered schools. 29 USC 2618(a)(1). Employers should apply the general regulations governing the return to work of an employee transferred to an alternative position during a period of intermittent or reduced leave schedule. 29 CFR 825.204(e).

9. Impact of Intermittent or Reduced Leave Schedule on Other FMLA Requirements

The taking of FMLA leave on an intermittent or reduced leave schedule basis impacts on other FMLA rights and requirements, most notably employee eligibility, notice, medical certification, and return to work issues. While these issues are discussed in more detail in other chapters, the following presents a quick overview of this subject.

a. Eligibility

In the federal sector, the determination of whether an employee is eligible for FMLA leave is determined at leave commencement. In order to determine when leave commences, it is necessary to determine what constitutes leave. Remarkably, the term "leave" is not defined in the statues or regulations for purposes of the FMLA.

The DOL issued an advisory opinion, however, that defines leave for purposes of eligibility as a period or periods of absence(s) for the same covered condition during the course of a 12–month leave year. DOL WH FMLA Advisory Opinion No. 112 (Sept. 11, 2000). In so doing, the DOL essentially adopted the decision of the district court in *Barron v. Runyon*, 11 F. Supp. 2d 676 (E.D. Va. 1998). Pursuant to that definition, employee eligibility for FMLA leave is determined at the commencement of a period of FMLA leave for the same covered condition during the course of a leave year. Where FMLA leave is taken intermittently or on a reduced leave schedule basis for the same covered condition, eligibility is calculated once on the occasion of the first intermittent or reduced leave schedule absence in the series of absences. Eligibility is not calculated for each of the multiple absences when FMLA leave is taken on an intermittent or reduced leave schedule basis.

It is unclear whether the DOL's interpretation will be adopted for purposes of Title II, the CAA, or the PEOAA. [The impact of FMLA leave taken on an intermittent or reduced leave schedule basis is discussed more fully in Chapter 5, "Employee Eligibility for Leave."]

b. Notice

An employee must provide timely and adequate notice of the need for FMLA leave. When FMLA leave is taken on an intermittent or reduced leave schedule basis, additional requirements govern how often an employee must give notice of the need for leave, and the content of that notice. [Chapter 8, "Notice Requirements," discusses employee notice requirements involving FMLA leave on an intermittent and reduced leave schedule.]

c. Medical Certification

To support a request for FMLA leave based on the employee's own serious health condition, or to care for a covered family member with a serious health condition, an employer may require an employee to provide a medical certification. The certification should identify whether FMLA leave is to be taken on an intermittent or reduced leave schedule basis and, if so, the probable duration of the leave, the probable number and interval between treatments, actual or estimated dates of treatment, and periods of known recovery. [For a further discussion of medical certification requirements when FMLA leave is taken on an intermittent or reduced leave schedule basis, see Chapter 9, "Documentation Requirements."]

d. Return to Work

Employers generally have the right to require an employee returning from FMLA leave to furnish a medical certificate attesting to the employee's fitness to return to duty. The employer's right to require a fitness for duty certification is, in some instances, circumscribed where FMLA leave is taken on an intermittent or reduced leave schedule basis. [The rules governing fitness for duty certifications of employees taking FMLA leave on an intermittent or reduced leave schedule basis are discussed more fully in Chapter 13, "Return to Work from Leave."]

C. LEAVE SCHEDULING IN AGENCIES WITH MIXED FMLA RESPONSIBILITIES

Agencies whose workforce consists of a mixture of employees covered by different FMLA leave scheduling requirements must exercise great care to ensure that it is correctly applying the applicable FMLA rules. Because of differences in the various federal sector FMLA requirements, an agency with a majority of employees covered by Title II of the Act that simply applies those rules to all employees, including those covered by Title I, may quickly find itself in violation of the law. An agency that rotely applies the requirements of Title II may also be losing greater opportunities to control FMLA leave offered by application of the requirements of Title I.

CHAPTER 11
SUBSTITUTION OF PAID LEAVE

I. OVERVIEW

Generally, FMLA leave is unpaid. *See* 29 USC 2612(c) (Title I); 29 CFR 825.207(a) (same); 5 USC 6382(c) (Title II); 5 CFR 630.1205(a) (same); 2 USC 1312(a)(1) (the CAA); S. Res. 242, Cong. Rec. S3959, S3965 (April 23, 1996); 29 CFR 825.207(a) (same); 3 USC 412(a)(1) (PEOAA); *see Repa v. Roadway Express, Inc.*, 477 F.3d 938, 940-41 (7th Cir. 2007) (employer is not required to pay an employee while the employee is on FMLA leave); *Chubb v. City of Omaha, Nebraska*, 424 F.3d 831, 834 (8th Cir. 2005); *Tippens v. Airnet Systems, Inc.*, No. 2:05-CV-421, 2007 U.S. Dist. LEXIS 23808, at *15 & n.2 (S.D. Ohio March 30, 2007); *Hendricks v. Compass Group USA, Inc.*, No. 4:03CV79AS, 2006 U.S. Dist. LEXIS 64433, at *5-6 (N.D. Ind. Aug. 29, 2006); *Dortman v. ACO Hardware, Inc.*, 405 F. Supp. 2d 812, 820 (E.D. Mich. 2005); *Lines v. City of Ottawa, Kansas*, No. 02–2248–KHV, 2003 U.S. Dist. LEXIS 10203, at *15 (D. Kan. June 16, 2003) (FMLA guarantees 12 weeks of unpaid leave). However, all four federal sector FMLA statutes permit the use of paid leave in substitution for, or to run concurrently with, unpaid FMLA leave. The circumstances under which paid leave may be used in conjunction with unpaid FMLA leave, what accrued paid leave may be used, and who gets to make the election to use paid leave, however, differ depending on what federal sector FMLA statute applies.

Section II of this chapter discusses paid leave substitution, including what accrued paid leave may be used in substitution of unpaid FMLA leave, the limitations on paid leave substitution, and compensatory time off. Section III addresses temporary disability leave and workers' compensation as paid leave. Section IV will address the effect paid leave substitution has on various FMLA procedures such as notice and documentation. Finally, Section V will discuss the mixed responsibilities under the FMLA and paid leave substitution.

II. PAID LEAVE

In the federal sector, unpaid FMLA leave may run in conjunction with paid leave in two circumstances: (1) an eligible employee may substitute accrued paid leave for unpaid FMLA leave; or (2) FMLA leave may run concurrently with an absence occasioned by an eligible employee's workplace injury for which he or she is receiving workers' compensation, or pursuant to a federal employer's temporary disability benefit plan. A review of each follows.

A. SUBSTITUTION OF ACCRUED PAID LEAVE

Under certain circumstances, the FMLA permits an eligible federal employee to substitute accrued paid leave for unpaid FMLA leave. *See* 29 USC 2612(d) (Title I); 29 CFR 825.207(a) (same); 5 USC 6382(d) (Title II); 5 CFR 630.1205(b) (same); 2 USC 1312(a)(1) (incorporating § 102 of Title I, 29 USC 2612 (CAA); S. Res. 242, Cong. Rec. S3959, S3965 (April 23, 1996); 29 CFR 825.207(a) (same); 3 USC 412(a)(1) (incorporating § 102 of Title I, 29 USC 2612 (PEOAA). The substitution provisions are intended to allow for the specified paid leave that has accrued but not yet been taken by an employee to be substituted for the unpaid leave required under the FMLA, in order to mitigate the financial impact of wage loss due to family and temporary medical leave. Preamble, 29 CFR 825.207.

1. Election of Paid Leave

Under Title I, Title II, the CAA and the PEOAA, an eligible employee may choose to substitute accrued paid leave for unpaid FMLA leave. *See* 29 USC 2612(d)(2)(A) (Title I); 29 CFR 825.207(a) (same); 5 USC 6382(d) (Title II); 5 CFR 630.1205(b) (same); 2 USC 1312(a)(1) (CAA); S. Res. 242, Cong. Rec. S3959, S3965 (April 23, 1996); 29 CFR 825.207(a) (same); 3 USC 412(a)(1) (PEOAA); *see Repa v. Roadway Express, Inc.*, 477 F.3d 938, 940-41 (7th Cir. 2007); *Bloom v. Metro heart Group of St. Louis, Inc.*, 440 F.3d 1025, at *13 (8th Cir. 2006).

If an eligible employee does not choose to substitute accrued paid leave, under Title I, the CAA and the PEOAA, the employer may require the employee to substitute accrued paid leave for FMLA leave. *See* 29 USC 2612(d)(2)(A) (Title I);

29 CFR 825.207(a) (same); 2 USC 1312(a)(1) (CAA); S. Res. 242, Cong. Rec. S3959, S3965 (April 23, 1996); 29 CFR 825.207(a) (same); 3 USC 412(a)(1) (PEOAA); *see also Repa v. Roadway Express, Inc.*, 477 F.3d 938, 940-41 (7th Cir. 2007); *Stentz v. City of Republic, Missouri*, 448 F.3d 1008, 1010 (8th Cir. 2006) (FMLA grants an employer the power to require an employee to substitute any accrued sick leave for FMLA leave); *Bloom v. Metro heart Group of St. Louis, Inc.*, 440 F.3d 1025 (8th Cir. 2006); *Dortman v. ACO Hardware, Inc.*, 405 F. Supp. 2d 812, 820 (E.D. Mich. 2005).

If the employer elects to give the employee paid leave in lieu of unpaid leave, the employee is not entitled to an additional period of unpaid leave after exhausting the 12-week period of paid leave. 29 USC 2612(d)(2)(B); *see Lines v. City of Ottawa, Kansas*, No. 02-2248-KHV, 2003 U.S. Dist. LEXIS 10203, at n.9 (D. Kan. June 16, 2003); *see also Miller v. Personal-Touch of Virginia, Inc.*, 342 F. Supp. 2d 499, 511 (E.D. Va. 2004) (an employer may require the employee to substitute any period of accrued vacation, sick, or other leave for any part of the 12-week period of FMLA leave); *Pellegrino v. County of Orange*, 313 F. Supp. 2d 303, 319, n.9 (S.D.N.Y. 2004) (FMLA permits employers to require their employees to exhaust FMLA leave before taking any other leave to which they might be statutorily or contractually entitled); *Strykowski v. Rush North Shore Medical Center*, No. 02 C 0778, 2003 U.S. Dist. LEXIS 13206, at *15 (N.D. Ill. July 30, 2003) (FMLA permits employers to require employees to substitute any accrued paid vacation leave for FMLA leave).

The only decision of consequence regarding the substitution of paid leave since the publication of the *FMLA Guide* is *Miller v. Personal-Touch of Virginia, Inc.*, 342 F. Supp. 2d 499, 511 (E.D. Va. 2004). That case turned on whether plaintiff could elect to take accrued paid leave first and then take unpaid FMLA leave for the same FMLA-qualifying reason. The court held that plaintiff could not stack unpaid FMLA leave on top of paid leave for the same FMLA-qualifying reason so that she received more than 12 weeks of leave, at least where the employee was provided with adequate written notice that the employer considers the leave as FMLA-qualifying. In that circumstance, if an employee decides to use any accrued paid leave for the same reason during that period, such decision constitutes an employee election to substitute paid leave that will run concurrently with unpaid FMLA leave, whether or not that was the intention of the employee.

Plaintiff Yolanda Miller was employed as a private duty nurse supervisor for Personal-Touch. At all relevant times to the events at issue in the case, Miller was eligible for unpaid FMLA leave and accrued 144 hours of paid leave in the form of vacation, sick leave, floating holidays, and personal days. In March 2002, Miller learned that she was pregnant with an expected due date of November 27, 2002. Miller subsequently informed her employer on August 1, 2002, of her need to take leave due to her pregnancy and the birth of her child.

On September 24, 2002, Miller met with a representative of Personal-Touch where she completed a request for FMLA leave. At this meeting the parties discussed the substitution of accrued paid leave for unpaid FMLA leave. Miller came away from the meeting with the belief that she could decline to substitute accrued paid leave for unpaid FMLA leave and instead run the two forms of leave consecutively. Personal-Touch contended that before, during, and after that meeting it advised plaintiff that if she elected to substitute paid leave for unpaid FMLA leave, the paid leave would run concurrent with the 12 weeks of FMLA leave. On September 24, 2002, plaintiff signed and submitted the FMLA request form with the start and end dates left blank.

On September 26, 2002, plaintiff informed Personal-Touch that her doctor placed her on bed rest for the last two months of her pregnancy. The FMLA request form was completed with FMLA leave set to begin September 26, 2002, and end December 19, 2002. Again, plaintiff insisted that she was advised that she could first use accrued paid leave and then, and only then, would FMLA leave begin. She claimed that no one ever advised her when her FMLA leave would begin. Personal-Touch claimed that Miller was given a copy of the completed FMLA Request Form.

Plaintiff was absent from work on full bed rest until she delivered her son on November 25, 2002. Personal-Touch called plaintiff on December 11, 2002, and advised Miller that her FMLA leave would end on December 19, 2002, and that if she could not return to work her job could not be guaranteed. Personal-Touch followed up this telephone conversation with a letter of confirmation the following day. Plaintiff was released to return to work by her doctor on January 6, 2003. By that time, Personal-Touch had already terminated her.

Plaintiff filed suit alleging that her termination violated the FMLA. She claimed that had her paid leave been used in addition to, and not in place of, her unpaid FMLA leave, she could have remained on leave until January 20, 2003. Alternatively, plaintiff argued that Personal-Touch permitted her to take unpaid FMLA leave intermittently with her accrued paid leave. Under either the substitution or the intermittent leave argument, plaintiff concluded that Personal-Touch wrongfully substituted her accrued paid leave for unpaid FMLA leave.

The court initially found that Personal-Touch properly notified Miller that her FMLA leave commenced at the start of her bed rest, not sometime later after she exhausted her paid leave. In pertinent part, the FMLA request form she signed on September 24, 2002, specifically provided that "the requested leave will be counted against your annual FMLA leave entitlement." *Id.* at 507. Because it gave proper written notice to Miller that it would count all of the leave taken due to her pregnancy toward her FMLA entitlement, Personal-Touch was permitted to consider all such leave as FMLA leave, regardless of whether it was paid. According to the court, in this case plaintiff admitted that she elected to use paid leave during the period covered by FMLA leave. The interspersion of paid and unpaid leave periods for her pregnancy, the court found, completely undermined plaintiff's professed belief that she used all of her paid leave first and then, and only then, would she be permitted to use her 12 weeks of FMLA leave.

The court concluded that "substitution of paid leave under the FMLA is not intended to extend the total leave period beyond the [12] weeks guaranteed under the FMLA." *Id.* at. 512. "The court concludes that the taking of any leave for an FMLA qualifying reason, when the employee has notice that the leave is being taken for this reason and decides to use paid leave during this period, constitutes an elected substitution of paid leave, in spite of the plaintiff's belief to the contrary." *Id.* Title II prohibits an employer from requiring an employee to substitute paid leave for any or all of the period covered by unpaid FMLA leave. 5 CFR 630.1205(d); *see AFGE, Council of Marine Corps Locals Council 240 and US Dept. of Navy*, 51 FLRA 49, 51 (FLRA Aug. 29, 2005).

a. Order of Election

The FMLA statutes that allow either an eligible employee or employer to elect to substitute an employee's accrued paid leave (Title I, the CAA, and the PEOAA), do not prioritize who, the employee or the employer, has the initial right to elect substitution of paid leave for unpaid FMLA leave. Rather, the statutes merely provide that an "eligible employee may elect, or an employer may require the employee, to substitute" any accrued paid leave for any part of the 12-week unpaid FMLA leave entitlement. 29 USC 2612(d)(2); *see* 2 USC 1312(a)(1) (incorporating § 102 of the FMLA, 29 USC 2612); 3 USC 412 (a)(1) (same).

The regulations implementing the FMLA clarify the order election. In the first instance, an eligible employee gets to choose whether he or she wishes to substitute paid leave for unpaid FMLA leave. If an employee does not choose to substitute accrued paid leave, the employer has the right to require the employee to substitute accrued paid leave for FMLA leave. 29 CFR 825.207(a) (Title I); S. Res. 242, Cong. Rec. S3959–S3997 (April 23, 1996); 29 CFR 825.207(a) (CAA). An employee always has the right to request, in the first instance, that appropriate paid leave be substituted. Preamble, 29 CFR 825.207. If the employee does not initially request substitution of available paid leave, the employer retains the right to require it. *Id.* Of course, because an employer *may* require paid leave substitution does not mean that an employer *must* require paid leave substitution. If the employer elects not to require paid leave substitution, the employee retains the paid leave for use in the future.

An employer may not override an employee's initial election to substitute appropriate paid leave for FMLA leave, nor place any other limitations on its use. For example, an employer could not require that an employee who has elected to substitute available paid leave for FMLA leave use that paid leave only in full day increments. Preamble, 29 CFR 825.207. At the same time, in the absence of other limiting factors (such as more generous leave terms pursuant to employer policy or a collective bargaining agreement), where an employee does not initially elect substitution of available paid leave, the employee must accept the employer's decision to require substitution, even where the employee opposes the employer's imposition of paid leave substitution. *Id.*

Note that an employee's affirmative decision not to elect to substitute paid leave for unpaid leave is not protected from being overridden by an employer. Quite the opposite. If an eligible employee fails to elect to substitute paid leave for unpaid FMLA leave, the employer may require the employee to substitute available paid leave, the employee's wishes or objections notwithstanding.

If neither the employee nor the employer elects to substitute paid leave for unpaid FMLA leave as permitted, the employee remains entitled to all the paid leave which is earned or accrued under the terms of the employer's paid leave policies. 29 CFR 825.207(f) (Title I); S. Res. 242, Cong. Rec. S3959, S3966 (April 23, 1996); 29 CFR 825.207(f) (CAA); *see Stentz v. City of Republic, Missouri*, 448 F.3d 1008, 1010 (8th Cir. 2006). This suggests that unpaid FMLA leave is the default where neither the employee nor the employer elects substitution of paid leave for unpaid FMLA leave.

Generally speaking, to reduce absenteeism, it is in the interest of an employer to limit the amount of leave available to an employee. In the FMLA context, where an absence meets the requirements of both the FMLA and available paid leave, an employer is well advised to exercise its option, if available, and elect to have the paid leave substituted for the unpaid FMLA leave. The unwanted depletion of an employee's paid leave balance for FMLA leave may also deter or limit marginal requests for FMLA leave. Employees generally dislike depleting their vacation leave, especially when required to and against their wishes.

By the same token, because an employer cannot override an employee's election that paid leave not be substituted for unpaid FMLA leave, it is incumbent on employees and their representatives to clearly notify the employer of their wishes regarding paid leave substitution. Absent clear instructions by the employee on paid leave substitution, the employer decides the issue. Absent controlling employer policy, the employee's subsequent objections will not defeat an employer's election to substitute the employee's accrued paid leave for unpaid FMLA leave. In practical terms, if an employee fails to notify the employer that he or she does not wish to have the paid leave substituted, an employer can require that the available employee's annual leave be used for the absence.

b. Choice Among Paid Leave Balances

For purposes of election, the FMLA does not specifically address whether the right of an employee or employer to substitute available paid leave includes the right to select a specific paid leave balance over others that may be available. For example, an employee with both an available sick leave balance and annual leave balance may elect to substitute annual leave for unpaid FMLA leave for planned surgery resulting in an overnight stay in a hospital. While sick leave would appear more appropriate given the reason for the absence, the employee may wish to use annual leave because, in this example, the end of the leave year is approaching and the employee needs to use his annual leave or lose it. Again, there is nothing specific in the regulations that would require the employee to use the available leave that sounds most appropriate given the reason for the absence. The only requirement in the regulations is that the leave be earned or accrued and that the employee must meet the usual requirements of the paid leave plan. *See* 29 CFR 825.207(a)–(c).

The prohibition against an employer placing limitations on the use of the paid leave initially elected by the employee would appear to bar an employer from switching an employee's explicit election of one type of available paid leave for another. Preamble, 29 CFR 825.207. *But see Haggard v. Farmers Ins. Exchange*, 1996 U.S. Dist. LEXIS 4078 (D. Or. March 26, 1996) (employer did not violate the FMLA by substituting unpaid FMLA leave with paid leave from accrued vacation time rather than from her paid sick leave balance as requested).

Similarly, an employer would appear able to require an employee to use one type of available paid leave over others, where the employee initially fails to make an election on paid leave substitution. For example, an employer could require an employee needing hospitalization to use available annual leave rather than available sick leave if the employee initially failed to elect to substitute paid leave for unpaid FMLA. The fact that the employee would prefer that the employer use her available sick leave rather than her more precious annual leave is immaterial. *See, e.g.,* Preamble, 29 CFR 825.207 (employee must accept employer's decision to elect paid leave substitution, even though the employee would desire a different result).

Of course, like the employee, the employer would have to elect a paid leave balance that is available in accordance with employer policy. *See* 29 CFR 825.207(a)–(c). By policy or collective bargaining agreement, an employer may limit its ability to elect paid leave in substitution for unpaid FMLA leave. For example, an employer may have a collective bargaining agreement that provides that only an employee can elect to use annual leave in substitution for FMLA leave.

Another limitation is the prohibitions against interference with FMLA rights or discrimination for exercising the same. That is, an employer that elects to substitute the use of annual leave rather than the sick leave preferred by the employee should not be doing so in order to punish the employee for exercising his or her rights under the FMLA. One way to avoid this is for an employer to have a consistently applied policy identifying the order in which it will draw on accrued leave balances when the employer elects to substitute paid leave for unpaid FMLA leave.

There is an argument that the substituted leave selected by an employee or employer must be related to the reason for the leave. In the preamble to the final regulations implementing Title I, 29 CFR 825.207, the Department of Labor repeatedly used the term "appropriate paid leave" when describing an employee and employer's right of substitution. The final regulations themselves refer to "earned or accrued" paid leave. *See* 29 CFR 825.207(a)–(c). Because the term "appropriate" does not necessarily have the same meaning as earned or accrued, the argument could be made that "appropriate paid leave" limits what paid leave can be drawn upon to the most obvious type of leave available given the nature of the reason for the absence. For example, an employee absent due to illness covered by the employer's sick leave policy might be limited to using the sick leave policy in substitution for unpaid FMLA leave rather than annual leave. This is because sick leave is the more appropriate type of paid leave, given the nature of the request.

Given the plain language of the regulations, it is not recommended that arguments be made relying on the use of the term "appropriate" in the Preamble to the final regulations implementing Title I. The difference in terms suggests that an argument could be made.

c. Who Makes the Election?

The issue here is whether the right to make an election is limited to the employee or employer, or whether others may make the election. This is likely to arise in a situation where others are attempting to act on the employee's behalf. It does not appear that others may make the election to substitute paid leave for unpaid FMLA leave.

Under Title I, the CAA, and the PEOAA, the right to elect to substitute paid leave rests initially with an eligible employee and, under certain circumstances, with the employer. See 29 CFR 825.207(a); S. Res. 242, Cong. Rec. S3959, S3965 (April 23, 1996); 29 CFR 825.207(f) (CAA). Under Title I, the right to elect to substitute available paid leave for unpaid FMLA leave rests exclusively with the employee. 5 CFR 630.1205(b), (d). The terms "employee" and "employer" are specifically defined in the respective statutes and implementing regulations. See 29 USC 2611(2) (eligible employee), § 2611(4) (employer defined); 29 CFR 825.108 (public agency employer defined); 825.800 (eligible employee); 5 USC 6381(1) (employee defined); 5 CFR 630.1201(b)(I) (employee defined); 2 USC 1301(3)–(9) (employee and employer defined); S. Res. 242, Cong. Rec. S3959, S3961 (April 23, 1996); 29 CFR 825.110 (eligible employees); 3 USC 401(a)(3) (employee defined), § 401(a)(4) (employing office defined).

For further discussion of who are covered employees and employers under the federal sector FMLA statutes, see Chapters 2 through 4.

Nowhere in these definitions does the term "employee" include anyone acting on behalf of the employee. In contrast, some of the federal sector FMLA statutes allow a spokesperson for the employee to notify the employer of the employee's need for FMLA leave. 29 CFR 825.208(a) (Title I); S. Res. 242, Cong. Rec. S3959, S3966 (April 23, 1996); 29 CFR 825.208(a) (CAA). Title I does not appear to have a similar provision. Specifically, the regulation, 29 CFR 208(a), provides:

> The employer's designation decision must be based only on information received from the employee or the employee's spokesperson (e.g., if the employee is incapacitated, the employee's spouse, adult child, parent, doctor, etc., may provide notice to the employer of the need to take FMLA leave).

The quoted provision is contained in the section of the implementing regulations addressing the employer's obligation to designate leave, paid or unpaid, as FMLA–qualifying. The immediate problem is that the employer is supposed to designate leave, paid or unpaid, based on information obtained from the employee or the employee's spokesperson regarding the need to take leave. Whether an employee needs to take FMLA leave is not the same as whether an employee needing FMLA leave wants to substitute available paid leave for unpaid FMLA leave. Further, only the employee or employer can make an election to substitute paid leave for unpaid FMLA leave, not an employee's spokesperson.

In the absence of specific direction, it is unclear what an employer should do when faced with a request by a spokesperson for an employee electing to substitute paid leave for unpaid FMLA leave. Similarly, if an employer accedes to a spokesperson's representation that the employee wants to substitute paid leave, it is unclear what effect an employee's subsequent rescission of that request would have.

Undoubtedly, there will be courts that will read 29 CFR 208(a) to encompass the right of an employer to rely on the representations of a spokesperson for an employee regarding the election to substitute paid leave for unpaid FMLA leave. They will argue in favor of allowing spokespersons to make substitution elections for incapacitated employees based on the regulatory language, its placement in 29 CFR 825.208 governing employer designation of leave as paid or unpaid, as well as fairness. Here, the argument is that in the absence of a spokesperson being permitted to elect for an incapacitated employee, the employer, by operation of 29 CFR 825.207(a), is authorized to make the election. Some courts will feel that it is unfair for an incapacitated employee to lose his or her right to make an election because he or she is physically incapable of doing so, not because he or she does not want to make an election and is able to make an election through a spokesperson.

The argument works well when the employee agrees with the election made by the spokesperson. Where, however, the employee disagrees with the election made by the spokesperson, the argument loses some of its appeal. Courts will then have to decide whether an employer following the direction of a spokesperson nevertheless violated the FMLA if the employee subsequently disagrees with the election made. Of course, courts could protect employers by simply binding the employee to the election made by the spokesperson, even when the employee subsequently disagrees with the election.

Additionally, allowing spokespersons to make the paid leave substitution election for the employee will necessarily result in litigation over the actual or apparent authority of the spokesperson to make the election for the employee and the question of whether the employer acted reasonably when it acted in reliance on the spokesperson's representations. Again, this will likely come up where the employee disagrees with the election made by the spokesperson. This, in turn, will raise issues of the scope of an employer's duty to investigate whether the spokesperson is a *bona fide* representative of the employee, and what evidence might be needed to establish that the employer conducted a reasonable inquiry as to the spokesperson's authority. These issues could be avoided if the employee is the only person with the authority to make the substitution election, as provided by the regulations.

There will be others that strictly read the regulations to prohibit an employer from relying on anyone other than the employee from making the paid leave substitution election. Presumably, courts that do not allow employers to follow the election as communicated by a spokesperson will treat the situation as if the employee did not make an initial election whether to substitute paid leave for unpaid FMLA leave. In those instances, by operation of 29 CFR 825.205(a), the employer is empowered to make the substitution election, even against the wishes of the employee.

d. Notice of Election

The manner and adequacy of the employee's notice to the employer of his or her election to substitute or not substitute paid leave for unpaid FMLA leave is not addressed in the federal sector FMLA statutes or implementing regulations. If the employee's election decision is deemed to be part of the employee's larger obligation to notify his or her employer of the need for FMLA leave, or at least analogous to such notice, then the general rules governing the manner and adequacy of an employee's notice of the need for FMLA leave should apply to the employee's decision to substitute paid leave for unpaid FMLA leave. [For a further discussion of employee notice obligations, see Chapter 8, "Notice Requirements."]

Several courts have addressed the adequacy of the employee's notice in the context of an election to substitute paid leave for unpaid FMLA leave, reaching opposite conclusions. In *Price v. City of Fort Wayne*, 117 F.3d 1022 (7th Cir. 1997), the Seventh Circuit found that a plaintiff's request for paid sick leave only provided her employer with sufficient information regarding her need for FMLA leave. The court rejected the City's argument that by requesting only paid leave, and failing to ask for unpaid leave, the employee foreclosed the inference that she might be requesting FMLA leave. According to the court, it was incumbent upon the employer to seek further information to determine if the employee wanted her absence covered by the protections of the FMLA. In essence, the court held that a request only for sick leave could constitute an election to substitute paid leave for unpaid FMLA leave where the leave otherwise meets the requirements of the FMLA.

The district court in *Walthall v. Fulton County School District et al.*, 18 F. Supp. 2d 1378, 1383–1384 (N.D. Ga. 1998), *aff'd without op.*, 192 F.3d 131 (11th Cir. 1999), disagreed with result reached by the Seventh Circuit in *Price*. In that case, the district court found that the employee's election to take paid sick leave precluded her ability to subsequently claim that the leave should have been covered by the FMLA. According to the court, at 1383:

> The Act provides that the employee may "elect" to substitute paid leave for unpaid FMLA leave. The regulations provide that the employee may "choose" to substitute paid leave for FMLA leave. The Act does not require clairvoyance on the part of the employer. *Satterfield v. Wal–Mart Stores*, 135 F.3d 973, 980 (5th Cir. 1988). The Act is not intended to "constitute a trap for employers who fail to divine unspoken (or even unthought) requests for [FMLA] leave." *Paasch v. City of Safety Harbor*, 915 F. Supp. 315, 321 (M.D. Fla. 1995), *aff'd* 78 F.3d 600 (11th Cir. 1996). Following the Seventh Circuit's [in *Price*] construction of the Act would require clairvoyance on the part of employers and make the Act a trap for the unwary.

The court went on to hold that "[w]here the Plaintiff has an option of claiming paid sick leave or FMLA leave, the employee must make an election to be covered by the Act.... The Act should not be interpreted to give every terminated employee the right to retroactively claim that his or her sick leave should be considered FMLA leave, thereby supporting a claim pursuant to the Act's non-discrimination provisions." *Id.* at 1384.

The decision of the court in *Walthall* is partially explained by its view, which is not universally shared, that the paid leave is mutually exclusive of unpaid FMLA leave. As set forth more fully in Subsection 2 of this section, under this view, a decision to substitute paid leave for unpaid FMLA leave means that the absence at issue is no longer covered by the FMLA. Other courts believe that paid leave substitution means that unpaid FMLA leave runs concurrently with the substituted paid leave.

In conclusion, the regulations and courts have failed to clarify the manner and adequacy of notice that an employee must give the employer regarding the election to substitute or not substitute paid leave for unpaid FMLA leave. Prudence suggests that the notice provisions for requesting FMLA leave should apply to employee substitution elections. As set forth more fully in Chapter 8, "Notice Requirements," however, there is some confusion about what constitutes adequate employee notice of the need for FMLA leave. Perhaps the regulatory agencies could clarify this area by issuing further guidance.

e. Timing of Election

(1) Title II

Title II of the Act provides that an employee must notify the employer of his or her intent to substitute paid leave for unpaid FMLA leave prior to the date that such paid leave commences. 5 CFR 630.1205(e). This necessarily means that an eligible federal employee covered by Title II of the FMLA does not have to make the substitution election at the time that the employee requests FMLA leave. As set forth more fully in Chapter 8, "Notice Requirements," Title II requires that an eligible employee give at least a 30-calendar-day notice where the need for FMLA leave is foreseeable. 5 CFR 630.1206(a). Where the need for leave is not foreseeable, Title II requires that an eligible employee give notice within a reasonable period of time appropriate to the circumstances. 5 CFR 1206(c). A Title II employee is also prohibited from retroactively substituting paid leave for unpaid FMLA leave already taken. 5 CFR 630.1205(e).

(2) Title I, the CAA, and the PEOAA

Unfortunately, the regulations implementing Title I, the CAA, and the PEOAA do not contain a bright-line rule similar to that provided in Title II regarding when an employee must make the election regarding the substitution of paid leave for unpaid FMLA leave. Rather, the timing of the election under these statutes appears tied to an employer's awareness of whether leave may qualify for FMLA protections. This awareness by the employer, in turn, is premised on the employee's obligation to timely notify the employer of the need for FMLA leave. The end result is that the time within which an employee must make an initial substitution election is something of a moving target, depending on the awareness of the employer. In certain circumstances, an employee may be permitted to elect substitution of paid leave after completing his or her absence and returning to work. [The notice obligations of employees and employers are addressed more fully in Chapter 8, "Notice Requirements."]

Generally, it appears that an employee is required to make an election to substitute paid leave for unpaid leave at the time the employee or the designated spokesperson gives notice of the need for leave. This result is suggested based on the requirement that an employer's decision to substitute paid leave for unpaid FMLA leave, or that paid leave taken under an existing leave plan be counted as FMLA leave, must be made within two business days of the time the employee gives notice of the need for leave. 29 CFR 825.208(c). Because employers only get to exercise their right to make a substitution election when employees have failed to make their own initial substitution election, the two-day limitation placed on employers would appear to act as a limitation on the time period during which employees have to make their initial election.

Under certain circumstances, employees appear to have additional time to make their election to substitute paid leave for unpaid FMLA leave, including [the ability to make reverse elections wherein the employee has taken paid leave and subsequently seeks to substitute or impose FMLA protections on that leave. These results are suggested by the interplay of the regulations governing employee notice and employer responsibilities to designate leave, paid or unpaid, as FMLA-qualifying. [Employee notice and employer designation responsibilities are addressed more fully in Chapter 8, "Notice Requirements."]

The two-day requirement measured from the employee's request for leave for an employer to decide whether to require that paid leave is to be substituted for unpaid leave, or that paid leave taken under an existing leave plan be counted as FMLA leave, is relaxed where the employer does not initially have sufficient information to make a determination. Here, an employer may delay the decision to require an employee to substitute paid leave for unpaid FMLA leave until the time when the employer determines that the leave qualifies as FMLA leave. 29 CFR 825.208(c). This may not occur until after leave has commenced. *Id.* In all circumstances, however, once an employer has acquired knowledge that leave, paid or unpaid, is being taken for an FMLA-covered reason, the employer must promptly (within two business days absent extenuating circumstances) notify the employee that paid leave is designated and will be counted as FMLA leave. 29 CFR 825.208(b)(1).

Again, because an employer's ability to require an employee to substitute paid leave for unpaid FMLA leave is not triggered until the employee fails to make an initial election, and the employer is unable to require an employee to substitute paid leave until sufficient information is provided to determine if the employee's leave qualifies as FMLA leave, the requirements suggest that an employee would be able to make an initial substitution election up until the time the employer gains sufficient information to determine whether to designate the leave as FMLA-qualifying.

This logic appears to be borne out in the reverse election regulations. In a reverse election an employee has taken paid leave and subsequently wants FMLA protections for that paid leave. For example, an employee, Terry, takes two weeks of annual leave to go skiing. In the middle of the second week, Terry informs the employer that she broke her leg at the beginning of the second week, and that she needs an extension of leave for a period of hospitalization and to recover. Until Terry provided her midweek notice, the employer was unaware that Terry's absence might be covered by the FMLA. Once notified, the employer had two days to designate the leave, paid or unpaid, as FMLA-qualifying. In this example, Terry is entitled to FMLA leave from the beginning of the second week through the extension of leave. 29 CFR 208(d).

Similarly, an employee who took two days of sick leave advised the employer on his return to work that the leave was for a reason covered by the FMLA. The employer may retroactively cover the sick leave with the protections of the FMLA. 29 CFR 825.208(e)(1).

f. Employee Election of Paid Leave, Not FMLA Leave

The issue here is the effect of an affirmative decision by an eligible employee to forgo FMLA protections by requesting that the leave be covered by use of accrued paid leave only. There appears to be conflict between the outcome required by the implementing regulations and the way in which the courts have handled these matters.

Under the regulations implementing Title I, the CAA, and the PEOAA, because the employee has not elected to substitute paid leave for unpaid FMLA leave, the employer has the option of requiring the use of paid leave. 29 CFR 825.207(a). If the employer does not elect to substitute paid leave for unpaid FMLA leave, the leave is covered as unpaid FMLA leave only, and the employee retains the use of the accrued paid leave. 29 CFR 825.207(f). Essentially, the regulations do not give an employee the option of affirmatively and consciously electing to forgo the benefits of the FMLA (thereby reserving protected leave for later use) in favor of accrued paid leave, knowing that the use of unprotected leave could result in disciplinary action. On this point, the DOL regulations are paternalistic.

As set forth more fully in Subsection 2 of this section, several courts have held that an employee's election to take paid leave precluded application of unpaid FMLA leave to the same absence. This construction of the FMLA is not universally held. It would, however, allow federal employees the limited ability to choose whether they wanted to use FMLA benefits for a particular absence or risk using paid leave benefits only, knowing that an employer could issue discipline for that absence. Of course, unwary federal employees who simply neglect to elect FMLA benefits when choosing to use a paid leave option could unwittingly subject themselves to discipline as, under the construction of some courts, their absence would not be protected by the FMLA.

The issue is discussed more fully in the following subsection.

2. Substitution

Unfortunately, the key term "substitute" is undefined in the FMLA or in the implementing regulations. It is unfortunate because the term is susceptible to at least two interpretations. See, e.g., *Strickland v. Water Works and Sewer Board of the City of Birmingham*, 239 F.3d 1199, 1204 (11th Cir. 2001) (characterizing the FMLA's use of the term "substitute" as an "inartful and unfortunate use of language"). Taken literally, an employee who substitutes or replaces accrued paid leave for unpaid FMLA leave arguably is no longer protected by the FMLA. Rather, her absence is governed by the employer's leave program on which the accrued paid leave was drawn. As the absence is not protected by the FMLA, it could be the subject of discipline.

Alternatively, a narrower interpretation would limit the scope of the term "substitute" to the payment of wages only. Essentially, under this narrower interpretation, FMLA leave would run concurrently with the employer's paid leave program. An employee who elected to substitute paid leave for unpaid FMLA leave would receive pay by drawing on available accrued paid leave, but would retain the protections of the FMLA. Under this interpretation, a federal employer would run afoul of the FMLA by subjecting an eligible employee to discipline for an absence protected by the FMLA, even when an election was made to substitute available paid leave.

The few courts that have had the opportunity to address the meaning of "substitute" have reached opposite conclusions. In *Strickland v. Water Works and Sewer Board of the City of Birmingham*, 239 F.3d 1199, 1205 (11th Cir. 2001), the circuit court held that, taken together, the provisions of Title I of the FMLA provide that an employee who substitutes paid leave for unpaid FMLA leave means that the FMLA leave runs concurrently with the unpaid FMLA leave.

In *Strickland*, company policy required employees to exhaust accrued paid leave before they could use FMLA leave. The district court held that Strickland's discharge for the day he was absent due to illness was not protected by the FMLA because the company had lawfully substituted accrued paid sick leave for FMLA leave in accordance with 29 CFR 825.207(a) and (e). *Strickland v. The Water Works and Sewer Board of the City of Birmingham, Alabama*, No. CV-98-B-0374-S, 1999 U.S. Dist. LEXIS 22488, at 11–12. (N.D. Ala. Sept. 15, 1999), *vacated, remanded*, 239 F.3d 1199 (11th Cir. 2001). Because paid leave was substituted for unpaid FMLA leave, the district court concluded that Strickland was not entitled to the protections of the FMLA.

On appeal, the Eleventh Circuit reversed the decision of the district court. According to the Appellate Court, the "district court misinterpreted the FMLA as permitting employers with paid sick leave policies to choose whether an employee's FMLA-qualifying absence will be either unpaid but protected by the Act, or paid but unprotected." *Strickland*, 239 F.3d at 1204. Characterizing the district court's misinterpretation as understandable given the "inartful and unfortunate use of language in the FMLA and its accompanying regulations" regarding substitution, the Appellate Court, based on consideration of the context of the substitution provisions and the purpose of the FMLA, concluded that the substitution language did not make paid sick leave and unpaid FMLA leave mutually exclusive. *Id.* at 1204–1205. Rather, the court held:

> These provisions, taken together, make clear that an employer who is subject to the FMLA and also offers a paid sick leave policy has two options when an employee's leave qualifies both under the FMLA and under the employer's paid leave policy: the employer may either permit the employee to use his FMLA leave and paid sick leave sequentially, or the employer may require that the employee use his FMLA leave entitlement and his paid sick leave concurrently. The Water Works Board adopted the latter option. Neither Congress nor the Department of Labor could have intended by using the substitution language, to allow employers to evade the FMLA by providing their employees with paid sick leave benefits. Otherwise, when an employee misses work for an illness that qualifies under both his employer's paid sick leave policy and the FMLA, his employer could elect to have the absence count as paid sick leave rather than FMLA leave and would then be free to discharge him without running afoul of the Act.

Accord Stentz v. City of Republic, Missouri, 448 F.3d 1008, 1010 (8th Cir. 2006); *Tippens v. Airnet Systems, Inc.*, No. 2:05-CV-421, 2007 U.S. Dist. LEXIS 23808, at *14 (S.D. Ohio March 30, 2007) (employer may permit an employee to use FMLA leave and other accrued leave sequentially or may require that the two run concurrently).

Reaching the opposite conclusion, the circuit court in *Thornton v. BASF*, No. 99–2243, 2000 U.S. App. LEXIS 15909 (4th Cir. July 11, 2000), held that the employer did not violate the FMLA when it terminated plaintiff for excessive absenteeism following her return to work from a 13-week absence for a serious heart condition. BASF did not classify the plaintiff's absence as protected by the FMLA. Rather, as specifically requested by plaintiff, BASF provided plaintiff with paid short–

term disability benefits pursuant to company policy. Rejecting the plaintiff's argument that BASF violated the FMLA by unilaterally electing not to classify her leave as FMLA leave, the court held that, in light of her affirmative request for paid short-term disability benefits, her absence was not FMLA-protected.

Short-term disability benefits are technically not the same as accrued paid leave available for substitution. *See* 29 CFR 825.207(d)(1). Technicalities aside, however, short-term disability benefits are treated the same as paid leave substitution.

The affirmative election of paid leave benefits by an employee led courts in two other cases to find that an employee taking paid sick leave was in lieu of unpaid FMLA leave, absent further indication from the employee that he wanted the paid leave to run concurrently with the unpaid FMLA leave. *See Solis et al. v. Phillips Puerto Rico Core, Inc.*, No. 98-1879 (CCC), 2000 U.S. Dist. LEXIS 1763 (D. P.R. Jan. 13, 2000); *Walthall v. Fulton County School District et al.*, 18 F. Supp. 2d 1378, 1381-1384 (N.D. Ga. 1998).

The district court in *Solis* based its decision on what it termed the "greater benefit theory." In that case, the "greater benefit" was plaintiff's receipt of paid sick leave for 13 days of absence following surgery for a thyroid condition. According to the court, by accepting paid leave, the plaintiff was precluded from receiving unpaid leave under the FMLA. Candidly, though, the rationale for this conclusion is a bit murky. According to the court, "[s]ince leaves at Phillips run concurrently [including FMLA leave], Solis cannot claim them at the same time." *Solis*, 2000 U.S. Dist. LEXIS at *28. According to the 1988 edition of the Merriam-Webster dictionary, "concurrent" is defined as "operating or occurring at the same time." I am at a loss as to what the *Solis* court meant.

A clearer explanation for the conclusion that paid leave and unpaid FMLA leave are mutually exclusive was offered by the court in *Walthall*. In that case, the district court held that an employee who elected paid sick leave without contemporaneously indicating that she also wanted the leave to be covered by the FMLA failed to provide adequate notice to her employer of the need for FMLA leave. *Walthall*, 18 F. Supp. 2d at 1383. As such, the leave was not covered by the FMLA, even though it otherwise met the criteria for coverage. *Id*. The court reasoned that an "election" requires an affirmative choice by an employee: coverage under paid leave policies or coverage under the Act. *Id*. at 1384. The court noted that there are significant advantages to an employee not to elect FMLA coverage for an absence. *Id*. at 1383-1384. It also rejected the argument that a request only for paid sick leave automatically constitutes a request for FMLA coverage. *Id*.

3. Accrued Paid Leave

As applied to the federal sector, the FMLA permits the use of accrued paid leave in substitution for unpaid FMLA leave. This section addresses what accrued paid leave may be used in substitution for unpaid FMLA leave. The four FMLA statues applicable to the federal sector differ on what accrued paid leave is available for substitution. Generally speaking, employees covered by Title II of the FMLA have less choice on what paid leave balances may be substituted for unpaid FMLA leave than federal employees covered by Title I, the CAA, and the PEOAA.

a. Title II

Under 5 USC 6382(d), an eligible employee may elect to substitute any of the employee's accrued or accumulated annual or sick leave for any part of the 12-week period of unpaid FMLA leave. Employers are not, however, required to provide paid sick leave in any situation in which the employer would not normally provide paid sick leave. *Id*. In other words, if an employee chooses to substitute paid sick leave for unpaid leave under the FMLA, he or she may only do so in those situations where the use of sick leave would otherwise be permitted by law or regulation.

Pursuant to the 5 CFR 630.1205(b), an eligible employee may elect to substitute the following paid leave for any or all of the period of leave without pay taken as FMLA leave:

- Accrued annual or sick leave under Subchapter I of Chapter 63 of Title 5
- Advanced annual or sick leave
- Leave made available to an employee under the Voluntary Leave Transfer Program or the Voluntary Leave Transfer Bank Program consistent with Subparts I and J of Part 630 of this chapter

The regulations implementing Title II do not permit an employee to draw on any other accrued leave that may be available and applicable in substitution for unpaid FMLA leave. For example, if the terms of a collective bargaining agreement provided a more generous variety of leave then the types of leave identified in 5 CFR 630.1205(b), such leave would arguably not be available to the employee for substitution. A counter argument is that the statutory language in Title II, as opposed to the regulatory language, prohibits the substitution of accrued paid sick leave only to situations where the employer would not normally provide such paid leave. 5 USC 6382(d). Arguably, the more expansive terms of collective bargaining agreement or, for that matter, the practices of an employer would fit within that definition even if the paid leave balances were outside of those identified in 5 CFR 1205(b).

While paid leave substitution is restricted under Title I to certain types of leave, there is no restriction on the running of unpaid FMLA leave concurrently with paid leave that is not accrued, but is available as a matter of law or employer policy, such as compensatory time off, workers' compensation, and temporary disability leave programs.

Annual and sick leave in the federal government is governed by Chapter 63 of Title 5, 5 USC 6301 *et seq*. Postal employees and others who are not considered employees within the meaning of Title 5 are governed by other regulations, employer rules, and the terms of negotiated collective bargaining agreements.

(1) Annual Leave

Annual leave is generally provided to employees for rest, for recreation, and for personal and emergency purposes. The current Title 5–based federal leave system allows covered employees to accrue and accumulate annual leave to use for paid absences from work. Annual leave accrual rates increase based on the number of years of federal service, with employees with less than three years of service accruing up to 13 days of annual leave each leave year. By comparison, covered employees with 15 or more years of service may accumulate up to 26 days of paid annual leave each leave year. 5 USC 6303(a)(1)–(3).

Annual leave can be accumulated and carried forward from one leave year to the next, generally up to a maximum of 30 days. 5 USC 6304(a). Employees who were working outside the United States, its territories or possessions, may accumulate up to 45 days of annual leave. 5 USC 6304(b); 5 CFR 630.302. Employees holding Senior Executive Service positions may accumulate up to 90 days of annual leave. 5 USC 6304(f); 5 CFR 630.301. The phrase "use it, or lose it" describes the situation faced by a federal employee with annual leave in excess of the maximum accumulation amount that may be carried over from one year to the next.

A federal employee's right to use accrued annual leave is generally not absolute. While an employee's request to use accrued annual leave generally may not be denied based on the reason the employee wants to use the leave, a federal employer may restrict when an employee uses annual leave. Federal agencies may regulate how and when an employee may request to use accrued annual leave. For example, employer policy will often require that an employee's request for annual leave must be submitted on a specific form, and, except in emergency situations, be approved in advance. Pursuant to applicable collective bargaining agreements, annual leave is sometimes regulated so that more senior employees have first choice for preferred annual leave periods.

While federal supervisors should not deny an employee's request for accrued annual leave for frivolous or discriminatory reasons, they may deny annual leave to meet the legitimate work needs of the employer. For example, during the height of the tax season, the IRS is likely to deny most requests for annual leave in order to timely process tax returns.

Similarly, an employer generally has the right to deny annual leave where the employee failed to follow all of the employer procedural requirements for perfecting annual leave. For example, a federal supervisor has the right to deny a request for annual leave that was not made on the usual form required for such leave. Of course, because an employer has the right to deny a request for paid FMLA leave does not mean that it must do so in all instances where an employee, for example, fails to follow all of the technicalities for requesting annual leave. Rights are like options: they may be exercised by the party holding the option, but they are not required to be exercised. Moreover, the denial of paid leave is not the same as the denial of unpaid FMLA leave.

(2) Sick Leave

Sick leave is available for an employee's own illness or injury, as well as the sickness and injury of certain covered family members. The amount of sick leave an employee may accrue depends on whether the individual is a full- or part-time employee. A full-time employee accumulates sick leave at the rate of four hours per pay period, or 13 days per leave year. 5 USC 6307(a). Part-time employees earn a pro-rated amount of sick leave based on the number of hours they have served in a pay status. 5 USC 6307(d)(3)(B); 5 CFR 630.406. There is no limit on the amount of sick leave that an employee may accumulate and carry forward to succeeding leave years. 5 USC 6307(b).

There are eight (8) instances under Title 5 where a federal employee may request to use accrued paid sick leave. These eight instances are divided into four categories: (1) situations involving the employee's own illness; (2) situations where the employee is not ill, but is needed to care for a covered family member who is ill; (3) situations where neither the employee nor a covered family member is ill; and (4) situations involving medical charity to others.

(a) Employee's Own Illness

Pursuant to 5 CFR 630.401(a)(1), (2), and (5), an employer must grant sick leave to an employee when the employee:

- receives medical, dental, or optical examination or treatment;
- is incapacitated for the performance of duties by physical or mental illness, injury, pregnancy, or childbirth;
- would, as determined by the health authorities having jurisdiction or by a health care provider, jeopardize the health of others by his or her presence on the job because of exposure to a communicable disease.

Unfortunately, most of the key terms in these provisions are undefined. For example, the regulations fail to define what constitutes a medical, dental, or optical examination or treatment. For that matter, the regulations fail to define what an examination or treatment means for purposes of sick leave. Presumably, only a defined health care provider can conduct medical, dental, or optical examinations and provide treatment. For purposes of the annual and sick leave provisions, a health care provider is defined, by cross reference to 5 CFR 630.1202 (an OPM FMLA regulation), as follows:

- A licensed Doctor of Medicine or Doctor of Osteopathy or a physician who is serving on active duty in the uniformed services and is designated by the uniformed service to conduct examinations under this subpart
- Any health care provider recognized by the Federal Employees Health Benefits Program or who is licensed or certified to conduct examinations under this subpart
- A health care provider as defined in paragraph (2) of this definition who practices in a country other than the United States, who is authorized to practice in accordance with the laws of that country, and who is performing within the scope of his or her practice as defined under such law
- A Christian Science practitioner listed with the First Church of Christ, Scientist, in Boston, Massachusetts
- A Native American, including an Eskimo, Aleut, and Native Hawaiian, who is recognized as a traditional healing practitioner by native traditional religious leaders who practices traditional healing methods as believed, expressed, and exercised in Indian religions of the American Indian, Eskimo, Aleut, and Native Hawaiians

For a further discussion of who constitutes a health care provider for purposes of the FMLA, see Chapter 7, "Covered Conditions."

"Incapacitated" is another critical term that is not defined in the sick leave regulations. Does the employee have to be completely incapacitated from performing all of her duties, essential and non-essential, in order to exercise her rights to sick leave, or will incapacity from performing some, but not all, of the employee's duties suffice? The difference may be critical for purposes of the substitution of paid sick leave with unpaid FMLA leave. For example, the level of incapacity necessary to invoke the protections of the FMLA was the inability to perform a single essential job function. If the level of incapacity for paid sick leave were complete incapacity, an employee who was not completely incapacitated would not be able to substitute paid sick leave for unpaid FMLA leave.

To clarify this area, OPM needs to define key sick leave terms, or, better yet, cross-reference these terms with equivalent terms in the OPM FMLA regulations. This will avoid unnecessary confusion and litigation.

"Communicable disease" is another key undefined term. According to the preamble to the final OPM regulations, 59 Fed. Reg. 62266, 62268 (Dec. 2, 1994), the absence of a definition was deliberate:

> We have not attempted to define the term "communicable disease," however, because the key determination that has to be made is not whether a particular illness constitutes a "communicable disease," but whether an employee's exposure to the illness would jeopardize the health of other employees. This determination can be made only by the health authorities having jurisdiction or a health care provider.

If, as indicated, the term "communicable disease" has no independent meaning, OPM should not use it. The terms "disease" and "communicable disease" are medical terms of art. If, as appears to be the case, OPM is solely focused on the communicable nature of any illness that an employee is exposed to in the workplace, then OPM should use the broader term "illness" rather than communicable disease to avoid unnecessary confusion.

Note that an employee is entitled to sick leave due to exposure to a communicable disease even though the employee may not, him or herself, be incapacitated by the illness. For example, an employee who is exposed to an individual with tuberculosis may not be ill or otherwise exhibit any symptoms of the illness. As defined, the employee would still be entitled to paid sick leave, as required by health care authorities.

In all of the above instances, there is no restriction on the amount of sick leave available to an employee for his or her own illness or exposure to an illness. For example, an employee exposed to a communicable disease such as tuberculosis would be permitted to use available sick leave for the entire period of time during which health care authorities having jurisdiction or a health care provider determines that an employee's exposure to a communicable disease would jeopardize the health of other employees. Preamble, 59 Fed. Reg. 62266 at 62268.

(b) To Care For An Ill Covered Family Member

With the 1994 enactment of the Federal Employees Family Friendly Leave Act (FEFFLA), 5 USC 6301 *et seq.*, federal employees (as defined in 5 USC 2105) were allowed to use a limited amount of sick leave to care for covered family members, and for purposes relating to the death of a covered family member. 5 USC 6307(d)(2). As originally enacted, the amount of sick leave available under the FEFFLA was limited to 40 hours in any year, plus up to an additional 64 hours in any year, but only to the extent the use of such additional hours did not cause the amount of accrued sick leave available to the employee to fall below 80 hours. 5 USC 6307(d)(3)(A).

On May 24, 1999, President Clinton issued a memorandum directing OPM to expand the use of paid sick leave for family care purposes. OPM obliged, issuing final regulations effective June 20, 2000. 65 Fed. Reg. 37,234 (June 13, 2000). The revised regulations substantially expand the sick leave available to a covered employee. The regulations are divided into two parts: (1) those addressing non-serious health conditions; and (2) those addressing serious health conditions. For purposes of paid sick leave, the same family members are covered under both branches. The family members covered for paid sick leave, however, are not the same as those covered for purposes of FMLA leave.

"Family member" means a spouse, and parents thereof; children, including adopted children, and spouses thereof; parents; brothers and sisters and spouses thereof; and any individual related by blood or affinity whose close association with the employee is the equivalent of a family relationship. 5 USC 6307(d)(1); 5 CFR 630.201(b).

Note that the only family members covered by Title II of the FMLA (in fact, all of the FMLA statutes) are a parent, son or daughter, and a spouse. 5 USC 6381(3), (6); 5 CFR 630.1202. Because it applies to a more limited range of family members, FMLA leave will not apply in every instance where an employee is entitled to paid sick leave to care for a covered family member with a serious health condition. For example, an employee requests leave to care for the spouse of a sister with a serious health condition. The employee is entitled to paid sick leave for this purpose. Because, however, the spouse of a sister is not a covered individual within the meaning of the FMLA, the employee would not be entitled to FMLA leave for the same absence. As such, without the protections of the FMLA, the employee could be subject to discipline for the time spent on paid sick leave.

The converse, however, is also not automatically true. That is, simply because the definition of a covered family member for purposes of paid sick leave is broader than that of Title II of the FMLA, it does not follow that meeting the definition of a "parent," "spouse," or "children" for purposes of paid sick leave automatically means the employee meets the definition of those terms under Title II of the FMLA. The reason for this is simple: the terms are defined differently. For example, for purposes of receipt of paid sick leave, a covered family member includes children, without restriction. Under the FMLA, on the other hand, a covered son or daughter is defined in terms biological or non-biological relationship, age (above or below 18), and disability (for adult children incapable of self-care). 5 USC 6381(6). An employee who wanted leave to care for a 35-year-old, non-disabled child for a medical examination would be entitled to paid sick leave, but not FMLA leave for the same absence. [For a further discussion of covered individuals under the FMLA, see Chapter 6, "Covered Family Members."]

Paid sick leave is available for an employee to care for a covered family member with a non-serious health condition in two instances: (1) the employee provides care for a family member who is incapacitated by a medical or mental condition; or (2) the employee provides care for a family member receiving medical, dental, or optical examination or treatment. 5 CFR 630.401(3)(I).

Again, key terms are left undefined. For example, what does it mean for an employee to "provide care for" a family member? The answer is not found in the regulations. OPM, however, has indicated that caring for a family member includes psychological comfort as well as physical care, including being with the family member during a hospital stay or while being examined in a doctor's office. Preamble, 65 Fed. Reg. 37,234 (June 13, 2000). This appears to be the same as the Title I FMLA definition of needed to care for. *See, e.g.,* 29 CFR 825.116.

The terms "incapacitated" and "medical or mental condition" are also undefined. Regarding the former, the lack of a definition gives rise to the question of exactly how incapacitated does the family member have to be in order for the employee to exercise his or her right to take paid sick leave? Are we talking near death or the sniffles? For that matter, incapacitated from doing what? Note that for an employee to receive paid sick leave for his or her own illness, the employee must be incapacitated "for the performance of duties." 5 CFR 630.401(a)(2). In comparison, there is no condition on the incapacitation of a family member. Presumably, an employee is entitled to paid sick leave to care for a brother whose illness incapacitated the brother from baiting a fishing hook in Bermuda. The check on this type of abuse is an employer's ability to request medical documentation supporting the employee's request for paid sick leave for family purposes. 5 CFR 630.403. Reliance on the ability to request a medical certificate in support of leave as a means of protection against employee abuse rests on the dubious assumption that health care providers are neutral.

The failure of OPM to define what constitutes a "medical or mental condition" is also unnecessarily problematic. Is a medical or mental condition the same or different from a "physical or mental illness"? The former applies to covered family members, while the latter applies to an employee's own incapacitating illness. *Compare* 5 CFR 630.401(a)(2) *with* 5 CFR 630.401(a)(3)(I). If the terms do mean the same thing, why not either use the same terms, or indicate that they mean the same thing? If they mean different things, how about defining the difference? Again, the availability of supporting medical certification from a health care provider is, presumably, to stem employee abuse. 5 CFR 630.403. The criticism of the lack of clear definitions for key terms is not merely a parsing of words. Under Title II of the FMLA (in fact, under all FMLA statutes), employers are legally obligated to grant applicable and available paid sick leave in substitution for unpaid leave at the request of an employee. The lack of clarity of key terms for paid sick leave to care for covered family members simply makes it more difficult for employers to determine whether the illness claimed by the employee constitutes both a serious health condition within the meaning of the FMLA, and paid sick leave for a medical or mental condition. The difficulty stems from differences between the key terms of the FMLA and the key terms for paid sick leave.

For example, under Title II the term "incapacity" is defined as the inability to work, attend school, or perform other regular daily activities because of a serious health condition or treatment for or recovery from a serious health condition. 5 CFR 1202 (definition of incapacity). For purposes of paid sick leave, the term "incapacitated" is undefined. As undefined, incapacitated could be construed to have the same meaning as it does when used in the FMLA. On the other hand, it may mean something completely different. The safe course is for employers to interpret these key, undefined sick leave terms broadly. Where the facts meet the definition of corollary FMLA terms, the employee's request for paid sick leave should be granted. Where they do not, the employee may only be entitled to paid sick leave, and not to FMLA leave.

Note that a covered family member need not always be incapacitated or even ill for an employee to be entitled to paid sick leave to attend to a family member receiving medical, dental, or optical examination or treatment. 5 CFR 630.401(a)(3)(I). As discussed more fully in Chapter 7, "Covered Conditions," while an employee may be entitled to FMLA leave for non-routine medical examination, the employee generally has to have a serious health condition in order to qualify for leave for a medical examination.

Paid sick leave is also available to an employee to provide care to a covered family member who is incapacitated due to a serious health condition. 5 CFR 630.401(3)(ii). A "serious health condition" for purposes of paid sick leave is defined by incorporation of the FMLA definition of the same term. 5 CFR 630.201 (definition of serious health condition). As such, an employer's determination that a covered family member has a serious health condition for purposes of the FMLA will concurrently establish coverage for purposes of paid sick leave. [For a further discussion of what constitutes a serious health condition within the meaning of the FMLA, see Chapter 7, "Covered Conditions."]

(c) Paid Sick Leave When No One is Sick: Adoptions and Funeral Arrangements

An employee must be granted paid sick leave in two instances when no one is sick: (1) to make arrangements necessitated by the death of a family member or to attend the funeral of a family member; and (2) to be absent from duty for purposes relating to the adoption of a child, including appointments with adoption agencies, social workers, and attorneys; court proceedings; required travel; and any other activities necessary to allow the adoption to proceed. 5 CFR 630.401(a)(4), (6). In these two situations, neither the employee nor a covered family member needs to be ill.

Potentially, an employee may be granted paid sick leave in three other instances when no one is sick (although someone may be sick): (1) an employee's absence to undergo a medical, dental, or optical examination; (2) an employee's absence to attend the medical, dental, or optical examination of a covered family member; and (3) an employee's absence due to exposure to a communicable disease. 5 CFR 630.401(a)(1), (3)(I), and (5). This section concentrates on the two areas identified above where an employee is entitled to paid sick leave where illness is not a variable.

Paid sick leave is available for an employee to make funeral arrangements or attend the funeral of a covered family member. As the covered family member is deceased, he or she no longer has a serious health condition within the meaning of the FMLA. That is, FMLA leave applies to the serious health conditions of the living. *See, e.g., Lange v. Showbiz Pizza Time, Inc.*, 12 F. Supp. 2d 1150, 1154 (D. Kan. 1998) (under Title I, because a serious health condition within the meaning of the FMLA contemplates only medical conditions affecting the living, the defendant did not violate the FMLA when it denied the plaintiff additional leave to care for his mother's affairs after her death). Query whether the use of the conjunctive "or" could be interpreted to mean that an employee must elect whether to use paid sick leave on the death of a family member either to make funeral arrangements or to attend the funeral, not both.

Note that this type of leave is not solely for the bereavement of the employee. It is to make or attend funeral arrangements. Arguably, the leave is also not available for an employee to "wrap up" the affairs of the deceased. Rather, by its terms, leave is limited to making arrangements for, or attending the funeral of, a deceased family member only. It also differs from paid funeral leave to attend a memorial service of an immediate relative who died as a result of injury while serving as a member of the armed forces in a combat zone, although these may overlap. 5 CFR 630.801–804. Of course, an employee who is incapacitated with grief as a result of the death of a family member would, all things being equal, be entitled to paid sick leave for his or her own illness.

As funeral leave does not involve an individual with a serious health condition, it would not meet the requirements of a covered condition for purposes of FMLA leave. As such, funeral leave would not be a basis for paid leave substitution for unpaid FMLA leave.

Paid sick leave for adoption is available to both the adoptive mother and father. Preamble, 60 Fed. Reg. 26,977, 26,977–26,978 (May 22, 1995). There does not appear to be any limitation prohibiting both parents, even if working for the same federal employer, to take the full amount of leave available to each, and to take the leave at the same time. Paid sick leave for adoption is not, however, available for bonding time between the new parents and the adopted child. Preamble, 60 Fed. Reg. at 26,978. According to OPM, annual leave and leave without pay are the appropriate means to secure time to bond with the newly–adopted child.

Adoption is a covered condition for purposes of FMLA leave. 5 CFR 630.1203(a)(2). It is defined as the legal process in which an individual becomes the legal parent of another's child. 5 CFR 630.1202 (definition of adoption). Title II, however, does not define an adoption with the same specificity as the paid sick leave provisions in terms of meeting with social workers, attorneys, etc. As such, paid sick leave may be substituted for unpaid FMLA leave for an adoption only where visits to social workers, attorneys, and the other items mentioned in the paid sick leave provisions are part of the legal process for an adoption. If a visit to a social worker, for instance, is not part of the legal process for an adoption, the employee may be paid sick leave for that visit, but the visit may not be covered by the FMLA.

(d) Paid Leave for Organ or Bone-Marrow Donation

Pursuant to 5 USC 6327, each calendar year, an employee of an executive agency is entitled to paid leave, separate from sick or annual leave, of:

- up to 7 days each calendar year to serve as a bone-marrow donor;
- up to 30 days of paid leave each calendar year to serve as an organ donor.

Depending on the circumstances, the act of donating an organ or bone marrow may constitute a serious health condition within the meaning of the FMLA, typically because an overnight stay in a hospital is involved. As such, this paid leave would appear to be available as a basis of substitution for unpaid FMLA leave. Not so fast, though. Under Title II, the only paid leave that is available for substitution for unpaid FMLA leave is found in Subchapter I of Chapter 63 of Title 5. 5 USC 6382(d). Leave for organ and bone marrow donation is contained in Subchapter II of Chapter 63 of Title 5, 5 USC 6327. It is not, therefore, available to employees covered by Title II of the Act. It might, however be available to employees covered by Title I of the Act. Title I does not specifically limit the available paid leave that may be used in substitution. As long as the paid leave to be substituted is available and may be used under general employer rules for the leave at issue, Title I would permit leave substitution.

Here, as long as the Title I employee works for an executive agency, the individual would be able to use paid organ and bone-marrow leave in substitution for unpaid FMLA leave, in those circumstances that meet the requirements of the FMLA and for organ and bone-marrow leave.

(e) Amount of Paid Sick Leave Available

The amount of paid sick leave available to an employee and, therefore, available for paid leave substitution, depends on the reason for the sick leave. An employee, however, may not substitute any more sick or annual leave than he or she has available. 5 USC 6382(d); 5 CFR 630.1205(b)(1).

There is no restriction on the amount of available paid sick leave that an employee may use for: (1) his or her own incapacitating illness; (2) for the employee to receive medical, dental, or optical examination or treatment; or (3) for adoption-related purposes. There are, however, restrictions on the amount of paid sick leave available for an employee's use to provide care for a covered family member. In total, a full-time employee may not use more than a total of 480 hours of sick leave (or, in the case of a part-time employee or an employee with an uncommon tour of duty, an amount of sick leave equal to 12 times the average number of hours in his or her scheduled tour of duty each week) for all family care purposes due to illness or to make funeral arrangements. 5 CFR 630.401(c)(3).

The paid sick leave regulations establish a minimum amount of paid sick leave available to an employee for family care purposes each leave year. That minimum amount may increase if certain conditions are met, up to the maximum allowable for family care purposes, 480 hours for a full-time employee.

The minimum amount of paid sick leave that a full-time employee may use to provide care for a family member who is incapacitated due to a medical or serious health condition; to attend a medical examination or treatment with the family member; or to make arrangements for, or attend the funeral of, a family member, is 40 hours of leave each leave year. 5 CFR 630.401(d)(1). A part-time employee or an employee with an uncommon tour of duty is entitled to the average number of hours in his or her regularly scheduled administrative workweek. *Id.*

A full-time employee may use more than the minimum amount of accrued and accumulated sick leave up to the maximum provided only if he or she maintains a sick leave balance of at least 80 hours. 5 CFR 630.401(d)(2). In the case of a part-time employee or an employee with an uncommon tour of duty, two times the average number of hours in his or her regularly scheduled administrative workweek. *Id.* To be entitled to the maximum amount of accrued sick leave, an employee must maintain this additional leave balance during any period of time during which the employee is using more than his or her basic entitlement (*i.e.* 40 hours in the case of a full-time employee). 5 CFR 630.401(d)(2), (e). Only the first 40 hours (or a proportional amount for an employee on a part-time schedule or uncommon tour of duty) may be advanced. 5 CFR 630.401(d)(3). Sick leave may not be advanced to an employee for the purpose of meeting this additional minimum leave balance. 5 CFR 630.401(d)(3), (e).

Where a full-time employee maintains a minimum balance of accrued and accumulated sick leave of at least 80 hours (or a pro-rated amount for part-time employees), a full-time employee may use up to 480 hours of available paid sick leave during a leave year to care for a covered family member incapacitated with a serious health condition. 5 CFR 630.401(c)(1). In the case of a part-time employee or an employee with an uncommon tour of duty, an amount of sick leave is calculated to equal 12 times the average number of hours in his or her scheduled tour of duty each week during a leave year. *Id.* If the number of hours in the employee's tour of duty is changed during the leave year, the employee's entitlement to use sick leave for this purpose is recalculated based on the employee's new tour of duty. 5 CFR 630.401(g).

In two instances, subtractions from the maximum total amount of paid sick leave available to an employee to care for a covered family member with a serious health condition must be made. 5 CFR 630.401(c)(2). First, any sick leave used by an employee during the leave year to provide care for a family member who is incapacitated due to a medical or mental condition or to attend to a family member receiving medical, dental, or optical examination or treatment must be subtracted from the maximum amount of leave available to an employee to care for a covered family member with a serious health condition. Paid sick leave used by an employee to make arrangements for, or attend the funeral of, a family member, must also be subtracted from the amount of leave available to an employee to care for a family member with a serious health condition. 5 CFR 630.401(c)(2).

Conversely, if the employee has used his entire allotment of paid sick leave to care for a family member with a serious health condition, the employee is not entitled to use any additional paid sick leave to make arrangements for or attend the funeral of a family member, to take a family member for a medical exam or treatment, or to care for a family member who is incapacitated due to a medical or mental condition. 5 CFR 630.401(c)(2).

A full-time employee who seeks to use paid leave to care for a family member who does not have a serious health condition, or to make arrangements for, or attend, the funeral of a family member, is limited to 40 hours (five days) of paid leave each leave year. 5 CFR 630.401(d)(2). That amount is pro-rated for part-time employees or employees with an uncommon tour of duty. *Id.* If that employee has accrued and accumulated a minimum of 80 hours of paid leave (or a pro-rated amount for other than full-time employees), the employee may use up to a maximum of 104 hours (13 days) of leave for these purposes. 5 CFR 630.401(b), (d)(2).

Examples

The following examples illustrate the operation of the above paid sick leave rules.

Example 1:   A full-time employee uses 13 days (104 hours) of sick leave for family care purposes early in the leave year (leave year one). On April 1, the employee requests additional sick leave to care for her mother-in-law with a serious health condition. Since the employee has already used the 13-day (104-hour) entitlement to sick leave to care for a family member under § 630.401(a)(3)(I), she may use only nine weeks and two days (376 hours) of sick leave in the same leave year to care for a family member with a serious health condition. The employee only gets to use that amount if she has at least 80 hours of accrued and available sick leave. As of the beginning of the next leave year (leave year two), the employee has a new entitlement to use up to 13 days (104 hours) of sick leave for general family care or funeral purposes and a new entitlement to use up to 480 hours of sick leave to care for a family member with a serious health condition.

Example 2:   A full-time employee used three days (24 hours) of sick leave to attend the funeral of her grandmother in January. The employee then requested an additional four weeks (160 hours) of sick leave to care for her grandfather, who had pneumonia, a serious health condition. The employee used 184 hours of sick leave for all family care purposes. She has a remaining entitlement to ten days (80 hours) of sick leave for general family care purposes or up to seven weeks and two days (296 hours) of sick leave to care for a family member with a serious health condition, provided she has at least 80 hours of accrued sick leave in her sick leave account.

(3)   Advanced Annual or Sick Leave

Under Title II, an employee may substitute paid annual or sick leave for unpaid FMLA leave that the employee has not accrued or accumulated. An employee may substitute unpaid FMLA leave with advanced annual or sick leave approved under the same terms and conditions that apply to any other employee who requests advanced annual or sick leave. 5 USC 6382(d); 5 CFR 630.1205(b)(2).

Advances of both annual leave and sick leave are permitted. The approval of an appropriate official is required to effectuate an advance; such approvals are generally limited to special circumstances. Advances of leave are generally not made if it is known at the time of a request that the employee will not return to duty. Advances of annual leave may not exceed the amount of annual leave that earned during the remainder of the leave year. Advanced sick leave may not exceed 90 days.

There are limitations on the use of advanced sick leave to meet the 80-hour (or pro-rata equivalent for part-time employees or employees on an uncommon tour of duty) minimum balance necessary to secure the availability of the maximum amount of accrued sick leave for certain family care purposes. 5 CFR 630.401(d)(2)(e).

(4) Leave Transfer

Leave made available to an employee under the Voluntary Leave Transfer Program or the Voluntary Leave Transfer Bank Program may be the subject of an employee election to substitute paid leave for unpaid FMLA leave. 5 USC 6382(d); 5 CFR 630.1205(b)(3).

(a) Voluntary Leave Transfer Program

The Voluntary Leave Transfer Program allows an employee to donate unused accrued annual leave for the medical emergency needs of another employee who has exhausted all of his or her available leave. Under the Voluntary Leave Transfer Program, covered employees experiencing their own or a family member's medical emergency who have exhausted all of their available leave may receive donations of unused accrued annual leave from fellow employees to help offset the hardship resulting from the medical emergency. 5 CFR 630.901(a). The term "family member" is defined the same under sick leave for family care purposes. 5 CFR 630.902 (definition of family member).

At its most basic, the Voluntary Leave Transfer Program requires each federal employer to establish and administer procedures to permit the voluntary transfer of annual leave in the event of a medical emergency. 5 CFR 630.903. A medical emergency means a medical condition of an employee or a family member of such employee that is likely to require an employee's absence from duty for a prolonged period of time and result in a substantial loss of income to the employee because of the unavailability of paid leave. 5 CFR 630.902 (definition of medical emergency). The medical emergency has to last at least 24 hours (or, in the case of a part-time employee or an employee with an uncommon tour of duty, at least 30 percent of the average number of hours in the employee's biweekly scheduled tour of duty). 5 CFR 905(c).

An employee makes written application to his or her employer to become a leave recipient. 5 CFR 630.904(a). The application must identify the individual requesting the leave, give the reasons transferred leave is needed, including a brief description of the nature, severity, and anticipated duration of the medical emergency, and if it is recurring, the approximate frequency of the medical emergency affecting the potential leave recipient, and any information that may be required by the potential leave recipient's employer, including a certification from one or more physicians, or other appropriate experts, with respect to the medical emergency. 5 CFR 630.904.

The employer must notify the individual applying for the leave transfer within ten calendar days (excluding Saturdays, Sundays, and legal public holidays) as to whether the application for leave is approved. 5 CFR 630.905(d), (e).

An employee donates unused and accrued annual leave by submitting a voluntary request to his or her employer that a specified number of hours of his or her accrued annual leave account be transferred to the annual leave account of a specified leave recipient. 5 CFR 630.906(a). The donated leave goes directly into the account of the requesting employee, not the requesting employee's supervisor. 5 CFR 630.906(d).

A leave recipient is restricted in how transferred annual leave may be used. 5 CFR 630.909. The employee may only use the transferred annual leave for the medical emergency for which the transfer was sought. 5 CFR 630.909(a). In each pay period, the receiving employee must first use any accrued annual and sick leave before transferred annual leave is used. 5 CFR 630.909(b). The transferred annual leave is subject to all of the conditions and requirements generally imposed on such leave. 5 CFR 630.909(c). Transferred annual leave may also be substituted retroactively for any period of LWOP or used to liquidate indebtedness for any period of advanced leave (annual or sick) that began on or after the date fixed by the employer as the beginning of the medical emergency. 5 CFR 630.909(d).

When the medical emergency affecting a leave recipient terminates, the transfer of annual leave to the recipient ends, and any unused transferred annual leave is restored to the leave donors. 5 CFR 630.910(c).

The Voluntary Leave Transfer Program applies to officers and federal employees covered by the annual and sick leave provisions of Subchapter I of Chapter 63 of Title 5. 5 CFR 630.901. Covered employees are defined by reference to 5 USC 6301(2). [For a further discussion of the definition of employee for purposes of the FMLA, see Chapter 4, "Federal Employees Covered by the FMLA."]

(b) Voluntary Leave Transfer Bank

A Voluntary Leave Transfer Bank allows leave bank members to pool unused accrued annual leave into a fund available to all members who have exhausted their own leave and are in need of additional leave for their own medical emergency or the medical emergency of a family member. The Leave Transfer Bank differs from the Leave Transfer Program in that in the former, the donating employees pool their money for the benefit of a large number of potential member recipients. In the Leave Transfer Program, the employees donate the leave to specifically identified individual recipients.

The Voluntary Leave Transfer Bank shares many similarities with the Voluntary Leave Transfer Program. Key terms such as "medical emergency" and "family member" are defined the same as in the Voluntary Leave Transfer Program. 5 CFR 630.1002 (defining medical emergency and family member). Because the unused accrued annual leave is pooled rather than distributed individually, contributions to the Bank are handled differently than under the Voluntary Leave Transfer Program. For example, there is a limited open season when membership in the bank is permitted. 5 CFR 630.1004(d).

To receive accrued annual leave from the Leave Bank, the recipient must submit an application establishing that the medical emergency will require an absence from duty of at least 24 hours (or a lesser, pro rata amount for employees on a part-time schedule or uncommon tour of duty). 5 CFR 630.1007(b). The leave bank board must provide timely written notification to the applicant on the action. 5 CFR 630.1007(d).

The same restrictions on the use of transferred annual leave apply to leave withdrawn from a leave bank. A leave recipient may only use leave withdrawn from a leave bank for the medical emergency for which the leave was approved. 5 CFR 630.1009(a). The leave recipient is required to use any accrued annual and sick leave (if applicable) before using annual leave withdrawn from a leave bank. 5 CFR 630.1009(b). The approval and use of annual leave withdrawn from a leave bank is subject to all of the usual conditions for the use of annual leave. 5 CFR 630.1009(c). Annual leave withdrawn from a leave bank may also be used retroactively as a substitute for any period of leave without pay or used to liquidate indebtedness for any period of advanced leave that began on or after the onset of the medical emergency. 5 CFR 630.1009(d). Unpaid FMLA leave is run as leave without pay.

The relationship of the FMLA and the voluntary leave transfer and leave bank programs are best illustrated with an example. Assume an employee invokes his entitlement to FMLA leave as a result of a medical emergency. This employee does not have any paid leave available and therefore applies for donated leave under his employer's leave transfer program. Approximately two to three weeks later, the employee is approved as a leave recipient and receives donated annual leave. Under the voluntary leave transfer and leave bank programs, the employee may retroactively substitute paid leave for leave without pay beginning on the date the emergency began, consistent with 5 CFR 630.906(e) and 630.1009(d). The 12-month period and the 12-week entitlement to leave under the FMLA begin on the date the employee first invoked FMLA leave. The employee receives the benefits and protections of both the FMLA and the voluntary leave transfer program simultaneously.

b. Title I, the CAA, and the PEOAA

An eligible employee may elect, or an employer may require the employee, to substitute any accrued paid vacation, personal, or family leave of the employee for all or part of the employee's annual 12-week FMLA entitlement for the birth, placement of a child for adoption or foster care, or care for a spouse, child, or parent with a serious health condition, or for the employee's own serious health condition. 29 USC 2612(d)(2)(A); 29 CFR 825.207(a)–(c); 2 USC 1312(a)(1) (incorporating § 102 of Title I of the FMLA, 29 USC 2612); S. Res. 242, Cong. Rec. S3959, S3965 (April 23, 1996); 29 CFR 825.207(a) (CAA); 3 USC 412(a)(1) (incorporating § 102 of Title I of the FMLA, 29 USC 2612); *see Dotson v. BRP US, Inc.*, No. 06-cv-4004-JPG, 2007 U.S. Dist. LEXIS 6832, at *14 & n.1 (S.D. Ill. Jan. 31, 2007) (perfectly permissible under the FMLA for an employer to count an individual's paid vacation, personal or medical or sick leave toward the 12-week leave period mandated by the statute).

An employer is not required to substitute accrued paid sick or medical leave in any situation in which the employer would not normally provide any such paid leave. 29 USC 2612(d)(2)(B); 29 CFR 825.207(b)–(c); 2 USC 1312(a)(1) (incorporating § 102 of Title I of the FMLA, 29 USC 2612); S. Res. 242, Cong. Rec. S3959, S3965–S3966 (April 23, 1996); 29 CFR 825.207(b)–(c); 3 USC 412(a)(1) (incorporating § 102 of Title I of the FMLA, 29 USC 2612).

(1) Family Leave

The term "family leave" as used in the FMLA, 29 CFR 825.207(b), S. Res. 242, Cong. Rec. S3959, S3965 (April 23, 1996); 29 CFR 825.207(b), refers to paid leave provided by the employer covering the particular circumstances for which the employee seeks leave for either:

- Birth of a child and to care for such child;
- Placement of a child for adoption or foster car; or
- Care for a spouse, child or parent with a serious health condition.

Employers are not required to have a paid family leave plan. If they do, however, to the extent it applies to the situation faced by the eligible employee, accrued family leave is available in substitution for unpaid FMLA leave. For example, if the employer's leave plan allows use of family leave to care for a child but not for a parent, the employer is not required to allow accrued family leave to be substituted for FMLA leave used to care for a parent. 29 CFR 825.207(b); S. Res. 242, Cong. Rec. S3959–S3997 (April 23, 1996); 29 CFR 825.207(b).

Unlike Title II, Title I does not restrict the paid leave available for substitution to the leave identified in Subchapter I of Chapter 63 of Title 5. Every accrued paid leave balance is potentially available in substitution for unpaid FMLA leave. The only limitation placed by Title I on the paid leave available for substitution of unpaid FMLA leave is the use restrictions of the paid leave plan.

In the federal sector, Title I employees are entitled to substitute accrued and accumulated paid leave to provide care for family members only to the extent that the employer provides paid family leave to Title I employees. It is by no means a given that Title I employees share the same annual and sick leave benefits as Title II employees. Employees covered by the paid sick and annual leave benefits of Title 5 are defined in reference to 5 USC 2105. 5 USC 6301(2)(A). That section also specifically excludes from coverage most of the employees who fall within the provisions of Title II. 5 USC 6301(2)(B). [For a more detailed discussion of which employees are covered by Title I and Title II of the FMLA, see Chapter 4, "Federal Employees Covered by the FMLA."]

Whether paid annual or sick leave benefits are available to care for a family member of a Title I employee, a review of employer policies is required. Some agencies, like the Postal Service, are completely governed by Title I of the FMLA. Paid annual and sick leave provisions that may be available for family care purposes are set forth in collective bargaining agreements and the Employee and Labor Relations Manual (ELM). In federal agencies with mixed employee populations, most covered by Title II and some covered by Title I, employer policy will govern the extent of paid leave available for substitution of unpaid FMLA leave.

(2) Medical or Sick Leave

Substitution of paid accrued medical or sick leave may be made for any otherwise unpaid FMLA needed to care for a family member or the employee's own serious health condition. 29 CFR 825.207(c); S. Res. 242, Cong. Rec. S3959–S3997 (April 23, 1996); 29 CFR 825.207(c). Substitution of paid sick or medical leave may be elected to the extent the circumstances meet the employer's usual requirements for the use of sick or medical leave. 29 CFR 825.207(c); S. Res. 242, Cong. Rec. S3959, S3965–S3966 (April 23, 1996); 29 CFR 825.207(c); *see Chase v. Flinn*, No. 04-1500 (RHK/JSM), 2005 U.S. Dist. LEXIS 39322, at *20-21 (D. Minn. Dec. 5, 2005). An employer is not required to allow substitution of paid sick or medical leave for unpaid FMLA leave "in any situation" where the employer's uniform policy would not normally allow such paid leave. 29 CFR 825.207(c); S. Res. 242, Cong. Rec. S3959, S3965–S3966 (April 23, 1996); 29 CFR 825.207(c); *see Chase v. Flinn*, No. 04-1500 (RHK/JSM), 2005 U.S. Dist. LEXIS 39322, at *20-21 (D. Minn. Dec. 5, 2005). An employee, therefore, has a right to substitute paid medical or sick leave to care for a seriously ill family member only if the employer's leave plan allows paid leave to be used for that purpose. 29 CFR 825.207(c); S. Res. 242, Cong. Rec. S3959–S3997 (April 23, 1996); 29 CFR 825.207(c). Similarly, an employee does not have a right to substitute paid medical or sick leave for a serious health condition that is not covered by the employer's leave plan. 29 CFR 825.207(c); S. Res. 242, Cong. Rec. S3959, S3965–S3966 (April 23, 1996); 29 CFR 825.207(c).

The extent of accrued paid medical and sick leave available for substitution with unpaid FMLA leave is governed by employer policies and the terms of applicable collective bargaining agreements. Title I federal employees do not, as a matter of law, automatically receive the same benefits as employees who fall within the definition of paid sick and annual leave in Title 5.

Employees must abide by existing procedures for requesting paid leave to be entitled to paid leave concurrent with FMLA leave. In *Chase v. Flinn*, No. 04-1500 (RHK/JSM), 2005 U.S. Dist. LEXIS 39322, at *20-21 (D. Minn. Dec. 5, 2005), the court found that the employer did not interfere with the employee's FMLA rights by refusing to designate FMLA leave as paid sick leave. The employer established that the employee failed to perfect his right to sick leave in accordance with employer leave policies. Specifically, the sick leave policy required the employee to provide sick leave documents to his immediate supervisor. The employee forwarded the documents directly to the employer's medical department. The court found that by doing so the employee failed to perfect his right to paid sick leave.

(3) Vacation or Personal Leave

Substitution of paid accrued vacation or personal leave may be made for any otherwise unpaid FMLA needed to care for a family member or the employee's own serious health condition. 29 CFR 825.207(c); S. Res. 242, Cong. Rec. S3959, S3965–S3966 (April 23, 1996); 29 CFR 825.207(c). Paid vacation or personal leave, including leave earned or accrued under plans allowing paid time off, may be substituted, at either the employee's or the employer's option, for any qualified FMLA leave. 29 CFR 825.207(e); S. Res. 242, Cong. Rec. S3959, S3966 (April 23, 1996); 29 CFR 825.207(e). The employer may place no limitations on substitution of paid vacation or personal leave for these purposes. 29 CFR 825.207(e); S. Res. 242, Cong. Rec. S3959, S3966 (April 23, 1996); 29 CFR 825.207(e).

The extent of accrued paid medical and sick leave available for substitution with unpaid FMLA leave is governed by employer policies and the terms of applicable collective bargaining agreements. Title I federal employees do not, as a matter of law, automatically receive the same benefits as employees who fall within the definition of paid sick and annual leave in Title 5.

III. COMPENSATORY OVERTIME, WORKERS' COMPENSATION, TEMPORARY DISABILITY LEAVE, FLEXIBLE WORK SCHEDULE CREDIT HOURS, AND UNEMPLOYMENT COMPENSATION

This section addresses the effect of FMLA leave on an eligible employee's receipt of compensatory overtime in lieu of overtime wages, receipt of workers' compensation benefits as a result of an on–the–job injury, or receipt of temporary disability benefits pursuant to company policy.

A. COMPENSATORY OVERTIME

Compensatory time off or "comp time" is paid time off the job which is earned and accrued by an employee in lieu of immediate cash payment for work in excess of the statutory hours for which overtime compensation is required by § 7 of the Fair Labor Standards Act (FLSA), 29 USC 207(o). Comp time is not a form of accrued paid leave that an employer may require an employee to substitute for unpaid FMLA leave. 29 CFR 825.207(l); S. Res. 242, Cong. Rec. S3959, S3966 (April 23, 1996); 29 CFR 825.207(l) (same). It is also not a benefit provided by an employer. Preamble, 29 CFR 825.207. Rather, it is an alternative form of paying public employees (only) for overtime hours worked. *See* DOL WH FMLA Advisory Opinion No. 34 (April 12, 1994).

1. Title II

Compensatory time off in lieu of overtime pay is generally available throughout the federal government. Title II has adopted the reasoning of the DOL that comp time off is not accrued paid leave available for substitution with unpaid FMLA leave. Preamble, Substitution of Paid Leave, 5 CFR 1205 (applying DOL's arguments to comp time earned under 5 USC 5543). Title II does permit substitution of paid leave for FMLA leave in limited circumstances. 5 USC 6382(d). Those circumstances do not include available compensatory time off. However, as we have seen under Title I and the CAA, compensatory time off is generally not considered paid leave. As such, the limitations on paid leave substitution set forth in 5 USC 6382(d) should not prohibit an employee from requesting that comp time be used for an FMLA covered reason, just as it is permitted by Title I and the CAA. *See* 5 CFR 551.101 (OPM's regulations on compensatory time off implement the FLSA as applied to the federal sector).

Compensatory time off with pay in lieu of overtime pay is allowed for irregular or occasional work at the employer's discretion. 5 CFR 551.531(a). When permitted under employer flexible work schedule programs, time off with pay in lieu of overtime pay is also permitted, at the discretion of the employer, for regularly scheduled or irregular or occasional overtime. 5 CFR 551.531(b).

Both exempt and nonexempt employees who are covered by the definition of "employee" at 5 USC 5541(2) are permitted to take paid comp time in lieu of overtime pay. An employee for purposes of 5 USC 5541(2) means and employee of:

- An executive employer;
- The Government of the District of Columbia;
- The Judicial Branch, the Botanic Garden, the Office of the Architect of the Capitol, who occupies a position subject to Chapter 51 and Subchapter III of Chapter 53 of Title 5.

Excluded from the definition of employee under 5 USC 5541(2) are:

- A justice or judge of the United States;
- The head of an employer other than the Government of the District of Columbia;
- A member of the Metropolitan Police or Fire Department of the District of Columbia;
- A member of the U.S. Secret Service Uniformed Division, and member of the U.S. Park Police, other than for purposes of § 5545(a) and 5546;
- A student–employee defined by § 5351 of Title 5;
- An employee outside the continental United States or in Alaska who is paid in accordance with local native prevailing wage rates for the area of employment;
- An employee of the Tennessee Valley Authority;
- An individual to whom § 1291(a) of Title 50, Appendix, applies;
- An employee of a federal land bank, a federal intermediate credit bank, or a bank of cooperatives;
- An employee whose pay is fixed and adjusted from time to time in accordance with prevailing rates under Subchapter IV of Chapter 53 of this Title, or by a wage board or similar administrative authority;
- An employee of the Transportation Corps of the Army on a vessel operated by the United States, a vessel employee of the Environmental Science Services Administration, or a vessel employee of the Department of the Interior;
- A "teacher" or an individual holding a "teaching position" as defined by § 901 of Title 20;
- A Foreign Service Officer;
- A member of the Senior Foreign Service;
- A member of the Senior Executive Service;
- A member of the FBI and Drug Enforcement Administration Senior Executive Service.

Compensatory time off can also be approved for a "prevailing rate employee," as defined at 5 USC 5342(2), but there is no authority to require that any prevailing rate (wage) employee be compensated for irregular or occasional overtime work by granting compensatory time off. A prevailing rate employee is a person employed in or under a recognized trade or craft, or other skilled mechanical craft, or in an unskilled, semi-skilled, or skilled manual labor occupation, and any other person, including a foreman and a supervisor, in a position having trade, craft, or labor experience and knowledge as the paramount requirement. 5 USC 5342(2)(A).

Agencies may require that an FLSA exempt employee (as defined at 5 USC 5541(2)) receive compensatory time off in lieu of overtime pay for irregular or occasional overtime work, but only for those FLSA exempt employees whose rate of basic pay is above the rate for GS–10, step 10. 5 CFR 551.114(c). Mandatory compensatory time off is not permitted for prevailing rate employees or in lieu of FLSA overtime pay. 5 CFR 551.531(c). Compensatory time off may be approved, but not required, in lieu of regularly scheduled overtime work only for employees, including prevailing rate employees, who are directed to work overtime hours under flexible work schedules 5 USC 6123(a)(3).

An employer may set time limits for an FLSA exempt or nonexempt employee to take compensatory time off. 5 CFR 551.531(d). An employer may provide that an FLSA exempt employee who earns compensatory time off will lose entitlement to compensatory time off and overtime pay if it is not used within employer time limits, unless the failure was due to an exigency of the service beyond the employee's control. 5 CFR 550.114(d). For nonexempt employees, if the compensatory time off is not requested or taken within the employer established time limits, the employee must be paid for overtime work at the overtime rate in effect for the work period in which it was earned. 5 CFR 551.531(d).

The calculation of compensatory time off is equal to the amount of overtime earned by performing overtime. 5 CFR 551.531(e).

2. Title I

Federal employees who are included in the Title 5 definition of an employee for purposes of comp time generally do not enjoy the right to compensatory time off in lieu of overtime wages. Comp time is not available to these federal employees because they are not included within the definition of a covered "public employer" within the meaning of § 7(o) of the FLSA, 29 USC 207(o). That section permits public agencies, defined as a State, a political subdivision of a State, or an interstate governmental employer, under certain, limited circumstances, to substitute compensatory time off in lieu of a federal employee being paid time–and–a–half for overtime. 29 CFR 825.207(l); 29 CFR 553.21. Note that the definition of a public agency covered by § 7(o) of the FLSA does not include federal agencies.

Compensatory time is accumulated at a rate of not less than one–and–one–half hours for each overtime hour worked. 29 CFR 825.207(l); 5 CFR 553.22(b). There are limitations on the number of comp time hours an employee may accrue depending on whether the employee works in fire protection or law enforcement (480 hours) or elsewhere for a public agency (240 hours). 29 CFR 825.207(l); 5 CFR 553.24.

A covered state or local public employee may request to use his or her balance of compensatory time for an FMLA reason. 29 CFR 825.207(l). If the public employer permits the accrual to be used in compliance with the FLSA, 29 CFR 553.25, the absence, which is paid from the employee's accrued compensatory time account, may not be counted against the employee's FMLA leave entitlement. 29 CFR 825.207(l).

3. The CAA

With one exception, CAA–covered employees may not receive compensatory time in lieu of overtime compensation. 2 USC 1313(a)(3). The exception would permit the accrual of comp time in lieu of immediate payment of overtime wages for covered employees whose work schedules directly depend on the schedule of the House of Representatives or the Senate. 2 USC 1313(c)(3). The Board of Directors of the Office of Compliance was directed to issue regulations comparable to the provisions of the FLSA that apply to CAA–covered employees who have irregular work schedules. *Id.*

Under CAA Board regulations, employing offices are authorized to provide compensatory time off, instead of overtime pay, for covered employees whose work schedules directly depend on the schedule of the House of Representatives and the Senate. A covered employee's work schedule *directly depends* on the schedule of the House or the Senate if the eligible employee:

- performs work that directly supports the conduct of business in the chamber, and
- work hours that regularly change in response to the schedule of the House and the Senate.

Compensatory time off may be provided in lieu of overtime pay for any hours worked in excess of 60 hours in a workweek by a covered employee whose schedule directly depends on the schedule of the House or the Senate. Accordingly, the employing office must provide:

- pay, at the rate of time–and–a–half, for all hours in excess of 40 and up to 60 in a workweek, and

- pay or time off, at the rate of time–and–a–half, for all hours in excess of 60 in a workweek.

Compensatory time off, if any is authorized under applicable law, may be accrued and used for an FMLA reason. S. Res. 242, Cong. Rec. S3959, S3966 (April 23, 1996); 29 CFR 825.207(I). Compensatory time off is not a form of accrued paid leave that an employing office may require the employee to substitute for unpaid FMLA leave. S. Res. 242, Cong. Rec. S3959, S3966 (April 23, 1996); 29 CFR 825.207(I). If the employing office permits the accrual of compensatory time to be used in compliance with applicable Board regulations, the absence, which is paid from the employee's accrued compensatory time account, may not be counted against the employee's FMLA leave entitlement. S. Res. 242, Cong. Rec. S3959, S3966 (April 23, 1996); 29 CFR 825.207(I)

4. PEOAA

Like the CAA but with one exception, the PEOAA does not permit covered employees to receive compensatory time in lieu of overtime compensation. 3 USC 413(a)(3). The PEOAA permits the President or designee to issue regulations that would permit the accrual of compensatory time in lieu of overtime pay for covered employees whose work schedules directly depend on the schedule of the President or the Vice President.

B. WORKERS' COMPENSATION

Although FMLA leave may run concurrently with workers' compensation leave, because workers' compensation leave is both paid and not considered accrued paid leave, technically the FMLA provisions governing paid leave substitution do not apply. 29 CFR 825.207(d)(2); S. Res. 242, Cong. Rec. S3959, S3966 (April 23, 1996); 29 CFR 825.207(d)(2); DOL WH FMLA Advisory Opinion No. 92 (Dec. 12, 1997); see Repa v. Roadway Express, Inc., 477 F.3d 938, 941 (7th Cir. 2007); Hendricks v. Compass Group USA, Inc., No. 4:03CV79AS, 2006 U.S. Dist. LEXIS 64433, at *5-6 (N.D. Ind. Aug. 29, 2006).

Workers' compensation leave is not a form of accrued paid leave within the meaning of the FMLA. See 60 Fed. Reg. 2180, 2205–06 (1995); Preamble, 29 CFR 825.207. Workers' compensation is a statutory entitlement, payments of which are drawn from funds provided by the employers, but administered, in the case of federal employers, by the federal government. Leave under a workers' compensation law is also not considered "unpaid leave" within the meaning of the FMLA. 29 CFR 825.207(d)(2); S. Res. 242, Cong. Rec. S3959, S3966 (April 23, 1996); 29 CFR 825.207(d)(2). Workers' compensation is paid leave. Because workers' compensation is not a form of paid leave offered by an employer, and because it is not unpaid, the FMLA provisions governing paid leave substitution do not apply to employees receiving workers' compensation benefits. 29 CFR 825.207(d)(2); S. Res. 242, Cong. Rec. S3959, S3966 (April 23, 1996); 29 CFR 825.207(d)(2); DOL WH FMLA Advisory Opinion No. 92 (Dec. 12, 1997).

Because the FMLA's paid leave substitution provisions do not apply where an employee elects to receive workers' compensation payments, the employee may *not* elect, nor may the employer *require* the employee, to exhaust any form of paid leave provided by the employer during any portion of the absence covered by the workers' compensation payments. 60 Fed. Reg. 2180, 2205–06 (1995), Preamble, 29 CFR 825.207; DOL WH FMLA Advisory Opinion No. 92 (Dec. 12, 1997); see Hendricks v. Compass Group USA, Inc., No. 4:03CV79AS, 2006 U.S. Dist. LEXIS 64433, at *5-6 (N.D. Ind. Aug. 29, 2006). An employee may not take accrued paid leave concurrently with both workers' compensation and FMLA leave. Hendricks v. Compass Group USA, Inc., No. 4:03CV79AS, 2006 U.S. Dist. LEXIS 64433, at *5-6 (N.D. Ind. Aug. 29, 2006).

Although the paid leave substitution provisions do not apply to leaves of absence covered by workers' compensation, the FMLA allows employers to count workers' compensation leave toward an employee's 12–week FMLA leave entitlement, provided the on–the–job illness or injury constitutes a serious health condition within the meaning of the FMLA. 29 CFR 825.207(d)(2); S. Res. 242, Cong. Rec. S3966, S3997 (April 23, 1996); 29 CFR 825.207(d)(2); DOL WH FMLA Advisory Opinion No. 92 (Dec. 12, 1997); DOL WH FMLA Advisory Opinion No. 43 (Aug. 24, 1994); DOL WH FMLA Advisory Opinion No. 42, #5 (Aug. 23, 1994); see Hassell v. American Signature, Inc., No. 2:06cv518, 2006 U.S. Dist. LEXIS 87475, at *2 & n.1 (E.D. Va. Dec. 1, 2006). The FMLA provides that a serious health condition may result from injury to an employee "on or off" the job. 29 CFR 825.207(d)(2); S. Res. 242, Cong. Rec. S3959, S3966 (April 23, 1996); 29 CFR 825.207(d)(2). Of course, in order to count the workers' compensation leave towards an employee's FMLA leave entitlement, the employer must properly designate the leave at the beginning of the absence as required by the FMLA implementing regulations. 29 CFR 825.207(d)(2); S. Res. 242, Cong. Rec. S3959, S3966 (April 23, 1996); 29 CFR 825.207(d)(2).

For example, Tonya works as a paralegal with the Transportation Security Administration (TSA) on a one-year not-to-exceed assignment. She injures her back carrying boxes of documents for a large class action lawsuit. Tonya tends to overdo things. She dutifully files a claim for workers' compensation benefits while on leave recuperating. Her injury constitutes a serious health condition within the meaning of the FMLA. In addition to receiving workers' compensation benefits, Tonya would not be entitled to also receive accrued paid sick leave for the same period of time. Because workers' compensation leave is not unpaid leave, the FMLA substitution provisions do not apply. *See, e.g.,* DOL WH FMLA Advisory Opinion No. 92 (Dec. 12, 1997).

Similarly, the TSA would not be able to require Tonya to substitute any accrued paid vacation, personal, medical, or sick leave for any part of the absence that is covered by workers' compensation. 60 Fed. Reg. 2180, 2205–06 (1995), Preamble to 29 CFR 825.207; DOL WH FMLA Advisory Opinion No. 92 (Dec. 12, 1997). The TSA can, however, count the time Tonya was on workers' compensation leave toward her 12-week FMLA entitlement, provided the TSA meets all of the employer requirements of the FMLA. *See* DOL WH FMLA Advisory Opinion No. 42, #5 (Aug. 23, 1994).

As will be discussed in more detail in Chapter 13, "Return to Work from Leave," and Chapter 16, "Interaction of the FMLA with Other Federal Laws, Employer Practices, and Collective Bargaining Agreements," an employer is precluded from requiring an employee to return to work prematurely from leave concurrently covered by workers' compensation and the FMLA, if the employee remains unable to perform any one or more of the essential functions of the original position, and the employee has not yet exhausted his or her full FMLA leave entitlement. 29 CFR 825.207(d)(2); S. Res. 242, Cong. Rec. S3959, S3966 (April 23, 1996); 29 CFR 825.207(d)(2). The reference point for determining the employee's essential job functions is the position held by the employee when the employee gave notice of the need for leave or leave commencement, whichever is earlier. 60 Fed. Reg. 2180, 2205–06 (1995), Preamble to 29 CFR 825.207.

On the other hand, the FMLA does not prevent the continuation of lawful policies under workers' compensation programs that discontinue wage replacement payment if and when an employee refuses to accept a medically-approved light duty assignment. 29 CFR 825.207(d)(2); S. Res. 242, Cong. Rec. S3959, S3966 (April 23, 1996); 29 CFR 825.207(d)(2). In that case, the employee may continue on FMLA leave where the employee cannot perform one or more of the essential functions of the employee's former position, and the employee or employer would have the right to elect to substitute appropriate paid leave, or continue on unpaid FMLA leave, until the employee has exhausted his or her 12-week FMLA leave entitlement. 29 CFR 825.207(d)(2); S. Res. 242, Cong. Rec. S3959, S3966 (April 23, 1996); 29 CFR 825.207(d)(2).

For example, TSA finds and offers Tonya a medically approved light duty job within her limitations. Tonya cannot lift more than one pound, and an essential function of her paralegal responsibilities involves handling large boxes of documents. Tonya declines the light duty job. Knowing that her workers' compensation benefits will be cut, Tonya requests that her accrued sick leave be substituted for unpaid FMLA leave to cover the remaining 4 weeks of her recovery. Because Tonya used only two weeks of her 12-week FMLA entitlement, and because she has more than four weeks of sick leave accrued, the remaining four weeks are covered by the FMLA and/or (depending on what court you are following) paid sick leave.

Similarly, if Tonya declined a medically approved light duty job within her medical restrictions, she would lose workers' compensation benefits. If she did elect to substitute paid leave for unpaid FMLA leave for the remaining 4 weeks of her recovery, TSA could require Tonya to exhaust her accrued paid leave, including paid vacation, personal, medical or sick leave.

C. TEMPORARY DISABILITY LEAVE

Generally speaking, the federal government does not have temporary disability leave programs. These programs exist mainly in the private sector. Because, however, some federal employing entities may have temporary disability plans, the matter is discussed more fully below.

Payments provided under employer plans covering temporary disabilities (whether provided voluntarily through insurance or under a self-insured plan, or required to meet legally mandated disability provisions (e.g., pregnancy disability laws) are treated the same as workers' compensation payments. 60 Fed. Reg. 2180, 2205–06 (1995), Preamble to 29 CFR 825.207; *see Repa v. Roadway Express, Inc.*, 477 F.3d 938, 940-41 (7th Cir. 2007). Leave under a temporary disability plan, whether public or private, is not a form of accrued paid leave within the meaning of the FMLA. DOL WH FMLA Advisory Opinion No. 92 (Dec. 12, 1997). Nor is leave under a temporary disability plan unpaid leave within the meaning of the FMLA. *Id., citing* 29 CFR 825.207(d)(1); *see Repa*, 477 F.3d at 940-41. Because the leave pursuant to a temporary disability plan is not a form of paid leave offered by an employer, and because it is not unpaid, the FMLA provisions governing paid leave substitution do not apply to employees receiving workers' compensation benefits. 29 CFR 825.207(d)(1); S. Res. 242, Cong. Rec. S3959, S3966 (April 23, 1996); 29 CFR 825.207(d)(1); DOL WH FMLA Advisory Opinion No. 92 Dec. 12, 1997); *see Repa*, 477 F.3d at 940-41.

Because the paid leave substitution provisions do not apply, an employee receiving payments from a paid disability plan may *not* elect, nor may the employer *require* the employee, to exhaust any form of paid leave provided by the employer during any portion of the absence covered by paid temporary disability leave. 60 Fed. Reg. 2180, 2205–06 (1995), Preamble to 29 CFR 825.207. However, the employer may designate the leave as FMLA leave for purposes of both the temporary disability benefit plan and the 12-week FMLA leave entitlements. 29 CFR 825.207(d)(1); S. Res. 242, Cong. Rec. S3959, S3966 (April 23, 1996); 29 CFR 825.207(d)(1); *see Repa*, 477 F.3d at 940-41; *Skelton v. The Health Alliance*, No. 1:04cv797, 2006 U.S. Dist. LEXIS 74073, at *10 & n.2 (S.D. Ohio Oct. 11, 2006) (disability leave for the birth of a child is to be considered FMLA leave and counted in the 12 weeks of leave permitted by the FMLA). The unpaid FMLA leave and the paid disability plan leave run concurrently, provided, of course, that all conditions are met for FMLA leave coverage and coverage under the paid temporary disability leave plan. 29 CFR 825.207(d)(1); S. Res. 242, Cong. Rec. S3959, S3966 (April 23, 1996); 29 CFR 825.207(d)(1); *see Repa*, 477 F.3d at 940-41.

The prohibition on paid leave substitution when an employee is on disability leave is not limited to disability leave for the birth of a child. In *Repa v. Roadway Express, Inc.*, 477 F.3d 938, 941 (7th Cir. 2007), the court found that 825.207(d)(1) is not limited to disability leave for the birth of a child. Repa was receiving paid disability leave for a workplace injury in accordance with the employer's Loss of Time Benefit policy. The court also rejected the argument that 825.207(d)(1) did not apply because the paid disability program was provided by a third party and not the employer. As such, Roadway Express violated the FMLA when it required the employee to substitute paid leave for unpaid FMLA leave where the employee was on paid disability leave.

For example, our heroine, Tonya, instead of suffering from a workplace injury, is now eight months pregnant. Due to complications, Tonya's physician wants her to take leave for the month before and after her pregnancy. Paid leave for childbirth is available for Tonya under the employer's temporary disability leave policy. Tonya elects to receive paid leave under the disability leave plan. Disability leave for the birth of a child would generally be considered FMLA leave for a serious health condition and counted toward the 12 weeks of leave permitted under the FMLA. 29 CFR 825.207(d)(1); S. Res. 242, Cong. Rec. S3959, S3966 (April 23, 1996); 29 CFR 825.207(d)(1). TSA could count the entire period of absence when Tonya was on paid disability for the birth of her child toward Tonya's 12-week FMLA entitlement.

TSA could not, however, require Tonya to substitute paid vacation, personal, medical, or sick leave for any part of the absence that is covered by payments under the TSA temporary disability leave plan. Again, disability leave is not considered accrued paid leave subject to the paid leave substitution provisions. For the same reason, Tonya would be precluded from relying on the FMLA's substitution provisions to insist upon receiving both temporary disability payments and accrued paid leave benefits during the absence. *See* DOL WH FMLA Advisory Opinion No. 92 (Dec. 12, 1997).

D. FLEXIBLE WORK SCHEDULE AND ACCRUED CREDIT HOURS

Flexible work schedules involve work arrangements in which fixed times of arrival and departure are replaced by a working day composed of two different types of work time: *core time* and *flexible time*. 5 USC 6122(a); 5 CFR Part 610. Core time is the period of the day in which all employees are expected to be at work, typically from 9:00 or 9:30 a.m. to 3:00 or 3:30 p.m. Flexible time is that part of the work day within which a participating employee may choose his or her time of arrival and departure, based on the particular needs and requirements of the position. At all times, the employee must meet basic work-hour requirements, generally 80 hours each biweekly pay period. The employee can meet the basic work-hour requirements with any combination of work hours, leave, compensatory time off, or credit hours.

Some flexible work-hour programs allow employees to earn credit hours for any work hour in excess of the basic work-hour requirement. This allows the employee to vary the length of the workdays or weeks. Credit hours are earned in lieu of overtime pay. An employee may carry over a maximum of 24 credit hours from pay period to pay period.

These earned credit hours may not be substituted for unpaid FMLA leave. Rather, under Title II, they are treated the same as compensatory time off. Preamble, 5 CFR 1205, Substitution of Paid Leave (OPM indicates that accrued credit hours under a flexible work schedule should be treated the same as compensatory time off, and may not be used in substitution for unpaid FMLA leave). The lack of availability of accrued flexible work schedule credit hours as a substitute for unpaid FMLA leave is also evident in that Title II limits paid leave substitution to leave in Subchapter I of Chapter 63 of Title 5, 6 USC 6301 *et seq.* Flexible Work Schedules, on the other hand, are addressed in Subchapter II of Chapter 61 of Title 5, 5 USC 6122.

For purposes of the FMLA, although earned flexible workplace schedule credit hours may not be used in substitution for FMLA leave, they may be used to cover leave for FMLA purposes. Under DOL's interpretation, adopted by Title II, an employer may not deduct available FMLA leave from an eligible employee who chooses to use flexible work schedule credit hours in lieu of unpaid FMLA leave.

E. UNEMPLOYMENT COMPENSATION

Another alternative to the use of accrued paid leave in substitution of unpaid FMLA leave is the use of state unemployment compensation funds. During his 1999 commencement speech at Grambling State University and in a May 1999 Executive Memorandum, President Clinton directed the Department of Labor to develop model legislation to permit states to use surplus unemployment insurance funds to subsidize parents who use the FMLA to care for a newborn or newly adopted child. President Clinton explained the need for this legislation by noting the results of a 1996 study by the Commission on Family and Medical Leave showing that "lost pay was the most significant barrier to parents taking advantage of unpaid leave after the birth or adoption of a child. This new step will help to give states the ability to eliminate a significant barrier that parents face in taking leave." 1999 Memorandum.

President Clinton's proposal was met with predictable cheers from most proponents of paid family leave, and jeers from business groups. Steven K. Wisensale, Family Leave Policy: the Political Economy of Work and Family in America 192–93 (2001). The US Department of Labor issued final unemployment compensation/parental leave regulations effective August 14, 2000. 65 Fed. Reg. 37,209–37,227 (June 13, 2000). The regulations are codified at 20 CFR Part 604.

The purpose of the final regulations was to allow state unemployment fund monies to provide partial wage replacement to mothers and fathers on FMLA leave following the birth or adoption of a child. 20 CFR 604.1. A state's participation in the program was voluntary. 20 CFR 604.2. If the state chooses to provide birth and adoption unemployment compensation, all individuals covered by the state's unemployment compensation must be covered by the birth and adoption compensation program. 20 CFR 604.20. The program was described as experimental.

Under the program, parents are eligible for birth or adoption unemployment compensation during the one-year period commencing with the week in which their child is born or placed with them for adoption. 20 CFR 604.20. Weeks preceding the week of the birth or placement and weeks following the end of the one-year period are not compensable. 20 CFR 604.21. The experimental program came complete with model State legislation to commence the program and a question and answer format addressing various issues. Note that the program does not require the illness of anyone: not mother, father, newborn, or adopted child. It essentially allows mothers and fathers time off for bonding with their newborn or newly adopted child.

A number of states followed suit with proposals for the use of unemployment compensation surpluses for FMLA purposes. Wisensale, Family Leave Policy at 194–211 (2001). None of the proposals, however, were enacted. 67 Fed. Reg. at 72,122. ("Since the Department [of Labor] made the BAA–UC experiment available in 2000, no state has elected to participate.")

On December 4, 2002, the DOL issued a notice of proposed rulemaking to remove the final Birth and Adoption Unemployment Compensation (BAA–UC) regulations. 67 Fed. Reg. at 72,122–72,126 (Dec. 4, 2002). In response to litigation alleging that the BAA–UC law was inconsistent with federal UC law, the DOL conducted a review of its BAA–UC regulations. Based on that review, the DOL concluded that "the BAA–UC experiment is poor policy and is a misapplication of federal UC law relating to the requirement that UC recipients be 'able and available' for work." 67 Fed. Reg. at 72,122. The period for written comments closed on February 3, 2003. It would appear likely that the BAA–UC experiment has come to an end.

IV. EFFECT OF PAID LEAVE ON FMLA PROCEDURAL REQUIREMENTS

This section will address the impact of an employee's receipt of paid leave benefits, whether by the employee's own election or employer requirement, on FMLA procedural requirements.

A. TITLE I, THE CAA AND THE PEOAA

1. Paid Leave Substitution

The substitution of paid leave for unpaid leave may lessen the burden of meeting FMLA procedural requirements regarding notice and certification. Because of this, employers need to think carefully before requiring an employee to substitute paid leave for unpaid FMLA leave as they may, for example, be relieving the employee from responsibilities to provide medical certification that the employer would rather retain. Paid leave substitution will never result in an increase in the difficulty of meeting the notice and certification requirements of the FMLA.

a. Less Stringent Paid Leave Procedural Requirements

When an employee elects, or an employer requires, substitution of paid leave (of any type) for unpaid FMLA leave under circumstances permitted by the FMLA regulations, and the employer's notice and certification requirements for taking the substituted paid leave are less stringent than the requirements of the FMLA, only the less stringent requirements may be imposed. 29 CFR 825.207(h); S. Res. 242, Cong. Rec. S3959, S3966 (April 23, 1996); 29 CFR 825.207(h). As an exception to this rule, when accrued paid vacation or personal leave is substituted for unpaid FMLA leave for a serious health condition within the meaning of the FMLA, an employee may be required to comply with any less stringent medical certification requirements of the employer's sick leave program. 29 CFR 825.207(h); S. Res. 242, Cong. Rec. S3959, S3966 (April 23, 1996); 29 CFR 825.207(h). An employee who complies with an employer's less stringent leave plan requirements in such cases may not have leave for an FMLA purpose delayed or denied on the grounds that the employee has not complied with the stricter requirements of the FMLA. 29 CFR 825.207(h); S. Res. 242, Cong. Rec. S3959, S3966 (April 23, 1996); 29 CFR 825.207(h). [An employee's notice obligations are addressed more fully in Chapter 8, "Notice Requirements."]

Initially, it must be noted that the regulations fail to give guidance on how to judge whether an employer's paid leave procedural requirements (e.g. notice and certification) are less stringent than those of the FMLA. The judgment could be made any number of ways. For example, the judgment could be made based on a comparison of a particular FMLA requirement against a specific employer paid leave notice or certification requirement, or the absence thereof, at issue. Although by no means clear, this would appear to be the method of comparison intended. See 29 CFR 825.302(g) (for example, if an employee or employer elects to substitute paid vacation leave for unpaid FMLA leave, and the employer's paid vacation leave plan imposes no prior notification requirements for taking such vacation leave, no advance notice may be required for the FMLA taken in these circumstances).

Alternatively, the judgment could be based on comparing the employer's paid leave notice and procedural requirements against the FMLA requirements as a whole. In this scenario, as long as any employer paid leave notice or certification requirement was less stringent than any comparable FMLA procedural requirement, the standard would arguably be met. It would not be necessary for the particular certification or notice provision at issue to be less stringent for 29 CFR 825.207. This interpretation is of little benefit to employees as they would always enjoy the benefits of the less stringent substituted paid leave standard at issue. Employers, however, might find this a useful interpretation.

As a consequence of the above-identified rules, the impact of paid leave substitution on FMLA notice and certification requirements is something of a mixed bag for employees and employers. On the one hand, employers who have not stiffened their paid leave notice and medical certification provisions may think they are being tough by requiring an employee to substitute paid annual leave for FMLA leave, only to discover that they have substantially degraded their ability to get useful medical documentation to support that leave. In that case, the employer would only be able to require that the employee satisfy the less stringent medical certification requirements for sick leave. If the employer's sick leave documentation requirements did not, for example, include a process for obtaining a second or third medical opinion like that under the FMLA, a good argument could be made that the employer is precluded from challenging the flimsy documentation provided. When faced with an employee requesting essentially indefinite intermittent FMLA leave with dubious medical documentation (e.g. a general practitioner certifying a psychiatric claim), employers will want to have every option available to challenge that leave.

Employers should carefully scrutinize their existing paid leave notice and certification requirements so that they maximize their right to require notice and medical documentation similar to that provided under Title I of the FMLA. In order to avoid discrimination claims, policy changes must apply to all employees. That is, the paid leave notice and documentation policy cannot be aimed only at those who take paid leave in conjunction with unpaid FMLA leave, as that would be discriminatory.

In *Solovey v. Wyoming Valley Health Care System*, 396 F. Supp. 2d 534, 537-38 (M.D. Pa. Oct. 13, 2005), the court found that the employer's two week notification policy in order to use accrued paid vacation time violated the FMLA because it diminished the employee's right to use paid vacation time when the employee's need to use that time is not foreseeable. In so holding, the court relied on the language in 29 CFR 825.207(e), that "no limitation" may be placed by the employer on substitution of paid vacation time which an employee opts to substitute for qualified FMLA leave. In contrast, the court noted that an employee who substitutes accrued medical or sick leave must meet the employer's usual requirements for use of that leave. Because that provision did not reference vacation leave, the court stated that it took "no limitations" to mean just that. On the other hand, the paid leave substitution provisions may also be interpreted in a way that relieves employers from onerous FMLA procedural requirements as well. A strict reading of 29 CFR 825.207(h) reveals that it is not, as written, limited to employees. Rather, by its terms the regulation provides that if paid leave is substituted for unpaid FMLA by election of either the employee or employer, only the employer's less stringent notice and certification requirements apply. Since FMLA notice and certification requirements apply to both employees and employers, it would appear that the election to substitute paid leave for unpaid FMLA leave could lighten the notice burden on employers.

For example, under Title I, the CAA, and the PEOAA, an employer is required to provide an employee with written notice detailing the specific expectations and obligations of the employee and explain any consequences of a failure to meet these obligations. 29 CFR 825.301(b)(1); S. Res. 242, Cong. Rec. S3959, S397 (April 23, 1996); 29 CFR 825.301(b)(1). In the event an employer fails to provide the written notice to an employee as required, an employer is prohibited from taking any action against the employee for failure to comply with any of the many provisions required to be set forth in the written notice. 29 CFR 825.301(f); S. Res. 242, Cong. Rec. S3959, S3971 (April 23, 1996); 29 CFR 825.301(f). Given the broad scope of information that is required to be in the employer's written notice, this is a fairly steep penalty.

Where paid leave is substituted for unpaid leave, however, only the less stringent notice and certification requirements of the employer's paid leave policy may be imposed. Absent any language in the implementing regulations suggesting that the imposition of the less stringent employer procedural requirements is limited to employees, it would appear that an employer could relieve itself from having to meet the rigorous FMLA notice requirements by simply not including those as part of the paid leave policy at issue. Potentially, an employer could craft paid leave notice and certification provisions that were at least as stringent as those of the FMLA regarding employee obligations, but considerably less stringent than what the FMLA requires of employers.

Candidly, this is a somewhat literal and, perhaps, aggressive reading of 29 CFR 825.207(h). The tone of the comments contained in the preamble suggests that DOL may have meant to lighten the burden of meeting the notice and certification requirements of employees. *See* 60 Fed. Reg. 2180, 2205–06 (1995), Preamble to 29 CFR 825.207. On the other hand, if this is what the drafters of the regulation meant, they should have simply stated as such.

b. More Stringent Paid Leave Procedural Requirements

The FMLA does not prohibit an employer from imposing notice or certification requirements for paid leave that meet or exceed the procedural requirements of the FMLA. Again, the FMLA requires an employer to grant an eligible employee unpaid leave, provided all of the requirements are met. The FMLA does not require that an employer provide any paid leave for reasons that might also meet one of the conditions covered by the FMLA. The provision of paid leave is completely discretionary with the employer. Of course, an employer could not manipulate its paid and unpaid leave policies so as to discriminate against employees on FMLA leave by treating them less favorably than employees under similar circumstances who have elected not to take FMLA leave.

Where the paid leave policy of an employer has more stringent notice and certification requirements than those required by the FMLA, an employee who wishes to receive pay for the FMLA absence must meet those more stringent requirements. If the employee does not meet the more stringent requirements to receive pay pursuant to the employer's paid leave policy, as long as the employee meets all of the requirements to perfect his claim for FMLA leave (including the FMLA's employee notice and certification requirements), the employee is entitled to unpaid FMLA leave for the absence.

Note that where paid leave is substituted for unpaid FMLA leave, if the employer's notice and certification requirements are less strict than the FMLA's comparable requirements, the FMLA's requirements drop down to the level of the less strict employer requirements. The opposite, however, is not true. Where the employer's paid leave notice and certification requirements exceed those of the FMLA, the FMLA's procedural requirements do not increase to meet the substituted procedural requirements of the employer. Rather, the FMLA's requirements remain the same. As long as the employee meets the FMLA's notice and certification requirements, all things being equal, the employee is entitled to unpaid FMLA leave. To be paid, the employee would have to meet the more stringent employer paid leave requirements.

B. TITLE II

Unlike under Title I, the CAA, and the PEOAA, the substitution of paid leave for unpaid FMLA leave under Title II has no impact on the notice and certification requirements of the FMLA. Specifically, Title II's notice and certification requirements are not lowered to meet an employer's less stringent paid leave notice and certification requirements. Rather, the statute and implementing regulations clearly provide that in order for an employee to be entitled to substituted paid leave, the employee must meet all of the requirements for that paid leave. *See* 5 USC 6382(b)(1); 5 CFR 630.1205(b)(1)–(3). Whether those paid leave requirements are less or more stringent than those of Title II of the FMLA is not mentioned as being relevant to the inquiry.

As a result, under Title II an employer determines whether an employee has met the notice and certification requirements of the FMLA by reference to Title II's standards on those issues only. The notice and certification standards for paid leave are not relevant to the inquiry of Title II coverage. Rather, the procedural standards for paid leave are only relevant in determining whether the employee may be paid for the absence that is also covered by the FMLA. This is very different from how Title II, the CAA, and the PEOAA treat the interaction of paid leave with unpaid FMLA leave for purposes of meeting the FMLA's notice and certification requirements.

V. MIXED FMLA RESPONSIBILITIES AND PAID LEAVE SUBSTITUTION

The workforce of virtually all federal employers consist of a mixture of FMLA coverage. Many Title 5 federal agencies contain full-time employees covered by Title II of the Act, as well as temporary and part-time employees who are covered by Title I of the FMLA. To avoid inadvertent violations of the FMLA, federal employers need to know and apply the correct FMLA requirements to each individual who may be requesting FMLA leave. Because of the differences in the four federal sector FMLA laws, an employer that simply applies one FMLA law across the board to all employees runs the considerable risk of violating that person's rights, and incurring liability as a result.

Differences in the rules regarding paid leave substitution is a prime area where a lack of care on the part of an employer can result in liability for violations of the FMLA laws. For example, take a typical Title 5 employer whose workforce is mainly covered by Title II of the Act. The employer, however, like most, hires some part-time and temporary help along the way. Assume that these part-time employees are covered by Title I of the FMLA and are otherwise eligible for FMLA leave. Seasonal firefighters are a good example of a short-term workforce that tends to come back year after year and, therefore, would meet the Title I eligibility requirements.

For paid leave substitution under Title II, an eligible employee has to separately meet the requirements for the paid annual or sick leave, and the requirements for FMLA leave, including procedural requirements such as notice and documentation. A Title I employee, on the other hand, may not have to separately meet the requirements of both the FMLA and the available paid leave. Regarding procedural requirements, if the paid leave requirements are less demanding than those of the FMLA, only the lesser paid leave requirements apply.

Assume a Title 5 employer is not aware of its differing FMLA responsibilities. This employer would then simply apply the Title II rules to its entire workforce. All employees of this employer are, therefore, required to separately meet the procedural requirements for paid leave and for unpaid FMLA leave. In terms of the majority of Title II employees in its workforce, the employer is behaving legally. If, however, the notice or other procedural requirements for paid leave are less stringent than those for FMLA leave (typically, this occurs for annual leave), the employer will violate the rights of Title I employees if it requires the employee to meet the more burdensome procedural requirements of the FMLA. Again, this is because Title I requires employers to apply any less stringent procedural requirements where paid leave is substituted for unpaid FMLA leave.

A Title 5 employer that violates the rights of a Title I employee is subject to the remedies under Title I of the Act. That may mean spending the time and money to defend a federal lawsuit, the payment of back wages or other out-of-pocket expenses, and legal fees, which can quickly add up. More importantly, in addition to the employer, Title I allows suits against individual managers and supervisors who interfere with an employee's FMLA rights.

CHAPTER 12
MAINTENANCE OF BENEFITS

I. OVERVIEW

The FMLA provides certain protections to eligible employees who take FMLA leave. These protections include a prohibition on the loss of any benefits an employee has accrued before FMLA leave commences, and an employee's right to retain accrued benefits on his or her return from FMLA leave. They also include the right to maintain certain health benefits during the pendency of their FMLA leave of absence.

Section II, "Retention of Accrued Employment Benefits", of this chapter discusses the rules regarding the retention of accrued benefits during FMLA leave. The "Maintenance of Health Benefits" is discussed in Section III. Section IV addresses, "Employee Payment of Health Benefit Premiums While on FMLA Leave." The "Consequences of Employee Failure to Make Timely Health Benefit Plan Premium Payments" are discussed in Section V. The recovery of employee benefit premiums paid by the employer during the pendency of FMLA leave is discussed in Section VI, "Employee Recovery of Costs of Maintaining Health Care Coverage." Finally, the maintenance of employee benefits in agencies with mixed FMLA responsibilities is addressed in Section VII, "Mixed Responsibilities of Employing Agencies to Maintain Employment Benefits During FMLA Leave", of this chapter.

II. RETENTION OF ACCRUED EMPLOYMENT BENEFITS

A. GENERAL RULE

The right to retain accrued employment benefits while on FMLA leave is universally recognized in all federal–sector FMLA laws, with nearly identical language.

1. Title II

Title II prohibits the loss of any employment benefit accrued prior to the date when FMLA leave commenced. 5 USC 6384(b); 5 CFR 630.1208(c). Rather, an eligible employee who takes FMLA leave has the right, upon return from such leave, to be restored to the same or an equivalent position with equivalent benefits, pay, status, and other terms and conditions of employment. 5 USC 6384(a); 5 CFR 630.1208(a)(2), (4). [For a discussion of an employee's rights on return from FMLA leave, see Chapter 13, "Return to Work From Leave."]

2. Title I

The taking of FMLA leave shall not result in the loss of any employment benefit accrued prior to the date on which leave commenced. 29 USC 2614(a)(2); 29 CFR 825.215(d)(3). On his or her return from FMLA leave, an eligible employee has the right to be restored to the same or an equivalent position with equivalent benefits, pay, status, and other terms and conditions of employment. 29 USC 2614(a)(1); 29 CFR 825.215(d)(1). See DOL WH FMLA Advisory Opinion No. 25 (January 10, 1994).

3. CAA

By incorporation of § 104 of Title I of the FMLA, 29 USC 2614, the CAA prohibits the loss of any employment benefits accrued prior to the date on which leave commences as a consequence of an employee taking FMLA leave. 2 USC 1312(a)(1); S. Res. 242, Cong. Rec. S3959, S3966 (April 23, 1996); 29 CFR 825.215(d)(2). On return from FMLA leave, an employee is entitled to be restored to the same or an equivalent position with equivalent benefits, pay, status, and other terms and conditions of employment. 2 USC 1312(a)(1); S. Res. 242, Cong. Rec. S3959, S3966 (April 23, 1996); 29 CFR 825.215(d)(1).

4. PEOAA

By incorporation of § 104 of Title I of the FMLA, 29 USC 2614, the CAA prohibits the loss of any employment benefits accrued prior to the date on which leave commences as a consequence of an employee taking FMLA leave. 3 USC 412(A)(1). Similarly, on his or her return from FMLA leave, an employee is entitled to be restored to the same or an equivalent position with equivalent benefits, pay, status, and other terms and conditions of employment. 3 USC 412(a)(1).

B. DEFINITIONS

To better understand this section, common terms will be defined. Differences, if any, between the federal sector FMLA laws will be noted in each definition.

1. Employment Benefits

a. Title I, the CAA, and the PEOAA

The term "employment benefits" is similarly defined in Title I and, by incorporation, the CAA and the PEOAA. *See* 29 USC 2611(5) (Title I); 2 USC 1312(a)(1) (incorporating Title I definitions into CAA); 3 USC 412(a)(1) (incorporating Title I definitions into PEOAA).

Employment benefits means all benefits provided or made available to employees by an employer, including group life insurance, health insurance, disability insurance, sick leave, annual leave, educational benefits, and pensions, regardless of whether such benefits are provided by a practice or written policy of an employer or through an "employee benefit plan," as defined in section 3(3) of the Employee Retirement Income Security Act of 1974 (29 USC 1002(3)). 29 USC 2611(5) (Title I); 2 USC 1312(a)(1); 3 USC 412(a)(1).

The term "employment benefits" is also defined in the regulations implementing Title I, the CAA, and the PEOAA. Essentially, the implementing regulations repeat the statutory definition. *See* 29 CFR 825.215(d) (defining benefits), 29 CFR 825.800 (employment benefits defined); S. Res. 242, Cong. Rec. S3959, S3966, S3977 (April 23, 1996); 29 CFR 825.215(d) (defining benefits); 29 CFR 825.800 (defining employment benefits).

The DOL broadly interprets employment benefits to include all benefits, including attendance, safety, or production bonuses to which the employee is entitled. DOL WH FMLA Advisory Opinion No. 93 (February 6, 1994) (despite its discretionary nature, paid administrative leave for physical fitness is a benefit within meaning of the FMLA); DOL WH FMLA Advisory Opinion No. 79 (Feb. 23, 1996) (safety incentive bonus); DOL WH FMLA Advisory Opinion No. 56 (March 28, 1995) (weekly bonus for attendance); DOL WH FMLA Advisory Opinion No. 31 (March 21, 1994) (bonuses premised on perfect attendance or perfect safety held to be "employment benefits" within the meaning of FMLA).

However, the regulations add to the statutory definition by identifying what is not considered an employment benefit. According to the regulations, non-employment-related obligations paid by employees through voluntary deductions such as supplemental insurance are not included in the term "employment benefits," citing 29 CFR 825.209(a). 29 CFR 825.800 (defining employment benefits); S. Res. 242, Cong. Rec. S3959, S3966, S3977 (April 23, 1996); 29 CFR 825.800 (defining employment benefits); *see* DOL WH FMLA Advisory Opinion No. 6 (Oct. 1, 1993) (disability insurance not a health benefit that an employer must maintain during FMLA leave); *see also Goodman v. Town of Farmington Bd. of Ed.*, No. 3:01cv1609 (CFD), 2005 U.S. Dist. LEXIS 33734, at *9 & n.3 (D. Conn. Dec. 6, 2005) (employer not required to maintain an employee's life insurance coverage during FMLA leave).

b. Title II

Although it uses the term, Title II does not specifically define employment benefits in either the statute or the implementing regulations. However, at several points, the regulations give examples of what constitutes employment benefits as: "e.g., life insurance, health benefits, retirement coverage, and leave accrual." *See* 5 CFR 630.1204(d)(3); 630.1208(b)(4).

According to my handy Fifteenth Edition of the Blue Book, the signal *e.g.* indicates that the cited authority states the proposition; other authorities also state the proposition, but citation to them would not be helpful or useful. That is, *e.g.*

means you are being given some, but not necessarily all, examples of the stated proposition (in this case, the meaning of employment benefits). OPM should seriously consider defining this key term so that covered employees and employing agencies know what constitutes an employment benefit for purposes of determining what benefits are accrued at the time of leave commencement, as well as when the employee returns to work from FMLA leave. Leaving the term undefined simply invites unnecessary litigation.

2. Accrued Benefits

The term "accrued" is not defined in any of the federal sector FMLA statutes or implementing regulations. By implication, the term appears to mean the level of benefits earned as of the time of leave commencement. *See* 29 CFR 825.215(d)(1) ("At the end of an employee's FMLA leave, benefits must be resumed in the same manner and at the same levels as provided when the leave began."); 5 CFR 630.1208(c); S. Res. 242, Cong. Rec. S3959, S3966 (April 23, 1996); 29 CFR 825.215(d)(1). By referencing the level of employment benefits, the term "accrued" does not appear to require that the employee have an immediate right to exercise the employment benefit. That is, an employee is allowed to bank partial credit toward earned benefits. *See* DOL WH FMLA Advisory Opinion No. 56 (Mar. 28, 1995) (employer's policy of giving pro-rata share of attendance-based bonus to employee who took FMLA leave was permissible because policy recognized partial time accrued toward bonus before FMLA leave commenced); DOL WH FMLA Advisory Opinion No. 25 (Jan. 10, 1994) (employee must receive partial credit for pre-existing condition for the amount of time satisfied prior to starting leave as accrued benefit).

For example, Kirk has worked on and off for the federal government for ten years. Under the prevailing annual leave formula, Kirk earns approximately one hour of annual leave for every 13 hours of work. If Kirk worked ten hours, he would not accumulate an hour of annual leave. He would be three hours shy. If Kirk took FMLA leave, he would be credited the ten hours he worked toward the one hour of annual leave. Stated differently, Kirk would not lose the ten hours he had worked toward accruing one hour of annual leave because he took FMLA leave, even though he had not perfected his right to the one hour of annual leave at the time his FMLA leave commenced.

3. Leave Commencement

Under all of the federal FMLA statutes, the prohibition against the loss of any accrued employment benefits is determined as of the commencement of FMLA leave. The terms "leave" and "commenced" are not defined by any of the federal sector FMLA statutes and regulations. As set forth more fully in Chapter 5, "Employee Eligibility for Leave," the failure to define these key terms has resulted in problems with the application of the FMLA. Knowing when FMLA leave "commences" would appear to be a prerequisite to accurately determining what employment benefits have accrued as of leave commencement.

A problem in this area arises when an employee takes more than one FMLA-covered absence related to the same underlying condition. As set forth more fully in Chapter 10, "Leave Amount and Scheduling," an eligible employee may take FMLA leave in any of three ways: (1) in one continuous block of time; (2) intermittently, e.g., more than one absence for the same underlying covered condition; and (3) on a reduced leave schedule, which, again, is more than one absence for the same underlying covered condition. It is clear that when leave is taken in a single block of time, FMLA leave commences when the absence begins. The beginning of this single absence fixes the time when accrued employment benefits are determined.

Problems also arise when FMLA is used intermittently or on a reduced leave schedule related to the same underlying covered condition. With multiple, related absences the question of when FMLA leave commence arises. Is each related absence treated separately for purposes of determining whether leave has commenced? Alternatively, should only the first in the series of related absences be regarded as the FMLA leave commencement date? The base issue here is whether leave is synonymous with absence or a series of related absences.

The DOL addressed the issue in the context of employee eligibility under Title I. *See* DOL WH FMLA Advisory Opinion No. 112 (Sept. 11, 2000). According to the DOL:

> The issue then is what the term "leave" means—whether it encompasses all leave for the same serious health condition, or whether each intermittent leave absence for the same condition is considered separate leave under the Act and regulations.

As with the accrual of employment benefits, the 1,250 work hours requirement for employee eligibility for FMLA leave is determined at leave commencement. See 29 CFR 825.110(a)(2). Obviously, to determine when leave commences it is necessary to know what constitutes leave.

The DOL concluded, based on its review of the legislative history of Title I, that leave encompasses all leave for the same serious health condition. In so finding, the DOL agreed with the analysis and conclusion of the district court in *Barron v. Runyon*, 11 F. Supp. 2d 676 (E.D. Va. 1998). Like the DOL, the court in *Barron* concluded that, in the context of multiple absences for the same underlying covered condition, leave commenced as of the first absence for the same underlying condition during each 12–month leave year.

Applying the DOL–approved definition of leave to the determination of what employment benefits have accrued to the employee taking intermittent or reduced schedule FMLA leave as of leave commencement, yields the following unsatisfactory results:

- Assume an employee is diagnosed with an FMLA–qualifying chronic condition, such as Multiple Sclerosis (MS), that results in the employee needing intermittent leave due to the episodic nature of the condition. Assume further that the agency uses the calendar year as the 12–month FMLA leave year. The employee takes intermittent leave due to the MS on January 1–3, and again on December 29–30 of the same year. Otherwise, the employee worked a full schedule. Since, according to the DOL, the "leave" commenced on January 1, the only benefits that accrued to the employee are those that were available to the employee on that day. The employee would not be entitled to any benefits that accrued between his or her initial return from leave on January 4 and the second intermittent absence on December 29 because, under the DOL fiction, all intermittent/reduced leave schedule FMLA leave is considered a single leave period that only ends when the employee returns to work on December 31, when FMLA leave is no longer needed.

- Assume the same facts as in the first example and, in addition, assume that the employee requests FMLA leave for up to six weeks for another serious health condition that requires major surgery and a subsequent period of recovery (e.g., a hysterectomy). In this example, FMLA leave begins on May 1 of the same leave year. The introduction of a second FMLA leave absence for a different covered condition, according to the DOL, creates a second point in time (May 1) when FMLA leave commences. In this scenario, the employee would be credited with all employment benefits accrued up to May 1. Now, with the introduction of a second use of FMLA leave, the employee receives credit for employment benefits accrued up to May 1. With only one illness, the employee only receives credit for accrued benefits as of January 1.

- Assume the same facts as in the second example except, at the time of the second and different FMLA–qualifying circumstance, the employee does not meet the 1,250–hour eligibility test. In this situation, the employee would not be entitled to FMLA leave for that (i.e. second) reason. Because no FMLA leave commenced on May 1, the employee is only entitled to employment benefits that accrued as of January 1, the first day of his or her first FMLA absence.

It is assumed that the above is not what the DOL meant when it tied the determination of what employment benefits have accrued to FMLA leave commencement. Rather, it is assumed that, in this instance, the drafters of the statute and the regulations equated leave with the commencement of every FMLA absence. In that way, accrued benefits accumulate between related as well as unrelated FMLA absences.

The base problem is the lack of a coherent definition of leave, a rather surprising fact given that the sum and substance of the FMLA is about that very term. It also arises from the fact that the implementing regulations appear to use leave as synonymous with absence in some circumstances (such as here, I would contend), and in other situations the DOL uses leave as meaning a series of related absences, such as for employee eligibility.

The ability of DOL, OPM and the other FMLA regulatory bodies to fix this issue by changing the regulations is somewhat circumscribed in that the determination of eligibility and employment benefit accrual at leave commencement is assigned by statute. As DOL started down this road with the issuance of DOL WH FMLA Advisory Opinion No. 112 (Sept. 11, 2000), it would appear incumbent on DOL to fix the problem created. Absent credible support in the legislative record, it does not appear that the answer lies in defining leave differently for purposes of eligibility and employment benefit accrual, to name just two of many instances where the term "leave" is used in the implementing regulations.

As for the other FMLA regulatory agencies, they should consider distancing themselves from the DOL position while thinking through this matter. The DOL, OPM, and the other federal sector FMLA regulatory agencies should get together and come up with a uniform solution to the leave definition problem.

Employing agencies should, nevertheless, continue to credit employees with employment benefits they earn pursuant to agency policy and practice. The FMLA implementing regulations recognize that employers must comply with an agency employment benefit program, plan, or collective bargaining agreement that provides greater FMLA leave entitlements to employees than those provided by the Act. 29 CFR 700(a), (c) (Title I); 5 CFR 630. 1210(a);); S. Res. 242, Cong. Rec. S3959, S3966 (April 23, 1996); 29 CFR 825.700(a)–(b) (CAA). If permitted by agency paid or unpaid leave policies, the accrual of employment benefits during the period of an employee's intermittent or reduced leave schedule FMLA leave would be such a greater benefit.

C. ACCRUAL OF SENIORITY AND EMPLOYMENT BENEFITS DURING FMLA LEAVE

1. Title I, the CAA, and the PEOAA

The FMLA does not require the accrual of any seniority or employment benefits during any period of FMLA leave. 29 USC 2614(a)(3)(A). See DOL WH FMLA Advisory Opinion No. 56 (March 28, 1995); DOL WH FMLA Advisory Opinion No. 54 (February 22, 1995); DOL WH FMLA Advisory Opinion No. 24 (January 6, 1994). The implementing regulations have modified the statutory requirement to limit the prohibition to any period of *unpaid* FMLA leave. 29 CFR 825.215(d)(2), (5); S. Res. 242, Cong. Rec. S3959, S3966 (April 23, 1996); 29 CFR 825.215(d)(2). If, however, employees on paid or unpaid leave were entitled to accrue seniority or employment benefits as a matter of agency policy, then employees on FMLA leave would also be so entitled. 29 CFR 700(a), (c); S. Res. 242, Cong. Rec. S3959, S3966 (April 23, 1996); 29 CFR 825.700(a)–(b). That is, an employee's entitlement to the accrual of seniority or employment benefits during FMLA leave, whether paid or unpaid, will be strictly based upon the employer's established policies of accruing seniority or employment benefits during any absence where paid or unpaid leave applies. DOL WH FMLA Advisory Opinion No. 109 (Sept. 8, 2000) (citing 29 USC 2614(3) and 29 CFR 825.215(d)(2) and (5)). To do otherwise would be considered a discriminatory action by the employer against the employee on FMLA leave, which is prohibited by 29 CFR 825.220(c). DOL WH FMLA Advisory Opinion No. 42, No. 11 (Aug. 23, 1994); DOL WH FMLA Advisory Opinion No. 24 (Jan. 6, 1994).

The DOL illustrates the above rules, DOL WH FMLA Advisory Opinion No. 109 (Sept. 8, 2000), with the following examples:

- If the employer's established leave policies do not permit the accrual of seniority during an unpaid leave of absence, this same policy would apply to unpaid leave covered by the FMLA. The employer in the same example would be in compliance so long as the returning employee is restored to the same level of seniority that the employee accrued prior to the commencement of FMLA leave.

- If the employer's established leave policies provide for the accrual of seniority during an absence where paid leave benefits have been applied, then the employer must permit, consistent with its policies, the accrual of seniority during the portion of FMLA leave where paid leave benefits (i.e. vacation, personal, sick/medical leave, or family) are substituted for unpaid FMLA leave.

- If the employer's established policies do not permit the accrual of seniority during an absence covered by a state workers' compensation plan, nothing in the FMLA will require the employer to modify its policies to permit the accrual of seniority during the workers' compensation absence that also qualifies for and is designated as FMLA leave. This position would also apply where an employee on FMLA leave receives concurrently paid disability leave benefits and the accrual of seniority under the employer's established policies is not permitted.

The DOL issued a number of advisory opinions interpreting the above for Title I. Because the CAA and the PEOAA incorporate § 104, 29 USC 2614(a)(3)(A), The DOL's advisory opinions on this point bear some consideration when interpreting the substantively identical provisions of the CAA and the PEOAA.

In *Petty v. Carolina Biological Supply and Med. Life Ins*. Co., No. 1:05CV00954, 2006 U.S. Dist. LEXIS 63615, at *20-21 (M.D. N.C. Sept. 5, 2006), the court found that life insurance was a benefit the employee accrued prior to taking FMLA leave. If the employer's policy permitted an employee to maintain life insurance while they were on leave, life insurance coverage had to be maintained during FMLA leave. If, however, the employer's policy revoked coverage from employees on leave, then the employer was not required to maintain life insurance coverage during FMLA leave.

Absent more generous employer–unpaid leave policies, the DOL has opined that vacation time, sick leave, or longevity for pay purposes do not accumulate during a period of unpaid FMLA leave. See DOL WH FMLA Advisory Opinion No. 109 (Sept. 8, 2000); DOL WH FMLA Advisory Opinion No. 102 (Mar. 26, 1999) (employer plan that denied employees who did not work a minimum number of days from receiving vacation pay did not violate the FMLA by excluding time spent on FMLA leave); DOL WH FMLA Advisory Opinion No. 42, No. 11 (Aug. 23, 1994) (vacation leave, sick leave, longevity); DOL WH FMLA Advisory Opinion No. 24 (Jan. 6, 1994) (sick leave); accord Henry v. Fulton County Bd. of Ed., No. 1:05-CV-2008-TWT, 2006 U.S. Dist. LEXIS 74062, at *8 & n.2 (N.D. Ga. Oct. 10, 2006), aff'd, 2007 U.S. App. LEXIS 15874 (11th Cir. July 3, 2007) (sick days do not accrue during FMLA leave). Time on FMLA leave generally does not count toward pension plan credit. DOL WH FMLA Advisory Opinion No. 54 (Feb. 22, 1995). An employer is not required to continue paying a cash benefit in lieu of health and welfare benefits during any period of unpaid FMLA leave. DOL WH FMLA Advisory Opinion No. 1 (June 15, 1993) (vacation pay).

2. Title II

Like Title I, Title II does not mandate the accrual of any employment benefits during any period of FMLA leave. 5 USC 6384(c)(1); 5 CFR 630.1208(d)(1). Unlike Title I, however, Title II does not automatically preclude the accumulation of seniority during the employee's FMLA absence. Neither the OPM regulations nor the preamble to those regulations explain whether the absence of seniority indicates that seniority continues to accumulate during the pendency of an employee's FMLA absence, whether paid or unpaid. Unless seniority is viewed as an "employment benefit" (an undefined term in Title II), it would appear that Title II requires the accumulation of seniority while the employee is on FMLA leave.

Regarding "employment benefits," the absence of a definition of the term under Title II makes it somewhat difficult for an employing agency to determine what accrues and what does not accrue. The implementing regulations cite life insurance, health benefits, retirement coverage, and leave accrual as examples of employment benefits. 5 CFR 630.1208(b)(4). A more comprehensive definition of employment benefits would be helpful to employing agencies.

D.   GREATER BENEFITS PROTECTION

All of the federal FMLA laws permit employing agencies to provide more generous employment benefits than the legal minimum.

Employers are both permitted to provide, and required to abide by, any employment benefit program that provides more generous family or medical leave rights of employees than the rights established by the FMLA. 29 CFR 825.700(a) (Title I); 5 CFR 630.120(a) (Title II); S. Res. 242, Cong. Rec. S3959, S3966 (April 23, 1996); 29 CFR 825.700(a); see DOL WH FMLA Advisory Opinion No. 56 (March 38, 1995) (employer policy may permit accrual of benefits beyond the minimum requirements of FMLA). Conversely, the rights established by the FMLA may not be diminished by any employment benefit program or plan, including the provisions of a collective bargaining agreement. 29 CFR 825.700(a); 5 CFR 630.1210b); S. Res. 242, Cong. Rec. S3959, S3966 (April 23, 1996); 29 CFR 825.700(a).

If an employer provides greater unpaid FMLA leave rights than are afforded by the FMLA, the employer is not required to extend additional rights afforded by the FMLA, such as maintenance of health benefits. 29 CFR 825.700(a); S. Res. 242, Cong. Rec. S3959, S3966 (April 23, 1996); 29 CFR 825.700(a); see Miller v. Personal–Touch of Virginia, Inc., 342 F. Supp. 2d 499, 2004 U.S. Dist. LEXIS 22583, at *18 (E.D. Va. 2004), aff'd, 2005 U.S. App. LEXIS 24240 (4th Cir. 2005); Nusbaum v. CB Richard Ellis, Inc., 171 F. Supp. 2d 377, 383 (D.N.J. 2001); Hite v. Biomet, Inc., 53 F. Supp. 2d 1013, 1018 (N.D. Ind. 1999).

Title II does not contain similar language.

Employers are also permitted to provide leave policies that are more generous than those provided under the FMLA. 29 CFR 825.700(b); 5 CFR 630.1210(c); S. Res. 242, Cong. Rec. S3959, S3966 (April 23, 1996); 29 CFR 825.700(b). Under Title II, an agency's adoption of more generous leave policies may not provide entitlement to paid time off in an amount greater than that otherwise authorized by law or provide sick leave in any situation in which sick leave would not normally be allowed by law or regulation. 5 CFR 630.1210(c). Neither Title I, the CAA, nor the PEOAA contain this limitation.

III. MAINTENANCE OF HEALTH BENEFITS

A. HEALTH PLANS DEFINED

Three different types of health plans are addressed in the federal sector FMLA regulations governing maintenance of health plans during the period an eligible employee is on FMLA leave.

1. Group Health Plan

Title I and the CAA define "group health plan" the same. Specifically, a group health plan is defined by reference to the Internal Revenue Code of 1986, 26 USC 5000(b)(1). 29 CFR 825.209(a), 825.800; S. Res. 242, Cong. Rec. S3959, S3967 (April 23, 1996); 29 CFR 825.209(a), 825.800. It means a plan of, or contributed to by, an employer (including a self-insured plan) to provide health care (directly or otherwise) to the employer's employees, former employees, or the families of such employees or former employees. 26 USC 5000(b)(1); 29 CFR 825.800 (group health plan defined); S. Res. 242, Cong. Rec. S3959, S3977 (April 23, 1996); 29 CFR 825.800 (same).

The regulations at 29 CFR 825.800 (group health plan defined); S. Res. 242, Cong. Rec. S3959, S3977 (April 23, 1996); 29 CFR 825.800, go on to identify what is not a group health plan:

> For purposes of the FMLA the term "group health plan" shall not include an insurance program providing health coverage under which employees purchase individual policies from insurers provided that:
>
> (1) No contributions are made by the employer;
>
> (2) Participation in the program is completely voluntary for employees;
>
> (3) The sole functions of the employer with respect to the program are, without endorsing the program, to permit the insurer to publicize the program to employees, to collect premiums through payroll deductions and to remit them to the insurer;
>
> (4) the employer receives no consideration in the form of cash or otherwise in connection with the program, other than reasonable compensation, excluding profit, for administrative services actually rendered in connection with payroll deduction; and
>
> (5) The premium charged with respect to such coverage does not increase in the event the employment relationship terminates.

Essentially, the term "group health plan" does not include non-employment-related health benefits paid directly by employees through voluntary deductions, e.g., individual life insurance or disability insurance. An employer is not responsible for maintaining or restoring these non-group health benefits for employees who take FMLA leave. *See* Preamble, 29 CFR 825.209; 825.213(b). *See* DOL WH FMLA Advisory Opinion No. 19 (Dec. 6, 1993) (employer plan allowing employees covered by insurance from another source to receive weekly cash supplement in lieu of insurance is not a group health plan that needs to be maintained during FMLA leave).

2. FEHBP

Title II and the CAA require maintenance of health benefits provided by the Federal Employees Health Benefits Program (FEHBP). FEHBP was created in 1959 by the Federal Employees Health Benefits Act, Public Law 86-382. *Nat. Assoc. of Postal Supervisors v. U.S.*, 21 Cl. Ct. 310, 314, n. 5 (Cl. Ct. 1990). The Act was passed "to bring the Government abreast of most private employers...." *Id.* At the time, comprehensive group health insurance was available in the private sector but not to federal employees. *Id.* Congress designed FEHBP to provide federal employees with a variety of health insurance options. *Id.* FEHBP is the nation's largest employer-sponsored health insurance program. 2002 Federal Personnel Guide 64 (24th ed. 2002).

OPM oversees FEHBP. *Nat. Assoc. of Postal Supervisors v. U.S.*, 21 Cl. Ct. 310, 314, n. 5 (Cl. Ct. 1990). Commercial insurance carriers and other organizations that wish to sponsor health plans for federal employees must apply to OPM. *Id.* OPM reviews the applications and decides who may enter FEHBP. *Id.* OPM's regulations governing the administration of the FEHBP are contained in 5 CFR Part 890.

Not all federal employees are entitled to participate in FEHBP. Those excluded from coverage are identified in 5 CFR 890.102(c). Those excluded from participation include a number of employees covered by Title I of the FMLA. *See* 5 CFR 890.102(c)(1) (certain employees serving temporary appointments of less than one year); 890.102(c)(2) (certain individuals whose employment is less than six months); and 890.102(c)(3) (an intermittent employee).

3. Multi-Employer Health Plan

Title I and the CAA include special health benefits maintenance rules governing multi-employer benefits plans, which will be discussed more fully in a subsequent subpart of this chapter. Title I and the CAA, 29 CFR 825.211(a), S. Res. 242, Cong. Rec. S3959, S3968 (April 23, 1996); 29 CFR 825.211(a), define a multi-employer health plan as:

> a plan to which more than one employer is required to contribute, and which is maintained pursuant to one or more collective bargaining agreements between employee organization(s) and the employers.

Again, Title II does not address multi-employer health benefit plans.

B. GENERAL RULE REQUIRING MAINTENANCE OF HEALTH BENEFITS DURING FMLA LEAVE

The continuation of health benefits while an employee is on FMLA leave is the right of all federal sector employees. Employees may, however, waive that right during an FMLA absence. While similar, the rules requiring the continuation of health care coverage are sufficiently different that they will be treated separately.

1. Title I

Under Title I there are two types of health plans specifically addressed by the regulations: (1) group health plans; and (2) multi-employer health plans.

a. Group Health Plans

During any FMLA leave, an employer must maintain the employee's coverage under any group health plan on the same conditions as coverage as though the employee was continuously employed during the entire leave period. 29 USC 2614(c); 29 CFR 825.209(a); *see Goodman et. al. v. Town of Farmington Bd. of Ed.*, No. 3:01cv1609 (CFD), 2005 U.S. Dist. LEXIS 33734, at *9 & n.3 (D. Conn. Dec. 6, 2005). This means that, if an employer normally pays a portion of an employee's group health plan premiums prior to the employee's taking FMLA leave, the employer must continue to pay the employer share of the premiums during the FMLA leave at the same rate, i.e., as if the employee continued to work instead of taking leave. DOL WH FMLA Advisory Opinion No. 23 (Dec. 28, 1993); DOL WH FMLA Advisory Opinion No. 1 (June 15, 1993). An employer that has an existing group health plan may not offer an employee an option that does not provide for maintenance of health benefits overage during any period of FMLA leave. DOL WH FMLA Advisory Opinion No. 13 (Nov. 2, 1993) (employer option to employee to maintain full medical coverage during FMLA leave or accept 50% of the cost of in lieu in the form of deferred compensation violates Act).

A few points are noteworthy. First, under Title I, covered employers, including federal agencies, are required to maintain group health benefit coverage while the employee is on FMLA leave. The rule applies to the entire federal government. 29 CFR 825.209(a) ("All employers covered by [Title I] of the FMLA, including public agencies, are subject to the Act's requirement to maintain health coverage."). However, an employee may elect not to retain group health coverage. *See* 29 CFR 825.209(e).

Second, the rule does not distinguish employees on unpaid FMLA leave from employees who have substituted paid leave for unpaid leave. In all cases, employing agencies are required to maintain the group health coverage of employees on FMLA leave.

Finally, the rule is limited to group health plans, a defined term (refer to Section III, A, 1, above).

b. Multi-Employer Health Plans

During the duration of an eligible employee's FMLA leave, group health coverage under a multi-employer plan must be maintained at the same level of coverage and benefits applicable to the employee at the time FMLA leave commenced. 29 CFR 825.211(c); S. Res. 242, Cong. Rec. S3959, S3968 (April 23, 1996); 29 CFR 825.211(c). *See* DOL WH FMLA Advisory Opinion No. 14 (Nov. 13, 1993).

An employer whose employees are provided health benefits through operation of a multi-employer plan must continue to make contributions during FMLA leave unless the employer demonstrates that the employee would not otherwise have been employed. DOL WH FMLA Advisory Opinion No. DOL WH FMLA Advisory Opinion No. 14 (Nov. 13, 1993). To maintain health benefits coverage under multi-employer health plans for employees on FMLA leave, the employer must make adequate contributions on behalf of the employee as through the employee was continuously employed for the duration of FMLA leave. DOL WH FMLA Advisory Opinion No. 30 (March 18, 1994). If the multi-employer health plan contains an explicit FMLA provision for maintaining coverage, such as through pooled contributions by all employers party to the plan, the employer must make arrangements to ensure that up to 12 weeks of coverage in any 12-month period is maintained for employees on FMLA leave. *Id*. An employee using FMLA leave cannot be required to use banked hours or pay a greater premium than the employee would have been required to pay if the employee had been continuously employed. *Id*.

How an employer ensures adequate contributions to maintain benefits coverage on behalf of employees on FMLA leave is not addressed in the regulations. *Id*. The regulations encourage plans to develop rules that would accommodate this FMLA requirement. *Id*. Translation for employing agencies: you figure it out.

c. Fraud Exception

An employee who fraudulently obtains FMLA leave from an employer is not protected by the FMLA's job protection or maintenance of health benefits provisions. 29 CFR 825.312(g); *see Chalimoniuk v. Interstate Brands Corp.*, 172 F. Supp. 2d 1055, 1058 (S.D. Ind. 2001); *Chavez v. Lawrence & Frederick, Inc.*, No. 97 C 4535, 1999 U.S. Dist. LEXIS 16361, at *9 (N.D. Ill. Oct. 12, 1999); *Salgado v. CDW Computer Centers, Inc.*, No. 97 C 1975, 1998 U.S. Dist. LEXIS 1374, at *24 (N.D. Ill. Feb. 5, 1998).

2. Title II

An employee enrolled in a health benefits plan who is placed on a leave without pay status as a result of entitlement to FMLA leave may elect to continue his or her health benefits enrollment while on FMLA leave without pay and arrange to pay the appropriate employee contributions into the Employees Health Benefits Fund. 5 USC 6386; 5 CFR 630.1209.

First, note that the continuation of health benefits during the pendency of FMLA leave is at the option of the employee. The employee could opt not to continue health benefits coverage, and the employing agency would not have to continue health coverage. Of course, if the employee does not opt out of continuation of health benefits, they must be maintained.

Note further that the option is limited to employees currently enrolled in a health plan under the Federal Employees Health Benefits Program (FEHBP). Presumably, that means that an employing agency is not required to provide health benefits coverage to employees who are not currently enrolled in the FEHBP program. The obligation is to *continue* health care coverage, not provide coverage where none exists.

Third, the option of the employee to elect not to pursue continuation of health care coverage only applies when the leave is unpaid. Neither the statute nor the regulations discuss what happens when the employee has substituted paid leave for unpaid FMLA leave. Presumably, the employing agency would continue health benefits coverage pursuant to the exiting paid leave policy selected in substitution for unpaid FMLA leave.

Finally, Title II specifically refers to health benefits plans under the Federal Employees Health Benefits Program. Title II does not mention any other health plans, such as group health or multi-employer health benefits plans.

3. CAA

The third variation on this theme is contained in the FMLA, as applied by the CAA. During any FMLA leave period, the employing office must maintain the employee's coverage under the FEHBP or any group health plan on the same conditions as coverage would have been provided if the employee had been continuously employed during the entire leave period. S. Res. 242, Cong. Rec. S3959, S3967 (April 23, 1996), 825.209(a). All employing offices are subject to the requirements of the FMLA, as made applicable by the CAA, to maintain health coverage. *Id.*

Note that the CAA is limited to employing offices, as defined in that Act. By comparison, Title I applies to the entire federal government as a public agency, and Title II applies to any federal employee who is enrolled in a FEHBP.

Second, continuation of health coverage is mandatory; an employee does not have the option not to retain coverage.

Third, two different health care coverage's are involved: FEHBP and a group health plan.

These terms are addressed immediately below.

Finally, like Title I, the CAA regulation does not distinguish between employees on unpaid FMLA leave and those who have elected to substitute paid leave for unpaid FMLA leave.

C. SCOPE OF HEALTH BENEFITS THAT MUST BE PROVIDED DURING LEAVE

The FMLA rules governing the health benefits that must be provided during an employee's leave are substantially similar, although some differences exist.

1. General Rule

a. Title I, the CAA, and the PEOAA

(1) Group Health Plans

The same group health benefits provided to an employee prior to taking FMLA leave must be maintained during FMLA leave. 29 CFR 825.209(b); S. Res. 242, Cong. Rec. S3959, S3967 (April 23, 1996); 29 CFR 825.209(b). During a period of FMLA leave, an employer must maintain coverage under any group health plan at the level and under the conditions coverage would have been provided if the employee had continued to be employed continuously during the leave. Preamble, 29 CFR 825.209; *see Goodman et. al. v. Town of Farmington Bd. of Ed.*, No. 3:01cv1609 (CFD), 2005 U.S. Dist. LEXIS 33734, at *9 & n.3 (D. Conn. Dec. 6, 2005).

For example, if family member coverage is provided to an employee, family member coverage must be maintained during the FMLA leave. 29 CFR 825.209(b); S. Res. 242, Cong. Rec. S3959, S3967 (April 23, 1996); 29 CFR 825.209(b). Similarly, benefit coverage during FMLA leave for medical care, surgical care, hospital care, dental care, eye care, mental health counseling, substance abuse treatment, etc., must be maintained during FMLA leave if provided in an employer's group health plan, including a supplement to a group health plan, whether or not provided through a flexible spending account or other component of a cafeteria plan. 29 CFR 825.209(b); S. Res. 242, Cong. Rec. S3959, S3967 (April 23, 1996); 29 CFR 825.209(b).

(2) Multi-Employer Health Plans

As with group health plans, Title I requires that an employing agency maintain during FMLA leave the same multi-employer health benefits provided to an employee prior to taking FMLA leave. 29 CFR 825.211(b); S. Res. 242, Cong. Rec. S3959, S3968 (April 23, 1996); 29 CFR 825.11(b). This regulation would appear to be in complete accord with the nearly identical provision governing group health plans. *See* 29 CFR 825.209.

b. Title II

The scope of health benefits to be maintained during the pendency of an employee's FMLA leave under Title II is less than clear. The scope could be the same, or it might be less, depending on how you read the implementing regulations and the interplay of leave without pay and the FEHBP.

In support of maintenance of the same level of benefits, the regulations provide that an employee enrolled in a health benefits plan under the FEHBP who is placed in a leave without pay status as a result of FMLA leave may elect to continue his or her health benefits enrollment. 5 CFR 630.1209. Obviously, this suggests maintenance of the *status quo*.

In support of a potentially lower level of benefits, the regulations provide, in pertinent part, that a restored employee is not entitled to any benefit other than a benefit to which the employee would have been entitled had the employee not taken leave. 5 CFR 630.1208(d)(2). The regulations continue: the "same entitlements and limitations in law and regulations that apply to the benefits of employment of an employee in a leave without pay status apply to any employee taking of FMLA leave without pay, except where different entitlements and limitations are specifically provided in this subpart." 5 CFR 630.1208(e).

The first question is whether the specific health benefits regulation set forth in 5 CFR 630.1209 constitutes a different entitlement and limitation than that contained in 5 CFR 630.1208(d) and (e). This, in turn, depends on whether the continuation of health benefits *(i.e.* at the level *before* the employee takes FMLA/leave without pay) during the pendency of an employee's FMLA absence (§ 630.1209) is at a level different than the level would have been if the employee had not taken FMLA leave, but was on leave without pay for the same period (§ 630.1208(e)). If the level is different, § 630.1209 controls, which would appear to maintain the *status quo*. If the level of health benefits is not different, then § 630.1208(e) controls. Depending on how FEHBP treats individuals on leave without pay, the employee taking FMLA leave may be entitled to the same or less health benefits during the pendency of unpaid FMLA leave.

Having made the distinction, it appears likely that § 630.1209 would be considered a different entitlement, and an employee who elects to continue FEHBP health benefits while on leave without pay would continue to receive health benefits at the same level the employee enjoyed immediately before going on FMLA leave.

2. Effect of Changes in Health Plan Coverage

a. Title I, the CAA, and the PEOAA

(1) Group Health Plans

An employer that provides a new health plan or benefits or that changes health benefits or plans while an employee is on FMLA leave must provide the new or changed plan/benefits to the same extent as if the employee were not on leave. 29 CFR 825.209(c); S. Res. 242, Cong. Rec. S3959, S3967 (April 23, 1996); 29 CFR 825.209(b). For example, if an employer changes a group health plan so that dental care becomes covered under the plan, an employee on FMLA leave must be given the same opportunity as other employees to receive (or obtain) the dental care coverage. 29 CFR 825.209(c); S. Res. 242, Cong. Rec. S3959, S3967 (April 23, 1996); 29 CFR 825.209(b). Any other plan changes (e.g., in coverage, premiums, deductibles, etc.), which apply to all employees of the workforce, would also apply to an employee on FMLA leave. 29 CFR 825.209(c); S. Res. 242, Cong. Rec. S3959, S3967 (April 23, 1996); 29 CFR 825.209(b).

The underlying rationale for the above is that an employer, during a period of FMLA leave, must maintain coverage under any group health plan at the level and under the conditions coverage would have been provided if the employee had been continuously employed. Preamble, 29 CFR 825.209. If changes are made to the plan or program during an employee's FMLA leave, those changes form the conditions at which coverage would have been provided had the employee been continuously employed, and apply to the employee on FMLA leave, provided, of course, the changes do not decrease any existing benefit the employee enjoyed before starting FMLA leave.

(2) Multi-Employer Health Plans

The section of the regulations addressing multi-employer health plans does not address the effect of changes on plan coverage and benefits during an employee's FMLA leave absence. 29 CFR 825.211; S. Res. 242, Cong. Rec. S3959, S3968 (April 23, 1996); 29 CRF 825.211(b). Given the specificity with which the regulations address this issue regarding group health plan benefits, 29 CFR 825.209(c); S. Res. 242, Cong. Rec. S3959, S3968 (April 23, 1996); 29 CFR 825.209(c), the absence of similar regulations governing multi-employer health plans suggests that those rules do not apply to multi-employer plans.

On the other hand, in the Preamble to the final regulations, 29 CFR 825.211, the DOL stated the following:

> Coverage by the group health plan must be maintained at the level coverage would have been provided if the employee continued to be employed instead of taking FMLA leave. As discussed elsewhere in these regulations, this means, for example, that if, but for being on leave, an employee would have been laid off, the employee's rights under FMLA, including the requirement to maintain group health plan a coverage, are whatever they would have been had the employee not been on leave when the layoff occurred.

By referencing other regulations (the only other similar regulations being § 825.209), and clearly indicating that the right to maintain benefits is determined as if the employee were not on FMLA leave, if an employee who was not on leave would be entitled to take advantage of changes in benefits and coverage, the employee on FMLA leave would also have that right. That is, the Preamble to 29 CFR 825.211 appears to incorporate the group health plan requirement that changes to plan coverage and benefits must also be provided to an employee covered by a multi-employer health plan during the employee's FMLA absence.

b. Title II

Unlike Title I, Title II does not expressly address changes in health benefit plan coverage during the pendency of an employee's FMLA leave. Cobbling together several regulations suggests that, as a practical matter, the result would be the same as under Title I.

First, the option to continue enrollment under the FEHBP while an employee is on FMLA leave without pay suggests that such enrollment is subject to whatever changes or modifications that might occur to the FEHBP health plan or program. 5 CFR 630.1209. The regulations certainly do not prohibit changes to FEHBP health plans during the pendency of an employee's FMLA leave, except that such changes cannot reduce the level of benefits enjoyed by the employee prior to taking FMLA leave. 5 CFR 630.1208(a)(2).

Second, an employee who is restored to duty from FMLA leave is entitled to the same or equivalent position with equivalent benefits. 5 CFR 630.1208(a)(2). An employee returning from FMLA leave is not entitled to any benefit other than the benefits the employee would have been entitled to, had the employee not taken FMLA leave. 5 CFR 630.1208(d)(2). Again, this suggests that if changes are made to employment benefits during the pendency of FMLA leave, the employee on FMLA leave has the same entitlement to the changed benefits as if the employee had not taken leave.

3. Employer Notice to Employee of Health Plan Changes

a. Title I, the CAA, and the PEOAA

(1) Group Health Plans

Employers must notify employees on FMLA leave of any opportunity to change plans or benefits. 29 CFR 825.209(d); S. Res. 242, Cong. Rec. S3959, S3967 (April 23, 1996); 29 CFR 825.209(d). For example, if the group health plan permits an employee to change from a single to family coverage upon the birth of a child or to otherwise add new family members, such a change in benefits must be made available while an employee is on FMLA leave. 29 CFR 825.209(d); S. Res. 242, Cong. Rec. S3959, S3967 (April 23, 1996); 29 CFR 825.209(d). If the employee requests the changed coverage it must be provided by the employer. 29 CFR 825.209(d); S. Res. 242, Cong. Rec. S3959, S3967 (April 23, 1996); 29 CFR 825.209(d).

The regulations do not indicate when or how the employee must be notified. Presumably, an employing agency should notify the employee on FMLA leave within sufficient time to enable the employee to make a timely election of the change in benefits. Employers would be well-advised to provide such notification in writing, even if only to confirm oral notification. To accomplish this, employing agencies should ensure that they have accurate, up-to-date address and contact information before the employee goes out on FMLA leave.

(2) Multi-Employer Health Plans

The implementing regulations do not directly require an employer to provide an eligible employee with notice of changes in multi-employer health plan benefits during the pendency of FMLA leave. Given the presence of such a notice requirement for group health plans, 29 CFR 825.209(d), the absence of this requirement in the implementing regulations for multi-employer health plans suggests, as a matter of regulatory construction, that employers need notify eligible employees covered by multi-employer health plans of any changes in plan coverage during FMLA leave.

While the above makes sense as a matter of statutory construction, employers should proceed with caution. The explanatory language in the preamble to the final regulations suggests that employees on FMLA leave should be treated like an employee who had not taken FMLA leave for purposes of continuation of multi-employer plan benefits. If an employee who had not taken FMLA leave would have been notified of changes to multi-employer plan benefits, the employee on FMLA leave should be treated the same.

b. Title II

Title II does not address or otherwise impose an obligation on an employing agency to notify an employee of changes to health plans during the pendency of an FMLA leave absence.

D. ELECTION TO FOREGO GROUP HEALTH COVERAGE

All federal sector employees may elect not to continue health plan benefits during FMLA leave.

1. Title I, the CAA, and the PEOAA

a. Group Health Plans

An employee may choose not to retain group health plan coverage during FMLA leave. 29 CFR 825.209(e); S. Res. 242, Cong. Rec. S3959, S3967 (April 23, 1996); 29 CFR 825.209(e). See DOL WH FMLA Advisory Opinion No. 64 (June 21, 1995). However, when an employee returns from FMLA leave, the employee is entitled to reinstatement on the same terms as prior to taking the leave, including family or dependent coverages, without any qualifying period, physical examination, exclusion of pre-existing conditions, or to wait for an open season. 29 CFR 825.209(e); 825.212(c); S. Res. 242, Cong. Rec. S3959, S3967–S3968 (April 23, 1996); 29 CFR 825.209(e); 825.212(c). [Issues arising on an employee's return to work from FMLA leave are discussed more fully in Chapter 13, "Return to Work from Leave."]

Because employing agencies are required to reinstate employees to health care coverage on the same terms as before the employee took FMLA leave, employers frequently decide to pay the employee's share of health premiums, if any, during the pendency of the leave to avoid any changes in the employee's health care coverage that might result if the policy were allowed to lapse.

b. Multi-Employer Health Plans

There is no provision in the regulations that would allow an employee to elect to discontinue multi-employer health plan coverage. Rather, the regulations unequivocally provide that during the duration of an employee's FMLA leave, health plan coverage must be maintained. 29 CFR 825.211(c); S. Res. 242, Cong. Rec. S3959, S3967 (April 23, 1996); 29 CFR 825.209(e).

Based on statements made by DOL in the preamble to the final regulations, 29 CFR 825.211, it could be argued that an employee on FMLA leave has the same rights to continuance of health benefits as if the employee had not gone on FMLA leave. If an employee who is not on FMLA leave had the option to discontinue multi-employer health benefits coverage, the employee on FMLA leave should enjoy the same right. That is, the right to continue FMLA leave coverage necessarily includes the right to discontinue such coverage.

The DOL might consider clearing this area up with some supplemental regulations or interpretive guidance.

2. Title II

Under Title II, an employee may certainly elect to forgo continuation of health benefits during the pendency of his or her FMLA leave. 5 USC 6386; 5 CFR 630.1209. An employee who takes FMLA leave is also entitled, on return to the agency, to the same employment benefits made available to the employee in his or her previous position (e.g., life insurance, health benefits, retirement coverage, and leave accrual). 5 CFR 630.1208(b)(4). [For a further discussion of return to work issues, see Chapter 13, "Return to Work from Leave."]

E. CESSATION OF HEALTH BENEFITS DURING FMLA LEAVE

Under certain circumstances, an employer may terminate health benefits coverage during an employee's FMLA absence.

1. Title I, the CAA, and the PEOAA

a. Group Health Plans

Pursuant to 29 CFR 825.209(f); S. Res. 242, Cong. Rec. S3959, S3967–S3968 (April 23, 1996), 825.209(f), an employer's obligation to maintain health benefits coverage during FMLA leave (and to restore the employee to the same or equivalent position on the conclusion of that leave) ceases in three circumstances:

- If and when the employment relationship would have terminated if the employee had not taken FMLA leave;
- An employee informs the employer of his or her intent not to return from leave;
- The employee fails to return from FMLA leave or continues on leave after exhausting his or her FMLA leave entitlement in the 12-month period.

There are two exceptions to this rule that may require continued group health benefits coverage. First, if temporary continued coverage of group health benefits is required pursuant to the Consolidated Omnibus Budget Reconciliation Act of 1986 (COBRA), an employer may not terminate health benefits coverage. Second, for certain key employees (as discussed below), different rules govern an employer's obligation to continue group health coverage. 29 CFR 825.209(f); S. Res. 242, Cong. Rec. S3959, S3967 (April 23, 1996); 29 CFR 825.209(f).

(1) Termination of Employee During FMLA Leave

An employee on FMLA leave has no greater right to employment than if the employee had not taken FMLA leave. 29 CFR 825.312(d); S. Res. 242, Cong. Rec. S3959, S3974 (April 23, 1996); 29 CFR 825.312(d). As a result, if the job of the employee would have been eliminated, such as through a department-wide downsizing, layoff, or other nondiscriminatory reason (including discipline for performance or conduct) not related to the employee's use of FMLA leave, the employer's obligation to continue group health benefits ceases along with the job. *See* Preamble, 29 CFR 825.209, 825.312.

The regulations do not explicitly discuss when the employer may terminate the employee's group health coverage, particularly where the employer may know before the employee takes FMLA leave that the employee, for example, will be laid off during the leave period. In the absence of regulatory language permitting an employer to terminate group health benefits before the actual layoff, employers would be wise to wait until the nondiscriminatory action (layoff, downsizing, termination for cause, etc.) actually occurs before terminating group health benefits.

Remember, where an employee is being terminated, COBRA may require the continuation of group health benefits. In that case, the FMLA group health benefits obligations fall by the wayside and COBRA governs the continuation of group health benefits. *See* DOL WH FMLA Advisory Opinion No. 64 (June 21, 1995) (discussion of COBRA benefits and the FMLA). [For a discussion of the interaction of the FMLA with COBRA benefits on the termination of an employee, see Chapter 16, "Interaction of the FMLA with Other Federal Laws, Employer Practices, and Collective Bargaining Agreements."]

(2) Notice of Employee Intent Not to Return From FMLA Leave

An employer who has been advised by the employee before or during leave that the employee does not intend to return from work may terminate group health benefits, including before the employee starts FMLA leave if the employer is so informed before the leave starts. 29 CFR 825.209(f); S. Res. 242, Cong. Rec. S3959, S3967–S3968 (April 23, 1996); 29 CFR 825.209(f); see DOL WH FMLA advisory Opinion No. 1 (June 15, 1993). In this instance, the regulations specifically permit an employer to terminate group health benefits before the employee is even on FMLA leave. Of course, an employer is not required to terminate health benefits at this time.

The employee must give unequivocal notice of his or her intention not to return to work from FMLA leave. 29 CFR 825.312(e); S. Res. 242, Cong. Rec. S3959, S3974 (April 23, 1996); 29 CFR 825.312(e). The term "unequivocal" means leaving no doubt; clear; unambiguous. Webster's Ninth New Collegiate Dictionary (Merriam-Webster 1983). An employee who states that she does not think or does not believe that she will be returning to work has not given "unequivocal" notice of intent not to return to work. Prudent employing agencies should request such employee notification in writing. If the employee does not provide such notice in writing, the agency should send a letter by regular and certified mail confirming the employee's unequivocal notice of intent not to return to work before terminating the employee and his or her group health benefits. The letter should also give the employee a few days to make objections before any employer action is taken.

Finally, if the employee has substituted paid leave for unpaid FMLA leave, the employer must maintain group health benefits even if the employee has given unequivocal notice of his or her intent not to return to work from FMLA leave. 29 CFR 825.312(d), (e); S. Res. 242, Cong. Rec. S3959, S3974 (April 23, 1996); 29 CFR 825.312(d), (e).

b. Multi-Employer Health Plans

Pursuant to 29 CFR 825.211(e), coverage under multi-employer health plans during an employee's FMLA leave may be terminated in the same three ways as under group health plans (29 CFR 825.209(f)):

- The employee's FMLA leave entitlement is exhausted;

- The employer can show that the employee would have been laid off and the employment relationship terminated;

- The employee provides unequivocal notice of intent not to return to work.

By cross-referencing 29 CFR 825.209(f), the examples and interpretations given to that regulation apply to interpretations of 29 CFR 825.211(e) regarding the cessation of continued multi-employer health plan coverage of an eligible employee on FMLA leave.

A fourth way that employee coverage under a multi-employer health plan may legally cease was discussed in DOL WH FMLA Advisory Opinion No. 14 (Nov. 13, 1993). If the employer whose employees receive benefits pursuant to a multi-employer plan ceases activity and all employees on that job are laid off, the employer may discontinue contributions on behalf of an employee taking unpaid FMLA leave if the employer can demonstrate the employee would not have continued to be employed by either the employer or another employer who is a member of the same plan. Id.

If, on the other hand, the employer closes one worksite, lays off all employees, but moves those employees to another site to continue employment, the employer must continue to make contributions on behalf of the employees taking FMLA leave as it is reasonable to assume the employee would have continued at the alternative site as well. Id.

2. Title II

Title II does not specifically address the termination of health benefits during an employee's FMLA leave. Generically, Title II provides that an employee is not entitled to any right, benefit, or position of employment other than any right, benefit, or position to which the employee would have been entitled had the employee not taken FMLA leave. 5 USC 6384(c)(2); 5 CFR 630.1208(d)(2). At a minimum, the termination of health benefits under Title II would be governed by existing agency policy. For example, if agency policy allowed the termination of health benefits where an employee gave unequivocal notice that he or she was resigning, the same rule would apply to an employee who is on FMLA leave.

F. CESSATION OF HEALTH BENEFITS OF A KEY EMPLOYEE

If a "key employee" does not return from FMLA leave when notified by the employer that substantial or grievous economic injury will result from his or her reinstatement, the employee's entitlement to group health plan benefits continues unless and until the employee: (a) advises the employer that the employee does not desire restoration to employment at the end of the leave period; (b) FMLA leave entitlement is exhausted; or (c) reinstatement is actually denied. 29 CFR 825.209(g); S. Res. 242, Cong. Rec. S3959, S3967–S3968 (April 23, 1996); 29 CFR 825.209(g). [A full discussion of the key employees may be found in Chapter 13, "Return to Work from Leave."] What follows below is the abridged version in order to understand the interplay between the maintenance of group health benefits and key employees

The concept of a key employee does not exist in Title II. It is, however, recognized in Title I, the CAA, and the PEOAA. A "key employee" is a salaried FMLA–eligible employee who is among the highest paid ten percent of all the employees employed by the employer within 75 miles of the employee's worksite. 29 CFR 825.217(a); S. Res. 242, Cong. Rec. S3959, S3970 (April 23, 1996); 29 CFR 825.217(a). An employer may deny job restoration to a key employee if such denial is necessary to prevent substantial and grievous economic injury to the operations of the employer. 29 CFR 825.216(c); S. Res. 242, Cong. Rec. S3959, S3970 (April 23, 1996); 29 CFR 825.216(c).

Essentially, an employer who has determined that restoration of the key employee to employment will cause "substantial and grievous economic injury" to the operations of the employer has the right to deny reemployment to the key employee. 29 CFR 825.218(a); S. Res. 242, Cong. Rec. S3959, S3970 (April 23, 1996); 29 CFR 825.218(a). The employer must notify the employee of this determination, including the consequences with respect to reinstatement and maintenance of health benefits. 29 CFR 825.219(a); S. Res. 242, Cong. Rec. S3959, S3970 (April 23, 1996); 29 CFR 825.219(a). If the key employee has already begun FMLA leave and does not return to work in response to the employer's notification of intent to deny restoration, the employee continues to be entitled to maintenance of health benefits and the employer may not recover its cost of health benefit premiums. 29 CFR 825.219(c); S. Res. 242, Cong. Rec. S3959, S3970 (April 23, 1996); 29 CFR 825.219(c).

IV. EMPLOYEE PAYMENT OF HEALTH BENEFIT PREMIUMS WHILE ON FMLA LEAVE

This section addresses the rules governing an employee's payment of his or her share of any health benefit plan premiums during FMLA leave.

A. TITLE II

Title II provides that an employee enrolled in FEBHP who takes FMLA leave may elect to continue health benefits enrollment and arrange to pay currently into the Employees' Health Benefits Fund the appropriate employee contributions. 5 USC 6386; 5 CFR 630.1209. Employee premium contributions must be made consistent with 5 CFR 890.502. 5 CFR 630.1209.

In pertinent part, § 890.502 sets out procedures governing an employee's payment of health premiums when an employee enters a leave without pay status (LWOP). 5 CFR 890.502(b). Again, under Title II, unless paid leave is substituted, FMLA leave is run as leave without pay. 5 CFR 1205(a).

1. Agency Notice to Employee of Options

As soon as the employing office knows that an employee whose premium payments cannot be made because the employee will have or has leave without pay status, the employing office must provide the employee written notice of the options and consequences for the payment of health care premiums to ensure continued health care coverage. 5 CFR 890.502(b)(1). If the employing office cannot give the written notice to the employee directly, the notice must be mailed by first class mail. Id.

The notice indicates that the employee may either discontinue health benefits plan coverage during the period of leave without pay, or elect to continue coverage by choosing one of two available options. 5 CFR 890.502(b)(2). The employee's election must be in the form of a signed writing, which is received by the employing office within 31 days from receipt of the agency's notification. Id. If the employee fails to timely provide the written statement to the agency, absent unusual circumstances, the agency may terminate the health benefits enrollment. 5 CFR 890.502(b)(3), (4).

2. Employee Premium Payment Options

The employee may elect to pay the premiums on either a current basis, or on a delayed basis upon the employee's return to work from leave without pay. 5 CFR 890.502(b)(2)(i)–(ii).

a. Current Payment Method

An employee may agree to make health plan premium payments directly to the agency on a current basis. 5 CFR 890.502(b)(2)(I). The employee must agree that if he or she does not pay the premiums, upon returning to employment or upon pay becoming sufficient to cover the premiums, the employing office will deduct, in addition to the current pay period's premiums, an amount equal to the premiums for a pay period during which the employee was in LWOP status. *Id.* The employing office will continue to use this method to deduct the accrued unpaid premiums from salary until the debt is recovered in full. The employee must also agree that if he or she does not return to work or the employing office cannot recover the debt in full from salary, the employing office may recover the debt from whatever other sources it normally has available for recovery of a debt to the United States. *Id.*

b. Payment Plan Method

An employee may agree to make payments upon returning to employment or upon pay becoming sufficient to cover the premiums. Then the employing office will deduct, in addition to the current pay period's premiums, an amount equal to the premiums for a pay period during which the employee was in LWOP status. 5 CFR 890.502(b)(2)(ii). The employing office will continue using this method to deduct salary until the debt is recovered in full. *Id.* The employee must also agree that if he or she does not return to work or the employing office cannot recover the debt in full from salary, the employing office may recover the debt from whatever other sources it normally has available for recovery of a debt to the United States. *Id.*

3. Termination of Health Benefits

The employing office must give the employee written notice of termination. 5 CFR 890.502(b)(3). Terminations of enrollment are retroactive to the end of the last pay period in which the premium was withheld from pay. 5 CFR 890.502(b)(5). The employee and covered family members, if any, are entitled to the temporary extension of coverage for conversion and may convert to an individual contract for health benefits. *Id.*

B. TITLE I, THE CAA AND THE PEOAA

Title I, the CAA, and the PEOAA address three types of health benefits plans: (1) group health benefits; (2) multi-employer benefit plans; and (3) FEHBP. They also address other non–group health benefit plans. Each of these areas will be discussed in more detail below in terms of payment of health benefit premiums during the pendency of an employee's FMLA leave.

1. Group Health Plan Benefits

Group health plan benefits must be maintained on the same basis as coverage would have been provided if the employee had been continuously employed during the period of FMLA leave. Continuation of group health plan benefits on the same basis includes the requirement that the employee continue to pay his share, if any, of group health plan premiums, during the FMLA leave period. 29 CFR 825.210(a); S. Res. 242, Cong. Rec. S3959, S3967 (April 23, 1996); 29 CFR 825.210(a).

a. Changes to Premium Rates

If premiums are raised or lowered, the employee will be required to pay the new premium rates. 29 CFR 825.210(a); S. Res. 242, Cong. Rec. S3959, S3967 (April 23, 1996), 825.210(a). Note, however, that in the preamble to the final regulations, the DOL indicates that employers cannot increase the employee's share of premiums during unpaid FMLA leave. Preamble, 29 CFR 825.210. Presumably, the rationale for such a prohibition is that a change in the percentage of premiums paid by the employee compared with those paid by the employer would violate the rule that group health plan benefits must be maintained at the same level as the employee had before taking FMLA leave.

Conversely, in the same section of the preamble, the DOL appears to contradict itself. The DOL states that "[a]ny changes to premium rates and levels of coverages or other conditions of the plan that apply to the employer's active workforce also apply to eligible employees on FMLA leave." Preamble, 29 CFR 825.210. Presumably, an increase in the premium percentage paid by employees would be enforceable as long as that change applied to all employees in the workforce, including employees on FMLA leave.

Until this matter is clarified by the DOL, employing agencies would be well-advised to limit changes in group health plans to, at most, changes in premium payments. It is reasonably clear that this would be allowed.

b. Substitution of Paid Leave

If the FMLA leave is substituted paid leave, the employee's share of premiums must be paid by the method used during any paid leave, presumably as a payroll deduction. 29 CFR 825.210(b); S. Res. 242, Cong. Rec. S3959, S3967 (April 23, 1996); 29 CFR 825.210(b).

Note the loose regulatory language used in this regulation. Presumably, the regulation means that if an employee or employer elects to substitute paid leave for unpaid FMLA leave, the rules governing premium payments are governed by the paid leave *actually selected and applied* in substitution. This is not what the regulations say, however. As stated, if paid leave is substituted, premium payments are governed by the method applied during *any paid leave*. That raises the specter that an employee or employer could elect the easiest or the hardest paid leave premium payment plan, even if it is not the paid leave category actually applied in substitution for unpaid FMLA leave.

c. Unpaid FMLA Leave

An employer, pursuant to § 825.210(c); S. Res. 242, Cong. Rec. S3959, S3967 (April 23, 1996); 29 CFR 825.210(c), may require employees to pay their share of premium payments in any of the following five ways:

- Payment would be due at the same time as it would be made if by payroll deduction;

- Payment would be due on the same schedule as payments are made under COBRA;

- Payment would be prepaid pursuant to a cafeteria plan at the employee's option;

- The employer's existing rules for payment by employees on "leave without pay" would be followed, provided that such rules do not require prepayment (i.e. prior to the commencement of the leave) of the premiums that will become due during a period of unpaid FMLA leave or payment of higher premiums than if the employee had continued to work instead of taking leave;

- Another system voluntarily agreed to between the employer and the employee, which may include prepayment of premiums (e.g., through increased payroll deductions when the need for the FMLA leave is foreseeable).

The employer may require that the employee pay his or her share of premium payments to the employer or to the insurance carrier. 29 CFR 825.210(c); S. Res. 242, Cong. Rec. S3959, S3967 (April 23, 1996), 825.210(c). An employer may not, however add additional charges to employee premium payments for administrative expenses. S. Res. 242, Cong. Rec. S3959, S3967 (April 23, 1996); 29 CFR 825.210(c). Nor may an employer require an employee who takes FMLA leave to pay more for maintaining group health insurance during the employee's FMLA leave than the employee normally pays when working. DOL WH FMLA Advisory Opinion No. 23 (Dec. 28, 1993). It would appear safe to assume that the prohibition on employers from charging an administrative fee for processing premium payments would also extend to any employer charges, however labeled.

d. Employer Notice

An employer must provide the employee with advance written notice of the terms and conditions governing employee payment of their share of group health plan premiums payments. 29 CFR 825.210(d); 825.310(b)(1)(iv); S. Res. 242, Cong. Rec. at S3968, S3974 (April 23, 1996); 29 CFR 825.210 (d); 825.310(b)(1)(iv). [For a further discussion of employer notice obligations, see Chapter 8, "Notice Requirements."]

e. Limitation on Requirements

According to the DOL regulations, an employer may not require more of an employee using FMLA leave than the employer requires of other employees on leave without pay. 29 CFR, 825.210(e); S. Res. 242, Cong. Rec. S3959, S3968 (April 23, 1996); 29 CFR 825.210 (e).

This is certainly one of the more bizarre DOL regulations. While housed in the section governing how an employee on FMLA leave pays his or her share of group health premiums, there is nothing in the regulation itself that suggests that it is limited to that topic. In fact, there is nothing in the regulation itself to suggest that it has anything to do with that topic.

The preamble to the final DOL regulations suggests a tie to premium payments. According to the Preamble to 29 CFR 825.210:

> Employers must give employees advance written notice of the terms of payment of such premiums during FMLA leave, and an employer may not apply more stringent requirements to an employee on FMLA leave than required of employees on other forms of unpaid leave under the terms of the Interim Final Rule.

It is unclear what the rule is stating. Viewed narrowly, the rule may mean that an employee on unpaid FMLA leave, for purposes of payment of group health premiums, must be treated the same as any other employee on any type of unpaid leave, again, in terms of payment of group health plan premiums.

Under a broader interpretation, the rule could be read as saying an employee on FMLA leave, whether paid or unpaid, may not be required to meet any more stringent requirements for payment of group health plan premiums than an employee on LWOP. Such a rule would, essentially, undermine the employee's having to adhere to more demanding premium payment requirements where paid leave is substituted for unpaid FMLA leave, thereby negating 29 CFR 825.209(c).

Finally, under the broadest interpretation, the regulation is not restricted to employee premium payments during FMLA leave, and applies to all aspects (e.g., notice, certification, etc.) where paid leave is substituted for unpaid FMLA leave. It is unlikely that the last two interpretations are what the DOL meant. Still, loose regulatory language breeds litigation.

f. OWCP

An employee who is receiving payments as a result of a workers' compensation injury must make arrangements with the employer for payment of group health plan benefits when simultaneously taking FMLA leave. 29 CFR 825.210(f); S. Res. 242, Cong. Rec. S3959, S3968 (April 23, 1996); 29 CFR 825.210(f).

2. Multi-Employer Health Benefit Plans

Like group health plans, the provisions governing multi-employer health benefit plans require an employee on FMLA leave to make premium contributions during the pendency of FMLA leave. An employer using FMLA leave cannot, however, be required to use "banked" hours or to pay a greater premium than the employee would have been required to pay if the employee had been continuously employed. 29 CFR 825.211(d); S. Res. 242, Cong. Rec. S3959, S3968 (April 23, 1996); 29 CFR 825.211(d). In addition to the rate of contribution being the same, the DOL indicated that the employee must pay the rate at the same schedule, at the same wage or salary, and otherwise under the same terms and conditions as he or she normally worked before going on leave, unless a contrary result can be clearly demonstrated by the employer (or by the plan, where appropriate). Preamble, 29 CFR 825.211.

The preamble language suggests that employers and employees have limited options when it comes to employee payment of premiums. Unlike group health plans, it appears that the only option an employer and employee have on employee payment of his or her share of multi-employer health plan premiums during FMLA leave is the same schedule and manner of payment that governed before the employee took FMLA leave.

3. FEHBP

In addition to group health plan and multi-employer health plan payments, the CAA includes the requirement that employer's maintain FEHBP health benefits for employees enrolled in that program.

Title I does not address employee FEHBP premium payments directly. S. Res. 242, Cong. Rec. S3959, S3967 (April 23, 1996); 29 CFR 825.209(a). Rather, the only reference in the CAA regarding an employee's obligation to continue making his or her share of premium payments during the pendency of FMLA leave is that FEHBP coverage must be maintained on the same conditions as coverage would have been provided if the employee had been continuously employed during the entire leave period. S. Res. 242, Cong. Rec. S3959, S3967 (April 23, 1996); 29 CFR 825.209(a). There is no indication that the CAA rules governing employee payment of health premiums pursuant to a group or multi-employer health plan apply to employees covered by FEHBP. Apparently, only FEHBP premium payment rules apply.

4. Other Health Benefit Plans

Maintenance of health insurance policies (e.g., supplemental life insurance, disability insurance, etc.) which are not a part of the employer's group health plan, as described in 825.209(a)(1), are the sole responsibility of the employee. The employee and the insurer should make necessary arrangements for payment of premiums during the period of unpaid FMLA leave. 29 CFR 825.210(e); S. Res. 242, Cong. Rec. S3959, S3968 (April 23, 1996); 29 CFR 825.210(e).

V. CONSEQUENCES OF EMPLOYEE FAILURE TO MAKE TIMELY HEALTH PLAN PREMIUM PAYMENTS

A. TERMINATION OF EMPLOYER MAINTENANCE OBLIGATIONS

1. Title II

Title 5 CFR 890.502(b) governs the continuation of FEHBP benefits when a Title II covered employee is on unpaid FMLA leave. Interestingly, there is no clear provision in the regulation that terminates the continuation of health benefits coverage in the event that an employee fails to make the premium payments. Unfortunately, the regulations on this point are unnecessarily fuzzy.

Termination of FEHBP health benefits during leave without pay is addressed in 5 CFR 890.502(b)(5). This section provides, in pertinent part, that "terminations of FEHBP enrollment under paragraphs (b)(2) and (3) of this section are retroactive to the end of the last pay period in which the premium was withheld from pay." Paragraph (b)(2), 5 CFR 890.502(b)(2), requires that employees who wish to continue health benefits coverage during a period of leave without pay (such as unpaid FMLA leave) must make a written election from two available options. Termination of health benefits for failure to make premium payments is not, however, addressed in paragraph (b)(2). In fact, paragraph (b)(2) does not set forth any grounds for termination of the continuation of health benefits once a written election is perfected by the employee. Instead, paragraph (b)(2) requires an employee to agree that if he or she does not return to work or the employing office cannot recover the unpaid premium debt in full from salary, the employing office may recover the debt from whatever other sources it normally has available for recovery of a debt to the United States. 5 CFR 890.502(b)(2)(I), (ii).

Because paragraph (b)(2) does not provide for the termination of FEHBP coverage where an employee fails to make premium payments, the language in paragraph (b)(5), 5 CFR 890.502(b)(5), indicating that terminations of enrollment under paragraph (b)(2) are retroactive, is curious. Presumably, paragraph (b)(5) allows for the termination of FEHBP enrollment during a period of unpaid FMLA leave where the employee fails to make premium payments. Otherwise, paragraph (b)(5) makes no sense as it refers to terminations made pursuant to paragraph (b)(3), which paragraph contains no provision for termination of FEHBP enrollment.

Read in combination, paragraphs (b)(3) and (b)(5) appear to provide that agencies may terminate FEHBP benefits where the employee does not return to work or the employing office cannot recover the premium debt in full from salary, and that debt is owed by the employee as a debt to the United States, which may be recovered from whatever sources it normally has available for recovery of a debt to the United States.

Alternatively, as written, an employee who timely elects to continue FEHBP payments during a period of leave without pay, such as unpaid FMLA leave, would have those benefits continue, whether the employee actually continues making payments or not. That is, the failure of an employee to make premium payments is not, of itself, a reason for termination of FEHBP health benefits continuation. Rather, the unpaid premiums simply become a debt the employee owes to the United States, which is collected in the normal course.

Paragraph (b)(3) provides that if the employee fails to return the signed continuation of health benefits election form within 31 days after the day he or she receives notice from the employer of the need for continued coverage, absent circumstances beyond the employee's control, the employing office must terminate the employee's enrollment in FEHB. 5 CFR 890.502(b)(3). The employing office must notify the employee in writing of the termination. *Id*. Termination of enrollment under paragraph (b)(3) is retroactive to the end of the last pay period in which the premium was withheld from pay. 5 CFR 890.502(b)(5).

The employee and covered family members, if any, are entitled to the temporary extension of coverage for conversion and may convert to an individual contract for health benefits. 5 CFR 890.502(b)(5). An employee whose coverage has been terminated may enroll upon his or her return to duty in a pay status in a position in which the employee is eligible for coverage under FEHBP. *Id*.

2. Title I, the CAA, and the PEOAA

a. Group Health Plan

An employer's obligation to continue group health insurance coverage ceases under the FMLA if an employee's premium payment is more than 30 days late. 29 CFR 825.212(a)(1); S. Res. 242, Cong. Rec. S3959, S3968 (April 23, 1996); 29 CFR 825.212(a). The 30–day period may be extended pursuant to an established employer policy providing a longer grace period. 29 CFR 825.212(a)(1), (2); S. Res. 242, Cong. Rec. S3959, S3968 (April 23, 1996), 825.212(a)(1), (2); *see*, DOL WH FMLA Advisory Opinion No. 42, #8 (Aug. 23, 1996).

(1) Employer Notice of Health Benefits Termination

To drop an employee's health insurance coverage for untimely premium payments, the employing agency must provide written notice to the employee that the payment has not been received. 29 CFR 825.212(a)(1); S. Res. 242, Cong. Rec. S3959, S3968 (April 23, 1996); 29 CFR 825.212(a). Such notice must be mailed to the employee at least 15 days before the coverage is to cease, advising that coverage will be dropped on a specified date at last 15 days after the date of the letter unless the payment has been received by that date. *Id*.; *see* DOL WH FMLA Advisory Opinion No. 64 (June 21, 1995).

The regulations assume that the employer knows the whereabouts of the employee. If so, the employing agency should send the letter to the address where it knows the employee currently resides. If the employer does not know where the employee currently resides, the employing agency would be well–advised to make reasonable efforts to find this information. Contact at the last known address of record, emergency contact numbers, workplace friends, and union representatives, if any, should be made in order to locate the employee. That search should be documented. If all else fails and the employee's current address remains unknown, the letter should be sent to the last known address of record.

b. Retroactive Termination

Generally, an employer may not retroactively terminate employee health coverage for employee nonpayment of his or her share of premium payments. Specifically, coverage for the employee may be terminated at the end of the 30–day grace period, provided the required 15–day notice has been given. 29 CFR 825.212(a)(1); S. Res. 242, Cong. Rec. S3959, S3968 (April 23, 1996); 29 CFR 825.212(a).

For example, an employee misses a health benefits premium payment while out on unpaid FMLA leave. The employing agency must send out the notice of termination of benefits within 15 days of when it intends to terminate benefits. Since it is in the employing agency's economic interest to terminate benefits as soon as possible (to relieve itself of having to pay its share of premium payments), the employing agency would be well–advised, absent a more generous unpaid leave policy, to send out the termination notice within a few days of the missed payment (allowing for the possibility that receipt of the payment was delayed in the mail). The employing agency would then be in a position to terminate health benefits coverage on day 31 (more than 30 days late) from when the premium payment was due.

Where, however, the employer has established policies regarding other forms of unpaid leave that provide for the employer to cease coverage retroactively to the date the unpaid premium payment was due, the employer may drop the employee from coverage retroactively in accordance with that policy, provided the 15-day notice was given. 29 CFR 825.212(a)(1); S. Res. 242, Cong. Rec. S3959, S3968 (April 23, 1996); 29 CFR 825.212(a).

3. Multi-Employer Health Plans

There is no special FMLA provision that addresses the consequences to an employee who fails to make required multi-employer health care premium payments during the course of FMLA leave. The FMLA does provide, however, that coverage under a multi-employer health plan must be maintained at the level of coverage that would have been provided if the employee continued in his employment instead of taking FMLA leave. That being the case, it suggests that the consequences of an employee's failure to make premium payments during unpaid FMLA leave are governed by the terms of the multi-employer health plan.

4. FEHBP

There are no special rules governing the consequences for the failure of a CAA employee to make FEHBP premium payments during the course of FMLA leave. Rather, the FMLA regulations provide that an employer has no obligation regarding the maintenance of a health insurance policy that is not a group health plan. S. Res. 242, Cong. Rec. S3959, S3968 (April 23, 1996); 29 CFR 825.212(a)(2).

B. OTHER CONSEQUENCES

1. Non-Group Health Plans

An employer has no obligation regarding the maintenance of a health insurance policy that is not a group health plan. 29 CFR 825.212(a)(2); S. Res. 242, Cong. Rec. S3959, S3968 (April 23, 1996); 29 CFR 825.212(a)(2).

2. Continuation of Other FMLA Obligations

Where an employee's group health benefits coverage is terminated for non-payment of premiums, all other obligations of an employing agency under the FMLA would continue. 29 CFR 825.212(a)(3); S. Res. 242, Cong. Rec. S3959, S3968 (April 23, 1996), 825.212(a)(3). For example, an employing agency would continue to have an obligation to reinstate an employee on return from FMLA leave. *Id.*

3. Employer Payment of Employee Premiums

An employing agency may elect to pay the employee's share of missed group health benefits premium payments. 29 CFR 825.212(b); S. Res. 242, Cong. Rec. S3959, S3968 (April 23, 1996), 825.212(b). There does not appear to be any requirement that the employing agency first obtain the employee's permission to make such premium payments. An employer may recover the employee's share of any premium payments missed by the employee for any FMLA leave period during which the employing agency maintains health coverage by paying the employee's share. 29 CFR 825.212(b); S. Res. 242, Cong. Rec. S3959, S3968 (April 23, 1996); 29 CFR 825.212(b). *See* DOL FMLA Advisory Opinion No. 42, #8 (Aug. 23, 1994); DOL WH FMLA Advisory Opinion No. 11 (Nov. 2, 1993).

The regulations do not provide specific guidance regarding how the employer recoups the premium payments it advanced to the employee. According to the DOL, the employer and the employee should make arrangements for repayment that do not unduly impact the employee's financial condition, such as periodic payroll deduction. DOL WH FMLA Advisory Opinion No. 11 (Nov. 2, 1993).

Employing agencies faced with the potential loss of health benefits to an employee due to the employee's failure to pay his or her share of the premium payments will often pay the premiums themselves to ensure the resumption of such benefits when the employee returns to work from FMLA leave. Again, the statute and regulations make the employer responsible for maintaining group health benefits during periods of FMLA leave and the restoration of all benefits when the employee returns from leave. DOL WH FMLA Advisory Opinion No. 11 (Nov. 2, 1993). In consideration of the employer's potential dilemma when the employee fails or is unable to make co-payments for premiums during unpaid leave, the regulations provide that the employer may unilaterally decide to pay the premiums for not only group health insurance but also other benefits such as life insurance, disability insurance, etc., thereby avoiding any lapse in coverage. *Id.*

This provision enables the employer to meet the obligation to restore full benefits upon the employee's return to work and to avoid any requirements of the insurance carrier that may be imposed in the event coverage is allowed to lapse, such as waiting periods, requirements to submit for a physical, or limitations that might be imposed regarding new preexisting conditions of the employee. *Id.*

4. Re-Qualification of Group Health Plan Benefits

As set forth more fully in Chapter 13, "Return to Work from Leave," if group health coverage lapses because an employee has not made required premium payments, upon the employee's return to work from FMLA leave, the employing agency must still restore the employee to coverage and benefits equivalent to those the employee would have had if the leave had not been taken and the premium payments hand not been missed, including family or dependent care coverage. 29 CFR 825.212(c); S. Res. 242, Cong. Rec. S3959, S3968 (April 23, 1996); 29 CFR 825.212(c). In such a case, an employee may not be required to meet any qualification requirements imposed by the plan, including any new preexisting condition waiting period, waiting for an open season, or passing a medical examination to obtain reinstatement of group health benefit coverage. 29 CFR 825.212(c); S. Res. 242, Cong. Rec. S3959, S3968 (April 23, 1996); 29 CFR 825.212(c). *See* DOL FMLA Advisory Opinion No. 64 (June 21, 1995); DOL FMLA Advisory Opinion No. 42, #8 (Aug. 23, 1994); DOL WH FMLA Advisory Opinion No. 11 (Nov. 2, 1993).

For example, let's say that before an employee takes FMLA leave he or she satisfied the pre-existing conditions limitation period for a particular condition, and the employee is not considered to have a preexisting condition when the employee commences FMLA leave. While on leave, the employee has no disability coverage and suffers from an entirely different condition. The employee returns to work on the conclusion of FMLA leave. The question is whether a new pre-existing conditions limitation would be imposed for the new condition, or would the employee receive partial credit for both conditions for the amount of time satisfied prior to starting the leave?

An employee who has partially satisfied the pre-existing conditions limitation period prior to commencing FMLA leave need only satisfy the remainder upon return from leave. A new pre-existing conditions limitation period could not be imposed in the example cited. The employee must receive partial credit toward both conditions for the amount of time satisfied prior to starting the leave. Because the taking of FMLA leave cannot result in the loss of any employment benefit accrued prior to the date on which the leave commenced, plans may not impose new pre-existing conditions limitations periods or "start the limitation period clock ticking again" after each FMLA leave. DOL WH FMLA Advisory Opinion No. 25 (Jan. 10, 1994).

It has been noted that this provision may give preferential treatment to eligible employees who take FMLA leave over employees who do not take FMLA leave, who drop health benefit coverage, and who are subject to reinstatement rules requiring waiting periods and medical examinations. Preamble, 29 CFR 825.212. In response, the DOL has not denied that those who take FMLA leave may receive preferential treatment in terms of re-qualifying for group health benefits. Rather, the DOL argued that the FMLA provides that the taking of FMLA leave will not result in the loss of any employment benefit accrued prior to the date on which the leave commenced. This includes entitlement to the same level and coverage of group health benefits as the employee enjoyed prior to taking FMLA leave. *Id.*

Because of the prohibition against re-qualification, many employers simply pay the employee's share of any missed employee premiums, and collect the money from the employee. By doing it this way, employers avoid the prospect of their health insurance company refusing to reinstate the returning employee absent a medical examination. In that event, the employer would be in violation of the Act, not the health insurance company.

VI. EMPLOYER RECOVERY OF COSTS OF MAINTAINING HEALTH CARE COVERAGE

This section addresses the ability of an employing agency to recover costs it incurred for maintaining health care coverage during FMLA leave.

A. TITLE II

The employee's payment of his or her share of health care premiums for a period of unpaid FMLA leave under Title II is governed by 5 CFR 890.502. Under this section, an employee incurs indebtedness due the United States in the amount of the employee's withholding required for each pay period that health benefits withholdings or direct premium payments are not made but during which the enrollment continues. 5 CFR 890.502(a). The employing office may recovery the debt from whatever other sources it normally has available for recovery of a debt to the United States. 5 CFR 890.502(b)(2)(i), (ii).

B. TITLE I, THE CAA, AND THE PEOAA

The ability to recover health care premium costs incurred by an employing agency for maintaining health benefits coverage during FMLA leave depends on the type of benefit involved: (1) group health care; (2) multi-employer; (3) FEHBP, and (4) self-insured employers.

1. Group Health Plans

a. General Rule

An employing agency is entitled under certain circumstances to recover premiums that the employer paid for maintaining coverage for the employee during any period of unpaid FMLA leave if the employee fails to return from FMLA leave. 29 USC 2614(c)(2); 2 USC 1312(a) (adopting 29 USC 2614 for the CAA); 3 USC 412(a) (same for PEOAA).

(1) Recovery of Payments Made on Behalf of Employee

An employing agency may recover the employee's share of any premium payments missed by the employee for any FMLA leave period during which the employer maintains health coverage by paying the employee's share after the premium payment is missed. 29 CFR 825.212(b), 825.213(a).

(2) Recovery of Employing Agency's Share of Premiums

An employing agency may also recover its share of health plan premiums during a period of unpaid FMLA leave from an employee if the employee fails to return to work after the employee's FMLA leave entitlement has been exhausted or expires. 29 CFR 825.213(a); S. Res. 242, Cong. Rec. S3959, S3968 (April 23, 1996); 29 CFR 825.213(a); *see Jines v. Evans Motors, Inc.*, 292 F. Supp. 2d 1130, 1139 (N.D. Ind. 2003).

b. Amount of Recovery

The regulations do not provide specific guidance regarding how the employer recoups the premium payments it advanced to the employee. According to the DOL, the employer and the employee should make arrangements for repayment that do not unduly impact the employee's financial condition, such as periodic payroll deduction. DOL WH FMLA Advisory Opinion No. 11 (Nov. 2, 1993).

In the event that employee and the employer cannot reach agreement on the amount proposed by the employer to be deducted from the employee's wages, the DOL has opined that the arrangements for repayment should be reasonable and not impose unreasonable hardships or difficulties on either party. DOL WH FMLA Advisory Opinion No. 65 (July 13, 1995). For example, the employer should not attempt to recover payments all at once by deducting the entire amount due from the employee's first paycheck. On the other hand, the employee should not attempt to stretch payments out over an unreasonably long time. The DOL would view additional deductions equal to a regular group health plan premium as reasonable. *Id.*

c. Exceptions

An employing agency may not recover any group health premiums it paid, whether on behalf of the employee or its own share, for one (or more) of two reasons:

(1) Serious Health Conditions

If the employee did not return to work from FMLA leave due to the continuation, recurrence, or onset of a serious health condition of the employee or the employee's family member, which would otherwise entitle the employee to leave under the FMLA, the employer may not recover any health care premiums it paid during unpaid FMLA leave. 29 USC 2614(c)(2)(B)(I); 29 CFR 825.213(a)(1); 2 USC 1312(a) (adopting 29 USC 2614 for the CAA); S. Res. 242, Cong. Rec. S3959, S3968 (April 23, 1996); 29 CFR 825.213(a)(1); 3 USC 412(a) (same for PEOAA); see DOL WH FMLA Advisory Opinion No. 42, #6 (Aug. 23, 1994).

(2) Other Circumstances

An employer is precluded from recovering premium payments paid by the employer to maintain group health care coverage during a period of unpaid FMLA leave where the employee fails to return to work due to other circumstances beyond the employee's control. 29 USC 2614(c)(2)(B)(ii); 29 CFR 825.213(a)(2); 2 USC 1312(a) (adopting 29 USC 2614 for the CAA); S. Res. 242, Cong. Rec. S3959, S3968 (April 23, 1996), 20 CFR 825.213(a)(2); 3 USC 412(a) (same for PEOAA). *See* DOL WH FMLA Advisory Opinion No. 42, #6 (Aug. 23, 1994); *see Jines v. Evans Motors, Inc.*, 292 F. Supp. 2d 1130, 1139 (N.D. Ind. 2003).

Examples of situations that fit within the broad definition of "other circumstances beyond the employee's control", as set forth in 29 CFR 825.213(a)(2); Cong. Rec. S3959, S3968 (April 23, 1996); 29 CFR 825.213(a)(2), include:

- Where a parent chooses to stay home with a newborn child who has a serious health condition;
- An employee's spouse is unexpectedly transferred to a job location more than 75 miles from the employee's worksite;
- A relative or individual other than an immediate family member has a serious health condition and the employee is needed to provide care;
- The employee is laid off while on leave;
- The employee is a "key employee" who decided not to return to work upon being notified of the employer's intention to deny restoration because of substantial and grievous economic injury to the employer's operations and is not reinstated by the employer.

Examples of circumstances that would not meet the definition of "circumstances beyond the employee's control", as set forth in 29 CFR 825.213(a)(2); S. Res. 242, Cong. Rec. S3959, S3968 (April 23, 1996); 29 CFR 825.213(a)(2), include:

- Where an employee desires to remain with a parent in a distant city even though the parent no longer requires the employee's care;
- A parent chooses not to return to work to stay home with a well newborn.

In *Jines*, the court found that an employer's termination of an employee before the expiration of the employee's FMLA leave was outside of the employee's control that would negate the employer's claim for recovery of premium payments.

d. When Has An Employee "Returned to Work"?

An employee who returns to work for at least 30 calendar days is considered to have "returned to work." 29 CFR 825.213(a)(2); S. Res. 242, Cong. Rec. S3959, S3968 (April 23, 1996); 29 CFR 825.213(a)(2). There are two exceptions to the general rule. An employee who transfers directly from taking FMLA leave to retirement, or who retires during the first 30 days after the employee returns to work, is deemed to have returned to work. 29 CFR 825.213(c); S. Res. 242, Cong. Rec. S3959, S3968 (April 23, 1996); 29 CFR 825.213(c).

For example, an employee is granted 12 weeks of unpaid FMLA leave to take care of an adopted child. However, when the employee is scheduled to return to work, he only works for four days and then informs the company he is quitting to stay home with the child. Can the employer recover from the employee the costs of the health care benefits from the period that the employee was out on leave?

The answer is yes, with certain limitations. Pursuant to 29 CFR 825.213, an employer may recover its share of health plan premiums during a period of unpaid FMLA leave from an employee if the employee fails to return to work after the employee's FMLA leave entitlement has been exhausted or expires, unless the reason the employee dos not return is due to the continuation, recurrence, or onset of a serious health condition that would entitle the employee to leave under FMLA, or due to other circumstances beyond the employee's control. An employee who returns to work for at least 30 calendar days is considered to have returned to work for purposes of FMLA and the employee would no longer have any responsibility to reimburse the employer for group health insurance premiums paid while on unpaid FMLA leave.

Here, the employee did not return to work for the minimum 30 days to avoid repayment of health insurance premiums. Nor does it appear that the reason the employee quit work was due to a serious health condition or other circumstance beyond his control. As such, the employer may collect the health insurance premiums the employer paid during the pendency of the employee's FMLA leave. *See* DOL FMLA Advisory Opinion No. 42, #6 (Aug. 23, 1994).

An employer will be unable to collect health insurance premium payments made during an employee's FMLA leave period even though the employee retires retroactive to before the employee commenced FMLA leave, and before FMLA leave benefits were exhausted. According to the DOL, a decision subsequent to the granting of an FMLA leave request approving disability retirement with a retroactive effective date for purposes of receiving pension benefits does not preempt or extinguish in any way the employee's statutory rights under the FMLA, including the right to have group health benefits maintained under the same terms for the duration of the protected leave period. If, as here, the employee cannot return to work at the end of the leave period due to the continuation a of serious health condition, the employer cannot recover premium payments. *See* DOL WH FMLA Advisory Opinion No. 26 (Jan. 14, 1994).

e. Medical Certification of a Serious Health Condition

When an employee fails to return to work because of the continuation, recurrence, or onset of a serious health condition, thereby precluding the employer from recovering its (share of) health benefit premium payments made on the employee's behalf during a period of unpaid FMLA leave, the employer may require medical certification of the employee's or family member's serious health condition. 29 CFR 825.213(a)(3); S. Res. 242, Cong. Rec. S3959, S3968 (April 23, 1996), 825.213(a)(3). Unless requested, a medical certification is not required. 29 CFR 825.213(a)(3); S. Res. 242, Cong. Rec. S3959, S3968 (April 23, 1996); 29 CFR 825.213(a)(3). [For an extensive discussion of medical certification requirements in support of a request for FMLA leave, see Chapter 9, "Documentation Requirements."]

The employee is required to provide medical certification in response to an employer's request within 30 days from the date of the employer's request. 29 CFR 825.213(a)(3); S. Res. 242, Cong. Rec. S3959, S3968 (April 23, 1996); 29 CFR 825.213(a)(3). An employee may use the medical certification form developed by the DOL for this purpose. 29 CFR 825.213(a)(3); S. Res. 242, Cong. Rec. S3959, S3968 (April 23, 1996); 29 CFR 825.213(a)(3). By use of the permissive "may," the implication is that other medical forms are acceptable.

The regulations fail to identify what information may be required of the employee in this medical certification. By referring only to the section of the regulations referencing the optional medical certification form, the regulations fail to identify what medical information an employer is entitled to receive. In addition to referencing the optional form, the regulations should have cited to 29 CFR 825.306(b), which identifies what information an employer is entitled to receive for purposes of a medical certification. This failure will no doubt cause unnecessary litigation as employers attempt to obtain more medical information than is generally permitted or, conversely, employee's attempt to provide medical certifications with as little information as possible.

The regulations also do not provide a mechanism for an employer to challenge the certification provided by the employee. Unlike a medical certification to support a request for FMLA leave, there is no second or third medical opinion process available for purposes of recovering premium payments. The absence of a challenge mechanism can also result in mischief. For example, consider an employee who fails to return to work due to the continuation of the serious health condition of stress. He provides a medical certification as requested by his employer in support of his claim and the certification is signed by his podiatrist. Exactly what a podiatrist knows about psychiatric conditions is unclear. According to the regulations, the employer eats the costs of health care premiums.

For that matter, the medical certification provision of 29 CFR 825.213(a)(3) does not say the certification has to be from a health care provider, as defined in the FMLA. As such, the medical certification the employer arguably has to accept in support of an employee's failure to return from work due to a serious health condition could be signed by anyone, including the employee.

While employing agencies will likely play it safe and limit the medical information requested to that allowed in 29 CFR 825.306(b), and while it is likely that the overwhelming majority of employees to provide sufficient medical information from a qualified health care provider, the absence of specificity in these regulations (easily accomplished by cross-reference to other provisions) is disturbing.

If the employee fails to timely provide medical certification responsive to an employer's request, or the reason for not returning to work does not meet the test of circumstances beyond the employee's control, the employer may recover 100% of the health benefit premiums it paid during the period of unpaid FMLA leave.

f. Substituted Paid Leave

When an employee elects or an employer requires paid leave to be substituted for FMLA leave, the employer may not recover its share of health insurance or other non-health benefit premiums for any period of FMLA leave covered by paid leave. 29 CFR 825.213(a)(3); S. Res. 242, Cong. Rec. S3959, S3968 (April 23, 1996); 29 CFR 825.213(a)(3).

g. OWCP and Other Forms of Compensation

Because paid leave provided under a plan covering temporary disabilities (including workers' compensation) is not unpaid, recovery of health insurance premiums does not apply to such paid leave. 29 CFR 825.213(a)(3); S. Res. 242, Cong. Rec. S3959, S3968 (April 23, 1996); 29 CFR 825.213(a)(3).

2. Multi-Employer Health Plans

The FMLA regulations do not address the recovery by an employing agency of premium payments made by the employer to continue health benefits during an employee's FMLA leave, including in the event the employee fails to return to work from such leave.

3. FEHBP

The FMLA regulations governing the CAA do not address the recovery of premium payments made by an employing agency to continue health care coverage during an employee's FMLA leave. Presumably, such recovery is governed by 5 CFR 890.502, and is treated like any other debt owed by an employee to the United States.

4. Self-Insured Health Plans

The amount that self-insured employers may recover is limited to only the employer's share of allowable premiums as would be calculated under COBRA, excluding the two percent fee for administrative costs. 29 CFR 825.213(e); S. Res. 242, Cong. Rec. S3959, S3968 (April 23, 1996); 29 CFR 825.213(e).

5. Other Non-Group Health Benefits

Under some circumstances an employing agency may elect to maintain other benefits (e.g., life insurance, disability insurance, etc.) by paying the employee's share or premiums during periods of unpaid FMLA leave. 29 CFR 825.213(b); S. Res. 242, Cong. Rec. S3959, S3968 (April 23, 1996); 29 CFR 825.213(b). For example, to ensure that the employer can meet its responsibilities to provide equivalent benefits to the employee upon return from unpaid FMLA leave, it may be necessary that premiums be paid continuously to avoid a lapse of coverage. If the employer elects to maintain such benefits during the leave, at the conclusion of leave, the employer is entitled to recover only the costs incurred for paying the employee's share of any premiums, whether or not the employee returns to work. 29 CFR 825.213(b); S. Res. 242, Cong. Rec. S3959, S3968 (April 23, 1996); 29 CFR 825.213(b). The employer is not entitled to charge an administration or other fee for covering such premium payments.

6. Method of Collection

When an employee fails to return to work, any health and non-health benefit premiums that an employer is permitted to recover, considered as a debt owed by the non-returning employee to the employer. 29 CFR 825.213(f); S. Res. 242, Cong. Rec. S3959, S3968 (April 23, 1996); 29 CFR 825.213(f). The employer may recover the costs through deduction from any sums due to the employee (e.g., unpaid wages, vacation pay, profit sharing, etc.), provided such deductions do not otherwise violate applicable federal wage payment or other laws. Alternatively, the employer may initiate legal action against the employee to recover such costs. 29 CFR 825.213(f); S. Res. 242, Cong. Rec. S3959, S3968 (April 23, 1996); 29 CFR 825.213(f).

7. Effect of Debt on Existing Obligations

The existence of a debt owed by the employee to the employer for premium payments caused by the employee's failure to return to work does not alter the employer's responsibilities for health benefit coverage and, under a self-insurance plan, payment of claims incurred during the period of FMLA leave. 29 CFR 825.213(f); S. Res. 242, Cong. Rec. S3959, S3968 (April 23, 1996); 29 CFR 825.213(f).

VII. MIXED RESPONSIBILITIES OF EMPLOYING AGENCIES TO MAINTAIN EMPLOYMENT BENEFITS DURING FMLA LEAVE

Federal agencies with mixed FMLA responsibilities must be mindful of the different legal requirements and opportunities available under the federal sector FMLA laws applicable to their workforce. An agency, for example, that simply applies the benefits requirements of Title II to all of its employees, including those covered by Title I, may quickly run afoul of very different legal requirements mandated by Title II of the FMLA. It may also miss opportunities available under Title I that are not available under Title II.

The same is true for unions and other organizations representing the interests of federal employees. Ensuring agency legal compliance and the availability of more advantageous FMLA rights and benefits for employees requires a thorough understanding of the similarities and differences between the federal sector FMLA laws, particularly between Titles I and II of the FMLA.

For example, Title II does not specifically impose an obligation on employing agencies to notify employees of any changes to health benefit plans. An employing agency that abided by Title II and did not notify employees of health plan benefit changes might find itself in violation Title I, which specifically requires employing agencies to notify employees covered by that law of changes to group health benefit plans.

The collection of premiums paid by the employer in lieu of payments by the employee during the pendency of FMLA leave includes another trap for the unwary agency. Title I contains two exceptions where an employing agency is prohibited from collecting premium payments that it paid for the employee during the pendency of FMLA leave. These exceptions are not contained in Title II. A Title II agency that was unaware of these exceptions and that attempted to collect premiums due title-covered employees in circumstances where the premiums were legally excluded would be in violation of the law. The agency and individual supervisors could face an expensive lawsuit, be subject to damages, and have to pay attorney fees and costs.

There are also a number of opportunities in Title I that may be more advantageous to employees and employing agencies than are the opportunities in Title II. For example, regarding the availability of paid leave in substitution of unpaid FMLA leave, Title I permits employing agencies to have more generous benefit provisions than the minimum required by the FMLA, without restriction. Title II, on the other hand, limits the amount of paid leave time off that may be substituted for unpaid FMLA leave to the amount of leave legally available. Unions and employing agencies representing Title I employees should consider bargaining with employing agencies for the availability of more paid leave than the legal limit applicable to Title II employees.

Similarly, Title II employees are limited to health benefits pursuant to the FEHBP. Title I employees, on the other hand, are not limited to health benefits offered by the FEHBP. This may present opportunities to employing agencies, unions, and other organizations representing employees.

For employing agencies, it is clear under Title I that seniority does not accrue to an employee on FMLA leave, absent a more generous agency policy. Under Title II, it is less clear whether seniority accrues during FMLA leave.

Under Title I, employing agencies have 5 options to collect premium payments paid on behalf of a Title I-covered employee on FMLA leave. Under Title II, there are only two options available for an agency to recoup premium payments from an employee.

Title I also contains special provisions regarding the termination of health benefits of so-called key employees. These provisions may be advantageous to employing agencies. Title II does not recognize key employees.

Given the differences in minimum legal requirements and opportunities available, employing agencies, unions, and other organizations representing employees are well advised to closely scrutinize what FMLA laws apply to any given federal employee in agencies with mixed FMLA responsibilities.

CHAPTER 13
RETURN TO WORK FROM LEAVE

I. OVERVIEW

The right of an eligible employee to take FMLA leave is of little value without the concomitant right to return to work on the conclusion of that leave. The FMLA protects the right of eligible federal sector employees to return to work from FMLA leave. To perfect that right, the employee must meet certain preconditions. Employers also have stringent responsibilities they must fulfill as part of the process of accepting an employee's return to work from FMLA leave. The return to work requirements, while substantially similar for federal sector employees, are by no means identical.

Section II, "Employees' Rights On Return To Work From FMLA Leave", of this chapter addresses the basic rules governing an employee's right to return to work from FMLA leave. Section III discusses what employees must do in order to perfect their right to return to work, "Employee's Perfection of Right to Return to Work." The circumstances in which an employer has an affirmative right to deny job restoration to an employee on FMLA leave are addressed in Section IV, "Limitations on an Employer's Obligation to Reinstate an Employee." The return to work rights of so-called "Key Employees" are discussed in Section V. Special rules governing job restoration of certain school employees are set forth in Section VI, "Special Rules Governing Certain Schools." Finally, the responsibilities of agencies whose workforces contain a mixture of FMLA coverages are discussed in Section VII, "Agencies with Mixed FMLA Responsibilities."

II. EMPLOYEES' RIGHTS ON RETURN TO WORK FROM FMLA LEAVE

An eligible federal employee who takes FMLA leave for the intended purpose of the leave is entitled, on return from such leave, to be restored by the employer to the same position the employee held when the leave commenced, or an equivalent position, with equivalent benefits, pay and other terms and conditions of employment. 29 USC 2614(a); 29 CFR 825.214(a); 5 USC 6384(a); 5 CFR 630.1208(a); 2 USC 1312(a)(1) (incorporating 29 USC 2614 into CAA); S. Res. 242, Cong. Rec. S3959, S3969 (April 23, 1996); 29 CFR 825.214(a); 3 USC 412(a)(1) (incorporating 29 USC 2614 into PEOAA); *see Harrell v. USPS*, 445 F.3d 913, 919 (7th Cir. 2006); *Sista v. CDC IXIS North Am., Inc.*, 445 F.3d 161, 174 (2d Cir. 2006); *Edgar v. JAC Products, Inc.*, 443 F.3d 501, 506 (6th Cir. 2005); *Fogelman v. Greater Hazelton Health Alliance*, 122 Fed. Appx. 521 (3d Cir. 2004) (stating general rule under Title I); *accord Hanger v. Lake County*, 390 F.3d 579 (8th Cir. 2004); *Mitchell v. Dutchmen Mfg. Inc.*, 389 F.3d 746, 748 (7th Cir. 2004); *Dressler v. Community Service Communications, Inc.*, 275 F. Supp. 2d 17 (1st Cir. 2004); *Haley v. Alliance Compressor LLC*, 391 F.3d 644 (5th Cir. 2004); *Hoge v. Honda of America Mfg., Inc.*, 384 F.3d 238 (6th Cir. 2004); *Montgomery v. State of Maryland*, 72 Fed. Appx. 17 (4th Cir. 2003); *Conoshenti v. Pub. Serv. Elec. & Gas Co.*, 364 F.3d 135, 141 (3d Cir. 2004) (stating general rule under Title I); *Rice v. Sunrise Express, Inc.*, 209 F.3d 1008 (7th Cir. 2000), *cert. denied*, 531 U.S. 1012 (2000); *Hicks v. Leroy's Jewelers, Inc. et al.*, No. 98-6596, 2000 U.S. App. LEXIS 17568 (6th Cir. July 17, 2000) (same); *Green v. Alcan Aluminum Corp.*, No. 98-3775, 1999 U.S. App. LEXIS 30158 (6th Cir. 1999); *Reynolds v. Phillips & Temro Industries, Inc.*, 195 F.3d 411, 413-14 (8th Cir. 1999); *Tardie v. Rehabilitation Hospital of Rhode Island et al.*, 168 F.3d 538, 543 (1st Cir. 1999); *Watkins v. J&S Oil Co., Inc.*, 164 F.3d 55, 59 (1st Cir. 1998); *Douglas v. E.G. Baldwin & Associates, Inc.*, 150 F.3d 604, n. 2 (6th Cir. 1998); *Diaz v. Fort Wayne Foundry Corp.*, 131 F.3d 711 (7th Cir. 1997); *Donahoo v. Master Data Center*, 282 F. Supp. 2d 540, 551 (E.D. Mich. 2003).

An employee is entitled to reinstatement even if the employer has replaced the employee or restructured his or her position to accommodate the employee's absence. 29 CFR 825.214(a). *See Cline v. Home Quality Management, Inc.*, No. 01-9016-CIV-MOORE, 2004 U.S. Dist. LEXIS 5475, at *16 (S.D. Fla. March 18, 2004).

An employer who refused to restore an eligible employee to the same or equivalent position upon his return from FMLA leave violated the FMLA. *Hillstrom v. Best Western TLC Hotel*, 265 F. Supp. 2d 117, 126 (D. Mass. 2003), *aff'd*, 354 F.3d 27 (1st Cir. 2003).

The rights and obligations governing a federal employee's return to work from FMLA leave differ depending on which FMLA statute and regulations apply.

A. EMPLOYEE RETURN TO WORK FROM LEAVE

The job restoration provisions of all federal sector versions of the FMLA share three common elements: (1) the right is limited to current eligible employees; (2) the term "return" is undefined; and (3) the term "leave" is undefined.

1. Current Eligible Employee

a. Title I, the CAA, and the PEOAA

The right of a federal employee to return to work from leave under these statutes is limited to "any eligible employee" who takes FMLA leave. 29 USC 2614(a); 2 USC 1312(a)(1) (incorporating 29 USC 2614 into CAA); 3 USC 412(a)(1) (incorporating 29 USC 2614 into PEOAA); see Hillstrom v. Best Western TLC Hotel, 265 F. Supp. 2d 117, 126 (D. Mass. 2003), aff'd, 354 F.3d 27 (1st Cir. 2003); Parker v. Hahnemann University Hospital et al., 234 F. Supp. 2d 478, n.13 (D. N.J. 2002) (FMLA entitled eligible employee's reinstatement); Holmes v. E.Spire Communications, Inc. et al., 135 F. Supp. 2d 657, 664 (D. Md. March 15, 2001) (FMLA provides that an eligible employee is entitled upon return from FMLA leave, to be restored to the same or an equivalent position); Lempres v. CBS, Inc., 916 F. Supp. 15, 19 (D. D.C. 1996) (FMLA provides eligible employees, with certain exceptions, the right to reinstatement to their former position or an equivalent one upon return from approved FMLA leave). Unfortunately, the regulations implementing this clear statutory requirement garble this issue. The regulatory language has omitted any reference to an "eligible" employee. Rather, the regulations speak in terms of "an employee." 29 CFR 825.214(a); S. Res. 242, Cong. Rec. S3959, S3969 (April 23, 1996); 29 CFR 825.214(a).

It would appear that the regulations should be read to limit the right to job restoration to eligible employees. The comments to the final Title I regulations contained in the Preamble to 29 CFR 825.214, repeat the rule, including the reference to "an eligible employee." Preamble, 29 CFR 825.214.

The absence of a reference to an "eligible" employee in the job restoration regulations gives rise to the argument that employees who did not meet the eligibility requirements for FMLA leave would nonetheless have a right to be returned to work from that leave. As set forth more fully in Chapter 5, "Employee Eligibility for Leave," in several instances the implementing regulations require an employer to grant FMLA leave to an ineligible employee. The United States Supreme court struck down one of these regulations as unconstitutional.

Under the regulations, an employer is required to grant FMLA leave to an ineligible employee where the employer either mistakenly confirms eligibility, or fails to timely advise the employee whether he or she is eligible for FMLA leave. 29 CFR 825.110(d); S. Res. 242, Cong. Rec. S3959, S3961–S3962 (April 23, 1996); 29 CFR 825.110(d). Similarly, the regulations provide that an employee receives the full protections of the Act when an employer fails to timely advise an employee whether it has designated the leave, paid or unpaid, as FMLA leave. 29 CFR 825.208(c); S. Res. 242, Cong. Rec. S3959, S3966–S3967 (April 23, 1996); 29 CFR 825.208(c). The U.S. Supreme Court struck down a similar penalty regulation in § 825.700(a) as unconstitutional. Ragsdale v. Wolverine World Wide, Inc., 535 U.S. 81, 122 S. Ct. 1155, 152 L. Ed. 2d 167 (2002).

In all likelihood, the Supreme Court's decision in Ragsdale vitiated the continued viability of the above regulations allowing FMLA leave to apply to non–eligible employees. [For a further discussion of this issue, see Chapter 5, "Employee Eligibility for Leave."] As such, the right to return to work from FMLA leave should only apply to eligible employees. Employers faced with arguments to the contrary should cite the specific language of the statute and the language in the Preamble to the final regulations implementing Title I that the right is only enjoyed by eligible employees. Additionally, employers may argue that, pursuant to the Supreme Court's decision in Ragsdale, to the extent that the regulatory language may be read as requiring an employer to return a non–eligible employee from FMLA leave with all of the rights granted to eligible employees, the regulation is unconstitutional as it extends FMLA rights beyond the express intent of Congress.

The Tenth Circuit has addressed this issue. In Dimond v. J.C. Penny, Inc., 116 F.3d 489 (10th Cir. 1997), the court affirmed judgment for the employer. The plaintiff was erroneously granted FMLA leave even though he did not satisfy the 12–month eligibility test. He worked for J.C. Penny for 10 months at the time he requested and was granted FMLA leave. J.C. Penny terminated Dimond during his absence from work. Although he acknowledged that he did not work the requisite 12 months to qualify for FMLA leave benefits, Dimond argued that because J.C. Penny had mistakenly provided him benefits under the Act, it should be estopped from relying in his ineligibility with regard to the Act's other benefits, chiefly the right to return to work at the end of this 12 weeks of leave. The court held that estoppel did not apply because the doctrine is based on reasonable reliance, and plaintiff's reliance could not be reasonable as he plainly was not eligible for FMLA leave.

By referencing any eligible employee, the FMLA limits job restoration rights to current employees. Former employees do not have a right to return to work from FMLA leave. *Walthall v. Fulton County School District,* No. 1:96–CV–2881, 1998 U.S. Dist. LEXIS 16832 (N.D. Ga. Sept. 23, 1998), *aff'd without op.*, 192 F.3d 131 (11th Cir. 1999) (employee not entitled to reinstatement to her former or an equivalent position upon conclusion of FMLA leave because plaintiff resigned, obviating any FMLA–based obligation on the part of employer to reinstate employee*); see also Watkins v. J&S Oil Co.*, 165 F.3d 55 (1st Cir. 1998) (whether an employee voluntarily resigned before attempting to return to work is one of fact for the fact finder). [A further discussion of the impact of an employee's notice that he or she does not intend to return to work from FMLA leave is contained in Section IV of this chapter, "Special Rules Governing Certain Schools."]

Of course, employers may be required to return an employee to work from leave pursuant to employer policy, including the terms of a collective bargaining agreement. In those cases, the return to work of an employee who is not eligible within the meaning of the FMLA is governed solely by employer policy, not the FMLA.

b. Title II

The statutory and regulatory language in Title II is consistent. It also does not specifically limit the right to job restoration to an eligible employee.

Any employee who takes FMLA leave is entitled, on return from FMLA leave, to the same or an equivalent position, with equivalent benefits, pay, status, and other terms and conditions of employment. 5 USC 6384(a); 5 CFR 630.1208(a). Unlike the regulations implementing Title I, the CAA, and the PEOAA, there is no dispute under Title II that the right to return to work from FMLA leave is limited to "eligible" employees. First, the Statute defines employee to include the eligibility requirements. 5 USC 6381(1)(A). [For a further discussion of the eligibility requirements under Title II, see Chapter 5, "Employee Eligibility for Leave."]

Second, the regulations implementing Title II do not contain penalty provisions similar to those set forth in 29 CFR 825.110(d) and 825.208(c). As a result, an employer's mistaken notice of eligibility, or failure to timely notify the employee of eligibility, or that it has designated the leave as FMLA leave, will not result in an otherwise ineligible employee being granted FMLA leave by operation of law. Under Title II, only eligible employees have the right to return to work from FMLA leave.

Like Title I, the CAA, and the PEOAA, the use of the term "employee" in Title II suggests that the right to return to work from FMLA leave is limited to current employees. Employees who resign or who otherwise permanently depart from employment (i.e., they die) during the pendency of FMLA leave would not have an FMLA right to return to work.

Employees covered by Title II who are not eligible for FMLA leave benefits but who were mistakenly granted FMLA leave would not have a right to return to work from that leave under Title II. Rather, their return to work from leave is governed by applicable employer policy, including the terms of a collective bargaining agreement.

2. Leave

The right to job restoration is triggered by an employee's return from FMLA leave. What constitutes FMLA leave, therefore, is critical in determining when an employee returns from that leave.

a. Title I, the CAA, and the PEOAA

The term "leave" is not defined in the Statute or the implementing regulations. For purposes of Title I eligibility, the DOL has defined leave as the taking of all FMLA leave for the same covered condition. *See* DOL WH FMLA Advisory Opinion No. 112 (Sept. 11, 2000). If leave is taken in a single block of time for the same covered condition, that absence is considered FMLA leave. If, on the other hand, FMLA leave were taken intermittently or on a reduced leave schedule for the same covered condition, the entire series of separate absences would constitute a single period of FMLA leave. *See Covey v. Methodist Hospital of Dyersburg, Inc.*, 56 F. Supp. 2d 965, 968 (W.D. Tenn. 1999) (employee who was taking

FMLA leave on reduced leave schedule was not entitled to job restoration until the need for such schedule has ended; where plaintiff's restrictions are permanent, employee will never return from FMLA leave, and employer was justified in transferring employee permanently to position that better accommodates employee's need for reduced leave schedule). For example, an eligible employee needs to take a week of FMLA leave to care for a parent with a serious health condition. For purposes of an employee's return to work, the week of leave for the same covered condition constitutes the FMLA leave period. On conclusion of that leave, the employee's right to return to work is implicated.

If the employee were to take FMLA in two hour increments once a week over the course of months to care for a parent with a serious health condition, the entire series of absences, not any single absence within the series, is considered a single period of FMLA leave. As such, the employee's right to job restoration would be implicated only on the conclusion of the last FMLA absence in the series. In our example, if the employee took 16 absences of two hours apiece over the course of three months, FMLA leave would encompass the entire series of 12 absences. The leave would end with the conclusion of the sixteenth and last FMLA absence.

Under this definition of leave, an eligible employee could take FMLA leave for several different reasons during the same time period. In our example above, the employee is considered to be on FMLA leave for the entire 16-week period to care for a parent with a serious health condition. In that same 16-week time period, the employee could claim a single day of FMLA leave for his or her own serious health condition, and two four-hour days to care for a covered child with a serious health condition. During the same 16-week period, the employee has three different periods of FMLA leave running. On the conclusion of each of those three different FMLA leave periods, the employee will have rights and obligations to job restoration.

b. Title II

Title II, like Title I, the CAA, and the PEOAA, does not define what constitutes FMLA leave. In all likelihood, the OPM will follow the lead of the DOL and define leave as linking all absences to the same covered condition. Because of its impact on the rules governing an employee's return from FMLA leave, as well as a number of other rules, OPM needs to identify what constitutes leave for purposes of Title II.

3. Return

An eligible employee's right to restoration to the same or equivalent position is triggered on the employee's return from FMLA leave. Not surprisingly, it is less than clear what that means.

a. Title I, the CAA, and the PEOAA

(1) Defined

There is no specific definition provided to determine when an employee "returns from [FMLA] leave." Common sense suggests that an eligible employee returns from leave when the FMLA leave has concluded. *See Hoge v. Honda of America Mfg., Inc.*, 384 F.3d 238 (6th Cir. 2004); *Oatman v. Fuji Photo Film U.S.A., Inc.*, No. 3:00-CV-2116-R, 2002 U.S. Dist. LEXIS 2644 (N.D. Tex. Feb. 15, 2002), *aff'd*, 2002 U.S. App. LEXIS 24826 (5th Cir. 2002), *cert. denied*, 538 U.S. 978 2003) (under FMLA, plaintiff must show that he was eligible to be reinstated to his position of employment when his FMLA leave expired). Ordinarily, this is not an issue because the employer and employee will communicate and establish a return date for an employee taking FMLA leave. In such cases, the timing of the employee's "return" will not be at issue, and the restoration entitlement will arise when the employee returns in a timely manner and in a physical condition to perform the essential functions of the job s/he left, after providing the fitness-for-duty medical certification, if required. *Hoge v. Honda of America Mfg., Inc.*, 384 F.3d 238 (6th Cir. 2004).

The above definition is supported by statutory language governing the maintenance of health benefits during the pendency of FMLA leave. In discussing when an employer may recover premium payments that an employer paid for maintaining group health coverage during unpaid FMLA leave, the Statute provides that "the employee fails to return from leave under § 102 after the period of leave to which the employee is entitled has expired." 29 USC 2614(c)(2)(A); 2 USC 1312(a)(1) (incorporating 29 USC 2614 into CAA); 3 USC 412(a)(1) (incorporating 29 USC 2614 into PEOAA). [For a further discussion of the rights and obligations governing the maintenance of health benefits during the pendency of FMLA leave, see Chapter 12, "Maintenance of Benefits."] Comments in the preamble to the final DOL regulations lend further support that "return from leave" means at the conclusion of FMLA leave. Preamble, 29 CFR 825.214 ("In the Department's view the contractor would have the responsibilities as the primary employer of the employee for job *restoration at the conclusion of the employee's FMLA leave.*") (emphasis supplied).

The statute and regulations are unclear whether the phrase "return from leave" has the same meaning as "return to work." In some places the statute uses the phrase "return from leave." *See* 29 USC 2614(c)(2)(A). In other instances, however, the statute uses the term "return to work." *See* 29 USC 2614(c)(2)(b), (3)(a). It is unclear from both the statute and the legislative history whether the terms have separate meanings or are used interchangeably. Based on my reading, it appears that the statute is using the terms interchangeably.

The regulations appear to interchange the phrase "return from leave" with "return to work." *See* Preamble, 29 CFR 825.214 (in addressing comments by Sommer & Barnard that regulations did not address employer's obligation to reinstate an employee who returns from work before the planned expiration of the scheduled FMLA leave, DOL did not distinguish return from leave with return to work, but simply added that the issue was addressed in another regulation). Of course, this makes sense, as the basic tenet of FMLA leave is the right to be absent from work, and to return to work on the conclusion of FMLA leave. That is, implicit in the phrase "on return from leave," is the destination of that return: work.

The term "return to work" is defined for purposes of the FMLA maintenance of benefits rules. An employee who returns to work for at least 30 calendar days is considered to have returned to work. 29 CFR 825.213(c); S. Res. 242, Cong. Rec. S3959, S3966–S3968 (April 23, 1996); 29 CFR 825.213(c). An employee who transfers directly from taking FMLA leave to retirement, or who retires during the first 30 days after the employee returns to work, is defined to have returned to work from FMLA leave. 29 CFR 825.213(c); S. Res. 242, Cong. Rec. S3959, S3966–S3968 (April 23, 1996); 29 CFR 825.213(c).

If return from leave means the same as return to work, interesting results occur. For example, if an employee is not considered to have returned to work on the conclusion of FMLA leave until the passage of 30 calendar days, it follows that the employee does not have the immediate right to the same or equivalent position for the first 30 calendar days the employee is back at work. For purposes of the FMLA, absent retirement, until 30 calendar days have passed the employee has not yet returned to work.

This 30-day window before an eligible employee is considered to have returned to work appears relatively unrestricted. The rules governing an employee's transfer to an alternative position during a period of intermittent or FMLA leave on a reduced leave schedule would not apply during this 30-day period. Those rules only apply to accommodate an employee who currently needs FMLA leave. They require that the alternative position must have equivalent pay and benefits, but need not have equivalent duties. 29 CFR 825.204(c). Because, by definition, the employee no longer needs FMLA leave, the limitations that the alternative position must have equivalent pay and benefits would not apply.

The FMLA leave period could not be extended because an employee may not be required to take more FMLA than necessary to address the circumstances that precipitated the need for leave. 29 CFR 825.203(c)(2). If, for example, the employee originally needed intermittent FMLA leave for his or her own serious health condition, on the conclusion of that condition the employee would no longer need FMLA leave. In that case, the rules governing transfer to an alternative position arguably do not apply. Because an employee is not considered to have returned to work until the passage of 30 calendar days after the employee has physically returned to work, the rules requiring an employer to provide equivalent pay and benefits, but not duties, in an alternative position would not extend into this 30-day period.

Assuming that return from leave means the same thing as return to work, employers should not treat the 30-day window as a free-for-all where they can require employees who have physically returned from FMLA leave to suffer placement in positions that do not provide equivalent pay, benefits, or terms and conditions of employment. The rules prohibiting an employer from discriminating against an employee for exercising rights under the FMLA still apply. Employers should treat this period as a time to prepare the organization to receive the employee back into his or her former or an equivalent position.

If the employee can be returned to the same position within these 30 days, the employee should be returned as soon as practical. Agencies should not delay the employee's return to the same or an equivalent position for 30 days just because they can. If the employee cannot be returned to the same or an equivalent position immediately, to avoid claims of discrimination or retaliation for exercising FMLA rights, agencies are well-advised to structure the job so that the employee is receiving equivalent pay, benefits, and duties, if possible.

Of course, the above interpretation depends on the phrase "on return from leave" having the same meaning as "return to work." Nothing from the DOL or others appears to indicate that the phrases do not mean the same thing. Quite the opposite is true. Most treat the employees return from leave as commencing the first day the employee is able to show up back at work. Employers would be safe to follow that rule, at least for purposes of the return to work rules. However, that would not be a safe course to follow for purposes of collecting benefit premiums the employer paid on behalf of an employee during the pendency of FMLA leave.

Employers faced with accusations that they failed to immediately return an employee to the same or an equivalent position should consider the above argument as a defense. Unions and other organizations representing employees should consider bargaining for employer rules that require an employee's immediate return to work on the conclusion of FMLA leave to the same or an equivalent position. Employers are not prohibited from offering more generous leave benefits than the minimum required by the FMLA.

(2) What Constitutes an Employee's Return: Physical Presence or Notice?

The FMLA does not require that an employee show up on the employer's doorstep in order to qualify as having returned to work from FMLA leave. A telephone call on or before the expiration of FMLA leave appears to be the minimum effort required to satisfy this requirement. See *Duty v. Norton–Alcoa Proppants*, 293 F.3d 481, 494 (8th Cir. 2002) (employee attempted to return to work by telephoning employer on the day after his FMLA leave expired to find out what was expected of him in order to return to work); *Watkins v. J & S Oil Co., Inc.*, 164 F.3d 55, 59 (1st Cir. 1998); *Barry v. Wing Mem. Hosp.*, 142 F. Supp. 2d 161, 165–66 (D. Mass. 2001); see, e.g., *Routes v. Henderson*, 58 F. Supp. 2d 959, 992 (S.D. Ind. 1999) (court held that employee's contact with supervisor in which he asked to be restored to position he held constituted attempt to exercise right to return to work from FMLA leave; manner of employee contact not disclosed). In *Watkins*, the First Circuit ejected a *per se* rule that would require an employee on FMLA leave to actually show up to work on or before the expiration of the 12 weeks of FMLA leave in order to perfect the FMLA right to job restoration. Citing 29 CFR 825.309, which requires only that an employee express a continuing desire to return to work in order for the employer's obligation to maintain health benefits, the court held that the employee returned from FMLA leave at the time of his last telephone call wherein the employee expressed a continuing desire to return to his former position.

(3) Employee's Obligation to Return

The regulations do not address the permissible time frame in which an employee who has not exhausted his or her 12 weeks of FMLA leave must return to work on the expiration of the need for FMLA leave. In *Brown v. J.C. Penny Corporation*, 924 F. Supp. 1158, 1163 (S.D. Fla. 1996), the court held that the employee relinquished his FMLA right to return to work from FMLA leave by failing to return to work until one month after his father's death from a serious health condition. The employee had originally taken FMLA leave to care for his father. After his father's death, the employee remained on leave to take care of his father's affairs. The court rejected the plaintiff's argument that taking care of his affairs after his father's death was covered by the FMLA. The father's serious health condition, the court ruled, ended with his death.

The court in *Brown* did not impose a minimum time period within which all employees must return to work from FMLA leave in order to enjoy the job restoration provisions of the FMLA. Nor did it impose a reasonable period of time. Employees whose need for FMLA leave has ceased are well advised to contact their employer as soon as practicable of their wish to return to work. Ideally, this should be done while the employee is still on FMLA leave. Technically, if the need for leave has ceased, the employee is no longer on FMLA leave. The right to return to work under the FMLA is predicated on the return being from FMLA leave. While the DOL and some courts may allow an employee a reasonable period of time to contact the employer or physically return to work after FMLA leave has expired, that period of time is likely to be narrowly construed.

In *Lindsey v. Gardner's Supermarket*, No. 1:98–CV–162–JAD, 1999 U.S. Dist. LEXIS 7526 (N.D. Miss. May 10, 1995), the district court held that the supermarket did not violate the FMLA when it discharged the employee after the employee failed to report for work on a specified return date, without prior notice of explanation that the employee could not return to work that day.

In *Warrant v. Aetna Life Insurance Co.*, No. 3:97–CV–1030–R, 1999 U.S. Dist. LEXIS 12849 (N.D. Tex. Aug. 13, 1999), the district court held that Aetna did not violate the FMLA when it ordered the employee to immediately return to work on receipt of a medical release indicating that the employee could return to work immediately. The employee returned to work as instructed, got ill, and was taken to the hospital. The employee claimed that Aetna violated the FMLA by prematurely ordering her to return to work. The court rejected this claim, finding that Aetna was entitled to rely on the medical release provided by the employee's health care provider.

(4) Employer Delay of an Employee's Return to Work

Employers may desire a brief delay to prepare the workplace for the return of the employee. For example, if a temporary employee was appointed in the employee's position, the employer may wish a short delay in the return of the employee in order to move or release that temporary employee. An employer might also wish a short delay in order to prepare an equivalent position for the employee.

Neither the FMLA statutes nor the implementing regulations permit an employer to delay the return of an employee on the conclusion of that employee's need for FMLA leave, except where the employer requires a fitness-for-duty certification or another FMLA exception specifically sanctions the delay in job restoration. Such certifications and exceptions are discussed later in this chapter. The statue provides that an employee who takes leave for the intended purpose is entitled, on return from such leave, to be restored to their same or an equivalent position. 29 USC 2614(a)(1). The term "return from FMLA leave" is undefined. Presumably, it means when the employee no longer needs FMLA leave.

An employer may, however, require an employee who is returning earlier than expected to provide reasonable notice (i.e., within two business days) of the changed circumstances where foreseeable. 29 CFR 825.309(c); S. Res. 242, Cong. Rec. S3959, S3973–S3975 (April 23, 1996); 29 CFR 825.309(c). Note that the notice provision only applies where the changed circumstances necessitating an earlier than expected return to work is foreseeable. Presumably, when the changed circumstances are not foreseeable, the employee may simply show up to work, and the employer has to cope with that return as best as it can, without violating the FMLA.

The requirement that an employee notify an employer of an early return to work does not set forth a penalty should the employee neglect to provide notice, such as a two-day delay in the employee's return to work. It is unclear whether the employer could adopt such a penalty for violation of a published notice requirement. Any delay in an employee's return to work could not be charged against the employee's 12-week FMLA leave entitlement where the employee has signaled that he or she no longer needs FMLA leave. An employer cannot require an employee to take more FMLA leave than is necessary to address the employee's FMLA need for leave. As a result, any administrative delay in the employee's return to work would have to be charged to some other form of leave.

An employer does not have a reasonable period of time within which to return an employee from FMLA leave to his or her same or an equivalent position. Rather, with two exceptions, an employee must be immediately returned to his or her same or equivalent position on the conclusion of FMLA leave. The two exceptions permitting an employer to delay the return of an employee from FMLA leave to his or her same or equivalent position are: (1) until the employee receives a requested fitness-for-duty medical certification, 29 CFR 825.310(f); and (2) where the employer did not have reasonable notice of an employee's return from FMLA leave because the employee took either more or less leave than anticipated, 29 CFR 825.309(c), 825.312(e).

The court in *Hoge v. Honda of America Mfg., Inc.*, 384 F.3d 238 (6th Cir. 2004), addressed whether an employer can delay the return of an employee from FMLA leave for a reasonable period of time. Hoge took FMLA leave for back surgery. During her leave, Hoge called Honda and requested an extension of her FMLA leave to recover from surgery. Both requests were granted. The parties disputed the date of her anticipated return. Plaintiff appeared and attempted to work on June 27, 2000. Honda did not restore her to her same or an equivalent position that day. Honda returned her to an equivalent position on July 31, 2000. Plaintiff sued Honda alleging that the delay in returning her to work from FMLA leave violated the job restoration provisions of the FMLA. The district court agreed, awarding Hoge monetary damages, attorney fees, and costs. Honda appealed.

On appeal, Honda argued that the FMLA required Honda to reinstate plaintiff to her employment position or an equivalent position only within a reasonable time, not immediately, and that Honda did so in this case. Honda pointed to the absence of language on the issue in the FMLA. It also argued that the FMLA should be read *in para materia* with the ADA, and employers must be afforded a reasonable amount of time to evaluate whether an employee is disabled, to identify reasonable accommodations, and to minimize potential liability under other federal and state laws. Honda claimed that plaintiff's physical limitations, her unanticipated return, and the significant changes made by Honda to its production processes during a "model changeover" reasonably prevented Honda from restoring plaintiff to work until July 31, 2000. The Sixth Circuit disagreed.

The court declined to read a reasonableness element into the timing of when a returning employee is entitled to job restoration under the FMLA where such an element does not exist in the text of the statute. The court found that the text of the FMLA was clear regarding the timing of the return of an employee from FMLA leave. The court observed:

> The FMLA's test, set forth in more detail above, provides than an employee returning from FMLA leave "shall be entitled, *on return from such leave*...to be restored by the employer" to his prior position or an equivalent position with the same conditions of employment. 29 U.S.C. § 2614(a). The plain meaning of "on return from such leave" is not ambiguous and, contrary to Honda's argument, will not be construed to mean "within a reasonable time after the employee is able to return from such leave." If an employee returning from FMLA leave can perform the essential functions of his previous or an equivalent position, the right to restoration is triggered on the employee's timely return from leave. 29 U.S.C. § 2614(a); 29 C.F.R. § 825.214(b). If Congress had intended to permit employers to restore employees within a reasonable time after their need for FMLA leave had ended, it would have so stated.... The clear import of this language requires restoration upon return, unless one of the specific limitations or exceptions applies. (Citations omitted).

The court continued that "reasonable delay" to afford an employer the opportunity to find the employee a suitable position would force the employee to take more FMLA leave as required and would interfere with an employee's exercise of FMLA rights. *Id.*

The court dismissed Honda's argument that the FMLA should be read *in para materia* with the ADA to afford employers a reasonable period of time to find a position as a reasonable accommodation, noting that the leave provisions of the FMLA are wholly distinct from the reasonable accommodation obligations of employers covered by the ADA. *Id.*

Where the employee's return date is uncertain or changes, the FMLA regulatory scheme dictates the timing of an employee's "return" from FMLA leave. In such cases, employers are entitled to reasonable notice of an employee's return (29 CFR 825.309(c)):

> It may be necessary for an employee to take more leave than originally anticipated. Conversely, an employee may discover after beginning leave that the circumstances have changed and the amount of leave originally anticipated is no longer necessary. An employee may not be required to take more FMLA leave than necessary to resolve the circumstances that precipitated the need for leave. In both of these situations, the employer may require that the employee provide the employer with reasonable notice (i.e., within two business days) of the changed circumstance where foreseeable. The employer may also obtain information on such changed circumstances through requested status reports.

Section 825.312(e) of the DOL FMLA regulations further provides: "If the employee is able to return to work earlier than anticipated, the employee shall provide the employer two business days notice where feasible; the employer is required to restore the employee once such notice is given." *Id.*

Because *Hoge's expected return date was unclear*, the parties disputed whether Honda should have known that she would report for work on June 27. The analysis of the Sixth Circuit in that regard, is instructive:

> If her early return from approved leave was not anticipated, then the regulations governing an employee's early return from FMLA leave apply. Under 29 C.F.R. §§ 825.309(c) and 825.312(e), Plaintiff was required to provide Honda reasonable notice (i.e., two business days) that she would be returning sooner than expected. Thus, by showing up for work at the beginning of the work day, Hoge put Honda on reasonable notice that she was ready and capable of returning to the position that she left (with the accommodation of her physical limitations associated with her back injury) or its equivalent.

> If Honda did not have reasonable notice of Hoge's return date, it was not required to permit Plaintiff to return to work until June 29, 2000, two business days after receiving notice of her willingness and ability to return to work. Conversely, if Honda did have reasonable notice that Hoge's extension of FMLA leave was to end on June 26, 2000, it was required to restore her to a door line position or an equivalent on June 27, 2000, because it does not dispute that Hoge was capable of performing the essential functions of such position.

Id. Under *Hoge*, an employer generally may not delay an employee's return to work where it either knows or had reasonable notice of the return date. It is possible that reasonable notice could include an employee simply showing up for work unannounced. Where, however, an employer does not have reasonable notice of an employee's return date, the employer is permitted to delay the employee's "return" from FMLA leave to the same or an equivalent position for up to two business days.

Employers are well advised to plan ahead for the employee's return to work from FMLA leave. Whether the employee will be placed in his or her former position or an equivalent position should be decided early on, and contingencies made in the event the employee returns to work earlier or later than expected. Given the absence of direction on this issue, agencies should avoid delaying an employee's return to work from FMLA leave unless specifically permitted to do so by a recognized FMLA exception.

b. Title II

Title II fails to define when an employee is considered to have returned from FMLA leave. Like Title I, the CAA, and the PEOAA, Title II premises an employee's right to be restored by the employer to the same or an equivalent position "upon the return" of the employee from FMLA leave. 5 USC 6384(a). The implementing regulations refine this to read "upon [the employee's] return to the employer [from FMLA leave]." 5 CFR 630.1208. Title II does not otherwise define what the terms "return to the employer" or "return to work" mean. It does not require a minimum period of time (e.g., 30 calendar days) before the employee is considered to have returned to work. As a result, Title II does not share the same problems and opportunities as do Title I, the CAA, and the PEOAA, as a result of requiring a minimum period of physical presence at work before the employee who has returned to work from FMLA leave is legally considered to have returned in order for the right to the same or an equivalent position to apply.

Return to the employer certainly means the physical return of the employee to work following a period of FMLA leave. It is unclear, however, whether return means notice of return, as was concluded by one case interpreting Title I. It is also unclear whether a brief delay by the employer in returning the employee would be tolerated under Title II. Arguably, because the right to be returned to the same or an equivalent position is tied to the employee's return to the employer, the right does not apply until the employee so returns. The regulation does not on its face prohibit an employer from delaying the employee's return to work. Of course, the anti-discrimination provisions would prohibit any such delay that was not for legitimate, nondiscriminatory reasons.

B. SAME OR EQUIVALENT POSITION

All eligible federal employees who have returned to work from FMLA leave are entitled to be returned to the same or equivalent position. Although similar, those rights are not uniform throughout the federal sector.

1. Same Position

a. Title I, the CAA, and the PEOAA

On return from FMLA leave, an eligible employee is entitled to be restored by the employer to the position of employment held by the employee when the leave commenced, or to an equivalent position. 29 USC 2614(a)(1); 2 USC 1312(a)(1) (incorporating 29 USC 2614 into CAA); 3 USC 412(a)(1) (incorporating 29 USC 2614 into PEOAA); *see Csicsmann v. Sallada*, 211 Fed. Appx. 163 (4th Cir. 2006).

An employee does not have an absolute entitlement to restoration to his or her pre-leave position after taking FMLA leave. *Csicsmann v. Sallada*, 211 Fed. Appx. 163 (4th Cir. 2006); *Yashenko v. Harrah's NC Casino, Co.*, 446 F.3d 541, 549 (4th Cir. 2006); *Foraker v. Apollo Group, Inc.*, No. CV-04-2614-PHX-DGC, 2007 U.S. Dist. LEXIS 38676, at *10 (D. Az. May 25, 2007).

An employee is entitled to reinstatement to the same position even if the employer replaced the employee or restructured the position to accommodate the employee's absence. 29 CFR 825.214(a); S. Res. 242, Cong. Rec. S3959, S3969 (April 23, 1996); 29 CFR 825.214(a); *see Cline v. Home Quality Management, Inc.*, No. 01-9016-CIV-MOORE, 2004 U.S. Dist. LEXIS 5475, at *16 (S.D. Fla. March 18, 2004); *Parker v. Hahnemann University Hospital et al.*, 234 F. Supp. 2d 478, n.13 (D. N.J.

2002); *Hanna v. Pay-And-Save, Inc. et al.*, No. 5:00-CV-430-C, 2001 U.S. Dist. LEXIS 20095 (N.D. Tex. Dec. 5, 2001); *Madison v. The Sherwin William Co.*, 158 F. Supp. 2d 854, 858-59 (N.D. Ill. April 6, 2001); *Brown v. J.C. Penny Corporation*, 924 F. Supp. 1158, 1163 (S.D. Fla. 1996). However, the fact that an employer has permanently filled the employee's former position is not, in itself, a violation of the Statute. Because an employee may also be returned to an equivalent position, the FMLA does not require that an employee be returned to the exact position that he or she held prior to embarking on FMLA leave. *Brown v. J.C. Penny Corporation*, 924 F. Supp. at 1163.

The statutes and regulations do not, however, provide any further guidance on what constitutes the employee's same position. An employee who is offered return from FMLA leave to the same position has no right to refuse that offer, and the employer has no obligation to accede to the employee's request to be returned to a different job. *Williams v. SAAD's Healthcare*, No. 99-1070-BH-S, 2000 U.S. Dist. LEXIS 4180 (S.D. Ala. March 16, 2000).

As defined, an employee is only entitled to return to the same position held prior to commencement of the FMLA leave at issue. This is true even where the employee was transferred to another position that better accommodated the employee's need for intermittent or FMLA leave on a reduced leave schedule. 29 CFR 825.204(e); S. Res. 242, Cong. Rec. S3959, S3965 (April 23, 1996); 29 CFR 825.204(e). If the employer already moved the employee from his or her permanent position to another position before the employee requested FMLA leave, the employee would only be entitled to be returned to the position held prior to the start of FMLA leave.

For example, Gary's permanent position with the Postal Service is Senior Real Estate Attorney at Headquarters. Gary takes a detail as a manager with the Facilities Service Office at Headquarters. During his detail, Gary requests six weeks of FMLA leave to care for a parent who unexpectedly came down with a serious health condition. When his parent recovers, Gary seeks to return to work. Pursuant to the FMLA, Gary is entitled to be returned to the position he held on detail, or an equivalent position, as it was the position he held at the commencement of FMLA leave.

It is clear that Gary would not be entitled to return to his permanent position from FMLA leave. The FMLA right to return to work is limited to the position the employee held prior to the commencement of FMLA leave. Of course, employer policy, including the terms of a collective bargaining agreement, and/or other federal laws might provide greater rights and require that Gary be returned to his permanent position if, for example, his detail ended during the course of his FMLA leave. It would be a very unusual federal case where a federal employee on a detail would effectively lose his or her permanent position as a result of going out on FMLA. In *Colpean v. Ajilon, LLC*, No. 05-73710, 2007 U.S. Dist. LEXIS 23344, at *21-24 (E.D. Mich. March 30, 2007), the court found that the employer returned the employee to the same position the employee held at the time leave commenced. At the time, the employer had the employee in an unassigned, non-pay status for a week or two. Prior to that, she had been employed on a temporary assignment for several years. The court found that the employee's return to the unassigned, non-pay status the employee held at leave commencement was all that was required by the FMLA.

While undefined, placement of the employee in the same position held prior to leave commencement requires that the position, pay, benefits, and other terms and conditions of employment be essentially what they were when the employee commenced FMLA leave, unless greater benefits have been added during the period of FMLA leave. Placement of an employee on return from FMLA leave in the same position but with reduced or adversely altered pay, benefits, or other terms and conditions of employment is violative of the Act. *Cooper v. Olin Corporation, Winchester Division*, 246 F.3d 1083, 1090 (8th Cir. 2001) (restoration of salary, title and benefits does not necessarily constitute restoration to the same position within the meaning of 29 USC 2614(a)(1)(A) when the job duties and essential functions of the newly assigned position are materially different from those of the employee's pre-leave position). *But see Robinson v. Overnite Transportation Co.*, No. 95-3067, 1997 U.S. App. LEXIS 6574 (4th Cir. April 9, 1997) (court noted absence of support for the plaintiff's position that his return to same position but with imposition of probationary period following an accident fundamentally altered the nature of his position).

The FMLA does not require that an employer first attempt to place the returning employee in the same position from which the employee commenced FMLA leave, and, if that is not possible, only then may an employer place the employee in an equivalent position. *See* Preamble, 29 CFR 825.214 (DOL lacks authority to require employer to first attempt to place a returning employee in same position before placement in equivalent position). *See Watkins v. J&S Oil Co., Inc. et al.*, 164 F.3d 55 (1st Cir. 1998) (employer not required under FMLA to return the plaintiff to his former management position, employer was required, however, to afford the employee equivalent work and compensation under the Act). Unless the employer has a policy or practice requiring otherwise, both alternatives are equally available to an employer.

This would appear to be the case even if the employee's position remained open, and the employee wanted to be returned to the same position rather than an equivalent position. Of course, such a decision on the part of an employer must be for legitimate, nondiscriminatory reasons and not as a form of illegal retaliation or discrimination because the employee exercised rights under the FMLA.

Unions and other organizations representing the interests of employees should consider bargaining for a requirement that employees have the option of which job they would like to be returned to from FMLA leave: (1) their permanent job; (2) their same job; (3) or an equivalent job. Alternatively, a uniform order of return could be established. For example, all employees returning from FMLA leave are first returned to their same position. If that position is not available, then the employee is returned to an equivalent position.

b. Title II

Under Title II, an employee returning to work from FMLA leave is entitled to be returned to the same position held by the employee when the leave commenced. 5 USC 6384(a)(1); 5 CFR 630.1208(a)(1). This is the same right as enjoyed by employees covered by Title I, the CAA, and the PEOAA. Like those statutes, Title II does not further define what constitutes the employee's same position.

Where an employee is placed in an alternative position to accommodate the need for FMLA leave on an intermittent or reduced leave schedule basis, the employee is entitled on returning from such leave, to be returned to his or her permanent position or an equivalent position. 5 CFR 630.1204(c). This is different than the entitlement enjoyed by employees covered by Title I, the CAA, and the PEOAA, where the employer is only required to return the employee to the position held prior to leave commencement, whether or not that is the employee's permanent position.

The regulations are confusing on this point. In pertinent part, 5 CFR 630.1204(c) provides:

> Upon returning from [FMLA leave on an intermittent or reduced leave schedule basis], the employee shall be entitled to be returned to his or her permanent position or an equivalent position, as provided in § 630.1208(a).

The confusion stems from the fact that § 630.1208(a) does not require an employee returning from FMLA leave to be returned to his or her permanent position. Rather, it requires that the employee be restored to the position he or she held prior to leave commencement, which might be the employee's permanent position; it also might not be.

This linkage of two regulations with different terminology also confuses the issue of what position is used to determine whether the employer legally placed the employee into an equivalent position: the employee's permanent position or the position the employee held prior to leave commencement, even if that is not the employee's permanent position.

Presumably, the regulation should be read as requiring an employee returning to work from an alternative position that better accommodates the need for intermittent or FMLA leave on a reduced leave schedule to be placed in his or her permanent position or a position equivalent to the permanent position. If the employer has not placed the employee in an alternative position to accommodate intermittent or leave on a reduced leave schedule, then the employee is returned to the position the employee held at the time of leave commencement. That is true whether this was the employee's permanent position or not.

Of course, one could also argue that the right to return to work in all instances is to the employee's permanent position, no matter how FMLA leave is taken. The problem with this view is that the statutory language says otherwise. Indeed, the fact that the Statute only speaks in terms of return to the position the employee held at the time of leave commencement would appear to undermine any argument in favor of a return to the employee's permanent position. That suggests that 5 CFR 630.1204(c) may be susceptible to an argument that it is constitutionally invalid.

Of course, employer policy, including the terms of a collective bargaining agreement, and the requirements of other laws may require that the employee ultimately be returned to the permanent position in lieu of termination where, for example, the temporary position held by the employee at the commencement of FMLA leave has ceased to exist.

2. Equivalent Position

As an alternative to return to the same position the employee held at the commencement of FMLA leave, employers are permitted to return the employee to an equivalent position. While substantially similar, the federal sector FMLA laws define an equivalent position differently.

Note that the requirement that an equivalent position include equivalent pay, benefits, and other terms and conditions of employment applies equally to situations where the employee was returned to the same position, or an equivalent one. The point of all of the specificity to determine equivalence is to get the employee in a position that is nearly identical to the position held before commencing FMLA leave. As such, those rules apply equally when determining whether an employer has complied with the FMLA by returning the employee to the same position held.

a. Equivalency Generally

(1) Title I, the CAA, and the PEOAA

An equivalent position is one that is virtually identical to the employee's former position in terms of pay, benefits and working conditions, including privileges, prerequisites and status. 29 CFR 825.215(a); S. Res. 242, Cong. Rec. S3959, S3969 (April 23, 1996); 29 CFR 825.215(a); *see Smith v. East Baton Rouge Parish School Bd.*, 453 F.3d 650, 651 (5th Cir. 2006); *Hanger v. Lake County*, 390 F.3d 579 (8th Cir. 2004) (citing general Title I rule); *accord Mitchell v. Dutchmen Mfg. Inc.*, 389 F.3d 746, 748 (7th Cir. 2004); *Hoge v. Honda of America Mfg., Inc.*, 384 F.3d 238 (6th Cir. 2004); *Montgomery v. State of Maryland*, 72 Fed. Appx. 17 (4th Cir. 2003); *Cooper v. Olin Corporation, Winchester Division*, 246 F.3d 1083, 1090 (8th Cir. 2001); *Douglas v. E.G. Baldwin & Associates, Inc.*, 150 F.3d 604, n. 2 (6th Cir. 1998); *LaFortune v. Fiber Materials, Inc.*, No. 03-275-P-H, 2004 U.S. Dist. LEXIS 21405, at *12 (D. Me. Oct. 25, 2004); *Oby v. Baton Rouge Marriott*, 329 F. Supp 2d 772 (M.D. La. 2004); *Felix v. Sun Microsystems, Inc.*, No. JFM-03-1304, 2004 U.S. Dist. LEXIS 7508, at *39 (D. Md. April 12, 2004); *Sabatino v. Flik International Corp.*, 286 F. Supp. 2d 327, 337 (S.D.N.Y. 2003); *Donahoo v. Master Data Center*, 282 F. Supp. 2d 540, 551 (E.D. Mich. 2003); *Hillstrom v. Best Western TLC Hotel*, 265 F. Supp. 2d 117, 126 (D. Mass. 2003), *aff'd*, 354 F.3d 27 (1st Cir. 2003); *Farina v. Compuware Corp.*, No. CV-98-722-HX-ROS, 2003 U.S. Dist. LEXIS 5983 (D. Az. March 31, 2003); *Parker v. Hahnemann University Hospital et al.*, 234 F. Supp. 2d 478, n. 12 (D. N.J. 2002).

The FMLA entitles an employee to an equivalent position, not a position of the employee's choice. *Foraker v. Apollo Group, Inc.*, No. CV-04-2614-PHX-DGC, 2007 U.S. Dist. LEXIS 38676, at *12 (D. Az. May 25, 2007).

As explained in the FMLA's legislative history (Report from the Committee on Labor and Human Resources (S.5), Report 103-3, January 27, 1993, p. 29), the standard for evaluating job equivalence under the FMLA parallels Title VII's general prohibition against job discrimination (42 USC 2000e-2(a)(1)), which prohibits "discriminat[ion]…with respect to [an employee's] compensation, terms, conditions, or privileges of employment," and is intended to be interpreted similarly:

> The committee recognizes that it will not always be possible for an employer to restore an employee to the precise position held before taking leave. On the other hand, employees would be greatly deterred from taking leave without assurance that upon return from leave, they will be reinstated to a genuinely equivalent position. Accordingly, the bill contains an appropriately stringent standard for assignment of employees returning from leave to jobs other than the precise position that they previously held.

First, the standard of "equivalence"—not merely "comparability" or "similarity"—necessarily requires a correspondence to the duties and other terms and conditions and privileges of an employee's previous position. Second, the standard encompasses all "terms and conditions" of employment, not just those specified. In *Csicsmann v. Sallada*, 211 Fed. Appx. 163 (4th Cir. 2006), the Fourth Circuit found that the pre- and post-leave positions were equivalent because the "concrete and measurable aspects of Csicsmann's positions were exactly the same." It was undisputed that Csicsmann's salary, title, bonus eligibility, health care, and retirement benefits remained unchanged in his new position. He continued to work the same schedule and at the same physical office.

An equivalent position need not be identical to the pre-leave position. In *Watkins v. J&S Oil Co., Inc. et al.*, 164 F.3d 55, 59 (1st Cir. 1998), the First Circuit described the equivalent requirement "to mean that which is substantially equal or similar, not necessarily identical or exactly the same. The employer may take into account the employee's physical capabilities in determining the equivalent work and compensation involved." A position may be equivalent even though it differs in some respects from the employee's pre-leave position. *Foraker v. Apollo Group*, No. CV-04-2614-PHX-DGC, 2007 U.S. Dist. LEXIS 38676, at 812 (D. Az. May 25, 2007).

Whether a post-leave position is equivalent to the employee's pre-leave position does not depend on the number of paragraphs in the job description. *Foraker*, 2007 U.S. Dist. LEXIS 38676, at 812 (rejecting employee complaint that job description contains only 6 numbered paragraphs where his pre-leave job description had ten paragraphs). In *Hillstrom v. Best Western TLC Hotel*, 265 F. Supp. 2d 117, 126–127 (D. Mass. 2003), aff'd, 354 F.3d 27 (1st Cir. 2003), the court addressed whether by "same or equivalent position" the FMLA means that the employee must be returned to a position identical in all respects to the one he left, or does it mean a position that is substantially similar in its conditions of employment? The statute itself, the court noted, did not answer the question, and the attendant regulation "is of several minds on the subject." The court contrasted 29 CFR 825.215(a), which requires that the positions be "virtually identical," with subsections (e) and (f), which define equivalence in terms of "substantially similar duties, conditions, responsibilities, and status, and excludes *de minimis* and intangible aspects of the job." On return from FMLA leave the employee resumed his position running the Rooms Division of the hotel with the same pay and benefits, but with a different title. He also lost his private office, reported to a new manager, and lost supervisor responsibility for a maintenance engineer. The court found that the change in title and reassignment of the maintenance engineer in the chain of command were *de minimis*. It concluded that, "[o]n balance, I cannot believe that Congress in enacting the FMLA, intended to make a federal case out of office space."

In *Lempres v. CBS, Inc.*, 916 F. Supp. 15, 20 (D. D.C. 1996), the district court held that CBS did not refuse to restore the plaintiff to an equivalent position on her return from FMLA leave when it refused to provide the plaintiff assurances of permanent employment or assurances that a certain position will have some permanence to it. Because the plaintiff worked for CBS under an employment contact of determinable length prior to FMLA leave, she was not entitled to assurance of job permanence on return from FMLA leave. As she was not told the terms, responsibilities, benefits, title, or salary would be changed on her return from FMLA leave in any way from those provided by her pre–leave employment contract, the plaintiff was not entitled to receive any further assurance of job security.

The determination whether the position offered is equivalent is generally a question of fact for the jury. *Watkins v. J&S Oil Co.*, 164 F.3d 55, 60 (1st Cir. 1998); *Parker v. Hahnemann University Hospital et al.*, 234 F. Supp. 2d 478, n.13 (D. N.J. 2002).

Cobain v. Destination Hotels & Resorts, No. S-05-2248 FCD DAD, 2007 U.S. Dist. LEXIS 40077, at *65-66 (E.D. Ca. June 1, 2007), presented a twist on the usual situation. The employee argued that the employer should have returned him to the comparable Marketing Coordinator position to his pre-leave Marketing Manager position on his return from FMLA leave. In the interim, the company was bought out and the Marketing Manager position was eliminated. The employee applied for the newly created Marketing Coordinator position, but was not selected. The court found that Marketing Coordinator position was not equivalent to the employee's pre-leave position because it paid $10,000 a year less, it was not a supervisory position, and did not perform the same functions as the employee's pre-leave position. Because it was not equivalent, the court found the employer was not required by the FMLA to reinstate the employee into the Marketing Coordinator position. Usually, the employee argues that a position is not equivalent, whereas the employer argues that it is. In *Cobain*, the employee argued that the position was equivalent and the employer argued that it was not.

(2) Title II

Equivalency, for purposes of Title II is not generally defined in the statute or the regulations. Nor is the concept of "equivalence" tied to the interpretation given to that term under Title VII of the Civil Rights Act, as is the case under Title I. Rather, for purposes of Title II, the concept of "equivalence" is defined more mechanically by reference to equivalent pay, benefits, status, and terms and conditions of employment, as set forth in the regulations.

b. Equivalent Pay, Including Bonuses

(1) Title I, the CAA, and the PEOAA

An employee returned to work from FMLA leave is entitled to have the same or an equivalent opportunity for pay, bonuses, profit sharing, and other similar discretionary and non–discretionary payments. 29 CFR 825.215(e)(3); S. Res.

242, Cong. Rec. S3959, S3969 (April 23, 1996); 29 CFR 825.215(e)(3); *see Csicsmann v. Sallada*, 211 Fed. Appx. 163 (4th Cir. 2006); *Douglas v. E.G. Baldwin & Associates, Inc.*, 150 F.3d 604, n. 2 (6th Cir. 1998).

The requirement that an employee who is placed in an equivalent position on return from FMLA leave receive equivalent pay includes entitlement to any unconditional pay increases, which may have occurred during the FMLA leave period, such as cost of living increases. 29 CFR 825.215(c)(1); S. Res. 242, Cong. Rec. S3959, S3969 (April 23, 1996); 29 CFR 825.215(c)(1). An employee would not be entitled to pay increases conditioned on seniority, length of service, or work performed during FMLA leave, unless it is the employer's policy or practice to do so with respect to other employees on leave without pay. 29 CFR 825.215(c)(1); S. Res. 242, Cong. Rec. S3959, S3969 (April 23, 1996); 29 CFR 825.215(c)(1). In these cases, absent a more beneficial employer policy, any pay increase would be granted on a pro rata basis including the employee's seniority, length of service, and work performed, etc., excluding the period of unpaid FMLA leave. 29 CFR 825.215(c)(1); S. Res. 242, Cong. Rec. S3959, S3969 (April 23, 1996); 29 CFR 825.215(c)(1). This is simply another way of acknowledging that an employee retains all employment benefits accrued up to the commencement of FMLA leave on return from that leave. It also recognizes that an employee may not be penalized for taking FMLA leave.

The right to be restored to a position with equivalent pay includes entitlement to a position with the same or equivalent pay premiums, such as shift differential. 29 CFR 825.215(c)(1); S. Res. 242, Cong. Rec. S3959, S3969 (April 23, 1996); 29 CFR 825.215(c)(1). If an employee departed from a position averaging ten hours of overtime (and corresponding overtime pay) each week, an employee is ordinarily entitled to such a position on return from FMLA leave. 29 CFR 825.215(c)(1); S. Res. 242, Cong. Rec. S3959, S3969 (April 23, 1996); 29 CFR 825.215(c)(1).

Bonuses must be considered in determining whether an employer returned the employee to an equivalent position. 29 CFR 825.215(c)(2); S. Res. 242, Cong. Rec. S3959, S3969 (April 23, 1996); 29 CFR 825.215(c)(1). Like premium pay, the right to be restored to a position with equivalent pay generally includes entitlement to a position with the same or equivalent bonuses. The FMLA, however, makes some distinctions between employers' bonus plans. *Csicsmann v. Sallada*, 211 Fed. Appx. 163 (4th Cir. 2006).

Many employers pay bonuses in different forms to employees for job–related performance such as for perfect attendance, safety (absence of injuries or accidents on the job) and exceeding production goals. 29 CFR 825.215(c)(2); S. Res. 242, Cong. Rec. S3959, S3969 (April 23, 1996); 29 CFR 825.215(c)(2). *See generally Sommer v. The Vanguard Group*, 461 F.3d 397, 400 (3d Cir. 2006). Bonuses for perfect attendance and safety do not require performance by the employee but rather contemplate the absence of occurrences. 29 CFR 825.215(c)(2); S. Res. 242, Cong. Rec. S3959, S3969 (April 23, 1996); 29 CFR 825.215(c)(2); *see Golden v. Chautauqua Airlines, Inc.*, No. 1:05-cv-786-RLY-TAB, 2007 U.S. Dist. LEXIS 22052, at *31-34 (S.D. Ind. March 26, 2007). To the extent an employee who takes FMLA leave meets all the qualifications to receive these types of bonuses up to the point that FMLA leave begins, the employee must continue to qualify for this entitlement upon returning from FMLA leave. 29 CFR 825.215(c)(2); S. Res. 242, Cong. Rec. S3959, S3969 (April 23, 1996); 29 CFR 825.215(c)(2). *See generally Sommer*, 461 F.3d at 400.

For example, if the employer offers a bonus of any kind for perfect attendance during the course of a calendar year, the fact that the employee took the maximum 12 workweeks of FMLA leave during that period could not be held against the employee. The employee would be still be entitled to a bonus for perfect attendance just like any other employee who actually worked every single day. 29 CFR 825.215(c)(2); S. Res. 242, Cong. Rec. S3959, S3969 (April 23, 1996); 29 CFR 825.215(c)(2); *see Sommer*, 461 F.3d at 400; *Golden*, 2007 U.S. Dist. LEXIS 22052, at *32.

In *Payton v. Federal Express, Corp.*, No. 1:06-CV-0033, 2006 U.S. Dist. LEXIS 68207, at 10-13 (M.D. Pa. Sept. 22, 2006), the Fed Ex attendance policy required employees to attend work at least 96.92% of the time. An employee who fell below the 96.92% ration was subject to discipline. Payton took 30 days of approved FMLA leave to care for his wife who experienced pregnancy-related complications. At the time, he had an attendance ratio of 96.5%, which was below acceptable levels. Fed Ex deducted the FMLA leave from the base days used to calculate the annual attendance ratio. As re-calculated, Fed Ex informed Payton that he was at 96.52%, which is below satisfactory. Payton received his second disciplinary notice. He was terminated a few months later after receiving his third disciplinary notice. Payton sued, alleging that his termination violated the FMLA because Fed Ex improperly counted his FMLA leave against his attendance percentage. The court agreed with Payton. The court noted that although Fed Ex subtracted 30 days from the denominator (from 260 to 230 days), it failed to adjust the numerator accordingly. The adjustment reduced the number of "no fault" days available to Payton. By doing so, Fed Ex counted the FMLA leave absences against the "no fault" attendance policy in violation of 825.220(c).

The lesson of *Payton* is that employers need people in HR who know how to do math.

A monthly production bonus, on the other hand, does require performance by the employee. 29 CFR 825.215(c)(2); S. Res. 242, Cong. Rec. S3959, S3969 (April 23, 1996); 29 CFR 825.215(c)(2). If the employee is on FMLA leave during any part of the period for which the bonus is computed, the employee is entitled to the same consideration for the bonus as other employees on paid or unpaid leave (as appropriate). 29 CFR 825.215(c)(2); S. Res. 242, Cong. Rec. S3959, S3969 (April 23, 1996); 29 CFR 825.215(c)(2); *see Sommer*, 461 F.3d at 400.

A bonus program based on production goals, quality standards, company performance, and/or an employee's hours/weeks worked constitutes a production bonus in the DOL regulations and may be prorated for absences under the FMLA. *See id.* at 404-405; *Golden*, 2007 U.S. Dist. LEXIS 22052, at *31; *Dierlam v. Wesley Jessen Corp.*, 222 F. Supp. 2d 1052 (N.D. Ill. 2002).

Employers are not required to calculate production bonuses of employees who take unpaid forms of leave the same as those who take paid leave. In *Sommer v. The Vanguard Group*, 461 F.3d 397, 400 (3d Cir. 2006), the employee argued that the FMLA (825.215(c)(2)) requires that an employee on FMLA leave be entitled to the same consideration for a bonus as other employees on paid or unpaid leave. Because Vanguard did not prorate the production bonus of an employee on paid vacation or sick leave, it could prorate the bonus of an employee taking FMLA leave. The court rejected the argument, noting that it would put Sommer in a better position than he would have been in had he not taken FMLA leave, which is not required by the FMLA. Sommer took short term disability leave, which under the employer's policy would result in the proration of his bonus. *Accord Golden v. Chautauqua Airlines, Inc.*, No. 1:05-cv-786-RLY-TAB, 2007 U.S. Dist. LEXIS 22052, at *32-34 (S.D. Ind. March 26, 2007);

(2) Title II

An employee returned to an equivalent position is entitled to equivalent pay. 5 CFR 630.1208(a). Equivalent pay includes an equivalent grade or pay level, including any applicable locality-based comparability payment under 5 USC 5304. 5 CFR 630.1208(b)(2). Equivalent pay also includes (5 CFR 630.1208(b)(2):

- Any special rate of pay for law enforcement officers or special pay adjustments for law enforcement officers under Sections 403 and 404 of the Federal Employees Pay Comparability Act of 1990 (Pub. L. 101–509), respectively;

- Continued rate of pay under Subpart G of Part 531 of this Chapter; and

- Special salary rate under 5 USC 5305 or similar provision of law.

To be equivalent, the same or equivalent opportunity for premium pay consistent with applicable law and regulations under 5 CFR Part 550, Subpart A, or 5 CFR Part 551, Subpart E must be available to the employee who has returned to work from FMLA leave and is place in the same or an equivalent position. 5 CFR 630.1208(b)(6).

Equivalency further requires the same or equivalent opportunity for within-grade increase, performance award, incentive award, or other similar discretionary and non-discretionary payments, consistent with applicable laws and regulations. 5 CFR 630.1208(b)(5).

c. Equivalent Benefits

On return from FMLA leave an eligible federal employee placed in an equivalent position is entitled to the same or equivalent benefits to the employee's former position.

(1) Title I, the CAA, and the PEOAA

At the end of an employee's FMLA leave, benefits must be resumed in the same manner and at the same levels as provided when the leave began, and subject to any changes in benefit levels that may have taken place during the period of FMLA leave affecting the entire workforce, unless otherwise elected by the employee. 29 CFR 825.215(d)(1); S. Res. 242, Cong. Rec. S3959, S3969 (April 23, 1996); 29 CFR 825.215(d)(1).

Benefits include all benefits provided or made available to employees by an employer, including group life insurance, health insurance, disability insurance, sick leave, annual leave, educational benefits, and pensions, regardless of whether such benefits are provided by a practice or written policy of an employer though an employee benefit plan as defined in § 3(3) of the Employee Retirement Income Security Act of 1974, 29 USC 1002(3). 29 CFR 825.215(d); S. Res. 242, Cong. Rec. S3959, S3969 (April 23, 1996); 29 CFR 825.215(d); *Lempres v. CBS, Inc.*, 916 F. Supp. 15, 20 (D. D.C. 1996).

On return from FMLA leave, an employee cannot be required to requalify for any benefits the employee enjoyed before FMLA leave began (including family and dependent coverages). 29 CFR 825.215(d)(1); S. Res. 242, Cong. Rec. S3959, S3969 (April 23, 1996); 29 CFR 825.215(d)(1). For example, if an employee was covered by a life insurance policy before taking leave but is not covered or coverage lapses during the period of unpaid FMLA leave (perhaps the employee neglected to pay his share of the premiums), the employee cannot be required to meet any qualifications, such as taking a physical examination, in order to requalify for life insurance upon return from leave. 29 CFR 825.215(d)(1); S. Res. 242, Cong. Rec. S3959, S3969 (April 23, 1996); 29 CFR 825.215(d)(1); *see Aleman v. U-Haul Co. of Illinois, Inc.*, No. 06 C 0726, 2007 U.S. Dist. LEXIS 36504, at *18-19 (N.D. Ill. May 18, 2007). Because of this rule, most employers are well advised to modify current benefit policies in order to restore employees to equivalent benefits upon return from FMLA leave, including the payment of the employee's share of premiums, subject to recovery, during the period of FMLA leave. 29 CFR 825.215(d)(1); S. Res. 242, Cong. Rec. S3959, S3969 (April 23, 1996); 29 CFR 825.215(d)(1).

An employee may, but is not entitled to, accrue any additional benefits or seniority during unpaid FMLA leave. Benefits accrued at the time leave began, however, (e.g., paid vacation, sick or personal leave to the extent not substituted for FMLA leave) must be available to the employee upon return from FMLA leave. 29 CFR 825.215(d)(1); S. Res. 242, Cong. Rec. S3959, S3969 (April 23, 1996); 29 CFR 825.215(d)(1); *see Chubb v. City of Omaha, Nebraska*, 424 F.3d 831 (8th Cir. 2005). [For a further discussion of the accrual and maintenance of benefits while an employee is on FMLA leave, see Chapter 12 "Maintenance of Benefits."]

In *Chubb v. City of Omaha*, 424 F.3d 831, 832-833 (8th Cir. 2005), the employee argued that he was not restored to an equivalent position because he was denied an annual leave bonus. The City of Omaha awards a police officer who does not take more than 40 hours of sick leave in a year with 2 hours of additional annual leave for each pay period during a year in which the officer had at least 1000 hours of accrued sick leave. Chubb had at least 1000 hours of accrued sick leave in 2003. He took more than 40 hours (three weeks) of FMLA-sick leave that year, and the City denied him the annual leave bonus when he returned to work. The court agreed that the City had the right to deny Chubb the annual leave bonus because he took paid sick leave concurrently with FMLA leave. The court also rejected Chubb's argument that the City required him to take paid leave. The court noted that the City gave Chubb the choice of annual or sick leave. Had he chosen annual leave, Chubb would have retained the right to his annual leave bonus. He voluntarily elected sick leave, thereby ceding his claim to the annual leave bonus. The court also noted that the City could have required Chubb to substitute paid sick leave.

Employers must treat employees on unpaid FMLA leave as if they continued to work, for purposes of changes to benefit plans. 29 CFR 825.215(d)(5); S. Res. 242, Cong. Rec. S3959, S3969 (April 23, 1996); 29 CFR 825.215(d)(5). Employees are entitled to changes in benefit plan, except those that may be dependent on seniority or accrual during the leave period, immediately upon return from leave or to the same extent they would have qualified if no leave had been taken. 29 CFR 825.215(d)(5); S. Res. 242, Cong. Rec. S3959, S3969 (April 23, 1996); 29 CFR 825.215(d)(5). For example, if the benefit plan is predicated on a pre-established number of hours worked each year and the employee does not have sufficient hours as a result of taking unpaid FMLA leave, the benefit is lost.

Finally, with respect to pension and other retirement plans, any period of unpaid FMLA leave shall not be treated as or counted toward a break in service for purposes of vesting and eligibility to participate. 29 CFR 825.215(d)(4); S. Res. 242, Cong. Rec. S3959, S3969 (April 23, 1996); 29 CFR 825.215(d)(4); *see Vitale v. Latrobe Area Hospital*, 420 F.3d 278, 286 (3d Cir. 2005). Also, if the plan requires an employee to be employed on a specific date in order to be credited with a year of service for vesting, contributions or participation purposes, an employee on unpaid FMLA leave on that date is deemed to have been employed on that date. 29 CFR 825.215(d)(4); S. Res. 242, Cong. Rec. S3959, S3969 (April 23, 1996); 29 CFR 825.215(d)(4). However, unpaid FMLA leave periods need not be treated as credited service for purposes of benefit accrual, vesting and eligibility to participate. 29 CFR 825.215(d)(4); S. Res. 242, Cong. Rec. S3959, S3969 (April 23, 1996); 29 CFR 825.215(d)(4); *see Vitale*, 420 F.3d at 286.

(2) Title II

On return to the employer from FMLA leave, an employee is entitled to the same or equivalent benefits as the employee enjoyed before commencing leave. Specifically, the regulations provide that an employee is entitled to the same employment benefits made available to the employee in his or her previous position (e.g., life insurance, health benefits, retirement coverage, and leave accrual). 5 CFR 630.1208(b)(4).

It is worth noting that the regulations implementing Title II do not go into the level of detail regarding the requirement of equivalent benefits as do the regulations implementing Title I, the CAA, and the PEOAA. For example, the regulations implementing Title II do not address an employee's entitlement to any changes in benefit plans that occurred during the period of FMLA leave. Given the broad language contained in the Statute and regulations that an employee returning from FMLA leave is entitled to an equivalent position with equivalent benefits, agencies are well advised to apply the specific instances identified in Title I, the CAA, and the PEOAA to employees covered by Title II.

d. Equivalent Terms and Conditions of Employment

(1) Title I, the CAA, and the PEOAA

An equivalent position must have substantially similar duties, conditions, responsibilities, privileges and status as the employee's original position. 29 CFR 825.215(e); S. Res. 242, Cong. Rec. S3959, S3969 (April 23, 1996); 29 CFR 825.215(e); *see Hanger v. Lake County*, 390 F.3d 579 (8th Cir. 2004); *LaFortune v. Fiber Materials, Inc.*, No. 03–275–P–H, 2004 U.S. Dist. LEXIS 21405, at *11 (D. Me. Oct. 25, 2004); *Oby v. Baton Rouge Marriott*, 329 F. Supp 2d 772 (M.D. La. 2004); *Felix v. Sun Microsystems, Inc.*, No. JFM–03–1304, 2004 U.S. Dist. LEXIS 7508, at *39 (D. Md. April 12, 2004); *Sabatino v. Flik International Corp.*, 286 F. Supp. 2d 327, 337 (S.D.N.Y. 2003).

A position is not equivalent simply because it has the same salary. Working conditions, including privileges, perquisites and status, are also to be considered when analyzing whether positions are equivalent. *Vlahos v. Schroeffel*, No. 02-CV-0139 (DLI), 2006 U.S. Dist. LEXIS 95814, at *14-15 (E.D.N.Y. March 6, 2006).

Equivalent terms and conditions of employment also include (29 CFR 825.215(e)(1)–(4); S. Res. 242, Cong. Rec. S3959, S3969 (April 23, 1996); 29 CFR 825.215(e)(1)–(4)):

- Reinstatement to the same or a geographically proximate worksite (i.e., one that does not involve a significant increase in commuting time or distance);
- Return to the same shift or the same or an equivalent work schedule.

See Csicsmann v. Sallada, 211 Fed. Appx. 163 (4th Cir. 2006); *Douglas v. E.G. Baldwin & Associates, Inc.*, 150 F.3d 604, n.2 (6th Cir. 1998) (employee ordinarily entitled to return to the same shift or the same or an equivalent work schedule); *Farina v. Compuware Corp.*, No. CV-98-722-HX-ROS, 2003 U.S. Dist. LEXIS 5983 (D. Az. March 31, 2003) (geographically proximate worksite); *Parker v. Hahnemann University Hospital et al.*, 234 F. Supp. 2d 478, n. 13 (D. N.J. 2002) (question of fact precluding summary judgment whether offered positions were equivalent where they required work on evenings and weekends and because they were subordinate in status to pre–leave position).

The regulations are confusing regarding the determination of whether an equivalent worksite is appropriate, as the term is described in both geographic ("geographically proximate") and temporal (significant increase in "commuting time") terms. One could have a geographically proximate worksite that, because of the lack of availability of public transportation, might be far more difficult to reach, resulting in a significant increase in commuting time. Given the inherent potential for conflict, employers are well advised to consider both as requirements (geographic proximity and commute time) when determining if the return of an employee to a different location will pass the equivalency test.

The regulations also fail to define what would constitute a geographically proximate worksite, or a significant increase in commuting time. For that matter, the regulations fail to identify from what vantage point this is judged: the subjective belief of the employee; the opinion of the employer; or the hypothetical reasonable person. Absent an agreed upon vantage point to judge this issue, employers should attempt to come to agreement with the employee on this issue before the employee is placed at the new worksite. Absent agreement, agencies should consider the propriety of the move from the view of a reasonable person in the position of the returning employee.

In *Robinson v. Overnite Transportation Co.*, No. 95-3067, 1997 U.S. App. LEXIS 6574 (4th Cir. April 9, 1997), the circuit court rejected the plaintiff's argument that the imposition of a probationary period in accordance the company's policy following an accident fundamentally changed the nature of his position at Overnite. The court noted that Robinson failed to cite any authority for the proposition that the imposition of a period of probation changed the nature of his position as a truck driver such that it would not be deemed equivalent under § 214(a) of the FMLA. Additionally, the court noted that Robinson was placed on probation because he violated safety rules and caused a serious accident, not because he had taken leave as a result of injuries sustained in the accident.

The loss of supervisory responsibilities and a private office was sufficient to deny summary judgment to the employer in *LaFortune v. Fiber Materials, Inc.*, No. 03-275-P-H, 2004 U.S. Dist. LEXIS 21405, at *11, n.3 (D. Me. Oct. 25, 2004). The court noted that an equivalent position is not simply a position with equivalent pay and benefits, but includes equivalent working conditions as well. *But see Hillstrom v. Best Western TLC Hotel*, 265 F. Supp. 2d 117, 126–127 (D. Mass. 2003), *aff'd*, 354 F.3d 27 (1st Cir. 2003) (loss of private office and some supervisor responsibilities *de minimis*).

An employee was not entitled to a specified number of higher level acting supervisory assignments on return from FMLA leave. In *Clemons v. Potter*, No. 3:05-cv-35-J-32TEM, 2007 U.S. Dist. LEXIS 42061, at *4-6 (D. Fla. June 11, 2007), the employee, a supervisor, was returned to his pre-leave position with the same pay and benefits. The employee argued that, because he served as an acting manager prior to taking FMLA leave, he was entitled to be named an acting manager on a specified number of occasions after his return. The court disagreed. The court noted that service as an acting manager was not a specified part of Clemons' job description nor was it an established benefit of holding his supervisory position. Moreover, prior to taking FMLA leave, Clemons was not guaranteed selection as an acting manager on any scheduled or predictable basis. The court concluded that the acting manager position was "not an emolument of Clemons'" supervisor position. The FMLA's job restoration rules, did not, therefore, require the employer to provide Clemons with a specified number of acting manager assignments.

In *Donahoo v. Master Data Center*, 282 F. Supp. 2d 540, 551 (E.D. Mich. 2003), the court found that, even if the two positions carried equal pay and benefits, the data-entry job offered to the plaintiff on her return from FMLA leave was not of equal status to the computer analyst position she held prior to taking FMLA leave. According to the court, a data-entry job is not as sophisticated, nor does it require a similar level of training and education, as a computer analyst.

In *Martin v. Inhabitants of the City of Biddeford*, No. 02-122-P-H, 2003 U.S. Dist. LEXIS 5375, at *44 (D. Me. April 1, 2003), the court found sufficient evidence of a change in working conditions, including perquisites and status, after the employee returned from FMLA leave to preclude awarding summary judgment to the employer. On her return from leave, the employee assumed her former position with the same pay and benefits. The only change discernable from the facts is that telephone calls regarding court matters continued to be routed to the person who replaced her during leave rather than to her.

Employers can get themselves in trouble if they try to ease the burden on an employee returning from FMLA leave. In *Johnson v. Campbell Mithun*, 401 F. Supp. 2d 964, 971-72 (D. Minn. Nov. 29, 2005), Johnson took FMLA leave as a result of incapacity associated with her multiple sclerosis. At the time, she was the Vice President and Creative Director of the Packaged Food Group for the defendant's advertising business. She was extensively involved with a large commercial project for an Italian client. While she was on leave her employer reassigned the project to someone else. On her return from leave, her manager did not give her the project back. Her manager substantially reduced her workload, and what she was given was low-level work even though higher level work was available. Johnson's supervisor stated that he wanted to "ease" her back into work even though she never asked to be eased back into work. Her supervisor told her that she would get more work in a month, which never materialized. The court concluded that there was sufficient evidence in the record that Johnson was not returned to an equivalent position to deny summary judgment to the employer.

(2) Title II

An equivalent position under Title II requires equivalent terms and conditions of employment. 5 CFR 630.1208(a)(1). Equivalent terms and conditions of employment include:

- The same commuting area (§ 630.1208(b));
- The same type of appointment, work schedule, status, and tenure (§ 630.1208(b)(3)); and

- The same or equivalent opportunity for training or education benefits consistent with applicable laws and regulations, including any training that an employee may be required to complete to qualify for his or her previous position (§ 630.1208(b)(7)).

The regulations clearly allow for a returning employee to be placed in an equivalent position that is not physically located at the same location as the employee's former position. The regulations, however, do not define what constitutes the same commuting area. It could mean that the new worksite must be in the same geographic area as the employee's former worksite. Alternatively, it could mean that, as long as the new worksite is approximately the same distance or commuting time as the old site, the location is equivalent, even if it is in the opposite direction of the old worksite. Finally, commuting area could be interpreted more broadly, so that time and distance from the employee's residence is largely immaterial, as long as the new worksite is within the same commuting area.

It is recommended that employers keep the time and commuting distance as close to what the employee enjoyed before taking FMLA leave when determining if the new worksite is within the same commuting area. Equivalency serves as a proxy for what the employee originally had before FMLA leave.

Note that Title I, the CAA, and the PEOAA prohibit significant increases in commuting time or distance from the employee's former site. The standard under Title II is that the new worksite must be in the same commuting area. It is unclear whether these are the same standards.

Title II, like the other federal sector FMLA statutes, defines equivalent terms and conditions to include an equivalent work schedule and status. Status is undefined. Title II contains several iterations of equivalent terms and conditions of employment not found in Title I, the CAA, and the PEOAA. For example, Title II requires return to the same type of appointment and tenure. 5 CFR 630.1208(b)(3). Arguably, however, based on the broad definition of equivalence contained in Title I, the CAA, and the PEOAA, these requirements would also be applicable to Title I federal employees. Note that the terms "appointment," "tenure," and "status" are undefined.

e. *De Minimis,* Intangible, or Immeasurable Aspects of Job

(1) Title I, the CAA, and the PEOAA

The requirement that an employee be restored to the same or equivalent job with the same or equivalent pay, benefits, and terms and conditions of employment does not extend to *de minimis* or intangible aspects of the job. 29 CFR 825.215(f); S. Res. 242, Cong. Rec. S3959, S3969 (April 23, 1996); 29 CFR 825.215(f); *see Csicsmann v. Sallada*, 211 Fed. Appx. 163 (4th Cir. 2006); *Smith v. East Baton Rouge Parish School Bd.* 453 F.3d 650, 651 (5th Cir. 2006); *Tanganelli v. Talbots, Inc.*, 169 Fed. Appx. 123 (3d Cir. 2006); *Mitchell v. Dutchmen Mfg. Inc.*, 389 F.3d 746, 748 (7th Cir. 2004); *Montgomery v. State of Maryland*, 266 F.3d 334, 341-42 (4th Cir. 2003), *vacated on other grounds*, 535 U.S. 1075, 122 S. Ct. 1958 (2002); *Douglas v. E.G. Baldwin & Associates, Inc.*, 150 F. 3d 604, n.2 (6th Cir. 1998); *Oby v. Baton Rouge Marriott*, 329 F. Supp 2d 772 (M.D. La. 2004); *Felix v. Sun Microsystems, Inc.*, No. JFM–03–1304, 2004 U.S. Dist. LEXIS 7508, at *39 (D. Md. April 12, 2004); *Sabatino v. Flik International Corp.*, 286 F. Supp. 2d 327, 337 (S.D.N.Y. 2003); *Donahoo v. Master Data Center*, 282 F. Supp. 2d 540, 551 (E.D. Mich. 2003); *Hillstrom v. Best Western TLC Hotel,* 265 F. Supp. 2d 117, 127 (D. Mass. 2003), *aff'd*, 354 F.3d 27 (1st Cir. 2003).

The regulations fail to define what aspects of an employee's former position would be considered *de minimis* or intangible. Several courts, however, have fleshed this out somewhat.

The post–leave assignment of new tasks involving small hand tools for a limited period of time each day was found to be the type of *de minimis*, intangible, and immeasurable aspects of the job excluded by 29 CFR 825.215(f). *Mitchell v. Dutchmen Mfg. Inc.*, 389 F.3d 746, 748 (7th Cir. 2004) (requiring employee to use new hand tools in production of recreational vehicles is a *de minimis* change).

A requirement that an employee, who returns from FMLA leave, undergo additional training in order to perform in an equivalent position does not establish that the employer failed to return the employee to an equivalent position. *Oby v. Baton Rouge Marriott*, 329 F. Supp 2d 772 (M.D. La. 2004).

In *Oby*, the employee was the manager of all housekeepers at the Baton Rouge Marriott prior to taking FMLA leave. On her return from FMLA leave, the employer offered plaintiff the position of food and beverage manager at the

Baton Rouge Marriott at her same salary (which was more than the current food and beverage manager was making), employment benefits, and other terms and conditions of employment. Plaintiff declined the position. Plaintiff alleged that the food and beverage manager position was not equivalent to her former position because she would have to train for this position since she had no experience as a food and beverage manager. She also claimed that the position violated her religious beliefs against selling alcohol, and that Marriott was setting her up to fail. The court noted that plaintiff failed to produce any evidence that the positions were not identical, they both involved supervisory duties and both had the same goal and responsibility: customer service in and maintenance of the Baton Rouge Marriott in a managerial capacity. The court characterized plaintiff's arguments as "either based on plaintiff's subjective beliefs or intangible aspects of the job" and ruled in favor of the employer's motion for summary judgment.

The mere fact that the post-return equivalent job is in a different salary grade than the job held prior to taking FMLA leave is *de minimis* when the evidence shows that all the aspects of the job, including the salary, were identical or nearly identical. *Felix v. Sun Microsystems, Inc.*, No. JFM-03-1304, 2004 U.S. Dist. LEXIS 7508, at *39 (D. Md. April 12, 2004).

In *Felix*, the employee held the position of Individual Contributor Program Manager, level E-12. Upon his return from FMLA leave, Felix was offered an Individual Contributor Program Manager position, level E-10, but at the same salary and with the same benefits as his former position. The evidence established that the job titles and job descriptions were basically the same. The two positions had equivalent duties and responsibilities. Both E-10 and E-12 employees are eligible for promotions to director positions. According to the court, the only evidence presented by plaintiff that the two positions were not equivalent was his view that the new job was a demotion from his previous position. The court found such evidence wanting, holding that a plaintiff "must point to specific elements of the new job that are different from the old job, such as the salary, promotional opportunities, duties, or conditions of employment."

An employee's failure to substantiate her claim that her post-leave position was not equivalent to her pre-FMLA leave position led the court in *Sabatino v. Flik International Corp.*, 286 F. Supp. 2d 327, 337 (S.D.N.Y. 2003), to find that the differences between the positions, i.e., hours, location, job responsibility, and promotional opportunity, were *de minimis*. Prior to taking leave, plaintiff was an assistant manager. She was offered a manager position, which she turned down. The court found *de minimis* that her new position was ten miles away from her former position. It noted that plaintiff claimed that the hours of work were different, but could not recall what her hours of work had been. Similarly, although she claimed that the job responsibilities and promotional opportunities were not the same, she failed, beyond summary assertion, to set forth any evidence to suggest that the post-leave position was not equal to her pre-leave position. Absent specific facts, the court awarded summary judgment in favor of the employer on plaintiff's failure to reinstate FMLA claim.

A change in job title and reduction of opportunity to travel to other schools to help with bookkeeping and assignment to one school was found to be *de minimis* where the employee retained the same salary and had substantially the same job duties *Smith v. East Baton Rouge Parish School Bd.*, 453 F.3d 650, 652 (5th Cir. 2006).

In *Hillstrom v. Best Western TLC Hotel*, 265 F. Supp. 2d 117, 126-127 (D. Mass. 2003), *aff'd*, 354 F.3d 27 (1st Cir. 2003), the court found that the change in title and reassignment of the maintenance engineer in the chain of command were *de minimis* changes.

According to one court, a warm greeting on the employee's return to work is a *de minimis* or intangible aspect of the job that is not required by the FMLA. *Borner v. Zale Lipsky University Hospital*, No. CA-3:01-CV-227-R, 2002 U.S. Dist. LEXIS 4787 (N.D. Tex. March 20, 2002).

Being kept "out of the loop" was held an intangible or *de minimis* aspect of the job. *Noyer v. Viacom, Inc. et al.*, No. 97-CIV-6989, 1998 U.S. Dist. LEXIS 17602 (S.D.N.Y. Nov. 5, 1998). The fact that employee did not receive the store keys for a week, was not invited to a meeting (which she was permitted to attend) or the fact that a schedule the employee created was discarded were *de minimis* or intangible aspects of the job. *Tanganelli v. Talbots, Inc.*, 169 Fed. Appx. 123 (3d Cir. 2006).

In *Noyer*, the plaintiff was the former Senior Vice President of Communications for Nickelodeon. She claimed that she resigned shortly after returning from a four-month FMLA-covered maternity leave because her job responsibilities were significantly reduced. On her return, Noyer resumed her same title, salary, benefits, office, and duty to report to the same Nickelodeon president as she had when she left.

The plaintiff's responsibilities were to address the communications aspects of problems arising out of conflicting business relations between defendants Nickelodeon, Viacom, and MTV Networks with a United Kingdom satellite distributor. Without her input, the plaintiff learned that the president of Nickelodeon and the CEO of MTV decided to solicit the assistance of an outside consultant on the issue. The plaintiff scaled back the use of this consultant before she went on maternity leave. The plaintiff also learned that a meeting took place with the consultant, the CEO of MTV, and the president of Nickelodeon in which it was decided to "leak" a news story to the press regarding the dispute with the UK Company. Believing that she was purposely kept out of the loop, the plaintiff quit when she was advised of the decision to leak the news story a few days after the story appeared.

In rejecting the plaintiff's contention that her position was marginalized on her return from FMLA leave, the district court noted that the decision to make the leak was outside of her purview as it was made by the CEO of MTV Networks, whom the plaintiff neither served nor reported to. The MTV Networks Chairman had no duty, the court found, to consult with her at all on anything, including this issue. Moreover, the court rejected the plaintiff's contention that her boss, the president of Nickelodeon, failed to inform her about everything that was going on with the project that she was assigned. The court found that, even if the non-disclosure was deliberate, it did not violate the FMLA. Rather, the court held that the plaintiff had no entitlement in her position to the contents of confidential decisions taken by MTV Networks at the highest level regarding MTV Networks' corporate strategy. As such, the court found that the plaintiff was, in effect, demanding a right to which she was not entitled prior to her FMLA leave, which is not a violation of the FMLA.

The above suggests that all rights and entitlements of the employee's former position will be examined, including the right to be overruled by those at higher levels in the organization.

Note the potential contradiction in the regulations on this point. On the one hand, the regulations clearly require that an employee be restored to the same or an equivalent position, including "privileges, perquisites and status." On the other hand, the regulations say that the entitlement does not extend to "intangible, immeasurable aspects of the job." If status means prestige, then it is an intangible, immeasurable aspect of the job. If it means relative rank in relation to others, then it is more akin to position, which is tangible.

If the term "status" is a right enjoyed by an employee on return from FMLA leave, it behooves regulatory bodies to define the term so that employers are on notice of what is required of them. It is unfair to provide that any violation of the implementing regulations constitutes a violation of the FMLA, while at the same time critical terms, including actionable rights, are left undefined.

In *Csicsmann v. Sallada*, 211 Fed. Appx. 163 (4th Cir. 2006), the Fourth Circuit rejected the employee's argument that his post-leave position was not equivalent because it was less prestigious and less visible than his pre-leave position. The court opined that "these are the intangible aspects of the position appropriately excluded from an equivalency determination."

In *Montgomery v. Maryland et al.*, 266 F.3d 334, 341–42 (4th Cir. 2001), *vacated on other grounds*, 535 U.S. 1075, 122 S. Ct. 1958 (2002), the circuit court stated that the employee's "complaint focuses on precisely the sorts of *de minimis*, intangible, and immeasurable aspects of a job that the regulations specifically exclude." For example, the employee alleged that her duties formerly were "truly administrative," but now are "the simplest, most menial of clerical functions: answer the phone, taking messages, typing simple correspondence, and the like." The plaintiff held the position of Administrative Aide Stenographer both before and after FMLA leave. She further alleged, while she used to have "her own work area," now she must work in a "room shared with another employee." Finally, she contends that she has diminished job security. Addressing these issues, the court noted that:

> Montgomery's other complaints, such as the alleged reduction in the complexity of her tasks and the sharing of workspace, also fall within the excluded *de minimis* category. The difference between "truly administrative tasks" and "answering the phone, taking messages, typing simple correspondence," is not of sufficient magnitude, especially given the equivalent pay grade, increment level, and administrative classification, to constitute an FMLA violation. And the difference between having one's own work space and having to share space with on another person is not of such import as to implicate the protections of the governing federal law.

Other courts have found that the loss of a personal workspace on return from FMLA leave is an intangible or *de minimis* aspect of the job. *See Devine v. Prudential Ins. Co. of America*, No. 03-3791 (FLW), 21, 22, 23, 24, 25, 2007 U.S. Dist. LEXIS 46856, at *89-91 (D. N.J. June 28, 2007): *Hillstrom v. Best Western TLC Hotel*, 265 F. Supp. 2d 117, 126–127 (D. Mass. 2003) (court "cannot belief that Congress, in enacting the FMLA, intended to make a federal case out of office space"), *aff'd*, 354

F.3d 27 (1st Cir. 2003). *But see LaFortune v. Fiber Materials, Inc.*, No. 03-275-P-H, 2004 U.S. Dist. LEXIS 21405, at *11, n. 3 (D. Me. Oct. 25, 2004) (loss of office cited as evidence that employee not returned to same or equivalent position).

The view that the loss of one's own work space and having to share space with another person is *de minimis* and therefore unprotected by the Act, seems dubious. It is unlikely that a federal trial judge returning from FMLA leave who was told that he or she now had to share an office would consider this an intangible benefit of the job. Agencies would be well-advised to return employees who enjoyed a private office or cubicle to a like space on return from FMLA leave.

(2) Title II

Title II also excludes intangible or immeasurable aspects of the job. 5 CFR 630.1208(b)(5). Note that, unlike Title I, *de minimis* aspects of the job are not excluded from the definition of an "equivalent position," as long as they are measurable or tangible.

That leads to a second observation: what is meant by measurable or tangible aspects of a job? It is possible, after all, to measure subjective beliefs as well as objective facts. In any event, the regulations fail to identify what aspects of the job are and are not tangible or measurable.

f. Lapsed Qualification for the Job; Licenses

(1) Title I, the CAA, and the PEOAA

If an employee is no longer qualified for the position because of the employee's inability to attend a necessary course, renew a license, fly a minimum number of hours, etc., as a result of taking FMLA leave, the employee must be given a reasonable opportunity to fulfill those conditions upon return to work. 29 CFR 825.215(b); S. Res. 242, Cong. Rec. S3959, S3969 (April 23, 1996); 29 CFR 825.215(b).

The regulations do not provide any guidance on what constitutes a reasonable opportunity. One court has opined that requiring an employer to wait three months for a delivery employee to recover his driver's license would not be reasonable. *Jewell v. Reid's Confectionary Co.*, No. 01-119-B-S, 2001 U.S. Dist. LEXIS 19212 (D. Me. Nov. 21, 2001).

In *Geromanos v. Columbia Univ., College of Physicians and Surgeons*, 322 F. Supp. 2d 420, 427 (S.D.N.Y. 2004), the court found that plaintiff was not entitled to reinstatement following FMLA leave because she was unable to perform all of the essential functions of her job due to the lapse of a mandatory nursing license. The court noted that 75% of the employee's job was involved with patient care and required the nursing license. The employee's 12 weeks of FMLA leave expired in June, and the earliest she could get her nursing license renewed was in October. The court did not specifically discuss the FMLA requirement that the employee be given a reasonable opportunity on return from FMLA leave to meet the licensure requirement. Implicitly, the court may be saying that the four-month period between when her FMLA leave expired and when she could obtain her nursing license was unreasonable where 75% of her job required a nursing license.

In *Fejes v. Gilpin Ventures, Inc.*, 960 F. Supp. 1487 1 (D. Colo. 1997), the district court denied an employer's motion for summary judgment due to the existence of material issues of fact whether the employer provided the employee a reasonable opportunity to renew her gaming license which expired while she was out on FMLA leave.

Nothing in the regulations suggests that an employer may deny an employee's return to work until the employee requalifies for the same or an equivalent position on return from FMLA leave. Quite the opposite is true. The regulations specifically provide that the employee is to be given a reasonable opportunity to fulfill those lapsed conditions on return to work. As a result, employers are required to return an employee who is not qualified for the job, and must provide the employee with the same or equivalent pay, benefits, and terms and conditions of employment while the employee attempts to requalify to actually perform work.

An employer would be prevented from requiring an employee who is prohibited from performing his or her job until a license or other similar qualification is renewed to transfer to another position or from changing that employee's duties. The regulations simply do not provide an employer with an exception from the duty to return the employee to the same or an equivalent position where the employee can no longer perform the position because of the loss of a license or other certification. As the employer may be legally, contractually, or ethically prohibited from allowing the employee to perform the job without a required license, the employer faces the prospect of violating the FMLA by abiding by the other laws if it does not allow the employee to perform those duties. Of course, an employee could, however, voluntarily agree to such a change in the job until he or she re-qualifies for a license, etc. Moreover, employer policy may address what happens to an employee who is no longer qualified for perform the job due to lack of certification or licensure. If the employer has such a policy, it should be followed. If not, the employer should consider enacting such a policy in order to avoid treating an employee returning from FMLA leave differently than those who have not taken FMLA leave.

The fact that the employee is given a reasonable opportunity to cure the loss of a license or other qualification standard suggests that entitlement is not open ended. That is, after a reasonable number of tries and/or time, if the employee fails to regain the license or certification, the FMLA entitlement to return to work would appear to lapse. Employer policy or practice would solely govern the employee's terms and conditions of employment at that point, at least with respect to the failure to have a required license, certification, or meet some other qualification requirement for the job.

If the reason for the loss of a required license was not due to the FMLA leave, but was for other reasons, the requirement that an employer provide a returning an employee a reasonable opportunity to regain the license does not apply. That was the conclusion of the district court in *Jewell v. Reid's Confectionary Co.*, No. 01-119-B-S, 2001 U.S. Dist. LEXIS 19212 (D. Me. Nov. 21, 2001). In that case, the plaintiff worked as a delivery driver for Reid's Confectionary Company. He took FMLA leave as a result of suffering two heart attacks. While on FMLA leave, the state of Maine suspended his driver's license for a five-month period as a result of his having a defibrillator implanted in his chest following the two heart attacks. Jewell's doctor cleared him to return to work, stating that he could perform all of his job activities, including driving. At the time of his return to work, however, his driver's license remained suspended by the state of Maine. Reid's Confectionary Company refused to reinstate Jewell because he could not drive. Jewell sued, alleging violation of the FMLA. Citing 29 CFR 825.215(b), Jewell alleged that his employer should have reinstated him and allowed him a reasonable opportunity to regain his driver's license.

Rejecting Jewell's argument, the court found that a close reading of § 825.215(b) reveals that it only applies if the license was lost as a result of the leave. In other words, § 825.215(b) provides an opportunity for an employee to re-qualify for the previous position if the absence from work caused the loss of licensure. Here, the regulation did not apply because Jewell's loss of his driver's license was the direct result of his illness, rather than a collateral result of his absence from work. The state of Maine suspended his driver's license because of the implanted defibrillator. Because the loss of his license was not the direct result of his use of FMLA leave, the court held that Jewell was not entitled to a reasonable opportunity to regain it pursuant to § 825.215(b). The court granted dismissal of Jewell's suit.

(2) Title II

Title II also requires an employer to provide a returning employee with an opportunity to requalify for his or her previous position. 5 CFR 630.1208(b)(7). Specifically, as part of the entitlement to an equivalent position on return to the employer from FMLA leave, the employer must also provide the same or equivalent opportunity for training or education benefits consistent with applicable regulations, including any training that an employee may be required to complete to qualify for his or her previous position. *Id*.

The opportunity to receive training to requalify for the employee's previous position appears less generous than the similar regulation governing employees covered by Title I, the CAA, and the PEOAA. Arguably, whatever rendered the Title II employee unqualified for the previous employment must be susceptible to training. If training can ameliorate the loss of a license or other certification necessary to qualify for the employee's previous position, then the employer must afford the employee the opportunity to take such training. Note, however, that the employer's obligation to afford the employee the opportunity to requalify is not an independent right, but falls under the general requirement that the employer provide the same or equivalent opportunity for training or education benefits. This arguably narrows the scope considerably. If a course or license preparation class is not available locally, and the employer's practice is limited to affording employees local training opportunities only, the employer arguably would not be obliged to send the employee to the same course offered at a site on the other side of the country.

The regulations do not address what happens if the employee is no longer qualified for the previous position and the lack of qualification cannot be rectified through training. For example, flying a minimum number of hours.

The regulations are more generous than those under Title I in terms of the opportunity that must be afforded to the employee to receive training in order to meet the qualification standards of his or her previous position. Under Title I, an employee is given a reasonable opportunity to requalify. Under Title II, the regulations omit reasonableness as a qualifier. Arguably, that means the employer must provide the employee with every available effort to requalify, without time or other limitations, except those that go beyond current employer policy or practice.

The regulations also say nothing about precluding the employee from returning to work because he or she is no longer qualified for the former position, and will not be able to take a training course, perform a certain number of activities, or work the requisite period of time until some weeks or months after job restoration. This issue is addressed more fully later in this chapter.

3. Voluntary Move to Alternative Position; Light Duty

The FMLA does not prohibit an employer from accommodating an employee's request to be restored to a different shift, schedule, or position that better suits the employee's personal needs on return from leave. 29 CFR 825.215(e)(5); S. Res. 242, Cong. Rec. S3959, S3969 (April 23, 1996); 29 CFR 825.215(e)(5); *see Hoge v. Honda of America Mfg., Inc.*, 384 F.3d 238 (6th Cir. 2004); *Wright v. Owens–Illinois, Inc.*, No. 2:02–cv–223–LJM–WGH, 2004 U.S. Dist. LEXIS 8538, at *21 (S.D. Ind. May 14, 2004). An employer may also offer the employee a promotion to a better position. 29 CFR 825.215(e)(5); S. Res. 242, Cong. Rec. S3959, S3969 (April 23, 1996); 29 CFR 825.215(e)(5). However, an employer may not induce an employee to accept a different position against the employee's wishes. 29 CFR 825.215(e)(5); S. Res. 242, Cong. Rec. S3959, S3969 (April 23, 1996); 29 CFR 825.215(e)(5).

Absent voluntary consent, an employer may not require an employee to return to a light duty position. Preamble, 29 CFR 825.215. Again, an employee who is able to perform all of the essential functions of his or her position on return from FMLA leave has the right to return to the same or an equivalent position. An employer may have a program under which an employee could voluntarily return to duty before he or she is able to perform all the essential functions of the job. Preamble, 29 CFR 825.215. In such a case, because an employee cannot waive his or her FMLA rights, the employee's right to be restored to his or her original or an equivalent position would continue until 12 weeks have passed in the applicable 12–month period, including all FMLA leave and the light duty period for which the employee would otherwise have been on leave. Preamble, 29 CFR 825.215; *see Hoge*, 384 F.3d 238; *Wright*, 2004 U.S. Dist. LEXIS 8538, at *21.

4. Reasonable Accommodation

Unlike the ADA or the Rehabilitation Act, the FMLA does not require an employer to reasonably accommodate an employee's serious health condition to facilitate the employee's return to work from FMLA leave. *See* 29 CFR 825.702(a), 825.214(b); S. Res. 242, Cong. Rec. S3959, S3969, S3976 (April 23, 1996); 29 CFR 825.702(a); *see Battle v. UPS, Inc.*, 438 F.3d 856, 864-65 (8th Cir. 2006); *Fogelman v. Greater Hazleton Health Alliance*, 122 Fed. Appx. 521 (3d Cir. 2004) (finding no violation of the FMLA where employee admitted that she could not return to work at the conclusion of 12 weeks of FMLA leave without reasonable accommodation, which is not required by FMLA); *Conroy v. Township of Lower Merion*, 77 Fed. Appx. 556 (3d Cir. 2003), *cert denied*, 124 S. Ct. 2872 (2004) (critical question is whether employee required an accommodation to perform the essential functions of her job or an equivalent job; if so, then the employer had no duty to restore her to her position after she took FMLA leave); *Tardie v. Rehabilitation Hospital of Rhode Island et al.*, 168 F.3d 538, 544 (1st Cir. 1999) (section 825.214(b), unlike the ADA, omits the qualifying language "with or without reasonable accommodation"; the regulation goes on to state that the employer may have obligations under the ADA, but this reminder does not import the "reasonable accommodation" qualifier into the FMLA context); *Henry v. Fulton County Bd. of Ed.*, No. 1:05-CV-2008-TWT, 2006 U.S. Dist. LEXIS 74062, at *12 (N.D. Ga. Oct. 10, 2006), *aff'd*, 2007 U.S. App. LEXIS 74062 (11th Cir. July 3, 2007).

This is true even if the employer terminated the employee before the FMLA leave period expired. *Lombardo v. Air Products & Chemicals, Inc.*, No. 05-1120, 2006 U.S. Dist. LEXIS 46077, at *21-22 (E.D. Pa. July 7, 2006); *Passauer v. Quest Diagnostics, Inc.*, No. CCB-03-159, 2004 U.S. Dist. LEXIS 6966, at n.3 (D. Md. April 22, 2004) (FMLA does not require that the employer accommodate any restrictions or limitations an employee might have following medical leave); *Strykowski v. Rush North Shore Medical Center*, No. 02 C 0778, 2003 U.S. Dist. LEXIS 13206, at *19–20 (N.D. Ill. July 30, 2003) (unlike the ADA, FMLA job restoration regulation omits the qualifying "with or without reasonable accommodation" language); *St. Hilaire v. Minco Products, Inc.*, 288 F. Supp. 2d 999, 1098 (D. Minn. 2003) (FMLA does not require an employer to allow an employee to stay in a position that the employee cannot perform); *Alifano v. Merck & Co., Inc. et al.*, 175 F. Supp. 2d 792 (E.D. Pa. Dec. 7, 2001); *Jewell v. Reid's Confectionary Co.*, 172 F. Supp. 2d 212, 220 (D. Me. 2001) (rejecting argument that § 825.215(b) language essentially creates an ADA–style accommodation duty); *Reinehimer v. Cemcolift, Inc.*, No. 98–562, 2001 U.S. Dist. LEXIS 1165 (E.D. Pa. Feb. 1, 2001), *aff'd*, 292 F.3d 375 (3d Cir. 2002) (unlike requirements of ADA, Cemcolift was not required by FMLA to provide employee with an accommodation (such as wearing a respirator) to enable him to perform the essential functions of his position); *Williams v. SAAD's Healthcare*, No. 99–1070–BH–S, 2000 U.S. Dist. LEXIS 4180 (S.D. Ala. March 16, 2000) (unlike the ADA, § 825.214(b) omits the qualifying "with or without reasonable accommodation" language); *Kephart v. Cherokee County, North Carolina*, 52 F. Supp. 2d 607, 608 (W.D. N.C. 1999), *rev'd on other grounds, remanded*, No. 99-1789, 2000 U.S. App. LEXIS 18924 (4th Cir. Aug. 4, 2000) (FMLA did not require employer to hire assistant instead of replacing key employee; court found that this "argument is tantamount to requiring the County to make a 'reasonable accommodation' during Plaintiff's FMLA leave, something the Act does not require"), *aff'd in part, rev'd on other grounds*, 229 F.3d 1142 (4th Cir. 2000); *Ellis v. Mohenis Servs.*, No. 96–6307, 1998 U.S. Dist. LEXIS 13219 (E.D. Pa. Aug. 24, 1998);

In *Deery v. Port Auth. Transit Corp.*, No. 05-1353, 2006 U.S. Dist. LEXIS 62870, at *12 & n.6 (D.N.J. Aug. 23, 2006), the employee could perform all of the essential functions of his job with one "minor" exception, he wanted to be moved to another supervisor. The court found that the FMLA did not require the employer to accommodate the employee in order to allow the employee to return to work.

Of course, employers may have an obligation to reasonably accommodate the employee pursuant to the ADA. 29 CFR 825.214(b); S. Res. 242, Cong. Rec. S3959, S3969 (April 23, 1996); 29 CFR 825.214(b); *see Battle v. UPS, Inc.*, 438 F.3d 856, 864-65 (8th Cir. 2006) (any duty to accommodate employee is governed solely by the ADA, not FMLA); *Deery v. Port Auth. Transit Corp.*, No. 05-1353, 2006 U.S. Dist. LEXIS 62870, at *12 & n.6 (D.N.J. Aug. 23, 2006); *Williams v. SAAD's Healthcare*, No. 99–1070–BH–S, 2000 U.S. Dist. LEXIS 4180 (S.D. Ala. March 16, 2000) (section 825.214(b) states that an employer may have obligations under the ADA, but this reminder does not import the 'reasonable accommodation' qualifier into the FMLA context). In order for the duty to reasonably accommodate to apply, the employee attempting to return to work from FMLA leave must be disabled within the meaning of the Rehabilitation Act.

5. Greater Employer Benefits

An employer may provide leave benefits that exceed the minimum requirements of the FMLA. 29 CFR 825.700(a); S. Res. 242, Cong. Rec. S3959, S3969, S3976 (April 23, 1996); 29 CFR 825.214(b), 825.700(a). An employer must observe any employment benefit program or plan that provides greater family or medical leave rights to employees than the rights established by the FMLA. 29 CFR 825.700(a); S. Res. 242, Cong. Rec. S3959, S3976 (April 23, 1996); 29 CFR 825.700(a).

In the context of return to work, while an employer is not obligated by the FMLA to reasonably accommodate an employee who is unable to perform all of the essential functions of the position on return from FMLA leave, an employer's more generous FMLA leave policies may require such accommodation. *See Conti v. CSX International*, No. 02–1658, 2003 U.S. Dist. LEXIS 2520 (E.D. Pa. Feb. 14, 2003) (noting absence of binding legal precedent under FMLA that if an employer has a policy to provide reasonable accommodations to employees, a court must ignore the policy; if the defendant had such a policy, and refused to apply it to the plaintiff, the court opined that such evidence may be relevant in developing a trial record; summary judgment on the issue denied).

Other courts, however, have held that, even if the employer provided more generous FMLA leave benefits as a matter of policy, § 825.700 does not provide an FMLA cause of action for the alleged violation of these more generous leave policies. For example, in *Holmes v. E.Spire Communications, Inc. et al.*, 135 F. Supp. 2d 657, 666–68 (D. Md. 2001), the district court rejected the plaintiff's argument that her FMLA right to return to work continued beyond 12 weeks where she had not exhausted her employer's more generous maternity benefits, citing 29 CFR 825.700. Citing *Rich v. Delta Air Lines, Inc.*, 921 F. Supp. 767, 773 (N.D. Ga. 1996), the court held that § 825.700 does not, and could not, create a federal cause of action under the FMLA to enforce the voluntary employer policies of providing benefits that exceed those required by the FMLA.

C. JOINT EMPLOYERS

Joint employment is a concept limited to Title I, the CAA, and the PEOAA. It is not recognized in Title II. Basically, joint employment occurs where two or more entities exercise some control over the work or working conditions of the employee on FMLA leave. *See* 29 CFR 825.106(a); S. Res. 242, Cong. Rec. S3959, S3961 (April 23, 1996); 29 CFR 825.106(a). The classic example of a joint employment relationship is when a temporary or leasing employer supplies employees to a secondary employer. 29 CFR 825.106(a); S. Res. 242, Cong. Rec. S3959, S3961 (April 23, 1996); 29 CFR 825.106(a). [For a further discussion of joint employment, see Chapter 3, "FMLA Coverage of the Federal Government."]

Joint employment relationships are characterized by a primary and secondary employer. The primary employer has the authority to hire and fire, assign or place the employee, make payroll, and provide employment benefits. 29 CFR 825.106(a); S. Res. 242, Cong. Rec. S3959, S3961 (April 23, 1996); 29 CFR 825.106(a). The temporary or leasing employer that supplies employees is generally considered to be the primary employer. 29 CFR 825.106(a); S. Res. 242, Cong. Rec. S3959, S3961 (April 23, 1996); 29 CFR 825.106(a). The secondary employer would be the employer that is using the services of the employee, as contracted or leased through the temporary help or employee leasing employer.

Job restoration on the conclusion of FMLA leave is the responsibility of the primary employer. 29 CFR 825.106(a); S. Res. 242, Cong. Rec. S3959, S3961 (April 23, 1996); 29 CFR 825.106(a); *see Mahoney v. Nokia, Inc.*, 444 F. Supp. 2d 1246, 1257 (M.D. Fla. July 28, 2006), *aff'd*, 2007 U.S. App. LEXIS 1246 (11th Cir. June 11, 2007). The secondary employer is responsible for accepting the employee returning from FMLA leave if the secondary employer continues to use a replacement employee from the temporary or leasing employer, and the employer chooses to place the employee with the secondary employer. 29 CFR 825.106(a); S. Res. 242, Cong. Rec. S3959, S3961 (April 23, 1996); 29 CFR 825.106(a); *see Mahoney*, 444 F. Supp. 2d at 1257.

Note that the primary employer, the temporary or leasing employer in this example, must always accept the return of the employee from FMLA leave, assuming all other conditions are met. The primary employer is not, however, required to re-employ the returned employee with the secondary employer. For the employee to be returned to the secondary employer, two conditions must be met: (1) the secondary employer must be using a replacement employee from the temporary or leasing employer; and (2) the temporary or leasing employer must choose to send the employee back to the secondary employer. If both conditions are met, the secondary employer must accept the return of the employee from FMLA leave.

The return to work obligations of a temporary help employer are illustrated in *Colpean v. Ajilon, LLC*, No. 05-73710, 2007 U.S. Dist. LEXIS 23344, at *21-24 (E.D. Mich. March 30, 2007). Colpean was a temporary IT employee with Ajilon. She was placed in an assignment with Daimler Chrysler (DC). DC notified Ajilon that it no longer needed Colpean. At the same time, Colpean was planning to take 12 weeks of FMLA-maternity leave. Before she took leave, Colpean's assignment with DC ended. She returned to Ajilon in a non-pay status for a week or two before she took FMLA leave. When she returned from leave, Ajilon placed her in a non-pay status. Colpean insisted that Ajilon should have returned her to work with DC. The court disagreed. The court found that Ajilon returned Colpean to the position she held at the time her leave commenced. Because she was not working for DC at the time, Ajilon did not have to return her to a position with DC.

The return to work obligations of an employer hiring employees through a union hall is addressed in *Klich v. Gabe's Construction Co.*, No. 05-C-1262, 2007 U.S. Dist. LEXIS 11988, at *42-44 (E.D. Wis. Feb. 20, 2007). The court found that Klich was not an employee of Gabe's, but was an employee of the local steamfitters union. He worked out of the union hiring hall for Gabe's when work was available. For the ten-year period prior to his FMLA leave, Klich worked for Gabe's. The court found that, as an employee of the steamfitters, Klich was not entitled to be returned to work with Gabe's, but rather was only entitled to be returned to the union list for consideration in hiring. Requiring Gabe's to place Klich on a project after his surgery would be providing greater rights and benefits of employment than Klich was entitled to prior to his surgery.

III. EMPLOYEES' PERFECTION OF RIGHT TO RETURN TO WORK

An eligible employee's right to job restoration on the conclusion of the need for FMLA leave is not absolute. Certain conditions must be met in order for an employee to perfect the FMLA right to return to work. *Pharakhone v. Nissan North America, Inc. et al.*, 324 F.3d 405 (6th Cir. 2003) (FMLA right to reinstatement is not absolute); *Kohls v. Beverly enterprises Wisconsin, Inc.*, 259 F.3d 799, 804 (7th Cir. 2001) (same); *Routes v. Henderson*, 58 F. Supp. 2d 959, 977 (S.D. Ind. 1999) (FMLA permits employers to condition employee's right to restoration, such as requirement of fitness-for-duty certification). Failure to meet these conditions may deprive an employee of an FMLA right to be restored to the same or equivalent position on return from FMLA leave. Of course, the employee may enjoy an independent right to return to work pursuant to employer policy, including the terms of a collective bargaining agreement, or other legal right to be returned to work.

A. EMPLOYEE IS UNABLE TO PERFORM ALL ESSENTIAL JOB FUNCTIONS

1. Title I, the CAA, and the PEOAA

An employee who is unable to perform an essential function of the previous position because of a physical or mental condition, including the continuation of a serious health condition, has no right to restoration to the same or an equivalent position under the FMLA. 29 CFR 825.214(a); S. Res. 242, Cong. Rec. S3959, S3969 (April 23, 1996); 29 CFR 825.214(a); *see Harrell v. USPS*, 445 F.3d 913, 919 (7th Cir. 2006), *cert. denied*, 127 S. Ct. 845 (2006); *Sista v. CDC IXIS North Am., Inc.*, 445 F.3d 161, 174 (2d Cir. 2006); *Edgar v. JAC Products, Inc.*, 443 F.3d 501, 506, 509-510 (6th Cir. 2005); *Bloom v. Metro Heart Group of St. Louis, Inc.*, 440 F.3d 1025, 1030 (8th Cir. 2006); *Johnson v. Houston's Restaurant, Inc.*, 167 Fed. Appx. 393 (5th Cir. 2006); *Joostberns v. UPS, Inc.*, 166 Fed. Appx. 783 (6th Cir. 2006); *Coburn v. Parker Hannifin*, 429 F.3d 325, 332 (1st Cir. 2005); *Brumbalough v. Camelot Care Centers, Inc.*, 427 F.3d 996, 1001 (6th Cir. 2005), *Fogelman v. Greater Hazleton Health Alliance*, 122 Fed. Appx. 521 (3d Cir. 2004); *Hoge v. Honda of America Mfg., Inc.*, 384 F.3d 238 (6th Cir. 2004) (FMLA right to job restoration does not arise unless the returning employee is able to perform the essential functions of the position or an equivalent); *Conroy v. Township of Lower Merion*, 77 Fed. Appx. 556 (3d Cir. 2003), *cert denied*, 124 S. Ct. 2872 (2004) (because employee could not perform all essential job functions on return from FMLA leave, employee had no FMLA right to job restoration. As such, employer's request that employee submit to an IME did not interfere with her FMLA rights because she had no FMLA right to return to work at all); *Rinehimer v. Cemcolift, Inc.*, 292 F.3d. 375, 384 (3d Cir. 2002); *Spangler v. Federal Home Loan Bank of Des Moines*, 278 F.3d 847, 851 (8th Cir. 2002); *Hicks v. Leroy's Jewelers, Inc. et al.*, No. 98–6596, 2000 U.S. App. LEXIS 17568 (6th Cir. July 17, 2000); *Reynolds v. Phillips & Temro Industries, Inc.*, 195 F.3d 411, 413–14 (8th Cir. 1999); *Sarno v. Douglas Elliman–Gibbons & Ives, Inc.*, 183 F.3d 155, 161–62 (2nd Cir. 1999); *Tardie v. Rehabilitation Hospital of Rhode Island et al.*, 168 F.3d 538, 543 (1st Cir. 1999); *Ruff v. DePaul U.*, No. 07 C 156, 2007 U.S. Dist. LEXIS 25065, at *10-11 (N.D. Ill. April 4, 2007); *Sheaffer v. County of Chatam*, 337 F. Supp. 2d 709 (M.D. N.C. 2004) (courts have held that a plaintiff does not state a cause of action for failure to reinstate when he is unable to return to work at the end of the 12–week period); *Geromanos v. Columbia Univ., College of Physicians and Surgeons*, 322 F. Supp. 2d 420, 427 (S.D.N.Y. 2004) (plaintiff had no right to reinstatement because she was incapable of performing the essential functions of her position at the end of the 12 weeks); *Pasley v. City of Dallas*, No. 3:01–CV–1194–K, 2004 U.S. Dist. LEXIS 10998, at *25 (N.D. Tex. June 1, 2004) (no right to reinstatement, as more than 12 weeks elapsed between the time she started FMLA leave and when she was cleared to return to work). An employee has no FMLA right to restoration to another position if the employee is unable to perform the essential functions of the position he or she held when leave began. *Lombardo v. Air Products & Chemicals, Inc.*, No. 05-1120, 2006 U.S. Dist. LEXIS 46077, at *17 (E.D. Pa. July 7, 2006).

This is true even if the employer terminated the employee before the FMLA leave period expired. *Lombardo v. Air Products & Chemicals, Inc.*, No. 05-1120, 2006 U.S. Dist. LEXIS 46077, at *17 (E.D. Pa. July 7, 2006).

Nor would the FMLA require an employer to create a position that does not exist for an employee who is unable to perform the functions of his or her former position at the end of FMLA leave. 29 CFR 825.214(b); S. Res. 242, Cong. Rec. S3959, S3969 (April 23, 1996); 29 CFR 825.214(b); *see Johnson v. Houston's Restaurant, Inc.*, 167 Fed. Appx. 393 (5th Cir. 2006); *Oatman v. Fuji Photo Film U.S.A., Inc.*, No. 3:00–CV–2116–R, 2006 U.S. App. LEXIS 3962 (N.D. Tex. Feb. 15, 2002); *Williams v. SAAD's Healthcare*, No. 99–1070–BH–S, 2000 U.S. Dist. LEXIS 4180 (S.D. Ala. March 16, 2000) (dismissing FMLA claims based on employer's refusal to provide alternative employment, as this is clearly not required under the FMLA); *Jewell v. Reid's Confectionary Co.*, 172 F. Supp. 2d 212, 220 (D. Me. 2001) (employee failed to present evidence suggesting he was physically able to resume his normal job duties on the expiration of leave, and who did not even contact his employer to inquire about returning to work at the end of the leave period, has no FMLA right to be restored to prior or similar position, including a job involving light duty work); *Soletro v. National Fed. of Independent Business*, 130 F. Supp. 2d 906, 911 (N.D. Ohio 2001); DOL WH FMLA Advisory Opinion No. 47 (Oct. 17, 1994). An employer may, however, have additional compliance obligations with respect to the employee under other federal laws (the Rehabilitation Act, Title VII of the Civil Rights Act), or the more generous provisions afforded by employer policy, including the requirements of a collective bargaining agreement. 29 CFR 825.214(b), 825.700; DOL WH FMLA Advisory Opinion No. 47 (Oct. 17, 1994).

Courts have precluded FMLA claims where the employee was no longer able to perform a wide variety of essential job functions on return to work from FMLA leave. For example, an employee whose job required him to work a certain number of hours was not entitled to a right to return to work with restrictions limiting the number of hours that he could work. *See Tardie v. Rehabilitation Hospital of Rhode Island et al.*, 168 F.3d 538, 543 (1st Cir. 1999); *Alifano v. Merck & Co., Inc. et al.*, 175 F. Supp. 2d 792 (E.D. Pa. Dec. 7, 2001); *Voskuil v. Environmental Health Center-Dallas, et. al*, No. 3:96–CV–0683–D,

1997 U.S. Dist. LEXIS 23565 (N.D. Tex. Aug. 19, 1997) (employee restricted to four hours a day at time of expiration of 12 weeks of FMLA leave was unable to perform all essential job functions entitling employee to job restoration under FMLA). Restrictions on an employee's ability to travel in a job that required extensive travel brought the employee outside the return to work provisions of the FMLA. *Alifano v. Merck & Co., Inc. et al.*, 175 F. Supp. 2d 792 (E.D. Pa. Dec. 7, 2001).

Some courts do not require reinstatement where the employee can not perform the essential functions of his or her former position at the end of FMLA leave because of lifting restrictions. *Reynolds v. Phillips & Temro Industries, Inc.*, 195 F.3d 411, 414 (8th Cir. 1999); *Lombardo v. Air Products & Chemicals, Inc.*, No. 05-1120, 2006 U.S. Dist. LEXIS 46077, at *17 (E.D. Pa. July 7, 2006); *Passauer v. Quest Diagnostics, Inc.*, No. CCB-03-159, 2004 U.S. Dist. LEXIS 6966, at *8 (D. Md. April 22, 2004) (employee with warehouse job who was unable to lift more than 30 pounds on return from FMLA leave was unable to perform all the essential functions of the job and, therefore, did not have an FMLA right to job restoration); *Strykowski v. Rush North Shore Medical Center*, No. 02 C 0778, 2003 U.S. Dist. LEXIS 13206, at *19–20 (N.D. Ill. July 30, 2003) (10–pound lifting restriction rendered respiratory therapist unable to perform essential job function to lift, carry, and push medium to heavy objects); *Soletro v. National Fed. of Independent Business*, 130 F. Supp. 2d 906, 911 (N.D. Ohio 2001). Of course, if lifting is not an essential function of the job, an employee returning to work before 12 weeks of FMLA leave expire with lifting restrictions would have to be reinstated. *See Greenlee v. Christus Spohn Health Sys. Corp.*, No. C-06-123, 2007 U.S. Dist. LEXIS 398, at 814-15 (S.D. Tex. Jan. 4, 2007).

In *Joostberns v. UPS, Inc.*, 166 Fed. Appx. 783 (6th Cir. 2006), the Sixth Circuit found a driver's inability to operate heavy machinery while on prescription medication sufficient to preclude reinstatement. A foreman who worked in an environment with dust and fumes could not perform the essential functions of his position where he was released to return to full–time duty, except he had to avoid dust and fumes. *Rinehimer v. Cemcolift, Inc.*, 292 F.3d. 375, 384 (3d Cir. 2002).

An employee's total disability at the time her FMLA leave expiration precluded an FMLA right to return to work. *Green v. Alcan Aluminum Corp.*, No. 98–3775, 1999 U.S. App. LEXIS 30158 (6th Cir. 1999); *Madison v. The Sherwin Williams Co.*, 158 F. Supp. 2d 854, 858 (N.D. Ill. 2001) (employee could not perform essential functions of former position, or any position remaining at Chicago facility); *Barry v. Wing Mem. Hosp.*, 142 F. Supp. 2d 161, 165–66 (D. Mass. 2001); *Soletro v. National Fed. of Independent Business*, 130 F. Supp. 2d 906, 911 (N.D. Ohio 2001)

In V*oskuil v. Environmental Health Center–Dallas et. al*, No. 3:96–CV–0683–D, 1997 U.S. Dist. LEXIS 23565 (N.D. Tex. Aug. 19, 1997), the district court addressed whether a full–time employee was entitled to job restoration from FMLA leave even though she could only work four hours a day. Plaintiff maintained that, notwithstanding this restriction, she could perform the essential functions of her job as Director of Human Resources because it was classified as an exempt position. The plaintiff argued that exempt employees are only required to complete assignments, do not have specific hourly constraints, and can even be part–time under certain conditions. Rejecting these arguments, the court found an absence of any evidence that would support the conclusion that the plaintiff could perform the job responsibilities of a full–time job in four–hour days regardless of strict hourly constraints. As such, the employer had no duty to offer the plaintiff a full–time position at the expiration of her 12–week FMLA leave period.

Few courts have explored the contours of what constitute "essential job functions" for purposes of determining whether an employee is entitled to return to work from FMLA leave. Some courts have relied on concepts developed in interpreting the ADA and the Rehabilitation Act. At least one court has suggested otherwise. *Duty v. Norton–Alcoa Proppants*, 293 F.3d 481, 495 (8th Cir. 2002); *Villareal v. The Scooter Store-San Antonio Ltd.*, No. SA-04-CA-0194, 2005 U.S. Dist. LEXIS 6019, at *5 & n.6 (W.D. Tex. April 1, 2005).

The Eighth Circuit in *Duty*, 293 F.3d at 495, addressed the standard for determining whether an employee was capable of performing the essential functions of the position on return from FMLA leave as follows:

> To determine whether an employee is capable of performing the essential functions of his job for purposes of FMLA entitlement, we do not utilize the same criteria outlined by the ADA and the courts interpreting it. *See Stekloff v. St. John's Mercy Health Sys.*, 218 F.3d 858, 861 (8th Cir. 2000). Rather, because "the declared purpose of the FMLA and its legislative history" are concerned with maintaining job security, an FMLA inquiry examining the employee's ability to perform the essential functions of his job focuses "on [his] ability to perform those functions in [his] current environment." *Stekloff,* 218 F.3d at 861-62.

The court later clarified that, in the FMLA context, this determination was limited to a demonstration that Duty was able to perform the essential functions of his former job. The court then applied its reasoning that Duty was capable of performing the essential functions of his position for purposes of disability law to the FMLA claim. *Duty*, 293 F.3d at 495. By so doing, the court appears to sanction limited application of the principles developed in interpreting essential job functions, for purposes of the ADA and the Rehabilitation Act in the FMLA context. In the return to work context, an evaluation is limited to whether the employee can fulfill the essential job functions of the employee's pre–FMLA leave position.

In finding that the ability to work more than a 40–hour week was an essential function of the position at issue, the First Circuit in *Tardie v. Rehabilitation Hospital of Rhode Island, et al.*, 168 F.3d 538, 544 (1st Cir. 1999), referenced language in the position description that the individual must have "sufficient endurance to perform tasks over long periods of time." The position description did not specifically identify the ability to work a set number of hours as an essential function. The court also credited statements made by Tardie in her deposition regarding the frequency with which she worked long hours. The court did not credit Tardie's offer of a payroll check showing a salary based on a 40–hour workweek. The court opined that, as a salaried employee, the employer was not required to keep records on the hours she actually worked in the performance of her job. Interestingly, in addressing arguments over the essential functions of her job, the court referenced cases interpreting "essential functions" for purposes of the ADA.

In *Brumbalough v. Camelot Care Centers, Inc.*, 427 F.3d 996, 1003 (6th Cir. 2005), the Sixth Circuit considered whether limitations on travel and the ability to work more than 40 hours a week was an essential function of the State Clinical Director position. The court noted that the determination whether functions are "essential" is a question of fact. A court must engage in a highly fact-specific inquiry and base its determination on more than statements in a job description. The determination should reflect the actual functions and circumstances of the particular enterprise. The court went on to find material issues of fact in dispute whether extensive travel or the ability to work more than 40 hours a week was an essential function of the position. The court noted the absence of the ability to work more than 40 hours from the position description as one factor.

Applying ADA principles, the court in *Villareal v. The Scooter Store-San Antonio Ltd.*, No. SA-04-CA-0194, 2005 U.S. Dist. LEXIS 6019, at *5 & n.6 (W.D. Tex. April 1, 2005), found that the employee was unable to perform the essential function of being able to get along with supervisors and co-workers and, therefore, did not have the right to job restoration.

In *Routes v. Henderson*, 58 F. Supp. 2d 959, 977 (S.D. Ind. 1999), the district court addressed whether an employee returning to work from FMLA leave was able to perform all of the essential functions of the pre–leave position, such that the employee had an FMLA right to return to work. The Postal Service argued that the employee was not entitled to job restoration because he was not available to work seven days a week. The Postal Service contended that being available to work seven days a week was an essential function of Routes' pre–leave position as a part–time flexible clerk. The plaintiff's physician supplied a medical note releasing Routes to return to work, which indicated that it would be better if he only worked five days a week. *Routes*, 58 F. Supp. 2d at 970.

Addressing what constitutes an essential function, the court (*Routes*, 58 F. Supp. 2d at 992–93) noted that:

> The term "function" in essential function, however, complicates the analysis because it traditionally refers to physical functions of the job, such as the ability to lift certain weights, or perform certain movements. Here, the function is more like a requirement—to be available to work on any seven days of a week for the convenience of the employer. Given that the employer was engaged in the business of delivering the public's mail on a timely basis, and that the volume of mail to be handled can vary widely over time, it is essential to the function of the post office that certain employees are available to be scheduled on a flexible basis corresponding to postal demands.

As further support for a finding that availability to work seven days a week was an essential function of his position, the court noted the provisions of the governing collective bargaining agreement (CBA). The CBA specifically provided that part–time flexible clerks must be available for work seven days a week. The court also noted the testimony of the postmaster that he informed all part–time flexible clerks of this requirement, and that Routes understood this requirement.

The court also noted that a written job description showing this requirement as an essential function would have been given "substantial deference." *Routes*, 58 F. Supp. 2d at 993. As support for this proposition, the court cited several cases interpreting the ADA. The court noted "There is no doubt an employer is entitled to define the essential functions of a position." *Id*. Unfortunately for the Postal Service, the requirement that a part-time flexible employee be available to work seven days a week is not set forth in a written job description.

The Postal Service's claim that being available to work seven days a week was an essential job function was weakened, the court opined, by the fact that Routes was not replaced for six months after he attempted to return to work. *Id*. Nevertheless, the court held that availability to work seven days a week was essential to the operation of the post office in Nashville and, therefore, is an essential function of Routes' position. *Id*.

Having determined that availability to work seven days a week was an essential job function, the court turned to whether the Postal Service demonstrated that Routes was not capable of performing that function when he contacted the employer to return to work. The court concluded that the Postal Service had failed. The evidence relied on by the Postal Service, the doctor's note releasing Routes to return to work did not unequivocally state that Routes was not available to work seven days a week. Rather, it provided that Routes could be available to work seven days a week—only that it would be better if he did not actually work more than five days a week. This evidence, according to the court, "falls far short of proving that Routes could no longer perform an essential function of the job. If the Postal Service was not satisfied with the medical documentation provided, it should have availed itself of the second and third opinion process." *Routes*, 58 F. Supp. at 993–94. The court concluded that the "inability to perform an essential function" exception to the right to restoration did not apply. *Id*.

Moss v. Formosa Plastics Corp., 99 F. Supp. 2d 737 (M.D. La. 2000), involved an employee in a safety-sensitive position who was subject to severe epileptic seizures resulting in unconsciousness. After a severe seizure where he was unconscious for approximately 40 minutes, Formosa involuntarily placed Moss on FMLA leave. Moss subsequently saw a series of physicians at the direction of Formosa, two of whom opined that Moss could not safely return to work because of his epilepsy. Moss also saw his owns physicians, one indicated that Moss was fit to return to work, the other said he was not. Formosa suggested that Moss seek out a third opinion regarding his ability to return to work. The physician initially indicated that Moss was fit to return to work, but should avoid working on ladders or at heights. The same doctor wrote another note indicating that Moss was "ok to return to work—but should not be responsible for managing toxic chemicals." Formosa terminated Moss's employment. Moss sued, alleging that Formosa should have returned him to work from FMLA leave.

In awarding summary judgment to the employer, the district court considered whether Moss was able to perform the essential functions of the position of control panel operator. The court credited the testimony of the employer that an essential function of the plaintiff's position, Panel Board Operator in Formosa's Caustic Chlorine Plant, involved the coordination of plant-wide emergency response measures. Because he sometimes worked alone and had to act quickly in the event of an emergency, the court found that "it is clear that an employee in Moss's position must be alert at all times." The court then reviewed the various medical notes, most of which said that Moss could not safely perform the functions of his position. Regarding the two doctor's notes from Moss's physicians, the court examined both notes together to conclude that Moss was not able to perform the essential functions of his job because of his condition. Specifically, the court held that the control panel operator was required to be alert in the case of an emergency, and Moss's condition preventing him from doing so.

Several courts reject employee arguments that the employer's wrongful conduct somehow exacerbated his or her medical problems, thus preventing the employee from returning to work before the expiration of the 12 weeks of FMLA leave. *See Edgar v. JAC Products, Inc.*, 443 F.3d 501 (6th Cir. 2006); *Farrell v. Tri-County Met. Transport. District of Oregon*, No. CV 04-296-PA, 2006 U.S. Dist. LEXIS 30257, at *5-6 (D. Or. May 15, 2006); *Barry v. Wing Mem. Hosp.*, 142 F. Supp. 2d 161 (D. Mass. 2001).

Of course, if an employee were physically able to return to work upon the expiration of FMLA leave, an employer would be liable for failing to restore the employee to the same or an equivalent position. *Holmes v. E.Spire Communications, Inc. et al.*, 135 F. Supp. 2d 657, 664 (D. Md. March 15, 2001).

Finally, where an employee is unable to return to work from FMLA leave after 12 weeks, the employee's return, if any, is governed by employer policies. *See Becksondorf v. Schwemann Giant Super Markets, Inc.*, No. 95-3822 § "K" (3), 1997 U.S. Dist. LEXIS 5693 (E.D. La. April 21, 1997), *aff'd without op.*, 134 F.3d 369 (5th Cir. 1997).

2. Title II

Title II does not contain a provision that requires that an employee be able to perform all essential job functions of the previous position as a condition for the employer to return the employee to work.

The regulations generally provide that an employee returning from FMLA leave is not entitled to any right, benefit, or position to which the employee would have been entitled had the employee not taken the leave. 5 CFR 1208(d)(2). They also provide that an employee is not entitled to be returned to the same or equivalent position if the employee would not otherwise have been employed in that position at the time the employee returns from leave. 5 CFR 630.1208(f). Unfortunately, no examples are provided, either directly in the regulations or in the comments to the final regulations.

A third regulation might also apply. Title II permits an employer to require an employee returning from FMLA leave to provide a medical certification that the employee is able to perform the essential functions of his or her position. 5 CFR 630.1208(h). The rule spells out what may happen if the employee delays or fails to supply the requested medical certification. Ironically, the regulation fails to say what happens if the doctor writes on the medical certification that the employee is incapable of performing any of the essential job functions.

Section 630.1208(f) may come into play if employer policy or practice would not return an employee to the same or an equivalent position when the employee is unable to perform an essential function of the job, then the employee would not have an FMLA right to return to work. The provisions of the Rehabilitation Act might apply, if the employee were disabled within the meaning of the law, but the employee would not have a right to be returned to work under the FMLA or employer policy.

B. FITNESS-FOR-DUTY MEDICAL CERTIFICATIONS

The FMLA permits an employer under certain circumstances to require an employee to provide a medical certification regarding his or her ability to return to work.

1. Title I, the CAA, and the PEOAA

a. General Rule

As a condition of restoring an employee whose FMLA leave was due to the employee's own serious health condition, an employer may have a uniformly-applied policy or practice that requires all similarly-situated employees (i.e., same occupation, same serious health condition) who take leave for such conditions to obtain and present certification from the employee's health care provider that the employee is able to resume work. 29 USC 2614(a)(4); 29 CFR 825.310(a); 2 USC 1312(a)(4) (incorporating 29 USC 2614 into CAA); S. Res. 242, Cong. Rec. S3959, S3974 (April 23, 1996); 29 CFR 825.310(a). 3 USC 412(a)(1) (incorporating 29 USC 2614 into PEOAA); *see Killian v. Yorozu Automotive Tennessee, Inc.*, 454 F.3d 549, 555 (6th Cir. 2006); *Drago v. Jenne*, 453 F.3d 1301, 1306-1307 (11th Cir. 2006); *Harrell v. USPS*, 445 F.3d 913, 920 (7th Cir. 2006), cert. denied, 127 S. Ct. 845 (2006); *Bloom v. Metro Heart Group of St. Louis, Inc.*, 440 F.3d 1025, 1030 (8th Cir. 2006); *Buettner v. North Oklahoma County Mental Health Center*, 158 Fed. Appx. 81 (10th Cir. 2005); *Brumbalough v. Camelot Care Centers, Inc.*, 427 F.3d 996, 1001 (6th Cir. 2005); *Hoge v. Honda of America Mfg., Inc.*, 384 F.3d 238 (6th Cir. 2004); *Cooper v. Olin Corporation, Winchester Division*, 246 F.3d 1083, 1090 (8th Cir. 2001); *Matthews v. Fairview Health Services*, No. 01-2151-ADM/AJB, 2003 U.S. Dist. LEXIS 5901 (D. Minn. April 7, 2003); *Rogers v. New York University*, 250 F. Supp. 2d 310 (S.D.N.Y. 2002); *Conroy v. Township of Lower Merion et al.*, No. 00-CV-3528, 2001 U.S. Dist. LEXIS 11460 (E.D. Pa. Aug. 7, 2001); *Underhill v. Willamina Lumber Co. et al.*, No. 98-630-AS, 1999 U.S. Dist. LEXIS 9722 (D. Ore. June 17, 1999); *Routes v. Henderson*, 58 F. Supp. 2d 959, 977 (S.D. Ind. 1999); *Johnson v. USPS*, No. 1:97-CV-794, 1999 U.S. Dist. LEXIS 7981, at n. 14 (W.D. Mich. May 26, 1999); *Burton v. Neumann*, No. 97-8061-CIV-HURLEY, 1999 U.S. Dist. LEXIS 16122 (S.D. Fla. April 8, 1999); *Hensley v. Baptist Hospital of East Tennessee, Inc. et al.*, No. 3:96-CV-789, 1997 U.S. Dist. LEXIS 22515 (E.D. Tenn. Oct. 27, 1997); *Wagner v. Texas A&M University et al.*, 939 F. Supp. 1297, 1324-25 (S.D. Tex. 1996).

An example of a uniformly applied practice is when an employer states that any employee absent for a specified number of days must submit a fitness-for-duty certification before returning to work. *Routes v. Henderson*, 58 F. Supp. 2d 959, 977 (S.D. Ind. 1999).

The uniform practice need only apply to employees on FMLA leave. In *Bloom v. Metro Heart Group of St. Louis, Inc.*, 440

F.3d 1025, 1030 (8th Cir. 2006), the employee argued that the fitness-for-duty requirement was not uniform because it only applied to employees on FMLA leave, and not to employees on non-FMLA leave. The court disagreed. According to the clear language of the FMLA, the fitness-for-duty requirement applies only to employees who have taken FMLA leave.

An employer fails to establish the existence of a uniform policy or practice by simply mentioning the existence of the policy. *Nott v. Woodstock Care Center, Inc. et al.*, No. C-3-99-133, 2001 U.S. Dist. LEXIS 22655, at *26 (S.D. Ohio March 21, 2001) (moving brief mentioned existence of uniform "policy" requiring fitness-for-duty certification on return from FMLA leave, but failed to produce policy, insufficient evidence of existence of policy).

Nothing in the FMLA permits an employer to require that the fitness to return to duty certification be from a health care provider that is a specialist in the applicable field, as opposed to a general practitioner. *Matthews v. Fairview Health Services*, No. 01-2151-ADM/AJB, 2003 U.S. Dist. LEXIS 5901 (D. Minn. April 7, 2003) (fitness to return to duty certification from internist rather than cardiology specialist sufficient to clear employee to return to work from FMLA leave).

An employer did not violate the Act when it elected to rely on the written fitness-for-duty certification of one of the employee's health care providers over the oral certification of another of the employee's health care providers. In *Rogers v. New York University*, 250 F. Supp. 2d 310 (S.D.N.Y. 2002), the employee was seeing two therapists for psychological issues during her FMLA leave absence. When apprised that her FMLA leave was about to run out and that she needed to return to work with a written certification of fitness for duty in order to preserve her job, both health care providers contacted NYU. One health care provider submitted a written certification indicating that the employee would not be fit to return to duty for one or two months. The other left several phone messages that failed to indicate that the employee was able to return to work or when. The court held that NYU was within its rights to rely on the written certification, which had some specificity, over the ambiguous telephone messages.

The FMLA generally does not permit an employer to require an employee to submit to an employer approved health care provider before the employee returns to work from FMLA leave. Preamble, 29 CFR 310. The Statute provides that the employee must only provide the employer with certification from the employee's health care provider to qualify to return to work. *Id*. As stated by the court in *Albert v. Runyon*, 6 F. Supp. 2d 57 (D. Mass. 1998):

> The FMLA does not authorize an employer to make its own determination of whether an employee is fit to return from FMLA leave following recovery from a serious health condition. Rather, an employer must rely on the evaluation done by the employee's own clinician and return the employee to work without delay upon receipt of medical certification, which need only be a simple statement of an employee's ability to return.

See Matthews v. Fairview Health Services, No. 01-2151-ADM/AJB, 2003 U.S. Dist. LEXIS 5901 (D. Minn. April 7, 2003).

An employer is not entitled to certification of fitness to return to duty when the employee takes intermittent leave. 29 CFR 825.310(g); S. Res. 242, Cong. Rec. S3959, S3974 (April 23, 1996); 29 CFR 825.310(g). Note that the prohibition is absolute. An employer is prohibited from requesting a return to work certification after any absences during the course of a period of intermittent leave. It is also prohibited from requesting fitness-for-duty certification on the conclusion of intermittent leave.

Note also that FMLA leave on a reduced leave schedule is not subject to the prohibition. An employer could request a return to work certification from an employee on the conclusion of FMLA leave taken on a reduced leave schedule for the employee's own serious health condition. An employer would not, however, be able to request a return to work certification until the reduced leave schedule has run its course.

The fitness-for-duty certification must be provided contemporaneously with the employee's ability to return to work. *Burkett v. Beaulieu Group, LLC*, 382 F. Supp. 2d 1376, 1380-81 (N.D. Ga. Aug. 16, 2005), *aff'd*, 168 Fed. Appx. 895 (11th Cir. 2006) (rejecting employee argument that recertification provided a month before the employee returned to work constituted fitness-for-duty certification); *Barnes v. Ethan Allen*, Inc., 356 F. Supp. 2d 1306, 1311-12 (S.D. Fla. 2005), *aff'd*, 2005 U.S. App. LEXIS 18931 (11th Cir. 2005) (certification suggesting employee could return to work in 4-6 weeks was not a fitness-for-duty certification. Fitness-for-duty certification must be "relevant to the employees' condition at the time FMLA leave is concluded"; allowing six-week old note to qualify as fitness-for-duty certification is not reasonable under FMLA).

b. Contents and Form of Certification

A return to work certification under the FMLA need only be a simple statement of an employee's ability to resume work. 29 USC 2614(a)(4); 29 CFR 825.310(c); S. Res. 242, Cong. Rec. S3959, S3974 (April 23, 1996); 29 CFR 825.310(c); see *Brumbalough v. Camelot Care Centers, Inc.*, 427 F.3d 996, 1003 (6th Cir. 2005); *Cooper v. Olin Corporation, Winchester Division*, 246 F.3d 1083, 1090 (8th Cir. 2001); *Porter v. United States Alumoweld Co., Inc.*, 125 F.3d 243, 247 (4th Cir. 1997); *Carpo v. Wartburg Lutheran Home for the Aging*, No. 05 CV 1169 (JG), 2006 U.S. Dist. LEXIS 74856, at *7-8 (E.D.N.Y. Oct. 16, 2006); *Burkett v. Beaulieu Group, LLC*, 382 F. Supp. 2d 1376, 1380-81 (N.D. Ga. Aug. 16, 2005), *aff'd*, 168 Fed. Appx. 895 (11th Cir. 2006); *Routes v. Henderson*, 58 F. Supp. 2d 959, 996, n.23 (S.D. Ind. 1999); *Albert v. Runyon*, 6 F. Supp. 2d 57 (D. Mass. 1998); DOL WH FMLA Advisory Opinion No. 113 (Sept. 11, 2000); *Matthews v. Fairview Health Services*, No. 01–2151–ADM/AJB, 2003 U.S. Dist. LEXIS 5901 (D. Minn. April 7, 2003); *Rogers v. New York University*, 250 F. Supp. 2d 310 (S.D.N.Y. 2002); DOL WH FMLA Advisory Opinion No. 58 (April 28, 1995). As such, the proper elements of a restoration certification differ somewhat from the certification of a serious health condition under 29 USC 2613. *Cooper v. Olin Corporation, Winchester Division*, 246 F.3d 1083, 1090 (8th Cir. 2001).

Just how short a health care provider's statement can be is illustrated in *Underhill v. Willamina Lumber Co. et al.*, No. 98–630–AS, 1999 U.S. Dist. LEXIS 9722 (D. Ore. June 17, 1999). In that case, the court held that the following signed statement from the employee's health care provider satisfied the fitness–for–duty certification requirements of the FMLA: "pt. may return back to work."

A fitness–for–duty certification must be in writing, and must unambiguously state the employee is capable of returning to work and when. See *Burkett v. Beaulieu Group, LLC*, 382 F. Supp. 2d 1376, 1380-81 (N.D. Ga. Aug. 16, 2005), *aff'd*, 168 Fed. Appx. 895 (11th Cir. 2006) (certification must be an unconditional release of the plaintiff to return to work); *Rogers v. New York University*, 250 F. Supp. 2d 310 (S.D.N.Y. 2002) (ambiguous telephone messages by treating physician failed to satisfy FMLA fitness-for-duty requirements as it was not in writing, failed to clearly state that employee was medically able to return to work and when, as opposed to merely stating that losing her job would be damaging to her).

In *Bloom v. Metro Heart Group of St. Louis, Inc.*, 440 F.3d 1025, 1030 (8th Cir. 2006), the employee failed to submit a fitness-for-duty certification. The employee argued that the employer should have relied on her physician's statement in the discussion section of a report she submitted as the equivalent of a fitness-for-duty certification. The Eighth Circuit found the following language ambiguous:

> Whatever direction or energies her previous treating physicians think best for her, it should be carried on by them in her behalf.
>
> If she were working, I would not be able to determine any medical basis to restrict her work activities as a sonographer/electrocardiographer/ultrasound technician.

The court found the language "too vague and conditional" to constitute a statement that Bloom was fit-for-duty.

In *Brumbalough v. Camelot Care Centers, Inc.*, 427 F.3d 996, 1003 (6th Cir. 2005), the court found the following health care provider statement sufficient: "Linda Brumbalough may return to work on 8/13/01. She should only work a 40-55 hour week and limit her out of town travel to 1 day."

A certification that an employee "may attempt return to work" was an adequate certification that the employee was able to resume work. *Carpo v. Wartburg Lutheran Home for the Aging*, No. 05 CV 1169 (JG), 2006 U.S. Dist. LEXIS 74856, at *7-8 (E.D.N.Y. Oct. 16, 2006). In *Carpo*, the court opined that by stating that the employee "may attempt to return to work" the doctor conveyed that, as a medical matter, Carpo was able to resume her work as a nutritionist. The qualifying language "may attempt" did not intimate that Carpo was incapable of resuming the full duties of her position. Rather, it conveyed that the doctor was not absolutely certain, but, because it was very likely that she could, it was safe for her to try. In so holding, the court rejected the employer's argument that the return to work certification had to unequivocally state that Carpo was "capable of resuming the full duties of her position."

A return to work fitness–for–duty certification that failed to state that the employee is "fully able to resume performing the essential functions of the employee's position," as required by the employer's FMLA Standard Operating Procedure, was found to be insufficient to meet the requirements of 29 USC 2614(a)(4). *Burton v. Neumann*, No. 97–8061–CIV–HURLEY, 1999 U.S. Dist. LEXIS 16122 (S.D. Fla. April 8, 1999). *But see Carpo v. Wartburg Lutheran Home for the Aging*, No. 05

CV 1169 (JG), 2006 U.S. Dist. LEXIS 74856, at *9-10 (E.D.N.Y. Oct. 16, 2006) (FMLA does not require a definitive statement that an employee is able to return to her "full duties").

The employee submitted a certification from her physician entitled "to whom it may concern" that stated that "there is no medical reason why [plaintiff] cannot continue to be employed at this time." The court's decision was undoubtedly influenced by the fact that the employee was on notice of what the contents of the certification should say as the employer had previously given the employee a copy of the policy.

An employer may seek certification only with regard to the particular serious health condition that caused the employee's need for FMLA leave. 29 CFR 825.310(c); S. Res. 242, Cong. Rec. S3959, S3974 (April 23, 1996); 29 CFR 825.310(c); see Hoge v. Honda of America Mfg., Inc., 384 F.3d 238 (6th Cir. 2004); Routes v. Henderson, 58 F. Supp. 2d 959, 996, n. 23 (S.D. Ind. 1999); DOL WH FMLA Advisory Opinion No. 113 (Sept. 11, 2000); DOL WH FMLA Advisory Opinion No. 58 (April 28, 1995). For example, an employer cannot require the certification to address the returning employee's general state of health. In fact, given the brevity of the required certification, the rule that the certification is limited to the serious health condition at issue is largely superfluous. A certification that simply states that the employee is fit to return to duty is satisfactory, even though it does not mention anything about the employee's condition. *Underhill v. Willamina Lumber Co. et al.*, No. 98–630–AS, 1999 U.S. Dist. LEXIS 9722 (D. Ore. June 17, 1999) (certification stating, "pt. may return to work" held sufficient).

Once an employee submits a statement from her health care provider which indicates that she may return to work, the employer's duty to reinstate the employee is triggered. *Brumbalough v. Camelot Care Centers, Inc.*, 427 F.3d 996, 1004 (6th Cir. 2005),

c. Clarification of Certification

An employer may, under limited circumstances, make further inquiries regarding the contents of the fitness–for–duty certification proffered by the employee. A health care provider employed by the employer may contact the employee's health care provider, with the employee's permission, for purposes of clarification of the employee's fitness to return to work. 29 CFR 825.310(c); S. Res. 242, Cong. Rec. S3959, S3974 (April 23, 1996); 29 CFR 825.310(c); see Cooper v. Olin Corporation, Winchester Division, 246 F.3d 1083, 1090 (8th Cir. 2001); Matthews v. Fairview Health Services, No. 01–2151–ADM/AJB, 2003 U.S. Dist. LEXIS 5901 (D. Minn. April 7, 2003); DOL WH FMLA Advisory Opinion No. 113 (Sept. 11, 2000); DOL WH FMLA Advisory Opinion No. 58 (April 28, 1995). However, no additional information may be acquired, and clarification may be requested only for the serious health condition for which FMLA leave was taken. 29 CFR 825.310(c); S. Res. 242, Cong. Rec. S3959, S3974 (April 23, 1996); 29 CFR 825.310(c); see DOL WH FMLA Advisory Opinion No. 113 (Sept. 11, 2000); DOL WH FMLA Advisory Opinion No. 58 (April 28, 1995).

An employer may not delay the employee's reinstatement to work while requesting or waiting for clarification. 29 CFR 825.310(e); S. Res. 242, Cong. Rec. S3959, S3974 (April 23, 1996); 29 CFR 825.310(e); see Cooper v. Olin Corporation, Winchester Division, 246 F.3d 1083, 1090 (8th Cir. 2001); Matthews v. Fairview Health Services, No. 01–2151–ADM/AJB, 2003 U.S. Dist. LEXIS 5901 (D. Minn. April 7, 2003); Underhill v. Willamina Lumber Co. et al., No. 98–630–AS, 1999 U.S. Dist. LEXIS 9722 (D. Ore. June 17, 1999); Albert v. Runyon, 6 F. Supp. 2d 57, 63 (D. Mass. 1998).

Combined with the extremely limited scope of the certification, the lack of ability to obtain additional information reduces the utility of the clarification option. Basically, an employer can, with the employee's permission, obtain clarification of whatever happens to be on the fitness–for–duty certification. Clarification will often devolve into deciphering illegible handwriting.

Courts are divided whether the fitness-for-duty clarification procedure is permissive or mandatory. Several courts have excused an employer's failure to use the clarification process when provided an ambiguous fitness-for-duty certification. For example, as set forth more fully below, in *Conroy v. Township of Lower Merion et al.*, No. 00–CV–3528, 2001 U.S. Dist. LEXIS 11460 (E.D. Pa. Aug. 7, 2001), the district court held that an employer did not violate the Act when it required an employee to follow the clarification procedures of the governing collective bargaining agreement to submit an independent medical examination where the certification submitted by the employee's health care provider was unclear and confusing. A supervisor's unauthorized contact with the employee's health care provider to clarify a fitness–for–duty certification did not constitute an actionable violation of the FMLA. *Hensley v. Baptist Hospital of East Tennessee, Inc. et al.*, No. 3:96–CV–789, 1997 U.S. Dist. LEXIS 22515 (E.D. Tenn. Oct. 27, 1997). Even assuming that the supervisor did not have the plaintiff's permission to contact the plaintiff's health care provider, the court held that it failed to see a substantive violation of the Act. The court noted that the plaintiff was granted the leave covered by the certificate, she was paid sick leave benefits during this time, and she was restored to her position on return from leave without delay. The supervisor called to see if plaintiff could return-to-work sooner rather than later.

At least one court found that an employer's failure to seek clarification of an ambiguous fitness-for-duty certification interfered with the employee's FMLA rights. In *Carpo v. Wartburg Lutheran Home for the Aging*, No. 05 CV 1169 (JG), 2006 U.S. Dist. LEXIS 74856, at *14 (E.D.N.Y. Oct. 16, 2006), the court found that the employer violated the FMLA when it failed to seek clarification of the employee's fitness-for-duty certification. The court rejected the employer's argument that the use of the word "may" in the regulation rendered the use of the clarification procedure permissive. The court opined:

> The job security of employees returning to work with good-faith but arguably insufficient certifications should not depend on the beneficence of the employer. Without explicit guidance from the statute or regulations, I will not adopt an interpretation so contrary to Congress's stated purpose of protecting the jobs of employees with temporary health problems. The FMLA and its implementing regulations nowhere permit an employee to refuse restoration to an employee upon submission of a timely but inadequate fitness-for-duty report. This omission has significance.
>
> ****
>
> Of course, the FMLA nowhere explicitly prohibits termination of employees with timely but inadequate certifications, and I have little doubt that a fitness-for-duty report can be so facially inadequate that no amount of "clarification" from its author would be sufficient to entitle the employee to return to work. But when, as here, an employer claims to find ambiguity in a return-to-work certificate that the issuing doctor can usefully clarify, the default rule, in keeping with the Congressional purpose, is that the employee must be allowed to remain on the payroll while clarification is sought.

d. Effect of Terms of Collective Bargaining Agreement

If the terms of a collective bargaining agreement govern an employee's return to work, those provisions still apply when an employee returns to work from FMLA leave. 29 CFR 825.310(b); S. Res. 242, Cong. Rec. S3959, S3974 (April 23, 1996); 29 CFR 825.310(c); see *Harrell v. USPS*, 445 F.3d 913, 919-20 (7th Cir. 2006), *cert. denied*, 127 S. Ct. 845 (2006); *Underhill v. Willamina Lumber Co. et al.*, No. 98–630–AS, 1999 U.S. Dist. LEXIS 9722 (D. Ore. June 17, 1999); DOL WH FMLA Advisory Opinion No. 113 (Sept. 11, 2000); DOL WH FMLA Advisory Opinion No. 58 (April 28, 1995). What this provision means is unclear. The lack of clarity results from the inconsistent interpretations given to this provision by the DOL, which wrote it, and the courts that have interpreted it.

For the DOL, if the terms of a collective bargaining agreement, for instance, require a fitness–for–duty examination or more information than a short, simple statement that the employee is able to return to work, then those terms apply, with two conditions. *See* DOL WH FMLA Advisory Opinion No. 113 (Sept. 11, 2000). The first condition is that the fitness–for–duty examination must be job–related and consistent with business necessity, as required by the Americans with Disabilities Act (ADA). *Id*.; *see Harrell*, 445 F.3d at 919. For example, even if the terms of a collective bargaining agreement allowed for a fitness–for–duty examination, an attorney covered by that agreement could not be required to submit to a medical examination or inquiry just because her leg had been amputated. The essential functions of an attorney's job do not require use of both legs; therefore such an inquiry would not be job related. 29 CFR 825.310(b); S. Res. 242, Cong. Rec. S3959, S3974 (April 23, 1996); 29 CFR 825.310(b). On the other hand, an employer may require a warehouse laborer, whose back impairment affects the ability to lift, to be examined by an orthopedist before the employee is returned to work, as required by the terms of an applicable collective bargaining agreement. The employer would not, however, be permitted to require the employee to submit to an HIV test where the test is not related to either the essential functions of his or her job or to his or her impairment. 29 CFR 825.310(b); S. Res. 242, Cong. Rec. S3959, S3974 (April 23, 1996); 29 CFR 825.310(b).

The second condition, which will be discussed more fully below, addresses the employer's obligation to notify an employee of the return to work certification and fitness–for–duty procedures. The FMLA notification procedures establish the minimum notice due even when a collective bargaining agreement establishes the return–to–work certification requirements. DOL WH FMLA Advisory Opinion No. 113 (Sept. 11, 2000).

In order for the exception to apply, the collective bargaining agreement must apply to the employee returning from FMLA leave. *Albert v. Runyon*, 6 F. Supp. 2d 57 (D. Mass. 1998) (exceptions allowing employer to impose additional conditions on employee returning from FMLA leave pursuant to a valid state or local law or collective bargaining agreement did not apply where the employee, a district manager, was not subject to terms of collective bargaining agreement).

Employers may not, under the umbrella of the collective bargaining agreement exception, provide an employee with less return-to-work rights than the minimum required by the FMLA. DOL WH FMLA Advisory Opinion No. 58 (April 28, 1995). *See also* 29 CFR 825.220(d). For example, a collective bargaining agreement, which provides for reinstatement to a position that is not equivalent because of seniority (e.g., provides lesser pay), is superseded by the FMLA. DOL WH FMLA Advisory Opinion No. 58 (April 28, 1995).

Finally, nothing in the FMLA prevents employers from amending existing leave and benefit programs, provided they comply with the FMLA. If a collective bargaining agreement does not have a return to work certification procedure, the employer may implement such a procedure provided that it complies with the FMLA and that implementation of the procedure complies with all applicable requirements under federal law, including the requirement that management bargain in good faith with collective bargaining representative over these terms. DOL WH FMLA Advisory Opinion No. 58 (April 28, 1995).

The courts are split whether an employer may impose more stringent return-to-work certification requirements pursuant to a collective bargaining agreement than the short, simple statement permitted by the FMLA. The Seventh and Eighth Circuits have found that an employer may require an employee to abide by the more stringent return-to-work requirements of a collective bargaining agreement. *See Harrell v. USPS*, 445 F.3d 913, 920-927 (7th Cir. 2006), *cert. denied*, 127 S. Ct. 845 (2006); *Harris v. Emergency Providers, Inc. et al.*, 51 Fed. Appx. 600 (8th Cir. 2002).

In *Harrell v. USPS*, 445 F.3d 913, 920-927 (7th Cir. 2006), *cert. denied*, 127 S. Ct. 845 (2006), Postal Service policy, incorporated into the national collective bargaining agreement, required employees out on medical leave for certain reasons or for a certain length of time to submit more medical information as a prerequisite for the employee to be cleared to return to work by the medical department. Harrell provided a short statement of his ability to return to work, but refused to provide the more detailed information. As a result, he was eventually terminated. The court agreed with the Postal Service that an employer may impose more stringent return-to-work certification requirements on an employee if those requirements are incorporated into a collective bargaining agreement.

in *Harris v. Emergency Providers, Inc. et al.*, 51 Fed. Appx. 600 (8th Cir. 2002), held that the employer's demand that the employee undergo a fitness-for-duty examination, as permitted by the governing collective bargaining agreement, did not violate the FMLA where the employee failed to show that the fitness-for-duty requirement was inconsistently applied.

In *Conroy v. Township of Lower Merion et al.*, No. 00-CV-3528, 2001 U.S. Dist. LEXIS 11460 (E.D. Pa. Aug. 7, 2001), the district court held that an employer did not violate the Act when it invoked its own practice set forth in the governing collective bargaining agreement conditioning reemployment on an employee's obtaining an independent medical examination (IME) where the certification provided by the employee's health care provider was unclear. The FMLA, the court held, allows a collective bargaining agreement (CBA) to establish its own procedures for an employee's return to work and these procedures can supersede those of the FMLA, provided the provisions of the CBA did not compromise the protections afforded to the employee pursuant to the FMLA. Where a provision of the CBA is more restrictive than that of the FMLA, the FMLA will supersede the CBA. The court held that the practice at issue did not interfere with rights guaranteed by the FMLA. According to the court in *Conroy*:

> The FMLA simply entitled an employee to resume her employment. *See* 29 USC 2614. It does not, however, ensure a particular administrative procedure for returning to work. Therefore, as Defendant is merely implementing a policy for handling situations where a certification is unclear, these practices do not restrict or even affect Plaintiff's rights under the FMLA. Even though requiring an IME creates an additional step for Plaintiff, Defendant covers the cost of the IME and this practice does not alter the standard for Plaintiff's eligibility or make it more difficult for Plaintiff to be deemed qualified to return.

The case is interesting in that it cites the FMLA regulation (29 CFR 825.310(a)) that if clarification is needed, a health care provider for the employer, with the employee's permission, may consult with the employee's health care provider rather than seek an additional examination. It then ignores the regulation, and holds that the employer was justified by the

CBA to subject the employee to the company's requirement to undergo an IME as the means of clarification, where that route is permitted by a CBA.

In *Routes v. Henderson*, 58 F. Supp. 2d 959, 994–95 (S.D. Ind. 1999), the court came to virtually the opposite conclusion than the Eighth Circuit in *Harris* and the DOL regarding the interplay between the return to work requirements of the FMLA and the requirements of a valid collective bargaining agreement (CBA). In that case, the Postal Service argued that it had the right to require Routes to undergo a fitness–for–duty examination as a condition of returning him to work from FMLA leave. The court disagreed on three grounds. First, the court found that the CBA at issue did not contain a specific provision that governed the return to work of an employee on leave due to a serious health condition. Rather, the CBA referenced the continued effectiveness of the Postal Service handbooks and manuals. The court found that the vagueness and generality of this language "make it unlikely to take precedence over the more specifically–worded FMLA subparagraph in § 2614(a)(4)." *Routes*, 58 F. Supp. at 994.

Second, the court argued that, as a guaranteed substantive statutory right, the right of restoration could not be easily diminished or abrogated by a collective bargaining agreement. *Id*. The correct reading of the provision, according to the court, was that the FMLA did not diminish the obligation of the employer to comply with any collective bargaining agreement that provides greater family or medical leave rights to employees than the rights established in the FMLA. *Id*., citing 29 USC 2652(a). Any other reading would allow an employer to diminish the right of restoration established in the FMLA through the implementation of more restrictive return to work policies pursuant to a collective bargaining agreement.

Finally, the court indicated that if it were to interpret the CBA as incorporating the Postal Service's more restrictive return to work policies, it would amount to allowing the union to waive its members' substantive statutory right to restoration after FMLA leave, without them knowing it. The court declined to interpret § 2614(a)(4) as authorizing such a general waiver.

As an interesting side note, in addition to reaching the opposite conclusion, the opinion of the DOL, DOL WH FMLA Advisory Opinion No. 113 (Sept. 11, 2000), directly involved the Postal Service, and was issued over a year after the court's decision in *Routes*.

e. DOT Requirements

In *Matthews v. Fairview Health Services*, No. 01–2151–ADM/AJB, 2003 U.S. Dist. LEXIS 5901 (D. Minn. April 7, 2003), the court addressed the interaction of return to work fitness–for–duty certification requirements of the FMLA with Department of Transportation (DOT) regulations entitling an employer to subject an employee to a medical examination where the physical qualification of the employee to operate a commercial vehicle is in question.

In *Matthews*, the plaintiff was a part–time truck driver/materials handler. His position entailed driving, loading and unloading carts 20 hours per week. The physical requirements specified an ability to lift and carry up to 50 pounds occasionally, to push and pull on wheels 74 or fewer pounds frequently, and to push and pull on wheels between 75 and 100 pounds occasionally. The driving component was subject to DOT regulations, which requires drivers of commercial motor vehicles to meet specific physical qualifications (49 CFR 391.41).

In October, Fairview granted Matthews FMLA leave for the installation of a pacemaker. Pursuant to policy, employees returning to work from FMLA leave must present medical documentation substantiating their ability to resume work prior to reinstatement. Matthews provided Fairview a return–to–work certification from his physician. The release stated that Matthews could return to work without restriction, but that he should not work more than 40 hours in a two–week period. On receipt, Fairview informed Matthews that he needed to undergo a DOT physical before returning to his position.

Matthews attended the DOT physical, which was conducted by a physician selected by Fairview. Prior to the DOT physical, Fairview notified the physician that Matthews had taken FMLA leave to have a pacemaker inserted, and that he was returned to work without restrictions, but that he should not work more than 40 hours during the first two weeks. Fairview provided the physician with a description of Matthews's job duties, and asked for an evaluation whether he could fully perform his job.

After examining him, the physician conducting the DOT physical found that Matthews passed the DOT requirements.

In a handwritten note, the doctor stated that he would not approve him for full duty as set forth in the job description, particularly regarding lifting issues.

When Matthews sought to resume work, Fairview informed him that he had to provide a work release from a cardiologist before he would be reinstated. Matthews subsequently filed suit, alleging that Fairview failed to return him to work in his same or an equivalent position. Matthews argued that the original note from his physician clearing him to return to work without restrictions triggered Fairview's duty to restore him to his job without further delay. Fairview countered that, in light of the applicable DOT regulations, it was justified in demanding fitness-for-duty certification from a cardiac specialist.

After finding that the original note provided by his physician adequately cleared Matthews to return to work, the court turned to the question of whether the DOT rules permitted Fairview to request additional, specific certification of Matthews' health condition. The court answered in the negative.

According to the court, the DOT regulations relied on by Fairview (49 CFR 391.45) "make no reference to FMLA reinstatement. Neither do they explicitly allow it to refuse nor condition driver certification based on reservations about non-driving aspects of a position, on clearance from a specialist. For DOT purposes," the court continued, "certification is complete upon the medical examiners finding and properly recording that the employee is 'physically qualified' to drive a commercial motor vehicle.... No requirement of evaluation of non-driving responsibilities appears on the face of these regulations, nor does any explicit authorization to delay reinstatement or certification based on non-driving criteria."

Here, the court found that Matthews met the DOT specifications, as indicated in the form signed by the physician who conducted the DOT examination. As such, Matthews was authorized, for purposes of the DOT, to return to work as a commercial truck driver. However, Fairview's solicitation of the DOT physician's opinion regarding full performance of the lifting, pushing, and pulling requirements of the position and its resultant demand for documentation from a cardiologist prior to restoring Matthews to his position, the court found, represented an independent medical judgment beyond that necessary to meet the regulatory requirements of the DOT, and was unsupported by the FMLA. In fact, the court concluded that, while likely done in good faith and for legitimate safety concerns, "this type of medical assessment by an employer is prohibited by the FMLA."

Note that the court did not find that an employer was prohibited from conditioning an employee's return to work on the requirement that the employee undergo an actual fitness-for-duty physical, in accordance with DOT requirements. What the court said was that DOT requirements are limited to driving only, and do not extend to other, non-driving aspects of the job.

Similarly, the court did not generally hold that an employer was prohibited from delaying an employee's return to work from FMLA leave until the employee undergoes the DOT physical. Implicitly, the court found that the delay was permissible to secure certification from a health care provider that the employee met the DOT physical requirements for driving. Further delay to obtain additional certification from a health care specialist on non-driving issues, the court found, was not covered by DOT requirements and, therefore, violated the employee's right to job restoration.

f. Interaction With ADA-Approved Medical Examinations

The FMLA conditionally permits an employer to request a fitness-for-duty certification consisting of a simple statement attesting to an eligible employee's ability to return to work. The ADA, on the other hand, in certain circumstances allows an employer to require an employee to undergo a more comprehensive medical examination as a condition of returning an employee to work. How these two provisions interact when the absence is covered by the FMLA is the topic of this section. Basically, there is a split in the courts regarding the appropriate interplay of the ADA and the FMLA regarding return to work fitness-for-duty requirements.

The ADA prohibits an employer from requiring a medical examination or making inquiries of an employee concerning whether the employee is an "individual with a disability or as to the nature or severity of the disability unless such examination or inquiry is shown to be job-related and consistent with business necessity." 42 USC 12112(d)(4). To determine whether a medical examination meets these requirements, the EEOC regulations, 20 CFR Part 1630, App. 1630.14(c) provide clarification as follows:

This provision permits employers to make inquiries or require medical examinations (fitness-for-duty exams) when there is a need to determine whether an employee is still able to perform the essential functions of his or her job.

Further, § 9.4 of the EEOC Technical Assistance Manual on the Employment Provisions of the ADA provides the following: "If a worker has an on-the-job injury which appears to affect his/her ability to do essential job functions, a medical examination or inquiry is job-related and consistent with business necessity."

In *Porter v. United States Alumoweld Co., Inc.*, 125 F.3d 243, 247 (4th Cir. 1997), the court held that the employer did not violate the FMLA when it required an employee returning to work from an on-the-job injury to undergo functional capacity evaluation as a condition of the employee's return to work. The employee submitted a certification from his physician that stated that the employee was able to return to work safely and without any limitations. When the employee failed to undergo the functional capacity examination, he was fired. The employee sued, alleging violation of the FMLA. Specifically, he contended that Alumoweld violated the FMLA by requiring him to undergo the fitness-for-duty exam. He argued that, pursuant to the FMLA, he submitted the requisite fitness-for-duty certification, which need only be a simple statement of an employee's ability to return to work.

The court disagreed. "Porter," the court held, "fails to recognize that the FMLA certification is a health verification distinct from the ADA prescribed exam. In fact, the FMLA implies that an employee may be required to meet the fitness requirements of that Act and the ADA. Similarly, the requirements under the Americans with Disabilities Act (ADA) that any return-to-work physical be job-related must be complied with." *Id*. According to the court:

> Under Porter's reading of the FMLA, that Act would be violated every time an employer requested a fitness-for-duty examination under the ADA, a request which requires the disclosure of more medical information than would be available from the FMLA's "simple statement of an employee's ability to return to work." We reject Porter's attempt to so restrict the operation of the ADA.

Id. The decision of the Fourth Circuit in *Porter* was rejected by the district court in *Underhill v. Willamina Lumber Co. et al.*, No. 98–630–AS, 1999 U.S. Dist. LEXIS 9722 (D. Ore. June 17, 1999). In rejecting the decision of the Fourth Circuit, the court in *Underhill* relied on the decision in *Albert v. Runyon*, 6 F. Supp. 2d 57 (D. Mass. 1998). The issue in *Albert* was whether an employer could require an employee to submit to a fitness-for-duty examination before allowing the employee to return to work. *Albert*, 6 F. Supp. 2d at 63. The *Albert* court stated that while the FMLA allows for additional clarification, an employer may not force an employee to submit to further examination before allowing her to return to work. *Id*. The employer in that case, the Postal Service, argued in the alternative that it was permitted to require a fitness-for-duty examination as a pre-condition to reinstatement pursuant to a uniform policy and in accordance with the ADA.

Addressing the appropriate interplay between the independent fitness-for-duty examination allowed by the ADA and the return to work provisions of the FMLA, the *Albert* court noted, "There, of course, is no logical reason that an examination which does not violate the ADA cannot violate the FMLA—indeed, it would not be surprising to find that the prohibitions of these different statutes are not co-extensive." *Albert*, 6 F. Supp. 2d at 67–68. This observation by the *Albert* court is the opposite of what the Fourth Circuit opined in *Porter*.

The *Albert* court rejected the employer's contention that the FMLA should be read to allow pre-reinstatement medical examinations that are consistent with the ADA but adopted the ADA requirements that any fitness-for-duty examination allowed under the FMLA be job-related and consistent with business necessity. *Underhill*, 1999 U.S. Dist. LEXIS 9722, at *24. In summary, the court in *Albert*, 6 F. Supp. 2d at 69, stated:

> The ADA and the FMLA do not conflict if the ADA's business necessity requirement requires more than employee's having taken FMLA leave. In sum, an employer may not order an employee returning from FMLA leave to submit to a fitness-for-duty because of that leave, or because of an underlying condition that the employee's health care provider has certified will not interfere with the employee's ability to work, or because the employer views the certification as inadequate for its own purposes. An employer only has a sufficient "business need" to examine a returning employee where the employee's ongoing limitations may interfere with her ability to work.

The court in *Underhill* adopted the reasoning and the holding enunciated in *Albert*. It found that the employer violated the FMLA when it refused to return him to work out of concern for the effects of his taking prescription medication even though the employee tendered a fitness-for-duty certification from a health care provider permitting the employee to return to work without restrictions. The employer wanted a second opinion on the safety of returning the employee to his job as a sawmill operator. [For a further discussion of the interaction of the FMLA with the ADA and Rehabilitation Act, see Chapter 16, "Interaction of the FMLA with Other Federal Laws, Employer Practices, and Collective Bargaining Agreements."]

g. Cost of Certification

The cost of the certification is borne by the employee and the employee is not entitled to be paid for the time or travel costs spent in acquiring the return to work fitness–for–duty certification. 29 CFR 825.310(d); S. Res. 242, Cong. Rec. S3959, S3974 (April 23, 1996); 29 CFR 825.310(d). *See Underhill v. Willamina Lumber Co. et al.*, No. 98–630–AS, 1999 U.S. Dist. LEXIS 9722 (D. Ore. June 17, 1999). In response to comments made to the proposed final regulations that the fitness–for–duty certification should be obtained at the employer's expense, the DOL (Preamble, 29 CFR 825.310) stated:

> The statute clearly requires the employer to bear the costs of the second and third medical opinions. The Congress made no such provision for recertification or fitness–for–duty certifications. The Department is unable to assign these costs to the employer in the absence of statutory language.

Of course, employer policy or the terms of a collective bargaining agreement may provide more generous leave benefits, such as paying the employee for the time spent obtaining a fitness–for–duty certification, and/or the cost of the certification. Unions and other organizations representing the interests of employees frequently bargain to obtain employer payment for some or all of the costs to obtain a fitness–for–duty certification.

h. Employer Notice Requirements

In order to require an employee to submit a return to work fitness–for–duty medical certification, an employer must notify the employee of this obligation. *Murray v. Cannon Valley Cooperative*, No. Civ. 05-1836 (JNE/JJG), 2006 U.S. Dist. LEXIS 93215, at *13 (D. Minn. Dec. 26, 2006). An employer may be required to provide such notice to the employee in three different ways.

(1) Employee Handbook

If the employer has a handbook explaining employment policies and benefits, the handbook should explain the employer's general policy regarding any requirement for fitness–for–duty certification to return to work. 29 CFR 825.310(e); S. Res. 242, Cong. Rec. S3959, S3974 (April 23, 1996); 29 CFR 825.310(e). Note that the requirement that an employer provide notice if it has a handbook is somewhat less demanding than the general rule governing notice where the employee has written policies. 29 CFR 825.301(a); S. Res. 242, Cong. Rec. S3959, S3971 (April 23, 1996); 29 CFR 825.301(a). Under the general rule, if an employer has any written guidance concerning employee benefits and leave rights, such as an employee handbook, the employer must include information on FMLA rights and responsibilities and the employer's FMLA policies into those documents. 29 CFR 825.301(a); S. Res. 242, Cong. Rec. S3959, S3971 (April 23, 1996); 29 CFR 825.301(a). [For a further discussion of the employer's general notice obligations, see Chapter 8, "Notice Requirements."]

(2) Individual Notice

An employer must include in the notice that employers are required to give each employee pursuant to § 825.301(b)(1), a statement advising the employee that a fitness–for–duty certification to return to work from FMLA leave is required. 29 CFR 825.310(e); S. Res. 242, Cong. Rec. S3959, S3974 (April 23, 1996); 29 CFR 825.310(e). This notice must be given to the employee no less often than the first time in each six–month period that an employee gives notice of the need for FMLA leave (if FMLA leave is taken during the six–month period). 29 CFR 825.301(c); S. Res. 242, Cong. Rec. S3959, S3971 (April 23, 1996); 29 CFR 825.301(c). The notice must be given within a reasonable period of time after notice of the need for FMLA leave is provided by the employee. 29 CFR 825.301(c); S. Res. 242, Cong. Rec. S3959, S3971 (April 23, 1996); 29 CFR 825.301(c). If FMLA leave has already begun, the employer should notify the employee by mail to the employee's address of record. 29 CFR 825.301(c); S. Res. 242, Cong. Rec. S3959, S3971 (April 23, 1996); 29 CFR 825.301(c). [For a further discussion of this notice requirement, see Chapter 8, "Notice Requirements."]

An employer's request that it would need a medical release from all of the doctors who treated the employee during his hospitalization, not just his foot doctor, was an adequate request as a condition of returning to work. *Buettner v. North Oklahoma County Mental Health Center*, 158 Fed. Appx. 81 (10th Cir. 2005).

(3) Specific Notice

In addition to inclusion into an employer's employee handbook and notice at least twice a leave year, the regulations require an employer to provide notice a third way. Specifically, the regulations (29 CFR 825.310(e); S. Res. 242, Cong. Rec. S3959, S3974 (April 23, 1996); 29 CFR 825.310(e)) provide:

> Specific notice shall also be given to any employee from whom fitness–for–duty certification will be required either at the time notice of the need for leave is given or immediately after leave commences and the employer is advised of the medical circumstances requiring the leave, unless the employee's condition changes from one that did not previously require certification pursuant to the employer's practice or policy.

Murray v. Cannon Valley Cooperative, No. Civ. 05-1836 (JNE/JJG), 2006 U.S. Dist. LEXIS 93215, at *13 (D. Minn. Dec. 26, 2006).

The regulation suffers from several infirmities. First, by using the term "specific notice," the regulations presumably mean notice that the employee will be required to provide a fitness–for–duty certification as a condition of returning to work from FMLA leave. Additionally, the means or method of notice is not specified. Agencies are well advised to provide such notice in writing to the last address of record. If the employee is a member of a bargaining unit, consideration should be given to serving the bargaining unit representative with notice in addition to service at the employee's last address of record.

The second and more important issue is the employer's obligation if the condition raised in the modifying language exists. That is, take for example that "the employee's condition changes from one that did not previously require certification pursuant to the employer's practice or policy." It is unclear whether the existence of this condition obviates the employer's duty to provide the required specific notice altogether, or whether it is delayed because the employee, for example, started out on annual leave (which does not have a medical certification requirement) but later changed to FMLA leave during the course of the same leave. As written, it would appear that requirement to provide specific notice is obviated if the condition is met.

Third, it is unclear exactly what is being required. This confusion results from the modifying language after the comma. The modifying language after the comma raises two interpretive issues. The first issue is whether the language after the comma modifies the entire preceding sentence, or simply the part that begins "or immediately after leave commences and the employer is advised…." Given the context, it would appear that the modifier is limited to the second scenario only

Absent evidence that an employer gave an employee timely, specific notice that a fitness-for-duty certification was required before the employee could return to work from FMLA leave, an employer may not delay an employee's return to work pending submission of a fitness-for-duty certification. *Murray v. Cannon Valley Cooperative*, No. Civ. 05-1836 (JNE/JJG), 2006 U.S. Dist. LEXIS 93215, at *13 (D. Minn. Dec. 26, 2006) (employee informed for first time of fitness-for-duty requirement on day he was cleared to return to work; employer required him to obtain certification, delayed his return to work for 3 weeks, and then terminated him).

In *Bobel v. Bolingbrook Park District*, No. 05 C 2482, 2006 U.S. Dist. LEXIS 44851 (N.D. Ill. June 19, 2006), the court found that the employer's failure to provide specific notice that a fitness-for-duty certification was required within the time frame specified in 825.301(c) did not interfere with the employee's FMLA rights where the employee had reasonable notice of the requirement before the expiration of his FMLA leave.

i. Failure to Provide Certification

An employer may delay restoration to employment until an employee submits a required fitness–for–duty certification, unless the employer has failed to provide the employee with the required notices. 29 CFR 825.310(f); S. Res. 242, Cong. Rec. S3959, S3974 (April 23, 1996); 29 CFR 825.310(f); *see Killian v. Yorozu Automotive Tennessee, Inc.*, 454 F.3d 549, 555 (6th Cir. 2006); *Drago v. Jenne*, 453 F.3d 1301, 1306-1307 (11th Cir. 2006); *Murray v. Cannon Valley Cooperative*, No. Civ. 05-

1836 (JNE/JJG), 2006 U.S. Dist. LEXIS 93215, at *13 (D. Minn. Dec. 26, 2006); *Nott v. Woodstock Care Center, Inc. et al.*, No. C–3–99–133, 2001 U.S. Dist. LEXIS 22655, at *26 (S.D. Ohio March 21, 2001) (failure of employer to designate Nott's leave as FMLA precludes employer from requiring her to provide medical certification, citing 29 CFR 825.310(f)).

In *Drago v. Jenne*, 453 F.3d 1301, 1306-1307 (11th Cir. 2006), the employee returned to work earlier than anticipated. The employer directed him to take another two days of leave and return to work with a fitness for duty certification, which he did. The court found that the requirement did not interfere with Drago's FMLA rights. The employee failed to notify his employer of the anticipated duration of his leave. The FMLA also allows an employer to delay restoration until the employee provides a medical certification, which it did. The court found the employer had a uniform policy requiring returning employees to provide a fitness-for-duty certification.

If the employee fails to provide either a fitness for duty certification or a new medical certification for a serious health condition at the time FMLA leave is concluded, the employee may be terminated. 29 CFR 825.311(c); *see Killian v. Yorozu Automotive Tennessee, Inc.*, 454 F.3d 549, 555 (6th Cir. 2006); *Burkett v. Beaulieu of America, Inc.*, 168 Fed. Appx. 895 (11th Cir. 2006); *Buettner v. North Oklahoma County Mental Health Center*, 158 Fed. Appx. 81 (10th Cir. 2005); *Brumbalough v. Camelot Care Centers, Inc.*, 427 F.3d 996, 1001 (6th Cir. 2005); *Garcia v. Crown Services, Inc.*, No. 04-C-879, 2006 U.S. Dist. LEXIS 60281, at *24 (E.D. Wis. Aug. 15, 2006) (employee's failure to provide fitness-for-duty certification as requested by employer was valid reason to terminate her employment).

An employee who asks for an extension of leave is still on FMLA leave. As the employee has not returned to work, the fitness-for-duty certification requirement does not apply. *See Killian v. Yorozu Automotive Tennessee, Inc.*, 454 F.3d 549, 555 (6th Cir. 2006).

j. Second or Third Opinions

Generally, second or third opinions are not available to an employer to challenge the adequacy of the fitness–for–duty certification. 29 CFR 825.310(e); S. Res. 242, Cong. Rec. S3959, S3974 (April 23, 1996); 29 CFR 825.310(e). *See Matthews v. Fairview Health Services*, No. 01–2151–ADM/AJB, 2003 U.S. Dist. LEXIS 5901 (D. Minn. April 7, 2003). In explaining unavailability of second or third opinions for fitness–for–duty certifications, the DOL offered the following (Preamble, 29 CFR 825.310) reasoning:

> The statue expressly provides for second and third medical opinions regarding the original medical certification. No such provision is contained in the statute for the fitness–for–duty certification. The Department [of Labor] is unable to incorporate this suggestion [favoring second and third opinions for return–to–duty certifications] in the Final Rule.

To be valid in determining fitness for a return to duty, a second or third opinion process would have to be required pursuant to a collective bargaining agreement. An employer might be better served, however, in setting up a process whereby, in addition to a certification supplied by the employee's health care provider, the employer may also direct the employee to a health care provider of the employer's choosing as a condition of return to work. Obviously, the collective bargaining agreement should also provide that a health care provider should clear the employee to return to work before the employee is provided job restoration.

k. Unfit to Return to Duty

If the return to work fitness–for–duty certification indicates that the employee is not fit to return to work, the employee has no FMLA right to return to work from leave. 29 CFR 825.214(b); S. Res. 242, Cong. Rec. S3959, S3969 (April 23, 1996); 29 CFR 825.312(b).

When an employee is unable to return to work after FMLA leave because of the continuation, recurrence, or onset of the employee's or family member's serious health condition, thereby preventing the employer from recovering its share of health benefit premium payments made on the employee's behalf during a period of unpaid FMLA leave, the employer may require medical certification of the employee's or family member's serious health condition. 29 CFR 825.310(h); S. Res. 242, Cong. Rec. S3959, S3974 (April 23, 1996); 29 CFR 825.310(h). The cost of this certification is borne by the employee and the employee is not entitled to be paid for the time or travel costs spent in acquiring this certification. 29

CFR 825.310(h); S. Res. 242, Cong. Rec. S3959, S3974 (April 23, 1996); 29 CFR 825.310(h). [For a further discussion of this issue, see Chapter 9, "Documentation Requirements," and Chapter 12, "Maintenance of Benefits."]

I. Fitness-for-Duty Exams After Employee Has Returned to Work

The FMLA does not prohibit employers from requiring an employee to submit to an examination after returning to work from FMLA leave. Preamble, 29 CFR 825.310. In pertinent part, the preamble provides:

> The regulations do not prohibit the employer from requiring the employee to submit to an examination after returning to work, provided such examination is job related and consistent with business necessity in accordance with ADA guidelines.

A natural reading of the above would suggest that the FMLA does prohibit examinations after an employee returns to work if the examination is not job related or consistent with business necessity in accordance with the ADA. That would be an incorrect reading of this poorly written guidance. The ADA (which technically does not apply to the federal government, 42 USC 12111(5)(B)(I) ("the term 'employer' does not include…the United States"), prohibits post-hire employee medical examinations unless they are job related and consistent with business necessity. There is no specific FMLA rule that governs the situation, as suggested, where the employee is not on FMLA leave, but back at work. The only viable claim in that case would be of discrimination and retaliation for exercising FMLA rights, which is different than the situation presented in the Preamble.

After an employee has returned to work from FMLA leave, an employer may require the employee to undergo a medical examination on the first day of the employee's return to work. Preamble, 29 CFR 825.310. Several courts, however, have held that an employer may not rely solely on the taking of FMLA leave or pre-FMLA leave behavior (which the court noted only appeared as a reason once litigation ensured) as the justification for a post-reinstatement fitness-for-duty examination. *Routes v. Henderson*, 58 F. Supp. 2d 959, 995–96 (S.D. Ind. 1999); *Albert v. Runyon*, 6 F. Supp. 2d 57 (D. Mass. 1998). Rather, an employer may only rely on an employee's post-reinstatement behavior to justify a fitness-for-duty examination for an employee who recently returned from FMLA leave. *Id.* Alternatively, if the employer can show that the employee's prior conduct, unrelated to the underlying temporarily disabling medical condition, would have justified a fitness-for-duty examination, then such an examination would be justified. However, when an employee's pre-leave conduct and medical certification are adequate to satisfy the requirements of the FMLA, the employer may not take actions against the employee merely because the certification does not satisfy the employer's more restrictive standards. *Routes*, 58 F. Supp. 2d at 996 (*citing Albert*, 6 F. Supp. 2d at 66). After an employee has returned to work from FMLA leave, the propriety of a fitness-for-duty examination is governed by the Americans with Disabilities Act. *Ward v. Merck & Co., Inc.*, No. 04-CV-5996, 2006 U.S. Dist. LEXIS 437, at *19 (E.D. Pa. Jan. 10, 2006), *aff'd*, 2007 U.S. App. LEXIS 6024 (3d Cir. 2007).

Additionally, to avoid a claim of disability discrimination, the examination must be job-related and consistent with business necessity. Great care needs to be exercised, as the disability discrimination requirements in this area are tricky. Managers and supervisors are well advised to consult with counsel before requiring a medical examination of an employee on the first day of his or her return from FMLA leave.

2. Title II

a. General Rule

Title II permits employers in certain circumstances to require an employee to provide a medical certification from the employee's health care provider indicating that the employee is able to perform the essential functions of his or her position. 5 CFR 630.1208(h). The availability of this requirement is limited to situations where FMLA leave was taken due to the employee's own serious health condition. *Id.* The requirement that an employee must provide written certification from a health care provider must also be pursuant to a uniformly applied employer practice or policy that requires all similarly situated employees (i.e., same occupation, same serious health condition) to provide such certification. 5 CFR 630.1208(h).

In many respects, the rule mirrors the entitlement contained in 5 USC 6384(d) of Title 5, 5 USC 6384(d). In pertinent part, that Statute provides

As a condition of restoration, the employer may have a uniformly applied practice or policy that requires each such employee to receive certification from the health care provider of the employee that the employee is able to resume work.

An employer may not require a medical certification to return to work during the period an employee takes leave intermittently or under a reduced leave schedule. 5 CFR 630.1208(h). Unlike Title I, this formulation extends the prohibition to reduced schedule leave in addition to intermittent leave. However, Title II does not prohibit an employer from requiring an employee to provide a medical certification that the employee can perform all essential job functions on return from work. Rather, the regulation merely prohibits agencies from requiring employees using FMLA leave on an intermittent or reduced leave schedule basis to submit medical certifications of fitness to return to duty after each intermittent or reduced leave schedule absence. The regulation requires the employer to wait until the employee signals that he or she no longer needs intermittent or FMLA leave on a reduced leave schedule. On the occasion of the employee returning from the last absence intermittent or reduced leave schedule absence, the employer may require the employee to submit a medical certification of fitness to resume all essential job functions.

b. Scope of Certification

Like Title I, Title II limits the scope of information to the serious health condition of the employee that gave rise to the need for FMLA leave. Preamble, 5 CFR 630.1208. Title II allows for far more information in the medical certification than the short statement permitted by Title I, the CAA, and the PEOAA.

Under Title II, the same conditions for verifying the adequacy of a medical certification in 29 CFR 630.1207(c), 5 CFR 1207(c), apply to the medical certification to return to work. 5 CFR 630.1208(h). Specifically, by cross reference to subparagraph (b) of the same section, 5 CFR 630.1207(c) permits an employer to require an employee as a condition of return from FMLA leave to provide a complete medical certification, with all of the information normally required for a medical certification to support the need for FMLA leave. The only limitations are that an employer may not require any personal or confidential information in the written medical certification other than that required by 5 CFR 630.1207(b).

The apparent application of the general rule governing the contents of a medical certification for certification of fitness to return to duty is puzzling. None of the permissible contents of a medical certification address the fitness of an employee to return to work from FMLA leave. *See* 5 CFR 630.1207(b). Rather, the general medical certification seeks information on what leave is needed. Therefore, incorporation of the general certification contents rule would appear inconsequential.

The regulation specifically provides that an employer is entitled to a medical certification from the health care provider of the employee that the employee is able to perform the essential functions of his or her position. 5 CFR 630.1208(h). While the regulations, unlike Title I, do not talk in terms of a short statement of ability to return to work, it would appear that this is closer to the case than a full–blown medical certification.

The regulations also do not specify how much time the employee has to respond to a request for medical certification regarding the fitness of an employee to return to duty from FMLA leave. Generally, an employee has no later than 15 calendar days to provide a medical certification in response to an employer request. Where that is not practical, the employee must provide the certification within a reasonable time, but no later than 30 calendar days after the date the employer requests such medical certification. 5 CFR 630.1207(h). [For a further discussion of employee responses to employer requests for medical certification, see Chapter 9, "Documentation Requirements."]

Absent a given time frame, employers should apply a reasonable period of time. What will be reasonable will depend on the facts of each case. As a guide, the employer should consider applying the time frame governing the production of medical certifications generally, e.g., 15 calendar days, up to a maximum of 30 calendar days. It would be hard to argue that application of the general rule to return to work fitness–for–duty certifications was unreasonable.

c. Clarification

If an employee submits a completed certification signed by the health care provider, the employer may not request new information from the health care provider. 5 CFR 630.1207(c). However, a health care provider representing the employer, including a health care provider employed by the employer or under administrative oversight of the employer, may contact the health care provider who completed the medical certification, with the employee's permission, for purposes of clarifying the medical certification. 5 CFR 630.1207(c).

Again, the regulations do not specifically identify what is the permissible scope of the contents of the return to work certification. As such, it would appear difficult to determine whether such certification is complete, for purposes of the clarification rule. Agencies that wish to play it conservatively should determine if the certification is complete based on whether it provides that the employee is "able to perform the essential functions of his or her position." 5 CFR 630.1208(h). In order to ensure that the health care provider knows what the essential functions of the employee's position are, the employer should require the employee to provide the health care provider with the job description or other document identifying the essential functions of the position. Consider also requiring that the health care provider acknowledge receipt of that document in the health care provider's return to work certification.

Note that the employer should not directly contact the health care provider, at least not without the employee's permission, in order to deliver the job description document. Employers are restricted from contacting the employee's health care provider. While this would not constitute an attempt at clarification, and, therefore would arguably fall outside the prohibition, it remains a risky proposition.

d. Collective Bargaining Agreements

Title II does not contain a provision allowing employers to apply the more stringent return to work requirements set forth in an applicable collective bargaining agreement.

e. Cost

An employer is required to pay the expenses incurred by the employee in obtaining the written medical certification of fitness to resume all essential functions on return to duty. 5 CFR 630.1208(l). In response to a comment objecting to this requirement, OPM stated, "[s]ince the request for medical certification to return to work is at the discretion and direction of the employer, the employer assumes the responsibility to pay the expenses." Preamble, 5 CFR 630.1208. It is unclear what constitutes expenses. Generally speaking, pay is usually not referred to as an employee's expense. Rather, the terms may refer to the cost of the certification, and travel costs, including mileage, parking, tolls, etc.

f. Notice Requirements

Title II also requires an employer to notify an employee if he or she will be required to provide a return to work medical certification as a condition of being entitled to return to work on the conclusion of FMLA leave. The requirement under Title II, however, is very different than comparative requirements under Title I, the CAA, and the PEOAA.

If an employer requires an employee to obtain written medical certification of fitness to return to full duty, the regulations require that the employer "shall notify the employee of this requirement before leave commences, or to the extent practicable in emergency situations." 5 CFR 630.1208(l). The regulations do not specify how notice is to be accomplished.

The lack of specificity in the regulations governing notice of an employee's obligation to provide a return-to-work medical certification is mirrored in the general notice regulations under Title II. According to the regulations, each employer shall inform its employee of the entitlements and responsibilities under the FMLA, including the requirements and obligations of employees. 5 CFR 630.1203(g). The OPM discussed the means of meeting that requirement in the preamble to the final regulations (5 CFR 630.1203) as follows:

> To meet this requirement, agencies may wish to provide employee's access to the FMLA and OPM's implementing regulations or employer policies or guidance on implementing the FMLA. Also, agencies may provide employees access to OPM's fact sheet and brochure, "Federal Employees Entitlements Under the Family and Medical Leave Act of 1993" or "Family-Friendly Leave Policies for Federal Employees."

The parched regulatory guidance provided by Title II regarding employer notice to employees of the obligation to provide a fitness-for-duty medical certification in order to return to work is disappointing, to say the least. On the other hand, the lack of guidance affords agencies and employees the opportunity to enact sensible employee notice policies on this issue.

(1) Employee Handbook

Title II does not specifically require that an employer include a statement in an employee handbook, manual, or other documents addressing leave and benefits regarding the obligation to provide medical certification that an employee can perform all essential job functions before being returned to work from FMLA leave. It also does not prohibit publication in employee handbooks or manuals.

Since agencies must include a statement addressing this, and other FMLA rights and responsibilities in any employee handbook, manual, or other written documents addressing benefits and leave for Title I employees, agencies should include a similar statement for employees covered by Title II. Care needs to be taken in the preparation of these materials as the rights and obligations enjoyed by employees covered by Title I, the CAA, and the PEOAA, are not the same as those enjoyed by employees covered by Title II. A single uniform statement that does not clearly address these differences may result in miscommunication and other problems for agencies.

Finally, this is an area in which unions and other organizations representing employees should bargain to obtain more specific FMLA notice obligations than are provided in the regulations. Employers should generally welcome more specificity in this weak area of the Title II regulations.

(2) Individual Notice

The Title II regulations do not require agencies to provide individual notice to employees at least once every six months that they are required, as a condition of returning to work from FMLA leave, to provide a fitness–for–duty medical certification.

Although not required, agencies should seriously consider adopting a method for periodically informing their employees of their FMLA rights and obligations, including return to work medical certification requirements, if any. Agencies could apply the Title I method to Title II employees, as the employer will have to build a system for ensuring compliance with that section anyway. Alternatively, agencies could include this as part of a formal training program, so that a record of the training received by each employee is maintained. If it does this, however, it must still comply with all of the notice requirements for employees covered by Title I. Again, this is an area that is ripe for further definition pursuant to the terms of a collective bargaining agreement.

(3) Specific Notice

Title II of the regulations does not require that specific notice be provided to each employee at the time that FMLA leave commences. It is also not prohibited by the regulations. Agencies should seriously consider developing a form or forms setting forth the respective FMLA rights and responsibilities of the different categories of employees (e.g., Title I or Title II in most agencies). The form would include notice of the rights and obligations governing the employee's return to work, and would, at minimum, be provided to the employee at the last known address of record shortly after the employer is informed that the employee is requesting FMLA leave. Providing notice every time an employee requests FMLA leave will go a long way to ensure that the employer satisfies the vague notice requirements of Title II.

g. Failure to Provide Documentation

If an employee attempts to return to work without the required medical certification, an employer may delay the return of an employee until acceptable medical certification is provided. 5 CFR 630.1208(h). During this period of delay, an employer may grant the employee's request for appropriate leave. Preamble, 5 CFR 630.1208. Note that the time an employee's return to work was delayed until receipt of a medical certification would normally not be considered FMLA leave. At this point in time, the employee is essentially saying that FMLA leave is no longer needed and he or she is ready to return to work. This will likely be verified by the medical certification that is eventually provided by the employee.

If the employee refuses to request non–FMLA leave until the medical certification is provided, or does not provide the required certification (see below), the employer may use the procedures provided under 5 CFR Part 752 to place the employee on enforced leave, suspend the employee, or remove the employee, as appropriate. Preamble, 5 CFR 630.1208.

The consequences of an employee's complete failure to provide a medical certification of the fitness to return to duty are both clearly defined and significant under Title II. An employee who does not provide medical certification signed by the health care provider that includes all of the required information is not entitled to FMLA leave. 5 CFR 630.1208(l). Moreover, an employee's failure or refusal to provide a written medical certification as a condition of return to work from FMLA leave may be grounds for appropriate disciplinary or adverse action. 5 CFR 630.1208(l).

The regulations do not require that an employer delay the employee's return to duty at all, except in those circumstances when the minimum time has not run for the employee to provide the documentation. The use of the term "may" is permissive. An employer may delay the employee's restoration to duty until it receives the requested certification, or it may not. This is an area where more generous employer policies on return to work, including the terms of a collective bargaining agreement often allow an employee additional time to provide the medical documentation then the minimum required by the FMLA.

h. Second and Third Opinions

The second and third opinion process for challenging the validity of the certification is not available on the certification of an employee's ability to return to work. 5 CFR 630.1208(h). As a practical matter that means that the employer is stuck with the certification it receives from the employee. In that sense, Title II and Title I, the CAA, and the PEOAA are the same on this issue.

i. Unfit for Duty

As set forth more fully in Section III.A. of this chapter, "Employee is Unable to Perform All Essential Job Functions", the regulations do not provide for what happens if the certification submitted by the employee indicates that the employee is not able to perform the essential functions of his or her position. Unlike Title I, Title II does not condition an employee's return from FMLA leave.

The regulations generally provide that an employee returning from FMLA leave is not entitled to any right, benefit, or position to which the employee would have been entitled, had the employee not taken the leave. 5 CFR 1208(d)(2). They also provide that an employee is not entitled to be returned to the same or equivalent position if the employee would not otherwise have been employed in that position at the time the employee returns from leave. 5 CFR 630.1208(f). Unfortunately, no examples are shared by the writers, either directly in the regulations or in the comments to the final regulations.

A third regulation might also apply. Title II permits an employer to require an employee returning from FMLA leave to provide a medical certification that the employee is able to perform the essential functions of his or her position. 5 CFR 630.1208(h). The rule spells out what may happen if the employee delays or fails to supply the requested medical certification. Ironically, the regulation fails to say what happens if the doctor writes on the medical certification that the employee is incapable of performing any of the essential job functions.

This is where § 630.1208(f) comes into play. If employer policy or practice would not return an employee to the same or an equivalent position where the employee is unable to perform an essential function of the job, then the employee would not have an FMLA right to return to work. However, if, as is likely the case, employer policy or practice, including the terms of a collective bargaining agreement, provide for the return of an employee from leave who is unable to perform the essential functions of the position, such as in a light or limited duty position, then the employee would have a non–FMLA right to return to work.

The provisions of the Rehabilitation Act might also apply, if the employee were disabled within the meaning of the law. In that case, the employer would have to consider reasonable accommodation of the employee. There, the employee's right to return to work would be governed by employer policy and the Rehabilitation Act, not the FMLA. As set forth more fully in Chapter 16, "Interaction of the FMLA with Other Federal Laws, Employer Practices, and Collective Bargaining Agreements," an employee may simultaneously have an FMLA right to return to duty, and a right to reasonable accommodation under the Rehabilitation Act when the employee's ailment constitutes a serious health condition and a disability.

j. Medical Examination After the Employee Returns to Work

There are no specific FMLA regulations that govern when an employer may require an employee who has just returned from FMLA leave to submit to a medical examination.

Agencies, however, often question the ability of an employee to return to work, as certified by the employee's health care provider. Since, however, the employer is prohibited from requiring an employee to undergo a second or third medical opinion on a fitness to return to duty certification, employees often look for the first opportunity on the employee's return to work to require the employee to undergo an employer–directed medical examination.

If an employee submits a medical certification but the employer believes that the employee is not fully recovered when he or she returns to work, may be a danger to himself or herself or others, or is a disruptive force in the worksite, the employer may take action under 5 CFR Part 752 or other appropriate disciplinary authority. Preamble, 5 CFR 630.1208. If the employer believes that additional medical documentation would be helpful in determining appropriate action, the employer may offer a medical or psychiatric examination under 5 CFR 339.302. Preamble, 5 CFR 630.1208.

Additionally, Subpart C of Part 339, 5 CFR 301–306, addresses the authority of an employer to require any employee to undergo medical or psychiatric examination. In pertinent part, the regulations (5 CFR 339.301(b)–(c)) provide:

> Subject to [5 CFR] § 339.103 [EEOC Requirements], an employer may require an individual who has applied for or occupies a position which has medical standards or physical requirements or which is part of an established medical evaluation program, to report for a medical examination:
>
> (1) Prior to appointment or selection (including reemployment on the basis of full or partial recovery from a medical condition); or
>
> ....
>
> (3) Whenever there is a direct question about an employee's continued capacity to meet the physical or medical requirements of a position.

To comply with the requirements of the Rehabilitation Act, a post–hire medical examination must be job-related and consistent with business necessity. *See* 42 USC 12112(d)(4).

C. EXHAUSTION OF FMLA LEAVE

1. Title I, the CAA, and the PEOAA

In order to have an FMLA right to return to work, the employee must return to work before the employee exhausts his or her 12 weeks of FMLA leave. *See Edgar v. JAC Products, Inc.*, 443 F.3d 501, 506, 512 (6th Cir. 2005); *Hicks v. Leroy's Jewelers, Inc. et al.*, No. 98–6596, 2000 U.S. App. LEXIS 17568 (6th Cir. July 17, 2000) (an employee on approved FMLA leave has no right to job restoration under the Act if she fails to return to work 12 weeks after her leave began); *McGregor v. AutoZone, Inc.*, 180 F.3d 1305, 1308 (11th Cir. 1999); *Cehrs v. Northeast Ohio Alzheimer's Research Ctr.*, 155 F.3d 775, 784–85 (6th Cir. 1998); *Geromanos v. Columbia Univ., College of Physicians and Surgeons*, 322 F. Supp. 2d 420, 427, 428–29 (S.D.N.Y. 2004) (if an employee does not seek to return to work before the expiration of her FMLA leave, the employer is not under an express statutory duty to reinstate her); *Wright v. Owens–Illinois, Inc.*, No. 2:02–cv–223–LJM–WGH, 2004 U.S. Dist. LEXIS 8535, at *29 (S.D. Ind. May 14, 2002) (FMLA job restoration entitlement generally expires after 12 weeks); *Sabatino v. Flik International Corp.*, 286 F. Supp. 2d 327, 338 (S.D.N.Y. 2003) (employer not obligated to reinstate plaintiff to any job under the FMLA where employee was out for more than the protected 12 weeks of leave); *Phillips v. Leroy–Somer North America et al.*, No. 01–1046–T, 2003 U.S. Dist. LEXIS 5349 (W.D. Tenn. March 28, 2003); *Howell v. Standard Motor Products, Inc.*, No. 4:99–CV–987–E, 2001 U.S. Dist. LEXIS 12332 (N.D. Tex. Aug. 10, 2001); *Gray v. Sears, Roebuck & Co., Inc.*, 131 F. Supp. 2d 895, 901 (S.D. Tex. 2001) (dismissing the plaintiff's FMLA claim where plaintiff did not return to work immediately after the end of his leave period); *Dean v. Methodist Hosp. of Dallas*, 1998 U.S. Dist. LEXIS 18573 (N.D. Tex. 1998) (granting summary judgment against employee who did not seek to return to work until two months after end of 12–week FMLA leave entitlement); *Santos v. Shields Health Group*, 996 F. Supp. 87, 93 (D. Mass. 1998); *Voskuil v. Environmental Health Center–Dallas et al.*, No. 3:96–CV–0683–D, 1997 U.S. Dist. LEXIS 23565 (N.D. Tex. Aug. 19, 1997).

The DOL addressed this matter in the preamble to the final regulations (Preamble, 29 CFR 825.309) as follows:

> Three commentators requested clarification regarding the employee's status when the employee fails to return at the conclusion of the leave or after 12 weeks of absence.
>
> If the employee does not return to work at the conclusion of the planned leave, the employee should give the employer reasonable notice of the need for an extension if less than 12 weeks of FMLA leave have [been] exhausted in the 12-month period. If the employee is unable to or does not return to work at the end of 12 weeks of FMLA leave, all entitlements and rights under FMLA cease at that time; the employee is no longer entitled to any further restoration rights under FMLA, and the employer is no longer required to maintain group health benefits pursuant to FMLA.

An employee, who continues on leave after the expiration of his or her 12-week FMLA entitlement expires, may be terminated at any time without violating the FMLA. *Dortman v. ACO Hardware, Inc.*, 405 F. Supp. 2d 812, 822 (E.D. Mich. 2005). Note, however, that several courts have found that an employee, who has exhausted his or her 12-week FMLA entitlement, may still assert a retaliation claim when they are denied job restoration. *See Coburn v. Parker Hannifin*, 429 F.3d 325, 333 (1st Cir. 2005); *Hunt v. Rapides Healthcare Sys., LLC*, 277 F.3d 757, 768-69 (5th Cir. 2001).

Where an employee takes more than 12 weeks of leave pursuant to an employer's policy, the employee is only entitled (under the FMLA) to return to work to the same or an equivalent position if the employee is able to return to work during the time designated as FMLA leave. *Farina v. Compuware Corp.*, 256 F. Supp. 2d 1033 (D. Az. 2003). For example, if the employer provides more than 12 weeks of leave as a matter of policy, an employee who remains on leave after the exhaustion of 12 weeks of FMLA leave loses the FMLA right to job restoration. The employee's rights, if any, to job restoration are governed solely by the employer's policies, not the FMLA. *Dogmanits v. Capital Blue Cross*, 413 F. Supp. 2d 452, 462-63 (E.D. Pa. 2005). An employer's failure to abide by the requirement to notify the employee of the rights and obligations under the FMLA, particularly that the employee must return to work before the 12 workweeks of FMLA leave has expired, has led some courts to excuse the employee's failure to timely return to work. *See Duty v. Norton–Alcoa Proppants*, 293 F.3d 481, 493–94 (8th Cir. 2002) (affirming use of equitable estoppel to prevent employer from claiming that employee's FMLA leave exceeded 12 weeks where employer's letter erroneously informed employee that entire 34-week sick leave qualified for FMLA leave); *Santosuosso v. Novocare Rehab.*, No. 04-2923 (JEI), 2006 U.S. Dist. LEXIS 88938, at *14-18 (D.N.J. Nov. 22, 2006); *Sherry v. Protections, Inc.*, 981 F. Supp. 1133, 1134 (N.D. Ill. 1997).

Other courts have not excused an employee's failure to return to work due to an employer's failure to provide notice of FMLA rights and obligations, where the employee has received his or her 12 weeks of FMLA leave. *See Ragsdale v. Wolverine Worldwide, Inc.*, 535 U.S. 81, 122 S. Ct. 1155, 152 L. Ed. 2d 167 (2002); *McGregor v. AutoZone, Inc.*, 180 F.3d 1305, 1307 (11th Cir. 1999); *Sarno v. Douglas Elliman–Gibbons & Ives, Inc.*, 183 F.3d 155, 161–62 (2d Cir. 1999) (explaining that if, at the end of the FMLA's twelve week leave period, an employee is unable to perform the essential functions of her former job, then any lack of notice of the statutory 12 week limitation on FMLA leave found not rational would be found to have impeded the employee's return to work); *Phillips v. Leroy–Somer North America et al.*, No. 01–1046–T, 2003 U.S. Dist. LEXIS 5349 (W.D. Tenn. March 28, 2003); *Hill v. Steven Motors, Inc.*, 228 F. Supp. 2d 1247, 1258 (D. Kan. 2002), aff'd, 2004 U.S. App. LEXIS 8849 (10th Cir. 2004) (employee who received 22 weeks of leave not injured by lack of notice when evidence established that she was physically unable to return to work within 12 weeks); *Howell v. Standard Motor Products, Inc.*, No. 4:99–CV–987–E, 2001 U.S. Dist. LEXIS 12332 (N.D. Tex. Aug. 10, 2001); *Williams v. SAAD's Healthcare*, No. 99–1070–BH–S, 2000 U.S. Dist. LEXIS 4180 (S.D. Ala. March 16, 2000); *Santos v. Shields Health Group*, 996 F. Supp. 87, 93 (D. Mass. 1998). [For a further discussion of the affect of an employer's failure to notify an employee of FMLA rights and obligations, see Chapter 8, "Notice Requirements."]

Similarly, when an employer fails to designate the leave year, the employee receives the benefit of the most generous leave year provisions. This will likely extend the leave year so that the employee's return to work from FMLA leave is now timely. *See Bachelder v. Am West Airlines*, 259 F.3d 1112, 1127–28 (9th Cir. 2001). *But see Phillips v. Leroy–Somer North America et al.*, No. 01–1046–T, 2003 U.S. Dist. LEXIS 5349 (W.D. Tenn. March 28, 2003). [For a further discussion of this issue, see Chapter 10, "Leave Amount and Scheduling."]

2. Title II

Title II does not specifically state that in order to enjoy the FMLA right to return to work from FMLA leave, the employee must exercise that right before the 12 weeks of FMLA leave are exhausted. It would appear, however, implicit in the notion that once all FMLA leave is exhausted, the right to return to work is governed exclusively by employer policy or practice for the type of non–FMLA leave the employee is on at the time of return.

D. EMPLOYEE NOTICE OBLIGATIONS OF RETURN TO WORK

Employees may be obligated to advise agencies of their intent to return to work from FMLA leave. An employee's unequivocal notice of intent not to return to work from FMLA leave, moreover, greatly impacts an employer's continuing FMLA obligations to that employee.

1. Periodic Status Reports

a. Title I, the CAA, and the PEOAA

An employer may have a non–discriminatory policy that requires an employee on FMLA leave to report periodically on the employee's status and intent to return to work. 29 CFR 825.309(a); S. Res. 242, Cong. Rec. S3959, S3974 (April 23, 1996); 29 CFR 825.309(a); see Jones v. USPS, No. 20 0-3054, 2007 U.S. App. LEXIS 13790, at *2-3 (Fed. Cir. June 11, 2007); *Meadows v. Texar Fed. Credit Union*, No. 5:05CV158, 2007 U.S. Dist. LEXIS 4456, at *51 (E.D. Jan. 22, 2007); *Pande v. Chevron Corp.*, No. 04-5107 CW, 2007 U.S. Dist. LEXIS 3247, at *25 (N.D. Ca. Jan. 17, 2007). An employer may not use this entitlement to require status reports in a manner that is burdensome and disruptive to the employee while on FMLA leave. Preamble, 29 CFR 825.309. The employer's policy must take into account all of the relevant facts and circumstances related to the individual's leave situation. 29 CFR 825.309(a); S. Res. 242, Cong. Rec. S3959, S3974 (April 23, 1996); 29 CFR 825.309(a); see *Meadows v. Texar Fed. Credit Union*, No. 5:05CV158, 2007 U.S. Dist. LEXIS 4456, at *83 (E.D. Jan. 22, 2007); *Ryl-Kuchar v. Care Centers, Inc.*, No. 05-3223, 2006 U.S. Dist. LEXIS 87853, at *15 (N.D. Ill. Dec. 4, 2006). The intent is that such requests be reasonable under the circumstances. Preamble, 29 CFR 825.309. An employer who misuses or abuses this provision may be found to have engaged in prohibited acts under the Statute. Preamble, 29 CFR 825.309.

In *Pande v. Chevron Corp.*, No. 04-5107 CW, 2007 U.S. Dist. LEXIS 3247, at *25 (N.D. Ca. Jan. 17, 2007), the court found that the employer's requirement that employees on FMLA leave report once every 30 days on their status and intent to return to work did not violate the FMLA.

The regulations do not address what constitutes a periodic status report. Nor do the regulations provide specific rules governing the method and form of the request and response. Presumably, the employer's policy on this matter may address these requirements. As such, the employer should be able to specify that the periodic status report must be provided in writing within a specified, reasonable period of time after the request. With respect to the employee's return to duty, employer policy should also be able to require the employee to indicate a commitment to return to duty, as well as an actual or estimated return date.

Note that, while the regulations require that the agencies policy be applied in a non–discriminatory manner, they do not require the policy to be uniformly-applied. You will recall that an employer may require a return to work fitness–for–duty certification, but only pursuant to a uniformly applied policy or practice. 29 CFR 825.310(a).

The regulations do not indicate what happens if an employee fails to timely provide responsive information pursuant to an employer's request for a periodic status report on the employee's intent to return to work. Presumably, employer policy can specify a penalty. Moreover, it could be argued that, like notice or a medical certification, the penalty for an employee's failure to provide a requested periodic status report is the loss of FMLA protections for all or part of the leave at issue. *See, e.g.,* 29 CFR 825.311(b). The FMLA provides extraordinary protections to employees who abide by their responsibilities. Employees who do not abide by their FMLA responsibilities, in turn, should not reap FMLA protection.

Gilliam v. United Parcel Service, Inc., 233 F.3d 969 (7th Cir. 2000), addressed a similar issue. There, an employee took time off to be with his finance after she delivered their child. The governing collective bargaining agreement provided that an employee who failed to report to work for three consecutive days and who does not notify the employer by the beginning of the scheduled starting time on the third day is in violation of company attendance policy and may be disciplined. Gilliam told his supervisor he would be back "in a few days." *Id.* at 971. Gilliam's supervisor understood this to mean a few calendar days. Gilliam, however, thought that his leave had an indefinite duration. He did not try to contact his supervisor for a week. Gilliam was terminated pursuant to the terms of the collective bargaining agreement for job abandonment. He filed suit, alleging that the failure to return him to work violated the FMLA.

The Seventh Circuit affirmed the decision of the district court that the return–to–work notice provisions of the collective bargaining agreement did not violate the FMLA. On the contrary, the court cited § 825.302(d) of the DOL FMLA regulations, providing that "An employer may...require an employee to comply with the employer's usual and customary notice and procedural requirements for requesting leave." *Id*. The court found that, at UPS, the usual and customary notice and procedural requirements mandated that Gilliam notify his supervisor no later than the beginning of the third working day of leave when Gilliam will return to work. Nothing in the FMLA, the court held, prevents an employer from enforcing a rule requiring employees on FMLA leave to keep the employer informed about the employee's plans to return to work.

The decision does not specifically address the FMLA regulation on periodic status reports. It does provide, however, that an employer may require periodic status reports from an employee as a matter of policy. It was this policy that Gilliam violated. The penalty for that violation was termination.

It is not clear what notice an employer must provide to an employee indicating that periodic status reports while on FMLA leave of intent to return to work may be required. If the employer adopts a period status report requirement as policy, it would appear that this must be included in any employee handbook, manual, or other written materials regarding leave and benefits. 29 CFR 825.301(a)(1); S. Res. 242, Cong. Rec. S3959, S3971 (April 23, 1996); 29 CFR 825.301(a). Agencies may, but are not required to, include notice of the requirement to provide periodic status reports of intent to return to work in the required individual employee notice of FMLA rights and obligations. 29 CFR 825.301(b)(2); S. Res. 242, Cong. Rec. S3959, S3971 (April 23, 1996); 29 CFR 825.301(b)(2).

Unions and other organizations representing employees are generally opposed to such employer policies. As such, agencies should expect these entities to keep such policies out and, if unsuccessful in that endeavor, to limit the scope of such policies by placing conditions on the frequency of requests, lengthening the time frame for responses, and minimizing the penalty for an employee's failure to timely respond.

An employer is not obligated to require an employee to report periodically while on FMLA leave. In *Jones v. USPS*, No. 20 0-3054, 2007 U.S. App. LEXIS 13790, at *2-3 (Fed. Cir. June 11, 2007), the employee argued that his employer had the responsibility to require him to report on his status one he was on leave. had they done so, the employee argued that he would have found out that he could not remain on FMLA leave once he was no longer needed to care for his wife. The court disagreed, noting that the regulations "permissive language neither imposes a duty upon Jones' employer, not relieves him of his responsibility to take advantage of FMLA leave only when he was "needed to care for" his wife.

b. Title II

Title II permits agencies to require employees to provide periodic status reports. An employer may require an employee to report periodically to the employer on his or her status and intention to return to work. 5 CFR 630.1208(j). An employer's policy to require such reports must take into account all of the relevant facts and circumstances of the employee's situation. *Id*.

The regulations do not address the penalty for an employee's failure to provide a requested periodic status report. The penalties for failure to abide by the general notification requirements would not apply, as the periodic status report requirement is not housed in the general notice regulation. 5 CFR 630.1208(l) (employee who does not comply with the notification requirements in § 630.120 is not entitled to FMLA leave; the period status report requirement is contained in § 630.1208(j)).

Arguably, employer policy could govern this matter. 5 CFR 630.1208(j). The regulation provides that periodic status reports are governed by employer policy. Nothing in the regulation prohibits that policy from having a penalty provision, provided it takes into account all of the attendant circumstances. On the other hand, an argument could be made that any penalty imposed by employer policy would violate the FMLA because such penalty would diminish FMLA entitlements. 5 CFR 630.1211(b). In this case, the entitlement that would be diminished would be the lack of penalty for an employee's failure to provide a periodic status report.

2. Notice of Intent to Return to Work Earlier than Anticipated

a. Title I, the CAA, and the PEOAA

An employee may discover after beginning leave that the circumstances have changed and the amount of leave originally anticipated is no longer necessary. 29 CFR 825.309(c); S. Res. 242, Cong. Rec. S3959, S3973-74 (April 23, 1996); 29 CFR 825.309(c). See *Killian v. Yorozu Automotive Tennessee, Inc.*, 454 F.3d 549, 554-555 (6th Cir. 2006); *Stuart v. Regis Corp.*, No. 1:05CV00016DAK, 2006 U.S. Dist. LEXIS 46719, at *14 (D. Ut. July 10, 2006). In that situation, an employer may require that the employee provide the employer reasonable notice (i.e., within two business days) of the changed circumstances, where foreseeable. 29 CFR 825.309(c); S. Res. 242, Cong. Rec. S3959, S3973-74 (April 23, 1996); 29 CFR 825.309(c). See *Killian v. Yorozu Automotive Tennessee, Inc.*, 454 F.3d 549, 554-555 (6th Cir. 2006); *McLaughlin v. Innovative Logistics Group, Inc.*, No. 05-72305, 2007 U.S. Dist. LEXIS 6363, at *18 (E.D. Pa. Jan. 30, 2007). The employer may also obtain information on such changed circumstances through requested status reports. 29 CFR 825.309(c); S. Res. 242, Cong. Rec. S3959, S3973-74 (April 23, 1996); 29 CFR 825.309(c).

In the Preamble to the final regulations, the DOL described the two-day requirement as the minimum period to provide notice required by the employee where early return to work is foreseeable. Preamble, 29 CFR 825.309. By describing this as the minimum period, the Preamble suggests that reasonable notice may require more than two business days of notice, depending on the circumstances.

The term "foreseeable" is not defined. That is, how far in advance does some event have to be known before it is determined to be "foreseeable." Presumably, in the absence of a stated minimum period of time, something that I learn about today that will happen tomorrow is, by definition, foreseeable when I learn of it today.

Reasonable notice is measured from the date of the changed circumstances. It is unclear whether this means the date the employee became aware of the changed circumstances, or the date of the actual changed circumstances. For example, an employee suffers a serious health condition requiring the use of a prosthesis before the employee may return to work. The employee is scheduled to receive the prosthesis in one month. Unexpectedly, the employee is informed that the prosthesis will be available in two weeks. The question is whether the two-day notice period (assuming it applies) runs from the date the employee learned that the prosthesis is arriving earlier than expected, or the date the prosthesis actually arrives. The linkage of the term "foreseeable" with "changed circumstances" suggests that the two-day notice period begins to run when the employee becomes aware of the change, not when the change actually occurs.

In *Killian v. Yorozu Automotive Tennessee, Inc.*, 454 F.3d 549, 554-555 (6th Cir. 2006), the court found that the employee provided reasonable notice of her need for an extended period of leave when she contacted her employer six full days before the expiration of her original leave. Under the regulations, the court opined that Killian could have waited four more days before notifying her employer that she needed a leave extension.

The regulations fail to address whether reasonable notice is required where the early return to work is not foreseeable. For example, an employee is on intermittent FMLA to care for a seriously ill parent. The leave is expected to last several months. The parent unexpectedly dies as a result of complications from surgery. Wishing to return to work immediately, the employee simply shows up at the worksite. The employer, in the meantime, has hired a replacement, and has not otherwise prepared to accept the employee's return. If the regulations required reasonable notice, the employer would have at least a few days to get organized to accept the return of the employee.

Assuming two days notice of an early return to work is provided, the question arises whether the employer may continue to designate those two days as FMLA leave or not. The two-day notice rule does not alter the basic rule that an employer may not require an employee to take more FMLA leave than is necessary to resolve the circumstance that precipitated the need for leave. 29 CFR 825.309(c); S. Res. 242, Cong. Rec. S3959, S3973-74 (April 23, 1996); 29 CFR 825.309(c). If the employee continues to need FMLA leave during the notice period, the employer could count that time against the employee's FMLA leave entitlement. If, on the other hand, the employee attempts to return to work before the planned expiration of the scheduled FMLA leave (i.e., the employee no longer needs FMLA leave) without advance notice to the employer, the employer may keep the employee out on leave, but may not count the time against the employee's FMLA leave entitlement. Preamble, 29 CFR 214.

Finally, the status reports referenced in this regulation appear to refer to the requirement that, on request, an employee must provide periodic status reports of his or her intent to return to work. 29 CFR 825.309(a); S. Res. 242, Cong. Rec.

S3959, S3973 (April 23, 1996), 825.309(a). The evidence that status reports are the same as periodic status reports, not a new type of report, is confirmed in the preamble to the final DOL regulations. After addressing the two-day notice requirement of § 825.309(c), the DOL stated "[a]lso, an employer may obtain such information in periodic status reports from the employee." Preamble, 29 CFR 825.214. The quoted language is nearly identical to that last sentence of 29 CFR 825.309(c); S. Res. 242, Cong. Rec. S3959, S3973-74 (April 23, 1996); 29 CFR 825.309(c).

b. Title II

Title II does not provide any special rules governing an employee's earlier than expected return to duty from FMLA leave. These rules may, however, be enacted as part of an employer's policies requiring an employee to report periodically on his or her status and intention to return to work. 5 CFR 630.1208(j). An employer's policy requiring such reports must take into account all of the relevant facts and circumstances of the employee's situation. *Id.* In addition to not hassling an employee while on FMLA leave with repeated requests for period status reports, there is nothing in that language that would prohibit an employer from requiring an employee returning from FMLA earlier than expected to provide a minimum period of advance notice, if that is practicable under all of the circumstances.

Agencies might consider such a policy, particularly if they hire temporary replacements or otherwise take action that might need some lead time to unwind before accepting an employee's return from FMLA leave. Remember, the notice period may give agencies some breathing room to get ready to accept the return of the employee to the same or an equivalent position. Absent a short notice period, agencies might find themselves in violation of the FMLA if they are not ready to accept an employee's immediate return from FMLA leave to the same or an equivalent position.

3. Unequivocal Notice of Intent Not to Return to Work

a. Title I, the CAA, and the PEOAA

If an employee gives unequivocal notice of intent not to return to work from FMLA leave, the employer's obligations under the FMLA to maintain health benefits (subject to COBRA requirements) and to restore the employee cease. 29 CFR 825.309(b); S. Res. 242, Cong. Rec. S3959, S3973 (April 23, 1996); 29 CFR 825.309(b). *See Henry v. Fulton County Bd. of Ed.*, No. 1:05-CV-2008-TWT, 2006 U.S. Dist. LEXIS 74062, at *13 (N.D. Ga. Oct. 10, 2006), *aff'd*, 2007 U.S. App. LEXIS 15874 (11th Cir. July 3, 2007); *Goodman v. Town of Farmington Bd. of Ed.*, No. 3:01cv1609(CFD), 2005 U.S. Dist. LEXIS 33734, at 9 (D. Ut. Dec. 6, 2005). These obligations, however, do continue if an employee indicates that he or she may be unable to return to work but expresses a continuing desire to do so. 29 CFR 825.309(b); S. Res. 242, Cong. Rec. S3959, S3973 (April 23, 1996); 29 CFR 825.309(b). *See Goodman v. Town of Farmington Bd. of Ed.*, No. 3:01cv1609(CFD), 2005 U.S. Dist. LEXIS 33734, at 9 (D. Ut. Dec. 6, 2005). In that case, the employee's notice cannot be said to be "unequivocal."

The regulations do not define when notice is considered to be unequivocal. In the preamble to the final regulations (Preamble, 29 CFR 825.309), the DOL addressed the meaning of the term "unequivocal" as follows:

> The definition of this term [unequivocal] is that it is understandable in only one way with no expression of uncertainty, i.e., distinct, plain, absolute, clear.

The DOL has opined that the failure of an employee to provide a periodic status report of intent to return to work as requested by an employer does not constitute unequivocal notice of intent not to return to work in all cases. Preamble, 29 CFR 825.309. According to the DOL:

> The determination would depend upon all the facts in the specific cases. The commenter assumes that the employee has received a notice (requesting periodic status report). Perhaps the employee is in another city caring for a parent and does not receive a request mailed to the employee's home. It is simply not possible to state a general rule regarding this circumstances; it is dependent on all the facts. Clearly, the failure to respond does not constitute unequivocal notice in all cases.

The regulations also do not require that such notice be written or oral. As such, as long as it is unequivocal, the notice of intent not to return to work may be either oral or in writing. *See* Preamble, 29 CFR 825.309 (explaining that the term "unequivocal" has nothing to do with whether notice is written or verbal).

b. Title II

There are no special rules under Title II governing an employee's unequivocal notice of intent not to return from FMLA leave. The regulations do provide, however, that an employee on unpaid FMLA leave is entitled to the same entitlements and limitation in law and regulations of an employee in a leave without pay status. 5 CFR 630.1208(e). An employee is also not entitled to any right, benefit, or position of employment other than any right, benefit, or position to which the employee would have been entitled had the employee not taken FMLA leave. The employee who gives unequivocal notice of intent not to return from FMLA leave should not be treated better than any other employee on leave who gives notice that they are not coming back to work.

4. Form of Employee Notice

In *Burton v. Neumann*, No. 97-8061-CIV-HURLEY, 1999 U.S. Dist. LEXIS 16122 (S.D. Fla. April 8, 1999), the district court found that an employee failed to perfect her right to return to work when the employee failed to file an "intent to return to work" form required by the employer's policy before the expiration of 12 week of the start of FMLA leave. The requirement was contained in a policy that was previously provided to the employee. Pursuant to that policy, the failure to submit the notice may be considered a voluntary resignation. When the employee failed to submit the letter of intent to return to work, the employer acted as if the employee had resigned. The plaintiff had otherwise indicated her desire to return to work, just not on the form provided. According to the court, "the fact remains that [the] plaintiff was told to fill out a particular form and did not do so." The case is interesting, as it does not tie its decision to any particular DOL regulation permitting an employer to require a written notice of intent to return to work on a particular form under penalty of termination. This is not a big surprise, as there is no such regulation.

IV. LIMITATIONS ON AN EMPLOYER'S OBLIGATION TO REINSTATE AN EMPLOYEE

A. OVERVIEW

Assuming an employee otherwise satisfies all of the preconditions for return to work from FMLA leave (e.g., the employee is able to perform all essential job functions), he provided timely notice or periodic status reports of his intent to return to work, and tendered a fitness-for-duty certification as requested, there may be additional reasons why an employer may not have to accept the return of an employee from FMLA leave. This section addresses those limitations.

B. GENERAL RULE

An employee who takes FMLA leave has a substantive right to be returned to the same or an equivalent position on the completion of that leave. 29 USC 2614(a)(1)(A); 29 CFR 825.214(a). The right is not, however, absolute. *Sista v. CDC IXIS North Am., Inc.*, 445 F.3d 161, 174 (2d Cir. 2006); *Thornberry v. McGehee Desha County Hosp.*, 403 F.3d 972, 978 (8th Cir. 2005); *Taylor v. The Union Institute et al.*, 30 Fed. Appx. 443 (6th Cir. 2002) (right to return to work from FMLA leave not absolute); *Gerking v. Wabash Ford/Sterling Truck Sales, Inc.*, No. IP-IP00-0495-C-B/K, 2002 U.S. Dist. LEXIS 17365 (S.D. Ind. Sept. 6, 2002).

An employee has no greater right to reinstatement or to other benefits and conditions of employment than if the employee had been continuously employed during the FMLA leave period. 29 USC 2614(a)(3); 29 CFR 825.216(a); 2 USC 1312(a)(1) (incorporating 29 USC 2614 into CAA); 5 USC 6284 (c)(2); S. Res. 242, Cong. Rec. S3959, S3969 (April 23, 1996); 29 CFR 825.3216(a); 3 USC 412(a)(1) (incorporating 29 USC 2614 into PEOAA); *see Campbell v. Gambro Healthcare, Inc.*, 478 F.3d 1282 (10th Cir. 2007); *Holpp v. Integrated Communications Corp.*, 214 Fed. Appx. 176 (3d Cir. 2007); *Sista v. CDC IXIS North Am., Inc.*, 445 F.3d 161, 174 (2d Cir. 2006); *Thornberry v. McGehee Desha County Hosp.*, 403 F.3d 972, 978 (8th Cir. 2005); *Hoge v. Honda of America Mfg., Inc.*, 384 F.3d 238 (6th Cir. 2004) (an employee returning from FMLA leave is not entitled to restoration unless he would have continued to be employed if he had not taken FMLA leave; an employer need not restore an employee who would have lost his job or been laid off even if he had not taken FMLA leave); *Conoshenti v. Pub. Serv. Elec. & Gas Co.*, 364 F.3d 135, 141 (3d Cir. 2004) (if an employee is discharged during or at the end of a protected leave for a reason unrelated to the leave, there is no right to reinstatement); *Smith v. Diffee Ford-Lincoln-Mercury, Inc.*, 298 F.3d 955, 963 (10th Cir. 2002); *Taylor v. the Union Institute et al.*, 30 Fed. Appx. 443 (6th Cir. 2002); *Kohls v. Beverly Enterprises Wisconsin, Inc.*, 259 F.3d 799, 804 (7th Cir. 2001); *Santos v. Knitgoods Workers' Union Local 155 et al.*, 252 F.3d 175, 178 (2nd Cir. 2001); *Strickland v. Water Works and Sewer Board of the City of Birmingham*, 239 F.3d

1199, 1208 (11th Cir. 2001); *Rice v. Sunrise Express, Inc. et al.*, 217 F.3d 492 493 (7th Cir. 2000); *Renaud v. Wyoming Dept. of Family Services et al.*, 203 F.3d 723, 732 (10th Cir. 2000); *Kariotis v. Navistar Int'l Transp. Corp.*, 131 F.3d 672, 681 (7th Cir. 1997); *Martin v. Brevard County Public Schools*, No. 6:05-cv-971-Orl-22RS, 2007 U.S. Dist. LEXIS 9910, at *28 (M.D. Fla. Feb. 13, 2007); *Hayes v. U.S. Bancorp Piper Jaffray Inc.*, No. 03-4208 (RHK/AJB), 2004 U.S. Dist. LEXIS 18667, at *37-38 (D. Minn. Sept. 16, 2004); *Geromanos v. Columbia Univ., College of Physicians and Surgeons*, 322 F. Supp. 2d 420, 427, 428-29 (S.D.N.Y. 2004); *Maldonado v. Frio County, Texas*, No. SA-02-CA-1046-XR, 2004 U.S. Dist. LEXIS 10723, at *11 (W.D. Tex. June 1, 2004) (an employer is entitled to dismiss an employee for any lawful reason at any time, whether before, during, or after an employee requests or takes leave pursuant to the FMLA, as long as the employer does not discriminate or retaliate against the employee for requesting or taking such leave). Attempts at limiting the reach of the omnibus exception to the duty to restore an employee to return to work from FMLA leave have proved unsuccessful. Employees have argued that the omnibus exception does not apply where the employee was on FMLA leave when the adverse action occurred. They argue that, by its terms, the exception only applies to a "restored employee." See *Sylvester v. Dead River Co.*, 260 F. Supp. 2d 181 (D. Me. 2003). The argument is contradicted by the DOL implementing regulations, *see* 29 CFR 825.216(a)(1) and 825.312(d), as well as the courts. *Ogborn v. United Food & Commercial Workers Union, Local No. 881*, 305 F.3d 763, 768 (7th Cir. 2002); *Kosakow v. New Rochelle Radiology Assocs.*, 274 F.3d 706, 733 (2d Cir. 2001); *Taylor v. The Union Institute et al.*, 30 Fed. Appx. 443 (6th Cir. 2002); *Kohls v. Beverly Enterprises Wisconsin, Inc.*, 259 F.3d 799, 804-07 (7th Cir. 2000); *Sylvester v. Dead River Co.*, 260 F. Supp. 2d 181 (D. Me. 2003).

C. EXAMPLES OF THE GENERAL RULE

The regulations implementing Title I, the CAA, and the PEOAA address a number of examples where the general rule that an employee on FMLA leave does not enjoy any greater right to return to work than if the employee had not taken FMLA leave. The Preamble to Title I adds several more examples. Because the general rule is universally recognized throughout federal sector for purposes of the FMLA, these examples should apply with equal force to all federal agencies.

1. Discipline; Termination

The taking of FMLA leave does not immunize an employee from discipline for conduct or performance problems. An employee may be subject to discipline, including removal, while on FMLA leave. See *Gambini v. Total Renal Care, Inc.*, 480 F. 3d 950 (9th Cir. 2007) (employer may terminate an employee during leave if the employer would have made the same decision had the employee not taken leave); *Holpp v. Integrated Communications Corp.*, 214 Fed. Appx. 176 (3d Cir. 2007); *Sista v. CDC IXIS North Am., Inc.*, 445 F.3d 161, 174 (2d Cir. 2006); *Conoshenti v. Pub. Serv. Elec. & Gas Co.*, 364 F.3d 135, 141 (3d Cir. 2004) (if an employee is discharged during or at the end of a protected leave for a reason unrelated to the leave, there is no right to reinstatement); *Spangler v. Federal Home Loan Bank of Des Moines*, 278 F.3d 847, 853 (8th Cir. 2002); *Santos v. Knitgoods Workers' Union Local 155 et al.*, 252 F.3d 175, 178-79 (2nd Cir. 2001) (employer did not have FMLA obligation to pay employee unused sick leave benefits where employee was terminated for non-FMLA reasons during FMLA leave, when employer policy would not normally provide unused sick leave benefits to employee on termination); *Renaud v. Wyoming Dept. of Family Services et al.*, 203 F.3d 723, 732 (10th Cir. 2000) (termination of employee while on FMLA in alcohol treatment program valid where termination was for using alcohol on the job, not the use of FMLA leave); *Kohls v. Beverly Enterprises Wisconsin, Inc.*, 259 F.3d 799, 806 (7th Cir. 2001) (mismanaging money and other performance problems legitimate reason for termination independent of FMLA leave); *Bailey v. Amsted Industries, Inc.*, 172 F.3d 1041, 1045-46 (8th Cir. 1999) (employee cannot claim protection from the FMLA for disciplinary action as a result of absences that are not attributable to his serious health condition); *Schreiber v. Chicago Mercantile Exchange, Inc.*, No. 03 C 8568, 2004 U.S. Dist. LEXIS 23108, at *17 (N.D. Ill. Nov. 15, 2004); *Maldonado v. Frio County, Texas*, No. SA-02-CA-1046-XR, 2004 U.S. Dist. LEXIS 10723, at *11 (W.D. Tex. June 1, 2004) (termination of employee for documented performance problems after employee requested and was approved to take FMLA leave, but before she began FMLA leave, did not violate the FMLA); *Blohm v. Dillard's Inc. et al.*, 95 F. Supp. 2d 473 480 (E.D. N.C. 2000); *Clark v. New York State Electric & Gas Corp.*, 67 F. Supp. 2d 63, 80 (N.D.N.Y. 1999), *aff'd*, 216 F.3d 1071 (2d Cir. 2000) (it is not unlawful to terminate an employee while they are on FMLA leave, provided the taking of FMLA leave was not the cause for termination); *Santos v. Knitgoods Workers' Union Local 155*, 1999 U.S. Dist. LEXIS 9036 (S.D.N.Y. June 15, 1999), *aff'd*, 252 F.3d 175 (2d Cir. 2001).

The rule applies to civil service employees covered by Title II of the FMLA. See *Abramson v. DHS*, No. DC-0752-06-0587-I-1, 2006 MSPB LEXIS 5366, at *15 (Sept. 22, 2006) (taking of FMLA leave does not prohibit an employer from proceeding with appropriate action under part 432 or part 752).

Remember, an employee on FMLA leave is entitled to no greater right of employment than if the leave was not taken. Provided the employer's policies do not discriminate against those who take FMLA leave, are applied uniformly to similarly situated employees, and violate no other laws, regulations, or collective bargaining agreements that are applicable, sanctions such as discharge for misconduct may continue to be applied to the employee on FMLA leave for actionable offenses as if the employee continued to work. Preamble, 29 CFR 825.216; Preamble, 5 CFR 1208.

For example, if an employee was unsuccessful in improving performance during an opportunity period to improve and invoked the entitlement to FMLA leave immediately following the opportunity period, the employer may issue the proposal and decision notices for removal based on unacceptable performance and effect the action just as it normally would. There is no obligation to wait until the employee has returned from FMLA leave in order to proceed with an otherwise valid adverse or performance-based action. Preamble, 5 CFR 630.1208. Of course, agencies may not remove or otherwise discipline an employee based on the use of leave under the FMLA. *Id.*

Similarly, the fact that the poor performance was caused by the same illness that gave rise to the need for FMLA leave does not protect the employee from dismissal for performance deficiencies or give the employee the right to return to work and demonstrate improved performance when not ill. See *Thornberry v. McGehee Desha County Hosp.*, 403 F.3d 972, 978 (8th Cir. 2005); *McBride v. Citgo Petroleum Corp.*, 281 F.3d 1099, 1108 (10th Cir. 2002); *Knepp v. Overhead Door Corp.*, No. 1:03-CV-1993, 2005 U.S. Dist. LEXIS 41165, at *15-18 (M.D. Pa. Aug. 16, 2005) (conduct related to substance abuse).

The fact that the FMLA leave permitted an employer to discover the conduct or performance problems that resulted in the disciplinary action taken against the employee "cannot logically be a bar to the employer's ability to fire the deficient employee." *Kohls v. Beverly Enterprises Wisconsin, Inc.*, 259 F.3d 799, 806 (7th Cir. 2001); *accord Campbell v. Gambro Healthcare, Inc.*, 478 F.3d 1282 (10th Cir. 2007).

In *Conoshenti v. Pub. Serv. Elec. & Gas Co.*, 364 F.3d 135, 141 (3d Cir. 2004), the Third Circuit affirmed the award of summary judgment to the employer even though the employer cited periods of time covered by the FMLA as the basis for the employee's termination. In that case, the employee was on a last chance agreement (LCA) which provided that any violation of the LCA would automatically constitute just cause and he would be fired. Conoshenti was absent from work for 92 days, well beyond the 12 weeks of FMLA leave to which he was entitled. Applying a shifting burden-of-proof scheme, the court initially found that the inclusion of the FMLA period in the termination notice constituted direct evidence that Conoshenti's FMLA leave was impermissibly relied on as a factor in the discharge decision. The burden of proof shifted to PSE&G to demonstrate the absence of but-for causation. The court agreed with PSE&G that Conoshenti would have been discharged absent any consideration of his 12 weeks of FMLA-protected leave. Once his 12 weeks of FMLA expired, Conoshenti's first absence violated the LCA, subjecting him to immediate discharge.

An employee was held to have no right to job restoration where her continued employment was conditioned on her completion of an accredited substance abuse treatment program and submission of weekly progress reports, and she failed to complete the treatment program. *Geromanos v. Columbia Univ., College of Physicians and Surgeons*, 322 F. Supp. 2d 420, 427, 428–29 (S.D.N.Y. 2004).

The termination of an employee after the employee's sole client expressed serious concerns about the employee's performance and suggested that their continued business could be at risk if the employee continued to manage the account, was for a reason other than the employee's use of FMLA leave and, therefore, did not violate the Act. *Holpp v. Integrated Communications Corp.*, 214 Fed. Appx. 176 (3d Cir. 2007).

Termination of an employee who, while on FMLA leave, stopped into work to pick up paperwork and engaged in a heated confrontation with his supervisor, was for a reason other than the use of FMLA. *Reinhart v. Mineral Technologies, Inc.*, No. 05-4203, 2006 U.S. Dist. LEXIS 89279, at *41-42 & n.11 (E.D. Pa. Nov. 27, 2006).

The circuits are split concerning whether the employer or the employee bears the burden of proof to establish that the employer would have taken action against the employee irrespective of the employee taking FMLA leave. The Tenth and Eleventh Circuits have held that once an employee proves that he or she was denied reinstatement after FMLA leave, the employer must prove that the employee would have been laid off anyway for some other reason. *Smith v. Diffe Ford Lincoln–Mercury, Inc.*, 298 F.3d 955, 962–63 (10th Cir. 2002); *Parris v. Miami Herald Publ'g Co.*, 216 F.3d 1298 (11th Cir. 2000); *O'Connor v. PCA Family Health Plan, Inc.*, 200 F.3d 1349 (11th Cir. 2000). The Seventh Circuit places the burden of proof on the employee. *Kohls v. Beverly Enterprises Wisconsin, Inc.*, 259 F.3d 799, 805 (7th Cir. 2001); *Rice v. Sunrise Express, Inc.*, 217 F.3d 1008, 1016–19 (7th Cir.), cert. denied, 531 U.S. 1012, 121 S. Ct. 567 (2000).

In *Sista v. CDC IXIS North Am., Inc.*, 445 F.3d 161, 174 (2d Cir. 2006), the Second Circuit indicated that an employer must be able to show that an employee would not otherwise have been employed at the time reinstatement is requested in order to deny restoration to employment. There, the employer established that Sista was terminated for threatening his supervisor. The court found that Sista failed to demonstrate that the employer's reason for terminating him was pretextual, and that the real reason was his exercise of FMLA rights.

In *Gerking v. Wabash Ford/Sterling Truck Sales, Inc.*, No. IP–IP00–0495–C–B/K, 2002 U.S. Dist. LEXIS 17365 (S.D. Ind. Sept. 6, 2002), the district court found that the employer failed to establish that the employee did not have a right to return from FMLA leave because the employee would have been fired for sexual harassment. The court phrased the issue as whether the employer *would* have fired Gerking for harassment had Gerking not been on FMLA leave, not whether the employer *could* have fired Gerking. The court noted Wabash's failure to offer evidence that it fired employees in similar circumstances to establish that it would have fired Gerking. In contrast, the court credited contrary evidence offered by Gerking that the policy was not enforced in the past.

In *Strickland v. Water Works and Sewer Bd. Of the City of Birmingham*, 239 F.3d 1199, 1208 (11th Cir. 2001), the circuit court found sufficient material facts in dispute to reverse the award of summary judgment to the employer and remand the matter for further development of the record. In that case, the employer argued that it terminated the plaintiff, not because he took FMLA leave, but because of his failure to follow his supervisor's directions in handling a customer's water bill. The problem with that argument, the court noted, was that the letter the employer wrote to the employee terminating his employment made no mention of the unsatisfactory handling of the customer's complaint. Rather, it referenced his insubordination and "walking off the job" on a certain day, the events of which are in dispute. The employee claimed that those events included his taking FMLA leave.

Employers who intend to rely on the omnibus exception to defend against claims that adverse actions taken against an employee who has exercised rights under the FMLA must be prepared to offer evidence that they have taken similar action under similar circumstances against employees who have not taken FMLA leave.

Employers that are found to have relied on an employee's taking of FMLA leave as a factor in the issuance of discipline or termination during FMLA leave are in violation of the Act. *See Smith v. Diffee Ford–Lincoln–Mercury, Inc.*, 298 F.3d 955, 961 (10th Cir. 2002); *Kohls v. Beverly Enterprises Wisconsin, Inc.*, 259 F.3d 799, 806 (7th Cir. 2001).

2. Layoff/RIF

If an employee is laid off during the pendency of FMLA leave and employment terminated, the employer's responsibility to continue FMLA leave, maintain group health plan benefits, and restore the employee cease at the time the employee is laid off, provided the employer has no continuing obligations under a collective bargaining agreement or otherwise. 29 CFR 825.216(a); S. Res. 242, Cong. Rec. S3959, S3969 (April 23, 1996); 29 CFR 825.216(a); *see Taylor v. The Union Institute et al.*, 30 Fed. Appx. 443 (6th Cir. 2002) (layoff decision based on employee's historical and consistently below average recruiting performance, not including period when employee was on FMLA leave, sufficient non–FMLA reason for layoff decision); *Parris v. The Miami Herald Publishing Co.*, 216 F.3d 1298, 1301 (11th Cir. 2000); *O'Connor v. PCA Family Health Plan, Inc.*, 200 F.3d 1349, 1354 (11th Cir. 2000) (RIF); *Ilhardt v. Sara Lee Corp.*, 118 F.3d 1151, 1157 (7th Cir. 1997) (employer had no obligation to reinstate employee after FMLA leave ended because an employer's responsibility to reinstate an employee ceased at the time employee was laid off in a RIF); *Schreiber v. Chicago Mercantile Exchange, Inc.*, No. 03 C 8568, 2004 U.S. Dist. LEXIS 23108, at *17 (N.D. Ill. Nov. 15, 2004); *Hayes v. U.S. Bancorp Piper Jaffray Inc.*, No. 03–4208 (RHK/AJB), 2004 U.S. Dist. LEXIS 18667, at *37–38 (D. Minn. Sept. 16, 2004); *Price v. Washington Hospital Center*, 321 F. Supp. 2d 38, 45 (D.D.C. 2004) (elimination of position during a RIF while employee was on FMLA leave did not violate employee's FMLA rights); *Sylvester v. Dead River Co.*, 260 F. Supp. 2d 181 (D. Me. 2003) (decision to restructure organization in preparation of sale of business where employee worked which preceded employee's need for FMLA leave was non–FMLA reason justifying employee's termination during FMLA leave); *Manarel v. Mothers Work, Inc.*, No. 01–Civ.–0235 (JSR), 2002 U.S., Dist. LEXIS 5541 (S.D.N.Y. March 29, 2002); *Madison v. The Sherwin William Co.*, 158 F. Supp. 2d 854, 858–59 (N.D. Ill. April 6, 2001).

Nor is an employer required to transfer an employee whose position has been eliminated in a restructuring simply because the employee requested FMLA leave. In *Skrjanc v. Great Lakes Power Serv. Co.*, 272 F.3d 309, 314 (6th Cir. 2001), the circuit court found that the FMLA does not give an employee a freestanding right to be considered for a transfer if the employee did not have such right before requesting FMLA leave. Absent evidence of a policy or practice allowing employees whose positions have been eliminated to apply for other jobs within the company, the fact that an employee requested FMLA leave a month before the restructuring does not give the employee any more right to a transfer than if the employee never requested FMLA leave. It would be a violation of the Act, however, if employees who requested FMLA leave were given less rights to a transfer than employees who never requested or used FMLA leave.

Whether the employee's pre-leave position was eliminated in a restructuring so that the employee does not have an FMLA right to return to work may depend in part on how an employer addressed the duties of that eliminated position. If the employer distributed the duties of the position to others during the employee's FMLA leave, the employee may not have been eliminated for purposes of the FMLA, and the employee may have a right to return to work. 29 C. F.R. § 825.214(a) (an employee is entitled to such reinstatement even if the employer replaced the employee or restructured his or her position to accommodate the employee's absence).

This situation typically arises when an employer learns, during the course of an employee's FMLA-leave absence, that they can handle the duties of the position without the employee. To save money, the employer eliminates the employee's job during FMLA leave, distributes the job duties to others, and then refuses to reinstate the employee once the need for FMLA leave has ended. In this case, the omnibus exception would not apply, and the employee may have a right to return to work. See *Parker v. Hahnemann University Hospital et al.*, 234 F. Supp. 2d 478, n. 13 (D. N.J. 2002) (denying summary judgment where evidence was submitted that employee's pre-leave job was not eliminated, and employer considered how the position worked without her when they decided to eliminate her employment); *Brenlla v. Lasorsa Buick Pontiac Chevrolet, Inc.*, No. 00-CIV-5207 (JCF), 2002 U.S. Dist. LEXIS 9358 (S.D.N.Y. May 28, 2002) (ample evidence to support jury's conclusion that Brenlla's termination and the consolidation of positions were not motivated by legitimate business concerns).

On the other hand, if the position were slated for elimination before the employee went on leave, by operation of the omnibus exception, the enactment of that change during an employee's FMLA leave would not give the employee the right to return to work from FMLA leave to a position that no longer existed. *Parris v. the Miami Herald Publishing Co.*, 216 F.3d 1298, 1302–03 (11th Cir. 2000) (denying summary judgment where the proof that the decision to eliminate the employee's pursuant to a restructuring was unclear due to contradictory personnel forms, a lack of notification to the employee, and potential disparate application of the rules). In *Dressler v. Community Service Communications, Inc.*, 275 F. Supp. 2d 17 (1st Cir. 2004), the court found that an employee's loss of the leadership of the human resources unit to a new director during a period in which the employee was taking intermittent FMLA leave did not violate the job restoration requirements of the FMLA. The court reasoned that the change in circumstances would have occurred regardless of whether the employee took FMLA leave and, as such, the FMLA does not protect him against such change. As support, the court noted that the employee's performance had deteriorated; the company was creating a number of other new division directors during the same period thereby requiring managers to report to new chiefs; and the company was independently interested in expanding the capability of the human resource unit to include organizational development, a skill that the employee did not possess. According to the court, "[t]here were thus substantial reasons for the company to introduce a new director, other than Dressler, to have the division."

In *Hayes v. U.S. Bancorp Piper Jaffray Inc.*, No. 03-4208 (RHK/AJB), 2004 U.S. Dist. LEXIS 18667, at *37–38 (D. Minn. Sept. 16, 2004), the employee's position was eliminated in the fifth round of a reduction in force. The court found that the employer established that the elimination of plaintiff's position while she was on FMLA leave was unrelated to her taking leave. The employee did not contest the fact that her "Pod" was one of the least profitable, and that she was lacking in decisiveness, assertiveness, and presence on the trading floor.

In *Schreiber v. Chicago Mercantile Exchange, Inc.*, No. 03 C 8568, 2004 U.S. Dist. LEXIS 23108, at *17 (N.D. Ill. Nov. 15, 2004), the employer granted Schreiber's request for 12 weeks of FMLA leave. At the time of her request, the employer was reorganizing in preparation for an Initial Public Offering (IPO) of stock. Pursuant to a number of meetings, a new organizational chart was constructed and several new positions were added to the division where plaintiff worked. Plaintiff's job was eliminated as a result of the reorganization. She was the only person in her division to lose her job as a result of the reorganization. The employer concluded that plaintiff did not have enough work to do and that her job duties could easily be shifted to others. Schrieber was notified that her position was eliminated two days before she was to return to work from FMLA leave. A year and a half after her position was eliminated, an administrative position was posted in her former division. She applied, but did not get the job. Plaintiff sued, alleging that her termination violated her FMLA right to job restoration. Finding no evidence to cast doubt on the legitimate reason provided by her employer for terminating Schreiber, the court found that CME was under no obligation to reinstate her once her position was eliminated.

In *Donahoo v. Master Data Center*, 282 F. Supp. 2d 540, 551 (E.D. Mich. 2003), the court noted that, while 29 CFR 825.216 only explicitly applies to an employer's denial of restoration of employment, it would seem to apply by analogy to the denial of restoration to an equivalent position. There, the court found material issues of fact regarding the employer's motivation for eliminating plaintiff's original, pre-leave position precluded summary judgment.

In *O'Connor v. PCA Family Health Plan, Inc.*, 200 F.3d 1349, 1354 (11th Cir. 2000), the circuit court rejected the plaintiff's attempt to establish that the employer acted in a discriminatory manner when it removed two other employees on FMLA leave from a final RIF roster while failing to do the same for her. Finding the argument to be without merit, the court opined that: "PCA's voluntary adoption of an employment policy designed to avoid legal entanglements (ironically unsuccessful) does not expand the scope of legally enforceable employment protection beyond that which the statute affords. If anything, PCA's oversight of O'Connor's name and failure to remove it from the final RIF roster only indicates that O'Connor's FMLA status played no part in PCA's decision to discharge her."

The term "otherwise" would fall into the category of more generous employer leave benefits pursuant to a policy or practice. 29 CFR 825.700(a); S. Res. 242, Cong. Rec. S3959, S3976 (April 23, 1996); 29 CFR 825.700(a). Stated differently, an employee who invokes his or her entitlement to FMLA leave is not immune from the impact of reduction in force before, during, or after the period of FMLA leave. Preamble, 5 CFR 630.1208.

An employee may not be restored to an equivalent position if written notification is provided that the equivalent position will be affected by a reduction in force where the employee's previous position is not affected by the reduction in force. 5 CFR 630.1208(g). Similarly, restoration to a job slated for lay-off when the employee's original position is not, would not meet the requirements of being returned to work to an equivalent position. 29 CFR 825.215(f); S. Res. 242, Cong. Rec. S3959, S3969 (April 23, 1996); 29 CFR 825.215(f).

The circuits are split on the question of who bears the burden of proof. *See Hayes v. U.S. Bancorp Piper Jaffray Inc.*, No. 03-4208 (RHK/AJB), 2004 U.S. Dist. LEXIS 18667, at *37–38 (D. Minn. Sept. 16, 2004). Some courts require that an employer bear the burden of proving that an employee would have been laid off during the FMLA leave period and, therefore, would not be entitled to restoration. 29 CFR 825.216(a)(1); *see Donahoo v. Master Data Center*, 282 F. Supp. 2d 540, 553 (E.D. Mich. 2003).

3. Shift Eliminated/Overtime Reduced

If an employer has eliminated a shift, or reduced overtime, an employee would not be entitled to return to work that shift or to a position with the original amount of overtime. 29 CFR 825.216(a)(2); S. Res. 242, Cong. Rec. S3959, S3969 (April 23, 1996); 29 CFR 825.216(a)(2). However, if a position on, for example, a night shift is filled by another employee during the pendency of FMLA leave, the employee returning to work is entitled to return to the same shift on which he was employed before taking FMLA leave. 29 CFR 825.216(a)(2); S. Res. 242, Cong. Rec. S3959, S3969 (April 23, 1996); 29 CFR 825.216(a)(2).

4. Employee Hired for Specific Term or Project

If an employee was hired for a specific term or only to perform work on a discrete project, the employer has no obligation to restore the employee if the employment term or project is over and the employer would not otherwise have continued to employ the employee. 29 CFR 825.216(b); S. Res. 242, Cong. Rec. S3959, S3969 (April 23, 1996); 29 CFR 825.216(b);. *see Martin v. Brevard County Public Schools*, No. 6:05-cv-971-Orl-22RS, 2007 U.S. Dist. LEXIS 9910, at *30 (M.D. Fla. Feb. 13, 2007) (employee hired for a one-year contract had no right to reinstatement to his prior position because the term of the employment contract expired by the time he sought reinstatement).

On the other hand, if an employee was hired to perform work on a contract, and after the contract period the contract was awarded to another contractor, the successor contractor may be required to restore the employee if it is a successor employer within the meaning of the FMLA. 29 CFR 825.216(b); S. Res. 242, Cong. Rec. S3959, S3969 (April 23, 1996); 29 CFR 825.216(b). [For a further discussion of successor employers, see Chapter 3, "FMLA Coverage of the Federal Government."]

5. Workers' Compensation

If the absence was covered by workers' compensation and the FMLA, and after 12 weeks of FMLA leave the employee is unable to return to work at all, or is unable to perform all essential job functions of his or her former position, the employee no longer has the protections of the FMLA and must look to the workers' compensation statute or the Rehabilitation Act for any relief or protections, including the right to return to work. 29 CFR 825.216(d); S. Res. 242, Cong. Rec. S3959, S3969 (April 23, 1996); 29 CFR 825.216(d); *see Clark v. New York State Electric & Gas Corp.*, 67 F. Supp. 2d 63, 80 (N.D.N.Y. 1999), *aff'd*, 216 F.3d 1071 (2d Cir. 2000).

6. Probationary Periods

Under certain circumstances, probationary periods may be extended because of a period of FMLA leave. A probationary period may also be imposed on an employee's return from FMLA leave. Again, an employee is not entitled to any greater employment benefits because he or she exercised rights under the FMLA leave; employees just may not lose any benefits enjoyed by other employees.

Regarding the former, absent a more generous employer policy or the contrary requirements of a collective bargaining agreement, probationary periods may be extended as a result of an employee taking FMLA leave. As stated in the preamble to the final OPM regulations, 5 CFR 630.1208:

> If an employee is in an LWOP status during the probationary period, the probationary period will be extended by the amount of LWOP in excess of 22 days. Therefore, depending upon the duration of the LWOP, the length of an employee's probationary period could be extended by the FMLA leave. If so, the employee would still be in a probationary status upon his or her return to work. However, an employee who invokes his or her entitlement to leave under the FMLA is not protected from termination during probation if the employer decides to terminate the individual's employment during probation. For example, if an employer notified a probationary employee with ten months of service that he or she was to be removed due to misconduct, and the employee invoked his or her FMLA entitlement, the employer would not need to wait until the FMLA leave was exhausted (and the employee completed probation) before taking action.

The same rules would apply to employers covered by Title I, the CAA, and the PEOAA. In light of this rule, unions and other organizations representing the interests of employees generally attempt to bargain so that the probationary periods continue to run during the course of the probationary employee's FMLA absence. Agencies, on the other hand, generally take the opposite view.

As with discipline, probationary periods may be imposed on an employee's return to work if, but for the taking of FMLA leave, the employee would have been placed on probation, usually for violation of employer policies. *See Robinson v. Overnite Transportation Co.*, No. 95–3067, 1997 U.S. App. LEXIS 6574 (4th Cir. April 9, 1997) (placement of truck driver on probationary period on return to work from FMLA leave did not violate the Act where placement was made pursuant to company policy following driving accident when plaintiff fell asleep at the wheel).

7. Outside Employment

If the employer has a uniformly applied policy governing outside or supplemental employment, such a policy may continue to apply to an employee while on FMLA leave. 29 CFR 825.312(h); S. Res. 242, Cong. Rec. S3959, S3974 (April 23, 1996); 29 CFR 825.312(h); *see Pharakhone v. Nissan North America, Inc. et al.*, 324 F.3d 405 (6th Cir. 2003); *Worster v. Carlson Wagonlit Travel, Inc.*, No. 3:02CV167 (EBB), 2005 U.S. Dist. LEXIS 33285, at *2 & n.1 (D. Conn. July 6, 2005). An employee who violates a uniformly–applied policy against working while on FMLA leave is not entitled to reinstatement if the employee would have lost his or her job for violating the work rule even if the employee hand not taken FMLA leave. *Pharakhone v. Nissan North America, Inc. et al.*, 324 F.3d 405 (6th Cir. 2003).

To be "uniformly-applied," an employer's policy prohibiting outside employment during FMLA leave does not have to prohibit outside employment in all circumstances. In *Worster v. Carlson Wagonlit Travel, Inc.*, No. 3:02CV167 (EBB), 2005 U.S. Dist. LEXIS 33285, at *2 & n.1 (D. Conn. July 6, 2005), the employer's policy prohibited outside employment when an employee was on full-time FMLA leave, but not when the employee took intermittent FMLA leave. The employee was caught working while on full-time FMLA leave. Worster argued that the employer's policy was not "uniformly-applied" and, therefore, invalid, because it prohibited outside employment when an employee was on full time FMLA leave but allowed outside employment when FMLA leave was taken intermittently. The court disagreed. The court noted that the regulation does not differentiate between intermittent and full-time FMLA leave, but "neither does it proscribe an employer from making such a distinction and them applying it uniformly."

An employer's decision to terminate an employee for violation of company policy prohibiting the employee from working elsewhere while she was on paid leave concurrent with FMLA leave is not a *per se* violation of the FMLA, and does not constitute interference with the employee's FMLA rights. In *Geromanos v. Columbia Univ., College of Physicians and Surgeons*, 322 F. Supp. 2d 420, 432–433 (S.D.N.Y. 2004), the employee was fired for working as a part-time Lamaze instructor during FMLA leave. According to the court, the employer "had a right to place whatever restrictions it chose on the conditions of its program for paid leave, and its decision to limit plaintiff's ability to work while ostensibly disabled was not contrary to the FMLA."

In *Gray v. USPS*, 97 MSPR 617 (2004), *aff'd*, 2005 U.S. App. LEXIS 10961 (Fed. Cir. June 9, 2005), the Board sustained the removal of a Postal employee for working a second job while on FMLA/sick leave. The employee failed to obtain prior approval to work his second job while on sick leave as required by Postal Service policy. An employer that does not have such a policy may not deny benefits to which an employee is entitled under the FMLA on this basis unless the FMLA was fraudulently obtained, as in paragraph (g) of this section. 29 CFR 825.312(h); S. Res. 242, Cong. Rec. S3959, S3974 (April 23, 1996); 29 CFR 825.312(h). Implicit in this exception to the right to reinstatement from FMLA leave is the right of employers to have a uniformly applied policy that prohibits an employee from working at another job while on FMLA leave.

8. Fraud

An employee who takes leave under § 102 "for the intended purpose of the leave" is entitled to job restoration. 29 USC 2614(a)(1). An employee who secures FMLA leave by means of fraud is not entitled to FMLA protections. 29 CFR 825.312(g); S. Res. 242, Cong. Rec. S3959, S3974 (April 23, 1996); 29 CFR 825.312(h); see *Kariotis v. Navistar Int'l Transp. Corp.*, 131 F.3d 672, 681 (7th Cir. 1997); *Chalimoniuk v. Interstate Brands Corp.*, 172 F. Supp. 2d 1055, 1058 (S.D. Ind. 2001); *Madison v. The Sherwin Williams Co.*, 158 F. Supp. 2d 854, 858 (N.D. Ill. 2001); *Worster v. Carlson Wagonlit Travel, Inc.*, No. 3:02CV167 (EBB), 2005 U.S. Dist. LEXIS 33285, at *2 & n.1 (D. Conn. July 6, 2005); *Chavez v. Lawrence & Frederick, Inc.*, No. 97 C 4535, 1999 U.S. Dist. LEXIS 16361, at *9 (N.D. Ill. Oct. 12, 1999); *Salgado v. CDW Computer Centers, Inc.*, No. 97 C 1975, 1998 U.S. Dist. LEXIS 1374, at *24 (N.D. Ill. Feb. 5, 1998).

In *Kariotis*, the plaintiff claimed that the defendant-employer violated the return-to-work provisions of the FMLA. The United States Court of Appeals for the Seventh Circuit held that an employer could lawfully terminate an employee suspected of fraud who was on FMLA leave in the same way that an employer would lawfully terminate an employee for similar reasons who had been working during the same time. In *Baltuskonis v. U.S. Airways, Inc.*, 60 F. Supp. 2d 445, 448 (E.D. Pa. 1999), the district court upheld the termination of an employee for providing an altered doctor's note in support of that leave. The district court rejected the employee's argument that the short period of time between the employee's request for FMLA leave and the termination suggested a discriminatory intent on the part of the employer. Rather, the court held that the employee's termination for providing an altered doctor's note in support of the leave was a legitimate, nondiscriminatory reason justifying termination.

In *LeBouef v. New York University Medical Center*, No. 98-Civ.-0973 (JSM), 2000 U.S. Dist. LEXIS 18263 (S.D.N.Y. Dec. 20, 2000), the district court upheld the termination of an employee for fraudulent use of sick leave. In that case, the employee was granted FMLA leave concurrent with paid sick leave. The leave was schedule to begin a week before the employee was to undergo surgery. The employee claimed he needed the leave a week before surgery because he was in pain and he feared further injury. During this week, the employee admitted that he attended his daughter's christening and attended a traffic court proceeding. Under NYU policy, sick leave was available only for illness. The policy excluded the use of sick leave for personal business and child-rearing responsibilities. In light of the employee's admissions and NYU's paid leave policies, the court found that defendant had a legitimate, nondiscriminatory reason for terminating plaintiff.

Courts have also found that employers did not violate the Act where they terminated employees who the employer in good faith, albeit mistakenly, believed secured FMLA leave through fraud. *Kariotis v. Navistar Int'l Transp. Corp.*, 131 F.3d 672, 681 (7th Cir. 1997); *Worster v. Carlson Wagonlit Travel, Inc.*, No. 3:02CV167 (EBB), 2005 U.S. Dist. LEXIS 33285, at

*9-12 (D. Conn. July 6, 2005); *Williamson v. Parker Hannifin Corp.*, 208 F. Supp. 2d 1248 (N.D. Ala. 2002) (employee's failure to rebut evidence that employee went camping rather than care for gravely ill parent as claimed justified employer's removal of employee as leave was not for intended purposes).

V. KEY EMPLOYEES

Agencies with employees covered by Title I, and employing offices within the meaning of the CAA and the PEOAA enjoy a narrow exemption covering certain high level employees from the FMLA's general requirement to restore an employee to employment after FMLA. This exemption is not recognized for employees covered by Title II of the FMLA. As such, what follows only applies to agencies or employing offices with employees covered by Title I, the CAA, and the PEOAA.

The real world viability of this exemption in the federal government is, at best, questionable. However, because, the exemption is available to federal agencies, and employing offices covered by the CAA and the PEOAA, the subject is addressed in detail below.

A. OVERVIEW

An employer or employing office is not required by the FMLA to return certain highly compensated or key employees to work from FMLA leave where:

(1) the exemption is limited to a salaried eligible employee who is among the highest paid ten percent of the employer's workforce within 75 miles of the facility where employed;

(2) the denial of restoration to employment (but not the taking of the leave) must be necessary to prevent "substantial and grievous economic injury" to the employer's operations;

(3) the employer has notified the employee of its intent to deny restoration under this exemption at the time the employer determines that such grievous economic injury would occur; and

(4) the employer must allow the employee an opportunity to elect to return to work after receiving the notice from the employer.

29 USC 2614(b); 2 USC 1312(a)(1) (incorporating 29 USC 2614 into CAA); 3 USC 412(a)(1) (incorporating 29 USC 26214 into PEOAA). *See* Preamble, 29 CFR 825.217; *see Kephart v. Cherokee County, North Carolina*, No. 99-1789, 2000 U.S. App. LEXIS 18924 (4th Cir. Aug. 4, 2000); *Meadows v. Texar Fed. Credit Union*, No. 5:05CV158, 2007 U.S. Dist. LEXIS 4456, at *51 (E.D. Jan. 22, 2007). *Oby v. Baton Rouge Marriott*, 329 F. Supp. 2d 772 (M.D. La. 2004); *O'Grady v. Catholic Health Partners Services*, No. 00-C-7144, 2002 U.S. Dist. LEXIS 2182 (N.D. Ill. Feb. 13, 2002); DOL WH FMLA Advisory Opinion No. 50 (Nov. 23, 1994) (addressing basic rule for key employees).

These factors are addressed more fully below.

B. KEY EMPLOYEE DEFINED

A key employee is a salaried, FMLA-eligible employee who is among the highest paid ten percent of all employees employed by the employer within 75 miles of the employee's worksite. 29 USC 2614(b)(2); 29 CFR 825.217(a); S. Res. 242, Cong. Rec. S3959, S3970 (April 23, 1996), 825.217(a); *see Kephart v. Cherokee County, North Carolina*, No. 99-1789, 2000 U.S. App. LEXIS 18924 (4th Cir. Aug. 4, 2000); *Meadows*, 2007 U.S. Dist. LEXIS 4456, at *51 (E.D. Jan. 22, 2007); *Oby*, 329 F. Supp. 2d 772 (no dispute, employee was "key" employee as she had third highest salary at the Baton Rouge Marriott); *O'Grady*, 2002 U.S. Dist. LEXIS 2182.

1. Salaried Employee

A salaried employee is one who is paid on a salary basis. For purposes of Title I, "paid on a salary basis" is defined by cross-reference to 29 CFR 541.118. *See* 29 CFR 825.217(b). For the CAA, "paid on a salary basis" is defined by reference to Part 541 of the Board's regulations implementing § 203 of the CAA (2 USC 1313). S. Res. 242, Cong. Rec. S3959, S3970 (April 23, 1996); 29 CFR 825.217(b). These cross-referenced regulations both define employees who may qualify as exempt from the minimum wage and overtime requirements of the FLSA as executive, administrative, and professional employees. 29 CFR 825.217(b); S. Res. 242, Cong. Rec. S3959, S3970 (April 23, 1996); 29 CFR 825.217(b); *see O'Grady v. Catholic Health Partners Services*, No. 00–C–7144, 2002 U.S. Dist. LEXIS 2182 (N.D. Ill. Feb. 13, 2002).

2. Employer; Employing Office

The key employee regulations do not define what constitutes an "employer" (Title I), or "employing office" (the CAA).

a. Title I

In the preamble to the final regulations implementing Title I, the DOL indicated that the definition of the term "employer" contained in 29 CFR 825.104 would control. Preamble, 29 CFR 825.217. The particular issue addressed by the DOL had to do with a situation involving a parent and subsidiary. Preamble, 29 CFR 825.217.

The reference to § 825.104 as the means for defining what constitutes an employer for purposes of determining a key employee leads to some interesting results. First, it appears that the calculation of whether a particular employer has key employees must take into account all federal employees within 75 miles of the particular worksite, not just the ten percent of the highest paid employees of that employer. Second, individual employees are considered covered employers within the meaning of § 824.105, if they act directly or indirectly in the interest of an employer to any of the employer's employees. 29 CFR 825.104(a), (d). [For a further discussion of who is a covered employer within the meaning of the FMLA, see Chapter 3, "FMLA Coverage of the Federal Government."]

Regarding the first argument, § 825.104 defines all public agencies as covered employers. 29 CFR 825.104(a). A "public employer" is defined as the government of the United States. 29 CFR 825.108(a). Because an employer is defined in terms of the United States government as a whole and not a particular federal public employer, the calculation of whether a particular employee is within the highest paid ten percent of all federal employees within 75 miles of that employee's worksite is nearly impossible to achieve. While most agencies exempt basic employee information, including name, duty station, and salary, from the protections of the Privacy Act, the logistics involved with gathering this information on anything close to a timely basis arguably renders this interpretation of the key employee exemption nearly impossible to effectuate.

The key employee exemption, however, would appear very much available to agencies based on the second definition of an employer, pursuant to § 825.104. A covered employer under the FMLA includes "any person who acts directly or indirectly in the interests of an employer to any of the employer's employees." 29 CFR 825.104(d). Since relatively low–level management officials will meet this definition, it follows that individual supervisors within a particular federal employer at a particular location may meet this definition. As a result, for all practical purposes, each location of every federal employer may be considered to be an employer within the meaning of Title I of the FMLA. Given that level of locality, it is possible that an individual supervisor, strapped with a limited budget and little flexibility, could argue that the return of a key employee would cause substantial and grievous economic injury.

This is another example where the definition of employer for liability purposes completely breaks down for other purposes. The fact of the matter is that, in most federal agencies, low and middle level managers have virtually no authority over hiring and budgets. Identifying these individuals as FMLA employers is, therefore, a legal fiction much divorced from de facto reality.

b. CAA

The calculation of whether an employee is a key employee for purposes of the CAA is made by reference to an employing office. S. Res. 242, Cong. Rec. S3959, S3970 (April 23, 1996); 29 CFR 825.217(c). An "employing office" is defined in the CAA, 2 USC 1301(4), as:

- the personal office of a member of the House of Representatives or of a Senator;
- a committee of the House of Representatives or the Senate or a joint committee;
- any other office headed by a person with the final authority to appoint, hire, discharge, and set the terms, conditions, or privileges of the employment of an employee of the House of Representatives or the Senate;

- the Capitol Guide Board; the Capitol Police Board, the Congressional Budget Office, the Office of the Architect of the Capitol, the Office of the Attending Physician, the Office of Compliance, and the Office of Technology.

Because the CAA regulations, unlike Title I, define an "employing office" in terms of each individual employing office that falls under the CAA, the calculation of the highest paid ten percent of employees is limited to employees of that particular employing office within 75 miles of the employees' worksite. It would not include any other employees covered by another employing office subject to the CAA. For example, Vicki works for a committee of the House. To determine whether she is a key employee, Vickie's pay would be compared with the pay of all other members of the same House committee within 75 miles of Vickie's worksite, which is Washington D.C. Even though there are many other employees of many other House and Senate committees within 75 miles of Vicki's worksite, their pay would not be included to determine whether Vickie was in the top ten percent of the highest paid employees for her committee. Again, Vicki's employing office, by definition, is her committee, not all other committees or entities covered by the CAA.

3. Calculation of Highest Paid Ten Percent

A key employee is an employee in the highest paid top ten percent of all employees, both salaried and non-salaried, who are employed by the employer within 75 miles of the worksite. 29 USC 2614(b)(2); 29 CFR 825.217(c); 2 USC 1312(a)(1) (incorporating 29 USC 2614 into CAA); S. Res. 242, Cong. Rec. S3959, S3970 (April 23, 1996); 29 CFR 825.217(c); 3 USC 412(a)(1) (incorporating 29 USC 26214 into PEOAA). The employer counts all employees at the worksite, including those are eligible and ineligible for FMLA leave. 29 CFR 825.217(c); S. Res. 242, Cong. Rec. S3959, S3970 (April 23, 1996); 29 CFR 825.217(c); *see O'Grady v. Catholic Health Partners Services*, No. 00-C-7144, 2002 U.S. Dist. LEXIS 2182 (N.D. Ill. Feb. 13, 2002) (absent evidence presented by the employer, court found a genuine issue of fact whether the employee was properly classified as a key employee, given the possibility that many hourly employees may have had yearly incomes far above the plaintiff's).

The determination of which employees at the worksite are among the highest paid ten percent is made based on year-to-date earnings divided by weeks worked by the employee (including weeks in which paid leave was taken). 29 CFR 825.217(c)(1); S. Res. 242, Cong. Rec. S3959, S3970 (April 23, 1996); 29 CFR 825.217(c)(1). Earnings include wages, premium pay (including overtime, shift differential pay), incentive pay (e.g., commissions), and nondiscretionary and discretionary bonuses. 29 CFR 825.217(c)(1); S. Res. 242, Cong. Rec. S3959, S3970 (April 23, 1996); 29 CFR 825.217(c)(1). Earnings do not include incentives whose value is determined at some future date, e.g., stock options, or benefits or perquisites. 29 CFR 825.217(c)(1); S. Res. 242, Cong. Rec. S3959, S3970 (April 23, 1996); 29 CFR 825.217(c)(1).

4. When the "Key Employee" Determination is Made

The determination of whether a salaried employee is among the highest paid ten percent is made at the time the employee gives notice of the need for FMLA leave. 29 USC 2614(b)(1)(B); 29 CFR 825.217(c)(2); 2 USC 1312(a)(1) (incorporating 29 USC 2614 into CAA); S. Res. 242, Cong. Rec. S3959, S3970 (April 23, 1996); 29 CFR 825.217(c)(2); 3 USC 412(a)(1) (incorporating 29 USC 26214 into PEOAA).

C. SUBSTANTIAL AND GRIEVOUS ECONOMIC INJURY

The Achilles' Heel of the applicability of the key employee exemption to federal agencies is whether the return of that employee would cause substantial and grievous economic injury to the employer or office.

1. General Rule

To deny restoration to a key employee, the employer or employing office must establish that restoring the employee would cause "substantial and grievous economic injury" to the employer's operations. 29 CFR 2614(b)(1)(A); 29 CFR 825.218(a); 2 USC 1312(a)(1) (incorporating 29 USC 2614 into CAA); S. Res. 242, Cong. Rec. S3959, S3970 (April 23, 1996), 825.218(a); 3 USC 412(a)(1) (incorporating 29 USC 26214 into PEOAA); *see Meadows v. Texar Fed. Credit Union*, No. 5:05CV158, 2007 U.S. Dist. LEXIS 4456, at *51 (E.D. Jan. 22, 2007).

Note that it is the return of the key employee from FMLA leave, not the loss of the employee due to taking leave that causes the substantial and grievous economic injury. 29 CFR 825.218(a); S. Res. 242, Cong. Rec. S3959, S3970 (April 23, 1996); 29 CFR 825.218(a); *see Kephart v. Cherokee County, North Carolina*, No. 99–1789, 2000 U.S. App. LEXIS 18924, at *8 (4th Cir. Aug. 4, 2000); *Meadows*, 2007 U.S. Dist. LEXIS 4456, at *51; *O'Grady v. Catholic Health Partners Services*, No. 00–C–7144, 2002 U.S. Dist. LEXIS 2182 (N.D. Ill. Feb. 13, 2002) (restoration may be denied only when restoration itself—not the employee's absence—will cause substantial and grievous economic injury).

2. When the Determination is Made

The statute and the regulations are at odds when the determination is made that restoring the key employee would cause "substantial and grievous economic injury" to the employer's operations. *Kephart v. Cherokee County, North Carolina*, 52 F. Supp. 2d 607, 608 (W.D. N.C. 1999), *rev'd on other grounds, remanded*, No. 99-1789, 2000 U.S. App. LEXIS 18924 (4th Cir. Aug. 4, 2000). The Statute requires the employer to provide notice to the employee as soon as such determination is made that substantial and grievous injury would result from the return of the employee. 29 USC 2614(b)(1)(B). Obviously, in order to notify the employee, the employer must have made the determination. The implementing regulations require that the determination be made at the time restoration is sought. *Kephart v. Cherokee County, North Carolina*, 52 F. Supp. 2d 607, 609 (W.D. N.C. 1999), *rev'd on other grounds, remanded*, No. 99-1789, 2000 U.S. App. LEXIS 18924 (4th Cir. Aug. 4, 2000). In *Kephart*, the district court applied both the statutory and regulatory standard in finding that the employer, both at the time of its determination that the plaintiff was a key employee, and at the time he requested reinstatement, considered the economic impact of returning the employee. *Kephart*, 52 F. Supp. 2d at 611.

3. Standard of Determination

Due to the fact-specific nature of the determination, a precise test cannot be set for the level of hardship or injury to the employer that must be sustained. 29 CFR 825.218(c); S. Res. 242, Cong. Rec. S3959, S3970 (April 23, 1996); 29 CFR 825.218(c); *see Kephart v. Cherokee County, North Carolina*, No. 99–1789, 2000 U.S. App. LEXIS 18924 (4th Cir. Aug. 4, 2000); *Meadows*, 2007 U.S. Dist. LEXIS 4456, at *51; *Oby v. Baton Rouge Marriott*, 329 F. Supp. 2d 772 (M.D. La. 2004); *O'Grady*, 2002 U.S. Dist. LEXIS 2182; *Kephart v. Cherokee County, North Carolina*, 52 F. Supp. 2d 607, 609 (W.D. N.C. 1999), *rev'd on other grounds*, No. 99–1789, 2000 U.S. App. LEXIS 18924 (4th Cir. Aug. 4, 2000).

If the reinstatement of a key employee threatens the economic viability of the employer (Title I) or employing office (CAA), that would constitute substantial and grievous economic injury. 29 CFR 825.218(c); S. Res. 242, Cong. Rec. S3959, S3970 (April 23, 1996); 29 CFR 825.218(c); *see Kephart v. Cherokee County, North Carolina*, No. 99–1789, 2000 U.S. App. LEXIS 18924 (4th Cir. Aug. 4, 2000); *Meadows*, 2007 U.S. Dist. LEXIS 4456, at *51; *Oby*, 329 F. Supp. 2d 772.

A lesser injury, which causes substantial long-term economic injury, would also be sufficient. 29 CFR 825.218(c); S. Res. 242, Cong. Rec. S3959, S3970 (April 23, 1996); 29 CFR 825.218(c); *see Kephart v. Cherokee County, North Carolina*, No. 99–1789, 2000 U.S. App. LEXIS 18924 (4th Cir. Aug. 4, 2000); *Meadows v. Texar Fed. Credit Union*, No. 5:05CV158, 2007 U.S. Dist. LEXIS 4456, at *53 (E.D. Jan. 22, 2007); *Oby v. Baton Rouge Marriott*, 329 F. Supp. 2d 772, 2004 U.S. Dist. LEXIS 15426, at *28 (M.D. La. 2004).

Minor inconveniences and costs that an employer or employing office would experience in the normal course of doing business would not constitute substantial and grievous economic injury. 29 CFR 825.218(c); S. Res. 242, Cong. Rec. S3959, S3970 (April 23, 1996); 29 CFR 825.218(c); *see Kephart v. Cherokee County, North Carolina*, No. 99–1789, 2000 U.S. App. LEXIS 18924 (4th Cir. Aug. 4, 2000); *Meadows*, 2007 U.S. Dist. LEXIS 4456, at *53; *O'Grady v. Catholic Health Partners Services*, No. 00–C–7144, 2002 U.S. Dist. LEXIS 2182 (N.D. Ill. Feb. 13, 2002). When evaluating whether substantial and grievous economic injury will occur as a result of restoring a key employee to work following FMLA leave, an employer or employing office may take into account its ability to temporarily replace (or temporarily do without) the employee on FMLA leave. 29 CFR 825.218(b); S. Res. 242, Cong. Rec. S3959, S3970 (April 23, 1996); 29 CFR 825.218(b). If permanent replacement is unavoidable, the cost of then reinstating the employee can be considered in evaluating whether substantial and grievous economic injury will occur from restoration; in other words, the effect on the operations of the company of reinstating the employee in an equivalent position. 29 CFR 825.218(b); S. Res. 242, Cong. Rec. S3959, S3970 (April 23, 1996); 29 CFR 825.218(b); *see Kephart v. Cherokee County, North Carolina*, No. 99–1789, 2000 U.S. App. LEXIS 18924 (4th Cir. Aug. 4, 2000).

The court in *Oby v. Baton Rouge Marriott*, 329 F. Supp. 2d 772, 2004 U.S. Dist. LEXIS 15426, at *28 (M.D. La. 2004), found that the Baton Rouge Marriott would have suffered substantial and grievous economic injury had it reinstated plaintiff to the position of executive housekeeper. As evidence, the court noted that plaintiff was replaced and the cost of paying each of the two executive housekeepers $41,000 per year would cause the Baton Rouge Marriott substantial and grievous economic injury. The court's decision may be better explained by plaintiff's failure to present any evidence to rebut the employer's evidence that it would have suffered substantial and grievous economic injury had it reinstated plaintiff. It is difficult to imagine circumstances where the denying the reinstatement of a key employee in the federal government would threaten the economic viability of the federal government as a whole, an individual federal employer, or an employing office. It is equally hard to imagine that substantial long-term economic injury would result from the return of a key employee to the same or equivalent federal position. Certainly, this is more likely to happen in the smaller employing offices governed by the CAA and the PEOAA. These offices have strict, limited budgets that may be relatively inflexible. If an employing office were to permanently replace a key employee, it may not have the financial flexibility to reemploy that individual. Of course, that position depends on the assumption that busting a limited budget for an employing office is equivalent to substantial long-term economic injury. Clearly that is debatable.

For example, in *Kephart v. Cherokee County, North Carolina*, 52 F. Supp. 2d 607, 608 (W.D. N.C. 1999), *rev'd on other grounds, remanded*, No. 99-1789, 2000 U.S. App. LEXIS 18924 (4th Cir. Aug. 4, 2000), the district court found that a county employer sustained its burden of establishing that the return of a "key employee," the county tax assessor, would cause "substantial and grievous economic injury" to the employer under the circumstances. In support of its conclusion, the court cited the fact that the county assessor was one of the highest paid ten percent employees in the county, that he took leave just before the crush of tax season, that the position had to be filled to get the tax bills out, and, by statute, once the position was filled the appointment would be for the remainder of the term. The county could not, therefore, use a temporary assessor. Moreover, if the tax bills did not get out on time, the economic viability of the county would be placed in jeopardy. The limited budget of the county, moreover, did not permit the hiring of a temporary employee, or the rehiring of the plaintiff; the funds simply were not budgeted. According to the court, "[a]lthough no case law has yet defined 'substantial and grievous economic injury,' the court finds the facts of this situation fit into the definition as a matter of law." *Kephart*, 52 F. Supp. 2d at 610–11.

On appeal, the Fourth Circuit reversed finding that the existence of a material issue of fact precluded the award of summary judgment to the county. Specifically, the court held that deposition testimony established that in December 1996 when the plaintiff requested reinstatement, the county could have returned the individual who replaced the plaintiff to her original position, because she had only an interim appointment as tax assessor, and reinstated the plaintiff to the position of tax assessor with no resulting economic injury. Under the DOL regulations, after an employer has notified a key employee that substantial and grievous economic injury would result from the employee's reinstatement, "an employee is still entitled to request reinstatement at the end of the leave period." 29 CFR 825.219(d). At that point, the employer must again determine whether there will be substantial and grievous economic injury from reinstatement based on the facts at that time. The court held that on remand the county must show that, based on the facts in December 1996 when the plaintiff requested reinstatement, substantial and grievous economic injury would have resulted from the plaintiff's reinstatement.

Under the broad definition of employer under Title I, the prospect that the return of a single key employee would wreak substantial long-term economic injury to the federal government as a whole, or even a single federal employer, would appear remote. If, however, a single supervisor, more than likely an SES-level manager who would have key employees under his or her responsibility, is considered an employer for purposes of the FMLA, the argument that the return of a key employee would result in substantial and grievous economic injury has a higher probability of success, given the budget restrictions that this SES manager may be operating under.

4. Comparison with ADA "Undue Hardship Standard"

The "substantial and grievous economic injury" test under the FMLA is different from and more stringent than, the ADA's "undue hardship" standard for reasonable accommodation. 29 CFR 825.218(d); S. Res. 242, Cong. Rec. S3959, S3970 (April 23, 1996); 29 CFR 825.218(d); *see Kephart v. Cherokee County, North Carolina*, No. 99-1789, 2000 U.S. App. LEXIS 18924 (4th Cir. Aug. 4, 2000). The DOL explained the difference (Preamble, 29 CFR 825.218) as follows:

> FMLA creates a narrow exception to the reinstatement rights of a key employee, whereas ADA's standard provides a measure of the reasonableness of any accommodation. Additionally, the definitions of the two terms suggest that "substantial and grievous economic injury" is more stringent than "undue hardship." The FMLA rules define "substantial and grievous economic injury" to include "substantial long-term injury." Undue hardship is

defined as "significant difficulty or expense" (see Appendix to 29 CFR Part 1630.2(p)). Accordingly, the final rule is revised to clarify that the two standards are, in fact, different, and that the FMLA's standard is more stringent than the ADA's "undue hardship" standard.

D. EMPLOYER NOTICE TO KEY EMPLOYEE

Agencies and employing offices have three notice obligations that must be satisfied to exercise the key employee exemption and deny job restoration following FMLA leave. [For a discussion of the employer's obligations to notify employees of their rights and responsibilities under the FMLA, see Chapter 8, "Notice Requirements."]

1. Initial Notice of Key Employee Qualification and Consequences

a. General Rule

An employer who believes that reinstatement may be denied to a key employee, must give written notice to the employee at the time the employee gives notice of the need for FMLA leave (or when FMLA leave commences, if earlier) that he or she qualifies as a key employee. 29 CFR 825.219(a), 825.301(b)(1)(vi); S. Res. 242, Cong. Rec. S3959, S3970–71 (April 23, 1996); 29 CFR 825.219(a), 825.301(b)(1)(vi); see *Kephart v. Cherokee County, North Carolina*, No. 99–1789, 2000 U.S. App. LEXIS 18924 (4th Cir. Aug. 4, 2000); *Meadows v. Texar Fed. Credit Union*, No. 5:05CV158, 2007 U.S. Dist. LEXIS 4456, at *53–54 (E.D. Jan. 22, 2007); *Banks, v. CBOCS West, Inc.*, No. 1 C 795, 2006 U.S. Dist. LEXIS 13930, at *5-6 (N.D. Ill. Feb. 1, 2006); *Oby v. Baton Rouge Marriott*, 329 F. Supp. 2d 772 (M.D. La. 2004); *Panza v. The Grappone Companies, Inc. et al.*, No. 99–221–M, 2000 U.S. Dist. LEXIS 16390 (D. N.H. Oct. 20, 2000); *Woodford v. Community Action of Greene County, Inc. et al.*, 103 F. Supp. 2d 97, 100–101 (N.D. N.Y. 2000).

At the same time, the employer must also fully inform the employee of the potential consequences with respect to reinstatement and maintenance of health benefits if the employer should determine that substantial and grievous economic injury to the employer's operations would occur if the employee is reinstated from FMLA leave. 29 CFR 825.219(a), 825.301(b)(1)(vi); S. Res. 242, Cong. Rec. S3959, S3970–71 (April 23, 1996); 29 CFR 825.219(a), 825.301(b)(1)(vi); see *Kephart v. Cherokee County, North Carolina*, No. 99–1789, 2000 U.S. App. LEXIS 18924 (4th Cir. Aug. 4, 2000); *Meadows v. Texar Fed. Credit Union*, No. 5:05CV158, 2007 U.S. Dist. LEXIS 4456, at *53–54 (E.D. Jan. 22, 2007); *Oby v. Baton Rouge Marriott*, 329 F. Supp. 2d 772 (M.D. La. 2004); *Panza v. The Grappone Companies, Inc. et al.*, No. 99–221–M, 2000 U.S. Dist. LEXIS 16390 (D. N.H. Oct. 20, 2000) (the term "notice" refers to both the notice of status as a key employee and notice of decision not to restore); *Woodford v. Community Action of Greene County, Inc. et al.*, 103 F. Supp. 2d 97, 100–101 (N.D.N.Y. 2000).

b. When and How Initial Notice Must be Provided

The initial notice must be in writing. 29 CFR 825.219(a); S. Res. 242, Cong. Rec. S3959, S3970 (April 23, 1996); 29 CFR 825.219(a); see *Meadows*, 2007 U.S. Dist. LEXIS 4456, at *53–54; *Oby*, 329 F. Supp. 2d 772; *Panza*, 2000 U.S. Dist. LEXIS 16390 (written notice).

The regulations require that an employer must "give" the written notice to the employee. It is unclear how an employer must give the notice to the employee. The regulations do, however, specify that personal service or service by certified mail is required for the notice that the employer has determined that substantial and grievous economic injury would result from the return of the employee. 29 CFR 825.218(b); S. Res. 242, Cong. Rec. S3959, S3970 (April 23, 1996); 29 CFR 825.219(b). Where notice of substantial and economic injury is made at the same time as the notice of qualification as a key employee, service of both notices should be accomplished certified mail or in person.

The FMLA does not specify when an employer must notify the employee that the employer considers him or her to be a key employee. *Woodford v. Community Action of Greene County, Inc. et al.*, 103 F. Supp. 2d 97, 100–101 (N.D.N.Y. 2000). The regulations implementing the Statute indicate that such notice must be made at the time leave is requested. 29 CFR 825.219(a); S. Res. 242, Cong. Rec. S3959, S3970 (April 23, 1996); 29 CFR 825.219(b). The employer must inform the employee when the employee gives notice of the need for FMLA leave (or when FMLA leave commences, if earlier). *Oby*, 329 F. Supp. 2d 772. If such notice cannot be given immediately because of the need to determine whether the employee is a key employee, it must be given as soon as practicable after being notified of a need for leave (or the commencement of leave, if earlier). *Id.*

In *Woodford v. Community Action of Greene County, Inc. et al.*, 103 F. Supp. 2d 97, 100–101 (N.D.N.Y. 2000), the court held that an interval of two or three days between the plaintiff's request for leave and the written notice that the plaintiff was a key employee and reinstatement would be denied was "not so great as to place Defendants in violation of the CFR's requirement that the employer give written notice 'as soon as practicable' after the request for leave."

When notice of qualification as a key employee will be made separately from the notice of the determination of substantial and grievous economic injury (because, for example, the employer needs more time to make a determination on substantial and grievous economic injury), the regulations do not provide a method for service of the notice. To play it safe, an employer should either personally serve the notice or send it certified mail. If personal service is selected, the employer should require the employee to sign a form signifying that he or she has received the notice. If the employee refuses, have a witness watch the hand delivery.

Under the key employee regulations, an employer has three opportunities to provide the initial notice of key employee qualification and consequences to the employee. An employer must provide the initial written notice either at the time the employee gives notice of the need for FMLA leave, or when FMLA leave commences, if earlier. 29 CFR 825.219(a); S. Res. 242, Cong. Rec. S3959, S3970 (April 23, 1996); 29 CFR 825.219(a).

If the employer needs to determine whether the employee is a key employee, the employer may provide the initial written notice as soon as practicable after being notified of the need for FMLA leave, or the commencement of leave, if earlier. 29 CFR 825.219(a); S. Res. 242, Cong. Rec. S3959, S3970 (April 23, 1996); 29 CFR 825.219(a). It should be noted that the key employee regulations require that the initial notice be given every time a key employee requests leave when the employer believes that reinstatement may be denied.

The general employer notice regulations require notice to every employee regarding, among other things, the employee's status as a key employee, and the potential consequences that restoration may be denied. 29 CFR 825.301(b)(1)(vi); S. Res. 242, Cong. Rec. S3959, S3971 (April 23, 1996); 29 CFR 825.301(b)(1)(vi); *see Wilson v. Lemington Home for the Aged*, 159 F. Supp. 2d 186, 193 (W.D. Pa. 2001). This notice must also be in writing, but need only be given once during each six-month period, on the occasion of the employee first request for FMLA leave during that period. 29 CFR 825.301(c); S. Res. 242, Cong. Rec. S3959, S3971 (April 23, 1996); 29 CFR 825.301(c). It would appear that this notice is in addition to the notice specifically required by the key employee regulations.

c. Consequences of Failure to Provide Initial Notice

An employer who fails to provide timely initial notice will lose the right to deny restoration, even if substantial and grievous economic injury will result from reinstatement. 29 CFR 825.219(a); S. Res. 242, Cong. Rec. S3959, S3970 (April 23, 1996); 29 CFR 825.219(a); *see Kephart v. Cherokee County, North Carolina*, No. 99–1789, 2000 U.S. App. LEXIS 18924 (4th Cir. Aug. 4, 2000); *Oby v. Baton Rouge Marriott*, 329 F. Supp. 2d 772, 2004 U.S. Dist. LEXIS 15426, at *28 (M.D. La. 2004); *Panza v. The Grappone Companies, Inc. et al.*, No. 99–221–M, 2000 U.S. Dist. LEXIS 16390 (D. N.H. Oct. 20, 2000) (defendants precluded as a matter of law from seeking refuge in 29 USC 2614(b) for failure to restore key employee where defendants did not inform the plaintiff that he qualified as a key employee).

The penalty imposed for violation of the notice provision is unconscionable and highly susceptible to constitutional challenge. If the employer was correct when it designated the return of this key employee as a threat to the economic viability of the firm, forcing the employer to take the employee back as a penalty for a delay in getting the employee the initial key notice not only punishes the employer, but also punishes the other employees as well as the returning employee if the firm goes under.

Because the key employee exemption is not generally viable in the federal sector, application of the rule that forces employers to return key employees for minor notice violations would probably not have the same degree of impact on a federal employer as it would on a small private sector employer.

In the wake of the Supreme Court's decision in *Ragsdale v. Wolverine World-Wide Inc.*, 535 U.S. 81, 152 L. Ed. 2d 167, 122 S. Ct. 1155 (2002), the penalty provision of the initial notice required for key employees appears to be in jeopardy of being found invalid. In that case, the Supreme Court struck down the portion of 29 CFR 825.700(a) that penalized employers for failing to notify employees that leave was being counted against the employee's 12-week FMLA leave entitlement. As a penalty, the leave the employee took could not be counted toward the employee's 12 weeks of FMLA leave, effectively extending the amount of FMLA leave available to an employee beyond the 12-week statutory maximum.

Here, many of the same factors cited by the Supreme Court in *Ragsdale* apply to the penalty imposed for violation of the initial key employee notice provision. First, as in *Ragsdale*, the regulations' automatic presumption of an impairment of FMLA rights as a result of an employer's failure to timely inform an employee of an FMLA key employee designation, runs contrary to the statute's remedial scheme, which places the burden of proving a real impairment on the employee. Second, the penalty imposed, substantial and grievous economic injury by forcing the return of the key employee, does not bear a substantial relation to the harm suffered by the employee, which might be a minor delay in receipt of such notice. Finally, compared with the $100 fine imposed for failure to display the FMLA poster (the only penalty provision for a failure to provide notice contained in the Statute), the infliction of substantial and grievous economic injury on the employer is unreasonable.

2. Notice of Substantial and Grievous Economic Injury

a. General Rule

As soon as an employer makes a good faith determination, based on the facts available, that substantial and grievous economic injury to its operations will result if a key employee who has given notice of the need for FMLA leave or is using FMLA leave is reinstated, the employer must notify the employee in writing of its determination, that it cannot deny FMLA leave, and that it intends to deny restoration to employment on completion of the FMLA leave. 29 USC 2614(b)(1)(B); 29 CFR 825.219(b); S. Res. 242, Cong. Rec. S3959, S3970 (April 23, 1996); 29 CFR 825.219(b); *see Meadows v. Texar Fed. Credit Union*, No. 5:05CV158, 2007 U.S. Dist. LEXIS 4456, at *54 (E.D. Jan. 22, 2007).

This notice must explain the basis for the employer's finding that substantial and grievous economic injury will result, and, if leave has commenced, must provide the employee a reasonable time in which to return to work, taking into account the circumstances, such as the length of leave and the urgency of the need for the employee to return to work. 29 CFR 825.219(b); S. Res. 242, Cong. Rec. S3959, S3970 (April 23, 1996); 29 CFR 825.219(b); *see Meadows v. Texar Fed. Credit Union*, No. 5:05CV158, 2007 U.S. Dist. LEXIS 4456, at *53–54 (E.D. Jan. 22, 2007). This notification does not constitute termination, as the employee is still entitled to work for the employer, but the individual's original position may no longer be available. *Kelley v. DecisionOne Corporation*, Case Nos. 00–CV–32, 00–CV–968, 2000 U.S. Dist. LEXIS 17508 (E.D. Pa. Dec. 7, 2000), aff'd, 276 F.3d 577 (3d Cir. 2001).

b. Timing and Manner of Notice

An employer must provide the notice of substantial and grievous economic injury "as soon as" the determination is made. 29 CFR 825.219(b); S. Res. 242, Cong. Rec. S3959, S3970 (April 23, 1996); 29 CFR 825.219(b); *see Meadows*, 2007 U.S. Dist. LEXIS 4456, at *53–54. It is anticipated that an employer will ordinarily be able to give such notice prior to the employee starting leave. 29 CFR 825.219(b); S. Res. 242, Cong. Rec. S3959, S3970 (April 23, 1996); 29 CFR 825.219(b); *see Meadows*, 2007 U.S. Dist. LEXIS 4456, at *53–54.

It is unclear what "as soon as" means in terms of days. In other contexts, "as soon as practicable" means within two business days, absent extenuating circumstances. *See* 29 CFR 825.110(d); S. Res. 242, Cong. Rec. S3959, S3962 (April 23, 1996); 29 CFR 825.110(d). There is nothing in the regulations to indicate that as soon as determined means the same thing as soon as practicable. Clearly, as soon as determined means a relatively short period of time. *See Woodford v. Community Action of Greene County, Inc. et al.*, 103 F. Supp. 2d 97, 100–101 (N.D.N.Y. 2000) (court held that an interval of two or three days between the plaintiff's request for leave and written notice that the plaintiff was a key employee and reinstatement would be denied was "not so great as to place Defendants in violation of the CFR's requirement that the employer give written notice 'as soon as practicable' after the request for leave").

This notice must be served either in person or by certified mail. 29 CFR 825.219(b); S. Res. 242, Cong. Rec. S3959, S3970 (April 23, 1996); 29 CFR 825.219(b); *see Meadows*, 2007 U.S. Dist. LEXIS 4456, at *53–54. Note that if this notice is available at the same time as the notice that the employee qualifies as a key employee, service should be obtained both by certified mail and in person.

c. Consequences of Employer Failure to Provide Notice

While § 825.219(b) does not contain its own penalty provision, it appears that the prior penalty provision applies to both the initial notice and substantial and grievous economic injury notice. Refer above to the discussion of the penalty provision for the initial notice of key employee designation.

3. Notice of Denial of Restoration

a. General Rule

A key employee retains the right to request reinstatement at the end of the FMLA leave period. 29 CFR 825.219(d); S. Res. 242, Cong. Rec. S3959, S3970 (April 23, 1996); 29 CFR 825.219(d); *see Kephart v. Cherokee County, North Carolina*, No. 99–1789, 2000 U.S. App. LEXIS 18924 (4th Cir. Aug. 4, 2000). An employee may request reinstatement even if he or she failed to return to work after receipt of the notice that substantial and grievous economic injury will result if the employee is reinstated to employment. 29 CFR 825.219(d); S. Res. 242, Cong. Rec. S3959, S3970 (April 23, 1996); 29 CFR 825.219(d). If the employee requests reinstatement, the employer must again determine whether there will be substantial and grievous economic injury from reinstatement, based on the facts at that time. 29 CFR 825.219(d); S. Res. 242, Cong. Rec. S3959, S3970 (April 23, 1996); 29 CFR 825.219(d).; *see Kephart v. Cherokee County, North Carolina*, No. 99–1789, 2000 U.S. App. LEXIS 18924 (4th Cir. Aug. 4, 2000).

b. Timing and Method of Notice

If it is determined that substantial and grievous economic injury will result, the employer must notify the employee in writing of the denial of restoration. The notification must be made in person or by certified mail. No time limit is set for providing this notice.

c. Consequences of Failure to Provide Notice

The regulations do not provide a penalty for an employer's failure to provide this notice. In *Banks, v. CBOCS West, Inc.*, No. 1 C 795, 2006 U.S. Dist. LEXIS 13930, at *5-6 (N.D. Ill. Feb. 1, 2006), the employer notified the employee of his status as a key employee, but failed to notify Banks of its decision to deny restoration. The court allowed the employee of to proceed with his claim that he was demoted in retaliation for requesting FMLA leave.

E. RIGHTS OF KEY EMPLOYEES

1. Return to Work

As part of the employer's notice of substantial and grievous economic injury, an employer must notify an employee whose FMLA leave has already commenced that the employee has a reasonable period of time on receipt of the employer's notice in which to return to work. 29 CFR 825.219(b); S. Res. 242, Cong. Rec. S3959, S3970 (April 23, 1996); 29 CFR 825.219(b). In determining what constitutes a reasonable period of time, the employer must take into account the circumstances, such as the length of the leave and the urgency of the need for the employee to return to work. 29 CFR 825.219(b); S. Res. 242, Cong. Rec. S3959, S3970 (April 23, 1996); 29 CFR 825.219(b).

The regulation does not specifically require an employee to notify the employer that he or she has elected to return to work. Rather, it simply requires a return within a reasonable period of time.

Agencies should not set an arbitrary deadline as the reasonable period for the employee to return to work. For example, agencies should not apply the same rule to everyone, or simply make up a rule that, say, ten days seems reasonable. An employer must be able to demonstrate that it took all of the facts into consideration in determining what a reasonable period of time would be.

The rules do not specify what happens if the employer blocks an employee's return to work by imposing an unreasonable or arbitrary period of time for the employee to return. Presumably, the employer will be found to have interfered with the employee's FMLA rights, and, at the end of the day, the employer may have to accept the return of the employee, with back pay, benefits, and payment of attorney fees. Agencies, therefore, need to act reasonably in determining what constitutes a reasonable period of time when a key employee elects to return to work from FMLA leave.

2. Maintenance of Health Benefits

If an employee elects not to return to work in response to the employer's notification of intent to deny restoration, the employee continues to be entitled to maintenance of health benefits and the employer may not recover its cost of health benefit plan premiums. 29 CFR 825.219(b); S. Res. 242, Cong. Rec. S3959, S3970 (April 23, 1996); 29 CFR 825.219(b). [For a further discussion of an employer's obligations to maintain health care benefits during the course of FMLA leave, see Chapter 12, "Maintenance of Benefits."] A key employee's rights under the FMLA continue unless and until the employee either gives notice that he or she no longer wishes to return to work, or the employer actually denies reinstatement at the conclusion of the leave period. 29 CFR 825.219(b); S. Res. 242, Cong. Rec. S3959, S3970 (April 23, 1996); 29 CFR 825.219(b). Again, the regulations do not require an employee to notify the employer of his or her intent not to return to work from FMLA leave.

F. BURDEN OF PROOF

The key employee defense to job restoration is an affirmative defense. *Kephart v. Cherokee County, North Carolina*, No. 99-1789, 2000 U.S. App. LEXIS 18924 (4th Cir. Aug. 4, 2000). Defendants have the burden of proving: (1) notice of intent to terminate; (2) a showing of "substantial and grievous economic injury to the operations of the employer"; and (3) a showing that the plaintiff was within the top ten percent of employees in wage earnings. *Id*. The first and third elements require objective showings; however, the second element is inherently subjective—just the type of issue juries were designed to resolve. *Id*. Note that the court later resolved this issue as a matter of law in favor of the employer. *See Kephart v. Cherokee County, North Carolina*, 52 F. Supp. 2d 607, 611 (W.D.N.C. 1999), *rev'd on other grounds*, No. 99-1789, 2000 U.S. App. LEXIS 18924 (4th Cir. Aug. 4, 2000).

VI. SPECIAL RULES GOVERNING CERTAIN SCHOOLS

A. OVERVIEW

Title I and the CAA have special rules that apply to employees of certain schools. Title II does not contain special rules for school employees. What follows addresses the special FMLA rules for employees of certain schools pursuant to Title I and the CAA.

B. APPLICATION

1. Covered Schools

Under Title I, the FMLA applies to any "local educational employer," as defined in § 1471(12) of the Elementary and Secondary Education Act of 1965, 20 USC 2891(12), and any eligible employee of the employer. 29 USC 2618(a)(1)(A); 29 CFR 825.600(a). It also applies to any private elementary or secondary school and an eligible employee of the school. 29 USC 2618(a)(1)(B); 29 CFR 825.600(a). The special school rule does not apply to other kinds of educational institutions, such as colleges and universities, trade schools, and preschools. 29 CFR 825.600(a).

The special school provisions of Title I of the FMLA are not directly incorporated into the CAA. 2 USC 1312(a)(1) (incorporating §§ 101 through 105 of the FMLA, 29 USC 2611 through §2615; the special school provisions in Title I are set forth in § 108, 29 USC 2618). Nevertheless, regulations implementing the CAA include special rules governing certain school employees. S. Res. 242, Cong. Rec. S3959, S3975 (April 23, 1996); 29 CFR 825.600-604.

2. Covered School Employees

Different rules apply to different employees of covered schools.

a. Instructional Employees

Special school rules affecting the taking of intermittent leave or leave on a reduced leave schedule, or leave near the end of an academic term only apply to "instructional employees." 29 CFR 825.600(c); S. Res. 242, Cong. Rec. S3959, S3975

(April 23, 1996), 825. 600(c). Covered instructional employees are those whose principal function is to teach and instruct students in a class, a small group, or an individual setting. 29 CFR 825.600(c); S. Res. 242, Cong. Rec. S3959, S3975 (April 23, 1996); 29 CFR 825.600(c). The cited regulations further provide that the term includes:

- Teachers
- Athletic coaches
- Driving instructors
- Special education assistants, such as signers for the hearing impaired.

Those excluded from the definition of instructional employees (29 CFR 825.600(c); S. Res. 242, Cong. Rec. S3959, S3975 (April 23, 1996); 29 CFR 825. 600(c)) include:

- Teacher assistants or aides who do not have as their principal job actual teaching or instructing
- Counselors
- Psychologists
- Curriculum specialists
- Cafeteria workers
- Maintenance workers
- Bus drivers.

b. All Employees

The special rules, which apply to restoration to an equivalent position, apply to all employees of local educational agencies. 29 CFR 825.600(c); S. Res. 242, Cong. Rec. S3959, S3975 (April 23, 1996); 29 CFR 825. 600(c).

C. RETURN TO WORK RIGHTS

Generally, an employee must be restored to the same or an equivalent position when FMLA leave is no longer needed. That rule is modified in certain instances for instructional employees of covered schools.

1. Intermittent Leave or Leave on a Reduced Leave Schedule

The right of an instructional school employee to return to work from FMLA leave taken on an intermittent or reduced leave schedule basis is unchanged by the special school rules. As set forth more fully in Chapter 10, "Leave Amount and Scheduling," the special school rules in this area allow agencies more flexibility in handling such requests, but do not alter the agencies obligations to accept an employee returning from FMLA leave taken on an intermittent or reduced leave schedule.

This special rule applies to eligible instructional employees when the following conditions (29 CFR 825.601a)(1); S. Res. 242, Cong. Rec. S3959, S3975 (April 23, 1996); 29 CFR 825. 601(a)(1)) are met:

- Intermittent or Reduced Schedule FMLA leave is needed;
- Due to a serious health condition;
- The leave is foreseeable based on planned medical treatment; and
- The employee would be on leave for more than 20 percent of the total number of working days over the period the leave would extend.

Where the above conditions are met, the school employer may require the employee to choose either to: (1) take leave for a period or periods of a particular duration, not greater than the duration of the planned treatment; or (2) transfer temporarily to an available alternative position for which the employee is qualified, has equivalent pay and benefits and better accommodates recurring periods of leave than does the employee's regular position. 29 CFR 825.601a)(1); S. Res. 242, Cong. Rec. S3959, S3975 (April 23, 1996); 29 CFR 825.601(a)(1).

The term "periods of a particular duration" means a block or blocks of time beginning no earlier than the first day for which leave is needed, and may include an uninterrupted period of leave. 29 CFR 825.601a)(2); S. Res. 242, Cong. Rec. S3959, S3975 (April 23, 1996); 29 CFR 825.601(a)(2). There is no other restriction on the employee's ability to return to work under either option.

2. Leave Near the End of Academic Term

There are special rules that apply where an instructional employee begins FMLA leave more than five weeks before the end of an academic term, less than five weeks before the end of an academic term, and less than three weeks before the end of an academic term. These rules place restrictions on an employee's unfettered ability to return to work on the conclusion of the need for FMLA leave.

a. Leave Taken More Than Five Weeks From End of Academic Term

Where an instructional employee begins FMLA leave more than five weeks before the end of the academic term, the school (29 USC 2618(d)(1); 29 CFR 825.602(a)(1); S. Res. 242, Cong. Rec. S3959, S3975 (April 23, 1996); 29 CFR 825. 601(a)(1)) may require the employee to continue taking leave until the end of the term (i.e., delay return to work) when:

- The leave will last at least three weeks; and
- The employee would return to work during the three-week period before the end of the term.

"Academic term" means the school semester, which typically ends near the end of the calendar year and the end of the spring each school year. 29 CFR 825.602(b); S. Res. 242, Cong. Rec. S3959, S3975 (April 23, 1996); 29 CFR 825.602(b). In no case may a school have more than two academic terms or semesters each year for purposes of the FMLA. 29 CFR 825.602(b); S. Res. 242, Cong. Rec. S3959, S3975 (April 23, 1996); 29 CFR 825.602(b).

b. Leave Taken Less Than Five Weeks From End of Academic Term

Where an eligible instructional employee takes FMLA leave for a purpose other than the employee's own serious health condition during the five-week period before the end of an academic term, the school (29 USC 2618(d)(2); 29 CFR 825.602(a)(2); S. Res. 242, Cong. Rec. S3959, S3975 (April 23, 1996); 29 CFR 825. 601(a)(2)) may require the employee to continue taking leave until the end of the academic term if:

- The leave will last more than two weeks; and
- The employee will return to work during the two-week period before the end of the academic term.

c. Leave Begins Less Than Three Weeks Before End of Academic Term

Where the employee begins FMLA leave for a purpose other than the employee's own serious health condition during the three-week period before the end of a academic term, and the leave will last more than five working days, the employer may require the employee to continue taking leave until the end of the academic term. 29 USC 2618(d)(3); 29 CFR 825.602(a)(3); S. Res. 242, Cong. Rec. S3959, S3975 (April 23, 1996); 29 CFR 825. 601(a)(3)).

d. Leave Calculation and Return to Work

Where an employee is required to take leave until the end of an academic term, only the period of leave until the employee is ready and able to return to work may be charged against the employee's FMLA leave entitlement. 29 CFR 825.603(b); S. Res. 242, Cong. Rec. S3959, S3975 (April 23, 1996), 825. 603(b). The reason for this is that, because the employer has the option not to require the employee to stay on FMLA leave until the end of the school term, any additional leave required by the employer to end of the school term is not counted as FMLA leave. 29 CFR 825.603(b); S. Res. 242, Cong. Rec. S3959, S3975 (April 23, 1996); 29 CFR 825.603(b). The school is also required to maintain the employee's group health insurance and restore the employee to the same or equivalent job, including other benefits, at the conclusion of this extended, non–FMLA leave period to the end of the academic term.

D. EQUIVALENT POSITION

All eligible school employees have the right to be returned to their same or an equivalent position on the conclusion of FMLA leave. Restoration to an equivalent position, however, is treated differently than is generally required under 29 CFR 825.215; S. Res. 242, Cong. Rec. S3959, S3969 (April 23, 1996); 29 CFR 825. 215.

1. General Rule

The determination of how an employee is to be restored to an equivalent position on return from FMLA leave is made on the basis of "established school board policies and practices, private school policies and practices, and collective bargaining agreements." 29 USC 2618(e); 29 CFR 825.604; S. Res. 242, Cong. Rec. S3959, S3975 (April 23, 1996); 29 CFR 825. 604.

Any established policy that is used as a basis to restore an employee to an equivalent position must provide substantially the same protections as provided in the Act for reinstated employees. 29 CFR 825.604 (*citing* 29 CFR 825.215); S. Res. 242, Cong. Rec. S3959, S3975 (April 23, 1996); 29 CFR 825.604. In other words, the policy or collective bargaining agreement must provide for restoration to an equivalent position with equivalent conditions of employment. 29 CFR 825.604; S. Res. 242, Cong. Rec. S3959, S3975 (April 23, 1996); 29 CFR 825.604. For example, an employee may not be restored to a position requiring additional licensure or certification. 29 CFR 825.604; S. Res. 242, Cong. Rec. S3959, S3975 (April 23, 1996); 29 CFR 825.604.

The regulations do not define what "substantially the same protections" means. Clearly, "substantially the same" does not mean identical or exactly the same. School employers, therefore, would appear to have more leeway in returning an employee to an equivalent position than is normally required. For example, while as a general matter restoration must be to a geographically proximate location, a school board policy or collective bargaining agreement may deviate from this requirement provided the deviation does not result in substantially less employee protections. Preamble, 29 CFR 825.604.

The regulations do not specify what happens in the event the school board policy or collective bargaining agreement is found not to provide substantially the same protections as the general rules governing return to an equivalent position. Presumably, the school employer will be found in violation of the FMLA.

School employers, unions, and organizations representing school employees will want to carefully review school policies and collective bargaining agreements governing the placement of an employee in an equivalent position on return from FMLA leave.

It is unclear whether an employee who is restored to the same position held prior to taking FMLA requires exactly the same terms and condition of employment, or whether substantially the same terms and conditions would be sufficient. As worded, the regulation applies the substantially the same language only to an equivalent position. However, an equivalent position is merely a proxy for the same position. If an equivalent position need only be substantially similar to the former position, it raises the question whether the terms and conditions of employment of the same position need only be substantially the same.

2. Notice to Employees

The regulations require that the established policies or collective bargaining agreements used as a basis for restoration must be in writing, must be made known to the employee prior to taking FMLA leave, and must clearly explain the employee's restoration rights upon return from leave. 29 CFR 825.604; S. Res. 242, Cong. Rec. S3959, S3975 (April 23, 1996); 29 CFR 825.604.

The regulations do not specify what happens if the school employer fails to provide timely or adequate notice, as required. Presumably, the school employer would not be allowed to rely on the special exemption. In that case, it is unclear whether the general requirement that the employee be returned to an equivalent position comes into play (i.e., § 825.215), or whether some other penalty is imposed.

VII. AGENCIES WITH MIXED FMLA RESPONSIBILITIES

Most agencies have employees covered by Titles I and II of the Act. The majority of employees in these mixed agencies are covered by Title II, with a minority covered by Title I. Agencies should not, however, assume that application and compliance with the requirements of Title II of the Act will automatically meet the similar sounding requirements of Title I. In many instances that is simply not the case. Similarly, compliance with the requirements of Title I does not guarantee compliance with the mandates of Title II.

For example, under Title I, the employee's right to return to work is to the position that the employee held when FMLA leave commenced. Under Title II, the right to return to work on the conclusion of FMLA leave is to the employee's permanent position. An employee's permanent position may not be the same as the position that an employee held immediately preceding the commencement of FMLA leave. Therefore, an employer that dutifully applied the Title II requirements to all employees, and returned a Title I employee to his or her permanent position instead of the position the employee held immediately preceding leave commencement, would be in violation of Title I of the Act.

Under Title II, where an employee is returned to an equivalent position, that position must be in the same commuting area. The comparable requirement under Title I provides that the equivalent position must not result in a significant increase in commuting time. While adherence to the commuting requirements of Title II will likely not result in a violation of Title I, the reverse is not necessarily true. An equivalent position that does not significantly increase commuting time for purposes of Title I may violate Title II's requirement that the employee be placed in an equivalent position in the "same" commuting area.

Major differences between Titles I and II involve fitness–for–duty certifications. Title II permits an employer to require the employee to submit to a full-blown medical certification, addressing all of the permissible contents, as a condition of return to work from FMLA leave. Title I, on the other hand, generally requires employers to accept a short statement from the employee's health care provider that the employee is able to return to work. An exception allows Title I employers to apply the fitness–for–duty certification requirements contained in a collective bargaining agreement. Title II does not recognize such an exception.

An employer that applies the Title II fitness–for–duty certification requirement seeking a great deal of medical information regarding Title I employees will violate Title I of the Act every time. Moreover, a Title II employer with a collective bargaining agreement with more strict fitness–for–duty certification requirements will miss an opportunity to manage FMLA leave if it applies the Title II rule to employees covered by Title I because Title II does not recognize such the collective bargaining agreement exception.

The notice provisions of Titles I and II governing fitness–for–duty certifications are dramatically different. Title I has very specific requirements mandating notice to employees that a fitness–for–duty requirement is required as a condition of all employees to return from FMLA leave. Such notice must be included in any written employee handbooks, manuals, or other written material about employee leave and benefits. It must also be provided to each employee every time a request for FMLA leave is made.

Title II, on the other hand, requires notice of a fitness–for–duty requirement, but fails to specify exactly how such notice is to be accomplished. Title II does not specifically require that notice be included in an employee handbook or manual. Nor does it require that specific notice of the requirement that a fitness–for–duty certification is required as a condition of an employee's return from FMLA leave be given to each employee every time FMLA leave is requested. Application of the loose notice requirements of Title II to employees covered by Title I will almost certainly result in an agencies violation of Title I of the Act.

Moreover, an employer that follows the dictates of either Title I or Title II may be missing opportunities to control and therefore diminish the impact of FMLA absences on the workforce. For example, Title I does not require an employer to return an employee to work who is unable to perform all of the essential functions of his or her position on return from leave. There is no such requirement under Title II. While the opportunity for a federal employer to prohibit an employee who is unable to perform all essential functions on return from FMLA leave is more limited than in the private sector, it is not extinct. At minimum, an employer could move to dismiss a claim that the employee's return violated the FMLA. The employer could argue that a Title I employee does not have an FMLA right to return to work if he or she is unable to perform all essential job functions. While the employee may have contractual or other claims if return from leave is denied, the claim will not be based in the Title I of the FMLA, which includes individual supervisor liability, attorney fees, and double damages.

Unlike Title I, Title II does not have special rules addressing so-called key employees or certain school employees. These rules give agencies options to manage the FMLA leave of certain employees. While these options need not be exercised in every case, they do provide management some ability to control the use of FMLA leave by certain Title I employees that is not present under Title II.

The return to work rules of the major FMLA provisions contain substantial differences. Such differences create a minefield for unwary federal agencies who assume that adherence to the requirements of Title II necessarily results in compliance with Title I. The key to avoiding FMLA leave violations and costly litigation is to analyze every request for FMLA leave carefully. Knowing which FMLA leave requirements apply to the employee requesting leave is the first step in that process.

CHAPTER 14
RECORD-KEEPING REQUIREMENTS

I. OVERVIEW

This chapter addresses special record-keeping requirements mandated of employing agencies by the FMLA. Only employing agencies covered by Titles I and II of the Act are mandated to make, keep and preserve FMLA records. Neither the CAA nor the PEOAA contain special FMLA record-keeping requirements.

Section II, "Title I Record-Keeping Requirements", addresses the FMLA record keeping requirements of Title I. "Title II Record-Keeping Requirements" are discussed in Section III, and "FMLA Record-Keeping Under The CAA and The PEOAA" is addressed in Section IV. The rules regarding "Disclosure of FMLA Records" are addressed in Section V. Finally, Section VI, "Mixed Agency FMLA Responsibilities and Record Keeping", addresses record-keeping requirements in agencies with mixed FMLA responsibilities.

II. TITLE I RECORD-KEEPING REQUIREMENTS

A. GENERAL OBLIGATIONS

Covered employers are required to make, keep, and preserve records pertaining to compliance with Title I in accordance with § 11(c) of the Fair Labor Standards Act, 29 USC 211(c), and in accordance with regulations issued by DOL. 29 USC 2616(b). Under the FLSA, the DOL may require a covered employer, by regulations or for enforcement purposes, to:

- make, keep, and preserve any records of the persons employed relating to these persons wages, hours, and other conditions and practices of employment;
- preserve these records for the prescribed time periods;
- prove reports.

The special FMLA record-keeping regulations of Title I are set forth in 29 CFR 825.500.

B. REQUIRED RECORDS

Title I requires covered employers to create and retain two types of records: (1) nonmedical and (2) medical.

1. Nonmedical Records

The type of nonmedical FMLA records that must be maintained is dependent on whether a covered employer has eligible employees.

a. Employing Agencies Without Eligible Employees

The basic Title I record-keeping requirement covers employing agencies with no *eligible employees*. Employee eligibility under Title I has three components: (1) the employee must have been employed by the employing agency for at least 12 months; (2) the employee must have been employed for at least 1,250 hours of service during the 12-month period immediately preceding leave commencement; and (3) the employee must be employed at a worksite with at least 50 employees within 75 miles. 29 CFR 825.110. [For a further discussion of employee eligibility, see Chapter 5, "Employee Eligibility for Leave."]

A covered employing agency that does not employ any eligible employees must maintain basic payroll and identifying employee data, including name, address, and occupation; rate or basis of pay and terms of compensation; daily and weekly hours worked per pay period; additions to or deductions from wages; and total compensation paid. 5 CFR 825.500(d). This is basically the same information already required to be kept pursuant to the FLSA. Preamble, 29 CFR 825.207. According to the DOL, this information is required to enable a covered employer to determine employee eligibility. *Id.*

As set forth more fully in Chapter 3, "FMLA Coverage of the Federal Government," the entire U. S. Government is considered to be a covered employer within the meaning of the FMLA. *See* 29 CFR 108(a) (defining a covered public agency employer under Title I of the FMLA as including the government of the United States). As such, all federal employers, even those without any Title I–covered, eligible employees, are subject to the Title I requirement to maintain certain basic payroll information. While the FLSA requires maintenance of this information already, it is yet another example that the reach of Title I of the FMLA extends to all federal agencies.

b. Employing Agencies With Eligible Employees

Employing agencies with eligible employees have added record-keeping responsibilities beyond basic information requirements. A covered employer who has eligible employees must, pursuant to 29 CFR 825.500(c), maintain records that disclose the following information:

- Basic payroll and identifying employee data, including name, address, and occupation; rate or basis of pay and terms of compensation; daily and weekly hours worked per pay period; additions to or deductions from wages; and total compensation.

- Dates FMLA leave is taken by FMLA eligible employees (e.g. available from time records, requests for leave, etc., if so designated). Leave must be designated in records as FMLA leave; leave so designated may not include leave required under State law or an employer plan which is not also covered by the FMLA.

- The hours of FMLA leave, if the leave is taken by eligible employees in increments of less than one full day.

- Copies of employee notices of leave furnished to the employer under the FMLA, if in writing, and copies of all general and specific notice given to employees as required under the FMLA and these regulations (*see* 825.301(b)). Copies may be maintained in employee personnel files.

- Any documents (including written and electronic documents) describing employee benefits or employer policies and practices regarding the taking of paid and unpaid leaves.

- Premium payments of employee benefits.

- Records of any dispute between the employer and an eligible employee regarding designation of leave as FMLA leave, including any written statement from the employer or employee of the reasons for the designation and for the disagreement.

See Uthell v. Mid-Illinois Concrete, Inc., No. 05-4034-JLF, 2006 U.S. Dist. LEXIS 89314, at *11-12 (S.D. Ill. Dec. 11, 2006); *Dupee v. Klaff's, Inc.*, 462 F. Supp. 2d 244, 249 (D. Conn. 2006).

When an employing agency has Title I eligible employees, the regulations require that certain records be kept regarding the FMLA activities of those employees, as well as general information not specifically tied to any particular eligible employee. For example, dates FMLA leave is taken, the amount of time spent on FMLA leave, and disputes regarding FMLA designation are tied only to eligible employees. 29 CFR 825.500(c)(2), (3), and (7). An employer that fails to keep such records would be in violation of the Act. *Slaughter v. American Building Maintenance Co. of New York*, 64 F. Supp. 2d 319, 330, n. 9 (S.D.N.Y. 1999).

In *Dupee v. Klaff's, Inc.*, 462 F. Supp. 2d 244, 249 (D. Conn. 2006), the employee moved for an adverse inference instruction to be given at trial on the basis of the alleged disappearance of doctor's notices excusing him from work for medical reasons from his personnel file. The court denied the motion without prejudice absent evidence that the notes were, in fact, provided. The court opined that the misplacement or destruction of the doctor's notes may have violated the FMLA's record keeping requirements.

Additionally, records covering all employees, not just eligible employees, must be kept regarding basic employee information, employee notice information, employee benefits, and premium payments of employee benefits. 29 CFR 825.500(c)(1), (4), (5), and (6).

2. Medical Records

Records and documents relating to medical certification, recertifications or medical histories of employees or employees' family members, created for purposes of the FMLA, must be maintained by an employing agency as confidential medical records. 29 CFR 825.500(g); *see George v. Russell Stover Candies, Inc.*, 106 Fed. Appx. 946 (6th Cir. 2004); *Dupee v. Klaff's, Inc.*, 462 F. Supp. 2d 244, 249 (D. Conn. 2006); *O'Reilly v. Rutgers, The State University*, No. 04-5787 (FSH), 2006 U.S. Dist. LEXIS 2341, at *18-23 (D. N.J. Jan. 19, 2006), *aff'd*, 2007 U.S. App. LEXIS 9530 (3d Cir. April 25, 2007); *Kitts v. General Tel. North, Inc.*, No. 2:04-cv-173, 2005 U.S. Dist. LEXIS 20421, at *37-39 (S.D. Ohio Sept. 19, 2005). FMLA medical records must be maintained separately from an employee's usual personnel records. *Id.*

Medical records created for purposes of the FMLA and the ADA must be maintained in conformance with the ADA's confidentiality requirements, except that, pursuant to 29 CFR 825.500(g)(1)–(3):

- Supervisors and managers may be informed regarding necessary restrictions on the work or duties of an employee and necessary accommodations;

- First aid and safety personnel may be informed (when appropriate) if the employee's physical or medical condition might require emergency treatment, and;

- Government officials investigating compliance with the FMLA (or other pertinent law) must be provided relevant information on request.

Under the ADA, medical records are required to be kept confidential. To accomplish this, the ADA requires covered employers to collect and maintain employee medical records separate from other personnel records. 29 CFR 1630.14(c)(1), (d)(1). The ADA regulations contain the same limited exceptions to medical record confidentiality as those identified above for the FMLA. 29 CFR 1630.14(c)(1)(i)–(iii), (d)(1)(i)–(iii).

As currently written, it is unclear that the added requirement to maintain medical records in conformance with the ADA where the records invoke both the FMLA and ADA is applicable to federal employers. By its express terms, the ADA does not apply to the federal government. *See* 42 USC 12111(5)(B)(I); 29 CFR 1630.2(e)(2)(I). Rather, federal employees are covered by the employment protection provisions of the Rehabilitation Act of 1973, 29 USC 701, 704. It is noted, however, that the ADA regulations are strikingly similar to the FMLA regulations regarding medical records. In *O'Reilly v. Rutgers, The State University*, No. 04-5787 (FSH), 2006 U.S. Dist. LEXIS 2341, at *21 (D.N.J. Jan. 19, 2006), *aff'd*, 2007 U.S. App. LEXIS 9530 (3d Cir. April 25, 2007), the district court noted approvingly of the method of storage used by Rutgers. In that case, medical information was maintained by each department head. Only two individuals, the department head and the department administrators, had regular access to the department's personnel records. The personnel records were kept in a locked file cabinet, in a locked closet, in a locked office. Rutgers kept medical records separate from other personnel records. Medical records were kept in separate, sealed envelopes marked confidential. According to the court, "[t]he limited access and tight security practiced by Rutgers are more than sufficient to protect the information contained in Ms. O'Reilly's HCP certification."

3. Joint Employment

In a joint employment relationship, what records an employing agency must maintain depends on whether the record is of a primary employee or secondary employee. 29 CFR 825.500(e). As set forth more fully in Chapter 3, "FMLA Coverage of the Federal Government," primary employees are those employees who are directly employed by the federal employing agency. Secondary employees, on the other hand, are those who are employed by the federal employing agency through an intermediary, such as a temporary agency or employee leasing company. The secondary employee is directly employed by the temporary agency, but is doing work for the federal employer.

Regarding primary employees, the regulations provide that employing agencies are required to keep all records required by the provisions governing employers with eligible employees. 29 CFR 825.500(e). Presumably, this means that an employing agency need only keep basic information on employees who are not eligible for FMLA leave under Title I, and more detailed information on primary employees who are eligible for FMLA leave. 5 CFR 825.500(c).

With respect to secondary employees, federal employing agencies are only required to keep the basic personnel information identified in § 825.500(c)(1). *See* 29 CFR 825.500(e). The DOL concluded that other records were not necessary because the secondary employer's responsibilities in a joint employment relationship are only to reinstate the employee under the circumstances set forth in § 825.106(a) and to not violate any of the prohibited acts of the statute. Preamble, 29 CFR 825.500.

4. FLSA-Exempt Employees and FMLA Record Keeping

An employing agency is not required to keep a record of the actual hours worked by FMLA-eligible employees who are exempt from the overtime provisions of the FLSA, provided that (1) eligibility for FMLA leave is presumed for any employee employed for at least 12 months; and (2) with respect to employees taking FMLA leave intermittently or on a reduced leave schedule, the employer and employee agree on the employee's normal work schedule or average hours worked each week and reduce the agreement to a written record. 29 CFR 825.500(f). The written record of this agreement must be maintained in the form and for the terms of all FMLA records. The form and terms of FMLA records is addressed in Subsection C of this section.

The regulations raise several issues. First, the regulations do not clearly indicate whether the presumption of eligibility can be rebutted. This would appear to be the case based on the language in 29 CFR 825.110(c). In pertinent part, this regulation places the burden on the employer to show that an FLSA-exempt employee has not worked the requisite 1,250 hours. In the event that the employee is unable to meet this burden, the employee is deemed to meet the 1,250-hour eligibility test, citing § 825.500(f). 29 CFR 825.110(c).

Similarly, the regulation also fails to explain whether a covered employer can rebut the third criteria for Title I eligibility: that at least 50 employees be employed within 75 miles of the worksite of the employee requesting FMLA leave. *See* 29 CFR 825.110(a)(3). Presumably, the price an employing agency pays for avoiding the creation and maintenance of work-hour records on FLSA-exempt, FMLA-eligible employees is a waiver of its ability to challenge employee eligibility. This is not an insignificant cost.

Third, the scope of 825.500(f) is not entirely clear. The use of the conjunctive "and" suggests that the two conditions contained in the regulation are linked. That is, an employing agency need not create and maintain FMLA records regarding FLSA-exempt employees who are eligible for FMLA leave where the employees take intermittent or reduced schedule leave, if the additional conditions are met. Because the exception to the requirement to create and maintain records is limited to situations involving intermittent or reduced schedule leave only, it follows that employing agencies must create and keep records of actual hours worked where FMLA leave is taken in a block of time by FLSA-exempt, FMLA-eligible employees.

Fourth, in order to avoid the record-keeping requirement, in addition to agreeing to presume that the employee is eligible for FMLA leave, the employing agency must reach written agreement with the employee regarding the employee's normal schedule or average hours worked each week. Although there is no time frame attached to this requirement, employing agencies are well advised to get this agreement as soon as possible. It is unclear what would happen to an agency if it were unable to reach such an agreement on the employees' normal schedule or average weekly hours of work and the employee returned to work. Presumably, the employing agency would be in violation of the Act, as it would not have work-hour records on this employee.

Similarly, it is also unclear what happens if the employee unreasonably refuses to enter into a written agreement on this subject. In the absence of any penalty language in the regulations, an employee's refusal to enter a written agreement with the employer will result in the employing agency's obligation to create and maintain a record of work hours on this FLSA-exempt employee, at least if the employee is eligible for FMLA leave and seeks intermittent or reduced schedule leave.

Finally, the regulations do not say what happens if an employing agency decides to keep work-hour records on FLSA-exempt employees. Presumably, the employee loses the presumption of eligibility.

5. Employee Transfers and FMLA Record Keeping

Unlike Title II, there is no provision in the DOL regulations governing the transfer of FMLA record information to other federal agencies in the event a that Title I employee were to leave her position with one federal agency and move to another federal agency. Federal employers are well advised to ensure that the receiving agency receives from the losing agency sufficient FMLA information to determine whether the employee is eligible for FMLA leave. As discussed in Chapter 5, "Employee Eligibility for Leave," for purposes of Title I eligibility, the entire U.S. Government is considered a single employer. This means that an agency hiring a Title I employee who has worked for other federal agencies must actively obtain information from those agencies regarding the time the employee has spent with the federal government, as well as the hours worked in the 12 months preceding the hiring.

As set forth more fully below, the FMLA information that is required to be divulged by 5 CFR 630.1211(c)(1)–(2) is insufficient for the needs of an agency receiving a Title I employee who has worked for the federal government in the past. Specifically, the beginning and ending dates of the employee's 12-month period may be of little value because Title I allows an employer to choose from several methods of determining how an employee's 12-month FMLA leave year period is calculated. If the method selected by the receiving federal agency for calculating the Title I employee's 12-month FMLA leave year differs from the information required to be disclosed by 5 CFR 630.1211(c)(1), the latter information will be of virtually no use.

Knowing the number of leave hours the employee has taken may be useful to determine how many FMLA leave hours the Title I employee has remaining in the leave year. 5 CFR 630.1211(c)(2). I say "may" because there is nothing in the DOL or OPM regulations that recognizes that FMLA leave taken as a Title II employee during a leave year is subtracted from the employee's leave account if the employee moves to a different agency and becomes a Title I employee. While that certainly makes sense, there is simply nothing in the regulations that prohibits an employee from insisting that such a move effectively restarts the FMLA clock, providing a new 12-week entitlement to FMLA leave no matter how much leave the employee has taken. [For further discussion of how much FMLA leave an employee may take, see Chapter 10, "Leave Amount and Scheduling."]

More importantly, the FMLA information required to be transferred by 5 CFR 630.1211 does not address eligibility issues. The employee's OPF and Form 50s contained therein will almost certainly indicate the periods of prior federal employment, which should assist all federal employers in determining whether the employee meets the 12 months of employment eligibility test. What that information will not show, however, is how many hours the employee worked in the 12 months preceding the transfer or hiring. This information addresses the 1,250-hour eligibility requirement of Title I, which draws on all federal employment for this purpose.

Federal agencies hiring employees covered by Title I should make an effort to obtain work-hours information from any federal agency where the employee worked within 12 months of the hiring or transfer. An agency that does not make this effort and denies a request for FMLA leave based on incomplete information, such as that required to be transferred pursuant to 5 CFR 630.1211(c), runs the considerable risk of being found in violation of the Act.

C. FORM OF RECORDS AND RETENTION PERIOD

Title I sets out rules regarding the form, location, and retention period of FMLA records. These rules are discussed below.

1. Form of Records

No particular order or form of records is required by Title I of the FMLA. 29 CFR 825.500(b). Nor are covered employers required to revise their computerized payroll or personnel records systems to comply. *Id*. Employing agencies must, however, keep Title I FMLA records in a form that is readily available to the DOL upon request. The records may be maintained in computer form provided that the records can be made available for transcription or copying. *Id*. Similarly, the FMLA records may also be kept on microfilm or another basic source document of an automated data processing memory, provided that adequate resources are made available by the employer. The data must be clear and identifiable by date or pay period, and that extensions or transcriptions of the information are available on the request of DOL. *Id*.

As a practical matter, while the DOL regulations do not require covered employers to create separate record-keeping systems to keep track of FMLA leave usage, many covered employers have found it necessary to do just that. Some, such as the Postal Service, have created their own in-house attendance tracking systems, including FMLA leave. Others have purchased FMLA tracking software available from a number of private vendors.

The FMLA does not prohibit an employer from retroactively creating handwritten records. In *Brown v. Dollar General*

Stores, Ltd., No. 1:04CV-107-M, 2006 U.S. Dist. LEXIS 6746, at *15 & n.4 (W.D. Ky. Feb. 21, 2006), the employer discovered that a number of absences covered by the FMLA were not recorded as FMLA leave in the employers records. As a result of the audit, it was discovered that the employee exhausted his FMLA leave. The employer notified the employee that his FMLA was exhausted and requested that he return to work. The employee was subsequently terminated when he did not return to work. The employee sued, alleging that "retroactive, handwritten record-keeping does not create the kind of reliable records contemplated by the Act." The court disagreed, noting that 29 CFR 825.500(b) does not require any particular form of records. The court found that the employer's alteration of the records as a result of the audit was permissible.

2. Location of Records

How FMLA records are actually stored will depend on whether the records are medical or nonmedical.

Title I medical certifications, recertifications, and medical histories of employees or employees' family members are considered confidential medical records that must be maintained separate from the employee's general personnel file. 29 CFR 825.500(g); *see Dupee v. Klaff's, Inc.*, 462 F. Supp. 2d 244, 249 (D. Conn. 2006).

Regarding nonmedical FMLA records, the regulations do not require that these records be stored separately from an employee's general personnel file. With one exception, the regulations do not identify how nonmedical records may be maintained. Records regarding employee and employer FMLA notice obligations may be maintained in the employee's personnel files. *Dupee*, 462 F. Supp. 2d at 249. Of course, when you have only one instance where the regulations indicated that nonmedical information may be kept in an employee's personnel file, it calls into question whether other nonmedical information can be similarly stored. The lack of clear guidance notwithstanding, covered employers may include nonmedical FMLA information in an employee's personnel file.

The non-medical information may, however, be stored in automated record-keeping systems, provided the FMLA information is readily retrievable by individual employees. That is, covered employers are not required to centralize the nonmedical FMLA information in employee personnel folders.

3. Retention Period

Covered employers must keep and maintain all FMLA records for at least three years. 29 CFR 825.500(b); *see Rucker v. Lee Holding Co.*, 471 F.3d 6, n.5 (1st Cir. 2006). This period coincides with the three-year statute of limitations for an employee to file a private lawsuit alleging a willful violation of the FMLA. 29 CFR 825.4000(a)(2)(b). [For a further discussion of enforcement of Title I of the FMLA, see Chapter 15, "Prohibited Acts, Enforcement, and Remedies."]

III. TITLE II RECORD-KEEPING REQUIREMENTS

A. GENERAL OBLIGATIONS

Title II of the FMLA requires covered employing agencies to maintain records on employees who take FMLA leave. 5 CFR 630.1211(a). The stated purpose for requiring employing agencies to maintain FMLA information is so that: "OPM can evaluate the use of family and medical leave by Federal employees and provide the Congress and others with information about the use of this entitlement." *Id.* This would appear to be different from the unstated reason for the maintenance of FMLA data under Title I, which claims to be for DOL enforcement purposes.

B. REQUIRED RECORDS

Like Title I, the FMLA records that Title II requires the maintenance of may also be divided into medical and nonmedical records.

1. Nonmedical Records

At a minimum, Title II (5 CFR 630.1211(b)(1)–(4)) requires that each agency must maintain the following records regarding each employee who takes FMLA leave:

- The employee's rate of basic pay, as defined in 5 CFR 550.103;
- The occupational series for the employee's position;
- The number of hours of FMLA leave taken, including any paid leave substituted for FMLA leave without pay;
- Whether the leave was taken under 630.1203(a)(1) (birth of son or daughter), 630.1201(a)(2) (adoption/foster care placement of son or daughter), 630.1201(a)(1)(3) (serious health condition of covered family member), or 630.1201(a)(4) (serious health condition of employee).

Note that the above records must be maintained on employees who have taken FMLA leave. To take FMLA leave, an employee must meet the eligibility requirements. Therefore, under Title II, employing agencies are only required to maintain the identified FMLA records of eligible employees who have, in fact, taken FMLA leave.

2. Medical Records

To ensure security and confidentiality, employing agencies must safeguard written medical certifications, recertification's, second and third medical opinions, and return to work medical certifications regarding an employee's request for, or return from, FMLA leave about individuals in accordance with Subpart A or Part 293 of this chapter. 5 CFR 630.1207(k). The reference to safeguarding the medical records of individuals would appear to cover the medical records of family members of covered employees. It is unclear whether the regulation contains a misprint. It might have been intended to read: in accordance with subpart A *of* part 293.

As written, Subpart A of the OPM regulations implementing Chapter 63 of Title 5, 5 CFR 630.101, provides, essentially, that each agency is responsible for maintaining records of individual employee leave in accordance with methods prescribed by the General Accounting Office. Other than being perhaps a general delegation of authority to covered agencies, the cited regulation is of little assistance in establishing a uniform federal practice on how medical records should be kept. As written, the regulation suggests that employing agencies are free to develop whatever practices they wish to ensure the security and confidentiality of medical records.

Alternatively, 5 CFR 630.1207(k) might have meant to refer to Subpart A of Part 293. That would appear to make more sense. Part 293 of the regulations implementing Title 5, 5 CFR Part 293, contain the OPM requirements for agency maintenance of personnel records. Subpart A of Part 293 sets forth the basic policies on maintenance of Personnel Records. 5 CFR 293.101–108. In pertinent part, Subpart A places the burden on each covered agency to establish administrative, technical, and physical controls to protect information in personnel records from unauthorized access, use, modification, destruction, or disclosure. 5 CFR 293.101(a). Subpart A defines a covered "agency" as any executive department, military department, government corporation, government-controlled corporation, or other establishment in the executive branch of the government (including the Executive Office of the President), or any independent regulatory agency. 5 CFR 293.102 (definition of agency).

Personnel records must be stored in metal filing cabinets, which are locked when the records are not in use, or in a secured room. Alternative storage facilities may be employed provided they furnish an equivalent or greater degree of security than do these methods. 5 CFR 293.106(b). The regulations go on to limit access to personnel records to the subject of the record and employees whose official duties require access to personnel records. The regulations also require that a record be kept of the removal of personnel records from storage areas. *Id*. Safeguards for automated records are governed by 5 CFR 293.107.

Subpart A of Part 293, 5 CFR 293.101–108 is not, however, the most natural group of regulations one would consider to govern the security and confidentiality of FMLA medical records. Part E of Subpart 293, 5 CFR 293.501–511, specifically addresses Employee Medical File System Records. This system defines employees by cross-reference to 5 USC 2105. 5 CFR 293.502. This would effectively exclude federal employees covered by Title I of the Act. [For a discussion of employee coverage under the FMLA, see Chapter 4 "Federal Employees Covered by the FMLA."]

If 5 CFR 630.1207(k) meant to refer to Subpart A of Part 293, then FMLA records would be covered for confidentiality and security purposes as nonmedical records. If, on the other hand, § 630.1207(k) meant all of Part 293, the FMLA medical certification records would appear to fit more naturally into Subpart E of Part 293, 5 CFR 293.501–511, governing the security and confidentiality of medical records.

Further clarification from OPM on this issue is needed. In the meantime, employing agencies are well advised to apply the added security of the regulations governing medical records to covered employees.

3. Joint Employment

Perhaps because the concept of "joint employment" is not addressed in Title II, there are no regulations differentiating between the record-keeping responsibilities of primary and secondary employers, as in Title I.

4. FLSA-Exempt Employees and FMLA Record Keeping

Unlike Title I, there are no special record-keeping regulations in Title II addressing record-keeping issues involving FLSA-exempt employees. This is not surprising since the eligibility criteria for Title II employees do not contain a minimum work-hours requirement as does Title I.

5. Employee Transfers and FMLA Record Keeping

When an employee transfers to a different agency, the losing agency is required to provide the gaining agency with information on FMLA leave taken by the employee during the 12 months prior to the date of transfer. 5 CFR 630.1211(c). Specifically, the losing agency must provide: (1) the beginning and ending dates of the employee's 12-month period, as determined under 5 CFR 630.1203(c); and (2) the number of hours of FMLA leave taken during the employee's 12-month period. 5 CFR 630.1211(c)(1)–(2). An employee's 12-month period begins on the date an employee first takes FMLA leave, and continues for 12 months. 5 CFR 630.1203(c).

It is not clear how the term "agency" is being defined. Presumably, it means any federal employer. Federal agencies are well advised to make sure they receive this information from the losing federal agency to ensure timely compliance with Title II of the FMLA, for those employees covered by Title II.

C. FORM OF RECORDS AND RECORDS RETENTION

Title II does not set out its own rules regarding the form, location, and retention period of FMLA records. For FMLA medical records, as set forth above, these terms are addressed by incorporation of 5 CFR Part 293. Presumably, in the absence of specific FMLA regulations, the nonmedical FMLA records are governed by general personnel records provisions of 5 CFR Part 293, as supplemented by agency policies and procedures.

IV. FMLA RECORD-KEEPING UNDER THE CAA AND THE PEOAA

The CAA and the PEOAA do not address any special FMLA record-keeping requirements. Both Statues incorporate §§ 101 through 105 of Title I of the FMLA (29 USC 2611-15). 2 USC 1312(a)(1) (CAA); 3 USC 412(a)(1) (PEOAA). The requirement for covered employers to maintain FMLA records is contained in § 106 of Title I of the FMLA, 29 USC 2616.

The regulations implementing the CAA and the PEOAA do not include any special FMLA record keeping requirements. While these regulations generally follow the DOL's Title I FMLA regulations, they do not include a counterpart to 29 CFR 825.500 regarding retention of FMLA records.

V. DISCLOSURE OF FMLA RECORDS

This section addresses the rules governing the disclosure of FMLA records. Disclosures are divided into two categories: (1) government inspection of agency FMLA records, and (2) other disclosures. Because neither the CAA nor the PEOAA have specific regulations governing the maintenance or disclosure of FMLA records, what follows will address the requirements under Title I and Title II of the FMLA, as well as other laws.

A. GOVERNMENT INSPECTION OF FMLA RECORDS

1. DOL

Under Title I, employing agencies must make the required FMLA records available to representatives of the DOL at their request for inspection, copying, and transcription. 29 USC 2616(c); 29 CFR 825.500(b). DOL generally cannot require an employer or any plan, fund, or program to submit to the DOL any books or records more than once during any 12-month period. 5 USC 2616(c). However, if the DOL has reasonable cause to believe that an employer has violated the Act or the DOL FMLA regulations, the DOL may request inspection of FMLA records more frequently than once during any 12-month period. *Id.*

An employer does not have an obligation under 825.500 to disclose FMLA records to an employee. Section 825.500 obligates an employer to disclose FMLA records to the U.S. Department of Labor only. *Slentz v. City of Republic, Missouri*, 448 F.3d 1008, 1011-1012 (8th Cir. 2006).

2. OPM

Under Title II, OPM's access to FMLA records is broader still than DOL's authority under Title I. So that it can evaluate the use of family and medical leave by federal employees and provide the Congress and others with information about the use of this entitlement, covered agencies are required to submit to OPM FMLA records "as OPM may require." 5 CFR 630.1211(a).

3. Other Government Agencies

Government agencies other than those directly involved with the regulation of federal FMLA leave and benefits (e.g. DOL and OPM) may be entitled to review employee FMLA records as part of their investigative powers and regulatory function. For example, the National Labor Relations Board may seek to review information from the Postal Service as part of an investigation of an NLRB complaint. Similarly, OSHA may have the authority to review employee FMLA records as part of an investigation into workplace safety. Again, the authority of agencies who are not directly involved with the regulation of federal sector FMLA leave and benefits to review employee FMLA records is governed by that agency's investigatory authority and the Privacy Act.

Employing agencies that are asked to disclose employee FMLA records are well advised to consult counsel before releasing such information.

B. OTHER DISCLOSURES

Employee FMLA records may also be sought by any number of other individuals and entities. Disclosure of FMLA records to employees and third parties are governed by the Privacy Act and the Freedom of Information Act.

1. Privacy Act

Generally speaking, federal sector FMLA records are personnel records governed by the Privacy Act of 1974, 5 USC 552a. The Privacy Act governs the collection, maintenance, use and disclosure of personnel information by the Federal Government. While many of the specifics of the Privacy Act are well beyond the scope of this book, a few provisions should be mentioned.

Broadly speaking, FMLA records on individual employees are generally maintained as part of a "system of records" under the Privacy Act. A system of records is defined as a group of records under the control of any agency from which information is retrieved by the name of the individual or by some identifying number, symbol, or other identifying particular assigned to the individual. 5 USC 552a(a)(5). If you recall, both Title I and Title II require the creation and maintenance of individualized FMLA records.

The Privacy Act permits individual agency employees access to their own FMLA records, provided such records are contained in a "system of records." 5 USC 552a(d)(1). The individual also has a limited right to amend erroneous records.

5 USC 552a(d)(2). One of the easiest ways to ensure compliance with the Privacy Act is to obtain a release signed by the employee permitting the agency to disclose the records to identified third parties.

Generally, the Privacy Act prohibits disclosure of personnel information, including FMLA information, to third parties, without the written consent of the individual whose record is being sought. 5 USC 552a(b). There are a dozen exceptions to this rule, four of which will be addressed because of the frequency in which they arise.

The Privacy Act was enacted to safeguard the public from unwarranted dissemination of personal information contained in agency records. The Privacy Act accomplishes this by generally prohibiting nonconsensual disclosure of any information retrieved from a protected record, unless that information falls into one of a number of statutory exceptions. *Doe v. USPS*, 317 F.3d 339, 342 (D.C. Cir. 2003) (citing *Bartel v. FAA*, 725 F.2d 1403, 1407–1408 (D.C. Cir. 1984)).

The interaction of the FMLA, the Privacy Act, and the medical confidentiality provisions of the Americans with Disabilities Act ("ADA"), 42 USC 12112(d)4)(B), was addressed by the Circuit Court for the District of Columbia in *Doe v. USPS*, 317 F.3d 339, 340–341 (D.C. Cir. 2003). The court found sufficient material evidence in dispute to reverse an award of summary judgment to the Postal Service on Doe's claims that a Postal supervisor's disclosure of information on his FMLA medical certification form violated the confidentiality provisions of the Privacy Act and the Rehabilitation Act.

In *Doe*, after missing several weeks of work due to illness, plaintiff filled out a Department of Labor Form WH 380, the medical certification form, in order to have his absence covered by the FMLA. On the form, Doe's doctor stated that Doe had "AIDS related complex" and "chronic HIV infection." On his return to work, Doe learned that his HIV status had become common knowledge among his coworkers, many of whom commented to him about it. Several identified Doe's management-level supervisor as the source of the information. Doe filed suit alleging that the disclosure of his confidential medical information by management violated the Privacy Act and the medical confidentiality provisions of the Americans with Disabilities Act (ADA), 42 USC 12112(d).

The district court awarded summary judgment to the Postal Service on both claims, concluding that: (1) Doe failed to raise a genuine issue of material fact as to whether a Postal Service employee improperly disclosed information retrieved from his medical records in violation of the Privacy Act, and (2) the FMLA forms were not an employer inquiry subject to the ADA's medical confidentiality requirement. The employee appealed the award of summary judgment to the DC Circuit.

With respect to Doe's Privacy Act claim, the Postal Service did not dispute that Doe's FMLA certification form was contained in an agency record subject to the Privacy Act's confidentiality requirements. Nor did the Postal Service argue that the information on the form qualified for one of the statutory exceptions permitting disclosure. The Postal Service argued that Doe failed to offer sufficient evidence that a Postal employee disclosed information about Doe's medical information from information the employee obtained from Doe's medical certification form. The court disagreed. In support of its determination that Doe produced sufficient evidence, albeit circumstantial, to defeat summary judgment, the court cited: (1) the testimony of several coworkers who identified a management official as the source of the medical information about Doe; (2) the alleged disclosures by a supervisor regarding his HIV condition occurred after Doe submitted his FMLA form; and (3) in the normal course of business the alleged disclosing supervisor reviewed leave requests, including FMLA requests.

Doe's Rehabilitation Act claim also rested on his contention that the Postal Service supervisor improperly disclosed the contents of his FMLA form. The Rehabilitation Act, which generally prohibits federal government employers from discriminating on the basis of disability, also forbids such employers from disclosing employees' private medical records, incorporating by reference the medical examination confidentiality provision of the ADA, 42 USC 12112(d). *See* 29 USC 791(g), 794(d). The provision generally prohibits employer inquiries into employee's medical conditions, with two exceptions: (1) voluntary medical examinations, which are part of an employee health program available to employees at that worksite, and (2) inquiries into the ability of an employee to perform job-related functions. The court found that the Postal Service's request that Doe support his request for FMLA leave with medical certification constituted an "employer inquiry" within the meaning of the ADA confidentiality provisions. As such, the ADA required that the information disclosed by Doe in the FMLA certification form "spreads no farther than necessary to satisfy the legitimate needs of both the employer and employee." *Id*. The court found sufficient evidence in the record to suggest that the Postal Service violated that requirement to defeat summary judgment.

Doe reminds federal employers that they need to safeguard FMLA information from unwarranted disclosure or face costly and time-consuming litigation.

a. Need to Know Within the Agency

Pursuant to 5 USC 552(b)(1), employees within a federal agency who have a need to know FMLA information as part of their official duties have a right to access that information for those official purposes. For example, an agency that employs FMLA coordinators whose function is to manage FMLA leave would have a right to access individual FMLA records without first obtaining the individual's written permission in order to fulfill their function as FMLA coordinator.

b. Routine Uses

The Privacy Act allows agencies to create so-called "routine uses" that permit disclosure of the record for purposes compatible with the purpose for which the record is collected. 5 USC 552a(b)(3). Agencies invariably publish the various records that make up the personnel system of records, as well as the routine uses for which an agency can disclose the records without the prior written consent of the employee whose record is being disclosed. The routine use exception is potentially very broad. The routine uses of each agency should be consulted to determine whether a disclosure of FMLA information was in violation of the Act. Nine times out of ten, if no other exception applies, the agency will have created dozens of routine uses, at least one of which will apply. For example, a typical routine use allows union representing bargaining unit employees of the federal agency access to a great deal of otherwise confidential employee FMLA information.

c. Congress

The Privacy Act allows disclosure of FMLA information (provided, of course, that it is contained in a system of records) to the House or Senate, or a committee, subcommittee, or joint committee thereof. 5 USC 552a(b)(9). This section does not authorize an agency to disclose Privacy Act protected information to an individual member of Congress acting on his or her own behalf or on behalf of a constituent. *See* OMB Guidelines, 40 Fed. Reg. 28948, 28955 (1975). Because of the complexities of the FMLA, Congressional inquires on behalf of constituent federal employees is common.

d. Court Order

An agency may release Privacy Act protected information without first obtaining the written consent of the individual whose record is sought pursuant to the order of a court of competent jurisdiction. 5 USC 552a(b)(11). A judge must specifically approve a court order. *See Doe v. DiGenova*, 779 F.2d 74, 77–85 (D.C. Cir. 1985). A subpoena is generally not a court order. Frequently, when an employee is divorcing or is involved in a lawsuit due to an injury, one of the attorneys in the mix fills out a form subpoena and serves the agency. Because this subpoena is not typically a court order signed by a judge, it is not a legitimate basis for disclosing the Privacy Act information being sought.

A second issue here is what constitutes a court of competent jurisdiction. While the law on this is somewhat tricky, it is reasonably clear that a state court is rarely going to be a court of competent jurisdiction over a nonparty federal agency. For example, employees A and B are divorcing in state court. Employee B secures a court order from the state directing the federal agency employer to release Privacy Act protected personnel records of employee A. Because a state court is not a court of competent jurisdiction over a federal agency, the federal agency could refuse to release the information. CAUTION: When dealing with judges, state or federal, federal agencies would be well-advised to get agency counsel involved before declining to provide court-ordered personnel information on the ground that the court lacks jurisdiction.

2. Freedom of Information Act (FOIA)

Some third parties attempt to obtain personnel information about a federal employee through a request under the FOIA. Exemption 6 of the FOIA, 5 USC 552b(6), exempts from disclosure all information about an individual contained in "personnel and medical files and similar files" when disclosure of the information would "constitute a clearly unwarranted invasion of personnel privacy." The case law interpreting this exemption is complex. Agency counsel should be consulted before this exemption from disclosure is used to prohibit access to an employee's FMLA records. That said, it is very unlikely that individual employee FMLA records will be released under FOIA. FOIA generally cannot be used as an end-run on the Privacy Act.

3. Disclosure to Supervisors

The FMLA does not prohibit an employer from requiring an employee to submit medical certification to the employee's immediate supervisor. Courts uniformly reject employee arguments that submission of the medical certification to an immediate supervisor violates the confidentiality provisions of the FMLA.

In *O'Reilly v. Rutgers, The State University*, No. 04-5787 (FSH), 2006 U.S. Dist. LEXIS 2341, at *18-23 (D.N.J. Jan. 19, 2006), *aff'd*, 2007 U.S. App. LEXIS 9530 (3d Cir. April 25, 2007), the employee refused to submit her FMLA medical certification to her immediate supervisor rather than to Rutgers' medical staff for approval as required by Rutgers policy. O'Reilly argued that Rutgers violated the record-keeping provisions of 825.500, which require that an employer keep FMLA medical records confidential. O'Reilly argued that 825.500 prohibits managers and supervisors from reviewing FMLA requests and accompanying health care provider certifications in the first instance. The court disagreed. Based on a plain reading of the regulations, the court found that employers may exempt supervisors and managers from the regulations confidentiality requirements in certain circumstances where those individuals are not already privy to an employee's medical information through the leave approval process. The FMLA does not, however, impose such a restriction. Plaintiff's fear, the court concluded, that her medical information might be wrongfully disclosed does not permit her to refuse to submit her medical certification to her employer. Having refused to provide her employer with a medical certification, the court found that O'Reilly was not entitled to FMLA leave.

In *Kitts v. General Tel. North, Inc.*, No. 2:04-cv-173, 2005 U.S. Dist. LEXIS 20421, at *37-39 (S.D. Ohio Sept. 19, 2005), the employers supervisor and, later, a security investigator, confronted the employee on her return from leave regarding the reason for her absence. In both instances, the employee lied. Kitts had a psychiatric condition that she did not want to reveal. She argued that she was not obligated by the FMLA to disclose confidential medical information in her responses. As such, her responses to the questioning at issue could not be held against her, even if they were outright lies. The court disagreed. The court noted that the employee could not cite to any section of the FMLA or its regulations that provides employees with a right to medical privacy, or gives them the right to refuse to truthfully answer questions concerning the FMLA. The FMLA allows employers to disclose information about the employee's medical condition prior to approving leave. "While employers may enact policies restricting who, within the company, may have access to that information, nothing in the FMLA imposes a similar restriction." Because the employee could not point to a company policy prohibiting her supervisor and the security officer from questioning her regarding the reason for her absence, the questioning did not violate the FMLA.

In *George v. Russell Stover Candies, Inc.*, 106 Fed. Appx. 946 (6th Cir. 2004), plaintiff alleged that Russell Stover's policy requiring employees to call-in to request FMLA leave rather than request such leave directly from her supervisor violated her FMLA-protected right to confidentiality because other employees had access to the call-in system and could learn confidential information regarding any FMLA-qualifying health conditions underlying those absences. The court found that it need not and did not express an opinion on this issue because plaintiff conceded that Russell Stover's policy did not prohibit plaintiff from directly informing her supervisor of her need for leave or require employees to disclose the specific details of any illness underlying their absence via the call-in system.

4. Constitutional Right to Privacy

Several courts have addressed employee constitutional challenges to the requirement that an employee submit FMLA medical certification to his or her immediate supervisor rather than a member of the medical staff for approval. Courts have uniformly found that an employer does not violate an employee's constitutional right to privacy by requiring him or her to return his or her FMLA medical certification form to the supervisor.

In *O'Reilly v. Rutgers, The State University*, No. 04-5787 (FSH), 2006 U.S. Dist. LEXIS 2341, at *18-23 (D.N.J. Jan. 19, 2006), *aff'd*, 2007 U.S. App. LEXIS 9530 (3d Cir. April 25, 2007), the employee argued that Rutgers violated her constitutional right to privacy by requiring her to submit her FMLA medical certification (from her psychiatrist) to her immediate supervisor rather than separate medical staff at Rutgers. The constitutional right to privacy extends to protect an individual's interest in avoiding disclosure of personal matters, including medical information. *Whalen v. Roe*, 429 U.S. 589, 599, 97 S. Ct. 869 (1977). However, an individual's right to control access to his or her medical history is not absolute and public health or other public concerns may support access to facts an individual might otherwise chose to withhold. *U.S. v. Westinghouse*, 638 F.2d 570, 578 (3d Cir. 1980).

Under *Westinghouse*, 638 F.2d at 578, whether a constitutional violation occurred depends on:

> The type of record requested, the information it does or might contain, the potential for harm in any subsequent non-consensual disclosure, the injury from disclosure to the relationship in which the record was generated, the adequacy of safeguards to prevent unauthorized disclosure, the degree of need for access, and whether there is an express statutory mandate, articulated public policy, or other recognizable public interest militating toward access.

The court found that the FMLA certification was limited in scope and far less detailed than the medical records considered in Westinghouse (which allowed access to OSHA-related medical records). Second, Rutgers had effective security to protect against unauthorized access. Third, the FMLA specifically authorizes employers to request health care provider certifications from employees requesting leave. "This express statutory mandate is precisely the kind that will weight in favor of access and against a finding of privacy violation." *O'Reilly*, 2006 U.S. Dist. LEXIS 2341, at *22. Submitting medical information in support of an FMLA claim may be considered a waiver of the right to complete confidentiality. *Id*.

In *Dodge v. Trustees of the National Gallery of Art*, 326 F. Supp. 2d 1, 17 (D. D.C. 2004). plaintiff alleged that the defendants violated his constitutional rights by releasing his son's FMLA medical records to his immediate supervisor to evaluate his request for FMLA leave. The issue arose when Dodge refused to work mandatory overtime citing his prior approval for FMLA leave. To investigate plaintiff's refusal to work mandatory overtime, Dodge's supervisor reviewed information regarding plaintiff's approved application for FMLA leave. The information included a letter from Dodge's son's physician substantiating the need for FMLA leave. Dodge previously notified the National Gallery Personnel Office that he considered the physician's letter confidential and insisted that it not be shared with his supervisor. The supervisor took disciplinary action against Dodge for his refusal to work mandatory overtime after concluding that plaintiff's FMLA status did not excuse him from mandatory overtime.

The court held that the defendants did not improperly release the plaintiff's FMLA submissions, which included his son's medical records. The court found that by voluntarily submitting his son's medical records, the plaintiff essentially waived his right to keep these records confidential from his supervisor, who was reviewing the plaintiff's FMLA status. The court found that the release of the plaintiff's FMLA submissions to his supervisor, including his son's medical records, fell within 29 CFR 825.500(g). That provision provides "[s]upervisors and managers may be informed regarding necessary restrictions on the work or duties of an employee and necessary accommodations." The court observed:

> For the plaintiff's supervisor to decide whether the plaintiff could be excused from his mandatory overtime work duties due to his FMLA leave status, the supervisor had to understand and evaluate the urgency of the plaintiff's family conditions. In order to determine the urgency and nature of the plaintiff's FMLA justification, the supervisor had no choice but to examine the son's medical records since it was his son's medical condition that was excusing plaintiff from work related obligations. The plaintiff cannot now legitimately argue that the defendant exceeded its authority in "turning over the complete medical records relating to one of the employee's family members." For the plaintiff to assume that defendants could make a well warranted decision without these documents is infeasible.

VI. MIXED AGENCY FMLA RESPONSIBILITIES AND RECORD KEEPING

The record–keeping requirements of Title I and Title II of the Act are not the same. Federal agencies that have employees covered by Title I of the Act are well advised to comply with the record–keeping requirements of Title I for those employees. Indeed, Title I of the Act has record–keeping requirements covering all federal employers whether they have eligible Title I employees or not. Except for federal employers covered by the CAA and PEOAA, all federal agencies must follow the record–keeping requirements of both Title I and Title II. A federal agency that has Title I employees but only follows the record–keeping requirements of Title II is violating the law.

If the failure of an agency to follow all applicable the record–keeping requirements results in a denial of FMLA leave or other violation of the Act, individual supervisors as well as the federal agency as a whole could be faced with the cost and hassle of defending an expensive lawsuit. Additionally, the failure of a federal agency to comply with the requirements of all applicable record–keeping regulations could easily be found to be a willful violation, subjecting the individual manager and employing agency to double damages.

CHAPTER 15
PROHIBITED ACTS, ENFORCEMENT, AND REMEDIES

I. OVERVIEW

All federal employers are prohibited from interfering with the exercise of any right provided by the FMLA. Some federal employers are also prohibited from discriminating against any individual for using FMLA leave, opposing any employer practice made unlawful by the Act, or for engaging in protected activity in furtherance of the enforcement of the Act. Violations of the FMLA are enforced differently under each federal sector variant of the FMLA, as are the remedies available.

Section II, "Prohibited Acts", addresses what acts are prohibited under the FMLA. Knowing what acts are prohibited by the various federal sector variants of the FMLA is important because such violations form the bedrock of any claim for enforcement and action for damages. The differing systems for enforcing employee FMLA rights and employer FMLA responsibilities are addressed in Section III, "Enforcement." Section IV discusses the "Remedies", if any, available to an aggrieved employee or other individual for federal employer violations of the FMLA. Finally, Section V, "Miscellaneous Litigation Matters", explores various litigation issues that arise in some cases pursuant to the enforcement of FMLA rights.

Substantial differences exist between the federal sector variants of the FMLA regarding what is prohibited, how violations are enforced, and what remedies are available to aggrieved employees.

II. PROHIBITED ACTS

All federal sector variants of the FMLA prohibit certain employer conduct that interferes with FMLA rights and benefits. What conduct is prohibited, however, differs depending on which federal sector variant of the FMLA applies to the aggrieved employee or other individual claiming a violation. This section explores what constitutes prohibited conduct under each of the four federal sector FMLA laws.

A. TITLE I, THE CAA AND THE PEOAA

1. Introduction

Section 105 of Title I of the FMLA (29 USC 2615) addresses the employer acts, that are prohibited by the FMLA. The CAA and PEOAA, respectively, incorporate § 105 of Title I of the FMLA. *See* 2 USC 1312(a)(1) (CAA); 3 USC 412(a)(1) (PEOAA).

DOL issued regulations implementing § 105 for purposes of Title I, and the Board of Directors of the Office of Compliance for purposes of the CAA. *See* 29 CFR 825.220 (Title I); S. Res. 242, Cong. Rec. S3959, S3970–71 (April 23, 1996); 29 CFR 825.220. Although permitted by the Statute, neither the President nor a designee have issued regulations implementing the incorporated prohibited acts provisions of § 105 of Title I. *See* 3 USC 412(c)(1). In the absence of implementing regulations, the PEOAA requires that the "the most relevant substantive executive agency regulation promulgated to implement the statutory provision at issue" must be applied by the administrative agency adjudicating a claim. 3 USC 455. As § 105 of Title I is specifically incorporated into the PEOAA for purposes of the FMLA, the DOL regulations (specifically, 29 CFR 825.220) apply to the PEOAA.

2. General Rule

Section 105 of Title I of the FMLA (29 USC 2615) provides:

(a) Interference With Rights.—

Exercise of rights. It shall be unlawful for any employer to interfere with, restrain, or deny the exercise of or the attempt to exercise, any right provided under this Title.

Discrimination. It shall be unlawful for any employer to discourage or in any other manner discriminate against any individual for opposing any practice made unlawful by this Title.

(b) Interference with Proceedings or Inquiries. It shall be unlawful for any person to discharge or in any other manner discriminate against any individual because such individual—

(1) Has filed any charge, or has instituted or caused to be instituted any proceeding, under or related to this Title;

(2) Has given or is about to give, any information in connection with any inquiry or proceeding relating to any right provided under this Title; or

(3) Has testified, or is about to testify, in any inquiry or proceeding relating to any right provided under this Title.

The FMLA prohibits an employer from "interfering with, restraining, or denying the exercise of or the attempt to exercise, any right provided" under the FMLA, and may not discharge or discriminate in any way against an employee for opposing practices that are unlawful under the FMLA. 29 USC 2615; 29 CFR 825.220; *see Hite v. Vermeer Mfg., Co.*, 446 F.3d 858, 865 (8th Cir. 2006); *Kauffman v. Federal Express Corp.*, 426 F.3d 880, 884 (7th Cir. 2005); *Hoffman v. Professional Med Team*, 394 F.3d 414 (6th Cir. 2005); *Humenny v. Genex Corp., Inc.*, 390 F.3d 901, 905 (6th Cir. 2004); *Edmonsond v. The Brookwood Community*, 114 Fed. Appx. 148 (5th Cir. 2004) (under the FMLA, an employer may not penalize an employee for exercise of FMLA rights); *Dressler v. Community Service Communications, Inc.*, 115 Fed. Appx. 452 (1st Cir. 2004); *Muriekes v. Boeing Co.*, 111 Fed. Appx. 483 (9th Cir. 2004); *Hoge v. Honda of America Mfg., Inc.*, 384 F.3d 238 (6th Cir. 2004); *Slaughter–Cooper v. Kelsey Sybold Med. Group. P.A.*, 379 F.3d 285 n.14 (5th Cir. 2004); *Walker v. Elmore County Bd. of Ed.*, 379 F.3d 1249 (11th Cir. 2004); *Bones v. Honeywell Intl., Inc.*, 366 F.3d 869, 877 (10th Cir. 2004); *Brenneman v. MedCentral Health System*, 366 F.3d 412, 422 (6th Cir. 2004), cert. denied, 534 U.S. 1146 (2005); *Potenza v. City of New York*, 365 F.3d 165, 167 (2d Cir. 2004); *Conoshenti v. Public Service Elec. & Gas Co.*, 364 F.3d 135, 141 (3d Cir. 2004); *Sherrod v. Philadelphia Gas Works*, 57 Fed. Appx. 68 (3d Cir. 2003); *Hunt v. Rapides Healthcare System, LLC*, 277 F.3d 757, 763, n.5 (5th Cir. 2001); *Smith v. Bellsouth Telecommunications, Inc.*, 273 F.3d 1303, 1306 (11th Cir. 2001); *Bachelder v. America West Airlines, Inc.*, 259 F.3d 1112, 1122 (9th Cir. 2001); *Cooper v. Olin Corp.*, 246 F.3d 1083, 1090 (8th Cir. 2001); *Mardis v. Central Nat. Bank & Trust of Enid*, 173 F.3d 864 (table), 1999 U.S. App. LEXIS 7261, at *5 (10th Cir. April 15, 1999); *Hodgens v. General Dynamics Corp.*, 144 F.3d 151, 160, n. 3 (1st Cir. 1998). As modified by implementing regulations, if any, the CAA and PEOAA incorporate the above prohibitions for purposes of employees covered by those laws. *See* 2 USC 1312(a)(1)(CAA); 3 USC 412(a)(1) (PEOAA). A review of each of these prohibited acts, as animated by the implementing regulations, follows.

3. Interference

The FMLA prohibits two forms of interference: (1) an employer is prohibited from interfering with FMLA rights; and (2) it is unlawful for any person to discharge or in any other manner discriminate against any individual because such individual filed a charge, instituted or caused to be instituted an FMLA proceeding, has given or is about to give information in connection with an FMLA inquiry or proceeding, or testified or is about to testify in an FMLA inquiry or proceeding. 29 USC 2615(a), (b); 29 CFR 825.220(a)(1), (3); *see Conoshenti*, 364 F.3d at 141; *Thomas v. Pearle Vision, Inc.*, 251 F.3d 1132, 1138 (7th Cir. 2001); *Lewis v. Harper Hospital*, 241 F. Supp. 2d 769, 772–73 (E.D. Mich. 2002); *Shtab v. The Greate Bay Hotel and Casino, Inc.*, 173 F. Supp. 2d 255, 260–63 (D.N.J. 2001); *Schoeber v. SMC Pneumatics Inc.*, No. IP99-1285-C-T/G, 2000 U.S. Dist. LEXIS 12478, at *18 (S.D. Ind. Aug. 21, 2000); *LeGrand v. Village of McCook*, No. 96-C-5951, 1998 U.S. Dist. LEXIS 5230, at *19, n.5 (N.D. Ill. April 15, 1998); *Bryant v. Delbar Products, Inc. et al.*, 18 F. Supp. 2d 799, 802 (M.D. Tenn. 1998); *Lacoparra v. Pergament Home Centers, Inc.*, 982 F. Supp. 213, 220 (S.D.N.Y. 1997) (an employer's failure to provide an employee with statutorily–required notice of the FMLA policies constitutes actionable interference where it causes the employee to forfeit FMLA protections).

The Statute does not define the meaning of "interfering with, restraining, or denying the exercise or attempt to exercise FMLA rights." *Sherrod v. Philadelphia Gas Works*, 57 Fed. Appx. 68 (3d Cir. 2003) (FMLA does not define interference); *McKinzie v. Sprint/United Management Co.*, No. 03–2348–GTV, 2004 U.S. Dist. LEXIS 23417, at *28 (D. Kan. Nov. 16, 2004). The DOL (and CAA) implementing regulations, however, broadly define interference as any violation of the Act or the implementing regulations. *George v. Russell Stover Candies, Inc.*, 106 Fed. Appx. 946 (6th Cir. 2004); *Brenneman v. MedCentral Health System*, 366 F.3d 412, 422 (6th Cir. 2004), cert. denied, 2005 U.S. LEXIS 1474 (U.S. 2005); *Conoshenti v. Pub. Serv. Elec. & Gas Co.*, 364 F.3d 135, 142 (3d Cir. 2004); *Liu v. Amway Corp.*, 347 F.3d 1125, 1133 (9th Cir. 2003); *Dittle v.*

USPS, No. 04–146 (PAM/RLE), 2005 U.S. Dist. LEXIS 1487, at *14 (D. Minn. Feb. 2, 2005); *Regan v. Natural Resources Group, Inc.*, 345 F. Supp. 2d 1000, 1010 (D. Minn. 2004); *Paulson v. Superior Plating, Inc.*, No. 03-3118 (RHK/AJB), 2004 U.S. Dist. LEXIS 19383, at *10 (D. Minn. Sept. 27, 2004); *Dressler v. Community Service Communications, Inc.*, 275 F. Supp. 2d 17, n.11 (D. Me. Aug. 6, 2003), *aff'd*, 115 Fed. Appx. 452 (1st Cir. 2004).

The implementing regulations (29 CFR 825.220(b); S. Res. 242, Cong. Rec. S3959, S3970 (April 23, 1996); 29 CFR 825.220(b)) however, broadly define these terms:

> Any violations of the Act or of these regulations constitute interfering with, restraining, or denying the exercise of rights provided by the Act.

See Bachelder v. America West Airlines, Inc., 259 F.3d 1112, 1125 (9th Cir. 2001); *Cooper v. Olin Corp.*, 246 F.3d 1083, 1090 (8th Cir. 2001); *Hodgens v. General Dynamics Corp.*, 144 F.3d 151, 160 n.3 (1st Cir. 1998); *Kent v. Maryland Transp. Auth.*, No. CCB-06-2351, 2006 U.S. Dist. LEXIS 94832, at *10 (D. Md. Dec. 21, 2006), *aff'd*, 2007 U.S. App. LEXIS 16228 (4th Cir. July 9, 2007); *Hillstrom v. Best Western TLC Hotel*, 265 F. Supp. 2d 117, 2003 U.S. Dist. LEXIS 8854, at *22 (D. Mass. May 28, 2003), *aff'd*, 354 F.3d 27 (1st Cir. 2003); *Wilson v. Lemington Home for the Aged*, 159 F. Supp. 2d 186, 194 (W.D. Pa. 2001) (an employer's failure to provide notice to an employee of FMLA rights and responsibilities constitutes actionable interference with FMLA rights); *Schoeber v. SMC Pneumatics, Inc.*, No. IP 99-1285-C T/G, 2000 U.S. Dist. LEXIS 19088 (Dec. 4, 2000) (an employer's erroneous instruction to an employee that only a certain health care provider could fill out the medical certification not required by Act constitutes an act of interference); *Maxwell v. GTE Wireless Service Corp.*, 121 F. Supp. 2d 649, 657 (N.D. Ohio 2000); *Blohm v. Dillards Inc. et al.*, 95 F. Supp. 2d 473, 479 (E.D.N.C. 2000); *Goodwin-Haulmark v. Menninger Clinic, Inc.*, 76 F. Supp. 2d 1235, 1241 (D. Kan. 1999); *Bryant v. Delbar Products, Inc. et al.*, 18 F. Supp. 2d 799, 802 (M.D. Tenn. 1998) (an employer interfered with FMLA rights by assessing an "occurrence" under absenteeism policy for leave covered by FMLA); *LeGrand v. Village of McCook*, No. 96-C-5951, 1998 U.S. Dist. LEXIS 5230, at *12 (N.D. Ill. April 15, 1998) (an employer letter that required less than 15 days to submit medical certification and failed to identify deficiencies in prior certification, as required by the DOL implementing regulations, interfered with the employee's FMLA rights); *Hensley v. Baptist Hospital of East Tennessee, Inc. et al.*, No. 3:96-cv-789, 1997 U.S. Dist. LEXIS 22515, at *32 (E.D. Tenn. Oct. 27, 1997).

Examples of what constitutes "interfering with" the exercise of employee FMLA rights include:

> Refusal to authorize FMLA leave;
>
> Discouraging an employee from using FMLA leave;
>
> Manipulation by a covered employer to avoid responsibilities under the FMLA.

29 CFR 825.220(b); S. Res. 242, Cong. Rec. S3959, S3970 (April 23, 1996); 29 CFR 825.220(b)); *see Stallings v. Hussmann Corp.*, 447 F.3d 1041, 1050 (8th Cir. 2006); *Brenneman v. MedCentral Health System*, 366 F.3d 412, 422 (6th Cir. 2004), *cert. denied*, 543 U.S. 1146 (2005); *Potenza v. City of New York*, 365 F.3d 165, 167 (2d Cir. 2004); *Conoshenti v. Pub. Serv. Elec. & Gas Co.*, 364 F.3d 135, 142 (3d Cir. 2004); *Liu v. Amway Corp.*, 347 F.3d 1125, 1133 (9th Cir. 2003); *Sherrod v. Philadelphia Gas Works*, 57 Fed. Appx. 68 (3d Cir. 2003); *Thomas v. Pearle Vision, Inc.*, 251 F.3d 1132, 1138 (7th Cir. 2001) (discouraging eligible employees from exercising FMLA rights prohibited); *Hicks v. LeRoy's Jewelers, Inc.*, 225 F.3d 659 (table), 2000 U.S. App. LEXIS 17568, at *11, n.6 (6th Cir. July 17, 2000), *cert. denied*, 531 U.S. 1146 (2001); *Robinson v. Overnite Transp. Co.*, 110 F.3d 60 (table), No. 95-3067, 1997 U.S. App. LEXIS 6574, at *23 (4th Cir. April 9, 1997) (under interim regulations); *Bila v. Radioshack Corp.*, No. 03-10177-BC, 2004 U.S. Dist. LEXIS 24649, at *24 (E.D. Mich. Nov. 23, 2004); *McKinzie v. Sprint/United Management Co.*, No. 03-2348-GTV, 2004 U.S. Dist. LEXIS 23417, at *28 (D. Kan. Nov. 16, 2004). An employer interferes with the exercise of protected FMLA rights when, due to circumstances imposed by the employer, employees become reluctant to exercise their rights for fear of being fired or disciplined. *Stallings v. Hussmann Corp.*, 447 F.3d 1041, 1050 (8th Cir. 2006).

In *Bachelder v. America West Airlines, Inc.*, 259 F.3d 1112, 1123 (9th Cir. 2001), the court looked to interpretations of § 8(a)(1) of the National Labor Relations Act because "Section 2615's language of 'interference with' and 'restraint of' the exercise of the rights it guarantees to employees largely mimics that of the NLRA." It should be noted that neither the legislative or regulatory history of the FMLA refers to the NLRA as a model for "interference" claims.

Actionable interference in violation of the FMLA may occur in a wide variety of settings. *See Goodwin-Haulmark v. Menninger Clinic, Inc.*, 76 F. Supp. 2d 1235, 1242 (D. Kan. 1999) (forcing the plaintiff to choose between resignation and working without FMLA leave interfered with the plaintiff's rights by discouraging an employee from using FMLA leave); *Vorhees v. Time Warner Cable National Division*, No. 98–1460, 1999 U.S. Dist. LEXIS 13227, at *17–18 (E.D. PA. Aug. 30, 1999) (creation and advertisement of position that included some of the plaintiff's job duties while the plaintiff was on FMLA leave sufficient to defeat summary judgment on employee claim that employer interfered with the employee's FMLA rights); *Herman v. Princeton City School*, No. 1–C–96–358, 1997 U.S. Dist. LEXIS 22250 (S.D. Ohio Sept. 23, 1997) (requiring an employee to pay the employer's share of health plan premium payments during FMLA leave constituted actionable interference).

An employer interfered with an employee's FMLA rights when a supervisor falsely advised the employee, without adequate investigation, that the only option available to the employee needing leave to care for his seriously ill mother was to resign. *Williams v. Ill. Dept. of Corrections*, No. 05-cv-4227-JPG, 2007 U.S. Dist. LEXIS 17119, at *18-19 (S.D. Ill. March 9, 2007). In other cases, employer conduct was found not to interfere with employee FMLA rights. In *LeGrand v. Village of McCook*, No. 96–C–5951, 1998 U.S. Dist. LEXIS 5230, at *12 (N.D. Ill. April 15, 1998), the court found that an employer posting a notice to all department personnel in several locations stating that if the employee, or anyone purporting to represent the employee, were to first make contact, the signatory of the memorandum should be contacted. The court rejected the argument that the posting of the memorandum constituted actionable interference with the employee's FMLA rights as there was no evidence that it hampered the employee's ability to litigate her claims. *See also Dodgens v. Kent Mfg. Co.*, 955 F. Supp. 560, 564 (D.S.C. 1997) (the employer calling the employee out on FMLA leave twice and asking the employee to take a demotion did not constitute actionable interference claim under the FMLA).

An employer's refusal to authorize FMLA leave does not always constitute actionable interference with FMLA rights. In *Regan v. Natural Resources Group, Inc.*, 345 F. Supp. 2d 1000, 1010 (D. Minn. 2004), the employee alleged that the employer interfered with his FMLA rights by laying him off while on FMLA leave. The employee alleged that the employer should have allowed him to remain on FMLA leave. Citing 29 CFR 825.216(a)(1), the court found that the employer's FMLA responsibilities ceased at the time the employee was laid off. The employer was, therefore, not required to continue providing the employee with FMLA leave.

Similarly, the fact that an employer notifies an employee of his or her termination during FMLA leave does not necessarily constitute actionable interference. *Geromanos v. Columbia Univ., College of Physicians and Surgeons*, 322 F. Supp. 2d 420, 428 (S.D.N.Y. 2004) (employee may be terminated while on medical leave as long as the taking of FMLA leave was not the cause for the termination).

An employer's request that an employee provide weekly progress reports on the employee's treatment while on FMLA leave to attend rehabilitation program for alcoholism did not constitute interference in violation of the FMLA. In *Geromanos v. Columbia Univ., College of Physicians and Surgeons*, 322 F. Supp. 2d 420, 428 (S.D.N.Y. 2004), the court found that such progress reports were not medical certifications within the meaning of the FMLA, but were required in order for plaintiff to comply with the company's paid leave program. The court found that it was both reasonable and permissible for an employer to condition paid leave on an employee's submission of progress reports.

The court in *Geromanos v. Columbia Univ., College of Physicians and Surgeons*, 322 F. Supp. 2d 420, 428 (S.D.N.Y. 2004), also held that the employer did not interfere with plaintiff's FMLA rights by refusing to allow her to work another job while on FMLA leave. The court found that Columbia's decision to terminate plaintiff for violation of the company's prohibition on outside work during paid leave did not constitute interference with her right to FMLA leave. The FMLA did not require the employer to provide plaintiff with pay while on FMLA leave, and was therefore free to impose conditions on matters such as outside work as a condition of providing paid leave. Geromanos was terminated by her employer, in part, because she was working as a part–time Lamaze instructor during FMLA leave in violation of company policy. *Accord Pharakhone v. Nissan North America, Inc.*, 324 F.3d 405 (6th Cir. 2003) (termination for violation of company policy prohibiting employee from working while on FMLA leave did not violate FMLA anti–interference provisions).

Retaliation against an employee who has taken FMLA leave constitutes actionable interference in violation of § 2615(a)(1) as well as illegal retaliation under § 2615(a)(2). *Rigodon v. Deutsche Bank Securities*, No. 04 Civ. 2548 (GEL), 2004 U.S. Dist. LEXIS 22385, at *7 (S.D.N.Y. Nov. 1, 2004) (limitation or denial of overtime and adverse work schedule modification after an employee returns from FMLA leave may constitute interference with FMLA rights).

Of course, if the adverse employment action at issue is unrelated to the employee's exercise of FMLA rights, an employee's interference claim will fail. *Bones v. Honeywell Intl., Inc.*, 366 F.3d 869, 877 (10th Cir. April 23, 2004) (a reason for dismissal that is unrelated to a request for FMLA leave will not support recovery under an interference theory). In *Bones*, the court noted that it was uncontested that the employee violated the employer's absence policy, and that this was the reason he was terminated. The court observed, "Bones' request for an FMLA leave does not shelter her from the obligation, which is the same as that of any other Honeywell employee, to comply with Honeywell's employment policies, including its absence policy."

In a third group of cases, courts have declined to find actionable interference with FMLA rights for technical violations of the DOL regulations. *See Smith v. Eastman Kodak Co. et al.*, No. 95–4677 (DRD), 1999 U.S. Dist. LEXIS 17506 (D.N.J. Oct. 7, 1999), *aff'd*, 2001 U.S. App. LEXIS 15652 (3d Cir. 2001) (an employee who received all FMLA leave to which the employee was entitled did not have an FMLA claim for the employer's failure to inform employee of FMLA rights); *Fisher v. State Farm Mut. Auto. Ins. Co.*, 999 F. Supp. 866, 871 (E.D. Tex. 1998), *aff'd without op.*, 176 F.3d 479 (5th Cir. 1999) (no cause of action for technical violation of the FMLA), *aff'd without opinion*, 176 F.3d 479, 1999 U.S. App. LEXIS 5516 (5th Cir. 1999); *Hensley v. Baptist Hospital of East Tennessee, Inc. et al.*, No. 3:96–cv–789, 1997 U.S. Dist. LEXIS 22515, at *32 (E.D. Tenn. Oct. 27, 1997) (court declined to find substantive violation of the anti–interference provisions of the FMLA based on the employer's telephone call to the employee's physician without the employee's permission, where the employee was given FMLA leave and was returned to work without delay); *Dodgens v. Kent Mfg. Co.*, 955 F. Supp. 560, 565 (D.S.C. 1997) ("Court would be elevating form over substance to permit this claim [failure to explain FMLA benefits and leave rights in employee handbook] to go forward in light of the fact that Dodgens received all of the leave benefits that he was guaranteed pursuant to the FMLA").

In *Dowell v. Indiana Heart Physicians, Inc.*, NO. 1:03–cv–1410–DFH–TAB, 2004 U.S. Dist. LEXIS 26433, at *28 (S.D. Ind. Dec. 22, 2004), the employer contacted the employee's physician to clarify a medical certification without first gaining the employee's permission as required by 29 CFR 825.307(a). The court nevertheless found that the employee failed to state a viable claim for damages because he had not submitted evidence demonstrating that the errant physician contact interfered with his FMLA rights. The court noted that the employer did not try to influence or dissuade the doctor regarding the employee's FMLA leave request.

A co-worker complaint to another co-worker about the plaintiff's taking FMLA leave is not a violation of the FMLA. *Bahr v. Penn. Dept. of Public Welfare*, No. 3:05cv2617, 2007 U.S. Dist. LEXIS 13299, at *9 (M.D. Pa. Feb. 27, 2007).

a. Adequate Employee Notice Requirement

The circuits are split over whether the employee must establish that he or she gave proper notice of a need for FMLA leave in order to establish an FMLA interference claim. The Tenth Circuit has held that whether an employee provided proper notice of the need for FMLA leave is separate from the analysis of the substantive claim that an employer interfered with the exercise of an employee's FMLA rights. *Bones v. Honeywell Intl., Inc.*, 366 F.3d 869, 877 (10th Cir. April 23, 2004). The Sixth Circuit has explicitly made employee notice part of its test for interference with FMLA rights. *See Cavin v. Honda of Am. Mfg., Inc.*, 346 F.3d 713, 719–722 (6th Cir. 2003); *Sherrod v. Philadelphia Gas Works*, 57 Fed. Appx. 68 (3d Cir. 2003) (the employer who denied FMLA leave so the employee could care for grandmother did not interfere with the employee's FMLA rights where the employee failed to notify the employer that the grandmother raised the employee when the employee was a child, making the grandmother *in loco parentis*); *Robinson v. Overnite Transp. Co.*, 110 F.3d 60 (table), No. 95–3067, 1997 U.S. App. LEXIS 6574, at *23 (4th Cir. April 9, 1997) (the employer did not interfere with the employee's FMLA rights where the employee failed to provide the employer adequate notice of need for FMLA leave); *Hobart v. Behavioral Connections of Wood County, Inc.*, No. 3:03CV7313, 2004 U.S. Dist. LEXIS 12051, at *18 (N.D. Ohio July 1, 2004) (finding sufficient evidence that the employee put the employer on notice of the need for FMLA leave to deny summary judgment to the employer); *Brock v. United Grinding Technologies, Inc. et al.*, 257 F. Supp. 2d 1089, 1104–1105 (S.D. Ohio 2003) (no unlawful interference with FMLA rights where an employee failed to give sufficient notice that absences might qualify for FMLA leave); *Howard v. Garage Door Group, Inc.*, 197 F. Supp. 2d 1297, 1309 (D. Kan. 2002), *aff'd*, 2005 U.S. App. LEXIS 3509 (10th Cir. 2005) (where an employee never requested leave, the employer did not interfere with the employee's FMLA rights by failing to notify the employee of her potential eligibility for FMLA benefits at the time of the employee's discharge).

Similarly, an employer does not interfere with an employee's FMLA rights by denying leave when the employee's request referred to a medical condition that a prior "negative" certification had established was not covered by the FMLA. *Stoops v. One Call Communications, Inc.*, 141 F.3d 309, 3313-14 (7th Cir. 1998).

b. Employer Notice Failures as Interference

Courts have found an employer's failure to notify an employee of FMLA rights and responsibilities to constitute actionable interference. *See Wilson v. Lemington Home for the Aged*, 159 F. Supp. 2d 186, 194 (W.D. Pa. 2001) (employer failure to provide notice to the employee of FMLA rights and responsibilities constitutes actionable interference with FMLA rights); *Goodwin-Haulmark v. Menninger Clinic, Inc.*, 76 F. Supp. 2d 1235, 1241 (D. Kan. 1999) (failure to post notice and include summary of FMLA rights in the employee handbook cited as FMLA violations); *Herman v. Princeton City School*, No. 1-C-96-358, 1997 U.S. Dist. LEXIS 22250 (S.D. Ohio Sept. 23, 1997). *But see Dodgens v. Kent Mfg. Co.*, 955 F. Supp. 560, 565 (D.S.C. 1997) ("Court would be elevating form over substance to permit this claim [failure to explain FMLA benefits and leave rights in employee handbook] to go forward in light of the fact that Dodgens received all of the leave benefits that he was guaranteed pursuant to the FMLA").

Other courts have held that, in order for there to be actionable interference, the employee must have forfeited FMLA rights because of the lack of notice. *See Conoshenti v. Pub. Serv. Elec. & Gas Co.*, 364 F.3d 135, 141 (3d Cir. 2004); *Sisturn v. Time-Warner Cable*, No. 02-CV-8023, 2004 U.S. Dist. LEXIS 16681, at *42–46 (E.D. Pa. Aug. 19, 2004), *Geromanos v. Columbia Univ., College of Physicians and Surgeons*, 322 F. Supp. 2d 420, 428 (S.D.N.Y. 2004); *Schober v. SMC Pneumatics, Inc.*, No. IP 99-1285-CT/G, 2000 U.S. Dist. LEXIS 19088 (S.D. Ind. Dec. 4, 2000) (an employer giving misleading or incorrect information to an employee about the employee's FMLA rights constitutes interference if the incorrect information causes the employee to forfeit FMLA protections); *Covey v. Methodist Hospital of Dyersburg, Inc.*, 56 F. Supp. 2d 965, 968-69 (W.D. Tenn. 1999) (to prevail on failure to inform claim, the employee had to demonstrate (1) defendants failed to correctly inform the employee of FMLA rights; and (2) that failure causes the employee to forfeit protections provided by the Act); *Jefferies v. Dept. of Navy*, 78 MSPR 255 (1998); *Gross v. Dept. of Justice*, 77 MSPR 83 (1997) (the appellant failed to show that he was harmed by the agency's failure to inform him of his rights and responsibilities under the FMLA).

An employee who is unable to show prejudice resulting from an employer's failure to notify the employee that leave has been designated as FMLA leave fails to state an FMLA interference claim. In *Wright v. Owens-Illinois, Inc.*, 2:02-cv-223-LJM-WGH, 2004 U.S. Dist. LEXIS 8535, at *20 (S.D. Ind. May 14, 2004), the court found that the plaintiff could not establish prejudice from the employer's failure to notify the employee that his ten weeks of medical leave and eight weeks of light duty had been designated as FMLA leave. The court opined that "the lack of notice of FMLA designation is irrelevant if a plaintiff cannot make a showing of prejudice. Wright cannot connect the lack of notice to any prejudice because he would not have been able to return to his position even if Owens promptly notified him that his 10-week leave and 'light duty' assignment counted as FMLA leave." Plaintiff was placed on permanent medical restriction that would prevent him from ever performing the essential functions of his job, and he received more than 12 weeks of FMLA leave.

An employer may violate the anti-interference provisions of the FMLA by enforcement of a company policy that violates the requirements of the FMLA. In *Cavin v. Honda of America Mfg., Inc.*, 346 F.3d 713, 726 (6th Cir. 2003), Cavin alleged that Honda interfered with his FMLA rights by failing to recognize certain absences as covered by the FMLA. Honda argued that it properly denied FMLA status to the disputed absences because Cavin failed to properly notify Honda of his need for FMLA leave. Pursuant to Honda policy, Cavin was required to request FMLA leave within three days of his unforeseeable absence due to a motorcycle accident. Finding Honda's notice requirements for foreseeable FMLA leave stricter than those contemplated by the FMLA, the court found that Honda interfered with Cavin's right to FMLA leave by denying FMLA leave status because Cavin did not comply with the time limits imposed by Honda policy.

In *Bila v. RadioShack Corp.*, No. 03-10177-BC, 2004 U.S. Dist. LEXIS 24649, at *22-24 (E.D. Mich. Nov. 23, 2004), the court found that an employee's FMLA interference claim based on erroneous advice he initially received that he was not eligible for FMLA leave due to the anticipated birth of a child failed where the employee ultimately received all of the FMLA leave that he requested.

The FMLA was not, however, intended to enable an employee to sue for an employer's failure to give notice, unless such failure impeded the exercise of FMLA rights. Where plaintiff was medically unable to return to work at the conclusion of 12 weeks of FMLA leave, and where the employee could not have structured her leave in any different fashion if the employer had provided timely notice, the employee fails to state an interference claim within the meaning of the FMLA. *Miller v. Personal-Touch of Virginia, Inc.*, 342 F. Supp. 2d 499, 513 (E.D. Va. Nov. 2, 2004). [An employer's notice obligations are addressed in Chapter 8, "Notice Requirements."]

c. Employer Actions That "Chill" Employee FMLA Rights

Neither the statute nor the implementing regulations define what it means to be "discouraged" from exercising rights under the FMLA. *Sabbrese v. Lowe's Home Centers, Inc.*, 320 F. Supp. 2d 311, 327 (W.D. Pa. June 9, 2004). Where an employer's actions provide a strong disincentive against an employee taking FMLA leave, the employer violates the FMLA. *McKinzie v. Sprint/United Management Co.*, No. 03-2348-GTV, 2004 U.S. Dist. LEXIS 23417, at *28 (D. Kan. Nov. 16, 2004). Courts in several recent decisions have addressed employee allegations of employer actions that discourage or chill employee FMLA rights.

The courts are split regarding whether an employee may bring an interference claim for employer conduct that could "chill" an employee's desire to take FMLA leave. *Compare Bachelder v. America West Airlines, Inc.*, 259 F.3d 1112, 1124 (9th Cir. 2001) (employer acts that "chill" an employees' willingness to exercise those rights constitutes unlawful "interference" or "restraint"); *Shtab v. The Greate Bay Hotel and Casino, Inc.*, 173 F. Supp. 2d 255, 267-68 (D.N.J. 2001) (where authorization for FMLA leave was denied after leave occurred, noting that a jury could conclude that employer's suggestion that employee take different date of leave chilled the plaintiff's assertion of rights under FMLA); *Williams v. Shenango, Inc.*, 986 F. Supp. 309, 320-321 (W.D. Pa. 1997) (where the employer denied request for FMLA leave and suggested that the employee take leave on a different week, but retroactively approved leave after it was taken, a reasonable person could conclude that the employer interfered with FMLA rights) *with Keller v. Putnam Fiduciary Trust Co. et al.*, 238 F.3d 5, 10 (1st Cir. 2000) (not every comment about problems created by the use of FMLA leave can fairly be treated as an adverse employment action violative of the FMLA); *Mardis v. Central Nat. Bank & Trust of Enid*, 173 F.3d 864 (table), No. 98-6056, 1999 U.S. App. LEXIS 7261, at *8 (10th Cir. April 15, 1999) (threatening an employee with absolute forfeiture of accrued but unused vacation and sick leave might indeed establish a violation of the FMLA. However, mere postponement of a scheduled vacation and temporary restriction of use of vacation leave with no ultimate loss of accrued benefits, would likely not constitute actionable discouragement); *Sweeney v. West*, 149 F.3d 550, 556 (7th Cir. 1998) (not all comments about problems created by use of FMLA leave are actionable violations of the FMLA); *Burch v. WDAS AM/FM, AM.FM Inc.*, No. 00-4852, 2002 U.S. Dist. LEXIS 12290, at *27 (E.D. Pa. July 1, 2002) (where an employee was not denied leave, the employer's failure to promptly respond to the employee's e-mail and periodic reminders about overdue reports and other matters required of the employee in the ordinary course of work not prohibited conduct); *Alifano v. Merck & Co., Inc.*, 175 F. Supp. 2d 792 (E.D. Pa. 2001) (the plaintiff could not bring claim for interference in the absence of any adverse employment action where the employer allegedly discouraged but did not deny leave); *Hensley v. Baptist Hospital of East Tennessee, Inc. et al.*, No. 3:96-cv-789, 1997 U.S. Dist. LEXIS 22515, at *32 (E.D. Tenn. Oct. 27, 1997) (court declined to find substantive violation of the anti-interference provisions of the FMLA based on the employer's telephone call to the employee's physician without the employee's permission, where the employee was given FMLA leave and was returned to work without delay); *Dodgens v. Kent Mfg. Co.*, 955 F. Supp. 560, 565 (D.S.C. 1997) ("Court would be elevating form over substance to permit this claim to go forward in light of the fact that Dodgens received all of the leave benefits that he was guaranteed pursuant to the FMLA").

Sarcastic and derogatory comments about an employee's need to take time off from work continues to be a ripe area for FMLA interference claims. Where an employee, subjected to sarcastic or derogatory comments, continues to request and receive FMLA, several recent court decisions have found that such conduct did not dissuade or chill the employee from exercising FMLA rights. In *Dittle v. USPS*, No. 04-146 (PAM/RLE), 2004 U.S. Dist. LEXIS 1487, at *22 (D. Minn. Feb. 2, 2005), the court found that a supervisor's comments, "some people use FMLA to get out of work," and reminders that the employee had taken more sick leave and had more FMLA call-ins than any other employee, although characterized as inappropriate, were ultimately found not to constitute actionable interference with FMLA rights. The court found no evidence that the comments dissuaded plaintiff from requesting and taking FMLA leave.

Similarly, in *McKinzie v. Sprint/United Management Co.*, No. 03-2348-GTV, 2004 U.S. Dist. LEXIS 23417, at *28 (D. Kan. Nov. 16, 2004), plaintiff's supervisor made remarks in staff meetings and in an e-mail message that either explicitly or implicitly cast doubt on the legitimacy of plaintiff's need for approved intermittent FMLA leave for panic attacks. Because plaintiff was allowed to take FMLA leave each time she needed to do so, the court found that plaintiff failed to demonstrate that her supervisor's conduct discouraged her from taking FMLA leave or created any kind of chilling effect.

A supervisor's attempt to dissuade an employee from taking more FMLA leave shortly after his transfer into the office failed to demonstrate actionable interference with FMLA rights where the employee actually received all of the FMLA leave he requested. *Bila v. RadioShack Corp.*, No. 03-10177-BC, 2004 U.S. Dist. LEXIS 24649, at *22-24 (E.D. Mich. Nov. 23, 2004).

Statements from a supervisor of how important the employee was to the company and that the company really needed him did not discourage the employee from taking FMLA leave. *Bailey v. Miltope Corp.*, No. 2:05-cv-1061-MEF (WO), 2007 U.S. Dist. LEXIS 1760, at *22-23 (M.D. Ala. Jan. 8, 2007).

An employer's suggestion that an employee could work from home rather than take FMLA leave could constitute discouragement. *Butler v. IntraCare Hosp., N.*, Civ. No. H-05-2854, 2006 U.S. Dist. LEXIS 75297, at *4 (S.D. Tex. Oct. 4, 2006).

Derogatory comments and overt hostility on the part of an employee's supervisor toward an employee's medical condition and need for leave was cited by the court in *Lukacinsky v. Panasonic Service Co.*, No. 03–40141–FDS, 2004 U.S. Dist. LEXIS 25846, at ** 25, 54 (D. Mass. Nov. 29, 2004), as evidence of a willful FMLA violation, thereby extending the statute of limitations from two to three years to initiate a civil action. The supervisor's conduct was also cited as strong evidence of pretext, contributing to the defeat of the employer's motion for summary judgment on plaintiff's FMLA retaliation claim.

The denial and reduction in available overtime and adverse work schedule modifications in retaliation for an employee taking FMLA leave may constitute actionable interference with FMLA rights. *Rogodon v. Deuthsche Bank Securities, Inc.*, 04 Civ. 2548 (GEL), 2004 U.S. Dist. LEXIS 22385, at *8–11 (S.D.N.Y. Nov. 1, 2004).

A two-week notice policy discourages employees from taking FMLA leave if the need for leave is unforeseeable because they could have to go two weeks without pay. *Solovey v. Wyo. Valley Health Care Sys. Hosp.*, 396 F. Supp. 2d 534, 540 (M.D. Pa. 2005).

Disciplining an employee for taking FMLA–protected intermittent leave is sufficient to discourage or chill an employee from exercising FMLA rights. In *Sabbrese v. Lowe's Home Centers, Inc.*, 320 F. Supp. 2d 311, 326–331 (W.D. Pa. 2004), Loew's issued plaintiff a disciplinary warning for leaving his department without notifying a supervisor. Plaintiff was a known diabetic who was required to control his blood sugar to avoid fainting and nausea. His condition was approved by his employer for intermittent FMLA leave. There was no dispute that plaintiff left his department because his blood sugar level dropped, and he needed to eat to control his blood sugar. The court characterized plaintiff's leaving to go on his lunch break as intermittent FMLA leave. In rejecting the employer's motion for summary judgment, the court observed that "[d]isciplining Sabbrese for taking permitted leave, however, is arguably a more egregious 'chilling' of his rights under the FMLA because he was actually penalized for exercising [his] right to take intermittent leave when medically necessary."

Mischaracterizing an employee's leave, denying requests for FMLA leave and extensions of leave, and using her protected FMLA leave as a factor in its decision to terminate the employee was found sufficient by the Ninth Circuit in *Liu v. Amway Corp.*, 347 F.3d 1125, 1133 (9th Cir. 2003), to survive the employer's motion for summary judgment. According to the court: "An employer has discouraged an employee from taking FMLA leave when his or her supervisor interferes with the length and dates of leave, including denying leave out right." The mischaracterization of her leave as personal leave rather than FMLA leave, the court found, deprived Liu of rights under the FMLA. By designating her leave as "personal," she was subject to the control and discretion of her supervisor in taking leave that she had a statutory right to take.

Of course, an employee who receives disciplinary warnings for absences not covered by the FMLA fails to make a viable FMLA claim. *Khan v. Federal Reserve Bank of New York*, 02 Civ. 8893 (JCF), 2005 U.S. Dist. LEXIS 1543, at *42 (S.D.N.Y. Feb. 2, 2005).

d. Manipulation

The regulations provide examples of impermissible employer manipulation to avoid FMLA responsibilities. Although substantially the same, the examples differ somewhat between Title I, the CAA, and the PEOAA. For purposes of Title I (29 CFR 825.220(b)(1)–(3)), interference in the form of manipulation by a covered employer to avoid FMLA responsibilities includes:

(1) Transferring employees from one worksite to another for the purpose of reducing worksites, or to keep worksites, below the 50–employee threshold for employee eligibility under the Act;

(2) Changing the essential functions of the job in order to preclude the taking of leave; and

(3) Reducing the hours available to work in order to avoid employee eligibility.

See *Conoshenti v. Pub. Serv. Elec. & Gas Co.*, 364 F.3d 135, n.12 (3d Cir. 2004); *Dressler v. Community Service Communications, Inc.*, 275 F. Supp. 2d 17, n.11 (D. Me. 2003), *aff'd*, 115 Fed. Appx. 452 (1st Cir. 2004).

Manipulation cases have included situations where an employer misinforms or fails to inform an employee of the existence of FMLA rights, or imposes adverse employment actions in anticipation of the employee's request for FMLA leave in order to make such leave unavailable. *Dressler v. Community Service Communications, Inc.*, 275 F. Supp. 2d 17, n. 11 (D. Me. 2003), *aff'd*, 115 Fed. Appx. 452 (1st Cir. 2004) (*citing LaCoparra v. Pergament Home Ctrs., Inc.*, 982 F. Supp. 213, 220 (S.D.N.Y. 1997)). However, the manipulation of the facts to avoid paying for sick leave, rather than to avoid FMLA responsibilities, has been held to be unprotected by the FMLA. *Hicks v. LeRoy's Jewelers, Inc.*, 225 F.3d 659 (table), 2000 U.S. App. LEXIS 17568, at *11, n. 6 (6th Cir. July 17, 2000), *cert. denied* 531 U.S. 1146 (2001).

In *Norman v. Southern Guaranty Ins. Co.*, 191 F. Supp. 2d 1321, 1331 (M.D. Ala. 2002), the court addressed the employee's claim that the employer's failure to calculate the 12 weeks of FMLA leave in such a way that the employee avoided violation of the employer's absenteeism policies constituted unlawful interference. In that case, by designating the employee's leave time at the end of the applicable 12-month period as FMLA, the employer was able to apply its internal absenteeism policy in such a way as to terminate her (for violation of the policy). If the employer had designated her FMLA-qualifying leave at the beginning of the applicable period, the employee would not be in violation of the company absenteeism policy. The employee argued that by calculating the employee's leave as it did, the employer manipulated the leave to avoid responsibilities under the Act. The court disagreed. It found that there is "simply nothing in the FMLA or its enforcement regulations that affirmatively requires that an employer always designate FMLA leave in such a manner that the employee would not be in violation of the employer's leave policy." *Norman*, 191 F. Supp. at 1331. However, the court went on to find that an employer that intentionally applies its company policies in such a way as to interfere with or retaliate against an employee for exercising rights under the FMLA might be liable under the FMLA. Such liability, however, would require some element of intent by the employer to frustrate or avoid FMLA responsibilities. Because it requires intent, the issue was considered as a discrimination claim rather than an interference claim.

The CAA FMLA regulations include Title I examples 2 and 3, but not example number 1. S. Res. 242, Cong. Rec. S3959, S3970 (April 23, 1996); 29 CFR 825.220(b)). The first example of manipulation in the Title I regulations was not included in the comparable CAA regulations because the CAA does not include a minimum employee worksite complement to determine employee eligibility. Title I does.

To be eligible for FMLA leave, an employee covered by Title I must meet three requirements: (1) the employee must have been employed by the employer for at least 12 months; (2) the employee must have been employed at least 1,250 hours of service during the 12 months immediately preceding leave commencement; and (3) the employee must be employed at a worksite where 50 or more employees are employed by the employer within 75 miles of that worksite. 29 CFR 825.110(a)(1)–(3). Eligibility for FMLA leave for employees covered by the CAA has two preconditions: (1) the employee has been employed by a CAA employing office for 12 months; and (2) the employee has been employed for at least 1,250 hours during the previous 12 months. S. Res. 242, Cong. Rec. S3959, S3961 (April 23, 1996); 29 CFR 825.110(a).

For the same reason, the first example of employer manipulation would not apply to employees covered by the PEOAA. Like the CAA, the PEOAA does not include a minimum employee worksite complement as a precondition to eligibility for FMLA leave. *See* 3 USC 412(a)(2)(B). [Employee eligibility is addressed more fully in Chapter 5, "Employee Eligibility for Leave."]

e. Denial of Restoration and Interference

The different forms of prohibited conduct carry different burdens of proof, some easier to prove than others. Such differences drive employees to fit the facts of one type of case into the easier proof scheme of another. Such a case was addressed by the court in *Dressler v. Community Service Communications, Inc.*, 275 F. Supp. 2d 17, n.11 (D. Me. 2003), *aff'd*, 115 Fed. Appx. 452 (1st Cir. 2004). There, the court addressed the plaintiff's argument that he was denied restoration to his former position when he was laid off during his use of intermittent leave. According to the court:

> Dressler's firing–as–a–denial–of–restoration–argument is simply a clever way of trying to shortcut his burden of persuading the Court that sufficient evidence exists in the record for a fact finder to reject Commtel's justification and to conclude, instead, that Dressler was terminated in retaliation for exercising his FMLA rights. For this

reason, I conclude that the theory Dressler advances in his memorandum of law does not make out a [Section] 2615(a) interference claim, only a retaliation claim masquerading as one. After all, the entire impetus of Dressler's case is that he was fired because of his need for FMLA leave in 2001.

The court went on to treat the claim as a retaliation case, and applied the tougher *McDonnell Douglas* shifting proof scheme. The employee failed to meet his burden of proof to defeat summary judgment.

Other courts have held that the refusal to restore an eligible employee to the same or an equivalent position upon his or her return from FMLA leave violates the anti-interference provisions of the FMLA. See *Hackett v. Clifton Gunderson*, LLC, No. 03 C 6046, 2004 U.S. Dist. LEXIS 21919, at *19 (N.D. III. Nov. 4, 2004); *LaFortune v. Fiber Materials, Inc.*, No. 03-275-P-H, 2004 U.S. Dist. LEXIS 21405, at *10 (D. Me. Oct. 25, 2004) (loss of supervisor responsibilities and private office sufficient evidence to allow fact finder to conclude that new position is not equivalent to former position); *Hillstrom v. Best Western TLC Hotel*, 265 F. Supp. 2d 117 (D. Mass. 2003), *aff'd*, 354 F.3d 27 (1st Cir. 2003).

In *Hoge v. Honda of America MFG., Inc.*, 384 F.3d 238 (6th Cir. 2004), the court found that an employer's failure to return an employee to work within two days of the conclusion of her FMLA leave interfered with her rights in violation of the FMLA. [The case is addressed more fully in Chapter 13.]

The First Circuit in *Dressler v. Community Service Communications, Inc.*, 115 Fed. Appx. 452 (1st Cir. 2004), affirmed the lower court's decision awarding summary judgment to the employer regarding his FMLA claim for failure to restore the employee to the same or an equivalent position.

In *Ashe v. Aronov Homes, Inc.*, 354 F. Supp. 2d 1251 (M.D. Ala. 2004), language in the memorandum prepared by the employer regarding plaintiff's termination citing his return from a lengthy FMLA leave absence was sufficient to defeat the employer's motion of summary judgment on the employee's interference claim alleging that the employer violated the FMLA by not restoring him to the same or an equivalent position. The employer alleged that it terminated plaintiff for reasons unrelated to FMLA usage, but the court noted the absence of any reference to such independent reason in the memorandum justifying the employee's termination.

4. Discrimination

Three types of discrimination are prohibited by the statutes and implementing regulations: (1) use; (2) opposition to unlawful practices; and (3) participation in protected activities. Each of these forms of discrimination is addressed separately below.

a. Use of FMLA Leave

(1) General Rule

An employer is prohibited from discriminating against employees or prospective employees who have used FMLA leave. 29 CFR 825.220(c); S. Res. 242, Cong. Rec. S3959, S3970 (April 23, 1996); 29 CFR 825.220(c); see *Conoshenti v. Pub. Serv. Elec. & Gas Co.*, 364 F.3d 135, 141-142 (3d Cir. 2004); *Spurlock v. Peterbilt Motors Co., Inc.*, 58 Fed. Appx. 630 (6th Cir. 2003) (the employer may not retaliate against an employee for taking leave under the FMLA); *Chandler v. Specialty Tires of Am. Inc.*, 283 F.3d 818, 825 (6th Cir. 2002); *Smith v. BellSouth Telecommunications, Inc.*, 273 F.3d 1303, 1307-14 (11th Cir. 2001); *Brungart v. BellSouth Telecommunications, Inc.*, 231 F.3d 791, 798 (11th Cir. 2000), cert. denied, 532 U.S. 1037 (2001); *King v. Preferred Technical Group*, 166 F.3d 887, 891 (7th Cir. 1999); *Duckworth v. Pratt & Whitney, Inc.*, 152 F.3d 1, 10-11 (1st Cir. 1998); *Hodgens v. General Dynamics Corp.*, 144 F.3d 151, 160 n.4 (1st Cir. 1998); *Gordon v. Trustees of Governors State U.*, No. 06 C 4957, 2007 U.S. Dist. LEXIS 31864, at *11-12 (N.D. III. April 26, 2007); *Ungerfleider v. Fleet Mortgage Group of Fleet Bank*, 329 F. Supp. 2d 343, (D. Conn. 2004); *Bradley v. Mary Rutan Hospital Assoc.*, 322 F. Supp. 2d 926, 937 (S.D. Ohio 2004); *Ariba v. Owens-Illinois, Inc. et al.*, No. 1:02CV00111, 2003 U.S. Dist. LEXIS 9429, at *14 (M.D.N.C. June 4, 2003); *Schoeber v. SMC Pneumatics Inc.*, No. IP99-1285-C-T/G, 2000 U.S. Dist. LEXIS 12478, at n. 7 (S.D. Ind. Aug. 21, 2000); *Hillstrom v. Best Western TLC Hotel*, 265 F. Supp. 2d 117 (D. Mass. 2003), *aff'd*, 354 F.3d 27 (1st Cir. 2003).

The rule does not appear to be obviously grounded in any provision in the statute. See *Hodgens v. General Dynamics Corp.*, 144 F.3d 151, 160 n.4 (1st Cir. 1998) (FMLA does not explicitly make it unlawful to discriminate against an employee for use of FMLA leave); *Ariba v. Owens-Illinois, Inc.* et al., No. 1:02CV00111, 2003 U.S. Dist. LEXIS 9429, at *14 (M.D.N.C.

June 4, 2003); *Schoeber v. SMC Pneumatics Inc.*, No. IP99–1285–C–T/G, 2000 U.S. Dist. LEXIS 12478, at n.7 (S.D. Ind. Aug. 21, 2000); *Dodgens v. Kent Mfg., Co.*, 955 F. Supp. 560, 565 (D.S.C. 1997) (cause of action for retaliatory discharge available even though not specifically provided for under § 2617).

There are two anti-discrimination provisions in Title I, §§ 105(a)(2) and 105(b), 29 USC 2615(a)(2), (b). Neither expressly prohibits discrimination based on the use of FMLA leave. Respectively, those sections prohibit discrimination for opposing unlawful practices and for participation in enforcement proceedings. The argument could be made that § 825.220(c) is grounded in the anti-interference provisions of the Act, 29 USC 2615(a)(1). That is, discrimination, by its very nature, interferes with, restrains, or denies the exercise or attempt to exercise FMLA rights. The structure of the DOL implementing regulations reinforces this interpretation. The lead-in language in § 825.220(a) provides, in pertinent part, that the FMLA prohibits interference with employee rights under the law.

In *Bachelder v. America West Airlines, Inc.*, 259 F.3d 1112, 1124–25 (9th Cir. 2001), the Ninth Circuit held that the part of § 825.220(c) that prohibits an employer from using the taking of FMLA leave as a negative factor actually pertains to the "interference with the exercise of FMLA rights" section of the Statute, § 2615(a)(1), and not the anti-retaliation and anti-discrimination sections, §§ 2615(a)(2) and (b). Accordingly, the court applied the burden of proof used for interference claims, not the burden of proof scheme used for FMLA retaliation or discrimination claims. *See Hodgens v. General Dynamics Corp.*, 144 F.3d 151, 159–160 (1st Cir. 1998) (discrimination for "use" of FMLA leave grounded in § 2615(a)(1) as a form of "interference"). Some other forms of discrimination are listed as examples of such interference. *See* 29 CFR 825.220(a); S. Res. 242, Cong. Rec. S3959, S3970 (April 23, 1996); 29 CFR 825.220(a).

Unfortunately, there is nothing in the regulatory development that specifies the statutory source for the anti-discrimination for "use" rule. The absence of such direct linkage may encourage employers to challenge the validity of the rule. Several courts, however, have found § 825.220(c) to be valid. *See Hodgens v. General Dynamics Corp.*, 144 F.3d 151, 160 n.4 (1st Cir. 1998) (FMLA does not explicitly make it unlawful to discriminate against an employee for use of FMLA leave); *Schoeber v. SMC Pneumatics Inc.*, No. IP99–1285–C–T/G, 2000 U.S. Dist. LEXIS 12478, at n.7 (S.D. Ind. Aug. 21, 2000); *Hillstrom v. Best Western TLC Hotel*, 265 F. Supp. 2d 117 (D. Mass. 2003) (although FMLA does not explicitly make it unlawful to retaliate against an employee for exercising rights under the FMLA, Act was clearly intended to provide such protection).

The term "discriminating" is not defined for purposes of this provision. It is, therefore, unclear whether the term refers to discrimination in the formal Title VII sense of disparate treatment or disparate impact theories, or whether a more generic form of "discrimination" is intended. As with the many other undefined terms throughout the implementing regulations, the lack of definition of the key term "discriminating" leaves open the possibility for creative arguments by advocates for employers and employees on the meaning of the regulation.

Note that the rule applies to "employees or prospective employees." It is not limited to "eligible employees." An "employee" is a defined term under the Act. 29 USC 2611(3); 2 USC 1312(a)(1) (incorporating § 101 of Title I, 29 USC 2611, into the CAA). The term "prospective employee" is not defined. Presumably, it means an applicant for employment. There is some evidence that this may be the case as the DOL Comments accompanying issuance of the final implementing regulations indicate that "prospective employee" was added to address employer inquires of FMLA usage by job applicants. *See* Preamble, 29 CFR 825.220. Since, however, virtually anyone can be a "prospective" employee, an argument could be made that the regulation applies to those who have not formally applied for a position with a covered federal employer. For example, an individual who has used FMLA leave does not apply for a position with a federal agency because it is known that management in this federal agency does not hire those who have used FMLA leave. In that sense, the individual who did not apply could be a prospective employee.

As discussed in Section III of this chapter, "Enforcement", the coverage of "employees or prospective employees" from employer prohibited acts does not provide complete protection. While the enforcement mechanisms are different for each federal sector FMLA leave, essentially, there are two choices for enforcement: (1) filing a civil action in court; or (2) filing a complaint with an administrative body that investigates the claim. Civil actions are limited to "eligible employees." Administrative complaints must be filed by employees or persons acting on behalf of the employee. The regulations say nothing about prospective employees being able to file administrative complaints or civil actions.

This anti-discrimination rule is limited to situations where FMLA leave has already been used. By its terms, it would not apply to prospective situations where an employee has unsuccessfully attempted to use FMLA leave. For example, an employee's request for FMLA leave is denied. Subsequently, the employee is denied a preferred assignment by management. The employee suspects that the denial was due to the prior request for FMLA leave. By its terms, such a discrimination claim would not be available as there was no "use" of FMLA leave. However, as discussed previously, the denial of FMLA leave could be the basis for an interference claim. The denial of FMLA leave could also be the basis of a discrimination claim under the "opposition" theory.

The regulations illustrate the rule with three examples:

1) If an employee on leave without pay would otherwise be entitled to full benefits (other than health benefits) the same benefits would be required to be provided to an employee on unpaid FMLA leave.

2) By the same token, employers cannot use the taking of FMLA leave as a negative factor in employment actions, such as hiring, promotions or disciplinary actions.

3) FMLA leave cannot be counted under "no fault" attendance policies.

29 CFR 825.220(c); S. Res. 242, Cong. Rec. S3959, S3970 (April 23, 1996); 29 CFR 825.220(c); see *Hite v. Vermeer Mfg., Co.*, 446 F.3d 858, 865 (8th Cir. 2006) (negative factor); *Brenneman v. Medical Health System*, 366 F.3d 412, 422 (6th Cir. 2004), cert. denied, 2005 U.S. LEXIS 1474 (U.S. 2005); *Conoshenti v. Pub. Serv. Elec. & Gas Co.*, 364 F.3d 135, 141–142 (3d Cir. 2004); *Liu v. Amway Corp.*, 347 F.3d 1125, 1133 (9th Cir. 2003); *Cavin v. Honda of America Mfg., Inc.*, 346 F.3d 713, 726 (6th Cir. 2003) (negative factor); *Darby v. Bratch et al.*, 287 F.3d 673, 679–80 (8th Cir. 2002); *Bachelder v. America West Airlines, Inc.*, 259 F.3d 1112, 1122 (9th Cir. 2001) (upholding validity of § 825.220(c)); *King v. Preferred Technical Group*, 166 F.3d 887, 891 (7th Cir. 1999) (negative factor); *Hodgens v. General Dynamics Corp.*, 144 F.3d 151, 159–160 (1st Cir. 1998); *Stoops v. One Call Communications, Inc.*, 141 F.3d 309, 312 (7th Cir. 1998) (FMLA–qualifying leave may not be counted against an employee under an employer's "no fault" attendance policy); *Bauer v. Varity Dayton–Walther Corp.*, 118 F.3d 1109, 1111 (6th Cir. 1997) (no fault attendance policy); *Hackett v. Clifton Gunderson, LLC*, No. 03 C 6046, 2004 U.S. Dist. LEXIS 21919, at *21 (N.D. Ill. Nov. 4, 2004) (negative factor); *Bradley v. Mary Rutan Hospital Assoc.*, 322 F. Supp. 2d 926, 937 (S.D. Ohio 2004); *Geromanos v. Columbia Univ., College of Physicians and Surgeons*, 322 F. Supp. 2d 420, 427 (S.D.N.Y. 2004) (negative factor); *Wright v. Owens–Illinois, Inc.*, 2:02–cv–223–LJM–WGH, 2004 U.S. Dist. LEXIS 8535, at *20 (S.D. Ind. May 14, 2004); *Roberts v. Owens–Illinois, Inc.*, 2:02–cv–207–LJM–WGH, 2004 U.S. Dist. LEXIS 8534, at *15 (S.D. Ind. May 14, 2004).

Neither past nor anticipated FMLA leave may be used as grounds for an adverse action. *Baugher v. Dekko Heating Technologies*, 92 Fed. Appx. 328 (7th Cir. 2004). However, an employer is not obliged to keep an individual on the payroll so that s/he can take future FMLA leave. *Baugher v. Dekko Heating Technologies*, 92 Fed. Appx. 328 (7th Cir. 2004) (employee discharged for longstanding performance deficiencies plus an episode of perceived dishonesty did not have actionable retaliation claim).

A brief review of these examples follows.

(2) Benefits

To avoid violating the "use" discrimination provisions of the FMLA, employers must provide an employee on FMLA leave, paid or unpaid, with the same benefits as an employee who is on non–FMLA leave, paid or unpaid. According to the Comments to the final DOL regulations, "FMLA's anti–discrimination provisions were interpreted in the Interim Final Rule to prohibit an employer from requiring more of an employee who took FMLA leave than the employer requires of employees who take other forms of paid or unpaid leave (e.g., requirements to furnish written notice or certification for use of leave)." Preamble, 29 CFR 825.220. When an employee or employer elects to substitute paid leave (of any type) for unpaid FMLA leave, and the employer's procedural requirements for taking that kind of leave are less stringent than the requirements for FMLA (e.g., notice or certification requirements), only the less stringent requirements may be imposed. 29 CFR 825.207(h); S. Res. 242, Cong. Rec. S3959, S3966 (April 23, 1996); 29 CFR 825.207(h).

In *Ghattas Trust v. Unumprovident Life Ins.*, No. 1:03cv1614A (JCC), 2004 U.S. Dist. LEXIS 26753, at *33 (E.D. Va. Oct. 5, 2004), the employer adopted a group life insurance plan with a provision that excluded any employee who was on leave when the plan took effect. Employees on FMLA leave would be grandfathered under the old plan, but excluded from the new plan. The court found that by grandfathering the old life insurance benefits, the employer satisfied the requirement of the FMLA to return the employee to the position with the same benefits as prior to taking FMLA leave. The court also noted that 29 USC 2614(a)(3) provides that restored employees are not entitled to the accrual of any employment benefit during any period of FMLA leave, or any right, benefit, or position of employment other than what the employee would have been entitled to had he or she not taken leave. [For a further discussion of the affect of an employer's paid or unpaid leave policies on FMLA leave, see Chapter 11, "Substitution of Paid Leave."]

(3) Negative Factor

The term "negative factor" is undefined. The term "employment action" is also not formally defined, but illustrated with examples. The examples are of tangible employment actions, such as hiring, promotions, or disciplinary actions. It is unclear whether "employment action" is limited to tangible employment actions, or whether intangible (e.g., minor) "employment actions" are also included. For example, Title VII has been interpreted not to cover various intangible employment actions, such as so-called oral "discussions" given by management to an employee. *See White v. Postmaster General,* EEOC Request No. 01921696, 3306/E1 (1992). By regulation, the EEOC will generally not consider allegations of discrimination based on proposed employment actions. *See* 29 CFR 1613.215(a)(2).

Absent further direction, employers might argue that only tangible "employment actions" are covered by the "use" discrimination regulation, citing the examples provided. *See also Darby v. Bratch et al.,* 287 F.3d 673, 679–80 (8th Cir. 2002) (reversing the district court after finding that the plaintiff did suffer adverse employment action when she was told upon returning to work that she would not be promoted, she was disciplined for FMLA absences, and failure to be rehired); *Keller v. Putnam Fiduciary Trust Co. et al.,* 238 F.3d, 5, 10 (1st Cir. 2001) (noting that not every comment about problems created by use of FMLA leave constitutes an adverse employment action violating the FMLA; what is prevented is adverse action against the employee for using protected leave).

Advocates for employees, on the other hand, could argue that the lack of definition combined with the broad remedial purpose of the Act suggests that even intangible employment actions may be covered. The cases addressed previously on the "chilling" of employee rights would support such an argument. Similarly, minor employment actions might also constitute impermissible "interference with" an employee's FMLA rights. As we will see, however, in the "Remedies" section of this chapter, the courts are less inclined to entertain civil suits where the employee has not suffered an injury–in–fact.

What does appear to be clear, however, is that the use of FMLA leave cannot be held against an employee for hiring, promotions, or discipline. Agencies need to be very careful to screen out FMLA leave usage from decisions regarding promotions, transfers, bonuses, special assignments, and other employment actions. This can come about in two ways. First, the employee's own absenteeism record could be used as part of the decision process for an employment action. Second, the absenteeism record of the unit under the supervision of a particular manager could be used for employment decisions or the performance evaluation of a particular manager. If, for example, a factor in a manager's performance evaluation included the absenteeism rate of the unit he or she managed, a negative performance evaluation and concomitant reduced bonus could violate the FMLA if FMLA leave were not factored out before the employment decision is made. *See Keller v. Putnam Fiduciary Trust Co. et al.,* 238 F.3d 5, 10 (1st Cir. 2001) (notation in review accompanying low performance evaluation that the employee's "attendance was unpredictable," where an employee took approved FMLA leave during the rating period, noted in decision, but forfeited because it was only raised on appeal).

An employee who was coached (the first step in the company's progressive discipline policy) and ultimately removed in part for the employee's failure to abide by the company's attendance policy (which the court found violated the FMLA) constituted a "negative factor" for purposes of the FMLA because it contributed to the employer's decision to terminate the employee. *Cavin v. Honda of America Mfg., Inc.,* 346 F.3d 713, 726 (6th Cir. 2003).

Finally, the taking of FMLA leave does not immunize an employee from adverse employment actions independent of FMLA leave usage. The regulations clearly provide that the FMLA does not entitle any employee to any right, benefit, or position of employment other than any right, benefit, or position of employment to which the employee would have been entitled if the employee had not taken leave under the FMLA. 29 CFR 825.216(a), 825.312(d); S. Res. 242, Cong. Rec. S3959, S3969–70, S3974 (April 23, 1996); 29 CFR 825.216(a), 825.312(d). As succinctly stated by the DOL in the Comments to the final Title I regulations, "FMLA cannot be used by employees as a 'shield' to avoid legitimate discipline." Preamble, 29 CFR 825.220; *see Burton v. Buckner Children and Family Services, Inc.,* No. 3:02–CV–0415–P, 2003 U.S. Dist. LEXIS 8951, at *17 (N.D. Tex. Mary 28, 2003) (the employee is not immunized from any and all adverse employment actions merely because she was taking FMLA leave); *see, e.g., Mummert v. Vencor, Inc. et al.,* 21 Fed. Appx. 710 (9th Cir. 2001) (a jury instruction that the employer's termination of an employee during the employee's FMLA leave necessarily violates the Act does not correctly state the law). Of course, employers may be put to the test to prove that the adverse employment action was taken for reasons independent of the taking of FMLA leave.

(4) "No Fault" Attendance Policies and Attendance-Based Bonus Plans

A "no fault" attendance policy that counts FMLA leave as an absence or occurrence violates the FMLA. 29 CFR 825.220(c); S. Res. 242, Cong. Rec. S3959, S3970 (April 23, 1996); 29 CFR 825.220(c); *see Stoops v. One Call Communications, Inc.*, 141 F.3d 309, 312 (7th Cir. 1998); DOL WH FMLA Advisory Opinion No. 31 (March 21, 1994) (discussing no fault attendance policies); DOL WH FMLA Advisory Opinion No. 2 (Aug. 16, 1993) (leave taken for a FMLA required reason may not be counted in any manner under "no fault" attendance policies).

The term "'no fault' attendance policies" is not defined by the regulations. Essentially, a "no fault" attendance policy is one that attaches penalties to absences or "occurrences" no matter what the reason for the absence. Generally, under a "no fault" attendance policy, progressive discipline attaches when an employee accumulates a pre-determined number of absences, up to termination. "No fault" attendance policies also generally include a provision that reduces the number of absence points or occurrences when an employee goes for a designated period of time (e.g., 90 days) without a recordable absence. *See* DOL WH FMLA Advisory Opinion No. 100 (Jan. 12, 1999) (describing a "no fault" attendance policy).

While an FMLA absence can never be counted as an incident or occurrence for purposes of a "no fault" attendance policy, FMLA leave does not automatically count toward the reduction of absence points or occurrences pursuant to such a policy. Whether "no fault" absence points or occurrences are deducted will depend on the employer's paid or unpaid leave policies. Again, the Act does not provide an employee greater rights to other benefits and conditions of employment than if the employee had been continuously working during the FMLA leave period. 29 CFR 825.216(a), 825.312(d); S. Res. 242, Cong. Rec. S3959, S3969–70, S3974 (April 23, 1996); 29 CFR 825.216(a), 825.312(d). With respect to the reduction of absence points or occurrences pursuant to an employer's "no fault" attendance policy, the DOL provides the following example (DOL WH FMLA Advisory Opinion No. 100 Jan. 12, 1999)):

> In the first example, if the employee was on unpaid FMLA leave and the employer's policy does not permit the accrual of benefits or seniority during any unpaid leave, upon return to work the employer would only be obligated to restore the employee to the same or an equivalent position to what the employee had prior to the start of leave. If the employee had 45 days without a recordable incident at the time the unpaid FMLA leave commenced, the employer would be obligated to restore the employee to this number of days credited without an incident. The employer could neither count the FMLA leave period toward an attendance control policy for potential termination, nor credit the unpaid FMLA leave toward the recordable time for dropping such points.

> In the second example, if FMLA leave was covered by paid leave (or unpaid leave) that provides for the accrual of benefits and seniority, then the FMLA leave could be credited towards the time free of a recordable incident. In this example, the FMLA leave could not be counted as an occurrence or incident for purposes of the "no fault" attendance policy. FMLA leave may never be counted as an occurrence or incident pursuant to a "no fault" attendance policy.

Closely related to the issue of "no fault" attendance policies are attendance-based bonus policies. Many employers pay bonuses in different forms to employees for job-related performance such as for perfect attendance, the absence of on-the-job injuries or accidents, and exceeding production goals. 29 CFR 825.215(c)(2); S. Res. 242, Cong. Rec. S3959, S3969 (April 23, 1996); 29 CFR 825.215(c)(2). As discussed in Chapter 12, "Maintenance of Benefits," and Chapter 13, "Return to Work from Leave," these various bonus programs interact with the FMLA in different ways. With respect to bonuses based on attendance in particular, such bonuses "do not require performance by the employee but rather contemplate the absence of occurrences. To the extent an employee who takes FMLA leave had met all the requirements for…[the] bonus before FMLA leave began, the employee is entitled to continue this entitlement upon return from FMLA leave, that is, the employee may not be disqualified for the bonus(es) for the taking of FMLA leave. *See* § 825.220(b) and (c)." 29 CFR 825.215(c)(2); S. Res. 242, Cong. Rec. S3959, S3969 (April 23, 1996); 29 CFR 825.215(c)(2); *see Estes v. Meridian One Corporation, et al.*, 6 Fed. Appx. 142 (4th Cir. 2001) (commission on sales earned while the employee was on FMLA leave analogous to production bonus because commissions were paid based on monthly sales record performance).

b. Opposition to Unlawful Practices

(1) General Rule

The second form of FMLA anti-discrimination prohibits employers from discriminating against individuals for opposing unlawful FMLA practices. Specifically, the Statute provides:

> It shall be unlawful for any employer to discharge or in any other manner discriminate against any individual for opposing any practice made unlawful by this Title.

29 USC 2615(a)(2); 2 USC 1312(a)(1) (incorporating 29 USC 2615 into CAA); 3 USC 412(a)(1) (incorporating § 29 USC 2615 into PEOAA); *see Walker v. Elmore County Bd. of Ed.*, 379 F.3d 1249 (11th Cir. 2004) (the Act prohibits an employer from retaliating against an employee who attempts to exercise any FMLA-created right); *Aubuchon v. Knauf Fiberglass, GMBH*, 359 F.3d 950, 954 (7th Cir. 2004); *Levine v. The Children's Museum of Indianapolis, Inc.*, 61 Fed. Appx. 298 (7th Cir. 2003); *Smith v. Memorial Hosp. Corp., et. al.*, 302 F.3d 827, 832 (8th Cir. 2002); *Wood v. Handy & Harman Co.*, No. 05-CV-TCK-FHM, 2006 U.S. Dist. LEXIS 81186, at *10 & n.1 (N.D. Okla. Nov. 6, 2006); *Bradley v. Mary Rutan Hospital Assoc.*, 322 F. Supp. 2d 926, 937 (S.D. Ohio 2004).

The implementing regulations slightly modify the statutory definition. For purposes of Title I, the DOL regulation (29 CFR 825.220(a)(2)) provides:

> An employer is prohibited from discharging or in any other way discriminating against any person (whether or not an employee) for opposing or complaining about any unlawful practice under the Act.

The comparable regulation implementing the FMLA for purposes of the CAA (S. Res. 242, Cong. Rec. S3959, S3969 (April 23, 1996); 29 CFR 825.220(a)(2)) provides:

> An employing office is prohibited from discharging or in any other way discriminating against any covered employee (whether or not an eligible employee) for opposing or complaining about any unlawful practice under the FMLA as made applicable by the CAA.

As with many other FMLA regulations, Title I uses the term "employer," whereas the CAA uses the term "employing office." Both terms are defined by their respective statutes and regulations. Generally speaking, an "employing office" within the meaning of the CAA is a smaller work unit than "employer" for purposes of Title I. [For a further discussion of the terms "employer" and "employing office" for FMLA purposes, see Chapter 3, "FMLA Coverage of the Federal Government."]

More significantly, the anti-discrimination provisions for opposition to unlawful conduct are more narrowly defined for purposes of the CAA than for Title I. The CAA prohibits discrimination for opposition conduct to covered employees, whether or not they are eligible. The CAA term "covered employee" means (2 USC 1301(3)) any employee of:

- The House of Representatives;
- The Senate;
- The Capitol Guide Service;
- The Capitol Police;
- The Congressional Budget Office;
- The Office of the Architect of the Capitol;
- The Office of the Attending Physician;
- The Office of Compliance; or
- The Office of Technology Assessment.

See S. Res. 242, Cong. Rec. S3959, S3969 (April 23, 1996); 29 CFR 825.220(a)(3)(iii), 825.220(e).

Discrimination for opposing unlawful practices under Title I, in contrast, covers any "person," whether or not the person is an employee. The term "person" is defined in the Statute as having the same meaning as given such term in § 3(a) of the Fair Labor Standards Act of 1938, 29 USC 1002(3). See 29 USC 2611(8). According to the DOL implementing regulations, "person" means an individual, partnership, association, corporation, business trust, legal representative, or any organized group of persons, and includes a public agency. 29 CFR 825.800 (definition of "person"). A job applicant or former employee is not specifically included within the regulatory definition of "person."

The DOL regulations also inexplicably reiterate, "individuals, not merely employees, are protected from retaliation for opposing (e.g., file a complaint about) any practice which is unlawful under the Act." 29 CFR 825.220(e). The term "individuals" is not defined. Presumably, it means the same thing as "person." The counter argument, of course, is that if the DOL meant "person," a defined term, it would have used that term. By using "individual," an undefined term, the implication is that it means something different than "person." For example, since an applicant or former employee is not included in the definition of a "person," it could be argued that they constitute an "individual" for purposes of gaining protection under the "opposition" clause.

The protections afforded by the "opposition" clause, whether to a "person" or "individual," apply to any individual or entity, such as a union, whether employed or not employed by the agency. That would include prospective employees, such as job applicants. Under the CAA, discrimination is prohibited against employees covered by the CAA. Because applicants and former employees are included within the definition of "employee" (S. Res. 242, Cong. Rec. S3959, S3976 (April 23, 1996); 29 CFR 825.800 (definition of "employee")), the CAA "opposition clause" would apply to those individuals as well.

(2) Legislative and Regulatory History

According to the legislative history, the "opposition" provision of § 105(a)(2) of Title I, 29 USC 2615(a)(2), was "derived from Title VII of the Civil Rights Act of 1964 (42 USC 2000e-3(a)) and is intended to be construed in the same manner. Under § 105(a) of this Act, as under Title VII of the Civil Rights Act, an employee is protected against employer retaliation for opposing any practice that he or she reasonably believes to be a violation. S. Rep. 103-3, p. 34.

The DOL (Preamble, 29 CFR 825.220) used slightly different language to describe the protections afforded by the "opposition" clause of § 105(a)(2) of the FMLA. The opposition clause "is derived from Title VII of the Civil Rights Act of 1964 and is intended, according to the legislative history, to be construed in the same manner. FMLA provides the same sorts of protections to workers who oppose, protest, or attempt to correct alleged violations of the FMLA as are provided to workers under Title VII."

Presumably, the rationale of the above legislative history will also apply to the comparable "opposition" clause anti-discrimination provisions of the CAA. As a result, case law interpreting reprisal or retaliation cases under Title II should be relevant to FMLA "opposition" clause cases. [This issue will be addressed more fully in a later section of this chapter regarding "Burden of Proof."]

(3) Opposition

Neither the Statute nor the regulations define what would constitute protected "opposition" or "complaining" conduct. Filing a complaint about unlawful conduct is cited as an example of protected opposition conduct. See 29 CFR 825.220(e); S. Res. 242, Cong. Rec. S3959, S3969 (April 23, 1996); 29 CFR 825.220(e). Presumably, the means or form of opposition used by the individual seeking the protections of the "opposition" clause will be judged pursuant to the anti-retaliation provisions of Title VII.

Typically, a plaintiff engages in the necessary "protected activity" simply by taking or requesting FMLA leave. *Wood v. Handy & Harman Co.*, No. 05-CV-TCK-FHM, 2006 U.S. Dist. LEXIS 81186, at *10 & n.1 (N.D. Okla. Nov. 6, 2006). Protected activity has also been found to include a supervisor's refusal to deliver a letter from human resources to an employee indicating that the employee's leave to care for her ill husband did not qualify as FMLA leave. *Wood v. Handy & Harman Co.*, No. 05-CV-TCK-FHM, 2006 U.S. Dist. LEXIS 81186, at *12 (N.D. Okla. Nov. 6, 2006).

In *Hoffman v. Professional Med Team*, 394 F.3d 414 (6th Cir. 2005), the Sixth Circuit declined to decide whether the plaintiff's heated exchanges with her supervisor regarding a medical certification supporting her request for FMLA leave consisted of "opposition" within the meaning of the FMLA. Because the district court did not commit clear error in concluding that legitimate motives prompted the employer to terminate Hoffman, the court found it unnecessary to address the issue. Ironically, the legitimate reason for discharge sustained by the Sixth Circuit was plaintiff's profanity-laced exchange with her supervisor regarding the FMLA medical certification form. The district court found the employee's profanity-laced comments to be protected opposition activity.

(4) Reasonable Belief of Unlawful Conduct

Individuals, and not merely employees, are protected if they oppose any practice that they reasonably believe to be a violation of the Act or regulations. 29 CFR 825.220(e); S. Res. 242, Cong. Rec. S3959, S3969 (April 23, 1996); 29 CFR 825.220(e); see Wood v. Handy & Harman Co., No. 05-CV-TCK-FHM, 2006 U.S. Dist. LEXIS 81186, at *13 (N.D. Okla. Nov. 6, 2006).

An employee need only have a reasonable belief that the conduct was unlawful. Wood v. Handy & Harman Co., No. 05-CV-TCK-FHM, 2006 U.S. Dist. LEXIS 81186, at *13-14 (N.D. Okla. Nov. 6, 2006). It is not necessary that the conduct at issue actually be unlawful. *Id.* at *13.

(5) Scope of Prohibition

The regulations do not further define the scope of the prohibition against discharging or otherwise discriminating against any person for opposing unlawful conduct. As written, the prohibition against discrimination in retaliation for opposition activity is absolute. That would appear to include forms of retaliation that do not amount to tangible employment actions. Here again, however, the interpretations by the EEOC and the courts of the anti-retaliation provisions of Title VII of the Civil Rights Act can be used as a guide.

(6) Enforcement

While the statutes and implementing regulations extend the protections of the "opposition" clause to any person (in the case of Title I) or any covered person (for the CAA), not all of the potential individuals covered by these protections can enforce their rights. Specifically, as set forth more fully in the "Enforcement" section of this chapter, under Title I, only employees can file a complaint with the DOL alleging a violation of the FMLA. 29 CFR 825.400(a)(1)-(2). While a Title I employee can initiate a civil action, employers are only liable for damages to eligible employees. 29 USC 2617(1). Title I shuts out non-employees from bringing suit for violations of the FMLA. The CAA, on the other hand, allows covered employees to either initiate an administrative action or a civil action. S. Res. 242, Cong. Rec. S3959, S3975 (April 23, 1996), 29 CFR 825.400(a).

Several recent cases have addressed whether ineligible employees can bring a retaliation action against an employer. In *Humenny v. Genex Corp., Inc.*, 390 F.3d 901, 905 (6th Cir. 2004), the Sixth Circuit addressed the retaliation complaint of a former employee. The employee argued that the statute's use of the terms "employee" and "individual" indicate that the retaliation provisions apply regardless of whether an employee is eligible for FMLA leave. The court disagreed. The Sixth Circuit reasoned that both the statute and the implementing regulations prohibit retaliation based on the exercise of any rights provided by the Act. Because the plaintiff was not an eligible employee, she never exercised or attempted to exercise any "rights" provided to her by the FMLA.

In *Walker v. Elmore County Bd. of Ed.*, 379 F.3d 1249 (11th Cir. 2004), the issue on appeal was whether a request for maternity leave made by an employee who is ineligible at the time of her request constitutes an attempt to exercise a FMLA right within the meaning of the FMLA anti-retaliation provisions. The court held that Walker's claim failed because, as an ineligible employee, she was not protected by the FMLA. The court found that this was not a situation where an ineligible employee requests FMLA leave to commence after the employee reaches eligibility. Rather, in *Walker*, the employee was ineligible both at the time she requested leave and when leave was scheduled to commence. The court concluded that the FMLA "does not protect an attempt to exercise a right that is not provided by FMLA, i.e., the right to leave before one becomes eligible therefore."

Enforcement actions under the CAA are limited to "covered employees," the same individuals protected by the "opposition" anti-discrimination provisions. 2 USC 1402. Therefore, unlike Title I, the CAA does not promise protections to persons, such as non-employees, that have no right under the FMLA to enforce violations of their FMLA rights.

c. Participation

(1) General Rule

The FMLA prohibits discrimination for interference with, or participation in, inquiries regarding FMLA rights. Specifically, the Act provides:

> It shall be unlawful for any person to discharge or in any other manner discriminate against any individual because such individual—
>
>> has filed any charge, or has instituted or caused to be instituted any proceedings, under or related to this Title;
>>
>> has given, or is about to give, any information in connection with any inquiry or proceeding relating to any right provided under this Title; or
>>
>> has testified, or is about to testify, in any inquiry or proceeding relating to any right provided under this Title.

29 USC 2615(b); 2 USC 1312(a)(1) (incorporating 29 USC 2615 into CAA); 3 USC 412(a)(1) (incorporating 29 USC 2615 into PEOAA); *see Conoshenti v. Pub. Serv. Elec. & Gas Co.*, 364 F.3d 135, 141 (3d Cir. 2004); *Bachelder v. America West Airlines, Inc.*, 259 F.3d 1112, 1123 n.8 (9th Cir. 2001).

The implementing regulations substantially follow the statutory language, with a few notable modifications. 29 CFR 825.220(a)(3); S. Res. 242, Cong. Rec. S3959, S3969 (April 23, 1996); 29 CFR 825.220(a)(3). With respect to Title I, the DOL regulations provide:

> All persons (whether or not employers) are prohibited from discharging or in any other way discriminating against any person (whether or not an employee) because that person has
>
>> (i) Filed any charge, or has instituted (or caused to be instituted) any proceeding under or related to this Act;
>>
>> (ii) Given, or is about to give, any information in connection with an inquiry or proceeding relating to a right under this Act;
>>
>> (iii) Testified, or is about to testify, in any inquiry or proceeding relating to a right under this Act.

See LeGrand v. Village of McCook, No. 96–C–5951, 1998 U.S. Dist. LEXIS 5230, at *12 (N.D. Ill. April 15, 1998).

The Title I regulations indicate that "all persons" includes non–employers. They also indicate that the individual discriminated against can be any person, including non–employees. Such refinements are not obvious from the statutory language. Again, the term "person" is defined to include an individual, partnership, association, corporation, business trust, legal representative, or any organized group of persons, and includes a public agency. 29 CFR 825.800 (definition of "person").

The CAA regulations (S. Res. 242, Cong. Rec. S3959, S3969 (April 23, 1996); 29 CFR 825.220(a)(3)) implementing 29 USC 2615(b) provides:

> All employing offices are prohibited from discharging or in any other way discriminating against any covered employee (whether or not an eligible employee) because that covered employee has—
>
>> (i) Filed any charge, or has instituted (or caused to be instituted) any proceeding under or related to the FMLA, as made applicable by the CAA;
>>
>> (ii) Given, or is about to give, any information in connection with an inquiry or proceeding relating to a right under the FMLA, as made applicable by the CAA; or
>>
>> (iii) Testified, or is about to testify, in any inquiry or proceeding relating to a right under the FMLA, as made applicable by the CAA.

A closer review of key statutory and regulatory language regarding the prohibition against participation discrimination follows after a brief review of the legislative and regulatory history.

(2) Legislative and Regulatory History

Section 105(b), 29 USC 2615(b), is modeled on § 15(a)(3) of the Fair Labor Standards Act of 1938 (29 USC 215(a)(3)) and "is similarly intended to achieve the objective of protecting employees who file charges or otherwise participate in proceedings under this [T]itle and of promoting the integrity of such inquiries or proceedings." S. Rep. 103-3, pp. 34-35.

Given these roots, cases interpreting § 105(b) of the Fair Labor Standards Act would appear to be applicable for purposes of applying the "participation" anti-discrimination provisions of the FMLA.

(3) Persons vs. Employing Offices

Scope accounts for most of the material differences between the regulations implementing the "participation" anti-discrimination provisions for purposes of Title I and the CAA. Title I prohibits "all persons," including non-employers, from engaging in discrimination for participation in FMLA-related inquiries. Again, a "person" is broadly defined to include individuals, corporations, associations, business trusts, legal representatives, public agencies, and "any organized group of persons." 29 CFR 825.800 (definition of "person"). The CAA, on the other hand, limits the scope of the prohibition to discrimination by an "employing office." The term "employing office" is defined by the CAA to specifically named public entities. 2 USC 1301(3)). The CAA, unlike Title I, would not cover discrimination by non-CAA-covered employing offices for participation in covered FMLA inquires. Title seeks to prohibit all such discrimination, whether or not the discriminating entity is covered by Title I or is an employer.

(4) Discriminating

As set forth in the legislative history of Title I, the term "discrimination" is modeled after § 105(b), 29 USC 2615(b), of the Fair Labor Standards Act of 1938 (29 USC 215(a)(3)). A review of that provision is beyond the scope of this book. What is noteworthy about the statutory and regulatory language is the absence of any reference to whether such discrimination is limited to tangible employment actions, such as discharge, or whether it also applies to discrimination involving intangible employment actions as well. Again, the case law under § 105(b) of the FLSA is a good place to begin this inquiry.

Even if § 105(b) of the FLSA limits "participation" discrimination to tangible employment benefits, it does not necessarily follow that FMLA is so limited. That is, simply because 29 USC 2615(b) is "modeled" after § 105(b) of the FLSA does not mean that the FMLA cannot be interpreted differently, for example, to include intangible employment actions. Neither the Statute nor the implementing regulations place any limits on the meaning of "discriminating." The broader the meaning of "discriminating," the more employment actions will fit within the prohibition.

In *LeGrand v. Village of McCook*, No. 96-C-5951, 1998 U.S. Dist. LEXIS 5230, at *12 (N.D. Ill. April 15, 1998), the court found that an employer did not violate the Act when a manager posted a notice in several locations indicating that employees should not discuss any aspect of LeGrand's employment without authorization; this did not constitute actionable discrimination because that person instituted an FMLA-related proceeding. The court noted that such postings did not forbid employees from talking to the employee or her representative, but merely required prior authorization before doing so. Moreover, LeGrand did not allege that she had even tried to talk with anyone, or that anyone had declined to talk to her because of the posting.

(5) Individuals vs. Covered Employees

The difference in scope of the implementing regulations is also illustrated in what victims of "participation" discrimination are covered by Title I and the CAA. Title I broadly includes "any person" within the scope of its protections against discrimination for participation in FMLA-related inquiries. Again, "person" is a broadly defined term that includes non-employees, let alone non-eligible employees. As such, "person" would cover prospective employees, such as job applicants.

The CAA, on the other hand, limits the scope of the "participation" anti-discrimination provisions to any "covered employee." The term "covered employee" is defined as only including employees of the nine specified "employing offices" covered by the CAA. 2 USC 1301(3)). A "covered employee" would include employees, whether eligible for FMLA leave or not. A "covered employee" would not, however, include non-CAA persons, including employees from other federal agencies. Since "employee" is defined as including applicants and former employees (S. Res. 242, Cong. Rec. S3959, S3967 (April 23, 1996); 29 CFR 825.800 (definition of "employee")), those individuals would appear to be included within the definition of a "covered employee."

(6) Charges and Proceedings

Three forms of protected "participation" are protected from discrimination by Title I, the CAA, and the PEOAA. One form of protected "participation" involves the filing of any charge or institution of any proceeding under or related to the FMLA. 29 USC 2615(b)(1); 29 CFR 825.220(a)(3)(I); S. Res. 242, Cong. Rec. S3959, S3969 (April 23, 1996); 29 CFR 825.220(a)(3)(I); *see LeGrand v. Village of McCook*, No. 96-C-5951, 1998 U.S. Dist. LEXIS 5230, at *12 (N.D. Ill. April 15, 1998). A few differences between the statutes and key undefined terms are noteworthy.

The terms "charge," "institution," and "proceedings" are undefined in the Statute and implementing regulations. The use of the term "charge" is particularly interesting since the term is not used for purposes of enforcement of FMLA rights. Pursuant to Title I, the DOL is empowered to receive, investigate and attempt to resolve "complaints." 29 USC 2617(b)(1). Alternatively, an eligible employee may file a "civil action" against an employer for violations of § 105 of Title I. 29 USC 2617(b)(1).

For purposes of the CAA, the terms "charge" and "institution," while used, are also undefined. Enforcement of FMLA rights for purposes of the CAA requires administrative exhaustion, which is begun by a request for counseling. 2 USC 1401. Specifically, the Statute provides, "To commence a proceeding, a covered employee alleging a violation of a law made applicable under part A of Title II shall request counseling of the Office [of Compliance]." 2 USC 1402(a).

Absent a specific definition, and with an eye toward how similar terms may be defined for purposes of the FLSA, 29 USC 2915(b), "charge" and "institution" should certainly be read as including a "complaint," "civil action," and a "request for counseling." Presumably, a "charge" could mean any accusation of wrongdoing in violation of the respective FMLA laws, including informal complaints, grievances pursuant to a collective bargaining agreement, and charges made that are reported in the press.

A broad reading of "charge," "institution," and "proceeding" would also appear warranted given the statutory and regulatory language that such actions may take place "under or related to" the respective version of the FMLA. Actions "under" the FMLA would seem to cover the use of enforcement actions provided by the respective federal sector FMLA statutes. Actions "related to" charges or proceedings under the respective FMLA statutes would appear to cover virtually any dispute resolution process used to hear complaints or resolve allegations of unlawful FMLA conduct.

A question remains whether the term "filed" regarding charges limits the scope of the protection to formal dispute resolution systems. The term "file" is a rather formalistic way to describe making informal complaints, writing a Congressman, or contacting the press to complain. In any event, the lack of a definition for what "filed" means suggests that point can be argued and litigated any number of ways.

(7) Information

Giving information in connection with an inquiry or proceeding relating to a right under the FMLA is also considered protected activity. The phrase "about to give" information suggests a close temporal proximity between the unlawful conduct when the "information" was to be given in connection with an inquiry or proceeding. The litigation question will be how close in time must someone be in order to meet the "is about to give" standard. There is, however, no stated temporal limit on the meaning of "is about to give."

The phrase "any information" is undefined. It does not, on its face, require that the information be relevant or truthful to the inquiry or proceeding. The only requirement is that the information have some undefined connection to an "inquiry or proceeding" relating to an FMLA right. Presumably, the naming of an employee as a witness or someone with knowledge would suffice for such a connection, no matter whether the information the individual has is relevant.

The term "inquiry" is not defined by the Statute or implementing regulations. Again, the term may be defined for purposes of the FLSA, 29 USC 2915(b). Regulations and cases interpreting that provision should be reviewed for any guidance as those terms are applied to the FMLA. Otherwise, an "inquiry" should probably be construed broadly to include formal and informal inquiries (and proceedings) relating to rights under the Act. Such a broad interpretation would certainly include grievance–arbitration procedures pursuant to the terms of a collective bargaining agreement. They would also arguably include internal investigation and dispute resolution systems used by covered federal employers.

(8) Testimony

The observations stated above for inquires are generally applicable to the use of the terms "testified, or is about to testify." The terms are undefined for purposes of the FMLA. The terms may be defined for purposes of the FLSA, 29 USC 2915(b). Regulations and cases interpreting that provision should be reviewed for guidance as those terms are applied to the FMLA. At least one definition of "testimony" is a "solemn declaration usually made orally by a witness under oath in response to interrogation by a lawyer or authorized public official." Webster's Ninth New Collegiate Dictionary (Merriam–Webster, Inc., 1988) (definition of "testimony"). An alternative definition offered by the same dictionary is "a firsthand authentication of a fact." The former definition would limit the scope of this version of the "participation" anti–discrimination provision. The latter definition is broad enough to cover almost any informal conversation.

(9) Enforcement

While the statutes and implementing regulations extend the protections of the "participation" clause to any person (in the case of Title I) or any covered person (for the CAA), not all of the potential individuals covered by these protections can enforce their rights. Specifically, as set forth more fully in the "Enforcement" section of this chapter, under Title I, only employees can file a complaint with the DOL alleging a violation of the FMLA. 29 CFR 825.400(a)(1)–(2). While a Title I employee can initiate a civil action, employers are only liable for damages to eligible employees. 29 USC 2617(1). Title I shuts out non–employees from bringing suit for violations of the FMLA. The CAA, on the other hand, allows covered employees to either initiate an administrative action or a civil action. S. Res. 242, Cong. Rec. S3959, S3975 (April 23, 1996); 29 CFR 825.400(a).

Enforcement actions under the CAA are limited to a "covered employee," the same individuals who are protected by the "participation" anti–discrimination provisions. 2 USC 1402. Therefore, unlike Title I, the CAA does not promise protections to non–employees that have no FMLA right to enforce violations of those rights.

5. Waiver

a. General Rule

Employers cannot waive, nor may employers induce employees to waive their rights under the FMLA. 29 CFR 825.220(d); Res. 242, Cong. Rec. S3959, S3969 (April 23, 1996); 29 CFR 825.220(d); see *Taylor v. Progress Energy, Inc.*, No. 04-1525, 2007 U.S. App. LEXIS 15846, at *4 (4th Cir. July 3, 2007); *Conoshenti v. Pub. Serv. Elec. & Gas Co.*, 364 F.3d 135, 141 (3d Cir. 2004); *Faris v. Williams WPC–1, Inc. et al.*, 332 F.3d 316, 320–323 (5th Cir. 2003); *Sanders v. May Dept. Stores Co.*, 315 F.3d 940, 945 (8th Cir. 2003), cert. denied, 123 S. Ct. 2608, 156 L. Ed. 2d 627 (2003); *Thornton v. BASF*, 217 F.3d 840 (table), 2000 U.S. App. LEXIS 15909, at *6 (4th Cir. July 11, 2000); *Dougherty v. TEVA Pharmaceuticals USA, Inc.*, No. 05-2336, 2007 U.S. Dist. LEXIS 27200 (E.D. Pa. April 9, 2007); *Artis v. Palos Community Hospital*, No. 02 C 8855, 2004 U.S. Dist. LEXIS 20150, at *19 (N.D. Ill. Sept. 23, 2004); *Wright v. Owens–Illinois, Inc.*, 2:02–cv–223–LJM–WGH, 2004 U.S. Dist. LEXIS 8535, at *20 (S.D. Ind. May 14, 2004); *Roberts v. Owens–Illinois, Inc.*, 2:02–cv–207–LJM–WGH, 2004 U.S. Dist. LEXIS 8534, at *15 (S.D. Ind. May 14, 2004); *Lewis v. Harper Hospital*, 241 F. Supp. 2d 769, 772–73 (E.D. Mich. 2002). For example, employees (or their collective bargaining representatives) cannot "trade off" the right to take FMLA leave against some other benefit offered by the employer. 29 CFR 825.220(d); Res. 242, Cong. Rec. S3959, S3969 (April 23, 1996); 29 CFR 825.220(d).

b. Regulatory Development

The anti–waiver provision was the subject of a number of comments prior to the publication of the final DOL regulations. Specifically, the commentator's were concerned that the "no waiver of rights" provision would prohibit allowance of waivers and releases in connection with settlement of FMLA claims and as part of a severance package (as allowed under Title VII and ADEA claims, for example). Preamble, 29 CFR 825.220. In response, the DOL stated:

> The Department has given careful consideration to the comments received on this section and has concluded that prohibitions against employees waiving their rights constitute sound public policy under the FMLA, as is also the case under other labor standards such as the FLSA.

The DOL went on to address two exceptions to the no–wavier rule, which are addressed more fully below. The upshot of the regulatory history is that the DOL intention in promulgating § 825.220(d) was to prohibit the waiver of FMLA claims by employees, at least to the same extent that other labor laws, such as the FLSA, prohibit such waiver.

c. Waiver or Rights

Section 825.220(d) does not define "waive." By example, it would appear that "waive" means the same thing as a "trade off" of FMLA rights for other benefits offered by the employer. An employee's election to take personal leave under the employer's leave policy rather than unpaid FMLA leave was held to not constitute an unlawful "trade off" of FMLA rights. *See Sanders v. May Dept. Stores Co.*, 315 F.3d 940, 945 (8th Cir. 2003) (to avoid medical certification requirement of FMLA, an employee undergoing sex change operation chose personal leave, which did not require certification), *cert. denied* 123 S. Ct. 2608, 156 L. Ed. 2d 627 (2003); *see, e.g., Thornton v. BASF*, 217 F.3d 840 (table), 2000 U.S. App. LEXIS 15909 (4th Cir. July 11, 2000) (not deciding whether the employer's policy compelling the employee to chose between earned short term disability benefits and FMLA protections was unlawful, where employee did not actually consider or exercise such a choice).

The courts are split on the scope of the FMLA's prohibition on the "waiver of rights." *See Taylor v. Progress Energy, Inc.*, No. 04-1525, 2007 U.S. App. LEXIS 15846, at *4 (4th Cir. July 3, 2007); *Faris v. Williams WPC-1, Inc.*, 332 F.3d 316 (5th Cir. 2003); *Dougherty v. TEVA Pharms. USA, Inc.*, No. 05-2336, 2007 U.S. Dist. LEXIS 27200 (E.D. Pa. April 11, 2007). The split centers on what constitutes an FMLA "right." Specifically, the split addresses whether the anti-waiver provision prohibits an employee from waiving their right to sue for FMLA violations as part of a severance agreement.

In *Faris v. Williams WPC–1, Inc. et al.*, 332 F.3d 316, 320–323 (5th Cir. 2003), the Fifth Circuit concluded that Section 825.220(d)'s prohibition against waivers applied only to "substantive rights" under the FMLA, such as the right to leave, reinstatement, etc., rather than to proscriptive rights (i.e., one's remedies), which may be waived. In that case, the employer terminated the employee citing poor performance. The employer offered the employee the equivalent of a month's salary to sign a release waiving her rights to pursue all claims against the employer. The release did not specifically mention the FMLA. The employee signed the release, took the money, and has never offered to return the payment. The employee subsequently sued the employer alleging that her termination violated the anti–retaliation provisions of the FMLA. The district court denied summary judgment to the employer on the grounds that the FMLA dictated that FMLA claims could not be waived. On interlocutory appeal, the Fifth Circuit reversed.

The court began its analysis by emphasizing the "proper focus is on the meaning of the phrase 'rights under the FMLA.'". 332 F.3d at 320. It concluded that this phrase (when read in the context of the regulation as a whole) referred only to the substantive protections of the FMLA. This was so because the, nowhere did the regulation describe, for example, a "cause of action for discrimination as an FMLA right." *Id.* at 321. A cause of action for damages, the court noted, is not mentioned in § 825.220(d) as a "right" that cannot be waived. *Faris*, 332 F.3d at 320–21. The court concluded that "rights" that may not be waived are distinct from the means of protecting those rights, such as a cause of action for discrimination. "A plain reading of the regulation is that it prohibits prospective waiver of rights, not the post–dispute settlement of claims." *Faris*, 332 F.3d at 321.

In *Dougherty v. TEVA Pharmaceuticals USA, Inc.*, No. 05-2336, 2007 U.S. Dist. LEXIS 27200, at *8 (E.D. Pa. April 9, 2007), the court held that Section 825.220(d) does not prohibit an employee from waiving past FMLA claims as part of a severance agreement or settlement. It would, however, prohibit an employee from prospectively waiving or settling all substantive and procedural FMLA rights.

The court in *Doughtery* rejected the *Faris* view that Section 825.220(d) distinguished between either substantive or proscriptive rights, or between prospective and retrospective rights. The court found that 825.220(d) prohibits the prospective waiver of both proscriptive (the right to sue) and substantive rights. 2007 U.S. Dist. LEXIS 27200, at *21-22. However, the court went on to find that an employee can elect to retroactively waive (or settle) a claim that has accrued because the employee is not waiving any proscriptive or substantive rights under the FMLA. "This is so because the decision to bring a claim (i.e., exercise one's proscriptive rights) is not a separate right under the Act. And Section 825.220(d) only prohibits the waiver of *rights under* the FMLA." The court continued:

> In other words, the decision to bring a claim (saying that you are going to exercise your right to sue) is not a separate right under the FMLA. Nowhere does the FMLA (or regulation) mandate that an aggrieved employee *must* exercise her proscriptive rights and bring an FMLA claim. An employee's decision to exercise her proscriptive rights is an independent one that she alone must make. Thus, the decision to excuse the FMLA's proscriptive protections stands apart from the FMLA. That right (the decision whether to file suit or not) arises only when an employer has violated the FMLA. So it can't be a right "under the FMLA" because it doesn't exist in the absence of an FMLA violation (whereas the proscriptive right to protect against FMLA violations does). So by settling a past FMLA claim, the employee still retains all of her substantive rights and remedies (proscriptive rights) under the FMLA. After a settlement, an employer cannot, for example, deny her of FMLA leave. And if it does, the employee always has a remedy (proscriptive right) under the FMLA to challenge that action. Entering into a settlement or severance agreement, therefore, doesn't change anything for the employee in terms of rights under the FMLA- she still remains all of them.

The Fourth Circuit in *Taylor v. Progress Energy, Inc.* (*Taylor II*), No. 04-1525, 2007 U.S. App. LEXIS 15846 (4th Cir. July 3, 2007), held that 825.220(d) prohibits the prospective and retrospective waiver of all FMLA rights (substantive and proscriptive), unless the waiver has the prior approval of the U.S. Department of Labor or a court. In so doing, the Fourth Circuit rejected the rejected *Faris* and *Dougherty*. In so holding, the court confirmed its analysis in *Taylor v. Progress Energy, Inc.* (*Taylor I*), 415 F.3d 364 (4th Cir. 2005), vacated, no. 04-1525, 2006 U.S. App. LEXIS 15744 (4th Cir. June 14, 2006). The court vacated its earlier decision when the Secretary of Labor filed an *amicus* brief in support of the company's petition for rehearing *en banc*. The DOL disagreed with the court's interpretation of 825.220(d) in *Taylor I*, In agreement with *Daugherty*, the DOL argued that 825.220(d) prohibited only the prospective waiver of FMLA rights.

In *Taylor II*, the court initially found that "rights under the FMLA" includes claims. There are three categories of "rights under the FMLA," substantive, proscriptive, and remedial. Substantive rights include an employee's right to take a certain amount of unpaid medical leave each year and the right to reinstatement following such leave. Proscriptive rights include an employee's right not to be discriminated or retaliated against for exercising substantive rights. The remedial right is an employee's right to bring a claim or action to recover damages or obtain equitable relief from an employer that violates the FMLA. The regulations, by specifying "rights under the FMLA," therefore refers to *all* rights under the FMLA, including the right to bring an action or claim for a violation of the Act.

The DOL urged the court to consider the decision in *Daughterty*. The court in *Taylor II* found that the reasoning behind the *Daughtery* decision "does not withstand close analysis." 2007 U.S. App. LEXIS 15846 at 10. *Taylor* found that the *Daugherty* erred when it found that the ability to bring an FMLA claim is "a kind of right," but not a "right under the FMLA." According to *Taylor II,* the decision "ignores FMLA's text." The FMLA explicitly makes the "right… to bring an action" or claim for violation a right under the Act. *See* 29 USC §§ 2617(a)(2), (a)(4). Moreover, Daughtery "confuses the decision to exercise rights with the waiver of rights. The regulation, *Taylor II* observed, does not prevent an employee from deciding not to exercise her FMLA rights. However, an employee who signs a release or settlement agreement does more than decide not to exercise her right to sue; "she relinquishes the right entirely." While section 200(d) does not prevent an employee from deciding not to exercise the right to sue, it does prevent her from waiving or relinquishing that right. Finally, the court rejected DOL's argument that its reading is consistent with well-accepted policy disfavoring prospective waivers of rights, but encouraging settlement of claims in employment law. The court noted that the settlement or waiver of claims is not permitted when it would thwart the legislative policy which the law was designed to effectuate. The FMLA, like the FLSA, provides a minimum floor of protection for employees. Private settlements of FMLA claims undermine Congress's objective of imposing uniform minimum standards.

It is clear that the FMLA prohibits the wavier of substantive FMLA rights. With respective to proscriptive rights (i.e., the right to sue), the picture is less clear. The DOL abandoned its one-time support of the decision in *Faris* because it would allow an employee to prospectively waive both proscriptive and remedial rights. Employers outside of the Fifth Circuit should avoid the prospective waiver of all FMLA rights. The DOL believes that an employee may retrospectively release or settle FMLA proscriptive rights (the right to sue) that have already accrued. The Fourth Circuit, in a persuasive opinion, found that retrospective waivers of proscriptive rights (i.e., settlements) are prohibited, unless secured with the assistance of the DOL or a court. Employers, wherever located, are well-advised to exercise great caution in this area and secure the assistance of counsel before entering into any FMLA settlement that is not supervised by a court, the DOL or, for the CAA, the Office of Administration.

As if to prove that caution is required in this area, in *Mitrow v. Verizon Communications, Inc.*, No. 3:05cv64, 2007 U.S. Dist. LEXIS 28829, at *48-49 (M.D. Pa. April 19, 2007), the court allowed an employee to proceed with an FMLA civil suit even though the employer and employee worked out a settlement through the U.S. Department of Labor. By the settlement, the employer retroactively granted FMLA coverage for the absence at issue. The employer argued that, because received the required FMLA coverage, she did not suffer any prejudice, and was not entitled to judgment. To do otherwise, the employer argued, would render the conciliation agreement meaningless and would discourage other employers from participating in the conciliation process. The court disagreed. The court opined that, because the employer initially refused to provide the employee with coverage, and the employer was forced to settle a claim it originally denied through the involvement of the DOL, the employee could maintain suit. Taken to its logical conclusion, any employer that initially disagrees with an employee's claim that the FMLA was violated forever forfeits the right to settle the claim, even if that settlement is achieved with the assistance of the Department of Labor.

In *Dierlam v. Wesley Jessen Corp.*, 222 F. Supp. 2d 1052, 1055–56 (N.D. Ill. 2002), the court held that an employee who signed a separation agreement with a broad waiver of claims provision (waiving all claims, pending or potential, arising out of employment), was violative of the anti–waiver provisions of the FMLA and, therefore, unenforceable. The court's decision was based largely on the similar decision of the court in *Bluitt v. Eval Co. of America, Inc.*, 3 F. Supp. 2d 761, 763 (S.D. Tex. 1998).

An FMLA "right" an employee may not waive by contract is the statute of limitations to initiate an FMLA claim. In *Lewis v. Harper Hospital*, 241 F. Supp. 2d 769, 772–73 (E.D. Mich. 2002), the governing employment contract provided that an employee would not commence any action or other legal proceeding relating to employment or the termination from employment more than six months after the complained of event. The contract specifically provided that the employee voluntarily waive any statute of limitations to the contrary. The court concluded that the imposition of a six-month statute of limitations on FMLA claims in lieu of the statutory limitations period of two or three years, constituted interference with the employee's FMLA rights.

The prohibition on an employee's ability to waive FMLA rights seems even more implausible under the CAA, which requires administrative exhaustion of an employee's FMLA claim through counseling and mediation. 2 USC 1401–1403. If an employee cannot compromise the undefined FMLA "rights" in these dispute resolution forums, exactly what is the purpose of counseling and mediation? Absent the ability of both parties to engage in compromise, the process of "counseling" and "mediation" would appear to be a waste of time, at least. If the "counseling" or "mediation" actually works as intended, resulting in compromise by all parties, the process amounts to an institutionalized practice encouraging the systemic violation of § 825.220(d). Applying *Taylor II*, if the settlement is supervised by the CAA Office of Administration it should be valid.

d. Employee

Section 825.220(d) prohibits an "employee" from waiving his or her FMLA rights. This raises the question of whether "employee" is limited to current employees, or whether it extends to prospective or former employees. At least one court questioned whether § 825.220(d) extends to individuals other than current employees. *See Faris v. Williams WPC–1, Inc. et al.*, 332 F.3d 316, 319–320 (5th Cir. 2003).

In *Faris*, the court noted that Title I defines "employee" by reference to the FLSA, 29 USC 203(e). 29 USC 2611(3). The court found the FLSA definition of "employee," ("any individual employed by an employer") to be "completely circular and explains nothing." *Faris*, 332 F.3d at 319 *(quoting Nationwide Mut. Ins. Co. v. Darden*, 503 U.S. 318, 323, 117 L. Ed. 2d 581, 112 S. Ct. 1344 (1992)). The court noted that "employee" as used in the FMLA was ambiguous because in various contexts it refers only to current employees, but in others situations it refers to former employees. *Faris*, 332 F.3d at 320. As such, the court reviewed the context in which "employee" is used to see whether the wavier prohibition applies to retaliation claims. After reviewing § 825.220, the court concluded, "there are strong indications that 'employee' refers only to current employees. It certainly cannot be said that the usage unambiguously encompasses former employees." *Faris*, 332 F.3d at 320.

Other courts have also concluded that "employee" is ambiguous in the FMLA context. *See Smith v. BellSouth Telecomms*

Inc., 273 F.3d 1303, 1307–13 (11th Cir. 2001) (finding "employee" ambiguous and deferring to the DOL's interpretation that the term includes prospective employees for purposes of discrimination claims); *Duckworth v. Pratt & Whitney, Inc.*, 152 F.3d 1, 9–11 (1st Cir. 1998) (same); 29 CFR 825.220(c) (prohibiting employers from discriminating against "employees and prospective employees" who have used FMLA leave).

e. Collective Bargaining Representative

The FMLA provides that the rights established for employees under the Act "shall not be diminished by any collective bargaining agreement or any employment benefit program or plan." 29 USC 2653. Notably, this section of Title I is not incorporated into the CAA or the PEOAA for purposes of the FMLA. This considerably muddies the status of the prohibition against waiver by a collective bargaining representative for purposes of the PEOAA and the CAA.

The PEOAA and CAA incorporate § 105 of Title I, 29 USC 2615. Section 825.220(d) of the DOL regulations, 29 CFR 825.220(d), implements the statutory prohibitions contained in § 105 of Title I. Section 825.220(d) clearly prohibits waiver of FMLA rights by collective bargaining representatives. However, that reference (to a collective bargaining representative) does not appear to be traceable to § 105 of Title I (29 USC 2615), but to § 402(b) of Title I (29 USC 2652(b)). Section 105 of Title I does not address or otherwise mention the term "waiver."

The PEOAA has not issued its own regulations implementing the FMLA. As such, by operation of law, the PEOAA applies, to the extent necessary and appropriate, the most relevant substantive executive regulation promulgated to implement the statutory provision at issue. 3 USC 455. Generally, those are the regulations implementing Title I, the Act that is specifically referenced and major provisions which are incorporated into the PEOAA. Given the fact that the PEOAA does not incorporate § 402(b) of Title I, an argument could be made that it would be inappropriate to apply that provision. Since § 825.220(d) of the Title I implementing regulations draw on § 402(b) of the Statute regarding the prohibition of waiver of FMLA rights by collective bargaining representatives, an argument could be made that the references to waiver by collective bargaining representatives in § 825.220(d) should not apply to the PEOAA. Of course, given the presence of the language in the enforcement regulations implementing § 105 of Title I, the argument could be made that those regulations would fully apply to the PEOAA.

The matter is either cleared (or rendered more complicated) in the CAA by the presence of implementing regulations comparable to § 825.700(a) of Title I that clearly prohibit a collective bargaining representative from diminishing an employee's FMLA rights. S. Res. 242, Cong. Rec. S3959, S3970, S3976 (April 23, 1996); 29 CFR 825.220(d), 825.700(a). The problem, again, is that the prohibition on a collective bargaining representative's ability to diminish an employee's FMLA rights is founded in § 402(b) of the Title I, which was not incorporated into the CAA. Nor is there any other provision of the FMLA provisions of the CAA that otherwise address the interaction of the FMLA with collective bargaining rights. The end result being that arguments can be made that the CAA "no waiver" provisions, at least as they apply to collective bargaining representatives, are invalid as they lack a statutory foundation. The counter argument, of course, is that the regulations were a valid exercise under *Chevron*, and they clearly prohibit the waiver of FMLA rights by collective bargaining unit representatives. Litigation to follow.

f. Light Duty Exception

A limited exception to the "no waiver" of FMLA rights provisions permits an employee's voluntary and uncoerced acceptance (not as a condition of employment) of a "light duty" assignment while recovering from a serious health condition. 29 CFR 825.220(d), 825.702(d)(2); S. Res. 242, Cong. Rec. S3959, S3970, S3976 (April 23, 1996); 29 CFR 825.220(d), 825.702(d)(2); *see Artis v. Palos Community Hospital*, No. 02 C 8855, 2004 U.S. Dist. LEXIS 20150, at *19 (N.D. Ill. Sept. 23, 2004); *Wright v. Owens–Illinois, Inc.*, 2:02–cv–223–LJM–WGH, 2004 U.S. Dist. LEXIS 8535, at *22 (S.D. Ind. May 14, 2004); *Roberts v. Owens–Illinois, Inc.*, 2:02–cv–207–LJM–WGH, 2004 U.S. Dist. LEXIS 8534, at *16 (S.D. Ind. May 14, 2004).

The "light duty" exception allows an employee on FMLA leave to return to work by voluntarily accepting a "light duty" or different assignment. Preamble, 29 CFR 825.220. Where an employee accepts a "light duty" or other assignment while still recovering from a serious health condition, the employee's right to restoration to the same or an equivalent position is available up to the maximum of 12 weeks in any given FMLA leave year, including all FMLA leave taken and the period of "light duty." 29 CFR 825.220(d); S. Res. 242, Cong. Rec. S3959, S3970 (April 23, 1996); 29 CFR 825.220(d). [Return to work issues are addressed in Chapter 13, "Return to Work from Leave." The calculation of the amount of FMLA leave available to an employee is addressed in Chapter 10, "Leave Amount and Scheduling."]

The term "light duty" is not defined. Presumably, a "light duty" job is one that has different or lesser essential job functions than the position the employee held at the time of leave commencement. Similarly, the term "voluntary and uncoerced" are also undefined. The use of the term "acceptance" implies that the "light duty" exception also permits an employer to make an offer of a "light duty" or other position. Absent this exception, such an offer would otherwise constitute an impermissible "inducement" of a waiver of an FMLA right, in this case the right to take FMLA leave.

In *Artis v. Palos Community Hospital*, No. 02 C 8855, 2004 U.S. Dist. LEXIS 20150, at *19 (N.D. Ill. Sept. 23, 2004), the employee alleged that her acceptance of a light duty position was not voluntary because the employer failed to inform her that she could take unpaid FMLA leave instead. The court characterized the plaintiff's evidence as "thin" regarding whether her acceptance of a light duty position was not voluntary. Plaintiff did not allege that she was coerced in her deposition and admitted that she was given a copy of the hospital's temporary limited duty policy, which presented unpaid FMLA leave as an option in addition to paid temporary limited duty. The court went on to find that, even assuming that she had involuntarily taken limited duty in lieu of unpaid FMLA leave, the court held that she did not have a viable FMLA claim because there was no deprivation of FMLA rights.

g. Early Retirement

Section 825.220 of the implementing regulations do not address the affect of the "no waiver" of FMLA rights rule on early out or other early retirement incentive plans. The matter is, however, addressed in the comments accompanying the publication of the final DOL Title I FMLA regulations. As explained in the comments (Preamble, 29 CFR 825.220):

> Such [early out] windows are typically open for a limited period of time and require all employees accepting the offer to be off the payroll by a certain date. If employees on FMLA leave have the right to participate in an early retirement program, but may continue to have and assert leave rights, the leave rights could adversely affect administration of the early retirement program.

With respect to early-out programs, "an employee on FMLA leave may be required to give up his or her remaining FMLA leave entitlement to take an early-out offer from" his or her employer. Preamble, 29 CFR 825.220. According to the DOL, "[u]nder these circumstances, FMLA rights would cease because the employment relationship ceases, and the employee would not otherwise have continued employment."

Moreover, an employer is not required to extend an early-out window to accommodate employees who are out on FMLA leave. However, the employer must afford employees who are out on FMLA leave the same opportunity, if any, to avail themselves of any such offer that would have been made available if the employee had not been on FMLA leave. Preamble, 29 CFR 825.220. [For a further discussion of an employer's duty to make benefits available to an employee on FMLA leave, see Chapter 12, "Maintenance of Benefits."]

6. Posting Violations

As set forth more fully in Chapter 8, "Notice Requirements," Title I requires all covered federal employers to post and keep posted in conspicuous places a notice of FMLA rights. 29 USC 2619; 29 CFR 825.300. Neither the CAA nor the PEOAA require a similar posting. The posting requirement of Title I is contained in § 109 of the Act, which is not incorporated into the CAA and the PEOAA for purposes of the FMLA. *See* 2 USC 1312(a)(1) (CAA); 3 USC 412(a)(1) (PEOAA).

a. General Rule

Every employer covered by Title I of the FMLA is required to post and keep posted on its premises, in conspicuous places where employees are employed, whether or not it has any "eligible" employees, a notice explaining the Act's provisions and providing information concerning the procedures for filing complaints of violations of the Act with the Wage and Hour Division of the DOL. 29 USC 2619(a); 29 CFR 825.300(a). The notice must be posted prominently where it can be readily seen by employees and applicants for employment. 29 USC 2619(a); 29 CFR 825.300(a). The poster and the text must be large enough to be easily read and contain fully legible text. 29 CFR 825.300(a). Where an employer's workforce is comprised of a significant portion of workers who are not literate in English, the employer shall be responsible for providing the notice in a language in which the employees are literate. 29 CFR 825.300(c). The DOL makes available copies of the required poster in both English and Spanish.

b. Violations

A covered federal employer that does not post the required notice will violate the FMLA. Any violation of the Act or of the implementing regulations constitutes interfering with, restraining, or denying the exercise of rights provided by the Act. 29 CFR 825.220(b). [The consequences for such a violation are addressed in the "Enforcement" and "Remedies" sections of this chapter. They were also previously discussed in Chapter 8, "Notice Requirements."]

B. TITLE II

1. Introduction

Title II also bars actions that interfere with an employee's FMLA rights. Unlike Title I, the CAA, and the PEOAA, however, Title II does not define these prohibited acts in great detail. There are no OPM regulations specifically implementing the statutory language governing prohibited conduct.

2. General Rule

According the statute (5 USC 6385(b)):

> An employee shall not directly or indirectly intimidate, threaten, or coerce, or attempt to intimidate, threaten, or coerce, any other employee for the purpose of interfering with the exercise of any rights that such other employee may have under this Subchapter. 5 U.S.C. § 6385(a).

"Intimidate, threaten, or coerce" is defined to include–

> promising to confer or conferring any benefit (such as appointment, promotion, or compensation); or

> taking or threatening to take any reprisal (such as deprivation of appointment, promotion, or compensation).

Again, the regulations issued by the OPM to implement Title II of the FMLA do not address the statutory prohibitions contained in 5 USC 6385. No explanation is given either in the regulations or the comments accompanying publication of the interim or final OPM implementing regulations for the absence of regulations addressing the prohibited acts section of Title II.

If an agency erroneously interferes with an employee's right to leave under the FMLA, any resulting adverse action is in violation of the law and may not be sustained. *Jones v. Dept. of the Navy*, No. DC-0752-06-0092-I-2, 2006 MSPB LEXIS 5031, at *4-5 (Sept. 5, 2006); *Fisher v. DHHS*, No. DC-0752-05-0280-I-1, 2005 MSPB LEXIS 2653, at *8 (June 3, 2005), *rev. denied*, 101 MSPR (131 (2005); *Ramey v. USPS*, 70 MSPR 463, 467 (1996).

3. Employee

By its terms, Title II prohibits coercion, direct or indirect, by an employee against another employee. The term "employee" is defined as having the same meaning as "employee" for purposes of § 2105 of Title 5, 5 USC 2105. 5 USC 6385(b). As addressed more fully in Chapter 4, "Federal Employees Covered by the FMLA," § 2105 applies to certain appointed officers or individuals in the civil service, as well as certain employees of the U.S. Naval Academy, military exchanges, and reserves in the armed forces, under certain circumstances. 5 USC 2105.

The limitation of the anti–coercion provisions of Title II to "employees" as defined by 5 USC 2105 is interesting in several respects. First, Title II generally defines a covered "employee" by reference to 5 USC 6301(2). 5 USC 6381(1)(A). Section 6301(2), 5 USC 6301(2), includes § 2105 of Title 5 within its definition. 5 USC 6301(2)(A). However, it also in includes two more groups to the definition of "employee." 5 USC 6381(1)(A). These groups include certain employees of armed forces NAFI organizations, and certain employees of the Veterans Health Administration. [For a further discussion of this issue, see Chapter 4, "Federal Employee's Covered by the FMLA."]

Because more positions are covered by the general Title II definition of "employee" in § 6301(2) of Title 5 than are covered by § 2105 of that same Title, it follows that there are employees covered by Title II that are not covered by the anti–

coercion protections of Title II. Such employees could freely discriminate against other employees, or be the subject of discrimination by Title II employees, without engaging in unlawful conduct. That seems like a problem (and one that could easily be patched by OPM implementing regulations).

The limitation to "employees" in the Title II anti-coercion provisions leaves employees of federal agencies or entities with a mixture of FMLA coverage's unprotected from coercion by non-Title II employees. For example, an individual employed at the U.S. Naval Academy in the midshipman's barbershop is covered by Title II. 5 USC 2105(b). Assume that the U.S. Naval Academy is commanded by a member of the uniformed services. Title II does not cover a member of the uniformed services. 5 USC 2101(1). As a result, Title II covered employees of the Naval Academy who are coerced, intimidated, threatened for the purpose of interfering with their right to take FMLA leave by the highest ranking official of the Naval Academy, technically, would not have been coerced in violation of the Title II.

By the same token, a Title II employee could deliberately interfere with a Title I employee's FMLA rights through coercion, threats, and intimidation, and such conduct, reprehensible as it may be, is not prohibited by the anti-coercion provisions of § 6385 of Title II. This scenario is far more likely to occur as most federal agencies are predominately staffed with employees within the meaning of 5 USC 2105 of the Act, not Title II. Of course, as set forth above, Title I of the Act protects employees covered by that Act against prohibited conduct perpetrated by any "person," which is broad enough to cover all other federal employees, including Title II employees.

4. Intimidate, Threaten, or Coerce

The Act makes it impermissible for a Title II employee to "directly or indirectly" intimidate, threaten or coerce another Title II employee regarding FMLA rights. The Act does not define or otherwise illustrate what would constitute a "direct or indirect" prohibited act. The facts of each case will have to be reviewed to determine whether the prohibited act was direct or indirect.

The term "intimidate, threaten, or coerce" is illustrated by two examples of prohibited conduct. It does not, however, appear that these examples exhaust the possibilities that may satisfy "intimidate, threaten, or coerce."

Moreover, Title II prohibits the "attempt" to intimidate, threaten, or coerce a Title II employee. "Attempt" is not defined or otherwise illustrated.

5. Intent

For the purpose of interfering with the exercise of FMLA rights it is not enough that a Title II (§ 2105 only) employee, directly or indirectly, attempt or actually intimidate, threaten, or coerce another Title II (§ 2105 only) employee regarding FMLA rights. Rather, the Title II anti-coercion provisions appear to impose an intent element into the equation. Such intimidation, threats, or coercion are only impermissible if the actions of the Title II (§ 2105 only) employee was "for the purpose of interfering with the exercise of" the other Title II (§ 2105 only) employee's FMLA rights. Again, there is no guidance offered on what this may entail. Presumably, however, in order to have a "purpose of interfering with the exercise of" FMLA rights, the party doing the intimidating, threatening, or coercion has to be aware of those rights, and must be aware that the Title II employee in question is at least attempting to "exercise" FMLA rights. The way that the anti-coercion language of § 6385 is written arguably rewards management ignorance of Title II employee FMLA rights.

III. ENFORCEMENT

The means of enforcing FMLA rights is different for each of the four federal sector variants of the FMLA. There are profound differences between the federal sector FMLA statues in the ability of aggrieved federal employees to enforce their FMLA rights. Some federal employees are limited to filing grievances pursuant to internal agency procedures or collective bargaining agreements. Other enforcement procedures require extensive administrative exhaustion. Several give employees the right to file a civil lawsuit in federal court. Knowing how any given federal employee's FMLA rights are vindicated is just as important as knowing the substance of those rights.

A. TITLE I

1. Introduction

Title I of the FMLA provides two avenues of redress for FMLA violations. One avenue is for an aggrieved employee to file an administrative complaint with the U.S. Department of Labor. The other avenue available for relief for employer FMLA violations is for the aggrieved employee to initiate a civil action in federal court. Also available as a third avenue of redress is the ability of employees to seek enforcement of FMLA rights through non–FMLA enforcement mechanisms. For example, an aggrieved employee might use an internal agency dispute resolution procedure, or grievance procedures pursuant to the terms of an applicable collective bargaining agreement. Under limited circumstances, an employee may also adjudicate FMLA violations by means of an EEO complaint or MSPB appeal. In certain circumstances, an employee may concurrently use more than one of these avenues of redress to prosecute a claim of unlawful activity in violation of the FMLA.

The relevant statutory provisions include 29 USC 2616 and 2617. The relevant DOL regulations may be found at 29 CFR 825.400 and 825.500.

2. Employee Complaints to the U.S. Department of Labor

a. Introduction

The DOL receives, investigates, and attempts to resolve employee complaints of unlawful conduct in violation of Title I of the FMLA. The DOL does not, however, conduct administrative hearings regarding FMLA claims. If an informal resolution of an employee's FMLA complaint is not achieved, the DOL can bring suit against the federal employer. More likely, given the stretched resources of the DOL, the agency will advise the employee that it has found a violation and that the employee has the right to initiate his or her own civil action.

b. Filing Administrative Complaints with DOL

(1) General Rule

The DOL "shall receive, investigate, and attempt to resolve complaints of violation of § 105 in the same manner that the Secretary [of Labor] receives, investigates, and attempts to resolve complaints of violations of § 6 and 7 of the FLSA (29 USC 206 and 207)." 29 USC 2617(b); *see Ogborn v. United Food and Commercial Workers, Local No. 881 et al.*, No. 98 C 4623, 2000 U.S. Dist. LEXIS 14092, at n.16 (N.D. Ill. Sept. 25, 2000), *aff'd*, 305 F.3d 763 (7th Cir. 2002); *Cox v. AutoZone, Inc.*, 990 F. Supp. 1369, 1373 (M.D. Ala. 1998); *McGregor v. Autozone, Inc.*, 180 F.3d 1305 (11th Cir. 1999). As discussed in the preceding section of this chapter, § 105 of Title I, 29 USC 2615, sets forth what employer acts are prohibited by the FMLA.

According to the legislative history (S. Rep. 103–3, January 27, 1933, p. 35):

> The FMLA's enforcement scheme is modeled on the enforcement scheme of the FLSA, which has been in effect since 1938. Thus the FMLA creates no new agency or enforcement procedures, but instead relies on the time-tested FLSA procedures already established by the Department of Labor.

The above language is also reflected in the Preamble accompanying the publication of the final DOL regulations. Preamble, 29 CFR 825.400–404. The statement notwithstanding, enforcement procedures (undoubtedly no different than those in effect for the FLSA) are set forth in §§ 400 through 404 of the DOL implementing regulations, 29 CFR 825.400–404.

(2) Effect of Filing DOL Complaint on Right to Bring Private Civil Action

The filing of a complaint of FMLA violations with the Secretary of Labor does not preclude an employee from concurrently filing a private civil action regarding the same issue. *Wilson v. Dallas Independent School District*, No. CA3: 97–CV–0281–BC, 1998 U.S. Dist. LEXIS 1415, at *8–14 (N.D. Tex. Jan. 30, 1998). An employee's right to file a private action will terminate only when the Secretary files a civil action seeking relief for the employee. *Id.*

(3) Process for Filing Administrative Complaints

(a) Who May File

An employee or another person on behalf of the employee may file an administrative complaint with the DOL. 29 CFR 825.400(a)(1); see *Ogborn*, 2000 U.S. Dist. LEXIS 14092, at n.16; *Wilson v. Dallas Independent School District*, No. CA3: 97-CV-0281-BC, 1998 U.S. Dist. LEXIS 1415, at *8 (N.D. Tex. Jan. 30, 1998). In response to comments prior to the publication of the final regulations, the DOL addressed (Preamble, 29 CFR 825.400–404) the filing of complaints by others:

> The Department [of Labor], in its enforcement of the FLSA, has accepted complaints from employees as well as other persons who may have knowledge of the circumstances (e.g., a relative of the employee, a Collective Bargaining Unit representative, a competitor, etc.).

By its terms, the regulation allows the filing of a complaint by another "person." "Person" is a defined term under Title I. The Statute defines a "person" as having the same meaning as "person" for purposes of § 3(a) of the FLSA, 29 USC 203(a). 29 USC 2611(8). "Person" means an individual, partnership, association, corporation, business trust, legal representative, or any organized group of persons. 29 USC 203(a); 29 CFR 825.800 (definition of "person"). Given such a broad definition, a "person" would certainly include a relative of the employee, a Collective Bargaining Unit representative, as well as others who may have knowledge of the circumstances.

If another "person" files the administrative complaint, that "person" must be filing "on behalf of" the employee. The term "on behalf of" is not explained. Again, FLSA interpretations of this phrase should apply. The phrase "on behalf of" suggests (at least to me) that the person filing has some awareness of the unlawful acts directed against a particular employee, and is filing on behalf of that employee (rather than for his or her own interests or benefit).

The limitation on the filing of administrative complaints with the DOL to employees or other persons acting on behalf of the employee necessarily excludes anyone who is not in one of those two categories. "Employee" is defined in Title I of the FMLA by reference to the definition of that term in the FLSA (29 USC 203(e)). 29 USC 2611(3). The regulations implementing Title I repeat the FLSA definition of "employee." 29 CFR 825.800 (definition of "employee"). Absent from the Title I definition of "employee" is any reference to applicants for employment, as well as any other non-employees. As you may recall, the Title I "prohibited acts" regulations included prospective employees and persons, whether or not employees, within the protections of the Act. See 29 CFR 825.220(a)(2), (3), (c). Unless these other non-employee "persons" are filing an administrative complaint "on behalf of" a covered "employee," they would not have the right to file an administrative complaint with the DOL alleging a violation of the FMLA. Of course, if § 203(e) of the FLSA has been interpreted to include applicants or other non-employees, that would likely be the case under Title I.

(b) Where to File

An administrative complaint alleging a violation of the FMLA may be filed in person, by mail or by telephone with the national or any local office of the Wage and Hour Division, Employment Standards Administration, U.S. Department of Labor. 29 CFR 825.401(a). Addresses and telephone numbers of local DOL Wage and Hour Offices may be found in the telephone book or on the DOL's web page, www.dol.gov.

(c) Form of Complaint

There is not an official DOL FMLA complaint form that must be used. Further, the DOL does not require that the complaint adhere to any particular form, except that the complaint must (1) be in writing, and (2) include a full statement of the alleged unlawful acts and/or omissions, with pertinent dates. 29 CFR 825.401(c).

(d) Time Frame for Filing Administrative Complaint

An administrative complaint should be filed with the DOL within a reasonable time of when the employee discovers that his or her FMLA rights have been violated. 29 CFR 825.401(b). In no event may an administrative complaint be filed more than two years after the action that is alleged to be a violation of the FMLA occurred, or three years in the case of a willful violation. *Id*. The referenced two- and three-year time periods reflect the statute of limitations for an employee or the Secretary of Labor to initiate a civil action for violation of the FMLA. *See* 29 USC 2617(b)(3), 2617(c)(1)–(2). The statute of limitations will be addressed more fully later in this chapter.

The general rule governing the time frame for filing an administrative complaint is interesting on two accounts. First, by its terms, the regulation only applies to employees. There is no mention of another "person" acting "on behalf of" the aggrieved employee. One could read such an omission as exempting complaints filed by other "persons" acting on the employee's behalf from the time limitations. Presumably this was not what was meant and the omission of other "persons" who may file administrative complaints from the limitations period was inadvertent.

The second interesting aspect of the DOL administrative limitations period is that an FMLA complaint could be late even though it is filed within the two- or three-year statutory limitations period. The regulations require an employee to file an administrative complaint within a "reasonable time" of discovery of the alleged violation of FMLA rights. Where discovery is immediate, an employee who waits for close to two or three years before contacting the DOL may be deemed by DOL to have failed to file within a "reasonable time." The DOL administrative process is not a prerequisite for initiating a civil action, so if the DOL declined to investigate an employee's administrative complaint because it was not filed within a "reasonable time," the employee would still be able to file a civil action, provided that this is done within the relevant two- or three-year period.

(e) Post–Complaint Process

Generally speaking, complaints of FMLA violations are filed with a local office of the DOL Wage and Hours Division. On receipt and review for timeliness, a Wage and Hour investigator is assigned to the complaint. Assignments are generally not made on a first come, first serve basis. Rather, they are made based on an assessment of the seriousness of the alleged violations.

After the case has been assigned, the investigator often contacts the complainant (the employee or other person, typically a Collective Bargaining Representative or the employee's attorney) to clarify the allegations and obtain additional information that was not available from the written administrative complaint. The investigator is not, however, required to initiate the investigation by contacting the complaining party.

As part of the DOL investigation, the Wage and Hour investigator will contact the employer. The scope and authority of such investigation, as well as employer responsibilities, is addressed more fully below. More often than not, the investigator attempts to informally resolve the complaint before the conclusion of the investigation. If informal resolution fails, a decision is made regarding whether Wage and Hour will refer the matter to the DOL Solicitor, who may initiate a civil action. If, as is often the case, the DOL decides not to initiate its own civil action, the complainant will be informed of that decision. The complainant will also be informed that he or she has the right to initiate his or her own civil action against the employer to seek redress for the alleged unlawful practices. Again, a complainant need not exhaust administrative remedies with the DOL before initiating a private civil action.

c. Investigative Authority

(1) General Authority

The Secretary of Labor is authorized to conduct investigations to ensure compliance with Title I of the FMLA. 29 USC 2616(a). The DOL's authority to conduct FMLA investigations is governed by § 11(a) of the FLSA (29 USC 211(a)). 29 USC 2616(a). In pertinent part, FLSA § 11(a) provides:

> The Administrator or his designated representative may investigate and gather data regarding the wages, hours, and other conditions and practices of employment in any industry subject to his chapter, and may enter and inspect such places and such records (and make such transcriptions thereof), question such employees, and investigate such facts, conditions, practices, or matters as he may deem necessary or appropriate to determine whether any person has violated any provision of this chapter, or which may aid in the enforcement of the provisions of this chapter.

Pursuant to this authority, the DOL Wage and Hour Division may conduct investigations in two general situations: (1) routine investigations; and (2) investigations of complaints of alleged violations of the FMLA. *See* 29 USC 2617(b) (authority to investigate and resolve FMLA administrative complaints). Generally, however, the Wage and Hours Division hardly ever conducts routine investigations of employers because of the scarcity of resources and the high number of investigations prompted by complaints of unlawful conduct. Understand, however, that the DOL can exercise the authority described below without the necessity of a complaint of unlawful conduct.

(2) Enter and Inspect

As part of the investigation of a complaint of unlawful conduct in violation of the FMLA, the DOL is legally authorized to enter the agency's premises in order to obtain records, question employees, and otherwise gather facts as part of its investigation. Frequently, however, an on-site inspection is not conducted. Rather, in the typical case involving the allegations of a single employee, the investigator may call the employer, explain the allegations, and ask for the written position of the agency regarding the allegations. Interviews and requests for records, if any, are also frequently taken by telephone in lieu of an on-site investigation.

Where an on-site investigation is deemed appropriate, the DOL investigator is not obligated to arrange a time and place with the employer for the on-site inspection, although that is most often the practice. Employers should be aware that the DOL investigator might simply "show up" and demand entry, records, copies of records, and to question employees, including management. In that event, the federal employer is well advised to immediately contact agency counsel on how best to proceed. Where a DOL investigator contacts the federal employer to make arrangements for an on-site FMLA investigation, the agency should be mindful that this is a courtesy and that requests for an unreasonable delay in the initiation of the on-site investigation will likely not be accommodated.

Generally, the on-site investigation will take place at the facility where the alleged violation occurred. If more than one facility is involved, or if the alleged violation is a policy or practice that applies to more than a single facility, all such facilities where the unlawful conduct occurred or the unlawful policy applies are fair game for an on-site investigation.

(3) Question Employees

The investigator may ask to interview employees, including members of management, as part of the on-site investigation. Employers may, but are not required to, make employees available to the DOL investigator on its premises during work hours. Many employers elect not to make employees available to the DOL investigator during work hours as a means of controlling the information provided by the employer, particularly by management. Managers who are interviewed by the DOL investigator are viewed as speaking for the employer. Of course, an employer cannot prohibit an employee from speaking with the DOL investigator off-premises during non-work hours. That is frequently what happens, particularly regarding interviews conducted with non-managerial colleagues of the complaining employee. Ultimately, whether it is in the best interests of an employer to allow the DOL investigator to conduct on-site interviews with employees regarding alleged violations or compliance with the FMLA is a matter that should be raised with agency counsel before the investigator arrives.

If management decides to allow interviews of management representatives, management generally has the right to attend those interviews. Management generally does not have the right to attend interviews of the complaining party or of non-management employees.

(4) Authority to Review FMLA Records

Whether routine or prompted by a complaint of unlawful activity, a DOL investigator is authorized to inspect and copy relevant records maintained by the employer regarding the FMLA. 29 USC 2616(a), 2717(b)(1). The scope of the records is limited to reasonableness and relevancy. This, of course, will depend on the facts of each case. The point is that the DOL is not permitted to go on a fishing expedition by examining every piece of paper maintained by management, whether related to the FMLA or not.

As discussed more fully in Chapter 14, "Record Keeping Requirements," Title I of the FMLA mandates that employers keep certain records for purposes of compliance with the FMLA. 29 USC 2626(b); 29 CFR 825.500. Government officials investigating compliance with the FMLA (or other pertinent law) must be provided the records for inspection and copying by representatives of the DOL on request. 29 CFR 825.500(b). The DOL does not mandate how employers keep their records, as long as adequate viewing equipment is available. 29 CFR 825.500(b). Copies must be clear and identifiable by date or pay period. 29 CFR 825.500(b).

Agency counsel should be consulted before any records or copies of records are provided to the DOL investigator.

(5) Subpoena Power and Employer Refusals to Cooperate with DOL Investigation

For purposes of a DOL investigation, whether a routine investigation or one prompted by a complaint of unlawful conduct, regarding the FMLA, the Secretary of Labor has the subpoena authority provided under § 9 of the FLSA (29 USC 209). 29 USC 2616(d). Section 9 of the FLSA provides:

> For the purpose of any hearing or investigation provided for in this Chapter, the provisions of Sections 49 and 50 of Title 15 (relating to the attendance of witnesses and the production of books, papers, and documents), are made applicable to the jurisdiction, powers, and duties of the Administrator, the Secretary of Labor, and the industry committees.

To obtain employer records, the DOL investigator usually serves an administrative subpoena on the employer for the records it seeks. The DOL may issue the administrative subpoena to inspect the employer's records without a search warrant. *Donovan v. Lone Steer, Inc.*, 464 U.S. 408, 104 S. Ct. 769, 78 L. Ed. 2d 567 (1984). The DOL's subpoena must be limited in scope to what is reasonable and relevant, and describe with sufficient specificity the documents to be provided. *Oklahoma Press Pub. Co. v. Walling*, 327 U.S. 186, 66 S. Ct. 494, 90 L. Ed. 614 (1946). The DOL is prohibited from issuing the administrative subpoena arbitrarily or capriciously. *Newmark v & Co. v. Wirtz*, 330 F.2d 576 (2nd Cir. 1964).

If an employer refuses to comply with an administrative subpoena, the DOL may seek enforcement by the federal courts. *Oklahoma Press Pub. Co. v. Walling*, 327 U.S. 186, 66 S. Ct. 494, 90 L. Ed. 614 (1946). The subpoenaed employer is entitled to question the reasonableness of the subpoena before suffering any penalties for refusal to comply, and objections to the subpoena may be raised in an action filed in the federal district court. *Donovan v. Lone Steer, Inc.*, 464 U.S. 408, 104 S. Ct. 769, 78 L. Ed. 2d 567 (1984). However, it is not a defense for an employer objecting to a DOL administrative subpoena to allege an infringement of constitutional rights. *Donovan v. Mehlenbacher*, 652 F.2d 228 (2d Cir. 1981). The employer bears the burden of proving the unreasonableness of the DOL administrative subpoena. *Donovan v. Mehlenbacher*, 652 F.2d 228 (2nd Cir. 1981).

An employer that refuses to obey an order of a federal court enforcing the DOL administrative subpoena may be cited for civil contempt. *Durkin v. Fisher*, 204 F.2d 930 (7th Cir. 1953), *cert. denied*, 346 U.S. 897 (1953); *Walling v. Etweiler Bros.*, 58 F. Supp. 201 (D. Id. 1944), *aff'd* 157 F.2d 841 (9th Cir. 1946), *cert denied*, 330 U.S. 819, 67 S. Ct. 676, 91 Led. 1270 (1947). Employers in civil contempt of a federal court order can find themselves facing substantial fines and other nasty penalties.

Before an employer decides to refuse to comply with a DOL administrative subpoena, agency counsel should be consulted.

(6) Completion of the Investigation

Generally, on the conclusion of the investigation the DOL investigator holds a conference with the employer to discuss the findings of the investigation. The DOL investigator identifies what he or she believes to be violations and proposes the action the employer would need to take to come into compliance with the FMLA. At this conference an employer can provide additional facts, clear up discrepancies, and assert defenses. More than one closing conference is possible, particularly where new facts or defenses have been introduced requiring further investigation or consideration.

Once the investigation has closed and all discussions regarding a settlement have been exhausted without an agreement, if the DOL believes that the employer violated the Act it must decide whether to forward the matter to the DOL Solicitor. The Solicitor may then bring a civil action against the employer, or simply advise the employee that it found a violation and that the employee has a right to file a civil action to seek redress. Given the high volume of FMLA complaints handled by the DOL, very few individual employee complaints are forwarded to the DOL Solicitor. Rather, class complaints involving systemic employer FMLA violations pursuant to an unlawful policy or practice are more likely to be forwarded to the DOL Solicitor.

d. DOL Supervised Settlements

The enforcement provisions of the FMLA, 29 USC 2617, direct the DOL to resolve FMLA complaints in the same manner it resolves complaints under the FLSA, 29 USC 216. *Mion v. Aftermarket Tool & Equipment Group*, 990 F. Supp. 535, 539 (W.D. Mich. 1997). The FLSA authorizes the DOL "to supervise the payment of the unpaid minimum wages or the unpaid overtime compensation owing to any employee or employees…and the agreement of any employee to accept such payment shall upon payment in full constitute a waiver by such employee of any right he may have under [S]ubsection (b) of this [S]ection to unpaid minimum wages or unpaid overtime compensation and an additional equal amount as liquidated damages." 29 USC 216(c). The DOL, therefore, has the same authority to supervise a binding settlement and waiver under the FMLA as it has under the FLSA. *Mion*, 990 F. Supp. at 540. As such, where the DOL supervises the settlement of an employee's FMLA claim, such settlement is binding on the employee, and the employee will be deemed to have waived the right to pursue a claim by way of a private civil action. *Id.* at 539–541.

Three factors govern whether the DOL will be considered to have supervised the resolution of a claim: (1) DOL supervision; (2) resolution of the claim; and (3) acceptance of the DOL-supervised resolution by the employee. *Id.* at 540–41. In *Mion*, the employee was arguing against the DOL supervised settlement as she wanted to pursue a private civil action as she believed that she was owed substantially more money than she recovered in the DOL settlement.

Courts have found the requisite DOL supervision where the employer and the DOL exchanged a letter, call, memo, and visit (*Torreblanca v. Naas Foods, Inc.*, No. F 78-163, 1980 U.S. Dist. LEXIS 13893 (N.D. Ind. Feb. 25, 1980) (FLSA case)), and where the DOL met with the employer, received employer correspondence, and supplied WH–58 release forms (*Cuevas v. Monroe Street City Club*, 752 F. Supp. 1405, 1416 (N.D. Ill. 1990) (FLSA case)). In *Mion*, the court found that the DOL supervised the claim where the parties agreed that the DOL investigated the claim, determined the amount owed, and forwarded WH–58 release forms to Aftermarket to be signed by Mion. The court also noted that there was evidence of communications between the DOL and Aftermarket by letter, a fax, and a phone call. *Mion*, 990 F. Supp. at 440.

Mion argued that the DOL did not resolve her claim in accordance with the damage provisions of § 2617(a)(1)(A) because the $310.18 recovered was well below what she intended to establish at trial. *Id.* at 440. Disagreeing, the court stated:

> However, the fact that the DOL recommends a settlement amount lower than that to which a plaintiff believes she is entitled is incidental to the nature of settlements. As the Court noted in *Walton v. United Consumers Club, Inc.*, 786 F.2d 303 (7th Cir. 1986), "the statute is concerned with settlements, and a settlement is a compromise—the employee surrenders his opportunity to get 100 cents on the dollar, in exchange for a smaller payment with certainty." *Id.* at 305 (referring to 29 U.S.C. § 216(c)). In addition, a plaintiff who accepts a DOL supervised settlement waives her right to an equivalent amount in liquidated damages under [Section] 2617(a)(1)(A)(iii). See *Torreblanca*, 1980 U.S. Dist. LEXIS 13893, 1980 WL 2100, at *3 (holding under FLSA, 29 U.S.C. § 216(c)).

Finally, the court addressed whether Mion had agreed to the DOL–supervised back wage payment of $310.18. The mere cashing of a check issued under a DOL–supervised settlement does not release the employee's claims where the DOL did not send out the applicable release forms. *Id.* at 540 (citing *Walton v. United Consumers Club, Inc.*, 786 F.2d 303, 307 (7th Cir. 1986)). However, the DOL may indicate its assent to a settlement by sending out the applicable release forms. *Walton*, 786 F.2d at 306. Similarly, a § 216(c) wavier applies where the DOL supplied, and the employee signed, WH–58 release forms. *Mion*, 990 F. Supp. at 440 (citing *Cuevas v. Monroe Street City Club*, 752 F. Supp. 1405, 1415–16 (N.D. Ill. 1990)). Moreover, where an employee cashes the employer's check, the DOL's supplying of WH–58 forms effectuates the waiver, even if the employee does not sign the release forms. *Mion*, 990 F. Supp. at 440 (citing *Heavenridge v. Ace-Tex Corp.*, No. 92-75610, 1993 U.S. Dist. LEXIS 21129, at *3 (E.D. Mich. Sept. 3, 1993) (plain language of WH–58 predicated employee's waiver on acceptance of back wages rather than on employee's signature).

Applying the above rules to the case at hand, the court in *Mion* found that because Aftermarket paid the full amount identified by the DOL as due, and where Mion cashed the check, the terms of the release were met, even though Mion never signed the WH–58 release form. As a result, the court granted Aftermarket's motion for summary judgment on the issue of Mion's waiver of her FMLA claims. *Mion*, 990 F. Supp. at 541.

e. Civil Actions Brought by the DOL

The Solicitor of Labor may appear for and represent the Secretary of Labor on any litigation to enforce the provisions of the FMLA. 29 USC 2617(e). The DOL Solicitor may bring an action in any court of competent jurisdiction to recover damages pursuant to § 2617(a)(1)(A) of Title 29 (29 USC 2617(a)(1)(A)). 29 USC 2617(b)(2); *see Reich v. Midwest Plastic Engineering, Inc.*, No. 1:94–CV–525, 1995 U.S. Dist. LEXIS 8772, at *7 (W.D. Mich. June 6, 1995). The DOL Solicitor may also seek injunctive relief. 29 USC 2617(d); *see Reich v. Midwest Plastic Engineering, Inc. et al.*, 934 F. Supp. 266, 268 (W.D. Mich. 1996), *aff'd without opinion*, 113 F.3d 1235 (6th Cir. 1997). When the DOL brings a civil action on behalf of an employee, the employee's right to bring his or her own private civil action on the same issue terminates. 29 USC 2617(a)(4); *see Wilson v. Dallas Independent School District*, No. CA3: 97–CV–0281–BC, 1998 U.S. Dist. LEXIS 1415, at *8–14 (N.D. Tex. Jan. 30, 1998).

As with a private right of action brought by an employee, a civil action must be brought by the DOL Solicitor within two years after the date of the last event constituting the alleged violation. 29 USC 2617(c)(1). Where the violation of the FMLA was "willful," the DOL Solicitor must file suit no later than three years from the date of the last event constituting the alleged violation. 29 USC 2617(c)(2).

The prospect of a federal lawsuit funded and financed by the Government of the United States in the form of the DOL Solicitor is not to be underestimated. On the other hand, in addition to in-house counsel, most federal agencies are represented by the United States Department of Justice in federal court litigation. While Justice is rarely pleased with the idea of defending inter-agency lawsuits, that is its charge. The point is that, while the threat of a DOL Solicitor lawsuit is daunting to many employers, particularly those in the private sector with limited resources, such a threat is not of the same character when directed at federal agencies, which generally do have the resources to defend themselves. As such, federal agencies are usually in a better position to "push back" on a DOL threat of litigation made in the course of settlement negotiations.

f. Posting Violations

(1) General Rule

As with any other violations, posting violations may be discovered by the DOL as part of a rare routine investigation. More likely, however, posting violations may have been confirmed after an investigation of an employee or union complaint of an unlawful FMLA practice (e.g., not having the required poster posted in conspicuous places where employees and applicants may see the poster). *See, e.g.*, 29 CFR 825.300 (general posting requirement).

If a representative of the DOL determines that an employer has committed a willful violation of the posting requirement, and that the imposition of a civil money penalty for such violation is appropriate, the representative may issue and serve a notice of penalty on the employer in person or by certified mail. 29 CFR 825.402. Where service by certified mail is not accepted, notice will be deemed to be received on the date of attempted delivery. *Id.* Where service is not accepted, the DOL may also serve the notice of civil penalty by regular mail. *Id.* The civil monetary penalty for willful violation of the posting requirement is up to $100 for each separate offense. 29 USC 2619(b); 29 CFR 825.300(b).

(2) Employer Appeals of Civil Penalty

An employer may appeal the assessment of a civil monetary penalty from the Wage and Hour Regional Administrator for the region in which the alleged violation(s) occurred. 29 CFR 825.403(a). If the employer does not timely appeal the issuance of a civil monetary penalty for a posting violation, the notice of penalty constitutes the final ruling for the Secretary of Labor. *Id.* That means the employer has no other means of challenging the civil penalty.

To file an appeal, an employer must file a petition with the Wage and Hour Administrator for the region in which the alleged violation(s) occurred. 29 CFR 825.403(b). The petition does not have to be in any particular form, but pursuant to 29 CFR 825.404(b) it must be: (1) in writing; (2) contain the legal and factual bases for the petition; and (3) must be mailed to the Regional Administrator within 15 days of receipt of the notice of penalty.

An employer may also request an oral hearing on the appeal of the civil penalty. 29 CFR 825.403(b). If such an appeal is heard, the oral hearing will be conducted by telephone. *Id.*

The decision of the Regional Administrator constitutes the final order of the Secretary of Labor regarding the appeal of the civil monetary penalty. 29 CFR 825.403(c). There is no additional avenue of appeal after the decision of the Regional Administrator.

3. Private Right of Action

A second avenue of redress available to aggrieved employees for violation of the FMLA is for the employee to file a private civil action against the federal employer. The requirements for such suits are addressed below.

a. General Rule

Section 107 of the FMLA, 29 USC 2617(a)(2), sets forth the FMLA requirements to maintain a civil action for violations of Title I of the Act, and provides:

> An action to recover the damages or equitable relief prescribed in paragraph (1) civil action to recover certain damages and equitable relief may be maintained against any employer (including a public agency) in any Federal or State Court of competent jurisdiction by any one or more employees for and in behalf of—
>
> (A) the employees; or
>
> (B) the employees and other employees similarly situated.

See *Smith v. BellSouth Telecommunications, Inc.*, 273 F.3d 1303, 1306 (11th Cir. 2001); *Smith v. Virgin Islands Port Authority*, No. 2002-227, 2005 U.S. Dist. LEXIS 56, at *34 (D.V.I. Jan. 2, 2005); *Wheeler v. Pioneer Dev. Services, Inc.*, 349 F. Supp 2d 158 (D. Mass. 2004); *Rosteutcher v. MidMichigan Physicians Group*, 332 F. Supp. 2d 1049, 1063 (E.D. Mich. 2004); *Kallen v. DOD*, No. 1:03-CV-1634-JDT-TAB, 2004 U.S. Dist. LEXIS 19576, at *5 (S.D. Ind. Aug. 11, 2004); *Holliday v. Vacationland Federal Credit Union*, No. 3:03 CV 7493, 2004 U.S. Dist. LEXIS 5655, at *6 (N.D. Ohio April 5, 2004).

According to the legislative history, the civil enforcement scheme of Title I of the FMLA is modeled on the enforcement scheme of the FLSA. S. 103-3, p. 35. "Thus, the FMLA creates no new agency or enforcement procedures, but instead relies on the time-tested FLSA procedures already established by the Department of Labor." S. 103-3, p. 35. Clearly, case law interpreting the FLSA enforcement scheme should be consulted for purposes of civil enforcement of the FMLA.

There is no administrative exhaustion requirement mandated by the FMLA before a federal employee covered by Title I may initiate a private civil action against a federal employer for violation(s) of the FMLA. See *Kingsby v. Potter*, No. 06CV0679, 2007 U.S. Dist. LEXIS 13214, at *18 (E.D. Wis. Feb. 26, 2007); *Barrett v. Detroit Heading, LLC*, No. 05-72341, 2006 U.S. Dist. LEXIS 55230, at *4 (E.D. Mich. Aug. 9, 2006) (union employee not required to file grievance before initiating civil action); *Ogborn v. United Food and Commercial Workers, Local No. 881 et al.*, No. 98 C 4623, 2000 U.S. Dist. LEXIS 14092 (N.D. Ill. Sept. 25, 2000), aff'd, 305 F.3d 763 (7th Cir. 2002); *Wilson v. Dallas Independent School District*, No. CA3:97-CV-0281-BC, 1998 U.S. Dist. LEXIS 1415, at *12-14 (N.D. Tex. Jan. 30, 1998); *Shannon v. City of Philadelphia*, 1999 U.S. Dist. LEXIS 2428 (E.D. Pa. March 5, 1993); *Krohn v. Forsting*, 11 F. Supp. 2d 1082, 1085 (E.D. Mo. 1998); *Danfelt v. Bd. of County Commissioners of Washington County*, 998 F. Supp. 606, 609 (D. Md. 1998); *Spurlock v. NYNEX*, 949 F. Supp. 1022, 1030 (W.D.N.Y. 1996). Similarly, an employee may file an administrative complaint with the Secretary of Labor and a private right of action concurrently. *Wilson v. Dallas Independent School District*, 1998 U.S. Dist. LEXIS 1415, at *12-14.

b. Who May Initiate a Private Action?

By its terms, a private civil action for violations of the FMLA may only be brought by an employee. An "employee" is a term defined in the Statute and implementing regulations. *See* 29 USC 2611(3); 29 CFR 825.800 (definition of "employee"). While broad, the definition is not limitless. Specifically, an "employee" does not include prospective employees or applicants. *See* 29 CFR 825.800 (definition of "employee"). Nor does the definition of "employee" include other non-employees, such as former employees. As such, one would think that non-employees who are covered by the "prohibited acts" provisions of the FMLA do not have the right to file a private civil action against the offending employer under the FMLA. *See* 29 CFR 825.220(a)(2)-(3), (c). Pursuant to the doctrine of sovereign immunity, because a federal employer may only be sued where specifically permitted (i.e., sovereign immunity has been waived), non-employees who have been subject to unlawful FMLA conduct in violation of the "prohibited acts" provisions of the FMLA will very likely be unable to successfully bring a private action in federal court against the federal employer.

Notwithstanding the fact that the statutory and regulatory definition of "employee" under Title I does not include former or prospective employees, the DOL regulations do include prospective employees within the protections from discrimination for use of FMLA leave. 29 CFR 825.220(c). Two circuits have upheld this regulation where a former employee alleged that the decision not to rehire was the result of discrimination for use of FMLA leave. *See Smith v. Telecommunications, Inc.*, 273 F.3d 1303, 1307–1314 (11th Cir. 2001) ("Since the provision of the FMLA that affords a private right of action to 'employees' is ambiguous, and the Department of Labor regulation prohibiting an employer from considering an employee's past use of FMLA leave in hiring decisions is a reasonable interpretation of the [S]tatute, we must afford that regulation *Chevron* deference"); *Duckworth v. Pratt & Whitney, Inc.*, 152 F.3d 1, 10–11 (1st Cir. 1998).

The term "employee" is not defined as including a union or collective bargaining representative. Therefore, a union or collective bargaining representative *per se* should not be able to file a civil action against a federal employer. *See New York Metro Area Postal Union v. Potter*, No. 00–Civ. 8538 (LTS)(RLE), 2003 U.S. Dist. LEXIS 4904, at *6–8 (S.D.N.Y. March 31, 2003) (a union may not sue an employer for violation of the FMLA).

Typically, the plaintiff in an FMLA retaliation case is an employee who took or attempted to take FMLA leave and then suffered an adverse action. The FMLA also permits an eligible employee to bring suit for retaliation for "opposing" an employer's treatment of another employee. *See Wood v. Handy & Harman Co.*, No. 05-CV-TCK-FHM, 2006 U.S. Dist. LEXIS 81186, at *10 & n.1 (N.D. Okla. Nov. 6, 2006).

Note that, while an employee or employees must bring the civil action, the civil action may be on behalf of other employees besides the one(s) initiating the civil litigation. This would appear to permit class action litigation. *See Bond v. Abbott Laboratories*, 188 F.3d 506 (table), 1999 U.S. App. LEXIS 22242, at *2 (6th Cir. Sept. 9, 1999) (FMLA case allowed to proceed as class action on issue of whether employer's attendance control policy violated FMLA on its face); *Cox v. AutoZone, Inc.*, 990 F. Supp. 1369, 1373, n.7 (M.D. Ala. 1998) (class actions are possible under the FMLA), *aff'd, McGregor v. Autozone, Inc.*, 180 F.3d 1305 (11th Cir. 1999). In class action litigation, one or more employees allege that an employer has engaged in systematic violations of the FMLA rights against other similarly situated employees. Typically, this occurs because the employer has a policy or practice that violates the FMLA every time that policy or practice is used, which could be on a daily basis.

Generally, only an "eligible employee" may initiate a private right of action for violation of the FMLA. *Humenny v. Genex Corp., Inc.*, 390 F.3d 901, 904 (6th Cir. 2004) ("Where a plaintiff does not qualify as an 'eligible employee,' the court lacks jurisdiction to decide the FMLA case"); *Walker v. Elmore County Bd. of Ed.*, 379 F.3d 1249, 1253 (11th Cir. 2004); *see Morrison v. Amway Corp. et. al.*, 323 F.3d 920, 927–28 & n.10 (11th Cir. 2003).

In *Humenny*, the employee argued that the reference to "employee" and "individual" in 29 USC 2615(a)(1)–(2) indicated that satisfaction of the eligibility requirements was not a prerequisite to sue for FMLA violations. Disagreeing, the court found that a close reading of the statute demonstrated that employers were prohibited from retaliating against employees for the exercise of a "right," and only eligible employees could exercise FMLA rights.

c. When Must a Private Civil Action Be Initiated?

(1) General Rule

A civil action to enforce FMLA rights generally must be filed within two years after the date of the last event constituting the alleged violation. 29 USC 2617(c)(1); *see Williams v. Northwest Airlines, Inc.*, 53 Fed. Appx. 350 (6th Cir. 2002*), cert. denied,* 123 S. Ct. 2224 (2003); *Williams v. Schuller International, Inc. et al.*, 29 Fed Appx. 306 (6th Cir. 2002) (normal limitations period for FMLA action is two years); *Melvin v. Knoll, Inc. et al.*, 21 Fed. Appx. 305 (6th Cir. 2001) (two-year statute of limitations applies to most claims under FMLA); *Butler v. Owens–Brockway Plastic Products, Inc.*, 199 F.3d 314, 317 (6th Cir. 1999); *Nero v. Industrial Molding Corp.*, 167 F.3d 921, 929 n.4 (5th Cir. 1999*); Rigel v. Wilks*, No. 1:03-CV-971, 2006 U.S. Dist. LEXIS 93659, at *41 (M.D. Pa. Dec. 28, 2006); *Murray v. Walgreens Co.*, No. CIV-05-1125-M, 2006 U.S. Dist. LEXIS 27310, at *3 (D. Okl. April 14, 2006); *Ungerfleider v. Fleet Mortgage Group of Fleet Bank*, 329 F. Supp. 2d 343, 2004 U.S. Dist. LEXIS 15760, at *50 (D. Conn. 2004) (FMLA claim time barred where it was filed almost three years from employee's resignation); *Fernandez v. IBP, Inc.*, No. SA–02–CV–1161-XR, 2004 U.S. Dist. LEXIS 13494 (W.D. Tex. July 19, 2004); *Rivera v. Caribbean Refrescos, Inc.*, No. 02–2499 (DRD), 2004 U.S. Dist. LEXIS 17230, at *47 (D.P.R. May 26, 2004); *Passauer v. Quest Diagnostics, Inc.*, No. CCB-03-159, 2004 U.S. Dist. LEXIS 6966, at *5 (D. Md. April 22, 2004); *Porter v. NYU School of Law et al.*, No. 99 Civ. 4693 (TPG), 2003 U.S. Dist. LEXIS 14674, at *14 (S.D.N.Y. Aug. 25, 2003), *aff'd*, 392 F.3d 530 (2d Cir. 2004); *Rhoades v. Stewart Enterprises, Inc. et al.*, No. 01–5044, 2003 U.S. Dist. LEXIS 550, at *16 (E.D. Pa. Jan. 7, 2003)

In the case of a "willful" violation of § 105 of Title I (29 USC 2615), a civil action may be brought within three years of the date of the last event constituting the alleged violation. 29 USC 2617(c)(2); *see Williams v. Northwest Airlines, Inc.*, 53 Fed. Appx. 350 (6th Cir. 2002*), cert. denied,* 123 S. Ct. 2224 (2003); *Williams v. Schuller International, Inc. et al.*, 29 Fed Appx. 306 (6th Cir. 2002); *Melvin v. Knoll, Inc. et al.*, 21 Fed. Appx. 305 (6th Cir. 2001); *Butler v. Owens–Brockway Plastic Products, Inc.*, 199 F.3d 314, 317 (6th Cir. 1999); *Nero v. Industrial Molding Corp.*, 167 F.3d 921, 929, n.4 (5th Cir. 1999); *Rigel v. Wilks*, No. 1:03-CV-971, 2006 U.S. Dist. LEXIS 93659, at *41 (M.D. Pa. Dec. 28, 2006); *Murray v. Walgreens Co.*, No. CIV-05-1125-M, 2006 U.S. Dist. LEXIS 27310, at *3 (D. Okl. April 14, 2006); *Ungerfleider v. Fleet Mortgage Group of Fleet Bank*, 329 F. Supp. 2d 343, 2004 U.S. Dist. LEXIS 15760, at *51 (D. Conn. 2004) (three-year statute of limitations not applicable; plaintiff failed to provide facts showing that violation was "willful"); *Passauer v. Quest Diagnostics, Inc.*, No. CCB–03–159, 2004 U.S. Dist. LEXIS 6966, at *5 (D. Md. April 22, 2004); *Fernandez v. IBP, Inc.*, No. SA–02–CV–1161-XR, 2004 U.S. Dist. LEXIS 13494 (W.D. Tex. July 19, 2004); *Porter v. NYU School of Law et al.*, No. 99 Civ. 4693 (TPG), 2003 U.S. Dist. LEXIS 14674, at *14 (S.D.N.Y. Aug. 25, 2003), *aff'd*, 392 F.3d 530 (2d Cir. 2004). The FMLA does not provide a standard for determining willfulness. *Williams v. Schuller International, Inc. et al.*, 29 Fed Appx. 306 (6th Cir. 2002); *Packard v. Continental Airlines, Inc.*, 24 Fed. Appx. 960 (10th Cir. 2001), *cert denied,* 536 U.S. 923 (2002); *Rigel*, 2006 U.S. Dist. LEXIS 93659, at *41 (FMLA does not define "willful"). Courts have applied the "willful" standard first developed by the Supreme Court for age discrimination claims in *Trans World Airlines, Inc. v. Thurston*, 469 U.S. 111, 128–129, 83 L. Ed. 2d 523, 105 S. Ct. 613 (1985). There, the Supreme Court held that a violation was "willful" if "the employer either knew or showed reckless disregard for the matter of whether its conduct was prohibited by the ADEA." *This standard was subsequently adopted for willful violations of the Fair Labor Standards Act. See McLaughlin v. Richland Shoe Co.*, 486 U.S. 128, 133, 100 L. Ed. 2d 115, 108 S. Ct. 1677 (1988) (adopting the *Thurston* standard for the two-tiered statute of limitations in the Fair Labor Standards Act); *Williams v. Schuller International, Inc. et al.*, 29 Fed Appx. 306 (6th Cir. 2002); *Packard v. Continental Airlines, Inc.*, 24 Fed. Appx. 960 (10th Cir. 2001), *cert. denied,* 536 U.S. 923 (2002). (citing *McLaughlin v. Richland Shoe Co.*, 486 U.S. 128, 133, 100 L. Ed. 2d 115, 108 S. Ct. 1677 (1988)).

Courts have since applied the similar standard of "willfulness" by reference to the FLSA or ADEA cases for purposes of the FMLA. *See Hoffman v. Professional Med Te*am, 394 F.3d 414 (6th Cir. 2005) (applying ADEA willful standard); *Packard*, 24 Fed. Appx. 960 (applying reckless disregard standard); *Williams v. Northwest Airlines, Inc.*, 53 Fed. Appx. 350 (6th Cir. 2002*), cert. denied* 123 S. Ct. 2224 (2003) (citing *McLaughlin v. Richland Shoe Co.*, 486 U.S. 128, 132–35, 100 L. Ed. 2d 115, 108 S. Ct. 1677 (1988)); *Nero v. Industrial Molding Corp.*, 167 F.3d 921, 929 n. 4 (5th Cir. 1999) (indicating that reckless disregard standard applies to determine willfulness in Fifth Circuit); *Rigel*, 2006 U.S. Dist. LEXIS 93659, at *42; *Ungerfleider*, 329 F. Supp. 2d 243 (applying FLSA willful standard).

The ADA and FLSA standards appear similar. Under the ADEA willfulness standard, an employer that intentionally or recklessly violates the FMLA is deemed to have acted willfully. *Hoffman v. Professional Med Te*am, 394 F.3d 414 (6th Cir. 2005). The FLSA standard for willfulness is that the employer either knew or showed reckless disregard for the matter of whether its conduct was prohibited by the statute. *Ungerfleider*, 329 F. Supp. 2d 343 (applying FLSA willful standard); *Fernandez*, 2004 U.S. Dist. LEXIS 13494 (FLSA case law); *Passauer*, 2004 U.S. Dist. LEXIS 6966, at *5; *Porter*, 2003 U.S. Dist. LEXIS 14674, at *14 (applying reckless disregard standard of Supreme Court in *Richland Shoe*); *Hoffman*, 2003 U.S. Dist. LEXIS 11913, at *24–29 (to prove willful violation, the plaintiff must show either (1) employer knew that its refusal to accept the plaintiff's certification form as tendered violated the FMLA; or (2) the employer's actions showed a reckless disregard for the matter in light of the FMLA Statute*); Rhoades v. Stewart Enterprises, Inc. et al.*, No. 01–5044, 2003 U.S. Dist. LEXIS 550, at *16 (E.D. Pa. Jan. 7, 2003) (willfulness established by showing employer knew or showed reckless disregard for matter of whether employer's actions were prohibited by the FMLA); *Hanger v. Lake County et al.*, No. 01–1506 (RHK/RLE), 2002 U.S. Dist. LEXIS 25403, at *15–16 (D. Minn. Dec. 31, 2002), *aff'd*, 390 F.3d 579 (8th Cir. 2004); *Edwards v. Ford Motor Co. et al.*, 179 F. Supp. 2d 714, 719 (W.D. Ky. 2001) (evidence must show more than Ford's mere negligent violation of a particular obligation of the FMLA; willful conduct in the FMLA context is viewed as an employer that knows its conduct to be wrong or has shown reckless disregard for the matter in light of the statute).

The burden is on the employee to establish a "willful" violation. *Williams v. Northwest Airlines, Inc.*, 53 Fed. Appx. 350 (6th Cir. 2002*), cert. denied,* 123 S. Ct. 2224 (2003); *Melvin v. Knoll, Inc. et al.*, 21 Fed. Appx. 305 (6th Cir. 2001); *Porter v. NYU School of Law et al.*, No. 99 Civ. 4693 (TPG), 2003 U.S. Dist. LEXIS 14674, at *21 (S.D.N.Y. Aug. 25, 2003),), *aff'd*, 392 F.3d 530 (2d Cir. 2004) (employee failed to establish willful violation); *Hoffman v. Professional Med Team*, No. 1:01–CV–3, 2003 U.S. Dist. LEXIS 11913, at *24–29 (W.D. Mich. June 5, 2003), *aff'd*, 394 F.3d 414 (6th Cir. 2004); *Rhoades v. Stewart Enterprises, Inc. et al.*, No. 01–5044, 2003 U.S. Dist. LEXIS 550, at *16 (E.D. Pa. Jan. 7, 2003).

Mere negligence on the part of the employer is insufficient to establish "willful" conduct. *Packard v. Continental Airlines, Inc.*, 24 Fed. Appx. 960 (10th Cir. 2001*), cert denied,* 536 U.S. 923 (2002); *Rigel v. Wilks*, No. 1:03-CV-971, 2006 U.S. Dist. LEXIS

93659, at *41 (M.D. Pa. Dec. 28, 2006). To demonstrate that the employer willfully violated the FMLA, a plaintiff must show more than his request for leave was "bungled." *Rigel,* 2006 U.S. Dist. LEXIS 93659, at *48.

The courts will want evidence, such as employee testimony, to establish that an employer knew what it was doing violated the FMLA. *See id.* at *42–43 (a 'willful' violation requires a showing that the employer either knew or showed reckless disregard for the matter of whether its conduct was prohibited by statute); *Hoffman v. Professional Med Team*, No. 1:01–CV–3, 2003 U.S. Dist. LEXIS 11913, at *29 (W.D. Mich. June 5, 2003), aff'd, 394 F.3d 414 (6th Cir. 2004).

An employer's understanding of the FMLA and its related regulations are important in discerning whether it "know or showed reckless disregard" for whether it was violating the statute. *Rigel,* 2006 U.S. Dist. LEXIS 93659, at *43. An employer does not act in "reckless disregard" of FMLA requirements where the employer's interpretation of the requirements of the FMLA is not "wholly inconsistent with the language of the law." *Hoffman,* 2003 U.S. Dist. LEXIS 11913, at *24–29. That leaves open the possibility that the employer's interpretation of what is required by the FMLA could be legally incorrect, but not "willful" because it was not "wholly inconsistent" with the language of the law.

In *Porter v. NYU School of Law et al.,* No. 99 Civ. 4693 (TPG), 2003 U.S. Dist. LEXIS 14674, at *14–21 (S.D.N.Y. Aug. 25, 2003), aff'd, 392 F.3d 530 (2d Cir. 2004), the district court reviewed the plaintiff's allegation that NYU had "willfully" interfered with his FMLA rights when it denied his request for leave and terminated his employment. The focus of the review centered on the employee's allegations that NYU had procedurally violated the Act in three ways: (1) NYU failed to explain how his application for FMLA leave was deficient and did not permit him more time to submit additional materials; (2) NYU failed to schedule a third medical opinion examination; and (3) NYU failed to notify him of the status of his FMLA application before terminating him. The court rejected all of these allegations. The court recited uncontested facts that NYU made multiple contacts with the employee regarding deficiencies with the original certification provided, allowed plaintiff additional time to provide a complete certification, and gave him the form to do so. Second, NYU was not legally required to schedule a third examination, as the requirement was permissive, not mandatory. Finally, NYU had notified the plaintiff that the results of the second medical examination revealed that he could return to work. NYU offered the employee more time to provide additional medical documentation, but he never did. The court concluded that Porter failed to demonstrate a "willful" violation by NYU of his rights under the FMLA that would entitle him to the Act's three-year statute of limitations.

Similarly, the court in *Hoffman v. Professional Med Team*, No. 1:01–CV–3, 2003 U.S. Dist. LEXIS 11913, at *24–29 (W.D. Mich. June 5, 2003), aff'd, 394 F.3d 414 (6th Cir. 2004), also focuses on whether the employer properly applied FMLA procedural requirements regarding the handling of medical certification. There, the employee provided a medical certification that indicated that the plaintiff had a serious health condition, but did not require FMLA leave. The employer advised the employee of the contradictory nature of the certification, and gave the employee a number of opportunities to correct it. That did not happen. Absent evidence that the employer knew that the certification was, in fact, valid, the court held that the employee failed to establish that the employer knew it was violating the FMLA. The court also opined that the employee had failed to establish that the employer showed a reckless disregard for the matter in light of the FMLA. The court stated that "[w]hile the Court need not reach the question of whether PMT's interpretation of what constitutes a complete and adequate certification was correct, the Court finds that the PMT's interpretation was not wholly inconsistent with the plain language of the FMLA, the regulations construing the FMLA, and the Seventh Circuit's opinion in *Stoops,* as discussed above. The Plaintiff failed to show that PMT met the second prong of the 'willful violation' test."

Neither the Statute nor the implementing regulations address when an FMLA cause of action accrues, beyond the "date of the last event constituting the violation." A claimant's cause of action under the FMLA accrues when the employer violates the employee's rights under the Statute. *Hanger v. Lake County et al.,* No. 01–1506 (RHK/RLE), 2002 U.S. Dist. LEXIS 25403, at *13 (D. Minn. Dec. 31, 2002), aff'd, 390 F.3d 579 (8th Cir. 2004) *(citing Moore v. Payless Shoe Source, Inc.*, 139 F.3d 1210, 1214 (8th Cir. 1998) (holding that an alleged failure to designated workers' compensation leave as FMLA leave "occurred and accrued" at the time the leave should have been properly designated.

Where the FMLA claim is based on termination, the employee's FMLA claim accrues on the date of termination. *Williams v. Northwest Airlines, Inc.*, 53 Fed. Appx. 350 (6th Cir. 2002*), cert. denied,* 123 S. Ct. 2224 (2003); *Butler v. Owens–Brockway Plastic Products, Inc.*, 199 F.3d 314, 317 (6th Cir. 1999) (termination was last unlawful act from which calculation of statute of limitations is to be made); *Hillstrom v. Best Western TLC Hotel,* 265 F. Supp. 2d 117, 128, n.17 (D. Mass. 2003), aff'd, 354 F.3d 27 (1st Cir. 2003) (last act of termination occurred within two years of filing complaint),

In *Garner v. Calcione et al.*, 173 F.3d 855 (table), 1999 U.S. App. LEXIS 4716 (6th Cir. March 16, 1999), the court held that the civil action was time barred because both the denial of leave and the plaintiff's termination occurred more than three years before the civil action was filed. Where an FMLA claim is based on a "failure to restore" theory, the last event constituting the violation occurs on the date the employee is returned to work, albeit in a non-equivalent position. *Hanger v. Lake County et al.*, No. 01-1506 (RHK/RLE), 2002 U.S. Dist. LEXIS 25403, at *13 (D. Minn. Dec. 31, 2002), aff'd, 390 F.3d 579 (8th Cir. 2004).

Absent evidence that the deciding official knew the reason for plaintiff's absence or that plaintiff allegedly received a leave of absence, the plaintiff failed to establish that the employer acted knowingly and recklessly. *Fernandez v. IBP, Inc.*, No. SA-02-CV-1161-XR, 2004 U.S. Dist. LEXIS 13494 (W.D. Tex. July 19, 2004).

Courts routine reject enforcement of employment contracts limiting the time an employee has to file suit for violation of the FMLA. *See Grosso v. Federal Express Corp.*, 467 F. Supp. 2d 449, 456 (E.D. Pa. Dec. 19, 2006); *Lewis v. Harper Hosp.*, 241 F. Supp. 2d 769, 772-73 (E.D. Mich. 2002) (six-month contractual limitations period impermissibly interfered with federal rights under FMLA); *Woods v. DaimlerChrysler*, No. 4:02CV834 CDP, 2003 U.S. Dist. LEXIS 26849, at *4 (E.D. Mo. Dec. 2, 2003) (six-month limitations clause unenforceable to bar FMLA claim), aff'd, 409 F.3d 984 (8th Cir. 2005); *Henegar v. Daimler-Chrysler Corp.*, 280 F. Supp. 2d 680, 682 n.1 (E.D. Mich. 2003) (same); *Wineman v. Durkee Lakes Hunting & Fishing Club, Inc.*, 352 F. Supp. 2d 815, 823 (E.D. Mich. 2005). *But see Badgett v. Federal Express Corp.*, 378 F. Supp. 2d 613, 624-25 (M.D.N.C. 2005) (six-month limitations clause upheld and FMLA claim denied as untimely).

Failure to file within the requisite statute of limitations bars the action or claims as untimely. *Melvin v. Knoll, Inc. et al.*, 21 Fed. Appx. 305 (6th Cir. 2001); *Garner v. Calcione et al.*, 173 F.3d 855 (table), 1999 U.S. App. LEXIS 4716 (6th Cir. March 16, 1999); *Porter v. NYU School of Law et al.*, No. 99 Civ. 4693 (TPG), 2003 U.S. Dist. LEXIS 14674, at *14 (S.D.N.Y. Aug. 25, 2003), aff'd, 392 F.3d 530 (2d Cir. 2004); *Bui v. IBP, Inc.*, 205 F. Supp. 2d 1181, 1184-85 (D. Kan. 2002), aff'd, 34 Fed. Appx. 653 (10th Cir. 2002), *Gray v. Sears, Roebuck & Co., Inc.*, 131 F. Supp. 2d 895, 901 (S.D. Tex. 2001) (because more than three years have passed on all of the employee's FMLA claims except failure to reinstate, statute of limitations has run on all but failure to reinstate claim).

(2) Extending the Time Period for Filing a Civil Action

Courts have recognized exceptions to the statute of limitations that effectively extend the period of time for an individual to file a civil action. Those exceptions include equitable tolling and continuing violations. It is unclear whether the continuing violations doctrine applies to FMLA claims. *See Packard v. Continental Airlines, Inc.*, 24 Fed. Appx. 960 (10th Cir. 2001), *cert. denied* 536 U.S. 923 (2002) (assuming without deciding equitable tolling and continuing violations theory applies to FMLA claims); *Hanger v. Lake County et al.*, No. 01-1506 (RHK/RLE), 2002 U.S. Dist. LEXIS 25403 (D. Minn. Dec. 31, 2002), aff'd, 390 F.3d 579 (8th Cir. 2004) (same).

"The continuing violations doctrine is premised on the equitable notion that the statue of limitations should not begin to run until a reasonable person would be aware that his or her rights have been violated." *Hanger*, 2002 U.S. Dist. LEXIS 25403 (quoting *Martin v. Nannie & Newborns, Inc.*, 3 F.3d 1410, 1415, n. 6 (10th Cir. 1993))

There are four critical elements to establishing a continuing violation: (1) there must be a series of related incidents or personnel actions; (2) at least one of those incidents or personnel actions must have occurred within the statute of limitations (e.g., two years, or three years for a willful violation); and (3) the individual was not reasonably aware that the incidents or personnel actions were discriminatory; and (4) once aware of the discriminatory nature of the incidents or personnel actions, the individual timely filed his or her civil action. *See United Airlines v. Evans*, 431 U.S. 553, 97 S. Ct. 1885, 52 L. Ed. 2d 571 (1977) (Title VII claim). Generally discrete acts, such as a failure to promote, do not constitute a series of related incidents or personnel actions. *Hanger v. Lake County et al.*, No. 01-1506 (RHK/RLE), 2002 U.S. Dist. LEXIS 25403 (D. Minn. Dec. 31, 2002) (citing *High v. University of Minnesota*, 236 F.3d 909 (8th Cir. 2000), aff'd, 390 F.3d 579 (8th Cir. 2004). The court in *Hanger* opined that it was "highly unlikely" that the continuing violations theory would apply to a failure-to-restore claim as such a claim involved a discrete act. *Hanger*, 2002 U.S. Dist. LEXIS 25403 ("This Court has never applied the continuing violations doctrine to a discrete act, such as failure to promote, and we decline to do so now.").

In order to apply equitable tolling, some circuits require that the failure of an employee to timely file a civil action must be a consequence of either a deliberate design by the employer or of actions that the employer should unmistakably have understood would cause the employee to delay filing a complaint. *Id.* (*citing Dring v. McDonnell Douglas Corp.*, 58 F.3d 1323, 1327–28 (8th Cir. 1995)). In *Hanger*, the court found that there was no evidence that the employee was unaware of the alleged FMLA violation (failure to restore to work) or that Lake County thwarted her efforts to file suit. Accordingly, even if the "FMLA were susceptible to a continuing violations theory, Hanger could not avail herself of it."

Filing a discrimination charge with the EEOC has also been held not to toll the statute of limitations for an FMLA claim. *Shannon v. City of Philadelphia*, No. 98–5277, 1999 U.S. Dist. LEXIS 2428, n. 4 (E.D. Pa. March 5, 1999) (decision bolstered by fact that FMLA does not require the plaintiff to pursue any administrative remedies before filing in federal court).

Similarly, the court in *Bui v. IBP, Inc.*, 205 F. Supp. 2d 1181, 1184–85 (D. Kan. 2002), *aff'd*, 34 Fed. Appx. 653 (10th Cir. 2002), held that the relation back doctrine of Rule 15 of the Federal Rules of Civil Procedure did not render timely an otherwise untimely FMLA civil complaint by construing it as an amendment to a prior, but separate, civil action. Rule 15 of the Federal Rules of Civil Procedures provides in pertinent part: "An amendment of a pleading relates back to the date of the original pleading when…the claim or defense asserted in the amended pleading arose out of the conduct, transaction, or occurrence set forth or attempted to be set forth in the original pleading.…" Fed. R. Civ. P. 15(c)(3). The court held that Rule 15 does not apply where a party is not seeking to "amend" or "supplement" the original pleading, but rather files a separate lawsuit. *Bui*, 205 F. Supp. 2d at 1185 (*citing Benge v. United States*, 17 F.3d 1286, 1288 (10th Cir. 1994)).

d. Who Is the Defendant in a Private Civil Action for Violation of the FMLA?

A private civil action to recover damages or for equitable relief for violation(s) of the FMLA may be brought against an "employer." As set forth more fully in Chapter 3, "FMLA Coverage of the Federal Government," an "employer" is a defined term under the FMLA. 29 USC 2611(4); 29 CFR 825.104, 106–109, 825.800 (definition of "employer"). In pertinent part, an "employer" includes: (1) any person acting, directly or indirectly, in the interest of a covered employer; or (2) any public agency. 29 CFR 825.104(a).

A "public agency" is defined in § 3(x) of the FLSA, 29 USC 203(x). 29 USC 2617(a)(2), 2611(4)(A)(iii); 29 CFR 825.108. A "public agency" is defined to include the Government of the United States, or an agency of the United States. 29 CFR 825.108(a). The regulation does not indicate any order of preference between an individual agency and the Government of the United States as a whole. For purposes of filing a pleading, presumably an employee suing an agency in federal court could name either the Government of the United States or the agency, or both. The lack of an order of preference between an agency and the Government of the United States is more of a problem when addressing the eligibility requirements for Title I employees. [For a discussion of this issue, see Chapter 5, "Employee Eligibility for Leave."]

The FMLA's definition of "employer" is the same as the FLSA, 29 USC 203(d), insofar as it includes any person who acts directly or indirectly in the interest of an employer to any of the employer's employees. As such, the majority of courts have looked to the FLSA definition of "employer" for purposes of the FMLA. *See Modica v. Clare Taylor, et. al.*, 465 F.3d 174, 186 (5th Cir. 2006); *Darby v. Bratch*, 287 F.3d 673, 680–81 (8th Cir. 2002) (courts addressing whether FMLA claim can be brought against public officials in their individual capacities have analyzed this issue by comparing the definition of employer under the FMLA with the definition of employer under the FLSA); *Wascura v. Carver*, 169 F.3d 683, 685-87 (11th Cir. 1999) (interpreting "employer" for FMLA by reference to FLSA definition of same term); *Johnson v. Fayett County, Tennessee et al.*, No. 03–2018 D, 2003 U.S. Dist. LEXIS 11838 (W.D. Tenn. July 8, 2003); *Cantley v. Simmons et al.*, 179 F. Supp. 2d 654, 656–58 (S.D. W.Va. 2002); *Morrow v. Putnam et al.*, 142 F. Supp. 2d 1271 (D. Nev. 2001); *Longstreeth v. Copple et al.*, 101 F. Supp. 2d 776, 778–79 (N.D. Iowa 2000) (collecting cases); *Buser v. Southern Food Service, Inc. et al.*, 73 F. Supp. 2d 556, 561–62 (M.D.N.C. 1999) (collecting cases); *Kilvitis v. County of Luzerne et al.*, 52 F. Supp. 2d 403, 411–13 (M.D. Pa. 1999) (collecting cases); *Freemon v. Foley*, 911 F. Supp. 326, 330 (N.D. Ill. 1995).

A minority of courts has looked to Title VII, or internally to the FMLA to determine the meaning of "employer" for purposes of the FMLA. *See Carter v. Rental Uniform Serv. of Culpeper, Inc.*, 977 F. Supp. 753, 759 (W.D. Va. 1997) (applying Title VII principles); *Frizzell v. Southwest Motor Freight*, 906 F. Supp. 441, 449 (E.D. Tenn. 1995), *aff'd in part, rev'd in part on other grounds, remanded*, 154 F.3d 641 (6th Cir. 1998) (same); *Johnson v. Runyon et al.*, No. 1:97–CV–794, 1999 U.S. Dist. LEXIS 5748 (W.D. Mich. April 22, 1999).

In the comments accompanying publication of the final regulations (Preamble, 29 CFR 825.202), the DOL observed: "Under established FLSA case law, corporate officers, managers and supervisors acting in the interest of an employer can be held individually liable for violations of the FMLA." *See, e.g., Reich v. Circle C Investments, Inc.*, 998 F.2d 324 (5th Cir.

1993); *Dole v. Elliot Travel & Tours, Inc.*, 942 F.2d 962 (6th Cir. 1991); *see Darby v. Bratch*, 287 F.3d 673, 680–81 (8th Cir. 2002) (implementing regulations of the FMLA recognize similarities of the FMLA and FLSA definitions of employer); *Evans v. Henderson et al.*, No. 99 C 8332, 2000 U.S. Dist. LEXIS 11907 (N.D. Ill. Aug. 16, 2000) (same).

Most circuit courts have held that the FLSA extends liability to management personnel in their individual capacities. *See Modica v. Clare Taylor, et. al.*, 465 F.3d 174, 186-87 (5th Cir. 2006); *Baystate Alternative Staffing, Inc. v. Herman*, 163 F.3d 668, 676–79 (1st Cir. 1998); *United States Dep't of Labor v. Cole Enters., Inc.*, 62 F.3d 775, 778–79 (6th Cir. 1995); *Brock v. Hamad*, 867 F.2d 804, 808 (4th Cir. 1989); *Riordan v. Kempiners*, 831 F.2d 690, 694 (7th Cir. 1987); *Donovan v. Grim Hotel Co.*, 747 F.2d 966, 971–72 (5th Cir. 1984*)*, *cert. denied, Grim Hotel Co., v. Brock*, 471 U.S. 1124 (1985*); Donovan v. Sovereign Security, Ltd.*, 726 F.2d 55, 59 (2d Cir. 1984). *But see Darby Bratch*, 287 F.3d 673, 681–82 (8th Cir. 2002) (although finding in favor of individual liability pursuant to terms of FMLA, court noted that in prior decision, which it did not alter, it assumed that there was no individual liability under FLSA); *Wascura v. Carver*, 169 F.3d 683 (11th Cir. 1999) (following prior circuit decision holding public agency employees not individually liable under FLSA).

Notwithstanding the statutory and regulatory definitions of the FMLA, the courts are split on whether managers or supervisors are "employers" who may be sued in their individual capacities for violations of the FMLA. This division is further split depending on whether the individual manager or supervisor works in the public or private sectors. In both the public and private sectors, the majority of courts have held that individual supervisors or managers may be liable in their individual capacities for violations of the FMLA. A minority of courts have found no individual public supervisor/manager liability. *See generally* Ann K. Wooster, *Individual Liability Under Family and Medical Leave Act (29 USC 2601 et. seq.)*, 170 ALR Fed 561 (2001); David R. Mellon, *Individual Liability as an "Employer" Under the Family and Medical Leave Act*, 22 Am. J. Trial Advoc. 449 (1998); Michael L. Ripple, *Supervisors Beware: The Family and Medical Leave Act May Be Hazardous to Your Health*, 16 J. Contemp. Health L. & Policy 273 (1999).

With respect to managers and supervisors of public agencies, the majority of courts have recognized individual managers and supervisors as "employers" subject to suit in their individual capacities. *See Modica*, 465 F.3d at 186; *Darby*, 287 F.3d at 680–81 (plain language of statute defines "employer" to include persons acting in interests of employer, and court saw no reason to distinguish employers in the public sector from those in the private sector on this issue*); Hibbs v. U.S. et al.*, 273 F.3d 844, 871–72 (9th Cir. 2001), *aff'd on other grounds* 538 U.S. 721 (2003) (agreeing that some supervisor employees can be sued as employers under the FMLA, but determining which supervisors qualify "is not a straight forward matter"); *Luder v. Endicott*, 253 F.3d 1020, 1022 (7th Cir. 2001) (in finding, pursuant to FLSA, that individual public supervisors are liable as FMLA "employers," court distinguished *Wascura* as inconsistent with *Hafer v. Melo*, 502 U.S. 21, 28, 116 L. Ed. 2d 301, 112 S. Ct. 358 (1991)); *Sheaffer v. County of Chatham*, 337 F. Supp. 2d 709 (M.D.N.C. 2004); *Johnson v. Fayett County, Tennessee et al.*, No. 03–2018 D, 2003 U.S. Dist. LEXIS 11838 (W.D. Tenn. July 8, 2003) (court respectfully disagreed with minority view expressed in *Wascura* and joins the judicial majority, which has found that public officials may be held liable under the FMLA in their individual capacities); *Cantley v. Simmons et al.*, 179 F. Supp. 2d 654, 656–58 (S.D. W.Va. 2002); *Carter v. USPS*, 157 F. Supp. 2d 726, 728 (W.D. Ky. 2001); *Morrow v. Putnam*, 142 F. Supp. 2d 1271 (D. Nev. 2001) (disagreeing with *Wascura* and stating public officials in their individual capacities are employers under the FLSA and FMLA); *Mosley v. Douglas County Correctional Center et al.*, No. 8:99CV78, 2000 U.S. Dist. LEXIS 6810, at *5–8 (D. Neb. May 17, 2000); *Kilvitis v. County of Luzerne*, 52 F. Supp. 2d 403, 416 (M.D. Pa. 1999); *Meara v. Bennett*, 27 F. Supp. 2d 288, 291 (D. Mass. 1998) (case involving a public official defendant found that the language of the FMLA "clearly suggests that individuals are contemplated as defendants"); *Clay v. City of Chicago*, No. 96 C 3684, 1997 U.S. Dist. LEXIS 1458 (N.D. Ill. Feb. 11, 1997) (denying motion to dismiss public official defendant where allegations could be read to infer that public official "exercised" supervisory authority over" plaintiff); *Waters v. Baldwin County et al.*, 936 F. Supp. 860, 863–64 (S.D. Ala. 1996); *Knussman v. State of Maryland*, 935 F. Supp. 659, 664 (D. Md. 1996), *aff'd in part, rev'd in part on other grounds*, 272 F.3d 625 (4th Cir. 2001) (FMLA case involving public official defendant; "Liability of individual defendants in their individual capacities is not foreclosed by the FMLA.").

Others have found that public managers and supervisors are not liable for violations of the FMLA in their individual capacities. *See Mitchell v. Chapman*, 343 F.3d 811 (6th Cir. 2003), *cert. denied*, 124 S. Ct. 2908 (2004); *Lizzi v. Alexander et al.*, 255 F.3d 128, 136–138 (4th Cir. 2001), *cert. denied*, 534 U.S. 1081 (2002); *Wascura v. Carver*, 169 F.3d 683 (11th Cir. 1999), *cert. denied*, 534 U.S. 1081 (2002) (holding public officials in their individual capacities are not employers under FLSA or the FMLA); *Billings v. Cape Cod Child Dev. Program, Inc.*, 270 F. Supp. 2d 175, n.1 (D. Mass. July 15, 2003) (dismissing claims against individual defendants after finding that FMLA permits suit against employer only, not against supervisory-level employees); *Johnson v. Rinaldi et al.*, No. 1:99CV170, 2001 U.S. Dist. LEXIS 9833, at *19–20 (M.D.N.C. April 13, 2001) (following *Keene*); *Keene v. Rinaldi*, 127 F. Supp. 2d 770, 778 (M.D.N.C. 2000) (magistrate judge's thoroughly researched recommendation that public supervisors in their individual capacities are not "employers" within the meaning of the FMLA and, therefore, may not be sued in their individual capacities); *Frizzell v. Southwest Motor Freight*, 906 F. Supp. 441, 449 (E.D. Tenn. 1995), *aff'd in part, rev'd in part, remanded*, 154 F.3d 641 (6th Cir. 1998) (no individual liability under the FMLA after analogizing FMLA to Title VII). Interestingly, the reasoning of each of these courts differs. Note that, as indicated above, other district courts in the Fourth and Eleventh Circuits have found in favor of individual liability.

The decision of the Fourth Circuit in *Lizzie* that state officials may not be sued in their individual capacities for alleged violations of the FMLA rests largely on Eleventh Amendment issues. *Lizzie*, 255 F.3d at 136–138. In this context, the Eleventh Amendment issues relate to the ability of the federal government to apply the FMLA to state governments. Relying on Supreme Court decisions interpreting the Eleventh Amendment, the court opined that the real party in interest where individual state officials are named as defendants is the state because the individuals took actions on their official capacities. Because the real party in interest is the state, the individual defendants, like the state, were immune from suit pursuant to the Eleventh Amendment. In light of the Supreme Court's recent decision in *Nev. Dept. of Human Res. v. Hibbs*, 123 S. Ct. 1972, 155 L. Ed 2d 953 (2003), that the Eleventh Amendment does not bar application of at least part of Title I of the FMLA to the states, it is questionable how much, if anything, is left of the immunity of state public officials to FMLA claims in their individual capacities.

In holding that a public official sued in his individual capacity is not an "employer" under the FMLA, the Eleventh Circuit in *Wascura* held that "employer" should be interpreted consistently with the similar definition set forth in FLSA. Because the Eleventh Circuit had previously held that FLSA does not allow recovery against government employees sued in their individual capacity, the court was compelled to find the same for purposes of the FMLA. It should be noted that one district court within the Eleventh Circuit has declined to follow the court's decision in *Wascura*. See *Waters v. Baldwin County et al.*, 936 F. Supp. 860, 863–64 (S.D. Ala. 1996).

In *Keene*, the court reasoned that individual managers and supervisors of the Postal Service were not "employers" within the meaning of the FMLA based on its reading of the FMLA definition of "public agency." For *Keene*, the FMLA definition of "employer" differed from the FLSA definition of that term, thereby undermining the rationale of the decisions of other courts that have ruled that supervisors may be individually liable based on similarities between the FMLA and the FLSA. According to the court (127 F. Supp. 2d at 774–75), "the starting point for this inquiry begins with the Statute and the definition of who can be an employer under the Act."

The FMLA (29 USC 2611(4)) defines "employer" in the following manner.

> (4) Employer
>
> > (a) In general
> >
> > The term "employer"—
> >
> > > (i) means any person engaged in commerce or in any industry or activity affecting commerce that employs 50 or more employees for each working day during each of 20 or more calendar workweeks in the current or preceding calendar year;
> > >
> > > (ii) includes any person who acts, directly or indirectly, in the interest of an employer to any of the employees of such employer; and any successor in interest of an employer;
> > >
> > > (iii) includes any "public agency," as defined in Section 203(x) of this Title; and
> > >
> > > (iv) includes the General Accounting Office and the Library of Congress.

According to the court in *Keene*, individual liability was possible for the private sector pursuant to the definitions in §§ 2611(4)(A)(I) and (ii). Public employers, however, are covered FMLA "employers" in Subsections 2611(4)(A)(iii) and (iv) entirely apart from Subsections 2611(4)(A)(I) and (ii), which cover only private employers. Subsections 2611(4)(a)(iii) and (iv) do not include "any person who acts, directly or indirectly, in the interest of an employer to any employees of such employer." The order of the subsections and the fact that the reference to an individual acting on behalf of an employer was not placed in the definition, strongly suggested to the court that individual liability only applied in the private sector, not to persons working for public agencies. *Keene*, 127 F. Supp. 2d at 776.

In support of its interpretation, the court in *Keene* also noted that the DOL regulations defining "employer" covered by

Title I refer to corporate officers, but not individuals working for public agencies. *Id.* at 776 (*citing* 29 CFR 825.104(d)). Moreover, the regulation that addressed public agency liability (29 CFR 825.108) does not mention individual liability. Finally, the court argued allowing suit against individual managers and supervisors made more sense in the private sector to ensure payment of damages where the identity of the employer may be unclear, which would not be the case with a public agency employer.

For an almost point-by-point rebuttal to *Keene*, see *Cantley v. Simmons*, 179 F. Supp. 2d 654 (S.D. W.Va. 2002) and *Morrow v. Putnam*, 142 F. Supp. 2d 1271 (D. Nev. 2001).

Similar to *Keene*, the court in *Johnson v. Runyon et al.*, No. 1:97-CV-794, 1999 U.S. Dist. LEXIS 7981 (W.D. Mich. April 22, 1999), focused on the FMLA definition of a "public agency" as an employer in finding that Postal Service managers and supervisors could not be sued in their individual capacity. Like *Keene*, the court concluded that neither individual supervisors nor the Postmaster General fit within the definition of "public agency" as defined by the FMLA and FLSA. Unlike *Keene*, the court applied the doctrine of sovereign immunity to preclude suit against the individually named defendants. Pursuant to the principles of sovereign immunity, the United States can be sued only when it has given its express consent, and any waiver must be express, clear, and unequivocal. The court concluded that while a covered "public agency" could be sued, individual managers and supervisors of that agency, because they were not included within the FMLA definition of "public agency," could not be sued.

Finally, in an interesting recent case involving the private sector, the court in *Ariba v. Owens-Illinois, Inc. et al.*, No. 1:02CV00111, 2003 U.S. Dist. LEXIS 9429, at *17 (M.D.N.C. June 4, 2003), held that because § 2615(a) specifically prohibits "employers" from engaging in prohibited conduct, and because there is no reference in the Statute or in § 825.220(c) to agents of any employer, or to any person, the court dismissed the plaintiff's retaliatory discharge claim against all individually named defendant managers as a matter of law. It is unclear why the court did not refer to the statutory or regulatory definition of "employer," which does arguably include individuals acting on behalf of their employer.

Like the public sector, the majority of courts have recognized that individual managers and supervisors in the private sector may be held liable as "employers" for violations of the FMLA. *See Longstreth v. Copple*, 101 F. Supp. 2d 776 (N.D. Iowa 2000) (holding private sector managers in their individual capacities are employers under FMLA); *Buser v. S. Food Serv., Inc.*, 73 F. Supp. 2d 556, 561 (M.D.N.C. 1999); *Carpenter v. Refrigeration Sales Corp. et al.*, 49 F. Supp. 2d 1028, 1031 (N.D. Ohio 1999); *Bryant v. Delbar Products, Inc. et al.*, 18 F. Supp. 2d 799, 807-808 (M.D. Tenn. 1998); *Mercer v. Borden*, 11 F. Supp. 2d 1190 (C.D. Cal. 1998); *Rupnow v. TRC, Inc. et al.*, 999 F. Supp. 1047, 1048 n.2 (N.D. Ohio 1998); *Stubl v. T.A. Systems, Inc.*, 984 F. Supp. 1075, 1083 (E.D. Mich. 1997); *Beyer v. Elkay Mfg. Col. et al.*, No. 97 C 50067, 1997 U.S., Dist. LEXIS 14459 (N.D. Ill. Sept. 19, 1997); *Norris v. North American Publishing Co. et al.*, No. 96-8662, 1997 U.S. Dist. LEXIS 2352 (E.D. Pa. Feb. 28, 1997); *Johnson v. A.P. Products, Ltd. et al.*, 934 F. Supp. 625, 628629 (S.D.N.Y. 1996); *Freemon v. Foley*, 911 F. Supp. 326, 332 (N.D. Ill. 1995); *Reich v. Midwest Plastic Engineering, Inc. et al.*, No. 1:94-CV-525, 1995 U.S. Dist. LEXIS 8772, at *13-16 (W.D. Mich. June 6, 1995); *McKiernan v. Smith-Edwards-Dunlap Co. et al.*, No. 95-1175, 1995 U.S. Dist. LEXIS 6822, at *10 (E.D. Pa. May 17, 1995).

A minority of courts have rejected individual supervisor liability. *See Wascura v. Carver*, 169 F.3d 683 (11th Cir. 1999) (holding public officials in their individual capacities are not employers under FLSA or the FMLA); *Ariba v. Owens-Illinois, Inc. et al.*, No. 1:02CV00111, 2003 U.S. Dist. LEXIS 9429, at *17 (M.D.N.C. June 4, 2003) (because § 2615(a) specifically prohibits "employers" from engaging in prohibited conduct, and because there is no reference in the Statute or in § 825.220(c) to agents of any employer, or to any person, court dismissed the plaintiff's retaliatory discharge claim against all individually named defendant managers as a matter of law); *Frizzell v. Southwest Motor Freight*, 906 F. Supp. 441, 449 (E.D. Tenn. 1995), *rev'd on other grounds*, 154 F.3d 641 (6th Cir. 1998) (no individual liability under the FMLA after analogizing FMLA to Title VII); *Johnson v. Runyon*, No. 1:97-CV-794, 1999 U.S. Dist. LEXIS 7981 (W.D. Mich. April 22, 1999).

Because the majority of courts hold that an individual manager or supervisor may be liable in his or her individual capacity as an FMLA-covered "employer" does not mean that he or she will be liable. To be liable as an FMLA-covered "employer," the individual managers and supervisors must have exercised some authority or control over the complaining employee regarding FMLA leave. Again, an employer is defined as including "any person who acts, directly or indirectly, in the interest of an employer to any of the employees of such employer." 29 USC 2611(4)(A)(ii)(I). Courts have looked to the FLSA to determine what constitutes acting "directly or indirectly" in the interests of an employer to any of the employees of the employer. *See Buser v. Southern Food Service, Inc. et al.*, 73 F. Supp. 2d 556, 563-64 (M.D.N.C. 1999);

Kilvitis v. County of Luzerne et al., 52 F. Supp. 2d 403, 412–13 (M.D. Pa. 1999) (collecting FLSA cases); *Knussman v. State of Maryland*, 935 F. Supp. 659, 664–65 (D. Md. 1996), *aff'd in part, rev'd in part on other grounds*, 272 F.3d 625 (4th Cir. 2001); *Johnson v. A.P. Products, Ltd. et al.*, 934 F. Supp. 625, 628–29 (S.D.N.Y. 1996); *Freemon v. Foley*, 911 F. Supp. 326, 330–32 (N.D. Ill. 1995).

The standard for making this determination under the FLSA differs somewhat in each circuit. Generally, to be found liable as an "employer" under the FMLA, an individual must have had supervisory authority over the complaining party and responsibility, in whole or in part, for the alleged violation. *Kilvitis v. County of Luzerne et al.*, 52 F. Supp. 2d 403, 412–13 (M.D. Pa. 1999); *Rupnow v. TRC, Inc.*, 999 F. Supp. 1047, 1048 (N.D. Ohio 1998) (a supervisor who exercises sufficient control over the plaintiff's ability to take protected leave may be individually liable under FMLA); *Bryant v. Delbar Prods., Inc.*, 18 F. Supp. 2d 799, 808 (M.D. Tenn. 1998) (FMLA extends individual liability to those who control a plaintiff's ability to take leave); *Divizio v. Elmwood Care, Inc.*, No. 97-8365, 1998 U.S. Dist. LEXIS 8398 (N.D. Ill. May 28, 1998) (a supervisor who exercises control over an employee's leave may be held individually liable under FMLA); *Clay v. City of Chicago*, No. 96 C 3684, 1997 U.S. Dist. LEXIS 1458 (N.D. Ill. Feb. 11, 1997); *Beyer v. Elkay Mfg., Co.*, No. 97-50067, 1997 U.S. Dist. LEXIS 14459 (N.D. Ill. Sept. 19, 1997) (supervisors may be individually liable under FMLA if they had some control over the plaintiff's ability to take leave); *Johnson v. A.P. Products, Ltd. et al.*, 934 F. Supp. 625, 628–29 (S.D.N.Y. 1996) (applying economic realities test); *Freemon v. Foley*, 911 F. Supp. 326, 330–32 (N.D. Ill. 1995).

The individual manager or supervisor need not have exclusive control over all day-to-day affairs of the employee, as long as he or she possess control over the aspect of employment alleged to have been violated. *Freemon*, 911 F. Supp. at 330–32.

Courts have found a variety of actions by managers and employers sufficient evidence that the manager or supervisor acted, directly or indirectly, in the interests of the employer so that the individual was considered to be an "employer" within the meaning of the FMLA. *See Evans v. Henderson et al.*, No. 99 C 8332, 2000 U.S. Dist. LEXIS 11907 (N.D. Ill. Aug. 16, 2000) (allegation that managers participated in the plaintiff's termination sufficient to subject them to individual liability under FMLA; where no allegations were directed at Postmaster General and another employee, the complaint against them was dismissed); *Buser v. Southern Food Service, Inc.*, 73 F. Supp. 2d 556, 564–65 (M.D.N.C. 1999) (VP of employer that made ultimate decision to terminate the plaintiff is "employer" within meaning of FMLA); *Kilvitis v. County of Luzerne et al.*, 52 F. Supp. 2d 403, 416 (M.D. Pa. 1999) (signing of termination letter); *Carpenter v. Refrigeration Sales Corp. et al.*, 49 F. Supp. 2d 1028, 1031 (N.D. Ohio 1999) (head of HR department who administered FMLA, spoke to the employee about illness, and, most significantly, made decision to terminate her, "employer" for purposes of FMLA); *Bryant v. Delbar Products, Inc. et al.*, 18 F. Supp. 2d 799, 808–809 (M.D. Tenn. 1998) (manager with responsibility for all personnel matters of the plant, including the power to grant leave to the plaintiff, who discussed the plaintiff's absenteeism problems with the plaintiff more than once, who discussed termination with the manager who eventually authorized the plaintiff's termination, and who, in fact, fired the plaintiff, is an "employer" under FMLA); *Clay v. City of Chicago*, No. 96 C 3684, 1997 U.S. Dist. LEXIS 1458 (N.D. Ill. Feb. 11, 1997) (individuals who informed Clay on return from FMLA leave that the plaintiff was being replaced as HR director and demoted sufficient allegation of intent to sue as individuals to defeat motion to dismiss).

Absent an allegation that an individual manager or supervisor exercised some control over the plaintiff's ability to take leave or otherwise engaged in conducted violative of the Act, such managers or supervisors are not "employers" within the meaning of the FMLA. *Evans v. Henderson et al.*, No. 99 C 8332, 2000 U.S. Dist. LEXIS 11907 (N.D. Ill. Aug. 16, 2000) (absent allegations of misconduct, Postmaster General and another employee dismissed as individual employers within meaning of FMLA); *Cooper v. Harbour Inns of Baltimore, Inc.*, No. L-98-2173, 2000 U S. Dist. LEXIS 4284 (D. Md. March 20, 2000) (an employee's supervisor could not be held individually liable under FMLA since technician had produced no evidence to show supervisor was involved in any way with nursing home's decision to terminate her); *Johnson v. A.P. Products, Ltd. et al.*, 934 F. Supp. 625, 629 (S.D.N.Y. 1996); *Freemon v. Foley*, 911 F. Supp. 326 (N.D. Ill. 1995) (temporary supervisor did not exercise sufficient control over employee's ability to take protected leave to qualify as FMLA "employer").

As a practical matter, this means that an employee or employees may sue either or both the agency or an individual supervisor or supervisors involved with the unlawful FMLA conduct at issue. Many employees like the idea of being able to sue an individual supervisor or manager as a way to extract redress directly from the individual(s) who caused the employee damages. In fact, the ability of an employee to sue individual supervisors is a frequent threat made by employees and unions to individual supervisors and managers. Although the ability to sue individual managers and supervisors gives an employee the appearance of empowerment, and may even cause some managers and supervisors to make doubly sure that their FMLA decisions are correct, in many respects the ability to sue individual managers and supervisors is a classic case of "less than meets the eye."

Because decisions, right or wrong, involving requests for FMLA leave are made during the "course and scope" of federal employment, the overwhelming majority of individual managers and supervisors in the federal sector who are sued will receive Justice Department representation. Those few that do not will likely have their legal fees paid for by the Justice Department or the agency. As such, the individual manager or supervisor will rarely feel the financial strain of the cost of litigation.

Similarly, even if damages are awarded to an employee against an individual manager or supervisor, there is nothing in the Act that would prohibit an agency from reimbursing the manager or supervisor. Agencies are inclined to do this for a number of reasons. For example, the FMLA is not an easy statute to understand or administer. An individual manager or supervisor who, in good faith, made an errant FMLA decision on behalf of the agency, should not personally suffer financial ruin. This is particularly true where the agency has provided little or no FMLA training to the manager or supervisor. Moreover, it may be very difficult to attract and retain new employees to management if they know that, along with the promotion, comes potential financial ruin if they make a wrong FMLA decision.

Of course, individual managers and supervisors in public agencies are not guaranteed that, ultimately, the agency will back them up and pay for costs and damages in the event of an adverse decision in an employee FMLA lawsuit. Associations and other organizations representing federal managers and supervisors should seriously consider pressing the agency for guarantees of reimbursement. Alternatively, they might advocate that agencies pay for employment liability insurance for individual federal managers and supervisors.

e. Courts of Competent Jurisdiction

In the federal sector, only federal courts are courts of competent jurisdiction over federal employers. Employees who have decided to initiate a civil action against their employer for FMLA violations should do so by filing their complaint with the clerk of the relevant federal district court. The first response of the government where a federal employee has initially filed a FMLA complaint against a federal employer in state court will be an action to remove the complaint to federal district court. Employees should consult with counsel before initiating an FMLA civil action to ensure, among other things, that they are filing their suit in the correct federal court.

In *Minard v. ITC Deltacom Communications, Inc.*, 447 F.3d 352 (5th Fir. 2006), the court held that the FMLA eligibility requirement that an employee must be employed at a worksite having at least 50 employees within 75 miles is not a limit on the federal courts' subject matter jurisdiction, but instead is an essential ingredient of an FMLA claim for relief. The district court dismissed the employee's lawsuit for lack of subject matter jurisdiction because the employee was not an "eligible employee" within the meaning of the FMLA. The Fifth Circuit, relying on the Supreme Court's decision in *Arbaugh v. Y & H Corp.*, 126 S. Ct. 1235, 163 L. Ed. 2d 1097 (2006), reversed, finding that the employee-numerocity requirement is an element of an FMLA claim, not a limit on the federal court's subject matter jurisdiction. The court remanded the matter to the district court to determine whether the employer should be equitably estopped from denying the employee FMLA protections where the employer told the employee that she was an FMLA-eligible employee.

f. Limitations on Bringing a Private Civil Action

An employee may not bring or maintain a civil action against a federal employer for damages or injunctive relief for violations of the FMLA in two circumstances, both involving intervention by the Secretary of Labor. An employee may not bring or maintain a civil action against a federal employer under Title I where the Secretary of Labor files a complaint to recover damages owing to the eligible employee. 29 USC 2617(a)(4)(B); *see Ogborn v. United Food and Commercial Workers, Local No. 881 et al.*, No. 98 C 4623, 2000 U.S. Dist. LEXIS 14092, at n. 16 (N.D. Ill. Sept. 25, 2000), *aff'd* 305 F.3d 763 (7th Cir. 2002), (if the Secretary of Labor files an action seeking damages or payments for the employee, the employee is preempted from filing his or her own action). For example, where an employee files both a complaint with the DOL and filed a civil action for damages, if the DOL decided to bring a civil action on behalf of the employee and filed a civil suit, by operation of the Statute, the employee's individual lawsuit terminates. More than likely, an employer will file a motion to dismiss the employee's civil action, leaving the DOL's civil suit to proceed.

The second limitation on an employee's ability to maintain his or her own private civil action against a federal employer occurs when the Secretary of Labor files a complaint for injunctive relief to compel a federal employer to cease delay in payment of an award of damages. 29 USC 2617(a)(4)(A). For example, a federal employee is awarded damages by a court for FMLA violations. The employer proceeds to delay payment of the award, giving one excuse after another. An employee, on his or her own, could go into court and seek to enforce the award. Where, however, the Secretary of Labor files a complaint to compel the employer to make payment to the employee, the employee's individual efforts to enforce the award terminate. This second scenario is more likely to occur in the private sector, and should be relatively rare in the federal sector.

4. Other Enforcement Avenues

FMLA rights may be enforced, directly or indirectly, by means other than those provided by the Act. These other means of redress may be used in substitution for, or in addition to, the statutory means addressed above. Of course, use of a means of enforcement other than that provided by Title I of the FMLA will be governed by the procedural and substantive rules and requirements of that forum. What follows is a general overview of other potential avenues of enforcement. Whether these avenues are available in any given situation will, of course, depend on the agency and the facts of each case.

a. Grievance Process

There are generally two types of grievance or dispute resolution processes available in the federal sector: (1) those required pursuant to the terms of a collective bargaining agreement; and (2) internal agency grievance procedures that are not tied to a collective bargaining agreement.

Regarding the former, most collective bargaining agreements contain a grievance–arbitration process for the resolution of workplace disputes. Typically, the scope of what may be grieved in this process is broadly worded to include disputes, differences, disagreements, or complaints between the parties related to wages, hours, and conditions of employment. As a form of leave, disputes regarding FMLA leave generally fall within "wages, hours, and conditions of employment." Of course, only members of the bargaining unit covered by a particular collective bargaining agreement may avail themselves of the grievance process afforded by the collective bargaining agreement. Managers and supervisors are not members of any bargaining unit.

Agencies often have their own internal dispute resolution where employees can grieve complaints about various work issues. Again, this system is not mandated by the terms of a collective bargaining agreement. Generally, the internal agency grievance process defines which employees may use the process and for what topics. Employees who have access to a grievance process pursuant to the terms of a collective bargaining agreement are frequently excluded from also being able to use the separate agency grievance process. Managers and supervisors typically have access to the internal agency grievance process.

The agency grievance process also defines what subjects may be heard in the process. Generally speaking, the subjects that may be heard in the agency grievance process are more limited than what could typically be heard pursuant to the terms of a collective bargaining agreement. Disputes regarding FMLA leave, however, would typically be a subject that an internal agency grievance process would entertain. The rules of each internal agency grievance process should be consulted to determine whether a complaint regarding FMLA leave by the employee might be heard in that process.

A bargaining unit employee is not required to grieve his or her FMLA claim before he or she may file a civil lawsuit. *Barrett v. Detroit Heading, LLC*, No. 05-72341, 2006 U.S. Dist. LEXIS 55230, at *4 (E.D. Mich. Aug. 9, 2006).

b. MSPB

A claim that a federal employer violated an employee's FMLA rights is not an independent basis for Board jurisdiction. A federal employee may, however, raise violation of the FMLA in connection with other adverse actions that the Board does have jurisdiction over. *See Bogumill v. OPM*, 168 F.3d 1320 (table), 1998 U.S. App. LEXIS 18750, at *4 (Fed. Cir. Aug. 13, 1998); *Mann v. Haigh*, 120 F.3d 34, 37 (4th Cir. 1997); *Gray v. USPS*, 97 MSPR 617 (Oct. 22, 2004), aff'd, 2005 U.S. App. LEXIS 10961 (Fed. Cir. June 9, 2005) (removal); *Vaughn–Johnson v. Army*, No. DC-0752-04-0449-I-1, 2004 MSPB LEXIS 1511 (Aug. 17, 2004) (removal); *Hite v. USPS*, Docket No. AT-0752-04-598-I-1, 2004 MSPB LEXIS 1300 (Aug. 9, 2004), *pet. denied*, 98 MSPR 677 (2005), *rev. dismissed*, 2005 U.S. App. LEXIS 18289 (Fed. Cir. 2005), aff'd, 2006 U.S. App. LEXIS 4134 (Fed. Cir. 2006) (removal); *Bradshaw v. VA*, No. SF3443-04-0468-I-1, 2004 MSPB LEXIS 1603 (Sept. 8, 2004), aff'd, 2005 U.S.

App. LEXIS 8485 (Fed. Cir. 2005); *Lau v. USPS*, 87 MSPR 647 (2001) (FMLA claims dismissed because, as non–preference eligible employee of the Postal Service, the Board did not have jurisdiction over her adverse action appeal); *Moore v. USPS*, 83 MSPR 533 (1999); *Ellshoff v. DOI*, 76 MSPR 54 (1997), *rev'd on other grounds, remanded*, 78 MSPR 615 (1998); *Ramey v. USPS*, 70 MSPR 463 (1996), *aff'd*, 178 F.3d 1312 (table), 1999 U.S. App. LEXIS 657 (Fed. Cir. Jan. 8, 1999). Where an employee brings an FMLA claim to the Board, the burden of proving a violation is on the agency, not the employee. *Davis v. VA*, No. CH-0752-06-0724-I-1, 2006 MSPB LEXIS 7394, at *13 (Dec. 12, 2006); *Bhatti v. DHS*, No. SF-0752-06-0036-I-1, 2006 U.S. MSPB LEXIS 41, at *9 (Feb. 9, 2006); *Cole v. DHHS*, No DC-0752-05-0457-I-1, 2005 MSPB LEXIS 6825, at *6 (Nov. 1, 2005); *Ellshoff v. Dept. of the Interior*, 76 MSPR 54, 74 (1997), *pet. denied*, 98 MSPR 677 (2005), *rev. dismissed*, 2005 U.S. App. LEXIS 18289 (Fed. Cir. 2005), *aff'd*, 2006 U.S. App. LEXIS 4134 (Fed. Cir. 2006).

Where the facts, either specifically raised by the appellant or otherwise shown by the record evidence, implicate the FMLA relative to a leave-related charge, the Board will consider and apply the FMLA without shifting the burden of proof to the appellant. *Davis v. VA*, 2006 MSPB LEXIS 7394, at *13; *Cole v. DHHS*, 2005 MSPB LEXIS 6825, at *6; *Fairley v. USPS*, 82 MSPR 588, 591 (1999); *Ellshoff*, 76 MSPR at 74.

Thus, where the appellant raises nonfrivilous factual allegations reasonably relating to an FMLA claim, or the agency's evidence or other allegations otherwise show that FMLA-qualifying leave was involved, the administrative judge has the responsibility to develop the record evidence as necessary and appropriate. *Davis v. VA*, 2006 MSPB LEXIS 7394, at *13; *Cole v. DHHS*, 2005 MSPB LEXIS 6825, at *6.

The appellant must merely present sufficient evidence to trigger consideration of the absences under the FMLA. *Davis v. VA*, No. CH-0752-06-0724-I-1, 2006 MSPB LEXIS 7394, at *13 (Dec. 12, 2006); *Cole v. DHHS*, No DC-0752-05-0457-I-1, 2005 MSPB LEXIS 6825, at *6 (Nov. 1, 2005); *Fairley v. USPS*, 82 MSPR 588, 591 (1999). The agency then bears the burden of proving that it properly denied FMLA leave in taking a leave-based action against the employee. *Davis v. VA*, 2006 MSPB LEXIS 7394, at *13-14; *Cole v. DHHS*, 2005 MSPB LEXIS 6825, at *6; *Williams v. Dept. of the Navy*, No. DC-0752-05-0431-I-1, 2005 MSPB LEXIS 6866, at *2-3 (Oct. 17, 2005), *pet. denied*, 101 MSPR 133 (2006); *Fisher v. DHHS*, No. DC-0752-05-0280-I-1, 2005 MSPB LEXIS 2653, at *8 (June 3, 2005), *rev. denied*, 101 MSPR 131 (2005).

An allegation of AWOL must be scrutinized in light of the appellant's rights under the FMLA. *Bhatti v. DHS*, No. SF-0752-06-0036-I-1, 2006 MSPB LEXIS 41, at *9 (Feb. 9, 2006), *rev. denied*, 102 MSPR 485 (2006).

For an excellent analysis of employee appeal rights to the MSPB, see Peter Broida, *A Guide to Merit Systems Protection Board Law and Practice* (Dewey Publications, Inc. 2007).

c. EEOC

While the FMLA prohibits certain acts of discrimination involving the exercise of FMLA rights, the EEOC does not have plenary jurisdiction over claims of unlawful conduct under the FMLA. The EEOC hears federal sector cases involving claims of discrimination based on age, color, disability, national origin, race, religion, and sex pursuant to Title VII of the Civil Rights Act of 1964, as amended, the Rehabilitation Act of 1973, as amended, and the Age Discrimination in Employment Act, as amended. The EEOC would not, therefore, have jurisdiction over a claim that an employee was unlawfully discriminated against in violation of the provisions of the FMLA. *See Eldridge v. Potter*, 2003 EEOPUB LEXIS 3870 n.2 (2003) (an employee cannot use the EEO Complaint process to lodge a collateral attack on another proceeding, citing *Wills v. DOD*, EEOC Request No. 05970596 (July 30, 1998); *Kleinman v. USPS*, EEOC Request No. 05940585 (Sept. 22, 1994); *Lingad v. USPS*, EEOC Request No. 05930106 (June 25, 1993)).

The EEOC would, however, have jurisdiction to hear a claim that FMLA leave or other FMLA benefits were unlawfully denied because of the employee's age, color, disability, national origin, race, religion, or sex, or in retaliation for engaging in activity protected by the anti–discrimination laws. *Holland v. Potter*, 01A33409, 2003 EEOPUB LEXIS 4733 (2003) (discriminatory denial of FMLA leave based on disability states a claim within purview of EEOC regulations, citing *Shannon v USPS*, EEOC Request No. 05970764 (July 6, 1996). The legitimacy of the denial of FMLA leave or other benefits would almost certainly be reviewed (presumably, the employer would defend by arguing that it acted in accordance with the FMLA, a legitimate, non–discriminatory reason). Ultimately, however, the EEOC's decision should rest on whether the employee established that he or she was discriminated against based on a protected category (age, color, disability, national origin, race, religion, or sex). The decision would not rest on whether or not the employer abided by the requirements of the FMLA. *See generally Ramsey v. Potter*, 2003 EEPUB LEXIS 4170 (2003) (reviewing employee allegations of Title VII retaliation in the form of requests for medical documentation, fill out forms, and interrupt FMLA leave to submit to an investigative interview); *Dinndorf v. Potter*, 2003 EEOPUB LEXIS 3857 (2003) (alleging discrimination based on disability and retaliation for prior EEO activity when FMLA leave was denied); *Eldridge v. Potter*, 2003 EEOPUB LEXIS 3870 n.2 (2003) (allegation of denial of sick leave in violation of Title VII, Rehabilitation Act, and ADEA stated valid EEO claim not impermissible collateral attack on the FMLA). [The interaction of the FMLA with other laws is addressed more fully in the Chapter 16.] For an in-depth review of the federal sector EEO process, see Ernest C. Hadley, *A Guide to Federal Sector Equal Employment Law & Practice* (Dewey Publications, Inc. 2007).

d. Unfair Labor Practice Charges

Filing an unfair labor practice charge with the National Labor Relations Board (NLRB) is another alternative means for indirectly adjudicating FMLA claims available to Postal Service employees who are members of collective bargaining units. Labor-management relations in the Postal Service, unlike most federal agencies, are governed by the National Labor Relations Act of 1935 (NLRA), as amended 29 USC 141 et. seq. *See* 39 USC 1203. The NLRB enforces the provisions of the NLRA.

In pertinent part, the NLRA guarantees the right of employees to form, join, or assist labor organizations, and to bargain collectively with their employers through representatives of their choosing regarding the terms and conditions of their employment. 29 USC 157. To ensure that employees can freely choose their own representatives for the purpose of collective bargaining, or to choose not to be represented, the NLRA establishes a procedure by which they can exercise their choice at a secret-ballot election conducted by the NLRB. Further, to protect the rights of employees and employers, the NLRA also defines certain practices by employers and unions as unfair labor practices.

Section 8(a) of the Act (29 USC 158(a)) identifies the unfair labor practices of employers. Under the NLRA, an employer is prohibited from:

- Interfering with, restraining, or coercing employees in the exercise of their section 7 (29 USC 157) rights to organize, form, join, or assist a labor organization;

- To dominate or interfere with the formation or administration of any labor organization (prohibiting so-called "company unions");

- To discriminate in regard to hiring, tenure, or any term or condition of employment to encourage or discourage membership in any labor organization;

- To discharge or otherwise discriminate against an employee because the employee has filed charges or given testimony under the Act; and

- To refuse to bargain in good faith about wages, hours, and other conditions of employment with the duly authorized collective bargaining representative.

The NLRA also prohibits as unfair labor practices certain conduct by labor organizations. 29 USC 158(b).

An employee who believes that he or she is aggrieved by an unfair labor practice of an employer files an unfair labor practice charge with the appropriate NLRB Regional Office. Generally, an unfair labor practice charge must be filed with the Regional Office within six months of the occurrence of the unfair labor practice. 29 USC 160(b). The charge may be filed by an employee or labor organization. The General Counsel and the staff of the Regional Office investigate and prosecute unfair labor practice cases. If the investigation reveals a potential violation of the NLRA, the NLRB regional office may try to informal or formally resolve the matter. If that is not successfully, the Regional Office issues an unfair labor practice complaint to the employer, which begins the start of formal administrative litigation. Such litigation can culminate in a hearing before and a decision of an administrative law judge.

The NLRB does not have primary jurisdiction to investigate and prosecute claims of employer violations of the FMLA. Under Title I that is the responsibility of the DOL. Rather the NLRB may consider a claim that an employer has violated the FMLA where it is framed as an unfair labor practice within the meaning of the NLRA. For example, the Postal Service's FMLA policy is set forth in § 515 of the Employee and Labor Relations Manual (ELM). As with other employee handbooks and manuals, the ELM is incorporated into the terms of the governing collective bargaining agreements between the Postal Service and the various unions through Article 19. Because the substantive provisions of the FMLA have been incorporated into the terms of collective bargaining agreement, a violation of the FMLA may also constitute a violation of the collective bargaining agreement. Violations of the terms of Postal Service collective bargaining agreements by management may, therefore, constitute unfair labor practices within the meaning of the NLRA, specifically sections 8(a)(1) (interference with section 7 rights) and 8(a)(5) (refusal to bargain in good faith), 29 USC 158(a)(1), (5).

The advantage to a Postal Service employee or union filing an unfair labor practice charge with the Board is that the matter is investigated and prosecuted at the expense of the government, not the union or employee. Moreover, a Board charge can be filed at the same time an employee files a complaint with the DOL and/or files a civil action. The disadvantages are that most unfair labor practice charges filed with the NLRB alleging individual violations of the FMLA will never be investigated or otherwise prosecuted. To conserve resources, the NLRB will defer matters for resolution pursuant to the applicable collective bargaining agreement. While the NLRB maintains an open file on the matter, for all practical purposes, the issue has been stayed while the claim works its way through the parties' grievance process. That could take years. The NLRB, however, is less inclined to defer claims of unfair labor practices to the grievance arbitration process where systemic violations are alleged. Other disadvantages of using the NLRB to adjudicate FMLA claims is that unfair labor practice charges must be filed within 6 months of the occurrence, which is significantly less than the 2 or 3 years allowed by Title I of the FMLA for filing a civil action. Moreover, while the NLRB will take into consideration the goals of the charging party, the NLRB runs the investigation and litigation. The charging party is not in control. Finally, while the substance of the FMLA claim forms the heart of the unfair labor practice allegation, resolution of the claim is made on whether the NLRA has been violated. As such, the NLRB route is an indirect method for resolving FMLA claims.

The NLRB has addressed Postal Service FMLA claims. *See USPS and National Association of Letter Carriers*, 339 NLRB No. 150, 2003 NLRB LEXIS 491 (2003) (finding unlawful pattern and practice of failing to provide requested relevant information to union, including FMLA information regarding a grievant/member of the bargaining unit of the requesting union, in violation of sections 8(a)(1) and (5) of the NLRA).

B. TITLE II

1. General Rule

Title II of the FMLA grants covered employees essentially the same substantive rights to FMLA leave as those granted to employees covered by Title I. *Mann v. Haigh*, 120 F.3d 34, 37 (4th Cir. 1997); *Gardner v. United States et al.*, No. 96–1467 (EGS), 1999 U.S. Dist. LEXIS 2195, at *22 (D.D.C. Jan. 29, 1999); *Keen v. Brown*, 958 F. Supp. 70, 72 (D. Ct. 1997). Unlike Title I, however, neither Title II nor the OPM implementing regulations contain a process for enforcing the prohibitions against employee intimidation, threats, or coercion, contained in 5 USC 6385. *Mann*, 120 F.3d at 37 (no private right of action in federal court); *Keen*, 958 F. Supp. at 72 (Title II regulations do not reference any means of enforcement). The legislative history of the Act suggests that employees covered by Title II may enforce their FMLA rights pursuant to existing grievance procedures. Specifically, the House Committee Report (H.R. 103-8 (II), p. 51, 103rd Congress, 1st Session, Parts 1 and 2, February 2, 1993) states that the Committee:

> believes that the provisions of [the FMLA] affecting federal employees can be adequately enforced using existing grievance procedures established by a collective bargaining agreement or by agency management.

See Keen, 958 F. Supp. at 73–74 (*quoting* House Report).

The interim OPM regulations implementing Title II reiterate that an employee who believes that an agency has not fully complied with the FMLA rights contained in Title II and the OPM regulations "may file a grievance under an agency's administrative grievance procedures or negotiated grievance procedures." 58 Fed. Reg. 39596, 39602 (July 23, 1993). *See Keen*, 958 F. Supp. at 72 (quoting same). The reference to enforcement of Title II employee FMLA rights by use of an agency or collective bargaining agreement grievance process is not mentioned in the preamble to the final OPM regulations. *See* 61 Fed. Reg. 6441 (December 5, 1996).

The House Committee Report also indicated its expectation that the Office of Special Counsel (OSC) will "aggressively pursue any violation" of Title II of the FMLA pursuant to its responsibilities for investigation of the civil service laws. H.R. Rep. 103-8 (II). Essentially, OSC serves as an investigator and prosecutor of certain defined prohibited federal personnel practices. The principal investigative and prosecutorial functions of the OSC are set forth in 5 USC 1214, 1215, and 1216. These functions were summarized by the MSPB in *Marren v. Dept. of Justice*, 51 MSPR 632, 637 n. 4 (1991):

The functions of the OSC are: To conduct prohibited personnel practice investigations to see whether employee complaints of improper management actions are valid; to use the results of these investigations to seek corrective action form the agency and, if the agency fails to take action, from the MSPB; to seek injunctive relief, known as a stay, that will restore the employee who alleges to be a victim of prohibited personnel practice to his or her job while a corrective action petition is being prepared or being considered; to prosecute disciplinary action complaints against Federal employees who engage in prohibited personnel practices, who violate orders of the MSPB, or who violate statutes related to the merit system, such as the Hatch Act; and to screen whistleblowing disclosures and order agency investigations of the substance of allegations. *See* 5 USC 1206.

The role of the Office of Special Counsel of the Merit Systems Protection Board is beyond the scope of this book. For an in-depth review of these functions, see Peter Broida, *A Guide to the Merit Systems Protection Board Law and Practice*, Chapter 13 (Dewey Publications, Inc. 2007).

The limitation of enforcement of FMLA rights by Title II-covered employees to grievance procedures and resort to OSC has been criticized as grossly insufficient. *See* James M. Eisenmann, Federal Employees' Unenforceable and Illusory Rights Under the Family and Medical Leave Act of 1993, 4 BNA Employment Discrimination Reports, Analysis & Perspective (April 12, 1995). Essentially, the criticism is that federal employees covered by Title II are treated disparately in terms of enforcement and remedies for violations of the FMLA. Federal employees covered by Title I and the CAA may enforce violations of the FMLA by filing a private civil action for damages in federal court or, in the case of the CAA, through administrative review before the agency with appellate review by a federal court. Use of an internal agency grievance process was derided as an unsatisfactory means for a Title II employee to seek redress of FMLA violations as such processes do not provide for review by outside third party neutral or judicial review. Rather, higher-level management generally rubber-stamps the actions of lower-level line management. "In short, a federal employee's right to file a grievance with his/her agency pales in comparison to the right to file a suit in court or, as for the congressional employees, the right to file a administrative complaint with an adjudicatory hearing, subject to court review. In most federal agencies, the grievance procedure involves no hearings, no oral presentations, no right to examine or cross examine witnesses, and, significantly, no review of the grievance decisions by an outside neutral party."

The availability of OSC as a vehicle for enforcement of FMLA rights was criticized as not providing non-unionized employees with a meaningful right of enforcement. The OSC, the article maintained, has been criticized by Congress for failure to "aggressively" investigate violations of the civil service laws. Moreover, with respect to the MSPB, a federal employee could only raise FMLA violations as an affirmative defense to an otherwise appealable adverse action, greatly limiting the availability of enforcement. Finally, even if the MSPB heard the case, the Board has no authority to award damages for FMLA violations.

Finally, it was unclear whether an arbitrator could award damages, attorney fees, or other monetary relief for violations of Title II of the FMLA. Absent a waiver of sovereign immunity, it was likely that monetary relief for violations would not be available to remedy violations of the Title II of the FMLA.

The solution proposed was that Congress needed to amend the FMLA to provide all federal employees the enforcement and remedial rights Congress gave to employees covered by Title I and the CAA. "Until Congress makes these changes, federal employees will be left with a law that cannot be enforced." To date, Congress has not modified the enforcement or remedial provisions of Title II of the FMLA.

2. Federal Court

The FMLA does not afford an employee covered by Title II of the FMLA the right to file a private civil action in federal court to address violations of the law. *See Bogumill v. OPM*, 168 F.3d 1320 (table), 1998 U.S. App. LEXIS 18750, at *4 (Fed. Cir. Aug. 13, 1998); *Mann v. Haigh*, 120 F.3d 34, 37 (4th Cir. 1997); *Gibson-Michaels v. Blair*, No. 06-1940 (RMU), 2007 U.S. Dist. LEXIS 32564, at *8-9 (D.D.C. May 3, 2007); *Giesken v. VA*, No. 06-14901-BC, 2007 U.S. Dist. LEXIS 31971, at 3 (E.D. Mich. May 2, 2007); *Kallen v. DOD*, No. 1:03-CV-1634-JDT-TAB, 2004 U.S. Dist. LEXIS 19576, at *5 (S.D. Ind. Aug. 11, 2004); *Sullivan-Obst v. Powell*, 300 F. Supp. 2d 85, 99 (D.D.C. 2004); *Gardner v. United States et al.*, No. 96-1467 (EGS), 1999 U.S. Dist. LEXIS 2195, at *22 (D.D.C. Jan. 29, 1999); *Wilson v. Dallas Independent School District*, No. CA3:97-CV-0281-BC, 1998 U.S. Dist. LEXIS 1415, at *12 (N.D. Tex. Jan. 30, 1998); *Keen v. Brown*, 958 F. Supp. 70, 72-75 (D. Conn. 1997); *Sutherland v. Bowles*, No. 94-71570, 1995 U.S. Dist. LEXIS 11018 (E.D. Mich. Jan. 17, 1995).

Courts have rejected employee arguments that a private right of action is implied under Title II, or is otherwise available under different federal laws. *Mann v. Haigh*, 120 F.3d 34, 37 (4th Cir. 1997) (no implicit right of action); *Gardner v. United States et al.,* No. 96-1467 (EGS), 1999 U.S. Dist. LEXIS 2195, at *22 (D.D.C. Jan. 29, 1999) (same); *Keen v. Brown*, 958 F. Supp. 70, 72–75 (D. Conn. 1997) (same). To determine whether a private right of action should be implied under a particular statute, courts focus on the question of congressional intent: whether there is any indication of legislative intent, implicit or explicit, to create a remedy or to deny one. *Keen*, 958 F. Supp. at 73 (*citing Cannon v. Univ. Chicago*, 441 U.S. 677, 730, 60 L. Ed. 2d 560, 99 S. Ct. 1946 (1979); *Health Care Plan Inc. v. Aetna Life Ins. Co.*, 966 F.3d 738, 740 (2d Cir. 1992)). After reviewing the legislative and regulatory history, the court in *Keen* concluded that the evidence clearly indicated that Congress did not intend to provide a private enforcement mechanism for employees covered by Title II. *Keen,* 958 F. Supp. at 74.

Moreover, Title II of the FMLA does not expressly waive sovereign immunity. Except for situations in which the Constitution itself authorizes suit against the federal government, a suit against the federal government is permissible only if Congress consented to suit. *Mann v. Haigh*, 120 F.3d 34, 37 (4th Cir. 1997) (*citing Army & Air Force Exch. Serv. v. Sheehan*, 456 U.S. 728, 734, 72 L. Ed. 2d 20, 102 S. Ct. 2118 (1982)). Absent a waiver, sovereign immunity shields the federal government and its agencies from suit. *Keen*, 958 F. Supp. at 73 (*citing FDIC v. Meyer*, 510 U.S. 471, 476, 114 S. Ct. 996, 127 L. Ed. 2d 308 (1994)). Any waiver of sovereign immunity must be unequivocal. *Keen*, 958 F. Supp. at 37 *citing DOE v. Ohio*, 503 U.S. 6–7, 613, 118 L. Ed. 2d 255, 112 S. Ct. 1627 (1992). No express wavier of sovereign immunity exists allowing an employee to file a private action for violations of Title II. *Mann*, 120 F.3d at 37; *Keen v. Brown*, 958 F. Supp. 70, 74 (D. Conn. 1997).

Similarly, courts have rejected arguments that the Administrative Procedures Act (APA) provides a right of action to employees covered by Title II for violations of the FMLA. *Mann v. Haigh*, 120 F.3d 34, 37 (4th Cir. 1997); *Keen v. Brown*, 958 F. Supp. 70, 74 (D. Conn. 1997). Section 702 of the APA states that "[a] person suffering a legal wrong because of agency action…is entitled to seek judicial review thereof." 5 USC 702. The Civil Service Reform Act (CSRA) is the exclusive remedy for federal employees challenging agency actions. Accordingly, a federal employee covered by Title II may not process his or her FMLA claim through the APA, as the APA has been preempted by the CSRA. *Mann*, 120 F.3d at 37; *Keen*, 958 F. Supp. at 74, 75-77. The CSRA preempts an APA claim even where the employment action is not subject to review by the CSRA. *Mann*, 120 F.3d at 37 (*citing United States v. Fausto*, 484 U.S. 439, 455, 98 L. Ed. 2d 830, 108 S. Ct. 668 (1988)).

Absent judicial review, an employee who does not have a MSPB right of appeal is left with internal agency grievance appeals for his or her FMLA claim. *See Mann*, 120 F.3d at 37.

3. MSPB

An employee covered by Title II of the FMLA may raise violations of the FMLA before the MSPB, but only in connection with adverse actions over which the MSPB otherwise has jurisdiction. *Bogumill v. OPM*, 168 F.3d 1320 (table), 1998 U.S. App. LEXIS 18750, at *4 (Fed. Cir. Aug. 13, 1998); *Moore v. USPS*, 83 MSPR 533 (1999); *Landahl v. Commerce*, 83 MSPR 40 (1999), *aff'd,* 10 Fed. Appx. 950 (Fed. Cir. 2001); *Burge v. Dept. of Air Force*, 82 MSPR 75 (1999), *aff'd,* 7 Fed. Appx. 931 (Fed. Cir. 2001); *Ellshoff v. DOI*, 76 MSPR 54 (1997), *rev'd on other grounds, remanded*, 78 MSPR 615 (1998); *Ramey v. USPS*, 70 MSPR 463 (1996) *aff'd* 178 F.3d 1312 (table), 1999 U.S. App. LEXIS 657 (Fed. Cir. Jan. 8, 1999).

An exploration of what employees and adverse actions are within the jurisdiction of the MSPB is beyond the scope of this book. The reader is referred to Peter Broida, *A Guide to Merit Systems Protection Board Law and Practice*, Chapter 1 (Dewey Publications, Inc. 2007).

4. Unfair Labor Practice Charges

The FMLA claims of certain federal sector bargaining unit employees may be reviewed as an unfair labor practice charge by the Federal Labor Relations Authority (FLRA). The Federal Service–Labor–Management Relations Statute (Title VII of the Civil Service Reform Act of 1978, 5 USC 7101–7135) governs labor–management relations in most of the federal sector. The FLRA enforces the terms of the Federal Service–Labor–Management Relations Statute (FSLMRS). A full exploration of the labor–management rights of employees covered by the FSLMRS is beyond the scope of this book. What follows is an overview of the pertinent features of that law as may be relevant to claims of violation of the FMLA.

The FSLMRS applies to employees of certain executive agencies, including nonappropriated fund instrumentalities, the Library of Congress, the Government Printing Office, and the Smithsonian Institution. 5 USC 7103. Employees not covered include those of the General Accounting Office, the Federal Bureau of Investigation, the Central Intelligence

Agency, the Tennessee Valley Authority, the Federal Labor Relations Authority, the Federal Service Impasses Panel, or the United States Secret Service. 5 USC 7103. Labor-management relations in the Postal Service is governed by the National Labor Relations Act.

In certain respects, the FSLMRS mirrors the rights and protections afforded by the NLRA discussed above in connection with Title I. The FSLMRS protects the right of covered employees to form, join, or assist any labor organization, and the right to engage in collective bargaining. 5 USC 7102. The FSLMRS also prohibits certain employer and union conduct as unfair labor practices. 5 USC 7116.

Unfair labor practices of agencies within the meaning of the FSLMRS (5 USC 7116) are:

- Interference with, restraint, or coercion of any employee in the exercise by the employee of any right provided by the FSLMRS;

- Encouragement or discouragement of membership in any labor organization by discrimination in connection with hiring, tenure, promotion, or other conditions of employment;

- To sponsor, control, or otherwise assist any labor organization;

- To discipline or otherwise discriminate against an employee because the employee has filed a complaint, affidavit, or petition, or has given any information or testimony as required by the FSLMRS;

- To refuse to consult or negotiate in good faith with a labor organization.

The FSLMRS also prohibits certain labor organization conduct as unfair labor practices. 5 USC 7116.

An aggrieved employee or union may file a charge with a local FLRA office alleging that an agency or labor organization has committed an unfair labor practice. 5 USC 7118. Generally, such unfair labor practice charges must be filed within 6 months of the occurrence, but that period may be extended under certain circumstances. 5 USC 7118. The FLRA General Counsel investigates the charge and may issue a complaint alleging an unfair labor practice. 5 USC 7118. If the complaint is not resolved informally or formally, the matter may culminate in an administrative hearing. 5 USC 7118.

The unfair labor practice procedures of the FSLMRS are similar to those of the NLRA. As such, like the NLRA, the process may be employed under certain circumstances to indirectly review claims of FMLA violations. The previous discussion addressing unfair labor practice charges involving FMLA claims before the NLRB under Title I should be consulted as a guide to what might be possible before the FLRA.

C. CAA

1. Introduction

The CAA contains an administrative and judicial dispute-resolution process for, among others, FMLA claims. Generally, the process requires employees to exhaust administrative remedies through a counseling and mediation process. At the conclusion of those processes, an employee has the right to elect to proceed with the FMLA claim in a hearing conducted by the Office of Compliance. Alternatively, an employee may file a private civil action for damages in federal court. *See* 2 USC 1401.

a. Office of Compliance

The Office of Compliance (Office) is responsible for the administration of the CAA administrative and judicial dispute resolution process. The CAA established the Office as an independent office within the legislative branch of the federal government. 2 USC 1381(a). The Office is composed of a five member Board of Directors, one of whom serves as Chair, appointed jointly by the Speaker of the House of Representatives, the Majority Leader of the Senate, and the Minority Leaders of the House of Representatives and the Senate, 2 USC 1381(b)-(c). Members of the Board of Directors serve part-time for staggered terms of up to five years. 2 USC 1381(e). The Board and Office are subject to oversight (except with respect to individual cases) by the Senate Committees on Rules and Administration and Government Affairs, and the Committee on House Oversight of the House of Representatives. 2 USC 1381(l).

The Office is also composed of an Executive Director, Deputy Executive Directors for the House and Senate, a General Counsel, and attorneys and other staff. 2 USC 1382. The Executive Director acts as the Chief Operating Officer of the Office with overall responsibility for carrying out the mandate of the Office. 2 USC 1382(a)(4). The responsibilities of the Deputy Executive Directors and General Counsel are also set forth in the Statute. 2 USC 1382(b)–(c).

The Office is charged with providing alternative dispute resolution procedures, and adjudicative hearings and appeals for covered legislative branch employees. *See Billinger v. OPM*, 82 MSPR 195 (1999), *rev'd on other grounds, remanded*, 206 F.3d 1401 (Fed. Cir. 2000). It is also responsible for providing education and information on the CAA to members of Congress, other employing offices, and employees of the legislative branch. The Office of General Counsel enforces the provisions of the CAA relating to health and safety and public access requirements for the disabled, including conducting periodic compliance inspections, and investigation and prosecution of claims. Additionally, the General Counsel investigates and prosecutes unfair labor practice claims under the CAA. *See* 2 USC 1331, 1341.

b. FMLA Complaints

The Office issues annual reports to Congress regarding issues and complaints handled. Some of these reports are available on the Office of Compliance website at www.compliance.gov/reports. CAA employee inquiries and complaints regarding FMLA leave appear to make up a relatively modest number of the total inquiries and complaints reported by the Office. For example, in the Report to Congress for calendar year 2000, the Office reported that 16 of 235 covered employee contacts involved the FMLA. *See* Office of Compliance § 301(H) Report to Congress: January 1, 2000–December 31, 2000, p. 2. Of the 105 requests for counseling reported that year, six involved the FMLA. *Id*. Although the Report is less than clear, it does not appear that FMLA leave was the basis for any employee complaint.

The Report to Congress for calendar year 1999 is similarly devoid of a significant number of FMLA issues. The Office reported that of the 296 contacts made by the over 20,000 CAA-covered employees, only 33 of them involved the FMLA. *See* Office of Compliance § 301(H) Report to Congress (January 1, 1993–December 31, 1999), p. 3. Of the 330 requests for counseling filed that year, one involved FMLA rights. *Id*., at p. 5. It appears from the report that the one FMLA complaint was referred to mediation and was subsequently the subject of one of the nine complaints filed with the Office. *Id*. at p. 6. It is unclear from the Report what subsequently happened to the FMLA complaint.

2. Complaint Procedure

a. Exclusive Procedure

The CAA dispute-resolution procedures are the exclusive means available to commence an administrative or judicial proceeding to remedy a violation of the rights and protections afforded under the CAA, including the FMLA. 2 USC 1361(d)(1). The lone exception to that rule allows a covered employee under § 206 of the CAA (2 USC 1316) to also use the provisions of Chapter 43 of Title 38 (38 USC Chapter 4301 *et. seq.*) that are applicable to the employee. 2 USC 1361(d)(2). Chapter 43 of Title 38 is generally known as the Uniformed Services Employment and Reemployment Rights Act (USERRA). USERRA generally addresses rights and protections relating to veterans' employment and reemployment. Essentially, an employee under USERRA may either directly petition the Secretary of Labor or file an appeal with the MSPB regarding a claim that the employee has been denied employment or restoration to employment by reason of military service. *See* USC 4322, 4324. Employee enforcement rights under USERRA are addressed in Peter Broida, *A Guide to Merit Systems Protection Law and Practice*, Chapter 1 (Dewey Publications, Inc. 2007).

As the exclusive system for resolving FMLA complaints, it does not appear that the CAA generally allows employees covered by a collective bargaining unit to resolve FMLA disputes through any grievance-arbitration system. Employees of the Office of the Architect of the Capitol and of the Capitol Police have a limited right to grieve violations, including FMLA violations. 2 USC 1401. This right will be addressed below.

b. Counseling

(1) General Rule

To commence a proceeding, a covered employee alleging a violation of the FMLA must request counseling by the Office.

2 USC 1402(a); *see Halcomb v. Office of the Senate Sergeant–At–Arms of the United States Senate*, 209 F. Supp. 2d 175, 178, n. 3 (D.D.C. 2002); *Moore v. Capitol Guide Board et al.*, 982 F. Supp. 35, 38 (D.D.C. 1997). The request for counseling must be made no later than 180 days after the date of the alleged violation. *Id.* The period of counseling is 30 days, unless the employee and the Office agree to reduce the period. 2 USC 1402(b). The 30–day counseling period begins on the date the request for counseling is received. *Id.* The Office notifies the employee in writing when the counseling period has ended. 2 USC 1402(c).

The doctrine of equitable tolling has been held to apply to excuse an employee's untimely request for counseling. *Halcomb v. Office of the Senate Sergeant–At–Arms of the United States Senate*, 209 F. Supp. 2d 175, 178 (D.D.C. 2002); *Thompson v. Capitol Police Bd.*, 120 F. Supp. 2d 78, 79 (D.D.C. 2000), *aff'd*, 22 Fed. Appx. 14 (D.C. Cir. 2001). The court in *Thompson* reasoned that, like Title VII, "the CAA provision that specifies a time for filing charges appears in a separate section from the one covering jurisdiction, and does not make any mention of jurisdiction." Nevertheless, even though the *Thompson* court held that equitable tolling principles are applicable to the CAA, it dismissed the plaintiff's claim because he failed to present any evidence that his situation was an "extraordinary and carefully circumscribed instance suitable for equitable tolling." *Thompson,* 120 F. Supp. 2d at 83.

(2) Key Terms

A request for counseling must be made by a "covered employee." The term "covered employee" is a defined term that means any employee of an identified "employing office" of Congress covered by the CAA. *See* 2 USC 1301(3). Individuals who are not "covered employees" within the meaning of the CAA cannot initiate a claim with the Office for unlawful FMLA conduct. That the definition of "employee" includes an applicant for employment and a former employee. 2 USC 1301(4). Neither "employee" nor "covered employee" include unions, employee associations, or others within the meaning of those terms. It is at best an open question whether a union could initiate a proceeding by requesting counseling for an FMLA violation. On the other hand, there is nothing in the regulation prohibiting one covered employee (e.g., a union representative) from requesting counseling on behalf of another covered employee.

There is no indication how an employee must make the request for counseling. Absent further instructions, it would appear that such a request need not be in writing, and may be done orally.

It is unclear how the "counseling" is conducted by the Office. Nor is there any indication of what form the product of that counseling would take. Presumably, the counseling is designed to resolve the issue at the lowest possible level. It is unclear whether resolution would take the form of a written settlement.

(3) Availability of Grievance Process

In the case of an employee (including applicants and former employees) of the Office of the Architect of the Capitol or of the Capitol Police, the Executive Director of the Office, after receiving a request for counseling, may recommend that the employee use the grievance procedures of the Architect of the Capitol or the Capitol Police for resolution of the employee's grievance for a specific period of time, which shall not count against the time available for counseling or mediation. 2 USC 1401.

A few observations are in order. First, note that this proviso applies to any employee, not "covered employee," of the Office of the Architect of the Capitol or of the Capitol Police. Second, a request for counseling is still required to initiate a proceeding. Only after counseling is requested does the Executive Director of the Office recommend that the employee use the grievance procedure. Third, it is unclear whether the "recommendation" of the Executive Director is binding, or whether the employee may decline the recommendation in favor of proceeding with the counseling. Note that proceeding in the grievance process is not a decision that may be unilaterally made by the employee or union. It first requires a recommendation by the Executive Director of the Office.

Finally, if the employee accepts the recommendation of the Executive Director and proceeds in the grievance process, the request for counseling is not dismissed. Rather, the administrative process is stayed and does not count against the time for counseling and mediation. There is nothing in the Statute that indicates what happens if the matter is resolved in the grievance process. Presumably, the complaint is moot and the request for counseling is dismissed or closed. If, however, the complaint is not completely resolved to the satisfaction of the employee in the grievance process, presumably the employee could return to counseling. There is no indication in the Statute for the process of re-instituting the counseling process on conclusion of the grievance process. There is nothing in the Statute indicating that an employee is precluded from proceeding with counseling even if he or she received everything he or she was entitled to in the grievance process.

If counseling results in a settlement, such settlement must be reduced to writing, and be approved by the Office Executive Director before becoming effective. 2 USC 1414. Presumably, the same rule applies to settlements in the referenced grievance processes.

(4) Confidentiality

All counseling is strictly confidential, except that the Office and a covered employee may agree to notify the employing office of the allegations. 2 USC 1416(a).

c. Mediation

(1) General Rule

Within 15 days after receipt by the employee of the notice of the end of the counseling period, the covered employee who alleged a violation of the FMLA (as applied by the CAA) must file a request for mediation with the Office. 2 USC 1403(a); see *Halcomb v. Office of the Senate Sergeant-At-Arms of the United States Senate*, 209 F. Supp. 2d 175, 178, n. 3 (D.D.C. 2002); *Moore v. Capitol Guide Board et al.*, 982 F. Supp. 35, 38 (D.D.C. 1997). Presumably, a covered employee would only be afforded the opportunity to request mediation if counseling were unsuccessful. The Statute does not require that the request for mediation be in writing.

(2) Mediation Process

The parties to CAA mediation may include the Office, the covered employee, the employing office, and one or more individuals appointed by the Executive Director after considering recommendations by organizations composed primarily of individuals experienced in adjudicating or arbitrating personnel matters. 2 USC 1403(b)(1). The Statute does not indicate who selects what parties will attend the mediation. Mediation involves meetings with the parties separately or jointly for the purpose of resolving the dispute between the covered employee and the employing office. 2 USC 1403.

If the mediation results in a settlement, such settlement must be reduced to writing, and be approved by the Office Executive Director before becoming effective. 2 USC 1414.

No individual, who is appointed by the Executive Director to mediate, may conduct or aid in an administrative hearing conducted under § 405 with respect to the same matter or shall be subject to subpoena or any other compulsory process with respect to the same matter. 2 USC 1403(d).

(3) Mediation Period

The mediation period lasts 30 days beginning on the date the request for mediation is received by the Office. 2 USC 1403(c). The mediation period may be extended for an additional period at the joint request of the covered employee and the employing office. 2 USC 1403(c). The use of the words "may" and "request" suggests that someone makes a decision on a joint request to extend the mediation, although the Statute does not identify who would make such a decision. Presumably, a representative of the Office makes a decision on a joint request for an extension. It is also unclear whether each extension is for another 30-day period, or whether the parties (or the unnamed deciding official) can jointly stipulate to some other period.

The Office must notify the covered employee and the employing office when the mediation period has ended. 2 USC 1403. The Statute does not require that notice of the conclusion of the mediation period be in writing. Presumably, however, it is in writing since receipt of the notice of the end of the mediation period triggers the start of the period in which the covered employee must elect to file an administrative complaint or file a civil action in federal court. 2 USC 1404. There is no indication that the notice signaling the end of the mediation period necessarily means that the mediation did not achieve a settlement, although that is presumably the case.

(4) Confidentiality

All mediation is strictly confidential. 2 USC 1416(b).

d. Election of Proceedings

A CAA-covered employee whose FMLA claim was not successfully resolved after counseling and mediation has the right to elect whether to continue to prosecute the claim administratively, or to file a civil action in federal court. Specifically, the Statute (2 USC 1404) provides:

> Not later than 90 days after a covered employee received notice of the end of the period of mediation, but no sooner than 20 days after receipt of such notification, such covered employee may either:
>
> (1) file a complaint with the Office in accordance with Section 405, or
>
> (2) file a civil action in accordance with Section 408 in the United States district court for the district in which the employee is employed or for the District of Columbia.

See *Moore v. Capitol Guide Board et al.,* 982 F. Supp. 35, 38 (D.D.C. 1997).

No explanation is provided for the 30-day waiting period from receipt of the notice of the end of the mediation period before a covered employee may make his or her election. Presumably, a covered employee who "jumps the gun" and files before the 30-day period may have the administrative or federal civil action dismissed for failure to timely exhaust administrative remedies. In such a case, the employee should simply be able to cure the exhaustion issue by re-filing within the permitted 60-day window.

Where an employee files early during the initial 30-day window, an employing office might consider waiting until the closure of the 60-day period to re-file before moving to dismiss the claim for failure to timely exhaust administrative remedies. In that case, the employee's claim should be dismissed as untimely, and the employee would not be able to timely re-file after the expiration of the 60-day period. Equitable considerations might sway a Hearing Officer or a district court to allow such re-filing even though it would be untimely. There is a wealth of federal court case law dealing with claims of discrimination in the federal sector (mostly the Postal Service) on these timeliness issues that might be of some assistance.

3. Election of a Section 405 Administrative Complaint

a. General Rule

A covered employee may, upon the completion of mediation under § 403, file a complaint with the Office. 2 USC 1405(a). The respondent to the complaint is the employing office that is either involved in the violation, or in which the violation is alleged to have occurred, and about which mediation was conducted. 2 USC 1405(a)(1)–(2). The difference in the two variations is not further explained.

Note that only a covered employee is permitted to file a complaint with the Office. The Statute does not, by its terms, specify that a particular form of complaint be used or that it be in writing. Nor does the Statute limit complaints to situations where the mediation effort did not result in an acceptable settlement.

b. Hearing Officer

Upon the filing of a complaint, the Executive Director of the Office must appoint an independent hearing officer to consider the complaint and render a decision. 2 USC 1405(c)(1). The Executive Director must select hearing officers on a rotational or random basis from master lists consisting (2 USC 1405(c)(1), (2)) of:

> Members of the bar of a state or the District of Columbia and retired judges of the United States Courts who are experienced in adjudicating the kinds of personnel and other matters for which hearings may be held under the Act, and

Individuals who are experts in technical matters relating to accessibility and usability by persons with disabilities or technical matters relating to occupational safety and health.

In developing lists, the Executive Director of the Office must consider candidates recommended by the Federal Mediation and Conciliation Service or the Administrative Conference of the United States. 2 USC 1405(b)(2).

Members of the House or Senate, the head of an employing office, a member of the Board of Directors of the Office, or a covered employee may not be appointed to be a CAA hearing officer. 2 USC 1405(c)(1).

Hearing officers may be appointed as full-time employees of the Office. 2 USC 1405(c)(1). Alternatively, the selection of hearing officers may be made on the basis of specialized expertise needed for particular matters. *Id.*

c. Dismissal

A hearing officer may dismiss any claim that the hearing officer finds to be frivolous or that fails to state a claim upon which relief may be granted. Presumably, this means that a hearing officer could do this on his or her own motion without the necessity of a motion by an employing office; an employing office could file a motion to dismiss a claim based on these grounds as well. The terms "frivolous" and "failure to state a claim" are not defined or otherwise illustrated.

d. Discovery

Reasonable prehearing discovery may be permitted at the discretion of the hearing officer. 2 USC 1405(e). The Statute does not further define "discovery." While ultimately left to the discretion of the hearing officer, given the requirement that non-technical expert hearing officers be members of a bar association or a retired judge of the United States Courts, it would appear very likely that discovery permitted by the Federal Rules of Civil Procedure (interrogatories, deposition, requests for production of documents, and admissions) will serve as a general guide on the type of prehearing discovery permitted. Presumably, the party or parties wishing to conduct discovery should file a motion requesting prehearing discovery, detailing exactly what discovery the party desires and why.

e. Subpoenas

At the request of a party, a hearing officer may issue subpoenas for the attendance of witnesses and for the production of correspondence, books, papers, documents, and other records. 2 USC 1405(f)(1). The attendance of witnesses and the production of records may be required from any place within the United States. *Id.* Subpoenas must be served in accordance with Rule 45(b) of the Federal Rules of Civil Procedure.

Some people served with a CAA subpoena may object to providing the requested information. If a person refuses, on the basis of relevance, privilege, or other objection, to testify in response to a question or to produce records in connection with a proceeding before a hearing officer, the hearing officer must rule on the objection. 2 USC 1405(f)(2). At the request of the witness or any party, the hearing officer may refer the ruling to the Office Board of Directors for review. *Id.* On the hearing officer's own volition, the hearing officer may also refer the ruling on an objection by a witness or party to the Board of Directors. *Id.*

If a person fails to comply with a subpoena issued by a CAA hearing officer, the Office Board of Directors may authorize the General Counsel to apply, in the name of the Office, to an appropriate United States district court for an order requiring that person to appear before the hearing officer to give testimony or produce records. 2 USC 1405(f)(3). The application for a court order may be made within the judicial district where the hearing is conducted, or where that person is found, resides, or transacts business. *Id.* Any failure to obey a lawful order of the district court issued pursuant to § 405 of the CAA (2 USC 1405(f)(3)(A)) may be held by such court to be in civil contempt.

There is no indication how the Board is alerted in order to authorize the General Counsel to apply for a district court order. Presumably, this is done by the hearing officer, either on his or her own volition, or on the motion of a party.

Service of process in an action to enforce a CAA hearing officer subpoena in federal district court, or contempt proceedings in the event the person fails to comply with a lawful order of district court, may be served in any judicial district in which the person refusing or failing to comply, threatening to refuse or not to comply, resides, transacts business, or may be found. 2 USC 1405(f))(3)(B). Subpoenas for witnesses who are required to attend such proceedings may run into any other district. *Id.*

f. Conduct of Hearing

The Statute does not set forth a mandatory process for how the actual hearing is handled. Nor does it address rules of evidence. Presumably, the conduct of the hearing is at the discretion of the hearing officer. Given the presence of attorneys and retired judges as hearing officers, it is very likely that such hearings will at least assume the form of employment arbitration, with relaxed rules of evidence. Some former federal judges, however, may insist on strict adherence to the rules of evidence. Again, this will likely depend on the inclination of the hearing officer.

Hearing officers are guided by judicial decisions interpreting the laws made applicable by § 102 (2 USC 1302), and by decisions of the Office Board of Directors. 2 USC 1405(h). Title I of the FMLA is one of the laws listed under § 102 of the CAA. *See* 2 USC 1302(5).

There is nothing in the Statute to indicate whether the hearing is transcribed. Nor is it apparent whether the hearing is open to the public.

g. Settlement

If a settlement is reached, such settlement must be reduced to writing, and be approved by the Office Executive Director before becoming effective. 2 USC 1414.

h. Decision

Hearing officers issue written decisions. 2 USC 1405(g). The written decision must be issued as expeditiously as possible, but in no case in more than 90 days after the conclusion of the hearing. *Id.*

The Statute proscribes that the written decision address certain matters. The decision must (2 USC 1405(g)):

- state the issues raise in the complaint;
- describe the evidence in the record;
- contain findings of fact and conclusions of law;
- make a determination whether a violation has occurred; and
- order such remedies as are appropriate pursuant to Title II of the CAA.

The Office transmits the written decision to the parties. 2 USC 1405(g). That implies that the hearing officer submits his or her decision to the Office rather than directly to the parties. The Office also records the decision. *Id.*

If a decision is not appealed under § 406 to the Office Board of Directors, the decision is considered a final decision of the Office. 2 USC 1405(g).

i. Appeal to Office Board of Directors

An employee or employing office aggrieved by the decision of the hearing officer may file a petition for review by the Office Board of Directors. 2 USC 1406(a). Such appeal must be filed within 30 days after entry of the decision in the records of the Office. *Id.* There is no indication in the Statute how an aggrieved party confirms the date when the hearing officer's decision has been entered in the records of the Office. Nor does the Statute provide that the appeal must be in writing, or be in a particular form.

The parties to the hearing upon which the decision of the hearing officer was made are provided a reasonable opportunity to be heard, through written submission and, at the discretion of the Office Board of Directors, through oral argument. 2 USC 1406(b). The Statute does not provide particulars regarding the time frame for providing such written submissions, page limitations, or the form of the submission. Nor does the Statute address the right of a party to submit a reply or response to the other party. Presumably, these details are provided to the parties by the Office Board of Directors.

The standard of review of the Office Board of Directors on an appeal of a CAA hearing officer decision is set forth in the Statute. According to the Statute (2 USC 1406(c):

> The Board shall set aside a decision of a hearing officer if the Board determines that the decision was—
>
>> arbitrary, capricious, an abuse of discretion, or otherwise not consistent with law;
>>
>> not made consistent with required procedures; or
>>
>> unsupported by substantial evidence.

The above standards are not further defined or explained. Presumably, case law interpreting these terms for purposes of appellate review of a trial court decision would be of some assistance in framing these issues.

In making its determination, the Office Board of Directors reviews the whole record, or those parts of it cited by a party. 2 USC 1406(d). The Office Board will take due account of the rule of prejudicial error. *Id.* The rule of prejudicial error is not otherwise explained. Again, the "rule of prejudicial error" as applied in the federal courts will likely be applied. Presumably, to review the "record" requires a hearing transcript.

The Office Board of Directors will issue a written decision setting forth the reasons for its decision. 2 USC 1406(e). The decision may affirm, reverse, or remand to the hearing officer for further proceedings. *Id.* A decision that does not require further proceedings before a hearing officer shall be entered in the records of the Office as a final decision. *Id.*

j. Judicial Review of Office Board of Director Decisions

A petition for review to the United States Court of Appeals for the Federal Circuit is available to a party aggrieved by a final decision of the Office Board of Directors. Such petitions are also available in other circumstances, as set for more fully below. The petition for review must be filed no later than 90 days after the entry in the Office of a final decision of the Board of Directors. 2 USC 1407(c)(3).

The United States Court of Appeals for the Federal Circuit has jurisdiction over any proceeding commenced by a petition of 2 USC 1407(a)(1)(A)–(C)) by:

(A) a party aggrieved by a final decision of the Board under Section 406(e) in cases arising under Part A of Title II,

(B) a charging individual or a respondent before the Board who files a petition under Section 210(d)(4),

(C) The General Counsel or a respondent before the Board under Section 215(c)(5), or

(D) The General Counsel or a respondent before the Board who files a petition under Section 220(c)(3).

For purposes of the FMLA, only Subsection (A) above is applicable. Section 210(d)(4), 2 USC 1331(d)(4), addresses rights and protections under the ADA relating to public services and accommodations. Section 215(5), 2 USC 11341(c)(5), addresses OSHA rights and protections, and § 220(c)(3), 2 USC 1351(c)(3), addresses rights under the Federal Service Labor Management Relations Act.

With respect to petition by an aggrieved party from a final decision of the Office Board of Directors, the Court of Appeals for the Federal Circuit has exclusive jurisdiction to set aside, suspend (in whole or in part), to determine the validity of, or otherwise review the final decision of the Board. 2 USC 1407(a)(1).

The United States Court of Appeals for the Federal Circuit also has jurisdiction over any petition of the Office General Counsel, filed in the name of the Office and at the direction of the Board of Directors, to enforce a final decision of a hearing officer pursuant to § 405(g), or the final decision of the Board of Directors pursuant to § 406(e). 2 USC 1407(a)(2).

The Office is the respondent before the Court of Appeals for the Federal Circuit in an appeal from the final decision of the Office Board of Directors. 2 USC 1407(b)(1). Any other party before the Board of Directors may also be named as a respondent to the petition before the Court of Appeals for the Federal Circuit by filing a notice of election with the court within 30 days after service of the petition. *Id.* Note that the Statute implies that the aggrieved party from a final decision of the Office Board of Directors must serve a copy of the petition to the Court of Appeals for the Federal Circuit on the other parties before the Board.

The party whom the Office of General Counsel has determined failed to comply with the final decision of a CAA hearing officer or Office Board of Directors pursuant to §§ 405(g) and 406(e) of the CAA is the respondent to an enforcement petition filed with the Court of Appeals for the Federal Circuit filed by the Office General Counsel. 2 USC 1407(b)(1)(C).

A party before the Office Board of Directors on appeal of a final decision of a hearing officer may intervene in an action before the Court of Appeals for the Federal Circuit where the party was not named as a respondent. 2 USC 1407(b)(2).

Judicial review by the Court of Appeals for the Federal Circuit of a final decision of the Office Board of Directors is governed by Chapter 158 of Title 28, United States Code. 2 USC 1407(c). The Statute lists four exceptions to the application of Chapter 158 of Title 28 to judicial review of final decisions of the Office Board of Directors (2 USC 1407(c)(1)–(4)):

1. With respect to Section 2344 of Title 28, United States Code, service of a petition in any proceeding in which the Office is a respondent shall be on the General Counsel rather than on the Attorney General;

2. The provisions of Section 2348 of Title 28, United States Code, on the authority of the Attorney General, shall not apply;

3. The petition for review shall be filed no later than 90 days after entry in the Office of a final decision under Section 406(e); and

4. The Office shall be an "agency" as the term is used in Chapter 158 of Title 28, United States Code.

The CAA provides the standard of review to be used by the Court of Appeals for the Federal Circuit on petitions from the final decision of the Office Board of Directors. According to the Statute (2 USC 1407(d)):

> To the extent necessary for decision in a proceeding commenced under Subsection (a)(1) and when presented, the Court shall decide all relevant questions of law and interpret constitutional and statutory provisions. The Court shall set aside a final decision of the Board if it is determined that the decision was—
>
> arbitrary, capricious, an abuse of discretion, or otherwise not consistent with law;
>
> not made consistent with required procedures; or
>
> unsupported by substantial evidence.

In making its determination, the Court of Appeals for the Federal Circuit is required to review the record, or those parts of it cited by a party, and due account must be taken of the rule of prejudicial error. 2 USC 1407(e).

4. Private Right to File a Civil Action

As an alternative to an administrative appeal to the Office Board of Directors, a covered employee may file a civil action after completing counseling and mediation. 2 USC 1404(2).

a. General Rule

A CAA–covered employee may file a civil action in the United States district court for the district in which the employee is employed or for the District of Columbia alleging a violation of the FMLA. 2 USC 1404, 1408(a); *see Moore v. Capitol Guide Board et al.*, 982 F. Supp. 35, 38 (D.D.C. 1997). In order to file such a civil action, the employee must have exhausted his or her administrative remedies by completing the required counseling and mediation. 2 USC 1408(a); *see Halcomb v. Office of the Senate Sergeant–At–Arms of the United States Senate*, 209 F. Supp. 2d 175, 178 (D.D.C. 2002). *Moore v. Capitol Guide Board et al.*, 982 F. Supp. 35, 38 (D.D.C. 1997). A court will dismiss a civil action where an employee fails to first exhaust the administrative remedies. *Halcomb v. Office of the Senate Sergeant–At–Arms of the United States Senate*, 209 F. Supp. 2d 175, 178 (D.D.C. 2002). The civil action that may be commenced by a covered employee may only seek redress for a violation for which the employee has completed counseling and mediation. 2 USC 1408(a); *see Halcomb v. Office of the Senate Sergeant–At–Arms of the United States Senate*, 209 F. Supp. 2d 175, 179 (D.D.C. 2002) (because it was not addressed in counseling and mediation as required, the plaintiff's retaliation claim was dismissed). Similarly, a civil action may not be commenced against CAA–covered employing offices that were not a party to the counseling and mediation sessions regarding the claim. *Moore v. Capitol Guide Board et al.*, 982 F. Supp. 35, 38 (D.D.C. 1997) (the employee, not Office of Compliance, bears responsibility for identifying proper respondents for administrative exhaustion).

b. Time to File Suit

The civil action must be filed in the federal district court no later than 90 days after the covered employee receives notice of the end of the period of mediation, but no sooner than 30 days after receipt of such notification. 2 USC 1404(2). The employing office alleged to have committed the violation, or in which the violation is alleged to have occurred, is the named defendant in the litigation. 2 USC 1408(b); *see Moore v. Capitol Guide Board et al.*, 982 F. Supp. 35, 38 (D.D.C. 1997) (civil action may not be commenced against CAA–covered employing offices who were not a party to the counseling and mediation sessions regarding the claim).

In *Moore*, the court addressed who was a proper party defendant in a claim arising under the CAA. The Statute permits a covered employee to bring a civil action against the "employing office alleged to have committed the violation, or in which the violation is alleged to have occurred." 2 USC 1408(b). Moore, a former employee of the Capitol Guide, brought suit alleging employment discrimination against seven CAA–covered employing offices. She named as defendants, the Office of the Architect of the Capitol, the Office of the Sergeant-At-Arms of the House of Representatives, the Committee on House Administration of the House of Representatives, the Office of the Secretary of the Senate, the Committee on Rules and Administration of the Senate, and the Office of the Sergeant-at-Arms and Doorkeeper of the Senate. *Moore*, 982 F. Supp. at 36. Moore claimed that each of the named defendants was her "employer" within the meaning of the FMLA. *Moore*, 982 F. Supp. at 38. Six of the seven defendants moved for dismissal claiming that they were not the plaintiff's "employer" within the meaning of the FMLA.

The court held that a covered employee could only bring suit under the CAA against one of the nine employing office listed under the CAA. *Moore*, 982 F. Supp. at 39, n.5. Moore, the court found, could only bring suit against the single employing office responsible for the alleged violation. *Id*. The court's decision relied on the statutory language that a covered employee may bring suit under the CAA only against "*the* employing office" alleged to have committed the violation, or in which the violation is alleged to have occurred." *Id*. at 39 (emphasis supplied). The court concluded that, contrary to her claims, Moore was only the employee of the Capitol Guide Service, not the other named defendants. *Moore*, 982 F. Supp. at 39–40. Because Moore is not an "employee" of any of the defendants except the Capitol Guide Service, they cannot be considered to be her "employing office." *Id*. at 40. As such, they were incorrectly named as defendants and the court dismissed them from the case.

c. Right to Jury Trial

Finally, a right to a jury trial may be demanded by any party to the civil litigation, where a jury trial would be available in an action against a private defendant under the relevant law made applicable by this Act. 2 USC 1408(c). Although not specifically provided in the Statute itself, courts have interpreted Title I of the FMLA to permit a jury trial against a private defendant.

5. Miscellaneous CAA Enforcement Provisions

a. Judicial Review of CAA Regulations

The CAA allows a court to review the validity of CAA–issued regulations in limited circumstances. 2 USC 1409 (except as provided in this section, the validity of regulations issued under this Act are not subject to judicial review). Where a petition of a final decision of the Office Board of Directors is made to the Court of Appeals for the Federal Circuit, or where a covered employee files a civil action in federal district court after completing mediation and counseling, the court may review the validity of any CAA–issued regulation. 2 USC 409. Such review must be conducted in accordance with Subparagraphs (A) through (D) of § 706(2) of Title 5, United States Code. *Id*. An exception to that general rule involves CAA regulations approved by a joint resolution under § 304(c), 2 USC 1384(c). 2 USC 1409. Where regulations were issued pursuant to a joint resolution, the court reviewing the validity of such regulations must do so in accordance with § 706(2)(B) of Title 5, United States Code. 2 USC 1409.

The FMLA regulations were not issued pursuant to a joint resolution of the House and Senate. By Senate Resolution 242 (April 15, 1996), the Senate agreed to the proposed FMLA regulations. *See* S. Res. 242, Cong. Rec. (April 23, 1996) 29 CFR S3959–S3997. The House had previously passed its own resolution.

If the court determines that the regulation is invalid, the court must apply, to the extent necessary and appropriate, the most relevant substantive executive agency regulation promulgated to implement the statutory provisions with respect to which the invalid regulation was issued. 2 USC 1409. Again, as the CAA regulations implementing the FMLA specifically incorporate identified sections of Title I of the FMLA, 2 USC 1312(a)(1), the DOL regulations implementing those sections would appear to be the most relevant substantive executive agency regulations promulgated that would apply.

b. Other Judicial Review Prohibited; Wavier of Sovereign Immunity

Except as expressly authorized by §§ 407, 408, and 409 (2 USC 1404, 1408, and 1409), the compliance or noncompliance with the provisions of the CAA and any action taken pursuant to this Act shall not be subject to judicial review. 2 USC 1410. *See Payne v. Meeks*, 200 F. Supp. 2d 200 (E.D.N.Y. 2002) (comprehensive statutory scheme established by Congress in CAA to govern rights of congressional employees precluded a *Bivens* claim asserted by a former employee of a U.S. Representative); *Harris et al. v. Office of the Architect of the Capitol*, 16 F. Supp. 2d 8, 9 (D.D.C. 1998) (CAA held exclusive means for adjudicating employment claims of covered employees; court lacked jurisdiction over claims brought under individual statutes incorporated into CAA). This provision of the Statute would appear to clearly preclude adjudication of claims of violation of the FMLA, as applied by the CAA, by any means other than the method prescribed by the CAA. Unless specifically permitted by the Statute, that would appear to preclude grievances, unfair labor practice charges, and other litigation that seeks a determination whether an employing office violated the terms of the FMLA.

Similarly, the authority to bring judicial proceedings under §§ 405(f)(3) (enforcement of subpoenas), 407 (judicial review of a decision of the Office Board of Directors), and 408 (civil action by covered employee), 2 USC 1405(f)(3), 1407, and 1408, shall not constitute a waiver of sovereign immunity for any other purpose. 2 USC 1413. It also does not constitute a waiver of:

> The privileges of any Senator or Member of the House of Representatives under [A]rticle I, [S]ection 6, [C]lause 1, of the Constitution, or a waiver of any power of either the Senate or the House of Representatives under the Constitution, including under [A]rticle I, [S]ection 5, [C]lause 3, or under the rules of either House relating to records and information within its jurisdiction.

2 USC 1413.

Congress may be willing to allow individual managers in the public and private sectors covered by Title I to be sued in their individual capacities for FMLA violations, but they made doubly sure that no one would mistakenly assume that Congress exposed themselves to individual suit for violations of the FMLA.

c. Expedited Supreme Court Review of Certain Appeals

An appeal may be taken directly to the Supreme Court of the United States from an interlocutory or final judgment, decree, or order of a court upon the constitutionality of any provision of the CAA. 2 USC 1412(a). The Supreme Court, if it has not previously ruled on the question, may accept jurisdiction over the appeal, advance the appeal on the docket, and expedite the appeal to the greatest extent possible. 2 USC 1412(b).

In *Office of Senator Mark Dayton v. Hanson*, No. 06-618, 2007 U.S. LEXIS 5903 (May 21, 2007), the U.S. Supreme Court found that it lacked jurisdiction to consider an appeal of a decision of the Federal Circuit affirming the denial of Senator Dayton's motion to dismiss a former employee's lawsuit alleging violations of the FMLA, the ADA, and the FLSA. The Senator's Office moved to dismiss the suit based on a claim of immunity under the Constitution's *Speech or Debate Clause*. The Supreme Court found that the Federal Circuit's decision did not constitute a "ruling upon the constitutionality" of any provision of the Congressional Accountability Act. The district courts minute order denying the motion to dismiss did not state any grounds for decision. Therefore, that order "[was] not a constitutional holding." The Court of Appeals' opinion rejected the appellant's argument that forcing Senator Dayton to defend against the allegations would necessarily contravene the *Speech or Debate Clause*, although it leaves open the possibility that the *Speech or Debate Clause* may limit the scope of the proceedings in some respects. The Supreme Court found that "[n]either of those holdings qualifies as a ruling on the validity of the Act itself." The Supreme Court rejected the argument advanced by the Senator that the Court of Appeals' decision amounts to a ruling that the CAA is constitutional as applied.

d. Settlements

Any settlement entered into by the parties through a process described in § 401 (2 USC 1401) must be in writing and does not become effective unless it is approved by the Office Executive Director. 2 USC 1414. The processes described in § 401 are counseling, mediation, an administrative appeal on the conclusion of mediation, or a civil action, and judicial review of such actions. *See* 2 USC 1401. Such process also applies to FMLA claims.

e. Confidentiality

The CAA provides rules of confidentiality that are applicable to the various processes for enforcement of the Act. 2 USC 1416. They are:

(a) Counseling.—All counseling shall be strictly confidential, except that the Office and a covered employee may agree to notify the employing office of the allegations.

(b) Mediation.—All mediation shall be strictly confidential.

(c) Hearings and Deliberations.—Except as provided in Subsections (d), (e), and (f), all proceedings and deliberations of hearing officers and the Board, including any related records, shall be confidential. This Subsection shall not apply to proceedings under Section 215, but shall apply to deliberations of hearing officers and the Board under that section.

(d) Release of Records for Judicial Action.—The records of hearing officers and the Board may be made public if required for the purpose of judicial review under Section 407.

(e) Access by Committees of Congress.—At the discretion of the Executive Director, the Executive Director may provide to the Committee on Standards of Official Conduct of the House of Representatives and the Select Committee on Ethics of the Senate access to the records of the hearings and decisions of the hearing officers and the Board, including all written and oral testimony in the possession of the Office. The Executive Director shall not provide such access until the Executive Director has consulted with the individual filing the complaint at issue, and until a final decision has been entered under Section 405(g) or Section 406(e).

(f) Final Decisions.—A final decision entered under Section 405(g) or Section 406(e) shall be made public if it is in favor of the complaining covered employee, or in favor of the charging party under Section 210, or if the decision reverses a decision of a hearing officer which had been in favor of the covered employee or charging party. The Board may make public any other decision at its discretion.

Section 405(g) of the CAA, 2 USC 1405(g), is a final decision of a hearing officer. Section 406(e), 2 USC 406(e), is a final decision of the Office Board of Directors. Section 210 of the CAA, 2 USC 1331, involves public accommodation or persons with disabilities, not the FMLA.

f. Savings Provisions

The savings provisions of the CAA address the treatment of claims that existed before the effective date of the Act and/or the opening of the Office for receipt of counseling or mediation requests. The savings provisions are divided into those applying for employees of the House of Representatives and Senate, and employees of the Architect of the Capitol. These two parts are, in turn, divided into claims arising before the effective date of § 201 of the CAA, and those arising between the effective date and the opening of the Office. Section 506 of the CAA, 2 USC 1435, sets forth the treatment of these claims. The reader is advised that these provisions should be consulted if the claim at issue arose prior to approximately January 1996.

D. PEOAA

1. Introduction

The enforcement rights of employees covered by the PEOAA are similar to, although by no means identical to, the rights of employees covered by the CAA. Administrative remedies in the form of counseling and mediation must be exhausted before an employee may initiate an administrative appeal or a civil action in federal court.

A review of the PEOAA enforcement procedures follows.

2. Complaint Procedure

a. Overview

The procedures (3 USC 451) for consideration of alleged violations of the PEOAA consists of:

Counseling and mediation as provided in § 452; and

Election, as provided in § 453, of either:

an administrative proceeding as provided in § 453(1) and judicial review as provided in § 1296 of Title 28; or

a civil action in a district court of the United States as provide in § 1346(g) of Title 28.

The basic structure is similar to the enforcement process for the CAA. There is an administrative exhaustion requirement of counseling and mediation. Following the required administrative exhaustion, the covered employee has a right to elect between an administrative process (with judicial review), or to proceed directly to federal court.

Note that only a "covered employee" has the right to enforce PEOAA rights, including FMLA rights. A "covered employee" is a defined term that means an employee (including an applicant for employment and a former employee) of an employing office. 3 USC 401(a)(2)–(3). The term "employing office" is defined (3 USC 401(a)(4)) as:

each office, agency, or other component of the Executive Office of the President;

the Executive Residence at the White House; and

the official residence (temporary or otherwise) of the Vice President.

Additionally, for purposes of the FMLA, a "covered employee" must also be an "eligible employee," as that term is defined by the PEOAA FMLA regulations. 3 USC 401(b)(2), 412(a)(2)(B).

b. Exclusive Procedure

Generally, no person may commence an administrative or judicial proceeding to seek a remedy for rights and protections afforded by the PEOAA except as provided in this chapter and in §§ 1296 and 1346(g) of Chapter 179 of Title 28. 3 USC 435(d)(1). Sections 1296 and 1346(g) of Title 28 (28 USC 1296, 1346(g)) address the right of a covered employee to judicial review of PEOAA FMLA claims.

The one exception to the general rule allows a covered veteran employee under § 416 (3 USC 416) to also use any provisions of Chapter 43 of the title applicable to the employee. 3 USC 435(d)(2). Section 416 of the PEOAA addresses the rights and protections relating to veterans' employment and reemployment. 3 USC 416.

As the exclusive procedure, employees covered by the PEOAA are precluded from enforcing their FMLA rights in any other forum, or by any other means. If a PEOAA covered employee were to attempt to enforce FMLA rights in another forum, the employing office would likely move for dismissal of the claim citing this section and the doctrine of sovereign immunity. Similarly, a covered employee who attempted to vindicate his or her PEOAA FMLA rights by filing a federal civil court action outside of the exclusive means of enforcement provided by the PEOAA will likely have the case summarily dismissed.

3. Counseling and Mediation

a. General Rule

The President, or the designee of the President, shall by regulation establish procedures substantially similar to those under §§ 402 and 403 of the Congressional Accountability Act of 1995 for the counseling and mediation of alleged violations of a law made applicable by the PEOAA, such as the FMLA. 3 USC 452(a).

All counseling and mediation required by the PEOAA is strictly confidential. 3 USC 456(a)–(b). Regarding counseling only, with the consent of the parties, the employing office may be notified of the counseling. 3 USC 456(a).

b. Exhaustion Requirement

A covered employee who has not exhausted counseling and mediation under the PEOAA is ineligible to make any election under § 453 or otherwise pursue any further form of relief under the PEOAA. 3 USC 452(a).

4. Election of Proceedings

Pursuant to § 453 of the PEOAA, 3 USC 453, a covered employee, no later than 90 days after a covered employee receives a notice of the end of the period of mediation, but no sooner than 30 days after receipt of such notification, may either—

> file a complaint with the appropriate agency, as determined under § 454; or

> file a civil action under § 1346(g) of Title 28.

The election to proceed administratively or by filing a civil action is comparable to the election provided by the CAA. However, as set forth more fully below, the similarities end here.

5. Election of Administrative Appeal

a. General Rule

The MSPB is the agency that will adjudicate an employee's claim that an employing office violated the FMLA. 3 USC 454(a). The complaint in an action involving a violation of the FMLA (as applied by the PEOAA) "shall be processed under the procedures specified by the President, or the designee of the President, in such regulations as the President or designee may issue." 3 USC 454(a).

b. Exceptions

An exception to the general rule addresses claims of discrimination under §§ 411 and 417 of the PEOAA (3 USC 411 and 417). 3 USC 454(b)(1)–(2). As these sections do not address the FMLA they will not be discussed any further.

c. MSPB Consideration of Appeal

Where a covered employee has elected to appeal his or her FMLA claim to the MSPB following counseling and mediation, if the President, or the designee of the President, has not issued a regulation on a matter for which this chapter requires a regulation to be issued, the MSPB must apply, to the extent necessary and appropriate, the most relevant substantive executive agency regulation promulgated to implement the statutory provision at issue in the proceeding.

In this case, regulations implementing the FMLA for purposes of the PEOAA have not been issued. Since the PEOAA incorporates specific sections of Title I of the Act, the DOL regulations implementing those regulations should be the most relevant substantive executive agency regulations relied upon by the MSPB to implement the FMLA for purposes of the PEOAA. *See* 3 USC 412(a)(1) (incorporating specified sections of Title I of the FMLA into the PEOAA).

d. Judicial Review

A party aggrieved by a final decision of the MSPB regarding a PEOAA FMLA claim may petition the United States Court of Appeals for the Federal Circuit for review. 28 USC 1296(a)(1). Such petition must be filed within 30 days after the date that the petitioner receives notice of the final MSPB decision. 28 USC 1296(b). Absent further limitation, it would appear that a covered employee or employing office could file a petition for review with the United States Court of Appeals for the Federal Circuit.

In any proceeding under § 1296 of Title 28 (28 USC 1296), if the President, the designee of the President, or the Federal Labor Relations Authority has not issued a regulation on a matter for which Chapter 5 of Title 3 requires a regulation to be issued, the court shall apply, to the extent necessary and appropriate, the most relevant substantive executive agency regulation promulgated to implement the statutory provision at issue in the proceeding. 28 USC 3903.

Neither the President, or a designee of the President, nor the FLRA has issued regulations implementing the FMLA for purposes of the PEOAA. The PEOAA, however, has incorporated specific sections of Title I of the FMLA into the PEOAA. 3 USC 412(a)(1). As such, the regulations implementing these provisions would appear to be the most relevant substantive executive agency regulations that a court should apply.

6. Election to File Civil Action

a. General Rule

After completion of counseling and mediation, a covered employee may elect to file a civil action under § 1346(g) of Title 28, 28 USC 1346(g). Section 1346(g) of Title 28 vests exclusive jurisdiction in the federal district courts, subject to the provisions of Chapter 179, over any civil action commenced by a covered employee under § 453(2) of Title 3, 3 USC 453(2). 28 USC 1346(g). That would include PEOAA FMLA claims. The covered employee must file a civil action no later than 90 days after the covered employee receives notice of the end of the period of mediation, but no sooner than 30 days after receipt of such notice. 3 USC 453.

In a PEOAA FMLA action under § 1346(g) of Title 28 (28 USC 1346(g)), the defendant is the employing office alleged to have committed the violation involved. 28 USC 3901(a).

b. Venue

Pursuant to 28 USC 1413, a civil action under § 1346(g) of Title 28 (28 USC 1346(g)) may be brought in either:

The United States District Court for the district in which the employee is employed; or

In the United States District Court for the District of Columbia.

c. Jury Trials

Where a covered employee makes a timely election after counseling and mediation to initiate a civil action in an appropriate federal district court, the covered employee or the employing office may demand a jury trial where a jury trial is available in an action against a private defendant under the relevant law made applicable by Chapter 5 of Title 3 (which includes the FMLA). 28 USC 3901(b). Title I has been interpreted by the courts as providing a jury trial. As such, jury trials should be available to PEOAA employees alleging violations of the FMLA.

d. Effect of Failure to Issue Regulations

In any proceeding under § 1346(g) of Title 28 (28 USC 1346(g)), if the President, the designee of the President, or the Federal Labor Relations Authority has not issued a regulation on a matter for which Chapter 5 of Title 3 requires a regulation to be issued, the court shall apply, to the extent necessary and appropriate, the most relevant substantive executive agency regulation promulgated to implement the statutory provision at issue in the proceeding. 28 USC 3903.

Neither the President, or a designee of the President, nor the FLRA has issued regulations implementing the FMLA for purposes of the PEOAA. The PEOAA, however, has incorporated specific sections of Title I of the FMLA into the PEOAA. 3 USC 412(a)(1). As such, the regulations implementing these provisions would appear to be the most relevant substantive executive agency regulations that a court should apply.

7. Miscellaneous PEOAA Enforcement Provisions

a. Judicial Review of PEOAA Regulations

As the PEOAA has not issued regulations implementing the FMLA, this provision is not yet relevant for purposes of the FMLA. In the event regulations are issued implementing the FMLA for purposes of the PEOAA, the Statute (28 USC 3902) provides the following regarding judicial review of the validity of such regulations:

> In any proceeding under Section 1296 or Section 1346(g) of this Title (28 USC 1296, 1346(g)) in which the application of a regulation issued under Chapter 5 of Title 3 is at issue, the court may review the validity of the regulation in accordance with the provisions of Subparagraphs (A) through (D) of Section 706(2) of Title 5. If the court determines that the regulation is invalid, the court shall apply, to the extent necessary and appropriate, the most relevant substantive executive agency regulation promulgated to implement those statutory provisions with respect to which invalid regulation was issued. Except as provided in this section, the validity of regulations issued under this Chapter is not subject to judicial review.

b. Expedited Supreme Court Review of Certain Appeals

An appeal may be taken directly to the Supreme Court of the United States from any interlocutory or final judgment, decree, or order of a court upon the constitutionality of any provision of Chapter 5 of Title 3. 28 USC 3904(a). That would include PEOAA FMLA rights.

The Supreme Court "shall, if it has not previously ruled on the question, accept jurisdiction over such an appeal, advance the appeal on the docket, and expedite the appeal to the greatest extent possible." 28 USC 3904(b).

IV. REMEDIES

The remedies available for redress of unlawful conduct in violation of the FMLA differ substantially under the four federal sector variants of the FMLA.

A. TITLE I

1. Introduction

Title I of the FMLA provides for two alternative forms of damages for actual monetary losses suffered by an eligible employee as a result of the unlawful actions of a covered federal employer. The Act also provides for interest on such damages, and attorney fees and costs. Finally, the Act permits an award of equitable relief, such as employment, reinstatement, and promotions, that may have been illegally denied in violation of the FMLA.

2. Damages

An aggrieved eligible employee or the Secretary of Labor may bring a civil action for damages for an employer that has engaged in prohibited acts in violation of § 105 (29 USC 2615) of Title I of the FMLA. 29 USC 2617(a), (b)(2).

a. Lost Wages, Salary, Employment Benefits, and Other Compensation

(1) General Rule

If a covered employer violates the prohibited acts provisions of § 105 of Title I of the FMLA (29 USC 2615), the Act allows any eligible employee affected to recover damages equal to: "Any wages salary, employment benefit, or other compensation denied or lost to such employee by reason of the violation." 29 USC 2617(a)(1)(A)(i)(I); *see also Rodgers v. City of Des Moines*, 435 F.3d 904, 909 (8th Cir. 2006); *Beeber v. Williams College*, 430 F. Supp. 2d 18, 22 (D. Mass. 2006); 29 CFR 825.400(c).

An employee must suffer a tangible loss of wages, salary, employment benefits or other compensation in order to be entitled to damages for unlawful conduct in violation of the FMLA. 29 CFR 825.400(c). *See Coker v. McFaul*, No. 06-3587, 2007 U.S. App. LEXIS 16565, at *17, 2007 Fed. Appx. 0466N (6th Cir. June 29, 2007); *Roberson v. Game Stop, Inc.*, No. 3:03-CV-2816-H, 2005 U.S. Dist. LEXIS 858, at *12 (N.D. Tex. Jan. 20, 2005); *Sheaffer v. County of Chatham*, No. 337 F. Supp. 2d 709 (M.D.N.C. 2004) (dismissing request for damages that exceeds the permissible scope of the FMLA); *Bila v. RadioShack Corp.*, No. 03-10177-BC, 2004 U.S. Dist. LEXIS 24649, at *39 (E.D. Mich. Nov. 23, 2004); *Ghattas Trust v. Unumprovident Life Ins.*, No. 1:03cv1614A (JCC), 2004 U.S. Dist. LEXIS 26753, at *33 (E.D. Va. Oct. 5, 2004); *Roberts v. Owens-Illinois, Inc.*, No. 2:02-cv-207-LJM-WGH, 2004 U.S. Dist. LEXIS 8534, at *25 (S.D. Ind. May 14, 2004); *Carlsen v. Green Thumb, Inc.*, No. 01-2076 (JRT/RLE), 2004 U.S. Dist. LEXIS 12497, at *11 (D. Minn. May 21, 2004); *Dillaway v. Ferrante*, No. 02-715 (JRT/JSM), 2003 U.S. Dist. LEXIS 23468, at *27 (D. Minn. Dec. 9, 2003); *Coleman v. Potomac Electric Power Co.*, 281 F. Supp. 2d 250, 254 (D.D.C. 2003). In *Roberts v. Owens-Illinois, Inc.*, No. 2:02-cv-207-LJM-WGH, 2004 U.S. Dist. LEXIS 8534, at *25 (S.D. Ind. May 14, 2004), the court found that plaintiff failed to state a claim for relief for violation of the FMLA because she suffered no actual monetary losses. In that case, the employer reinstated the employee with back pay and paid for her medical expenses until the date she returned to work.

The legislative history indicates that the "relief provided in FMLA also parallels the provisions of the FLSA." S.103-3, p. 35.

(2) Key Terms

(a) Eligible Employee

Damages for lost wages, salary, employment benefits, other compensation are only available to an "eligible employee." *Morrison v. Amway Corp. et al.*, 323 F.3d 920, 927 (11th Cir. 2003) (eligible employee status under the FMLA is a threshold jurisdictional question that also appears to be a *prima facie* element for recovery); *Smith v. Virgin Islands Port Authority*, No. 2002-227, 2005 U.S. Dist. LEXIS 5, at *34 (D.V.I. Jan. 2, 2005); *Keen v. Brown*, 958 F. Supp. 70, 72 (D. Ct. 1997) (enforcement remedies in Title I apply only to "eligible employees"). An "eligible employee" is a defined term requiring the individual to meet three requirements involving length of service with the federal employer, the working of a minimum number of hours preceding the commencement of FMLA leave, and working at a worksite with a minimum number of employees within a specified geographic area. 29 USC 2611(2); 29 CFR 825.110, 825.111. [Employee eligibility is addressed more fully in Chapter 5, "Employee Eligibility for Leave."]

The limitation of the availability of damages to eligible employees is in contrast to the broader language used to describe those protected against employer actions prohibited by the Act, as well as who can file an administrative complaint with the DOL or file a civil action. The Act and implementing regulations extend the prohibited acts provisions of the FMLA to any "person" or "individual." *See* 29 USC 2615(a)(3), (b); 29 CFR 825.220(a)(2), (3). The DOL is empowered to accept and investigate complaints of unlawful FMLA practices from "employees." 29 CFR 825.400(a)(1). Indeed, the DOL regulations indicate that an "employee" is entitled to file a civil action for violation of the FMLA. 29 CFR 825.400(a)(2).

For all practical purposes, since the right to obtain relief for an employer's violation of the FMLA is limited to "eligible employees," only "eligible employees" are protected from unlawful employer conduct under the Act.

(b) Wages and Salary

Neither the statute nor the DOL regulations define "wages" or "salary." As commonly understood, "wages" means the receipt of payment for labor or other services rendered in the employment context. *See* Merriam Webster's Ninth New Collegiate Dictionary (Merriam-Webster, Inc. 1988). "Salary" is defined as fixed compensation for regularly paid for services. *See* Merriam Webster's Ninth New Collegiate Dictionary (Merriam-Webster, Inc. 1988). Clearly, "wages" and "salary" refer to compensation within an employment relationship.

(c) Employment Benefits

The term "employment benefits" is defined in the Statute and regulations. It means all benefits provided or made available to employees by an employer, including group life insurance, health insurance, disability insurance, sick leave, annual leave, educational benefits, and pensions, regardless of whether such benefits are provided by a practice or written policy of an employer or through an "employee benefit plan." 29 USC 2611(5); 29 CFR 825.800 (definition of "employment benefits"). The term does not include non-employment related obligations paid by employees through voluntary deductions such as supplemental insurance. 29 CFR 825.800 (definition of "employment benefits").

In *Herman v. Princeton City School*, No. 1-C-96-358, 1997 U.S. Dist. LEXIS 22250 (S.D. Ohio Sept. 23, 1997), the court ordered the employer to reimburse the employee for the employer's portion of the health plan premium payments that the employees were required to make during FMLA leave.

Again, as suggested by the term itself, "employment benefits" arises out of an employment relationship.

(d) Other Compensation

The term "other compensation" is not defined by the Statute or the DOL implementing regulations. The term "other" is certainly vague and susceptible to broad interpretation. However, application of basic cannons of statutory construction suggest that "other compensation" has a more limited meaning. As explained in Kelly N. Honohan, *Note: Remedying the Liability Limitation Under the Family and Medical Leave Act*, 70 B.U. L. Rev. 1043 (October, 1999):

> Employing the canon of statutory construction *ejusdem generis*, when a general phrase—e.g., "other compensation"—follows in a series of specific terms—e.g., "wages, salary, and employment benefits"—the general phrase should be construed as referring to matters similar to those more specific terms.

Additionally, the rule of *noscitur a sociis* provides that a word in a Statute should be defined in light of the words with which it is associated. *Nero v. Industrial Modling Corp.*, 167 F.3d 921, 930 (5th Cir. 1999); Kelly N. Honohan, *Note: Remedying the Liability Limitation Under the Family and Medical Leave Act*, 70 B.U. L. Rev. 1043 (October, 1999), n.72 (citing *Jarrecki v. G.D. Searle & Co.*, 367 U.S. 303, 307 (1961)).

Applying these doctrines of statutory construction, "other compensation" should be construed to mean economic benefits, like wages, salary, or employment benefits, resulting or arising out of an employment relationship. *See* Kelly N. Honohan, *Note: Remedying the Liability Limitation Under the Family and Medical Leave Act*, 70 B.U. L. Rev. 1043, 1054 (October, 1999).

The majority of courts that have addressed the meaning of "other compensation" have followed the cannons of statutory construction and required that the "other compensation" lost as a result of unlawful conduct required a *quid pro quo* exchange between the employees and their employers. *See Nero v. Industrial Modling Corp.*, 167 F.3d 921, 930 (5th Cir. 1999) ("other compensation" does not include consequential damages, such as out-of-pocket expenses for moving and job search); *Barrilleaux v. Thayer Lodging Group, Inc.*, No. 97-3252 § E/5, 1998 U.S. Dist. LEXIS 14597, at *3 (E.D. La. Sept. 11, 1998) (child care and parental care costs not included in "other compensation" where an employee is claiming lost wages, salary and benefits); *Dawson v. Leewood Nursing Home, Inc.*, 14 F. Supp. 2d 828, 833 (E.D. Va. 1998); *Lloyd v. Wyoming Valley Health Care Sys., Inc.*, 994 F. Supp 288, 291 (M.D. Pa. 1998); *McAnnally v. Wyn South Molded Prods., Inc.*, 912 F. Supp. 512, 513 (N.D. Ala. 1996).

Damages for emotional distress have been rejected as a form of "other compensation." *Lloyd v. Wyoming Valley Health Care Sys., Inc.*, 994 F. Supp. 288, 291 (M.D. Pa. 1998) (court rejected the plaintiff's argument that "other compensation" should be interpreted to include damages for emotional distress).

(e) Forms of Wages, Salary, Employment Benefits, and Other Compensation

i) Back Pay

Of course, in order to recover back pay and interest on back pay, the employer's violation of the FMLA must have been the cause for the loss of wages. In *Tornberg v. Business Interlink Service, Inc.*, 237 F. Supp. 2d 778, 789 (E.D. Mich. 2002), the court declined to award the employee damages for lost wages where the employer's violation, failure to pay the employer's share of premiums and cancellation of his medical coverage, did not cause the plaintiff's lost wages. The FMLA violation did not involve the employee's termination or the refusal of the employer to reinstate the employee on the conclusion of FMLA leave. Rather, the three weeks of lost wages claimed by the employee resulted from his resigning and finding a new job.

The calculation of back wages was described in *Mummert v. Vencor, Inc. et al.*, 21 Fed. Appx. 710 (9th Cir. 2001). There, the court found that back wages were the difference between what the employee would have earned and what the employee did earn once the employee found substitute employment at the same rate of pay, regardless of the length of the underlining ordered leave. The employer had argued that, since it could have fired the employee after the 10-day FMLA leave period, the back wages should only be for the 10 days of leave.

An award of back pay need not include the period of time the employee was on FMLA leave, which is unpaid. *Barrilleaux v. Thayer Lodging Group, Inc.*, No. 97-3252 § E/5, 1998 U.S. Dist. LEXIS 14597, at *7 (E.D. La. Sept. 11, 1998); *see, e.g., Smith v. Diffee Ford-Lincoln-Mercury, Inc.*, 298 F.3d 955, 962 (10th Cir. 2002) (damages limited to benefits the employee would have received had the employer not interfered with her right to reinstatement following FMLA leave).

Events subsequent to an employer's unlawful FMLA conduct may serve to cut off an employer's liability to an employee for back pay. For example, a valid discharge subsequent to a discriminatory act has been held to cut off an employer's liability for back pay arising out of the unlawful FMLA conduct occurring prior to the discharge. *Hite v. Biomet, Inc.*, 53 F. Supp. 2d 1013, 1025-26 (N.D. Ind. 1999). According to the court, "[t]his is logical because the valid termination of an employee severs the employment relationship and the obligations which compose such a relationship. In this way, the employer's liability is limited since the valid termination is, essentially, a superseding cause which relieves it from further liability for back pay awards." *Id.* (citations omitted); *see Lapham v. Vanguard Cellular Systems, Inc.*, 102 F. Supp. 2d 266 (M.D. Pa. 2000) (same).

The rejection of an employer's unconditional job offer generally ends the accrual of back pay damages. *Barrilleaux v. Thayer Lodging Group, Inc.*, No. 97-3252 § E/5, 1998 U.S. Dist. LEXIS 14597, at *7 (E.D. La. Sept. 11, 1998) (citing *Ford Motor Co. v. EEOC*, 458 U.S. 219, 241, 102 S. Ct. 3057, 3070, 73 L. Ed. 2d 721 (1982)). The court in *Barrilleaux* reasoned that, while Ford considered the matter in terms of Title II, there was no reason that the analysis would not apply to the FMLA. A number of courts have created an exception for "special circumstances." *Barrilleaux v. Thayer Lodging Group, Inc.*, No. 97-3252 § E/5, 1998 U.S. Dist. LEXIS 14597, at *7. Numerous courts have concluded that a plaintiff's reasonable rejection of an offer of reinstatement is such a "special circumstance." *Id.* (citing *Pierce v. F.R. Tripler & Co.*, 955 F.2d 820 (2d Cir. 1992); *Graefenhain v. Pabst Brewing Co.*, 870 F.2d 1198, 1203 (7th Cir. 1989), *Taylor v. Teletype Corp.*, 648 F.2d 1129, 1139 (8th Cir.), *cert. denied*, 454 U.S. 969, 102 S. Ct. 515, 70 L. Ed. 2d 386 (1981); *Lewis v. Federal Prison Indus., Inc.*, 953 F.2d 1277, 1279 (11th Cir. 1992)). The court in *Barrilleaux* found that the reasonableness of the employee's rejection of the offer was a matter for the trier of fact. *Id.* at *9.

Courts are split regarding whether an award of back pay under the FMLA is subject to deductions for income taxes, social security, Medicare, and other similar withholdings. *Compare Longstreth v. Copple*, 101 F. Supp. 2d 776 (N.D. Iowa 2000) *with Churchill v. Star Enterprises*, 3 F. Supp. 2d 622, 624-25 (E.D. Pa. 1998), *aff'd on other grounds*, 183 F.3d 184 (3d Cir. 1999). In *Longstreth*, the defendants, the former employer and an individual manager of the employer, made an Offer of Judgment to the plaintiff. The offer was for $40,000. When it was accepted, the actual monetary amount paid was reduced by deductions for federal and state income taxes, and other deductions required by law. The employee filed a motion arguing that deductions should not have been made. Had the offer been made solely by the former employer, the court opined that deductions for federal and state taxes, etc., would have been required. *Longstreth*, 101 F. Supp. at 778. However, because the Offer did not include language indicating that the amount was for MCI wages, they were not. Moreover, because the offer came from two defendants, one offer did not pay wages but was only liable for damages, the court could not apportion the $40,000 for purposes of making deductions. As such, the court required that the Offer of Judgment be paid in full without deduction.

In *Churchill*, the court held that a jury verdict awarding damages in favor of the plaintiff "does not and cannot represent wages for services performed since [the plaintiff] performed none during the relevant time frame." Therefore, the court concluded, "no withholding is mandated under federal or state law." *Churchill*, 3 F. Supp. 2d at 624-25. In so holding, the court found that two IRS rulings holding that back pay payments to former employees for discrimination were considered "wages" subject to deductions contradicted the plain language of the FMLA. The court concluded that it must follow the language of the Statute.

ii) Overtime

In *Thorson v. Gemini, Inc. et al.*, 205 F.3d 370, 384 (8th Cir. 2000), *cert. denied*, 531 U.S. 871 (2000), the court rejected as "little more than guesswork" the plaintiff's claim that the district court erred when it excluded from the back pay award any amount for lost overtime hours. The plaintiff argued that, because he worked an average of sixty-five hours of overtime in 1992 and 1993, the court should have added 65 hours of overtime in the award of back pay for overtime the employee would have worked in each of the next four years. In deciding not to award the requested overtime hours, the court found that Thorson's claim that she would have worked had she remained with Gemini was speculative.

iii) Front Pay

As an equitable remedy, courts have awarded front pay to compensate employees for violations of the FMLA. *See Smith v. Diffe Ford-Lincoln-Mercury, Inc.*, 298 F.3d 955, 964 (10th Cir. 2002); *Nichols v. Ashland Hospital Corp. et al.*, 251 F.3d 496, 503-504 (4th Cir. 2001); *Thorson v. Gemini, Inc. et al.*, 205 F.3d 370 384 (8th Cir. 2000), *cert. denied*, 531 U.S. 871 (2000); *Cline v. Wal-Mart Stores, Inc.*, 144 F.3d 294, 307 (4th Cir. 1998). While back pay compensates the victim of discrimination for lost wages and benefits before trial, front pay is intended to compensate for loses after trial. *Smith v. Diffe Ford-Lincoln-Mercury, Inc.*, 298 F.3d 955, 964 (10th Cir. 2002); *Palma v. Pharmedica Communications, Inc.*, No. 3:00CV1128 (HBF), 2003 U.S. Dist. LEXIS 21227, at *2 (D. Conn. Sept. 30, 2003).

Reinstatement is generally the preferred equitable remedy over front pay because the latter can result in a windfall to a plaintiff. *See Nichols*, 251 F.3d 496; *Miller v. AT&T*, 83 F. Supp. 2d 700 (S.D. W.Va. 2000), *aff'd on other grounds*, 250 F.2d 820 (4th Cir. 2001) (front pay inappropriate where employee went back to school and, as a result, changed career goals); *McCoy v. Orleans Parish School Bd.*, No. 02-2510 Section "R" (3), 2004 U.S. Dist. LEXIS 6843, at *6 (E.D. La. April 19, 2004); *Palma*, 2003 U.S. Dist. LEXIS 21227, at *2 (the decision to award front pay is discretionary, and a request for front pay may be denied if the court finds that the back pay award is sufficient to make the plaintiff whole).

Generally, as an equitable remedy, the calculation and award of front pay is the responsibility of the court, not a jury. *See Taylor v. Invacare Corp.*, 64 Fed. Appx. 516 (6th Cir. 2003); *Smith v. Diffe Ford-Lincoln-Mercury, Inc.*, 298 F.3d 955, 964 (10th Cir. 2002); *Nichols*, 251 F.3d at 503-504; *Hardin v. Caterpillar, Inc.*, 227 F.3d 268, 269 (5th Cir. 2000); *Thorson*, 205 F.3d at 384; *Passauer v. Quest Diagnostics, Inc.*, No. CCB-03-159, 2004 U.S. Dist. LEXIS 6966, at *5 (D. Md. April 22, 2004); *Palma*, 2003 U.S. Dist. LEXIS 21227, at *16 (the award of front pay is in the sound discretion of the court).

Where, however, legal and equitable issues in the same case involve common issues of fact, such questions of fact are submitted to the jury, and the court in resolving equitable issues is then bound by the jury's findings. *Smith v. Diffe Ford-Lincoln-Mercury, Inc.*, 298 F.3d 955, 965 (10th Cir. 2002).

In order to qualify for front pay, a plaintiff must have been diligent in seeking comparable employment and under no circumstances can the award be based on speculation. *Palma*, 2003 U.S. Dist. LEXIS 21227, at *2. In *Palma*, the court found that front pay was not warranted where the plaintiff was made whole by an award of compensatory and liquidated damages in the amount of $280,000, and plaintiff did not seek other employment during the four years following her illegal termination.

Courts will not award front pay where the claims are too speculative. *See Thorson v. Gemini, Inc. et al.*, 205 F.3d 370, 384-85 (8th Cir. 2000), *cert. denied*, 531 U.S. 871 (2000). In *Thorson*, the plaintiff challenged the district court's award of front pay on several grounds. First, she claimed that front pay should have included one year's overtime pay and one year's profit sharing. *Thorson*, 205 F.3d at 384-85. The Eighth Circuit held that the district court did not abuse its discretion in not including amounts for overtime and profit sharing in the front pay award. These amounts were speculative and would require the court, in the case of profit sharing, to predict that the company would be profitable and the amount of profit sharing.

The court in *Thorson* also rejected the plaintiff's challenge to the period and the wage differential used by the district court for calculating front pay. The plaintiff argued that she should be entitled to front pay for 12 years instead of for one year. She also claimed that front pay should have been calculated based on a $2.12 per hour wage differential based on the last job she had before trial. The district court judge had set the wage differential at $ 0.96 for one year of straight time based on the job she held the longest between the discriminatory act and trial. *Thorson*, 205 F.3d at 385. The Eighth Circuit agreed with the trial court, finding that the job used by the trial court was more like the one she had with Gemini than the last job she held for a week with the larger pay differential. The court also credited the trial judge's calculation that the plaintiff's salary at that comparison job would have matched her salary at Gemini within a year if she had not voluntarily left the position.

iv) Commissions

Commissions earned on sales while an employee is on FMLA leave is a form of "other compensation" recoverable as damages pursuant to 29 USC 2617(a)(1)(A)(i)(I). *Estes v. Meridian One Corporation, et. al.*, 6 Fed. Appx. 142 (4th Cir. 2001).

v) Bonuses

In *Dierlam v. Wesley Jessen Corp.*, 222 F. Supp. 2d 1052, 1056–57 (N.D. Ill. 2002), the court awarded as damages an amount equivalent to a "stay bonus" provided to employees who remained employed and actively working for the company for a one-year period of time during which ownership of the employer was in transition. The plaintiff stayed, but took 12 weeks of approved FMLA leave during the one-year bonus period. The company prorated the bonus to reflect the employee's 12-week FMLA leave absence. The employee sued, alleging that the reduction in the bonus violated the FMLA. In agreement, the court found that the "stay bonus" was like a bonus for perfect attendance or safety that did not require performance by the employee but rather contemplated the absence of occurrences. *Dierlam*, 222 F. Supp. 2d at 1056 (*citing* 29 CFR 215(c)). "As such, [Section] 825.215(c) makes the stay bonus one for which Dierlam may not be disqualified, either partially or wholly, for the taking of FMLA leave." *Dierlam*, 222 F. Supp. at 1057. The court concluded that the plaintiff was entitled to the full amount of the stay bonus, plus interest, attorney fees and costs. *Id.*

vi) Profit Sharing

Damages for lost profit sharing have been held to be recoverable as damages for violations of the FMLA. In *Thorson v. Gemini, Inc. et al.*, 205 F.3d 370, 384–85 (8th Cir. 2000), *cert. denied*, 531 U.S. 871 (2000), the court awarded amounts for lost profit sharing as part of the back pay award. The court declined to award future amounts for lost profit sharing as part of the front pay award as too speculative.

vii) Benefits

Employers who have failed to pay the employer's share of premium payments during an employee's FMLA leave have been required to pay as damages the amount of the premium payments made by the employee. *See Herman v. Princeton City School*, No. 1–C–96–358, 1997 U.S. Dist. LEXIS 22250 (S.D. Ohio Sept. 23, 1997) (the employer was required to reimburse the amount of the employer's share of premium payments the employer required each employee to make during FMLA leave).

In *Tornberg v. Business Interlink Service, Inc.*, 237 F. Supp. 2d 778, 789 (E.D. Mich. 2002), the court declined to award $ 729.30 in interest on the medical bills from the time they were incurred by the employee until the employer finally paid the employee. The court opined that payment of interest to the employee for medical bills that should have been paid, not to the employee, but to medical providers, would be a windfall.

Lost vacation time that an employee was forced to use as a result of the denial of FMLA leave arguably falls within the definition of "any wages, salary, employment benefits, or other compensation denied or lost to such employee by reason of a violation of the FMLA." *Carlsen v. Green Thumb, Inc.*, No. 01–2076 (JRT/RLE), 2004 U.S. Dist. LEXIS 12497, at *1 (D. Minn. May 21, 2004).

A very different result regarding vacation time was found in *Whitney v. Wal-Mart Stores, Inc.*, No. 03–65–P–H, 2004 U.S. Dist. LEXIS 5237, at *10 (D. Me. March 30, 2004). There, the employee's position required that he work from 48 to 52 hours a week. The employee's medical provider restricted plaintiff from working more than 40 hours a week with two consecutive days off. The medical provider subsequently increased that amount to 45 hours a week with two consecutive days off. Because he could not work the full hours of his position, plaintiff was not allowed to return to work. Plaintiff argued that Wal-Mart have been allowed him to hold his original position indefinitely by using FMLA leave and vacation leave for a period until he received a new 12 weeks of FMLA leave. He argued that he was entitled to damages for the hours over 45 per week until he was reinstated in his original job. The court disagreed. Notably, the court held that the FMLA does not require an employer to continue to employ a person in a particular position indefinitely after that individual becomes unable to work the full number of hours required. The court also rejected evidence supporting plaintiff's theory of damages because it was not disclosed during discovery.

(3) Punitive and Emotional Distress Damages

Title I of the FMLA is silent on the prevailing plaintiff's recovery of emotional or punitive damages. *Montgomery v. State of Maryland et al.*, 266 F.3d 334, 341 (4th Cir. 2001), *vacated and remanded on other grounds*, 535 U.S. 1075 (2002) ("The FMLA text nowhere provides, however, for recovery of damages for emotional distress"); *Beeber v. Williams College*, 430 F. Supp. 2d 18, 22 (D. Mass. 2006); *Hite v. Biomet, Inc.*, 53 F. Supp. 2d 1013, 1024, n.13 (N.D. Ind. 1999).

The FMLA does not provide for the recovery of emotional or punitive damages. *See Rodgers v. City of Des Moines*, 435 F.3d 904, 909 (8th Cir. 2006); *Brumbalough v. Camelot Care Ctrs., Inc.*, 427 F.3d 996, 1007 (6th Cir. 2005); *Montgomery v. State of Maryland et al.*, 266 F.3d 334, 341 (4th Cir. 2001) (consequential and emotional distress damages not recoverable under FMLA), *vacated and remanded on other grounds*, 535 U.S. 1075 (2002); *Graham v. State Farm Mut. Ins. Co.* 193 F.3d 1274, 1284 (11th Cir. 1999) (damages not recoverable for mental distress); *Nero v. Industrial Molding Corp.*, 167 F.3d 921, 930 (5th Cir. 1999) (damages for mental anguish not available under FMLA); *Beeber*, 430 F. Supp. 2d at 22; *Ammons–Lewis v. Metropolitan Water Reclamation District of Greater Chicago*, No. 03 C 0885, 2004 U.S. Dist. LEXIS 21917, at *26 (N.D. Ill. Nov. 1, 2004), *aff'd*, 488 F.3d 739 (7th Cir. 2007); *Sheaffer v. County of Chatham*, 337 F. Supp. 2d 709 (M.D.N.C. 2004); *Roberts v. Owens–Illinois, Inc.*, No. 2:02–cv–207–LJM–WGH, 2004 U.S. Dist. LEXIS 8534, at *25 (S.D. Ind. May 14, 2004); *Dillaway v. Ferrante*, No. 02–715 (JRT/JSM), 2003 U.S. Dist. LEXIS 23468, at *16 (D. Minn. Dec. 9, 2003); *Coleman v. Potomac Electric Power Co.*, 281 F. Supp. 2d 250, 254 (D.D.C. 2003); *Metzler v. Federal Home Loan Bank of Topeka*, No. 03–4024–SAC, 2003 U.S. Dist. LEXIS 17971, at *3 (D. Kan Sept. 10, 2003) (punitive damages, damages for pain and suffering, and unenumerated economic losses are not recoverable under the FMLA). The logic of the majority is clear: since the FMLA specifically lists the kinds of recovery available, all of which relate to actual monetary damages, the statute simply does not permit recovery for emotional distress. *Beeber*, 430 F. Supp. 2d at 22.

The Eighth Circuit originally held that emotional distress damages were available for violations of the FMLA. In *Duty v. Norton–Alcoa Proppants*, 293 F.3d 481, 496 (8th Cir. 2002), the court found that, pursuant to 29 USC 2617(a)(1)(A)(i)(I), the district court had properly instructed the jury to assess damages actually sustained by Duty, including lost wages and fringe benefits as well as compensation for "mental anguish, loss of dignity, and other intangible injuries." The court concluded that there was sufficient evidence in the record to support the jury's compensatory damages award, "including Duty's and his wife's testimony that Duty suffered emotionally after losing his job." *Id*. Relying on *Duty*, several district courts also allowed damages for emotional distress for violation of the FMLA. *See also Billings v. Cape Cod Child Dev. Program, Inc.*, 270 F. Supp. 2d 175 (D. Mass. 2003) (dismissing state claim for intentional infliction of emotional distress after finding FMLA allows recovery of emotional distress damages in FMLA termination cases); *Beyer v. Elkay Mfg. Col. et al.*, No. 97 C 50067, 1997 U.S. Dist. LEXIS 14459 (N.D. Ill. Sept. 19, 1997) (in dicta, court stated,"…FMLA allows for compensatory and punitive damages…"). The Eighth Circuit has since changed course, holding that "the reference to emotional distress damages in *Duty* is probably mistaken and not sound law." *Rodgers v. City of Des Moines*, 435 F.3d 904, 908 (8th Cir. 2006); *Beeber*, 430 F. Supp. 2d at 22.

The court in *Dillaway v. Ferrante*, No. 02–715 (JRT/JSM), 2003 U.S. Dist. LEXIS 23468, at *27 (D. Minn. Dec. 9, 2003), declined to find that emotional distress damages were available as "other compensation" for a violation of the FMLA. Dillaway relied on a decision of the Eighth Circuit in *Duty v. Norton–Alco Proppants*, 293 F.3d 481, 496 (8th Cir. 2002). The court found that plaintiff's reading of *Duty* as permitting emotional distress damages was not unreasonable. The court, however, found that *Duty* did not specifically find that emotional distress damages were available under the FMLA. Rather, those damages were available under another applicable statute. The court followed the majority of decisions finding that compensation for mental anguish is not available for FMLA violations.

b. Actual Monetary Losses Other Than Lost Wages, Salary, Employment Benefits, and Other Compensation

(1) General Rule

In a case in which wages, salary, employment benefits, or other compensation have not been denied or lost to the employee, an employer who violates § 105 is liable to any affected eligible employee for any actual monetary losses sustained by the employee as a direct result of the violation, such as the cost of providing care, up to a sum equal to 12 weeks of wages or salary for the employee. 29 USC 2617(a)(1)(A)(i)(II); 29 CFR 825.400(c); *see Rodgers v. City of Des Moines*, 435 F.3d 904, 909 (8th Cir. 2006); *Coleman v. Potomac Electric Power Co.*, 281 F. Supp. 2d 250, 254 (D.D.C. 2003);

Hite v. Biomet, Inc., 53 F. Supp. 2d 1013, 1024 (N.D. Ind. 1999); *Barrilleaux v. Thayer Lodging Group, Inc.*, No. 97–3252 § E/5, 1998 U.S. Dist. LEXIS 14597, at *3 (E.D. La. Sept. 11, 1998). Again, such damages only come into consideration where the employee is not claiming any lost wages, salary, or benefits as a result of the employer's FMLA violation. *Hite v. Biomet, Inc.*, 53 F. Supp. 2d 1013, 1024 (N.D. Ind. 1999); *Barrilleaux*, 1998 U.S. Dist. LEXIS 14597, at *3 (§ 2617 provides two separate avenues to recover damages. An employee claiming lost wages, salary, and benefits can only recover those damages, and not the non–wage/salary/benefits damages provided by § 2617(A)(i)(II)).

An employee does not have standing to bring an FMLA claim for injuries not resulting in lost salary, employment benefits, or other tangible benefits. *Roberson v. Game Stop, Inc.*, No. 3:03–CV–2816–H, 2005 U.S. Dist. LEXIS 858, at *12 (N.D. Tex. Jan. 20, 2005); *Ammons–Lewis v. Metropolitan Water Reclamation District of Greater Chicago*, No. 03 C 0885, 2004 U.S. Dist. LEXIS 21917, at *26 (N.D. Ill. Nov. 1, 2004), *aff'd*, 488 F.3d 739 (7th Cir. 2007); *Roberts v. Owens–Illinois, Inc.*, No. 2:02–cv–207–LJM–WGH, 2004 U.S. Dist. LEXIS 8534, at *25 (S.D. Ind. May 14, 2004); *Coleman v. Potomac Electric Power Co.*, 281 F. Supp. 2d 250, 254 (D.D.C. 2003) (recovery under the FMLA is unambiguously limited to actual monetary losses).

As an example, the Statute and regulations cite the cost of providing care incurred by the eligible employee who was denied leave, as the type of actual monetary loss (other than wages, salary, employment benefits, or other compensation) that an employee would be entitled to receive as damages, up to the cap of 12 weeks of wages or salary. *See* 29 USC 2617(a)(1)(A)(i)(II); 29 CFR 825.400(c).

(2) Key Terms

(a) Wages or Salary

The terms "wages" and "salary" are not defined by the Statute and regulations. As the remedial provisions of the FMLA are modeled after the FLSA, to the extent those terms are defined by the FLSA, those definitions should apply. Otherwise, the common dictionary understanding of "wages" or "salary" should suffice.

The absence of a definition for "wages" or salary" greatly impacts the ability to calculate the statutory cap on this type of damages. The cap on actual monetary losses suffered by an eligible employee is based on an employee's "wages" or "salary." Moreover, no time frame is given for such a calculation. The Statute does not provide that the 12–week wage/salary cap is calculated on the employee's average earnings over a defined period of time (e.g., 12 weeks, 6 months, or a year).

Moreover, the use of the term "or" may be problematic where an eligible employee's base salary is supplemented with various bonuses. Presumably, the Statute meant to include all employee wage or salary compensation as the basis for this calculation. Again, the use of the conjunctive "or" makes it appear that an employee with a base salary and other wages (e.g., bonuses) must make some sort of election for purposes of calculating the damage limit.

Note that the 12–week damage cap only includes the amount of "wages" or "salary." The value of employment benefits and "other compensation" is not included in the 12–week damage cap. The exclusion of these terms necessarily lowers the total amount of damages available to an employee for an employer's violation of the Act.

(b) Actual Monetary Loss

The phrase "actual monetary loss" is not defined or otherwise described, with the exception of the provision of the example of "the cost of providing care." Since, however, the loss must be both actual and monetary, it would appear that this provision would not include damages for emotional distress. Using the "cost of providing care" example as a guide, it would appear that an "actual monetary loss" is one that involves out–of–pocket expense to an employee.

(c) Direct Result

The Statute does not explain the term "direct result" for purposes of the actual monetary damages suffered by an eligible employee. Presumably, "direct result" means actual out of pocket expenses or indebtedness incurred by the employee as a result of the employer's unlawful actions. It is unclear how "indirect" an expense may become before it is no longer counted as an actual monetary loss sustained by the employee, for purposes of damages recoverable for an FMLA violation. For example, if an employer unlawfully denies an employee FMLA leave so that the employee must use insurance benefits to cover the cost of care, if insurance premiums increase because of that use, it is unclear if the premium increase is an "actual monetary loss" suffered by an employee recoverable as damages.

Out-of-pocket medical expenses incurred by an employee whose health benefits were cut off during the medical leave of absence she was required to take after being denied FMLA leave were not recoverable where the employee would have lost insurance coverage if she were granted FMLA leave anyway. *Ammons-Lewis v. Metropolitan Water Reclamation District of Greater Chicago*, No. 03 C 0885, 2004 U.S. Dist. LEXIS 21917, at *26 (N.D. III. Nov. 1, 2004), *aff'd*, 488 F.3d 739 (7th Cir. 2007).

In *Coleman v. Potomac Electric Power Co.*, 281 F. Supp. 2d 250, 254 (D.D.C. 2003), the court rejected plaintiff's argument that he was entitled to overtime losses as such losses were not due to the FMLA violation, but by other alleged wrongdoing on the part of the employer which was being pursued by the union in the grievance procedure.

Similarly, if an eligible employee is unlawfully denied FMLA leave, and the employee suffers emotional distress because of such denial (e.g., the leave was to care for an ill parent who died before the employee could get there), it is unclear whether medical expenses incurred for psychological care incurred by the employee would be considered to be a "direct result" of the unlawful conduct.

By comparison, damages for lost wages, salary, employment benefits, or other compensation does not have the "direct result" component. Presumably, such damages may be a direct or indirect result of the unlawful conduct of the employer.

Again, as the FLSA was used as a guide for the remedial provisions of Tile I, to the extent these terms have been interpreted for purposes of the FLSA, they should be consulted for purposes of the remedial provisions of Title I of the FMLA.

(3) The Problem of Requiring Actual Monetary Losses

The requirement that an eligible employee suffer actual losses, whether in the form of lost wages, salary, employment benefits, or other compensation, or in actual monetary losses other than lost wages, salary, etc., has been criticized as all too frequently allowing employers to engage in unlawful conduct without consequence. *See* Kelly N. Hoonah, *Note: Remedying the Liability Limitation Under the Family and Medical Leave Act*, 79 B.U. L. Rev. 1043 (October, 1999). The issue was summarized in the *Note Id.* at 1049) as follows:

> While some employees may successfully recover lost wages or salary under the Act's provisions, other employee's appearing to fall within the Act's ambit may nevertheless be ineligible for relief. If the FMLA provides a remedy only when an individual sustains a covered loss, then the employee who is entitled to take leave but whose request is denied may have no remedy under the FMLA. Similarly, the employee who takes leave but encounters discrimination upon returning to work may have no remedy, as the employee may not have lost any wages, salary, or employment benefits. The Statute provides that employees can recover "any actual monetary losses sustained…such as the cost of providing care." But what about employees who have not incurred such costs? Like employees who sustain actual monetary losses, these employees appear to have suffered a violation of their rights. They would fail to qualify for a remedy under the Act, however, unless they quit or took leave without permission and sued for back pay, or unless their employers fired them for taking leave. Many employees would likely choose to avoid these consequences.

The Note found that the lack of a remedy in situation where the employee was denied FMLA rights but did not suffer actual damages ran counter to the purpose of the Act to provide eligible employees the right to balance the demands of the workplace with the needs of families by entitling employees to take reasonable, protected leave. 79 B.U. L. Rev. at 1064–65. The Note recommended that the FMLA be amended to allow for actual and emotional distress damages to ensure employer compliance with the FMLA. *Id.*

c. Prejudgment Interest

To the award of covered damages, an eligible employee is also entitled to receive interest calculated at the prevailing rate. 29 USC 2617(a)(1)(A)(ii), 2617(b)(2); 29 CFR 825.400(c); *see Smith v. Diffee Ford-Lincoln-Mercury, Inc.*, 298 F.3d 955, 964 (10th Cir. 2002); *Coleman v. Potomac Electric Power Co.*, 281 F. Supp. 2d 250, 254 (D.D.C. 2003); *Rice v. Sunrise Express, Inc.*, 237 F. Supp. 2d 962, 969–971 (N.D. Ind. 2002); *Johnson v. Honda of America Mfg., Inc.*, 221 F. Supp. 2d 853, 858 (S.D.

Ohio 2002); *Herman v. Princeton City School*, No. 1–C–96–358, 1997 U.S. Dist. LEXIS 22250 (S.D. Ohio Sept. 23, 1997) (interest on award at prevailing rate); *Hite v. Biomet, Inc.*, 53 F. Supp. 2d 1013, 1024 (N.D. Ind. 1999) (prejudgment interest available).

The award of prejudgment interest to a prevailing plaintiff is mandatory. *Bella v. Lasorda Buick Pontiac Chevrolet, Inc. et al.*, No. 00–Civ. 5207 (JCF), 2002 U.S. Dist. LEXIS 9358, at *38 (S.D.N.Y. May 28, 2002). A prevailing party who was only awarded nominal damages is entitled to prejudgment interest. *McDonnell v. Miller Oil Co.*, 134 F.3d 638, 640 (4th Cir. 1998).

Absent a showing of actual monetary losses, the employee is not entitled to prejudgment interest. *Coleman v. Potomac Electric Power Co.*, 281 F. Supp. 2d 250, 254 (D.D.C. 2003).

Neither the Statute nor the regulations identify how the prevailing rate of interest is calculated. *Rice v. Sunrise Express, Inc.*, 237 F. Supp. 2d 962, 969 (N.D. Ind. 2002). As a result, courts have used a variety of methods for calculating the award of prejudgment interest in FMLA cases. For example, in the Seventh Circuit, prejudgment interest is calculated using the prime rate unless either there is a statutory defined rate or the district court engages in "refined rate–setting" directed at determining a more accurate market rate for interest. *Id.* (calculation of prejudgment interest based on post–judgment rate of interest erroneous in Seventh Circuit). Several courts have calculated prejudgment interest based on the rate for governing awards for post judgment interest in 28 USC 1961. *See Brenlla v. Lasorsa Buick Pontiac Chevrolet, Inc. et al.*, No. 00–Civ. 5207 (JCF), 2002 U.S. Dist. LEXIS 9358, at *38 (S.D.N.Y. May 28, 2002) (applying rate in 29 USC 1961, compounded annually); *Herman v. Princeton City School*, No. 1–C–96–358, 1997 U.S. Dist. LEXIS 22250 (S.D. Ohio Sept. 23, 1997) (the court calculated prevailing interest based on the effective Equivalent Coupon Issue Yield as of the date of the Order, the rate used by the Clerk of the district court to calculate post–judgment interest).

The court in *Morris v. VCW, Inc.*, No. 95–0737–CV–W–3–6, 1996 U.S. Dist. LEXIS 19201, at *16 (W.D. Mo. Dec. 26, 1996) held that the calculation of prejudgment interest was a matter for the jury, not the judge. Because evidence regarding interest was not presented to the jury, the court denied the employee's request for prejudgment interest.

d. Liquidated Damages

(1) General Rule

An employer who violates § 105 (prohibited acts) of Title I is also liable to any eligible employee affected for an additional amount as liquidated damages. 29 USC 2617(a)(1)(A)(iii), 2617(b)(2); 29 CFR 825.400(c); *see Taylor v. Invacare Corp.*, 64 Fed. Appx. 516 (6th Cir. 2003); *Mummert v. Vencor, Inc. et al.*, 21 Fed. Appx. 710 (9th Cir. 2001); *Young v. Sears Roebuck & Co.*, No. 2005-224, 2007 U.S. Dist. LEXIS 51930, at *20-21 (E.D. Ky. July 17, 2007); *Cobb v. Contract Transport, Inc.*, No. 04-305-KSF, 2007 U.S. Dist. LEXIS 45043, at *3 (E.D. Ky. June 21, 2007); *McIntyre v. Advance Auto Parts*, No. 1:04 CV 1857, 2007 U.S. Dist. LEXIS 1944, at *48 (N.D. Ohio Jan. 10, 2007); *Palma v. Pharmedica Communications, Inc.*, No. 3:00CV1128 (HBF), 2003 U.S. Dist. LEXIS 21227, at *2 (D. Conn. Sept. 30, 2003); *Miller v. G.B. Sales & Service, Inc.*, No. 02–70758, 2003 U.S. Dist. LEXIS 19450, at *4 (E.D. Mich. Sept. 29, 2003); *Metzler v. Federal Home Loan Bank of Topeka*, No. 03–4024–SAC, 2003 U.S. Dist. LEXIS 17971, at *3 (D. Kan Sept. 10, 2003).

The amount of "liquidated damages" is equal to the sum of the damages for lost wages, salary, etc., or actual monetary losses (as set forth in 29 USC 2617(a)(1)(A)(I)), and interest (as set forth in 29 USC 2617(a)(1)(A)(ii)). *See Wilkerson v. AutoZone, Inc.*, No. 04-6220, 2005 U.S. App. LEXIS 22492, at *15 (6th Cir. Oct. 17, 2005); *Taylor v. Invacare Corp.*, 64 Fed. Appx. 516 (6th Cir. 2003); *Smith v. Diffee Ford–Lincoln–Mercury, Inc.*, 298 F.3d 955, 964 (10th Cir. 2002) (adding liquidated damages to the awards of back pay and prejudgment interest effectively doubles the size of the award); *Thorson v. Gemini, Inc. et al.*, 205 F.3d 370, 383 (8th Cir. 2000), *cert. denied*, 531 U.S. 871 (2000); *Nero v. Industrial Molding Corp.*, 167 F.3d 921, 925, n. 2, 928 (5th Cir. 1999); *Cobb v. Contract Transport, Inc.*, No. 04-305-KSF, 2007 U.S. Dist. LEXIS 45043, at *3 (E.D. Ky. June 21, 2007); *Young v. Sears Roebuck & Co.*, No. 2005-224, 2007 U.S. Dist. LEXIS 51930, at *20-21 (E.D. Ky. July 17, 2007);. *McIntyre*, 2007 U.S. Dist. LEXIS 1944, at *27; *Dillaway v. Ferrante*, No. 02–715 (JRT/JSM), 2003 U.S. Dist. LEXIS 23468, at *27 (D. Minn. Dec. 9, 2003); *Palma.*, 2003 U.S. Dist. LEXIS 21227, at *2; *Metzler*, 2003 U.S. Dist. LEXIS 17971, at *3.

Courts may reduce an award of liquidated damages to only compensatory damages if the employer proves to the satisfaction of the court that the act or omission that violated § 2615 was in good faith, and that the employer had reasonable grounds for believing the act or omission was not in violation of the FMLA. *Wilkerson*, 2005 U.S. App. LEXIS

22492, at *15; *McIntyre*, 2007 U.S. Dist. LEXIS 1944, at *27; *Cobb*, 2007 U.S. Dist. LEXIS 45043, at *3; *Young*, 2007 U.S. Dist. LEXIS 51930, at *20-21 (E.D. Ky. July 17, 2007); *Palma*, 2003 U.S. Dist. LEXIS 21227, at *2; *G.B. Sales & Service, Inc.*, 2003 U.S. Dist. LEXIS 19450, at *11.

Courts considering liquidated damages under the FMLA have looked to cases under the FLSA. *See Cobb*, 2007 U.S. Dist. LEXIS 45043, at *3-4; *Palma*, 2003 U.S. Dist. LEXIS 21227, at *3.

An employee who suffers actual monetary losses may also be entitled to liquidated damages equal to those losses. 29 USC 2617(a)(1)(A)(iii); *see Coleman v. Potomac Electric Power Co.*, 281 F. Supp. 2d 250, 254 (D.D.C. 2003). Conversely, absent a showing of actual monetary losses, the employee is not entitled to liquidated damages. *Coleman*, 281 F. Supp. 2d at 254.

Absent an actual covered monetary loss resulting from a violation of the FMLA, an employee is not entitled to liquidated damages. *Spurlock v. Postmaster General*, 19 Fed. Appx. 338 (6th Cir. 2001); *Tornberg v. Business Interlink Services, Inc.*, 237 F. Supp. 2d 778, 789 (E.D. Mich. 2002).

(2) Defense of Good Faith and Reasonable Grounds

Employers who violate § 105 by engaging in prohibited conduct may nevertheless avoid an award of liquidated damages provided they establish to the satisfaction of the court that the act or omission which violated § 105 was in good faith and the employer had reasonable grounds for believing that the act or omission was not a violation of § 105. 29 USC 2617(a)(1)(A)(iii); 29 CFR 825.400(c); *see Taylor v. Invacare Corp.*, 64 Fed. Appx. 516 (6th Cir. 2003); *Smith v. Diffee Ford–Lincoln–Mercury, Inc.*, 298 F.3d 955, 964 (10th Cir. 2002); *Duty v. Norton–Alcoa Proppants*, 293 F.3d 481, 497 (8th Cir. 2002); *Cobb*, 2007 U.S. Dist. LEXIS 45043, at *3; *Young*, 2007 U.S. Dist. LEXIS 51930, at *20-21; *Dillaway*, 2003 U.S. Dist. LEXIS 23468, at *27; *Chenoweth v. Wal–Mart Stores, Inc.*, 159 F. Supp. 2d 1032, 1039 (S.D. Ohio 2001); *Morris v. VCW, Inc.*, No. 95–0737–CV–W–3–6, 1996 U.S. Dist. LEXIS 19201, at *5 (W.D. Mo. Dec. 26, 1996) (defense established by convincing showing by employer that violation was in good faith and objectively reasonable). Liquidated damages are considered compensatory rather than punitive in nature. *Palma*, 2003 U.S. Dist. LEXIS 21227, at *2.

The employer bears the burden of establishing, by plain and substantial evidence, subjective good faith and objective reasonableness.

If an employer proves its defense of good faith and reasonable belief, the court, in its discretion, may reduce the amount of liability to the amount of regular damages, as determined under clauses (I) (damages) and (ii) (interest) of § 107 (29 USC 2617(a)(1)(A), (ii)). A court may not exercise its discretion to reduce or eliminate liquidated damages unless the employer first sustains its burden to prove both good faith and reasonable grounds. *Arban v. West Publishing Corp.*, 345 F.3d 390, 407-08 (6th Cir. 2003); *Chandler v. Specialty Tires of America (Tennessee)*, 283 F.3d 818, 827 (6th Cir. 2002) (employers must show both good faith and reasonable grounds for the act or omission in order for a district court to consider reduction in liquidated damages); *Thorson v. Gemini, Inc. et al.*, 205 F.3d 370, 383 (8th Cir. 2000), *cert. denied*, 531 U.S. 871 (2000); *Nero v. Industrial Molding Corp.*, 167 F.3d 921, 928 (5th Cir. 1999); *Cobb v. Contract Transport, Inc.*, No. 04-305-KSF, 2007 U.S. Dist. LEXIS 45043, at *3 (E.D. Ky. June 21, 2007); *Chenoweth v. Wal–Mart Stores, Inc.*, 159 F. Supp. 2d 1032, 1039 (S.D. Ohio 2001).

Note that employers are liable for liquidated damages in every case, absent successful assertion of the good faith/reasonable belief defense. *Nero*, 167 F.3d at 929, n. 4 ("Doubling of an award is the norm under the FMLA, because a plaintiff is awarded liquidated damages in addition to compensation lost"); *Cobb*, 2007 U.S. Dist. LEXIS 45043, at *3 (strong presumption favors award of liquidated damages); *Herman v. Princeton City School*, No. 1–C–96–358, 1997 U.S. Dist. LEXIS 22250 (S.D. Ohio Sept. 23, 1997) (court awarded liquidated damages as a matter of course without fanfare or discussion for violation of the FMLA).

Neither the Act or regulations define or otherwise explain what would constitute "good faith" or an employer's "reasonable grounds for believing" that its conduct was not prohibited by the FMLA. *Nero*, 167 F.3d at 928 (FMLA does not, by its terms, provide guidance as to what constitutes "good faith"); *see Morris v. VCW, Inc.*, No. 95–0737–CV–W–3–6, 1996 U.S. Dist. LEXIS 19201, at *5 (W.D. Mo. Dec. 26, 1996) (neither FMLA nor implementing regulations establish parameters by which to assess validity of a stated "good faith" defense). For purposes of the reduction of FMLA damages involving employees of local educational agencies, the legislative history of the Act identifies advice of counsel, collective bargaining agreement, and compliance with valid state and local laws, the laws referenced in § 108(b), and regulations or policies promulgated by the DOL, as factors tending to establish that the covered educational employer had reasonable grounds for believing that it was not acting in violation of the FMLA. S. Rep. 103-3, p. 37. Perhaps some of the same considerations (state or local law would not generally not be a basis for an excuse as such laws generally do not apply to the federal government) would animate the good faith/reasonable grounds determination for non–educational facilities.

According to the legislative history, the remedial provisions of the FMLA parallel the provisions of the FLSA. *See* S. Rep. 103-3, p. 35. Like the FMLA, the FLSA also provides that an employer "shall" be liable for damages and liquidated damages, and both statutes (the FMLA and FLSA) provide that, if good faith is proven, the district court "may" reduce the amount of liquidated damages. *See* 29 USC 216(b) (providing damages under FLSA); *Id.* at 260 (providing good faith defense of liquidated damages under FLSA). As such, courts have interpreted "good faith" for purposes of the FMLA the same as that term has been defined for purposes of the FLSA. *Nero*, 167 F.3d at 928; *Frizzell v. Southwest Motor Freight*, 154 F.3d 641, 644 (6th Cir. 1998) (citing S. Rep. No. 103-3, that remedial provisions of FMLA parallel those of FLSA); *Morris v. VCW, Inc.*, No. 95-0737-CV-W-3-6, 1996 U.S. Dist. LEXIS 19201, at *6-10 (W.D. Mo. Dec. 26, 1996) (applying FLSA principles to determine "good faith" for purposes of liquidated damages).

Under the FLSA, a district court may not exercise its discretionary authority to reduce or to eliminate a liquidated damages award unless the employer first sustains its burden of showing that its failure to obey the Statute was in "good faith." *Nero*, 167 F.3d at 928; *Chenoweth*, 159 F. Supp. 2d at 1039. The employer's burden of establishing FLSA "good faith" has been described as substantial. *Vega v. Gasper*, 36 F.3d 417, 427 (5th Cir. 1994). Moreover, even if a trial court is satisfied that an employer acted both in good faith and reasonably, in an FLSA case a trial court may still award liquidated damages at its discretion in any amount up to the maximum amount allowed. *Nero*, 167 F.3d at 929 n. 4, citing, *Mireles v. Frio Foods, Inc.*, 899 F.2d 1407, 1417, n. 8 (5th Cir. 1990).

Because the award of liquidated damages is the norm under the FMLA, a "district court's discretion to reduce liquidated damages 'must be exercised consistently with the strong presumption under the Statute in favor of doubling.'" *Nero*, 167 F.3d at 929 (*quoting Shea v. Galaxie Lumber Constr. Co., Ltd.*, 152 F.3d 729, 733 (7th Cir. 1998)); *Palma v. Pharmedica Communications, Inc.*, No. 3:00CV1128 (HBF), 2003 U.S. Dist. LEXIS 21227, at *2 (D. Conn. Sept. 30, 2003) (same).

Relying on FLSA case law, the court in *Morris v. VCW, Inc.*, No. 95-0737-CV-W-3-6, 1996 U.S. Dist. LEXIS 19201, at *9 (W.D. Mo. Dec. 26, 1996), described the burden on employers to perfect the defense to a claim for FMLA liquidated damages as follows:

> To avoid a liquidated damages award, defendant bears the burden of establishing that it acted with subjective good faith and that it had an objectively reasonable belief its conduct did not violate the law. *See Thomas v. Howard Univ. Hosp.*, 309 U.S. App. D.C. 93, 39 F.3d 370, 372-73 (D.C. Cir. 1994); *Hultgren v. County of Lancaster*, 913 F.2d 498, 509 (8th Cir. 1990). The good faith requirement demands that the defendant establish that it honestly intended to ascertain the dictates of the FMLA and to act in conformance with it. *See Cross v. Arkansas Forestry Comm'n*, 938 F.2d 912, 917-18 (8th Cir. 1991) (subsequent history omitted); *Marshall v. Brunner*, 668 F.2d 748, 753 (8th Cir. 1982).

Bald assertions by an employer that it was acting in good faith, standing alone, are insufficient to preclude an award of liquidated damages. *Morris v. VCW, Inc.*, No. 95-0737-CV-W-3-6, 1996 U.S. Dist. LEXIS 19201, at *10 (W.D. Mo. Dec. 26, 1996). Good faith has both an objective and subjective component. *Id.* at *13. It requires both that the employer subjectively believed it acted in good faith, and that such belief was objectively reasonable. *Id.*

Moreover, good faith requires some duty to investigate potential liability under the FMLA. *Morris*, 1996 U.S. Dist. LEXIS 19201, at *10 (*citing Barcellona v. Tiffany English Pub*, 597 F.2d 464, 469 (5th Cir. 1979)). An employer cannot claim good faith when it "blindly operate[s] a business without making any investigation as to [its] responsibilities" under the FMLA. *Id.* Successfully establishing reasonable grounds for the conduct taken generally requires a showing that the employer relied on a reasonable, although erroneous, interpretation of the Act or its implementing regulations. *Morris*, 1996 U.S. Dist. LEXIS 19201, at *5, *citing, Thomas v. Howard Univ. Hosp.*, 39 F.3d 370, 373 (D.C. Cir. 1994). Nor does a misunderstanding as to the Act's requirements provide reasonable grounds to excuse violation of the law. *Morris*, 1996 U.S. Dist. LEXIS 19201, at *10 (*citing Crenshaw v. Quarles Drilling Corp.*, 798 F.2d 1345, 1351 (10th Cir. 1986)).

An employer does not have to consult with an attorney regarding the requirements of the FMLA to establish that it acted in good faith. *Cobb v. Contract Transport, Inc.*, No. 04-305-KSF, 2007 U.S. Dist. LEXIS 45043, at *3 (E.D. Ky. June 21, 2007). In

Cobb, the court found that the employer acted in good faith when it consulted with the DOL statute and regulations to ascertain whether the employee was eligible for FMLA coverage.

The determination of "good faith" for purposes of liquidated damages is distinct from "willful" conduct for purposes of the statute of limitations. *Nero v. Industrial Molding Corp.*, 167 F.3d 921, 929 n. 4 (5th Cir. 1999). In *Nero*, the employer argued that "good faith" should be read together with the word "willful" in the FMLA. *Id*. Both the FMLA and FLSA contain these terms, and "willful" has been defined as "reckless disregard" of an employee's rights for purposes of the FLSA. *Id*. (citing *Peters v. City of Shreveport*, 818 F.2d 1148, 1168 (5th Cir. 1987)). The court in *Nero* declined to incorporate the "reckless disregard" standard for willful conduct into the liability provisions of 29 USC 2617. *Id*. According to the court, "there is no indication that the word 'willful' in the limitations provision has any bearing on the good faith defense in the liability provision." *Id*.

Courts have found lack of good faith and reasonableness where employers act out of ignorance of the requirements of the FMLA. In *Morris v. VCW, Inc.*, No. 95–0737–CV–W–3–6, 1996 U.S. Dist. LEXIS 19201, at *5 (W.D. Mo. Dec. 26, 1996), the court concluded that the employer did not establish that it acted in good faith and reasonably, so as to avoid imposition of liquidated damages. In so holding, the court noted that the company president's limited understanding or knowledge of the requirements of the Act prior to terminating the employee for requesting leave, the lack of any evidence that the company president reviewed the requirements of the FMLA or relied on legal advice prior to terminating the employee was a lack of good faith. Even assuming that the company president honestly misunderstood the situation, the court concluded that objective reasonableness could not be found. The court noted that it was not reasonable for the employer to assume that the doctor who wrote the employee's note did not exercise professional judgment. According to the court, the company president's "hard-driving conduct may, in some contexts, be good for business. The angry violation of Leave Act entitlement was not in good faith, and clearly subjects the employer to double damages."

A similar conclusion was reached by the court in *Chandler Specialty Tires of America (Tennessee), Inc.*, 283 F.3d 818, 827 (6th Cir. 2002). In that case, the court found that, even assuming the employer had a good faith belief that the employee was not covered by the FMLA, the employer's belief was not reasonable. The human resources manager testified that he had no experience with the FMLA the day he fired the employee, that he made no inquiries into her request for leave, and that he made no independent effort to check information supplied regarding the employee's status. Rather, the employer's decision to terminate employee was based on an eight-minute conversation with the employee's supervisor.

Good faith requires more than a showing of ignorance of the prevailing law or uncertainty about its development. It is not enough to show that a violation was not purposeful. Nor is good faith demonstrated by the absence of complaints on the part of employees or conformity with industry-wide practice. Good faith requires that an employer first take active steps to ascertain the dictates of the law and then efforts to comply with them. *Palma v. Pharmedica Communications, Inc.*, No. 3:00CV1128 (HBF), 2003 U.S. Dist. LEXIS 21227, at *2 (D. Conn. Sept. 30, 2003); *Miller v. G.B. Sales & Service, Inc.*, No. 02–70758, 2003 U.S. Dist. Lexis 19450, at *11 (E.D. Mich. Sept. 29, 2003).

An employer's claim that it was confused that an employee was requesting a reasonable accommodation rather than a reduced work schedule under the FMLA did not constitute "reasonable grounds" for believing that the employer was not interfering with the employee's FMLA rights. *Verhoff v. Time Warner Cable, Inc.*, No. 3:05CV7277, 2007 U.S. Dist. LEXIS 37590, at *2 (N.D. Ohio May 23, 2007). The court in *Verhoff* observed, "[w]hile employers are certainly affected by a host of laws and regulations that must be upheld under the statute, it is certainly no excuse that the legal framework for employers is too complex or confusing."

Neither good faith nor reasonable grounds for the act or omission were established where the employer terminated an employee for taking half days of FMLA leave six weeks after the DOL advised the employer that denial of half-day medical leave was a violation of the FMLA, and where the employer admitted that it made no independent effort to determine the law. *Palma*, 2003 U.S. Dist. LEXIS 21227, at *2.

An employer who "never gave the FMLA any thought" nor consulted a professional about employment law or about firing an employee before terminating the plaintiff for taking FMLA leave does not act in good faith or reasonably to justify a reduction by the court in the amount of liquidated damages awarded by the jury. *Dillaway v. Ferrante*, No. 02–715 (JRT/JSM), 2003 U.S. Dist. LEXIS 23468, at *27 (D. Minn. Dec. 9, 2003).

Evidence of not acting in good faith cited by other courts has included refusing to return an employee to work until the employee functioned at 100% capacity, rather than the correct determination of whether the employee can perform the essential functions of the position. *Duty v. Norton–Alcoa Proppants*, 293 F.3d 481, 497 (8th Cir. 2002). An employer's violation of its own policy was found to be fatal to its claim of acting in good faith. *Mummert v. Vencor, Inc. et al.*, 21 Fed. Appx. 710 (9th Cir. 2001).

Similarly, courts have cited a variety of factors in finding that the employer acted in good faith and had reasonable grounds for believing that its actions were not violative of the Act sufficient to deny an award of liquidated damages. *See Taylor v. Invacare Corp.*, 64 Fed. Appx. 516 (6th Cir. 2003) (court equated "good faith" with not acting in "bad faith." Court noted that employer believed that it was firing employee because of attendance and performance problems unrelated to his FMLA–protected absences); *Thorson v. Gemini, Inc. et al.*, 205 F.3d 370, 383 (8th Cir. 2000), *cert. denied*, 531 U.S. 871 (2000) (newness of the law, the employer's attempts to obtain a copy of the DOL interim regulations, the employee's history of excessive and disruptive absences, and district court's prior adjudication, without the benefit of the DOL's 1996 opinion letter that reversed its prior position minor illnesses are not serious health conditions, that the employer did not violate the Act, was compelling evidence that the employer had an objectively reasonable belief that its termination of employee was not violative of the FMLA); *Miller v. AT&T*, 83 F. Supp. 2d 700 (S.D. W.Va. 2000), *aff'd on other grounds*, 250 F.3d 820 (4th Cir. 2001) (employer not subject to liquidated damages where it held good faith and reasonable belief that flu did not constitute FMLA–covered "serious health condition" at time it terminated employee).

Because it must establish both good faith and that it acted reasonably, an employer that establishes good faith but not reasonableness has not perfected the conditions of a trial court to consider a reduction of liquidated damages. *Taylor*, 64 Fed. Appx. 516 (district court did not abuse discretion in refusing to reduce liquidated damages award where it found that employer, while acting in good faith, did not act reasonably; employer applied no fault attendance policy to FMLA absence, something strictly prohibited by the DOL regulations); *Chandler Specialty Tires of America (Tennessee), Inc.*, 283 F.3d 818, 827 (6th Cir. 2002) (Even assuming employer had a good faith belief that employee was not covered by the FMLA, that belief was unreasonable: HR manager testified he had no experience with the FMLA the day he fired the employee, that he made no inquiries into her request for leave, and he made no independent effort to check information supplied regarding the employee's status, and that the decision to terminate employee was based on an eight–minute conversation with employee's supervisor.).

Of course, an employer who establishes the good faith defense and thereby avoids liquidated damages is still liable for actual damages sustained by the employee as a result of the employer's violation of the Act. *Bachelder v. America West Airlines, Inc.*, 259 F.3d 1112, 1130 (9th Cir. 2001).

In *Atchley v. the Nordam Group, Inc. et al.*, 180 F.3d 1143, 1151–52 (10th Cir. 1999), the court held that an award of liquidated damages for violation of the FMLA and punitive damages for violation of Title II did not amount to an impermissible double recovery. There, the Pregnancy Discrimination Act and FMLA claims both addressed the failure of the employer to reinstate the employee after giving birth.

Employers with management practicing the "shoot, ready, aim" school of discipline will not only likely find themselves in violation of the substantive entitlements of the FMLA, but will almost certainly be unable to credibly seek reduction in the award of liquidated damages. Disciplinary actions based on attendance, or the use of attendance as a "negative factor" for other employment decisions, must be closely scrutinized to avoid violations of the FMLA. Any doubts about the validity of the action being contemplated should be resolved by running the matter through counsel.

e. Miscellaneous Rules on Title I Damages

(1) Special Rules Concerning Employees of Local Educational Agencies

Title I of the FMLA provides a means for covered local educational employers to argue for a reduction in damages. The Statute (29 USC 2618(f)) provides:

> If a local educational agency or private elementary or secondary school that has violated this Title proves to the satisfaction of the court that the agency, school, or department had reasonable grounds for believing that the underlying act or omission was not a violation of this Title, such court may, in the discretion of the court, reduce the amount of the liability provided for under Section 107(a)(1)(A) to the amount and interest determined under Clauses (I) and (ii), respectively, of such action.

It is unclear exactly what this means. It appears to mean that a covered local educational employer may be relieved of having to pay any liquidated damages if it establishes that it had reasonable grounds to believe that the underlying act or omission was not a violation of the FMLA. In that sense, this rule is similar, although not identical, to the defense generally available to covered employers to avoid liquidated damages. See 29 USC 2617(a)(1)(iii). One difference between the general defense to a claim for liquidated damages and the defense available to covered local educational employers is that the former requires a showing that the employer was both acting in good faith and had reasonable grounds to believe that the act or omission was not a violation of § 105 of Title I. Local educational employers, on the other hand, need only establish that they had reasonable grounds to believe they were not violating the law. They are not required meet the additional requirement of acting in good faith.

The legislative history of the Act identifies advice of counsel, collective bargaining agreements, and compliance with valid state and local laws, the laws referenced in § 108(b), and regulations or policies promulgated by the DOL, as factors tending to establish that the covered educational employer had reasonable grounds for believing that it was not acting in violation of the FMLA. S. Rep. 103–3, p. 37.

(2) Damages Recovered by the Secretary of Labor

Any sums recovered in a civil action by the Secretary of Labor against an employer for violation of the FMLA must be held in a special deposit account and will be paid, on order of the Secretary, directly to each employee affected. 29 USC 2617(b)(3). Any such sums not paid to an employee because of inability to do so within a period of three years is deposited into the Treasury of the United States as miscellaneous receipts. *Id.*

3. Equitable Relief

a. Private Civil Action

In addition to covered damages and interest, an employer who engages in acts prohibited by Title I of the FMLA is also liable to any eligible employee affected (29 USC 2617(A)(1)(B)) for:

> Such equitable relief as may be appropriate, including employment, reinstatement, and promotion.

See Nichols v. Ashland Hospital Corp. et al., 251 F.3d 496, 503–504 (4th Cir. 2001); *Herman v. Princeton City School*, No. 1–C–96–358, 1997 U.S. Dist. LEXIS 22250 (S.D. Ohio Sept. 23, 1997). According to the legislative history, "this section is intended to provide employees with the right to pursue all varieties of equitable relief, including preliminary relief." S. Rep. 103–3, p. 36.

Equitable relief, such as injunctive relief, either requires an employer to do something (e.g., rehire an employee wrongly fired in violation of the FMLA), or stop doing something that the employer is currently doing (e.g., continued enforcement of an employer policy that violates the FMLA rights of employees). *See Walker v. UPS, Inc.*, 240 F.3d 1268, 1277 (10th Cir. 2001); *Herman*, 1997 U.S. Dist. LEXIS 22250 (awarding equitable relief in form of injunction prohibiting employer from committing further violations of 29 USC 2615 by (I) failing to place posters required by 29 USC 2619 in appropriate locations in each of its buildings or (ii) otherwise interfering with its employees' exercise of their rights under the FMLA).

In *Knussman v. Maryland et al.*, 935 F. Supp. 659, 668 (D. Md. 1996), *aff'd in part, rev'd in part on other grounds*, 272 F.3d 625 (4th Cir. 2001), the district court rejected defense arguments that the term "including" limited equitable relief to employment, reinstatement, and promotion. The employer also argued that, because the Secretary of Labor could seek injunctive relief, the plaintiffs were precluded from doing so. In *Knussman*, the plaintiffs sought to require the defendants to promulgate and notify the employees of a written FMLA policy, post information regarding employee FMLA leave rights, refrain from retaliating against the plaintiff in any way, and granting the plaintiff 12 weeks of parental leave. The court found that a fair reading of § 2617(a)(1)(B) authorizes the court to award appropriate equitable relief, and that there is nothing in the Statute or its legislative history demonstrating that "including" is a word of limitation. Moreover, the court found that the fact that the Secretary of Labor may bring an action for injunctive relief does not preclude an individual employee from seeking the same relief. *Knussman*, 935 F. Supp. at 668–69.

Equitable relief is not available where the employee has not suffered actual damages. *Rodgers v. City of Des Moines*, 435 F.3d 904, 909 (8th Cir. 2006); *Walker v. UPS, Inc.*, 240 F.3d 1268, 1277 (10th Cir. 2001).

b. Secretary of Labor

As indicated previously in the "Enforcement" section of this chapter, the Secretary of Labor may seek injunctive relief in the district courts of the United States to: (1) restrain violation of § 105, including the restraint of any withholding of payment of wages, salary, employment benefits, or other compensation, plus interest, found by the court to be due to eligible employees; or (2) to award such other equitable relief as may be appropriate, including employment, reinstatement, and promotion. 29 USC 2617(d)(1)–(2); see Reich v. Midwest Plastic Engineering, Inc. et al., 934 F. Supp. 266, 268 (W.D. Mich. 1996), aff'd without opinion 113 F.3d 1235 (6th Cir. 1997). FLSA case law governs the DOL's request for injunctive relief. Id. The Sixth Circuit has explained that the purpose of issuing an injunction under the FLSA is to effectuate "general compliance" by "preventing recurring violations." Id. citing Martin v. Funtime, Inc., 963 F.2d 110, 113 (6th Cir. 1992). The DOL is entitled to some, although not "unbridled," discretion in requesting injunctive relief. Id. As such, seeking injunctive relief to prevent future violations of the Act is justifiable prosecutorial action under the Act. "Current compliance is not necessarily sufficient ground to deny relief." Reich, 934 F. Supp. at 928.

The fact that the Secretary of Labor may seek injunctive relief does not preclude an employee from seeking the same relief in a private civil action. Knussman v. Maryland et al., 935 F. Supp. 659, 668–69 (D. Md. 1996), aff'd in part, rev'd in part on other grounds, 272 F.3d 625 (4th Cir. 2001).

4. Attorney's Fees and Costs

a. General Rule

In an action to recover damages or equitable relief for violation of § 105 of Title I, in addition to any judgment awarded to the plaintiff, the court shall allow a reasonable attorney's fee, reasonable expert witness fees, and other costs of the action to be paid by the defendant. 29 USC 2617(a)(1)(B)(3), 2617(b)(2); 29 CFR 825.400(c); see Bryant v. Dollar General Corp., No. 3:05-0840, 2007 U.S. Dist. LEXIS 46397, at *1 (M.D. Tenn. June 26, 2007); Coleman v. Potomac Electric Power Co., 281 F. Supp. 2d 250, 254 (D.D.C. 2003); Hite v. Biomet, Inc., 53 F. Supp. 2d 1013, 1024 (N.D. Ind. 1999) (attorney fees available).

Statutory damages are a prerequisite to interest, liquidated damages, and attorney fees. Coleman, 281 F. Supp. 2d at 254. In Coleman v. Potomac Electric Power Co., 281 F. Supp. 2d 250, 254 (D.D.C. 2003), the court held that plaintiff was not entitled to attorney fees because he was not entitled nor was he awarded a judgment for FMLA violations. Prior to filing suit, an arbitrator returned plaintiff to work with full back pay and benefits. Because he suffered no actual monetary loss as a result of the employer's FMLA violation, the court found that the employee was not entitled to judgment. Absent judgment in his favor, the employee was not entitled to an award of attorney fees.

With the exception of the allowance of expert witness fees, this provision is modeled after § 216(b) of the FLSA, "and therefore should be interpreted in the same way as the FLSA." S. Rep. 103–3, p. 36. According to the federal courts, the award of attorney fees under the FLSA is mandatory and unconditional. Id. A court has no discretion to deny fees to a prevailing plaintiff; its discretion extends only to the amount allowed. Id. (citing Shelton v. Ervin, 830 F.2d 182, 184 (11th Cir. 1987); United Slate, Tile and Composition Roofers v. G & M Roofing, 732 F.2d 495, 501 (6th Cir. 1984); Graham v. Henegar, 640 F.2d 732, 736 (5th Cir. 1981) (en blanc); see also Hagelthorn v. Kennecott Corp., 710 F.2d 76, 86 (2d Cir. 1983)).

The requirement that a defendant pay reasonable expert fees was included in direct response to the Supreme Court's holding in West Virginia University Hospitals, Inc. v. Casey, 111 S. Ct. 1138 (1991). S. Rep. 103–3, p. 36. In that case, the Court made clear that expert witness fees will be awarded only if explicitly authorized by statute. Id.

b. Attorneys' Fees

As under FLSA, an award of attorney fees to a prevailing party in an FMLA case is mandatory, although the trial court has broad discretion in determining the actual amount of the award. Estes v. Meridian One Corp. et al., 6 Fed. Appx. 142 (4th Cir. 2001); see McDonnell v. Miller Oil Co., Inc., 134 F.3d 638, 641 (4th Cir. 1998); Sherry v. Protection, Inc., 14 F. Supp. 2d 1055, (N.D. Ill. 1998) (award of attorney fees mandatory).

Notwithstanding the reference in the legislative history to a "prevailing" party, one circuit correctly noted that 29 USC 2617(a)(3) does not contain an express reference to the term "prevailing party." Bond v. Abbott Labs., 188 F.3d 506 (table),

1999 U.S. App. LEXIS 22242, at *11 (6th Cir. Sept. 9, 1999). Nevertheless, the court concluded: "The plain language of the fee-shifting provision of the FMLA requires the award of attorneys' fees in cases only where a violation of the FMLA is established." *Bond v. Abbott Labs.*, 188 F.3d 506 (table), 1999 U.S. App. LEXIS 22242, at *11 (6th Cir. Sept. 9, 1999). Other courts have used the term "prevailing party" to describe the FMLA requirement for attorney fees and costs. *See Hoge v. Honda of America Mfg., Inc.*, No. 2:00-CV-995, 2003 U.S. Dist. LEXIS 4068, at *3 (S.D. Ohio March 3, 2003). But see *Sherry v. Protection, Inc.*, 14 F. Supp. 2d 1055 (N.D. Ill. 1998) (suggesting that an employee may be eligible for fees even when requirements of a prevailing party are not met). A party "prevails" when actual relief on the merits of the claim materially alters the legal relationship between the parties. *See Farrar v. Hobby*, 506 U.S. 103, 111, 121 L. Ed. 2d 494, 113 S. Ct. 566 (1992).

A plaintiff who fails to establish a violation of the FMLA is not a "prevailing party" entitled to attorney fees. *Bond v. Abbott Labs.*, 188 F.3d 506 (table), 1999 U.S. App. LEXIS 22242, at *11 (6th Cir. Sept. 9, 1999); *Dawson v. Leewood Nursing Home, Inc.*, 14 F. Supp. 2d 828, 1998 U.S. Dist. Lexis 12142 (E.D. Va. Aug. 5, 1998) (FMLA requires that attorney fees be awarded when a violation of the Act is established but only in addition to a judgment. Accordingly, we find that where there is no reasonable likelihood of a judgment being awarded, there can be no basis upon which attorney fees are recoverable); *Schmitt v. Beverly Health and Rehab, Servs.*, Inc., 962 F. Supp. 1379 (D. Kan 1997) (plaintiff not entitled to recover attorney fees when FMLA claim is dismissed for failure to state a claim).

Such violation, moreover, must actually interfere with employee FMLA rights; mere technical violations of the Act will not support an award of attorney fees. *Bond v. Abbott Labs.*, 188 F.3d 506 (table), 1999 U.S. App. LEXIS 22242, at *11 (6th Cir. Sept. 9, 1999) (where inadequate employer notice provided to the employees prior to the revision of a attendance control program did not lead any employee to forfeit rights under the FMLA, and where no employee was wrongly denied FMLA leave or disciplined for FMLA leave, the employer's failure to comply with FMLA's notice requirements did not interfere with the employee's statutory rights and, as a result, the plaintiff was not entitled to attorney fees); see, e.g., *Williams v. Toyota Motor Mfg., Kentucky, Inc.*, 224 F.3d 840, 845 n. 2 (6th Cir. 2000) (not deciding whether the employee who could show a technical violation but no damages would be entitled to recover attorney fees).

Attorneys' fees have, however, been awarded where a plaintiff has won only nominal damages pursuant to a finding that the employer violated the FMLA. *See Wilson v. Dallas Independent School District*, No. CA3:97-CV-0281-BC, 1998 U.S. Dist. LEXIS 1415, at *8 (N.D. Tex. Jan. 30, 1998) (attorney fees available even where nominal damages awarded). *But see McDonnell v. Miller Oil Co.*, 134 F.3d 638, 640 (4th Cir. 1998) (reversing district court determination that award of $19,698.91 in attorney fees was mandated by the Statute despite the fact that the plaintiff was only awarded $2.10 in damages; circuit court indicated that trial court did not appear aware that it had discretion to reduce attorney fee award in light of limited victory at trial). It should be noted that "nominal damages" generally means a $1 award. *See e.g., Rice v. Sunrise Express, Inc.*, 237 F. Supp. 2d 962, 974 n. 11 (N.D. Ind. 2002) (citing *Farrar v. Hobby*, 506 U.S. 103, 113 S. Ct. 566, 121 L. Ed. 2d 494 (1992); *Morimanno v. Taco Bell*, 979 F. Supp. 791 (N.D. Ind. 1997) (discussing nominal versus *de minimis* damages). Courts have awarded large attorney fee awards where a plaintiff has been awarded very small amounts in damages. *See Rice v. Sunrise Express, Inc.*, 237 F. Supp. 2d 962, 971–78 (N.D. Ind. 2002) ($129,663.60 in attorney fees awarded where the plaintiff received only $720 in damages for FMLA violations).

The FMLA does not authorize an award of attorney fees to a prevailing defendant, only to a successful plaintiff. *Billings v. Cape Cod Child Dev. Program, Inc.*, 270 F. Supp. 2d 175 (D. Mass. 2003). In *Billings*, the successful employer argued that it should be entitled to an award of attorney fees pursuant to 28 USC 1927, which provides:

> Any attorney or other person admitted to conduct cases in any court of the United States or any Territory thereof who so multiplies the proceedings in any case unreasonably and vexatiously may be required by the court to satisfy personally the excess costs, expenses, and attorneys' fees reasonably incurred because of such conduct.

The court declined to award attorney fees to the defendant after concluding that there was nothing vexatious about the litigation. The term *vexatious* means intended to harass. Webster's Ninth New Collegiate Dictionary (Merriam-Webster, Inc., 1988). The possibility that an employer might be able to secure attorney fees and costs, at least in federal court actions, should be sobering to plaintiffs and their counsel.

To assess the reasonableness of attorney fees under the FMLA, courts have applied the familiar two-step lodestar process applied in Title VII cases. First, the court must determine the "lodestar" figure by taking the proven number of hours reasonably expended on the litigation multiplied by the attorney's reasonable hourly rate. Second, the court may adjust the lodestar to reflect relevant considerations peculiar to the subject litigation. *See Bryant v. Dollar General*

Corp., No. 3:05-0840, 2007 U.S. Dist. LEXIS 46397, at *2 (M.D. Tenn. June 26, 2007); *Hoge v. Honda of America Mfg., Inc.*, No. 2:00–CV–995, 2003 U.S. Dist. LEXIS 4068, at *3 (S.D. Ohio March 3, 2003); *Rice v. Sunrise Express, Inc.*, 237 F. Supp. 2d 962, 971–78 (N.D. Ind. 2002); *Brenlla v. Lasora Buick Pontiac Chevrolet, Inc. et al.*, No. 00 Civ. 5207 (JCF), 2002 U.S. Dist. LEXIS 9358, at *42 (S.D.N.Y. May 28, 2002); *Sheppard v. Honda of America Mfg., Inc.*, 160 F. Supp. 2d 860, 874–76 (S.D. Ohio. 2001); *Cookston v. Miller Freeman, Inc.*, No.3:98–CV–2106–D, 1999 U.S. Dist. LEXIS 14381 (N.D. Tex. Sept. 14, 1999); *Barrilleaux v. Thayer Lodging Group, Inc.*, No. 97–3252 § E/1, 1999 U.S. Dist. LEXIS 9073 (E.D. La. June 14, 1999); *Mora v. Chem–Tronics, Inc.*, No. 97–CV–0851–J (JFS), 1999 U. S. Dist. Lexis 10752 (S.D. Cal. July 7, 1999).

The primary concern in considering a motion for attorney fees is that the award be reasonable. That is, an award should adequately compensate counsel yet avoid producing a windfall to the lawyer. *Hoge v. Honda of America Mfg., Inc.*, Case o. 2:00–CV–995, 2003 U.S. Dist. LEXIS 4068, at *3 (S.D. Ohio March 3, 2003); *Sheppard v. Honda of America Mfg., Inc.*, 160 F. Supp. 2d 860, 874–76 (S.D. Ohio. 2001).

With respect to the calculation of the lodestar, a "reasonable" hourly rate should reflect the "market rate" for the attorney's services. *Rice v. Sunrise Express, Inc.*, 237 F. Supp. 2d 962, 972 (N.D. Ind. 2002); *Brenlla v. Lasora Buick Pontiac Chevrolet, Inc. et al.*, No. 00 Civ. 5207 (JCF), 2002 U.S. Dist. LEXIS 9358, at *43 (S.D.N.Y. May 28, 2002); *Barrilleaux v. Thayer Lodging Group, Inc.*, No. 97–3252 § E/1, 1999 U.S. Dist. LEXIS 9073, at *4 (E.D. La. June 14, 1999).

The attorney's experience and expertise also factor in to the determination of a "reasonable" hourly rate. *Rice v. Sunrise Express, Inc.*, 237 F. Supp. 2d 962, 922–73, n. 9 (N.D. Ind. 2002); *Brenlla v. Lasora Buick Pontiac Chevrolet, Inc. et al.*, No. 00 Civ. 5207 (JCF), 2002 U.S. Dist. LEXIS 9358, at *43 (S.D.N.Y. May 28, 2002); *Sheppard v. Honda of America Mfg., Inc.*, 160 F. Supp. 2d 860, 875 (S.D. Ohio. 2001).

Generally, a fee applicant demonstrates the reasonableness of the hourly rate by submitting affidavits from local practitioners who verify that the rates charged are within the local applicable market rate. *Bryant v. Dollar General Corp.*, No. 3:05-0840, 2007 U.S. Dist. LEXIS 46397, at *1 (M.D. Tenn. June 26, 2007); *Rice v. Sunrise Express, Inc.*, 237 F. Supp. 2d 962, 972 (N.D. Ind. 2002) citing *Spegon v. Catholic Bishop of Chicago*, 175 F.3d 544, 556 (7th Cir. 1999).

Similarly, a party opposing the reasonableness of the hourly rate sought by the prevailing party generally does so by submitting affidavits of attorneys with similar experience stating that the rates sought greatly exceed the rates those attorneys would ordinarily charge in similar cases. *Rice v. Sunrise Express, Inc.*, 237 F. Supp. 2d 962, 972 (N.D. Ind. 2002) (citation omitted). In many instances, the reasonableness of the hourly rate is not contested. See *Rice v. Sunrise Express, Inc.*, 237 F. Supp. 2d 962, 922 (N.D. Ind. 2002); *Barrilleaux v. Thayer Lodging Group, Inc.*, No. 97–3252 § E/1, 1999 U.S. Dist. LEXIS 9073, at *4, n.3 (E.D. La. June 14, 1999); *Morris v. VCW, Inc.*, No. 95–0737–CV–W–3–6, 1996 U.S. Dist. LEXIS 19201, at *19 (W.D. Mo. Dec. 26, 1996).

Once the lodestar is calculated, the second inquiry conducted by the court is to determine whether adjustments will be made to the lodestar amount. A number of courts have applied the 12–factor test developed by the Fifth Circuit in *Johnson v. Georgia Highway Express, Inc.*, 488 F.2d 714, 717–19 (5th Cir. 1974). See *Hoge v. Honda of America Mfg., Inc.*, No. 2:00–CV–995, 2003 U.S. Dist. LEXIS 4068, at *4, n. 1 (S.D. Ohio. March 3, 2003); *Shepherd v. Honda of America Mfg., Inc.*, 160 F. Supp. 2d 860, 875, n. 4 (S.D. Ohio 2001); *Barrilleaux v. Thayer Lodging Group, Inc.*, No. 97–3252 § E/1, 1999 U.S. Dist. LEXIS 9073, at *2 (E.D. La. June 14, 1999); *Cookston v. Freeman, Inc.*, No. 3:98–CV–2106–D, 1999 WL 714760 (N.D. Tex. Sept. 14, 1999); *Mora v. Chem–Tronics, Inc.*, 5 WH Cases 2d 1122 (S.D. Cal. 1999). Courts in other FMLA cases have reviewed the lodestar calculation without reference to the 12–factor test. See *Rice v. Sunrise Express, Inc.*, 237 F. Supp. 2d 962, 922 (N.D. Ind. 2002); *Brenlla v. Lasora Buick Pontiac Chevrolet, Inc. et al.*, No. 00 Civ. 5207 (JCF), 2002 U.S. Dist. LEXIS 9358, at *43 (S.D.N.Y. May 28, 2002).

The 12–factor test used by some courts is (*Hoge v. Honda of America Mfg., Inc.*, No. 2:00–CV–995, 2003 U.S. Dist. LEXIS 4068, at *4 n. 1 (S.D. Ohio. March 3, 2003)):

> The time and labor required by a given case;
>
> The novelty and difficulty of the questions presented;
>
> The skill needed to perform the legal service properly;
>
> The preclusion of employment by the attorney due to acceptance of the case;

The customary fee;

Whether the fees are fixed or contingent;

Time limitations imposed by the client or the circumstances;

The amount involved and the results obtained;

The experience, reputation, and ability of the attorneys;

The 'undesirability' of the case;

The nature and length of the professional relationship with the client; and

Awards in similar cases.

See Reed v. Rhodes, 179 F.3d 453, 471–72, n. 3 (6th Cir. 1999); *Kerr v. Screen Guild Extras, Inc.,* 526 F.2d 67, 70 (9th Cir. 1975); *Johnson v. Georgia Hwy. Express, Inc.,* 488 F.2d 714, 717–19 (5th Cir. 1974).

The most critical factor in calculating a reasonable fee award is the degree of success obtained, and when a plaintiff has achieved only partial or limited success, the product of hours reasonably expended on the litigation as a whole multiplied by a reasonable hourly rate may be an excessive amount. *Bryant v. Dollar General Corp.,* No. 3:05-0840, 2007 U.S. Dist. LEXIS 46397, at *2 (M.D. Tenn. June 26, 2007); *Rice v. Sunrise Express, Inc.,* 237 F. Supp. 2d 962, 972 (N.D. Ind. 2002) citing *Hensley v. Eckerhart,* 461` U.S. 424, 436, 76 Led. 2d 40, 103 S. Ct. 1933 (1983).

In *Bryant v. Dollar General Corp.,* No. 3:05-0840, 2007 U.S. Dist. LEXIS 46397, at *1 (M.D. Tenn. June 26, 2007), the court found some of the hours billed excessive. For example, the court found 4 hours to draft the complaint excessive "inasmuch as the Complaint is a relatively simple recital of Plaintiff's version of the facts and spans only four pages." The court found that 23.8 hours spent summarizing the deposition excessive, and a type of clerical work that should have been handled by a paralegal. The court also found 19 hours claimed to prepare the motion for attorney fees excessive. The court noted a five percent cap on an attorney fee petition. That is, the amount claimed for preparing the attorney fee petition should not exceed 5% of the hours spent on the whole case. The fact that the amount of attorney fees generated is disproportionate to the amount of damages awarded does not necessarily foreclose the recovery of fees. Rather, proportionality is a factor that a court may consider in determining the reasonableness of a fee request. *Hoge v. Honda of America Mfg., Inc.,* No. 2:00–CV–995, 2003 U.S. Dist. LEXIS 4068, at *4, n. 1 (S.D. Ohio. March 3, 2003) (collecting cases). In *Hoge,* the employee won a judgment of $3,781.20 in damages, and was awarded $18,112.50 in attorney fees, not including costs. The court declined to reduce the attorney fee award based on a proportionality argument.

In *Rice v. Sunrise Express, Inc.,* 237 F. Supp. 2d 962, 972 (N.D. Ind. 2002), the plaintiff was awarded $720 in damages. She had originally claimed approximately $12,000 in damages. Given the limited nature of her victory, the court reduced by 20% the plaintiff's original request for $162,000 in attorney fees, to $129,663.60. The 20% reduction was previously offered by plaintiff. The court's decision rested heavily on the importance of the fee award in civil rights cases. *Rice,* 237 F. Supp. 2d at 975–76.

In *Morris v. VCW, Inc.,* Case O. 95–0737–CV–W–3–6, 1996 U.S. Dist. LEXIS 19201 (W.D. Mo. Dec. 26, 1996), the court awarded $80,000 in attorney fees to the prevailing plaintiff. The plaintiff was also awarded $19,376 in actual damages, which was doubled with the additional award of liquidated damages.

For those who don't believe that FMLA cases can get expensive, the court in *Mora v. Chem–Tronics, Inc.,* 5 WH Cases 2d 1122 (S.D. Cal. 1999), awarded a prevailing plaintiff $391,279.78 in attorney fees alone.

Just as a reminder, under Title I, individual managers and supervisors may be liable as FMLA "employers." That means that these large damage and attorney fee awards for violation of the FMLA can be assessed against an individual manager or supervisor.

c. Costs

(1) General Rule

A prevailing employee may recover certain costs of litigation. 29 USC2617(a)(3). *See Hoge v. Honda of America Mfg., Inc.*, No. 2:00–CV–995, 2003 U.S. Dist. LEXIS 4068, at *3 (S.D. Ohio March 3, 2003). Although not specifically authorized by the Statute, courts have also awarded costs to a prevailing defendant in FMLA cases. *See Ogborn v. United Food and Commercial Workers Union, Local No. 881*, 305 F.3d 763, 769–70 (7th Cir. 2002); *Billings v. Cape Cod Child Dev. Program, Inc.*, 270 F. Supp. 2d 175 (D. Mass., 2003) (indicating that Rule 54 (d) of the Federal Rules of Civil Procedure permits such an award of costs to a prevailing party, and that Congress "evinced no intent in enacting the FMLA to override the presumption of Rule 54(d)"); *Rice v. Sunrise Express, Inc.*, 237 F. Supp. 2d 962, 978–79 (N.D. Ind. Nov. 13, 2002) (calculation of costs based on Rule 54(d) of Federal Rules of Civil Procedure in tandem with 28 USC 1920).

The courts have not settled on the scope of taxable costs that may be recovered by a prevailing party. Most courts permit the prevailing party on an FMLA claim to recover costs as permitted by Rule 54 (d) of the Federal Rules of Civil Procedure, as modified by 28 USC 1920. The argument could be made, however, that the FMLA permits reimbursement of costs beyond those permitted by Rule 54(d) and 28 USC 1920. The legislative history indicates that the remedial provisions of the FMLA parallel those of the FLSA, 29 USC 216(b), and should be interpreted the same as the FLSA. S. Rep. 103–3, p. 36. Some courts have interpreted the FLSA as allowing the recovery of costs beyond those normally allowed under Fed. R. Civ. P. 54(d) and 28 USC 1920. *See Smith v. Diffee Ford–Lincoln–Mercury, Inc.*, 298 F.3d 955, 968–69 (10th Cir. 2002) citing *Herold v. Hajoca Corp.*, 864 F.2d 317, 323 (4th Cir. 1988), *cert. denied*, 490 U.S. 1107, 104 L. Ed. 2d 1022, 109 S. Ct. 3159 (1989) (holding that FLSA's costs provision authorizes an award of costs as part of "reasonable attorney's fee," which would not be authorized under Rule 54 or 28 USC 1920); *Colunga v. Young*, 722 F. Supp. 1479, 1488 (W.D. Mich. 1989), *aff'd*, 914 F.2d 255 (6th Cir. 1990) (holding that while travel and telephone expenses are not recoverable under Rule 54 or 28 USC 1920, they are recoverable under the remedial and more broadly interpreted cost–shifting aspect of FLSA). Under the FLSA, reasonable out–of–pocket expenses are included within costs. *Smith v. Diffee Ford–Lincoln–Mercury, Inc.*, 298 F.3d 955, 968–69 (10th Cir. 2002) citing *Shorter v. Valley Bank & Trust Co.*, 678 F. Supp. 714, 726 (N.D. Ill. 1988). In *Diffee*, the court could not discern what claimed out–of–pocket expenses were at issue and remanded the matter for further clarification. *Diffee*, 298 F.3d at 969.

Like many areas involving the FMLA, employees and agencies are well advised to consult case law interpreting the remedial provisions of the FLSA to determine the potential scope of taxable costs that may be recoverable to an employee for violation of the FMLA.

Courts addressing costs in the context of the FMLA have done so by referencing Rule 54(d) of the Federal Rules of Civil Procedure and 28 USC 1920. Rule 54(d) creates a presumption favoring the award of costs to the prevailing party. *Rice v. Sunrise Express, Inc.*, 237 F. Supp. 2d 962, 978–79 (N.D. Ind. Nov. 13, 2002) (citing *Coyne-Delany Co., Inc. v. Capital Dev. Bd.*, 717 F.2d 385, 1983 U.S. App. LEXIS 24074 (7th Cir. 1983)).

The legislative history of the FMLA suggests that the award of costs might be mandatory. *See, e.g.*, S. Rep. 103–3, p. 36 ("…the award of attorney's fees under the FLSA is unconditional. A court has no discretion to deny fees to a prevailing plaintiff; its discretion extends only to the amount allowed"). Trial courts, however, possess wide discretion to determine whether expenses claimed by the prevailing party are actually taxable costs. *Rice v. Sunrise Express, Inc.*, 237 F. Supp. 2d 962, 978–79 (N.D. Ind. Nov. 13, 2002) citing *Deimer v. Cincinnati Sub-Zero Products, Inc.*, 58 F.3d 341, 345 (7th Cir. 1995). Courts must carefully scrutinize a prevailing party's bill of costs. *Rice v. Sunrise Express, Inc.*, 237 F. Supp. 2d 962, 978–79 (N.D. Ind. Nov. 13, 2002) citing *Farmer v. Arabian Am. Oil Co.*, 379 U.S. 227, 235, 13 L. Ed. 2d 248, 85 S. Ct. 411 (1964).

In *Fiato v. Keala*, 191 Fed. Appx. 551 (9th Cir. 2006), the court affirmed the award of costs to the employer who secured summary judgment. Addressing the employee's challenge to the award of costs, the court noted that Federal Rule of Civil Procedure 54(d)(1) allows district courts to award costs unless otherwise provided by statute. While the FMLA addresses costs, the court found the provision inapplicable. The FMLA provision governing costs applies only where an employee seeks damages from an employer. Where, as here, a court awards costs to an employer against an employee, the award is governed solely by Rule 54(d)(1).

(2) Recoverable Costs

In determining what costs may be recovered by a prevailing party, Rule 54(d) works in tandem with 28 USC 1920. Costs outside those enumerated in § 1920 have been disallowed by some courts. *Rice v. Sunrise Express, Inc.*, 237 F. Supp. 2d 962, 978–79 (N.D. Ind. Nov. 13, 2002) *citing In re San Juan Plaza Hotel Fire Litigation*, 995 F.2d 956, 964 (1st Cir. 1993). The taxable costs that may be recovered by a prevailing part as specified in 28 USC 1920 include fees for:

Clerk fees;

Transcripts;

Printing;

Witnesses;

Copies of papers "necessarily" used in the case;

Docketing fees;

Compensation of court appointed experts and interpreters.

See Rice v. Sunrise Express, Inc., 237 F. Supp. 2d 962, 978 (N.D. Ind. Nov. 13, 2002).

Fees of the Clerk include filing fees as well as fees for the service of the summons and subpoenas. *Rice*, 237 F. Supp. 2d at 979. Transcript fees for depositions, as well as fees for court conferences, have been held covered. *Id*. Fees for daily transcripts are within the discretion of the court. *Id*. (citing *Farmer v. Arabian Am. Oil Co.*, 379 U.S. 227, 235, 13 L. Ed. 2d 248, 85 S. Ct. 411 (1964)); *see also Hoge v. Honda of America Mfg., Inc.*, No. 2:00–CV–995, 2003 U.S. Dist. LEXIS 4068, at *8 (S.D. Ohio March 3, 2003) (costs for filing fee and court reporters' fees for attending deposition, as well as fees for obtaining transcripts recoverable); *Brenlla v. Larosa Buick Pontiac Chevrolet, Inc. et al.*, No. 00 Civ. 5207 (JCF), 2002 U.S. Dist. LEXIS 9358, at *48 (S.D.N.Y. May 28, 2002) (awarding fees for service of subpoenas, service of the complaint, and transcripts).

Costs for enlargements and exhibits are recoverable, but only when they are an essential aid to understanding the issue in the case. *Rice*, 237 F. Supp. 2d at 979 (citing *Antonson v. United Armored Services, Inc.*, 2002 U.S. Dist. LEXIS 8039, at *2 (N.D. Ill. May 3, 2002)); *Bd. of Trustees of Underwood Neuhaus Co., Inc.*, 1995 U.S. Dist. LEXIS 1058 (N.D. Ill. Jan. 25, 1995). Taxable costs of printing do not include the costs of printing Supreme Court briefs. *Rice.*, 237 F. Supp. 2d at 979.

Photocopying expenses are recoverable under 29 USC 1920(4) if the copies were reasonably necessary for the use in the case. *Rice*, 237 F. Supp. 2d at 979 (citing *M.T. Bonk Co. v. Milton Bradley Co.*, 945 F.2d 1404, 1410 (7th Cir. 1991)); *see also Hoge v. Honda of America Mfg., Inc.*, No. 2:00–CV–995, 2003 U.S. Dist. LEXIS 4068, at *8 (S.D. Ohio March 3, 2003) (costs for photocopying recoverable). Extra copies of filed papers are not necessary, but are for the convenience of the attorneys, and the cost of extra copies is not taxable. *Rice*, 237 F. Supp. 2d at 979 (citing *Haroco, Inc. v. Am. Bank and Trust Co. of Chicago*, 38 F.3d 1429, 1441 (7th Cir. 1994)).

In the Seventh Circuit, the per page charges for in–house copying may not exceed the charges of an outside print shop unless the party can demonstrate why the higher in–house charge is appropriate. *Rice*, 237 F. Supp. 2d at 979 (citing *Manley v. City of Chicago*, 236 F.3d 392, 398 (7th Cir. 1991)). The court in *Sunrise* found that local print shops charged $0.10 per page. Absent further evidence justifying charges of $0.20 and $ 0.25 submitted by the plaintiff, the court reduced the taxable printing costs to $0.10 per page. *Id.* at 979.

Costs under Rule 54(d)(1) and 28 USC 1920 include witness fees. *See* 28 USC 1920(3). In addition, 28 USC 1821 limits the witness fee authorized by § 1920 to $40 per day, plus actual expenses for travel by common carrier, as well as a per diem allowance where an overnight stay is required, up to a maximum amount prescribed by the Administrator of the General Services. *Rice*, 237 F. Supp. 2d at 979 (citing 28 USC 1821(b)–(d)). The fee includes mileage costs. *Id.* at 979.

Note that the FMLA specifically provides for the recovery of expert witness fees. 29 USC 2617(a)(3). Expert witness fees are exempt from the witness reimbursement restrictions of Rule 54(d) and 28 USC 1920, including the $40 per day cap. *See, e.g., Brenlla v. Larosa Buick Pontiac Chevrolet, Inc. et al.*, No. 00 Civ. 5207 (JCF), 2002 U.S. Dist. LEXIS 9358, at *48 (S.D.N.Y. May 28, 2002) ($2000 fee for consultation with doctor, who testified at trial, found to be both reasonable and a reimbursable cost); *Shepard v. Honda of America Mfg., Inc.*, 160 F. Supp. 2d 860, 875–76 (S.D. Ohio 2001) (although noting

Rule 54(d) limitation on witness fees to $40 per day, court awarded $3,122.50 for expert witness fees to the plaintiff who was successful on merits of ADA and FMLA claims).

Finally, because it is not listed in 28 USC 1920 as a compensable cost, mediation expenses are not compensable. *Rice,* 237 F. Supp. 2d at 979.

Costs were reimbursed for expenses incurred for computerized legal research and messenger service in *Brenlla v. Larosa Buick Pontiac Chevrolet, Inc. et al.,* No. 00 Civ. 5207 (JCF), 2002 U.S. Dist. LEXIS 9358, at *48 (S.D.N.Y. May 28, 2002) (request was unopposed).

5. MSPB Remedies

The remedies discussed above are available to an employee or the Secretary of Labor by way of filing a civil lawsuit against the employer in federal court. As set forth earlier in the "Enforcement" section of this chapter, however, certain federal employees covered by Title I may appeal leave-related discipline, including FMLA leave, to the MSPB.

FMLA leave is not an independent basis for Board jurisdiction. Rather, a violation of the FMLA may be asserted by an employee as grounds for invalidating a leave-related adverse action that is appealable to the Board. Both the employee and the adverse action must be within the Board's jurisdiction. *Bogumill v. OPM,* 168 F.3d 1320 (table), 1998 U.S. App. LEXIS 18750, at *4 (Fed. Cir. Aug. 13, 1998); *Lau v. USPS,* 87 MSPR 647 (2001) (Board did not have jurisdiction over FMLA claims because Postal employee is not a preference-eligible employee or otherwise entitled to appeal an adverse action to the Board); *Moore v. USPS,* 83 MSPR 533 (1999); *Landahl v. Dept. of Commerce,* 83 MSPR 40 (1999), *aff'd,* 10 Fed. Appx. 950 (Fed. Cir. 2001); *Burge v. Dept. of Air Force,* 82 MSPR 75 (1999), *aff'd,* 7 Fed. Appx. 931 (Fed. Cir. 2001); *Ellshoff v. DOI,* 76 MSPR 54 (1997); *Ramey v. USPS,* 70 MSPR 463 (1996), *aff'd,* 178 F.3d 1312 (table), 1999 U.S. App. LEXIS 657 (Fed. Cir. Jan. 8, 1999).

For the most part, the below cases address certain Postal employees with adverse action appeal rights to the Board. Employees of the Postal Service are covered by Title I of the FMLA. *See Jennifer v. USPS,* Docket No. PH-0752-00-0344-I-2, 2001 MSPB LEXIS 1298 & n.6 (2001); *Young v. USPS,* 79 MSPR 25, n. 4 (1998); *Ramey v. USPS,* 70 MSPR 463, n.1 (1996), *aff'd,* 178 F.3d 1312 (table), 1999 U.S. App. LEXIS 657 (Fed. Cir. Jan. 8, 1999), *modified on other grounds, Ellshoff v. Dept. of Interior,* 76 MSPR 54, 73–74 (1997). As set forth more fully in Chapter 4, "Federal Employees Covered by the FMLA," other federal employees are covered by Title I of the FMLA as well. For an excellent analysis of what federal employees have MSPB appeal rights, and what adverse actions are appealable to the Board, see Peter Broida, *A Guide to Merit Systems Protection Board Law and Practice* (Dewey Publications, Inc. 2007).

The Board has held that it has jurisdiction over an adverse action involving a leave-related issue involving the FMLA even if the appellant could have sought enforcement of his or her FMLA rights in other forums. *Moore v. USPS,* 83 MSPR 533 (1999) (rejecting USPS argument that Board did not have jurisdiction because the appropriate forum for the appellant's FMLA claims is either the DOL or a federal district court pursuant to 29 CFR 825.400).

The agency bears the burden of proving that, in taking a leave-related disciplinary action, it properly denied an "eligible" employee leave under the FMLA. *Williams v. Dept. of Air Force,* 89 MSPR 484 (2001); *Covington v. Dept. of Army,* 85 MSPR 612 (2000) (agency has burden of proof that it did not interfere with appellant's FMLA rights in taking its leave-related action); *Moore v. USPS,* 83 MSPR 533 (1999); *Fairley v. USPS,* 82 MSPR 588 (1999); *Garnder v. USPS,* 79 MSPR 9 (1998); *Byers v. USPS,* 78 MSPR 456 (1998); *Jefferies v. Dept. of Navy,* 78 MSPR 255 (1998); *Gross v. Dept. of Justice,* 77 MSPR 83 (1997); *Ellshoff v. Dept. of Interior,* 76 MSPR 54, 73–74 (1997). Where an appellant raises nonfrivolous factual allegations reasonably relating to an FMLA claim, or the agency's evidence or allegations otherwise show that FMLA-qualifying leave was involved, the administrative judge has the responsibility to develop the record evidence as necessary and appropriate. *Williams v. Dept. of Air Force,* 89 MSPR 484 (2001); *Fairley v. USPS,* 82 MSPR 588 (1999).

Prior to *Ellshoff,* the Board treated an FMLA claim as an affirmative defense and the burden of proving that the defense was placed on the appellant. *Fairley v. USPS,* 82 MSPR 588 (1999); *Ramey v. USPS,* 70 MSPR 463, 467 (1996) *aff'd* 178 F.3d 1312 (table), 1999 U.S. App. LEXIS 657 (Fed. Cir. Jan. 8, 1999). In *Ellshoff,* the Board found that there was no basis for treating the FMLA differently from any other leave-related statute, and found that "where the facts, either specifically raised by the appellant or otherwise shown by record evidence, implicate the FMLA relative to a leave related charge, the Board will consider and apply the FMLA without shifting the burden of proof to the appellant." *Ellshoff,* 76 MSPR at 73.

The Board has addressed a number of MSPB appeals involving FMLA claims filed by employees covered by Title I of the Act. *Jenifer v. USPS*, Docket No. PH-0752-00-0344-I-2, 2001 MSPB LEXIS 1298, n. 6 (2001) (nonprecedential decision of MSPB regional office) (removal for exceeding permissible number of unscheduled absences as agreed to in last chance agreement sustained); *Hamilton v. USPS*, 84 MSPR 635 (1999) (affirming agency removal of employee for failure to meet attendance requirements of position due to seven unscheduled absences even though FMLA protected some specifications); *Moore v. USPS*, 83 MSPR 533 (1999) (petition for enforcement of Board order canceling removal and ordering reinstatement, with back pay and all other appropriate relief); *Fairley v. USPS,* 82 MSPR 588 (1999) (vacating prior Board decision affirming removal for AWOL and failure to be regular in attendance and remanding appeal for further consideration of FMLA on absences at issue in light of Board's decision in *Ellshoff*); *Nolan v. USPS*, 80 MSPB 241 (1998) (Board has jurisdiction over constructive suspension allegation resulting from an employee not allowed to return to work from FMLA leave when desired due to delay in processing return to work certification requirements); *Young v. USPS*, 79 MSPR 25, n. 4 (1998) (although removal for AWOL partially covered by FMLA, Board sustained removal for absences not so covered); *Garnder v. USPS,* 79 MSPR 9 (1998) (vacating and remanding for further consideration of FMLA claims removal of employee for violating terms of last chance agreement setting maximum number of unscheduled absences); *Byers v. USPS,* 78 MSPR 456 (1998) (removal for failure to be regular in attendance sustained even though certain specifications regarding absences were not, as such absences were covered by the FMLA).

The Board cases involving Title I employees are interesting in several respects. First, many Board decisions cite as support federal court case law interpreting Title I of the FMLA. *See Hamilton v. USPS*, 84 MSPR 635 (1999) *citing Robbins v. Bureau of Nat'l Affairs, Inc.*, 896 F. Supp. 18, 20-21 (D.D.C. 1995) (addressing whether the employee met the 1250-hour test for eligibility; *Young v. USPS*, 79 MSPR 25 (1998) *citing Manual v. Westlake Polymers Corp.* 66 F.3d 758, 761-63 (5th Cir. 1995); *Brown v. J.C. Penney Corp.*, 924 F. Supp. 1158, 1161-63 (S.D. Fla. 1996)). While this is not a surprising development given that the Board and the courts are interpreting the same statute and implementing regulations, it nevertheless is noteworthy as it strongly suggests that the Board may be receptive to other arguments based on federal case law interpretations of Title I of the FMLA.

In the several cases where it found that the agency interfered with an employee's FMLA rights by including FMLA-covered leave as a basis for leave-related discipline, the Board did not utilize (or reference) the burden of proof scheme used by the majority of courts for FMLA interference claims. *See Jenifer v. USPS*, Docket No. PH-0752-00-0344-I-2, 2001 MSPB LEXIS 1298 (2001) (nonprecedential decision of MSPB regional office); *Hamilton v. USPS*, 84 MSPR 635 (1999); *Young v. USPS*, 79 MSPR 25, n. 4 (1998); *Byers v. USPS,* 78 MSPR 456 (1998). Rather, the Board in these cases appeared to simply assess the available facts without the benefit of a proof scheme.

The inclusion of FMLA leave as part of leave-related discipline was not fatal to the adverse action taken by the agency. Rather, the Board applied its usual rule sustaining a charge where there is proof that one or more, but not all, supporting specifications have been met. *Jenifer v. USPS*, Docket No. PH-0752-00-0344-I-2, 2001 MSPB LEXIS 1298 (2001) (nonprecedential decision of MSPB regional office); *Hamilton v. USPS*, 84 MSPR 635 (1999); *Young v. USPS*, 79 MSPR 25, n. 4 (1998); *Byers v. USPS,* 78 MSPR 456 (1998).

Finally, in *Moore v. USPS*, 83 MSPR 533 (1999), the Board addressed the interplay between the Back Pay Act and the FMLA. There, the appellant sought enforcement of a prior Board order directing the Postal Service to cancel the his removal, reinstate him, and to pay him back pay, with interest, and other benefits pursuant to the Back Pay Act. *Moore v. USPS*, 83 MSPR 533 (1999). The appellant claimed that the Postal Service violated the order by finding him ineligible for FMLA leave shortly after his return to work. One of the requirements for Title I eligibility is that the employee have worked at least 1,250 hours in the 12-month period immediately preceding leave commencement. Because he had been removed, appellant had not worked the requisite 1,250 hours prior to leave commencement. The appellant argued, and the administrative judge agreed, that the appellant should have been credited with the hours he would have worked as part of the Board order to reinstate him with full back pay and benefits. According to the administrative judge, "but for the agency's unwarranted personnel action, the appellant would have worked 1,250 hours prior to the date he made the leave request." *Id.* At 539.

In pertinent part, the Postal Service argued that the Back Pay Act does not require an agency to, in effect, "deem" an employee eligible for FMLA leave where, as here, the employee did not meet the statutory requirements for entitlement to FMLA leave because he did not work the requisite hours for leave eligibility. The Board held that the Back Pay Act applies to preference eligible employees, and provides, *Id.* At 538 *quoting* 5 USC 5596(b)(1)(B), that:

> An employee of an agency who...is found by appropriate authority under applicable law, rule, regulation, or

collective bargaining agreement, to have been affected by an unjustified or unwarranted personnel action which has resulted in the withdrawal or reduction of all or part of the pay, allowances, or differentials of the employee...(B) *for all purposes, is deemed to have performed service for the agency during that period [for which the employee received back pay]...*

(Emphasis supplied).

The Postal Service argued that the language of the Back Pay Act applies to traditional benefits of employment like leave, health insurance, and life insurance, not statutory rights. The Board rejected these arguments. The Board did not see such a distinction in the language of the Act nor did it perceive any meaningful conceptual difference between an employee's eligibility for leave rights created by the FMLA and the employee's eligibility for qualifications for other types of leave rights created by other statues and regulations. In point, the Board held that the "for all purposes" language of the Back Pay Act included eligibility for FMLA leave. According to the Board; *Moore*, 83 MSPR at 540:

> Although the Back Pay Act and the FMLA were enacted for different purposes, their terms affecting the same subject matter must be construed harmoniously and consistently with one another, if reasonably possible. *See Woodyard–Hamilton v. Office of Personnel Management,* 64 M.S.P.R. 150, 154 (1991); *see also* Singer, Sutherland Statutory Construction § 57.01 (5th Ex. 1992). The Back Pay Act states that "for all purposes" an employee is deemed to have performed service during the period for which the employee received back pay, and the FMLA states that an employee must have performed 1,250 hours of service during the 12 months period to the date of the leave request. The question before us is whether the phrase "for all purposes" under the Back Pay Act and the FMLA require an affirmative answer. We find that the remedial purpose of the Back Pay Act encompasses the eligibility requirements of the FMLA. We find that the remedial purposes of the Back Pay Act and the FMLA require an affirmative answer. Therefore, the appellant is an eligible employee under the FMLA and the agency, by refusing to consider the appellant's requests for FMLA leave, failed to restore him to the *status quo ante* pursuant to the Board's final decision at 78 M.S.P.R. 31. *See Kerr,* 726 F.2d at 733.

Outside of the Back Pay Act context, courts have rejected the argument that an employee who has been returned to work with back pay and benefits also receives credit as if the employee had worked the back pay hours for purposes of FMLA leave eligibility. *See Plumley v. Southern Container, Inc.,* No. 00–140–P–C, 2001 U.S. Dist. LEXIS 16040 (D. Me. Oct. 9, 2001).

The Board in *Moore* did one more interesting thing. After determining (erroneously, as it turns out) that the employee was not eligible for FMLA leave, the Postal Service terminated Moore for AWOL and failure to follow leave reporting instructions. The Board found that this second removal violated the FMLA as Moore was incapacitated during this period of time due to a chronic serious health condition. As a remedy, the Board ordered the Postal Service to cancel this second removal action and restore the employee to work, with back pay, interest, and other benefits pursuant to the Back Pay Act. Appellant was also apprised of his right to request attorney fees. What is noteworthy is that the remedies awarded were pursuant to the Back Pay Act and Board law, not the FMLA. Apparently no argument was made for liquidated damages, which is permissible under the FMLA.

B. TITLE II

1. Introduction

Neither the Statute nor the OPM implementing regulations address what remedies, if any, are available to an employee covered by Title II for an employer's violation of the FMLA.

2. General Rule

As addressed in the "Enforcement" section of this chapter, the legislative and regulatory history of Title II and the OPM regulations indicate that grievance procedures, both internal agency procedures and those pursuant to the terms of a collective bargaining agreement, were the means available to a covered employee to seek redress for violations of Title II of the FMLA. As such, in the absence of remedial provisions in Title II or the OPM implementing regulations, sovereign immunity would appear to bar recovery for damages for violation of the FMLA, except as permitted by agency policy, including the terms of a collective bargaining agreement. That is, the recovery of damages is limited to whatever is allowed to an employee who uses the grievance system at issue, whether internal agency or pursuant to the terms of a collective bargaining agreement. If these systems allow for awards non-wage, out-of-pocket expenses, liquidated damages, attorney fees, and expert witness fees, such should also be available to employees alleging violation of Title II of the FMLA. More than likely, however, the internal agency grievance process does not allow for recovery of these types of losses. Grievance systems contained in collective bargaining agreements may also provide for the types of damages and other losses that may be recovered by a grievant.

3. MSPB

As indicated previously in the "Enforcement" section of this chapter, federal employees with MSPB appeal rights for covered adverse actions may raise the issue of violation of the FMLA. *Bogumill v. OPM*, 168 F.3d 1320 (table), 1998 U.S. App. LEXIS 18750, at *4 (Fed. Cir. Aug. 13, 1998); *Moore v. USPS*, 83 MSPR 533 (1999), *pet. dismissed*, 85 MSPR 249 (1999); *Landahl v. Dept. of Commerce*, 83 MSPR 40 (1999), *aff'd*, 10 Fed. Appx. 950 (Fed. Cir. 2001); *Burge v. Dept. of Air Force*, 82 MSPR 75 (1999), *aff'd*, 7 Fed. Appx. 931 (Fed. Cir. 2001); *Ellshoff v. DOI*, 76 MSPR 54 (1997), *rev'd on other grounds, remanded*, 78 MSPR 615 (1998); *Ramey v. USPS*, 70 MSPR 463 (1996), *aff'd*, 178 F.3d 1312 (table), 1999 U.S. App. LEXIS 657 (Fed. Cir. Jan. 8, 1999).

The Board has held that it has jurisdiction over an adverse action involving a leave-related issue involving the FMLA even if the appellant could have sought enforcement of his or her FMLA rights in other forums. *Moore v. USPS*, 83 MSPR 533 (1999) (rejecting USPS argument that the Board did not have jurisdiction because the appropriate forum for the appellant's FMLA claims is either the DOL or a federal district court pursuant to 29 CFR 825.400).

The agency bears the burden of proving that, in taking a leave-related disciplinary action, it properly denied an "eligible" employee leave under the FMLA. *Williams v. Dept. of Air Force*, 89 MSPR 484 (2001); *Covington v. Dept. of Army*, 85 MSPR 612 (2000) (agency has burden of proof that it did not interfere with appellant's FMLA rights in taking its leave-related action), *pet. denied*, 90 MSPR 24(2001), *review dismissed*, 2002 U.S. App. LEXIS 2559 (Fed. Cir. 2002); *Moore v. USPS*, 83 MSPR 533 (1999), *pet. dismissed*, 85 MSPR 249 (1999); *Fairley v. USPS*, 82 MSPR 588 (1999); *Garnder v. USPS*, 79 MSPR 9 (1998), *pet. denied*, 83 MSPR 91 (1999); *Byers v. USPS*, 78 MSPR 456 (1998); *Jefferies v. Dept. of Navy*, 78 MSPR 255 (1998); *Gross v. DOJ*, 77 MSPR 83 (1997); *Ellshoff v. Dept. of Interior*, 76 MSPR 54, 73-74 (1997), *rev'd on other grounds, remanded*, 78 MSPR 615 (1998). Where an appellant raises nonfrivolous factual allegations reasonably relating to an FMLA claim, or the agency's evidence or allegations otherwise show that FMLA-qualifying leave was involved, the administrative judge has the responsibility to develop the record evidence as necessary and appropriate. *Williams v. Dept. of Air Force*, 89 MSPR 484 (2001); *Fairley v. USPS*, 82 MSPR 588 (1999).

Prior to *Ellshoff*, the Board treated an FMLA claim as an affirmative defense and the burden of proving that the defense was placed on the appellant. *Fairley v. USPS*, 82 MSPR 588 (1999); *Ramey v. USPS*, 70 MSPR 463, 467 (1996) *aff'd* 178 F.3d 1312 (table), 1999 U.S. App. LEXIS 657 (Fed. Cir. Jan. 8, 1999). In *Ellshoff*, the Board found that there was no basis for treating the FMLA differently from any other leave-related statute, and found "that where the facts, either specifically raised by the appellant or otherwise shown by record evidence, implicate the FMLA relative to a leave related charge, the Board will consider and apply the FMLA without shifting the burden of proof to the appellant." *Ellshoff*, 76 MSPR at 73.

The Board has addressed a number of MSPB appeals involving FMLA claims filed by employees covered by Title II of the Act. *See Williams v. Dept. of Air Force*, 89 MSPR 484 (2001) (sustaining removal after finding that the employee's sleep apnea did not constitute a serious health condition within the meaning of the FMLA as it did not incapacitate him for duty during the relevant time period); *Covington v. Dept. of Army*, 85 MSPR 612 (2000), *pet. denied*, 90 MSPR 24(2001), *review dismissed*, 2002 U.S. App. LEXIS 2559 (Fed. Cir. 2002) (nonfrivolous allegation established that appellant was not AWOL, and that agency breached settlement agreement when it charged her with AWOL and by removing her); *Landahl v. Dept. of Commerce*, 83 MSPR 40 (1999) (appellant raised a nonfrivolous allegation that his resignation was coerced in violation of his rights to leave under the FMLA, entitling him to a jurisdictional hearing on the voluntariness of his resignation) *aff'd* 10 Fed. Appx. 950 (Fed. Cir. 2001); *Young v. Dept. of Veterans Affairs*, 83 MSPR 187 (1999) (sustaining removal of appellant for AWOL); *Burge v. Dept. of Air Force*, 82 MSPR 75 (1999) (remand to AJ to develop more evidence whether removal for AWOL violated FMLA); *Jefferies v. Dept. of Navy*, 78 MSPR 255 (1998) (removal for AWOL and failure to follow leave procedures sustained after finding that the appellant failed to provide adequate medical documentation to support his claim for FMLA leave); *Gross v. Dept. of Justice*, 77 MSPR 1997) (ordering cancellation of 20-day suspension for AWOL where the employee's absence due to a family medical emergency was covered by the FMLA); *Ellshoff v. Dept.*

of *Interior*, 76 MSPR 54 (1997), *rev'd on other grounds, remanded*, 78 MSPR 615 (1998) (ordering cancellation of removal for AWOL after finding that the appellant's leave was covered by FMLA); *Joos v. Dept. of Treasury*, 74 MSPR 684 (1997) (Board found the agency not in compliance with last chance settlement agreement where the agency removed the appellant for excessive absences where such absences were covered by the FMLA).

Board litigation reveals several interesting points. In several cases, the Board applied cases or regulations interpreting Title I of the Act to employees covered by Title II. In *Ellshoff v. Dept. of Interior*, 76 MSPR 54 (1997), *rev'd on other grounds, remanded*, 78 MSPR 615 (1998), the Board held that a Title II employee need not explicitly invoke the FMLA in requesting FMLA–qualifying leave, citing *Manual v. Westlake Polymers Corp.* 66 F.3d 758, 762 (5th Cir. 1995), a Title I case. The Board justified its determination that *Manual* was "persuasive authority" on this point by finding "that the notice provisions under Title I and Title II are identical in material respects." The decision was based on the OPM interim regulations, which the Board found were silent on this issue. As set forth in Chapter 8, "Notice Requirements," the Board's observation that the notice provisions governing Title I and Title II are "identical in material respects" is a gross overstatement.

The Board in *Ellshoff* also cited the Title I decision in *Manual v. Westlake Polymers Corp.* 66 F.3d 758, 762 (5th Cir. 1995) for the proposition that the final OPM regulations implementing Title II do not apply retroactively. Rather, because the matter arose during the pendency of the OPM interim regulations, the case was governed by the interim regulations. The OPM interim regulations were effective from July 23, 1993 through January 5, 1997. The final OPM FMLA regulations became effective on January 6, 1997.

In *Burge v. Dept. of Air Force*, 82 MSPR 75 (1999), *pet. denied*, 86 MSPR 688 (2000), the appellant untimely submitted a medical certification in support of his request for FMLA leave. The Board noted "the FMLA implementing regulations at 5 CFR Part 630, which apply to federal employees, do not list any circumstances under which an untimely submission may be accepted by an agency." The Board, however, went on to both note and apply (by analogy) 29 CFR 825.305(b), which allows untimely submission of medical documentation (by employees in the private sector and Postal Service) where timely submission is not practical under the circumstances, despite the employee's diligent, good faith efforts. The Board held that this "same standard applies in determining whether a federal employee's untimely medical certification should be considered under the FMLA."

The Board's willingness to resort to Title I regulations and case law to fill "gaps" in the OPM regulations raises interesting possibilities for both agencies and employees.

In *Young v. Dept. of Veterans Affairs*, 83 MSPR 187 (1999), the Board sustained the agency's removal of the appellant for AWOL. In so doing, the Board found that the appellant was not entitled to leave under the FMLA for the AWOL period, as his 12 weeks of FMLA leave had expired before the AWOL period. The Board held that "[b]ecause the appellant's unpaid leave lasted for more than 12 weeks, the FMLA does not preclude sustaining the charge of excessive use of unpaid leave here." The rule is the same under Title I. That is, an agency cannot interfere with a right that has already expired.

Several other observations regarding the Board's Title II decisions are worth noting. First, none of the decisions use (or even mention) the burden of proof scheme for interference and discrimination claims developed by the courts interpreting Title I. This would appear to be a prime area for incorporation of Title I case law.

The Board has also not applied or otherwise addressed remedies available under the FMLA for violation of that Act. This is understandable for employees covered by Title II since, as discussed earlier in this chapter, neither the Statute nor regulations provide for any remedies. Rather, the Board has applied its traditional remedies where it finds that an agency has failed to sustain its leave–related discipline. For example, in *Gross v. Dept. of Justice*, 77 MSPR 83 (1997), the Board applied its usual remedies of ordering the agency to cancel the adverse action, restore the employee to employment, pay the appellant back pay, with interest, and restore other benefits. The Board also notified the appellant of his right to reimbursement for reasonable attorney fees and costs, and directed the employee to file a petition for attorney fees and costs within 35 calendar days. *See Ellshoff v. Dept. of Interior*, 76 MSPR 54 (1997), *rev'd on other grounds, remanded*, 78 MSPR 615 (1998),

Similarly, in *Joos v. Dept. of Treasury*, 74 MSPR 684 (1997), the Board ordered the agency to rescind its placement of appellant on AWOL status and his subsequent removal action, required that the appellant be placed on LWOP during the period in question, directed the agency to expunge all indications of the action from the appellant's records, and ordered the agency to pay $4,000 in attorney fees.

C. CAA

1. Introduction

The remedies available under the CAA are the same as those available under Title I.

2. General Rule

The remedy for violation of § 202(a) of CAA FMLA (2 USC 1312(a)) "shall be such remedy, including liquidated damages, as would be appropriate if awarded under paragraph (1) of § 107(a) of the Family and Medical Leave Act of 1993 (29 USC 2617(a)(1))." 2 USC 1312(b). Section 202(a) of the CAA FMLA incorporates §§ 101 through 105 (29 USC 2611–2615) of Title I of the FMLA. 2 USC 1312(a)(1).

Section 107(a) of Title I of the FMLA (29 USC 2617(a)(1)) permits an eligible employee to recover damages for:

> The amount of any wages, salary, employment benefits, or other compensation denied or lost to such employee by reason of the violation;
>
> In a case in which wages, salary, employment benefits, or other compensation have not been denied or lost to the employee, any actual monetary losses sustained by the employee as a direct result of the violation, such as the cost of providing care, up to a sum equal to 12 weeks of wages or salary for the employee;
>
> Interest on the above amounts;
>
> Liquidated damages, unless the employer can establish that the employer acted in good faith and had reasonable grounds for believing that the act or omission was not violative of the FMLA;
>
> Such equitable relief as may be appropriate, including employment, reinstatement, and promotion; and
>
> Attorney's fees, expert witness fees, and costs.

The reader is referred to the section of this chapter addressing "Remedies" under Title I of the FMLA, as the provisions regarding a civil action by employees therein apply to the FMLA as applied through the CAA. What does not apply are the Title I provisions regarding complaints and civil actions involving the Secretary of Labor.

3. Civil Penalties and Punitive Damages

The CAA specifically prohibits the award of civil penalties or punitive damages with respect to any claim under the CAA, which could include FMLA claims. 2 USC 1361(c). Note, again, that the CAA permits liquidated damages, where appropriate, for violations of the FMLA as applied by the CAA. 2 USC 1312(b).

4. Payments

Awards and settlements pursuant to the CAA, including awards and settlements involving the CAA FMLA, may only be paid by funds that have been appropriated to an account of the Office of the Treasury of the United States for payment of awards and settlements of employing offices. 2 USC 1415(a). The CAA authorizes the appropriation for such accounts such sums as may be necessary to pay for such awards and settlements. 2 USC 1415(a), (c). Funds in the account are not available for payment of awards and settlements involving the GAO, the GPO or the Library of Congress. 2 USC 1415(c).

D. PEOAA

1. Introduction

The PEOAA, like the CAA, applies the remedies available for violation of Title I of the FMLA to FMLA claims arising under the PEOAA.

2. General Rule

The remedy for violation of Subsection (a), 3 USC 412(a)), "shall be such remedy, including liquidated damages, as would be appropriate, if awarded under paragraph (1) of § 107(a) of the Family and Medical Leave Act of 1993." 3 USC 412(b). Subsection (a), 3 USC 412(a), incorporates §§ 101–105, 29 USC 2611–2615, of Title I of the FMLA into the PEOAA for purposes of the PEOAA FMLA.

Paragraph (a)(1) of § 107 of the FMLA, 29 USC 2617(a)(1), provides the following remedies to (in the case of the PEOAA) a covered employee:

> The amount of any wages, salary, employment benefits, or other compensation denied or lost to such employee by reason of the violation;

> In a case in which wages, salary, employment benefits, or other compensation have not been denied or lost to the employee, any actual monetary losses sustained by the employee as a direct result of the violation, such as the cost of providing care, up to a sum equal to 12 weeks of wages or salary for the employee;

> Interest on the above amounts;

> Liquidated damages, unless the employer can establish that the employer acted in good faith and had reasonable grounds for believing that the act or omission was not violative of the FMLA;

> Such equitable relief as may be appropriate, including employment, reinstatement, and promotion; and

> Attorney's fees, expert witness fees, and costs.

29 USC 2617(a)(1)–(4).

The reader is referred to the section of this chapter addressing "Remedies" under Title I of the FMLA, as the provisions regarding a civil action by employees therein apply to the FMLA as applied through the CAA. What does not apply are the Title I remedy provisions regarding complaints and civil actions involving the Secretary of Labor.

3. Attorney's Fees, Expert Witness Fees, Costs, and Interest

It is clear that a prevailing party in a PEOAA FMLA claim is entitled to an award of attorney fees, expert witness fees, costs, and interest. What is unclear, however, is the standard to be used to determine such an award of attorney fees, expert witness fees, costs, and interest under the PEOAA.

The FMLA provisions of the PEOAA specifically incorporate certain remedial provisions of Title I of the FMLA, including those provisions addressing attorney fees, expert witness fees, costs, and interest. The legislative history of the remedial provisions of Title I of the FMLA indicate that attorney fees are interpreted pursuant to § 216(b) of the FLSA, and are to be interpreted in the same way as the FLSA. S. Rep. 103–3, p. 36. The legislative history also indicates that expert witness fees are included as a result of a decision of the Supreme Court to the affect that expert witness fees are not recoverable unless specifically authorized by statute. S. Rep. 103–3, p. 36. Interest is calculated at the prevailing rate. 29 USC 2617(a)(1)(ii).

Pursuant to the PEOAA, Title 28 was modified by adding Chapter 179. Section 3905 of Title 28 (29 USC 3905) addresses the award of attorney fees, expert witness fees, and costs. Specifically, in judicial actions under § 1296 or § 1346(g) involving PEOAA claims, including FMLA claims, "the court may award attorney's fees, expert fees, and other costs as would be appropriate if awarded under § 706(k) of the Civil Rights Act of 1964." 28 USC 3905. Interest in these judicial proceedings is calculated pursuant to § 717(d) of the Civil Rights Act of 1964. 28 USC 3905.

One way to interpret this apparent contradiction is that the Title I method of calculation applies while the covered employee prosecutes a PEOAA FMLA claim before the MSPB. Once in court, however, the calculation of attorney fees, expert fees, costs, and interest is made in accordance with the requirements of Title 28. Of course, this makes little sense. Another way to address this is for the MSPB and courts to simply apply the Title I methodology throughout, notwithstanding the contrary requirements of Title 28. More than likely, the courts will split on which methodology applies. Advocates should prepare to argue both methods of calculation.

4. Civil Penalties and Punitive Damages

Like the CAA, the PEOAA, except as otherwise provided in this chapter, prohibits the award of a civil penalty or punitive damages with respect to any claim under the PEOAA, including FMLA claims. 3 USC 435(c); 28 USC 3905(c). Note that the PEOAA FMLA allows claims for liquidated damages. 3 USC 412(b).

5. Payments

The payment of judgments, awards, or settlements pursuant to the PEOAA, including FMLA claims, is made pursuant to 28 USC 3906, which provides:

> A judgment, award, or compromise settlement against the United States under this Chapter (including interest and costs) shall be paid—
>
> (1) under Section 1304 of Title 31, if it arises out of an action commenced in district court of the United States (or any appeal therefrom); or
>
> (2) out of amounts otherwise appropriate or available to the office involved, if it arises out of an appeal from an administrative proceeding under Chapter 5 of Title 3.

V. MISCELLANEOUS LITIGATION MATTERS

A. INTRODUCTION

The following addresses a number of civil litigation issues involving FMLA claims. As such, these issues currently involve claims under Title I, and will undoubtedly directly impact civil litigation of FMLA claims arising under the CAA and the PEOAA. Indirectly, some of these issues, such as burden of proof, may migrate into the decisional processes of the MSPB, arbitration decisions, and other agency dispute resolution systems, thereby impacting even Title II claims.

B. FMLA CLAIM OF DECEASED

In *Collins v. OSF Health Care System, et. al.*, 262 F. Supp. 2d 959 (C.D. Ill. 2003), the court held that a husband could not bring suit against an employer for FMLA violations in his individual capacity. In his capacity as executor of the estate of his wife's estate, however, the husband could maintain a timely filed FMLA claim against the employer.

C. REMOVAL

Title I of the FMLA permits an employee to initiate a civil action in any federal or state court of competent jurisdiction. 29 USC 2617(a)(2). In the federal sector, only the federal courts are courts of competent jurisdiction. If, however, if a civil action is initiated in a state court, it may be removed to an appropriate federal district court as an action arising under the laws of the United States. *See Eastus v. Blue Bell Creameries, L.P.*, 97 F.3d 100 (5th Cir. 1996) (affirming district court decision removing FMLA case to federal court based on federal question jurisdiction); *Henriquez v. Royal Sonesta, Inc.*, 1996 U.S. Dist. LEXIS 4616 (E.D. La. April 10, 1996) (court denied the plaintiff's motion to remand to case back to state court, finding that matter based solely on claims brought under FMLA was properly removed to federal court on the basis of federal question jurisdiction); *Ladner v. Alexander and Alexander, Inc.*, 879 F. Supp. 598 (W.D. La. 1995).

D. ADMINISTRATIVE EXHAUSTION

Exhaustion is not required for an employee to initiate a civil action under Title I. *Ogborn v. United Food and Commercial Workers, Local No. 881 et al.*, No. 98 C 4623, 2000 U.S. Dist. LEXIS 14092 (N.D. Ill. Sept. 25, 2000); *Shannon v. City of Philadelphia*, Case No 98–3277, 1999 U.S. Dist. LEXIS 2428 (E.D. Pa. March 5, 1993); *Krohn v. Forsting*, 11 F. Supp. 2d 1082, 1085 (E.D. Mo. 1998); *Danfelt v. Bd. of County Commissioners of Washington County*, 998 F. Supp. 606, 609 (D. Md. 1998); *Spurlock v. NYNEX*, 949 F. Supp. 1022, 1030 (W.D.N.Y. 1996).

E. ARBITRATION OF FMLA CLAIMS

Many private sector employers require prospective employees to sign employment agreements in which, among other things, the employee agrees to submit any disputes arising out of employment to arbitration. Most courts that have addressed the enforcement of such agreements have held that they bind employees to arbitrate their FMLA claims rather than pursue a civil action. See *O'Neil v. Hilton Head Hospital*, 115 F.3d 272 (4th Cir. 1997); *Mandel v. SCI Illinois Services, Inc. et al.*, No. 02 C 8979, 2003 U.S. Dist. LEXIS 13408 (N.D. Ill. Aug. 1, 2003); *Reece v. Commercial Credit Corp.*, 955 F. Supp. 567 (D.S.C. 1997). *Satarino v. A.G. Edwards & Sons, Inc.*, 941 F. Supp. 609 (N.D. Tex. 1996).

In *Jones v. Fujitsu Network Communications, Inc.*, 81 F. Supp. 2d 688, 692 (N.D. Tex. 1999), the court declined to enforce the provision in an employment agreement requiring arbitration that required the employee to pay for half the cost of arbitration. However, because there was a severability clause, the court enforced the requirement that the employee must arbitrate the FMLA claim. Had there not been a severability clause, it is likely that the court would not have required arbitration.

Courts have split on whether a bargaining unit employee must first submit his or her FMLA claim through the grievance arbitration process. *Compare Brown v. TWA*, 127 F.3d 337 (4th Cir. 1997) (FMLA claims arbitrable under collective bargaining agreement where agreement explicitly incorporated statutory provisions of FMLA into agreement); *Smith v. CPC Foodservice*, 955 F. Supp. 84 (N.D. Ill. 1997) (a former employee alleging his termination violated the FMLA required to arbitrate claim pursuant to collective bargaining agreement rather than bringing it in federal court, where collective bargaining agreement specifically referred to FMLA and contained broad, mandatory grievance–arbitration provisions); *Jessie v. Carter Health Care Center, Inc.*, 930 F. Supp. 1174 (E.D. Ky. 1996) (the plaintiff's claims barred by the employee's failure to pursue available remedies through grievance–arbitration procedure of governing collective bargaining agreement); *with McGinnis v. Wonder Chemical Co.*, No. 95–4384, 1995 U.S. Dist. LEXIS 18909 (E.D. Pa. Dec. 21, 1995) (the court refused to dismiss employee's FMLA claims on the ground that the employee failed to arbitrate claims pursuant to collective bargaining agreement).

Title II does not permit a civil action for the enforcement of FMLA rights. As such, there is no administrative exhaustion requirement prior to bringing a federal civil action.

Administrative exhaustion is required under the CAA and the PEOAA before an employee may institute a civil action.

F. ISSUE PRECLUSION OR COLLATERAL ESTOPPEL

Issue preclusion or collateral estoppel, bars the re-litigation of an issue of law or fact that was raised, litigated, and actually decided by a judgment in a prior proceeding between the parties, if the determination of that issue was essential to the judgment, regardless of whether or not the two proceedings are based on the same claim. *Kosakow v. New Rochelle Radiology Associates, P.C.*, 88 F. Supp. 2d 199, 210 (S.D.N.Y. 2000), vacated, remanded, 274 F.3d 760 (2d Cir. 2001); see also *Shtab v. The Greate Bay Hotel and Casino, Inc.*, 173 F. Supp. 2d 255, 260–63 (D.N.J. 2001) (issue preclusion "prevents re-litigation of a particular fact or legal issue that was litigated in an earlier action," citing *Seborowski v. Pittsburgh Press Co.*, 188 F.3d 163, 169 (3d Cir. 1999). (The purpose of claim preclusion is to avoid piecemeal litigation of claims arising from the same events. *Churchill v. Star Enterprises et al.*, 183 F.3d 184, 194 3d Cir. 1999). The bottom line on issue preclusion involving the FMLA is that such awards *may* be binding on subsequent court litigation, provided all conditions are met. In the arbitration context, it is not easy to meet all conditions for the application of the doctrine of issue preclusion.

Issue preclusion applies to issues resolved in arbitration proceedings. *Shtab*, 173 F. Supp. 2d at 261 citing *Seborowski*, 183 F.3d at 169; *Gruntal*, 854 F. Supp. at 337. It also applies where employee claims have been addressed in an administrative forum prior to the initiation of civil litigation. See *Kosakow v. New Rochelle Radiology, Associates, P.C.*, 88 F. Supp. 2d 1999 (S.D.N.Y. 2000), vacated, remanded, 274 F.3d 760 (2d Cir. 2001) (claims filed with New York State Department of Human Rights subject of issue preclusion).

The Third Circuit addressed claim preclusion involving the FMLA in *Churchill v. Star Enterprises et al.*, 183 F.3d 184, 189 (3rd Cir. 1999) ("this case seems to present the first application in any court of appeals of claim preclusion barring the assertion of claims following a case already litigated under the FMLA"). As stated by the Third Circuit (183 F.3d at 194):

> Claim preclusion gives dispositive effect to a prior judgment if a particular issue, although not litigated, could have been raised in the earlier proceeding. Claim preclusion requires: (1) a final judgment on the merits in a

prior suit involving; (2) the same parties or their privities; and (3) a subsequent suit based on the same cause of action.

See also DeCointio v. Westchester County Medical Center, 821 F.2d 111, 117 (2d Cir. 1987), *cert. denied*, 484 U.S. 965 1987) ("The issue must have been material to the first action or proceeding and essential to the decision rendered therein… and it must be on the point actually to be determined in the second action or proceeding such that 'a different judgment in the second would destroy or impair rights or interests established in the first.'"); *Shtab*, 173 F. Supp. 2d at 261. (the doctrine of issue preclusion applies where: (1) the identical issue was decided in a prior adjudication; (2) there was a final judgment on the merits; (3) the party against whom the doctrine is asserted was a party or in privities with a party to the prior adjudication; and (4) the party against whom it is asserted had a full and fair opportunity to litigate the issue in the prior adjudication).

In *Churchill*, the Third Circuit addressed claim preclusion where an employee had filed two separate lawsuits arising out of the same common facts. *Churchill*, 183 F.3d at 187. The first lawsuit addressed FMLA claims. The second lawsuit addressed claims under the ADA and a state anti–discrimination law. Applying the doctrine of claim preclusion, the district court dismissed the second lawsuit. On appeal, the Third Circuit affirmed the dismissal of the case pursuant to the doctrine of claim preclusion. The court held that different legal theories did not mean that claim preclusion did not apply. *Churchill*, 183 F.3d at 195. Moreover, while there were some differences in the factual allegations, because the thrust of the two complaints remained practically identical, the court concluded that the claims were the same.

Claim preclusion may also apply where the prior action was administratively adjudicated. The court in *Shtab v. The Greate Bay Hotel and Casino, Inc.*, 173 F. Supp. 2d 255, 260–63 (D.N.J. 2001), addressed what affect, if any, a prior adjudication of FMLA issues in arbitration had on subsequent litigation of the same FMLA issue in a federal court action. Because arbitrations are not conducted in courts of law and arbitrators are not bound by the same rules of evidence and procedures that judges are, issue preclusion based on a prior arbitration is permissible but not mandatory. *Shtab*, 173 F. Supp. 2d at 261 citing *Osula v. Community College of Philadelphia*, No. 00–98, 2000 U.S. Dist. LEXIS 11609 (E.D. Pa. Aug. 15 2000). An arbitration award is not considered "final" for purposes of issue preclusion absent judicial confirmation of the award, *Gruntal*, 854 F. Supp. at 337, and, for this reason, unconfirmed arbitral awards have been denied preclusive effect in subsequent litigation. *Shtab*, 173 F. Supp. 2d at 261 citing *Leddy v. Standard Drywall, Inc.*, 875 F.2d 383, 385 (2nd Cir. 1989); *Singer v. Tappan Co.*, 593 F.2d 545, 549 (2nd Cir. 1979); *Gruntal*, 854 F. Supp. at 338–39; *Scott v. Snelling and Snelling, Inc.*, 732 F. Supp. 1034, 1039 (N.D. Cal. 1990).

The Supreme Court has not addressed the preclusive effect of an adverse arbitration award on the rights bestowed by the FMLA. *Shtab*, 173 F. Supp. 2d at 261. However, in other contexts, the Supreme Court has held that adverse arbitral decisions do not necessarily preclude an employee's subsequent litigation of his or her federal statutory claims in a judicial forum. *See e.g., McDonald v. City of West Branch*, 466 U.S. 284, 292, 80 L. Ed. 2d 302, 104 S. Ct. 1799 (1984) (a discharged police officer was not precluded by an adverse arbitration decision from pursuing his § 1983 claim in federal court); *Barrentine v. Arkansas–Best Freight System*, 450 U.S. 728, 67 L. Ed. 2d 641, 101 S. Ct. 1437 (1981) (FLSA); *Alexander v. Gardner–Denver Co.*, 415 U.S. 36, 39 L. Ed. 2d 147, 94 S. Ct. 1011 (1974) (Title VII). The Supreme Court based its decision on three factors. First, the expertise an arbitrator brings to the resolution of claims "pertains primarily to the law of the shop, not the law of the land." *McDonald*, 466 U.S. at 290; *Gardner–Denver*, 415 U.S. at 57. Second, in a dispute over provisions in a collective bargaining agreement, "the union has exclusive control over the 'manner and extent to which an individual grievance is presented.'" *McDonald*, 466 U.S. at 291; *Gardner–Denver*, 415 U.S. at 58, n. 19. As a result, the union might make different strategic choices or present some claims less vigorously than would the employee. *McDonald*, 466 U.S. at 291; *Gardner–Denver*, 415 U.S. at 58. Finally, "arbitral fact–finding" is generally not equivalent to judicial fact–finding, thus, "according preclusive effect to arbitration awards in [Section] 1983 actions would severely undermine the protection of federal rights." *McDonald*, 466 U.S. at 292.

Applying the above factors, the court in *Shtab* found against issue preclusion and in favor of allowing the employee's federal suit to proceed. The court noted that, although the arbitrator reached the FMLA claim, the formal issue in the arbitration related only to interpretation of the seniority provisions of the collective bargaining agreement. *Shtab*, 173 F. Supp. 2d at 262. The court also noted that Shtab was not a party to the arbitration and was not represented by counsel. *Id*. Third, significant issues under the FMLA were not addressed in the arbitration. Finally, the arbitration decision was never judicially confirmed. The court concluded that the arbitration award should not be given preclusive effect in subsequent litigation. *Shtab*, 173 F. Supp. 2d at 263; *see also Slaughter v. American Building Maintenance Co.*, 64 F. Supp. 2d 319, 330–31 (S.D.N.Y. 1999) (an arbitrator's decision that an employee's termination was justified under the collective bargaining agreement did not collaterally estop the employee from bringing a FMLA claim because the issues addressed in each were distinct and the notice requirement under the agreement and the FMLA were different).

In *Kosakow v. New Rochelle Radiology Associates*, P.C., 274 F.3d 706, 727-36 (2d Cir. 2001), the Second Circuit vacated and remanded the decision of the district court that the employee was collaterally estopped from litigating her FMLA claims in federal court because she already presented her case to a state administrative agency, and the agency determined that there was no probable cause to believe that Kosakow's termination was the result of discrimination. Applying the analysis of the Supreme Court in *Univ. of Tenn. V. Elliott*, 478 U.S. 788, 106 S. Ct. 3220 (1986), the Second Circuit concluded that Kosakow did not have a full and fair opportunity to litigate her FMLA issue in her case before the state administrative agency. The court noted the absence of discovery, the informality of the administrative hearing, including the inability to confront witnesses, and because the Kosakow was not represented by counsel in the prior proceeding.

In *Dillaway v. Ferrante*, No. 02–715 (JRT/JSM), 2003 U.S. Dist. LEXIS 23468, at *16 (D. Minn. Dec. 9, 2003), the court addressed the preclusive effect on an FMLA claim of an employee–favorable arbitration decision. The court initially noted that, in the typical case (where the employee either failed to submit his or her complaint to arbitration or suffered an adverse arbitration decision), there is no collateral estoppel effect of employee–adverse arbitration decisions. Plaintiff argued that, because he won, collateral estoppel should apply. Disagreeing, the court followed cases that found that the same policy reasons for not giving the arbitration preclusive effect apply when the plaintiff attempts to use a prior arbitration award against the defendant. The court concluded that it was not bound by the prior arbitration decision.

G. PLEADINGS

A number of courts have addressed the minimum facts which must be plead in order for a complaint in federal court to survive a motion to dismiss for failure to state a claim. The essential elements of an FMLA claim that an employee must address in his or her complaint are:

The plaintiff was an eligible employee under the FMLA;

That the plaintiff's employer is covered by FMLA;

That plaintiff was entitled to leave or other benefits or protections pursuant to the FMLA;

That the employer engaged in some conduct prohibited by the FMLA.

See *Arbia v. Owens–Illinois, Inc. et al.*, No. 1:02CV0011, 2003 U.S. Dist. LEXIS 9429, at *15 (M.D.N.C. June 4, 2003) (the plaintiff plead facts sufficient to establish an FMLA retaliatory discharge claim by providing that she was an employee of the defendant, she provided a doctor's note about her medical condition, she was granted FMLA leave by the employer, and she received written reprimand upon her return from FMLA leave); *Collins v. OSF Healthcare Systems, et. al.*, 262 F. Supp. 2d 959, at *9 (C.D. Ill. May 20, 2003); *Wilson v. Ameritech*, No. 01 C 9511, 2003 U.S. Dist. LEXIS 8033, at *16 (N.D. Ill. May 12, 2003); *Reddinger v. Hospital Central Services, Inc.*, 4 F. Supp. 2d 405, 411 (E.D. Pa. 1998); *LeGrand v. Village of McCook*, No. 96–C–5951, 1998 U.S. Dist. LEXIS 5230, at *12 (N.D. Ill. April 15, 1998); *Dormeyer v. Comerica Bank–Illinois*, 1997 U.S. Dist. LEXIS 10260, at *4–6 (N.D. Ill. July 11, 1997); *Mitchell v. Continental Plastic Containers, Inc.*, No. C–1–97–412, 1998 U.S. Dist. LEXIS 21465, at *9 (S.D. Ohio March 3, 1998); *Boyce v. New York City Mission Society*, 963 F. Supp. 290 (S.D.N.Y. 1997); *Schmitt v. Beverly Health and Rehabilitation Services, Inc.*, 962 F. Supp. 1379, 1381–82 (D.K an. 1997); *Spurlock v. NYNEX*, 949 F. Supp. 1022, 103–33 (W.D.N.Y. 1996); *Blumental v. Murray et al.*, 946 F. Supp. 623, 626 n. 4 (N.D. Ill. 1996); *Procopia v. Castrol Indust. North America, Inc.*, No. 96–5234, 1996 U.S. Dist. LEXIS 17418 (E.D. Pa. Nov. 21, 1996); *Bildy v. Examination Management Services*, No. 96 C 3553, 1996 U.S. Dist. LEXIS 14539 (N.D. Ill. Oct. 2, 1996); *Burke v. NALCO Chemical Co.*, No. 96 C 981, 1996 U.S. Dist. Lexis 10190 (N.D. Ill. July 17, 1996).

In *McCoy v. Orleans Parish School Bd.*, No. 02–2510 Section "R" (3), 2004 U.S. Dist. LEXIS 6843, at *6 (E.D. La. April 19, 2004), the court denied the employer's motion *in limine* and the motion to strike plaintiff's FMLA retaliation claim. The employer contended that a retaliation claim was not set forth in the complaint. The court noted that Rule 8 of the Federal Rules of Civil Procedure requires only a short and plain statement of the claim showing that the pleader is entitled to relief. Read in its entirety, the court concluded that plaintiff's complaint states a claim against the employer for retaliation by demoting her from "Principal" to "Principal on Special Assignment" because of her use of FMLA leave. According to the court, "this basic recitation of facts is enough to allege that OPSB retaliated against her for taking [ ] FMLA–approved sick leave."

H. SERVICE OF PROCESS

The FMLA does not provide for nationwide service of process. *Pelchat v. Sterilite Corp.*, 931 F. Supp. 939, 943 (D.N.H. 1996).

I. JURY TRIAL

The FMLA does not expressly provide for the right to a jury trial. *Davis v. Henderson*, No. 99–3028, 2000 U.S. App. LEXIS 31946, at *4–5 (6th Cir. Dec. 4, 2000); *Frizzell v. Southwest Motor Freight*, 154 F.3d 641, 643 (6th Cir. 1998); *Helmly v. Stone Container Corp. et al.*, 957 F. Supp. 1274, 1275 (S.D. Ga. 1997). The courts that have directly addressed the issue are split.

The Sixth Circuit has held that there is no right to a jury trial against the Government of the United States. *Davis v. Henderson*, No. 99–3028, 2000 U.S. App. LEXIS 31946, at *4–5 (6th Cir. Dec. 4, 2000). According to the court:

> Even when Congress waives sovereign immunity, it does not simultaneously concede to a jury trial. Congress has provided for a general waiver of the Postal Service's sovereign immunity, but that general waiver did not create a right to a jury trial. The Second Circuit explained that Congress has granted "broad waivers of immunity [that have] subjected the federal government and its agencies to many types of liability and process…[but] the waiver of sovereign immunity does not, by itself, grant a right to trial by jury in an [action] against the federal government." *Young v. United States Postal Service*, 869 F.2d 158, 159 (2nd Cir. 1989) (citations omitted). The Supreme Court has held that the right to a jury trial against an agency of the United States can only exist if Congress "clearly and unequivocally" grants such a right by statute. *Lehman v. Nakshian*, 453 U.S. 156, [162, 69 L. Ed. 2d 548, 101 S. Ct. 2698 (1981)].

The decision of the Sixth Circuit is significant because it is the only circuit to directly find a right to a jury trial for FMLA claims. *Frizzell v. Southwest Motor Freight*, 154 F.3d 64, 643 (6th Cir. 1998). The decision in *Davis* effectively limits the right to a jury trial for FMLA claims to the private sector, absent an explicit Congressional waiver. *See Davis v. Henderson*, No. 99–3028, 2000 U.S. App. LEXIS 31946, at *4–5 (6th Cir. Dec. 4, 2000) ("Regardless of whether there is a right to a jury trial under the FMLA against a private defendant, [the] appellant has no right to a jury trial against the Postal Service").

At least one other court has held that a plaintiff does not have a right to a jury trial under the FMLA. *Hicks v. Maytag Corp.*, No. 1:95–cv–5, 1995 U.S. Dist. LEXIS 21708, at *11 (E.D. Tenn. July 13, 1995). In *Hicks*, the court reasoned, "the FMLA envisions only equitable remedies. Further, [the] FMLA does not provide a statutory right to a jury trial." *Id*. The decision in *Hicks* has been criticized by other courts. *See Bryant v. Delbar Products, Inc.*, 18 F. Supp. 2d 799, 810 (M.D. Tenn. 1998); *Helmly v. Stone Container Corp.*, 957 F. Supp. 1274, 1276 (S.D. Ga. 1997).

The majority of courts that have addressed the issue have concluded that there is a right to a jury under the FMLA, at least with respect to some claims. *See Frizzell v. Southwest Motor Freight*, 154 F.3d 641, 643 (6th Cir. 1998) (the court cited legislative history and fact that FMLA was modeled after FLSA, which provides for jury trials, in finding a right to jury trial under FMLA); *Whitney v. Wal–Mart Stores, Inc.*, No. 03–65–P–H, 2004 U.S. Dist. LEXIS 5237, at *10 (D. Me. March 30, 2004); *Mora v. Chem–tronics, Inc.*, 16 F. Supp. 2d 1192 (S.D. Ca. 1998); *Bryant v. Delbar Prods., Inc.*, 18 F. Supp. 2d 799, 8090810 (M.D. Tenn. 1998) (right to jury trial on issue of back pay and liquidated damages; equitable issues, such as reinstatement and front pay, decided by the court); *Hemly v. Stone Container Corp.*, 957 F. Supp. 1274, 1275 (S.D. Ga. 1997); *Souders v. Fleming Cos.*, 960 F. Supp. 218, 218 (D. Neb. 1997) (jury trial on issue of liability and back pay, but the court would decide equitable issues such as reinstatement and front pay).

Additionally, a number courts, although not directly addressing the issue, have referenced FMLA cases as having been tried to juries. *See Taylor v. Invacare Corp.*, 64 Fed. Appx. 516 (6th Cir. 2003) (affirming jury award of damages for FMLA violations); *Smith v. Diffee Ford–Lincoln–Mercury, Inc.*, 298 F.3d 955 (10th Cir. 2002) (affirming jury verdict in favor of the plaintiff and award of damages); *Mummert v. Vencor Inc. et al.*, 21 Fed. Appx. 710 (9th Cir. 2001) (the court could not say that jury's FMLA verdict was not supported by "substantial evidence"); *Duty v. Norton–Alcoa Proppants*, 293 F.3d 481, 496–501 (8th Cir. 2002) (affirming jury award of damages for FMLA violations*); Estes v. Meridian One Corp. et al.*, 6 Fed. Appx. 142 (4th Cir. 2001) (affirming jury award of damages*); Hachmann v. Time Warner Entertainment Co.*, 151 F.3d 591 (7th Cir. 1998) (affirming jury verdict in FMLA case in favor of the plaintiff); *Cline v. Wal–Mart Stores*, 144 F.3d 294 (4th Cir. 1998) (as a form of equitable relief, determination of front pay in a damages award under FMLA should be made by district court, not jury; the court remanded jury award on front pay and liquidated damages, but let stand jury award on back pay); *McDonnell v. Mobil Oil Corp.*, 134 F.3d 638 (4th Cir. 1998) (jury found violation of FMLA for failure to offer the employee same or equivalent position on return from FMLA leave); *Hopson v. Quitman Country Hospital*, 126 F.3d 635 (5th Cir. 1997) (whether the employee gave notice as soon as practicable, whether an employee made reasonable effort to schedule leave so as not to disrupt the employer's operations, and what constitutes change in circumstances are questions of fact for jury to decide

J. BURDEN OF PROOF

1. General Rule

As discussed in the "Enforcement" section of this chapter, Title I employees are authorized under 29 USC 2617(a) to bring a civil action to recover damages for violation of § 2615. Courts have recognized two theories for recovery on FMLA claims under § 2615: the interference/entitlement theory and the retaliation/discrimination theory. *See Coker v. McFaul*, No. 06-3587, 2007 U.S. App. LEXIS 16565, at *17, 2007 FED App. 0466N (6th Cir. June 29, 2007); *Kauffman v. Federal Express Corp.*, 426 F.3d 880, 884 (7th Cir. 2005); *Hoffman v. Professional Med Team*, 394 F.3d 414 (6th Cir. 2005); *Hoge v. Honda of America Mfg., Inc.*, 384 F.3d 238 (6th Cir. 2004*); Walker v. Elmore County Bd. of Ed.*, 379 F.3d 1249, 1251 (11th Cir. 2004); *Zsenyuk v. City of Arson*, 99 Fed. Appx. 794 (9th Cir. 2004); *Potenza v. City of New York*, 365 F.3d 165, 167 (2d Cir. 2004); *Dry v. Boeing Co.*, 92 Fed. Appx. 675 (10th Cir. 2004); *Cooke v. C. Bean Transport, Inc.*, 72 Fed. Appx. 740 (10th Cir. 2003); *Liu v. Amway Corp.*, 347 F.3d 1125 (9th Cir. 2003); *Smith v. Diffee Ford–Lincoln–Mercury, Inc.*, 298 F.3d 955, 960 (10th Cir. 2002); *Hunt v. Rapides Health Care, System, LLC*, 277 F.3d 757, 762–63 (5th Cir. 2001); *Bachelder v. America West Airlines, Inc.*, 259 F.3d 1112, 1122 (9th Cir 2001); *Strickland v. Water Works and Sewer, Bd. of City of Birmingham*, 239 F.3d 1199, 1206–1207, n.9 (11th Cir. 2001) (FMLA does not clearly delineate those two claims with the labels "interference" and "retaliation," those are the labels courts have used in describing an employee's claims under the Act"); *King v. Preferred Technical Group*, 166 F. 3d 887, 891 (7th Cir. 1999); *Hodgens v. General Dynamics Corp.*, 144 F.3d 151, 159–60 (1st Cir. 1998).

The theories have been found to be broad, interrelated, and non–exclusive. *Smith v. Diffee Ford–Lincoln–Mercury, Inc.*, 298 F.3d 955, 960 (10th Cir. 2002); *Bachelder v. America West Airlines, Inc.*, 259 F.3d 1112, 1122 (9th Cir 2001); *Gordon v. Trustees of Governors State U.*, No. 06 C 4957, 2007 U.S. Dist. LEXIS 31864, at *7 (N.D. Ill. April 26, 2007); *Cagle v. Finishmaster, Inc.*, No. 1:03–cv–0265–JDT–WTL, 2004 U.S. Dist. LEXIS 26714, at *28 (S.D. Ind. Dec. 23, 2004); *Bradley v. Mary Rutan Hospital Assoc.*, 322 F. Supp. 2d 926, 937 (S.D. Ohio 2004); *Dillaway v. Ferrante*, No. 02–715 (JRT/JSM), 2003 U.S. Dist. LEXIS 23468, at *11 (D. Minn. Dec. 9, 2003) (the lines between the two categories are not hard and fast).

The two types of FMLA claims can be asserted simultaneously. *Ash v. Aronov Homes, Inc.*, No. 2:03–cv–840–F, 2004 U.S. Dist. LEXIS 26900, at *28 (M.D. Ala. Oct. 15, 2004).

The distinction between interference/prescriptive claims and retaliation-discrimination/proscriptive claims is important in terms of the burden of proof. *Dillaway v. Ferrante*, No. 02–715, 2003 U.S. Dist. LEXIS 23468, at *10 (D. Minn. Dec. 9, 2003). The difference between prescriptive and proscriptive approaches inheres in the relevance of the employer's intent. *Potenza v. City of New York*, 365 F.3d 165, 167 (2d Cir. 2004).

The discrimination/retaliation theory requires proof of discriminatory intent whereas an interference claim requires only proof that the employer denied the employee his or her entitlements under the Act. *Kauffman v. Federal Express Corp.*, 426 F.3d 880, 884 (7th Cir. 2005); *Gordon v. Trustees of Governors State U.*, No. 06 C 4957, 2007 U.S. Dist. LEXIS 31864, at *7 (N.D. Ill. April 26, 2007). The burden of proof for violation of § 2615(a)(1) interference claims has been described as a much simpler standard than the burden–shifting approach commonly used in § 2615(a)(2) retaliation/discrimination claims. *Zsenyuk v. City of Carson*, 99 Fed. Appx. 794 (9th Cir. 2004).

Courts find the current state of FMLA law regarding the burden of proof confusing. *Bradley v. Mary Rutan Hospital Assoc.*, 322 F. Supp. 2d 926, 938 (S.D. Ohio 2004). The confusion stems from the failure of both parties and courts to identify which section(s) of the statute plaintiffs base their claims on and instead use labels such as "interference," "discrimination," or "retaliation." As observed by the court in *Bradley*, 322 F. Supp. 2d at 938:

> Courts use different, sometimes conflicting, frameworks for analyzing the claims, as illustrated by the case law cited in the parties' cross–motions. The courts often do not make clear, however, whether the framework they establish and/or employ should apply only to factually similar cases, only to cases bearing the same label, or only to claims arising under the specific statutory section(s). Accordingly, while several frameworks have been created, often it is impossible to discern when a particular framework should apply, especially when the parties do as they did here, and argue different frameworks, labels and sections.

The court in *Bradley* went on to develop a single burden of proof scheme for all claims brought by a plaintiff alleging that his/her employer used the FMLA leave against the employee in some unlawful way. In such cases, the plaintiff has the burden of establishing by a preponderance of the evidence that:

1. She is an "eligible employee," 29 USC 2611(2);

2. Defendant is an "employer," 29 USC 2611(4);

3. She was entitled to take leave for one of the reasons set forth in 29 USC 2612(a)(1);

4. She gave proper notice of her intention to take leave, 29 CFR 825.302; and

5. The employer somehow used the leave against her and in an unlawful manner, as provided in either the statute or regulations.

The court noted that the above framework was not very different from the one adopted by the Sixth Circuit in *Cavin v. Honda of Am. Mfg.*, 346 F.3d 713, 719 (6th Cir. 2003) for so-called interference claims. *Bradley v. Mary Rutan Hospital Assoc.*, 322 F. Supp. 2d 926, 940, n. 16 (S.D. Ohio, 2004). According to the court, the only difference between the two standards was the exclusion of an additional element cited by the *Cavin* court requiring the employee to establish that the employer denied the employee FMLA benefits to which he was entitled. The *Bradley* court was uncomfortable with the term "benefit" based on the facts with which it was presented.

In defense, an employer can show how the plaintiff cannot meet one or more of the five elements by a preponderance of the evidence. The *Bradley* court rejected a shifting burden of proof scheme. *Bradley v. Mary Rutan Hospital Assoc.*, 322 F. Supp. 2d 926, 940 (S.D. Ohio, 2004).

Applying the facts to this new standard, the court in *Bradley* found that plaintiff failed to establish that she was entitled to leave for her own medical condition. She did, however, establish that she was entitled to leave to care for her husband with a serious health condition. The court found that she provided timely and adequate notice of her need for FMLA leave to care for her husband. The court found the existence of genuine issues of fact precluding summary judgment regarding the last element, whether the employer used plaintiff's FMLA leave against her.

It will be interesting to watch whether other courts follow *Bradley* and create a single burden of proof scheme that is arguably applicable to facts that traditionally would give rise to interference or retaliation claims.

A review of the burdens of proof attendant with the two established theories follows.

2. Interference/Entitlement Theory

The entitlement or interference theory is derived from the FMLA's creation of substantive rights. *Smith v. Diffee Ford–Lincoln–Mercury, Inc.*, 298 F.3d 955, 960 (10th Cir. 2002). It arises from 29 USC 2615(a): "it shall be unlawful for any employer to interfere with, restrain, or deny the exercise of or the attempt to exercise, any right provided in this subchapter." *Hoffman v. Professional Med Team*, 394 F.3d 414 (6th Cir. 2005); *Hoge v. Honda of America MFG., Inc.*, 384 F.3d 238 (6th Cir. 2004); *Zsenyuk v. City of Carson*, 99 Fed. Appx. 794 (9th Cir. 2004); *Dry v. Boeing Co.*, 92 Fed. Appx. 675 (10th Cir. 2004); *Diffee Ford–Lincoln–Mercury, Inc.*, at 960.

The FMLA entitlements, as set forth in 29 USC 2612(a), 2614(a), include the right of certain employees to take up to 12 works of leave for protected reasons, and the right of an employee to return to his or her job or an equivalent job at the conclusion of that FMLA leave. *Diffee Ford–Lincoln–Mercury, Inc.*, 298 F.3d at 960; *Bachelder v. America West Airlines, Inc.*, 259 F.3d 1112, 1122 (9th Cir 2001); *Nero v. Industrial Molding Corp.*, 167 F.3d 921, 927 (5th Cir. 1999); *Peters v. Community Action Committee, Inc., of Chambers–Tallapossa–Coosa*, 977 F. Supp. 1428, 1432 (M.D. Ala. 1997). These rights have been described as essentially prescriptive, "setting substantive floors" for conduct by employer, and creating "entitlements for employees." *Thomas v. Pearle Vision, Inc.*, 251 F.3d 1132, 1139 (7th Cir. 2001); *Strickland v. Water Works and Sewer Board. of the City of Birmingham*, 239 F.3d 1199, 1206–07 (11th Cir. 2001); *Hodgens v. General Dynamics Corp.*, 144 F.3d 151, 159 (1st Cir. 1998); *Diaz v. Fort Wayne Foundry Corp.*, 131 F.3d 711, 712–13 (7th Cir. 1997); *Snelling v. Clarian Health Partners, Inc.*, 184 F. Supp. 2d 838, 845 (S.D. Ind. 2002).

If an employer interferes with the FMLA-created right to covered leave or to reinstatement following the leave, a deprivation of this right is a violation regardless of the employer's intent. *See Coker v. McFaul*, No. 06-3587, 2007 U.S. App.

LEXIS 16565, at *18, 2007 FED App. 0466N (6th Cir. June 29, 2007); *Kauffman v. Federal Express Corp.*, 426 F.3d 880, 884 (7th Cir. 2005); *Hoffman*, 394 F.3d 414; *Hoge.*, 384 F.3d 238; *Cooke v. C. Bean Transport, Inc.*, 72 Fed. Appx. 740 (10th Cir. 2003); *Dry*, 92 Fed. Appx. 675; *Potenza v. City of New York*, 365 F.3d 165, 167 (2d Cir. 2004); *Diffee Ford–Lincoln–Mercury, Inc.*, 298 F.3d at 960; *Strickland v. Water Works and Sewer, Bd. of City of Birmingham*, 239 F.3d 1199, 1208 (11th Cir. 2001); *King v. Preferred Technical Group*, 166 F. 3d 887, 891 (7th Cir. 1999); *Hodgens v. General Dynamics Corp.*, 144 F.3d 151, 159–60 (1st Cir. 1998).

As stated by the First Circuit in *Hodgens* (144 F.3d at 159):

> As to these [prescriptive] rights, therefore, the employee need not show that the employer treated other employees less favorably, and an employer may not defend its interference with the FMLA's substantive rights on the ground that it treats all employees equally poorly without discriminating. In such cases, the employer's subjective intent is not relevant. The issue is simply whether the employer provided its employee the entitlements set forth in the FMLA—for example, a [12]-week leave or reinstatement after taking a medical leave. Because the issue is the right to an entitlement, the employee is due the benefits if the statutory requirements are satisfied, regardless of the intent of the employer. (citations omitted).

See also Ogborn v. United Food and Commercial Workers Union, Local No. 881, et. al., 305 F.3d 763, 769 (7th Cir. 2002) (in a suit charging violations of the substantive, as opposed to the anti–discrimination, provisions of the FMLA, proof of pretext is neither necessary nor sufficient to show a violation of the statute).

As such, an employer's good faith or lack of knowledge that its conduct violates the FMLA does not protect it from liability under the interference theory. *Liu v. Amway Corp.*, 347 F.3d 1125, 1135 (9th Cir. 2003).

To prevail on an FMLA claim based on the interference/entitlement theory, an employee need only establish by a preponderance of the evidence entitlement to the FMLA benefits claimed. *Hoffman v. Professional Med Team*, 394 F.3d 414 (6th Cir. 2005); *Hoge v. Honda of America Mfg., Inc.*, 384 F.3d 238 (6th Cir. 2004); *Dry v. Boeing Co.*, 92 Fed. Appx. 675 (10th Cir. 2004); *Smith v. Diffee Ford–Lincoln–Mercury, Inc.*, 298 F.3d 955, 960 (10th Cir. 2002); *Bachelder v. America West Airlines, Inc.*, 259 F.3d 1112, 1122 (9th Cir 2001); *Diaz v. Ft. Wayne Foundry Corp.* 131 F.3d 711, 713 (7th Cir. 1997); *Mueller v. J.P. Morgan Chase & Co.*, No. 1:05 CV 560, 2007 U.S. Dist. LEXIS 20828, at *36 & n.12 (N.D. Ohio March 23, 2007).

Courts have come up with different formulations for a plaintiff's *prima facie* case involving § 2615(a)(1) interference claims depending on the deprivation of rights at issue. In the Sixth Circuit, an employee must demonstrate that: (1) he was an eligible employee; (2) the defendant was an employer as defined under the FMLA; (3) he was entitled to leave under the FMLA; (4) he gave the employer notice of his intention to take leave; and (5) the employer denied him FMLA benefits to which he was entitled. *Coker v. McFaul*, 2007 FED App. 0466N (6th Cir. June 29, 2007). This inquiry "is an objective one divorced from the employer's motives, with the central question being simply whether the employee was entitled to the FMLA benefits at issue." *Id.*

In the Tenth Circuit, to establish a *prima facie* case based on a § 2615(a)(1) interference theory, an employee must demonstrate: (1) FMLA leave entitlement; (2) denial of substantive rights under the FMLA; and (3) a causal connection between the two. *Dry v. Boeing Co.*, 92 Fed. Appx. 675 (10th Cir. 2004).

In *Zsenyuk v. City of Carson*, 99 Fed. Appx. 794 (9th Cir. 2004), the Ninth Circuit held that a plaintiff with a § 2615(a)(1) interference case must establish by a preponderance of the evidence that: (1) he took FMLA–protected leave; (2) he suffered adverse employment actions; and (3) the adverse actions were causally related to his FMLA leave.

In *Hoge v. Honda of America MFG., Inc.*, 384 F.3d 238 (6th Cir. 2004), the court asserted that plaintiff must establish that her employer interfered with a FMLA right to medical leave or to reinstatement following FMLA leave. According to the court, Hoge must establish that: (1) she was an eligible employee; (2) Honda is a covered employer; (3) she was entitled to leave under the FMLA; (4) she gave Honda notice of her intent to take leave, and (5) Honda denied her FMLA benefits or interfered with FMLA rights to which she was entitled. *Accord McIntyre v. Advance Auto Parts*, No. 1:04 CV 1857, 2007 U.S. Dist. LEXIS 1944, at *27 (N.D. Ohio Jan. 10, 2007); *Bila v. RadioShack Corp.*, No. 03–10177–BC, 2004 U.S. Dist. LEXIS 24649, at *23 (E.D. Mich. Nov. 23, 2004).

Causation was the focus of a number of FMLA interference cases. In *Zsenyuk v. City of Carson*, 99 Fed. Appx. 794 (9th Cir. 2004), the court found that the employee failed to raise a genuine issue regarding causation. Zsenyuk alleged that he suffered a number of instances of adverse employment actions after taking a month of FMLA–protected leave. The court, however, found that the incidents complained of were the product of an investigation of the plaintiff's conduct which began before he requested and received FMLA leave. Plaintiff's reliance on the temporal proximity of his use of FMLA leave and the instances of alleged harassment, the court found, was nullified by the fact that the investigation pre-dated his FMLA leave. Because he offered no evidence that the conduct of and result of the investigation were influenced by his exercise of FMLA rights, the court concluded that plaintiff failed to establish a viable FMLA interference claim. Summary judgment was awarded to the City of Carson.

In *Gordon v. Bd. of Trustees of Governors State U.*, No. 06 C 495, 2007 U.S. Dist. LEXIS 31864, at *12 & n.1 (N.D. Ill. April 26, 2007), the court found that the employer had ample cause to terminate the employee for her refusal to perform tasks she believed were beneath her skill level and shouting at her supervisor.

In *Cagle v. Finishmaster, Inc.*, No. 1:03-cv-0265-JDL-WTL, 2004 U.S. Dist. LEXIS 26714, at *29 (S.D. Ind. Dec. 23, 2004), the decision to terminate plaintiff was made several days before the employee initially requested FMLA leave. The court observed that "[t]his sequence of events is fatal to Cagle's substantive-rights claim."

Employee failures to perfect entitlement to FMLA leave have also been the cause of a number of decisions adverse to plaintiffs. For example, in *Dry v. Boeing Co.*, 92 Fed. Appx. 675 (10th Cir. 2004), the court found that the employee's failure to timely provide necessary medical documentation to support his request for FMLA leave as required rendered his absences outside of the protections of the FMLA. Conversely, an employer's delay in processing the employee's FMLA paperwork may constitute actionable interference, even if the employee's FMLA leave request is ultimately approved. *Mueller v. J.P. Morgan Chase & Co.*, No. 1:05 CV 560, 2007 U.S. Dist. LEXIS 20828, at *37-40 (N.D. Ohio March 23, 2007).

An employee's failure to provide timely and adequate notice of the need for FMLA leave is another example where an employee's failure to perfect entitlement to FMLA leave resulted in the downfall of his § 2615(a)(1) interference claim. For example, in *Cagle v. Finishmaster, Inc.*, No. 1:03-cv-0265-JDL-WTL, 2004 U.S. Dist. LEXIS 26714, at *29 (S.D. Ind. Dec. 23, 2004), the court found that Cagle did not provide legally sufficient notice of his need for FMLA leave. Based on the on-going communication between Cagle and his physician, the court determined that Cagle's need for leave was foreseeable, yet, he failed to include dates or the anticipated duration of the leave in his initial e-mail notice as required.

An employee who affirmatively refuses FMLA leave coverage at the time leave is requested is precluded from arguing at trial that his or her employer interfered with the employee's right to FMLA leave. *Bailey v. Southwest Gas Co.*, 275 F.3d 1181, 1185 (9th Cir. 2002); *Sharer v. State of Oregon*, No. 04-CV-1690-BR, 2007 U.S. Dist. LEXIS 24925, at *26-30 (D. Ore. March 30, 2007).

To be entitled to FMLA benefits and protections, an employee must meet the FMLA eligibility requirements. An employee who does not meet the FMLA eligibility requirements does not have a viable FMLA claim. *Walker v. Elmore County Bd. of Ed.*, 379 F.3d 1249, 1253 (11th Cir. Aug. 5, 2004) (request for FMLA leave made by ineligible employee for leave that would begin when employee would still be ineligible is not protected by the FMLA).

An employee does not have a viable FMLA claim where they have received all of the FMLA benefits they are entitled to and, in that instance, a court will dismiss an employee's FMLA interference claim. In *Rosteutcher v. MidMichigan Physicians Group*, 332 F. Supp. 2d 1049, 1063-1064 (E.D. Mich. 2004), an employee who was separated after she returned from FMLA leave to her former position did not have a viable interference claim for failure to restore her to her position.

Of course, when employees do allege sufficient facts that their FMLA rights have been violated, courts are reluctant to dismiss their case. For example, an employer's reference to an employee's "lengthy illness" in the memorandum justifying the employee's removal was sufficient to raise genuine issues of fact that the employee was denied the FMLA right to job restoration at the conclusion of FMLA leave and to preclude summary judgment. *Ashe v. Aronov Homes, Inc.*, 354 F. Supp. 2d 1251 (M.D. Ala. 2004).

There is a split in the circuits over the proper standard of proof for FMLA retaliation claims. *See Conoshenti v. Pub. Serv. Elec. & Gas Co.*, 364 F.3d 135, 147, n.9 (3d Cir. 2004). The split appears to result because retaliation for taking FMLA leave does not come within the literal scope of § 2615(a)(2). *Id*. Section 2615(a)(2) makes it unlawful to retaliate "against any individual for opposing any practice made unlawful by the [FMLA]," and § 2615(b) makes it "unlawful to retaliate against any individual for participating in any inquiry or proceeding related to the FMLA." 29 USC 2615(a)(2), (b).

The circuits are split three ways on this issue. The Second, Third, Sixth and Tenth Circuits have held that an employee's claim that he was discharged in retaliation for having taken FMLA leave is analyzed pursuant to the retaliation theory of § 2615(a)(2). *Potenza v. City of New York*, 365 F.3d 165, 167–168 (2d Cir. 2004); *Conoshenti v. Pub. Serv. Elec. & Gas Co.*, 364 F.3d 135, 147, n. 9 (3d Cir. 2004) (citing *Arban v. West Publish. Corp.* 345 F.3d 390, 401 (6th Cir. 2003) and *Smith v. Diffee Ford–Lincoln–Mercury, Inc.*, 298 F.3d 955, 960 (10th Cir. 2002) (same)). The First, Seventh, Ninth, and Eleventh Circuits have held that FMLA retaliatory discharge claims arise from § 2615(a)(1) and 29 CFR 825.220(c) as interference claims. *Conoshenti*, 364 F.3d at 147, n.9 (citing *Strickland v. Water Works & Sewer Bd.*, 239 F.3d 1199, 1206 (11th Cir. 2001)); *Bachelder v. American West Airlines, Inc.*, 259 F.3d 1112, 1125 (9th Cir. 2001); *King v. Preferred Technical Group*, 166 F.3d 887, 891 (7th Cir. 1999); *Hodgens v. General Dynamic Corp.*, 144 F.3d 151, 159–60 (1st Cir. 1998)).

Direct or indirect evidence, or both, may be used by an employee to establish a § 2615(a)(1) interference claim. However, no scheme shifting burden of production back and forth is required. *Bachelder v. American West Airlines, Inc.*, 259 F.3d 1112, 1125 (9th Cir. 2001).

In *Conoshenti v. Pub. Serv. Elec. & Gas Co.*, 364 F.3d 135, 147 n. 9 (3d Cir. 2004), the court applied the direct evidence standard set forth by the Supreme Court in *Price Waterhouse v. Hopkins*, 490 U.S. 228, 109 S. Ct. 1775 (1989). "Direct evidence" means evidence sufficient to allow the jury to find that "the decision makers placed substantial negative reliance on [the protected activity] in reaching their decision" to fire him. *Connors v. Chrysler Fin. Corp.*, 160 F.3d 971, 976 (3d Cir. 1998) (quoting *Price Waterhouse*, 490 U.S. at 277, 109 S. Ct. 1775)). Under the *Price Waterhouse* framework, when an FMLA plaintiff alleging unlawful termination presents "direct evidence" that his FMLA leave was a substantial factor in the decision to fire him, the burden of persuasion on the issue of causation shifts, and the employer must prove that it would have fired plaintiff even if it had not considered the FMLA leave. *Conoshenti*, 364 F.3d at 147 (3d Cir. 2004).

The court in *Conoshenti* found that plaintiff established direct evidence that his FMLA leave was a substantial factor in the decision to terminate him. The evidence consisted of the termination letter and supporting documents that referenced his entire absence, including absences covered by the FMLA. However, because it was uncontested that plaintiff violated the terms of a last chance agreement that provided that any violation would be automatic just cause for termination, the court concluded that the employer would have discharged Conoshenti for reasons unrelated to his use of FMLA leave.

The significance of a broad reading of the anti–interference/entitlement provisions is that employer intent is not issue. If the employee establishes that he or she was eligible and entitled to FMLA leave (or to be returned from FMLA leave), and such leave or restoration was denied, absent a legitimate non–discriminatory reason (e.g., the employee was fired or laid off for reasons having nothing to do with the FMLA), the employer loses the case. Employers should expect to see a marked increase in the use of the interference/entitlement theory as employees seek to avoid having to provide discriminatory animus on the part of the employer.

Because an employee who has taken FMLA leave is not entitled to any greater employment rights than if he or she had not taken FMLA leave, an employer who terminates an employee for legitimate reasons independent of the taking of FMLA leave does not interfere with an employee's FMLA rights. See *Moran v. Wal–Mart Corp.*, No. 5:02–CV–096–C, 2003 U.S. Dist. LEXIS 5099, at *11–14 (N.D. Tex. April 1, 2003) (although court found no question that employee was entitled to FMLA leave, employer did not interfere with employee right to take FMLA leave where intervening investigation revealed employee had engaged in theft; employee's termination before she started FMLA leave, therefore, did not violate the FMLA).

An employer does not interfere with an employee's FMLA claim by investigating suspected FMLA abuse. *Hoskins v. Pridgeon & Clay, Inc.*, No. 1:05-CV-816, 2007 U.S. Dist. LEXIS 24674, at *34-35 (W.D. Mich. April 3, 2007); *Kitts v. Gen. Tel. North*, No. 2:04-CV-173, 2005 U.S. Dist. LEXIS 20421, at *11 (S.D. Ohio Sept. 19, 2005).

3. Retaliation/Discrimination Theory

The retaliation/discrimination theory is the second type of theory recognized to recover for violations of the FMLA. The theory is grounded in 29 USC 2615(a)(2), which makes it unlawful for an employer "to discharge or in any other manner discriminate against any individual for opposing any practice made unlawful by this subchapter." *Hoffman v. Professional Med Team*, 394 F.3d 414 (6th Cir. 2005); *Dry v. Boeing Co.*, 92 Fed. Appx. 675 (10th Cir. 2004); *Schreiber v. Chicago Mercantile Exchange, Inc.*, No. 03 C 8568, 2004 U.S. Dist. LEXIS 23108, at *9 (N.D. Ill. Nov. 14, 2004).

This theory is characterized as proscriptive in nature, as it proscribes or prohibits certain employer conduct. *Hoge v.*

Honda of America Mfg., Inc., 384 F.3d 238 (6th Cir. 2004); *Sheaffer v. County of Chatham,* 337 F. Supp. 2d 709, 726 (M.D.N.C. Sept. 17, 2004); *McCoy v. Orleans Parish School Bd.,* No. 02-2510 Section "R" (3), 2004 U.S. Dist. LEXIS 6843, at *8 (E.D. La. April 19, 2004).

The Act itself does not on its face encompass a claim for retaliation based on an employee's exercise of her right to FMLA leave. *Voorhees v. Time Warner Cable Nat. Div.,* No. 98-1460, 1999 U.S. Dist. LEXIS 13227, at *9 (E.D. Pa Aug. 30, 1999). The DOL regulations (29 CFR 825.220(c)), however, have interpreted § 2615(a)(2) as encompassing a cause of action for an employee's use of FMLA leave. *Hodgens v. General Dynamics Corp.,* 144 F.3d 151, 159-60, n.4 (1st Cir. 1998); *Arbia v. Owens-Illinois, Inc. et al.,* No. 1:02CV00111, 2003 U.S. Dist. LEXIS 9429, at *13-14 (M.D.N.C. June 4, 2003); *Snelling v. Clarian Health Partners, Inc.,* 184 F. Supp. 2d 838, 846 (S.D. Ind. 2002); *Voorhees v. Time Warner Cable Nat. Div.,* No. 98-1460, 1999 U.S. Dist. LEXIS 13227, at *9 (E.D. Pa Aug. 30, 1999).

29 CFR 220(c) provides:

> An employer is prohibited from discriminating against employees or prospective employees who have used FMLA leave. For example, if an employee on leave without pay would otherwise be entitled to full benefits (other than health benefits). The same benefits would be required to be provided to an employee on unpaid FMLA leave. By the same token, employers cannot use the taking of FMLA leave as a negative factor in employment actions, such as hiring, promotions or disciplinary actions; nor can FMLA leave be counted under "no fault" attendance policies.

Because the Statute and implementing regulations prohibit discrimination, they have been referred to as proscriptive provisions. *See Hunt v. Rapides Healthcare System,* LLC, 277 F.3d 757, 769 (5th Cir. 2001); *Thomas v. Pearle Vision, Inc.,* 251 F.3d 1132, 1139-40 (7th Cir. 2001); *Hodgens v. General Dynamics Corp.,* 144 F.3d 151, 159-60 (1st Cir. 1998).

A plaintiff need not establish a violation of the substantive, prescriptive provisions (i.e., an interference/entitlement claim) of the FMLA to allege a violation of the prescriptive provisions. *See Hunt v. Rapides Healthcare System,* LLC, 277 F.3d 757, 769 (5th Cir. 2001). The FMLA's protection against retaliation is not limited to periods in which an employee is on FMLA leave, but encompasses the employer's conduct both during and after the employee's FMLA leave. *Id.*

Most courts analyze retaliation-discrimination claims pursuant to the burden of proof schemes initially developed for Title VII cases in *McDonnell Douglas v. Burdine,* 411 U.S. 792, 93 S. Ct. 1817 (1973) and *Price Waterhouse v. Hopkins,* 490 U.S. 228, 109 S. Ct. 1775 (1989). *See LePore v. Lanvision Systems, Inc.,* 113 Fed. Appx. 449 (3d Cir. 2004); *Slaughter-Cooper v. Kelsey Seybold Med. Group, P.A.,* 379 F.3d 285, 291 n.13 (5th Cir. 2004); *Potenza, v City of New York,* 365 F.3d 165 (2nd Cir. 2004); *Spurlock v. Peterbilt Motors Co., Inc.,* 58 Fed. Appx. 630 (6th Cir. 2003); *Strickland v. Water Works And Sewer Bd. of the City of Birmingham,* 239 F.3d 1199, 1207 (11th Cir. 2001); *King v. Preferred Tech, Group,* 166 F.3d 887, 891 (7th Cir. 1999); *Hodgens v. General Dynamics Corp.,* 144 F.3d 151, 160-61 (1st Cir. 1998); *Worster v. Carlson Wagon Lit Travel, Inc.,* No. 3:02CV167 (EBB), 2005 U.S. Dist. LEXIS 1274, at *33 (D. Conn. Jan. 4, 2005), *aff'd,* 2006 U.S. App. LEXIS 3615 (2d Cir. 2006) (*McDonnell Douglas* burden shifting analysis applies to FMLA retaliation claims); *Schreiber v. Chicago Mercantile Exchange, Inc.,* No. 03 C 8568, 2004 U.S. Dist. LEXIS 23108, at *9 (N.D. Ill. Nov. 14, 2004); *LaFortune v. Fiber Materials, Inc.,* No. 03-275-P-H, 2004 U.S. Dist. LEXIS 21405, at *14 (D. Me. Oct. 25, 2004) (First Circuit adopted *McDonnell Douglas* burden shifting framework for analysis of FMLA retaliation claims); *Sheaffer v. County of Chatham,* 337 F. Supp. 2d 709, 726 (M.D.N.C. Sept. 17, 2004) (Fourth Circuit *in dicta* has suggested that the *McDonnell Douglas* burden-shifting test applies to FMLA retaliation claims).

The Ninth Circuit reserved judgment on whether the *McDonnell Douglas* analysis would be applicable in an anti-retaliation action under § 2615(a)(2). *Liu v. Amway Corp.,* 347 F.3d 1125, 1136, n.10 (9th Cir. 2003). In *Oby v. Baton Rouge Marriott,* 329 F. Supp. 2d 772, 782 (M.D. La. 2004), the court, following Fifth Circuit precedent, applied a modified *McDonnell Douglas* approach for mixed-motive cases absent direct evidence of discrimination.

A plaintiff may provide FMLA retaliation by direct evidence, as set forth in *Price Waterhouse v. Hopkins,* 490 U.S. 228, 244-46, 104 L. Ed. 2d 268, 109 S. Ct. 1775(1989), or indirectly through the burden-shifting analysis set forth by the Supreme Court in *McDonnell Douglas Corp. v. Green,* 411 U.S. 792, 36 L. Ed. 2d 668, 93 S. Ct. 1817 (1973). *Spurlock v. Peterbilt Motors Co., Inc.,* 58 Fed. Appx. 630 (6th Cir. 2003); *Strickland v. Water Works And Sewer Bd. of the City of Birmingham,* 239 F.3d 1199, 1207 (11th Cir. 2001); *Hodgens v. General Dynamics Corp.,* 144 F.3d 151, 160-61 (1st Cir. 1998); *Cagle v. FinishMaster, Inc.,* No. 1:03-cv-0265-JDT-WTL, 2004 U.S. Dist. LEXIS 26714, at *33-34 (S.D. Ind. Dec. 23, 2004); *Bila v. RadioShack Corp.,* No. 03-10177-BC, 2004 U.S. Dist. LEXIS 24649, at *27-28 (E.D. Mich. Nov. 23, 2004); *Schreiber v. Chicago Mercantile Exchange,*

Inc., No. 03 C 8568, 2004 U.S. Dist. LEXIS 23108, at *9 (N.D. Ill. Nov. 14, 2004); *Ashe v. Aronov Homes, Inc.*, 354 F. Supp. 2d 1251 (M.D. Ala. 2004); *Rosteutcher v. MidMichigan Physicians Group*, 332 F. Supp. 2d 1049, 1064 (E.D. Mich. 2004).

Under the *Price Waterhouse* framework, when a FMLA plaintiff alleging unlawful termination presents "direct evidence" that his FMLA leave was a substantial factor in the decision to fire him, the burden of persuasion on the issue of causation shifts, and the employer must prove that it would have fired the plaintiff even if it had not considered the FMLA leave. *Conoshenti v. Pub. Serv. Elec. & Gas Co.*, 364 F.3d 135, 147 (3d Cir. 2004). This burden requires the employer to convince the trier-of-fact that it is more likely than not that the decision would have been the same absent consideration of the illegitimate factor. The employer need not isolate the sole cause for the decision; rather it must demonstrate that with the illegitimate factor removed from the calculus, sufficient business reasons would have induced it to take the same employment action. This evidentiary scheme essentially requires the employer to place the employee in the same position he or she would have occupied absent discrimination. *Id.* at 147–148 (3d Cir. 2004) (quoting *Price Waterhouse*, 490 U.S. at 276–77, n.11).

To establish impermissible evidence through direct evidence, the plaintiff must provide evidence that is "so revealing of discriminatory animus" that it proves the existence of discrimination without inference or presumption. *Wilson v. Lemington Home for the Aged*, 159 F. Supp. 2d 186, 195 (W.D. Pa. 2001) (citing *Armbruster v. Unisys Corp.*, 32 F.3d 768, 778–79 (3rd Cir. 1994)). The plaintiff's evidence must show that "decision makers placed substantial negative reliance on an illegitimate criterion in reaching their decision." *Wilson*, 159 F. Supp. 2d at 195 (citing *Price Waterhouse*, 490 U.S. at 277 (J. O'Connor concurring in the judgment). If the plaintiff does provide such evidence, the defendant must rebut it by proving that even if the discrimination was a "motivating factor" in the adverse employment decision, the defendant would have made the same employment decision regardless of its discriminatory animus." *Wilson*, 159 F. Supp. 2d at 195.

A plaintiff attempting to prove discrimination by direct evidence faces a "high hurdle." *LePore v. Lanvision Systems, Inc.*, 113 Fed. Appx. 449 (3d Cir. 2004). Specifically, the evidence must demonstrate that the "decision makers placed substantial negative reliance on an illegitimate criterion in reaching their decision." *Id.* In these so-called mixed-motive cases, courts apply the analysis developed by the Supreme Court in *Price Waterhouse v. Hopkins*, 490 U.S. 228, 109 S. Ct. 1775 (1989). *Conoshenti v. Pub. Serv. Elec. & Gas Co.*, 364 F.3d 135, 147 (3d Cir. 2004).

In *LePore*, plaintiff argued that comments made by her supervisor that she might not want to come back to work after giving birth and to proactively seek child care as her job required travel were not direct evidence of discrimination. The court noted plaintiff's admission that the comments were not discriminatory. The court concluded that Lepore "has not cleared the high evidentiary hurdle of *Price Waterhouse*. Her mixed motives claim was therefore properly rejected."

In *Cagle v. FinishMaster, Inc.*, No. 1:03-cv-0265-JDT-WTL, 2004 U.S. Dist. LEXIS 26714, at *35 (S.D. Ind. Dec. 23, 2004), the court found that the proximity in timing of an employee's request for FMLA leave and his termination five days later failed to establish direct evidence linking his FMLA leave request and the adverse action. According to the court, "mere temporal proximity between the protected activity and the action alleged to have been taken in retaliation will rarely be sufficient in and of itself to create a triable issue." In *Cagle*, the court found that the employer decided to terminate plaintiff before she notified the employer of the need for FMLA leave.

In *Wilson v. Lemington Home for the Aged*, 159 F. Supp. 2d 186, 195 (W.D. Pa. 2001), the court found direct evidence of discriminatory intent in the employer's letter of termination to the employee. *Wilson*, 159 F. Supp. 2d at 195. The letter indicates that the plaintiff was deemed to have voluntarily quit by failing to provide the requisite medical certification pursuant to the defendant's FMLA policy. *Id.* In violation of the notice requirements of the FMLA, however, the court found that the employer had failed to provide the plaintiff with specific notice of her FMLA rights and obligations, including the obligation to provide a medical certification in support of her request for FMLA leave. Because it violated the notice provisions, and where it cited those provisions as the reason for determining that the employee had quit, the court found this to be direct evidence of discriminatory animus.

In the absence of direct evidence of the employer's discriminatory intent, courts have applied the *McDonnell Douglas* burden-shifting framework. See *Smith v. Memorial Hosp. Corp., et al.*, 302 F.3d 827, 832 (8th Cir. 2002); *Nichols v. Ashland Hosp. Corp.*, 251 F.3d 496, 502 (4th Cir. 2001); *Hunt v. Rapides Healthcare Systems, LLC*, 277 F.3d 757, 768 (5th Cir. 2001); *Skrjanc v. Great Lakes Power Service Co.*, 272 F.3d 309, 315 (6th Cir. 2001); *Strickland v. Water Works And Sewer Bd. of the City of Birmingham*, 239 F.3d 1199, 1207 (11th Cir. 2001); *King v. Preferred Technical Group*, 166 F.3d 887, 891 (7th Cir. 1999); *Hodgens v. General Dynamics Corp.*, 144 F.3d 151, 160–61 (1st Cir. 1998 *McDonnell Douglas* allocates the burdens of production and persuasion in accordance with a three-step procedure. *See McDonnell Douglas*, 411 U.S. at 802-04. Under that framework, a plaintiff employee must carry the initial burden of coming forward with sufficient evidence to establish a *prima facie* case of discrimination or retaliation. *See Texas Dept. of Community Affairs v. Burdine*, 450 U.S. 248, 252-53, 67 L. Ed. 2d 207, 101 S. Ct. 1089 (1981). If the employee does so, then the burden shifts to the employer to articulate some legitimate, nondiscriminatory reason for the action taken against the employee sufficient to raise a genuine issue of fact as to whether it discriminated against the employee. *McDonnell Douglas*, 411 U.S. at 802; *see Burdine*, 450 U.S. at 253. The employer "must clearly set forth, through the introduction of admissible evidence, the reasons for the [adverse action]. The explanation provided must be legally sufficient to justify a judgment for the [employer]." *Burdine*, 450 U.S. at 255. If the employer's evidence creates a genuine issue of fact, the presumption of discrimination drops from the case, and the plaintiff retains the ultimate burden of showing that the employer's stated reason for taking the adverse action was in fact pretext for retaliating against the employee for having taken protected FMLA leave. *King v. Preferred Technical Group*, 166 F.3d 887, 891-92 (7th Cir. 1999); *Hodgens v. General Dynamics Corp.*, 144 F.3d 151, 160-61 (1st Cir. 1998).

Under the *McDonnell Douglas* burden-shifting analysis, to establish a *prima facie* case of retaliation, a plaintiff must demonstrate: (1) the employee engaged in protected conduct; (2) the employee suffered an adverse employment action; and (3) there is a casual connection between the protected activity and the adverse employment decision. *See LePore v. Lanvision Systems, Inc.*, 113 Fed. Appx. 449 (3d Cir. 2004); *Doebele v. Sprint/United Management Co., et. al.*, 342 F.3d 1117 (10th Cir. 2003); *Strickland v. Water Works and Sewer Bd. of the City of Birmingham*, 239 F.3d 1199, 1207 (11th Cir. 2001); *King v. Preferred Technical Group*, 166 F.3d 887, 891-92 (7th Cir. 1999); *Michels v. Sunoco Home Comfort Service*, No. 04-1906, 2004 U.S. Dist. LEXIS 25152, at *10 (E.D. Pa. Dec. 10, 2004); *Bila v. RadioShack Corp.*, No. 03-10177-BC, 2004 U.S. Dist. LEXIS 24649, at *27-28 (E.D. Mich. Nov. 23, 2004); *LaFortune v. Fiber Materials, Inc.*, No. 03-275-P-H, 2004 U.S. Dist. LEXIS 21405, at *14 (D. Me. Oct. 25, 2004); *Ashe v. Aronov Homes, Inc.*, 354 F. supp. 2d 1251 (M.D. Ala. 2004); *Sheaffer v. County of Chatham*, 337 F. Supp. 2d 709, 726 (M.D.N.C. 2004); *Rosteutcher v. MidMichigan Physicians Group*, 332 F. Supp. 2d 1049, 1064 (E.D. Mich. 2004); *Sahadi v. Per-Se Technologies, Inc.*, 280 F. Supp. 2d 689 (E.D. Mich. 2003).

The *prima facie* case burden is "quite easy to meet." *Hodgens*, 144 F.3d at 159. The burden of establishing a *prima facie* case is not onerous, and the showing is easily made. *LaFortune v. Fiber Materials, Inc.*, No. 03-275-P-H, 2004 U.S. Dist. LEXIS 21405, at *19 (D. Me. Oct. 25, 2004).

Courts have invariably described the employee's *prima facie* case differently. The Second Circuit in *Potenza v. City of New York*, 365 F.3d 165, 168 (2d Cir. 2004), described the elements of the employee's *prima facie* FMLA retaliation claim as: (1) the employee exercised rights protected under the FMLA; (2) he was qualified for his position; (3) he suffered an adverse employment action; and (4) the adverse employment action occurred under circumstances giving rise to an inference of retaliatory intent. *Accord Worster v. Carlson Wagon Lit. Travel, Inc.*, No. 3:02CV167 (EBB), 2005 U.S. Dist. LEXIS 1274, at *33 (D. Conn. Jan. 4, 2005).

In *Bila v. RadioShack Corp.*, No. 03-10177-BC, 2004 U.S. Dist. LEXIS 24649, at *27-28 (E.D. Mich. Nov. 23, 2004), the court added a requirement that the employee establish that the employer knew about the employee's protected activity.

Some courts have added a requirement that the employee demonstrate that, after engaging in protected activity, only he, and not any similarly situated employee who did not engage in FMLA protected activity, was subjected to an adverse employment action even though he was performing his job in a satisfactory manner. *LePore*, 113 Fed. Appx. 449; *Cagle v. FinishMaster, Inc.*, No. 1:03-cv-0265-JDT-WTL, 2004 U.S. Dist. LEXIS 26714, at *34 (S.D. Ind. Dec. 23, 2004); *Schreiber v. Chicago Mercantile Exchange, Inc.*, No. 03 C 8568, 2004 U.S. Dist. LEXIS 23108, at *9 (N.D. Ill. Nov. 15, 2004); *Skiles v. Eli Lilly and Co.*, No. IP 01-1535-C H/K, 2003 U.S. Dist. LEXIS 11374, at *31 (S.D. Ind. June 18, 2003) (applying new rule for proving retaliation under indirect method announced in *Stone v. City of Indianapolis Public Utilities Div.*, 281 F.3d 640, 644 (7th Cir. 2002)).

In *Oby v. Baton Rouge Marriott*, 329 F. Supp. 2d 772, 785-786 (M.D. La. 2004), the court, following Fifth Circuit precedent, applied a modified *McDonnell Douglas* approach for mixed-motive cases absent direct evidence of discrimination. Under this scheme, the plaintiff must first still demonstrate a *prima facie* case of discrimination. The defendant then must articulate a legitimate, non-discriminatory reason for its decision to terminate the plaintiff; and, if the defendant meets its burden of production, the plaintiff must then offer sufficient evidence to create a genuine issue of material fact either: (1) that the defendant's reason is not true, but is instead a pretext for discrimination; or (2) that the defendant's reason, while true, is only one of the reasons for its conduct, and another "motivating factor" is the plaintiff's protected characteristic. If a plaintiff demonstrates that the protected characteristic was a motivating factor in the employment decision, it then falls to the defendant to prove that it would haven taken the same adverse action regardless of discriminatory animus. If the employer fails to carry this burden, plaintiff prevails.

A similar format applied the first two elements of the *prima facie* case, but then split the third, giving the employee the choice of either establishing that the employee was treated less favorably than an employee who had not requested leave under the FMLA, or the adverse decision was made because she took FMLA leave. *See Hunt v. Rapides Healthcare Systems, LLC*, 277 F.3d 757, 768 (5th Cir. 2001); *Wesley v. One Price Clothing Stores, Inc.*, No. 4:02–CV–834–A, 2003 U.S. Dist. LEXIS 14221, at *11 (N.D. Tex. Aug. 15, 2003); *Jarjoura v. Ericsson, Inc.*, 266 F. Supp. 2d 519, 528 (N.D. Tex. 2003), *aff'd*, 2003 U.S. App. LEXIS (5th Cir. 2003).

Still others have added an element that the employer knew of the employee's exercise of FMLA rights. *See Brungart v. BellSouth Telecommunications, Inc.*, 231 F.3d 791, 799 (11th Cir. 2000), *cert. denied*, 532 U.S. 1037 (2001); *Bryant v. Delbar Prods., Inc.*, 18 F. Supp. 2d 799, 809–10 (M.D. Tenn. 1998).

In addition to any FMLA cases, employers and employees will want to consult the latest iteration of the *prima facie* case for a Title VII retaliation claim in their circuit.

a. Adverse Employment Action

In order to establish a *prima facie* case of FMLA retaliation–discrimination, an employee must establish that they suffered an adverse employment action as a result of the exercise of FMLA rights. The Supreme Court's decision in *Burlington Northern & Santa Fe Railway Co., v. White*, 126 S. Ct. 2405, 165 L. Ed. 2d 345 (2006), a Title IV case, has impacted this determination. There, the Supreme Court, 126 S. Ct. at 2412-15, explained:

> The anti-retaliation provision protects an individual not from all retaliation, but from retaliation that produces an injury or harm... In our view, a plaintiff must show that a reasonable employee would have found the challenged action materially adverse, "which in this context means it might well have 'dissuaded a reasonable worker from engaging in protected activity.'"

Several courts have applied the standard enunciated in *Burlington Northern* to FMLA retaliation claims. *See Metzler v. Federal Home Loan Bank of Topeka*, 464 F.3d 1164, 1171 n.2 (10th Cir. 2006); *Grosso v. Federal Express Corp.*, 467 F. Supp. 2d 449, 458-59 (E.D. Pa. Dec. 19, 2006); *Foraker v. Apollo Group, Inc.*, 2006 U.S. Dist. LEXIS 85737, at *2 (D. Ariz. Nov. 22, 2006); *Campbell v. Wash. County Pub. Library*, 2006 U.S. Dist. LEXIS 64397, at *6 (S.D. Ohio Sept. 8, 2006), *aff'd*, 2007 U.S. App. LEXIS 17393 (6th Cir. 2007).

Applying *Burlington Northern*, the reassignment of a preferred truck did not constitute an adverse employment action to support an FMLA retaliation claim. *Grosso v. Federal Express Corp.*, 467 F. Supp. 2d 449, 458-59 (E.D. Pa. 2006) (broken air conditioning in assigned truck for a few weeks would not dissuade a reasonable worker from taking FMLA leave; reassignment of employee to harder driving route with the worst truck in fleet was "materially adverse"; failure to extend personal leave beyond 90 days not materially adverse).

Prior to *Burlington Northern*, courts applied different standards to determine whether the employee suffered an adverse employment action for purposes of an FMLA discrimination/retaliation claim. Some courts require that only "ultimate employment decisions, such as to hire, discharge, refuse to promote, can constitute an adverse employment action." *Hunt v. Rapides Healthcare Systems, LLC*, 277 F.3d 757, 768 (5th Cir. 2001); *Sheaffer v. County of Chatham*, 337 F. Supp. 2d 709, 727 (M.D.N.C. 2004); *see, e.g., King v. Preferred Technical Group*, 166 F.3d 887, 893 (7th Cir. 1999) (termination met adverse employment action requirement).

An adverse employment action necessarily encompasses all tangible employment actions, such as hiring, firing, failing to promote, reassignment or a decision causing a significant change in benefits. *Lipscomb v. Electronic Data Systems, Corp.*, 462 F. Supp. 2d 581, 588 (D. Del. 2006).

Other courts include "stripping the employee of any work–related privileges, refusing to consider the employee's request for transfer or promotion, removing the employee from a position, threats of retaliation for protected activity, and reassignment to a remote cubicle" as adverse actions. It also includes a loss of status. *LaFourtune v. Fiber Materials, Inc.*, No. 03–275–P–H, 2004 U.S. Dist. LEXIS 21405, at *16 (D. Me. Oct. 25, 2004). The decisions invariably track the prevailing position taken by the circuit court in Title VII cases.

Courts differ on what constitutes an adverse employment action. For example, job transfers may or may not constitute an adverse employment action. The issue was recently vetted in *Worster v. Carlson Wagon Lit. Travel, Inc.*, No. 3:02CV167 (EBB), 2005 U.S. Dist. LEXIS 1274, at *33 (D. Conn. Jan. 4, 2005), *aff'd*, 2006 U.S. App. LEXIS 3615 (2d Cir. 2006). There, the court focused on whether the transfer had a materially adverse affect on the employee's career. According to the court:

> Transfers that do not result in a demotion through loss of pay, rank, title or significant job responsibilities do not ordinarily constitute adverse actions. *See Galabya v. New York City Bd. Of Educ.*, 202 F.3d 636, 641 (2d Cir. 2000) ("[A] transfer is an adverse employment action if it results in a change in responsibilities so significant as to constitute a setback to the plaintiff's career."). However, "an involuntary transfer may constitute an adverse employment action if the plaintiff shows that the transfer created a materially significant disadvantage with respect to the terms of [his] employment." *Williams v. R.H. Donnelley Corp.*, 368 F.3d 123, 128 (2d Cir. 2004).

The district court in *Worster* concluded that plaintiff's assignment to the Pearson account did not materially disadvantage Worster's employment. The court noted that while plaintiff alleged that he was dissatisfied with the transfer and argued that the account position was less flexible and a lower-level position, plaintiff did not establish that he suffered loss of pay, rank, or title. While his responsibilities changed as a result of the transfer, the position was only temporary and plaintiff admitted that it was for business reasons. According to the court, "[a] business reason does not need to be good or even wise. It simply has to be nondiscriminatory."

The court in *LaFourtune v. Fiber Materials, Inc.*, No. 03-275-P-H, 2004 U.S. Dist. LEXIS 21405, at *16 (D. Me. Oct. 25, 2004), found a layoff to be an adverse employment action. Similarly, firing an employee constitutes an adverse employment action. *Sheaffer v. County of Chatham*, 337 F. Supp. 2d 709, 727 (M.D.N.C. Sept. 17, 2004).

A claim of hostile work environment, however, has been found to raise a material issue of fact whether the employee suffered an adverse employment action. *See Hite v. Biomet, Inc.*, 38 F. Supp. 2d 720, 741 (N.D. Ind. 1999).

Employer requests for leave verification and notice are not adverse actions or retaliatory employment actions. *Manns v. ArvinMeritor, Inc.*, 291 F. Supp. 2d 655, 661 (N.D. Ohio 2003). "An employer can make reasonable requests for leave verification and notice (even for a single day)—it need not simply accept an employee's say-so that he needs and has taken FMLA leave on a particular day." This is so even if the need for leave will be on an intermittent basis, the employee must still show the need for leave on a specific date. *Id.*

Finally, courts have held that verbal reprimands and threats of termination do not constitute adverse employment actions. *See Boriski v. City of College Station*, 65 F. Supp. 2d 493 (S.D. Tex. 1999); *Mistretta v. Volusia County Dept. of Corrections*, 61 F. Supp. 2d 1255 (M.D. Fla. 1999).

b. Causal Connection

To establish a casual link between the employee's exercise of FMLA rights and the adverse action, the employee must prove that an employers' retaliatory motive played a part in the adverse employment action. *Hite v. Vermeer Mfg., Co.*, 446 F.3d 858, 865 (8th Cir. 2006);

An employee must show that the protected activity and the adverse action were not "wholly unrelated." *Brungart v. BellSouth Telecommunications, Inc.*, 231 F.3d 791, 799 (11th Cir. 2000) *cert. denied*, 532 U.S. 1037 (2001); *Ashe v. Aronov Homes, Inc.*, 354 F. Supp. 2d 1251 (M.D. Ala. 2004); *Norman v. Southern Guaranty Ins. Co.*, 191 F. Supp. 2d 1321, 1332 (M.D. Ala. 2002). In order to show that two things were not entirely unrelated, the plaintiff must generally show that the decision-maker was aware of the protected conduct at the time of the adverse employment action. *Brungart v. BellSouth Telecommunications, Inc.*, 231 F.3d 791, 799 (11th Cir. 2000), *cert. denied*, 532 U.S. 1037 (2001); *Norman v. Southern Guaranty Ins. Co.*, 191 F. Supp. 2d 1321, 1332 (M.D. Ala. 2002). Other courts have held that the employee must demonstrate that the employer would not have taken the adverse action but for the employee's protected activity. *King v. Preferred Technical Group*, 166 F.3d 887, 892 7th Cir. 1999); *Routes v. Henderson*, 58 F. Supp. 2d 959, 979 (S.D. Ind. 1999). The employee does not need to establish that his or her protected activity was the sole reason for the employer's adverse action to establish a causal link. *Sherrod v. American Airlines*, 132 F.3d 1112, 1122 (5th Cir. 1998); *Bryant v. Delbar Products, Inc.*, 18 F. Supp. 2d 799, 809 (M.D. Tenn. 1998) (causal connection established where one of several absences cited as basis for discipline was covered by FMLA).

A plaintiff's burden to demonstrate a casual connection between an employee's FMLA leave and an adverse action is minimal, and courts are expected to draw reasonable inferences from any credible evidence that the plaintiff puts forth. *Mueller v. J.P. Morgan Chase & Co.*, No. 1:05 CV 560, 2007 U.S. Dist. LEXIS 20828, at *52 (N.D. Ohio March 23, 2007).

This burden may be established in two ways: (1) a close temporal proximity between the protected conduct and the adverse action; or (2) by showing that the employer gained knowledge of the employee's protected conduct at a point temporally proximate to the adverse action. *Ashe v. Aronov Homes, Inc.*, 354 F. Supp. 2d 1251 (M.D. Ala. 2004); *accord Hite v. Vermeer Mfg., Co.*, 446 F.3d 858, 865 (8th Cir. 2006) (employee can establish a causal link between her protected activity and the adverse employment action through the timing of the two events). An employee may establish a causal relationship between the adverse employment action and the employee's engagement in FMLA protected activities by direct or, more typically, indirect evidence. Direct evidence of a causal relationship has been found where an employer complained about FMLA-covered absences. *See Smith v. BellSouth Telecommunications, Inc.*, 273 F.3d 1301, 1314 (11th Cir. 2001) (staffing manager notes that former employee's file was marked as not eligible for rehire, "took a lot of FMLA" sufficient to defeat employer motion for summary judgment); *Maxwell v. GTE Wireless Service Corp.*, 121 F. Supp. 2d 649, 658 (N.D. Ohio 2000) (Maxwell presented direct evidence of a causal connection between the FMLA leave to care for his son, and his termination by employer statements complaining about the employee's absences to care for his child, and the manager was going to take action against the employee as a result); *Routes v. Henderson*, 58 F. Supp. 2d 959 (S.D. Ind. 1999) (causal link established by evidence that employer developed a negative attitude toward the plaintiff after he took FMLA leave).

Generally, however, an employee relies on the timing of the adverse employment action following the employee's engagement in FMLA protected activities to establish causation for purposes of the employee's *prima facie* case. Courts have regularly found that an employee satisfied the causation requirement where there is a close temporal proximity between the protected conduct and the adverse employment action. *See Smith v. Memorial Hosp. Corp., et al.*, 302 F.3d 827, 832–33 (8th Cir. 2002) (extremely close temporal proximity of 2 weeks sufficient to establish requisite causation); *Brungart v. BellSouth Telecommunications, Inc.*, 231 F.3d 791, 799 (11th Cir. 2000) (close proximity in time can establish casual connection) *cert. denied*, 532 U.S. 1037 (2001); *Glekln v. Democratic Nat. Campaign Committee*, 199 F.3d 1365 (D.C. Cir. 2000) (timing between an employee's notifying an employer of pregnancy and adverse decision established causal connection for *prima facie* case of FMLA retaliation); *King v. Preferred Technical Group*, 166 F.3d 887 (7th Cir. 1999); *Hodgens v. General Dynamics Corp.*, 144 F.3d 151, 168 (1st Cir. 1998); *Arbia v. Owens-Illinois, Inc. et al.*, No. 1:02CV00111, 2003 U.S. Dist. LEXIS 9429, at *15 (M.D.N.C. June 4, 2003) (written reprimand on return from FMLA leave); *Darboe v. Staples, Inc., et. al.*, 243 F. Supp. 2d 5, 15–16 (S.D.N.Y. 2003) (employee first told of demotion shortly after return from FMLA leave established tight temporal sequence sufficient to establish causal connection); *Norman v. Southern Guaranty Ins. Co.*, 191 F. Supp. 2d 1321, 1332–33 (M.D. Ala. 2002) (an employee presented with a memorandum warning her of excessive absenteeism on the day she returned to work established causation. *Wilson v. Lemington Home of the Aged*, 159 F. Supp. 2d 186, 195 (W.D. Pa. 2001) (approximately two-week interval between request for leave and termination letter established casual connection by virtue of temporal proximity). Of course, if the temporal proximity between the adverse employment action and the employee's protected FMLA activities are not close, the employee will not establish the casual element of the *prima facie* case for FMLA retaliation. For example, in *Hillstrom v. Best Western TLC Hotel*, 265 F. Supp. 2d 117, 2003 U.S. Dist. LEXIS 8854, at *29 (D. Mass. May 28, 2003), *aff'd*, 354 F.3d 27 (1st Cir. 2003), the court found that the 15-month period that separated the employee's use of FMLA leave and his termination, without more, was "simply too extended a time period to support a casual connection between his protected absence and Phipps' decision to fire him." Similarly, in *Mistretta v. Volusia County Dept. of Corrections*, 61 F. Supp. 2d 1255 (M.D. Fla. 1999), the court held that the one-year gap between the use of FMLA leave and the employee's termination precluded a finding of a casual connection between the two events based on timing. *See also Spurlock v. Peterbilt Motors Co. Inc.*, 58 Fed. Appx. 630 (6th Cir. 2003) (several year interval between the plaintiff's use of FMLA leave and discharge, without more, insufficient to establish causal relationship); *Schlater v. Eaton Corp.*, No. 1:02-CV-10003, 2003 U.S. Dist. LEXIS 14366, at *15 (S.D. Iowa May 7, 2003) (6-month time period between beginning of plaintiff's leave and termination is too remote to establish a temporal connection that might support an inference of causation).

Courts are split as to whether timing alone between the protected activity and the adverse action can establish the necessary causal link. Many courts have held that temporal proximity alone may be sufficient to establish the necessary causal connection. *LaFourtune v. Fiber Materials, Inc.*, No. 03-275-P-H, 2004 U.S. Dist. LEXIS 21405, at 16 (D. Me. Oct. 25, 2004); *Ashe v. Aronov Homes, Inc.*, 354 F. Supp. 2d 1251 (M.D. Ala. 2004).

Cases in which temporal proximity alone was found sufficient to create an inference of a causal link have uniformly held that the temporal proximity must be "very close." *Hite v. Vermeer Mfg., Co.*, 446 F.3d 858, 866 (8th Cir. 2006). Where temporal proximity is weak, even these courts require additional information to establish causation. *LaFourtune*, 2004 U.S. Dist. LEXIS 21405, at *19 (11–month interval between lay off and return from FMLA requires more evidence of causation).

Absent additional evidence, relatively short intervals between protected activity and an adverse employment action lack the requisite temporal proximity for purposes of causation. *See Potenza, v City of New York*, 365 F.3d 165 (2nd Cir. 2004) (while a two–month interval between employee's return to work from FMLA leave and removal did not completely vitiate a retaliation claim, absent additional evidence of discriminatory intent the court affirmed award of summary judgment for employer). Where the adverse action occurs the day the employee returns from FMLA leave and cites the leave as the basis for the action, the employee will easily satisfy his/her *prima facie* case. *See Ashe*, 2004 U.S. Dist. LEXIS 26900, at *30.

Other courts have held that proximity in time between an employee's exercise of FMLA rights and an adverse action, standing alone, will usually not provide sufficient evidence of causation to survive summary judgment. *See Hite v. Vermeer Mfg., Co.*, 446 F.3d 858, 866 (8th Cir. 2006) (mere coincidence of timing is rarely sufficient to establish causation element); *Strickland v. Water Works and Sewer Bd. of the City of Birmingham*, 239 F.3d 1199, 1207–08 (11th Cir. 2001); *Brungart v. BellSouth Telecommunications, Inc.*, 231 F.3d 791, 799 (11th Cir. 2000), *cert. denied*, 532 U.S. 1037 (2001) ("That requirement rests upon common sense. A decision maker cannot have been motivated to retaliate by something unknown to him"); *Gordon v. Bd. of Trustees of Governors State U.*, No. 06 C 495, 2007 U.S. Dist. LEXIS 31864, at *12 & n.1 (N.D. Ill. April 26, 2007); *Bila v. RadioShack Corp.*, No. 03–10177–BC, 2004 U.S. Dist. LEXIS 24649, at *27–28 (E.D. Mich. Nov. 23, 2004); *Rosteutcher v. MidMichigan Physicians Group*, 332 F. Supp. 2d 1049, 1064 (E.D. Mich. 2004). These courts apply a "timing–plus" test. *Rosteutcher v. MidMichigan Physicians Group*, 332 F. Supp. 2d 1049, 1064 (E.D. Mich. 2004). Pursuant to that test, the combination of proximity in time with other evidence can suggest a causal connection sufficient to establish a *prima facie* case of retaliation. *Id.*

Where temporal proximity alone is insufficient to establish causation, an employee may prove causation by providing evidence of the employer's discriminatory comments. *Hite v. Vermeer Mfg., Co.*, 446 F.3d 858, 866 (8th Cir. 2006); *Bila v. RadioShack Corp.*, No. 03–10177–BC, 2004 U.S. Dist. LEXIS 24649, at *27–28 (E.D. Mich. Nov. 23, 2004); *Rosteutcher v. MidMichigan Physicians Group*, 332 F. Supp. 2d 1049, 1064 (E.D. Mich. 2004); *LaFourtune v. Fiber Materials, Inc.*, No. 03–275–P–H, 2004 U.S. Dist. LEXIS 21405, at *19 (D. Me. Oct. 25, 2004).

In *Hodgens v. General Dynamics Corp.*, 144 F.3d 151, 165 (1st Cir. 1998), the court credited toward the establishment of the employee's *prima facie* case comments made by the employee's supervisor warning the employee that he was taking "too much time off" shortly after taking several days off for surgery. *See e.g., Doeble v. Sprint/United Management Co., et. al.*, No. 01–3372, 2003 U.S. App. LEXIS 18012, at *51 (10th Cir. Aug. 28, 2003) (pretext established by evidence of management remarks adverse to employee's use of FMLA leave); *Tamayo v. DeLoitee & Touche, LLP*, Civ. No. 05-3364 (WHW), 2007 U.S. Dist. LEXIS 2878 at *23 (D.N.J. Jan. 16, 2007) (temporal proximity and evidence of ongoing antagonism supported casual link); *Bila v. RadioShack Corp.*, No. 03–10177–BC, 2004 U.S. Dist. LEXIS 24649, at *27–28 (E.D. Mich. Nov. 23, 2004); *English v. Baptist Healthcare System, Inc.*, No. 3:01CV–92–H, 2003 U.S. Dist. LEXIS 921, at *19 (W.D. Ky. Jan, 22, 2003) (casual connection established by temporal proximity plus supervisor statements indicating resentment over plaintiff's use of FMLA leave).

However, in *Schafer v. Querrey & Harrow, Ltd.*, No. 01 C 3908, 2002 U.S. Dist. LEXIS 3695, at *8 (N.D. Ill. March 7, 2002), the district court held that occasional offensive comments are not relevant in an employment suit unless the plaintiff can show that the person making the comments is the same person who made the adverse employment decision. The employee in *Schafer* was unable to establish that the individual making the pregnancy–related offensive remarks was the individual who later made the adverse action decision

Evidence of an employer's awareness of the employee's protected FMLA activities may be established by direct or circumstantial evidence. *Strickland v. Water Works and Sewer Bd. of the City of Birmingham*, 239 F.3d 1199, 1207–08, n.10 (11th Cir. 2001); *Brungart v. BellSouth Telecommunications, Inc.*, 231 F.3d 791, 799 (11th Cir. 2000) (temporal proximity of adverse action to employee's FMLA protected activities serves as indirect evidence of employer's awareness), *cert. denied*, 532 U.S. 1037 (2001).

Causation may also be established by demonstrating disparate treatment. In *Schreiber v. Chicago Mercantile Exchange, Inc.*, No. 03 C 8568, 2004 U.S. Dist. LEXIS 23108, at *11 (N.D. Ill. Nov. 14, 2004), plaintiff was terminated as part of a mini–RIF.

The court held that in a RIF case, the employee need not establish that similarly situated employees were treated more favorably. Rather, the employee need only show that the employee's duties were absorbed by the remaining employees who had not exercised FMLA rights. Because some of the remaining employees who absorbed plaintiff's job duties had exercised FMLA rights, the court concluded that plaintiff failed to establish her *prima facie* case of FMLA retaliation. An employee may shorten the gap between the protected activity and the adverse action by showing that shortly after he or she engaged in protected activity, the employer took escalating adverse and retaliatory action against her. *Hite v. Vermeer Mfg., Co.*, 446 F.3d 858, 866 (8th Cir. 2006).

Close temporal proximity may be defeated where there is undisputed proof that the employer had no knowledge of the protected activity at the time the decision was made. *Ashe v. Aronov Homes, Inc.*, 354 F. Supp. 2d 1251 (M.D. Ala. 2004). In *Strickland v. Water Works and Sewer Bd. of the City of Birmingham*, 239 F.3d 1199 (11th Cir. 2001), the Eleventh Circuit held that, even where only nine days passed between leave and the decision to fire him, an employee who failed to establish that he gave his employer adequate notice of the need for FMLA leave could not satisfy the requirement that his employers were aware of his protected activities at the time it decided to take the adverse employment action. *Id.* at 1207–08.

Courts have held that where the decision to take the adverse employment action was made before the protected activity (e.g., request for or use of FMLA leave), the casual element of the employee's *prima facie* case cannot be met, and the claim fails. *See Burch v. WDAS AM/FM, AM.FM Inc. et al.*, No. 00–4852, 2002 U.S. Dist. LEXIS 12290, at *32 (E.D. Pa. July 1, 2002) ("One cannot reasonably conclude that the plaintiff was terminated for something which occurred after the decision to terminate him was made").

Employees have been held not to establish the requisite casual connection between protected FMLA leave and discipline where the adverse action involves discipline for absences beyond those protected by the FMLA. *See Hypes v. First Commerce Corp.*, 134 F.3d 721, 725–26 (5th Cir. 1998); *Enright v. CGH Med.* Center, No. 96–C–50224, 1999 U.S. Dist. LEXIS 370 (N.D. Ill. Jan. 12, 1999) (despite reference to FMLA leave in supervisor's notes, evidence established that employee was disciplined or unplanned sick days not FMLA absences); *Boriski v City of College Station*, 65 F. Supp. 2d 493, 514 (S.D. Tex. 1999); *Summerville v. Esco Co.*, 52 F. Supp. 2d 804, 812–14 (W.D. Mich. 1999); *Dodgens v. Kent Mfg., Co.*, 955 F. Supp. 560–563–66 (D.S.C. 1997).

c. Employer's Legitimate Non–Discriminatory Reason

Under the *McDonnell Douglas* proof scheme, once it has been determined that an employee has met his or her *prima facie* case, the burden shifts to the employer to offer a legitimate nondiscriminatory reason for the adverse employment action. *Smith v. BellSouth Telecommunications, Inc.*, 273 F.3d 1303, 1314 (11th Cir. 2001); *King v. Preferred Technical Group*, 166 F.3d 887, 893 (7th Cir. 1999); *Snelling v. Clarian Health Partners, Inc.*, 184 F. Supp. 2d 838, 848 (S.D. Ind. 2002).

The employer's burden at this stage is 'relatively light: it is satisfied if the defendant articulates any legitimate reason for the adverse employment action; the defendant need not prove that the articulated reason actually motivated the action.'" *Wilson v. Lemington Home of the Aged*, 159 F. Supp. 2d 186, 195 (W.D. Pa. 2001) (quoting *Krouse v. American Sterilizer Co.*, 126 F.3d 494, 500 (3rd Cir. 1997)); *see also King v. Preferred Technical Group*, 166 F.3d 887, 893 (7th Cir. 1999) (quoting *Texas Dept. of Community Affairs v. Burdine*, 450 U.S. 248, 254, 67 L. Ed. 2d 207, 101 S. Ct. 1089 (1981)); *Swanson v. Senior Resource Connection*, 254 F. Supp. 2d 945, 958 (S.D. Ohio 2003) (employer's burden at second stage of *McDonnell Douglas* frameworks of analysis is not onerous, and only requires it to articulate a good-faith, non-discriminatory justification for its actions); *Glunt v. GES Exposition Services, Inc. et al.*, 123 F. Supp. 2d 847, 872 (D. Md. 2000). If the defendant carries this burden of production, the presumption raised by the *prima facie* case is rebutted, and drops from the case. *King v. Preferred Technical Group*, 166 F.3d 887, 893 (7th Cir. 1999) (quoting *Texas Dept. of Community Affairs v. Burdine*, 450 U.S. 248, 255 & n. 10, 67 L. Ed. 2d 207, 101 S. Ct. 1089 (1981)).

Generally, an employer establishes the burden of production by explaining that the adverse employment action was taken due to conduct or performance deficiencies unrelated to the exercise for rights protected by the FMLA. Remember, the FMLA does not provide an employee any greater employment rights than the employee would have had if FMLA leave had not been not taken. 29 USC 2614(a)(3); 29 CFR 825.312(d); *see Rice v. Sunrise Express*, 209 F.3d 1008, 1017 (7th Cir. 2000); *Ogborn v. United Food and Commercial Workers, Local No. 881 et al.*, No. 98 C 4623, 2000, U.S. Dist. LEXIS 14092, at *33–34 (N.D. Ill. Sept. 25, 2000), *aff'd*, 305 F.3d 763 (7th Cir. 2002). As such, the FMLA does not prohibit an employer from terminating an employee, including one on FMLA leave, on any ground other than in retaliation for or because of exercising rights under the FMLA. *Ogborn v. United Food and Commercial Workers, Local No. 881 et al.*, No. 98 C 4623, 2000 U.S. Dist. LEXIS 14092, at *33–34 (N.D. Ill. Sept. 25, 2000) (collecting cases), *aff'd*, 305 F.3d 763 (7th Cir. 2002).

Employers have been found to satisfy their burden of production by claiming that the employee would have been disciplined or discharged anyway for performance problems. *See Hoffman v. Professional Med Team*, 394 F.3d 414 (6th Cir. 2005) (employee's discharge for use of profanity while arguing with her supervisor about her FMLA request found to be legitimate basis for adverse action); *Baugher v. Dekko Heating Technologies*, 92 Fed. Appx. 328 (7th Cir. 2004) (no reasonable juror could conclude on this record that the reason for Baugher's discharge was actual or anticipated FMLA leave, rather than longstanding deficiencies in performance plus an episode of perceived dishonesty); *Spurlock v. Peterbilt Motors Co. Inc.*, 58 Fed. Appx. 630 (6th Cir. 2003) (termination resulted from continued unsatisfactory performance); *King v. Preferred Technical Group*, 166 F.3d 887, 893 (7th Cir. 1999) (legitimate nondiscriminatory reason established by the employer's claim that collective bargaining agreement required the termination of the employee who did not return to work on expiration of leave of absence); *Bila v. RadioShack Corp.*, No. 03-10177-BC, 2004 U.S. Dist. LEXIS 24649, at *27–28 (E.D. Mich. Nov. 23, 2004) (insubordination and failure to get along with supervisors found to be legitimate, non-discriminatory reasons for adverse action); *Skiles v. Eli Lilly and Co.*, No. IP 01-1535-C H/K, 2003 U.S. Dist. LEXIS 11374, at *33–35 (S.D. Ind. June 18, 2003) (performance deficiencies); *Jarjoura v. Ericsson, Inc.*, 266 F. Supp. 2d 519, 528 (N.D. Tex. 2003), *aff'd*, 2003 U.S. App. (misuse of government credit card); *Norman v. Southern Guaranty Ins. Co.*, 191 F. Supp. 2d 1321, 1332–33 (M.D. Ala. 2002) (an employer's assertion that the employee's excessive absences met the employer's burden of production at this stage); *Wilson v. Lemington Home of the Aged*, 159 F. Supp. 2d 186, 195 (W.D. Pa. 2001) (court assumed the employer met burden of production where the employer indicated that it terminated the employee because it believed that she had quit as evidenced by the fact that the employee removed all her personal items from her office); *Glunt v. GES Exposition Services, Inc. et al.*, 123 F. Supp. 2d 847, 872 (D. Md. 2000) (poor job performance qualifies as a legitimate, nondiscriminatory reason to demote an employee); *Ogborn*, 2000 U.S. Dist. LEXIS 14092, at *33–34 (the plaintiff would have been discharged regardless of taking FMLA leave because of his deficient job performance regarding processing grievances).

Courts have also accepted excessive absenteeism as a legitimate, non-discriminatory reason justifying discipline. *See Bailey v. Amsted Indus., Inc.*, 172 F.3d 1041, 1045–46 (8th Cir. 1999); *Hypes v. First Commerce Corp.*, 134 F.3d 721, 725 (5th Cir. 1998); *Morgan v. Hilti, Inc.*, 108 F.3d 1319, 1325 (10th Cir. 1997). Other courts have refused to accept an employer's proffer of absenteeism as a legitimate, non-discriminatory reason for an adverse action where it might include leave protected by the FMLA. *Doebele v. Sprint/United Management Co.*, 342 F.3d 1117 (10th Cir. 2003) (discharge based in part on attendance problems, most of which were covered by FMLA, held sufficient evidence of pretext); *Brice-Northard v. Sports Authority*, No. 97-7275, 1998 U.S. Dist. LEXIS 20408 (S.D. Fla. Aug. 13, 1998) (denying summary judgment to employer where it was unclear whether FMLA absences were included in performance evaluation); *Williams v. Shenango, Inc.*, 986 F. Supp. 309, 321–22 (W.D. Pa. 1997) (inclusion of FMLA protected absences on discipline record could lead reasonable persons to conclude that employee was retaliated against for exercising FMLA rights).

Falsification of a job application has been held to be a legitimate reason for an employer to terminate an employee. *See Aubuchon v. Knauf Fiberglass, GMBH*, 359 F.3d 950 (7th Cir. 2004) (company policy that mandated discharge for falsification of job application formed legitimate grounds for discharge where there was no evidence that the policy was applied more harshly to employees who exercised FMLA rights).

In *McBride v. Citgo Petroleum Corp.*, 281 F.3d 1099 (10th Cir. 2002), the court held that the FMLA does not protect an employee from discipline for performance problems caused by the same serious health condition that gave rise to the need for protected FMLA leave. The FMLA, the Tenth Circuit held, only protects an employee's right to take and return from FMLA leave. Performance problems caused by her illness are not protected by the FMLA.

The automatic termination of an employee by operation of the terms of a contract was found to be a legitimate, non-discriminatory reason to justify the employee's termination. In *Slaughter-Cooper v. Kelsey Seybold Med. Group, P.A.*, 379 F.3d 285, 291, n. 13 (5th Cir. 2004), the employee was a physician working under an employment contract. The contract contained an automatic termination clause that was triggered if the employee became disabled and unable to work for longer than three months. Plaintiff was injured in an off-duty accident and was unable to work for more than three months. This time, however, was covered by the FMLA. Absent evidence of pretext, the court found that the automatic termination of her employment by contract did not violate the anti-retaliation provisions of the FMLA.

The anti-retaliation provisions of the FMLA have also been held only to apply to retaliation for protected FMLA activities, not general office politics. In *D'Amico v. Compass Groups USA, Inc. et al.,* 198 F. Supp. 2d 18 (D. Mass. 2002), *aff'd,* 52 Fed. Appx. 524 (1st Cir. 2002), the court awarded summary judgment to the employer dismissing the plaintiff's FMLA retaliation claims because the retaliation was due to the employee's "going over" his supervisor's head, not for taking FMLA leave. According to the court, "churlish and insensitive behavior by a supervisor, however regrettable, and however harmful to an employee, is not conduct falling within the prohibitions of the [FMLA] anti-discrimination laws."

d. Honest Belief Defense

A number of courts have recognized an employer's defense to a claim of unlawful discrimination or retaliation that the employer honestly, albeit mistakenly, believed at the time it took the adverse action in question that the employee had procured the FMLA leave by fraud. *See Medley v. Polk Co.,* 260 F.3d 1202, 1207–1208 (10th Cir. 2001); *Kariotis v. Navistar Int'l Transp. Corp.* 131 F.3d 672, 680–81 (7th Cir. 1997); *Williamson v. Parker Hannifin Corp.,* 208 F. Supp. 2d 1248 (N.D. Ala. 2002); *Wesley v. One Price Clothing Stores, Inc.,* No. 4:02–CV–834–A, 2003 U.S. Dist. LEXIS 14221 (N.D. Tex. Aug. 15, 2003); *Moughari v. Publix Super Markets,* No. 4:97cv212–WS, 1998 U.S. Dist. LEXIS 8951 (N.D. Fla.); *Stonum v. U.S. Airways, Inc.,* 83 F. Supp. 2d 894, 903, n.12 (S.D. Ohio 1999); *see also Snelling Clarian Health Partners, Inc.,* 184 F. Supp. 2d 838, 848 (S.D. Ind. 2002) ("honest belief" defense would apply even where employer's reasons for adverse action were foolish, trivial, or even baseless, as long as employer honestly believed reasons; material issues of fact precluded application of honest belief defense).

The Seventh Circuit in *Kariotis,* 131 F.3d at 680–81, explained the rationale behind the honest belief defense as follows:

> Discrimination statutes allow employers to discharge employees for almost any reason whatsoever (even a mistaken but honest belief) as long as the reason is not illegal discrimination. Thus, when an employee is discharged because of an employer's honest mistake, federal anti-discrimination laws offer no protection. Likewise, when an employer discharges an employee because of inefficient work habits, excess absenteeism, an unacceptable attitude with customers and coworkers, or for a myriad of other reasons, anti-discrimination laws do not come into play.

*****

> The problem for Kariotis [the employee] is that Navistar [the employer] has demonstrated that it honestly believed she was not on legitimate FMLA leave [.]

Similarly, in *Slaughter–Cooper v. Kelsey Seybold Med. Group, P.A.,* 379 F.3d 285, 291, n. 13 (5th Cir. 2004), plaintiff, who had recently returned to work from FMLA leave, was terminated for instructing a subordinate to deflect all phone calls that day by telling callers that she was busy and could not come to the phone. Plaintiff argued that her subordinate either misunderstood or misrepresented what she said. As such, the adverse action was improper. The court opined that:

> [N]either the FMLA nor any federal statute forbids substantively *mistaken* decisions. The question is whether the adverse action rests on a ground forbidden by federal law.... Firing someone who misrepresented availability during working hours does not violate any rule of federal law; and if (as is undeniable on this record) the persons who made the decision actually believed that Baugher told Slagle to stymie callers, it is impossible to deem the action a pretext for discrimination or an episode of retaliation.

See also Hoffman v. Professional Med Team, 394 F.3d 414 (6th Cir. 2005) (dispute over disciplinary actions is not concerned with whether the employee's purported misconduct actually occurred, but whether it sincerely motivated the employer's adverse action decision).

The district court in *Moughari v. Publix Super Markets* (1998 U.S. Dist. LEXIS 8951 at *2) opined that:

> Moughari was not using his [FMLA] leave time [for the birth of a child] for its intended purposes and was not being candid with his mangers about his leave. Such termination did not constitute a violation of the FMLA whether or not Moore's [Moughari's district manager] conclusion about Moughari's alleged improper use of leave time was correct, whether or not Moughari was on FMLA leave at the time, and whether or not Publix failed to properly advise Moughari about his FMLA rights. *See Kariotis v. Navistar Int'l Transp. Corp.,* 131 F.3d 672 (7th Cir. 1979).

An employer is not required to interview the employee or the employee's witnesses in order to obtain the benefit of the "honest belief" rule. *Hoskins v. Pridgeon & Clay, Inc.*, No. 1:05-CV-816, 2007 U.S. Dist. LEXIS 24674, at *25 (W.D. Mich. April 3, 2007). There is no requirement that the decisional process used by the employer be optimal or that it leave no stone unturned. *Smith v. Chrysler Corp.*, 155 F.3d 799, 807 (6th Cir. 1998); *Hoskins v. Pridgeon & Clay, Inc.*, No. 1:05-CV-816, 2007 U.S. Dist. LEXIS 24674, at *25 (W.D. Mich. April 3, 2007).

An employer need not prove that an employee committed FMLA fraud in order to fit within the honest belief rule. "A requirement that the employer be able to demonstrate that the employee engaged in misconduct in order to obtain the benefit of the "honest belief" rule would eviscerate the rule itself. *Hoskins v. Pridgeon & Clay, Inc.*, No. 1:05-CV-816, 2007 U.S. Dist. LEXIS 24674, at *28 (W.D. Mich. April 3, 2007).

Of course, if an employee really did fraudulently obtain FMLA leave, that would also be a legitimate, nondiscriminatory reason for taking disciplinary action. *See LeBoeuf v. NYU Med. Center,* No. 98–Civ.–0973 (JSM), 2000 U.S. Dist. LEXIS 18263 (S.D.N.Y. Dec. 20, 2000) (termination of an employee who took FMLA leave in conjunction with paid sick leave was terminated after it was learned that, in violation of the employer's policy, the employee took more leave than necessary for illness in order to attend to personal and family matters).

e. Pretext

Once a defendant has proffered a legitimate non-retaliatory reason for the adverse employment action, a plaintiff must present evidence from which a jury could determine that the adverse employment action was in retaliation for exercising rights under the FMLA and not for the legitimate reason proffered by the defendant. *Bila v. RadioShack Corp.*, No. 03–10177–BC, 2004 U.S. Dist. LEXIS 24649, at *33 (E.D. Mich. Nov. 23, 2004).

To satisfy this burden, a plaintiff may either discredit the proffered reason with direct or circumstantial evidence or by adducing direct or circumstantial evidence that discrimination was more likely than not a motivating cause of the adverse employment action. *See Doebele v. Sprint/United Management Co.*, 342 F.3d 1117 (10th Cir. 2003); *Wilson v. Lemington Home For the Aged*, 159 F. Supp. 2d 186, 196 (W.D. Pa. 2001); *Ogborn v. United Food and Commercial Workers, Local No. 881 et al.*, No. 98 C 4623, 2000 U.S. Dist. LEXIS 14092, at *36 (N.D. Ill. Sept. 25, 2000), *aff'd*, 305 F.3d 763 (7th Cir. 2002). With respect to the former, some courts require that an employee show: (a) that the proffered reason had no basis in fact, (b) that the proffered reason did not actually motivate the decision, or (c) that the reason was an insufficient reason to motivate the adverse action. *Ogborn*, 2000 U.S. Dist. LEXIS 14092, at *36.

The evidence which a plaintiff can present in an attempt to establish that a defendant's stated reasons are pretextual may take a variety of forms, and a plaintiff may not be required to pursue any particular means of demonstrating that the employer's stated reasons are pretextual. *See Doebele v. Sprint/United Management Co.*, 342 F.3d 1117 (10th Cir. 2003) (direct and circumstantial evidence permitted to establish pretext).

Temporal proximity of the adverse action and the FMLA activity has been held to establish pretext. For example, in *Darboe v. Staples, Inc., et. al.*, 243 F. Supp. 2d 5, 15–16 (S.D.N.Y. 2003), to defeat summary judgment, the court found that the temporal proximity between the use of FMLA leave and the employee's demotion shortly after returning to work was alone sufficient to establish pretext. *See also Smith v. Memorial Hosp. Corp., et al.*, 302 F.3d 827, 832 (8th Cir. 2002) (although it is possible that strong evidence of a *prima face* case can establish pretext, employers explanation for termination for performance deficiencies required additional evidence beyond mere temporal proximity, which plaintiff failed to provide).

Where, however, it is established that the employee violated company policy (the reason given by the employer for the employee's termination), timing alone will not establish pretext. For example, in *Jarjoura v. Ericsson, Inc.*, 266 F. Supp. 2d 519, 528 (N.D. Tex. 2003), *aff'd*, 2003 U.S. App. LEXIS 25515 (5th Cir. 2003), the district court found that plaintiff failed to establish that the employer's explanation that it terminated the employee for violation of his company credit card and company cell phone was pretextual. The court found that that Jarjoura violated company policy by using his company credit card for non-business related purchases on several occasions. 266 F. Supp. at 530. The court rejected the plaintiff's argument that the timing of his termination shortly after he was placed on FMLA leave established pretext. According to the court, in light of the clear evidence that Jarjoura violated Ericsson's company credit card policy, the mere fact that this violation was discovered shortly after he was placed on FMLA leave, without more, does not, standing alone, establish pretext sufficient to defeat summary judgment for the employer. 266 F. Supp. 2d at 531. According to the court (266 F. Supp. 2d at 528–29):

"[A] plaintiff's *prima facie* case, combined with sufficient evidence to find that the employer's asserted justification is false, may permit the trier of fact to conclude that the employer unlawfully discriminated," and may therefore be enough to prevent summary judgment or judgment as a matter of law. This showing, however, is not always enough to prevent summary judgment in favor of the employer. By way of example, an employer would be entitled to summary judgment "if the records conclusively revealed some other, nondiscriminatory reason for the employer's decision, or if the plaintiff created only a weak issue of fact as to whether the employer's reason was untrue and there was abundant and uncontroverted independent evidence that no discrimination had occurred."

(Citations omitted).

Courts have held that an employer's proffered reason for taking an adverse employment action is pretextual if the adverse action considered, or may have considered, the use of FMLA leave. *See Doebele v. Sprint/United Management Co.*, 342 F.3d 1117 (10th Cir. 2003); *Sahadi v. Per–Se Technologies, Inc.*, 280 F. Supp. 2d 689 (E.D. Mich. 2003) (adverse action based on history of absences, some of which were covered by the FMLA, sufficient to establish pretext); *Sharpe v. MCI Telecommunications, Corp.*, 19 F. Supp. 2d 483, 490 (E.D.N.C. 1998); *Williams v. Shenango, Inc.*, 986 F. Supp. 309, 322 (W.D. Pa. 1997); *Miller v. Galen of Florida*, No. 96–248–CIV–T–17–E, 1997 U.S. Dist. LEXIS 17901 (M.D. Fla. June 19, 1997). *But see Hodgens v. General Dynamics Corp.*, 144 F.3d 151, 167 (1st Cir. 1998) (court declined to rely on reference to excessive absences after FMLA leave to establish pretext where there were other unprotected absences sufficient to justify adverse employment action).

Courts have split on the treatment of negative comments about an employee's use of FMLA leave as evidence of employer pretext for the adverse action. Some courts have cited such comments in support of a finding of pretext. *See Doebele v. Sprint/United Management Co.*, 342 F.3d 1117 (10th Cir. 2003). Other courts have discounted such comments for a variety of reasons. *See Hodgens v. General Dynamics Corp.*, 144 F.3d 151, 167 (1st Cir. 1998) (notwithstanding negative comments about employee's use of FMLA leave in supervisor's notes, court held unprotected absence sufficient to justify adverse employment action); *Burke v. Health Plus of Michigan, Inc.*, No. 01–10335–BC, 2003 U.S. Dist. LEXIS 290, at *17 (E.D. Mich. Jan. 7, 2003) (holding that taking an adverse employment action against an employee because of her medical condition is distinct from retaliation because she declared her intention to take, or actually took, unpaid FMLA leave. The former does not constitute a violation of the FMLA, and the plaintiff has not shown that the latter occurred here. Supervisor had stated that if plaintiff went on leave, he would be stuck doing her job); *Bond v. Sterling, Inc.*, 77 F. Supp. 2d 300 (N.D.N.Y. 1999) (statement that "we are not a family oriented company, we are a business" held insufficient to establish pretext where employee was terminated for failure to attend a meeting while on FMLA leave); *Rocky v. Columbia Lawnwood Reg. Med. Center*, 54 F. Supp. 2d 1159, 1171 (S.D. Fla. 1999) (supervisors statement five months prior to termination for excessive absences that if plaintiff did not stop taking time off to care for son she would be fired considered isolated and remote); *McGarity v. Mary Kay Cosmetics*, No. 3:96–CV–3413–R, 1998 U.S. Dist. LEXIS 1150 (N.D. Tex. Jan. 21, 1998) (supervisors stated disapproval of a man who would take FMLA leave for the birth of a child and expressing that co-workers would "get" the plaintiff on his return from FMLA leave, found insufficient to support inference that plaintiff's suspension was in retaliation for taking FMLA leave given plaintiff's workplace error and three-month time span between discipline and comments).

Finally, courts have found evidence of pretext where the employee's stated reasons are contradicted by the record. For example, in *English v. Baptist Healthcare System, Inc.*, No. 3:01CV–92–H, 2003 U.S. Dist. LEXIS 921, at *19 (W.D. Ky. Jan. 22, 2003), the court found pretext based on a combination of adverse supervisor comments about the employee's use of FMLA leave and contradictions in the reason for a transfer. The employer had originally argued that it transferred the employee because of a lack of work. It subsequently denied that reason and offered a different justification, the employee's inability to perform the job.

K. APPLICABLE REGULATIONS

To determine whether an employer has interfered with or discriminated against an employee within the meaning of the FMLA, it is necessary to know what implementing regulations apply. The DOL issued interim regulations to implement the FMLA on June 4, 1993, which went into effect on August 5, 1993. *See* 58 Fed. Reg. 31794. Subsequently, the DOL issued final regulations effective April 6, 1995. The majority of courts have held that the final regulations do not apply retroactively. Rather, where the issues in a case arose during the time the interim regulations were in effect, those regulations apply, even if the case is not heard until after the effective date of the final DOL regulations. *See Victorelli v.*

Shadyside Hospital, 128 F.3d 184, 186 (3d Cir. 1997); *Gay v. Gilman Paper Co.*, 125 F.3d 1432, 1434 & n.4 (11th Cir. 1997); *Bauer v. Varity Dayton-Walter Corp.*, 118 F.3d 1109, 1112 & n.1 (6th Cir. 1997); *Manuel v. Westlake Polymers, Corp.*, 66 F.3d 758, 761 & n.2 (5th Cir. 1995); *Robinson v. Overnite Transp., Co.*, 110 F.3d 60 (table), 1997 U.S. App. LEXIS 6574, at n.4 (4th Cir. April 9, 1997).

In the absence of its own implementing regulations and requirement that it follow, essentially, the regulations implementing Title I, the PEOAA courts interpreting the PEOAA are also likely to follow the Title I case law rejecting retroactive application of the final DOL FMLA regulations where a case arose during a time when the interim regulations were in effect.

For purposes of Title II, the MSPB has also applied the OPM interim regulations in effect at the time of the alleged FMLA violations, not the subsequently issued final OPM regulations implementing Title II. *See Burge v. Dept. of Air Force*, 82 MSPR 75, n. 3 (1999), *pet. denied*, 86 MSPR 688 (2000) ("Although the Office of Personnel Management (OPM) has issued final FMLA regulations effective January 6, 1997, the applicable regulations here are the interim regulations issued by OPM on July 23, 1993, that were in effect at the time of the agency's October 1, 1996, action."); *Gross v. Dept. of Justice*, 77 MSPR 83, 86 n. 2 (1997) (same); *Ellshoff v. Dept. of Interior*, 76 MSPR 54 n. 3 (1997), *rev'd on other grounds, remanded*, 78 MSPR 615 (1998) (*citing Manuel v. Westlake Polymers Corp.*, 66 F.3d 758, 761 n. 2, 762-63 (5th Cir. 1995)); *Crutchfield v. Dept. of Navy*, 73 MSPR 444, n. 3 (1997) (*citing Manuel v. Westlake Polymers Corp.*, 66 F.3d 758, 761 n. 2, 762-63 (5th Cir. 1995)).

Finally, the final regulations implementing the FMLA for purposes of the CAA were approved on April 15, 1996. Presumably, the CAA will follow suit and not apply the final implementing regulations retroactively.

L. NOMINAL DAMAGES

The courts are split on the availability of nominal damages for violation of the FMLA. Several circuits have held that nominal damages are not available. *See Montgomery v. State of Maryland et al.*, 266 F.3d 334, 341 (4th Cir. 2001), *vacated and remanded on other grounds*, 535 U.S. 1075 (2002) (because the plaintiff only sought damages for emotional distress, which are not recoverable, the court dismissed the plaintiff's complaint against two individual supervisors for failure to state a claim for which relief was available); *Spurlock v. Postmaster General*, 19 Fed. Appx. 338 (6th Cir. 2001) (absent actual damages, an employee does not have a viable FMLA claim); *Walker v. UPS, Inc.*, 240 F.3d 1268, 1277 (10th Cir. 2001) (absent actual damages, the plaintiff had no grounds for obtaining equitable relief); *Carlsen v. Green Thumb, Inc.*, No. 01-2076 (JRT/RLE), 2004 U.S. Dist. LEXIS 12497, at *12-13 (D. Minn. May 21, 2004).

Other courts have, however, allowed nominal damages. *See McDonnell v. Miller Oil Co.*, 134 F.3d 638, 640 (4th Cir. 1998); *Wilson v. Dallas Independent School District*, No. CA3:97-CV-0281-BC, 1998 U.S. Dist. LEXIS 1415, at *8 (N.D. Tex. Jan. 30, 1998) (attorney fees and prejudgment interest available even where nominal damages awarded).

M. MITIGATION

Neither the Statute nor the implementing regulations require an aggrieved employee to mitigate his or her damages in order to be entitled to receive a full award of back pay for an employer's violation of the FMLA. Courts, however, have required mitigation of damages in order for an aggrieved employee to receive a full back pay award. *See Taylor v. Invacare Corp.*, 64 Fed. Appx. 516 (6th Cir. 2003); *Nichols v. Ashland Hosp. Corp.*, 251 F.3d 496 (4th Cir. 2001); *Miller v. AT&T Corp.*, 250 F.3d 820 (4th Cir. 2001); *Thorson v. Gemini, Inc. et al.*, 205 F.3d 370, 385 (8th Cir. 2000), *cert. denied*, 531 U.S. 871 (2000); *Sherman v. Al/FOCS, Inc.*, 113 F. Supp. 2d 65 (D. Mass. 2000).

The burden of showing lack of mitigation is on the defendant. *Taylor v. Invacare Corp.*, 64 Fed. Appx. 516 (6th Cir. 2003); *Nichols v. Ashland Hosp. Corp.*, 251 F.3d 496 (4th Cir. 2001); *Snow v. Health South Corp.*, No. IP00-0151 C-M/S, 2001 U.S. DST. LEXIS 5534 (S.D. Ind. March 21, 2001). The defendant must show that substantially equivalent positions were available and the plaintiff failed to use reasonable diligence in seeking them out. *Id.*; *see Snow v. Health South Corp.*, No. IP00-0151 C-M/S, 2001 U.S. Dist LEXIS 5534 (S.D. Ind. March 21, 2001).

In *Taylor v. Invacare Corp.*, 64 Fed. Appx. 516 (6th Cir. 2003), the court held that the defendant failed to establish that the employee had not mitigated his damages. General evidence that unemployment was low and jobs plentiful was found insufficient. Rather, the defendant was required to establish that jobs were plentiful for men of Taylor's age, skill and experience. The court also noted that the defendant did not offer any evidence that Taylor should have started his own business in order to mitigate damages. According to the court, self–employment, if undertaken in good faith, may be a reasonable alternative to seeking other comparable employment for purposes of mitigation. *Id.* at n. 9 *citing Hawkins v. 1115 Legal Service Care*, 163 F.3d 684, 696 (1998) (collection cases).

In *Thorson v. Gemini, Inc.* 205 F.3d 370, 385 (8th Cir. 2000), *cert. denied*, 531 U.S. 871 (2000), the plaintiff challenged the Magistrate's reduction of her back pay award for failure to mitigate. The court reduced the award not only by the amounts she actually earned or, in the case of unemployment compensation, collected during the back pay period, but also because of decisions she twice made to quit employment voluntarily regarding the working conditions of those positions was not unreasonable. According to the court, "Given Thorson's post–Gemini work history (and her surprising inability to find entry–level work even in the booming economy until her unemployment insurance expired, twice), it could be argued that the Magistrate Judge was generous in not reducing the back pay award further for Thorson's failure to mitigate." *Id.*

The court in *Sherman v. Al/FOCS, Inc.*, 113 F. Supp. 2d 65 (D. Mass. 2000), addressed the duty to accept a non–equivalent position and mitigation. There, the employee was unlawfully terminated from work shortly after returning from FMLA leave. The employer offered the former employee positions that were not substantially equivalent to the position the employee had held. The employer argued that the employee's refusal to accept these positions demonstrated a failure to mitigate damages. The district court disagreed, and awarded damages including full back pay, liquidated damages, interest and attorney fees.

An employee is only required to make a good faith effort in order to meet the requirement to mitigate damages. The employee need not actually be successful in securing other employment in order to be entitled to a full award of back pay. *See Miller v. AT&T Corp.* 250 F.3d 820 (4th Cir. 2001) (a former employee awarded full back pay after finding that she diligently sought alternative employment for five months before deciding to enroll in college; award included time she spent in college); *Snow v. Health South Corp.*, No. IP00–0151 C–M/S, 2001 U.S. Dist LEXIS 5534 (S.D. Ind. March 21, 2001) (the employer failed to establish that the plaintiff did not exercise reasonable diligence in seeking alternative employment in light of her circumstances and the job market where the employee developed a career in real estate rather than find a position in her former health care administration field).

N. AFTER ACQUIRED EVIDENCE

The Sixth Circuit in *Edgar v. JAC Products, Inc.*, 443 F.3d 502, 511 (6th Cir. 2006), recently addressed whether evidence of an employee's medical condition, acquired by the employer after the adverse employment decision is taken, can be used by the employer to justify the action. The district court refused to consider the employer's post-judgment medical evidence that the employee was unable to return to work before the expiration of their 12-week FMLA leave entitlement. The district court rejected the evidence, reasoning that because the information was not available at the time the employer decided to terminate Edgar, it would not be considered at trial. Although it affirmed the decision of the district court, the Sixth Circuit addressed the consideration of after-acquired evidence in FMLA cases concluding that the consideration of after-acquired evidence depends on the FMLA theory of liability. After-acquired evidence may be considered in interference/entitlement cases. In discrimination/retaliation cases, the consideration is more limited. Where the medical information known to the employer prior to the adverse action decision shows that the employee could not return within 12 weeks, an employer may rely on after-acquired evidence to rebut the employee's *prima facie* case of discrimination. Where the employer learns of the employee's inability to return to work only after the adverse action, an employer in a discrimination/retaliation cannot rely on after-acquired evidence as a defense to liability, but may use it to limit damages.

The MSPB recently held that it would no longer accept or consider medical evidence at hearing that the employee failed to provide in support of his or her request for FMLA leave. The Board explained that its position on the issue changed because the FMLA "contains its own mechanism for resolving a dispute regarding the sufficiency of medical evidence submitted in support a leave request." *Dias v. VA*, 102 MSPR 53 (2006), *appeal dismissed*, 2006 U.S. App. LEXIS 28961 (Fed. Cir. 2006), *vacated, reinstated*, 2006 U.S. App. LEXIS 32257 (Fed. Cir. 2006), *aff'd*, 2007 U.S. App. LEXIS 11530 (Fed. Cir. 2007).

CHAPTER 16
INTERACTION OF THE FMLA WITH OTHER FEDERAL LAWS, EMPLOYER PRACTICES, AND COLLECTIVE BARGAINING AGREEMENTS

I. OVERVIEW

The leave benefits and protections provided by the FMLA must be considered in the broader context of existing federal employment laws, agency practices, and the terms of applicable collective bargaining agreements. Existing federal employment laws, such as the Pregnancy Discrimination Act, the Rehabilitation Act, and the Americans with Disabilities Act, directly address the availability of leave benefits to employees in certain circumstances. It is, therefore, important to understand how the FMLA interacts with these existing federal employment laws regarding an employee's entitlement to leave. Similarly, it is it is important to understand how employer practices and the terms of applicable collective bargaining agreements interact with the minimum requirements of the FMLA.

Section II of this chapter addresses the interaction of the FMLA with other federal employment laws. Agency leave practices and the terms of collective bargaining agreements on the FMLA are addressed in Section III.

II. OTHER FEDERAL LAWS

A. INTRODUCTION

The FMLA is not the only federal employment law that provides employees with entitlement to job-protected leave. Existing federal anti-discrimination and other federal laws may require an employer to provide, and entitle a federal employee to receive, leave from work for reasons other than those established by the FMLA. In some instances, these other reasons for leave may overlap with the entitlements and benefits of the FMLA. This section will address how the FMLA interacts with the other major federal laws regarding employee entitlement to leave in circumstances involving, or similar to those covered by, the FMLA.

B. GENERAL RULE

The interaction of the FMLA with other federal employment laws involving leave is addressed differently by the four federal sector variants of the FMLA. Some address the interaction in both the Statute and regulations, others only in the regulations, and still others do not address the subject at all.

1. Title I

Title I addresses the interaction of the FMLA with existing anti-discrimination laws in both the Statute and the DOL implementing regulations. Section 401(a) of Title I (29 USC 2651(a)) provides:

> Nothing in this Act or any amendment made by this Act shall be construed to modify or affect any Federal or State law prohibiting discrimination on the basis of race, religion, color, national origin, sex, age, or disability.

See Cavin v. Honda of America Mfg., Inc., 138 F. Supp. 2d 987, 993 (S.D. Ohio March 28, 2001); *O'Hare v. Mt. Vernon Bd. of Education*, 16 F. Supp. 2d 868, 895 (S.D. Ohio 1998); *Cehrs v. Northeast Ohio Alzheimer Research Center et al.*, 959 F. Supp. 441, 449, n.8 (N.D. Ohio 1997), *aff'd in part, rev'd and remanded in part on other grounds*, 155 F.3d 775 (6th Cir. 1998); *Urbano v. Continental Airlines, Inc.*, No. H-95-3508, 1996 U.S. Dist. LEXIS 20412, at *12 (S.D. Tex. Nov. 1, 1996) (addressing elements of proof for FMLA retaliation claim by applying Title VII standards), *aff'd,* 138 F.3d 204 (5th Cir. 1998); DOL WH

FMLA Advisory Opinion No. 82 (July 31, 1996); DOL WH FMLA Advisory Opinion No. 47 (Oct. 17, 1994); DOL WH FMLA Advisory Opinion No. 29 (Feb. 7, 1994); DOL WH FMLA Advisory Opinion No. 28 (Jan. 31, 1994).

The FMLA's legislative history explains that nothing in the FMLA may be read to affect or amend Title VII of the Civil Rights Act of 1964, as amended by the Pregnancy Discrimination Act. S. Rep. 103-3, 103d Cong., 1st Sess. 38 (1993). *See* 29 CFR 825.702(a). Similarly, the FMLA is not "not intended to modify or to affect the Rehabilitation Act of 1973, as amended, the regulations concerning employment which have been promulgated pursuant to that [S]tatute, or the Americans With Disabilities Act of 1990, or the regulations issued under that [A]ct." S. Rep. 103-3, 103d Cong., 1st Sess. 38 (1993); *see* 29 CFR 825.702(a). The legislative history explains that the "purpose of the FMLA is to make leave available to eligible employees and employers within its coverage, and not to omit already existing rights and protections." S. Rep. 103-3, 103d Cong., 1st Sess. 38 (1993); *see* 29 CFR 825.702(a).

The DOL implementing regulations have interpreted the above directives of the Statute and legislative history to require that an employer "provide leave under whichever statutory provision provides the greater benefits to employees." 29 CFR 825.702(a); *see Rogers v. New York University*, 250 F. Supp. 2d 310, 315 (S.D.N.Y. 2002); *Vincent v. Wells Fargo Guard Services, Inc. of Florida*, 3 F. Supp. 2d 1405, 1420 (S.D. Fla. 1998); DOL WH FMLA Advisory Opinion No. 82 (July 31, 1996); DOL WH FMLA Advisory Opinion No. 55 (March 10, 1995); DOL WH FMLA Advisory Opinion No. 29 (Feb. 7, 1994). Specifically, the comments accompanying the publication of the final DOL regulations (Preamble, 29 CFR 825.702) explain:

> Comments from U.S. Senators Dodd and Kerry (sponsors of both FMLA and ADA), in a letter to the EEOC dated November 22, 1993, make clear that congressional intent was for both Acts to be applied with whichever statutory provision provides the greater rights to employees. In keeping with the statutory intent, FMLA [Section] 401 should not be interpreted in any way as limiting or forcing an election of rights under FMLA or ADA. Similarly, comments from U.S. Representatives Williams and Ford (Committee on Education and Labor), in a letter to the EEOC dated November 19, 1993, explained that congressional intent, in the case of an employee with a serious health condition under FMLA who is also a qualified individual with a disability under ADA, was for the FMLA and ADA to be applied in a manner that assured the most generous provisions of both would apply. The statutes provide simultaneous protection and at all times an employer is required to comply with both laws. The Department concurs with this interpretation of the FMLA as it relates to the ADA and other discrimination laws. In summary, providing the "more beneficial" rights or protections does not undermine an employer's obligation to observe the requirements of both statutes. Satisfying any or all FMLA requirements, including granting an employee 12 weeks of leave and restoring the employee to the same job, does not absolve an employer of any potential ADA responsibilities to that employee (and vice versa).

Given the clear directive in Title I that the FMLA does not trump the requirements of other federal anti-discrimination laws, and that an employer is required to provide the "greater benefit" to the employee when the FMLA and another federal anti-discrimination laws apply, employers must exercise great care to determine what federal laws apply to each request, and which laws provide the "greater benefit." Unfortunately, but for a few examples, neither the Statute nor the implementing regulations fully explain the parameters of the "greater benefits" theory. We will address the examples of this theory when addressing the Rehabilitation Act/ADA and workers' compensation issues.

2. Title II

Title II of the Act does not address the interaction of the FMLA with other federal employment laws. However, the OPM regulations implementing Title II do address the issue. The regulations (5 CFR 630.1210(d)) provide:

> The entitlements under [S]ections 6381 and 6387 of Title 5, United States Code, and this [S]ubpart do not modify or otherwise affect any Federal law prohibiting discrimination. If the entitlements under [S]ections 6381 through 6387 of Title 5, United States Code, and this [S]ubpart conflict with any Federal law prohibiting discrimination, an agency must comply with whichever statute provides greater entitlements to employees.

Clearly, Title II, like Title I, applies the "greater benefits" theory where the FMLA and another federal anti-discrimination law apply to the same situation. The comments accompanying the final OPM regulations provide some examples to illustrate the concept. The examples will be addressed in later sections of this chapter.

3. CAA

The CAA does not address the interaction of the FMLA with other federal anti-discrimination laws. The CAA incorporates §§ 101 through 105 and 107 of the Title I FMLA into the CAA. 2 USC 1312(a)(1), (b). Section 401(a) of Title I, 29 USC 2651(a), addresses the affect of the FMLA on other federal anti-discrimination laws. Again, that section is not incorporated into the CAA. Nor does the CAA independently have a similar provision.

The regulations implementing the FMLA for purposes of the CAA do, however, address the interaction of the FMLA with other federal employment laws. S. Res. 242, Cong. Rec. S3959, S3976 (April 23, 1996); 29 CFR 825.702. As we have seen with other subjects, the CAA FMLA regulations are nearly identical to the DOL regulations implementing Title I. The CAA FMLA regulations provide, in pertinent part, that "[n]othing in FMLA modifies or affects any applicable law prohibiting discrimination on the basis of race, religion, color, national origin, sex, age, or disability (e.g. Title VII of the Civil Rights Act of 1964, as amended by the Pregnancy Discrimination Act), as made applicable by the CAA." S. Res. 242, Cong. Rec. S3959, S3976 (April 23, 1996); 29 CFR 825.702(a). Section 201 of the CAA, 2 USC 1311, incorporates identified sections of Title VII, the Age Discrimination in Employment Act of 1967, the Rehabilitation Act of 1973, and the Americans with Disabilities Act of 1990.

The CAA FMLA regulations also require employing offices to apply the greater benefits theory. Specifically, an "employing office must therefore provide leave under whichever statutory provision provides the greater rights to employees." S. Res. 242, Cong. Rec. S3959, S3976 (April 23, 1996); 29 CFR 825.702(a).

4. PEOAA

The PEOAA does not address the interaction of the FMLA with other federal anti-discrimination laws. The PEOAA incorporates §§ 101 through 105 and 107 of the Tile I FMLA into the PEOAA. 3 USC 412(a)(1), (b). Section 401(a) of Title I, 29 USC 2651(a), addresses the affect of the FMLA on other federal anti-discrimination laws. Again, that section is not incorporated into the PEOAA, nor does the PEOAA independently have a similar provision.

Regulations implementing the FMLA for purposes of the PEOAA have not been issued. As such, the PEOAA does not address the interaction of the FMLA with other federal anti-discrimination laws. In that case, the argument could be made that the "greater benefit" theory does not apply to employees covered by the PEOAA. The requirements of the FMLA and other applicable federal anti-discrimination law would, therefore, apply separately without consideration of which law provides the greater benefit to the employee.

Although not formally incorporated into the PEOAA, the implementing regulations of the other federal sector variants of the FMLA will likely be applied to the PEOAA. The PEOAA provides that, in the event that implementing regulations have not been issued, administrative agencies or courts adjudicating PEOAA FMLA claims (the MSPB) must apply, to the extent necessary and appropriate, the most relevant substantive executive agency regulation promulgated to implement the statutory provision at issue in the proceeding. *See* 3 USC 455; 28 USC 3903. Read together, these provisions could be interpreted to permit the MSPB or a court to apply the implementing regulations of Titles I or II, or the CAA regarding the interaction of the FMLA with other laws into the PEOAA.

A contrary interpretation would be that, because both statutes condition the ability of a court or administrative agency to reference other implementing regulations "to implement the statutory provision at issue," the PEOAA could not rely on regulations addressing the interaction of the FMLA with other federal anti-discriminations laws. Again, the PEOAA does not incorporate § 401(a) of Title I, which addresses the interaction of the FMLA with other federal employment laws. As such, the implementing regulations of Title I, Title II, and the PEOAA arguably would not apply.

It is likely that courts and administrative agencies interpreting the FMLA for purposes of the PEOAA will apply the substance of the implementing regulations of Title I, Title II, or the CAA regarding the interaction of the FMLA with other federal anti-discrimination laws.

C. REHABILITATION ACT/ADA

The coordination of FMLA leave with leave required as a reasonable accommodation pursuant to the Rehabilitation Act/ADA is vexing. Separately, both laws are very difficult to properly administer. Where these laws overlap, the potential for misunderstanding and misapplication resulting in violations of one or both laws dramatically increases.

A federal sector employee who suffers from a serious illness may be eligible for leave both under the FMLA and under the Rehabilitation Act/ADA. The FMLA entitles eligible employees to take up to 12 weeks of job-protected FMLA leave a year when their own serious health condition renders them unable to perform one or more essential functions of their job. The Rehabilitation Act/ADA requires employers to reasonably accommodate qualified disabled employees unless such accommodation would cause the employer undue hardship. Leave is a form of Rehabilitation Act/ADA reasonable accommodation.

The high potential for interaction of the FMLA with the Rehabilitation Act/ADA is reflected in the legislative history of § 401 of the Act (29 USC 2651) as well as the implementing regulations. The legislative history devotes an entire paragraph to the interaction of the FMLA with the Rehabilitation Act and the ADA. See S. Rep. 103-3, 103d Congress, 1st Sess. 38 (1993). The FMLA was "not intended to modify or to affect" the requirements of the Rehabilitation Act or the ADA. Rather, the "leave provisions of the Family and Medical Leave Act are wholly distinct from the reasonable accommodation obligations of employers covered under the American s with Disabilities Act...or the Federal government itself." S. Rep. 103-3, 103d Congress, 1st Sess. 38 (1993); see Hatchett v. Philander Smith College et al., 251 F.3d 670, 675, n. 4 (8th Cir. 2001); Ellis v. Mohenis Services, Inc., et al., No. 96-6307, 1998 U.S. Dist. LEXIS 13219, at *15 (E.D. Pa. Aug. 24, 1998); Vincent v. Wells Fargo Guard Services, Inc. of Florida, 3 F. Supp. 2d 1405, 1420 (S.D. Fla. 1998); DOL WH FMLA Advisory Opinion No. 97 (July 10, 1998); Cehrs v. Northeast Ohio Alzheimer Research Center et al., 959 F. Supp. 441, 449, n.8 (N.D. Ohio 1997), aff'd in part, rev'd in part, remanded, 155 F.3d 775 (6th Cir. 1998) (leave provisions of FMLA wholly distinct from reasonable accommodation obligations of ADA).

Fully, seven of nine of the examples of the interaction of the FMLA with other laws contained in the DOL implementing regulations address the interaction of the FMLA with the Rehabilitation Act/ADA. See 29 CFR 702(b)-(f). Two of the three explanatory paragraphs contained in the OPM comments accompanying the final Title I regulations address the interaction of the FMLA with the Rehabilitation Act. See Preamble, 5 CFR 630.1210 (greater leave entitlements).

To avoid liability under one or both laws, determining when an employee falls under the benefits and protections of the FMLA and the Rehabilitation Act/ADA, and what obligations provide the "greater benefit" to the employee, requires careful consideration by federal employers. What follows is a basic introduction to the Rehabilitation Act/ADA and a comparison of key requirements of those laws with the FMLA. For a more in-depth review of the requirements of the Rehabilitation Act and ADA, the reader is referred to Ernest C. Hadley, *A Guide to Federal Sector Disability Discrimination Law and Practice* (Dewey Publications, Inc. 2006).

1. Basics of Rehabilitation Act/ADA

The Rehabilitation Act of 1973, 29 USC 791 *et seq.*, prohibits federal agencies and other employers receiving federal funding from discriminating against "handicapped individuals" on the basis of disability. In 1992, the Rehabilitation Act (29 USC 791(g)) was amended to incorporate the standards of Title I of the Americans with Disabilities Act. As a result, the term "disabilities" has replaced the original Rehabilitation Act term "handicapped."

Section 12112(a) of the ADA (42 USC 12112(a)) generally prohibits discrimination against qualified individuals with disabilities with regard to "job application procedures, the hiring, advancement or discharge of employees, employee compensation, job training, and other terms, conditions and privileges of employment." The ADA defines an individual with a disability as one who: (1) has a physical or mental impairment that substantially limits one or more of the individual's major life activities; (2) has a record of such impairment; or (3) is regarded as having such an impairment. 42 USC 12102(2); *see also* 29 USC 706(8)(B). A "qualified individual with a disability" is an individual who meets the prerequisites for the job and can perform the essential functions of the position with or without reasonable accommodation. 42 USC 12111(8). The ADA does not define the term "essential job functions." The EEOC implementing regulations define "essential functions" of a job as "the fundamental job duties of the employment position the individual with a disability holds or desires." 29 CFR 1630.2(n). Factors considered by the EEOC in determining the existence of an "essential job function" include, but are not limited to: (1) the reason the position exists is to perform that function; (2) there are a limited number of employees among whom the performance of that function can be distributed; or (3) the function is so highly specialized that an individual is hired for his or her expertise or ability to perform the particular function. 29 CFR 1630(n)(i)-(iii). The business judgment of the employer on what functions are essential is also a factor that is considered, although it is not dispositive of the issue. *See* 29 CFR 1630.2(n)(3)(I) (listing the employer's judgment as one of seven factors to be considered in determining whether a particular function is essential).

Disability-based employment discrimination under Title I of the ADA includes an employer's failure to make reasonable accommodation to the known physical or mental limitations of an otherwise qualified applicant or employee with a disability, unless the employer can show that the accommodation would impose an undue hardship on the operation of its business. 42 USC 12112(b)((5). *See* DOL WH FMLA Advisory Opinion No. 97 (July 10, 1998); DOL WH FMLA Advisory Opinion No. 55 (March 10, 1995). Reasonable accommodation may include "job restructuring, part-time employment or modified work schedules." 42 USC 12111(9)(B). The EEOC implementing regulations suggest that "permitting the use of accrued paid leave or providing additional unpaid leave are acceptable forms of reasonable accommodation, at least where there is no accommodation that would allow the employee to do the job currently." 29 CFR 1630.2(o).

Note that leave as an ADA reasonable accommodation is disfavored. The EEOC implementing regulations suggest that an employer must first attempt to accommodate the otherwise qualified employee with a disability in his or her current position. Only where accommodation in the employee's current job is unsuccessful do the EEOC regulations suggest that leave is an acceptable form of accommodation. Under the FMLA, leave is the primary benefit afforded to employees. The FMLA does not require, indeed prohibits, an employer from making accommodations that would negate an eligible employee's entitlement to FMLA leave.

Moreover, leave as a reasonable accommodation under the Rehabilitation Act/ADA is frequently denied based on the conclusion of many courts that an employee in need of leave is not a "qualified individual with a disability" entitled to reasonable accommodation. At the core of such decisions is the belief, held by a majority of courts, that regular and predictable attendance is an essential job function of most jobs. *See Waggoner v. Olin Corp.*, 169 F.3d 481, 487 (7th Cir. 1999); *Corr v. MTA Long Island Bus.*, No. 98-9417, 1999 U.S. App. LEXIS 25058, at *4 (2d Cir. Oct. 7, 1999); *Corder v. Lucent Technologies, Inc.*, 162 F.3d 924 (7th Cir. 1998); *Nesser v. Trans World Airlines, Inc.*, 160 F.3d 442 (8th Cir. 1998); *Moore v. Payless Shoe Source, Inc.*, 139 F.3d 1210, 1213 (8th Cir. 1998); *Hypes on Behalf of Hypes v. First Commerce Corp.*, 134 F.3d 721 (5th Cir. 1998); *Halperin v. Abacus Tech. Corp.*, 128 F.3d 191, 198 (4th Cir. 1997); *Rogers v. Int'l. Marine Terminals, Inc.*, 87 F.3d 755, 759 (5th Cir. 1996); *Carr v. Reno*, 23 F.3d 525, 530 (D.C. Cir. 1994); *Tyndall v. Nat'l. Educ. Centers*, 31 F.3d 209, 213 (4th Cir. 1994); *Jackson v. Veterans Admin.*, 22 F.3d 277, 278 (11th Cir. 1994). The conundrum was explained as follows:

> However, proving that one is qualified for a job while seeking leave as a reasonable accommodation poses a fundamental difficulty. The facts that demonstrate the inability to attend work on a standard schedule and the need for time off from work are the same facts courts rely on to conclude that the individual is unqualified for the position and entitled to no accommodation under the ADA. Courts reason that because the ADA protects only employees who can work despite their disability, an employee who seeks leave for work as a form of reasonable accommodation because he cannot work regularly may be unable to meet his initial burden of showing that he is qualified for the job.

James A. Passamano, *Article: Employee Leave Under the Americans with Disabilities Act and the Family and Medical Leave Act*, 38 S. Tex. L. Rev. 861, 870 (July 1997); *see also* Megan G. Rosenberger, *Article: Absenteeism and the ADA: The Limits and the Loopholes*, 50 Cath. U. L. Rev. 957 (Summer 2001); Stacy A. Hickox, *Article: Absenteeism Under the Family and Medical Leave Act and the Americans With Disabilities Act*, 50 DePaul L. Rev. 183 (Fall 2000).

Several courts have found that FMLA leave can be used to demonstrate that an employee cannot perform the essential functions of the job because he or she is unable to fulfill the position's attendance requirements. *See Praigrod v. St. Mary's Med. Center*, No. 3:05-cv-JDT-WGH, 2007 U.S. Dist. LEXIS 4506, at *820 (S.D. Ind. Jan. 19, 2007); *Payne v. Fairfax County*, No. 1:05cv1446, 2006 U.S. Dist. LEXIS 79725, at *24-26 (E.D. Va. Nov. 1, 2006).

Notwithstanding the presumption held by a majority of courts of regular and predictable attendance as an essential job function, reasonable accommodation in the form of temporary leave has been held to be a requirement of the Rehabilitation Act/ADA. *See Rascon v. US West Communications, Inc.*, 143 F.3d 1324, 1334 (10th Cir. 1998) (granting request for 30-days leave to employee who previously had taken 90 days of leave held a reasonable accommodation); *Myers v. Hose*, 50 F.3d 278, 284 (4th Cir. 1995); *Powers v. Polygram Holdings, Inc.*, 40 F. Supp. 2d 195, 200-01 (S.D.N.Y. 1999); *Fritz v. Mascotech Auto. Sys. Group*, 914 F. Supp. 1481, 1491 (E.D. Mich. 1996); *Carlson v. Inacom Corp.*, 885 F. Supp. 1314 (D. Neb. 1995); *Soodman v. Wildman, Harrold, Allen & Dixon*, No. 95-C-3834, 1997 U.S. Dist. LEXIS 1495, at *22 (N.D. Ill. Feb. 7, 1997).

Employers are not, however, required to provide an employee with an indefinite leave of absence as a Rehabilitation Act/ADA reasonable accommodation. *See Gantt v. Wilson Sporting Goods Co.*, 143 F.3d 1042, 1047 (6th Cir. 1998); *Monette v. Electronic Data Sys. Corp.*, 90 F.3d 1173 (6th Cir. 1996); *Hudson v. MCI Telecoms. Corp.*, 87 F.3d 1167 (10th Cir. 1996); *Rogers v. Int. Marine Terminals*, 87 F.3d 755 (5th Cir. 1996); *Myers v. Hose*, 50 F.3d 278, 283 (4th Cir. 1995); *Mitchell v. Washington School Dis*trict, 992 F. Supp. 395 (S.D.N.Y. 1998), *aff'd,* 190 F.3d 1 (2d Cir. 1999). Depending on the circumstances, leave up to a year pursuant to the employer's short-term disability policy could be a required reasonable accommodation protected by the ADA. *See Nunes v. Wal-Mart Stores, Inc.*, 164 F.3d 1243, 1245-46 (9th Cir. 1999); *Gannt v. Wilson Sporting Goods Co.*, 143 F.3d 1042, 1047 (6th Cir. 1998).

Leave as a form of reasonable accommodation, while required by the Rehabilitation Act/ADA, has had limited success in the courts. Still, federal employers need to analyze every potential FMLA/Rehabilitation Act/ADA request for leave as reasonable accommodation based on the facts and circumstances involved.

2. Key Requirements

a. Covered Employers

The FMLA and Rehabilitation Act/ADA apply to all federal sector employers. The application, however, is not uniform. The anti-discrimination provisions of the Rehabilitation Act/ADA directly apply to covered employees of any executive agency and the United States Postal Service. 29 USC 794(a). The Rehabilitation Act/ADA applies to employees of Congress through the CAA, 2 USC 1311(a)(3), and employees of the Executive Office of the President through the PEOAA, 3 USC 411(a)(3).

Unlike the uniformly applied anti-discrimination provisions of the Rehabilitation Act/ADA, four different variants of the FMLA apply to different segments of the federal workforce. Some, like the FMLA through the CAA and the PEOAA, apply only to certain covered employees of identified employing offices. Others, like the FMLA as applied by Titles I and II of the Act, do not define themselves in terms of covered employing offices. Rather, they define coverage more in terms of what employees of the government of the United States are included within the jurisdiction of each Title. There are substantial similarities and differences in critical terms and requirements of the four federal sector variants of the FMLA. For purposes of determining whether the FMLA and/or the Rehabilitation Act/ADA apply to any given situation and, if so, which provides the "greater benefits," federal agencies must make sure that they compare the uniform requirements of the Rehabilitation Act/ADA with the applicable federal sector variant of the FMLA.

b. Eligibility for Leave

The qualifications for the benefits and protections offered by the FMLA and Rehabilitation Act/ADA are different. Under the Rehabilitation Act/ADA, an employee need only meet the definition of a "qualified individual with a disability" to gain the protections of the Act. A "qualified individual with a disability" means an individual with a disability who, with or without reasonable accommodation, can perform the essential functions of the employment position that such individual holds or desires. 42 USC 12111(8). For the Rehabilitation Act/ADA, qualification for the benefits and protections of the Act is not based on tenure with the employer. Rather, a disabled employee need only demonstrate that he or she is able to perform all essential job functions before he or she is covered and eligible for leave as a reasonable accommodation.

Qualification for leave under the FMLA, in contrast, is tenure-based. As discussed more fully in Chapter 5, "Employee Eligibility for Leave," employee eligibility for FMLA leave differs under the four federal sector variants of the FMLA. The criteria used under all of the federal sector variants, however, include a minimum one-year period of employment with the agency or government of the United States. In addition to the one-year minimum period of employment, other variants of the FMLA require that the employee have worked a minimum of 1,250 hours in the 12-month period preceding commencement of the leave. Finally, one federal sector variant of the FMLA (Tile I) also adds a requirement that a minimum number of employees be employed at the worksite of the employee requesting leave. An employee who meets the applicable eligibility requirements may be, all things being equal, entitled to take FMLA leave for a covered condition. Unlike the Rehabilitation Act/ADA, the ability of the employee to perform the essential functions of the position at the time of leave commencement is not required. On the contrary, to qualify for FMLA leave, an employee must be able to establish that he or she cannot perform one or more essential job functions due to a covered serious health condition.

c. Basic Entitlement

At the most basic level, all of the federal sector variants of the FMLA provide eligible employees with up to 12 weeks of job-protected leave each 12-month leave year for certain covered conditions. The Act also requires employers to maintain health benefits during an employee's absence on FMLA leave. On the conclusion of the employee's leave, the Act requires the employer to return the employee to the same or an equivalent position. Many of these issues are addressed separately in subsequent subsections of this chapter. Unlike the ADA, the FMLA does not require an employer to reasonably accommodate an employee. *Alifano v. Merck & Co., Inc. et al.*, 175 F. Supp. 2d 792, 795 (E.D. Pa. Dec. 7, 2001).

In contrast, the Rehabilitation Act/ADA does not place a defined limit on the amount of leave that a federal employer may be required to provide to a qualified individual with a disability as a reasonable accommodation. An employer must provide leave to an otherwise qualified individual with a disability as a reasonable accommodation up to the point where it constitutes an undue hardship to the employer. *See* 29 CFR 825.702(b); *see also Rogers v. New York University*, 250 F. Supp. 2d 310, 315 (S.D.N.Y. 2002). Undue hardship, particularly in the federal sector, will frequently require an agency to accommodate an employee's leave in excess of the 12 weeks mandated by the FMLA. Notwithstanding the absence of a statutory or regulatory cap on the amount of leave that may be required by the Rehabilitation Act/ADA as a reasonable accommodation, the obligation to provide leave is not limitless. If undue hardship is not reached, an employee needing large amounts of leave may be found to be unable to perform the essential functions of his or her position, negating the agencies obligation to reasonably accommodate the employee.

d. Covered Conditions

The conditions entitling a covered employee to leave under the FMLA or Rehabilitation Act/ADA differ, but may overlap. However, while they may overlap, a "serious health condition" under the FMLA and a "disability" under the Rehabilitation Act/ADA are different concepts that must be analyzed separately. 29 CFR 825.702(b); *see Berry v. T-Mobile USA, Inc.*, 490 F.3d 1211 (10th Cir. 2007); *Burnett v. LFW, Inc.*, 472 F.3d 471, 483 (7th Cir. 2006); *Hurlbert v. St. Mary's Health Care System, Inc.*, 439 F.3d 1286, 1295 (11th Cir. 2006); *Rhoads v. FDIC et al.*, 257 F.3d 373, 387, n.12 (4th Cir. 2001), *cert. denied*, 535 U.S. 933 (2002); *Stekloff v. St. John's Mercy Health Systems*, 218 F.3d 858, 861 (8th Cir. 2000) (an employee who is unable to work in one job due to serious health condition establishes incapacity whereas under ADA, the employee would have to show inability to work a broad range of jobs to establish that he or she is disabled in the major life activity of working); *Carlson v. Rent-A-Center, Inc.*, 237 F. Supp. 2d 114, 124, n.8 (D. Me. 2002); *Ellis v. Mohenis Services, Inc. et al.*, No. 96-6307, 1998 U.S. Dist. LEXIS 13219, at *15 (E.D. Pa. Aug. 24, 1998) (an employee who has a "serious health condition" for purposes of the FMLA is not necessarily "disabled" under the ADA); *Vincent v. Wells Fargo Guard Services, Inc. of Florida*, 3 F. Supp. 2d 1405, 1420 (S.D. Fla. 1998); *Odessey v. Comcast Cablevision of Maryland, L.P.*, No. S 96-3468, 1998 U.S. Dist. LEXIS 21946, at *2 (D. Md. April 17, 1998) (although the plaintiff was found to have a FMLA "serious health condition," it did not rise to the level of a disability within the coverage of ADA); *George v. Associated Stationers et al.*, 932 F. Supp. 1012, 1016 (N.D. Ohio 1996); DOL WH FMLA Advisory Opinion No. 97 (July 10, 1998) (FMLA leave provisions wholly distinct from ADA reasonable accommodation requirements); DOL WH FMLA Advisory Opinion No. 55 (March 10, 1995) (same); DOL WH FMLA Advisory Opinion No. 47 (Oct. 17, 1994) (FMLA, unlike ADA, does not require an employer to reasonably accommodate an employee returning from FMLA leave who is unable to perform all essential job functions).

Because differences between an FMLA "serious health condition" and an ADA "disability," an employer's suggestion that an employee apply for FMLA leave due to a known serious health condition is not evidence that the employer "regarded" the employee as being disabled within the meaning of the ADA. *See Berry v. T-Mobile USA, Inc.*, 490 F.3d 1211 (10th Cir. 2007).

For purposes of reasonable accommodation, the Rehabilitation Act/ADA defines a "disability" as "a physical or mental impairment that substantially limits one or more of an individual's major life activities." 42 USC 1202(2). Whether an individual is substantially limited in a major life activity is determined with reference to (A) the nature and severity of the impairment; (B) the duration or expected duration of the impairment, and (C) the actual or expected permanent or long-term impact of the impairment. 29 CFR 1630.2(j).

Specifically excluded from the definition of a Rehabilitation Act/ADA "disability" (29 USC 706(8)) are:

- Individuals who are currently engaging in the illegal use of drugs, when a covered entity acts on the basis of such use;

- Sex-related behaviors, including homosexuality, bisexuality, transvestism, transexualism, pedophilia, exhibitionism, voyeurism, gender identity disorders that are not the result of physical impairments, and other sexual behavior disorders;

- Compulsive gambling;

- Kleptomania;

- Pyromania.

Moreover, the regulations generally exclude pregnancy from the definition of disability. 29 CFR 1630.2(h); *see also Brown v. Postmaster General*, 01842361 (1986). However, complications caused by pregnancy, childbirth, or related medical conditions may render the condition a "disability" within the meaning of the Rehabilitation Act/ADA. *See* 29 CFR 1604.10(b).

The determination of whether an impairment rises to the level of a "substantial limitation of a major life activity" takes into consideration the duration of the impairment. The EEOC has issued interpretive guidance that provides, in relevant part, "temporary, non-chronic impairments of short duration, with little or no long-term impact or permanent impact, are usually not disabilities." 29 CFR App. 1630 (2002) (*Interpretive Guidance on Title I of the Americans with Disabilities Act); see also Navarro v. Pfizer Corp.*, 261 F.3d 90, 96 (1st Cir. 2001). On the other hand, an impairment need not be permanent or incurable in order to be considered a substantial limitation on a major life activity within the meaning of the Rehabilitation Act/ADA.

The exclusion of less serious, short-term conditions from consideration as a substantial limitation of a major life activity within the meaning of the Rehabilitation Act/ADA is contained in the EEOC's Compliance Manual. Section 902 of the Compliance Manual provides an extensive definition of the term "disability." Section 902.4(d) of the Compliance Manual addresses the duration requirement. In relevant part, that section provides:

> Generally, conditions that last for only a few days or weeks and have no permanent or long-term effects on an individual's health are not substantially limiting impairments. Examples of such transitory conditions are common colds, influenza, and most broken bones and sprains. The mere fact that an individual may have required absolute bed rest or hospitalization for such a condition does not alter the transitory nature of the condition. Even the necessity of surgery, without more, is not sufficient to raise a short-term condition to the level of a disability.

Moreover, recent decisions of the Supreme Court have significantly narrowed the scope of "disability" for purposes of the Rehabilitation Act/ADA. In *Sutton v. United Air Lines, Inc.*, 527 U.S. 471, 482 (1999), the Court held that the effects of mitigating measures (e.g. glasses for those with limited vision) must be factored into the determination whether an employee was disabled within the meaning of the ADA. In *Toyota Motor Manufacturing Kentucky, Inc.*, 122 S. Ct. 681, 691 (2002), the Court ruled that the test for determining whether a physical or mental impairment substantially limits one or more major life activities was measured in terms of the ability to perform tasks central to most people's lives, not the ability to perform the tasks of a particular job. For example, if carpal tunnel syndrome restricts an individual's ability to perform repetitive assembly line work but does not restrict the individual's ability to perform everyday functions like driving, dressing, and shopping, then it does not qualify as a protected disability under the ADA. *Id.* at 692.

As discussed more fully in Chapter 7, "Covered Conditions," the FMLA provides that an eligible employee has the right to 12 weeks of job-protected leave each leave year where the employee, or a covered family member, has a serious health condition. In the case of the employee's own serious health condition, the condition must render the employee unable to perform any one or more of the essential functions of the employee's position. When the employee needs leave to care for a covered family member with a serious health condition, the condition must incapacitate the covered family member from working, or from performing other regular daily activities.

A "serious health condition" is defined as:

- *Inpatient care*: any period of incapacity or any subsequent treatment in connection with such inpatient care.

- +*three days incapacity and health care provider treatment(s)*: any period of incapacity of more than three consecutive calendar days, and any subsequent treatment or period of incapacity relating to the same condition, that also involves: (1) treatment two or more times by a health care provider; or (2) treatment by a health care provider on one occasion followed by a regimen of continuing treatment under the supervision of a health care provider.

- *Pregnancy or prenatal care*: any period of pregnancy or for prenatal care.

- *Chronic serious health conditions*: any period of incapacity or treatment for such incapacity due to a chronic serious health condition. A "chronic serious health condition" is one that; (1) requires periodic visits for treatment by a health care provider; (2) continues over an extended period of time; and (3) may cause episodic rather than a continuing period of incapacity. Examples include asthma, diabetes, and epilepsy.

- *Permanent/long-term conditions*: any period of incapacity that is permanent or long term for which treatment may not be effective.

- *Multiple health care provider treatments*: any absence to receive multiple treatments by a health care provider for: (1) restorative surgery after an accident or other injury; or (2) for a condition that would likely result in an absence of more than three consecutive calendar days if left untreated. Examples include kidney dialysis, chemotherapy, and physical therapy for severe arthritis.

While both the FMLA and the Rehabilitation Act/ADA cover certain health conditions, there are a number of differences in the types of conditions covered by each Act. First, the ADA specifically excludes a number of health conditions that are specifically included as covered conditions within the meaning of the FMLA. For example, absent complications, pregnancy is not considered to be a disability. Any period of incapacity due to pregnancy is, however, a covered condition entitling an eligible employee to FMLA leave.

Similarly, the Rehabilitation Act/ADA durational requirement will exclude many health conditions from consideration as a disability. The FMLA, on the other hand, specifically includes many health conditions of very short duration. For example, a condition that necessitates an employee to spend an overnight stay in a hospital is considered to be a serious health condition within the meaning of the FMLA. Absent permanent or long term effects, a condition that may cause an overnight stay in a hospital is cited as an example of the type of short-term impairment that does not constitute a substantial limitation of a major life activity and, therefore, a disability. Most of the FMLA definitions of a covered "serious health condition" involve, at the low end, very short periods of incapacity to qualify for FMLA coverage (e.g. "any period of incapacity").

The Rehabilitation Act/ADA definition of disability also does not contain many of the limitations imposed by the FMLA for a "serious health condition." For example, except for inpatient care, all of the FMLA "serious health care" definitions require "continuing treatment by a health care provider." The ADA has no such requirement. An employee can meet the definition of a "qualified individual with a disability" even though he or she is not under the continuing treatment of a health care provider. The FMLA also has very specific definitions for who is considered to be a health care provider for purposes of FMLA leave. Again, this issue is not addressed by the ADA.

In terms of the seriousness of a health condition for coverage as a "serious health condition" and/or "disability," the FMLA and the Rehabilitation Act/ADA share the same continuum. The FMLA almost exclusively occupies the lower end of the spectrum populated by very short-term illnesses. The extreme lower end of the spectrum, involving very minor illnesses is covered by sick leave only. The Rehabilitation Act/ADA covers more serious health conditions that involve a higher degree of permanency and duration such that they constitute a substantial limitation of a major life activity. The FMLA also covers this part of the spectrum along with the Rehabilitation Act/ADA. The FMLA includes within the definition of a serious health condition chronic serious health conditions and long-term and permanent conditions. Depending on the facts, these serious health conditions may also constitute Rehabilitation Act/ADA covered disabilities. For that matter, there is nothing preventing an employee from spending two months in a hospital, rather than the minimum overnight stay. The point being that virtually all of the FMLA "serious health condition" definitions potentially can reach the level of permanency and duration such that they may also be considered to be a disability. Conversely, an employee who is disabled within the meaning of the Rehabilitation Act/ADA will very likely meet at least one of the FMLA-covered serious health conditions. The facts of each case will have to be closely scrutinized in order to confirm coverage under the FMLA and/or Rehabilitation Act/ADA.

In *Hurlbert v. St. Mary's Health Care System, Inc.*, 439 F. 3d. 1286, 1295 (11th Cir. 2006), the Eleventh Circuit found that the district court erred when it equated the "inability to work" under the FMLA with the ADA inquiry into whether a person is unable to perform the major life function of working. Hurlbert took FMLA leave from his paramedic job at St. Mary's, but continued to work his second job as a firefighter during leave. Applying the ADA standard, the district court found that Hurlbert was not incapacitated within the meaning of the FMLA because he was not prohibited from performing a broad range of jobs, including his fire fighting job. The Eleventh Circuit ruled that the district court erred by applying the ADA standard. Under the FMLA, whether Hurlbert was incapacitated due to a serious health condition was determined based on his current job, even if that job was the only one Hurlbert was unable to perform.

e. Covered Individuals

An eligible employee's right to FMLA leave is broader than reasonable accommodation leave under the Rehabilitation Act/ADA because FMLA leave is available for the serious health condition of both the employee and a covered family member. As set forth more fully in Chapter 6, "Covered Family Members," family members covered by the FMLA for purposes of an employee's entitlement to leave include a spouse, parent, son or daughter. The Rehabilitation Act/ADA does not provide for leave as a reasonable accommodation for a non-disabled employee to provide care for a disabled family member. *See Tyndall v. Nat. Educ. Ctrs., Inc.*, 31 F.3d 209, 214 (4th Cir. 1994); 29 CFR 1630.8. An employer's obligation to provide reasonable accommodation under the Rehabilitation Act/ADA is limited to disabled employees.

The ADA does, however, contain an anti-discrimination provision that makes it unlawful for an employer to discriminate against a qualified individual because of that individual's relationship or association with an individual known to have a disability. *See* 42 USC 12112(b)(4). The relationships within the protections of this provision extend beyond those of the FMLA, and could include persons who are not family members at all. Again, however, this prohibition does not require an employer to reasonably accommodate an employee in the form of providing the employee leave to care for this individual. However, this provision would prohibit an employer from treating the employee disparately by denying leave for the employee to care for an individual with a disability in circumstances where the employer would not otherwise deny the leave because, for example, the employer generally has no interest in what the employee does on leave (e.g. annual leave).

f. Undue Hardship

The FMLA, unlike the Rehabilitation Act/ADA, does not excuse an employer's obligation to provide leave to an eligible employee for a covered serious health condition because the request would pose a burden on the employer. As an entitlement statute, the FMLA requires that a covered employer allow an eligible employee to take job-protected leave where the employee has met all of the preconditions for such leave. The burden placed on the employer as a result of the employee's FMLA absence(s) does not directly factor into the determination of the employee's right to take FMLA leave. Employees taking leave on an intermittent or reduced leave schedule basis are, however, supposed to attempt to arrange their absences to minimize disruption to the employer's operations.

The right of an otherwise qualified individual with a disability to take leave as a reasonable accommodation pursuant to the Rehabilitation Act/ADA is conditioned on such leave not imposing an undue burden or hardship on the operations of the employer. 42 USC 12112(b)(5)(A). The ADA defines "undue hardship" at 42 USC 12111(10)(A) as "an action requiring significant difficulty or expenses, when considered in light of the factors" enumerated in the Statute. The enumerated ADA "undue hardship" factors (42 USC 12111(10)(B)) are:

- The nature and cost of the accommodation needed;
- The overall financial resources of the facility or facilities involved in the provision of the reasonable accommodation;
- The number of persons employed at such facility;
- The effect on expenses and resources, or the impact otherwise of such accommodation upon the operation of the facility;
- The overall financial resources of the covered entity;

- The overall size of the business entity with respect to the number of employees;

- The number, type and location of its facilities;

- The type of operation or operations of the covered entity, including the composition, structure, and functions of the workforce of such entity; and

- The geographic separateness, administrative, or fiscal relationship of the facility or facilities in question to the covered entity.

Additional guidance regarding the term "undue hardship" may be found in the Appendix to the ADA implementing regulations, 29 CFR Part 1630, App. at § 1630.2(p).

The EEOC has opined that an employer may take into consideration FMLA leave already taken by the employee when deciding whether ADA accommodation leave in excess of the FMLA 12 weeks poses an undue hardship. Preamble, 29 CFR § 825.702. The Equal Employment Opportunity Commission addressed this issue in a Fact Sheet (*U.S. Equal Employment Opportunity Commission Fact Sheet, The Family and Medical Leave Act, the Americans with Disabilities Act, and Title VII of the Civil Rights Act of 1964* (Nov. 1995)) as follows:

12. Q: Does the FMLA's limit of 12 workweeks of leave in a 12-month period mean that the ADA also limits employees to 12 weeks of leave per year?

A: No. The FMLA does not mean that more than 12 weeks of unpaid leave automatically imposes an undue hardship for purposes of the ADA. An otherwise qualified individual with a disability is entitled to more than 12 weeks of unpaid leave as a reasonable accommodation if the additional leave would not impose an undue hardship on the operation of the employer's business. To evaluate whether the additional leave would impose an undue hardship, the employer may consider the impact on its operations caused by the employee's initial 12-week absence, along with the undue hardship factors specified in the ADA. *See* 29 CFR 1630.2(p).

The *EEOC's Enforcement Guidance: Reasonable Accommodations and Undue Hardship Under the Americans with Disabilities Act*, EEOC Notice No. 915.002 (March 1, 1999), addresses undue hardship and employee leave as a reasonable accommodation:

Providing leave to an employee who is unable to provide a fixed date of return is a form of reasonable accommodation. However, if an employer is able to show that the lack of a fixed return date causes an undue hardship, then it can deny the leave. In certain circumstances, undue hardship will derive from the disruption to the operations of the entity that occurs because the employer can neither plan for the employee's return nor permanently fill the position. If an employee cannot provide a fixed date of return, and an employer determines that it can grant such leave at the time without causing undue hardship, the employer has the right to require, as part of the interactive process, that the employee provide periodic updates on his/her condition and possible date of return. After receiving these updates, employers may reevaluate whether continued leave constitutes an undue hardship.

Courts and the EEOC have held that reasonable accommodation in the form of leave for an indefinite period of time imposes an undue hardship on the employer, barring the requirement for leave as a reasonable accommodation. *See Fernandez v. Secretary of Treasury*, 03940025 (1994). Similarly, courts and the EEOC have held that erratic, intermittent absences also impose an undue hardship on employers. *See Rabago v. Secretary of Veterans Affairs*, 01940834 (1994). Of course, whether leave as a reasonable accommodation will constitute an undue hardship is a fact-driven issue unique to each case.

g. Notice

The FMLA and Rehabilitation Act/ADA differ on the obligation of employees to request leave. They also differ on the obligations of employers to inform employees of their rights and responsibilities. For that matter, as addressed in Chapter 8, "Notice Requirements," the various federal sector variants of the FMLA do not mandate the same employee and employer notice obligations.

Generically, the FMLA requires that an eligible employee make a timely request for leave that adequately informs the employer that need for leave may be covered by the FMLA. Timeliness of the request is measured based on whether the need for leave is foreseeable. To be adequate, an employee (with the exception of Title II-covered employees) need not invoke the FMLA by name or otherwise indicate that the employee desires FMLA leave. The employee need only provide sufficient facts explaining why the employee needs the leave so that the employer may determine whether the leave is covered by the FMLA. The timeliness and adequacy of employee notice may also be affected by whether paid leave has been substituted for unpaid FMLA leave.

The Rehabilitation Act/ADA does not contain any specific employee notice requirements. There are no temporal limitations on the right of an otherwise qualified individual with a disability to request a reasonable accommodation. An employee is required to request a reasonable accommodation. *See EEOC: Enforcement Guidance on Reasonable Accommodation and Undue Hardship Under the Americans With Disabilities Act*. An employee, however, need not invoke the Rehabilitation Act/ADA by name or use the term reasonable accommodation, but may use plain English to make a request for accommodation. *Id*. Where the need for an accommodation is obvious and an employee who is not so accommodated is performing poorly, then the employer should offer an accommodation before taking performance-based adverse action against the employee. *Id*.

The notice obligations imposed on employers differ substantially under the FMLA and the Rehabilitation Act/ADA. Again, differences in the various federal sector variants of the FMLA notwithstanding, generally, the employer notice obligations are substantial and very specific. The FMLA may require covered employers to (1) post an FMLA poster; (2) include an FMLA policy statement as part of any employee handbook, manual, or other written material regarding leave and benefits; (3) provide written guidance to the employee in the absence of an employee handbook or manual; (4) periodically provide specific written notice of FMLA rights and responsibilities; (5) inform the employee whether he or she is eligible for FMLA leave; (6) inform the employee whether the employer has designated the leave, paid or unpaid, as FMLA leave; (7) provide written notice of any medical certification/fitness-for-duty requirements; and (8) notify the employee of key employee status. See Chapter 8, "Notice Requirements"; *see also* Lawrence P. Postal, *Sailing the Employment Law Bermuda Triangle*, 18 The Labor Lawyer 165, 172 (Fall 2002).

The ADA/Rehabilitation Act, in contrast, merely requires employers to post a notice that describes the provisions of the ADA. 42 USC 12115. The EEOC has created a compliant poster, which is available on their website. There are no other formal employer notice requirements governing the rights of disabled employees generally.

It is unclear whether employer notice of FMLA leave rights is an example of a "greater right" such that a federal employer would be obligated to inform the employee of those rights if the leave at issue was covered both by the FMLA and the Rehabilitation Act/ADA. The situation is complicated by the fact that "greater benefits" is undefined. Nor do the examples provided in the DOL implementing regulations address employer notice requirements as a "greater benefit." *See* 29 CFR 825.7-2(b)-(f). If employer notice of FMLA rights were considered the "greater benefits" when compared to the meager Rehabilitation Act/ADA notice requirements, the employer would be obligated to abide by the FMLA notice requirements where the employee's request for leave was covered by both the FMLA and the Rehabilitation Act/ADA. The safer course for an employer is to abide by all of the notice requirements of the FMLA, whether or not the employee's request is also covered by the Rehabilitation Act/ADA.

h. Medical Documentation

Both the FMLA and the Rehabilitation Act/ADA permit an employer to request medical certification from an employee in support of a request for leave. While strict under both statutes, the standards for medical certification differ.

Under the ADA, for current employees, an employer is generally prohibited from making inquiries into the nature and extent of an employee's disability, except where such inquires are job-related and consistent with business necessity. 42 USC 12112(d)(4)(A); 29 CFR 1630.14(c)(1). An employer may verify an employee's disability and/or request for reasonable accommodation in two ways: (1) require the employee to submit medical documentation from the employee's health care provider; or (2) require the employee to submit to a medical examination.

Consistent with the ADA, an employer may require a current employee to verify the existence of a claimed disability and that an accommodation is warranted by submitting documentation from the employee's treating health care provider. *EEOC Enforcement Guidance: Disability-Related Inquiries and Medical Examinations of Employees Under the Americans with Disabilities Act* (July 27, 2000). An employer may not request documentation in response to a request for reasonable accommodation when (1) both the disability and the need for reasonable accommodation are obvious or (2) the individual has already provided the employer with sufficient information to substantiate that he or she has a disability and needs the accommodation requested. *Id*.

According to the *EEOC's Enforcement Guidance on Medical Examinations*, an employee's medical documentation may be insufficient:

- If the documentation does not establish that the employee has an ADA disability (e.g. a condition that substantially limits a major life activity) or if the documentation does not justify the need for reasonable accommodation;

- The health care professional does not have the expertise to give an opinion about the employee's medical condition;

- The information does not specify the functional limitations due to the disability;

- Other factors indicate that the information provided is not credible or is fraudulent.

An employer also has the option of providing an employee's health care provider with a list of questions if the employee signs a limited release for this purpose. *See EEOC Enforcement Guidance on Reasonable Accommodations and Undue Hardship Under the Americans with Disabilities Act*, EEOC Notice No. 915.002 (March 1, 1999).

Alternatively, the Rehabilitation Act/ADA permits an employer to require a current employee to submit to a medical examination by a health care provider selected by the employer when (1) there is a need to determine whether the employee is able to perform essential job functions; or (2) it is necessary to the reasonable accommodation process. *See* 29 CFR 1630.14(c); 29 CFR App. § 1630.14(c).

As addressed more fully in Chapter 9, "Documentation Requirements," the FMLA allows employers to request that an employee provide a medical certification in order to substantiate the need for FMLA leave due to his or her own serious health condition, or the serious health condition of a covered family member. *See* 29 USC 2613(c). The certification must be from the employee's own health care provider (if the need for FMLA leave is due to the employee's own serious health condition), or the health care provider of the covered family member with a serious health condition. Unlike the Rehabilitation Act/ADA, the medical information that an employer is entitled to receive for this purpose is specifically prescribed by the FMLA. As such, the FMLA regulations generally prohibit an employer from requiring more medical information than what is permitted. *See* 29 CFR 825.306. Where the need for FMLA leave is due to the employee's own serious health condition, an employer may provide the employee's health care provider with a description of the essential functions of the employee's position.

The FMLA generally does not permit an employer to require an employee (or covered family member) to submit to a medical examination to confirm the employee's need for FMLA leave. However, an employer may require that the individual with the serious health condition (either the employee or a covered family member) submit to a second opinion medical examination by a health care provider of the employer's choosing if the employer has reason to doubt the validity of the initial medical certification provided by the employee. If the results of the examination of the second health care opinion provider differs from the initial certification, an employer may require examination by a third health care opinion provider, which is final and binding on all parties regarding the employee's request for FMLA leave. The third health care provider is jointly selected by the employer and the employee.

Generally, in terms of medical certification supporting a request for leave that may be covered by both the FMLA and the Rehabilitation Act/ADA, the "greater benefits" to employees appears to be provided by the FMLA. The FMLA does not permit, at least as an initial matter, an employee to submit to a medical examination to confirm the existence of a serious health condition requiring leave. Moreover, the prescribed information that an employer is entitled to receive to confirm the need for FMLA leave is likely to be less than what would fall within the broader Rehabilitation Act/ADA parameters of "job-related and consistent with business necessity." Accordingly, employers might consider a two-step process where an employee is entitled to the protections of the FMLA and the Rehabilitation Act/ADA. The employee who claims a disability would first be subjected to the scrutiny permitted by the FMLA; if he or she passes muster under that test and then exhausts his or her FMLA leave, he or she could be subjected to the possibly more comprehensive examination or inquiries permitted under the ADA before additional leave could be required as a reasonable accommodation. *See* Jana Howard Carey, Sandra S. Fink, *How the ADA and FMLA Interact with an Employer's Policies Concerning Absenteeism and Leave Due to Employee Medical Conditions*, C874 ALI–ABA 269 (ALI–ABA 1993).

Finally, a question that frequently arises is whether an employer's request for medical certification under the FMLA to determine whether the employee has a covered "serious health condition" runs afoul of the ADA restrictions on disability-related inquires of employees. Answering the question in the negative, the EEOC in *Fact Sheet: The Family and Medical Leave Act, the Americans With Disabilities Act, and Title VII of the Civil Rights Act of 1964* (Nov. 1995) explained:

> 10. Q: Is there a conflict between the FMLA provision allowing employers to ask for certification that an employee has a serious health condition and the ADA restrictions on disability-related inquiries of employees?
>
> A: No. When an employee requests leave under the FMLA for a serious health condition, employers will not violate the ADA by asking for the information specified in the FMLA certification form. The FMLA form only requests information relating to the particular serious health condition, as defined in the FMLA, for which the employee is seeking leave. An employer is entitled to know why an employee, who otherwise should be at work, is requesting time off under the FMLA. If the inquires are strictly limited in this fashion, they would be "job-related and consistent with business necessity" under the ADA.

The above guidance by the EEOC, although addressing Title I of the FMLA, should equally apply to the other federal sector variants of the FMLA.

i. How Leave May Be Taken

The FMLA and the Rehabilitation Act/ADA differ on the manner in which leave is actually taken. As addressed more fully in Chapter 10, "Leave Amount and Scheduling," the FMLA entitles an eligible employee to take his or her 12 weeks of FMLA leave for a covered condition in a single block, intermittently, or on a reduced leave schedule basis. "Intermittent leave" is leave taken in separate blocks of time due to a single qualifying covered condition. 29 CFR 825.203(a). A "reduced leave schedule" is a leave schedule that reduces an employee's usual number of working hours per workweek, or hours per workday. *Id.* An eligible employee generally has the right under the FMLA to take leave on an intermittent or reduced leave schedule basis for the employee's own serious health condition, if medically necessary, and to provide care for a covered family member with a serious health condition. 29 CFR 825.203, 825.205.

The right of an eligible employee to take leave on an intermittent or reduced leave schedule basis is subject to two conditions. If the leave is for planned medical treatments:

- The employee must attempt to schedule such leave to minimize disruption to the employer's operations (29 CFR 825.302(e)); and

- The employer can temporarily transfer the employee to another position with the same pay and benefits (29 CFR 825. 203, 825.204).

Reasonable accommodation under the Rehabilitation Act/ADA would include leave on an intermittent or reduced leave schedule basis, subject to a defense of undue hardship by an employer. *See* 42 USC 12111(9)(A)-(B) (modified work schedules are permissible forms of reasonable accommodation). Unlike the FMLA, the Rehabilitation Act/ADA does not require an employee to attempt to schedule the leave to minimize disruption to his or her employer's operations.

Nor does the ADA permit an employer to automatically transfer an employee to an equivalent position that might better accommodate a modified work schedule. On the contrary, an employer must first attempt to accommodate the employee in his or her current position. If that is not possible or would cause undue hardship to the employer, the Rehabilitation Act allows an employer to transfer an employee to an equivalent, vacant position. 29 CFR 1630.2(o). *See also* 29 CFR 825.702(b). If no equivalent position is available, the Rehabilitation Act/ADA permits an employer to reassign the employee as a reasonable accommodation to a lower graded and pay position. The FMLA, on the other hand, requires that reassignment be to a position of equivalent pay and benefits.

The Rehabilitation Act/ADA is also far less welcoming to the accommodation of sporadic leave than the FMLA. Again, when the conditions are met, the FMLA requires an employer to permit an employee to take leave on an intermittent basis. The Rehabilitation Act/ADA also permits intermittent leave as a reasonable accommodation, subject to a defense of undue hardship on the employer. Courts interpreting the Rehabilitation Act/ADA have been receptive to employer claims of undue hardship for accommodation involving the sporadic, unpredictable use of leave. *See Waggoner v. Olin Corp.*, 169 F.3d 481, 484 (7th Cir. 1999) (ADA does not require employers to accommodate erratic, unexplained absences because attendance is a requirement of most jobs); *Jackson v. Veteran's Administration*, 22 F.3d 277, 278-79 (11th Cir. 1994) (because of sporadic, unpredictable basis of absences, the employee could not perform essential job function of the job—presence on the job); *Palazzolo v. Galen Hospitals, of Texas, Inc.*, No. 1:96-cv-2550-TWT, 1997 U.S.

Dist. LEXIS 21915 (N.D. Ga. Nov. 25, 1997); *Gore v. G.T.E. South*, 917 F. Supp. 1564, 1572–73 (M.D. Ala. 1996) (the employer need not accommodate unpredictable absences); *Walders v. Garrett*, 765 F. Supp. 303, 313 (E.D. Va. 1991) (the employer need not allow employee to work when feeling well if it would unacceptably reduce efficiency), *aff'd*, 956 F.2d 1163 (4th Cir. 1992); *Santiago v. Temple U.*, 739 F. Supp. 974, 979 (E.D. Pa. 1990) (holding that requiring accommodation of unpredictable excessive absenteeism unreasonable), *aff'd without opinion*, 928 F.2d 396 (3d Cir. 1991). *But see Dutton v. Johnson County Bd. of County Commissioners*, 859 F. Supp. 498 (D. Kan. 1994) (despite sporadic absences, it is a question of fact whether other accommodations were available where absences were not excessive and employee's performance did not suffer).

In *Hatchett v. Philander Smith College et al.*, 251 F.3d 670, 675 n.4 (8th Cir. 2001), the court held that the FMLA did not require an employer to return an employee to work on an intermittent or reduced leave schedule basis when the employee was unable to perform all of the essential functions of the job while at work. The employee had argued that such leave would allow her to "work harden" back to the full capacity. The court pointed out that the FMLA does not require reasonable accommodation of a returning employee who is unable to perform all essential job functions.

Of course, whether accommodation of unpredictable absences will cause undue hardship to a particular federal employer will depend on the facts of each case.

j. Paid Leave Substitution

Both the FMLA and the Rehabilitation Act/ADA allow the use of paid leave. Under the Rehabilitation Act/ADA, available paid leave may be used as a reasonable accommodation. An employer, however, is not required to provide additional paid leave. *See EEOC Enforcement Guidance on Reasonable Accommodation and Undue Hardship Under the Americans with Disabilities Act*, p. 25 (March 2, 1999).

As discussed more fully in Chapter 11, "Substitution of Paid Leave," the four federal sector variants of the FMLA allow for substitution of accrued and available paid leave for unpaid FMLA leave, although the circumstances differ somewhat regarding who may elect paid leave substitution. For Title I, the CAA, and the PEOAA, either the employee or employer may elect to substitute paid leave for unpaid FMLA leave. Under Title II, only the employee may elect to substitute paid leave for unpaid FMLA leave.

k. Maintenance of Benefits During Leave

Health benefits' protections during an employee's leave differs under the FMLA and the Rehabilitation Act/ADA. As discussed more fully in Chapter 12, "Maintenance of Benefits," the FMLA generally requires employers to maintain group health benefits under the same terms offered to the employees who are not on leave. On return to work from FMLA leave, an employee is entitled to the same or equivalent group health benefits as he or she enjoyed before taking leave. The group health benefits of a full-time employee who takes FMLA leave on an intermittent or reduced leave schedule basis must be maintained at the full-time employee level. The level of group health benefits may not be reduced even though the employee is only working the equivalent of a part-time schedule.

In terms of maintenance of health benefits coverage, the protections afforded by the Rehabilitation Act/ADA are less generous than those of the FMLA. The ADA prohibits an employer from discriminating against a qualified individual with a disability in terms of benefit coverage. 42 USC 12112(b)(4); 29 CFR 1630.4(f). For example, an employer must receive the same type and level of benefits as a similarly situated, non-disabled employee. Unlike the FMLA, this equivalency requirement is not measured by what benefits the otherwise qualified individual with a disability enjoyed prior to leave. Rather, equivalency is measured at the time of accommodation. A full-time employee who becomes a part-time employee because of the use of leave as a reasonable accommodation is only entitled to whatever health benefits a non-disabled, part-time employee would receive pursuant to employer policy.

The DOL and CAA implementing regulations (29 CFR 825.702(c)(1); S. Res. 242, Cong. Rec. S3959, S3976 (April 23, 1996); 29 CFR 825.702(c)(1)) illustrate how the FMLA and Rehabilitation Act/ADA interact in this situation with respect to a qualified individual with a disability:

> A reasonable accommodation under the ADA might be accomplished by providing an individual with a disability with a part-time job with no health benefits, assuming the employer did not ordinarily provide health insurance

for part-time employees. However, FMLA would permit an employee to work a reduced leave schedule until the equivalent of 12 workweeks of leave were used, with group health benefits maintained during this period.

See DOL WH FMLA Advisory Opinion No. 97 (July 10, 1998); DOL WH FMLA Advisory Opinion No. 82 (July 31, 1996); DOL WH FMLA Advisory Opinion No. 55 (March 10, 1995).

The implementing regulations go on to illustrate the above rule (29 CFR § 825.702(c)(2); S. Res. 242, Cong. Rec. S3959, S3976 (April 23, 1996); 29 CFR 825.702(c)(2)) as follows:

> If the same [full-time] employee needed to work part-time (a reduced leave schedule) after returning to his or her same job, the employee would still be entitled under FMLA to have group health plan coverage maintained for the remainder of the two-week equivalent of FMLA leave entitlement, notwithstanding an employer policy that part-time employees do not receive health insurance. This employee would be entitled under the ADA to reasonable accommodations to enable the employee to perform the essential functions of the part-time position. In addition, because the employee is working a part-time schedule as a reasonable accommodation, the employee would be shielded from FMLA's provision for temporary assignment to a different alternative position. Once the employee has exhausted his or her remaining FMLA leave entitlement while working the reduced (part-time) schedule, if the employee is a qualified individual with a disability, and if the employee is unable to return to the same full-time position at that time, the employee might continue to work part-time as a reasonable accommodation, barring undue hardship; the employee would then be entitled to only those employment benefits ordinarily provided by the employer to part-time employees.

As regards the maintenance of benefits rules of the FMLA and the Rehabilitation Act/ADA, the greater benefit to employees is found under the FMLA rules. As demonstrated by the above DOL/CAA examples, as long as an employee is on FMLA leave, he or she retains the greater benefits regarding the maintenance of health benefits afforded by the FMLA, even if the employee is a qualified individual with a disability and the leave is also considered a reasonable accommodation. Because 12 workweeks of FMLA leave taken intermittently can continue for long periods of time, it is possible that an employee would not lose entitlement to full-time group health benefits even though he or she has been working a part-time schedule for years.

I. Return to Work

An employee's reinstatement to work following leave is addressed by both the FMLA and the Rehabilitation Act/ADA. Not surprisingly, the statues have different standards.

As described in the *EEOC Fact Sheet: The Family and Medical Leave Act, the Americans with Disabilities Act, and Title VII of the Civil Rights Act of 1964* (Nov. 1995):

> 14. Q: What are employees' reinstatement rights under the ADA and the FMLA?
>
> A: Under the ADA, the employee is entitled to return to the same job unless the employer demonstrates that holding the job open would impose an undue hardship.
>
> In some instances, an employee may request more leave under the ADA even after the employer has communicated that it cannot hold the employee's job open any longer (i.e. there is undue hardship). In this situation, the ADA-covered employer must see if it has a vacant, equivalent position for which the employee is qualified and to which the employee can be reassigned without undue hardship to continue his/her leave. If an equivalent position is not available, the employer must look for a vacant position at a lower level. Continued accommodation is not required if a vacant position at a lower level is also unavailable.
>
> In other instances, an employer may hold the original position open, and the employee may want to return to work, but may be unable to perform an essential function of the original position even with reasonable accommodation. Under the ADA, the employer must then consider reassignment, first to a vacant equivalent position for which the individual is qualified and, if one is unavailable, to vacant position at a lower level. Further accommodation is not required if a vacant position at a lower level is also unavailable.

As addressed more fully in Chapter 13, "Return to Work from Leave," an employer is required to return an employee from FMLA leave to the same or to an equivalent position. In order to perfect a right to reinstatement, an employee must return from work before the 12 weeks of FMLA leave has been exhausted. Moreover, an employee does not have an FMLA right to return to work from FMLA leave where the employee is unable to perform all essential job functions of the same or equivalent position. Nor does the FMLA require an employer to reasonably accommodate an employee returning from FMLA leave who is unable to perform all essential job functions. Of course, such accommodation may be required by more generous agency policies, the terms of any applicable collective bargaining agreement or, if the employee is disabled, by the Rehabilitation Act/ADA.

Under the FMLA, an employer may also refuse to reinstate an employee from FMLA leave if the employee has failed to provide a medical or fitness for duty certification, because the employee's position has been eliminated for non-discriminatory reasons, or because the employee has been terminated, again for reasons unrelated to the use of FMLA leave. *See* 29 CFR 825.312. Under some federal sector variants of the FMLA, there are additional limitations on the return to work of certain school and "key" employees from FMLA leave. The FMLA does not have an "undue" burden defense *per se* to avoid reinstatement of an employee from FMLA leave. The "key employee" exception under some of the federal sector variants of the FMLA would permit an employer from returning a so-called "key" employee where the return of the employee would cause the employer "substantial and grievous" economic injury. *See* 29 CFR 825.217, 825.218.

Both the ADA and the FMLA permit an employer to require an employee returning from leave to provide a fitness-for-duty certification. As described in the *EEOC's Enforcement Guidance: Disability Related Inquiries and Medical Examinations of Employees Under the Americans with Disabilities Act* (July 27, 2000), fitness for duty certifications upon an employee's return to work must be job related and consistent with business necessity, and are only permitted when:

- There is a need to determine whether an employee is still able to perform the essential functions of the job;
- The employee may pose a direct threat;
- It is necessary to the reasonable accommodation process; or
- It is required by applicable federal, state, or local law.

Under the ADA, the employer may elect to choose the physician to perform the fitness-for-duty examination, or accept a medical certification of fitness to return to duty from the employee's health care provider.

Generally, the FMLA permits employers to require an employee to provide a fitness-for-duty certification from the employee's health care provider as a condition of reinstatement. In order to require an employee to provide a fitness-for-duty certification, the following conditions (29 CFR 825.310(a), 825.301(c)) must be met:

- The employer must have a uniformly applied practice or policy for all employees, not just those returning from FMLA leave;
- Notice of a fitness-for-duty must be included in any employee handbook or other written materials addressing leave and benefits; and
- Written notice must be given to the employee of the obligation to provide a fitness-for-duty certification as a condition of reinstatement.

The FMLA requires that any return to work fitness-for-duty certification must comply with the ADA requirement that it be limited only to information regarding the health condition that caused the need for FMLA leave. *See* 29 CFR 825.301(c), 825.702(e). Fitness-for-duty certifications cannot be required where the employee is using intermittent leave. If the employee fails to timely provide a requested fitness-for-duty certification, the employer may delay the employee's reinstatement until certification is provided. If the certification is never provided, the employer may deny FMLA leave and take disciplinary action against the employee for the absence pursuant to existing agency policy.

The DOL and CAA implementing regulations (29 CFR 825.702(c)(2), (4); S. Res. 242, Cong. Rec. S3959, S3976 (April 23, 1996); 29 CFR 825.702(c)(2), (4)) illustrate the interaction of the FMLA and Rehabilitation Act/ADA reinstatement issues as follows:

> (2) A qualified individual with a disability who is also an "eligible employee" entitled to FMLA leave requests [ten] weeks of medical leave as a reasonable accommodation, which the employer grants because it is not an undue hardship. The employer advises the employee that the [ten] weeks of leave is also being designated as

FMLA leave and will count toward the employee's FMLA leave entitlement. This designation does not prevent the parties from also treating the leave as a reasonable accommodation and reinstating the employee into the same job, as required by the ADA, rather than an equivalent position under the FMLA, [as] that is the greater right available to the employee. At the same time, the employee would be entitled under FMLA to have the employer maintain group health plan coverage during the leave, as the requirement provides the greater right to the employee.

(4) At the end of the FMLA leave entitlement, an employer is required under FMLA to reinstate the employee in the same or an equivalent position, with equivalent pay and benefits, to which the employee held when leave commenced. The employer's FMLA obligations would be satisfied if the employer offered the employee an equivalent full-time position. If the employee were unable to perform the essential functions of that equivalent position even with reasonable accommodation, because of a disability, the ADA may require the employer to make a reasonable accommodation at that time by allowing the employee to work part-time or by reassigning the employee to a vacant position, barring undue hardship.

In the second scenario, the employee would not have had an FMLA right to be reinstatement because he or she was unable to perform the essential functions of the job. If, on the other hand, the employee were also disabled within the meaning of the Rehabilitation Act/ADA, the employee would have a right to reinstatement because the greater benefit bestowed by those laws would require reinstatement and reasonable accommodation, barring undue hardship.

m. Confidentiality of Medical Records

Both the FMLA and the ADA require employers to keep medical information confidential. Under the Rehabilitation Act/ADA, employers must keep all medical information on employees confidential. 29 CFR 1630.14(b)(1). In order to ensure confidentiality, the medical records must be kept in a file separate from personnel files and in a separate locked cabinet. 29 CFR 1630.14(c). Access to employee medical records is limited to certain individuals with a legitimate need to know such information. The EEOC regulations (29 CFR 1630.14(b)(1)(i)–(iii); 29 CFR App. § 1630.14(b)) identify the following individuals and circumstances that would permit access to employee medical records:

- Decision-makers involved in the hiring process to ensure that employment decisions are made consistent with the ADA;
- Supervisors and managers may be told about necessary restrictions on the work and duties of the employee and about necessary accommodations;
- First aid and safety personnel may be informed if the disability might require emergency treatment;
- Government officials investigating compliance with the ADA must be given relevant information on request;
- Employers may give information to state workers' compensation offices, state second injury funds, or workers' compensation insurance carriers in accordance with state workers' compensation laws; and
- Employers may use the information for insurance purposes.

Note that the Rehabilitation Act/ADA confidentiality provisions generally preclude telling co-workers and others about an employee's disabilities, including as a part of an explanation for reasonable accommodations afforded to the employee. In *Enforcement Guidance: Americans with Disabilities Act and Psychiatric Disabilities*, EEOC Notice No. 915.002 (March 25, 1997), the EEOC explained that, if asked, an employer may not disclose medical information concerning an individual with a disability to co-workers (who generally do not have a legitimate reason to know this information). Nor may an employer tell co-workers, and others without a legitimate reason to know, whether the employer is providing a reasonable accommodation to a particular individual. The employer may simply state in response to such questions that it is "acting for legitimate business reasons or in compliance with federal law."

As discussed more fully in Chapter 9, "Documentation Requirements," and Chapter 14, "Record Keeping Requirements," the medical confidentiality requirements of the four federal sector variants of the FMLA are not uniform. All FMLA variants, however, substantially mirror the confidentiality protections afforded by the Rehabilitation Act/ADA. Title I of the FMLA specifically incorporates the ADA confidentiality protections. *See* 5 CFR 630.1207(j).

The medical confidentiality provisions of Title I, the CAA, and the PEOAA substantially follow the requirements of the Rehabilitation Act/ADA. Records and documents relating to medical certifications, recertifications or medical histories of employees or employees' family members, created for purposes of the FMLA, must be maintained as confidential medical records in files separate from the employee's usual personnel files. *See* 29 CFR 825.500(g). Where the ADA is also applicable, the medical records must be maintained in conformance with ADA confidentiality requirements. 29 CFR 825.500(g). In that case, the ADA exceptions to confidentiality apply. 29 CFR 825.500(g)(1)–(3).

In a *Fact Sheet* regarding the Family and Medical Leave Act, the Americans with Disabilities Act, and Title VII of the Civil Rights Act of 1964 (November, 1995), the EEOC addressed the maintenance of a single confidential medical file for purposes of the FMLA and the ADA:

> 11. Q: May an employer keep a single confidential medical file for each employee, separate from the usual personnel file, for medical documentation under both the ADA and the FMLA?
>
> A: Yes. An employer may keep a single confidential medical file, separate from the usual personnel file, containing both FMLA and ADA medical information if the employer follows the ADA confidentiality standards. This includes following the ADA interpretations of those confidentiality exceptions that are set forth in both the ADA and the FMLA regulations. For example, employers may not give supervisors and managers unlimited access to the medical files. However, employers may give supervisors and managers information concerning necessary work restrictions and accommodations.

Again, in accordance with ADA standards, a single confidential employee medical file would have to be maintained separate from the employee's usual personnel files and, with respect to physical files, in a separate locked cabinet.

An employee who is both eligible for FMLA leave and disabled within the meaning of the Rehabilitation Act/ADA may not, in lieu of FMLA leave, be required by his or her employer to take another position as a reasonable accommodation. As explained by the DOL and CAA implementing regulations (29 CFR 825.702(d)(1); S. Res. 242, Cong. Rec. S3959, S3976 (April 23, 1996); 29 CFR 825.702(d)(1)):

> If FMLA entitles an employee to leave, an employer may not, in lieu of FMLA leave, *require* an employee to take a job with a reasonable accommodation. However, ADA may require an employer to offer an employee the opportunity to take such a position. An employer may not change the essential functions of the job in order to deny FMLA leave. *See* § 825.220(b).

See Johnson v. USPS, Case No 1:97–CV–794, 1999 U.S. Dist. LEXIS 7981, at n. 18 (W.D. Mich. May 26, 1999); DOL WH FMLA Advisory Opinion No. 17 (Nov. 15, 1993).

An employee may, however, voluntarily end his or her leave and accept such an alternative position, provided that the offer and acceptance is uncoerced. Preamble, 29 CFR 825.702. The employee would then retain the right to be restored to the position held by the employee at the time the FMLA leave was requested (or commenced) until 12 weeks have passed, including all FMLA leave taken and the period the employee returned to "light duty." *Id.*

Finally, when an employer violates both the FMLA and the ADA, an employee may be able to recover under either or both statutes, but may not be awarded double relief for the same loss. *See* 29 CFR 825.702(a).

D. PREGNANCY DISCRIMINATION ACT OF 1978

Pregnancy, childbirth, and prenatal care are covered conditions for purposes of FMLA leave. See Chapter 7, "Covered Conditions." Leave due to pregnancy and pregnancy-related conditions may also be covered by the Pregnancy Discrimination Act of 1978 (PDA), 42 USC 2000e(k). This subsection will compare and contrast the leave provisions of the PDA with those of the FMLA.

1. Overview of PDA

The FMLA does not modify or affect the leave requirements imposed on employers by Title VII of the Civil Rights Act of 1964, as amended by the Pregnancy Discrimination Act of 1978 (PDA). *See* S. Rep. 103–3, 103d Cong., 1st Sess. 38 (1993); 29 CFR 825.702(a); S. Res. 242, Cong. Rec. S3959, S3976 (April 23, 1996); 29 CFR 825.702(a). The PDA amended the Title VII definition of sex discrimination to include any discrimination based on childbirth, pregnancy, or related health conditions. *Green v. New Balance Athletic Shoe, Inc.*, 182 F. Supp. 2d 128, 134 (D. Me. 2002); *Vargas v. Globetrotters Engineering Corp.*, 4 F. Supp. 2d 780, 784 (N.D. Ill. 1998).

In pertinent part, the PDA (42 USC 2000-e(k)) provides:

> The terms "because of sex" or "on the basis of sex" include, but are not limited to, because of or on the basis of pregnancy, childbirth, or related medical conditions; and women affected by pregnancy, childbirth, or related medical conditions shall be treated the same for all employment-related purposes, including receipt of benefits under fringe benefit programs, as other persons not so affected but similar in their ability or inability to work, and nothing in [S]ection 2000e-2(h) of this [T]itle shall be interpreted to permit otherwise.

The Pregnancy Discrimination Act of 1978 (PDA), was Congress' reaction to the Supreme Court's decision in *General Electric v. Gilbert*, 429 U.S. 125 (1976). There, the Court held that the exclusion of pregnancy from an employer's comprehensive disability insurance plan did not constitute sexual discrimination within the meaning of Title VII of the Civil Rights Act of 1964. The Court's rationale was that discrimination on the basis of pregnancy was not the same as discrimination on the basis of sex because pregnancy was not a condition that affected all women. *See* Sean Stewart, *Note and Comments: PDA, FMLA, and Beyond: A Brief Look at Past, Present, and Future Sex Discrimination Laws and Their Effects on the Teaching Profession*, 2003 BYU Educ. & L. J. 835, 839–40, n.26 (2003); David W. Wilhelmus and Mary Tiede Wilhelmus, *The Interaction of the Americans with Disabilities Act, the Family and Medical Leave Act, and the Pregnancy Discrimination Act and Their Impact on Libraries*, 88 Law Libr. J. 231, 235 (Spring 1996).

As an amendment to Title VII, the PDA applies to virtually all employers in the federal sector. Section 717(a) of Title VII, 42 USC 2000e16(a) provides:

> All personnel actions affecting employees or applicants for employment (except with regard to aliens employed outside the limits of the United States) in military departments as defined in [S]ection 102 of Title 5, in executive agencies as defined in [S]ection 105 of Title 5 (including employees and applicants for employment who are paid from nonappropriated funds), in the United States Postal Service and the Postal Rate Commission, in those units of Government of the District of Columbia having positions in the competitive service, and in those units of the judicial branches of the Federal Government having positions in the competitive service, and in the Government Printing Office, the General Accounting Office, and the Library of Congress shall be made free from discrimination based on race, color, religion, sex, or national origin.

The PDA applies to employees of employing offices covered by the CAA, 2 USC 1302(2), 1311(a)(1), and the PEOAA, 3 USC 402(2), 411(a)(1).

The EEOC has developed regulations to implement the PDA. 29 CFR Part 1604. According to those regulations, the "basic principle of the Act is that women affected by pregnancy and related conditions must be treated the same as other applicants and employees on the same basis of their ability and inability to work." 29 CFR Part 1604, Appendix, Introduction. The EEOC went on (29 CFR Part 1604, Appendix, Introduction), in pertinent part, to explain:

> [A woman] usually cannot be forced to go on leave as long as she can still work. If other employees who take disability leave are entitled to get their jobs back when they are able to work again, so are women who have been unable to work because of pregnancy.

> In the area of fringe benefits, such as disability benefits, sick leave and health insurance, the same principle applies. A woman unable to work for pregnancy related reasons is entitled to disability benefits or sick leave on the same basis as employees unable to work for other medical reasons. Also, any health insurance provided must cover expenses for pregnancy-related conditions on the same basis as expenses for other medical conditions.

The PDA does not *per se* require agencies to grant leave to an employee due to pregnancy, childbirth, or related conditions. *EEOC Fact Sheet: The Family and Medical Leave Act, the Americans with Disabilities Act, and Title VII of the Civil Rights Act of 1964* (Nov. 1995), Q&A #22. Rather, the PDA requires agencies to treat pregnancy and pregnancy-related conditions the same as non-pregnancy conditions under agency policies and practices. *EEOC Fact Sheet: The Family and Medical Leave Act, the Americans with Disabilities Act, and Title VII of the Civil Rights Act of 1964* (Nov. 1995), Q&A #20. *See Cabrera v. Trataros Const. Inc.*, 184 F. Supp. 2d 149 (D.P.R. 2002) (PDA does not require employers to make accommodations for its pregnant employees; employers can treat pregnant women as badly as they treat similarly affected but nonpregnant employees).

The EEOC regulations make it a *prima facie* violation of Title VII for an agency to have a "written or unwritten policy or practice that excludes from employment applicants or employees because of pregnancy, childbirth or related medical conditions." 29 CFR § 1604(a). The EEOC regulations go on to explain that written or unwritten employment policies and practices involving matters such as the commencement and duration of leave, the availability of extension, the accrual of seniority and other benefits and privileges, reinstatement, and payment under any health or disability insurance or sick leave plan, formal or informal, must be applied to disability due to pregnancy, childbirth, or related medical conditions on the same terms and conditions as they are applied to other disabilities. 29 CFR 1604.10(b).

The regulations issued by the EEOC to implement the PDA clarified the equivalency requirements in a question and answer format. Regarding leave, the EEOC questions and answers (29 CFR Part 1604, Appendix), in pertinent part, provide:

5. Q. If, for pregnancy-related reasons, an employee is unable to perform the functions of her job, does the employer have to provide her an alternative job?

    A. An employer is required to treat an employee temporarily unable to perform the functions of her job because of her pregnancy-related condition in the same manner as it treats other temporarily disabled employees, whether by providing modified tasks, alternative assignments, disability leaves, leaves without pay, etc. For example, a woman's primary job function may be the operation of a machine and, incidental to that function, she may carry materials to and from the machine. If other employees temporarily unable to lift are relieved of these functions, pregnant employees also unable to lift must be temporarily relieved of the function.

6. Q. What procedures may an employer use to determine whether to place on leave as unable to work a pregnant employee who claims she is able to work or deny leave to a pregnant employee who claims that she is disabled from work?

    A. An employer may not single out pregnancy-related conditions for special procedures for determining an employee's ability to work. However, an employer may use any procedure used to determine the ability of all employees to work. For example, if an employer requires its employees to submit a doctor's statement concerning their inability to work before granting leave or paying sick benefits, the employer may require employees affected by pregnancy-related conditions to submit such statement. Similarly, if an employer allows its employees to obtain doctor's statements from their personal physicians for absences due to other disabilities, it must accept doctor's statements from personal physicians for absences and return dates connected with pregnancy-related disabilities.

7. Q. Can an employer have a rule that prohibits an employee from returning to work for a predetermined length of time after childbirth?

    A. No.

8. Q. If an employee has been absent from work as a result of a pregnancy-related condition and recovers, may her employer require her to remain on leave until after her baby is born?

    A. No. An employee must be permitted to work at all times during pregnancy when she is able to perform her job.

9. Q. Must an employer hold open the job of an employee who is absent on leave because she is temporarily disabled by pregnancy-related conditions?

    A. Unless the employee on leave has informed the employer that she does not intend to return to work, her job must be held open for her return on the same basis as jobs are held open for employees on sick or disability leave for other reasons.

The EEOC distinguishes between leave for pregnancy and leave for childcare after the female employee is medically able to return to work. Specifically, the EEOC regulations provide (29 CFR Part 1604, Appendix):

18. Q. Must an employee grant leave to a female employee for childcare purposes after she is medically able to return to work following leave necessitated by pregnancy, childbirth, or related medical conditions?

    A. While leave for child care purposes is not covered by the Pregnancy Discrimination Act, ordinarily Title VII principles would require that leave for childcare purposes be granted on the same basis as leave which is granted to employees for other non-medical reasons. For example, if an employer allows its employees to take leave without pay or accrued annual leave for travel or education which is not job related, the same type of leave must be granted to those who wish to remain on leave for infant care, even though they are medically able to work.

See Cal. Fed. Sav. & Loan v. Guerra, 479 U.S. 272, 289 (1987) (care for a newborn child not covered under the PDA, only time missed due to birth); *Barnes v. Hewlett-Packard Co.*, 846 F. Supp. 442 (D. Md. 1994) (same); *Record v. Mill Neck Manor Lutheran School for Deaf*, 611 F. Supp. 905 (E.D.N.Y. 1985) (same); *Baffuto-Fein v. Pfizer, Inc.*, No. 91 Civ. 3063 (TPG), 1993 U.S. Dist. LEXIS 12214 (S.D.N.Y. 1993) (termination of employee who, while physically able to return to work following her pregnancy, did not do so on the agreed date due to childcare issues, did not violate the PDA).

By including the PDA under the umbrella of Title VII, aggrieved employees may pursue damages against agencies pursuant to disparate treatment or disparate impact theories. *Dormeyer v. Comerica Bank-Illinois et al.*, 223 F.3d 579, 583 (7th Cir. 2000); *Green v. New Balance Athletic Shoe, Inc.*, 182 F. Supp. 2d 128, 134-35 (D. Me. 2002). Disparate treatment addresses intentional discrimination based on pregnancy or pregnancy-related conditions. Disparate impact claims, on the other hand, do not require an employee to prove intentional discrimination. Rather, facially neutral leave policies that have disparate impact on women due to pregnancy or pregnancy-related conditions may violate Title VII. *See Scherrr v. Woodland Sch. Community Dist.*, 867 F.2d 974 (7th Cir. 1988) (claim seeking leave of absence based on pregnancy discrimination in violation of PDA may be based on theory of disparate impact as well as disparate treatment).

The long and the short of the PDA is that agencies must ensure that their leave policies do not treat pregnancy and pregnancy-related conditions differently from other medical conditions. 29 CFR 825.702(f).

2. Comparison of PDA and FMLA

The PDA differs from the FMLA in many substantive respects. The primary difference is that the FMLA mandates a minimum amount of job-protected leave to eligible employees for certain covered conditions, including pregnancy, childbirth, and for prenatal care. The PDA, in contrast, requires employers to treat employees who are pregnant or have pregnancy-related impairments no differently than other similarly situated employees. *See Green v. New Balance Athletic Shoe, Inc.*, 182 F. Supp. 2d 128, 134-35 (D. Me. 2002). The PDA does not mandate leave or set detailed minimum requirements as does the FMLA. Such requirements are largely derived from existing agency leave policies, which the PDA does not even require an agency to have.

What follows are a few examples to illustrate the differences between the FMLA and the PDA regarding leave for pregnancy, childbirth, and pregnancy-related conditions. The facts of each case will have to be examined to determine if both the FMLA and PDA apply and, if so, which statute provides the "greater benefits" in terms of leave.

a. Eligibility

Specific differences between the PDA and the FMLA include eligibility requirements. Under the PDA, there is no formal eligibility requirement as there is under the FMLA. As such, a leave policy that complies with the FMLA may violate the PDA. An employee is protected by the PDA regardless of how long the employee has worked for the agency. All federal sector variants of the FMLA, in contrast, require at least 12 months of employment in order for the employee to be considered eligible for FMLA leave. Some federal sector variants also require for FMLA leave eligibility a minimum number of work hours and employees at the worksite of the employee requesting FMLA leave. An agency policy that denies pregnancy leave during the first year of employment, but provides leave for other medical conditions, would discriminate against pregnant women in violation of the PDA. *The Family and Medical Leave Act, the Americans with Disabilities Act, and Title VII of the Civil Rights Act of 1964* (Nov. 1995), Q&A #21. Additionally, a neutral policy that prohibits an employee from taking sick leave or short-term disability leave during the first year of employment could have a disparate impact on women and violate Title VII.

As stated by in the DOL FMLA regulations (29 CFR 825.702(f)):

> Under title VII of the Civil Rights Act of 1964, as amended by the Pregnancy Discrimination Act, an employer should provide the same benefits for women who are pregnant as the employer provides to other employees with short-term disabilities. Because Title VII does not require employees to be employed for less than 12

months by the employer (and, therefore, not an "eligible" employee under FMLA) may not be denied maternity leave if the employer normally provides short-term disability benefits to employees with the same tenure who are experiencing other short-term disabilities.

All of the federal sector variants of the FMLA require an agency to provide leave under whichever statutory provision requires the greater rights to employees. In terms of eligibility, the PDA provides the "greater benefit" as there are no minimum statutory requirements that an employee must meet in order for entitlement to the benefits and protections of the PDA to apply.

b. Excessive Absences

In stark contrast to the entitlement to 12 weeks of job-protected leave provided to eligible employees for covered conditions by the FMLA, the PDA does not require an agency to provide any job-protected leave for pregnancy or pregnancy-related conditions. The PDA only requires that agencies not treat leave for pregnancy or pregnancy-related conditions disparately than leave for similar medical conditions. Agencies, therefore, would not violate the PDA by taking disciplinary action against employees for absences caused by pregnancy or pregnancy-related conditions, provided that the agency took similar disciplinary action against non-pregnant employees who missed a comparable amount of work. *See Stout v. Baxter Healthcare Corp.*, 282 F.3d 856 (5th Cir. 2002) (PDA does not protect pregnant employee from discharge for absence from work even if absence is due to pregnancy or complications of pregnancy, unless absences of non-pregnant employees are overlooked); *Dormeyer v. Comerica Bank-Illinois et al.*, 223 F.3d 579, 583 (7th Cir. 2000) (collecting cases); *Armindo v. Padlocker, Inc.*, 209 F.3d 1319 (11th Cir. 2000) (PDA not violated by employer who fires pregnant employee for excessive absences, unless employer overlooks comparable absences of non-pregnant employees); *Troy v. Bay State Computer Group, Inc.*, 141 F.3d 378 (1st Cir. 1998) (PDA is not medical leave act, and employer would not automatically be liable for sex discrimination for discharging employee for poor attendance under standard applies to other employees, even if poor record were due to pregnancy complications).

In contrast, the FMLA prohibits an agency from using the taking of FMLA leave as a basis for disciplinary action. Where the leave at issue involves pregnancy or is pregnancy-related and is covered by both the PDA and the FMLA, the FMLA provides the "greater benefit."

c. Intermittent/Reduced Leave Schedule

Generally, an employee is entitled to take FMLA leave on an intermittent or reduced leave schedule for pregnancy, childbirth, or prenatal care, with some conditions. See Chapter 10, "Leave Amount and Scheduling." This is not necessarily the case under the PDA. Again, the PDA does not require an agency to provide leave at all for pregnancy or pregnancy-related conditions. Rather, the PDA requires that an agency provide leave for pregnancy or pregnancy-related conditions to the same extent that it provides leave for similar medical conditions. For example, in *Spina v. Management Recruiters of O'Hare*, 764 F. Supp. 519 (N.D. Ill. 1991), a pre-FMLA case, the court held that an employer did not violate the PDA when it refused to reduce the employee's work schedule from four to three days a week due to the employee's pregnancy-related health problems. In so holding, the court rejected the employee's disparate treatment argument, noting that male workers who were allowed to work reduced hours when they were having medical problems were not similarly situated. *See also Gleklen v. Democratic Congressional Campaign Committee, Inc.*, 199 F.3d 1365 (D.C. Cir. 2000) (termination of an employee who refused to work full-time schedule found not in violation of PDA or FMLA).

In these cases, the greater benefit would be under the FMLA which, if all preconditions are met, would require an agency to provide a reduced work schedule for an employee's pregnancy or pregnancy-related conditions, up to the 12 week maximum leave entitlement each leave year. How the agency treated non-pregnant employees is not relevant for purpose of FMLA entitlement to leave.

d. Return to Work

The FMLA generally requires that an eligible employee be returned to the same or an equivalent position on return from FMLA leave. See Chapter 13, "Return to Work from Leave." The PDA, in contrast, does not require an agency to return an employee to the same or an equivalent position from leave due to pregnancy or a pregnancy-related condition. Again, the PDA simply prohibits an employer from treating an employee worse than nonpregnant employees returning from leave for similar medical conditions. If an agency's policy did not require reinstatement to the same position on return from medical leave, the PDA would not require an employer to return an employee from leave due to pregnancy to the same position. *See Grayson v. Wickes Corp.*, 450 F. Supp. 1112 (N.D. Ill. 1978), *aff'd*, 607 F.2d 1194 (7th Cir. 1979); *Soreo-Yasher v. First Office Mgmt.*, 926 F. Supp. 646 (N.D. Ohio 1996) (permanent replacement of an employee not violative of PDA), *aff'd*, 129 F.3d 1265 (6th Cir. 1997). Of course, if an employer returned nonpregnant employees to their same positions on conclusion of leave but did not do the same for employees returning from maternity leave, the agency would violate the PDA. *See Garner v. Wal-Mart Stores*, 807 F.2d 1536 (11th Cir. 1987); *Communications Workers of America v. Illinois Bell Tel. Co.*, 509 F. Supp. 6 (N.D. Ill. 1980).

Where both the FMLA and the PDA apply to an employee's leave due to pregnancy, childbirth, or pregnancy related conditions, whether the FMLA or the PDA provides the "greater benefit" in terms of return to work (or other benefits) will depend on the facts of each case. If the agency's maternity leave policy does not require the placement of pregnant or nonpregnant employees in their same or an equivalent position, then the FMLA would likely provide the "greater benefit." If the agency's policy required the employee to return to work in the same position, an employer could violate the PDA by returning the employee to an equivalent position as permitted by the FMLA.

E. TITLE VII OF THE CIVIL RIGHTS ACT OF 1964

In addition to the protections afforded by the Rehabilitation Act/ADA and the PDA, the FMLA does not modify or affect any federal law prohibiting discrimination on the basis of race, religion, color, national origin, sex, age, or disability. *See* 29 USC 2651(a); 29 CFR 825.70-2(a). These would include the anti-discrimination protections of Title VII of the Civil Rights Act of 1964 (Title VII), as amended, and the Age Discrimination in Employment Act of 1973 (ADEA), as amended. 29 CFR 825.70-2(a).

Neither Title VII nor the ADEA require an agency to give employees leave. Rather, these anti-discrimination laws prohibit agencies from discriminating against employees on the basis of age, race, color, religion, sex, or national origin in terms of leave in general, including the administrative of family medical leave. The EEOC explained the protections in *Fact Sheet: The Family and Medical Leave Act, the Americans with Disabilities Act, and Title VII of the Civil Rights Act of 1964* (Nov. 1995) as follows:

> 22. Q. Does Title VII require covered employers to give employees leave to care for an ill child or family member?
>
> A. Title VII in itself does not require employers to give employees leave to care for an ill child or family member. However, Title VII prohibits covered employers from discriminating on the basis of race, color, religion, sex, or national origin when they administer family leave.
>
> For example, if an employer allowed a woman but not a man to take 12 weeks of leave to care for a newly adopted or placed child, the man would have a Title VII cause of action because the employer administered family leave in a discriminatory way based on gender.
>
> As another example, if an employer allowed a women to take [three] weeks of childcare leave in addition to leave necessary to recuperate from childbirth, but declined to permit a man to take [three] weeks of childcare leave, the man would have a Title VII cause of action because the employer administered family leave in a discriminatory way based on gender.

As discussed in Chapter 15, "Prohibited Acts, Enforcement, and Remedies," allegations of discriminatory application of FMLA leave by federal agencies in violation of Title VII has been addressed by the EEOC in a number of cases.

F. WORKERS' COMPENSATION

A "serious health condition" within the meaning of the FMLA may result from a workplace injury. As such, FMLA leave may coincide with absences covered by the Federal Employee's Compensation Act (FECA), 5 USC 8101 *et seq. See* 29 CFR §§ 825.207(d)(2) (an employee's FMLA leave entitlement may run concurrently with a workers' compensation absence when the injury is one that meets the criteria for a serious health condition), 825.702(d)(2); S. Res. 242, Cong. Rec. S3959, S3966, S3976 (April 23, 1996); 29 CFR 825.207(d)(2) (same), 825.702(d)(2); *see* DOL WH FMLA Advisory Opinion No. 42 (Aug. 23, 1994), Q&A #5. The period of time an employee is on workers' compensation status may be counted against the 12-week FMLA leave entitlement available to eligible employees, provided all other requirements of FMLA are complied with during the period of absence. DOL WH FMLA Advisory Opinion No. 42 (Aug. 23, 1994), Q&A #5. For example, as required by the FMLA, health benefits must be maintained under the same terms and conditions as if the employee continued to work. *Id.*

FECA is not a federal anti-discrimination law. Rather, FECA is an entitlement program that provides monetary compensation, medical care and assistance, vocational rehabilitation, and reemployment rights to federal employees who sustain injuries as a result of their employment with the federal government in lieu of allowing the injured employee to sue the employer in tort. Because it is not a federal anti-discrimination law, the FMLA and FECA need not be compared for purposes of determining which law in a given situation provides greater rights to employees. *See* 29 CFR 825.702(a). Rather, employees who incur a workplace injury must separately satisfy the requirements of both FECA and the FMLA in order to obtain the benefits and protections of either or both laws.

A comprehensive review of the requirements of FECA is beyond the scope of this book. What follows is a brief overview of FECA. Several areas of interaction of the FMLA with FECA are also addressed.

1. FECA

In general, FECA covers all employees and civilian officers of the government of the United States. The DOL Office of Workers' Compensation Programs administers FECA. In pertinent part, FECA benefits cover any employee workplace injury, including the aggravation of a pre-existing injury or illness. Employees generally must file an injury compensation claim within three years of the occurrence. FECA benefits include payment of all medical expenses and vocational rehabilitation costs, wage replacement based on the employee's partial or total disability, scheduled awards for permanent loss of use or bodily disfigurement, job protection, and a right to re-instatement for one-year to the same or an equivalent job as the one they held prior to disablement. After a year, the employee has the right to priority consideration in job placement.

Additional information about FECA may be found in Publication CA-810, *Injury Compensation for Federal Employees*, and in Publication CA-550, *Federal Injury Compensation: Questions and Answers About the Federal Employees' Compensation Act* (Superintendent of Documents, Government Printing Office, Washington, DC 20402).

2. FECA/FMLA Interaction

The DOL and CAA implementing regulations address several areas where the FMLA interacts with FECA as a result of a workplace injury to an employee that also constitutes a serious health condition within the meaning of the FMLA. These areas, which have been discussed in more detail in previous chapters of this book, are briefly addressed below.

a. Paid Leave Substitution

FMLA leave is generally unpaid. In contrast, absences covered by FECA are generally paid. Where FMLA leave for an employee's own serious health condition is due to a workplace injury covered by FECA, and the employee is receiving FECA wage replacement payments, the FMLA leave is, for all intents and purposes, treated as if it were paid leave. *See* 29 CFR 825.207(d)(2); S. Res. 242, Cong. Rec. S3959, S3966 (April 23, 1996); 29 CFR 825.207(d)(2) (same). As such, the paid leave substitution provisions of the FMLA do not apply. *See* 29 CFR 825.207(d)(2); S. Res. 242, Cong. Rec. S3959, S3966 (April 23, 1996); 29 CFR 825.207(d)(2). This prevents a double recovery by the employee (receipt of workers' compensation plus accrued paid leave). Once the employee's worker's compensation benefits cease, however, the paid leave substitution provisions of the FMLA may be applied. *See* 29 CFR 825.207(d)(2); S. Res. 242, Cong. Rec. S3959, S3966 (April 23, 1996); 29 CFR 825.207(d)(2). [Paid leave substitution is addressed in Chapter 11, "Substitution of Paid Leave."]

b. Maintenance of Health Benefits During FMLA Leave

The FMLA generally requires an agency to maintain group health benefits at the same levels and on the same terms and conditions during an employee's FMLA leave absence. Maintenance of health benefits on the same terms and conditions includes the requirement that employees pay their share of health care premium payments. Where an employee is receiving payments as a result of a workers' compensation injury, the employee must make arrangements with the employer for payment of group health plan benefits when simultaneously taking unpaid FMLA leave. 29 CFR 825.210(f);

S. Res. 242, Cong. Rec. S3959, S3968 (April 23, 1996); 29 CFR 825.210(f). [Maintenance of Health Benefits during FMLA leave is addressed in Chapter 12, "Maintenance of Benefits."]

c. Medical Information

As discussed in Chapter 9, "Documentation Requirements," the FMLA strictly proscribes when and what information may be obtained from an employee's health care provider. Agencies are generally not allowed to request or require additional information beyond that which is permitted by the DOL implementing regulations. Agencies are also generally prohibited from contacting the employee's health care provider without the employee's prior consent. *See* 29 CFR 825.307(a). An exception to this rule permits the employer or a representative of the employer to have direct contact with the employee's workers' compensation health care provider where an employee is on FMLA leave running concurrently with a workers' compensation absence, and the provisions of the workers' compensation statute permit such direct contact. 29 CFR 825.307(a)(1); S. Res. 242, Cong. Rec. S3959, S3973 (April 23, 1996); 29 CFR 825.307(a)(1). [FMLA limitations on employee contact with an employee's health care provider are addressed in Chapter 9, "Documentation Requirements."]

d. Light Duty

An agency may not require an employee whose absence is covered by both the FMLA and FECA to take a light duty position offered pursuant to FECA. If the employer offers such a position, the employee is permitted but not required to accept the position. 29 CFR 825.207(d)(2), 825.220(d), 825.702(d)(2); S. Res. 242, Cong. Rec. S3959, S3966, S3971, S3976 (April 23, 1996); 29 CFR 825.207(d)(2), 825.220(d), 825.702(d)(2); *see Johnson v. USPS*, Case No 1:97–CV–794, 1999 U.S. Dist. LEXIS 7981, at n.18 (W.D. Mich. May 26, 1999); DOL WH FMLA Advisory Opinion No. 75 (Nov. 14, 1995); DOL WH FMLA Advisory Opinion No. 55 (March 10, 1995); DOL WH FMLA Advisory Opinion No. 38 (July 21, 1994). If the employee declines to take the light duty position, the employee may no longer qualify for payments for workers' compensation. The employee remains, however, entitled to continue on FMLA leave until the employee is either able to return to the same or equivalent position left or until the 12-week FMLA leave entitlement is exhausted. 29 CFR 825.207(d)(2), 825.702(d)(2). 29 CFR 825.207(d)(2), 825.702(d)(2); S. Res. 242, Cong. Rec. S3959, S3966, S3976 (April 23, 1996); 29 CFR 825.207(d)(2), 825.702(d)(2); *see Johnson v. USPS*, Case No 1:97–CV–794, 1999 U.S. Dist. LEXIS 7981, at n. 18 (W.D. Mich. May 26, 1999); DOL WH FMLA Advisory Opinion No. 75 (Nov. 14, 1995); DOL WH FMLA Advisory Opinion No. 55 (March 10, 1995); DOL WH FMLA Advisory Opinion No. 38 (July 21, 1994). [Reinstatement of an employee from FMLA leave is addressed in Chapter 13, "Return to Work from Leave."]

G. FAMILY FRIENDLY LEAVE ACT

FMLA leave is generally unpaid. As discussed in Chapter 11, "Substitution of Paid Leave," accrued paid leave may be substituted for unpaid FMLA leave. The Family Friendly Leave Act, 5 USC 6301 *et seq.*, permits certain federal employees (as defined in 5 USC 2105) to use a limited amount of paid sick leave to care for a covered family member, and for purposes relating to the death of a covered family member. 5 USC 6307(d)(2). The purposes for which paid sick leave may be used to care for a covered family member under the Family Friendly Leave Act include situations that may also constitute serious health conditions entitling certain eligible federal employees (those covered by Title II of the Act) to FMLA leave. [The reader is referred to Chapter 11, "Substitution of Paid Leave," for a more detailed discussion of the interaction of the FMLA with the Family Friendly Leave Act.]

H. UNIFORMED SERVICES EMPLOYMENT AND REEMPLOYMENT RIGHTS ACT

The Department of Labor has issued a Fact Sheet (a copy of which is provided in the Appendix of this book) clarifying the affect of covered military service on an employee's eligibility for FMLA leave under Title I of the Act. Essentially, the DOL has interpreted the Uniformed Services Employment and Reemployment Rights Act (USERRA) to require employers to count active duty service toward the 12 months and 1,250 hours of service requirements for purposes of FMLA eligibility.

As discussed in Chapter 5, "Employee Eligibility for Leave," to be entitled to FMLA leave an employee must meet certain eligibility requirements. The eligibility requirements differ among the four federal sector variants of the FMLA. Two of the eligibility requirements are affected by USERRA. All of the federal sector variants of the FMLA require that the employee have worked for the employer for at least 12 months prior to the commencement of leave. In addition to that requirement, Title I, the CAA, and the PEOAA require that an employee have completed at least 1,250 hours of service (i.e. work) prior to leave commencement. For purposes of the 12 months of employment, any time the employee is on the payroll basically counts toward meeting this eligibility requirement, including leave. The 1,250-hours of service requirement, in contrast, only counts time actually spent working. Thus, time spent on leave, paid or unpaid, generally does not count toward meeting the requisite 1,250 hours of service.

The USERRA, 38 USC 4301 *et seq.*, is a federal law that provides reemployment rights for veterans and members of the National Guard and Reserve following qualifying military service. It also prohibits employer discrimination against any person on the basis of that person's past military service, current military obligations or intent to join one of the uniformed services. Pertinent to the FMLA, USERRA also provides that service members who have concluded their tours of duty and who are reemployed by their employers are entitled to all benefits of employment they would have obtained if they had remained at work.

The DOL has interpreted the entitlement to "all benefits of employment" to include the accrual of time toward FMLA entitlement. The DOL reasoned that, but for the military service, the service member would have been employed and would have worked. Along with the Fact Sheet, the DOL issued a memorandum addressing USERRA-FMLA Questions and Answers (July 25, 2002), a copy of which is set forth in the appendix to this book. In pertinent part, the USERRA-FMLA Questions and Answers provide as follows:

> 5. How should the 12-month FMLA requirement be calculated for returning service members?
>
> USERRA requires that a person reemployed under its provisions be given credit for any months he or she would have been employed *but for* the military service in determining eligibility for FMLA leave. A person reemployed following military service should be given credit for the period of military service toward the months-of-employment eligibility requirement. Each month served performing military service counts as a month actively employed by the employer. For example, someone who has been employed by an employer for [nine] months is ordered to active military service for [nine] months after which he or she is reemployed. Upon reemployment, the person must be considered to have been employed by the employer for more than the required 12 months ([nine] months actually employed plus [nine] months while serving in the military service) for purposes of FMLA eligibility. It should be noted that the 12 months of employment do not have to be consecutive to meet this FMLA requirement.
>
> 6. How should the 1,250 hours-of-service requirement be calculated for returning service members?
>
> An employee returning after military service should be credited with the hours-of-service that would have been performed *but for* the period of military service in determining FMLA eligibility. Accordingly, a person reemployed following military service has the hours that would have been worked for the employer added to any hours actually worked during the previous 12-month period to meet the 1,250 hour requirement. In order to determine the hours that would have been worked during the period of military service, the employee's pre-service work schedule can generally be used for calculations. For example, an employee who works 40 hours per week for the employer returns to employment following 20 weeks of military service and requests leave under the FMLA. To determine the person's eligibility, the hours he or she would have worked during the period of military service (29 x 40 + 800 hours) must be added to the hours actually worked during the 12-month period prior to the start of the leave to determine if the 1,250-hour requirement is met.

Because the above was issued by the DOL, it technically applies only to employees covered by Title I. Because the PEOAA does not have its own FMLA implementing regulations, but incorporates the section of Title I addressing eligibility, it is very likely that the above interpretation already applies to employees and employing offices covered by the PEOAA. For the same reason, it seems highly likely that this interpretation will also be applied to employees and employers covered by the CAA. There does not appear to be any obvious reason why this interpretation would not be picked up for employees covered by Title II.

I. DEPARTMENT OF TRANSPORTATION REQUIREMENTS

1. Title I

The Tenth Circuit in *Cooke v. C. Bean Transport, Inc.*, 72 Fed. Appx. 740 (10th Cir. 2003), addressed the interaction of the Department of Transportation (DOT) fitness requirements for commercial truck drivers and FMLA fitness–to–return–to–duty medical certification requirements. DOT regulations requiring medical examination and certification of physical ability to operate a commercial motor vehicle state that "any driver whose ability to perform his normal duties has been impaired by a physical or mental injury or disease," must be medically examined and certified prior to operating a commercial motor vehicle. 49 CFR 391.45; *see Cooke v. C. Bean Transport, Inc.*, 72 Fed. Appx. 740 (10th Cir. 2003). The purpose of the DOT physical examination is to determine whether a driver has any condition that may "affect the driver's ability to operate a commercial motor vehicle safely." 49 CFR 391.43(f). Under the FMLA, a fitness–for–duty certification "need only be a simple statement of an employee's ability to return to work." 29 CFR 825.310(c).

In *Cooke v. C. Bean Transport, Inc.*, 72 Fed. Appx. 740 (10th Cir. 2003), plaintiffs, a team of commercial truck drivers, alleged that, in violation of the FMLA, Cooke was impermissibly required to undergo an additional physical examination before his employer allowed him to return to work. The court, citing *Porter v. United States Alumoweld, Co., Inc.*, 125 F.3d 243, 247 (4th Cir. 1997) (holding that an employer does not violate the FMLA by requiring an employee to submit to an ADA–required fitness–for–duty exam), held that C. Bean's enforcement of DOT regulations by requiring Cooke to submit to a DOT physical examination did not violate the FMLA.

III. EMPLOYER PRACTICES AND COLLECTIVE BARGAINING AGREEMENTS

A. INTRODUCTION

The FMLA interacts with existing agency policies in two ways: (1) an employer may provide more generous family and medical leave benefits than the minimum required by the Act; and (2) the FMLA is affected by existing agency leave policies. Moreover, the treatment of more generous and existing agency family and medical leave act policies differs among the four federal sector variants of the FMLA.

B. TITLE I AND THE CAA

1. General Rule

Title I of the Act (29 USC 2652(a)–(b)) provides that:

> (a) More Protective. Nothing in this Act or any amendment made by this Act shall be construed to diminish the obligation of an employer to comply with any collective bargaining agreement or any employment benefit program or plan that provides greater family or medical leave rights to employees than the rights established under this Act or any amendment made by this Act.
>
> (b) Less Protective. The rights established for employees under this Act or any amendment made by this Act shall not be diminished by any collective bargaining agreement or any employment benefit program or plan.

See Fulham v. HSBC Bank USA, No. 99 Civ. 11054 (JGK), 2001 U.S. Dist. LEXIS 13570, at *26 (S.D.N.Y. Sept. 6, 2001); *Holmes v. E–Sire Communications, Inc.*, 135 F. Supp. 2d 657, 666–67 (D. Md. 2001); *Donnellan v. N.Y. City Transit Authority*, No. 98 Civ. 1096 (BSJ), 1999 U.S. Dist. LEXIS 11103, at *7, n. 5 (S.D.N.Y. July 22, 1999); DOL WH FMLA Advisory Opinion No. 103 (March 26, 1999); DOL WH FMLA Advisory Opinion No. 102 (March 26, 1999); DOL WH FMLA Advisory Opinion No. 100 (Jan. 12, 1999); DOL WH FMLA Advisory Opinion No. 97 (July 10, 1998); DOL WH FMLA Advisory Opinion No. 91 (Dec. 9, 1997); DOL WH FMLA Advisory Opinion No. 58 (April 28, 1995); DOL WH FMLA Advisory Opinion No. 33 (March 29, 1994) (§ 402 of the FMLA does not preclude a union's right to collectively bargain greater benefits than those afforded under the Act. In the instant case, the subject union could negotiate that substitution of accrued paid leave as an election of the employee *only*).

Section 403 of Title I (29 USC 2653) goes on to encourage employers to provide more generous family or medical leave policies:

> Nothing in this Act or any amendment made by this Act shall be construed to discourage employers from adopting or retaining leave policies more generous than any policies that comply with the requirements under this Act or any amendment made by this Act.

See *Ragsdale v. Wolverine World Wide, Inc.*, 535 U.S. 81, 122 S. Ct. 1155, 1164, 152 L. Ed. 2d 167 (2002); *McGregor v. AutoZone, Inc.*, 180 F.3d 1305, 1308 (11th Cir. 1999); *Ruder v. Maine General Med. Center*, 204 F. Supp. 2d 16, 2002 U.S. Dist. LEXIS 8564, at *11 (D. Me. May 10, 2002); *Chan v. Loyola U. Med. Center*, No. 97 C 3170, 1999 U.S. Dist. LEXIS 18456, at *13, n. 5 N.D. Ill. Nov. 23, 1999); *Covey v. Methodist Hosp. of Dyersburg, Inc.*, 56 F. Supp. 2d 965, 970 (W.D. Tenn. 1999); *Barron v. Runyon*, 11 F. Supp. 2d 676, 679 (D. Va. 1998); *Santos v. Shields Health Group*, 996 F. Supp. 87, 93 (D. Mass. 1998); *Kruse v. LaGuardia Hospital*, No. 95–CV–4467 (JG), 1996 U.S. Dist. LEXIS 22433, at *6 (E.D.N.Y. Nov. 7, 1996); DOL WH FMLA Advisory Opinion No. 81 (June 18, 1996); *McKiernan v. Smith–Edwards–Dunlap Co. et al.*, No. 95–1175, 1995 U.S. Dist. LEXIS 6822, at *6 (E.D. Pa. May 17, 1995); DOL WH FMLA Advisory Opinion No. 43 (Aug. 24, 1994).

Sections 402 and 403 of Title I, 29 USC 2952, 2653, are not sections incorporated by reference into the CAA for purposes of the FMLA. *See* 2 USC 1312(a)(1), (b) (CAA). However, the requirement that employing offices covered by the CAA must observe any collective bargaining agreement or employment benefit program or plan that provides greater rights than those established by the FMLA and, conversely, may not diminish FMLA rights, is set forth in the regulations implementing the FMLA for the CAA. *See* S. Res. 242, Cong. Rec. S3959, S3976 (April 23, 1996); 29 CFR 825.700(a).

The statutory requirements are further clarified in the DOL and CAA regulations implementing the FMLA. 29 CFR 825.700(a); S. Res. 242, Cong. Rec. S3959, S3976 (April 23, 1996); 29 CFR 825.700(a).

2. Greater Family or Medical Leave Benefits

Neither the Statute nor the legislative history describe or otherwise explain what is meant by "greater family or medical leave rights." The DOL and CAA regulations implementing the FMLA, however, provide additional (although by no means overwhelming) clarification on this issue. In pertinent part, the regulations (29 CFR 825.700(a); S. Res. 242, Cong. Rec. S3959, S3976 (April 23, 1996); 29 CFR 825.700(a)) provide:

> An employer must observe any employment benefit program or plan that provides greater family or medical leave rights to employees than the rights established by the FMLA.
>
> ****
>
> If an employer provides greater leave rights than are afforded by FMLA, the employee is not required to extend additional rights afforded by FMLA, such as maintenance of health benefits (other than through COBRA), to the additional leave period not covered by FMLA.

See DOL WH FMLA Advisory Opinion No. 915 (Dec. 9, 1997).

The CAA uses the term "employing office" instead of "employer." It also adds to the parenthetical reference to COBRA the phrase "or 5 USC 8905a, whichever is applicable." S. Res. 242, Cong. Rec. S3959, S3976 (April 23, 1996); 29 CFR 825.700(a).

Comments accompanying the publication of the final DOL regulations implementing Title I add further insight. The comments (Preamble, 29 CFR 825.700) noted the following question and answer:

> [W]hether "more generous" family or medical leave provided pursuant to contract or an employer policy may be counted against an employee's 12–week FMLA leave entitlement under circumstances where either the employees would not yet be eligible for FMLA leave, or the leave is for a reason that does not qualify as FMLA leave (e.g. employers adopt leave policies that mirror FMLA but relax eligibility requirements or the definition of serious health condition, or expand the "family member" definition to include in–laws and domestic partners). To reduce the incentive for employers to eliminate "more generous" policies, these commenter's contend that DOL should allow employers to count such leave towards FMLA leave entitlements.

The DOL responded to the question (Preamble, 29 CFR 825.700) as follows:

> Leave granted under circumstances that do not meet FMLA's coverage, eligibility, or specified reasons for FMLA–

qualifying leave may not be counted against FMLA's 12-week entitlement. However, employers may designate paid leave as FMLA leave and offset the maximum entitlement under the employer's more generous policies to the extent the leave qualifies as FMLA leave.

In the example given, "more generous" is defined as meaning outside the basic requirements of the Act. For example, an agency policy that permitted family or medical leave for the serious health condition of a brother or sister would be "more generous" than the FMLA as it would permit leave in circumstances wholly outside of the benefits and protections of the FMLA. Similarly, a policy that lowered the eligibility requirement for FMLA leave from 1,250 hours of work to 800 hours would be "more generous" as any leave taken prior to the employee's reaching the statutory 1,250 hours of eligibility requirement would fall wholly outside of the benefits and protections of the Act. *See also Barron v. Runyon*, 11 F. Supp. 2d 676, 679 (D. Va. 1998) (USPS policy applying FMLA benefits before effective date of Act more generous policy).

By falling wholly outside the benefits and protections of the Act, the leave taken is not covered by the FMLA. As such, it may not be counted against an eligible employee's 12-week FMLA leave entitlement. Nor do other benefits and protections required by the FMLA leave, such as maintenance of health benefits, extend (as a matter of law pursuant to 29 USC 2652(a) and 29 CFR 825.700(a)) to family or medical leave that falls wholly outside of the FMLA. Rather, such leave is a creature of agency policy, and the benefits and protections afforded by that policy apply, not the FMLA. If the agency policy did not, for example, protect such leave from counting as a negative factor for purposes of discipline, then such leave could count against the employee. *See* DOL WH FMLA Advisory Opinion No. 91 (Dec. 9, 1997) (the employer permitted to provide more than 12 weeks of family or medical leave. Where an employer by policy annually provides 14 weeks of family or medical leave, employer would be *obligated under its own leave policies* to extend benefits for 14 weeks). *See* DOL WH FMLA Advisory Opinion No. 103 (March 26, 1999) (same, involving an employer's policy allowing up to 52 weeks of leave).

Similarly, an employee does not have a cause of action under the FMLA (§ 825.700) for employer violation of the provisions of an employer's more generous family or medical leave provisions. In *Fulham v. HSBC Bank USA*, No. 99 Civ. 11054 (JGK), 2001 U.S. Dist. LEXIS 13570, at *26 (S.D.N.Y. Sept. 6, 2001) (*quoting Rich v. Delta Air Lines, Inc.*, 921 F. Supp. 767, 773–74 (N.D. Ga. 1996)), the court explained:

> The purpose of this regulation [29 C.F.R. § 825.700(a)] is to ensure that the FMLA is not interpreted to abrogate any currently existing employee benefit plan. Therefore, if an employer has a plan or program more generous than the FMLA, than the FMLA will not supersede or reduce those more generous benefits, which the employer has chosen to provide. In essence, the regulation is merely a truism that emphasizes that employers are legally bound by valid contractual agreements made with their employees regarding employment benefits. An employer's contractual obligations are distinct, however, from the regulation at issue and the FMLA itself.

See Devine v. Prudential Ins. Co. of America, No. 03-3971 (FLW), 21, 22, 23, 24, 25, 2007 U.S. Dist. LEXIS 46856, at *83-86 (D. N.J. June 28, 2007), *Willi v. American Airlines, Inc.*, No. 4:05-CV-453-Y, 2007 U.S. Dist. LEXIS 41429, at *10 (N.D. Tex. June 7, 2007); *Panto v. Palmer Dialysis Center/Total Renal Care*, No. 01–6013, 2003 U.S. Dist. LEXIS 5663, at *20 (E.D. Pa. April 7, 2003); *Green v. New Balance Athletic Shoe, Inc.*, 182 F. Supp. 2d 128, 135 (D. Me. 2002). *Holmes v. E–Spire Communications, Inc.*, 135 F. Supp. 2d 657, 666–67 (D. Md. 2001); *Covey v. Methodist Hosp. of Dyersburg, Inc.*, 56 F. Supp. 2d 965, 971–72 (W.D. Tenn. 1999); *Barron v. Runyon*, 11 F. Supp. 2d 676, 679 (D. Va. 1998); *Pert v. Value RX*, No. 96-73153, 1996 U.S. Dist. LEXIS 17748, at *2 (E.D. Mich. Oct. 9, 1996),

In *Panto v. Palmer Dialysis Center/Total Renal Care*, No. 01–6013, 2003 U.S. Dist. LEXIS 5663, at *20 (E.D. Pa. April 7, 2003), company policy provided that leaves of absence would be administered in compliance with the FMLA. The policy further provided that an employee's qualified leave of absence, upon approval, may be extended for an additional three months (not to exceed a total of six months). The employee argued that defendant was estopped from asserting that Panto's leave was confined to 12 weeks because defendant's policy allowed for up to six months of medical leave under the FMLA. The court disagreed. The court found that, although the employer's policy contemplated an additional three months of "qualified leave of absence," any such leave beyond 12 weeks was not covered by the FMLA, and the FMLA does not create a federal cause of action to enforce voluntary employer policies providing benefits that exceed those required by the FMLA.

In *Devine v. Prudential Ins. Co. of America*, No. 03-3971 (FLW), 21, 22, 23, 24, 25, 2007 U.S. Dist. LEXIS 46856, at *83-86 (D.N.J. June 28, 2007), the court rejected the argument that the employer violated the FMLA when it failed to return the employee to her same or an equivalent position where she was out in excess of 12 weeks (nearly 5 months) pursuant to the employer's more generous leave program. The court agreed with the opinion of the court in *Pert v. Value RX*, No. 96-73153, 1996 U.S. Dist. LEXIS 17748, at *2 (E.D. Mich. Oct. 9, 1996), that the FMLA requirement that the FMLA does not diminish an employer's obligation to comply with more generous family or medical leave benefits did not give an employee a cause of action under the FMLA for violation of contractual benefits in excess of those required by the FMLA.

In *Willi v. American Airlines, Inc.*, No. 4:05-CV-453-Y, 2007 U.S. Dist. LEXIS 41429, at *10 (N.D. Tex. June 7, 2007), the court rejected the argument that employees who did not meet the eligibility requirements of the FMLA could bring a cause of action for violation of the FMLA where the employer's policy extended family and medical leave benefits to non-eligible employees. The court opined that "the fact that American established a policy that defined employee-leave rights more generously than the FMLA does not create an FMLA cause of action."

The lesson here, particularly for employees and organizations that represent the interests of employees, is that obtaining more generous family or medical leave benefits pursuant to agency policy or the terms of a collective bargaining agreement does not affect FMLA coverage. FMLA coverage is dictated by statute, as interpreted by valid implementing regulations. Only Congress can formally broaden the FMLA's reach by, for example, lowering the eligibility requirements. Agency policy or the terms of a collective bargaining agreement cannot broaden the reach of the FMLA. Rather, the FMLA permits an agency to provide more generous family or medical leave benefits as a matter of agency policy. As such, a violation of a more generous agency policy would generally not constitute grounds for a claim of interference or discrimination within the meaning of the FMLA in violation of 29 USC 2652(a) and 29 CFR 825.700(a). *See Barron v. Runyon*, 11 F. Supp. 2d 676, 679 (D. Va. 1998) (USPS policy adopting FMLA provisions before Act became effective for the agency granted more generous leave benefits as a matter of policy, but did not change legally effective date of FMLA to the agency).

Of course, there is nothing preventing an agency from applying the benefits and protections of the FMLA to its more generous family or medical leave policy. In that case, the agency would be bound by the requirements of the FMLA even as to the more generous family or medical leave policies, but only as a matter of policy. An aggrieved employee would not be able to sue an employer for a violation of the FMLA where the more generous policy is not formally covered by the FMLA. The employee would, however, be able to allege violations of agency policy, and enforce the same by the means generally available for violations of agency leave policies.

Examples of more generous leave provisions have included reinstatement rights to employees who are unable to perform all essential job functions at the end of their 12 weeks of job–protected FMLA leave and partial pay pursuant to an employer's short–term disability plan. *See* DOL WH FMLA Advisory Opinion No. 97 (July 10, 1998) (more generous employer return to work policy); DOL WH FMLA Advisory Opinion No. 43 (Aug. 24, 1994) (the DOL example of a "more generous" benefit employer short–term disability leave plan that included partial pay).

3. Less Protection

The FMLA sets the minimum requirements covered employers must meet to be in compliance with the law. It is, therefore, no surprise that the Act (Title I, anyway) and the implementing regulations (Title I and the CAA) prohibit the diminution of the minimum FMLA leave rights and protections by agency policy or the terms of a collective bargaining agreement. 29 USC 2652(b); 29 CFR 825.700(a); S. Res. 242, Cong. Rec. S3959, S3976 (April 23, 1996); 29 CFR 825.700(a); *see Marrero v. Camden County Bd. of Social Services et al.*, 164 F. Supp. 2d 455, 463–64 (D.N.J. 2001) ("Simply put, where an employer's internal policies conflict with the provisions of the FMLA, the FMLA controls and an employee need only comply with the requirements of the Act to invoke its protections."); *Conroy v. Township of Lower Merion et al.*, No. 00–CV–3528, 2001 U.S. Dist. LEXIS 11460, at *7 (E.D. Pa. Aug. 7, 2001); *Donnellan v. N.Y. City Transit Authority*, No. 98 Civ. 1096 (BSJ), 1999 U.S. Dist. LEXIS 11103, at *8, n. 5 (S.D.N.Y. July 22, 1999); *George v. Associated Stationers et al.*, 932 F. Supp. 1012, 1017 (N.D. Ohio 1996); *Reich v. Midwest Plastic Engineering, Inc.*, No. 1:94–CV–525, 1995 U.S. Dist. LEXIS 8772, at *12 (W.D. Mich. June 6, 1995); *McKiernan v. Smith–Edwards–Dunlap Co.*, No. 95–1175, 1995 U.S. Dist. LEXIS 6822, at *12 (E.D. Pa. May 17, 1995); *Alaska Airlines, Inc. et al., v. Oregon Bureau of Labor et al.*, 884 F. Supp. 393, 396 (D. Ore. March 13, 1995), *aff'd*, 122 F.3d 812 (9th Cir. 1997).

For example, a provision of a collective bargaining agreement that provides for reinstatement to a position that is not equivalent because of seniority (e.g. provides lesser pay) is superseded by the FMLA. S. Res. 242, Cong. Rec. S3959, S3976 (April 23, 1996); 29 CFR 825.700(a). Generally, neither employees nor collective bargaining representatives can waive employee FMLA rights. 29 CFR 825.220(d); S. Res. 242, Cong. Rec. S3959, S3971 (April 23, 1996); 29 CFR 825.220(d); *see also Marrero v. Camden County Bd. of Social Services et al.*, 164 F. Supp. 2d 455, 463–64 (D. N.J. 2001) (the employer's policy and collective bargaining agreement that required an employee to provide medical certification where leave exceeded five days held invalid as it conflicted with FMLA requirement that the employer request certification and allow the employee 15 calendar days in which to comply).

The minimum requirements of the FMLA are set forth in Title I and the CAA, and more particularly in the regulations implementing those statutes. As addressed more fully in Chapter 15, "Prohibited Acts, Enforcement, and Remedies," any violation of the Act or of the implementing regulations constitutes interfering with, restraining, or denying the exercise of rights provided by the FMLA. 29 CFR 825.220(b); S. Res. 242, Cong. Rec. S3959, S3976 (April 23, 1996); 29 CFR 825.220(b).

4. Modifications to Employee Family or Medical Leave Benefits

The FMLA does not prohibit a covered employer or employing office within the meaning of Title I and the CAA from amending existing leave and employee benefit programs, provided it complies with the FMLA. 29 CFR 825.700(b); S. Res. 242, Cong. Rec. S3959, S3976 (April 23, 1996); 29 CFR 825.700(a); *see* DOL WH FMLA Advisory Opinion No. 58 (April 28, 1995). Covered employers are, therefore, permitted to adopt more generous family or medical leave policies. Conversely, they are also permitted to modify or get rid of more generous policies, provided that whatever policy is ultimately adopted meets the minimum requirements of the FMLA. *See* DOL WH FMLA Advisory Opinion No. 5 (Sept. 27, 1993).

Of course, the FMLA regulations do not supplant an agency's obligation to abide by other legal or contractual requirements governing changes in terms and conditions of federal employment. For example, where an agency is a party to a collective bargaining agreement with a union, changes to terms and conditions of employment involving employee leave and benefit plans generally must be bargained with the union before they are implemented. *See* DOL WH FMLA Advisory Opinion No. 58 (April 28, 1995) (where "collective bargaining agreement does not have a return to work certification procedure, employer may implement such a procedure *provided* that it complies with FMLA and, *provided further*, that implementation of the procedure complies with all applicable requirements under Federal and State law (including the National Labor Relations Act)").

5. Existing Family and Medical Leave Act Policies

Agency leave polices greatly impact the rights and benefits of the afforded by the FMLA. The regulations implementing the FMLA require the existence of certain agency leave policies before FMLA rights may be exercised. For example, the ability of an agency to condition an employee's return to work from FMLA leave on submission of a fitness–for–duty medical certification is premised on the existence of a uniformly–applied policy or practice that requires all similarly–situated employees who take leave for such conditions to obtain and present such a certification. *See* 29 CFR 2614(a)(4); 29 CFR 825.310(a). Return to work medical certifications are discussed in Chapters 9, "Documentation Requirements," and 13, "Return to Work from Leave." Absent such a uniformly applied policy or practice, an FMLA employer would not be able to exercise the FMLA right to require a return–to–work fitness–for–duty medical certification. The ability of an agency to take disciplinary action against an employee for substance abuse is also conditioned on the existence of an agency policy permitting same. *See* 29 CFR 825.112(g).

Other FMLA regulations have built a certain amount of flexibility into the requirements of the Act (Title I, the CAA, and the PEOAA) to apply employer leave and attendance policies. Generally, this flex lowers the bar for an employee to meet the requirements of the Act. For example, the FMLA requires an employee to provide advance notice of a need for FMLA leave depending on whether the need for leave is foreseeable. See Chapter 8, "Notice Requirements." An Agency's paid and unpaid leave polices may, however, lower the amount of advance notice of a need for FMLA leave an employee is required to provide. The implementing regulations prohibit an employer from requiring an employee to meet the stricter FMLA notice requirements where the agency's leave policy or the terms of a collective bargaining agreement allow less advance notice to the employer. 29 CFR 825.302(g). For example, if an employee or employer elects to substitute paid vacation leave for unpaid FMLA leave, and the employer's paid vacation leave plan imposes no prior notification requirements for taking vacation leave, no advance notice may be required for FMLA leave taken in these circumstances. 29 CFR 825.302(g).

The FMLA implementing regulations also occasionally allow agency policies to increase the minimum FMLA requirements. In our previous example of a return–to–work fitness for duty medical certification, generally such certifications may only be a simple statement of an employee's ability to return to work. 29 CFR 825.310(c). However, if the terms of a collective bargaining agreement govern an employee's return to work, those provisions apply. 29 CFR 825.310(b). The DOL has interpreted that regulation to permit an agency to require returning employees to submit to a fitness-for-duty medical evaluation and provide a far more detailed medical certification of the employee's fitness to return to duty from FMLA leave, where such is required by the terms of a governing collective bargaining agreement. *See* DOL WH FMLA Advisory Opinion No. 113 (Sept. 11, 2000).

Federal sector FMLA employers, unions, employee associations and employees need to be aware that agency leave policies may impact FMLA requirements. As such, agency leave policies need to be closely scrutinized against the minimum FMLA leave requirements in order to determine if lower or higher agency leave policies affect FMLA rights, or whether agency policies have been superseded by the minimum requirements of the FMLA. Knowing where agency leave policies add flexibility to the FMLA requirements also allows agencies, union, and employee associations to craft FMLA leave policies that are more beneficial to their interests.

6. Collective Bargaining Agreements

The terms of collective bargaining agreements clearly form part of an agency's policies. That notwithstanding, the interaction of the terms of collective bargaining agreements with the FMLA is separately mentioned in some of the statutes and implementing regulations at several points. The following briefly addresses FMLA regulations in addition to the regulations addressing more or less generous family or medical leave benefits discussed above.

a. Effective Date of the FMLA

The existence of a collective bargaining agreement initially delayed application of Title I of the FMLA to covered employers. Title I of the FMLA generally became effective for employers on August 5, 1993. For employers with collective bargaining agreements in effect on August 5, 1993, the Act did not become effective until February 5, 1994. *See* 29 USC 825.102(a), 825.700(c)(1).

b. Intermittent Leave and Employee Transfers

Where an eligible employee requires FMLA leave on an intermittent or reduced leave schedule basis, an employer is permitted to transfer the employee to an available alternative position that better accommodates the employee's need for recurring leave. 29 CFR 825.204(a); S. Res. 242, Cong. Rec. S3959, S3964 (April 23, 1996); 29 CFR 825.204(a). Such transfers "may require compliance with any applicable collective bargaining agreement." 29 CFR 825.204(b); S. Res. 242, Cong. Rec. S3959, S3964 (April 23, 1996); 29 CFR 825.204(b).

c. Multi-Employer Health Plans

The requirement that an employer continue health benefits during the pendency of an employee's FMLA leave absence includes benefits provided pursuant to multi-employer health plans. Title I and the CAA define a multi-employer health plan as a plan to which more than one employer is required to contribute, and which is maintained pursuant to one or more collective bargaining agreement(s) between employee organization(s) and the employers. 29 CFR 825.211(a); S. Res. 242, Cong. Rec. S3959, S3968 (April 23, 1996); 29 CFR 825.211(a). Special FMLA requirements are attached to maintenance of health benefits pursuant to such collectively bargained, multi-employer health plans. See Chapter 12, "Maintenance of Benefits."

d. Reinstatement of Laid-Off Employees

Generally, an employee has no greater right to reinstatement or to other benefits and conditions of employment than if the employee had been continuously employed during the FMLA leave period. 29 CFR 825.216(a); S. Res. 242, Cong. Rec. S3959, S3969 (April 23, 1996); 29 CFR 825.216(a). If an employee is laid off during the course of taking FMLA leave and employment is terminated, the employer's responsibility to continue FMLA leave, maintain group health plan benefits and restore the employee cease at the time the employee is laid off, unless the employer has continuing obligations under a collective bargaining agreement or otherwise. 29 CFR 825.216(a)(1); S. Res. 242, Cong. Rec. S3959, S3969 (April 23, 1996); 29 CFR 825.216(a)(1).

e. Waiver of Rights

The FMLA specifically prohibits the collective bargaining representative of an employee from waiving his or her FMLA rights as a "trade off" for other benefits. 29 CFR 825.220(d); S. Res. 242, Cong. Rec. S3959, S3971 (April 23, 1996); 29 CFR 825.220(d). *See Faris v. Williams WPC–I, Inc. et al.,* 332 F.3d 316, 320 (5th Cir. 2003). [Waiver of FMLA rights is addressed in Chapter 15, "Prohibited Acts, Enforcement, and Remedies."]

f. Medical Certification

The terms of a collective bargaining agreement govern an employee's return to work from leave. 29 CFR 825.310(b); S. Res. 242, Cong. Rec. S3959, S3974 (April 23, 1996); 29 CFR 825.310(b).

g. Special School Rules

The restoration of an instructional employee to an equivalent position on return to FMLA leave may be made on the basis of "established school policies and practices, and collective bargaining agreements." 29 CFR 825.604; S. Res. 242, Cong. Rec. S3959, S3975 (April 23, 1996); 29 CFR 825.604. *See* DOL WH FMLA Advisory Opinion No. 80 (April 24, 1996).

C. PEOAA

Section 402 of the Title I, 29 USC 2952, is not one of the sections incorporated by reference into the PEOAA for purposes of the FMLA, 3 USC 412(a)(1), (b) (PEOAA). Nor have regulations been adopted by the President or the designee of the President to implement the FMLA for purposes of the PEOAA. Because the PEOAA does not adopt § 402 of Title the FMLA, and in the absence of its own implementing regulations, it is unclear whether the PEOAA FMLA permits an employing office to provide (as a matter of policy) more generous family or medical leave benefits than the minimum required by the FMLA. Similarly, even if the PEOAA FMLA allows an employing office to provide more generous family or medical leave polices than are required by the Act, it is unclear whether such policies would be covered by the FMLA or not. Again, the absence of implementing regulations addressing the affect of more generous family or medical leave provisions similar to those provided by the DOL and CAA is the cause of such confusion.

Notwithstanding the absence of guidance by the PEOAA, it is likely that the MSPB and courts interpreting the FMLA for purposes of the PEOAA will apply the Title I and/or CAA FMLA regulations addressing more generous employer family or medical leave benefits. The PEOAA provides that, in the absence of its own implementing regulations, the MSPB or courts must apply, "to the extent necessary and appropriate, the most relevant substantive executive agency regulation promulgated to implement the statutory provision at issue in the proceeding." 3 USC 455; 28 USC 3903. One could interpret such language as permitting the MSPB or the court to apply § 402 of Title I and/or § 825.700(a) of the DOL or CAA regulations where the issue involved the affect of more generous family or medical leave benefits pursuant to the policy of a PEOAA employing office with the minimum requirements of the FMLA.

Finally, given the incorporation into the PEOAA of specified sections of Title I of the FMLA, it would appear clear that providing less family or medical leave benefits than the minimum required by those incorporated sections of Title I of the FMLA, as clarified by the DOL implementing regulations and as interpreted by the courts, would appear to violate the FMLA. The absence of incorporation of § 402(b) of the Title I (29 USC 2652(b)), therefore, would not allow PEOAA employing offices to provide by policy less FMLA protection than afforded by the incorporated Act.

D. TITLE II

In most respects, Title II follows the lead of Title I when it comes to agency policies or practices providing more or less generous family or medical leave benefits.

1. General Rule

Title II of the FMLA does not address an agency's adoption of more generous family and medical leave benefits than the minimum required by the Act. The OPM regulations (5 CFR 630.1210(a)), however, do provide that:

> An agency shall comply with any collective bargaining agreement or any agency employment benefit program or plan that provides greater family or medical leave than those provided under this subpart.

An exception to that general rule, it prohibits agencies from adopting leave policies more generous than those provided by the FMLA, except that such policies may not provide entitlement to paid time off in an amount greater than that otherwise authorized by law or provide sick leave in any situation in which sick leave would not normally be allowed by law or regulation. 5 CFR 630.1210(c).

The OPM regulations do not define or otherwise illustrate what it means by "more generous" family or medical leave benefits. Nor do the OPM regulations define or otherwise address the affect that the adoption of more generous family or leave benefits has on the FMLA. Unlike the DOL, the comments to the final OPM regulations do not provide examples that demonstrate whether Title II of the FMLA covers these more generous family or medical leave policies, or whether, like Title I, these more generous leave policies are only covered by agency policy. That is, an employee aggrieved by a violation of a more generous family or medical leave policy would only be able to grieve a violation of the policy, not a violation of the FMLA. Presumably, like Title I, an employee aggrieved by an agency violation of a more generous family or medical leave policy would not be able to allege a violation of § 630.1210(a) of Title II, but would be limited to grieving violation of agency policy.

2. Less Generous

The OPM regulations prohibit an agency from diminishing FMLA entitlements by any employment benefit program or plan, or by any collective bargaining agreement. 5 CFR 630.1210(b). No further explanation is provided to illustrate the operation of this regulation. Presumably, an agency policy that provides less family or medical leave benefits under circumstances covered by the FMLA would be in violation of this prohibition.

3. Amendments

Agencies with employees covered by Title II are not prevented from amending their family or medical leave policies, provided the policies comply with the requirements of this Subpart. 5 CFR 630.1210(a). Presumably, that means that agencies can amend their family or medical leave polices in any way as long as the minimum requirements of the FMLA are met. For example, an agency whose existing policy simply mirrors the minimum requirements of the FMLA could provide more generous family or medical leave benefits. Conversely, an agency with exceedingly generous family or medical leave policies could degrade those policies, provided that what remains meets the minimum requirements of the FMLA.

Finally, there is nothing in the OPM regulations to suggest that agencies are relieved of their responsibilities to amend existing agency family or medical leave policies in accordance with the usual legal and collective bargaining agreement requirements for amending agency leave policies. For example, agencies generally are required to bargain with appropriate collective bargaining unit representatives over changes in terms and conditions of employment affecting bargaining unit employees before implementing such changes.

4. Existing Family and Medical Leave Act Policies

As discussed above regarding Title I and the CAA, agency leave policies, including the terms of collective bargaining agreements, affect the operation of Title II of the FMLA. The presence of agency policies is required in some instances in order for certain FMLA rights to apply. For example, for an agency to have the authority to require an employee returning from FMLA leave to submit a fitness–for–duty medical certification, the agency must first have a uniformly applied policy or practice requiring same under similar circumstances. 5 USC 6384(d); 5 CFR 630.1208(h). An agency's "usual and customary" policies that are less burdensome than the requirements may also apply for employee notification of the need for FMLA leave. 5 CFR 630.1206(e). As such, agencies and employees must carefully review the Title II requirements to determine the interaction of agency leave policies with the requirements of the FMLA.

5. Collective Bargaining Agreements

Other than diminution of FMLA benefits, neither Title II nor the OPM implementing regulations specifically address the interaction of the FMLA with collective bargaining agreements. It is, therefore, unclear how Title II interacts with the terms of collective bargaining agreements in situations comparable to those identified above for Title I, the PEOAA, and the CAA. Presumably, the terms of collective bargaining agreements will be treated the same as agency policies in terms of interaction with Title II of the FMLA.

APPENDIX

WH Publication 1420: Your Rights Under the Family and Meidcal Leave Act of 1993 783

WH-381: Employer Response to Employee Request for Family or Medical Leave 785

DOL USERRA-FMLA July 22, 2002 Memorandum 787

DOL USERRA-FMLA Questions and Answers 791

Your Rights
under the
Family and Medical Leave Act of 1993

FMLA requires covered employers to provide up to 12 weeks of unpaid, job-protected leave to "eligible" employees for certain family and medical reasons. Employees are eligible if they have worked for their employer for at least one year, and for 1,250 hours over the previous 12 months, and if there are at least 50 employees within 75 miles. The FMLA permits employees to take leave on an intermittent basis or to work a reduced schedule under certain circumstances.

Reasons for Taking Leave:

Unpaid leave must be granted for *any* of the following reasons:
- to care for the employee's child after birth, or placement for adoption or foster care;
- to care for the employee's spouse, son or daughter, or parent who has a serious health condition; or
- for a serious health condition that makes the employee unable to perform the employee's job.

At the employee's or employer's option, certain kinds of *paid* leave may be substituted for unpaid leave.

Advance Notice and Medical Certification:

The employee may be required to provide advance leave notice and medical certification. Taking of leave may be denied if requirements are not met.
- The employee ordinarily must provide 30 days advance notice when the leave is "foreseeable."
- An employer may require medical certification to support a request for leave because of a serious health condition, and may require second or third opinions (at the employer's expense) and a fitness for duty report to return to work.

Job Benefits and Protection:

- For the duration of FMLA leave, the employer must maintain the employee's health coverage under any "group health plan."
- Upon return from FMLA leave, most employees must be restored to their original or equivalent positions with equivalent pay, benefits, and other employment terms.
- The use of FMLA leave cannot result in the loss of any employment benefit that accrued prior to the start of an employee's leave.

Unlawful Acts by Employers:

FMLA makes it unlawful for any employer to:
- interfere with, restrain, or deny the exercise of any right provided under FMLA:
- discharge or discriminate against any person for opposing any practice made unlawful by FMLA or for involvement in any proceeding under or relating to FMLA.

Enforcement:

- The U.S. Department of Labor is authorized to investigate and resolve complaints of violations.
- An eligible employee may bring a civil action against an employer for violations.

FMLA does not affect any Federal or State law prohibiting discrimination, or supersede any State or local law or collective bargaining agreement which provides greater family or medical leave rights.

For Additional Information:

If you have access to the Internet visit our FMLA website: **http://www.dol.gov/esa/whd/fmla.** To locate your nearest Wage-Hour Office, telephone our Wage-Hour toll-free information and help line at 1-866-4USWAGE (1-866-487-9243): a customer service representative is available to assist you with referral information from 8am to 5pm **in your time zone;** or log onto our Home Page at **http://www.wagehour.dol.gov.**

U.S. Department of Labor
Employment Standards Administration
Wage and Hour Division
Washington, D.C. 20210

WH Publication 1420
Revised August 2001

*U.S. GOVERNMENT PRINTING OFFICE 2001-476-344/49051

Employer Response to Employee
Request for Family or Medical Leave
(Optional Use Form -- See 29 CFR § 825.301)

U.S. Department of Labor
Employment Standards Administration
Wage and Hour Division

(Family and Medical Leave Act of 1993)

OMB No. : 1215-0181
Expires : 08-31-07

Date: _____

To: _____
(Employee's Name)

From: _____
(Name of Appropriate Employer Representative)

Subject: REQUEST FOR FAMILY/MEDICAL LEAVE

On _____ , you notified us of your need to take family/medical leave due to:
       (Date)

☐ The birth of a child, or the placement of a child with you for adoption or foster care; or

☐ A serious health condition that makes you unable to perform the essential functions for your job: or

☐ A serious health condition affecting your ☐ spouse, ☐ child, ☐ parent, for which you are needed to provide care.

You notified us that you need this leave beginning on _____ and that you expect
                                                              (Date)
leave to continue until on or about _____ .
                                            (Date)

Except as explained below, you have a right under the FMLA for up to 12 weeks of unpaid leave in a 12-month period for the reasons listed above. Also, your health benefits must be maintained during any period of unpaid leave under the same conditions as if you continued to work, and you must be reinstated to the same or an equivalent job with the same pay, benefits, and terms and conditions of employment on your return from leave. If you do not return to work following FMLA leave for a reason other than: (1) the continuation, recurrence, or onset of a serious health condition which would entitle you to FMLA leave; or (2) other circumstances beyond your control, you may be required to reimburse us for our share of health insurance premiums paid on your behalf during your FMLA leave.

This is to inform you that: *(check appropriate boxes; explain where indicated)*

1. You are ☐ eligible ☐ not eligible for leave under the FMLA.

2. The requested leave ☐ will ☐ will not be counted against your annual FMLA leave entitlement.

3. You ☐ will ☐ will not be required to furnish medical certification of a serious health condition. If required, you must furnish certification by _____ *(insert date)* (must be at least 15 days after you are notified of this requirement), or we may delay the commencement of your leave until the certification is submitted.

4. You may elect to substitute accrued paid leave for unpaid FMLA leave. We ☐ will ☐ will not require that you substitute accrued paid leave for unpaid FMLA leave. If paid leave will be used, the following conditions will apply: *(Explain)*

Form WH-381
Rev. June 1997

5. (a) If you normally pay a portion of the premiums for your health insurance, these payments will continue during the period of FMLA leave. Arrangements for payment have been discussed with you, and it is agreed that you will make premium payments as follows: *(Set forth dates, e.g., the 10th of each month, or pay periods, etc. that specifically cover the agreement with the employee.)*

   (b) You have a minimum 30-day *(or, indicate longer period, if applicable)* grace period in which to make premium payments. If payment is not made timely, your group health insurance may be cancelled, *provided* we notify you in writing at least 15 days before the date that your health coverage will lapse, or, at our option, we may pay your share of the premiums during FMLA leave, and recover these payments from you upon your return to work. We ☐ will ☐ will not pay your share of health insurance premiums while you are on leave.

   (c) We ☐ will ☐ will not do the same with other benefits (*e.g.*, life insurance, disability insurance, etc.) while you are on FMLA leave. If we do pay your premiums for other benefits, when you return from leave you ☐ will ☐ will not be expected to reimburse us for the payments made on your behalf.

6. You ☐ will ☐ will not be required to present a fitness-for-duty certificate prior to being restored to employment. If such certification is required but not received, your return to work may be delayed until certification is provided.

7. (a) You ☐ are ☐ are not a "key employee" as described in § 825.217 of the FMLA regulations. If you are a "key employee:" restoration to employment may be denied following FMLA leave on the grounds that such restoration will cause substantial and grievous economic injury to us as discussed in § 825.218.

   (b) We ☐ have ☐ have not determined that restoring you to employment at the conclusion of FMLA leave will cause substantial and grievous economic harm to *us*. *(Explain (a) and/or (b) below. See §825.219 of the FMLA regulations.)*

8. While on leave, you ☐ will ☐ will not be required to furnish us with periodic reports every _____ _____ *(indicate interval of periodic reports, as appropriate for the particular leave situation)* of your status and intent to return to work *(see § 825.309 of the FMLA regulations)*. If the circumstances of your leave change and you are able to return to work earlier than the date indicated on the reverse side of this form, you ☐ will ☐ will not be required to notify us at least two work days prior to the date you intend to report to work.

9. You ☐ will ☐ will not be required to furnish recertification relating to a serious health condition. *(Explain below. if necessary, including the interval between certifications as prescribed in §825.308 of the FMLA regulations.)*

This optional use form may be used to satisfy mandatory employer requirements to provide employees taking FMLA leave with Written notice detailing spectfic expectations and obligations of the employee and explaining any consequences of a failure to meet these obligations. (29 CFR 825.301(b).)

Note: Persons are not required to respond to this collection of information unless it displays a currently valid OMB control number.

Public Burden Statement

We estimate that it will take an average of 5 minutes to complete this collection of information, including the time for reviewing instructions. searching existing data sources, gathering and maintaining the data needed, and completing and reviewing the collection of information. If you have any comments regarding this burden estimate or any other aspect of this collection of information, including suggestions for reducing this burden. send them to the Administrator, Wage and Hour Division, Department of Labor, Room S-3502. 200 Constitution Avenue, N.W., Washington. D.C. 20210.

DO NOT SEND THE COMPLETED FORM TO THE OFFICE SHOWN ABOVE.

U.S. Department of Labor Assistant Secretary for
Veteran's Employment and Training
Washington, D.C. 20210

JUL 2 2 2002

MEMORANDUM FOR: REGIONAL SOLICITORS;
VETERANS' EMPLOYMENT AND TRAINING SERVICE
REGIONAL ADMINISTRATORS AND DIRECTORS;
WAGE AND HOUR DIVISION REGIONAL
ADMINISTRATORS AND DISTRICT DIRECTORS

FROM: EUGENE SCALIA
Solicitor of Labor

FREDERICO JUARBE JR.
Assistant Secretary
Veterans' Employment and Training

TAMMY D. MCCUTCHEN
Administrator
Wage and Hour Division

SUBJECT: Protection of Uniformed Service Members' Rights to
Family and Medical Leave

The purpose of this memorandum is to advise staff of the three agencies regarding the rights of reemployed members of the uniformed services to family and medical leave under the provisions of the Family and Medical Leave Act of 1993, 29 U.S.C. §§ 2601-2654 (FMLA), and the Uniformed Services Employment and Reemployment Rights Act of 1994, 38 U.S.C. §§ 4301-4333 (USERRA). This memorandum also provides guidance regarding coordination between the Department of Labor's Wage and Hour Division field staff (WHD) and the Veterans' Employment and Training Service (VETS) field staff on cases involving this issue.

Over 90,000 members of the National Guard and Reserve have been called up since the President's declaration of a national emergency following the attacks of September 11, 2001. As these service members conclude their tours of duty and return to civilian employment, it is important for employers to recognize that USERRA requires that returning veterans receive all benefits of employment that they would have obtained if they had been continuously employed. One such benefit is eligibility for leave under the FMLA.

Under the FMLA, an "eligible employee" is entitled to 12 workweeks of leave during any 12-month period because of childbirth, adoption or foster care, or a serious health condition of the employee or certain family members. The FMLA provides that, to be eligible for family or medical leave, an employee must work for a covered employer, must have worked for the employer for at least 12 months and must have worked at least 1250 hours for that employer during the 12-month period prior to the start of the leave. The requirement of 1250 hours worked applies to persons employed by private employers, state and local governments, and the Postal Service.

A member of the National Guard or Reserve who is absent from employment for an extended period of time due to military service and who requests FMLA leave shortly after returning to civilian employment may not have actually worked for his or her employer for a total of 12 months or may not have performed 1250 hours of actual work with the employer in the 12 months prior to the start of the FMLA leave. Thus, the question may arise as to whether the time and hours that the employee would have worked but for his or her military service should be combined with the time employed and the hours actually worked for an employer to meet the 12-months of employment and the 1250 hours eligibility requirements.

For example, suppose that an employee who normally works a 40-hour week leaves civilian employment on November 5, 2001, to serve a tour of duty in Afghanistan, and is reemployed by the same civilian employer on June 10, 2002. On July 1, 2002, the employee begins FMLA leave, at which time the employee has only 840 hours of actual work performed for the civilian employer in the twelve months prior to the leave request (18 weeks prior to the military service, and 3 weeks following reemployment, at 40 hours per week). If the employee is otherwise eligible for FMLA leave, the 1240 hours that the employee would have worked but for his or her service in Afghanistan (31 weeks at 40 hours per week) should be added to the 840 hours actually worked, for a total of 2080 hours for purposes of determining FMLA eligibility.

Under USERRA, a person who is reemployed is entitled to the rights and benefits that he (or she) would have attained if he had remained continuously employed.[1] The "rights and benefits" protected by USERRA include those provided by employers and those required by statute, such as the right to leave under FMLA. Accordingly, a returning service member would be entitled to FMLA leave if the hours that he or she would have worked for the civilian employer during the period of military service would have met the FMLA eligibility threshold. Therefore, in determining whether a veteran meets the FMLA eligibility requirement, the months employed and the hours that were actually worked for the civilian employer should be combined with the months and hours that would have been worked during the twelve months prior to the start of the leave requested but for the military service.

Recognition of the rights and responsibilities established by USERRA will facilitate reentry into the workforce by those who stood ready to serve our nation. To assure that reemployed service members receive family and medical leave benefits that they are entitled to, all WHD and VETS investigators should follow the guidance in this memorandum when dealing with inquiries involving family and medical leave rights for such service members. WHD will refer to VETS any complaint in which this interpretation may be determinative along with a written determination that the information provided by the complainant appears, on its face, to indicate that: 1) the reason for leave qualifies as leave under the FMLA; 2) the employer is covered by

---

[1] However, a service member would not be entitled to rights and benefits that are considered as a form of short-term compensation, such as accrued vacation.

the FMLA; and 3) the service member would have been eligible for FMLA but for his or her military service. If the complainant in such a case meets USERRA's eligibility criteria (i.e., notice given, duration and nature of service, timely return/application), VETS will open a USERRA case. For cases opened directly with VETS in which the USERRA eligibility criteria are met, VETS will seek a written determination from WHD regarding the FMLA eligibility issues. With respect to cases opened directly by VETS or cases opened upon referral from WHD, VETS State Directors and WHD District Directors will coordinate as necessary to investigate and resolve these complaints. A request for assistance from one Director to another will constitute a delegation of authority to the other to assist in the conduct of the investigation.

USERRA-FMLA QUESTIONS AND ANSWERS
7/25/02
THE EFFECT OF THE UNIFORMED SERVICES EMPLOYMENT AND REEMPLOYMENT RIGHTS ACT ON LEAVE ELIGIBILITY UNDER THE FAMILY AND MEDICAL LEAVE ACT

1. **What is the Uniformed Services Employment and Reemployment Rights Act (USERRA)?**

   USERRA is a Federal law that provides reemployment rights for veterans and members of the National Guard and Reserve following qualifying military service. It also prohibits employer discrimination against any person on the basis of that person's past military service, current military obligations or intent to join one of the uniformed services. Enacted in 1994, USERRA traces its roots to 1940. It is codified at 38 U.S.C. § 4301 to § 4333.

2. **What is the Family and Medical Leave Act (FMLA)?**

   FMLA is a Federal law that provides "eligible" employees of a covered employer the right to take up to 12 workweeks of unpaid, job-protected leave, during any 12 months, for the birth and care of a newborn, adoption or foster care, or a serious health condition of the employee or certain family members. An "eligible" employee is one who meets certain requirements specified in the statute. FMLA was enacted in 1993 and is codified at 29 U.S.C. § 2601 to § 2654 and at 5 U.S.C. § 6381 to § 6387, relating to Federal civil service employees.

3. **What are the leave eligibility provisions of the FMLA?**

   In order to be eligible for leave under the FMLA, employees must meet several eligibility criteria. Two of these criteria affected by USERRA are: (1) the person must have been employed by the employer for at least 12 months; and (2) the person must have worked at least 1250 hours for that employer during the 12 month period preceding the start of the leave. The requirement of 1250 hours worked applies to persons employed by private employers, state and local governments, and the Postal Service.

4. **What effect does USERRA have on these requirements?**

   USERRA requires that service members who conclude their tours of duty and who are reemployed by their civilian employers receive all benefits of employment that they would have obtained if they had been continuously employed, except those benefits that are considered a form of short-term compensation, such as accrued paid vacation. If a service member had been continuously employed, one such benefit to which he or she might have been entitled is leave under the FMLA. The service member's eligibility will depend upon whether the service member would have met the eligibility requirements outlined above had he or she not performed military service.

5. **How should the 12-month FMLA requirement be calculated for returning service members?**

    USERRA requires that a person reemployed under its provisions be given credit for any months he or she would have been employed *but for* the military service in determining eligibility for FMLA leave. A person reemployed following military service should be given credit for the period of military service towards the months-of-employment eligibility requirement. Each month served performing military service counts as a month actively employed by the employer. For example, someone who has been employed by an employer for 9 months is ordered to active military service for 9 months after which he or she is reemployed. Upon reemployment, the person must be considered to have been employed by the employer for more than the required 12 months (9 months actually employed plus 9 months while serving in the military service) for purposes of FMLA eligibility. It should be noted that the 12 months of employment do not have to be consecutive to meet this FMLA requirement.

6. **How should the 1250 hours-of-service requirement be calculated for returning service members?**

    An employee returning after military service should be credited with the hours-of-service that would have been performed *but for* the period of military service in determining FMLA eligibility. Accordingly, a person reemployed following military service has the hours that would have been worked for the employer added to any hours actually worked during the previous 12-month period to meet the 1250 hour requirement. In order to determine the hours that would have been worked during the period of military service, the employee's pre-service work schedule can generally be used for calculations. For example, an employee who works 40 hours per week for the employer returns to employment following 20 weeks of military service and requests leave under the FMLA. To determine the person's eligibility, the hours he or she would have worked during the period of military service ($20 \times 40 = 800$ hours) must be added to the hours actually worked during the 12-month period prior to the start of the leave to determine if the 1250-hour requirement is met.

7. **Where can I get more information about USERRA?**

    The Department of Labor's Veterans' Employment and Training Service (VETS) administers USERRA, provides technical assistance/educational outreach, and investigates complaints. Information about USERRA is available on the VETS Web site. The address is http://www.dol.gov/vets/. There you will find USERRA information as well as a directory of local VETS offices.

This is one of a series of fact sheets highlighting U.S. Department of Labor programs. It is intended as a general description only and does not carry the force of legal opinion.

INDEX

Active duty physicians
   Healthcare provider :: 247

ADA :: 747, 768
   Benefits, maintenance :: 759
   Covered conditions :: 751
   Covered employers :: 750
   Covered individuals :: 754
   Eligibility for leave :: 750
   Entitlements :: 751
   Intermittent/reduced leave :: 758
   Leave scheduling :: 758
   Medical certification :: 756
   Medical records, confidential :: 762
   Notice requirements :: 755
   Paid leave substitution :: 759
   Pregnancy Discrimination Act :: 763
   Return to work :: 760
   Undue hardship :: 754

Adequacy of notice
   Based on covered condition types :: 321
   Employee must request leave :: 315
   Inability to provide notice :: 323
   Invoking FMLA by name :: 317
   Need for FMLA leave :: 307
   Notice issues :: 324
   Prior FMLA covered condition :: 319
   Providing FMLA leave forms :: 323
   Truthful information :: 322
   Vague requests :: 317

Adoption
   Age 18 or over
      CAA :: 145
      PEOAA :: 145
      Title I :: 145
      Title II :: 147
   Block leave scheduling :: 441
   CAA :: 141
   Covered condition :: 5, 134, 141
   Definition :: 146
   Entitlement condition :: 2
   Intermittent/reduced leave :: 146, 148, 444
   Leave conclusion
      CAA :: 145
      PEOAA :: 145
      Title I :: 145
      Title II :: 148
   PEOAA :: 141
   Placement :: 141, 146
   Pre-adoption leave
      CAA :: 144
      PEOAA :: 144
      Title I :: 144
      Title II :: 147
   Source
      CAA :: 144
      PEOAA :: 144
      Title I :: 144

      Title II :: 147
   Stepchildren
      CAA :: 145
      PEOAA :: 145
      Title I :: 145
      Title II :: 147
   Title I :: 141
   Title II :: 146
   Twelve month leave year :: 408, 416

Agency obligation to reinstate
   Discipline :: 589
   Fraud :: 595
   Layoff/RIF :: 591
   Outside employment :: 594
   Overtime reduced :: 593
   Probationary periods :: 594
   Return to work :: 588
   Shift eliminated :: 593
   Specific term or project :: 593
   Termination :: 589
   Workers' compensation :: 594

Agricultural Stabilization and Conservation Service :: 56

Alien employee
   Title II exclusions :: 62

Allergies
   Serious health condition :: 240

Army and AF Exchange Service :: 57

Army and AF Motion Picture Service :: 57

Atomic Energy Commission :: 47

Benefits
   [see Health benefits]
   Accrual of benefits
      CAA :: 509
      PEOAA :: 509
      Title I :: 509
      Title II :: 510
   Accrual of seniority
      CAA :: 509
      PEOAA :: 509
      Title I :: 509
      Title II :: 510
   Accrued benefits, definition :: 507
   ADA :: 759
   Employee handbooks :: 287
   Employee notice requirement :: 331
   Employment benefits, definition :: 506
   FECA :: 769
   Greater protection :: 510
   Group health plan changes :: 287
   Leave commencement, definition :: 507
   Maintenance of :: 10, 505
   Notice requirements :: 286

   Premium payments :: 287
   Rehabilitation Act :: 759
   Retention of accrued benefits :: 505
   Return to work, equivalent :: 549
   Workers' compensation :: 769
   Written notice :: 287

Bereavement leave
   Serious health condition :: 159

Birth and care of a newborn
   CAA :: 201
   PEOAA :: 201
   Title I :: 201
   Title II :: 204

Birth of a child
   Because of the birth :: 134, 138
   Block leave scheduling :: 441
   CAA :: 134
   Childcare :: 137
   Childcare availability, Title II :: 140
   Covered condition :: 5, 134
   Documentation
      CAA :: 136
      PEOAA :: 136
      Title I :: 136
      Title II :: 140
   Entitlement condition :: 2
   Foster care placement :: 444
   Intermittent/reduced leave :: 137, 141, 444
   Leave conclusion
      CAA :: 136
      PEOAA :: 136
      Title I :: 136
      Title II :: 139
   Multiple births
      CAA :: 137
      PEOAA :: 137
      Title I :: 137
      Title II :: 140
   Paid leave
      CAA :: 138
      PEOAA :: 138
      Title I :: 138
      Title II :: 141
   PEOAA :: 134
   Prenatal care :: 135
      CAA :: 135
      PEOAA :: 135
      Title I :: 135
      Title II :: 139
   Return to work early
      CAA :: 137
      Title I :: 137
      Title II :: 140
      PEOAA :: 137
   Title I :: 134
   Title II :: 138
   To care for, definition :: 134, 138

Twelve month leave year :: 408, 416

Block leave scheduling :: 440
   Adoption :: 441
   Birth of a child :: 441
   Foster care placement :: 441
   Serious health condition :: 441
   Smallest increments :: 440

Brothers and sisters
   Family member not covered :: 130

Burden of proof
   Discrimination theory :: 729
   Entitlement theory :: 726
   Interference theory :: 726
   Retaliation theory :: 729

CAA :: 1
   Accrued paid leave substitution :: 491
   Adequacy of need for leave notice :: 307
   Adoption :: 141
      12 mo. period :: 145
      age 18 or over :: 145
      source :: 144
      stepchildren :: 145
   Basic medical certification information :: 355
   Birth and care of newborn :: 201
   Birth of child :: 134
      12 mo. period :: 136
      childcare :: 137
      documentation :: 136
      multiple births :: 137
      paid leave :: 138
      return to work :: 137
   Changes in health coverage :: 515
   Chronic serious health condition :: 205
      episodic :: 209
      healthcare provider :: 208
   Circumstances permitting medical recertification :: 390
   Collective bargaining agreement :: 772
   Compensatory overtime :: 495
   Congressional employees :: 62
   Copies, 2nd/3rd opinions :: 379
   Coverage and eligibility :: 38
   Covered employee :: 4, 64
      defined :: 64, 66, 95
   Covered employer :: 35
   Eligibility requirements :: 4, 66
   Eligible employee, defined :: 66
   Employee eligibility notice :: 272
   Employee rights and obligations :: 263
   Employer practices :: 772
   Employer requirements
      FMLA poster :: 258
      leave designation :: 274
      written guide :: 259, 262
   Employer to confirm eligibility :: 272
   Employing office, defined :: 66, 76, 95
   Enforcement :: 677
   Essential functions, documentation :: 168
   Failure to provide medical certification :: 385
   Failure to provide need for leave notice :: 325
   Familial relationship, documentation :: 401
   Family leave outside the US :: 97
   Forego health benefits coverage :: 517
   Foreseeable need for leave :: 291
   Foster care placement :: 148
      12 mo. period :: 150
      age 18 and over :: 150
      duration :: 150
      multiple :: 150
      pay :: 150
      source :: 149
   Furloughs, effect on 12 months :: 78
   Health benefit
      employee payment :: 521
      during leave :: 514
      recovering cost :: 528
   Healthcare provider :: 208, 220, 241, 339
   Hours in preceding 12 months :: 97
   Hours of service, 1250 hours :: 95
   Hours worked :: 95
   House of Representatives :: 1
   Incapacity, treatment :: 188
   Inpatient care :: 174
   Integrated employer test :: 36
   Interaction with federal laws :: 747
   Intermittent/reduced leave :: 137, 146, 151, 251, 441
   Job restoration :: 38
   Joint employment :: 37, 76, 96
   Leave
      effect on 12 mo. :: 77
      effect on 1250 hours. :: 96
   Leave commencement :: 78, 97
   Level of care :: 160
   Light duty :: 166
   Long term incapacity :: 213
   Managers and supervisors :: 36
   Manner of notice, need for leave :: 301
   Medical certification :: 162, 336
      2nd opinion :: 372
      3rd opinion :: 376
      Christian Science :: 375
      clarification :: 370
      contents :: 354
      employer notice :: 341
      incomplete :: 364
      paid leave :: 357
      provided :: 348
      request :: 347
   Medical recertification :: 388
      form :: 395
      notice :: 396
      payment :: 396
      time frame :: 395
   Mental illness :: 237
   Military leave :: 77, 96
   Multiple employers :: 36
   Multiple treatments :: 218
   Need for leave notice :: 291
   Nonconsecutive employment :: 77
   Notice of leave designation :: 276
   Notice requirements :: 6
      benefits :: 286
      health benefits :: 516
      joint employment :: 289
      key employees :: 288, 332
      leave year calculation :: 285
      paid leave :: 479
      recordkeeping :: 290
   Other caregivers :: 159
   Permanent incapacity :: 213
   Pre-adoption leave :: 144
   Pre-foster care placement :: 149
   Pregnancy :: 197
   Prenatal care :: 135, 197, 200
   Presidential appointed officer :: 63
   Primary-secondary employer :: 37
   Prohibited acts :: 39, 625
   Provisional leave, 2nd/3rd opinions :: 376
   Reasonable accommodation :: 166
   Record-keeping requirements :: 618
   Remedies :: 718
   Return to work
      equivalent
         benefits :: 549
         pay :: 547
         position :: 546
         terms :: 551
      medical certification :: 565
      same position :: 543
   RIFs, effect on 12 mo. :: 77
   Scope of health benefits during leave :: 514
   Second opinion, payment :: 375
   Selection of provider, 3rd opinion :: 378
   Senate :: 1
   Serious health condition :: 155, 180, 197, 205, 213, 218
   Substance abuse :: 230
      treatment :: 232
   Successor-in-interest :: 36, 76, 96
   Teachers, hours worked :: 97
   Third opinion, payment :: 378
   To care for, documentation :: 162
   Traveling care :: 161
   Twelve month leave year :: 408
   Twelve months employment :: 76
   Twelve workweeks calculation :: 421
   Unable to perform :: 163, 164
   USERRA :: 77, 96
   Workweek marriage penalty :: 433

Cancerous growth removal
   Serious health condition :: 240

Capitol Guide Service
   Covered employee :: 4, 64
   Covered employer :: 35

Capitol Police
   Covered employee :: 4, 64
   Covered employer :: 35

Care for a newborn child
   [see Birth of a child]
   Covered condition :: 5
   Entitlement condition :: 2

Chief of mission
  Title II exclusions :: 63
Childcare availability
  Birth of child
    CAA :: 137
    PEOAA :: 137
    Title I :: 137
    Title II :: 140
Chiropractors :: 243
Christian Science
  Healthcare provider :: 244, 248
Chronic serious health condition
  CAA :: 205
  Definition :: 207, 212
  Episodic incapacity
    CAA :: 209
    PEOAA :: 209
    Title I :: 209
    Title II :: 213
  Extended period, Title II :: 213
  Incapacity :: 206, 211
    any period :: 206, 211, 219, 223
  Medical recertification
    CAA :: 390
    exceptions
      CAA :: 391
      PEOAA:: 391
      Title I :: 391
      Title II :: 398
    PEOAA:: 390
    Title I :: 390
    Title II :: 398
  PEOAA :: 205
  Periodic visits :: 207, 212
  Recurring episodes, Title II :: 213
  Serious health condition :: 205
  Title I :: 205
  Title II :: 210
  Treatment :: 206, 211
CIA proprietary corporations :: 55
Civil action
  Enforcement, CAA :: 685
Civil litigation issues :: 720
  Administrative exhaustion :: 720
  Applicable regulations :: 741
  Arbitration of FMLA claims :: 721
  Burden of proof :: 725
  Claim of deceased :: 720
  Collateral estoppel :: 721
  Issue preclusion :: 721
  Jury trial :: 724
  Mitigation :: 742
  Nominal damages :: 742
  Pleadings :: 723
  Removal :: 720
  Service of process :: 724
Civil service appointment
  Title II :: 50

Civil service employees
  Appointing official :: 52
  Appointment :: 50
  Authorized official :: 52
  Covered employee :: 49
  Performs a federal function :: 53
  Title II :: 49
  Under federal supervision :: 53
Civilian in military department
  Covered employee :: 43
  NAFI :: 43
  Title I :: 43
Clinical psychologists :: 243
Clinical social workers :: 244
Coast Guard exchanges :: 57
Collective bargaining agreements
  CAA :: 777
  Interaction :: 772
    CAA :: 772
    PEOAA :: 778
    Title I :: 772
    Title II :: 778
  Intermittent leave :: 777
  Laid-off employees :: 777
  Multiple employers :: 777
  Return to work :: 778
  School employees :: 778
  Title I :: 777
    effective date of FMLA :: 777
  Title II :: 779
  Transfers :: 777
  Waiver of rights :: 778
Compensatory overtime
  Paid leave substitution :: 493
    CAA :: 495
    PEOAA :: 496
    Title I :: 495
    Title II :: 493
Competitive service
  Covered employee :: 49
Complications
  Cosmetic treatments :: 230
  Minor illnesses :: 226
Confirm employee's eligibility
  Eligibility is met :: 273
  Employer requirements :: 272
  Leave commences :: 273
  Notice requirements :: 272
  Not yet eligible :: 272
Congressional Budget Office
  Covered employee :: 4, 64
  Covered employer :: 35
Congressional employees :: 62
Continuing treatment
  Chronic health condition, Title II :: 210
  Definition :: 179

  Title II :: 194
  Incapacity :: 181, 194
  More than 3 days
    CAA :: 181, 185
    PEOAA :: 181, 185
    Title I :: 181, 185
    Title II :: 193, 194
  Multiple treatments :: 218
  Pregnancy, Title II :: 203
  Prenatal care :: 200
  Regulatory developments
    chronic :: 205, 210
    long-term :: 214, 216
    more than 3 days :: 181, 193
    multiple :: 219, 222
    permanent :: 214, 216
  Serious health condition :: 179
  Substance abuse, Title II :: 237
Cooperative Extension Service :: 56
Cosmetic treatments :: 230
Council of Economic Advisors
  Covered employee :: 4
  Covered employer :: 39
Covered condition :: 5, 133
  ADA :: 751
  Adoption :: 5, 134, 141
  Agencies with mixed variant :: 254
  Birth of child :: 5, 134
  Care of newborn :: 5
  Foster care placement :: 5, 134, 148
  Rehabilitation Act :: 751
  Serious health condition :: 5, 154, 155
Covered employee
  Agricultural Stabilization and
    Conservation Service :: 56
  Army and AF Exchange Service :: 57
  Army and AF Motion Picture Service :: 57
  Atomic Energy Commission :: 47
  CAA :: 4, 64, 66
  Capitol Guide Service :: 4, 64
  Capitol Police :: 4, 64
  CIA proprietary corporations :: 55
  Civil service employees :: 49
  Civilian in military department :: 43
  Coast Guard exchanges :: 57
  Congressional Budget Office :: 4, 64
  Cooperative Extension Service :: 56
  Council of Economic Advisors :: 4
  Definition :: 3, 41
  Executive Office of the President :: 4
  Executive Residence at the White House :: 4
  Executive branch :: 44
  Federal Home Loan Mortgage
    Corporation :: 45
  Federal Reserve :: 46
  Foreign Service employees :: 59
  General Accounting Office :: 47
  Government Printing Office :: 4
  House of Representatives :: 4, 64
  Intermittent appointment :: 4, 43

Judicial branch :: 4, 49
Legislative branch :: 4, 49
Marine Corps exchanges :: 57
NAFI :: 43, 57
National Guard :: 43
National Security Council :: 4
Naval Academy employees :: 57
Navy exchanges :: 57
Navy ship's stores ashore :: 57
Office Architect of the Capitol :: 4, 64
Office National Drug Control Policy :: 4
Office of Attending Physician :: 4, 64
Office of Management and Budget :: 4
Office of Policy Development :: 4
Office of the Vice President :: 4
Office of Compliance :: 4, 64
Office of Technology :: 4, 64
Part-time employees :: 4
PBGC :: 45
PEOAA :: 4, 64, 67
Senate :: 4, 64
Teachers for DOD :: 58
Temporary appointment :: 4
Tennessee Valley Authority :: 45
Title I :: 4, 41
Title II :: 4, 49, 66
US Tax Court :: 4
Veterans Health Administration :: 58
White House Office :: 4

Covered employer :: 3, 21
ADA :: 750
CAA :: 35
Capitol Guide Service :: 35
Capitol Police :: 35
Congressional Budget Office :: 35
Council of Economic Advisors :: 39
Definition :: 21
Executive Office of the President :: 39
Executive Residence at the White House :: 39
House of Representatives :: 35
Integrated employer test :: 25, 36
Integrated enterprise test :: 24
Job restoration :: 33, 38
Joint employment :: 28, 37
Joint employment eligibility :: 33, 38
Joint employment test :: 24, 36
Joint ventures :: 24
Leased employees :: 24
Managers and supervisors :: 22, 36
Mixed responsibilities :: 39
Multiple employers :: 24, 36
National Security Council :: 39
Office of Compliance :: 35
Office of Management and Budget :: 39
Office of National Drug Control Policy :: 39
Office of Policy Development :: 39
Office of Technology :: 35
Office of the Architect of the Capitol :: 35
Office of the Attending Physician :: 35
Office of the Vice President :: 39
PEOAA :: 39

Public agency :: 21
Rehabilitation Act :: 750
Senate :: 35
Successor-in-interest :: 22
Temporary employees :: 24
Title I :: 21
Title II :: 34, 35
Title V :: 35

Covered family members :: 5, 117
Disability, physical or mental :: 125
Documentation :: 132, 401
In Loco Parentis :: 122, 131
Medical certification :: 162, 170
Paid leave substitute, Title II :: 485
Parent :: 129
Pre-existing disability :: 126
Son or daughter :: 122
    18 or over :: 124
    age requirement. :: 124
    current :: 123
    definition :: 122
    relationship :: 122
    self-care :: 124
    under 18 :: 124
Spouse :: 117
    civil union :: 119
    definition :: 117
    divorce :: 119
    domestic partners :: 120
    marriage :: 117
Substance abuse
    CAA :: 234
    PEOAA :: 234
    Title I :: 234
    Title II :: 237

Covered individuals :: 5, 117
ADA :: 754
Rehabilitation Act :: 754

DC government employees
Title I :: 61
Title II exclusions :: 60, 61

Deemed eligible :: 111
Eligibility confirmed, misrepresentation :: 115
Estoppel :: 112
    collateral :: 116
    equitable :: 112
Interference standard :: 112, 116
Notice
    eligibility is met :: 110, 273
    leave commences :: 111, 273
    not yet eligible :: 111, 273
Penalty provision in courts :: 111
Silence, misrepresentation :: 114
Title I :: 110

Defense of Marriage Act
Full Faith and Credit Clause :: 120
Marriage, defined :: 121
Spouse :: 120
    defined :: 121

Dentists :: 243

Designation of FMLA leave
Employer requirements :: 274
    CAA :: 274
    PEOAA :: 284
    Title I :: 274
    Title II :: 284
Failure to provide notice :: 280
Manner of notice :: 279
Notice requirements :: 274
Timing of notice :: 276

Determining employee numbers
Eligible/non-eligible employee :: 100
Fifty employees within 75 miles :: 99
Title I :: 99
US Government as single employer :: 100

Direct supervision
Definition
    CAA :: 208
    PEOAA :: 208
    Title I :: 208
    Title II :: 212
Nurse, Physician's Assistant :: 208

Disability
Pregnancy :: 201
Physical or mental
    case law :: 127
    definition :: 125
    major life activity, definition :: 125
    son or daughter, 18 or over :: 125

Disclosure of records :: 618
Congress :: 621
Court order :: 621
DOL :: 619
Freedom of Information Act :: 621
Government inspection :: 619
Need to know within an agency :: 621
OPM :: 619
Other government agencies :: 619
Privacy Act :: 619
Routine uses :: 621

Discrimination
Prohibited acts :: 634

Doctors
Healthcare provider
    CAA :: 243
    PEOAA :: 243
    Title I :: 243
    Title II :: 247

Documentation :: 335
ADA :: 756
Agencies with mixed variant :: 404
Birth of child
    CAA :: 136
    PEOAA :: 136
    Title I :: 136
    Title II :: 140
Count eligibility requirement, Title I :: 103

Covered family members :: 132, 401
Employee maintained on payroll :: 103
Essential functions
    CAA :: 168
    PEOAA :: 168
    Title I :: 168
    Title II :: 172
Establish familial relationship :: 401
Evidence of care :: 162
Familial relationship
    CAA :: 401
    PEOAA :: 401
    Title I :: 401
    Title II :: 402
Fifty employees within 75 miles :: 103
Fitness to return to duty :: 7, 401
Health benefits, medical certification :: 530
Hours of service, 1250 hours :: 92
Intermittent/reduced leave :: 455
Medical certification :: 7, 162, 170, 335
Medical recertification :: 7, 388
Rehabilitation Act :: 756
Serious health condition :: 249
Status reports :: 7, 401

DOL complaints :: 653
Civil actions by DOL :: 658
DOL supervised settlements :: 658
Filing :: 653
    effect on civil action :: 653
    process :: 654
Investigative authority :: 655
Posting violations :: 659

EEOC
Enforcement :: 672

Eligibility for leave
ADA :: 750
Pregnancy Discrimination Act :: 766
Rehabilitation Act :: 750

Eligibility requirements :: 65
CAA :: 4, 66
Count eligibility requirement, Title I :: 98
Deemed eligible :: 110
Employee :: 4
Employee eligibility :: 104
Employer coverage :: 104
Fifty employees within 75 miles :: 98
General eligibility notice rule :: 110
Hours of service, 1250 hours :: 78
Lowered by company policy :: 90, 103
PEOAA :: 4, 67
Qualifications :: 4
Title I :: 4, 65, 110
Title II :: 5, 66

Eligible employee
CAA :: 66
PEOAA :: 67
Title I :: 65
Title II :: 66

Employee
Definition :: 3, 41, 66, 67

Eligibility
    Employer requirements :: 272
    CAA :: 272
    PEOAA :: 273
    Title I :: 272
    Title II :: 274
    Intermittent/reduced leave :: 470
    Notice requirements :: 272
    CAA :: 272
    Title I :: 272
    Title II :: 274
    PEOAA :: 273
Notice requirements :: 6, 290
    Adequacy of notice :: 307
    CAA :: 307
    PEOAA :: 307
    Title I :: 307
    Title II :: 324
    Changed circumstances
    CAA :: 328
    PEOAA :: 328
    Title I :: 328
    Title II :: 329
    Failure to provide notice :: 325
    CAA :: 325
    PEOAA:: 325
    Title I :: 325
    Title II :: 327
    Joint employment :: 333
    Maintenance of benefits :: 331
    Manner of notice
    CAA :: 301
    PEOAA :: 301
    Title I :: 301
    Title II :: 306
    Manner of providing notice :: 301
    Miscellaneous requirements :: 328
    Need for FMLA leave :: 291
    Need for leave notice :: 291, 307
    CAA :: 291
    PEOAA :: 291
    Title I :: 291
    Title II :: 298
    Not to return to work :: 587
    Paid leave substitution :: 329, 478, 479
    Periodic status reports :: 584
    Return to work :: 331, 584
        early :: 586
        form of notice :: 588
    Schedule, consult employer :: 329
    School employees :: 333
    Rights and obligations
    Changes to notice :: 266
    Employer's duty, questions :: 269
    Employer's notice failure :: 269
    Employer requirements
    CAA :: 263
    PEOAA :: 271
    Title I :: 263
    Title II :: 271
    Frequency of notice :: 266
    Language of notice :: 265
    Manner of notice :: 266

    Medical certification :: 343
    Notice contents :: 264
    Notice of fitness for duty requirement :: 267
    Notice of medical certification requirement :: 267
    Notice requirements :: 263, 343
    CAA :: 263
    PEOAA :: 271
    Title I :: 263
    Title II :: 271
    Timing of notice :: 266
    Written guidance :: 263, 343

Employee maintained on payroll
Documentation :: 103
Proof :: 103

Employer interference
Hours worked, Title I :: 89

Employer notice requirements :: 6, 255
Before leave commences :: 111
Eligibility is met notice :: 110
Eligibility requirement, Title I :: 110
Failure to pay health benefit :: 525
Fitness-for-duty
    CAA :: 574
    PEOAA :: 574
    Title I :: 574
    Title II :: 579
Health benefit, employee payment :: 522
Health benefit options :: 520
Health plan changes :: 516
Medical certification :: 341
    CAA :: 341
    PEOAA :: 341
    Title I :: 341
    Title II :: 346
Not yet eligible notice :: 110

Employer practices
Amendments to benefits :: 779
Existing FMLA policy
    CAA :: 776
    Title I :: 776
    Title II :: 779
Greater benefits :: 773
Interaction :: 772
    CAA :: 772
    PEOAA :: 778
    Title I :: 772
    Title II :: 778
Less protection
    CAA :: 775
    Title I :: 775
    Title II :: 779
Modification to benefits :: 776

Employer requirements
Deemed eligible :: 273
Designation of FMLA leave :: 274
Employee eligibility :: 272

Employee rights and obligations :: 263, 343
FMLA poster :: 255
Written guidance :: 342
    absence :: 259, 262, 342

Enforcement :: 11, 625, 652
CAA :: 677
Civil action
    CAA :: 685
    PEOAA :: 691
Complaint processing
    CAA counseling :: 678
    CAA mediation :: 680
Complaint procedure
    CAA :: 678
    PEOAA :: 689
Confidentiality, CAA :: 688
Counseling, PEOAA :: 690
EEOC, Title I :: 672
Election of appeal, PEOAA :: 690
Employee complaint to DOL :: 653
    civil actions :: 658
    filing :: 653
    investigation authority :: 655
    post violation :: 659
    supervised settlements :: 658
Grievance process :: 671
Judicial review
    CAA regulations :: 686
    PEOAA :: 691
        regulations :: 692
Mediation, PEOAA :: 690
MSPB
    PEOAA :: 690
    Title I :: 671
    Title II :: 676
Office of Compliance, CAA :: 677
PEOAA :: 689
Private right of action :: 660
Savings provisions, CAA :: 688
Section 405 complaint, CAA :: 681
Settlements, CAA :: 688
Supreme Court review
    CAA :: 687
    PEOAA:: 692
Title I :: 653
Title II :: 674
    federal court :: 675
Unfair labor practice charges :: 673, 676
Wavier of sovereign immunity :: 687

Entitlement conditions :: 2
Adoption :: 2
Birth of child :: 2
Care of newborn :: 2
Foster care :: 2
Serious health condition :: 2

Entitlements :: 2, 8
ADA :: 751
Rehabilitation Act :: 751
Successor-in-interest :: 23

Episodic incapacity
Chronic health condition
    CAA :: 209
    PEOAA :: 209
    Title I :: 209
    Title II :: 213

Essential functions
Definition :: 165, 170, 171
Documentation
    CAA :: 168
    PEOAA :: 168
    Title I :: 168
    Title II :: 172
Position held
    CAA :: 167
    PEOAA :: 167
    Title I :: 167
    Title II :: 172
Serious health condition :: 167, 172

Essential job functions
Definition :: 165, 171

Estoppel
Collateral
    deemed eligible :: 112, 116
Equitable
    deemed eligible :: 112
    eligibility confirmed,
        misrepresentation :: 115
    silence, misrepresentation :: 114

Evidence of care, documentation
CAA :: 162
PEOAA :: 162
Title I :: 162
Title II :: 170

Exclusions
Employees of DC government :: 60
Temporary or intermittent employees :: 60
Title II :: 60

Executive Office of the President
Covered employee :: 4
Covered employer :: 39
Variant :: 2

Executive Residence at the White House
Covered employee :: 4
Covered employer :: 39

Executive branch
Covered employee :: 44
Independent establishment :: 46
Variant :: 1

Executive department :: 44
Covered employee :: 44

Extended period of time
Chronic health condition, Title II :: 213

Familial relationship
Documentation to establish :: 401

CAA :: 401
PEOAA :: 401
Title I :: 401
Title II :: 402

Family Friendly Leave Act :: 485, 770

Family member not covered :: 130
Brothers and sisters :: 130
Grandparents :: 130
Parents-in-law :: 130

Farm Credit Administration :: 62

FDIC :: 46

FECA :: 768, 769
Benefits, maintenance :: 769
Light duty :: 770
Medical information :: 770
Paid leave substitution :: 769

Federal Home Loan Mortgage Corporation :: 45

Federal laws
Interaction :: 745
    CAA :: 747
    PEOAA :: 747
    Title I :: 745
    Title II :: 746

FEFFLA :: 485, 770

FEHPB
Definition :: 511
Failure to pay, termination :: 526
Health benefits premium payments :: 524
Healthcare provider :: 247
Recovering cost of benefits :: 531

FERC
Healthcare provider :: 47

Fifty employees within 75 miles
Determination :: 99
Determining employee numbers :: 99
Distance measurement :: 104
Documentation :: 103
Effect of leave on :: 100
Eligibility requirements :: 98
Eligible/non-eligible employee :: 100
Employee eligibility :: 104
Employer coverage :: 104
General worksite rule :: 105
Joint employment :: 102
    worksite :: 108
Laid-off employees :: 101
Leave of absence :: 101
Lowered by company policy :: 103
Military leave, Title I :: 102
No fixed worksite :: 106
Outside the US, Title I :: 103
Part-time employees :: 101
Personal residence worksite :: 107
Proof :: 103
Resignations :: 101
Separate facilities, worksite :: 106

Single or multiple locations :: 105
Suspensions :: 101
Teachers, Title I :: 103
US Government as single employer :: 100
Worksite, definition :: 105

Fitness to return to duty
[see Return to Duty]
Documentation :: 7, 401

FLSA-exempt employees
Fluctuating workweek :: 465
Intermittent/reduced leave :: 464
Record keeping
    Title I :: 614
    Title II :: 618
Salary basis test, exemption :: 464
Title II :: 465
Twelve workweeks calculation :: 428

FLSA principles
Development :: 80
Hours worked :: 80
    exclusions :: 82
Lunch or meal breaks :: 81
Off-duty work time :: 81
On-call time :: 82
On-duty work time :: 80
Rest periods, breaks :: 81
Suffer or permit to work :: 80

FMLA
Background :: 1, 2, 13
Covered under :: 3
Eligibility requirements :: 4, 65
Enforcement and remedies :: 11
Entitlements :: 2
Interaction with
    collective bargaining :: 772
    employer practice :: 772
    federal laws :: 745
Purpose :: 2
Qualifications :: 3
Variants :: 1

FMLA poster
Employer requirements :: 255
    CAA :: 258
    PEOAA :: 258
    Title I :: 255
    Title II :: 258
Notice requirements :: 255

Foreign Service employees :: 59

Foster care
Definition :: 148, 152

Foster care placement
Age 18 or over
    CAA :: 150
    PEOAA :: 150
    Title I :: 150
    Title II :: 153
Block leave scheduling :: 441
CAA :: 148

Covered condition :: 5, 134, 148
Entitlement condition :: 2
Intermittent/reduced leave :: 151, 154
Leave conclusion
    CAA :: 150
    PEOAA :: 150
    Title I :: 150
    Title II :: 153
Minimum duration
    CAA :: 150
    PEOAA :: 150
    Title I :: 150
    Title II :: 153
Multiple placements
    CAA :: 150
    PEOAA :: 150
    Title I :: 150
    Title II :: 153
Pay
    CAA :: 150
    PEOAA :: 150
    Title I :: 150
    Title II :: 153
PEOAA :: 148
Pre-placement leave
    CAA :: 149
    PEOAA :: 149
    Title I :: 149
    Title II :: 153
Source
    CAA :: 149
    PEOAA :: 149
    Title I :: 149
    Title II :: 153
Title I :: 148
Title II :: 152
Twelve month leave year :: 408, 416

Furloughs
Title I :: 89

General Accounting Office
Independent establishment :: 47

Government corporation
Covered employee :: 44
Definition :: 45
Federal Home Loan Mortgage
    Corporation :: 45
Mixed-ownership :: 45
PBGC :: 45
Tennessee Valley Authority :: 45
Title I :: 44
Wholly owned by the government :: 45

Government Printing Office :: 4

Grandparents
Family member not covered :: 130

Grievance process
Enforcement :: 671

Group health plans
Cessation of benefits during leave :: 518
Changes in coverage :: 515

Definition :: 511
Employee premium payment :: 521
Employer notice of changes :: 516
Failure to pay, termination :: 525
Forego coverage :: 517
Health benefits during leave :: 512
Recovering cost of benefits :: 528
Return to work :: 529
Scope of health benefits during leave :: 514

Health benefits
Agencies with mixed variant :: 532
Cessation during FMLA leave :: 518
    CAA :: 518
    key employees :: 520
    PEOAA :: 518
    Title I :: 518
    Title II :: 519
Changes
    employer notice :: 516
    in coverage
        CAA :: 515
        PEOAA :: 515
        Title I :: 515
        Title II :: 516
    notice :: 516
During leave
    CAA :: 514
    Title I :: 512
    Title II :: 513
Effect of paid leave :: 522
Employee payment :: 520
    CAA :: 521
    employee premium :: 526
    limitation :: 523
    PEOAA :: 521
    Title I :: 521
    Title II :: 520
Failure to pay
    promptly :: 524
    termination :: 524
FEHPB :: 511
    premium payments :: 524
Forego coverage :: 517
Group health plans :: 511
Health plans, defined :: 511
Key employees :: 605
Maintenance :: 511
    during leave :: 512
Medical certification :: 530
Multi-employer health plans :: 512
Non-group health plans :: 526, 531
Other plans, premium payments :: 524
Recovering cost of benefits :: 527
    CAA :: 528
    collection :: 532
    debt effect :: 532
    PEOAA :: 528
    Title I :: 528
    Title II :: 528
Return to work, requalification :: 527
Scope of benefits during leave :: 514
Self-insured health plans :: 531

Substitution of paid leave :: 531
Termination, Title II :: 521
Workers' compensation :: 523, 531

Healthcare provider
Active duty physicians :: 247
Authorized to practice, definition :: 242
Chiropractors :: 243
Christian Science :: 244, 248
Clinical psychologist :: 243
Clinical social work :: 244
Definition :: 241, 339
    CAA :: 241
    PEOAA :: 241
    Title I :: 241
    Title II :: 247
Dentists :: 243
Doctors
    CAA :: 243
    PEOAA :: 243
    Title I :: 243
    Title II :: 247
FEHPB healthcare provider :: 247
In another country
    CAA :: 246
    PEOAA :: 246
    Title I :: 246
    Title II :: 248
Licensed federal and state, Title II :: 248
Medical certification
    CAA :: 339
    PEOAA :: 339
    Title I :: 339
    Title II :: 340
Multiple treatments
    CAA :: 220
    PEOAA :: 220
    Title I :: 220
    Title II :: 224
Native American, Title II :: 248
Nurse midwives :: 244
Nurse practitioners :: 244
Osteopaths :: 243
Podiatrists :: 243
Recognized by employer :: 245
Recognized by group plan manager :: 245
Scope of authorized practice :: 242
Serious health condition :: 241
Substance abuse, treatment :: 233, 237
Treatments :: 189, 195, 233, 237
    CAA :: 208
    incapacity :: 189, 195
    PEOAA :: 208
    Title I :: 208
    Title II :: 212

HIPAA
Medical certification :: 403

History of the FMLA
Amendments :: 19
Background :: 13
Creation of the FMLA :: 16
Economic :: 18
Family leave outside the US :: 15
FMLA 1987 :: 17
FMLA 1989 :: 17
FMLA 1991 :: 17
FMLA 1993 :: 18
Parental care responsibility :: 14
PDLA :: 16
PMLA :: 17
Single parent families :: 14
Social :: 13
State family leave laws :: 15
Time demands :: 13
Women :: 13

Hours of service, 1250 hours
Documentation :: 92
Effect of leave on :: 96
Eligibility requirements :: 78
    CAA :: 95
    PEOAA :: 98
    Title I :: 78
    Title II :: 95
Employer interference Title I :: 89
Joint employment
    CAA :: 96
    Title I :: 90
Layover time, Title I :: 86
Leave commences
    CAA :: 97
    Title I :: 93
Lowered by company policy :: 90
Military leave
    CAA :: 96
    Title I :: 84
Outside the US
    CAA :: 97
    Title I :: 91
Pre/postliminary activities :: 85
Preceding 12 months
    CAA :: 97
    Title I :: 93
Proof :: 92
Successor-in-interest
    CAA :: 96
    Title I :: 91
Suspensions and terminations :: 87
Teachers
    CAA :: 97
    Title I :: 91
Training, Title I :: 87
USERRA
    CAA :: 96
    Title I :: 84

Hours worked
CAA :: 95
Effect of furloughs, Title I :: 89
Effect of layoffs, Title I :: 89
FLSA principles :: 80
Overtime or premium pay :: 83
Paid or unpaid leave , Title I :: 83
PEOAA :: 98
Pre/postliminary activities, Title I :: 85
Title I :: 79, 98
Union business, Title I :: 85

House of Representatives
Covered employee :: 4, 64
Covered employer :: 35
Variant :: 1

Illegal appointments :: 60

In Loco Parentis :: 122
Exception :: 131
Son or daughter :: 122
Stepchildren
    CAA :: 145
    PEOAA :: 145
    Title I :: 145
    Title II :: 147

Incapacity
Chronic serious health condition :: 206, 211
Continuing treatment :: 181, 194
Definition :: 174, 181, 194
Episodic
    CAA :: 209
    PEOAA :: 209
    Title I :: 209
    Title II :: 213
Healthcare provider :: 189, 195
Inpatient care :: 174
More than 3 days
    CAA :: 185
    PEOAA :: 185
    Title I :: 185
    Title II :: 194
Multiple treatment, over 3 days :: 221, 224
Permanent or long term :: 213
Pregnancy :: 198, 203
Prenatal care :: 198, 203
Serious health condition :: 174, 180, 181, 193, 194
Subsequent treatment :: 189, 195
Treatment
    CAA :: 188
    PEOAA :: 188
    Title I :: 188
    Title II :: 194

Independent establishment
Atomic Energy Commission :: 47
Covered employee :: 44
Executive branch :: 46
Factors :: 46
General Accounting Office :: 47
Parts of larger executive departments :: 47
Title I :: 44

Inpatient care
CAA :: 174
Cosmetic treatments :: 230
Examples
    CAA :: 177
    PEOAA :: 177
    Title I :: 177
    Title II :: 178
Hospice :: 176
Hospital :: 176

Illness :: 176
Impairment :: 176
Incapacity :: 174
Injury :: 176
Overnight stay :: 176
PEOAA :: 174
Physical or mental condition :: 176
Residential medical care facility :: 176
Serious health condition :: 174, 178
Subsequent incapacity :: 177
Subsequent treatment :: 177
Title I :: 174
Title II :: 178
Treatment :: 175

Integrated employer test
CAA :: 36
Covered employer :: 25, 36
Multiple employers :: 25, 36
Title I :: 25

Integrated enterprise test
Covered employer :: 24
Multiple employers :: 24
Title I :: 24

Interference
Prohibited acts :: 626

Interference standard
Deemed eligible :: 112, 116

Intermittent appointment
Covered employee :: 4, 43
Title I :: 43

Intermittent/reduced leave
ADA :: 758
Adoption :: 444
  CAA :: 146
  PEOAA :: 146
  Title I :: 146
  Title II :: 148
Birth of a child :: 444
  CAA :: 137
  PEOAA :: 137
  Title I :: 137
  Title II :: 141
Documentation :: 455
Equivalent position
  CAA :: 460
  PEOAA :: 460
  Title I :: 460
  Title II :: 458
  transfer :: 457
FLSA-exempt employees :: 464
Foster care placement :: 444
  CAA :: 151
  PEOAA :: 151
  Title I :: 151
  Title II :: 154
Impact on
  eligibility :: 470
  medical certification requirements :: 470
  notice requirements :: 470
  return to work requirements :: 471
Intermittent leave definition
  CAA :: 442
  PEOAA :: 442
  Title I :: 442
  Title II :: 441
Leave amount :: 466
Leave increments :: 462, 463
Leave scheduling :: 441
Medical certification :: 455
Medical need
  CAA :: 251, 447
  definition :: 251
  PEOAA :: 251, 447
  Title I :: 251, 447
  Title II :: 253, 447
Medical recertification :: 393
  exception :: 394
Other requirements
  CAA :: 252
  PEOAA :: 252
  Title I :: 252
  Title II :: 253
Pregnancy Discrimination Act :: 767
Reduced leave definition :: 443
Rehabilitation Act :: 758
School employees :: 467, 606
Serious health condition :: 250, 445, 456
  avoid disruption :: 449
  CAA :: 251, 456
  medical necessity :: 446
  notice :: 453
  PEOAA :: 251, 456
  Title I :: 251, 456
  Title II :: 253, 456
Uses of leave :: 252

Job restoration
CAA :: 38
Covered employer :: 33, 38
Joint employers :: 33, 38
Primary-secondary employer :: 33, 38
Title I :: 33

Joint employers
Job restoration :: 33, 38
Multiple employers :: 27, 37
Primary-secondary employer :: 32, 37
Prohibited acts :: 34, 39
Return to work :: 559

Joint employment
CAA :: 37, 76, 96
Count eligibility requirement, Title I :: 102
Coverage and eligibility :: 33, 38
Covered employer :: 28, 37
Economic realities test :: 28
Employee notice requirement :: 333
Fifty employees within 75 miles :: 102
Hours of service, 1250 hours :: 90, 96
Hours worked
  CAA :: 96
  Title I :: 90
Multiple employers :: 28, 37
Notice requirements :: 289
Record keeping
  Title I :: 613
  Title II :: 618
Temporary employees :: 28, 37
Title I :: 27, 28, 67, 90
Twelve months employment :: 67, 74, 76
Worksite :: 108

Joint employment test
CAA :: 36
Covered employer :: 24, 36
Multiple employers :: 24
Title I :: 24

Judicial branch :: 4

Judiciary
Covered employee :: 48

Key employees
Burden of proof :: 605
Calculation of highest paid 10% :: 598
Cessation of health benefits :: 520
Definition :: 596
Denial of restoration notice :: 604
Determination :: 598
Employer :: 597
Initial qualification notice :: 601
Notice requirements :: 288, 332, 601
Return to work :: 596
Rights :: 604
  health benefits :: 605
  return to work :: 604
Salaried employee :: 596
Substantial/grievous injury :: 598
  notice :: 603

Layoffs
Count eligibility requirement, Title I :: 101
Effect 1250 hours, Title I :: 89

Layover time
Hours of service, 1250 hours :: 86
Hours worked, Title I :: 86

Leave
Amount :: 407
  leave year :: 8, 407
  workweek :: 8, 407
Available
  serious health condition :: 197
Conclusion
  adoption
    CAA :: 145
    PEOAA :: 145
    Title I :: 145
    Title II :: 148
  birth of child
    CAA :: 136
    PEOAA :: 136
    Title I :: 136
    Title II :: 139
  foster care
    CAA :: 150
    PEOAA :: 150

Title I :: 150
Title II :: 153
Covered individuals :: 5
Effect on 12 months
    CAA :: 77
    Title I :: 69
    Title II :: 74
Effect on 1250 hours
    CAA :: 96
    Title I :: 83
Effect on count requirement, Title I :: 100
Of absence
    effect on count requirement :: 101
Scheduling :: 8, 439
    ADA :: 758
    Agencies with mixed variant :: 471
    block leave :: 440
        adoption :: 441
        birth :: 441
        foster care :: 441
        serious health condition :: 441
    intermittent/reduced leave definition :: 441, 444
    CAA :: 442
    PEOAA :: 442
    Title I :: 442
    Title II :: 441
    reduced leave definition :: 443
    rehabilitation Act :: 758
    smallest increments of block leave :: 440
Substitution of paid leave :: 9, 473
Year
    [see Twelve month leave year]
    leave amount :: 8
    notice requirements :: 285
        itle II :: 286

Legislative branch :: 4

Light duty
FECA :: 770
Serious health condition :: 166, 171
Workers' compensation :: 770

Manner of notice
Employer policies effect on :: 305, 307
Foreseeable need
    CAA :: 302
    PEOAA :: 302
    Title I :: 302
    Title II :: 307
Need for FMLA leave :: 301
Not foreseeable need :: 303
Who may provide notice
    CAA :: 301
    PEOAA :: 301
    Title I :: 301
    Title II :: 306

Marine Corps exchanges :: 57

Marriage :: 117
Definition :: 121

Medical certification :: 7, 335
ADA :: 756
ADA approved examination :: 572
CAA :: 336
Christian Science
    CAA :: 375
    PEOAA :: 375
    Title I :: 375
    Title II :: 382
Clarification :: 369
    CAA :: 370
    PEOAA :: 370
    Title I :: 370
    Title II :: 371
Contents :: 354
    basic certification information
        CAA :: 355
        PEOAA :: 355
        Title I :: 355
        Title II :: 359
    CAA :: 354
    DOH WH 380 :: 362
    employee's serious health condition
        CAA :: 357
        PEOAA :: 357
        Title I :: 357
        Title II :: 360
    family member's serious health condition :: 357, 360
    PEOAA :: 354
    Title I :: 354, 361
    Title II :: 358, 361
Covered family members :: 162, 170
DOL WH 380 :: 362
Employee rights and obligations :: 343
Employer notice requirements :: 341
Employer policies effect on :: 353, 354, 358, 360
Employer requirements
    CAA :: 341
    fitness-for-duty :: 574, 579
    PEOAA :: 341
    Title I :: 341
    Title II :: 346
Employer written guidance :: 342
Employer's notice failure :: 344
Essential functions
    CAA :: 168
    PEOAA :: 168
    Title I :: 168
    Title II :: 172
Failure to satisfy requirements :: 385
    CAA :: 385
    PEOAA :: 385
    Title I :: 385
    Title II :: 387
Fitness-for-duty :: 565
Foreseeable need :: 349
Health benefits :: 530
Healthcare provider :: 339
    CAA :: 339
    PEOAA :: 339
    Title I :: 339

Title II :: 340
HIPAA :: 403
Incomplete :: 364
    CAA :: 364
    PEOAA :: 364
    Title I :: 364
    Title II :: 369
Intermittent/reduced leave :: 455, 470
Not foreseeable need :: 349
Paid leave substitute
    CAA :: 357
    PEOAA :: 357
    Title I :: 357
    Title II :: 360
Payment, 2nd opinion
    CAA :: 375
    PEOAA :: 375
    Title I :: 375, 383
    Title II :: 383
Payment, 3rd opinion
    CAA :: 378
    PEOAA :: 378
    Title I :: 378
    Title II :: 385
PEOAA :: 336
Preliminary leave designation :: 352, 354
Problems :: 363
    absence estimates :: 363
    basis for care :: 364
    essential function :: 364
    leave duration estimates :: 363
    medical facts :: 363
Provided
    time limits :: 348
        CAA :: 348
        PEOAA :: 348
        Title I :: 348
        Title II :: 353
Rehabilitation Act :: 756
Request
    serious health condition :: 530
    time limits :: 347
        CAA :: 347
        PEOAA :: 347
        Title I :: 347
        Title II :: 348
Return to work :: 565
Second opinion
    CAA :: 372
    PEOAA :: 372
    Title I :: 372
    Title II :: 381
Second/third opinion :: 372
    entitled :: 375, 383
    time frame :: 383
Serious health condition :: 162, 170, 249
Third opinion
    CAA :: 376
    PEOAA :: 376
    Title I :: 376
    Title II :: 384
Title I :: 336
Title II :: 338

Written guidance, absence :: 342
Medical need
Definition :: 251
Intermittent/reduced leave :: 251, 253
Medical recertification
CAA :: 388
Chronic conditions
CAA :: 390
exceptions
CAA :: 391
PEOAA :: 391
Title I :: 391
Title II :: 398
PEOAA :: 390
Title I :: 390
Title II :: 398
Circumstances permitting
CAA :: 390
PEOAA :: 390
Title I :: 390
Title II :: 398
Documentation :: 7, 388
Failure to provide medical recertification :: 397, 401
Forms
CAA :: 395
PEOAA :: 395
Title I :: 395
Title II :: 400
Incapacity exceeds 30 days :: 391
exception :: 392
Intermittent/reduced leave :: 393
executive :: 394
Long-term conditions
CAA :: 390
exceptions
CAA :: 391
PEOAA :: 391
Title I :: 391
Title II :: 398
PEOAA :: 390
Title I :: 390
Title II :: 398
Notice of requirement
CAA :: 396
PEOAA :: 396
Title I :: 396
Title II :: 400
Other circumstances
CAA :: 394
exceptions
CAA :: 394
PEOAA :: 394
Title I :: 394
Title II :: 399
PEOAA :: 394
Title I :: 394
Title II :: 398
Payment
CAA :: 396
PEOAA :: 396
Title I :: 396

Title II :: 400
PEOAA :: 388
Pregnancy
CAA :: 390
exceptions
CAA :: 391
PEOAA :: 391
Title I :: 391
Title II :: 398
PEOAA :: 390
Title I :: 390
Title II :: 398
Second/third opinion prohibited :: 396
Title II :: 400
Selection of provider
CAA :: 395
PEOAA :: 395
Title I :: 395
Title II :: 399
Time frame
CAA :: 395
PEOAA :: 395
Title I :: 395
Title II :: 399
Title I :: 388
Title II :: 398
Medical records, confidentiality
ADA :: 762
Rehabilitation Act :: 762
Medical treatment
Definition :: 168, 173
Serious health condition :: 168, 173
Mental illness
Serious health condition :: 237, 239
Military leave
CAA :: 77, 96
Title I :: 69, 84, 102
Title II :: 75
Minor illnesses :: 225
Complications :: 226
Serious health condition :: 227
Mixed variants agencies
Covered conditions :: 254
Documentation :: 404
Employer notice requirements :: 290
Health benefits :: 532
Leave scheduling :: 471
Notice requirements :: 334
Paid leave substitution :: 502
Record-keeping requirements :: 623
Return to work :: 609
Twelve month leave year :: 417
Twelve workweek calculation :: 439
MSPB
Enforcement :: 671, 676
PEOAA :: 690
Remedies
Title I :: 713

Title II :: 716
Multi-employer health plans
Cessation of benefits during leave :: 519
Changes in coverage :: 515
Definition :: 512
Employee premium payment :: 523
Employer notice of changes :: 517
Failure to pay, termination :: 526
Forego coverage :: 517
Health benefits during leave :: 513
Recovering cost of benefits :: 531
Scope of health benefits during leave :: 514
Multiple births
CAA :: 137
PEOAA :: 137
Title I :: 137
Title II :: 140
Multiple employers
CAA :: 36
Coverage and eligibility :: 33, 38
Covered employer :: 24, 36
Integrated employer test :: 25, 36
Integrated enterprise test :: 24
Joint employers :: 27, 37
Joint employment :: 28, 37
Joint employment test :: 24, 36
Joint ventures :: 24, 27, 37
Leased employees :: 27
Prohibited acts :: 34, 39
Temporary employees :: 27
Multiple treatments
Absence, definition :: 219, 223
Absence to receive :: 219, 223
CAA :: 218
Continuing treatment :: 218
Healthcare provider
CAA :: 220
PEOAA :: 220
Title I :: 220
Title II :: 224
Incapacity, over 3 days :: 221, 224
PEOAA :: 218
Recovery :: 220
Restorative surgery :: 221, 224
Serious health condition :: 223
Title I :: 218
Title II :: 222
NAFI
Civilian in military department :: 43
Covered employee :: 43, 57
defined :: 43
Title I :: 43
Title II :: 57
National Guard :: 43
National Security Council
Covered employee :: 4
Covered employer :: 39

Naval Academy employees
  Covered employee :: 57
  Title II :: 57
    exclusions :: 63

Navy exchanges :: 57

Navy ship's stores ashore :: 57

Need for FMLA leave
  Adequacy of notice :: 307
    CAA :: 307
    PEOAA :: 307
    Title I :: 307
    Title II :: 324
  Employee notice requirement :: 291
  Employee requirements :: 328
  Notice
    employer policies effect on :: 296, 300
    failure to provide :: 325
      CAA :: 325
      PEOAA:: 325
      Title I :: 325
      Title II :: 327
    foreseeable need
      CAA :: 291
      PEOAA :: 291
      Title I :: 291
      Title II :: 298
    manner of providing :: 301
      CAA :: 301
      PEOAA :: 301
      Title I :: 301
      Title II :: 306
    not foreseeable need
      CAA :: 294
      PEOAA :: 294
      Title I :: 294
      Title II :: 299
    timing of notice :: 291, 307
      CAA :: 291
      PEOAA :: 291
      Title I :: 291
      Title II :: 298

Nonconsecutive employment
  CAA :: 77
  Title I :: 68
  Title II :: 74
  Twelve months employment :: 68, 74, 77

Notice requirements :: 6, 255
  ADA :: 755
  Benefits :: 286
    CAA :: 286
    PEOAA :: 286
    Title I :: 286
    Title II :: 288
  CAA :: 6
  Confirm eligibility :: 272
  Deemed eligible :: 273
  Designation of FMLA leave :: 274
  Eligibility is met
    CAA :: 273
    deemed eligible :: 110, 273

    general eligibility notice rule :: 110
    Title I :: 273
  Employee :: 6, 290
    eligibility :: 272
      CAA :: 272
      PEOAA :: 273
      Title I :: 272
      Title II :: 274
    rights and obligations :: 263, 343
  Employer :: 6, 255
  Failure to pay health benefit :: 525
  Fitness-for-duty
    CAA :: 574
    PEOAA :: 574
    Title I :: 574
    Title II :: 579
  FMLA poster :: 255
    CAA :: 258
    PEOAA :: 258
    Title I :: 255
    Title II :: 258
  Health benefit
    employee payment :: 522
    options :: 520
  Health plan changes :: 516
  Intermittent/reduced leave :: 453, 470
  Joint employment :: 289
  Key employees :: 288, 332, 601
    CAA :: 288, 332
    denial of restoration :: 604
    initial notice :: 601
    PEOAA :: 288, 332
    substantial and grievous injury :: 603
    Title I :: 288, 332
  Leave commences
    CAA :: 273
    deemed eligible :: 111, 273
    general eligibility notice rule :: 111
    Title I :: 273
  Leave designation
    CAA :: 274
    PEOAA :: 284
    Title I :: 274
    Title II :: 284
  Leave year calculations :: 285
    CAA :: 285, 411
    PEOAA :: 285, 411
    Title I :: 285, 411
    Title II :: 286
  Miscellaneous employer
    requirements :: 285
  Mixed variants agencies :: 334
  Not to return to work :: 587
  Not yet eligible
    CAA :: 272
    deemed eligible :: 111, 273
    general eligibility notice rule :: 110
    Title I :: 272
  PEOAA :: 6
  Periodic status reports :: 584
  Posting violations :: 650
  Record keeping :: 289, 290
  Rehabilitation Act :: 755

  Return to work
    early :: 586
    employee :: 584
    form of notification :: 588
  School employees :: 608
  Timing of leave designation :: 276
  Title I :: 6
  Title II :: 6
  Written guidance :: 259
    absence :: 262
    CAA :: 259, 262
    PEOAA :: 261, 263
    Title I :: 259, 262
    Title II :: 261, 263

Nurse, physician's assistants
  Direct supervision :: 208

Nurse midwives :: 244

Nurse practitioners :: 244

Office of Compliance
  Covered employee :: 4, 64
  Covered employer :: 35
  Enforcement, CAA :: 677

Office of Inspector General :: 46

Office of Management and Budget
  Covered employee :: 4
  Covered employer :: 39

Office of National Drug Control Policy
  Covered employee :: 4
  Covered employer :: 39

Office of Policy Development
  Covered employee :: 4
  Covered employer :: 39

Office of Technology
  Covered employee :: 4, 64
  Covered employer :: 35

Office of the Architect of the Capitol
  Covered employee :: 4, 64
  Covered employer :: 35

Office of the Attending Physician
  Covered employee :: 4, 64
  Covered employer :: 35

Office of the Vice President
  Covered employee :: 4
  Covered employer :: 39

Osteopath :: 243

Overnight stay
  Inpatient care :: 176
  Serious health condition :: 176

Paid leave substitution :: 9, 473
  Accrued credit hours :: 498
  Accrued paid leave :: 482
    CAA :: 491
    PEOAA :: 491
    Title I :: 491

Title II :: 482
ADA :: 759
Adoption arrangements :: 487
Advanced leave, Title II :: 489
Agencies with mixed variant :: 502
Annual leave, Title II :: 483
Birth of child
    CAA :: 138
    PEOAA :: 138
    Title I :: 138
    Title II :: 141
Compensatory overtime :: 493
    CAA :: 495
    PEOAA :: 496
    Title I :: 495
    Title II :: 493
Covered family member, Title II :: 485
Election
    not FMLA benefits :: 480
    timing :: 479
Employee notice requirement :: 329, 478
    CAA :: 329, 479
    PEOAA:: 329, 479
    Title I :: 329, 479
    Title II :: 329, 479
Employee's own illness :: 484
Family leave :: 492
FECA :: 769
Flexible work schedule :: 498
Funeral arrangements :: 487
Medical certification
    CAA :: 352, 357
    PEOAA :: 352, 357
    Title I :: 352, 357
    Title II :: 354, 360
Medical leave :: 492
Organ/bone-marrow donation :: 488
Personal leave :: 493
Procedural requirements :: 500
    CAA :: 500
    PEOAA :: 500
    Title I :: 500
    Title II :: 502
Rehabilitation Act :: 759
Sick leave
    amount, Title II :: 488
    CAA :: 492
    PEOAA :: 492
    Title I :: 492
    Title II :: 483
Substitution, definition :: 481
Temporary disability leave :: 497
Unemployment compensation :: 499
Vacation leave
    CAA :: 493
    PEOAA :: 493
    Title I :: 493
Voluntary Leave Transfer Bank :: 491
Voluntary Leave Transfer Program :: 490
Workers' compensation :: 769

Paid or unpaid leave
  Hours worked, Title I :: 83

Panama Canal Commission
  Title II exclusions :: 62

Parent
  Covered family member :: 129
  Definition :: 129
  Multiple parents :: 129
  Relationship, current or past :: 129
  Serious health condition :: 156, 169

Parents-in-law
  Family member not covered :: 130

Part-time employee
  Count eligibility requirement, Title I :: 101
  Covered employee :: 4, 42
  Fifty employees within 75 miles :: 101
  Title I :: 42, 61
  Title II exclusions :: 61
  Twelve workweeks calculation :: 425

PBGC
  Covered employee :: 45
  Government corporation :: 45
  Title I :: 45

PDA
  [see Pregnancy Discrimination Act]

PDLA :: 16

PEOAA :: 2
  Accrued paid leave substitution :: 491
  Adequacy of need for leave notice :: 307
  Adoption :: 141
    12 month period :: 145
    age 18 or over :: 145
    source :: 144
    stepchildren :: 145
  Basic medical certification
    information :: 355
  Birth and care of newborn :: 201
  Birth of child :: 134
    12 month period :: 136
    childcare :: 137
    documentation :: 136
    multiple births :: 137
    paid leave :: 138
    return to work :: 137
  Changes in health coverage :: 515
  Chronic serious health condition :: 205
    episodic :: 209
    healthcare provider :: 208
  Circumstances permitting medical
    recertification :: 390
  Collective bargaining agreements :: 778
  Compensatory overtime :: 496
  Copies, 2nd/3rd opinions :: 379
  Covered employee :: 4, 64
    defined :: 64, 67
  Covered employer :: 39
  Eligibility requirements :: 4, 67
  Eligible employee, defined :: 67
  Employee eligibility notice :: 273
  Employee rights and obligations :: 271
  Employer practices :: 778

Employer requirements
  FMLA poster :: 258
  leave designation :: 284
  written guide :: 261, 263
Employing office, defined :: 67, 78
Enforcement :: 689
Essential functions, documentation :: 168
Executive Office of the President :: 2
Failure to provide
  medical certification :: 385
  need for leave notice :: 325
Familial relationship, documentation :: 401
Forego health benefits coverage :: 517
Foreseeable need for leave :: 291
Foster care placement :: 148
  12 month period :: 150
  age 18 and over :: 150
  duration :: 150
  multiple :: 150
  pay :: 150
  source :: 149
Health benefit
  employee payment :: 521
  recovering cost :: 528
Healthcare provider :: 208, 220, 241, 339
Hours of service, 1250 hours :: 98
Hours worked :: 98
Incapacity, treatment :: 188
Inpatient care :: 174
Interaction with federal laws :: 747
Intermittent/reduced leave :: 137, 146, 151, 251, 441
Level of care :: 160
Light duty :: 166
Long term incapacity :: 213
Manner of notice, need for leave :: 301
Medical certification :: 162, 336
  2nd opinion :: 372
  3rd opinion :: 376
  Christian Science :: 375
  clarification :: 370
  employer notice :: 341
  incomplete :: 364
  paid leave :: 357
  provided :: 348
  contents :: 354
  request :: 347
Medical recertification :: 388
  form :: 395
  notice :: 396
  payment :: 396
  time frame :: 395
Mental illness :: 237
Multiple treatments :: 218
Need for leave notice :: 291
Notice requirements :: 6
  benefits :: 286
  health benefits :: 516
  joint employment :: 289
  key employees :: 288, 332
  leave year calculation :: 285
  paid leave :: 479
  record keeping :: 290

Other caregivers :: 159
Permanent incapacity :: 213
Pre-adoption leave :: 144
Pre-foster care placement :: 149
Pregnancy :: 197
Prenatal care :: 135, 197, 200
Prohibited acts :: 625
Provisional leave, 2nd/3rd opinions :: 376
Reasonable accommodations :: 166
Record-keeping requirements :: 618
Remedies :: 718
Return to work
  equivalent
    benefits :: 549
    pay :: 547
    position :: 546
    terms :: 551
  medical certification :: 565
  same position :: 543
Scope of health benefits during leave :: 514
Second opinion, payment :: 375
Selection of provider, 3rd opinion :: 378
Serious health condition :: 155, 180, 197, 205, 213, 218
Substance abuse :: 230
  treatment :: 232
Third opinion, payment :: 378
To care for, documentation :: 162
Traveling care :: 161
Twelve month leave year :: 408
Twelve months employment :: 78
Twelve workweeks calculation :: 421
Unable to perform :: 163, 164
Workweek marriage penalty :: 433

Period of incapacity
Definition :: 174

Periodic visits
Chronic serious health condition :: 207, 212

Permanent or long term
Incapacity :: 213
  CAA :: 213
  PEOAA :: 213
  Title I :: 213
  Title II :: 216
Serious health condition :: 213

PMLA :: 17

Podiatrists :: 243

Postal Rate Commission
Covered employee :: 42
Title I :: 42
Title II exclusions :: 63
Variant :: 1

Posting violations
Prohibited acts :: 650

Pre-adoption leave
CAA :: 144
PEOAA :: 144
Title I :: 144

Title II :: 147

Pre-foster care placement
CAA :: 149
PEOAA :: 149
Title I :: 149
Title II :: 153

Pre/postliminary activities
Hours worked, Title I :: 85

Pregnancy
As a disability :: 201
CAA :: 197
Incapacity :: 198, 203
  any period :: 198, 203
Medical recertification
  CAA :: 390
  exception
    CAA :: 391
    PEOAA :: 391
    Title I :: 391
    Title II :: 398
  PEOAA :: 390
  Title I :: 390
  Title II :: 398
PEOAA :: 197
Serious health condition :: 197, 203
Title I :: 197
Title II :: 203
Treatment :: 199, 203

Pregnancy Discrimination Act
ADA :: 763
Eligibility for leave :: 766
Excessive absences :: 767
Intermittent/reduced leave :: 767
Rehabilitation Act :: 763
Return to work :: 767

Prenatal care
Birth of child
  CAA :: 135
  PEOAA :: 135
  Title I :: 135
  Title II :: 139
CAA :: 197, 200
Incapacity :: 198, 203
  any period :: 198, 203
PEOAA :: 197, 200
Serious health condition :: 135, 197, 203
Title I :: 197, 200
Title II :: 203, 204
Treatment :: 199, 203

President appointed officer
CAA :: 63
Title I :: 62
Title II exclusions :: 62, 63

President designated officer
Title I :: 63
Title II exclusions :: 63

Primary-secondary employer
CAA :: 37

Job restoration :: 33, 38
Responsibilities :: 32, 37
Title I :: 32

Private contractors :: 60

Private right of action
Courts of competent jurisdiction :: 670
Defendant :: 665
Enforcement :: 660
Extending time for filing :: 664
Limitations :: 670
When to initiate :: 661
Who may initiate :: 660

Prohibited acts :: 625
CAA :: 39, 625
Discrimination
  attendance :: 638
  benefits :: 636
  CAA :: 634
  definition :: 643
  negative factor :: 637
  opposing unlawful acts :: 639
  participation :: 642
  PEOAA :: 634
  Title I :: 634
  use of leave :: 634
Interference
  actions that chill :: 631
  CAA :: 626
  denial of restoration :: 633
  employee notice :: 629
  employer notice :: 630
  manipulation :: 632
  PEOAA :: 626
  Title I :: 626
Joint employers :: 34, 39
PEOAA :: 625
Posting violations :: 650
Title I :: 34, 625
Title II
  employee definition :: 651
  intent :: 652
  intimidate, threaten, or coerce :: 652
Waiver
  CAA :: 645
  collective bargaining representative :: 649
  definition :: 646
  early retirement :: 650
  employee :: 648
  light duty exception :: 649
  PEOAA :: 645
  regulatory developments :: 645
  rights :: 646
  Title I :: 645

Public agency
Definition :: 21
Title I :: 21

Qualifications
Documentation :: 7
Eligibility requirements :: 4

For protection under FMLA :: 3
Leave :: 5
Notice requirements :: 6

Radio Free Europe :: 46

Reasonable accommodation
Light duty
   CAA :: 166
   PEOAA :: 166
   Title I :: 166
   Title II :: 171
Return to work :: 558
Serious health condition :: 166, 171

Record-keeping requirements :: 611
Agencies with mixed variant :: 623
CAA :: 618
Disclosure
   Congress :: 621
   court order :: 621
   FOIA :: 621
   need to know :: 621
   of records :: 618
   Privacy Act :: 619
   routine uses :: 621
   to DOL :: 619
   to government agencies :: 619
   to OPM :: 619
FLSA-exempt
   Title I :: 614
   Title II :: 618
Form of records
   Title I :: 615
   Title II :: 618
Government inspection :: 619
Joint employment
   Title I :: 613
   Title II :: 618
Location of records, Title I :: 616
Medical
   Title I :: 613
   Title II :: 617
Nonmedical
   eligible employ :: 612
   non- eligible employee :: 611
   Title I :: 611
   Title II :: 616
Notice requirements :: 289, 290
PEOAA :: 618
Retention of records
   Title I :: 616
   Title II :: 618
Title I :: 611
Title II :: 616
Transfers
   Title I :: 614
   Title II :: 618

Recurring episodes
Chronic health condition, Title II :: 213

Regulatory developments
Chronic health condition
   CAA :: 205

PEOAA :: 205
Title I :: 205
Title II :: 210
Long term incapacity
   CAA :: 214
   PEOAA :: 214
   Title I :: 214
   Title II :: 216
More than 3 days
   CAA :: 181
   PEOAA :: 181
   Title I :: 181
   Title II :: 193
Multiple treatments
   CAA :: 219
   PEOAA :: 219
   Title I :: 219
   Title II :: 222
Permanent incapacity
   CAA :: 214
   PEOAA :: 214
   Title I :: 214
   Title II :: 216

Rehabilitation Act :: 747
Benefits, maintenance :: 759
Covered conditions :: 751
Covered employers :: 750
Covered individuals :: 754
Eligibility for leave :: 750
Entitlements :: 751
Intermittent/reduced leave :: 758
Leave scheduling :: 758
Medical certification :: 756
Medical records, confidential :: 762
Notice requirements :: 755
Paid leave substitution :: 759
Pregnancy Discrimination Act :: 763
Return to work :: 760
Undue hardship :: 754

Relationship requirement
Son or daughter :: 122

Remedies :: 11, 625, 692
Attorney fees
   PEOAA :: 719
   Title I :: 707
CAA :: 718
Civil penalties
   CAA :: 718
   PEOAA :: 720
Costs
   PEOAA :: 719
   Title I :: 711
   recoverable :: 712
Damages, Title I :: 692
   back pay :: 694
   benefits :: 694, 697
   bonuses :: 697
   commissions :: 697
   compensation :: 694
   education agencies :: 705
   emotional distress :: 698

   front pay :: 696
   liquidated :: 701
   monetary loss :: 698
   overtime :: 696
   prejudgment interest :: 700
   profit sharing :: 697
   punitive :: 698
   wages and salary :: 693
Equitable relief, Title I :: 706
   civil action :: 706
   Secretary of Labor :: 707
Interest, PEOAA :: 719
MSPB
   Title I :: 713
   Title II :: 716
Payments
   CAA :: 718
   PEOAA :: 720
PEOAA :: 718
Punitive damages
   CAA :: 718
   PEOAA :: 720
Title I :: 692
Title II :: 715
Witness fees, PEOAA :: 719

Reservist in armed forces
Title II exclusions :: 63

Resignations
Effect on count requirement :: 101

Restorative surgery
Multiple treatments :: 221, 224
Serious health condition :: 221, 224, 240

Retroactive leave :: 278, 330

Return to work :: 535
ADA :: 760
Agencies with mixed variant :: 609
Alternative position :: 558
Bonuses :: 547
Collective bargaining agreement
   CAA :: 569
   PEOAA :: 569
   Title I :: 569
   Title II :: 579
Current eligible employee :: 536
   CAA :: 536
   PEOAA :: 536
   Title I :: 536
   Title II :: 537
De Minimis/intangible job :: 553
Employee notice requirement :: 331, 584
   CAA :: 332
   PEOAA:: 332
   Title I :: 332
   Title II :: 332
Employee rights :: 535
Employees perfection of right :: 560
Employer delay of return :: 541
Employer notice requirements
   CAA :: 574
   PEOAA:: 574

Title I :: 574
Title II :: 579
Entitlement :: 11
Equivalent
  benefits :: 549
    CAA :: 549
    PEOAA :: 549
    Title I :: 549
    Title II :: 551
  pay :: 547
    CAA :: 547
    PEOAA :: 547
    Title I :: 547
    Title II :: 549
  terms and conditions :: 551
    CAA :: 551
    PEOAA :: 551
    Title I :: 551
    Title II :: 552
Essential job functions
  CAA :: 561
  PEOAA :: 561
  Title I :: 561
  Title II :: 565
Exhaustion of leave
  CAA :: 582
  PEOAA :: 582
  Title I :: 582
  Title II :: 583
Fitness-for-duty :: 565
FMLA leave :: 537
  CAA :: 537
  PEOAA :: 537
  Title I :: 537
  Title II :: 538
Form of employee notice :: 588
Greater employer benefits :: 559
Group health plans :: 529
Health benefits, requalification :: 527
Intermittent/reduced leave :: 471
Joint employers :: 559
Key employees :: 596
Lapsed qualifications, license :: 556
Light duty :: 558
Limitations on agency obligation :: 588
Medical certifications :: 565
  2nd/3rd opinions
    CAA :: 576
    PEOAA :: 576
    Title I :: 576
    Title II :: 581
  ADA :: 572
  after return
    CAA :: 577
    PEOAA :: 577
    Title I :: 577
    Title II :: 582
  CAA :: 565
  clarification
    CAA :: 568
    PEOAA :: 568
    Title I :: 568
    Title II :: 578

  contents and form
    CA :: 567
    PEOAA :: 567
    Title I :: 567
    Title II :: 578
  cost
    CAA :: 574
    PEOAA :: 574
    Title I :: 574
    Title II :: 579
  DOT requirements :: 571
  failure to provide
    CAA :: 575
    PEOAA :: 575
    Title I :: 575
    Title II :: 580
  PEOAA :: 565
  scope, Title II :: 578
  Title I :: 565
  Title II :: 577
Notice :: 540
  not to return :: 587
Obligation to return :: 540
Periodic status reports :: 584
Physical presence :: 540
Position :: 543
  equivalent :: 546
    CAA :: 546
    PEOAA :: 546
    Title I :: 546
    Title II :: 547
  same
    CAA :: 543
    PEOAA :: 543
    Title I :: 543
    Title II :: 545
Pregnancy Discrimination Act :: 767
Reasonable accommodation :: 558
Rehabilitation Act :: 760
Return, definition
  CAA :: 538
  PEOAA :: 538
  Title I :: 538
  Title II :: 543
School employees :: 605
  equivalent position :: 608
  instructional :: 605
  intermittent leave :: 606
  near end of term :: 607
  notice :: 608
  reduced leave :: 606
Unfit
  CAA :: 576
  PEOAA :: 576
  Title I :: 576
  Title II :: 581

Return to work, early
Birth of child
  CAA :: 137
  PEOAA :: 137
  Title I :: 137
  Title II :: 140

Notice of intent
  CAA :: 586
  PEOAA :: 586
  Title I :: 586
  Title II :: 587

School employees
Collective bargaining agreement :: 778
Covered employees :: 605
Covered schools :: 605
Employee notice requirement :: 333
Instructional employees :: 605
Intermittent/reduced leave :: 467, 606
Leave near end of term :: 607
Notice requirements :: 333
Return to work :: 605
  equivalent position :: 608
  rights :: 606

Second/third opinion
Copies
  CAA :: 379
  PEOAA :: 379
  Title I :: 379
  Title II :: 385
Entitlement :: 375, 383
Exclusivity :: 379
Medical certification :: 372
  CAA :: 396
  Christian Science :: 375, 382
  PEOAA :: 396
  Title I :: 396
  Title II :: 400
Preliminary designation
  CAA :: 376
  PEOAA :: 376
  Title I :: 376
  Title II :: 383
Provisional leave
  CAA :: 376
  PEOAA :: 376
  Title I :: 376
  Title II :: 383
Refusal to cooperate :: 381
Return to work :: 576, 581
Time frame, Title II :: 383

Second opinion
Medical certification
  CAA :: 372
  PEOAA :: 372
  Title I :: 372
  Title II :: 381
Payment
  CAA :: 375
  PEOAA :: 375
  Title I :: 375
  Title II :: 383

Section 405 administrative complaint :: 681
Appeal to Office Board of Directors :: 683
Conduct of hearing :: 683
Decision :: 683
Discovery :: 682

Dismissal :: 682
Hearing officer :: 681
Judicial review, Office Board of Directors :: 684
Settlement :: 683
Subpoenas :: 682

Senate
Covered employee :: 4, 64
Covered employer :: 35
Variant :: 1

Serious health condition
Allergies :: 240
Bereavement leave :: 159
Block leave scheduling :: 441
By medical condition :: 249
CAA :: 155
Chronic :: 205, 210
    CAA :: 205
    PEOAA :: 205
    Title I :: 205
    Title II :: 210
Combined conditions :: 238
Continuing treatment :: 179
Cosmetic treatments :: 230
Covered condition :: 5, 154, 155
Covered family member :: 2, 117, 155
Definition :: 179
    CAA :: 174, 180, 197, 205, 213, 218
    PEOAA :: 174, 180, 197, 205, 213, 218
    Title I :: 174, 180, 197, 205, 213, 218
    Title II :: 178, 193, 203, 210, 216, 222
Documentation :: 249
Employee :: 2
    CAA :: 163
    medical certification
        CAA :: 357
        PEOAA :: 357
        Title I :: 357
        Title II :: 360
    PEOAA :: 163
    Title I :: 163
    Title II :: 170
Entitlement condition :: 2
Essential functions :: 170, 171
Essential job functions :: 165, 167, 171, 172
Evidence :: 249
Family member, medical certification :: 357, 360
Healthcare provider :: 241
    CAA :: 241
    PEOAA :: 241
    Title I :: 241
    Title II :: 247
Illegal substance, definition :: 236
Incapacity :: 174, 181, 194
    CAA :: 180
    PEOAA :: 180
    Title I :: 180
    Title II :: 193
        treatment :: 188, 194
Inpatient care :: 174, 177, 178
Intermittent/reduced leave :: 250, 445

Leave available :: 197
Legislative history :: 179
Level of care
    CAA :: 160
    PEOAA :: 160
    Title I :: 160
    Title II :: 170
Light duty :: 166, 171
Long term incapacity :: 213, 216
    CAA :: 213
    PEOAA :: 213
    Title I :: 213
    Title II :: 216
Medical certification :: 2, 249, 530
Medical treatment
    CAA :: 168
    PEOAA :: 168
    Title I :: 168
    Title II :: 173
Mental illness :: 237, 239
Minor illnesses
    exceptions :: 227
    excluded :: 225
Multiple treatments :: 218, 222, 223
    absence :: 219, 223
    CAA :: 218
    PEOAA :: 218
    recovery :: 220
    Title I :: 218
    Title II :: 222
Other caregivers
    CAA :: 159
    PEOAA :: 159
    Title I :: 159
    Title II :: 169
Overnight stay :: 176
Parent
    CAA :: 156
    PEOAA :: 156
    Title I :: 156
    Title II :: 169
PEOAA :: 155
Permanent incapacity :: 213, 216
    CAA :: 213
    PEOAA :: 213
    Title I :: 213
    Title II :: 216
Permanent or long term :: 213
Pregnancy
    CAA :: 197
    PEOAA :: 197
    Title I :: 197
    Title II :: 203
Prenatal care :: 200
    CAA :: 135, 197
    PEOAA :: 135, 197
    Title I :: 135, 197
    Title II :: 203, 204
Reasonable accommodation :: 166, 171
Regimen of continuing treatment :: 239
Removal of cancerous growth :: 240
Restorative surgery :: 221, 224, 240
Routine exams, excluded :: 239

Son or daughter
    CAA :: 156
    PEOAA :: 156
    Title I :: 156
    Title II :: 169
Special issues :: 225
    cosmetic :: 230
    minor illness :: 225
Spouse
    CAA :: 156
    PEOAA :: 156
    Title I :: 156
    Title II :: 169
Stepchildren
    CAA :: 145
    PEOAA :: 145
    Title I :: 145
    Title II :: 147
Substance abuse :: 230
    CAA :: 230
    definition :: 231, 236
    PEOAA :: 230
    Title I :: 230
    Title II :: 236
Title I :: 155
Title II :: 169
To care for the living :: 159
Traveling care
    CAA :: 161
    PEOAA :: 161
    Title I :: 161
    Title II :: 170
Treatment :: 175
Types of conditions :: 173
Unable to perform
    CAA :: 163, 164
    PEOAA :: 163, 164
    Title I :: 163, 164
    Title II :: 170, 171

Smithsonian Institution
Covered employee :: 46

Son or daughter
Age 18 or over :: 124
Age requirement :: 124
Covered family member :: 122
Current :: 123
Definition :: 122
Disability, physical or mental :: 125
Incapable of self-care :: 124
In Loco Parentis :: 122
Pre-existing disability :: 126
Relationship requirement :: 122
Serious health condition :: 156, 169
Under age 18 :: 124

Source of adoption
CAA :: 144
PEOAA :: 144
Title I :: 144
Title II :: 147

Spouse
Civil union :: 119

Covered family member :: 117
Defense of Marriage Act :: 120
Definition :: 121
Divorce :: 119
Domestic partners :: 120
Marriage :: 117
    common-law :: 118
Serious health condition :: 156, 169

State officials :: 60

Status reports
Documentation :: 7, 401

Stepchildren
Adoption
    CAA :: 145
    PEOAA :: 145
    Title I :: 145
    Title II :: 147
Serious health condition :: 145, 147

Subsequent treatment
Incapacity
    CAA :: 189
    PEOAA :: 189
    Title I :: 189
    Title II :: 195

Substance abuse :: 230, 235
Covered family members :: 234, 237
Definition
    CAA :: 231
    PEOAA :: 231
    Title I :: 231
    Title II :: 236
Discipline :: 233
Drug testing, return to work :: 235
Healthcare provider
    CAA :: 233
    PEOAA :: 233
    Title I :: 233
    Title II :: 237
Serious health condition :: 230
    CAA :: 230
    PEOAA :: 230
    Title I :: 230
    Title II :: 236
Treatment
    CAA :: 232
    PEOAA :: 232
    Title I :: 232
    Title II :: 237

Substitution of paid leave
[see Paid leave substitution]
Election :: 473
    choice of balance :: 476
    made by who :: 477
    notice :: 478
    order :: 475
Recovering cost of benefits :: 531

Successor-in-interest
CAA :: 36, 76, 96
Covered employer :: 22

Entitlements :: 23
Factors to determine :: 23
Hours worked, Title I :: 91
Responsibilities :: 23
Title I :: 68, 91
Title II :: 74
Twelve months employment :: 68, 74, 76

Supervisor liability :: 1, 36
Covered employer :: 22

Suspensions
Effect on count requirement :: 101
Hours worked, Title I :: 87

Teachers
Count eligibility requirement, Title I :: 103
Hours worked
    CAA :: 97
    Title I :: 91

Teachers for DOD
Covered employee :: 58
Definition :: 58
Teaching position, definition :: 58
Title II :: 58

Temporary appointment
Covered employee :: 4

Temporary construction employees
Title II exclusions :: 61

Temporary disability leave
Paid leave substitution :: 497

Temporary or intermittent employees
Title II exclusions :: 60, 61

Tennessee Valley Authority :: 45

Terminations
Hours worked, Title I :: 87

Third opinion
Medical certification
    CAA :: 376
    PEOAA :: 376
    Title I :: 376
    Title II :: 384
Payment
    CAA :: 378
    PEOAA :: 378
    Title I :: 378
    Title II :: 385
Selection of provider
    CAA :: 378
    PEOAA :: 378
    Title I :: 378
    Title II :: 384

Time limits
Medical certification
    provided :: 348
    CAA :: 348
    PEOAA :: 348
    Title I :: 348
    Title II :: 353

request :: 347
    CAA :: 347
    PEOAA :: 347
    Title I :: 347
    Title II :: 348

Title I :: 1
Accrued paid leave substitution :: 491
Adequacy of need for leave notice :: 307
Adoption :: 141
    12 mo. period :: 145
    age 18 or over :: 145
Adoption
    source :: 144
    stepchildren :: 145
Atomic Energy Commission :: 47
Basic medical certification information :: 355
Birth and care of newborn :: 201
Birth of child :: 134
    12 mo. period :: 136
    childcare :: 137
    documentation :: 136
    multiple births :: 137
    paid leave :: 138
    return to work :: 137
Changes in health coverage :: 515
Chronic serious health condition :: 205
    episodic :: 209
    healthcare provider :: 208
Circumstances permitting medical recertification :: 390
Civilian in military department :: 43
Clarification, PEOAA :: 370
Collective bargaining agreement :: 772
Compensatory overtime :: 495
Congressional employees :: 62
Copies, 2nd/3rd opinions :: 379
Count eligibility
    determined :: 99
    requirement :: 98
Coverage and eligibility :: 33
Covered employee :: 4, 41
    defined :: 41
Covered employer :: 21
Deemed eligible :: 110
Eligibility requirements :: 4, 65, 110
Eligible employee, defined :: 65
Employee
    eligibility notice :: 272
    maintained on payroll :: 99, 103
    of DC government :: 61
    rights and obligations :: 263
Employer
    interference, hours :: 89
    practices :: 772
    requirements
        FMLA poster :: 255
        leave designation :: 274
        to confirm eligibility :: 272
        written guide :: 259, 262
Enforcement :: 653
Executive branch :: 1, 44

Failure to provide
    medical certification :: 385
    need for leave notice :: 325
Familial relationship, documentation :: 401
Family leave outside the US :: 72, 91, 103
Farm Credit Administration :: 62
Federal Reserve :: 46
Federal Home Loan Mortgage
    Corporation :: 45
Fifty employees within 75 miles :: 98
Forego health benefits coverage :: 517
Foreseeable need for leave :: 291
Foster care
    12 mo. period :: 150
    age 18 and over :: 150
    duration :: 150
    multiple :: 150
    pay :: 150
    placement :: 148
    source :: 149
Furloughs
    effect on 12 mo. :: 70
    effect on 1250 hours :: 89
Government corporation :: 44
Health benefits
    during leave :: 512
    employee payment :: 521
    recovering cost :: 528
Healthcare provider :: 208, 220, 241, 339
Hours in preceding 12 months :: 93
Hours of service, 1250 hours :: 78
Hours worked :: 79, 98
    proof :: 92
Incapacity, treatment :: 188
Inpatient care :: 174
Integrated employer test :: 25
Interaction with federal laws :: 745
Intermittent/reduced leave :: 137, 146, 151, 251, 441
Intermittent appointment :: 43
Job restoration :: 33
Joint employers :: 27
Joint employment :: 28, 67, 90
Layoffs, effect 1250 hours :: 89
Layover time :: 86
Leave commencement :: 71, 93
    effect on 1250 hours. :: 83
    effect on 12 months :: 69
    effect on count requirement :: 100
Level of care :: 160
Light duty :: 166
Long term incapacity :: 213
Manner of notice, need for leave :: 301
Medical certification :: 336
    2nd opinion :: 372
    3rd opinion :: 376
    Christian Science :: 375
    clarification :: 370
    contents :: 354, 361
    employer notice :: 341
    incomplete :: 364
    paid leave :: 357
    provided :: 348
    request :: 347
Medical recertification :: 388
    form :: 395
    notice :: 396
    payment :: 396
    time frame :: 395
Mental illness :: 237
Military leave :: 69, 84, 102
Multiple employers :: 24
Multiple treatments :: 218
NAFI :: 43
National Guard :: 43
Need for leave notice :: 291
Nonconsecutive employment :: 68
Notice of leave designation :: 276
Notice requirements :: 6
    benefits :: 286
    health benefits :: 516
    joint employment :: 289
    key employees :: 288, 332
    leave year calculation :: 285
    paid leave :: 479
    record keeping :: 290
Other caregivers :: 159
Overtime or premium pay :: 83
Part-time employees :: 42, 61
PBGC :: 45
Permanent incapacity :: 213
Postal Rate Commission :: 1, 42
Pre-adoption leave :: 144
Pre-foster care placement :: 149
Pre/postliminary activities :: 85
Pregnancy :: 197
Prenatal care :: 135, 197, 200
President appointed officer :: 62
President designated officer :: 63
Primary-secondary employer :: 32
Prohibited acts :: 34, 625
Provisional leave, 2nd/3rd opinions :: 376
Public agency :: 21
Reasonable accommodations :: 166
Record-keeping requirements :: 611
    form :: 615
    location :: 616
    medical :: 613
    nonmedical :: 611
    retention :: 616
    transfers :: 614
Remedies :: 692
Return to work
    equivalent
        benefits :: 549
        pay :: 547
        position :: 546
        terms :: 551
    medical certification :: 565
    same position :: 543
RIFs, effect on 12 months :: 70
Scope of health benefits during leave :: 514
Second opinion, payment :: 375
Selection of provider, 3rd opinion :: 378
Serious health condition :: 155, 180, 197, 205, 213, 218
Substance abuse :: 230
    treatment :: 232
Successor-in-interest :: 68, 91
Suspensions and terminations :: 87
Teachers :: 103
    hours worked :: 91
Tennessee Valley Authority :: 45
Third opinion, payment :: 378
To care for, documentation :: 162
Training :: 87
Traveling care :: 161
Twelve month leave year :: 408
Twelve months employment :: 67
Twelve workweeks calculation :: 421
Unable to perform :: 163, 164
Union business, hours worked :: 85
USERRA :: 69, 84
US Government as single employer :: 67, 100
USPS :: 1, 42
Worksite, definition :: 105
Workweek marriage penalty :: 433

Title II :: 1

Accrued paid leave substitution :: 482
Adequacy of need for leave notice :: 324
Adoption :: 146
    12 month period :: 148
    age 18 or over :: 147
    source :: 147
    stepchildren :: 147
Army and AF Exchange Service :: 57
Army and AF Motion Picture Service :: 57
Basic medical certification information :: 359
Because of the birth :: 138
Birth and care of newborn :: 204
Birth of child :: 138
    12 month period :: 139
    childcare :: 140
    documentation :: 140
    multiple births :: 140
    paid leave :: 141
    return to work :: 140
Changes in health coverage :: 516
Chronic serious health condition :: 210
    healthcare provider :: 212
    episodic :: 213
    extended time :: 213
    recurring :: 213
CIA proprietary corporations :: 55
Circumstances permitting medical recertification :: 398
Civil Service Employees :: 49
Coast Guard exchanges :: 57
Collective bargaining agreement :: 778
Compensatory overtime :: 493
Cooperative Extension Service :: 56
Copies, 2nd/3rd opinions :: 385
Covered employee :: 4, 49
    defined :: 49, 66
Covered employer :: 34, 35
Eligibility requirements :: 5, 66

Employee
    definition :: 73
    eligibility notice :: 274
    rights and obligations :: 271
Employer
    practices :: 778
    requirements
        FMLA poster :: 258
        leave designation :: 284
        written guide :: 261, 263
Enforcement :: 674
Essential functions, documentation :: 172
Exception, 12 month leave year :: 408
Exclusions :: 60, 61
    alien employee :: 62
    Chief of mission :: 63
    congressional employees :: 62
    employees of DC government :: 60, 61
    Farm Credit Administration :: 62
    Naval Academy employees :: 63
    Panama Canal Commission :: 62
    part-time employees :: 61
    Postal Rate Commission :: 63
    President appointed officer :: 62, 63
    President designated officer :: 63
    reservist in armed forces :: 63
    temporary employees :: 61
        construction employees :: 61
        or intermittent employees :: 60
    USPS :: 63
Failure to provide
    medical certification :: 387
    need for leave notice :: 327
Familial relationship, documentation :: 402
Forego health benefits coverage :: 518
Foreign Service employees :: 59
Foreseeable need for leave :: 298
Foster care placement :: 152
    12 month period :: 153
    age 18 and over :: 153
    duration :: 153
    multiple :: 153
    pay :: 153
    source :: 153
Furloughs, effect on 12 months :: 76
Health benefits
    during leave :: 513
    employee payment :: 520
Healthcare provider :: 212, 224, 247, 340
Hours of service, 1250 hours :: 95
Incapacity, Treatment :: 194
Inpatient care :: 178
Interaction with federal laws :: 746
Intermittent/reduced leave :: 141, 148, 154, 253, 441
Leave
    commencement :: 76
    effect on 12 month :: 74
Level of care :: 170
Light duty :: 171
Long term incapacity :: 216
Manner of notice, need for leave :: 306
Marine Corps exchanges :: 57

Medical certification :: 162, 170, 338
    2nd opinion :: 381
    3rd opinion :: 384
    Christian Science :: 382
    clarification :: 371
    contents :: 358, 361, 362
    DOL WH 380 :: 362
    employer notice :: 346
    incomplete :: 369
    paid leave :: 360
    provided :: 353
    request :: 348
Medical recertification :: 398
    form :: 400
    notice :: 400
    payment :: 400
    time frame :: 399
Mental illness :: 239
Military leave :: 75
Multiple treatments :: 222
NAFI :: 57
Naval Academy employees :: 57
Navy exchanges :: 57
Navy ship's stores ashore :: 57
Need for leave notice :: 298
Nonconsecutive employment :: 74
Notice requirements :: 6
    benefits :: 288
    leave year calculations :: 286
    paid leave :: 479
    record keeping :: 290
Other caregivers :: 169
Permanent incapacity :: 216
Pre-adoption leave :: 147
Pre-foster care placement :: 153
Pregnancy :: 203
Prenatal care :: 139, 203, 204
Prohibited acts :: 651
Provisional leave, 2nd/3rd opinion :: 383
Reasonable accommodation :: 171
Record keeping
    medical :: 617
    nonmedical :: 616
    requirements :: 616
    transfers :: 618
Remedies :: 715
Return to work
    equivalent
        benefits :: 551
        pay :: 549
        position :: 547
        terms :: 552
    medical certification :: 577
    same position :: 545
RIFs, effect on 12 months :: 75
Scope of health benefits during leave :: 514
Second opinion, payment :: 383
Selection of provider, 3rd opinion :: 384
Serious health condition :: 169, 193, 203, 210, 216, 222
Substance abuse :: 236
    treatment :: 237
Successor-in-interest :: 74

Teachers for DOD :: 58
Termination, effect on :: 75
Third opinion, payment :: 385
Time frame, 2nd/3rd opinion :: 383
Traveling care :: 170
Twelve month leave year :: 407, 408
Twelve months employment :: 73
Twelve workweeks calculation :: 418
Unable to perform :: 170, 171
USERRA :: 75
Veterans Health Administration :: 58

Title V :: 1
Covered employer :: 35
House of Representatives :: 1
Senate :: 1

Title VII :: 768

Training
Hours of service, 1250 hours :: 87
Hours worked, Title I :: 87

Treatment
By a healthcare provider :: 189, 195, 233, 237
Chronic serious health condition :: 206, 211
Definition :: 175
    CAA :: 188
    PEOAA :: 188
    Title I :: 188
Healthcare provider
    CAA :: 208
    PEOAA :: 208
    Title I :: 208
    Title II :: 212
Inpatient care :: 175
Pregnancy :: 199, 203
Prenatal care :: 199, 203
Schedule, consult employer :: 329
Serious health condition :: 175
Substance abuse
    CAA :: 232
    PEOAA :: 232
    Title I :: 232
    Title II :: 237

Twelve month leave year :: 407
Adoption
    CAA :: 416
    PEOAA :: 416
    Title I :: 416
    Title II :: 408
Agencies with mixed variant :: 417
Birth of a child
    CAA :: 416
    PEOAA :: 416
    Title I :: 416
    Title II :: 408
CAA :: 408
    12 month period options :: 408
    calendar or fixed year :: 409
    change calculation method :: 411
    measured forward :: 409
    rolling back :: 410

uniform application :: 410
Employer policy effects on :: 417
Failure to select calculation method :: 415
Foster care placement
    Title I :: 416
    Title II :: 408
Notice requirements :: 411
PEOAA :: 408
    12 month period options :: 408
    calendar or fixed year :: 409
    change calculation method :: 411
    measured forward :: 409
    rolling back :: 410
    uniform application :: 410
Title I :: 408
    12 month period options :: 408
    calendar or fixed year :: 409
    change calculation method :: 411
    measured forward :: 409
    rolling back :: 410
    uniform application :: 410
Title II :: 407

Twelve months employment
CAA :: 76
Calculating :: 67
Effect of furloughs
    CAA :: 78
    Title I :: 70
    Title II :: 76
Effect of leave on :: 69, 74, 77
Effect of RIFs
    CAA :: 77
    Title I :: 70
    Title II :: 75
Effect of termination
    CAA :: 77
    Title I :: 70
    Title II :: 75
Eligibility requirements
    CAA :: 76
    PEOAA :: 78
    Title II :: 73, 76
Former employees, Title I :: 72
Joint employment :: 67, 74, 76
Leave commences
    CAA :: 78
    Title I :: 71, 78
    Title II :: 76
Military leave
    CAA :: 77
    Title I :: 69
    Title II :: 75
Nonconsecutive employment :: 68, 74, 77
Outside the US, Title I :: 72, 103
PEOAA :: 78
Successor-in-interest :: 68, 74, 76
Title I :: 67
Title II :: 73
USERRA
    CAA :: 77
    Title I :: 69
    Title II :: 75

US Government as single employer :: 67

Twelve workweeks calculation :: 417
Agencies with mixed variant :: 439
Amount of leave available :: 418
    CAA :: 421
    PEOAA :: 421
    Title I :: 421
    Title II :: 418
Business action temporary ceased :: 430
Calculation start point :: 423
Employer policy
    CAA :: 438
    effects on :: 437
    PEOAA :: 438
    Title I :: 438
    Title II :: 437
FLSA-exempt employees :: 428
Holidays :: 429
Key terms, Title II :: 418
Leave amount, Title II :: 419
Limit on leave amount :: 420
Marriage penalty :: 433
Overtime hours :: 430
Part-time or variable hours :: 425
Spouses in same agency :: 433
Temporal period absence
    CAA :: 423
    PEOAA :: 423
    Title I :: 423
    Title II :: 420
Timing of calculation, Title II :: 420
Work schedule
    CAA :: 422
    changes :: 431
    definition
    PEOAA :: 422
    Title I :: 422
Work schedules that vary :: 426

Undue hardship
ADA :: 754
Rehabilitation Act :: 754

Unemployment compensation
Paid leave substitution :: 499

Union business :: 85
Hours worked, Title I :: 85

USERRA :: 770
CAA :: 77, 96
Hours of service, 1250 hours :: 84, 96
Title I :: 69, 84
Title II :: 75
Twelve months employment :: 69, 75, 77

USPS
Covered employee :: 42, 48
Title I :: 42
Title II exclusions :: 63
Variant :: 1

US Tax Court :: 4

Variants :: 1, 21
CAA :: 1
PEOAA :: 2
Title I :: 1
Title II :: 1
Title V :: 1

Veterans Health Administration :: 58

Voluntary Leave Transfer Bank :: 491

Voluntary Leave Transfer Program :: 490

Waiver
Prohibited acts :: 645

WARN Act :: 105

WH 380-Certification of Health Care Provider :: 362

White House :: 48

White House Office :: 4

Workers' compensation :: 768
Benefits, maintenance :: 769
FECA :: 768
Health benefits :: 531
    payment :: 523
Light duty :: 770
Medical information :: 770
Paid leave substitution :: 496
Return to work :: 594

Worksite
Definition :: 105
Joint employment :: 108
No fixed worksite :: 106
Personal residence :: 107
Separate facilities :: 106
Single or multiple locations :: 105

Workweek
[see Twelve workweeks calculation]
Leave amount :: 8

Written guidance
Employee rights and obligations :: 263, 343
Employer requirements :: 259, 262
    CAA :: 259, 262
    PEOAA :: 261, 263
    Title I :: 259, 262
    Title II :: 261, 263
Medical certification, employer notice :: 342
Notice requirements :: 259, 262

NOTES

NOTES

NOTES

NOTES

NOTES

NOTES

NOTES

NOTES